Traditions & Encounters

CONNECT WITH THE

Stories

OF HISTORY

Students will readily engage with the past when they see that history is the work of real people. Bentley and Ziegler enliven world history through the vivid tales of merchants, missionaries, monarchs, explorers, conquerors, and commoners across cultures:

In 629 . . . in defiance of the [Chinese] emperor [Tang Taizong], a young Buddhist monk slipped past imperial watchtowers under cover of darkness and made his way west. His name was Xuanzang, and his destination was India, homeland of Buddhism . . . [where he would] visit the holy sites of Buddhism, and . . . learn about Buddhism from the purest sources. Xuanzang could not have imagined the difficulties he would face. Immediately after his departure from China, his guide abandoned him in the Gobi desert. After losing his water bag and collapsing in the heat, Xuanzang made his way to the oasis town of Turpan on the silk roads . . . [Then] Xuanzang crossed three of the world's highest mountain ranges—the Tian Shan, Hindu Kush, and Pamir ranges—and lost one-third of his party. . . . Yet Xuanzang persisted and arrived in India in 630. By the time of his return [to Chang'an] in 645, Xuanzang had logged more than 16,000 kilometers (10,000 miles) on the road.

MAP 12.1
The silk roads, 200 B.C.E.–300 C.E.
Note the extent of the land and sea routes known collectively as the silk roads.
Consider the political and economic conditions that would be necessary for regular travel and trade across the silk roads.

- Vivid stories keep students involved and help them to get the most from their study of world history.
- Clear, vibrant, precise maps with extended captions—entirely redesigned for this edition—help students put the experiences of individual historical actors in geographical context.

CONNECT TO THE

Experience

OF HISTORY

Students will experience history interactively:

- With *Connect History*—a visual, auditory, and interactive online experience—students no longer skim a text passively for facts and dates to memorize. They engage with what they read through hands-on activities, and they expand upon and apply what they learn in the process.
- Through its features, *Traditions & Encounters* emphasizes the point that history is not just a collection of facts. It is rather a creative effort based on detective work of historians examining evidence from the past and the analysis of themes that cross cultural boundary lines.
- New "Thinking About Traditions" and "Thinking About Encounters" boxes pose critical-thinking questions about the ways these twin themes play out across cultures and time periods.
- Images—paintings, mosaics, photos, posters, sculptures, architecture, and the like—draw students into the related narrative, and extended captions help them learn how to analyze visual clues to the past.

thinking about **TRADITIONS**

Competing Christianities

The Byzantine empire and western Europe inherited the same Christianity from the late Roman empire. How did Christianity develop along distinct lines in the two regions? What influences contributed to the development of such different understandings of Christianity?

CONNECT TO

Success

IN HISTORY

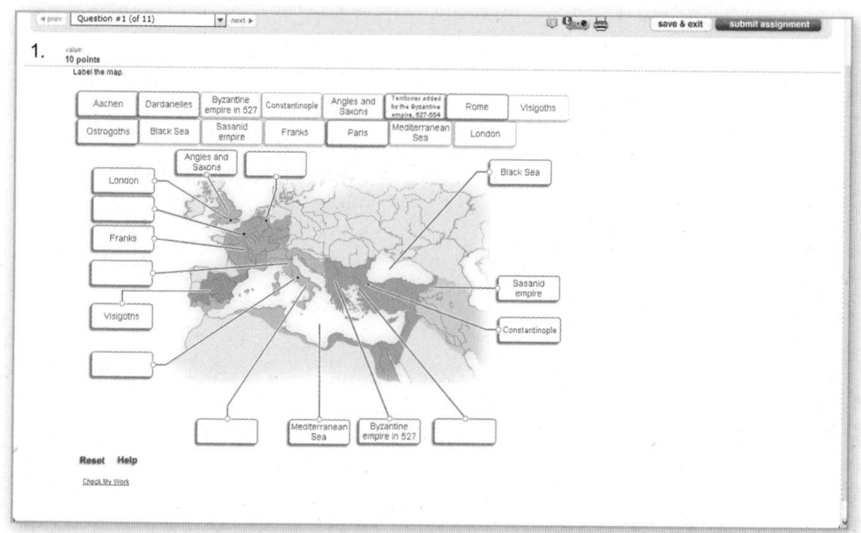

Connect History paves a path to student success:

- *Connect History,* a groundbreaking digital learning solution, helps students study more effectively—confirming what they know and pushing their learning further through engaging activities.
- *Connect History* works in tandem with questions accompanying image captions and primary sources in each chapter and builds a personalized study plan for each student.
- *Connect History* builds critical-thinking skills by placing students in a historical "critical mission" scenario and asking them to examine, evaluate, and analyze relevant data to support a recommended action.
- *Connect History* includes tools for understanding maps and geography, analyzing primary source documents, and writing a research paper (including documenting sources and avoiding plagiarism).

Traditions & Encounters

A Global Perspective on the Past

AP* Edition

Jerry H. Bentley
University of Hawai`i

Herbert F. Ziegler
University of Hawai`i

Reinforced Binding

What does it mean?

This textbook is widely adopted by colleges and universities yet it is frequently used in high school for teaching Advanced Placement,* honors and electives courses. Since high schools frequently adopt for several years, it is important that a textbook can withstand the wear and tear of usage by multiple students. To ensure durability, McGraw-Hill has elected to manufacture this textbook in compliance with the "Manufacturing Standards and Specifications for Textbook Administrators" (MSST) published by the National Association of State Textbook Administrators (NASTA). The MSST manufacturing guidelines provide minimum standards for the binding, paper type, and other physical characteristics of a text with the goal of making it more durable.

The McGraw·Hill Companies

Published by McGraw-Hill, an imprint of The McGraw-Hill Companies, Inc., 1221 Avenue of the Americas, New York, NY 10020.

This book is printed on acid-free paper.

2 3 4 5 6 7 8 9 10 DOW 15 14 13 12 11

ISBN: 978-0-07-659438-2
MHID: 0-07-659438-6

Vice President Editorial: *Michael Ryan*
Publisher: *Christopher Freitag*
Sponsoring Editor: *Matthew Busbridge*
Executive Marketing Manager: *Stacy Best Ruel*
Executive Director of Development: *Lisa Pinto*
Senior Developmental Editor: *Mikola De Roo*
Editorial Coordinators: *Elena Mackawgy, Jaclyn Mautone*
Senior Production Editor: *Carey Eisner*
Art Editor: *Robin Mouat*
Cartography: *Mapping Specialists and Mary Swab*
Design Manager: *Jeanne Schreiber*
Interior Designer: *Amanda Kavanagh*
Cover Designer: *Kirk DouPonce, DogEared Design*
Manager, Photo Research: *Brian J. Pecko*
Buyer II: *Tandra Jorgensen*
Composition: *9/12 Garamond Book by Thompson Type*
Printing: *R.R. Donnelley*

Cover: Painted limestone sculpture of a scribe: © Erich Lessing/Art Resource, NY; 13th cent. illustration of a Muslim traveler passing a lively agricultural village on camel: © Art Resource, NY; Lucas Cranach painting of Martin Luther, 1525: © Scala/Art Resource, NY; Image of Mohandas Ghandi: © Bettmann/Corbis; Omnipotent Technology: © Sanford/Agliolo/Corbis; Illustration of Dona Marina translating for Hernan Cortez entering an alliance with Tlaxcala ruler: Benson Latin American Collection, General Libraries, University of Texas at Austin; Earth: © istockphoto .com/7nuit

Library of Congress Cataloging-in-Publication Data

Bentley, Jerry H., 1949–
Traditions & encounters : a global perspective on the past / Jerry Bentley, Herbert Ziegler. — 5th ed.
v. cm.
Includes bibliographical references and index.
ISBN-13: 978-0-07-659438-2 (hardcover : alk. paper)
ISBN-10: 0-07-659438-6 (hardcover : alk. paper)

1. World history. 2. Intercultural communication—History. I. Ziegler, Herbert F., 1949– II. Title. III. Title: Traditions and encounters.
D20.B42 2011
909—dc22

2010036144

The Internet addresses listed in the text were accurate at the time of publication. The inclusion of a Web site does not indicate an endorsement by the authors or McGraw-Hill, and McGraw-Hill does not guarantee the accuracy of the information presented at these sites.

www.glencoe.com

brief contents

part 4

part 5

part 6

part 7

contents

part 1

part 2

AP Themes: The Formation of Classical Societies, 500 B.C.E. to 500 C.E. 128

part 3

AP Themes: The Postclassical Era, 500 to 1000 C.E. 256

part 5

AP Themes: The Origins of Global Interdependence, 1500 to 1800 462

part 6

AP Themes: An Age of Revolution, Industry, and Empire, 1750 to 1914 618

好他是還

maps

sources from the past

preface

Since its first edition, *Traditions & Encounters* has broken new ground. It has explored the grand scheme of world history as a product of real-life human beings pursuing their individual and collective interests. It has also offered a global perspective on the past by focusing on both the distinctive characteristics of individual societies and the connections that have linked the fortunes of different societies. It has combined a clear chronological framework with the twin themes of tradition and encounter, which help to make the unwieldy story of world history both more manageable and more engaging. From the beginning, *Traditions & Encounters* has offered an inclusive vision of the global past—one that is meaningful and appropriate for the interdependent world of contemporary times.

With this fifth edition, *Traditions & Encounters* takes another bold step and becomes the first truly interactive world history program by integrating an engaging text narrative with an innovative online learning platform, *Connect History.** The narrative and analysis of world history presented in *Traditions & Encounters* are now married to *Connect History*'s hands-on online activities, an adaptive diagnostic, and additional pedagogy, primers, and resources. The result is a unique learning environment that promotes active student learning, student success, and better course results.
(*A fully integrated e-book is included in *Connect Plus History.*)

How does *Traditions & Encounters* help students comprehend what they read?

Traditions & Encounters connects students to the story of world history.

A Cohesive Organization that Frames Global History into Seven Eras. How is it possible to make sense of the entire human past? Given the diversity of human societies, gathering and organizing the sheer mass of information in a meaningful way is a daunting challenge for any world history survey course. *Traditions & Encounters* addresses this challenge through its seven-part chronological organization, which enables students to understand the development of the world through time while also exploring broader, big-picture thematic issues in world history.

Captivating Stories of World History, in Geographical Context. Chapter-opening "Eyewitness" vignettes and an engaging narrative of the people and processes that have shaped world history work together with a highly praised map program to lend a strong framework to historical knowledge—clearly connecting the *who* and the *what* of world history (individual human actors, networks of communication and exchange, significant events, and global processes) to the *when* and the *where* (the chronological and geographical context).

The Quest for Political Order
The Early Byzantine Empire
Muslim Conquests and Byzantine Revival
The Rise of the Franks
The Age of the Vikings
Economy and Society in Early Medieval Europe
The Two Economies of Early Medieval Europe
Social Development in the Two Worlds of Christendom
The Evolution of Christian Societies in Byzantium and Western Europe
Popes and Patriarchs
Monks and Missionaries
Two Churches

EYEWITNESS:
Emperor Charlemagne and His Elephant

In the year 802 C.E., an unusual traveler arrived at Aachen (in modern Germany), capital of the western European empire ruled by Charlemagne. The traveler was a rare albino elephant, a diplomatic gift from the Abbasid caliph Harun al-Rashid to Charlemagne. The elephant—whom Harun named Abu al-Abbas, in honor of the Abbasid dynasty's founder—was born in India and went to Baghdad with his trainer in about 798. From Baghdad the animal accompanied an embassy overland through Syria and Egypt to a port on the Tunisian coast, then sailed across the Mediterranean to Portovenere (near Genoa in northern Italy), and finally trekked across the Alps and overland to Charlemagne's court. Abu al-Abbas must have shivered through the cold, damp winters of Europe. Yet he enjoyed swimming in the Rhine River, and until his death in 810, he amazed and delighted all who beheld him.

Charlemagne was not a friend of Islam. At the battle of Tours (732 C.E.), his grandfather, Charles Martel, had defeated a Muslim army that ventured into Frankish territory after Muslim forces had conquered most of the Iberian peninsula. Charlemagne himself fought Muslims in an unsuccessful effort to restore Christian rule in northern Spain. One of the battles from his campaign provided the raw material for a popular poetic work called the *Song of Roland*. Nevertheless, in spite of his personal religious preferences, Charlemagne found it both necessary and convenient to have diplomatic dealings with Harun al-Rashid.

Charlemagne dispatched at least three embassies to Baghdad and received three in return. The embassies dealt with several issues: the safety of Christian pilgrims and merchants traveling in Abbasid-controlled Syria and Palestine, Charlemagne's relations with Muslim neighbors, and policy toward the Byzantine empire, which stood between western Europe and the Abbasid caliphate. Charlemagne's realm was weak and poor compared with the Abbasid empire, but for about half a century, it seemed that Charlemagne and his successors might be able to reestablish a centralized imperial state in western Europe. His dealings with Harun al-Rashid—and the unusual odyssey of the elephant Abu al-Abbas—reflected a general recognition that Charlemagne had the potential to establish a western European empire similar to the Byzantine and Abbasid realms.

327

Online Activities in *Connect History* Turn Reading about World History into a Hands-On, Sensory Learning Experience. The activities in *Connect History,* a new Web-based assignment and assessment platform, are based on the narrative content of *Traditions & Encounters,* so they build on what students learn from reading the text and push them to explore that knowledge at greater depth. Making full use of the Web's flexibility as a learning platform, the activities in *Connect History* take a range of forms—textual, audio, and visual—and address multiple learning styles. Some exercises require students to interact with and analyze images and primary sources; others prompt students to compare and contrast the political structures or religious beliefs of different cultures they've been reading about; still others assess students' knowledge of chronology or geography. Across the board, these activities prompt active dialogue between student and text. Further, *Connect History* for AP students provides AP-style chapter and part questions as well as two complete practice exams. As a result, students go beyond reading to engagement and interaction with the tools of world history as well as developing their test-taking skills.

How does *Traditions & Encounters* guide students from seeing history as an assortment of facts to a hands-on, interactive engagement with the past?

Traditions & Encounters connects students to the experience of world history.

A Pair of Themes Organize the Complexity of Global Human Experience. Since its first edition, *Traditions & Encounters* has used its title's twin themes to bring focus to the vastness of world history. The "tradition" theme draws attention to the distinctive political, social, economic, and cultural traditions that the world's peoples have devised to organize their societies and guide their affairs:

> *What forms of political leadership have different peoples devised?* • *How have the world's peoples exploited natural resources to provide themselves with food, shelter, and other necessities?* • *What forms of social organization have different peoples developed, on the basis of birth, class, wealth, gender, ethnicity, or other criteria?* • *What kinds of religious beliefs have the world's peoples espoused, which scientific and philosophical ideas have they explored, and what artistic and cultural practices have they pursued?*

The "encounter" theme directs attention to the networks of transportation, communication, and exchange that have linked individual societies to one another through processes of cross-cultural interaction:

> *Why have individuals left their own societies to explore the larger world?* • *What kinds of relationships did they establish with their counterparts in other societies?* • *What networks of transportation, communication, and exchange did they construct to sustain interactions among different societies?* • *What effects did these exchanges have on the societies that engaged in dealings with one another?*

Through new chapter-level and part-level features, the hallmark twin themes of *Traditions & Encounters* emerge in greater clarity than ever before in this fifth edition. As a result, students have resources that enable them to move beyond the facts of history and examine the past critically, analyze causes and effects, and recognize similarities and differences across world regions and time periods. By digging deeper into the implications of world history's stories—not just the *who,* the *what,* and the *where,* but also the *why* and the *how*—students can make sense of the human past.

***Connect History* Activities, Learning Scenarios, and Intellectual Tools that Hone Students' Analytical Skills.** *Connect History* offers a range of online resources and assignments designed to cultivate the skills that enable students to think like historians—from geography diagnostics and primary source tutorials to exercises in the critical analysis of historical images, artifacts, and primary sources. These tools help students read maps, understand geography, question primary sources and other historical evidence, and develop the skills of analysis and synthesis.

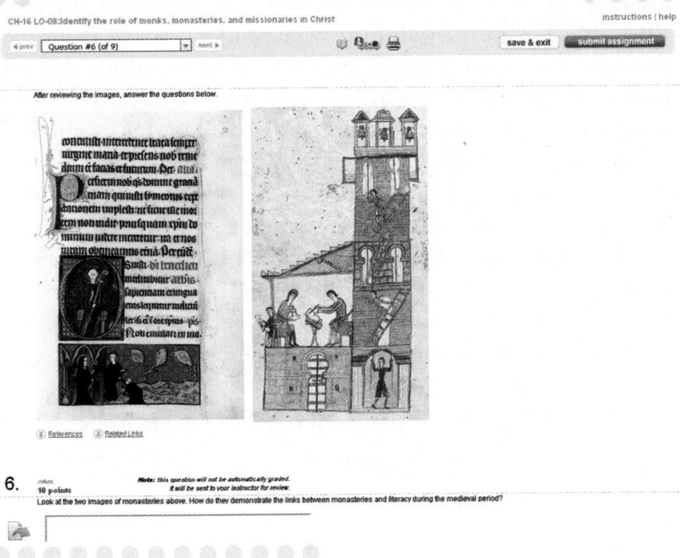

How does *Traditions & Encounters* enable students to comprehend reading assignments, think critically about important issues, and prepare for essays and exams?

Traditions & Encounters connects students to success in your world history course.

Comprehensive Chapter-Ending Pedagogy and Current Scholarship. Chronology boxes outline each chapter's most important dates and events. "In Perspective" sections, chapter-ending summaries, offer brief overviews of significant developments. "For Further Reading" sections, fully updated for the fifth edition, mention the most important works available about the chapter's topics and serve as a resource for further study or research projects. A running pronunciation guide appearing at the bottom of pages and an end-of-book glossary help students with unfamiliar names and terms.

Digital Assignments that Assess and Improve Students' Knowledge Base. The groundbreaking digital tools in *Connect History* enable students reading *Traditions & Encounters* to create a personalized study plan tailored to their own learning styles. By using the online diagnostics, exercises, and activities that *Connect History* provides for every chapter of *Traditions & Encounters,* students can clearly identify what they know well and what they need to study more carefully. The interactivity and assessment feedback of *Connect History* reinforces what students read, ensuring that they genuinely understand events and their sequence, key historical developments in chronological and geographical context, important concepts, and cause-and-effect relationships. As a result, students not only read more, but they also devote their studying time and energy to the most useful issues, and they are able to think and write critically about what they read.

CHANGES FOR THE FIFTH EDITION

PART 1: The Early Complex Societies, 3500 to 500 B.C.E.

CHAPTER 1: Before History

Revised discussions of early Homo sapiens *and* Homo erectus *use of language and communication, and expanded discussion on origins of agriculture*

CHAPTER 5: Early Society in East Asia

Expanded discussion of iron weapons in the Zhou dynasty

CHAPTER 6: Early Societies in the Americas and Oceania

Expanded discussion of migrations to the Americas and Oceania and revised discussion of Olmec influence in Mesoamerica

PART 2: The Formation of Classical Societies, 500 B.C.E. to 500 C.E.

CHAPTER 7: The Empires of Persia

Revised discussion of Xerxes' Persian rule in Mesopotamia and Egypt

CHAPTER 8: The Unification of China

Revised and expanded discussion of the Qin and Han emperors' bureaucracy and Ban Zhao's treatise

CHAPTER 9: State, Society, and the Quest for Salvation in India

New discussion of Ghandara-style art

CHAPTER 10: Mediterranean Society: The Greek Phase

Revised discussion of Socrates and new discussion of Greek contributions to the sciences and mathematics

CHAPTER 11: Mediterranean Society: The Roman Phase

New discussion of sea lanes and expanded discussion of Mediterranean trade

CHAPTER 12: Cross-Cultural Exchanges on the Silk Roads

Expanded discussion of the monsoon system and the spread of disease caused by maritime travel

PART 3: The Postclassical Era, 500 to 1000 C.E.

CHAPTER 13: The Expansive Realm of Islam

Revised and expanded discussion of Abbasid capital Baghdad and cultural adaptation

A brand-new "Sources from the Past," Al-Muqaddasi on Iraq in the late tenth century

CHAPTER 14: The Resurgence of Empire in East Asia

New discussion of Wu Zhao and the spread of Buddhism in China

CHAPTER 16: The Two Worlds of Christendom

A "Sources from the Past" included in Chapter 13 in the previous edition, Benjamin of Tudela on the Caliph's Court at Baghdad, now appears in this new chapter.

PART 4: The Acceleration of Cross-Cultural Interaction, 1000 to 1500 C.E.

CHAPTER 17: Nomadic Empires and Eurasian Integration

New discussion of nomadic pastoralists in Central Asia

A brand-new "Sources from the Past," William of Rubruck on Gender Relations among the Mongols

CHAPTER 18: States and Societies of Sub-Saharan Africa

New discussion of Jenne-jeno and revised discussion of the effects of the slave trade in sub-Saharan Africa

CHAPTER 19: The Increasing Influence of Europe

New discussion of the decline of the Byzantine empire and revised discussion of Christian influence during the High Middle Ages, the Bogomils and Cathars heresies, and the Crusades of 1095

PART 5: The Origins of Global Interdependence, 1500 to 1800

CHAPTER 22: Transoceanic Encounters and Global Connections

Revised discussion of the effects of the Columbian exchange of food crops, goods and animals, and world population growth

CHAPTER 23: The Transformation of Europe

New discussion of notable female scientists, including Émilie du Châtelet, and their contributions to the sciences during the sixteenth and seventeenth centuries

A brand-new "Sources from the Past," an excerpt from John Locke's An Essay Concerning Human Understanding

CHAPTER 24: New Worlds: The Americas and Oceania

New discussion of the effects of race and ethnicity on social hierarchy in colonial society

CHAPTER 27: The Islamic Empires

Revised discussion of the Ottoman Empire of early modern times and the three Islamic ruling empires

PART 6: An Age of Revolution, Industry, and Empire, 1750 to 1914

CHAPTER 28: Revolutions and National States in the Atlantic World

Revised and expanded discussion of revolutionary wars in America, France, and Haiti

CHAPTER 32: The Building of Global Empires

Expanded and revised discussion of the English East India Company and the Indian rebellion

A brand-new "Sources from the Past," The Royal Niger Company Mass-Produces Imperial Control in Africa

PART 7: Contemporary Global Realignments, 1914 to the Present

CHAPTER 33: The Great War: The World in Upheaval

A brand-new "Sources from the Past," Memorandum of the General Syrian Congress

CHAPTER 34: An Age of Anxiety

A brand-new "Sources from the Past," Joseph Stalin on the First Five-Year Plan

CHAPTER 36: New Conflagrations: World War II and the Cold War

New discussion of the medical mistreatment of POWs during the cold war

CHAPTER 38: A World without Borders

New discussion of the cold war, and revised discussion of globalization, developing economies, and climate change in the contemporary world

Two brand-new "Sources from the Past": an excerpt on climate change from Al Gore's An Inconvenient Truth, *and Aung San Suu Kyi's Politics and Family: The Hope of and for Girl Children*

NEW FEATURES AND CHANGES THROUGHOUT THE TEXT

AP Content. This new edition of *Traditions and Encounters* offers a variety of AP-specific content. Each Part begins with an opener focusing on the AP World History Themes. These pages also show how the Key Concepts and Historical Thinking Skills are addressed in each part of the book. Additionally, we have included critical thinking questions called Assessing the AP Themes at the end of each part.

"Thinking About" features. New "Thinking About Traditions" and "Thinking About Encounters" boxes focus on historical elements that highlight how the twin themes of traditions and encounters play out across cultures and time periods. Each box ends with related critical-thinking questions around these two forces that have shaped world history.

New primary sources. Eight brand-new "Sources from the Past," along with a wealth of resources in *Connect History* provide students with plenty of opportunities for critical analyses of primary sources. The primary sources new to this edition: Al-Muqaddasi, on Iraq in the Late Tenth Century; William of Rubruck on Gender Relations among the Mongols; an excerpt from John Locke's *An Essay Concerning Human Understanding;* The Royal Niger Company Mass-Produces Imperial Control in Africa; Memorandum from the General Syrian Congress; Joseph Stalin on the First Five-Year Plan; an excerpt on climate change from Al Gore's *An Inconvenient Truth,* and Aung San Suu Kyi's "Politics and Family: The Hope of and for Girl Children."

New part-ending features. "State of the World" assesses the global themes covered during the preceding chapters, giving students a thematic big-picture snapshot—both textually and visually using a combined global map and timeline—of the world during a particular period.

New map program. An entirely redesigned map program offers superior clarity, better topographical information, and greater global geographical precision and context with more vivid and distinct use of color and new globe locator icons within regional maps to better orient students. Extended captions with critical-thinking questions enrich students' understanding of the relationship between geography and history.

Fresh, inviting design for visual engagement and ease of use. An engaging, modern, and vivid design with new images and extended captions draws students into the narrative, provides visual cues for remembering content, and makes content easier to parse and digest.

Streamlined organization. Reorganization of content reduces the total number of chapters in the text, making the individual volumes more manageable to teach in one semester.

A new Chapter 16, "The Two Worlds of Christendom," combines elements of former Chapters 13 and 17 and places Europe in a more global perspective.

Elimination of the prior edition's Chapter 38 ("The Bipolar World") integrates the events of the cold war more seamlessly and clearly into coverage of World War II (Chapter 36, "New Conflagrations: World War II") and post–World War II decline of imperialist empires (Chapter 37, "The End of Empire").

OUTSTANDING FEATURES OF

Traditions & Encounters

FIFTH EDITION:

more emphasis on critical thinking and analysis

thinking about ENCOUNTERS

Trading-Post Empires
Trading-post empires provided the most prominent spaces for cross-cultural interactions between Europeans, Africans, and Asians. Trading posts also limited European intrusion into Africa and Asia, especially in contrast to the settlement empires of the Americas. What characterized the relations between, for example, the Portuguese and the inhabitants of the Indian Ocean basin? Why were Europeans confined to such posts?

thinking about TRADITIONS

Empires and Their Roads
All the classical empires invested resources in the building of roads and transportation networks that helped them to integrate their vast territories into manageable societies. Compare the road system of the Roman empire with those of the Persian, Han, and Mauryan empires. How did Roman roads complement Mediterranean sea lanes to link regions of the empire?

NEW

"Thinking About Traditions" and "Thinking About Encounters" boxes

These brief boxes—one of each in every chapter—spotlight instances in which the traditions and encounters themes arise in specific historical contexts. Each box ends with critical-thinking questions that prompt reflection about the roles of traditions and encounters in shaping the global past.

NEW

"Sources From the Past"

Every chapter showcases primary source documents—letters, journal entries, political tracts, philosophical reflections, religious writings, and other relevant primary sources. Each source concludes with a critical-thinking question that prompts students to explore the issues raised in the document. The fifth edition includes eight brand-new "Sources from the Past"—including Stalin's thoughts about his First Five-Year Plan and an excerpt from Al Gore's *An Inconvenient Truth.* Together with a wealth of resources in *Connect History,* students have numerous opportunities for critical analyses of primary sources.

sources from the past

The Royal Niger Company Mass-Produces Imperial Control in Africa

The 1880s proved a crucial time for sub-Saharan African societies and European imperial adventurers. European nations at the Berlin Conference set forth the rules by which they would partition and rule African states, and then those nations—such as Great Britain—commissioned companies like the Royal Niger Company to assert imperial prerogatives. To fend off French competitors in the Niger River delta, the British-controlled Royal Niger Company had local rulers sign its "standard treaty," a mass-produced, fill-in-the-blank treaty that essentially ceded trade and political control to the company, and thus to Britain, in what became the British colony of Nigeria.

We, the undersigned Chiefs of _________, with the view to the bettering of the condition of our country and our people, do this day cede to the Royal Niger Company, for ever, the whole of our territory from _________.

We also give to the said Royal Niger Company full power to settle all native disputes arising from any cause whatever, and we pledge ourselves not to enter into any war with other tribes without the sanction of the said Royal Niger Company.

We understand that the said Royal Niger Company have full power to mine, farm, and build in any portion of our country.

We bind ourselves not to have any intercourse with any strangers or foreigners except through the said Royal Niger Company.

In consideration of the foregoing, the said Royal Niger Company (Chartered and Limited) bind themselves not to interfere with any of the native laws or customs of the country, consistently with the maintenance of order and good government.

The said Royal Niger Company agree to pay native owners of land a reasonable amount for any portion they may require.

The said Royal Niger Company bind themselves to protect the said Chiefs from the attacks of any neighboring aggressive tribes.

The said Royal Niger Company also agree to pay the said Chiefs _________ measures native value.

We, the undersigned witnesses, do hereby solemnly declare that the _________ Chiefs whose names are placed opposite their respective crosses have in our presence affixed their crosses of their own free will and consent, and that the said _________ has in our presence affixed his signature.

Done in triplicate at _________, this _________ day of _________, 188__.

Declaration by interpreter I, _________, of _________, do hereby solemnly declare that I am well acquainted with the language of the country, and that on the _________ day of _________, 188__, I truly and faithfully explained the above Agreement to all the Chiefs present, and that they understood its meaning.

For Further Reflection

- What did this "standard treaty" promise to Nigerian leaders, and what was expected in return? Given language barriers and imperial greed, do you believe Nigerians received true and faithful explanations of the treaty's meaning?

Source: Alfred J. Andrea and James H. Overfield, eds. *The Human Record: Sources of Global History,* 3rd ed., vol. 2. Boston: Wadsworth, 1998, pp. 299–300.

strong support for the AP themes discussed in each era

part 3

THE POSTCLASSICAL ERA 500 TO 1000 C.E.

Chapter 21 ▪ Reaching Out: Expanding Horizons of Cross-Cultural Interaction 459

Assessing AP Themes

For Further Reading

NEW
Part Openers

Each Part Opener in this new AP Edition of *Traditions and Encounters,* written by Ane Lintvedt-Dulac and reviewed by the textbook author, Jerry Bentley, has been written to demonstrate how the chapters relate to the AP Themes. In addition, we have added icons  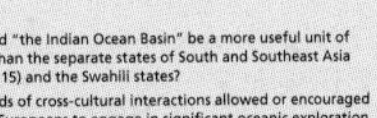 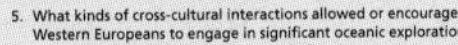 to show where the Historical Thinking Skills are addressed. These part openers will help students better see the connection between the themes, Historical Thinking Skills, and Key Concepts.

NEW
Assessing AP Themes

These thought provoking questions were added to this AP Edition to help students and teachers connect the content in each part to the AP World History Themes. These questions provide excellent preparation for the AP Exam.

A World on the Point of Global Integration

When Christopher Columbus and his crew sailed across the Atlantic Ocean in 1492, the world's peoples were no strangers to long-distance travels and meetings, nor were cross-cultural interactions and exchanges foreign experiences for them. Peoples of the world's three major geographical zones—the eastern hemisphere, the western hemisphere, and Oceania—had been dealing for thousands of years with counterparts from different societies. Even as they built their own distinctive political, social, economic, and cultural traditions, the world's peoples also engaged the larger world beyond their own societies. Their interactions were often hostile or unpleasant, taking the form of raids, wars, campaigns of imperial expansion, or transmissions of epidemic diseases. Yet their engagements frequently took more peaceful and beneficial forms, as trade, missionary activity, technological diffusion, and the spread of agricultural crops linked peoples of different societies.

Until 1492, however, long-distance travels and cross-cultural interactions took place mostly within the world's three broad regions. With rare and fleeting exceptions, peoples of the eastern hemisphere, the western hemisphere, and Oceania kept to their own parts of the world. They rarely possessed nautical technologies that would have enabled them to cross the earth's oceans regularly and carry on sustained relationships with peoples across the waters. Even when sufficient nautical technologies were available, the costs, dangers, and uncertain prospects of transoceanic voyaging mostly discouraged mariners from making efforts to venture beyond their own zones.

Developments of the era 1000 to 1500 were the immediate context for efforts to cross the world's largest bodies of water. Even as they carried out brutal campaigns of conquest, peoples of nomadic pastoral societies forged links between settled agricultural societies throughout Eurasia and created a demand for continuing relationships, particularly commercial relationships. While Turkish and Mongol peoples wielded more influence than any of their nomadic ancestors in Eurasia, Muslim Arab and Persian merchants drew the societies of sub-Saharan Africa increasingly into interaction with others of the eastern hemisphere. The region of the eastern hemisphere with the most to gain from transoceanic voyaging was western Europe, which otherwise had few good routes providing access to lands to the south and east. Thus, even though mariners from China, India, Persia, the Pacific islands, and other lands also possessed effective nautical technologies, it is not surprising that western European peoples most energetically and most systematically explored opportunities to establish maritime networks of travel, transport, trade, communication, and exchange.

In the year 1500 the world stood on the brink of a new era in the experience of humankind. Peoples of the world's three major geographical zones—the eastern hemisphere, the western hemisphere, and Oceania—were poised to enter into permanent and sustained interaction. The results of their engagements were profitable or beneficial for some peoples but difficult or disastrous for others. It is impossible to comprehend them except in context of the acceleration of cross-cultural interaction in the era 1000 to 1500.

460

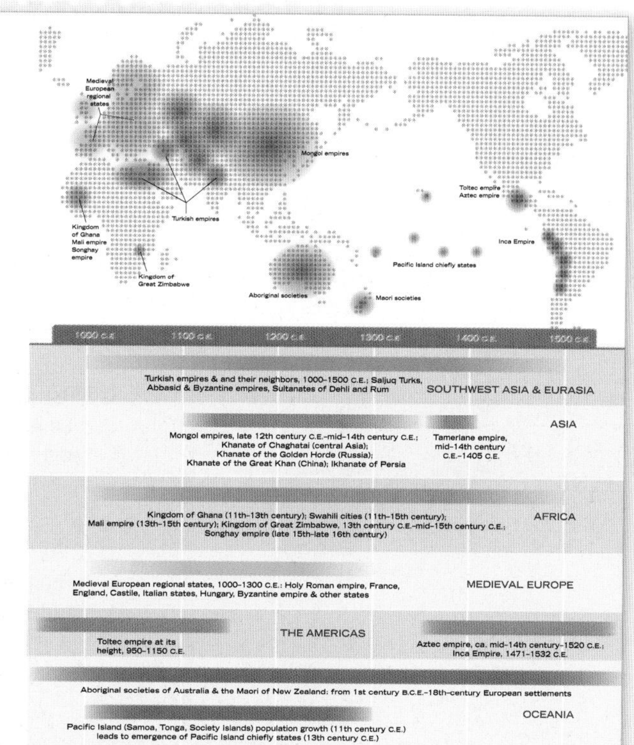

NEW

"State of the World" Part Closers

Each part now ends with a "State of the World" essay, which reassesses the global themes and includes a global map and timeline. These new pages provide a comprehensive review of the preceding chapters. For the AP student, these pages are an excellent tool to make comparisons between different regions of the world during the same era.

A watercolor painting from sixteenth-century Iran depicts a caravan of pilgrims traveling to Mecca while making the hajj. In what ways did the hajj facilitate social and business relationships?

Integrated Illustrations Program

Images that personalize the past by depicting everyday individuals at work and play are well integrated with the larger narrative, enhancing and supporting the themes of traditions and encounters.

- Critical-thinking questions enable students to analyze illustrations in the historical and cultural contexts discussed in the text.

a visual program that deepens the understanding of world history

NEW
Maps Program

The entire map program has been redesigned to make topographical features clearer and boundaries more distinct. Regional maps include new globe locator icons that place individual regions in global context.

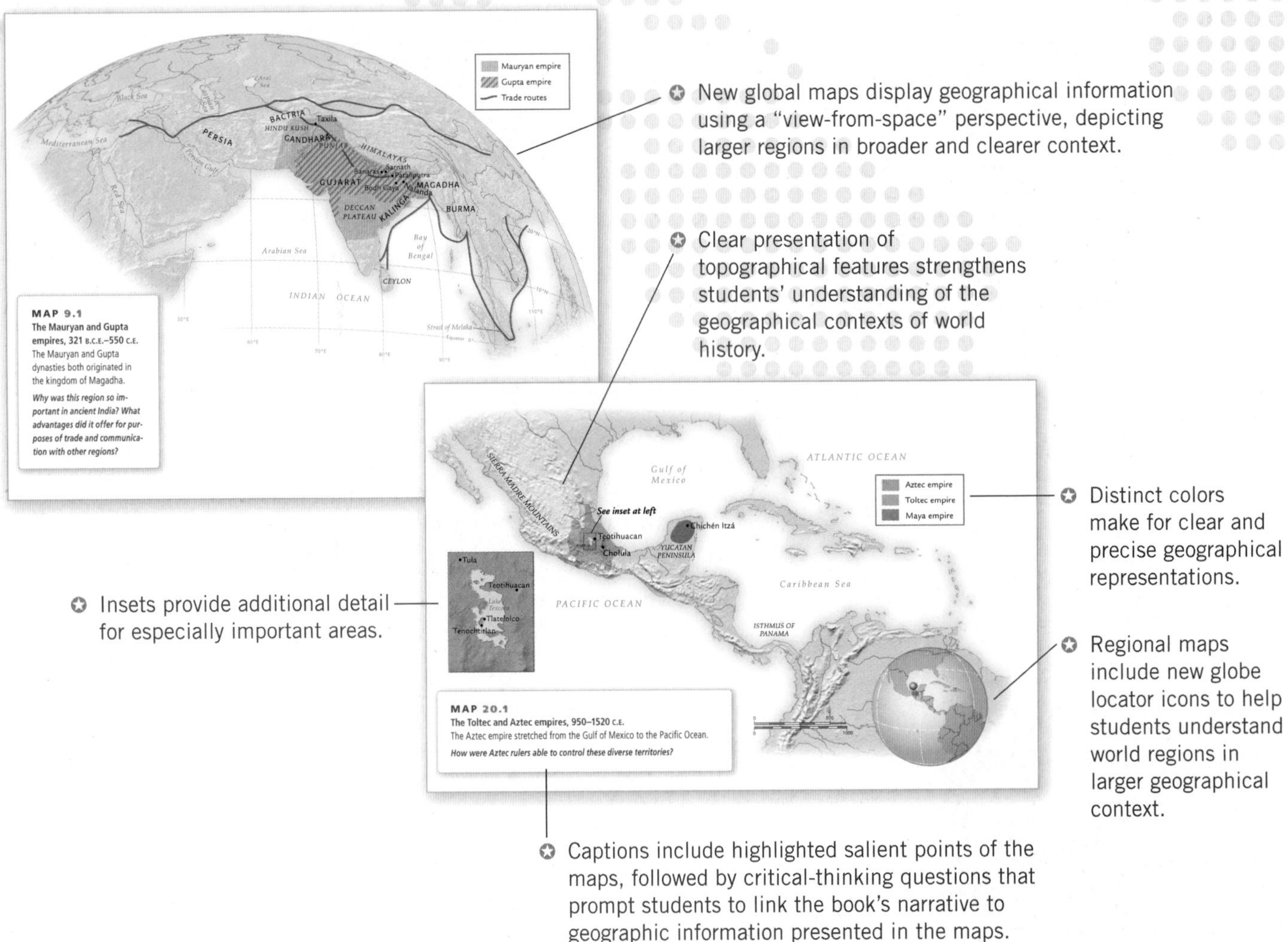

MAP 9.1
The Mauryan and Gupta empires, 321 B.C.E.–550 C.E.
The Mauryan and Gupta dynasties both originated in the kingdom of Magadha.
Why was this region so important in ancient India? What advantages did it offer for purposes of trade and communication with other regions?

MAP 20.1
The Toltec and Aztec empires, 950–1520 C.E.
The Aztec empire stretched from the Gulf of Mexico to the Pacific Ocean.
How were Aztec rulers able to control these diverse territories?

a brief note on usage

This book qualifies dates as B.C.E. ("Before the Common Era") or C.E. ("Common Era"). In practice, B.C.E. refers to the same epoch as B.C. ("Before Christ"), and C.E. refers to the same epoch as A.D. (*Anno Domini,* a Latin term meaning "in the year of the Lord"). As historical study becomes a global, multicultural enterprise, however, scholars increasingly prefer terminology that does not apply the standards of one society to all the others. Thus reference in this book to B.C.E. and C.E. reflects emerging scholarly convention concerning the qualification of historical dates.

Measurements of length and distance appear here according to the metric system, followed by their English-system equivalents in parentheses.

The book transliterates Chinese names and terms into English according to the *pinyin* system, which has largely displaced the more cumbersome Wade-Giles system. Transliteration of names and terms from other languages follows contemporary scholarly conventions.

supplements

AP PRACTICE BOOKLET

This supplemental booklet provides students with two practice tests based on the new AP World History Course Description. This booklet provides AP students with a chance to prepare for the new AP exam format. It also provides students with helpful hints and background information about the new exam. The answers to the practice exams, including Free-Response Questions, are located on the Online Learning Center.

PRIMARY SOURCE INVESTIGATOR FOR ADVANCED PLACEMENT

McGraw-Hill's Primary Source Investigator (PSI) is available online at www.glencoe.com/psi and gives AP students and teachers access to more than 650 primary and secondary sources, including documents, images, maps, and videos correlated to the chapter content. Additionally, there is a new primary source questioning strategy section and a complete set of Document-based Questions to develop skills for the AP exam.

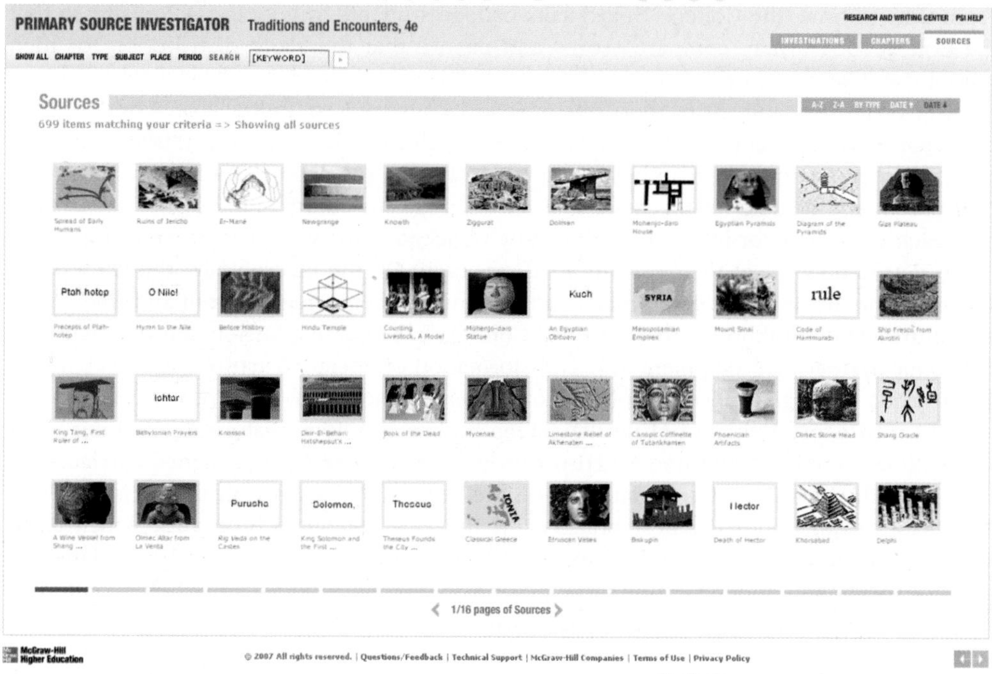

ONLINE LEARNING CENTER

The Online Learning Center (www.glencoe.com/bentleyAP5) includes a computerized test bank, PowerPoint slides, and a wealth of AP-specific content, including a variety of multiple-choice and essay questions to use as practice in preparation for the AP exam. The password-protected teacher side of the Online Learning Center contains the AP Teacher's Manual, Test Bank files, and other valuable materials to help teachers design and enhance the course. The teacher side of the OLC also provides teachers with rubrics to use in grading the Assessing AP Themes questions located at the end of each part, as well as rubrics to the AP specific questions located on the PSI and answers to the practice tests in the AP Practice Booklet.

about the AP world history course

COURSE THEMES AND STRUCTURE

The Advanced Placement (AP) program was created by the College Board, which also developed the SAT exam. The AP World History course descriptions and exams are written by the AP World History Development Committee, which consists of college history professors and high school teachers with experience teaching the AP World History course. This committee has studied the World History course descriptions from hundreds of university professors to determine which concepts to include in the AP World History course descriptions and the focus of the AP World History exams. The College Board requires audits of high school courses with the AP designation to ensure that the high school curriculum meets standards equivalent to the best practices of college World History courses. From time to time, the College Board asks college students to take the AP exam, so that the College Board may compare scores and ensure that the score distribution for high school test-takers is appropriate.

Between 2006 and 2010, the College Board convened committees of World History professors and experienced AP teachers to tweak the original course description in order to align the course with collegiate best practices and make the course description both more transparent and flexible for teachers. The redesigned Curriculum Framework has six Periods, each with three, or in one case four, Key Concepts. This will make it easier for teachers to decide how to set their priorities for coverage. On the macro-scale, the five Course Themes (Interaction Between Humans and the Environment; Development and Interaction of Cultures; State-Building, Expansion and Conflict; Creation, Expansion and Interaction of Economic Systems; Development and Transformation of Social Structures) are unchanged, and provide the organizational tools for teachers and students to analyze the content. The nine World History Habits of Mind have been replaced by four Historical Thinking Skills that will be common to all three AP History courses as each of the redesigned curricula are launched. The inclusion of and emphasis on the Historical Thinking Skills aligns the three AP History exams with the best practices of the best collegiate programs, which teach students how to use the distinctive analytical skills of historians. For world historians, the skills of seeing and understanding large patterns of change, and learning how to compare historical events over time and space, are particularly significant.

PERIODS IN THE REDESIGNED CURRICULUM FRAMEWORK

The periods, which form the backbone of the course, are essentially the same as they have been in previous years. There are four minor changes: suggested coverage time has been adjusted slightly; the Foundations period (c. 8000 B.C.E. to c. 600 C.E.) has been broken into two periods; "circa" or "c." has been added to the dates; and the period 1750 to 1914 has been adjusted to c. 1750 to c. 1900.

The earliest part of human history has been given its own period (Period 1: Technological and Environmental Transformations, to c. 600 B.C.E.). It is only to be given 5% of the course coverage, however. This changes the emphasis of the course to a more modern bias. What used to be the Foundations Era, receiving 20% of the coverage time, is now

5% for Period 1 and 15% for Period 2. The shift is the emphasis: don't spend much time on the pre-Classical history. All the other Periods should receive 20% of course coverage.

"Circa" has been added to all the dates of all the Periods in order in increase or encourage flexibility with dates. Teachers should feel free to play with the beginning and end dates of the Periods if it makes the teaching of the Key Concepts more effective. For example, one can teach the establishment of Islam in Period 2 (c. 600 B.C.E. to c. 600 C.E.) even though it's not established as a significant religion until a century later. Thematically, however, it belongs with the teaching of the other world religions. Along the same lines, 1914 had been changed to c. 1900 simply because 1914 was the only event-specific date in the course chronology. Teachers are free to teach the causes of the Great War as part of the c. 1750–c. 1900 period or the c. 1900 to the Present period, as they see fitting into the themes they are emphasizing. If there's a question about where a significant event should be placed, Theme should trump Chronology. Teachers need to be transparent about this, and explain what they are doing to the students. It will not matter where the Great War is placed, for example, in the scoring of an essay, as long as the student can explain it as either the logical end of Imperialism or the logical beginning of the destructive 20th century, or both.

KEY CONCEPTS IN THE REDESIGNED CURRICULUM FRAMEWORK

The most significant change in the AP Course Description is the development of the Key Concepts. Each Period has three Key Concepts (and c. 1750–c. 1900 has four). These Key Concepts should help teacher and students focus on the most important themes of a particular Period. They should simplify the task of organizing what materials one must teach, and how one can organize and present that material in a coherent way. The Key Concepts are also Global in nature, thus helping teachers and students to rise above the minutia and tie specific events to larger global processes. The Key Concepts also lend themselves to creating essay questions for classroom assessment purposes. Below is the list of Key Concepts as provided by the College Board:

Key Concepts:

1.1. Big Geography and the Peopling of the Earth
1.2. The Neolithic Revolution and Early Agricultural Societies
1.3. The Development and Interactions of Early Agricultural, Pastoral and Urban Societies
2.1. The Development and Codification of Religious and Cultural Traditions
2.2. The Development of States and Empires
2.3. Emergence of Transregional Networks of Communication and Exchange
3.1. Expansion and Intensification of Communication and Exchange Networks
3.2. Continuity and Innovation of State Forms and Their Interactions
3.3. Increased Economic Productive Capacity and Its Consequences
4.1. Globalizing Networks of Communication and Exchange
4.2. New Forms of Social Organization and Modes of Production
4.3. State Consolidation and Imperial Expansion
5.1. Industrialization and Global Capitalism
5.2. Imperialism and Nation-State Formation
5.3. Nationalism, Revolution and Reform
5.4. Global Migration
6.1. Science and the Environment
6.2. Global Conflicts and Their Consequences
6.3. New Conceptualizations of Global Economy, Society and Culture

Throughout the Curriculum Framework, examples of historical content are provided. The required content is indicated. There are also suggestions for content, usually in parentheses or indicated in a sidebar note. These suggestions are meant to give teachers permission to explore a particular Key Concept in a variety of ways or in greater depth.

HISTORICAL THINKING SKILLS IN THE REDESIGNED CURRICULUM FRAMEWORK

The nine Habits of Mind in the earlier Course Description booklets have been replaced by four Historical Thinking Skills in the redesigned Curriculum Framework. In fact, all three AP history courses (World, US, and European) will use the same Historical Thinking Skills to teach historical analysis and research. The Historical Thinking Skills are: Crafting Historical Arguments from Historical Evidence; Applying Chronological Reasoning Skills; Applying Comparison and Contextualization Skills; and Applying Historical Interpretation and Synthesis.

The AP World History exam is designed to evaluate how well students have learned to think like historians, not merely test them on content knowledge. The Curriculum Framework on the AP Central website has the best descriptions of how the four Historical Thinking Skills are applied to World History in particular. What follows here is a brief summation of those explanations.

1. **Crafting Historical Arguments from Historical Evidence.** Students will need to be taught how to write an analytical essay and to identify and evaluate a historical argument. This means, ideally, that students will be exposed to both reading and writing of historical arguments in each of the Periods studied. Students will also have to be able to interpret, draw inferences, and assess the validity of historical documents. Students should be exposed to as many documents of as many different types as possible in the course of the AP World History class. Historians work with documents, not textbooks, after all.
2. **Chronological Reasoning.** Students will need to assess patterns of Change and Continuity over Time. This is the essence of all historical study. One of the essay questions on the AP exam is a CCOT question. Students do not need to memorize endless lists of dates for AP World History. Instead, they need to internalize the logic of the Periods or the periodization of the course. The test essays are structured by these periods and the Key Concepts that drive them.
3. **Comparison and Contextualization.** In some ways, comparison is the easiest Historical Thinking Skill to learn. AP students need to be able to compare within one society or among several societies; and to compare across time and space. To contextualize, however, is a more difficult skill. Students need to be able to take the history of a specific region and show how it fits into the larger story of world history as a whole. For example, how does the history of trade along the Silk roads in the Post-Classical period fit into the larger world historical themes of "Creation, Expansion and Interaction of Economic Systems" and "Development and Interaction of Cultures"?
4. **Applying Historical Interpretation and Synthesis.** World historians have to be careful not to impose the values and viewpoints (interpretations) of their own societies on the many different societies they are studying, and understand that each society may interpret the past in its own way. As for the skill of synthesis in world history, is it possible to bring many different regional histories into a single narrative of world history?

The AP World History Curriculum has been tweaked, not changed dramatically. The four Historical Thinking Skills and the Key Concepts of each period have been written to help clarify the vast scope and sequence of the course. The new Curriculum Framework should be easier to understand and should give teachers more leeway in the content they teach while focusing students on the big picture of key world-historical skills.

AP WORLD HISTORY CHRONOLOGICAL CORRELATION

Period	Pages
Period 1: Technological and Environmental Transformations, to c. 600 B.C.E.	
• Key Concept 1.1. Big Geography and the Peopling of the Earth	
I. Archeological evidence indicates that during the Paleolithic era, hunting-foraging bands of humans gradually migrated from their origin in East Africa to Eurasia, Australia and the Americas, adapting their technology and cultures to new climate regions.	2, 3, 7, 10–15
• Key Concept 1.2. The Neolithic Revolution and Early Agricultural Societies	
I. Beginning about 10,000 years ago, the Neolithic Revolution led to the development of new and more complex economic and social systems.	2, 3, 16–19, 22, 23, 53
II. Agriculture and pastoralism began to transform human societies.	2, 3, 17–22
• Key Concept 1.3. The Development and Interactions of Early Agricultural, Pastoral, and Urban Societies	
I. Core and foundational civilizations developed in a variety of geographical and environmental settings where agriculture flourished.	2, 3, 25–27, 49–65, 72–76, 87–104, 109–111, 116–118
II. The first states emerged within core civilizations	2–6, 26–37, 43–45, 49–65, 102
III. Culture played a significant role in unifying states through laws, language, literature, religion, myths and monumental art.	2–3, 27–29, 32, 33, 35, 37–41, 43, 53, 55, 53–65, 73, 74, 76–84, 97–102, 109–111, 128, 129, 142–145
Period 2: Organization and Reorganization of Human Societies, c. 600 B.C.E. to 600 C.E.	
• Key Concept 2.1. The Development and Codification of Religious and Cultural Traditions	
I. Codifications and further developments of existing religious traditions provided a bond among the people and an ethical code to live by.	77–84, 128, 129, 144, 145, 182–185, 226, 227
II. New belief systems and cultural traditions emerged and spread, often asserting universal truths.	128, 129, 150–154, 179–182, 204–208, 225–229
III. Belief systems affected gender roles (such as Buddhism's encouragement of a monastic life or Confucianism's emphasis on filial piety).	162, 229
IV. Other religious and cultural traditions continued parallel to the codified, written belief systems in core civilizations.	67, 68, 97, 98, 128, 129
V. Artistic expressions, including literature and drama, architecture, and sculpture, show distinctive cultural developments.	111, 112, 115, 128, 129, 182–185, 194, 197, 207, 222, 223

• Key Concept 2.2. The Development of States and Empires	
I. The number and size of imperial societies grew dramatically by imposing political unity on areas where previously there had been competing states.	111–116, 118, 128, 129, 132–138, 156–162, 170–174, 194–201, 215–220
II. Empires and states developed new techniques of imperial administration based, in part, on the success of earlier political forms.	128, 129, 134, 135, 138, 139, 141, 142, 156–160, 171, 172, 215–220
III. Imperial societies displayed unique social and economic dimensions.	112, 115, 116, 128, 129, 134, 139, 159, 162, 164, 165, 171, 172, 175–177, 193, 201, 203, 204, 214, 222–225, 329, 330
IV. The Roman, Han, Maurya and Gupta empires created political, cultural and administrative difficulties that they could not manage, which eventually led to their decline, collapse and transformation into successor empires or states.	128, 129, 161–165, 174, 244, 245, 247–250
• Key Concept 2.3. Emergence of Transregional Networks of Communication and Exchange	
I. Land and water routes created transregional trade, communication and exchange networks in the Eastern Hemisphere, while separate networks connected the peoples and societies of the Americas somewhat later.	118, 128, 129, 194, 195, 235–239, 374–377
II. New technologies facilitated long-distance communication and exchange.	128, 129, 235, 270, 271, 312–314
III. Alongside the trade in goods, the exchange of people, technology, religious and cultural beliefs, food crops, domesticated animals, and disease pathogens developed across far-flung networks of communication and exchange.	128, 129, 135 140, 182, 229, 239–244
Period 3: Regional and Transregional Interactions, c. 600 C.E. to c. 1450	
• Key Concept 3.1. Expansion and Intensification of Communication and Exchange Networks	
I. Improved transportation technologies and commercial practices led to an increased volume of trade, and expanded the geographical range of existing and newly active trade networks.	256, 257, 267–272, 282–286, 289, 292, 293, 298, 299, 311–313, 323, 324, 350, 351, 364, 365, 374–375, 379, 380, 397–401, 415–418, 423
II. The movement of peoples caused environmental and linguistic effects.	121–123, 256, 257, 270, 334–336, 350, 351, 354, 372–375, 379
III. Cross-cultural exchanges were fostered by the intensification of existing, or the creation of new, networks of trade and communication.	256, 257, 264–266, 277, 278, 281, 282, 291–292, 296–298, 320–324, 350, 351, 361, 362, 376–382, 416, 417, 435–440
IV. There was continued diffusion of crops and pathogens throughout the Eastern Hemisphere along the trade routes.	256, 257, 268, 269, 288, 366, 372, 445–447

• Key Concept 3.2. Continuity and Innovation of State Forms and Their Interactions	
I. Empires collapsed and were reconstituted; in some regions new state forms emerged.	111, 112, 256, 257, 267, 268, 275–277, 283–285, 299–301, 308, 309, 328–332, 366, 397, 418, 425
II. Interregional contacts and conflicts between states and empires encouraged significant technological and cultural transfers, for example between Tang China and the Abbasids, across the Mongol empires and during the Crusades.	256, 257, 293, 294, 350, 351, 364, 365, 412
• Key Concept 3.3. Increased Economic Productive Capacity and Its Consequences	
I. Innovations stimulated agricultural and industrial production in many regions.	256, 257, 268, 269, 288, 290, 291, 313, 314, 350, 351, 397, 412, 418, 443
II. The fate of cities varied greatly, with periods of significant decline, and with periods of increased urbanization buoyed by rising productivity and expanding trade networks.	256, 257, 289, 290, 350, 351, 366, 398, 399, 436, 437, 445–447
III. Despite significant continuities in social structures and in methods of production, there were also some important changes in labor management and in the effect of religious conversion on gender relations and family life.	256, 257, 272, 273, 285, 286, 290, 298, 299, 343, 344, 350, 351, 354–356, 382–385, 400–404, 427
Period 4: Global Interactions, c. 1450 to c. 1750	
• Key Concept 4.1. Globalizing Networks of Communication and Exchange	
I. In the context of the new global circulation of goods, there was an intensification of all existing regional trade networks that brought prosperity and economic disruption to the merchants and governments in the trading regions of the Indian Ocean, Mediterranean, Sahara and overland Eurasia.	462, 463,465–468, 477, 478, 550, 551
II. European technological developments in cartography and navigation built on previous knowledge developed in the classical, Islamic and Asian worlds, and included the production of new tools (such as the astrolabe or revised maps), innovations in ship designs (such as caravels), and an improved understanding of global wind and currents patterns—all of which made transoceanic travel and trade possible.	462, 463, 468, 469
III. Remarkable new transoceanic maritime reconnaissance occurred in this period.	462–463, 470–475, 537, 541–545, 580

IV. The new global circulation of goods was facilitated by royal chartered European monopoly companies that took silver from Spanish colonies in the Americas to purchase Asian goods for the Atlantic markets, but regional markets continued to flourish in Afro-Eurasia by using established commercial practices and new transoceanic shipping services developed by European merchants.	462, 463, 475–477, 488, 489, 510, 511, 533–535
V. The new connections between the Eastern and Western hemispheres resulted in the Columbian Exchange.	462, 463, 486–489
VI. The increase in interactions between newly connected hemispheres and intensification of connections within hemispheres expanded the spread and reform of existing religions and created syncretic belief systems and practices.	462, 463, 494, 495, 539–541, 556, 588, 605, 606
VII. As merchants' profits increased and governments collected more taxes, funding for the visual and performing arts, even for popular audiences, increased.	450–452, 497, 584, 588–590, 600, 604
• Key Concept 4.2. New Forms of Social Organization and Modes of Production	
I. Traditional peasant agriculture increased and changed, plantations expanded, and demand for labor increased. These changes both fed and responded to growing global demand for raw materials and finished products.	462, 463, 482, 483, 534–536, 539–540, 558–568, 582
II. As new social and political elites changed, they also restructured new ethnic, racial and gender hierarchies.	462, 463, 503, 504, 511, 512, 533, 534, 562–564, 575, 582, 586, 587
• Key Concept 4.3. State Consolidation and Imperial Expansion	
I. Rulers used a variety of methods to legitimize and consolidate their power.	421, 462, 463, 503–505, 547–578, 587, 588, 597–600, 605–608
II. Imperial expansion relied on the increased use of gunpowder, cannons and armed trade to establish large empires in both hemispheres.	462, 463, 476–478, 481–483, 529–532, 574–576, 596–598, 600–603
III. Competition over trade routes (such as Omani-European rivalry in the Indian Ocean or piracy in the Caribbean), state rivalries (such as the Thirty Years War or the Ottoman-Safavid conflict) and local resistance (such as bread riots) all provided significant challenges to state consolidation and expansion.	462, 463, 483, 497, 498
Period 5: Industrialization and Global Interaction, c. 1750 to c. 1900	
• Key Concept 5.1. Industrialization and Global Capitalism	
I. Industrialization fundamentally changed how goods were produced.	618, 619, 652–659, 665, 666, 714, 715, 726, 727

II. New patterns of global trade and production developed that further integrated the global economy as industrialists sought raw materials and new markets for the increasing amount of goods produced in their factories.	618, 619, 671–673, 691, 693, 694, 717–719, 741
III. To facilitate investments at all levels of industrial production, financiers developed and expanded various financial institutions.	512, 513, 637, 659
IV. There were major developments in transportation and communication, including railroads, steamships, telegraphs and canals.	655, 659
V. The development and spread of global capitalism led to a variety of responses.	618, 619, 667–671, 707, 710, 711, 714, 722–727
VI. The ways in which people organized themselves into societies also underwent significant transformations in industrialized states due to the fundamental restructuring of the global economy.	618, 619, 660–667
• Key Concept 5.2. Imperialism and Nation-State Formation	
I. Industrializing powers established transoceanic empires.	693–695, 717–719, 736–746
II. Imperialism influenced state formation and contraction around the world.	481–483, 618, 619, 645, 646, 678–682, 724–727, 741, 742, 747
III. New racial ideologies, especially Social Darwinism, facilitated and justified imperialism.	752
• Key Concept 5.3. Nationalism, Revolution and Reform	
I. The rise and diffusion of Enlightenment thought that questioned established traditions in all areas of life often preceded the revolutions and rebellions against existing governments.	517, 518, 618, 619, 622–624
II. Beginning in the 18th century, peoples around the world developed a new sense of commonality based on language, religion, social customs and territory. These newly imagined national communities linked this identity with the borders of the state, while governments used this idea to unite diverse populations.	641, 642
III. The spread of Enlightenment ideas and increasing discontent with imperial rule propelled reformist and revolutionary movements.	565, 618, 619, 624–629, 631–637, 670, 671, 680, 710, 712, 719–724, 737
IV. The global spread of Enlightenment thought and the increasing number of rebellions stimulated new transnational ideologies and solidarities.	618, 619, 637–640, 668–670, 696
• Key Concept 5.4. Global Migration	
I. Migration in many cases was influenced by changes in demography in both industrialized and unindustrialized societies that presented challenges to existing patterns of living.	618, 619, 661–663

II. Migrants relocated for a variety of reasons.	618, 619, 663, 664, 689–691
III. The large-scale nature of migration, especially in the 19th century, produced a variety of consequences and reactions to the increasingly diverse societies on the part of migrants and the existing populations.	618, 619, 690, 691, 697
Period 6: Accelerating Global Change and Realignments, c. 1900 to the Present	
• Key Concept 6.1. Science and the Environment	
I. Researchers made rapid advances in science that spread throughout the world, assisted by the development of new technology.	760, 761, 794, 795, 881, 892, 898, 902, 903, 920, 921
II. Humans fundamentally changed their relationship with the environment.	760, 761, 903–905
III. Disease, scientific innovations and conflict led to demographic shifts.	662, 663, 760, 761, 770, 771, 845, 847, 848, 853, 905, 908–910
• Key Concept 6.2. Global Conflicts and Their Consequences	
I. Europe dominated the global political order at the beginning of the 20th century, but both land-based and transoceanic empires gave way to new forms of transregional political organization by the century's end.	717–724, 760, 761, 778, 779, 781–785, 814–816, 868–871, 874–876
II. Emerging ideologies of anti-imperialism contributed to the dissolution of empires.	815, 816, 824, 825, 867–871, 876, 877, 879, 880, 882, 886
III. Political changes were accompanied by major demographic and social consequences.	760, 761, 777, 783–785, 850–853, 867, 868, 919, 921
IV. Military conflicts occurred on an unprecedented global scale.	760, 761,765–767, 773–777, 836–842, 853–860, 894–896
V. Although conflict dominated much of the 20th century, many individuals and groups—including states—opposed this trend. Some individuals and groups, however, intensified the conflicts.	760, 761, 815, 868, 878, 879, 882, 885, 886, 910, 911
• Key Concept 6.3. New Conceptualizations of Global Economy, Society and Culture	
I. States, communities and individuals became increasingly interdependent, a process facilitated by the growth of institutions of global governance.	760, 761, 783, 854, 896, 897, 899, 900, 901, 912, 913
II. People conceptualized society and culture in new ways; some challenged old assumptions about race, class, gender and religion, often using new technologies to spread reconfigured traditions.	760, 761, 874, 913, 914
III. Popular and consumer culture became global.	n/a

AP WORLD HISTORY THEMATIC CORRELATION

Theme	Chapters/Pages
Theme 1: Interaction Between Humans and the Environment	
• Demography and disease	pp. 2, 17, 20, 22, 50, 67, 72, 116, 120; throughout Chapter 12; pp. 288–289, 311, 341–342, 351, 366, 372–373, 399, 430, 436, 446–447, 467, 475, 486–487, 508; throughout Chapter 24; pp. 558, 565, 579–580, 587, 604–605, 661–663, 744–745, 781; throughout Chapter 38
• Migration	pp. 7–9, 17; throughout Chapter 2; pp. 50, 52, 65–67, 76–77, 88; throughout Chapter 6; pp. 132, 170, 249, 299–300, 310, 315, 354–358, 372–374, 388, 417, 430–431, 488, 550, 642, 657, 663–664; throughout Chapter 30; pp. 716, 744–745, 750–751, 871, 917–921
• Patterns of settlement	Throughout Chapters 1–4; pp. 88–89, 101–104; throughout Chapter 6; p. 132
• Technology	Throughout Chapters 1, 2, 29, 38
Theme 2: Development and Interaction of Cultures	
• Religions	pp. 20, 38–39; throughout Chapters 3, 4; pp. 106–107, 112–114, 132, 136, 142–145; throughout Chapter 9; pp. 201, 206–208, 211–212, 225–229, 239–243; throughout Chapter 13; pp. 294–295, 300, 302, 306, 320–324, 356, 358, 361–365, 385–388, 405–407, 421–422, 426–427, 539–541, 556–557, 589, 605–607, 610, 680, 793
• Belief systems, philosophies and ideologies	pp. 150–155, 516–519; throughout Chapter 28; pp. 667–671, 778; throughout Chapter 34
• Science and technology	Throughout Chapter 3; p. 76; throughout Chapter 5; pp. 119–122, 160–163, 189–190, 222–223, 257, 270, 288–292, 332, 338–339, 356, 398, 442–445, 468–469, 507–508, 514–516, 581, 611, 734–736, 770–771, 857–860, 883, 903
• The arts and architecture	pp. 14–15, 31, 37, 91, 100–101, 109–112, 115, 151, 157, 165–166, 175, 182–183, 189–190, 203, 207, 300, 320, 448, 450–453, 566–567, 584, 589–590, 607, 695, 793, 795–797

Theme 3: State-Building, Expansion and Conflict	
• Political structures and forms of governance	pp. 27–33, 52–57, 73–74, 88–94; throughout Chapter 6; pp. 132–138, 156–162, 170–174; throughout Chapters 10–12; pp. 264–268, 282–288, 306–310, 320–322; throughout Chapters 16–20; pp. 447–450, 475–486, 498–508, 529–533, 550–555, 572–578, 585–587; throughout Chapters 27, 28, 31, 32; pp. 778–779; throughout Chapters 35, 37
• Empires	pp. 28–32, 132–138, 156–162, 170–174, 217–220, 244–250, 329–332; throughout Chapter 17; pp. 418–419, 475–486, 498–908, 528–531, 572–578; throughout Chapters 27, 31, 32
• Nations and nationalism	pp. 641–646, 753–754, 765, 777, 782, 787, 804, 807–810, 814–819, 823–825, 870–875, 882–883
• Revolts and revolutions	pp. 165–166, 245, 384–385, 502, 512–516, 536, 549, 565–567; throughout Chapter 28; pp. 670, 688–700, 706; throughout Chapter 31; pp. 737, 751, 777–780, 802, 816, 860, 876–877, 880–883, 893–894
• Regional, transregional, and global structures and organizations	pp. 783–785, 819–820, 839, 854–855, 872; throughout Chapter 38
Theme 4: Creation, Expansion and Interaction of Economic Systems	
• Agricultural and pastoral production	Throughout Chapter 1; pp. 36–37; throughout Chapters 3–6; pp. 138, 141, 162, 172, 221, 254, 257, 268–270, 288–290, 310–311, 351, 354–355, 372, 341–342, 372, 379, 398, 412; throughout Chapter 20; pp. 442–443, 487, 538–539, 558, 579, 587–588, 604, 803–804, 823
• Trade and commerce	pp. 14, 32–33, 40–41, 50, 59–62, 73–74, 101–102, 110–112, 116, 123, 131–132, 138, 142, 171–175, 190–195, 200–203, 221–223, 229, 234–239, 260, 270–272, 282–283, 288–294, 305–308, 311, 320, 337–339, 350, 355, 364, 372–379, 388, 399–402, 412, 418–419, 423, 428–429, 436–439, 462, 467–468, 476–479, 488–489, 525–526, 543, 559–561, 580–581, 605, 672–673, 899–900

• Labor systems	pp. 34–35, 39, 96–97, 140–141, 165, 194, 196, 203–204, 224–225, 271–272, 337–341, 384–385, 511–512; throughout Chapters 24, 25; pp. 573–574, 582, 633, 637–639; throughout Chapter 29; pp. 681–683, 696–968, 713–714, 741, 750–751, 823–825, 849, 907, 920
• Industrialization	p. 619; throughout Chapter 29
• Capitalism and socialism	pp. 494, 508–513, 652, 659, 667–671, 761, 802–804, 816–819, 826, 855, 857, 879–880, 892–896
Theme 5: Development and Transformation of Social Structures	
• Gender roles and relations	pp. 10–11, 15–16, 35, 59, 67, 79–80, 96–99, 140, 162, 175–176, 193, 203, 207, 223–224, 272–273, 290, 339–340, 355–366, 383–384, 402–404, 419–422, 427, 440–441, 515–516, 519, 533–534, 562–563, 578–579, 603–604, 621, 629, 638–640, 650–652, 655, 666–670, 696–697, 700, 773, 775, 808–809, 812–814, 836, 847, 852–854, 879, 886–887, 911, 914–918
• Family and kinship	pp. 35–36, 79, 97–99, 139, 151, 175–176, 203–204, 223–225, 244, 260, 290, 358, 373–374, 382–383, 512, 557–558, 565, 578–579, 665–667, 905, 907
• Racial and ethnic constructions	pp. 76–77, 533–534, 566–567; throughout Chapter 32; pp. 808–810, 824–825, 849–852, 871, 878–879
• Social and economic classes	pp. 10–11, 20–21, 26, 32–35, 45, 57–59, 74–75, 77–78, 94–97, 109, 112, 123, 132, 140–141, 143, 156, 164–165, 193, 213–217, 224, 245, 266–267, 288, 300–301, 340–341, 355, 382–385, 392 400–404, 419–421, 426–427, 430–432, 511–512, 573–574, 582–583, 587–588, 627–629, 663, 665–667, 713–714, 724–726, 823

about the authors

Jerry H. Bentley is professor of history at the University of Hawai`i and editor of the *Journal of World History.* He has written extensively on the cultural history of early modern Europe and on cross-cultural interactions in world history. His research on the religious, moral, and political writings of the Renaissance led to the publication of *Humanists and Holy Writ: New Testament Scholarship in the Renaissance* (1983) and *Politics and Culture in Renaissance Naples* (1987). His more recent research has concentrated on global history and particularly on processes of cross-cultural interaction. His book *Old World Encounters: Cross-Cultural Contacts and Exchanges in Pre-Modern Times* (1993) studies processes of cultural exchange and religious conversion before modern times, and his pamphlet *Shapes of World History in Twentieth-Century Scholarship* (1996) discusses the historiography of world history. His current interests include processes of cross-cultural interaction and cultural exchange in modern times.

Herbert F. Ziegler is an associate professor of history at the University of Hawai`i. He has taught world history since 1980 and currently serves as director of the world history program at the University of Hawai`i. He also serves as book review editor of the *Journal of World History.* His interest in twentieth-century European social and political history led to the publication of *Nazi Germany's New Aristocracy* (1990). He is at present working on a study that explores from a global point of view the demographic trends of the past ten thousand years, along with their concomitant technological, economic, and social developments. His other current research project focuses on the application of complexity theory to a comparative study of societies and their internal dynamics.

acknowledgments

Many individuals have contributed to this book, and the authors take pleasure in recording deep thanks for all the comments, criticism, advice, and suggestions that helped to improve the work. The editorial team at McGraw-Hill did an outstanding job of keeping the authors focused on the project. Special thanks go to Chris Freitag, Lisa Pinto, Matthew Busbridge, Mika De Roo, Arthur Pomponio, Carey Eisner, Stacy Best Ruel, Elena Mackawgy, Jaclyn Mautone, Sarah Remington, Robin Mouat, Jeanne Schreiber, and Brian J. Pecko, who provided crucial support by helping the authors work through difficult issues and solve the innumerable problems of content, style, and organization that arise in any project to produce a history of the world. Many colleagues at the University of Hawai`i and elsewhere aided and advised the authors on matters of organization and composition. Finally, we would like to express our appreciation for the advice of the following individuals, who read and commented on the fifth edition, as well as previous editions of *Traditions & Encounters*.

Manuscript Reviewers

Heather J. Abdelnur
Blackburn College

Henry Abramson
Florida Atlantic University

Wayne Ackerson
Salisbury University

Roger Adelson
Arizona State University

Sanjam Ahluwalia
Northern Arizona University

William Alexander
Norfolk State University

Alfred Andrea
University of Vermont

Ed Anson
University of Arkansas at Little Rock

Henry Antkiewicz
East Tennessee State University

Maria Arbelaez
University of Nebraska at Omaha

Peter Arnade
University of California, San Marcos

Karl Bahm
University of Wisconsin, Superior

Vaughan Baker
University of Louisiana at Lafayette

Gene Barnett
Calhoun Community College

Beth Allison Barr
Baylor University

Ian Barrow
Middlebury College

Dixee Bartholomew-Feis
Buena Vista University

Mike Balyo
Chemeketa Community College

Guy Beckwith
Auburn University

Lynda Bell
University of California, Riverside

Norman Bennett
Boston University

Houri Berberian
California State University, Long Beach

Robert Blackey
California State University, San Bernardino

David Blaylock
Eastern Kentucky University

Wayne Bodle
Indiana University of Pennsylvania

Beau Bowers
Central Piedmont Community College

Connie Brand
Meridian Community College

Michael Brescia
State University of New York, Fredonia

Brian T. Brownson
Murray State University

Samuel Brunk
University of Texas, El Paso

Deborah Buffton
University of Wisconsin, La Crosse

Maureen Burgess
Colorado State University

Rainer Buschmann
Hawai`i Pacific University

Sharon L. Bush
LeMoyne-Owen College

Antonio Calabria
University of Texas, San Antonio

Lewis Call
California Polytechnic State University, San Luis Obispo

Thomas Callahan, Jr.
Rider University

Alice-Catherine Carls
University of Tennessee at Martin

Kay Carr
Southern Illinois University

James Carroll
Iona College

Carol Carter
University of Central Arkansas

Tom Carty
Springfield College

Bruce Castleman
San Diego State University

Douglas Catterall
Cameron University

Douglas Chambers
University of Southern Mississippi, Hattiesburg

Choi Chatterjee
California State University, Los Angeles

Orazio Ciccarelli
University of Southern Mississippi

Andrew Clark
University of North Carolina at Wilmington

Hugh R. Clark
Ursinus College

Harold Cline
Middle Georgia College

Tim Coates
College of Charleston

Joan Coffey
Sam Houston State University

Daniel Connerton
North Adams State

Keith Cox
California State University

Bruce Cruikshank
Hastings College

Graciella Cruz-Tara
Florida Atlantic University

Lynn Curtright
Tallahassee Community College

Richard Cusimano
University of Louisiana at Lafayette

Ken Czech
St. Cloud State University

Francis K. Danquah
Southern University

Touraj Daryaee
California State University, Fullerton

Jon Davidann
Hawai`i Pacific University

Allen Davidson
Georgia Southern University

Denise Z. Davidson
Georgia State University

Brian Davies
University of Texas, San Antonio

John Davis
Radford University

Thomas Davis
Virginia Military Institute

Elisa Denlinger
University of Wisconsin, La Crosse

Stewart Dippel
University of the Ozarks

Kevin Dougherty
University of Southern Mississippi

Ross Doughty
Ursinus College

Cathi Dunkle
Mid-Michigan Community College

Ross Dunn
San Diego State University

Peter Dykema
Arkansas Tech University

Lane Earns
University of Wisconsin, Oshkosh

Christopher Ehret
University of California, Los Angeles

Laura Endicott
Southwestern Oklahoma State

Nancy Erickson
Erskine College

James Evans
Southeastern Community College

David Fahey
Miami University

Edward Farmer
University of Minnesota

James David Farthing
Oklahoma Baptist University

Lanny Fields
California State University, San Bernardino

Allan Fisher
Michigan State University

Robert Frankle
University of Memphis

Bonnie Frederick
Washington State University

Karl Friday
University of Georgia

Amy Froide
University of Tennessee, Chattanooga

James Fuller
University of Indianapolis

Jessie Ruth Gaston
California State University, Sacramento

Kurt Gingrich
Radford University

Robert Gomez
San Antonio College

Paul Goodwin
University of Connecticut, Storrs

Matthew Gordon
Miami University of Ohio

Steve Gosch
University of Wisconsin, Eau Claire

Andrew Goss
University of New Orleans

Joseph Gowaskie
Rider University

Sherry Sanders Gray
Mid-South Community College

Brian Gurian
Harrisburg Area Community College

John Haag
University of Georgia

Dr. John Haas
Cerritos College

Raymond J. Haberski, Jr.
Marian College

Jeffrey Hamilton
Baylor University

Michael Hamm
Centre College

Travis Hanes III
University of North Carolina—Wilmington

Eric J. Hanne
Florida Atlantic University

Preston Hardy, Jr.
University of Tennessee, Martin

Stephen Harmon
Pittsburg State University

Alice K. Harris
University of California, Davis

Russell Hart
Hawai`i Pacific University

John Hayden
Southwestern Oklahoma State

Randolph Head
University of California, Riverside

Mary Hedberg
Saginaw Valley State University

Gerald Herman
Northeastern University

David Hertzel
Southwestern Oklahoma State

Udo Heyn
California State University, Los Angeles

Kathryn Hodgkinson
The Hockaday School

Caroline Hoefferle
Wingate University

Peter Hoffenberg
University of Hawai`i, Manoa

Blair Holmes
Brigham Young University

Mary Hovanec
Cuyahoga Community College

Scott Howlett
Saddleback Community College

Kailai Huang
Massachusetts College of Liberal Arts

J. Sanders Huguenin
University of Science and Arts of Oklahoma

Richard Hume
Washington State University

Carol Sue Humphrey
Oklahoma Baptist University

Alfred Hunt
State University of New York

Rebecca C. Huskey
Georgia State University

Raymond Hylton
J. Sergeant Reynolds Community College

W. Scott Jessee
Appalachian State University

Phyllis Jestice
University of Southern Mississippi, Hattiesburg

Eric F. Johnson
Kutztown University of Pennsylvania

Cheryl Johnson-Odim
Loyola University

Kimberley Jones-de Oliveira
Long Island University

Jonathan Judaken
University of Memphis

Theodore Kallman
Delta College

Alan Karras
University of California, Berkeley

Thomas Kay
Wheaton College

Charles Keller
Pittsburgh State University

David L. Kenley
Elizabethtown College

Winston Kinsey
Appalachian State University

Cengiz Kirli
Purdue University

Mark Klobas
Scottsdale Community College

Paul Knoll
University of Southern California

Keith Knuuti
University of Hawai`i, Hilo

Kenneth Koons
Virginia Military Institute

Cheryl Koos
California State University, Los Angeles

Cynthia Kosso
Northern Arizona University

Zoltan Kramer
Central Washington University

James Krokar
DePaul University

Glenn Lamar
University of Louisiana at Lafayette

Lisa Lane
Miracosta College

George Lankevich
Bronx Community College

Dennis Laumann
University of Memphis

Donald Layton
Indiana State University

Loyd Lee
SUNY-New Paltz

Jess LeVine
Brookdale Community College

Keith Lewinstein
Bridgewater State University

Richard Lewis
St. Cloud State University

Yi Li
Tacoma Community College

Tony Litherland
Oklahoma Baptist University

Paul Lococo, Jr.
Leeward Community College

James Long
Colorado State University

David Longfellow
Baylor University

Christine E. Lovasz-Kaiser
University of Southern Indiana

Ben Lowe
Florida Atlantic University

Jared Ludlow
Brigham Young University, Hawai`i

Herbert Luft
Pepperdine Univeristy

Lu Lui
University of Tennessee—Knoxville

Paul Madden
Hardin-Simmons University

Moira Maguire
University of Arkansas, Little Rock

Farid Mahdavi
San Diego State University

Dorothea A. L. Martin
Appalachian State University

Tracey Martin
Benedictine University

Ken Mason
Santa Monica College

Robert Mathews
Northshore Community College

Laura E. Mayhall
The Catholic University of America

William Maynard
Arkansas State University

Robert McCormick
University of South Carolina—Spartanburg

Jeff McEwen
Chattanooga State Technical College

Randall McGowen
University of Oregon

Adam McKeown
Columbia University

John McNeill
Georgetown University

James McSwain
Tuskegee University

Pamela McVay
Ursuline College

John Mears
Southern Methodist University

Daniel Miller
Calvin College

Monserrat Miller
Marshall University

Laura Mitchell
University of Texas, San Antonio
David Montgomery
Brigham Young University
Garth Montgomery
Radford University
George Moore
San Jose State University
Gloria Morrow
Morgan State University
David Mungello
Baylor University
Jeffrey Myers
Avila College
Peter Nayenga
St. Cloud State University
Ruth Necheles-Jansyn
Long Island University
Virginia Carolyn Neel
(aka Carolyn Neel)
Arkansas Tech University
Eric Nelson
Missouri State University
Marian Nelson
University of Nebraska
Wing Chung Ng
University of Texas at San Antonio
C. Brid Nicholson
Kean University
Janise Nuckols
Windward Community College
Deanne Nuwer
University of Southern Mississippi, Hattiesburg
Greg O'Brien
University of Southern Mississippi, Hattiesburg
Thomas F. O'Brien
University of Houston
Agnes A. Odinga
Minnesota State University, Mankato
Veena Talwar Oldenburg
Baruch College
Brian O'Neil
University of Southern Mississippi
Patricia O'Niell
Central Oregon Community College
Samuel Oppenheim
California State University, Stanislaus
John Oriji
California Polytechnic State University, San Luis Obispo
Anne Osborne
Rider University
James Overfield
University of Vermont
Keith Pacholl
State University of West Georgia
Melvin Page
East Tennessee State University
Loretta Pang
Kapiolani Community College
Jean Paquette
Lander University
Jotham Parsons
University of Delaware
Denis Paz
University of North Texas
Patrick Peebles
University of Missouri—Kansas City
Peter W. Petschauer
Appalachian State University
Phyllis Pobst
Arkansas State University
Elizabeth Pollard
San Diego State University
Jon Porter
Franklin College
Carl J. Post
Essex County College
Clifton Potter
Lynchburg College
David Price
Santa Fe Community College
Rebecca Pulju
Kent State University
Alfonso Quiroz
Bernard M. Baruch College, CUNY
Julie Rancilio
Kapi`olani Community College
Stephen Rapp
Georgia State University
Vera Reber
Shippensburg University
John Reid
Georgia Southern University
Thomas Renna
Saginaw Valley State University
Diana Reynolds
Point Loma Nazarene University
Douglas Reynolds
Georgia State University
Ira Rice
Ball State University
Cheryl Riggs
California State University, San Bernardino
John Ritter
Chemeketa Community College
Leonard R. Ronaldson
Robert Morris University
Lynn Rose
Truman State University
Aviel Roshwald
Georgetown University
Chad Ross
East Carolina University
Dan Russell
Springfield College
Eric Rust
Baylor University
John Ryan
Kansas City Kansas Community College
Pamela G. Sayre
Henry Ford Community College
Cristofer Scarboro
King's College
William Schell
Murray State University
Daryl Schuster
University of Central Florida
Jane Scimeca
Brookdale Community College
Gary Scudder
Georgia Perimeter College
Kimberly Sebold
University of Maine, Presque Isle
Michael J. Seth
James Madison University
Tara Sethia
California State University, Pomona
Howard Shealy
Kennesaw State College
Nancy Shoemaker
University of Connecticut, Storrs
MaryAnn Sison
University of Southern Mississippi, Hattiesburg
Jonathan Skaff
Shippensburg University
David Smith
California State Polytechnic University, Pomona
Michael Smith
Purdue University
Roland Spickerman
University of Detroit—Mercy

Wendy St. Jean
Springfield College

Michelle Staley
East Mississippi Community College

Tracy Steele
Sam Houston State University

Richard Steigmann-Gall
Kent State University, Kent

John Steinberg
Georgia Southern University

Heather Streets
Washington State University

Laichen Sun
California State University, Fullerton

Roshanna Sylvester
California State University, Fullerton

Stephen Tallackson
Purdue University, Calumet

Lenette S. Taylor
Kent State University

John Thornton
Millersville University

Robert Tignor
Princeton University

Elisaveta B. Todorova
University of Cincinnati

James Tueller
Brigham Young University, Hawai`i

Kirk Tyvela
Ohio University

Michael G. Vann
California State University, Sacramento

Tom Velek
Mississippi University for Women

Deborah Vess
Georgia College and State University

John Voll
Georgetown University

Sandra Wagner-Wright
University of Hawai`i, Hilo

Mark Wasserman
Rutgers University

Jeff Wasserstrom
Indiana University—Bloomington

Mary Watrous-Schlesinger
Washington State University, Pullman

Theodore Weeks
Southern Illinois University

Guy Wells
Kent State University

Robert Wenke
University of Washington

Sally West
Truman State University

Sherri West
Brookdale Community College

Michael J. Whaley
Lindenwood University

Scott Wheeler
West Point

Joe Whitehorne
Lord Fairfax Community College

S. Jonathan Wiesen
Southern Illinois University, Carbondale

Anne Will
Skagit Valley Community College

Richard Williams
Washington State University

Allen Wittenborn
San Diego State University

David Wittner
Utica College

William Wood
Point Loma Nazarene University

John Woods
University of Chicago

Anand Yang
University of Utah

Ping Yao
California State University, Los Angeles

C. K. Yoon
James Madison University

Herb Zettl
Springfield College

Design Reviewers

Wayne Ackerson
Salisbury University

Hussein A. Amery
Colorado School of Mines

Michael Balyo
Chemeketa Community College

Carolyn Neel
Arkansas Tech University

C. Brid Nicholson
Kean University

Carl J. Post
Essex County College

Julie Rancilio
Kapi`olani Community College

Leah Renold
Texas State University

Pamela G. Sayre
Henry Ford Community College

Linda Bregstein Scherr
Mercer County Community College

Michael J. Seth
James Madison University

Elisaveta B. Todorova
University of Cincinnati

Michael G. Vann
California State University, Sacramento

Michael J. Whaley
Lindenwood University

Carlton Wilson
North Carolina Central University

Marc Zayac
Georgia Perimeter College

Connect History Board of Advisors

Clare Balawajder
Thomas Nelson Community College

Brett Berliner
Morgan State University

Jeff Bowersox
University of Southern Mississippi

Sue Gronewold
Kean University

Andrew P. Haley
University of Southern Mississippi

Linda Bregstein Sherr
Mercer County Community College

Brian Ulrich
Shippensburg University

Connect History Reviewers

Jennifer Foray
Purdue University

Aimee Harris-Johnson
El Paso Community College

Andrew Lewis
American University

Christine E. Lovasz-Kaiser
University of Southern Indiana

David Mock
Tallahassee Community College

Stuart Smith III
Germanna Community College

AP Reviewers

Elaine Evans
Charles Hart
Constance Hines
Branden Schield
Patrick Whelan

part 1

THE EARLY COMPLEX SOCIETIES, 3500 TO 500 B.C.E.

The first chapter in this textbook is called "Before History." What the authors mean by this is before *written* history. For most of human existence, humans didn't need to write. We could speak, we could draw, and we could create all sorts of useful tools, but we didn't need to use a written script. Someone would remember the information or see the drawing and explain it orally. HTS 1 To understand pre-written history, historians have to use fossils, cave drawings, and other physical objects (anthropological evidence). In AP World History, you are going to be asked to use many types of evidence to draw conclusions about what people were doing and thinking, how they were living and dying, as well as where they were going and why.

Archeological evidence shows us that humans (*Homo sapiens*) have existed for approximately 200,000 years. For 95 percent of this time, we hunted and gathered (or foraged) for food, organized in small kinship-based groups, gradually migrating by foot and boat from East Africa to all habitable continents. To adapt to the challenges of different geographical settings, including Ice Ages, humans developed tools. They shared or spread technologies and beliefs as they traveled and settled in particular places. These unwritten but crucial parts of human history are covered in the AP Key Concept of Big Geography (understanding the basic structures of the earth) and the Peopling of the Earth (how and why some humans migrated out of Africa). HTS 2 In the twenty-first century, we still need to understand how and why humans migrate—what pushes people out of their homeland, what pulls them to new places, and how people adapt to and change the environment in which they live.

The slow rate of change in human patterns of living sped up about 10,000 years ago. Some foragers on the Eurasian, African, and American continents began to settle in one place. Some raised plants and tamed animals (farmers), some just tamed animals and continued to migrate (pastoralists), while many remained foragers. Farming, or the domestication of plants and animals, ultimately changed almost every aspect of human life and the planet on which we live. The advent of farming is called the *Neolithic Revolution* by most historians, who use the date 8000 B.C.E. as a very general beginning point for modern human history. In AP World History, you are going to be asked to look for common characteristics and patterns of organization between these first settled communities in Eurasia, Africa, the Americas, and the Pacific Islands (Oceania).

Farming was (and is) much more work than foraging, but the benefits were potentially huge. Surplus food could be stored in a shed or house for later use. Surplus food meant healthier people and therefore larger populations. Some people within these larger populations could leave farming and take up specialized tasks like making storage vessels and tools or being warriors, and then trade their services for food. These artisans (skilled workers) settled into small village centers, then small towns, and finally cities by about 3000 B.C.E.

AP World History will focus primarily on people living in societies based on cities and their surrounding farmlands, called *urban-based complex societies* or *civilizations.* By the date 600 B.C.E., which ends Period 1 in AP World History, all the major types of political organization have appeared for the first time: foraging communities, farming and pastoralist communities, cities and city-states, kingdoms, and empires. These foundational civilizations, sometimes called "river civilizations," are the first complex societies you will study and compare. Remember, though, that the Olmecs in Mesoamerica and the Chavin in Andean mountains of South America weren't on rivers, so the term is a bit misleading. Nevertheless, societies in Mesopotamia, Egypt, the Indus River valley, the Yellow River valley, and in the Americas can be compared in terms of certain core characteristics: their cities, complex institutions (such as government bureaucracies, armies, and religious hierarchies), multi-layered social structures, record-keeping abilities, and organized long-distance trading relationships. Keeping track of people, ideas, money, and merchandise required record-keeping in these complex societies. This allows historians to evaluate written evidence in addition to archeological evidence to analyze ancient human societies.

In the original human forager societies, men and women only owned what they could carry and everyone did the same basic tasks within their gender roles. In farming, pastoralist, and urban-based societies, however, humans could own more and had specialized tasks that not everyone could do. Historians think that these new patterns of life led to the creation of *social classes*—some people being perceived as more important or more successful than other people—based on land and animal ownership, occupation, gender, and age. AP World History will ask you to evaluate to what extent these patterns of complex societies, and especially these patterns of social classes, remain with us today.

Culture often played a significant role in unifying different peoples in these early states through laws, language, literature, religion, myths, and monumental art. New religious beliefs including the Vedic/Hindu religion, Hebrew monotheism, and Zoroastrianism appeared in these early societies and had significant influence in later periods.

Most humans were still foragers in this early time period. Urban-based societies were the exception, not the rule, and they were not located very close to one another. And yet, there seems to have been some interactions between some of them, for example between the Mesopotamians and the Indus River valley peoples. Historians look for evidence of civilizations interacting peacefully through trade and travel or aggressively through military contacts and conquests. Why? Because merchants, missionaries, and the military spread goods, cultural and religious ideas, technologies and diseases between cities, and this introduced changes into societies. Look for the trade routes and who travels upon them as you study the civilizations in this era, and don't forget to watch for the pastoralists, who often served as the "truckers" along the trade routes.

These patterns of development and interaction, developed independently on four continents, and will continue to resonate in later periods in AP World History. Because this is the first time in human history we see patterns like these, historians sometimes call this very early period in human history—the Foundations period.

Before History

chapter 1

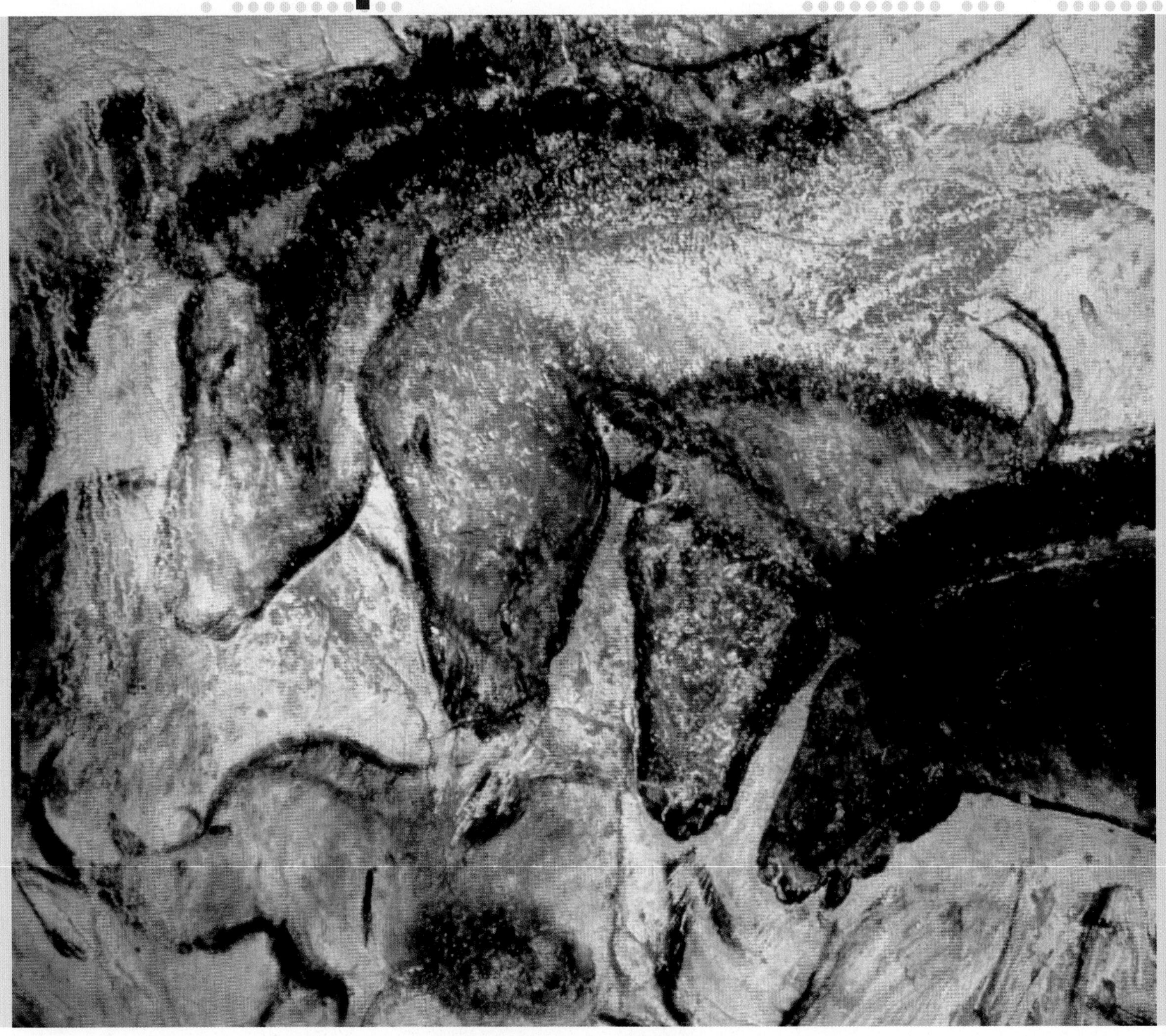

A quartet of horses depicted about thirty thousand years ago in a painting from the Chauvet cave in southern France.

EYEWITNESS:
Lucy and the Archaeologists

Throughout the evening of 30 November 1974, a tape player in an Ethiopian desert blared the Beatles' song "Lucy in the Sky with Diamonds" at top volume. The site was an archaeological camp at Hadar, a remote spot about 320 kilometers (200 miles) northeast of Addis Ababa. The music helped fuel a spirited celebration: earlier in the day, archaeologists had discovered the skeleton of a woman who died 3.2 million years ago. Scholars refer to this woman's skeleton as AL 288-1, but the woman herself has become by far the world's best-known prehistoric individual under the name Lucy.

At the time of her death, from unknown causes, Lucy was age twenty-five to thirty. She stood just over 1 meter (about 3.5 feet) tall and probably weighed about 25 kilograms (55 pounds). After she died, sand and mud covered Lucy's body, hardened gradually into rock, and entombed her remains. By 1974, however, rain waters had eroded the rock and exposed Lucy's fossilized skeleton. The archaeological team working at Hadar eventually found 40 percent of Lucy's bones, which together form one of the most complete and best-preserved skeletons of any early human ancestor. Later searches at Hadar turned up bones belonging to perhaps as many as sixty-five additional individuals, although no other collection of bones from Hadar rivals Lucy's skeleton for completeness.

Analysis of Lucy's skeleton and other bones found at Hadar demonstrates that the earliest ancestors of modern human beings walked upright on two feet. Erect walking is crucial for human beings because it frees their arms and hands for other tasks. Lucy and her contemporaries did not possess large or well-developed brains—Lucy's skull was about the size of a small grapefruit—but unlike the neighboring apes, which used their forelimbs for locomotion, Lucy and her companions could carry objects with their arms and manipulate tools with their dexterous hands. Those abilities enabled Lucy and her companions to survive better than many other species. As the brains of our human ancestors grew larger and more sophisticated—a process that occurred over a period of several million years—human beings learned to take even better advantage of their arms and hands and established flourishing communities throughout the world.

According to geologists the earth came into being about 4.5 billion years ago. The first living organisms made their appearance hundreds of millions of years later. In their wake came increasingly complex creatures such as fish, birds, reptiles, and mammals. About forty million years ago, short, hairy, monkeylike animals began to populate tropical regions of the world. Humanlike cousins to these animals began to appear only four or five million years ago, and our species, *Homo sapiens,* about two hundred thousand years ago.

Even the most sketchy review of the earth's natural history clearly shows that human society has not developed in a vacuum. The earliest human beings inhabited a world already well stocked with flora and fauna, a world shaped for countless eons by natural rhythms that governed the behavior of all the earth's creatures. Human beings made a place for themselves in this world, and over time they demonstrated remarkable ingenuity in devising ways to take advantage of the earth's resources. Indeed, it has become clear in recent years that the human animal has exploited the natural environment so thoroughly that the earth has undergone irreversible changes.

A discussion of such early times might seem peripheral to a book that deals with the history of human societies, their origins, development, and interactions. In conventional terminology, *prehistory* refers to the period before writing, and *history* refers to the era after the invention of writing enabled human communities to record and store information. It is certainly true that the availability of written documents vastly enhances the ability of scholars to understand past ages, but recent research by archaeologists and evolutionary biologists has brightly illuminated the physical and social development of early human beings. It is now clear that long before the invention of writing, human beings made a place for their species in the natural world and laid the social, economic, and cultural foundations on which their successors built increasingly complex societies.

THE EVOLUTION OF *HOMO SAPIENS*

During the past century or so, archaeologists, evolutionary biologists, and other scholars have vastly increased the understanding of human origins and the lives our distant ancestors led. Their work has done much to clarify the relationship between human beings and other animal species. On one hand, researchers have shown that human beings share some remarkable similarities with the large apes. This point is true not only of external features, such as physical form, but also of the basic elements of genetic makeup and body chemistry—DNA, chromosomal patterns, life-sustaining proteins, and blood types. In the case of some of these elements, scientists have been able to observe a difference of only 1.6 percent between the DNA of human beings and that of chimpanzees. Biologists therefore place human beings in the order of primates, along with monkeys, chimpanzees, gorillas, and the various other large apes.

On the other hand, human beings clearly stand out as the most distinctive of the primate species. Small differences in genetic makeup and body chemistry have led to enormous differences in levels of intelligence and ability to exercise control over the natural world. Human beings developed an extraordinarily high order of intelligence, which enabled them to devise tools, technologies, language skills, and other means of communication and cooperation. Whereas other animal species adapted physically and genetically to their natural environment, human beings altered the natural environment to suit their needs and desires—a process that began in remote prehistory and continues in the present day. Over the long term, too, intelligence endowed humans with immense potential for social and cultural development.

The Hominids

A series of spectacular discoveries in east Africa has thrown valuable light on the evolution of the human species. In Tanzania, Kenya, Ethiopia, and other places, archaeologists have unearthed bones and tools of human ancestors going back about five million years. The Olduvai Gorge in Tanzania and Hadar in Ethiopia have yielded especially rich remains of individuals like the famous Lucy. These individuals probably represented several different species belonging to the genus ***Australopithecus*** ("the southern ape"), which flourished in east Africa during the long period from about four million to one million years ago.

Australopithecus In spite of its name, *Australopithecus* was not an ape but, rather, a hominid—a creature belonging to the family Hominidae, which includes human and humanlike species. Evolutionary biologists recognize *Australopithecus* as a genus standing alongside *Homo* (the genus in which biologists place modern human beings) in the family of hominids. Compared with our species, *Homo sapiens,* Lucy and other australopithecines would seem short, hairy, and limited in intelligence. They stood something over 1 meter (3 feet) tall, weighed 25 to 55 kilograms (55 to 121 pounds), and had a brain size of about 500 cubic cen-

Australopithecus (ah-strah-loh-PITH-uh-kuhs)

timeters. (The brain size of modern humans averages about 1,400 cc.)

Compared with other ape and animal species, however, australopithecines were sophisticated creatures. They walked upright on two legs, which enabled them to use their arms independently for other tasks. They had well-developed hands with opposable thumbs, which enabled them to grasp tools and perform intricate operations. They almost certainly had some ability to communicate verbally, although analysis of their skulls suggests that the portion of the brain responsible for speech was not very large or well developed.

The intelligence of australopithecines was sufficient to allow them to plan complex ventures. They often traveled deliberately—over distances of 15 kilometers (9.3 miles) and more—to obtain the particular kinds of stone that they needed to fashion tools. Chemical analyses show that the stone from which australopithecines made tools was often available only at sites distant from the camps where archaeologists discovered the finished tools. Those tools included choppers, scrapers, and other implements for food preparation. With the aid of their tools and intelligence, australopithecines established themselves securely throughout most of eastern and southern Africa.

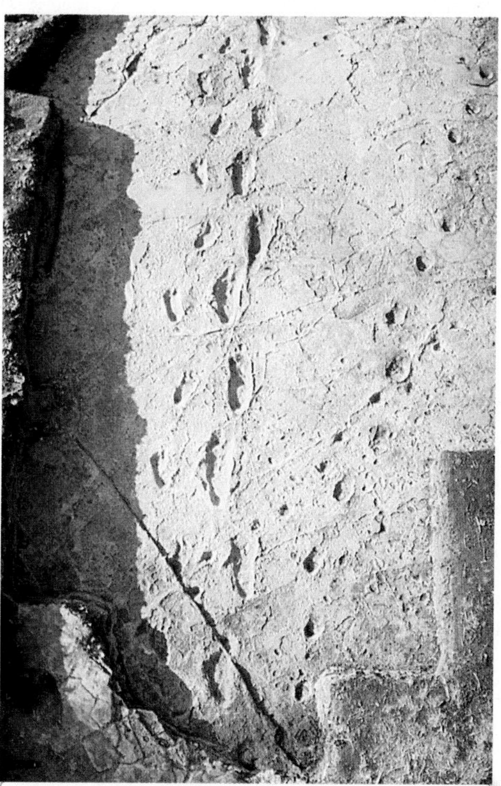

Fossilized footprints preserved near Olduvai Gorge in modern Tanzania show that hominids walked upright some 3.5 million years ago. These prints came from an adult walking on the left and a child on the right.

Homo erectus By about one million years ago, australopithecines had disappeared as new species of hominids possessing greater intelligence evolved and displaced their predecessors. The new species belonged to the genus *Homo* and thus represented creatures considerably different from the australopithecines. Most important of them was *Homo erectus*—"upright-walking human"—who flourished from about two million to two hundred thousand years ago. *Homo erectus* possessed a larger brain than the australopithecines—the average capacity was about 1,000 cc—and fashioned more sophisticated tools as well. To the australopithecine choppers and scrapers, *Homo erectus* added cleavers and hand axes, which not only were useful in food preparation but also provided protection against predators. *Homo erectus* also learned how to start and tend fires, which furnished the species with a means to cook food, a defense against large animals, and a source of artificial heat.

Even more important than tools and fire were intelligence and the ability to communicate complex ideas. *Homo erectus* individuals did not have the physiological means to enunciate the many sounds that are essential for sophisticated language, but they were able to devise plans, convey their intentions, and coordinate their activities. Archaeologists have found many sites that served as camps where *Homo erectus* groups congregated and collected food. They came together at these sites, bringing meat from small animals that they hunted as well as the plants and nuts that they gathered. They probably also scavenged the meat of large animals that had fallen prey to lions and other predators. The large quantities of food remains that archaeologists have excavated at these sites indicate that *Homo erectus* individuals had the ability to organize their activities and communicate plans for obtaining and distributing food.

Migrations of *Homo erectus*

With effective tools, fire, intelligence, and communication abilities, *Homo erectus* gained increasing control over the natural environment and introduced the human species into widely scattered regions. Whereas australopithecines had not ventured beyond eastern and southern Africa, *Homo erectus* migrated to north Africa and the Eurasian landmass. Almost two million years ago, *Homo erectus* groups moved to southwest Asia and beyond to Europe, south Asia, east Asia, and southeast Asia. By two hundred thousand years ago, they had established themselves throughout the temperate zones of the eastern hemisphere, where archaeologists have unearthed many specimens of their bones and tools.

Homo sapiens

Like *Australopithecus,* though, *Homo erectus* faded with the arrival of more intelligent and successful human species. *Homo sapiens* ("consciously thinking human") evolved about two hundred thousand years ago and has skillfully adapted to the natural environment ever since. Early *Homo sapiens* already possessed a large brain—one approaching the size of modern human brains. More important than the size of the brain, though, is its structure: the modern human brain is especially well developed in the frontal regions, where conscious, reflective thought takes place. This physical feature provided *Homo sapiens* with an enormous advantage.

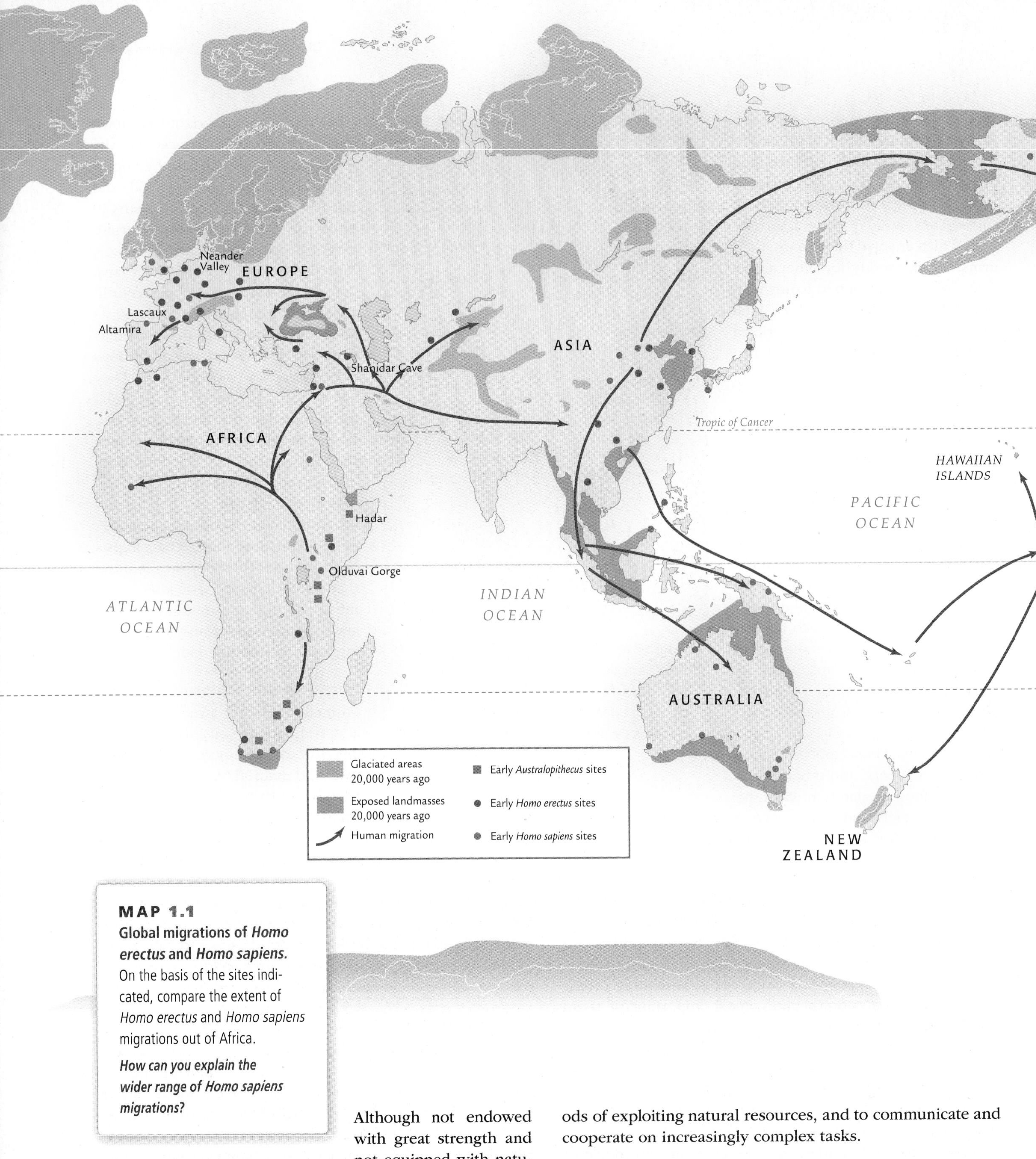

MAP 1.1
Global migrations of *Homo erectus* and *Homo sapiens*.
On the basis of the sites indicated, compare the extent of *Homo erectus* and *Homo sapiens* migrations out of Africa.
How can you explain the wider range of Homo sapiens migrations?

Although not endowed with great strength and not equipped with natural means of attack and defense—claws, beaks, fangs, shells, venom, and the like—*Homo sapiens* possessed a remarkable intelligence that provided a powerful edge in the contest for survival. It enabled individuals to understand the structure of the world around them, to organize more efficient methods of exploiting natural resources, and to communicate and cooperate on increasingly complex tasks.

Language Furthermore, between about one hundred thousand and fifty thousand years ago, *Homo sapiens* evolved a combination of physiological traits that was unique among animal species—a throat with vocal cords and a separate mouth cavity with a tongue, which enabled them

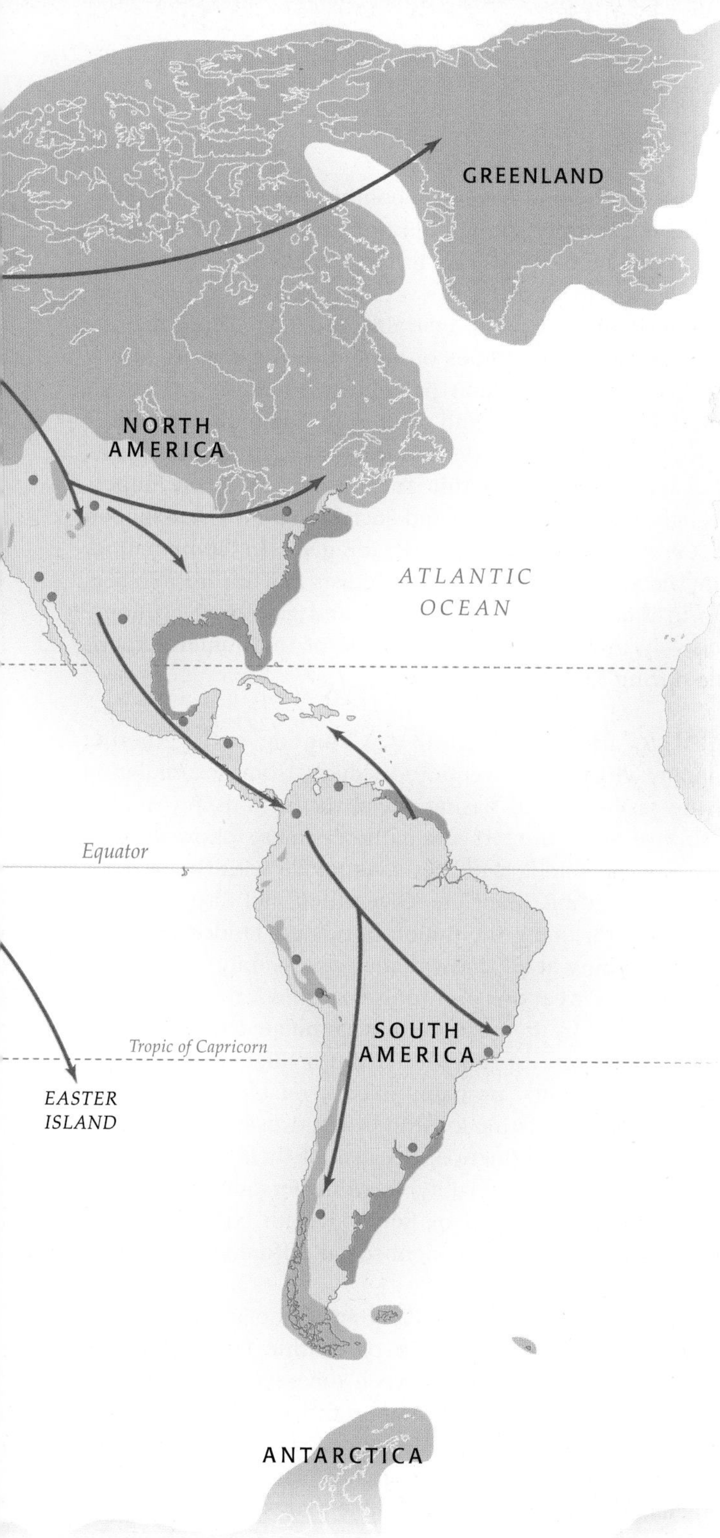

to enunciate hundreds of distinct sounds. Over time, *Homo sapiens* articulated those sounds into spoken languages that were endlessly flexible and that enabled individuals to communicate messages that were far more complex, more detailed, and more precise than those of *Homo erectus* and other human species. High intelligence and flexible language made for a powerful combination that enhanced the ability of *Homo sapiens* to thrive in the world.

Migrations of *Homo sapiens* Intelligence and language enabled *Homo sapiens* to adapt to widely varying environmental conditions and to establish the species securely throughout the world. Beginning about one hundred thousand years ago, communities of *Homo sapiens* spread throughout the eastern hemisphere and populated the temperate lands of Africa, Europe, and Asia, where they encountered *Homo erectus* groups that had inhabited those regions for several hundred thousand years. *Homo sapiens* soon moved beyond the temperate zones, though, and established communities in progressively colder regions—migrations that were possible because their intelligence allowed *Homo sapiens* to fashion warm clothes from animal skins and to build effective shelters against the cold.

Between sixty thousand and fifteen thousand years ago, *Homo sapiens* extended the range of human population even further. Several ice ages cooled the earth's temperature during that period, resulting in the concentration of water in massive glaciers, the lowering of the world's sea levels, and the exposure of land bridges that linked Asia with regions of the world previously uninhabited by humans. Small bands of individuals crossed those bridges and established communities in the islands of Indonesia and New Guinea, and some of them went farther to cross the temporarily narrow straits of water separating southeast Asia from Australia.

The Peopling of the World *Homo sapiens* arrived in Australia about sixty thousand years ago, perhaps even earlier. Somewhat later, beginning as early perhaps as twenty-five thousand years ago, other groups took advantage of land bridges linking Siberia with Alaska and established human communities in North America. From there they migrated throughout the western hemisphere. By about fifteen thousand years ago, communities of *Homo sapiens* had appeared in almost every habitable region of the world.

This peopling of the world was a remarkable accomplishment. No other animal or plant species has autonomously made its way to all habitable parts of the world. Some species, such as rats and roaches, have tagged along with humans and established themselves in distant homes. Other animals and plants—dogs and horses, for example, and wheat and potatoes—have found their way to new lands because humans intentionally transported them. Only *Homo sapiens,* however, has been able to make a home independently in all parts of the world.

The Natural Environment Their intellectual abilities enabled members of the *Homo sapiens* species to recognize problems and possibilities in their environment and then to take action that favored their survival. At sites of early settlements, archaeologists have discovered increasingly sophisticated tools that reflect *Homo sapiens'* progressive control over the environment. In addition to the choppers, scrapers, axes, and other tools that earlier species possessed, *Homo sapiens* used knives, spears, and bows and arrows. Individuals made dwellings for themselves in caves and in hutlike shelters fabricated from wood, bones, and animal skins. In cold regions *Homo sapiens* warmed themselves with fire and cloaked themselves in the skins of animals. Mounds of ashes discovered at their campsites show that in especially cold regions, they kept fires burning continuously during the winter months. *Homo sapiens* used superior intelligence, sophisticated tools, and language to exploit the natural world more efficiently than any other species the earth had seen.

Indeed, intelligent, tool-bearing humans competed so successfully in the natural world that they brought tremendous pressure to bear on other species. As the population of *Homo sapiens* increased, large mammal species in several parts of the world became extinct. Mammoths and the woolly rhinoceros disappeared from Europe, giant kangaroos from Australia, and mammoths, mastodons, and horses from the Americas. Archaeologists believe that changes in the earth's climate altered the natural environment enough to harm those species. In most cases, however, human hunting probably helped push large animals into extinction. Thus, from their earliest days on earth, members of the species *Homo sapiens* became effective and efficient competitors in the natural world—to the point that they threatened the very survival of other large but less intelligent species.

"This peopling of the world was a remarkable accomplishment. No other animal or plant species has autonomously made its own way to all habitable parts of the world."

PALEOLITHIC SOCIETY

By far the longest portion of the human experience on earth is the period historians and archaeologists call the paleolithic era, the "old stone age." The principal characteristic of the paleolithic era was that human beings foraged for their food: they scavenged meat killed by predators or hunted wild animals or gathered edible products of naturally growing plants. The paleolithic era extended from the evolution of the first hominids until about twelve thousand years ago, when groups of *Homo sapiens* in several parts of the world began to rely on cultivated crops to feed themselves.

Economy and Society of Hunting and Gathering Peoples

In the absence of written records, scholars have drawn inferences about paleolithic economy and society from other kinds of evidence. Archaeologists have excavated many sites that open windows on paleolithic life, and anthropologists have carefully studied hunting and gathering societies in the contemporary world. In the Amazon basin of South America, the tropical forests of Africa and southeast Asia, the deserts of Africa and Australia, and a few other regions as well, small communities of hunters and gatherers follow the ways of our common paleolithic ancestors. Although contemporary hunting and gathering communities reflect the influence of the modern world—they are by no means exact replicas of paleolithic societies—they throw important light on the economic and social dynamics that shaped the experiences of prehistoric foragers. In combination, then, the studies of both archaeologists and anthropologists help to illustrate how the hunting and gathering economy decisively influenced all dimensions of the human experience during the paleolithic era.

Relative Social Equality A hunting and gathering economy virtually prevents individuals from accumulating private property and basing social distinctions on wealth. To survive, most hunters and gatherers must follow the animals that they stalk, and they must move with the seasons in search of edible plant life. Given their mobility, it is easy to see that, for them, the notion of private, landed property has no meaning at all. Individuals possess only a few small items such as weapons and tools that they can carry easily as they move. In the absence of accumulated wealth, hunters and gatherers of paleolithic times, like their contemporary descendants, probably lived a relatively egalitarian existence. Social distinctions no doubt arose, and some individuals became influential because of their age, strength, courage, intelligence, fertility, force of personality, or some other trait. But personal or family wealth could not have served as a basis for permanent social differences.

Relative Gender Equality Some scholars believe that this relative social equality in paleolithic times extended even further, to relations between the sexes. All members of a paleolithic group made important contributions to the survival of the community. Men traveled on sometimes distant hunting expeditions in search of large animals while women and children gathered edible plants, roots, nuts, and fruits from the area near the group's camp. Meat from the hunt was the most highly prized item in the paleolithic diet, but plant foods were essential to survival. Anthropologists calculate that in modern hunting and gathering societies, women contribute more calories to the community's diet than do the men. As a source of protein, meat represents a crucial supplement to the diet. But plant products sustain the men during hunting expeditions and feed the entire community when the hunt does not succeed. Because of the thorough interdependence of the sexes from the viewpoint of food production, paleolithic society probably did not encourage the domination of one sex by the other—certainly not to the extent that became common later.

sources from the past

Richard E. Leakey on the Nature of *Homo sapiens sapiens*

Richard E. Leakey (1944–) has spent much of his life searching for the fossilized remains of early hominids in east Africa. While seeking to explain the evolutionary biology of hominids, Leakey offered some reflections on the nature and distinctive characteristics of our species.

What are we? To the biologist we are members of a subspecies called *Homo sapiens sapiens,* which represents a division of the species known as *Homo sapiens.* Every species is unique and distinct: that is part of the definition of a species. But what is particularly interesting about our species? . . .

Our forelimbs, being freed from helping us to get about, possess a very high degree of manipulative skill. Part of this skill lies in the anatomical structure of the hands, but the crucial element is, of course, the power of the brain. No matter how suitable the limbs are for detailed manipulation, they are useless in the absence of finely tuned instructions delivered through nerve fibres. The most obvious product of our hands and brains is technology. No other animal manipulates the world in the extensive and arbitrary way that humans do. The termites are capable of constructing intricately structured mounds which create their own "air-conditioned" environment inside. But the termites cannot choose to build a cathedral instead. Humans are unique because they have the capacity to *choose* what they do.

Communication is a vital thread of all animal life. Social insects such as termites possess a system of communication that is clearly essential for their complex labours: their language is not verbal but is based upon an exchange of chemicals between individuals and on certain sorts of signalling with the body. In many animal groups, such as birds and mammals, communicating by sound is important, and the posture and movement of the body can also transmit messages. The tilting of the head, the staring or averted eyes, the arched back, the bristled hair or feathers: all are part of an extensive repertoire of animal signals. In animals that live in groups, the need to be able to communicate effectively is paramount.

For humans, body language is still very important but the voice has taken over as the main channel of information-flow. Unlike any other animal, we have a spoken language which is characterized by a huge vocabulary and a complex grammatical structure. Speech is an unparalleled medium for exchanging complex information, and it is also an essential part of social interaction in that most social of all creatures, *Homo sapiens sapiens.*

All the points I have mentioned are characteristics of a very intelligent creature, but humans are more than just intelligent. Our sense of justice, our need for aesthetic pleasure, our imaginative flights, and our penetrating self-awareness, all combine to create an indefinable spirit which I believe is the "soul."

For Further Reflection

- Granting that *Homo sapiens* possesses distinctive characteristics and enjoys unique abilities, as Leakey has eloquently suggested, to what extent does human membership in the larger animal kingdom help explain human experiences in the world?

Source: Richard E. Leakey. *The Making of Mankind.* New York: E. P. Dutton, 1981, pp. 18, 20.

A hunting and gathering economy has implications not only for social and sexual relations but also for community size and organization. The foraging lifestyle of hunters and gatherers dictates that they mostly live in small bands, which today include about thirty to fifty members. Larger groups could not move efficiently or find enough food to survive over a long period. During times of drought or famine, even small bands have trouble providing for themselves. Individual bands certainly have relationships with their neighbors—agreements concerning the territories that the groups exploit, for example, or arrangements to take marriage partners from each others' groups—but the immediate community is the focus of social life.

The survival of hunting and gathering bands depends on a sophisticated understanding of their natural environment. In contemporary studies, anthropologists have found that hunting and gathering peoples do not wander aimlessly about hoping to find a bit of food. Instead, they exploit the environment systematically and efficiently by timing their movements to coincide with the seasonal migrations of the animals they hunt and the life cycles of the plant species they gather.

Big-Game Hunting Archaeological remains show that early peoples also went about hunting and gathering in a purposeful and intelligent manner. Although almost anyone could take a small, young, or wounded animal, the hunting of big game posed special challenges. Large animals such as elephant, mastodon, rhinoceros, bison, and wild cattle were not only strong and fast but also well equipped to defend themselves and even attack their human hunters. *Homo sapiens* fashioned special tools, such as sharp knives, spears, and bows and arrows, and devised special tactics for hunting these animals. The hunters wore disguises such as animal skins and coordinated their movements so as to attack game simultaneously from several directions. They sometimes even started fires or caused disturbances to stampede herds into swamps or enclosed areas where hunters could kill them more easily. Paleolithic hunting was a complicated venture. It clearly demonstrated the capacity of early human communities to pool their uniquely human traits—high intelligence, ability to make complicated plans, and sophisticated language and communications skills—to exploit the environment.

Paleolithic Settlements In regions where food resources were especially rich, a few peoples in late paleolithic times abandoned the nomadic lifestyle and established permanent settlements. The most prominent paleolithic settlements were those of Natufian society in the eastern Mediterranean (modern-day Israel and Lebanon), Jomon society in central Japan, and Chinook society in the Pacific northwest region of North America (including the modern states of Oregon and Washington and the Canadian province of British Columbia). As early as 13,500 B.C.E., Natufians collected wild wheat and took animals from abundant antelope herds. From 10,000 to 300 B.C.E., Jomon settlers harvested wild buckwheat and developed a productive fishing economy. Chinook society emerged after 3000 B.C.E. and flourished until the mid-nineteenth century C.E., principally on the basis of wild berries, acorns, and massive salmon runs in local rivers. Paleolithic settlements had permanent dwellings, sometimes in the form of longhouses that accommodated several hundred people, but often in the form of smaller structures for individual families. Many settlements had populations of a thousand or more individuals. As archaeological excavations continue, it is becoming increasingly clear that paleolithic peoples organized complex societies with specialized rulers and craftsmen in many regions where they found abundant food resources.

Statue of a Neandertal man based on the study of recently discovered bones. How does his knifelike tool compare with the tools used by *Homo erectus?*

Neandertal (nee-ANN-duhr-tawl)

Paleolithic Culture

Neandertal Peoples Paleolithic individuals did not limit their creative thinking to strictly practical matters of subsistence and survival. Instead, they reflected on the nature of human existence and the world around them. The earliest evidence of reflective thought comes from sites associated with **Neandertal** peoples, named after the Neander valley in western Germany where their remains first came to light. Neandertal peoples flourished in Europe and southwest Asia

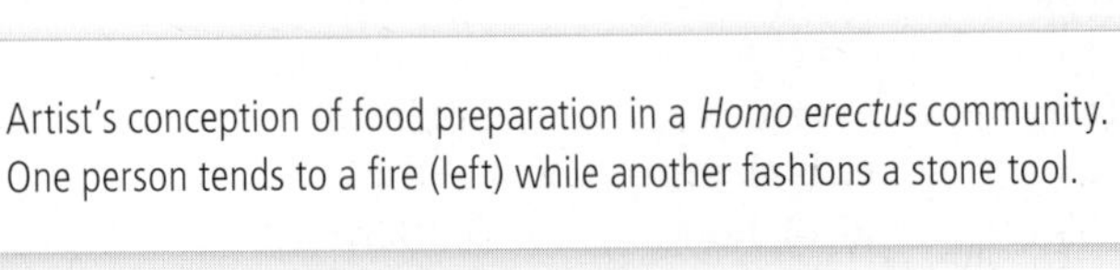

Artist's conception of food preparation in a *Homo erectus* community. One person tends to a fire (left) while another fashions a stone tool.

between about two hundred thousand and thirty-five thousand years ago. Most scholars regard Neandertal peoples as members of a distinct human species known as *Homo neandertalensis.* For about ten millennia, from forty-five thousand to thirty-five thousand years ago, Neandertal groups inhabited some of the same regions as *Homo sapiens* communities, and members of the two species sometimes lived in close proximity to each other. DNA analysis suggests that there was little if any interbreeding between the two species, but it is quite likely that individuals traded goods between their groups, and it is possible that Neandertal peoples imitated the technologies and crafts of their more intelligent cousins.

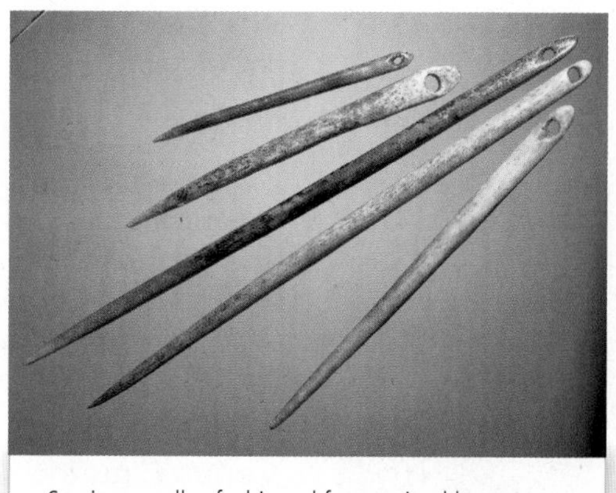

Sewing needles fashioned from animal bones about fifteen thousand years ago.

At several Neandertal sites, archaeologists have discovered signs of careful, deliberate burial accompanied by ritual observances. Perhaps the most notable is that of Shanidar cave, located about 400 kilometers (250 miles) north of Baghdad in modern-day Iraq, where survivors laid the deceased to rest on beds of freshly picked wildflowers and then covered the bodies with shrouds and garlands of other flowers. At other Neandertal sites in France, Italy, and central Asia, survivors placed flint tools and animal bones in and around the graves of the deceased. It is impossible to know precisely what Neandertal peoples were thinking when they buried their dead in that fashion. Possibly they simply wanted to honor the memory of the departed, or perhaps they wanted to prepare the dead for a new dimension of existence, a life beyond the grave. Whatever their intentions, Neandertal peoples apparently recognized a significance in the life and death of individuals that none of their ancestors had appreciated. They had developed a capacity for emotions and feelings, and they cared for one another even to the extent of preparing elaborate resting places for the departed.

The Creativity of *Homo sapiens* *Homo sapiens* was much more intellectually inventive and creative than *Homo neandertalensis.* Many scholars argue that *Homo sapiens* owed much of the species's intellectual prowess to the ability to construct powerful and flexible languages for the communication of complex ideas. With the development of languages, human beings were able both to accumulate knowledge and to transmit it precisely and efficiently to new generations. Thus it was not necessary for every individual human being to learn from trial and error or from direct personal experience about the nature of the local environment or the best techniques for making advanced tools. Rather, it was possible for human groups to pass large and complex bodies of information along to their offspring, who then were able to make immediate use of it and furthermore were in a good position to build on inherited information by devising increasingly effective ways of satisfying human needs and desires.

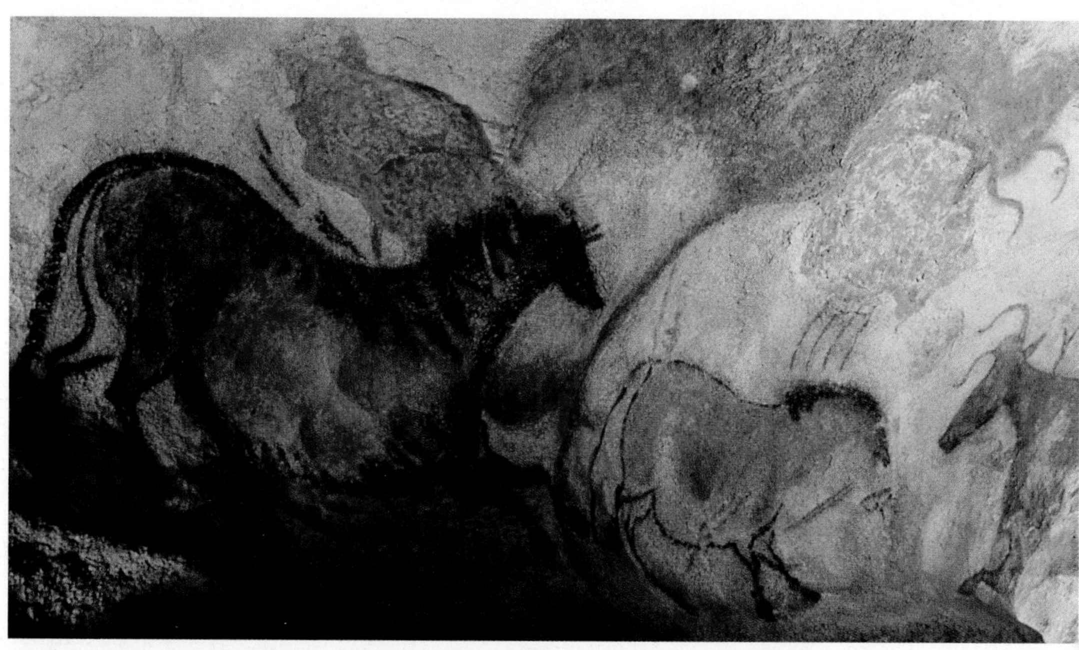

Cave painting from Lascaux in southern France, perhaps intended to help hunters gain control over the spirits of large game animals. To what extent do you think a painting can "capture" an animal?

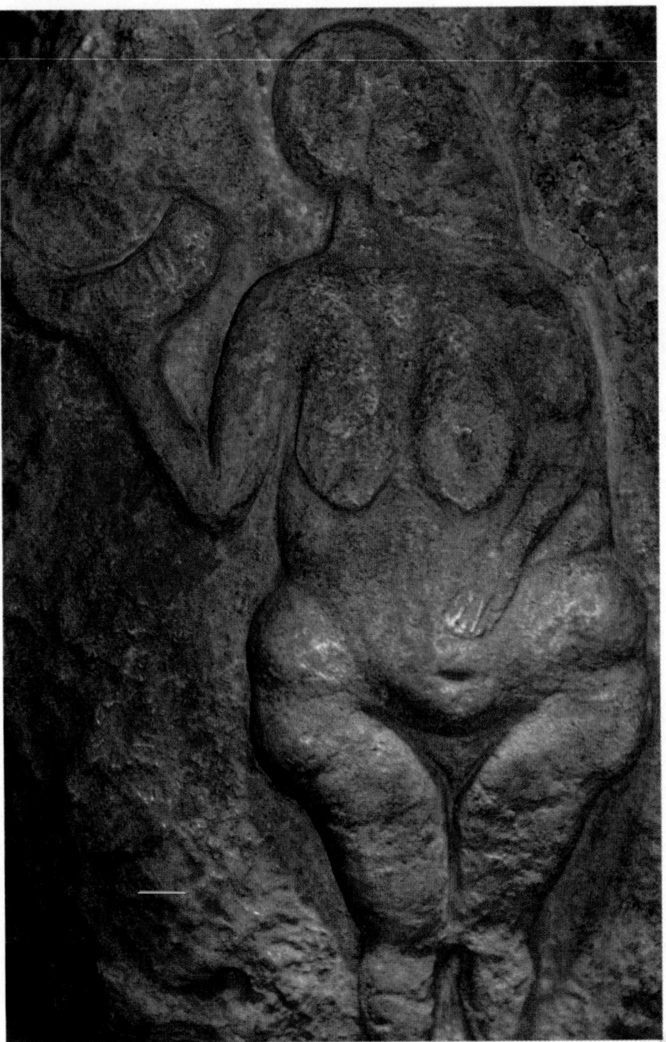

Venus figurine from southern France. This image, carved on a cave wall about twenty-five thousand years ago, depicts a woman of ample proportions. The exaggerated sexual features suggest that paleolithic peoples fashioned this and similar figurines out of an interest in fertility.

From its earliest days on the earth, *Homo sapiens* distinguished itself as a creative species. At least 200,000 years ago, *Homo sapiens* was producing stone blades with long cutting edges. By 140,000 years ago, early humans had learned to supplement their diet with shellfish from coastal waters, and they had developed networks with neighbors that enabled them to trade high-quality obsidian stone over distances sometimes exceeding 300 kilometers (185 miles). By 110,000 years ago, they had devised means of catching fish from deep waters. By 100,000 years ago, they had begun to fashion sharp tools such as sewing needles and barbed harpoons out of animal bones. Somewhat later they invented spear-throwers—small slings that enabled hunters to hurl spears at speeds upwards of 160 kilometers per hour (100 miles per hour). About 50,000 to 40,000 years ago, they were fabricating ornamental beads, necklaces, and bracelets, and shortly thereafter they began painting images of human and animal subjects. About 10,000 years ago, they invented the bow and arrow, a weapon that dramatically enhanced the power of human beings with respect to other animal species.

Venus Figurines The most visually impressive creations of early *Homo sapiens* are the Venus figurines and cave paintings found at many sites of early human habitation. Archaeologists use the term *Venus figurines*—named after the Roman goddess of love—to refer to small sculptures of women, usually depicted with exaggerated sexual features. Most scholars believe that the figures reflect a deep interest in fertility. The prominent sexual features of the Venus figurines suggest that the sculptors' principal interests were fecundity and the generation of new life—matters of immediate concern to paleolithic societies. Some interpreters speculate that the figures had a place in ritual observances intended to increase fertility.

Cave Paintings Paintings in caves frequented by early humans are the most dramatic examples of prehistoric art. The known examples of cave art date from about thirty-four thousand to twelve thousand years ago, and most of them are in caves in southern France and northern Spain. In that region alone, archaeologists have discovered more than one hundred caves bearing prehistoric paintings. The best-known are Lascaux in France and Altamira in Spain. There, prehistoric peoples left depictions of remarkable sensitivity and power. Most of the subjects were animals, especially large game such as mammoth, bison, and reindeer, although a few human figures also appear.

thinking about TRADITIONS

Intelligence, Language, and the Emergence of Cultural Traditions

High intelligence and sophisticated language enabled *Homo sapiens* to devise clever ways of exploiting natural resources and passing knowledge along to their descendants. Later generations did not have to reinvent methods of providing for themselves but, rather, could learn earlier techniques and find ways to enhance them. In what ways did intelligence and language enable early *Homo sapiens* to create traditions of reflection about the relationship between human beings and the natural world?

Two cave paintings (here and next page) produced five to six thousand years ago illustrate the different roles played by men and women in the early days of agriculture. Here women harvest grain.

As in the case of the Venus figurines, the explanation for the cave paintings involves a certain amount of educated guesswork. It is conceivable that early artists sometimes worked for purely aesthetic reasons—to beautify their living quarters. But many examples of cave art occur in places that are almost inaccessible to human beings—deep within remote chambers, for example, or at the end of long and constricted passages. Paintings in such remote locations presumably had some other purpose. Most analysts believe that the prominence of game animals in the paintings reflects the artists' interest in successful hunting expeditions. Thus cave paintings may have represented efforts to exercise sympathetic magic—to gain control over subjects (in this case, game animals) by capturing their spirits (by way of accurate representations of their physical forms). Although not universally accepted, this interpretation accounts reasonably well for a great deal of the evidence and has won widespread support among scholars.

Whatever the explanation for prehistoric art, the production of the works themselves represented conscious and purposeful activity of a high order. Early artists compounded pigments and manufactured tools. They made paints from minerals, plants, blood, saliva, water, animal fat, and other available ingredients. They used mortar and pestle for grinding pigments and mixing paints, which they applied with moss, frayed twigs and branches, or primitive brushes fabricated from hair. The simplicity and power of their representations have left deep impressions on modern critics ever since the early twentieth century, when their works became widely known. The display of prehistoric artistic talent clearly testifies once again to the remarkable intellectual power of the human species.

THE NEOLITHIC ERA AND THE TRANSITION TO AGRICULTURE

A few societies of hunting and gathering peoples inhabit the contemporary world, although most of them do not thrive because agricultural and industrial societies have taken over environments best suited to a foraging economy. Demographers estimate the current number of hunters and gatherers to be about thirty thousand, a tiny fraction of the world's human population of more than six billion. The vast majority of the world's peoples, however, have crossed an economic threshold of immense significance. When human beings brought plants under cultivation and animals under domestication, they dramatically altered the natural world and steered human societies in new directions.

The Origins of Agriculture

Neolithic Era The term *neolithic era* means "new stone age," as opposed to the old stone age of paleolithic times. Archaeologists first used the term *neolithic* because of refinements in tool-making techniques: they found polished stone tools in neolithic sites, rather than the chipped implements characteristic of paleolithic sites. Gradually, however, archaeologists became aware that something more fundamental than tool production distinguished the neolithic from the paleolithic era. Polished stone tools occurred in sites where peoples relied on cultivation, rather than foraging, for their subsistence. Today the term *neolithic era* refers to the early stages of agricultural society, from about twelve thousand to six thousand years ago.

Global Climate Change Agriculture was almost impossible and indeed inconceivable until about fifteen thousand years ago. During the ice ages, the earth was much colder and drier than it is today, and furthermore, it experienced wild fluctuations of temperature and rainfall. In any given year, sun and rain might have brought abundant harvests, but frigid and arid conditions might ruin crops for the next decade or more. Thus agriculture would have been an unreliable and even foolhardy venture. After the ice ages, the earth entered an era of general warming, increased rainfall, and more stable climatic conditions. Neolithic peoples soon took advantage of those conditions by encouraging the growth of edible plants and bringing wild animals into dependence upon human keepers.

Gender Relations and Agriculture Many scholars believe that women most likely began the systematic care of plants. As the principal gatherers in foraging communities, women became familiar with the life cycles of plants and noticed the effects of sunshine, rain, and temperature on vegetation. Hoping for larger and more reliable supplies of food, women in neolithic societies probably began to nurture plants instead of simply collecting available foods in the wild. Meanwhile, instead of just stalking game with the intention of killing it for meat, neolithic men began to capture animals and domesticate them by providing for their needs and supervising their breeding. Over a period of decades and centuries, those practices gradually led to the formation of agricultural economies.

Independent Inventions of Agriculture Agriculture—including both the cultivation of crops and the domestication of animals—emerged independently in several different parts of the world. The earliest evidence of agricultural activity discovered so far dates to the era after 9000 B.C.E., when peoples of southwest Asia (modern-day Iraq, Syria, and Turkey) cultivated wheat and barley while domesticating sheep, goats, pigs, and cattle. Between 9000 and 7000 B.C.E., African peoples inhabiting the southeastern margin of the Sahara desert (modern-day Sudan) domesticated cattle, sheep, and goats while cultivating sorghum. Between 8000 and 6000 B.C.E., peoples of sub-Saharan west Africa (in the vicinity of modern Nigeria) also began independently to cultivate yams, okra, and black-eyed peas. In east Asia, residents of the Yangzi River valley began to cultivate rice as early as 6500 B.C.E., and their neighbors to the north in the Yellow River valley raised crops of millet and soybeans after 5500 B.C.E. East Asian peoples also kept pigs and chickens from an early date, perhaps 6000 B.C.E., and they later added water buffaloes to their domesticated stock. In southeast Asia the cultivation of taro, yams, coconut, breadfruit, bananas, and citrus fruits, including oranges, lemons, limes, tangerines, and grapefruit, dates from probably 3000 B.C.E. or earlier.

Peoples of the western hemisphere also turned independently to agriculture. Inhabitants of Mesoamerica (central Mexico) cultivated maize (corn) as early as 4000 B.C.E., and they later added a range of additional food crops, including beans, peppers, squashes, and tomatoes. Residents of the central Andean region of South America (modern Peru) cultivated potatoes after 3000 B.C.E., and they later added maize and beans to their diets. It is possible that the Amazon River valley was yet another site of independently invented agriculture, this one centering on the cultivation of manioc, sweet potatoes, and peanuts. Domesticated animals were much less prominent in the Americas than in the east-

Men herd domesticated cattle in the early days of agriculture. This painting and the one on the preceding page are both in a cave at Tassili n'Ajjer in modern-day Algeria.

ern hemisphere. Paleolithic peoples had hunted many large species to extinction: mammoths, mastodons, and horses had all disappeared from the Americas by 7000 B.C.E. (The horses that have figured so prominently in the modern history of the Americas all descended from animals introduced to the western hemisphere during the past five hundred years.) With the exception of llamas, alpacas, and guinea pigs of the Andean regions, most American animals were not well suited to domestication.

thinking about ENCOUNTERS

Migrations and the Early Spread of Agriculture
Ever since *Homo erectus* left Africa almost two million years ago and established communities in the Eurasian continent, human beings have been migratory creatures, quick to search for opportunities in lands beyond the horizon. Whenever humans moved to new lands, they carried their technologies with them and introduced new ways of exploiting natural resources. In what ways did early human migrations help explain the early spread of agriculture?

The Early Spread of Agriculture Once established, agriculture spread rapidly, partly because of the methods of early cultivators. One of the earliest techniques, known as slash-and-burn cultivation, involved frequent movement on the part of farmers. To prepare a field for cultivation, a community would slash the bark on a stand of trees in a forest and later burn the dead trees to the ground. The resulting weed-free patch was extremely fertile and produced abundant harvests. After a few years, however, weeds invaded the field, and the soil lost its original fertility. The community then moved to another forest region and repeated the procedure. Migrations of slash-and-burn cultivators helped spread agriculture throughout both eastern and western hemispheres. By 6000 B.C.E., for example, agriculture had spread from its southwest Asian homeland to the eastern shores of the Mediterranean and the Balkan region of eastern Europe, and by 4000 B.C.E. it had spread farther to western Europe north of the Mediterranean.

While agriculture radiated out from its various hearths, foods originally cultivated in only one region also spread widely, as merchants, migrants, or other travelers carried knowledge of those foods to agricultural lands that previously had relied on different crops. Wheat, for example, spread from its original homeland in southwest Asia to Iran and northern India after 5000 B.C.E. and farther to northern China perhaps by 3000 B.C.E. Meanwhile, rice spread from southern China to southeast Asia by 3000 B.C.E. and to the Ganges River valley in India by 1500 B.C.E. African sorghum reached India by 2000 B.C.E., while southeast Asian bananas took root in tropical lands throughout the Indian Ocean basin. In the western hemisphere, maize spread from Mesoamerica to the southwestern part of the United States by 1200 B.C.E. and farther to the eastern woodlands region of North America by 100 C.E.

Agriculture involved long hours of hard physical labor—clearing land, preparing fields, planting seeds, pulling weeds, and harvesting crops. Indeed, agriculture probably required more work than paleolithic foraging: anthropologists calculate that modern hunting and gathering peoples spend about four hours per day in providing themselves with food and other necessities, devoting the remainder of their time to rest, leisure, and social activities. Yet agriculture had its own appeal in that it made possible the production of abundant food supplies. Thus agriculture spread widely, eventually influencing the lives and experience of almost all human beings.

Early Agricultural Society

In the wake of agriculture came a series of social and cultural changes that transformed human history. Perhaps the most important change associated with early agriculture was a population explosion. Spread thinly across the earth in paleolithic times, the human species multiplied prodigiously after agriculture increased the supply of food. Historians estimate that before agriculture, about 10,000 B.C.E., the earth's human population was four million. By 5000 B.C.E., when agriculture had appeared in a few world regions, human population had risen to about five million. Estimates for later dates demonstrate eloquently the speed with which, thanks to agriculture, human numbers increased:

Year	Human Population
3000 B.C.E.	14 million
2000 B.C.E.	27 million
1000 B.C.E.	50 million
500 B.C.E.	100 million

Emergence of Villages and Towns Their agricultural economy and rapidly increasing numbers encouraged neolithic peoples to adopt new forms of social organization. Because they devoted their time to cultivation rather than foraging, neolithic peoples did not continue the migratory life of their paleolithic predecessors but, rather, settled near their fields in permanent villages. One of the earliest known neolithic villages was Jericho, site of a freshwater oasis north of the Dead Sea in present-day Israel, which came into existence before 8000 B.C.E. Even in its early days, Jericho may have had two thousand residents—a vast crowd compared with a paleolithic hunting band. The residents farmed mostly wheat and barley with the aid of water from the oasis. During the earliest days of the settlement, they kept no domesticated animals, but they added meat to their diet by hunting local game animals. They also engaged in a limited amount of trade, particularly in salt and obsidian, a hard, volcanic glass from which ancient peoples fashioned knives and blades. About 7000 B.C.E., the residents surrounded their circular mud huts with a formidable wall and moat—a sure sign that the wealth concentrated at Jericho had begun to attract the interest of human predators.

Specialization of Labor The concentration of large numbers of people in villages encouraged specialization of labor. Most people in neolithic villages cultivated crops or kept animals. Many also continued to hunt and forage for wild plants. But a surplus of food enabled some individuals to concentrate their time and talents on enterprises that had nothing to do with the production of food. The rapid development of specialized labor is apparent from excavations carried out at one of the best-known neolithic settlements, Çatal Hüyük. Located in south-central Anatolia (modern-day Turkey), Çatal Hüyük was occupied continuously from 7250 to 5400 B.C.E., when residents abandoned the site. Originally a small and undistinguished neolithic village, Çatal Hüyük grew into a bustling town, accommodating about five thousand inhabitants. Archaeologists have uncovered evidence that residents manufactured pots, baskets, textiles, leather, stone and metal tools, wood carvings, carpets, beads, and jewelry among other products. Çatal Hüyük became a prominent village partly because of its close proximity to large obsidian deposits. The village probably was a center of production and trade in obsidian tools: archaeologists have discovered obsidian that originated near Çatal Hüyük at sites throughout much of the eastern Mediterranean region.

Three early craft industries—pottery, metallurgy, and textile production—illustrate the potential of specialized labor in neolithic times. Neolithic craftsmen were not always the original inventors of the technologies behind those industries: the Jomon society of central Japan produced the world's first known pottery, for example, about 10,000 B.C.E. But neolithic craftsmen expanded dramatically on existing practices and supplemented them with new techniques to fashion natural products into useful items. Their enterprises reflected the conditions of early agricultural society: either the craft industries provided tools and utensils needed by cultivators, or they made use of cultivators' and herders' products in new ways.

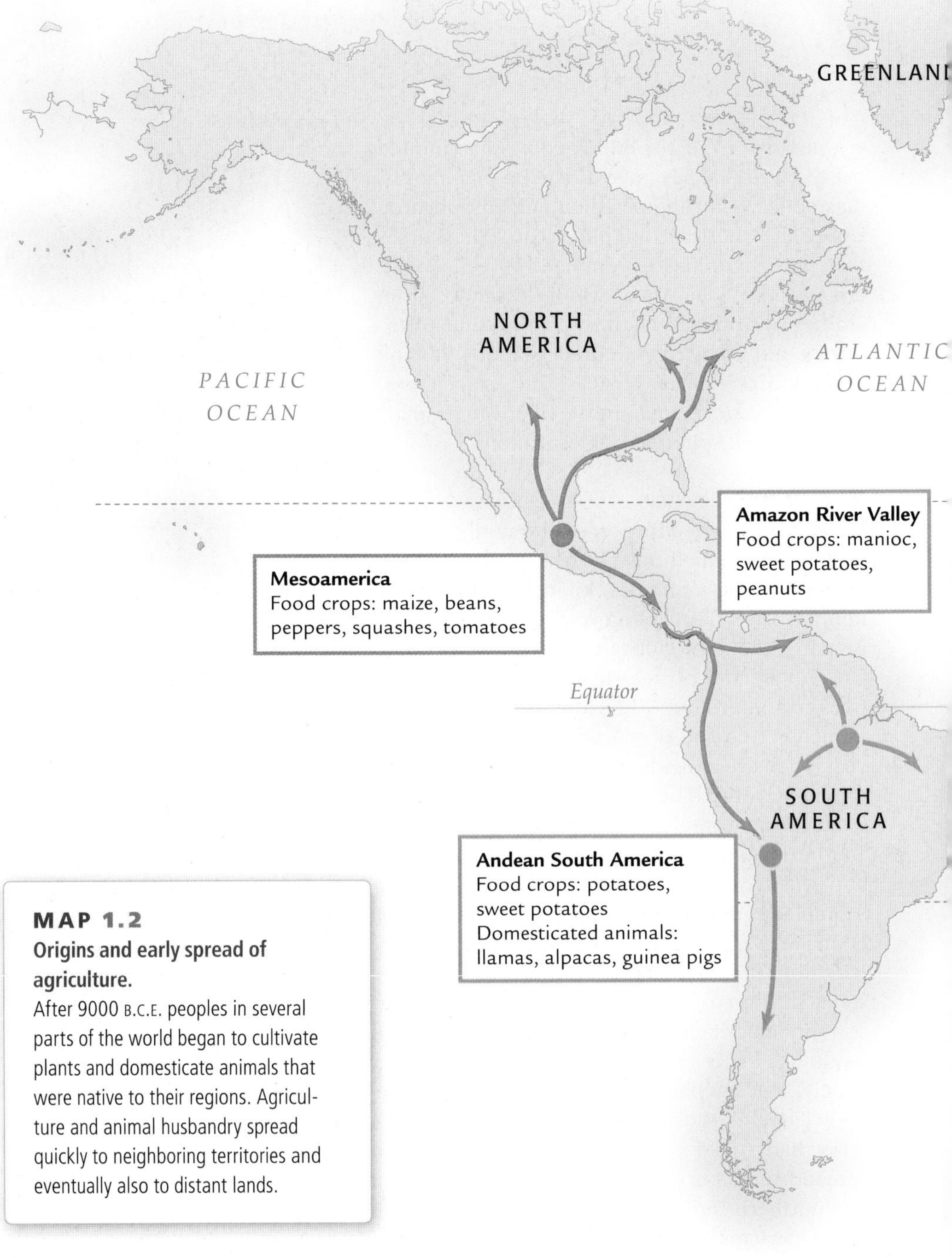

MAP 1.2
Origins and early spread of agriculture.
After 9000 B.C.E. peoples in several parts of the world began to cultivate plants and domesticate animals that were native to their regions. Agriculture and animal husbandry spread quickly to neighboring territories and eventually also to distant lands.

Pottery The earliest of the three craft industries to emerge was pottery. Paleolithic hunters and gatherers had no use for pots. They did not store food for long periods of time, and in any case lugging heavy clay pots around as they moved from one site to another would have been inconvenient. A food-producing society, however, needs containers to store surplus foods. By about 7000 B.C.E., neolithic villagers in several parts of the world had discovered processes that transformed malleable clay into fire-hardened,

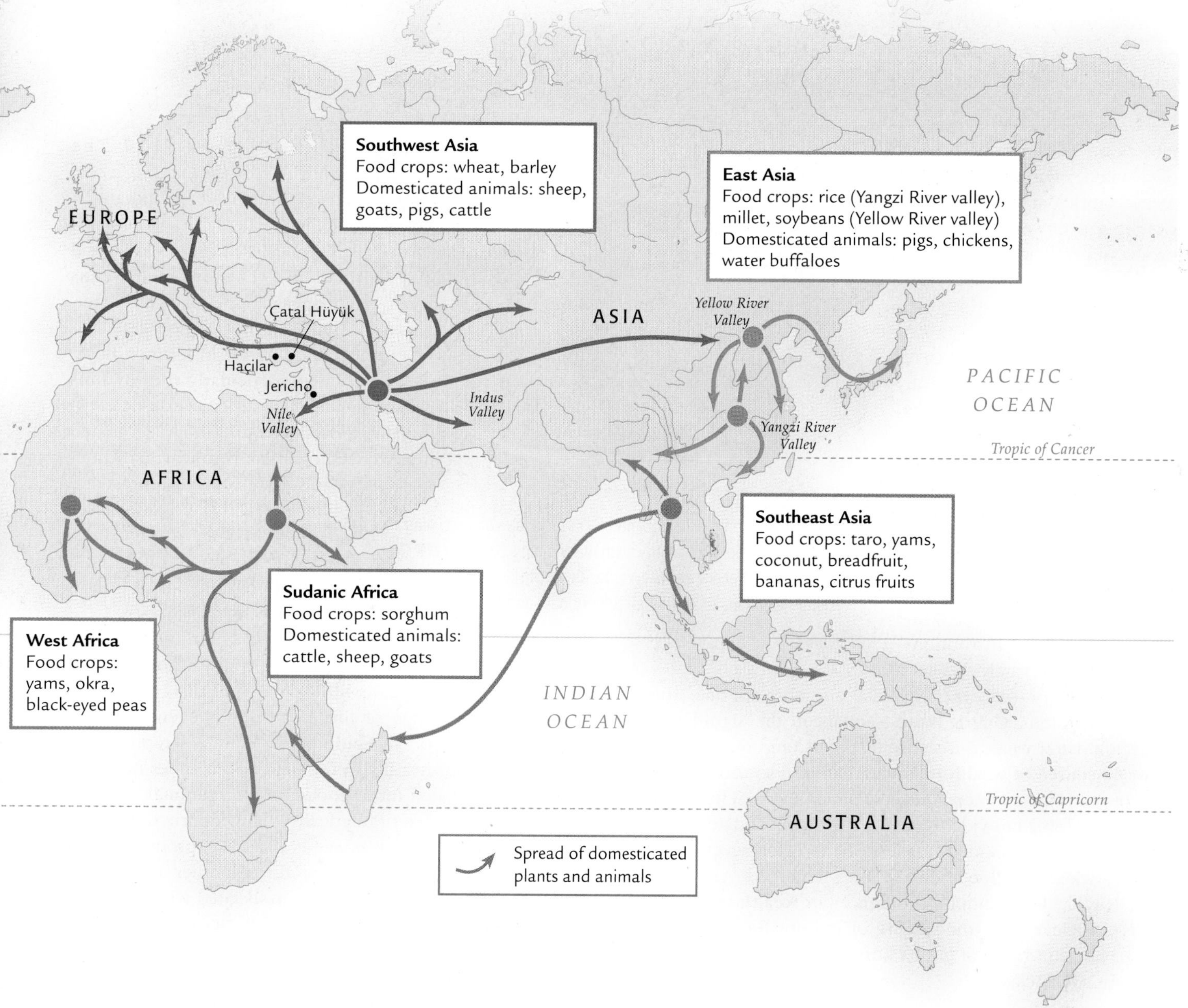

waterproof pottery capable of storing dry or liquid products. Soon thereafter, neolithic craftsmen discovered that they could etch designs into their clay that fire would harden into permanent decorations and furthermore that they could color their products with glazes. As a result, pottery became a medium of artistic expression as well as a source of practical utensils.

Metalworking Metallurgy soon joined pottery as a neolithic industry. The earliest metal that humans worked with systematically was copper. In many regions of the world, copper occurs naturally in relatively pure and easily malleable form. By hammering the cold metal, it was possible to turn it into jewelry and simple tools. By 6000 B.C.E., though, neolithic villagers had discovered that they could use heat to extract copper from its ores and that when heated to high temperatures, copper became much more workable. By 5000 B.C.E., they had raised temperatures in their furnaces high enough to melt copper and pour it into molds. With the technology of smelting and casting copper, neolithic communities were able to make not only jewelry and decorative items but also tools such as knives, axes, hoes, and weapons. Moreover, copper metallurgy served as a technological foundation on which later neolithic craftsmen developed expertise in the working of gold, bronze, iron, and other metals.

Textile Production Because natural fibers decay more easily than pottery or copper, the dating of textile production is not certain, but fragments of textiles survive from as early as 6000 B.C.E. As soon as they began to raise crops and keep animals, neolithic peoples experimented with techniques of selective breeding. Before long they had bred strains of plants and animals that provided long, lustrous, easily worked fibers. They then developed technologies for spinning the fibers into threads and weaving the threads into cloth. The invention of textiles was probably the work of women, who were able to spin thread and weave fabrics at home while nursing and watching over small children. Textile production quickly became one of the most important enterprises in agricultural society.

Social Distinctions and Social Inequality

The concentration of people into permanent settlements and the increasing specialization of labor provided the first opportunity for individuals to accumulate considerable wealth. Individuals could trade surplus food or manufactured products for gems, jewelry, and other valuable items. The institutionalization of privately owned landed property—which occurred at an uncertain date after the introduction of agriculture—enhanced the significance of accumulated wealth. Because land was (and remains) the ultimate source of wealth in any agricultural society, ownership of land carried enormous economic power. When especially successful individuals managed to consolidate wealth in their families' hands and kept it there for several generations, clearly defined social classes emerged. Already at Çatal Hüyük, for example, differences in wealth and social status are clear from the quality of interior decorations in houses and the value of goods buried with individuals from different social classes.

Pottery vessel from Haçilar in Anatolia in the shape of a reclining deer, produced about the early sixth millennium B.C.E. Long after they began to practice agriculture, residents of Haçilar and other neolithic communities continued to hunt deer and other game.

Neolithic Culture

Quite apart from its social effects, agriculture left its mark on the cultural dimension of the human experience. Because their lives and communities depended on the successful cultivation of crops, neolithic farmers closely observed the natural world around them and noted the conditions that favored successful harvests. In other words, they developed a kind of early applied science. From experience accumulated over the generations, they acquired an impressive working knowledge of the earth and its rhythms. Agricultural peoples had to learn when changes of season would take place: survival depended on the ability to predict when they could reasonably expect sunshine, rain, warmth, and freezing temperatures. They learned to associate the seasons with the different positions of the sun, moon, and stars. As a result, they accumulated a store of knowledge concerning relationships between the heavens and the earth, and they made the first steps toward the elaboration of a calendar, which would enable them to predict with tolerable accuracy the kind of weather they could expect at various times of the year.

Religious Values

The workings of the natural world also influenced neolithic religion. Paleolithic communities had already honored, and perhaps even worshiped, Venus figurines in hopes of ensuring fertility. Neolithic religion reflected the same interest in fertility, but it celebrated particularly the rhythms that governed agricultural society—birth, growth, death, and regenerated life. Archaeologists have unearthed thousands of neolithic representations of gods and goddesses in the form of clay figurines, drawings on pots and vases, decorations on tools, and ritual objects.

The neolithic gods included not only the life-bearing, Venus-type figures of paleolithic times but also deities associated with the cycle of life, death, and regeneration. A pregnant goddess of vegetation, for example, represented neolithic hopes for fertility in the fields. Sometimes neolithic worshipers associated these goddesses with animals such as frogs or butterflies that dramatically changed form during the course of their lives, just as seeds of grain sprouted, flourished, died, and produced new seed for another agricultural cycle. Meanwhile, young male gods associated with bulls and goats represented the energy and virility that participates in the creation of life.

Some deities were associated with death: many neolithic goddesses possessed the power to bring about decay and destruction. Yet physical death was not an absolute end. The procreative capacities of gods and goddesses resulted in the births of infant deities who represented the regeneration of life—freshly sprouted crops, replenished stocks of domestic animals, and infant human beings to inaugurate a new biological cycle. Thus neolithic religious thought clearly reflected the natural world of early agricultural society.

The Origins of Urban Life

Within four thousand years of its introduction, agriculture had dramatically transformed the face of the earth. Human beings multiplied prodigiously, congregated in densely populated quarters, placed the surrounding lands under cultivation, and domesticated several species of animals. Besides altering the physical appearance of the earth, agriculture transformed the lives of human beings. Even a modest neolithic village dwarfed a paleolithic band of a few dozen hunters and gatherers. In larger villages and towns, such as Jericho and Çatal Hüyük, with their populations of several thousand people, their specialized labor, and their

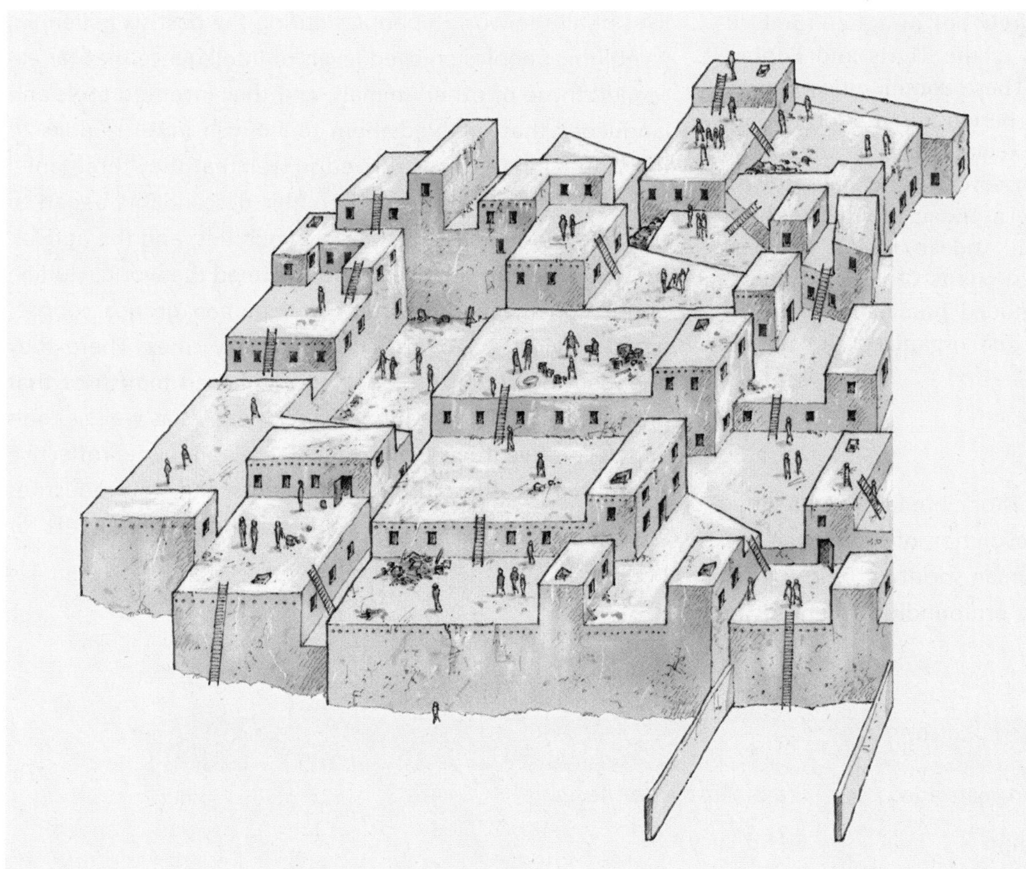

Artist's conception of Jericho, one of the world's first towns with defensive walls. Jericho had no streets and no ground-level doors or windows that might have provided easy access for predators and invaders. Residents entered their homes from rooftops and pulled ladders up behind them.

craft industries, social relationships became more complex than would have been conceivable during paleolithic times. Gradually, dense populations, specialized labor, and complex social relations gave rise to an altogether new form of social organization—the city.

Emergence of Cities Like the transition from foraging to agricultural society, the development of cities and complex societies organized around urban centers was a gradual process rather than a well-defined event. Because of favorable location, some neolithic villages and towns attracted more people and grew larger than others. Over time, some of those settlements evolved into cities. What distinguished early cities from their predecessors, the neolithic villages and towns?

Even in their early days, cities differed from neolithic villages and towns in two principal ways. In the first, cities were larger and more complex than neolithic villages and towns. Çatal Hüyük featured an impressive variety of specialized crafts and industries. With progressively larger populations, cities fostered more intense specialization than any of their predecessors among the neolithic villages and towns. Thus it was in cities that large classes of professionals emerged—individuals who devoted all their time to efforts other than the production of food. Professional craft workers refined existing technologies, invented new ones, and raised levels of quality and production. Professional managers also appeared—governors, administrators, military strategists, tax collectors, and the like—whose services were necessary to the survival of the community. Cities also gave rise to professional cultural specialists such as priests, who maintained their communities' traditions, transmitted their values, organized public rituals, and sought to discover meaning in human existence.

In the second, whereas neolithic villages and towns served the needs of their inhabitants and immediate neighbors, cities decisively influenced the political, economic, and cultural life of large regions. Cities established marketplaces that attracted buyers and sellers from distant parts. Brisk trade, conducted over increasingly longer distances, promoted economic integration on a much larger scale than was possible in neolithic times. To ensure adequate food supplies for their large populations, cities also extended their claims to authority over their hinterlands, thus becoming centers of political and military control as well as economic influence. In time, too, the building of temples and schools in neighboring regions enabled the cities to extend their cultural traditions and values to surrounding areas.

The earliest known cities grew out of agricultural villages and towns in the valleys of the Tigris and Euphrates rivers in modern-day Iraq. These communities crossed the urban threshold during the period about 4000 to 3500 B.C.E. and soon dominated their regions. During the following centuries, cities appeared in several other parts of the world, including Egypt, northern India, northern China, central Mexico, and the central Andean region of South America. Cities became the focal points of public affairs—the sites from which leaders guided human fortunes, supervised neighboring regions, and organized the world's earliest complex societies.

inperspective

In many ways the world of prehistoric human beings seems remote and even alien. Yet the evolution of the human species and the development of human society during the paleolithic and neolithic eras have profoundly influenced the lives of all the world's peoples during the past six millennia. Paleolithic peoples enjoyed levels of intelligence that far exceeded those of other animals, and they invented tools and languages that enabled them to flourish in all regions of the world. Indeed, they thrived so well that they threatened their sources of food. Their neolithic descendants began to cultivate food to sustain their communities, and the agricultural societies that they built transformed the world. Human population rose dramatically, and human groups congregated in villages, towns, and eventually cities. There they engaged in specialized labor and launched industries that produced pottery, metal goods, and textiles as well as tools and decorative items. Thus intelligence, language, reflective thought, agriculture, urban settlements, and craft industries all figure in the legacy that prehistoric human beings left for their descendants. ●

CHRONOLOGY	
4 million–1 million years ago	Era of *Australopithecus*
3.5 million years ago	Era of Lucy
2.5 million–200,000 years ago	Era of *Homo erectus*
200,000 B.C.E.	Early evolution of *Homo sapiens*
200,000–35,000 B.C.E.	Era of Neandertal peoples
13,500–10,500 B.C.E.	Natufian society
10,000–8000 B.C.E.	Early experimentation with agriculture
10,000–300 B.C.E.	Jomon society
8000 B.C.E.	Appearance of agricultural villages
4000–3500 B.C.E.	Appearance of cities
3000 B.C.E.–1850 C.E.	Chinook society

For Further Reading

Elizabeth Wayland Barber. *Women's Work: The First 20,000 Years.* New York, 1994. Fascinating study of prehistoric and ancient textiles, which the author argues was a craft industry dominated by women from the earliest times.

Peter Bellwood. *First Farmers: The Origins of Agricultural Societies.* Oxford, 2005. A comprehensive and comparative review of early agriculture and its effects.

David Christian. *Maps of Time: An Introduction to Big History.* Berkeley, 2004. A brilliant study that considers human history in the context of natural history since the big bang.

Mark Nathan Cohen. *The Food Crisis in Prehistory: Overpopulation and the Origins of Agriculture.* New Haven, 1977. Contends that overpopulation and food shortages encouraged human communities to resort to cultivation.

———. *Health and the Rise of Civilization.* New Haven, 1989. Argues that human groups faced new dietary problems and diseases as they relied on agriculture and congregated in urban settings.

Jared Diamond. *Guns, Germs, and Steel: The Fates of Human Societies.* New York, 1997. A wide-ranging book that throws fresh light particularly on the invention and early spread of agriculture.

Margaret Ehrenberg. *Women in Prehistory.* London, 1989. Brings archaeological discoveries to bear on questions of sex and gender relations in prehistoric times.

Marija Gimbutas. *The Civilization of the Goddess.* San Francisco, 1991. A controversial but often insightful book especially valuable for its analysis of prehistoric art and religion.

———. *The Goddesses and Gods of Old Europe.* London, 1982. A provocative examination of the religions of paleolithic Europe.

R. Dale Guthrie. *The Nature of Paleolithic Art.* Chicago, 2005. Examines paleolithic art in the context of human physiology and argues that much paleolithic art reflected interests in food and sex.

Donald C. Johanson and Maitland A. Edey. *Lucy: The Beginnings of Humankind.* New York, 1981. Fascinating account of the discovery of Lucy and the scholarly controversies that ensued.

Richard G. Klein. *The Dawn of Human Culture.* New York, 2002. Places the development of human consciousness in the context of evolutionary history.

James Mellaart. *Çatal Hüyük: A Neolithic Town in Anatolia.* New York, 1967. Discussion of Çatal Hüyük by its excavator.

Kathy D. Schick and Nicholas Toth. *Making Silent Stones Speak: Human Evolution and the Dawn of Technology.* New York, 1993. Fascinating examination of stone tools and paleolithic technology.

Bruce D. Smith. *The Emergence of Agriculture.* New York, 1995. Concentrates on the initial domestication of plant and animal species in world regions where agriculture originated.

Christopher Stringer and Clive Gamble. *In Search of the Neanderthals: Solving the Puzzle of Human Origins.* New York, 1993. Excellent, well-illustrated study of Neandertal peoples and their relationship to modern human beings.

Erik Trinkaus and Pat Shipman. *The Neandertals: Changing the Image of Mankind.* New York, 1993. Insightful account of the discovery, study, and interpretation of Neandertal remains.

Nicholas Wade. *Before the Dawn: Recovering the Lost History of Our Ancestors.* New York, 2006. Excellent synthesis of studies on human evolution.

Early Societies in Southwest Asia and the Indo-European Migrations

chapter 2

A wall relief from an Assyrian palace of the eighth century B.C.E. depicts Gilgamesh as a heroic figure holding a lion.

EYEWITNESS:
Gilgamesh: The Man and the Myth

By far the best-known individual of ancient Mesopotamian society was a man named Gilgamesh. According to historical sources, Gilgamesh was the fifth king of the city of Uruk. He ruled about 2750 B.C.E.—for a period of 126 years, according to one semilegendary source—and he led his community in its conflicts with Kish, a nearby city that was the principal rival of Uruk. Historical sources record little additional detail about Gilgamesh's life and deeds.

But Gilgamesh was a figure of Mesopotamian mythology and folklore as well as history. He was the subject of numerous poems and legends, and Mesopotamian bards made him the central figure in a cycle of stories known collectively as the *Epic of Gilgamesh.* As a figure of legend, Gilgamesh became the greatest hero figure of ancient Mesopotamia. According to the stories, the gods granted Gilgamesh a perfect body and endowed him with superhuman strength and courage. He was "the man to whom all things were known," a supremely wise individual who "saw mysteries and knew secret things." The legends declare that he constructed the massive city walls of Uruk as well as several of the city's magnificent temples to Mesopotamian deities.

The stories that make up the *Epic of Gilgamesh* recount the adventures of this hero and his cherished friend Enkidu as they sought fame. They killed an evil monster, rescued Uruk from a ravaging bull, and matched wits with the gods. In spite of their heroic deeds, Enkidu offended the gods and fell under a sentence of death. His loss profoundly affected Gilgamesh, who sought for some means to cheat death and gain eternal life. He eventually found a magical plant that had the power to confer immortality, but a serpent stole the plant and carried it away, forcing Gilgamesh to recognize that death is the ultimate fate of all human beings. Thus, while focusing on the activities of Gilgamesh and Enkidu, the stories explored themes of friendship, loyalty, ambition, fear of death, and longing for immortality. In doing so they reflected the interests and concerns of the complex, urban-based society that had recently emerged in Mesopotamia.

Productive agricultural economies supported the development of the world's first complex societies, in which sizable numbers of people lived in cities and extended their political, social, economic, and cultural influence over large regions. The earliest urban societies so far known emerged during the early fourth millennium B.C.E. in southwest Asia, particularly in Mesopotamia.

As people congregated in cities, they needed to find ways to resolve disputes—sometimes between residents within individual settlements, other times between whole settlements themselves—that inevitably arose as individual and group interests conflicted. In search of order, settled agricultural peoples recognized political authorities and built states throughout Mesopotamia. The establishment of states encouraged the creation of empires, as some states sought to extend their power and enhance their security by imposing their rule on neighboring lands.

Apart from stimulating the establishment of states, urban society in Mesopotamia also promoted the emergence of social classes, thus giving rise to increasingly complex social and economic structures. Cities fostered specialized labor, and the resulting efficient production of high-quality goods in turn stimulated trade. Furthermore, early Mesopotamia also developed distinctive cultural traditions as Mesopotamians invented a system of writing and supported organized religions.

Mesopotamian and other peoples regularly interacted with one another. Mesopotamian prosperity attracted numerous migrants, such as the ancient Hebrews, who settled in the region's cities and adopted Mesopotamian ways. Merchants such as the Phoenicians, who also embraced Mesopotamian society, built extensive maritime trade networks that linked southwest Asia with lands throughout the Mediterranean basin. Some Indo-European peoples also had direct dealings with their Mesopotamian contemporaries, with effects crucial for both Indo-European and Mesopotamian societies. Other Indo-European peoples never heard of Mesopotamia, but they employed Mesopotamian inventions such as wheels and metallurgy when undertaking extensive migrations that profoundly influenced historical development throughout much of Eurasia from western Europe to India and beyond. Even in the earliest days of city life, the world was the site of frequent and intense interaction between peoples of different societies.

THE QUEST FOR ORDER

During the fourth millennium B.C.E., human population increased rapidly in Mesopotamia. Inhabitants had few precedents to guide them in the organization of a large-scale society. At most they inherited a few techniques for keeping order in the small agricultural villages of neolithic times. By experimentation and adaptation, however, they created states and governmental machinery that brought political and social order to their territories. Moreover, effective political and military organization enabled them to build regional empires and extend their authority to neighboring peoples.

Mesopotamia: "The Land between the Rivers"

The place-name *Mesopotamia* comes from two Greek words meaning "the land between the rivers," and it refers specifically to the fertile valleys of the Tigris and Euphrates rivers in modern-day Iraq. Mesopotamia receives little rainfall, but the Tigris and Euphrates brought large volumes of freshwater to the region. Early cultivators realized that by tapping these rivers, building reservoirs, and digging canals, they could irrigate fields of barley, wheat, and peas. Small-scale irrigation began in Mesopotamia soon after 6000 B.C.E.

Sumer Artificial irrigation led to increased food supplies, which in turn supported a rapidly increasing human population while also attracting migrants from other regions. Human numbers grew especially fast in the land of Sumer in the southern half of Mesopotamia. It is possible that the people known as the Sumerians already inhabited this land in the sixth millennium B.C.E., but it is perhaps more likely that they were later migrants attracted to the region by its agricultural potential. In either case, by about 5000 B.C.E. the Sumerians were constructing elaborate irrigation networks that helped them realize abundant agricultural harvests. By 3000 B.C.E. the population of Sumer was approaching one hundred thousand—an unprecedented concentration of people in ancient times—and the Sumerians were the dominant people of Mesopotamia.

Semitic Migrants While supporting a growing population, the wealth of Sumer also attracted migrants from other regions. Most of the new arrivals were Semitic peoples—so called because they spoke tongues in the Semitic family of languages, including Akkadian, Aramaic, Hebrew, and Phoenician. (Semitic languages spoken in the world today include Arabic and Hebrew, and African peoples speak many other languages related to Semitic tongues.) Semitic peoples were nomadic herders who went to Mesopotamia

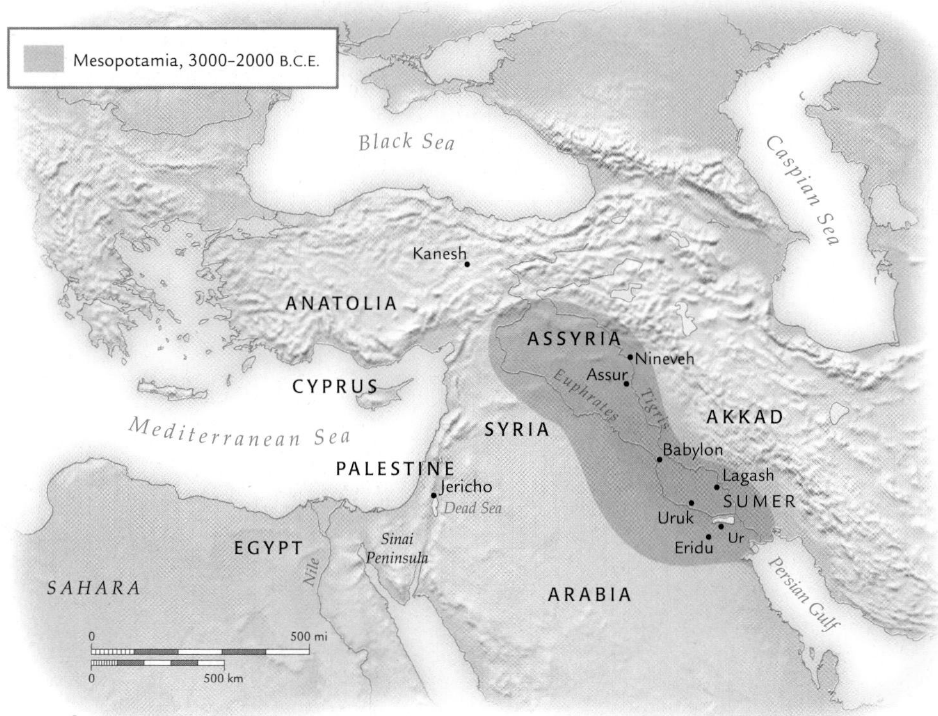

MAP 2.1
Early Mesopotamia, 3000–2000 B.C.E.
Note the locations of Mesopotamian cities in relation to the Tigris and Euphrates rivers.

In what ways were the rivers important for Mesopotamian society?

from the Arabian and Syrian deserts to the south and west. They often intermarried with the Sumerians, and they largely adapted to Sumerian ways.

Beginning around 4000 B.C.E., as human numbers increased in southern Mesopotamia, the Sumerians built the world's first cities. These cities differed markedly from the neolithic villages that preceded them. Unlike the earlier settlements, the Sumerian cities were centers of political and military authority, and their jurisdiction extended into the surrounding regions. Moreover, bustling marketplaces that drew buyers and sellers from near and far turned the cities into economic centers as well. The cities also served as cultural centers where priests maintained organized religions and scribes developed traditions of writing and formal education.

Sumerian City-States For almost a millennium, from 3200 to 2350 B.C.E., a dozen Sumerian cities—Eridu, Ur, Uruk, Lagash, Nippur, Kish, and others—dominated public affairs in Mesopotamia. These cities all experienced internal and external pressures that prompted them to establish states—formal governmental institutions that wielded authority throughout their territories. Internally, the cities needed to maintain order and ensure that inhabitants cooperated on community projects. With their expanding populations, the cities also needed to prevent conflicts between urban residents from escalating into serious civic disorder. Moreover, because agriculture was crucial to the welfare of urban residents, the cities all became city-states: they not only controlled public life within the city walls but also extended their authority to neighboring territories and oversaw affairs in surrounding agricultural regions.

While preserving the peace, government authorities also organized work on projects of value to the entire community. Palaces, temples, and defensive walls dominated all the Sumerian cities, and all were the work of laborers recruited and coordinated by government authorities such as Gilgamesh, whom legendary accounts credit with the building of city walls and temples at Uruk. Particularly impressive were the ziggurats—distinctive stepped pyramids that housed temples and altars to the principal local deity. In the city of Uruk, a massive ziggurat and temple complex went up about 3200 B.C.E. to honor the fertility goddess Inanna. Scholars have calculated that its construction required the services of fifteen hundred laborers working ten hours per day for five years.

Even more important than buildings were the irrigation systems that supported productive agriculture and urban society. As their population grew, the Sumerians expanded their networks of reservoirs and canals. The construction, maintenance, and repair of the irrigation systems required the labor of untold thousands of workers. Only recognized government authorities had the standing to draft workers for this difficult labor and order them to participate in

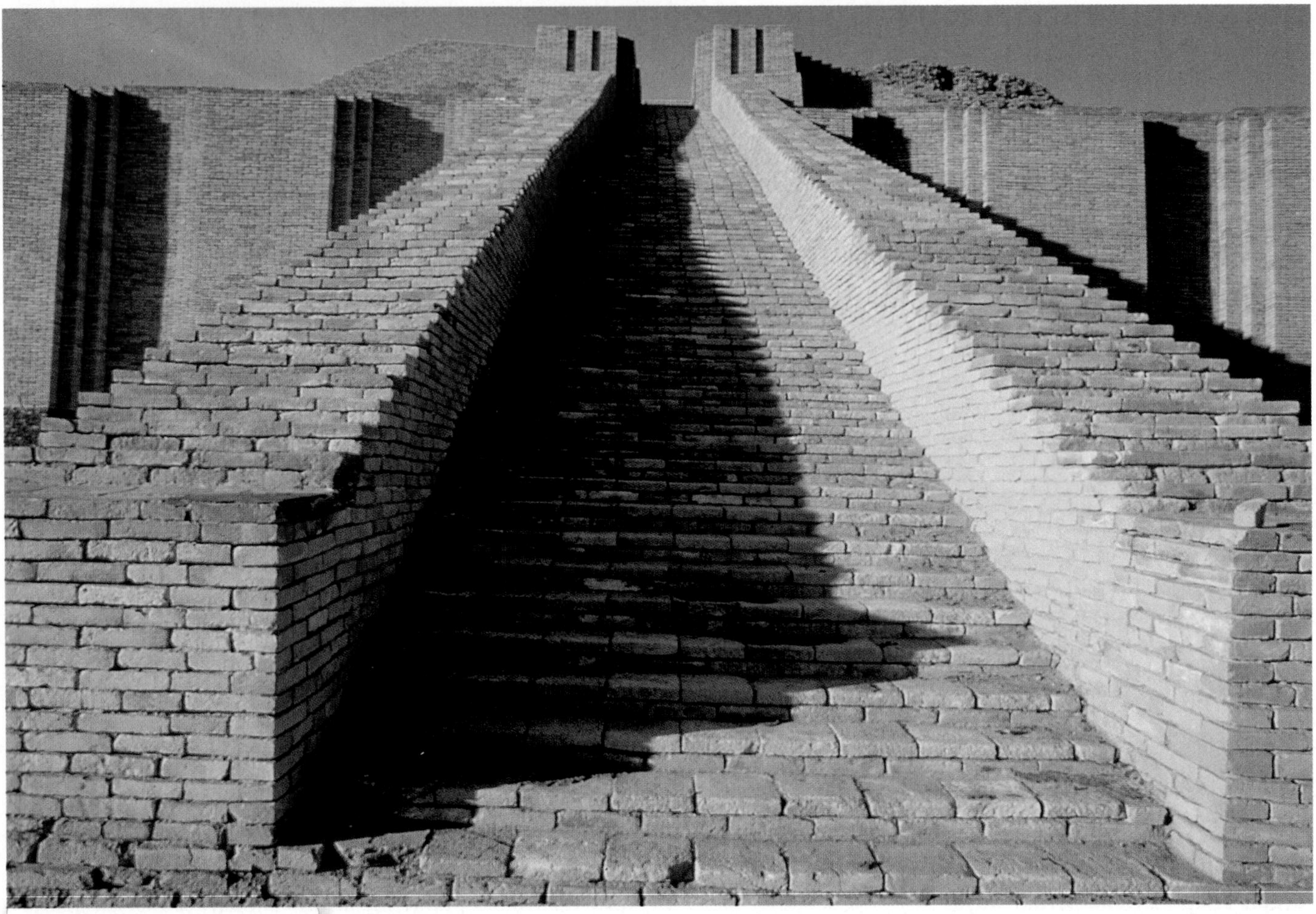

Rising more than 30 meters (100 feet), the massive temple of the moon god Nanna-Suen (sometimes known as Sin) dominated the Sumerian city of Ur. Constructing temples of this size required a huge investment of resources and thousands of laborers. As some of the largest human-built structures of the time, how might such temples have impressed Mesopotamian peoples?

such large-scale projects. Even when the irrigation systems functioned perfectly, recognized authority was still necessary to ensure equitable distribution of water and to resolve disputes.

In addition to their internal pressures, the Sumerian cities faced external problems. The wealth stored in Sumerian cities attracted the interest of peoples outside the cities. Mesopotamia is a mostly flat land with few natural geographic barriers. It was a simple matter for raiders to attack the Sumerian cities and take their wealth. The cities responded to that threat by building defensive walls and organizing military forces. The need to recruit, train, equip, maintain, and deploy military forces created another demand for recognized authority.

Sumerian Kings The earliest Sumerian governments were probably assemblies of prominent men who made decisions on behalf of the whole community. When crises arose, assemblies yielded their power to individuals who possessed full authority during the period of emergency. These individual rulers gradually usurped the authority of the assemblies and established themselves as monarchs. By about 3000 B.C.E. all Sumerian cities had kings who claimed absolute authority within their realms. In fact, however, the kings generally ruled in cooperation with local nobles, who came mostly from the ranks of military leaders who had displayed special valor in battle. By 2500 B.C.E. city-states dominated public life in Sumer, and city-states such as Assur and Nineveh had also begun to emerge in northern Mesopotamia.

The Course of Empire

Once they had organized effective states, Mesopotamians ventured beyond the boundaries of their societies. As early as 2800 B.C.E., conflicts between city-states often led to war, as aggrieved or ambitious kings sought to punish or conquer their neighbors. Sumerian accounts indicate that the king of

Kish, a city-state located just east of Babylon, extended his rule to much of southern Mesopotamia after 2800 B.C.E., for example, and Sumerian poems praised King Gilgamesh for later liberating Uruk from Kish's control. In efforts to move beyond constant conflicts, a series of conquerors worked to establish order on a scale larger than the city-state by building empires that supervised the affairs of numerous subject cities and peoples. After 2350 B.C.E. Mesopotamia fell under the control of several powerful regional empires.

Sargon of Akkad These regional empires emerged as Semitic peoples such as the Akkadians and the Babylonians of northern Mesopotamia began to overshadow the Sumerians. The creator of empire in Mesopotamia was Sargon of Akkad, a city near Kish and Babylon whose precise location has so far eluded archaeologists. A talented administrator and brilliant warrior, Sargon (2370–2315 B.C.E.) began his career as a minister to the king of Kish. About 2334 B.C.E. he organized a coup against the king, recruited an army, and went on the offensive against the Sumerian city-states. He conquered the cities one by one, destroyed their defensive walls, and placed them under his governors and administrators. As Sargon's conquests mounted, his armies grew larger and more professional, and no single city-state could withstand his forces.

Empire: A New Form of Political Organization Sargon's empire represented a historical experiment, as the conqueror worked to devise ways and means to hold his possessions together. He relied heavily on his personal presence to maintain stability throughout his realm. For much of his reign, he traveled with armies, which sometimes numbered more than five thousand, from one Mesopotamian city to another. The resulting experience was quite unpleasant for the cities he visited, because their populations had to provide food, lodging, and financial support whenever Sargon and his forces descended upon them. That inconvenience naturally generated considerable resentment of the conqueror and frequently sparked local rebellions. In a never-ending search for funds to support his army and his government, Sargon also seized control of trade routes and supplies of natural resources such as silver, tin, and cedar wood. By controlling and taxing trade, Sargon obtained financial resources to maintain his military juggernaut and transform his capital of Akkad into the wealthiest and most powerful city in the world. At the high point of his reign, his empire embraced all of Mesopotamia, and his armies had ventured as far afield as the Mediterranean and the Black Sea.

For several generations Sargon's successors maintained his empire. Gradually, though, it weakened, partly because of chronic rebellion in city-states that resented imperial rule, partly also because of invasions by peoples hoping to seize a portion of Mesopotamia's fabulous wealth. By about 2150 B.C.E. Sargon's empire had collapsed altogether. Yet the memory of his deeds, recorded in legends and histories as well as in his works of propaganda, inspired later conquerors to follow his example.

Hammurabi and the Babylonian Empire Most prominent of the later conquerors was the Babylonian Hammurabi (reigned 1792–1750 B.C.E.), who styled himself "king of the four quarters of the world." The Babylonian empire dominated Mesopotamia until about 1600 B.C.E. Hammurabi improved on Sargon's administrative techniques by relying on centralized bureaucratic rule and regular taxation. Instead of traveling from city to city with an army both large and hungry, Hammurabi and his successors ruled from Babylon (located near modern Baghdad) and stationed deputies in the territories they controlled. Instead of confiscating supplies and other wealth in the unfortunate regions their armies visited, Hammurabi and later rulers instituted less ruinous but more regular taxes collected by their officials. By these means Hammurabi developed a more efficient and predictable government than his predecessors and also spread its costs more evenly over the population.

Hammurabi's Laws Hammurabi also sought to maintain his empire by providing it with a code of law. Sumerian rulers had promulgated laws perhaps as early as 2500 B.C.E., and Hammurabi borrowed liberally from his predecessors in compiling the most extensive and most complete Mesopotamian law code. In the prologue to his laws, Hammurabi proclaimed that the gods had chosen him "to promote the welfare of the people, . . . to cause justice to prevail in the land, to destroy the wicked and evil, [so] that the strong might not oppress the weak, to rise like the sun over the people, and to light up the land." Hammurabi's laws established high standards of behavior and stern punishments for violators. They prescribed death penalties for murder, theft, fraud, false accusations, sheltering of runaway slaves, failure to

Bronze bust of a Mesopotamian king often thought to represent Sargon of Akkad. The sculpture dates to about 2350 B.C.E. and reflects high levels of expertise in the working of bronze.

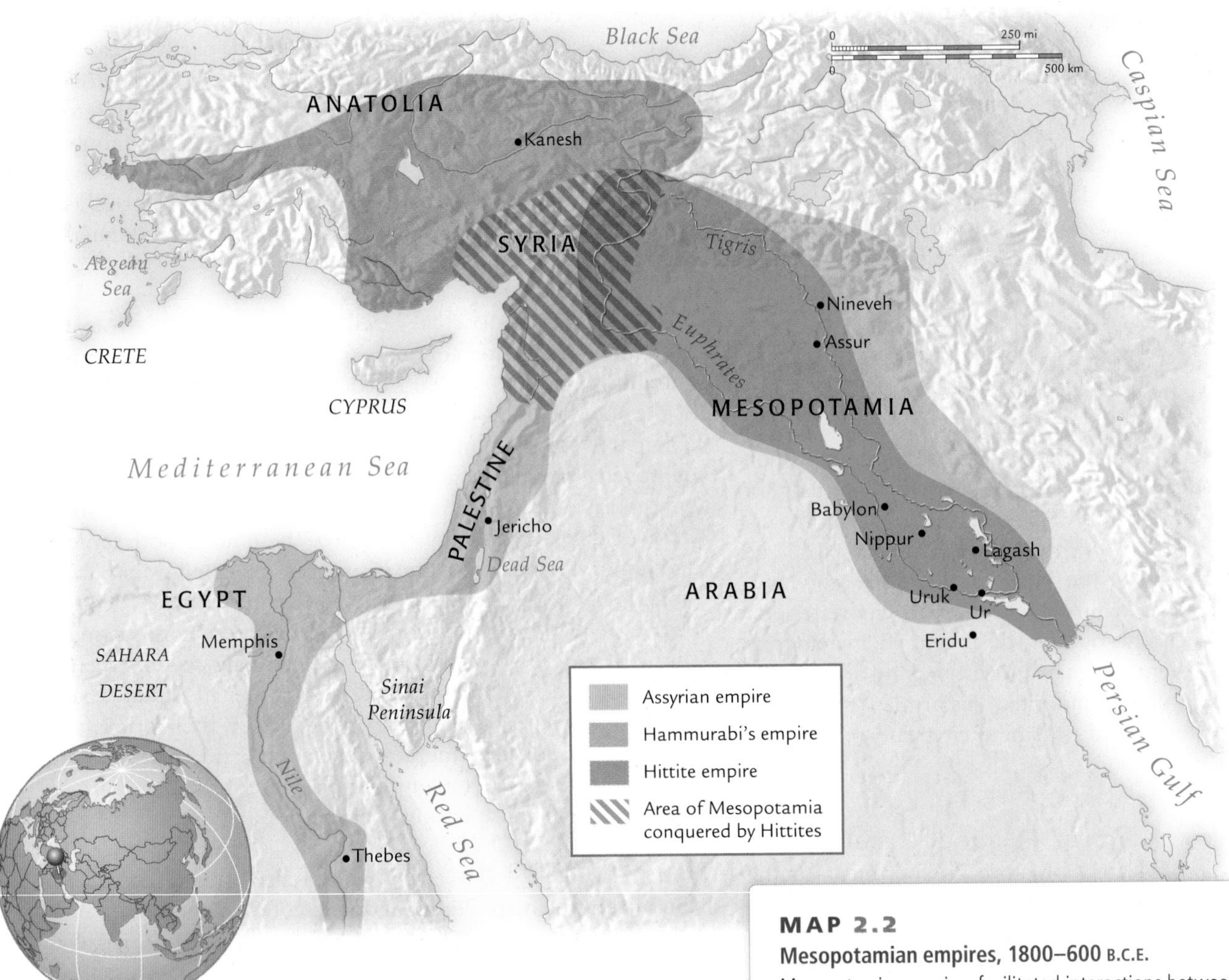

MAP 2.2
Mesopotamian empires, 1800–600 B.C.E.
Mesopotamian empires facilitated interactions between peoples from different societies.

Consider the various land, river, and sea routes by which peoples of Mesopotamia, Anatolia, and Egypt were able to communicate with one another in the second and first millennia B.C.E.

obey royal orders, adultery, and incest. Civil laws regulated prices, wages, commercial dealings, marital relationships, and the conditions of slavery.

The code relied heavily on the principle of ***lex talionis,*** the "law of retaliation," whereby offenders suffered punishments resembling their violations. But the code also took account of social standing when applying this principle. It provided, for example, that a noble who destroyed the eye or broke the bone of another noble would have his own eye destroyed or bone broken, but if a noble destroyed the eye or broke the bone of a commoner, the noble merely paid a fine in silver. Local judges did not always follow the prescriptions of Hammurabi's code: indeed, they frequently relied on their own judgment when deciding cases that came before them. Nevertheless, Hammurabi's laws established a set of standards that lent some degree of cultural unity to the far-flung Babylonian empire.

lex talionis (lehks tah-lee-oh-nihs)

Despite Hammurabi's administrative efficiencies and impressive law code, the wealth of the Babylonian empire attracted invaders, particularly the Hittites, who had built a powerful empire in Anatolia (modern-day Turkey), and about 1595 B.C.E. the Babylonian empire crumbled before Hittite assaults. For several centuries after the fall of Babylon, southwest Asia was a land of considerable turmoil, as regional states competed for power and position while migrants and invaders struggled to establish footholds for themselves in Mesopotamia and neighboring regions.

The Later Mesopotamian Empires

Imperial rule returned to Mesopotamia with the Assyrians, a hardy people from northern Mesopotamia who had built a compact state in the Tigris River valley during the nineteenth century B.C.E. Taking advantage of their location on trade routes running both north-south and east-west, the Assyrians built flourishing cities at Assur and Nineveh. They built a powerful and intimidating army by organizing their forces into standardized units and placing them under the command of professional officers. The Assyrians appointed these officers because of merit, skill, and bravery rather than noble birth or family connections. They supplemented infantry with cavalry forces and light, swift, horse-drawn chariots, which they borrowed from the Hittites. These chariots were devastating instruments of war that allowed archers to attack their enemies from rapidly moving platforms. Waves of Assyrian chariots stormed their opponents with a combination of high speed and withering firepower that unnerved the opponents and left them vulnerable to the Assyrian infantry and cavalry forces.

The Assyrian Empire After the collapse of the Babylonian empire, the Assyrian state was one among many jockeying for power and position in northern Mesopotamia. After about 1300 B.C.E. Assyrians gradually extended their authority to much of southwest Asia. They made use of recently invented iron weapons to strengthen their army, which sometimes numbered upward of fifty thousand troops who pushed relentlessly in all directions. At its high point, during the eighth and seventh centuries B.C.E., the Assyrian empire embraced not only Mesopotamia but also Syria, Palestine, much of Anatolia, and most of Egypt. King Assurbanipal, whose long reign (668–627 B.C.E.) coincided with the high tide of Assyrian domination, went so far as to style himself not only "king of Assyria" but also, grandiosely, "king of the universe."

Like most other Mesopotamian peoples, the Assyrians relied on the administrative techniques pioneered by their Babylonian predecessors, and they followed laws much like those enshrined in the code of Hammurabi. They also preserved a great deal of Mesopotamian literature in huge libraries maintained at their large and lavish courts. At his magnificent royal palace in Nineveh, for example, King Assurbanipal maintained a vast library that included thousands of literary scholarly texts as well as diplomatic correspondence and administrative records. Indeed, Assurbanipal's library preserved most of the Mesopotamian literature that has survived to the present day, including the *Epic of Gilgamesh*.

The Assyrian empire brought wealth, comfort, and sophistication to the Assyrian heartland, particularly the cities of Assur and Nineveh, but elsewhere Assyrian domination was extremely unpopular. Assyrian rulers faced intermittent rebellion by subjects in one part or another of their empire, the very size of which presented enormous administrative challenges. Ultimately, a combination of internal unrest and external assault brought their empire down in 612 B.C.E.

This handsome basalt stele shows Hammurabi receiving his royal authority from the sun god, Shamash. Some four thousand lines of Hammurabi's laws are inscribed below. Why would it have been useful to associate Hammurabi with divine powers?

Nebuchadnezzar and the New Babylonian Empire For half a century, from 600 to 550 B.C.E., Babylon once again dominated Mesopotamia during the New Babylonian empire, sometimes called the Chaldean empire. King Nebuchadnezzar (reigned 605–562 B.C.E.) lavished wealth and resources on

thinking about TRADITIONS

The Invention of Politics
Mesopotamians conducted some of the world's first experiments in organizing sustainable communities for large numbers of people living in densely populated spaces. What methods of political and social organization did they adopt? How and why did they change their political order over time? What role did written law codes play in consolidating Mesopotamian political and social traditions?

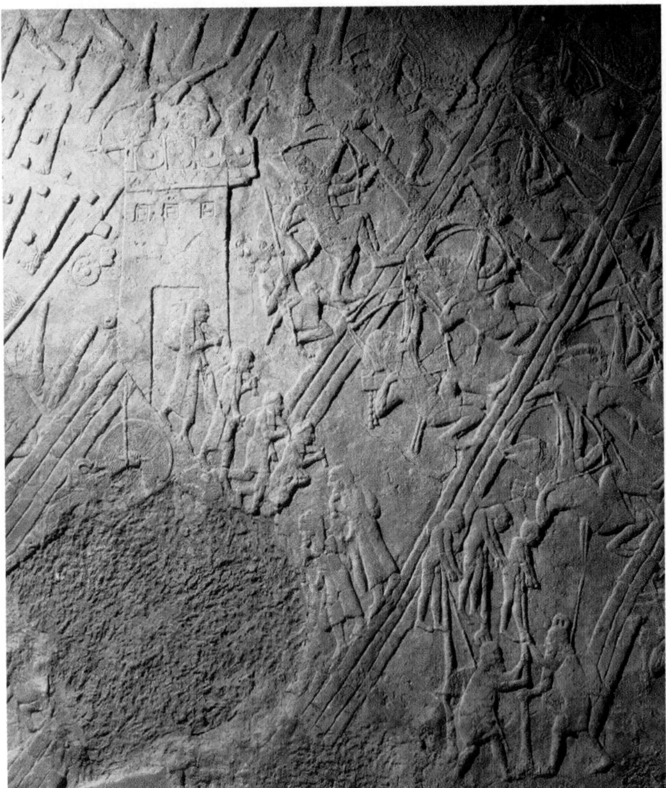

An alabaster relief sculpture from the eighth century B.C.E. depicts Assyrian forces besieging a city and dispatching defeated enemy soldiers. Assyrian royal palaces commonly featured similar wall reliefs celebrating victories of the Assyrian armies.

his capital city. Babylon occupied some 850 hectares (more than 2,100 acres), and the city's defensive walls were reportedly so thick that a four-horse chariot could turn around on top of them. Within the walls there were enormous palaces and 1,179 temples, some of them faced with gold and decorated with thousands of statues. When one of the king's wives longed for flowering shrubs from her mountain homeland, Nebuchadnezzar had them planted in terraces above the city walls, and the hanging gardens of Babylon have symbolized the city's luxuriousness ever since.

By that time, however, peoples beyond Mesopotamia had acquired advanced weapons and experimented with techniques of administering large territories. By the mid-sixth century B.C.E., Mesopotamians largely lost control of their affairs, as foreign conquerors absorbed them into their empires.

THE FORMATION OF A COMPLEX SOCIETY AND SOPHISTICATED CULTURAL TRADITIONS

With the emergence of cities and the congregation of dense populations in urban spaces, specialized labor proliferated. The Mesopotamian economy became increasingly diverse, and trade linked the region with distant peoples. Clearly defined social classes emerged, as small groups of people concentrated wealth and power in their hands, and Mesopotamia developed into a patriarchal society that vested authority largely in adult males. While building a complex society, Mesopotamians also allocated some of their resources to individuals who worked to develop sophisticated cultural traditions. They invented systems of writing that enabled them to record information for future retrieval. Writing soon became a foundation for education, science, literature, and religious reflection.

Economic Specialization and Trade

When large numbers of people began to congregate in cities and work at tasks other than agriculture, they vastly expanded the stock of human skills. Craftsmen refined techniques inherited from earlier generations and experimented with new ways of doing things. Pottery, textile manufacture, woodworking, leather production, brick making, stonecutting, and masonry all became distinct occupations in the world's earliest cities.

Bronze Metallurgy Metallurgical innovations ranked among the most important developments that came about because of specialized labor. Already in neolithic times, craftsmen had fashioned copper into tools and jewelry. In pure form, however, copper is too soft for use as an effective weapon or as a tool for heavy work. About 4000 B.C.E. Mesopotamian metalworkers discovered that if they alloyed copper with tin, they could make much harder and stronger implements. Experimentation with copper metallurgy thus led to the invention of bronze. Because both copper and tin were relatively rare and hence expensive, most people could not afford bronze implements. But bronze had an immediate impact on military affairs, as craftsmen turned out swords, spears, axes, shields, and armor made of the recently invented metal. Over a longer period, bronze also had an impact on agriculture. Mesopotamian farmers began to use bronze knives and bronze-tipped plows instead of tools made of bone, wood, stone, or obsidian.

Iron Metallurgy After about 1000 B.C.E. Mesopotamian craftsmen began to manufacture effective tools and weapons with iron as well as bronze. Experimentation with iron metallurgy began as early as the fourth millennium B.C.E., but early efforts resulted in products that were too brittle for heavy-duty uses. About 1300 B.C.E. craftsmen from Hittite society in Anatolia (discussed later in this chapter) developed techniques of forging exceptionally strong iron tools and weapons. Iron metallurgy soon spread throughout Anatolia, Mesopotamia, and other regions as well, and Assyrian conquerors made particularly effective use of iron weapons in building their empire. Because iron deposits are much cheaper and more widely available than copper and tin, the ingredients of bronze, iron quickly became the metal of choice for weapons and tools.

The Wheel While some craftsmen refined the techniques of bronze and iron metallurgy, others devised efficient means of transportation based on wheeled vehicles and sailing ships, both of which facilitated long-distance trade. The first use of wheels probably took place about 3500 B.C.E., and Sumerians were building wheeled carts by 3000 B.C.E. Wheeled carts and wagons enabled people to haul heavy loads of bulk goods—such as grain, bricks, or metal ores—over much longer distances than human porters or draft animals could manage. The wheel rapidly diffused from Sumer to neighboring lands, and within a few centuries it was in common use throughout Mesopotamia and beyond.

Shipbuilding Sumerians also experimented with technologies of maritime transportation. By 3500 B.C.E. they had built watercraft that allowed them to venture into the Persian Gulf. By 2300 B.C.E. they were trading regularly with merchants of Harappan society in the Indus River valley of northern India (discussed in chapter 4), which they reached by sailing through the Persian Gulf and the Arabian Sea. Until about 1750 B.C.E. Sumerian merchants shipped woolen textiles, leather goods, sesame oil, and jewelry to India in exchange for copper, ivory, pearls, and semiprecious stones. During the time of the Babylonian empire, Mesopotamians traded extensively with peoples in all directions: they imported silver from Anatolia, cedar-wood from Lebanon, copper from Arabia, gold from Egypt, tin from Persia, lapis lazuli from Afghanistan, and semiprecious stones from northern India.

Trade Networks Archaeological excavations have shed bright light on one Mesopotamian trade network in particular. During the early second millennium B.C.E., Assyrian merchants traveled regularly by donkey caravan some 1,600 kilometers (1,000 miles) from their home of Assur in northern Mesopotamia to Kanesh (modern Kültepe) in Anatolia. Surviving correspondence shows that during the forty-five years from 1810 to 1765 B.C.E., merchants transported at least eighty tons of tin and one hundred thousand textiles from Assur and returned from Kanesh with no less than ten tons of silver. The correspondence also shows that the merchants and their families operated a well-organized business. Merchants' wives and children manufactured textiles in Assur and sent them to their menfolk who lived in trading colonies at Kanesh. The merchants responded with orders for textiles in the styles desired at Kanesh.

The Emergence of a Stratified Patriarchal Society

Social Classes Agriculture enabled human groups to accumulate wealth, and distinctions between the more and less wealthy appeared already in neolithic villages such as Jericho and Çatal Hüyük. With increasingly specialized labor and long-distance trade, however, cities provided many more opportunities for the accumulation of wealth. Social distinctions in Mesopotamia became much more sharply defined than those of neolithic villages.

In early Mesopotamia the ruling classes consisted of kings and nobles who won their positions because of their valor and success as warriors. The early kings of the Sumerian cities made such a deep impression on their contemporaries that legends portrayed them as offspring of the gods. According to many legends, for example, Gilgamesh of Uruk, the son of a goddess and a king, was two-thirds divine and one-third human. Some legends recognized him as a full-fledged god. Large-scale construction projects ordered by the kings and the lavish decoration of capital cities also reflected the high status of the Mesopotamian ruling classes. All the Mesopotamian cities boasted massive city walls and imposing public buildings.

A silver model of a boat discovered in a royal tomb at Ur throws light on Sumerian transportation of grain and other goods on the rivers, canals, and marshes of southern Mesopotamia about 2700 B.C.E.

PART 1

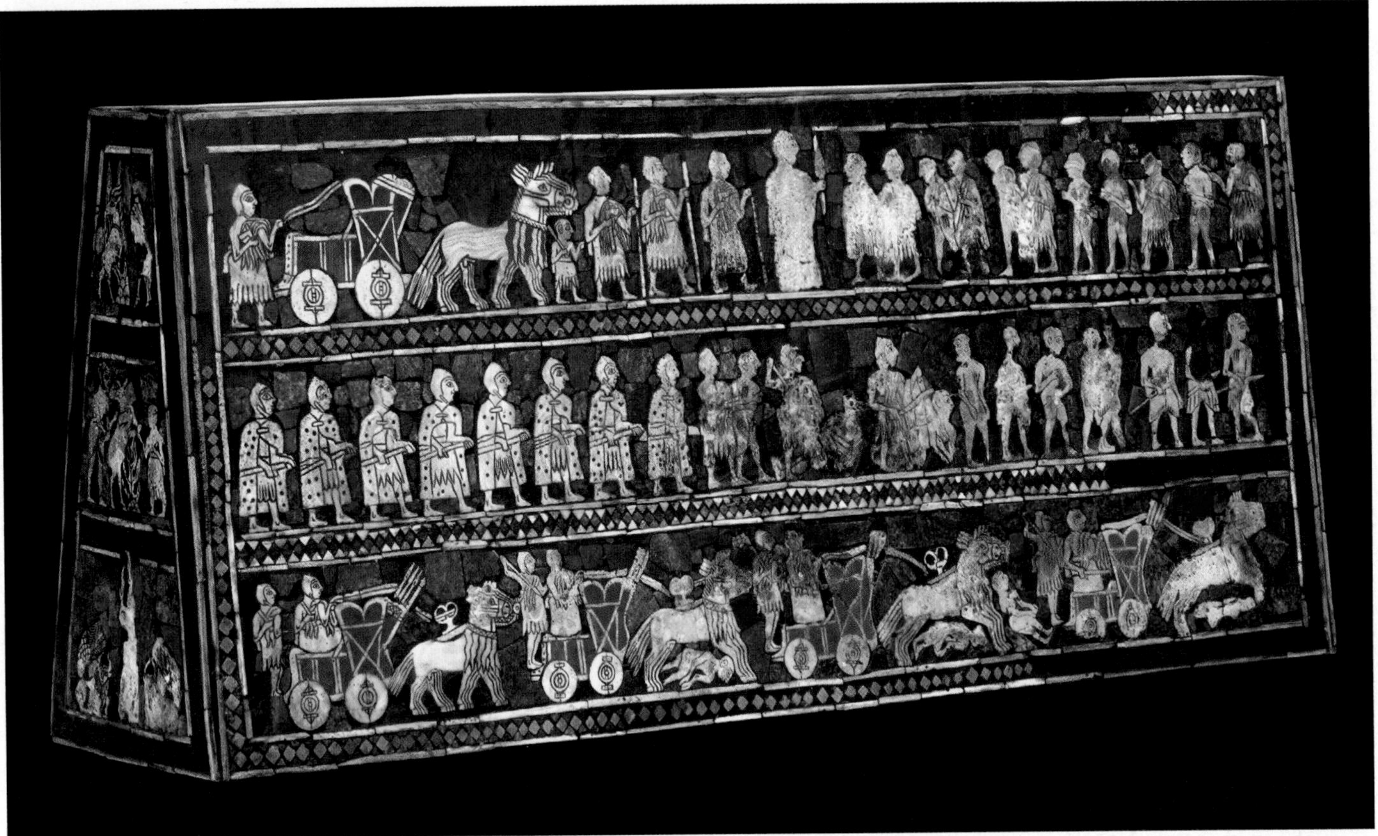

The Royal Standard of Ur, produced about 2700 B.C.E., depicts diners at an elaborate banquet with musicians (top rank) as well as common folk who bring fish, goats, sheep, cattle, and agricultural produce for the affair. How do these figures give us insight into life among the Sumerians?

Temple Communities Closely allied with the ruling elites were priests and priestesses, many of whom were younger relatives of the rulers. The principal role of the priestly elites was to intervene with the gods to ensure good fortune for their communities. In exchange for those services, priests and priestesses lived in temple communities and received offerings of food, drink, and clothing from city inhabitants. Temples also generated income from vast tracts of land that they owned and large workshops that they maintained. One temple community near the city of Lagash employed six thousand textile workers between 2150 and 2100 B.C.E. Other temple communities cultivated grains, herded sheep and goats, and manufactured leather, wood, metal, and stone goods. Because of their wealth, temples provided comfortable livings for their inhabitants, and they also served the needs of the larger community. Temples functioned as banks where individuals could store wealth, and they helped underwrite trading ventures to distant lands. They also helped those in need by taking in orphans, supplying grain in times of famine, and providing ransoms for community members captured in battle.

Apart from the ruling and priestly elites, Mesopotamian society included less privileged classes of free commoners, dependent clients, and slaves. Free commoners mostly worked as peasant cultivators in the countryside on land owned by their families, although some also worked in the cities as builders, craftsmen, or professionals, such as physicians or engineers. Dependent clients had fewer options than free commoners because they possessed no property. Dependent clients usually worked as agricultural laborers on estates owned by others, including the king, nobles, or priestly communities, and they owed a portion of their production to the landowners. Free commoners and dependent clients all paid taxes—usually in the form of surplus agricultural production—that supported the ruling classes, military forces, and temple communities. In addition, when conscripted by ruling authorities, free commoners and dependent clients also provided labor services for large-scale construction projects involving roads, city walls, irrigation systems, temples, and public buildings.

Slaves Slaves came from three main sources: prisoners of war, convicted criminals, and heavily indebted individuals who sold themselves into slavery to satisfy their obligations. Some slaves worked as agricultural laborers on the estates of nobles or temple communities, but most were domestic servants in wealthy households. Many masters granted slaves their freedom, often with a financial gift, after several years of good service. Slaves with accommodating masters sometimes even engaged in small-scale trade and earned enough money to purchase their freedom.

Patriarchal Society While recognizing differences of rank, wealth, and social status, Mesopotamians also built a patriarchal society that vested authority over public and private affairs in adult men. Within their households men decided the work that family members would perform and made marriage arrangements for their children as well as any others who came under their authority. Men also dominated public life. Men ruled as kings, and decisions about policies and public affairs rested almost entirely in men's hands.

Hammurabi's laws throw considerable light on sex and gender relations in ancient Mesopotamia. The laws recognized men as heads of their households and entrusted all major family decisions to their judgment. Men even had the power to sell their wives and children into slavery to satisfy their debts. In the interests of protecting the reputations of husbands and the legitimacy of offspring, the laws prescribed death by drowning as the punishment for adulterous wives, as well as for their partners, while permitting men to engage in consensual sexual relations with concubines, slaves, or prostitutes without penalty.

Women's Roles In spite of their subordinate legal status, women made their influence felt in Mesopotamian society. At ruling courts women sometimes advised kings and their governments. A few women wielded great power as high priestesses who managed the enormous estates belonging to their temples. Others obtained a formal education and worked as scribes—literate individuals who prepared administrative and legal documents for governments and private parties. Women also pursued careers as midwives, shopkeepers, brewers, bakers, tavern keepers, and textile manufacturers. There are no records of women serving as rulers or holding high-level administrative positions.

During the second millennium B.C.E., Mesopotamian men progressively tightened their control over the social and sexual behavior of women. To protect family fortunes and guarantee the legitimacy of heirs, Mesopotamians insisted on the virginity of brides at marriage, and they forbade casual socializing between married women and men outside their family. By 1500 B.C.E. and probably even earlier, upper-class women in Mesopotamian cities had begun to wear veils when they ventured beyond their own households to discourage the attention of men from other families. This concern to control women's social and sexual behavior spread throughout much of southwest Asia and the Mediterranean basin, where it reinforced patriarchal social structures.

Cuneiform tablet from Ur dating from 2900 to 2600 B.C.E. It records deliveries of barley to a temple.

The Development of Written Cultural Traditions

The world's earliest known writing came from Mesopotamia. Sumerians invented a system of writing about the middle of the fourth millennium B.C.E. to keep track of commercial transactions and tax collections. They first experimented with pictographs representing animals, agricultural products, and trade items—such as sheep, oxen, wheat, barley, pots, and fish—that figured prominently in tax and commercial transactions. By 3100 B.C.E. conventional signs representing specific words had spread throughout Mesopotamia.

Cuneiform Writing A writing system that depends on pictures is useful for purposes such as keeping records, but it is a cumbersome way to communicate abstract ideas. Beginning about 2900 B.C.E. the Sumerians developed a more flexible system of writing that used graphic symbols to represent sounds, syllables, and ideas as well as physical objects. By combining pictographs and other symbols, the Sumerians created a powerful writing system.

When writing, a Sumerian scribe used a stylus fashioned from a reed to impress symbols on wet clay. Because the stylus left lines and wedge-shaped marks, Sumerian writing is known as *cuneiform,* a term that comes from two Latin words meaning "wedge-shaped." When dried in the sun or baked in an oven, the clay hardened and preserved a permanent record of the scribe's message. Babylonians, Assyrians, and other peoples later adapted the Sumerians' script to their languages, and the tradition of cuneiform writing continued for more than three thousand years. Thousands of clay tablets with cuneiform writing survive to the present day. Although it entered a period of decline in the fourth century B.C.E. after the arrival of Greek alphabetic script, in which each written symbol represents a distinct, individual sound, scribes continued to produce cuneiform documents into the early centuries C.E.

Education Most education in ancient times was vocational instruction designed to train individuals to work in specific trades and crafts. Yet Mesopotamians also established formal schools, since it required a great deal of time and concentrated effort to learn cuneiform writing. Most of those who learned to read and write became scribes or government officials. A few pursued their studies further and became priests,

sources from the past

Hammurabi's Laws on Family Relationships

By the time of Hammurabi, Mesopotamian marriages had come to represent important business and economic relationships between families. Hammurabi's laws reflect a concern to ensure the legitimacy of children and to protect the economic interests of both marital partners and their families. While placing women under the authority of their fathers and husbands, the laws also protected women against unreasonable treatment by their husbands or other men.

128: If a seignior [a lord or a man of property] acquired a wife, but did not draw up the contracts for her, that woman is no wife.

129: If the wife of a seignior has been caught while lying [i.e., having sexual relations] with another man, they shall bind them and throw them into the water. If the husband of the woman wishes to spare his wife, then the king in turn may spare his subject.

130: If a seignior bound the (betrothed) wife of a(nother) seignior, who had no intercourse with a male and was still living in her father's house, and he has lain in her bosom and they have caught him, that seignior shall be put to death, while that woman shall go free.

131: If a seignior's wife was accused by her husband, but she was not caught while lying with another man, she shall make affirmation by god and return to her house. . . .

138: If a seignior wishes to divorce his wife who did not bear him children, he shall give her money to the full amount of her marriage-price [money or goods that the husband paid to the bride's family in exchange for the right to marry her] and he shall also make good to her the dowry [money or goods that the bride brought to the marriage] which she brought from her father's house and then he may divorce her.

139: If there was no marriage-price, he shall give her one mina of silver as the divorce-settlement.

140: If he is a peasant, he shall give her one-third mina of silver.

141: If a seignior's wife, who was living in the house of the seignior, has made up her mind to leave in order that she may engage in business, thus neglecting her house (and) humiliating her husband, they shall prove it against her; and if her husband has then decided on her divorce, he may divorce her, with nothing to be given her as her divorce-settlement upon her departure. If her husband has not decided on her divorce, her husband may marry another woman, with the former woman living in the house of her husband like a maidservant.

142: If a woman so hated her husband that she has declared, "You may not have me," her record shall be investigated at her city council, and if she was careful and was not at fault, even though her husband has been going out and disparaging her greatly, that woman, without incurring any blame at all, may take her dowry and go off to her father's house.

143: If she was not careful, but was a gadabout, thus neglecting her house (and) humiliating her husband, they shall throw that woman into the water.

For Further Reflection

- Discuss the extent to which Hammurabi's various provisions on family relationships protected the interests of different groups—husbands, wives, and the family itself.

Source: James B. Pritchard, ed. *Ancient Near Eastern Texts Relating to the Old Testament.* Princeton: Princeton University Press, 1955, pp. 171–72.

physicians, or professionals such as engineers and architects. Formal education was by no means common, but already by 3000 B.C.E., literacy was essential to the smooth functioning of Mesopotamian society.

Though originally invented for purposes of keeping records, writing clearly had potential that went far beyond the purely practical matter of storing information. Mesopotamians relied on writing to communicate complex ideas about the world, the gods, human beings, and their relationships with one another. Indeed, writing made possible the emergence of a distinctive cultural tradition that shaped Mesopotamian values for almost three thousand years.

Astronomy and Mathematics Literacy led to a rapid expansion of knowledge. Mesopotamian scholars devoted themselves to the study of astronomy and mathematics—crucial sciences for agricultural societies. Knowledge of astronomy helped them prepare accurate calendars, which in turn enabled them to chart the rhythms of the seasons and determine the appropriate times for planting and harvesting crops. They used their mathematical skills to survey agricultural lands and allocate them to the proper owners or tenants. Some Mesopotamian conventions persist to the present day: Mesopotamian scientists divided the year into twelve months, for example, and they divided the

In this terra-cotta relief tablet from the Babylonian empire, Gilgamesh (left, with knife) and his companion Enkidu (right, with knife) overcome an evil guardian of the deep forests during their adventure on the earth.

hours of the day into sixty minutes, each composed of sixty seconds.

The *Epic of Gilgamesh* Mesopotamians also used writing to communicate abstract ideas, investigate intellectual problems, and reflect on human beings and their place in the world. Best known of the reflective literature from Mesopotamia is the *Epic of Gilgamesh*. Parts of this work came from the Sumerian city-states, but the whole epic, as known today, was the work of compilers who lived after 2000 B.C.E. during the days of the Babylonian empire. In recounting the experiences of Gilgamesh and Enkidu, the epic explored themes of friendship, relations between humans and the gods, and especially the meaning of life and death. The stories of Gilgamesh and Enkidu resonated so widely that for some two thousand years—from the time of the Sumerian city-states to the fall of the Assyrian empire—they were the principal vehicles for Mesopotamian reflections on moral issues.

THE BROADER INFLUENCE OF MESOPOTAMIAN SOCIETY

While building cities and regional states, Mesopotamians deeply influenced the development and experiences of peoples living far beyond Mesopotamia. Often their wealth and power attracted the attention of neighboring peoples. Sometimes Mesopotamians projected their power to foreign lands and imposed their ways by force. Occasionally migrants left Mesopotamia and carried their inherited traditions to new lands. Mesopotamian influence did not completely transform other peoples and turn them into carbon copies of Mesopotamians. On the contrary, other peoples adopted Mesopotamian ways selectively and adapted them to their needs and interests. Yet the broader impact of Mesopotamian society shows that, even in early times, complex agricultural societies organized around cities had strong potential to influence the development of distant human communities.

Hebrews, Israelites, and Jews

The best-known cases of early Mesopotamian influence involved Hebrews, Israelites, and Jews, who preserved memories of their historical experiences in an extensive collection of sacred writings. Hebrews were speakers of the ancient Hebrew language. Israelites formed a branch of Hebrews who settled in Palestine (modern-day Israel) after 1200 B.C.E. Jews descended from southern Israelites who inhabited the kingdom of Judah. For more than two thousand years, Hebrews, Israelites, and Jews interacted constantly with Mesopotamians and other peoples as well, with profound consequences for the development of their societies.

The Early Hebrews The earliest Hebrews were pastoral nomads who inhabited lands between Mesopotamia and Egypt during the second millennium B.C.E. As Mesopotamia prospered, some Hebrews settled in the region's cities. According to the Hebrew scriptures (the Old Testament of the Christian Bible), the Hebrew patriarch Abraham came from the Sumerian city of Ur, but he migrated to northern Mesopotamia about 1850 B.C.E., perhaps because of disorder in Sumer. Abraham's descendants continued to recognize many of the deities, values, and customs common to Mesopotamian peoples. Hebrew law, for example, borrowed the principle of *lex talionis* from Hammurabi's code. The Hebrews also told the story of a devastating flood that had destroyed all early human society. Their account was a variation on similar flood stories related from the earliest days of Sumerian society. One early version of the story made its way into the *Epic of Gilgamesh*. The Hebrews altered the story and adapted it to their own interests and purposes, but their familiarity with the flood story shows that they participated fully in the larger society of Mesopotamia.

Migrations and Settlement in Palestine The Hebrew scriptures do not offer reliable historical accounts of early times, but they present memories and interpretations of Hebrew experience from the perspectives of later religious leaders who collected oral reports and edited them into a body of writings after 800 B.C.E. According to those scriptures, some Hebrews migrated to Egypt during the eighteenth century B.C.E. About 1300 B.C.E., however, this branch of the Hebrews departed under the leadership of Moses and went to Palestine. Organized into a loose federation of twelve tribes, these Hebrews, known as the Israelites, fought bitterly with other inhabitants of Palestine and carved out a territory for themselves. Eventually the

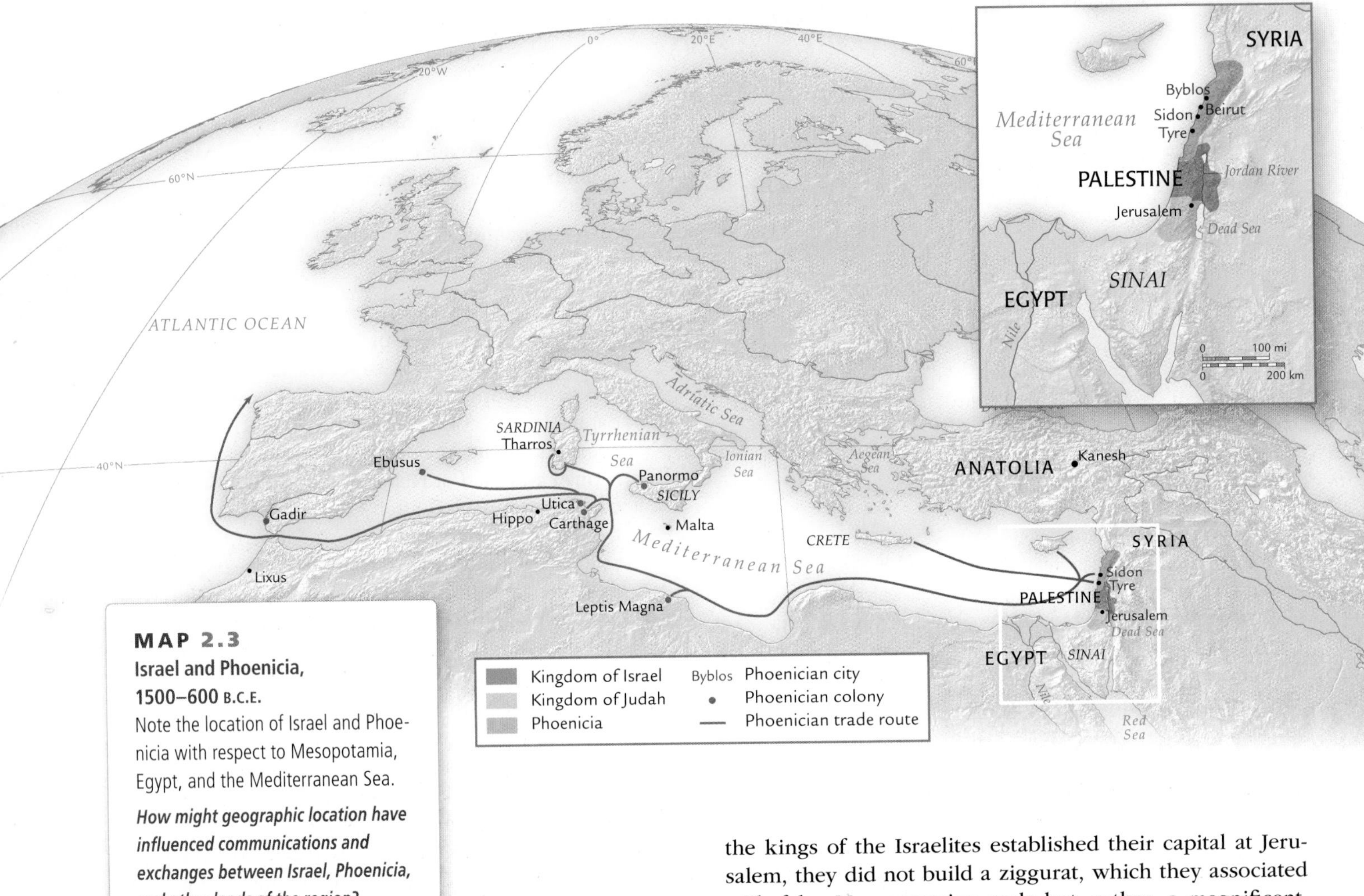

MAP 2.3
Israel and Phoenicia, 1500–600 B.C.E.
Note the location of Israel and Phoenicia with respect to Mesopotamia, Egypt, and the Mediterranean Sea.
How might geographic location have influenced communications and exchanges between Israel, Phoenicia, and other lands of the region?

Israelites abandoned their inherited tribal structure in favor of a Mesopotamian-style monarchy that brought the twelve tribes under unified rule. During the reigns of King David (1000–970 B.C.E.) and King Solomon (970–930 B.C.E.), Israelites dominated the territory between Syria and the Sinai peninsula. They built an elaborate and cosmopolitan capital city at Jerusalem and entered into diplomatic and commercial relations with Mesopotamians, Egyptians, and Arabian peoples.

Moses and Monotheism The Hebrew scriptures also teach that after the time of Moses, the religious beliefs of the Israelites developed along increasingly distinctive lines. The early Hebrews had recognized many of the same gods as their Mesopotamian neighbors: they believed that nature spirits inhabited trees, rocks, and mountains, for example, and they honored various deities as patrons or protectors of their clans. Moses, however, embraced monotheism: he taught that there was only one god, known as **Yahweh,** who was a supremely powerful deity, the creator and sustainer of the world. All other gods, including the various Mesopotamian deities, were impostors—figments of the human imagination rather than true and powerful gods. When the kings of the Israelites established their capital at Jerusalem, they did not build a ziggurat, which they associated with false Mesopotamian gods but, rather, a magnificent, lavishly decorated temple in honor of Yahweh.

Although he was the omnipotent creator of the universe, Yahweh was also a personal god. He expected his followers to worship him alone, and he demanded that they observe high moral and ethical standards. In the Ten Commandments, a set of religious and ethical principles that Moses announced to the Israelites, Yahweh warned his followers against destructive and antisocial behaviors such as lying, theft, adultery, and murder. A detailed and elaborate legal code prepared after Moses's death instructed the Israelites to provide relief and protection for widows, orphans, slaves, and the poor. Between about 800 and 400 B.C.E., the Israelites' religious leaders compiled their teachings in a set of holy scriptures known as the Torah (Hebrew for "doctrine" or "teaching"), which laid down Yahweh's laws and outlined his role in creating the world and guiding human affairs. The Torah taught that Yahweh would reward individuals who obeyed his will and punish those who did not. It also taught that Yahweh would reward or punish the whole community collectively, according to its observance of his commandments.

Historical and archaeological records tell a less colorful story than the account preserved in the Hebrew scriptures. Archaeological evidence shows that Israelites maintained communities in the hills of central Palestine after 1200 B.C.E. and that they formed several small kingdoms in the region

Yahweh (YAH-way)

after 1000 B.C.E. There are signs of intermittent conflicts with neighboring peoples, but there is no indication that Israelites conquered all of Palestine. On the contrary, they interacted and sometimes intermarried with other peoples of the region. Like their neighbors, they learned to use iron to fabricate weapons and tools. They even honored some of the deities of other Palestinian peoples: the Hebrew scriptures themselves mention that the Israelites worshiped gods other than Yahweh. The recognition of Yahweh as the only true god seems to have emerged about the eighth century B.C.E. rather than in the early days of the Hebrews' history.

Assyrian and Babylonian Conquests The Israelites placed increasing emphasis on devotion to Yahweh as they experienced a series of political and military setbacks. Following King Solomon's reign, tribal tensions led to the division of the community into a large kingdom of Israel in the north and a smaller kingdom of Judah in the land known as Judea to the south. During the ninth century B.C.E., the kingdom of Israel came under pressure of the expanding Assyrian empire and even had to pay tribute to Assyrian rulers. In 722 B.C.E. Assyrian forces conquered the northern kingdom and deported many of its inhabitants to other regions. Most of these exiles assimilated into other communities and lost their identity as Israelites. The kingdom of Judah retained its independence only temporarily: founders of the New Babylonian empire toppled the Assyrians, then looked south, conquered the kingdom of Judah, and destroyed Jerusalem in 586 B.C.E. Again, the conquerors forced many residents into exile. Unlike their cousins to the north, however, most of these Israelites maintained their religious identity, and many of the deportees eventually returned to Judea, where they became known as Jews.

Ironically, perhaps, the Israelites' devotion to Yahweh intensified during this era of turmoil. Between the ninth and sixth centuries B.C.E., a series of prophets urged the Israelites to rededicate themselves to their faith and obey Yahweh's commandments. These prophets were moral and social critics who blasted their compatriots for their materialism, their neglect of the needy, and their abominable interest in the fertility gods and nature deities worshiped by neighboring peoples. The prophets warned the Israelites that unless they mended their ways, Yahweh would punish them by sending conquerors to humiliate and enslave them. Many Israelites took the Assyrian and Babylonian conquests as proof that the prophets accurately represented Yahweh's mind and will.

The Early Jewish Community The exiles who returned to Judea after the Babylonian conquest did not abandon hope for a state of their own, and indeed they organized several small Jewish states as tributaries to the great empires that dominated southwest Asia after the sixth century B.C.E. But the returnees also built a distinctive religious community based on their conviction that they had a special relationship with Yahweh, their devotion to Yahweh's teachings as expressed in the Torah, and their concern for justice and righteousness. These elements enabled the Jews to maintain a strong sense of identity as a people distinct from Mesopotamians and others, even as they participated fully in the development of a larger complex society in southwest Asia. Over the longer term, Jewish monotheism, scriptures, and moral concerns also profoundly influenced the development of Christianity and Islam.

The Phoenicians

North of the Israelites' kingdom in Palestine, the Phoenicians occupied a narrow coastal plain between the Mediterranean Sea and the Lebanon Mountains. They spoke a Semitic language, referring to themselves as

An Assyrian relief sculpture depicts King Jehu of Israel paying tribute to King Shalmaneser III of Assyria about the middle of the ninth century B.C.E.

Canaanites and their land as Canaan. (The term *Phoenician* comes from early Greek references.)

The Early Phoenicians Ancestors of the Phoenicians migrated to the Mediterranean coast and built their first settlements sometime after 3000 B.C.E. They did not establish a unified monarchy but, rather, organized a series of independent city-states ruled by local kings. The major cities—Tyre, Sidon, Beirut, and Byblos—had considerable influence over their smaller neighbors, and during the tenth century B.C.E. Tyre dominated southern Phoenicia. Generally speaking, however, the Phoenicians showed more interest in pursuing commercial opportunities than in state building or military expansion. Indeed, Phoenician cities were often subject to imperial rule from Egypt or Mesopotamia.

Phoenician Trade Networks Though not a numerous or militarily powerful people, the Phoenicians influenced societies throughout the Mediterranean basin because of their maritime trade and communication networks. Their meager lands did not permit development of a large agricultural society, so after about 2500 B.C.E. the Phoenicians turned increasingly to industry and trade. They traded overland with Mesopotamian and other peoples, and they provided much of the cedar timber, furnishings, and decorative items that went into the Israelites' temple in Jerusalem. Soon the Phoenicians ventured onto the seas and engaged also in maritime trade. They imported food and raw materials in exchange for high-quality metal goods, textiles, pottery, glass, and works of art that they produced for export. They enjoyed a special reputation for brilliant red and purple textiles colored with dyes extracted from several species of mollusc that were common in waters near Phoenicia. They also supplied Mesopotamians and Egyptians with cedar logs from the Lebanon Mountains for construction and shipbuilding.

The Phoenicians were excellent sailors, and they built the best ships of their times. Between 1200 and 800 B.C.E., they dominated Mediterranean trade. They established commercial colonies in Rhodes, Cyprus, Sicily, Sardinia, Spain, and north Africa. They sailed far and wide in search of raw materials such as copper and tin, which they used to make bronze, as well as more exotic items such as ivory and semiprecious stones, which they fashioned into works of decorative art. Their quest for raw materials took them well beyond the Mediterranean: Phoenician merchant ships visited the Canary Islands, coastal ports in Portugal and France, and even the distant British Isles, and adventurous Phoenician mariners made exploratory voyages to the Azores Islands and down the west coast of Africa as far as the Gulf of Guinea.

Like the Hebrews, the Phoenicians largely adapted Mesopotamian cultural traditions to their own needs. Their gods, for example, mostly came from Mesopotamia. The Phoenicians' most prominent female deity was Astarte, a fertility goddess known in Babylon and Assyria as Ishtar. Like the Mesopotamians, the Phoenicians associated other deities with mountains, the sky, lightning, and other natural phenomena. Yet the Phoenicians did not blindly follow Mesopotamian examples: each city built temples to its favored deities and devised rituals and ceremonies to honor them.

Alphabetic Writing The Phoenicians' tradition of writing also illustrates their creative adaptation of Mesopotamian practices to their own needs. For

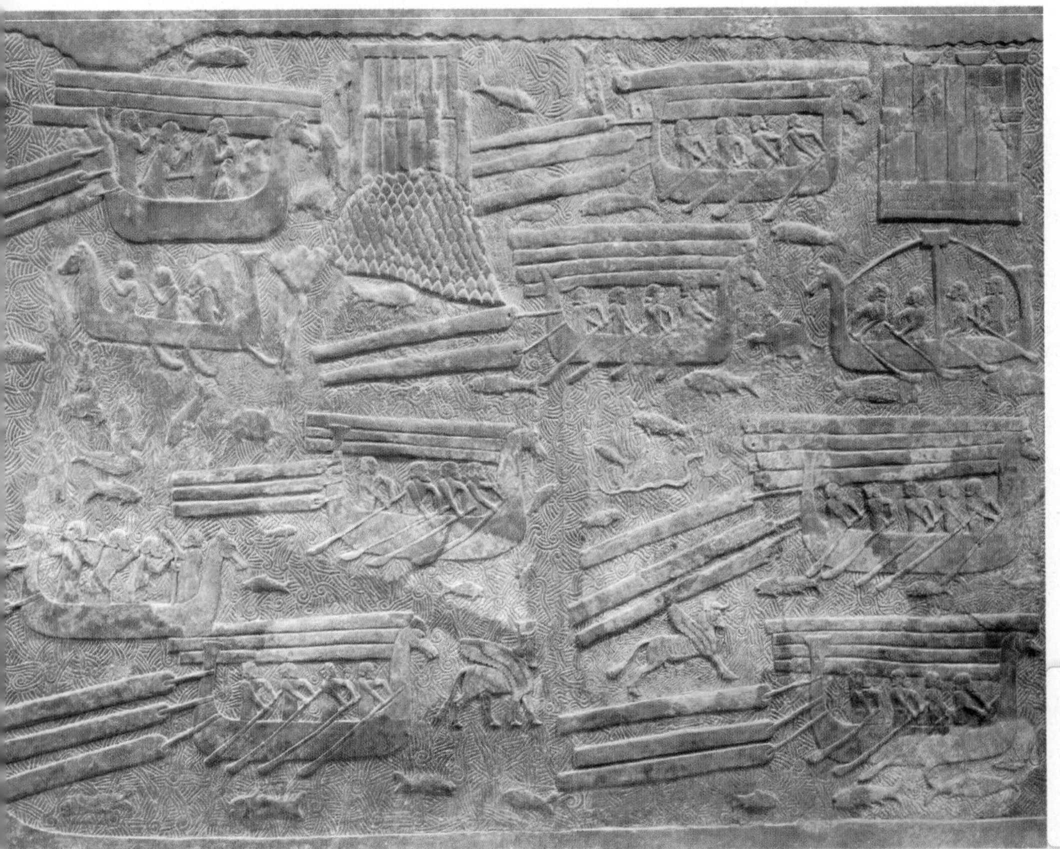

A relief sculpture from an Assyrian palace depicts Phoenician ships transporting cedar logs, both by towing them and by hauling them on top of the boats.

sources from the past

Israelites' Relations with Neighboring Peoples

When Solomon succeeded David as king of the Israelites, he inherited a state at peace with neighboring peoples, and he was able to construct a temple to Yahweh. To do so, however, he needed to establish trade relations with neighboring peoples, since the Israelites did not have the raw materials or construction skills to build a large and magnificent temple. Thus he dealt with Hiram, king of the Phoenician city of Tyre, who provided timber and construction workers and also helped Solomon obtain gold, precious stones, and decorative items for the temple.

And Hiram king of Tyre sent his servants unto Solomon, for he had heard that they had anointed him king in the room of his father, for Hiram was ever a lover of David. And Solomon sent to Hiram, saying, "Thou knowest how David my father could not build a house [temple] in the name of the Lord his God because of the wars which were about him on every side, until the Lord put [his enemies] under the soles of his feet. But now the Lord my God hath given me rest on every side, so that there is neither adversary nor evil occurring. And behold, I plan to build a house in the name of the Lord my God. . . . Now therefore command thou that they hew me cedar trees out of Lebanon, and my servants shall be with thy servants, and unto thee will I give hire for thy servants according to all that thou shalt appoint, for thou knowest that there is not among us any that has skill to hew timber like the Sidonians [Phoenicians].". . .

And Hiram sent to Solomon, saying, "I have considered the things which thou sent to me for, and I will do all thy desire concerning timber of cedar, and concerning timber of fir. My servants shall bring them down from Lebanon unto the sea, and I will convey them by sea in floats unto the place that thou shalt appoint me, and will cause them to be discharged there, and thou shalt receive them, and thou shalt accomplish my desire, in giving food for my household." So Hiram gave Solomon cedar trees and fir trees according to all his desire. And Solomon gave Hiram twenty thousand measures of wheat for food for his household, and twenty measures of pure oil. Thus gave Solomon to Hiram year by year. And the Lord gave Solomon wisdom, as he promised him, and there was peace between Hiram and Solomon, and they two made a league together.

And king Solomon raised a levy out of all Israel, and the levy was thirty thousand men. And he sent them to Lebanon, ten thousand a month in turns. A month they were in Lebanon, and two months at home. . . . And the king commanded, and they brought great stones, costly stones, and hewed stones, to lay the foundation of the house. And Solomon's builders and Hiram's builders did hew them, and the stonemasons. So they prepared timber and stones to build the house. . . .

And king Solomon made a navy of ships in Eziongeber [a port on the Gulf of Aqaba]. And Hiram sent in the navy his servants, shipmen that had knowledge of the sea, with the servants of Solomon. And they came to Ophir [probably southern Arabia or Ethiopia], and fetched from thence gold, four hundred and twenty talents, and brought it to king Solomon. . . .

And the navy of Hiram, that brought gold from Ophir, brought in from Ophir great plenty of almug trees and precious stones. And the king made of the almug trees pillars for the house of the Lord.

For Further Reflection

- In what ways does the Hebrew scriptural discussion of Solomon's temple portray the Israelites as participants in a larger world of diplomatic, commercial, and cultural interaction?

Source: 1 Kings 5:1–18, 9:26–28, 10:11–12 (Authorized Version). (Translation slightly modified.)

a millennium or more, they relied on cuneiform writing to preserve information, and they compiled a vast collection of religious, historical, and literary writings. (Most Phoenician writing has perished, although some fragments have survived.) After 2000 B.C.E. Syrian, Phoenician, and other peoples began experimenting with simpler alternatives to cuneiform. By 1500 B.C.E. Phoenician scribes had devised an early alphabetic script consisting of twenty-two symbols representing consonants—the Phoenician alphabet had no symbols for vowels. Learning twenty-two letters and building words with them was much easier than memorizing the hundreds of symbols employed in cuneiform. Because alphabetic writing required much less investment in education than did cuneiform writing, more people were able to become literate than ever before.

Alphabetic writing spread widely as the Phoenicians traveled and traded throughout the Mediterranean basin. About the ninth century B.C.E., for example, Greeks modified the Phoenician alphabet and added symbols representing vowels. Romans later adapted the Greek alphabet to their language and passed it along to their cultural heirs in Europe. In later centuries alphabetic writing spread to central Asia, south Asia, southeast Asia, and ultimately throughout most of the world.

Phoenician, Greek, Hebrew, and Roman letters.

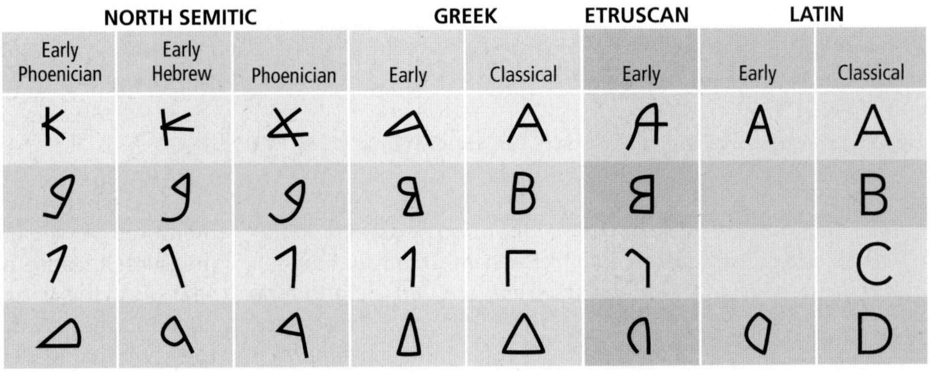

NORTH SEMITIC			GREEK		ETRUSCAN	LATIN	
Early Phoenician	Early Hebrew	Phoenician	Early	Classical	Early	Early	Classical

THE INDO-EUROPEAN MIGRATIONS

After 3000 B.C.E. Mesopotamia was a prosperous, productive region where peoples from many different communities mixed and mingled. But Mesopotamia was only one region in a much larger world of interaction and exchange. Mesopotamians and their neighbors all dealt frequently with peoples from regions far beyond southwest Asia. Among the most influential of these peoples in the third and second millennia B.C.E. were those who spoke various Indo-European languages. Their migrations throughout much of Eurasia profoundly influenced historical development in both southwest Asia and the larger world as well.

Indo-European Origins

Indo-European Languages During the eighteenth and nineteenth centuries, linguists noticed that many languages of Europe, southwest Asia, and India featured remarkable similarities in vocabulary and grammatical structure. Ancient languages displaying these similarities included Sanskrit (the sacred language of ancient India), Old Persian, Greek, and Latin. Modern descendants of these languages include Hindi and other languages of northern India, Farsi (the language of modern Iran), and most European languages, excepting only a few, such as Basque, Finnish, and Hungarian. Because of the geographic regions where these tongues are found, scholars refer to them as Indo-European languages. Major subgroups of the Indo-European family of languages include Indo-Iranian, Greek, Balto-Slavic, Germanic, Italic, and Celtic. English belongs to the Germanic subgroup of the Indo-European family of languages.

After noticing linguistic similarities, scholars sought a way to explain the close relationship between the Indo-European languages. It was inconceivable that speakers of all these languages independently adopted similar vocabularies and grammatical structures. The only persuasive explanation for the high degree of linguistic coincidence was that speakers of Indo-European languages were all descendants of ancestors who spoke a common tongue and migrated from their original homeland. As migrants established separate communities and lost touch with one another, their languages evolved along different lines, adding new words and expressing ideas in different ways. Yet they retained the basic grammatical structure of their original speech, and they also kept much of their ancestors' vocabulary, even though they often adopted different pronunciations (and consequently different spellings) of the words they inherited from the earliest Indo-European language.

The Indo-European Homeland The original homeland of Indo-European speakers was probably the steppe

TABLE 1.1 Similarities in Vocabulary Indicating Close Relationships between Select Indo-European Languages

English	German	Spanish	Greek	Latin	Sanskrit
father	vater	padre	pater	pater	pitar
one	ein	uno	hen	unus	ekam
fire	feuer	fuego	pyr	ignis	agnis
field	feld	campo	agros	ager	ajras
sun	sonne	sol	helios	sol	surya
king	könig	rey	basileus	rex	raja
god	gott	dios	theos	deus	devas

region of modern-day Ukraine and southern Russia, the region just north of the Black Sea and the Caspian Sea. The earliest Indo-European speakers built their society there between about 4500 and 2500 B.C.E. They lived mostly by herding cattle, sheep, and goats, while cultivating barley and millet in small quantities. They also hunted horses, which flourished in the vast grasslands of the Eurasian steppe stretching from Hungary in the west to Mongolia in the east.

Horses Because they had observed horses closely and learned the animals' behavioral patterns, Indo-European speakers were able to domesticate horses about 4000 B.C.E. They probably used horses originally as a source of food, but they also began to ride them soon after domesticating them. By 3000 B.C.E. Sumerian knowledge of bronze metallurgy and wheels had spread north to the Indo-European homeland, and soon thereafter Indo-European speakers devised ways to hitch horses to carts, wagons, and chariots. The earliest Indo-European language had words not only for cattle, sheep, goats, and horses, but also for wheels, axles, shafts, harnesses, hubs, and linchpins—all of the latter learned from Mesopotamian examples.

The possession of domesticated horses vastly magnified the power of Indo-European speakers. Once they had domesticated horses, Indo-European speakers were able to exploit the grasslands of southern Russia, where they relied on horses and wheeled vehicles for transport and on cattle and sheep for meat, milk, leather, and wool. Horses also enabled them to develop transportation technologies that were much faster and more efficient than alternatives that relied on cattle, donkey, or human power. Furthermore, because of their strength and speed, horses provided Indo-European speakers with a tremendous military advantage over peoples they encountered. It is perhaps significant that many groups of Indo-European speakers considered themselves superior to other peoples: the terms *Aryan, Iran,* and *Eire* (the official name of the modern Republic of Ireland) all derive from the Indo-European word *aryo,* meaning "nobleman" or "lord."

PART 1

Indo-European Expansion and Its Effects

The Nature of Indo-European Migrations Horses also provided Indo-European speakers with a means of expanding far beyond their original homeland. As they flourished in southern Russia, Indo-European speakers experienced a population explosion, which prompted some of them to move into the sparsely inhabited eastern steppe or even beyond the grasslands altogether. The earliest Indo-European society began to break up about 3000 B.C.E., as migrants took their horses and other animals and made their way to new lands. Intermittent migrations of Indo-European peoples continued until about 1000 C.E. Like early movements of other peoples, these were not mass migrations so much as gradual and incremental processes that resulted in the spread of Indo-European languages and ethnic communities, as small groups of people established settlements in new lands, which then became foundations for further expansion.

The Hittites Some of the most influential Indo-European migrants in ancient times were the Hittites. About 1900 B.C.E. the Hittites migrated to the central plain of Anatolia, where they imposed their language and rule on the region's inhabitants. During the seventeenth and sixteenth centuries B.C.E., they built a powerful kingdom and established close relations with Mesopotamian peoples. They traded with Babylonians and Assyrians, adapted cuneiform writing to their Indo-European language, and accepted many Mesopotamian deities into their pantheon. In 1595 B.C.E. the Hittites toppled the mighty Babylonian empire, and for several centuries thereafter they were the dominant power in southwest Asia. Between 1450 and 1200 B.C.E., their authority extended to eastern Anatolia, northern Mesopotamia, and Syria down to Phoenicia. After 1200 B.C.E. the unified Hittite state dissolved, as waves of invaders attacked societies throughout the eastern Mediterranean region. Nevertheless, a Hittite identity survived, along with the Hittite language, throughout the era of the Assyrian empire and beyond.

A stone carving from about 1200 B.C.E. depicts a Hittite chariot with spoked wheels during a lion hunt. A horse pulls the chariot bearing one driver and one archer.

War Chariots The Hittites were responsible for two technological innovations—the construction of light, horse-drawn war chariots and the refinement of iron metallurgy—that greatly strengthened their society and influenced other peoples throughout much of the ancient world. Sumerian armies had sometimes used heavy chariots with solid wooden wheels, but they were so slow and cumbersome that they had limited

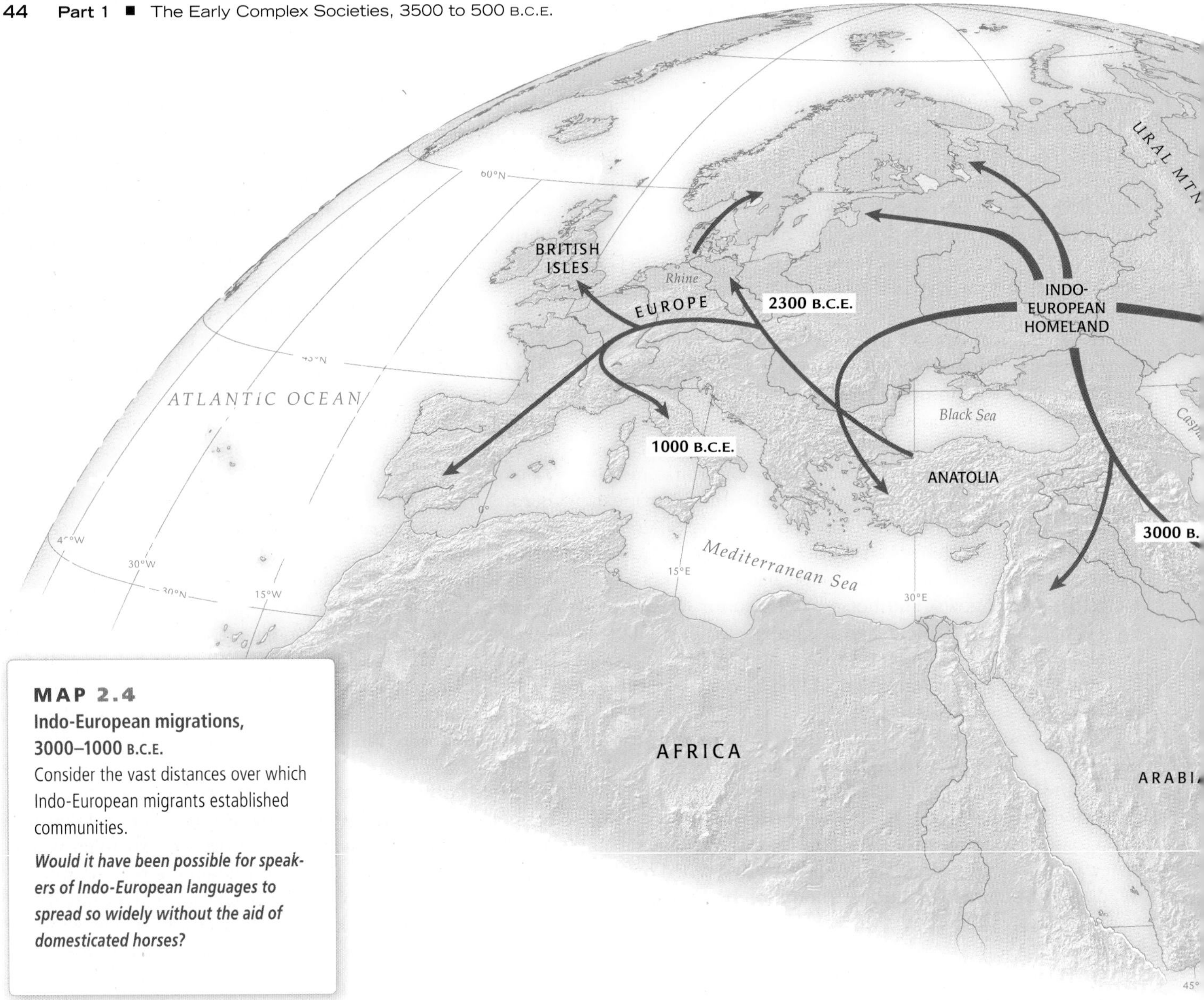

MAP 2.4
Indo-European migrations, 3000–1000 B.C.E.
Consider the vast distances over which Indo-European migrants established communities.
Would it have been possible for speakers of Indo-European languages to spread so widely without the aid of domesticated horses?

military value. About 2000 B.C.E. Hittites fitted chariots with recently invented spoked wheels, which were much lighter and more maneuverable than Sumerian wheels. The Hittites' speedy chariots were crucial in their campaign to establish a state in Anatolia. Following the Hittites' example, Mesopotamians soon added chariot teams to their armies, and Assyrians made especially effective use of chariots in building their empire. Indeed, chariot warfare was so effective—and its techniques spread so widely—that charioteers became the elite strike forces in armies throughout much of the ancient world from Rome to China.

Iron Metallurgy After about 1300 B.C.E. the Hittites also refined the technology of iron metallurgy, which enabled them to produce effective weapons cheaply and in large quantities. Other peoples had tried casting iron into molds, but cast iron was too brittle for use as tools or weapons. Hittite craftsmen discovered that by heating iron in a bed of charcoal, then hammering it into the desired shape, they could forge strong, durable implements. Hittite methods of iron production diffused rapidly—especially after the collapse of their kingdom in 1200 B.C.E. and the subsequent dispersal of Hittite craftsmen—and eventually spread throughout all of Eurasia. (Peoples of sub-Saharan Africa independently invented iron metallurgy.) Hittites were not the original inventors either of horse-drawn chariots or of iron metallurgy: in both cases they built on Mesopotamian precedents. But in both cases they clearly improved on existing technologies and introduced innovations that other peoples readily adopted.

Indo-European Migrations to the East While the Hittites were building a state in Anatolia, other Indo-European speakers migrated from the steppe to different regions. Some went east into central Asia, venturing as far as the Tarim Basin (now western China) by 2000 B.C.E. Stunning evidence of those migrations came to light recently when archaeologists excavated burials of individuals with European features in China's Xinjiang province. Because

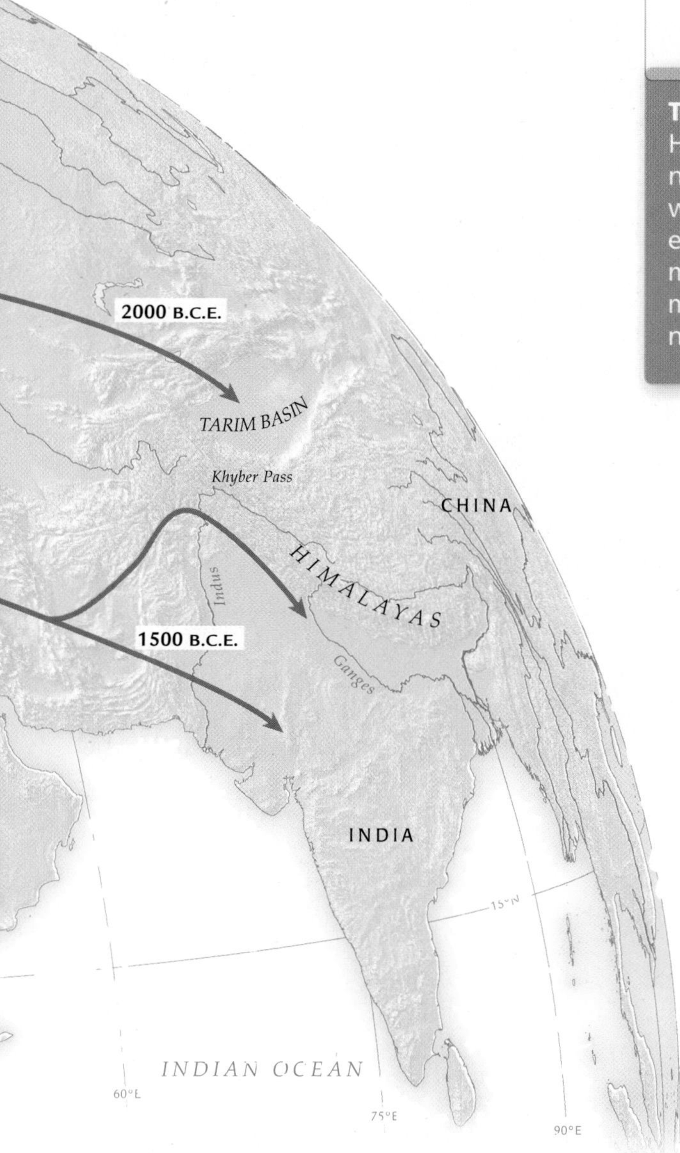

thinking about ENCOUNTERS

Technological Diffusion and Its Effects
Human beings have usually been quick to borrow useful technologies from other peoples and combine them with their own ways of doing things. Consider the effects when early speakers of Indo-European languages brought wheeled vehicles and metallurgy from Mesopotamia together with their own domesticated horses. To what extent did the combination of technologies make Indo-European migrations possible?

PART 1

of the region's extremely dry atmosphere, the remains of some deceased individuals are so well preserved that their fair skin, light hair, and brightly colored garments are still clearly visible. Descendants of these migrants survived in central Asia and spoke Indo-European languages until well after 1000 C.E., but most of them were later absorbed into societies of Turkish-speaking peoples.

Indo-European Migrations to the West Meanwhile, other Indo-European migrants moved west. One wave of migration took Indo-European speakers into Greece after 2200 B.C.E., with their descendants moving into central Italy by 1000 B.C.E. Another migratory wave established an Indo-European presence farther to the west. By 2300 B.C.E. some Indo-European speakers had made their way from southern Russia into central Europe (modern Germany and Austria), by 1200 B.C.E. to western Europe (modern France), and shortly thereafter to the British Isles, the Baltic region, and the Iberian peninsula. These migrants depended on a pastoral and agricultural economy: none of them built cities or organized large states. For most of the first millennium B.C.E., however, Indo-European Celtic peoples largely dominated Europe north of the Mediterranean, speaking related languages and honoring similar deities throughout the region. They recognized three principal social groups: a military ruling elite, a small group of priests, and a large class of commoners. Most of the commoners tended herds and cultivated crops, but some also worked as miners, craftsmen, or producers of metal goods. Even without large states, Celtic peoples traded copper, tin, and handicrafts throughout much of Europe.

Indo-European Migrations to the South Yet another, later wave of migrations established an Indo-European presence in Iran and India. About 1500 B.C.E. the Medes and Persians migrated into the Iranian plateau, while the Aryans began filtering into northern India. Like the Indo-European Celts in Europe, the Medes, Persians, and Aryans herded animals, cultivated grains, and divided themselves into classes of rulers, priests, and commoners. Unlike the Celts, though, the Medes, Persians, and Aryans soon built powerful states (discussed in later chapters) on the basis of their horse-based military technologies and later their possession also of iron weapons.

inperspective

Building on neolithic foundations, Mesopotamian peoples constructed societies much more complex, powerful, and influential than those of their predecessors. Through their city-states, kingdoms, and regional empires, Mesopotamians created formal institutions of government that extended the authority of ruling elites to all corners of their states, and they occasionally mobilized forces that projected their power to distant lands. They generated several distinct social classes. Specialized labor fueled productive economies

A pair of harnessed bulls produced by Indo-European speaking Hittites about the eighteenth century B.C.E. Indo-European speakers made effective use of horses, but they also herded cattle, sheep, and goats.

and encouraged the establishment of long-distance trade networks. They devised systems of writing, which enabled them to develop sophisticated cultural traditions. They deeply influenced other peoples, such as the Hebrews and the Phoenicians, throughout southwest Asia and the eastern Mediterranean basin. They had frequent dealings also with Indo-European peoples. Although Indo-European society emerged far to the north of Mesopotamia, speakers of Indo-European languages migrated widely and established societies throughout much of Eurasia. Sometimes they drew inspiration from Mesopotamian practices, and sometimes they developed new practices that influenced Mesopotamians and others as well. Thus, already in remote antiquity, the various peoples of the world profoundly influenced one another through cross-cultural interaction and exchange. ●

CHRONOLOGY

3200–2350 B.C.E.	Era of Sumerian dominance in Mesopotamia
3000 B.C.E.–1000 C.E.	Era of Indo-European migrations
2350–1600 B.C.E.	Era of Babylonian dominance in Mesopotamia
2334–2315 B.C.E.	Reign of Sargon of Akkad
1792–1750 B.C.E.	Reign of Hammurabi
1700–1200 B.C.E.	Era of Hittite dominance in Anatolia
1000–612 B.C.E.	Era of Assyrian dominance in Mesopotamia
1000–970 B.C.E.	Reign of Israelite King David
970–930 B.C.E.	Reign of Israelite King Solomon
722 B.C.E.	Assyrian conquest of the kingdom of Israel
605–562 B.C.E.	Reign of Nebuchadnezzar
600–550 B.C.E.	New Babylonian empire
586 B.C.E.	New Babylonian conquest of the kingdom of Judah

For Further Reading

David W. Anthony. *The Horse, the Wheel, and Language: How Bronze-Age Riders from the Eurasian Steppes Shaped the Modern World.* Princeton, 2007. Brilliant study of early Indo-European speakers and the uses they made of domesticated horses.

Maria Eugenia Aubet. *The Phoenicians and the West: Politics, Colonies, and Trade.* Trans. by M. Turton. Cambridge, 1993. A scholarly synthesis based on archaeological finds as well as written records.

Elizabeth Wayland Barber. *The Mummies of Ürümchi.* New York, 1999. Brings archaeological evidence to bear on the early Indo-European migrations, especially those to the Tarim Basin.

———. *Women's Work: The First 20,000 Years.* New York, 1994. Fascinating study of ancient textiles, which the author argues was a craft industry dominated by women from the earliest times.

Trevor Bryce. *The Kingdom of the Hittites.* New ed. Oxford, 2005. A solid, scholarly account of Hittite history, with an emphasis on political issues.

———. *Life and Society in the Hittite World.* Oxford, 2002. Complements Bryce's political history by exploring social and economic issues.

Israel Finkelstein and Neil Asher Silberman. *The Bible Unearthed: Archaeology's New Vision of Ancient Israel and the Origin of Its Sacred Texts.* New York, 2001. Interprets the Hebrew scriptures and early Israelite history in light of numerous archaeological discoveries.

Andrew George, trans. *The Epic of Gilgamesh.* London, 1999. A careful study and fresh translation of the best-known Mesopotamian literary work prepared on the basis of recently discovered texts.

Pita Kelekna. *The Horse in Human History.* Cambridge, 2009. Fascinating analysis of horses' roles in human history.

J. P. Mallory and Victor H. Mair. *The Tarim Mummies: Ancient China and the Mystery of the Earliest Peoples from the West.* London, 2000. A cautious analysis of the Indo-European migrants to the Tarim Basin, drawing heavily on linguistic evidence.

Sabatino Moscati, ed. *The Phoenicians.* New York, 1988. A lavishly illustrated volume with essays by experts on all dimensions of Phoenician society and history.

Hans J. Nissen and Peter Heine. *From Mesopotamia to Iraq: A Concise History.* Chicago, 2009. An authoritative discussion of ancient Mesopotamia viewed in the context of the longer history of Iraq.

Joan Oates. *Babylon.* London, 1979. Well-illustrated and authoritative examination of ancient Babylonian society.

J. N. Postgate. *Early Mesopotamia: Society and Economy at the Dawn of History.* London, 1992. Outstanding synthesis that draws on both archaeological and textual sources.

James B. Pritchard, ed. *Ancient Near Eastern Texts Relating to the Old Testament.* 2 vols. 3rd ed. Princeton, 1975. Important collection of primary sources in translation, emphasizing parallels between the ancient Hebrews and other peoples.

Michael Roaf. *Cultural Atlas of Mesopotamia and the Ancient Near East.* New York, 1990. Richly illustrated volume with well-informed essays on all dimensions of Mesopotamian history.

Georges Roux. *Ancient Iraq.* 3rd ed. London, 1992. A well-written and engaging survey of Mesopotamian political, social, economic, and cultural history.

Marc van de Mieroop. *A History of the Ancient Near East, ca. 3000–323 B.C.* Oxford, 2004. A concise and readable history of ancient Mesopotamia and neighboring societies.

Early African Societies and the Bantu Migrations

chapter 3

Anubis, the jackal-headed Egyptian god of mummification, prepares the mummy of a deceased worker for burial. This painting comes from the wall of a tomb built about the thirteenth century B.C.E.

PART 1

EYEWITNESS:
Herodotus and the Making of a Mummy

For almost three thousand years, Egyptian embalmers preserved the bodies of deceased individuals through a process of mummification. Egyptian records rarely mention the techniques of mummification, but the Greek historian Herodotus traveled in Egypt about 450 B.C.E. and briefly explained the craft. The embalmer first used a metal hook to draw the brain of the deceased out through a nostril and then removed the internal organs through an incision made alongside the abdomen, washed them in palm wine, and sealed them with preservatives in stone vessels. Next, the embalmer washed the body, filled it with spices and aromatics, and covered it for about two months with natron, a naturally occurring salt substance. When the natron had extracted all moisture from the body, the embalmer cleansed it again and wrapped it with strips of fine linen covered with resin. Adorned with jewelry, the preserved body then went into a coffin bearing a painting or sculpted likeness of the deceased.

Careful preservation of the body was only a part of the funerary ritual for prominent Egyptians. Ruling elites, wealthy individuals, and sometimes common people as well laid their deceased to rest in expensive tombs equipped with furniture, tools, weapons, and ornaments that the departed would need in their next lives. Relatives periodically brought food and wine to nourish the deceased, and archaeologists have discovered soups, beef ribs, pigeons, quail, fish, bread, cakes, and fruits among those offerings. Artists decorated some tombs with elegant paintings of family members and servants, whose images accompanied the departed into a new dimension of existence.

Egyptian funerary customs were reflections of a prosperous agricultural society. Food offerings consisted mostly of local agricultural products, and scenes painted on tomb walls often depicted workers preparing fields or cultivating crops. Moreover, bountiful harvests explained the accumulation of wealth that supported elaborate funerary practices, and they also enabled some individuals to devote their efforts to specialized tasks such as embalming. Agriculture even influenced religious beliefs. Many Egyptians believed fervently in a life beyond the grave, and they likened the human experience of life and death to the agricultural cycle in which crops grow, die, and come to life again in another season.

As Mesopotamians built a productive agricultural society in southwest Asia and as Indo-European peoples introduced domesticated horses to much of Eurasia, cultivation and herding also transformed African societies. African agriculture first took root in the Sudan, then moved into the Nile River valley and also to most parts of sub-Saharan Africa. Agriculture flourished particularly in the fertile Nile valley, and abundant harvests soon supported fast-growing populations. That agricultural bounty underwrote the development of Egypt, the most prosperous and powerful of the early agricultural societies in Africa, and also of Nubia, Egypt's neighbor to the south.

Distinctive Egyptian and Nubian societies began to take shape in the valley of the Nile River during the late fourth millennium B.C.E., shortly after the emergence of complex society in Mesopotamia. Like their Mesopotamian counterparts, Egyptians and Nubians drew on agricultural surpluses to organize formal states, support specialized laborers, and develop distinctive cultural traditions. Like Mesopotamians again, Egyptian and Nubian residents of the Nile valley had regular dealings with peoples from other societies. They drew inspiration for political and social organization both from Mesopotamia and from their African neighbors to the south. They also traded actively with Mesopotamians, Phoenicians, Africans, and others as well. Political and economic competition sometimes led to military conflicts with peoples of other societies: on several occasions when they enjoyed great wealth and power, both Egyptians and Nubians embarked on campaigns of imperial conquest, but when their power waned, they found themselves intermittently under attack from the outside.

Indeed, like their counterparts in Mesopotamia, Egyptian and Nubian societies developed from their earliest days in a larger world of interaction and exchange. Just as Mesopotamians, Hittites, Hebrews, and Phoenicians influenced one another in southwest Asia, inhabitants of the Nile valley mixed and mingled with Mesopotamians, Phoenicians, and other peoples from the eastern Mediterranean, southwest Asia, and sub-Saharan Africa. Just as Indo-European peoples migrated to new lands and established communities that transformed much of Eurasia, Bantu peoples migrated from their original homeland in west Africa and established settlements that brought profound change to much of sub-Saharan Africa. By no means were Egypt and Nubia isolated centers of social development. Like Mesopotamia, Egypt in particular was a spectacularly prosperous society, but like Mesopotamia again, Egypt was only one part of a much larger world of interacting societies.

EARLY AGRICULTURAL SOCIETY IN AFRICA

Egypt was the most prominent of early African societies, but it was by no means the only agricultural society, nor even the only complex, city-based society of ancient Africa. On the contrary, Egypt emerged alongside Nubia and other agricultural societies in sub-Saharan Africa. Indeed, agricultural crops and domesticated animals reached Egypt from sub-Saharan Africa by way of Nubia as well as from southwest Asia. Favorable geographic conditions enabled Egyptians to build an especially productive agricultural economy that supported a powerful state, while Nubia became home to a somewhat less prosperous but nonetheless sophisticated society. After taking shape as distinctive societies, Egypt had regular dealings with both eastern Mediterranean and southwest Asian peoples, and Nubia linked Egypt and the eastern Mediterranean basin with the peoples and societies of sub-Saharan Africa.

Climatic Change and the Development of Agriculture in Africa

African agriculture emerged in the context of gradual but momentous changes in climatic conditions. About 10,000 B.C.E., after the end of the last ice age, the area now occupied by the Sahara desert was mostly a grassy steppe land with numerous lakes, rivers, and streams. Climatic and geographic conditions were much like those of the Sudan region—not the modern state of Sudan but, rather, the extensive transition zone of savanna and grassland that stretches across the African continent between the Sahara to the north and the tropical rain forest to the south. Grasses and cattle flourished in that environment. Many human inhabitants of the region lived by hunting wild cattle and collecting wild grains, while others subsisted on fish and aquatic resources from the region's waters.

Early Sudanic Agriculture After about 9000 B.C.E., peoples of the eastern Sudan domesticated cattle and became nomadic herders, while they continued to collect wild grains. After 7500 B.C.E. they established permanent settlements and began to cultivate sorghum, a grain still widely grown in the contemporary world for human and animal consumption. Meanwhile, after about 8000 B.C.E., inhabitants of the western Sudan began to cultivate yams in the region between the Niger and Congo rivers. Sudanic agriculture became increasingly diverse over the following centuries: sheep and goats arrived from southwest Asia after 7000 B.C.E., and Sudanic peoples began to cultivate gourds, watermelons, and cotton after 6500 B.C.E.

Agricultural productivity enabled Sudanic peoples to organize small-scale states. By about 5000 B.C.E. many Sudanic peoples had formed small monarchies ruled by kings who were viewed as divine or semidivine beings. For several thousand years, when Sudanic peoples buried their deceased kings, they also routinely executed a group of royal servants and entombed them along with the king so that they could continue to meet their master's needs in another life. Sudanic peoples also developed religious beliefs that reflected their agricultural society. They recognized a single divine force as the source of good and evil, and they associated it with rain—a matter of concern for any agricultural society.

Climatic Change After 5000 B.C.E. the northern half of Africa experienced a long-term climatic change that profoundly influenced social organization and agriculture throughout the region. Although there was considerable fluctuation, the climate generally became much hotter and drier than before. The Sahara desert, which as late as 5000 B.C.E. had been cool and well watered enough to support human, animal, and vegetable life, became increasingly arid and uninhabitable. This process of desiccation turned rich grasslands into barren desert, and it drove both humans and animals to more hospitable regions. Many Sudanic cultivators and herders gathered around remaining bodies of water such as Lake Chad. Some moved south to the territory that is now northern Uganda. Others congregated in the valley of the Nile River, the principal source of water flowing through north Africa.

The Nile River Valley Fed by rain and snow in the high mountains of east Africa, the Nile, which is the world's longest river, courses some 6,695 kilometers (4,160 miles) from its source at Lake Victoria to its outlet through the delta to the Mediterranean Sea. Each spring, rain and melting snow swell the river, which surges north through the Sudan and Egypt. Until the completion of the high dam at Aswan in 1968, the Nile's accumulated waters annually flooded the plains downstream. When the waters receded, they left behind a layer of rich, fertile muck, and those alluvial deposits supported a remarkably productive agricultural economy throughout the Nile River valley.

Egypt and Nubia: "Gifts of the Nile"

Agriculture transformed the entire Nile River valley, with effects that were most dramatic in Egypt. In ancient times, Egypt referred not to the territory embraced by the modern state of Egypt but, rather, to the ribbon of land bordering the lower third of the Nile between the Mediterranean and

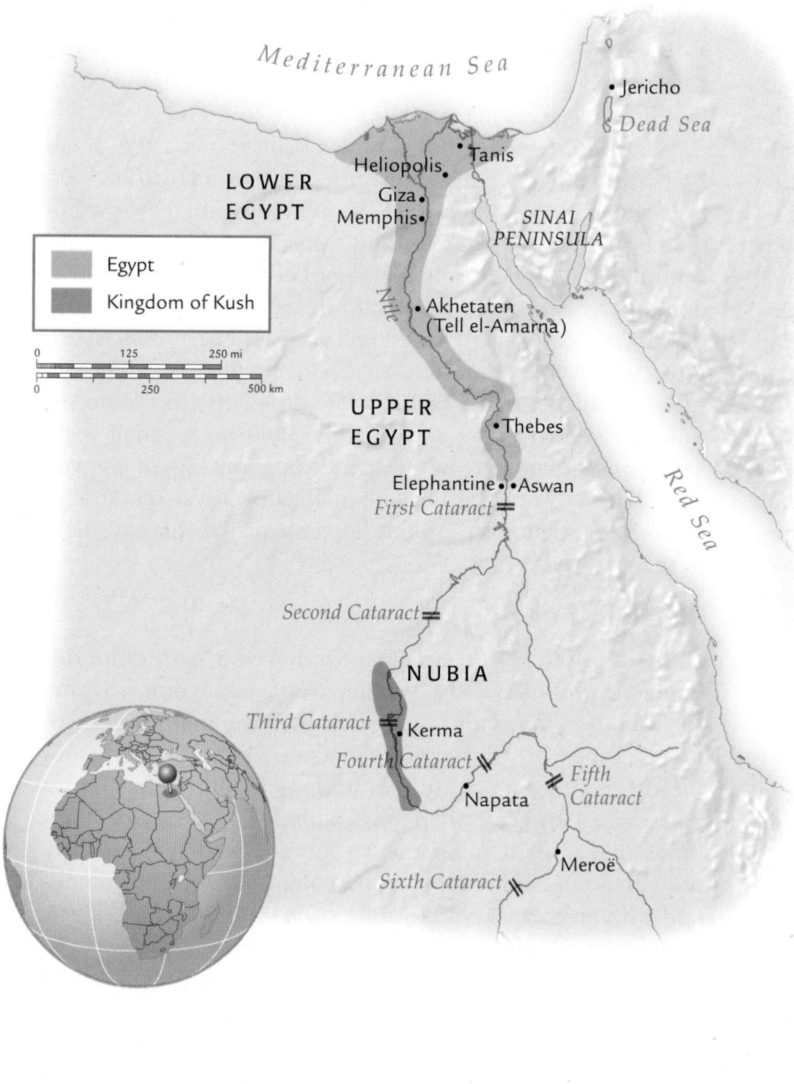

MAP 3.1
The Nile valley, 3000–2000 B.C.E.
Note the difference in size between the kingdom of Egypt and the kingdom of Kush.

What geographic conditions favored the establishment of large states north of the first cataract of the Nile River?

the river's first cataract (an unnavigable stretch of rapids and waterfalls) near Aswan. Egypt enjoyed a much larger floodplain than most of the land to the south known as Nubia, the middle stretches of the Nile valley between the river's first and sixth cataracts. As the Sahara became increasingly arid, cultivators flocked to the Nile valley and established societies that depended on intensive agriculture. Because of their broad floodplains, Egyptians were able to take better advantage of the Nile's annual floods than the Nubians to the south, and they turned Egypt into an especially productive agricultural region that was capable of supporting a much larger population than were Nubian lands. Because of its prosperity, the Greek historian Herodotus proclaimed Egypt the "gift of the Nile." If he had known more about Nubia, Herodotus might well have realized that it too was a gift of the Nile, even if it was less prosperous.

A painting from the tomb of a priest who lived about the fifteenth century B.C.E. depicts agricultural workers plowing and sowing crops in southern Egypt.

Early Agriculture in the Nile Valley Geography ensured that both Egypt and Nubia would come under the influence of the Mediterranean basin to the north and sub-Saharan Africa to the south, since the Nile River links the two regions. About 10,000 B.C.E., migrants from the Red Sea hills in northern Ethiopia traveled down the Nile valley and introduced to Egypt and Nubia the practice of collecting wild grains. They also introduced a language ancestral to Coptic, the language of ancient Egypt, to the lower reaches of the Nile valley. After 5000 B.C.E., as the African climate grew hotter and drier, Sudanic cultivators and herders moved down the Nile, introducing Egypt and Nubia to African crops such as gourds and watermelons as well as animals domesticated in the Sudan, particularly cattle and donkeys. About the same time, wheat and barley from Mesopotamia reached Egypt and Nubia by traveling up the Nile from the Mediterranean.

Both Egyptians and Nubians relied heavily on agriculture at least by 5000 B.C.E. Egyptian cultivators went into the floodplains in the late summer, after the recession of the Nile's annual flood, sowed their seeds without extensive preparation of the soil, allowed their crops to mature during the cool months of the year, and harvested them during the winter and early spring. With less extensive floodplains, Nubians relied more on prepared fields and irrigation by waters diverted from the Nile. As in Mesopotamia, high agricultural productivity led to a rapid increase in population throughout the Nile valley. Demographic pressures soon forced Egyptians in particular to develop more intense and sophisticated methods of agriculture. Cultivators moved beyond the Nile's immediate floodplains and began to grow crops on higher ground that required plowing and careful preparation. They built dikes to protect their fields from floods and catchment basins to store water for irrigation. By 4000 B.C.E. agricultural villages dotted the Nile's shores from the Mediterranean in the north to the river's fourth cataract in the south.

Political Organization As in Mesopotamia, dense human population in Egypt and Nubia brought a need for formal organization of public affairs. Neither Egypt nor Nubia faced the external dangers that threatened Mesopotamia, since the Red Sea, the Mediterranean Sea, and hostile deserts discouraged foreign invaders in ancient times. Nevertheless, the need to maintain order and organize community projects led both Egyptians and Nubians to create states and recognize official authorities. By 4000 B.C.E. agricultural villages along the Nile traded regularly with one another and cooperated in building irrigation networks.

The earliest Egyptian and Nubian states were small kingdoms much like those instituted in the Sudan after 5000 B.C.E. Indeed, it is likely that the notion of divine or semidivine rulers reached Egypt and Nubia from the eastern and central Sudan, where rulers had earlier founded small kingdoms to govern their agricultural and herding communities. In any case, small kingdoms appeared first in southern Egypt and Nubia after 4000 B.C.E. During the following centuries, residents living farther down the Nile (to the north) founded similar states, so that by 3300 B.C.E. small local kingdoms organized public life throughout Egypt as well as Nubia. As in the earlier Sudanic states, royal servants in these Nile kingdoms routinely accompanied deceased rulers to their graves.

The Unification of Egypt

Menes After 3100 B.C.E. Egypt followed a path quite different from those of the smaller Nubian kingdoms. Drawing on agricultural and demographic advantages, Egyptian rulers forged all the territory between the Nile delta and the river's first cataract into a unified kingdom much larger and more powerful than any other Nile state. Tradition holds that unified rule came to Egypt about 3100 B.C.E. in the person of a conqueror named Menes (sometimes identified with an early Egyptian ruler called Narmer). Menes was an ambitious minor official from southern Egypt (known as Upper Egypt, since the Nile flows north) who rose to power and extended his authority north and into the delta (known as Lower Egypt). According to tradition, Menes founded the city of Memphis, near modern Cairo, which stood at the junction of Upper and Lower Egypt. Memphis served as Menes' capital and eventually became the cultural as well as the political center of ancient Egypt.

Menes and his successors built a centralized state ruled by the pharaoh, the Egyptian king. The early pharaohs claimed to be gods living on the earth in human form, the owners and absolute rulers of all the land. In that respect, they continued the tradition of divine kingship inherited from the early agricultural societies of the Sudan. Indeed, as late as 2600 B.C.E., deceased pharaohs took royal servants with them to the grave. Egyptians associated the early pharaohs with Horus, the sky god, and they often represented the pharaohs together with a falcon or a hawk, the symbol of Horus. Later they viewed rulers as offspring of Amon, a sun god, so that the pharaoh was a son of the sun. They considered the ruling pharaoh a human sun overseeing affairs on the earth, just as Amon was the sun supervising the larger cosmos, and they believed that after his death the pharaoh actually merged with Amon. Artistic representations also depict pharaohs as enormous figures towering over their human subjects.

Menes, unifier of Egypt, prepares to sacrifice an enemy. He wears the crown of Upper Egypt, and the falcon representing the god Horus oversees his actions in this relief carving on a votive tablet. Two fallen enemies lie at the bottom of the tablet.

The Archaic Period and the Old Kingdom The power of the pharaohs was greatest during the first millennium of Egyptian history—the eras known as the Archaic Period (3100–2660 B.C.E.) and the Old Kingdom (2660–2160 B.C.E.). The most enduring symbols of their authority and divine status are the massive pyramids constructed during the Old Kingdom as royal tombs, most of them during the century from 2600 to 2500 B.C.E. These enormous monuments stand today at Giza, near Cairo, as testimony to the pharaohs' ability to marshal Egyptian resources. The largest is the pyramid of Khufu (also known as Cheops), which involved the precise cutting and fitting of 2.3 million limestone blocks weighing up to 15 tons each, with an average weight of 2.5 tons. Scholars estimate that construction of Khufu's pyramid required the services of some eighty-four thousand laborers working eighty days per year (probably during the late fall and winter, when the demand for agricultural labor was light) for twenty years. Apart from the laborers, hundreds of architects, engineers, craftsmen, and artists also contributed to the construction of the pyramids.

Relations between Egypt and Nubia Even after the emergence of the strong pharaonic state that took Egypt on a path different from those followed by other Nile societies, the fortunes of Egypt and Nubia remained closely intertwined. Egyptians had strong interests in Nubia for both political and commercial reasons: they were wary of Nubian kingdoms that might threaten Upper Egypt, and they desired products such as gold, ivory, ebony, and precious stones that were available only from southern lands. Meanwhile, Nubians had equally strong interests in Egypt: they wanted to protect their independence from their large and powerful neighbor to the north, and they sought to profit by controlling trade down the Nile.

The Early Kingdom of Kush Tensions led to frequent violence between Egypt and Nubia throughout the Archaic Period and the Old Kingdom. The early pharaohs organized at least five military campaigns to Nubia between 3100 and 2600 B.C.E. Pharaonic forces destroyed the Nubian kingdom of Ta-Seti soon after the unification of Egypt, leading to Egyptian domination of Lower Nubia (the land between the first and second cataracts of the Nile) for more than half a millennium, from about 3000 to 2400 B.C.E. That Egyptian presence in the north forced Nubian leaders to concentrate their efforts at political organization farther to the south in Upper Nubia. By about 2500 B.C.E. they had established a powerful kingdom, called Kush, with a capital at Kerma, about 700 kilometers (435 miles) south of Aswan. Though not as powerful as united Egypt, the kingdom of Kush was a formidable and wealthy state that dominated the upper reaches of the Nile and occasionally threatened southern Egypt.

Funerary sculpture from a tomb in Upper Egypt dating from about 2200–2000 B.C.E. depicts Nenu, a Nubian mercenary soldier who served in the Egyptian army, together with his Egyptian wife, their two sons, a servant, and two pet dogs.

In spite of constant tension and frequent hostilities, numerous diplomats and explorers traveled from Egypt to Nubia in search of political alliances and commercial relationships, and many Nubians sought improved fortunes in Egypt. Around 2300 B.C.E., for example, the Egyptian explorer Harkhuf made four expeditions to Nubia. He returned from one of his trips with a caravan of some three hundred donkeys bearing exotic products from tropical Africa, as well as a dancing dwarf, and his cargo stimulated Egyptian desire for trade with southern lands. Meanwhile, Nubian peoples looked for opportunities to pursue in Egypt. By the end of the Old Kingdom, Nubian mercenaries were quite prominent in Egyptian armies. Indeed, they often married Egyptian women and assimilated into Egyptian society.

Turmoil and Empire

The Hyksos After the Old Kingdom declined, Egyptians experienced considerable and sometimes unsettling change. A particularly challenging era of change followed from their encounters with a Semitic people whom Egyptians called the **Hyksos** ("foreign rulers"). Little information survives about the Hyksos, but it is clear that they were horse-riding nomads. Indeed, they probably introduced horses to Egypt, and their horse-drawn chariots, which they learned about from Hittites and Mesopotamians, provided them with a significant military advantage over Egyptian forces. They enjoyed an advantage also in their weaponry: the Hyksos used bronze weapons and bronze-tipped arrows, whereas

Hyksos (HICK-sohs)

thinking about **TRADITIONS**

Environment, Climate, and Agriculture

Agriculture is possible only if environmental and climatic conditions are tolerably favorable for the cultivation of crops. What environmental and climatic conditions made it possible for Egyptians and Nubians to build agricultural societies in the Nile River valley? To what extent can environmental and climatic conditions help explain why the agricultural societies of Egypt and Nubia developed along different lines?

MAP 3.2

Imperial Egypt, 1400 B.C.E.

Compare the territory ruled by the New Kingdom with the earlier kingdom of Egypt as represented in Map 3.1.

Why was the New Kingdom able to expand so dramatically to the north and south? Why did it not expand also to the east and west?

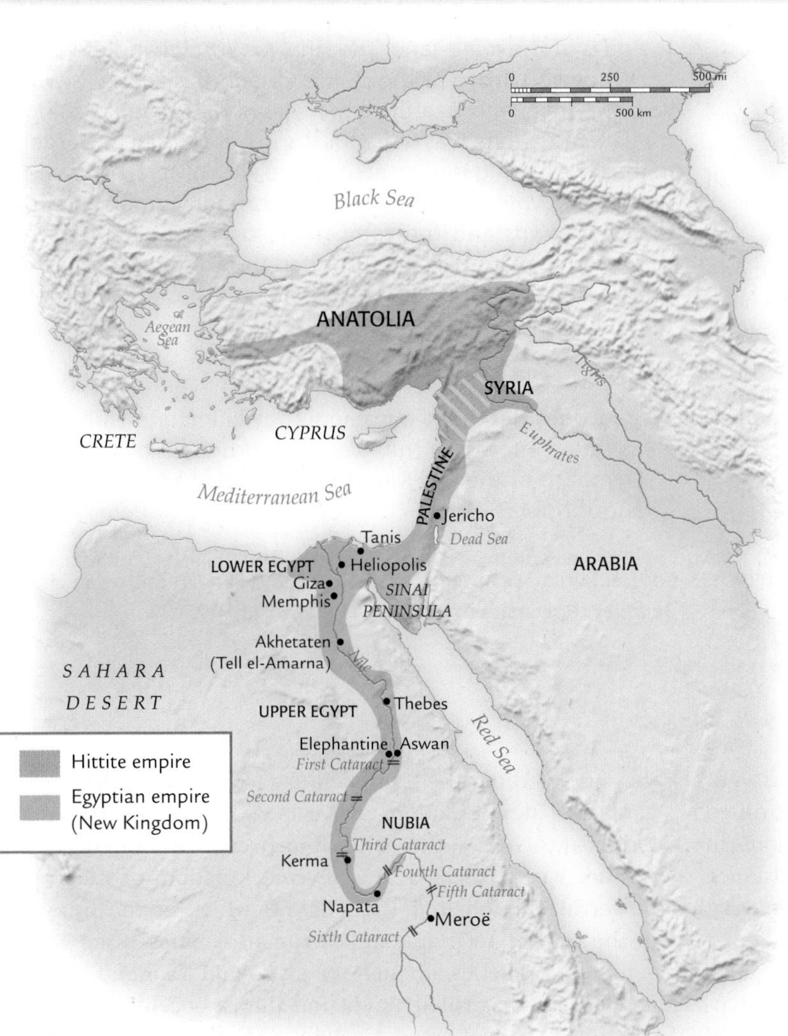

Egyptians relied mostly on wooden weapons and arrows with stone heads. About 1674 B.C.E. the Hyksos captured Memphis and levied tribute throughout Egypt.

Hyksos rule provoked a strong reaction especially in Upper Egypt, where disgruntled nobles organized revolts against the foreigners. They adopted horses and chariots for their own military forces. They also equipped their troops with bronze weapons. Working from Thebes and later from Memphis, Egyptian leaders gradually pushed the Hyksos out of the Nile delta and founded a powerful state known as the New Kingdom (1550–1070 B.C.E.).

The New Kingdom Pharaohs of the New Kingdom presided over a prosperous and productive society. Agricultural surpluses supported a population of perhaps four million people as well as an army and an elaborate bureaucracy that divided responsibilities among different offices. One department oversaw the court and royal estates, for example, while others dealt with military forces, state-recognized religious cults, the treasury, agricultural affairs, local government, and the administration of conquered territories. Pharaohs of the New Kingdom did not build enormous pyramids as did their predecessors of the Old Kingdom, but they erected numerous temples, palaces, and monumental statues to advertise their power and authority.

Egyptian Imperialism Pharaohs of the New Kingdom also worked to extend Egyptian authority well beyond the Nile valley and the delta. After expelling the Hyksos, they sought to prevent new invasions by seizing control of regions that might pose threats in the future. Most vigorous of the New Kingdom pharaohs was Tuthmosis III (reigned 1479–1425 B.C.E.). After seventeen campaigns that he personally led to Palestine and Syria, Tuthmosis dominated the coastal regions of the eastern Mediterranean as well as north Africa. Rulers of the New Kingdom also turned their attention to the south and restored Egyptian dominance in Nubia. Campaigning as far south as the Nile's fifth cataract, Egyptian armies destroyed Kerma, the capital of the kingdom of Kush, and crushed a series of small Nubian states that had arisen during the period of Hyksos rule. Thus for half a millennium Egypt was an imperial power throughout much of the eastern Mediterranean basin and southwest Asia as well as most of the Nile River valley.

sources from the past

Harkhuf's Expeditions to Nubia

Many Egyptians wrote brief autobiographies that they or their descendants had carved into their tombs. One of the most famous autobiographies from the Old Kingdom is that of Harkhuf, a royal official who became governor of Upper Egypt before 2300 B.C.E. The inscriptions in his tomb mention his four expeditions to Nubia to seek valuable items and report on political conditions there. The inscriptions also include the text of a letter from the boy-pharaoh Neferkare expressing his appreciation for Harkhuf's fourth expedition and his desire to see the dancing dwarf that Harkhuf brought back from Nubia.

The majesty of [Pharaoh] Mernere, my lord, sent me together with my father . . . to [the Upper Nubian kingdom of] Yam to open the way to that country. I did it in seven months; I brought from it all kinds of beautiful and rare gifts, and was praised for it greatly.

His majesty sent me a second time alone. . . . I came down [the Nile] bringing gifts from that country in great quantity, the likes of which had never before been brought back to this land [Egypt]. . . .

Then his majesty sent me a third time to Yam. . . . I came down with three hundred donkeys laden with incense, ebony, . . . panther skins, elephant's tusks, throw sticks, and all sorts of good products.

[The letter of Pharaoh Neferkare to Harkhuf:] Notice has been taken of this dispatch of yours which you made for the King at the Palace, to let one know that you have come down in safety from Yam with the army that was with you. You have said in this dispatch of yours that you have brought all kinds of great and beautiful gifts. . . . You have said in this dispatch of yours that you have brought a pygmy of the god's dances from the land of the horizon-dwellers [the region of Nubia southeast of Egypt], like the pygmy whom the [royal official] Bawerded brought from Punt [Ethiopia and Somalia] in the time of King Isesi. You have said to my majesty that his like has never been brought by anyone who [visited] Yam previously.

Truly you know how to do what your lord loves and praises. Truly you spend day and night planning to do what your lord loves, praises, and commands. His majesty will provide you many worthy honors for the benefit of your son's son for all time, so that all people will say, when they hear what my majesty did for you: "Does anything equal what was done for the sole companion Harkhuf when he came down from Yam, on account of the vigilance he showed in doing what his lord loved, praised, and commanded?"

Come north to the residence at once! Hurry and bring with you this pygmy whom you brought from the land of the horizon-dwellers live, hale, and healthy, for the dances of the god, to gladden the heart, to delight the heart of King Neferkare who lives forever! When he goes down with you into the ship, get worthy men to be around him on deck, lest he fall into the water! When he lies down at night, get worthy men to lie around him in his tent. Inspect ten times at night! My majesty desires to see this pygmy more than the gifts of the mine-land [the Sinai peninsula] and of Punt!

When you arrive at the residence and this pygmy is with you live, hale, and healthy, my majesty will do great things for you, more than was done for the [royal official] Bawerded in the time of King Isesi, in accordance with my majesty's wish to see this pygmy. Orders have been brought to the chief of the new towns and the companion, overseer of priests to command that supplies be furnished from what is under the charge of each from every storage depot and every temple that has not been exempted.

For Further Reflection

- How does Harkhuf's autobiography illuminate early Egyptian interest in Nubia and the processes by which Egyptians of the Old Kingdom developed knowledge about Nubia?

Source: Miriam Lichtheim, ed. *Ancient Egyptian Literature,* 3 vols. Berkeley: University of California Press, 1973, 1: 25–27.

After the New Kingdom, Egypt entered a long period of political and military decline. Just as Hyksos rule provoked a reaction in Egypt, Egyptian rule provoked reactions in the regions subdued by pharaonic armies. Local resistance drove Egyptian forces out of Nubia and southwest Asia, then Kushite and Assyrian armies invaded Egypt itself.

The Revived Kingdom of Kush By 1100 B.C.E. Egyptian forces were in full retreat from Nubia. After they vacated the region, about the tenth century B.C.E., Nubian leaders organized a new kingdom of Kush with a capital at Napata, located just below the Nile's fourth cataract. By the eighth century B.C.E., rulers of this revived kingdom of Kush were powerful enough to invade Egypt, which at the time was in the grip of religious and factional disputes. King Kashta conquered Thebes about 760 B.C.E. and founded a Kushite dynasty that ruled Egypt for almost a century. Kashta's successors consolidated Kushite authority in Upper Egypt,

A wall painting from the tomb of an Egyptian imperial official in Nubia depicts a delegation of Nubians bringing tribute in the forms of exotic beasts, animal skins, and rings of gold. Why might these unusual gifts have been welcome tribute for Egyptians?

claimed the title of pharaoh, and eventually extended their rule to the Nile delta and beyond.

Meanwhile, as Kushites pushed into Egypt from the south, Assyrian armies equipped with iron weapons bore down from the north. During the mid-seventh century B.C.E., while building their vast empire, the Assyrians invaded Egypt, campaigned as far south as Thebes, drove out the Kushites, and subjected Egypt to Assyrian rule. After the mid-sixth century B.C.E., like Mesopotamia, Egypt fell to a series of foreign conquerors who built vast empires throughout southwest Asia and the eastern Mediterranean region, including Egypt and north Africa.

THE FORMATION OF COMPLEX SOCIETIES AND SOPHISTICATED CULTURAL TRADITIONS

As in Mesopotamia, cities and the congregation of dense populations encouraged the emergence of specialized labor in the early agricultural societies of Africa. This development was particularly noticeable in Egypt, but specialized labor was a prominent feature also of societies in the southern reaches of the Nile River valley. Clearly defined social classes emerged throughout the Nile valley, and both Egyptians and Nubians built patriarchal societies that placed authority largely in the hands of adult males. The Egyptian economy was especially productive, and because of both its prosperity and its geographic location, Egypt figured as a center of trade, linking lands in southwest Asia, the eastern Mediterranean, and sub-Saharan Africa. Meanwhile, like southwest Asia, the Nile valley was a site of sophisticated cultural development. Writing systems appeared in both Egypt and Nubia, and writing soon became a principal medium of literary expression and religious reflection as well as a means for preserving governmental records and commercial information.

The Emergence of Cities and Stratified Societies

Cities of the Nile Valley: Egypt Cities were not as prominent in early societies of the Nile River valley as they were in ancient Mesopotamia. In the Nile valley, populations clustered mostly in numerous agricultural villages that traded regularly with their neighbors up and down the river. Nevertheless, several major cities emerged and guided affairs in both Egypt and Nubia. The conqueror Menes founded Memphis as early as 3100 B.C.E. Because of its location at the head of the Nile delta, Memphis was a convenient site for a capital: Menes and many later pharaohs as well ruled over a unified Egypt from Memphis. Besides the capital, other cities played important roles in Egyptian affairs. Thebes, for example, was a prominent political center even before the unification of Egypt. After unification, Thebes

Building pyramids and other large structures involved heavy work, especially by the less privileged classes. Here an Egyptian manuscript painting produced about 1000 B.C.E. depicts a supervisor overseeing a group of laborers as they drag a sled loaded with building blocks.

became the administrative center of Upper Egypt, and several pharaohs even took the city as their capital. Heliopolis, meaning "City of the Sun," was the headquarters of a sun cult near Memphis and a principal cultural center of ancient Egypt. Founded about 2900 B.C.E., Heliopolis reached the height of its influence during the New Kingdom, when it was the site of an enormous temple to the sun god Re. Yet another important city was Tanis on the Nile delta. At least by the time of the Middle Kingdom, and perhaps even earlier, Tanis was a bustling port and Egypt's gateway to the Mediterranean.

Cities of the Nile Valley: Nubia Nubian cities are not as well known as those of Egypt, but written records and archaeological excavations both make it clear that powerful and prosperous cities emerged in the southern Nile valley as well as in Egypt. The most prominent Nubian cities of ancient times were Kerma, Napata, and Meroë. Kerma, located just above the Nile's third cataract, was the capital of the earliest kingdom of Kush. For a millennium after its foundation about 2500 B.C.E., Kerma dominated both river and overland routes between Egypt to the north and Sudanic regions to the south. The fortunes of Kerma waxed and waned as Egypt and Kush contended with each other for power in Nubia, but it remained an influential site until its destruction about 1450 B.C.E. by the aggressive armies of Egypt's expansive New Kingdom. About the tenth century B.C.E., Napata emerged as the new political center of Nubia. Located just below the Nile's fourth cataract, Napata was more distant from Egypt than Kerma and hence less vulnerable to threats from the north. After King Kashta and his successors conquered Egypt, Napata enjoyed tremendous prosperity because of the wealth that flowed up the Nile to the Kushite capital. About the middle of the seventh century B.C.E., after Assyrian forces expelled the Kushites and asserted imperial control in Egypt, the capital of Kush moved farther south, this time to Meroë, located between the Nile's fifth and sixth cataracts about 1,600 kilometers (1,000 miles) from the southern border of Egypt. Meroë presided over a flourishing kingdom of Kush that enjoyed great prosperity because of its participation in Nile trade networks until its gradual decline after about 100 C.E.

Social Classes In Egypt and Nubia alike, ancient cities were centers of considerable accumulated wealth, which encouraged the development of social distinctions and hierarchies. Like the Mesopotamians, ancient Egyptians recognized a series of well-defined social classes. Egyptian peasants and slaves played roles in society similar to those of their Mesopotamian counterparts: they supplied the hard labor that made complex agricultural society possible. The organization of the ruling classes, however, differed considerably between Mesopotamia and Egypt. Instead of a series of urban kings, as in Mesopotamia, Egyptians recognized the pharaoh as a supreme central ruler. Because the pharaoh was theoretically an absolute ruler, Egyptian society had little room for a noble class like that of Mesopotamia. Instead of depending on nobles who owed their positions to their birth, Egypt relied on professional military forces and an elaborate bureaucracy of administrators and tax collectors who served the central government. Thus, in Egypt much more than in Mesopotamia, individuals of common birth could attain high positions in society through government service.

Surviving information illuminates Egyptian society much better than Nubian, but it is clear that Nubia also was the site of a complex, hierarchical society in ancient times. Meroë, for example, was home to government officials, priests, craftsmen, merchants, laborers, and slaves. Cemeteries associated with Nubian cities clearly reveal social and

> "The most enduring symbols of the [pharaoh's] authority and divine status are the massive pyramids."

economic distinctions. Tombs of wealthy and powerful individuals were often elaborate structures—comfortable dwelling places tastefully decorated with paintings and filled with expensive goods such as gold jewelry, gems, fine furniture, and abundant supplies of food. In keeping with the ancient traditions of Sudanic kingship, many royal tombs became the final resting places also of servants ritually executed so that they could tend to the needs of their master in death. Graves of commoners were much simpler, although they usually contained jewelry, pottery, personal ornaments, and other goods to accompany the departed.

Patriarchal Society Like their Mesopotamian counterparts, both Egyptian and Nubian peoples built patriarchal societies that vested authority over public and private affairs in their men. Women of upper elite classes oversaw the domestic work of household servants. Below the level of the upper elites, even in wealthy households, women routinely performed domestic work, which included growing vegetables, grinding grain, baking bread, brewing beer, spinning thread, and weaving textiles. Elite men enjoyed comfortable positions as scribes or government officials, while men of lower classes worked as agricultural laborers, potters, carpenters, craftsmen, or fishermen. Both men and women were able to accumulate property, including slaves, and pass wealth along to their children. Men alone, however, were the governors of households and the larger society as a whole. With rare exceptions men were the rulers in both Egyptian and Nubian states, and decisions about government policies and public affairs rested mostly in men's hands.

Women's Influence in Egypt and Nubia Yet women made their influence felt in ancient Egyptian and Nubian societies much more than in contemporary Mesopotamia. In Egypt, women of the royal family frequently served as regents for young rulers. Many royal women also used their status to influence policy, sometimes going so far as to participate in plots to manipulate affairs in favor of their sons or even in palace rebellions seeking to unseat a pharaoh. In one notable case, a woman took power as pharaoh herself: Queen Hatshepsut (reigned 1473–1458 B.C.E.) served as coruler with her stepson Tuthmosis III. The notion of a female ruler was unfamiliar and perhaps somewhat unsettling to many Egyptians. In an effort to present her in unthreatening guise, a monumental statue of Queen Hatshepsut depicts her wearing the stylized beard traditionally associated with the pharaohs. In Nubia, in contrast, there is abundant evidence of many women rulers in the kingdom of Kush, particularly during the period when Meroë was the capital. Some ruled in their own right, others reigned jointly with male kings, and many governed also in the capacity of a regent known as the *kandake* (root of the name Candace). Meanwhile, other women wielded considerable power as priestesses in the numerous religious cults observed in Egypt and Nubia. A few women also obtained a formal education and worked as scribes who prepared administrative and legal documents for governments and private parties.

Economic Specialization and Trade

With the formation of complex, city-based societies, peoples of the Nile valley were able to draw on a rapidly expanding stock of human skills. Bronze metallurgy made its way from Mesopotamia to both Egypt and Nubia, and Sudanic peoples independently developed a technology of iron production that eventually spread to most parts of sub-Saharan Africa. Pottery, textile manufacture, woodworking, leather production, stonecutting, and masonry all became distinct occupations in cities throughout the Nile valley. Specialized labor and the invention of efficient transportation technologies encouraged the development of trade networks that linked the Nile valley to a much larger world.

Bronze Metallurgy Nile societies were much slower than their Mesopotamian counterparts to adopt metal tools and weapons. Whereas the production of bronze flourished in Mesopotamia by 3000 B.C.E., use of bronze implements became widespread in Egypt only after the seventeenth century B.C.E., when the Hyksos relied on bronze weapons to impose their authority on the Nile delta. After expelling the Hyksos, Egyptians equipped their forces with bronze weapons, and the imperial armies of Tuthmosis and other pharaohs of the New Kingdom carried up-to-date bronze weapons like those used in Mesopotamia and neighboring lands. As in Mesopotamia, and other lands as well, the high cost of copper and tin kept bronze out of the hands of most people. Royal workshops closely monitored supplies of the valuable metal: officers weighed the bronze tools issued to workers at royal tombs, for example, to ensure that craftsmen did not shave slivers off them and divert expensive metal to personal uses.

A wall painting produced about 1300 B.C.E. shows Egyptian goldsmiths fashioning jewelry and decorative objects for elite patrons. Early experience with gold metallurgy prepared craftsmen to work with bronze and iron when knowledge of those metals reached Egypt.

Iron Metallurgy Bronze was even less prominent in Nubian societies than in Egypt. Indeed, Nubia produced little bronze, since the region was poor in copper and tin, and so relied on imports from the north. During the centuries after 1000 B.C.E., however, the southern Nile societies made up for their lack of bronze with the emergence of large-scale production of iron. The Hittites had developed techniques for forging iron in Anatolia about 1300 B.C.E., but iron metallurgy in Africa arose independently from local experimentation with iron ores, which are plentiful in sub-Saharan Africa. The earliest traces of African iron production discovered by archaeologists date from about 900 B.C.E. in the Great Lakes region of east Africa (modern-day Burundi and Rwanda) and also on the southern side of Lake Chad (in modern-day Cameroon). It is quite possible that African peoples produced iron before 1000 B.C.E. From the Great Lakes region and the Sudan, iron metallurgy quickly spread throughout most of sub-Saharan Africa. Furnaces churned out iron implements both in Nubia and in west Africa at least by 500 B.C.E. Meroë in particular became a site of large-scale iron production. Indeed, archaeologists who excavated Meroë in the early twentieth century C.E. found enormous mounds of slag still remaining from ancient times.

A wooden model found in a tomb shows how Egyptians traveled up and down the Nile River. Produced about 2000 B.C.E., this sculpture depicts a relatively small boat with a mast, sail, rudder, and poles to push the vessel through shallow waters as the figure in front gauges the water's depth. Many wall and tomb paintings confirm the accuracy of this model.

Transportation Nile craftsmen also worked from the early days of agricultural society to devise efficient means of transportation. Within Egypt, the Nile River greatly facilitated transportation, and Egyptians traveled up and down the river before 3500 B.C.E. Because the Nile flows north, boats could ride the currents from Upper to Lower Egypt. Meanwhile, prevailing winds blow almost year-round from the north, so that by raising a sail, boats could easily make their way upriver from Lower to Upper Egypt. Soon after 3000 B.C.E. Egyptians sailed beyond the Nile into the Mediterranean, and by about 2000 B.C.E. they had thoroughly explored the waters of the Red Sea, the Gulf of Aden, and the western portion of the Arabian Sea. Egyptians also made use of Mesopotamian-style wheeled vehicles for local transport, and they relied on donkey caravans for transport between the Nile valley and ports on the Red Sea.

In Nubia, navigation on the Nile was less convenient than in Egypt because unnavigable cataracts made it necessary to transport goods overland before continuing on the river. Moreover, sailing ships heading upriver found it difficult to negotiate a long stretch of the Nile around the fourth cataract because winds blow the same direction as the currents. Thus, although Nubian societies were able to make some use of the Nile for purposes of transportation, they had to rely more than Egyptians on overland transport by wheeled vehicles and donkey caravan.

Trade Networks In both Egypt and Nubia, specialized labor and efficient means of transportation encouraged the development of long-distance trade. Egypt was in special need of trade because the land enjoys few natural resources other than the Nile. Irregular exchanges of goods between Egypt and Nubia took place in early times, perhaps 4000 B.C.E. or even before. By the time of the Old Kingdom, trade flowed regularly between Egypt and Nubia. The cities of Aswan and Elephantine at the southern border of Egypt reflected that trade in their very names: Aswan took its name from the ancient Egyptian word *swene,* meaning "trade," and Elephantine owed its name to the large quantities of elephant ivory that passed through it while traveling down the Nile from Nubia to Egypt. Apart from ivory, exotic African goods such as ebony, leopard skins, ostrich feathers, gemstones, gold, and slaves went down the Nile in exchange for pottery, wine, honey, and finished products from Egypt. Among the most prized Egyptian exports were fine linen textiles woven from the flax that flourished in the Nile valley as well as high-quality decorative and ornamental objects such as boxes, furniture, and jewelry produced by skilled artisans. Commerce linked Egypt and Nubia throughout ancient times, even when tensions or hostilities complicated relations between the two societies.

Egyptian merchants looked north as well as south. They traded with Mesopotamians as early as 3500 B.C.E., and after 3000 B.C.E. they were active throughout the eastern Mediter-ranean basin. Egyptian commerce in the Mediterranean

Queen Hatshepsut's fleet takes on cargo at Punt. Stevedores (dockworkers who load and unload ships) carry jars of aromatics and trees with carefully wrapped roots onto the Egyptian vessels. In the bottom panel, ships loaded with cargo prepare to depart.

thinking about ENCOUNTERS

Interactions between Egypt and Nubia

The geography of the long Nile River valley ensured that the lands of Egypt and Nubia would have frequent dealings with each other. Consider the different forms of engagement that brought Egypt and Nubia into interaction with each other: diplomatic missions, military expeditions, and trading relationships. What kinds of effects did these different forms of engagement have in both Egypt and Nubia?

sometimes involved enormous transfers of goods. Since Egypt has few trees, for example, all wood came from abroad. Pharaohs especially prized aromatic cedar for their tombs, and Egyptian ships regularly imported huge loads from Lebanon. One record of about 2600 B.C.E. mentions an expedition of forty ships hauling cedar logs. In exchange for cedar Egyptians offered gold, silver, linen textiles, leather goods, and dried foods such as lentils.

Maritime Trade: Egypt and Punt After the establishment of the New Kingdom, Egyptians also traded through the Red Sea and the Gulf of Aden with an east African land they called Punt—probably modern-day Somalia and Ethiopia. From Punt they imported gold, ebony, ivory, cattle, aromatics, and slaves. The tomb of Queen Hatshepsut bears detailed illustrations of a trading expedition to Punt about 1450 B.C.E. Paintings in the tomb show large Egyptian ships bearing jewelry, tools, and weapons to Punt and then loading the exotic products of the southern land, including apes, monkeys, dogs, a panther, and myrrh trees with their roots carefully bound in bags. Thus, as in southwest Asia, specialization of labor and efficient technologies of transportation not only quickened the economies of complex societies in Egypt and Nubia but also encouraged their interaction with peoples of distant lands.

Early Writing in the Nile Valley

Hieroglyphic Writing Writing appeared in Egypt at least by 3200 B.C.E., possibly as a result of Mesopotamian influence. As in Mesopotamia, the earliest Egyptian writing was pictographic, but Egyptians soon supplemented their pictographs with symbols representing sounds and ideas. Early Greek visitors to Egypt marveled at the large and handsome pictographs that adorned Egyptian monuments and buildings. Since the symbols were particularly prominent on temples, the visitors called them *hieroglyphs,* from two Greek words meaning "holy inscriptions." Quite apart from monument inscriptions, hieroglyphic writing survives on sheets of papyrus, a paper-like material fashioned from the insides of papyrus reeds, which flourish along the Nile River. The hot, dry climate of Egypt has preserved not only mummified bodies but also large numbers of papyrus texts bearing administrative and commercial records as well as literary and religious texts.

Although striking and dramatic, hieroglyphs were also somewhat cumbersome. Egyptians went to the trouble of using hieroglyphs for formal writing and monument inscriptions, but for everyday affairs they commonly relied on the hieratic ("priestly") script, a simplified, cursive form of hieroglyphs. Hieratic appeared in the early centuries of the third millennium B.C.E., and Egyptians made extensive use of the script for more than three thousand years, from about 2600 B.C.E. to 600 C.E. Hieratic largely disappeared after the middle of the first millennium C.E., when Egyptians adapted the Greek alphabet to their language and developed alphabetic scripts known as the demotic ("popular") and Coptic ("Egyptian") scripts. Hieratic, demotic, and Coptic scripts all survive mostly in papyrus texts but occasionally also in inscriptions.

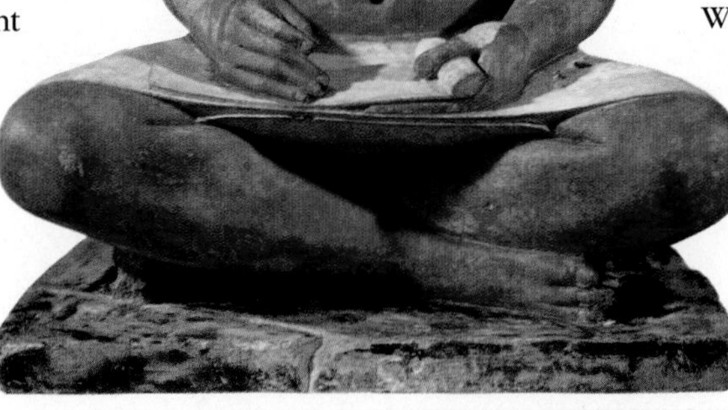

A painted limestone sculpture from the Old Kingdom depicts an Egyptian scribe writing on papyrus. How did formal education and literacy influence social distinctions and the development of social classes in ancient Egypt?

Education Formal education and literacy brought handsome rewards in ancient Egypt. The privileged life of a scribe comes across clearly in a short work known as "The Satire of the Trades." Written by a scribe exhorting his son to study diligently, the work detailed all the miseries associated with eighteen different professions: metalsmiths stunk like fish; potters grubbed in the mud like pigs; fishermen ran the risk of sudden death in the jaws of the Nile's ferocious crocodiles. Only the scribe led a comfortable, honorable, and dignified life.

Nubian peoples spoke their own languages, although many individuals were fully conversant in Egyptian as well as their native tongues, but all early writing in Nubia was Egyptian hieroglyphic writing. Indeed, over the centuries Egypt wielded great cultural influence in Nubia, especially during times when Egyptian political and military influence was strong in southern lands. Egyptian political and military officials often erected monuments and inscribed them with accounts in hieroglyphics of their deeds in Nubia. Similarly, Egyptian priests traveled regularly to Nubia, organized temples devoted to Egyptian gods, and promoted their beliefs in hieroglyphics. Egyptian influence was very strong in Nubia also during the eighth and seventh centuries B.C.E. when the kings of Kush ruled Egypt as pharaohs and sponsored extensive trade, travel, and communication between Egypt and Nubia.

Meroitic Writing Nubian inscriptions continued to appear in Egyptian hieroglyphic writing as late as the first century C.E. After about the fifth century B.C.E., however, Egyptian cultural influence declined noticeably in Nubia. After the transfer of the Kushite capital from Napata to Meroë, Nubian scribes even devised an alphabetic script for the Meroitic language. They borrowed Egyptian hieroglyphs but used them to represent sounds rather than ideas and so created a flexible writing system. Many Meroitic inscriptions survive, both on monuments and on papyrus. To date, however, scholars have not been able to understand Meroitic writing. Although they have ascertained the sound values of the alphabet, the Meroitic language itself is so different from other known languages that no one has been able to decipher Meroitic texts.

The Development of Organized Religious Traditions

Amon and Re Like their counterparts in other world regions, Egyptians and Nubians believed that deities played prominent roles in the world and that proper cultivation of the gods was an important community responsibility. The principal gods revered in ancient Egypt were Amon and Re. Amon was originally a local Theban deity associated with the sun, creation, fertility, and reproductive forces, and Re was a sun god worshiped at Heliopolis. During the Old Kingdom, priests associated the two gods with each other and honored them in the combined cult of Amon-Re. At Heliopolis, a massive temple complex supported priests who tended to the cult of Amon-Re and studied the heavens for astronomical purposes. When Egypt became an imperial power during the New Kingdom, some devotees suggested that Amon-Re might even be a universal god who presided over all the earth.

Aten and Monotheism For a brief period the cult of Amon-Re faced a monotheistic challenge from the god Aten, another deity associated with the sun. Aten's champion was Pharaoh Amenhotep IV (reigned 1353–1335 B.C.E.), who changed his name to Akhenaten in honor of his preferred deity. Akhenaten considered Aten the world's "sole god, like whom there is no other." Thus, unlike the priests of Amon-Re, most of whom viewed their god as one among many, Akhenaten and others devoted to Aten considered their deity the one and only true god. Their faith represented one of the world's earliest expressions of monotheism—the belief that a single god rules over all creation.

Akhenaten built a new capital city called Akhetaten ("Horizon of Aten," located at modern Tell el-Amarna), where broad streets, courtyards, and open temples allowed unobscured vision and constant veneration of the sun. He also dispatched agents to all parts of Egypt with instructions to encourage the worship of Aten and to chisel out the names of Amon, Re, and other gods from inscriptions on temples and public buildings. As long as Akhenaten lived, the cult of Aten flourished. But when the pharaoh died, traditional priests mounted a fierce counterattack, restored the cult of Amon-Re to privileged status, and nearly annihilated the worship and even the memory of Aten.

Mummification Whereas Mesopotamians believed with Gilgamesh that death brought an end to an individual's existence, many Egyptians believed that death was not an end so much as a transition to a new dimension of existence. The yearning for immortality helps to explain the Egyptian practice of mummifying the dead. During the Old Kingdom, Egyptians believed that only the ruling elites would survive the grave, so they mummified only pharaohs and their close relatives. Later, however, other royal officials and wealthy individuals merited the posthumous honor of mummification. During the New Kingdom, Egyptians came to think

"The yearning for immortality helps to explain the Egyptian practice of mummifying the dead."

of eternal life as a condition available to normal mortals as well as to members of the ruling classes. By the time the Greek historian Herodotus described the process of mummification in the fifth century B.C.E., many wealthy families were able to help their deceased relatives attain immortality by preserving their bodies. Mummification never became general practice in Egypt, but with or without preservation of the body, a variety of religious cults promised to lead individuals of all classes to immortality.

Cult of Osiris The cult of Osiris attracted particularly strong popular interest. According to the myths surrounding the cult, Osiris's evil brother Seth murdered him and scattered his dismembered parts throughout the land, but the victim's loyal wife, Isis, retrieved his parts and gave her husband a proper burial. Impressed by her devotion,

sources from the past

The Great Hymn to Aten

After the death of Pharaoh Akhenaten, priests of Amon destroyed temples to Aten and all public inscriptions singing his praises. Yet many private inscriptions survived in tombs of priests and royal officials who died while in service at the new royal capital of Akhetaten. In excavating these tombs, archaeologists have brought to light many texts praising Aten and outlining the monotheistic beliefs surrounding his cult. Most famous of these inscriptions is the text known as "The Great Hymn to Aten."

Splendid you rise in heaven's lightland,
O living Aten, creator of life!
When you have dawned in eastern lightland,
You fill every land with your beauty.
You are beauteous, great radiant,
High over every land;
Your rays embrace the lands,
To the limit of all that you made. . . .

When you set in western lightland,
Earth is in darkness as if in death;
One sleeps in chambers, heads covered,
One eye does not see another.
Were they robbed of their goods,
That are under their heads,
People would not remark it.
Every lion comes from its den,
All the serpents bite;
Darkness hovers, earth is silent,
As their maker rests in lightland.

Earth brightens when you dawn in lightland.
When you shine as Aten of daytime;
As you dispel the dark,
As you cast your rays,
The Two Lands [of Upper Egypt and Lower Egypt]
are in festivity.
Awake they stand on their feet,
You have roused them;
Bodies cleansed, clothed,
Their arms adore your appearance.
The entire land sets out to work. . . .
How many are your deeds,
Though hidden from sight,
O Sole God beside whom there is none!
You made the earth as you wished, you alone,
All peoples, herds, and flocks;
All upon earth that walk on legs,
All on high that fly on wings,
The lands of Khor and Kush,
The land of Egypt. . . .

Your rays nurse all fields,
When you shine they live, they grow for you;
You made the seasons to foster all that you made,
Winter to cool them, heat that they taste you.
You made the far sky to shine therein,
To behold all that you made;
You alone, shining in your form of living Aten,
Risen, radiant, distant, near.
You made millions of forms from yourself alone,
Towns, villages, fields, the river's course;
All eyes observe you upon them,
For you are the Aten of daytime on high.

For Further Reflection

- As conceived in "The Great Hymn to Aten," what was the role of Aten as creator and sustainer of life on earth?

Source: Miriam Lichtheim, ed. *Ancient Egyptian Literature*, 3 vols. Berkeley: University of California Press, 1976, 2: 96–99.

the gods restored Osiris to life—not to physical human life among mortals, however, but to a different kind of existence as god of the underworld, the dwelling place of the departed. Because of his death and resurrection, Egyptians associated Osiris with the Nile (which flooded, retreated, and then flooded again the following year) and with their crops (which grew, died, and then sprouted and grew again.)

Egyptians also associated Osiris with immortality and honored him through a religious cult that demanded observance of high moral standards. As lord of the underworld, Osiris had the power to determine who deserved the blessing of immortality and who did not. Following their deaths, individual souls faced the judgment of Osiris, who had their hearts weighed against a feather symbolizing justice. Those with heavy hearts carrying a burden of evil and guilt did not merit immortality, whereas those of pure heart and honorable deeds gained the gift of eternal life. Thus Osiris's cult held out hope of eternal reward for those who behaved according to high moral standards, and it cast its message in terms understandable to cultivators in early agricultural society.

Osiris, Egyptian god of the underworld (seated at right), receives a recently deceased individual, while attendants weigh the heart of another individual against a feather to determine if the person is deserving of immortality. This illustration comes from a papyrus copy of the *Book of the Dead* that was buried with a royal mummy.

Nubian Religious Beliefs Nubian peoples observed their own religious traditions, some of which they probably inherited from the early agricultural societies of the Sudan, but little written information survives to throw light on their religious beliefs. The most prominent of the Nubian deities was the lion-god Apedemak, often depicted with a bow and arrows, who served as war god for the kingdom of Kush. Another deity, Sebiumeker, was a creator god and divine guardian of his human devotees.

Alongside native traditions, Egyptian religious cults were quite prominent in Nubia, especially after the aggressive pharaohs of the New Kingdom imposed Egyptian rule on the southern lands. Nubian peoples did not mummify the remains of their deceased, but they built pyramids similar to those of Egypt, although smaller, and they embraced several Egyptian gods. Amon was the preeminent Egyptian deity in Nubia as in Egypt itself: many Nubian temples honored Amon, and the kings of Kush portrayed themselves as champions of the Egyptian god. Osiris was also popular in Nubia, where he sometimes appeared in association with the native deity Sebiumeker. In the early days after their introduction, Egyptian cults were most prominent among the Nubian ruling classes. Gradually, however, Egyptian gods attracted a sizable following, and they remained popular in Nubia until the sixth century C.E. They did not displace native gods so much as they joined them in the Nubian pantheon. Indeed, Nubians often identified Egyptian gods with their own deities or endowed the foreign gods with traits important in Nubian society.

An elaborate gold ring from a tomb at Meroë, dating probably to the third century C.E., depicts a deity named Sebiumeker (sometimes referred to as Sebewyemeker). Although often associated with Osiris, Sebiumeker was a Meroitic god with no exact counterpart in Egypt.

BANTU MIGRATIONS AND EARLY AGRICULTURAL SOCIETIES OF SUB-SAHARAN AFRICA

Like their counterparts in southwest Asia, Egyptian and Nubian societies participated in a much larger world of interaction and exchange. Mesopotamian societies developed under the strong influences of long-distance trade, diffusions of technological innovations, the spread of cultural traditions, and the far-flung migrations of Semitic and Indo-European peoples. Similarly, quite apart from their dealings with southwest Asian and Mediterranean peoples, Egyptian and Nubian societies developed in the context of widespread interaction and exchange in sub-Saharan Africa. The most prominent processes unfolding in sub-Saharan Africa during ancient times were the migrations of Bantu-speaking peoples and the establishment of agricultural societies in regions where Bantu speakers settled. Just as Sudanic agriculture spread to the Nile valley and provided an economic foundation for the development of Egyptian and Nubian societies, it also spread to most other regions of Africa south of the Sahara and supported the emergence of distinctive agricultural societies.

The Dynamics of Bantu Expansion

The Bantu Among the most influential peoples of sub-Saharan Africa in ancient times were those who spoke Bantu languages. The original Bantu language was one of many related tongues in the larger Niger-Congo family of languages widely spoken in west Africa after 4000 B.C.E. (Niger-Congo languages include also those spoken by Mande, Kru, Wolof, Yoruba, Igbo, and other peoples.) The earliest Bantu speakers inhabited a region embracing the eastern part of modern Nigeria and the southern part of modern Cameroon. Members of this community referred to themselves as *bantu* (meaning "persons" or "people"). The earliest Bantu speakers settled mostly along the banks of rivers, which they navigated in canoes, and in open areas of the region's forests. They cultivated yams and oil palms, which first came under cultivation by early agricultural peoples in the western Sudan, and in later centuries they also adopted crops that reached them from the eastern and central Sudan, particularly millet and sorghum. They also kept goats and raised guinea fowl. They lived in clan-based villages headed by chiefs who conducted religious rituals and represented their communities in dealings with neighboring villages. They traded regularly with hunting and gathering peoples who inhabited the tropical forests. Formerly called pygmies, these peoples are now referred to as forest peoples. Bantu cultivators provided these forest peoples with pottery and stone axes in exchange for meat, honey, and other forest products.

Bantu Migrations Unlike most of their neighbors, the Bantu displayed an early readiness to migrate to new territories. By 3000 B.C.E. they were slowly spreading south into the west African forest, and after 2000 B.C.E. they expanded rapidly to the south toward the Congo River basin and east toward the Great Lakes, absorbing local populations of hunting, gathering, and fishing peoples into their agricultural societies. Over the centuries, as some groups of Bantu speakers settled and others moved on to new territories, their languages differentiated into more than five hundred distinct but related tongues. (Today, more than ninety million people speak Bantu languages, which collectively constitute the most prominent family of languages in sub-Saharan Africa.) Like the Indo-European migrations discussed in chapter 2, the Bantu migrations were not mass movements of peoples. Instead, they were intermittent and incremental processes that resulted in the gradual spread of Bantu languages and ethnic communities, as small groups moved to new territories and established settlements, which then became foundations for further expansion. By 1000 C.E. Bantu-speaking peoples occupied most of Africa south of the equator.

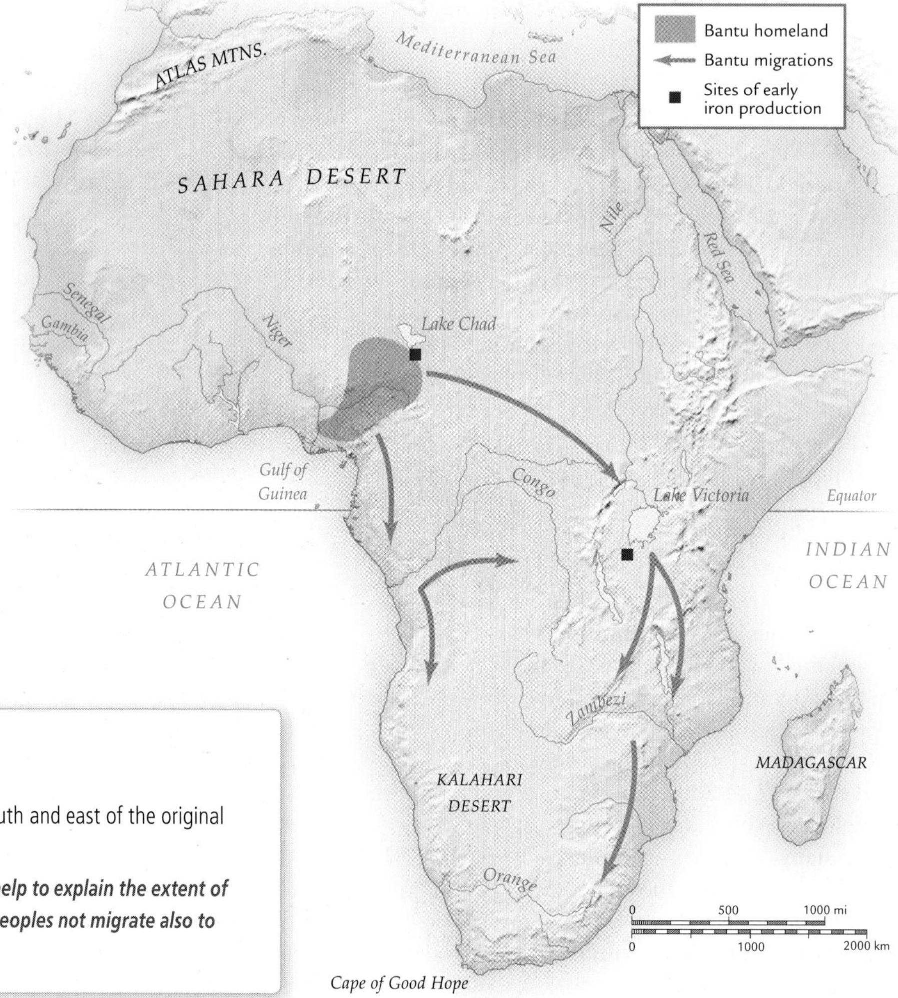

MAP 3.3
Bantu migrations, 2000 B.C.E.–1000 C.E.
Note that Bantu migrations proceeded to the south and east of the original homeland of Bantu-speaking peoples.

To what extent do technological considerations help to explain the extent of the Bantu migrations? Why did Bantu-speaking peoples not migrate also to the north and west of their homeland?

The precise motives of the early Bantu migrants remain shrouded in the mists of time, but it seems likely that population pressures drove the migrations. Two features of Bantu society were especially important for the earliest migrations. First, Bantu peoples made effective use of canoes in traveling the networks of the Niger, Congo, and other rivers. Canoes enabled Bantu to travel rapidly up and down the rivers, leapfrogging established communities and establishing new settlements at inviting spots on riverbanks. Second, agricultural surpluses enabled the Bantu population to increase more rapidly than the populations of hunting, gathering, and fishing peoples whom they encountered as they moved into new regions. When settlements grew uncomfortably large and placed strains on available resources, small groups left their parent communities and moved to new territories. Sometimes they moved to new sites along the rivers, but they often moved inland as well, encroaching on territories occupied by forest peoples. Bantu migrants placed pressures on the forest dwellers, and they most likely clashed with them over land resources. They learned a great deal about local environments from the forest peoples, however, and they also continued to trade regularly with them. Indeed, they often intermarried and absorbed forest peoples into Bantu agricultural society.

"As some groups of Bantu speakers settled and others moved on to new territories, their languages differentiated into more than five hundred distinct but related tongues."

Iron and Migration After about 1000 B.C.E., the pace of Bantu migrations quickened, as Bantu peoples began to produce iron tools and weapons. Iron tools enabled Bantu cultivators to clear land and expand the zone of agriculture more effectively than before, and iron weapons strengthened the hand of Bantu groups against adversaries and competitors for lands or other resources. Thus iron metallurgy supported rapid population growth among the Bantu while also lending increased momentum to their continuing migrations, which in turn facilitated the spread of iron metallurgy throughout most of sub-Saharan Africa.

Early Agricultural Societies of Sub-Saharan Africa

Several smaller migrations took place alongside the spread of Bantu peoples in sub-Saharan Africa. Between 3500 and 1000 B.C.E., southern Kushite herders pushed into parts of east Africa (modern-day Kenya and Tanzania), while Sudanese cultivators and herders moved into the upper reaches of the Nile River (now southern Sudan and northern Uganda). Meanwhile, Mande-speaking peoples who cultivated African rice established communities along the Atlantic estuaries of west Africa, and other peoples speaking Niger-Congo languages spread the cultivation of okra from forest regions throughout much of west Africa.

PART 1

Spread of Agriculture Among the most important effects of Bantu and other migrations was the establishment of agricultural societies throughout most of sub-Saharan Africa. Between 1000 and 500 B.C.E., cultivators extended the cultivation of yams and grains deep into east and south Africa (modern-day Kenya, Malawi, Mozambique, Zimbabwe, and South Africa), while herders introduced sheep and cattle to the region. About the same time, Bantu and other peoples speaking Niger-Congo languages spread the intensive cultivation of yams, oil palms, millet, and sorghum throughout west and central Africa while also introducing sheep, pigs, and cattle to the region. By the late centuries B.C.E., agriculture had reached almost all of sub-Saharan Africa except for densely forested regions and deserts.

As cultivation and herding spread throughout sub-Saharan Africa, agricultural peoples built distinctive societies and cultural traditions. Most Bantu and other peoples as well lived in communities of a few hundred individuals led by chiefs. Many peoples recognized groups known as age sets, or age grades, consisting of individuals born within a few years of one another. Members of each age set jointly assumed responsibility for tasks appropriate to their levels of strength, energy, maturity, and experience. During their early years, for example, members of an age set might perform light public chores. At maturity, members jointly underwent elaborate initiation rites that introduced them to adult society. Older men cultivated fields and provided military service, while women tended to domestic chores and sometimes traded at markets. In later years, members of age sets served as community leaders and military officers.

Religious Beliefs African cultivators and herders also developed distinctive cultural and religious traditions. Both Sudanic and Niger-Congo peoples (including Bantu speakers), for example, held monotheistic religious beliefs by 5000 B.C.E. Sudanic peoples recognized a single, impersonal divine force that they regarded as the source of both good and evil. They believed that this divine force could take the form of individual spirits, and they often addressed the divine force through prayers to intermediary spirits. The divine force itself, however, was ultimately responsible for rewards and punishments meted out to human beings. For their part, Niger-Congo peoples recognized a single god originally called Nyamba who created the world and established the principles that would govern its development and then stepped back and allowed the world to proceed on its own. Individuals did not generally address this distant creator god directly but, rather, offered their prayers to ancestor spirits and local territorial spirits believed to inhabit the world and influence the fortunes of living humans. Proper attention to these spirits would ensure good fortune, they believed, whereas their neglect would bring punishment or adversity from disgruntled spirits.

Individual communities did not always hold religious beliefs in the precise forms just outlined. Rather, they frequently borrowed elements from other communities and adapted their beliefs to changing circumstances or fresh understandings of the world. Migrations of Bantu and other peoples in particular resulted in a great deal of cultural mixing and mingling, and religious beliefs often spread to new communities in the wake of population movements. After 1000 B.C.E., for example, as they encountered Sudanic peoples and their reverence of a single divine force that was the source of good and evil, many Bantu peoples associated the god Nyamba with goodness. As a result, this formerly distant creator god took on a new moral dimension that brought him closer to the lives of individuals. Thus, changing religious beliefs sometimes reflected widespread interactions among African societies.

inperspective

Like other world regions, Africa was a land in which peoples of different societies regularly traded, communicated, and interacted with one another from ancient times. African agriculture and herding first emerged in the Sudan, then spread both to the Nile River valley and to arable lands throughout sub-Saharan Africa. Agricultural crops and domesticated animals from southwest Asia soon made their way into the Nile valley. With its broad floodplains, Egypt became an especially productive land, while Nubia supported a smaller but flourishing society. Throughout the Nile valley, abundant agricultural surpluses supported dense populations and supported the construction of prosperous societies with sophisticated cultural traditions. Elsewhere in sub-Saharan Africa, populations were less dense, but the migrations of Bantu and other peoples facilitated the spread of agriculture, and later iron metallurgy as well, throughout most of the region. Meanwhile, the Nile River served as a route of trade and communication linking Egypt and the Mediterranean basin to the north with the Sudan and sub-Saharan Africa to the south. Only in the context of migration, trade, communication, and interaction is it possible to understand the early development of African societies. ●

CHRONOLOGY

9000 B.C.E.	Origins of Sudanic herding
7500 B.C.E.	Origins of Sudanic cultivation
3100 B.C.E.	Unification of Egypt
3100–2660 B.C.E.	Archaic Period of Egyptian history
2660–2160 B.C.E.	Egyptian Old Kingdom
2600–2500 B.C.E.	Era of pyramid building in Egypt
2500–1450 B.C.E.	Early kingdom of Kush with capital at Kerma
2000 B.C.E.	Beginnings of Bantu migrations
1550–1070 B.C.E.	Egyptian New Kingdom
1479–1425 B.C.E.	Reign of Pharaoh Tuthmosis III
1473–1458 B.C.E.	Reign of Queen Hatshepsut (coruler with Tuthmosis III)
1353–1335 B.C.E.	Reign of Pharaoh Amenhotep IV (Akhenaten)
900 B.C.E.	Invention of iron metallurgy in sub-Saharan Africa
760 B.C.E.	Conquest of Egypt by King Kashta of Kush

For Further Reading

Elizabeth Wayland Barber. *Women's Work: The First 20,000 Years.* New York, 1994. Fascinating study of ancient textiles, which the author argues was a craft industry dominated by women from the earliest times.

Stanley Burstein, ed. *Ancient African Civilizations: Kush and Axum.* Princeton, 1998. Brings together the principal Greek and Latin writings on the kingdoms of Kush and Axum.

Basil Davidson. *Lost Cities of Africa.* Rev. ed. Boston, 1970. Popular account with discussions of Kush and Meroë.

Christopher Ehret. *An African Classical Age: Eastern and Southern Africa in World History, 1000 B.C. to A.D. 400.* Charlottesville, Va., 1998. A pathbreaking volume focusing on eastern and southern Africa and drawing on both linguistic and archaeological evidence.

———. *The Civilizations of Africa: A History to 1800.* Charlottesville, Va., 2001. An important contribution that views Africa in the context of world history.

John L. Foster. *Ancient Egyptian Literature: An Anthology.* Austin, 2001. A useful and readily accessible selection of literary works from ancient Egypt.

Zahi Hawass. *Silent Images: Women in Pharaonic Egypt.* New York, 2000. A prominent archaeologist draws on both textual and artifactual evidence in throwing light on women's experiences in ancient Egypt.

T. G. H. James. *Pharaoh's People: Scenes from Life in Imperial Egypt.* London, 1984. Draws on archaeological and literary scholarship in reconstructing daily life in ancient Egypt.

Barry J. Kemp. *Ancient Egypt: Anatomy of a Civilization.* New York, 2006. Wide-ranging and reflective analysis emphasizing Egyptian identity.

Timothy Kendall, ed. *Kerma and the Kingdom of Kush, 2500–1500 B.C.: The Archaeological Discovery of an Ancient Nubian Empire.* Washington, D.C., 1997. Well-illustrated volume that focuses on the city of Kerma and its role in ancient Nubian society.

Roderick James McIntosh. *The Peoples of the Middle Niger: The Island of Gold.* Oxford, 1998. Fascinating volume emphasizing the environmental context of west African history.

Catharine H. Roehrig, Renée Dreyfus, and Cathleen A. Keller, eds. *Hatshepsut: From Queen to Pharaoh.* New York, 2005. Brilliantly illustrated volume focusing on the reign of the New Kingdom's female pharaoh.

Jan Vansina. *Paths in the Rainforests: Toward a History of Political Tradition in Equatorial Africa.* Madison, 1990. A brilliant synthesis concentrating on central Africa by one of the world's foremost historians of Africa.

Derek A. Welsby. *The Kingdom of Kush: The Napatan and Meroitic Empires.* London, 1996. Draws on both written and archaeological sources in tracing the development of ancient Nubia and charting its relationship with Egypt.

Early Societies in South Asia

chapter 4

Sandstone bust of a distinguished man, perhaps a priest-king, from Mohenjo-daro.

Harappan Society

Foundations of Harappan Society

Harappan Society and Culture

The Indo-European Migrations and Early Aryan India

The Aryans and India

Origins of the Caste System

The Development of Patriarchal Society

Religion in the Vedic Age

Aryan Religion

The Blending of Aryan and Dravidian Values

EYEWITNESS:
Indra, War God of the Aryans

For a god, Indra was quite a rambunctious fellow. According to the stories told about him by the Aryans, Indra had few if any peers in fighting, feasting, or drinking. The Aryans were a herding people who spoke an Indo-European language and who migrated to south Asia in large numbers after 1500 B.C.E. In the early days of their migrations they took Indra as their chief deity. The Aryans told dozens of stories about Indra and sang hundreds of hymns in his honor.

One story had to do with a war between the gods and the demons. When the gods were flagging, they appointed Indra as their leader, and soon they had turned the tide against their enemies. Another story, a favorite of the Aryans, had to do with Indra's role in bringing rain to the earth—a crucial concern for any agricultural society. According to this story, Indra did battle with a dragon who lived in the sky and hoarded water in the clouds. Indra first slaked his thirst with generous drafts of *soma,* a hallucinogenic potion consumed by Aryan priests, and then attacked the dragon, which he killed by hurling thunderbolts at it. The dragon's heavy fall caused turmoil both on earth and in the atmosphere, but afterward the rains filled seven rivers that flowed through northern India and brought life-giving waters to inhabitants of the region.

The Aryans took Indra as a leader against earthly as well as heavenly foes. They did not mount a planned invasion of India, but as they migrated in sizable numbers into south Asia, they came into conflict with Dravidian peoples already living there. When they clashed with the Dravidians, the Aryans took the belligerent Indra as their guide. Aryan hymns praised Indra as the military hero who trampled enemy forces and opened the way for the migrants to build a new society.

For all his contributions, Indra did not survive permanently as a prominent deity. As Aryan and Dravidian peoples mixed, mingled, interacted, and intermarried, tensions between them subsided. Memories of the stormy and violent Indra receded into the background, and eventually they faded almost to nothing. For a thousand years and more, however, Aryans looked upon the rowdy, raucous war god as a ready source of inspiration as they sought to build a society in an already occupied land.

Tools excavated by archaeologists show that India was a site of human occupation at least two hundred thousand years ago, long before the Aryans introduced Indra to south Asia. Between 8000 and 5000 B.C.E., cultivators built a neolithic society west of the Indus River, in the region bordering on the Iranian plateau, probably as a result of Mesopotamian influence. By 7000 B.C.E. agriculture had taken root in the Indus River valley. Thereafter agriculture spread rapidly, and by about 3000 B.C.E. Dravidian peoples had established neolithic communities throughout much of the Indian subcontinent. The earliest neolithic settlers cultivated wheat, barley, and cotton, and they also kept herds of cattle, sheep, and goats. Agricultural villages were especially numerous in the valley of the Indus River. As the population of the valley swelled and as people interacted with increasing frequency, some of those villages evolved into bustling cities, which served as the organizational centers of Indian society.

Early cities in India stood at the center of an impressive political, social, and cultural order built by Dravidian peoples on the foundation of an agricultural economy. The earliest urban society in India, known as Harappan society, brought wealth and power to the Indus River valley. Eventually, however, it fell into decline, possibly because of environmental problems, just as large numbers of Indo-European migrants moved into India from central Asia and built a very different society. For half a millennium, from about 1500 to 1000 B.C.E., the Indian subcontinent was a site of turmoil as the migrants struggled with Dravidian peoples for control of the land and its resources. Gradually, however, stability returned with the establishment of numerous agricultural villages and regional states. During the centuries after 1000 B.C.E., Aryan and Dravidian peoples increasingly interacted and intermarried, and their combined legacies led to the development of a distinctive society and a rich cultural tradition.

HARAPPAN SOCIETY

Like early agricultural societies in Mesopotamia and Egypt, Harappan society—named after Harappa, one of its two chief cities—developed in the valley of a river, the Indus, whose waters were available for irrigation of crops. As agricultural yields increased, the population also grew rapidly, and by about 3000 B.C.E. neolithic villages were evolving into thriving cities.

Unfortunately, it is impossible to follow the development of Harappan society in detail for two reasons. One is that many of the earliest Harappan physical remains are inaccessible. Silt deposits have raised the level of the land in the Indus valley, and the water table has risen correspondingly. Because the earliest Harappan remains lie below the water table, archaeologists cannot excavate them or study them systematically. The earliest accessible remains date from about 2500 B.C.E., when Harappan society was already well established. As a result, scholars have learned something about Harappa at its high point, but little about the circumstances that brought it into being or the conditions of life during its earliest days.

A second problem that handicaps scholars who study Harappan society is the lack of deciphered written records. Harappans had a system of writing that used about four hundred symbols to represent sounds and words, and archaeologists have discovered thousands of clay seals, copper tablets, and other artifacts with Harappan inscriptions. Scholars consider the language most likely a Dravidian tongue related to those currently spoken in central and southern India, but they have not yet succeeded in deciphering the script. As a result, the details of Harappan life remain hidden behind the veil of an elaborate pictographic script. The understanding of Harappan society depends entirely on the study of material remains that archaeologists have uncovered since the 1920s.

Foundations of Harappan Society

The Indus River If the Greek historian Herodotus had known of Harappan society, he might have called it the "gift of the Indus." Like the Nile, the Indus draws its waters from rain and melting snow in towering mountains—in this case, the Hindu Kush and the Himalayas, the world's highest peaks. As the waters charge downhill, they pick up enormous quantities of silt, which they carry for hundreds of kilometers. Like the Nile again, the Indus then deposits its burden of rich soil as it courses through lowlands and loses its force. Today, a series of dams has largely tamed the Indus, but for most of history it spilled its waters annually over a vast floodplain, sometimes with devastating effect. Much less predictable than the Nile, the Indus has many times left its channel altogether and carved a new course to the sea.

Despite its occasional ferocity, the Indus made agricultural society possible in northern India. The most important food crops and domesticated animals came to the region from Mesopotamia. Early cultivators in the Indus River valley sowed wheat and barley in September, after the flood receded, and harvested their crops the following spring. Inhabitants of the valley supplemented their harvests of wheat and barley with meat from herds of cattle, sheep, and goats. Their diet also included poultry: cultivators in the Indus valley kept flocks of the world's first domesticated chickens. Indus valley inhabitants cultivated cotton probably before 5000 B.C.E., and fragments of dyed cloth dating to about 2000 B.C.E. testify to the existence of a cotton textile industry.

As in Mesopotamia and Egypt, agricultural surpluses in India vastly increased the food supply, stimulated population growth, and supported the establishment of cities and specialized labor. Between 3000 and 2500 B.C.E., Dravidian peoples built a complex society that dominated the Indus River valley until its decline after 1900 B.C.E. The agricultural surplus of the Indus valley fed two large cities, Harappa and Mohenjo-daro, as well as subordinate cities and a vast agricultural hinterland. Archaeologists have excavated about seventy Harappan settlements along the Indus River. Harappan society embraced much of modern-day Pakistan and part of northern India as well—a territory about 1.3 million square kilometers (502,000 square miles)—and thus was considerably larger than either Mesopotamian or Egyptian society.

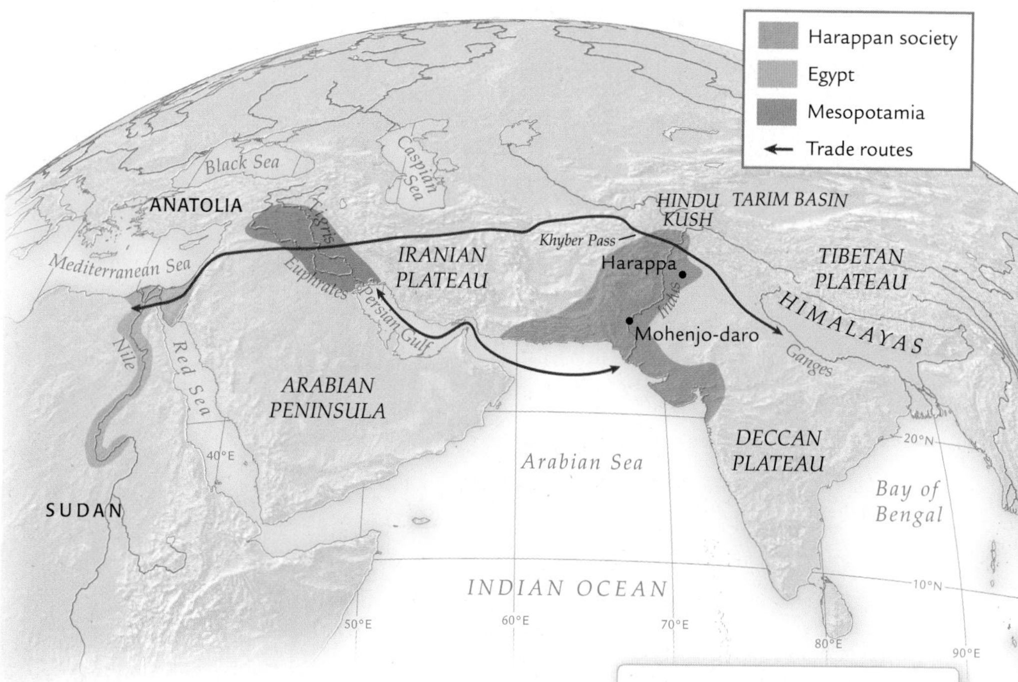

MAP 4.1
Harappan society and its neighbors, ca. 2000 B.C.E.
Compare Harappan society with its Mesopotamian and Egyptian contemporaries with respect to size.

What conditions would have been necessary to enable trade to flow between the Indus River valley and Mesopotamia?

Political Organization No evidence survives concerning the Harappan political system. Archaeological excavations have turned up no evidence of a royal or imperial authority. It is possible that, like the early Sumerian city-states, the Harappan cities were economic and political centers for their own regions. Because of their large size, however, Harappa and Mohenjo-daro were especially prominent in Harappan society even if they did not dominate the Indus valley politically or militarily. The population of Mohenjo-daro was thirty-five to forty thousand, and Harappa was probably slightly smaller. Archaeologists have discovered the sites of about 1,500 Harappan settlements, but none of the others approached the size of Harappa or Mohenjo-daro.

Harappa and Mohenjo-Daro Both Harappa and Mohenjo-daro had city walls, a fortified citadel, and a large granary, suggesting that they served as centers of political authority and sites for the collection and redistribution of taxes paid in the form of grain. The two cities represented a considerable investment of human labor and other resources: both featured marketplaces, temples, public buildings, extensive residential districts, and broad streets laid out on a carefully planned grid so that they ran north-south or east-west. Mohenjo-daro also had a large pool, perhaps used for religious or ritual purposes, with private dressing rooms for bathers.

The two cities clearly established the patterns that shaped the larger society: weights, measures, architectural styles, and even brick sizes were consistent throughout the land, even though the Harappan society stretched almost 1,500 kilometers (932 miles) from one end to the other. This standardization no doubt reflects the prominence of Harappa and Mohenjo-daro as powerful and wealthy cities whose influence touched all parts of Harappan society. The high degree of standardization was possible also because the Indus River facilitated trade, travel, and communications among the far-flung regions of Harappan society.

Specialized Labor and Trade Like all complex societies in ancient times, Harappa depended on a successful agricultural economy. But Harappans also engaged in trade, both domestic and foreign. Pottery, tools, and decorative items produced in Harappa and Mohenjo-daro found their way to all corners of the Indus valley. From neighboring peoples in Persia and the Hindu Kush mountains, the Harappans obtained gold, silver, copper, lead, gems, and semiprecious stones. During the period about 2300 to 1750 B.C.E., they also traded with Mesopotamians, exchanging Indian copper, ivory, beads, and semiprecious stones for Sumerian wool, leather, and olive oil. Some of that trade may

This aerial view of the excavations at Mohenjo-daro illustrates the careful planning and precise layout of the city. What does the city's layout suggest about the planning abilities of the city's builders?

have gone by land over the Iranian plateau, but most of it probably traveled by ships that followed the coastline of the Arabian Sea between the mouth of the Indus River and the Persian Gulf.

Harappan Society and Culture

Like societies in Mesopotamia and Egypt, Harappan society generated considerable wealth. Excavations at Mohenjo-daro show that at its high point, from about 2500 to 2000 B.C.E., the city was a thriving economic center with a population of about forty thousand. Goldsmiths, potters, weavers, masons, and architects, among other professionals, maintained shops that lined Mohenjo-daro's streets. Other cities also housed communities of jewelers, artists, and merchants.

Social Distinctions The wealth of Harappan society, like that in Mesopotamia and Egypt, encouraged the formation of social distinctions. Harappans built no pyramids, palaces, or magnificent tombs, but their rulers wielded great authority from the citadels at Harappa and Mohenjo-daro. It is clear from Harappan dwellings that rich and poor lived in very different styles. In Mohenjo-daro, for example, many people lived in one-room tenements in barrackslike structures, but there were also individual houses of two and three stories with a dozen rooms and an interior courtyard, as well as a few large houses with several dozen rooms and multiple courtyards. Most of the larger houses had their own wells and built-in brick ovens. Almost all houses had private bathrooms with showers and toilets that drained into city sewage systems. The water and sewage systems of Mohenjo-daro were among the most sophisticated of the ancient world, and they represented a tremendous investment of community resources.

In the absence of deciphered writing, Harappan beliefs and values are even more difficult to interpret than politics and society. Archaeologists have discovered samples of Harappan writing dating as early as 3300 B.C.E., and they have recovered hundreds of seals bearing illustrations and written inscriptions. Scholars have been able to identify several symbols representing names or words, but not enough to understand the significance of the texts. Even without written texts, however, material remains shed some tantalizing light on Harappan society. A variety of statues, figurines, and illustrations carved onto seals reflect a tradition of representational art as well as expertise in gold, copper, and bronze metallurgy. A particularly striking statue is a bronze figurine of a dancing girl discovered at Mohenjo-daro. Provocatively posed and clad only in bracelets and a necklace, the figure expresses a remarkable suppleness and liveliness.

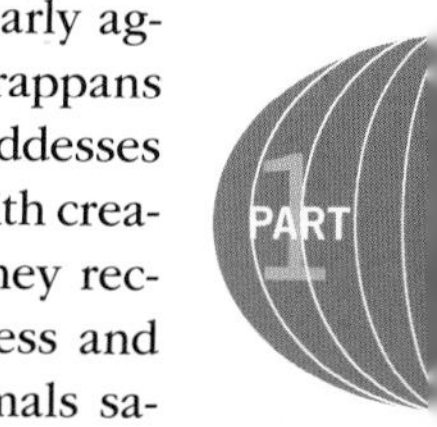

A bronze statuette produced at Mohenjo-daro between 3000 and 1500 B.C.E. depicts a lithe dancing girl.

Fertility Cults Harappan religion reflected a strong concern for fertility. Like other early agricultural societies, Harappans venerated gods and goddesses whom they associated with creation and procreation. They recognized a mother goddess and a horned fertility god, and they held trees and animals sacred because of their associations with vital forces. For lack of written descriptions, it is impossible to characterize Harappan religious beliefs more specifically. Many scholars believe, however, that some Harappan deities survived the collapse of the larger society and found places later in the Hindu pantheon. Fertility and procreation are prominent concerns in popular Hinduism, and scholars have often noticed similarities between Harappan and Hindu deities associated with those values.

Harappan Decline Sometime after 1900 B.C.E., Harappan society entered a period of decline. One prominent theory holds that ecological degradation was a major cause of decline. Harappans deforested the Indus valley to clear land for cultivation and to obtain firewood. Deforestation led to erosion of topsoil and also to reduced amounts of rainfall. Over hundreds of years—perhaps half a millennium or more—most of the Indus valley became a desert, and agriculture is possible there today only with the aid of artificial irrigation. Those climatic and ecological changes reduced agricultural yields, and Harappan society faced a subsistence crisis during the centuries after 1900 B.C.E.

It is also likely that natural catastrophes—periodic flooding of the Indus River or earthquakes—weakened Harappan society. Archaeologists found more than thirty unburied human skeletons scattered about the streets and buildings of Mohenjo-daro. No sign of criminal or military violence accounts for their presence, but a sudden flood or earthquake could have trapped some residents who were unable to flee the impending disaster. In any case, by about 1700 B.C.E., the populations of Harappa and Mohenjo-daro had abandoned the cities as mounting difficulties made it impossible to sustain complex urban societies. Some of the smaller, subordinate cities outlived Harappa and Mohenjo-daro, but by about 1500 B.C.E., Harappan cities had almost entirely collapsed.

The carving on a seal discovered at Mohenjo-daro depicts a man wearing cattle horns and meditating while surrounded by both domestic and wild animals. The figure may well represent a Harappan deity.

Decline of the cities, however, did not mean the total disappearance of Harappan social and cultural traditions. In many ways, Harappan traditions survived the decline of the cities, because peoples from other societies adopted Harappan ways for their own purposes. Cultivation of wheat, barley, and cotton continued to flourish in the Indus valley long after the decline of Harappan society. Harappan deities and religious beliefs intrigued migrants to India and found a home in new societies. Eventually, cities themselves returned to south Asia, and, in some cases, Harappan urban traditions may even have inspired the establishment of new cities.

THE INDO-EUROPEAN MIGRATIONS AND EARLY ARYAN INDIA

During the second millennium B.C.E., as Harappan society declined, bands of foreigners filtered into the Indian subcontinent and settled throughout the Indus valley and beyond. Most prominent were nomadic and pastoral peoples speaking Indo-European languages who called themselves Aryans ("noble people"). By 1500 B.C.E. or perhaps somewhat earlier, they had begun to file through the passes of the Hindu Kush mountains and establish small herding and agricultural communities throughout northern India.

Their migrations took place over several centuries: by no means did the arrival of the Aryans constitute an invasion or an organized military campaign. It is likely that Indo-European migrants clashed with Dravidians and other peoples already settled in India, but there is no indication that the Aryans conquered or destroyed Harappan society. By the time the Indo-Europeans entered India, internal problems had already brought Harappan society to the point of collapse. During the centuries after 1500 B.C.E., Dravidian and Indo-European peoples intermarried, interacted, and laid social and cultural foundations that would influence Indian society to the present day.

"Cattle did not become sacred, protected animals (as they are today among the Hindus) until many centuries after the Aryans' arrival."

The Aryans and India

The Early Aryans When they entered India, the Aryans practiced a limited amount of agriculture, but they depended much more heavily on a pastoral economy. They kept sheep and goats, but they especially prized their horses and herds of cattle. Horses were quite valuable because of their expense and relative rarity: horses do not breed well in India, so it was necessary for Aryans to replenish their supplies of horseflesh by importing animals from central Asia. Like their Indo-European cousins to the north, the Aryans harnessed horses to carts and wagons to facilitate transportation, and they also hitched them to chariots, which proved to be devastating war machines when deployed against peoples who made no use of horsepower. Meanwhile, cattle became the principal measure of wealth in early Aryan society. The Aryans consumed both dairy products and beef—cattle did not become sacred, protected animals (as they are today among Hindus) until many centuries after the Aryans' arrival—and they often calculated prices in terms of cattle. Wealthy individuals in early Aryan society usually owned extensive herds of cattle.

The Vedas The early Aryans did not use writing, but they composed numerous poems and songs. Indeed, they preserved extensive collections of religious and literary works by memorizing them and transmitting them orally from one generation to another in their sacred language, Sanskrit. (For everyday communication, the Aryans relied on a related but less formal tongue known as Prakrit, which later evolved into Hindi, Bengali, Urdu, and other languages currently spoken in northern India.) The earliest of those orally transmitted works were the Vedas, which were collections of hymns, songs, prayers, and rituals honoring the various gods of the Aryans. There are four Vedas, the earliest and most important of which is the *Rig Veda,* a collection of 1,028 hymns addressed to Aryan gods. Aryan priests compiled the *Rig Veda* between about 1400 and 900 B.C.E., and they committed it to writing, along with the three later Vedas, about 600 B.C.E.

The Vedas represent a priestly perspective on affairs: the word *veda* means "wisdom" or "knowledge" and refers to the knowledge that priests needed to carry out their functions. While transmitting religious knowledge, however, the Vedas also shed considerable light on early Aryan society in India. In view of their importance as historical sources, scholars refer to Indian history during the millennium between 1500 and 500 B.C.E. as the Vedic age.

The Vedic Age The Vedas reflect a boisterous society in which the Aryans clashed repeatedly with the Dravidians and other peoples already living in India. The Vedas refer frequently to conflicts between Aryans and indigenous peoples whom the Aryans called *dasas,* meaning "enemies" or "subject peoples." The Vedas identify Indra, the Aryan war god and military hero, as one who ravaged citadels, smashed dams, and destroyed forts the way age consumes cloth garments. These characterizations suggest that the Aryans clashed frequently with the Dravidians of the Indus valley, attacking their cities and wrecking the irrigation systems that had supported agriculture in Harappan society. It is clear that Aryans often had friendly relations with Dravidian peoples: they learned about the land, for example, and adopted Dravidian agricultural techniques when they settled in villages. Nevertheless, competition over land and resources fueled intermittent conflict between Aryan and Dravidian peoples.

The Aryans also fought ferociously among themselves. They did not have a state or common government but, rather, formed hundreds of chiefdoms organized around herding communities and agricultural villages. Most of the chiefdoms had a leader known as a *raja*—a Sanskrit term related to the Latin word *rex* ("king")—who governed in collaboration with a council of village elders. Given the large number of chiefdoms, there was enormous potential for conflict in Aryan society. The men of one village often raided the herds of their neighbors—an offense of great significance, since the Aryans regarded cattle as the chief form of wealth in their society. Occasionally, too, ambitious chiefs sought to extend their authority by conquering neighbors and dominating the regions surrounding their communities.

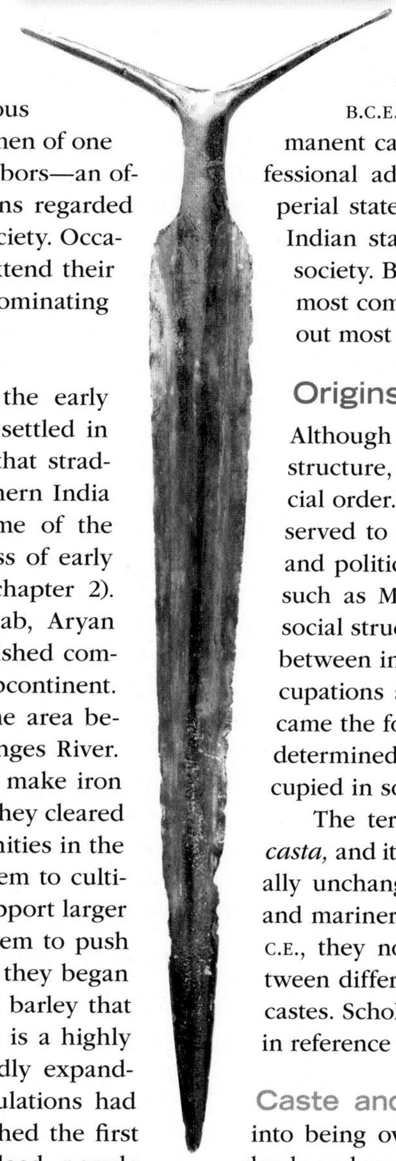

This bronze sword manufactured by Aryan craftsmen was a much stronger and more effective weapon than the lighter swords of Harappan defenders.

Aryan Migrations in India During the early centuries of the Vedic age, Aryan groups settled in the Punjab, the upper Indus River valley that straddles the modern-day border between northern India and Pakistan. These migrations were some of the most prominent waves in the larger process of early Indo-European migrations (discussed in chapter 2). After establishing themselves in the Punjab, Aryan migrants spread east and south and established communities throughout much of the Indian subcontinent. After 1000 B.C.E. they began to settle in the area between the Himalayan foothills and the Ganges River. About that same time they learned how to make iron tools, and with axes and iron-tipped plows they cleared forests and established agricultural communities in the Ganges valley. Iron implements enabled them to cultivate more land, produce more food, and support larger communities, which in turn encouraged them to push deeper into the Ganges River valley. There they began to cultivate rice rather than the wheat and barley that were staple crops in the Punjab. Since rice is a highly productive crop, it provided food for rapidly expanding populations. By about 750 B.C.E., populations had increased enough that Aryans had established the first small cities in the Ganges River valley. Indeed, population became so dense in northern India that some Aryans decided to move along and seek their fortunes elsewhere. By 500 B.C.E. Aryan groups had migrated as far south as the northern Deccan, a plateau region in the southern cone of the Indian subcontinent about 1,500 kilometers (950 miles) south of the Punjab.

Changing Political Organization As they settled into permanent communities and began to rely more on agriculture than herding, the Aryans gradually lost the tribal political organization that they had brought into India and evolved more formal political institutions. In a few places, especially in the isolated hilly and mountainous regions of northern India, councils of elders won recognition as the principal sources of political authority. They directed the affairs of small republics—states governed by representatives of the citizens. In most places, though, chiefdoms developed into regional kingdoms. Between 1000 and 500 B.C.E., tribal chiefs worked increasingly from permanent capitals and depended on the services of professional administrators. They did not build large imperial states: not until the fourth century B.C.E. did an Indian state embrace as much territory as Harappan society. But they established regional kingdoms as the most common form of political organization throughout most of the subcontinent.

Origins of the Caste System

Although they did not build a large-scale political structure, the Aryans constructed a well-defined social order. Indeed, in some ways their social hierarchy served to maintain the order and stability that states and political structures guaranteed in other societies, such as Mesopotamia, Egypt, and China. The Aryan social structure rested on sharp hereditary distinctions between individuals and groups, according to their occupations and roles in society. Those distinctions became the foundation of the caste system, which largely determined the places that individuals and groups occupied in society.

The term *caste* comes from the Portuguese word *casta,* and it refers to a social class of hereditary and usually unchangeable status. When Portuguese merchants and mariners visited India during the sixteenth century C.E., they noticed the sharp, inherited distinctions between different social groups, which they referred to as castes. Scholars have employed the term *caste* ever since in reference to the Indian social order.

Caste and *Varna* The caste system did not come into being overnight. Rather, caste identities developed slowly and gradually as the Aryans established settlements throughout India. When the Aryans first entered India, they probably had a fairly simple society consisting of herders and cultivators led by warrior-chiefs and priests. As they settled in India, however, growing social complexity and interaction with Dravidian peoples prompted them to refine their social distinctions. The Aryans used the term *varna,* a Sanskrit word meaning "color," to refer to the major social classes. This terminology suggests that social distinctions arose partly from differences in complexion between the Aryans, who referred to themselves as "wheat-colored," and the darker-skinned Dravidians. Over time Aryans and

Dravidians mixed, mingled, interacted, and intermarried to the point that distinguishing between them was impossible. Nevertheless, in early Vedic times differences between the two peoples probably prompted Aryans to base social distinctions on Aryan or Dravidian ancestry.

Social Distinctions in the Late Vedic Age After about 1000 B.C.E. the Aryans increasingly recognized four main *varnas: brahmins* (priests); *kshatriyas* (warriors and aristocrats); *vaishyas* (cultivators, artisans, and merchants); and *shudras* (landless peasants and serfs). Some centuries later, probably about the end of the Vedic age, they added the category of the *untouchables*—people who performed dirty or unpleasant tasks, such as butchering animals or handling dead bodies, and who theoretically became so polluted from their work that their very touch could defile individuals of higher status. A late hymn of the *Rig Veda,* composed probably around 1000 B.C.E., offers a priestly perspective on *varna* distinctions. According to the hymn, the gods created the four *varnas* during the early days of the world and produced brahmins and kshatriyas as the most honorable human groups that would lead their societies. Thus during the late Vedic age the recognition of *varnas* and theories of their origins had the effect of enhancing the status and power of priestly and aristocratic classes.

Subcastes and *Jati* Until about the sixth century B.C.E., the four *varnas* described Vedic society reasonably well. Because they did not live in cities and did not yet pursue many specialized occupations, the Aryans had little need for a more complicated social order. Over the longer term, however, a much more elaborate scheme of social classification emerged. As Vedic society became more complex and generated increasingly specialized occupations, the caste system served as the umbrella for a complicated hierarchy of subcastes known as *jati.* Occupation largely determined an individual's *jati:* people working at the same or similar tasks in a given area belonged to the same subcaste, and their offspring joined them in both occupation and *jati* membership. By the eighteenth and nineteenth centuries C.E., in its most fully articulated form, the system featured several thousand *jati,* which prescribed individuals' roles in society in minute detail. Brahmins alone divided themselves into some 1,800 *jati.* Even untouchables belonged to *jati,* and some of them looked down upon others as far more miserable and polluted than themselves.

Castes and subcastes deeply influenced the lives of individual Indians through much of history. Members of a *jati* ate with one another and intermarried, and they cared for those who became ill or fell on hard times. Elaborate rules dictated forms of address and specific behavior appropriate for communication between members of different castes and subcastes. Violation of *jati* rules could result in expulsion from the larger group. That penalty was serious, since an outcaste individual could not function well and sometimes could not even survive when shunned by all members of the larger society.

Caste and Social Mobility The caste system never functioned in an absolutely rigid or inflexible manner but, rather, operated so as to accommodate social change. Indeed, if the system had entirely lacked the capacity to change and reflect new social conditions, it would have disappeared. Individual vaishyas or shudras occasionally turned to new lines of work and prospered on the basis of their initiative, for example, and individual brahmins or kshatriyas sometimes fell on hard times, lost their positions of honor, and moved down in the social hierarchy. More often, however, social mobility came about as the result of group rather than individual efforts, as members of *jati* improved their condition collectively. Achieving upward mobility was not an easy matter—it often entailed moving to a new area or at least taking on a new line of work—but the possibility of improving individual or group status helped to dissipate tensions that otherwise might have severely tested Indian society.

The caste system also enabled foreign peoples to find a place in Indian society. The Aryans were by no means the only foreigners to cross the passes of the Hindu Kush and enter India. Many others followed them over the course of the centuries and, upon arrival, sooner or later organized themselves into well-defined groups and adopted caste identities.

By the end of the Vedic age, caste distinctions had become central institutions in Aryan India. Whereas in other lands, states and empires maintained public order, in India the caste system served as a principal foundation of social organization. Individuals have often identified more closely with their *jati* than with their cities or states, and castes have played a large role in maintaining social discipline in India.

The Development of Patriarchal Society

While building an elaborate social hierarchy on the foundations of caste and *varna* distinctions, the Aryans also constructed a strongly patriarchal social order on the basis

thinking about TRADITIONS

Comparing Societies and Understanding Their Differences
Harappans and Aryans built very different political and social traditions in south Asia. What were the main differences between the two societies with respect to political, social, and economic organization? How might you account for such different forms of political, social, and economic organization in the same land?

sources from the past

The *Rig Veda* on the Origin of the Castes

Priests compiled the Rig Veda *over a period of half a millennium, and the work inevitably reflects changing conditions of Aryan India. One of the later hymns of the* Rig Veda *offers a brief account of the world's creation and the origin of the four castes (varnas). The creation came when the gods sacrificed Purusha, a primeval being who existed before the universe and brought the world with all its creatures and features into being. The late date of this hymn suggests that the Aryans began to recognize the four castes about 1000 B.C.E. The hymn clearly reflects the interests of the brahmin priests who composed it.*

A thousand heads hath Purusha, a thousand eyes, a thousand feet.

He covered earth on every side and spread ten finger's breadth beyond.

This Purusha is all that hath been and all that is to be,

The Lord of Immortality which waxes greater still by food.

So mighty is his greatness; yea, greater than this is Purusha.

All creatures are one-fourth of him, [the other] three-fourths [of him are] eternal life in heaven. . . .

When the gods prepared the sacrifice with Purusha as their offering,

Its oil was spring, the holy gift was autumn; summer was the wood. . . .

From that great general sacrifice the dripping fat was gathered up.

He formed the creatures of the air, and animals both wild and tame.

From that great general sacrifice [sages] and [ritual hymns] were born.

Therefrom were [spells and charms] produced; the Yajas [a book of ritual formulas] had its birth from it.

From it were horses born; from it all creatures with two rows of teeth.

From it were generated [cattle], from it the goats and sheep were born.

When they divided Purusha, how many portions did they make?

What do they call his mouth, his arms? What do they call his thighs and feet?

The *brahmin* was his mouth, of both his arms was the *kshatriya* made.

His thighs became the *vaishya,* from his feet the *shudra* was produced.

The moon was gendered from his mind, and from his eye the sun had birth;

Indra and Agni [the god of fire] from his mouth were born, and Vayu [the wind] from his breath.

Forth from his navel came mid-air; the sky was fashioned from his head;

Earth from his feet, and from his ear the regions. Thus they formed the worlds.

For Further Reflection

- How does this passage from the *Rig Veda* compare with accounts of the world's creation offered by other religious and scientific traditions?

Source: Ralph T. Griffith, trans. *The Hymns of the Rigveda,* 4 vols., 2nd ed. Benares: E. J. Lazarus, 1889–92, 4:289–93. (Translation slightly modified.)

of gender distinctions. At the time of their migrations into India, men already dominated Aryan society. All priests, warriors, and tribal chiefs were men, and the Aryans recognized descent through the male line. Women influenced affairs within their families but enjoyed no public authority. By maintaining and reinforcing gender distinctions, the Aryans established a patriarchal social order that stood alongside the caste system and *varna* hierarchy as a prominent feature of their society.

As the Aryans settled in agricultural communities throughout India, they maintained a thoroughly patriarchal society. Only males could inherit property, unless a family had no male heirs, and only men could preside over family rituals that honored departed ancestors. Because they had no priestly responsibilities, women rarely learned the Vedas, and formal education in Sanskrit remained almost exclusively a male preserve.

The *Lawbook of Manu* The patriarchal spokesmen of Vedic society sought to place women explicitly under the authority of men. During the first century B.C.E. or perhaps somewhat later, an anonymous sage prepared a work and attributed it to Manu, founder of the human race according to Indian mythology. Much of the work, known as the *Lawbook of Manu,* dealt with proper moral behavior and social relationships, including sex and gender relationships. Although composed after the Vedic age, the *Lawbook of Manu* reflected the society constructed earlier under

Aryan influence. The author advised men to treat women with honor and respect, but he insisted that women remain subject to the guidance of the principal men in their lives—first their fathers, then their husbands, and, finally, if they survived their husbands, their sons. The *Lawbook* also specified that the most important duties of women were to bear children and maintain wholesome homes for their families.

Sati Thus, like Mesopotamian, Egyptian, and other early agricultural societies, Vedic India constructed and maintained a deeply patriarchal social order. One Indian custom demonstrated in especially dramatic fashion the dependence of women on their men—the practice of ***sati*** (or *suttee*), by which a widow voluntarily threw herself on the funeral pyre of her deceased husband to join him in death. Although widows occasionally entered the fires during the Vedic age and in later centuries, sati never became a popular or widely practiced custom in India. Nevertheless, moralists often recommended sati for widows of socially prominent men, since their example would effectively illustrate the devotion of women to their husbands and reinforce the value that Indian society placed on the subordination of women.

This greenish-blue schist (metamorphic rock) carving illustrates the devotion of a mother to her child.

RELIGION IN THE VEDIC AGE

As the caste system emerged and helped to organize Indian society, distinctive cultural and religious traditions also took shape. The Aryans entered India with traditions and beliefs that met the needs of a mobile and often violent society. During the early centuries after their arrival in India, those inherited traditions served them well as they fought to establish a place for themselves in the subcontinent. As they spread throughout India and mixed with the Dravidians, however, the Aryans encountered new religious ideas that they considered intriguing and persuasive. The resulting fusion of Aryan traditions with Dravidian beliefs and values laid the foundation for Hinduism, a faith immensely popular in India and parts of southeast Asia for more than two millennia.

Aryan Religion

As in Mesopotamia, Egypt, and other lands, religious values in India reflected the larger society. During the early centuries following their migrations, for example, the Aryans spread through the Punjab and other parts of India, often fighting with the Dravidians and even among themselves. The hymns, songs, and prayers collected in the *Rig Veda* throw considerable light on Aryan values during this period.

Aryan Gods The chief deity of the *Rig Veda* was Indra, the boisterous and often violent character who was partial both to fighting and to strong drink. Indra was primarily a war god. The Aryans portrayed him as the wielder of thunderbolts who led them into battle against their enemies. Indra also had a domestic dimension: the Aryans associated him with the weather and especially with the coming of rain to water the crops and the land. The Aryans also recognized a host of other deities, including gods of the sun, the sky, the moon, fire, health, disease, dawn, and the underworld. The preeminence of Indra, however, reflects the instability and turbulence of early Vedic society.

Although the Aryans accorded high respect to Indra and his military leadership, their religion did not neglect ethics. They believed that the god Varuna presided over the sky from his heavenly palace, where he oversaw the behavior of mortals and preserved the cosmic order. Varuna and his helpers despised lying and evil deeds of all sorts, and they afflicted malefactors with severe punishments, including disease and death. They dispatched the souls of serious evildoers to the subterranean House of Clay, a dreary and miserable realm of punishment, while allowing souls of the virtuous to enter the Aryan heaven known as the World of the Fathers.

Ritual Sacrifices Yet that ethical concern was a relatively minor aspect of Aryan religion during early Vedic times. Far more important from a practical point of view was the proper performance of ritual sacrifices by which the Aryans hoped to win the favor of the gods. By the time the Aryans entered India, those sacrifices had become complex and elaborate affairs. They involved the slaughter of dozens and sometimes even hundreds of specially prepared animals—cattle, sheep, goats, and horses from the Aryans' herds—as priests spoke the sacred and mysterious chants and worshipers partook of soma, a hallucinogenic concoction that produced sensations of power and divine inspiration. The Aryans believed that during the sacrificial event their gods visited the earth and joined the worshipers in ritual eating and drinking. By pleasing the gods with frequent and large sacrifices, the Aryans expected to gain divine support that would ensure military success, large families, long life, and abundant herds of cattle. But those rewards required constant attention to religious ritual: proper honor for the gods called for households to have brahmins perform no fewer than five sacrifices per day—a time-consuming and expensive obligation.

sati (suh-tee)

Accompanied by an attendant bearing his banner and weapons, Indra, chief deity of the *Rig Veda,* rides an elephant that carries him through the clouds, while a king and a crowd of people in the landscape below worship a sacred tree.

PART 1

Spirituality Later in the Vedic age, Aryan religious thought underwent a remarkable evolution. As the centuries passed, many Aryans became dissatisfied with the sacrificial cults of the Vedas, which increasingly seemed like sterile and mechanical rituals rather than a genuine means of communicating with the gods. Even brahmins sometimes became disenchanted with rituals that did not satisfy spiritual longings. Beginning about 800 B.C.E. many thoughtful individuals left their villages and retreated to the forests of the Ganges valley, where they lived as hermits and reflected on the relationships between human beings, the world, and the gods. They contemplated the Vedas and sought mystical understandings of the texts, and they attracted disciples who also thirsted for a spiritually fulfilling faith.

These mystics drew considerable inspiration from the religious beliefs of Dravidian peoples, who often worshiped nature spirits that they associated with fertility and the generation of new life. Dravidians also believed that human souls took on new physical forms after the deaths of their bodily hosts. Sometimes souls returned as plants or animals, sometimes in the bodily shell of newborn humans. The notion that souls could experience transmigration and reincarnation—that an individual soul could depart one body at death and become associated with another body through a new birth—intrigued thoughtful people and encouraged them to try to understand the principles that governed the fate of souls. As a result, a remarkable tradition of religious speculation emerged.

The Blending of Aryan and Dravidian Values

The Upanishads Traces of that tradition appear in the Vedas, but it achieved its fullest development in a body of works known as the **Upanishads,** which began to appear late in the Vedic age, about 800 to 400 B.C.E. (Later Upanishads continued to appear until the fifteenth century C.E., but the most important were those composed during the late Vedic age.) The word *upanishad* literally means "a sitting in front of," and it refers to the practice of disciples gathering before a sage for discussion of religious issues. Most of the disciples were men, but not all. Gargi Vakaknavi, for example, was a woman who drove the eminent sage Yajnavalkya to exasperation because he could not answer her persistent questions. The Upanishads often took the form of dialogues that explored the Vedas and the religious issues that they raised.

Brahman, the Universal Soul The Upanishads taught that appearances are deceiving, that individual human beings in fact are not separate and autonomous creatures. Instead, each person participates in a larger cosmic order and forms a small part of a universal soul, known as *Brahman.* Whereas the physical world is a theater of change, instability, and illusion, Brahman is an eternal, unchanging, permanent foundation for all things that exist—hence the only genuine reality. The authors of the Upanishads believed that individual souls were born into the physical world not once, but many times: they believed that souls appeared most often as humans, but sometimes as animals, and possibly even occasionally as plants or other vegetable matter. The highest goal of the individual soul, however, was to escape this cycle of birth and rebirth and enter into permanent union with Brahman.

Teachings of the Upanishads The Upanishads developed several specific doctrines to explain this line of thought. One was the doctrine of *samsara,* which held that upon death, individual souls go temporarily to the World of the Fathers and then return to earth in a new incarnation. Another was the doctrine of *karma,* which accounted for the specific incarnations that souls experienced. The *Brhadaranyaka Upanishad* offers a succinct explanation of the workings of karma: "Now as a man is like this or like that, according as he acts and according as he behaves, so will he be: a man of good acts will become good, a man of bad acts, bad. He becomes pure by pure deeds, bad by bad deeds." Thus individuals who lived virtuous lives and fulfilled all their duties could expect rebirth into a purer and more honorable existence—for example, into a higher and more distinguished caste. Those who accumulated a heavy burden of karma, however, would suffer in a future incarnation by

Upanishads (oo-PAHN-ee-shahds)

sources from the past

The *Mundaka Upanishad* on the Nature of Brahman

Indian commentators often spoke of the Mundaka Upanishad *as "the shaving Upanishad" because, like a razor, it cut off errors arising in the mind. Its purpose was to teach knowledge of Brahman, which it held was not accessible through sacrifices, rites, or even worship. Only proper instruction would bring understanding of Brahman.*

Brahma was before the gods were, the Creator of all, the Guardian of the Universe. The vision of Brahman, the foundation of all wisdom, he gave in revelation to his first-born son Atharvan.

That vision and wisdom of Brahman given to Atharvan, he in olden times revealed to Angira. And Angira gave it to Satyavaha, who in succession revealed it to Angiras.

Now there was a man whose name was Saunaka, owner of a great household, who, approaching one day Angiras with reverence, asked him this question: "Master, what is that which, when known, all is known?" The Master replied: Sages say there are two kinds of wisdom, the higher and the lower.

The lower wisdom is in the four sacred *Vedas,* and in the six kinds of knowledge that help to know, to sing, and to use the *Vedas:* definition and grammar, pronunciation and poetry, ritual and the signs of heaven. But the higher wisdom is that which leads to the Eternal [i.e., Brahman].

He is beyond thought and invisible, beyond family and colour. He has neither eyes nor ears; he has neither hands nor feet. He is everlasting and omnipresent, infinite in the great and infinite in the small. He is the Eternal whom the sages see as the source of all creation.

Even as a spider sends forth and draws in its thread, even as plants arise from the earth and hairs from the body of man, even so the whole creation arises from the Eternal.

By *Tapas,* the power of meditation, Brahman attains expansion and then comes primeval matter. And from this comes life and mind, the elements and the worlds and the immortality of ritual action.

From that Spirit [Brahman] who knows all and sees all, whose *Tapas* is pure vision, from him comes [the god] Brahma, the creator, name and form and primal matter. . . .

This is the truth: As from a fire aflame thousands of sparks come forth, even so from the Creator an infinity of beings have life and to him return again.

But the spirit of light above form, never-born, within all, outside all, is in radiance above life and mind, and beyond this creation's Creator.

From him comes all life and mind, and the senses of all life. From him comes space and light, air and fire and water, and this earth that holds us all.

The head of his body is fire, and his eyes the sun and the moon; his ears, the regions of heaven, and the sacred *Vedas* his word. His breath is the wind that blows, and this whole universe is his heart. The earth is his footstool. He is the Spirit that is in all things.

From him comes the sun, and the source of all fire is the sun.

From him comes the moon, and from this comes the rain and all herbs that grow upon earth. And man comes from him, and man unto woman gives seed; and thus an infinity of beings come from the Spirit supreme. . . .

From him the oceans and mountains; and all rivers come from him. And all herbs and the essence of all whereby the Inner Spirit dwells with the elements: all come from him.

For Further Reflection

- How does the understanding of the world as articulated in the *Mundaka Upanishad* compare and contrast with the view outlined in the story of Purusha's sacrifice as told in the selection from the *Rig Veda* presented earlier?

Source: Juan Mascaró, trans. *The Upanishads.* London: Penguin, 1965, pp. 75–78.

being reborn into a difficult existence, or perhaps even into the body of an animal or an insect.

Even under the best of circumstances, the cycle of rebirth involved a certain amount of pain and suffering that inevitably accompany human existence. The authors of the Upanishads sought to escape the cycle altogether and attain the state of *moksha,* which they characterized as a deep, dreamless sleep that came with permanent liberation from physical incarnation. That goal was difficult to reach, since it entailed severing all ties to the physical world and identifying with the ultimate reality of Brahman, the universal soul. The two principal means to *moksha* were asceticism and meditation. By embarking on a regime of extreme asceticism—leading extremely simple lives and denying themselves all pleasure—individuals could purge themselves of desire for the comforts of the physical world. By practicing yoga, a form of intense and disciplined meditation, they could concentrate on the nature of Brahman and its relationship to their souls. Diligent efforts, then, would enable individuals to achieve *moksha* by separating themselves from

A cave painting from an undetermined age, perhaps several thousand years ago, shows that early inhabitants of India lived in close company with other residents of the natural world.

the physical world of change, illusion, and incarnation. Then their souls would merge with Brahman, and they would experience eternal, peaceful ecstasy.

Religion and Vedic Society Just as brahmin theories about the origins of *varna* distinctions reflected Aryan society about 1000 B.C.E., so the religious views of the Upanishads dovetailed with the social order of the late Vedic age. Indeed, modern commentators have sometimes interpreted the worldview of the Upanishads—particularly the doctrines of samsara and karma—as a cynical ideology designed to justify the social inequalities imposed by the caste system. The doctrines of samsara and karma certainly reinforced the Vedic social order: they explained why individuals were born into their castes—because they had behaved virtuously or badly during a previous incarnation—and they encouraged individuals to observe their caste duties in hopes of enjoying a more comfortable and honorable incarnation in the future.

It would be overly simplistic, however, to consider these doctrines merely efforts of a hereditary elite to justify its position and maintain its hegemony over other classes of society. The sages who gave voice to these doctrines were conscientiously attempting to deal with genuine spiritual and intellectual problems. To them the material world seemed supremely superficial—a realm of constant change and illusion offering no clear sign as to the nature of ultimate reality. It seemed logical to suppose that a more real and substantial world stood behind the one that they inhabited. Greek philosophers, Christian theologians, and many others have arrived at similar positions during the course of the centuries. It should come as no great surprise, then, that the authors of the Upanishads sought ultimate truth and certain knowledge in an ideal world that transcends our own. Their formulation of concepts such as samsara and karma represented efforts to characterize the relationship between the world of physical incarnation and the realm of ultimate truth and reality.

The Upanishads not only influenced Indian thought about the nature of the world but also called for the observance of high ethical standards. They discouraged greed, envy, gluttony, and all manner of vice, since those traits indicated excessive attachment to

thinking about ENCOUNTERS

Cross-Cultural Encounters and Religious Change
Aryans who migrated into south Asia held distinctive religious beliefs that differed greatly from those of the native peoples of the region. Yet, by the end of the Vedic age, Aryans had abandoned some of their ancestors' most prominent beliefs. How is it possible to explain the transformation of Aryan religious beliefs? What role might interactions between Aryan and Dravidian peoples have played in the formation of new religious views?

the material world and insufficient concentration on union with the universal soul. The Upanishads advocated honesty, self-control, charity, and mercy. Most of all, they encouraged the cultivation of personal integrity—a self-knowledge that would incline individuals naturally toward both ethical behavior and union with Brahman. The Upanishads also taught respect for all living things, animal as well as human. Animal bodies, after all, might well hold incarnations of unfortunate souls suffering the effects of a heavy debt of karma. Despite the evil behavior of these souls in their earlier incarnations, devout individuals would not wish to cause them additional suffering or harm. A vegetarian diet thus became a common feature of the ascetic regime.

inperspective

Like sub-Saharan African and other regions of Eurasia, south Asia was a land of cross-cultural interaction and exchange even in ancient times. Knowledge of agriculture made its way to the Indian subcontinent as early as 7000 B.C.E., probably from southwest Asia, and a productive agricultural economy made it possible for Dravidian peoples to build a sophisticated society in the Indus River valley and to trade with peoples as far away as Mesopotamia. The arrival of Aryan migrants led to intense and systematic interactions between peoples of markedly different social and cultural traditions. Although they no doubt often engaged in conflicts, they also found ways of dealing with one another and living together in a common land. By the end of the Vedic age, the merging of Aryan and Dravidian traditions had generated a distinctive Indian society. Agriculture and herding had spread with the Aryans to most parts of the Indian subcontinent. Regional states maintained order over substantial territories and established kingship as the most common form of government. The caste system not only endowed social groups with a powerful sense of identity but also helped to maintain public order. A distinctive set of religious beliefs explained the world and the role of human beings in it, and the use of writing facilitated further reflection on spiritual and intellectual matters. ●

CHRONOLOGY	
8000–7000 B.C.E.	Beginnings of agriculture in south Asia
2500–2000 B.C.E.	High point of Harappan society
1900 B.C.E.	Beginning of Harappan decline
1500 B.C.E.	Beginning of Aryan migration to India
1500–500 B.C.E.	Vedic age
1400–900 B.C.E.	Composition of the *Rig Veda*
1000 B.C.E.	Early Aryan migrations into the Ganges River valley
1000 B.C.E.	Emergence of *varna* distinctions
1000–500 B.C.E.	Formation of regional kingdoms in northern India
800–400 B.C.E.	Composition of the principal Upanishads
750 B.C.E.	Establishment of first Aryan cities in the Ganges valley
500 B.C.E.	Early Aryan migrations to the Deccan Plateau

For Further Reading

Bridget and Raymond Allchin. *The Rise of Civilization in India and Pakistan.* Cambridge, 1982. A detailed and authoritative survey of early Indian society based largely on archaeological evidence.

F. R. Allchin. *The Archaeology of Early Historic South Asia: The Emergence of Cities and States.* Cambridge, 1995. A collection of scholarly essays on the roles of cities and states in ancient India.

A. L. Basham. *The Wonder That Was India.* New York, 1954. A popular survey by a leading scholar of ancient India.

Ainslie T. Embree, ed. *Sources of Indian Tradition.* 2 vols. 2nd ed. New York, 1988. An important collection of primary sources in translation.

Walter A. Fairservis. *The Roots of Ancient India.* 2nd ed. Chicago, 1975. A judicious analysis of ancient Indian society, especially Harappan society, based on archaeological excavations.

Jonathan Mark Kenoyer. *Ancient Cities of the Indus Valley Civilization.* Oxford, 1998. A well-illustrated volume that synthesizes recent archaeological and linguistic scholarship on Harappan society.

J. P. Mallory. *In Search of the Indo-Europeans: Language, Archaeology, and Myth.* London, 1989. Carefully reviews modern theories about early Indo-European speakers in light of both the linguistic and the archaeological evidence.

Juan Mascaró, trans. *The Upanishads.* London, 1965. A superb English version of selected Upanishads by a gifted translator.

William H. McNeill and Jean W. Sedlar, eds. *Classical India.* Oxford, 1969. A useful collection of primary sources in translation.

Gregory Possehl, ed. *Ancient Cities of the Indus.* New Delhi, 1979. Collection of scholarly essays that bring the results of archaeological research to bear on Harappan society.

———, ed. *Harappan Civilization: A Recent Perspective.* 2nd ed. New Delhi, 1993. Offers a variety of revisionist interpretations of Harappan society.

Shereen Ratnagar. *Trading Encounters: From the Euphrates to the Indus in the Bronze Age.* New Delhi, 2004. Relies on archaeological discoveries in examining commercial relations between Harappan society and Mesopotamia.

———. *Understanding Harappa: Civilization in the Greater Indus Valley.* New Delhi, 2001. Focuses on archaeological evidence.

Romila Thapar. *Early India: From the Origins to A.D. 1300.* Berkeley, 2003. A fresh view by one of the leading scholars of early Indian history.

Mortimer Wheeler. *Civilizations of the Indus Valley and Beyond.* London, 1966. A clear and succinct survey by a leading archaeologist.

———. *My Archaeological Mission to India and Pakistan.* London, 1976. Reflections and personal experiences of the former Head of the Archaeological Survey of India.

Stanley Wolpert. *A New History of India.* 7th ed. New York, 2004. A concise and readable survey of Indian history.

Early Society in East Asia

chapter 5

A rectangular bronze cooking vessel from the Shang dynasty features human faces as decorations on all four sides.

PART 1

EYEWITNESS:
King Yu and the Taming of the Yellow River

Ancient Chinese legends tell the stories of heroic figures who invented agriculture, domesticated animals, taught people to marry and live in families, created music, introduced the calendar, and instructed people in the arts and crafts. Most important of these heroes were three sage-kings—Yao, Shun, and Yu—who laid the foundations of Chinese society. King Yao was a towering figure, sometimes associated with a mountain, who was extraordinarily modest, sincere, and respectful. Yao's virtuous influence brought harmony to his family, the larger society, and ultimately all the states of China. King Shun succeeded Yao and continued his work by ordering the four seasons of the year and instituting uniform weights, measures, and units of time.

Most dashing of the sage-kings was Yu, a vigorous and tireless worker who rescued China from the raging waters of the flooding Yellow River. Before Yu, according to the legends, experts tried to control the Yellow River's floods by building dikes to contain its waters. The river was much too large and strong for the dikes, however, and when it broke through them it unleashed massive floods. Yu abandoned the effort to dam the Yellow River and organized two alternative strategies. He dredged the river so as to deepen its channel and minimize the likelihood of overflows, and he dug canals parallel to the river so that floodwaters would flow harmlessly to the sea without devastating the countryside.

The legends say that Yu worked on the river for thirteen years without ever returning home. Once, he passed by the gate to his home and heard his wife and children crying out of loneliness, but he continued on his way rather than interrupt his flood-control work. Because he tamed the Yellow River and made it possible to cultivate rice and millet, Yu became a popular hero. Poets praised the man who protected fields and villages from deadly and destructive floods. Historians reported that he led the waters to the sea in a manner as orderly as lords proceeding to a formal reception. Eventually, Yu succeeded King Shun as leader of the Chinese people. Indeed, he founded the Xia dynasty, the first ruling house of ancient China.

The legends of Yao, Shun, and Yu no doubt exaggerated the virtues and deeds of the sage-kings. Agriculture, arts, crafts, marriage, family, government, and means of water control developed over an extended period of time, and no single individual was responsible for introducing them into China. Yet legends about early heroic figures reflected the interest of a people in the practices and customs that defined their society. At the same time, the moral thinkers who transmitted the legends used them to advocate values they considered beneficial for their society. By exalting Yao, Shun, and Yu as exemplars of virtue, Chinese moralists promoted the values of social harmony and selfless, dedicated work that the sage-kings represented.

Groups of the early human species *Homo erectus* made their way to east Asia as early as eight hundred thousand years ago. At that early date they used stone tools and relied on a hunting and gathering economy like their counterparts in other regions of the earth. As in Mesopotamia, Egypt, and India, however, population pressures in east Asia encouraged communities to experiment with agriculture. Peoples of southern China and southeast Asia domesticated rice after about 7000 B.C.E., and by 5000 B.C.E. neolithic villages throughout the valley of the Yangzi River (Chang Jiang) depended on rice as the staple item in their diet. During the same era, millet came under cultivation farther north, in the valley of the Yellow River (Huang He), where neolithic communities flourished by 5000 B.C.E. In later centuries wheat and barley made their way from Mesopotamia to northern China, and by 2000 B.C.E. they supplemented millet as staple foods of the region.

Agricultural surpluses supported numerous neolithic communities throughout east Asia. During the centuries after 3000 B.C.E., residents of the Yangzi River and Yellow River valleys lived in agricultural villages and communicated and traded with others throughout the region. During the second millennium B.C.E., they began to establish cities, build large states, and construct distinctive social and cultural traditions. Three dynastic states based in the Yellow River valley brought much of China under their authority and forged many local communities into a larger Chinese society. Sharp social distinctions emerged in early Chinese society, and patriarchal family heads exercised authority in both public and private affairs. A distinctive form of writing supported the development of sophisticated cultural traditions. Meanwhile, Chinese cultivators had frequent dealings with peoples from other societies, particularly with nomadic herders inhabiting the grassy steppes of central Asia. Migrating frequently on the steppes, nomadic peoples linked China with lands to the west and brought knowledge of bronze and iron metallurgy, horse-drawn chariots, and wheeled vehicles to east Asia. As in early Mesopotamia, Egypt, and India, then, complex society in east Asia promoted the development of distinctive social and cultural traditions in the context of cross-cultural interaction and exchange.

POLITICAL ORGANIZATION IN EARLY CHINA

As agricultural populations expanded, villages and towns flourished throughout the Yellow River and **Yangzi** River valleys. Originally, those settlements looked after their own affairs and organized local states that maintained order in small territories. By the late years of the third millennium B.C.E., however, much larger regional states began to emerge. Among the most important were those of the **Xia,** Shang, and **Zhou** dynasties, which progressively brought much of China under their authority and laid a political foundation for the development of a distinctive Chinese society.

Yangzi (YAHNG-zuh)
Xia (SHYAH)
Zhou (JOH)

Early Agricultural Society and the Xia Dynasty

The Yellow River Like the Indus, the Yellow River is boisterous and unpredictable. It rises in the mountains bordering the high plateau of Tibet, and it courses almost 4,700 kilometers (2,920 miles) before emptying into the Yellow Sea. It takes its name, Huang He, meaning "Yellow River," from the vast quantities of light-colored loess soil that it picks up along its route. Loess is an extremely fine, powder-like soil that was deposited on the plains of northern China, as well as in several other parts of the world, after the retreat of the glaciers at the end of the last ice age, about twelve thousand to fifteen thousand years ago. So much loess becomes suspended in the Yellow River that the water turns yellow and the river takes on the consistency of a soup. The soil gradually builds up, raising the riverbed and forcing the water out of its established path. The Yellow River periodically unleashes a tremendous flood that devastates fields, communities, and anything else in its way. The Yellow River has altered its course many times and has caused so much destruction that it has earned the nickname "China's Sorrow."

Yet geographic conditions have also supported the development of complex society in China. During most years, there is enough rainfall for crops, so early cultivators had no need to build complex irrigation systems like those of Mesopotamia. They invested a great deal of labor, however, in dredging the river and building dikes, in a partially successful effort to limit the flood damage. Loess soil is extremely fertile and easy to work, so even before the introduction of metal tools, cultivators using wooden implements could bring in generous harvests.

Pottery bowl from the early Yangshao era excavated at Banpo, near modern Xi'an. The bowl is fine red pottery decorated with masks and fishnets in black.

Yangshao Society and Banpo Village

Abundant harvests in northern China supported the development of several neolithic societies during the centuries after 5000 B.C.E. Each developed its own style of pottery and architecture, and each likely had its own political, social, and cultural traditions. Yangshao society, which flourished from about 5000 to 3000 B.C.E. in the middle region of the Yellow River valley, is especially well known from the discovery in 1952 of an entire neolithic village at Banpo, near modern Xi'an. Excavations at Banpo unearthed a large quantity of fine painted pottery and bone tools used by early cultivators in the sixth and fifth millennia B.C.E.

As human population increased, settlements like that at Banpo cropped up throughout much of China, in the valley of the Yangzi River as well as the Yellow River. In east Asia, as in other parts of the world, the concentration of people in small areas brought a need for recognized authorities who could maintain order, resolve disputes, and organize public works projects. Village-level organization sufficed for purely local affairs, but it did little to prevent or resolve conflicts between villages and did not have the authority to organize large-scale projects in the interests of the larger community.

Chinese legends speak of three ancient dynasties—the Xia, the Shang, and the Zhou—that arose before the Qin and Han dynasties brought China under unified rule in the third century B.C.E. The Xia, Shang, and Zhou dynasties were hereditary states that extended their control over progressively larger regions, although none of them embraced all the territory claimed by later Chinese dynasties. Large numbers of written accounts survive to throw light on the Zhou dynasty, which scholars have long recognized as a historical ruling house. Until recently, however, information about the Xia and Shang dynasties came from legendary accounts that scholars mostly did not trust. As a result, many historians dismissed reports of the Xia and the Shang dynasties as mythical fantasies. Only in the later twentieth century did archaeological excavations turn up evidence that the Xia and the Shang were indeed historical dynasties rather than figments of ancient imaginations.

The Xia Dynasty

Archaeological study of the Xia dynasty is still in its early stages. Nevertheless, during the past few decades, archaeological discoveries have suggested that the Xia dynasty made one of the first efforts to organize public life in China on a large scale. Although it was not the only early state in China, the Xia was certainly one of the more vigorous states of its time. Most likely the dynasty came into being about 2200 B.C.E. in roughly the same region as the Yangshao society. By extending formal control over this region, the Xia dynasty established a precedent for hereditary monarchical rule in China.

Ancient legends credit the dynasty's founder, the sage-king Yu, with the organization of effective flood-control projects: thus here, as in Mesopotamia and Egypt, the need to organize large-scale public works projects helped to establish recognized authorities and formal political institutions. Although no information survives about the political institutions of the Xia, the dynasty's rulers probably exercised power throughout the middle Yellow River valley by controlling the leaders of individual villages. The dynasty encouraged the founding of cities and the development of metallurgy, since the ruling classes needed administrative centers and bronze weapons to maintain their control. The recently excavated city of Erlitou, near Luoyang, might well have been the capital of the Xia dynasty. Excavations have shown that the city featured a large, palace-type structure as well as more modest houses, pottery workshops, and a bronze foundry.

The Shang Dynasty

According to the legends, the last Xia king was an oppressive despot who lost his realm to the founder of the Shang dynasty. In fact, the Xia state did not entirely collapse and did

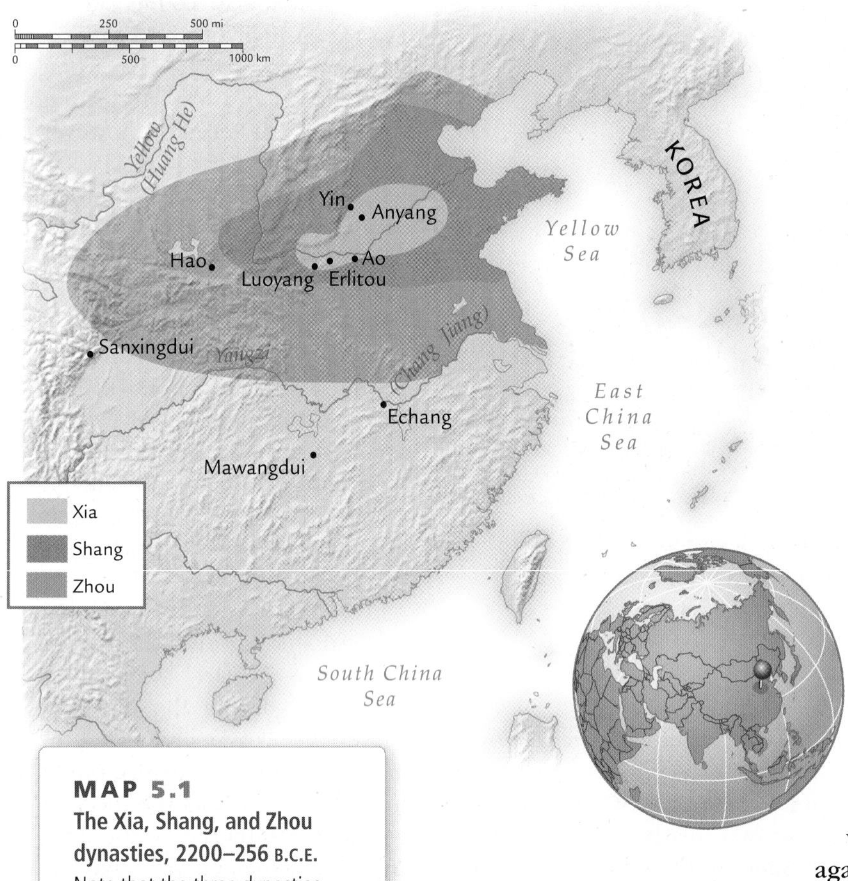

MAP 5.1
The Xia, Shang, and Zhou dynasties, 2200–256 B.C.E.
Note that the three dynasties extended their territorial reach through time.
How might technological considerations explain the increasing size of early Chinese states?

not disappear so much as it gave way gradually before the Shang, which arose in a region to the south and east of the Xia realm. Tradition assigns the Shang dynasty to the period 1766 to 1122 B.C.E., and archaeological discoveries have largely confirmed those dates. Because the Shang dynasty left written records as well as material remains, the basic features of early Chinese society come into much clearer focus than they did during the Xia.

Bronze Metallurgy and Horse-Drawn Chariots

Technology helps to explain the rise and success of the Shang dynasty. Bronze metallurgy transformed Chinese society during Shang times and indeed may well have enabled Shang rulers to displace the Xia dynasty. Bronze metallurgy went to China from southwest Asia, together with horses, horse-drawn chariots, carts, wagons, and other wheeled vehicles. This collection of related technologies traveled to China as well as India with the early Indo-European migrants (discussed in chapter 2), some of whom made their way to the Tarim Basin (now **Xinjiang** province in western China) as early as 2000 B.C.E. Early Chinese chariots were close copies of Indo-European chariots from the Iranian plateau, and ancient Chinese words for wheels, spokes, axles, and chariots all derived from Indo-European roots.

Bronze metallurgy reached China before the Shang dynasty, and indeed the Xia dynasty had already made limited use of bronze tools and weapons. But Shang ruling elites managed to monopolize the production of bronze in the Yellow River valley by controlling access to copper and tin ores. They also dramatically expanded production by employing government craftsmen to turn out large quantities of bronze axes, spears, knives, and arrowheads exclusively for the Shang rulers and their armies. Control over bronze production strengthened Shang forces against those of the Xia and provided them with arms far superior to stone, wood, and bone weapons wielded by their rivals.

Shang nobles also used bronze to make fittings for their horse-drawn chariots, which began to appear in China between about 1500 and 1200 B.C.E. Like the Aryans in India, Shang warriors used these vehicles to devastating effect against adversaries who lacked horses and chariots. With their arsenal of bronze weapons, Shang armies had little difficulty imposing their rule on agricultural villages and extending their influence throughout much of the Yellow River valley. Meanwhile, because the ruling elites did not permit free production of bronze, potential rebels or competitors had little hope of resisting Shang forces and even less possibility of displacing the dynasty.

Shang kings extended their rule to a large portion of northeastern China centered on the modern-day province of Henan. Like state builders in other parts of the world, the kings claimed a generous portion of the surplus agricultural production from the regions they controlled and then used that surplus to support military forces, political allies, and others who could help them maintain their rule. Shang rulers clearly had abundant military force at their disposal. Surviving records mention armies of 3,000, 5,000, 10,000, and even 13,000 troops, and one report mentions the capture of 30,000 enemy troops. Although those numbers are probably somewhat inflated, they still suggest that Shang rulers maintained a powerful military machine.

Shang Political Organization Like their Xia predecessors, Shang rulers also relied on a large corps of political allies. They did not rule a highly centralized state. Rather, their authority rested on a vast network of walled towns whose local rulers recognized the authority of the Shang kings. During the course of the dynasty, Shang kings may have con-

Xinjiang (sing-jyahng)

A tomb from the early Zhou dynasty containing the remains of horses and war chariots, which transformed military affairs in ancient China. Survivors sacrificed the horses and buried them along with the chariots for use by the tomb's occupant after his death.

trolled one thousand or more towns. Apart from local rulers of those towns, others who shared the agricultural surplus of Shang China included advisors, ministers, craftsmen, and metalsmiths, who in their various ways helped Shang rulers shape policy or spread their influence throughout their realm.

Shang society revolved around several large cities. According to tradition, the Shang capital moved six times during the course of the dynasty. Though originally chosen for political and military reasons, in each case the capital also became an important social, economic, and cultural center—the site not only of administration and military command but also of bronze foundries, arts, crafts, trade, and religious observances.

The Shang Capital at Ao Excavations at two sites have revealed much about the workings of the Shang dynasty. The Shang named one of its earliest capitals Ao, and archaeologists have found its remains near modern Zhengzhou. The most remarkable feature of this site is the city wall, which originally stood at least 10 meters (33 feet) high, with a base some 20 meters (66 feet) thick. The wall consisted of layer upon layer of pounded earth—soil packed firmly between wooden forms and then pounded with mallets until it reached rocklike hardness before the addition of a new layer of soil on top. This building technique, still used in the countryside of northern China, can produce structures of tremendous durability. Even today, for example, parts of the wall of Ao survive to a height of 3 to 4 meters (10 to 13 feet). The investment in labor required to build this wall testifies to the ability of Shang rulers to mobilize their subjects: modern estimates suggest that the wall required the services of ten thousand laborers working almost twenty years.

The Shang Capital at Yin Even more impressive than Ao is the site of Yin, near modern Anyang, which was the capital during the last two or three centuries of the Shang dynasty. Archaeologists working at Yin have identified a complex of royal palaces, archives with written documents, several residential neighborhoods, two large bronze foundries, several workshops used by potters, woodworkers, bone carvers, and other craftsmen, and scattered burial grounds.

Eleven large and lavish tombs constructed for Shang kings, as well as other, more modest, tombs, have received particular attention. Like the resting places of the Egyptian pharaohs, most of these tombs attracted grave robbers soon after their construction. Enough remains, however, to show that the later Shang kings continued to command the high respect enjoyed by their predecessors at Ao. The graves included thousands of objects—chariots, weapons, bronze goods, pottery, carvings of jade and ivory, cowry shells (which served both as money and as exotic ornamentation), and sacrificial victims, including dogs, horses, and scores of human beings intended to serve the deceased royals in another existence. One tomb alone contained skeletons of more than three hundred sacrificial victims—probably wives, servants, friends, and hunting companions—who joined the Shang king in death.

Jade figurines excavated at Anyang from the tomb of Fu Hao, who was one of the consorts of the Shang king Wu Ding. The carvings represent servants who would tend to Fu Hao's needs after death.

The Tomb of Lady Fu Hao Most important of the tombs at Yin is the sepulcher of Fu Hao, one of sixty-four consorts (wives) of the Shang king Wu Ding, who ruled in the thirteenth century B.C.E. Fu Hao's resting place is the only tomb at Yin to escape the notice of grave robbers—perhaps because it was located in the Shang palace rather than in the cemetery that held other royal tombs. In any case, after her burial about 1250 B.C.E., Fu Hao's tomb remained undisturbed for more than three thousand years until Chinese archaeologists discovered it and excavated it in 1976.

Fu Hao was King Wu Ding's favorite consort, and her tomb reflected her status. It contained 468 bronze objects, including 130 weapons, 23 bells, and 4 mirrors. In combination, the bronze items in her tomb weighed about 1,600 kilograms (3,500 pounds). Metalsmiths would have required 11 tons of ore to produce these objects. In an age when bronze was extremely expensive and hence rare, Fu Hao and the Shang royal family were conspicuous consumers of that valuable commodity. Quite apart from bronzewares, Fu Hao's tomb contained 755 jade carvings, 564 bone carvings, 5 finely carved ivory cups, 11 pottery objects, and 6,900 cowry shells. Moreover, the tomb held the remains of six dogs and the skeletons of sixteen human beings—sacrificial victims buried with Fu Hao to guard her and attend to her needs after death. Fu Hao's unlooted tomb has thrown valuable light on the Shang dynasty and the resources that were available to residents of the royal court.

Beyond the Yellow River Valley Like the Xia state, the Shang realm was only one of many that organized public life in ancient China. Legendary and historical accounts paid special attention to the Xia and Shang dynasties because of their location in the Yellow River valley, where the first Chinese imperial states rose in later times. But archaeological excavations are making it clear that similar states dominated other regions at the same time the Xia and Shang ruled the Yellow River valley. Recent excavations, for example, have unearthed evidence of a very large city at Sanxingdui in modern-day Sichuan province (southwestern China). Occupied about 1700 to 1000 B.C.E., the city was roughly contemporaneous with the Shang dynasty, and it probably served as capital of a regional kingdom. Like their Xia and Shang counterparts, tombs at Sanxingdui held large quantities of bronze, jade, stone, and pottery objects, as well as cowry shells and elephant tusks, that indicate close relationships with societies in the valleys of both the Yangzi River and the Yellow River.

The Zhou Dynasty

Little information survives to illustrate the principles of law, justice, and administration by which Shang rulers maintained order. They did not promulgate law codes such as those issued in Mesopotamia but, rather, ruled by proclamation or decree, trusting their military forces and political allies to enforce their will. The principles of ancient Chinese politics and statecraft become more clear in the practices of the Zhou dynasty, which succeeded the Shang as the preeminent political authority in northern China. Dwelling in the Wei River valley of northwestern China (modern Shaanxi province), the Zhou were a tough and sinewy people who battled Shang forces in the east and nomadic raiders from the steppes in the west. Eventually, the Zhou allied with the Shang and won recognition as kings of the western regions. Because they organized their allies more effectively than the Shang, however, they gradually eclipsed the Shang dynasty and ultimately displaced it altogether.

Rise of the Zhou Shang and Zhou ambitions collided in the late twelfth century B.C.E. According to Zhou accounts, the last Shang king was a criminal fool who gave himself over to wine, women, tyranny, and greed. As a result, many of the towns and political districts subject to the Shang transferred their loyalties to the Zhou. After several unsuccessful attempts to discipline the Shang king, Zhou forces seized the Shang capital of Yin, beheaded the king, and replaced his administration with their own state in 1122 B.C.E. The new rulers allowed Shang heirs to continue governing small districts but reserved for themselves the right to oversee affairs throughout the realm. The new dynasty ruled most of northern and central China, at least nominally, until 256 B.C.E.

The Mandate of Heaven In justifying the deposition of the Shang, spokesmen for the Zhou dynasty articulated a set of principles that have influenced Chinese thinking about government and political legitimacy over the long term. The Zhou theory of politics rested on the assumption that earthly events were closely related to heavenly affairs. More specifically, heavenly powers granted the right to govern—the "mandate of heaven"—to an especially deserving individual known as the son of heaven. The ruler then served as a link between heaven and earth. He had the duty to govern conscientiously, observe high standards of honor and justice, and maintain order and harmony within his realm. As long as he did so, the heavenly powers would approve of his work, the cosmos would enjoy a harmonious and well-balanced stability, and the ruling dynasty would retain its mandate to govern. If a ruler failed in his duties, however, chaos and suffering would afflict his realm, the cosmos would fall out of balance, and the displeased heavenly powers would withdraw the mandate to rule and transfer it to a more deserving candidate. On the basis of that reasoning, spokesmen for the new dynasty explained the fall of the Shang and the transfer of the mandate of heaven to the Zhou. From that time until the twentieth century C.E., Chinese ruling houses routinely invoked the doctrine of the mandate of heaven to justify their rule, and emperors habitually took the title "son of heaven."

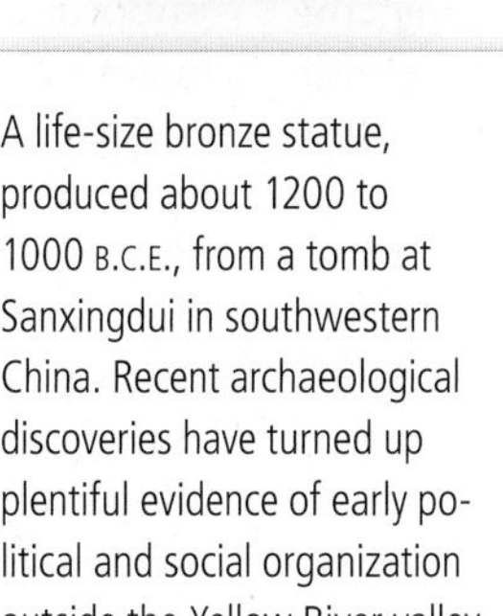

A life-size bronze statue, produced about 1200 to 1000 B.C.E., from a tomb at Sanxingdui in southwestern China. Recent archaeological discoveries have turned up plentiful evidence of early political and social organization outside the Yellow River valley.

Political Organization The Zhou state was much larger than the Shang. In fact, it was so extensive that a single central court could not rule the entire land effectively, at least not with the transportation and communication technologies available during the second and first millennia B.C.E. As a result, Zhou rulers relied on a decentralized administration: they entrusted power, authority, and responsibility to subordinates who in return owed allegiance, tribute, and military support to the central government.

During the early days of the dynasty, that system worked reasonably well. The conquerors continued to rule the Zhou ancestral homeland from their capital at Hao, near modern Xi'an, but they allotted possessions in conquered territories to relatives and other allies. The subordinates ruled their territories with limited supervision from the central government. In return for their political rights, they visited the Zhou royal court on specified occasions to demonstrate their continued loyalty to the dynasty, they delivered taxes and tribute that accounted for the major part of Zhou finances, and they provided military forces that the kings deployed in the interests of the Zhou state as a whole. When not already related to their subordinates, the Zhou rulers sought to arrange marriages that would strengthen their ties to their political allies.

Weakening of the Zhou Despite their best efforts, however, the Zhou kings could not maintain control indefinitely over this decentralized political system. Subordinates gradually established their own bases of power: they ruled their territories not only as allies of the Zhou kings but also as long-established and traditional governors. They set up regional bureaucracies, armies, and tax systems, which allowed them to consolidate their rule and exercise their authority. They promulgated law codes and enforced them with their own forces. As they became more secure in their rule, they also became more independent of the Zhou dynasty itself. Subordinates sometimes ignored their obligations to appear at the royal court or deliver tax proceeds. Occasionally, they refused to provide military support or even turned their forces against the dynasty in an effort to build up their regional states.

Iron Metallurgy Technological developments also worked in favor of subordinate rulers. The Shang kings had largely monopolized the production of bronze weapons by controlling the sources of copper and tin, but because of technological changes, Zhou rulers were unable to control metal production as closely as their predecessors. During the first millennium B.C.E., the technology of iron metallurgy spread to China and gradually made bronze weapons obsolete. Because iron ores are cheaper, more abundant, and more widely distributed than copper and tin, Zhou kings were unable to control access to them. Their subordinates moved quickly to establish ironworks and outfit their forces with iron weapons that were just as effective as those employed by Zhou armies. Thus iron weapons enabled subordinates to resist the central government and pursue their own interests.

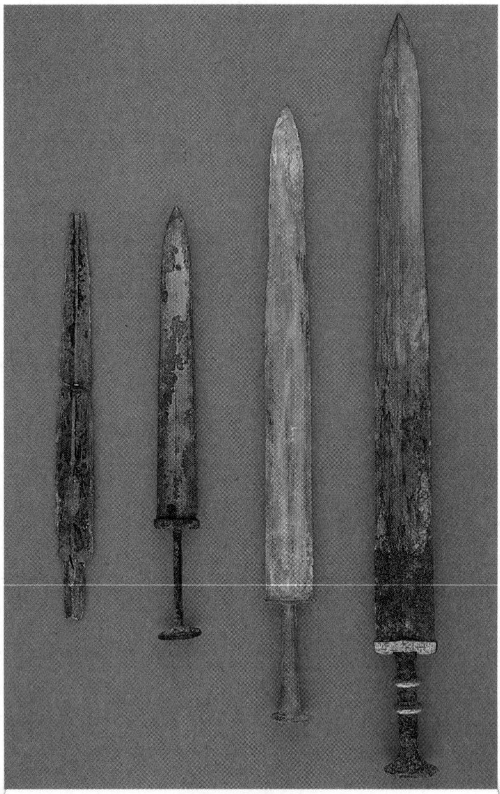

The Zhou dynasty saw development of sword design that resulted in longer, stronger, and more lethal weapons. Relatively inexpensive iron swords, like those depicted here, contributed to political instability and chronic warfare during the late Zhou dynasty.

In the early eighth century B.C.E., the Zhou rulers faced severe problems that brought the dynasty to the point of collapse. In 771 B.C.E. nomadic peoples invaded China from the west. They came during the rule of a particularly ineffective king who did not enjoy the respect of his political allies. When subordinates refused to support the king, the invaders overwhelmed the Zhou capital at Hao. Following that disaster, the royal court moved east to Luoyang in the Yellow River valley, which served as the Zhou capital until the end of the dynasty.

In fact, the political initiative had passed from the Zhou kings to their subordinates, and the royal court never regained its authority. By the fifth century B.C.E., territorial princes ignored the central government and used their resources to build, strengthen, and expand their states. They fought ferociously with one another in hopes of establishing themselves as leaders of a new political order. So violent were the last centuries of the Zhou dynasty that they are known as the Period of the Warring States (403–221 B.C.E.). In 256 B.C.E. the Zhou dynasty ended when the last king abdicated his position under pressure from his ambitious subordinate the king of Qin. Only with the establishment of the Qin dynasty in 221 B.C.E. did effective central government return to China.

SOCIETY AND FAMILY IN ANCIENT CHINA

In China, as in other parts of the ancient world, the introduction of agriculture enabled individuals to accumulate wealth and preserve it within their families. Social distinctions began to appear during neolithic times, and after the establishment of the Xia, Shang, and Zhou dynasties the distinctions became even sharper. Throughout China the patriarchal family emerged as the institution that most directly influenced individuals' lives and their roles in the larger society.

The Social Order

Ruling Elites Already during the Xia dynasty, but especially under the Shang and the early Zhou, the royal family and allied noble families occupied the most honored positions in Chinese society. They resided in large, palatial compounds made of pounded earth, and they lived on the agricultural surplus and taxes delivered by their subjects. Because of the high cost of copper and tin, bronze implements were beyond the means of all but the wealthy, so the conspicuous consumption of bronze by ruling elites clearly set them apart from less privileged classes. Ruling elites possessed much of the bronze weaponry that ensured military strength and political hegemony, and through their subordinates and retainers they controlled most of the remaining bronze weapons available in northern China. They also supplied their households with cast-bronze utensils—pots, jars, wine cups, plates, serving dishes, mirrors, bells, drums, and vessels used in ritual ceremonies—which were beyond the means of less privileged people. These utensils often featured elaborate, detailed decorations that indicated remarkable skill on the part of the artisans who built the molds and cast the metal. Expensive bronze utensils bore steamed rice and rich dishes of fish, pheasant, poultry, pork, mutton, and rabbit to royal and aristocratic tables, whereas less privileged classes relied on clay pots and consumed much simpler fare, such as vegetables and porridges made of millet, wheat, or rice. Ruling elites consumed bronze in staggering quantities: the tomb of Marquis Yi of Zeng, a provincial governor of the late Zhou dynasty, contained a collection of bronze weapons and decorative objects that weighed almost 11 tons.

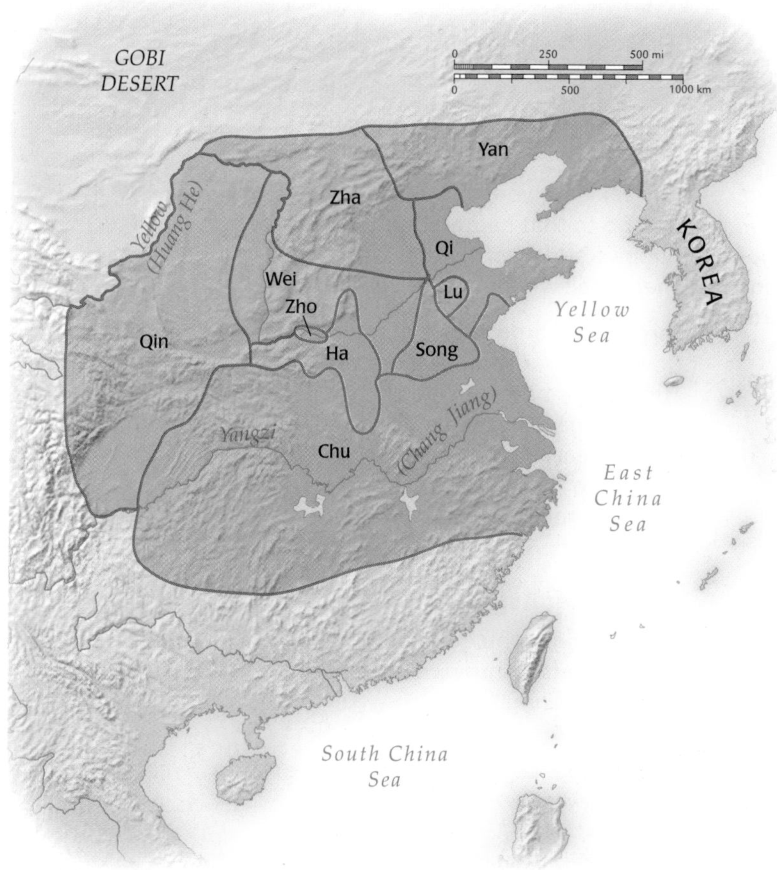

MAP 5.2
China during the Period of the Warring States, 403–221 B.C.E.
Early Zhou rulers used iron tools and weapons to create a sizable kingdom. As knowledge of iron production spread, however, political and military leaders were able to establish several regional states that competed for power and territory.

A privileged class of hereditary aristocrats rose from the military allies of Shang and Zhou rulers. Aristocrats possessed extensive land holdings, and they worked at administrative and military tasks. By Zhou times many of them lived in cities where they obtained at least an elementary education, and their standard of living was much more refined than that of the commoners and slaves who worked their fields and served their needs. Manuals of etiquette from Zhou times instructed the privileged classes in decorous behavior and outlined the proper way to carry out rituals. When dining in polite company, for example, the cultivated aristocrat should show honor to the host and refrain from gulping down food, swilling wine, making unpleasant noises, picking teeth at the table, and playing with food by rolling it into a ball.

Specialized Labor A small class of free artisans and craftsmen plied their trades in the cities of ancient China. Some, who worked almost exclusively for the privileged classes, enjoyed a reasonably comfortable existence. During the Shang dynasty, for example, bronzesmiths often lived in houses built of pounded earth. Although their dwellings were modest, they were also sturdy and relatively expensive to build because of the amount of labor required for pounded-earth construction. Jewelers, jade workers, embroiderers, and

The delicate design of this bronze wine vessel displays the high level of craftsmanship during the late Shang dynasty. Why would objects like this appeal particularly to elite classes?

sources from the past

Peasants' Protest

Peasants in ancient China mostly did not own land. Instead, they worked as tenants on plots allotted to them by royal or aristocratic owners, who took sizable portions of the harvest. In the following poem from the Book of Songs, *a collection of verses dating from Zhou times, peasants liken their lords to rodents, protest the bite lords take from the peasants' agricultural production, and threaten to abandon the lords' lands for a neighboring state where conditions were better.*

Large rats! Large rats!
Do not eat our millet.
Three years have we had to do with you.
And you have not been willing to show any regard for us.
We will leave you,
And go to that happy land.
Happy land! Happy land!
There shall we find our place.

Large rats! Large rats!
Do not eat our wheat.
Three years have we had to do with you.
And you have not been willing to show any kindness to us.
We will leave you,
And go to that happy state.
Happy state! Happy state!
There shall we find ourselves aright.

Large rats! Large rats!
Do not eat our springing grain!
Three years have we had to do with you,
And you have not been willing to think of our toil.
We will leave you,
And go to those happy borders.
Happy borders! Happy borders!
Who will there make us always to groan?

For Further Reflection

- How might you go about judging the extent to which these verses throw reliable light on class relations in ancient China?

Source: James Legge, trans. *The Chinese Classics,* 5 vols. London: Henry Frowde, 1893, 4:171–72.

manufacturers of silk textiles also benefited socially because of their importance to the ruling elites.

Merchants and Trade There is little information about merchants and trade in ancient China until the latter part of the Zhou dynasty, but archaeological discoveries show that long-distance trade routes reached China during Shang and probably Xia times as well. Despite the high mountain ranges and forbidding deserts that stood between China and complex societies in India and southwest Asia, trade networks linked China with lands to the west and south early in the third millennium B.C.E. Jade in Shang tombs came from central Asia, and military technology involving horse-drawn chariots came through central Asia from Mesopotamia. Shang bronzesmiths worked with tin that came from the Malay peninsula in southeast Asia, and cowry shells came through southeast Asia from Burma and the Maldive Islands in the Indian Ocean. The identity of the most important trade items that went from China to other lands is not clear, but archaeologists have unearthed a few pieces of Shang pottery from Mohenjo-daro and other Harappan sites.

Meanwhile, Chinese mariners began to probe nearby waters for profitable sea routes. Legendary accounts credit King Yu, the supposed founder of the Xia dynasty, with the invention of sails. There is no archaeological indication of Chinese sails before about 500 B.C.E., but there is abundant evidence that Chinese mariners used large oar-propelled vessels before 2000 B.C.E. These watercraft supported fishing and trade with offshore islands even before the emergence of the Xia dynasty. By the time of the Shang dynasty, Chinese ships were traveling across the Yellow Sea to Korea. During the Zhou dynasty, shipbuilding emerged as a prominent business all along coastal China, and mariners had discovered how to navigate their vessels by the stars and other heavenly bodies.

Peasants Back on the land, a large class of semiservile peasants populated the Chinese countryside. They owned no land but provided agricultural, military, and labor services for their lords in exchange for plots to cultivate, security, and a portion of the harvest. They lived like their neolithic predecessors in small subterranean houses excavated to a depth of about 1 meter (3 feet) and protected from the elements by thatched walls and roofs. Women's duties included mostly indoor activities such as wine making, weaving, and cultivation of silkworms, whereas men spent most of their time outside working in the fields, hunting, and fishing.

Few effective tools were available to cultivators until the late Zhou dynasty. They mostly relied on wooden digging sticks and spades with bone or stone tips, which were

A wooden digging stick with two prongs was the agricultural tool most commonly used for cultivation of loess soils in the Yellow River valley.

strong enough to cultivate the powdery loess soil of northern China; bronze tools were too expensive for peasant cultivators. Beginning about the sixth century B.C.E., however, iron production increased dramatically in China, and iron plows, picks, spades, hoes, sickles, knives, and rakes all came into daily use in the countryside.

Slaves There was also a sizable class of slaves, most of whom were enemy warriors captured during battles between the many competing states of ancient China. Slaves performed hard labor, such as the clearing of new fields or the building of city walls, that required a large workforce. During the Shang dynasty, but rarely thereafter, hundreds of slaves also figured among the victims sacrificed during funerary, religious, and other ritual observances.

Family and Patriarchy

Throughout human history the family has served as the principal institution for the socialization of children and the preservation of cultural traditions. In China the extended family emerged as a particularly influential institution during neolithic times, and it continued to play a prominent role in the shaping of both private and public affairs after the appearance of the Xia, Shang, and Zhou states. Indeed, the early dynasties ruled their territories largely through family and kinship groups.

Veneration of Ancestors One reason for the pronounced influence of the Chinese family is the veneration of ancestors, a practice with roots in neolithic times. In those early days agricultural peoples in China diligently tended the graves and memories of their departed ancestors. They believed that spirits of their ancestors passed into another realm of existence from which they had the power to support and protect their surviving families if the descendants displayed proper respect and ministered to the spirits' needs. Survivors buried tools, weapons, jewelry, and other material goods along with their dead. They also offered sacrifices of food and drink at the graves of departed relatives. The strong sense of ancestors' presence and continuing influence in the world led to an equally strong ethic of family solidarity. A family could expect to prosper only if all its members—the dead as well as the living—worked cooperatively toward common interests. The family became an institution linking departed generations to the living and even to those yet unborn—an institution that wielded enormous influence over both the private and the public lives of its members.

In the absence of organized religion or official priesthood in ancient China, the patriarchal head of the family presided at rites and ceremonies honoring ancestors' spirits. As mediator between the family's living members and its departed relatives, the family patriarch possessed tremendous authority. He officiated not only at ceremonies honoring ancestors of his household but also at memorials for collateral and subordinate family branches that might include hundreds of individuals.

Patriarchal Society Chinese society vested authority principally in elderly males who headed their households. Like its counterparts in other regions, Chinese society took on a strongly patriarchal character—one that intensified with the emergence of large states. During neolithic times Chinese men wielded public authority, but they won their rights to it by virtue

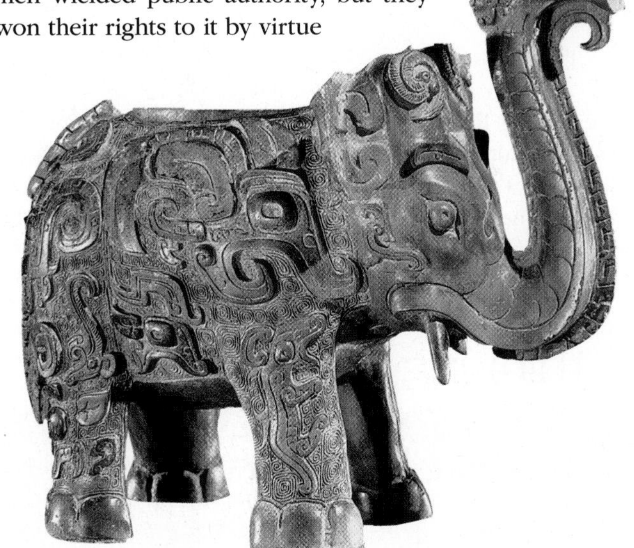

When burying their departed kin, survivors placed bronze ritual vessels with food and drink in the tombs. In the tombs of wealthy individuals, those vessels sometimes took elaborate shapes.

sources from the past

Family Solidarity in Ancient China

A poem from the Book of Songs *illustrates clearly the importance of family connections in ancient China.*

The flowers of the cherry tree—
Are they not gorgeously displayed?
Of all the men in the world
There are none equal to brothers.

On the dreaded occasions of death and burial,
It is brothers who greatly sympathize.
When fugitives are collected on the heights and low grounds,
They are brothers who will seek one another out.

There is the wagtail on the level height—
When brothers are in urgent difficulties,
Friends, though they may be good
Will only heave long sighs.

Brothers may quarrel inside the walls [of their own home],
But they will oppose insult from without,
When friends, however good they may be,
Will not afford help.

When death and disorder are past,
And there are tranquillity and rest,
Although they have brothers,
Some reckon them not equal to friends.

Your dishes may be set in array,
And you may drink to satiety.
But it is when your brothers are all present
That you are harmonious and happy, with child-like joy.

Loving union with wife and children
Is like the music of lutes.
But it is the accord of brothers
That makes the harmony and happiness lasting.

For the ordering of your family,
For the joy in your wife and children,
Examine this and study it—
Will you not find that it is truly so?

For Further Reflection

- To what extent does other archaeological and historical evidence corroborate the views expressed in these verses about the importance of family in ancient China?

Source: James Legge, trans. *The Chinese Classics,* 5 vols. London: Henry Frowde, 1893, 4:250–53. (Translation slightly modified.)

of the female line of their descent. Even if it did not vest power and authority in women, this system provided solid reasons for a family to honor its female members. As late as Shang times, two queens posthumously received the high honor of having temples dedicated to their memories.

thinking about TRADITIONS

Comparing Traditions of Patriarchal Society
Early agricultural societies in Mesopotamia, Egypt, India, and China all adopted strong patriarchal traditions of social organization. Compare the specific features of the patriarchal order that emerged in each of these societies. Why did peoples in very different world regions all build social orders that vested public authority in men and that strictly controlled the behavior of women?

Women's Influence Women occasionally played prominent roles in public life during Shang times. Fu Hao, for example, the consort of King Wu Ding whose tomb has thrown important light on Shang royal society, ventured beyond the corridors of the Shang palace to play prominent roles in public life. Documents from her tomb indicate Fu Hao supervised her estate and presided over sacrificial ceremonies that were usually the responsibility of men who were heads of their households. She even served as general on several military campaigns and once led thirteen thousand troops in a successful operation against a neighboring state.

During the later Shang and Zhou dynasties, however, women came to live increasingly in the shadow of men. Large states brought the military and political contributions of men into sharp focus. The ruling classes performed elaborate ceremonies publicly honoring the spirits of departed ancestors, particularly males who had guided their families and led especially notable lives. Gradually, the emphasis on men became so intense that Chinese society lost its matrilineal character. After the Shang dynasty, not even queens and empresses merited temples dedicated exclusively to their memories: at most, they had the honor of being remembered in association with their illustrious husbands.

EARLY CHINESE WRITING AND CULTURAL DEVELOPMENT

Organized religion did not play as important a role in ancient China as it did in other early societies. Early Chinese myths and legends explained the origins of the world, the human race, agriculture, and the various arts and crafts. But Chinese thinkers saw no need to organize those ideas into systematic religious traditions. They often spoke of an impersonal heavenly power—*tian* ("heaven"), the agent responsible for bestowing and removing the mandate of heaven on rulers—but they did not recognize a personal supreme deity who intervened in human affairs or took special interest in human behavior. Nor did ancient China support a large class of priests like those of Mesopotamia, Egypt, and India who mediated between human beings and the gods. A few priests conducted ritual observances in honor of royal ancestors at royal courts, but for the most part family patriarchs represented the interests of living generations to the spirits of departed ancestors.

In that environment, then, writing served as the foundation for a distinctive secular cultural tradition in ancient China. Chinese scribes may have used written symbols to keep simple records during Xia times, but surviving evidence suggests that writing came into extensive use only during the Shang dynasty. As in other lands, writing in east Asia quickly became an indispensable tool of government as well as a means of expressing ideas and offering reflections on human beings and their world.

Oracle Bones and Early Chinese Writing

In Mesopotamia and India, merchants pioneered the use of writing. In China, however, the earliest known writing served the interests of rulers rather than traders. Writing in China goes back at least to the early part of the second millennium B.C.E. Surviving records indicate that scribes at the Shang royal court kept written accounts of important events on strips of bamboo or pieces of silk. Unfortunately, almost all those materials have perished, along with their messages. Yet one medium employed by ancient Chinese scribes has survived the ravages of time to prove beyond doubt that writing figured prominently in the political life of the Shang dynasty. Recognized just over a century ago, inscriptions on so-called oracle bones have thrown tremendous light both on the Shang dynasty and on the early stages of Chinese writing.

Oracle Bones Oracle bones were the principal instruments used by fortune-tellers in ancient China. In other early societies, specialists forecast the future by examining the entrails of sacrificed animals, divining the meaning of omens or celestial events such as eclipses, studying the flight of birds, or interpreting weather patterns. In China, diviners used specially prepared broad bones, such as the shoulder blades of sheep or turtle shells. They inscribed a question on the bone and then subjected it to heat, either by placing it into a fire or by scorching it with an extremely hot tool. When heated, the bone developed networks of splits and cracks. The fortune-teller then studied the patterns and determined the answer to the question inscribed on the bone. Often the diviner recorded the answer on the bone, and later scribes occasionally added further information about the events that actually came to pass.

During the nineteenth century C.E., peasants working in the fields around Anyang discovered many oracle bones bearing inscriptions in archaic Chinese writing. They did not recognize the writing, but they knew they had found an unusual and valuable commodity. They called their finds "dragon bones" and sold them to druggists, who ground them into powder that they resold as an especially potent medicine. Thus an untold number of oracle bones went to the relief of aches, pains, and ills before scholars recognized their true nature. During the late 1890s dragon bones came to the attention of historians and literary scholars, who soon determined that the inscriptions represented an early and previously unknown form of Chinese writing. Since then, more than two hundred thousand oracle bones have come to light.

Most of the oracle bones have come from royal archives, and the questions posed on them clearly reveal the day-to-day concerns of the Shang royal court. Will the season's harvest be abundant or poor? Should the king attack his enemy or not? Will the queen bear a son or a daughter? Would it please the royal ancestors to receive a sacrifice of animals—or perhaps of human slaves? During the reign of King Wu Ding, no fewer than 1,300 oracle bones recorded questions about the prospects for rain. Taken together, bits of information preserved on the oracle bones have allowed historians to piece together an understanding of the political and social order of Shang times.

Early Chinese Writing Even more important, the oracle bones offer the earliest glimpse into the tradition of Chinese writing. The earliest form of Chinese writing, like Sumerian and Egyptian writing, was the pictograph—a conventional or stylized representation of an object. To represent complex or abstract notions, the written language often combined various pictographs into an ideograph. Thus, for

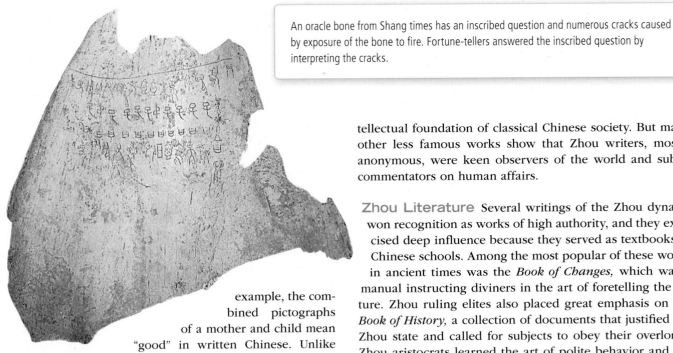

An oracle bone from Shang times has an inscribed question and numerous cracks caused by exposure of the bone to fire. Fortune-tellers answered the inscribed question by interpreting the cracks.

example, the combined pictographs of a mother and child mean "good" in written Chinese. Unlike most other languages, written Chinese did not include an alphabetic or phonetic component.

The characters used in contemporary Chinese writing are direct descendants of those used in Shang times. Scholars have identified more than two thousand characters inscribed on oracle bones, most of which have a modern counterpart. (Contemporary Chinese writing regularly uses about five thousand characters, although thousands of additional characters are also used for technical and specialized purposes.) Over the centuries, written Chinese characters have undergone considerable modification: generally speaking, they have become more stylized, conventional, and abstract. Yet the affinities between Shang and later Chinese written characters are apparent at a glance.

Thought and Literature in Ancient China

The political interests of the Shang kings may have accounted for the origin of Chinese writing, but once established, the technology was available for other uses. Because Shang writing survives only on oracle bones and a small number of bronze inscriptions—all products that reflected the interests of the ruling elite that commissioned them—evidence for the expanded uses of writing comes only from the Zhou dynasty and later times.

A few oracle bones survive from Zhou times, along with a large number of inscriptions on bronze ceremonial utensils that the ruling classes used during rituals venerating their ancestors. Apart from those texts, the Zhou dynasty also produced books of poetry and history, manuals of divination and ritual, and essays dealing with moral, religious, philosophical, and political themes. Best known of these works are the reflections of Confucius and other late Zhou thinkers (discussed in chapter 8), which served as the intellectual foundation of classical Chinese society. But many other less famous works show that Zhou writers, mostly anonymous, were keen observers of the world and subtle commentators on human affairs.

Zhou Literature Several writings of the Zhou dynasty won recognition as works of high authority, and they exercised deep influence because they served as textbooks in Chinese schools. Among the most popular of these works in ancient times was the *Book of Changes,* which was a manual instructing diviners in the art of foretelling the future. Zhou ruling elites also placed great emphasis on the *Book of History,* a collection of documents that justified the Zhou state and called for subjects to obey their overlords. Zhou aristocrats learned the art of polite behavior and the proper way to conduct rituals from the *Book of Etiquette,* also known as the *Book of Rites.*

"Scholars have identified more than two thousand characters inscribed on oracle bones, most of which have a modern counterpart."

The *Book of Songs* Most notable of the classic works, however, was the *Book of Songs,* also known as the *Book of Poetry* and the *Book of Odes,* a collection of verses on themes both light and serious. Though compiled and edited after 600 B.C.E., many of the 311 poems in the collection date from a much earlier period and reflect conditions of the early Zhou dynasty. Some of the poems had political implications because they recorded the illustrious deeds of heroic figures and ancient sage-kings, and others were hymns sung at ritual observances. Yet many of them are charming verses about life, love, family, friendship, eating, drinking, work, play, nature, and daily life that offer reflections on human affairs without particular concern for political or social conditions. One poem, for example, described a bride about to join the household of her husband:

> The peach tree is young and elegant;
> Brilliant are its flowers.
> This young lady is going to her future home,
> And will order well her chamber and house.

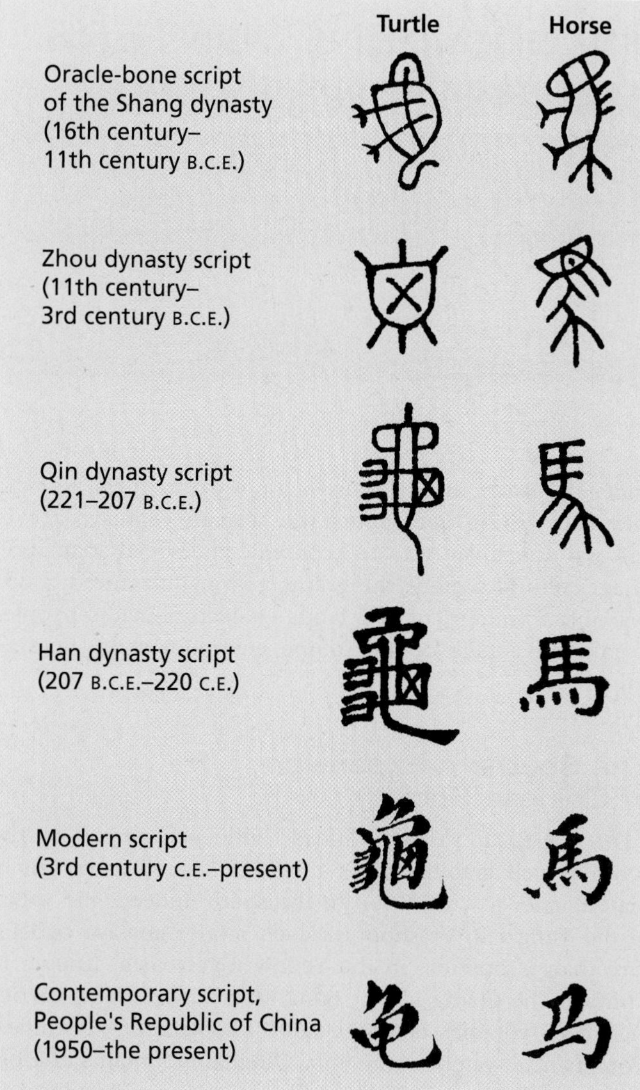

The evolution of Chinese characters from the Shang dynasty to the present.

The peach tree is young and elegant;
Abundant will be its fruit.
This young lady is going to her future home,
And will order well her house and chamber.

The peach tree is young and elegant;
Luxuriant are its leaves.
This young lady is going to her future home,
And will order well her family.

Destruction of Early Chinese Literature The *Book of Songs* and other writings of the Zhou dynasty offer only a small sample of China's earliest literary tradition, for most Zhou writings have perished. Those written on delicate bamboo strips and silk fabrics have deteriorated: records indicate that the tomb of one Zhou king contained hundreds of books written on bamboo strips, but none of them survive. Other books fell victim to human enemies. When the imperial house of **Qin** ended the chaos of the Period of the Warring States and brought all of China under tightly centralized rule in 221 B.C.E., the victorious emperor ordered the destruction of all writings that did not have some immediate utilitarian value. He spared works on divination, agriculture, and medicine, but he condemned those on poetry, history, and philosophy, which he feared might inspire doubts about his government or encourage an independence of mind. Only a few items escaped, hidden away for a decade or more until scholars and writers could once again work without fear of persecution. These few survivors represent the earliest development of Chinese literature and moral thought.

ANCIENT CHINA AND THE LARGER WORLD

Towering mountains, forbidding deserts, and turbulent seas stood between China and other early societies of the eastern hemisphere. These geographic features did not entirely prevent communication between China and other lands, but they hindered the establishment of direct long-distance trade relations such as those linking Mesopotamia with Harappan India or those between the Phoenicians and other peoples of the Mediterranean basin. Nevertheless, like other early societies, ancient China developed in the context of a larger world of interaction and exchange. Trade, migration, and the expansion of Chinese agricultural society all ensured that peoples of the various east Asian and central Asian societies would have regular dealings with one another. Chinese cultivators had particularly intense relations—sometimes friendly and sometimes hostile—with their neighbors to the north, the west, and the south.

Chinese Cultivators and Nomadic Peoples of Central Asia

From the valley of the Yellow River, Chinese agriculture spread to the north and west. The dry environment of the steppes limited expansion in these directions, however, since harvests progressively diminished to the point that agriculture became impractical. During the Zhou dynasty, the zone of agriculture extended about 300 kilometers (186 miles) west of Xi'an, to the eastern region of modern Gansu province.

Steppe Nomads As they expanded to the north and west, Chinese cultivators encountered nomadic peoples who had built pastoral societies in the grassy steppe lands

Qin (chihn)

of central Asia. These lands were too arid to sustain large agricultural societies, but their grasses supported large herds of horses, cattle, sheep, goats, and yaks. After Indo-European peoples in the western steppes began to ride domesticated horses, about 4000 B.C.E., they were able to herd their other animals more effectively and push deeper into the steppes. By 2900 B.C.E., after learning the techniques of bronze metallurgy, they had introduced heavy wagons into the steppes, and by 2200 B.C.E. their wagons were increasingly prominent in the steppe lands east of the Ural Mountains. After about 1000 B.C.E. several clusters of nomadic peoples organized powerful herding societies on the Eurasian steppes.

thinking about ENCOUNTERS

Chinese Cultivators and Their Nomadic Neighbors
For about three millennia, Chinese cultivators and nomadic pastoralists confronted each other in the zone where lands that were capable of supporting agriculture blended into the arid and grassy steppes. How can you best characterize the relationship between Chinese cultivators and nomadic pastoralists? What were the effects of those interactions in both Chinese and nomadic societies?

Nomadic Society Nomadic peoples did little farming, since the arid steppe did not reward efforts at cultivation. Instead, the nomads concentrated on herding their animals, driving them to regions where they could find food and water. The herds provided meat and milk as well as skins and bones from which the nomads fashioned clothes and tools. Because nomadic peoples ranged widely over the grassy steppes of central Asia, they served as links between agricultural societies to the east and west. They were prominent intermediaries in trade networks spanning central Asia. They also brought knowledge of bronze metallurgy and horse-drawn chariots from southwest Asia. Nomadic peoples depended on agricultural societies for grains and finished products, such as textiles and metal goods, which they could not readily produce for themselves. In exchange for these products, they offered horses, which flourished on the steppes, and their services as links to other societies.

Despite this somewhat symbiotic arrangement, Chinese and nomadic peoples always had tense relations. Indeed, they often engaged in bitter wars, since the relatively poor but hardy nomads frequently fell upon the rich agricultural society at their doorstep and sought to seize its wealth. At least from the time of the Shang dynasty, and probably from the Xia as well, nomadic raids posed a constant threat to the northern and western regions of China. The Zhou state grew strong enough to overcome the Shang partly because Zhou military forces honed their skills waging campaigns against nomadic peoples to the west. Later, however, the Zhou state almost crumbled under the pressure of nomadic incursions compounded by disaffection among Zhou allies and subordinates.

Nomadic peoples did not imitate Chinese ways. The environment of the steppe prevented them from cultivating crops, and the need to herd their animals made it impossible for them to settle permanently in towns or to build cities. Nomadic peoples did not adopt Chinese political or social traditions but, rather, organized themselves into clans under the leadership of charismatic warrior-chiefs. Nor did they use writing until about the seventh century C.E. Yet pastoral nomadism was an economic and social adaptation to agricultural society: the grains and manufactured goods available from agricultural lands enabled nomadic peoples to take advantage of the steppe environment by herding animals.

The Southern Expansion of Chinese Society

The Yangzi Valley Chinese influence spread to the south as well as to the north and west. There was no immediate barrier to cultivation in the south: indeed, the valley of the Yangzi River supports even more intensive agriculture than is possible in the Yellow River basin. Known in China as the Chang Jiang ("Long River"), the Yangzi carries enormous volumes of water 6,300 kilometers (3,915 miles) from its headwaters in the lofty Qinghai mountains of Tibet to its mouth near the modern Chinese cities of Nanjing and Shanghai, where it empties into the East China Sea. The moist, subtropical climate of southern China lent itself readily to the cultivation of rice: ancient cultivators sometimes raised two crops of rice per year.

There was no need for King Yu to tame the Yangzi River, which does not bring devastating floods like those of the Yellow River. But intensive cultivation of rice depended on the construction and maintenance of an elaborate irrigation system that allowed cultivators to flood their paddies and release the waters at the appropriate time. The Shang and Zhou states provided sources of authority that could supervise a complex irrigation system, and harvests in southern China increased rapidly during the second and first millennia B.C.E. The populations of cultivators' communities surged along with their harvests.

As their counterparts did in lands to the north and west of the Yellow River valley, the indigenous peoples of southern China responded in two ways to the increasing prominence of agriculture in the Yangzi River valley. Many

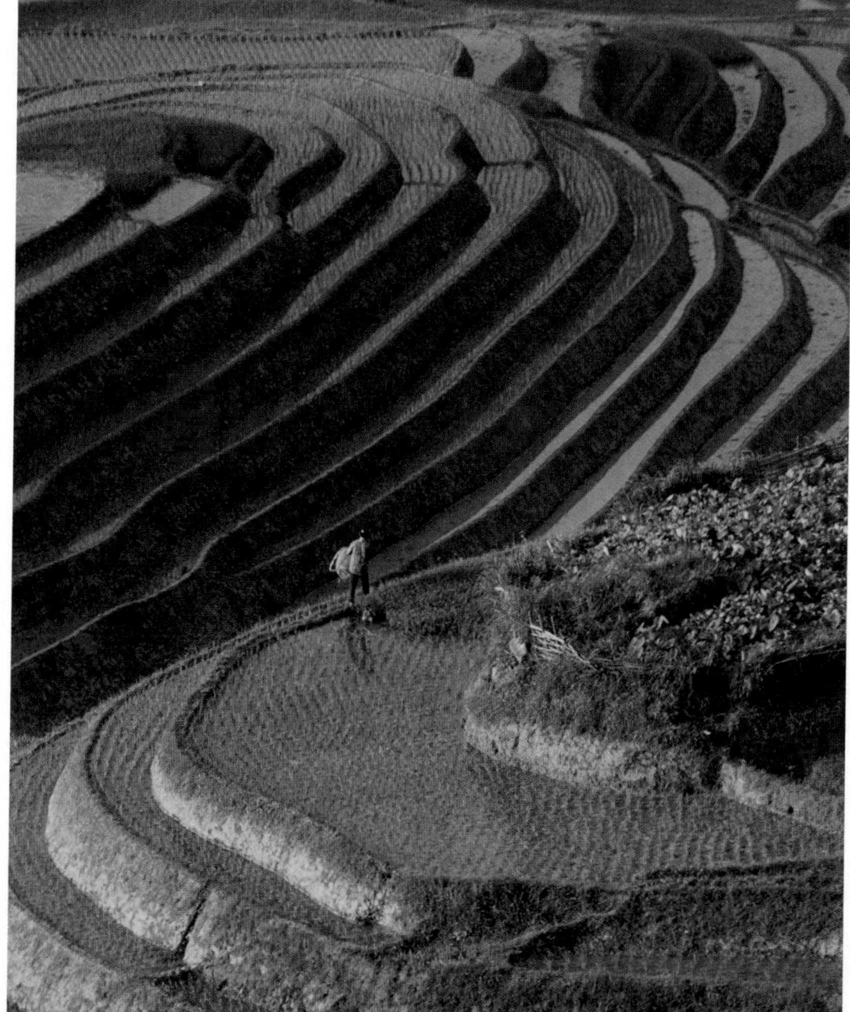

Terraced rice paddies in the river valleys of southern China have long produced abundant harvests.

PART 1

became cultivators themselves and joined Chinese agricultural society. Others continued to live by hunting and gathering: some moved into the hills and mountains, where conditions did not favor agriculture, and others migrated to Taiwan or southeast Asian lands such as Vietnam and Thailand, where agriculture was less common.

The State of Chu Agricultural surpluses and growing populations led to the emergence of cities, states, and complex societies in the Yangzi as well as the Yellow River valley. During the late Zhou dynasty, the powerful state of Chu, situated in the central region of the Yangzi, governed its affairs autonomously and challenged the Zhou for supremacy. By the end of the Zhou dynasty, Chu and other states in southern China were in regular communication with their counterparts in the Yellow River valley. They adopted Chinese political and social traditions as well as Chinese writing, and they built societies closely resembling those of the Yellow River valley. Although only the northern portions of the Yangzi River valley fell under the authority of the Shang and Zhou states, by the end of the Zhou dynasty all of southern China formed part of an emerging larger Chinese society.

inperspective

Agricultural peoples in east Asia built complex societies that in broad outline were much like those to the west. Particularly in the valleys of the Yellow River and the Yangzi River, early Chinese cultivators organized powerful states, developed social distinctions, and established sophisticated cultural traditions. Their language, writing, beliefs, and values differed considerably from those of their contemporaries in other societies, and these cultural elements lent a distinctiveness to Chinese society. In spite of formidable geographic obstacles in the form of deserts, mountain ranges, and extensive bodies of water, inhabitants of ancient China managed to trade and communicate with peoples of other societies. As a result, wheat cultivation, bronze and iron metallurgy, horse-drawn chariots, and wheeled vehicles all made their way from southwest Asia to China in ancient times. Thus, in east Asia as in other parts of the eastern hemisphere, agriculture demonstrated its potential to provide a foundation for large-scale social organization and to support interaction and exchange between peoples of different societies. ●

CHRONOLOGY	
5000–3000 B.C.E.	Yangshao society
2200–1766 B.C.E.	Xia dynasty
1766–1122 B.C.E.	Shang dynasty
1122–256 B.C.E.	Zhou dynasty
403–221 B.C.E.	Period of the Warring States

For Further Reading

Cyril Birch, ed. *Anthology of Chinese Literature.* 2 vols. New York, 1965. Collection of literary sources in translation.

Kwang-chih Chang. *The Archaeology of Ancient China.* 4th ed. New Haven, 1986. Brings the results of archaeological excavations to bear on ancient Chinese history.

———. *Early Chinese Civilization: Anthropological Perspectives.* Cambridge, Mass., 1976. Essays by a distinguished archaeologist.

———. *Shang Civilization.* New Haven, 1980. Based on archaeological research.

Nicola di Cosmo. *Ancient China and Its Enemies: The Rise of Nomadic Power in East Asian History.* Cambridge, 2002. An insightful study analyzing the emergence of pastoral nomadism and relations between Chinese cultivators and nomadic peoples in ancient times.

Jacques Gernet. *Ancient China from the Beginnings to the Empire.* Trans. by R. Rudorff. London, 1968. A brief popular survey of early Chinese society.

Cho-yun Hsu. *Ancient China in Transition: An Analysis of Social Mobility, 722–222 B.C.* Stanford, 1965. A scholarly examination of social change during the later Zhou dynasty.

——— and Katheryn M. Linduff. *Western Chou Civilization.* New Haven, 1988. Draws on both literary sources and archaeological discoveries in offering a comprehensive study of the early Zhou dynasty.

David N. Keightley, ed. *The Origins of Chinese Civilization.* Berkeley, 1983. An important collection of scholarly articles dealing with all aspects of early Chinese society.

Owen Lattimore. *Inner Asian Frontiers of China.* 2nd ed. New York, 1951. Fascinating analysis of the relationship between Chinese and nomadic peoples of central Asia by a geographer who traveled through much of central Asia in the early twentieth century.

Michael Loewe and Edward L. Shaughnessy, eds. *The Cambridge History of Ancient China: From the Origins of Civilization to 221 B.C.* Cambridge, 1999. Presents fourteen detailed essays by leading scholars.

Victor H. Mair, Nancy S. Steinhardt, and Paul R. Goldin, eds. *Hawai`i Reader in Traditional Chinese Culture.* Honolulu, 2005. An imaginative selection of primary sources in English translation.

Jessica Rawson. *Ancient China: Art and Archaeology.* New York, 1980. An outstanding and well-illustrated volume with especially strong treatment of archaeological discoveries.

Robert L. Thorp. *China in the Early Bronze Age: Shang Civilization.* Philadelphia, 2006. Authoritative synthesis of archaeological studies that places the Shang dynasty in its historical context.

William Watson. *Early Civilization in China.* New York, 1966. Well-illustrated popular account dealing with the period from prehistoric times to the Zhou dynasty.

Early Societies in the Americas and Oceania

chapter 6

In this wall painting from a Maya temple, dignitaries converse among themselves during a ceremony.

Early Societies of Mesoamerica

The Olmecs

Heirs of the Olmecs: The Maya

Maya Society and Religion

Heirs of the Olmecs: Teotihuacan

Early Societies of South America

Early Andean Society and the Chavín Cult

Early Andean States: Mochica

Early Societies of Oceania

Early Societies in Australia and New Guinea

The Peopling of the Pacific Islands

EYEWITNESS:
Chan Bahlum Spills Blood to Honor the Gods

In early September of the year 683 C.E., a Maya man named Chan Bahlum grasped a sharp obsidian knife and cut three deep slits into the skin of his penis. He inserted into each slit a strip of paper made from beaten tree bark so as to encourage a continuing flow of blood. His younger brother Kan Xul performed a similar rite, while other members of his family also drew blood from their bodies.

The bloodletting observances of September 683 C.E. were political and religious rituals, acts of deep piety performed as Chan Bahlum presided over funeral services for his recently deceased father, Pacal, king of the Maya city of Palenque in the Yucatan peninsula. The Maya believed that the shedding of royal blood was essential to the world's survival. Thus, as Chan Bahlum prepared to succeed his father as king of Palenque, he let his blood flow copiously.

Throughout Mesoamerica, Maya and other peoples performed similar rituals for a millennium and more. Maya rulers and their family members regularly spilled their blood by opening wounds with obsidian knives, stingray spines, or sharpened bones. Men commonly drew blood from the penis, like Chan Bahlum, and women often drew from the tongue. Both sexes occasionally drew blood also from the earlobes, lips, or cheeks, and they sometimes increased the flow by pulling long, thick cords through their wounds.

This shedding of blood was so crucial to Maya rituals because of its association with rain and agriculture. According to Maya priests, the gods had shed their blood to water the earth and nourish crops of maize, and they expected human beings to honor them by imitating their sacrifice. By spilling human blood the Maya hoped to please the gods and ensure that life-giving waters would bring bountiful harvests to their fields. By inflicting painful wounds not just on their enemies but on their own bodies as well, the Maya demonstrated their conviction that bloodletting rituals were essential to the coming of rain and the survival of their agricultural society.

Early societies in the Americas and Oceania developed independently and differed considerably from their counterparts in the eastern hemisphere. Human migrants reached both regions long after human groups had established populations in most other world regions. In fact, migrations to the Americas and Oceania represented some of the last episodes in the long process by which *Homo sapiens* established populations in all habitable parts of the world.

Human foragers reached the Americas, Australia, and New Guinea during ice ages when glaciers locked up much of the earth's water, causing sea levels all over the world to decline precipitously—sometimes by as much as 300 meters (984 feet). For thousands of years, temporary land bridges linked regions that both before and after the ice ages were separated by the seas. One land bridge linked Siberia with Alaska. Another joined the continent of Australia with the island of New Guinea, while low sea levels also exposed large stretches of land connecting Sumatra, Java, and other Indonesian islands to the peninsula of southeast Asia. The temporary land bridges enabled human migrants to walk right into previously unpopulated regions and start new communities.

The establishment of human populations in the Pacific islands was a much later development. Only about six thousand years ago did the ancestors of the Polynesians invent highly maneuverable sailing canoes and build a body of nautical expertise that allowed them to populate the islands of the vast Pacific Ocean. By about 700 C.E. these remarkable sailors had found their way to every speck of land in the world's largest ocean, which covers one-third of the earth's surface.

Oceans separated the Americas and Oceania from the eastern hemisphere and from each other. By no means, however, did the early human inhabitants of the Americas and Oceania lead completely isolated lives. To the contrary, there were frequent and sometimes regular interactions between peoples of different societies within the Americas and within Oceania. Moreover, there were sporadic but significant contacts between Asian peoples and Pacific islanders and also between Pacific islanders and native peoples of the Americas. It is likely that at least fleeting encounters took place as well between peoples of the eastern and western hemispheres, although little evidence survives on the nature of encounters in early times. Yet even as they dealt frequently with peoples of other societies, the first inhabitants of the Americas and Oceania established distinctive societies of their own, like their counterparts in the eastern hemisphere.

Indeed, despite their different origins and their distinctive political, social, and cultural traditions, peoples of the Americas and Oceania built societies that in some ways resembled those of the eastern hemisphere. Human communities independently discovered agriculture in several regions of North America and South America, and migrants introduced cultivation to the inhabited Pacific islands as well. With agriculture came increasing populations, settlement in towns, specialized labor, formal political authorities, hierarchical social orders, long-distance trade, and organized religious traditions. The Americas also generated large, densely populated societies featuring cities, monumental public works, imperial states, and sometimes traditions of writing as well. Thus, like their counterparts in the eastern hemisphere, the earliest societies of the Americas and Oceania reflected a common human tendency toward the development of increasingly complex social forms.

EARLY SOCIETIES OF MESOAMERICA

Much is unclear about the early population of the Americas by human communities. The first large wave of migration from Siberia to Alaska probably took place about 13,000 B.C.E. But small numbers of migrants may have crossed the Bering land bridge earlier, and it is also possible that some migrants reached the western hemisphere by watercraft, sailing or drifting with the currents from northeast Asia down the west coast of North America. In the view of some scholars, it is also possible that some migrants crossed the Atlantic Ocean and established communities on the eastern coast of North America. Several archaeological excavations at widely scattered sites in both North America and South America have yielded remains that scholars date to 15,000 B.C.E. or earlier, suggesting that at least a few human groups made their way to the Americas before the beginning of large-scale migration from Siberia. In any case, after 13,000 B.C.E. migrants arrived in large numbers, and they quickly populated all habitable regions of the western hemisphere. By 9500 B.C.E. they had reached the southernmost part of South America, more than 17,000 kilometers (10,566 miles) from the Bering land bridge.

The earliest human inhabitants of the Americas lived exclusively by hunting and gathering. Beginning about 8,000 B.C.E., however, it became increasingly difficult for them to survive by foraging. Large game animals became scarce, partly because they did not adapt well to the rapidly warming climate and partly because of overhunting by expanding human communities. By 7500 B.C.E. many species of large animals in the Americas were well on the road to extinction. Some human communities relied on fish and small game to supplement foods that they gathered. Others turned to agriculture, and they gave rise to the first complex societies in the Americas.

The Olmecs

Early Agriculture in Mesoamerica By 8000 to 7000 B.C.E., the peoples of Mesoamerica—the region from the central portion of modern Mexico to Honduras and El Salvador—had begun to experiment with the cultivation of squashes, manioc, beans, chili peppers, avocados, and gourds. By 4000 B.C.E. they had discovered the agricultural potential of maize, which soon became the staple food of the region. Later they added tomatoes to the crops they cultivated. Agricultural villages appeared soon after 3000 B.C.E., and by 2000 B.C.E. agriculture had spread throughout Mesoamerica.

Early Mesoamerican peoples had a diet rich in cultivated foods, but they did not keep as many animals as their counterparts in the eastern hemisphere. Their domesticated animals included turkeys and small, barkless dogs, both of which they consumed as food. They had no cattle, sheep, goats, or swine, so far less animal protein was available to them than to their counterparts in the eastern hemisphere. In addition, most large animals of the western hemisphere were not susceptible to domestication, so Mesoamericans were unable to harness the energy of animals such as horses and oxen that were prominent in the eastern hemisphere. Human laborers prepared fields for cultivation, and human porters carried trade goods on their backs. Mesoamericans had no need for wheeled vehicles, which would have been useful only if draft animals were available to pull them.

Ceremonial Centers Toward the end of the second millennium B.C.E., the tempo of Mesoamerican life quickened as elaborate ceremonial centers with monumental pyramids, temples, and palaces arose alongside the agricultural villages. The first of these centers were not cities like those of early societies in the eastern hemisphere. Permanent residents of the ceremonial centers included members of the ruling elite, priests, and a few artisans and craftsmen who tended to the needs of the ruling and priestly classes. Large numbers of people gathered in the ceremonial centers on special occasions to observe rituals or on market days to exchange goods, but most people then returned to their homes in neighboring villages and hamlets.

Olmecs: The "Rubber People" Agricultural villages and ceremonial centers arose in several regions of Mesoamerica. The earliest known and the most thoroughly studied of them appeared on the coast of the Gulf of Mexico, near the modern Mexican city of Veracruz, which emerged as the nerve center for Olmec society. Historians and archaeologists have systematically studied Olmec society only since the 1940s, and many questions about the Olmecs remain unanswered. Even their proper name is unknown: the term

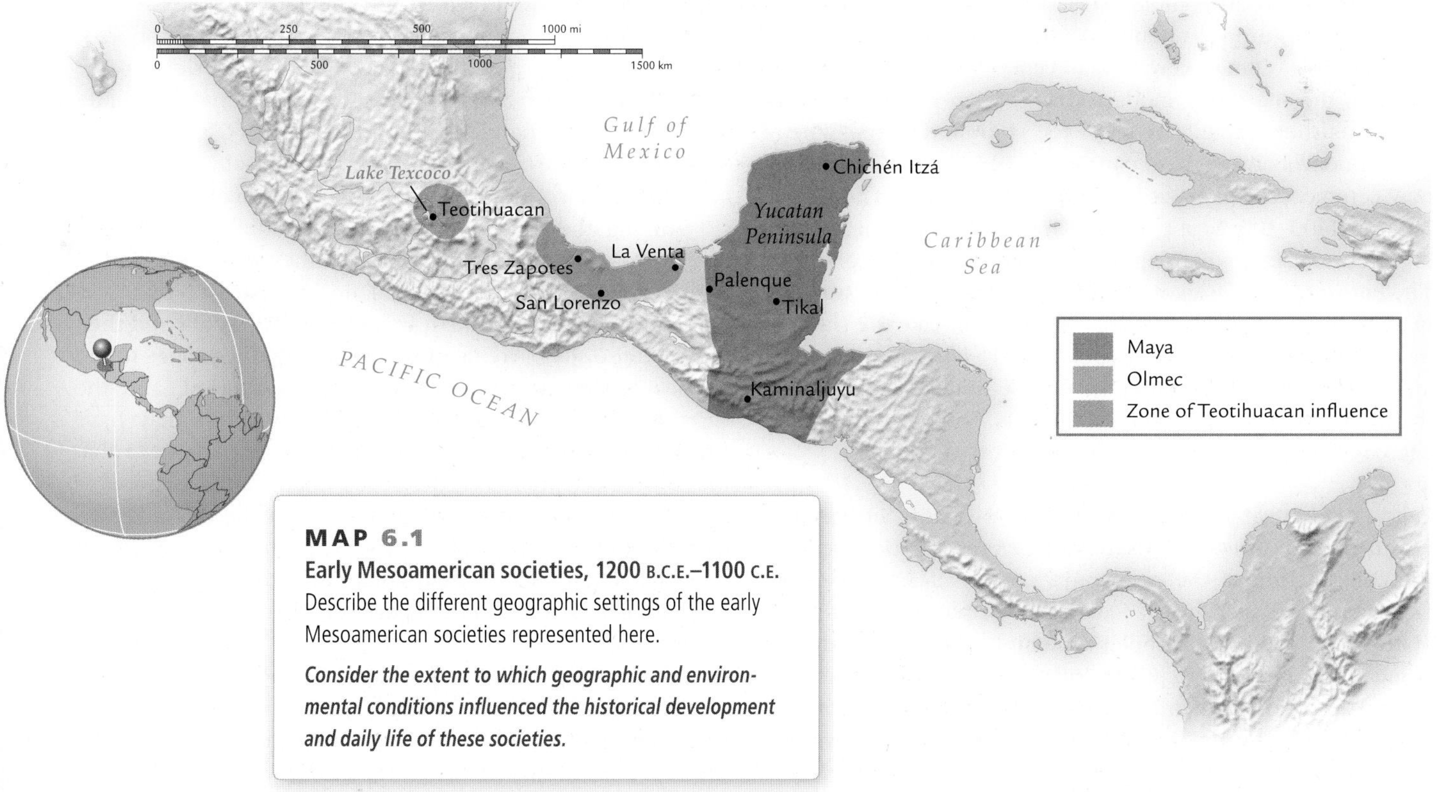

MAP 6.1
Early Mesoamerican societies, 1200 B.C.E.–1100 C.E.
Describe the different geographic settings of the early Mesoamerican societies represented here.

Consider the extent to which geographic and environmental conditions influenced the historical development and daily life of these societies.

Colossal Olmec head carved from basalt rock between 1000 and 600 B.C.E. and discovered at La Venta. Olmecs carved similar heads for their ceremonial centers at San Lorenzo and Tres Zapotes. Why might Olmecs have taken the trouble to carve and move such massive sculptures?

Olmec (meaning "rubber people") did not come from the ancient people themselves, but derives instead from the rubber trees that flourish in the region they inhabited. Nevertheless, some of the basic features of Olmec society have become reasonably clear, and it is certain that Olmec cultural traditions influenced all complex societies of Mesoamerica until the arrival of European peoples in the sixteenth century C.E.

The first Olmec ceremonial center arose about 1200 B.C.E. on the site of the modern town of San Lorenzo, and it served as their capital for some four hundred years. When the influence of San Lorenzo waned, leadership passed to new ceremonial centers at La Venta (800–400 B.C.E.) and Tres Zapotes (400–100 B.C.E.). These sites defined the heartland of Olmec society, where agriculture produced rich harvests. The entire region receives abundant rainfall, so there was no need to build extensive systems of irrigation. Like the Harappans, however, the Olmecs constructed elaborate drainage systems to divert waters that otherwise might have flooded their fields or destroyed their settlements. Some Olmec drainage construction remains visible and effective today.

Olmec Society Olmec society was probably authoritarian in nature. Untold thousands of laborers participated in the construction of the ceremonial centers at San Lorenzo, La Venta, and Tres Zapotes. Each of the principal Olmec sites featured an elaborate complex of temples, pyramids, altars, stone sculptures, and tombs for rulers. Common subjects delivered a portion of their harvests for the maintenance of the elite classes living in the ceremonial centers and provided labor for the various large-scale construction projects.

Indeed, common subjects labored regularly on behalf of the Olmec elite—not only in building drainage systems and ceremonial centers but also in providing appropriate artistic adornment for the capitals. The most distinctive artistic creations of the Olmecs were colossal human heads—possibly likenesses of rulers—sculpted from basalt rock. The largest of these sculptures stands 3 meters (almost 10 feet) tall and weighs some 20 tons. In the absence of draft animals and wheels, human laborers dragged enormous boulders from quarries, floated them on rafts to points near their destinations, dragged them to their intended sites, and then positioned them for the sculptors. The largest sculptures required the services of about one thousand laborers. Apart from the colossal heads, the Olmec capitals featured many other large stone sculptures and monumental buildings that required the services of laborers by the hundreds and thousands. Construction of the huge pyramid at La Venta, for example, required some eight hundred thousand man-days of labor.

Trade in Jade and Obsidian Olmec influence extended to much of the central and southern regions of modern Mexico and beyond that to modern Guatemala and El Salvador. The Olmecs spread their influence partly by military force, but trade was a prominent link between the Olmec heartland and the other regions of Mesoamerica. The Olmecs produced large numbers of decorative objects from jade, which they had to import. In the absence of any metal technology, they also made extensive use of obsidian from which they fashioned knives and axes with wickedly sharp cutting edges. Like jade, obsidian came to the Gulf Coast from distant regions in the interior of Mesoamerica. In exchange for the imports, the Olmecs traded small works of art fashioned from jade, basalt, or ceramics and perhaps also local products such as animal skins.

Among the many mysteries surrounding the Olmecs, one of the most perplexing concerns the decline and fall of their society. The Olmecs systematically destroyed their ceremonial centers at both San Lorenzo and La Venta and then deserted the sites. Archaeologists studying these sites found statues broken and buried, monuments defaced, and the capitals themselves burned. Although intruders may have ravaged the ceremonial centers, many scholars believe that the Olmecs deliberately destroyed their capitals, perhaps because of civil conflicts or doubts about the effectiveness and legitimacy of the ruling classes. In any case, by about 400 B.C.E. Olmec society had fallen on hard times, and soon thereafter societies in other parts of Mesoamerica eclipsed it altogether.

Nevertheless, Olmec traditions deeply influenced later Mesoamerican societies. Olmecs made astronomical observations and created a calendar to help them keep track of the seasons. They invented a system of writing, although unfortunately little of it survives beyond calendrical inscriptions. They also carried out rituals involving human sacrifice and invented a distinctive ball game. Later Mesoamerican peoples adopted all these Olmec traditions as well as their cultivation of maize and their construction of ceremonial centers with temple pyramids. The later and better-known societies of Mesoamerica stood largely on Olmec foundations.

Olmec ceremonial axe head carved from jade about 800 to 400 B.C.E. Jaguar features, such as those depicted here, are prominent in Olmec art.

Heirs of the Olmecs: The Maya

During the thousand years following the Olmecs' disappearance about 100 B.C.E., complex societies arose in several Mesoamerican regions. Human population grew dramatically, and ceremonial centers cropped up at sites far removed from the Olmec heartland. Some of them evolved into genuine cities: they attracted large populations of permanent residents, embarked on ambitious programs of construction, maintained large markets, and encouraged increasing specialization of labor. Networks of long-distance trade linked the new urban centers and extended their influence to all parts of Mesoamerica. Within the cities themselves, priests devised written languages and compiled a body of astronomical knowledge. In short, Mesoamerican societies developed in a manner roughly parallel to their counterparts in the eastern hemisphere.

The Maya The earliest heirs of the Olmecs were the Maya, who created a remarkable society in the region now occupied by southern Mexico, Guatemala, Belize, Honduras, and El Salvador. The highlands of Guatemala offer fertile soil and excellent conditions for agriculture. Permanent villages began to appear there during the third century B.C.E. The most prominent of them was Kaminaljuyú, located on the site of modern Guatemala City. Like the Olmec capitals, Kaminaljuyú was a ceremonial center rather than a true city, but it dominated the life of other communities in the region. Some twelve thousand to fifteen thousand laborers worked to build its temples, and its products traveled the trade routes as far as central Mexico. During the fourth century C.E., Kaminaljuyú fell under the economic and perhaps also the political dominance of the much larger city of **Teotihuacan** in central Mexico and lost much of its influence in Maya society.

After the fourth century, Maya society flourished mostly in the poorly drained Mesoamerican lowlands, where thin, tropical soils quickly lost their fertility. To enhance the agricultural potential of the region, the Maya built terraces designed to trap silt carried by the numerous rivers passing through the lowlands. By artificially retaining rich earth, they dramatically increased the agricultural productivity of their lands. They harvested maize in abundance, and they also cultivated cotton from which they wove fine textiles highly prized both in their own society and by trading partners in other parts of Mesoamerica. Maya cultivators also raised cacao, the large bean that is the source of chocolate. Cacao was a precious commodity consumed mostly by nobles in Maya society. They whisked powdered cacao into water to create a stimulating beverage, and they sometimes even ate the bitter cacao beans as snacks. The product was so valuable that Maya used cacao beans as money.

Tikal From about 300 to 900 C.E., the Maya built more than eighty large ceremonial centers in the lowlands—all with pyramids, palaces, and temples—as well as numerous smaller settlements. Some of the larger centers attracted dense populations and evolved into genuine cities. Foremost among them was Tikal, the most important Maya political center between the fourth and the ninth centuries C.E. At its height, roughly 600 to 800 C.E., Tikal was a wealthy and bustling city with a population approaching forty thousand. It boasted enormous paved plazas and scores of temples, pyramids, palaces, and public buildings. The Temple of the Giant Jaguar, a stepped pyramid rising sharply to a height of 47 meters (154 feet), dominated the skyline and represented Tikal's control over the surrounding region, which had a population of about five hundred thousand.

The Maya organized themselves politically into scores of small city-kingdoms. Tikal was probably the largest, but Palenque and Chichén Itzá also were sizable states. The smaller kingdoms had populations between ten thousand and thirty thousand. Maya kings often bore menacing names such as Curl Snout, Smoking Frog, and Stormy Sky. Especially popular were names associated with the jaguar, the most dangerous predator of the Mesoamerican forests. Prominent Maya kings included Great Jaguar Paw, Shield Jaguar, Bird Jaguar, and Jaguar Penis (meaning the progenitor of other jaguar-kings).

Maya Warfare Dazzled by Maya architecture and sculpture, scholars of earlier generations thought these kingdoms

Teotihuacan (tay-uh-tee-wah-KAHN)

Temple of the Giant Jaguar at Tikal, which served as funerary pyramid for Lord Cacao, a prominent Maya ruler of the late sixth and early seventh centuries C.E. Why might a Maya ruler wish to associate himself with a jaguar?

were peaceful states that promoted artistic and scientific endeavors. Since the 1970s, however, historians and archaeologists have deciphered thousands of previously unreadable inscriptions that have dramatically transformed understanding of Maya politics. Combined with fresh archaeological discoveries, these sources make it clear that the Maya kingdoms fought constantly with one another. Victors generally destroyed the peoples they defeated and took over their ceremonial centers, but the purpose of Maya warfare was not so much to kill enemies as to capture them in hand-to-hand combat on the battlefield. Warriors won enormous prestige when they brought back important captives from neighboring kingdoms. They stripped captives of their fine dress and symbols of rank, and sometimes they kept high-ranking captives alive for years, displaying them as trophies. Ultimately, however, most captives ended their lives either as slaves or as sacrificial victims to Maya gods. High-ranking captives in particular often underwent ritual torture and sacrifice in public ceremonies on important occasions.

Chichén Itzá Bitter conflicts between small kingdoms were sources of constant tension in Maya society. Only about the ninth century C.E. did the state of Chichén Itzá in the northern Yucatan peninsula seek to dampen hostile instincts and establish a larger political framework for Maya society. The rulers of Chichén Itzá preferred to absorb captives and integrate them into their own society rather than annihilate them or offer them up as sacrificial victims. Some captives refused the opportunity and went to their deaths as proud warriors, but many agreed to recognize the authority of Chichén Itzá and participate in the construction of a larger society. Between the ninth and eleventh centuries C.E., Chichén Itzá organized a loose empire that brought a measure of political stability to the northern Yucatan.

Maya Decline By about 800 C.E., however, most Maya populations had begun to desert their cities. Within a century Maya society was in full decline everywhere except the northern Yucatan, where Chichén Itzá continued to flourish. Historians have suggested many possible causes of the decline, including invasion by foreigners from Mexico, internal dissension and civil war, failure of the system of water control leading to diminished harvests and demographic collapse, ecological problems caused by destruction of the forests, the spread of epidemic diseases, and natural catastrophes such as earthquakes. Possibly several problems combined to destroy Maya society. It is likely that debilitating civil conflict and excessive siltation of agricultural terraces caused particularly difficult problems for the Maya. In any case, the population declined, the people abandoned their cities, and long-distance trade with central Mexico came to a halt. Meanwhile, the tropical jungles of the lowlands encroached upon human settlements and gradually smothered the cities, temples, pyramids, and monuments of a once-vibrant society.

Maya Society and Religion

Apart from the kings and ruling families, Maya society included a large class of priests who maintained an elaborate calendar and transmitted knowledge of writing, astronomy, and mathematics. A hereditary nobility owned most land and cooperated with the kings and priests by organizing military forces and participating in religious rituals. Maya merchants came from the ruling and noble classes. Their travels had strong political overtones, since they served not only as traders but also as ambassadors to neighboring lands and allied peoples. Moreover, they traded mostly in exotic and luxury goods, such as rare animal skins, cacao beans, and finely crafted works of art, which rulers coveted as signs of special status. Apart from the ruling and priestly elites, Maya society generated several other distinct social classes. Professional architects and sculptors oversaw construction of large monuments and public buildings. Artisans specialized in the production of pottery, tools, and cotton textiles. Large classes of peasants and slaves fed the entire society and provided physical labor for the construction of cities and monuments.

The Maya built upon the cultural achievements of their Olmec predecessors. Maya priests studied astronomy and mathematics, and they devised both a sophisticated calen-

A vivid mural from a temple in the small Maya kingdom of Bonampak (in the southern part of modern Mexico) depicts warriors raiding a neighboring village to capture prisoners who will become sacrificial victims.

dar and an elaborate system of writing. They understood the movements of heavenly bodies well enough to plot planetary cycles and predict eclipses of the sun and moon. They invented the concept of zero and used a symbol to represent zero mathematically, which facilitated their manipulation of large numbers. By combining their astronomical observations and mathematical reasoning, Maya priests calculated the length of the solar year at 365.242 days—about seventeen seconds shorter than the figure reached by modern astronomers.

The Maya Calendar Maya priests constructed the most elaborate calendar of the ancient Americas. Its complexity reflected a powerful urge to identify meaningful cycles of time and to understand human events in the context of those cycles. The Maya calendar interwove two kinds of year: a solar year of 365 days governed the agricultural cycle, and a ritual year of 260 days governed daily affairs by organizing time into twenty "months" of thirteen days apiece. The Maya believed that each day derived certain specific characteristics from its position in both the solar and the ritual calendar and that the combined attributes of each day would determine the fortune of activities undertaken on that day. It took fifty-two years for the two calendars to work through all possible combinations of days and return simultaneously to their respective starting points, so 18,980 different combinations of characteristics could influence the prospects of an individual day. Maya priests carefully studied the various opportunities and dangers that would come together on a given day in hopes that they could determine which activities were safe to initiate. Apart from calculating the prospects of individual days, the Maya attributed especially great significance to the fifty-two-year periods in which the two calendars ran. They believed that the end of a cycle would bring monumental changes and that ultimately the world would end after one such cycle.

Maya Writing While building on the calendrical calculations of the Olmecs, the Maya also expanded upon their predecessors' tradition of written inscriptions. In doing so they created the most flexible and sophisticated of all the early American systems of writing. The Maya script contained both ideographic elements (like Chinese characters) and symbols for syllables. Scholars have begun to decipher this script only since the 1960s, and it has become clear that writing was just as important to the Maya as it was to early complex societies in the eastern hemisphere. Maya scribes wrote works of history, poetry, and myth, and they also kept genealogical, administrative, and astronomical records. Most Maya writing survives today in the form of inscriptions on temples and monuments, but scribes produced untold numbers of books written on paper made from beaten tree bark or on vellum made from deerskin. When Spanish conquerors and missionaries arrived in Maya lands in the sixteenth century C.E., however, they destroyed all the books they could find in hopes of undermining native religious beliefs. Today only four books of the ancient Maya survive, all dealing with astronomical and calendrical matters.

Maya Religious Thought Surviving inscriptions and other writings shed considerable light on Maya religious and cultural traditions. The *Popol Vuh,* a Maya creation myth, taught that the gods had created human beings out of maize and water, the ingredients that became human flesh and blood. Thus Maya religious thought reflected the fundamental role of agriculture in their society, much like religious thought in early complex societies of the eastern hemisphere. Maya priests also taught that the gods kept the world going and maintained the agricultural cycle in exchange for honors and sacrifices performed for them by human beings.

In this stone relief sculpture, a Maya king from Yaxchilán (between Tikal and Palenque in the southern Yucatan peninsula) holds a torch over a woman from the royal family as she draws a thorn-studded rope through a hole in her tongue, so as to shed her blood in honor of the Maya gods.

Bloodletting Rituals The most important of those sacrifices involved the shedding of human blood, which the Maya believed would prompt the gods to send rain to water their crops of maize. Some bloodletting rituals centered on war captives. Before sacrificing the victims by decapitation, their captors cut off the ends of their fingers or lacerated their bodies so as to cause a copious flow of blood in honor of the gods. Yet the Maya did not look upon those rituals simply as opportunities to torture their enemies. The frequent and voluntary shedding of royal blood, as in the case of Chan Bahlum's self-sacrifice at Palenque, testifies to the depth of Maya convictions that they inhabited a world created and sustained by deities who expected honor and reverence from their human subjects.

The Maya Ball Game Apart from the calendar and sacrificial rituals, the Maya also inherited a distinctive ball game from the Olmecs. The game sometimes pitted two men against each other, but it often involved teams of two to four members—mostly men, although there is evidence that women sometimes played the game as well. The object of the game was for players to score points by propelling a rubber ball through a ring or onto a marker without using their hands. The Maya used a ball about 20 centimeters (8 inches) in diameter. Made of solid baked rubber, the ball was both heavy and hard—a blow to the head could easily cause a concussion—and players needed great dexterity and skill to maneuver it accurately using only their feet, legs, hips, torso, shoulders, or elbows. The game was extremely popular: almost all Maya ceremonial centers, towns, and cities had stone-paved courts on which players performed publicly.

The Maya played the ball game for several reasons. Sometimes individuals competed for sporting purposes, and sometimes players or spectators laid bets on the outcome of contests between professionals. The ball game figured also in Maya political affairs as a ritual that honored the conclusion of treaties. High-ranking captives often engaged in forced public competition in which the stakes were their very lives: losers became sacrificial victims and faced torture and execution immediately following the match. Alongside some ball courts were skull racks that bore the severed heads of losing players. Thus Maya concerns to please the gods by shedding human blood extended even to the realm of sport.

Heirs of the Olmecs: Teotihuacan

While the Maya flourished in the Mesoamerican lowlands, a different society arose to the north in the highlands of Mexico. For most of human history, the valley of central Mexico, situated some two kilometers (more than a mile) above sea level, was the site of several large lakes fed by the waters coming off the surrounding mountains. Most of the lakes have disappeared during the past two or three centuries as a result of environmental changes and deliberate draining of

thinking about TRADITIONS

Agriculture and the Maya Way of Life

A productive agricultural economy was the foundation of Maya society. In many ways, Maya social and cultural traditions reflected the significance of agriculture to the Maya way of life. What roles did mathematics, astronomy, calendar making, religious beliefs, and even bloodletting rituals play in Maya agricultural society?

their waters. In earlier times, however, their abundant supplies of fish and waterfowl attracted human settlers. The lakes also served as sources of freshwater and as transportation routes linking communities situated on their shores.

The earliest settlers in the valley of Mexico did not build extensive irrigation systems, but they channeled some of the waters from the mountain streams into their fields and established a productive agricultural society. Expanding human population led to the congregation of people in cities and the emergence of a complex society in the Mesoamerican highlands. The earliest center of that society was the large and bustling city of Teotihuacan, located about 50 kilometers (31 miles) northeast of modern Mexico City.

A limestone altar carved in 796 C.E. depicts two Maya kings playing a ritual ball game to celebrate the negotiation of an agreement.

The City of Teotihuacan

Teotihuacan was probably a large agricultural village by 500 B.C.E. It expanded rapidly after about 200 B.C.E., and by the end of the millennium its population approached fifty thousand. By the year 100 C.E., the city's two most prominent monuments, the colossal pyramids of the sun and the moon, dominated the skyline. The Pyramid of the Sun is the largest single structure in Mesoamerica. It occupies nearly as much space as the pyramid of Khufu in Egypt, though it stands only half as tall. At its high point, about 400 to 600 C.E., Teotihuacan was home to almost two hundred thousand inhabitants, a thriving metropolis with scores of temples, several palatial residences, neighborhoods with small apartments for the masses, busy markets, and hundreds of workshops for artisans and craftsmen.

The organization of a large urban population, along with the hinterland that supported it, required a recognized source of authority. Although Teotihuacan generated large numbers of books and records that perhaps would have shed light on the character of that authority, they unfortunately perished when the city itself declined. Paintings and murals suggest that Teotihuacan was a theocracy of sorts. Priests figure prominently in the works of art, and scholars interpret many figures as representations of deities. Priests were crucial to the survival of the society, since they kept the calendar and ensured that planting and harvesting took

Aerial view of Teotihuacan, looking toward the Pyramid of the Moon (top center) from the Pyramid of the Sun (bottom left). Shops and residences occupied the spaces surrounding the main street and the pyramids.

place at the appropriate seasons. Thus it would not have been unusual for them to govern Teotihuacan in the name of the gods, or at least to cooperate closely with a secular ruling class.

The Society of Teotihuacan Apart from rulers and priests, Teotihuacan's population included cultivators, artisans, and merchants. Perhaps as many as two-thirds of the city's inhabitants worked during the day in fields surrounding Teotihuacan and returned to their small apartments in the city at night. Artisans of Teotihuacan were especially famous for their obsidian tools and fine orange pottery, and scholars have identified numerous workshops and stores where toolmakers and potters produced and marketed their goods within the city itself. The residents of Teotihuacan also participated in extensive trade and exchange networks. Professional merchants traded their products throughout Mesoamerica. Archaeologists have found numerous samples of the distinctive obsidian tools and orange pottery at sites far distant from Teotihuacan, from the region of modern Guatemala City in the south to Durango and beyond in the north.

Until about 500 C.E. there was little sign of military organization in Teotihuacan. The city did not have defensive walls, and works of art rarely depicted warriors. Yet the influence of Teotihuacan extended to much of modern Mexico and beyond. The Maya capital of Kaminaljuyú, for example, fell under the influence of Teotihuacan during the fourth century C.E. Although the rulers of Teotihuacan may have established colonies to protect their sources of obsidian and may have undertaken military expeditions to back up their authority throughout central Mexico, the city's influence apparently derived less from military might than from its ability to produce fine manufactured goods that appealed to consumers in distant markets.

Cultural Traditions Like the Maya, the residents of Teotihuacan built on cultural foundations established by the Olmecs. They played the ball game, adapted the Olmec calendar to their own uses, and expanded the Olmecs' graphic symbols into a complete system of writing. Unfortunately, only a few samples of their writing survive in stone carvings. Because their books have all perished, it is impossible to know exactly how they viewed the world and their place in it. Works of art suggest that they recognized an earth god and a rain god, and it is certain that they carried out human sacrifices during their religious rituals.

Decline of Teotihuacan Teotihuacan began to experience increasing military pressure from other peoples around 500 C.E. Works of art from this period frequently depicted eagles, jaguars, and coyotes—animals that Mesoamericans associated with fighting and military conquest. After about 650 C.E. Teotihuacan entered a period of decline. About the middle of the eighth century, invaders sacked and burned the city, destroying its books and monuments. After that catastrophe most residents deserted Teotihuacan, and the city slowly fell into ruin.

EARLY SOCIETIES OF SOUTH AMERICA

By about 12,000 B.C.E., hunting and gathering peoples had made their way across the narrow isthmus of Central America and into South America. Those who migrated into the region of the northern and central Andes mountains hunted deer, llama, alpaca, and other large animals. Both the mountainous highlands and the coastal regions below benefited from a cool and moist climate that provided natural harvests of squashes, gourds, and wild potatoes. Beginning about 8000 B.C.E., however, the climate of this whole region became increasingly warm and dry, and the changes placed pressure on natural food supplies. To maintain their numbers, the human communities of the region began to experiment with agriculture. Here, as elsewhere, agriculture encouraged population growth, the establishment of villages and cities, the building of states, and the elaboration of organized cultural traditions. During the centuries after 1000 B.C.E., the central Andean region generated complex societies parallel to those of Mesoamerica.

"The most important of these sacrifices involved the shedding of human blood, which the Maya believed would prompt the gods to send rain to water their crops of maize."

Early Andean Society and the Chavín Cult

Although they were exact contemporaries, early Mesoamerican and Andean societies developed largely independently. The heartland of early Andean society was the region now occupied by the states of Peru and Bolivia. Geography discouraged the establishment of communications between the Andean region and Mesoamerica. Neither the Andes mountains nor the lowlands of modern Panama and Nicaragua offered an attractive highway linking the two regions. Several agricultural products and technologies diffused slowly from one area to the other: cultivation of maize and squashes spread from its Mesoamerican home to the central Andean region while Andean gold, silver, and copper metallurgy traveled north to Mesoamerica.

Geography conspired even against the establishment of communications within the central Andean region. Deep

MAP 6.2
Early societies of Andean South America, 1000 B.C.E.–700 C.E.
The early societies of Andean South America occupied long, narrow territories between the Andes Mountains and the Pacific Ocean.

Why did these societies not occupy territories to the east?

valleys crease the western flank of the Andes mountains, as rivers drain waters from the highlands to the Pacific Ocean, so transportation and communication between the valleys has always been difficult. Nevertheless, powerful Andean states sometimes overcame the difficulties and influenced human affairs as far away as modern Ecuador and Colombia to the north and northern Chile to the south.

Early Agriculture in South America Most of the early Andean heartland came under cultivation between 2500 and 2000 B.C.E., and permanent settlements dotted the coastal regions in particular. The earliest cultivators of the region relied on beans, peanuts, and sweet potatoes as their main food crops. Their most important domesticated animals were camel-like llamas and alpacas, which provided them with both meat and wool, and which also served as pack animals in some areas of the Andean highlands. They also cultivated cotton, which they used to make fishnets and textiles. The rich marine life of the Pacific Ocean supplemented agricultural harvests, enabling coastal peoples to build an increasingly complex society. Settlements probably appeared later in the Andean highlands than in the coastal regions, but many varieties of potato supported agricultural communities in the highlands after about 2000 B.C.E. By 1800 B.C.E. Andean peoples were constructing canals and irrigation systems to support cultivation on the dry lands at the mouths of the western Andean valleys. They also had begun to fashion distinctive styles of pottery and to build temples and pyramids in large ceremonial centers.

The Chavín Cult Shortly after the year 1000 B.C.E., a new religion appeared suddenly in the central Andes. The Chavín cult, which enjoyed enormous popularity during the period 900 to 800 B.C.E., spread through most of the territory occupied by modern Peru and then vanished about 300 B.C.E. Unfortunately, no information survives to indicate the precise significance of the cult, nor even its proper name: scholars have named it after the modern town of Chavín de Huántar, one of the cult's most prominent sites. One theory suggests that the cult arose when maize became an important crop in South America. The capacity of maize to support large populations might well have served as the stimulus for the emergence of a cult designed to promote fertility and abundant harvests. In any case, the large temple complexes and elaborate works of art that accompanied the cult demonstrate its importance to those who honored it. Devotees produced intricate stone carvings representing their deities with the features of humans and wild animals such as jaguars, hawks, eagles, and snakes. The extensive distribution of the temples and carvings shows that the Chavín cult seized the imagination of agricultural peoples throughout the central Andean region.

During the era of the Chavín cult, Andean society became increasingly complex. Weavers produced elaborate and intricately designed textiles of both cotton and wool (from llamas and alpacas) using looms that they braced with straps around their backs. Artisans manufactured large, light, and strong fishnets from cotton string. Craftsmen experimented with minerals and discovered techniques of gold, silver, and copper metallurgy. They mostly fashioned metals into pieces of jewelry or other decorative items but also made small tools out of copper.

Early Cities There is no evidence to suggest that Chavín cultural and religious beliefs led to the establishment of a state or any organized political order. Indeed, they probably inspired the building of ceremonial centers rather than the making of true cities. As the population increased and society became more complex, however, cities began to appear shortly after the disappearance of the Chavín cult. Beginning about 200 B.C.E. large cities emerged at the modern-day sites of Huari, Pucara, and Tiahuanaco. Each of these early Andean cities had a population exceeding ten thousand, and each also featured large public buildings, ceremonial plazas, and extensive residential districts.

Many Mochica pots portray human figures and often depict distinctive characteristics of individuals or typical scenes from daily life. This pot represents two women helping a man who consumed a little too much maize beer.

Early Andean States: Mochica

Political and Economic Integration of the Andean Valleys Along with cities there appeared regional states. The earliest Andean states arose in the many valleys on the western side of the mountains. These states emerged when conquerors unified the individual valleys and organized them into integrated societies. They coordinated the building of irrigation systems so that the lower valleys could support intensive agriculture, and they established trade and exchange networks that tied the highlands, the central valleys, and the coastal regions together. Each region contributed products to the larger economy of the valley: from the highlands came potatoes, llama meat, and alpaca wool; the central valleys supplied maize, beans, and squashes; and the coasts provided sweet potatoes, fish, and cotton.

This organization of the Andean valleys into integrated economic zones did not come about by accident. Builders of early Andean states worked deliberately and did not hesitate to use force to consolidate their domains. Surviving stone fortifications and warriors depicted in works of art testify that the early Andean states relied heavily on arms to introduce order and maintain stability in their small realms.

The Mochica State Because early Andean societies did not make use of writing, their beliefs, values, and ways of life remain largely unknown. One of the early Andean states, however, left a remarkable artistic legacy that allows a glimpse into the life of a society otherwise almost entirely lost. The Mochica state had its base in the valley of the Moche River, and it dominated the coasts and valleys of northern Peru during the period about 300 to 700 C.E. Mochica painting survives largely on pottery vessels, and it offers a detailed and expressive depiction of early Andean society in all its variety.

Many Mochica ceramics take the form of portraits of individuals' heads. Others represent the major gods and the various subordinate deities and demons. Some of the most interesting depict scenes in the everyday life of the Mochica people: aristocrats embarking on a hunting party, warriors leading captives bound by ropes, women working in a textile factory under the careful eye of a supervisor, rulers receiving messengers or ambassadors from neighboring states, and beggars looking for handouts on a busy street. Even in the absence of writing, Mochica artists left abundant evidence of a complex society with considerable specialization of labor.

Mochica was only one of several large states that dominated the central Andean region during the first millennium C.E. Although they integrated the regional economies of the various Andean valleys, none of those early states was able to impose order on the entire region or even to dominate a portion of it for very long. The exceedingly difficult geographic barriers posed by the Andes mountains presented challenges that ancient technology and social organization simply could not meet. In addition, during the sixth and seventh centuries C.E., climatic fluctuations brought a long series of severe droughts to the Andean region. As a result, by the end of the first millennium C.E., Mochica and several other Andean societies had disappeared, and Andean society exhibited regional differences much sharper than those of Mesoamerica and early complex societies in the eastern hemisphere.

EARLY SOCIETIES OF OCEANIA

Human migrants entered Australia and New Guinea at least by 60,000 years before the present, and possibly earlier than that. They arrived in watercraft—probably rafts, or perhaps canoes fitted with sails—but because of the low sea levels of that era, the migrants did not have to cross large stretches of open ocean. Those earliest inhabitants of Oceania also migrated—perhaps over land when sea levels were still low—to the Bismarcks, the Solomons, and other small island groups near New Guinea. Beginning about 5,000 years ago, seafaring peoples from southeast Asia visited the northern coast of New Guinea for purposes of trade. Some of them settled there, but many others ventured farther and established communities in the island groups of the western Pacific Ocean. During the centuries that followed, their descendants sailed large, oceangoing canoes throughout the Pacific basin, and by the middle centuries of the first millennium C.E., they had established human communities in all the habitable islands of the Pacific Ocean.

Early Societies in Australia and New Guinea

Human migrants reached Australia and New Guinea long before any people had begun to cultivate crops or keep herds of domesticated animals. Inevitably, then, the earliest inhabitants of Australia and New Guinea lived by hunting and gathering their food. For thousands of years, foraging peoples probably traveled back and forth between Australia and New Guinea. Those migrations ceased about ten thousand years ago when rising seas separated the two lands. After that time, human societies in Australia and New Guinea followed radically different paths. The aboriginal peoples of Australia maintained hunting and gathering societies until large numbers of Europeans established settler communities there in the nineteenth and twentieth centuries C.E. New Guinea peoples, however, turned to agriculture: beginning about 3000 B.C.E. the cultivation of root crops such as yams and taro and the keeping of pigs and chickens spread rapidly throughout the island.

Early Hunting and Gathering Societies in Australia Like hunting and gathering peoples elsewhere, the aboriginal Australians lived in small, mobile communities that undertook seasonal migrations in search of food. Over the centuries, they learned to exploit the resources of the various ecological regions of Australia. Plant foods, including fruits, berries, roots, nuts, seeds, shoots, and green leaves, constituted the bulk of their diet. In the tropical region of Cape York in northern Australia, they consumed no fewer than 141 species of plants. Aboriginal peoples found abundant plant life even in the harsh desert regions of interior Australia. In the vicinity of modern Alice Springs in central Australia, for example, they included about 20 species of greens and 45 kinds of seeds and nuts in their diet. They also used at least 124 plants as medicines, ointments, and drugs. To supplement their plant-based diet, they used axes, spears, clubs, nets, lassos, snares, and boomerangs to bring down animals ranging in size from rats to giant kangaroos, which grew to a height of 3 meters (almost 10 feet), and to catch fish, waterfowl, and small birds.

Austronesian Peoples The earliest inhabitants of New Guinea foraged for food, like their neighbors to the south. About five thousand years ago, however, a process of social and economic change began to unfold in New Guinea. The agents of change were seafaring peoples from southeast Asia speaking Austronesian languages, whose modern linguistic relatives include Malayan, Indonesian, Filipino, Polynesian, and other Oceanic languages as well as the Malagasy language of Madagascar and the tongues spoken by the indigenous peoples of Taiwan and southern China. Austronesian-speaking peoples possessed remarkable seafaring skills. They sailed the open ocean in large canoes equipped with outriggers, which stabilized their craft and

Windjana figures (cloud and rain spirits) loom from a rock painting produced about twelve thousand years ago by inhabitants of the Chamberlain Gorge region in western Australia.

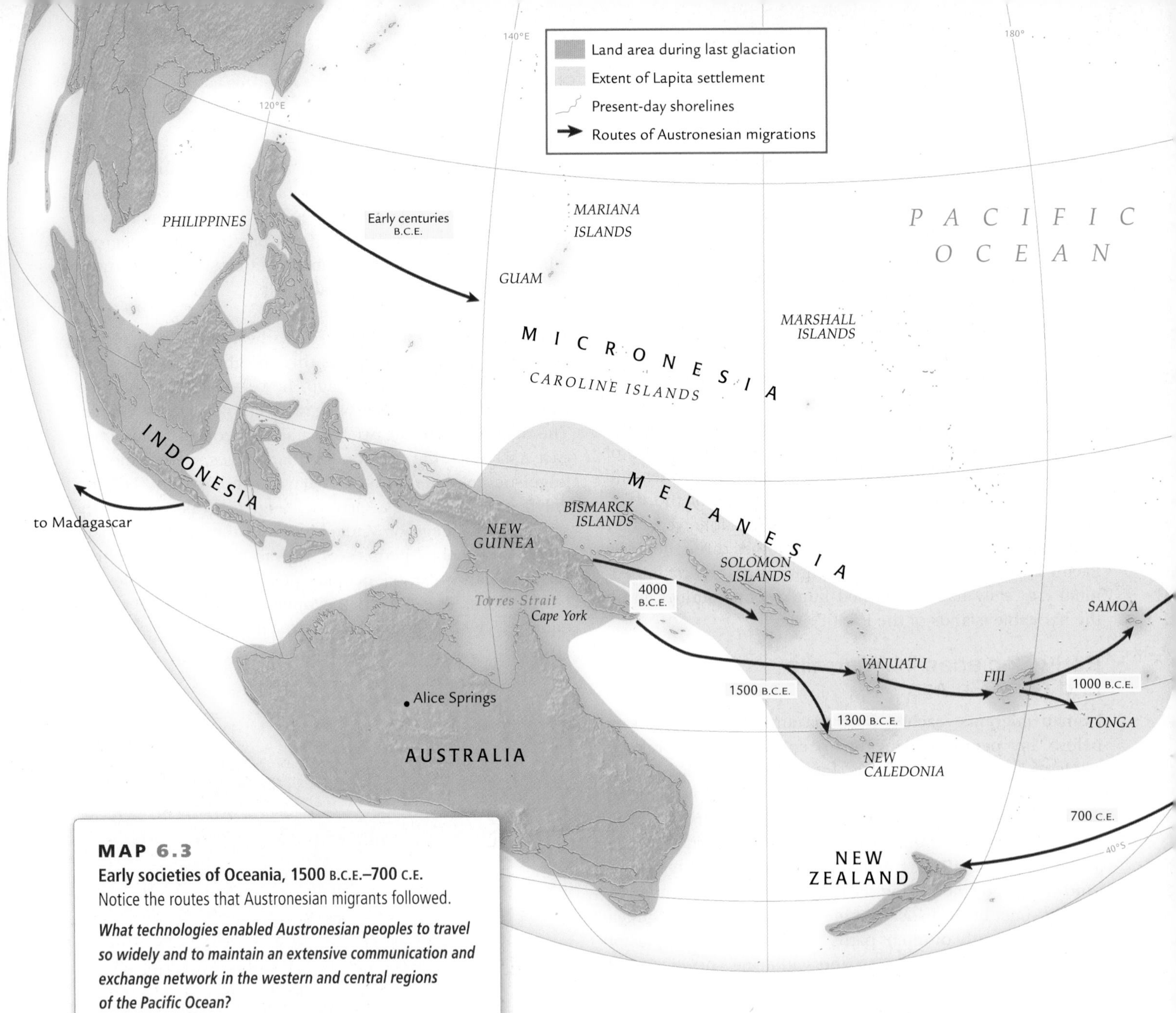

MAP 6.3
Early societies of Oceania, 1500 B.C.E.–700 C.E.
Notice the routes that Austronesian migrants followed.

What technologies enabled Austronesian peoples to travel so widely and to maintain an extensive communication and exchange network in the western and central regions of the Pacific Ocean?

reduced the risks of long voyages. By paying close attention to winds, currents, stars, cloud formations, and other natural indicators, they learned how to find distant lands reliably and return home safely. Beginning about 3000 B.C.E. these mariners visited the northern coast of New Guinea, where they traded with the indigenous peoples and established their own communities.

Early Agriculture in New Guinea Austronesian seafarers came from societies that depended on the cultivation of root crops and the herding of animals. When they settled in New Guinea, they introduced yams, taro, pigs, and chickens to the island, and the indigenous peoples themselves soon began to cultivate crops and keep animals. Within a few centuries agriculture and herding had spread to all parts of New Guinea. Here, as in other lands, agriculture brought population growth and specialization of labor: after the change to agriculture, permanent settlements, pottery, and carefully crafted tools appeared throughout the island.

Separated from New Guinea only by the narrow Torres Strait, the aboriginal peoples of northern Australia knew about the cultivation of foodstuffs, since they had occasional dealings with traders from New Guinea. Agriculture even spread to the islands of the Torres Strait, but it did not take root in Australia until the arrival of European peoples in the late eighteenth century C.E. Meanwhile, Austronesian-speaking peoples who introduced agriculture and herding to New Guinea sailed their outrigger canoes farther and established the first human settlements in the islands of the Pacific Ocean.

The Peopling of the Pacific Islands

The hunting and gathering peoples who first inhabited Australia and New Guinea also established a few settlements

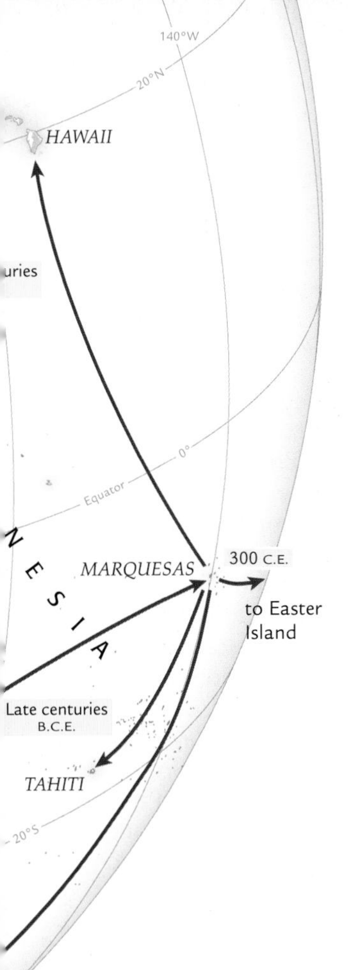

Austronesian mariners sailed double-hulled voyaging canoes much like those from Ra`iatea in the Society Islands, drawn in 1769 by an artist who accompanied Captain James Cook on his first voyage in the Pacific Ocean. How might the hulls, the sails, the deck, and other features of the canoe depicted here have facilitated travel and migration over the open ocean?

in the Bismarck and Solomon island groups east of New Guinea. They ventured to those islands during the era when the seas were low and sailing distances from New Guinea were consequently very short. They did not have the maritime technology, however, to sail far beyond the Solomons to the more distant islands in the Pacific Ocean. Even if they had, the small Pacific islands, with limited supplies of edible plants and animals, would not have supported communities of foragers.

Austronesian Migrations to Polynesia Austronesian-speaking peoples possessed a sophisticated maritime technology as well as agricultural expertise, and they established settlements in the islands of the Pacific Ocean. They sailed large, oceangoing canoes with twin hulls joined by a deck on which they carried supplies. When they found uninhabited lands, their food crops and domesticated animals enabled them to establish agricultural societies in the islands. Once they had established coastal settlements in New Guinea, Austronesian seafarers sailed easily to the Bismarck and Solomon islands, perhaps in the interests of trade. From there they undertook exploratory voyages that led them to previously unpopulated islands.

This reconstructed Lapita pot discovered in New Caledonia features the distinctive stamped design characteristic of all Lapita pottery.

By about 1500 B.C.E. Austronesian mariners had arrived at Vanuatu (formerly called New Hebrides) and New Caledonia, by 1300 B.C.E. at Fiji, and by 1000 B.C.E. at Tonga and Samoa. During the late centuries of the first millennium B.C.E., they established settlements in Tahiti and the Marquesas. From there they launched ventures that took them to the most remote outposts of Polynesia—the territory falling in the triangle with Hawai`i, Easter Island, and New Zealand at the points—which required them to sail over thousands of nautical miles of blue water. They reached the islands of Hawai`i in the early centuries C.E., Easter Island by 300 C.E., and the large islands of New Zealand by 700 C.E.

Austronesian Migrations to Micronesia and Madagascar While one branch of the Austronesian-speaking peoples populated the islands of Polynesia, other branches sailed in different directions. From the Philippines some ventured to the region of Micronesia, which includes small islands and atolls such as the Mariana, Caroline, and

sources from the past

The Voyage of Ru

Numerous chants and stories of Pacific islanders preserve the memory of ancient seafarers who built oceangoing canoes, equipped them with supplies, and sailed off in search of new lands. Many of the mariners mentioned in those stories set out from Havai`i (modern-day Ra`iatea near Tahiti). The stories mention several motives for the voyages: overpopulation, social tensions, and thirst for adventure. The following selection explains how the navigator Ru undertook a voyage from Havai`i to the previously uninhabited island of Aitutaki in the Southern Cook Islands.

Although not of royal blood, Ru was a man of good standing. He was a peace-loving man, but ambitious of becoming a leader, and [he] viewed with concern the quickly-increasing population of the island.

Moved by a quarrel over the headship of his clan, Ru began to make plans. He decided to build a large seaworthy canoe and call together his friends and relations, and try to persuade enough of them to join him in searching for an uninhabited island somewhere toward the setting sun, where he felt sure he would find land and become a great chief. [He persuaded his four younger brothers, his four wives, and twenty young women from the ruling family of Havai`i to accompany him] . . .

A search was then made for two large *tamanu* trees suitable for a canoe for the voyage. The making of this canoe was a lengthy process, for the trees had to be felled and hewn out with stone adzes. When finished to Ru's satisfaction, the two hulls were hauled down to the beach and lashed together. . . . Some further days were spent training for the coming voyage. The canoe and the mat-sails were tested, and much time was spent handling and paddling the canoe until the crew were proficient. For two days friends and relatives assisted in gathering enough food for the voyage. *Taro, puraka* [pig], *kuru* [breadfruit], and a large supply of water were put on board. All record of how the water was carried has been lost. Some say it was carried in coconuts.

The next morning, the wind being favorable, Ru decided to set sail. The whole island came to say farewell to the twenty-nine voyagers. The reef was cleared, the sails were hoisted, and the canoe was headed toward the west, Ru taking the steering oar, and his brother Verituamaroa standing in the bows as pilot. Though conditions were favorable for the first two days, the women were sick as soon as the canoe was out of sight of the land. On the third day heavy clouds banked up, the wind, which had changed round, now blew strongly from the west, and the sea was so rough that the women and men had to take turns bailing the canoe; she was riding heavily owing to the hulls being new and deeply laden. [The voyaging party survived the storm] . . .

Favorable weather was met for the next two days and each night Ru checked his course by a star. On the third afternoon after the storm, Verituamaroa, who was still in the bows of the canoe, cried out that he could see land ahead. It was thought that he might have been deceived by a bank of clouds, but soon they could clearly see the break of waves on the reef. All now gazed eagerly at the new land. After a search a suitable passage was found [through the reef], the sails were taken down, and the women were ordered to paddle the canoe in. . . .

Finding the island uninhabited, Ru divided it among the twenty young women, as they were of royal blood and consequently had first claim to the land. Ru told them that they were as mats on the floor, as other canoes were bound to come sooner or later bringing men with them. On these mats the men would sleep, and from them this new land would be populated.

For Further Reflection

- What does Ru's story suggest about the nature of social and gender relations in early Pacific islands populations?

Source: Drury Low. "The Story of Ru's Canoe and the Discovery and Settlement of Aitutaki." *Journal of the Polynesian Society* 43 (1934): 17–24.

Marshall islands of the western Pacific. Yet others looked west from their homelands in Indonesia, sailed throughout the Indian Ocean, and became the first human settlers of the large island of Madagascar off the east African coast. Malagasy, the principal language of modern-day Madagascar, is clearly identifiable as an Austronesian tongue.

The Lapita Peoples The earliest Austronesian migrants to sail out into the Pacific Ocean and establish settlements in Pacific islands are known as the Lapita peoples. No one knows what they called themselves: the name *Lapita* comes from a beach in New Caledonia where some of the earliest recognizable Lapita artifacts came to the attention of

thinking about ENCOUNTERS

Human Migration to the Pacific Islands
The establishment of human communities in the Pacific islands was the last phase of the long process by which *Homo sapiens* populated the habitable regions of the earth. In all likelihood, the islands of New Zealand were the last sizable lands that human beings reached. What combinations of technology and supplies were necessary for Austronesian mariners to sail to the remote Pacific islands?

archaeologists. It is clear, however, that between about 1500 and 500 B.C.E., Lapita peoples maintained communication and exchange networks throughout a large region extending about 4,500 kilometers (2,800 miles) from New Guinea and the Bismarck Archipelago to Samoa and Tonga.

Wherever they settled, Lapita peoples established agricultural villages where they raised pigs and chickens and introduced the suite of crops they inherited from their Austronesian ancestors, including yams, taro, breadfruit, and bananas. They supplemented their crops and domesticated animals with fish and seaweed from nearby waters, and they soon killed off most of the large land animals and birds (some of which, in the absence of natural predators, had evolved into flightless species) that were suitable for human consumption. They left abundant evidence of their presence in the form of their distinctive pottery decorated with stamped geometric designs.

For about one thousand years, Lapita peoples maintained extensive networks of trade and communication across vast stretches of open ocean. Their agricultural settlements were largely self-sufficient, but they placed high value on some objects from distant islands. Their pottery was a principal item of long-distance exchange, as was high-quality obsidian, which they sometimes transported over thousands of kilometers, since it was available at only a few sites of Lapita settlement. Other trade items brought to light by archaeologists include shell jewelry and stone tools. It is likely that Lapita peoples also traded feathers, foodstuffs, and spouses, although evidence for those exchanges does not survive in the archaeological record. In any case, it is clear that like their counterparts in other regions of the world, the earliest inhabitants of the Pacific islands maintained regular contacts with peoples well beyond their societies.

Chiefly Political Organization After about 500 B.C.E. Lapita trade networks fell into disuse, probably because the various Lapita settlements had grown large enough that they could supply their own needs and concentrate on the development of their own societies. By the middle part of the first millennium B.C.E., Lapita and other Austronesian peoples had established hierarchical chiefdoms in the Pacific islands. Leadership passed from a chief to his eldest son, and near relatives constituted a local aristocracy. Contests for power and influence between ambitious subordinates frequently caused tension and turmoil, but the possibility of migration offered an alternative to conflict. Dissatisfied or aggrieved parties often built voyaging canoes, recruited followers, and set sail with the intention of establishing new settlements in uninhabited or lightly populated islands. Indeed, the spread of Austronesian peoples throughout the Pacific islands came about partly because of population pressures and conflicts that encouraged small parties to seek fresh opportunities in more hospitable lands.

Over the longer term, descendants of Lapita peoples built strong, chiefly societies, particularly on large islands with relatively dense populations like those of the Tongan, Samoan, and Hawaiian groups. In Hawai`i, for example, militarily skilled chiefs cooperated closely with priests, administrators, soldiers, and servants in ruling their districts, which might include a portion of an island, an entire island, or even several islands. Chiefs and their retinues claimed a portion of the agricultural surplus produced by their subjects, and they sometimes required subjects to deliver additional products, such as fish, birds, or timber. Apart from organizing public life in their own districts, chiefs and their administrators vied with the ruling classes of neighboring districts, led public ritual observances, and oversaw irrigation systems that watered the taro plants that were crucial to the survival of Hawaiian society. Eventually, the chiefly and aristocratic classes became so entrenched and powerful that they regarded themselves as divine or semidivine, and the law of the land prohibited common subjects from even gazing directly at them.

inperspective

Little writing survives to illuminate the historical development of early societies in the Americas and Oceania. Thus it is impossible to offer the sort of richly detailed account of their political organization, social structures, and cultural traditions that historians commonly provide for societies of the eastern hemisphere. Nevertheless, it is clear that migrations to the Americas and Oceania represented continuations of population movements that began with *Homo erectus* and early *Homo sapiens,* resulting eventually in the establishment of human communities in all habitable parts of the earth. Moreover, it is clear that the earliest inhabitants of the Americas and Oceania built productive and vibrant societies whose development roughly paralleled that of their counterparts in the eastern hemisphere. Many communities depended on an agricultural economy, and with their surplus production they supported dense populations, engaged in specialized labor, established formal political authorities, constructed hierarchical social orders, carried on long-distance trade, and formed distinctive cultural traditions. The early historical development of the Americas and Oceania demonstrates once again the tendency of agriculture to encourage human communities to construct ever more elaborate and complex forms of social organization. ●

CHRONOLOGY

AMERICAS	
13,000 B.C.E.	Human migration to North America from Siberia
8000–7000 B.C.E.	Origins of agriculture in Mesoamerica
4000 B.C.E.	Origins of maize cultivation in Mesoamerica
3000 B.C.E.	Origins of agriculture in South America
1200–100 B.C.E.	Olmec society
1000–300 B.C.E.	Chavín cult
200 B.C.E.–750 C.E.	Teotihuacan society
300–1100 C.E.	Maya society
300–700 C.E.	Mochica society
OCEANIA	
60,000 B.C.E.	Human migration to Australia and New Guinea
3000 B.C.E.	Origins of agriculture in New Guinea
3000 B.C.E.	Austronesian migrations to New Guinea
1500–500 B.C.E.	Lapita society
1500 B.C.E.–700 C.E.	Austronesian migrations to Pacific islands

Assessing AP Themes

1. How and why did early humans migrate from their places of origin? Consider what historians call the push-pull factors.
2. Compare the economies and social structures of the hunting and gathering peoples with the urban-based societies.
3. How did technological developments help humans to adapt to different environments and regions? Consider both forager societies as well as urban-based societies in this era.
4. What are the general characteristics of urban-based societies? Why is each characteristic necessary?
5. Compare the political, social, and religious structures/institutions of the early river civilizations.
6. What circumstances contributed to peaceful or to conflict-ridden relations between pastoralists and urban-based societies?

For Further Reading

Peter Bellwood. *The Polynesians: Prehistory of an Island People.* Rev. ed. London, 1987. Well-illustrated popular account emphasizing the origins and early development of Polynesian societies.

Geoffrey Blainey. *Triumph of the Nomads: A History of Aboriginal Australia.* Melbourne, 1975. A sympathetic account of Australia before European arrival, well informed by archaeological discoveries.

Michael D. Coe. *The Maya.* 4th ed. London, 1987. Well-illustrated popular account by one of the world's leading scholars of the Maya.

———. *The Olmec World: Ritual and Rulership.* Princeton, 1996. Presents essays on the Olmecs along with lavish illustrations of their art.

Richard A. Diehl. *The Olmecs: America's First Civilization.* London, 2004. The best brief introduction to Olmec society.

David Freidel, Linda Schele, and Joy Parker. *Maya Cosmos: Three Thousand Years on the Shaman's Path.* New York, 1993. Fascinating investigation of Maya conceptions of the world and their continuing influence in the present day.

K. R. Howe. *The Quest for Origins: Who First Discovered and Settled the Pacific Islands?* Honolulu, 2003. Reviews the numerous theories advanced to explain the arrival of human populations and the establishment of human societies in the remote islands of the Pacific Ocean.

Patrick V. Kirch. *The Lapita Peoples: Ancestors of the Oceanic World.* Cambridge, Mass., 1997. Thorough discussion of Lapita society drawing heavily on the author's own research.

———. *On the Road of the Winds: An Archaeological History of the Pacific Islands before European Contact.* Berkeley, 2000. A valuable synthesis of scholarship by the foremost contemporary archaeologist of the Pacific islands.

David Lewis. *We, the Navigators: The Ancient Art of Landfinding in the Pacific.* Honolulu, 1973. Fascinating reconstruction of traditional methods of noninstrumental navigation used by seafaring peoples of the Pacific islands.

Charles C. Mann. *1491: New Revelations of the Americas before Columbus.* New York, 2006. Summarizes a great deal of archaeological research on the pre-Columbian Americas.

Simon Martin and Nikolai Grube. *Chronicle of the Maya Kings and Queens: Deciphering the Dynasties of the Ancient Maya.* London, 2000. Offers an important synthesis of Maya political history on the basis of both inscriptions and archaeological discoveries.

Michael E. Mosley. *The Incas and Their Ancestors: The Archaeology of Peru.* Rev. ed. London, 2001. A comprehensive survey of Andean history through the era of the Incas.

Linda Schele and David Freidel. *A Forest of Kings: The Untold Story of the Ancient Maya.* New York, 1990. Draws heavily on deciphered inscriptions in reconstructing the history of the ancient Maya.

Linda Schele and Mary Ellen Miller. *The Blood of Kings: Dynasty and Ritual in Maya Art.* New York, 1986. A richly illustrated volume that explores Maya society through works of art and architecture as well as writing.

Dennis Tedlock, trans. *Popol Vuh: The Definitive Edition of the Mayan Book of the Dawn of Life and the Glories of Gods and Kings.* New York, 1985. The best translation of the *Popol Vuh,* with an excellent introduction.

David Webster. *The Fall of the Ancient Maya: Solving the Mystery of the Maya Collapse.* London, 2002. A careful and readable analysis of the difficulties that confronted Maya society.

State of the World

A World with Crops and Herds, Cities and States, Writing and Religion

High intelligence and sophisticated language enabled *Homo sapiens* to establish communities throughout the world. *Homo sapiens* made adjustments that were necessary to survive and flourish in almost every terrestrial environment: mountain, valley, coastline, grassland, desert, rain forest, tundra, and more. Everywhere they went, human beings found ways to exploit locally available resources and use them in the interests of their communities. By about fifteen thousand years ago, *Homo sapiens* already ranked as a highly successful competitor among the species inhabiting the earth.

Yet the paleolithic era was only the beginning of human prominence in the world. After the adoption of agriculture, human beings dramatically increased their presence and influence in the world. They progressively claimed lands and devoted them to the cultivation of plants and the maintenance of domesticated animals. They made many plant and animal species dependent upon human masters, and they exploited those species for purposes of satisfying human needs and making human life more agreeable.

The implications of agriculture were enormous. With abundant supplies of food available to them, human populations surged, and the size of human communities grew to proportions that would have been inconceivable to paleolithic foragers. Villages dotted the landscapes of early agricultural societies, and towns emerged at strategic sites where trading was convenient or valuable resources were readily available. In regions of high agricultural production and large populations, cities served as nerve centers guiding political, economic, and cultural affairs both within their own limits and in neighboring territories. These cities were the first sites of experimentation in the art of organizing large numbers of people living together in densely populated spaces. The implications of agriculture extended further to the organization of sizable regions under the supervision of formal states. Only with surplus foods produced by cultivators were states able to provide for the rulers, armies, administrators, and other specialists who were essential to their survival.

Food surpluses also made it possible for agricultural societies to support intellectual specialists. The invention of writing magnified human intelligence by enabling the precise communication of information, ideas, and reflections. By 500 B.C.E. scribes and scholars in several world regions had generated libraries of written works and used writing to expand intellectual boundaries by engaging in speculation about the nature of reality, the meaning of life, and the relationship between human beings and the various gods recognized in their different societies.

The invention of agriculture ranks alongside the mastery of fire and the process of industrialization as one of the most important turning points in human history. Within a few thousand years, agriculture transformed a world in which small, foraging bands of *Homo sapiens* competed directly with other animal species into a world in which human groups claimed ever larger shares of the earth's resources for their own use.

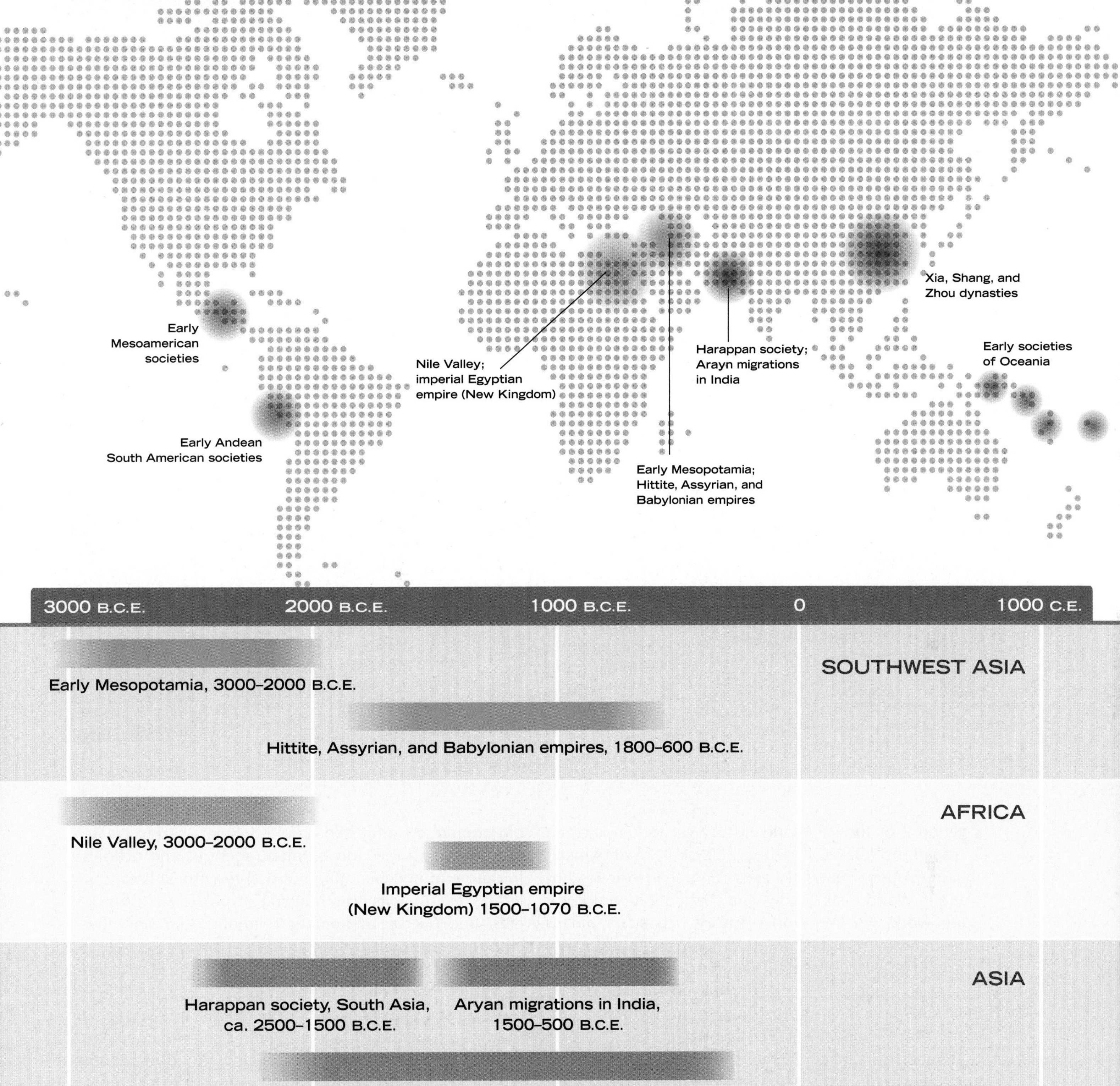

SOUTH AMERICA

Early Mesoamerican societies, 1200 B.C.E.–1100 C.E.

Early Andean South American societies, 1000 B.C.E.–700 C.E.

OCEANIA

Early societies of Oceania, ca. 1500 B.C.E.–700 C.E.

part 2

THE FORMATION OF CLASSICAL SOCIETIES, 500 B.C.E. TO 500 C.E.

Period 2 of the AP World History curriculum is often called the "Classical" period. "Classical" used to mean the Greco-Roman roots of western European societies, but we're in World History now, and that definition doesn't quite work. For AP World History, "classical" means something that has become traditional and has staying-power: it is really old but still hangs around today and still influences people in important ways. Starting around 500 B.C.E., humans came up with sophisticated governments, interregional trade networks, social structures that made some people more important that others, and belief systems that still exist today. By c. 500 C.E., the world's first empires had all collapsed, thus ending the so-called "Classical" period. Surprisingly, many of the structures and beliefs of our modern world were created in the thousand years between c. 500 B.C.E. and c. 500 C.E.

In Period 2 of the AP curriculum, one of the three significant themes you will investigate concerns the similarities, differences, and uniquenesses of the imperial governments of Persia, China, India, Greece and Rome, Mesoamerica and the Andean region of South America. Each of these empires grew by taking over competing states. Rulers then had to figure out how to govern, protect the borders, and exploit huge amounts of land and big populations they had acquired. Rulers had to create huge bureaucracies (government agencies and officials in charge of implementing policies) to enforce laws, collect taxes, supervise the building of public works' projects, and oversee diplomatic relations. And since the empires were built by conquest, there had to be large and well-organized militaries to either conquer or maintain the borders and peace within those borders. Since the easiest way to move an army around was on paved roads, each of these classical empires spent money and manpower on building and maintaining road networks. For navies water routes were key, and port cities had to be maintained.

Conquest was one way to get to know another culture, but so was trade. The second major theme of Period 2 is the emergence of trade and communications networks with peoples in other regions (transregional networks). You will need to know where and why certain trade routes existed, who traveled along them, and with whom these traders did business. Pay particular attention when nomadic/pastoralist people are mentioned. They often functioned as the "truckers" of the trade routes, and were important links in commercial networks. They occasionally invaded the empires as well.

These routes were land-based and water-based. Deserts, oceans, and rivers are not barriers but gates if one has the appropriate technology. Watch for the innovative technologies that were used and spread along the trade routes. Watch also for unintended consequences of movement along the trade routes. Diseases hitchhiked with the travelers and their goods, and wreaked havoc periodically. HTS 4 Epidemics, or even pandemics,

broke out in most of the major empires in the later years of this period, and contributed to the destruction of the Han, Roman, and Gupta empires. HTS 3 This is the Period when we see the beginnings of "globalization" for good and bad.

People moved more than merchandise and diseases along the trade routes. HTS 2 Ideas traveled as well, and in this period and the next, you will need to watch carefully for the spread of religious traditions out of their home regions and into new areas. In the Foundations era, we saw people develop religions and belief systems to explain the natural world around them—animism, shamanism, polytheism, ancestor worship (veneration), and the early phases of what become Hinduism and Judaism. The third major theme of Period 2 is the development and codification (organization, writing down or solidifying rules) of religious and cultural traditions. Judaism and Hinduism continued to mature and by the end of this period, believers had common sets of practices, scriptures, and beliefs. HTS 2 Along with older belief systems, new belief systems emerged in Period 2 and remain significant until today—Buddhism, Confucianism, Daoism, and Christianity. These old and new belief systems helped people make sense of the natural world and often provided universal answers to human questions about how to behave personally, one's responsibilities to other people, and what happens when people die.

Each of the classical societies or civilizations developed distinct, unique cultural traditions. A society's art, architecture, drama, and sculpture tell historians a lot about a people's values, beliefs, interests, and technological abilities. HTS 4 These cultural "documents" sometimes show us the human side of a long-dead society—its sense of humor, for example, or what standards of beauty might have been. These cultural documents also provide examples when historians look for evidence of one society learning and adopting information or styles from another society. We can see merchants bringing their religious ideas to new places along their trade routes, and then the local people combining their old beliefs into the new ones, in a process called syncretism (blending). Historians have found evidence of this syncretism in buildings and artwork as well as written works.

What really interests historians is what happens when two or three themes such as trade routes, religion, and codification of cultural and political institutions are put in motion simultaneously. In Period 2, we see evidence that rulers claimed to be gods or blessed (mandated) by ancestors and were therefore considered all powerful. HTS 4 These rulers usually made their divine status well known. It is evidenced in both writings and on public monuments. HTS 3 Another trend of overlapping themes includes the spread of religious ideas by missionaries traveling along the trade routes, which were originally built for the military.

If you lived in a classical imperial society, you were identified with a specific social class, and you knew perfectly well who was above you and who was below you on the social scale. All the classical civilizations divided their societies into groups of landowners, unskilled workers, artisans (skilled craftsmen), merchants, military and government bureaucrats, and slaves. All the classical societies were patriarchal, meaning that men were more important and had more rights than women. As you read about each classical society, be sure you understand how their social structure was organized; how religions helped to reinforce these social structures; if there was something unique about a particular society's way of organizing its people into classes; and the responsibilities of and taxes owed by each social class. HTS 4 And don't forget to watch for conflict between the classes—it's often partially responsible for toppling these classical empires.

The Empires of Persia

chapter 7

An enameled tile frieze created about 515 B.C.E. depicts a group of life-size Persian archers at the palace of King Darius in Susa.

EYEWITNESS:
King Croesus and the Tricky Business of Predicting the Future

The Greek historian Herodotus relished a good story, and he related many a tale about the Persian empire and its conflicts with other peoples, including Greeks. One story had to do with a struggle between Cyrus, leader of the expanding Persian realm, and Croesus, ruler of the powerful and wealthy kingdom of Lydia in southwestern Anatolia. Croesus noted the growth of Persian influence with concern and asked the Greek oracle at Delphi whether to go to war against Cyrus. The oracle, which had a reputation for delivering ambiguous predictions, responded that an attack on Cyrus would destroy a great kingdom.

Overjoyed, Croesus lined up his allies and prepared for war. In 546 B.C.E. he launched an invasion and seized a small town, provoking Cyrus to engage the formidable Lydian cavalry. The resulting battle was hard fought but inconclusive. Because winter was approaching, Croesus disbanded his troops and returned to his capital at Sardis, expecting Cyrus to retreat as well. But Cyrus was a vigorous and unpredictable warrior, and he pursued Croesus to Sardis. When he learned of the pursuit, Croesus hastily assembled an army to confront the invaders. Cyrus threw it into disarray, however, by advancing a group of warriors mounted on camels, which spooked the Lydian horses and sent them into headlong flight. Cyrus's army then surrounded Sardis and took the city after a siege of only two weeks. Croesus narrowly escaped death in the battle, but he was taken captive and afterward became an advisor to Cyrus. Herodotus could not resist pointing out that events proved the Delphic oracle right: Croesus's attack on Cyrus did indeed lead to the destruction of a great kingdom—his own.

The victory over Lydia was a major turning point in the development of the Persian empire. Lydia had a reputation as a kingdom of fabulous wealth, partly because it was the first land to use standardized coins with values guaranteed by the state. Taking advantage of its coins and its geographic location on the Mediterranean, Lydia conducted maritime trade with Greece, Egypt, and Phoenicia as well as overland trade with Mesopotamia and

Persia. Lydian wealth and resources gave Cyrus tremendous momentum as he extended Persian authority to new lands and built the earliest of the vast imperial states of classical times.

Classical Persian society began to take shape during the sixth century B.C.E. when warriors conquered the region from the Indus River to Egypt and southeastern Europe. Their conquests yielded an enormous realm much larger than the earlier Babylonian or Assyrian empires. The very size of the Persian empire created political and administrative problems for its rulers. Once they solved those problems, however, a series of Persian-based empires governed much of the territory between India and the Mediterranean Sea for more than a millennium—from the mid-sixth century B.C.E. until the early seventh century C.E.—and brought centralized political organization to many distinct peoples living over vast geographic spaces.

In organizing their realm, Persian rulers relied heavily on Mesopotamian techniques of administration, which they adapted to their own needs. Yet they did not hesitate to create new institutions or adopt new administrative procedures. In the interest of improved communications and military mobility, they also invested resources in the construction of roads and highways linking the regions of the empire. As a result of those efforts, central administrators were able to send instructions throughout the empire, dispatch armies in times of turmoil, and ensure that local officials would carry out imperial policies.

The organization of the vast territories embraced by the classical Persian empires had important social, economic, and cultural implications. High agricultural productivity enabled many people to work at tasks other than cultivation: classes of bureaucrats, administrators, priests, craftsmen, and merchants increased in number as the production and distribution of food became more efficient. Meanwhile, social extremes became more pronounced: a few individuals and families amassed enormous wealth, many led simple lives, and some fell into slavery. Good roads fostered trade within imperial borders, and Persian society itself served as a commercial and cultural bridge between Indian and Mediterranean societies. As a crossroads, Persia served not only as a link in long-distance trade networks but also as a conduit for the exchange of philosophical and religious ideas. Persian religious traditions did not attract many adherents beyond the imperial boundaries, but they inspired religious thinkers subject to Persian rule and also influenced Judaism, Christianity, and Islam.

THE RISE AND FALL OF THE PERSIAN EMPIRES

The empires of Persia arose in the arid land of Iran. For centuries Iran had developed under the shadow of the wealthier and more productive Mesopotamia to the west while absorbing intermittent migrations and invasions of nomadic peoples coming out of central Asia to the northeast. During the sixth century B.C.E., rulers of the province of Persia in southwestern Iran embarked on a series of conquests that resulted in the formation of an enormous empire. For more than a millennium, four ruling dynasties—the **Achaemenids** (558–330 B.C.E.), the Seleucids (323–83 B.C.E.), the Parthians (247 B.C.E.–224 C.E.), and the Sasanids (224–651 C.E.)—maintained a continuous tradition of imperial rule in much of southwest Asia.

The Achaemenid Empire

The Medes and the Persians The origins of classical Persian society trace back to the late stages of Mesopotamian society. During the centuries before 1000 B.C.E., two closely related peoples known as the **Medes** and the Persians migrated from central Asia to Persia (the southwestern portion of the modern-day state of Iran), where they lived in loose subjection to the Babylonian and Assyrian empires. The Medes and the Persians spoke Indo-European languages, and their movements were part of the larger Indo-European migrations. They shared many cultural traits with their distant cousins, the Aryans, who migrated into India. They were mostly pastoralists, although they also practiced a limited amount of agriculture. They organized themselves by clans rather than by states or formal political institutions, but they recognized leaders who collected taxes and delivered tribute to their Mesopotamian overlords.

Though not tightly organized politically, the Medes and the Persians were peoples of considerable military power. As descendants of nomadic peoples from central Asia, they possessed the equestrian skills common to many steppe peoples. They were expert archers, even when mounted on their horses, and they frequently raided the wealthy lands of Mesopotamia. When the Assyrian and Babylonian empires weakened in the sixth century B.C.E., the Medes and the Persians embarked on a vastly successful imperial venture of their own.

Cyrus Cyrus the Achaemenid (reigned 558–530 B.C.E.) launched the Persians' imperial venture. In some ways Cyrus was an unlikely candidate for that role. He came

Achaemenid (ah-KEE-muh-nid)
Medes (meeds)

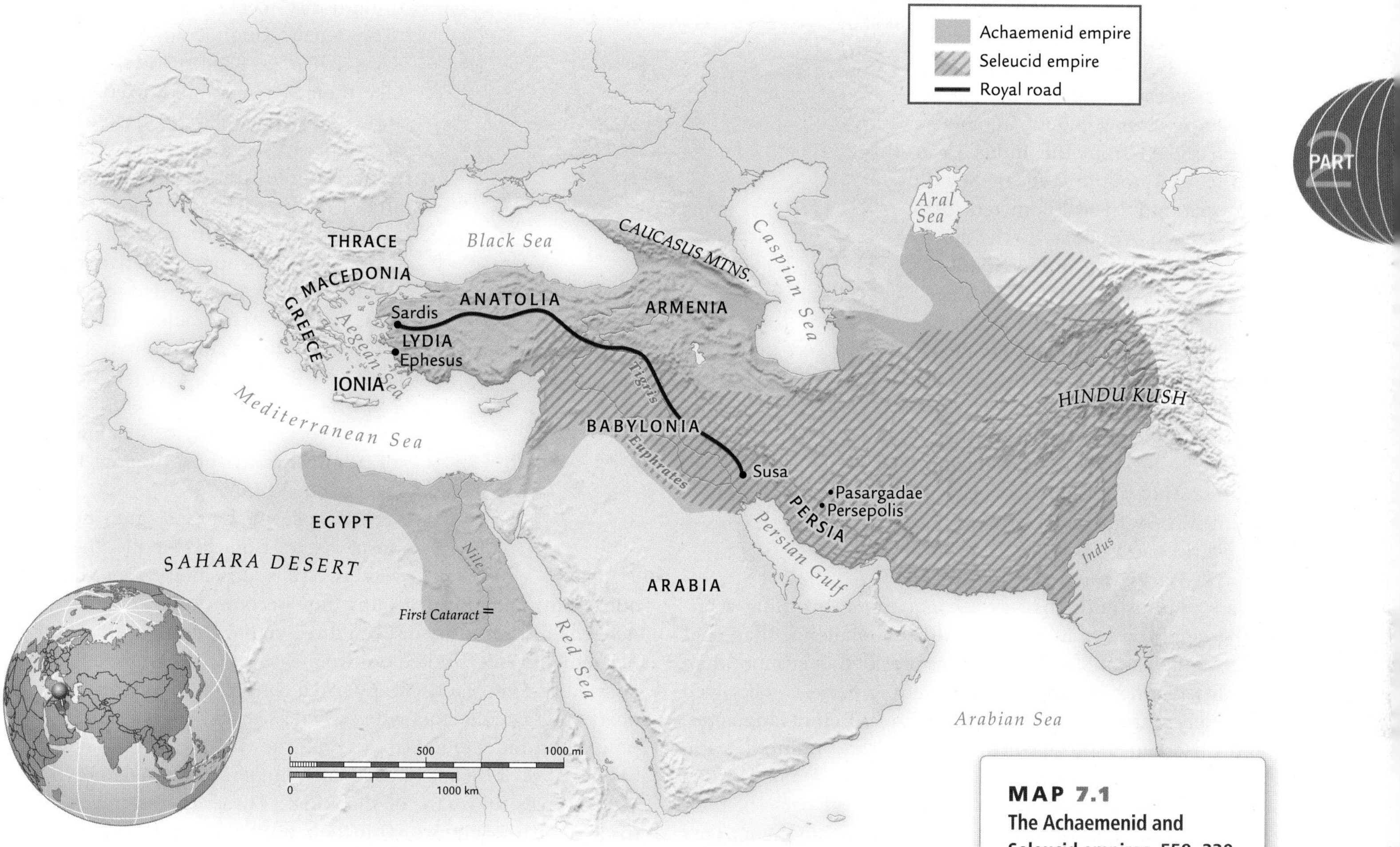

MAP 7.1
The Achaemenid and Seleucid empires, 558–330 B.C.E. and 323–83 B.C.E.
Compare the size of the Achaemenid empire with the earlier Mesopotamian and Egyptian empires discussed in chapters 2 and 3.
What role did the Royal Road and other highways play in the maintenance of the Achaemenid empire?

from a mountainous region of southwestern Iran, and in reference to the region's economy, his contemporaries often called him Cyrus the Shepherd. Yet Cyrus proved to be a tough, wily leader and an outstanding military strategist. His conquests laid the foundation of the first Persian empire, also known as the Achaemenid empire because its rulers claimed descent from Cyrus's Achaemenid clan.

Cyrus's Conquests In 558 B.C.E. Cyrus became king of the Persian tribes, which he ruled from his mountain fortress at Pasargadae. In 553 B.C.E. he initiated a rebellion against his Median overlord, whom he crushed within three years. By 548 B.C.E. he had brought all of Iran under his control, and he began to look for opportunities to expand his influence. In 546 B.C.E. he conquered the powerful kingdom of Lydia in Anatolia (modern-day Turkey). Between 545 B.C.E. and 539 B.C.E., he campaigned in central Asia and Bactria (modern Afghanistan). In a swift campaign of 539 B.C.E., he seized Babylonia, whose vassal states immediately recognized him as their lord. Within twenty years Cyrus went from minor regional king to ruler of an empire that stretched from India to the borders of Egypt.

Cyrus no doubt would have mounted a campaign against Egypt, the largest and wealthiest neighboring state outside his control, had he lived long enough. But in 530 B.C.E. he fell, mortally wounded, while protecting his northeastern frontier from nomadic raiders. His troops recovered his body and placed it in a simple tomb, which still stands, that Cyrus had prepared for himself at his palace in Pasargadae.

Darius Cyrus's empire survived and expanded during the reigns of his successors. His son Cambyses (reigned 530–522 B.C.E.) conquered Egypt in 525 B.C.E. and brought its wealth into Persian hands. The greatest of the Achaemenid emperors, Darius (reigned 521–486 B.C.E.), extended the empire both east and west. His armies pushed into northwestern India as far as the Indus River, absorbing the northern Indian kingdom of Gandhara, while also capturing Thrace,

Macedonia, and the western coast of the Black Sea in southeastern Europe. By the late sixth century, Darius presided over an empire stretching some 3,000 kilometers (1,865 miles) from the Indus River in the east to the Aegean Sea in the west and 1,500 kilometers (933 miles) from Armenia in the north to the first cataract of the Nile River in the south. This empire embraced mountains, valleys, plateaus, jungles, deserts, and arable land, and it touched the shores of the Arabian Sea, Aral Sea, Persian Gulf, Caspian Sea, Black Sea, Red Sea, and Mediterranean Sea. With a population of some thirty-five million, Darius's realm was by far the largest empire the world had yet seen.

The tomb of Cyrus at Pasargadae—one of the few Achaemenid monuments that have survived to the present.

Yet Darius was more important as an administrator than as a conqueror. Governing a far-flung empire was a much more difficult challenge than conquering it. The Achaemenid rulers presided over more than seventy distinct ethnic groups, including peoples who lived in widely scattered regions, spoke many different languages, and observed a profusion of religious and cultural traditions. To maintain their empire, the Achaemenids needed to establish lines of communication with all parts of their realm and design institutions that would enable them to tax and administer their territories. In doing so, they not only made it possible for the Achaemenid empire to survive but also pioneered administrative techniques that would outlast their dynasty and influence political life in southwestern Asia for centuries to come.

Persepolis Soon after his rise to power, Darius began to centralize his administration. About 520 B.C.E. he started to build a new capital of astonishing magnificence at Persepolis, near Pasargadae. Darius intended Persepolis to serve not only as an administrative center but also as a monument to the Achaemenid dynasty. Structures at Persepolis included vast reception halls, lavish royal residences, and a well-protected treasury. From the time of Darius to the end of the Achaemenid dynasty in 330 B.C.E., Persepolis served as the nerve center of the Persian empire—a resplendent capital bustling with advisors, ministers, diplomats, scribes, accountants, translators, and bureaucratic officers of all descriptions. Even today, massive columns and other ruins bespeak the grandeur of Darius's capital.

Achaemenid Administration: The Satrapies The government of the Achaemenid empire depended on a finely tuned balance between central initiative and local administration. The Achaemenid rulers made great claims to authority in their official title—"The Great King, King of Kings, King in Persia, King of Countries." Like their Mesopotamian predecessors, the Achaemenids appointed governors to serve as agents of the central administration and oversee affairs in the various regions. Darius divided his realm into twenty-three satrapies—administrative and taxation districts governed by satraps. Yet the Achaemenids did not try to push direct rule on their subjects: most of the satraps were Persians, but the Achaemenids recruited local officials to fill almost all administrative posts below the level of the satrap.

Because the satraps often held posts distant from Persepolis, there was always a possibility that they might ally with local groups and become independent of Achaemenid authority or even threaten the empire itself. The Achaemenid rulers relied on two measures to discourage that possibility. First, each satrapy had a contingent of military officers and tax collectors who served as checks on the satraps' power and independence. Second, the rulers created a new category of officials—essentially imperial spies—known as "the eyes and ears of the king." These agents traveled throughout the empire with their own military forces conducting surprise audits of accounts and procedures in the provinces and collecting intelligence reports. The division of provincial responsibilities and the institution of the eyes and ears of the king helped the Achaemenid rulers maintain control over a vast empire that otherwise might easily have split into a series of independent regional kingdoms.

Taxes, Coins, and Laws Darius also sought to improve administrative efficiency by regularizing tax levies and standardizing laws. Cyrus and Cambyses had accepted periodic "gifts" of tribute from subject lands and cities. Though often lavish, the gifts did not provide a consistent and reliable source of income for rulers who needed to finance a large bureaucracy and army. Darius replaced irregular tribute payments with formal tax levies. He required each satrapy to pay a set quantity of silver—and in some cases a levy of horses or slaves as well—deliverable annually to the imperial court. Darius followed the example of the Lydian king Croesus and issued standardized coins—a move that fostered trade. In an equally important initiative begun in the year 520 B.C.E., he sought to bring the many legal systems of his empire closer to a single standard. He did not abolish the existing laws of individual lands or peoples, nor did he impose a uniform law code on his entire empire. But he directed legal experts to study and codify the laws

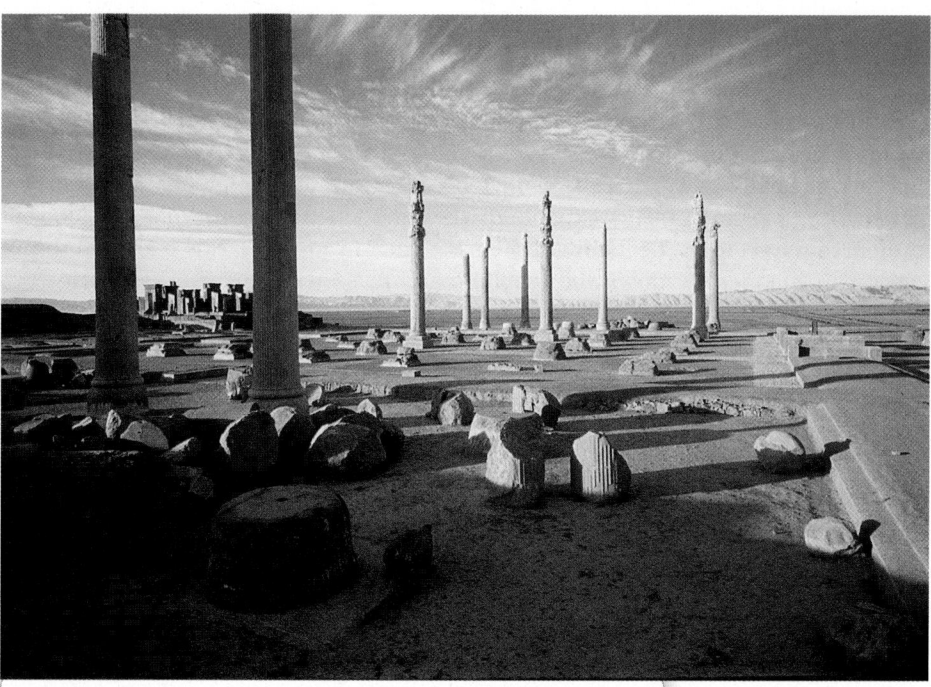

Ruins of Persepolis, showing the imperial reception hall and palaces. The columns rise about 19 meters (62 feet) and once supported a massive roof.

of his subject peoples, modifying them when necessary to harmonize them with the legal principles observed in the empire as a whole.

Roads and Communications Alongside their administrative and legal policies, the Achaemenid rulers took other measures to knit their far-flung realm into a coherent whole. They built good roads across their realm, notably the so-called Persian Royal Road—parts of it paved with stone—that stretched about 2,575 kilometers (1,600 miles) from the Aegean port of Ephesus to Sardis in Anatolia, through Mesopotamia along the Tigris River, to Susa in Iran, with an extension to Pasargadae and Persepolis. Caravans took some ninety days to travel this road, lodging at inns along the well-policed route.

The imperial government also organized a courier service and built 111 postal stations at intervals of 40 to 50 kilometers (25 to 30 miles) along the Royal Road. Each station kept a supply of fresh horses and food rations for couriers, who sometimes traveled at night as well as during daylight hours. Scholars estimate that these couriers were able to carry urgent messages from one end of the Royal Road to the other in two weeks' time. The Greek historian Herodotus spoke highly of these imperial servants, and even today the United States Postal Service takes his description of their efforts as a standard for its employees: "Neither snow nor rain nor heat nor gloom of night stays these couriers from the swift completion of their appointed rounds." The Achaemenids also improved existing routes between Mesopotamia and Egypt, and they built new roads linking Persia with northern India, Mesopotamia, Anatolia, Syria, and Egypt. In combination, these imperial highways stretched approximately 13,000 kilometers (8,000 miles). In addition to improving communications, these roads facilitated trade, which helped to integrate the empire's various regions into a larger economy.

thinking about TRADITIONS

Sinews of the Persian Empire

Maintenance of large empires depended upon elaborate networks of transportation, communication, and administration. What were the most important elements enabling the Achaemenids to hold their empire together? Consider especially the roles of the imperial capital, the satrapies, the imperial bureaucracy, the eyes and ears of the king, and the Persian Royal Road.

Decline and Fall of the Achaemenid Empire

The Achaemenid Commonwealth The Achaemenids' roads and administrative machinery enabled them to govern a vast empire and extend Persian influences throughout their territories. Political stability made it possible to undertake extensive public works projects such as the construction of ***qanat*** (underground canals), which led to enhanced agricultural production and population growth. Iron metallurgy spread to all parts of the empire, and by the end of the Achaemenid dynasty, iron tools were common in Persian agricultural communities. Peoples in the various regions of the Achaemenid empire maintained their ethnic identities, but all participated in a larger Persian commonwealth.

Eventually, however, difficulties between rulers and subject peoples undermined the integrity of the Achaemenid empire. Cyrus and

qanat (kah-NAHT)

Darius both consciously pursued a policy of toleration in administering their vast multicultural empire: they took care to respect the values and cultural traditions of the peoples they ruled. In Mesopotamia, for example, they did not portray themselves as Persian conquerors but, rather, as legitimate Babylonian rulers and representatives of Marduk, the patron deity of Babylon. Darius also won high praise from Jews in the Achaemenid empire, since he allowed them to return to Jerusalem and rebuild the temple that Babylonian conquerors had destroyed in 587 B.C.E.

Darius's successor, Xerxes (reigned 486–465 B.C.E.), had more difficult relations with subject peoples. The burden of Persian rule became particularly heavy in Mesopotamia and Egypt—regions with sophisticated cultural traditions and long histories of independence—and subject peoples there frequently rose up in rebellion. Xerxes did not seek to impose specifically Persian values in Mesopotamia and Egypt, but he harshly repressed rebellions and thereby gained a reputation for cruelty and insensitivity to the concerns of subject peoples.

The Persian Wars The Achaemenids had an especially difficult time with their ethnic Greek subjects. Greeks inhabited many of the cities in Anatolia—particularly in the region of Ionia on the Aegean coast of western Anatolia—and they maintained close economic and commercial ties with their cousins in the peninsula of Greece itself. The Ionian Greeks fell under Persian domination during the reign of Cyrus. They became restive under Darius's Persian governors—"tyrants," the Greeks called them—who oversaw their affairs. In 500 B.C.E. the Ionian cities rebelled, expelled or executed their governors, and asserted their independence. Their rebellion launched a series of conflicts that Greeks called the Persian Wars (500–479 B.C.E.).

The conflict between the Ionian Greeks and the Persians expanded when the cities of peninsular Greece sent fleets to aid their kinsmen in Ionia. Darius managed to put down the rebellion and reassert Achaemenid authority, but he and his successors became entangled in a difficult and ultimately destructive effort to extend their authority to the Greek peninsula. In 490 B.C.E. Darius attempted to forestall future problems by mounting an expedition to conquer the wealthy Greek cities and absorb them into his empire. Though larger and much more powerful than the forces of the disunited Greek city-states, the Persian army had to contend with long and fragile lines of supply as well as a hostile environment. After some initial successes, the Persians suffered a rout at the battle of Marathon (490 B.C.E.), and they returned home without achieving their goals. Xerxes sent another expedition ten years later, but within eighteen months, it too had suffered defeat both on land and at sea and had returned to Persia.

For almost 150 years the Persian empire sparred intermittently with the Greek cities. The adversaries mounted small expeditions against each other, attacking individual cities or fleets, but they did not engage in large-scale campaigns. The Greek cities were too small and disunited to pose a serious challenge to the enormous Persian empire. Meanwhile, for

Stone carving from Persepolis showing an enthroned Darius (with his son Xerxes standing behind him) receiving a high court official, as incense burners perfume the air. In what ways does the official's posture indicate respect and submission to the emperor?

their part, the later Achaemenids had to concentrate on the other restive and sometimes rebellious regions of their empire and could not embark on new rounds of expansion.

A silver coin from the early Hellenistic period depicting the conqueror Alexander of Macedon.

Alexander of Macedon The standoff ended with the rise of Alexander of Macedon, often called Alexander the Great (discussed more fully in chapter 10). In 334 B.C.E. Alexander invaded Persia with an army of some forty-eight thousand tough, battle-hardened Macedonians. Though far smaller than the Persian army in numbers, the well-disciplined Macedonians carried heavier arms and employed more sophisticated military tactics than their opponents. As a result, they sliced through the Persian empire, advancing almost at will and dealing their adversaries a series of devastating defeats. In 331 B.C.E. Alexander shattered Achaemenid forces at the battle of Gaugamela, and within a year the empire founded by Cyrus the Shepherd had dissolved.

Alexander led his forces into Persepolis, confiscated the wealth stored in the imperial treasury there, paid his respects at the tomb of Cyrus in Pasargadae, and proclaimed himself heir to the Achaemenid rulers. After a brief season of celebration, Alexander and his forces ignited a blaze—perhaps intentionally—that destroyed Persepolis. The conflagration was so great that when archaeologists first began to explore the ruins of Persepolis in the eighteenth century, they found layers of ash and charcoal up to 1 meter (3 feet) deep.

The Achaemenid empire had crumbled, but its legacy was by no means exhausted. Alexander portrayed himself in Persia and Egypt as a legitimate successor of the Achaemenids who observed their precedents and deserved their honors. He retained the Achaemenid administrative structure, and he even confirmed the appointments of many satraps and other officials. As it happened, Alexander had little time to enjoy his conquests, because he died in 323 B.C.E. after a brief effort to extend his empire to India. But the states that succeeded him—the Seleucid, Parthian, and Sasanid empires—continued to employ a basically Achaemenid structure of imperial administration.

The Seleucid, Parthian, and Sasanid Empires

The Seleucids After Alexander died, his chief generals fought among themselves and struggled to take over the conqueror's realms. In Persia the victor was Seleucus, formerly commander of an elite guard corps in Alexander's army, who dominated the territories of the former Achaemenid empire and ruled them from 305 to 281 B.C.E. Like Alexander, Seleucus and his successors retained the Achaemenid systems of administration and taxation as well as the imperial roads and postal service. The **Seleucids** also founded new cities throughout the realm and attracted Greek colonists to occupy them. The migrants, who represented only a small fraction of the whole population of the empire, largely adapted to their new environment. Nonetheless, the establishment of cities greatly stimulated trade and economic development both within the Seleucid empire and beyond.

As foreigners, the Seleucids faced opposition from native Persians and especially their ruling classes. Satraps often revolted against Seleucid rule, or at least worked to build power bases that would enable them to establish their independence. The Seleucids soon lost their holdings in northern India, and the seminomadic Parthians progressively took over Iran during the third century B.C.E. The Seleucids continued to rule a truncated empire until 83 B.C.E., when Roman conquerors put an end to their empire.

The Parthians Meanwhile, the Parthians established themselves as lords of a powerful empire based in Iran that they extended to wealthy Mesopotamia. The Parthians had occupied the region of eastern Iran around Khurasan since Achaemenid times. They retained many of the customs and traditions of nomadic peoples from the steppes of central Asia. They did not have a centralized government, for example, but organized themselves politically through a federation of leaders who met in councils and jointly determined policy for all allied groups. They were skillful warriors, accustomed to defending themselves against constant threats from nomadic peoples farther east.

As they settled and turned increasingly to agriculture, the Parthians also devised an effective means to resist nomadic invasions. Because they had no access to feed grains, nomadic peoples allowed their horses to forage for food on the steppes during the winter. The Parthians discovered that if they fed their horses on alfalfa during the winter, their animals would grow much larger and stronger than the small horses and ponies of the steppes. Their larger animals could then support heavily armed warriors outfitted with metal armor, which served as an effective shield against the arrows of the steppe nomads. Well-trained forces of heavily armed cavalry could usually put nomadic raiding parties to flight. Indeed, few existing forces could stand up to Parthian heavy cavalry.

Seleucids (sih-LOO-sihds)

Gold sculpture of a nomadic horseman discharging an arrow. This figurine dates from the fifth or fourth century B.C.E. and might well represent a Parthian.

Parthian Conquests As early as the third century B.C.E., the Parthians began to wrest their independence from the Seleucids. The Parthian satrap revolted against his Seleucid overlord in 238 B.C.E., and during the following decades his successors gradually enlarged their holdings. Mithradates I, the Parthians' greatest conqueror, came to the throne about 171 B.C.E. and transformed his state into a mighty empire. By about 155 B.C.E. he had consolidated his hold on Iran and had also extended Parthian rule to Mesopotamia.

Parthian Government The Parthians portrayed themselves as enemies of the foreign Seleucids, as restorers of rule in the Persian tradition. To some extent that characterization was accurate. The Parthians largely followed the example of the Achaemenids in structuring their empire: they governed through satraps, employed Achaemenid techniques of administration and taxation, and built a capital city at Ctesiphon on the Euphrates River near modern Baghdad. But the Parthians also retained elements of their steppe traditions. They did not develop nearly so centralized a regime as the Achaemenids or the Seleucids but, rather, vested a great deal of authority and responsibility in their clan leaders. These men often served as satraps, and they regularly worked to build independent bases of power in their regions. They frequently mounted rebellions against the imperial government, though without much success.

For about three centuries the Parthians presided over a powerful empire between India and the Mediterranean. Beginning in the first century C.E., they faced pressure in the west from the expanding Roman empire. The Parthian empire as a whole never stood in danger of falling to the Romans, but on three occasions in the second century C.E. Roman armies captured the Parthian capital at Ctesiphon. Combined with internal difficulties caused by the rebellious satraps, Roman pressure contributed to the weakening of the Parthian state. During the early third century C.E., internal rebellion brought it down.

The Sasanids Once again, though, the tradition of imperial rule continued, this time under the **Sasanids,** who came from Persia and claimed direct descent from the Achaemenids. The Sasanids toppled the Parthians in 224 C.E. and ruled until 651 C.E., re-creating much of the splendor of the Achaemenid empire. From their cosmopolitan capital at Ctesiphon, the Sasanid "king of kings" provided strong rule from Parthia to Mesopotamia while also rebuilding an elaborate system of administration and founding or refurbishing numerous cities. Sasanid merchants traded actively with peoples to both east and west, and they introduced into Iran the cultivation of crops such as rice, sugarcane, citrus fruits, eggplant, and cotton that came west over the trade routes from India and China.

During the reign of Shapur I (239–272 C.E.), the Sasanids stabilized their western frontier and created a series of buffer states between themselves and the Roman empire. Shapur even defeated several Roman armies and settled the prisoners in Iran, where they devoted their famous engineering skills to the construction of roads and dams. After Shapur, the Sasanids did not expand militarily, but entered into a standoff relationship with the Kushan empire in the east and the Roman and Byzantine empires in the west. None of those large empires was strong enough to overcome the others, but they contested border areas and buffer states, sometimes engaging in lengthy and bitter disputes that sapped the energies of all involved.

These continual conflicts seriously weakened the Sasanid empire in particular. The empire came to an end in 651 C.E. when Arab warriors killed the last Sasanid ruler, overran his realm, and incorporated it into their rapidly expanding Islamic empire. Yet even conquest by external invaders did not end the legacy of classical Persia, since Persian administrative techniques and cultural traditions were so powerful that the Arab conquerors adopted them to use in building a new Islamic society.

IMPERIAL SOCIETY AND ECONOMY

Throughout the eastern hemisphere during the classical era, public life and social structure became much more compli-

Sasanids (suh-SAH-nids)

cated than they had been during the days of the early complex societies. Centralized imperial governments needed large numbers of administrative officials, which led to the emergence of educated classes of bureaucrats. Stable empires enabled many individuals to engage in trade or other specialized labor as artisans, craftsmen, or professionals of various kinds. Some of them accumulated vast wealth, which led to increased distance and tensions between rich and poor. Meanwhile, slavery became more common than in earlier times. The prominence of slavery had to do partly with the expansion of imperial states, which often enslaved conquered foes, but it also reflected the increasing gulf between rich and poor, which placed such great economic pressure on some individuals that they had to give up their freedom in order to survive. All those developments had implications for the social structures of classical societies in Persia as well as China, India, and the Mediterranean basin.

Social Development in Classical Persia

During the early days of the Achaemenid empire, Persian society reflected its origins on the steppes of central Asia. When the Medes and the Persians migrated to Iran, their social structure was similar to that of the Aryans in India, consisting primarily of warriors, priests, and peasants. For centuries, when they lived on the periphery and in the shadow of the Mesopotamian empires, the Medes and the Persians maintained steppe traditions. Even after the establishment of the Achaemenid empire, some of them followed a seminomadic lifestyle and maintained ties with their cousins on the steppes. Family and clan relationships were extremely important in the organization of Persian political and social affairs. Male warriors headed the clans, which retained much of their influence long after the establishment of the Achaemenid empire.

Imperial Bureaucrats The development of a cosmopolitan empire, however, brought considerable complexity to Persian society. The requirements of imperial administration,

MAP 7.2

The Parthian and Sasanid empires, 247 B.C.E.–651 C.E.

Note the location of the Parthian and Sasanid empires between the Mediterranean Sea and northern India.

What roles did these two empires play in facilitating or hindering communications between lands to their east and west?

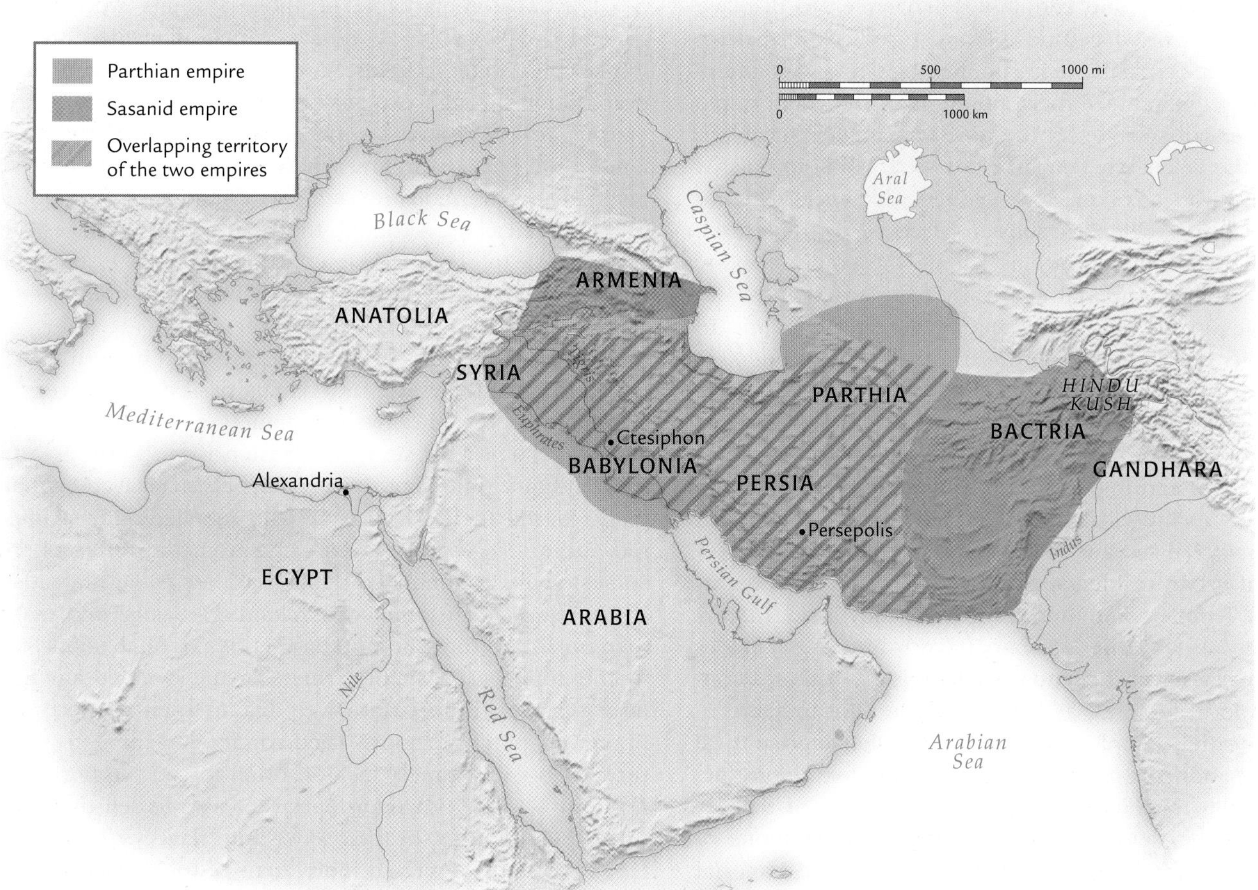

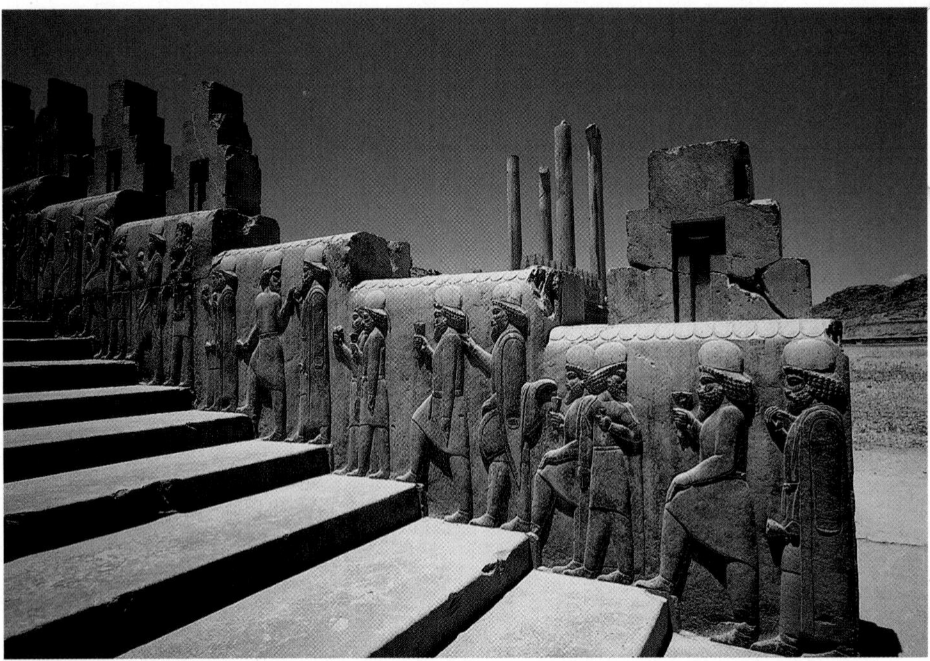

In this sculpture from Persepolis, Persian nobles dressed in fine cloaks and hats ascend the staircase leading to the imperial reception hall.

for example, called for a new class of educated bureaucrats who to a large extent undermined the position of the old warrior elite. The bureaucrats did not directly challenge the patriarchal warriors and certainly did not seek to displace them from their privileged position in society. Nevertheless, the bureaucrats' crucial role in running the day-to-day affairs of the empire guaranteed them a prominent and comfortable place in Persian society. By the time of the later Achaemenids and the Seleucids, Persian cities were home to masses of administrators, tax collectors, and record keepers. The bureaucracy even included a substantial corps of translators, who facilitated communications among the empire's many linguistic groups. Imperial survival depended on these literate professionals, and high-ranking bureaucrats came to share power and influence with warriors and clan leaders.

Free Classes The bulk of Persian society consisted of individuals who were free but did not enjoy the privileges of clan leaders and important bureaucrats. In the cities the free classes included artisans, craftsmen, merchants, and low-ranking civil servants. Priests and priestesses were also prominent urban residents, along with servants who maintained the temple communities in which they lived. In Persian society, as in earlier Mesopotamian societies, members of the free classes participated in religious observances conducted at local temples, and they had the right to share in the income that temples generated from their agricultural operations and from craft industries, such as textile production, that the temples organized. The weaving of textiles was mostly the work of women, who received rations of grain, wine, beer, and sometimes meat from the imperial and temple workshops that employed them.

In the countryside the free classes included peasants who owned land as well as landless cultivators who worked as laborers or tenants on properties owned by the state, temple communities, or other individuals. Free residents of rural areas had the right to marry and move as they wished, and they could seek better opportunities in the cities or in military service. Because the Persian empires embraced a great deal of parched land that received little rainfall, work in the countryside involved not only cultivation but also the building and maintenance of irrigation systems.

The most remarkable of those systems were underground canals known as *qanat,* which allowed cultivators to distribute water to fields without losing large quantities to evaporation through exposure to the sun and open air. Numerous *qanat* crisscrossed the Iranian plateau in the heartland of the Persian empire, where extreme scarcity of water justified the enormous investment of human labor required to build the canals. Although they had help from slaves, free residents of the countryside contributed much of the labor that went into the excavation and maintenance of the *qanat.*

Slaves A large class of slaves also worked in both the cities and the countryside. Individuals passed into slavery by two main routes. Most were prisoners of war who became slaves as the price of survival. These prisoners usually came from military units, but the Persians also enslaved civilians who resisted their advance or who rebelled against imperial authorities. Other slaves came from the ranks of free subjects who accumulated debts that they could not satisfy. In the cities, for example, merchants, artisans, and craftsmen borrowed funds to purchase goods or open shops, and in the countryside small farmers facing competition from large-scale cultivators borrowed against their property and liberty to purchase tools, seed, or food. Failure to repay those debts in a timely fashion often forced the borrowers not only to forfeit their property but also to sell their children, their spouses, or themselves into slavery.

Slave status deprived individuals of their personal freedom. Slaves became the property of an individual, the state, or an institution such as a temple community: they worked at tasks set by their owners, and they could not move or marry at will, although existing family units usually stayed together. Most slaves probably worked as domestic servants or skilled laborers in the households of the wealthy, but at least some slaves cultivated their owners' fields in the countryside. State-owned slaves provided much of the manual labor for large-scale construction projects such as roads, irrigation systems, city walls, and palaces.

In Mesopotamia, temple communities owned many slaves who worked at agricultural tasks and performed administrative chores for their priestly masters. During the mid- to late sixth century B.C.E., a slave named Gimillu served the temple community of Eanna in Uruk, and his career is relatively well-known because records of his various misadventures survive in archives. Gimillu appeared in numerous legal cases because he habitually defrauded his masters, pocketed bribes, and embezzled temple funds. Yet he held a high position in the temple community and always managed to escape serious punishment. His career reveals that slaves sometimes had administrative talents and took on tasks involving considerable responsibility. Gimillu's case clearly shows that slaves sometimes enjoyed close relationships with powerful individuals who could protect them from potential enemies.

Economic Foundations of Classical Persia

Agriculture was the economic foundation of classical Persian society. Like other classical societies, Persia needed large agricultural surpluses to support military forces and administrative specialists as well as residents of cities who were artisans, crafts workers, and merchants rather than cultivators. The Persian empires embraced several regions of exceptional fertility—notably Mesopotamia, Egypt, Anatolia, and northern India—and they prospered by mobilizing the agricultural surpluses of those lands.

Agricultural Production Barley and wheat were the grains cultivated most commonly in the Persian empires. Peas, lentils, mustard, garlic, onions, cucumbers, dates, apples, pomegranates, pears, and apricots supplemented the cereals in diets throughout Persian society, and beer and wine were the most common beverages. In most years agricultural production far exceeded the needs of cultivators, making sizable surpluses available for sale in the cities or for distribution to state servants through the imperial bureaucracy. Vast quantities of produce flowed into the imperial court from state-owned lands cultivated by slaves or leased out to tenants in exchange for a portion of the annual harvest. Even though they are incomplete, surviving records show that, for example, in 500 B.C.E., during the middle period of Darius's reign, the imperial court received almost eight hundred thousand liters of grain, quite apart from vegetables, fruits, meat, poultry, fish, oil, beer, wine, and textiles. Officials distributed some of that produce to the imperial staff as wages in kind, but much of it also found its way into the enormous banquets that Darius organized for as many as ten thousand guests. Satraps and other high officials lived on a less lavish scale than the Persian emperors but also benefited from agricultural surpluses delivered to their courts from their own lands.

Standardized Coins Agriculture was the economic foundation of the Persian empires, but the empires had the effect of encouraging rapid economic development and trade. By ensuring political stability and maintaining an elaborate network of roads, Achaemenid rulers laid solid foundations for economic prosperity and secure transportation of trade goods. Trade benefited also from the invention of standardized coins, which first appeared in the Anatolian kingdom of Lydia. Beginning about 640 B.C.E. the kings of Lydia

Tribute bearers from lands subject to Achaemenid rule bring rams, horses, and fabrics to the imperial court at Persepolis. Representatives of twenty-three lands offered tribute at the imperial new year festival.

issued coins of precisely measured metal and guaranteed their value. It was much simpler for merchants to exchange standardized coins than to weigh ingots or bullion when transacting their business. As a result, standardized coins quickly became popular and drew merchants from distant lands to Lydian markets. When Cyrus defeated the forces of King Croesus and absorbed Lydia into his expanding realm, he brought the advantages of standardized coins to the larger Achaemenid empire. Markets opened in all the larger cities of the empire, and the largest cities, such as Babylon, also were home to banks and companies that invested in commercial ventures.

Trade Long-distance trade grew rapidly during the course of the Persian empires and linked lands from India to Egypt in a vast commercial zone. Trade traveled both over land routes, including newly constructed highways such as the Persian Royal Road, and over sea lanes through the Red Sea, the Persian Gulf, and the Arabian Sea. The various regions of the Persian empires all contributed particular products to the larger imperial economy. India supplied gold, ivory, and aromatics. Iran and central Asia provided lapis lazuli, turquoise, and other semiprecious stones. Mesopotamia and Iran were sources of finished products such as textiles, mirrors, and jewelry. Anatolia supplied gold, silver, iron, copper, and tin. Phoenicia contributed glass, cedar, timber, and richly dyed woolen fabrics. Spices and aromatics came from Arabia. Egypt provided grain, linen textiles, and papyrus writing materials as well as gold, ebony, and ivory obtained from Nubia. Greek oil, wine, and ceramics also made their way throughout the empire and even beyond its borders.

Long-distance trade became especially prominent during the reigns of Alexander of Macedon and his Seleucid successors. The cities they established and the colonists they attracted stimulated trade throughout the whole region from the Mediterranean to northern India. Indeed, Greek migrants facilitated cultural as well as commercial exchanges by encouraging the mixing and mingling of religious faiths, art styles, and philosophical speculation throughout the Persian realm.

RELIGIONS OF SALVATION IN CLASSICAL PERSIAN SOCIETY

Cross-cultural influences were especially noticeable in the development of Persian religion. Persians came from the family of peoples who spoke Indo-European languages, and their earliest religion closely resembled that of the Aryans of India. During the classical era, however, the new faith of Zoroastrianism emerged and became widely popular in Iran and to a lesser extent also in the larger Persian empires. Zoroastrianism later influenced the beliefs and values of Judaism, Christianity, and Islam as well. During the late centuries of the classical era, from about 100 to 500 C.E., three missionary religions—Buddhism, Christianity, and Manichaeism—also found numerous converts in the Persian empire.

Zarathustra and His Faith

The earliest Persian religion centered on cults that celebrated outstanding natural elements and geographic features such as the sun, the moon, water, and especially fire. Persians recognized many of the same gods as the ancient Aryans, and their priests performed sacrifices similar to those conducted by the brahmins in India. The priests even made ceremonial use of a hallucinogenic agent called *haoma* in the same way that the Aryans used soma, and indeed the two concoctions were probably the same substance. Like the Aryans, the ancient Persians glorified strength and martial virtues, and the cults of both peoples sought principally to bring about a comfortable material existence for their practitioners.

Zarathustra During the classical era Persian religion underwent considerable change, as moral and religious thinkers sought to adapt their messages to the circumstances of a complex, cosmopolitan society. One result was the emergence of Zoroastrianism, which emerged from the teachings of Zarathustra. Though Zarathustra was undoubtedly a historical person and the subject of many early stories, little certain information survives about his life and career. It is not even clear exactly when he lived: many scholars date his life to the late seventh and early sixth centuries B.C.E., but many others believe he flourished sometime between 1200 and 1000 B.C.E. He came from an aristocratic family, and he probably was a priest who became disenchanted with the traditional religion and its concentration on bloody sacrifices and mechanical rituals. In any case, when he was about twenty years old, Zarathustra left his family and home in search of wisdom. After about ten years of travel, he experienced a series of visions and became convinced that the supreme god, whom he called Ahura Mazda (the "wise lord"), had chosen him to serve as his prophet and spread his message.

> *"Zoroastrians have often summarized their moral teachings in the simple formula 'good words, good thoughts, good deeds.'"*

The *Gathas* Like his life, Zarathustra's doctrine has proven to be somewhat elusive for modern analysts. Many of the earliest Zoroastrian teachings have perished, because the priests, known as magi, at first transmitted them orally. Only during the Seleucid dynasty did magi begin to preserve religious texts in writing, and only under the Sasanids did they compile their scriptures in a holy book

known as the Avesta. Nevertheless, many of Zarathustra's compositions survive, since magi preserved them with special diligence through oral transmission. Known as the *Gathas,* Zarathustra's works were hymns that he composed in honor of the various deities that he recognized. Apart from the *Gathas,* ancient Zoroastrian literature included a wide variety of hymns, liturgical works, and treatises on moral and theological themes. Though some of these works survive, the arrival of Islam in the seventh century C.E. and the subsequent decline of Zoroastrianism resulted in the loss of most of the Avesta and later Zoroastrian works.

A gold clasp or button of the fifth century B.C.E. with the symbol of Ahura Mazda, a Zoroastrian deity, as a winged god.

Zoroastrian Teachings Zarathustra and his followers were not monotheists. They recognized Ahura Mazda as a supreme deity, an eternal and beneficent spirit, and the creator of all good things. But Zarathustra also spoke of six lesser deities, whom he praised in the *Gathas.* Furthermore, he believed that Ahura Mazda engaged in a cosmic conflict with an independent adversary, an evil and malign spirit known as Angra Mainyu (the "destructive spirit" or the "hostile spirit"). Following a struggle of some twelve thousand years, Zarathustra believed, Ahura Mazda and the forces of good would ultimately prevail, and Angra Mainyu and the principle of evil would disappear forever. At that time individual human souls would undergo judgment and would experience rewards or punishments according to the holiness of their thoughts, words, and deeds. Honest and moral individuals would enter into a heavenly paradise, whereas demons would fling their evil brethren into a hellish realm of pain and suffering.

Popularity of Zoroastrianism Zarathustra did not call for ascetic renunciation of the world in favor of a future heavenly existence. To the contrary, he considered the material world a blessing that reflected the benevolent nature of Ahura Mazda. His moral teachings allowed human beings to enjoy the world and its fruits—including wealth, sexual pleasure, and social prestige—as long as they did so in moderation and behaved honestly toward others. Zoroastrians have often summarized their moral teachings in the simple formula "good words, good thoughts, good deeds."

Zarathustra's teachings began to attract large numbers of followers during the sixth century B.C.E., particularly among Persian aristocrats and ruling elites. Wealthy patrons donated land and established endowments for the support of Zoroastrian temples. The Achaemenid era saw the emergence of a sizable priesthood, whose members conducted religious rituals, maintained a calendar, taught Zoroastrian values, and preserved Zoroastrian doctrine through oral transmission.

Cyrus and Cambyses probably observed Zoroastrian rites, although little evidence survives to illustrate their religious preferences. Beginning with Darius, however, the Achaemenid emperors closely associated themselves with Ahura Mazda and claimed divine sanction for their rule. Darius ordered stone inscriptions celebrating his achievements, and in those monuments he clearly revealed his devotion to Ahura Mazda and his opposition to the principle of evil. He did not attempt to suppress other gods or religions, but tolerated the established faiths of the various peoples in his empire. Yet he personally regarded Ahura Mazda as a deity superior to all others.

In one of his inscriptions, Darius praised Ahura Mazda as the great god who created the earth, the sky, and humanity and who moreover elevated Darius himself to the imperial honor. With the aid of imperial sponsorship, Zoroastrian temples cropped up throughout the Achaemenid realm. The faith was most popular in Iran, but it attracted sizable followings also in Mesopotamia, Anatolia, Egypt, and other parts of the Achaemenid empire even though there was no organized effort to spread it beyond its original homeland.

Religions of Salvation in a Cosmopolitan Society

The arrival of Alexander of Macedon inaugurated a difficult era for the Zoroastrian community. During his Persian campaign, Alexander's forces burned many temples and killed numerous magi. Because at that time the magi still transmitted Zoroastrian doctrines orally, an untold number of hymns and holy verses disappeared. The Zoroastrian faith survived, however, and the Parthians cultivated it to rally support against the Seleucids. Once established in power, the Parthians observed Zoroastrian rituals, though they did not support the faith as enthusiastically as their predecessors had done.

Officially Sponsored Zoroastrianism During the Sasanid dynasty, however, Zoroastrianism experienced a revival. As self-proclaimed heirs to the Achaemenids, the Sasanids identified closely with Zoroastrianism and supported it zealously. Indeed, the Sasanids often persecuted other faiths if they seemed likely to become popular enough to challenge the supremacy of Zoroastrianism. With generous imperial backing, the Zoroastrian faith and the magi flourished as never before. Theologians prepared written versions of the holy texts and collected them in the Avesta.

sources from the past

Zarathustra on Good and Evil

Like many other religious faiths of classical times, Zoroastrianism encouraged the faithful to observe high moral and ethical standards. In this hymn from the Gathas, Zarathustra relates how Ahura Mazda and Angra Mainyu—representatives of good and evil, respectively—made choices about how to behave based on their fundamental natures. Human beings did likewise, according to Zarathustra, and ultimately all would experience the rewards and the punishments that their choices merited.

In the beginning, there were two Primal Spirits, Twins spontaneously active;
These are the Good and the Evil, in thought, and in word, and in deed:
Between these two, let the wise choose aright;
Be good, not base.

And when these Twin Spirits came together at first,
They established Life and Non-Life,
And so shall it be as long as the world shall last;
The worst existence shall be the lot of the followers of evil,
And the Good Mind shall be the reward of the followers of good.

Of these Twin Spirits, the Evil One chose to do the worst;
While the bountiful Holy Spirit of Goodness,
Clothing itself with the mossy heavens for a garment, chose the Truth;
And so will those who [seek to] please Ahura Mazda with righteous deeds, performed with faith in Truth. . . .

And when there cometh Divine Retribution for the Evil One,
Then at Thy command shall the Good Mind establish the Kingdom of Heaven, O Mazda,
For those who will deliver Untruth into the hands of Righteousness and Truth.

Then truly cometh the blow of destruction on Untruth,
And all those of good fame are garnered up in the Fair Abode,
The Fair Abode of the Good Mind, the Wise Lord, and of Truth!

O ye mortals, mark these commandments—
The commandments which the Wise Lord has given, for Happiness and for Pain;
Long punishment for the evil-doer, and bliss for the follower of Truth,
The joy of salvation for the Righteous ever afterwards!

For Further Reflection

- What assumptions does Zarathustra make about human nature and the capacity of human beings to make morally good choices through free will?

Source: D. J. Irani. *The Divine Songs of Zarathustra.* London: George Allen & Unwin, 1924.

They also explored points of doctrine and addressed difficult questions of morality and theology. Most people probably did not understand the theologians' reflections, but they flocked to Zoroastrian temples where they prayed to Ahura Mazda and participated in rituals.

The Zoroastrian faith faced severe difficulties in the seventh century C.E. when Islamic conquerors toppled the Sasanid empire. The conquerors did not outlaw the religion altogether, but they placed political and financial pressure on the magi and Zoroastrian temples. Some Zoroastrians fled their homeland under persecution and found refuge in India, where their descendants, known as Parsis ("Persians"), continue even today to observe Zoroastrian traditions. But most Zoroastrians remained in Iran and eventually converted to Islam. As a result, Zoroastrian numbers progressively dwindled. Only a few thousand faithful maintain a Zoroastrian community in modern-day Iran.

Other Faiths Meanwhile, even though Zoroastrianism ultimately declined in its homeland, the cosmopolitan character of the Persian realm offered it opportunities to influence other religious faiths. Numerous Jewish communities had become established in Mesopotamia, Anatolia, and Persia after the Hebrew kingdom of David and Solomon fell in 930 B.C.E. During the Seleucid, Parthian, and Sasanid eras, the Persian empire attracted merchants, emissaries, and missionaries from the whole region between the Mediterranean and India. Three religions of salvation—Buddhism, Christianity, and **Manichaeism,** all discussed in later chapters—found a footing alongside Judaism and attracted converts.

Manichaeism (man-ih-KEE-iz'm)

Darius faces Ahura Mazda, the Zoroastrian deity to whom he attributed his authority, as the various kings subject to him acknowledge him as their lord.

Indeed, Christianity and Manichaeism became extremely popular faiths in spite of intermittent rounds of persecution organized by Sasanid authorities.

Influence of Zoroastrianism While foreign faiths influenced religious developments in classical Persian society, Zoroastrianism also left its mark on the other religions of salvation. Jews living in Persia during Achaemenid times adopted several specific teachings of Zoroastrianism, which later found their way into the faiths of Christianity and Islam as well. Those teachings included the notion that an omnipotent and beneficent deity was responsible for all creation, the idea that a purely evil being worked against the creator god, the conviction that the forces of good will ultimately prevail over the power of evil after a climactic struggle, the belief that human beings must strive to observe the highest moral standards, and the doctrine that individuals will undergo judgment, after which the morally upright will experience rewards in paradise while evildoers will suffer punishments in hell. Those teachings, which have profoundly influenced Judaism, Christianity, and Islam, all derived ultimately from the faith of Zarathustra and his followers.

thinking about ENCOUNTERS

Religions on the Move

During the classical era, proponents of popular religions of salvation found opportunities to attract new adherents both in their homelands and beyond. How can you account for the presence in classical Persia of different religious traditions from different lands? To what extent did Persian ideas influence the development of other religious traditions?

inperspective

The Achaemenid empire inaugurated a new era of world history. The Achaemenids borrowed military and administrative techniques devised earlier by Babylonian and Assyrian rulers, but they applied those techniques on a much larger scale than did any of their Mesopotamian predecessors. In doing so they conquered a vast empire and then governed its diverse lands and peoples with tolerable success for more than two centuries. The Achaemenids demonstrated how it was possible to build and maintain a vast imperial state, and their example inspired later efforts to establish similar large-scale imperial states based in Persia and other Eurasian lands as well. The

Achaemenid and later Persian empires integrated much of the territory from the Mediterranean Sea to the Indus River into a commonwealth in which peoples of different regions and ethnic groups participated in a larger economy and society. By sponsoring regular and systematic interactions between peoples of different communities, the Persian empires wielded tremendous cultural as well as political, social, and economic influence. Indeed, Persian religious beliefs helped to shape moral and religious thought throughout much of southwest Asia and the Mediterranean basin. Zoroastrian teachings were particularly influential: although Zoroastrianism declined after the Sasanid dynasty, its doctrines strongly influenced the fundamental teachings of Judaism, Christianity, and Islam. ●

CHRONOLOGY

7th–6th centuries B.C.E.(?)	Life of Zarathustra
558–330 B.C.E.	Achaemenid dynasty
558–530 B.C.E.	Reign of Cyrus the Achaemenid
521–486 B.C.E.	Reign of Darius
334–330 B.C.E.	Invasion and conquest of the Achaemenid empire by Alexander of Macedon
323–83 B.C.E.	Seleucid dynasty
247 B.C.E.–224 C.E.	Parthian dynasty
224–651 C.E.	Sasanid dynasty

For Further Reading

Lindsay Allen. *The Persian Empire.* Chicago, 2005. A valuable survey of the Achaemenid empire with special attention to archaeological discoveries.

Mary Boyce, ed. *Textual Sources for the Study of Zoroastrianism.* Totowa, N.J., 1984. Sources in translation with numerous explanatory comments by the author.

———. *Zoroastrians: Their Religious Beliefs and Practices.* London, 1979. A survey of Zoroastrian history by a leading revisionist scholar.

Maria Brosius. *The Persians: An Introduction.* London, 2006. Perhaps the best short account of the Persian empires.

———. *Women in Ancient Persia, 559–331 B.C.* Oxford, 1996. Carefully examines both Persian and Greek sources for information about women and their role in Achaemenid society.

John Curtis and Nigel Tallis, eds. *Forgotten Empire: The World of Ancient Persia.* Berkeley, 2005. A lavishly illustrated collection of essays by experts on various aspects of the Achaemenid empire.

Muhammad A. Dandamaev and Vladimir G. Lukonin. *The Culture and Social Institutions of Ancient Iran.* Ed. by P. L. Kohl. Cambridge, 1989. Scholarly account that brings the results of Russian research to bear on the Achaemenid empire.

Jacques Duchesne-Guillemin. *The Hymns of Zarathustra.* London, 1952. A translation and commentary of Zarathustra's most important *Gathas.*

Richard C. Foltz. *Spirituality in the Land of the Noble: How Iran Shaped the World's Religions.* Oxford, 2004. Includes an accessible discussion of the Zoroastrian faith.

Richard N. Frye. *The Heritage of Central Asia: From Antiquity to the Turkish Expansion.* Princeton, 1996. Briefly sketches the history of various Iranian-speaking peoples in the steppes of central Asia as well as on the Iranian plateau.

———. *The Heritage of Persia.* Cleveland, 1963. A leading scholar's solid survey of Persia up to the Islamic conquest.

William W. Malandra. *An Introduction to Ancient Iranian Religion.* Minneapolis, 1983. Careful study of Zoroastrian textual sources.

Susan Sherwin-White and Amélie Kuhrt. *From Samarkhand to Sardis: A New Approach to the Seleucid Empire.* Berkeley, 1993. Detailed scholarly analysis of the Seleucid empire concentrating on political and economic matters.

Mark van de Mieroop. *A History of the Ancient Near East, ca. 3000–323 B.C.* Oxford, 2004. A concise and readable history that concludes with the Achaemenid empire.

Mortimer Wheeler. *Flames over Persepolis.* New York, 1968. Deals with Alexander's conquest of the Achaemenid empire and especially the spread of Greek art styles throughout the Persian empire.

Robert C. Zaehner. *The Dawn and Twilight of Zoroastrianism.* London, 1961. An important interpretation of Zoroastrianism that concentrates on the Achaemenid and Sasanid periods.

———, ed. *The Teachings of the Magi: A Compendium of Zoroastrian Beliefs.* London, 1956. Translations of texts by later Zoroastrian theologians.

The Unification of China

chapter 8

An eighteenth-century painting depicts the Han emperor discussing classical texts with Confucian scholars.

EYEWITNESS:
Sima Qian: Speaking Truth to Power in Han China

In the year 99 B.C.E., Chinese imperial officials sentenced the historian Sima Qian to punishment by castration. Like his father before him, Sima Qian was the official astrologer and historian at the court of the Han dynasty in Chang'an. For more than a decade, he had worked diligently on a project that he had inherited from his father—a history of China from earliest times to his own day. This project brought Sima Qian high prominence at the imperial court. When he spoke in defense of a dishonored general, his views attracted widespread attention. The emperor reacted furiously when he learned that Sima Qian had publicly expressed opinions that contradicted the ruler's judgment and ordered the historian to undergo his humiliating punishment.

Human castration was by no means uncommon in premodern times. Thousands of boys and young men of undistinguished birth underwent voluntary castration in China and many other lands as well in order to pursue careers as **eunuchs.** Ruling elites often appointed eunuchs, rather than nobles, to sensitive posts because eunuchs did not sire families and so could not build power bases to challenge established authorities. As personal servants of ruling elites, eunuchs sometimes came to wield enormous power because of their influence with rulers and their families.

Exemplary punishment was not an appealing alternative, however, to educated elites and other prominent individuals: when sentenced to punitive castration, Chinese men of honor normally avoided the penalty by taking their own lives. Yet Sima Qian chose to endure his punishment. In a letter to a friend, he explained that an early death by suicide would mean that a work that only he was capable of producing would go forever unwritten. To transmit his understanding of the Chinese past, then, Sima Qian opted to live and work in disgrace until his death about 90 B.C.E.

During his last years Sima Qian completed a massive work consisting of 130 chapters, most of which survive. He consulted court documents and the historical works of his

eunuchs (YOO-nihks)

predecessors, and when writing about his own age he supplemented those sources with personal observations and information gleaned from political and military figures who played leading roles in Chinese society. He composed historical accounts of the emperors' reigns and biographical sketches of notable figures, including ministers, statesmen, generals, empresses, aristocrats, scholars, officials, merchants, and rebels. He even described the societies of neighboring peoples with whom Chinese sometimes conducted trade and sometimes made war. The work of the disgraced but conscientious scholar Sima Qian provides the best information available about the development of early imperial China.

A rich body of political and social thought prepared the way for the unification of China under the Qin and Han dynasties. Confucians, Daoists, Legalists, and others formed schools of thought and worked to bring political and social stability to China during the chaotic years of the late Zhou dynasty and the Period of the Warring States. Legalist ideas contributed directly to unification by outlining means by which rulers could strengthen their states. The works of the Confucians and the Daoists did not lend themselves so readily to the unification process, but both schools of thought survived and profoundly influenced Chinese political and cultural traditions.

Like the Achaemenid rulers of classical Persia, the Qin and Han emperors built a powerful, centralized state on the foundation of a productive agricultural society. Like the Achaemenids, the Qin and Han emperors ruled through an elaborate bureaucracy, and they built an extensive network of roads that linked the various regions of their empire. The Qin and Han emperors went even further than their Persian counterparts in their efforts to foster cultural unity. They imposed a common written language throughout China and established an educational system based on Confucian thought and values. For almost 450 years the Qin and Han dynasties guided the fortunes of China and established a strong precedent for centralized imperial rule.

Especially during the Han dynasty, political stability was the foundation of economic prosperity. High agricultural productivity supported the development of iron and silk industries, and Chinese goods found markets in central Asia, India, the Persian empire, and even the Mediterranean basin. In spite of economic prosperity, however, later Han society experienced deep divisions between the small class of extremely wealthy landowners and the masses of landless poor. Those divisions eventually led to civil disorder and the emergence of political factions, which ultimately brought the Han dynasty to an end.

IN SEARCH OF POLITICAL AND SOCIAL ORDER

The late centuries of the Zhou dynasty brought political confusion to China and led eventually to the chaos associated with the Period of the Warring States (403–221 B.C.E.). During those same centuries, however, there also took place a remarkable cultural flowering that left a permanent mark on Chinese history. In a way, political turmoil helps to explain the cultural creativity of the late Zhou dynasty and the Period of the Warring States because it forced thoughtful people to reflect on the nature of society and the proper roles of human beings in society. Some sought to identify principles that would restore political and social order. Others concerned themselves with a search for individual tranquility apart from society. Three schools of thought that emerged during those centuries of confusion and chaos—Confucianism, Daoism, and Legalism—exercised a particularly deep influence on Chinese political and cultural traditions.

Confucius and His School

Confucius The first Chinese thinker who addressed the problem of political and social order in a straightforward and self-conscious way was Kong Fuzi (551–479 B.C.E.)—"Master Philosopher Kong," as his disciples called him, or Confucius, as he is known in English. He came from an aristocratic family in the state of Lu in northern China, and for many years he sought an influential post at the Lu court. But Confucius was a strong-willed man who often did not get along well with others. He could be quite cantankerous: he was known to lodge bitter complaints, for example, if someone undercooked or overcooked his rice. Not surprisingly, then, he refused to compromise his beliefs in the interest of political expediency, and he insisted on observing principles that frequently clashed with state policy. When he realized that he would never obtain anything more than a minor post in Lu, Confucius left in search of a more prestigious appointment elsewhere. For about ten years he traveled to courts throughout northern China, but he found none willing to accept his services. In 484 B.C.E., bitterly disappointed, he returned to Lu, where he died five years later.

Confucian Ideas Confucius never realized his ambition to become a powerful minister. Throughout his career, however, he served as an educator as well as a political advisor, and in that capacity he left an enduring mark on Chinese

society. He attracted numerous disciples who aspired to political careers. Some of his pupils compiled the master's sayings and teachings in a book known as the *Analects,* a work that has profoundly influenced Chinese political and cultural traditions.

Confucius's thought was fundamentally moral, ethical, and political in character. It was also thoroughly practical: Confucius did not address abstruse philosophical questions, because he thought they would not help to solve the political and social problems of his day. Nor did he deal with religious questions, because he thought they went beyond the capacity of mortal human intelligence. He did not even concern himself much with the structure of the state, because he thought political and social harmony arose from the proper ordering of human relationships rather than the establishment of state offices. In an age when bureaucratic institutions were not yet well developed, Confucius believed that the best way to promote good government was to fill official positions with individuals who were both well educated and extraordinarily conscientious. Thus Confucius concentrated on the formation of what he called *junzi*—"superior individuals"—who took a broad view of public affairs and did not allow personal interests to influence their judgments.

No contemporary portrait of Confucius survives, but artists have used their imaginations and depicted him in many ways over the years. This portrait of 1735 identifies Confucius as "the Sage and Teacher" and represents him in the distinctive dress of an eighteenth-century Confucian scholar-bureaucrat.

In the absence of an established educational system and a formal curriculum, Confucius had his disciples study works of poetry and history produced during the Zhou dynasty, since he believed that they provided excellent insight into human nature. He carefully examined the *Book of Songs,* the *Book of History,* the *Book of Rites,* and other works with his students, concentrating especially on their practical value for prospective administrators. As a result of Confucius's influence, literary works of the Zhou dynasty became the core texts of the traditional Chinese education. For more than two thousand years, until the early twentieth century C.E., talented Chinese seeking government posts proceeded through a cycle of studies deriving from the one developed by Confucius in the fifth century B.C.E.

For Confucius, though, an advanced education represented only a part of the preparation needed by the ideal government official. More important than formal learning was the possession of a strong sense of moral integrity and a capacity to deliver wise and fair judgments. Thus Confucius encouraged his students to cultivate high ethical standards and to hone their faculties of analysis and judgment.

Confucian Values Confucius emphasized several qualities in particular. One of them he called *ren,* by which he meant an attitude of kindness and benevolence or a sense of humanity. Confucius explained that individuals possessing *ren* were courteous, respectful, diligent, and loyal, and he considered *ren* a characteristic desperately needed in government officials. Another quality of central importance was *li,* a sense of propriety, which called for individuals to behave in conventionally appropriate fashion: they should treat all other human beings with courtesy, while showing special respect and deference to elders or superiors. Yet another quality that Confucius emphasized was ***xiao,*** filial piety, which reflected the high significance of the family in Chinese society. The demands of filial piety obliged children to respect their parents and other family elders, look after their welfare, support them in old age, and remember them along with other ancestors after their deaths.

Confucius emphasized personal qualities such as *ren, li,* and *xiao* because he believed that individuals who possessed those traits would gain influence in the larger society. Those who disciplined themselves and properly molded their characters would not only possess personal self-control but also have the power of leading others by example. Only through enlightened leadership by morally strong individuals, Confucius believed, was there any hope for the restoration of political and social order in China. Thus his goal was not simply the cultivation of personal morality for

xiao (SHAYOH)

sources from the past

Confucius on Good Government

Confucius never composed formal writings, but his disciples collected his often pithy remarks into a work known as the Analects *("sayings"). Referred to as "the Master" in the following excerpts from the* Analects, *Confucius consistently argued that only good men possessing moral authority could rule effectively.*

The Master said, "He who exercises government by means of his virtue may be compared to the north polar star, which keeps its place, while all the stars turn toward it. . . ."

The Master said, "If the people be led by laws, and uniformity be imposed on them by punishments, they will try to avoid the punishment, but will have no sense of shame.

"If they be led by virtue, and uniformity be provided for them by the rules of propriety, they will have the sense of shame, and moreover will become good. . . ."

The duke Ai asked, saying, "What should be done in order to secure the submission of the people?" Confucius replied, "Advance the upright and set aside the crooked, and then the people will submit. Advance the crooked and set aside the upright, and then the people will not submit."

Ji Kang asked how to cause the people to reverence their ruler, to be faithful to him, and to go on to seek virtue. The Master said, "Let him preside over them with gravity; then they will reverence him. Let him be filial and kind to all; then they will be faithful to him. Let him advance the good and teach the incompetent; then they will eagerly seek to be virtuous. . . ."

Zigong asked about government. The Master said, "The requisites of government are that there be sufficiency of food, sufficiency of military equipment, and the confidence of the people in their ruler."

Zigong said, "If it cannot be helped, and one of these must be dispensed with, which of the three should be foregone first?" "The military equipment," said the Master.

Zigong again asked, "If it cannot be helped, and one of the remaining two must be dispensed with, which of them should be foregone?" The Master answered, "Part with the food. From olden times, death has been the lot of all men; but if the people have no faith in their rulers, there is no standing for the state. . . ."

Ji Kang asked Confucius about government, saying, "What do you say to killing the unprincipled for the good of the principled?" Confucius replied, "Sir, in carrying on your government, why should you use killing at all? Let your evinced desires be for what is good, and the people will be good. The relation between superiors and inferiors is like that between the wind and the grass. The grass must bend when the wind blows across it. . . ."

The Master said, "When a prince's personal conduct is correct, his government is effective without the issuing of orders. If his personal conduct is not correct, he may issue orders, but they will not be followed."

For Further Reflection

- Compare Confucius's understanding of moral virtue with Zarathustra's notion of morality discussed in the previous chapter.

Source: James Legge, trans. *The Chinese Classics,* 7 vols. Oxford: Clarendon Press, 1893, 1:145, 146, 152, 254, 258–59, 266. (Translations slightly modified.)

its own sake but, rather, the creation of *junzi* who could bring order and stability to China.

Because Confucius expressed his thought in general terms, later disciples could adapt it to the particular problems of their times. Indeed, the flexibility of Confucian thought helps to account for its remarkable longevity and influence in China. Two later disciples of Confucius—Mencius and Xunzi—illustrate especially well the ways in which Confucian thought lent itself to elaboration and adaptation.

Mencius Mencius (372–289 B.C.E.) was the most learned man of his age and the principal spokesman for the Confucian school. During the Period of the Warring States, he traveled widely throughout China, consulting with rulers and offering advice on political issues. Mencius firmly believed that human nature was basically good, and he argued for policies that would allow it to influence society as a whole. Thus he placed special emphasis on the Confucian virtue of *ren* and advocated government by benevolence and humanity. This principle implied that rulers would levy light taxes, avoid wars, support education, and encourage harmony and cooperation. Critics charged that Mencius held a naively optimistic view of human nature, arguing that his policies would rarely succeed in the real world where human interests, wills, and ambitions constantly clash. Indeed, Mencius's advice had little practical effect during his lifetime. Over the long term, however, his ideas deeply influenced the Confucian tradition. Since about the tenth century C.E., many Chinese scholars have considered Mencius the most authoritative of Confucius's early expositors.

Xunzi Like Confucius and Mencius, Xunzi (298–238 B.C.E.) was a man of immense learning, but unlike his predecessors, he also served for many years as a government administrator. His practical experience encouraged him to develop a view of human nature that was less rosy than Mencius's view. Xunzi believed that human beings selfishly pursued their own interests, no matter what effects their actions had on others, and resisted making any contribution voluntarily to the larger society. He considered strong social discipline the best means to bring order to society. Thus whereas Mencius emphasized the Confucian quality of *ren,* Xunzi emphasized *li.* He advocated the establishment of clear, well-publicized standards of conduct that would set limits on the pursuit of individual interests and punish those who neglected their obligations to the larger society. Xunzi once likened human beings to pieces of warped lumber: just as it was possible to straighten out bad wood, so too it was possible to turn selfish and recalcitrant individuals into useful, contributing members of society. But the process involved harsh social discipline similar to the steam treatments, heat applications, hammering, bending, and forcible wrenching that turned warped wood into useful lumber.

Like Confucius and Mencius, however, Xunzi also believed that it was possible to improve human beings and restore order to society. This fundamental optimism was a basic characteristic of Confucian thought. It explains the high value that Confucian thinkers placed on education and public behavior, and it accounts also for their activist approach to public affairs. Confucians involved themselves in society: they sought government positions and made conscientious efforts to solve political and social problems and to promote harmony in public life. By no means, however, did the Confucians win universal praise for their efforts: to some of their contemporaries, Confucian activism represented little more than misspent energy.

Daoism

The Daoists were the most prominent critics of Confucian activism. Like Confucianism, Daoist thought developed in response to the turbulence of the late Zhou dynasty and the Period of the Warring States. But unlike the Confucians, the Daoists considered it pointless to waste time and energy on problems that defied solution. Instead of Confucian social activism, the Daoists devoted their energies to reflection and introspection, in hopes that they could understand the natural principles that governed the world and could learn how to live in harmony with them. The Daoists believed that over time, this approach would bring harmony to society as a whole, as people ceased to meddle in affairs that they could not understand or control.

Laozi and the *Daodejing* According to Chinese tradition, the founder of Daoism was a sage named Laozi who lived during the sixth century B.C.E. Although there probably was a historical Laozi, it is almost certain that several hands contributed to the *Daodejing* (*Classic of the Way and of Virtue*), the basic exposition of Daoist beliefs traditionally ascribed to Laozi, and that the book acquired its definitive form over several centuries. After the *Daodejing,* the most important Daoist work was the *Zhuangzi,* named after its author, the philosopher Zhuangzi (369–286 B.C.E.), who provided a well-reasoned compendium of Daoist views.

The *Dao* Daoism represented an effort to understand the fundamental character of the world and nature. The central concept of Daoism is *dao,* meaning "the way," more specifically "the way of nature" or "the way of the cosmos." *Dao* is an elusive concept, and the Daoists themselves did not generally characterize it in positive and forthright terms. In the *Daodejing,* for example, *dao* figures as the original force of the cosmos, an eternal and unchanging principle that governs all the workings of the world. Yet the *Daodejing* envisioned *dao* as a supremely passive force and spoke of it mostly in negative terms: *Dao* does nothing, and yet it accomplishes everything. *Dao* resembles water, which is soft and yielding, yet is also so powerful that it eventually erodes even the hardest rock placed in its path. *Dao* also resembles the cavity of a pot or the hub of a wheel: although they are nothing more than empty spaces, they make the pot and the wheel useful tools.

"Daoists devoted their energies to reflection and introspection, in hopes that they could understand the natural principles that governed the world."

If the principles of *dao* governed the world, it followed that human beings should tailor their behavior to its passive and yielding nature. To the Daoists, living in harmony with *dao* meant retreating from engagement in the world of politics and administration. Ambition and activism had not solved political and social problems. Far from it: human striving had brought the world to a state of chaos. The proper response to that situation was to cease frantic striving and live in as simple a manner as possible.

The Doctrine of *Wuwei* Thus early Daoists recognized as the chief moral virtue the trait of ***wuwei***—disengagement from the competitive exertions and active involvement in affairs of the world. *Wuwei* required that individuals refrain

wuwei (woo-WAY)

A jade statue produced about the tenth century C.E. depicts the sage Laozi on an ox. Legends reported that Laozi rode a blue ox from China to central Asia when spreading his teachings. Why would simple dress and transport be appropriate for Laozi?

from advanced education (which concentrated on abstruse trivialities) and from personal striving (which indicated excessive concern with the tedious affairs of the world). *Wuwei* called instead for individuals to live simply, unpretentiously, and in harmony with nature.

Wuwei also had implications for state and society: the less government, the better. Instead of expansive kingdoms and empires, the *Daodejing* envisioned a world of tiny, self-sufficient communities where people had no desire to conquer their neighbors or to trade with them. Indeed, even when people lived so close to the next community that they could hear the dogs barking and cocks crowing, they would be so content with their existence that they would not even have the desire to visit their neighbors!

Daoists subjected their philosophical rivals to ferocious attacks for dwelling on trivial and superficial issues instead of practicing *wuwei* and living in harmony with nature. Zhuangzi in particular possessed a caustic wit that he deployed effectively in mocking the Confucians and other philosophers for engaging in meaningless debates. Once, for example, he related a fable about a keeper of monkeys who ran low on food for his animals. He advised the monkeys that conditions forced him to cut their rations, so in the future he would bring them only three nuts in the morning and four in the afternoon. When the monkeys exploded in fury, the keeper relented and promised to bring four nuts in the morning and three in the afternoon—a proposal that the monkeys accepted with delight. The philosophers' fierce debates, Zhuangzi implied, were just as insignificant as the uproar over the monkeys' feeding schedule.

Political Implications of Daoism By encouraging the development of a reflective and introspective consciousness, Daoism served as a counterbalance to the activism and extroversion of the Confucian tradition. Indeed, Daoism encouraged the cultivation of self-knowledge in a way that appealed strongly to Confucians as well as to Daoists. Because neither Confucianism nor Daoism was an exclusive faith that precluded observance of the other, it has been possible through the centuries for individuals to study the Confucian curriculum and take administrative posts in the government while devoting their private hours to reflection on human nature and the place of humans in the larger world—to live as Confucians by day, as it were, and Daoists by night.

Legalism

Ultimately, neither Confucian activism nor Daoist retreat was able to solve the problems that plagued China during the Period of the Warring States. Order returned to China only after the emergence of a third school of thought—that of the Legalists—which promoted a practical and ruthlessly efficient approach to statecraft. Unlike the Confucians, the Legalists did not concern themselves with ethics, morality, or propriety. Unlike the Daoists, the Legalists cared nothing about principles governing the world or the place of human beings in nature. Instead, they devoted their attention exclusively to the state, which they sought to strengthen and expand at all costs.

Shang Yang Legalist doctrine emerged from the insights of men who participated actively in Chinese political affairs during the late fourth century B.C.E. Most notable of them was Shang Yang (ca. 390–338 B.C.E.), who served as chief minister to the duke of the Qin state in western China. His policies survive in a work entitled *The Book of Lord Shang,* which most likely includes contributions from other ministers as well as from Shang Yang himself. Though a clever and efficient administrator, Shang Yang also was despised and feared because of his power and ruthlessness. Upon the death of his patron, the duke of Qin, Shang Yang quickly fell: his enemies at court executed him, mutilated his body, and annihilated his family.

Han Feizi The most systematic of the Legalist theorists was Han Feizi (ca. 280–233 B.C.E.), a student of the Confucian scholar Xunzi. Han Feizi carefully reviewed Legalist ideas from political thinkers in all parts of China and synthesized them in a collection of powerful and well-argued essays on statecraft. Like Shang Yang, Han Feizi served as an advisor at the Qin court, and he too fell afoul of other ambitious men, who forced him to end his life by taking

sources from the past

Laozi on Living in Harmony with *Dao*

Committed Daoists mostly rejected opportunities to play active roles in government. Yet like the Confucians, the Daoists held strong views on virtuous behavior, and their understanding of dao *had deep political implications, as exemplified by the following excerpts from the* Daodejing.

The highest goodness is like water, for water is excellent in benefitting all things, and it does not strive. It occupies the lowest place, which men abhor. And therefore it is near akin to the *dao*. . . .

In governing men and in serving heaven, there is nothing like moderation. For only by moderation can there be an early return to the normal state of humankind. This early return is the same as a great storage of virtue. With a great storage of virtue there is nothing that may not be achieved. If there is nothing that may not be achieved, then no one will know to what extent this power reaches. And if no one knows to what extent a man's power reaches, that man is fit to be the ruler of a state. Having the secret of rule, his rule shall endure. Setting the tap-root deep, and making the spreading roots firm: this is the way to ensure long life to the tree. . . .

Use uprightness in ruling a state; employ indirect methods in waging war; practice non-interference in order to win the empire. . . .

The greater the number of laws and enactments, the more thieves and robbers there will be. Therefore the Sage [Laozi] says: "So long as I do nothing, the people will work out their own reformation. So long as I love calm, the people will right themselves. If only I keep from meddling, the people will grow rich. If only I am free from desire, the people will come naturally back to simplicity. . . ."

There is nothing in the world more soft and weak than water, yet for attacking things that are hard and strong, there is nothing that surpasses it, nothing that can take its place.

The soft overcomes the hard; the weak overcomes the strong. There is no one in the world but knows this truth, and no one who can put it into practice.

For Further Reflection

- To what extent did Daoists offer useful or practical political alternatives in the Period of the Warring States?

Source: Lionel Giles, trans. *The Sayings of Lao Tzu.* London: John Murray, 1905, pp. 26, 29–30, 41, 50. (Translations slightly modified.)

poison. The Legalist state itself thus consumed the two foremost exponents of Legalist doctrine.

Legalist Doctrine Shang Yang, Han Feizi, and other Legalists reasoned that the foundations of a state's strength were agriculture and armed forces. Thus Legalists sought to channel as many individuals as possible into cultivation or military service while discouraging them from pursuing careers as merchants, entrepreneurs, scholars, educators, philosophers, poets, or artists, since those lines of work did not directly advance the interests of the state.

The Legalists expected to harness subjects' energy by means of clear and strict laws—hence the name "Legalist." Their faith in laws distinguished the Legalists clearly from the Confucians, who relied on ritual, custom, education, a sense of propriety, and the humane example of benevolent *junzi* administrators to induce individuals to behave appropriately. The Legalists believed that those influences were not powerful enough to persuade subjects to subordinate their self-interest to the needs of the state. They imposed a strict legal regimen that clearly outlined expectations and provided severe punishment, swiftly administered, for violators. They believed that if people feared to commit small crimes, they would hesitate all the more before committing great crimes. Thus Legalists imposed harsh penalties even for minor infractions: individuals could suffer amputation of their hands or feet, for example, for disposing of ashes or trash in the street. The Legalists also established the principle of collective responsibility before the law. They expected all members of a family or community to observe the others closely, forestall any illegal activity, and report any infractions. Failing those obligations, all members of a family or community were liable to punishment along with the actual violator.

The Legalists' principles of government did not win them much popularity. Over the course of the centuries, Chinese moral and political philosophers have had little praise for the Legalists, and few have openly associated themselves with the Legalist school. Yet Legalist doctrine lent itself readily to practical application, and Legalist principles of government quickly produced remarkable results for rulers who adopted them. In fact, Legalist methods put an end to the Period of the Warring States and brought about the unification of China.

THE UNIFICATION OF CHINA

During the Period of the Warring States, rulers of several regional states adopted elements of the Legalist program. Legalist doctrines met the most enthusiastic response in the state of Qin, in western China, where Shang Yang and Han Feizi oversaw the implementation of Legalist policies. The Qin state soon dominated its neighbors and imposed centralized imperial rule throughout China. Qin rule survived only for a few years, but the succeeding Han dynasty followed the Qin example by governing China through a centralized imperial administration.

The Qin Dynasty

The Kingdom of Qin During the fourth and third centuries B.C.E., the Qin state underwent a remarkable round of economic, political, and military development. Shang Yang encouraged peasant cultivators to migrate to the sparsely populated state. By granting them private plots and allowing them to enjoy generous profits, his policy dramatically boosted agricultural production. By granting land rights to individual cultivators, his policy also weakened the economic position of the hereditary aristocratic classes. That approach allowed Qin rulers to establish centralized, bureaucratic rule throughout their state. Meanwhile, they devoted the newfound wealth of their state to the organization of a powerful army equipped with the most effective iron weapons available. During the third century B.C.E., the kingdom of Qin gradually but consistently grew at the expense of the other Chinese states. Qin rulers attacked one state after another, absorbing each new conquest into their centralized structure, until finally they had brought China for the first time under the sway of a single state.

The First Emperor In the year 221 B.C.E., the king of Qin proclaimed himself the First Emperor and decreed that his descendants would follow him and reign for thousands of generations. The First Emperor, Qin Shihuangdi (reigned 221–210 B.C.E.), could not know that his dynasty would last only fourteen years and in 207 B.C.E. would dissolve because of civil insurrections. Yet the Qin dynasty had a significance out of proportion to its short life. Like the Achaemenid empire in Persia, the Qin dynasty established a tradition of centralized imperial rule that provided large-scale political organization over the long term of Chinese history.

Like his ancestors in the kingdom of Qin, the First Emperor of China ignored the nobility and ruled his empire through a centralized bureaucracy. He governed from his

MAP 8.1
China under the Qin dynasty, 221–207 B.C.E.
Compare the size of Qin territories with those of earlier Chinese kingdoms depicted in Maps 5.1 and 5.2.
How is it possible to account for the greater reach of the Qin dynasty?

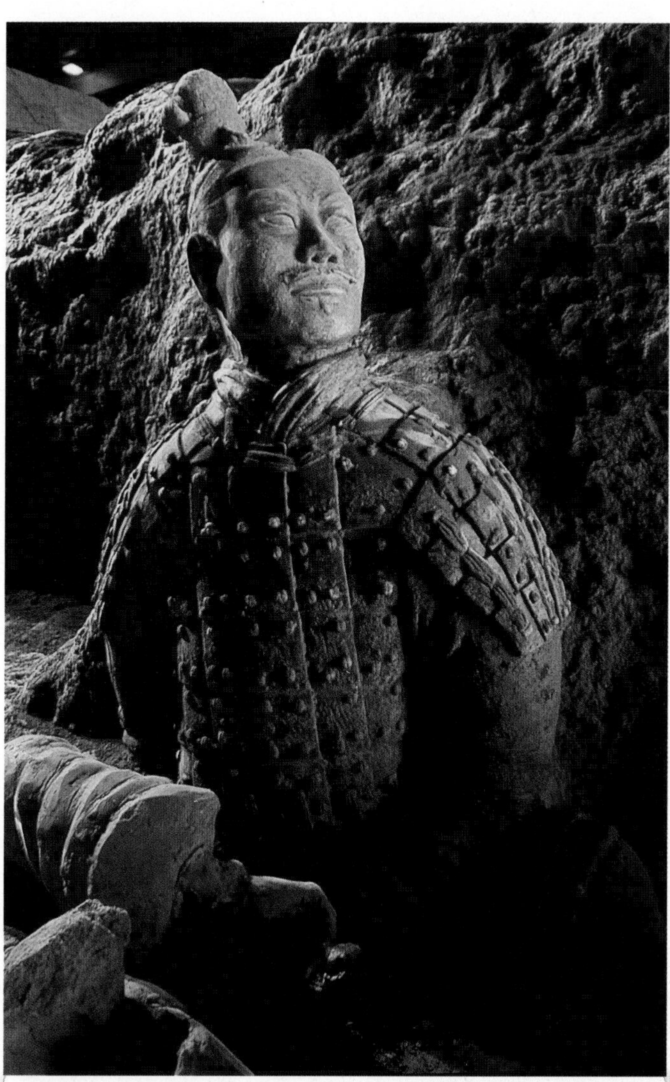
A life-size model of an infantryman suggests the discipline that drove the armies of Qin Shihuangdi, the self-proclaimed First Emperor of China.

capital at **Xianyang,** near the early Zhou capital of Hao and the modern city of Xi'an. The remainder of China he divided into administrative provinces and districts, and he entrusted the communication and implementation of his policies to officers of the central government who served at the pleasure of the emperor himself. He disarmed regional military forces and destroyed fortresses that might serve as points of rebellion or resistance. He built roads to facilitate communications and the movement of armies: his network of roads extended more than 6,800 kilometers (4,000 miles). He also drafted laborers by the hundreds of thousands to build defensive walls. Regional kings in northern and western regions of China had already constructed many walls in their realms in an effort to discourage raids by nomadic peoples. Qin Shihuangdi ordered workers to link the existing sections into a massive defensive barrier that was a precursor to the Great Wall of China.

The Burning of the Books It is likely that many Chinese welcomed the political stability introduced by the Qin dynasty, but by no means did the new regime win universal acceptance. Confucians, Daoists, and others launched a vigorous campaign of criticism. In an effort to reassert his authority, Qin Shihuangdi ordered execution for those who criticized his regime, and he demanded the burning of all books of philosophy, ethics, history, and literature. His decree exempted works on medicine, fortune-telling, and agriculture on the grounds that they had some utilitarian value. The emperor also spared the official history of the Qin state. Other works, however, largely went into the flames during the next few years.

The First Emperor took his policy seriously and enforced it earnestly. In the year following his decree, Qin Shihuangdi sentenced some 460 scholars residing in the capital to be buried alive for their criticism of his regime, and he forced many other critics from the provinces into the army and dispatched them to dangerous frontier posts. For the better part of a generation, there was no open discussion of classical literary or philosophical works. When it became safe again to speak openly, scholars began a long and painstaking task of reconstructing the suppressed texts. In some cases, scholars had managed, at great personal risk, to hide copies of the forbidden books, which they retrieved and recirculated. In other cases they reassembled texts that they had committed to memory. In many cases, however, works suppressed by Qin Shihuangdi simply disappeared.

Qin Centralization The First Emperor launched several initiatives that enhanced the unity of China. In keeping with his policy of centralization, he standardized the laws, currencies, weights, and measures of the various regions of China. Previously, regional states had organized their own legal and economic systems, which often conflicted with one another and hampered commerce and communications across state boundaries. Uniform coinage and legal standards encouraged the integration of China's various regions into a more tightly knit society than had ever been conceivable before. The roads and bridges that Qin Shihuangdi built throughout his realm, like those built in other classical societies, also encouraged economic integration: though constructed largely with military uses in mind, they served as fine highways for interregional commerce.

Standardized Script Perhaps even more important than his legal and economic policies was the First Emperor's standardization of Chinese script. Before the Qin dynasty, all regions of China used scripts derived from the one employed at the Shang court, but they had developed along

Xianyang (SHYAHN-YAHNG)

different lines and had become mutually unrecognizable. In hopes of ensuring better understanding and uniform application of his policies, Qin Shihuangdi mandated the use of a common script throughout his empire. The regions of China continued to use different spoken languages, as they do even today, but they wrote those languages with a common script—just as if Europeans spoke English, French, German, Italian, Russian, Spanish, and other languages but wrote them all down in Latin. In China, speakers of different languages use the same written symbols, but pronounce them and process them mentally in different ways. Nevertheless, the common script enables them to communicate in writing across linguistic boundaries.

In spite of his ruthlessness, Qin Shihuangdi ranks as one of the most important figures in Chinese history. The First Emperor established a precedent for centralized imperial rule, which remained the norm in China until the early twentieth century. He also pointed China in the direction of political and cultural unity, and with some periods of interruption, China has remained politically and culturally unified to the present day.

Tomb of the First Emperor Qin Shihuangdi died in 210 B.C.E. His final resting place was a lavish tomb constructed by some seven hundred thousand drafted laborers as a permanent monument to the First Emperor. Rare and expensive grave goods accompanied the emperor in burial, along with sacrificed slaves, concubines, and many of the craftsmen who designed and built the tomb. Qin Shihuangdi was laid to rest in an elaborate underground palace lined with bronze and protected by traps and crossbows rigged to fire at intruders. The ceiling of the palace featured paintings of the stars and planets, and a vast map of the First Emperor's realm, with flowing mercury representing its rivers and seas, decorated the floor. Buried in the vicinity of the tomb was an entire army of life-size pottery figures to guard the emperor in death. Since 1974, when scholars began to excavate the area around Qin Shihuangdi's tomb, more than fifteen thousand terra-cotta sculptures have come to light, including magnificently detailed soldiers, horses, and weapons.

The terra-cotta army of Qin Shihuangdi protected his tomb until recent times, but it could not save his successors or his empire. The First Emperor had conscripted millions of laborers from all parts of China to work on ambitious public works projects such as palaces, roads, bridges, irrigation systems, defensive walls, and his tomb. Although those projects increased productivity and promoted the in-

One detachment of the formidable, life-size, terra-cotta army buried in the vicinity of Qin Shihuangdi's tomb to protect the emperor after his death. The army consists of soldiers by the tens of thousands, along with weapons, horses, carts, and equipment. What does the construction of such a tomb suggest about Qin Shihuangdi's power and ability to command resources?

tegration of China's various regions, they also generated tremendous ill will among laborers compelled to leave their families and their lands. Revolts began in the year after Qin Shihuangdi's death, and in 207 B.C.E. waves of rebels overwhelmed the Qin court, slaughtering government officials and burning state buildings. The Qin dynasty quickly dissolved in chaos.

The Early Han Dynasty

Liu Bang The bloody end of the Qin dynasty might well have ended the experiment with centralized imperial rule in China. Although ambitious governors and generals could have carved China into regions and contested one another for hegemony in a reprise of the Period of the Warring States, centralized rule returned almost immediately, largely because of a determined commander named Liu Bang. Judging from the historian Sima Qian's account, Liu Bang was not a colorful or charismatic figure—indeed, he was a crude and somewhat oafish character with a large appetite for strong drink—but he was also a persistent man and a methodical planner. He surrounded himself with brilliant advisors and enjoyed the unwavering loyalty of his troops. By 206 B.C.E. he had restored order throughout China and established himself at the head of a new dynasty.

"The Han dynasty consolidated the tradition of centralized imperial rule that the Qin dynasty had pioneered."

Liu Bang called the new dynasty the Han, in honor of his native land. The Han dynasty turned out to be one of the longest and most influential in all of Chinese history. It lasted for more than four hundred years, from 206 B.C.E. to 220 C.E., although for a brief period (9–23 C.E.) a usurper temporarily displaced Han rule. Thus historians conventionally divide the dynasty into the Former Han (206 B.C.E.–9 C.E.) and the Later Han (25–220 C.E.).

The Han dynasty consolidated the tradition of centralized imperial rule that the Qin dynasty had pioneered. During the Former Han, emperors ruled from Chang'an, a cosmopolitan city near modern Xi'an that became the cultural capital of China. They mostly used wood as a building material, and later dynasties built over their city, so nothing of Han-era Chang'an survives. Contemporaries described Chang'an as a thriving metropolis with a fine imperial palace, busy markets, and expansive parks. During the Later Han, the emperors moved their capital east to Luoyang, also a cosmopolitan city second in importance only to Chang'an throughout much of Chinese history.

Early Han Policies During the early days of the Han dynasty, Liu Bang attempted to follow a middle path between the decentralized network of political alliances of the Zhou dynasty and the tightly centralized state of the Qin. Zhou decentralization encouraged political chaos, he thought, because regional governors were powerful enough to resist the emperor and pursue their own ambitions. Liu Bang thought that Qin centralization created a new set of problems, however, because it provided little incentive for imperial family members to support the dynasty.

Liu Bang tried to save the advantages and avoid the excesses of both Zhou and Qin dynasties. On the one hand, he allotted large landholdings to members of the imperial family, in the expectation that they would provide a reliable network of support for his rule. On the other hand, he divided the empire into administrative districts governed by officials who served at the emperor's pleasure in the expectation that he could exercise effective control over the development and implementation of his policies.

Liu Bang learned quickly that reliance on his family did not guarantee support for the emperor. In 200 B.C.E. an army of nomadic Xiongnu warriors besieged Liu Bang and almost captured him. He managed to escape—but without receiving the support he had expected from his family members. From that point forward, Liu Bang and his successors followed a policy of centralization. They reclaimed lands from family members, absorbed those lands into the imperial domain, and entrusted political responsibilities to an administrative bureaucracy. Thus, despite a brief flirtation with a decentralized government, the Han dynasty left as its principal political legacy a tradition of centralized imperial rule.

The Martial Emperor, Han Wudi Much of the reason for the Han dynasty's success was the long reign of the dynasty's greatest and most energetic emperor, Han Wudi, the "Martial Emperor," who occupied the imperial throne for fifty-four years, from 141 to 87 B.C.E. Han Wudi ruled his empire with vision and vigor. He pursued two policies in particular: administrative centralization and imperial expansion.

Han Centralization Domestically, Han Wudi worked strenuously to increase the authority and the prestige of the central government. He built an enormous bureaucracy to administer his empire, and he relied on Legalist principles of government. Like Qin Shihuangdi, Han Wudi sent imperial officers to implement his policies and maintain order in administrative provinces and districts. He also continued the Qin policy of building roads and canals to facilitate trade and communication between China's regions. To finance the vast machinery of his government, he levied taxes on agriculture, trade, and craft industries, and he established imperial monopolies on the production of essential goods such as iron and salt while placing the lucrative liquor industry under state supervision.

Model of a luxury chariot of the kind used by high imperial officials in the Qin and Han dynasties. Crafted from bronze with silver inlay, this model is about one-third life size.

In building such an enormous governmental structure, Han Wudi faced a serious problem of recruitment. He needed thousands of reliable, intelligent, educated individuals to run his bureaucracy, but education in China took place largely on an individual, ad hoc basis. Men such as Confucius, Mencius, and Xunzi accepted students and tutored them, but there was no system to provide a continuous supply of educated candidates for office.

The Confucian Educational System Han Wudi addressed that problem in 124 B.C.E. by establishing an imperial university that prepared young men for government service. Personally, the Martial Emperor was a practical man of affairs who cared little for learning. To demonstrate his contempt for academic pursuits, Liu Bang once emptied his bladder in the distinctive cap worn by Confucian scholars! Yet Han Wudi recognized that the success of his efforts at bureaucratic centralization would depend on a corps of educated officeholders. The imperial university took Confucianism—the only Chinese cultural tradition developed enough to provide rigorous intellectual discipline—as the basis for its curriculum. Ironically, then, while he relied on Legalist principles of government, Han Wudi ensured the long-term survival of the Confucian tradition by establishing it as the official imperial ideology. By the end of the Former Han dynasty, the imperial university enrolled more than three thousand students, and by the end of the Later Han, the student population had risen to more than thirty thousand.

Han Imperial Expansion While he moved aggressively to centralize power and authority at home, Han Wudi pursued an equally vigorous foreign policy of imperial expansion. He invaded northern Vietnam and Korea, subjected them to Han rule, and brought them into the orbit of Chinese society. He ruled both lands through a Chinese-style government, and Confucian values followed the Han armies into the new colonies. Over the course of the centuries, the

thinking about TRADITIONS

Confucians and Legalists
Han dynasty rulers drew on both Confucian and Legalist traditions in organizing their state. How were they able to combine such different schools of thought? How did Confucian and Legalist traditions reinforce each other in classical China?

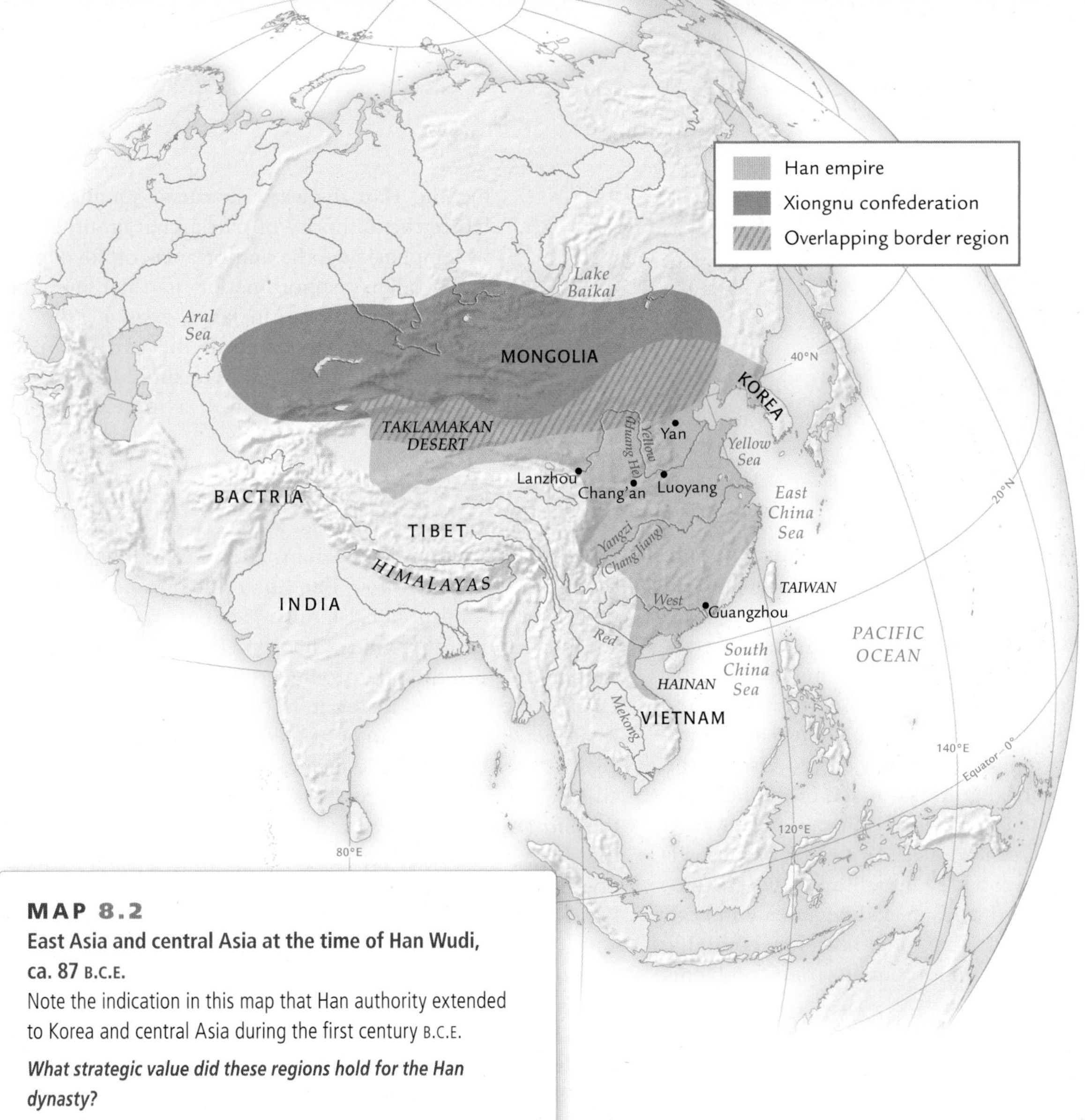

MAP 8.2
East Asia and central Asia at the time of Han Wudi, ca. 87 B.C.E.
Note the indication in this map that Han authority extended to Korea and central Asia during the first century B.C.E.
What strategic value did these regions hold for the Han dynasty?

PART 2

educational systems of both northern Vietnam and Korea drew their inspiration almost entirely from Confucianism.

The Xiongnu The greatest foreign challenge that Han Wudi faced came from the Xiongnu, a nomadic people from the steppes of central Asia who spoke a Turkish language. Like most of the other nomadic peoples of central Asia, the Xiongnu were superb horsemen. Xiongnu boys learned to ride sheep and shoot rodents at an early age, and as they grew older they graduated to larger animals and aimed their bows and arrows at larger prey. Their weaponry was not as sophisticated as that of the Chinese: their bows and arrows were not nearly as lethal as the ingenious and powerful crossbows wielded by Chinese warriors. But their mobility offered the Xiongnu a distinct advantage. When they could not satisfy their needs and desires through peaceful trade, they mounted sudden raids into villages or trading areas, where they commandeered food supplies or manufactured goods and then rapidly departed. Because they had no cities or settled places to defend, the Xiongnu could quickly disperse when confronted by a superior force.

During the reign of Maodun (210–174 B.C.E.), their most successful leader, the Xiongnu ruled a vast federation of nomadic peoples that stretched from the Aral Sea to the Yellow Sea. Maodun brought strict military discipline to the Xiongnu. According to Sima Qian, Maodun once instructed his forces to shoot their arrows at whatever target he himself selected. He aimed in succession at his favorite horse, one of his wives, and his father's best horse, and he summarily executed those who failed to discharge their arrows. When his forces reliably followed his orders, Maodun targeted his father, who immediately fell under a hail of arrows, leaving Maodun as the Xiongnu chief.

With its highly disciplined army, the Xiongnu empire was a source of concern to the Han emperors. During the early days of the dynasty, they attempted to pacify the Xiongnu by paying them tribute—providing them with food and finished goods in hopes that they would refrain from mounting raids in China—or by arranging marriages between the ruling houses of the two peoples in hopes of establishing peaceful diplomatic relations. Neither method succeeded for long.

thinking about ENCOUNTERS

Relations between Chinese and Xiongnu
Interaction between peoples of different societies can involve military conflict as well as more benign dealings, such as trade and exchanges of ideas. Why did Chinese and Xiongnu peoples engage in frequent hostilities rather than more peaceful interactions during the Han dynasty?

Han Expansion into Central Asia Ultimately, Han Wudi decided to go on the offensive against the Xiongnu. He invaded central Asia with vast armies—sometimes including as many as one hundred thousand troops—and brought much of the Xiongnu empire under Chinese military control. He pacified a long central Asian corridor extending almost to Bactria, which prevented the Xiongnu from maintaining the integrity of their empire and which served also as the lifeline of a trade network that linked much of the Eurasian landmass. He even planted colonies of Chinese cultivators in the oasis communities of central Asia. As a result of those efforts, the Xiongnu empire soon fell into disarray. For the moment, the Han state enjoyed uncontested hegemony in both east Asia and central Asia. Before long, however, economic and social problems within China brought serious problems for the Han dynasty itself.

FROM ECONOMIC PROSPERITY TO SOCIAL DISORDER

Already during the Xia, Shang, and Zhou dynasties, a productive agricultural economy supported the emergence of complex society in China. High agricultural productivity continued during the Qin and Han dynasties, and it supported the development of craft industries such as the forging of iron tools and the weaving of silk textiles. During the Han dynasty, however, China experienced serious social and economic problems as land became concentrated in the hands of a small, wealthy elite class. Social tensions generated banditry, rebellion, and even the temporary deposition of the Han state itself. Although Han rulers regained the throne, they presided over a much-weakened realm. By the early third century C.E., social and political problems had brought the Han dynasty to an end.

Productivity and Prosperity during the Former Han

Patriarchal Social Order The structure of Chinese society during the Qin and Han dynasties was similar to that of the Zhou era. Patriarchal households averaged five inhabitants, although several generations of aristocratic families sometimes lived together in large compounds. During the Han dynasty, moralists sought to enhance the authority of patriarchal family heads by emphasizing the importance of filial piety and women's subordination to their menfolk. The anonymous Confucian *Classic of Filial Piety,* composed probably in the early Han dynasty, taught that children should obey and honor their parents as well as other superiors and political authorities.

Ban Zhao, Woman Scholar An equally influential treatise was *Lessons for Women* by Ban Zhao (45–120 C.E.), perhaps the most famous woman scholar in Chinese history. Ban Zhao was born into a prominent literary and political family. Her father was a famous scholar and educator. One of her twin brothers was a powerful general, and the other followed in the footsteps of Sima Qian as the foremost historian of the later Han dynasty. Ban Zhao herself enjoyed an advanced education and argued in *Lessons for Women* that education should be available to all children—girls as well as boys. Yet Ban Zhao agreed with the *Classic of Filial Piety* and Confucian morality in general that the virtues most appropriate for women were humility, obedience, subservience, and devotion to their fathers, husbands, and sons. From the time of its composition around 100 C.E. to the early twentieth century, *Lessons for Women* was one of the most popular and most widely read statements on the role of women in Chinese society.

The vast majority of the Chinese population worked in the countryside cultivating grains and vegetables, which they harvested in larger quantities than ever before. In late Zhou times, cultivators often strengthened their plows with iron tips, but metalworkers did not produce enough iron to provide all-metal tools. During the Han dynasty the iron industry entered a period of rapid growth, and cultivators used not only plows but also shovels, picks, hoes, sickles, and spades with iron parts. The tougher implements enabled cultivators to produce more food and support larger populations than ever before. The agricultural surplus allowed many Chinese to produce fine manufactured goods and to engage in trade.

Iron Metallurgy The significance of the iron industry went far beyond agriculture. Chinese entrepreneurs had discovered how to make cast iron by the fourth century B.C.E., and production surged during the Han dynasty. The cast iron industry became so important that Emperor Han Wudi placed it under state control and created forty-six regional offices to supervise iron production. Han artisans experimented with production techniques and learned to craft fine utensils for both domestic and military uses. Iron pots, stoves, knives, needles, axes, hammers, saws, and other tools became standard fixtures in households that could not have afforded more expensive bronze utensils. The ready availability of iron also had important military implications.

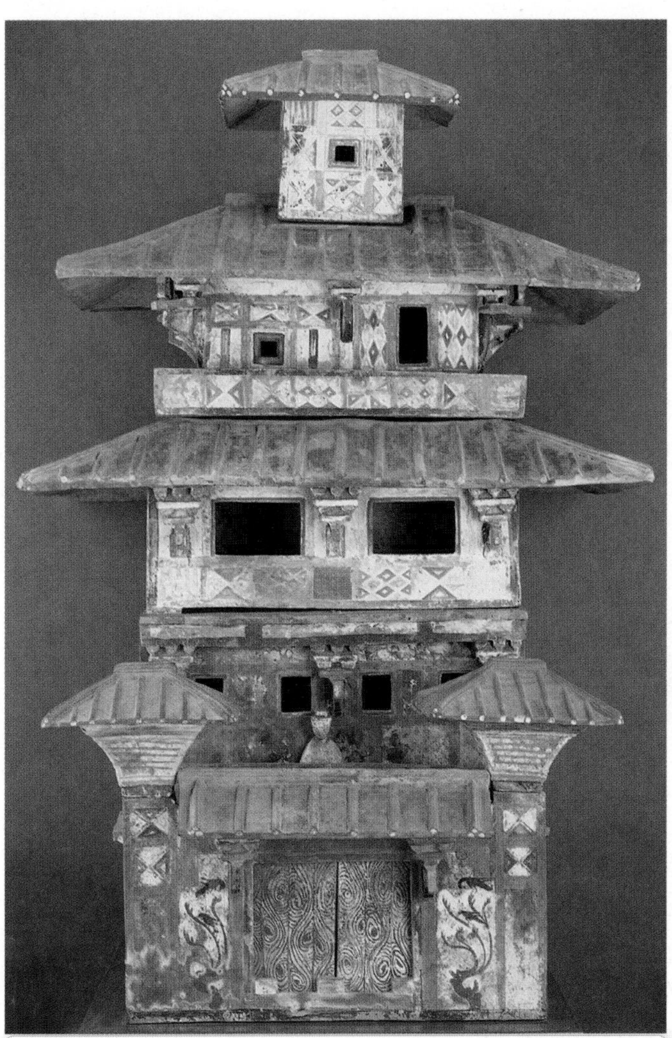
Clay model of an aristocratic house of the sort inhabited by a powerful clan during the Han dynasty. This model came from a tomb near the city of Guangzhou in southern China.

Craftsmen designed suits of iron armor to protect soldiers against arrows and blows, and the strength and sharpness of Han swords, spears, and arrowheads help to explain the success of Chinese armies against the Xiongnu and other nomadic peoples.

Silk Textiles Textile production—particularly sericulture, the manufacture of silk—became an especially important industry. The origins of sericulture date to the fourth millennium B.C.E., long before the ancient Xia dynasty, but only in Han times did sericulture expand from its original home in the Yellow River valley to most parts of China. It developed especially rapidly in the southern regions known today as Sichuan and Guangdong provinces, and the industry thrived after the establishment of long-distance trade relations with western lands in the second century B.C.E.

Although silkworms inhabited much of Eurasia, Chinese silk was especially fine because of advanced sericulture techniques. Chinese producers bred their silkworms, fed them on finely chopped mulberry leaves, and carefully unraveled their cocoons so as to obtain long fibers of raw silk that they wove into light, strong, lustrous fabrics. (In other lands, producers relied on wild silkworms that ate a variety of leaves and chewed through their cocoons, leaving only short fibers that yielded lower-quality fabrics.) Chinese silk became a prized commodity in India, Persia, Mesopotamia, and even the distant Roman empire. Commerce in silk and other products led to the establishment of an intricate network of trade routes known collectively as the silk roads (discussed in chapter 12).

Paper While expanding the iron and silk industries, Han craftsmen also invented paper. In earlier times Chinese scribes had written mostly on bamboo strips and silk fabrics but also inscribed messages on oracle bones and bronzewares. Probably before 100 C.E. Chinese craftsmen began to fashion hemp, bark, and textile fibers into sheets of paper, which was less expensive than silk and easier to write on than bamboo. Although wealthy elites continued to read books written on silk rolls, paper soon became the preferred medium for most writing.

Indeed, classical China was an incubator of technological innovation. Quite apart from their production of iron, silk, and paper, Chinese artisans found ways to improve on earlier technologies and also to devise entirely new inventions. Shortly before the time of the Qin and Han dynasties, for example, military engineers outfitted primitive crossbows, which had already been in use for several centuries, with a sophisticated trigger mechanism that turned them into powerful weapons. Meanwhile, others invented specially designed horse collars, which enabled cultivators to coax maximum power out of their draft animals. Somewhat later, about the first century C.E., nautical engineers invented the ship's rudder, which greatly simplified the steering of sailing vessels. These and other inventions contributed to high prosperity, especially during the early years of the Han dynasty.

Economic and Social Difficulties

In spite of general prosperity, China began to experience economic and social difficulties in the Former Han period. The military adventures and the central Asian policy of Han Wudi caused severe economic strain. Expeditions against the Xiongnu and the establishment of agricultural colonies in central Asia were extremely expensive undertakings, and they rapidly consumed the empire's surplus wealth. To finance his ventures, Han Wudi raised taxes and confiscated land and personal property from wealthy individuals, sometimes on the pretext that they had violated imperial laws. Those measures did not kill industry and commerce in China, but they discouraged investment in manufacturing

Han gentlemen sport luxurious silk gowns as they engage in sophisticated conversation. Wealthy individuals and ruling elites commonly dressed in silk, but peasants and others of the lower classes rarely if ever donned silk garments.

and trading enterprises, which in turn had a dampening effect on the larger economy.

Social Tensions Distinctions between rich and poor hardened during the course of the Han dynasty. Wealthy individuals wore fine silk garments, leather shoes, and jewelry of jade and gold, whereas the poor classes made do with rough hemp clothing and sandals. Tables in wealthy households held pork, fish, fowl, and fine aged wines, but the diet of the poor consisted mostly of grain or rice supplemented by small quantities of vegetables or meat. By the first century B.C.E., social and economic differences had generated serious tensions, and peasants in hard-pressed regions began to organize rebellions in hopes of gaining a larger share of Han society's resources.

Land Distribution A particularly difficult problem concerned the distribution of land. Individual economic problems brought on by poor harvests, high taxes, or crushing burdens of debt forced many small landowners to sell their

In Han times the wealthiest classes enjoyed the privilege of being buried in suits of jade plaques sewn together with gold threads, like the burial dress of Liu Sheng, who died in 113 B.C.E. at Manzheng in Hebei Province. Legend held that jade prevented decomposition of the deceased's body. Scholars have estimated that a jade burial suit like this one required ten years' labor. What does such a suit tell us about the lives of the Chinese elite during the Han dynasty?

property under unfavorable conditions or even to forfeit it in exchange for cancellation of their debts. In extreme cases, individuals had to sell themselves and their families into slavery to satisfy their creditors. Owners of large estates not only increased the size of their holdings by absorbing the property of their less fortunate neighbors but also increased the efficiency of their operations by employing cheap labor. Sometimes cheap laborers came in the form of slaves, other times in the form of tenant farmers who had to deliver as much as half their produce to the landowner for the right to till his property. In either case, the laborers worked on terms that favored the landlords.

By the end of the first century B.C.E., land had accumulated in the hands of a relatively small number of individuals who owned vast estates, while ever-increasing numbers of peasant cultivators led difficult lives with few prospects for improvement. Landless peasants became restive, and Chinese society faced growing problems of banditry and sporadic rebellion. Because the Han emperors depended heavily on the political cooperation of large landowners, however, they did not attempt any serious reform of the landholding system.

The Reign of Wang Mang Tensions came to a head during the early first century C.E. when a powerful and respected Han minister named Wang Mang undertook a thoroughgoing program of reform. In 6 C.E. a two-year-old boy inherited the Han imperial throne. Because the boy was unable to govern, Wang Mang served as his regent. Many officials regarded Wang as more capable than members of the Han family and urged him to claim the imperial honor for himself. In 9 C.E. he did just that: announcing that the mandate of heaven had passed from the Han to his family, he seized the throne. Wang Mang then introduced a series of wide-ranging reforms that have prompted historians to refer to him as the "socialist emperor."

The most important reforms concerned landed property: Wang Mang limited the amount of land that a family could hold and ordered officials to break up large estates, redistribute them, and provide landless individuals with property to cultivate. Despite his good intentions, the socialist emperor attempted to impose his policy without adequate preparation and communication. The result was confusion: landlords resisted a policy that threatened their holdings, and even peasants found its application inconsistent and unsatisfactory. After several years of chaos, Wang Mang faced the additional misfortune of poor harvests and famine, which sparked widespread revolts against his rule. In 23 C.E. a coalition of disgruntled landlords and desperate peasants ended both his dynasty and his life.

The Later Han Dynasty

Within two years a recovered Han dynasty returned to power, but it ruled over a weakened realm. The Later Han emperors even decided to abandon Chang'an, which had suffered grave damage during the years of chaos and rebellion, and establish a new capital at Luoyang. Nevertheless, during the early years of the Later Han, emperors ruled vigorously in the manner of Liu Bang and Han Wudi. They regained control of the centralized administration and reorganized the state bureaucracy. They also maintained the Chinese presence in central Asia, continued to keep the Xiongnu in submission, and exercised firm control over the silk roads.

The Yellow Turban Uprising The Later Han emperors did not seriously address the problem of land distribution that had helped to bring down the Former Han dynasty. The wealthy classes still lived in relative luxury while peasants worked under difficult conditions. The empire continued to suffer the effects of banditry and rebellions organized by desperate peasants with few opportunities to improve their lot. The Yellow Turban uprising—so named because of the distinctive headgear worn by the rebels—was a particularly serious revolt that raged throughout China and tested the resilience of the Han state during the late second century C.E.

A painted brick depicts a peasant working in the fields with a team of oxen and a wooden harrow. By the Han dynasty, many plows of this type had iron teeth. Produced in the third or fourth century C.E., this brick painting came from a tomb in Gansu Province in western China.

Though it dates from a somewhat later era, about the sixth century C.E., this cave painting from Dunhuang in Gansu Province (western China) offers some idea of the chaos that engulfed China as the Han dynasty crumbled.

Although the Later Han dynasty possessed the military power required to keep civil disorder under reasonable control, rebellions by the Yellow Turbans and others weakened the Han state during the second and third centuries C.E.

Collapse of the Han Dynasty The Later Han emperors were unable, however, to prevent the development of factions at court that paralyzed the central government. Factions of imperial family members, Confucian scholar bureaucrats, and court eunuchs sought to increase their influence, protect their own interests, and destroy their rivals. On several occasions, relations between the various factions became so strained that they made war against each other. In 189 C.E., for example, a faction led by an imperial relative descended on the Han palace and slaughtered more than two thousand beardless men in an effort to destroy the eunuchs as a political force. In that respect the attack succeeded. From the unmeasured violence of the operation, however, it is clear that the Later Han dynasty had reached a point of internal weakness from which it could not easily recover. Indeed, early in the next century, the central government disintegrated, and for almost four centuries China remained divided into several large regional kingdoms.

inperspective

The Qin state lasted for a short fourteen years, but it opened a new era in Chinese history. Qin conquerors imposed unified rule on a series of politically independent kingdoms and launched an ambitious program to forge culturally distinct regions into a larger Chinese society. The Han dynasty endured for more than four centuries and largely completed the project of unifying China. Han rulers built a centralized bureaucracy that administered a unified empire, thus establishing a precedent for centralized imperial rule in China. They also entered into a close alliance with Confucian moralists who organized a system of advanced education that provided recruits for the imperial bureaucracy. Moreover, on the basis of a highly productive economy stimulated by technological innovations, Han rulers projected Chinese influence abroad to Korea, Vietnam, and central Asia. Thus, like classical societies in Persia, India, and the Mediterranean basin, Han China produced a set of distinctive political and cultural traditions that shaped Chinese and neighboring societies over the long term. ●

CHRONOLOGY	
sixth century B.C.E.(?)	Laozi
551–479 B.C.E.	Confucius
403–221 B.C.E.	Period of the Warring States
390–338 B.C.E.	Shang Yang
372–289 B.C.E.	Mencius
298–238 B.C.E.	Xunzi
280–233 B.C.E.	Han Feizi
221–207 B.C.E.	Qin dynasty
206 B.C.E.–9 C.E.	Former Han dynasty
141–87 B.C.E.	Reign of Han Wudi
9–23 C.E.	Reign of Wang Mang
25–220 C.E.	Later Han dynasty

For Further Reading

Thomas J. Barfield. *The Perilous Frontier: Nomadic Empires and China.* Cambridge, Mass., 1989. A provocative analysis of the relations between Chinese and central Asian peoples.

Derk Bodde. *China's First Unifier: A Study of the Ch'in Dynasty as Seen in the Life of Li Ssu.* Leiden, 1938. Important study of the minister responsible for much of the Qin dynasty's policy.

Sebastian De Grazia, ed. *Masters of Chinese Political Thought from the Beginnings to the Han Dynasty.* New York, 1973. A valuable collection of primary sources in translation, all of them bearing on political themes.

Mark Elvin. *The Pattern of the Chinese Past.* Stanford, 1973. A remarkable analysis of Chinese history by an economic historian who brings a comparative perspective to his work.

Cho-yun Hsu. *Han Agriculture: The Formation of Early Chinese Agrarian Economy (206 B.C.–A.D. 220).* Seattle, 1980. Studies the development of intensive agriculture in Han China and provides English translations of more than two hundred documents illustrating the conditions of rural life.

Mark Edward Lewis. *The Early Chinese Empires: Qin and Han.* Cambridge, Mass., 2007. Emphasizes the long-term influence of imperial rule established by the Qin and Han dynasties.

Michael Loewe. *Everyday Life in Early Imperial China.* London, 1968. Deals with the social, economic, and cultural history of China during the Han dynasty.

———. *The Government of the Qin and Han Empires, 221 B.C.E.–220 C.E.* Indianapolis, 2006. A reliable survey by a leading scholar.

Victor H. Mair, trans. *Tao Te Ching: The Classic Book of Integrity and the Way.* New York, 1990. A fresh and lively translation of the Daoist classic *Daodejing,* based on recently discovered manuscripts.

Victor H. Mair, Nancy S. Steinhardt, and Paul R. Goldin, eds. *Hawai`i Reader in Traditional Chinese Culture.* Honolulu, 2005. An imaginative selection of primary sources in English translation.

Frederick W. Mote. *Intellectual Foundations of China.* 2nd ed. New York, 1989. A compact and concise introduction to the cultural history of classical China.

Michele Pirazzoli-t'Serstevens. *The Han Dynasty.* Trans. by J. Seligman. New York, 1982. An excellent and well-illustrated survey of Han China that draws on archaeological discoveries.

Benjamin I. Schwartz. *The World of Thought in Ancient China.* Cambridge, Mass., 1985. A synthesis of classical Chinese thought by a leading scholar.

Arthur Waldron. *The Great Wall of China: From History to Myth.* Cambridge, 1989. Places the modern Great Wall in the tradition of Chinese wall building from Qin times forward.

Arthur Waley, trans. *The Analects of Confucius.* New York, 1938. An English version of Confucius's sayings by a gifted translator.

———, trans. *Three Ways of Thought in Ancient China.* New York, 1940. Translations and comments on works from Confucian, Daoist, and Legalist traditions.

Burton Watson, trans. *Basic Writings of Mo Tzu, Hsün Tzu, and Han Fei Tzu.* New York, 1967. Translations of important political and social treatises from classical China.

———, trans. *Records of the Grand Historian.* Rev. ed. 2 vols. New York, 1993. Excellent translation of Sima Qian's history, the most important narrative source for Han China.

Wang Zhongshu. *Han Civilization.* Trans. by K. C. Chang. New Haven, 1982. A scholarly work that draws on both historical and archaeological research.

State, Society, and the Quest for Salvation in India

chapter 9

A limestone sculpture depicts a serene Buddha as he preaches a sermon to his followers.

EYEWITNESS:
Megasthenes: A Greek Perspective on Classical India

The earliest description of India by a foreigner came from the pen of a Greek ambassador named Megasthenes. As the diplomatic representative of the Seleucid emperor, Megasthenes lived in India for many years during the late fourth and early third centuries B.C.E., and he traveled throughout much of northern India. Although Megasthenes' book, the *Indika,* has long been lost, many quotations from it survive in Greek and Latin literature. These fragments clearly show that Megasthenes had great respect for the Indian land, people, and society.

Like travel writers of all times, Megasthenes included a certain amount of spurious information in his account of India. He wrote, for example, of ants the size of foxes that mined gold from the earth and fiercely defended their hoards from any humans who tried to steal them. Only by distracting them with slabs of meat, Megasthenes said, could humans safely make away with their treasure. He also reported races of monstrous human beings: some with no mouth who survived by breathing in the odors of fruits, flowers, and roots, others with feet pointing backward and eight toes per foot, and yet others with the heads of dogs who communicated by barking.

Beyond the tall tales, Megasthenes offered a great deal of reliable information. He portrayed India as a fertile land that supported two harvests of grain per year. He described the capital of Pataliputra as a rectangle-shaped city situated along the Ganges River and surrounded by a moat and a massive timber wall with 570 towers and sixty-four gates. He mentioned large armies that used elephants as war animals. He pointed out the strongly hierarchical character of Indian society (although he incorrectly held that there were seven instead of four main castes). He noted that two main schools of "philosophers" (Hindus and Buddhists) enjoyed special prominence as well as exemption from taxes, and he described the ascetic lifestyles and vegetarian diets followed by particularly devout individuals. In short, Megasthenes portrayed India as a wealthy land that supported a distinctive society with well-established cultural traditions.

In India as in Persia and China, the centuries after 500 B.C.E. witnessed the development of a classical society whose influence has persisted over the centuries. Its most prominent features were a well-defined social structure, which left individuals with few doubts about their position and role in society, and several popular religious traditions that helped to shape Indian beliefs and values. Two religions, Buddhism and Hinduism, also appealed strongly to peoples beyond the subcontinent.

Efforts to maintain an imperial government did not succeed nearly as well in India as they did in Persia and China. For the most part, classical India fell under the sway of regional kingdoms rather than centralized empires. Imperial regimes were crucial for the consolidation of Indian cultural traditions, however, because they sponsored cultural leaders and promoted their ideals throughout the subcontinent and beyond. The spread of Buddhism is a case in point: imperial support helped the faith secure its position in India and attract converts in other lands. Thus, even in the absence of a strong and continuing imperial tradition like that of Persia or China, the social and cultural traditions of classical India not only shaped the lives and experiences of the subcontinent's inhabitants but also influenced peoples in distant lands.

THE FORTUNES OF EMPIRE IN CLASSICAL INDIA

Following their migrations to India after 1500 B.C.E., the Aryans established a series of small kingdoms throughout the subcontinent. For centuries the rulers of those kingdoms fought constantly among themselves and sought to expand their states by absorbing others. By the sixth century B.C.E., wars of expansion had resulted in the consolidation of several large regional kingdoms that dominated much of the subcontinent. Despite strenuous efforts, none of these kingdoms was able to establish hegemony over the others. During the classical era, the Mauryan and the Gupta dynasties founded centralized, imperial states that embraced much of India, but neither empire survived long enough to establish centralized rule as a lasting feature of Indian political life.

The Mauryan Dynasty and the Temporary Unification of India

The unification of India came about partly as a result of intrusion from beyond the subcontinent. About 520 B.C.E. the Persian emperor Darius crossed the Hindu Kush mountains, conquered parts of northwestern India, and made the kingdom of Gandhara in the northern Punjab (northern modern-day Pakistan) a province of the Achaemenid empire. The establishment of Achaemenid authority in India introduced local rulers to Persian techniques of administration. Almost two centuries later, in 327 B.C.E., after overrunning the Persian empire, Alexander of Macedon crossed the Indus River and crushed the states he found there. Alexander remained in India only for a short time, and he did not make a deep impression on the Punjabi people: he departed after his forces mutinied in the year 325 B.C.E., and contemporary Indian sources did not even mention his name. Yet his campaign had an important effect on Indian politics and history, since he created a political vacuum in northwestern India by destroying the existing states and then withdrawing his forces.

Kingdom of Magadha Poised to fill the vacuum was the dynamic kingdom of Magadha, located in the central portion of the Ganges plain. Several regional kingdoms in the valley of the Ganges had become wealthy as workers turned forests into fields and trade became an increasingly prominent feature of the local economy. By about 500 B.C.E. Magadha had emerged as the most important state in northeastern India. During the next two centuries, the kings of Magadha conquered the neighboring states and gained control of Indian commerce passing through the Ganges valley as well as overseas trade between India and Burma passing across the Bay of Bengal. The withdrawal of Alexander from the Punjab presented Magadha with a rare opportunity to expand.

Chandragupta Maurya During the late 320s B.C.E., an ambitious adventurer named Chandragupta Maurya exploited that opportunity and laid the foundation for the Mauryan empire, the first state to bring a centralized and unified government to most of the Indian subcontinent. Chandragupta began by seizing control of small, remote regions of Magadha and then worked his way gradually toward the center. By 321 B.C.E. he had overthrown the ruling dynasty and consolidated his hold on the kingdom. He then moved into the Punjab and brought northwestern India under his control. Next he ventured beyond the Indus River and conquered the Greek state in Bactria—a large region straddling the border between modern Pakistan and Afghanistan, where Alexander of Macedon's Greek successors maintained a kingdom during the Seleucid era. By the end of the fourth century B.C.E., Chandragupta's empire embraced all of northern India from the Indus to the Ganges.

Chandragupta's Government A careful and systematic advisor named Kautalya devised procedures for the governance of Chandragupta's realm. Some of Kautalya's advice survives in the ancient Indian political handbook known as the *Arthashastra,* a manual offering detailed instructions

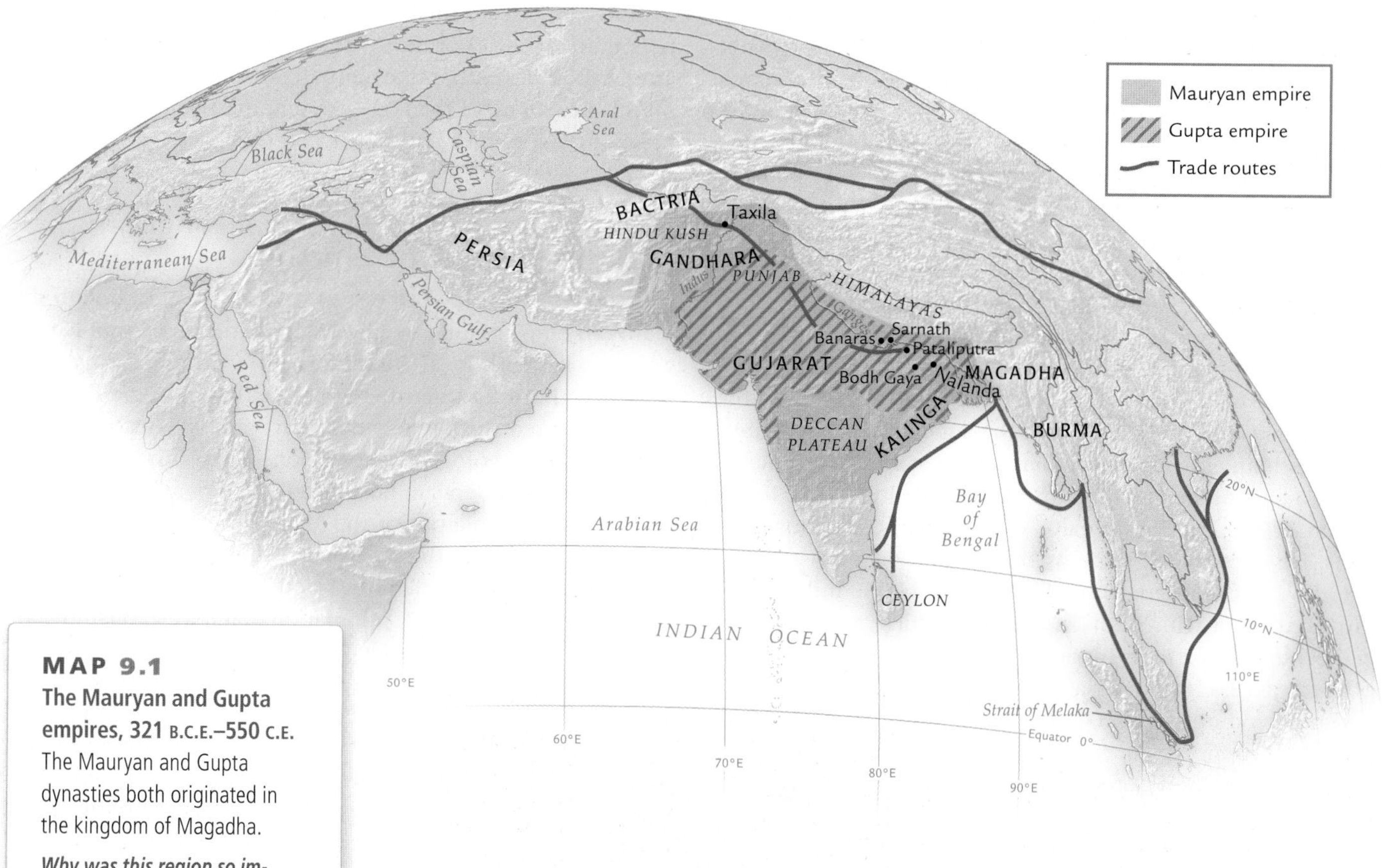

MAP 9.1
The Mauryan and Gupta empires, 321 B.C.E.–550 C.E.
The Mauryan and Gupta dynasties both originated in the kingdom of Magadha.

Why was this region so important in ancient India? What advantages did it offer for purposes of trade and communication with other regions?

on the uses of power and the principles of government. The *Arthashastra* outlined methods of administering the empire, overseeing trade and agriculture, collecting taxes, maintaining order, conducting foreign relations, and waging war. Kautalya also advised Chandragupta to make abundant use of spies, and he even included prostitutes in his stable of informants. Like the emperors of Persia and China, Chandragupta and Kautalya built a bureaucratic administrative system that enabled them to implement policies throughout the state.

Ashoka Maurya Tradition holds that Chandragupta abdicated his throne to become a monk and led such an ascetic life that he starved himself to death. Whether that report is true or not, it is certain that his son succeeded him in 297 B.C.E. and added most of southern India to the growing empire. The high point of the Mauryan empire, however, came during the reign of Chandragupta's grandson Ashoka.

Ashoka began his reign (268–232 B.C.E.) as a conqueror. When he came to power, the only major region that remained independent of the Mauryan empire was the kingdom of Kalinga (modern Orissa) in the east-central part of the subcontinent. In fact, Kalinga was not only independent of Mauryan rule but also actively hostile to its spread. The kingdom's resistance created difficulties for Ashoka because Kalinga controlled the principal trade routes, both by land and by sea, between the Ganges plain and southern India. Thus Ashoka's first major undertaking as emperor was to conquer Kalinga and bring it under Mauryan control, which he did in a bloody campaign in 260 B.C.E. By Ashoka's estimate, 100,000 Kalingans died in the fighting, 150,000 were driven from their homes, and untold numbers of others perished in the ruined land.

In spite of that campaign, Ashoka is much better known as a governor than as a conqueror. With Kalinga subdued, Ashoka ruled almost the entire subcontinent—only the southernmost region escaped his control—and he turned his attention to the responsible government of his realm. As heir to the administrative structure that Chandragupta and Kautalya had instituted, Ashoka ruled through a tightly organized bureaucracy. He established his capital at the fortified city of Pataliputra (near modern Patna), where a central administration developed policies for the whole empire. Pataliputra was a thriving and cosmopolitan city: the Greek ambassador Megasthenes reported that a local committee looked after the interests of foreigners in the city—and also carefully observed their movements. Ashoka went to great pains to ensure that his local subordinates implemented his policies. A central treasury oversaw the efficient collection of taxes—a hallmark of Kautalya's influence—which supported legions of officials, accountants, clerks, soldiers, and other imperial employees. Ashoka communicated his policies throughout his realm by inscribing edicts in natural stone formations or on pillars that he ordered erected. In these promulgations, known as the rock and pillar edicts, Ashoka issued imperial decrees, encouraged his subjects to observe Buddhist values, and expressed his intention to serve as a fair, just, and humane ruler.

As a result of Ashoka's policies, the various regions of India became well integrated, and the subcontinent benefited from both an expanding economy and a stable government. Ashoka encouraged the expansion of agriculture—the foundation of the empire's wealth—by building irrigation systems. He encouraged trade by building roads, most notably a highway of more than 1,600 kilometers (1,000 miles) linking Pataliputra with Taxila, the chief political and commercial center of northern India, which offered access to Bactria, Persia, and other points west. Ashoka also provided comforts for administrators, merchants, and other travelers by planting banyan trees to provide shade, digging wells, and establishing inns along the roads.

Decline of the Mauryan Empire Ashoka's policies did not long survive his rule, nor did his empire. Ashoka died in 232 B.C.E., and decline set in almost immediately. During its later years the Mauryan empire suffered from acute financial and economic difficulties. The empire depended on a strong army and a large corps of officials to administer imperial policy. Salaries for both soldiers and bureaucrats were expensive: Megasthenes said that in times of peace, military forces spent their time in idleness and drinking bouts while continuing to draw their pay. Eventually, those administrative costs outstripped the revenues that flowed into the central treasury. The later Mauryan emperors often resorted to the tactic of debasing their currency—reducing the amount of precious metal in a coin without reducing its nominal value. Because of their financial difficulties, they were unable to hold the realm together. They maintained control of the Ganges valley for some fifty years after Ashoka's death, but eventually they lost their grip even on this heartland of the Mauryan empire. By about 185 B.C.E. the Mauryan empire had disappeared.

As a symbol of his rule, Ashoka had this sculpture of four lions mounted atop a column about 20 meters (66 feet) tall. The lion capital is the official symbol of the modern Republic of India. Why might this sculpture more than two thousand years old be an attractive symbol for modern India?

The Emergence of Regional Kingdoms and the Revival of Empire

Bactrian Rule in Northwestern India Although the Mauryan empire came to an end, India did not crumble into anarchy. Instead, local rulers formed a series of kingdoms that brought order to large regions. Although regional kingdoms emerged throughout the subcontinent, historical records and archaeological excavations have thrown clearest light on developments in northern India. For almost two centuries after the collapse of the Mauryan empire, northwestern India fell under the rule of Greek-speaking conquerors from Bactria—Alexander of Macedon's imperial heirs who had mingled with local populations since establishing an independent Bactrian kingdom in the third century B.C.E. Indo-Greek forces invaded northern India as early as 182 B.C.E. and seized a large territory extending as far south as Gujarat. Bactria was a thriving commercial center linking lands from China in the east to the Mediterranean basin in the west, so Bactrian rule had the effect of promoting cross-cultural interaction and exchange in northern India. Large volumes of trade provided sources of revenue for the Bactrian rulers, and the city of Taxila flourished because of its strategic location on trade routes leading from northern India to Bactria. The northern region of Gandhara became a site of intense cultural as well as commercial exchange.

The Kushan Empire Beginning in the late second century B.C.E., several groups of nomadic conquerors from central Asia attacked Bactria and eventually put an end to the Indo-Greek kingdom there. The most successful of those conquerors were the Kushans, who ruled a sizable empire embracing much of northern India and central Asia from about 1 to 300 C.E. Under Kanishka, the most prominent of the

Archaeological excavations have unearthed parts of the defensive palisade, constructed of timbers almost 5 meters (16 feet) tall, that surrounded Pataliputra during Mauryan times.

Kushan emperors (reigned 78–103 C.E.), the Kushan empire included modern-day Pakistan, Afghanistan, and northern India to Gujarat and the central part of the Ganges valley.

Like the Indo-Greek Bactrians, the Kushans facilitated commerce between India and lands to the north. Indeed, the Kushan empire played a crucial role in the silk roads network (discussed in chapter 12) by pacifying much of the large region between Persia and China, thus making it possible for merchants to travel safely across long distances. Participation in extensive networks enabled Kushan rulers to serve as cultural intermediaries. They generously patronized Bactrian artists who employed Greek styles of painting and sculpture in the depiction of local subjects. This tradition, known as Ghandara style, was especially important for the early development of Buddhist art, because the Kushan rulers were enthusiastic proponents of Buddhism who frequently commissioned depictions of Buddhist figures. On several occasions the Kushans and other rulers of northern India faced ambitious kings who sought to expand their realms and imitate the Mauryas by building an empire based in the Indian subcontinent. Only with the Guptas, however, did any of them approach the realization of their imperial ambitions.

The Gupta Dynasty Like the Mauryas, the **Guptas** based their state in Magadha, a crucial region because of its wealth, its dominance of the Ganges valley, and its role as intermediary between the various regions of the subcontinent. The new empire arose on foundations laid by Chandra Gupta (not related to Chandragupta Maurya), who forged alliances with powerful families in the Ganges region and established a dynamic kingdom about the year 320 C.E. His successors, Samudra Gupta (reigned 335–375 C.E.) and Chandra Gupta II (reigned 375–415 C.E.), made the Magadhan capital of Pataliputra once again the center of a large empire. Between the two of them, Samudra Gupta and Chandra Gupta II conquered many of the regional kingdoms of India, and they established tributary alliances with others that elected not to fight. Only the Deccan Plateau and the southernmost part of the subcontinent remained outside the orbit of Gupta influence.

The Gupta empire was somewhat smaller in size than the Mauryan, and it also differed considerably in organization. Ashoka had insisted on knowing the details of regional affairs, which he closely monitored from his court at Pataliputra. The Guptas left local government and administration, and even the making of basic policy, in the hands of their allies in the various regions of their empire. When nomadic invaders threatened the empire during the later fifth century C.E., it split easily along the fault lines of the administrative regions. During the late fourth and early fifth centuries C.E., however, the Gupta dynasty brought stability and prosperity to the subcontinent. A Chinese Buddhist monk named Faxian traveled widely in India searching for texts of the Buddhist scriptures during the reign of Chandra Gupta II. In an account of his travels, Faxian reported that India was a prosperous land with little crime. It was possible to travel throughout the country, he said, without fear of molestation and even without official travel documents.

Guptas (GOOP-tahs)

Science and Mathematics Under conditions of political stability, Gupta prosperity sustained the work of scholars and enabled them to lay the foundations for sophisticated studies in the natural sciences and mathematics. Indian physicians developed techniques of plastic surgery, and astronomers determined that the earth is a sphere that rotates on its axis. Most influential of the scholars were the mathematicians. Advanced mathematics was possible because Indian numerals included a symbol for zero, which facilitates adoption of a place-value notation system, which in turn expedites mathematical computations. It is much simpler to multiply 19 × 84, for example, than XIX × LXXXIV. With their flexible numerals and their system of place-value notation, Indian mathematicians were able to carry out advanced algebraic calculations and anticipate the invention of calculus. Indian mathematicians calculated the value of *pi* to 3.1416 and the length of the solar year to 365.3586805 days. In the eighth century, Arab and Persian scholars encountered Indian mathematics and readily adopted what they called "Hindi numerals," which Europeans later termed "Arabic numerals," since they learned of them through Arab Muslims.

Gupta Decline Gupta administrative talents and cultural creativity were not a match, however, for the invasions of the White Huns, a nomadic people from central Asia who occupied Bactria during the fourth century C.E., and then prepared to cross the Hindu Kush mountains into India. For the first half of the fifth century, the Guptas repelled the Huns, but the defense cost them dearly in resources and eventually weakened their state. By the end of the fifth century, the Huns moved across the Hindu Kush almost at will and established several kingdoms in northern and western India.

The Gupta dynasty continued in name only: regional governors progressively usurped imperial rights and powers, and contemporary documents do not even record the names of all the later Gupta emperors. Once again, imperial government survived only for a short term in India. Not until the establishment of the Mughal dynasty in the sixteenth century C.E. did any state rule as much of India as the Mauryan and Gupta empires ruled. Memories of empire remained, to be sure, and there were periodic efforts to bring all of the subcontinent again under the control of a unified regime. But for the most part, large regional kingdoms dominated political life in India during the millennium between the Gupta and the Mughal dynasties.

Many surviving gold coins reflect the commercial vitality of northern India in the late first and early second centuries C.E. This one depicts the Buddha gesturing to his followers.

ECONOMIC DEVELOPMENT AND SOCIAL DISTINCTIONS

After spreading through the subcontinent, Aryan migrants turned increasingly from herding to agriculture. After about 1000 B.C.E., when they learned the techniques of iron metallurgy, they used iron axes and tools to advance into regions previously inaccessible to them, notably the jungle-covered valley of the Ganges River. The Aryans dispatched shudras, semifree serfs, to work in recently cleared fields, and from fertile lands they reaped large harvests. Agricultural surpluses supported the large-scale states such as the regional kingdoms and the Mauryan and Gupta empires that organized Indian public life. Agricultural surpluses also encouraged the emergence of towns, the growth of trade, and further development of the caste system.

Towns and Trade

Towns and Manufacturing After about 600 B.C.E. towns dotted the Indian countryside, especially in the northwestern corner of the subcontinent. These towns served the needs of a productive agricultural society by providing manufactured products for local consumption—pots, textiles, iron tools, and other metal utensils—as well as luxury goods such as jewelry destined for the wealthy and elite classes. Demand for manufactured products was very high, and some entrepreneurs organized businesses on a large scale. During Mauryan times, for example, a pottery manufacturer named Saddalaputta owned about five hundred workshops, whose products he distributed throughout the Ganges valley in his fleet of boats.

Flourishing towns maintained marketplaces and encouraged the development of trade. Within the subcontinent itself trade was most active along the Ganges River, although trade routes also passed through the Ganges delta east to Burma and down the east Indian coast to the Deccan and southern India. Roads built by Ashoka also facilitated overland commerce within the subcontinent.

Long-Distance Trade Meanwhile, the volume of long-distance trade also grew as large imperial states in China, southwest Asia, and the Mediterranean basin provided a political foundation enabling merchants to deal with their counterparts in distant lands. Direct political and military links with foreign peoples drew Indians into long-distance commercial relations. Beginning with Cyrus, the Achaemenid rulers of Persia coveted the wealth of India and included the northern kingdom of Gandhara as a province of their empire. The presence of Persian administrators in India and the building of roads between Persia and India facilitated commerce between the two lands. Alexander of Macedon's conquests helped to establish even more extensive trade networks by forging links between India and the Mediterranean basin by way of Bactria, Persia, and Anatolia.

From India, long-distance trade passed overland in two directions: through the Hindu Kush mountains and the Gandharan capital of Taxila to Persia and the Mediterranean basin, and across the silk roads of central Asia to markets in China. Cotton, aromatics, black pepper, pearls, and gems were the principal Indian exports, in exchange for which Indian merchants imported horses and bullion from western lands and silk from China.

Trade in the Indian Ocean Basin During the Mauryan era merchants continued to use land routes, but they increasingly turned to the sea to transport their goods. Seaborne trade benefited especially from the rhythms of the monsoon winds that govern weather and the seasons in the Indian Ocean basin. During the spring and summer the winds blow from the southwest, and during the fall and winter they come from the northeast. Once mariners recognized these rhythms, they could sail easily and safely before the wind to any part of the Indian Ocean basin.

As early as the fifth century B.C.E., Indian merchants had traveled to the islands of Indonesia and the southeast Asian mainland, where they exchanged pearls, cotton, black pepper, and Indian manufactured goods for spices and exotic local products. Many of those goods did not remain in India but, instead, traveled west through the Arabian Sea to the lands bordering the Persian Gulf and the Red Sea. Indian products also found markets in the Mediterranean basin. Indian pepper became so popular there that the Romans established direct commercial relations and built several trading settlements in southern India. Archaeologists working in southern India have unearthed hoards of Roman coins that testify to the large volume of trade between classical India and Mediterranean lands.

thinking about ENCOUNTERS

Routes to Encounters in Classical India
Interactions between peoples of different societies can take place only if there are ways for them to meet and communicate. How was it possible for Indians to overcome geographic obstacles posed by mountains and oceans to enter into trading relationships with other peoples?

Family Life and the Caste System

Gender Relations In the midst of urban growth and economic development, Indian moralists sought to promote stability by encouraging respect for strong patriarchal families and to promote the maintenance of a social order in which all members played well-defined roles. Most people lived with members of their nuclear family. Particularly among higher castes, however, several generations of a family often lived in large compounds ruled by powerful patriarchs. Literary works suggest that women were largely subordinate to men. The two great Indian epics, the ***Mahabharata*** and the ***Ramayana,*** commonly portrayed women as weak-willed and emotional creatures and exalted wives who devoted themselves to their husbands. In the *Ramayana,* for example, the beautiful Sita loyally followed her husband Rama into undeserved exile in a wild forest and remained faithful to him even during a long separation.

During the early centuries C.E., patriarchal dominance became more pronounced in India. By the Gupta era, child marriage was common: when girls were age eight or nine, their parents betrothed them to men

Buddhist art often depicted individuals as models of proper social relationships. Here a sculpture from a Buddhist temple at Karli, produced about the first century C.E., represents an ideal Buddhist married couple.

Mahabharata (mah-hah-BAH-rah-tah)
Ramayana (rah-mah-yah-nah)

PART 2

in their twenties. Formal marriage took place just after the girls reached puberty. Wives often came to dominate domestic affairs in their households, but the practice of child marriage placed them under the control of older men and encouraged them to devote themselves to family matters rather than to public affairs in the larger society.

Social Order After their arrival in India, the Aryans recognized four main castes or classes of people: brahmins (priests), kshatriyas (warriors and aristocrats), vaishyas (peasants and merchants), and shudras (serfs). Brahmins in particular endorsed this social order, which brought them honor, prestige, and sometimes considerable wealth as well. The growth of trade and the proliferation of industries, however, had deep implications for the larger structure of Indian society, since they encouraged further development of the caste system.

Castes and Guilds As trade and industrial activity expanded, new groups of artisans, craftsmen, and merchants appeared, many of whom did not fit easily in the established structure. Individuals working in the same craft or trade usually joined together to form a guild, a corporate body that supervised prices and wages in a given industry and provided for the welfare of members and their families. Guild members lived in the same quarter of town, socialized with one another, intermarried, and cared for the group's widows, orphans, and needy.

In effect, the guilds functioned as subcastes, known as *jati,* based on occupation. In fact, *jati* assumed much of the responsibility for maintaining social order in India. *Jati* regularly organized courts, through which they disciplined guild members, resolved differences, and regulated community affairs. Individuals who did not abide by group rules were liable to expulsion from the community. These outcastes then had to make their way through life—often by working as butchers, leather tanners, or undertakers or in other occupations deemed low and unclean—without the networks of support provided by *jati.* Thus Indian guilds and *jati* performed services that central governments provided in other lands. The tendency for individuals and their families to associate closely with others of the same occupation remained a prominent feature of Indian society well into modern times.

Wealth and the Social Order Beyond encouraging further development of the caste system, economic development in the subcontinent generated tremendous wealth, which posed a serious challenge to the social order that arose in India following the Aryan migrations. Traditional social theory accorded special honor to the brahmins and the kshatriyas because of the worthy lives they had led during previous incarnations and the heavy responsibilities they assumed as priests, warriors, and rulers during their current incarnations. Members of the vaishya and shudra castes, on the other hand, merited no special respect but, rather, had the obligation to work as directed by the higher castes. During the centuries after 600 B.C.E., however, trade and industry brought prosperity to many vaishyas and even shudras, who sometimes became wealthier and more influential in society than their brahmin and kshatriya contemporaries.

Economic development and social change in classical India had profound implications for the established cultural as well as the social order. The beliefs, values, and rituals that were meaningful in early Aryan

Jewel-bedecked flying goddesses drop flowers on the earth from their perch in the heavens. Their gems and personal adornments reflect the tastes of upper-class women during the Gupta dynasty. This painting on a rock wall, produced about the sixth century C.E., survives in modern Sri Lanka.

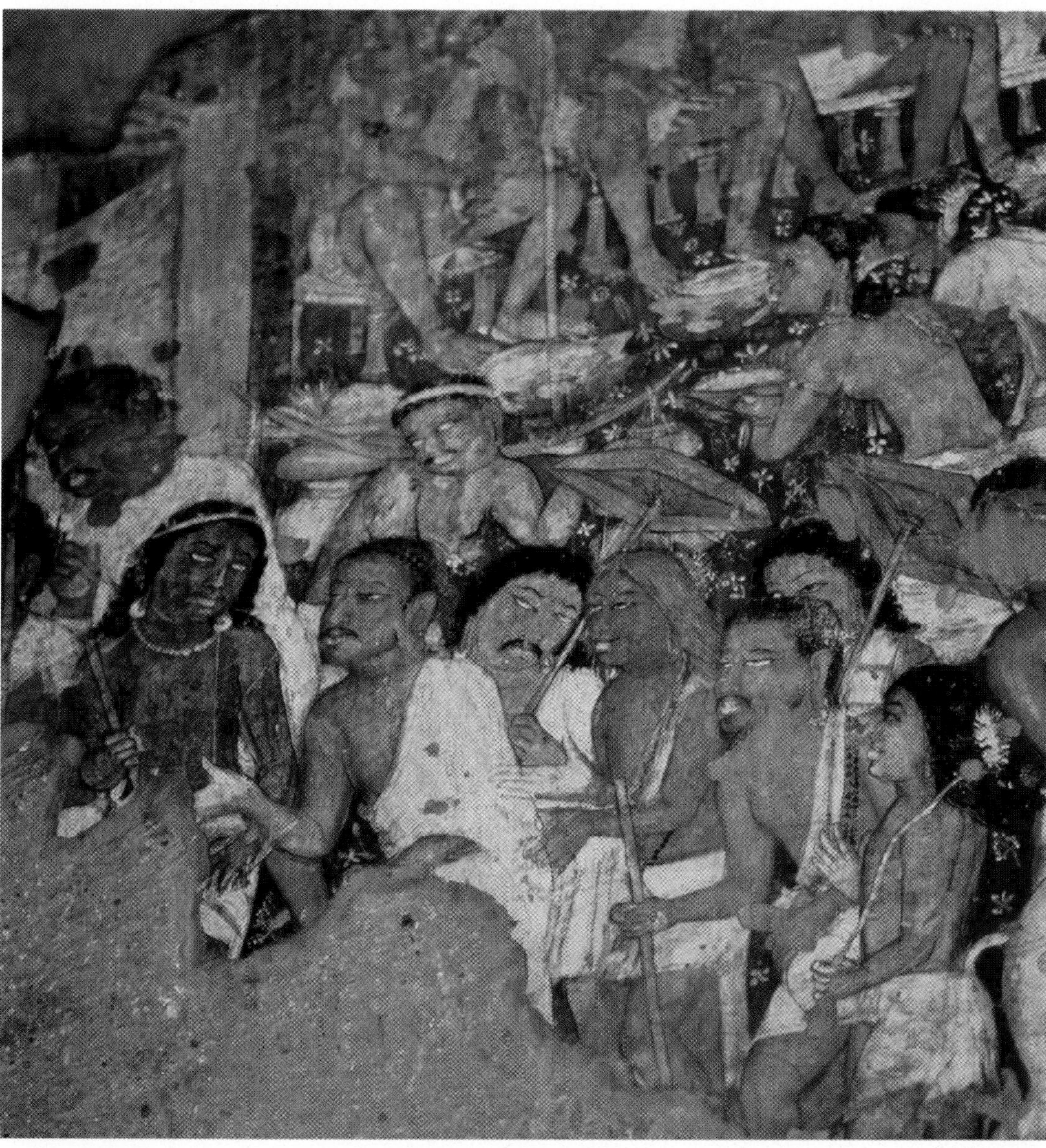

A painting produced in the sixth century C.E. in the Ajanta caves of central India depicts individuals of different castes, *jati,* and ethnic groups in a crowd scene.

society seemed increasingly irrelevant during the centuries after 600 B.C.E. Along with emerging towns, growing trade, increasing wealth, and a developing social structure, classical India saw the appearance of new religions that addressed the needs of the changing times.

RELIGIONS OF SALVATION IN CLASSICAL INDIA

Ancient Indian religion revolved around ritual sacrifices offered by brahmin priests in hopes that the gods would reward their loyal human servants with large harvests and abundant herds. Because the brahmins performed services deemed crucial for the survival of society, they enjoyed exemption from taxation. They also received hefty fees and generous gifts in return for their services. As the Indian economy developed, however, these services seemed less meaningful, especially to the newly wealthy classes of merchants and artisans. Many of these individuals came from the lower castes, and they resented the brahmins' pretensions to superiority.

During the sixth and fifth centuries B.C.E., a rash of new religions and philosophies rejected the brahmins' cults and appealed to the interests of new social classes. Some of them tended toward atheistic materialism: members of the Charvaka sect, for example, believed that the gods were figments of the imagination, that brahmins were charlatans who enriched themselves by hoodwinking others, and that human beings came from dust and returned to dust like any other animal in the natural world. The Charvakas' beliefs clearly reflected the increasingly materialistic character of Indian society and economy. Others, such as the Jains, the Buddhists, and the Hindus, turned to intense spirituality as an alternative to the mechanical rituals of the brahmins.

Jainism and the Challenge to the Established Cultural Order

Vardhamana Mahavira

Among the most influential of the new religions was **Jainism.** Although Jainist doctrines first appeared during the seventh century B.C.E., they became popular only when the great teacher Vardhamana Mahavira turned to Jainism in the late sixth century B.C.E. Mahavira ("the great hero") was born in northern India about 540 B.C.E. to a prominent kshatriya family. According to the semilegendary accounts of his life, he left home at the age of thirty to seek salvation by escaping from the cycle of incarnation. For twelve years he led an ascetic life wandering throughout the Ganges valley, after which he gained enlightenment. He abandoned all his worldly goods, even his clothes, and taught an ascetic doctrine of detachment from the world. For the next thirty years, until his death about 468 B.C.E., he expounded his thought to a group of dedicated disciples who formed a monastic order to perpetuate and spread his message. These disciples referred to Mahavira as *Jina* ("the conqueror"), and borrowing from this title his followers referred to themselves as *Jains.*

Vardhamana Mahavira with one of his disciples. Representations of the early Jains often depicted them in the nude because of their ascetic way of life.

Much of the inspiration for Jainist doctrine came from the Upanishads. Jains believed that everything in the universe—humans, animals, plants, the air, bodies of water, and even inanimate physical objects such as rocks—possessed a soul. As long as they remained trapped in terrestrial bodies, these souls experienced both physical and psychological suffering. Only by purification from selfish behavior could souls gain release from their imprisonment, shed the burdens of karma that they had accumulated during their various incarnations, and attain a state of bliss.

Jainist Ethics

Individuals underwent purification by observing the principle of **ahimsa,** or nonviolence to other living things or their souls. Devout Jain monks went to extremes to avoid harming the millions of souls they encountered each day. They swept the ground before them as they walked to avoid causing harm to invisible insects; they strained their drinking water through cloth filters to remove tiny animals they might unwittingly consume; they followed an abstemious and strictly vegetarian diet; they even wore masks and avoided making sudden movements so that they would not bruise or otherwise disturb the tiny souls inhabiting the surrounding air.

Jainist ethics were so demanding that few people other than devout monks could hope to observe them closely. The Jains believed that almost all occupations inevitably entailed violence of some kind: farming involved the killing of pests and the harvesting of living plants, for example, and crafts such as leather tanning depended on the slaughter of animals. Thus for most people Jainism was not a practical alternative to the religion of the brahmins.

Appeal of Jainism

For certain groups, however, Jainism represented an attractive alternative to the traditional cults. Jainist values and ethics had significant social implications. If all creatures possessed souls and participated in the ultimate reality of the world, it made little sense to draw sharp distinctions between different classes of human beings. As a result, the Jains did not recognize social hierarchies based on *varna* or *jati.* It is not surprising, then, that their faith became popular especially among members of lower castes who did not command much respect in the traditional social order, including merchants, scholars, and literary figures. In a typical day, individuals in these classes did little overt violence to other creatures or their souls, and they appreciated the spiritual sensitivity and the high moral standards that Jainism encouraged. They provided substantial lay support for the Jainist monks and helped to maintain the ideal of ahimsa as a prominent concern of Indian ethics. Indeed, the doctrine of ahimsa has been an especially influential teaching over the long term, both in India and beyond. Quite apart from some two million Indian individuals who maintain Jainist traditions in the present day, many Buddhists and Hindus recognize ahimsa as a fundamental element of their beliefs, and prominent reformers of the twentieth century C.E. such as

---

Jainism (JEYEN-iz'm)
ahimsa (uh-HIM-suh)

Mohandas K. Gandhi and Martin Luther King Jr. relied on the doctrine of ahimsa when promoting social reform by nonviolent means.

In spite of the moral respect it has commanded and the influence it has wielded through the centuries, however, Jainism has always been the faith of a small minority. It has simply been too difficult—or even impossible—for most people to observe. A more popular and practical alternative to the brahmins' cults came in the form of Buddhism.

A painting produced in the late fifth century C.E. depicts the Buddha seated under a pavilion as servants attend to his needs and anoint him with holy water.

Early Buddhism

Siddhartha Gautama Like Mahavira, the founder of Buddhism came from a kshatriya family, but he gave up his position and inheritance in order to seek salvation. His name was **Siddhartha Gautama,** born about 563 B.C.E. in a small tribal state governed by his father in the foothills of the Himalayas. According to early accounts, Gautama lived a pampered and sheltered life in palaces and parks, because his father had determined that Gautama would experience only happiness and would never know misery. He married his cousin and excelled in the program of studies that would prepare him to succeed his father as governor.

Eventually, however, Gautama became dissatisfied with his comfortable life. One day, according to an early legend, while riding toward a park in his chariot, Gautama saw a man made miserable by age and infirmity. When he asked for an explanation of this unsettling sight, Gautama learned from his chariot driver that all human beings grow old and weak. On later outings Gautama saw a sick man and a corpse, from whose fates he learned that disease and death were also inevitable features of the human condition. Finally Gautama noticed a monk traveling by foot in his distinctive dress, and he learned that some individuals withdraw from the active life of the world to lead holy lives and to perfect their spiritual qualities. In light of the misery he had previously witnessed, Gautama considered the monk a noble character and determined to take up an ascetic, wandering life for himself in the hope that it would help him to understand the phenomenon of suffering. Though not a strictly historical account, this story conveys well the Buddhist concern with suffering.

Gautama's Search for Enlightenment About 534 B.C.E. Gautama left his wife, his family, and the comforts of home to lead the existence of a holy man. He wandered throughout the Ganges valley searching for spiritual enlightenment and an explanation for suffering. He survived for a while by begging for his food but then abandoned society altogether to live as a hermit. He sought enlightenment first by means of intense meditation and later through the rigors of extreme asceticism. None of those tactics satisfied him. Then, according to Buddhist legends, as he sat one day beneath a large bo tree in Bodh Gaya, southwest of Pataliputra, Gautama decided that he would remain exactly where he was until he understood the problem of suffering. For forty-nine days he sat in meditation as various demons tempted him with pleasures and threatened him with terrors in efforts to shake his resolution. Eventually the demons withdrew, and Gautama prevailed. After forty-nine days under the bo tree, he received enlightenment: he understood both the problem of suffering and the means by which humans could eliminate it from the world. At that point, Gautama became the Buddha—"the enlightened one."

The Buddha and His Followers The Buddha publicly announced his doctrine for the first time about 528 B.C.E. at the Deer Park of Sarnath, near the Buddhist holy city of Banaras (modern Varanasi), in a sermon delivered to friends who had formerly been his companions in asceticism. Buddhists refer to this sermon as the "Turning of the Wheel of the Law" because it represented the beginning of the Buddha's quest to promulgate the law of righteousness. His teachings quickly attracted attention, and disciples came from all parts of the Ganges valley. He organized them

Siddhartha Gautama (sih-DHAR-tuh GOW-tau-mah)

into a community of monks who owned only their yellow robes and their begging bowls. They traveled on foot, preaching the Buddha's doctrine and seeking handouts for their meals. For more than forty years, the Buddha led his disciples throughout much of northern India in hopes of bringing spiritual enlightenment to others. About 483 B.C.E., at an age of some eighty years, he died after leaving his companions with a final message: "Decay is inherent in all component things! Work out your salvation with diligence!"

thinking about TRADITIONS

Religion and Society in Classical India
Jainism and Buddhism emerged in the context of a society undergoing rapid economic development. Would it have been likely for the teachings of these new religious movements to attract popular support during the Vedic age? Why might they have seemed attractive in the period after the sixth century B.C.E.?

Buddhist Doctrine: The Dharma The core of the Buddha's doctrine, known as the Four Noble Truths, teaches that all life involves suffering; that desire is the cause of suffering; that elimination of desire brings an end to suffering; and that a disciplined life conducted in accordance with the Noble Eightfold Path brings the elimination of desire. The Noble Eightfold Path calls for individuals to lead balanced and moderate lives, rejecting both the devotion to luxury often found in human society and the regimes of extreme asceticism favored by hermits and Jains. Specifically, the Noble Eightfold Path demands right belief, right resolve, right speech, right behavior, right occupation, right effort, right contemplation, and right meditation.

A moderate lifestyle characterized by quiet contemplation, thoughtful reflection, and disciplined self-control would enable Buddhists to reduce their desires for material goods and other worldly attractions, resulting eventually in detachment from the world itself. Ultimately, they believed that this lifestyle would lead them to personal salvation, which for Buddhists meant escape from the cycle of incarnation and attainment of *nirvana,* a state of perfect spiritual independence. Taken together, the teachings of the Four Noble Truths and the Noble Eightfold Path constitute the Buddhist *dharma*—the basic doctrine shared by Buddhists of all sects.

Appeal of Buddhism Like the Jains, the Buddhists sought to escape the cycle of incarnation without depending on the services of the brahmins. Like the Jains, too, they did not recognize social distinctions based on caste or *jati.* As a result, their message appealed strongly to members of lower castes. Because it did not demand the rigorous asceticism of Jainism, Buddhism became far more popular. Merchants were especially prominent in the ranks of the early Buddhists, and they often used Buddhist monasteries as inns when they traveled through northern India.

Apart from the social implications of the doctrine, there were several other reasons for the immense popularity of early Buddhism in India. One has to do with language. Following the example of the Buddha himself, early Buddhist monks and preachers avoided the use of Sanskrit, the literary language of the Vedas that the brahmins employed in their rituals, in favor of vernacular tongues that reached a much larger popular audience. Furthermore, early Buddhists recognized holy sites that served as focal points for devotion. Even in the early days of Buddhism, pilgrims flocked to Bodh Gaya, where Gautama received enlightenment, and the Deer Park of Sarnath, where as the Buddha he preached his first sermon. Also popular with the faithful were *stupas*—shrines housing relics of the Buddha and his first disciples that pilgrims venerated while meditating on Buddhist values.

Yet another reason for the early popularity of Buddhism was the organization of the Buddhist movement. From the days of the Buddha himself, the most enthusiastic and highly motivated converts joined monastic communities where they dedicated their lives to the search for enlightenment and salvation. Gifts and grants from pious lay supporters provided for the land, buildings, finances, and material needs of the monasteries. The monks themselves spent much of their time preaching, explaining the dharma to lay audiences, and encouraging their listeners to follow the Noble Eightfold Path in their daily lives. Over time, Buddhist monasteries became important institutions in Indian society. They served as banks for their communities, and they helped organize life in the Indian countryside by allocating their lands to individuals or groups of cultivators. Thus, during the centuries following the Buddha's death, monasteries wielded enormous social and economic as well as cultural influence in India.

Ashoka's Support The early Buddhist movement also benefited from the official patronage and support of the Mauryan dynasty. The precise reason for Ashoka's conversion to Buddhism is unclear. Early legends held that a devout Buddhist monk brought about Ashoka's conversion by dazzling him with supernatural powers. Ashoka's own account, as preserved in one of his edicts, explains that the emperor adopted Buddhism about 260 B.C.E. after the war against Kalinga. Saddened by the violence of the war and the suffering of the Kalingans, Ashoka said that he decided to pursue his aims henceforth by means of virtue, benevolence, and humanity rather than arms. Quite apart from his sincere religious convictions, it is likely that Ashoka found

Buddhism appealing as a faith that could lend unity to his culturally diverse and far-flung realm. In any case, in honor of ahimsa, the doctrine of nonviolence, Ashoka banned animal sacrifices in Pataliputra, gave up his beloved hunting expeditions, and eliminated most meat dishes from the tables of his court. Ashoka rewarded Buddhists with grants of land, and he encouraged them to spread their faith throughout India. He built monasteries and stupas and made pilgrimages to the holy sites of Buddhism. Ashoka also sent missionaries to Bactria and Ceylon (modern Sri Lanka), thus inaugurating a process by which Buddhism attracted large followings in central Asia, east Asia, and southeast Asia.

Mahayana Buddhism

From its earliest days Buddhism attracted merchants, artisans, and others of low rank in the traditional Indian social order. Its appeal was due both to its disregard for social classes and to its concern for ethical behavior instead of complicated ceremonies that seemed increasingly irrelevant to the lives and experiences of most people. Yet, even though it vastly simplified religious observances, early Buddhism made heavy demands on individuals seeking to escape from the cycle of incarnation. A truly righteous existence involved considerable sacrifice: giving up personal property, forsaking the search for social standing, and resolutely detaching oneself from the charms of family and the world. The earliest Buddhists thought that numerous physical incarnations, stretching over thousands of years, might be necessary before an individual soul would become pure enough to achieve salvation and pass into nirvana. Though perhaps more attractive than the religion of the brahmins, Buddhism did not promise to make life easy for its adherents.

PART 2

Development of Buddhism Between the third century B.C.E. and the first century C.E., however, three new

The famous Buddhist stupa at Sanchi, originally built by Ashoka and enlarged in later times, is a domed shrine—representing the dome of heaven over the earth—intended to contain sacred relics of the Buddha. The shrine is flanked by four entry gateways carved with intricate scenes from the Buddha's life; the pillars of the southern gateway, pictured here, are each crowned with four lions, a Buddhist symbol associated with strength and power.

developments in Buddhist thought and practice reduced obligations of believers, opened new avenues to salvation, and brought explosive popularity to the faith. In the first place, whereas the Buddha had not considered himself divine, some of his later followers began to worship him as a god. Thus Buddhism acquired a devotional focus that helped converts channel their spiritual energies and identify more closely with their faith. In the second place, theologians articulated the notion of the *bodhisattva* ("an enlightened being"). **Bodhisattvas** were individuals who had reached spiritual perfection and merited the reward of nirvana, but who intentionally delayed their entry into nirvana to help others who were still struggling. Some theologians taught that bodhisattvas could even perform good deeds on behalf of their less spiritually inclined brethren. Like Christian saints, bodhisattvas served as examples of spiritual excellence, and they provided a source of inspiration. Finally, Buddhist monasteries began to accept gifts from wealthy individuals and to regard the bequests as acts of generosity that merited salvation. Thus wealthy individuals could enjoy the comforts of the world, avoid the sacrifices demanded by early Buddhist teachings, and still ensure their salvation.

King Ashoka erected many stone pillars such as this handsome column, which stands 10 meters (32 feet) tall, to promote Buddhist teachings, direct travelers to holy sites, or commemorate significant events of the Buddha's life.

The Spread of Mahayana Buddhism

Because these innovations opened the road to salvation for large numbers of people, their proponents called their faith the ***Mahayana*** ("the greater vehicle," which could carry more people to salvation), as opposed to the *Hinayana* ("the lesser vehicle"), a pejorative term for the earlier and stricter doctrine known also as Theravada Buddhism. During the early centuries C.E., Mahayana Buddhism spread rapidly throughout India and attracted many converts from lay and wealthy classes. In later centuries Mahayana Buddhism became established also in central Asia, China, Japan, and Korea. The stricter Theravada faith did not disappear: it remained the dominant school of Buddhism in Ceylon, and in later centuries it spread also to Burma, Thailand, and other parts of southeast Asia. Since the first century C.E., however, most of the world's Buddhists have sought to ride the greater vehicle to salvation.

Nalanda

Mahayana Buddhism flourished partly because of educational institutions that efficiently promoted the faith. During the Vedic era, Indian education was mostly an informal affair involving a sage and his students. When Jains and Buddhists organized monasteries, however, they began to offer regular instruction and established educational institutions. Most monasteries provided basic education, and larger communities offered advanced instruction as well. Best known of all was the Buddhist monastery at Nalanda, founded during the Gupta dynasty in the Ganges River valley near Pataliputra. At Nalanda it was possible to study not only Buddhism but also the Vedas, Hindu philosophy, logic, mathematics, astronomy, and medicine. Nalanda soon became so famous as an educational center that pilgrims and students from foreign lands traveled there to study with the most renowned masters of Buddhist doctrine. By the end of the Gupta dynasty, several thousand students may have been in residence there.

The Emergence of Popular Hinduism

As Buddhism generated new ideas and attracted widespread popular interest, Hinduism underwent a similar evolution that transformed it into a popular religion of salvation. While drawing inspiration from the Vedas and the Upanishads, popular Hinduism increasingly departed from the older traditions of the brahmins. Like Mahayana Buddhism, Hinduism experienced changes in doctrine and observances that resulted in a faith that addressed the interests and met the needs of ordinary people.

The Epics

The great epic poems, the *Mahabharata* and the *Ramayana,* illustrate the development of Hindu values. Both works originated as secular tales transmitted orally during the late years of the Vedic age (1500–500 B.C.E.). Brahmin scholars revised them and committed them to writing probably during the early centuries C.E. The *Mahabharata* dealt with a bloody civil war for the control of northern India between two groups of cousins. Though originally a purely secular work, the brahmins made a prominent place in the poem for the god **Vishnu,** the preserver of the world who intervened frequently on behalf of virtuous individuals.

The *Ramayana* was originally a love and adventure story involving the trials faced by the legendary Prince Rama and his loyal wife, Sita. Rama went to great lengths to rescue Sita after the demon king of Ceylon kidnapped her, and his

---

bodhisattvas (BOH-dih-SAT-vuhs)
Mahayana (mah-huh-YAH-nah)
Vishnu (VISH-noo)

sources from the past

Ashoka as a Teacher of Humility and Equality according to the *Ashokavadana*

Following Ashoka's death, many legends circulated about the emperor, his life, his rule, and his devotion to Buddhism. About the second century C.E., anonymous editors collected many of those legends in a work known as the Ashokavadana (The Legend of Ashoka). *Though not historically reliable, the legend is valuable as a work showing how later generations revered Ashoka and made a hero of the Buddhist emperor. The following selection celebrates Ashoka's efforts to promote the Buddhist values of humility and the equality of believers in spite of their different caste origins.*

Not long after King Ashoka had come to have faith in the Teaching of the Buddha, he started honoring Buddhist monks, throwing himself at their feet wherever he saw them, in a crowd, or in a deserted place.

Now Ashoka had a minister named Yasas, and although he had the utmost faith in the Blessed One [the Buddha], he said, one day, to the king: "Your majesty, you ought not to prostrate yourself before wandering mendicants of every caste, and the Buddhist monks do come from all four castes."

To this Ashoka did not immediately respond. Sometime later, however, he told all his ministers that he needed to have the heads of various sorts of creatures, and he asked one of them to bring him the head of such and such an animal, and another to bring him the head of another animal, and so on. Finally, he ordered Yasas to bring him the head of a human being.

Now when the ministers had gathered all these heads, Ashoka ordered them to go to the market place and sell them. Soon, all of the heads had been sold, except Yasas's human head that no one would buy. Ashoka then told Yasas to give his head away, but, even though it was gratis, still no one would take it.

Ashamed at his lack of success, Yasas came back to Ashoka and said: "O king, the heads of cows, asses, sheep, deer, and birds—all were sold to people for a price; but no one would take this worthless human head, even free of charge."

"Why is that?" Ashoka asked his minister, "why wouldn't anyone accept this human head?"

"Because it disgusted them," Yasas replied.

"Oh?" said the king, "is it just this head that is disgusting or the heads of all human beings?"

"The heads of all humans," answered Yasas.

"What?" said Ashoka, "is my head disgusting as well?"

Out of fear, Yasas did not want to tell him the real fact of the matter, but the king ordered him to speak the truth, and finally he answered: "Yes."

After forcing this admission out of his minister, Ashoka then revealed to him his purpose in doing so: "You, sir, are obsessed with matters of form and superiority, and because of this attachment you seek to dissuade me from bowing down at the feet of the monks. But if I acquire some merit by bowing down a head so disgusting that no one on earth would take it, even free of charge, what harm is there in that? You, sir, look at the caste (*jati*) and not at the inherent qualities of the monks. Haughty, deluded, and obsessed with caste, you harm yourself and others."

For Further Reflection

- In what ways and for what reasons might this story from the *Ashokavadana* have appealed to various groups of early Buddhists?

Source: John S. Strong. *The Legend of King Ashoka: A Study and Translation of the* Ashokavadana. Princeton: Princeton University Press, 1983, pp. 234–36. (Translation slightly modified.)

alliance with Hanuman, general of the monkeys, led to exciting clashes with his enemies. Later brahmin editors made Rama an incarnation of Vishnu, and they portrayed Rama and Sita as the ideal Hindu husband and wife, devoted and loyal to each other even in times of immense difficulty.

The *Bhagavad Gita* A short poetic work known as the ***Bhagavad Gita*** ("song of the lord") best illustrates both the expectations that Hinduism made of individuals and the promise of salvation that it held out to them. The *Gita* was the work of many hands, and the date of its composition is uncertain. Scholars have placed it at various points between 300 B.C.E. and 300 C.E., and it most likely underwent several rounds of revision before taking on its final form about 400 C.E. Yet it eloquently evokes the cultural climate of India between the Mauryan and the Gupta dynasties.

The work is a self-contained episode of the *Mahabharata.* It presents a dialogue between Arjuna, a kshatriya warrior about to enter battle, and his charioteer Krishna, who was in fact a human incarnation of the god Vishnu. The immediate problem addressed in the work was Arjuna's reluctance to fight: the enemy included many of his friends

Bhagavad Gita (BUH-guh-vahd GEE-tuh)

and relatives, and even though he recognized the justice of his cause, he shrank from the conflict. In an effort to persuade the warrior to fight, Krishna presented Arjuna with several lines of argument. In the first place, he said, Arjuna must not worry about harming his friends and relatives, because the soul does not die with the human body. Arjuna's weapons did not have the power to touch the soul, so he could never harm or kill another person in any meaningful way.

Krishna also held that Arjuna's caste imposed specific moral duties and social responsibilities upon him. The duty of shudras was to serve, of vaishyas to work, of brahmins to learn the scriptures and seek wisdom. Similarly, Krishna argued, the duty of kshatriyas was to govern and fight. Indeed, Krishna went further and held that an individual's social responsibilities had spiritual significance. He told Arjuna that failure to fulfill caste duties was a grievous sin, whereas their observance brought spiritual benefits.

Finally, Krishna taught that Arjuna would attain everlasting peace and blessedness if he devoted himself to the love, adoration, and service of Krishna himself. Arjuna should abandon his selfish and superficial personal concerns and surrender to the deeper wisdom of the god. As a reward, wholehearted worship would bring Arjuna eternal salvation through unity with his god. Alongside understanding of the soul and caste duties, then, unquestioning faith and devotion would put Arjuna in the proper state of mind for the looming conflict by aligning his actions with divine wisdom and will. Krishna's teaching that faith would bring salvation helped inspire a tradition of ecstatic and unquestioning devotion in popular Hinduism.

Carving of a bodhisattva from the second or third century C.E. This carving perhaps represents Avalokitesvara, also known as the Lord of Compassion. Almost as perfect as the Buddha, Avalokitesvara had a reputation for protecting merchants and sailors, helping women conceive, and turning enemies into kind-hearted friends.

Hindu Ethics Hindu ethics thus differed considerably from those of earlier Indian moralists. The Upanishads had taught that only through renunciation and detachment from the world could individuals escape the cycle of incarnation. As represented in the *Bhagavad Gita,* however, Hindu ethical teachings made life much easier for the lay classes by holding out the promise of salvation precisely to those who participated actively in the world and met their caste responsibilities. To be sure, Krishna taught that individuals should meet their responsibilities in detached fashion: they should not become personally or emotionally involved in their actions, and they especially should not strive for material reward or recognition. Rather, they should perform their duties faithfully, concentrating on their actions alone, with no thought as to their consequences.

Other works by early Hindu moralists acknowledged even more openly than did the *Bhagavad Gita* that individuals could lead honorable lives in the world. Indeed, Hindu ethics commonly recognized four principal aims of human life: *dharma* (obedience to religious and moral laws), *artha* (the pursuit of economic well-being and honest prosperity), *kama* (the enjoyment of social, physical, and sexual pleasure), and moksha (the salvation of the soul). According to Hindu moral precepts, a proper balance of *dharma, artha,* and *kama* would help an individual to attain *moksha.*

As devotional Hinduism evolved and became increasingly distinct from the teachings of the Upanishads and the older traditions of the brahmins, it also enhanced its appeal to all segments of Indian society. Hinduism offered salvation to masses of people who, as a matter of practical necessity, had to lead active lives in the world and thus could not even hope to achieve the detachment envisioned in the Upanishads.

Popularity of Hinduism Hinduism gradually displaced Buddhism as the most popular religion in India. Buddhism remained strong through much of the first millennium C.E., and until about the eleventh century pilgrims traveled to India from as far away as China to visit the holy sites of Buddhism and learn about the faith in its original homeland. Within India, however, Buddhism grew remote from the popular masses. Later Buddhist monks did not seek to communicate their message to the larger society in the zealous way of their predecessors, but increasingly confined themselves to the comforts of monasteries richly endowed by wealthy patrons.

Meanwhile, devotional Hinduism also attracted political support and patronage, particularly from the Gupta emperors. The Guptas and their successors bestowed grants of land on Hindu brahmins and supported an educational system that promoted Hindu values. Just as Ashoka Maurya had advanced the cause of Buddhism, the Guptas and their successors later helped

sources from the past

Caste Duties according to the *Bhagavad Gita*

In urging Arjuna to enter battle, Krishna pointed out that Arjuna could not harm the immortal souls of his family and friends on the other side. Beyond that, however, Krishna emphasized the duty to fight that Arjuna inherited as a member of the kshatriya caste. Yet Krishna also counseled Arjuna to perform his duty in a spirit of detachment, not caring for victory or defeat.

As a man, casting off old clothes, puts on others and new ones, so the embodied self, casting off old bodies, goes to others and new ones. Weapons do not divide the self into pieces; fire does not burn it; waters do not moisten it; the wind does not dry it up. It is not divisible; it is not combustible; it is not to be moistened; it is not to be dried up. It is everlasting, all-pervading, stable, firm, and eternal. It is said to be unperceived, to be unthinkable, to be unchangeable. Therefore knowing it to be such, you ought not to grieve. But even if you think that the self is constantly born, and constantly dies, still, O you of mighty arms, you ought not to grieve thus. For to one that is born, death is certain; and to one that dies, birth is certain. Therefore about this unavoidable thing, you ought not to grieve. . . .

Having regard to your own duty, you ought not to falter, for there is nothing better for a kshatriya than a righteous battle. Happy those kshatriyas who can find such a battle—an open door to heaven! But if you will not fight this righteous battle, then you will have abandoned your own duty and your fame, and you will incur sin. All beings, too, will tell of your everlasting infamy; and to one who has been honored, infamy is a greater evil than death. Warriors who are masters of great chariots will think that you have abstained from the battle through fear, and having been highly thought of by them, you will fall down to littleness. Your enemies, too, decrying your power, will speak much about you that should not be spoken. And what, indeed, could be more lamentable than that? Killed, you will obtain heaven; victorious, you will enjoy the earth. Therefore arise, resolved to engage in battle. Looking on pleasure and pain, on gain and loss, on victory and defeat as the same, prepare for battle, and thus you will not incur sin. . . .

The state of mind that consists in firm understanding regarding steady contemplation does not belong to those who are strongly attached to worldly pleasures and power, and whose minds are drawn away by that flowery talk that is full of specific acts for the attainment of pleasures and power, and that promises birth as the fruit of actions—that flowery talk uttered by unwise ones who are enamored of Vedic words, who say there is nothing else, who are full of desires, and whose goal is heaven. . . .

Your business is with action alone, not by any means with the fruit of the action. Let not the fruit of action be your motive to action. Let not your attachment be fixed on inaction. Having recourse to devotion, perform actions, casting off all attachment, and being equable in success or ill success.

For Further Reflection

- How do these reflections on caste duties and detachment in the *Bhagavad Gita* compare and contrast with the moral and ethical teachings of Zarathustra and Confucius discussed in earlier chapters?

Source: *The Bhagavad Gita.* Trans. by Kashinath Trimbak Telang. In F. Max Müller, ed., *The Sacred Books of the East,* vol. 8. Oxford: Clarendon Press, 1908, pp. 45–48. (Translation slightly modified.)

Hinduism become the dominant religious and cultural tradition in India. By about 1000 C.E., Buddhism had entered a noticeable decline in India while Hinduism grew in popularity. Within a few centuries devotional Hinduism and the more recently introduced faith of Islam almost completely eclipsed Buddhism in its homeland.

in perspective

In India, as in classical Persia and China, a robust agricultural economy supported the creation of large-scale states and interregional trade. Although an imperial state did not become a permanent feature of Indian political life, the peoples of the subcontinent maintained an orderly society based on the caste system and regional states. Indian cultural and religious traditions reflected the conditions of the larger society in which they developed. Mahayana Buddhism and devotional Hinduism in particular addressed the needs of the increasingly prominent lay classes, and the two faiths profoundly influenced the religious life of Asian peoples over the long term of history. ●

CHRONOLOGY

563–483 B.C.E.	Life of Siddhartha Gautama, the Buddha
540–468 B.C.E.	Life of Vardhamana Mahavira
520 B.C.E.	Invasion of India by Darius of Persia
327 B.C.E.	Invasion of India by Alexander of Macedon
321–185 B.C.E.	Mauryan dynasty
321–297 B.C.E.	Reign of Chandragupta Maurya
268–232 B.C.E.	Reign of Ashoka Maurya
182 B.C.E.–1 C.E.	Bactrian rule in northern India
1–300 C.E.	Kushan empire in northern India and central Asia
78–103 C.E.	Reign of Kushan emperor Kanishka
320–550 C.E.	Gupta dynasty

For Further Reading

Roy C. Amore and Larry D. Shinn. *Lustful Maidens and Ascetic Kings.* New York, 1981. Translations of stories and moral tales from Hindu and Buddhist writings.

Karen Armstrong. *Buddha.* New York, 2001. An accessible introduction to the Buddha by a prominent scholar of Indian religions.

Jeannine Auboyer. *Daily Life in Ancient India.* Trans. by S. W. Taylor. London, 2002. An excellent introduction to Indian social history during the classical era.

A. L. Basham. *The Wonder That Was India.* 3rd ed. London, 2000. Popular and readable survey of premodern Indian history.

William Theodore De Bary, ed. *Sources of Indian Tradition.* 2 vols. 2nd ed. New York, 1988. Important collection of sources in translation.

Kautalya. *The Kautilya Arthashastra.* 3 vols. 2nd ed. Ed. by R. P. Kangle. Bombay, 1960–69. Translation of the most important political treatise of classical India.

Xinru Liu. *Ancient India and Ancient China: Trade and Religious Exchanges, A.D. 1–600.* Delhi, 1988. Important study exploring the early spread of Buddhism from India to central Asia and China.

Juan Mascaró, trans. *The Bhagavad Gita.* Harmondsworth, 1962. Brilliant and evocative English version by a gifted translator.

William H. McNeill and Jean W. Sedlar, eds. *Classical India.* New York, 1969. Collection of primary sources in translation.

Gregory Schopen. *Buddhist Monks and Business Matters: Still More Papers on Monastic Buddhism in India.* Honolulu, 2004. Focuses on the social and economic dimensions of early Buddhist monasticism.

Jean W. Sedlar. *India and the Greek World: A Study in the Transmission of Culture.* Totowa, N.J., 1980. Important study of relations between India and Greece, based on solid research.

K. M. Sen. *Hinduism.* London, 2005. Reissue of a classic interpretation with a new foreword by Amartya Sen drawing out the contemporary implications of the study.

John S. Strong. *The Legend of King Ashoka: A Study and Translation of the* Ashokavadana. Princeton, 1983. Valuable translation of an important early Buddhist account of King Ashoka's life and reign.

Romila Thapar. *Ashoka and the Decline of the Mauryas.* London, 1961. The best scholarly study of Ashoka and his reign.

———. *Early India: From the Origins to A.D. 1300.* Berkeley, 2003. A fresh view by one of the leading scholars of early Indian history.

Mortimer Wheeler. *Flames over Persepolis.* New York, 1968. Examines the influence of Greek and Persian traditions in northern India after the time of Alexander of Macedon.

Stanley Wolpert. *A New History of India.* 7th ed. New York, 2004. A concise and readable survey of Indian history.

Mediterranean Society: The Greek Phase

chapter 10

An Athenian vase produced in the late fifth century B.C.E. depicts Aphrodite, the Greek goddess of love (seated), with attendants at a garden party.

EYEWITNESS:
Homer: A Poet and the Sea

For a man who perhaps never existed, Homer has been a profoundly influential figure. According to tradition, Homer composed the two great epic poems of ancient Greece, the *Iliad* and the *Odyssey.* In fact, scholars now know that bards recited both poems for generations before Homer lived—the mid-eighth century B.C.E., if he was indeed a historical figure. Some experts believe that Homer was not a real man so much as a convenient name for several otherwise anonymous scribes who committed the *Iliad* and the *Odyssey* to writing. Others believe that a man named Homer had a part in preparing a written version of the epics, but that others also contributed significantly to his work.

Whether Homer ever really lived or not, the epics attributed to him deeply influenced the development of classical Greek thought and literature. The *Iliad* offered a Greek perspective on a campaign waged by a band of Greek warriors against the city of Troy in Anatolia during the twelfth century B.C.E. The *Odyssey* recounted the experiences of the Greek hero Odysseus as he sailed home after the Trojan war. The two works described scores of difficulties faced by Greek warriors—not only battles with Trojans but also challenges posed by deities and monsters, conflicts among themselves, and even psychological barriers that individuals had to surmount. Between them, the two epics preserved a rich collection of stories that literary figures mined for more than a millennium, reworking Homer's material and exploring his themes from fresh perspectives.

Quite apart from their significance as literary masterpieces, the *Iliad* and the *Odyssey* testify to the frequency and normality of travel, communication, and interaction in the Mediterranean basin during the second and first millennia B.C.E. Both works portray Greeks as expert and fearless seamen, almost as comfortable aboard their ships as on land, who did not hesitate to venture into the waters of what Homer called the "wine-dark sea" in pursuit of their goals. Homer lovingly described the sleek galleys in which Greek warriors raced across the waters, sometimes to plunder the slower but heavily laden cargo vessels that plied the Mediterranean sea lanes, more often to launch strikes at enemy targets. He even had Odysseus construct a sailing ship single-handedly when he was shipwrecked on an island inhabited only by a goddess. The *Iliad* and the *Odyssey* make it clear that maritime links touched peoples throughout the Mediterranean basin in Homer's time and, further, that Greeks were among the most prominent seafarers of the age.

Already during the second millennium B.C.E., Phoenician merchants had established links between lands and peoples at the far ends of the Mediterranean Sea. During the classical era, however, the Mediterranean basin became much more tightly integrated as Greeks, and later Romans as well, organized commercial exchange and sponsored interaction throughout the region. Under Greek and Roman supervision, the Mediterranean served not as a barrier but, rather, as a highway linking Anatolia, Egypt, Greece, Italy, France, Spain, north Africa, and even southern Russia (by way of routes through the Black Sea).

Ancient Greece differed from classical societies in other lands. Early in the classical era, the Greeks lived in autonomous city-states. Only after the late third century B.C.E. did they play prominent roles in the large, centralized empire established by their neighbors to the north in Macedon. Yet from the seventh through the second centuries B.C.E., the Greeks integrated the societies and economies of distant lands through energetic commercial activity over the Mediterranean sea lanes. They also generated a remarkable body of moral thought and philosophical reflection. Just as the traditions of classical Persia, China, and India shaped the cultural experiences of those lands, the traditions of the Greeks profoundly influenced the long-term cultural development of the Mediterranean basin, Europe, and southwest Asia as well.

EARLY DEVELOPMENT OF GREEK SOCIETY

Humans inhabited the Balkan region and the Greek peninsula from an early but indeterminate date. During the third millennium B.C.E., they increasingly met and mingled with peoples from different societies who traveled and traded in the Mediterranean basin. As a result, early inhabitants of the Greek peninsula built their societies under the influence of Mesopotamians, Egyptians, Phoenicians, and others active in the region. Beginning in the ninth century B.C.E., the Greeks organized a series of city-states, which served as the political context for the development of classical Greek society.

Minoan and Mycenaean Societies

Knossos During the late third millennium B.C.E., a sophisticated society arose on the island of Crete. Scholars refer to it as Minoan society, after Minos, a legendary king of ancient Crete. Between 2000 and 1700 B.C.E., the inhabitants of Crete built a series of lavish palaces throughout the island, most notably the enormous complex at Knossos decorated with vivid frescoes depicting Minoans at work and play. These palaces were the nerve centers of Minoan society: they were residences of rulers, and they also served as storehouses where officials collected taxes in kind from local cultivators. Palace officials devised a script known as Linear A, in which written symbols stood for syllables rather than words, ideas, vowels, or consonants. Although linguists have not yet been able to decipher Linear A, it is clear that Cretan administrators used the script to keep detailed records of economic and commercial matters.

Between 2200 and 1450 B.C.E., Crete was a principal center of Mediterranean commerce. Because of its geographic

A magnificent fresco from the town of Akrotiri on the island of Thera depicts a busy harbor, showing that Akrotiri traded actively with Crete and other Minoan sites. The volcanic eruption of Thera about 1628 B.C.E. destroyed Akrotiri.

location in the east-central Mediterranean, Crete received early influences from Phoenicia and Egypt. By 2200 B.C.E. Cretans were traveling aboard advanced sailing craft of Phoenician design. Minoan ships sailed to Greece, Anatolia, Phoenicia, and Egypt, where Cretan wine, olive oil, and wool were exchanged for grains, textiles, and manufactured goods. Archaeologists have discovered pottery vessels used as storage containers for Minoan wine and olive oil as far away as Sicily. After 1600 B.C.E. Cretans established colonies on Cyprus and many islands in the Aegean Sea, probably to mine local copper ores and gain better access to markets where tin was available.

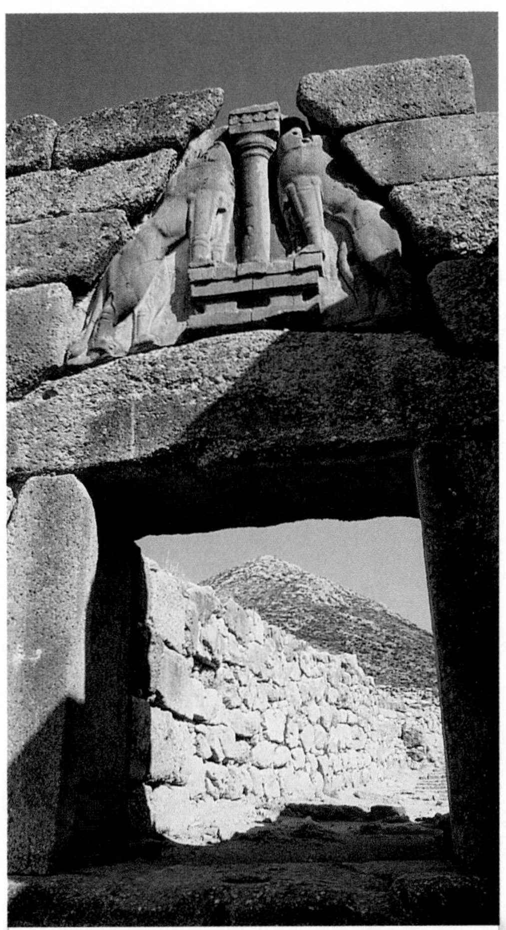
The Lion Gate at Mycenae illustrates the heavy fortifications built by Mycenaeans to protect their settlements.

Decline of Minoan Society After 1700 B.C.E. Minoan society experienced a series of earthquakes, volcanic eruptions, and tidal waves. Most destructive was a devastating volcanic eruption about 1628 B.C.E. on the island of Thera (Santorini) north of Crete. Between 1600 and 1450 B.C.E., Cretans embarked on a new round of palace building to replace structures destroyed by those natural catastrophes: they built luxurious complexes with indoor plumbing and drainage systems and even furnished some of them with flush toilets. After 1450 B.C.E., however, the wealth of Minoan society attracted a series of invaders, and Crete fell under foreign domination. Yet the Minoan traditions of maritime trade, writing, and construction deeply influenced the inhabitants of nearby Greece.

Mycenaean Society Beginning about 2200 B.C.E., migratory Indo-European peoples filtered over the Balkans and into the Greek peninsula. By 1600 B.C.E. they had begun to trade with Minoan merchants and visit Crete, where they learned about writing and large-scale construction. They adapted Minoan Linear A to their language, which was an early form of Greek, and devised a syllabic script known as Linear B. After 1450 B.C.E. they also built massive stone fortresses and palaces throughout the southern part of the Greek peninsula, known as the Peloponnesus. Because the fortified sites offered protection, they soon attracted settlers who built small agricultural communities. Their society is known as **Mycenaean,** after Mycenae, one of their most important settlements.

From 1500 to 1100 B.C.E., the Mycenaeans expanded their influence beyond peninsular Greece. They largely overpowered Minoan society, and they took over the Cretan palaces, where they established craft workshops. Archaeologists have unearthed thousands of clay tablets in Linear B that came from the archives of Mycenaean rulers in Crete as well as peninsular Greece. The Mycenaeans also established settlements in Anatolia, Sicily, and southern Italy.

Chaos in the Eastern Mediterranean About 1200 B.C.E. the Mycenaeans engaged in a conflict with the city of Troy in Anatolia. This Trojan war, which Homer recalled from a Greek perspective in his *Iliad,* coincided with invasions of foreign mariners in the Mycenaean homeland. Indeed, from 1100 to 800 B.C.E. chaos reigned throughout the eastern Mediterranean region. Invasions and civil disturbances made it impossible to maintain stable governments or even productive agricultural societies. Mycenaean palaces fell into ruin, the population sharply declined, and people abandoned most settlements. Many inhabitants of the Greek peninsula fled to the islands of the Aegean Sea, Anatolia, or Cyprus. Writing in both Linear A and Linear B disappeared. The boisterous character of the era comes across clearly in Homer's works. Though set in an earlier era, both the *Iliad* and the *Odyssey* reflect the tumultuous centuries after 1100 B.C.E. They portray a society riven with conflict, and they recount innumerable episodes of aggression, treachery, and violence alongside heroic bravery and courage.

The World of the Polis

The Polis In the absence of a centralized state or empire, local institutions took the lead in restoring political order in Greece. The most important institution was the city-state, or polis. The term *polis* originally referred to a citadel or fortified site that offered refuge for local communities during times of war or other emergencies. These sites attracted increasing populations, and many of them gradually became

Mycenaean (meye-seh-NEE-uhn)

lively commercial centers. They took on an increasingly urban character and extended their authority over surrounding regions. They levied taxes on their hinterlands and appropriated a portion of the agricultural surplus to support the urban population. By about 800 B.C.E. many *poleis* (the plural of polis) had become bustling city-states that functioned as the principal centers of Greek society.

The poleis took various political forms. Some differences reflected the fact that poleis emerged independently and elaborated their traditions with little outside influence. Others arose from different rates of economic development. A few poleis developed as small monarchies, but most were under the collective rule of local notables who ruled as oligarchs. Some poleis fell into the hands of generals or ambitious politicians—called "tyrants" by the Greeks—who gained power by irregular means. (The tyrants were not necessarily oppressive despots: indeed, many of them were extremely popular leaders. The term *tyrant* referred to their routes to power rather than their policies.) The most important of the poleis were Sparta and Athens, whose contrasting constitutions illustrate the variety of political styles in classical Greece.

Sparta Sparta was situated in a fertile region of the Peloponnesus. As their population and economy expanded during the eighth and seventh centuries B.C.E., the Spartans progressively extended their control over the Peloponnesus. In doing so, they reduced neighboring peoples to the status of *helots,* servants of the Spartan state. Although they were not chattel slaves, the helots also were not free. They could form families, but they could not leave the land. Their role in society was to provide agricultural labor and keep Sparta supplied with food. By the sixth century B.C.E., the helots

MAP 10.1
Classical Greece, 800–350 B.C.E.
Note the mountainous topography of the Greek peninsula and western Anatolia.
To what extent did geography encourage Greeks to venture into the Mediterranean Sea?

probably outnumbered the Spartan citizens by more than ten to one. With their large subject population, the Spartans were able to cultivate the Peloponnesus efficiently, but they also faced the constant threat of rebellion. As a result, the Spartans devoted most of their resources to maintaining a powerful and disciplined military machine.

Spartan Society In theory, Spartan citizens were equal in status. To discourage the development of economic and social distinctions, Spartans observed an extraordinarily austere lifestyle as a matter of policy. They did not wear jewelry or elaborate clothes, nor did they pamper themselves with luxuries or accumulate private wealth on a large scale. They generally did not even circulate coins made of precious metals but, instead, used iron bars for money. It is for good reason, then, that the adjective *spartan* refers to a lifestyle characterized by simplicity, frugality, and austerity.

A painted cup produced in Sparta about 550 B.C.E. depicts hunters attacking a boar. Spartans regarded hunting as an exercise that helped to sharpen fighting skills and aggressive instincts.

Distinction among the ancient Spartans came not by wealth or social status, but by prowess, discipline, and military talent, which the Spartan educational system cultivated from an early age. All boys from families of Spartan citizens left their homes at age seven and went to live in military barracks, where they underwent a rigorous regime of physical training. At age twenty they began active military service, which they continued until retirement. Spartan authorities also prescribed vigorous physical exercise for girls in hopes that they would bear strong children. When they reached age eighteen to twenty, young women married and had occasional sexual relations, but did not live with their husbands. Only at about age thirty did men leave the barracks and set up households with their wives and children.

By the fourth century B.C.E., Spartan society had lost much of its ascetic rigor. Aristocratic families had accumulated great wealth, and Spartans had developed a taste for luxury in food and dress. Nevertheless, Spartan society stood basically on the foundation of military discipline, and its institutions both reflected and reinforced the larger society's commitment to military values. In effect, Sparta sought to maintain public order—and discourage rebellion by the helots—by creating a military state that could crush any threat.

Athens In Athens as in Sparta, population growth and economic development caused political and social strain, but the Athenians relieved tensions by establishing a government based on democratic principles. Whereas Sparta sought to impose order by military means, Athens sought to negotiate order by considering the interests of the polis's various constituencies. Official positions were by no means open to all residents: only free adult males from Athens played a role in public affairs, leaving foreigners, slaves, and women with no direct voice in government. In seeking to resolve social problems, Athenians opened government offices to all male citizens and broadened the base of political participation in classical Greece.

Athenian Society During the seventh century B.C.E., an increasing volume of maritime trade brought prosperity to Attica, the region around Athens. The principal beneficiaries of that prosperity were aristocratic landowners, who also controlled the Athenian government. As their wealth grew, the aristocrats increased their landholdings and cultivated them with greater efficiency. Owners of small plots could not compete and fell heavily into debt. Competitive pressures often forced them to sell their holdings to aristocrats, and debt burdens sometimes overwhelmed them and pushed them into slavery.

By the early sixth century B.C.E., Attica had a large and growing class of people extremely unhappy with the structure of their society and poised to engage in war against their wealthy neighbors. Many poleis that experienced similar economic conditions suffered decades of brutal civil war between aristocrats and less privileged classes. In Athens, however, an aristocrat named Solon served as a mediator between classes, and he devised a solution to class conflict in Attica.

Solon and Athenian Democracy Solon forged a compromise between the classes. He allowed aristocrats to keep their lands—rather than confiscate them and redistribute them to landless individuals, as many of the less privileged preferred—but he cancelled debts, forbade debt slavery, and liberated those already enslaved for debt. To ensure that aristocrats would not undermine his reforms, Solon also provided representation for the common classes in the Athenian government by opening the councils of the polis to any citizen wealthy enough to devote time to public affairs, regardless of his lineage. Later reformers went even further. During the late sixth and fifth centuries B.C.E.,

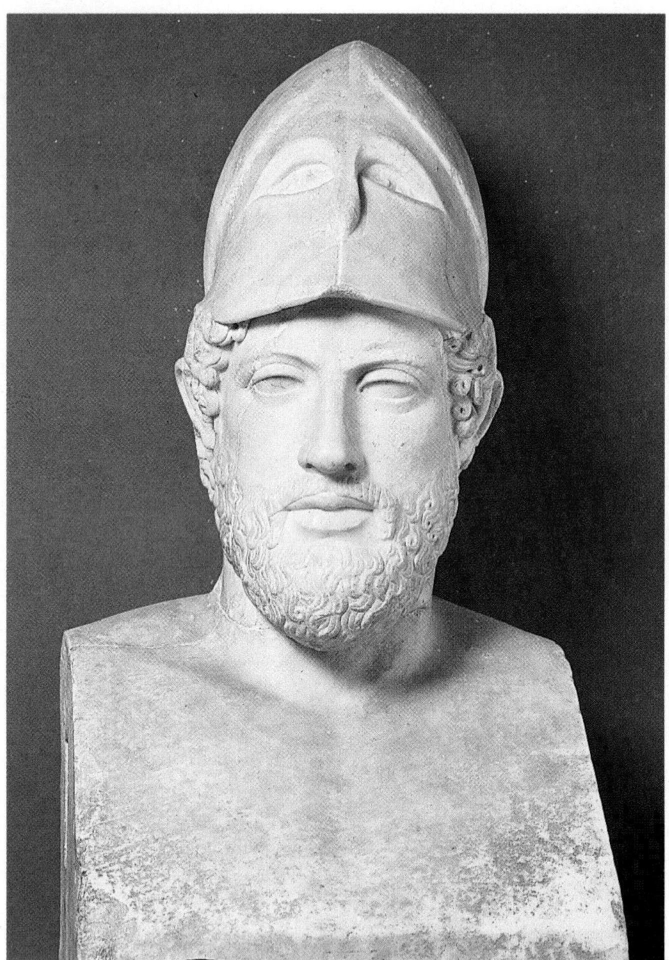

The image of Pericles, wearing a helmet that symbolizes his post as Athenian leader, survives in a Roman copy of a Greek statue.

Athenian leaders increased opportunities for commoners to participate in government, and they paid salaries to officeholders so that financial hardship would not exclude anyone from service.

Pericles Those reforms gradually transformed Athens into a democratic state. The high tide of Athenian power and prosperity came under the leadership of the statesman Pericles. Though he was of aristocratic birth, Pericles was the most popular Athenian leader from 461 B.C.E. until his death in 429 B.C.E. He wielded enormous personal influence in a government with hundreds of officeholders from the common classes, and he supported building programs that provided employment for thousands of construction workers and laborers. Under the leadership of Pericles, Athens became the most sophisticated of the poleis, with a vibrant community of scientists, philosophers, poets, dramatists, artists, and architects. Little wonder, then, that in a moment of civic pride, Pericles boasted that Athens was "the education of Greece."

GREECE AND THE LARGER WORLD

As the poleis prospered, Greeks became increasingly prominent in the larger world of the Mediterranean basin. They established colonies along the shores of the Mediterranean and the Black Sea, and they traded throughout the region. Eventually, their political and economic interests brought them into conflict with the expanding Persian empire. During the fifth century B.C.E., a round of intermittent war between the Greeks and the Persians ended in stalemate, but in the next century Alexander of Macedon toppled the Achaemenid empire. Indeed, Alexander built an empire stretching from India to Egypt and Greece. His conquests created a vast zone of trade and communication that encouraged commercial and cultural exchange on an unprecedented scale.

Greek Colonization

By about 800 B.C.E. the poleis were emerging as centers of political organization in Greece. During the next century increasing population strained the resources available in the rocky and mountainous Greek peninsula. To relieve population pressures, the Greeks began to establish colonies in other parts of the Mediterranean basin. Between the mid-eighth and the late sixth centuries B.C.E., they founded more than four hundred colonies along the shores of the Mediterranean Sea and the Black Sea.

The Greeks established their first colonies in the central Mediterranean during the early eighth century B.C.E. The most popular sites were Sicily and southern Italy, particularly the region around modern Naples, which was itself originally a Greek colony called Neapolis ("new polis"). These colonies provided merchants not only with fertile fields that yielded large agricultural surpluses but also with convenient access to the copper, zinc, tin, and iron ores of central Italy. By the sixth century B.C.E., Greek colonies dotted the shores of Sicily and southern Italy, and more Greeks lived in these colonies than in the Greek peninsula itself. By 600 B.C.E. the Greeks had ventured even farther west and established the important colony of Massalia (modern Marseilles) in what is now southern France.

Greek Colonies Greek colonies arose also in the eastern Mediterranean and the Black Sea. Hundreds of islands in the Aegean Sea beckoned to a maritime people such as the Greeks. Colonists also settled in Anatolia, where their Greek cousins had established communities during the centuries of political turmoil after 1100 B.C.E. During the eighth and seventh centuries B.C.E., Greeks ventured into the Black Sea in large numbers and established colonies all along its shores. These settlements offered merchants access to rich supplies of grain, fish, furs, timber, honey, wax, gold, and amber as well as slaves captured in southern Russia and transported to markets in the Mediterranean.

Unlike their counterparts in classical Persia, China, and India, the Greeks did not build a centralized imperial state.

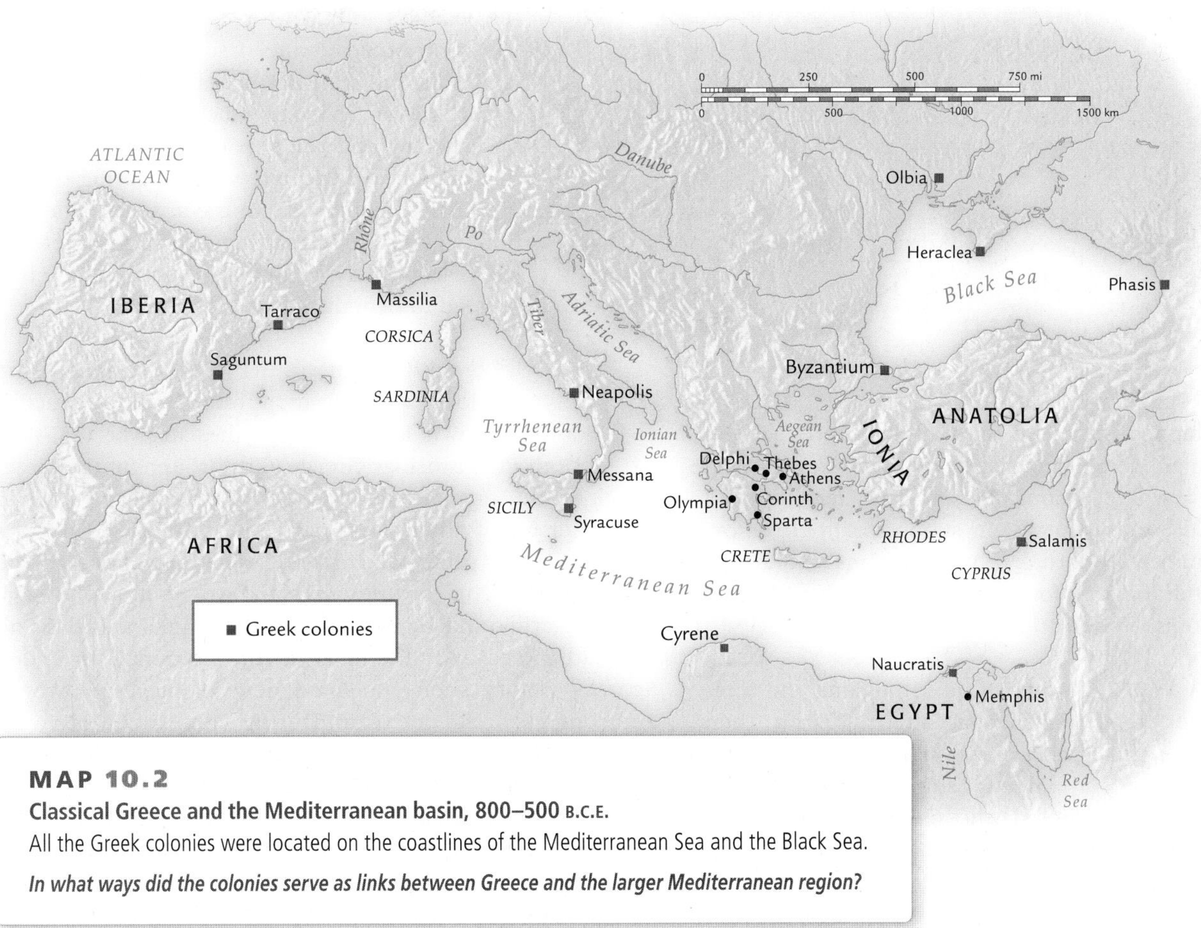

MAP 10.2
Classical Greece and the Mediterranean basin, 800–500 B.C.E.
All the Greek colonies were located on the coastlines of the Mediterranean Sea and the Black Sea.
In what ways did the colonies serve as links between Greece and the larger Mediterranean region?

Greek colonization was not a process controlled by a central government so much as an ad hoc response of individual poleis to population pressures. Colonies often did not take guidance from the poleis from which their settlers came but, rather, relied on their own resources and charted their own courses.

Effects of Greek Colonization

Nevertheless, Greek colonization sponsored more communication, interaction, and exchange than ever before among Mediterranean lands and peoples. From the early eighth century B.C.E., colonies facilitated trade between their regions and the poleis in peninsular Greece and Anatolia. At the same time, colonization spread Greek language and cultural traditions throughout the Mediterranean basin. Moreover, the Greek presence quickened the tempo of social life, especially in the western Mediterranean and the Black Sea. Except for a few urban districts surrounding Phoenician colonies in the western Mediterranean, these regions were home mostly to small-scale agricultural societies organized by clans. As Greek merchants brought wealth into these societies, local clan leaders built small states in areas such as Sicily, southern Italy, southern France, the Crimean peninsula, and southern Russia where trade was especially strong. Thus Greek colonization had important political and social effects throughout the Mediterranean basin.

Two Greek ships under sail, a merchant vessel (left) and a galley (right) powered by oars as well as sails.

Conflict with Persia

During the fifth century B.C.E., their links abroad brought the poleis of the Greek peninsula into direct conflict with the Persian empire in a long struggle known as the Persian Wars (500–479 B.C.E.). As the Persian emperors Cyrus

thinking about ENCOUNTERS

Political Implications of Greek Trade
The establishment of Greek colonies enlivened the larger Mediterranean basin. Discuss the effects that Greek colonies and trade brought to regions that previously had undergone little economic or political development. Why did trade have such wide-ranging effects?

and Darius tightened their grip on Anatolia, the Greek cities on the Ionian coast became increasingly restless. In 500 B.C.E. they revolted against Persian rule and expelled the Achaemenid administrators. In support of their fellow Greeks and commercial partners, the Athenians sent a fleet of ships to aid the Ionian effort. Despite that gesture, Darius repressed the Ionian rebellion by 493 B.C.E.

The Persian Wars To punish the Athenians and forestall future interference in Persian affairs, Darius then mounted a campaign against peninsular Greece. In 490 B.C.E. he sent an army and a fleet of ships to attack Athens. Although greatly outnumbered, the Athenians routed the Persian army at the battle of Marathon and then marched back to Athens in time to fight off the Persian fleet.

Ten years later Darius's successor, Xerxes, decided to avenge the Persian losses. In 480 B.C.E. he dispatched a force consisting of perhaps one hundred thousand troops and a fleet of one thousand ships to subdue the Greeks. The Persian army succeeded in capturing and burning Athens, but a Greek fleet led by Athenians shattered the Persian navy at the battle of Salamis. Xerxes himself viewed the conflict from a temporary throne set up on a hillside overlooking the narrow strait of water between Athens and the island of Salamis. The following year a Greek force at Plataea routed the Persian army, whose survivors retreated to Anatolia.

Greeks and Persians continued to skirmish intermittently for more than a century, although their conflict did not expand into full-scale war. The Persian rulers were unwilling to invest resources in the effort to conquer small and distant Greece, and after Xerxes' reign they faced domestic problems that prevented them from undertaking foreign adventures. For their part, the Greeks had neither the resources nor the desire to challenge the Persian empire, and they remained content with maintaining their independence.

The Delian League Once the Persian threat subsided, however, serious conflict arose among the Greek poleis themselves. After the Persian Wars, the poleis created an alliance known as the Delian League to discourage further Persian actions in Greece. Because of its superior fleet, Athens became the leader of the alliance. In effect, Athens supplied the league's military force, and the other poleis contributed financial support, which went largely to the Athenian treasury. Indeed, those contributions financed much of the Athenian bureaucracy and the vast construction projects that employed Athenian workers during the era of Pericles' leadership. In the absence of a continuing Persian threat, however, the other poleis resented having to make contributions that seemed to benefit only the Athenians.

The Peloponnesian War Ultimately, the tensions resulted in a bitter and destructive civil conflict known as the Peloponnesian War (431–404 B.C.E.). Both in peninsular Greece and throughout the larger Greek world, poleis divided into two armed camps under the leadership of Athens and Sparta, the most powerful of the poleis and the principal contenders for hegemony in the Greek world. The fortunes of war favored first one side, then the other, but by 404 B.C.E. the Spartans and their allies had forced the Athenians to unconditional surrender. Sparta's victory soon generated new jealousies, however, and conflicts broke out again. During the decades following Athenian surrender, hegemony in the Greek world passed to Sparta, Thebes, Corinth, and other poleis.

The Peloponnesian War was both a debilitating and a demoralizing conflict. The historian Thucydides wrote a detailed history of the war, and even though he was himself a loyal native of Athens, he did not hide the fact that Athenians as well as other parties to the conflict adopted brutal tactics. Athenians bullied smaller communities, disregarded the interests and concerns of other poleis, insisted that allies resolutely toe the Athenian line, and subjected insubordinate communities to severe punishments. When the small island of Melos refused to acknowledge the authority of Athens, for example, Thucydides reported that Athenian forces conquered the island, massacred all the men of military age, and sold the women and children into slavery. As a result of that and other atrocities, Athens lost its reputation as the moral and intellectual leader of the Greek people and gained notoriety as an arrogant, insensitive imperialist power. Meanwhile, as the Peloponnesian War divided and weakened the world of the Greek poleis, a formidable power took shape to the north.

The Macedonians and the Coming of Empire

The Kingdom of Macedon Until the fourth century B.C.E., the kingdom of Macedon was a frontier state north of peninsular Greece. The Macedonian population consisted partly of cultivators and partly of sheepherders who migrated seasonally between the mountains and the valleys. Although the Macedonians recognized a king, semiautonomous clans controlled political affairs.

Proximity to the wealthy poleis of Greece brought change to Macedon. From the seventh century B.C.E., the

Pericles organized the construction of numerous marble buildings, partly with funds collected from poleis belonging to the Delian League. Most notable of his projects was the Parthenon, located at the top of the Acropolis (the elevated fortress overlooking Athens). A temple dedicated to the goddess Athena, the Parthenon symbolizes the prosperity and grandeur of classical Athens.

Greek cities traded with Macedon. They imported grain, timber, and other natural resources in exchange for olive oil, wine, and finished products. Macedonian political and social elites, who controlled trade from their side of the border, became well acquainted with Greek merchants and their society.

Philip of Macedon During the reign of King Philip II (359–336 B.C.E.), Macedon underwent a thorough transformation. Philip built a powerful military machine that enabled him to overcome the traditional clans and make himself the ruler of Macedon. His military force featured an infantry composed of small landowners and a cavalry staffed by aristocrats holding large estates. During the fourth century B.C.E., both elements proved to be hardy, well trained, and nearly invincible.

When Philip had consolidated his hold on Macedon, he turned his attention to two larger prizes: Greece and the Persian empire. During the years following 350 B.C.E., Philip moved into northern Greece, annexing poleis and their surrounding territories. The poleis recognized the Macedonian threat, but the Peloponnesian War had poisoned the atmosphere so much that the poleis could not agree to form an alliance against Philip. Thus, as he moved into Greece, Philip faced nothing more than small forces patched together by shifting and temporary alliances. By 338 B.C.E. he had overcome all organized resistance and brought Greece under his control.

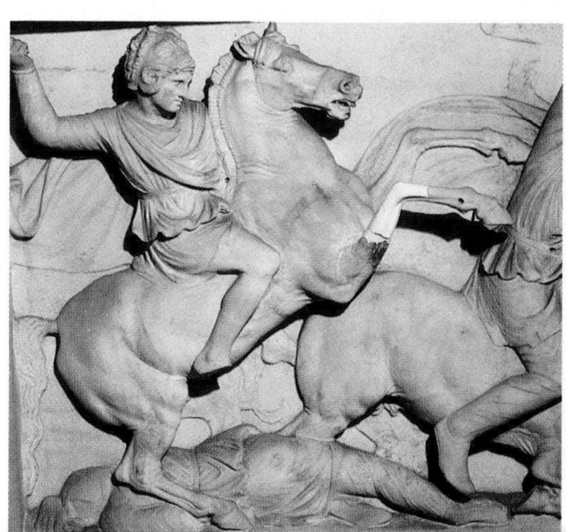

Wearing a lion skin around his head, Alexander the warrior plunges into battle with Persian forces in this carving on a stone sarcophagus.

Alexander of Macedon Philip intended to use his conquest of Greece as a launching pad for an invasion of Persia. He did not have the opportunity to carry out his plans, however, because an assassin brought him down in 336 B.C.E. The invasion of Persia thus fell to his son, the young Alexander of Macedon, often called Alexander the Great.

Alexander's Conquests At the age of twenty, Alexander succeeded Philip as ruler of an expanding empire. He soon began to assemble an army of about forty-eight thousand men to invade the Persian empire. Alexander was a brilliant strategist and an inspired leader, and he inherited a well-equipped, well-disciplined, highly spirited veteran force from his father. By 333 B.C.E. Alexander had subjected Ionia and Anatolia to his control; within another year he held Syria, Palestine, and Egypt; by 331 B.C.E. he controlled Mesopotamia and prepared to invade the Persian homeland. He took Pasargadae and burned the Achaemenid palace at Persepolis late in 331 B.C.E., and he pursued the dispirited Persian army for another year until the last Achaemenid ruler fell to an assassin. Alexander established himself as the new emperor of Persia in 330 B.C.E.

By 327 B.C.E. Alexander had larger ambitions: he took his army into India and crossed the Indus River, entering the Punjab. He subjected local rulers and probably would have continued to campaign in India except that his troops refused to proceed any farther from home. By 324 B.C.E. Alexander and his army had returned to Susa in Mesopotamia, where they celebrated their exploits in almost continuous feasting. Alexander busied himself with plans for governing his empire and for conducting further explorations. In June of 323 B.C.E., however, after an extended round of feasting and drinking, he suddenly fell ill and died at age thirty-three.

During the course of a meteoric career, Alexander proved to be a brilliant conqueror, but he did not live long enough to construct a genuine state for his vast realm or to develop a system of administration. He established cities throughout the lands he conquered and reportedly named about seventy of them Alexandria in his own honor. Alexander also toyed with some intriguing ideas about governing his empire, notably a scheme to marry his officers to Persian women and create a new ruling class of Greek, Macedonian, and Persian ancestry, but his early death prevented him from turning that plan into a coherent policy. So long

MAP 10.3

Alexander's empire, ca. 323 B.C.E.

Compare the boundaries of Alexander's empire with those of the Achaemenid empire as depicted in Map 7.1.

How was Alexander able to bring such extensive territories under his control?

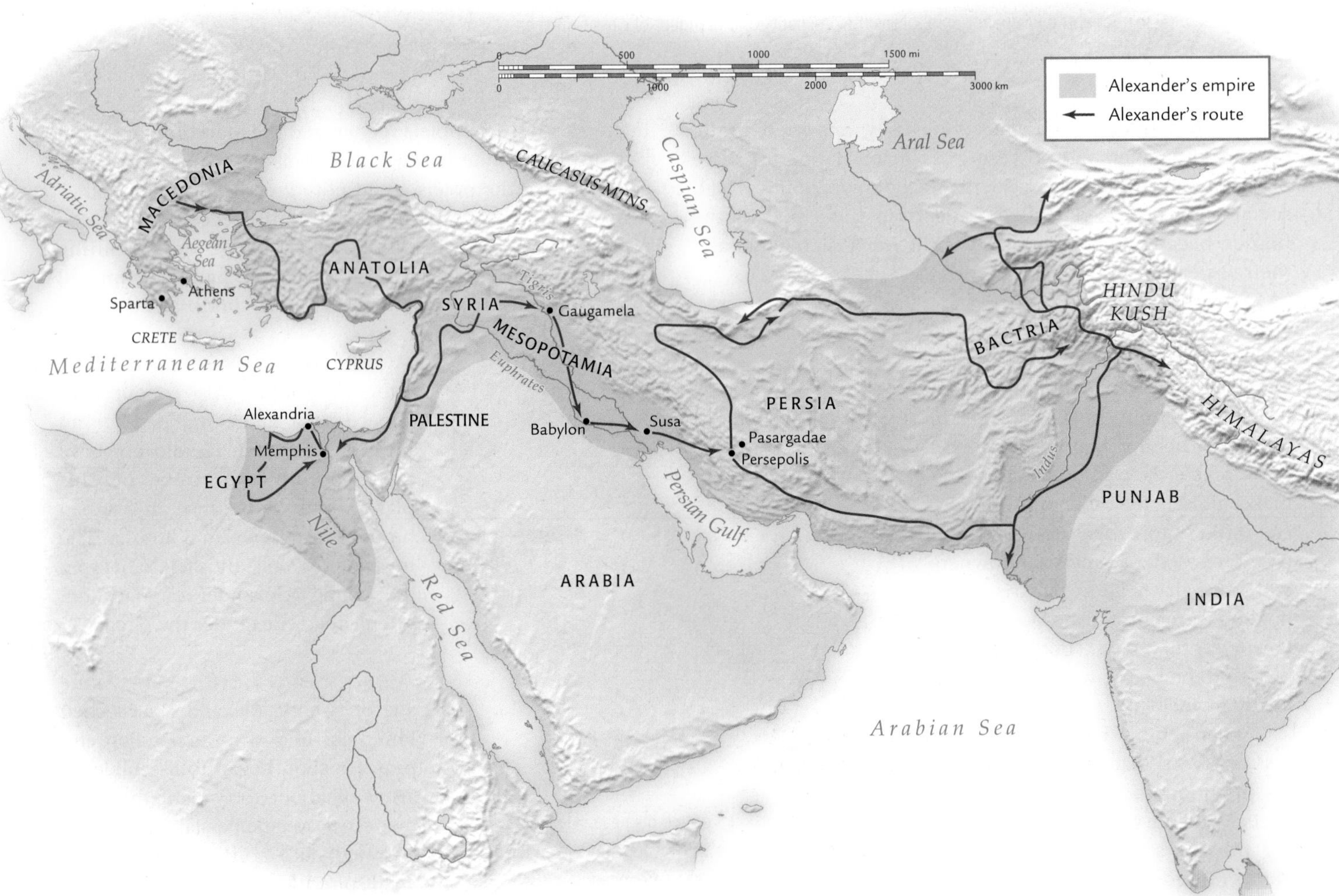

sources from the past

Arrian on the Character of Alexander of Macedon

One of the earliest surviving accounts of Alexander's life and career is that of Flavius Arrianus Xenophon, better known as Arrian. Although Greek, Arrian served in the armies of the early Roman empire and developed a strong interest in military history. About the middle of the second century C.E., *he composed his work on Alexander, drawing on contemporary accounts that no longer survive. Here he assesses Alexander's character.*

He had great personal beauty, invincible power of endurance, and a keen intellect; he was brave and adventurous, strict in the observance of his religious duties, and hungry for fame. Most temperate in the pleasures of the body, his passion was for glory only, and in that he was insatiable. He had an uncanny instinct for the right course in a difficult and complex situation, and was most happy in his deductions from observed facts. In arming and equipping troops and in his military dispositions he was always masterly. Noble indeed was his power of inspiring his men, of filling them with confidence, and, in the moment of danger, of sweeping away their fear by the spectacle of his own fearlessness. When risks had to be taken, he took them with the utmost boldness, and his ability to seize the moment for a swift blow, before his enemy had any suspicion of what was coming, was beyond praise. No cheat or liar ever caught him off his guard, and both his word and his bond were inviolable. Spending but little on his own pleasures, he poured out his money without stint for the benefit of his friends.

Doubtless, in the passion of the moment Alexander sometimes erred; it is true that he took some steps towards the pomp and arrogance of the Asiatic kings: but I, at least, cannot feel that such errors were very heinous, if the circumstances are taken fairly into consideration. For, after all, he was young; the chain of his successes was unbroken, and, like all kings, past, present, and to come, he was surrounded by courtiers who spoke to please, regardless of what evil their words might do. On the other hand, I do indeed know that Alexander, of all the monarchs of old, was the only one who had the nobility of heart to be sorry for his mistakes . . .

. . . As for his reputed heavy drinking, Aristoboulos [one of Alexander's generals who composed an account of the conqueror that was available to Arrian but that does not survive] declares that his drinking bouts were prolonged not for their own sake—for he was never, in fact, a heavy drinker—but simply because he enjoyed the companionship of his friends.

Anyone who belittles Alexander has no right to do so on the evidence only of what merits censure in him; he must base his criticism on a comprehensive view of his whole life and career. But let such a person, if blackguard Alexander he must, first compare himself with the object of his abuse: himself, so mean and obscure, and, confronting him, the great King with his unparalleled worldly success, the undisputed monarch of two continents [Europe and Asia], who spread the power of his name over all the earth. Will he dare to abuse him then, when he knows his own littleness and the triviality of his own pursuits, which, even so, prove too much for his ability?

It is my belief that there was in those days no nation, no city, no single individual beyond the reach of Alexander's name; never in all the world was there another like him, and therefore I cannot but feel that some power more than human was concerned in his birth; indications of this were, moreover, said to be provided at the time of his death by oracles; many people saw visions and had prophetic dreams; and there is the further evidence of the extraordinary way in which he is held, as no mere man could be, in honour and remembrance. Even today, when so many years have passed, there have been oracles, all tending to his glory, delivered to the people of Macedon.

For Further Reflection

- On the basis of Arrian's characterization, do you think Alexander had strong potential to become an effective governor as well as a talented conqueror?

Source: Arrian. *The Campaigns of Alexander.* Trans. by Aubrey de Sélincourt. Rev. by J. R. Hamilton. London: Penguin, 1971, pp. 395–98.

as he lived, he relied on established institutions such as the Persian satrapies to administer the lands he conquered.

The Hellenistic Empires

When Alexander died, his generals jockeyed for position in hopes of taking over choice parts of his realm, and by 275 B.C.E. they had divided the empire into three large states. Antigonus took Greece and Macedon, which his Antigonid successors ruled until the Romans established their authority in the eastern Mediterranean during the second century B.C.E. Ptolemy took Egypt, which the Ptolemaic dynasty ruled until the Roman conquest of Egypt in 31 B.C.E. Seleucus took the largest portion, the former Achaemenid empire stretching from Bactria to Anatolia, which his Seleucid successors

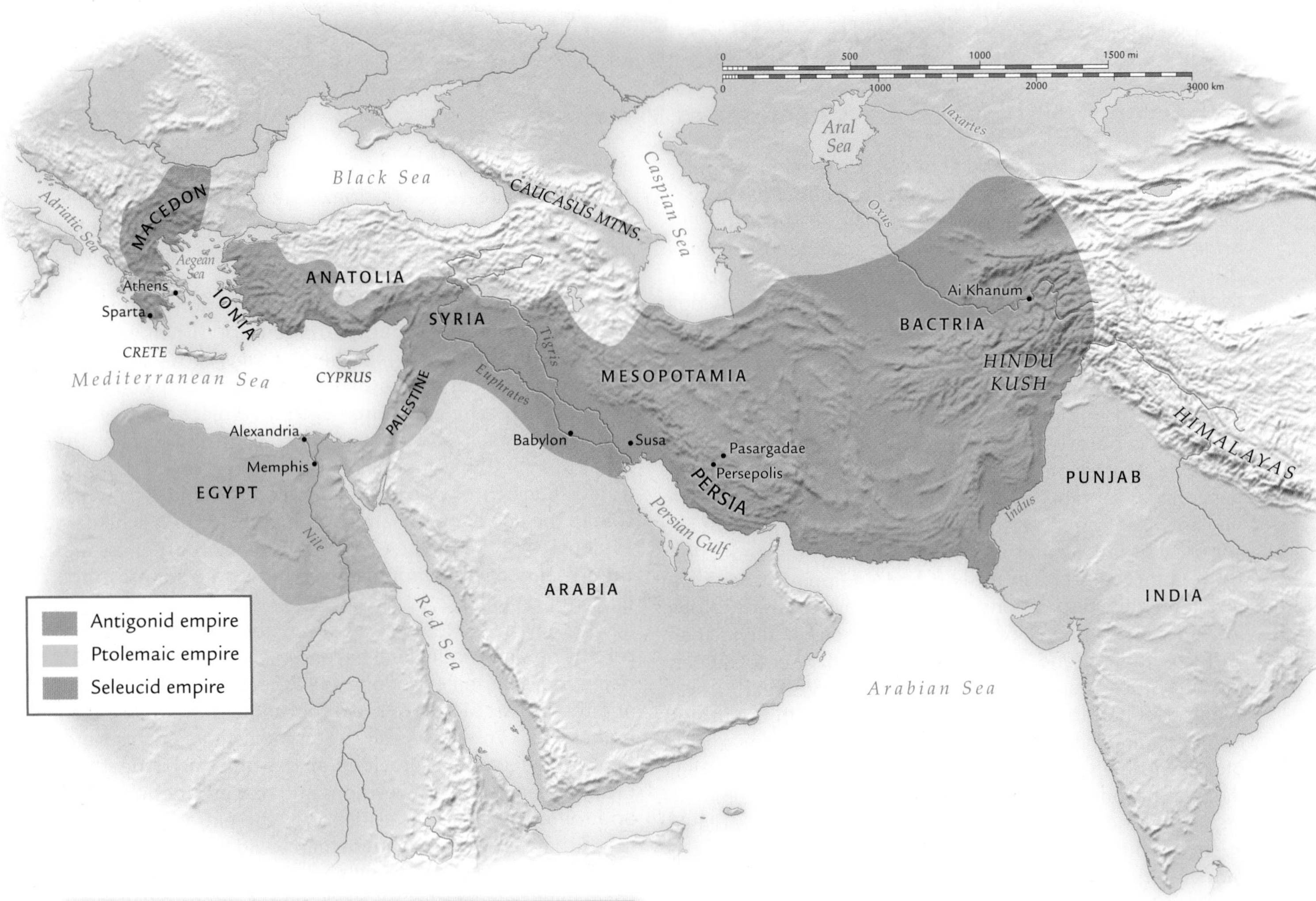

MAP 10.4
The Hellenistic empires, ca. 275 B.C.E.
Note the differences in size between the three Hellenistic empires.
Consider the geographical conditions and economic potential of the three empires.

ruled until the Parthians displaced them during the second century B.C.E.

The Hellenistic Era Historians refer to the age of Alexander and his successors as the Hellenistic age—an era when Greek cultural traditions expanded their influence beyond Greece (*Hellas*) to a much larger world. During the centuries between Alexander's death and the expansion of the Roman empire in the eastern Mediterranean, the Hellenistic empires governed cosmopolitan societies and sponsored interactions between peoples from Greece to India. Like imperial states in classical Persia, China, and India, the Hellenistic empires helped to integrate the economies and societies of distant regions. They facilitated trade, and they made it possible for beliefs, values, and religions to spread over greater distances than ever before.

The Antigonid Empire Although the Antigonid realm of Greece and Macedon was the smallest of the Hellenistic empires, it benefited handsomely from the new order. There was continual tension between the Antigonid rulers and the Greek cities, which sought to retain their independence by forming defensive leagues that stoutly resisted Antigonid efforts to control the Greek peninsula. The poleis often struck bargains with the Antigonids, offering to recognize their rule in exchange for tax relief and local autonomy. Internal social tensions also flared, as Greeks wrestled with the perennial problem of land and its equitable distribution. Yet cities such as Athens and Corinth flourished during the Hellenistic era as enormous volumes of trade passed through their ports. Moreover, the overpopulated Greek peninsula sent large numbers of colonists to newly founded cities, especially in the Seleucid empire.

The Ptolemaic Empire Perhaps the wealthiest of the Hellenistic empires was **Ptolemaic** Egypt. Greek and Macedonian overlords did not interfere in Egyptian society, but contented themselves with the efficient organization of agriculture, industry, and tax collection. They maintained the irrigation networks and monitored the cultivation of crops and the payment of taxes. They also established royal monopolies over the most lucrative industries, such as textiles, salt making, and the brewing of beer.

Alexandria Much of Egypt's wealth flowed to the Ptolemaic capital of Alexandria. Founded by Alexander at the mouth of the Nile, Alexandria served as the Ptolemies' administrative headquarters, but it became much more than a bureaucratic center. Alexandria's enormous harbor was able to accommodate 1,200 ships simultaneously, and the city soon became the most important port in the Mediterranean. Its wealth attracted migrants from all parts of the Mediterranean basin and beyond. Alongside Greeks, Macedonians,

> *"The city [Alexandria] was indeed an early megalopolis, where peoples of different ethnic, religious, and cultural traditions conducted their affairs."*

and Egyptians lived sizable communities of Phoenicians, Jews, Arabs, and Babylonians. and Egyptians lived sizable communities of Phoenicians, Jews, Arabs, and Babylonians. The city was indeed an early megalopolis, where peoples of different ethnic, religious, and cultural traditions conducted their affairs. Under the Ptolemies, Alexandria also became the cultural capital of the Hellenistic world. It was the site of the famous Alexandrian Museum—a state-financed institute of higher learning where philosophical, literary, and scientific scholars carried on advanced research—and of the equally famous Alexandrian Library, which supported the scholarship sponsored by the museum and which, by the first century B.C.E., boasted a collection of more than seven hundred thousand works.

The Seleucid Empire It was in the Seleucid realm, however, that Greek influence reached its greatest extent. The principal channels of that influence were the numerous cities that Alexander and his successors founded in the former Persian empire. Most of them were small settlements intended to serve as fortified sites or administrative centers, though some developed into thriving commercial centers. Greek and Macedonian colonists flocked to these cities, where they joined the ranks of imperial bureaucrats and administrators. Though few in number compared with the native populations, the colonists created a Mediterranean-style urban society that left its mark on lands as distant as Bactria and India. Emperor Ashoka of India had his edicts promulgated in Greek and Aramaic, the two most commonly used languages of the Hellenistic empires.

Greeks in Bactria Archaeological excavations have thrown considerable light on one of those Greek settlements—the Hellenistic colony at Ai Khanum on the Oxus River in ancient Bactria (modern-day Afghanistan). The colony at Ai Khanum was founded either by Alexander of Macedon or by Seleucus shortly after Alexander's death. As an integral part of the Seleucid empire, Bactria was in constant communication with Greece and the Mediterranean world. After about 250 B.C.E. the governors of Bactria withdrew from the Seleucid empire and established an independent Greek kingdom. Excavations at Ai Khanum show that the colony's inhabitants spoke the Greek language, dressed according to Greek fashions, read Greek literature and philosophy, and constructed buildings and produced works of art in Greek styles. At the same time, while honoring Greek gods at Greek shrines, residents of Ai Khanum also welcomed Persian and central Asian deities into their midst. Indeed, some Greeks even converted to Buddhism. Most prominent of the converts was King Menander, who ruled in Bactria approximately 160 to 135 B.C.E. In many ways, like the Achaemenids before them, the Hellenistic ruling classes constituted a thin, supervisory veneer over long-established societies that largely continued to observe inherited customs. Nevertheless, like classical states in Persia, China, and India, the Hellenistic empires brought distant lands into interaction by way of trade and cultural exchange.

THE FRUITS OF TRADE: GREEK ECONOMY AND SOCIETY

The geography of the Greek peninsula posed difficult challenges for its inhabitants: its mountainous terrain and rocky soil yielded only small harvests of grain, and the southern Balkan mountains hindered travel and communication. Indeed, until the construction of modern roads, much of Greece was more accessible by sea than by land. As a result, early Greek society depended heavily on maritime trade.

Trade and the Integration of the Mediterranean Basin

Trade Although it produced little grain, much of Greece is ideally suited to the cultivation of olives and grapes. After the establishment of the poleis, the Greeks discovered that they could profitably concentrate their efforts on the production of olive oil and wine. Greek merchants traded these products around the Mediterranean, returning with abundant supplies of grain and other items as well.

By the early eighth century B.C.E., trade had generated considerable prosperity in the Greek world. Merchants

---

Ptolemaic (TAWL-oh-may-ihk)

and mariners linked Greek communities throughout the Mediterranean world—not only those in the Greek peninsula but also those in Anatolia, the Mediterranean islands, and the Black Sea. The populations of all these communities grew dramatically, encouraging further colonization. In the colonies, merchants offered Greek olive oil and wine for local products. Grain came from Egypt, Sicily, and southern Russia, salted fish from Spain and Black Sea lands, timber and pitch from Macedon, tin from Anatolia, and slaves from Egypt and Russia. Merchant ships with a capacity of four hundred tons were common in the classical Mediterranean, and a few vessels had a capacity of one thousand tons. Some cities, such as Athens and Corinth, relied more on commerce than on agriculture for their livelihood and prosperity.

Commercial and Economic Organization Large volumes of trade promoted commercial and economic organization in the Mediterranean basin. In Greece, for example, shipowners, merchants, and moneylenders routinely formed partnerships to spread the risks of commercial ventures. Usually, a merchant borrowed money from a banker or an individual to purchase cargo and rented space from a shipowner, who transported the goods and returned the profits to the merchant. In the event of a shipwreck, the contract became void, leaving both the merchant and the lender to absorb their losses.

The production of cultivators and manufacturers filled the holds of Mediterranean merchant vessels. Manufacturers usually operated on a small scale, but there are records of pottery workshops with upward of sixty employees. One factory in fourth-century Athens employed 120 slaves in the manufacture of shields. Throughout the trading world of the Mediterranean basin, entrepreneurs established small businesses and offered their wares in the larger market.

Panhellenic Festivals Trade links between the Greek cities and their colonies contributed to a sense of a larger Greek community. Colonists recognized the same gods as their cousins in the Greek peninsula. They spoke Greek dialects, and they maintained commercial relationships with their native communities. Greeks from all parts gathered periodically to participate in panhellenic festivals that reinforced their common bonds. Many of those festivals featured athletic, literary, or musical contests in which individuals sought to win glory for their polis.

The Olympic Games Best known of the panhellenic festivals were the Olympic Games. According to tradition, in 776 B.C.E. Greek communities from all parts of the Mediterranean sent their best athletes to the polis of Olympia to engage in contests of speed, strength, and skill. Events included footracing, long jump, boxing, wrestling, javelin tossing, and discus throwing. Winners of events received olive wreaths, and they became celebrated heroes in their home poleis. The ancient Olympic Games took place every four years for more than a millennium before quietly disappearing from Greek life. So, although they were not united politically, by the sixth century B.C.E. Greek communities had nevertheless established a sense of collective identity.

Harvesting olives. In this painting on a vase, two men knock fruit off the branches while a third climbs the tree to shake the limbs, and another gathers olives from the ground.

During the Hellenistic era, trade drew the Greeks into an even larger world of commerce and communication as colonists and traders expanded the range of their operations throughout Alexander's empire and the realms that succeeded him. Caravan trade linked Persia and Bactria to the western regions of the Hellenistic world. Dependent on horses and donkeys, caravans could not transport heavy or bulky goods but, rather, carried luxury products such as gems and jewelry, perfumes and aromatic oils. These goods all had high value relative to weight so that merchants could feed themselves and their

thinking about TRADITIONS

Maintaining Identity in Dispersal

Greeks established a far-flung network of colonies in the Mediterranean and Black Sea regions, but they did not build a state or create political institutions to govern the affairs of all Greek-speaking peoples. How did their commercial institutions and cultural practices help Greek-speaking peoples to maintain a sense of common identity?

animals, pay the high costs of overland transport, and still turn a profit. Traffic in bulkier goods traveled the sea lanes of the Mediterranean, the Red Sea, the Persian Gulf, and the Arabian Sea.

Family and Society

Homer's works portrayed a society composed of heroic warriors and their outspoken wives. Strong-willed human beings clashed constantly with one another and sometimes even defied the gods in pursuing their interests. These aggressive and assertive characters depended on less flamboyant individuals to provide them with food and other necessities, but Homer had no interest in discussing the humdrum lives of farmers and their families.

A slave carrying a lantern guides his drunken master home following a party.

Patriarchal Society

With the establishment of poleis in the eighth century B.C.E., the nature of Greek family and society came into clearer focus. Like urban societies in southwest Asia and Anatolia, the Greek poleis adopted strictly patriarchal family structures. Male family heads ruled their households, and fathers even had the right to decide whether to keep infants born to their wives. They could not legally kill infants, but they could abandon newborns in the mountains or the countryside where they would soon die of exposure unless found and rescued by others.

Greek women fell under the authority of their fathers, husbands, or sons. Upper-class women living in poleis spent most of their time in the family home, and they ventured outside in the company of servants or chaperones and often wore veils to discourage the attention of men from other families. In most of the poleis, women could not own landed property, but they sometimes operated small businesses such as shops and food stalls. The only public position open to Greek women was that of priestess of a religious cult. Sparta was something of a special case when it came to gender relations: there women participated in athletic contests, went about town by themselves, joined in public festivals, and sometimes even took up arms to defend the polis. Even in Sparta, however, men were family authorities, and men alone determined state policies.

Sappho

Literacy was common among upper-class Greek women, and a few women earned reputations for literary talent. Most famous of them was the poet Sappho, who composed nine volumes of poetry around 600 B.C.E. Sappho, probably a widow from an aristocratic family, invited young women into her home for instruction in music and literature. Critics charged her with homosexual activity, and her surviving verse speaks of her strong physical attraction to young women. Greek society readily tolerated sexual relationships between men but frowned on female homosexuality. As a result, Sappho fell under a cloud of moral suspicion, and only fragments of her poetry survive.

Aristocratic families with extensive landholdings could afford to provide girls with a formal education, but in less privileged families all hands contributed to the welfare of the household. In rural families, men performed most of the outside work and women took care of domestic chores and wove wool textiles. In artisan families living in the poleis, both men and women often participated in businesses and maintained stands or booths in the marketplace.

Slavery

Throughout the Greek world, as in other classical societies, slavery was a prominent means of mobilizing labor. Slaves came from differing backgrounds. Some were formerly free Greeks who entered slavery because they could not pay their debts. Many came from the ranks of soldiers captured in war. A large number came from the peoples with whom the Greeks traded: slave markets at Black Sea ports sold seminomadic Scythians captured in Russia, and Egyptians provided African slaves from Nubia and other southern regions.

Greek law regarded all slaves as the private chattel of their owners, and the conditions of slaves' lives depended on the needs and the temperament of their owner. Physically powerful slaves with no special skills most often provided heavy labor in mines or on the estates of large landholders. Other unskilled slaves worked at lighter tasks as domestic servants or caretakers of their owners' children. Educated slaves and those skilled at some craft or trade had special opportunities. Their owners often regarded them as economic investments, provided them with shops, and allowed them to keep a portion of their earnings as an incentive and a reward for efficient work.

In some cases, slaves with entrepreneurial talent succeeded well enough in their businesses to win their freedom. A slave named Pasion, for example, worked first as a porter and then as a clerk at a prominent Athenian bank during the late fifth and early fourth centuries B.C.E. Pasion developed into a shrewd businessman who worked efficiently and turned considerable profits for his masters, who in turn entrusted him with greater responsibilities and rewarded him for successful efforts. Ultimately, Pasion gained his freedom, took over management of the bank, outfitted five warships from his own pocket, and won a grant of Athenian citizenship.

THE CULTURAL LIFE OF CLASSICAL GREECE

During the eighth and seventh centuries B.C.E., as Greek merchants ventured throughout the Mediterranean basin, they became acquainted with the sophisticated cultural traditions of Mesopotamia and Egypt. They learned astronomy, science, mathematics, medicine, and magic from the Babylonians as well as geometry, medicine, and divination from the Egyptians. They also drew inspiration from the myths, religious beliefs, art motifs, and architectural styles of Mesopotamia and Egypt. About 800 B.C.E. they adapted the Phoenician alphabet to their language: to the Phoenicians' consonants they added symbols for vowels and thus created an exceptionally flexible system for representing speech in written form.

Rational Thought and Philosophy

Greek Science and Mathematics As early as the seventh century B.C.E., Greek thinkers in the cosmopolitan cities of the Ionian coast were working with scientific and mathematical knowledge that reached them from Mesopotamia and Egypt. They did not accept the fanciful stories of the Greek myths, which attributed creation of the world to the gods. Rather, they inaugurated a tradition by which Greek scientists relied on observable evidence, rational thought, and human reason to explain the world as the result of natural processes. Thus, for example, the Ionian scientist Thales accurately predicted an eclipse of the sun that took place 28 May 585 B.C.E., and the Greek theorist Democritus suggested that all physical matter was composed of indivisible particles that he called *atoms.* The Ionian mathematician Pythagoras drew upon Babylonian ideas in developing a systematic approach to mathematics, and the Athenian physician Hippocrates worked to base medical practice on the understanding of human anatomy and physiology. Greek science was remarkable for its reliance on human reason to understand the world, and it served as a rich foundation for later scientific developments throughout the Mediterranean basin and beyond in both Christian Europe and the Muslim world.

Greek Philosophy Perhaps the most distinctive expression of classical Greek thought was philosophy, which brought the power of reason to bear on human issues as well as the natural world. The pivotal figure in the development of philosophy was Socrates (470–399 B.C.E.), a thoughtful and reflective Athenian driven by a powerful urge to understand human beings and human affairs in all their complexity. During his youth, Socrates studied the ideas of the Greek scientists, but he ultimately decided to focus his attention on human affairs rather than the natural world.

Socrates Socrates did not commit his thought to writing, but his disciple Plato later composed dialogues that represented Socrates' views. Nor did Socrates expound his views assertively: rather, he posed questions that encouraged reflection on human issues, particularly on matters of ethics and morality. He suggested that human beings could lead honest lives and that honor was far more important than wealth, fame, or other superficial attributes. He scorned those who preferred public accolades to personal integrity, and he insisted on the need to reflect on the purposes and goals of life. "The unexamined life is not worth living," he held, implying that human beings had an obligation to strive for personal integrity, behave honorably toward others, and work toward the construction of a just society.

In elaborating those views, Socrates often played the role of a gadfly who subjected traditional ethical teachings to critical scrutiny. This tactic outraged some of his fellow citizens, who brought him to trial on charges that he encouraged immorality and corrupted the Athenian youths who joined him in the marketplace to discuss moral and ethical issues. A jury of Athenian citizens decided that Socrates had indeed passed the bounds of propriety and condemned him to death. In 399 B.C.E. Socrates drank a potion of hemlock sap and died in the company of his friends.

Plato Socrates' influence survived in the work of his most zealous disciple, Plato (430–347 B.C.E.), and in Plato's disciple Aristotle (384–322 B.C.E.). Inspired by his mentor's reflections, Plato elaborated a systematic philosophy of great subtlety. He presented his thought in a series of dialogues in which Socrates figured as the principal speaker. In the earliest dialogues, written shortly after Socrates' death, Plato largely represented his mentor's views. As time passed, Plato gradually formulated his thought into a systematic vision of the world and human society.

The cornerstone of Plato's thought was his theory of Forms or Ideas. It disturbed Plato that he could not gain satisfactory intellectual control over the world. The qual-

Tradition holds that Socrates was not a physically attractive man, but this statue emphasizes his sincerity and simplicity. Judging from his clothing and posture, how might the sculptor have characterized Socrates?

sources from the past

Socrates' View of Death

In one of his earliest dialogues, the Apology, *Plato offered an account of Socrates' defense of himself during his trial before a jury of Athenian citizens. After the jury had convicted him and condemned him to death, Socrates reflected on the nature of death and reemphasized his commitment to virtue rather than to wealth or fame.*

And if we reflect in another way we shall see that we may well hope that death is a good thing. For the state of death is one of two things: either the dead man wholly ceases to be and loses all sensation; or, according to the common belief, it is a change and a migration of the soul unto another place. And if death is the absence of all sensation, like the sleep of one whose slumbers are unbroken by any dreams, it will be a wonderful gain. For if a man had to select that night in which he slept so soundly that he did not even see any dreams, and had to compare with it all the other nights and days of his life, and then had to say how many days and nights in his life he had slept better and more pleasantly than this night, I think that a private person, nay, even the great king of Persia himself, would find them easy to count, compared with the others. If that is the nature of death, I for one count it a gain. For then it appears that eternity is nothing more than a single night.

But if death is a journey to another place, and the common belief be true, that all who have died dwell there, what good could be greater than this, my judges? Would a journey not be worth taking if at the end of it, in the other world, we should be released from the self-styled judges of this world, and should find the true judges who are said to sit in judgment below? . . . It would be an infinite happiness to converse with them, and to live with them, and to examine them. Assuredly there they do not put men to death for doing that. For besides the other ways in which they are happier than we are, they are immortal, at least if the common belief be true.

And you too, judges, must face death with a good courage, and believe this as a truth, that no evil can happen to a good man, either in life, or after death. His fortunes are not neglected by the gods, and what has come to me today has not come by chance. I am persuaded that it is better for me to die now, and to be released from trouble. . . . And so I am hardly angry with my accusers, or with those who have condemned me to die. Yet it was not with this mind that they accused me and condemned me, but rather they meant to do me an injury. Only to that extent do I find fault with them.

Yet I have one request to make of them. When my sons grow up, visit them with punishment, my friends, and vex them in the same way that I have vexed you if they seem to you to care for riches or for anything other than virtue: and if they think that they are something when they are nothing at all, reproach them as I have reproached you for not caring for what they should and for thinking that they are great men when in fact they are worthless. And if you will do this, I myself and my sons will have received our deserts at your hands.

But now the time has come, and we must go hence: I to die, and you to live. Whether life or death is better is known to God, and to God only.

For Further Reflection

- How does Socrates' understanding of personal morality and its rewards compare and contrast with the Zoroastrian, Buddhist, and Hindu views discussed in earlier chapters?

Source: F. J. Church, trans. *The Trial and Death of Socrates,* 2nd ed. London: Macmillan, 1886, pp. 76–78. (Translation slightly modified.)

ity of virtue, for example, meant different things in different situations, as did honesty, courage, truth, and beauty. Generally speaking, for example, virtue required individuals to honor and obey their parents. But if a parent engaged in illegal behavior, virtue required offspring to denounce the offense and seek punishment. How was it possible, then, to understand virtue as an abstract quality? In seeking an answer to that question, Plato developed his belief that the world in which we live was not the only world—indeed, it was not the world of genuine reality, but only a pale and imperfect reflection of the world of Forms or Ideas. Displays of virtue or other qualities in the world imperfectly reflected the ideal qualities. Only by entering the world of Forms or Ideas was it possible to understand the true nature of virtue and other qualities. The secrets of that world were available only to philosophers—those who applied their rational faculties to the pursuit of wisdom.

Though abstract, Plato's thought had important political and social implications. In his dialogue *Republic,* for example, Plato sketched an ideal state that reflected his philosophical views. Because philosophers were in the best position to understand ultimate reality, and hence to design

A mosaic from the Italian town of Pompeii, near Naples, depicts Plato (standing at left) discussing philosophical issues with students. Produced in the early first century C.E., this illustration testifies to the popularity of Greek philosophy in classical Roman society.

policies in accordance with the Form or Idea of justice, he held that the best state was one where either philosophers ruled as kings or kings were themselves philosophers. In effect, then, Plato advocated an intellectual aristocracy: the philosophical elite would rule, and other, less intelligent, classes would work at functions for which their talents best suited them.

Aristotle During the generation after Plato, Aristotle elaborated a systematic philosophy that equaled Plato's work in its long-term influence. Though originally a disciple of Plato, Aristotle came to distrust the theory of Forms or Ideas, which he considered artificial intellectual constructs unnecessary for understanding the world. Unlike Plato, Aristotle believed that philosophers could rely on their senses to provide accurate information about the world and then depend on reason to sort out its mysteries. Like Plato, Aristotle explored the nature of reality in subtle metaphysical works, and he devised rigorous rules of logic in an effort to construct powerful and compelling arguments. But he also wrote on biology, physics, astronomy, psychology, politics, ethics, and literature. His work provided such a coherent and comprehensive vision of the world that his later disciples, the Christian scholastic philosophers of medieval Europe, called him "the master of those who know."

The Greek philosophers deeply influenced the development of European and Islamic cultural traditions. Until the seventeenth century C.E., most European philosophers regarded the Greeks as intellectual authorities. Christian and Muslim theologians alike went to great lengths to harmonize their religious convictions with the philosophical views of Plato and Aristotle. Thus, like philosophical and religious figures in other classical societies, Plato and Aristotle provided a powerful intellectual framework that shaped thought about the world and human affairs for two millennia and more.

Popular Religion

Because most Greeks of the classical era did not have an advanced education and did not chat with the philosophers on a regular basis, they did not rely on systems of formal logic when seeking to understand their place in the larger world. Instead, they turned to traditions of popular culture and popular religion that shed light on human nature and offered guidance for human behavior.

Greek Deities The Greeks did not recognize a single, exclusive, all-powerful god. Their Indo-European ancestors had attributed supernatural powers to natural elements such as sun, wind, and rain. Over the course of the centuries, the Greeks personified these powers and came to think of them as gods. They constructed myths that related the stories of the gods, their relations with one another, and their roles in bringing the world to its present state.

In the beginning, they believed, there was the formless void of chaos out of which emerged the earth, the mother and creator of all things. The earth then generated the sky, and together they produced night, day, sun, moon, and other natural phenomena. Struggles between the deities led to bitter heavenly battles, and ultimately Zeus, grandson of the earth and sky gods, emerged as paramount ruler of the divine realm. Zeus's heavenly court included scores of subordinate deities who had various responsibilities: the god Apollo promoted wisdom and justice, for example; the goddess Fortune brought unexpected opportunities and difficulties; and the Furies wreaked vengeance on those who violated divine law.

Religious Cults Like religious traditions in other lands, Greek myths sought to explain the world and the forces that shape it. They served also as foundations for religious cults that contributed to a powerful sense of community in classical Greece. Many of the cults conducted ritual observances that were open only to initiates. One especially popular cult known as the Eleusinian mysteries, for example, sponsored a ritual community meal and encouraged initiates to observe high moral standards.

Women's Cults Some cults admitted only women. Because women could not participate in legal and political life, the cults provided opportunities for them to play roles in society outside the home. The fertility cult of Demeter, goddess of grain, excluded men. In honor of Demeter, women gathered on a hill for three days, offered sacrifices to the goddess, and took part in a celebratory feast. This event occurred in October or November before the planting of grain and sought to ensure bountiful harvests.

The Cult of Dionysus Women were also the most prominent devotees of Dionysus, the god of wine, also known as Bacchus, although men sometimes joined in his celebration. During the spring of the year, when the vines produced their fruit, devotees retreated into the hills to celebrate Dionysus with song and dance. The dramatist Euripides offered an account of one such Dionysian season in his play *The Bacchae.* Euripides described the preparations for the festival and the celebrants' joyful march to the mountains. Spirited music and dance brought the devotees to such a state of frenzy that they fell on a sacrificial goat—and also a man hiding in the brush in an unwise effort to observe the proceedings—ripped the victims apart, and presented them as offerings to Dionysus. Though he was a skeptic who regarded much of Greek religion as sham and hypocrisy, Euripides nonetheless recognized that powerful emotional bonds held the Dionysian community together.

During the fifth century B.C.E., as the poleis strengthened their grip on public and political life, the religious cults became progressively more tame. The cult of Dionysus, originally one of the most unrestrained, became one of the most thoroughly domesticated. The venue of the rituals shifted from the mountains to the polis, and the nature of the observances changed dramatically. Instead of emotional festivals, the Dionysian season saw the presentation of plays that honored the traditions of the polis, examined relations between human beings and the gods, or reflected on problems of ethics and morality.

Tragic Drama This transformation of Dionysus's cult set the stage for the emergence of Greek dramatic literature as dramatists composed plays for presentation at annual theatrical festivals. Of the thousands of plays written in classical Greece, only a few survive: thirty-two tragedies and a dozen comedies have come down to the present in substantially complete form. Yet this small sample shows that the dramatists engaged audiences in subtle reflection on complicated themes. The great tragedians—Aeschylus, Sophocles, and Euripides—whose lives spanned the fifth century B.C.E., explored the possibilities and limitations of human action. To what extent could human beings act as responsible agents in society? What was their proper role when they confronted the limits that the gods or other humans placed on their activity? How should they proceed when the gods and human authorities presented them with conflicting demands?

Comic dramatists such as Aristophanes also dealt with serious issues of human striving and responsible behavior. They took savage delight in lampooning the public and political figures of their time. The comedians aimed to influence popular attitudes by ridiculing the foibles of prominent public figures and calling attention to the absurd consequences of ill-considered action.

Hellenistic Philosophy and Religion

As the Hellenistic empires seized the political initiative in the Mediterranean basin and eclipsed the poleis, Greek philosophy and religion lost their civic character. Because the poleis no longer controlled their destinies but, rather, figured as small elements in a large administrative machine, residents ceased to regard their polis as the focus of individual loyalties. Instead, they inclined toward cultural and religious alternatives that ministered to the needs and interests of individuals living in a large, cosmopolitan society.

The Hellenistic Philosophers The most popular Hellenistic philosophers—the Epicureans, the Skeptics, and the Stoics—addressed individual needs by searching for personal tranquility and serenity. Epicureans, for example, identified pleasure as the greatest good. By *pleasure* they did not mean unbridled hedonism but, rather, a state of quiet satisfaction that would shield them from the pressures of the Hellenistic world. Skeptics refused to take strong positions on political, moral, and social issues because they doubted the possibility of certain knowledge. Rather than engage in fruitless disputes, they sought equanimity and left contentious issues to others.

The most respected and influential of the Hellenistic philosophers were the Stoics, who considered all human beings members of a universal family. Unlike the Epicureans and the Skeptics, the Stoics did not seek to withdraw from the pressures of the world. Rather, they taught that individuals had the duty to aid others and lead virtuous lives. The Stoics believed that individuals could avoid anxieties caused by the pressures of Hellenistic society by concentrating their attention strictly on the duties that reason and nature demanded of them. Thus, like the Epicureans and the Skeptics, the Stoics sought ways to bring individuals to a state of inner peace and tranquility.

Religions of Salvation Although the philosophers' doctrines appealed to educated elites, religions of salvation enjoyed surging popularity in Hellenistic society. Mystery religions promised eternal bliss for initiates who observed their rites and lived in accordance with their doctrines. Some faiths spread across the trade routes and found followers far from their homelands. The Egyptian cult of Osiris, for example, became popular because it promised salvation for those who led honorable lives. Cults from Persia, Mesopotamia, Anatolia, and Greece also attracted disciples throughout the Hellenistic world.

Many of the mystery religions involved the worship of a savior whose death and resurrection would lead the way to eternal salvation for devoted followers. Some philosophers and religious thinkers speculated that a single god might rule the entire universe—just as Alexander and his successors governed enormous empires on earth—and that this god had a plan for the salvation of all humankind. Like the Hellenistic philosophies, then, religions of salvation addressed the interests of individuals searching for security in a complex world.

inperspective

Greek travelers linked the regions of the Mediterranean basin in classical times. Although they did not build a centralized empire, the Greeks dotted the Mediterranean and Black Sea shorelines with their colonies, and their merchant fleets stimulated both commercial and cultural interactions between peoples of distant lands. Greek merchants, soldiers, and administrators also played prominent roles in the vast empires of Alexander and the Hellenistic rulers. Quite apart from their political and economic significance, the Greeks also left a remarkably rich cultural legacy. Greek philosophy, literature, and science profoundly influenced the intellectual and cultural development of peoples from southwest Asia to western Europe. The Greek poleis and the Hellenistic cities provided nurturing environments for rational thought and academic pursuits, and the frequent travels of the Greeks promoted the spread of popular religious faiths throughout the Mediterranean basin and beyond. Like classical Persia, China, and India, the Mediterranean basin became an integrated world. ●

CHRONOLOGY	
2200–1100 B.C.E.	Minoan society
1600–1100 B.C.E.	Mycenaean society
800–338 B.C.E.	Era of the classical Greek polis
ca. 600 B.C.E.	Life of Sappho
500–479 B.C.E.	Persian Wars
490 B.C.E.	Darius's invasion of Greece
490 B.C.E.	Battle of Marathon
480 B.C.E.	Xerxes' invasion of Greece
480 B.C.E.	Battle of Salamis
479 B.C.E.	Battle of Plataea
470–399 B.C.E.	Life of Socrates
443–429 B.C.E.	Pericles' leadership in Athens
431–404 B.C.E.	Peloponnesian War
430–347 B.C.E.	Life of Plato
384–322 B.C.E.	Life of Aristotle
359–336 B.C.E.	Reign of Philip II of Macedon
336–323 B.C.E.	Reign of Alexander of Macedon

For Further Reading

Martin Bernal. *Black Athena: The Afroasiatic Roots of Classical Civilization.* 3 vols. New Brunswick, 1987–. Provocative and controversial study arguing for Egyptian and Semitic influences on early Greek society.

Sue Blundell. *Women in Ancient Greece.* Cambridge, Mass., 1995. A comprehensive survey of women and their roles in ancient Greek society.

Walter Burkert. *Babylon, Memphis, Persepolis: Eastern Contexts of Greek Culture.* Cambridge, Mass., 2004. Explores Mesopotamian, Egyptian, and Persian influences on Greek literature, philosophy, and science.

———. *The Orientalizing Revolution: Near Eastern Influence on Greek Culture in the Early Archaic Age.* Trans. by M. E. Pinder and W. Burkert. Cambridge, Mass., 1992. An important scholarly work tracing Mesopotamian influence in early Greece.

Lionel Casson. *The Ancient Mariners: Seafarers and Sea Fighters of the Mediterranean in Ancient Times.* 2nd ed. Princeton, 1991. Draws on discoveries of underwater archaeologists in reconstructing the maritime history of the ancient Mediterranean.

F. M. Cornford. *Before and After Socrates.* Cambridge, 1965. A short but brilliant synthesis of classical Greek philosophy.

Kenneth Dover. *The Greeks.* Austin, 1980. An engaging personal interpretation of classical Greece.

M. I. Finley. *Ancient Slavery and Modern Ideology.* Expanded ed. Princeton, 1998. Presents a thoughtful analysis of Greek and Roman slavery in light of modern slavery and contemporary debates.

Frank J. Frost. *Greek Society.* 2nd ed. Lexington, 1980. Concentrates on economic and social history from Mycenaean to Hellenistic times.

Frederick C. Grant, ed. *Hellenistic Religions: The Age of Syncretism.* Indianapolis, 1953. Fascinating collection of translated documents and texts that throw light on religious and philosophical beliefs of the Hellenistic era.

N. G. L. Hammond. *The Genius of Alexander the Great.* Chapel Hill, 1997. The best recent work on Alexander of Macedon.

W. V. Harris, ed. *Rethinking the Mediterranean.* New York, 2005. A collection of scholarly essays exploring issues that linked the various lands bordering the Mediterranean in premodern times.

Peregrine Horden and Nicholas Purcell. *The Corrupting Sea: A Study of Mediterranean History.* London, 2000. A challenging but important study of the Mediterranean basin.

Donald Kagan. *The Peloponnesian War.* New York, 2003. Synopsis of the debilitating conflict by the foremost contemporary scholar of the Peloponnesian War.

Sarah B. Pomeroy. *Goddesses, Whores, Wives, and Slaves: Women in Classical Antiquity.* New York, 1995. Outstanding study analyzing the status and role of women in classical Greece and Rome.

Susan Sherwin-White and Amélie Kuhrt. *From Samarkhand to Sardis: A New Approach to the Seleucid Empire.* Berkeley, 1993. Detailed scholarly analysis of the Seleucid empire concentrating on political and economic matters.

Mortimer Wheeler. *Flames over Persepolis.* New York, 1968. Examines the influence of Hellenistic artists in Persia, Bactria, and India.

Mediterranean Society: The Roman Phase

chapter 11

A marble relief sculpture of about 100 C.E. depicts a crew of men working in a treadmill that powers a crane used in construction of a Roman temple.

EYEWITNESS:
Paul of Tarsus and the Long Arm of Roman Law

About 55 C.E. Roman guards transported a prisoner named Paul of Tarsus from the port of Caesarea in Palestine to the city of Rome. The journey turned out to be more eventful than the travelers had planned. The party boarded a sailing ship loaded with grain and carrying 276 passengers as well. The ship departed in the fall—after the main sailing season, which ran from May through September—and soon encountered a violent storm. For two frightening weeks crew and passengers alike worked furiously to keep the ship afloat, jettisoning baggage, tackle, and cargo to lighten the load as wind and rain battered the vessel. Eventually, the ship ran aground on the island of Malta, where storm-driven waves destroyed the craft. Yet most of the passengers and crew survived, including Paul and his guards, who spent three months on Malta before catching another ship to Rome.

Paul had become embroiled in a dispute between Jews and early proponents of the fledgling Christian religion. Christianity first emerged as a sect of Judaism accepted by only a small number of individuals who regarded Jesus of Nazareth as a savior for the Jewish community. By the mid-first century C.E., Christianity was attracting numerous converts throughout the Mediterranean basin. Paul himself was a devout Jew from Anatolia who accepted Christian teachings and became a zealous missionary seeking converts from outside as well as within the Jewish community. Indeed, he was the principal figure in the development of Christianity from a Jewish sect to an independent religious faith. When a crowd of Paul's enemies attacked him in Jerusalem, where he was promoting his recently adopted faith, the resulting disturbance became so severe that authorities of the Roman imperial government intervened to restore order. Under normal circumstances Roman authorities would deliver an individual like Paul to the leaders of his ethnic community, and the laws and customs of that community would determine the person's fate.

Paul's case, however, was different. Knowing that Jewish leaders would condemn him and probably execute him, Paul asserted his rights as a Roman citizen. Although he had never traveled west of Greece, Paul had inherited Roman citizenship from his father. As a result, he had the right to appeal his case to Rome, and he did so. His appeal did not succeed. No record of his case survives, but tradition holds that imperial authorities executed him out of concern that Christianity threatened the peace and stability of the Roman state.

Paul's experience reflects the cosmopolitan character of the early Roman empire, which by the first century C.E. dominated the entire Mediterranean basin. Roman administrators oversaw affairs from Anatolia and Palestine in the east to Spain and Morocco in the west. Roman military forces maintained order in an empire with scores of different and sometimes conflicting ethnic and religious groups. Like many others, Paul of Tarsus traveled freely through much of the Roman empire in an effort to attract converts to Christianity. Indeed, except for the integration of the Mediterranean basin by the Roman empire, Paul's message and his faith might never have expanded beyond the small community of early Christians in Jerusalem.

Like the Phoenicians and the Greeks before them, the Romans established close links between the various Mediterranean regions. As they conquered new lands, pacified them, and brought them into their empire, the Romans enabled merchants, missionaries, and others to travel readily throughout the Mediterranean basin. The Romans differed from their Phoenician and Greek predecessors, however, by building an extensive land empire and centralizing the administration of their realm. At its high point the Roman empire dominated the entire Mediterranean basin and parts of southwest Asia, including Anatolia, Mesopotamia, Syria, Egypt, and north Africa, besides much of continental Europe, and even parts of Britain.

The Roman empire also served as a forum for the communication of philosophical ideas and religious beliefs. Educated elites often embraced sophisticated Hellenistic philosophies, particularly Stoicism, which found adherents throughout the Roman empire. The larger population took comfort in popular religious beliefs, many of which promised personal salvation to devout followers. Over the long term, Christianity was the most successful of the popular religions of salvation. The early Christians encountered harsh opposition and persecution from Roman officials. Yet the new faith took advantage of the Romans' well-organized imperial holdings and spread rapidly throughout the Mediterranean basin and beyond. Eventually, Christianity became the official religion of the Roman empire, and imperial sponsorship enabled Christianity to spread more effectively than before.

FROM KINGDOM TO REPUBLIC

Founded in the eighth century B.C.E., the city of Rome was originally a small city-state ruled by a single king. Late in the sixth century B.C.E., the city's aristocrats deposed the king, ended the monarchy, and instituted a republic—a form of government in which delegates represented the interests of various constituencies. The Roman republic survived for more than five hundred years, and it was under the republican constitution that Rome established itself as the dominant power in the Mediterranean basin.

The Etruscans and Rome

Romulus and Remus The city of Rome arose from origins both obscure and humble. According to the ancient legends, the city owed its existence to the flight of Aeneas, a refugee from Troy who migrated to Italy when Greek invaders destroyed his native land. Two of his descendants, the twins Romulus and Remus, almost did not survive infancy because an evil uncle abandoned them by the flooded Tiber River, fully expecting them to drown or die of exposure. But a kindly she-wolf found them and nursed them to health. The boys grew strong and courageous, and in 753 B.C.E. Romulus founded the city of Rome and established himself as its first king.

Modern scholars do not tell so colorful a tale, but they agree that Rome grew from humble beginnings. Beginning about 2000 B.C.E., bands of Indo-European migrants crossed the Alps and settled throughout the Italian peninsula. Like their distant cousins in India, Greece, and northern Europe, these migrants blended with the neolithic inhabitants of the region, adopted agriculture, and established tribal federations. Sheepherders and small farmers occupied much of the Italian peninsula, including the future site of Rome itself. Bronze metallurgy appeared about 1800 B.C.E. and iron about 900 B.C.E.

The Etruscans During the middle centuries of the first millennium B.C.E., Italy underwent rapid political and economic development. The agents of that development were the Etruscans, a dynamic people who dominated much of Italy between the eighth and the fifth centuries B.C.E. The Etruscans probably migrated to Italy from Anatolia. They settled first in Tuscany, the region around modern Florence, but they soon controlled much of the territory from the Po River valley in northern Italy to the region around modern Naples in the south. They built thriving cities and established political and economic alliances between their settlements. They manufactured high-quality bronze and iron goods, and they worked gold and silver into jewelry.

Paintings in Etruscan tombs often represent scenes from daily life. Illustrations in the Tomb of the Leopards in Tarquinia depict musicians playing pipes and lyre during a banquet.

They built a fleet and traded actively in the western Mediterranean. During the late sixth century B.C.E., however, the Etruscans encountered a series of challenges from other peoples, and their society began to decline. Greek fleets defeated the Etruscans at sea while Celtic peoples attacked them from Gaul (modern France).

The Kingdom of Rome The Etruscans deeply influenced the early development of Rome. Like the Etruscan cities, Rome was a monarchy during the early days after its foundation, and several Roman kings were Etruscans. The kings ruled Rome through the seventh and sixth centuries B.C.E., and they provided the city with paved streets, public buildings, defensive walls, and large temples.

Etruscan merchants drew a large volume of traffic to Rome, thanks partly to the city's geographic advantages. Rome enjoyed easy access to the Mediterranean by way of the Tiber River, but since it was not on the coast, it did not run the risk of invasion or attack from the sea. Already during the period of Etruscan dominance, trade routes from all parts of Italy converged on Rome. When Etruscan society declined, Rome was in a strong position to play a more prominent role both in Italy and in the larger Mediterranean world.

The Roman Republic and Its Constitution

Establishment of the Republic In 509 B.C.E. the Roman nobility deposed the last Etruscan king and replaced the monarchy with an aristocratic republic. At the heart of the city, they built the Roman forum, a political and civic center filled with temples and public buildings where leading citizens tended to government business. They also instituted a republican constitution that entrusted executive responsibilities to two consuls who wielded civil and military power. Consuls were elected by an assembly dominated by members of an elite class determined by birth known as the patricians, and they served one-year terms. The powerful Senate, whose members were patricians with extensive political experience, advised the consuls and ratified all major decisions. Because the consuls and the Senate both represented the interests of the patricians, there was constant tension between the hereditary elites and the common people, known as the plebeians.

Conflicts between Patricians and Plebeians During the early fifth century B.C.E., relations between the classes became so strained that the plebeians threatened to secede from Rome and establish a rival settlement. To maintain the integrity of the Roman state, the patricians granted plebeians the right to elect officials, known as tribunes, who represented their interests in the Roman government. Originally, plebeians chose two tribunes, but the number eventually rose to ten. Tribunes had the power to intervene in all political matters, and they possessed the right to veto measures that they judged unfair. In 449 B.C.E. patricians made a further concession to plebeians by promulgating Rome's first set of laws, known as the Twelve Tables, which drew upon Greek laws in establishing a framework for the social organization of the Roman state. The Twelve Tables served as the foundation for a long tradition of Roman law making.

Although the tribunes provided a voice in government for the plebeians, the patricians continued to dominate Rome. Tensions between the classes persisted for as long as the republic survived. During the fourth century B.C.E.,

Ruins of the Roman forum, where political leaders conducted public affairs during the era of the republic, still stand today.

plebeians became eligible to hold almost all state offices and gained the right to have one of the consuls come from their ranks. By the early third century, plebeian-dominated assemblies won the power to make decisions binding on all of Rome. Thus, like fifth-century Athens, republican Rome gradually broadened the base of political participation.

Constitutional compromises eased class tensions, but they did not solve all political problems confronted by the republic. When faced with civil or military crises, the Roman Senate appointed an official, known as a dictator, who wielded absolute power for a term of six months. By providing for strong leadership during times of extraordinary difficulty, the republican constitution enabled Rome to maintain a reasonably stable society throughout most of the republic's history. Meanwhile, by allowing various constituencies a voice in government, the constitution also helped to prevent the emergence of crippling class tensions.

The Expansion of the Republic

While the Romans dealt constructively with internal problems, external challenges mounted. During the fifth century B.C.E., for example, Rome faced threats not only from peoples living in the neighboring hills but also from the Etruscans. Beyond Italy were the Gauls, a powerful Celtic people who on several occasions invaded Italy. Between the fourth and second centuries B.C.E., however, a remarkable expansion of power and influence transformed Rome from a small and vulnerable city-state to the center of an enormous empire.

First the Romans consolidated their position in central Italy. During the fifth and early fourth centuries B.C.E., the Romans founded a large regional state in central Italy at the expense of the declining Etruscans and other neighboring peoples. Their conquests gave them access to the iron industry built by the Etruscans and greatly expanded the amount of land under Roman control.

During the later fourth century, the Romans built on their early conquests and emerged as the predominant power in the Italian peninsula. The Romans secured control of the peninsula partly because they established military colonies in regions they overcame and partly because of a generous policy toward the peoples they conquered. Instead of ruling them as vanquished subjects, the Romans often exempted them from taxation and allowed them to govern their internal affairs. Conquered peoples in Italy enjoyed the right to trade in Rome and take Roman spouses. Some gained Roman citizenship and rose to high positions in Roman society. The Romans forbade conquered peoples from making military or political alliances, except with Rome, and required them to provide soldiers and military support. Those policies provided the political, military, and diplomatic support Rome needed to put down occasional rebellions and to dominate affairs throughout the Italian peninsula.

Expansion in the Mediterranean With Italy under its control, Rome began to play a major role in the affairs of the larger Mediterranean basin and to experience conflicts with other Mediterranean powers. The principal power in the western Mediterranean during the fourth and third centuries B.C.E. was Carthage, located near modern Tunis. Originally established as a Phoenician colony, Carthage enjoyed a strategic location that enabled it to trade actively and build a strong regional empire in the western Mediterranean region. From the wealth generated by that commerce, Carthage became the dominant political power in north Africa (excluding Egypt), the southern part of the Iberian peninsula, and the western region of grain-rich Sicily as well. Meanwhile, the three Hellenistic empires that succeeded Alexander of Macedon continued to dominate the eastern Mediterranean: the Antigonids ruled Macedon, the Ptolemies ruled Egypt, and the Seleucids included wealthy Syria and Anatolia among their many possessions. The prosperity of the Hellenistic realms supported a thriving network of maritime commerce in the eastern Mediterranean, and as in the case of Carthage, commercial wealth enabled rulers to maintain powerful states and armies.

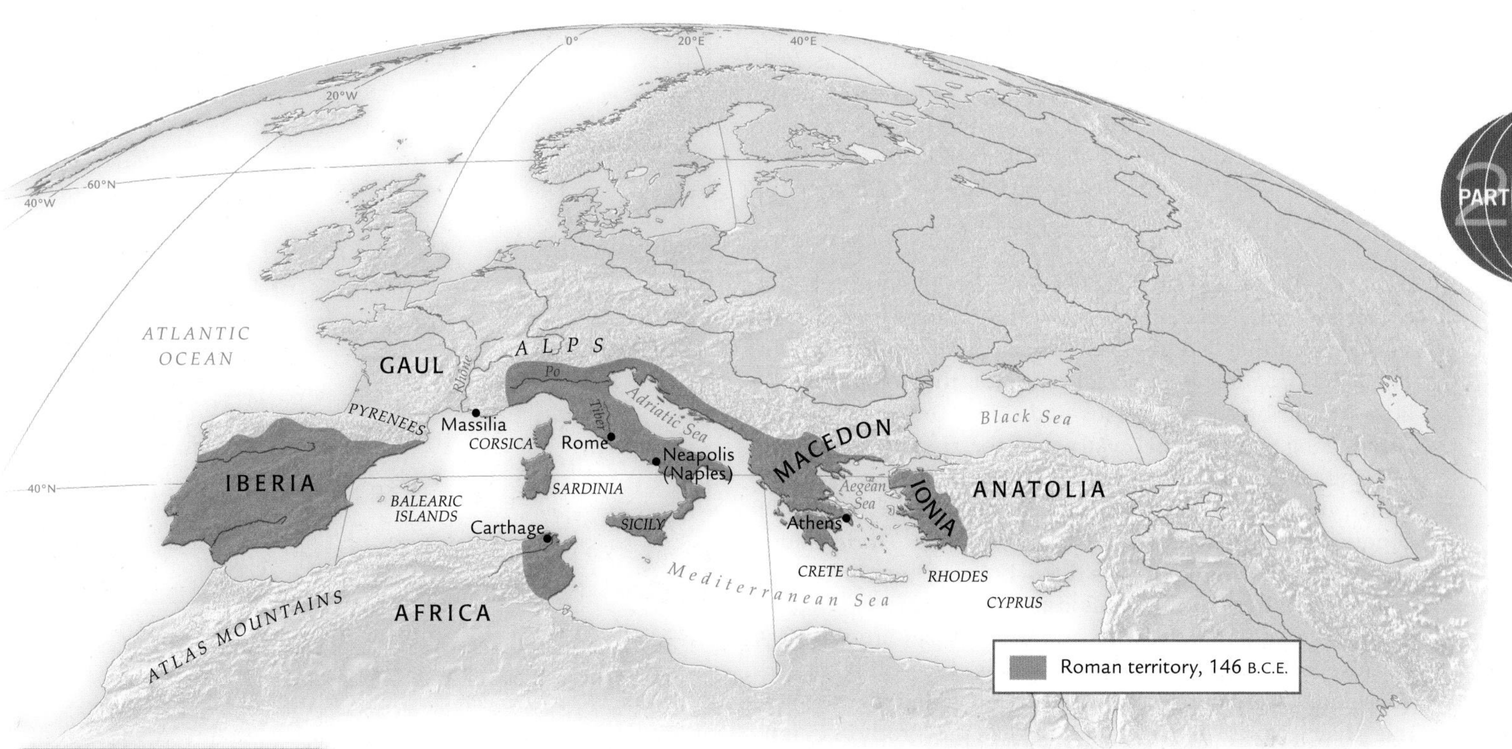

MAP 11.1
Expansion of the Roman republic to 146 B.C.E.
By the mid-second century B.C.E., the Roman republic controlled extensive territories outside Italy.

Consider the ways Roman expansion encouraged interactions and exchanges throughout the Mediterranean region.

The Punic Wars The Romans clashed first with Carthage. Between 264 and 146 B.C.E., they fought three devastating conflicts known as the Punic Wars with the Carthaginians. Friction first arose from economic competition, particularly over Sicily, the most important source of grain in the western Mediterranean. Later on, Romans and Carthaginians struggled for supremacy in the region. The rivalry ended after Roman forces subjected Carthage to a long siege, conquered the city, burned much of it to the ground, and forced some fifty thousand survivors into slavery. With their victory over Carthage, Romans became the dominant power brokers in the western Mediterranean region. Moreover, they annexed Carthaginian possessions in north Africa and Iberia—rich in grain, oil, wine, silver, and gold—and used those resources to finance continued imperial expansion.

Shortly after the beginning of the Carthaginian conflict, Rome became embroiled in disputes in the eastern Mediterranean. Conflict arose partly because pirates and ambitious local lords ignored the weakening Hellenistic rulers and threatened regional stability. On several occasions Roman leaders dispatched armies to protect the interests of Roman citizens and merchants, and those expeditions brought them into conflict with the Antigonids and the Seleucids. Between 215 and 148 B.C.E., Rome fought five major wars, mostly in Macedon and Anatolia, against Antigonid and Seleucid opponents. The Romans did not immediately annex lands in the eastern Mediterranean but, rather, entrusted them to allies in the region. Nevertheless, by the middle of the second century B.C.E., Rome clearly ranked as the preeminent power in the eastern as well as the western Mediterranean.

FROM REPUBLIC TO EMPIRE

Imperial expansion brought wealth and power to Rome, but wealth and power brought problems as well as benefits. Unequal distribution of wealth aggravated class tensions and gave rise to conflict over political and social policies. Meanwhile, the need to administer conquered lands efficiently strained the capacities of the republican constitution. During the first century B.C.E. and the first century C.E., Roman civil and military leaders gradually dismantled the republican constitution and imposed a centralized imperial form of government on the city of Rome and its empire.

Imperial Expansion and Domestic Problems

In Rome, as in classical China and Greece, patterns of land distribution caused serious political and social tensions.

Conquered lands fell largely into the hands of wealthy elites, who organized enormous plantations known as *latifundia.* Because they enjoyed economies of scale and often employed slave labor, owners of latifundia operated at lower costs than did owners of smaller holdings, who often had to mortgage their lands or sell out to their wealthier neighbors.

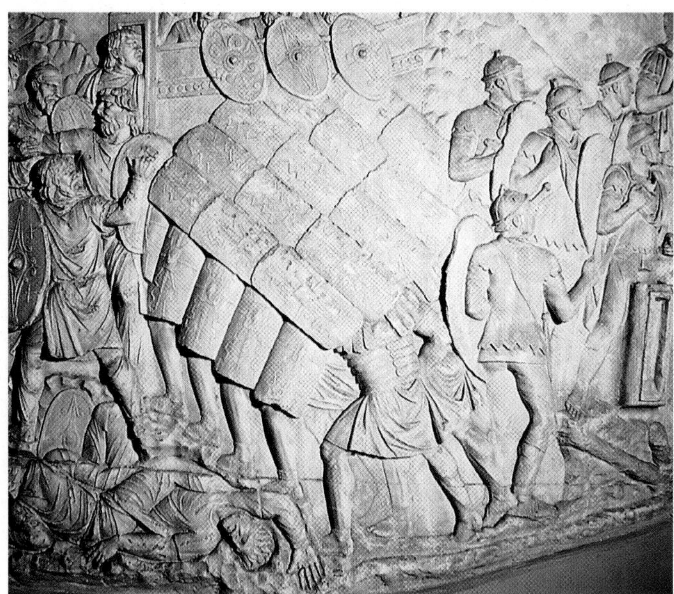

Roman expansion depended on well-equipped and highly disciplined military forces. In this detail from Trajan's Column, troops assume the siege formation known as the *testudo* (the "tortoise") by surrounding themselves with their shields to deflect defenders' missiles while approaching city walls.

The Gracchi Brothers During the second and first centuries B.C.E., relations between the classes became so strained that they led to violent social conflict and civil war. The chief proponents of social reform in the Roman republic were the brothers Tiberius and Gaius Gracchus. Just as Wang Mang, the imperial usurper of the Han dynasty, tried to bring about a redistribution of land resources in classical China, the Gracchi brothers worked to limit the amount of conquered land that any individual could hold. Those whose lands exceeded the limit would lose some of their property, which officials would then allocate to small farmers. Again, as in the case of Wang Mang, the Gracchi had little success because most members of the wealthy and ruling classes considered them dangerous radicals and found ways to stymie their efforts. Indeed, fearing that the brothers might gain influence over Roman affairs, their enemies assassinated Tiberius in 132 B.C.E. and executed Gaius on trumped-up charges in 121 B.C.E.

The experiences of the Gracchi brothers clearly showed that the constitution of the Roman republic, originally designed for a small city-state, might not be suitable for a large and growing empire. Formal political power remained in the hands of a small, privileged class of people in Rome, and their policies often reflected the interests of their class rather than the concerns of the empire as a whole. For the century following the assassinations of the Gracchi brothers, Roman politicians and generals jockeyed for power and position as they sought to mobilize support. Several military commanders began to recruit personal armies not from the ranks of small farmers—traditionally the core of the Roman army—but from landless rural residents and urban workers. Because these troops had no economic cushion to fall back on, they were intensely loyal to their generals and placed the interests of the army before those of the state. Most important of these generals were Gaius Marius, who sided with social reformers who advocated redistribution of land, and Lucius Cornelius Sulla, a veteran of several foreign campaigns who allied with the conservative and aristocratic classes.

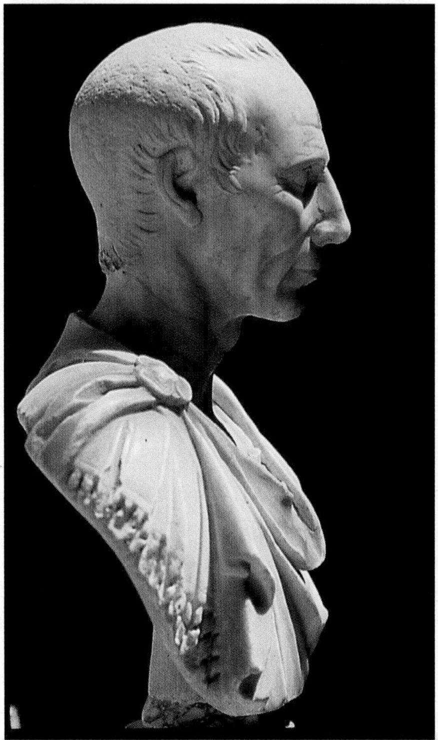

A bust of Julius Caesar depicts a trim conqueror and a canny political leader.

Civil War During the early first century B.C.E., Rome fell into civil war. In 87 B.C.E. Marius marched on Rome, placed the city under military occupation, and hunted down his political enemies. After Marius died the following year, Sulla made plans to take his place. In 83 B.C.E. he seized Rome and initiated a grisly slaughter of his enemies. Sulla posted lists naming proscribed individuals whom he labeled enemies of the state, and he encouraged the Roman populace to kill those individuals on sight and confiscate their properties. During a reign of terror that lasted almost five years, Sulla brought about the murder or execution of some ten thousand individuals. By the time Sulla died in 78 B.C.E., he had imposed an extremely conservative legislative program that weakened the influence of the lower classes and strengthened the hand of the wealthy in Roman politics.

Because Sulla's program did not address Rome's most serious social problems, however, it had no chance to succeed over a long term. Latifundia continued to pressure small farmers, who increasingly left the countryside and swelled the ranks of the urban lower classes. Poverty in the cities, especially Rome, led to periodic social eruptions when the price of grain rose or the supply fell. Meanwhile, the urban poor increasingly joined the personal armies of ambitious generals, who themselves posed threats to social and political stability. In this chaotic context Gaius Julius Caesar inaugurated the process by which Rome replaced its republican constitution with a centralized imperial form of government.

The Foundation of Empire

A nephew of the general Marius, Julius Caesar favored liberal policies and social reform. In spite of these well-known political sympathies, he escaped danger during the reign of Sulla and the conservatives who followed him. Caesar's survival was due in some measure to his youth—Sulla and his supporters simply did not consider Caesar to be a serious threat—but partly also to a well-timed excursion to Greece and the eastern Mediterranean. During the decade of the 60s B.C.E., Caesar played an active role in Roman politics. He spent enormous sums of money sponsoring public spectacles—such as battles between gladiators and wild animals—which helped him build a reputation and win election to posts in the republican government. This activity kept him in the public eye and helped to publicize his interest in social reform. During the next decade Caesar led a Roman army to Gaul, which he conquered and brought into the still-growing Roman empire.

The conquest of Gaul helped to precipitate a political crisis. As a result of his military victories, Caesar had become extremely popular in Rome. Conservative leaders sought to maneuver him out of power and regain the initiative for their own programs. Caesar refused to stand aside, and in 49 B.C.E. he turned his army toward Rome. By early 46 B.C.E. he had made himself master of the Roman state and named himself dictator—an office that he claimed for life rather than for the constitutional six-month term. Caesar then centralized military and political functions and brought them under his control. He confiscated property from conservatives and distributed it to veterans of his armies and other supporters. He launched large-scale building projects in Rome as a way to provide employment for the urban poor. He also extended Roman citizenship to peoples in the imperial provinces, and he even appointed Gauls to the Roman Senate.

Caesar's policies pointed the way toward a centralized, imperial form of government for Rome and its possessions, but the consolidation of that government had to wait for a new generation of leaders. Caesar's rule alienated many members of the Roman elite classes, who considered him a tyrant. In 44 B.C.E. they organized a plot to assassinate Caesar and restore the republic. They attacked Caesar and stabbed him to death in the Roman forum, but the restoration of an outmoded form of government was beyond their powers. Instead, they plunged Rome into a fresh round of civil conflict that persisted for thirteen more years.

Augustus When the struggles ended, power belonged to Octavian, a nephew and protégé of Julius Caesar and the dictator's adopted son. In a naval battle at Actium in Greece (31 B.C.E.), Octavian defeated his principal rival, Mark Antony, who had joined forces with Cleopatra, last of the Ptolemaic rulers of Egypt. He then moved quickly and efficiently to consolidate his rule. In 27 B.C.E. the Senate bestowed on him the title Augustus, a term with strong religious connotations suggesting the divine or semidivine nature of its holder. During his forty-five years of virtually unopposed rule, Augustus fashioned an imperial government that guided Roman affairs for the next three centuries.

Augustus's Administration Augustus's government was a monarchy disguised as a republic. Like Julius Caesar, Augustus ruled by centralizing political and military power. Yet he proceeded more cautiously than had his patron:

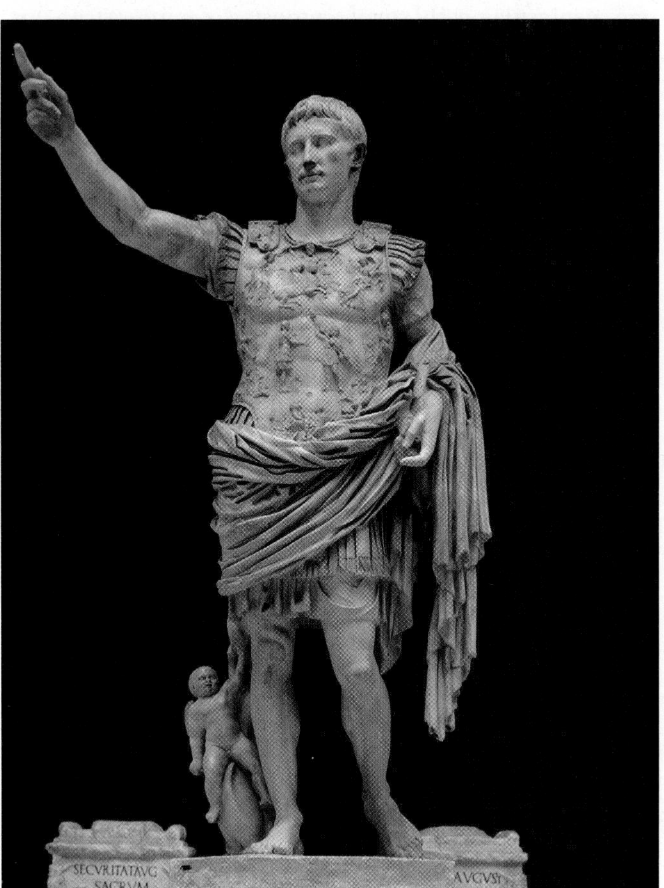

In this statue, which emphasizes his civil and military leadership in Rome, Augustus wears the uniform of a Roman general. How would you characterize the image of Augustus projected in this statue?

Augustus preserved traditional republican offices and forms of government and included members of the Roman elite in his government. At the same time, though, he fundamentally altered the nature of that government. He accumulated vast powers for himself and ultimately took responsibility for all important governmental functions. He reorganized the military system, creating a new standing army with commanders who owed allegiance directly to the emperor—a reform that eliminated problems caused during the late republic by generals with personal armies. He also was careful to place individuals loyal to him in all important positions. Augustus served as emperor until his death in 14 C.E. During his long reign he stabilized a land racked by civil war and enabled the institutions of empire to take root.

Continuing Expansion and Integration of the Empire

During the two centuries following Augustus's rule, Roman armies conquered distant lands and integrated them into a larger economy and society. During republican times Rome already held Italy, Greece, Syria, Gaul, and most of the Iberian peninsula, with small outposts in north Africa and Anatolia. By Augustus's reign imperial holdings included much of southeastern Europe, most of north Africa, including Egypt, and sizable territories in Anatolia and southwest Asia. At its high point, during the early second century C.E., the Roman empire embraced much of Britain as well as a continuous belt of possessions surrounding the Mediterranean and extending to rich agricultural regions inland, including Mesopotamia. After Octavian's conquest of Egypt in 30 B.C.E., Roman forces even made forays deep into the kingdom of Kush, and for more than three centuries they occupied a stretch of the Nile valley about 110 kilometers (70 miles) south of the river's first cataract near Aswan.

Roman expansion had especially dramatic effects in European lands embraced by the empire. Egypt, Anatolia, Syria, and Mesopotamia had long been sites of complex city-based societies, but Gaul, Germany, Britain, and Spain were sparsely populated lands occupied by cultivators who lived in small villages. When Roman soldiers, diplomats, governors, and merchants began to arrive in large numbers, they stimulated the development of local economies and states. They sought access to resources such as tin, and they encouraged local inhabitants to cultivate wheat, olives, and grapes. Local ruling elites allied with Roman representatives and used the wealth that came into their communities to control natural resources and build states on a much larger scale than ever before. Cities emerged where administrators and merchants conducted their business, and the tempo of European society noticeably quickened: Paris, Lyons, Cologne, Mainz, London, Toledo, and Segovia all trace their origins to Roman times.

The *Pax Romana* Within the boundaries of the Roman empire itself, a long era of peace facilitated economic and political integration from the first to the middle of the third century C.E. Augustus brought peace not only to Rome, by ending the civil disturbances that had plagued the city for more than a century, but also to the empire. His reign inaugurated the era known as the *pax romana* ("Roman peace") that persisted for two and a half centuries. In spite of occasional flare-ups, especially among conquered peoples who resented Roman rule, the *pax romana* facilitated trade and communication throughout the region from Mesopotamia to the Atlantic Ocean.

Roman Roads Like their Persian, Chinese, Indian, and Hellenistic counterparts, the Romans integrated their empire by building networks of transportation and communication. Since ancient times, Roman engineers have enjoyed a reputation as outstanding road builders. Roman engineers prepared a deep bed for their roads, edged them with curbs, provided for drainage, and then topped them off with large, flat paving stones. Their main roads were 6 to 8 meters (20 to 26 feet) wide—large enough to accommodate two-way traffic—and even roads winding through mountains were 2 to 3 meters (6 to 10 feet) wide. Builders placed milestones along the roads, and the imperial postal system maintained stations for couriers. The roads and postal system permitted urgent travel and messages to proceed with remarkable speed: Tiberius, successor of Augustus as Roman emperor, once traveled 290 kilometers (180 miles) in a single day over Roman roads.

"Roman engineers enjoyed a reputation as outstanding road builders."

Roads linked all parts of the Roman empire. One notable highway of more than 2,500 kilometers (1,554 miles) stretched along the northeast imperial frontier from the Black Sea to the North Sea, parallel to the Danube and Rhine Rivers. Another road linked Rome to the city of Gades (modern Cadiz) in southern Spain. A road of 4,800 kilometers (2,983 miles) ran parallel to the coast of north Africa, and numerous spurs reached south, enabling merchants and soldiers to range deep into the Sahara desert. Romans also built new roads that facilitated travel and trade in the eastern Mediterranean region. One route linked the port of Berenice on the Red Sea to Alexandria, and others linked the towns and ports of the eastern Mediterranean seaboard to Palmyra, a principal way station of caravan traffic coming west from central Asia. Scholars estimate the combined length of the Roman roads was greater than 80,000 kilometers (50,000 miles).

Sea Lanes Where roads came to the water's edge, Romans made use of sea lanes throughout the Mediterranean

MAP 11.2
The Roman empire, ca. 117 C.E.
Compare this map of the Roman empire at its height with Map 11.1 showing territories controlled by the Roman republic almost two centuries earlier.

How important was the Romans' extensive road network for the maintenance of their enormous empire?

Sea and the Black Sea. Established sea lanes linked ports from Syria and Palestine to Spain and north Africa. Indeed, the Mediterranean became essentially a Roman lake, which the Romans themselves called *mare nostrum* ("our sea"). Thus, by sea as well as by land, Romans found ways to maintain communications with all regions of their empire.

Roman Law Under conditions of political stability and the *pax romana,* jurists constructed an elaborate system of law. Romans began a tradition of written law in 449 B.C.E., when they promulgated the Twelve Tables as a basic law code for citizens of the early republic. As armies spread Roman influence throughout the Mediterranean, jurists worked to construct a rational body of law that would apply to all peoples under Roman rule. During the late republic and especially during the empire, the jurists articulated standards of justice and gradually applied them throughout Roman territory. They established the principle that defendants were innocent until proven guilty, and they ensured that defendants had a right to challenge their accusers before

thinking about TRADITIONS

Empires and Their Roads
All the classical empires invested resources in the building of roads and transportation networks that helped them to integrate their vast territories into manageable societies. Compare the road system of the Roman empire with those of the Persian, Han, and Mauryan empires. How did Roman roads complement Mediterranean sea lanes to link regions of the empire?

sources from the past

Tacitus on Corruption in the Early Roman Empire

Augustus's imperial regime and the pax romana *brought peace and stability to the Roman empire, but some contemporaries thought there was a darker side to the new imperial order. Cornelius Tacitus (56–120 C.E.) was a prominent aristocrat and the most important historian of the early Roman empire. In his* Annals, *written in the early second century C.E., Tacitus did not deny the "gift of peace," but he deplored the loss of political courage among Roman leaders after the establishment of the imperial regime.*

Famous writers have recorded Rome's early glories and disasters. The Augustan Age, too, had its distinguished historians. But then the rising tide of flattery exercised a deterrent effect. The reigns of [Augustus's successors as emperor] Tiberius, Gaius, Claudius, and Nero were described during their lifetimes in fictitious terms, for fear of the consequences; whereas the accounts written after their deaths were influenced by raging animosities. So I have decided to say a little about Augustus, with special attention to his last period, and then go on to the reign of Tiberius [14–37 C.E.] and what followed. . . .

[Augustus] seduced the army with bonuses, and his cheap food policy was successful bait for civilians. Indeed, he attracted everybody's goodwill by the enjoyable gift of peace. Then he gradually pushed ahead and absorbed the functions of the senate, the officials, and even the law. Opposition did not exist. War or judicial murder had disposed of all men of spirit. Upper-class survivors found that slavish obedience was the way to succeed, both politically and financially. They had profited from the revolution [the replacement of the republic by an imperial form of government], and so now they liked the security of the existing arrangement better than the dangerous uncertainties of the old regime. Besides, the new order was popular in the provinces. There, government by Senate and People was looked upon skeptically as a matter of sparring dignitaries and extortionate officials. The legal system had provided no remedy against these, since it was wholly incapacitated by violence, favouritism, and—most of all—bribery. . . .

Nobody had any immediate worries as long as Augustus retained his physical powers, and kept himself going, and his House, and the peace of the empire. But when old age incapacitated him, his approaching end brought hopes of change. A few people started idly talking of the blessings of freedom [i.e., discussing a return to the republic]. Some, more numerous, feared civil war; others wanted it. The great majority, however, exchanged critical gossip about candidates for the succession. . . .

Then two pieces of news became known simultaneously: Augustus was dead, and Tiberius was in control.

The new reign's first crime was the assassination of Agrippa Postumus [grandson of Augustus]. He was killed by a staff-officer—who found it a hard task, though he was a persevering murderer and the victim [was] taken by surprise unarmed. Tiberius said nothing about the matter in the senate. He pretended that the orders came from Augustus, who was alleged to have instructed the colonel in charge to kill Agrippa Postumus as soon as Augustus himself was dead. It is true that Augustus' scathing criticisms of the young man's behavior were undoubtedly what had prompted the senate to decree his banishment. But the emperor had never been callous enough to kill any of his relations, and that he should murder his own grandchild to remove the worries of a stepson seemed incredible. It would be nearer the truth to suppose that Tiberius because he was afraid, and Livia [Augustus's widow and mother of Tiberius by another man, but not the grandmother of Agrippa] through stepmotherly malevolence, loathed and distrusted the young Agrippa Postumus and got rid of him at the first opportunity. . . .

Meanwhile at Rome consuls, senate, knights, precipitately became servile. The more distinguished men were, the greater their urgency and insincerity. They must show neither satisfaction at the death of one emperor, nor gloom at the accession of another: so their features were carefully arranged in a blend of tears and smiles, mourning and flattery.

For Further Reflection

- How might a spokesperson from the Roman imperial court have responded to these views of Tacitus?

Source: Tacitus. *The Annals of Imperial Rome.* Rev. ed. Trans. by Michael Grant. Harmondsworth: Penguin, 1977, pp. 31–35.

a judge in a court of law. They also permitted judges to set aside laws that were unfair. Like transportation and communication networks, Roman law helped to integrate the diverse lands that made up the empire, and the principles of Roman law continued to shape Mediterranean and European society long after the empire had disappeared.

ECONOMY AND SOCIETY IN THE ROMAN MEDITERRANEAN

The rapid expansion of Roman influence and the imposition of Roman imperial rule brought economic and social changes to peoples throughout the Mediterranean basin.

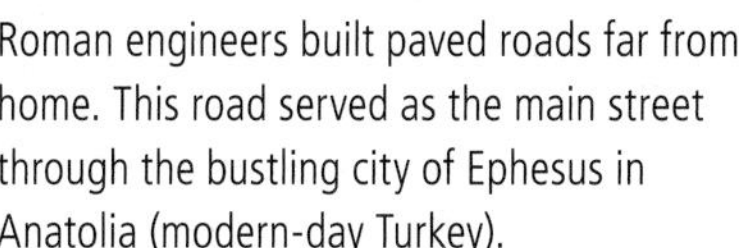

Roman engineers built paved roads far from home. This road served as the main street through the bustling city of Ephesus in Anatolia (modern-day Turkey).

Good roads and the *pax romana* encouraged trade between regions. Existing cities benefited handsomely from the wealth generated by trade, and in the lands they conquered, the Romans founded new cities to serve as links between local regions and the larger Mediterranean economy. Meanwhile, like most other peoples of classical times, the Romans built a strictly patriarchal society and made extensive use of slave labor.

Trade and Urbanization

Commercial Agriculture Like other classical societies, the Roman Mediterranean experienced economic development and social change as the state expanded and brought new regions into its network of trade and communication. Agricultural production, the economic foundation of the Roman empire, also underwent transformation with the expansion of empire and the growth of trade. Instead of planting crops for immediate local use, owners of latifundia concentrated on production for export. Grain from latifundia in north Africa, Egypt, and Sicily routinely found its way over the Roman roads and the Mediterranean sea lanes to the large cities of the empire. The ship that Paul of Tarsus boarded at Caesarea, for example, carried several hundred tons of wheat destined for consumers in Rome.

Commercial agriculture played an important role in the economic specialization and integration of the empire. Because it was possible to import grain at favorable prices from lands that routinely produced large surpluses, other regions could concentrate on the cultivation of fruits and vegetables or on the production of manufactured items. Greece, for example, concentrated on olives and grapevines. Syria and Palestine produced fruits, nuts, and wool fabrics. Gaul produced grain, supplied copper, and began to experiment with the cultivation of grapevines. Spain produced high-quality olive oil as well as wine, horses, and most of the precious metal used in the Roman empire. Italy became a center for the production of pottery, glassware, and bronze goods. Archaeologists have uncovered one pottery factory north of Rome that may have employed hundreds of workers and that had a mixing vat capable of holding more than 40,000 liters (10,568 gallons) of clay.

Mediterranean Trade Specialized production of agricultural commodities and manufactured goods set the stage for vigorous trade over the Mediterranean sea lanes. Roman military and naval power kept the seas largely free of pirates so that sizable cargoes could move safely over long distances, barring foul weather. As Roman military forces, administrators, tax collectors, and other officials traveled throughout the empire carrying out their duties, they joined the merchants in linking the Mediterranean's regions into a well-integrated network of communication and exchange. Archaeologists have discovered that even in remote rural areas, peasants routinely used high-quality pottery, ate food off fine tableware, consumed wines and oils imported from afar, and slept under tiled roofs. Beyond the Mediterranean, the port of Berenice on the Red Sea coast of Egypt offered access to the Indian Ocean and distant markets. Sometime about the first century C.E., an anonymous Roman subject composed a remarkable work called the *Periplus maris erythraei* (meaning a "sailing itinerary of the Red Sea"), which provided a description of the ports on the Red Sea itself as well as east African and Indian ports that Roman merchants commonly visited.

The City of Rome

Cities benefited handsomely from Mediterranean integration and played a prominent role in promoting economic and social change. Along with taxes, tributes, booty, and other wealth generated by military expansion, much of the profit from Mediterranean trade flowed to Rome, where it fueled remarkable urban development. In the first century C.E., some ten thousand statues decorated the city, along with seven hundred pools, five hundred fountains, and thirty-six monumental marble arches celebrating military victories and other achievements. The Roman state financed the construction of temples, bathhouses, public buildings, stadiums, and most important of all, aqueducts that brought fresh water into the city from the neighboring mountains. Construction projects benefited from the use of concrete, invented by Roman engineers during the republican era, which strengthened structures and allowed builders to meet high standards of precision required for plumbing and water control.

Construction provided employment for hundreds of thousands of workers. As a result, the population of Rome surged, and the city's economy experienced rapid growth. Shopkeepers, artisans, merchants, and bankers proliferated in the imperial capital. Economic development attracted large numbers of migrants from the countryside and from foreign lands. Most received low wages as laborers, construction workers, or servants, but those with skills sometimes found good employment as craftsmen. Some who went to Rome with a bit of money established successful businesses, and by hard work or good fortune, a few entrepreneurs became wealthy and respected businessmen.

Urban growth and development also took place beyond the capital. Some parts of the empire, such as Greece and Syria, had long-standing urban traditions. There trade and economic development brought additional prosperity. Elsewhere the Romans founded cities at strategic sites for purposes of government and administration, especially in Spain, Gaul, and Britain, which encouraged economic and social development at the far reaches of the empire.

Roman Cities and Their Attractions

As wealth concentrated in the cities, urban residents came to expect a variety of comforts not available in rural areas. Merchants traveling the roads and sea lanes brought delicacies and luxury items from all parts of the Roman empire: Spanish hams, oysters from British waters, fine wool cloaks from Gaul, and Syrian nuts, dates, and figs all made their way to consumers in Rome and other prosperous cities. Roman cities enjoyed abundant supplies of fresh water, sometimes brought from distant mountains by aqueducts, and elaborate sewage and plumbing systems. All sizable cities and even many smaller towns had public baths featuring hot and cold rooms, and often swimming pools and gymnasia as well. Underground sewers carried away wastewater.

Enormous circuses, stadiums, and theaters provided sites for the entertainment of the urban masses. Circuses were oval structures with tracks for chariot races, which

A wall painting from Stabiae (a small community near Pompeii destroyed by the eruption of Vesuvius in 79 C.E.) depicts an Italian harbor with ships, wharves, warehouses, markets, and decorative columns topped by statues.

Roman aqueducts were impressive products of Roman engineering. Many survive to the present day. This one carried water to the city of Nemausus in Gaul (modern Nîmes in France). The water flowed through a trough supported by the top layer of arches.

were wildly popular in the Roman empire. The Circus Maximus at Rome accommodated about 250,000 spectators. Entertainment in stadiums often took forms now considered coarse and cruel—battles to the death between gladiators or between humans and wild animals—but urban populations flocked to such events, which they looked on as exciting diversions from daily routine. The Roman Colosseum, a magnificent marble stadium and sports arena opened in 80 C.E., provided seating for about 50,000 spectators. The structure had a multicolored awning that protected viewers from sun and rain, and its construction was so precise that it was possible to flood the arena with water and stage mock naval battles within its walls.

Family and Society in Roman Times

The *Paterfamilias* Roman law vested immense authority in male heads of families. The Roman family consisted of an entire household, including slaves, free servants, and close relatives who lived together. Usually the eldest male ruled the household as *paterfamilias* ("father of the family"). Roman law gave the paterfamilias the authority to arrange marriages for his children, determine the work or duties they would perform, and punish them for offenses as he saw fit. He had rights also to sell them into slavery and even to execute them.

Although legally endowed with extraordinary powers, the Roman paterfamilias rarely ruled tyrannically over his charges. In fact, women usually supervised domestic affairs in Roman households, and by the time they reached middle age, women generally wielded considerable influence within their families. They helped select marriage partners for their offspring, and they sometimes played large roles in managing their families' financial affairs. Although Roman

From the days of the republic, residents of Rome consumed subsidized grain imported from distant territories. In this painting from a tomb, workers load grain onto a boat at the port of Ostia, at the mouth of the Tiber River, for transport upriver to the city of Rome.

law placed strict limits on the ability of women to receive inheritances, enforcement was inconsistent, and clever individuals found ways to evade the law or take advantage of its loopholes. During the third and second centuries B.C.E., as Roman expansion in the Mediterranean brought wealth to the capital, women came to possess a great deal of property. By the first century B.C.E., in spite of the authority legally vested in the paterfamilias, many women supervised the financial affairs of family businesses and wealthy estates.

Wealth and Social Change Increasing wealth had important consequences for Roman society. New classes of merchants, landowners, and construction contractors accumulated enormous private wealth and rivaled the old nobility for prominence. The newly rich classes built palatial houses with formal gardens and threw lavish banquets with rare and exotic foods such as boiled ostrich, parrot-tongue pie, and tree fungus served in a sauce of fish fat, jellyfish, and eggs. While wealthy classes probed culinary frontiers, cultivators and urban masses subsisted largely on porridge and vegetables occasionally supplemented by eggs, fish, sausage, or meat.

By the first century B.C.E., poverty had become a considerable problem in Rome and other large cities of the empire. Often unemployed, the urban masses sometimes rioted to express their dissatisfaction and seek improved conditions, and they readily provided recruits for private armies of ambitious generals such as Marius and Sulla. Imperial authorities never developed a true urban policy but, rather, sought to keep the masses contented with "bread and circuses"—subsidized grain and spectacular public entertainments.

Slavery Roman society made extensive use of slave labor: by the second century C.E., slaves may have represented as much as one-third of the population of the Roman empire. In the countryside they worked mostly on latifundia, though many labored in state quarries and mines. Rural slaves worked under extremely harsh conditions, often chained together in teams. Discontent among rural slaves led to several large-scale revolts, especially during the second and first centuries B.C.E. During the most serious uprising, in 73 B.C.E., the escaped slave Spartacus assembled an army of seventy thousand rebellious slaves. The Roman army dispatched eight legions, comprising more than forty thousand well-equipped, veteran troops, to quell the revolt.

In the cities, conditions were much less difficult than in the countryside. Female slaves commonly worked as domestic

A relief carving on a Roman monument depicts some slaves serving guests at a banquet (above), while others work in the kitchen (below). What does this carving suggest about the roles of slaves in Roman society?

servants while males toiled as servants, laborers, craftsmen, shopkeepers, or business agents for their owners. Slaves who had an education or possessed some particular talent had the potential to lead comfortable lives. The first-century Anatolian slave Epictetus even became a prominent Stoic philosopher. He spent much of his life studying with Rome's leading intellectuals, and he lectured to large audiences that included high Roman officials and perhaps even emperors.

More than their counterparts in rural areas, urban slaves could hope for manumission as a reward for a long term of loyal service: it was common, though not mandatory, for masters to free urban slaves about the time they reached age thirty. Until freed, however, slaves remained under the strict authority of their masters, who had the right to sell them, arrange their family affairs, punish them, and even execute them for serious offenses.

THE COSMOPOLITAN MEDITERRANEAN

The integration of the Mediterranean basin had important effects not only for the trade and economy of the Roman empire but also for its cultural and religious traditions. As travelers ventured throughout the Mediterranean basin, they became acquainted with other cultural and religious traditions. When migrants moved to Rome and other large cities, they often continued to observe their inherited traditions and thus contributed to the cosmopolitan cultural atmosphere of the empire. Roads and communication networks favored the spread of new popular religions. Most important of these over time was Christianity, which originated as a small and persecuted Jewish sect. Within three centuries, however, Christianity had become the official religion of the Roman empire and the predominant faith of the Mediterranean basin.

Greek Philosophy and Religions of Salvation

Roman Deities During the early days of their history, the Romans recognized many gods and goddesses, who they believed intervened directly in human affairs. Jupiter was the principal god, lord of the heavens. Mars was the god of war, Ceres the goddess of grain, Janus the god who watched the threshold of individual houses, and Vesta the goddess of the hearth. In addition to these major deities, most Roman households also honored tutelary deities, gods who looked after the welfare of individual families.

As the Romans expanded their political influence and built an empire, they encountered the religious and cultural traditions of other peoples. Often, they adopted the deities of other peoples and used them for their own purposes. From the Etruscans, for example, they learned of Juno, a goddess associated with women and marriage, and Minerva, the goddess of wisdom, as well as certain religious practices, such as divination of the future through examination of the internal organs of ritually sacrificed animals.

Greek Influence The Romans also drew inspiration from the Greek tradition of rational thought and philosophy. When the Romans established political hegemony in the eastern Mediterranean in the third and second centuries B.C.E., the most prominent school of thought in Hellenistic Greece was Stoicism. Recognizing that they lived in a large and interdependent world, the Stoics sought to identify a set of universal moral standards based on nature and reason that would transcend local ethical codes.

Cicero and Stoicism That approach to moral thought appealed strongly to Roman intellectuals, and thinkers such as Marcus Tullius Cicero (106–43 B.C.E.) readily adopted Stoic values. Cicero studied in Greece and became thoroughly acquainted with both classical and Hellenistic schools of thought. He was a persuasive orator, and he wrote clear, elegant, polished Latin prose. In adapting Hellenistic thought to Roman needs, Cicero drew heavily from the Stoics' moral and ethical teachings. His letters and treatises emphasized the individual's duty to live in accordance with nature and reason. He argued that the pursuit of justice was the individual's highest public duty, and he scorned those who sought to accumulate wealth or to become powerful through immoral, illegal, or unjust means. Through his speeches and especially his writings, Cicero helped to establish Stoicism as the most prominent school of moral philosophy in Rome.

A wall painting of the fourth century C.E. from a Christian catacomb depicts a group of pagan students gathered around their teacher, who presents a lesson in anatomy with the aid of a cadaver. This scene reflects the influence of Greek scientific and medical studies in the Roman empire.

This mithraeum—a shrine to the god Mithras—survives beneath the church of San Clemente in Rome. Benches accommodated worshipers. The sculpture on the altar depicts Mithras sacrificing a bull to the god Apollo.

Religions of Salvation Both educated elites and unschooled masses found comfort in religions of salvation that established their presence throughout the Mediterranean basin and beyond. Like Stoicism, these religions clearly reflected the political and social conditions of the Hellenistic period: in an imperial era, when close-knit city-states no longer served as a focus for individual loyalties, religions of salvation appealed to the popular masses by providing a sense of purpose and the promise of a glorious future existence.

These religions became prominent features of Mediterranean society during Hellenistic times and became increasingly noticeable in Rome during the late republic as migrants settled in the capital and brought their faiths with them. Under the Roman empire, religions of salvation flourished both in Rome and throughout the Mediterranean basin. Merchants, soldiers, and administrators carried their cults as they conducted their business, and missionaries traveled alongside them in search of converts. The roads of the empire and the sea lanes of the Mediterranean thus served not only as trade routes and lines of official communication but also as highways for religions of salvation, which traveled to all the ports and large cities of the empire.

Mithraism Among the most popular of these religions of salvation was **Mithraism,** a cult dedicated to the Persian deity Mithras. In Zoroastrian mythology, Mithras was a god closely identified with the sun and light. Roman soldiers serving in the Hellenistic world, particularly Anatolia, encountered the cult of Mithras and adapted it to their interests. They associated Mithras less with the sun than with military virtues such as strength, courage, and discipline, and the cult of Mithras quickly became exceptionally popular among the Roman armed forces.

The Mithraic religion provided divine sanction for human life and especially for purposeful moral behavior. It brought together a community that welcomed and nurtured like-minded individuals. Further, it offered hope for individuals who conscientiously observed the cult's teachings by promising them ecstatic and mysterious union with Mithras himself. During the late republic, Mithraic altars and temples appeared in military garrisons throughout the empire. During the early centuries C.E., administrators and merchants also became enchanted with Mithras, and his cult attracted followers among the male populations of all sizable communities and commercial centers in the Roman empire.

Cult of Isis The cult of Mithras did not admit women, but cults dedicated to the Anatolian mother goddess Cybele, the Egyptian goddess Isis, and other deities made a place for both men and women. Indeed, the cult of Isis may have been the most popular of all the Mediterranean religions of salvation before the rise of Christianity. Devotees built temples to Isis throughout the Roman empire, and they adored the Egyptian goddess as a benevolent and protective deity who nurtured her worshipers and helped them cope with the stresses of life in cosmopolitan society. Like the Mithraic religion, the cult of Isis and other religions of salvation attracted followers in Rome and other cities throughout the Mediterranean basin. The immense popularity of these religions of salvation provides a context that helps to explain the remarkable success of Christianity in the Roman empire.

Judaism and Early Christianity

The Jews and the Empire After the dissolution of the Jewish kingdom of David and Solomon in the tenth century

Mithraism (MITH-rah-iz'm)

thinking about ENCOUNTERS

Foreign Gods in the Roman Empire
How did foreign deities such as Mithras, Cybele, and Isis attract popular support in the Mediterranean basin? By what routes did these cults make their way into the Roman empire? Consider the roles of trade and imperial administration in the spread of religious traditions.

B.C.E., the Jewish people maintained their faith and their communities under various imperial regimes: Babylonian, Achaemenid, Alexandrian, Seleucid, and Roman. All these empires embraced many different ethnic and religious groups and mostly tolerated the cultural preferences of their subjects, providing that communities paid their taxes and refrained from rebellious activities. In an effort to encourage political loyalty, these empires often created state cults that honored their emperors as gods, and they sometimes called for subjects to participate in the cults and revere the emperor-gods.

That requirement created a serious problem for the strictly monotheistic Jews, who recognized only their god, Yahweh, as divine. Jews considered the pretensions of the state cults to be blasphemy, and many of them refused to pay homage to a mortal being who laid claim to divinity. Sometimes they even declined to pay taxes to regimes that required subjects to revere their emperors. Relations between Jews and imperial authorities became especially tense as the Romans extended their empire in the eastern Mediterranean region. Between the third century B.C.E. and the first century C.E., Jews in Palestine mounted several rebellions against their Seleucid and Roman overlords. Ultimately the resistance failed, and Roman forces decisively defeated the rebels during the Jewish War of 66 to 70 C.E.

The Essenes While some Jews actively fought the Romans, others founded new sects that looked for saviors to deliver them from subjection. The Essenes formed one such sect. In 1947 shepherds accidentally discovered some Essene writings known as the Dead Sea scrolls, which have shed fascinating light on the sect and its beliefs. The Essenes formed their community in Palestine during the first century B.C.E. They observed a strict moral code and participated in rituals designed to reinforce a sense of community: they admitted new members after a rite of baptism in water, and they took part in ritual community meals. They also looked for a savior who would deliver them from Roman rule and lead them in the establishment of a community in which they could practice their faith without interference.

Jesus of Nazareth The early Christians probably had little contact with the Essenes, but they shared many of the same concerns. The Christians formed their community around Jesus of Nazareth, a charismatic Jewish teacher whom they recognized as their savior. Born about the year 4 B.C.E., Jesus grew up at a time of high tension between Roman overlords and their Jewish subjects. He was a peaceful man who taught devotion to God and love for fellow human beings. He attracted large crowds because of a reputation for wisdom and miraculous powers, especially the ability to heal the sick.

Yet Jesus alarmed the Romans because he also taught that "the kingdom of God is at hand." To Jesus, the kingdom of God may well have referred to a spiritual realm in which God would gather those faithful to him. To Roman administrators, however, his message carried political overtones: an impending kingdom of God sounded like a threat to Roman rule in Palestine, especially since enthusiastic crowds routinely accompanied Jesus. In an effort to forestall a new round of rebellion, Roman administrators executed Jesus by fixing him to a cross in the early 30s C.E.

Jesus' Early Followers Jesus' crucifixion did not put an end to his movement. Even after his execution, Jesus' close followers strongly felt his presence and proclaimed that he had triumphed over death by rising from his grave. They called him "Christ," meaning "the anointed one," the savior who would bring individuals into the kingdom of God. They taught that he was the son of God and that his sacrifice served to offset the sins of those who had faith in him. They taught further that like Jesus, the faithful would survive death and would experience eternal life in the spiritual kingdom of God. Following Jesus' teachings, the early Christians observed a demanding moral code and devoted themselves uncompromisingly to God. They also compiled a body of writings—accounts of Jesus' life, reports of his followers' works, and letters outlining Christian teachings—that gained recognition as the New Testament. Together with the Jews' Hebrew scriptures, which Christians referred to as the Old Testament, the New Testament became the holy book of Christianity.

Paul of Tarsus Jesus and his earliest followers were all Jews. Beginning about the middle of the first century C.E., however, some Christians avidly sought converts from non-Jewish communities in the Hellenistic world and the Roman empire. The principal figure in the expansion of Christianity beyond Judaism was Paul of Tarsus, a Jew from Anatolia who zealously preached his faith, especially in the Greek-speaking eastern region of the Roman empire. Paul taught a Christianity that attracted the urban masses in the same way as other religions of salvation that spread widely in the Roman empire. His doctrine called for individuals to observe high moral standards and to place their faith ahead of personal and family interests. His teaching also explained the world and human history as the results of God's purposeful activity and so provided a framework of meaning

sources from the past

Jesus' Moral and Ethical Teachings

Several accounts of Jesus' life record the Sermon on the Mount in which Jesus challenged his followers to honor God and observe a demanding code of ethics. Here, Jesus explicitly instructed his listeners to reject moral and legal principles that southwest Asian peoples had followed since the third millennium B.C.E. and that the Babylonian emperor Hammurabi had enshrined in his famous code of laws about 1750 B.C.E. Jesus enjoined them to refrain from revenge against those who had caused them harm, for example, and instead to repay harm with kindness.

Blessed are the poor in spirit: for theirs is the kingdom of heaven. Blessed are they that mourn: for they shall be comforted. Blessed are the meek: for they shall inherit the earth. Blessed are they which do hunger and thirst after righteousness: for they shall be filled. Blessed are the merciful: for they shall obtain mercy. Blessed are the pure in heart: for they shall see God. Blessed are the peacemakers: for they shall be called the children of God. Blessed are they which are persecuted for righteousness's sake: for theirs is the kingdom of heaven. Blessed are ye when men shall revile you and persecute you and shall say all manner of evil against you falsely for my sake. Rejoice, and be exceeding glad: for great is your reward in heaven. . . .

Ye have heard that it hath been said, "An eye for an eye, and a tooth for a tooth." But I say unto you that ye resist not evil: but whosoever shall smite thee on thy right cheek, turn to him the other also. And if any man will sue thee at the law, and take away thy coat, let him have thy cloak also. And whosoever shall compel thee to go a mile, go with him two. Give to him that asketh thee, and from him that would borrow of thee turn not thou away.

Ye have heard that it hath been said, "Thou shalt love thy neighbour, and hate thine enemy." But I say unto you, love your enemies, bless them that curse you, do good to them that hate you, and pray for them which despitefully use you and persecute you, that ye may be the children of your Father which is in heaven: for he maketh his sun to rise on the evil and on the good, and sendeth rain on the just and on the unjust. . . .

Ask, and it shall be given you; seek, and ye shall find; knock, and it shall be opened unto you. For every one that asketh receiveth; and he that seeketh findeth; and to him that knocketh it shall be opened. What man is there of you, whom if his son ask bread, will he give him a stone? Or if he ask a fish, will he give him a serpent? If ye then, being evil, know how to give good gifts unto your children, how much more shall your Father which is in heaven give good things to them that ask him? Therefore all things whatsoever ye would that men should do to you, do ye even so to them.

For Further Reflection

- Compare and contrast Jesus' moral teachings with the Zoroastrian, Confucian, Daoist, Buddhist, Hindu, and Socratic views discussed in earlier chapters.

Source: Matthew 5:3–13, 5:38–45, 7:7–12 (Authorized Version). (Translation slightly modified.)

for individuals' lives. Furthermore, Paul's doctrine promised a glorious future existence for those who conscientiously observed the faith.

Like missionaries of other faiths, Paul was no stranger to Roman roads and Mediterranean sea lanes. He traveled widely in search of converts and made several journeys through Greece, Anatolia, Syria, and Palestine to visit fledgling Christian communities and offer them guidance. His last journey took him by ship from Palestine to Rome, where he took the opportunity to promote Christianity and seek converts for about two years before losing his appeal to the emperor and suffering execution.

Early Christian Communities For two centuries after the crucifixion of Jesus, there was no central authority for the fledgling church. Rather, individual communities selected supervisors, known as bishops, who oversaw priests and governed their jurisdictions according to their best understanding of Christian doctrine. As a result, until the emergence of Rome as the principal seat of church authority in the third century C.E., Christians held doctrinal views and followed practices that varied considerably from one community to the next: as different groups of people adopted Christianity, they interpreted Christian teachings in very different ways, just as different communities had earlier understood the cults of Mithras, Isis, and other deities in their own ways.

Early Christians generated a large number of writings to express their various understandings of Christianity and its implications. After the third century C.E., church authorities suppressed many of those writings and declared them heretical. Yet dozens of letters, gospels, and interpretative historical accounts survive to document the complexity and diversity of early Christian teachings. Some early Christians maintained that the faithful must accept specific doctrines, whereas others encouraged believers to find truth within themselves and express it in their own ways. Some religious leaders taught that Jesus had literally risen from the dead and come back to life, whereas others held that his resurrection was a spiritual rather than physical matter. Some communities forbade women to play active public roles in the church, but others allowed women to serve as priests. Some congregations permitted individuals to seek their own understanding of spiritual matters, but others insisted that access to spiritual truth was available only through properly ordained priests and bishops. Early Christianity was indeed a remarkably diverse faith. Only gradually did believers agree to recognize certain texts—the New Testament—as authoritative scripture and adopt them as fundamental guides for Christian doctrine and practice.

The Growth of Early Christianity Like the Jews from whose ranks they had sprung, the early Christians refused to honor the Roman state cults or revere the emperor as a god. As a result, Roman imperial authorities launched sporadic campaigns of persecution designed to eliminate Christianity as a threat to the empire. In spite of that repression, Christian numbers grew rapidly. During the first three centuries of the faith's existence, Christianity found its way to almost all parts of the Roman empire, and Christians established thriving communities throughout the Mediterranean basin and farther east in Mesopotamia and Iran. Rome itself had a sizable Christian population by 300 C.E.

The remarkable growth of Christianity reflected the new faith's appeal particularly to the lower classes, urban populations, and women. Christianity accorded honor and dignity to individuals who did not enjoy high standing in Roman society, and it endowed them with a sense of spiritual freedom more meaningful than wealth, power, or social prominence. Unlike the popular cult of Mithras, which admitted only men, Christianity taught the spiritual equality of the sexes and welcomed the contributions of both men and women. Like Mithraism and other religions of salvation, Christianity provided a sense of purpose and a promise of future glory for those who placed their faith in Jesus. Thus, although Christianity originated as a minor sect of Judaism, urban populations in the Roman empire embraced the new faith with such enthusiasm that by the third century C.E. it had become the most dynamic and influential religious faith in the Mediterranean basin.

inperspective

Under Roman influence, Mediterranean lands became a tightly integrated society. The Roman empire provided a political structure that administered lands as distant as Mesopotamia and Britain. Highly organized trade networks enabled peoples throughout the empire to concentrate on specialized agricultural or industrial production and to import foods and other goods that they did not produce themselves. Popular religions spread widely and attracted enthusiastic converts. Like Confucianism and Buddhism in classical China and India, rational philosophy and Christianity became prominent sources of intellectual and religious authority in the classical Mediterranean and continued to influence cultural development in the Mediterranean, Europe, and southwest Asia over the long term. ●

CHRONOLOGY	
753 B.C.E.	Founding of Rome, according to tradition
509 B.C.E.	Establishment of the Roman republic
264–146 B.C.E.	Roman expansion in the Mediterranean basin
106–43 B.C.E.	Life of Marcus Tullius Cicero
first century B.C.E.	Civil war in Rome
46–44 B.C.E.	Rule of Gaius Julius Caesar as dictator
31 B.C.E.–14 C.E.	Rule of Augustus
4 B.C.E.–early 30s C.E.	Life of Jesus of Nazareth
first century C.E.	Life of Paul of Tarsus
66–70 C.E.	Jewish War

For Further Reading

Keith R. Bradley. *Discovering the Roman Family: Studies in Roman Social History.* New York, 1991. A provocative analysis of Roman family life with illustrations from individual experiences.

———. *Slavery and Society at Rome.* Cambridge, 1994. An engaging and readable essay on slavery and its role in Roman society, with special attention to individual experiences.

Peter Brown. *The Rise of Western Christendom: Triumph and Diversity, A.D. 200–1000.* 2nd ed. Oxford, 2003. A landmark analysis of early Christian history by an unusually perceptive scholar.

Barry Cunliffe. *Greeks, Romans, and Barbarians: Spheres of Interaction.* New York, 1988. Draws on archaeological evidence in assessing the effects of the Roman presence in Gaul, Britain, and Germany.

M. I. Finley. *Ancient Slavery and Modern Ideology.* Expanded ed. Princeton, 1998. A thoughtful analysis of Greek and Roman slavery in light of modern slavery and contemporary debates.

A. H. M. Jones. *Augustus.* New York, 1970. A distinguished historian of ancient Rome provides the best study of Augustus and his career.

Paul MacKendrick. *The Mute Stones Speak: The Story of Archaeology in Italy.* New York, 1960. An older but engaging work with still valuable information on Roman architecture and construction techniques.

Ramsay MacMullen. *Christianizing the Roman Empire.* New Haven, 1984. Scholarly study of the processes by which Christianity became established in the Roman empire.

———. *Romanization in the Time of Augustus.* New Haven, 2000. Charts the diffusion of a Roman way of life throughout the empire.

Elaine Pagels. *Adam, Eve, and the Serpent.* New York, 1988. Provocative and fascinating analysis of early Christianity and its relationship with the Roman state.

———. *Beyond Belief: The Secret Gospel of Thomas.* New York, 2003. Explores some of the many diverse understandings of Christianity in the early years of the faith.

———. *The Gnostic Gospels.* New York, 1979. Fascinating reconstruction of some little-known early Christian communities.

Sarah B. Pomeroy. *Goddesses, Whores, Wives, and Slaves: Women in Classical Antiquity.* New York, 1975. Outstanding study analyzing the status and role of women in classical Greece and Rome.

Romolo Augusto Staccioli. *The Roads of the Romans.* Los Angeles, 2003. A well-illustrated volume that surveys the entire Roman road system.

Geza Vermes. *The Dead Sea Scrolls: Qumran in Perspective.* Rev. ed. London, 1994. A reliable introduction to scholarship on the Dead Sea scrolls and the community that produced them.

———. *The Dead Sea Scrolls in English.* 4th ed. London, 1995. Translations of the major texts from the Dead Sea scrolls that throw light on the Essenes and their beliefs.

Cross-Cultural Exchanges on the Silk Roads

chapter 12

An enameled glass goblet produced about the second century C.E. in Begram (modern-day Afghanistan) depicts a party harvesting dates in a grove of palms. The production technique is Roman, testifying to Mediterranean influence in central Asia.

EYEWITNESS:
Zhang Qian: An Early Traveler on the Silk Roads

In the year 139 B.C.E., the Chinese emperor Han Wudi sent an envoy named Zhang Qian on a mission to lands west of China. The emperor's purpose was to find allies who could help combat the nomadic Xiongnu, who menaced the northern and western borders of the Han empire. From captives he had learned that other nomadic peoples in far western lands bore grudges against the Xiongnu, and he reasoned that they might ally with Han forces to pressure their common enemy.

The problem for Zhang Qian was that to communicate with potential allies against the Xiongnu, he had to pass directly through lands they controlled. Soon after Zhang Qian left Han territory, Xiongnu forces captured him. For ten years the Xiongnu held him in comfortable captivity: they allowed him to keep his personal servant, and they provided him with a Xiongnu wife, with whom he had a son. When suspicions about him subsided, however, Zhang Qian escaped with his family and servant. He even had the presence of mind to keep with him the yak tail that Han Wudi had given him as a sign of his ambassadorial status. He fled to the west and traveled as far as Bactria, but he did not succeed in lining up allies against the Xiongnu. While returning to China, Zhang Qian again fell into Xiongnu hands but managed to escape after one year's detention when the death of the Xiongnu leader led to a period of turmoil. In 126 B.C.E. Zhang Qian and his party returned to China and a warm welcome from Han Wudi.

Although his diplomatic efforts did not succeed, Zhang Qian's mission had far-reaching consequences. Apart from political and military intelligence about western lands and their peoples, Zhang Qian brought back information of immense commercial value. While in Bactria about 128 B.C.E., he noticed Chinese goods—textiles and bamboo articles—offered for sale in local markets. Upon inquiry he learned that they had come from southwest China by way of Bengal. From that information he deduced the possibility of establishing trade relations between China and Bactria through India.

Han Wudi responded enthusiastically to that idea and dreamed of trading with peoples inhabiting lands west of China. From 102 to 98 B.C.E., he mounted an ambitious campaign that broke the power of the Xiongnu and pacified central Asia. His conquests simplified trade relations, since it became unnecessary to route commerce through India. The intelligence that Zhang Qian gathered during his travels thus contributed to the opening of the silk roads—the network of trade routes that linked lands as distant as China and the Roman empire—and more generally to the establishment of relations between China and lands to the west.

China and other classical societies imposed political and military control over vast territories. They promoted trade and communication within their own empires, bringing regions that had previously been self-sufficient into a larger economy and society. They also fostered the spread of cultural and religious traditions to distant regions, and they encouraged the construction of institutional frameworks that promoted the long-term survival of those traditions.

The influence of the classical societies did not stop at the imperial boundaries. Nearby peoples regarded their powerful neighbors with a mixture of envy and suspicion, and they sought to share the wealth that those neighbors generated. They pursued that goal by various means, both peaceful and violent, and relations with neighboring peoples, particularly nomadic peoples, became a major preoccupation of all the classical societies.

Beyond their relations with neighboring peoples, the classical societies established a broad zone of communication and exchange throughout much of the earth's eastern hemisphere. Trade networks crossed the deserts of central Asia and the breadth of the Indian Ocean. Long-distance trade passed through much of Eurasia and north Africa, from China to the Mediterranean basin, and to parts of sub-Saharan Africa as well.

This long-distance trade profoundly influenced the experiences of peoples and the development of societies throughout the eastern hemisphere. It brought wealth and access to foreign products, and it enabled peoples to concentrate their efforts on economic activities best suited to their regions. It facilitated the spread of religious traditions beyond their original homelands, since merchants carried their beliefs and sometimes attracted converts in the lands they visited. It also facilitated the transmission of disease: pathogens traveled the trade routes alongside commercial wares and religious faiths. Indeed, the transmission of disease over the silk roads helped bring an end to the classical societies, since infectious and contagious diseases sparked devastating epidemics that caused political, social, and economic havoc. Long-distance trade thus had deep political, social, and cultural as well as economic and commercial implications for classical societies.

LONG-DISTANCE TRADE AND THE SILK ROADS NETWORK

During the classical era, two developments reduced the risks associated with travel and stimulated long-distance trade. First, rulers invested heavily in the construction of roads and bridges. They undertook those expensive projects primarily for military and administrative reasons, but roads also had the effect of encouraging trade within individual societies and facilitating exchanges between different societies. And second, classical societies built large imperial states that sometimes expanded to the point that they bordered on one another: the campaigns of Alexander of Macedon, for example, brought Hellenistic and Indian societies into direct contact, and only small buffer states separated the Roman and Parthian empires. Even when they did not encounter each other so directly, classical empires pacified large stretches of Eurasia and north Africa. As a result, merchants did not face such great risk as in previous eras, the costs of long-distance trade dropped, and its volume rose dramatically.

Trade Networks of the Hellenistic Era

The tempo of long-distance trade increased noticeably during the Hellenistic era, partly because of the many colonies established by Alexander of Macedon and the Seleucid rulers in Persia and Bactria. Though originally populated by military forces and administrators, these settlements soon attracted Greek merchants and bankers who linked the recently conquered lands to the Mediterranean basin. The Seleucid rulers worked diligently to promote trade. They controlled land routes linking Bactria, which offered access to Indian markets, to Mediterranean ports in Syria and Palestine. Archaeologists have unearthed hundreds of coins, pieces of jewelry, and other physical remains, including Greek-style sculptures and buildings, that testify to the presence of Greek communities in Persia and Bactria during the Hellenistic era.

Parthian merchants and other travelers like the soldiers depicted here followed in the footsteps of their Achaemenid and Seleucid predecessors and became regular visitors to northern India. This gray schist carving from Gandhara dates from the second century B.C.E.

Like the Seleucids, the Ptolemies maintained land routes—in their case, routes going south from Egypt to the kingdom of Nubia and Meroë in east Africa—but they also paid close attention to sea lanes and maritime trade. They ousted pirates from sea lanes linking the Red Sea to the Arabian Sea and the Indian Ocean. They also built several new ports, the most important being Berenice on the Red Sea, and Alexandria served as their principal window on the Mediterranean.

The Monsoon System Even more important, perhaps, mariners from Ptolemaic Egypt learned about the monsoon winds that governed sailing and shipping in the Indian Ocean. During the summer the winds blow regularly from the southwest, whereas in the winter they blow from the northeast. Knowledge of these winds enabled mariners to sail safely and reliably to all parts of the Indian Ocean basin. During the second century B.C.E., Hellenistic mariners learned the rhythm of these winds from Arab and Indian seamen whose ancestors had sailed before the monsoons for centuries. Merchant seamen then established regular links by way of the Red Sea between India and Arabia in the east and Egypt and the Mediterranean basin in the west. The anonymous subject of the Roman empire who composed the *Periplus maris erythraei*—the sailing itinerary of the Red Sea mentioned in Chapter 11—understood the wind system of the Indian Ocean and described ports as far distant as east Africa and India that sailors could reach with the aid of the monsoons.

Establishment and maintenance of these trade routes was an expensive affair calling for substantial investment in military forces, construction, and bureaucracies to administer the commerce that passed over the routes. But the investment paid handsome dividends. Long-distance trade stimulated economic development within the Hellenistic realms themselves, bringing benefits to local economies throughout the empires. Moreover, Hellenistic rulers closely supervised foreign trade and levied taxes on it, thereby deriving income from even foreign products.

Trade in the Hellenistic World With official encouragement, a substantial trade developed throughout the Hellenistic world, from Bactria and India in the east to the Mediterranean basin in the west. Spices, pepper, cosmetics, gems, and pearls from India traveled by caravan and ship to Hellenistic cities and ports. Grain from Persia and Egypt fed urban populations in distant lands. Mediterranean wine, olive oil, jewelry, and works of art made their way to Persia and Bactria. And throughout the region from India to the Mediterranean, merchants conducted a brisk trade in slaves, largely kidnapping victims or prisoners of war.

Indeed, maritime trade networks through the Indian Ocean linked not only the large classical societies of Eurasia and north Africa but also smaller societies in east Africa. During the late centuries B.C.E., the port of Rhapta emerged as the principal commercial center on the east African coast. Archaeologists have not discovered the precise location of Rhapta, but it probably was located near modern Dar es Salaam in Tanzania. With increasing trade, groups of professional merchants and entrepreneurs emerged at Rhapta, and coins came into general use on the east African coast. Merchants of Rhapta imported iron goods such as spears, axes, and knives from southern Arabia and the eastern Mediterranean region in exchange for ivory, rhinoceros horn, tortoise shell, and slaves obtained from interior regions. Just as trade in the Mediterranean basin encouraged economic and political development in regions such as western Europe, far-flung commercial networks of the Hellenistic era fostered economic organization and the emergence of states in the distant lands that they brought into interaction.

The Silk Roads

The establishment of classical empires greatly expanded the scope of long-distance trade, as large portions of Eurasia and north Africa fell under the sway of one classical society or another. The Han empire maintained order in China and pacified much of central Asia, including a sizable corridor offering access to Bactria and western markets. The Parthian empire displaced the Seleucids in Persia and extended its authority to Mesopotamia. The Roman empire brought order to the Mediterranean basin. With the decline of the Mauryan dynasty, India lacked a strong imperial state, but the Kushan empire and other regional states provided stability and security, particularly in northern India, that favored long-distance trade.

Overland Trade Routes As the classical empires expanded, merchants and travelers created an extensive network of trade routes that linked much of Eurasia and north Africa. Historians refer to these routes collectively as the silk roads, since high-quality silk from China was one of the principal commodities exchanged over the roads. The overland silk roads took caravan trade from China to the Roman empire, thus linking the extreme ends of the Eurasian landmass. From the Han capital of Chang'an, the main silk road went west until it arrived at the Taklamakan desert, also known as the Tarim Basin. This desert is one of

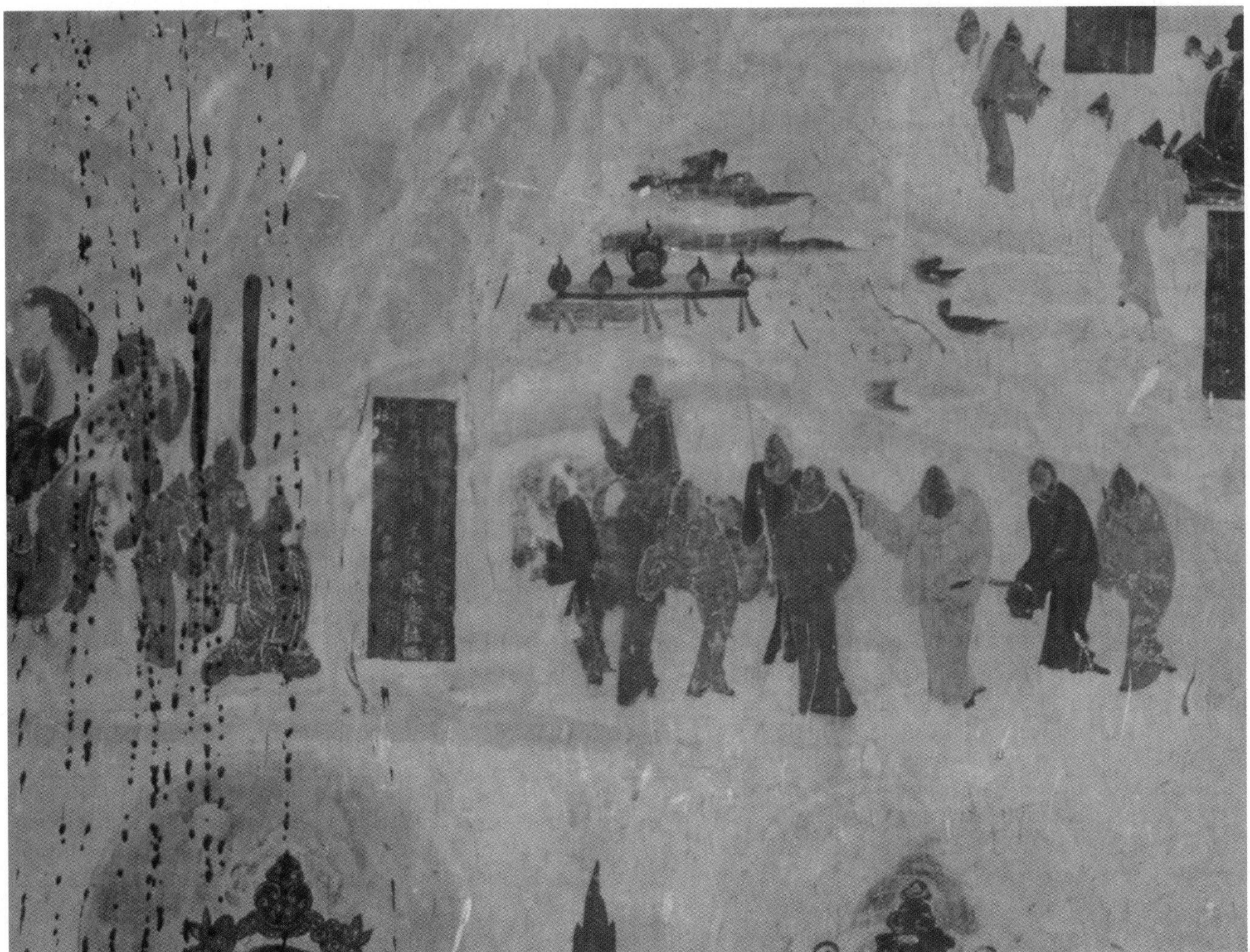

A cave painting from the late seventh century C.E. depicts the Chinese emperor Han Wudi (seated on horse) as he dispatches Zhang Qian (kneeling at left) on his mission to western lands in search of an alliance against the Xiongnu. Why did Zhang Qian's mission hold such great interest for the emperor?

the most dangerous and inhospitable regions of the earth: its very name, Taklamakan, warns that "he who enters does not come back out." The silk road then split into two main branches that skirted the desert proper and passed through oasis towns that ringed it to the north and south. The branches came together at Kashgar (now known as Kashi, located in the westernmost corner of modern China). From there the reunited road went west to Bactria, where a branch forked off to offer access to Taxila and northern India, while the principal route continued across northern Iran. There it joined with roads to ports on the Caspian Sea and the Persian Gulf and proceeded to Palmyra (in modern Syria), where it met roads coming from Arabia and ports on the Red Sea. Continuing west, it terminated at the Mediterranean ports of Antioch (in modern Turkey) and Tyre (in modern Lebanon).

Sea Lanes and Maritime Trade The silk roads also included a network of sea lanes that sustained maritime commerce throughout much of the eastern hemisphere. From Guangzhou in southern China, sea lanes through the South China Sea linked the east Asian seaboard to the mainland and the islands of southeast Asia. Routes linking southeast Asia with Ceylon (modern Sri Lanka) and India were especially busy during classical times. From India, sea lanes passed through the Arabian Sea to Persia and Arabia, and through the Persian Gulf and the Red Sea they offered access to land routes and the Mediterranean basin, which already possessed a well-developed network of trade routes.

Trade Goods A wide variety of manufactured products and agricultural commodities traveled over the silk roads. Generally speaking, silk and spices traveled west from

MAP 12.1
The silk roads, 200 B.C.E.–300 C.E.
Note the extent of the land and sea routes known collectively as the silk roads.

Consider the political and economic conditions that would be necessary for regular travel and trade across the silk roads.

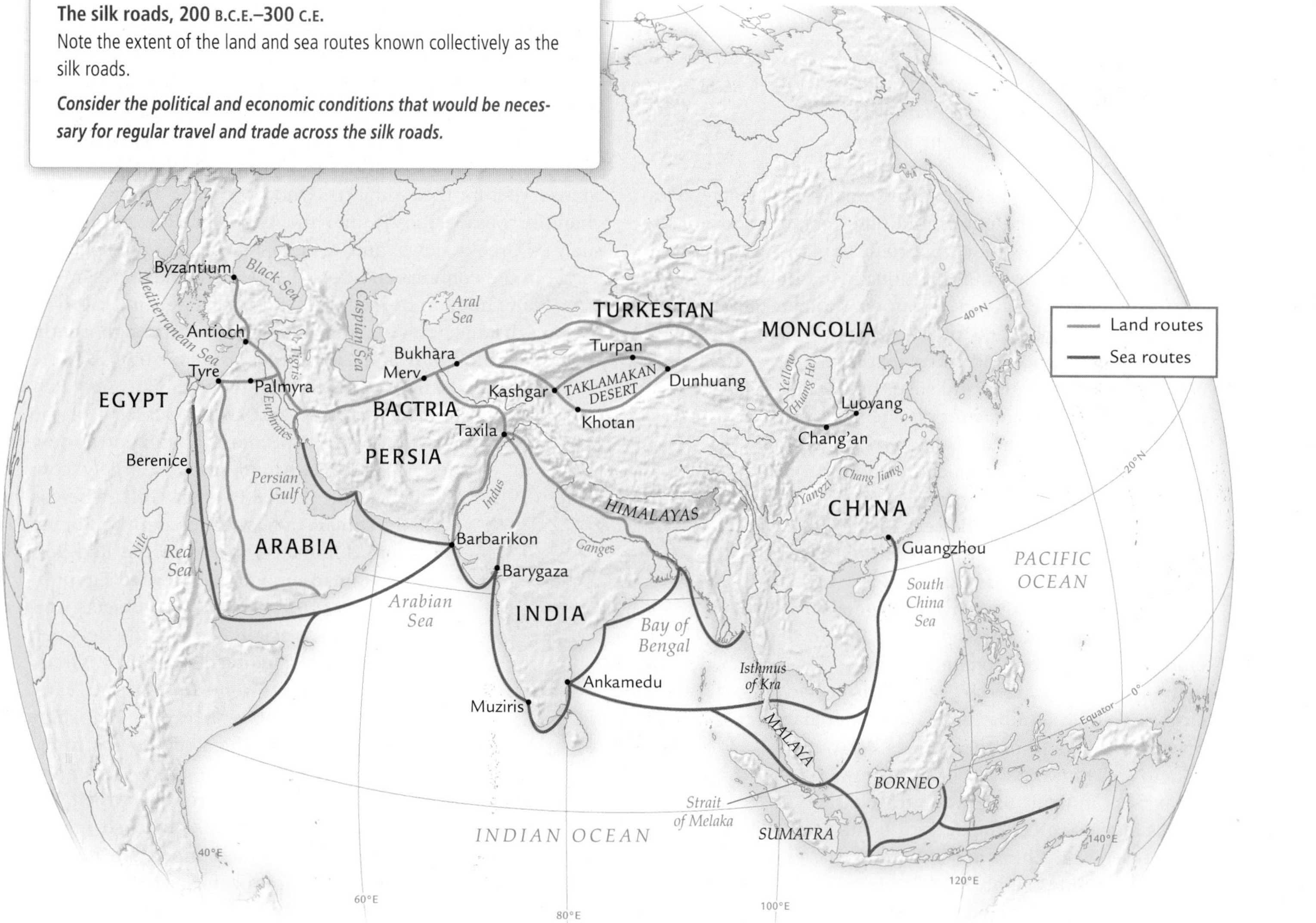

producers in southeast Asia, China, and India to consumers in central Asia, Iran, Arabia, and the Roman empire (including Egypt and north Africa as well as the European regions of the empire). Silk came mostly from China, the only land in classical times where cultivators and weavers had developed techniques for producing high-quality silk fabrics. The fine spices—cloves, nutmeg, mace, and cardamom—all came from southeast Asia. Ginger came from China, cinnamon from China and southeast Asia, pepper from India, and sesame oil from India, Arabia, and southwest Asia. Spices were extremely important commodities in classical times because they had many more uses than they do in the modern world. They served not only as condiments and flavoring agents but also as drugs, anesthetics, aphrodisiacs, perfumes, aromatics, and magical potions. Apart from spices, India exported cotton textiles and valuable exotic items such as pearls, coral, and ivory.

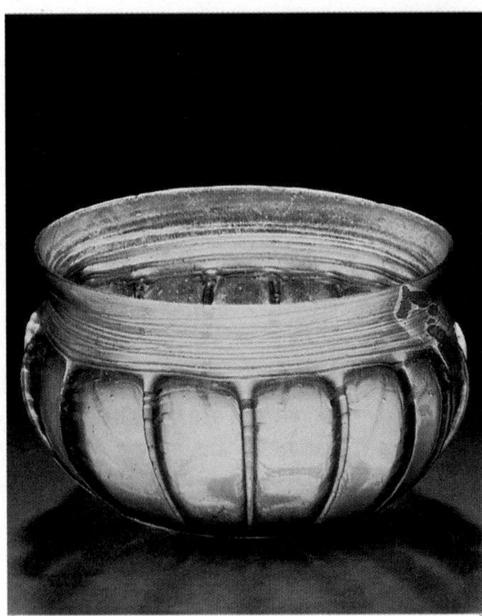

During the first century B.C.E., Romans developed advanced glass-blowing techniques that enabled them to produce wares such as this jar that were popular with wealthy consumers.

Central Asian and Mediterranean lands exchanged a variety of manufactured goods and other commodities for the silks and spices that they imported. Central Asia produced large, strong horses and high-quality jade, much prized in China by stone carvers. From the Roman empire came glassware, jewelry, works of art, decorative items, perfumes, bronze goods, wool and linen textiles, pottery, iron tools, olive oil, wine, and gold and silver bullion. Mediterranean merchants and manufacturers often imported raw materials such as uncut gemstones, which they exported as finished products in the form of expensive jewelry and decorative items.

Some individuals made very long journeys during classical times: Zhang Qian ventured from China as far west as Bactria; Chinese merchants traveled regularly to central Asia and Persia; several Indian embassies called on Roman emperors; Roman merchants traveled by sea at least as far east as southern India; and Malay merchant mariners sailed from the islands of southeast Asia to India and east Africa. On a few occasions individuals even traveled across much or all of the eastern hemisphere between China and the Roman empire. A Chinese ambassador named Gang Ying embarked on a mission to distant western lands in 97 C.E. and proceeded as far as Mesopotamia before reports of the long and dangerous journey ahead persuaded him to return home. And Chinese sources reported the arrival in 166 C.E. of a delegation claiming to represent the Roman emperor Marcus Aurelius. No information survives to throw light on the experiences of this party—or even to confirm its identity—but Roman subjects from Egypt or Syria might well have traveled as far as China in search of trading opportunities.

A Roman coin dated 189 C.E. depicts a merchant ship near the lighthouse at Alexandria. Ships like this one regularly picked up pepper and cinnamon from India along with other cargoes.

The Organization of Long-Distance Trade

Individual merchants did not usually travel from one end of Eurasia to the other. Instead, they handled long-distance trade in stages. On the caravan routes between China and Bactria, for example, Chinese and central Asian nomadic peoples dominated trade. Rarely if ever did they go farther west, however, because the Parthians took advantage of their power and geographic position to control overland trade within their boundaries and to reserve it for their subjects. Once it reached Palmyra, merchandise passed mostly into the hands of Roman subjects such as Greeks, Jews, and Armenians, who were especially active in the commercial life of the Mediterranean basin.

Meanwhile, on the seas, other peoples became involved in long-distance trade. From south China through southeast Asia to Ceylon and India, the principal figures were Malay and Indian mariners. In the Arabian Sea, Persians joined Egyptian and Greek subjects of the Roman empire as the most prominent trading peoples. The Parthian empire largely controlled trade in the Persian Gulf, whereas the Ptolemaic dynasty and later the Roman empire dominated affairs in the Red Sea. After Roman emperors absorbed Egypt in the first century C.E., their subjects carried on an especially brisk trade between India and the Mediterranean. The Greek geographer Strabo reported in the early first century C.E. that as many as 120 ships departed annually from the Red Sea for India. Most of those ships departed from the bustling port of Berenice, which Roman authorities considered so important that they maintained ten forts to guard its approaches. Archaeologists have unearthed the remains of a Roman trading outpost at Arikamedu, near modern Pondicherry in southern

India, and literary sources report that merchants subject to Roman rule established Indian colonies also at Muziris (near modern Cranganore), Barygaza (near modern Broach), Barbarikon (near modern Karachi), and other sites as well. Meanwhile, since the mid-first century C.E., the Romans also had dominated both the eastern and the western regions of *mare nostrum,* the Mediterranean.

It is impossible to determine the quantity or value of trade that passed over the silk roads in classical times, but it clearly made a deep impression on contemporaries. By the first century C.E., pepper, cinnamon, and other spices graced the tables of the wealthy classes in the Roman empire, where silk garments had become items of high fashion. Indeed, silk was in such demand that Roman merchants often stretched their supplies by unraveling the densely woven fabrics that came from China and then reweaving them into larger numbers of sheer garments that were sometimes so light as to be transparent. Some Romans fretted that see-through silk attire would lead to moral decay, and others worried that hefty expenditures for luxury items would ruin the imperial economy. In both cases, their anxieties testified to the powerful attraction of imported silks and spices for Roman consumers.

As it happened, long-distance trade did not cause moral or economic problems for the Roman empire or any other state in classical times. Indeed, it more likely stimulated rather than threatened local economies. Yet long-distance trade did not occur in a vacuum. Commercial exchanges encouraged cultural and biological exchanges, some of which had large implications for classical societies.

CULTURAL AND BIOLOGICAL EXCHANGES ALONG THE SILK ROADS

The silk roads served as magnificent highways for merchants and their commodities, but others also took advantage of the opportunities they offered to travel in relative safety over long distances. Merchants, missionaries, and other travelers carried their beliefs, values, and religious convictions to distant lands: Buddhism, Hinduism, and Christianity all traveled the silk roads and attracted converts far from their original homelands. Meanwhile, invisible travelers such as disease pathogens also crossed the silk roads and touched off devastating epidemics when they found fresh populations to infect. Toward the end of the classical era, epidemic disease that was spread over the silk roads caused dramatic demographic decline especially in China and the Mediterranean basin and to a lesser extent in other parts of Eurasia as well.

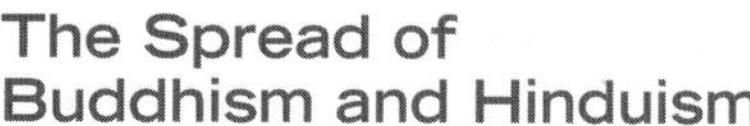

The Spread of Buddhism and Hinduism

By the third century B.C.E., Buddhism had become well established in northern India, and with the sponsorship of the emperor Ashoka it spread to Bactria and Ceylon. Buddhism was particularly successful in attracting merchants as converts. When they traveled, Buddhist merchants practiced their religion among themselves and explained it to others. Gradually, Buddhism made its way along the silk roads to Iran, central Asia, China, and southeast Asia.

Buddhism in Central Asia

Buddhism first established a presence in the oasis towns along the

A mosaic of the second century C.E. depicts a musician playing flutes and a dancer wearing a thin and revealing silk garment.

silk roads—notably Merv, Bukhara, Samarkand, Kashgar, Khotan, Kuqa, Turpan, and Dunhuang—where merchants and their caravans found food, rest, lodging, and markets. The oases depended heavily on trade for their prosperity, and they allowed merchants to build monasteries and invite monks and scribes into their communities. Because they hosted travelers who came from different lands, spoke different languages, and observed different religious practices, the oasis towns became cosmopolitan centers. As early as the second century B.C.E., many residents of the oases themselves adopted Buddhism, which was the most prominent religion of silk roads merchants for more than a millennium, from about 200 B.C.E. to 1000 C.E.

From the oasis communities Buddhism spread to the steppe lands of central Asia and to China. Nomadic peoples from the steppes visited the oases regularly to trade animal products from their herds for grains and manufactured items. They often found Buddhism intriguing, and in the early centuries C.E. they increasingly responded to its appeal. By the fourth century C.E., they had sponsored the spread of Buddhism throughout much of central Asia.

Buddhism in China By the first century B.C.E., Buddhism had also established a foothold in China. The earliest Buddhists in China were foreign merchants—Indians, Parthians, and central Asian peoples—who practiced their religion in the enclaves that Han dynasty officials allowed them to inhabit in Chang'an and other major cities. For several centuries Buddhism did not appeal very strongly to native Chinese. Yet the presence of monasteries and missionaries offered Buddhism the potential to attract Chinese converts. Beginning about the fifth century C.E., Chinese began to respond enthusiastically to Buddhism, which during the postclassical era became the most popular religion throughout all of east Asia, including Japan and Korea as well as China.

Buddhism and Hinduism in Southeast Asia As Buddhism spread north from India into central Asia and China, both Buddhism and Hinduism also began to attract a following in southeast Asia. Once again, merchants traveling the silk roads—in this case the sea lanes through the Indian Ocean—played prominent roles in spreading these religious traditions. Merchant mariners regularly plied the waters between India and southeast Asia during the late centuries B.C.E. By the first century C.E., clear signs of Indian cultural influence had appeared in southeast Asia. In Java, Sumatra, and other islands, as well as in the Malay peninsula and territories in modern Vietnam and Cambodia, rulers of southeast Asian states called themselves *rajas* ("kings"), in the manner of Indian rulers, and they adopted Sanskrit as a means of written communication. Many rulers converted to Buddhism, and others promoted the Hindu cults of Shiva and Vishnu. They built walled cities around lavish temples constructed in the Indian style. They appointed Buddhist or Hindu advisors, and they sought to enhance their authority by associating themselves with honored religious traditions.

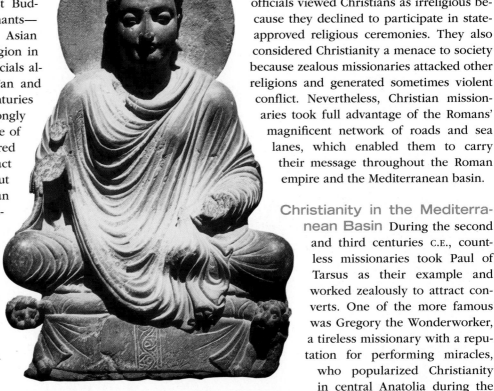

Early Buddhist sculpture in Bactria reflected the influence of Mediterranean and Greek artistic styles. This seated Buddha from the first or second century C.E. bears Caucasian features and wears Mediterranean-style dress.

The Spread of Christianity

Early Christians faced intermittent persecution from Roman officials. During the early centuries C.E., Roman authorities launched a series of campaigns to stamp out Christianity, since most Christians refused to observe the state cults that honored emperors as divine beings. Paradoxically, imperial officials viewed Christians as irreligious because they declined to participate in state-approved religious ceremonies. They also considered Christianity a menace to society because zealous missionaries attacked other religions and generated sometimes violent conflict. Nevertheless, Christian missionaries took full advantage of the Romans' magnificent network of roads and sea lanes, which enabled them to carry their message throughout the Roman empire and the Mediterranean basin.

Christianity in the Mediterranean Basin During the second and third centuries C.E., countless missionaries took Paul of Tarsus as their example and worked zealously to attract converts. One of the more famous was Gregory the Wonderworker, a tireless missionary with a reputation for performing miracles, who popularized Christianity in central Anatolia during the mid-third century C.E. Contemporaries reported that Gregory not only preached Christian doctrine but also expelled demons, moved boulders, diverted a river in flood, and persuaded

observers that he had access to impressive supernatural powers. Gregory and his fellow missionaries helped to make Christianity an enormously popular religion of salvation in the Roman empire. By the late third century C.E., in spite of continuing imperial opposition, devout Christian communities flourished throughout the Mediterranean basin in Anatolia, Syria, Palestine, Egypt, and north Africa as well as in Greece, Italy, Spain, and Gaul.

Christianity in Southwest Asia As Christianity became a prominent source of religious inspiration within the Roman empire, its missionaries also traveled the trade routes and found followers beyond the Mediterranean basin. By the second century C.E., sizable Christian communities flourished throughout Mesopotamia and Iran, and a few Christian churches had appeared as far away as India. Christians did not dominate eastern lands as they did the Roman empire, but they attracted large numbers of converts in southwest Asia. Indeed, beside Jews and Zoroastrians, Christians constituted one of the major religious communities in the region, and they remained so even after the seventh century C.E., when the Islamic religion favored by Arab Muslim conquerors began to displace the older religious communities.

Christian communities in Mesopotamia and Iran deeply influenced Christian practices in the Roman empire. To demonstrate utter loyalty to their faith, Christians in southwest Asia often followed strict ascetic regimes: inspired by Indian traditions, they abstained from sexual contact, refused fine foods and other comforts, and sometimes even withdrew from family life and society. These practices impressed devout Christians in the Roman empire. By the third century C.E., some Mediterranean Christians had begun to abandon society altogether and live as hermits in the deserts of Egypt, the mountains of Greece, and other isolated locations. Others withdrew from lay society but lived in

MAP 12.2
The spread of Buddhism, Hinduism, and Christianity, 200 B.C.E.– 400 C.E.
Compare the routes taken by Buddhism, Hinduism, and Christianity with the routes followed by merchants on silk roads depicted on Map 12.1.
How might you account for the similarities?

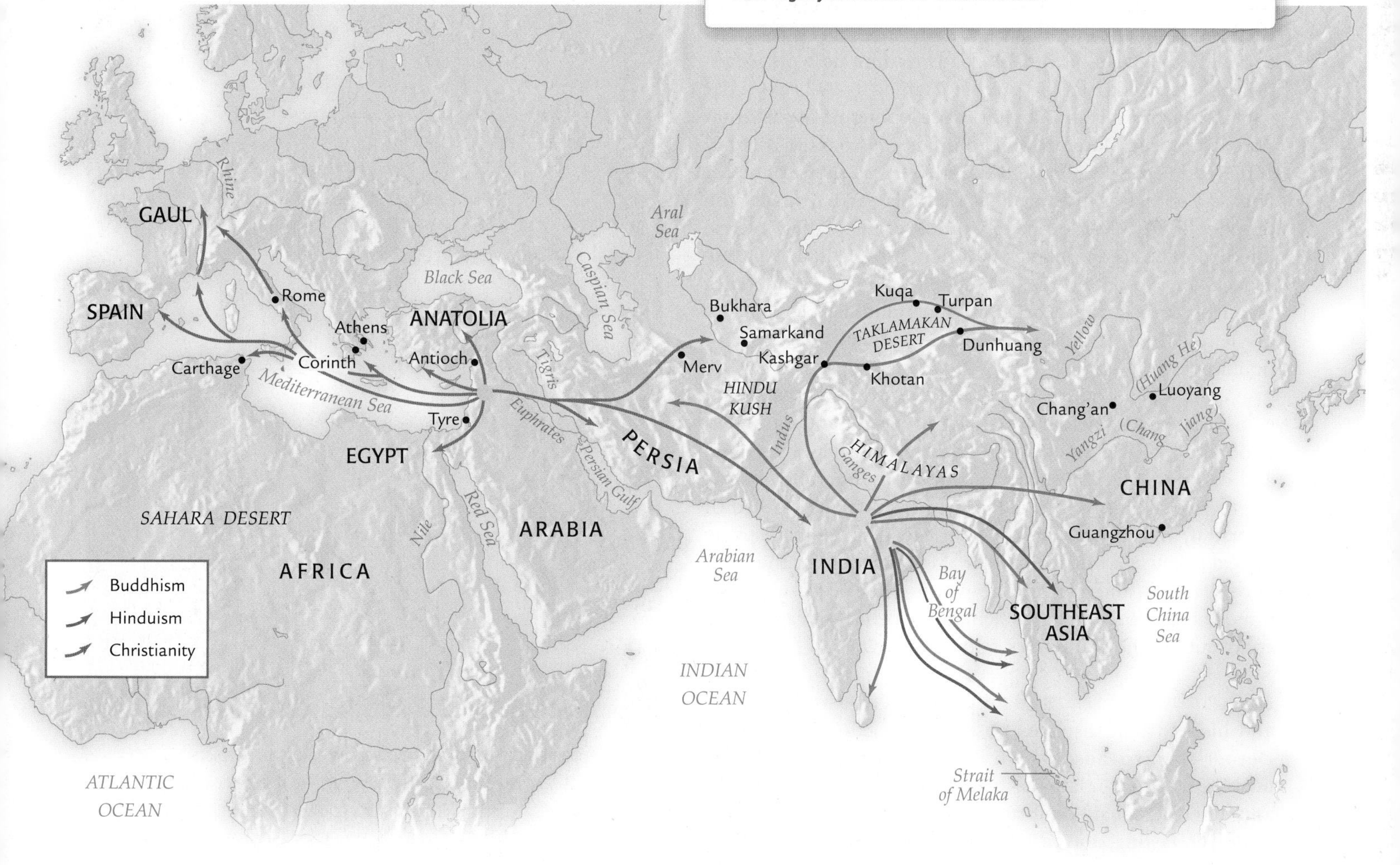

Buddhism
Hinduism
Christianity

communities of like-minded individuals who devoted their efforts to prayer and praise of God. Thus ascetic practices of Christians living in lands east of the Roman empire helped to inspire the formation of Christian monastic communities in the Mediterranean basin.

After the fifth century C.E., Christian communities in southwest Asia and the Mediterranean basin increasingly went separate ways. Most of the faithful in southwest Asia became Nestorians—followers of the Greek theologian Nestorius, who lived during the early fifth century and emphasized the human as opposed to the divine nature of Jesus. Mediterranean church authorities rejected Nestorius's views, and many of his disciples departed for Mesopotamia and Iran. They soon became prominent in local Christian communities, and they introduced a strong organizational framework to the church in southwest Asia. Although they had limited dealings with Mediterranean Christians, the Nestorians spread their beliefs east across the silk roads. Nestorian merchants took their version of Christianity with them on trade missions, and by the early seventh century they had established communities in central Asia, India, and China.

The Spread of Manichaeism

Mani and Manichaeism The explosive spread of Manichaeism dramatically illustrated how missionary religions made effective use of the silk roads trading network. Manichaeism derived from the prophet Mani (216–272 C.E.), a devout Zoroastrian from Babylon in Mesopotamia. Apart from Zoroastrianism, Mani drew deep influence from Christianity and Buddhism. He regarded Zarathustra as the prophet of Persia, Buddha as the prophet of India, and Jesus as the prophet of the Mediterranean world. Because of the intense interaction between peoples of different societies, Mani saw a need for a prophet for all humanity, and he promoted a blend of Zoroastrian, Christian, and Buddhist elements as a syncretic religion that would serve the needs of a cosmopolitan world.

Mani was a dualist: he viewed the world as the site of a cosmic struggle between the forces of light and darkness, good and evil. He associated light with spiritual awareness and darkness with the material world. He urged his followers to reject worldly pleasures, which entangled the spirit in matter, and rise toward the light. His doctrine had strong appeal because it offered a rational explanation for the presence of good and evil in the world while also providing a means for individuals to achieve personal salvation and contribute to the triumph of good over evil.

Manichaean Ethics Mani promoted an ascetic lifestyle and insisted that disciples observe high ethical standards. Devout Manichaeans, known as "the elect," abstained from marriage, sexual relations, fine clothing, meat, rich foods, and other personal comforts, dedicating themselves instead to prayer, fasting, and ritual observances. Less zealous Manichaeans, known as "hearers," led more conventional lives, but they followed a strict moral code and provided food and gifts to sustain the elect. All Manichaeans looked forward to individual salvation and eternal association with the forces of light and good.

Mani was a fervent missionary: he traveled widely to promote his beliefs, corresponded tirelessly with Manichaean adherents, and dispatched disciples to lands that he could not visit himself. He also created a Manichaean church with its own services, rituals, hymns, and liturgies. His doctrine attracted converts first in Mesopotamia, and before Mani's death it had spread throughout the Sasanid empire and into the eastern Mediterranean region. In spite of its asceticism, Manichaeism appealed especially strongly to merchants, who accepted the religion as hearers and supported the Manichaean church. By the end of the third century C.E., Manichaean communities had appeared in all the large cities and trading centers of the Roman empire.

A cave painting from about the seventh century C.E. depicts a group of devout Manichaean faithful, whose austere regimen called for them to dress in plain white garments and keep their hair uncut.

Decline of Manichaeism Manichaeism soon came under tremendous pressure. Zoroastrian leaders urged the Sasanid rulers to suppress Mani's movement as a threat to public order. Mani himself died in chains as a prisoner of the Sasanid emperor, who sought to use Zoroastrianism as a cultural foundation for the unification of his realm. Authorities in the Roman empire also persecuted Manichaeans, whom they suspected because of the religion's origins in the rival Sasanid empire. Indeed, during the fifth and sixth centuries, political authorities largely exterminated Manichaeism in the Mediterranean basin. Yet Manichaeism survived in central Asia, where it attracted converts among nomadic Turkish peoples who traded with merchants from China, India, and southwest Asia. Like Buddhism, Hinduism, and Christianity, then, Manichaeism relied on the trade routes of classical times to extend its influence to new lands and peoples.

The Spread of Epidemic Disease

While serving as routes for the distribution of trade goods and highways for the spread of religious beliefs, the roads and the sea lanes of the classical world also facilitated the movement of biological agents. The silk roads were the routes by which grapes, camels, and donkeys made their way from the Mediterranean region to China, while cherries, apricots, peaches, and walnuts traveled in the other direction, from central Asia and China to the Mediterranean. Alongside the fruits and nuts were some less welcome traveling companions—infectious and contagious diseases that sparked ferocious epidemics when they found their way to previously unexposed populations.

Information about human populations in classical times is scanty and full of gaps. Scholars often do not have records to work with and must draw inferences about population size from the area enclosed by city walls, the number of houses discovered in a settlement, the agricultural potential of a region, and similar considerations. As a result, population estimates for premodern societies are rough approximations rather than precise figures. Moreover, within a single society, individual regions often had very different demographic experiences. Nevertheless, even for classical times, the general outlines of population history are reasonably clear.

Epidemic Diseases During the second and third centuries C.E., the Han and Roman empires suffered large-scale outbreaks of epidemic disease. The most destructive diseases were probably smallpox and measles, and epidemics of bubonic plague may also have erupted. All three diseases are devastating when they break out in populations without resistance, immunity, or medicines to combat them. As disease ravaged the two empires, Chinese and Roman populations declined sharply.

During the reign of Augustus, the population of the Roman empire stood at about sixty million people. During the second century C.E., epidemics reduced Roman population by about one-quarter, to forty-five million. Most devastating was an outbreak of smallpox that spread throughout the Mediterranean basin during the years 165 to 180 C.E. The epidemic was especially virulent in cities, and it even claimed the life of the Roman emperor Marcus Aurelius (180 C.E.). In combination with war and invasions, continuing outbreaks caused a significant population decline during the third and fourth centuries: by 400 C.E. the number of Romans had fallen to perhaps forty million. During the fifth and early sixth centuries, the Roman population stabilized, but an epidemic of bubonic plague broke out in the mid-sixth century and caused a general population decline throughout the Mediterranean region.

Epidemics appeared slightly later in China than in the Mediterranean region. From fifty million people at the beginning of the millennium, Chinese population rose to sixty million in 200 C.E. As diseases found their way east, however, Chinese numbers fell back to fifty million by 400 C.E. and to forty-five million by 600 C.E. Thus by 600 C.E. both Mediterranean and Chinese populations had fallen by a quarter to a third from their high points during classical times.

Effects of Epidemic Diseases Demographic decline in turn brought economic and social change. Trade within the empires declined, and both the Chinese and the Roman economies contracted. Both economies also moved toward regional self-sufficiency: whereas previously the Chinese and Roman states had integrated the various regions of their empires into a larger network of trade and exchange, after about 200 C.E. they increasingly established several smaller regional economies that concentrated on their own needs instead of the larger imperial market. In the Roman empire, for example, the eastern Mediterranean regions of Anatolia, Egypt, and Greece continued to form a larger, integrated society, but regional economies increasingly emerged in western Mediterranean lands, including Italy, Gaul, Spain, and northwest Africa.

The demographic histories of classical Persia, India, and other lands are not as clear as they are for China and the Roman empire. Persia most likely experienced demographic, economic, and social problems similar to those that afflicted China and the Mediterranean basin. India may well have suffered from epidemic disease and population losses, although there is limited evidence for those troubles in south Asia. In

thinking about ENCOUNTERS

Silk Roads and Disease Roads
People who traded in silk also traded in germs. To what extent was the transmission of disease an inevitable result of long-distance travel and trade networks?

sources from the past

St. Cyprian on Epidemic Disease in the Roman Empire

St. Cyprian, bishop of Carthage, was an outspoken proponent of Christianity during the early and middle decades of the third century C.E. When epidemic disease struck the Roman empire in 251 C.E., imperial authorities blamed the outbreak on Christians who refused to honor pagan gods. Cyprian refuted that charge in his treatise On Mortality, *which described the symptoms of epidemic disease and reflected on its significance for the Christian community.*

It serves as validation of the [Christian] faith when the bowels loosen and drain the body's strength, when fever generated in bone marrow causes sores to break out in the throat, when continuous vomiting roils the intestines, when bloodshot eyes burn, when the feet or other bodily parts are amputated because of infection by putrefying disease, when through weakness caused by injuries to the body either mobility is impeded, or hearing is impaired, or sight is obscured. It requires enormous greatness of heart to struggle with resolute mind against so many onslaughts of destruction and death. It requires great loftiness to stand firm amidst the ruins of the human race, not to concede defeat with those who have no hope in God, but rather to rejoice and embrace the gift of the times. With Christ as our judge, we should receive this gift as the reward of his faith, as we vigorously affirm our faith and, having suffered, advance toward Christ by Christ's narrow path. . . .

Many of us [Christians] are dying in this epidemic—that is, many of us are being liberated from the world. The epidemic is a pestilence for the Jews and the pagans and the enemies of Christ, but for the servants of God it is a welcome event. True, without any discrimination, the just are dying alongside the unjust, but you should not imagine that the evil and the good face a common destruction. The just are called to refreshment, while the unjust are herded off to punishment: the faithful receive protection, while the faithless receive retribution. We are unseeing and ungrateful for divine favors, beloved brethren, and we do not recognize what is granted to us. . . .

How suitable and essential it is that this plague and pestilence, which seems so terrible and ferocious, probes the justice of every individual and examines the minds of the human race to determine whether the healthy care for the ill, whether relatives diligently love their kin, whether masters show mercy to their languishing slaves, whether physicians do not abandon those seeking their aid, whether the ferocious diminish their violence, whether the greedy in the fear of death extinguish the raging flames of their insatiable avarice, whether the proud bend their necks, whether the shameless mitigate their audacity, whether the rich will loosen their purse strings and give something to others as their loved ones perish all around them and as they are about to die without heirs.

For Further Reflection

- To what extent do you think St. Cyprian was effective in his efforts to bring inherited Christian teachings to bear on the unprecedented conditions he and his followers faced?

Source: Wilhelm von Hartel, ed. *S. Thasci Caecili Cypriani opera omnia* in *Corpus scriptorum ecclesiasticorum latinorum.* Vienna: 1868, vol. 3, pp. 305–6. (Translation by Jerry H. Bentley.)

east Asia and the Mediterranean basin, however, it is clear that epidemic disease seriously weakened Chinese and Roman societies. Indeed, epidemic disease contributed to serious instability in China after the collapse of the Han dynasty, and in weakening Mediterranean society, it helped bring about the decline and fall of the western Roman empire.

CHINA AFTER THE HAN DYNASTY

By the time epidemic diseases struck China, internal political problems had already begun to weaken the Han dynasty. By the late second century C.E., Han authorities had largely lost their ability to maintain order. Early in the third century C.E., the central government dissolved, and a series of autonomous regional kingdoms took the place of the Han state. With the disappearance of the Han dynasty, China experienced significant cultural change, most notably an increasing interest in Buddhism.

Internal Decay of the Han State

The Han dynasty collapsed largely because of internal problems that its rulers could not solve. One problem involved the development of factions within the ranks of the ruling elites. Marriage alliances between imperial and aristocratic families led to the formation of many factions whose members sought to advance their prospects in the imperial government and exclude others from important positions. That atmosphere led to constant infighting and backstabbing among the ruling elites, which in turn reduced the effectiveness of the central government.

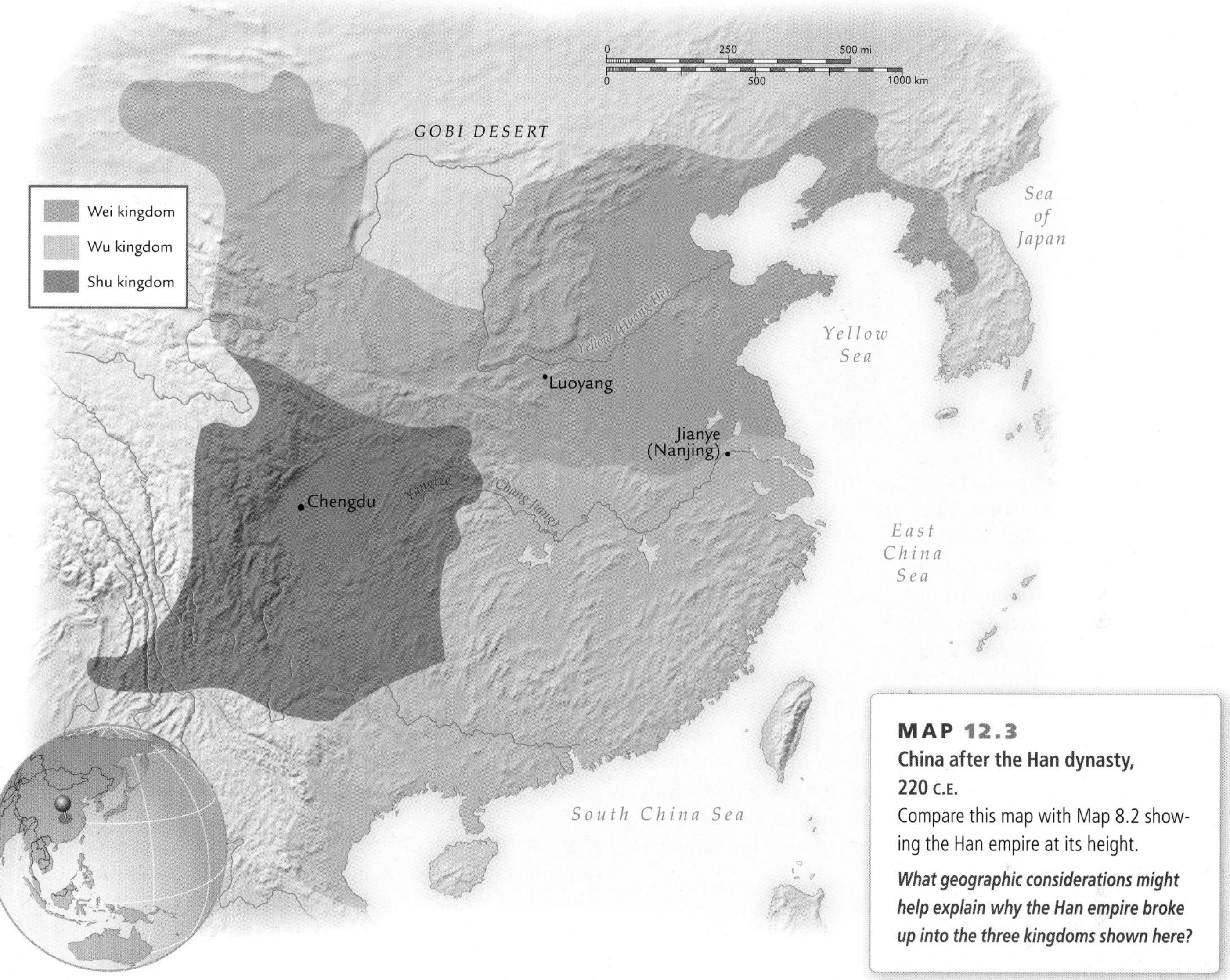

MAP 12.3
China after the Han dynasty, 220 C.E.
Compare this map with Map 8.2 showing the Han empire at its height.
What geographic considerations might help explain why the Han empire broke up into the three kingdoms shown here?

An even more difficult problem had to do with the perennial issue of land and its equitable distribution. At the turn of the millennium, the usurper Wang Mang had attempted to redistribute land in China, but his program did not survive his brief reign (9–23 C.E.). During the last two centuries of the Han dynasty, large landowners gained new influence in the government. They managed to reduce their share of taxes and shift the burden onto peasants. They even formed private armies to advance their class interests.

Peasant Rebellion Those developments provoked widespread unrest, particularly among peasants, who found themselves under increasing economic pressure with no means to influence the government. Pressures became particularly acute during the late second and third centuries when epidemics began to take their toll. In 184 C.E. peasant discontent fueled an immense uprising known as the Yellow Turban rebellion, so called because the rebels wore yellow headbands that represented the color of the Chinese earth and symbolized their peasant origins. Although authorities suppressed it after five years of fighting, the rebellion proved to be only the first in a series of insurrections that plagued the late Han dynasty.

Collapse of the Han Dynasty Meanwhile, Han generals increasingly usurped political authority. By 190 C.E. the Han emperor had become a mere puppet, and the generals effectively ruled the regions controlled by their armies. They allied with wealthy landowners of their regions and established themselves as warlords who maintained a kind of rough order based on force of arms. The generals continued to recognize an emperor for a short time, but in 220 C.E. they formally abolished the Han dynasty and divided the empire into three large kingdoms.

Once the dynasty had disappeared, large numbers of nomadic peoples migrated into China, especially the northern regions, and they helped to keep China disunited for more than 350 years. Between the fourth and sixth centuries C.E., nomadic peoples established large kingdoms that dominated much of northern China as well as the steppe lands.

After the collapse of the Han dynasty, China experienced social and economic difficulty. Wealthy classes often traveled in ox carts instead of more expensive, horse-drawn carriages. Archaeologists found this ceramic model of an ox cart in a tomb from the sixth century C.E.

Cultural Change in Post-Han China

In some ways, the centuries following the fall of the Han dynasty present a spectacle of chaos and disorder. One kingdom toppled another, only to fall in its turn to a temporary successor. War and nomadic invasions led to population decline in much of northern China. By the mid-fifth century, the region around Chang'an and Luoyang—the heartland of classical China—had experienced almost complete devastation because of armies that ravaged the region in search of food and plunder. Contemporaries reported that the Former Han capital of Chang'an had no more than one hundred households and that the Later Han capital of Luoyang resembled a trash heap more than a city.

Sinicization of Nomadic Peoples Beneath the disorderly surface of political events, however, several important social and cultural changes were taking place. First, nomadic peoples increasingly adapted to the Chinese environment. They took up agriculture and built permanent settlements. They married Chinese spouses and took Chinese names. They wore the clothes, ate the food, and adopted the customs of China. Some sought a formal Chinese education and became well versed in Chinese philosophy and literature. In short, nomadic peoples became increasingly sinicized, and as the generations passed, distinctions between peoples of nomadic and Chinese ancestry became less and less obvious. Partly because of that development, a new imperial dynasty was eventually able to reconstitute a centralized imperial state in north China.

Second, with the disintegration of political order, the Confucian tradition lost much of its credibility. The original goal of Confucius and his early followers was to find some means to move from chaos to stability during the Period of the Warring States. As long as Confucian methods and principles helped to maintain order, ruling elites and intellectual classes honored the Confucian tradition. When the Han dynasty collapsed, Confucianism seemed irrelevant.

Individuals who in earlier centuries might have committed themselves to Confucian values turned instead to Daoism and Buddhism. As in the Period of the Warring States, Daoism once again offered a way to find peace in a turbulent world. Originally, Daoism was a school of speculative philosophical thought that appealed mostly to an educated elite. After the fall of the Han, however, it became more a religious than a philosophical doctrine. Daoist sages not only promised salvation to those who observed their doctrines and rituals but also experimented with spices, herbs, and drugs to concoct elixirs or potions that supposedly conferred health and immortality. Daoism attracted widespread interest among a population afflicted by war and disease and became much more popular than before, especially because it faced less competition from the Confucian tradition.

Popularity of Buddhism Even more important than Daoism for Chinese cultural history was Buddhism. Until about the fourth century C.E., Buddhism was largely the faith of foreign merchants in China and attracted little interest on the part of native Chinese. After the fall of the Han empire, however, Buddhism received strong support from nomadic peoples who migrated into northern China and who in many cases had long been familiar with Buddhism in central Asia. Meanwhile, as a result of missionary efforts, the Indian faith began to attract a following among native Chinese as well. Indeed, between the fourth and sixth centuries C.E., Buddhism became well established in China. When a centralized imperial state took shape in the late sixth century C.E., Buddhism provided an important cultural foundation for the restoration of a unified political order.

THE FALL OF THE ROMAN EMPIRE

Moralists have often interpreted the fall of the Roman empire as a symbol of the transitory nature of human creations. Fascination with imperial Rome has encouraged the proliferation of theories—many of them quite silly—seeking to explain the fall of the empire as the result of some single, simple cause. By various accounts, the Roman empire declined and fell because of lead poisoning, radiation given off by bricks, immorality, or the rise of Christianity. Notwithstanding the zeal with which proponents have promoted pet theories, there was no single cause for the decline and fall of the Roman empire. Instead, a combination of internal problems and external pressures weakened the empire and brought an end to Roman authority in the western portion of the empire, whereas imperial rule continued until the fifteenth century C.E. in the eastern Mediterranean. In the Mediterranean basin as in China, imperial weakness and collapse coincided with significant cultural change, notably the increasing popularity of Christianity.

Sculpture of the tetrarchs, or four corulers of the Roman empire, during the late third century C.E.; from left, Galerius, Constantius, Diocletian, and Maximian. Do you think the tetrarchs were really such close companions as this sculpture suggests?

Internal Decay in the Roman Empire

The Barracks Emperors As in the case of the Han dynasty, internal political problems go a long way toward explaining the fall of the Roman empire. Like their Han counterparts, the Roman emperors faced internal opposition. During the half century from 235 to 284 C.E., there were twenty-six recognized emperors (and many others who staked temporary claims to the imperial office). Known as the "barracks emperors," most of them were generals who seized power, held it briefly, and then suddenly lost it when they were displaced by rivals or by their mutinous troops. Not surprisingly, most of the barracks emperors died violently: only one is known for sure to have succumbed to natural causes.

Apart from divisions and factions, the Roman empire faced problems because of its sheer size. Even during the best of times, when the emperors could count on abundant revenues and disciplined armed forces, the sprawling empire posed a challenge for central governors. After the third century, as epidemics spread throughout the empire and its various regions moved toward local, self-sufficient economies, the empire as a whole became increasingly unmanageable.

Diocletian The emperor Diocletian (reigned 284–305 C.E.) attempted to deal with this problem by dividing the empire into two administrative districts. The eastern district included the wealthy lands of Anatolia, Syria, Egypt, and Greece, and the western district embraced Italy, Gaul, Spain, Britain, and north Africa. A coemperor ruled each district with the aid of a powerful lieutenant, and Diocletian hoped the four officials, known as the *tetrarchs,* would be able to administer the vast empire more effectively than an individual emperor could. Diocletian was a skillful administrator. He managed to bring Rome's many armies, including unpredictable maverick forces, under firm imperial control. He also tried to deal with a crumbling economy by strengthening the imperial currency, forcing the government to adjust its expenditures to its income, and imposing price caps to dampen inflation. His economic measures were less successful than his administrative reforms, but they helped stabilize an economy ravaged by half a century of civil unrest.

Constantine Yet Diocletian's reforms also encouraged ambition among the four top corulers and their generals, and his retirement from the imperial office in 305 C.E. set off a round of internal struggles and bitter civil war. Already in 306 C.E. Constantine, son of Diocletian's coruler Constantius, moved to stake his claim as sole emperor. By 313 C.E. he had defeated most of his enemies, although he overcame his last rivals only in 324 C.E. Once he had consolidated his grip on power, Constantine ordered the construction of a new capital city, Constantinople, at a strategic site overlooking the Bosporus, the strait linking the Black Sea to the Sea of Marmara and beyond to the wealthy eastern Mediterranean.

After 330 C.E. Constantinople became the capital of a united Roman empire.

Constantine was an able emperor. With the reunion of the eastern and western districts of the empire, however, he and his successors faced the same sort of administrative difficulties that Diocletian had attempted to solve by dividing the empire. As population declined and the economy contracted, emperors found it increasingly difficult to marshal the resources needed to govern and protect the vast Roman empire. The need for protection against external threats became especially acute during the late fourth and early fifth centuries C.E.

Germanic Invasions and the Fall of the Western Roman Empire

Apart from internal problems, the Roman empire faced several formidable military threats. One arose on the empire's southeastern frontiers when the Sasanid dynasty toppled the Parthians in 224 C.E. and established a powerful state in Iran. Sasanid and Roman forces clashed repeatedly in Anatolia, Syria, and Mesopotamia as each side sought to consolidate its authority in border regions. Some of the conflicts dealt devastating blows. In the year 260 C.E., the Roman emperor Valerian fell captive to Sasanid forces. He spent his last few years at the Sasanid court in Ctesiphon, where his captors forced him to stoop and serve as a mounting stool when the Sasanid king wanted to ride his horse. (After his death, the Sasanids preserved Valerian's skin as a memento of their victory over the Romans.) Romans and Sasanids engaged in intermittent hostilities until the sixth century C.E., but a series of buffer states between the two empires reduced the intensity of conflict after the third century.

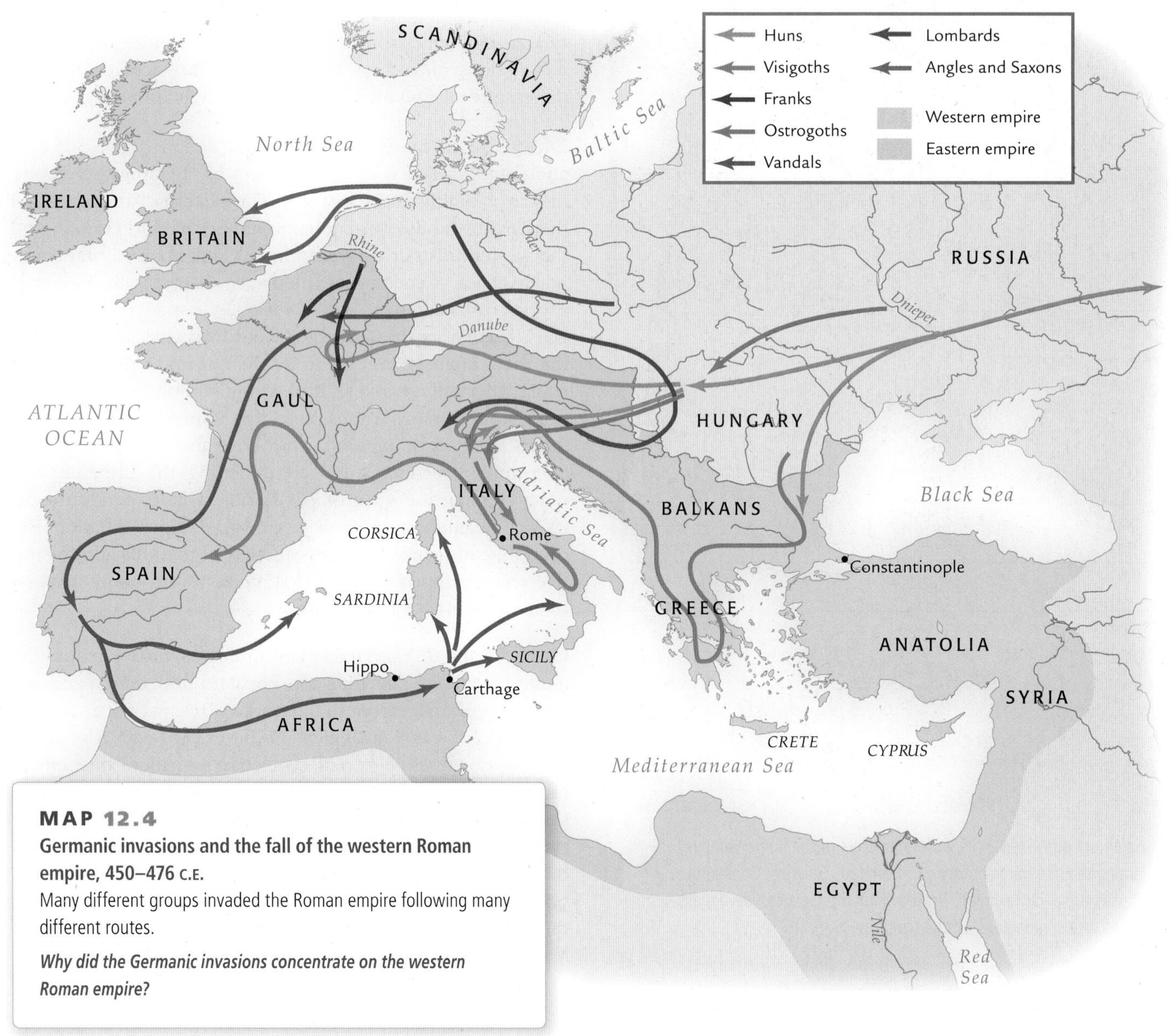

MAP 12.4
Germanic invasions and the fall of the western Roman empire, 450–476 C.E.
Many different groups invaded the Roman empire following many different routes.

Why did the Germanic invasions concentrate on the western Roman empire?

In this relief sculpture carved in the second century C.E., a clean-shaven Roman soldier battles bearded Germanic forces along the Danube river.

Migratory Germanic peoples posed a more immediate and serious military threat to the Roman empire. Indeed, during the fifth century C.E., Germanic invasions brought an end to Roman authority in the western half of the empire, although imperial rule survived for an additional millennium in the eastern Mediterranean.

Germanic Migrations Germanic peoples had migrated from their homelands in northern Europe and lived on the eastern and northern borders of the Roman empire since the second century C.E. Most notable were the Visigoths, who came originally from Scandinavia and Russia. Like the nomadic peoples who moved into northern China after the fall of the Han dynasty, the Visigoths settled, adopted agriculture, and drew deep inspiration from Roman society. They adapted Roman law to the needs of their society, for example, converted to Christianity, and translated the Bible into the Visigothic language. They also contributed large numbers of soldiers to the Roman armies. In the interests of social order, however, the Romans discouraged settlement of the Visigoths and other Germanic peoples within the empire, preferring that they constitute buffer societies outside imperial borders.

The Huns During the late fourth century, the relationship between Visigoths and Romans changed dramatically when the nomadic Huns began an aggressive westward migration from their homeland in central Asia. The Huns spoke a Turkish language, and they probably were cousins of the nomadic Xiongnu who inhabited the central Asian steppe lands west of China. During the mid-fifth century C.E., the warrior-king Attila organized the Huns into a virtually unstoppable military juggernaut. Under Attila, the Huns invaded Hungary, probed Roman frontiers in the Balkan region, menaced Gaul and northern Italy, and attacked Germanic peoples living on the borders of the Roman empire.

Collapse of the Western Roman Empire Attila did not create a set of political institutions or a state structure, and the Huns disappeared as a political and military force soon after his death in 453 C.E. By that time, however, the Huns had placed such pressure on Visigoths, Ostrogoths, Vandals, Franks, and other Germanic peoples that they streamed en masse into the Roman empire in search of refuge. Once inside imperial boundaries, they encountered little effective resistance and moved around almost at will. They established settlements throughout the western half of the empire—Italy, Gaul, Spain, Britain, and north Africa—where populations were less dense than in the eastern Mediterranean. Under the command of Alaric, the Visigoths even stormed and sacked Rome in 410 C.E. By the middle of the fifth century, the western part of the Roman empire was in shambles. In 476 C.E. imperial authority came to an ignominious end when the Germanic general Odovacer deposed Romulus Augustulus, the last of the Roman emperors in the western half of the empire.

Unlike the Han dynasty, the Roman empire did not entirely disintegrate: imperial authority survived for another millennium in the eastern half of the empire, known after the fifth century C.E. as the Byzantine empire. In the western half, however, Roman authority gradually dissolved, and nomadic peoples built successor states in regions formerly subject to Rome. Vandals and then Visigoths governed Spain, Franks ruled Gaul, Angles and Saxons invaded Britain, and Italy fell under the sway of a variety of peoples, including Visigoths, Vandals, and Lombards.

The colossal head of Constantine is one of the few remaining fragments from a marble statue that originally stood about 14 meters (46 feet) tall.

Cultural Change in the Late Roman Empire

In the Roman empire, as in China, the collapse of the imperial state coincided with important social and cultural changes. The Germanic peoples who toppled the empire looked to their own traditions for purposes of organizing society and government. When they settled in the regions of the former empire, however, they absorbed a good deal of Roman influence. They adapted Roman law to their needs, for example, thus preserving one of the most important features of Roman society. Over time, the mingling of Roman and Germanic traditions led to the emergence of an altogether new society—medieval Europe.

Prominence of Christianity

Christianity was perhaps the most prominent survivor of the western Roman empire. During the fourth century C.E., several developments enhanced its influence throughout the Mediterranean basin. In the first place, Christianity won recognition as a legitimate religion in the Roman empire. In 312 C.E., while seeking to establish himself as sole Roman emperor, Constantine experienced a vision that impressed on him the power of the Christian God. He believed that the Christian God helped him to prevail over his rivals, and in 313 he promulgated the Edict of Milan, which allowed Christians to practice their faith openly in the Roman empire. At some point during his reign, perhaps after his edict, Constantine converted to Christianity, and in the late fourth century the emperor Theodosius made Christianity the official religion of the Roman empire. By the mid-fourth century, Christians held important political and military positions, and imperial sponsorship helped their proponents attract more converts than ever before.

Christianity also began to attract thoughtful and talented converts who articulated a Christian message for the intellectual elites of the Roman empire. The earliest Christians had come largely from the ranks of ordinary working people, and their doctrine struck philosophers and the educated elites as both unsophisticated and unbelievable. During its first three centuries, Christianity grew as a popular religion of salvation favored by the masses, rather than as a reasoned doctrine of intellectual substance. During the fourth century, however, intellectual elites began to take more interest in Christianity.

St. Augustine

The most important and influential of these figures was St. Augustine (354–430 C.E.), bishop of the north African city of Hippo (modern-day Annaba in Algeria). Augustine had a fine education, and he was conversant with the leading intellectual currents of the day. During his youth he drew great inspiration from Stoicism and Platonism, and for nine years he belonged to a community of Manichaeans. Eventually, he became disillusioned with both Hellenistic philosophy and Manichaeism, and in 387 C.E., while studying in Italy, he converted to Christianity. For the remainder of his life, he worked to reconcile Christianity with Greek and Roman philosophical traditions, especially Platonism, and to articulate Christianity in terms that were familiar and persuasive to the educated classes. More than any others, Augustine's writings made Christianity an intellectually respectable alternative to Hellenistic philosophy and popular religions of salvation.

Besides winning the right to practice their religion openly and attracting intellectual talent, Christian leaders constructed an institutional apparatus that transformed a popular religion of salvation into a powerful church. In the absence of recognized leadership, the earliest Christians generated a range of conflicting and sometimes contradictory doctrines. Some taught that Jesus was a mortal human being, others that he was a god, and yet others that he was both human and divine. Some allowed women to serve as priests and attributed great powers to Jesus' mother, Mary, and others restricted church offices to men and conceived of Christian deities as males.

A manuscript illumination depicts St. Augustine holding a copy of his most famous work, *The City of God,* which sought to explain the meaning of history and the world from a Christian point of view.

The New Testament and the Emergence of Orthodox Christianity Early Christians might well have continued to express their understandings of their faith in individual ways. During the third and fourth centuries, however, as the Roman empire experienced political turmoil and underwent administrative changes, some church leaders sought doctrinal stability and worked to define essential tenets that all Christians must accept. As Christians became more prominent in the Roman empire, state authorities also promoted efforts to standardize teachings. Emperor Constantine himself pushed for a clear statement of Christian doctrine that he hoped would create a foundation for cultural unity in the Roman empire.

In search of clearly defined doctrine, church leaders conducted intense debates about the quality and authority of the numerous writings that the earliest Christians had generated. Those writings, which numbered in the scores or perhaps even hundreds, included gospels that told the story of Jesus' life, epistles that outlined the authors' views of moral and religious issues, and historical accounts that offered interpretations of early Christian experiences from different perspectives. By the late fourth century, church leaders were reaching consensus that twenty-seven short writings were more authoritative than the others, and they recognized these writings as canonical scriptures known later as the New Testament. By adopting a small number of writings as canonical, church leaders rejected many others as misguided, untruthful, or even heretical. As a result, they profoundly influenced the development of doctrine that most Christian authorities eventually came to recognize as the orthodox or correct teaching.

The Institutional Church To standardize their faith, Christian leaders also instituted a hierarchy of church officials. At the top were five religious authorities—the bishop of Rome and the **patriarchs** of Jerusalem, Antioch, Alexandria, and Constantinople—who resided in the most important spiritual and political centers of the Roman empire. These five authorities wielded roughly equal influence in the larger Christian community, although the bishop of Rome enjoyed somewhat greater prestige than the others. (His enhanced status derived both from his claim to be the spiritual descendant of Jesus' chief disciple, St. Peter, and from the fact that he had his seat at Rome, the original imperial capital.)

Subordinate to the five principal authorities were bishops, who presided over religious affairs in their districts, known as dioceses, which included all the prominent cities of the Roman empire. When theological disputes arose, the patriarchs and bishops assembled in church councils to determine which views would prevail as official doctrine. The councils at Nicaea (325 C.E.) and Chalcedon (451 C.E.), for example, took up the difficult and contentious issue of Jesus' nature. Delegates at the councils proclaimed that

thinking about TRADITIONS

The Evolution of Christianity

In the first century C.E., Christianity could claim only small numbers of believers from humble social classes. By the fourth century, a rapidly growing religious movement had attracted even emperors to its community. How did Christianity extend its appeal to political elites? How did Christianity change as a religious tradition between the first and the fourth centuries?

patriarch (PAY-tree-ahrk)

Jesus was both fully human and fully divine at the same time, in contrast to Nestorians, Arians, and other Christian groups who held that Jesus was either primarily human or primarily divine. The decisions and decrees of the church councils did not put an end to all debate, nor did they prevent new divisions and new grounds of contention from arising. Nevertheless, by defining the doctrines that most church authorities regarded as orthodox, council delegates left enduring influences on the beliefs and values of Christianity.

As Roman imperial authority crumbled, the bishop of Rome, known as the pope (from the Latin *papa,* meaning "father"), emerged as spiritual leader of Christian communities in the western regions of the empire. As the only sources of established and recognized authority, the popes and the bishops of other important cities organized local government and defensive measures for their communities. They also mounted missionary campaigns to convert Germanic peoples to Christianity. Although Roman imperial authority disappeared, Roman Christianity survived and served as a foundation for cultural unity in lands that had formerly made up the western half of the Roman empire.

inperspective

By 500 C.E. classical societies in Persia, China, India, and the Mediterranean basin had either collapsed or fallen into decline. Yet all the classical societies left rich legacies that shaped political institutions, social orders, and cultural traditions for centuries to come. Moreover, by sponsoring commercial and cultural relations between different peoples, the classical societies laid a foundation for intensive and systematic cross-cultural interaction in later times. After the third century C.E., the decline of the Han and Roman empires resulted in less activity over the silk roads than in the preceding three hundred years. But the trade routes survived, and when a new series of imperial states reestablished order throughout much of Eurasia and north Africa in the sixth century C.E., the peoples of the eastern hemisphere avidly resumed their crossing of cultural boundary lines in the interests of trade and communication. ●

CHRONOLOGY

3rd century B.C.E.	Spread of Buddhism and Hinduism to southeast Asia
2nd century B.C.E.	Introduction of Buddhism to central Asia
139–126 B.C.E.	Travels of Zhang Qian in central Asia
1st century B.C.E.	Introduction of Buddhism to China
2nd century C.E.	Spread of Christianity in the Mediterranean basin and southwest Asia
184 C.E.	Yellow Turban rebellion
216–272 C.E.	Life of Mani
220 C.E.	Collapse of the Han dynasty
284–305 C.E.	Reign of Diocletian
313–337 C.E.	Reign of Constantine
313 C.E.	Edict of Milan and the legalization of Christianity in the Roman empire
325 C.E.	Council of Nicaea
451 C.E.	Council of Chalcedon
476 C.E.	Collapse of the western Roman empire

Assessing AP Themes

1. What were/are the core beliefs, institutions, gender roles, and reach/spread of each of the world religions (including Islam)?
2. How did imperial states keep control of vast amounts of land and multi-ethnic populations?
3. What causes empires to collapse? Long-term, medium-term, short-term problems? Internal/external problems?
4. Where were the transregional trade routes (land and sea) located and what technologies were necessary for trade to flourish?
5. Who and what moved along the main transregional trade routes in this era? What were the significant consequences of these networks of exchange?

For Further Reading

Thomas J. Barfield. *The Perilous Frontier: Nomadic Empires and China.* Cambridge, Mass., 1989. Provocative study of the Xiongnu and other central Asian peoples.

Jerry H. Bentley. *Old World Encounters: Cross-Cultural Contacts and Exchanges in Pre-Modern Times.* New York, 1993. Studies the spread of cultural and religious traditions before 1500 C.E.

Peter Brown. *The Making of Late Antiquity.* Cambridge, Mass., 1978. Brilliant and evocative analysis of the cultural and religious history of the late Roman empire.

———. *The World of Late Antiquity, A.D. 150–750.* London, 1971. Well-illustrated essay concentrating on social and cultural themes.

Averil Cameron. *The Later Roman Empire, A.D. 284–430.* Cambridge, Mass., 1993. A lively synthesis.

———. *The Mediterranean World in Late Antiquity, A.D. 395–600.* London, 1993. Like its companion volume just cited, a well-informed synthesis.

Philip D. Curtin. *Cross-Cultural Trade in World History.* New York, 1984. A synthetic work that concentrates on merchant communities in distant lands and their roles in facilitating cross-cultural trade.

Edward Gibbon. *The Decline and Fall of the Roman Empire.* Many editions available. A classic account, still well worth reading, by a masterful historical stylist of the eighteenth century.

C. D. Gordon, ed. *The Age of Attila: Fifth-Century Byzantium and the Barbarians.* Ann Arbor, 1972. Translations of primary sources on the society and history of nomadic and migratory peoples.

Peter Heather. *The Fall of the Roman Empire: A New History of Rome and the Barbarians.* New York, 2007. A well-written synthesis.

Mark Edward Lewis. *China between Empires: The Northern and Southern Dynasties.* Cambridge, Mass., 2009. Discusses social and cultural change in China after the collapse of the Han dynasty.

Samuel Hugh Moffett. *A History of Christianity in Asia,* vol. 1. San Francisco, 1992. An important volume that surveys the spread of early Christianity east of the Roman empire.

Elaine Pagels. *Beyond Belief: The Secret Gospel of Thomas.* New York, 2003. Discusses the emergence of orthodox Christianity and the recognition of the New Testament as a body of canonical writings.

Joseph A. Tainter. *The Collapse of Complex Societies.* Cambridge, 1988. Scholarly review of theories and evidence bearing on the fall of empires and societies.

Jonathan Tucker. *The Silk Road: Art and History.* London, 2003. Lavishly illustrated volume exploring silk roads history and geography.

Mortimer Wheeler. *Flames over Persepolis.* New York, 1968. Well-illustrated volume dealing with the interactions of Greek, Persian, and Indian peoples during the Hellenistic era.

Roderick Whitfield, Susan Whitfield, and Neville Agnew. *Cave Temples of Mogao: Art and History on the Silk Road.* Los Angeles, 2000. Excellent brief discussion of the cave temples and archaeological remains at Dunhuang.

Susan Whitfield. *Life along the Silk Road.* Berkeley, 1999. Focuses on the experiences of ten individuals who lived or traveled along the silk roads.

Francis Wood. *The Silk Road: Two Thousand Years in the Heart of Asia.* Berkeley, 2002. A brilliantly illustrated volume discussing the history of the silk roads from antiquity to the twentieth century.

State of the World

A World with Capitals and Empires, Roads and Sea Lanes, Philosophies and Churches

Following the adoption of agriculture, the early complex societies demonstrated the remarkable potential of the human species. Building on foundations laid by the early complex societies, the classical societies scaled the size of human communities and the range of human influence up to dimensions that their ancestors could hardly have imagined. They inherited forms of social organization and techniques of statecraft from the early complex societies, but they made adjustments that enabled them to extend their reach far beyond individual regions to distant lands and peoples. The Achaemenid, Han, and Roman empires, for example, all borrowed forms of social organization from their predecessors, but all of them also dwarfed their forerunners and built impressive capital cities from which they supervised sprawling empires and held enormous territories together for centuries at a time.

The classical societies grew to such large geographic proportions that they all found it necessary to devote resources to the construction of roads and the discovery of reliable routes over the neighboring seas. Although expensive to build and maintain, transportation and communications networks served the rulers of classical societies as links between their capitals and the distant reaches of their empires. Roads and sea lanes functioned as the nerves of the classical societies.

Transportation and communications networks were not captives of individual societies. They eventually pointed beyond the boundaries of individual societies and offered access to a larger world. Rulers originally built roads to facilitate communications between their capitals and their provinces—and, if necessary, to send their armed forces to put down rebellions or ensure implementation of their policies. It is possible, however, that merchants made better use of the magnificent road systems of classical societies than did the rulers themselves. Merchants tied regions of the classical societies together by linking producers and consumers. Moreover, they put the classical societies in communication with one another by jumping their frontiers and creating trading relationships across much of the eastern hemisphere.

Merchants and their trade goods shared the roads and the sea lanes with other travelers, including agricultural crops, domesticated animals, and disease pathogens. Some of their more prominent traveling companions, though, were missionaries spreading the word about their beliefs. Building on traditions of writing and reflection inherited from their forerunners, the classical societies all generated cultural and religious traditions whose influences resonate more than two thousand years later. Confucianism, Buddhism, Greek science, rational philosophy, and Christianity have all changed dramatically since the time of their founders, none of whom would recognize their modern-day descendants. Nevertheless, their cultural and religious traditions have profoundly shaped the course of world history.

Rulers of the classical empires built the roads and sponsored exploration of the sea lanes, but merchants and missionaries were equal partners in the construction of the classical era of world history.

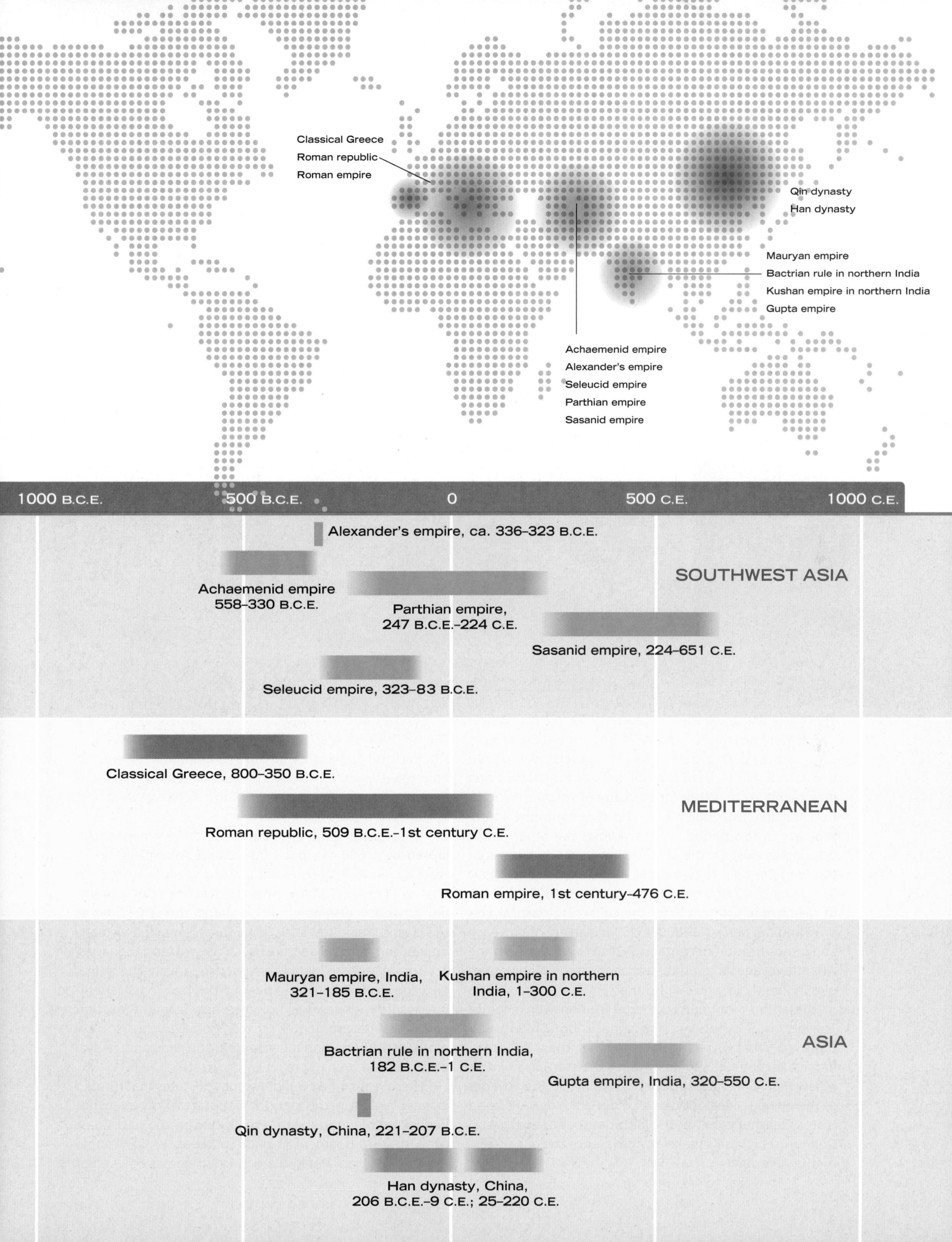
Classical Greece
Roman republic
Roman empire
Qin dynasty
Han dynasty
Mauryan empire
Bactrian rule in northern India
Kushan empire in northern India
Gupta empire
Achaemenid empire
Alexander's empire
Seleucid empire
Parthian empire
Sasanid empire
1000 B.C.E.
500 B.C.E.
0
500 C.E.
1000 C.E.
Alexander's empire, ca. 336–323 B.C.E.
SOUTHWEST ASIA
Achaemenid empire
558–330 B.C.E.
Parthian empire,
247 B.C.E.–224 C.E.
Sasanid empire, 224–651 C.E.
Seleucid empire, 323–83 B.C.E.
Classical Greece, 800–350 B.C.E.
MEDITERRANEAN
Roman republic, 509 B.C.E.–1st century C.E.
Roman empire, 1st century–476 C.E.
Mauryan empire, India,
321–185 B.C.E.
Kushan empire in northern
India, 1–300 C.E.
ASIA
Bactrian rule in northern India,
182 B.C.E.–1 C.E.
Gupta empire, India, 320–550 C.E.
Qin dynasty, China, 221–207 B.C.E.
Han dynasty, China,
206 B.C.E.–9 C.E.; 25–220 C.E.

part 3

THE POSTCLASSICAL ERA, 500 TO 1000 C.E.

This textbook uses a different dating (periodization) system than the AP World History Curriculum uses. In the AP Curriculum, Period 3 covers events from c. 600 to c. 1450—from the collapses of the world's first major empires to just *before* the age of Atlantic exploration starting with Columbus. The two hemispheres are separate in this period; neither knows the other places or peoples exist. In this text, however, the authors split this long period into two parts, Part 3 and Part 4. In Part 3, Bentley and Zeigler emphasize c. 500–c. 1000 as an era of major readjustment after the collapsing classical empires and the period c. 1000–c. 1500 as an era of outreach and intensification of contacts, which concludes with the Atlantic voyages that ultimately connect the globe's peoples in Part 4. So who's right, the AP World History folks or the authors of your textbook? The answer is, both! The historical events are the same in both interpretations. What differs is the emphasis; the AP Curriculum makes the Columbian voyages the starting point of a new Period 4 and Bentley and Zeigler see the voyages as the obvious conclusion of an older era. Your AP World History teacher can choose which date-set or interpretation to use; it won't make any difference to your success on the AP exam.

The period c. 600 to c. 1450 is often called the "Post-Classical" era because the themes from Period 2 (the classical era) are continued and amplified in Period 3. Your job is to track the continuities between Period 2 and Period 3 very carefully, while paying attention to the new features of the era.

The classical empires in Eurasia and the Americas collapsed by c. 600 C.E., but what replaced them? Some were replaced by new-and-improved versions of the old classical empires. Many post-classical imperial governments were reassembled along almost the same lines as the classical empires, social structures remained virtually intact, and cultural features such as written languages, art forms, and religions remained relatively the same. The "new-and-improved" part of the post-classical empires came with new technologies, new forms of taxation and other governmental powers, some tweaks to religious institutions, and much more trade and contact with other lands than had previously occurred.

There were, however, new types of states that formed in new places in this period. City-states flourished not just in the Mediterranean region, but on the East Coast of Africa, Mesoamerica, and Southeast Asia. People on the Arabian Peninsula launched massive wars of conquest, creating an Arab-speaking, predominantly Muslim world (called Dar al Islam) that stretched from the Iberian peninsula to western China, with the entire areas ruled, for a while, by a caliph. The Mongols, Central Asian pastoralists, controlled much of Eurasia for a time, ruled by interrelated khans. Nothing so grand replaced the fallen empires of Western Rome and Gupta India. Peoples in both regions settled on small kingdoms or principalities as a way to rule rather than an empire. HTS 3 In AP World History, you will need to know the locations of these states, the specifics of how they were ruled, and how states were connected to each other (peacefully or not).

Trade routes are as important as political rearrangements in Period 3. HTS 2 Although people in Afro-Eurasia and the Americas remained separate from each other in this period, within each hemisphere many more people and much more merchandise moved along trade routes. HTS 1 You will have to know the specifics of who and what was moving along these routes, and why. What were the new agricultural and transportation technologies and products? Who were the wealthy consumers with tastes for luxury goods? Who and where were the innovative merchants and trade organizations? Which governments sponsored commercial policies (minting coins and paper money) and useful infrastructure projects, like roads and canals? And while you're at it, watch out for the invaders—the Vikings, the Mongols, the Arabs, the Turkic peoples, the European Crusaders, the Mexica/Aztec. What important roles did they play, for better or worse, in the short-run and the long-run of world history?

HTS 2 It might useful to think of a spider's web when you evaluate the effects of massively increasing trade, which are both far-reaching and interconnected. For example, powerful new trading cities were created, in which foreign merchants set up communities. As a result there was a cross-fertilization of artistic, religious, linguistic, and cultural traditions between newcomers and inhabitants. Technology and science spread to new lands, creating powerful changes. Gunpowder weapons spread from China by the Mongol conquests through Dar al Islam, and from there into western Europe. Indian, Persian, Arab, and Greek science, math, and technologies located in universities and libraries within Dar al Islam slowly trickled into western Europe and formed the backbone of the Renaissance. Foods, diseases, and animals were transported by merchants from their places of origins to new lands, thereby dramatically changing agriculture and often dramatically affecting birth and death rates.

Merchants, missionaries, migrants, and military conquerors (the 4 Ms) spread religions and languages to new places. These religions and languages often were mixed (synthesized) and reinterpreted by the people in the visited or conquered lands. There are lots of examples of this cultural synthesis in Period 3, and AP students are asked frequently to explain the hows and whys and the significances of these syncretic (mixing or blending) processes. There are great architectural, literary, and artistic documents that illustrate this blending; they are important to AP World History, so watch for them in the photographs and document selections in the text.

It should be clear by now that you need to focus on the reasons for and consequences of increasing trade, contact, and wealth, but don't forget the people. HTS 3 As you go through these chapters, pay attention to what sorts of people do the work—who are the merchants, laborers, bankers, soldiers and sailors, and slaves? Watch for the new forms of coerced or forced labor developed in this period, especially serfdom and the mit'a system. Where do these people and their work "fit" into their society? How is one's position on the social ladder determined (who's on top, who's on bottom)? How do women fare in these post-classical societies? What was considered "women's work" and how much influence or power did women of different classes have on the "men's work"? Do newly-introduced religious beliefs improve or suppress the influence of women in a society? And always keep an eye on the pastoralist peoples—the Mongols, the Bantu, the Arabs, and Berbers; they are still big players in wars and trade.

HTS 1 More written documents have survived from post-classical period, and the ones that are highlighted in AP World History tend be travelers' writings. Why? Because these travelers comment on the people and practices in foreign lands, and they can tell us a lot about the extent of intercultural knowledge and understanding.

Finally, AP World History students have to understand the continuing importance of cities. HTS 3 Different cities have different missions in different societies. Much like comparing empires, it's possible to compare cities. Why do they rise and fall? Did the religious leaders in the region locate themselves in cities, and if so, why? Who ruled the cities, and were the cities important because they were political centers (capitals), or commercial or religious centers? Who lived in the cities, and where did they come from? Be prepared to explain the religious, commercial (trade), governmental, and cultural functions of at least two major cities in this period.

The Expansive Realm of Islam

chapter 13

A sixteenth-century Turkish manuscript depicts pilgrims praying at Mecca in the mosque surrounding the Ka'ba.

EYEWITNESS:
Season of the Mecca Pilgrimage

In 632 C.E. the prophet Muhammad visited his native city of Mecca from his home in exile at Medina, and in doing so he set an example that devout Muslims have sought to emulate ever since. Today the *hajj*—the holy pilgrimage to Mecca—draws Muslims by the hundreds of thousands from all parts of the world to Saudi Arabia. Each year Muslims travel to Mecca by land, sea, and air to make the pilgrimage and visit the holy sites of Islam.

In centuries past the numbers of pilgrims were smaller, but their observance of the hajj was no less conscientious. By the ninth century, pilgrimage had become so popular that Muslim rulers went to some lengths to meet the needs of travelers passing through their lands. With the approach of the pilgrimage season—the last month of the Islamic lunar calendar—crowds gathered at major trading centers such as Baghdad, Damascus, and Cairo. There they lived in tent cities, surviving on food and water provided by government officials, until they could join caravans bound for Mecca. Muslim rulers invested considerable sums in the maintenance of roads, wells, cisterns, and lodgings that accommodated pilgrims—as well as castles and police forces that protected travelers—on their journeys to Mecca and back.

The hajj was not only solemn observance but also an occasion for joy and celebration. Muslim rulers and wealthy pilgrims often made lavish gifts to caravan companions and others they met en route to Mecca. During her famous hajj of 976–977, for example, the Mesopotamian princess Jamila bint Nasir al-Dawla provided food and fresh green vegetables for her fellow pilgrims and furnished five hundred camels for handicapped travelers. She also purchased freedom for five hundred slaves and distributed fifty thousand fine robes among the common people of Mecca.

Most pilgrims did not have the resources to match Jamila's generosity, but for common travelers, too, the hajj became a special occasion. Merchants and craftsmen made acquaintances and arranged business deals with pilgrims from other lands. Students and scholars exchanged ideas during their weeks of traveling together. For all pilgrims, participation in ritual activities lent new meaning and significance to their faith.

The word *Islam* means "submission," signifying obedience to the rule and will of Allah, the only deity recognized in the strictly monotheistic Islamic religion. An individual who accepts the Islamic faith is a *Muslim,* meaning "one who has submitted." Though it began as one man's expression of unqualified faith in Allah, Islam quickly attracted followers and took on political and social as well as religious significance. During its first century, Islam reached far beyond its Arabian homeland, bringing Sasanid Persia and parts of the Byzantine empire into its orbit. By the eighth century the realm of Islam and the Byzantine empire stood as political and economic anchors of the postclassical world.

Early Islamic religious beliefs reflected the deep influence of Jewish and Christian traditions, while early Muslim society reflected the nomadic and mercantile Arabian society from which Islam arose. Over time, Muslims also drew inspiration from other societies and other cultural traditions. After toppling the Sasanid dynasty, Muslim conquerors adopted Persian techniques of government and finance to administer their lands. Persian literature, science, and religious values also found a place in Islamic society. During later centuries Muslims drew inspiration from Greek and Indian traditions as well. Thus Muslims did not invent a new Islamic society but, rather, fashioned it by blending elements from Arab, Persian, Greek, and Indian societies.

While drawing influence from other societies, however, Islam thoroughly transformed the cultural traditions that it absorbed. The expansive realm of Islam eventually provided a political framework for trade and diplomacy over a vast portion of the eastern hemisphere, from west Africa to the islands of southeast Asia. Many lands of varied cultural background thus became part of a larger society often called the *dar al-Islam*—an Arabic term that means the "house of Islam" and that refers to lands under Islamic rule.

A PROPHET AND HIS WORLD

Islam arose in the Arabian peninsula, and the new religion faithfully reflected the social and cultural conditions of its homeland. Desert covers most of the peninsula, and agriculture is possible only in the well-watered area of Yemen in the south and in a few other places, such as the city of Medina, where oases provide water. Yet human communities have occupied Arabia for millennia. Nomadic peoples known as bedouin kept herds of sheep, goats, and camels, migrating through the deserts to find grass and water for their animals. The bedouin organized themselves in family and clan groups. Individuals and their immediate families depended heavily on their larger kinship networks for support in times of need. In an environment as harsh and unforgiving as the Arabian desert, cooperation with kin often made the difference between death and survival. Bedouin peoples developed a strong sense of loyalty to their clans and guarded their common interests with determination. Clan identities and loyalties survived for centuries after the appearance of Islam.

Arabia also figured prominently in the long-distance trade networks of the postclassical era. Commodities arrived at ports on the Persian Gulf (near modern Bahrain), the Arabian Sea (near modern Aden), and the Red Sea (near Mecca) and then traveled overland by camel caravan to Palmyra or Damascus, which offered access to the Mediterranean basin. After the third century C.E., Arabia became an increasingly important link in trade between China and India in the east and Persia and Byzantium in the west. With the weakening of classical empires, trade routes across central Asia had become insecure. Merchants abandoned the overland routes in favor of sea lanes connecting with land routes in the Arabian peninsula. Trade passing across the peninsula was especially important for the city of Mecca, which became an important site of fairs and a stopping point for caravan traffic.

Muhammad and His Message

Muhammad's Early Life The prophet Muhammad came into this world of bedouin herders and worldly merchants. Born about 570 C.E. into a reputable family of merchants in Mecca, Muhammad ibn Abdullah lost both of his parents by the time he was six years old. His grandfather and uncle cared for him and provided him with an education, but Muhammad's early life was difficult. As a young man, he worked for a woman named Khadija, a wealthy widow whom he married about 595 C.E. Through this marriage he gained a position of some prominence in Meccan society, although he did not by any means enter the ranks of the elite.

By age thirty Muhammad had established himself as a merchant. He made a comfortable life for himself in Arabian society, where peoples of different religious and cultural traditions regularly dealt with one another. Most Arabs recognized many gods, goddesses, demons, and nature spirits whose favor they sought through prayers and sacrifices. Large communities of Jewish merchants also worked throughout Arabia, and, especially in the north, many Arabs had converted to Christianity by Muhammad's time. Although he was not deeply knowledgeable about Judaism or Christianity, Muhammad had a basic understanding of both traditions. He may even have traveled by caravan to Syria, where he would certainly have dealt with Jewish and Christian merchants.

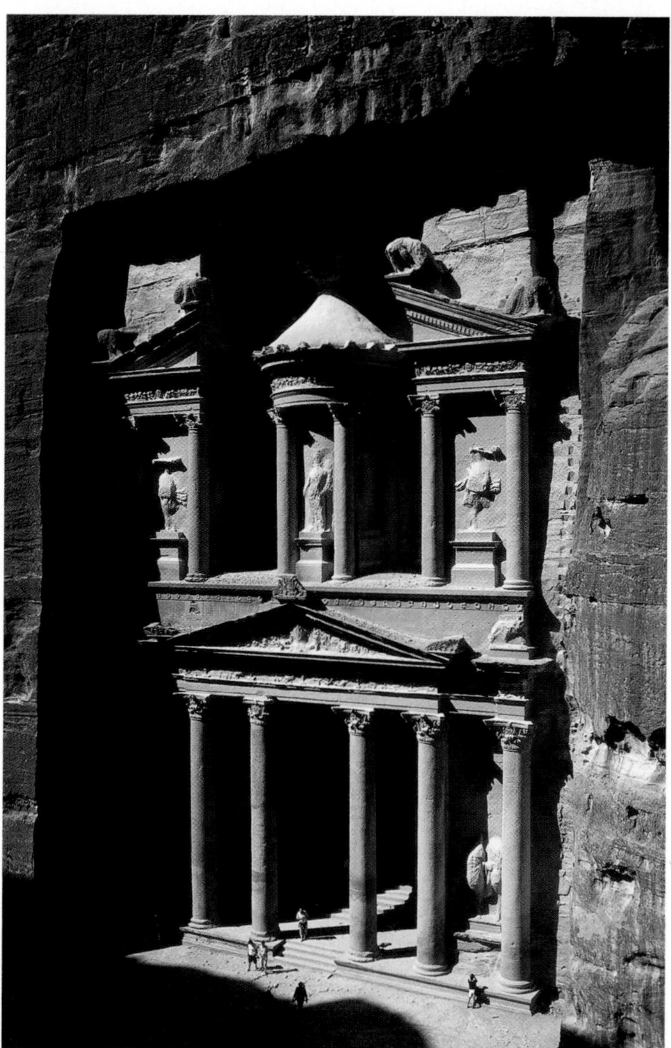

Some northern Arabs went to great lengths to demonstrate their devotion to Christianity. This structure, carved out of sheer rock along the wall of a ravine at Petra in modern-day Jordan, served as a monastery.

Muhammad's Spiritual Transformation About 610 C.E., as he approached age forty, Muhammad underwent a profound spiritual experience that transformed his life and left a deep mark on world history. His experience left him with the convictions that in all the world there was only one true deity, Allah ("God"), that he ruled the universe, that idolatry and the recognition of other gods amounted to wickedness, and that Allah would soon bring his judgment on the world, rewarding the righteous and punishing the wicked. Muhammad experienced visions, which he understood as messages or revelations from Allah, delivered through the archangel Gabriel (also recognized by Jews and Christians as a special messenger of God), instructing him to explain his views to others. He did not set out to construct a new religion by combining elements of Arab, Jewish, and Christian beliefs. In light of his cultural context, however, it is not surprising that he shared numerous specific beliefs with Jews and Christians—and indeed also with Zoroastrians, whose views had profoundly influenced the development of both Judaism and Christianity. In any case, in accordance with instructions transmitted to him by Gabriel, Muhammad began to expound his beliefs to his family and close friends. Gradually, others showed interest in his message, and by about 620 C.E. a zealous and expanding minority of Mecca's citizenry had joined his circle.

The Quran Muhammad originally presented oral recitations of the revelations he received during his visions. As the Islamic community grew, his followers prepared written texts of his teachings. During the early 650s devout Muslims compiled these written versions of Muhammad's revelations and issued them as the **Quran** ("recitation"), the holy book of Islam. A work of magnificent poetry, the Quran communicates in powerful and moving terms Muhammad's understanding of Allah and his relation to the world, and it serves as the definitive authority for Islamic religious doctrine and social organization.

Apart from the Quran, several other sources have provided moral and religious guidance for the Islamic community. Most important after the Quran are traditions known as *hadith,* which include sayings attributed to Muhammad and accounts of the prophet's deeds. Several collections of *hadith* appeared between the ninth and eleventh centuries C.E., and Muslim scholars have often taken them as guides for interpretation of the Quran. Regarded as less authoritative than the Quran and the *hadith,* but still important as inspirations for Islamic thought, were various additional early works describing social and legal customs, biographies of Muhammad, and pious commentaries on the Quran.

Muhammad's Migration to Medina

Conflict at Mecca The growing popularity of Muhammad's preaching brought him into conflict with the ruling elites at Mecca. Conflict centered on religious issues. Muhammad's insistence that Allah was the only divine power in the universe struck many polytheistic Arabs as offensive and dangerous as well, since it disparaged long-recognized deities and spirits thought to wield influence over human affairs. The tensions also had a personal dimension. Mecca's ruling elites, who were also the city's wealthiest merchants, took it as a personal affront and a threat to their position when Muhammad denounced greed as moral wickedness that Allah would punish.

Muhammad's attack on idolatry also represented an economic threat to those who owned and profited from the many shrines to deities that attracted merchants and pilgrims

Quran (koo-RAHN)

Current Islamic doctrine forbids artistic representations of Muhammad and Allah to prevent the worship of their images as idols. Although artists of previous centuries occasionally produced paintings of Muhammad, Islamic art has emphasized geometric design and calligraphy. This handsome page from a Quran written on vellum dates from the ninth or early tenth century.

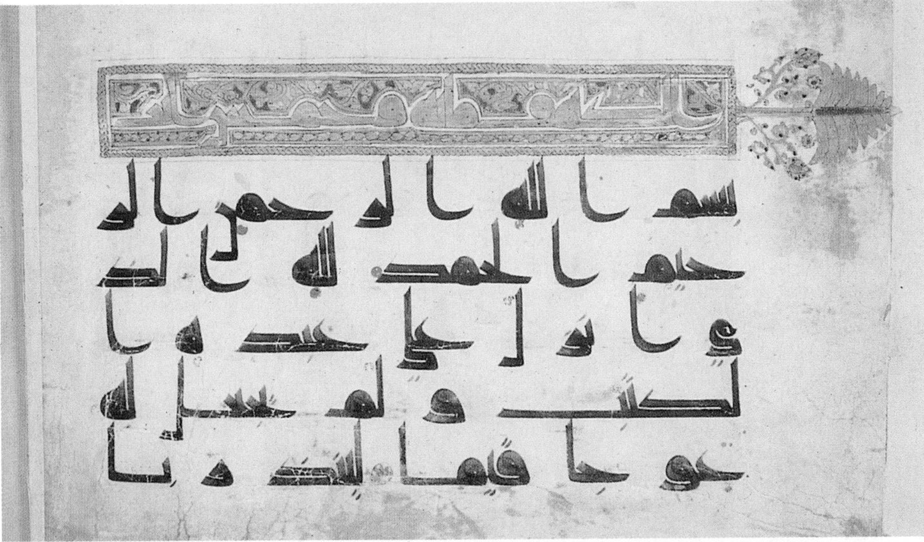

to Mecca. The best known of those shrines was a large black rock long considered to be the dwelling of a powerful deity. Housed in a cube-shaped building known as the **Ka'ba,** it drew worshipers from all over Arabia and brought considerable wealth to Mecca. As Muhammad relentlessly condemned the idolatry officially promoted at the Ka'ba and other shrines, the ruling elites of Mecca began to persecute the prophet and his followers.

The *Hijra* The pressure became so great that some of Muhammad's followers fled to Abyssinia (modern Ethiopia). Muhammad himself remained in Mecca until 622 C.E., when he too fled and joined a group of his followers in Yathrib, a rival trading city 345 kilometers (214 miles) north of Mecca. Muslims called their new home Medina ("the city," meaning "the city of the prophet"). Known as the *hijra* ("migration"), Muhammad's move to Medina serves as the starting point of the official Islamic calendar.

The *Umma* In Mecca, Muhammad had lived within the established political framework and concentrated on the moral and religious dimensions of his faith. In Medina he found himself at the head of a small but growing society in exile that needed guidance in practical as well as spiritual affairs. He organized his followers into a cohesive community called the *umma* ("community of the faithful") and provided it with a comprehensive legal and social code. He led this community both in daily prayers to Allah and in battle with enemies at Medina, Mecca, and other places. He looked after the economic welfare of the *umma*—sometimes by organizing commercial ventures and sometimes by launching raids against caravans from Mecca. Remembering the difficult days of his youth, he provided relief for widows, orphans, and the poor, and he made almsgiving a prime moral virtue.

The "Seal of the Prophets" Muhammad's understanding of his religious mission expanded during his years at Medina. He began to refer to himself as a prophet, indeed as the "seal of the prophets"—the final prophet through whom Allah would reveal his message to humankind. Muhammad accepted the authority of earlier Jewish and Christian prophets, including Abraham, Moses, and Jesus, and he held the Hebrew scriptures and the Christian New Testament in high esteem. He also accepted his predecessors' monotheism: Allah was the same omnipotent, omniscient, omnipresent, and exclusive deity as the Jews' Yahweh and the Christians' God. Muhammad taught, however, that the message entrusted to him offered a more complete revelation of Allah and his will than Judaism and Christianity had made available. Thus, while at Medina, Muhammad came to see himself consciously as Allah's final prophet: not simply as a devout man who explained his spiritual insights to a small circle of family and friends, but as the messenger who communicated Allah's wishes and his plan for the world to all humankind.

The Establishment of Islam in Arabia

Muhammad's Return to Mecca Throughout their sojourn at Medina, Muhammad and his followers planned ultimately to return to Mecca, which was both their home and the leading city of Arabia. In 629 C.E. they arranged with the authorities to participate in the annual pilgrimage to the Ka'ba, but they were not content with a short visit. In 630 they attacked Mecca and conquered the city. They forced the elites to adopt Muhammad's faith, and they imposed a government dedicated to Allah. They also destroyed the pagan shrines and replaced them with mosques, buildings that sought to instill a sense of sacredness and community where Muslims gathered for prayers. Only the Ka'ba escaped their efforts to cleanse Mecca of pagan monuments.

Muhammad and his followers denied that the Ka'ba was the home of a deity, but they preserved the black rock and

---

Ka'ba (KAH-buh)

sources from the past

The Quran on Allah and His Expectations of Humankind

The foundation of the Islamic faith is the understanding of Allah, his nature, and his plan for the world as outlined in the Quran. Through his visions Muhammad came to understand Allah as the one and only god, the creator and sustainer of the world in the manner of the Jews' Yahweh and the Christians' God. Those who rejected Allah and his message would suffer eternal punishment, but those who recognized and obeyed him would receive his mercy and secure his blessings.

In the name of Allah, most benevolent, ever-merciful.
All praise be to Allah,
Lord of all the worlds,
Most beneficent, ever-merciful,
King of the Day of Judgement.
You alone we worship, and to You
alone turn for help.
Guide us (O Lord) to the path that is straight,
The path of those You have blessed,
Not of those who have earned Your anger,
nor those who have gone astray. . . .

Verily men and women who have come to submission,
men and women who are believers,
men and women who are devout,
truthful men and women,
men and women with endurance,
men and women who are modest,
men and women who give alms,
men and women who observe fasting,
men and women who guard their private parts,
and those men and women who remember God a great deal,
for them God has forgiveness and a great reward.
No believing men and women have any choice in a matter
after God and His Apostle [i.e., Muhammad] have decided it.
Whoever disobeys God and His Apostle
has clearly lost the way and gone astray. . . .

O you who believe, remember God a great deal,
And sing His praises morning and evening.
It is He who sends His blessings on you,
as (do) His angels, that He may lead you out of darkness into light,
for He is benevolent to the believers. . . .

I call to witness
the early hours of the morning,
And the night when dark and still,
Your Lord has neither left you,
nor despises you.
What is to come is better for you
than what has gone before;
For your Lord will certainly give you,
and you will be content.
Did He not find you an orphan
and take care of you?
Did He not find you poor
and enrich you?
So do not oppress the orphan,
And do not drive
the beggar away,
And keep recounting the favours of your Lord. . . .

Say: "He is God
the one the most unique,
God the immanently indispensable.
He has begotten no one,
and is begotten of none.
There is no one comparable to Him."

For Further Reflection

- Compare the Quran's teachings on the relationship between Allah and human beings with the views of Zoroastrians, Jews, and Christians discussed in earlier chapters.

Source: *Al-Qur'an: A Contemporary Translation.* Trans. by Ahmed Ali. Princeton: Princeton University Press, 1984, pp. 11, 358, 359, 540, 559.

its housing as a symbol of Mecca's greatness. They allowed only the faithful to approach the shrine, and in 632 Muhammad himself led the first Islamic pilgrimage to the Ka'ba, thus establishing the hajj as an example for all devout Muslims. Building on the conquest of Mecca, Muhammad and his followers launched campaigns against other towns and bedouin clans, and by the time of the prophet's death in 632, shortly after his hajj, they had brought most of Arabia under their control.

The Five Pillars of Islam Muhammad's personal leadership decisively shaped the values and the development of the Islamic community. The foundation of Islam as elaborated by Muhammad consists of obligations known as the

A watercolor painting from sixteenth-century Iran depicts a caravan of pilgrims traveling to Mecca while making the hajj. In what ways did the hajj facilitate social and business relationships?

Five Pillars of Islam: (1) Muslims must acknowledge Allah as the only god and Muhammad as his prophet. (2) They must pray to Allah daily while facing Mecca. (3) They must observe a fast during the daylight hours of the month of Ramadan. (4) They must contribute alms for the relief of the weak and poor. (5) And, in honor of Muhammad's visits to Mecca in 629 and 632, those who are physically and financially able must undertake the hajj and make at least one pilgrimage to Mecca. During the centuries since its appearance, Islam has generated many schools and sects, each with its own particular legal, social, and doctrinal features. The Five Pillars of Islam, however, constitute a simple but powerful framework that has bound the *umma* into a cohesive community.

Jihad Some Muslims, though by no means all, have taken jihad as an additional obligation. The term ***jihad*** literally means "struggle," and Muslims have understood its imperatives in various ways. In one sense, jihad imposes spiritual and moral obligations on Muslims by requiring them to combat vice and evil. In another sense, jihad calls on Muslims to struggle against ignorance and unbelief by spreading the word of Islam and seeking converts to the faith. In some circumstances, jihad also involves physical struggle, obliging Muslims to take up the sword and wage war against unbelievers who threaten Islam.

Islamic Law: The *Sharia* Beyond the general obligations prescribed by the Five Pillars, Islamic holy law, known as the ***sharia,*** emerged during the centuries after Muhammad and offered detailed guidance on proper behavior in almost every aspect of life. Elaborated by jurists and legal scholars, the sharia drew its inspiration especially from the Quran and the early historical accounts of Muhammad's life and teachings. It offered precise guidance on matters as diverse as marriage and family life, inheritance, slavery, business and commercial relationships, political authority in the *dar al-Islam,* and crime. Through the sharia, Islam became more than a religious doctrine: it developed into a way of life complete with social and ethical values derived from Islamic religious principles.

THE EXPANSION OF ISLAM

After Muhammad's death the Islamic community might well have unraveled and disappeared. Muhammad had made no provision for a successor, and there was serious division within the *umma* concerning the selection of a new leader. Many of the towns and bedouin clans that had recently accepted Islam took the opportunity of Muhammad's death to renounce the fledgling religion, reassert their independence, and break free from Mecca's control. Within a short time, however, the Islamic community had embarked on a stunningly successful round of military expansion that ex-

thinking about TRADITIONS

The Prophet and the Principles of Islam
The Muslim community received the basic teachings of Islam through the prophet Muhammad. To what extent did the religious doctrines and social practices of Islam reflect the personal experiences of Muhammad? Consider Muhammad's understanding of Judaism and Christianity as well as his life, career, and family circumstances.

shari'a (shah-REE-ah)

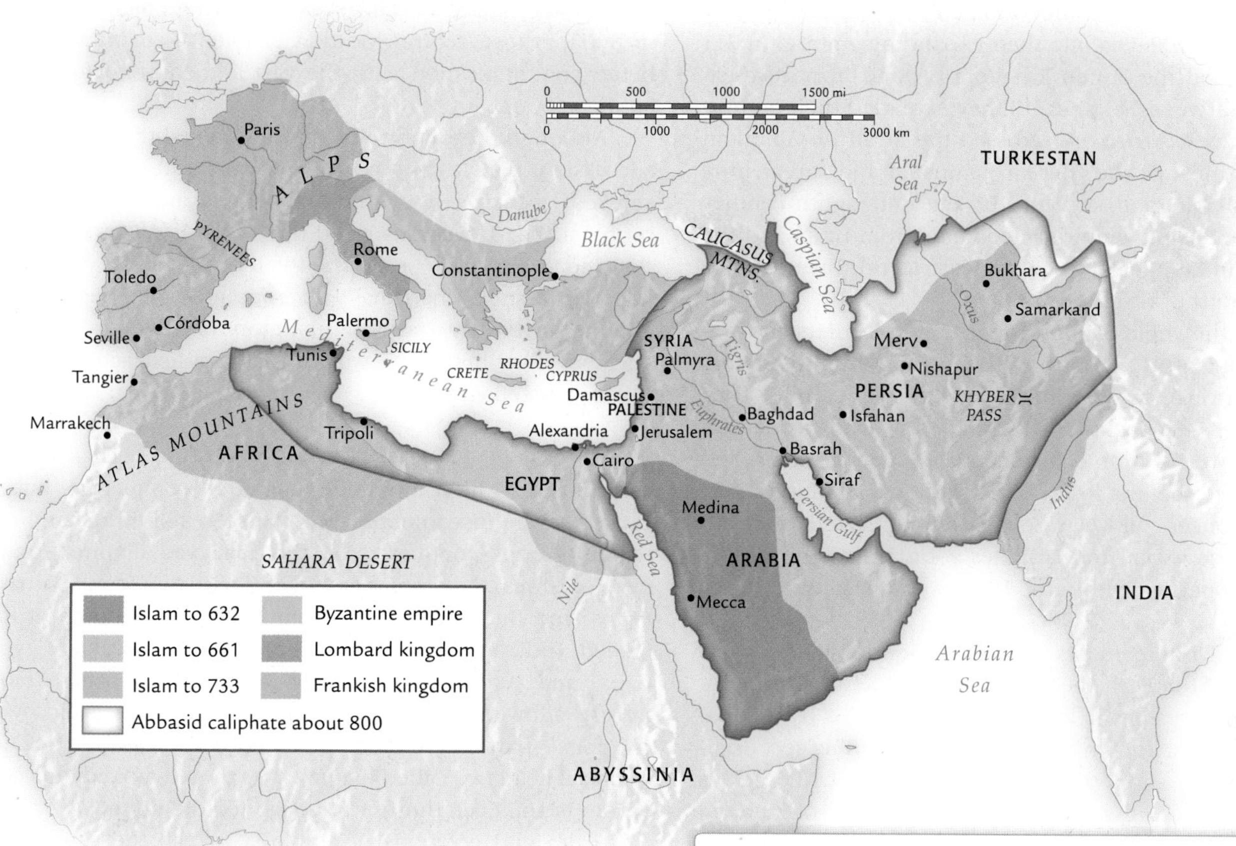

MAP 13.1
The expansion of Islam, 632–733 C.E.
During the seventh and eighth centuries, the new faith of Islam expanded rapidly and dramatically beyond its Arabian homeland.
How might you explain the spread of a new faith? What political and cultural effects followed from the expansion of Islam?

tended its political and cultural influence far beyond the boundaries of Arabia. Those conquests laid the foundation for the rapid growth of Islamic society.

The Early Caliphs and the Umayyad Dynasty

The Caliph Because Muhammad was the "seal of the prophets," it was inconceivable that another prophet should succeed him. Shortly after Muhammad's death his advisors selected **Abu Bakr,** a genial man who was one of the prophet's closest friends and most devoted disciples, to serve as *caliph* ("deputy"). Thus Abu Bakr and later caliphs led the *umma* not as prophets but as lieutenants or substitutes for Muhammad. Abu Bakr became head of state for the Islamic community as well as chief judge, religious leader, and military commander. Under the caliph's leadership, the *umma* went on the offensive against the towns and bedouin clans that had renounced Islam after Muhammad's death, and within a year it had compelled them to recognize Islam and the rule of the caliph.

The Expansion of Islam Indeed, during the century after Muhammad's death, Islamic armies ranged well beyond the boundaries of Arabia, carrying their religion and their authority to Byzantine and Sasanid territories and beyond. Although much less powerful than either the Byzantine empire or the Sasanid empire, Muslim armies fought with particular effectiveness because their leaders had forged previously competing tribal groups into a powerful state unified by their allegiance to Islam. Moreover, Muslim armies attacked at a moment when the Byzantine and Sasanid empires were exhausted from perennial conflicts with each other and when they also faced internal uprisings by overtaxed peasants and oppressed ethnic or religious minorities. Between 633 and 637 C.E., taking advantage of those difficulties, Muslim forces seized Byzantine Syria and Palestine and took most of Mesopotamia from the Sasanids. During the 640s they conquered Byzantine Egypt

Abu Bakr (ah-BOO BAHK-uhr)

and north Africa. In 651 they toppled the Sasanid dynasty and incorporated Persia into their expanding empire. In 711 they conquered the Hindu kingdom of Sind in northwestern India. Between 711 and 718 they extended their authority to northwest Africa and crossed the Strait of Gibraltar, conquering most of the Iberian peninsula and threatening the Frankish kingdom in Gaul. By the mid-eighth century an immense Islamic empire ruled lands from India and the central Asian steppe lands in the east to northwest Africa and Iberia in the west.

During this rapid expansion the empire's rulers encountered difficult problems of governance and administration. One problem had to do with the selection of caliphs. During the early decades after Muhammad's death, leaders of the most powerful Arab clans negotiated among themselves and appointed the first four caliphs. Political ambitions, personal differences, and clan loyalties complicated their deliberations, however, and disputes soon led to the rise of factions and parties within the Islamic community.

The Shia Disagreements over succession led to the emergence of the **Shia** sect, the most important and enduring of all the alternatives to the form of Islam observed by the majority of Muslims, known as Sunni Islam. The Shia sect originated as a party supporting the appointment of Ali and his descendants as caliphs. A cousin and son-in-law of Muhammad, Ali was a candidate for caliph when the prophet died, but support for Abu Bakr was stronger. Ali served briefly as the fourth caliph (656–661 C.E.), but his enemies assassinated him, killed many of his relatives, and imposed their own candidate as caliph. Partisans of Ali then organized the Shia ("party"), furiously resisted the victorious faction, and struggled to return the caliphate to the line of Ali. Although persecuted, the Shia survived and strengthened its identity by adopting doctrines and rituals distinct from those of the Sunnis ("traditionalists"), who accepted the legitimacy of the early caliphs. Shia partisans, for example, observed holy days in honor of their leaders and martyrs to their cause, and they taught that descendants of Ali were infallible, sinless, and divinely appointed to rule the Islamic community. Shia Muslims also advanced interpretations of the Quran that support the party's views, and the Shia itself has often served as a source of support for those who oppose the policies of Sunni leaders.

The Umayyad Dynasty After the assassination of Ali, the establishment of the **Umayyad** dynasty (661–750 C.E.) solved the problem of succession, at least temporarily. The Umayyads ranked among the most prominent of the Meccan merchant clans, and their reputation and network of alliances helped them bring stability to the Islamic community. Despite their association with Mecca, the Umayyads established their capital at Damascus, a thriving commercial city in Syria, whose central location enabled them to maintain better communication with the vast and still-expanding Islamic empire.

Although the Umayyads' dynasty solved the problem of succession, their tightly centralized rule and the favor they showed to their fellow Arabs generated an administrative problem. The Umayyads ruled the *dar al-Islam* as conquerors, and their policies reflected the interests of the Arab military aristocracy. The Umayyads appointed members of this elite as governors and administrators of conquered lands, and they distributed the wealth that they extracted among this privileged class.

Policy toward Conquered Peoples This policy contributed to high morale among Arab conquerors, but it caused severe discontent among the scores of ethnic and religious groups conquered by the Umayyad empire. Apart from Muslims, the empire included Christians, Jews, Zoroastrians, and Buddhists. Apart from Arabs and bedouin, it included Indians, Persians, Mesopotamians, Greeks, Egyptians, and nomadic Berbers in north Africa. The Arabs mostly allowed conquered peoples to observe their own religions—particularly Christians and Jews—but they levied a special head tax, called the *jizya,* on those who did not convert to Islam. Even those who converted did not enjoy access to wealth and positions of authority, which the Umayyads reserved almost exclusively for members of the Arab military aristocracy. This caused deep resentment among conquered peoples and led to restiveness against Umayyad rule.

Umayyad Decline Beginning in the early eighth century, the Umayyad caliphs became alienated even from other Arabs. They devoted themselves increasingly to luxurious living rather than to zealous leadership of the *umma,* and they scandalized devout Muslims by their casual attitudes toward Islamic doctrine and morality. By midcentury the Umayyad caliphs faced not only the resistance of the Shia, whose members continued to promote descendants of Ali for caliph, but also the discontent of conquered peoples throughout their empire and even the disillusionment of Muslim Arab military leaders.

The Abbasid Dynasty

Abu al-Abbas Rebellion in Persia brought the Umayyad dynasty to an end. The chief leader of the rebellion was Abu al-Abbas, a descendant of Muhammad's uncle. Although he was a Sunni Arab, Abu al-Abbas allied readily with Shias and with Muslims who were not Arabs, such as converts to Islam from southwest Asia. Particularly prominent among his supporters were Persian converts who resented the preference shown by the Umayyads to Arab Muslims. During the 740s Abu al-Abbas's party rejected Umayyad authority and seized control of Persia and Mesopotamia. In 750 his army shattered Umayyad forces in a huge battle. After-

---

Shia (SHEE-ah)
Umayyad (oo-MEYE-ahd)

The early expansion of Islam was a bloody affair. This illustration from an Arabic manuscript of the thirteenth century depicts a battle between Muhammad's cousin Ali and his adversaries.

ward, Abu al-Abbas invited the remaining members of the Umayyad clan to a banquet under the pretext of reconciling their differences. During the festivities his troops arrested the Umayyads and slaughtered them, effectively annihilating the clan. Abu al-Abbas then founded the **Abbasid** dynasty, which was the principal source of authority in the *dar al-Islam* until the Mongols toppled it in 1258 C.E.

The Abbasid Dynasty The Abbasid dynasty differed considerably from the Umayyad. For one thing, the Abbasid state was far more cosmopolitan than its predecessor. Even though they sprang from the ranks of conquering Arabs, Abbasid rulers did not show special favor to the Arab military aristocracy. Arabs continued to play a large role in government, but Persians, Egyptians, Mesopotamians, and others also rose to positions of wealth and power.

The Abbasid dynasty differed from the Umayyad also in that it was not a conquering dynasty. The Abbasids sparred intermittently with the Byzantine empire, they clashed frequently with nomadic peoples from central Asia, and in 751 they defeated a Chinese army at Talas River near Samarkand. The battle of Talas River was exceptionally important: it ended the expansion of China's Tang dynasty into central Asia (discussed in chapter 14), and it opened the door for the spread of Islam among Turkish peoples. Only marginally, however, did the Abbasids expand their empire by conquest. The *dar al-Islam* as a whole continued to grow during the Abbasid era, but the caliphs had little to do with the expansion. During the ninth and early tenth centuries, for example, largely autonomous Islamic forces from distant Tunisia mounted naval expeditions throughout the Mediterranean, conquering Crete, Sicily, and the Balearic Islands while seizing territories also in Cyprus, Rhodes, Sardinia, Corsica, southern Italy, and southern France. Meanwhile, Muslim merchants introduced Islam to southern India and sub-Saharan Africa (see chapter 18).

Abbasid Administration Instead of conquering new lands, the Abbasids largely contented themselves with administering the empire they inherited. Fashioning a government that could administer a sprawling realm with scores of linguistic, ethnic, and cultural groups was a considerable challenge. Before Muhammad, Arabs had no governments larger than city-states, nor did the Quran offer guidance for the administration of a huge empire. The Umayyad practice of allowing the Arab aristocracy to exploit subject lands and peoples had proven to be a failure. Thus Abu al-Abbas and his successors turned to long-standing Mesopotamian and Persian techniques of administration whereby rulers devised policies, built capital cities to oversee affairs, and organized their territories through regional governors and bureaucracies.

Baghdad Central authority emanated from the Abbasid court at Baghdad (capital of modern Iraq), a magnificent new city that the early Abbasid caliphs constructed near the Sasanid capital of Ctesiphon. By building this new center of government to replace the Umayyad capital at Damascus, the Abbasids associated themselves with the cosmopolitan environment of Mesopotamia. Baghdad was a round city protected by three round walls. At the heart of the city was the caliph's green-domed palace, from which instructions flowed to the distant reaches of the Abbasid realm. In

Abbasid (ah-BAH-sihd)

PART 3

the provinces, governors represented the caliph and implemented his political and financial policies.

Learned officials known as *ulama* ("people with religious knowledge") and *qadis* ("judges") set moral standards in local communities and resolved disputes. *Ulama* and *qadis* were not priests—Islam does not recognize priests as a distinct class of religious specialists—but they had a formal education that emphasized study of the Quran and the sharia. *Ulama* were pious scholars who sought to develop public policy in accordance with the Quran and sharia. *Qadis* heard cases at law and rendered decisions based on the Quran and sharia. Because of their moral authority, *ulama* and *qadis* became extremely influential officials who helped to ensure widespread observance of Islamic values. Apart from provincial governors, *ulama,* and *qadis,* the Abbasid caliphs kept a standing army, and they established bureaucratic ministries in charge of taxation, finance, coinage, and postal services. They also maintained the magnificent network of roads that the Islamic empire inherited from the Sasanids.

Harun al-Rashid The high point of the Abbasid dynasty came during the reign of the caliph Harun al-Rashid (786–809 C.E.). By the late eighth century, Abbasid authority had lost some of its force in provinces distant from Baghdad, but it remained strong enough to bring reliable tax revenues from most parts of the empire. Flush with wealth, Baghdad became a center of banking, commerce, crafts, and industrial production, a metropolis with a population of several hundred thousand people. According to stories from his time, Harun al-Rashid provided liberal support for artists and writers, bestowed lavish and luxurious gifts on his favorites, and distributed money to the poor and the common classes by tossing coins into the streets of Baghdad. Once, he sent an elephant and a collection of rich presents as gifts to his contemporary Charlemagne, who ruled the Carolingian empire of western Europe.

Abbasid Decline Soon after Harun al-Rashid's reign, the Abbasid empire entered a period of decline. Civil war between Harun's sons seriously damaged Abbasid authority, and disputes over succession rights became a recurring problem for the dynasty. Provincial governors took advantage of disorder in the ruling house by acting independently of the caliphs: instead of implementing imperial policies and delivering taxes to Baghdad, they built up local bases of power and in some cases actually seceded from the Abbasid empire. Meanwhile, popular uprisings and peasant rebellions, which often enjoyed the support of dissenting sects and heretical movements, further weakened the empire.

As a result of those difficulties, the Abbasid caliphs became mere figureheads long before the Mongols extinguished the dynasty in 1258. In 945, members of a Persian noble family seized control of Baghdad and established their clan as the power behind the Abbasid throne. Later, imperial authorities in Baghdad fell under the control of the Saljuq Turks, a nomadic people from central Asia who also invaded the Byzantine empire. In response to rebellions mounted by peasants and provincial governors, authorities in Baghdad allied with the Saljuqs, who began to enter the Abbasid realm and convert to Islam about the mid-tenth century. By the mid-eleventh century the Saljuqs effectively controlled the Abbasid empire. During the 1050s they took possession of Baghdad, and during the following decades they extended their authority to Syria, Palestine, and Anatolia. They retained Abbasid caliphs as nominal sovereigns, but for two centuries, until the arrival of the Mongols, the Saljuq *sultan* ("chieftain" or "ruler") was the true source of power in the Abbasid empire.

ECONOMY AND SOCIETY OF THE EARLY ISLAMIC WORLD

In the *dar al-Islam,* as in other agricultural societies, peasants tilled the land as their ancestors had done for centuries before them, while manufacturers and merchants supported a thriving urban economy. Here, as in other lands, the creation of large empires had dramatic economic implications. The Umayyad and Abbasid empires created a zone of trade, exchange, and communication stretching from India to Iberia. Commerce throughout this zone served as a vigorous economic stimulus for both the countryside and the cities of the early Islamic world.

New Crops, Agricultural Experimentation, and Urban Growth

The Spread of Food and Industrial Crops As soldiers, administrators, diplomats, and merchants traveled throughout the *dar al-Islam,* they encountered plants, animals, and agricultural techniques peculiar to the empire's various regions. They often introduced particularly useful crops to other regions. The most important of the transplants traveled west from India to Persia, southwest Asia, Arabia, Egypt, north Africa, Spain, and the Mediterranean islands of Cyprus, Crete, Sicily, and Sardinia. They included staple crops such as sugarcane, rice, and new varieties of sorghum and wheat; vegetables such as spinach, artichokes, and eggplants; fruits such as oranges, lemons, limes, bananas, coconuts, watermelons, and mangoes; and industrial crops such as cotton, indigo, and henna.

Effects of New Crops The introduction of these crops into the western regions of the Islamic world had wide-ranging effects. New food crops led to a richer and more varied diet. They also increased quantities of food available because they enabled cultivators to extend the growing season. In much of the Islamic world, summers are so hot and dry that cultivators traditionally left their fields fallow during that season. Most of the transplanted crops grew well in high heat, however, so cultivators in southwest Asia, north Africa, and other hot zones could till

In a thirteenth-century manuscript illustration, a fictional Muslim traveler passes a lively agricultural village. On the left a woman spins cotton thread. Sheep, goats, chickens, and date palms figure prominently in the local economy.

their lands year-round. The result was a dramatic increase in food supplies.

Some new crops had industrial uses. The most important of these was cotton, which became the basis for a thriving textile industry throughout much of the Islamic world. Indigo and henna yielded dyes that textile manufacturers used in large quantities.

Agricultural Experimentation Travel and communication in the *dar al-Islam* also encouraged experimentation with agricultural methods. Cultivators paid close attention to methods of irrigation, fertilization, crop rotation, and the like, and they outlined their findings in hundreds of agricultural manuals. Copies of these works survive in numerous manuscripts that circulated widely throughout the Islamic world. The combined effect of new crops and improved techniques was a far more productive agricultural economy, which in turn supported vigorous economic growth throughout the *dar al-Islam*.

Urban Growth Increased agricultural production contributed to the rapid growth of cities in all parts of the Islamic world from India to Spain. Delhi, Samarkand, Bukhara, Merv, Nishapur, Isfahan, Basra, Baghdad, Damascus, Jerusalem, Cairo, Alexandria, Palermo, Tunis, Tangier, Córdoba, and Toledo were all bustling cities, some with populations of several hundred thousand people. All these cities had flourishing markets supporting thousands of artisans, craftsmen, and merchants. Most of them were also important centers of industrial production, particularly of textiles, pottery, glassware, leather, iron, and steel.

One new industry appeared in Islamic cities during the Abbasid era: paper manufacture. Chinese craftsmen had

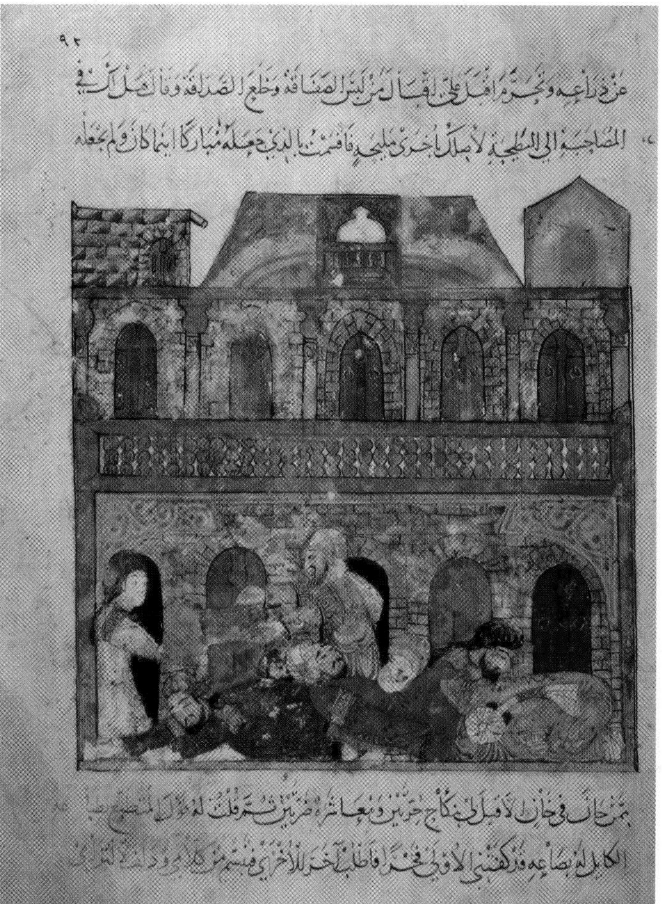

Caravanserais offered splendid facilities for caravan merchants, but they sometimes harbored dangers. In this illustration from a thirteenth-century manuscript, drugged merchants sleep soundly while burglars relieve them of their valuables.

made paper since the first century C.E., but their technology did not spread far beyond China until the eighth century. Paper was cheaper and easier to use than writing materials such as vellum sheets made from calfskin, and it soon became popular throughout the Islamic world. Paper facilitated the keeping of administrative and commercial records, and it made possible the dissemination of books and treatises in larger quantities than ever before. By the tenth century, mills produced paper in Persia, Mesopotamia, Arabia, Egypt, and Spain, and the industry soon spread to western Europe.

The Formation of a Hemispheric Trading Zone

From its earliest days Islamic society drew much of its prosperity from commerce. Muhammad himself was a merchant, and he held merchants in high esteem. According to early accounts of his life, Muhammad once said that honest merchants would stand alongside martyrs to the faith on the day of judgment. By the time of the Abbasid caliphate, elaborate trade networks linked all the regions of the Islamic world and joined it to a larger, hemispheric, economy.

Overland Trade When they overran the Sasanid empire, Muslim conquerors brought the prosperous trading cities of central Asia under control of the expanding *dar al-Islam*. Merv, Nishapur, Bukhara, and Samarkand were long-established commercial centers, and they made it possible for Muslim merchants to trade over a revived silk roads network extending from China in the east to the Mediterranean in the west. Thus Muslim merchants were able to take advantage of the extensive road networks originally built during the classical era by imperial authorities in India, Persia, and the Mediterranean basin. Umayyad and Abbasid rulers maintained the roads that they inherited because they provided splendid routes for military forces and administrative officials traveling through the *dar al-Islam*. But those same roads also made excellent highways for merchants as well as missionaries and pilgrims. Travel along the roads could be remarkably speedy and efficient. After the tenth century, for example, the Muslim rulers of Egypt regularly imported ice from the mountains of Syria to their palace in Cairo. Even during the summer months, they received five camel loads of ice weekly to cool their food and drink.

Camels and Caravans Overland trade traveled mostly by camel caravan. Although they are unpleasant and often uncooperative beasts, camels endure the rigors of desert travel much better than oxen, horses, or donkeys. Moreover, when fitted with a well-designed saddle, camels can carry heavy loads. During the early centuries C.E., the manufacture of camel saddles spread throughout Arabia, north Africa, southwest Asia, and central Asia, and camels became the favored beasts of burden in deserts and other dry regions. As camel transport became more common, the major cities of the Islamic world and central Asia built and maintained caravanserais—inns offering lodging for caravan merchants as well as food, water, and care for their animals.

Maritime Trade Meanwhile, innovations in nautical technology contributed to a steadily increasing volume of maritime trade in the Red Sea, Persian Gulf, Arabian Sea, and Indian Ocean. Arab and Persian mariners borrowed the compass from its Chinese inventors and used it to guide them on the high seas. From southeast Asian and Indian mariners, they borrowed the lateen sail, a triangular sail that increased a ship's maneuverability. From the Hellenistic Mediterranean they borrowed the astrolabe, an instrument that enabled them to calculate latitude.

Thus equipped, Arab and Persian mariners ventured throughout the Indian Ocean basin, calling at ports from

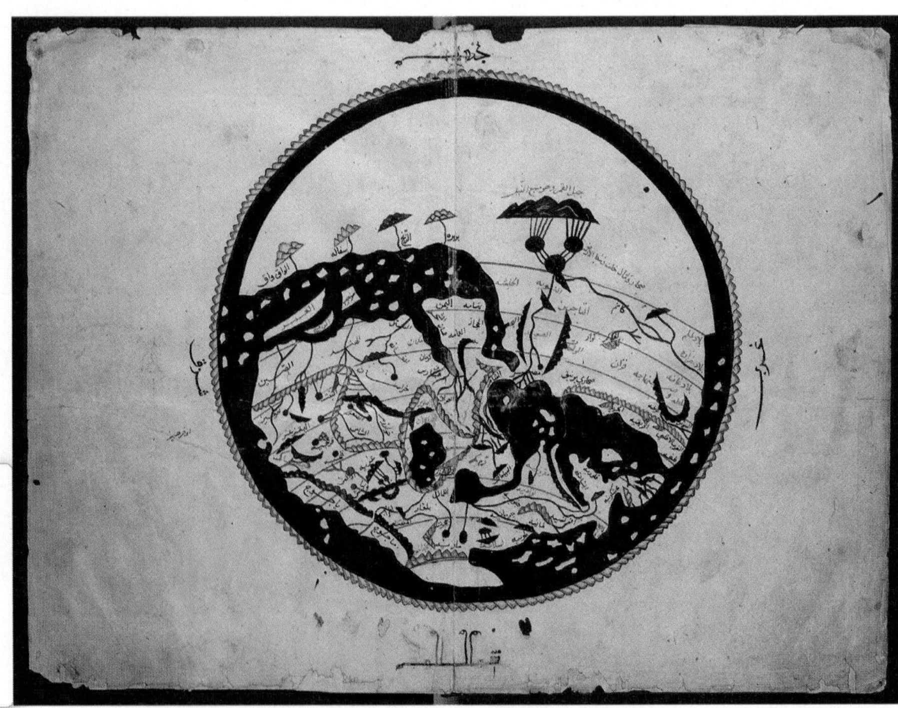

A map produced in the eleventh century by the Arab geographer al-Idrisi shows the lands known and reported by Muslim merchants and travelers. Note that, in accordance with Muslim cartographic convention, this map places south at the top and north at the bottom.

In this thirteenth-century manuscript illustration, merchants at a slave market in southern Arabia deal in black slaves captured in sub-Saharan Africa. Slaves traded in Islamic markets also came from Russia and eastern Europe.

southern China to southeast Asia, Ceylon, India, Persia, Arabia, and the eastern coast of Africa. The twelfth-century Persian merchant Ramisht of Siraf (a flourishing port city on the Persian Gulf) amassed a huge fortune from long-distance trading ventures. One of Ramisht's clerks once returned to Siraf from a commercial voyage to China with a cargo worth half a million dinars—gold coins that were the standard currency in the Islamic world. Ramisht himself was one of the wealthiest men of his age, and he spent much of his fortune on pious causes. He outfitted the Ka'ba with a Chinese silk cover that reportedly cost him eighteen thousand dinars, and he also founded a hospital and a religious sanctuary in Mecca.

Banks Banking also stimulated the commercial economy of the Islamic world. Banks had operated since classical antiquity, but Islamic banks of the Abbasid period conducted business on a much larger scale and provided a more extensive range of services than did their predecessors. They not only lent money to entrepreneurs but also served as brokers for investments and exchanged different currencies. They established multiple branches that honored letters of credit known as *sakk*—the root of the modern word *check*—drawn on the parent bank. Thus merchants could draw letters of credit in one city and cash them in another, and they could settle accounts with distant business partners without having to deal in cash.

The Organization of Trade Trade benefited also from techniques of business organization. Like banking, these techniques had precedents in classical Mediterranean society, but increasing volumes of trade enabled entrepreneurs to refine their methods of organization. Furthermore, Islamic law provided security for entrepreneurs by explicitly recognizing certain forms of business organization. Usually, Islamic businessmen preferred not to embark on solo ventures, since an individual could face financial ruin if an entire cargo of commodities fell prey to pirates or went down with a ship that sank in a storm. Instead, like their counterparts in other postclassical societies, Abbasid entrepreneurs often pooled their resources in group investments. If several individuals invested in several cargoes, they could distribute their risks and more easily absorb losses. Furthermore, if several groups of investors rented cargo space on several different ships, they spread their risks even more. Entrepreneurs entered into a variety of legally recognized joint endeavors during the Abbasid caliphate. Some involved simply the investment of money in an enterprise, whereas others called for some or all of the partners to play active roles in their business ventures.

As a result of improved transportation, expanded banking services, and refined techniques of business organization, long-distance trade surged in the early Islamic world. Muslim merchants dealt in silk and ceramics from China, spices and aromatics from India and southeast Asia, and jewelry and fine textiles from the Byzantine empire. Merchants also ventured beyond settled societies in China, India, and the

thinking about ENCOUNTERS

Religion and Agriculture

Is there any relationship between religious belief and agricultural practices? Consider the case of Muslim merchants who visited most regions of the eastern hemisphere and helped spread food and industrial crops to new lands. To what extent can the existence of a widely spread Muslim community help to explain this biological diffusion? To what extent might a similar diffusion have taken place in the absence of Islam?

Mediterranean basin to distant lands that previously had not engaged systematically in long-distance trade. They crossed the Sahara desert by camel caravan to trade salt, steel, copper, and glass for gold and slaves from the kingdoms of west Africa. They visited the coastal regions of east Africa, where they obtained slaves and exotic local commodities such as animal skins. They engaged in trade with Russia and Scandinavia by way of the Dnieper and Volga rivers and obtained high-value commodities such as animal skins, furs, honey, amber, and slaves as well as bulk goods such as timber and livestock. The vigorous economy of the Abbasid empire thus helped to establish networks of communication and exchange throughout much of the eastern hemisphere.

Al-Andalus The prosperity of Islamic Spain, known as al-Andalus, illustrates the far-reaching effects of long-distance trade during the Abbasid era. Most of the Iberian peninsula had fallen into the hands of Muslim Berber conquerors from north Africa during the early eighth century. The governors of al-Andalus were Umayyads who refused to recognize the Abbasid dynasty, and beginning in the tenth century they styled themselves caliphs in their own right rather than governors subject to Abbasid authority. Despite political and diplomatic tensions, al-Andalus participated actively in the commercial life of the larger Islamic world. The merchant-scholar al-Marwani of Córdoba, for example, made his hajj in 908 and then traveled to Iraq and India on commercial ventures. His profits amounted to thirty thousand dinars—all of which he lost in a shipwreck during his return home.

Imported crops increased the supply of food and enriched the diet of al-Andalus, enabling merchants and manufacturers to conduct thriving businesses in cities such as Córdoba, Toledo, and Seville. Ceramics, painted tiles, lead crystal, and gold jewelry from al-Andalus enjoyed a reputation for excellence and helped pay for imported goods and the building of a magnificent capital city at Córdoba. During the tenth century, Córdoba had more than 16 kilometers (10 miles) of lighted public roads as well as free Islamic schools, a gargantuan mosque, and a splendid library with four hundred thousand volumes.

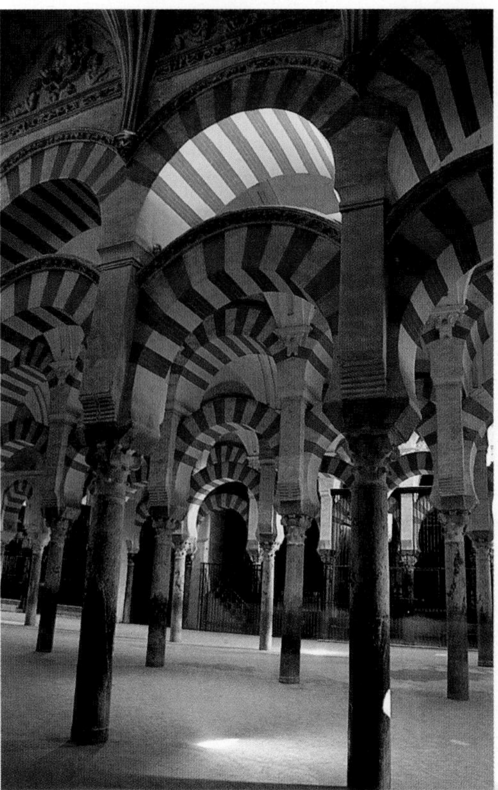

Interior of the mosque at Córdoba, originally built in the late eighth century and enlarged during the ninth and tenth centuries. One of the largest structures in the *dar al-Islam,* the mosque rests on 850 columns and features nineteen aisles.

The Changing Status of Women

A patriarchal society had emerged in Arabia long before Muhammad's time, but Arab women enjoyed rights not accorded to women in many other lands. They could legally inherit property, divorce husbands on their own initiative, and engage in business ventures. Khadija, the first of Muhammad's wives, managed a successful commercial business.

In some respects the Quran enhanced the security of women in Arabian society. It outlawed female infanticide, and it provided that dowries went directly to brides rather than to their husbands and male guardians. It portrayed women not as the property of their menfolk but as honorable individuals, equal to men before Allah, with their own rights and needs. Muhammad's kindness and generosity toward his wives, as related in early accounts of the prophet's life, also served as an example that may have improved the lives of Muslim women.

The Quran and Women For the most part, however, the Quran—and later the sharia as well—reinforced male dominance. The Quran and Islamic holy law recognized descent through the male line, and to guarantee proper inheritance, they placed a high premium on genealogical purity. To ensure the legitimacy of heirs, they subjected the social and sexual lives of women to the strict control of male guardians—fathers, brothers, and husbands. Though teaching that men should treat women with sensitivity and respect, the Quran and the sharia permitted men to take up to four wives, whereas women could have only one husband. The Quran and the sharia thus provided a religious and legal foundation for a decisively patriarchal society.

Veiling of Women When Islam expanded into the Byzantine and Sasanid empires, it encountered strong patriarchal traditions, and Muslims readily adopted long-standing customs such as the veiling of women. Social and family pressures had induced upper-class urban women to veil themselves in Mesopotamia as early as the thirteenth century B.C.E., and long before Muhammad the practice of veiling had spread to Persia and the eastern Mediterranean. As

a sign of modesty, upper-class urban women covered their faces and ventured outside their homes only in the company of servants or chaperones so as to discourage the attention of men. When Muslim Arabs conquered Mesopotamia, Persia, and eastern Mediterranean lands, they adopted the veiling of women. A conspicuous symbol of male authority thus found a prominent place in the early Islamic community.

The Quran served as the preeminent source of authority in the world of Islam, and it provided specific rights for Muslim women. Over the centuries, however, jurists and legal scholars interpreted the Quran in ways that progressively limited those rights and placed women increasingly under the control of male guardians. To a large extent the increased emphasis on male authority in Islamic law reflected the influence of the strongly hierarchical and patriarchal societies of Mesopotamia, Persia, and eastern Mediterranean lands as Islam developed from a local faith to a large-scale complex society.

ISLAMIC VALUES AND CULTURAL EXCHANGES

Since the seventh century C.E., the Quran has served as the cornerstone of Islamic society. Arising from a rich tradition of bedouin poetry and song, the Quran established Arabic as a flexible and powerful medium of communication. Even today Muslims regard the Arabic text of the Quran as the only definitive and reliable scripture: translations do not possess the power and authority of the original. When carrying their faith to new lands during the era of Islamic expansion, Muslim missionaries spread the message of Allah and provided instruction in the Quran's teachings, although usually they also permitted continued observance of pre-Islamic traditions. Muslim intellectuals drew freely from the long-established cultural traditions of Persia, India, and Greece, which they became acquainted with during the Umayyad and Abbasid eras.

The Formation of an Islamic Cultural Tradition

Muslim theologians and jurists looked to the Quran, stories about Muhammad's life, and other sources of Islamic doctrine in their efforts to formulate moral guidelines appropriate for their society. The body of civil and criminal law embodied in the sharia provided a measure of cultural unity for the vastly different lands of the Islamic world. Islamic law did not by any means erase the differences, but it established a common cultural foundation that facilitated dealings between peoples of various Islamic lands and that lent substance to the concept of the *dar al-Islam.*

Promotion of Islamic Values On a more popular level, *ulama, qadis,* and missionaries helped to bridge differences in cultural traditions and to spread Islamic values throughout the *dar al-Islam. Ulama* and *qadis* held positions at all Islamic courts, and they were prominent in the public life of all cities in the Islamic world. By resolving disputes according to Islamic law and ordering public observance of Islamic social and moral standards, they brought the values of the Quran and the sharia into the lives of peoples living far from the birthplace of Islam.

In this manuscript illustration a Muslim teacher (the figure with the open book) instructs students in a library near Baghdad in the fine points of Islamic law.

Formal educational institutions also promoted Islamic values. Many mosques maintained schools that provided an elementary education and religious instruction, and wealthy Muslims sometimes established schools and provided endowments for their support. By the tenth century institutions of higher education known as ***madrasas*** had begun to appear, and by the twelfth century they had become established in the major cities of the Islamic world. Muslim rulers often supported the madrasas in the interests of

madrasas (MAH-drahs-uhs)

recruiting literate and learned students with an advanced education in Islamic theology and law for administrative positions. Inexpensive paper enhanced scholars' ability to instruct students and disseminate their views.

Sufis Among the most effective Islamic missionaries were mystics known as Sufis. The term *Sufi* probably came from the patched woolen garments favored by the mystics. Sufis did not deny Islamic doctrine, and indeed many of them had an advanced education in Islamic theology and law. But they also did not find formal religious teachings to be especially meaningful. Thus, instead of concerning themselves with fine points of doctrine, Sufis worked to deepen their spiritual awareness. Most Sufis led pious and ascetic lives. Some devoted themselves to helping the poor. A few gave up their possessions and lived as mendicant beggars. Many sought a mystical, ecstatic union with Allah, relying on rousing sermons, passionate singing, or spirited dancing to bring them to a state of high emotion. Muslim theologians sometimes mistrusted Sufis, fearing that in their lack of concern for doctrine they would adopt erroneous beliefs. Nevertheless, after the ninth century Sufis became increasingly popular in Muslim societies because of their piety, devotion, and eagerness to minister to the needs of their fellow human beings.

Al-Ghazali Most important of the early Sufis was the Persian theologian al-Ghazali (1058–1111), who argued that human reason was too frail to understand the nature of Allah and hence could not explain the mysteries of the world. Only through devotion and guidance from the Quran could human beings begin to appreciate the uniqueness and power of Allah. Indeed, al-Ghazali held that philosophy and human reasoning were vain pursuits that would inevitably lead to confusion rather than understanding.

Sufi Missionaries Sufis were especially effective as missionaries because they emphasized devotion to Allah above mastery of doctrine. They sometimes encouraged individuals to revere Allah in their own ways, even if those ways did not have a basis in the Quran. They tolerated the continued observance of pre-Islamic customs, for example, as well as the association of Allah with deities recognized and revered in other faiths. The Sufis themselves led ascetic and holy lives, which won them the respect of the peoples to whom they preached. Because of their kindness, holiness, tolerance, and charismatic appeal, Sufis attracted numerous converts particularly in lands such as Persia and

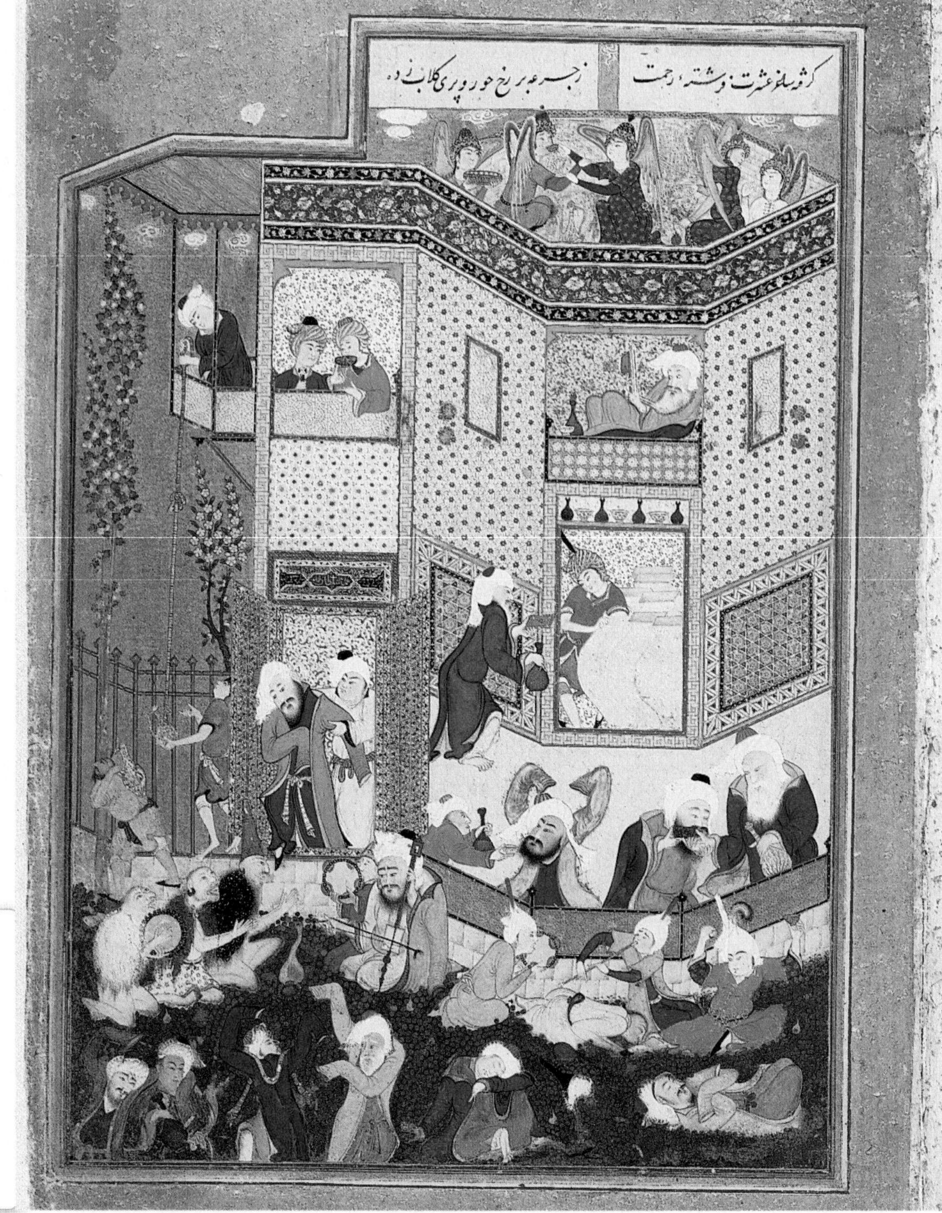

Through song, dance, and ecstatic experiences, sometimes enhanced by wine, Persian Sufis expressed their devotion to Allah, as in this sixteenth-century painting. How did Sufis facilitate the spread of Islam beyond Arabia?

India, where long-established religious faiths such as Zoroastrianism, Christianity, Buddhism, and Hinduism had enjoyed a mass following for centuries.

Hajj The symbol of Islamic cultural unity was the Ka'ba at Mecca, which from an early date attracted pilgrims from all parts of the Islamic world. The Abbasid caliphs especially encouraged observance of the hajj: they saw themselves as supreme leaders of a cohesive Islamic community, and as a matter of policy they sought to enhance the cultural unity of their realm. They built inns along the main roads to Mecca for the convenience of travelers, policed the routes to ensure the safety of pilgrims, and made lavish gifts to shrines and sites of pilgrimage. Individuals from far-flung regions of the Abbasid empire made their way to Mecca, visited the holy sites, and learned firsthand the traditions of Islam. Over the centuries those pilgrims spread Islamic beliefs and values to all parts of the Islamic world, and with the work of *ulama, qadis,* and Sufi missionaries, their efforts helped to make the *dar al-Islam* not just a name but also a reality.

Islam and the Cultural Traditions of Persia, India, and Greece

As the Islamic community expanded, Muslims of Arab ancestry interacted regularly with peoples from other cultural traditions, especially those of Persia, India, and Greece. In some cases, particularly in lands ruled by the Umayyad and Abbasid dynasties, large numbers of conquered peoples converted to Islam, and they brought elements of their inherited cultural traditions into Islamic society. In other cases, particularly in lands beyond the authority of Islamic rulers, Muslims became acquainted with the literary, artistic, philosophical, and scientific traditions of peoples who chose not to convert. Nevertheless, their traditions often held considerable interest for Muslims, who adapted them for their own purposes.

Translators and Travelers Muslims learned about different cultural traditions in several ways. The Abbasid dynasty officially supported the effort to acquire knowledge from other societies by inviting foreign scholars to the court at Baghdad and sponsoring translations of literary and scientific works from Greek, Latin, and Sanskrit into Arabic and Persian languages. By the tenth century Muslim as well as Jewish, Christian, and Zoroastrian translators had made a massive library of foreign knowledge available to Muslims. Meanwhile, Muslim merchants, missionaries, and other travelers compiled the most comprehensive body of geographic information ever assembled before European mariners made their way to all parts of the world after 1492. Drawing on Greek and Roman geographic knowledge as well as contemporary travelers' reports, Muslim geographers and cartographers produced maps, atlases, sea charts, and general descriptions of the world known to them, which included much of the eastern hemisphere. Particularly during its early centuries, the world of Islam was remarkably open to knowledge and ideas from other societies.

Persian Influences on Islam Persian traditions quickly found a place in Islamic society, since the culturally rich land of Persia fell under Islamic rule at an early date. Especially after the establishment of the Abbasid dynasty and the founding of its capital at Baghdad, Persian traditions deeply influenced Islamic political and cultural leaders. Persian administrative techniques, which Muslim conquerors borrowed from the Sasanid empire, were crucial for the organization of the imperial structure through which Umayyad and Abbasid rulers governed their vast empire. Meanwhile, Persian ideas of kingship profoundly influenced Islamic political thought. Muslim caliphs and regional governors drew readily on Persian views of kings as wise and benevolent but nonetheless absolute rulers.

Arab physicians made note of medicines used in Persian, Indian, and Greek societies and added more of their own. In this manuscript illustration, two physicians instruct a pharmacist in the preparation of medicines.

sources from the past

Al-Muqaddasi on Iraq in the Late Tenth Century

Al-Muqaddasi of Jerusalem was the leading scholar among the early Muslim geographers. He himself traveled from Morocco to northern India, and he gathered additional information from historians, merchants, and other travelers. About 985 he composed a massive book entitled The Best Divisions for Knowledge of the Regions *that presented a comprehensive geographic description of the* dar al-Islam. *In the following passages, al-Muqaddasi discusses Iraq and its major cities, which he considered quite admirable, even in an age of relative decline.*

This is the region of men of refinement, the fountainhead of scholars. The water is delightful, the air marvelous; it is the chosen place of the caliphs. It is the birthplace of . . . virtually every jurist, Reader [of the Quran], and litterateur; of nobles, sages, thinkers, ascetics, distinguished people; of charming and quick-witted people. Here is the birthplace of Abraham, the Companion of God, thither journeyed many noble Companions of the Prophet. Is not Basra there, which can be compared to the entire world? and Baghdad, praised by all mankind? sublime Kufa and Samarra? Its river [the Tigris] most certainly is of Paradise; and the dates of Basra cannot be forgotten. Its excellences are many and beyond count. The Sea of China [i.e., the Persian Gulf] touches its furthermost extremity, and the desert stretches along the edge of it. . . .

Yet it is the home of dissension and high prices, and every day it retrogresses; from injustice and taxes there is trouble, and distress. Its fruits are few, its vices many, and the oppression on the people is heavy. . . .

Basra is a distinguished capital; the Muslims founded it in the time of [the second caliph] Umar. He wrote to his Commander: "Build for the Muslims a city central to Fars and the country of the Arabs [i.e., midway between Persia and Arabia], towards the border of Iraq, on the Sea of China. So they agreed on the site of Basra, and the Arabs settled there. . . . For me, this town is superior to Baghdad, because of the prosperity here and the great number of pious people. . . .

The baths here are excellent. Fish and dates are here aplenty, besides meats, vegetables, grains, dairy products; the sciences and commerce flourish. Yet, good water is scarce, the air is constantly changing and baneful, and the people are amazingly given to riot. . . .

Baghdad is the metropolis of Islam. . . . Its people have distinctive characteristics of wittiness, charm, refinement, and correct scholarship. The climate is mild, and all that is good and beautiful is to be found there. Every skillful person comes from there, and every refinement is found there. Every heart yearns for it; every battle is fought over it, and every hand is raised to defend it. It is too renowned to need description, more glorious than we could possibly portray it, and is indeed beyond praise. . . .

It used to be the most beautiful possession of the Muslims, a most splendid city, far exceeding our description of it.

However, the authority of the caliphs declined, the city deteriorated, and the population dwindled. The City of Peace [a major district of Baghdad] is now desolate: the Mosque alone is frequented on Fridays, and otherwise the whole place is deserted. . . .

In these cities are many doctors of the law, readers of the Quran, litterateurs, eminent professional people, and kindly personages, especially in Baghdad and Basra. Preachers here are held in low estimation. Ice is brought hither from afar. The weather is cold in winter: sometimes water freezes at Basra, but commonly at Baghdad. . . .

The production of articles of commerce here is considerable. Have you not heard of the silks and linens of Basra, of the rare and exquisite articles produced there, and of its galbanum [an aromatic resin used in the production of perfumes]? It is a mine of pearls and gems, a port on the sea and an emporium on the land. Here are produced antimony, cinnabar, verdigris, and litharge of silver. Dates are exported from here to places far away, as well as henna, silk, essence of violet, and rosewater. . . . In the City of Peace elegant and varied apparel is made, and cloths of silk, and other materials. . . .

For Further Reflection

- Who might have read al-Muqaddasi's book? Why was his kind of descriptive geography a prominent field of scholarship during the Abbasid dynasty?

Source: Al-Muqaddasi. *The Best Divisions for Knowledge of the Regions.* Trans. by Basil Anthony Collins. Reading: Garnet, 1994, pp. 104, 106–8, 110, 114, 116–17. (Translation slightly modified.)

Persian influence was also noticeable in literary works from the Abbasid dynasty. Although Arabic served as the language of religion, theology, philosophy, and law, Persian was the principal language of literature, poetry, history, and political reflection. The verses of Omar Khayyam entitled the *Rubaiyat* ("quatrains") are widely known, thanks to a popular English translation by the Victorian poet Edward Fitzgerald, but many other writers composed works that in Persian display even greater literary elegance and originality. The marvelous collection of stories known as *The Ara-*

An illustration from a thirteenth-century, Arabic-language manuscript depicts the Greek philosopher Aristotle teaching three students about the astrolabe, an instrument that enabled the user to determine latitude.

bian Nights, or *The Thousand and One Nights,* for example, presented popular tales of adventure and romance set in the Abbasid empire and the court of Harun al-Rashid.

Indian Influences on Islam Indian mathematics, science, and medicine captured the attention of Arab and Persian Muslims who established Islamic states in northern India. The sophisticated mathematical tradition of Gupta India was attractive to Muslims both as a field of scholarship and for the practical purposes of reckoning and keeping accounts. Muslims readily adopted what they called "Hindi" numerals, which European peoples later called "Arabic" numerals, since they learned about them through Arab Muslims. Hindi numerals enabled Muslim scholars to develop an impressive tradition of advanced mathematics, concentrating on algebra (an Arabic word) as well as trigonometry and geometry. From a more practical point of view, Indian numerals vastly simplified bookkeeping for Muslim merchants working in the lively commercial economy of the Abbasid dynasty.

Muslims also found much to appreciate in the scientific and medical thought they encountered in India. With the aid of their powerful and flexible mathematics, Indian scholars were able to carry out precise astronomical calculations, which helped inspire the development of Muslim astronomy. Similarly, Indian medicine appealed to Muslims because of its treatments for specific ailments and its use of antidotes for poisons. Muslim visitors often railed against Indian religious beliefs—both Hindu and Buddhist—but they uniformly praised Indian mathematical, scientific, and medical thought, which they avidly adopted for their own uses and purposes.

Greek Influences on Islam Muslims also admired the philosophical, scientific, and medical writings of classical Greece. They became especially interested in Plato and Aristotle, whose works they translated and interpreted in commentaries. During the tenth and eleventh centuries, some Muslim philosophers sought to synthesize Greek and Muslim thought by harmonizing Plato with the teachings of Islam. They encountered resistance among conservative theologians such as the Sufi al-Ghazali, who considered Greek philosophy a completely unreliable guide to ultimate truth, since it relied on frail human reason rather than on the revelation of the Quran.

Partly in response to al-Ghazali's attacks, twelfth-century Muslim philosophers turned their attention more to Aristotle than to Plato. The most notable figure in this development was Ibn Rushd (1126–1198), *qadi* of Seville in the caliphate of Córdoba, who followed Aristotle in seeking to articulate a purely rational understanding of the world. Ibn Rushd's work not only helped to shape Islamic philosophy but also found its way to the schools and universities of western Europe, where Christian scholars knew Ibn Rushd as Averroes. During the thirteenth century his work profoundly influenced the development of scholasticism, the effort of medieval European philosophers to harmonize Christianity with Aristotelian thought.

Ibn Rushd's reliance on natural reason went too far for many Muslims, who placed more value on the revelations of the Quran than on the fruits of human logic. After the thirteenth century, Muslim philosophers and theologians who dominated the madrasas drew inspiration more from Islamic sources than from Greek philosophy. Platonic and Aristotelian influences did not disappear, but they lost favor in official seats of learning and fell increasingly under the shadow of teachings from the Quran and Sufi mystics. As they did with political and cultural traditions from Persia and India, Muslim thinkers absorbed Greek philosophy, reconsidered it, and used it to advance the interests of their society.

Quite apart from philosophy, Greek mathematics, science, and medicine appealed strongly to Muslims. Like their Indian counterparts, scholars in classical Greek and Hellenistic societies had developed elaborate traditions of scientific thought. Greek mathematics did not make use of Indian numerals, but it offered a solid body of powerful reasoning, particularly when dealing with calculations in algebra and geometry. Greek mathematics supported the development of astronomical and geographical scholarship, and studies of anatomy and physiology served as foundations for medical thought. Muslim scholars quickly absorbed those Greek traditions, combined them with influences from India, and used them all as points of departure for their studies. The result was a brilliant flowering of mathematical, scientific, and medical scholarship that provided Muslim societies with powerful tools for understanding the natural world.

inperspective

The prophet Muhammad did not intend to found a new religion. Instead, his intention was to express his convictions about Allah and perfect the teachings of earlier Jewish and Christian prophets by announcing a revelation more comprehensive than those Allah had entrusted to his predecessors. His message soon attracted a circle of devout and committed disciples, and by the time of his death most of Arabia had accepted Islam. During the two centuries following the prophet's death, Arab conquerors spread Islam throughout southwest Asia and north Africa and introduced their faith to central Asia, India, the Mediterranean islands, and Iberia. This rapid expansion of Islam encouraged the development of an extensive trade and communication network: merchants, diplomats, and other travelers moved easily throughout the Islamic world exchanging goods and introducing agricultural crops to new lands. Rapid expansion also led to encounters between Islam and long-established religious and cultural traditions such as Hinduism, Judaism, Zoroastrianism, Christianity, Persian literature and political thought, and classical Greek philosophy and science. Muslim thinkers readily adapted those earlier traditions to their needs. As a result of its expansion, its extensive trade and communication networks, and its engagement with other religious and cultural traditions, the *dar al-Islam* became one of the most prosperous and cosmopolitan societies of the postclassical world. ●

CHRONOLOGY	
570–632	Life of Muhammad
622	The *hijra*
632	Muhammad's *hajj*
650s	Compilation of the Quran
661–750	Umayyad dynasty
750–1258	Abbasid dynasty
786–809	Reign of Harun al-Rashid
1050s	Establishment of Saljuq control over the Abbasid dynasty
1058–1111	Life of al-Ghazali
1126–1198	Life of Ibn Rushd

For Further Reading

Muhammad Manazir Ahsan. *Social Life under the Abbasids.* New York, 1979. Draws on a wide range of sources in discussing dress, food, drink, housing, and daily life during the Abbasid era.

Jonathan P. Berkey. *The Formation of Islam: Religion and Society in the Near East, 600–1800.* Cambridge, 2003. Views the development of Islamic society in the context of relations between Muslims, Jews, and Christians.

Jonathan M. Bloom. *Paper before Print: The History and Impact of Paper in the Islamic World.* New Haven, 2001. Fascinating study exploring the production and uses of paper in the Islamic world before the adoption of printing technology.

Richard W. Bulliet. *The Camel and the Wheel.* New York, 1990. Pioneering study of the domestication of camels and transportation technologies based on camels.

Michael Cook. *Muhammad.* Oxford, 1983. A brief and accessible biography highlighting Muhammad's devout monotheism.

Fred McGraw Donner. *The Early Islamic Conquests.* Princeton, 1981. An important interpretation that emphasizes the significance of political and religious unity for early Muslim conquerors.

John Esposito. *Islam: The Straight Path.* 3rd ed. New York, 2005. The best brief introduction to Islam.

Richard C. Foltz. *Spirituality in the Land of the Noble: How Iran Shaped the World's Religions.* Oxford, 2004. Includes an accessible discussion of Persian influences on the Islamic faith.

Abu Hamid Muhammad al-Ghazzali. *The Alchemy of Happiness.* Trans. by Claude Field. Rev. by Elton L. Daniel. New York, 1991. Translation of one of the classic works of early Islamic religious and moral thought.

Ahmad Y. al-Hassan and Donald R. Hill. *Islamic Technology: An Illustrated History.* Cambridge, 1986. Thorough survey of Islamic science and technology, with attention both to original inventions and to elements borrowed by Muslims from other societies.

Mahmood Ibrahim. *Merchant Capital and Islam.* Austin, 1990. Examines the role of trade in Arabia during Muhammad's time and in early Islamic society.

Ira M. Lapidus. *A History of Islamic Societies.* Cambridge, 1988. Authoritative survey of Islamic history, concentrating on social and cultural issues.

Ilse Lichtenstadter. *Introduction to Classical Arabic Literature.* New York, 1974. A brief overview, accompanied by an extensive selection of texts in English translation.

M. Lombard. *The Golden Age of Islam.* Princeton, 2004. Concentrates on the social and economic history of the Abbasid period.

F. E. Peters. *The Hajj: The Muslim Pilgrimage to Mecca and the Holy Places.* Princeton, 1994. Draws on scores of travelers' reports in studying the Muslim practice through the ages of making a pilgrimage to Mecca.

———. *Muhammad and the Origins of Islam.* Albany, 1994. Excellent introduction to Muhammad's life and thought and the early days of his movement.

Al Qur'an: A Contemporary Translation. Trans. by Ahmed Ali. Princeton, 1984. A sensitive translation of the holy book of Islam.

Francis Robinson, ed. *The Cambridge Illustrated History of the Islamic World.* Cambridge, 1996. An excellent and lavishly illustrated introduction to Islam and the Muslim world.

Maxime Rodinson. *Islam and Capitalism.* Trans. by B. Pearce. New York, 1973. An influential volume that examines Islamic teachings on economic matters as well as economic practice in the Muslim world.

Ronald Segal. *Islam's Black Slaves: The Other Black Diaspora.* New York, 2001. A highly readable study of slavery in Islamic society.

Andrew M. Watson. *Agricultural Innovation in the Early Islamic World: The Diffusion of Crops and Farming Techniques, 700–1100.* Cambridge, 1983. Important scholarly study of the diffusion of food and industrial crops throughout the early Islamic world.

Michael Wolfe, ed. *One Thousand Roads to Mecca: Ten Centuries of Travelers Writing about the Muslim Pilgrimage.* New York, 1997. Presents selections from twenty-three accounts describing travelers' hajj experiences.

The Resurgence of Empire in East Asia

chapter 14

A painting on silk depicts anxious candidates taking the civil service examinations at the time of the emperor Song Renzong (reigned 1023–1031).

EYEWITNESS:
Xuanzang: A Young Monk Hits the Road

Early in the seventh century C.E., the emperor of China issued an order forbidding his subjects to travel beyond Chinese borders into central Asia. In 629, however, in defiance of the emperor, a young Buddhist monk slipped past imperial watchtowers under cover of darkness and made his way west. His name was **Xuanzang,** and his destination was India, homeland of Buddhism. Although educated in Confucian texts as a youth, Xuanzang had followed his older brother into a monastery where he became devoted to Buddhism. While studying the Sanskrit language, Xuanzang noticed that Chinese writings on Buddhism contained many teachings that were confusing or even contradictory to those of Indian Buddhist texts. He decided to travel to India, visit the holy sites of Buddhism, and study with the most knowledgeable Buddhist teachers and sages to learn about Buddhism from the purest sources.

Xuanzang could not have imagined the difficulties he would face. Immediately after his departure from China, his guide abandoned him in the Gobi desert. After losing his water bag and collapsing in the heat, Xuanzang made his way to the oasis town of Turpan on the silk roads. The Buddhist ruler of Turpan provided the devout pilgrim with travel supplies and rich gifts to support his mission. Among the presents were twenty-four letters of introduction to rulers of lands on the way to India, each one attached to a bolt of silk, five hundred bolts of silk and two carts of fruit for the most important ruler, thirty horses, twenty-five laborers, and another five hundred bolts of silk along with gold, silver, and silk clothes for Xuanzang to use as travel funds. After departing from Turpan, Xuanzang crossed three of the world's highest mountain ranges—the Tian Shan, Hindu Kush, and Pamir ranges—and lost one-third of his party to exposure and starvation in the Tian Shan. He crossed yawning gorges thousands of meters deep on footbridges fashioned from rope or chains, and he faced numerous attacks by bandits as well as confrontations with demons, dragons, and evil spirits.

Xuanzang (SHWEN-ZAHNG)

Yet Xuanzang persisted and arrived in India in 630. He lived there for more than twelve years, visiting the holy sites of Buddhism and devoting himself to the study of languages and Buddhist doctrine, especially at Nalanda, the center of advanced Buddhist education in India. He also amassed a huge collection of relics and images as well as 657 books, all of which he packed into 527 crates and transported back to China to advance the understanding of Buddhism in his native land.

By the time of his return in 645, Xuanzang had logged more than 16,000 kilometers (10,000 miles) on the road. News of the holy monk's efforts had reached the imperial court, and even though Xuanzang had violated the ban on travel, he received a hero's welcome and an audience with the emperor. Until his death in 664, Xuanzang spent his remaining years translating Buddhist treatises into Chinese and clarifying their doctrines. His efforts helped to popularize Buddhism throughout China.

Xuanzang undertook his journey at a propitious time. For more than 350 years after the fall of the Han dynasty, war, invasion, conquest, and foreign rule disrupted Chinese society. Toward the end of the sixth century, however, centralized imperial rule returned to China. The Sui and Tang dynasties restored order and presided over an era of rapid economic growth in China. Agricultural yields rose dramatically, and technological innovations boosted the production of manufactured goods. China ranked with the Abbasid and Byzantine empires as a political and economic anchor of the postclassical world.

For China the postclassical era was an age of intense interaction with other peoples. Chinese merchants participated in trade networks that linked most regions of the eastern hemisphere. Buddhism spread beyond its homeland of India, attracted a large popular following in China, and even influenced the thought of Confucian scholars. A resurgent China made its influence felt throughout east Asia: diplomats and armed forces introduced Chinese ways into Korea and Vietnam, and rulers of the Japanese islands looked to China for guidance in matters of political organization. Korea, Vietnam, and Japan retained their distinctiveness, but all three lands drew deep inspiration from China and participated in a larger east Asian society centered on China.

THE RESTORATION OF CENTRALIZED IMPERIAL RULE IN CHINA

During the centuries following the Han dynasty, several regional kingdoms made bids to assert their authority over all of China, but none possessed the resources to dominate its rivals over the long term. In the late sixth century, however, Yang Jian, an ambitious ruler in northern China, embarked on a series of military campaigns that brought all of China once again under centralized imperial rule. Yang Jian's Sui dynasty survived less than thirty years, but the tradition of centralized rule outlived his house. The Tang dynasty replaced the Sui, and the Song succeeded the Tang. The Tang and Song dynasties organized Chinese society so efficiently that China became a center of exceptional agricultural and industrial production. Indeed, much of the eastern hemisphere felt the effects of the powerful Chinese economy of the Tang and Song dynasties.

The Sui Dynasty

Establishment of the Dynasty Like Qin Shihuangdi some eight hundred years earlier, Yang Jian imposed tight political discipline on his state and then extended his rule to the rest of China. Yang Jian began his rise to power when a Turkish ruler appointed him duke of Sui in northern China. In 580 Yang Jian's patron died, leaving a seven-year-old son as his heir. Yang Jian installed the boy as ruler but forced his abdication one year later, claiming the throne and the Mandate of Heaven for himself. During the next decade Yang Jian sent military expeditions into central Asia and southern China. By 589 the house of Sui ruled all of China.

Like the rulers of the Qin dynasty, the emperors of the Sui dynasty (589–618 C.E.) placed enormous demands on their subjects in the course of building a strong, centralized government. The Sui emperors ordered the construction of palaces and granaries, carried out extensive repairs on defensive walls, dispatched military forces to central Asia and Korea, levied high taxes, and demanded compulsory labor services.

The Grand Canal The most elaborate project undertaken during the Sui dynasty was the construction of the Grand Canal, which was one of the world's largest waterworks projects before modern times. The second emperor, Sui Yangdi (reigned 604–618 C.E.), completed work on the canal to facilitate trade between northern and southern China, particularly to make the abundant supplies of rice and other food crops from the Yangzi River valley available to residents of northern regions. The only practical and economical way to transport food crops in large quantities was by water. But since Chinese rivers generally flow from west to east, only an artificial waterway could support a large volume of trade between north and south.

The Grand Canal was really a series of artificial waterways that ultimately reached from Hangzhou in the south to

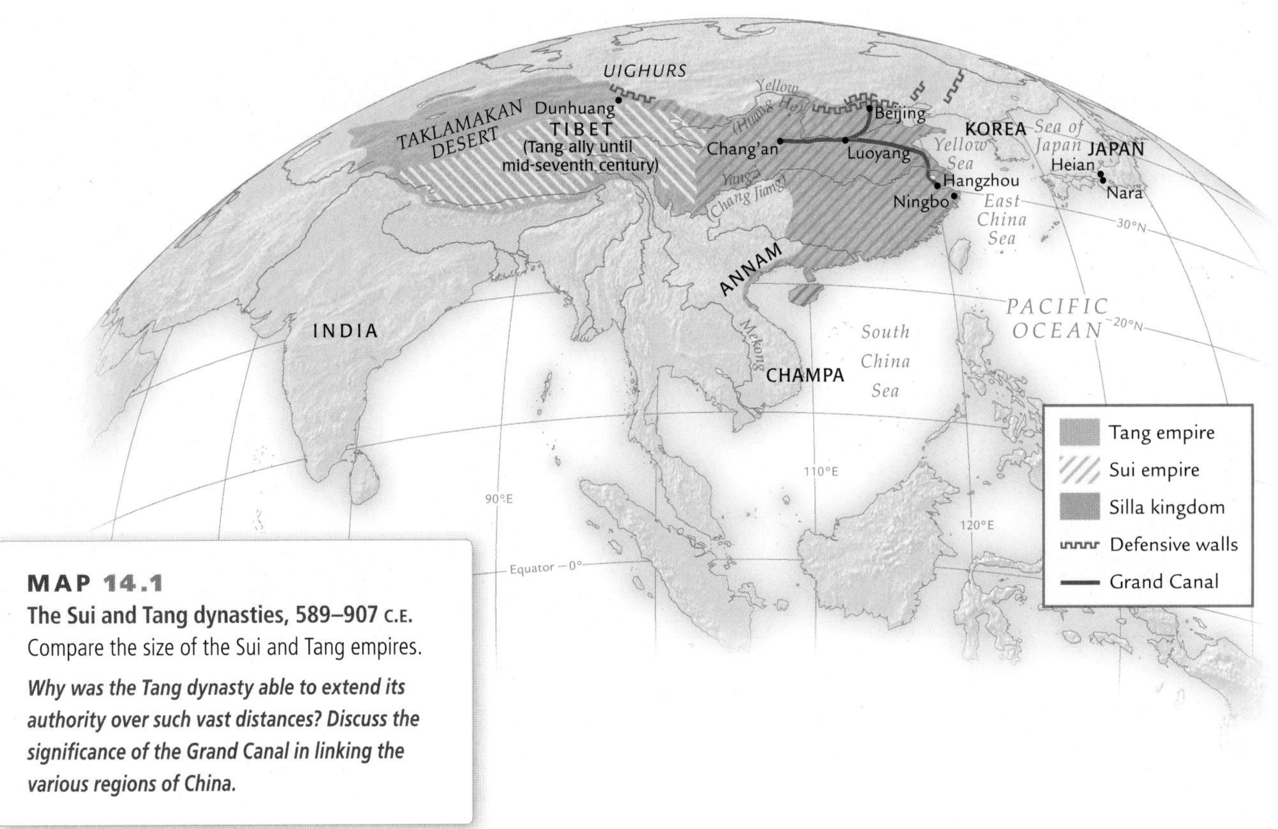

MAP 14.1
The Sui and Tang dynasties, 589–907 C.E.
Compare the size of the Sui and Tang empires.
Why was the Tang dynasty able to extend its authority over such vast distances? Discuss the significance of the Grand Canal in linking the various regions of China.

the imperial capital of Chang'an in the west to a terminus near modern Beijing in the north. Sui Yangdi used canals dug as early as the Zhou dynasty, but he linked them into a network that served much of China. When completed, the Grand Canal extended almost 2,000 kilometers (1,240 miles) and reportedly was forty paces wide, with roads running parallel to the waterway on either side.

Though expensive to construct, Sui Yangdi's investment in the Grand Canal paid dividends for more than a thousand years. It integrated the economies of northern and southern China, thereby establishing an economic foundation for political and cultural unity. Until the arrival of railroads in the twentieth century, the Grand Canal served as the principal conduit for internal trade. Indeed, the canal continues to function even today, although mechanical transport has diminished its significance as a trade route.

Sui Yangdi's construction projects served China well over a long term, but their dependence on high taxes and forced labor generated hostility toward his rule. The Grand Canal alone required the services of conscripted laborers by the millions. Military reverses in Korea prompted discontented subjects to revolt against Sui rule. During the late 610s, rebellions broke out in northern China when Sui Yangdi sought additional resources for his Korean campaign. In 618 a disgruntled minister assassinated the emperor and brought the dynasty to an end.

The Tang Dynasty

Soon after Sui Yangdi's death, a rebel leader seized Chang'an and proclaimed himself emperor of a new dynasty that he named Tang after his hereditary title. The dynasty survived for almost three hundred years (618–907 C.E.), and Tang rulers organized China into a powerful, productive, and prosperous society.

Tang Taizong Much of the Tang's success was due to the energy, ability, and policies of the dynasty's second emperor, **Tang Taizong** (reigned 627–649 C.E.). Taizong was both ambitious and ruthless: in making his way to the imperial throne, he murdered two of his brothers and pushed his father aside. Once on the throne, however, he displayed a high sense of duty and strove conscientiously to provide an effective, stable government. He built a splendid capital at Chang'an, and he saw himself as a Confucian ruler who heeded the interests of his subjects. Contemporaries reported that banditry ended during his reign, that the price of rice remained low, and that taxes levied on peasants amounted to only one-fortieth of the annual harvest—a 2.5 percent tax rate—although required rent payments and compulsory labor services meant that the effective rate of taxation was somewhat higher. These reports suggest that China enjoyed an era of unusual stability and prosperity during the reign of Tang Taizong.

Tang Taizong (TAHNG TEYE-zohng)

Barges make their way through a portion of the Grand Canal near the city of Wuxi in southern China. Built during the Sui dynasty, the waterways of the Grand Canal fostered the economic integration of northern and southern China.

Three policies in particular help to explain the success of the early Tang dynasty: maintenance of a well-articulated transportation and communications network, distribution of land according to the principles of the equal-field system, and reliance on a bureaucracy based on merit. All three policies originated in the Sui dynasty, but Tang rulers applied them more systematically and effectively than their predecessors had.

Transportation and Communications Apart from the Grand Canal, which served as the principal route for long-distance transportation within China, Tang rulers maintained an extensive communications network based on roads, horses, and sometimes human runners. Along the main routes, Tang officials maintained inns, postal stations, and stables, which provided rest and refreshment for travelers, couriers, and their mounts. Using couriers traveling by horse, the Tang court could communicate with the most distant cities in the empire in about eight days. Even human runners provided impressively speedy services: relay teams of some 9,600 runners supplied the Tang court at Chang'an with seafood delivered fresh from Ningbo, more than 1,000 kilometers (620 miles) away.

The Equal-Field System The equal-field system governed the allocation of agricultural land. Its purpose was to ensure an equitable distribution of land and to avoid the concentration of landed property that had caused social problems during the Han dynasty. The system allotted land to individuals and their families according to the land's fertility and the recipients' needs. About one-fifth of the land became the hereditary possession of the recipients, and the rest remained available for redistribution when the original recipients' needs and circumstances changed.

For about a century, administrators were able to apply the principles of the equal-field system relatively consistently. By the early eighth century, however, the system showed signs of strain. A rapidly rising population placed pressure on the land available for distribution. Meanwhile, through favors, bribery, or intimidation of administrators, influential families found ways to retain land scheduled for redistribution. Furthermore, large parcels of land fell out of the system altogether when Buddhist monasteries acquired them. Nevertheless, during the first half of the Tang dynasty, the system provided a foundation for stability and prosperity in the Chinese countryside.

Bureaucracy of Merit The Tang dynasty also relied heavily on a bureaucracy based on merit, as reflected by performance on imperial civil service examinations. Following the example of the Han dynasty, Sui and Tang rulers recruited government officials from the ranks of candidates who had progressed through the Confucian educational system and had mastered a sophisticated curriculum concentrating on the classic works of Chinese literature and philosophy. During the early Tang dynasty, most officeholders were aristocrats. By the late Tang era, however, when educational opportunities were widely available, officeholders came largely from the ranks of common families. The Confucian educational system and the related civil service served Chinese governments so well that, with modifications and an occasional interruption, they survived for thirteen centuries, disappearing only after the collapse of the Qing dynasty in the early twentieth century.

Military Expansion Soon after its foundation, the powerful and dynamic Tang state began to flex its military muscles. In the north, Tang forces brought Manchuria under imperial authority and forced the Silla kingdom in Korea to acknowledge the Tang emperor as overlord. To the south, Tang armies conquered the northern part of Vietnam. To the west they extended Tang authority as far as the Aral Sea and brought a portion of the high plateau of Tibet under Tang control. Territorially, the Tang empire ranks among the largest in Chinese history.

Tang Foreign Relations In an effort to fashion a stable diplomatic order, the Tang emperors revived the Han dynasty's practice of maintaining tributary relationships between China and neighboring lands. According to Chinese political theory, China was the Middle Kingdom, a powerful realm with the responsibility to bring order to subordinate lands through a system of tributary relationships. Neighboring lands and peoples would recognize Chinese emperors as their overlords. As tokens of their subordinate status, envoys from those states would regularly deliver gifts to the court of the Middle Kingdom and would perform the kowtow—a ritual prostration in which subordinates knelt before the emperor and touched their foreheads to the ground. In return, tributary states received confirmation of their authority as well as lavish gifts. Because Chinese authorities often had little real influence in these supposedly subordinate lands, there was always something of a fictional quality to the system. Nevertheless, it was extremely important throughout east Asia and central Asia because it institutionalized relations between China and neighboring lands, fostering trade and cultural exchanges as well as diplomatic contacts.

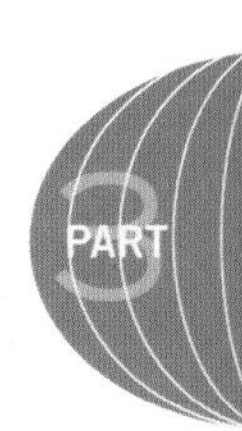

Tang Decline Under able rulers such as Taizong, the Tang dynasty flourished. During the mid-eighth century, however, casual and careless leadership brought the dynasty to a crisis from which it never fully recovered. In 755, while the emperor neglected public affairs in favor of music and his favorite concubine, one of the dynasty's foremost military commanders, An Lushan, mounted a rebellion and captured the capital at Chang'an, as well as the secondary capital at Luoyang. His revolt was short-lived: in 757 a soldier murdered An Lushan, and by 763 Tang forces had suppressed his army and recovered their capitals. But the rebellion left the dynasty in a gravely weakened state. Tang commanders were unable to defeat rebellious forces

In this wall painting from the tomb of a Tang prince, three Chinese officials (at left) receive envoys from foreign lands who pay their respects to representatives of the Middle Kingdom. The envoys probably come from the Byzantine empire, Korea, and Siberia. What features of their personal appearance and dress provide clues to the envoys' lands of origin?

sources from the past

The Poet Du Fu on Tang Dynasty Wars

The eighth century was a golden age of Chinese poetry. Among the foremost writers of the era was Du Fu (712–770 C.E.), often considered China's greatest poet. Born into a prominent Confucian family, Du Fu wrote in his early years about the beauty of the natural world. After the rebellion of An Lushan, however, he fell into poverty and experienced difficulties. Not surprisingly, poetry of his later years lamented the chaos of the late eighth century. In the following verses, Du Fu offered a bitter perspective on the wars that plagued China in the 750s and 760s.

A Song of War Chariots

The war-chariots rattle,
The war-horses whinny.
Each man of you has a bow and a quiver at his belt.
Father, mother, son, wife, stare at you going,
Till dust shall have buried the bridge beyond Chang'an.
They run with you, crying, they tug at your sleeves,
And the sound of their sorrow goes up to the clouds;
And every time a bystander asks you a question,
You can only say to him that you have to go.
. . . We remember others at fifteen sent north to guard the river
And at forty sent west to cultivate the camp-farms.
The mayor wound their turbans for them when they started out.
With their turbaned hair white now, they are still at the border,
At the border where the blood of men spills like the sea—
And still the heart of Emperor Wu is beating for war.
. . . Do you know that, east of China's mountains, in two hundred districts
And in thousands of villages, nothing grows but weeds,
And though strong women have bent to the ploughing,
East and west the furrows all are broken down?
. . . Men of China are able to face the stiffest battle,
But their officers drive them like chickens and dogs.
Whatever is asked of them,
Dare they complain?
For example, this winter
Held west of the gate,
Challenged for taxes,
How could they pay?
. . . We have learned that to have a son is bad luck—
It is very much better to have a daughter
Who can marry and live in the house of a neighbour,
While under the sod we bury our boys.
. . . Go to the Blue Sea, look along the shore
At all the old white bones forsaken—
New ghosts are wailing there now with the old,
Loudest in the dark sky of a stormy day.

For Further Reflection

- Assess the effects of war in the late Tang dynasty from the viewpoints of imperial rulers and individual subjects.

Source: Cyril Birch, ed. *Anthology of Chinese Literature,* 2 vols. New York: Grove Press, 1965, pp. 1:240–41.

by themselves, so they invited a nomadic Turkish people, the **Uighurs,** to bring an army into China. In return for their services, the Uighurs demanded the right to sack Chang'an and Luoyang after the expulsion of the rebels.

The Tang imperial house never regained control of affairs after this crisis. The equal-field system deteriorated, and dwindling tax receipts failed to meet dynastic needs. Imperial armies were unable to resist the encroachments of Turkish peoples in the late eighth century. During the ninth century a series of rebellions devastated the Chinese countryside. One uprising, led by the military commander Huang Chao, embroiled much of eastern China for almost a decade from 875 to 884. Huang Chao's revolt reflected and fueled popular discontent: he routinely pillaged the wealthy and distributed a portion of his plunder among the poor. In an effort to control the rebels, the Tang emperors granted progressively greater power and authority to regional military commanders, who gradually became the effective rulers of China. In 907 the last Tang emperor abdicated his throne, and the dynasty came to an end.

The Song Dynasty

Following the Tang collapse, warlords ruled China until the Song dynasty reimposed centralized imperial rule in the late tenth century. Though it survived for more than three centuries, the Song dynasty (960–1279 C.E.) never built a very powerful state. Song rulers mistrusted military leaders, and they placed much more emphasis on civil administration, industry, education, and the arts than on military affairs.

Uighurs (WEE-goors)

Song Taizu The first Song emperor, Song Taizu (reigned 960–976 C.E.), inaugurated this policy. Song Taizu began his career as a junior military officer serving one of the most powerful warlords in northern China. He had a reputation for honesty and effectiveness, and in 960 his troops proclaimed him emperor. During the next several years, he and his army subjected the warlords to their authority and consolidated Song control throughout China. He then persuaded his generals to retire honorably to a life of leisure so that they would not seek to displace him, and he set about organizing a centralized administration that placed military forces under tight supervision.

Song Taizu regarded all state officials, even minor functionaries in distant provinces, as servants of the imperial government. In exchange for their loyalty, Song rulers rewarded these officials handsomely. They vastly expanded the bureaucracy based on merit by creating more opportunities for individuals to seek a Confucian education and take civil service examinations. They accepted many more candidates into the bureaucracy than their Sui and Tang predecessors, and they provided generous salaries for those who qualified for government appointments. They even placed civil bureaucrats in charge of military forces.

Song Weaknesses The Song approach to administration resulted in a more centralized imperial government than earlier Chinese dynasties had enjoyed. But it caused two big problems that weakened the dynasty and eventually brought about its fall. The first problem was financial: the enormous Song bureaucracy devoured China's surplus production. As the number of bureaucrats and the size of their rewards grew, the imperial treasury came under tremendous pressure. Efforts to raise taxes aggravated the peasants, who mounted two major rebellions in the early twelfth century. By that time, however, bureaucrats dominated the Song administration to the point that it was impossible to reform the system.

The second problem was military. Scholar-bureaucrats generally had little military education and little talent for military affairs, yet they led Song armies in the field and made military decisions. It was no coincidence that nomadic peoples flourished along China's northern border throughout the Song dynasty. From the early tenth through the early twelfth century, the Khitan, a seminomadic people from Manchuria, ruled a vast empire stretching from northern Korea to Mongolia. During the first half of the Song dynasty, the Khitan demanded and received large tribute payments of silk and silver from the Song state to the south. In the early twelfth century, the nomadic Jurchen conquered the Khitan, overran northern China, captured the Song capital at Kaifeng, and proclaimed establishment of the Jin empire. Thereafter the Song dynasty moved its capital to the prosperous port city of Hangzhou and survived only in southern China, so that the latter part of the dynasty is commonly known as

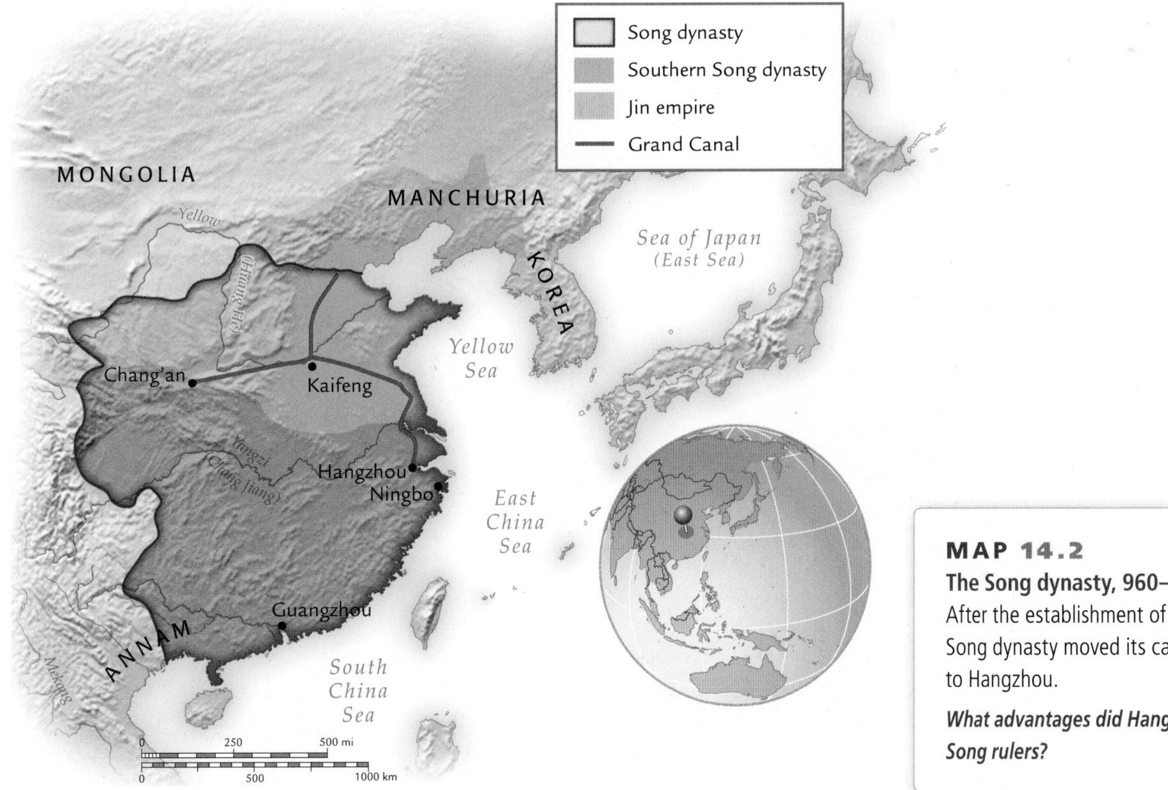

MAP 14.2
The Song dynasty, 960–1279 C.E.
After the establishment of the Jin empire, the Song dynasty moved its capital from Kaifeng to Hangzhou.
What advantages did Hangzhou offer to the Song rulers?

the Southern Song. This truncated Southern Song shared a border with the Jin empire about midway between the Yellow River and the Yangzi River until 1279, when Mongol forces ended the dynasty and incorporated southern China into their empire.

THE ECONOMIC DEVELOPMENT OF TANG AND SONG CHINA

Although the Song dynasty did not develop a particularly strong military capacity, it benefited from a remarkable series of agricultural, technological, industrial, and commercial developments that transformed China into the economic powerhouse of Eurasia. This economic development originated in the Tang dynasty, but its results became most clear during the Song, which presided over a land of enormous prosperity. The economic surge of Tang and Song times had implications that went well beyond China, since it stimulated trade and production throughout much of the eastern hemisphere for more than half a millennium, from about 600 to 1300 C.E.

Agricultural Development

Fast-Ripening Rice The foundation of economic development in Tang and Song China was a surge in agricultural production. Sui and Tang armies prepared the way for increased agricultural productivity when they imposed their control over southern China and ventured into Vietnam. In Vietnam they encountered strains of fast-ripening rice that enabled cultivators to harvest two crops per year. When introduced to the fertile fields of southern China, fast-ripening rice quickly resulted in an expanded supply of food. Like the *dar al-Islam,* Tang and Song China benefited enormously from the introduction of new food crops.

New Agricultural Techniques Chinese cultivators also increased their productivity by adopting improved agricultural techniques. They made increased use of heavy iron plows, and they harnessed oxen (in the north) and water buffaloes (in the south) to help prepare land for cultivation. They enriched the soil with manure and composted organic matter. They also organized extensive irrigation systems. These included not only reservoirs, dikes, dams, and canals but also pumps and waterwheels, powered by both animals and humans, that moved water into irrigation systems. Artificial irrigation made it possible to extend cultivation to difficult terrain, including terraced mountainsides—a development that vastly expanded China's agricultural potential.

Population Growth Increased agricultural production had dramatic results. One was a rapid expansion of the Chinese population. After the fall of the Han dynasty, the population of China reached a low point, about 45 million in

An illustration commissioned by the Song government shows peasants how to go about the laborious task of transplanting rice seedlings into a paddy flooded with water.

A twelfth-century painting depicts the spring festival as observed in the northern Song capital of Kaifeng. Porters, shopkeepers, peddlers, fortune-tellers, and Confucian scholars deep in conversation are all in view.

600 C.E. By 800 it had rebounded to 50 million, and two centuries later to 60 million. By 1127, when the Jurchen conquered the northern half of the Song state, the Chinese population had passed 100 million, and by 1200 it stood at about 115 million. This rapid population growth reflected both the productivity of the agricultural economy and the well-organized distribution of food through transportation networks built during Sui and Tang times.

Urbanization Increased food supplies encouraged the growth of cities. During the Tang dynasty the imperial capital of Chang'an was the world's most populous city, with perhaps as many as two million residents. During the Song dynasty, China was the most urbanized land in the world. In the late thirteenth century, Hangzhou, capital of the Southern Song dynasty, had more than one million residents. They supported hundreds of restaurants, noodle shops, taverns, teahouses, brothels, music halls, theaters, clubhouses, gardens, markets, craft shops, and specialty stores dealing in silk, gems, porcelain, lacquerware, and other goods. Hangzhou residents, like those in most cities, observed peculiar local customs. Taverns often had several stories, for example, and patrons gravitated to higher or lower stories according to their plans: those desiring only a cup or two of wine sat at street level, whereas those planning an extended evening of revelry sought tables on the higher stories.

As a capital, Hangzhou was something of a special case among cities, but during the Tang and Song eras, scores of Chinese cities boasted populations of one hundred thousand or more. Li Bai (701–761 C.E.), who was perhaps the most popular poet of the Tang era, took the social life of these Chinese cities as one of his principal themes. Li Bai mostly wrote light, pleasing verse celebrating life, friendship, and especially wine. (Tradition holds that the drunken poet died by drowning when he fell out of a boat while attempting to embrace the moon's reflection in the water.) The annual spring festival was an occasion dear to the heart of urban residents, who flocked to the streets to shop for new products, have their fortunes told, and eat tasty snacks from food vendors.

Another result of increased food production was the emergence of a commercialized agricultural economy. Because fast-ripening rice yielded bountiful harvests, many cultivators could purchase inexpensive rice and raise vegetables and fruits for sale on the commercial market. Cultivators specialized in crops that grew well in their regions, and they often exported their harvests to distant regions. By the twelfth century, for example, the wealthy southern province of Fujian imported rice and devoted its land to the production of lychees, oranges, and sugarcane, which fetched high prices in northern markets. Indeed, market-oriented cultivation went so far that authorities tried—with only limited success—to require Fujianese to grow rice so as to avoid excessive dependence on imports.

Patriarchal Social Structures With increasing wealth and agricultural productivity, Tang and especially Song China experienced a tightening of patriarchal social structures, which perhaps reflected a concern to preserve family fortunes through enhanced family solidarity. During the Song dynasty the veneration of family ancestors became much more elaborate. Instead of simply remembering ancestors and invoking their aid in rituals performed at home, descendants diligently sought the graves of their earliest traceable forefathers and then arranged elaborate graveside rituals in their honor. Whole extended families often traveled great distances to attend annual rituals venerating their ancestors—a practice that strengthened the sense of family identity and cohesiveness.

Foot Binding Strengthened patriarchal authority also helps to explain the popularity of foot binding, which spread widely during the Song era. Foot binding involved the tight wrapping of young girls' feet with strips of cloth that prevented natural growth of the bones and resulted in tiny, malformed, curved feet. Women with bound feet could not walk easily or naturally. Usually, they needed canes to walk by themselves, and sometimes they depended on servants to carry them around in litters. Foot binding never became universal in China, but many wealthy families and sometimes also peasant families bound the feet of their daughters to enhance their attractiveness and gain increased control over the girls' behavior. Like the practice of veiling women in Mediterranean and Muslim lands, foot binding placed women under tight supervision of their husbands or other male guardians, who then managed the women's affairs in the interests of the larger family.

Wu Zhao: The Lady Emperor Ironically, this era of strong patriarchal authority produced a rare female ruler. Wu Zhao (626–706 C.E.) was the daughter of a scholar-official. At the age of thirteen, she became a concubine at the court of Tang Taizong, where she attracted notice because of her intelligence, wit, and beauty. After Taizong's death, Wu Zhao became the concubine and later the wife of his successor. In 660 the emperor suffered a debilitating stroke, and Wu Zhao seized the opportunity to direct affairs as administrator of the court. In 690 she went further and claimed the imperial title for herself.

Confucian principles held that political leadership was a man's duty and that women should obey their fathers, husbands, and sons. Thus it was not surprising that factions emerged to oppose Wu Zhao's rule. The lady emperor, however, was resourceful in garnering support. She organized a secret police force to monitor dissident factions, and she ordered brutal punishment for those who stood in her way. She strengthened the civil service system as a way of undercutting aristocratic families that might attempt to displace her. She also generously patronized Buddhists, who returned the favor by composing treatises seeking to legitimize her rule. Although Confucian scholars reviled her, Wu Zhao was an energetic and effective ruler. She quashed rebellions, organized military campaigns, and opened the imperial administration to talented commoners who rose through the civil service system. She held on to her rule until age eighty, when opponents were finally able to force an ailing Wu Zhao to abdicate in favor of her son. Yet the lady emperor was unique as a woman who publicly and officially wielded power in a rigidly patriarchal society. Other women exercised influence indirectly or even "ruled from behind a screen," but Wu Zhao was the only woman in Chinese history to claim the imperial title and rule as emperor.

"She [Wu Zhao] strengthened the civil service system as a way of undercutting aristocratic families that might attempt to displace her."

Technological and Industrial Development

Porcelain Abundant supplies of food enabled many people to pursue technological and industrial interests. During the Tang and Song dynasties, Chinese crafts workers generated a remarkable range of technological innovations. During Tang times they discovered techniques of producing high-quality porcelain, which was lighter, thinner, and adaptable to more uses than earlier pottery. When fired with glazes, porcelain could also become an aesthetically appealing utensil and even a work of art. Porcelain technology gradually diffused to other societies, and Abbasid crafts workers in particular produced porcelain in large quantities. Yet demand for Chinese porcelain remained strong, and the Chinese exported vast quantities of porcelain during the Tang and Song dynasties. Archaeologists have turned up Tang and Song porcelain at sites all along the trade networks of the postclassical era: Chinese porcelain graced the tables of wealthy and refined households in southeast Asia, India, Persia, and the port cities of east Africa. Tang and

Song products gained such a reputation that fine porcelain has come to be known generally as *chinaware.*

Metallurgy Tang and Song craftsmen also improved metallurgical technologies. Production of iron and steel surged during this era, partly because of techniques that resulted in stronger and more useful metals. Chinese craftsmen discovered that they could use coke instead of coal in their furnaces and produce superior grades of metal. Between the early ninth and the early twelfth centuries, iron production increased almost tenfold according to official records, which understate total production. Most of the increased supply of iron and steel went into weaponry and agricultural tools: during the early Song dynasty, imperial armaments manufacturers produced 16.5 million iron arrowheads per year. Iron and steel also went into construction projects involving large structures such as bridges and pagodas. As in the case of porcelain technology, metallurgical techniques soon diffused to lands beyond China. Indeed, Song military difficulties stemmed partly from the fact that nomadic peoples quickly learned Chinese techniques and fashioned their own iron weapons for use in campaigns against China.

Gunpowder Quite apart from improving existing technologies, Tang and Song craftsmen invented entirely new products, tools, and techniques, most notably gunpowder, printing, and naval technologies. Daoist alchemists discovered how to make gunpowder during the Tang dynasty, as they tested the properties of various experimental concoctions while seeking elixirs to prolong life. They soon learned that it was unwise to mix charcoal, saltpeter, sulphur, and arsenic, because the volatile compound often resulted in singed beards and even destroyed buildings. Military officials, however, recognized opportunity in the explosive mixture. By the mid-tenth century, they were using gunpowder in bamboo "fire lances," a kind of flamethrower, and by the eleventh century they had fashioned primitive bombs.

The earliest gunpowder weapons had limited military effectiveness: they probably caused more confusion because of noise and smoke than damage because of their destructive potential. Over time, however, refinements enhanced their effectiveness. Knowledge of gunpowder chemistry quickly diffused through Eurasia, and by the late thirteenth century peoples of southwest Asia and Europe were experimenting with metal-barreled cannons.

Printing The precise origins of printing lie obscured in the mists of time. Although some form of printing may have predated the Sui dynasty, only during the Tang era did printing become common. The earliest printers employed block-printing techniques: they carved a reverse image of an entire page into a wooden block, inked the block, and then pressed a sheet of paper on top. By the mid-eleventh century, printers had begun to experiment with reusable, movable type: instead of carving images into blocks, they fashioned dies in the shape of ideographs, arranged them in a frame, inked them, and pressed the frame over paper sheets. Because formal writing in the Chinese language involved as many as forty thousand characters, printers often found movable type to be unwieldy and inconvenient, so they continued to print from wooden blocks long after movable type became available.

Printing made it possible to produce texts quickly, cheaply, and in huge quantities. By the late ninth century,

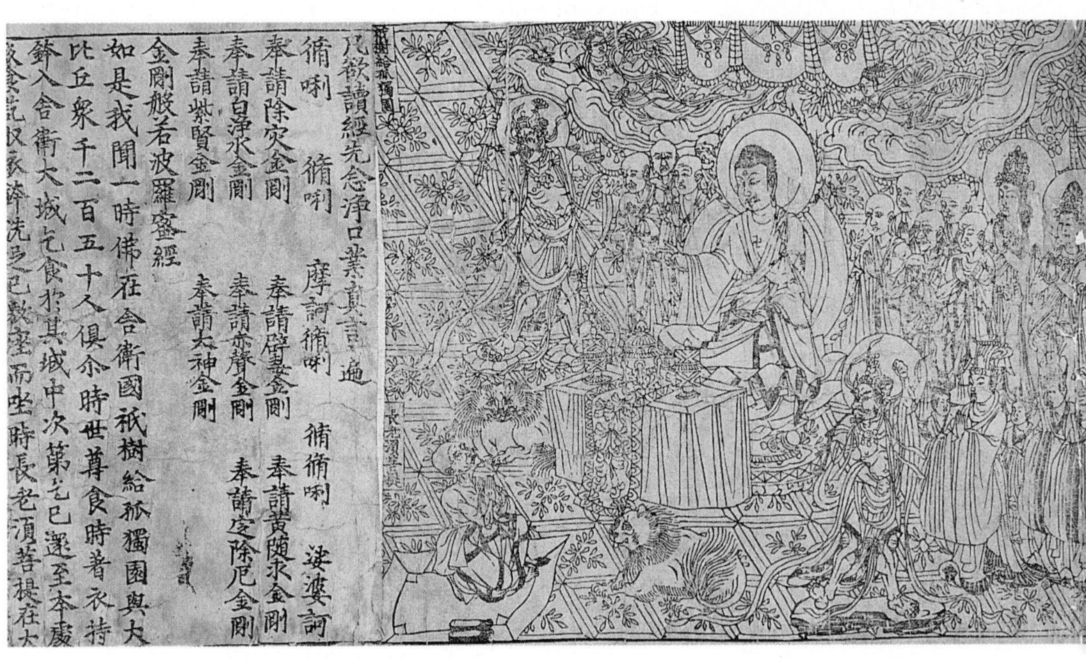
凡欲讀經先念淨口業真言遍
修唎 修唎 摩訶修唎 修修唎 娑婆訶
奉請除災金剛 奉請辟毒金剛 奉請黃隨求金剛
奉請白淨水金剛 奉請赤聲金剛 奉請定除災金剛
奉請紫賢金剛 奉請大神金剛
金剛般若波羅蜜經
如是我聞一時佛在舍衛國祇樹給孤獨園與大
比丘衆千二百五十人俱尒時世尊食時著衣持
鉢入舍衛大城乞食於其城中次第乞已還至本處
飯食訖收衣鉢洗足已敷座而坐時長老須菩提在大

A printed book from the twelfth century presents a Chinese translation of a Buddhist text along with a block-printed illustration of the Buddha addressing his followers.

printed copies of Buddhist texts, Confucian works, calendars, agricultural treatises, and popular works appeared in large quantities, particularly in southwestern China (modern Sichuan province). Song dynasty officials broadly disseminated printed works by visiting the countryside with pamphlets that outlined effective agricultural techniques.

thinking about TRADITIONS

Technology and Society
The Tang and Song dynasties were eras of dramatic technological development. To what extent did technological innovations reinforce the established features of Chinese political and social order? To what extent did they prompt fundamental change in Chinese traditions?

Naval Technology Chinese inventiveness extended also to naval technology. Before Tang times, Chinese mariners did not venture far from land. They traveled the sea lanes to Korea, Japan, and the Ryukyu Islands but relied on Persian, Arab, Indian, and Malay mariners for long-distance maritime trade. During the Tang dynasty, however, Chinese consumers developed a taste for the spices and exotic products of southeast Asian islands, and Chinese mariners increasingly visited those lands in their own ships. By the time of the Song dynasty, Chinese seafarers sailed ships fastened with iron nails, waterproofed with oils, furnished with watertight bulkheads, driven by canvas and bamboo sails, steered by rudders, and navigated with the aid of the "south-pointing needle"—the magnetic compass. Larger ships sometimes even had small rockets powered by gunpowder. Chinese ships mostly plied the waters between Japan and the Malay peninsula, but some ventured into the Indian Ocean and called at ports in India, Ceylon, Persia, and east Africa. Those long-distance travels helped to diffuse elements of Chinese naval technology, particularly the compass, which soon became the common property of mariners throughout the Indian Ocean basin.

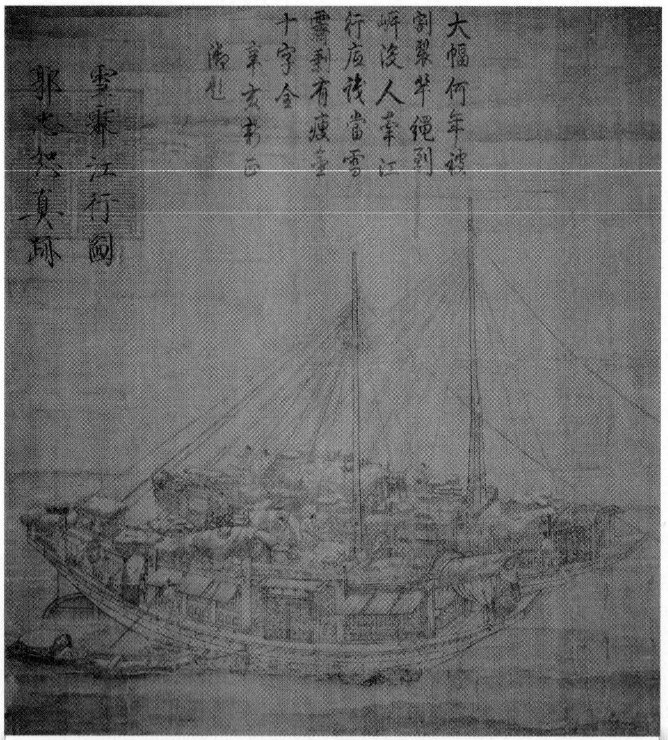

A detail from a Song-era painting on silk depicts two sturdy, broad-bottomed junks, the workhorses of the Chinese merchant fleet.

The Emergence of a Market Economy

Increased agricultural production, improved transportation systems, population growth, urbanization, and industrial production combined to stimulate the Chinese economy. China's various regions increasingly specialized in the cultivation of particular food crops or the production of particular manufactured goods, trading their products for imports from other regions. The market was not the only influence on the Chinese economy: government bureaucracies played a large role in the distribution of staple foods such as rice, wheat, and millet, and dynastic authorities closely watched militarily sensitive enterprises such as the iron industry. Nevertheless, millions of cultivators produced fruits and vegetables for sale on the open market, and manufacturers of silk, porcelain, and other goods supplied both domestic and foreign markets. The Chinese economy became more tightly integrated than ever before, and foreign demand for Chinese products fueled rapid economic expansion.

Financial Instruments Indeed, trade grew so rapidly during Tang and Song times that China experienced a shortage of the copper coins that served as money for most transactions. To alleviate the shortage, Chinese merchants developed alternatives to cash that resulted in even more economic growth. Letters of credit came into common use during the early Tang dynasty. Known as "flying cash," they enabled merchants to deposit goods or cash at one location and draw the equivalent in cash or goods elsewhere in China. Later developments included the use of promissory notes, which pledged payment of a given sum of money at a later date, and checks, which entitled the bearer to draw funds against cash deposited with bankers.

Paper Money The search for alternatives to cash also led to the invention of paper money. Wealthy merchants pioneered the use of printed paper money during the late ninth century. In return for cash deposits from their clients, they issued printed notes that the clients could redeem for merchandise. In a society short of cash, these notes greatly facilitated commercial transactions. Occasionally, however, because of temporary economic reverses or poor management, merchants were not able to honor their notes. The resulting discontent among creditors often led to disorder and sometimes even to riots.

By the eleventh century, however, the Chinese economy had become so dependent on alternatives to cash that it was impractical to banish paper money altogether. To preserve its convenience while forestalling public disorder, government authorities forbade private parties to issue paper money and reserved that right for the state. The first paper money printed under government auspices appeared in 1024 in Sichuan province, the most active center of early printing. By the end of the century, government authorities throughout most of China issued printed paper money—complete with serial numbers and dire warnings against the printing of counterfeit notes. Rulers of nomadic peoples in central Asia soon began to adopt the practice in their states.

Printed paper money caused serious problems for several centuries after its appearance. Quite apart from contamination of the money supply by counterfeit notes, government authorities frequently printed currency representing more value than they actually possessed in cash reserves—a practice not unknown in more recent times. The result was a partial loss of public confidence in paper money. By the late eleventh century, some notes of paper money would fetch only 95 percent of their face value in cash. Not until the **Qing** dynasty (1644–1911 C.E.) did Chinese authorities place the issuance of printed money under tight fiscal controls. In spite of abuses, however, printed paper money provided a powerful stimulus to the Chinese economy.

Foreign music and dance were very popular in the large cities of Tang China. This ceramic model depicts a troupe of musicians from southwest Asia performing on a platform mounted on a camel. Many such models survive from Tang times. Why were foreign performers so popular during the Tang dynasty?

A Cosmopolitan Society

Trade and urbanization transformed Tang and Song China into a prosperous, cosmopolitan society. Trade came to China both by land and by sea. Muslim merchants from the Abbasid empire and central Asia helped to revive the silk roads network and flocked to large Chinese trading centers. Even subjects of the Byzantine empire made their way across the silk roads to China. Residents of large Chinese cities such as Chang'an and Luoyang became quite accustomed to merchants from foreign lands. Indeed, musicians and dancers from Persia became popular entertainers in the cosmopolitan cities of the Tang dynasty. Meanwhile, Arab, Persian, Indian, and Malay mariners arriving by way of the Indian Ocean and South China Sea established sizable merchant communities in the bustling southern Chinese port cities of Guangzhou and Quanzhou. Contemporary reports said that the rebel general Huang Chao massacred 120,000 foreigners when he sacked Guangzhou and subjected it to a reign of terror in 879.

China and the Hemispheric Economy

Indeed, high productivity and trade brought the Tang and Song economy a dynamism that China's borders could not restrain. Chinese consumers developed a taste for exotic goods that stimulated trade throughout much of the eastern hemisphere. Spices from the islands of southeast Asia made their way to China, along with products as diverse as kingfisher feathers and tortoise shell from Vietnam, pearls and incense from India, and horses and melons from central Asia. Those items became symbols of a refined, elegant lifestyle—in many cases because of attractive qualities inherent in the commodities themselves but sometimes simply because of their scarcity and foreign provenance. In exchange for such exotic items, Chinese sent abroad vast quantities of silk, porcelain, and lacquerware. In central Asia, southeast Asia, India, Persia, and the port cities of east Africa, wealthy merchants and rulers wore Chinese silk and set their tables with Chinese porcelain. China's economic surge during the Tang and Song dynasties thus promoted trade and economic growth throughout much of the eastern hemisphere.

Qing (ching)

sources from the past

The Arab Merchant Suleiman on Business Practices in Tang China

The Arab merchant Suleiman made several commercial ventures by ship to India and China during the early ninth century C.E. In 851 an Arab geographer wrote an account of Suleiman's travels, describing India and China for Muslim readers in southwest Asia. His report throws particularly interesting light on the economic conditions and business practices of Tang China.

Young and old Chinese all wear silk clothes in both winter and summer, but silk of the best quality is reserved for the kings. . . . During the winter, the men wear two, three, four, five pairs of pants, and even more, according to their means. This practice has the goal of protecting the lower body from the high humidity of the land, which they fear. During the summer, they wear a single shirt of silk or some similar material. They do not wear turbans. . . .

In China, commercial transactions are carried out with the aid of copper coins. The Chinese royal treasury is identical to that of other kings, but only the king of China has a treasury that uses copper coins as a standard. These copper coins serve as the money of the land. The Chinese have gold, silver, fine pearls, fancy silk textiles, raw silk, and all this in large quantities, but they are considered commodities, and only copper coins serve as money.

Imports into China include ivory, incense, copper ingots, shells of sea turtles, and rhinoceros horn, with which the Chinese make ornaments. . . .

The Chinese conduct commercial transactions and business affairs with equity. When someone lends money to another person, he writes up a note documenting the loan. The borrower writes up another note on which he affixes an imprint of his index finger and middle finger together. Then they put the two notes together, roll them up, and write a formula at the point where one touches the other [so that part of the written formula appears on each note]. Next, they separate the notes and entrust to the lender the one on which the borrower recognizes his debt. If the borrower denies his debt later on, they say to him, "Present the note that the lender gave to you." If the borrower maintains that he has no such note from the lender, and denies that he ever agreed to the note with his fingerprints on it, and if the lender's note has disappeared, they say to him, "Declare in writing that you have not contracted this debt, but if later the lender brings forth proof that you have contracted this debt that you deny, you will receive twenty blows of the cane on the back and you will be ordered to pay a penalty of twenty million copper coins." This sum is equal to about 2,000 dinars [gold coins used in the Abbasid empire]. Twenty blows of the cane brings on death. Thus no one in China dares to make such a declaration for fear of losing at the same time both life and fortune. We have seen no one who has agreed when invited to make such a declaration. The Chinese are thus equitable to each other. No one in China is treated unjustly.

For Further Reflection

- In what ways might Chinese policies have encouraged business and trade during the Tang dynasty?

Source: Jean Sauvaget, ed. *Relation de la Chine et de l'Inde.* Paris, 1948, pp. 10–11, 15–16, 19–20. (Translated into English by Jerry H. Bentley.)

CULTURAL CHANGE IN TANG AND SONG CHINA

Interactions with peoples of other societies encouraged cultural change in postclassical China. The Confucian and Daoist traditions did not disappear. But they made way for a foreign religion—Mahayana Buddhism—and they developed along new lines that reflected the conditions of Tang and Song society.

The Establishment of Buddhism

Buddhist merchants traveling the ancient silk roads visited China as early as the second century B.C.E. During the Han dynasty their faith attracted little interest there: Confucianism, Daoism, and cults that honored family ancestors were the most popular cultural alternatives. After the fall of the Han, however, the Confucian tradition suffered a loss of credibility. The purpose and rationale of Confucianism was to maintain public order and provide honest, effective government. But in an age of warlords and nomadic invasions, it seemed that the Confucian tradition had simply failed. Confucian educational and civil service systems went into decline, and rulers sometimes openly scorned Confucian values.

Foreign Religions in China During the unsettled centuries following the fall of the Han dynasty, several foreign religions established communities in China. Nestorian Christians and Manichaeans settled in China, followed later by Zoroastrians fleeing the Islamic conquerors of Persia. Nestorians established communities in China by the late

sixth century. The emperor Tang Taizong issued a proclamation praising their doctrine, and he allowed them to open monasteries in Chang'an and other cities. By the mid-seventh century, Arab and Persian merchants had also established Muslim communities in the port cities of south China. Indeed, legend holds that an uncle of Muhammad built a small red mosque in the port city of Guangzhou. These religions of salvation mostly served the needs of foreign merchants trading in China and converts from nomadic societies. Sophisticated residents of Chinese cities appreciated foreign music and dance as well as foreign foods and trade goods, but most foreign religious traditions attracted little interest.

Dunhuang Yet Mahayana Buddhism gradually found a popular following in Tang and Song China. Buddhism came to China over the silk roads. Residents of oasis cities in central Asia had converted to Buddhism as early as the first or second century B.C.E., and the oases became sites of Buddhist missionary efforts. By the fourth century C.E., a sizable Buddhist community had emerged at Dunhuang in western China (modern Gansu province). Between about 600 and 1000 C.E., Buddhists built hundreds of cave temples in the vicinity of Dunhuang and decorated them with murals depicting events in the lives of the Buddha and the bodhisattvas who played prominent roles in Mahayana Buddhism. They also assembled libraries of religious literature and operated scriptoria to produce Buddhist texts. Missions supported by establishments such as those at Dunhuang helped Buddhism to establish a foothold in China.

Buddhism in China Buddhism attracted Chinese interest partly because of its high standards of morality, its intellectual sophistication, and its promise of salvation. Practical concerns also help to account for its appeal. Buddhists established monastic communities in China and accumulated sizable estates donated by wealthy converts. They cultivated those lands intensively and stored a portion of their harvests for distribution among local residents during times of drought, famine, or other hardship. Some monasteries engaged in banking or money-lending activities, and many others maintained schools that provided a basic education for local populations. Buddhist monasteries thus became important elements in the local economies of Chinese communities. Buddhism even had implications for everyday life in China. Buddhist monks introduced chairs into China: originally a

A tenth-century painting in a cave at Dunhuang depicts a monastery on Mt. Wutai in southern China, reputedly the earthly home of an influential bodhisattva and the site of numerous Buddhist monasteries.

piece of monastic furniture, the chair quickly became popular in secular society and found a place in domestic interiors throughout the land. Buddhist monks also introduced refined sugar into China and thus influenced both diet and cuisine.

In some ways, Buddhism posed a challenge to Chinese cultural and social traditions. Buddhist theologians typically took written texts as points of departure for elaborate, speculative investigations into metaphysical themes such as the nature of the soul. Among Chinese intellectuals, however, only the Confucians placed great emphasis on written texts, and they devoted their energies mostly to practical rather than metaphysical issues. Meanwhile, Daoists had limited interest in written texts of any kind. Buddhist morality called for individuals to strive for perfection by observing an ascetic ideal, and it encouraged serious Buddhists to follow a celibate, monastic lifestyle. In contrast, Chinese morality centered on the family unit and the obligations of filial piety, and it strongly encouraged procreation so that generations of offspring would be available to venerate family ancestors. Some Chinese held that Buddhist monasteries were economically harmful, since they paid no taxes, whereas others scorned Buddhism as an inferior creed because of its foreign origins.

Buddhism and Daoism Because of those differences and concerns, Buddhist missionaries sought to tailor their message to Chinese audiences. They explained Buddhist concepts in vocabulary borrowed from Chinese cultural traditions, particularly Daoism. They translated the Indian term *dharma* (the basic Buddhist doctrine) as *dao* ("the way" in the Daoist sense of the term), and they translated the Indian term *nirvana* (personal salvation that comes after an individual soul escapes from the cycle of incarnation) as *wuwei* (the Daoist ethic of noncompetition). While encouraging the establishment of monasteries and the observance of celibacy, they also recognized the validity of family life and offered Buddhism as a religion that would benefit the extended Chinese family: one son in the monastery, they taught, would bring salvation for ten generations of his kin.

Pilgrimage to India Monks and pilgrims helped popularize Buddhism in China. The monk Xuanzang (602–664 C.E.) was only one among hundreds of Chinese pilgrims who made the dangerous and difficult journey to India to visit holy sites and learn about Buddhism in its homeland. Xuanzang and other pilgrims returned to China with copies of treatises that deepened the understanding of Buddhism, and they were able to relate the teachings of Indian Buddhist masters to Chinese disciples.

Schools of Buddhism Over the years, monks and scholars organized several distinctive schools of Buddhism that appealed to Chinese tastes and interests. Buddhists of the Chan school (also known by its Japanese name, Zen) placed little emphasis on written texts but held intuition and sudden flashes of insight in high regard. Thus Chan Buddhists made a place for Daoist values in Chinese Buddhism. Even more popular than Chan Buddhism was the Pure Land school, which held out the prospect of personal salvation for those who devoted themselves to the Buddha. The lady emperor Wu Zhao herself followed Pure Land teachings, and she enthusiastically promoted the school—especially after friendly monks circulated a treatise predicting reincarnation of the Buddha as a female ruler. Wu Zhao eventually proclaimed herself the universal ruler and protector of Buddhism, and she sponsored the construction of monasteries and stupas throughout China.

This scroll painting depicts the return of the monk Xuanzang to China. His baggage included 657 books, mostly Buddhist treatises but also a few works on grammar and logic, as well as hundreds of relics and images.

A Japanese screen painting from the fourteenth century depicts a group of monks hard at work translating the Buddhist texts that the pilgrim Xuanzang transported from India to China.

Hostility to Buddhism In spite of its popularity, Buddhism met determined resistance from Daoists and Confucians. Daoists resented the popular following that Buddhists attracted, which resulted in diminished resources available for their tradition. Confucians despised Buddhists' exaltation of celibacy, and they denounced its teachings as alien superstition. They also condemned Buddhist monasteries as wasteful, unproductive burdens on society.

Persecution During the late Tang dynasty, Daoist and Confucian critics of Buddhism found allies in the imperial court. Beginning in the 840s the Tang emperors ordered the closure of monasteries and the expulsion of Buddhists as well as Zoroastrians, Nestorian Christians, and Manichaeans. Motivated largely by a desire to seize property belonging to foreign religious establishments, the Tang rulers did not implement their policy in a thorough way. Although it discouraged further expansion, Tang policy did not eradicate foreign faiths from China. Buddhism in particular enjoyed popular support that enabled it to survive. Indeed, it even influenced the development of the Confucian tradition during the Song dynasty.

Neo-Confucianism

The Song emperors did not persecute Buddhists, but they actively supported native Chinese cultural traditions in hopes of limiting the influence of foreign religions. They contributed particularly generously to the Confucian tradition. They sponsored the studies of Confucian scholars, for example, and subsidized the printing and dissemination of Confucian writings.

Confucians and Buddhism Yet the Confucian tradition of the Song dynasty differed from that of earlier times. The earliest Confucians had concentrated resolutely on practical issues of politics and morality, since they took the organization of a stable social order as their principal concern. Confucians of the Song dynasty studied the classic works of their tradition, but they also became familiar with the writings of Buddhists. They found much to admire in Buddhist thought. Buddhism not only offered a tradition of logical thought and argumentation but also dealt with issues, such as the

thinking about ENCOUNTERS

The Influence of a Determined Individual

After traveling to India in search of Buddhist knowledge and wisdom, the monk Xuanzang and other pilgrims helped to bring about cultural and religious change in China. To what extent can you attribute the spread of Buddhism to the efforts of individuals like Xuanzang? To what extent might general social conditions help to explain the popularity of Buddhism in China?

nature of the soul and the individual's relationship with the cosmos, not systematically explored by Confucian thinkers. Thus Confucians of the Song dynasty drew a great deal of inspiration from Buddhism. Because their thought reflected the influence of Buddhism as well as original Confucian values, it has come to be known as neo-Confucianism.

Zhu Xi The most important representative of Song neo-Confucianism was the philosopher **Zhu Xi** (1130–1200 C.E.). A prolific writer, Zhu Xi maintained a deep commitment to Confucian values emphasizing proper personal behavior and social harmony. Among his writings was an influential treatise entitled *Family Rituals* that provided detailed instructions for weddings, funerals, veneration of ancestors, and other family ceremonies. As a good Confucian, Zhu Xi considered it a matter of the highest importance that individuals play their proper roles both in their family and in the larger society.

Yet Zhu Xi became fascinated with the philosophical and speculative features of Buddhist thought. He argued in good Confucian fashion for the observance of high moral standards, and he believed that academic and philosophical investigations were important for practical affairs. But he concentrated his efforts on abstract and abstruse issues of more theoretical than practical significance. He wrote extensively on metaphysical themes such as the nature of reality. He argued in a manner reminiscent of Plato that two elements accounted for all physical being: *li,* a principle somewhat similar to Plato's Forms or Ideas that defines the essence of the being, and *qi,* its material form.

Neo-Confucian Influence Neo-Confucianism ranks as an important cultural development for two reasons. First, it illustrates the deep influence of Buddhism in Chinese society. Even though the neo-Confucians rejected Buddhist religious teachings, their writings adapted Buddhist themes and reasoning to Confucian interests and values. Second, neo-Confucianism influenced east Asian thought over a very long term. In China, neo-Confucianism enjoyed the status of an officially recognized creed from the Song dynasty until the early twentieth century, and in lands that fell within China's cultural orbit—particularly Korea, Vietnam, and Japan—neo-Confucianism shaped philosophical, political, and moral thought for half a millennium and more.

CHINESE INFLUENCE IN EAST ASIA

Like the *dar al-Islam,* Chinese society influenced the development of neighboring lands during postclassical times. Chinese armies periodically invaded Korea and Vietnam, and Chinese merchants established commercial relations with Japan as well as with Korea and Vietnam. Chinese techniques of government and administration helped shape public life in Korea, Vietnam, and Japan, and Chinese values and cultural traditions won a prominent place alongside native traditions. By no means did those lands become absorbed into China: all maintained distinctive identities and cultural traditions. Yet they also drew deep inspiration from Chinese examples and built societies that reflected their participation in a larger east Asian society revolving around China.

Korea and Vietnam

Chinese armies ventured into Korea and Vietnam on campaigns of imperial expansion as early as the Qin and Han dynasties. As the Han dynasty weakened, however, local aristocrats organized movements that ousted Chinese forces from both lands. Only during the powerful Tang dynasty did Chinese resources once again enable military authorities to mount large-scale campaigns. Although the two lands responded differently to Chinese imperial expansion, both borrowed Chinese political and cultural traditions and used them in their societies.

The Silla Dynasty During the seventh century, Tang armies conquered much of Korea before the native Silla dynasty rallied to prevent Chinese domination of the peninsula. Both Tang and Silla authorities preferred to avoid a long and costly conflict, so they agreed to a political compromise: Chinese forces withdrew from Korea, and the Silla king recognized the Tang emperor as his overlord. In theory, Korea was a vassal state in a vast Chinese empire. In practice, however, Korea was in most respects an independent kingdom, although the ruling dynasty prudently maintained cordial relations with its powerful neighbor.

Thus Korea entered into a tributary relationship with China. Envoys of the Silla kings regularly delivered gifts to Chinese emperors and performed the kowtow, but those concessions brought considerable benefits to the Koreans. In return for their recognition of Chinese supremacy, they received gifts more valuable than the tribute they delivered to China. Moreover, the tributary relationship opened the doors for Korean merchants to trade in China.

Chinese Influence in Korea Meanwhile, the tributary relationship facilitated the spread of Chinese political and cultural influences to Korea. Embassies delivering tribute to China included Korean royal officials who observed the workings of the Chinese court and bureaucracy and then organized the Korean court on similar lines. The Silla kings built a lavish new capital at their ancestral town of Kumsong (modern-day Kyongju in southeastern Korea), taking the Tang capital at Chang'an as their model. Silla rulers developed Kumsong from a small walled town with a few hundred families into a major capital with 179,000 households and nearly one million people. Their embassies to China included not only royal officials but also scholars who studied Chinese thought and literature and who took copies of Chinese writings back to Korea. Their efforts

---
Zhu Xi (ZHOO SHEE)

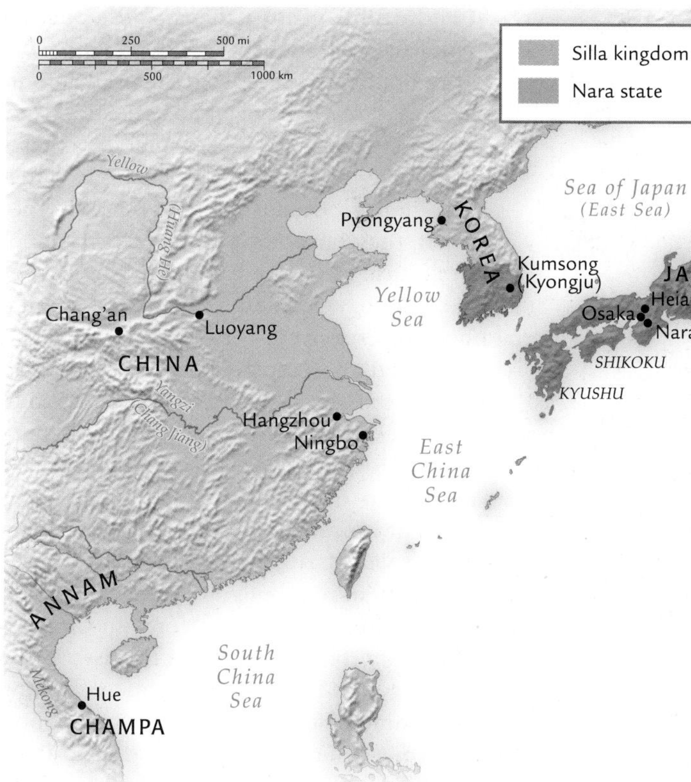

MAP 14.3
Borderlands of postclassical China: Korea, Vietnam, and Japan.
Note the geographic relationship of Korea, Vietnam, and Japan to China.
What geographic conditions help to account for the varying degrees of Chinese influence in Korea, Vietnam, and Japan?

helped to build Korean interest in the Confucian tradition, particularly among educated aristocrats. While Korean elite classes turned to Confucius, Chinese schools of Buddhism attracted widespread popular interest. Chan Buddhism, which promised individual salvation, won the allegiance of peasants and commoners.

China and Korea differed in many respects. Most notably, perhaps, aristocrats and royal houses dominated Korean society much more than was the case in China. Although the Korean monarchy sponsored Chinese schools and a Confucian examination system, Korea never established a bureaucracy based on merit such as that of Tang and Song China. Political initiative remained firmly in the hands of the ruling classes. Nevertheless, extensive dealings with its powerful neighbor ensured that Korea reflected the influence of Chinese political and cultural traditions.

China and Vietnam Chinese relations with Vietnam were far more tense than with Korea. When Tang armies ventured into the land that Chinese called Nam Viet, they encountered spirited resistance on the part of the Viet people, who had settled in the region around the Red River. Tang forces soon won control of Viet towns and cities, and they launched efforts to absorb the Viets into Chinese society, just as their predecessors had absorbed the indigenous peoples of the Yangzi River valley. The Viets readily adopted Chinese agricultural methods and irrigation systems as well as Chinese schools and administrative techniques. Like their Korean counterparts, Viet elites studied Confucian texts and took examinations based on a Chinese-style education, and Viet traders marketed their wares in China. Vietnamese authorities even entered into tributary relationships with the Chinese court. Yet the Viets resented Chinese efforts to dominate the southern land, and they mounted a series of revolts against Tang authorities. As the Tang dynasty fell during the early tenth century, the Viets won their independence and successfully resisted later Chinese efforts at imperial expansion to the south.

Like Korea, Vietnam differed from China in many ways. Many Vietnamese retained their indigenous religions in preference to Chinese cultural traditions. Women played a much more prominent role in Vietnamese society and economy than did their counterparts in China. Southeast Asian women had dominated local and regional markets for centuries, and they participated actively in business ventures closed to women in the more rigidly patriarchal society of China.

Chinese Influence in Vietnam Nevertheless, Chinese traditions found a place in the southern land. Vietnamese authorities established an administrative system and bureaucracy modeled on that of China, and Viet ruling classes prepared for their careers by pursuing a Confucian education. Furthermore, Buddhism came to Vietnam from China as well as India and won a large popular following. Thus, like Korea, Vietnam absorbed political and cultural influence from China and reflected the development of a larger east Asian society centered on China.

Early Japan

Chinese armies never invaded Japan, but Chinese traditions deeply influenced Japanese political and cultural development. The earliest inhabitants of Japan were nomadic peoples from northeast Asia who migrated to Japan about thirty-five thousand years ago. Their language, material culture, and religion derived from their parent society in northeast Asia. Later migrants, who arrived in several waves from the Korean peninsula, introduced cultivation of rice, bronze and iron metallurgy, and horses into Japan. As the population of the Japanese islands grew and built a settled agricultural society, small states dominated by aristocratic clans emerged. By the middle of the first millennium C.E., several dozen states ruled small regions.

Nara Japan The establishment of the powerful Sui and Tang dynasties in China had repercussions in Japan, where they suggested the value of centralized imperial government. One of the aristocratic clans in Japan insisted on its precedence over the others, although in fact it had never wielded effective authority outside its territory in central Japan. Inspired by the Tang example, this clan claimed imperial authority and introduced a series of reforms designed to centralize Japanese politics. The imperial house established a court modeled on that of the Tang, instituted a Chinese-style bureaucracy, implemented an equal-field system, provided official support for Confucianism and Buddhism, and in the year 710 moved to a new capital city at Nara (near modern Kyoto) that was a replica of the Tang capital at Chang'an. Never was Chinese influence more prominent in Japan than during the Nara period (710–794 C.E.).

Yet Japan did not lose its distinctive characteristics or become simply a smaller model of Chinese society. While adopting Confucian and Buddhist traditions from China, for example, the Japanese continued to observe the rites of Shinto, their indigenous religion, which revolved around the veneration of ancestors and a host of nature spirits and deities. Japanese society reflected the influence of Chinese traditions but still developed along its own lines.

The experiences of the Heian, Kamakura, and Muromachi periods clearly illustrate this point. In 794 the emperor of Japan transferred his court from Nara to a newly constructed capital at nearby Heian (modern Kyoto). During the next four centuries, Heian became the seat of a refined and sophisticated society that drew inspiration from China but also elaborated distinctively Japanese political and cultural traditions.

Heian Japan During the Heian period (794–1185 C.E.), local rulers on the island of Honshu mostly recognized the emperor as Japan's supreme political authority. Unlike their Chinese counterparts, however, Japanese emperors rarely ruled but, rather, served as ceremonial figureheads and symbols of authority. Effective power lay in the hands of the Fujiwara family, an aristocratic clan that controlled affairs from behind the throne through its influence over the imperial house and manipulation of its members.

Tang dynasty pottery figure of a Vietnamese dancer. Commercial and tributary relationships introduced southeast Asian performers to China, where sophisticated urban communities appreciated their exotic entertainment.

After the ninth century the Japanese political order almost continuously featured a split between a publicly recognized imperial authority and a separate agent of effective rule. This pattern helps to account for the remarkable longevity of the Japanese imperial house. Because emperors have not ruled, they have not been subject to deposition during times of turmoil: ruling parties and factions have come and gone, but the imperial house has survived.

The cultural development of Heian Japan also reflected both the influence of Chinese traditions and the elaboration of peculiarly Japanese ways. Most literature imitated Chinese models and indeed was written in the Chinese language. Boys and young men who received a formal education in Heian Japan learned Chinese, read the classic works of China, and wrote in the foreign tongue. Officials at court conducted business and kept records in Chinese, and literary figures wrote histories and treatises in the style popular in China. Even Japanese writing reflected Chinese influence, since scholars borrowed many Chinese characters and used them to represent Japanese words. They also adapted some Chinese characters into a Japanese syllabic script, in which symbols represent whole syllables rather than a single sound, as in an alphabetic script.

The Tale of Genji Because Japanese women rarely received a formal Chinese-style education, in Heian times aristocratic women made the most notable contributions to literature in the Japanese language. Of the many literary works that have survived from that era, none reflects Heian court life better than *The Tale of Genji.* Composed by Murasaki Shikibu, a lady-in-waiting at the Heian court who wrote in Japanese syllabic script rather than Chinese characters, this sophisticated work relates the experiences of a fictitious imperial prince named Genji. Living amid gardens and palaces, Genji and his friends devoted themselves to the cultivation of an ultra-refined lifestyle, and they became adept at mixing subtle perfumes, composing splendid verses in fine calligraphic hand, and wooing sophisticated women.

The Tale of Genji also offers a meditation on the passing of time and the sorrows that time brings to sensitive human beings. As Genji and his friends age, they reflect on past joys and relationships no longer recoverable. Their thoughts suffuse *The Tale of Genji* with a melancholy spirit that presents a subtle contrast to the elegant atmosphere of their surroundings at the Heian court. Because of her limited command of Chinese, Lady Murasaki created one of the most remarkable literary works in the Japanese language.

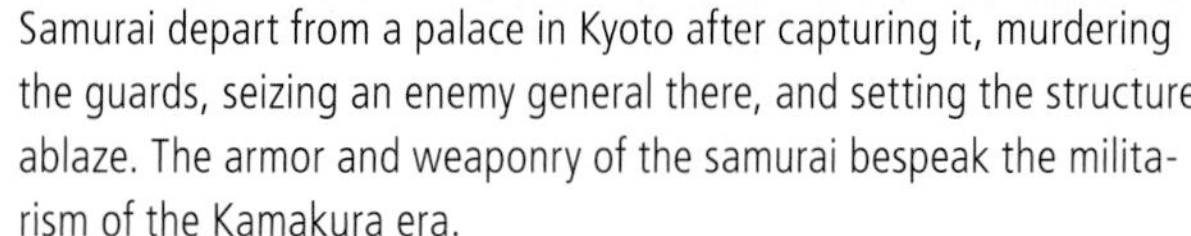

Samurai depart from a palace in Kyoto after capturing it, murdering the guards, seizing an enemy general there, and setting the structure ablaze. The armor and weaponry of the samurai bespeak the militarism of the Kamakura era.

Decline of Heian Japan As the charmed circle of aristocrats and courtiers led elegant lives at the imperial capital, the Japanese countryside underwent fundamental changes that brought an end to the Heian court and its refined society. The equal-field system gradually fell into disuse in Japan as it had in China, and aristocratic clans accumulated most of the islands' lands into vast estates. By the late eleventh century, two clans in particular—the Taira and the Minamoto—overshadowed the others. During the mid-twelfth century the two engaged in outright war, and in 1185 the Minamoto emerged victorious. The Minamoto did not seek to abolish imperial authority in Japan but, rather, claimed to rule the land in the name of the emperor. They installed the clan leader as *shogun*—a military governor who ruled in place of the emperor—and established the seat of their government at Kamakura, near modern Tokyo, while the imperial court remained at Kyoto. For most of the next four centuries, one branch or another of the Minamoto clan dominated political life in Japan.

Medieval Japan

Historians refer to the Kamakura and Muromachi periods as Japan's medieval period—a middle era falling between the age of Chinese influence and court domination of political life in Japan, as represented by the Nara and Heian periods, and the modern age, inaugurated by the Tokugawa dynasty in the sixteenth century, when a centralized government unified and ruled all of Japan. During this middle era, Japanese society and culture took on increasingly distinctive characteristics.

Political Decentralization In the Kamakura (1185–1333 C.E.) and Muromachi (1336–1573 C.E.) periods, Japan developed a decentralized political order in which provincial lords wielded effective power and authority in local regions where they controlled land and economic affairs. As these lords and their clans vied for power and authority in the countryside, they found little use for the Chinese-style bureaucracy that Nara and Heian rulers had instituted in Japan and still less use for the elaborate protocol and refined conduct that prevailed at the courts. In place of etiquette and courtesy, they valued military talent and discipline. The mounted warrior, the *samurai,* thus played the most distinctive role in Japanese political and military affairs.

The Samurai The samurai were professional warriors, specialists in the use of force and the arts of fighting. They served the provincial lords of Japan, who relied on the samurai both to enforce their authority in their own territories and to extend their claims to other lands. In return for those police and military services, the lords supported the samurai from the agricultural surplus and labor services of peasants working under their jurisdiction. Freed of obligations to feed, clothe, and house themselves and their families, samurai devoted themselves to hunting, riding, archery, and martial arts.

Thus, although it had taken its original inspiration from the Tang empire in China, the Japanese political order developed along lines different from those of the Middle Kingdom. Yet Japan clearly had a place in the larger east Asian society centered on China. Japan borrowed from China, among other things, Confucian values, Buddhist religion, a system of writing, and the ideal of centralized imperial rule. Though somewhat suppressed during the Kamakura and Muromachi periods, those elements of Chinese society not only survived in Japan but also decisively influenced Japanese development during later periods.

inperspective

The revival of centralized imperial rule in China had profound implications for all of east Asia and indeed for most of the eastern hemisphere. When the Sui and Tang dynasties imposed their authority throughout China, they established a powerful state that guided political affairs throughout east Asia. Tang armies extended Chinese influence to Korea, Vietnam, and central Asia. They did not invade Japan, but the impressive political organization of China prompted the islands' rulers to imitate Tang examples. Moreover, the Sui and Tang dynasties laid a strong political foundation for rapid economic development. Chinese society prospered throughout the postclassical era, partly because of technological and industrial innovation. Tang and Song prosperity touched all of China's neighbors, since it encouraged surging commerce in east Asia. Chinese silk, porcelain, and lacquerware were prized commodities among trading peoples from southeast Asia to east Africa. Chinese inventions such as paper, printing, gunpowder, and the magnetic compass found a place in societies throughout the eastern hemisphere as they diffused across the silk roads and the sea lanes. The postclassical era was an age of religious as well as commercial and technological exchanges: Nestorian Christians, Zoroastrians, Manichaeans, and Muslims all maintained communities in Tang China, and Buddhism became the most popular religious tradition in all of east Asia. During the postclassical era, Chinese social organization and economic dynamism helped to sustain interactions between the peoples of the eastern hemisphere on an unprecedented scale. ●

CHRONOLOGY	
589–618	Sui dynasty (China)
602–664	Life of Xuanzang
604–618	Reign of Sui Yangdi
618–907	Tang dynasty (China)
627–649	Reign of Tang Taizong
669–935	Silla dynasty (Korea)
710–794	Nara period (Japan)
755–757	An Lushan's rebellion
794–1185	Heian period (Japan)
875–884	Huang Chao's rebellion
960–1279	Song dynasty (China)
960–976	Reign of Song Taizu
1024	First issuance of government-sponsored paper money
1130–1200	Life of Zhu Xi
1185–1333	Kamakura period (Japan)
1336–1573	Muromachi period (Japan)

For Further Reading

Hugh R. Clark. *Community, Trade, and Networks: Southern Fujian Province from the Third to the Thirteenth Century.* Cambridge, 1991. Excellent scholarly study exploring the transformation of a region by trade and market forces.

Mark Elvin. *The Pattern of the Chinese Past.* Stanford, 1973. A brilliant analysis of Chinese history, concentrating particularly on economic, social, and technological themes.

Robert Finlay. *The Pilgrim Art: The Culture of Porcelain in World History.* Berkeley, 2010. Brilliant study outlining the Chinese invention of porcelain and the product's appeal in the larger world.

Karl Friday. *Samurai, Warfare and the State in Early Medieval Japan.* New York, 2004. A lively analysis with apt comparisons to medieval Europe.

Jacques Gernet. *Buddhism in Chinese Society: An Economic History from the Fifth to the Tenth Century.* Trans. by F. Verellen. New York, 1995. An important study emphasizing the economic and social significance of Buddhist monasteries in the Chinese countryside.

Peter D. Hershock. *Chan Buddhism.* Honolulu, 2005. An accessible introduction to Chan Buddhism focusing on four renowned masters.

Thomas P. Kasulis. *Shinto: The Way Home.* Honolulu, 2004. The best short introduction.

John Kieschnick. *The Impact of Buddhism on Chinese Material Culture.* Princeton, 2003. Fascinating scholarly study exploring the social effects of Buddhism in China.

Dieter Kuhn. *The Age of Confucian Rule: The Song Transformation of China.* Cambridge, Mass., 2009. Emphasizes social and economic developments.

Mark Edward Lewis. *China's Cosmopolitan Empire: The Tang Dynasty.* Cambridge, Mass., 2009. Perhaps the best single volume on Tang China.

Joseph Needham. *Science in Traditional China.* Cambridge, Mass., 1981. Essays on the history of Chinese science and technology.

Edward H. Schafer. *The Golden Peaches of Samarkand: A Study of T'ang Exotics.* Berkeley, 1963. Deals with relations between China and central Asian lands during the Tang dynasty.

———. *The Vermilion Bird: T'ang Images of the South.* Berkeley, 1967. Evocative study of relations between China and Vietnam during the Tang dynasty.

Tansen Sen. *Buddhism, Diplomacy, and Trade: The Realignment of Sino-Indian Relations, 600–1400.* Honolulu, 2003. A pathbreaking study exploring trade, diplomacy, and cultural exchanges between postclassical India and China.

Murasaki Shikibu. *The Tale of Genji.* 2 vols. Trans. by E. Seidensticker. New York, 1976. Fresh and readable translation of Lady Murasaki's classic work.

Pierre François Souyri. *The World Turned Upside Down: Medieval Japanese Society.* Trans. by K. Roth. New York, 2001. Reliable survey that places political developments in social and economic context.

H. Paul Varley. *Japanese Culture.* 4th ed. Honolulu, 2000. An authoritative analysis of Japanese cultural development from early times to the present.

James C. Y. Watt. *China: Dawn of a Golden Age, 200–750 A.D.* New York, 2004. Lavishly illustrated volume surveying the arts in postclassical China.

Roderick Whitfield, Susan Whitfield, and Neville Agnew. *Mogao: Art and History on the Silk Road.* Los Angeles, 2000. Excellent brief discussion of the cave temples and archaeological remains from Dunhuang.

Susan Whitfield. *Life along the Silk Road.* Berkeley, 1999. Focuses on the experiences of ten individuals who lived or traveled on the silk roads during the postclassical era.

Sally Hovey Wriggins. *The Silk Road Journey with Xuanzang.* Boulder, 2004. A fascinating and well-illustrated account of Xuanzang's journey to India and his influence on the development of Buddhism in China.

Arthur F. Wright. *Buddhism in Chinese History.* Stanford, 1959. A brief and incisive study of Buddhism in China by an eminent scholar.

Don J. Wyatt. *The Blacks of Premodern China.* Philadelphia, 2010. Pioneering study of Africans and other dark-skinned peoples in premodern China.

India and the Indian Ocean Basin

chapter 15

Kabir, the blind guru, weaves cloth while discussing religious matters with disciples.

EYEWITNESS: Buzurg Sets His Sights on the Seven Seas

Buzurg ibn Shahriyar was a tenth-century shipmaster from Siraf, a prosperous and bustling port city on the Persian Gulf coast. He probably sailed frequently to Arabia and India, and he may have ventured also to Malaya, the islands of southeast Asia, China, and east Africa. Like all sailors, he heard stories about the distant lands that mariners had visited, the different customs they observed, and the adventures that befell them during their travels. About 953 C.E. he compiled 136 such stories in his *Book of the Wonders of India.*

Buzurg's collection included a generous proportion of tall tales. He told of a giant lobster that seized a ship's anchor and dragged the vessel through the water, of mermaids and sea dragons, of creatures born from human fathers and fish mothers who lived in human society but had flippers that enabled them to swim through the water like fish, of serpents that ate cattle and elephants, of birds so large that they crushed houses, of a monkey that seduced a sailor, and of a talking lizard. Yet alongside the tall tales, many of Buzurg's stories accurately reflected the conditions of his time. One recounted the story of a king from northern India who converted to Islam and requested translations of Islamic law. Others reported on Hindu customs, shipwrecks, encounters with pirates, and slave trading.

Several of Buzurg's stories tempted readers with visions of vast wealth attainable through maritime trade. Buzurg mentioned fine diamonds from Kashmir, pearls from Ceylon, and a Jewish merchant who left Persia penniless and returned from India and China with a shipload of priceless merchandise. Despite their embellishments and exaggerations, his stories faithfully reflected the trade networks that linked the lands surrounding the Indian Ocean in the tenth century. Although Buzurg clearly thought of India as a distinct land with its own customs, he also recognized a larger world of trade and communication that extended from east Africa to southeast Asia and beyond to China.

Just as China served as the principal inspiration of a larger east Asian society in the postclassical era, India influenced the development of a larger cultural zone in south and southeast Asia. Yet China and India played different roles in their respective spheres of influence. In east Asia, China was the dominant power, even if it did not always exercise authority directly over its neighbors. In south and southeast Asia, however, there emerged no centralized imperial authority like the Tang dynasty in China. Indeed, although several states organized large regional kingdoms, no single state was able to extend its authority to all parts of the Indian subcontinent, much less to the mainland and islands of southeast Asia.

Though politically disunited, India remained a coherent and distinct society as a result of powerful social and cultural traditions: the caste system and the Hindu religion shaped human experiences and values throughout the subcontinent during the postclassical era. Beginning in the seventh century Islam also began to attract a popular following in India, and after the eleventh century Islam deeply influenced Indian society alongside the caste system and Hinduism.

Beyond the subcontinent, Indian traditions helped to shape a larger cultural zone extending to the mainland and islands of southeast Asia. Throughout most of the region, ruling classes adopted Indian forms of political organization and Indian techniques of statecraft. Indian merchants took their Hindu and Buddhist faiths to southeast Asia, where they attracted the interest first of political elites and then of the popular masses. Somewhat later, Indian merchants also helped to introduce Islam to southeast Asia.

While Indian traditions influenced the political and cultural development of southeast Asia, the entire Indian Ocean basin began to move toward economic integration during the postclassical era, as Buzurg ibn Shahriyar's stories suggest. Lands on the rim of the Indian Ocean retained distinctive political and cultural traditions inherited from times past. Yet innovations in maritime technology, development of a well-articulated network of sea lanes, and the building of port cities and entrepôts enabled peoples living around the Indian Ocean to trade and communicate more actively than ever before. As a result, peoples from east Africa to southeast Asia and China increasingly participated in the larger economic, commercial, and cultural life of the Indian Ocean basin.

ISLAMIC AND HINDU KINGDOMS

Like the Han and Roman empires, the Gupta dynasty came under severe pressure from nomadic invaders. From the mid-fourth to the mid-fifth century C.E., Gupta rulers resisted the pressures and preserved order throughout much of the Indian subcontinent. Beginning in 451 C.E., however, White Huns from central Asia invaded India and disrupted the Gupta administration. By the mid-sixth century, the Gupta state had collapsed, and effective political authority quickly devolved to invaders, local allies of the Guptas, and independent regional power brokers. From the end of the Gupta dynasty until the sixteenth century, when a Turkish people known as the Mughals extended their authority and their empire to most of the subcontinent, India remained a politically divided land.

The Quest for Centralized Imperial Rule

Northern and southern India followed different political trajectories after the fall of the Gupta empire. In the north, politics became turbulent and almost chaotic. Local states contested for power and territory, and northern India became a region of continuous tension and intermittent war. Nomadic Turkish-speaking peoples from central Asia frequently took advantage of that unsettled state of affairs to cross the Khyber Pass and force their way into India. They eventually found niches for themselves in the caste system and became completely absorbed into Indian society. Until processes of social absorption worked themselves out, however, the arrival of nomadic peoples caused additional disruption in northern India.

Harsha Even after the collapse of the Gupta dynasty, the ideal of centralized imperial rule did not entirely disappear. During the first half of the seventh century, King Harsha (reigned 606–648 C.E.) temporarily restored unified rule in most of northern India and sought to revive imperial authority. Harsha came to the throne of his kingdom in the lower Ganges valley at the age of sixteen. Full of energy and ambition, he led his army throughout northern India. His forces included twenty thousand cavalry, fifty thousand infantry, and five thousand war elephants, and by about 612 he had subdued those who refused to recognize his authority. He also made his presence felt beyond India. He extended his influence to several Himalayan states, and he exchanged a series of embassies with his contemporary, Emperor Tang Taizong of China.

Harsha enjoyed a reputation for piety, liberality, and even scholarship. He was himself a Buddhist, but he looked kindly on other faiths as well. He built hospitals and provided free medical care for his subjects. The Chinese pilgrim Xuanzang lived in northern India during his reign and reported that Harsha liberally distributed wealth to his subjects. On one occasion, Xuanzang said, the king and his aides doled out resources continuously for seventy-five days, making gifts to half a million people. Harsha also

MAP 15.1
Major states of postclassical India, 600–1600 C.E.
Several large rivers and river valleys offered opportunities for inhabitants of northern India.
How did peoples of southern India organize flourishing states and societies in the absence of major rivers?

generously patronized scholars and reportedly even wrote three plays himself.

Collapse of Harsha's Kingdom Despite his energy and his favorable reputation, Harsha was unable to restore permanent centralized rule. Since the fall of the Gupta dynasty, local rulers had established their authority too securely in India's regions for Harsha to overcome them. Harsha spent much of his reign on horseback traveling throughout his realm to solidify alliances with local rulers, who were virtually kings in their own lands. He managed to hold his loose empire together mainly by the force of his personality and his constant attention to political affairs. Ultimately, however, he fell victim to an assassin and left no heir to maintain his realm. His empire immediately disintegrated, and local rulers once again turned northern India into a battleground as they sought to enlarge their realms at the expense of their neighbors.

The Introduction of Islam to Northern India

The Conquest of Sind Amid nomadic incursions and contests for power, northern India also experienced the arrival of Islam and the establishment of Islamic states. Islam reached India by several routes. One was military: Arab forces entered India as early as the mid-seventh century, even before the establishment of the Umayyad caliphate, although their first expeditions were exploratory ventures rather than campaigns of conquest. In 711, however, a well-organized expedition conquered Sind, the Indus River valley in northwestern India, and incorporated it as a province of the expanding Umayyad empire. At mid-century, along with most of the rest of the *dar al-Islam,* Sind passed into the hands of the Abbasid caliphs.

Sind stood on the fringe of the Islamic world, well beyond the effective authority of the Abbasid caliphs. Much of its population remained Hindu, Buddhist, or Parsee, and it also sheltered a series of unorthodox Islamic movements. Infighting between Arab administrators eventually offered opportunities for local political elites to reassert Hindu authority over much of Sind. Yet the region remained nominally under the jurisdiction of the caliphs until the collapse of the Abbasid dynasty in 1258.

Merchants and Islam While conquerors brought Islam to Sind, Muslim merchants took their faith to coastal regions in both northern and southern India. Arab and Persian mariners had visited Indian ports for centuries before Muhammad, and their Muslim descendants dominated trade and transportation networks between India and western lands from the seventh through the fifteenth century. Muslim merchants formed small communities in all the major cities of coastal India, where they played a prominent role in Indian business and commercial life. They frequently married local women, and in many cases they also found places for themselves in Indian society. Thus Islam entered India's port cities in a more gradual but no less effective way than was the case in Sind. Well before the year 1000, for example, the Gujarat region housed a large Muslim population. Muslim merchants congregated there because of the port city of Cambay, the most important trading center in India throughout the millennium from 500 to 1500 C.E.

Turkish Migrants and Islam Islam also entered India by a third route: the migrations and invasions of Turkish-speaking peoples from central Asia. During the tenth century, several Turkish groups had become acquainted with Islam through their dealings with the Abbasid caliphate and had converted to the faith. Some of these Muslim Turks entered the Abbasid realm as mercenary soldiers or migrated into Byzantine Anatolia, and others moved into Afghanistan, where they established an Islamic state.

Mahmud of Ghazni Mahmud of Ghazni, leader of the Turks in Afghanistan, soon turned his attention to the rich land to the south. Mahmud was a complex figure. He was a patron of the arts who built Ghazni (near Kabul in modern-day Afghanistan) into a refined capital, where he supported historians, mathematicians, and literary figures at his court. At the same time, Mahmud was a determined and ruthless warrior who spent much of his time in the field with his armies. Between 1001 and 1027 he mounted seventeen raiding expeditions into India. Taking advantage of infighting between local rulers, he annexed several states in northwestern India and the Punjab. For the most part, however, Mahmud had less interest in conquering and ruling India than in plundering the wealth stored in its many well-endowed temples. Mahmud and his forces demolished hundreds of sites associated with Hindu or Buddhist faiths, and their campaigns hastened the decline of Buddhism in the land of its birth. They frequently established mosques or Islamic shrines on the sites of Hindu and Buddhist structures that they destroyed. Not surprisingly, however, Mahmud's raids did not encourage Indians to turn to Islam.

The Sultanate of Delhi During the late twelfth century, Mahmud's successors mounted a more systematic campaign to conquer northern India and place it under Islamic rule. By the early thirteenth century, they had conquered most of the Hindu kingdoms in northern India and established an Islamic state known as the sultanate of Delhi. The sultans established their capital at Delhi, a strategic site controlling access from the Punjab to the Ganges valley, and they ruled northern India, at least in name, for more than three centuries, from 1206 to 1526.

During the fourteenth century the sultans of Delhi commanded an army of three hundred thousand, and their state ranked among the most prominent in the Islamic world. They built mosques, shrines, and fortresses throughout their realm, and, like Mahmud of Ghazni, they were generous patrons of the arts and literature. Yet for the most part, the authority of the sultans did not extend far beyond Delhi. They often conducted raids in the Deccan region of southern India, but they never overcame Hindu resistance there. They had no permanent bureaucracy or administrative apparatus.

A fourteenth-century painting depicts the Turkish conqueror Mahmud of Ghazni as he dons a robe bestowed on him as a gift by the Abbasid caliph. Although Mahmud pursued independent policies, he always recognized the caliph as his overlord.

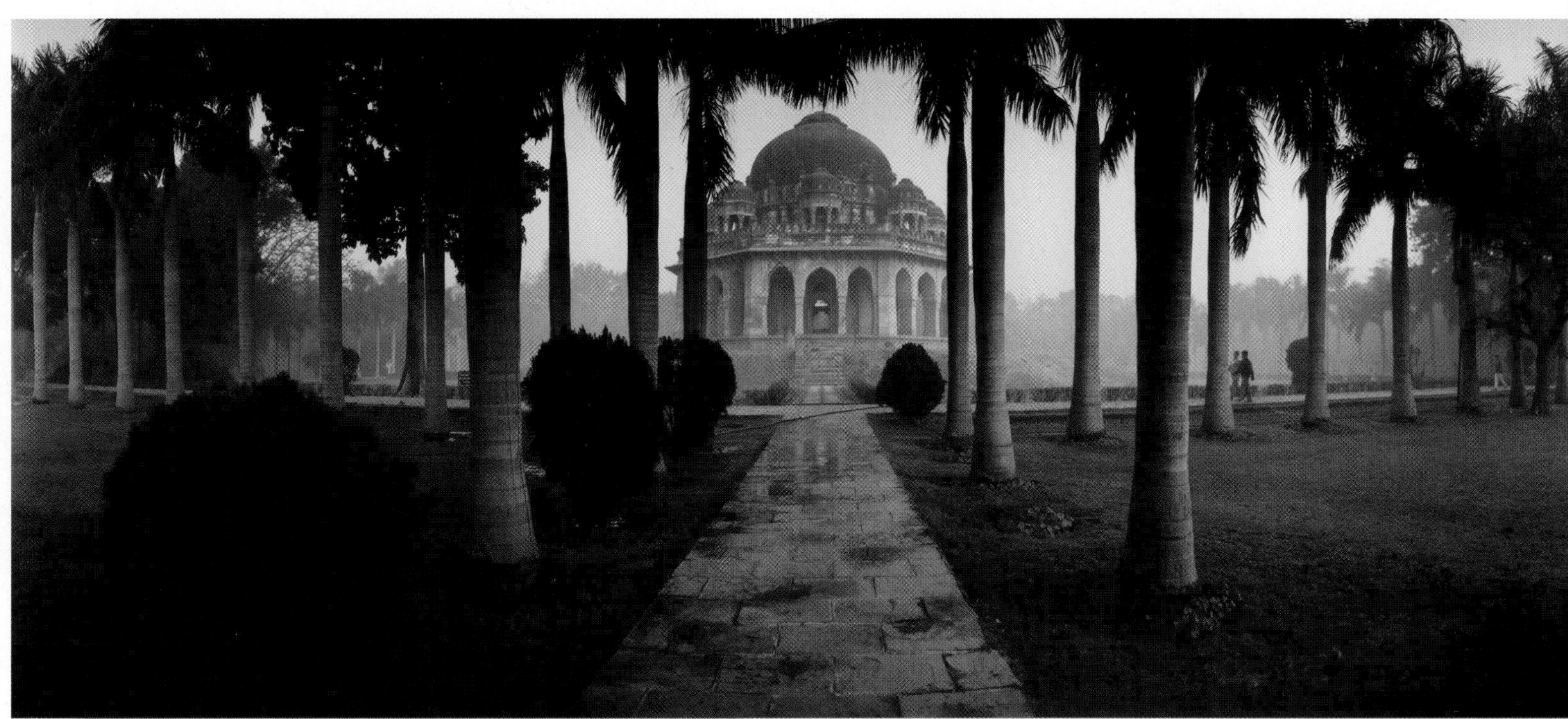

Lodi Gardens near Delhi is the cemetery of the Lodi sultans, the last dynasty to rule the sultanate of Delhi. Here a tomb reflects the introduction of Islamic architecture into India.

Even in northern India, they imposed a thin veneer of Islamic political and military authority on a land populated mostly by Hindus, and they depended on the goodwill of Hindu kings to carry out their policies and advance their interests in local regions. Indeed, they did not even enjoy comfortable control of their own court: of the thirty-five sultans of Delhi, nineteen perished at the hands of assassins. Nevertheless, the sultans prominently sponsored Islam and played a large role especially in the establishment of Islam in the Bengal region.

The Hindu Kingdoms of Southern India

Although it too remained politically divided, the southern part of the Indian subcontinent largely escaped the invasions, chronic war, and turmoil that troubled the north. Most Hindu rulers in the south presided over small, loosely administered states. Competition between states sometimes resulted in regional wars, but southern conflicts were less frequent, less intense, and less damaging than those that plagued the north.

The Chola Kingdom Although many regional states organized affairs in local jurisdictions, two kingdoms expanded enough to exercise at least nominal rule over much of southern India. The first was the Chola kingdom, situated in the deep south, which ruled the Coromandel coast for more than four centuries, from 850 to 1267 C.E. At its high point, during the eleventh century, Chola forces conquered Ceylon and parts of southeast Asia. Financed by the profits of trade, the Chola navy dominated the waters from the South China Sea to the Arabian Sea.

Chola rulers did not build a tightly centralized state: they allowed considerable autonomy for local and village institutions as long as they maintained order and delivered tax revenues on time. Chola rulers had less interest in building a powerful state than in realizing profits that came from their domination of trade in the Indian Ocean basin. Indeed, partly because of its loose institutional structure, the Chola state was in decline by the twelfth century. Native Sinhalese forces expelled Chola officials from Ceylon, and revolts erupted within southern India. The Chola realm did not entirely collapse, but by the early thirteenth century, much reduced in size and power, it had reverted to the status of one regional kingdom among many in southern India.

The Kingdom of Vijayanagar The second state that dominated much of southern India was the kingdom of **Vijayanagar,** based in the northern Deccan. The kingdom owed its origin to efforts by the sultans of Delhi to extend their authority to southern India. Exploratory forays by Turkish forces provoked a defensive reaction in the south. Officials in Delhi dispatched two brothers, Harihara and Bukka, to represent the sultan and implement court policies in the

Vijayanagar (vee-juh-yah-NAH-gahr)

The kings of Vijayanagar endowed their capital with splendid buildings and even provided these handsome domed stables for their elephants.

south. Although they had converted from their native Hinduism to Islam, Harihara and Bukka recognized an opportunity to establish themselves as independent rulers. In 1336 they renounced Islam, returned to their original Hindu faith, and proclaimed the establishment of an independent empire of Vijayanagar (meaning "city of victory"). Their unusual coup did not lead to hostilities between Muslims and Hindus: Muslim merchants continued to trade unmolested in the ports of southern India, as they had for more than half a millennium. But the Hindu kingdom of Vijayanagar was the dominant state in southern India from the mid-fourteenth century until 1565, when it fell to an alliance of Muslim kingdoms.

As in northern India, then, political division and conflict between states characterized southern India's political history in postclassical times. India did not generate the sort of large-scale, centralized, imperial state that guided the fortunes of postclassical societies in the eastern Mediterranean, southwest Asia, or China. States such as the sultanate of Delhi in northern India and the kingdoms of Chola and Vijayanagar in the south were not powerful enough to organize political life throughout the subcontinent. Nevertheless, on the basis of trade, common social structures, and inherited cultural traditions, a coherent and distinctive society flourished in postclassical India.

PRODUCTION AND TRADE IN THE INDIAN OCEAN BASIN

As in the Mediterranean, southwest Asia, and China, agricultural yields increased significantly in postclassical India, enabling large numbers of people to devote themselves to trade and manufacturing rather than the production of food. Trade forged links between the various regions of the subcontinent and fostered economic development in southern India. Trade also created links between India and distant lands, as merchants and manufacturers transformed the Indian Ocean basin into a vast zone of communication and exchange. The increasing prominence of trade and industry brought change to Indian society, as merchant and artisan guilds became stronger and more influential than before. Yet caste identities and loyalties also remained strong, and the caste system continued to serve as the most powerful organizing feature of Indian society.

Agriculture in the Monsoon World

The Monsoons Because of the rhythms of the monsoons, irrigation was essential for the maintenance of a large, densely populated, agricultural society. During the spring and summer, warm, moisture-laden winds from the southwest bring most of India's rainfall. During the autumn and winter, cool and very dry winds blow from the northeast. To achieve their agricultural potential, Indian lands required a good watering by the southern monsoon, supplemented by irrigation during the dry months. Light rain during the spring and summer months or short supplies of water for irrigation commonly led to drought, reduced harvests, and widespread famine.

Irrigation Systems In northern India, irrigation had been a fixture of the countryside since Harappan times, when cultivators tapped the waters of the Indus River. Later, as Aryans migrated into the Ganges River valley, they found plentiful surface water and abundant opportunities to build

irrigation systems. For the most part, however, southern India is an arid land without rivers like the Indus or the Ganges that can serve as sources for large-scale irrigation. Thus, as southern India became more densely populated, irrigation systems became crucial, and a great deal of energy and effort went into the construction of waterworks. Dams, reservoirs, canals, wells, and tunnels appeared in large numbers. Particularly impressive were monumental reservoirs lined with brick or stone that captured the rains of the spring and summer months and held them until the dry season, when canals carried them to thirsty fields. One such reservoir—actually an artificial lake constructed near Bhopal during the eleventh century—covered some 650 square kilometers (250 square miles). Projects of that size required enormous investments of human energy, both for their original construction and for continuing maintenance, but they led to significant increases in agricultural productivity.

"By 800 [C.E.] it [India's population] had increased almost 20 percent to 64 million..."

Population Growth As a result of that increased productivity, India's population grew steadily throughout the postclassical era. In 600 C.E., shortly after the fall of the Gupta dynasty, the subcontinent's population stood at about 53 million. By 800 it had increased almost 20 percent to 64 million, and by 1000 it had grown by almost an additional 25 percent to 79 million. During the following centuries the rate of growth slowed, as Indian numbers increased by 4 to 5 million individuals per century. Toward 1500, however, the rate of growth increased again, and by 1500 the subcontinent's population had reached 105 million.

Urbanization This demographic surge encouraged the concentration of people in cities. During the fourteenth century, the high point of the sultanate of Delhi, the capital city had a population of about four hundred thousand, which made it second only to Cairo among Muslim cities. Many other cities—particularly ports and trading centers, such as Cambay, Surat, Calicut, Quilon, and Masulipatam—had populations well over one hundred thousand. Cities in southern India grew especially fast, partly as a result of increasing agricultural productivity in the region.

Trade and the Economic Development of Southern India

Political fragmentation of the subcontinent did not prevent robust trade between the different states and regions of India. As the population grew, opportunities for specialized work became more numerous. Increased trade was a natural result of that process.

Internal Trade Most regions of the Indian subcontinent were self-sufficient in staple foods such as rice, wheat, barley, and millet. The case was different, however, with iron, copper, salt, pepper, spices, condiments, and specialized crops that grew well only in certain regions. Iron came mostly from the Ganges River valley near Bengal, copper mostly from the Deccan Plateau, salt mostly from coastal regions, and pepper from southern India. Those and other commodities sometimes traveled long distances to consumers in remote parts of the subcontinent. Pepper, saffron, and sugar were popular commodities in subcontinental trade, and even rice sometimes traveled as a trade item to northern and mountainous regions where it did not grow well.

Southern India and Ceylon benefited especially handsomely from this trade. As invasions and conflicts disrupted northern India, southern regions experienced rapid economic development. The Chola kingdom provided relative stability in the south, and Chola expansion in southeast Asia opened markets for Indian merchants and producers. Coastal towns such as Calicut and Quilon flourished, and they attracted increasing numbers of residents.

Temples and Society The Chola rulers allowed considerable autonomy to their subjects, and the towns and villages of southern India largely organized their own affairs. Public life revolved around Hindu temples that served as economic and social centers. Southern Indians used their growing wealth to build hundreds of elaborate Hindu temples, which organized agricultural activities, coordinated work on irrigation systems, and maintained reserves of surplus production for use in times of need. These temples also provided basic schooling for boys in the community, and larger temples offered advanced instruction as well. Temples often possessed large tracts of agricultural land, and they sometimes employed hundreds of people, including brahmins, attendants, musicians, servants, and slaves. To meet their financial obligations to employees, temple administrators collected a portion of the agricultural yield from lands subject to temple authority. Administrators were also responsible for keeping order in their communities and delivering tax receipts to the Cholas and other political authorities.

Temple authorities also served as bankers, made loans, and invested in commercial and business ventures. As a result, temples promoted the economic development of southern India by encouraging production and trade. Temple authorities cooperated closely with the leaders of merchant guilds in seeking commercial opportunities to exploit. The guilds often made gifts of land or money to temples by way of consolidating their relationship with the powerful economic institutions. Temples thus grew prosperous and became crucial to the economic health of southern India.

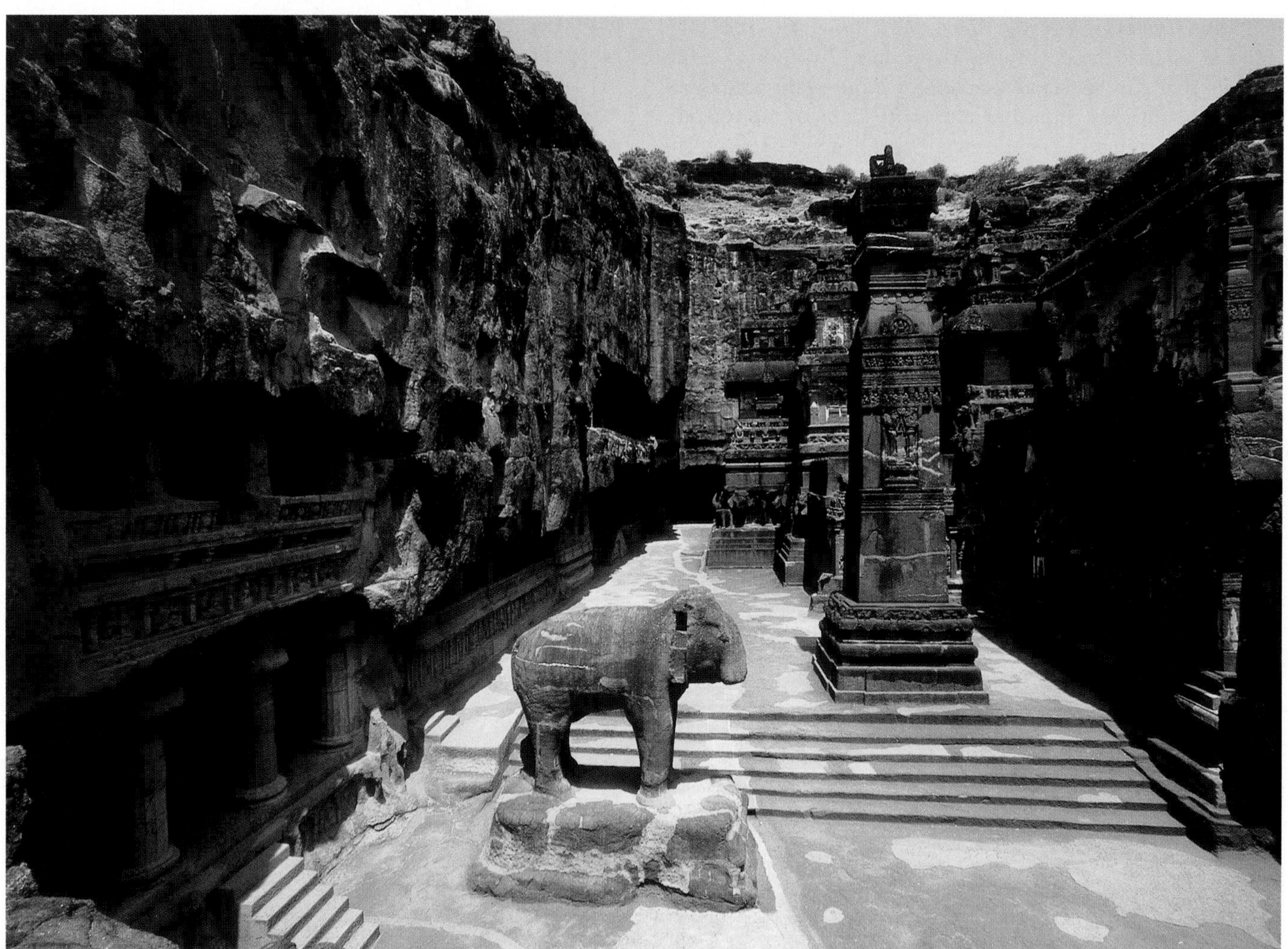

During the eighth century C.E., workers carved a massive temple out of sheer rock at Ellora in central India. Temple communities such as the one that grew up at Ellora controlled enormous resources in postclassical India. How did temple communities become wealthy institutions?

Cross-Cultural Trade in the Indian Ocean Basin

Indian prosperity sprang partly from the productivity of Indian society, but it depended also on the vast wealth that circulated in the commercial world of the Indian Ocean basin. Trade in the Indian Ocean was not new in postclassical times: Indian merchants had already ventured to southeast Asia during the classical era, and they dealt regularly with mariners from the Roman empire who traveled to India in search of pepper. During the postclassical era, however, larger ships and improved commercial organization supported a dramatic surge in the volume and value of trade in the Indian Ocean basin.

Dhows and Junks The earliest voyaging in the Indian Ocean followed the coastlines, but already in classical times mariners recognized the rhythms of the monsoons. Over time they built larger ships, which enabled them to leave the coasts behind and ply the blue waters of the Indian Ocean: the dhows favored by Indian, Persian, and Arab sailors averaged about one hundred tons burden in 1000 and four hundred tons in 1500. After the naval and commercial expansion of the Song dynasty, large Chinese and southeast Asian junks also sailed the Indian Ocean: some of them could carry one thousand tons of cargo.

As large, stable ships came into use, mariners increasingly entrusted their crafts and cargoes to the reasonably predictable monsoons and sailed directly across the Arabian Sea and the Bay of Bengal. In the age of sail, it was impossible to make a round trip across the entire Indian Ocean without spending months at distant ports waiting for the winds to change, so merchants usually conducted their trade in stages.

Emporia Because India stood in the middle of the Indian Ocean basin, it was a natural site for emporia and ware-

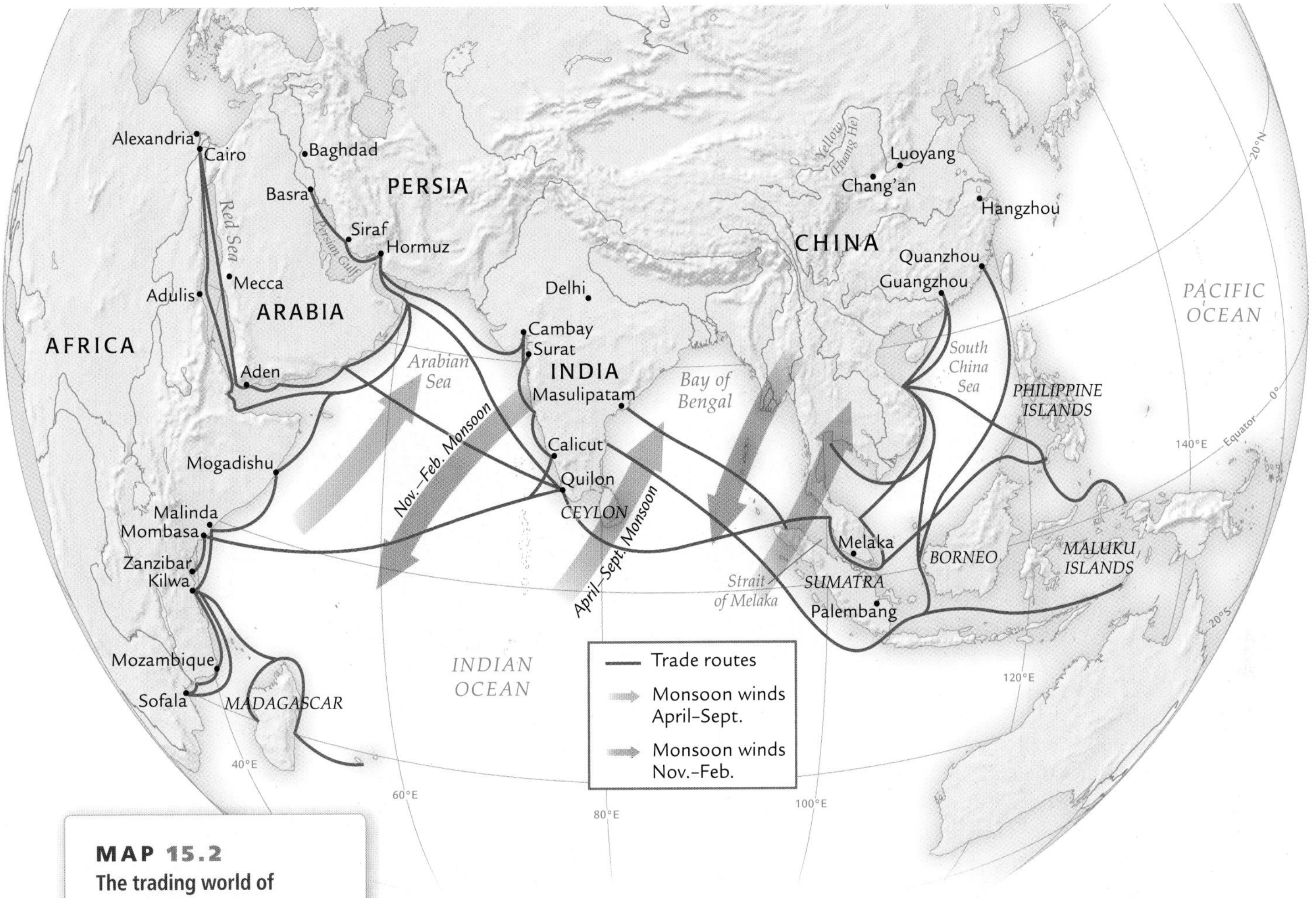

MAP 15.2
The trading world of the Indian Ocean basin, 600–1600 C.E.
Note the directions of seasonal winds in the Indian Ocean basin.
How would mariners take advantage of these winds to reach their destinations?

houses. Merchants coming from east Africa or Persia exchanged their cargoes at Cambay, Calicut, or Quilon for goods to take back west with the winter monsoon. Mariners from China or southeast Asia called at Indian ports and traded their cargoes for goods to ship east with the summer monsoon. Merchants also built emporia outside India: the storytelling mariner Buzurg ibn Shahriyar came from the emporium of Siraf on the Persian Gulf, a port city surrounded by desert that nevertheless enjoyed fabulous wealth because of its trade with China, India, and east Africa. Because of their central location, however, Indian ports became the principal clearinghouses of trade in the Indian Ocean basin, and they became remarkably cosmopolitan centers. Hindus, Buddhists, Muslims, Jews, and others who inhabited the Indian port cities did business with counterparts from all over the eastern hemisphere and swapped stories like those recounted by Buzurg ibn Shahriyar. In combination, the sea lanes and emporia of the Indian Ocean basin made up a network of maritime silk roads—a web of transportation, communication, and exchange that complemented the land-based silk roads and promoted interaction between peoples throughout much of the eastern hemisphere.

Particularly after the establishment of the Umayyad and Abbasid dynasties in southwest Asia and the Tang and Song dynasties in China, trade in the Indian Ocean surged. Indian merchants and mariners sometimes traveled to distant lands in search of marketable goods, but the carrying trade between India and points west fell mostly into Arab and Persian hands. During the Song dynasty, Chinese junks also ventured into the western Indian Ocean and called at ports as far away as east Africa. In the Bay of Bengal and the China seas, Malay and Chinese vessels were most prominent.

Specialized Production As the volume of trade in the Indian Ocean basin increased, lands around the ocean began to engage in specialized production of commodities for the commercial market. For centuries Indian artisans had enjoyed a reputation for the manufacture of fine cotton textiles,

Dhows fitted with lateen sails skim across the Indian Ocean much like their ancestors of the postclassical era.

which they produced in small quantities for wealthy consumers. In postclassical times their wares came into high demand throughout the trading world of the Indian Ocean basin. In response to that demand, Indian artisans built thriving local industries around the production of high-quality cotton textiles. These industries influenced the structure of the Indian economy: they created a demand for specific agricultural products, provided a livelihood for thousands of artisans, and enabled consumers to import goods from regions that specialized in the production of other commodities.

Alongside textiles, other specialized industries that emerged in postclassical India included sugar refining, leather tanning, stone carving, and carpet weaving. Iron and steel production also emerged as prominent industries. Indian artisans became well known especially for the production of high-carbon steel, which held a lethal cutting edge and consequently came into high demand for use in knives and swords. Other lands concentrated on the production of different manufactured goods and agricultural commodities: China produced silk, porcelain, and lacquerware; southeast Asian lands provided fine spices; incense, horses, and dates came from southwest Asia; and east Africa contributed gold, ivory, and slaves. Thus trade encouraged specialized production and economic development in all lands participating in the trade networks of the Indian Ocean basin: cross-cultural trade in postclassical times influenced the structure of economies and societies throughout much of the eastern hemisphere.

The Kingdom of Axum The experience of the kingdom of Axum (sometimes spelled Aksum) illustrates the potential of trade to support political as well as economic development. Founded in the highlands of northern Ethiopia about the first century C.E., Axum was originally a small kingdom whose merchants traded from the port of Adulis on the Red Sea. Axum soon displaced Kush as Egypt's principal link to southern lands and sent the Nubian kingdom into economic and political decline: about 360 C.E. Axumite forces even invaded Kush and destroyed the capital city of Meroë. During the fourth and fifth centuries, Axumites adopted Christianity and established a distinctive church that maintained relations with Christian communities in Egypt and the Mediterranean basin. During the sixth century Axum embarked on a round of territorial expansion, building an empire that included most of modern-day Ethiopia as well as Yemen in southern Arabia. Indeed,

thinking about ENCOUNTERS

Geography, Environment, and Trade
Commercial networks often link different environmental regions that are capable of producing different products because of local geographic conditions. What environmental zones did Indian Ocean networks reach? What geographic conditions favored the production of specific products in the various regions?

Mealtime for a Persian merchant and his two companions served by three women attendants in this ceiling decoration from the Ajanta caves in central India.

an Axumite army and elephant corps campaigned as far north as Mecca in the year 571 C.E., birth year of the prophet Muhammad.

During the seventh and eighth centuries, Arab conquerors sought to bring Axum into the expanding realm of Islam, but the kingdom maintained its independence and its Christian religion. Because neighboring lands mostly adopted Islam, Axum fell out of communication with other Christian societies. Nevertheless, Axumite merchants not only maintained commercial ties with distant lands, as ships from Adulis routinely sailed for India and the islands of southeast Asia, but also traded regularly with Muslim merchants in neighboring lands. From the sixth to the ninth century C.E., Adulis was perhaps the most prominent port in east Africa, funneling gold, ivory, and slaves from sub-Saharan Africa to Egypt, the eastern Mediterranean region, and the Indian Ocean basin. Thus, even though challenged by Muslim forces, Axum was able to maintain its independence and prosperity, largely because of its participation in trading networks of the Indian Ocean and Mediterranean Sea.

Caste and Society

The political, economic, and social changes of the postclassical era brought a series of challenges for India's caste system. Migrations, the growing prominence of Islam, economic development, and urbanization all placed pressures on the caste system as it had developed during the Vedic and classical eras. But the caste system has never been a rigid, unchanging structure. Rather, individuals and groups have continuously adjusted it and adapted it to new circumstances. Adjustments and adaptations of the postclassical era resulted in a caste system that was more complex than in earlier ages and that also extended its geographic reach deeper into southern India than ever before. In the absence of strong central governments, the caste system helped to maintain order in local communities by providing guidance on individuals' roles in society and their relationships with others.

Caste and Migration The caste system closely reflected changes in Indian society. It adapted to the arrival of migrants, for example, and helped to integrate them into Indian society. As Turkish peoples or Muslim merchants pursued opportunities in India, they gained recognition as distinct groups under the umbrella of the caste system. They established codes of conduct both for the regulation of behavior within their own groups and for guidance in dealing with members of other castes. Within a few generations their descendants had become absorbed into Indian society.

Caste and Social Change The caste system also accommodated the social changes brought about by trade and economic development. Indeed, the caste system influenced the lives of most people by helping to order their work and their relationships with other workers. The castes that individuals most closely identified with were the subcastes (*jati*), which often took the form of workers' guilds. As merchants and manufacturers became increasingly important in the larger economy, they organized powerful guilds to represent their interests. Merchant guilds in particular wielded political and economic influence, since their members enjoyed access to considerable wealth and contributed in large measure to the economic health of their states. Guild members forged group identities by working within the caste system. Merchants specializing in particular types of commerce, such as the silk, cotton, or spice trade, established themselves as distinct subcastes, as did artisans working in particular industries, such as the iron, steel, or leather business.

Expansion of the Caste System Besides becoming more complex, the caste system also extended its geographic reach. Caste distinctions first became prominent in northern India following Aryan migrations into the subcontinent. During the postclassical era, the caste system became securely established in southern India as well. Economic development aided that process by encouraging commercial relationships between southern merchants and their caste-conscious counterparts in the north. The emergence of merchant and craft guilds in southern regions strengthened the caste system, since guild members usually organized as a subcaste. Powerful temples also fostered caste distinctions. Caste-conscious brahmins who supervised the temples were particularly effective promoters of the system, since temples provided the only formal education available

sources from the past

Cosmas Indicopleustes on Trade in Southern India

Cosmas Indicopleustes was a Christian monk from Egypt who lived during the sixth century C.E. and traveled widely throughout north Africa and southwest Asia. On one of his trips, he ventured as far as India and Ceylon, which he described at some length in a work titled The Christian Topography. *Cosmas's account clearly shows that sixth-century India and Ceylon played prominent roles in the larger economy of the Indian Ocean basin.*

Ceylon lies on the other side of the pepper country [southern India]. Around it are numerous small islands all having fresh water and coconut trees. They nearly all have deep water close up to their shores. . . . Ceylon is a great market for the people in those parts. The island also has a church of Persian Christians who have settled there, and a priest who is appointed from Persia, and a deacon and a complete ecclesiastical ritual. But the natives and their kings are heathens. . . .

Since the island of Ceylon is in a central position, it is much frequented by ships from all parts of India and from Persia and Ethiopia, and it likewise sends out many of its own. And from the remotest countries—I mean China and other trading places—it receives silk, aloes, cloves, sandalwood, and other products, and these again are passed on to markets on this side, such as Male [the western coast of southern India], where pepper grows, and to Calliana [a port city near modern Bombay], which exports copper and sesame logs and cloth for making dresses, for it also is a great place of business. And also to Sind [Gujarat], where musk and castor and spice are procured, and to Persia and the Homerite country [Anatolia], and to Adule [in Ethiopia]. And this island [Ceylon] receives imports from all these markets that we have mentioned and passes them on to the remoter ports, while at the same time exporting its own produce in both directions. . . .

The kings of various places in India keep elephants. . . . They may have six hundred each, or five hundred, some more, some fewer. Now the king of Ceylon gives a good price both for the elephants and for the horses that he has. The elephants he pays for by the cubit [a unit of measurement equivalent to about half a meter or twenty inches]. For the height is measured from the ground, and the price is reckoned at so many gold coins for each cubit—fifty [coins] it may be, or a hundred, or even more. Horses they bring to him from Persia, and he buys them, exempting the importers of them from paying custom duties. The kings of the Indian subcontinent tame their elephants, which are caught wild, and employ them in war.

For Further Reflection

- How did Ceylon compare as a commercial center with Constantinople and Baghdad, as described by Benjamin of Tudela?

Source: Cosmas Indicopleustes. *The Christian Topography of Cosmas, an Egyptian Monk.* Trans. by J. W. McCrindle. London: Hakluyt Society, 1897, pp. 364–72. (Translation slightly modified.)

in most regions and also served as centers of local social life. By about the eleventh century C.E., caste had become the principal basis of social organization in southern India.

THE MEETING OF HINDU AND ISLAMIC TRADITIONS

The Indian cultural landscape underwent a thorough transformation during the postclassical era. Jainism and Buddhism lost much of their popular following. Neither belief completely disappeared from India, and indeed, a small community continues to observe each faith there even today. After 1000 C.E., however, Hindu and Islamic traditions increasingly dominated the cultural and religious life of India.

Hinduism and Islam differed profoundly as religious traditions. The Hindu pantheon made places for numerous gods and spirits, for example, whereas Islamic theology stood on the foundation of a firm and uncompromising monotheism. Yet both religions attracted large popular followings throughout the subcontinent, with Hinduism predominating in southern India and Islam in the north.

The Development of Hinduism

Toward the end of the first millennium C.E., Buddhism flourished in east Asia, central Asia, and parts of southeast Asia but came under great pressure in India. Like Mahayana Buddhism, both Hinduism and Islam promised salvation to devout individuals, and they gradually attracted Buddhists to their own communities. Invasions of India by Turkish peoples hastened the decline of Buddhism because the invaders looted and destroyed Buddhist stupas and shrines. In 1196 Muslim forces overran the city of Nalanda and ravaged the schools where Xuanzang and other foreign pilgrims had studied with the world's leading Buddhist philosophers and theologians. The conquerors torched Buddhist libraries and either killed or exiled thousands of monks living at

Southern Indian artists often portrayed Shiva in bronze sculptures as a four-armed lord of dancers. In this figure from the Chola dynasty, Shiva crushes with his foot a dwarf demon symbolizing ignorance. One hand holds a bell to awaken his devotees, another bears the fire used by Shiva as creator and destroyer of the world, and a third gestures Shiva's benevolence toward his followers.

Nalanda. Buddhism soon became a minor faith in the land of its birth.

Vishnu and Shiva Hinduism benefited from the decline of Buddhism. One reason for the increasing popularity of Hinduism was the remarkable growth of devotional cults, particularly those dedicated to Vishnu and Shiva, two of the most important deities in the Hindu pantheon. Vishnu was the preserver of the world, a god who observed the universe from the heavens and who occasionally entered the world in human form to resist evil or communicate his teachings. In contrast, Shiva was both a god of fertility and a destructive deity: he brought life but also took it away when its season had passed. Hindus associated many gods and goddesses with Vishnu and Shiva, and they recognized other cults that were altogether independent of these two. But the most popular devotional cults focused on veneration of Vishnu or Shiva.

Devotional Cults Hindus embraced the new cults warmly because they promised salvation. Devotional cults became especially popular in southern India, where individuals or family groups went to great lengths to honor their chosen deities. Often, cults originated when individuals identified Vishnu or Shiva with a local spirit or deity associated with a particular region or a prominent geographic feature. The famous cult of Shiva as lord of the dancers arose, for example, about the fifth or sixth century C.E. when devotees identified a stone long venerated locally in a southern Indian village as a symbol of Shiva. In the tenth century Chola kings took the dancing Shiva as their family god and spread the cult's popularity throughout southern India. By venerating images of Vishnu or Shiva, offering them food and drink, and meditating on the deities and their qualities, Hindus hoped to achieve a mystic union with the gods that would bring grace and salvation. As the cults proliferated, temples and shrines dotted the landscape of southern India. Veneration of Vishnu and Shiva gradually became popular among Hindus in northern as well as southern India.

Shankara The significance of Hinduism extended well beyond popular religion: it also influenced philosophy. Just as Buddhism, Christianity, and Islam influenced moral thought and philosophy in other lands, devotional Hinduism guided the efforts of the most prominent philosophers in postclassical India. Brahmin philosophers such as Shankara and Ramanuja took the Upanishads as a point of departure for subtle reasoning and sophisticated metaphysics. Shankara, a southern Indian devotee of Shiva who was active during the early ninth century C.E., took it upon himself to digest all sacred Hindu writings and harmonize their sometimes contradictory teachings into a single, consistent system of thought. In a manner reminiscent of Plato, Shankara held that the physical world was illusion—a figment of the imagination—and that ultimate reality lay beyond the physical senses. Although he was a worshiper of Shiva, Shankara mistrusted emotional services and ceremonies, insisting that only by disciplined logical reasoning could human beings understand the ultimate reality of Brahman, the impersonal world-soul of the Upanishads. Only then could they appreciate the fundamental unity of the world, which Shankara considered a perfectly understandable expression of ultimate reality, even though to human physical senses that same world appears chaotic and incomprehensible.

Ramanuja Ramanuja, a devotee of Vishnu who was active during the eleventh and early twelfth centuries C.E., challenged Shankara's uncompromising insistence on logic. Also a brahmin philosopher from southern India, Ramanuja's thought reflected the deep influence of devotional cults. According to Ramanuja, intellectual understanding of ultimate reality was less important than personal union with the deity. Ramanuja granted that intellectual efforts could lead to comprehension of reality, but he held that genuine bliss came from salvation and identification of individuals with their gods. He followed the *Bhagavad Gita* in recommending intense devotion to Vishnu, and he taught that by placing themselves in the hands of Vishnu, devotees would win the god's grace and live forever in his presence. Thus, in contrast to Shankara's consistent, intellectual system of thought, Ramanuja's philosophy pointed toward a Hindu theology of salvation. Indeed, his thought inspired the development of devotional cults throughout India, and it serves even today as a philosophical foundation for Hindu popular religion.

An elaborate open-air rock carving at Mamallapuram, south of modern Madras, celebrates the Ganges River as a gift from Shiva and other gods.

Islam and Its Appeal

The Islamic faith did not attract much immediate interest among Indians when it arrived in the subcontinent. It won gradual acceptance in merchant communities where foreign Muslim traders took local spouses and found a place in Indian society. Elsewhere, however, circumstances did not favor its adoption, since it often arrived in the cultural baggage of conquering peoples. Muslim conquerors generally reserved important political and military positions for their Arab, Persian, and Turkish companions. Only rarely did they allow Indians—even those who had converted to Islam—to hold sensitive posts. Thus, quite apart from the fact that they introduced a foreign religion radically different from those of the subcontinent, conquerors offered little incentive for Indians to convert to Islam.

Conversion to Islam Gradually, however, many Indians converted to Islam. By 1500 C.E. Indian Muslims numbered perhaps twenty-five million—about one-quarter of the subcontinent's population. Some Indians adopted Islam in hopes of improving their positions in society: Hindus of lower castes, for example, hoped to escape discrimination by converting to a faith that recognized the equality of all believers. In fact, Hindus rarely improved their social standing by conversion. Often, members of an entire caste or subcaste adopted Islam en masse, and after conversion they continued to play the same social and economic roles that they had before.

Sufis In India as elsewhere, the most effective agents of conversion to Islam were Sufi mystics. Sufis encouraged a personal, emotional, devotional approach to Islam. They did not insist on fine points of doctrine, and they sometimes even permitted their followers to observe rituals or venerate spirits not recognized by the Islamic faith. Because of their piety and sincerity, however, Sufi missionaries attracted individuals searching for a faith that could provide comfort and meaning for their personal lives. Thus, like Hinduism, Indian Islam emphasized piety and devotion. Even though Hinduism and Islam were profoundly different religions, they encouraged the cultivation of similar spiritual values that transcended the social and cultural boundary lines of postclassical India.

The Bhakti Movement In some ways, the gap between Hinduism and Islam narrowed in postclassical India because both religions drew on long-established and long-observed cultural traditions. Sufis, for example, often attracted schools of followers in the manner of Indian gurus, spiritual leaders who taught Hindu values to disciples who congregated around them. Even more important was the development of the *bhakti* movement, a cult of love and devotion that ultimately sought to erase the distinction be-

thinking about TRADITIONS

The Development of Hinduism and Islam
After the eleventh century C.E., Buddhism progressively declined in its original homeland, leaving Hinduism and Islam as the two main religious traditions prominent in India. How did Hinduism and Islam undergo change in the Indian cultural environment? To what extent might the two traditions have influenced each other?

sources from the past

The *Bhagavata Purana* on Devotion to Vishnu

With the development of devotional Hinduism in the post-classical era, religious leaders produced a body of literature known as the puranas, *texts that told stories about the gods and offered instructions in proper methods of worship. The most influential of these works is the* Bhagavata Purana ("Purana of the Lord"), *composed about the eighth or ninth century* C.E. *In the following selection the god Vishnu sometimes refers to himself in the third person as "the Lord" and sometimes speaks in the first person while instructing devotees how to worship him and support his cult.*

The teachers consider the utterance of the Lord's name as destructive of sin completely, even when the utterance is due to the name being associated with something else, or is done jocularly, or as a result of involuntary sound, or in derision. . . .

One should therefore resort to a teacher, desiring to know what constitutes the supreme welfare. . . . Taking the teacher as the deity, one should learn from him the practices characteristic of the Lord's devotees. . . . First, detachment from all undesirable associations, then, association with the good souls, compassion, friendliness, and due humility toward all beings, purity, penance, forbearance, silence, study of sacred writings, straightforwardness, continence, nonviolence, equanimity, seeing one's own Self and the Lord everywhere, seeking solitude, freedom from home, wearing clean recluse robes, satisfying oneself with whatever comes to one, faith in the scriptures of devotion and refraining from censure of those of other schools, subjugation of mind, speech, and action, truthfulness, quietude, restraint, listening to accounts of the Lord's advents, exploits, and qualities, singing of the Lord, contemplation of the Lord of wonderful exploits, engaging in acts only for His sake, dedicating unto the Lord everything—the rites one does, gifts, penance, sacred recital, righteous conduct and whatever is dear to one like one's wife, son, house, and one's own life—cultivating friendship with those who consider the Lord as their soul and master, service to the Lord and to the world and especially to the great and good souls, sharing in the company of fellow devotees the sanctifying glory of the Lord, sharing with them one's delight, satisfaction and virtues of restraint, remembering oneself and reminding fellow-worshipers of the Lord who sweeps away all sin; bearing a body thrilled with devotion and ecstatic experience of the Lord, now in tears with some thought of the Lord, now laughing, now rejoicing, now speaking out, now dancing, now singing, now imitating the Lord's acts, and now becoming quiet with the blissful experience of the Supreme—such are the devotees, who behave like persons not of this world. . . .

One should engage himself in singing of Me, praising Me, dancing with My themes, imitating My exploits and acts, narrating My stories or listening to them.

With manifold hymns of praise of Me, taken from the *Puranas* or from the local languages . . . , the devotee should praise and pray to Me that I bless him and prostrate himself completely before Me. With his head and hands at My feet, he should pray, "My lord, from the clutches of death [i.e., the cycle of birth and death], save me who have taken refuge under You." . . .

Whenever and wherever one feels like worshiping Me in images, etc., one should do so; I am, however, present in oneself and in all beings; for I am the Soul of everything. . . .

Having consecrated an image of Me one should build a firm temple for Me, and beautiful flower gardens around for conducting daily worship and festivals. For the maintenance of My worship, etc., in special seasons as well as every day, one should bestow fields, bazaars, townships, and villages, and thereby attain to My own lordship.

For Further Reflection

- Assess the extent to which the *Bhagavata Purana* builds on devotional teachings offered in the *Bhagavad Gita* discussed earlier.

Source: Ainslie T. Embree and Stephen Hay, eds. *Sources of Indian Tradition,* 2nd ed., 2 vols. New York: Columbia University Press, 1988, 1:325–26, 328.

tween Hinduism and Islam. The bhakti movement emerged in southern India during the twelfth century, and it originally encouraged a traditional piety and devotion to Hindu values. As the movement spread to the north, bhakti leaders increasingly encountered Muslims and became deeply attracted to certain Islamic values, especially monotheism and the notion of spiritual equality of all believers.

Guru Kabir The bhakti movement gradually rejected the exclusive features of both Hinduism and Islam. Thus guru Kabir (1440–1518), a blind weaver who was one of the most famous bhakti teachers, went so far as to teach that Shiva, Vishnu, and Allah were all manifestations of a single, universal deity, whom all devout believers could find within their own hearts. The bhakti movement did not succeed in

In India as in other lands, Sufi mystics were the most effective Muslim missionaries. This eighteenth-century painting depicts the Sufi Khwaja Khidr, beloved in Muslim communities throughout northern India as one associated with springtime, fertility, and happiness. Why would Sufis emphasize nonreligious values while promoting Islam?

harmonizing Hinduism and Islam. Nevertheless, like the Sufis, bhakti teachers promoted values that helped to build bridges between India's social and cultural communities.

THE INFLUENCE OF INDIAN SOCIETY IN SOUTHEAST ASIA

Just as China stood at the center of a larger east Asian society, India served as the principal source of political and cultural traditions widely observed throughout south and southeast Asia. For a millennium and more, southeast Asian peoples adapted Indian political structures and religions to local needs and interests. Although Indian armed forces rarely ventured into the region, southeast Asian lands reflected the influence of Indian society, as merchants introduced Hinduism, Buddhism, Sanskrit writings, and Indian forms of political organization. Beginning about the twelfth century, Islam also found solid footing in southeast Asia, as Muslim merchants, many of them Indians, established trading communities in the important port cities of the region. During the next five hundred years, Islam attracted a sizable following and became a permanent feature in much of southeast Asia.

The States of Southeast Asia

Indian Influence in Southeast Asia Indian merchants visited the islands and mainland of southeast Asia from an early date, perhaps as early as 500 B.C.E. By the early centuries C.E., they had become familiar figures throughout southeast Asia, and their presence brought opportunities for the native ruling elites of the region. In exchange for spices and exotic products such as pearls, aromatics, and animal skins, Indian merchants brought textiles, beads, gold, silver, manufactured metal goods, and objects used in political or religious rituals. Southeast Asian rulers used the profits from that trade to consolidate their political control.

Meanwhile, southeast Asian ruling elites became acquainted with Indian political and cultural traditions. Without necessarily giving up their own traditions, they borrowed Indian forms of political organization and accepted Indian religious faiths. On the model of Indian states, for example, they adopted kingship as the principal form of political authority. Regional kings in southeast Asia surrounded themselves with courts featuring administrators and rituals similar to those found in India.

Ruling elites also sponsored the introduction of Hinduism or Buddhism—sometimes both—into their courts. They embraced Indian literature such as the *Ramayana* and the *Mahabharata,* which promoted Hindu values, as well as treatises that explained Buddhist views on the world. They did not show much enthusiasm for the Indian caste system and continued to acknowledge the deities and nature spirits that southeast Asian peoples had venerated for centuries. But ruling elites readily adopted Hinduism and Buddhism, which they found attractive because the Indian faiths reinforced the principle of monarchical rule.

Funan The first state known to have reflected Indian influence in this fashion was Funan, which dominated the lower reaches of the Mekong River (including parts of modern Cambodia and Vietnam) between the first and the sixth centuries C.E. The rulers of Funan consolidated their grip on the Mekong valley and built a capital city at the port of Oc Eo. Funan grew wealthy because it dominated the Isthmus of Kra, the narrow portion of the Malay peninsula where merchants transported trade goods between China and India. (The short portage enabled them to avoid a long voyage around the Malay peninsula.) The rulers of Funan drew enormous wealth by controlling trade between China and India. They used their profits to construct an elaborate system of water storage and irrigation—so extensive that aerial photography still reveals its lines—that served a productive agricultural economy in the Mekong delta.

MAP 15.3
Early states of southeast Asia: Funan and Srivijaya, 100–1025 C.E.
Both Funan and Srivijaya relied heavily on maritime trade.

To what extent were they able to take advantage of the trading networks shown on Map 15.2?

As trade with India became an increasingly important part of Funan's economy, the ruling classes adopted Indian political, cultural, and religious traditions. They took the Sanskrit term *raja* ("king") for themselves and claimed divine sanction for their rule in the manner of Hindu rulers in India. They established positions for administrators and bureaucrats such as those found at Indian courts and conducted official business in Sanskrit. They introduced Indian ceremonies and rituals and worshiped Vishnu, Shiva, and other Hindu deities. They continued to honor local deities, particularly water spirits venerated widely throughout southeast Asia, but they eagerly welcomed Hinduism, which offered additional recognition and divine legitimacy for their rule. At first, Indian cultural and religious traditions were most prominent and most often observed at ruling courts. Over the longer term, however, those traditions extended well beyond ruling elites and won a secure place in southeast Asian society.

During the sixth century C.E., a bitter power struggle weakened Funan internally. Peoples from the north took advantage of that weakness, migrated to the lower Mekong valley in large numbers, and overwhelmed Funan. Chams settled in the southern portion of modern Vietnam, and Khmers dominated in the region occupied by modern Cambodia. By the late sixth century, Funan's intricate irrigation system had fallen into ruin, and Funan itself soon passed into oblivion.

Srivijaya After the fall of Funan, political leadership in southeast Asia passed to the kingdom of Srivijaya (670–1025 C.E.) based on the island of Sumatra. The kings of Srivijaya built a powerful navy and controlled commerce in southeast Asian waters. They compelled port cities in southeast Asia to recognize their authority, and they financed their navy and bureaucracy from taxes levied on ships passing through the region. They maintained an all-sea trade route between China and India, eliminating the need for the portage of trade goods across the Isthmus of Kra. As the volume of shipping increased in the postclassical era, the Srivijaya kingdom prospered until the expansive Chola kingdom of southern India eclipsed it in the eleventh century.

With the decline of Srivijaya, the kingdoms of Angkor (889–1431 C.E.), Singosari (1222–1292 C.E.), and Majapahit (1293–1520 C.E.) dominated affairs in southeast Asia. Many differences characterized these states. Funan had its base of operations in the Mekong valley, Srivijaya at Palembang in southern Sumatra, Angkor in Cambodia, and Singosari and Majapahit on the island of Java. Funan and Angkor were land-based states that derived most of their wealth from productive agricultural economies, whereas Srivijaya, Singosari, and Majapahit were island-based states that prospered because

MAP 15.4
Later states of southeast Asia: Angkor, Singosari, and Majapahit, 889–1520 C.E.
Angkor was a largely agricultural society, whereas Singosari and Majapahit were more active in maritime trade.

To what extent were these states able to take advantage of the trading networks shown on Map 15.2?

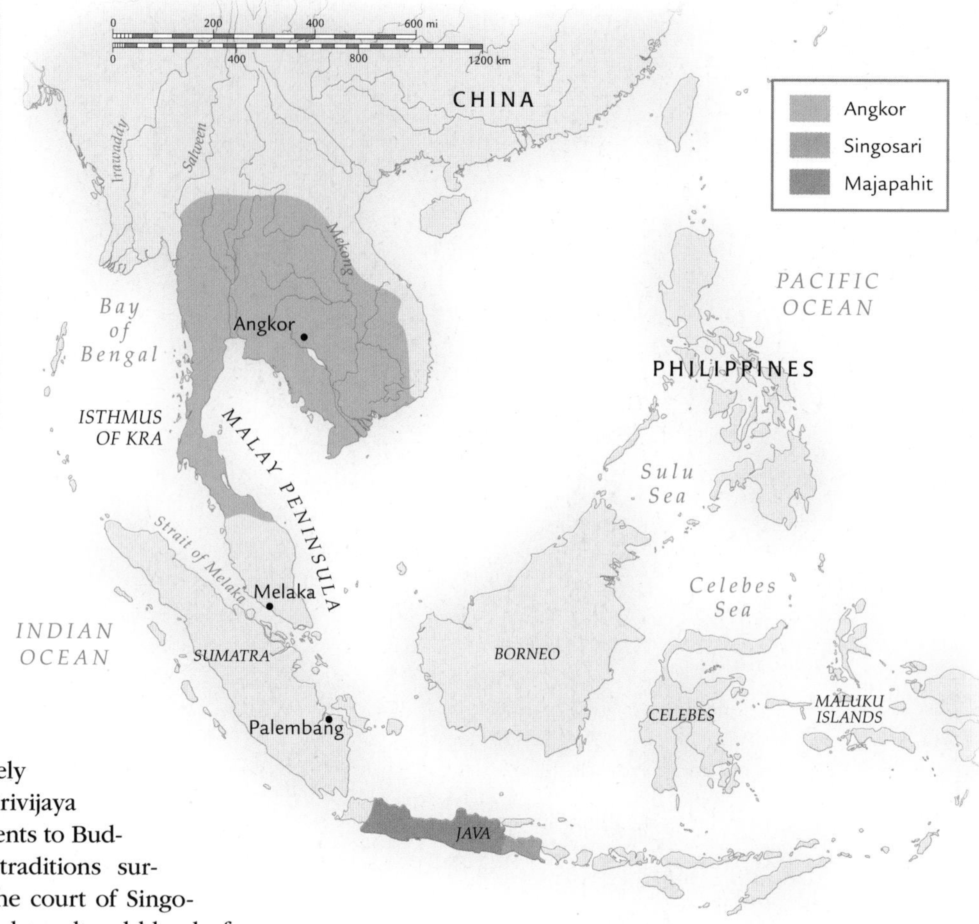

they controlled maritime trade. Funan and Majapahit were largely Hindu states, but the kings of Srivijaya and Angkor made deep commitments to Buddhism. Native southeast Asian traditions survived in all these states, and at the court of Singosari, religious authorities fashioned a cultural blend of Hindu, Buddhist, and indigenous values. Sculptures at the Singosari court depicted Hindu and Buddhist personalities, for example, but used them to honor local deities and natural spirits rather than Indian deities.

Angkor The magnificent monuments of Angkor testify eloquently to the influence of Indian traditions in southeast Asia. Beginning in the ninth century, kings of the Khmers began to build a capital city at Angkor Thom. With the aid of brahmin advisors from India, the kings designed the city as a microcosmic reflection of the Hindu world order. At the center, they built a temple representing the Himalayan Mount Meru, the sacred abode of Shiva, and surrounded it with numerous smaller temples representing other parts of the Hindu universe.

As the Khmers turned to Buddhism during the twelfth and thirteenth centuries, they added Buddhist temples to the complex, though without removing the earlier structures inspired by Hinduism. The entire complex formed a square with sides of about three kilometers (two miles), surrounded by a moat filled from the nearby Tonle Sap River. During the twelfth century the Khmer kings constructed a smaller but even more elaborate temple center at Angkor Wat, about one kilometer (just over half a mile) from Angkor Thom.

The Khmers abandoned Angkor in 1431 after Thai peoples invaded the capital and left much of it in ruins. Soon the jungle reclaimed both Angkor Thom and Angkor Wat, which remained largely forgotten until French missionaries and explorers rediscovered the sites in the mid-nineteenth century. Rescued from the jungle, the temple complexes of Angkor stand today as vivid reminders of the influence of Indian political, cultural, and religious traditions in southeast Asia.

The Arrival of Islam

Muslim merchants had ventured into southeast Asia by the eighth century, but only during the tenth century did they become prominent in the region. Some came from southern Arabia or Persia, but many were Indians from Gujarat or the port cities of southern India. Thus Indian influence helped to establish Islam as well as Hinduism and Buddhism in southeast Asia.

Conversion to Islam For several centuries Islam maintained a quiet presence in southeast Asia. Small communities of foreign merchants observed their faith in the port cities of the region but attracted little interest on the part of the native inhabitants. Gradually, however, ruling elites, traders,

Maritime trade flourished in southeast Asia during postclassical times. This ninth-century relief carving from the Buddhist temple at Borobodur in Java depicts a typical southeast Asian ship.

General view of the temple complex dedicated to Vishnu at Angkor Wat. These temples reflect the deep influence of Indian political, cultural, and religious traditions in southeast Asia.

and others who had regular dealings with foreign Muslims became interested in the faith. During the late thirteenth century, the Venetian traveler Marco Polo visited the island of Sumatra and noted that many residents of the towns and cities had converted to Islam, whereas those living in the countryside and the hills retained their inherited traditions.

Like Hinduism and Buddhism, Islam did not enter southeast Asia as an exclusive faith. Ruling elites who converted to Islam often continued to honor Hindu, Buddhist, or native southeast Asian traditions. They adopted Islam less as an exclusive and absolute creed than as a faith that facilitated their dealings with foreign Muslims and provided additional divine sanction for their rule. Rarely did they push their subjects to convert to Islam, although they allowed Sufi mystics to preach their faith before popular audiences. As in India, Sufis in southeast Asia appealed to a large public because of their reputation for sincerity and holiness. They allowed converts to retain inherited customs while adapting the message of Islam to local needs and interests.

Melaka During the fifteenth century the spread of Islam gained momentum in southeast Asia, largely because the powerful state of Melaka sponsored the faith throughout the region. Founded during the late fourteenth century by Paramesvara, a rebellious prince from Sumatra, Melaka took advantage of its strategic location in the Strait of Melaka, near modern Singapore, and soon became prominent in the trading world of southeast Asia. During its earliest days Melaka was more a lair of pirates than a legitimate state. By the mid-fifteenth century, however, Melaka had built a substantial navy that patrolled the waters of southeast Asia and protected the region's sea lanes. Melakan fleets compelled ships to call at the port of Melaka, where ruling authorities levied taxes on the value of their cargoes. Thus, like southeast Asian states of earlier centuries, Melaka became a powerful state through the control of maritime trade.

In one respect, though, Melaka differed significantly from the earlier states. Although it began as a Hindu state, Melaka soon became predominantly Islamic. About the mid-fifteenth century the Melakan ruling class converted to Islam. It welcomed theologians, Sufis, and other Islamic authorities to Melaka and sponsored missionary campaigns to spread Islam throughout southeast Asia. By the end of the fifteenth century, mosques had begun to define the urban landscapes of Java, Sumatra, and the Malay peninsula, and Islam had made its first appearance in the spice-bearing islands of Maluku and in the southern islands of the Philippine archipelago.

Thus, within several centuries of its arrival, Islam was a prominent feature in the cultural landscape of southeast Asia. Along with Hinduism and Buddhism, Islam helped link southeast Asian lands to the larger cultural world of India and to the larger commercial world of the Indian Ocean basin.

inperspective

With respect to political organization, India differed from postclassical societies in China, southwest Asia, and the eastern Mediterranean basin: India did not experience a return of centralized imperial rule such as that provided by the Tang and Song dynasties, the Umayyad and Abbasid dynasties, and the Byzantine empire. In other respects, however, India's development was similar to that of other postclassical societies. Increased agricultural production fueled population growth and urbanization, and trade encouraged specialized industrial production and rapid economic growth. The vigorous and voluminous commerce of the Indian Ocean basin influenced the structure of economies and societies from east Asia to east Africa. It brought prosperity especially to India, which not only contributed cotton, pepper, sugar, iron, steel, and other products to the larger hemispheric economy but also served as a major clearinghouse of trade. Like contemporary societies, postclassical India experienced cultural change, and Indian traditions deeply influenced the cultural development of other lands. Hinduism and Islam emerged as the two most popular religious faiths within the subcontinent, and Indian merchants helped to establish Hinduism, Buddhism, and Islam in southeast Asian lands. Throughout the postclassical era, India participated fully in the larger hemispheric zone of cross-cultural communication and exchange. ●

CHRONOLOGY	
1st to 6th century	Kingdom of Funan
606–648	Reign of Harsha
670–1025	Kingdom of Srivijaya
711	Conquest of Sind by Umayyad forces
early 9th century	Life of Shankara
850–1267	Chola kingdom
889–1431	Kingdom of Angkor
1001–1027	Raids on India by Mahmud of Ghazni
11th to 12th century	Life of Ramanuja
12th century	Beginning of the bhakti movement
1206–1526	Sultanate of Delhi
1336–1565	Kingdom of Vijayanagar
1440–1518	Life of guru Kabir

For Further Reading

Aziz Ahmad. *Studies in Islamic Culture in the Indian Environment.* Oxford, 1964. A scholarly analysis of the arrival of Islam and its effects in India.

Al-Biruni. *Alberuni's India.* 2 vols. Trans. by E. Sachau. London, 1910. English translation of al-Biruni's eleventh-century description of Indian customs, religion, philosophy, geography, and astronomy.

Buzurg ibn Shahriyar. *The Book of the Wonders of India: Mainland, Sea and Islands.* Trans. by G. S. P. Freeman-Grenville. London, 1981. Stories and tall tales of a tenth-century mariner who sailed frequently between Persia and India.

K. N. Chaudhuri. *Asia before Europe: Economy and Civilisation of the Indian Ocean from the Rise of Islam to 1750.* Cambridge, 1990. Controversial and penetrating analysis of economic, social, and cultural structures shaping societies of the Indian Ocean basin.

———. *Trade and Civilisation in the Indian Ocean: An Economic History from the Rise of Islam to 1750.* Cambridge, 1985. Brilliant analysis of the commercial life of the Indian Ocean basin by a prominent scholar.

Georges Coedès. *The Indianized States of Southeast Asia.* Trans. by S. B. Cowing. Honolulu, 1968. A careful survey that is still useful, though somewhat dated.

Ainslie T. Embree and Stephen Hay, eds. *Sources of Indian Tradition.* 2 vols. 2nd ed. New York, 1988. An important collection of primary sources in English translation.

Bernard Groslier and Jacques Arthaud. *Angkor: Art and Civilization.* Rev. ed. Trans. by E. E. Smith. New York, 1966. Well-illustrated summary, concentrating on the magnificent temple complexes at Angkor.

Kenneth R. Hall. *Maritime Trade and State Development in Early Southeast Asia.* Honolulu, 1985. Examines the link between long-distance trade and state building in southeast Asia.

Charles Higham. *The Civilization of Angkor.* London, 2001. Draws usefully on recent archaeological research in placing Angkor in historical context.

S. M. Ikram. *Muslim Civilization in India.* Ed. by A. T. Embree. New York, 1964. Important survey of Islam and its impact in India.

Michel Jacq-Hergoualc'h. *The Malay Peninsula: Crossroads of the Maritime Silk Road (100 B.C.–1300 A.D.).* Leiden, 2002. Scholarly study emphasizing the significance of maritime trade for southeast Asian societies.

Hermann Kulke and Dietmar Rothermund. *A History of India.* Totowa, N.J., 1986. A valuable interpretative synthesis of Indian history.

Eleanor Mannikka. *Angkor Wat: Time, Space, and Kingship.* Honolulu, 1996. A detailed analysis of the magnificent Cambodian temple complex from an architectural point of view.

Patricia Risso. *Merchants and Faith: Muslim Commerce and Culture in the Indian Ocean.* Boulder, 1995. Surveys the activities of Muslim merchants in the Indian Ocean basin from the seventh to the nineteenth century.

Tansen Sen. *Buddhism, Diplomacy, and Trade: The Realignment of Sino-Indian Relations, 600–1400.* Honolulu, 2003. A pathbreaking study exploring trade, diplomacy, and cultural exchanges between postclassical India and China.

Kernial Singh Sandhu. *Early Malaysia.* Singapore, 1973. Survey concentrating on the periods of Indian and Islamic influence in southeast Asia.

Burton Stein. *Vijayanagara.* Cambridge, 1989. A study of the southern Hindu kingdom concentrating on political and economic history.

Romila Thapar. *Early India: From the Origins to A.D. 1300.* Berkeley, 2003. A fresh view by one of the leading scholars of early Indian history.

Stanley Wolpert. *A New History of India.* 7th ed. New York, 2004. A concise and readable survey of Indian history.

The Two Worlds of Christendom

chapter 16

Pope Leo III crowns Charlemagne emperor in a manuscript illustration. The coronation symbolized the firm alliance between the Franks and the western Christian church.

EYEWITNESS:
Emperor Charlemagne and His Elephant

In the year 802 C.E., an unusual traveler arrived at Aachen (in modern Germany), capital of the western European empire ruled by Charlemagne. The traveler was a rare albino elephant, a diplomatic gift from the Abbasid caliph Harun al-Rashid to Charlemagne. The elephant—whom Harun named Abu al-Abbas, in honor of the Abbasid dynasty's founder—was born in India and went to Baghdad with his trainer in about 798. From Baghdad the animal accompanied an embassy overland through Syria and Egypt to a port on the Tunisian coast, then sailed across the Mediterranean to Portovenere (near Genoa in northern Italy), and finally trekked across the Alps and overland to Charlemagne's court. Abu al-Abbas must have shivered through the cold, damp winters of Europe. Yet he enjoyed swimming in the Rhine River, and until his death in 810, he amazed and delighted all who beheld him.

Charlemagne was not a friend of Islam. At the battle of Tours (732 C.E.), his grandfather, Charles Martel, had defeated a Muslim army that ventured into Frankish territory after Muslim forces had conquered most of the Iberian peninsula. Charlemagne himself fought Muslims in an unsuccessful effort to restore Christian rule in northern Spain. One of the battles from his campaign provided the raw material for a popular poetic work called the *Song of Roland.* Nevertheless, in spite of his personal religious preferences, Charlemagne found it both necessary and convenient to have diplomatic dealings with Harun al-Rashid.

Charlemagne dispatched at least three embassies to Baghdad and received three in return. The embassies dealt with several issues: the safety of Christian pilgrims and merchants traveling in Abbasid-controlled Syria and Palestine, Charlemagne's relations with Muslim neighbors, and policy toward the Byzantine empire, which stood between western Europe and the Abbasid caliphate. Charlemagne's realm was weak and poor compared with the Abbasid empire, but for about half a century, it seemed that Charlemagne and his successors might be able to reestablish a centralized imperial state in western Europe. His dealings with Harun al-Rashid—and the unusual odyssey of the elephant Abu al-Abbas—reflected a general recognition that Charlemagne had the potential to establish a western European empire similar to the Byzantine and Abbasid realms.

Historians refer to the period from about 500 to 1500 C.E. as the medieval period of European history—the "middle ages" falling between the classical era and modern times. During the early medieval period, from about 500 to 1000 C.E., European peoples recovered from the many problems that plagued the later Roman empire—epidemic disease, declining population, economic contraction, political turmoil, social unrest, and invasions by Germanic peoples. In doing so, they laid the foundations of European Christendom—a region that never experienced political unity but that adopted Christianity as the dominant source of cultural authority.

The two very different halves of medieval Christendom were the Byzantine empire in the eastern half of the Mediterranean basin and the Germanic states that succeeded the western Roman empire after its collapse in the fifth century C.E. The Byzantine empire was in fact a direct continuation of the Roman empire in the east. It did not extend its authority to the entire Mediterranean basin, but it inherited the most prosperous and productive regions of the classical Roman empire. Even after Muslim conquerors seized the wealthy provinces of Egypt and Syria in the seventh century, the Byzantine empire remained a political and economic powerhouse of the postclassical world. As a centralized imperial state like the Abbasid empire in southwest Asia or the Tang and Song dynasties in China, the Byzantine empire dominated the eastern Mediterranean and Black Sea regions. As an urbanized center of manufacturing, the Byzantine empire was also a highly productive society that both supported and benefited from trade throughout the eastern hemisphere.

Meanwhile, lands to the west of the Byzantine empire fell under the sway of invading peoples who dismantled the western part of the Roman empire and established a series of Germanic successor states. Charlemagne made heroic efforts to unify the western half of Christendom and establish a western counterpart to the Byzantine empire, but internal tensions and new rounds of invasions brought an early end to his own imperial creation. Thus, during the era 500 to 1000 C.E., western Christendom resembled postclassical India, where a restoration of imperial unity also turned out to be a fleeting experience, more than the Abbasid, Tang, Song, and Byzantine realms. When Charlemagne's empire dissolved, western European peoples fashioned alternatives to imperial rule by creating new decentralized forms of government that vested public authority mostly in local or regional rulers. At the same time, they also began a process of economic recovery by dramatically boosting agricultural production.

Both the Byzantine empire and the European states to the west inherited Christianity from the Roman empire, and rulers in both regions promoted Christianity as a cultural and moral foundation for their rule. After the eighth century C.E., however, political and religious tensions increasingly complicated relations between the two halves of the former Roman empire. Byzantine rulers bristled at the claims to empire made by Charlemagne and other western Christian rulers, and theologians in the two regions developed differing views on proper religious doctrine and practice. By the mid-eleventh century, the Byzantine and Roman churches had publicly and formally condemned each other. Byzantine missionaries promoted their brand of Christianity in Russia and other Slavic lands, while western Christians following the leadership of the popes in Rome spread their own views from the British Isles to Scandinavia and eastern Europe. Just as Abbasid leaders helped consolidate Islam as the principal cultural influence in the Muslim world, Byzantine and western Christians expanded the religious and moral authority of Christianity throughout Europe. In doing so, they created two worlds of Christendom.

THE QUEST FOR POLITICAL ORDER

The eastern half of the Roman empire suffered from invasions by Germanic peoples, but it did not collapse. The political challenge for rulers in this region—direct successors of the Roman emperors—was to restore order following the invasions. In the sixth century Byzantine rulers even tried to reestablish Roman authority throughout the Mediterranean basin. Their efforts fell short of that goal, and they soon lost considerable territories to expansive Muslim forces, but they nevertheless presided over a powerful society in the eastern Mediterranean region.

Political challenges were greater in lands to the west. Germanic invaders mostly passed through the eastern Roman empire, but they mostly settled down in western regions. Throughout Roman Europe and north Africa, Germanic invaders disrupted Roman authority, deposed Roman officials, and imposed new states of their own making. After two centuries of fighting, it looked as though one group of Germanic invaders, the Franks, might reestablish imperial authority in much of Roman Europe. If they had succeeded, they might have played a role similar to that of the Sui and Tang dynasties in China by reviving centralized imperial rule after a hiatus of several centuries. By the late ninth century, however, the Frankish empire had fallen victim to internal power struggles and a fresh series of devastating invasions. Political authority in western Europe then devolved to local and regional jurisdictions, whose leaders fashioned a decentralized political order.

The Early Byzantine Empire

The Byzantine empire takes its name from Byzantion—latinized as Byzantium—a modest market town and fishing village that occupied a site of enormous strategic significance. Situated on a defensible peninsula and blessed with a magnificent natural harbor known as the Golden Horn, Byzantion had the potential to control the Bosporus, the strait of water leading from the Black Sea to the Sea of Marmara and beyond to the Dardanelles, the Aegean Sea, and the Mediterranean. Apart from its maritime significance, Byzantion offered convenient access to the rich lands of Anatolia, southwestern Asia, and southeastern Europe. Sea lanes linked the city to ports throughout the Mediterranean basin.

The City of Constantine Recognizing its strategic value, the Roman emperor Constantine designated Byzantion the site of a new imperial capital, which he named Constantinople ("city of Constantine"). He built the new capital partly because the eastern Mediterranean was the wealthiest and most productive region of the Roman empire and partly because relocation enabled him to maintain close watch over both the Sasanid empire in Persia and the Germanic peoples who lived along the lower stretches of the Danube River. The imperial government moved to Constantinople after 330 C.E., and the new capital rapidly reached metropolitan dimensions. Constantine filled the city with libraries, museums, and artistic treasures, and he constructed magnificent marble palaces, churches, baths, and public buildings—all in an effort to create a new Rome fit for the ruler of a mighty empire. The city kept the name Constantinople until it fell to the Ottoman Turks (1453 C.E.), who renamed it Istanbul. By convention, however, historians refer to the realm

MAP 16.1
Successor states to the Roman empire, ca. 600 C.E.
Compare this map with Map 11.2 showing the Roman empire at its height.
How did the territories of the Byzantine empire differ from those of the classical Roman empire?

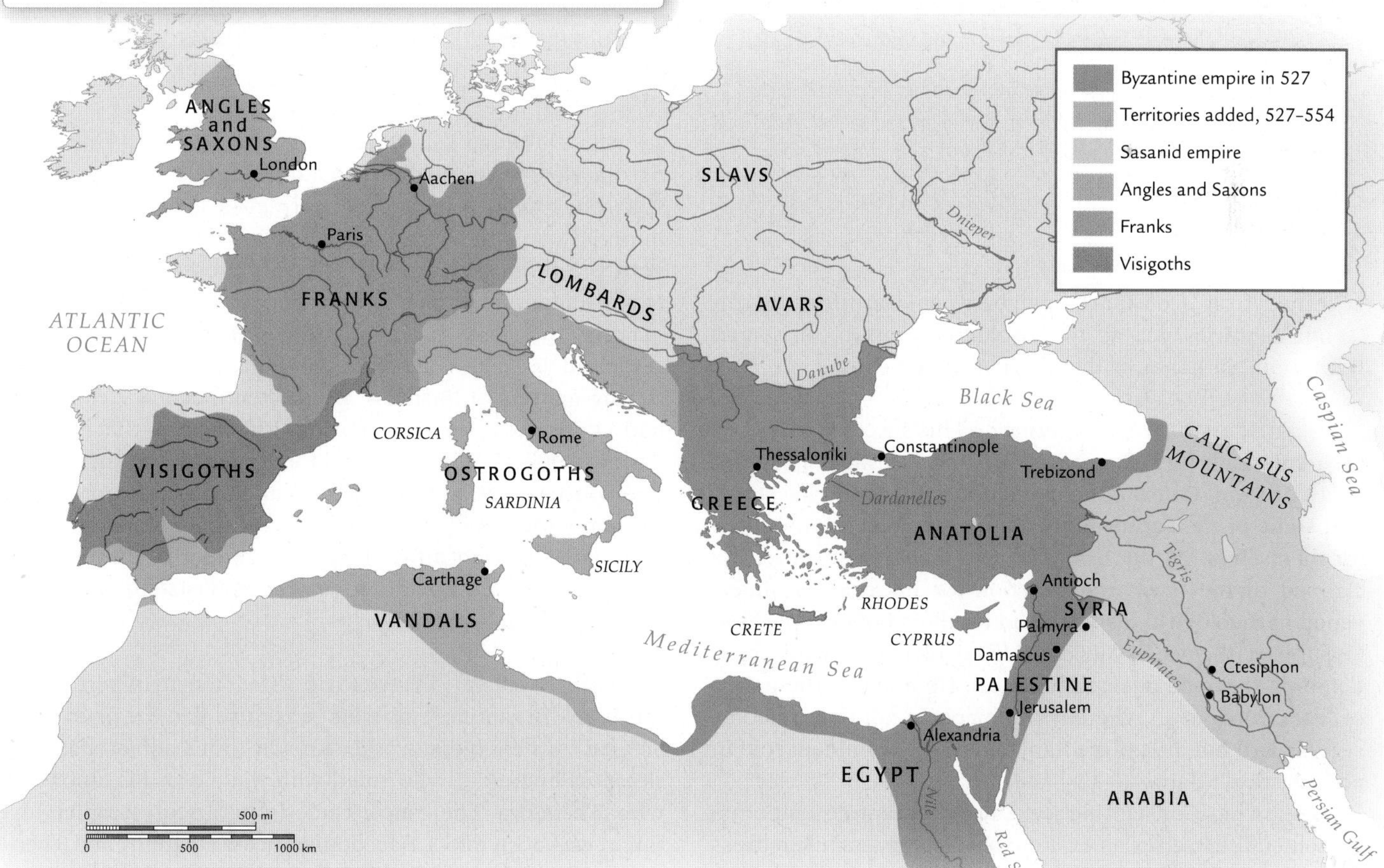

Justinian wears imperial purple robes in this mosaic, from the church of San Vitale in Ravenna, which depicts him in the company of ecclesiastical, military, and court officials.

governed from Constantinople between the fifth and fifteenth centuries C.E. as the Byzantine empire, or simply Byzantium, in honor of the original settlement.

Caesaropapism Constantine and his successors hedged their rule with the aura of divinity and awesome splendor. As a Christian, Constantine could not claim the divine status that some of the earlier Roman emperors had appropriated for themselves. As the first Christian emperor, however, he claimed divine favor and sanction for his rule. He intervened in theological disputes and used his political position to support the views he considered orthodox while condemning those he deemed heretical. He initiated the policy of "caesaropapism," whereby the emperor not only ruled as secular lord but also played an active and prominent role in ecclesiastical affairs.

Following Constantine's example, Byzantine emperors presented themselves as exalted, absolute rulers. Even dress and court etiquette testified to their lofty status. The emperors wore bejeweled crowns and dressed in magnificent silk robes dyed a dark, rich purple—a color reserved for imperial use and strictly forbidden to those not associated with the ruling house. High officials presented themselves to the emperor as slaves. When approaching the imperial majesty, they prostrated themselves three times and then ceremoniously kissed the imperial hands and feet before raising matters of business. By the tenth century engineers had contrived a series of mechanical devices that worked dazzling effects and impressed foreign envoys at the Byzantine court: imitation birds sang as ambassadors approached the emperor while mechanical lions roared and swished their tails. During an audience the imperial throne itself sometimes moved up and down to emphasize the awesome splendor of the emperor.

Justinian and Theodora The most important of the early Byzantine emperors was Justinian (reigned 527–565 C.E.), an energetic worker known to his subjects as "the sleepless emperor," who ruled with the aid of his ambitious wife, Theodora. The couple came from obscure origins: Justinian was born into a Macedonian peasant family, and Theodora, the daughter of a bear keeper in the circus, worked

The interior of the church of Hagia Sophia ("Holy Wisdom"), built by Justinian and transformed into a mosque in the fifteenth century. The dome rises almost 60 meters (197 feet) above the floor, and its windows allow abundant light to enter the massive structure.

as a striptease artist before meeting the future emperor. Yet both Justinian and Theodora were smart, strong-willed, and disciplined. Thanks to those qualities, Justinian received an education, found a position in the imperial bureaucracy, and mastered the intricacies of Byzantine finance. Theodora proved to be a sagacious advisor and a determined supporter of her emperor husband.

Like Constantine, Justinian lavished resources on the imperial capital. His most notable construction project was the church of Hagia Sophia ("holy wisdom"), a magnificent domed structure—later turned into a mosque by Ottoman conquerors—that ranks as one of the world's most important examples of Christian architecture. Visitors marveled at the church's enormous dome, which they likened to the heavens encircling the earth, and at the gold, silver, gems, and thousands of lamps that decorated and illuminated Hagia Sophia.

Justinian's Code Justinian's most significant political contribution was his codification of Roman law. The origins of Roman law went back to the times of the kings of Rome, and even though earlier scholars worked to codify the law, it had become a confusing mass of sometimes conflicting injunctions. Justinian ordered a systematic review of Roman law and issued the *Corpus iuris civilis* (*Body of the Civil Law*), which immediately won recognition as the definitive codification of Roman law. Updated by later emperors, Justinian's code has influenced civil law codes in most of Europe, in Japan, and in the state of Louisiana in the United States.

Byzantine Conquests Justinian's most ambitious venture was his effort to reconquer the western Roman empire from Germanic peoples and reestablish Roman authority throughout the Mediterranean basin. Between 533 and 565, Byzantine forces gained control over Italy, Sicily, much of northwestern Africa, and southern Spain. Yet Byzantium did not possess the resources to sustain a long-term occupation and consolidate those conquests. Shortly after Justinian's death, Byzantine forces abandoned Rome, leaving the city of Ravenna on Italy's Adriatic coast as the headquarters of Byzantine authority in the western Mediterranean. As a result, Ravenna possesses magnificent examples of Byzantine art and architecture, but Justinian's dream of reconstituting the old Roman empire soon faded into oblivion.

Muslim Conquests and Byzantine Revival

Justinian's efforts showed that the classical Roman empire was beyond recovery. While the emperor devoted his efforts to the western Mediterranean, the Sasanids threatened Byzantium from the east and Slavic peoples approached from the north. Later Byzantine emperors had no choice but to redeploy their resources to meet other threats.

Muslim Conquests After the seventh century C.E., the expansion of Islam (discussed in chapter 13) posed even more serious challenges to Byzantium. Shortly after Muhammad's death, Arab warriors conquered the Sasanid empire in Persia and overran large portions of the Byzantine empire as well. By the mid-seventh century, Byzantine Syria, Palestine, Egypt, and north Africa had fallen under Muslim rule. Muslim forces later subjected Constantinople itself to two prolonged sieges (in 674–678 and again in 717–718). Byzantium resisted this northward thrust of Islam partly because of advanced military technology. Byzantine forces used a weapon known as "Greek fire"—a nasty incendiary weapon compounded of sulphur, lime, and petroleum—which they launched at both the fleets and the ground forces of the invaders. Greek fire burned even when floating on water and thus created a hazard when deployed around wooden ships. On land it caused panic among enemy forces, since it was extremely difficult to extinguish and often burned troops to death. As a result of this defensive effort, the Byzantine empire retained its hold on Anatolia, Greece, and the Balkan region.

The *Theme* System Though diminished by Muslim conquests, the Byzantine empire was more manageable after the eighth century than was the far-flung realm of Justinian. Byzantine rulers responded to the threat of Islam with political and social adjustments that strengthened their reduced empire. Their most important innovation was the reorganization of Byzantine society under the *theme* system. They placed an imperial province called a *theme* under the authority of a general, who assumed responsibility for both its military defense and its civil administration. Generals received their appointments from the emperor, who closely monitored their activities to prevent decentralization of power and authority. Generals recruited armies from the ranks of free peasants, who received allotments of land for their military service.

Armies raised under the *theme* system were effective fighting forces, and they enabled Byzantium to expand its influence between the ninth and the twelfth centuries. During the tenth century Byzantine forces reconquered Syria and pushed their authority west into the Balkan region. By the mid-eleventh century, the Byzantine empire encompassed lands from Syria and Armenia in the east to southern Italy in the west, from the Danube River in the north to the islands of Cyprus and Crete in the south. Once again, Byzantium dominated the eastern Mediterranean region.

The Rise of the Franks

In the year 476 C.E., the Germanic general Odoacer deposed the last of the western Roman emperors. He did not claim the imperial title for himself, however, nor did he appoint anyone else as a replacement. The emperor's post simply remained vacant. Roman administrators and armies continued to function, temporarily, but urban populations declined as continuing invasions and power struggles disrupted trade and manufacturing. Deprived of legitimacy and resources

A manuscript illustration depicts Byzantine naval forces turning Greek fire on their Arab enemies.

supplied from Rome and other major cities, imperial institutions progressively weakened.

Germanic Kingdoms Gradually, a series of Germanic kingdoms emerged as successor states to the Roman empire. Visigoths, Ostrogoths, Lombards, Franks, and other Germanic peoples occupied imperial provinces, displacing Roman authorities and institutions. As they built successor states, Germanic peoples absorbed a great deal of Roman influence. Many of them converted to Christianity, for example, and others adapted Roman law to the needs of their own societies.

The Franks Most successful and most influential of the Germanic peoples were the Franks. By the early sixth century, the Franks had conquered most of Roman Gaul and emerged as the preeminent military and political power in western Europe. They also gained popular support when they abandoned their inherited polytheistic religion and converted to Christianity—a move that brought them the allegiance of the Christian population of the former Roman empire as well as support from the pope and the western Christian church.

In the eighth century the aristocratic clan of the Carolingians dramatically extended Frankish power. The Carolingian dynasty takes its name from its founder, Charles (*Carolus* in Latin)—known as Charles Martel ("Charles the Hammer") because of his military prowess. In 732 at the battle of Tours (in central France), he turned back a Muslim army that had ventured north from recently conquered Spain. His victory helped persuade Muslim rulers of Spain that it was not worthwhile for them to seek further conquests in western Europe.

A bronze statue depicts Charlemagne riding a horse and carrying an orb symbolizing his imperial authority.

Charlemagne The Frankish realm reached its high point under Charles Martel's grandson Charlemagne ("Charles the Great"), who reigned from 768 to 814. Like King Harsha in India, Charlemagne temporarily reestablished centralized imperial rule in a society disrupted by invasion and contests for power between ambitious local rulers. Like Harsha again, Charlemagne possessed enormous energy, and the building of the Carolingian empire was in large measure his personal accomplishment. Although barely literate, Charlemagne was quite intelligent. He spoke Latin, understood some Greek, and regularly conversed with learned men. He maintained diplomatic relations with the Byzantine empire and the Abbasid caliphate. The gift of the albino elephant Abu al-Abbas symbolized relations between the Carolingian and Abbasid empires, and until its death in 810, the animal accompanied Charlemagne on many of his travels.

When Charlemagne inherited the Frankish throne, his realm included most of modern France as well as the lands that now form Belgium, the Netherlands, and southwestern Germany. By the time of his death in 814, Charlemagne had extended his authority to northeastern Spain, Bavaria, and Italy as far south as Rome. He campaigned for thirty-two years to impose his rule on the Saxons of northern Germany and to repress their rebellions. Beyond the Carolingian empire proper, rulers in eastern Europe and southern Italy paid tribute to Charlemagne as imperial overlord.

Charlemagne's Administration Charlemagne built a court and capital at Aachen (in modern Germany), but like Harsha in India, he spent most of his reign on horseback, traveling throughout his realm to maintain authority. Constant travel was necessary because Charlemagne did not have the financial resources to maintain an elaborate bureaucracy or an administrative apparatus that could enforce his policies. Instead, he relied on aristocratic deputies, known

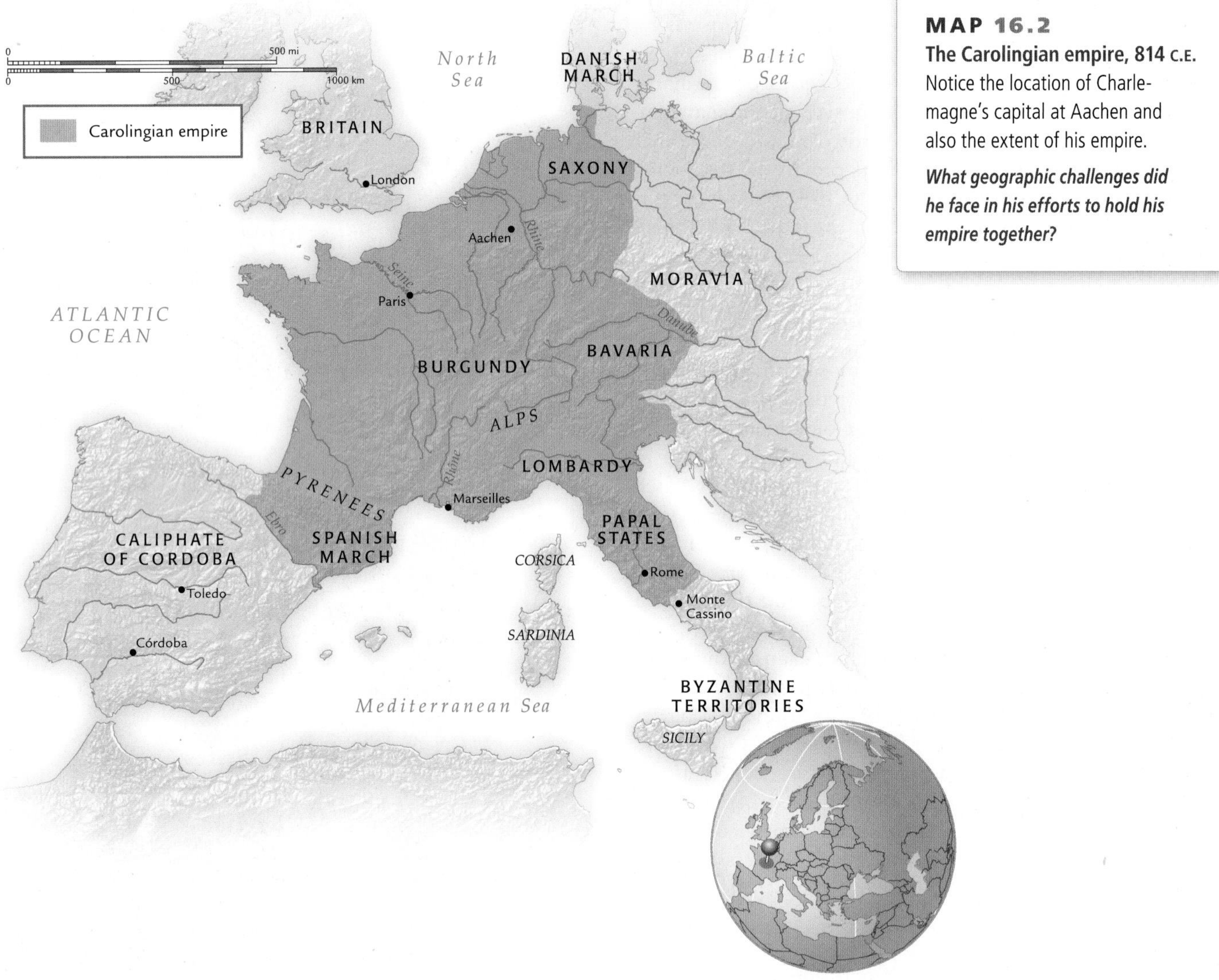

MAP 16.2
The Carolingian empire, 814 C.E.
Notice the location of Charlemagne's capital at Aachen and also the extent of his empire.
What geographic challenges did he face in his efforts to hold his empire together?

as counts, who held political, military, and legal authority in local jurisdictions. In an effort to keep the counts under control, Charlemagne instituted a group of imperial officials called the *missi dominici* ("envoys of the lord ruler"), who traveled annually to all jurisdictions and reviewed the accounts of local authorities.

Thus Charlemagne built the Frankish kingdom into an empire on the basis of military expeditions, and he began to outfit it with some centralized institutions. Yet he hesitated to call himself emperor because an imperial claim would constitute a direct challenge to the authority of the Byzantine emperors, who regarded themselves as the only legitimate successors of the Roman emperors.

Charlemagne as Emperor Only in the year 800 did Charlemagne accept the title of emperor. While campaigning in Italy, Charlemagne attended religious services conducted by Pope Leo III on Christmas Day. During the services, the pope proclaimed Charlemagne emperor and placed an imperial crown on his head. It is not certain, but it is possible that Charlemagne did not know of the pope's plan and that Leo surprised him with an impromptu coronation. Charlemagne had no desire for strained relations with the Byzantine emperors, who deeply resented his imperial title as a pretentious affront to their own dignity. In any case, Charlemagne had already built an imperial state, and his coronation constituted public recognition of his accomplishments.

The Age of the Vikings

If Charlemagne's empire had endured, Carolingian rulers might well have built a bureaucracy, used the *missi dominici* to enhance the authority of the central government, and reestablished imperial rule in western Europe. As it happened, however, internal disunity and external invasions brought the Carolingian empire to an early end.

The Oseberg ship, pictured here, is the best-preserved Viking vessel from the early middle ages. Built about 800 C.E., it served as a royal tomb until its discovery in 1903. A ship this size would accommodate about forty men.

Louis the Pious Charlemagne's only surviving son, Louis the Pious (reigned 814–840), succeeded his father and held the empire together. Lacking Charlemagne's strong will and military skills, however, Louis lost control of local authorities, who increasingly pursued their own interests. Moreover, Louis's three sons disputed the inheritance of the empire and waged bitter wars against one another. In 843 they divided the empire into three roughly equal portions and ruled as three kings. Thus, less than a century after its creation, the Carolingian empire dissolved.

Danish Vikings prepare to invade England in this manuscript illustration produced at an English monastery about 1130. The geographic range of Viking activity extended from England, France, northern Germany, and Russia to territories throughout the Mediterranean basin.

Invasions Even if internal divisions had not dismembered the Carolingian empire, external pressures might well have brought it down. Beginning in the late eighth century, three groups of invaders pillaged the Frankish realm in search of wealth stored in towns and monasteries. From the south came Muslims, who raided towns, villages, churches, and monasteries in Mediterranean Europe. Muslim invaders also conquered the island of Sicily and seized territories in southern Italy and southern France. From the east came the **Magyars,** descendants of nomadic peoples who had settled in Hungary. Expert horsemen, the Magyars raided settlements in Germany, Italy, and southern France. From the north came the Vikings, most feared of all the invaders, who began mounting raids in northern France even during Charlemagne's lifetime.

The Viking invasions were part of a much larger process of expansion by the Nordic peoples of Scandinavia. One cause of Norse expansion was probably population growth fueled by increased agricultural production in Scandinavia. The main cause, however, was the quest for wealth through trading and raiding in European lands to the south of Scandinavia. Norse expansion depended on a remarkable set of shipbuilding techniques and seafaring skills that Scandinavian mariners developed during the seventh and eighth centuries. They built rugged, shallow-draft boats outfitted both with sails, which enabled them to travel through the open ocean, and with oars, which enabled them to navigate rivers.

Vikings Many Norse seafarers were merchants seeking commercial opportunities or migrants seeking lands to settle and cultivate. Some, however, turned their maritime skills more toward raiding and plundering than trading or raising crops. These were the Vikings. The term *Viking* originally

Magyars (MAH-jahrs)

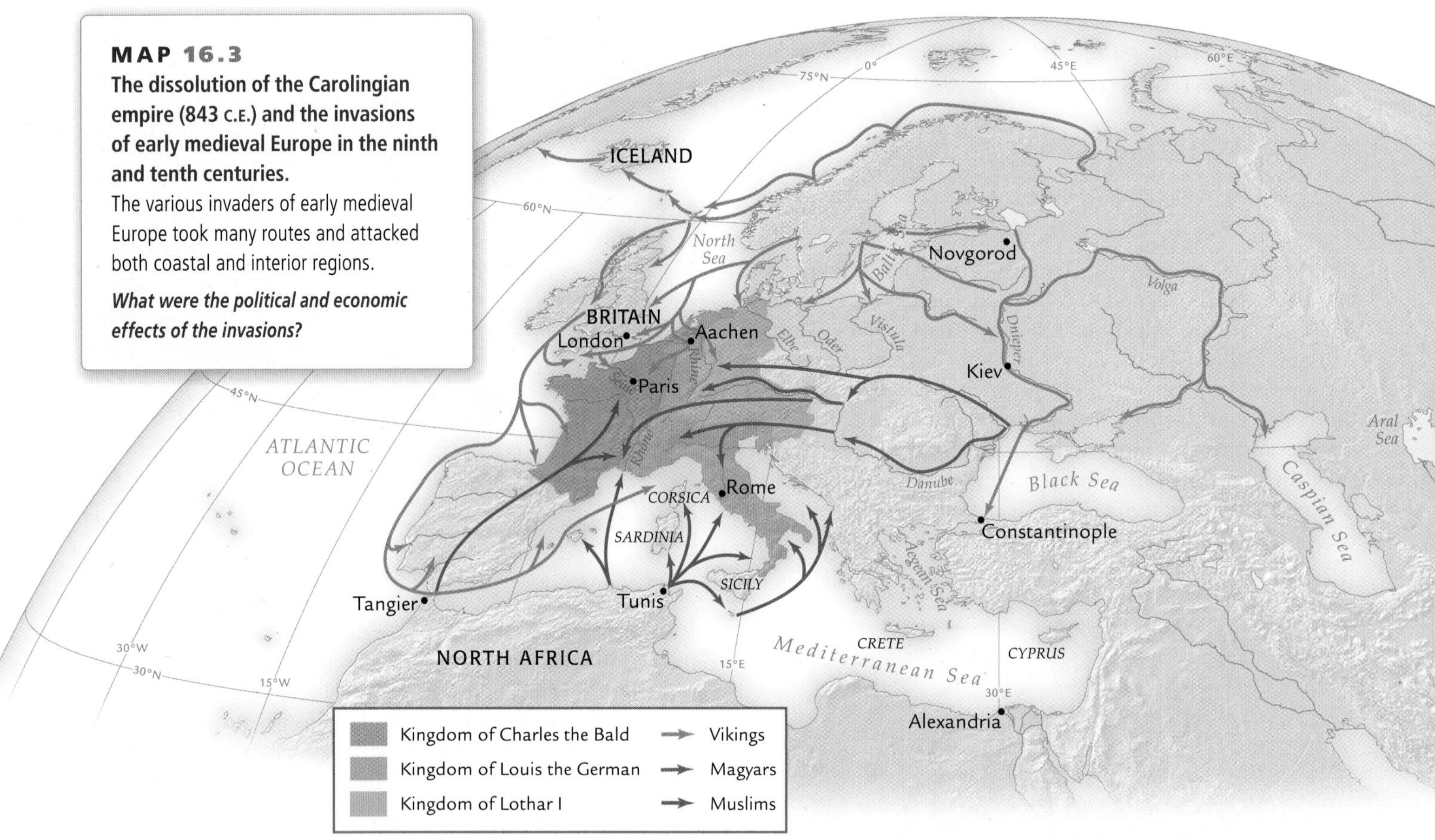

MAP 16.3
The dissolution of the Carolingian empire (843 C.E.) and the invasions of early medieval Europe in the ninth and tenth centuries.
The various invaders of early medieval Europe took many routes and attacked both coastal and interior regions.
What were the political and economic effects of the invasions?

referred to a group that raided the British Isles from their home at Vik in southern Norway. Over time, however, the term came to refer more generally to Norse mariners who mounted invasions and plundered settlements from Russia and eastern Europe to Mediterranean lands. With their shallow-draft boats, the Vikings were able to make their way up the many rivers offering access to interior regions of Europe. Vikings coordinated their ships' movements and timed their attacks to take advantage of the tides. Fleets of Viking boats with ferocious dragon heads mounted on their prows could sail up a river, surprise a village or a monastery far from the sea, and spill out crews of warriors who conducted lightning raids on unprepared victims.

The first Viking invaders began to attack unprotected monasteries in the 790s. Learning from experience, Viking forces mounted increasingly daring raids. In 844 C.E., more than 150 Viking ships sailed up the Garonne River in southern France, plundering settlements along the way. Sometimes Viking fleets attacked sizable cities: in 845, some 800 vessels appeared without warning before the city of Hamburg in northern Germany; in 885, a Viking force consisting of at least 700 ships sailed up the Seine River and besieged Paris; and in 994, an armada of about 100 ships sprinted up the Thames River and raided London. Some Vikings bypassed relatively close targets and ventured into the Mediterranean, where they plundered sites in the Balearic Islands, Sicily, and southern Italy. By following the Russian rivers to the Black Sea, other Vikings made their way to Constantinople, which they raided at least three times during the ninth and tenth centuries.

Devolution of Political Authority The Carolingians had no navy, no means to protect vulnerable sites, and no way to predict the movements of Viking raiders. Defense against the Magyars and the Muslims as well as the Vikings rested principally with local forces that could respond rapidly to invasions. Because imperial authorities were unable to defend their territories, the Carolingian empire became the chief casualty of the invasions. After the ninth century, political and military initiative in western Europe increasingly devolved to regional and local authorities.

The devolution of political authority took different forms in different lands. In England and Germany, regional kingdoms emerged and successfully defended territories more compact than the sprawling Carolingian empire. In France, the counts and other Carolingian subordinates usurped royal rights and prerogatives for themselves. The Vikings themselves established settlements in northern France and southern Italy, where they carved out small, independent states. Following a century of internal conflict and external invasion, the emergence of regional kingdoms and local authorities made it increasingly unlikely that imperial rule would return to western Europe. Like postclassical India but unlike postclassical societies in China, southwest Asia, and the eastern Mediterranean region, western Europe became a society of competing regional states. By putting an end to the ninth-century invasions and establishing a stable political order, these states laid a foundation for social, economic, and cultural development in later centuries.

ECONOMY AND SOCIETY IN EARLY MEDIEVAL EUROPE

Economic and social development in the two big provinces of Christendom mirrored their different political fortunes in the postclassical era. Byzantium was an economic powerhouse in the eastern Mediterranean region. The Byzantine countryside produced abundant agricultural surpluses, which supported large urban populations and fueled the work of manufacturers. Byzantine merchants participated in long-distance commercial networks that linked lands throughout the eastern hemisphere. Western Christendom, by contrast, experienced both a decline of agricultural production and a weakening of cities as repeated invasions disrupted economic and social as well as political affairs. By the tenth century, however, a measure of political stability served as a foundation for economic recovery, and western European peoples began to participate more actively in the larger trading world of the eastern hemisphere.

The Two Economies of Early Medieval Europe

The Byzantine Peasantry Byzantium was strongest when its large class of free peasants flourished. After adoption of the *theme* system in the eighth century, soldiers received allotments of land when they mustered out of the army. This arrangement supported a large and prosperous class of free peasants, who cultivated their land intensively in hopes of improving their families' fortunes. The free peasantry entered an era of gradual decline after the eleventh century as wealthy cultivators managed to accumulate large estates. For as long as it flourished, however, the free peasantry provided agricultural surpluses that served as the foundation for general prosperity in the Byzantine empire.

Manufacturing Agricultural surpluses supported manufacturing in Byzantium's cities, especially Constantinople, which was already a manufacturing megalopolis in classical times. The city was home to throngs of artisans and crafts workers, not to mention thousands of imperial officials and bureaucrats. Byzantine crafts workers enjoyed a reputation especially for their glassware, linen and woolen textiles, gems, jewelry, and fine work in gold and silver.

Silk In the sixth century, crafts workers added high-quality silk textiles to the list of products manufactured in the Byzantine empire. The Byzantine historian Procopius reported that two Christian monks from Persia traveled to China, where they observed the techniques of silk production, which at that time were unknown outside China. According to Procopius, the monks hollowed out their walking staffs and filled them with silkworm eggs, which they smuggled out of China, through their native land of Persia, and into the Byzantine empire. It is likely that Procopius simplified a more complex story by focusing attention on the monks, who by themselves could hardly have introduced a full-blown silk industry to Byzantium. The production of fine, Chinese-style silks required more than a few silkworm eggs. It called also for the mastery of sophisticated technologies and elaborate procedures that probably reached Byzantium by several routes.

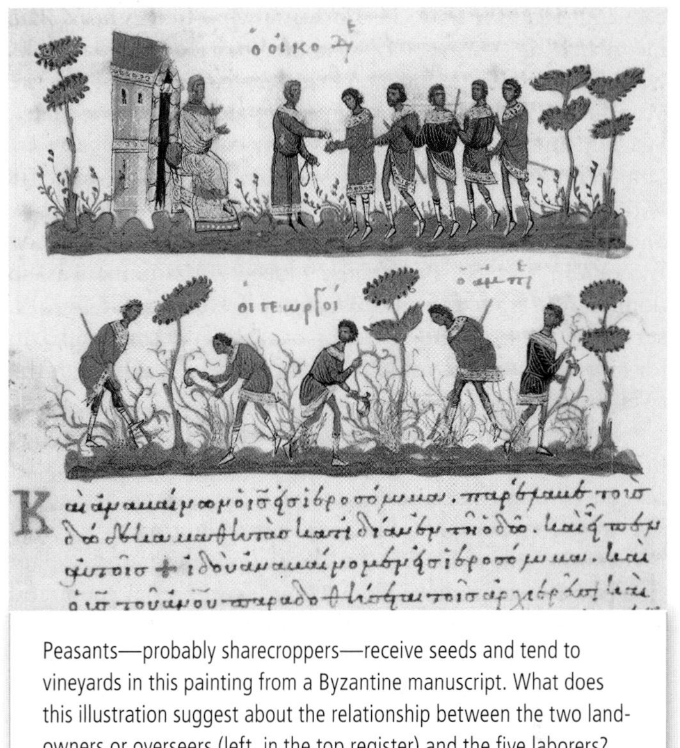

Peasants—probably sharecroppers—receive seeds and tend to vineyards in this painting from a Byzantine manuscript. What does this illustration suggest about the relationship between the two landowners or overseers (left, in the top register) and the five laborers?

In any case, silk textiles soon made major contributions to the Byzantine economy. By the late sixth century, Byzantine silks matched the quality of Chinese textiles, and Byzantium had become the principal supplier of the fashionable fabric to lands in the Mediterranean basin. The silk industry was so important to the Byzantine economy that the government closely supervised every step in its production and sale. Regulations allowed individuals to participate in only one activity—such as weaving, dyeing, or sales—to prevent the creation of a monopoly by a few wealthy or powerful entrepreneurs.

Byzantine Trade The Byzantine economy also benefited from trade. Sitting astride routes going east and west as well as north and south, Constantinople served as the main clearinghouse for trade in the western part of Eurasia. The merchants of Constantinople maintained commercial links with manufacturers and merchants in central Asia, Russia, Scandinavia, northern Europe, and the lands of the Black Sea and the Mediterranean basin. Even after the early Islamic conquests, Byzantine merchants traded regularly with their Muslim counterparts in Persia, Syria, Palestine, and Egypt except during periods of outright war between Byzantium and Muslim states. Indeed, Byzantium was so dominant in trade that the Byzantine gold coin, the *bezant,* served as the standard currency of the Mediterranean basin for more than half a millennium, from the sixth through the twelfth century.

Byzantium drew enormous wealth simply by controlling trade and levying customs duties on merchandise that passed through its lands. Moreover, Byzantium served as the western anchor of the Eurasian trading network that revived the silk roads of classical times. Silk and porcelain came to Constantinople from China, spices from India and southeast Asia. Carpets arrived from Persia and woolen textiles from western Europe, while timber, furs, honey, amber, and slaves came from Russia and Scandinavia. Byzantine subjects consumed some commodities from distant lands, but they redistributed most products, often after adding to their value by further processing—by fashioning jewelry out of gems imported from India, for example, or by dyeing raw woolen cloth imported from western Europe.

As Byzantium prospered, western Europe struggled to find its economic footing in an era of intermittent invasion and political turmoil, which disrupted both agricultural production and large-scale manufacturing. While dealing with political and military challenges, though, western Europeans also adopted a series of innovations that yielded increased agricultural production.

Heavy Plows One innovation involved a new kind of heavy plow that gradually replaced the light Mediterranean plows that had made their way north at the time of the Roman empire. In light, well-drained Mediterranean soils, cultivators used small wooden plows that broke the surface of the soil, created a furrow, and uprooted weeds. This type of plow made little headway in the heavy, moist soils of the north. After the eighth century a more serviceable plow came into use: a heavy tool equipped with iron tips and a mouldboard that turned the soil so as to aerate it thoroughly and break up the root networks of weeds. The heavy plow was a more expensive piece of equipment than the light Mediterranean plow, and it required cultivators to harness more energy to pull it through damp northern soils. Once hitched to oxen or draft horses, however, the heavy plow contributed to greater agricultural production.

As the heavy plow spread throughout western Europe, cultivators took several additional steps that increased agricultural production. They cleared new lands for cultivation and built ponds for fish. They constructed water mills, which enabled them to take advantage of a ready and renewable source of inanimate energy, thus freeing human and animal energy for other work. They employed a special horse collar, which allowed them to rely less on slow-moving oxen and more on speedier horses to pull their heavy plows. They increased cultivation of beans and other legumes, which enriched diets throughout western Chris-

In this twelfth-century manuscript illustration, a peasant guides a heavy, wheeled plow while his wife prods the oxen that pull the plow.

tendom. Thus western Europeans made numerous small adaptations that created a foundation for rural prosperity after 1000 C.E.

Trade in Western Christendom By no means did trade disappear from western Europe. Local markets and fairs offered opportunities for small-scale exchange, and itinerant peddlers shopped their wares from one settlement to another. Maritime trade flourished in the Mediterranean despite Muslim conquests in the region. Christian merchants from Italy and Spain regularly traded across religious boundary lines with Muslims of Sicily, Spain, and north Africa, who linked Europe indirectly with a larger world of communication and exchange.

Norse Merchant-Mariners Maritime trade flourished also in the North Sea and the Baltic Sea. Most active among the early medieval merchants in the northern seas were Norse seafarers, kinsmen of the Vikings. Norse traders followed the same routes as Viking raiders, and many individual mariners no doubt turned from commerce to plunder and back again as opportunities arose. Norse merchants called at ports from Russia to Ireland, carrying cargoes of fish and furs from Scandinavia, honey from Poland, wheat from England, wine from France, beer from the Low Countries, and swords from Germany. By traveling down the Russian rivers to the Black Sea, they were able to trade actively in both the Byzantine and the Abbasid empires. Thus, like Mediterranean merchants, but by different routes, Norse mariners linked western Europe with the world of Islam. Indeed, the Carolingian empire depended heavily on this connection: Norse merchants took Scandinavian products to the Abbasid empire and exchanged them for silver, which they traded at Carolingian ports for wine, jugs, glassware, and other products. The silver transported from the Abbasid empire by Norse merchants was a principal source of bullion used for minting coins in early medieval Europe and hence a crucially important element of the western European economy. Thus, even if western European merchants were not as numerous or prominent as their Byzantine counterparts, they nevertheless participated in the trading networks of the larger eastern hemisphere.

Social Development in the Two Worlds of Christendom

Byzantium: An Urban Society The Byzantine empire was rich in large, prosperous, cosmopolitan cities, including Alexandria, Antioch, and Damascus, to mention only a few. Indeed, until the Muslim conquests of the late seventh and eighth centuries, Byzantium was probably the world's most urbanized society, and residents of its cities enjoyed the benefits and observed urban traditions inherited from the classical Mediterranean world. Yet Constantinople had no rival among Byzantine cities. Subjects of the Byzantine empire referred to it simply as "the City." The heart of the City was the imperial palace, which employed twenty thousand workers as palace staff. Peacocks strutted through gardens filled with sculptures and fountains. Most famous of them was a gold fountain that spouted wine for imperial guests.

City Life Aristocrats maintained enormous palaces that included courtyards, reception halls, libraries, chapels, and quarters for members of the extended family as well as servants and slaves. In the fifth century Constantinople boasted 4,388 mansions, as well as 14 imperial and princely palaces. Women lived in separate apartments and did not receive male visitors from outside the household. Nor did they participate in banquets and parties, especially when wine flowed freely or when the affairs were likely to become so festive that they could compromise a woman's reputation. In Constantinople as well as other cities, upper-class women generally wore veils, like their Mediterranean ancestors from centuries past, to discourage the attention of men outside their own families.

Dwellings of less privileged classes were not so splendid. Artisans and crafts workers commonly lived in rooms above their shops, while clerks and government officials occupied multistory apartment buildings. Workers and the poor lived in rickety tenements where they shared kitchens and sanitary facilities with their neighbors.

Attractions of Constantinople Even for the poor, though, the City had its attractions. As the heir of Rome, Constantinople was a city of baths, which were sites of relaxation and exercise as well as hygienic bathing. Taverns and restaurants offered settings for social gatherings—checkers, chess, and dice games were especially popular activities at taverns—and theaters provided entertainment in the form of song, dance, and striptease. Mass entertainment took place in the Hippodrome, a large stadium adjacent to the imperial palace, where Byzantine subjects watched chariot races, athletic matches, contests

thinking about ENCOUNTERS

Northern Connections

During the postclassical era, Norse mariners found their way to most regions of Europe as well as the Abbasid empire and even ventured across the Atlantic Ocean to Greenland and North America. In what specific ways did Norse merchants and travelers create links between Europe and the larger world? What were the effects of those connections for Byzantine and western European peoples?

A manuscript illustration depicts one Byzantine woman weaving cloth (left) while another spins thread (right). Both women veil their hair for modesty. Women workers were prominent in Byzantine textile production.

between wild animals, and circuses featuring acts by clowns, jugglers, acrobats, and dwarfs.

Western Europe: A Rural Society Cities to the west had once offered similar pleasures, but they largely disappeared in the wake of Germanic invasions and the collapse of the western Roman empire in the late fifth century. The agricultural surplus of western Europe was sufficient to sustain local political elites but not substantial enough to support large, urban populations of artisans, crafts workers, merchants, and professionals. Towns survived, but they served more as economic hubs of surrounding regions than as vibrant centers integrating the economic activities of distant lands.

The Question of Feudalism How did the peoples of western Christendom reorganize their society after the collapse of the western Roman empire? Historians once used the term *feudalism* to characterize the political and social order of medieval Europe. They spoke routinely of a "feudal system" involving a neat hierarchy of lords and vassals, who collectively took charge of political and military affairs on the basis of personal relationships. Lords supposedly provided grants of land to their retainers in exchange for loyalty and military service. Over the years, scholarship has thoroughly undermined that view of medieval society, and historians have largely abandoned the concept of feudalism as a model that grossly oversimplifies a complex society. It is more accurate to view early medieval Europe as a society in which local political and military elites worked in various ad hoc ways to organize their territories and maintain social order. The arrangements they adopted had deep implications for the lives of political and military elites themselves and also for their relationships with commoners.

In the absence of an effective central authority such as an emperor, local notables or lords mobilized small private armies composed of armed retainers. Some of these lords were descendants of Carolingian or other ruling houses, and others were ambitious strongmen—essentially local warlords. Both the lords and their retainers were warriors with horses, weapons, and military expertise. Lords sometimes rewarded their retainers with grants of land or some other valuable, such as the right to income generated by a mill, the right to receive rents or payments from a village, or even a payment of money. In other cases, lords supported their retainers by maintaining them in their own households, where they provided equipment and training in military affairs. After the year 1000, lords increasingly hired their retainers, paying them for services on the basis of need. By one mechanism or another, lords and retainers constituted themselves as privileged political and military elites who dominated local regions.

Peasants Lords and retainers supported themselves and their families principally on the basis of the surplus agricultural production that they commandeered from a subject peasantry. Political and military elites obliged local peasants to provide labor services and payments of rents in kind, such as a portion of the harvest, a chicken, or a dozen eggs. Male peasants typically worked three days a week for their lords while also providing additional labor services during planting and harvesting season. Women peasants churned butter, made cheese, brewed beer, spun thread, wove cloth, or sewed clothes for their lords as well as for their own families. Some peasants also kept sheep or

sources from the past

The Wealth and Commerce of Constantinople

The Spanish rabbi Benjamin of Tudela traveled throughout Europe, north Africa, and southwest Asia between 1165 and 1173 C.E. He may have ventured as far as India, and he mentioned both India and China in his travel account. His main purpose was to record the conditions of Jewish communities, but he also described the many lands and about three hundred cities that he visited. His travels took place during an era of political decline for the Byzantine empire, yet he still found Constantinople a flourishing and prosperous city.

The circumference of the city of Constantinople is eighteen miles; half of it is surrounded by the sea, and half by land, and it is situated upon two arms of the sea, one coming from the sea of Russia [the Black Sea], and one from the sea of Sepharad [the Mediterranean].

All sorts of merchants come here from the land of Babylon, from the land of Shinar [Mesopotamia], from Persia, Media [western Iran], and all the sovereignty of the land of Egypt, from the land of Canaan [Palestine], and the empire of Russia, from Hungary, Patzinakia [Ukraine], Khazaria [southern Russia], and the land of Lombardy [northern Italy] and Sepharad [Spain].

Constantinople is a busy city, and merchants come to it from every country by sea or land, and there is none like it in the world except Baghdad, the great city of Islam. In Constantinople is the church of Hagia Sophia, and the seat of the pope of the Greeks, since Greeks do not obey the pope of Rome. There are also as many churches as there are days of the year. . . . And in this church [Hagia Sophia] there are pillars of gold and silver, and lamps of silver and gold more than a man can count.

Close to the walls of the palace is also a place of amusement belonging to the emperor, which is called the Hippodrome, and every year on the anniversary of the birth of Jesus the emperor gives a great entertainment there. And in that place men from all the races of the world come before the emperor and empress with jugglery and without jugglery, and they introduce lions, leopards, bears, and wild asses, and they engage them in combat with one another; and the same thing is done with birds. No entertainment like this is to be found in any other land. . . .

From every part of the Byzantine empire tribute is brought here every year, and they fill strongholds with garments of silk, purple, and gold. Like unto these storehouses and this wealth there is nothing in the whole world to be found. It is said that the tribute of the city amounts every year to 20,000 gold pieces, derived both from the rents of shops and markets and from the tribute of merchants who enter by sea or land.

The Greek inhabitants are very rich in gold and precious stones, and they go clothed in garments of silk and gold embroidery, and they ride horses and look like princes. Indeed, the land is very rich in all cloth stuffs and in bread, meat, and wine.

Wealth like that of Constantinople is not to be found in the whole world. Here also are men learned in all the books of the Greeks, and they eat and drink, every man under his vine and his fig-tree.

For Further Reflection

- How is it possible to account for the prosperity that Benjamin of Tudela found in Constantinople?

Source: Benjamin of Tudela. *The Itinerary of Benjamin of Tudela.* Trans. by M. N. Adler. London: H. Frowde, 1907. (Translation slightly modified.)

cattle, and their obligations to lords included products from their herds. Because lords provided peasants with land to cultivate and often with tools and animals as well, peasants had little opportunity to move to different lands. Indeed, they were commonly able to do so only with permission from their lords. They even had to pay fees for the right to marry a peasant who worked for a different lord.

Population During the fifth and sixth centuries, epidemic disease and political turmoil took a demographic toll in both Byzantium and western Europe. From a high point of about thirty-six million at the time of the Roman empire in 200 C.E., population fell to about twenty-six million in the year 600—nineteen million in Byzantium and seven million in western Europe. Population fluctuated dramatically over the next two centuries, as Byzantium lost territories to Muslims and western Europeans suffered repeated invasion. After the eighth century, however, both Byzantium and western Europe entered an era of demographic recovery. Political stability created a foundation for a more productive agricultural economy just as new food crops made their way from the Muslim world to Byzantium and Mediterranean Europe. Hard durum wheat, rice, spinach, artichokes, eggplant, lemons, limes, oranges, and melons brought increased calories and

sources from the past

Life on an Early Medieval Manor

Some useful insights into the lives and experiences of common people come from a decree known as the "Capitulary de Villis" issued by the emperor Charlemagne in 807 C.E. as a guide for stewards of Carolingian estates. The decree envisions a community with sophisticated agricultural and craft skills. Probably few estates observed all provisions of Charlemagne's decree, but the capitulary nonetheless communicates clearly how lords hoped to control their manors and profit from their production.

Each steward shall make an annual statement of all our income: an account of our lands cultivated by the oxen which our ploughmen drive and of our lands which the tenants of farms ought to plough; an account of the pigs, of the rents, of the obligations and fines; of the game taken in our forests without our permission; . . . of the mills, of the forest, of the fields, of the bridges, and ships; of the free men and the hundreds who are under obligations to our treasury; of markets, vineyards, and those who owe wine to us; of the hay, firewood, torches, planks, and other kinds of lumber; of the waste lands; of the fruits of the trees, of the nut trees, larger and smaller; of the grafted trees of all kinds; of the gardens; of the turnips; of the fish ponds; of the hides, skins, and horns; of the honey, wax; of the fat, tallow and soap; of the mulberry wine, cooked wine, mead, vinegar, beer, wine new and old; of the new grain and the old; of the hens and eggs; of the geese; the number of fishermen, [metal] smiths, sword-makers, and shoemakers; . . . of the forges and mines, that is iron and other mines; of the lead mines; . . . of the colts and fillies; they shall make all these known to us, set forth separately and in order, at Christmas, in order that we may know what and how much of each thing we have. . . .

[Stewards] must provide the greatest care, that whatever is prepared or made with the hands, that is, lard, smoked meat, salt meat, partially salted meat, wine, vinegar, mulberry wine, cooked wine . . . mustard, cheese, butter, malt, beer, mead, honey, wax, flour, all should be prepared and made with the greatest cleanliness. . . .

[Stewards should ensure] that in each of our estates, the chambers [living quarters] shall be provided with counterpanes, cushions, pillows, bed clothes, coverings for the tables and benches; vessels of brass, lead, iron and wood; andirons, chains, pot-hooks, adzes, axes, augers, cutlasses and all other kinds of tools, so that it shall never be necessary to go elsewhere for them, or to borrow them. And the weapons, which are carried against the enemy, shall be well cared for, so as to keep them in good condition; and when they are brought back they shall be placed in the chamber.

For our women's work they are to give at the proper time, as has been ordered, the materials, that is the linen, wool, woad, vermillion, madder, wool-combs, teasels, soap, grease, vessels and the other objects which are necessary.

Of the food products other than meat, two-thirds shall be sent each year for our own use, that is of the vegetables, fish, cheese, honey, mustard, vinegar, millet, panic [a grain similar to millet], dried and green herbs, radishes, and in addition of the wax, soap and other small products; and they shall tell us how much is left by a statement, as we have said above; and they shall not neglect this as in the past; because from those two-thirds, we wish to know how much remains.

Each steward shall have in his district good workmen, namely, blacksmiths, goldsmiths, silversmiths, shoemakers, [wood] turners, carpenters, sword-makers, fishermen, foilers [fine metalworkers], soap-makers, men who know how to make beer, cider, berry, and all other kinds of beverages, bakers to make pastry for our table, net-makers who know how to make nets for hunting, fishing and fowling, and the others who are too numerous to be designated.

For Further Reflection

- On the basis of the "Capitulary de Villis," how would you characterize the conditions of material life in the Carolingian countryside?

Source: *Translations and Reprints from the Original Sources of European History,* vol. 2. Philadelphia: University of Pennsylvania Press, 1900. (Translation slightly modified.)

dietetic variety that supported increasing populations. By the year 800 the two provinces of Christendom had a combined population of about twenty-nine million, which rose to about thirty-two million in 900 and thirty-six million in 1000—the level of the Roman empire's population some eight centuries earlier. Thus by the year 1000, both Byzantium and western Europe had built productive agricultural economies that sustained sizable and increasing populations.

THE EVOLUTION OF CHRISTIAN SOCIETIES IN BYZANTIUM AND WESTERN EUROPE

As heirs of the Roman empire, Byzantium and western Europe were both Christian societies. As in the cases of political, social, and economic affairs, though, the two big realms of Christendom created distinctive and ultimately competing

forms of their common religious inheritance. In both Byzantium and western Europe, Christianity served as the principal source of religious, moral, and cultural authority. Both lands supported ecclesiastical hierarchies with networks of monasteries. Both societies also worked to extend the reach of Christianity by sending missionaries to seek converts in northerly territories from Russia and Slavic lands to Scandinavia and the British Isles. By the year 1000 the twin heirs of Roman Christianity had laid the foundations for a large Christian cultural zone in the western part of the Eurasian continent that paralleled the Buddhist and Islamic cultural zones farther east. Yet even as they were promoting Christianity in their own societies and beyond, church authorities in Byzantium and western Europe fell into deep disagreement on matters of doctrine, ritual, and church authority. By the mid-eleventh century, their differences had become so great that church leaders formally denounced one another and established two rival communities: the Eastern Orthodox church in Byzantium and the Roman Catholic church in western Europe.

Popes and Patriarchs

Christianity had a more hierarchical organizational structure than any other major religious tradition. There was no pope of Buddhism, no patriarch in the Islamic world. Christianity, however, inherited a strong organizational structure from the time of the late Roman empire. In the early middle ages, the two most important Christian authorities were the bishop of Rome, known as the pope, and the patriarch of Constantinople.

The Papacy When the western Roman empire collapsed, the papacy survived and claimed continuing spiritual authority over all the lands formerly embraced by the Roman empire. At first the popes cooperated closely with the Byzantine emperors, who seemed to be the natural heirs of the emperors of Rome. Beginning in the late sixth century, however, the popes acted more independently and devoted their efforts to strengthening the western Christian church based at Rome and clearly distinguishing it from the eastern Christian church based at Constantinople.

Pope Gregory I The individual most responsible for charting an independent course for the Roman church was Pope Gregory I (590–604 C.E.), also known as Gregory the Great. As pope, Gregory faced an array of challenges. During the late sixth century, the Germanic Lombards campaigned in Italy, menacing Rome and the church in the process. Gregory mobilized local resources and organized the defense of Rome, thus saving both the city and the church. He also faced difficulties within the church, since bishops frequently acted as though they were supreme ecclesiastical authorities within their own dioceses. To regain the initiative, Gregory reasserted claims to papal primacy—the notion that the bishop of Rome was the ultimate authority for all the Christian church. Gregory also made contributions as a theologian. He emphasized the sacrament of penance, which required individuals to confess their sins to their priests and atone for them by penitential acts—a practice that enhanced the influence of the Roman church in the lives of individuals.

The Patriarchs The patriarchs of Constantinople were powerful officials, but they did not enjoy the independence of their brethren to the west. Following the tradition of caesaropapism inaugurated by the emperor Constantine in the fourth century, Byzantine emperors treated the church as a department of state. They appointed the patriarchs, and they instructed patriarchs, bishops, and priests to deliver sermons that supported imperial policy and encouraged obedience to imperial authorities. This caesaropapism was a source of tension between imperial and ecclesiastical authorities, and it also had the potential to provoke popular dissent when imperial views clashed with those of the larger society.

Iconoclasm The most divisive ecclesiastical policy implemented by Byzantine emperors was iconoclasm, inaugurated by Emperor Leo III (reigned 717–741 C.E.). Byzantium had a long tradition of producing icons—paintings of Jesus, saints, and other religious figures—many of which were splendid works of art. Most theologians took these icons as visual stimulations that inspired reverence for holy personages. Leo, however, became convinced that the veneration of images was sinful, tantamount to the worship of idols. In 726 C.E., he embarked on a policy of iconoclasm (which literally means "breaking of icons"), destroying religious images and prohibiting their use in churches. The policy immediately sparked protests and even riots throughout the empire, because icons were extremely popular among the laity. Debates about iconoclasm raged for more than a century. Only in 843 did Leo's followers abandon the policy of iconoclasm.

Monks and Missionaries

Consumed with matters of theology, ritual, and church politics, popes and patriarchs rarely dealt directly with the lay population of their churches. For personal religious instruction and inspiration, lay Christians looked less to the church hierarchy than to local monasteries.

Asceticism Christian monasticism grew out of the efforts of devout individuals to lead especially holy lives. Early Christian ascetics in Egypt, Mesopotamia, and Persia adopted extreme regimes of self-denial in order to focus all their attention on religious matters. Some lived alone as hermits. Others formed communes where they devoted themselves to the pursuit of holiness rather than worldly success. Many dedicated themselves to celibacy, fasting, and prayer.

Drawn by their reputation for piety, disciples gathered around these ascetics and established communities of men and women determined to follow their example. These communities became the earliest monasteries. During the early

This illustration from a psalter prepared about 900 C.E. depicts an iconoclast whitewashing an image of Jesus painted on a wall.

days of monasticism, each community developed its own rules, procedures, and priorities. The result was wild inconsistency: some monasteries imposed harsh and austere regimes of self-denial, and others offered little or no guidance.

St. Basil and St. Benedict Monasteries became much more influential when reformers provided them with discipline and a sense of purpose. The two most important reformers were the patriarch St. Basil of Caesarea (329–379 C.E.) in Byzantium and St. Benedict of Nursia (480–547 C.E.) in Italy. Both men prepared regulations for monasteries that provided for mild but not debilitating asceticism combined with meditation and work on behalf of the church. In both Basilian and Benedictine monasteries, individuals gave up their personal possessions and lived communal, celibate lives under the direction of the abbots who supervised the communities. Poverty, chastity, and obedience became the prime virtues for Basilian and Benedictine monks. At certain hours monks came together for religious services and prayers, dividing the remainder of the day into periods for study, reflection, and labor.

St. Scholastica Monasteries throughout Byzantium adopted the Basilian rule for their own use, while their counterparts in western Europe largely followed the rule of St. Benedict. Through the influence of St. Benedict's sister, the nun St. Scholastica (482–543 C.E.), an adaptation of the Benedictine rule soon provided guidance for the religious life of women living in convents.

Monasticism and Society Like Buddhist monasteries in Asian lands and charitable religious foundations in Muslim lands, Christian monasteries provided a variety of social services that enabled them to build close relations with local communities. Monks and nuns offered spiritual counsel to local laity, and they organized relief efforts by supplying food and medical attention at times of natural or other calamities. Monasteries and convents served both as orphanages and as inns for travelers. Sometimes they also provided rudimentary educational services for local communities.

Because of the various roles they played in the larger society, monasteries were particularly effective agents in the spread of Christianity. While providing social services, monks also zealously preached Christianity and tended to the spiritual needs of rural populations. For many people, a local neighboring monastery was the only source of instruc-

A fourteenth-century manuscript illustration shows St. Benedict with his crosier, the staff carried by abbots to symbolize their position (above), and meeting with two monks beside a fishpond at their monastery (below). What does the fishpond suggest about the economic significance of monasteries?

tion in Christian doctrine, and a local monastic church offered the only practical opportunity for them to take part in religious services. Through patience and persistence over decades and centuries, monks and nuns helped to instill Christian values in countless generations of European peasants.

Missionaries Some monks went beyond the bounds of their own society and sought to spread Christianity in the larger world. Indeed, one of the remarkable developments of the early middle ages was the creation of a large Christian cultural zone in the western part of the Eurasian continent.

Christianity was already well established in the Mediterranean region, but pagan Germanic and Slavic peoples occupied the more northerly parts of Europe. In the late sixth century, Pope Gregory I sent missionaries to England and targeted the pagan Germanic kings who ruled various parts of the island, hoping that their conversion would induce their subjects to adopt Christianity. This tactic largely succeeded: by the early seventh century Christianity enjoyed a stable foothold, and by 800 England was securely within the fold of the Roman church. The Franks and Charlemagne later sponsored efforts to extend Christianity to northern Germany and Scandinavia. They met spirited resistance from Germanic peoples, who had no desire to abandon their inherited gods or pagan beliefs, but by the year 1000 Christianity had won a sizable and growing following.

Meanwhile, Byzantine authorities sent missionaries to Balkan and Slavic lands. The most famous of the missionaries to the Slavs were Saints Cyril and Methodius, two brothers from Thessaloniki in Greece. During the mid-ninth century, Cyril and Methodius conducted missions in Bulgaria and Moravia (which included much of the modern Czech, Slovakian, and Hungarian territories). There they devised an alphabet, known as the Cyrillic alphabet, for the previously illiterate Slavic peoples. Though adapted from written Greek, the Cyrillic alphabet represented the sounds of Slavic languages more precisely than did the Greek, and it remained in use in much of eastern Europe until supplanted by the Roman alphabet in the twentieth century. In Russia and most other parts of the former Soviet Union, the Cyrillic alphabet survives to the present day.

North of Bulgaria another Slavic people began to organize large states: the Russians. About 989, at the urging of Byzantine missionaries, Prince Vladimir of Kiev converted to Christianity and ordered his subjects to follow his example. Vladimir was no paragon of virtue: he lauded drunkenness and reportedly maintained a harem of eight hundred girls. After his conversion, however, Byzantine influences flowed rapidly into Russia. Cyrillic writing, literacy, and Christian missions all spread quickly throughout Russia. Byzantine teachers traveled north to establish schools, and Byzantine priests conducted services for Russian converts. Thus Kiev served as a conduit for the spread of Byzantine cultural and religious influence in Russia.

Two Churches

Although they professed the same basic Christian doctrine, the churches of Constantinople and Rome experienced increasing friction after the sixth century. Tensions mirrored political strains, such as deep resentment in Byzantium after Charlemagne accepted the title of emperor from the pope in Rome. Yet church authorities in Constantinople and Rome also harbored different views on religious and theological issues. The iconoclastic movement of the eighth and ninth centuries was one focus of difference. Western theologians regarded religious images as perfectly appropriate aids to devotion and resented Byzantine claims to the contrary, whereas the iconoclasts took offense at the efforts of their Roman counterparts to have images restored in Byzantium.

Monasteries were the principal centers of literacy in western Europe during the early middle ages. In this manuscript illustration, one monk copies a manuscript, another makes geometric calculations, a third cuts parchment, two work on the building, and one more rings the bells that call monks and members of the surrounding community to religious services.

Religious Rivalry Over time the Christian churches based in Constantinople and Rome disagreed on many other points. Some ritual and doctrinal differences concerned forms of worship and the precise wording of theological teachings—relatively minor issues that in and of themselves need not have caused deep division in the larger Christian community. Byzantine theologians objected, for example, to the fact that western priests shaved their beards and used unleavened rather than leavened bread when saying Mass. Other differences concerned more substantive theological matters, such as the precise relationship between God, Jesus, and the Holy Spirit—all regarded as manifestations of God by most Christian theologians of the day.

Schism Alongside ritual and doctrinal differences, the Byzantine patriarchs and the Roman popes disputed their respective rights and powers. Patriarchs argued for the autonomy of all major Christian jurisdictions, including that of Constantinople, whereas popes asserted the primacy of Rome as the sole seat of authority for all Christendom. Ultimately, relations became so strained that the eastern and western churches went separate ways. In 1054 the patriarch and pope mutually excommunicated each other, each refusing to recognize the other's church as properly Christian. Despite efforts at reconciliation, the schism between eastern and western churches persists to the present day. In light of the schism, historians refer to the eastern Christian church after 1054 as the Eastern Orthodox church and its western counterpart as the Roman Catholic church.

inperspective

After the collapse of the western Roman empire, the two worlds of Christendom followed very different historical paths. Byzantium inherited a thriving economy, a set of governing institutions, an imperial bureaucracy, an established church, and a rich cultural tradition from classical Mediterranean society and the Roman empire. Even after the loss of territories to Muslim conquerors, Byzantium remained a powerful and productive society in the eastern Mediterranean region. By contrast, western Europe experienced turmoil in the face of repeated invasion, which thoroughly disrupted social and economic as well as political affairs. Only after the ninth century did western Europeans gradually manage to achieve political stability and lay the foundations for a more predictable and prosperous society. For all their differences, though, the two worlds of Christendom both advanced the construction of a large Christian cultural zone that paralleled the lands of Islamic and Buddhist influence to the east. This Christian cultural zone harbored different and competing versions of a common religion—like the Islamic cultural zone with both Sunni and Shia advocates or the Buddhist cultural zone with Mahayana as well as Theravada adherents—but Byzantium and western Europe both relied on religion as a foundation for cultural unity and made Christianity the most important source of cultural and moral authority throughout Europe. ●

thinking about TRADITIONS

Competing Christianities

The Byzantine empire and western Europe inherited the same Christianity from the late Roman empire. How did Christianity develop along distinct lines in the two regions? What influences contributed to the development of such different understandings of Christianity?

CHRONOLOGY	
313–337	Reign of Constantine
329–379	Life of St. Basil of Caesarea
476	Fall of the western Roman empire
480–547	Life of St. Benedict of Nursia
482–543	Life of St. Scholastica
527–565	Reign of Justinian
590–604	Reign of Pope Gregory I
717–741	Reign of Leo III
726–843	Iconoclastic controversy
732	Battle of Tours
751–843	Carolingian kingdom
768–814	Reign of Charlemagne
800	Coronation of Charlemagne as emperor
9th century	Missions of St. Cyril and St. Methodius to the Slavs
989	Conversion of Prince Vladimir of Kiev to Christianity
1054	Schism between Eastern Orthodox and Roman Catholic churches

Assessing AP Themes

1. What were the political, religious, and cultural changes and continuities from the now-extinct classical empires to the post-classical empires?
2. How did the empires of Dar al Islam change the dynamics of the political and economic systems of the eastern hemisphere?
3. What state policies, mercantile practices, and innovations in transportation contributed to the intensification of cross-cultural exchanges?
4. What were the significant cross-cultural exchanges that resulted from the intensification of trade and communication routes?
5. What were the cultural, religious, commercial, and governmental functions of at least two major cities in this time period?
6. Why could "the Indian Ocean Basin" be a more useful unit of analysis than the separate states of South and Southeast Asia and the Swahili states (from ch. 18)?
7. What were the changes in and continuities of labor forms, gender relations, and family structures from the previous era to this one?

For Further Reading

Marc Bloch. *Feudal Society.* 2 vols. Trans. by L. A. Manyon. Chicago, 1961. A classic interpretation concentrating on social and economic history.

Peter Brown. *The Rise of Western Christendom: Triumph and Diversity, A.D. 200–1000.* 2nd ed. Oxford, 2003. A landmark analysis of early Christian history.

Einhard and Notker the Stammerer. *Two Lives of Charlemagne.* Trans. by Lewis Thorpe. New York, 1969. Translations of two early biographies of Charlemagne.

Patrick J. Geary. *Before France and Germany: The Creation and Transformation of the Merovingian World.* 2nd ed. New York, 1997. Insightful study of Germanic societies in early medieval Europe.

Judith Herrin. *Byzantium: The Surprising Life of a Medieval Empire.* Princeton, 2009. A judicious survey of Byzantine history.

Richard Hodges and David Whitehouse. *Mohammed, Charlemagne, and the Origins of Europe: Archaeology and the Pirenne Thesis.* Ithaca, 1983. Views early medieval Europe in hemispheric context.

Michael McCormick. *Origins of the European Economy: Communications and Commerce, A.D. 300–900.* Cambridge, Mass., 2001. A comprehensive analysis that emphasizes the participation of early medieval Europe in a larger Mediterranean economy.

Procopius. *History of the Wars, Secret History, and Buildings.* Trans. by A. Cameron. New York, 1967. Translations of writings by the most important historian in the time of Justinian.

Susan Reynolds. *Fiefs and Vassals: The Medieval Evidence Reinterpreted.* Oxford, 1994. A densely written but important book offering a powerful scholarly critique of the concept of feudalism.

Mark Whittow. *The Making of Byzantium, 600–1025.* Berkeley, 1996. Emphasizes relations between Byzantium and neighboring societies.

State of the World

Revived Networks and New Cultural Zones

The establishment of classical societies was a remarkable feat of political and social organization. For about a millennium, a series of large, centralized imperial states dominated the temperate and subtropical zones of Eurasia and north Africa—by far the most densely populated part of the world at the time. The classical societies were fertile incubators of cultural and religious traditions, and they drove trade, missionary activity, and cross-cultural interaction throughout much of the eastern hemisphere.

When the classical societies declined and (mostly) collapsed, it was by no means certain that a network of interaction embracing much of the eastern hemisphere would survive. The reorganization of states and societies might well have taken place on a local or regional basis. Similarly, social and economic activity might have integrated compact territories rather than large empires. Cultural and religious leaders might have focused on the needs and interests of their own societies rather than dispatching missionaries to seek converts in distant lands. Indeed, Chinese, Indian, and western European societies reorganized themselves, at least temporarily, on smaller scales than in classical times.

Over the longer term, however, large-scale political and social organization returned to the eastern hemisphere, and by the year 1000 it served as a framework for even more intense and more widespread cross-cultural interaction than in earlier times. Three societies were particularly important for this development: the Byzantine empire in the eastern Mediterranean region, the Abbasid empire in southwestern Asia, and the revived Chinese empire under the Tang and Song dynasties. Those three societies generated so much economic production and so much demand for foreign products that they fueled hemispheric trade for half a millennium. They contributed to revival of the overland silk roads linking the most densely populated parts of Eurasia from the Mediterranean region through Muslim lands and India to China. Moreover, they sponsored the creation of an elaborate maritime network of sea lanes linking lands in all parts of the Indian Ocean basin.

The reconstitution of large-scale societies and extensive trading networks had dramatic cultural implications. During the half-millennium from 500 to 1000 C.E., advocates of Buddhism, Christianity, and Islam introduced writing and formal education to regions that had never seen them before. The three religious traditions themselves emerged as the dominant sources of cultural and moral inspiration in vast cultural zones embracing most of Eurasia and north Africa. Indeed, Islam began to influence cultural and religious life in sub-Saharan Africa as well. By the year 1000 the postclassical societies had spread their cultural traditions far more extensively than their classical predecessors, and they had laid the foundations for the long-term influence of Buddhism, Christianity, and Islam throughout most of the eastern hemisphere.

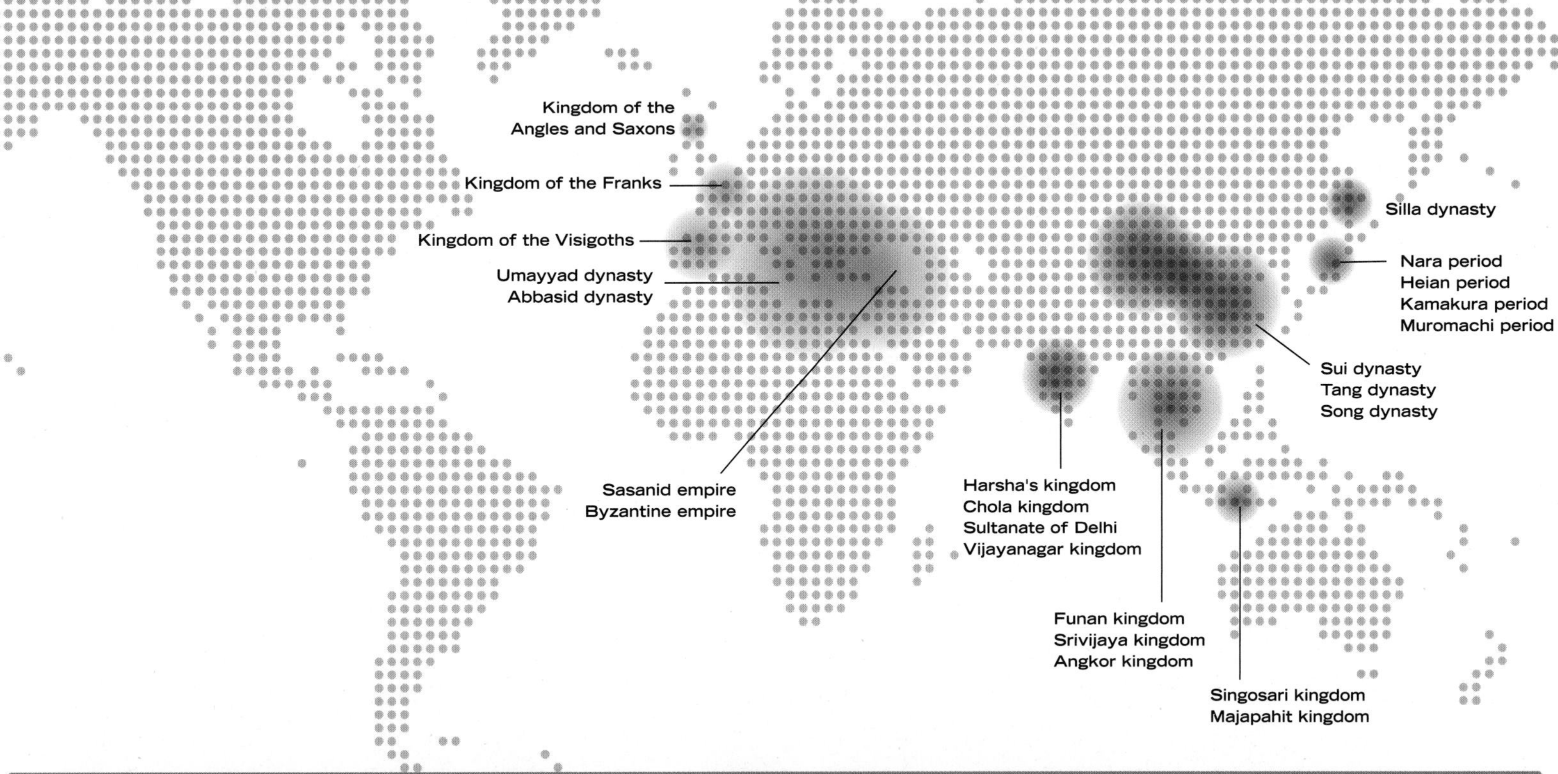

500 C.E. | 600 C.E. | 700 C.E. | 800 C.E. | 900 C.E. | 1000 C.E. | 1100 C.E. | 1200 C.E. | 1300 C.E. | 1400 C.E. | 1500 C.E. | 1600 C.E.

EAST ASIA

China: Sui dynasty, 589–618 C.E.

China: Tang dynasty, 618–907 C.E.

Korea: Silla dynasty, 669–935 C.E.

China: Song dynasty, 960–1279 C.E.

Japan: Nara period, 710–794 C.E.; Heian period, 794–1185 C.E.; Kamakura period, 1185–1333 C.E.; Muromachi period, 1336–1573 C.E.

India: Harsha's kingdom, 606–648 C.E.; Chola kingdom, 850–1267 C.E.; Sultanate of Delhi, 1206–1526 C.E.; Vijayanagar kingdom, ca. 1350–1565 C.E.

Funan kingdom, ca. 100 C.E.–ca. 599 C.E.; Srivijaya kingdom, 670–1025 C.E.; Angkor kingdom, 889–1431 C.E.; Singosari kingdom, 1222–1292 C.E.; Majapahit kingdom, 1293–1520 C.E.

SOUTHEAST ASIA

Sasanid empire, 224–641 C.E.; Byzantine empire, 5th–15th century C.E.

EUROPE & SOUTHWEST ASIA

Kingdoms of the Visigoths (ca. 470–early 8th century), Franks (late 5th century–early 8th century), and Angles and Saxons (5th century–mid-11th century)

AFRICA

Southwest Asia & northern Africa: Umayyad dynasty, 661–750 C.E.; Abbasid dynasty, 750–1258 C.E.

part 4

THE ACCELERATION OF CROSS-CULTURAL INTERACTION, 1000 TO 1500 C.E.

This set of chapters (17–20) concludes AP Period 3, c. 600 to c. 1450. Be sure you look back to the Part 3 opener on pages 256–257 to get a clearer picture of how Parts 3 and 4 come together on the AP exam. You will find that in these chapters you are going to explore the same themes and ideas introduced in Part 3 (chapters 13–16).

HTS 2 The period c. 600 to c. 1450 is often called the "Post-Classical" era because the themes from Period 2 (the classical era) are continued and amplified in Period 3. Your job is to track the continuities between Period 2 and Period 3 very carefully, while paying attention to the new features of the era.

Remember that the classical empires in Eurasia and the Americas collapsed by c. 600 C.E. One of the questions for this period of c. 600–c. 1450 is "what replaced them?" In this set of chapters (17–20), Bentley and Zeigler look at the end of the post-classical period for significant signs of political, economic, and religious power in the Mongol, Sub-Saharan African, western European, and Mesoamerican states. All four of these regions gained access to enormously profitable trade routes. HTS 3 In AP World History, you will need to know the locations of these powerful new states and how they conquered or acquired new significant power as well as the specifics of how these states were ruled, and how the states were connected to each other—by religion, war, trade, or diplomacy.

As you have already seen, it's not just merchandise that "travels" along the trade routes. Merchants, missionaries, migrants, and military conquerors were responsible for the spread of religion and language to new places where they were often mixed (synthesized) and reinterpreted. There are lots of examples of this cultural synthesis in Period 3, and AP students are frequently asked to explain the hows and whys and the significances of these syncretic processes. HTS 1 Remember, there are great architectural, literary, and artistic documents that illustrate this blending; they are important to AP World History, so watch for them in the photographs and document selections in the text.

Trade routes are as important as political rearrangements in Period 3. HTS 2 Although people in Afro-Eurasia and the Americas remained separate from each other in this period, within each hemisphere many more people and much more merchandise moved along trade routes.

You will have to know the specifics of who and what was moving along these routes, and why. What were the new agricultural and transportation technologies and products? Who were the wealthy consumers with tastes for luxury goods? Who and where were the innovative merchants and trade organizations? Which governments sponsored commercial policies (minting coins and paper money, for example) and useful infrastructure projects, like roads and canals? And while you're at it, watch out for the invaders—peoples like the Vikings, the Mongols, the Arabs, the Turkic peoples, the European Crusaders, the Mexica/Aztec. What important roles did they play in the short-run and the long-run of world history?

The peoples of Oceania and the Andean region of South America have unique attributes in this Period 3 of AP World History. Neither of these societies interacted with other societies as frequently as people in the other societies during this time period did. Both cleverly exploited their unusual environments and organized flourishing agricultural communities. Although they assembled a massive empire, the Inca economy was self-sufficient and did not engage in foreign trade, even with the Maya to their north. Look for the ways in which this makes the Inca unique in AP Period 3. Aided by their superior marine skills, the peoples of Oceania populated the vast array of Pacific islands, continuing the long human story of migration, bringing new peoples, animals, and plants to habitable parts of the planet.

It should be clear by now that you need to focus on the reasons for and consequences of increasing trade, contact, and wealth. It's also important not to forget the people. As you go through these post-classical chapters, pay attention to what sorts of people do the work—who are the merchants, the workers, the bankers, the soldiers and sailors, the slaves? New forms of coerced or forced labor were used in this period, so watch out for these, especially serfdom and the mit'a system. Where do these people and their work "fit" into their society? How is one's position on the social ladder determined (who's on top, who's on bottom)? How do women fare in these post-classical societies? What was considered "women's work" and how much influence or power did women of different classes have on the "men's work"? Do newly-introduced religious beliefs improve or suppress the influence of women in a society? And always keep an eye on the pastoralist peoples—the Mongols, the Bantu, the Arabs and Berbers; they are still big players in wars and trade.

More written documents have survived from the post-classical period, and the ones that are highlighted in AP World History tend be travelers' writings. Why? Because these travelers comment on the people and practices in foreign lands, and they can tell us a lot about the extent of intercultural knowledge and understanding.

Finally, AP World History students have to understand the continuing importance of cities and their growth. Different cities have different missions in different societies. Much like comparing empires, it's possible to compare cities. Why do they rise and fall? Did the religious leaders in the region locate themselves in cities, and if so, why? Who ruled the cities, and were the cities important because they were political centers (capitals), or commercial or religious centers? Who lived in the cities, and where did they come from? Were the cities centers of learning and the arts? Be prepared to explain the religious, commercial (trade), governmental, and cultural functions of at least two major cities in this period.

Nomadic Empires and Eurasian Integration

chapter 17

An elegant painting on silk by the thirteenth-century painter Liu Guandao depicts the Mongol emperor Khubilai Khan (center, in Chinese silks under Mongolian furs) with a hunting party bearing Mongolian bows, arrows, and satchels.

EYEWITNESS:
The Goldsmith of the Mongolian Steppe

Guillaume Boucher was a goldsmith who lived during the early and middle decades of the thirteenth century. At some point, perhaps during the 1230s, he left his native Paris and went to Budapest, which was then a part of the kingdom of Hungary. There he was captured by Mongol warriors campaigning in Hungary. The Mongols noticed and appreciated Boucher's talents, and when they left Hungary in 1242, they took him along with other skilled captives to their central Asian homeland.

For at least the next fifteen years, Boucher lived at the Mongol capital at Karakorum. Though technically a slave, he enjoyed some prestige. He supervised fifty assistants in a workshop that produced decorative objects of gold and silver for the Mongol court. His most ingenious creation was a spectacular silver fountain in the form of a tree. Four pipes, concealed by the tree's trunk, carried wines and other intoxicating drinks to the top of the tree and then dispensed them into silver bowls from which courtiers and guests filled their cups. Apart from his famous fountain, Boucher also produced statues in gold and silver, built carriages, designed buildings, and even sewed ritual garments for Roman Catholic priests who conducted services for Christians living at Karakorum and sought converts in the Mongol empire.

Boucher was by no means the only European living at the Mongol court. His wife was a woman of French ancestry whom Boucher had met and married in Hungary. The Flemish missionary William of Rubruck visited Karakorum in 1254, and during his sojourn there he encountered a Frenchwoman named Paquette who was an attendant to a Mongol princess, an artisan from Russia (Paquette's husband), an unnamed nephew of a French bishop, a Greek soldier, and an Englishman named Basil. Other European visitors to the Mongol court found Germans, Slavs, and Hungarians as well as Chinese, Koreans, Turks, Persians, and Armenians, among others. Many thirteenth-century roads led to Karakorum.

Nomadic peoples had made their influence felt throughout much of Eurasia as early as classical times. The Xiongnu confederation dominated central Asia and posed a formidable threat to the Han dynasty in China from the third to the first century B.C.E. During the second and third centuries C.E., the Huns and other nomadic peoples from central Asia launched the migrations that helped bring down the western Roman empire, and later migrations of the White Huns destroyed the Gupta state in India. Turkish peoples ruled a large central Asian empire from the sixth through the ninth century, and the Uighur Turks even seized the capital cities of the Tang dynasty in the mid-seventh century.

Between the eleventh and the fifteenth centuries, nomadic peoples became more prominent than ever before in Eurasian affairs. Turkish peoples migrated to Persia, Anatolia, and India, where they overcame existing authorities and established new states. During the thirteenth and fourteenth centuries, the Mongols established themselves as the most powerful people of the central Asian steppes and then turned on settled societies in China, Persia, Russia, and eastern Europe. By the early fourteenth century, the Mongols had built the largest empire the world has ever seen, stretching from Korea and China in the east to Russia and Hungary in the west.

Most of the Mongol states collapsed during the late fourteenth and fifteenth centuries, but the decline of the Mongols did not signal the end of nomadic peoples' influence on Eurasian affairs. Although a native Chinese dynasty replaced the Mongol state in China, the possibility of a Mongol revival forced the new dynasty to focus attention and resources on its central Asian frontier. Moreover, from the fourteenth through the seventeenth century, Turkish peoples embarked on new campaigns of expansion that eventually brought most of India, much of central Asia, all of Anatolia, and a good portion of eastern Europe under their domination.

The military campaigns of nomadic peoples were sometimes exceedingly destructive. Nomadic warriors often demolished cities, slaughtered urban populations, and ravaged surrounding agricultural lands. Yet those same forces also encouraged systematic peaceful interaction between peoples of different societies. Between the eleventh and the fifteenth centuries, like nomadic peoples of the Arabian and Saharan deserts, Turkish and Mongol peoples forged closer links than ever before between peoples of neighboring lands. By fostering cross-cultural communication and exchange on an unprecedented scale, the nomadic empires integrated the lives of peoples and the experiences of societies throughout much of the eastern hemisphere.

TURKISH MIGRATIONS AND IMPERIAL EXPANSION

Turkish peoples never formed a single, homogeneous group but, rather, organized themselves into clans and tribes that often fought bitterly with one another. Turkish clans and identities probably emerged after the Xiongnu confederation broke apart in the first and second centuries C.E. All Turkish peoples spoke related languages, and all were nomads or descendants of nomads. From modest beginnings they expanded their influence until they dominated not only the steppes of central Asia but also settled societies in Persia, Anatolia, and India.

Economy and Society of Nomadic Pastoralism

Nomadic Pastoralists and Their Animals

Nomadic peoples of central Asia were pastoralists who kept herds of animals—horses, sheep, goats, cattle, and camels. They built societies by adapting to the ecological conditions of arid lands. Central Asia does not receive enough rain to support large-scale agriculture, but grasses and shrubs flourish on the steppe lands. Maintenance of flocks required pastoral peoples of central Asia to move frequently. They drove their animals to lands with abundant grass and then moved them along as the animals thinned the vegetation. They did not wander aimlessly through the steppes but, rather, followed migratory cycles that took account of the seasons and local climatic conditions. They lived mostly off the meat, milk, and hides of their animals. They used animal bones for tools and animal dung as fuel for fires. They made shoes and clothes out of wool from their sheep and skins from their other animals. Wool was also the source of the felt that they used to fashion large tents called *yurts* in which they lived. They even prepared an alcoholic drink from animal products by fermenting mare's milk into a potent concoction known as *kumiss.*

The aridity of the climate and the nomadic lifestyle limited the development of human societies in central Asia. Only at oases did agriculture make it possible for dense populations to congregate. Settlements were few and small—and often temporary as well, since nomads carried their collapsible felt yurts with them as they drove their herds. Nomads often engaged in small-scale cultivation of millet or vegetables when they found sources of water, but the harvests were sufficient only to supplement animal products, not to sustain whole societies. Nomads also produced limited amounts of pottery, leather goods, iron weapons, and tools. Given their migratory habits, however, both intensive agriculture and large-scale craft production were practical impossibilities.

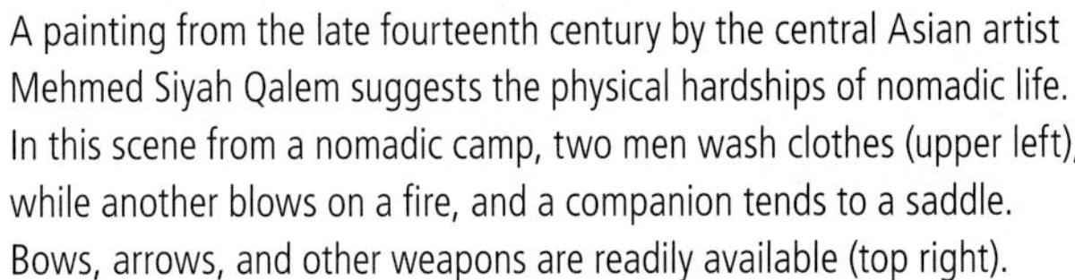
A painting from the late fourteenth century by the central Asian artist Mehmed Siyah Qalem suggests the physical hardships of nomadic life. In this scene from a nomadic camp, two men wash clothes (upper left), while another blows on a fire, and a companion tends to a saddle. Bows, arrows, and other weapons are readily available (top right).

Nomadic and Settled Peoples Thus nomads avidly sought opportunities to trade with settled peoples, and as early as the classical era brisk trade linked nomadic and settled societies. Much of that commerce took place on a small scale as nomads sought agricultural products and manufactured goods to satisfy their immediate needs. Often, however, nomads also participated in long-distance trade networks. Because of their mobility and their familiarity with large regions of central Asia, nomadic peoples were ideally suited to organize and lead the caravans that crossed central Asia and linked settled societies from China to the Mediterranean basin. During the postclassical era and later, Turkish peoples were especially prominent on the caravan routes of central Asia.

Nomadic Society Nomadic society generated two social classes: nobles and commoners. Charismatic leaders won recognition as nobles and thereby acquired the prestige needed to organize clans and tribes into alliances. Normally, nobles did little governing, since clans and tribes looked after their own affairs and resented interference. During times of war, however, nobles wielded absolute authority over their forces, and they dealt swiftly and summarily with those who did not obey orders.

The nobility was a fluid class. Leaders passed noble status along to their heirs, but the heirs could lose their status if they did not continue to provide appropriate leadership for their clans and tribes. Over the course of a few generations, nobles could return to the status of commoners who tended their own herds and followed new leaders. Meanwhile, commoners could win recognition as nobles by outstanding conduct, particularly by courageous behavior during war. Then, if they were clever diplomats, they could arrange alliances between clans and tribes and gain enough support to displace established leaders.

Gender Relations Adult males dominated nomadic pastoral societies, but women enjoyed much higher status than their counterparts in settled agricultural societies. In most nomadic pastoral societies, able-bodied men were frequently away from their herds on hunting expeditions or military campaigns. Thus women were primarily responsible for tending to the animals. Nomadic women were excellent horse riders and skilled archers: indeed, they sometimes fought alongside men in war. Because of their crucial economic roles, women wielded considerable influence in nomadic pastoral societies—sometimes as advisors with strong voices in family or clan matters and occasionally as regents or rulers in their own right.

sources from the past

William of Rubruck on Gender Relations among the Mongols

From 1253 to 1255 the French Franciscan missionary William of Rubruck traveled extensively in the recently established Mongol empire in hopes of converting the Mongols to Christianity. He was unsuccessful in his principal aim, but he met all the leading Mongol figures of the day, including the Great Khan Möngke. After his return to France, William composed a long account of his journey with descriptions of life on the steppes.

The married women make themselves very fine wagons. . . . One rich [Mongol] or Tartar has easily a hundred or two hundred such wagons with chests. Baatu [a prominent Mongol general and grandson of Chinggis Khan] has twenty-six wives, each of whom has a large dwelling, not counting the other, smaller ones placed behind the large one, which are chambers, as it were, where the maids live: to each of these dwellings belong a good two hundred wagons. . . .

One woman will drive twenty or thirty wagons, since the terrain is level. The ox- or camel-wagons are lashed together in sequence, and the woman will sit at the front driving the ox, which all the rest follow at the same pace. . . .

It is the women's task to drive the wagons, to load the dwellings on them and to unload again, to milk the cows, to make butter and *grut* [a kind of cheese], and to dress the skins and stitch them together, which they do with a thread made from sinew. They divide the sinew into tiny strands, and then twist them into a single long thread. In addition they stitch shoes, socks and other garments. They never wash clothes, for they claim that this makes God angry and that if they were hung out to dry it would thunder: in fact, they thrash anyone doing laundry and confiscate it. (They are extraordinarily afraid of thunder. In that event they turn out of their dwellings all strangers, and wrap themselves up in black felt, in which they hide until it has passed.) They never wash dishes either, but instead, when the meat is cooked, rinse the bowl in which they are to put it with boiling broth from the cauldron and then pour it back into the cauldron. In addition [the women] make the felt and cover the dwellings.

The men make bows and arrows, manufacture stirrups and bits, fashion saddles, construct the dwellings and wagons, tend the horses and milk the mares, churn the [*kumiss*] (that is, the mare's milk), produce the skins in which it is stored, and tend and load the camels. Both sexes tend the sheep and goats, and they are milked on some occasions by the men, on others by the women. The skins are dressed with curdled ewe's milk, thickened and salted.

For Further Reflection

- Why did women play such prominent social and economic roles in nomadic pastoral societies?

Source: William of Rubruck. *The Mission of Friar William of Rubruck.* Trans. by Peter Jackson. Ed. by Peter Jackson with David Morgan. London: Hakluyt Society, 1990, pp. 74, 90–91.

Nomadic Religion The earliest religion of the Turkish peoples revolved around shamans—religious specialists who possessed supernatural powers, communicated with the gods and nature spirits, invoked divine aid on behalf of their communities, and informed their companions of their gods' will. Yet many Turkish peoples became attracted to the religious and cultural traditions they encountered when trading with peoples of settled societies. They did not abandon their inherited beliefs or their shamans, but by the sixth century C.E. many Turks had converted to Buddhism, Nestorian Christianity, or Manichaeism. Partly because of their newly adopted religious and cultural traditions and partly because of their prominence in Eurasian trade networks, Turkish peoples also developed a written script.

Turkish Conversion to Islam Over the longer term, most Turks converted to Islam. The earliest converts were Turkish nomads captured in border raids by forces of the Abbasid caliphate in the early ninth century and integrated into the caliphate's armies as slave soldiers. The first large-scale conversion came in the late tenth century, when a Turkish ruling clan known as the Saljuqs turned to Islam and migrated to Iran in hopes of improving their fortunes through alliance with Abbasid authorities and service to the caliphate. Between the tenth and the fourteenth centuries, most Turkish clans on the steppes of central Asia also adopted Islam, and they carried the new religion with them when they expanded their political and military influence to new regions.

Military Organization That expansion took place when nomadic leaders organized vast confederations of peoples all subject, at least nominally, to a *khan* ("ruler"). In fact, khans rarely ruled directly but, rather, through the leaders of allied tribes. Yet when organized on a large scale, nomadic peoples wielded enormous military power, mostly because of their outstanding cavalry forces. Nomadic warriors learned to ride horses as children, and they had su-

thinking about TRADITIONS

Social Organization on the Steppes
Nomadic pastoral peoples organized their societies along lines very different from their counterparts in settled agricultural societies. To what extent did the natural environment and the demands of a pastoral economy influence social organization on the Eurasian steppe lands?

perior equestrian skills. Their arrows flew with deadly accuracy even when launched from the backs of galloping horses. Moreover, units of warriors coordinated their movements to outmaneuver and overwhelm their opponents.

Few armies were able to resist the mobility and discipline of well-organized nomadic warriors. When they found themselves at a disadvantage, they often were able to beat a hasty retreat and escape from their less speedy adversaries. With that military background, several groups of Turkish nomads began in the tenth century C.E. to seize the wealth of settled societies and build imperial states in the regions surrounding central Asia.

Turkish Empires in Persia, Anatolia, and India

Saljuq Turks and the Abbasid Empire Turkish peoples entered Persia, Anatolia, and India at different times and for different purposes. They approached Abbasid Persia much as Germanic peoples had earlier approached the Roman empire. From about the mid-eighth to the mid-tenth century, Turkish peoples lived mostly on the borders of the Abbasid realm, which offered abundant opportunities for trade. By the mid- to late tenth century, large numbers of Saljuq Turks served in Abbasid armies and lived in the Abbasid realm itself. By the mid-eleventh century the Saljuqs overshadowed the Abbasid caliphs. Indeed, in 1055 the caliph recognized the Saljuq leader Tughril Beg as *sultan* ("chieftain" or "ruler"). Tughril first consolidated his hold on the Abbasid capital at Baghdad, then he and his successors extended Turkish rule to Syria, Palestine, and other parts of the realm. For the last two centuries of the Abbasid state, the caliphs served as figureheads of authority while actual governance lay in the hands of the Turkish sultans.

Saljuq Turks and the Byzantine Empire While some Turkish peoples established themselves in Abbasid Persia, others turned their attention to the rich land of Anatolia, breadbasket of the Byzantine empire. Led by the Saljuqs, Turkish peoples began migrating into Anatolia in large numbers in the early eleventh century. In 1071, Saljuq forces inflicted a devastating defeat on the Byzantine army at Manzikert in eastern Anatolia and even took the Byzantine emperor captive. Following that victory, Saljuqs and other

A wall painting from a cave at Dunhuang, a major oasis on the silk roads, depicts a band of sword-wielding thieves (left) holding up a party of Turkish merchants (right). According to convention, the artist represented the Turks with pale skins, long noses, and deep-set eyes.

Turkish groups entered Anatolia almost at will. The peasants of Anatolia, who mostly resented their Byzantine overlords, often looked upon the Saljuqs as liberators rather than conquerors.

The migrants thoroughly transformed Anatolia. Turkish groups displaced Byzantine authorities and set up their own political and social institutions. They levied taxes on the Byzantine church, restricted its activities, and sometimes confiscated church property. Meanwhile, they welcomed converts to Islam and made political, social, and economic opportunities available to them. By 1453, when Ottoman Turks captured the Byzantine capital at Constantinople, Byzantine and Christian Anatolia had become largely a Turkish and Islamic land.

A carved statuette depicts a Turkish sultan of the thirteenth century, perhaps Tughril II or Tughril III, while at prayer.

Ghaznavid Turks and the Sultanate of Delhi While the Saljuqs spearheaded Turkish migrations in Abbasid Persia and Byzantine Anatolia, Mahmud of Ghazni led the Turkish Ghaznavids of Afghanistan in raids on lucrative sites in northern India. When the Ghaznavids began their campaigns in the early eleventh century, their principal goal was plunder. Gradually, though, they became more interested in permanent rule. They asserted their authority first over the Punjab and then over Gujarat and Bengal. By the thirteenth century, the Turkish sultanate of Delhi claimed authority over all of northern India. Several of the Delhi sultans conceived plans to conquer southern India and extend Muslim rule there, but none was able to realize those ambitions. The sultans faced constant challenges from Hindu princes in neighboring lands, and they periodically had to defend their northern frontiers from new Turkish or Mongol invaders. They maintained an enormous army with a large elephant corps, but those forces enabled them to hold on to their territories rather than to expand their empire.

Turkish rule had great social and cultural implications in India, as it did in Anatolia. Mahmud of Ghazni was a zealous foe of Buddhism and Hinduism alike, and he launched frequent raids on shrines, temples, and monasteries. His forces stripped Buddhist and Hindu establishments of their wealth, destroyed their buildings, and often slaughtered their residents and attendants as well. As Turkish invaders repressed Buddhism and Hinduism, they encouraged conversion to Islam and enabled their faith to establish a secure presence in northern India.

Though undertaken by different groups, for different reasons, and by different means, the Turkish conquests of Persia, Anatolia, and India represented part of a larger expansive movement by nomadic peoples. In all three cases, the formidable military prowess of Turkish peoples enabled them to move beyond the steppe lands of central Asia and dominate settled societies. By the thirteenth century, the influence of nomadic peoples was greater than ever before in Eurasian history. Yet the Turkish conquests represented only a prelude to an astonishing round of empire building launched by the Mongols during the thirteenth and fourteenth centuries.

THE MONGOL EMPIRES

For most of history the nomadic Mongols lived on the high steppe lands of eastern central Asia. Like other nomadic peoples, they displayed deep loyalty to kin groups organized into families, clans, and tribes. They frequently allied with Turkish peoples who built empires on the steppes, but they rarely played a leading role in the organization of states before the thirteenth century. Strong loyalties to kinship groups made it difficult for the Mongols to organize a stable society on a large scale. During the early thirteenth century, however, Chinggis Khan (sometimes spelled "Genghis Khan") forged the various Mongol tribes into a powerful alliance that built the largest empire the world has ever seen. Although the vast Mongol realm soon dissolved into a series of smaller empires—most of which disappeared within a century—the Mongols' imperial venture brought the societies of Eurasia into closer contact than ever before.

Chinggis Khan and the Making of the Mongol Empire

The unifier of the Mongols was Temüjin, born about 1167 into a noble family. His father was a prominent warrior who forged an alliance between several Mongol clans and seemed likely to become a powerful leader. When Temüjin was about ten years old, however, rivals poisoned his father and destroyed the alliance. Abandoned by his father's allies, Temüjin led a precarious existence for some years. He lived in poverty, since rivals seized the family's animals, and several times eluded enemies seeking to eliminate him as a potential threat to their own ambitions. A rival once captured him and imprisoned him in a wooden cage, but Temüjin made a daring midnight escape and regained his freedom.

Chinggis Khan's Rise to Power During the late twelfth century, Temüjin made an alliance with a prominent Mongol clan leader. He also mastered the art of steppe diplomacy, which called for displays of personal courage in battle, combined with intense loyalty to allies—as well as

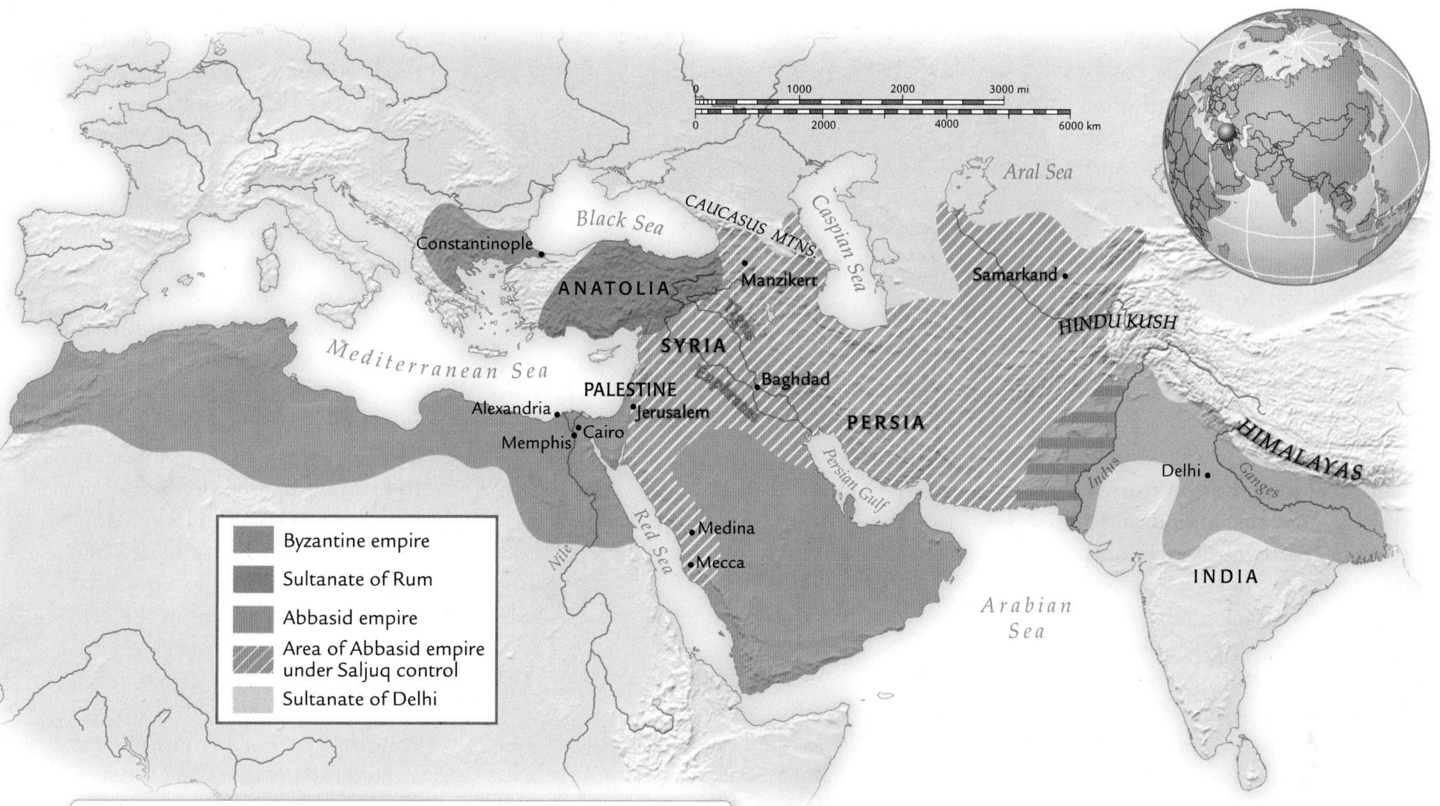

MAP 17.1
Turkish empires and their neighbors, ca. 1210 C.E.
After about 1000 C.E., nomadic Turkish peoples conquered and ruled settled agricultural societies in several regions of Eurasia and north Africa.

How were Turkish peoples able to venture so far from their central Asian homeland?

a willingness to betray allies or superiors to improve one's position—and the ability to entice previously unaffiliated tribes into cooperative relationships. Temüjin gradually strengthened his position, sometimes by forging useful alliances, often by conquering rival contenders for power, and occasionally by turning suddenly against a troublesome ally. He eventually brought all the Mongol tribes into a single confederation, and in 1206 an assembly of Mongol leaders recognized Temüjin's supremacy by proclaiming him Chinggis Khan ("universal ruler").

Mongol Political Organization Chinggis Khan's policies greatly strengthened the Mongol people. Earlier nomadic state builders had ruled largely through the leaders of allied tribes. Because of his personal experiences, however, Chinggis Khan mistrusted the Mongols' tribal organization. He broke up the tribes and forced men of fighting age to join new military units with no tribal affiliations. He chose high military and political officials not on the basis of kinship or tribal status but, rather, because of their talents or their loyalty to him. Chinggis Khan spent most of his life on horseback and did not establish a proper capital, but his successors built a sumptuous capital at Karakorum—present-day Har Horin, located about 300 kilometers (186 miles) west of the modern Mongolian capital of Ulaanbaatar. As command center of a growing empire, Karakorum symbolized a source of Mongol authority superior to the clan or the tribe.

The most important institution of the Mongol state was the army, which magnified the power of the small population. In the thirteenth century the Mongol population stood at about one million people—less than 1 percent of China's numbers. During Chinggis Khan's life, his army numbered only 100,000 to 125,000 Mongols, although allied peoples also contributed forces. How was it possible for so few people to conquer the better part of Eurasia?

Mongol Arms Like earlier nomadic armies, Mongol forces relied on outstanding equestrian skills. Mongols grew up riding horses, and they honed their skills by hunting and playing competitive games on horseback. Their bows, short enough for archers to use while riding, were also stiff, firing arrows that could fell enemies at 200 meters (656 feet). Mongol horsemen were among the most mobile forces of the premodern world, sometimes traveling more than 100 kilometers (62 miles) per day to surprise an enemy. Furthermore, the Mongols understood the psychological dimensions of warfare and used them to their advantage. If enemies surrendered without resistance, the Mongols usually spared their lives, and they provided generous treatment for artisans, crafts workers, and those with military skills. In the event of resistance, however, the Mongols ruthlessly slaughtered whole populations, sparing only a few, whom they sometimes drove before their armies as human shields during future conflicts.

Once he had united the Mongols, Chinggis Khan turned his army and his attention to other parts of central Asia and particularly to nearby settled societies. He attacked the various Turkish peoples ruling in Tibet, northern China, Persia, and the central Asian steppes. His conquests in central Asia were important because they protected him against the possibility that other nomadic leaders might challenge his rule. But the Mongol campaigns in China and Persia had especially far-reaching consequences.

This painting by a Chinese artist depicts Chinggis Khan at about age sixty. Though most of his conquests were behind him, Chinggis Khan's focus and determination are readily apparent in this portrait.

Mongol Conquest of Northern China Chinggis Khan himself extended Mongol rule to northern China, dominated since 1127 C.E. by the nomadic Jurchen people, while the Song dynasty continued to rule in southern China. The conquest of China began in 1211 C.E. when Mongol raiding parties invaded the Jurchen realm. Raids quickly became more frequent and intense, and soon they developed into a campaign of conquest. By 1215 the Mongols had captured the Jurchen capital near modern Beijing, which under the new name of Khanbaliq ("city of the khan") served also as the Mongol capital in China. Fighting between Mongols and Jurchen continued until 1234, but by 1220 the Mongols had largely established control over northern China.

Mongol Conquest of Persia While part of his army consolidated the Mongol hold on northern China, Chinggis Khan led another force to Afghanistan and Persia, ruled at that time by a successor to the Saljuqs known as the Khwarazm shah. In 1218 Chinggis Khan sought to open trade and diplomatic relations with the Khwarazm shah. The shah despised the Mongols, however, and he ordered his officials to murder Chinggis Khan's envoys and the merchants accompanying them. The following year Chinggis Khan took his army west to seek revenge. Mongol forces pursued the Khwarazm shah to an island in the Caspian Sea where he died. Meanwhile, they shattered the shah's army and seized control of his realm.

To forestall any possibility that the shah's state might survive and constitute a challenge to his own empire, Chinggis Khan wreaked destruction on the conquered land. The Mongols ravaged one city after another, demolishing buildings and massacring hundreds of thousands of people. Some cities never recovered. The Mongols also destroyed the delicate *qanat* irrigation systems that sustained agriculture in the arid region, resulting in severely reduced agricultural production. For centuries after the Mongol conquest, Persian chroniclers cursed the invaders and the devastation they visited upon the land.

By the time of his death in 1227, Chinggis Khan had laid the foundation of a vast and mighty empire. He had united the Mongols, established Mongol supremacy in central Asia, and extended Mongol control to northern China in the east and Persia in the west. Chinggis Khan was a conqueror, however, not an adminis-

A Persian manuscript illustration depicts Chinggis Khan and his cavalry in hot pursuit of retreating forces. On his road to power, Chinggis Khan depended not only on military might but also on strategic alliances with tribes and new political structures organized around loyalty and talent rather than tribal or kinship ties.

sources from the past

Marco Polo on Mongol Military Tactics

The Venetian Marco Polo traveled extensively through central Asia and China in the late thirteenth century, when Mongol empires dominated Asia. His book of travel writings is an especially valuable source of information about the Mongol age. Among other things, he described the Mongol way of making war.

Their arms are bows and arrows, sword and mace; but above all the bow, for they are capital archers, indeed the best that are known. . . .

When a Mongol prince goes forth to war, he takes with him, say, 100,000 men. Well, he appoints an officer to every ten men, one to every hundred, one to every thousand, and one to every ten thousand, so that his own orders have to be given to ten persons only, and each of these ten persons has to pass the orders only to another ten, and so on, no one having to give orders to more than ten. And every one in turn is responsible only to the officer immediately over him; and the discipline and order that comes of this method is marvellous, for they are a people very obedient to their chiefs. . . .

When they are going on a distant expedition they take no gear with them except two leather bottles for milk, a little earthenware pot to cook their meat in, and a little tent to shelter them from rain. And in case of great urgency they will ride ten days on end without lighting a fire or taking a meal. On such an occasion they will sustain themselves on the blood of their horses, opening a vein and letting the blood jet into their mouths, drinking till they have had enough, and then staunching it. . . .

When they come to an engagement with the enemy, they will gain the victory in this fashion. They never let themselves get into a regular medley, but keep perpetually riding round and shooting into the enemy. And as they do not count it any shame to run away in battle, they will sometimes pretend to do so, and in running away they turn in the saddle and shoot hard and strong at the foe, and in this way make great havoc. Their horses are trained so perfectly that they will double hither and thither, just like a dog, in a way that is quite astonishing. Thus they fight to as good purpose in running away as if they stood and faced the enemy because of the vast volleys of arrows that they shoot in this way, turning round upon their pursuers, who are fancying that they have won the battle. But when the Mongols see that they have killed and wounded a good many horses and men, they wheel round bodily and return to the charge in perfect order and with loud cries, and in a very short time the enemy are routed. In truth they are stout and valiant soldiers, and inured to war. And you perceive that it is just when the enemy sees them run, and imagines that he has gained the battle, that he has in reality lost it, for the Mongols wheel round in a moment when they judge the right time has come. And after this fashion they have won many a fight.

For Further Reflection

- In what ways do the military practices described by Marco Polo reflect the influence of the steppe environment on the Mongols?

Source: Marco Polo. *The Book of Ser Marco Polo,* 3rd ed. Trans. and ed. by Henry Yule and Henri Cordier. London: John Murray, 1921, pp. 260–63. (Translation slightly modified.)

trator. He ruled the Mongols themselves through his control over the army, but he did not establish a central government for the lands that he conquered. Instead, he assigned Mongol overlords to supervise local administrators and to extract a generous tribute for the Mongols' own uses. Chinggis Khan's heirs continued his conquests, but they also undertook the task of designing a more permanent administration to guide the fortunes of the Mongol empire.

The Mongol Empires after Chinggis Khan

Chinggis Khan's death touched off a struggle for power among his sons and grandsons, several of whom had ambitions to succeed the great khan. Eventually, his heirs divided Chinggis Khan's vast realm into four regional empires. The great khans ruled China, the wealthiest of Mongol lands. Descendants of Chaghatai, one of Chinggis Khan's sons, ruled the khanate of Chaghatai in central Asia. Persia fell under the authority of rulers known as the ilkhans, and the khans of the Golden Horde dominated Russia. The great khans were nominally superior to the others, but they were rarely able to enforce their claims to authority. In fact, for as long as the Mongol empires survived, ambition fueled constant tension and occasional conflict among the four khans.

Khubilai Khan The consolidation of Mongol rule in China came during the reign of Khubilai (sometimes spelled Qubilai), one of Chinggis Khan's grandsons. Khubilai was perhaps the most talented of the great conqueror's descendants. He unleashed ruthless attacks against his enemies, but he also took an interest in cultural matters and worked to improve the welfare of his subjects. He actively promoted Buddhism, and he provided support also for Daoists, Muslims, and Christians

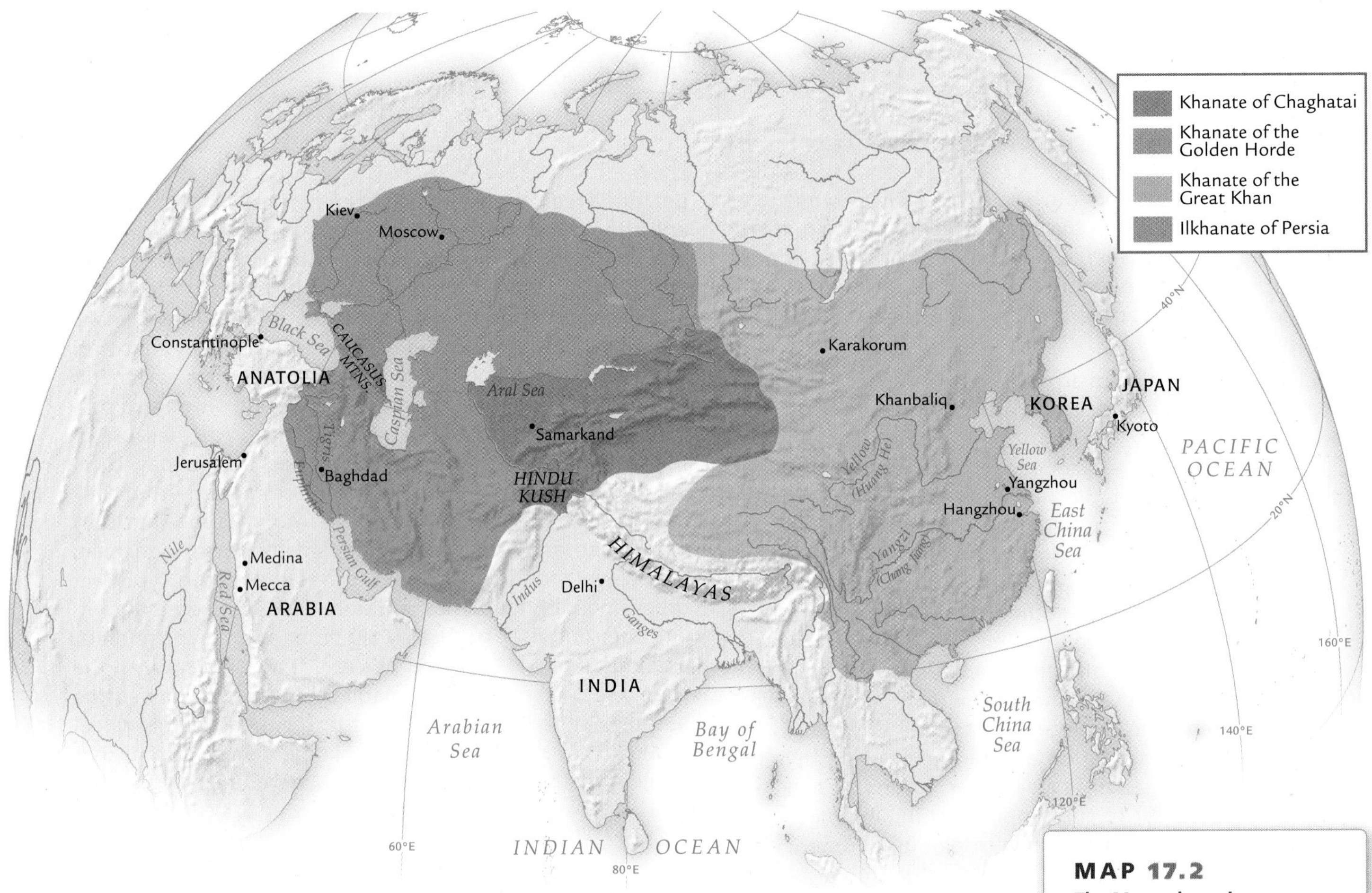

MAP 17.2
The Mongol empires, ca. 1300 C.E.
The Mongol empires stretched from Manchuria and China to Russia and eastern Europe.
In what ways did Mongol empires and Mongol policies facilitate trade, travel, and communication throughout Eurasia?

in his realm. The famous Venetian traveler Marco Polo, who lived almost two decades at Khubilai's court, praised him for his generosity toward the poor and his efforts to build roads. Though named great khan in 1260, Khubilai spent four years fighting off contenders. From 1264 until his death in 1294, Khubilai Khan presided over the Mongol empire at its height.

Mongol Conquest of Southern China Khubilai extended Mongol rule to all of China. From his base at Khanbaliq, he relentlessly attacked the Song dynasty in southern China. The Song capital at Hangzhou fell to Mongol forces in 1276, and within three years Khubilai had eliminated resistance throughout China. In 1279 he proclaimed himself emperor and established the **Yuan** dynasty, which ruled China until its collapse in 1368.

Beyond China, Khubilai had little success as a conqueror. During the 1270s and 1280s, he launched several invasions of Vietnam, Cambodia, and Burma as well as a naval expedition against Java involving five hundred to one thousand ships and twenty thousand troops. But Mongol forces did not adapt well to the humid, tropical jungles of southeast Asia. Pasturelands were inadequate for their horses, and the fearsome Mongol horsemen were unable to cope with the guerrilla tactics employed by the defenders. In 1274 and again in 1281, Khubilai also attempted seaborne invasions of Japan, but on both occasions typhoons thwarted his plans. The storm of 1281 was especially vicious: it destroyed about 4,500 Mongol vessels carrying more than one hundred thousand armed troops—the largest seaborne expedition before World War II. Japanese defenders attributed their continued independence to the *kamikaze* ("divine winds").

The Golden Horde As Khubilai consolidated his hold on east Asia, his cousins and brothers tightened Mongol control on lands to the west. Mongols of the group known as the Golden Horde overran Russia between 1237 and 1241 and then mounted exploratory expeditions into Poland, Hungary, and eastern Germany in 1241 and 1242. Mongols of the Golden Horde prized the steppes north of the Black Sea as prime pastureland for their horses. They maintained

Yuan (yoo-AHN)

The siege of Baghdad in 1258 C.E.: a Persian manuscript illustration depicts Mongol forces camped outside the city walls while residents huddle within. What role did catapults play in sieges like this?

a large army on the steppes from which they mounted raids into Russia. They did not occupy Russia, which they regarded as an unattractive land of forests, but they extracted tribute from the Russian cities and agricultural provinces. The Golden Horde maintained its hegemony in Russia until the mid-fifteenth century, when the princes of Moscow rejected its authority while building a powerful Russian state. By the mid-sixteenth century, Russian conquerors had extended their control to the steppes, but Mongol khans descended from the Golden Horde continued to rule the Crimea until the late eighteenth century.

The Ilkhanate of Persia While the Golden Horde established its authority in Russia, Khubilai's brother Hülegü toppled the Abbasid empire and established the Mongol **ilkhanate** in Persia. In 1258 he captured the Abbasid capital of Baghdad after a brief siege. His troops looted the city, executed the caliph, and massacred more than two hundred thousand residents by Hülegü's own estimate. From Persia, Hülegü's army ventured into Syria, but Muslim forces from Egypt soon expelled them and placed a limit on Mongol expansion to the southwest.

When the Mongols crushed ruling regimes in large settled societies, particularly in China and Persia, they discovered that they needed to become governors as well as conquerors. The Mongols had no experience administering complex societies, where successful governance required talents beyond the equestrian and military skills esteemed on the steppes. They had a difficult time adjusting to their role as administrators. Indeed, they never became entirely comfortable in the role, and most of their conquests fell out of their hands within a century.

Mongol Rule in Persia The Mongols adopted different tactics in the different lands that they ruled. In Persia they made important concessions to local interests. Although Mongols and their allies occupied the highest administrative positions, Persians served as ministers, provincial governors, and state officials at all lower levels. The Mongols basically allowed the Persians to administer the ilkhanate as long as they delivered tax receipts and maintained order.

Over time, the Mongols even assimilated to Persian cultural traditions. The early Mongol rulers of Persia mostly observed their native shamanism, but they tolerated all religions—including Islam, Nestorian Christianity, Buddhism, and Judaism—and they ended the privileges given Muslims during the Abbasid caliphate. Gradually, however, the Mongols themselves gravitated toward Islam. In 1295 Ilkhan Ghazan publicly converted to Islam, and most of the Mongols in Persia followed his example. Ghazan's conversion sparked large-scale massacres of Christians and Jews, and it signaled the return of Islam to a privileged position in Persian society. It also indicated the absorption of the Mongols into Muslim Persian society.

ilkhanate (EEL-kahn-ate)

Mongol Rule in China In China, by contrast, the Mongol overlords stood aloof from their subjects, whom they scorned as mere cultivators. They outlawed intermarriage between Mongols and Chinese and forbade the Chinese from learning the Mongol language. Soon after their conquest some of the victors went so far as to suggest that the Mongols exterminate the Chinese people and convert China itself into pastureland for their horses. Cooler heads eventually prevailed, and the Mongols decided simply to extract as much revenue as possible from their Chinese subjects. In doing so, however, they did not make as much use of native administrative talent as did their counterparts in Persia. Instead, they brought foreign administrators into China and placed them in charge. Along with their nomadic allies, the Mongols' administrative staff included Arabs, Persians, and perhaps even Europeans: Marco Polo may have served as an administrator in the city of Yangzhou during the reign of Khubilai Khan.

The Mongols also resisted assimilation to Chinese cultural traditions. They ended the privileges enjoyed by the Confucian scholars, and they dismantled the Confucian educational and examination system, which had produced untold generations of civil servants for the Chinese bureaucracy. They did not persecute Confucians, but they allowed the Confucian tradition to wither in the absence of official support. Meanwhile, to remain on good terms with subjects of different faiths, the Mongols allowed the construction of churches, temples, and shrines, and they even subsidized some religious establishments. They tolerated all cultural and religious traditions in China, including Confucianism, Daoism, Buddhism, and Christianity. Of Khubilai Khan's four wives, his favorite was Chabi, a Nestorian Christian.

The Mongols and Buddhism For their part the Mongols mostly continued to follow their native shamanist cults, although many of the ruling elite became enchanted with the Lamaist school of Buddhism that developed in Tibet. Lamaist Buddhism held several attractions for the Mongols. It made a prominent place for magic and supernatural powers, and in that respect it resembled the Mongols' shamanism. Moreover, Lamaist Buddhist leaders officially recognized the Mongols as legitimate rulers and went out of their way to court the Mongols' favor. They numbered the Mongols in the ranks of universal Buddhist rulers and even recognized the Mongol khans as incarnations of the Buddha. Thus it is not surprising that the Mongol ruling elites would find Lamaist Buddhism attractive.

The Mongols and Eurasian Integration

In building their vast empire, the Mongols brought tremendous destruction to lands throughout much of the Eurasian landmass. Yet they also sponsored interaction among peoples of different societies and linked Eurasian lands more directly than ever before. Indeed, Mongol rulers positively encouraged travel and communication over long distances. Recognizing the value of regular communications for their vast empire, Chinggis Khan and his successors maintained a courier network that rapidly relayed news, information, and government orders. The network included relay stations with fresh horses and riders so that messages could travel almost nonstop throughout Mongol territories. The Mongols' encouragement of travel and communication facilitated trade, diplomatic travel, missionary efforts, and movements of peoples to new lands.

The Mongols and Trade As a nomadic people dependent on commerce with settled agricultural societies, the Mongols worked to secure trade routes and ensure the safety of merchants passing through their territories. The Mongol khans frequently fought among themselves, but they maintained reasonably good order within their realms and allowed merchants to travel unmolested through their empires. As a result, long-distance travel and trade became much less risky than in earlier times. Merchants increased their commercial investments, and the volume of long-distance trade across central Asia dwarfed that of earlier eras. Lands as distant as China and western Europe became directly linked for the first time because of the ability of individuals to travel across the entire Eurasian landmass.

Diplomatic Missions Like trade, diplomatic communication was essential to the Mongols, and their protection of roads and travelers benefited ambassadors as well as merchants. Chinggis Khan destroyed the Khwarazm shah in Persia because the shah unwisely murdered the Mongol envoys Chinggis Khan dispatched in hopes of opening diplomatic and commercial relations. Throughout the Mongol era the great khans in China, the ilkhans in Persia, and the other khans maintained close communications by means of diplomatic embassies. They also had diplomatic dealings with rulers in Korea, Vietnam, India, western Europe, and other lands as well. Some diplomatic travelers crossed the entire Eurasian landmass. Several European ambassadors traveled to Mongolia and China to deliver messages from authorities seeking to ally with the Mongols against Muslim states in southwest Asia. Diplomats also traveled west: Rabban Sauma, a Nestorian Christian monk

thinking about ENCOUNTERS

Cultural Preferences of the Mongols
While building a massive Eurasian empire, Mongols encountered Muslims, Buddhists, Confucians, and representatives of other cultural traditions as well. Consider their reactions to these various traditions. Why might the Mongols have shown strong interest in some traditions but not others?

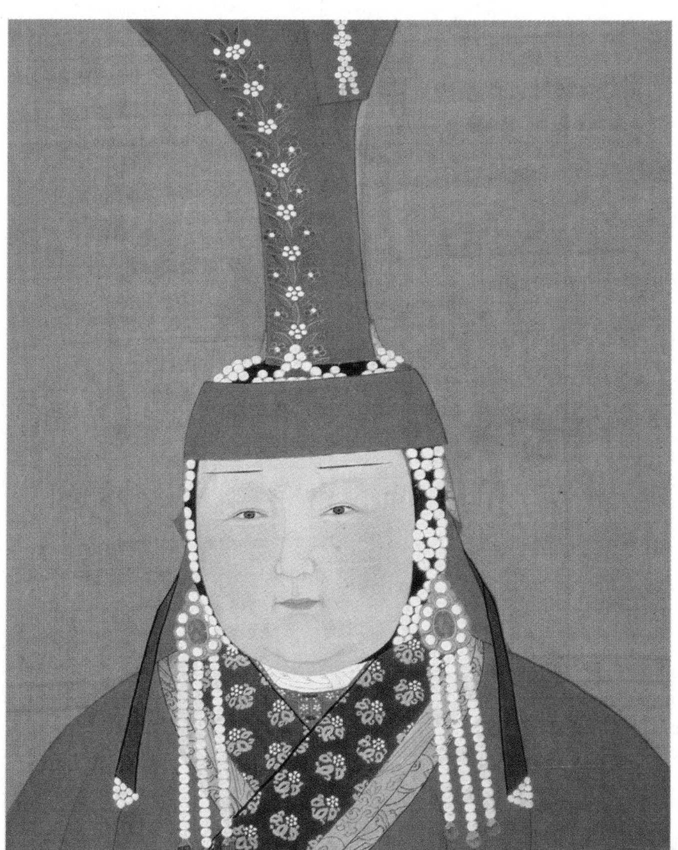

Chabi, a Nestorian Christian and the favorite wife of Khubilai Khan, wearing the distinctive headgear reserved for Mongol women of the ruling class.

born in Khanbaliq, visited Italy and France as a representative of the Persian ilkhan.

Missionary Efforts Like the silk roads in earlier times, Eurasian routes during the era of the Mongol empires served as highways for missionaries as well as merchants and diplomats. Sufi missionaries helped popularize Islam among Turkish peoples in central Asia, while Lamaist Buddhism from Tibet attracted considerable interest among the Mongols. Nestorian Christians, who had long been prominent in oasis communities throughout central Asia, found new opportunities to win converts when they went to China to serve as administrators for Mongol rulers there. Roman Catholic Christians also mounted missionary campaigns in China. (See chapter 21 for further discussion of travel during the Mongol era.)

Resettlement Another Mongol policy that encouraged Eurasian integration was the practice of resettling peoples in new lands. As a nomadic people, the Mongols had limited numbers of skilled artisans and educated individuals, but the more their empire expanded, the more they needed the services of specialized crafts workers and literate administrators. Mongol overlords recruited the talent they needed largely from the ranks of their allies and the peoples they conquered, and they often moved people far from their homelands to sites where they could best make use of their services. Among the most important of the Mongols' allies were the Uighur Turks, who lived mostly in oasis cities along the silk roads. The Uighurs were literate and often highly educated, and they provided not only many of the clerks, secretaries, and administrators who ran the Mongol empires but also units of soldiers who bolstered Mongol garrisons. Arab and Persian Muslims were also prominent among those who administered the Mongols' affairs far from their homelands.

Conquered peoples also supplied the Mongols with talent. When they overcame a city, Mongol forces routinely surveyed the captured population, separated out those with specialized skills, and sent them to the capital at Karakorum or some other place where there was demand for their services. From the ranks of conquered peoples came soldiers, bodyguards, administrators, secretaries, translators, physicians, armor makers, metalsmiths, miners, carpenters, masons, textile workers, musicians, and jewelers. After the 1230s the Mongols often took censuses of lands they conquered, partly to levy taxes and conscript military forces and partly to locate talented individuals. The Parisian goldsmith Guillaume Boucher was only one among thousands of foreign-born individuals who became permanent residents of the Mongol capital at Karakorum because of their special talents. Like their protection of trade and diplomacy, the Mongols' policy of resettling allies and conquered peoples promoted Eurasian integration by increasing communication and exchange between peoples of different societies.

Decline of the Mongols in Persia and China

Collapse of the Ilkhanate Soon after the long and prosperous reign of Khubilai Khan, the Mongols encountered serious difficulties governing Persia and China. In Persia excessive spending strained the treasury, and overexploitation of the peasantry led to reduced revenues. In the early 1290s the ilkhan tried to resolve his financial difficulties by introducing paper money and ordering all subjects to accept it for payment of all debts. The purpose of that measure was to drive precious metals into the hands of the government, but the policy was a miserable failure: rather than accept paper that they regarded as worthless, merchants simply closed their shops. Commerce ground to a halt until the ilkhan rescinded his order. Meanwhile, factional struggles plagued the Mongol leadership. The regime went into steep decline after the death of Ilkhan Ghazan in 1304. When the last of the Mongol rulers died without an heir in 1335, the ilkhanate itself simply collapsed. Government in Persia devolved to local levels until late in the fourteenth century when Turkish peoples reintroduced effective central government.

Decline of the Yuan Dynasty Mongol decline in China was a more complicated affair. As in Persia, it had an economic dimension. The Mongols continued to use the paper money that the Chinese had introduced during the Tang and Song dynasties, but they did not maintain adequate reserves of the bullion that backed up paper notes. The general population soon lost confidence in paper money, and prices rose sharply as a reflection of its diminished value. As in Persia, too, factions and infighting hastened Mongol decline in China. As the richest of the Mongol empires, China attracted the attention of ambitious warriors. Beginning in the 1320s power struggles, imperial assassinations, and civil war convulsed the Mongol regime in China.

Bubonic Plague Apart from financial difficulties and factional divisions, the Mongol rulers of China also faced an onslaught of epidemic disease. By facilitating trade and communications throughout Eurasia, the Mongols unwittingly expedited the spread of bubonic plague (discussed in chapter 21). During the 1330s plague erupted in southwestern China. From there it spread throughout China and central Asia, and by the late 1340s it had reached southwest Asia and Europe, where it became known as the Black Death. Bubonic plague sometimes killed half or more of an exposed population, particularly during the furious initial years of the epidemic, and it seriously disrupted economies and societies throughout much of Eurasia. In China depopulation and labor shortages that followed on the heels of epidemic plague weakened the Mongol regime. (Plague would also have caused serious problems for the Mongol rulers of Persia had the ilkhanate not collapsed before its arrival.)

The Mongols also faced a rebellious subject population in China. The Mongols stood apart from their Chinese subjects, who returned the contempt of their conquerors. Beginning in the 1340s southern China became a hotbed of peasant rebellion and banditry, which the Mongols could not control. In 1368 rebel forces captured Khanbaliq, and the Mongols departed China en masse and returned to the steppes.

Surviving Mongol Khanates Despite the collapse of the Mongol regimes in Persia and China, Mongol states did not completely disappear. The khanate of Chaghatai continued to prevail in central Asia, and Mongols posed a threat to the northwestern borders of China until the eighteenth century. Meanwhile, the khanate of the Golden Horde continued to dominate the Caucasus and the steppe lands north of the Black Sea and the Caspian Sea until the mid-sixteenth century when a resurgent Russian state brought the Golden Horde down. Like Mongols in China, however, Mongols in Russia continued to threaten until the eighteenth century, and Mongols who had settled in the Crimean peninsula retained their identity until Josef Stalin forcibly moved them to other parts of the Soviet Union in the mid-twentieth century.

AFTER THE MONGOLS

By no means did the decline of the Mongols signal the end of nomadic peoples' influence in Eurasia. As Mongol strength waned, Turkish peoples resumed the expansive campaigns that the Mongols had interrupted. During the late fourteenth and early fifteenth centuries, the Turkish conqueror Tamerlane built a central Asian empire rivaling that of Chinggis Khan himself. Although Tamerlane's empire foundered soon after his death, it deeply influenced three surviving Turkish Muslim states—the Mughal empire in India, the Safavid empire in Persia, and the Ottoman empire based in Anatolia—and also embraced much of southwest Asia, southeastern Europe, and north Africa.

Tamerlane the Whirlwind

The Lame Conqueror The rapid collapse of the Mongol states left gaping power vacuums in China and Persia. While the native Ming dynasty filled the vacuum in China, a self-made Turkish conqueror named Timur moved on Persia. Because he walked with a limp, contemporaries referred to him as Timur-i lang—"Timur the Lame," an appellation that made its way into English as Tamerlane.

Born about 1336 near Samarkand, Tamerlane took Chinggis Khan as his model. Like Chinggis Khan, Tamerlane came from a family of the minor nobility and had to make his own way to power. Like Chinggis Khan, too, he was a charismatic leader and a courageous warrior, and he attracted a band of loyal followers. During the 1360s he eliminated rivals to power, either by persuading them to join him as allies or by defeating their armies on the battlefield, and he won recognition as leader of his own tribe. By 1370 he had extended his authority throughout the khanate of Chaghatai and begun to build a magnificent imperial capital in Samarkand.

Tamerlane's Conquests For the rest of his life, Tamerlane led his armies on campaigns of conquest. He turned first to the region between Persia and Afghanistan, and he took special care to establish his authority in the rich cities so that he could levy taxes on trade and agricultural production. Next he attacked the Golden Horde in the Caucasus region and Russia, and by the mid-1390s he had severely weakened it. During the last years of the century, he invaded India and subjected Delhi to a ferocious sack: contemporary chroniclers reported, with some exaggeration, that for a period of two months after the attack not even birds visited the devastated city. Later, Tamerlane campaigned along the Ganges, although he never attempted to incorporate India into his empire. He opened the new century with campaigns in southwest Asia and Anatolia. In 1404 he began preparations for an invasion of China, and he was leading his army east when he fell ill and died in 1405.

Like his model Chinggis Khan, Tamerlane was a conqueror, not a governor. He spent almost his entire adult life planning and fighting military campaigns: he even had himself

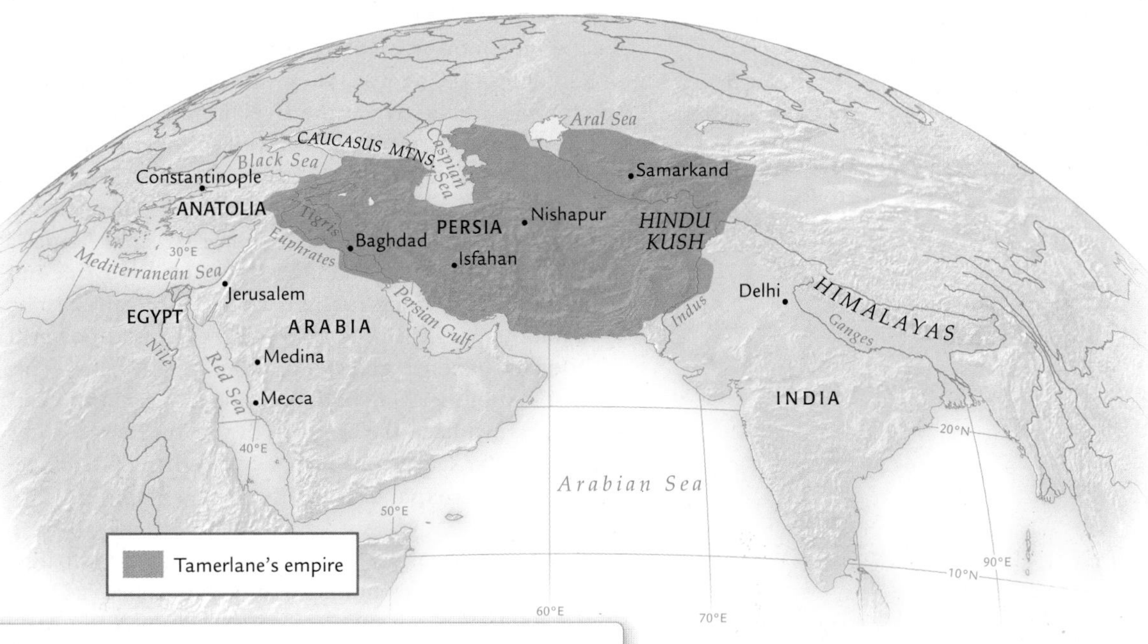

MAP 17.3

Tamerlane's empire, ca. 1405 C.E.

Notice the similarity between Tamerlane's empire and the ilkhanate of Persia outlined in Map 17.2.

To what extent do you think the cities and the administrative infrastructure of the region facilitated Tamerlane's efforts to control his empire?

Spoils from Tamerlane's campaigns and raids enriched the conqueror's capital at Samarkand. They financed, among other buildings, the magnificent tomb where Tamerlane's remains still rest.

carried around on a litter during his final illness, as he prepared to invade China. He did not create an imperial administration but, rather, ruled through tribal leaders who were his allies. He appointed overlords in the territories he conquered, but they relied on existing bureaucratic structures and simply received taxes and tributes on his behalf.

Tamerlane's Heirs Given its loose organization, it is not surprising that Tamerlane's empire experienced stresses and strains after the conqueror's death. Tamerlane's sons and grandsons engaged in a long series of bitter conflicts that resulted in the contraction of his empire and its division into four main regions. For a century after Tamerlane's death, however, they maintained control over the region from Persia to Afghanistan. When the last vestiges of Tamerlane's imperial creation disappeared, in the early sixteenth century, the Mughal, Safavid, and Ottoman empires that replaced it all clearly reflected the Turkish Muslim legacy of the lame conqueror.

The Foundation of the Ottoman Empire

Chapter 27 will discuss the Mughal empire in India and the **Safavid** empire in Persia, both of which emerged during the early sixteenth century as Tamerlane's empire finally dissolved. The early stages of Ottoman expansion predated Tamerlane, however, and the foundation of the Ottoman empire throws additional light on the influence of nomadic peoples during the period 1000 to 1500 C.E.

Osman After the Mongol conquest of Persia, large numbers of nomadic Turks migrated from central Asia to the ilkhanate and beyond to the territories in Anatolia that the Saljuq Turks had seized from the Byzantine empire. There they followed

Safavid (SAH-fah-vihd)

Although besieged by Ottoman forces, Constantinople received supplies from the sea for almost two months before Ottomans destroyed the city walls and completed their conquest of the Byzantine empire.

charismatic leaders who organized further campaigns of conquest. Among those leaders was Osman, who during the late thirteenth and early fourteenth centuries carved a small state for himself in northwestern Anatolia. In 1299 Osman declared independence from the Saljuq sultan and launched a campaign to build a state at the expense of the Byzantine empire. After every successful operation, Osman attracted more and more followers, who came to be known as Osmanlis or Ottomans.

Ottoman Conquests During the 1350s the Ottomans gained a considerable advantage over their Turkish rivals when they established a foothold across the Dardanelles at Gallipoli on the Balkan peninsula. The Ottomans quickly moved to expand the boundaries of their Balkan holdings. Byzantine forces resisted Ottoman incursions, but because of political fragmentation, ineffective government, and exploitation of the peasantry, the Ottomans found abundant local support. By the 1380s the Ottomans had become by far the most powerful people on the Balkan peninsula, and by the end of the century they were poised to capture Constantinople and take over the Byzantine empire.

Tamerlane temporarily delayed Ottoman expansion in the Byzantine realm. In 1402 Tamerlane's forces crushed the Ottoman army, captured the sultan, and subjected the Ottoman state to the conqueror's authority. After Tamerlane's death, Ottoman leaders had to reestablish their rule in their own realm. This undertaking involved both the repression of ambitious local princes who sought to build power bases at Ottoman expense and the defense of Ottoman territories against Byzantine, Venetian, and other Christian forces that sought to turn back the advance of the Turkish Muslims. By the 1440s the Ottomans had recovered their balance and begun again to expand in the Byzantine empire.

The Capture of Constantinople The campaign culminated in 1453 when Sultan Mehmed II, known as Mehmed the Conqueror, captured the Byzantine capital of Constantinople. After subjecting it to a sack, he made the city his own capital under the Turkish name of Istanbul. With Istanbul as a base, the Ottomans quickly absorbed the remainder of the Byzantine empire. By 1480 they controlled all of Greece and the Balkan region. They continued to expand throughout most of the sixteenth century as well, extending their rule to southwest Asia, southeastern Europe, Egypt, and north Africa. Once again, then, a nomadic people asserted control over a long-settled society and quickly built a vast empire.

inperspective

During the half millennium from 1000 to 1500 C.E., nomadic peoples of central Asia played a larger role than ever before in world history. As early as the second millennium B.C.E., they had periodically threatened states from China to the eastern Mediterranean region, and from classical times they had traded regularly and actively with peoples of settled societies. From 1000 to 1500 their relations with neighboring peoples changed, as they dominated affairs in most of Eurasia through their conquests and their construction of vast transregional empires. Turkish peoples built the most durable of the nomadic empires, but the spectacular conquests of the Mongols most clearly demonstrated the potential of nomadic peoples to project their formidable military power to settled agricultural societies. By establishing connections that spanned the Eurasian landmass, the nomadic empires laid the foundation for increasing communication, exchange, and interaction among peoples of different societies and thereby fostered the integration of the eastern hemisphere. The age of nomadic empires from 1000 to 1500 C.E. foreshadowed the integrated world of modern times. ●

CHRONOLOGY	
1055	Tughril Beg named sultan
1071	Battle of Manzikert
1206–1227	Reign of Chinggis Khan
1211–1234	Mongol conquest of northern China
1219–1221	Mongol conquest of Persia
1237–1241	Mongol conquest of Russia
1258	Mongol capture of Baghdad
1264–1279	Mongol conquest of southern China
1264–1294	Reign of Khubilai Khan
1279–1368	Yuan dynasty
1295	Conversion of Ilkhan Ghazan to Islam
1336–1405	Life of Tamerlane
1453	Ottoman capture of Constantinople

For Further Reading

S. A. M. Adshead. *Central Asia in World History.* New York, 1993. A provocative essay on central Asia and its place in the larger world.

Thomas T. Allsen. *Culture and Conquest in Mongol Eurasia.* Cambridge, 2001. Carefully studies the cultural exchanges sponsored by Mongol rulers, particularly those passing between China and Iran.

———. *Mongol Imperialism: The Policies of the Grand Qan Möngke in China, Russia, and the Islamic Lands, 1251–1259.* Berkeley, 1987. Scholarly analysis of Mongol empire building by Chinggis Khan's successors.

Thomas J. Barfield. *The Nomadic Alternative.* Englewood Cliffs, N.J., 1993. A sensitive study of nomadic societies in Africa and Eurasia by a leading anthropologist.

———. *The Perilous Frontier: Nomadic Empires and China.* Cambridge, Mass., 1989. Scholarly examination of the relationship between nomadic empires and Chinese society.

Vladimir N. Basilov, ed. *Nomads of Eurasia.* Trans. by M. F. Zirin. Los Angeles, 1989. Lavishly illustrated volume that presents translations of essays by Russian scholars on nomadic societies.

Carter Vaughn Findley. *The Turks in World History.* New York, 2005. A welcome volume that lucidly outlines the history of Turkish peoples and discusses relations between Turks and neighboring peoples.

Charles J. Halperin. *Russia and the Golden Horde: The Mongol Impact on Medieval Russian History.* Bloomington, 1985. An insightful study of the Golden Horde and its influence on Russian society.

Halil Inalcik. *The Ottoman Empire: The Classical Age, 1300–1600.* Trans. by N. Itzkowitz and C. Imber. New York, 1973. The best short introduction to early Ottoman history.

Peter Jackson. *The Mongols and the West, 1221–1410.* London, 2005. Offers a comprehensive review of military, diplomatic, commercial, and cultural relations between Mongol and European societies.

Paul Kahn, ed. *The Secret History of the Mongols: The Origin of Chingis Khan.* Adapted from the translation of F. W. Cleaves. San Francisco, 1984. A translation of the Mongols' history of their own society, adapted for modern readers.

Adam T. Kessler. *Empires beyond the Great Wall: The Heritage of Genghis Khan.* Los Angeles, 1993. Well-illustrated survey of nomadic states in central Asia from the Xiongnu to the Mongols.

Beatrice Forbes Manz. *The Rise and Rule of Tamerlane.* Cambridge, 1989. Scholarly analysis of Tamerlane's career and his empire.

David Morgan. *Medieval Persia, 1040–1797.* London, 1988. A brief and insightful survey concentrating on the eras of Turkish and Mongol dominance in Persia.

———. *The Mongols.* Oxford, 1986. Lucid and witty study: the best short work on the Mongols.

Morris Rossabi. *Khubilai Khan: His Life and Times.* Berkeley, 1988. Excellent scholarly study of the greatest of the great khans.

Arthur Waldron. *The Great Wall of China: From History to Myth.* Cambridge, 1989. Examines the role of defensive walls, including the Great Wall, in Chinese efforts to forestall raids by nomadic peoples of central Asia.

States and Societies of Sub-Saharan Africa

chapter 18

A bronze plaque from the kingdom of Benin depicts a local chief flanked by warriors and attendants.

EYEWITNESS:
The Lion Prince of Mali

A remarkable oral tradition preserves the story of the lion prince **Sundiata,** thirteenth-century founder of the Mali empire in west Africa. Oral traditions include stories, histories, epics, and other accounts transmitted by professional singers and storytellers known in Africa as griots. Until scholars began to collect and publish African oral traditions about the middle of the twentieth century, the story of Sundiata was available only when a griot recited it.

According to the oral tradition, Sundiata's father ruled a small west African kingdom in the northeastern part of what is now Guinea. Despite his royal parentage, Sundiata had a difficult childhood, since a congenitally defective leg left him partially crippled. When the old king died, his enemies invaded the kingdom and killed the royal offspring, sparing the child Sundiata because they thought his physical condition would prevent him from posing a threat to their ambitions. But Sundiata overcame his injury, learned to use the bow and arrow, and strengthened himself by hunting in the forest. As Sundiata grew stronger, his enemies began to fear him, and they forced him to seek refuge in a neighboring kingdom. While in exile, Sundiata distinguished himself as a warrior and assembled a powerful cavalry force staffed by loyal followers and allies.

About 1235 Sundiata returned to his homeland and claimed the throne. His cavalry slashed through the countryside, defeating his enemies almost at will. Within a few years he had overcome resistance, established the Mali empire, and consolidated his rule throughout the valley of the Niger River. Although he respected traditional religious beliefs and magical powers, Sundiata was also a Muslim, and he welcomed Muslim merchants from north Africa into his realm. He built a capital city at Niani, which soon became a thriving commercial center. Indeed, as a result of its control of the gold trade—and the political stability provided by Sundiata—the Mali empire became probably the wealthiest land in sub-Saharan Africa. For two centuries after Sundiata's death about 1260, the lion prince's legacy shaped the lives of west African peoples and linked west Africa with north Africa and the Mediterranean basin.

Sundiata (soon-JAH-tuh)

From the classical era forward, peoples from east Asia to the Mediterranean basin established extensive networks of trade and communication. African peoples living south of the Sahara desert participated in the larger economy of the eastern hemisphere, though not so fully as their counterparts in north Africa, who from ancient times were prominent in the trading world of the Mediterranean basin. Geographic conditions help to explain why trade and communication networks did not embrace sub-Saharan Africa as readily as they did other regions: the Sahara desert poses a formidable challenge to overland travelers from the north, the African coastlines offer few good natural harbors, and cataracts complicate travel up the continent's major rivers.

Nevertheless, like their Eurasian and north African counterparts, peoples of sub-Saharan Africa organized productive societies, built powerful states, and participated in large-scale networks of communication and exchange. Internal African processes drove much of that development. Between 1000 and 1500 C.E., in the wake of the Bantu and other migrations (discussed in chapter 3), peoples of sub-Saharan Africa continued to expand the amount of territory under cultivation and to establish agricultural societies. Furthermore, as their population increased, they organized states, developed centers of economic specialization, and carried on interregional trade. Alongside these internal processes, relations with other peoples of the eastern hemisphere also profoundly influenced the development of African societies. From the early centuries C.E. to 1500 and later as well, trade with lands of the Mediterranean and the Indian Ocean basins encouraged African peoples to organize their societies so as to produce commodities desired by consumers throughout much of the eastern hemisphere. This trade promoted urban development, the organization of large states and empires, and the introduction of new food crops and new religious beliefs into sub-Saharan Africa.

EFFECTS OF EARLY AFRICAN MIGRATIONS

By 1000 C.E. Bantu-speaking peoples had settled in most parts of Africa south of the equator, and Kushite, Sudanese, Mande, and other peoples had also established communities in lands far from their original homes. Some African peoples undertook small-scale migrations long thereafter, even into the nineteenth century. By about 1000, however, most of the migrations were complete, and for the next several centuries, African peoples built societies on the foundation of small communities that the Bantu and other migrations had generated.

Agriculture and Population Growth

The principal early result of the Bantu and other migrations was to spread agriculture and herding to almost all parts of Africa, excluding deserts and dense, equatorial rain forests. As they established agricultural societies, cultivators and herders displaced many of the hunting, gathering, and fishing peoples who previously inhabited sub-Saharan Africa and absorbed them into their societies. By about 500 B.C.E. most Bantu-speaking peoples had mastered the techniques of iron metallurgy, which enabled them to fashion iron axes, adzes, and hoes that facilitated further clearing of lands and extension of agriculture. By the early centuries C.E., cultivation and herding had reached the southernmost parts of Africa. Yams, sorghum, and millet were the dietary staples of many peoples in south Africa, and the indigenous Khoi people adopted cattle raising even before Bantu and Kushite herders moved into the region. Those developments resulted in increased agricultural production, rising population, and pressure for continuing migration to new territories.

Bananas The introduction of bananas to Africa encouraged a fresh migratory surge. First domesticated in southeast Asia, bananas entered Africa by way of sea lanes across the Indian Ocean. During the late centuries B.C.E., Malay seafarers from the islands that make up modern Indonesia sailed west beyond India, and by the early centuries C.E. they were exploring the east African coasts. Between about 300 and 500 C.E., they colonized the island of Madagascar and established banana cultivation there. (Apart from bananas, they brought Asian yams, taro, chickens, and southeast Asian cultural traditions. Malagasy, the language spoken on Madagascar even today, belongs to the Austronesian family of languages.) From Madagascar, bananas easily made the jump to the east African mainland. By 500 C.E. several varieties of bananas had become well established in Africa. They provided a nutritious supplement to Bantu diets and enabled the Bantu to expand into heavily forested regions where yams and millet did not grow well. Thus cultivation of bananas increased the supply of food available to the Bantu, enriched their diets, and allowed them to expand more rapidly than before.

Population Growth The population history of sub-Saharan Africa clearly reflects the significance of iron metallurgy and bananas. In 400 B.C.E., before iron working had deeply influenced the continent's societies, the population of sub-Saharan Africa stood at about 3.5 million. By the turn of the millennium, human numbers exceeded 11 million.

By 800 C.E., after banana cultivation had spread throughout the continent, the sub-Saharan population had climbed to 17 million. And by 1000, when the Bantu migrations had introduced agriculture and iron metallurgy to most regions of sub-Saharan Africa, the population had passed 22 million.

Bantu and Forest Peoples The continuing Bantu migrations, the expansion of Bantu population, and the establishment of new Bantu communities contributed to changes in relationships between Bantu and foraging peoples such as the forest dwellers of central Africa (the peoples once referred to as "pygmies"). In earlier times, the Bantu had often regarded the forest peoples as useful guides to environments that were unfamiliar to the Bantu, and oral traditions suggest that they relied on foragers' expert knowledge to learn about the possibilities that new environments offered. As Bantu populations surged, however, it became increasingly difficult for foragers to flourish. Some forest peoples joined the cultivators and effectively integrated into Bantu society. Others retreated into the forests, where they were able to sustain small-scale societies by becoming forest specialists and providing forest products such as animal skins in exchange for iron tools produced by neighboring Bantu communities.

African Political Organization

By 1000 C.E., after more than two millennia of migrations, the Bantu had approached the limits of their expansion. Because agricultural peoples already occupied most of the continent, migrating into new territories and forming new settlements was much more difficult than in previous centuries. Instead of migrating in search of new lands to cultivate, then, African peoples developed increasingly complex forms of government that enabled them to organize their existing societies more efficiently.

Kin-Based Societies Scholars have sometimes used the terms *stateless society* and *segmentary society* to refer to one form of social organization widely prevalent in Africa during and after the Bantu migrations. Although somewhat misleading, since they seem to imply that Bantu societies had little or no government, these terms accurately reflect the fact that early Bantu societies did not depend on an elaborate hierarchy of officials or a bureaucratic apparatus to administer their affairs. Instead, Bantu peoples governed themselves mostly through family and kinship groups.

Bantu peoples usually settled in villages with populations averaging about one hundred people. Male heads of families constituted a village's ruling council, which decided the public affairs for the entire group. The most prominent of the family heads presided over the village as a chief and represented the settlement when it dealt with neighboring peoples. A group of villages constituted a district, which became the principal focus of ethnic loyalties. Usually, there was no chief or larger government for the district. Instead, village chiefs negotiated on matters concerning two or more villages. Meanwhile, within individual villages, family and kinship groups disciplined their own members as necessary.

This type of organization lends itself particularly well to small-scale communities, but kin-based societies often grew to large proportions. Some networks of villages and districts organized the public affairs of several hundred thousand people. By the nineteenth century, for example, the Tiv people of Nigeria, numbering almost one million, conducted their affairs in a kin-based society built on a foundation of family and clan groups.

Early Cities: Jenne-jeno Meanwhile, Bantu-speaking peoples also established a vibrant urban society in the middle stretches of the Niger River, where low-lying lands forced the river into an inland delta. Equipped with iron tools, settlers arrived in the region during the late centuries B.C.E., and by 400 C.E. the settlement of Jenne-jeno ("Ancient Jenne," located

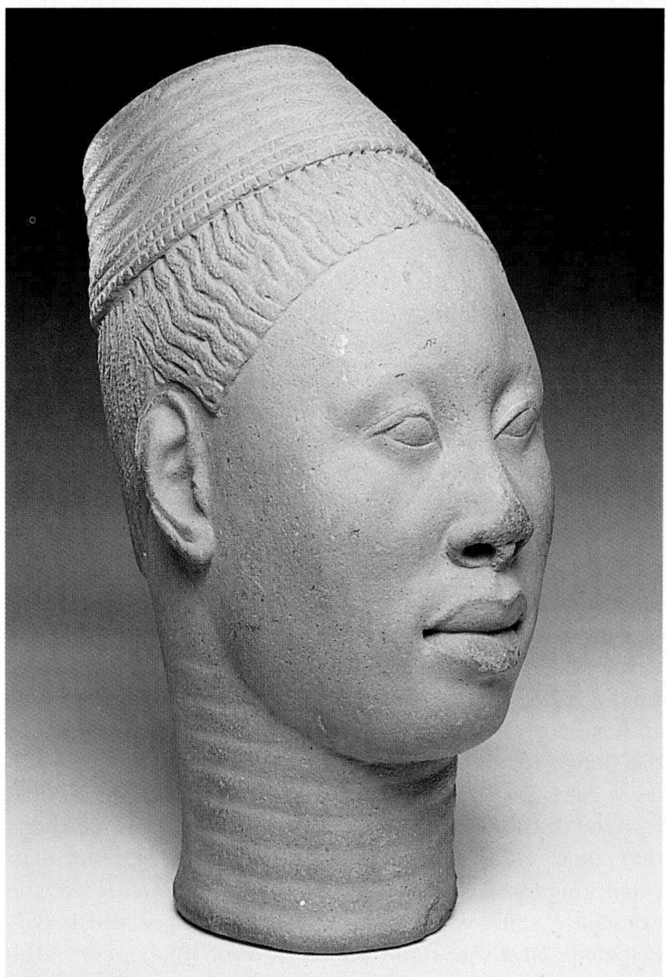

According to legend, this handsome terra-cotta head represents an ambitious warrior who usurped power in the small state of Ife (in modern Nigeria). Produced shortly after 1000 C.E., it testifies to the increasing tensions in sub-Saharan politics after the turn of the millennium.

just south of the modern city of Jenne in Mali) was emerging as a center of iron production and trade. Merchants of Jenne-jeno handled iron products as well as the region's abundant supplies of rice, fish, and domesticated animals, including cattle, sheep, and goats. They participated in an extensive trade network that reached from north Africa and the Mediterranean to the savannas and forests of central Africa. By the eighth century C.E., Jenne-jeno had become the principal commercial crossroads of west Africa. Although the city declined as west African kingdoms and empires arose in later centuries, it left a legacy of urban development in the region by inspiring the foundation of Timbuktu and other cities.

Chiefdoms After about 1000 C.E., many kin-based societies faced difficult challenges. Population growth strained resources, but few lands were available for migrants to settle. Conflicts between villages and districts became more frequent and more intense. Increased conflict encouraged Bantu communities to organize military forces for both offensive and defensive purposes, and military organization in turn encouraged the development of more formal structures of government. Many districts fell under the leadership of powerful chiefs, who overrode kinship networks and imposed their own authority on their territories. Some of these chiefs conquered their neighbors and consolidated their lands into small kingdoms. These local kingdoms emerged in several regions of sub-Saharan Africa after about 1000 C.E. The kingdoms of Ife and Benin, for example, arose in the forested regions of west Africa. Both realms were city-states in which the court and urban residents controlled the surrounding countryside through family relationships and political alliances. Both Ife and Benin also produced magnificent sculptures that put human faces and figures to the early history of sub-Saharan Africa. Local kingdoms appeared also in southern Africa and central Africa.

Kingdom of Kongo One of the most active areas of political development was the basin of the Congo River (also known as the Zaire River), a region where brisk economic development supported the emergence of large as well as small kingdoms. After about 1000 C.E. population pressures and military challenges encouraged kin-based societies in the Congo region to form small states embracing a few villages each. By 1200 conflict between these small states had resulted in the organization of larger, regional principalities that could resist political and military pressures better than small kingdoms could. One of the more prosperous of the Congolese states was the kingdom of Kongo, which participated actively in trade networks involving copper, raffia cloth, and nzimbu shells from the Atlantic Ocean. During the fourteenth century the kingdom of Kongo came to embrace much of the modern-day Republic of the Congo and Angola.

The central government of Kongo included the king and officials who oversaw military, judicial, and financial affairs. Beneath the central government were six provinces administered by governors, each of whom supervised several districts administered by subordinate officials. Within the districts, villages ruled by chiefs provided local government. Though not the only kingdom in sub-Saharan Africa, Kongo was perhaps the most tightly centralized of the early Bantu kingdoms. In most cases the king or other central administrators could appoint or replace local officials at will, and the central government maintained a royal currency system based on cowries, seashells that came from the Indian Ocean. The kingdom of Kongo provided effective organization from the fourteenth until the mid-seventeenth century, when Portuguese slave traders undermined the authority of the kings and the central government.

Kin-based societies did not disappear with the emergence of formal states. On the contrary, they survived into the nineteenth century in much of sub-Saharan Africa. Yet regional states and large kingdoms became increasingly prominent during the centuries after 1000 C.E. as Bantu and other African peoples responded to population pressures and military challenges facing their societies.

ISLAMIC KINGDOMS AND EMPIRES

While Bantu peoples organized societies on the basis of African traditions, merchants from north Africa and southwest Asia introduced Islam to sub-Saharan Africa. Islam arrived by two routes: it went to west Africa overland by trans-Saharan camel caravans, and it traveled to coastal east Africa over the sea lanes of the Indian Ocean in the vessels of merchant-mariners. After the eighth century C.E., Islam profoundly influenced the political, social, and economic development of sub-Saharan Africa as well as its cultural and religious development.

Trans-Saharan Trade and Islamic States in West Africa

The Sahara desert has never served as an absolute barrier to communication between human societies. Small numbers of nomadic peoples have lived in the desert itself ever since a process of desiccation created the Sahara beginning about 5000 B.C.E. Those nomads migrated around the desert and had dealings with other peoples settled on its fringes. Even in ancient and classical times, merchants occasionally organized commercial expeditions across the desert, although the value and volume of trade in the Mediterranean basin greatly exceeded that crossing the Sahara.

Camels The arrival of the camel quickened the pace of communication and transportation across the Sahara. Camels came to north Africa from Arabia, by way of Egypt and the Sudan, about the seventh century B.C.E. During the late centuries B.C.E., a special camel saddle, which took advantage of the animals' distinctive physical structure, also made its way to north Africa. Because a caravan took seventy to ninety days to cross the Sahara and because camels could travel long distances before needing water, they proved to

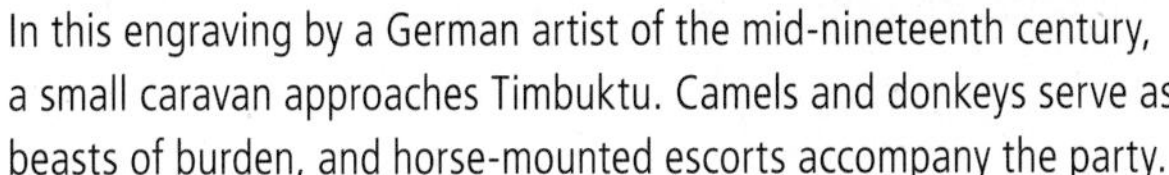
In this engraving by a German artist of the mid-nineteenth century, a small caravan approaches Timbuktu. Camels and donkeys serve as beasts of burden, and horse-mounted escorts accompany the party.

be useful beasts of burden in an arid region. After about 300 C.E., camels increasingly replaced horses and donkeys as the preferred transport animals throughout the Sahara as well as in the deserts of central Asia.

When Arab conquerors introduced Islam into north Africa during the seventh and eighth centuries, they also integrated the region into a rapidly expanding zone of commerce and communication. Thus it was natural for Muslims in north Africa to explore the potential of trade across the Sahara. By the late eighth century, Islamic merchants had trekked across the desert and established commercial relations with societies in sub-Saharan west Africa. There they found a series of long-established trading centers such as Gao, a terminus of caravan routes across the Sahara that offered access to the Niger River valley, which was a flourishing market for copper, ironware, cotton textiles, salt, grains, and carnelian beads.

The Kingdom of Ghana The principal state of west Africa at the time of the Muslims' arrival there was the kingdom of Ghana (not related to the modern state of Ghana), situated between the Senegal and Niger rivers in a region straddling the border between the modern states of Mali and Mauritania. Ghana emerged as a kingdom at an uncertain but early date: according to legends preserved by Arab travelers, as many as twenty-two kings ruled in Ghana before Muhammad and his companions embarked on the *hijra.* Ghana probably developed as a state during the fourth or fifth century C.E. when settled, agricultural peoples sought to protect their societies from the raids of camel-riding nomads who increasingly came out of the Sahara. When Muslims arrived in west Africa, the kingdom of Ghana was a regional state much like others that were emerging or soon would appear elsewhere in sub-Saharan Africa.

Gold Trade As trade and traffic across the desert increased, Ghana underwent a dramatic transformation. It became the most important commercial site in west Africa because it was the center for trade in gold, which was in high demand because of economic development and surging trade throughout the eastern hemisphere. Muslim merchants flocked to camel caravans traveling across the Sahara to Ghana in search of gold for consumers in the Mediterranean basin and elsewhere in the Islamic world. Ghana itself did not produce gold, but the kings procured nuggets from lands to the south—probably from the region around the headwaters of the Niger, Gambia, and Senegal rivers, which enjoyed the world's largest supply of gold available at the time. By controlling and taxing trade in the precious metal, the kings both enriched and strengthened their realm. Apart from gold, merchants from Ghana provided ivory and slaves for traders from north Africa. In exchange, they received horses, cloth, small manufactured wares, and salt—a crucial commodity in the tropics, but one that local sources could not supply in large quantities.

Koumbi-Saleh Integration into trans-Saharan trade networks brought enormous wealth and considerable power to Ghana. The kingdom's capital and principal trading site stood at Koumbi-Saleh, a small town today but a thriving commercial center with a population of some fifteen thousand to twenty thousand people when the kingdom was at its height, from the ninth to the twelfth century. Al-Bakri, a Spanish Muslim traveler of the mid-eleventh century, described Koumbi-Saleh as a flourishing site with buildings

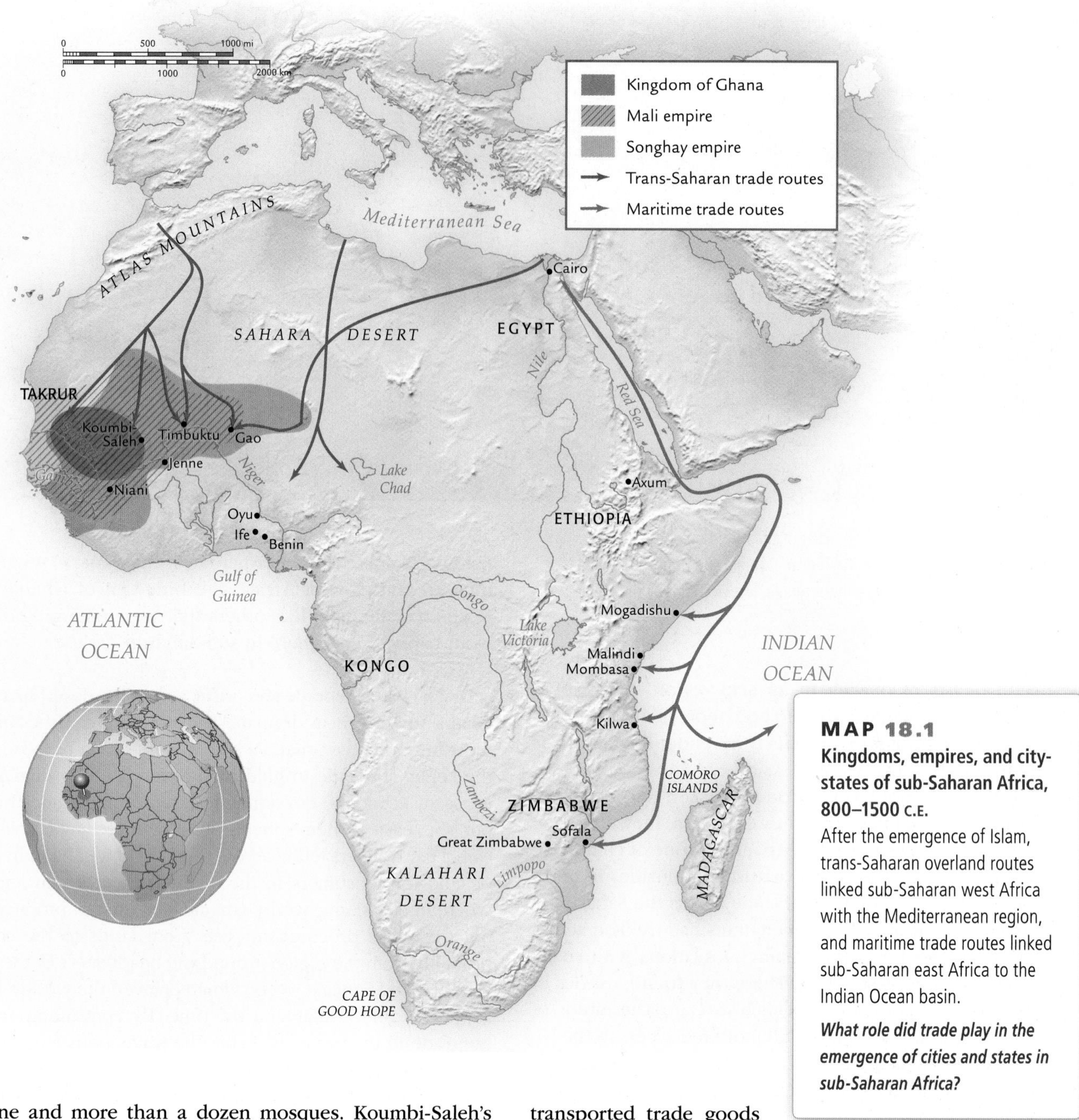

MAP 18.1
Kingdoms, empires, and city-states of sub-Saharan Africa, 800–1500 C.E.
After the emergence of Islam, trans-Saharan overland routes linked sub-Saharan west Africa with the Mediterranean region, and maritime trade routes linked sub-Saharan east Africa to the Indian Ocean basin.

What role did trade play in the emergence of cities and states in sub-Saharan Africa?

of stone and more than a dozen mosques. Koumbi-Saleh's wealth also supported a large number of *qadis* and Muslim scholars. From taxes levied on trade passing through Ghana, the kings financed a large army—al-Bakri reported that they could field two hundred thousand warriors—that protected the sources of gold, maintained order in the kingdom, kept allied and tributary states in line, and defended Ghana against nomadic incursions from the Sahara.

Islam in West Africa By about the tenth century, the kings of Ghana had converted to Islam. Their conversion led to improved relations with Muslim merchants from north Africa as well as Muslim nomads from the desert who transported trade goods across the Sahara. It also brought them recognition and support from Muslim states in north Africa. The kings of Ghana made no attempt to impose Islam forcibly on their society—unlike the neighboring kings of Takrur, who zealously campaigned for the conversion of their entire kingdom—nor did they accept Islam exclusively even for their own purposes. Instead, they continued to observe traditional religious customs: al-Bakri mentioned, for example, that native religious specialists practiced magic and kept idols in the woods surrounding the royal palace at Koumbi-Saleh. Even in the absence of efforts to impose Islam on Ghana, however, the faith attracted converts, particularly among those engaged in trade with Muslim merchants from the north.

As the kingdom expanded to the north, it became vulnerable to attacks by nomadic peoples from the Sahara who sought to seize some of the kingdom's wealth. During the early thirteenth century, raids from the desert weakened the kingdom, and it soon collapsed. Several successor states took over portions of Ghana's territory, but political leadership in west Africa fell to the powerful Mali empire, which emerged just as the kingdom of Ghana dissolved.

Sundiata The lion prince Sundiata (reigned 1230–1255) built the Mali empire during the first half of the thirteenth century after his return from exile. While away from home, he made astute alliances with local rulers, gained a reputation for courage in battle, and assembled a large army dominated by cavalry. By about 1235 he had consolidated his hold on the Mali empire, which expanded to include Ghana as well as other neighboring kingdoms in the regions surrounding the Senegal and Niger rivers. The empire included most of the modern state of Mali and extended also to lands now known as Mauritania, Senegal, Gambia, Guinea-Bissau, Guinea, and Sierra Leone.

This west African terra-cotta sculpture from the thirteenth or fourteenth century depicts a helmeted and armored warrior astride a horse with elaborate harness and head protection.

The Mali Empire and Trade

Mali benefited from trans-Saharan trade on an even larger scale than Ghana did. From the thirteenth until the late fifteenth century, Mali controlled and taxed almost all trade passing through west Africa. Enormous caravans with as many as twenty-five thousand camels linked Mali to north Africa. The capital city of Niani attracted merchants seeking to enter the gold trade, and market cities on the caravan routes such as Timbuktu, Gao, and Jenne became prosperous centers featuring buildings of brick and stone. Like the later kings of Ghana, the rulers of Mali honored Islam and provided protection, lodging, and comforts for Muslim merchants from the north. Although they did not force Islam on their realm, they encouraged its spread on a voluntary basis.

Mansa Musa The significance of trade and Islam for west Africa became clearest during the reign of Sundiata's grand-nephew Mansa Musa, who ruled Mali from 1312 to 1337, during the high point of the empire. Mansa Musa observed Islamic tradition by making his pilgrimage to Mecca in 1324–1325. His party formed a gargantuan caravan that included thousands of soldiers,

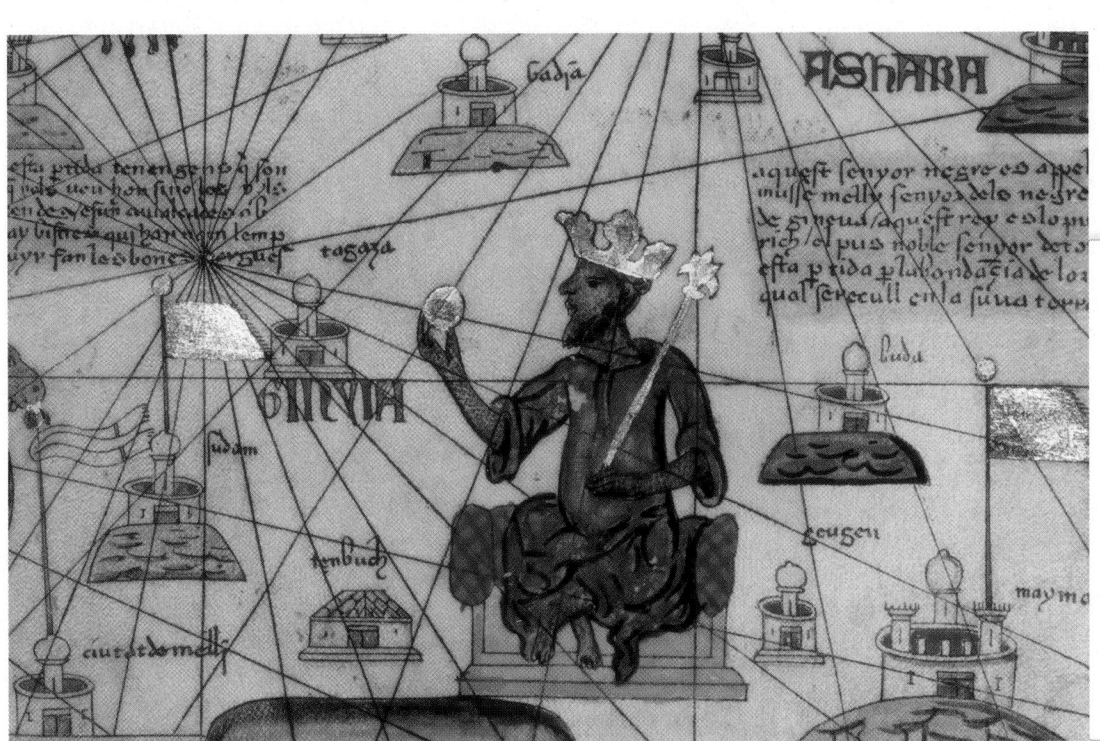

Mansa Musa enjoyed a widespread reputation as the wealthiest king in the world. On this map, prepared in 1375 by a cartographer from the Mediterranean island of Majorca, Mansa Musa holds a gold nugget about the size of a grapefruit. What does this illustration reveal about the image of west Africa in the Mediterranean world?

sources from the past

Sundiata and the Reconstruction of Niani

African griots tell many different versions of an oral tradition dealing with Sundiata and his establishment of the Mali empire. Some dwell on Sundiata's cunning and clever strategy, others on his courage and physical valor. After recounting his birth, childhood, and campaign to conquer Mali, some oral traditions emphasize Sundiata's connections with his birthplace and capital city, Niani. The following selection deals with Sundiata's restoration of stability and prosperity and especially his services to Niani.

The troops were marching along singing the "Hymn to the Bow," which the crowd took up. New songs flew from mouth to mouth. Young women offered the soldiers cool water and cola nuts. And so the triumphal march across Mali ended outside Niani, Sundiata's city.

It was a ruined town which was beginning to be rebuilt by its inhabitants. A part of the ramparts had been destroyed and the charred walls still bore the marks of fire. From the top of the hill, Djata [a nickname for Sundiata] looked on Niani, which looked like a dead city. . . . The survivors of the catastrophe were standing in rows on the Mali road. The children were waving branches, a few young women were singing, but the adults were mute. . . .

With Sundiata peace and happiness entered Niani. Lovingly Sogolon's son [i.e., Sundiata] had his native city rebuilt. He restored in the ancient style his father's old enclosure where he had grown up. People came from all the villages of Mali to settle in Niani. The walls had to be destroyed to enlarge the town, and new quarters were built for each kin group in the enormous army. . . .

In their new-found peace the villages knew prosperity again, for with Sundiata happiness had come into everyone's home. Vast fields of millet, rice, cotton, indigo, and fonio surrounded the villages. Whoever worked always had something to live on. Each year long caravans carried the taxes in kind [in the form of grains] to Niani. You could go from village to village without fearing brigands. A thief would have his right hand chopped off and if he stole again he would be put to the sword [in accordance with Islamic law].

New villages and new towns sprang up in Mali and elsewhere. "Dyulas," or traders, became numerous and during the reign of Sundiata the world knew happiness.

There are some kings who are powerful through their military strength. Everybody trembles before them, but when they die nothing but ill is spoken of them. Others do neither good nor ill and when they die they are forgotten. Others are feared because they have power, but they know how to use it and they are loved because they love justice. Sundiata belonged to this group. He was feared, but loved as well. He was the father of Mali and gave the world peace. After him the world has not seen a greater conqueror, for he was the seventh and last conqueror. He had made the capital of an empire out of his father's village, and Niani became the navel of the earth. In the most distant lands Niani was talked of and foreigners said, "Travellers from Mali can tell lies with impunity," for Mali was a remote country for many peoples.

The griots, fine talkers that they were, used to boast of Niani and Mali saying: "If you want salt, go to Niani, for Niani is the camping place of the [trans-Saharan] caravans. If you want gold, go to Niani, for Bouré, Bambougou, and Wagadou [sources of west African gold] work for Niani. If you want fine cloth, go to Niani, for the Mecca road passed by Niani. If you want fish, go to Niani, for it is there that the fishermen of Maouti and Djenné come to sell their catches. If you want meat, go to Niani, the country of the great hunters, and the land of the ox and the sheep. If you want to see an army, go to Niani, for it [is] there that the united forces of Mali are to be found. If you want to see a great king, go to Niani, for it is there that the son of Sogolon lives, the man with two names."

For Further Reflection

- To what extent was Sundiata's support for Islam an issue in the shaping of his reputation?

Source: D. T. Niane, ed. *Sundiata: An Epic of Old Mali.* Trans. by G. D. Pickett. Harlow, England: Longman, 1965, pp. 80–82.

attendants, subjects, and slaves as well as a hundred camels carrying satchels of gold. Mansa Musa bestowed lavish gifts on those who hosted him along the way, and during his three-month visit to Cairo, he distributed so much gold that the metal's value declined by as much as 25 percent on local markets.

Mansa Musa and Islam Mansa Musa drew great inspiration from his pilgrimage to Mecca, and upon return to Mali he took his religion even more seriously than before. He built mosques, particularly in the trading cities frequented by Muslim merchants, and he sent promising students to study with distinguished Islamic scholars in north Africa. He also established religious schools and brought in Arabian and north African teachers, including four descendants of Muhammad himself, to make Islam better known in Mali.

Within a century of Mansa Musa's reign, Mali would be in serious decline: factions crippled the central government,

thinking about TRADITIONS

Religion and Commerce
Adoption of Islam coincided with rapidly increasing trade in the early kingdoms and empires of west Africa. How can you account for the relationship between religion and commerce in this region?

provinces seceded from the empire, and military pressures came both from neighboring kingdoms and from desert nomads. By the late fifteenth century, the Songhay empire had completely overcome Mali. Yet Mansa Musa and other Mali rulers had established a tradition of centralized government that the Songhay realm itself would continue, and they had ensured that Islam would have a prominent place in west African society over the long term.

The Indian Ocean Trade and Islamic States in East Africa

While trans-Saharan caravan traffic linked west Africa to the larger trading world of the eastern hemisphere, merchant-mariners sailing the sea lanes of the Indian Ocean performed a similar service for coastal east Africa. Indian and Persian sailors had visited the east African coasts after about 500 B.C.E., and Hellenistic and Roman mariners sailed through the Red Sea en route to the same coasts. After the late centuries B.C.E., Malay seafarers also ventured into the western Indian Ocean from their island homelands in southeast Asia, and by the fourth and fifth centuries C.E. they had established colonies on the island of Madagascar. Those early visitors had limited opportunities to trade, however, since east African populations consisted mostly of hunting, gathering, and fishing peoples.

By the second century C.E., Bantu peoples had populated much of east Africa. They introduced agriculture, cattle herding, and iron metallurgy to the region, and here, as elsewhere in sub-Saharan Africa, they founded complex societies governed by small, local states. As their population increased, Bantu peoples founded settlements on the coasts and offshore islands as well as the interior regions of east Africa. Those coast dwellers supplemented their agricultural production with ocean fishing and maritime trade. They were the builders of **Swahili** society.

This fine piece of Chinese porcelain, probably produced in the fifteenth century, found its way into a Swahili tomb in modern Dar es Salaam, Tanzania.

The Swahili *Swahili* is an Arabic term meaning "coasters," referring to those who engaged in trade along the east African coast. The Swahili dominated the east African coast from Mogadishu in the north to Kilwa, the Comoro Islands, and Sofala in the south. They spoke Swahili, a Bantu language supplemented with words and ideas borrowed from Arabic. Swahili peoples developed different dialects, but they communicated readily among themselves because individuals frequently visited other Swahili communities in their oceangoing crafts. Indeed, all along the east African coast, Swahili society underwent similar patterns of development with respect to language, religion, architecture, and technology.

By the tenth century, Swahili society attracted increasing attention from Islamic merchants. From the interior regions of east Africa, the Swahili obtained gold, slaves, ivory, and exotic local products such as tortoise shells and leopard skins, which they traded for pottery, glass, and textiles that Muslim merchants brought from Persia, India, and China. The rapidly increasing volume and value of trade had large repercussions for Swahili states and societies, just as such changes had for west African societies.

The Swahili City-States By the eleventh and twelfth centuries, trade had brought tremendous wealth to coastal east Africa. By controlling and taxing trade within their jurisdictions, local chiefs strengthened their own authority and increased the influence of their communities. Gradually, trade concentrated at several coastal and island port cities that enjoyed sheltered or especially convenient locations: Mogadishu, Lamu, Malindi, Mombasa, Zanzibar, Kilwa, Mozambique, and Sofala. Each of those sites developed into a powerful city-state governed by a king who supervised trade and organized public life in the region.

The cities themselves underwent an impressive transformation. Villages in the interior regions of east Africa had buildings made of wood and dried mud, the principal materials used even for prominent structures such as mosques. By about the twelfth century, however, Swahili peoples began to construct much larger buildings of coral, and by the fifteenth century the main Swahili towns boasted handsome stone mosques and public buildings. Meanwhile, the ruling elites and wealthy merchants of Swahili trading cities dressed in silk and fine cotton clothes, and they set their tables with porcelain imported from China.

Swahili (swah-HEE-lee)

Kilwa Travelers' reports and recent archaeological discoveries have thrown especially clear light on the development of Kilwa, one of the busiest city-states on the east African coast. The earliest Bantu inhabitants of Kilwa relied mostly on fishing and engaged in a limited amount of trade between about 800 and 1000 C.E. During the next two centuries, they imported pottery and stoneware from other regions in east Africa and began to rely more on agriculture to support their growing numbers. By the early thirteenth century, Kilwans were prosperous enough to erect multistory stone buildings, and they used copper coins to facilitate economic transactions. Between 1300 and 1505, when Portuguese mariners subjected the city to a devastating sack, Kilwa enjoyed tremendous prosperity. The Moroccan traveler Ibn Battuta visited the city in 1331 and reported that Muslim scholars from Arabia and Persia lived at Kilwa and consulted regularly with the local ruler.

With a population of about twelve thousand, Kilwa was a thriving city that had many stone buildings and mosques. Residents imported cotton and silk textiles as well as perfumes and pearls from India, and archaeologists have unearthed a staggering amount of Chinese porcelain. Merchants of Kilwa imported those products in exchange for gold, slaves, and ivory obtained from interior regions. By the late fifteenth century, Kilwa exported about a ton of gold per year. Participation in Indian Ocean trade networks brought similar experiences to the other major Swahili cities.

In fact, the influence of long-distance trade passed well beyond the coasts to the interior regions of east Africa. Villagers in the interior did not enjoy the sumptuous lifestyles of the Swahili elites, but trade and the wealth that it brought underwrote the establishment of large and powerful kingdoms in east and central Africa.

Zimbabwe The best known of these kingdoms was Zimbabwe. The term *zimbabwe* refers simply to the dwelling of a chief. As early as the fifth and sixth centuries C.E., the region occupied by the modern states of Zimbabwe and Mozambique featured many wooden residences known throughout the land as *zimbabwe*. By the ninth century, chiefs had begun to build their *zimbabwe* of stone—indicating an increasingly complex and well-organized society that could invest resources in expensive construction projects. About the early thirteenth century, a magnificent stone complex known as Great Zimbabwe began to arise near Nyanda in the modern state of Zimbabwe. Within stone walls 5 meters (16 feet) thick and 10 meters (32 feet) tall, Great Zimbabwe was a city of stone towers, palaces, and public buildings that served as the capital of a large kingdom situated between the Zambesi and Limpopo rivers. At the time of its greatest extent, during the late fifteenth century, up to eighteen thousand people may have lived in the vicinity of the stone complex at Great Zimbabwe, and the kingdom stretched from the outskirts of the Swahili city of Sofala deep into the interior of south-central Africa.

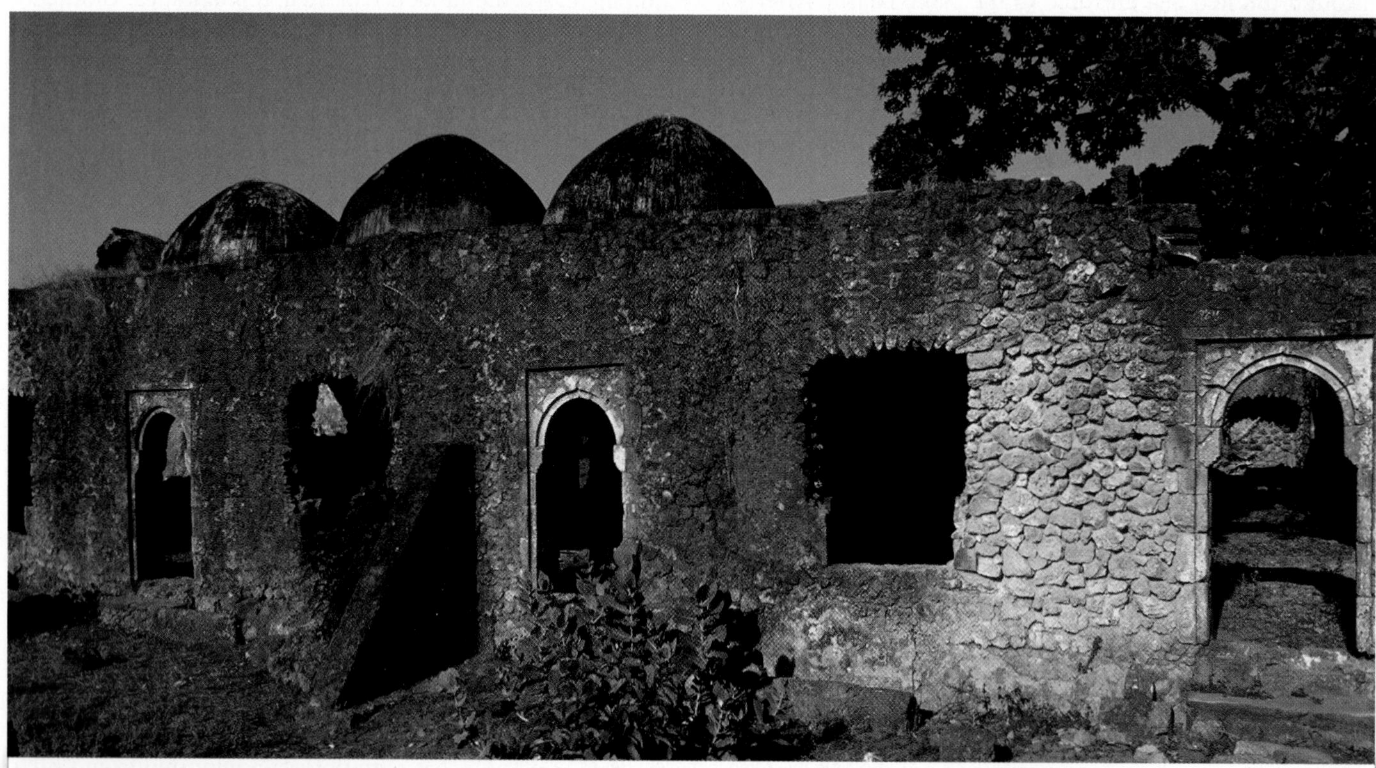

Ruins of Kilwa's Great Mosque, built during the thirteenth century, testify to the wealth that Indian Ocean trade brought to the city.

sources from the past

Ibn Battuta on Muslim Society at Mogadishu

During the fourteenth century the Moroccan jurist Ibn Battuta traveled throughout much of the eastern hemisphere. Twice he visited sub-Saharan Africa: in 1331, when he traveled along the Swahili coast, and in 1351–1352, when he visited the Mali empire. His account of his visit to the Swahili city of Mogadishu offers insight into the mercantile and social customs of the city as well as the hospitality accorded to distinguished visitors.

[Mogadishu] is a town of enormous size. Its inhabitants are merchants possessed of vast resources: they own large numbers of camels, of which they slaughter hundreds every day [for food], and also have quantities of sheep. In this place are manufactured the woven fabrics called after it, which are unequalled and exported from it to Egypt and elsewhere. It is the custom of the people of this town that, when a vessel reaches the anchorage, the *sumbuqs,* which are small boats, come out to it. In each *sumbuq* there are a number of young men of the town, each one of whom brings a covered platter containing food and presents it to one of the merchants on the ship saying "This is my guest," and each of the others does the same. The merchant, on disembarking, goes only to the house of his host among the young men, except those of them who have made frequent journeys to the town and have gained some acquaintance with its inhabitants; these lodge where they please. When he takes up residence with his host, the latter sells his goods for him and buys for him; and if anyone buys anything from him at too low a price or sells to him in the absence of his host, that sale is held invalid by them. This practice is a profitable one for them.

When the young men came on board the vessel in which I was, one of them came up to me. My companions said to him "This man is not a merchant, but a doctor of the law," whereupon he called out to his friends and said to them "This is the guest of the qadi." There was among them one of the qadi's men, who informed him of this, and he came down to the beach with a number of students and sent one of them to me. I then disembarked with my companions and saluted him and his party. He said to me "In the name of God, let us go to salute the Shaikh." "And who is the Shaikh?" I said, and he answered, "The Sultan," for it is their custom to call the sultan "the Shaikh." . . .

When I arrived with the qadi . . . at the sultan's residence, one of the serving-boys came out and saluted the qadi, who said to him "Take word to the intendant's office and inform the Shaikh that this man has come from the land of al-Hijaz [Arabia]." So he took the message, then returned bringing a plate on which were some leaves of betel and areca nuts, the same to the qadi, and what was left on the plate to my companions and the qadi's students. He brought also a jug of rose-water of Damascus, which he poured over me and over the qadi [i.e., over our hands], and said "Our master commands that he be lodged in the students' house," this being a building equipped for the entertainment of students of religion. . . .

We stayed there three days, food being brought to us three times a day, following their custom. On the fourth day, which was a Friday, the qadi and students and one of the Shaikh's viziers came to me, bringing a set of robes; these [official] robes of theirs consist of a silk wrapper which one ties round his waist in place of drawers (for they have no acquaintance with these), a tunic of Egyptian linen with an embroidered border, a furred mantle of Jerusalem stuff, and an Egyptian turban with an embroidered edge. They also brought robes for my companions suitable to their position. We went to the congregational mosque and made our prayers behind the *maqsura* [private box for the sultan]. When the Shaikh came out of the door of the *maqsura* I saluted him along with the qadi; he said a word of greeting, spoke in their tongue with the qadi, and then said in Arabic "You are heartily welcome, and you have honored our land and given us pleasure."

For Further Reflection

- From Ibn Battuta's report, how could you characterize the role of hospitality on the Swahili coast?

Source: H. A. R. Gibb, trans. *The Travels of Ibn Battuta, A.D. 1325–1354,* 4 vols. Cambridge: Hakluyt Society, 1958–94, 2:374–77.

Kings residing at Great Zimbabwe controlled and taxed the trade between the interior and coastal regions. They organized the flow of gold, ivory, slaves, and local products from sources of supply to the coast. Their control over those products enabled them to forge alliances with local leaders and to profit handsomely from commercial transactions. Just as the trans-Saharan trade encouraged the building of states and empires in west Africa, the Indian Ocean trade generated wealth that financed the organization of city-states on the coast and large kingdoms in the interior regions of east and central Africa.

Islam in East Africa In east Africa, again as in west Africa, trade brought cultural as well as political changes. Like their counterparts in west Africa, the ruling elites and the wealthy merchants of east Africa converted to the Islamic faith. They did not necessarily give up their religious and cultural traditions but, rather, continued to observe them for purposes of providing cultural leadership in their societies. By adopting Islam, however, they laid a cultural foundation for close cooperation with Muslim merchants trading in the Indian Ocean basin. Moreover, Islam served as a fresh source of legitimacy for their rule, since they gained recognition from Islamic states in southwest Asia, and their conversion opened the door to political alliances with Muslim rulers in other lands. Even though the conversion of elite classes did not bring about the immediate spread of Islam throughout their societies, it enabled Islam to establish a presence in east Africa under the sponsorship of some particularly influential patrons. The faith eventually attracted interest in larger circles and became one of the principal cultural and religious traditions of east Africa.

AFRICAN SOCIETY AND CULTURAL DEVELOPMENT

By the eleventh century C.E., Africa was a land of enormous diversity. The peoples of sub-Saharan Africa spoke some eight hundred different languages, and the continent supported a wide variety of societies and economies: mobile bands of hunting and gathering peoples, fishing peoples who lived alongside the continent's lakes and coasts, nomadic herders, subsistence farmers who migrated periodically to fresh lands, settled cultivators, and city-based societies that drew their livelihoods from mining, manufacturing, and trade. Although this diversity makes it difficult to speak of African society and cultural development in general terms, certain social forms and cultural patterns appeared widely throughout sub-Saharan Africa.

Social Classes

In kingdoms, empires, and city-states, such as Kongo, Mali, and Kilwa, respectively, African peoples developed complex societies with clearly defined classes: ruling elites, military nobles, administrative officials, religious authorities, wealthy merchants, artisans, business entrepreneurs, common people, peasants, and slaves. These societies more or less resembled those found in other settled, agricultural lands of Eurasia organized by powerful states.

In the small states and kin-based societies of sub-Saharan Africa, however, social structures were different. Small states often generated an aristocratic or ruling elite, and they always recognized a class of religious authorities. Outside the larger states and empires, however, generally speaking, kinship, sex and gender expectations, and age groupings were the principal considerations that determined social position in sub-Saharan Africa.

Kinship Groups Extended families and clans served as the main foundation of social and economic organization in small-scale agricultural societies. Unlike their counterparts in north Africa and Eurasia, sub-Saharan African peoples

An illustration from a seventeenth-century missionary account shows an African blacksmith (seated at right) working at his forge while an attendant (seated at left) uses a bellows to pump air into the furnace.

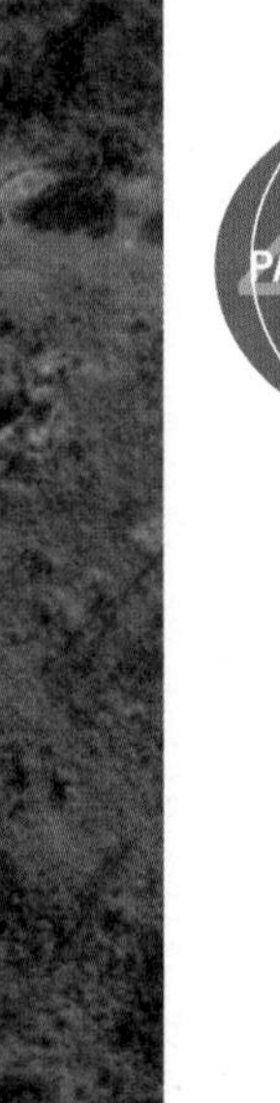

The massive stone complex of Great Zimbabwe, which featured very fine construction techniques, required the services of numerous expert masons and other craftsmen.

mostly did not recognize the private ownership of land. Instead, communities claimed rights to land and used it in common. The villages of sub-Saharan Africa, where most of the population lived, generally consisted of several extended family groups. Male heads of families jointly governed the village and organized the work of their own groups. They allocated portions of the communal lands for their relatives to cultivate and were responsible for distributing harvests equitably among all members of their groups. Thus most villagers functioned in society first as members of a family or a clan.

Sex and Gender Relations Sex and gender relations also influenced the roles individuals played in society. Sex largely determined work roles. Workers with special skills were mostly men. Leather tanning, for example, was the work of men who carefully guarded knowledge of their techniques and tanning compounds, which they passed down to their heirs. Iron working was a highly prestigious skill in many African societies because blacksmiths knew the secrets of turning ores into useful objects such as knives, hoes, spearheads, and swords. Blacksmiths often served as community leaders, and like leather tanners, they passed knowledge of their craft down to their heirs. Women in blacksmith families often served as potters for their communities. They too enjoyed special prestige because of their ability to transform ingredients from the earth into useful pottery vessels. Men usually undertook the heavy labor of clearing land and preparing it for cultivation. Both men and women participated in the planting and harvesting of crops, and women also tended to domestic chores and took primary responsibility for child rearing.

Women's Roles As in other societies, men largely monopolized public authority. Yet women in sub-Saharan Africa generally had more opportunities open to them than did their counterparts in other lands. Women enjoyed high honor as the sources of life. On at least a few occasions, women made their way to positions of power, and aristocratic women often influenced public affairs by virtue of their prominence within their families. Women merchants commonly traded at markets, and they participated actively in both local and long-distance trade in Africa. Sometimes women even engaged in combat and organized all-female military units.

The arrival of Islam did not change the status of women in sub-Saharan Africa as dramatically as it did in Arabia and southwest Asia. South of the Sahara, early converts to Islam came mostly from the ranks of the ruling elites and the merchant classes. Because it did not become a popular faith for several centuries after its introduction, Islam did not deeply influence the customs of most Africans. Even at royal courts where Islam attracted eager converts, Muslims of sub-Saharan Africa simply did not honor the same social codes as their counterparts in Arabia, southwest Asia, and north Africa. In a few societies upper-class Muslim women wore veils and led secluded lives. For the most part, however, Muslim women in sub-Saharan Africa socialized freely with men outside their immediate families, and they continued to appear and work openly in society in ways not permitted to women in other Islamic lands. Thus Islam did relatively little to curtail the opportunities available to women or to compromise their status in sub-Saharan Africa.

Age Grades Apart from kinship and expectations based on sex and gender roles, African society made a place for age groups that included all individuals within a given community born within a few years of one another. Historical linguistic analysis suggests that the recognition of those age grades, or age sets, arose in the early days of agricultural society in the Sudan, and it is clear that in many African societies the practice of grouping individuals into age grades has continued into recent times. Members of age grades performed tasks appropriate for their level of development, and they often bonded with one another to form tight circles of friends and political allies. Members of an age grade might provide labor for community projects, for example, or take joint responsibility for looking after village elders. They aided members who experienced adversities and helped one another at crucial junctures, such as marriage and the building of a new household. Thus age grades had the effect of establishing social ties that crossed the lines of family and kinship.

Slavery One class of individuals stood apart from the other social groups: slaves. As in other lands, the institution of slavery had a place in Africa since remote antiquity. Most slaves were captives of war. Others came from the ranks of debtors, suspected witches, and criminals. Within Africa most slaves probably worked as agricultural laborers, although many also worked as construction laborers, miners, or porters.

Slaves were a major form of personal wealth in sub-Saharan Africa. Since there was little if any private ownership of land, it was impossible for individuals to become wealthy through the accumulation of landholdings. On the basis of their slaves' labor, however, individuals were able to build wealth through increased agricultural production. Slaves also brought enhanced social status for their owners, so both slave holding and slave trading were prominent features of sub-Saharan African society.

Slave Trading After about the ninth century C.E., the expansion of the trans-Saharan and Indian Ocean trade networks stimulated increased traffic in African slaves. Muslim merchants provided access to markets in India, Persia, southwest Asia, and the Mediterranean basin, where the demand for slaves outstripped the supply available from eastern Europe, previously the main source of slaves. As a result, merchants from northern lands traded in sub-Saharan Africa not only for gold, ivory, and exotic local products but also for slaves.

In response to that demand, slave raiding became an increasingly prominent activity within Africa itself. Rulers of large-scale states and empires began to make war on smaller states and kin-based societies, which could not defend themselves effectively against better-organized neighbors, in search of captives destined for northern slave markets. In some years, ten thousand to twenty thousand Africans left their homes as slaves. During the mid-fourteenth century, the Moroccan traveler Ibn Battuta crossed the Sahara desert in a caravan that included six hundred slaves bound for north Africa and the Mediterranean basin. Mansa Musa of Mali set out on his pilgrimage to Mecca with five hundred slaves, many of whom he distributed along the way as gifts to his hosts. Other slaves departed from the coastal cities of east Africa for destinations in Persia and India.

". . . Moroccan traveler Ibn Battuta crossed the Sahara desert in a caravan that included 600 slaves bound for north Africa and the Mediterranean . . ."

The Zanj Revolt Records of this slave trade are scarce, but a lengthy uprising known as the Zanj revolt throws light on the nature of African slavery in Muslim lands. The term *Zanj* referred to black slaves from the Swahili coast. At least by the seventh century C.E., many Zanj slaves labored under extremely difficult conditions in southern Mesopotamia, where they worked on sugarcane plantations or cleared land of salt deposits to prepare it for cultivation. On several occasions they mounted revolts, which Muslim authorities promptly snuffed. Following a series of riots, in about 869 a rebel slave named Ali bin Muhammad organized about fifteen thousand Zanj slaves into an immense force that captured Basra, the most important city of southern Mesopotamia, and even established a rebel state in the region. Distracted by other threats, the Abbasid rulers of Mesopotamia turned their full attention to the rebellion only in 879, a full decade after it had begun. By 883 they had crushed the revolt, killed Ali bin Muhammad, and executed the other rebel leaders. Despite its ultimate collapse, the fourteen-year Zanj revolt clearly demonstrated that African slavery was a prominent feature of Muslim society.

Though smaller than the Atlantic slave trade of modern times, the Islamic slave trade was a sizable affair: between 750 and 1500 C.E., the number of African slaves transported to foreign lands may have exceeded ten million. The high demand led to the creation of networks within Africa that supplied slaves and served as a foundation for the Atlantic slave trade in later centuries.

African Religion

Peoples of sub-Saharan Africa developed a wide range of languages, societies, and cultural traditions. Religious beliefs and practices in particular took many forms. The continent's peoples referred to their deities by different names, told different stories about them, and honored them with different rituals. Yet certain features were common to many religions of sub-Saharan Africa. In combination, those features offer considerable insight into the cultural and religious climate of sub-Saharan Africa in premodern times.

Creator God Many African peoples had recognized a single, dominant creator god from the early days of Sudanic agriculture. Their beliefs did not persist unchanged through the centuries. On the contrary, they underwent considerable development as individual peoples learned about deities honored in other societies or as they sought their own improved understandings of the gods and their roles in the world. Nevertheless, many peoples recognized a single divine force or male god as the agent responsible for setting the world in motion and providing it with order. Some peoples believed that this god also sustained the world, intervening indirectly, through spirits, to influence the course of human affairs. Some considered this deity to be all-powerful, others regarded him as all-knowing, and many considered him both omnipotent and omniscient.

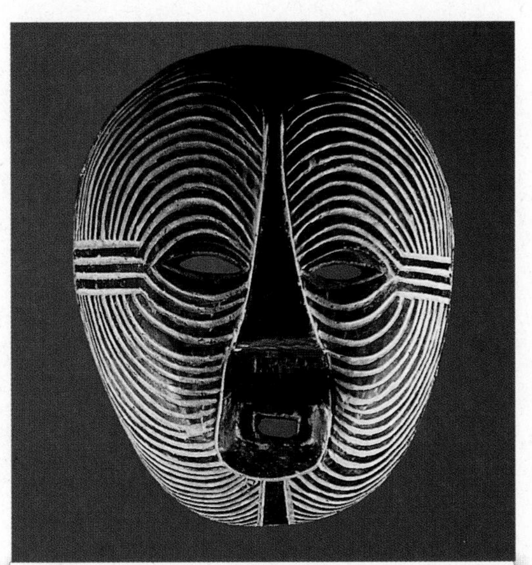

Entrancing and enthralling masks such as this one from Congo were essential to the proper observance of religious rituals, which often involved communicating with natural or animal spirits. In what ways do the features of this mask associate the diviner with powers not accessible to normal humans?

Lesser Deities and Spirits Apart from the superior creator god, Africans recognized many lesser deities and spirits often associated with the sun, wind, rain, trees, rivers, and other natural features. Unlike the creator god, these lesser deities participated actively in the workings of the world. They could confer or withhold benefits and bring favor or injury to humans. Similarly, most Africans believed that the souls of departed ancestors had the power to intervene in the lives and experiences of their descendants: the departed could shape events to the advantage of descendants who behaved properly and honored their ancestors and bring misfortune as punishment for evil behavior and neglect of their ancestors' memory. Much of the ritual of African religions focused on honoring deities, spirits, or ancestors' souls to win their favor or regain their goodwill. The rituals included prayers, animal sacrifices, and ceremonies marking important stages of life—such as birth, circumcision, marriage, and death.

Diviners Like other peoples of the world, Africans recognized classes of religious specialists—individuals who by virtue of their innate abilities or extensive training had the power to mediate between humanity and supernatural beings. Often referred to as diviners, they were intelligent people, usually men though sometimes women as well, who understood clearly the networks of political, social, economic, and psychological relationships within their communities. When afflicted by illness, sterility, crop failure, or some other disaster, individuals or groups consulted diviners to learn the cause of their misfortune. Diviners then consulted oracles, identified the causes of the trouble, and prescribed medicine, rituals, or sacrifices designed to eliminate the problem and bring about a return to normality.

For the most part, African religion concerned itself not with matters of theology but, rather, with the more practical business of explaining, predicting, and controlling the experiences of individuals and groups in the world. Thus African religion strongly emphasized morality and proper behavior as essential to the maintenance of an orderly world. Failure to observe high moral standards would lead to disorder, which would displease deities, spirits, and departed ancestors and ensure that misfortune befell the negligent parties. Because proper moral behavior was so important to their fortunes, family and kinship groups took responsibility for policing their members and disciplining those who fell short of expected standards.

The Arrival of Christianity and Islam

Alongside religions that concentrated on the practical matter of maintaining an orderly world, two religions of salvation won converts in sub-Saharan Africa—Christianity and Islam. Both arrived in Africa as foreign faiths introduced by foreign peoples, and in time the sub-Saharan adherents adapted both faiths to the needs and interests of their societies.

Early Christianity in North Africa

Christianity reached Egypt and north Africa during the first century C.E., soon after its appearance, as it attracted converts throughout the Mediterranean basin. Alexandria in Egypt became one of the most prominent centers of early Christian thought, and north Africa was the home of St. Augustine, among many other leaders of the fledgling church. Yet for several centuries Christianity remained a Mediterranean tradition whose appeal did not reach sub-Saharan Africa.

The Christian Kingdom of Axum

About the middle of the fourth century C.E., Christianity established a foothold in the kingdom of Axum, located in the highlands of modern Ethiopia. The first Axumite converts were probably local merchants who traded with Mediterranean Christians calling at the port of Adulis on the Red Sea. As missionaries visited Ethiopia, the kings of Axum also converted to Christianity, possibly in hopes of improving relations with their powerful neighbors to the north in Christian Egypt. Indeed, the kings of Axum were some of the first royal converts to Christianity, which they adopted shortly after the Roman emperor Constantine himself. Missionaries later es-

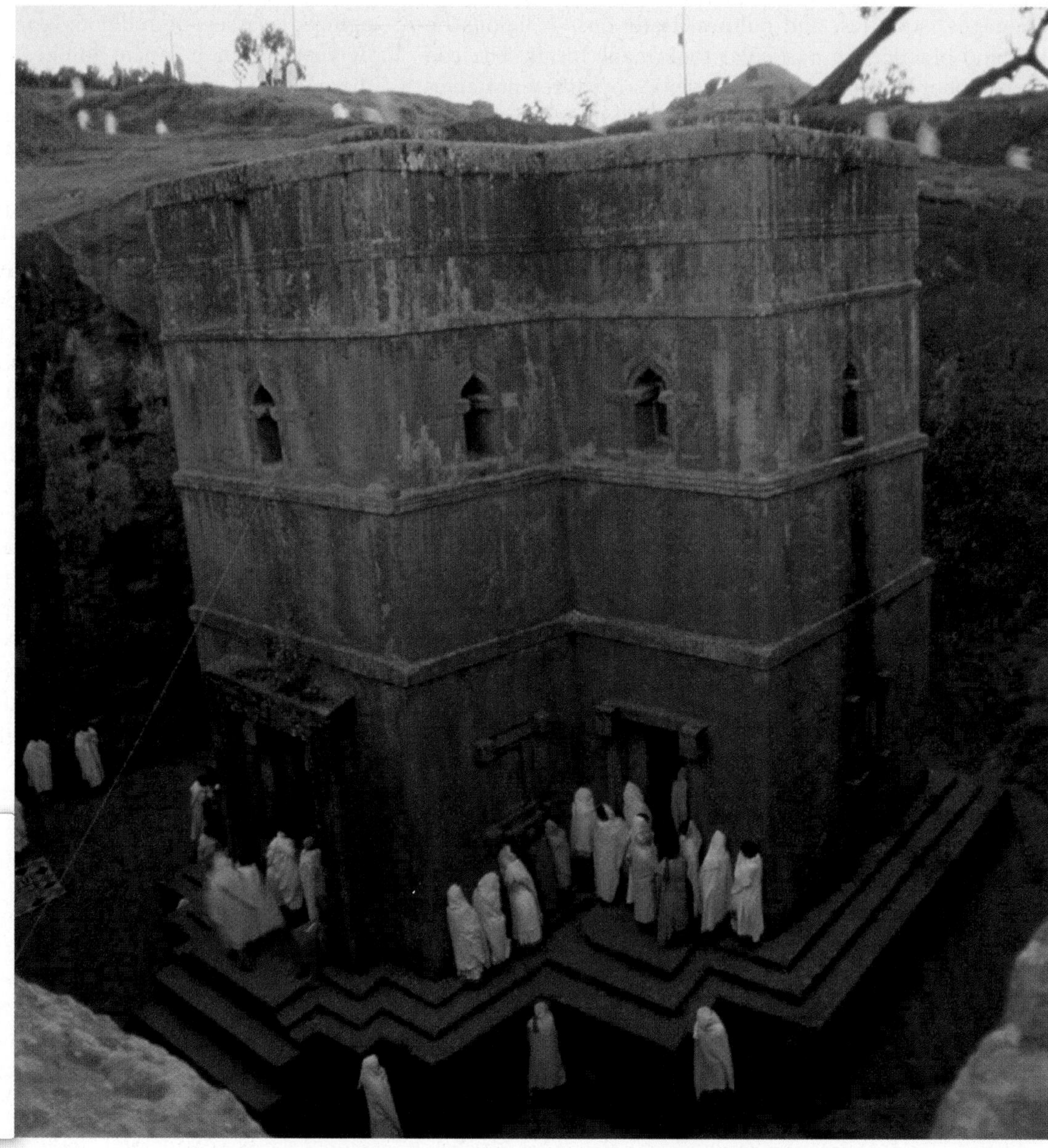

Worshipers gather at the church of St. George at Lalibela, Ethiopia, a massive structure in the form of a cross. Workers excavated the surrounding earth and then carved the church itself out of a rock.

tablished monasteries, translated the Bible into the Ethiopian language, and worked to popularize Christianity throughout the kingdom.

The fortunes of Christianity in Ethiopia reflected the larger political experience of the region. In the late seventh century C.E., the ruling house of Axum fell into decline, and during the next several centuries the expansion of Islam left an isolated island of Christianity in the Ethiopian highlands. During the twelfth century, however, a new ruling dynasty undertook a centralizing campaign and enthusiastically promoted Christianity as a foundation of cultural unity for the land. From the twelfth through the sixteenth century, Christianity enjoyed particular favor in Ethiopia. During the twelfth century, the Ethiopian kings ordered the carving of eleven massive churches out of solid rock—a monumental work of construction that required enormous resources and untold hours of labor. During the thirteenth century, rulers of Ethiopia's Solomonic dynasty claimed descent from the Israelite kings David and Solomon in an effort to lend additional biblical luster to their authority. The fictional work *Kebra Negast* (*The Glory of Kings*), which undertook to trace that lineage, has recently become popular among Rastafarians and devotees of reggae music in Ethiopia, Jamaica, and other lands as well. Meanwhile, Christianity retained its privileged status in Ethiopia until it fell out of favor following the socialist revolution of 1974.

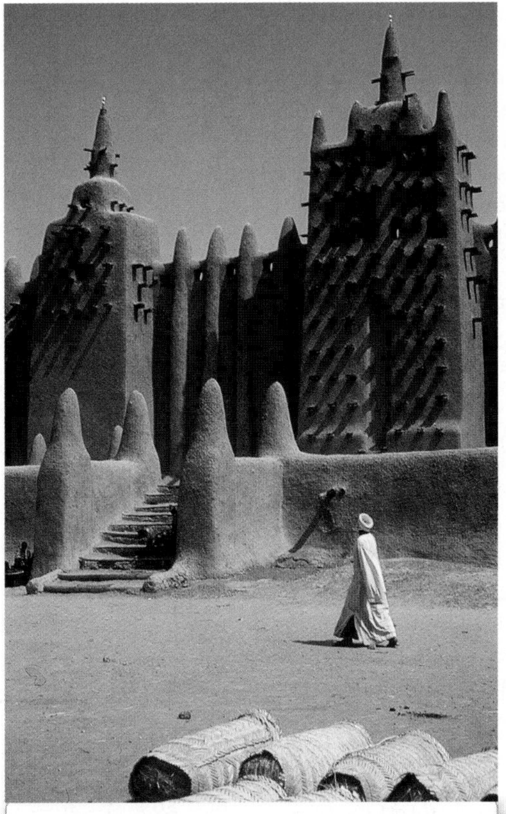

The magnificent mosque at Jenne, constructed in the fourteenth century, served as a principal center of Islamic education and scholarship in the Mali empire.

Ethiopian Christianity During the centuries after the Islamic conquests of Egypt, the Sudan, and northern Africa, Ethiopian Christians had little contact with Christians in other lands. As a result, although Ethiopian Christianity retained basic Christian theology and rituals, it increasingly reflected the interests of its African devotees. Ethiopian Christians believed that a large host of evil spirits populated the world, for example, and they carried amulets or charms for protection against these menacing spirits. The twelfth-century carved-rock churches themselves harked back to pre-Christian values, since rock shrines had been a prominent feature in Ethiopian religion from the second or perhaps even third millennium B.C.E. The rock churches absorbed that tradition into Ethiopian Christianity. Not until the sixteenth century, when Portuguese mariners began to visit Ethiopia en route to India, did Ethiopians reestablish relations with Christians from other lands.

In the meantime, Islam appealed strongly to ruling elites and merchants in sub-Saharan west Africa and coastal east Africa because it served as a cultural foundation for their business relationships with Muslim merchants from north Africa and southwest Asia. Nonetheless, African ruling elites and merchants did not convert to Islam purely for mercenary reasons. On the contrary, many converts often took Islam seriously. They built mosques, founded religious schools, invited experts in Islamic law into their lands, and displayed real enthusiasm for their adopted religion. Mansa Musa's pilgrimage to Mecca and his support of Islam in Mali represented a devotion to Islam shared by untold numbers of sub-Saharan Muslims.

African Islam Like Christianity, Islam in sub-Saharan Africa reflected the interests of local converts. Thus, as in India, southeast Asia, and other lands, Islam in sub-Saharan Africa made a place for the inherited traditions and beliefs of sub-Saharan Muslims. Africans who converted to Islam continued to take protective measures against the workings of evil spirits and witches, for example, and to participate in rituals designed to please nature deities and the spirits of departed ancestors.

thinking about ENCOUNTERS

Tensions between Old and New Values

When Christianity and Islam found their way to sub-Saharan Africa, they entered a cultural environment with long-established values and practices. Note the various ways Christianity and Islam underwent adjustment in sub-Saharan Africa. To what extent would it be likely for African peoples to abandon their inherited cultural traditions in favor of a wholly new alternative from a foreign land?

Islam and African Society Islam also had to accommodate African notions of proper relations between the sexes. When Ibn Battuta visited Mali in the mid-fourteenth century, he took deep offense at casual conversations that women had with men other than their husbands, and he became especially incensed when he observed women going about in public, even at the imperial court, dressed only in loincloths. Yet his hosts, even those who considered themselves pious Muslims, paid no heed to his railings and the lectures he delivered about the proper behavior and dress of women in Islamic society.

Indeed, during the early centuries after its introduction to the region, Islam supplemented rather than replaced the traditional religions of sub-Saharan Africa. West African merchants sometimes adopted Islam when they engaged actively in trade, since a common religion facilitated their dealings with Muslim merchants from other lands, but returned to their inherited traditions when they turned from mercantile to other pursuits. And ruling elites routinely continued to honor inherited religious traditions, which provided powerful sanctions for their rule, long after adopting Islam for the various advantages that it made available to them.

inperspective

States and societies of sub-Saharan Africa differed considerably from those in other parts of the eastern hemisphere. The foundations of most sub-Saharan societies were the agricultural economy and iron-working skills that Bantu and other peoples spread throughout most of the African continent. As these peoples migrated to new regions and established new communities, they usually based their societies on kin groups rather than the state structures that predominated elsewhere in the eastern hemisphere. When different societies came into conflict with one another, however, they increasingly established formal political authorities to guide their affairs. African peoples organized states of various sizes, some very small and others quite large. When they entered into commercial relationships with Muslim peoples in southwest Asia and north Africa, they also built formidable imperial states in west Africa and bustling city-states in coastal east Africa. These states had far-reaching implications for sub-Saharan societies because they depended on a regular and reliable flow of trade goods—particularly gold, ivory, and slaves—and they encouraged African peoples to organize themselves politically and economically to satisfy the demands of foreign Muslim merchants. Trade also had cultural implications because it facilitated the introduction of Islam, which together with native African traditions profoundly influenced the development of sub-Saharan societies. After the eighth century, ruling elites in both west Africa and coastal east Africa mostly accepted Islam and strengthened its position in their societies by building mosques, consulting Muslim advisors, and supporting Islamic schools. By 1500 C.E. African traditions and Islamic influences had combined to fashion a series of powerful, productive, and distinctive societies in sub-Saharan Africa. ●

CHRONOLOGY

4th century C.E.	Introduction of bananas to Africa
11th to 13th century	Kingdom of Ghana
11th to 15th century	Swahili cities
12th to 15th century	Kingdom of Great Zimbabwe
12th to 16th century	Christian kingdom of Axum
13th to 15th century	Mali empire
1230–1255	Reign of Sundiata
14th to 17th century	Kingdom of Kongo
1312–1337	Reign of Mansa Musa
1324–1325	Mansa Musa's pilgrimage to Mecca

For Further Reading

Ibn Battuta. *Ibn Battuta in Black Africa.* Ed. and trans. by Said Hamdun and Noel King. Princeton, 1998. Translations of travel accounts of visits to coastal east Africa and the empire of Mali by a famous fourteenth-century Moroccan traveler.

Paul Bohannan and Philip D. Curtin. *Africa and Africans.* 3rd ed. Prospect Heights, Ill., 1988. Exploration of themes in African history, society, and culture by an anthropologist and a historian.

Christopher Ehret. *An African Classical Age: Eastern and Southern Africa in World History, 1000 B.C. to A.D. 400.* Charlottesville, Va., 1998. A pathbreaking volume focusing on eastern and southern Africa and drawing on both linguistic and archaeological evidence.

———. *The Civilizations of Africa: A History to 1800.* Charlottesville, Va., 2002. An important contribution that views Africa in the context of world history.

J. F. P. Hopkins and N. Levtzion, eds. *Corpus of Early Arabic Sources for West African History.* Princeton, 2000. Translations of numerous important accounts by Muslim merchants and geographers who reported on conditions in west Africa before modern times.

Mark Horton and John Middleton. *The Swahili: The Social Landscape of a Mercantile Society.* Oxford, 2000. Useful survey that draws on both archaeological and written evidence.

Kairn A. Klieman. *"The Pygmies Were Our Compass": Bantu and Batwa in the History of West Central Africa, Early Times to c. 1900 C.E.* Portsmouth, N.H., 2003. Draws on archaeological, linguistic, oral, and ethnographic evidence to chart the changing relationships between Bantu and forest peoples.

Nehemia Levtzion. *Ancient Ghana and Mali.* London, 1973. Concentrates on the political, social, and cultural history of west African kingdoms and empires.

Ali A. Mazrui. *The Africans: A Triple Heritage.* Boston, 1986. Emphasizes the legacies of indigenous, Islamic, and Western influences on African history.

John S. Mbiti. *African Religions and Philosophy.* 2nd ed. London, 1990. A thorough and systematic study of traditional African religions in their cultural context.

Roderick James McIntosh. *The Peoples of the Middle Niger: The Island of Gold.* Oxford, 1998. Fascinating volume emphasizing the environmental context of west African history.

John Middleton. *The World of the Swahili: An African Mercantile Civilization.* New Haven, 1992. Rich scholarly analysis that places modern Swahili society and culture in its historical context.

D. T. Niane, ed. *Sundiata: An Epic of Old Mali.* 2nd ed. Trans. by G. D. Pickett. London, 2006. Translation of the story of Sundiata, founder of the Mali empire, as preserved in African oral tradition.

Alexandre Popovic. *The Revolt of African Slaves in Iraq.* Trans. by L. King. Princeton, 1999. Important study of the Zanj revolt of the ninth century.

Jan Vansina. *Paths in the Rainforests: Toward a History of Political Tradition in Equatorial Africa.* Madison, 1990. A brilliant synthesis of early African history by one of the world's foremost historians of Africa.

The Increasing Influence of Europe

chapter 19

Cloth merchants cut and sew woolen fabrics in a town market while customers shop.

EYEWITNESS:
From Venice to China and Back

In 1260 C.E. two brothers, Niccolò and Maffeo Polo, traveled from their native Venice to Constantinople. The Polo brothers were jewel merchants, and while in Constantinople, they decided to pursue opportunities farther east. They went first to Soldaia (modern Sudak), near Caffa on the Black Sea, and then to the trading cities of Sarai and Bulghar on the Volga River. At that point they might have returned home except that a war broke out behind them and prevented them from retracing their steps, so they joined a caravan and continued east. They spent three years in the great central Asian trading city of Bokhara, where they received an invitation to join a diplomatic embassy going to the court of Khubilai Khan. They readily agreed and traveled by caravan to the Mongol court, where the great khan received them and inquired about their land, rulers, and religion.

Khubilai was especially interested in learning more about Roman Catholic Christianity, most likely because he ruled a multicultural empire and wished to maintain harmony among the cultural and religious groups inhabiting his realm. Thus he asked the Polo brothers to return to Europe and request the pope to send learned theologians who could serve as authoritative sources of information on Christian doctrine. They accepted the mission and returned to Italy in 1269 as envoys of the great khan.

The Polo brothers were not able to satisfy the great khan's desire for expertise in Christian doctrine. The pope designated two missionaries to accompany the Polos, and the party set out in 1271, together with Niccolò's seventeen-year-old son, Marco Polo. Soon, however, the missionaries became alarmed at fighting along the route, and they decided to abandon the embassy and return to Europe. Thus only the Polos completed the journey, arriving at the Mongol court of Shangdu in 1274. Although they presented Khubilai with presents and letters from the pope rather than the requested missionaries, the great khan received them warmly and welcomed them to his court. In fact, they remained in China in the service of the great khan for the next seventeen years. Their mission gave rise to Marco Polo's celebrated account of his travels, and it signaled the reintegration of Europe into the political and economic affairs of the larger eastern hemisphere.

During the early middle ages, western Europe was a violent and disorderly land. The collapse of the western Roman empire and invasions by migratory peoples wrecked European society and economy. The Carolingian empire provided order only for a short time before a new series of invasions brought it down. As a result of the turmoil and disarray that plagued Europe during the half millennium from 500 to 1000 C.E., western Europeans played little role in the development of a hemispheric economy during the era dominated by the Tang, Song, Abbasid, and Byzantine empires.

During the early middle ages, however, Europeans laid the foundations of a more dynamic society. Regional states became the basis for a stable political order. New tools and technologies led to increased agricultural production and economic growth. The missionary efforts of the western Christian church brought cultural and religious unity to most of Europe. During the "high middle ages" of European history—the period from about 1000 to 1300 C.E.—European peoples built a vibrant and powerful society on the political, economic, and cultural foundations laid during the early middle ages.

Although the idea of empire continued to fascinate political thinkers and leaders, empire builders of the high middle ages did not manage to bring all of Europe under their control. Instead, local rulers organized powerful regional states. Increased agricultural production fueled rapid population growth. Economic expansion led to increased long-distance trade, enriched cities, and supported the establishment of new towns. Cultural and religious affairs also reflected the dynamism of the high middle ages, as European philosophers and theologians reconsidered traditional doctrines in light of fresh knowledge.

Political organization, demographic increase, and economic growth pushed Europeans once again into the larger world. European merchants began to participate directly in the commercial economy of the eastern hemisphere, sometimes traveling as far as China in search of luxury goods. Ambitious military and political leaders expanded the boundaries of Christendom by seizing Muslim-held territories in Spain and the Mediterranean islands. European forces even mounted a series of military crusades that sought to bring Islamic lands of the eastern Mediterranean basin under Christian control. They ultimately failed, but the crusades clearly demonstrated that Europeans were beginning to play a much larger role in the world than they had for the previous half millennium.

THE REGIONAL STATES OF MEDIEVAL EUROPE

Long after its disappearance the Roman empire inspired European philosophers, theologians, and rulers, who dreamed of a centralized political structure embracing all of Christian Europe. The Byzantine empire survived as the dominant power in the eastern Mediterranean region, where it flourished through the early eleventh century. By 1100 C.E., however, Byzantium experienced domestic social and economic difficulties as well as foreign pressure from both east and west. Even as Byzantium influenced the emergence of new states in Russia and eastern Europe, the empire itself gradually declined and in 1453 fell to Muslim Turkish invaders. As Byzantium weakened, western Europe underwent an impressive round of state building. Beginning in the late tenth century, German princes formed the so-called Holy Roman Empire, which they viewed as a Christian revival of the earlier Roman empire. Meanwhile, independent monarchies emerged in France and England, and other authorities ruled in the various regions of Italy and Spain. Thus medieval Europe was a political mosaic of independent and competing regional states.

The Late Byzantine Empire

Social and Economic Problems For about three centuries, the *theme* system (discussed in chapter 16) served the Byzantine empire well by supporting both a powerful army and a prosperous independent peasantry. About the eleventh century, however, wealthy landowners increasingly undermined the *theme* system by acquiring the properties of independent peasants and accumulating them into large estates. That development transformed formerly free peasants into a class of dependent agricultural laborers while reducing incentives for individuals to serve in Byzantine military forces. It also led to diminished tax receipts for the central government.

Challenges from the West As domestic problems mounted, Byzantium also faced fresh foreign challenges. From the west came representatives of a dynamic western Europe, where rapid economic development supported a round of military and political expansion. During the early eleventh century, Norman adventurers—descendants of Vikings who had settled on the Norman peninsula in northern France—carved out a regional state in southern Italy and expelled the last Byzantine authorities there. During

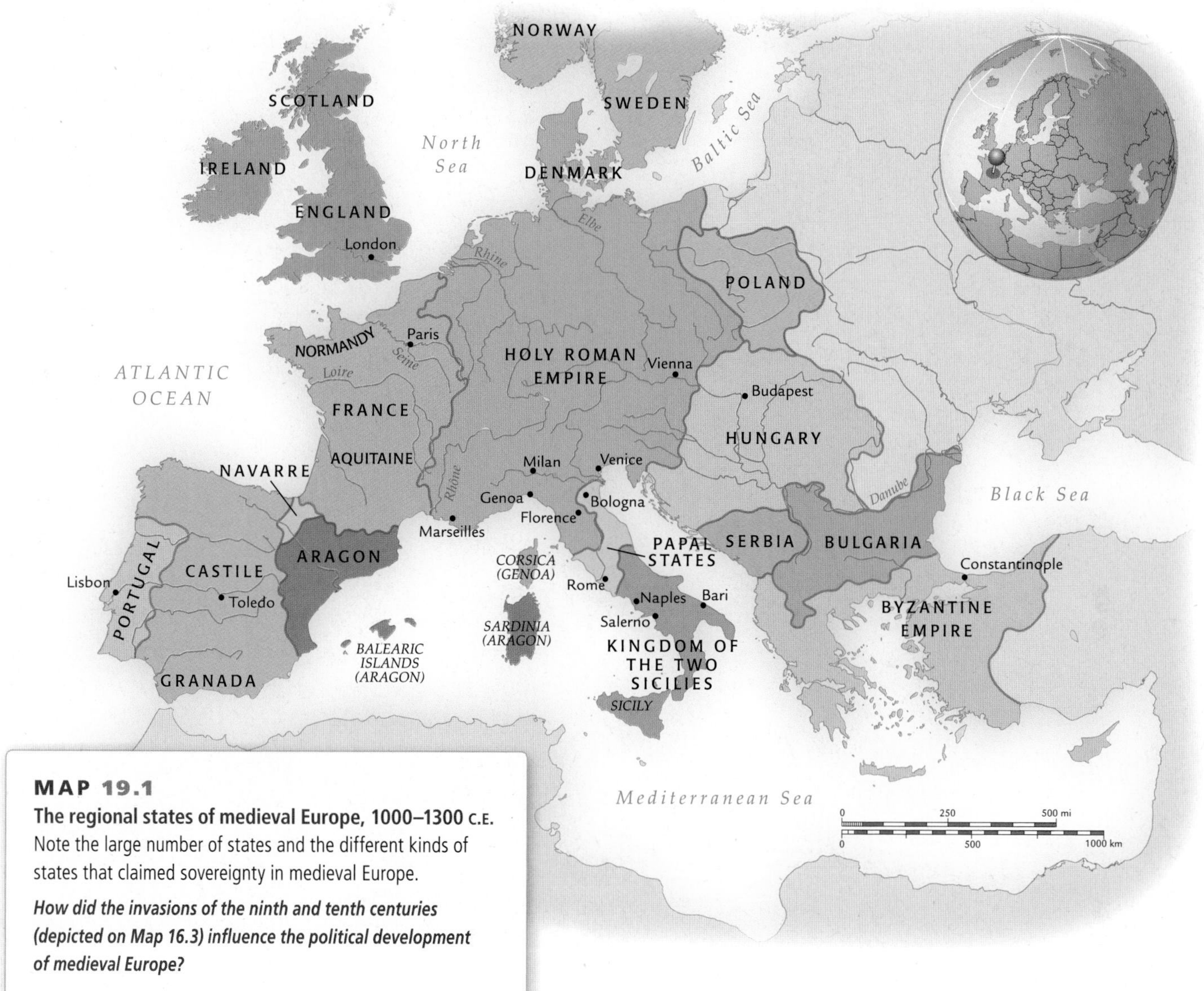

MAP 19.1
The regional states of medieval Europe, 1000–1300 C.E.
Note the large number of states and the different kinds of states that claimed sovereignty in medieval Europe.

How did the invasions of the ninth and tenth centuries (depicted on Map 16.3) influence the political development of medieval Europe?

the twelfth and thirteenth centuries, the Normans and other western European peoples mounted a series of crusades—vast military campaigns intended to recapture Jerusalem and other sites holy to Christians from Muslim rule—and took the opportunity to plunder the Byzantine empire. Venetian merchants even managed to hijack the fourth crusade (1202–1204 C.E.) from its original mission in the eastern Mediterranean and target Constantinople instead. Venetians had become prominent in the commercial life of the eastern Mediterranean, and they viewed the fourth crusade as an opportunity to strengthen their position against Byzantine competition. In 1204 the crusaders conquered Constantinople and subjected it to a devastating sack. Byzantine forces recaptured the city in 1261, but the humiliating destruction of the imperial capital dealt the empire a blow from which it never completely recovered.

Challenges from the East As Europeans advanced from the west, nomadic Turkish peoples invaded from the east. Most important among them were the Muslim Saljuqs, who beginning in the eleventh century sent waves of invaders into Anatolia, the agricultural heartland of the Byzantine empire. Given the military and financial problems of Byzantium, the Saljuqs found Anatolia ripe for plunder. In 1071 they handed the Byzantine army a demoralizing defeat at the battle of Manzikert. Byzantine forces then turned on each other in civil war, allowing the Saljuqs almost free rein in Anatolia. By the late twelfth century, the Saljuqs had seized much of Anatolia, while crusaders from western Europe held most of the remainder.

The loss of Anatolia sealed the fate of the Byzantine empire. A territorially truncated Byzantium survived until the mid-fifteenth century, but it enjoyed little autonomy and faced a series of challenges from Italian merchants, western European adventurers, and Turkish invaders. In 1453, following

During the sack of Constantinople in 1204, crusading forces seized and carted away Byzantine treasures of all sorts—including the great bronze horses that now stand over the entrance to St. Mark's basilica in Venice.

a long era of decline, the Byzantine empire came to an end when Ottoman Turks captured Constantinople and absorbed Byzantium's last remaining territories into their expanding realm.

The Holy Roman Empire

Otto I As the Carolingian empire faded during the ninth century, counts, dukes, and other local authorities took responsibility for providing order in their own regions. Gradually, some of them extended their influence beyond their own jurisdictions and built larger states. Otto of Saxony was particularly aggressive. By the mid-tenth century, he had established himself as king in northern Germany. He campaigned east of the Elbe River in lands populated by Slavic peoples (in what is now eastern Germany, western Poland, and the Czech Republic), and twice he ventured into Italy to quell political disturbances, protect the church, and seek opportunities in the south. In appreciation for his aid to the church, Pope John XII proclaimed Otto emperor in 962 C.E. Thus was born the Holy Roman Empire.

The imperial title had considerable cachet, and on several occasions energetic emperors almost transformed the Holy Roman Empire into a hegemonic state that might have reintroduced imperial unity to Europe. Conflict with the papacy, however, prevented the emperors from building a strong and dynamic state. Although the popes crowned the medieval emperors, their relations were usually tense, since both popes and emperors made large claims to authority in Christian Europe. Relations became especially strained when emperors sought to influence the selection of church officials, which the popes regarded as their own prerogative, or when emperors sought to extend their authority into Italy, where the popes had long provided political leadership.

Investiture Contest Neither the popes nor the emperors were strong enough to dominate the other, but the popes were able to prevent the emperors from building a powerful imperial state that would threaten the papacy as Europe's principal spiritual authority. The capacity of the papacy to weaken the empire became apparent during the Investiture Contest, a controversy over the appointment of church officials in the late eleventh and early twelfth centuries. From the earliest days of the Holy Roman Empire, imperial authorities had named important church officials to their positions, since the higher clergy provided political as well as religious services. In an effort to regain control of the clergy and ensure that church officials met appropriate spiritual criteria, Pope Gregory VII (1073–1085 C.E.) ordered an end to the practice of lay investiture—the selection and installation of church officials by lay rulers such as the emperors. When Emperor Henry IV (1056–1106 C.E.) challenged the pope's policy, Gregory excommunicated him and released his subjects from their duty to obey him. The German princes then took the opportunity to rebel against the emperor. Henry eventually regained control of the empire but only after beseeching Gregory's mercy while standing barefoot in the snow. Because of the pope's intervention in imperial affairs, however, the German princes won concessions that enhanced their independence and diminished the emperor's authority.

Frederick Barbarossa Popes and emperors clashed over their conflicting interests in Italy as well as over the appointment of church officials. Among the most vigorous of the medieval emperors was Frederick I, known as Frederick Barbarossa—"the red beard"—a vigorous and gallant man who reigned from 1152 to 1190 C.E. Working from his ancestral lands in southern Germany, Barbarossa sought to absorb the wealthy and increasingly urban region of Lombardy in northern Italy. Integration of Lombardy with his German holdings might have provided Barbarossa with the resources to control the German princes, build a powerful state, and dominate much of Europe. That prospect did not appeal to the popes, who marshaled support from other European states on behalf of the Italian cities. By the end of Barbarossa's reign, the papal coalition had forced the emperor to relinquish his rights in Lombardy. Once again, papal policies forestalled the transformation of the Holy Roman Empire into a powerful state.

Voltaire, the eighteenth-century French writer, once quipped that the Holy Roman Empire was "neither holy, nor Roman, nor an empire." Indeed, the Holy Roman Empire was an empire principally in name. In reality, it was a

King Louis IX (reigned 1226–1270), also known as St. Louis, helped to consolidate the Capetian hold on the French monarchy. In this fourteenth-century manuscript illustration, he hears the petitions of humble subjects (right), while hanged criminals (left) serve as a reminder of felony's results.

39,
HIC EXEVNT:CABALLI DENAVIBVS - ET HIC:MILITES: FESTINAVERVNT:HES

The Bayeux tapestry, a magnificent mural of woven linen about 70 meters (230 feet) long, depicts the Norman invasion and conquest of England in 1066. In this section Norman warriors sail across the English Channel and disembark in southern England.

regional state ruling Germany, though it also wielded influence intermittently in eastern Europe and Italy. In no sense, however, did the Holy Roman Empire restore imperial unity to western Europe.

Regional Monarchies in France and England

In the absence of an effective imperial power, regional states emerged throughout medieval Europe. In France and England, princes established regional monarchies on the basis of relationships between lords and their retainers.

Capetian France The French monarchy grew slowly from humble beginnings. When the last of the Carolingians died, in 987 C.E., the lords of France elected a minor noble named Hugh Capet to serve as king. Capet held only a small territory around Paris, and he was in no position to challenge his retainers, some of whom were far more powerful than the king himself. During the next three centuries, however, his descendants, known as the Capetian kings, gradually added to their resources and expanded their political influence. Relying on relationships between lords and retainers, they absorbed the territories of retainers who died without heirs and established the right to administer justice throughout the realm. By the early fourteenth century, the Capetian kings had gradually centralized power and authority in France.

The Normans The English monarchy developed quite differently. Its founders were the Normans. Though nominally subject to Carolingian and later to Capetian rulers, the dukes of Normandy in fact pursued their own interests with little regard for their lords. Within Normandy the dukes built a tightly centralized state in which all authority stemmed from the dukes themselves. The dukes also retained title to all land in Normandy, and in an effort to forestall conflicts of interest they strictly limited the right of their retainers to grant land to others. By the late tenth century, Norman lords had built a series of castles from which disciplined armies dominated their territories, and in the eleventh century they emerged as prominent political and military leaders throughout Europe and beyond to much of the Mediterranean basin as well.

Norman England In 1066 Duke William of Normandy invaded England, then ruled by descendants of the Angles, the Saxons, and other Germanic peoples who had migrated there during the fifth and sixth centuries. Following a speedy military victory, the duke, now known as William the Conqueror, introduced Norman principles of government and land tenure to England. While retaining many institutions of their Anglo-Saxon predecessors, the Norman kings of England ruled over a much more tightly centralized realm than did the Capetian kings of France.

Both the Capetians and the Normans faced challenges from retainers seeking to pursue independent policies or enlarge their powers at the expense of the monarchs. Both dynasties also faced external challenges: indeed, they often battled each other, since the Normans periodically sought to expand their possessions in France. On the basis of relationships between lords and retainers, however, both the Capetians and the Normans managed to organize regional monarchies that maintained order and provided reasonably good government.

Regional States in Italy and Iberia

Church Influence in Italy Regional states emerged also in other lands of medieval Europe, though not on such a large scale as the monarchies of France and England. In Italy, for example, no single regime controlled the entire peninsula. Rather, a series of ecclesiastical states, city-states, and principalities competed for power and position. In central Italy the popes had provided political leadership since the Carolingian era. Indeed, although the papacy was a spiritual rather than a political post, the popes ruled a good-sized territory in central Italy known as the Papal State. In northern Italy, too, the church influenced political affairs, since bishops of the major cities took much of the initiative in organizing public life in their regions. During the high middle ages, however, as the cities grew wealthy from trade and manufacturing, lay classes challenged the bishops and eventually displaced them as ruling authorities.

Italian States By about the twelfth century, a series of prosperous city-states—including Florence, Bologna, Genoa, Milan, and Venice—dominated not only their own urban districts but also the surrounding hinterlands. Meanwhile, in southern Italy, Norman adventurers—cousins of those who conquered Anglo-Saxon England—invaded territories still claimed by the Byzantine empire and various Muslim states. Norman adventurers first intervened in Italian affairs in the year 999, when a group of Norman pilgrims aided the people of Salerno as they fought off an attack by Muslim raiders. Other Normans later aided the city of Bari in its struggle for independence from Byzantine authority (1017–1018). When they learned that opportunities might be available for ambitious adventurers in an unstable region, Norman mercenaries soon made their way to southern Italy in large numbers. With papal approval and support, they overcame Byzantine and Muslim authorities, brought southern Italy into the orbit of Roman Catholic Christianity, and laid the foundations for the emergence of the powerful kingdom of Naples.

Christian and Muslim States in Iberia As in Italy, a series of regional states competed for power in the Iberian peninsula. From the eighth to the eleventh century, a series of Muslim states ruled most of the peninsula. Only in northern Spain did small Christian states hold sway, mostly in mountainous regions. Beginning in the mid-eleventh century, though, Christian adventurers from those states began to attack Muslim territories and enlarge their own domains. As in southern Italy, political and military instability attracted the attention of Norman adventurers, many of whom traveled to Spain and joined the armies of the Christian kingdoms as soldiers of fortune. By the late thirteenth century, the Christian kingdoms of Castile, Aragon, and Portugal controlled most of the Iberian peninsula, leaving only the small kingdom of Granada in Muslim hands.

With its Byzantine empire, Holy Roman Empire, regional monarchies, ecclesiastical principalities, city-states, and new states founded on conquest, medieval Europe might seem to present a chaotic and confusing political spectacle, particularly when compared with a land such as China, reunified by centralized imperial rule. Moreover, European rulers rarely

The Italian city-state of Florence grew rapidly during the high middle ages. This portrait of the city concentrates on the space enclosed by walls completed in the early fourteenth century.

sought to maintain the current state of affairs but, rather, campaigned constantly to enlarge their holdings at the expense of their neighbors. As a result, the political history of medieval Europe was a complicated affair. Yet the regional states of the high middle ages effectively tended to public affairs in limited regions. In doing so, they fashioned alternatives to a centralized empire as a form of political organization.

ECONOMIC GROWTH AND SOCIAL DEVELOPMENT

As regional states provided increasingly effective political organization, medieval Europe experienced dramatic economic growth and social development. The economic revival closely resembled the processes that in an earlier era had strengthened China, India, and the Islamic world. Increased agricultural production, urbanization, manufacturing, and trade transformed Europe into a powerful society and drew it once again into commercial relationships with distant lands.

Growth of the Agricultural Economy

As in China, India, and the Islamic world during the early postclassical era, a dramatic increase in agricultural yields was the foundation of economic growth and social development in medieval Europe. Several developments help to account for this increased agricultural production: the opening of new lands to cultivation, improved agricultural techniques, the use of new tools and technologies, and the introduction of new crops.

Expansion of Arable Land Beginning in the late tenth century, as local lords pacified their territories and put an end to invasions, Europe began to experience population pressure. In response serfs and monks cleared forests, drained swamps, and increased the amount of land devoted to agriculture. At first, some lords opposed those efforts, since they reduced the amount of land available for game preserves, where nobles enjoyed hunting wild animals. Gradually, however, the lords realized that expanding agricultural production would yield higher taxes and increase their own wealth. By the early twelfth century, lords were encouraging the expansion of cultivation, and the process gathered momentum.

Improved Agricultural Techniques Meanwhile, reliance on improved methods of cultivation and better agricultural technology led to significantly higher productivity. During the high middle ages, European cultivators refined and improved their techniques in the interests of larger yields. They experimented with new crops and with different cycles of crop rotation to ensure the most abundant harvests possible without compromising the fertility of the soil. They increased cultivation especially of beans, which not only provided dietary protein but also enriched the land because of their property of fixing nitrogen in the soils where they grow. They kept more domestic animals, which not only served as beasts of burden and sources of food but also enriched fields with their droppings. They dug ponds in which they raised fish, which provided yet another dietary supplement. By the thirteenth century, observation and experimentation with new crops and new techniques had vastly increased understanding of agricultural affairs. News of those discoveries circulated widely throughout Europe in books and treatises on household economics and agricultural methods. Written in vernacular languages for lay readers, these works helped to publicize innovations, which in turn led to increased agricultural productivity.

New Tools and Technologies During the high middle ages, European peoples expanded their use of water mills and heavy plows, which had appeared during the early middle ages, and also introduced new tools and technologies. Two simple items in particular—the horseshoe and the horse collar—made it possible to increase sharply the amount of land that cultivators could work. Horseshoes helped to prevent softened and split hooves on horses that tramped through moist European soils. Horse collars placed the burden of a heavy load on an animal's chest and shoulders rather than its neck and enabled horses to pull heavy plows without choking. Thus Europeans could hitch their plows to horses rather than to slower oxen and bring more land under the plow.

"By the early 12th century, lords were encouraging the expansion of cultivation, and the process gathered momentum."

New Crops Expansion of land under cultivation, improved methods of cultivation, and the use of new tools and technologies combined to increase both the quantity and the quality of food supplies. During the early middle ages, the European diet consisted almost entirely of grains and grain products such as gruel and bread. During the centuries from 1000 to 1300, meat, dairy products, fish, vegetables, and legumes such as beans and peas became much more prominent in the European diet, though without displacing grains as staple foods. Spain, Italy, and other Mediterranean lands benefited also from widespread cultivation of crops that had earlier been disseminated through the Islamic world: hard durum wheat, rice, spinach, artichokes, eggplant, lemons, limes, oranges, and melons all became prominent items in Mediterranean diets during the high middle ages.

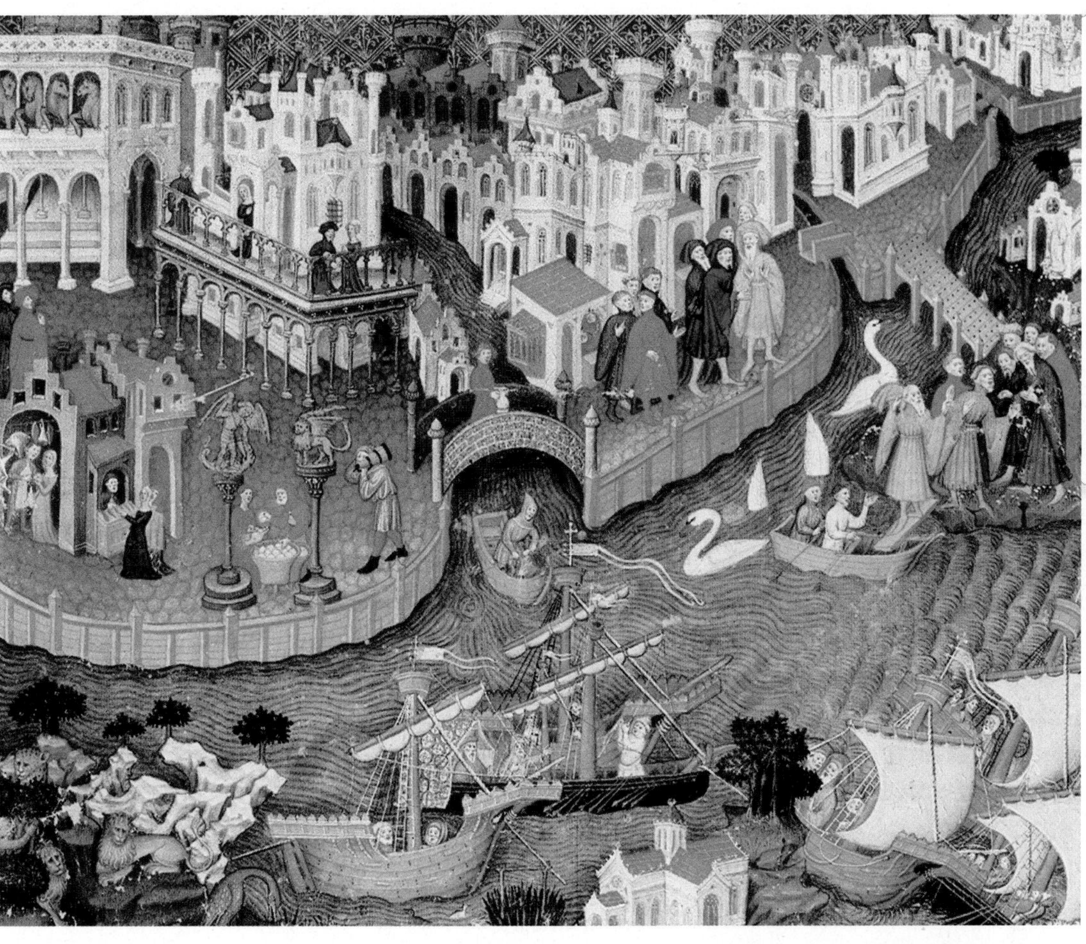

Venice, home of Marco Polo and a legion of merchants, drew enormous prosperity from trade. Street vendors, shopkeepers, and merchant ships figure prominently in this illustration from a fourteenth-century manuscript. How did its geographic location help Venice become a center of Mediterranean trade?

Population Growth As in other lands, increased agricultural productivity supported rapid population growth in medieval Europe. In 800 C.E., during the Carolingian era, European population stood at about twenty-nine million. By 1000, when regional states had ended invasions and restored order, it had edged up to thirty-six million. During the next few centuries, as the agricultural economy expanded, population surged. By 1100 it had reached forty-four million; by 1200 it had risen to fifty-eight million, an increase of more than 30 percent within one century; and by 1300 it had grown an additional 36 percent, to seventy-nine million. During the fourteenth century, epidemic plague severely reduced populations and disrupted economies in Europe as well as Asia and north Africa—a development discussed in chapter 21. Between 1000 and 1300, however, rapid demographic growth helped stimulate a vigorous revival of towns and trade in medieval Europe.

The Revival of Towns and Trade

Urbanization With abundant supplies of food, European society was able to support large numbers of urban residents—artisans, crafts workers, merchants, and professionals. Attracted by urban opportunities, peasants and serfs from the countryside flocked to established cities and founded new towns at strategically located sites. Cities founded during Roman times, such as Paris, London, and Toledo, became thriving centers of government and business, and new urban centers emerged from Venice in northern Italy to Bergen on the west coast of Norway. Northern Italy and Flanders (the northwestern part of modern Belgium) experienced especially strong urbanization. For the first time since the fall of the western Roman empire, cities began to play a major role in European economic and social development.

Textile Production The growth of towns and cities brought about increasing specialization of labor, which in turn resulted in a dramatic expansion of manufacturing and trade. Manufacturing concentrated especially on the production of wool textiles. The cities of Italy and Flanders in particular became lively centers for the spinning, weaving, and dyeing of wool. Trade in wool products helped to fuel economic development throughout Europe. By the twelfth century the counts of Champagne in northern France sponsored fairs that operated almost year-round and that served as vast marketplaces where merchants from all parts of Europe compared and exchanged goods.

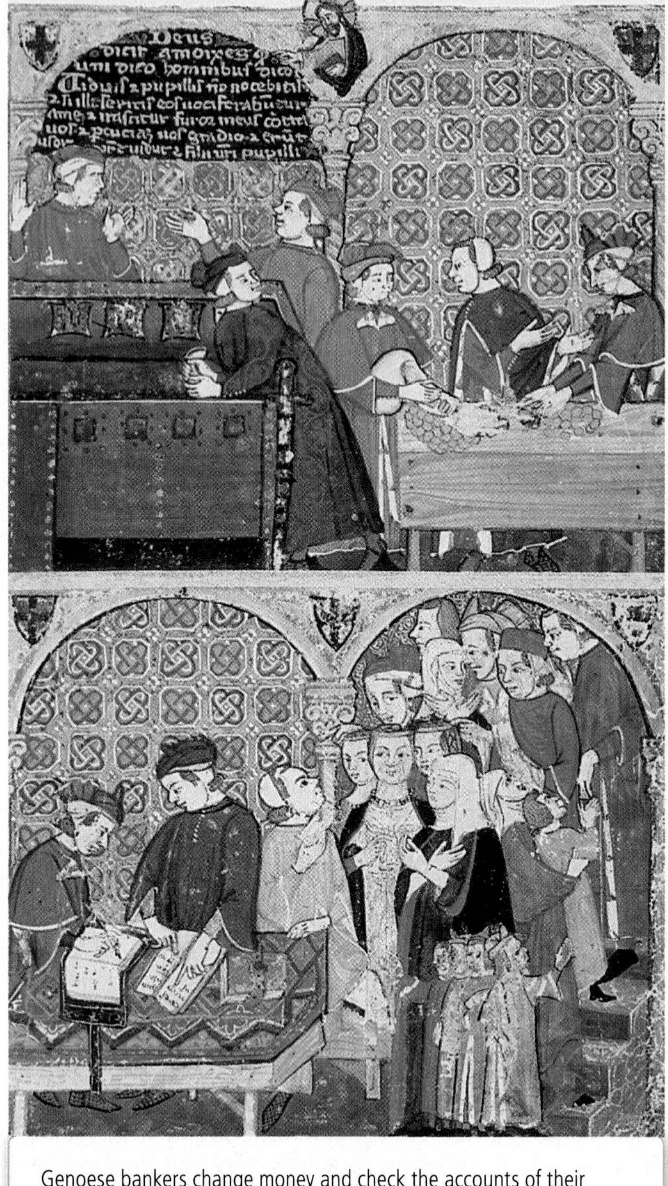

Genoese bankers change money and check the accounts of their clients in this fourteenth-century manuscript illustration.

Mediterranean Trade The revival of urban society was most pronounced in Italy, which was geographically well situated to participate in the trade networks of the Mediterranean basin. During the tenth century the cities of Amalfi and Venice served as ports for merchants engaged in trade with Byzantine and Muslim partners in the eastern Mediterranean. During the next century the commercial networks of the Mediterranean widened to embrace Genoa, Pisa, Naples, and other Italian cities. Italian merchants exchanged salt, olive oil, wine, wool fabrics, leather products, and glass for luxury goods such as gems, spices, silk, and other goods from India, southeast Asia, and China that Muslim merchants brought to eastern Mediterranean markets.

As trade expanded, Italian merchants established colonies in the major ports and commercial centers of the Mediterranean and the Black Sea. By the thirteenth century, Venetian and Genoese merchants maintained large communities in Constantinople, Alexandria, Cairo, Damascus, and the Black Sea ports of Tana, Caffa, and Trebizond. Caffa was the first destination of the Venetian brothers Niccolò and Maffeo Polo when they embarked on their commercial venture of 1260. Those trading posts enabled them to deal with Muslim merchants engaged in the Indian Ocean and overland trade with India, southeast Asia, and China. By the mid-thirteenth century the Polos and a few other Italian merchants were beginning to venture beyond the eastern Mediterranean region to central Asia, India, and China in search of commercial opportunities.

The Hanseatic League Although medieval trade was most active in the Mediterranean basin, a lively commerce grew up also in the northern seas. The Baltic Sea and the North Sea were sites of a particularly well-developed trade network known as the Hanseatic League, or more simply as the Hansa—an association of trading cities stretching from Novgorod to London and embracing all the significant commercial centers of Poland, northern Germany, and Scandinavia. The Hansa dominated trade in grain, fish, furs, timber, and pitch from northern Europe. The fairs of Champagne and the Rhine, the Danube, and other major European rivers linked the Hansa trade network with that of the Mediterranean.

Improved Business Techniques As in postclassical China and the Islamic world, a rapidly increasing volume of trade encouraged the development of credit, banking, and new forms of business organization in Europe. Bankers issued letters of credit to merchants traveling to distant markets, thus freeing them from the risk and inconvenience of carrying cash or bullion. Having arrived at their destinations, merchants exchanged their letters of credit for merchandise or cash in the local currency. In the absence of credit and banking, it would have been impossible for merchants to trade on a large scale.

Meanwhile, merchants devised new ways of spreading and pooling the risks of commercial investments. They entered into partnerships with other merchants, and they limited the liability of partners to the extent of their individual investments. The limitation on individual liability encouraged the formation of commercial partnerships, thus further stimulating the European economy.

Social Change

The Three Estates Medieval social commentators frequently held that European society embraced three estates or classes: "those who pray, those who fight, and those who work." Those who prayed were clergy of the Roman Catholic church. From lowly parish priests to bishops, cardinals,

sources from the past

Francesco Balducci Pegolotti on Trade between Europe and China

Francesco Balducci Pegolotti was an employee of a Florentine banking company. He traveled as far as London and Cyprus on bank business. Although he probably did not travel to Asia, Pegolotti learned about conditions that long-distance traders faced from many merchants who ventured far from home. About 1340 Pegolotti compiled their reports into a book of information and advice for merchants traveling to China from the port of Tana (modern Rostov) on the Sea of Azov.

In the first place, you must let your beard grow long and not shave. And at Tana you should furnish yourself with a dragoman [guide and interpreter]. And you must not try to save money in the matter of dragomen by taking a bad one instead of a good one. For the additional wages of the good one will not cost you so much as you will save by having him. And besides the dragoman it will be well to take at least two good men servants who are acquainted with the [Turkish] Cumanian tongue. . . .

The road you travel from Tana to Cathay [China] is perfectly safe, whether by day or by night, according to what the merchants say who have used it. Only if the merchant, in going or coming, should die upon the road, everything belonging to him will become the perquisite of the lord of the country in which he dies, and the officers of the lord will take possession of all. And in like manner if he die in Cathay. But if his brother be with him, or an intimate friend and comrade calling himself his brother, then to him they will surrender the property of the deceased, and so it will be rescued. . . .

Cathay is a province which contains a multitude of cities and towns. Among others there is one in particular, that is to say the capital city, to which is great resort of merchants, and in which there is a vast amount of trade; and this city is called Khanbaliq. And the said city hath a circuit of one hundred miles, and is all full of people and houses and of dwellers in the said city.

You may calculate that a merchant with a dragoman and two men servants and with goods to the value of twenty-five thousand golden florins should spend on his way to Cathay from sixty to eighty ingots of silver, and not more if he manages well; and for all the road back again from Cathay to Tana, including the expenses of living and the pay of servants, and all other charges, the cost will be about five ingots per head of pack animals, or something less. And you may reckon the ingot to be worth five golden florins. . . .

Anyone from Genoa or Venice wishing to go to the places above named and to make the journey to Cathay should carry linens with him, and if he visits Urgench [in modern Uzbekistan] he will dispose of these well. In Urgench he should purchase ingots of silver, and with these he should proceed without making any further investment, unless it be some bales of the very finest stuffs which go in small bulk, and cost no more for carriage than coarser stuffs would do.

Whatever silver the merchants may carry with them as far as Cathay the lord of Cathay will take from them and put into his treasury. And to merchants who thus bring silver they give that paper money of theirs in exchange. This is of yellow paper, stamped with the seal of the lord aforesaid. And this money is called balishi; and with this money you can readily buy silk and all other merchandise that you have a desire to buy. And all the people of the country are bound to receive it. And yet you shall not pay a higher price for your goods because your money is of paper. And of the said paper money there are three kinds, one being worth more than another, according to the value which has been established for each by that lord.

For Further Reflection

- On the basis of Pegolotti's report, how could you characterize the various commercial, financial, and economic risks faced by European merchants traveling to China and trading there?

Source: Henry Yule and Henri Cordier, eds. *Cathay and the Way Thither,* 2nd ed., 4 vols. London: Hakluyt Society, 1913–16, 3:151–55. (Translation slightly modified.)

and popes, the clergy constituted a spiritual estate owing its loyalty to the church rather than secular rulers. The fighters came from the ranks of nobles. They inherited their positions in society and received an education that concentrated on equestrian skills and military arts. Finally, there were those who worked—the vast majority of the population—who mostly cultivated land as peasants dependent for protection on their lords, those who fought.

The formula dividing society neatly into three classes captures some important truths about medieval Europe. It clearly reflects a society marked by political, social, and economic inequality: although they did not necessarily lead lives of luxury, those who prayed and those who fought enjoyed rights and honors denied to those who worked. Though bound by secular law, for example, clerics were members of an international spiritual society before they

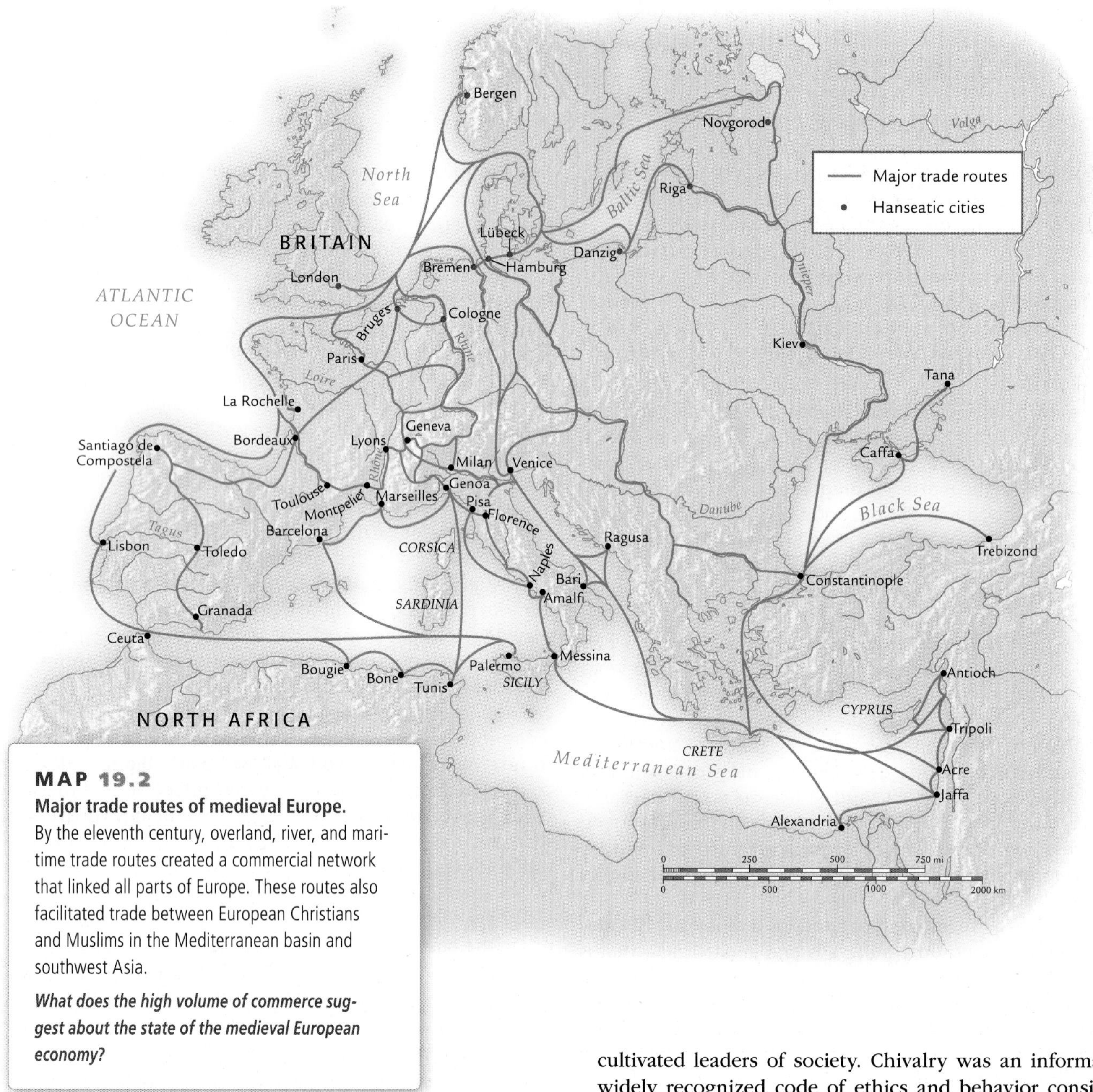

MAP 19.2
Major trade routes of medieval Europe.
By the eleventh century, overland, river, and maritime trade routes created a commercial network that linked all parts of Europe. These routes also facilitated trade between European Christians and Muslims in the Mediterranean basin and southwest Asia.

What does the high volume of commerce suggest about the state of the medieval European economy?

were subjects of a lord, and if they became involved in legal difficulties, they normally faced courts of law administered by the church rather than secular rulers. For their part the nobles mostly lived off the surplus production of dependent peasants and serfs.

Chivalry Yet, though expressing some truths, the formula overlooks processes that brought considerable change to medieval European society. Within the ranks of the nobles, for example, an emphasis on chivalry and courtly behavior gradually introduced expectations of high ethical standards and refined manners that encouraged warriors to become cultivated leaders of society. Chivalry was an informal but widely recognized code of ethics and behavior considered appropriate for nobles. Church officials originally promoted the chivalric code in an effort to curb fighting within Christendom. By the twelfth century the ritual by which a young man became initiated into the nobility as a knight commonly called for the candidate to place his sword upon a church altar and pledge his service to God. Thus, rather than seeking wealth and power, the noble who observed the chivalric code would devote himself to the causes of order, piety, and the Christian faith.

Troubadours Aristocratic women found the chivalric code much to their liking, and they went to some lengths to spread its values. Instead of emphasizing the code's religious dimensions, however, they promoted refined behavior and tender, respectful relations between the sexes. Reflections of their interests survive in the songs and poems of the troubadours, a class of traveling poets, minstrels, and entertainers whom aristocratic women enthusiastically patronized. The troubadours, who were most active in southern France and northern Italy, drew inspiration from a long tradition of love poetry produced in nearby Muslim Spain. Many troubadours visited the expanding Christian kingdoms of Spain, where they heard love poems and songs from servants, slaves, and musicians of Muslim ancestry. Enchanted by that refined literature, they began to produce similar verses for their own aristocratic patrons.

Eleanor of Aquitaine During the late twelfth and thirteenth centuries, troubadours traveled from one aristocratic court to another, where noblewomen rewarded them for singing songs and reciting verses that celebrated passionate love between a man and a woman. Troubadours flocked especially to Poitiers, where Eleanor of Aquitaine (1122–1204) liberally supported romantic poets and entertainers. Eleanor was the most celebrated woman of her day, and she used her influence to encourage the cultivation of good manners, refinement, and romantic love. The troubadours' performances did not instantly transform rough warriors into polished courtiers. Over the long term, however, the code of chivalry and the romantic poetry and song presented at aristocratic courts gradually softened the manners of the nobility.

A thirteenth-century manuscript illustration depicts two lute players: Muslim (left) and Christian (right). Muslim artists deeply influenced the poetry and music of the medieval troubadors.

Independent Cities Social change also touched those who worked. By the twelfth century the ranks of workers included not only peasants but also increasing numbers of merchants, artisans, crafts workers, and professionals such as physicians and lawyers, who filled the growing towns of medieval Europe. The expansion of the urban working population promoted the development of towns and cities as jurisdictions that fit awkwardly in the framework of the medieval political order. Because of their military power, lords could dominate small towns and tax their wealth. As towns grew larger, however, urban populations were increasingly able to resist the demands of nobles and guide their own affairs. By the late eleventh century, inhabitants of prosperous towns were demanding that local lords grant them charters of incorporation that exempted them from political regulation, allowed them to manage their own affairs, and abolished taxes and tolls on commerce within the urban district. Sometimes groups of cities organized leagues to advance their commercial interests, as in the case of the Hansa, or to protect themselves against the encroachments of political authorities.

Guilds The cities of medieval Europe were by no means egalitarian societies: cities attracted noble migrants as well as peasants and serfs, and urban nobles often dominated city affairs. Yet medieval towns and cities also reflected the interests and contributions of the working classes. Merchants and workers in all the arts, crafts, and trades organized guilds that regulated the production and sale of goods within their jurisdictions. By the thirteenth century the guilds had come to control much of the urban economy of medieval Europe. They established standards of quality for manufactured goods, sometimes even requiring members to adopt specific techniques of production, and they determined the prices at which members had to sell their products. In an effort to maintain a balance between supply and demand—and to protect their members' interests—they also regulated the entry of new workers into their groups.

Guilds had social as well as economic significance. They provided a focus for friendship and mutual support in addition to work. Guild members regularly socialized with one another, and prosperous guilds often built large halls where members held meetings, banquets, and sometimes boisterous drinking parties. Guilds came to the aid of members and their families by providing financial and moral support for those who fell ill. They also arranged funeral services for their deceased and provided support for survivors. Quite apart from regulating work, then, guilds constituted a kind of social infrastructure that made it possible for medieval cities to function.

Urban Women Women who lived in the countryside continued to perform the same kinds of tasks that their ancestors tended to in the early middle ages: household chores, weaving, and the care of domestic animals. But medieval towns

Women were prominent in the markets of medieval Europe and sometimes worked as bankers or tailors, as in this manuscript illustration.

and cities offered fresh opportunities for women as well as for men. In the patriarchal society of medieval Europe, few routes to public authority were open to women, but in the larger towns and cities women worked alongside men as butchers, brewers, bakers, candle makers, fishmongers, shoemakers, gemsmiths, innkeepers, launderers, money changers, merchants, and occasionally physicians and pharmacists. Women dominated some occupations, particularly those involving textiles and decorative arts, such as sewing, spinning, weaving, and the making of hats, wigs, and fur garments.

Most guilds admitted women into their ranks, and some guilds had exclusively female memberships. In thirteenth-century Paris, for example, there were approximately one hundred guilds. Six of them admitted only women, but eighty others included women as well as men among their members. The increasing prominence of women in European society illustrates the significance of towns and cities as agents of social change in medieval Europe.

EUROPEAN CHRISTIANITY DURING THE HIGH MIDDLE AGES

Throughout the middle ages, Christianity guided European thought on religious, moral, and ethical matters—Eastern Orthodox Christianity in the Byzantine empire and Roman Catholic Christianity in western Europe. Representatives of the Orthodox and Roman Catholic churches administered the rituals associated with birth, marriage, and death. Most of the art, literature, and music of the high middle ages drew inspiration from Christian doctrines and stories. Just as mosques and minarets defined the skylines of Muslim cities, the spires of churches and cathedrals dominated the landscape of medieval Europe, testifying visually to the importance of religion and the pervasive presence of the Eastern Orthodox and Roman Catholic churches.

Schools, Universities, and Scholastic Theology

During the early middle ages, European society was not stable and wealthy enough to support institutions of advanced education. Monasteries sometimes maintained schools that provided a rudimentary education, and political leaders occasionally supported scholars who lived at their courts, but very few schools offered formal education beyond an elementary level. In the absence of a widely observed curriculum or course of study, early medieval scholars drew their inspiration from the Bible and from major spokesmen of the early Christian church such as St. Augustine of Hippo.

Cathedral Schools During the high middle ages, economic development sharply increased the wealth of Europe and made more resources available for education. Meanwhile, an increasingly complex society created a demand for educated individuals who could deal with complicated political, legal, and theological issues. Beginning in the early eleventh century, bishops and archbishops in France and northern Italy organized schools in their cathedrals and invited well-known scholars to serve as master teachers. Schools in the cathedrals of Paris, Chartres, and Bologna in particular attracted students from all parts of Europe.

By the twelfth century the cathedral schools had established formal curricula based on writings in Latin, the official language of the Roman Catholic church. Instruction concentrated on the liberal arts, especially literature and philosophy. Students read the Bible and the writings of the church fathers, such as St. Augustine, St. Jerome, and St. Ambrose, as well as classical Latin literature and the few works of Plato and Aristotle that were available in Latin translation. Some cathedral schools also offered advanced instruction in law, medicine, and theology.

Universities About the mid-twelfth century, students and teachers organized academic guilds and persuaded political authorities to grant charters guaranteeing their rights. Student guilds demanded fair treatment for students from townspeople, who sometimes charged excessive rates for room and board, and called on their teachers to provide rigorous, high-quality instruction. Faculty guilds sought to vest teachers with the right to bestow academic degrees, which served as licenses to teach in other cities, and to control the curriculum in their institutions. These guilds had the effect of

transforming cathedral schools into universities. The first universities were those of Bologna, Paris, and Salerno—noted for instruction in law, theology, and medicine, respectively—but by the late thirteenth century, universities had appeared also in Rome, Naples, Seville, Salamanca, Oxford, Cambridge, and other cities throughout Europe.

A manuscript illustration depicts a professor, at top left, lecturing in a medieval German university. About half the students listen and take notes diligently, while the others catch up on their sleep or chat with friends.

The Influence of Aristotle The evolution of the university coincided with the rediscovery of the works of Aristotle. Western European scholars of the early middle ages knew only a few of Aristotle's minor works that were available in Latin translation. Byzantine scholars knew Aristotle in the original Greek, but they rarely had any dealings with their Roman Catholic counterparts. During the high middle ages, as commerce and communication increased between Byzantine Orthodox and Roman Catholic Christians, western Europeans learned about Aristotle's thought and obtained Latin translations from Byzantine philosophers. Western European scholars learned about Aristotle also through Muslim philosophers who appreciated the power of his thought and had most of his works translated into Arabic. Christian and Jewish scholars in Sicily and Spain became aware of those Arabic translations, which they retranslated into Latin. Although the resulting works had their flaws—since they filtered Aristotle's original Greek through both Arabic and Latin—they made Aristotle's thought accessible to Western European scholars.

Scholasticism: St. Thomas Aquinas During the thirteenth century, understanding of Aristotle's thought and Latin translations of his works spread throughout Europe, and they profoundly influenced almost all branches of thought. The most notable result was the emergence of scholastic theology, which sought to synthesize the beliefs and values of Christianity with the logical rigor of Greek philosophy. The most famous of the scholastic theologians was St. Thomas Aquinas (1225–1274), who spent most of his career teaching at the University of Paris. While holding fervently to his Christian convictions, St. Thomas believed that Aristotle had understood and explained the workings of the world better than any other thinker of any era. St. Thomas saw no contradiction between Aristotle and Christian revelation but, rather, viewed them as complementary authorities: Aristotle provided the most powerful analysis of the world according to human reason and Christianity explained the world and human life as the results of a divine plan. By combining Aristotle's rational power with the teachings of Christianity, St. Thomas expected to formulate the most truthful and persuasive system of thought possible.

In St. Thomas's view, for example, belief in the existence of God did not depend exclusively on an individual's faith. By drawing on Aristotle, St. Thomas believed, it was possible to prove rationally that God exists. Aristotle himself never recognized a personal deity such as the Jewish and Christian God, but he argued that a conscious agent had set the world in motion. St. Thomas borrowed Aristotle's arguments and identified the conscious agent with the Jewish and Christian God, who outlined his plan for the world in the Hebrew scriptures and the Christian New Testament. Thus, as expressed in the thought of St. Thomas Aquinas, scholastic theology represented the harmonization of Aristotle with Christianity and the synthesis of reason and faith. Like the neo-Confucianism of Zhu Xi or the Islamic philosophy of Ibn Rushd, scholastic theology reinterpreted inherited beliefs in light of the most advanced knowledge of the time.

Popular Religion

St. Thomas and the other scholastic theologians addressed a sophisticated, intellectual elite, not the common people of medieval Europe. The popular masses neither knew nor cared much about Aristotle. For their purposes, Christianity was important primarily as a set of beliefs and rituals that gave meaning to individual lives and that bound them together into coherent communities. Thus formal doctrine and theology did not appeal to popular audiences as much as the ceremonies and observances that involved individuals in the life of a larger community—and that also brought benefits in the form of supernatural aid or protection for an individual's crops or family.

Sacraments Popular piety generally entailed observance of the sacraments and devotion to the saints recognized by the Roman Catholic church. Sacraments are holy rituals that bring spiritual blessings on the observants. The church recognized seven sacraments, including baptism, matrimony, penance, and the Eucharist. Most important was the Eucharist, during which priests offered a ritual meal commemorating Jesus' last meal with his disciples before his trial and execution by Roman authorities. In addition to preparing individuals for salvation and symbolizing their membership in a holy community, the Eucharist had mundane uses: popular beliefs held that the sacrament would protect individuals from sudden death and advance their worldly interests.

Devotion to Saints Popular religion also took the form of devotion to the saints. According to church teachings, saints were human beings who had led such exemplary lives that God held them in special esteem. As a result, they enjoyed special influence with heavenly authorities and were able to intervene on behalf of individuals living in the world. Medieval Europeans constantly prayed for saints to look after their spiritual interests and to ensure their admission to heaven. Often, they also invoked the aid of saints who had reputations for helping living people as well as souls of the dead. Tradition held that certain saints could cure diseases, relieve toothaches, and guide sailors through storms to a port.

The Virgin Mary was a popular subject for devout medieval artists. Here a fourteenth-century stained glass window from the Notre Dame Cathedral in Evreux, France, represents the Virgin holding the infant Jesus in the company of an admirer.

The Virgin Mary During the high middle ages, the most popular saint was always the Virgin Mary, mother of Jesus, who personified the Christian ideal of womanhood, love, and sympathy, and who reportedly lavished aid on her devotees. According to a widely circulated story, the Virgin once even spared a criminal from hanging when he called upon her name. During the twelfth and thirteenth centuries, Europeans dedicated hundreds of churches and cathedrals to the Virgin, among them the splendid cathedral of Notre Dame ("Our Lady") of Paris.

Saints' Relics Medieval Europeans went to great lengths to express their adoration of the Virgin and other saints through veneration of their relics and physical remains, widely believed to retain the powers associated with those holy individuals. Churches assembled vast collections of relics, such as clothes, locks of hair, teeth, and bones of famous saints. Especially esteemed were relics associated with Jesus or the Virgin, such as the crown of thorns that Jesus reportedly wore during his crucifixion or drops of the Virgin's milk miraculously preserved in a vial. The practice of assembling relics clearly opened the door to fraud, but medieval Europeans avidly continued to admire and venerate saints' relics.

Pilgrimage Some collections of relics became famous well beyond their own regions. Like Muslims making the hajj, pilgrims trekked long distances to honor the saints the relics represented. Throughout the high middle ages, streams of pilgrims visited two European cities in particular—Rome in Italy and Compostela in Spain—and some ventured even farther to Jerusalem and the holy land of Christian origins. Rome was the spiritual center of western Christian society: apart from the popes and the central administration of the Roman Catholic church, the relics of St. Peter and St. Paul, the two most prominent apostles of early Christianity, rested in the churches of Rome. Compostela stood on the very periphery of Christian society, in a remote corner of northwestern Spain. Yet the relics of St. James preserved in the cathedral of Santiago de Compostela exercised a powerful attraction for the pious, who made Compostela the second-most popular pilgrimage destination of medieval Europe. Some devoted pilgrims also visited Jerusalem and the sites associated with the origins of Christianity: spiritual as well as commercial interests called Europeans into the larger world.

The making of pilgrimages became so common during the high middle ages that a travel industry emerged to serve the needs of pilgrims. Inns dotted the routes leading to popular churches and shrines, and guides shepherded groups of pilgrims to religious sites and explained their significance. There were even guidebooks that pointed out the major attractions along pilgrims' routes and warned them of difficult terrain and unscrupulous scoundrels who took advantage of visitors.

Reform Movements and Popular Heresies

Although veneration of the saints and the making of pilgrimages indicated a deep reservoir of piety, popular religion also reflected the social and economic development of medieval Europe. Particularly in western Europe, as wealth increased, several groups of particularly devout individuals feared that European society was becoming excessively materialistic. Even the Roman Catholic church seemed tainted by materialism. Benedictine monasteries, in which monks originally observed the virtues of poverty, chastity, and obedience, had in many cases become comfortable retreats where privileged individuals led leisurely lives. Meanwhile, the central administration of the Roman church expanded dramatically as lawyers and bureaucrats ran the church's affairs and sought ways to swell its treasury.

St. Francis of Assisi was the son of a wealthy merchant in central Italy, but he abandoned the comforts that he inherited and pledged himself to a life of poverty and preaching. Stories represented in this fresco from the basilica of St. Francis at Assisi report that he preached to the birds and encouraged them to sing in praise of God.

Dominicans and Franciscans The devout responded to this state of affairs in several ways. Working within the Roman church, some individuals organized movements designed to champion spiritual over materialistic values. Most prominent of them were St. Dominic (1170–1221) and St. Francis (1182–1226). During the thirteenth century St. Dominic and St. Francis founded orders of mendicants (beggars), known as the Dominican and Franciscan friars, who would have no personal possessions and would have to beg for their food and other needs from audiences to whom they preached. Mendicants were especially active in towns and cities, where they addressed throngs of recently arrived migrants whose numbers were so large that existing urban churches and clergy could not serve them well. The Dominicans and the Franciscans also worked zealously to combat heterodox movements and to persuade heretics to return to the Roman Catholic church.

Popular Heresy Whereas the Dominicans and the Franciscans worked within the church, others rejected the Roman Catholic church altogether and organized alternative religious movements. During the twelfth and thirteenth centuries in particular, several popular movements protested the increasing materialism of European society. The Waldensians, who were most active in southern France and northern Italy, despised the Roman Catholic clergy as

thinking about TRADITIONS

Prosperity and Its Problems

For three centuries following the year 1000, western Europe enjoyed a general rise in productivity and prosperity. This was an era of bustling towns, expanding trade, the establishment of universities, and the construction of massive cathedrals. Did prosperity bring problems in its wake? Why did Dominicans, Franciscans, and popular heretics criticize medieval European society? To what extent did they offer realistic solutions for the problems they identified?

sources from the past

Thomas of Celano on St. Francis of Assisi

Thomas of Celano was an early disciple of St. Francis. He joined the Franciscan Order about 1215, and in 1228, at the request of Pope Gregory IX, he composed a biography of St. Francis. His account emphasizes the transformation of St. Francis from a spoiled rich brat to a man of deep spirituality who made special efforts to help the poor.

In the city of Assisi, which lies at the edge of the Spoleto valley, there was a man by the name of Francis, who from his earliest years was brought up by his parents proud of spirit, in accordance with the vanity of the world; and imitating their wretched life and habits for a long time, he became even more vain and proud. . . .

These are the wretched circumstances among which the man whom we venerate today as a saint, for he truly is a saint, lived in his youth; and almost up to the twenty-fifth year of his age, he squandered and wasted his time miserably. Indeed, he outdid all his contemporaries in vanities and he came to be a promoter of evil and was more abundantly zealous for all kinds of foolishness. He was the admiration of all and strove to outdo the rest in the pomp of vainglory, in jokes, in strange doings, in idle and useless talk, in songs, in soft and flowing garments, for he was very rich, not however avaricious but prodigal, not a hoarder of money but a squanderer of his possession, a cautious business man but a very unreliable steward. On the other hand, he was a very kindly person, easy and affable, even making himself foolish because of it; for because of these qualities many ran after him, doers of evil and promoters of crime. . . .

[After his conversion] his greatest concern was to be free from everything of this world, lest the serenity of his mind be disturbed even for an hour by the taint of anything that was mere dust. He made himself insensible to all external noise, and bridling his external senses with all his strength and repressing the movements of his nature, he occupied himself with God alone. . . . He therefore frequently chose solitary places so that he could direct his mind completely to God; yet he was not slothful about entering into the affairs of his neighbors, when he saw the time was opportune, and he willingly took care of things pertaining to their salvation. For his safest haven was prayer; not prayer of a single moment, or idle or presumptuous prayer, but prayer of long duration, full of devotion, serene in humility. If he began late, he would scarcely finish before morning. Walking, sitting, eating, or drinking, he was always intent upon prayer. . . .

The father of the poor, the poor Francis, conforming himself to the poor in all things, was grieved when he saw some one poorer than himself, not because he longed for vainglory, but only from a feeling of compassion. And, though he was content with a tunic that was quite poor and rough, he very frequently longed to divide it with some poor person. But that this very rich poor man, drawn on by a great feeling of affection, might be able to help the poor in some way, he would ask the rich of this world, when the weather was cold, to give him a mantle or some furs. And when, out of devotion, they willingly did what the most blessed father asked of them, he would say to them: "I will accept this from you with the understanding that you do not expect ever to have it back again." And when he met the first poor man, he would clothe him with what he had received with joy and gladness. He bore it very ill if he saw a poor person reproached or if he heard a curse hurled upon any creature by anyone. . . .

For, he was accustomed to say: "Who curses a poor man does an injury to Christ, whose noble image he wears, the image of him who made himself poor for us in this world." Frequently, therefore, when he found the poor burdened down with wood or other things, he offered his own shoulders to help them, though his shoulders were very weak.

For Further Reflection

- In what ways did St. Francis's life experiences—his dissolute youth and his later concern for the poor—reflect the social and economic conditions of medieval Europe?

Source: Marion A. Habig, ed. *St. Francis of Assisi's Writings and Early Biographies: English Omnibus Sources for the Life of St. Francis.* Chicago: Franciscan Herald Press, 1972, pp. 229–31, 288–92.

immoral and corrupt, and they advocated modest and simple lives. They asserted the right of the laity to preach and administer sacraments—functions that the church reserved exclusively for priests—and they did not hesitate to criticize the church on the basis of biblical teachings. Although church authorities declared them heretical, the Waldensians continued to attract enthusiastic participants: a few Waldensians survive even today.

Bogomils and Cathars Some popular heresies flourished in both the Byzantine empire and western Europe. As long-distance trade networks linked Mediterranean lands, alternative religious ideas spread readily throughout the region. Reviving the dualistic views of the ancient Manichaeans, the Bogomils of Bulgaria and Byzantium viewed the world as a site of unrelenting, cosmic struggle between the forces of good and evil. In a quest for purity and spiritual perfection, they despised the material world and adopted an ascetic regime, renouncing wealth, marriage, and material pleasures. Their movement grew rapidly in the late tenth century, and in the eleventh century the Cathars (sometimes called Albigensians) were promoting similar views in southern France and northern Italy. Bogomils and Cathars rejected official churches, which they considered hopelessly corrupt, along with their priests and sacraments.

Both in Byzantium and in western Europe, established authorities took a dim view of these popular movements, which they regarded as threats to cultural stability. Beginning in the late eleventh century, government and church officials teamed up and mounted ruthless campaigns to destroy the Bogomils and the Cathars. By the fourteenth century, Bogomils and Cathars survived in a few remote regions, but their influence was decidedly on the wane.

THE MEDIEVAL EXPANSION OF EUROPE

During the high middle ages, the relationship between western European peoples and their neighbors underwent dramatic change. Powerful states, economic expansion, and demographic growth all strengthened European society, and church officials encouraged the colonization of pagan and Muslim lands as a way to extend the influence of Roman Catholic Christianity. Beginning about the mid-eleventh century, Europeans embarked on expansive ventures on several fronts: Atlantic, Baltic, and Mediterranean. Scandinavian seafarers ventured into the Atlantic Ocean, establishing colonies in Iceland, Greenland, and even for a short time North America. In the Baltic region, Europeans conquered and introduced

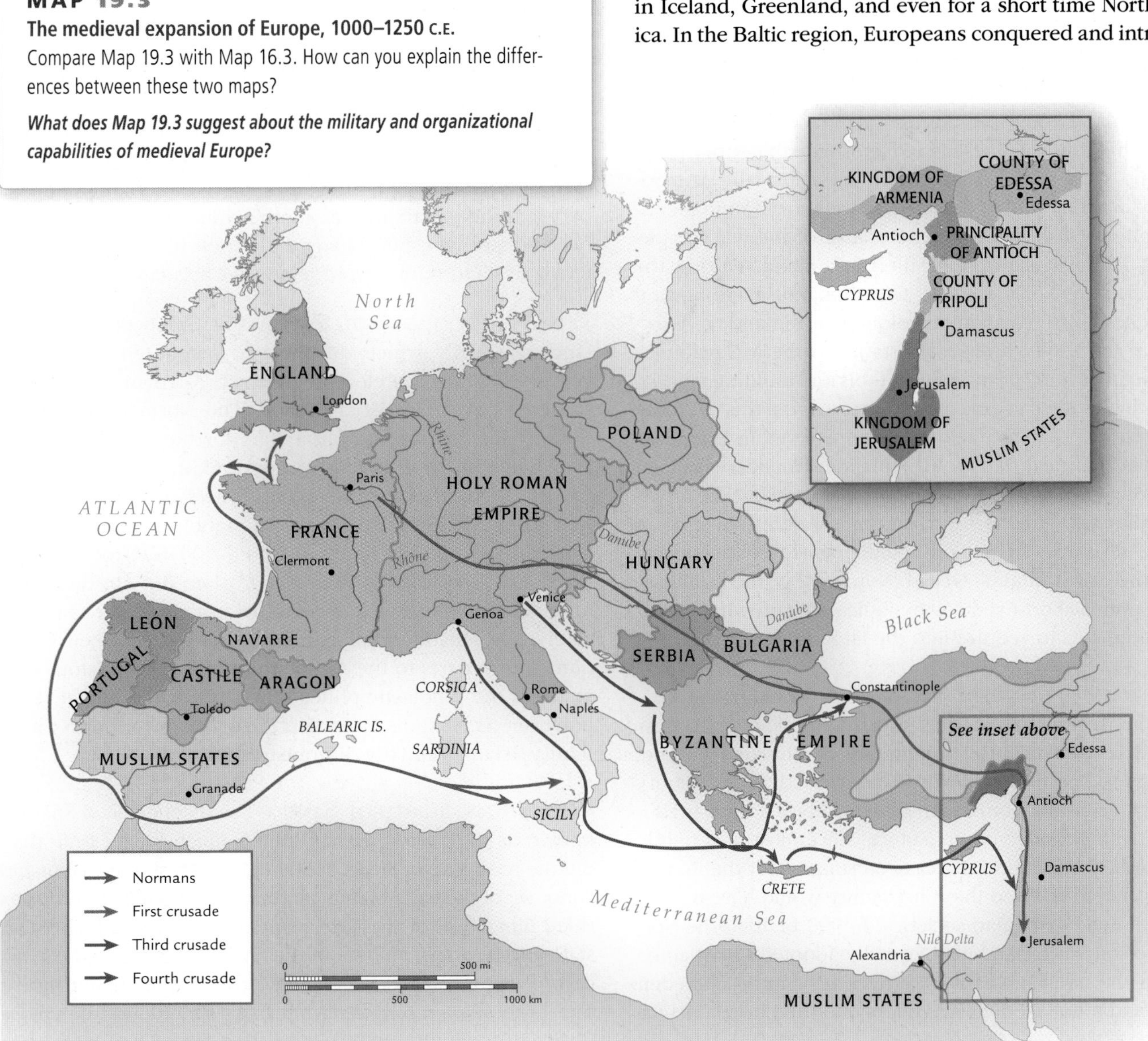

MAP 19.3
The medieval expansion of Europe, 1000–1250 C.E.
Compare Map 19.3 with Map 16.3. How can you explain the differences between these two maps?
What does Map 19.3 suggest about the military and organizational capabilities of medieval Europe?

Christianity to Prussia, Livonia, Lithuania, and Finland. In the Mediterranean basin, Europeans recaptured Spain and the Mediterranean islands that Muslims had conquered between the eighth and the tenth centuries. Finally, knights from all over Europe mounted enormous campaigns designed to seize the holy land of Palestine from Muslims and place it under Christian authority. As military ventures, the crusades achieved limited success, since they brought the holy land into Christian hands only temporarily. Nevertheless, the crusades signaled clearly that Europeans were beginning to play a much larger role in the affairs of the eastern hemisphere than they had during the early middle ages.

Atlantic and Baltic Colonization

Vinland When regional states began to emerge and protect western Europe from Viking raids during the ninth and tenth centuries, Scandinavian seafarers turned their attention to the islands of the North Atlantic Ocean. They occupied Iceland beginning in the late ninth century, and at the end of the tenth century a party led by Eric the Red discovered Greenland and established a small colony there. About 1000 C.E. his son Leif Ericsson led another exploratory party south and west of Greenland, arriving eventually at modern Newfoundland in Canada. There the party found plentiful supplies of fish and timber. Because of the wild grapes growing in the region, Leif called it Vinland. During the years following Leif's voyage, Greenlanders made several efforts to establish permanent colonies in Vinland.

Since the 1960s, archaeologists in northern Newfoundland have uncovered Scandinavian tools and building foundations dating to the early eleventh century. From this evidence and the stories of maritime ventures preserved in Scandinavian sagas, it is clear that the Greenlanders founded a colony in Newfoundland and maintained it for several decades. Ultimately, they left Vinland—or died there—since they did not have the resources to sustain a settlement over the stormy seas of the North Atlantic Ocean. Nonetheless, the establishment of even a short-lived colony indicated a growing capacity of Europeans to venture into the larger world.

Christianity in Scandinavia While Scandinavians explored the North Atlantic, the Roman Catholic church drew Scandinavia itself into the community of Christian Europe. The kings of Denmark and Norway converted to Christianity in the tenth century. Conversion of their subjects came gradually and with considerable resistance, since most held tightly to their inherited traditions. Yet royal support for the Roman Catholic church ensured that Christianity would have a place in Danish and Norwegian societies. In 999 or 1000 the Norwegian colony in Iceland also formally adopted Christianity. Between the twelfth and the fourteenth centuries, Sweden and Finland followed their neighbors into the Christian faith.

Crusading Orders and Baltic Expansion In the Baltic lands of Prussia, Livonia, and Lithuania, Christian authority arrived in the wake of military conquest. During the era of crusades, zealous Christians formed a series of hybrid, military-religious orders. The most prominent were the Templars, Hospitallers, and Teutonic Knights, who not only took religious vows but also pledged to devote their lives and efforts to the struggle against Muslims and pagans. The Teutonic Knights were most active in the Baltic region, where they waged military campaigns against the pagan Slavic peoples during the twelfth and thirteenth centuries. Aided by German missionaries, the Knights founded churches and monasteries in the territories they subdued. By the late thirteenth century, the Roman Catholic church had established its presence throughout the Baltic region, which progressively became absorbed into the larger society of Christian Europe.

The Reconquest of Sicily and Spain

The boundaries of Christian Europe also expanded in the Mediterranean basin. There, Europeans came into conflict with Muslims, whose ancestors had conquered the major Mediterranean islands and most of the Iberian peninsula between the eighth and the tenth centuries. As their society became stronger, Europeans undertook to reconquer those territories and reintegrate them into Christian society.

The Reconquest of Sicily Most important of the islands was Sicily, which Muslims had conquered in the ninth century. During the eleventh century, Norman warriors returned Sicily to Christian hands. The Norman adventurer Robert Guiscard carved out a state for himself in southern Italy while his brother Roger undertook the conquest of Sicily. By 1090, after almost twenty years of conflict, Roger had established his authority throughout the island. Missionaries and clergy soon appeared and reintroduced Roman Catholic Christianity to Sicily. Islam did not disappear immediately: Muslims continued to practice their faith privately, and Muslim scholars in Sicily introduced their Christian counterparts to the Arabic translations of Aristotle that inspired the scholastic philosophers. Over the longer term, however, as Muslims either left Sicily or converted to Christianity, Islam gradually disappeared from the island.

The *Reconquista* of Spain The reconquest of Spain—known as the ***reconquista***—took a much longer time than did the recapture of Sicily. Following the Muslim invasion and conquest of the early eighth century, the caliphate of Córdoba ruled almost all of the Iberian peninsula. A small Christian state survived in Catalonia in the far northeast, and the kingdom of León resisted Muslim advances in the far northwest. The process of *reconquista* began in the 1060s from those Christian toeholds. By 1085 Christian forces had pushed as far south as Toledo, and by 1150 they had recaptured Lisbon and established their authority over half of the peninsula.

reconquista (ray-kohn-KEE-stah)

Their successes lured reinforcements from France and England, and in the first half of the thirteenth century a new round of campaigns brought most of Iberia as well as the Balearic Islands into Christian hands. Only the kingdom of Granada in the far south of the peninsula remained Muslim. It survived as an outpost of Islam until 1492, when Christian forces mounted a campaign that conquered Granada and completed the *reconquista.*

The political, economic, and demographic strength of Christian Europe helps to explain the reconquests of Sicily and Spain as military ventures. Especially in the case of Spain, however, it is clear that religious concerns also helped to drive the *reconquista.* The popes and other leading clergy of the Roman Catholic church regarded Islam as an affront to Christianity, and they enthusiastically encouraged campaigns against the Muslims. When reconquered territories fell into Christian hands, church officials immediately established bishoprics and asserted Christian authority. They also organized campaigns to convert local populations. Dominican friars were especially active in Spain. They appealed to learned audiences by explaining Christianity in the terms of scholastic theology and arguments derived from Aristotle, whom Muslim intellectuals held in high esteem. When addressing popular audiences, they simply outlined the basic teachings of Christianity and urged their listeners to convert. With the establishment of Christian rule, the Roman Catholic church began to displace Islam in conquered Spain.

The crusades involved brutal conflict and atrocities from all sides. In this twelfth-century manuscript illustration, crusaders lob severed enemy heads at Muslims defending a fortress.

The Crusades

The term *crusade* refers to a holy war. It derives from the Latin word *crux,* meaning "cross," the device on which Roman authorities had executed Jesus. When a pope declared a crusade, warriors would "take up the cross" as a symbol of their faith, sew strips of cloth in the form of a cross on the backs of their garments, and venture forth to fight on behalf of Christianity. The wars that Christians fought against pagans in the Baltic and Muslims in the Mediterranean were crusades in this sense of the term, as was the campaign waged by Roman Catholic Christians against Cathar heretics in southern France. In popular usage, though, *crusades* generally refers to the huge expeditions that Roman Catholic Christians mounted in an effort to recapture Palestine, the land of Christian origins, and the holy city of Jerusalem from Muslim authorities.

Urban II Pope Urban II launched the crusades in 1095. Speaking at the Council of Clermont (in central France), Urban warned church leaders that Muslim Turks were threatening the eastern borders of Christendom. Indeed, the pope had recently received an urgent appeal from the Byzantine emperor, who requested military forces from western Europe to reinforce his own armies as Turkish invaders advanced toward Constantinople. Urban urged European princes to stabilize Christendom's borders and then go further to recapture Jerusalem and restore Christian rule to the holy land. He added emphasis to his appeal with the assertion that "Deus vult"—"God wills it!"

The First Crusade Shortly after Pope Urban announced the crusade, French and Norman nobles began to organize a military expedition to the holy land. In late 1096 the crusading armies began the long trek to Palestine. In 1097 and 1098 they captured Edessa, Antioch, and other strategic sites. In 1099 Jerusalem fell to the crusaders, who then proceeded to extend their conquests and carve conquered territories into Christian states.

Although the crusaders did not realize it, hindsight shows that their quick victories came largely because of division and disarray in the ranks of their Muslim foes. The crusaders' successes, however, encouraged Turks, Egyptians, and other Muslims to settle their differences, at least temporarily, in the interests of expelling European Christians from the eastern Mediterranean. By the mid-twelfth century, the crusader communities had come under tremendous pressure. The crusader state of Edessa fell to Turks in 1144, and the Muslim leader Salah al-Din, known to Europeans as Saladin, recaptured Jerusalem in 1187. Crusaders maintained several of their enclaves for another century, but Saladin's victories sealed the fate of Christian forces in the eastern Mediterranean.

Later Crusades Europeans did not immediately concede Palestine to the Muslims. By the mid-thirteenth century, they had launched five major crusades, but none of the later ventures succeeded in reestablishing a Christian presence in Palestine. The fourth crusade (1202–1204) was a particularly demoralizing affair, as crusaders ravaged Constantinople, the seat of Eastern Orthodox Christianity. Nevertheless, even though the later crusades failed in their principal objective, the crusading idea inspired European dreams of conquest in the eastern Mediterranean until the late sixteenth century.

A fourteenth-century manuscript illustration depicts Muslims burning captured crusaders at the stake.

Consequences of the Crusades As holy wars intended to reestablish Roman Catholic Christianity in the eastern Mediterranean basin, the crusades were wars of military and political expansion. Yet in the long run, the crusades were much more important for their social, economic, commercial, and cultural consequences. Even as European armies built crusader states in Palestine and Syria, European scholars and missionaries dealt with Muslim philosophers and theologians, and European merchants traded eagerly with their Muslim counterparts. The result was a large-scale exchange of ideas, technologies, and trade goods that profoundly influenced European development. Through their sojourns in Palestine and their regular dealings with Muslims throughout the Mediterranean basin, European Christians became acquainted with the works of Aristotle, Islamic science and astronomy, "Arabic" numerals (which Muslims had borrowed from India), and techniques of paper production (which Muslims had learned from China). They also learned to appreciate new food and agricultural products such as spices, granulated sugar, coffee, and dates as well as trade goods such as silk products, cotton textiles, carpets, and tapestries.

In the early days of the crusades, Europeans had little to exchange for those products other than rough wool textiles, furs, and timber. During the crusading era, however, demand for the new commodities increased throughout western Europe as large numbers of people developed a taste for goods previously available only to wealthy elites. Seeking to meet the rising demand for luxury goods, Italian merchants developed new products and marketed them in commercial centers and port cities such as Constantinople, Alexandria, Cairo, Damascus, Tana, Caffa, and Trebizond. Thus Niccolò, Maffeo, and Marco Polo traded in gems and jewelry, and other merchants marketed fine woolen textiles or glassware. By the thirteenth century, large numbers of Italian merchants had begun to travel well beyond Egypt, Palestine, and Syria to avoid Muslim intermediaries and to deal directly with the producers of silks and spices in India, China, and southeast Asia. Thus, although the crusades largely failed as military ventures, they encouraged the reintegration of western Europe into the larger economy of the eastern hemisphere.

thinking about ENCOUNTERS

The Historical Significance of the Crusades

Military campaigns commonly bring about death and destruction, and the crusades were no exception to the rule. Yet the crusades also prompted important cultural and intellectual exchanges. Taking into account their constructive as well as destructive consequences, how would you characterize the general historical significance of the crusades?

inperspective

From 1000 to 1300, Europe underwent thorough political and economic reorganization. Building on foundations laid during the early middle ages, political leaders founded a series of independent regional states. Despite the establishment of the Holy Roman Empire, they did not revive central imperial authority in western Europe. Regional states maintained good order and fostered rapid economic growth. Agricultural improvements brought increased food supplies, which encouraged urbanization, manufacturing, and trade. By the thirteenth century, European peoples traded actively throughout the Mediterranean, Baltic, and North Sea regions, and a few plucky merchants even ventured as far away as China in search of commercial opportunities. In the high middle ages, as in the early middle ages, Christianity was the cultural foundation of European society. The church prospered during the high middle ages, and advanced educational institutions such as cathedral schools and universities reinforced the influence of Christianity throughout Europe. Christianity even played a role in European political and military expansion, since church officials encouraged crusaders to conquer pagan and Muslim peoples in Baltic and Mediterranean lands. Thus between 1000 and 1300, western European peoples strengthened their own society and began in various ways to interact regularly with their counterparts in other regions of the eastern hemisphere. ●

CHRONOLOGY	
962	Coronation of Otto I as Holy Roman emperor
1056–1106	Reign of Emperor Henry IV
1066	Norman invasion of England
1073–1085	Reign of Pope Gregory VII
1096–1099	First crusade
1122–1204	Life of Eleanor of Aquitaine
1152–1190	Reign of Emperor Frederick Barbarossa
1170–1221	Life of St. Dominic
1182–1226	Life of St. Francis
1187	Recapture of Jerusalem by Saladin
1202–1204	Fourth crusade
1225–1274	Life of St. Thomas Aquinas
1271–1295	Marco Polo's trip to China
1453	Fall of Constantinople to Ottoman Turks

For Further Reading

Thomas Asbridge. *The Crusades.* New York, 2010. A breezy narrative history of the early crusades.

Robert Bartlett. *The Making of Europe: Conquest, Colonization, and Cultural Change, 950–1350.* Princeton, 1993. A well-documented examination of European expansion from a cultural point of view.

Marc Bloch. *Feudal Society.* 2 vols. Trans. by L. A. Manyon. Chicago, 1961. A classic interpretation concentrating on social and economic history that has decisively influenced the way historians think about medieval Europe.

Rosalind Brooke and Christopher Brooke. *Popular Religion in the Middle Ages: Western Europe, 1000–1300.* London, 1984. Well-illustrated essays on the faith of the masses.

Jean Gimpel. *The Medieval Machine: The Industrial Revolution of the Middle Ages.* New York, 1976. Explores the role of science and technology in the economy and society of medieval Europe.

David Herlihy. *Opera Muliebria: Women and Work in Medieval Europe.* New York, 1990. Examines women's roles both in their own households and in the larger society of medieval Europe.

Hubert Houben. *Roger II of Sicily: A Ruler between East and West.* Cambridge, 2002. Brief and clear account of Roger's reign with emphasis on the cultural exchanges that took place between Christians and Muslims in Norman Sicily.

Benjamin Z. Kedar. *Crusade and Mission: European Approaches toward the Muslims.* Princeton, 1984. Insightful scholarly analysis of European policies toward Muslims during the crusading era.

Robert S. Lopez. *The Commercial Revolution of the Middle Ages, 950–1350.* Englewood Cliffs, N.J., 1971. A succinct account of economic development during the high middle ages.

Hans Eberhard Mayer. *The Crusades.* 2nd ed. Oxford, 1988. Perhaps the best short history of the crusades.

Alex Metcalfe. *Muslims and Christians in Norman Sicily: Arabic Speakers and the End of Islam.* London, 2003. Scholarly study exploring the social, cultural, and linguistic dimensions of Sicilian history as the island made the transition from Muslim to Christian rule.

J. R. S. Phillips. *The Medieval Expansion of Europe.* Oxford, 1988. Excellent survey of European ventures in the larger world during the high and late middle ages.

Daniel Power, ed. *The Central Middle Ages.* Oxford, 2006. Seven leading scholars discuss aspects of medieval European history.

Susan Reynolds. *Fiefs and Vassals: The Medieval Evidence Reinterpreted.* Oxford, 1994. A powerful scholarly critique of the concept of feudalism.

Shulamith Shahar. *The Fourth Estate: A History of Women in the Middle Ages.* Trans. by C. Galai. London, 1983. Well-documented study of women and their status in medieval society.

Christopher Tyerman. *God's War: A New History of the Crusades.* Cambridge, Mass., 2006. A comprehensive review of crusades throughout Europe and the larger Mediterranean basin.

Elisabeth van Houts, ed. *The Normans in Europe.* Manchester, 2000. Presents English translations of sources illuminating Norman roles in medieval Europe.

Lynn White Jr. *Medieval Technology and Social Change.* Oxford, 1962. Pioneering study of technological diffusion and the role of technology in European economy and society.

Worlds Apart: The Americas and Oceania

chapter 20

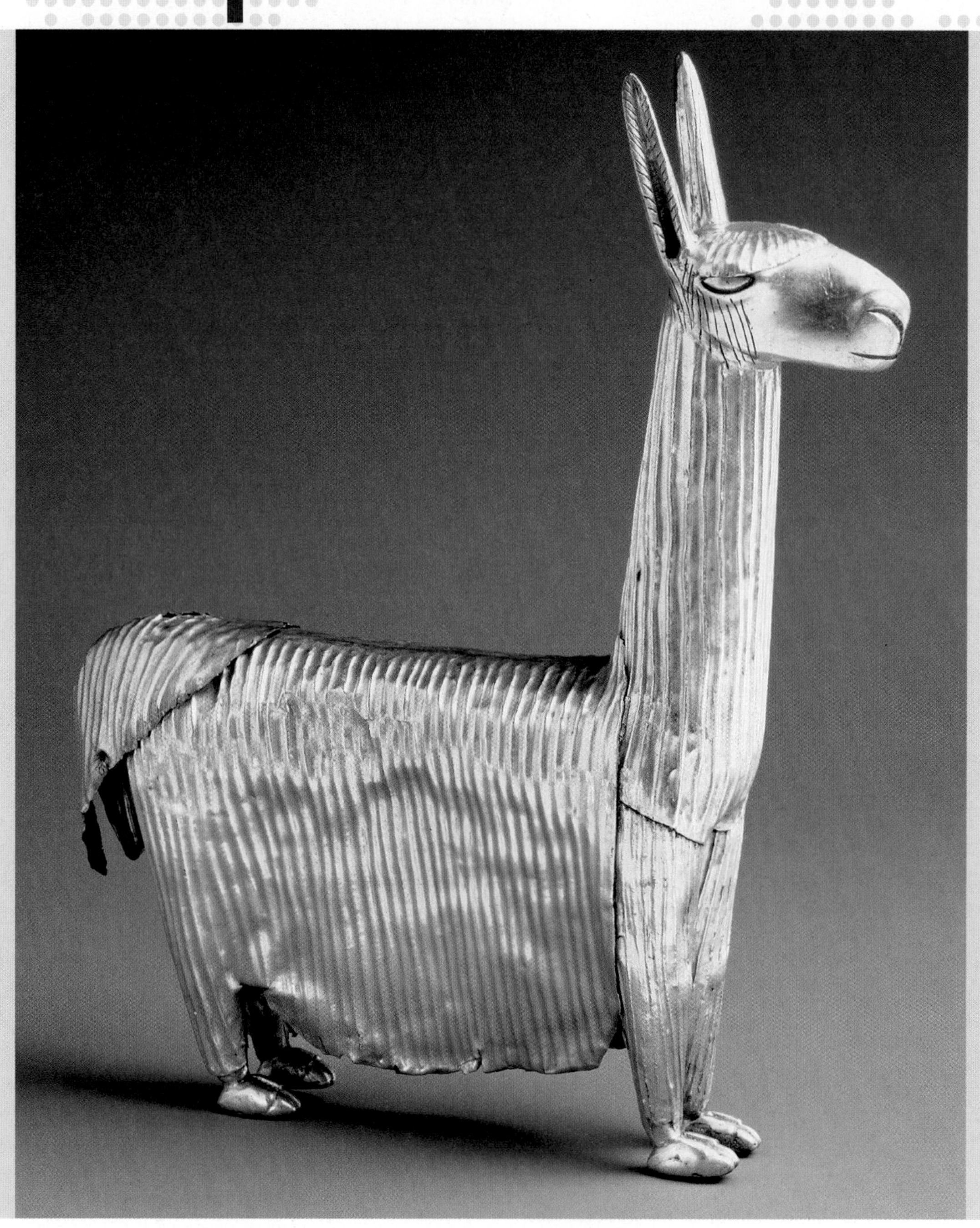

A handsome llama fashioned from silver sheet from Inca Peru.

EYEWITNESS:
First Impressions of the Aztec Capital

In November 1519 a small Spanish army entered **Tenochtitlan,** capital city of the Aztec empire. The Spanish forces came in search of gold, and they had heard many reports about the wealth of the Aztec empire. Yet none of those reports prepared them adequately for what they saw.

Years after the conquest of the Aztec empire, Bernal Díaz del Castillo, a soldier in the Spanish army, described Tenochtitlan at its high point. The city itself sat in the water of Lake Texcoco, connected to the surrounding land by three broad causeways, and as in Venice, canals allowed canoes to navigate to all parts of the city. The imperial palace included many large rooms and apartments. Its armory, well stocked with swords, lances, knives, bows, arrows, slings, armor, and shields, attracted Bernal Díaz's professional attention. The aviary of Tenochtitlan included eagles, hawks, parrots, and smaller birds in its collection, while jaguars, mountain lions, wolves, foxes, and rattlesnakes were noteworthy residents of the zoo.

To Bernal Díaz the two most impressive sights were the markets and the temples of Tenochtitlan. The markets astonished him because of their size, the variety of goods they offered, and the order that prevailed there. In the principal market at Tlatelolco, a district of Tenochtitlan, Bernal Díaz found gold and silver jewelry, gems, feathers, embroidery, slaves, cotton, cacao, animal skins, maize, beans, vegetables, fruits, poultry, meat, fish, salt, paper, and tools. It would take more than two days, he said, to walk around the market and investigate all the goods offered for sale. His well-traveled companions-in-arms compared the market of Tlatelolco favorably to those of Rome and Constantinople.

The temples also struck Bernal Díaz, though in a different way. Aztec temples were the principal sites of rituals involving human sacrifice. Bernal Díaz described his ascent to the top of the main pyramidal temple in Tenochtitlan, where fresh blood lay pooled around the stone that served as a sacrificial altar. He described priests with hair entangled and matted with blood. Interior rooms of the temple were so encrusted with blood, Bernal

Tenochtitlan (teh-NOCH-tee-tlahn)

Díaz reported, that their walls and floors had turned black, and the stench overcame even professional Spanish soldiers. Some of the interior rooms held the dismembered limbs of sacrificial victims, and others were resting places for thousands of human skulls and bones.

The contrast between Tenochtitlan's markets and its temples challenged Bernal Díaz and his fellow soldiers. In the markets they witnessed peaceful and orderly exchange of the kind that took place all over the world. In the temples, however, they saw signs of human sacrifice on a scale rarely matched, if ever, anywhere in the world. Yet by the cultural standards of the Aztec empire, there was no difficulty reconciling the commercial activity of the marketplaces with the human sacrifice of the temples. Both had a place in the maintenance of the world: trade enabled a complex society to function, while sacrificial rituals pleased the gods and persuaded them to keep the world going.

Although the peoples of Africa, Asia, and Europe interacted regularly before modern times, the indigenous peoples of the Americas had only sporadic dealings with their contemporaries across the oceans. Scandinavian seafarers established a short-lived colony in Newfoundland, and occasional ships from Europe and west Africa may have made their way to the western hemisphere. Before 1492, however, interaction between peoples of the eastern and western hemispheres was fleeting and random rather than a sustained and regular affair. During the period from 1000 to 1500 C.E., however, the peoples of North and South America, like their counterparts in the eastern hemisphere, organized large empires with distinctive cultural and religious traditions, and they created elaborate trade networks touching most regions of the American continents.

The indigenous peoples of Australia and the Pacific islands had irregular and sporadic dealings with peoples outside Oceania. Asian trade networks extended to the Philippines, the islands of Indonesia, and New Guinea. They even touched a few regions of northern Australia and the Mariana Islands, including Guam, but they did not extend to the more distant island societies of the Pacific Ocean. Pacific islanders themselves often sailed over the open ocean, creating and sustaining links between the societies of various island groups. They also had some dealings with the inhabitants of Asian and American lands bordering the Pacific Ocean. Like their counterparts in the western hemisphere, however, the indigenous peoples of Australia and the Pacific islands built self-sufficient societies that tended to their own needs. Even though they had extremely limited amounts of land and other natural resources to work with, by the thirteenth century C.E. they had established well-organized agricultural societies and chiefly states throughout the Pacific islands.

STATES AND EMPIRES IN MESOAMERICA AND NORTH AMERICA

Mesoamerica entered an era of war and conquest in the eighth century C.E. Great stores of wealth had accumulated in Teotihuacan, the largest early city in Mesoamerica. When Teotihuacan declined, it became a target for less-prosperous but well-organized forces from the countryside and northern Mexico. Attacks on Teotihuacan opened a long era of militarization and empire building in Mesoamerica that lasted until Spanish forces conquered the region in the sixteenth century. Most prominent of the peoples contesting for power in Mesoamerica were the Mexica, the architects of the Aztec empire.

The Toltecs and the Mexica

During the ninth and early tenth centuries, after the collapse of Teotihuacan, several regional states dominated portions of the high central valley of Mexico, the area surrounding Mexico City where agricultural societies had flourished since the late centuries B.C.E. Although these successor states and their societies shared the religious and cultural traditions of Teotihuacan, they fought relentlessly among themselves. Their capital cities all stood on well-defended hill sites, and warriors figured prominently in their works of art.

Toltecs With the emergence of the Toltecs and later the Mexica, much of central Mexico again came under unified rule. The Toltecs began to migrate into the area about the eighth century. They came from the arid land of northwestern Mexico, and they settled mostly at Tula, about 50 kilometers (31 miles) northwest of modern Mexico City. Though situated in a corner of the valley of Mexico that possesses thin soil and receives little rainfall, the Toltecs tapped the waters of the nearby River Tula to irrigate crops of maize, beans, peppers, tomatoes, chiles, and cotton. At its high point, from about 950 to 1150 C.E., Tula supported an urban population that might have reached sixty thousand people. Another sixty thousand lived in the surrounding region.

The Toltecs maintained a large and powerful army that campaigned periodically throughout central Mexico. They built a compact regional empire and maintained fortresses far to the northwest to protect their state from invasion by nomadic peoples. From the mid-tenth through the mid-twelfth century, they exacted tribute from subject peoples and transformed their capital into a wealthy city. Residents lived in spacious houses made of stone, adobe, or mud and sometimes covered their packed-earth floors with plaster.

Tula The city of Tula became an important center of weaving, pottery, and obsidian work, and residents imported large quantities of jade, turquoise, animal skins, exotic bird feathers, and other luxury goods from elsewhere in Mesoamerica. The Toltecs maintained close relations with societies on the Gulf coast as well as with the Maya of Yucatan. Indeed, Tula shared numerous architectural designs and art motifs with the Maya city of Chichén Itzá some 1,500 kilometers (932 miles) to the east.

Beginning about 1125 C.E. the Toltec empire faced serious difficulties as conflicts between the different ethnic groups living at Tula led to civil strife. By the mid-twelfth century, large numbers of migrants—mostly nomadic peoples from northwestern Mexico—had entered Tula and settled in the surrounding area. By 1175 the combination of civil conflict and nomadic incursion had destroyed the Toltec state. Archaeological evidence suggests that fire destroyed much of Tula about the same time. Large numbers of people continued to inhabit the region around Tula, but by the end of the twelfth century the Toltecs no longer dominated Mesoamerica.

The Mexica Among the migrants drawn to central Mexico from northwestern regions was a people who called themselves the Mexica, often referred to as Aztecs because they dominated the alliance that built the Aztec empire in the fifteenth century. (The term *Aztec* derives from *Aztlán*, "the place of the seven legendary caves," which the Mexica remembered as the home of their ancestors.) The Mexica arrived in central Mexico about the middle of the thirteenth century. They had a reputation for making trouble by kidnapping women from nearby communities and seizing land already cultivated by others. On several occasions their neighbors became tired of their disorderly behavior and forced them to move. For a century they migrated around central Mexico, jostling and fighting with other peoples and sometimes surviving only by eating fly eggs and snakes.

Tenochtitlan About 1345 the Mexica settled on an island in a marshy region of Lake Texcoco and founded the city that would become their capital—Tenochtitlan, on top of which Spanish conquerors later built Mexico City. Though inconvenient at first, the site offered several advantages. The lake harbored plentiful supplies of fish, frogs, and waterfowl.

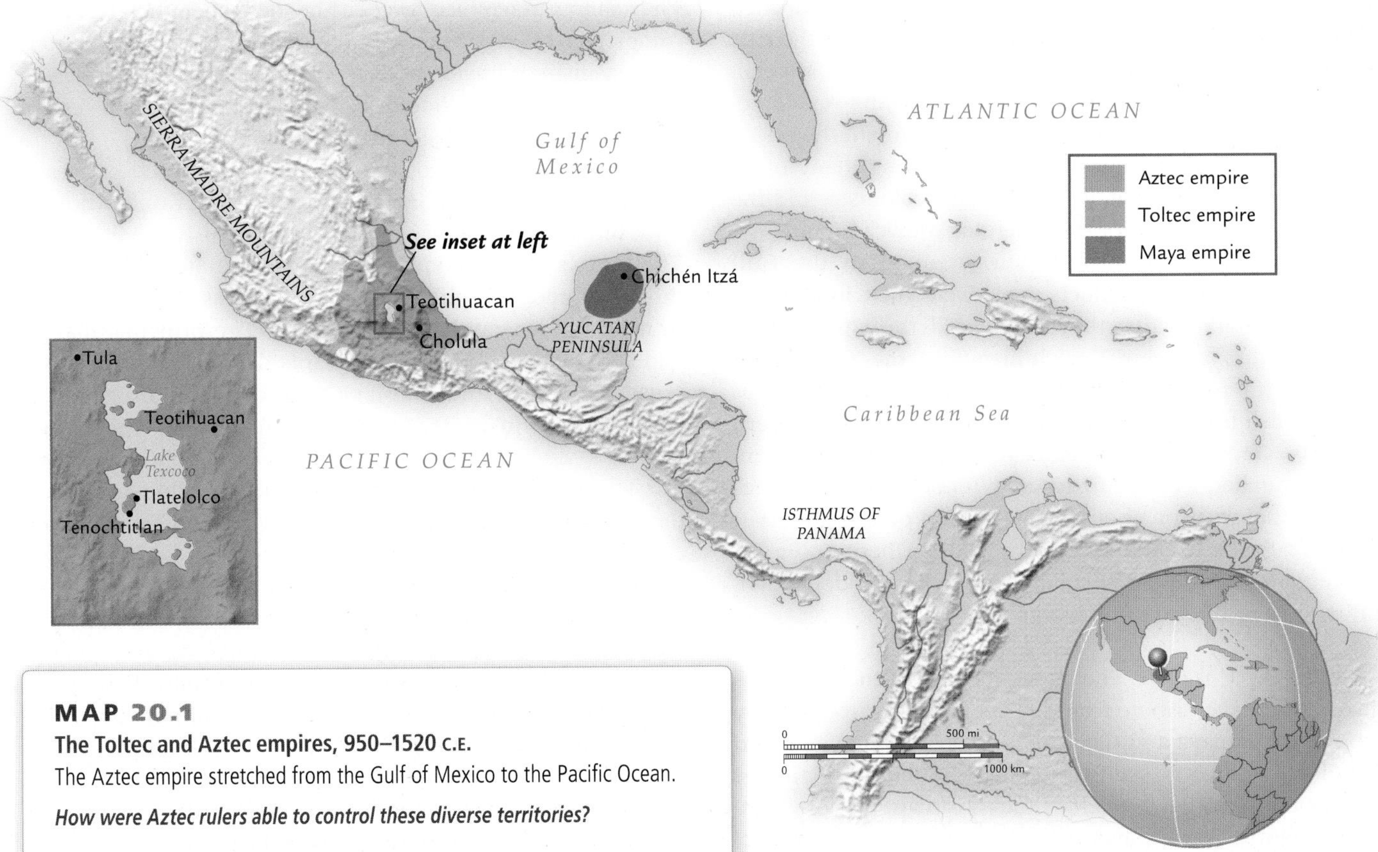

MAP 20.1
The Toltec and Aztec empires, 950–1520 C.E.
The Aztec empire stretched from the Gulf of Mexico to the Pacific Ocean.
How were Aztec rulers able to control these diverse territories?

Moreover, the lake enabled the Mexica to develop the *chinampa* system of agriculture. The Mexica dredged a rich and fertile muck from the lake's bottom and built it up into small plots of land known as *chinampas.* During the dry season, cultivators tapped water from canals leading from the lake to their plots, and in the temperate climate they grew crops of maize, beans, squashes, tomatoes, peppers, and chiles year-round. *Chinampas* were so fertile and productive that cultivators were sometimes able to harvest seven crops per year from their gardens. Finally, the lake served as a natural defense: waters protected Tenochtitlan on all sides, and Mexica warriors patrolled the three causeways that eventually linked their capital to the surrounding mainland.

Although the lakes of central Mexico have largely disappeared, a few *chinampas* survive, such as this one in Xochimilco, near modern Mexico City.

The Aztec Empire By the early fifteenth century, the Mexica were powerful enough to overcome their immediate neighbors and demand tribute from their new subjects. During the middle decades of the century, prodded by the military elite that ruled Tenochtitlan, the Mexica launched ambitious campaigns of imperial expansion. Under the rule of "the Obsidian Serpent" Itzcóatl (1428–1440) and Motecuzoma I (1440–1469), also known as Moctezuma or Montezuma, they advanced first against Oaxaca in southwestern Mexico. After conquering the city and slaying many of its inhabitants, they populated Oaxaca with colonists, and the city became a bulwark for the emerging Mexica empire.

The Mexica next turned their attention to the Gulf coast, whose tropical products made welcome tribute items in Tenochtitlan. Finally, they conquered the cities of the high plateaus between Tenochtitlan and the Gulf coast. About the mid-fifteenth century, the Mexica joined forces with two neighboring cities, Texcoco and Tlacopan (modern Tacuba), to create a triple alliance that guided the Aztec empire. Dominated by the Mexica and Tenochtitlan, the allies imposed their rule on about twelve million people and most of Mesoamerica, excluding only the arid northern and western regions and a few small pockets where independent states resisted the expanding empire.

Tribute and Trade The main objective of the triple alliance was to exact tribute from subject peoples. From nearby peoples the Mexica and their allies received food crops and manufactured items such as textiles, rabbit-fur blankets, embroidered clothes, jewelry, and obsidian knives. Tribute obligations were sometimes very oppressive for subject peoples. The annual tribute owed by the state of Tochtepec on the Gulf coast, for example, included 9,600 cloaks, 1,600 women's garments, 200 loads of cacao, and 16,000 rubber balls, among other items. Ruling elites entrusted some of these tribute items to officially recognized merchants, who took them to distant lands and exchanged them for local products. These included luxury items such as translucent jade, emeralds, tortoise shells, jaguar skins, parrot feathers, seashells, and game animals. The tropical lowlands also supplied vanilla beans and cacao—the source of cocoa and chocolate—from which Mexica elites prepared tasty beverages.

Unlike imperial states in the eastern hemisphere, the Aztec empire had no elaborate bureaucracy or administration. The Mexica and their allies simply conquered their subjects and assessed tribute, leaving local governance and the collection of tribute in the hands of the conquered peoples. The allies did not even maintain military garrisons throughout their empire. Nor did they keep a permanent, standing army. They simply assembled forces as needed when they launched campaigns of expansion or mounted punitive expeditions against insubordinate subjects. Nevertheless, the Mexica in particular had a reputation for military prowess, and fear of reprisal kept most subject peoples in line.

At the high point of the Aztec empire in the early sixteenth century, tribute from 489 subject territories flowed into Tenochtitlan, which was an enormously wealthy city. The Mexica capital had a population of about two hundred thousand people, and three hundred thousand others lived in nearby towns and suburban areas. The principal market had separate sections for merchants dealing in gold, silver, slaves, henequen and cotton cloth, shoes, animal skins, turkeys, dogs, wild game, maize, beans, peppers, cacao, and fruits.

The Spanish soldier Bernal Díaz del Castillo marveled at the sight before him when he first laid eyes on Tenochtitlan:

> And when we saw so many cities and villages built in the water and other great towns on dry land and that straight and level causeway going towards Mexico [Tenochtitlan], we were amazed . . . on account of the great towers and [temples] and buildings rising from the water, and all built of masonry. And some of our soldiers even asked whether the things that we saw were not a dream? It is not to be wondered at that I here write it

down in this manner, for there is so much to think over that I do not know how to describe it, seeing things as we did that had never been heard of or seen before, not even dreamed about.

Mexica Society

More information survives about the Mexica and their subjects than about any other people of the pre-Columbian Americas. A few Mexica books survived the Spanish conquest of the Aztec empire, and they offer direct testimony about the Mexica way of life. Moreover, a great deal of information survives from lengthy interviews conducted by Spanish missionaries with priests, elders, and other leaders of the Mexica during the mid-sixteenth century. Their reports fill many thick volumes and shed considerable light on Mexica society.

Social Structure Mexica society was rigidly hierarchical, with public honors and rewards going mostly to the military elite. The Mexica looked upon all males as potential warriors, and individuals of common birth could distinguish themselves on the battlefield and thereby improve their social standing. For the most part, however, the military elite came from the Mexica aristocracy. Men of noble birth received the most careful instruction and intense training in military affairs, and they enjoyed the best opportunities to display their talents on the battlefield.

Warriors The Mexica showered wealth and honors on the military elite. Accomplished warriors received extensive land grants as well as tribute from commoners for their support. The most successful warriors formed a council whose members selected the ruler, discussed public issues, and filled government positions. They ate the best foods—turkey, pheasant, duck, deer, boar, and rabbit—and they consumed most of the luxury items such as vanilla and cacao that came into Mexica society by way of trade or tribute. Even dress reflected social status in Mexica society. Sumptuary laws required commoners to wear coarse, burlaplike garments made of henequen but permitted aristocrats to drape themselves in cotton. Warriors enjoyed the right to don brightly colored capes and adorn themselves with lip plugs and eagle feathers after they captured enemies on the battlefield and brought them back to Tenochtitlan.

Mexica Women Women played almost no role in the political affairs of a society so dominated by military values, but they wielded influence within their families and enjoyed high honor as mothers of warriors. Mexica women did not inherit property or hold official positions, and the law subjected them to the strict authority of their fathers and their husbands. Women were prominent in the marketplaces, as well as in crafts involving embroidery and needlework. Yet Mexica society prodded them toward motherhood and homemaking.

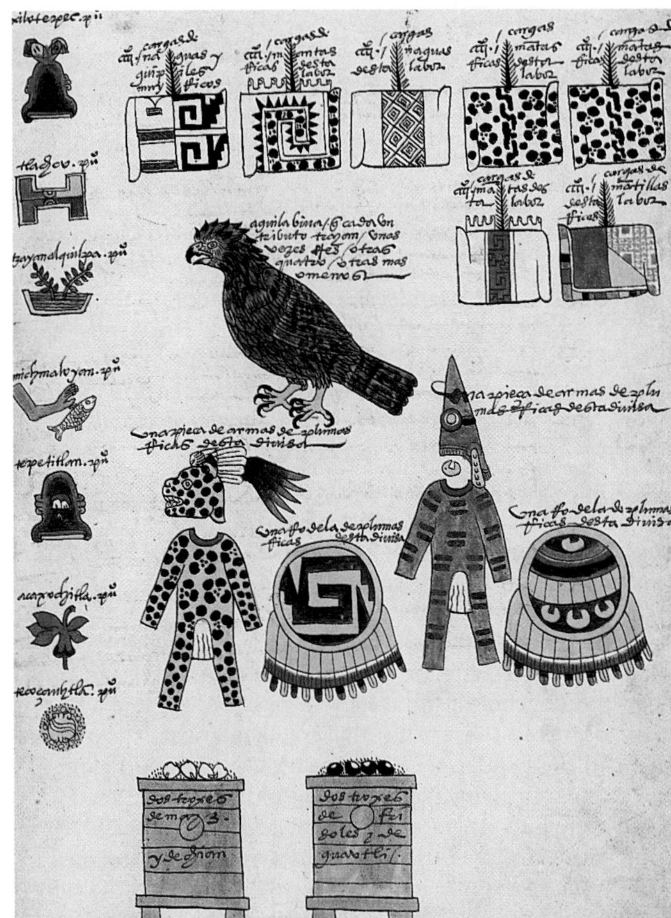

A Spanish copy of a Mexica list records tribute owed by six northwestern towns to the ruler Motecuzoma II. Each two years the towns delivered, among other items, women's skirts and blouses, men's shirts, warriors' armor and shields, an eagle, and various quantities of maize, beans, and other foods.

With the exception of a few who dedicated themselves to the service of a temple, all Mexica women married. Mexica values taught that their principal function was to bear children, especially males who might become distinguished warriors, and society recognized the bearing of children as equal to a warrior's capture of enemy in battle. Indeed, women who died in childbirth won the same fame as warriors who died valiantly on the battlefield. Even among the elite classes, Mexica women had the responsibilities of raising young children and preparing food for their families.

Priests In addition to the military aristocracy, a priestly class also ranked among the Mexica elite. Priests received a special education in calendrical and ritual lore, and they presided over religious ceremonies that the Mexica viewed as crucial to the continuation of the world. Priests read omens and explained the forces that drove the world, thereby

sources from the past

Mexica Expectations of Boys and Girls

Bernardino de Sahagún was a Franciscan missionary who worked to convert the native peoples of Mesoamerica to Christianity in the mid-sixteenth century. He interviewed Mexica elders and assembled a vast amount of information about their society before the arrival of Europeans. His records include the speeches made by midwives as they delivered infants to aristocratic families. The speeches indicate clearly the roles men and women were expected to play in Mexica society.

[To a newborn boy the midwife said:] "Heed, hearken: thy home is not here, for thou art an eagle, thou art an ocelot; thou art a roseate spoonbill, thou art a troupial. Thou art the serpent, the bird of the lord of the near, of the nigh. Here is only the place of thy nest. Thou hast only been hatched here; thou hast only come, arrived. Thou art only come forth on earth here. Here dost thou bud, blossom, germinate. Here thou becomest the chip, the fragment [of thy mother]. Here are only the cradle, thy cradle blanket, the resting place of thy head: only thy place of arrival. Thou belongest out there; out there thou hast been consecrated. Thou hast been sent into warfare. War is thy desert, thy task. Thou shalt give drink, nourishment, food to the sun, the lord of the earth. Thy real home, thy property, thy lot is the home of the sun there in the heavens. . . . Perhaps thou wilt receive the gift, perhaps thou wilt merit death [in battle] by the obsidian knife, the flowered death by the obsidian knife. . . ."

And if it were a female, the midwife said to her when she cut her umbilical cord: "My beloved maiden, my beloved noblewoman, thou has endured fatigue! Our lord, the lord of the near, of the nigh, hath sent thee. Thou hast come to arrive at a place of weariness, a place of anguish, a place of fatigue where there is cold, there is wind. . . . Thou wilt be in the heart of the home, thou wilt go nowhere, thou wilt nowhere become a wanderer, thou becomest the banked fire, the hearth stones. Here our lord planteth thee, burieth thee. And thou wilt become fatigued, thou wilt become tired; thou art to provide water, to grind maize, to drudge; thou art to sweat by the ashes, by the hearth."

Then the midwife buried the umbilical cord of the noblewoman by the hearth. It was said that by this she signified that the little woman would nowhere wander. Her dwelling place was only within the house; her home was only within the house; it was not necessary for her to go anywhere. And it meant that her very duty was drink, food. She was to prepare drink, to prepare food, to grind, to spin, to weave.

For Further Reflection

- How did gender roles and expectations of Mexica society compare with those of other settled, agricultural societies, such as China, India, the Islamic world, sub-Saharan Africa, and Europe?

Source: Bernardino de Sahagún. *Florentine Codex: General History of the Things of New Spain,* 13 vols. Trans. by Charles E. Dibble and Arthur J. O. Anderson. Salt Lake City: University of Utah Press, 1950–82, 7:171–73 (book 6, chapter 31).

wielding considerable influence as advisors to Mexica rulers. On a few occasions, priests even became supreme rulers of the Aztec empire: the ill-fated Motecuzoma II (reigned 1502–1520), ruler of the Aztec empire when Spanish invaders appeared in 1519, was a priest of the most popular Mexica cult.

Cultivators and Slaves The bulk of the Mexica population consisted of commoners who lived in hamlets cultivating *chinampas* and fields allocated to their families by community groups known as *calpulli.* Originally, *calpulli* were clans or groups of families claiming descent from common ancestors. With the passage of time, ancestry became less important to the nature of the *calpulli* than the fact that groups of families lived together in communities, organized their own affairs, and allocated community property to individual families. Apart from cultivating plots assigned by their *calpulli,* Mexica commoners worked on lands awarded to aristocrats or prominent warriors and contributed labor services to public works projects involving the construction of palaces, temples, roads, and irrigation systems. Cultivators delivered periodic tribute payments to state agents, who distributed a portion of what they collected to the elite classes and stored the remainder in state granaries and warehouses. In addition to these cultivators of common birth, Mexica society included a large number of slaves, who usually worked as domestic servants. Most slaves were not foreigners, but Mexica. Families sometimes sold younger members into servitude out of financial distress, and other Mexica were forced into slavery because of criminal behavior.

Artisans and Merchants Skilled artisans, particularly those who worked with gold, silver, cotton textiles, tropical bird feathers, and other items destined for consumption by the elite, enjoyed considerable prestige in Mexica society. Merchants specializing in long-distance trade occupied an important but somewhat more tenuous position

in Mexica society. Merchants supplied the exotic products such as gems, animal skins, and tropical bird feathers consumed by the elites and provided political and military intelligence about the lands they visited. Yet they often fell under suspicion as greedy profiteers, and aristocratic warriors frequently extorted wealth and goods from merchants who lacked powerful patrons or protectors.

Mexica Religion

When they migrated to central Mexico, the Mexica already spoke the Nahuatl language, which had been the prevalent tongue in the region since the time of the Toltecs. The Mexica soon adopted other cultural and religious traditions, some of which dated from the time of the Olmecs, shared by all the peoples of Mesoamerica. Most Mesoamerican peoples played a ball game in formal courts, for example, and maintained a complicated calendar based on a solar year of 365 days and a ritual year of 260 days. The Mexica enthusiastically adopted the ball game, and they kept a sophisticated calendar, although it was not as elaborate as the Maya calendar.

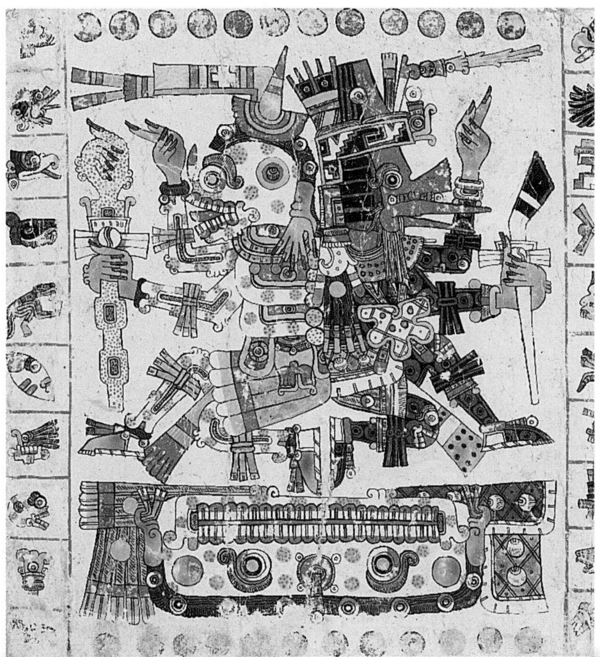

A Mexica manuscript known as the Codex Borgia depicts Quetzalcóatl (left) as the lord of life and Tezcatlipoca (right) as the god of death.

Mexica Gods The Mexica also absorbed the religious beliefs common to Mesoamerica. Two of their principal gods—Tezcatlipoca, "the Smoking Mirror," and Quetzalcóatl, "the Feathered Serpent"—had figured in Mesoamerican pantheons at least since the time of Teotihuacan, although different peoples knew them by various names. Tezcatlipoca was a powerful figure, the giver and taker of life and the patron deity of warriors, whereas Quetzalcóatl had a reputation for supporting arts, crafts, and agriculture.

Ritual Bloodletting Like their predecessors, the Mexica believed that their gods had set the world in motion through acts of individual sacrifice. By letting their blood flow, the gods had given the earth the moisture it needed to bear maize and other crops. To propitiate the gods and ensure the continuation of the world, the Mexica honored their deities through sacrificial bloodletting. Mexica priests regularly performed acts of self-sacrifice, piercing their earlobes or penises with cactus spines in honor of the primeval acts of their gods. The religious beliefs and bloodletting rituals clearly reflected the desire of the Mexica to keep their agricultural society going.

Huitzilopochtli Mexica priests also presided over the sacrificial killing of human victims. From the time of the Olmecs, and possibly even earlier, Mesoamerican peoples had regarded the ritual sacrifice of human beings as essential to the world's survival. The Mexica, however, placed much more emphasis on human sacrifice than their predecessors had. To a large extent the Mexica enthusiasm for human sacrifice followed from their devotion to the god Huitzilopochtli. Mexica warriors took Huitzilopochtli as their patron deity in the early years of the fourteenth century as they subjected neighboring peoples to their rule. Military success persuaded them that Huitzilopochtli especially favored the Mexica, and as military successes mounted, the priests of Huitzilopochtli's cult demanded sacrificial victims to keep the war god appeased.

Some of the victims were Mexica criminals, but others came as tribute from neighboring peoples or from the ranks of warriors captured on the battlefield during the many conflicts between the Mexica and their neighbors. In all cases, the Mexica viewed human sacrifice not as a gruesome form of entertainment but, rather, as a ritual essential to the world's survival. They believed that the blood of sacrificial victims sustained the sun and secured a continuing supply of moisture for the earth, thus ensuring that human communities would be able to cultivate their crops and perpetuate their societies.

thinking about TRADITIONS

The Mexica and Mesoamerican Bloodletting Rituals
The Mexica practiced bloodletting rituals much like those observed in Maya, Teotihuacan, Toltec, and other earlier Mesoamerican societies. Yet the Mexica shed human blood much more copiously than their predecessors. Why might the Mexica have emphasized this particular cultural tradition so much more strongly than earlier Mesoamerican peoples?

In this manuscript illustration an aide stretches a victim over a sacrificial altar while a priest opens his chest, removes the still-beating heart, and offers it to Huitzilopochtli. At the bottom of the structure, attendants remove the body of an earlier victim.

Peoples and Societies of the North

Beyond Mexico the peoples of North America developed a rich variety of political, social, and cultural traditions. Many North American peoples depended on hunting, fishing, and collecting edible plants. In the arctic and subarctic regions, for example, diets included sea mammals such as whale, seal, and walrus supplemented by land mammals such as moose and caribou. Peoples in coastal regions consumed fish, but in interior regions (the North American plains, for example), they hunted large animals such as bison and deer. Throughout the continent nuts, berries, roots, and grasses such as wild rice supplemented the meat provided by hunters and fishers. Like their counterparts elsewhere, hunting, fishing, and foraging peoples of North America built societies on a relatively small scale, since food resources in the wild would not support dense populations.

Pueblo and Navajo Societies In several regions of North America, agricultural economies enabled peoples to maintain settled societies with large populations. In what is now the American southwest, for example, Pueblo and Navajo peoples tapped river waters to irrigate crops of maize, which constituted as much as 80 percent of their diets. They also cultivated beans, squashes, and sunflowers, and they supplemented their crops with wild plants and small game such as rabbit. The hot and dry environment periodically brought drought and famine. Nevertheless, by about 700 C.E. the Pueblo and the Navajo began to construct permanent stone and adobe buildings. Archaeologists have discovered about 125 sites where agricultural peoples built such communities.

Iroquois Peoples Large-scale agricultural societies emerged also in the woodlands east of the Mississippi River. Woodlands peoples began to cultivate maize and beans during the early centuries C.E., and after about 800 these cultivated foods made up the bulk of their diets. They lived in settled communities, and they often surrounded their larger settlements with wooden palisades, which served as defensive walls. By 1000, for example, the Owasco people had established a distinct society in what is now upstate New York, and by about 1400 the five **Iroquois** nations (Mohawk, Oneida, Onondaga, Cayuga, and Seneca) had emerged from Owasco society. Women were in charge of Iroquois villages and longhouses, in which several related families lived together, and supervised cultivation of fields surrounding their settlements. Men took responsibility for affairs beyond the village—hunting, fishing, and war.

Iroquois (EAR-uh-kwoi)

Mound-Building Peoples The most impressive structures of the woodlands were the enormous earthen mounds that dotted the countryside throughout the eastern half of North America. Woodlands peoples used those mounds sometimes as stages for ceremonies and rituals, often as platforms for dwellings, and occasionally as burial sites. Modern agriculture, road building, and real estate development have destroyed most of the mounds, but several surviving examples demonstrate that they sometimes reached gigantic proportions.

Cahokia The largest surviving structure is a mound at Cahokia near East St. Louis, Illinois. More than 30 meters (100 feet) high, 300 meters (1,000 feet) long, and 200 meters (650 feet) wide, it was the third-largest structure in the western hemisphere before the arrival of Europeans. Only the temple of the sun in Teotihuacan and the temple of Quetzalcóatl in Cholula were larger. When the Cahokia society was at its height, from approximately 900 to 1250 C.E., more than one hundred smaller mounds stood within a few kilometers of the highest and most massive mound. Scholars have estimated that during the twelfth century, fifteen thousand to thirty-eight thousand people lived in the vicinity of the Cahokia mounds.

Trade Because peoples north of Mexico had no writing, information about their societies comes almost exclusively from archaeological discoveries. Burial sites reveal that mound-building peoples recognized various social classes, since they bestowed grave goods of differing quality and quantities on their departed kin. Archaeologists have shown, too, that trade linked widely separated regions and peoples of North America. An elaborate network of rivers—notably the Mississippi, Missouri, Ohio, and Tennessee rivers, along with their many tributaries—facilitated travel and trade by canoe in the eastern half of North America. Throughout the eastern woodlands, archaeologists have turned up stones with sharp cutting edges from the Rocky Mountains, copper from the Great Lakes region, seashells from Florida, minerals from the upper reaches of the Mississippi River, and mica from the southern Appalachian mountains. Indeed, the community at Cahokia probably owed its size and prominence to its location at the hub of North American trade networks. Situated near the confluence of the Mississippi, Missouri, and Ohio rivers, Cahokia was most likely the center of trade and communication networks linking the eastern woodlands of North America with the lower Mississippi valley and lands bordering the Gulf of Mexico.

STATES AND EMPIRES IN SOUTH AMERICA

South American peoples had no script and no tradition of writing before the arrival of Spanish invaders in the early sixteenth century. As a result, the experiences of early South American societies are much more difficult to recover than those of Mesoamerica, where writing had been in use since the fifth century B.C.E. Yet, from archaeological evidence and

Originally constructed about 1000 C.E., the Great Serpent Mound sits atop a ridge in modern Ohio. The serpent's coiled tail is visible at the left, while its open mouth holds an egg on the right. What uses might a ridgetop mound like this have served?

MAP 20.2
The Inca empire, 1471–1532 C.E.
The Incas built the largest empire in the pre-Columbian Americas.
How were they able to maintain control over their extensive realm?

information recorded by Spanish conquerors, it is possible to reconstruct much of the historical experience of Andean South America, which had been the site of complex societies since the first millennium B.C.E. As in Mesoamerica, cities and secular government in South America began to overshadow ceremonial centers and priestly regimes during the centuries from 1000 to 1500 C.E. Toward the end of the period, like the Mexica in Mesoamerica, the Incas built a powerful state, extended their authority over a vast region, and established the largest empire South America had ever seen.

The Coming of the Incas

After the disappearance of the Chavín and Moche societies, a series of autonomous regional states organized public affairs in Andean South America. The states frequently clashed, but rarely did one of them gain a long-term advantage over the others. For the most part they controlled areas either in the mountainous highlands or in the valleys and coastal plains.

Chucuito After the twelfth century, for example, the kingdom of Chucuito dominated the highlands region around Lake Titicaca, which straddles the border between modern Peru and Bolivia at about 4,000 meters (13,000 feet) of elevation. Chucuito depended on the cultivation of potatoes and the herding of llamas and alpacas—camel-like beasts that were the only large domesticated animals anywhere in the Americas before the sixteenth century. In elaborately terraced fields built with stone retaining walls, cultivators harvested potatoes of many colors, sizes, and tastes. Like maize in Mesoamerica, potatoes served as the staple of the highlanders' diet, which revolved around a potato-based stew enlivened by maize, tomatoes, green vegetables, peppers, chiles, and meat from llamas, alpacas, or tender, domesticated guinea pigs.

Apart from meat, llamas and alpacas provided the highlanders with wool, hides, and dung, widely used as fuel in a land with few trees. In exchange for potatoes and woolen textiles, the highlanders obtained maize and coca leaves from societies in lower valleys. They used maize to enhance their diet and to brew a beerlike beverage, and they chewed the coca leaves, which worked as a mild stimulant and enhanced stamina in the thin air of the high Andes. (When processed, coca leaves yield a much more powerful stimulant with addictive properties—cocaine.)

Chimu In the lowlands the powerful kingdom of Chimu (sometimes referred to as Chimor) emerged in the tenth century and expanded to dominate some 900 kilometers (560 miles) of the Peruvian coast for about a century before the arrival of the Incas in the mid-fifteenth century. Chimu governed a large and thriving society. Irrigation networks tapped the rivers and streams flowing from the Andes mountains, watered fields in the lowlands, and helped to generate abundant yields of maize and sweet potatoes. Judging from goods excavated at grave sites, Chimu society enjoyed considerable wealth and recognized clear distinctions between social classes.

Chimu's capital city, Chanchan, whose ruins lie close to the modern city of Trujillo, had a population that exceeded fifty thousand and may have approached one hundred thousand. Chanchan featured massive brick buildings, which indicated a capacity for mobilizing large numbers of people and resources for public purposes. The city's geography reflected a well-defined social order: each block belonged to an individual clan that supervised the affairs of its members and coordinated their efforts with those of other clans.

For several centuries, regional states such as Chucuito and Chimu maintained order in Andean South America. Yet, within a period of about thirty years, these and other regional states fell under the domination of the dynamic and expansive society of the Incas. The word *Inca* originally was the title of the rulers of a small kingdom in the valley of Cuzco, but in modern usage the term refers more broadly to those who spoke the Incas' Quechua language, or even to all subjects of the Inca empire.

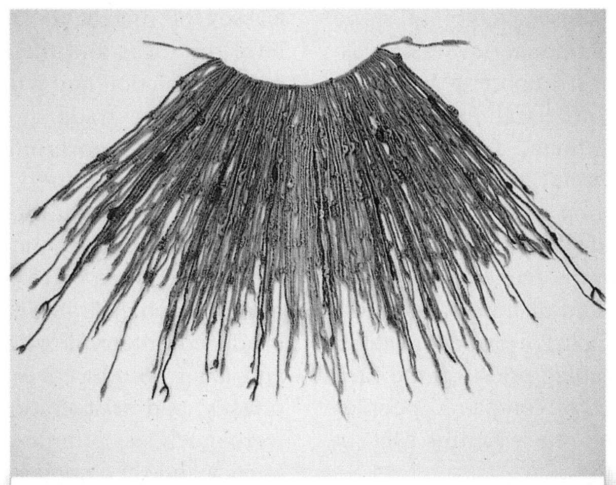

The different colors of quipu threads designated the different items recorded: population, animals, textiles, weapons, and perhaps even rulers and notable events of their reigns. People needed an advanced education to record and "read" information by quipu.

The Inca Empire After a long period of migration in the highlands, the Incas settled in the region around Lake Titicaca about the mid-thirteenth century. At first, they lived as one among many peoples inhabiting the region. About 1438, however, the Inca ruler Pachacuti (reigned 1438–1471) launched a series of military campaigns that vastly expanded the Incas' authority. Pachacuti ("Earthshaker") was a fierce warrior. According to Inca legends, he fought so furiously in one early battle that he inspired the stones in the field to stand up and combat his enemies. The campaigns of the Earthshaker were long and brutal. Pachacuti first extended Inca control over the southern and northern highlands and then turned his forces on the coastal kingdom of Chimu. Though well defended, Chimu had to submit to the Incas when Pachacuti gained control of the waters that supplied Chimu's irrigation system.

By the late fifteenth century, the Incas had built a huge empire stretching more than 4,000 kilometers (2,500 miles) from modern Quito to Santiago. It embraced almost all of modern Peru, most of Ecuador, much of Bolivia, and parts of Chile and Argentina as well. Only the tropical rain forests of the Amazon and other river valleys set a limit to Inca expansion to the east, and the Pacific Ocean defined its western boundary. With a population of about 11.5 million, the Inca empire easily ranked as the largest state ever built in South America.

The Incas ruled as a military and administrative elite. They led armies composed mostly of conquered peoples, and they staffed the bureaucracy that managed the empire's political affairs. But the Incas were not numerous enough to overwhelm their subjects. They routinely sought to encourage obedience among subject peoples by taking hostages from their ruling classes and forcing them to live at the Inca capital. When conquered peoples became restive or uncooperative, the Incas sent loyal subjects as colonists, provided them with choice land and economic benefits, and established them in garrisons to maintain order. When conquered peoples rebelled, Inca armies forced them to leave their homes and resettle in distant parts of the empire.

Inca Administration The vast Inca realm presented a serious administrative challenge to its rulers. The Inca administrative system was the invention of Pachacuti himself—the same Earthshaker who conquered the territories that made up the Inca empire. Toward the end of his reign, about 1463, Pachacuti entrusted military affairs to his son and settled in the highland village of Cuzco, where he designed a system of government to consolidate his conquests. He implemented taxes to support Inca rulers and administrators, and he organized a system of state-owned storehouses to stock agricultural surpluses and craft products such as textiles. He also began construction on an extensive network of roads that enabled Inca military forces and administrators to travel quickly to all parts of the empire.

Quipu In the absence of any script or system of writing, Inca bureaucrats and administrators relied on a mnemonic aid known as ***quipu*** to keep track of their responsibilities. Quipu consisted of an array of small cords of various colors and lengths, all suspended from one large, thick cord. Experts tied a series of knots in the small cords, which sometimes numbered a hundred or more, to help them remember certain kinds of information. Most quipu recorded statistical information having to do with population, state property, taxes, and labor services that communities owed to the central government. Occasionally, though, quipu also helped experts to remember historical information having to do with the establishment of the Inca empire, the Inca rulers, and their deeds. Although much more unwieldy and less flexible than writing, quipu enabled Inca bureaucrats to keep track of information well enough to run an orderly empire.

Cuzco Cuzco served as the administrative, religious, and ceremonial center of the Inca empire. When Pachacuti retired there, Cuzco was a modest village, but the conqueror soon transformed it into a magnificent capital that Incas considered "the navel of the universe." At the center was a huge plaza filled with glistening white sand transported from Pacific beaches to the high Andean city. Surrounding

---

quipu (KEE-poo)

the plaza were handsome buildings constructed of red stone cut so precisely by expert masons that no mortar was necessary to hold them together. The most important buildings sported gold facings, which threw off dazzling reflections when rays of the Andean sun fell on them.

Since Cuzco was primarily a capital and a ceremonial center, the city's permanent population was sizable but not enormous—perhaps forty thousand—but some two hundred thousand Inca subjects lived in the immediate vicinity. Apart from high-ranking imperial administrators, the most prominent permanent residents of Cuzco proper included the Inca rulers and high nobility, the high priests of the various religious cults, and the hostages of conquered peoples who lived with their families under the watchful eyes of Inca guardians.

Inca Roads A magnificent and extensive road system enabled the central government at Cuzco to communicate with all parts of the far-flung Inca empire and to dispatch large military forces rapidly to distant trouble spots. Two roads linked the Inca realm from north to south—one passing through the mountains, the other running along the coast. Scholars have estimated the combined length of those trunk routes at 16,000 kilometers (almost 10,000 miles). The combined length of the entire network of all Inca roads, including lesser thoroughfares as well as the major trunk routes, may have amounted to 40,000 kilometers (almost 25,000 miles).

Inca roads were among the best ever constructed before modern times. During the early sixteenth century, Spanish conquerors marveled at the roads—paved with stone, shaded by trees, and wide enough to accommodate eight horsemen riding abreast. A corps of official runners carried messages along the roads so that news and information could travel between Cuzco and the most distant parts of the empire within a few days. When the Inca rulers desired a meal of fresh fish, they dispatched runners from Cuzco to the coast, more than 320 kilometers (200 miles) away, and had their catch within two days. Like roads in empires in other parts of the world, the Incas' roads favored their efforts at centralization. Their roads even facilitated the spread of the Quechua language and their religious cult focusing on the sun, both of which became established throughout their empire.

Inca Society and Religion

Trade Despite those splendid roads, Inca society did not generate large classes of merchants and skilled artisans. On the local level the Incas and their subjects bartered surplus agricultural production and handcrafted goods among themselves. Long-distance trade, however, fell under the supervision of the central government. Administrators organized exchanges of agricultural products, textiles, pottery, jewelry, and craft goods, but the Inca state did not permit individuals to become independent merchants. In the absence of a market economy, there was no opportunity for a large class of professional, skilled artisans to emerge. Many individuals produced pottery, textiles, and tools for local consumption, and a few produced especially fine goods for the ruling, priestly, and aristocratic classes. But skilled crafts workers were much less prominent among the Incas than among the Mexica and the peoples of the eastern hemisphere.

Descendants prepare a ritual meal for a mummified Inca ruler (depicted in the background).

Ruling Elites The main classes in Inca society were the rulers, the aristocrats, the priests, and the peasant cultivators of common birth. The Incas considered their chief ruler a deity descended from the sun. In theory, this god-king owned all land, livestock, and property in the Inca realm, which he governed as an absolute and infallible ruler. Inca rulers retained their prestige even after death. Their descendants mummified the royal remains and regarded departed kings as intermediaries with the gods. Succeeding rulers often deliberated state policy in the presence of royal mummies so as to benefit from their counsel. Indeed, on the occasion of certain festivals, rulers brought out the mummified remains of their ancestors, dressed them in fine clothes, adorned them with gold and silver jewelry, honored them, and presented them with offerings of food and drink to maintain cordial relations with former rulers. Meanwhile, by way of tending to the needs of their living subjects, the Inca god-kings supervised a class of bureaucrats, mostly aristocrats, who allocated plots of land for commoners to cultivate on behalf of the state.

Aristocrats and Priests Like the ruling elites, Inca aristocrats and priests led privileged lives. Aristocrats consumed fine foods and dressed in embroidered clothes provided by common subjects. Aristocrats also had the right to wear large ear spools that distended their lobes so much that Spanish conquerors referred to them as "big ears." Priests often came from royal and aristocratic families. They led celibate and ascetic lives, but they deeply influenced Inca society because of their education and their responsibil-

ity for overseeing religious rituals. The major temples supported hundreds of priests, along with attendants and virgin women devoted to divine service who prepared ceremonial meals and wove fine ritual garments for the priestly staff.

Fulfilling her tribute duty to the Inca state, an Inca woman weaves woolen fabric on a loom attached to a tree.

Peasants The cultivators were mostly peasants of common birth who lived in communities known as *ayllu,* similar to the Mexicas' *calpulli,* which were the basic units of rural society. Ranging in size from small villages to larger towns, *ayllus* consisted of several families who lived together, sharing land, tools, animals, crops, and work. Peasants supported themselves by working on lands allocated to individual families by their *ayllu.* Instead of paying taxes or tribute, peasants also worked on state lands administered by aristocrats. Much of the production from these state lands went to support the ruling, aristocratic, and priestly classes. The rest went into state storehouses for public relief in times of famine and for the support of widows, orphans, and others unable to cultivate land for themselves. Apart from agricultural work, peasants also owed compulsory labor services to the Inca state. Men provided the heavy labor required for the construction, maintenance, and repair of roads, buildings, and irrigation systems. Women delivered tribute in the form of textiles, pottery, and jewelry. With the aid of quipu, Inca bureaucrats kept track of the labor service and tribute owed by local communities.

Inca Gods: Inti and Viracocha Members of the Inca ruling class venerated the sun as a god and as their major deity, whom they called Inti. They also recognized the moon, stars, planets, rain, and other natural forces as divine. Some Incas, including the energetic ruler Pachacuti, also showed special favor to the god Viracocha, creator of the world, humankind, and all else in the universe. The cult of the sun, however, outshone all the others. In Cuzco alone some four thousand priests, attendants, and virgin devotees served Inti, whose temple attracted pilgrims from all parts of the Inca empire. The first Spanish visitors to Cuzco reported that it took four hundred paces for them to walk around the temple complex, and they expressed amazement at its lavish decoration, including a golden sculpture of the sun encrusted with gems. Particularly astonishing to the visitors was an imitation garden in which grains of gold represented a field, which was planted with stalks of maize fabricated from gold and surrounded by twenty golden llamas with their attendants, also sculpted in gold. Priests of Inti and those serving other cults honored their deities with sacrifices, which in Inca society usually took the form of agricultural produce or animals such as llamas and guinea pigs rather than humans.

Moral Thought In addition to sacrifices and ritual ceremonies, Inca religion had a strong moral dimension. The Incas taught a concept of sin as a violation of the established social or natural order, and they believed in a life beyond death, during which individuals would receive rewards or punishments based on the quality of their earthly lives. Sin, they believed, would bring divine disaster both for individuals and for their larger communities. The Incas also observed rituals of confession and penance by which priests absolved individuals of their sins and returned them to the good graces of the gods.

THE SOCIETIES OF OCEANIA

Inhabitants of Oceania did not interact with peoples of different societies as frequently or systematically as did their counterparts in the eastern hemisphere, but they built and maintained flourishing societies of their own. The aboriginal peoples of Australia ventured over vast stretches of their continent and created networks of trade and exchange between hunting and gathering societies. Only in the far north, however, did they deal with peoples beyond Australia as they traded sporadically with merchants from New Guinea and the islands of southeast Asia. Meanwhile, throughout the Pacific Ocean, islanders built complex agricultural societies. By the time European mariners sailed into the Pacific Ocean in the sixteenth century, the larger island groups had sizable populations, hierarchical social orders, and hereditary chiefly rulers. In the central and western Pacific, mariners sailed regularly between island groups and established elaborate trade networks. Islanders living toward the eastern and western edges of the Pacific Ocean also had occasional dealings with American and Asian peoples, sometimes with significant consequences for the Pacific island societies.

The Nomadic Foragers of Australia

After the aboriginal peoples of Australia learned how to exploit the resources of the continent's varied regions, they led

MAP 20.3
The societies of Oceania.
Islands are much more numerous and much closer together in the western Pacific than in the eastern Pacific.

In what ways did proximity to or distance from other islands influence the development of Pacific island societies?

lives that in some ways changed little over the centuries. Unlike their neighbors to the north, they did not turn to agriculture. The inhabitants of New Guinea began to herd swine and cultivate root crops about 5000 B.C.E., and the inhabitants of islands in the Torres Strait (which separates Australia from New Guinea) took up gardening soon thereafter. Although aboriginal peoples of northern Australia must have known about foods cultivated in neighboring lands, they maintained nomadic, foraging societies until European peoples migrated to Australia in large numbers during the nineteenth and twentieth centuries.

Trade As a result of their mobile and nomadic way of life, aboriginal Australians frequently met and interacted with peoples of neighboring societies. Because Australia is a continent of enormous climatic and ecological diversity, different peoples enjoyed access to food and other resources unknown to others they encountered during their seasonal migrations. Even though as nomads they did not accumulate large quantities of material goods, groups regularly exchanged surplus food and small items when they met.

That sort of small-scale exchange eventually enabled trade goods to spread throughout most of Australia. Individuals did not travel along all the trade routes. Instead, trade goods passed from one aboriginal community to another until they came to rest in regions often distant from their origins. Pearly oyster shells were among the most popular trade items. Archaeologists have turned up many of these shells fashioned into jewelry more than 1,600 kilometers (1,000 miles) from the waters where the oysters bred. From interior regions came stone axe heads, spears, boomerangs, furs, skins, and fibers.

Aboriginal peoples occasionally traded foodstuffs, but with the exception of some root vegetables, those items were generally too perishable for exchange. Peoples on the north coast also engaged in a limited amount of trade with mariners from New Guinea and the islands of southeast Asia. Australian spears and highly prized pearly shells

went north in exchange for exotic items such as the striking flowers of the bird-of-paradise plant, stone clubs, decorative trinkets—and occasionally iron axes, much coveted by aboriginal peoples who had no tradition of metallurgy.

Cultural and Religious Traditions In spite of seasonal migrations, frequent encounters with peoples from other aboriginal societies, and trade over long distances, the cultural traditions of Australian peoples mostly did not diffuse much beyond the regions inhabited by individual societies. Aboriginal peoples paid close attention to the prominent geographic features of the lands around them. Rocks, mountains, forests, mineral deposits, and bodies of water were crucial for their survival, and they related stories and myths about those and other geographic features. Often, they conducted religious observances designed to ensure continuing supplies of animals, plant life, and water. Given the intense concern of aboriginal peoples with their immediate environments, their cultural and religious traditions focused on local matters and did not appeal to peoples from other regions.

The Development of Pacific Island Societies

By the early centuries C.E., human migrants had established agricultural societies in almost all the island groups of the Pacific Ocean. About the middle of the first millennium C.E., they ventured to the large islands of New Zealand—the last large, habitable region of the earth to receive members of the human species. After 1000 C.E., Polynesians inhabiting the larger Pacific islands grew especially numerous, and their surging population prompted remarkable social and political development.

Trade between Island Groups In the central and western regions of the Pacific, where several clusters of islands are relatively close to one another, mariners linked island societies. Regional trade networks facilitated exchanges of useful goods such as axes and pottery, exotic items such as shells and decorative ornaments, and sometimes even foodstuffs such as yams. Regional trade within individual island groups served social and political as well as economic functions, since it helped ruling elites establish and maintain harmonious relations with one another. In some cases, trade crossed longer distances and linked different island groups. Inhabitants of the Tonga, Samoa, and Fiji islands traded mats and canoes, for example, and also intermarried, thus creating political and social relationships.

Long-Distance Voyaging Elsewhere in Polynesia, vast stretches of deep blue water made it much more complicated to travel between different island groups and societies. As a result, regular trade networks did not emerge in the eastern Pacific Ocean. Nevertheless, mariners undertook lengthy voyages on an intermittent basis, sometimes with momentous results. After the original settlement of Easter Island about 300 C.E., for example, Polynesian mariners probably ventured to the western coast of South America,

A painting from 1825 shows several fishponds in active use near Honolulu in Hawai'i. How did ponds like these enable Hawaiians to catch more fish?

thinking about ENCOUNTERS

Maritime Encounters and Their Effects
Polynesian peoples inhabited tiny islands scattered throughout a vast ocean, and they necessarily relied on local resources to meet most of their needs. Yet they also sailed thousands of kilometers over open oceans to establish cultural contacts and trading relationships with inhabitants of other islands. What were the most important results of the encounters between residents of distant islands?

where they learned about the cultivation of sweet potatoes. Between about 400 and 700 C.E., mariners spread sweet potatoes throughout Polynesia and beyond to New Caledonia and Vanuatu. The new crop quickly became a prominent source of food in all the islands it reached. Sweet potatoes were especially important for the **Maori** population of New Zealand because the staple crops of the tropical Pacific did not flourish in the temperate climes of New Zealand. Thus long-distance voyages were responsible for the dissemination of sweet potatoes to remote islands situated thousands of kilometers from the nearest inhabited lands.

Another case of long-distance voyaging prompted social changes in the Hawaiian Islands. For centuries after the voyages that brought the original settlers to the islands in the early centuries C.E., there was little travel or communication between Hawai`i and other Polynesian societies. During the twelfth and thirteenth centuries, however, a series of two-way voyages linked Hawai`i with Tahiti and the Marquesas Islands. Memories of those voyages survive in oral traditions that relate the introduction into Hawai`i of new chiefly and priestly lines from Tahiti. Evidence for the voyages comes also from Hawaiian adoption of fishhook styles from Tahiti and words from the Tahitian language.

Population Growth

While undertaking regular or intermittent voyages over long distances, islanders throughout the Pacific Ocean also built productive agricultural and fishing societies. They cultivated taro, yams, sweet potatoes, bananas, breadfruit, and coconuts, and they kept domesticated chickens, pigs, and dogs. They also fed on abundant supplies of fish, which they caught by spear, net, and hook. After about the fourteenth century, as their population increased, the inhabitants of Hawai`i built ingenious fishponds that allowed small fry to swim from the ocean through narrow gates into rock-enclosed spaces but prevented larger fish from escaping. Fishponds enabled Hawaiians to harvest large quantities of mature fish with relative ease and thus contributed to the islanders' food supplies. The establishment of agricultural and fishing societies led to rapid population growth in all the larger Pacific island groups—Samoa, Tonga, the Society Islands (including Tahiti), and Hawai`i. In Hawai`i, the most heavily populated of the Polynesian island groups, the human population may have exceeded five hundred thousand when European mariners arrived in the late eighteenth century.

Dense populations sometimes led to environmental degradation and social strife on small islands with limited resources. Easter Island in particular was the site of dramatic problems arising from overpopulation. Polynesian migrants originally settled Easter Island in the early centuries C.E., and during the era from about 1100 to 1500, their descendants numbered about ten thousand. This population placed tremendous pressure on the island's resources and also competed fiercely among themselves for those resources. By 1500, having divided into hostile camps, islanders fought one another ferociously, engaging in brutal massacres of their enemies and the desecration of their bodies. As their society disintegrated, they sometimes resorted to cannibalism for lack of sufficient food.

Nan Madol

In other lands, dense populations promoted social organization on a scale never before seen in Oceania. On Pohnpei in the Caroline Islands, for example, the Sandeleur dynasty built a powerful state and organized construction of a massive stone palace and administrative center at Nan Madol. Built mostly during the period from 1200 to 1600, the complex included ninety-three artificial islets protected by seawalls and breakwaters on three sides.

Development of Social Classes

Indeed, beginning about the thirteenth century, expanding populations prompted residents of many Pacific islands to develop

A massive wall constructed of basalt rock protects a burial site at Nan Madol in Pohnpei.

Maori (MAU-ree)

sources from the past

Mo`ikeha's Migration from Tahiti to Hawai`i

A group of Polynesian oral traditions preserve memories of numerous two-way voyages between Tahiti and Hawai`i in the twelfth and thirteenth centuries. One of them has to do with Mo`ikeha, a high chief who left Tahiti because of domestic difficulties and migrated to Hawai`i, where he founded a new chiefly line. The legend recounts several voyages between Tahiti and Hawai`i. The following excerpts deal with Mo`ikeha's establishment as a chief in Hawai`i and the later arrival of his Tahitian son La`amaikahiki, who is credited with the introduction of Tahitian religious and cultural traditions to Hawai`i.

It was dark by the time they arrived [at the Hawaiian island of Kaua`i], so they did not land, instead, mooring their canoe offshore. Early the next morning the people saw this double-hulled canoe floating offshore with the kapu sticks of a chief aboard. The canoe was brought ashore and the travellers got off. Meanwhile the locals were gathering in a crowd to go surf-riding. . . . Among them were the two daughters of the ali`i nui [chief] of Kaua`i, Ho`oipoikamalanai and Hinauu.

Mo`ikeha and his companions saw the crowd and followed along to take part in the morning exercise. Mo`ikeha was a handsome man with dark reddish hair and a tall, commanding figure.

When Ho`oipoikamalanai and her sister saw Mo`ikeha, they immediately fell in love with him, and they decided to take him for their husband. Mo`ikeha in the meantime was also struck with the beauty and grace of the two sisters, and he, too, fell in love with them and decided to take one of them to be his wife. After enjoying the surf for a time, Ho`oipoikamalanai and her sister returned home and told their father about the new arrival and said: "We wish to take that young chief as a husband for one of us." The father approved.

Orders were issued that Mo`ikeha be brought to the house of the two ali`i women. Mo`ikeha and his company were sent for and brought in the presence of the king [the ali`i nui of Kaua`i]. The love of these young people being mutual, Ho`oipoikamalanai and Hinauu took Mo`ikeha to be their husband. Mo`ikeha became ali`i nui of Kaua`i after the death of his father-in-law. . . .

Mo`ikeha worked to make his two wives and five children happy, giving his undivided attention to the bringing up of his boys. He thought no more of Lu`ukia [his lover in Tahiti], but after a while, he began to feel a yearning desire to see his son La`amaikahiki, his child by his first wife Kapo. So he called his five sons together and said to them: "I'm thinking of sending one of you boys to bring your elder brother to Hawai`i." . . .

[After Mo`ikeha's son Kila sailed to Tahiti and found his elder half-brother] La`amaikahiki immediately prepared to accompany his brother to Hawai`i, as Mo`ikeha wished. La`amaikahiki took his priests and his god Lonoika`ouali`i, and set sail for Hawai`i with the men who had come with Kila. When they were approaching Kaua`i, La`amaikahiki began beating his drum. Mo`ikeha heard his drum and ordered everything, the land as well as the house, to be made ready for the reception of the chief La`amaikahiki. Upon the arrival of La`amaikahiki and Kila, the high priest of Kaua`i, Poloahilani, took La`amaikahiki and his god Lonoila`ouali`i ("Lono at the Chiefly Supremacy") to the heiau [temple]. It is said that La`amaikahiki was the first person to bring a god (akua) to Hawai`i. . . .

[After returning to Tahiti, then sailing again to Hawai`i, La`amaikahiki] set sail again, going up the Kona coast [of Hawai`i Island]. . . . It was on this visit that La`amaikahiki introduced hula dancing, accompanied by the drum, to Hawai`i. . . .

La`amaikahiki stayed a long time on Kaua`i teaching the people the art of dancing. From Kaua`i La`amaikahiki visited all the other islands of this group and thus the drum dance (hula ka`eke) spread to the other islands.

For Further Reflection

- How would you characterize the political, social, and cultural significance of two-way voyaging between Tahiti and Hawai`i?

Source: Teuira Henry and others. *Voyaging Chiefs of Havai`i.* Ed. by Dennis Kawaharada. Honolulu: Kalamaku Press, 1995, pp. 138–39, 144–46.

increasingly complex social and political structures. Especially on the larger islands, workers became more specialized: some concentrated on cultivating certain crops, and others devoted their efforts to fishing, producing axes, or constructing large, seagoing canoes. Distinct classes emerged as aristocratic and ruling elites decided the course of public affairs in their societies and extracted surplus agricultural production from those of common birth. The islands of Tonga, Tahiti, and Hawai`i had especially stratified societies with sharp distinctions between various classes of high chiefs, lesser chiefs, and commoners. Hawaiian society also recognized distinct classes of priests and skilled artisans, such as adze makers and canoe builders, ranking between the chiefly and common classes.

The Formation of Chiefly States In addition to distinct social classes, island societies generated strong political leadership. Ruling chiefs generally oversaw public affairs in portions of an island, sometimes in an entire island, and occasionally in several islands situated close to one another. In Tonga and Hawai`i, high chiefs frequently launched campaigns to bring additional islands under their control and create large centralized states. Rarely, however, were these militant chiefs able to overcome geographic and logistic difficulties and realize their expansionist ambitions before the nineteenth century.

Nevertheless, high chiefs guided the affairs of complex societies throughout Polynesia. They allocated lands to families, mobilized labor for construction projects, and organized men into military forces. They commanded enormous respect within their societies. In Hawai`i, for example, the classes of high chiefs known as *ali`i nui* intermarried, ate the best fish and other foods that were *kapu* ("taboo") to commoners, and had the right to wear magnificent cloaks adorned with thousands of bright red and yellow bird feathers. Indeed, a *kapu* forbade commoners to approach or even cast a shadow on the *ali`i nui*.

Polynesian Religion High chiefs worked closely with priests, who served as intermediaries between human communities and the gods. Gods of war and agriculture were common throughout the Pacific islands, but individual islands and island groups recognized deities particular to their own regions and interests. The most distinctive architecture of early Pacific societies was the ceremonial precinct and temple structure known as *marae* (or *heiau* in Hawaiian). *Marae* often had several terraced floors with a rock or coral wall designating the boundaries of the sacred space. In Tonga and Samoa, temples made of timber and thatched roofs served as places of worship, sacrifice, and communication between priests and the gods, whereas in eastern Polynesia religious ceremonies took place on platforms in open-air courtyards. The largest of those structures, the *marae* Mahaiatea on Tahiti, took the form of a step pyramid about 15 meters (49 feet) high with a base measuring 81 by 22 meters (266 by 72 feet).

Pacific island societies did not enjoy access to the range of technologies developed by continental peoples until the sixteenth and later centuries. Yet Pacific islanders cleverly exploited their environments, established productive agricultural economies, built elaborate, well-organized societies, and reached out when possible to engage in trade with their neighbors. Their achievements testify anew to the human impulses toward densely populated communities and interaction with other societies.

inperspective

The original inhabitants of the Americas and Oceania lived in societies that were considerably smaller than those of the eastern hemisphere. They did not possess the metallurgical technologies that enabled their counterparts to exploit the natural environment, nor did they possess the transportation technologies based on wheeled vehicles and domesticated animals that facilitated trade and communication among peoples of the eastern hemisphere. Nevertheless, long before they entered into sustained interaction with European and other peoples, they built complex societies and developed sophisticated cultural and religious traditions. Indigenous peoples established foraging, fishing, and agricultural societies throughout the Americas, and they fashioned tools from wood, stone, and bone that enabled them to produce enough food to support sizable communities. In Mesoamerica and Andean South America, they also built imperial states that organized public affairs on a large scale. The cultural and religious traditions of these imperial societies reflected their concern for agricultural production and the maintenance of complex social structures.

The original inhabitants of Australia and the Pacific islands built societies on a smaller scale than did the peoples of the Americas, but they too devised effective means of exploiting the natural environment and organizing flourishing communities. Australia was a continent of foraging nomadic peoples, whereas the Pacific islands supported densely populated agricultural societies. Although they had limited communication with peoples of the Americas or the eastern hemisphere, the peoples of Oceania traded and interacted regularly with their neighbors, and inhabitants of the Pacific islands sometimes undertook lengthy voyages to trade with distant island groups. ●

CHRONOLOGY

AMERICAS	
950–1150	High point of the Toltec empire
1175	Collapse of the Toltec empire
1250	Inca settlement near Cuzco
1345	Foundation of Tenochtitlan by the Mexica
1400	Emergence of the five Iroquois nations
1428–1440	Reign of the Aztec ruler Itzcóatl
1438–1471	Reign of the Inca ruler Pachacuti
1440–1469	Reign of the Aztec ruler Motecuzoma I
1502–1520	Reign of the Aztec ruler Motecuzoma II
1519	Arrival of Spanish conquerors in Mexico
OCEANIA	
11th century	Beginning of population growth in Pacific islands
12th century	Beginning of two-way voyages between Hawai`i and Tahiti and the Marquesas islands
13th century	Emergence of distinct social classes and chiefly states
14th century	Construction of fishponds in Hawai`i

For Further Reading

Peter Bellwood. *The Polynesians: Prehistory of an Island People.* Rev. ed. London, 1987. Well-illustrated popular account emphasizing the origins and early development of Polynesian societies.

Geoffrey Blainey. *Triumph of the Nomads: A History of Aboriginal Australia.* Melbourne, 1975. A sympathetic account of Australia before European arrival, well informed by archaeological discoveries.

Inga Clendinnen. *Aztecs: An Interpretation.* Cambridge, 1991. A brilliant re-creation of the Mexica world, concentrating on cultural and social themes.

George A. Collier, Renato I. Rosaldo, and John D. Wirth, eds. *The Inca and Aztec States, 1400–1800: Anthropology and History.* New York, 1982. Seventeen well-focused essays represent approaches that scholars have taken to the Inca and Aztec empires.

Nigel Davies. *The Ancient Kingdoms of Mexico.* Harmondsworth, 1983. Reliable popular account.

Hans Dietrich Disselhoff. *Daily Life in Ancient Peru.* Trans. by A. Jaffa. New York, 1967. A well-illustrated volume concentrating on social history that places Inca society in larger historical context.

Ben Finney. *Voyage of Rediscovery: A Cultural Odyssey through Polynesia.* Berkeley, 1994. Fascinating account of efforts to understand ancient Polynesian techniques of seafaring and migrations.

Ross Hassig. *Aztec Warfare: Imperial Expansion and Political Control.* Norman, Okla., 1988. A solid scholarly study of Mexica military affairs and their role in the building of the Aztec empire.

John Hyslop. *The Inka Road System.* New York, 1984. A careful archaeological study.

Patrick V. Kirch. *The Evolution of the Polynesian Chiefdoms.* Cambridge, 1984. Examines the development of Polynesian societies in light of archaeological discoveries.

———. *On the Road of the Winds: An Archaeological History of the Pacific Islands before European Contact.* Berkeley, 2000. A valuable synthesis of recent scholarship by the foremost contemporary archaeologist of the Pacific islands.

Miguel León-Portilla. *The Aztec Image of Self and Society: An Introduction to Nahua Culture.* Salt Lake City, 1992. An excellent guide to Mexica social and cultural history.

David Lewis. *We, the Navigators: The Ancient Art of Landfinding in the Pacific.* Honolulu, 1973. Fascinating reconstruction of traditional methods of noninstrumental navigation used by Pacific Islanders.

Charles C. Mann. *1491: New Revelations of the Americas before Columbus.* New York, 2006. Summarizes a great deal of archaeological research on the pre-Columbian Americas.

Michael E. Moseley. *The Incas and Their Ancestors: The Archaeology of Peru.* Rev. ed. London, 2001. A comprehensive survey of Andean history through the era of the Incas.

Lynda Norene Shaffer. *Native Americans before 1492: The Mound-building Centers of the Eastern Woodlands.* Armonk, N.Y., 1992. Places the mound-building societies in historical context.

Reaching Out: Expanding Horizons of Cross-Cultural Interaction

chapter 21

A giraffe from east Africa sent as a present to China in 1414 and painted by a Chinese artist at the Ming zoo.

EYEWITNESS:
On the Road with Ibn Battuta

One of the great world travelers of all time was the Moroccan legal scholar Ibn Battuta. Born in 1304 at Tangier, Ibn Battuta followed family tradition and studied Islamic law. In 1325 he left Morocco, perhaps for the first time, to make a pilgrimage to Mecca. He traveled by caravan across north Africa and through Egypt, Palestine, and Syria, arriving at Mecca in 1326. After completing his hajj, Ibn Battuta did not head for home but spent a year visiting Mesopotamia and Persia, then traveled by ship through the Red Sea and down the east African coast as far south as Kilwa. By 1330 he had returned to Mecca, but he did not stay there long. When he learned that the sultan of Delhi offered handsome rewards to foreign legal scholars, he set off for India. Instead of traveling there directly by sailing across the Arabian Sea, however, he followed a long and circuitous land route that took him through Egypt, Syria, Anatolia, Constantinople, the Black Sea, and the great trading cities of central Asia, Bokhara and Samarkand. Only in 1333 did he arrive in Delhi, from the north.

For the next eight years, Ibn Battuta remained in India, serving mostly as a *qadi* (judge) in the government of Muhammad ibn Tughluq, the sultan of Delhi. In 1341 Muhammad appointed him to head an enormous embassy to China, but a violent storm destroyed the party's ships as they prepared to depart Calicut for the sea voyage to China. All personal goods and diplomatic presents sank with the ships, and many of the passengers drowned. (Ibn Battuta survived because he was on shore attending Friday prayers at the mosque when the storm struck.) For the next several years, Ibn Battuta made his way around southern India, Ceylon, and the Maldive Islands, where he served as a *qadi* for the recently founded Islamic sultanate, before continuing to China on his own about 1345. He visited the bustling southern Chinese port cities of Quanzhou and Guangzhou, where he found large communities of Muslim merchants, before returning to Morocco in 1349 by way of southern India, the Persian Gulf, Syria, Egypt, and Mecca.

Still, Ibn Battuta's travels were not complete. In 1350 he made a short trip to the kingdom of Granada in southern Spain, and in 1353 he joined a camel caravan across the Sahara desert to visit the Mali empire, returning to Morocco in 1355. During his travels Ibn Battuta visited the equivalent of forty-four modern countries and logged more than 117,000 kilometers (73,000 miles). His account of his adventures stands with Marco Polo's book among the classic works of travel literature.

Between 1000 and 1500 C.E., the peoples of the eastern hemisphere traveled, traded, communicated, and interacted more regularly and intensively than ever before. The large empires of the Mongols and other nomadic peoples provided a political foundation for this cross-cultural interaction. When they conquered and pacified vast regions, nomadic peoples provided safe roads for merchants, diplomats, missionaries, and other travelers. Quite apart from the nomadic empires, improvements in maritime technology led to increased traffic in the sea lanes of the Indian Ocean and the South China Sea. As a result, long-distance travel became much more common than in earlier eras, and individual travelers such as Ibn Battuta and Marco Polo sometimes ventured throughout much of the eastern hemisphere.

Merchants and travelers exchanged more than trade goods. They diffused technologies and spread religious faiths. They also exchanged diseases and facilitated the spread of pathogens that caused widespread and deadly epidemics. During the middle decades of the fourteenth century, bubonic plague traveled the trade routes from western China to central Asia, southwest Asia, north Africa, and Europe. During its initial, furious onslaught, bubonic plague ravaged societies wherever it struck, and it continued to cause epidemics for three centuries and more.

Gradually, however, societies recovered from the plague. By the early fifteenth century, Chinese and western European peoples in particular had restabilized their societies and begun to renew cross-cultural contacts. In Europe, that effort had profound consequences for modern world history. As they sought entry to the markets of Asia, European mariners not only established direct connections with African and Asian peoples but also sailed to the western hemisphere and the Pacific Ocean. Their voyages brought the peoples of the eastern hemisphere, the western hemisphere, and Oceania into permanent and sustained interaction. Thus cross-cultural interactions of the period 1000 to 1500 pointed toward global interdependence, a principal characteristic of modern world history.

LONG-DISTANCE TRADE AND TRAVEL

Travelers embarked on long-distance journeys for a variety of reasons. Nomadic peoples ranged widely in the course of migrations and campaigns of conquest. East European and African slaves traveled involuntarily to the Mediterranean basin, southwest Asia, India, and sometimes even southern China. Buddhist, Christian, and Muslim pilgrims undertook extraordinary journeys to visit holy shrines. Three of the more important motives for long-distance travel between 1000 and 1500 C.E. were trade, diplomacy, and missionary activity. The cross-cultural interactions that resulted helped spread technological innovations throughout the eastern hemisphere.

Patterns of Long-Distance Trade

Merchants engaged in long-distance trade relied on two principal networks of trade routes. Luxury goods of high value relative to their weight, such as silk textiles and precious stones, often traveled overland on the silk roads used since classical times. Bulkier commodities, such as steel, stone, coral, and building materials, traveled the sea lanes of the Indian Ocean, since it would have been unprofitable to transport them overland. The silk roads linked all of the Eurasian landmass, and trans-Saharan caravan routes drew west Africa into the larger economy of the eastern hemisphere. The sea lanes of the Indian Ocean served ports in southeast Asia, India, Arabia, and east Africa while also offering access via the South China Sea to ports in China, Japan, Korea, and the spice-bearing islands of southeast Asia. Thus, in combination, land and sea routes touched almost every corner of the eastern hemisphere.

Trading Cities As the volume of trade increased, the major trading cities and ports grew rapidly, attracting buyers, sellers, brokers, and bankers from parts near and far. Khanbaliq (modern Beijing), Hangzhou, Quanzhou, Melaka, Cambay, Samarkand, Hormuz, Baghdad, Caffa, Cairo, Alexandria, Kilwa, Constantinople, Venice, Timbuktu, and many other cities had large quarters occupied by communities of foreign merchants. When a trading or port city enjoyed a strategic location, maintained good order, and resisted the temptation to levy excessive customs fees, it had the potential to become a major emporium serving long-distance trade networks. A case in point is Melaka (in modern Malaysia). Founded in the 1390s, within a few decades Melaka became the principal clearinghouse of trade in the eastern Indian Ocean. The city's authorities policed the strategic Strait of Melaka and maintained a safe market that welcomed all merchants and levied reasonable fees on goods exchanged there. By the end of the fifteenth century, Melaka had a

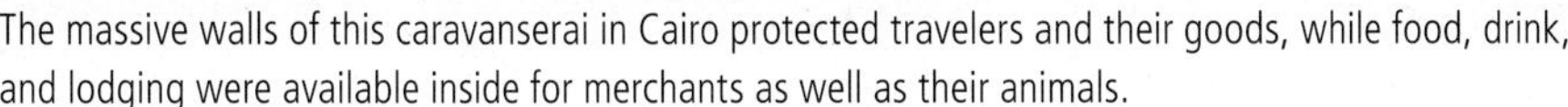

The massive walls of this caravanserai in Cairo protected travelers and their goods, while food, drink, and lodging were available inside for merchants as well as their animals.

population of some fifty thousand people, and in the early sixteenth century the Portuguese merchant Tomé Pires reported that more than eighty languages could be heard in the city's streets.

During the early and middle decades of the thirteenth century, the Mongols' campaigns caused economic disruption throughout much of Eurasia—particularly in China and southwest Asia, where Mongol forces toppled the Song and Abbasid dynasties. Mongol conquests inaugurated a long period of economic decline in southwest Asia where the conquerors destroyed cities and allowed irrigation systems to fall into disrepair. As the Mongols consolidated their hold on conquered lands, however, they laid the political foundation for a surge in long-distance trade along the silk roads. Merchants traveling the silk roads faced less risk of banditry or political turbulence than in previous times. Meanwhile, strong economies in China, India, and western Europe fueled demand for foreign commodities. Many merchants traveled the whole distance from Europe to China in pursuit of profit.

Marco Polo The best-known long-distance traveler of Mongol times was the Venetian Marco Polo (1253–1324). Marco's father, Niccolò, and uncle Maffeo were among the first European merchants to visit China. Between 1260 and 1269 they traveled and traded throughout Mongol lands, and they met Khubilai Khan as he was consolidating his hold on China. When they returned to China in 1271, seventeen-year-old Marco Polo accompanied them. The great khan took a special liking to Marco, who was a marvelous conversationalist and storyteller. Khubilai allowed Marco to pursue his mercantile interests in China and also sent him on numerous diplomatic missions, partly because Marco regaled him with stories about the distant parts of his realm. After seventeen years in China, the Polos decided to return to Venice, and Khubilai granted them permission to leave. They went back on the sea route by way of Sumatra, Ceylon, India, and Arabia, arriving in Venice in 1295.

A historical accident has preserved the story of Marco Polo's travels. After his return from China, Marco was captured and made a prisoner of war during a conflict between his native Venice and its commercial rival, Genoa. While imprisoned, Marco related tales of his travels to his fellow prisoners. One of them was a writer of romances, and he compiled the stories into a large volume that circulated rapidly throughout Europe.

In spite of occasional exaggerations and tall tales, Marco's stories deeply influenced European readers. Marco always mentioned the textiles, spices, gems, and other goods

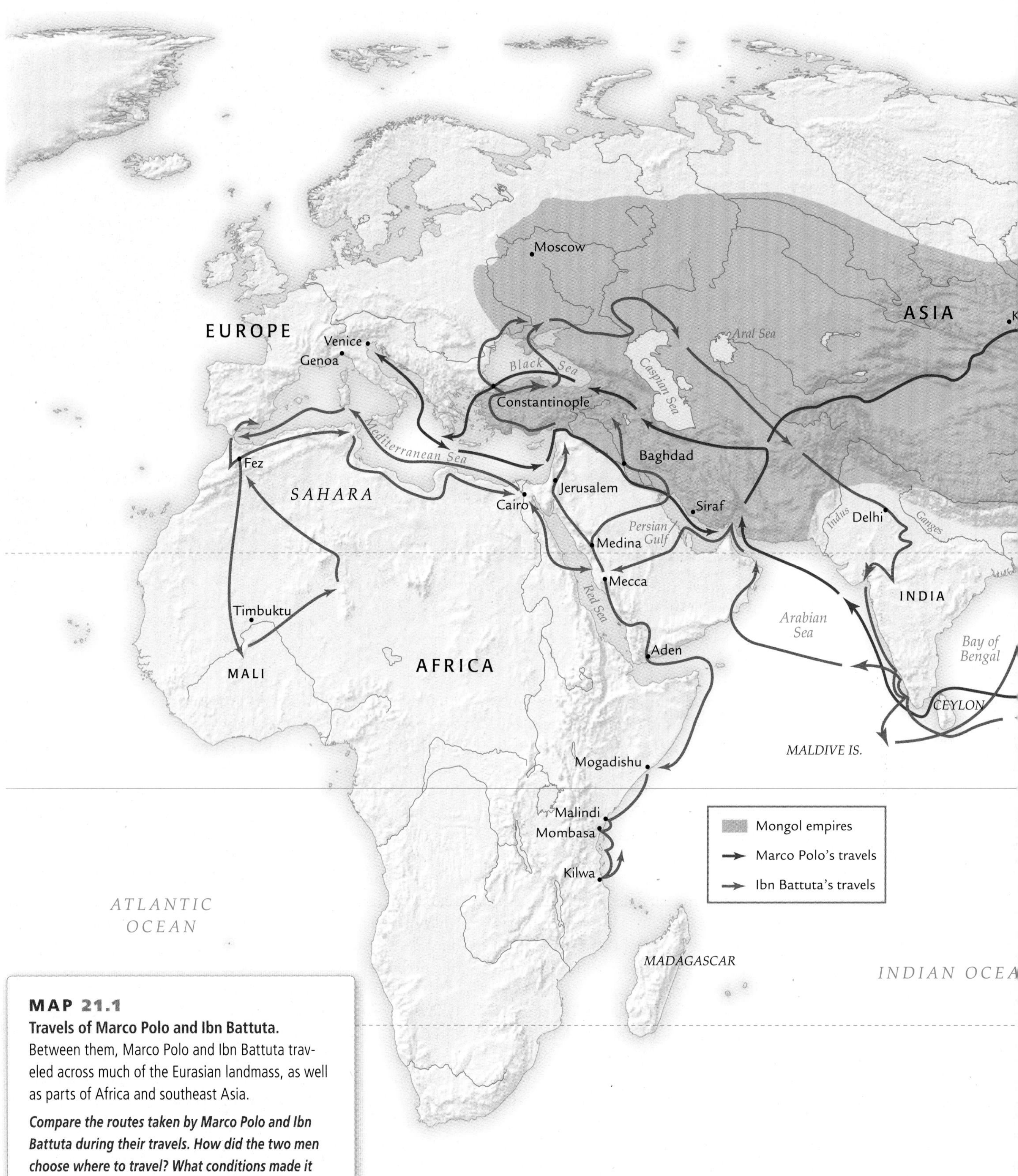

MAP 21.1

Travels of Marco Polo and Ibn Battuta.
Between them, Marco Polo and Ibn Battuta traveled across much of the Eurasian landmass, as well as parts of Africa and southeast Asia.

Compare the routes taken by Marco Polo and Ibn Battuta during their travels. How did the two men choose where to travel? What conditions made it possible for them to travel so far from their homes?

he observed during his travels, and European merchants took note, eager to participate in the lucrative trade networks of Eurasia. The Polos were among the first Europeans to visit China, but they were not the last. In their wake came hundreds of others, mostly Italians. In most cases, their stories do not survive, but their travels helped to increase European participation in the larger economy of the eastern hemisphere.

Political and Diplomatic Travel

Marco Polo came from a family of merchants, and merchants were among the most avid readers of his stories. Marco himself most likely collaborated closely with Italian merchants during his years in China. Yet his experiences also throw light on long-distance travel undertaken for political and diplomatic purposes. Khubilai Khan and the other Mongol rulers of China did not entirely trust their Chinese subjects and regularly appointed foreigners to administrative posts. In his account of his travels, Marco reported that Khubilai appointed him governor of the large trading city of Yangzhou. There is no independent evidence to confirm that claim, but Marco may well have filled some sort of administrative position. In addition, he represented Khubilai Khan's interests on diplomatic missions. To support himself in China, then, Marco supplemented his mercantile ventures with various official duties assigned to him by his patron, the great khan.

Mongol-Christian Diplomacy The emergence of elaborate trading networks and the establishment of vast imperial states created great demand for political and diplomatic representation during the centuries after 1000 C.E. The thirteenth century was a time of especially active diplomacy involving parties as distant as the Mongols and western Europeans, both of whom considered a military alliance against their common Muslim foes. As European Christians sought to revive the crusading movement and recapture Jerusalem from Muslim forces, the Mongols were attacking the Abbasid empire from the east. During the 1240s and 1250s, Pope Innocent IV dispatched a series of envoys who invited the Mongol khans to convert to Christianity and join Europeans in an alliance against the Muslims. The khans declined the invitation, proposing in reply that the pope and European Christians submit to Mongol rule or face destruction.

Rabban Sauma Although the early round of Mongol-European diplomacy offered little promise of cooperation, the Mongols later initiated another effort. In 1287 the Mongol ilkhan of Persia planned to invade the Muslim-held lands of southwest Asia, capture Jerusalem, and crush Islam as a political force in the region. In hopes of attracting support for the project, he dispatched Rabban Sauma, a Nestorian Christian priest born in the Mongol capital of Khanbaliq but of Turkish ancestry, as an envoy to the pope and European political leaders.

An illustration from a fourteenth-century French manuscript depicts Marco Polo picking pepper with local workers in southern India.

Rabban Sauma met with the kings of France and England, the pope, and other high officials of the Roman Catholic church. He enjoyed a fine reception, but he did not succeed in attracting European support for the ilkhan. Only a few years later, in 1295, Ghazan, the new ilkhan of Persia, converted to Islam, thus precluding any further possibility of an alliance between the Mongols of Persia and European Christians. Nevertheless, the flurry of diplomatic activity illustrates the complexity of political affairs in the eastern hemisphere and the need for diplomatic consultation over long distances.

The expansion of Islamic influence in the eastern hemisphere encouraged a different kind of politically motivated travel. Legal scholars and judges played a crucial role in Islamic societies, since the *sharia* prescribed religious observances and social relationships based on the Quran. Conversions to Islam and the establishment of Islamic states in India, southeast Asia, and sub-Saharan Africa created a demand for Muslims educated in Islamic law. After about the eleventh century, educated Muslims from southwest Asia and north Africa regularly traveled to recently converted lands to help instill Islamic values.

Ibn Battuta Best known of the Muslim travelers was Ibn Battuta (1304–1369). Islamic rulers governed most of the lands Ibn Battuta visited—including India, the Maldive Islands, the Swahili city-states of east Africa, and the Mali empire—but very few Muslims educated in the law were available in those lands. With his legal credentials Ibn Battuta had little difficulty finding government positions. As *qadi* and advisor to the sultan of Delhi, he supervised the affairs of a wealthy mosque and heard cases at law, which he strictly enforced according to Islamic standards of justice. On one occasion Ibn Buttuta sentenced a man to receive eighty lashes because he had drunk wine eight years earlier.

After leaving northern India, Ibn Battuta obtained a post as *qadi* in the Maldive Islands. There he heard cases at law and worked zealously to promote proper observance of Islam. He ordered lashings for men who did not attend Friday prayers, and he once sentenced a thief to lose his right hand in accordance with punishment prescribed by the *sharia*. He also attempted, unsuccessfully, to persuade island women to meet the standards of modesty observed in other Islamic lands by covering their breasts. In both east

sources from the past

Ibn Battuta on Customs in the Mali Empire

Long-distance travelers often encountered unfamiliar customs in foreign societies. The Moroccan traveler Ibn Battuta approved heartily when staying with hosts who honored the values of his own Muslim society, but he had little tolerance for those who did not. Here he describes what he witnessed at the sultan's court in the Mali empire.

The Blacks are the most respectful of people to their king and abase themselves most before him. They swear by him, saying *Mansa Sulaiman ki* [the law of Mansa Sulaiman, the Mali sultan]. If he summons one of them at his session in the cupola . . . the man summoned removes his robe and puts on a shabby one, takes off his turban, puts on a dirty skull-cap and goes in with his robe and his trousers lifted half way to his knees. He comes forward humbly and abjectly, and strikes the ground hard with his elbows. He stands as if he were prostrating himself in prayer, and hears what the Sultan says like this. If one of them speaks to the Sultan and he answers him, he takes his robe off his back, and throws dust on his head and back like someone making his ablutions with water. I was astonished that they did not blind themselves.

When the Sultan makes a speech in his audience those present take off their turbans from their heads and listen in silence. Sometimes one of them stands before him, recounts what he has done for his service, and says: "On such and such a day I did such and such, and I killed so and so on such and such a day." Those who know vouch for the truth of that and he does it in this way. One of them draws the string of his bow, then lets it go as he would do if he were shooting. If the Sultan says to him: "You are right" or thanks him, he takes off his robe and pours dust on himself. That is good manners among them. . . .

Among their good practices are their avoidance of injustice; there is no people more averse to it, and their Sultan does not allow anyone to practice it in any measure; [other good practices include] the universal security in their country, for neither the traveller nor the resident there has to fear thieves or bandits . . . their punctiliousness in praying, their perseverance in joining the congregation, and in compelling their children to do so; if a man does not come early to the mosque he will not find a place to pray because of the dense crowd; it is customary for each man to send his servant with his prayer-mat to spread it out in a place reserved for him until he goes to the mosque himself. . . . They dress in clean white clothes on Fridays; if one of them has only a threadbare shirt he washes it and cleans it and wears it for prayer on Friday. They pay great attention to memorizing the Holy Qur'an. . . .

Among their bad practices are that the women servants, slave-girls and young daughters appear naked before people, exposing their genitals. I used to see many like this in [the fasting month of] Ramadan, for it is customary for the *fararis* [commanders] to break the fast in the Sultan's palace, where their food is brought to them by twenty or more slave-girls, who are naked. Women who come before the Sultan are naked and unveiled, and so are his daughters. On the night of the twenty-seventh of Ramadan I have seen about a hundred naked slave-girls come out of his palace with food; with them were two daughters of the Sultan with full breasts and they too had no veil. They put dust and ashes on their heads as a matter of good manners. [Another bad practice:] Many of them eat carrion, dogs and donkeys.

For Further Reflection

- Discuss the various ways in which Islamic influences and established local customs came together in the Mali empire.

Source: H. A. R. Gibb, trans. *The Travels of Ibn Battuta, A.D. 1325–1354,* 4 vols. London: Hakluyt Society, 1958–94, 4:960, 965–66.

and west Africa, Ibn Battuta consulted with Muslim rulers and offered advice about government, women's dress, and proper relationships between the sexes. Like many legal scholars whose stories went unrecorded, Ibn Battuta provided guidance in the ways of Islam in societies recently converted to the faith.

Missionary Campaigns

Sufi Missionaries Islamic values spread not only through the efforts of legal scholars but also through the missionary activities of Sufi mystics. As in the early days of Islam, Sufis in the period from 1000 to 1500 ventured to recently conquered or converted lands and sought to win a popular following for the faith in India, southeast Asia, and sub-Saharan Africa. Sufis did not insist on a strict, doctrinally correct understanding of Islam but, rather, emphasized piety and devotion to Allah. They even tolerated continuing reverence of traditional deities, whom the Sufis treated as manifestations of Allah and his powers. By taking a flexible approach to their missions, the Sufis spread Islamic values without facing the resistance that unyielding and doctrinaire campaigns would likely have provoked.

Christian Missionaries Meanwhile, Roman Catholic missionaries also traveled long distances, in the interests of spreading Christianity. Missionaries accompanied the crusaders and other forces to all the lands where Europeans extended their influence after the year 1000. In lands where European conquerors maintained a long-term presence—such as the Baltic lands, the Balkan region, Sicily, and Spain—missionaries attracted converts in large numbers, and Roman Catholic Christianity became securely established. In the eastern Mediterranean region, however, where crusaders were unable to hold their conquests permanently, Christianity remained a minority faith.

The most ambitious missions sought to convert Mongols and Chinese to Roman Catholic Christianity. Until the arrival of European merchants and diplomats in the thirteenth century, probably no Roman Catholic Christian had ever ventured as far east as China, although Nestorian Christians from central Asia had maintained communities there since the seventh century. As more Europeans traveled to China, their expatriate communities created a demand for Roman Catholic services. Many of the Roman Catholic priests who traveled to China probably intended to serve the needs of those communities, but some of them also sought to attract converts.

John of Montecorvino Most active of the Roman Catholic missionaries in China was John of Montecorvino, an Italian Franciscan who went to China in 1291, became the first archbishop of Khanbaliq in 1307, and died there in 1328. While serving the community of Roman Catholic expatriates in China, John worked energetically to establish Christianity in the host society. He translated the New Testament and the book of Psalms into Turkish, a language commonly used at the Mongol court, and he built several churches in China. He took in young boys from Mongol and Chinese families, baptized them, and taught them Latin and Roman Catholic rituals. He claimed to have baptized six thousand individuals by 1305, and he invited the great khan himself to convert to Christianity. Although popular and widely respected among Europeans, Chinese, and Mongols alike, John attracted few Asian peoples to Christianity.

Caterina Vilioni, daughter of the Venetian merchant Domenico Vilioni, died in the Chinese trading city of Yangzhou in 1342. Her tombstone, which shows she was part of the Roman Catholic community in Yangzhou, came to light during a construction project in 1951.

Roman Catholic authorities in Europe dispatched many other priests and missionaries to China during the early fourteenth century, but like John of Montecorvino, they won few converts. Missions successfully established Christian communities in Scandinavia, eastern Europe, Spain, and the Mediterranean islands that European armies recaptured from Muslims during the centuries after 1000 C.E., but east Asia was too distant for the resources available to the Roman Catholic church. Moreover, east Asian peoples already possessed sophisticated religious and cultural traditions, so Christianity had little appeal. Nevertheless, Christian missions to China continued until the mid-fourteenth century, when the collapse of the Mongols' Yuan dynasty and the eruption of epidemic disease temporarily disrupted long-distance travel across Eurasia.

Long-Distance Travel and Cross-Cultural Exchanges

Cultural Exchanges Long-distance travel of all kinds, whether for commercial, political, diplomatic, or missionary purposes, encouraged cultural exchanges between peoples of different societies. Songs, stories, religious ideas, philosophical views, and scientific knowledge all passed readily among travelers who ventured into the larger world during the era from 1000 to 1500 C.E. The troubadours of western Europe, for example, drew on the poetry, music, and love songs of Muslim performers when developing the literature of courtly love. Similarly, European scientists avidly consulted their Muslim and Jewish counterparts in Sicily and Spain to learn about their understanding of the natural world.

Large numbers of travelers also facilitated agricultural and technological diffusion during the period from 1000 to 1500. Indeed, technological diffusion sometimes facilitated long-distance travel. The magnetic compass, for example, invented in China during the Tang or the Song dynasty, spread throughout the Indian Ocean basin during the eleventh century, and by the mid-twelfth century European mariners used compasses in the Mediterranean and the Atlantic Ocean. Diffusion of the compass was a boon to maritime trade, since it allowed mariners to sail over long stretches of deep water with confidence in their ability to find their destinations and return home safely.

Spread of Crops Long-distance journeys enabled Muslim travelers to introduce new food and commercial crops to sub-Saharan Africa. Food crops included citrus fruits and Asian strains of rice, which enriched diets in west Africa after the eleventh century. Muslims also introduced cotton to west Africa, and by 1100, cotton fab-

sources from the past

John of Montecorvino on His Mission in China

The Franciscan John of Montecorvino (1247–1328) served as a Roman Catholic missionary in Armenia, Persia, and India before going to China in 1291. There he served as priest to expatriate European Christians, and he sought to attract converts to Christianity from the Mongol and Chinese communities. In a letter of 8 January 1305 asking for support from his fellow Franciscans in Italy, John outlined some of his activities during the previous thirteen years.

[After spending thirteen months in India] I proceeded on my further journey and made my way to China, the realm of the emperor of the Mongols who is called the great khan. To him I presented the letter of our lord the pope and invited him to adopt the Catholic faith of our Lord Jesus Christ, but he had grown too old in idolatry. However, he bestows many kindnesses upon the Christians, and these two years past I have gotten along well with him. . . .

I have built a church in the city of Khanbaliq, in which the king has his chief residence. This I completed six years ago; and I have built a bell tower to it and put three bells in it. I have baptized there, as well as I can estimate, up to this time some 6,000 persons. . . . And I am often still engaged in baptizing.

Also I have gradually bought one hundred and fifty boys, the children of pagan parents and of ages varying from seven to eleven, who had never learned any religion. These boys I have baptized, and I have taught them Greek and Latin after our manner. Also I have written out Psalters for them, with thirty hymnals and breviaries [prayer books]. By help of these, eleven of the boys already know our service and form a choir and take their weekly turn of duty as they do in convents, whether I am there or not. Many of the boys are also employed in writing out Psalters and other suitable things. His Majesty the Emperor moreover delights much to hear them chanting. I have the bells rung at all the canonical hours, and with my congregation of babes and sucklings I perform divine service, and the chanting we do by ear because I have no service book with the notes. . . .

Indeed if I had but two or three comrades to aid me, it is possible that the emperor khan himself would have been baptized by this time! I ask then for such brethren to come, if any are willing to come, such I mean as will make it their great business to lead exemplary lives. . . .

I have myself grown old and grey, more with toil and trouble than with years, for I am not more than fifty-eight. I have got a competent knowledge of the language and script which is most generally used by the Tartars. And I have already translated into that language and script the New Testament and the Psalter and have caused them to be written out in the fairest penmanship they have, and so by writing, reading, and preaching, I bear open and public testimony to the law of Christ.

For Further Reflection

- To what extent did John of Montecorvino's missionary work reflect conditions different from those that motivated St. Francis of Assisi to found a mendicant order?

Source: Henry Yule and Henri Cordier, eds. *Cathay and the Way Thither,* 4 vols. London: Hakluyt Society, 1913–16, 3:45–50. (Translation slightly modified.)

rics had become popular with the ruling elites and wealthy merchants of the west African kingdoms. Cotton grew well in the savannas, and by 1500 it was the principal textile produced in sub-Saharan Africa.

Sugarcane Muslims were also instrumental in the continuing diffusion of sugarcane. Muslim merchants and other travelers had begun large-scale cultivation of sugarcane in southwest Asia and north Africa during the Abbasid caliphate. They experimented with the plant in west Africa but had limited success because of adverse environmental conditions.

After the twelfth century, however, Muslims facilitated the westward spread of sugarcane by acquainting European crusaders with crystallized sugar refined from cane. Up to that time Europeans had little access to refined sugar, and they relied on honey and fruits as sweeteners. They immediately appreciated the convenience of refined sugar. Italian entrepreneurs began to organize sugarcane plantations on Mediterranean islands such as Sicily, Cyprus, Crete, and Rhodes. Rapidly increasing demand for refined sugar encouraged investors to seek suitable locations throughout the Mediterranean basin. The cultivation of sugarcane had deep social and economic implications. Besides influencing local economic development in lands where it spread, it touched distant societies. Like their Muslim predecessors, European sugar producers often staffed their plantations with slave laborers, and the growth of plantations fueled an increasing demand for Muslim war captives and black Africans who could supply labor services.

Gunpowder Technologies Although Muslim merchants and travelers were especially prominent agents of

An illustration from a manuscript of 1282 depicts a Christian (left) playing chess with a Muslim (right). Chess was one of many cultural elements that passed from Muslim to Christian societies during the crusading era.

diffusion, Mongols also contributed to the process, notably by helping to spread gunpowder technologies west from China. Mongol invaders learned about gunpowder from Chinese military engineers in the early thirteenth century and soon incorporated gunpowder-based weapons into their arsenal: as early as 1214 Chinggis Khan's armies included an artillery unit. During the 1250s, as they campaigned in Persia and southwest Asia, the Mongols used catapults and trebuchets to lob gunpowder bombs into cities under siege. Muslim armies soon developed similar weapons in response.

By the mid-thirteenth century, gunpowder had reached Europe—possibly by way of Mongol-ruled Russia—and Europeans had begun to experiment with gunpowder-fueled rockets. By the early fourteenth century, armies from China to Europe possessed primitive cannons. Although not especially accurate, the weapons were powerful enough to blow holes in the defensive walls of cities under siege. Thus, with the assistance of Mongol warriors, gunpowder technology rapidly spread from its homeland in China across the entire Eurasian landmass.

Agricultural and technological diffusions of the era 1000 to 1500 were by no means unique processes in world history. For millennia, agricultural crops and technological skills had spread widely whenever peoples of different socie-

English forces besiege a French citadel during the Hundred Years' War (1337–1453). Note that the besiegers on the left side of this manuscript illustration employ cannons and smaller firearms that launch gunpowder bombs.

ties interacted with one another. Because of the particularly intense interactions of the period from 1000 to 1500, however, agricultural and technological diffusion profoundly influenced the lives of peoples throughout the eastern hemisphere. The spread of food crops enriched diets and supported increasing populations, and the spread of industrial crops such as cotton promoted economic development. The diffusion of the magnetic compass enabled mariners to sail the seas more safely and effectively, and the spread of gunpowder technology changed forever the nature of war.

CRISIS AND RECOVERY

As Eurasian peoples traveled over long distances, they not only exchanged trade goods, agricultural crops, and technological expertise but also unwittingly helped disease pathogens to spread. When diseases broke out among previously unexposed populations, they often caused deadly epidemics that severely disrupted whole societies. During the fourteenth century, bubonic plague erupted in epidemics that ravaged societies throughout most of Asia, Europe, and north Africa. Epidemic plague struck intermittently until the seventeenth century, but by the fifteenth century Chinese and European societies had begun to recover from its effects and wield their influence in the larger world.

Bubonic Plague

The Little Ice Age About 1300 C.E. a process of global climatic change caused temperatures to decline significantly and abruptly throughout much of the world. For more than five hundred years, the earth experienced a "little ice age," when temperatures were much cooler than in the era from

A painting of 1503 graphically communicates the horror felt by medieval Europeans when bubonic plague struck their communities. Here death takes away a cartload of victims while others die beside the road.

1000 to 1300 C.E. With markedly cooler temperatures and shorter growing seasons, agricultural production declined in many lands, leading to famine and sometimes even starvation. In some northerly lands, agriculture ceased to be a practical possibility: after the onset of the little ice age, Norse settlers abandoned the colonies they had occupied in Greenland since the tenth century.

Origins of Epidemic Bubonic Plague

As they struggled to cope with the cooling climate, peoples in much of the eastern hemisphere suddenly encountered a new challenge in the form of devastating epidemic disease. Bubonic plague spread from the Yunnan region of southwestern China, where it probably had been endemic for centuries. The plague bacillus infects rodents such as rats, squirrels, and prairie dogs, and fleas transmit the pathogen from one rodent to another. If rodent populations decline, fleas seek other hosts and sometimes spread the disease to human victims. In the early fourteenth century, Mongol military campaigns helped spread plague from Yunnan to China's interior: an epidemic in 1331 reportedly killed 90 percent of the population in Hebei province in northeastern China, near modern Beijing. During the 1350s epidemics broke out in widely scattered regions of China, and contemporaries reported that plague carried away two-thirds of the population in some afflicted areas.

Spread of Plague During the 1340s Mongols, merchants, and other travelers spread the disease along trade routes to points west of China. It thrived in the oases and trading cities of central Asia, where domestic animals and rodents provided abundant breeding grounds for fleas and the plague bacillus. By 1346 it had reached the Black Sea ports of Caffa and Tana. In 1347, Italian merchants fled plague-infected Black Sea ports and unwittingly spread the disease throughout the Mediterranean basin. By 1348, following the trade routes, plague had sparked epidemics in most of western Europe.

Wherever it appeared, bubonic plague struck with frightful effects. Victims developed inflamed lymph nodes, particularly in the neck, armpit, and groin areas, and most died within a few days after the onset of symptoms. Internal hemorrhaging often discolored the inflammations known as buboes—which gave rise to the term *bubonic*—and because of the black or purple swellings, Europeans referred to the plague as the "Black Death." Bubonic plague typically killed 60 to 70 percent of its human victims and had the potential to ravage a society within a few months. In some small villages and towns, disease wiped out the entire population. A spate of new births generally followed outbreaks of plague as societies tried to replenish their numbers, but plague also returned and claimed new victims. In Europe plague erupted intermittently from the 1340s until the late seventeenth century.

Some parts of the eastern hemisphere did not suffer directly from plague epidemics. The long, cold winters of Scandinavia discouraged the proliferation of plague-bearing

thinking about ENCOUNTERS

Long-Distance Travel and Cross-Cultural Exchanges
With the aid of long-distance travelers, many cultural traditions, technologies, and biological species spread widely through the eastern hemisphere: Islam, Christianity, gunpowder, the compass, sugarcane, bubonic plague, and others as well. Taking both a short-term and a long-term view, which do you consider the most important effects of long-distance travel in the era 1200 to 1500?

rodents and fleas, so the northernmost parts of Europe escaped the plague's worst effects. For reasons unknown, India also seems to have avoided serious difficulties. In fact, the Indian population grew from 91 million in the year 1300 to 97 million a century later and 105 million in 1500. Epidemics also largely bypassed sub-Saharan Africa, even though plague had long been endemic in the Great Lakes region of east Africa.

Population Decline In lands hard hit by plague, however, it took a century and more to begin recovery from the demographic consequences of epidemic disease. In 1300 China's population, already reduced by conflicts with the Mongols since the early thirteenth century, stood at eighty-five million. In 1400, after about seventy years of epidemic plague, Chinese numbers amounted to only seventy-five million. A century later demographic recovery was under way, and China's population rebounded to one hundred million.

European society also reeled from the effects of bubonic plague. From seventy-nine million in 1300, Europe's population dropped by almost 25 percent to sixty million in 1400. As in China, demographic recovery in Europe was under way in 1500 when the European population climbed to eighty-one million. Islamic societies in southwest Asia, Egypt, and north Africa also suffered devastating population losses, and demographic recovery took much longer there than in China and Europe. In Egypt human population probably did not reach preplague levels until the nineteenth century.

Social and Economic Effects Because of the heavy demographic toll that it levied, bubonic plague disrupted societies and economies throughout Eurasia and north Africa. Epidemics killed the young, the weak, and the old in especially high numbers, but they spared no group. Peasants and laborers, artisans and crafts workers, merchants and bankers, priests and nuns, rulers and bureaucrats all fell before the plague's onslaught. The disease caused severe labor shortages, which in turn generated social unrest.

In western Europe, for example, urban workers demanded higher wages, and many left their homes in search of better conditions. Political authorities responded by freezing wages and forbidding workers to leave their homes. For their part, peasants in the countryside also sought to improve their circumstances by moving to regions where landlords offered better terms. Landlords responded to that challenge by restricting the freedom of peasants to move and by reimposing labor requirements: in effect, the lords sought to reinstate conditions of serfdom that they had allowed to lapse before the arrival of plague. As a result of sharply conflicting interests, disgruntled workers and peasants mounted a series of rebellions that rocked both the towns and the countryside of western Europe. Authorities eventually extinguished the revolts but only after considerable social disruption and loss of life.

By the seventeenth century the plague had lost much of its ferocity. Epidemics occurred more sporadically, and they did not seriously diminish human populations. Since the 1940s, antibiotic drugs have brought the disease largely under control among human populations, although it survives in rodent communities throughout much of the world.

Ming artisans won worldwide fame for their blue-and-white porcelain, which inspired the founders of the Delft porcelain factory in the Netherlands. This covered jar dates from the early fifteenth century.

Recovery in China: The Ming Dynasty

By the mid-fourteenth century, the Mongols' Yuan dynasty was experiencing very difficult times. Financial mismanagement led to serious economic difficulties, and political conflicts led to assassinations and factional fighting among the Mongols. In 1368, with bubonic plague raging, the Yuan dynasty collapsed, and the Mongols departed China en masse and returned to the steppes, leaving China in a state of both demographic and political turmoil. An increasing birthrate soon helped to replenish human numbers. Political recovery accompanied the demographic rebound.

Hongwu When the Yuan dynasty fell, the governance of China returned to Chinese hands. The new emperor came from a family so poor that he spent much of his youth as a beggar. Orphaned, he entered a Buddhist monastery to assure himself of food, clothing, and shelter. Because of his size and strength, he came to the notice of military commanders, and he made his way through the ranks to lead the rebellious forces that toppled the Yuan dynasty. In 1368 he became Emperor Hongwu, and he proclaimed the establishment of the Ming ("brilliant") dynasty, which lasted until 1644.

Ming Centralization Hongwu immediately set about eliminating all traces of Mongol rule and establishing a government on the model of traditional Chinese dynasties. Like the founders of several earlier Chinese dynasties, Hongwu had little interest in scholarly matters, but he reestablished the Confucian educational and civil service systems to ensure a supply of talented officials and bureaucrats. At the same time, he moved to centralize authority more tightly than ever before in Chinese history. In 1380, when he suspected his chief minister of involvement in a treasonous plot, Hongwu executed the minister and his bureaucratic allies and also abolished the minister's position altogether. From that time forward the Ming emperors ruled directly, without the aid of chief ministers, and they closely supervised imperial affairs.

Mandarins and Eunuchs The Ming emperors insisted on absolute obedience to the policies and initiatives of the central government. They relied heavily on the mandarins, a special class of powerful officials sent out as emissaries of the central government to ensure that local officials implemented imperial policy. The Ming emperors also turned to eunuchs for governmental services. Earlier Chinese emperors, as well as rulers of other lands, had long relied on eunuchs, since they could not generate families and build power bases that might challenge ruling houses. In keeping with their centralizing policy, however, the Ming emperors employed eunuchs much more extensively than any of their predecessors, in the expectation that servants whose fortunes depended exclusively on the emperors' favor would work especially diligently to advance the emperors' interests.

The employment of mandarins and eunuchs enhanced the authority of the central government. The tightly centralized administration instituted by the early Ming emperors lasted more than five hundred years. Although the dynasty fell in 1644 to Manchu invaders, who founded the Qing dynasty, the Manchus retained the administrative framework of the Ming state, which largely survived until the collapse of the Qing dynasty in 1911.

Economic Recovery While building a centralized administration, the Ming emperors also worked toward economic recovery from nomadic rule and epidemic disease. The new rulers conscripted laborers to rebuild irrigation systems that had fallen into disrepair during the previous century, and agricultural production surged as a result. At the same time, they promoted the manufacture of porcelain, lacquerware, and fine silk and cotton textiles. Ming rulers did not actively promote trade with other lands, but private Chinese merchants eagerly sought commercial opportunities and conducted a thriving business marketing Chinese products in ports and trading cities from Japan to the islands of southeast Asia. Meanwhile, domestic trade surged within China, reflecting increasing productivity and prosperity.

Cultural Revival In addition to political and economic recovery, the Ming dynasty sponsored a kind of cultural revival in China. Emperor Hongwu tried to eradicate all signs of the recent nomadic occupation by discouraging the use of Mongol names and the wearing of Mongol dress. Ming emperors actively promoted Chinese cultural traditions, particularly the Confucian and neo-Confucian schools. Hongwu's successor, **Yongle,** organized the preparation of a vast encyclopedia that compiled all significant works of Chinese history, philosophy, and literature. This *Yongle Encyclopedia* ran to almost twenty-three thousand manuscript rolls, each equivalent to a medium-size book. The government originally planned to issue a printed edition of the encyclopedia but abandoned the project because of its enormous expense. Nevertheless, the *Yongle Encyclopedia* was a remarkable anthology, and it signaled the Ming rulers' interest in supporting native Chinese cultural traditions.

Yongle (YAWNG-leh)

Recovery in Europe: State Building

Demographic recovery strengthened states in Europe as it did in China. In Europe, however, political authority rested with a series of regional states rather than a centralized empire. By the late fifteenth century, states in Italy, Spain, France, England, and Russia had devised techniques of government that vastly enhanced their power.

During the later middle ages (1300–1500), internal problems as well as bubonic plague complicated European political affairs. The Holy Roman Empire survived in name, but after the mid-thirteenth century effective authority lay with the German princes and the Italian city-states rather than the emperor. In Spain descendants of Muslim conquerors held the kingdom of Granada in the southern portion of the Iberian peninsula. The kings of France and England sparred constantly over lands claimed by both. Their hostilities eventually resulted in the Hundred Years' War (1337–1453), a protracted series of intermittent campaigns in which the warring factions sought control of lands in France. Russia had even more difficult problems. In the late 1230s Mongol armies conquered the flourishing commercial center of Kiev, and descendants of Chinggis Khan extracted tribute from Russia for almost 250 years thereafter. In the fifteenth century, however, the Mongol states fell into disorder, giving rise to a vast power vacuum in Russia.

Taxes and Armies By the late fifteenth century, however, regional states in western Europe had greatly strengthened their societies, and some had also laid the foundations for the emergence of powerful monarchies. The state-building efforts of the later middle ages involved two especially important elements. The first was the development of fresh sources of finance, usually through new taxes levied directly on citizens and subjects, which supplemented the income that rulers received from their subordinates. The second was the maintenance of large standing armies, often composed of mercenary forces and equipped with gunpowder weapons, supported by state funds.

Italian States The state-building process began in Italy, where profits from industrial production and trade enriched the major cities. The principal Italian states—the city-states of Milan, Venice, and Florence, the papal state based in Rome, and the kingdom of Naples—needed large numbers of officials to administer their complex affairs. They also needed ready access to military forces that could protect

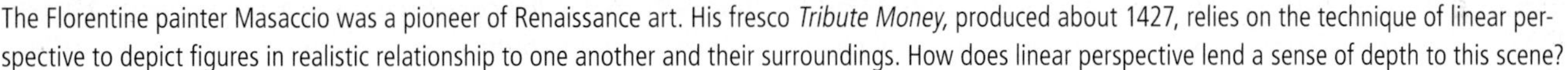

The Florentine painter Masaccio was a pioneer of Renaissance art. His fresco *Tribute Money*, produced about 1427, relies on the technique of linear perspective to depict figures in realistic relationship to one another and their surroundings. How does linear perspective lend a sense of depth to this scene?

their interests. Beginning as early as the thirteenth century, the Italian city-states financed those needs by levying direct taxes and issuing long-term bonds that they repaid from treasury receipts. With fresh sources of finance, the principal Italian states strengthened their authority within their own boundaries and between them controlled public affairs in most of the Italian peninsula.

France and England During the fourteenth and fifteenth centuries, Italian administrative methods made their way beyond the Alps. Partly because of the enormous expenses they incurred during the Hundred Years' War, the kings of France and England began to levy direct taxes and assemble powerful armies. The French kings taxed sales, hearths, and salt; their English counterparts instituted annual taxes on hearths, individuals, and plow teams. Rulers in both lands asserted the authority of the central government over the nobility. The English kings did not establish a standing army, but they were able to raise powerful forces when rebellion threatened public order. In France, however, King Louis XI (reigned 1461–1483) maintained a permanent army of about fifteen thousand troops, many of them professional mercenary soldiers equipped with firearms. Because the high expense of maintaining such forces was beyond the means of the nobility, Louis and his successors enjoyed a decisive edge over ambitious subordinates seeking to challenge royal authority or build local power bases.

Spain The process of state building was most dramatic in Spain, where the marriage in 1469 of Fernando of Aragon and Isabel of Castile united the two wealthiest and most important Iberian realms. Receipts from the sales tax, the primary source of royal income, supported a powerful standing army. Under Fernando and Isabel, popularly known as the Catholic Kings, Christian forces completed the *reconquista* by conquering the kingdom of Granada and absorbing it into their state. The Catholic Kings also projected their authority beyond Iberia. When a French army threatened the kingdom of Naples in 1494, they seized southern Italy, and by 1559 Spanish forces had established their hegemony throughout most of the Italian peninsula. Fernando and Isabel also sought to make a place for Spain in the markets of Asia by sponsoring Christopher Columbus's quest for a western route to China.

Russia State building took place in Russia as well as in western Europe. After the fourteenth century, as Mongol power waned, Russian princes sought to expand their territories. Most successful of them were the grand princes of Moscow. As early as the mid-fourteenth century, the princes began the process of "gathering the Russian land" by acquiring territories surrounding their strategically located commercial town of Moscow on the Volga River. In 1480 Grand Prince Ivan III (reigned 1462–1505), later known as Ivan the Great, stopped paying tribute to the Mongol khan. By refusing to acknowledge the khan's supremacy, Ivan in effect declared

Brunelleschi's magnificent dome on the cathedral of Florence dominates the city's skyline even today.

Russian independence from Mongol rule. He then made Moscow the center of a large and powerful state. His territorial annexations were impressive: Muscovy, the principality ruled from Moscow, almost tripled in size as he brought Russian-speaking peoples into his realm. The most important addition to his possessions came with the acquisition of the prosperous trading city of Novgorod. A hub of the lucrative fur trade and a member of the Hanseatic League of Baltic commercial cities, Novgorod was an autonomous city-state that governed its affairs through a town council. The city's merchants had strong ties to Poland and Lithuania to the west, and Ivan wanted to make sure that Novgorod's prosperity did not benefit neighboring states. Thus he demanded that the city acknowledge his authority. After crushing a futile uprising organized by Novgorod's merchants, he ended the city's independence in 1478 and absorbed it into the expansive Muscovite state. With the aid of Novgorod's wealth, Ivan was then able to build a strong centralized government modeled on the Byzantine empire. Indeed, Ivan went so far as to call himself *tsar* (sometimes spelled *czar*)—a Russianized form of the term *caesar,* which Byzantine rulers had borrowed from the classical Roman empire to signify their imperial status.

Competition between European states intensified as they tightened their authority in their territories. This competition led to frequent small-scale wars between European states, and it encouraged the rapid development of military and naval technology. As states sought technological advantages over their neighbors, they encouraged the refinement and improvement of weapons, ships, and sails. When one state acquired powerful weapons—such as personal firearms or ships equipped with cannons—neighboring states sought more advanced devices in the interests of security. Thus technological innovations vastly strengthened European armies just as they began to venture again into the larger world.

Recovery in Europe: The Renaissance

Demographic recovery and state-building efforts in Europe coincided with a remarkable cultural flowering known as

A painting by Venetian artists Gentile and Giovanni Bellini reflects Renaissance interests in the Muslim world. The painting depicts St. Mark (standing in the pulpit, left) preaching in Alexandria, Egypt. The audience includes Egyptians, Berbers, Turks, Persians, Ethiopians, and Mongols.

the Renaissance. The French word *renaissance* means "rebirth," and it refers to a round of artistic and intellectual creativity that took place from the fourteenth to the sixteenth century and that reflected the continuing development of a sophisticated urban society, particularly in western Europe. Painters, sculptors, and architects of the Renaissance era drew inspiration from classical Greek and Roman artists rather than from their medieval predecessors. They admired the convincing realism of classical sculpture and the stately simplicity of classical architecture. In their efforts to revive classical aesthetic standards, they transformed European art. Meanwhile, Renaissance scholars known as humanists looked to classical rather than medieval literary models, and they sought to update medieval moral thought and adapt it to the needs of a bustling urban society.

Italian Renaissance Art Just as they pioneered new techniques of statecraft, the Italian city-states also sponsored Renaissance innovations in art and architecture. In search of realistic depictions, Italian artists studied the human form and represented the emotions of their subjects. Italian painters such as Masaccio (1401–1428) and Leonardo da Vinci (1452–1519) relied on the technique of linear perspective to represent the three dimensions of real life on flat, two-dimensional surfaces. Sculptors such as Donatello (1386–1466) and Michelangelo Buonarotti (1475–1564) sought to depict their subjects in natural poses that reflected the actual workings of human muscles rather than in the awkward and rigid postures often found in earlier sculptures.

Renaissance Architecture Renaissance architects designed buildings in the simple, elegant style preferred by their classical Greek and Roman predecessors. Their most impressive achievement was the construction of domed buildings—awesome structures that enclosed large spaces but kept them open and airy under massive domes. Roman architects had built domes, but their technology and engineering did not survive the collapse of the Roman empire. Inspired by the Pantheon, a handsome Roman temple constructed in the second century C.E., the Florentine architect Filippo Brunelleschi (1377–1446) reinvented equipment and designs for a large dome. During the 1420s and 1430s, he oversaw the construction of a magnificent dome on the cathedral of Florence. Residents of Florence took Brunelleschi's dome as a symbol of the city's wealth and its leadership in artistic and cultural affairs.

The Humanists Like Renaissance artists and architects, scholars and literary figures known as humanists also drew inspiration from classical models. The term *humanist* referred to scholars interested in the humanities—literature, history, and moral philosophy. They had nothing to do with the secular and often antireligious interests of movements that go under the name humanism today: on the contrary, Renaissance humanists were deeply committed to Christianity. Several humanists worked diligently to prepare accurate texts and translations of the New Testament and other important Christian writings. Most notable of them was Desiderius Erasmus of Rotterdam (1466–1536), who in 1516 published the first edition of the Greek New Testament along with a revised Latin translation and copious annotations. Other humanists drew inspiration from the intense spirituality and high moral standards of early Christianity and promoted those values in their society.

Humanists scorned the dense and often convoluted writing style of the scholastic theologians. Instead, they preferred the elegant and polished language of classical Greek and Roman authors and the early church fathers, whose works they considered more engaging and more persuasive than the weighty tomes of medieval philosophers and theologians. Thus humanists such as the Florentine Francesco Petrarca, also known in English as Petrarch (1304–1374), traveled throughout Europe searching for manuscripts of classical works. In the monastic libraries of Italy, Switzerland, and southern France, they found hundreds of Latin writings that medieval scholars had overlooked. During the fifteenth century, Italian humanists became acquainted with Byzantine scholars and enlarged the body of classical Greek as well as Latin works available to scholars.

Humanist Moral Thought Classical Greek and Latin values encouraged the humanists to reconsider medieval ethical teachings. Medieval moral philosophers had taught that the most honorable calling was that of monks and nuns who withdrew from the world and dedicated their lives to prayer, contemplation, and the glorification of God, but the humanists drew inspiration from classical authors such as Cicero, who demonstrated that it was possible to lead a morally virtuous life while participating actively in the affairs of the world. Renaissance humanists argued that it was perfectly honorable for Christians to enter into marriage, business relationships, and public affairs, and they offered a spirited defense for those who rejected the cloister in favor of an active life in society. Humanist moral thought thus represented an effort to reconcile Christian values and ethics with the increasingly urban and commercial society of Renaissance Europe.

thinking about TRADITIONS

Comparative Cultural Revivals

Ming China and Renaissance Europe both experienced cultural revival in the fifteenth century. To what extent did their respective classical traditions influence cultural developments in the two lands? What were the effects of the cultural revivals in China and Europe?

Renaissance Europe and the Larger World Quite apart from their conscious effort to draw inspiration from classical antiquity, Renaissance art and thought also reflected increasing European participation in the affairs of the eastern hemisphere. As merchants linked Europe to the larger hemispheric economy, European peoples experienced increased prosperity that enabled them to invest resources in artistic production and support for scholarship. Renaissance painters filled their canvases with images of silk garments, ceramic vessels, lacquered wood, spice jars, foreign peoples, and exotic animals that had recently come to European attention. Princes and wealthy patrons commissioned hundreds of these paintings that brought a cosmopolitan look to their palaces, residences, and places of business.

This enchantment with the larger world extended also into the realm of ideas. The Italian humanist Giovanni Pico

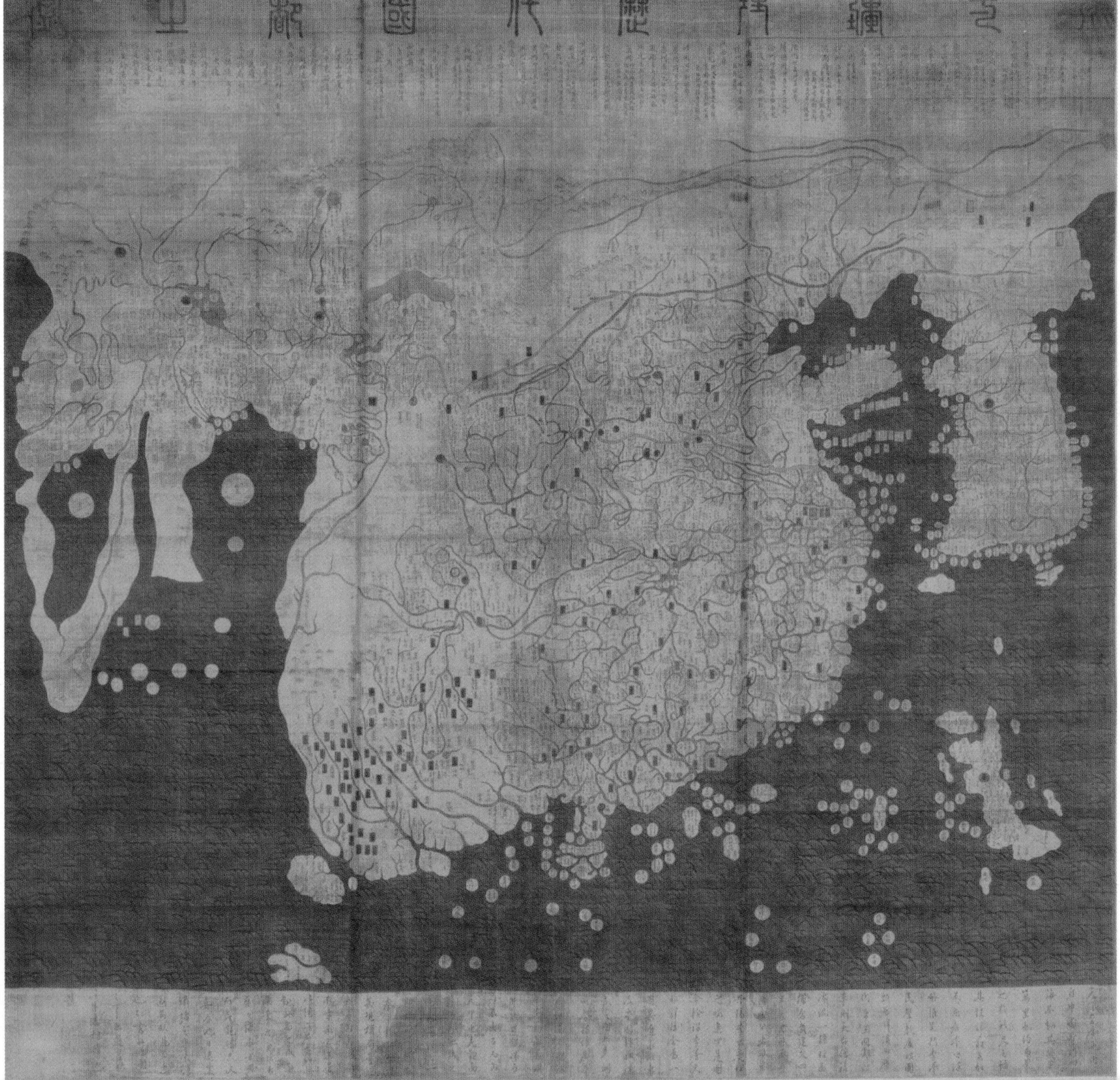

The Kangnido Map (1470) is one of the few surviving large-scale maps from east Asia before modern times. Produced in Korea, it draws on Chinese and Muslim sources, while exaggerating the size of the Korean peninsula.

della Mirandola (1463–1494) perhaps best reflected the enthusiasm of Renaissance scholars to comprehend the world beyond western Europe. In his exuberant *Oration on the Dignity of Man* (1486), Pico made a spirited effort to harmonize the divergent teachings of Plato, Aristotle, Judaism, Christianity, and Islam, not to mention Zoroastrianism and various occult and mystical traditions. His ambitious endeavor was ultimately unsuccessful: Pico had limited information about several of the traditions he sought to reconcile, and he sometimes offered superficial interpretations of doctrines that he imperfectly understood. Nevertheless, his *Oration* gave eloquent voice to the burning desire of many European scholars to understand the larger world. It is not surprising that just as Pico and other Renaissance humanists were undertaking that effort, European mariners were organizing expeditions to explore the lands and seas beyond Christendom.

EXPLORATION AND COLONIZATION

As peoples of the eastern hemisphere recovered from demographic collapse and restored order to their societies, they also sought to revive the networks of long-distance trade and communication that epidemic plague had disrupted. Most active in that effort were China and western Europe—the two societies that recovered most rapidly from the disasters of the fourteenth century. During the early Ming dynasty, Chinese ports accommodated foreign traders, and mariners mounted a series of enormous naval expeditions that visited almost all parts of the Indian Ocean basin. Meanwhile, Europeans ventured from the Mediterranean into the Atlantic Ocean, which served as a highway to sub-Saharan Africa and the Indian Ocean basin. By the end of the fifteenth century, Europeans not only had established sea lanes to India but also had made several return voyages to the American continents, thus inaugurating a process that brought all the world's peoples into permanent and sustained interaction.

The Chinese Reconnaissance of the Indian Ocean Basin

Having ousted the Mongols, the early Ming emperors were not eager to have large numbers of foreigners residing in China. Yet the emperors permitted foreign merchants to trade in the closely supervised ports of Quanzhou and Guangzhou, where they obtained Chinese silk, porcelain, and manufactured goods in exchange for pearls, gems, spices, cotton fabrics, and exotic products such as tortoise shells and animal skins. The early Ming emperors also refurbished the large Chinese navy built during the Song dynasty, and they allowed Chinese merchants to participate in overseas trading ventures in Japan and southeast Asia.

Zheng He's Expeditions Moreover, for almost thirty years, the Ming government sponsored a series of seven ambitious naval expeditions designed to establish a Chinese presence in the Indian Ocean basin. Emperor Yongle organized the expeditions for two main purposes: to impose imperial control over foreign trade with China and to impress foreign peoples with the power and might that the Ming dynasty had restored to China. Indeed, he might well have hoped to extend the tributary system, by which Chinese dynasties traditionally recognized foreign peoples, to lands in the Indian Ocean basin.

The expeditions took place between 1405 and 1433. Leading them was the eunuch admiral Zheng He, a Muslim from Yunnan in southwestern China who rose through the ranks of eunuch administrators to become a trusted advisor of Yongle. Zheng He embarked on each voyage with an awesome fleet of vessels complemented by armed forces large enough to overcome resistance at any port where the expedition called. On the first voyage, for example, Zheng He's fleet consisted of 317 ships accompanied by almost twenty-eight thousand armed troops. Many of these vessels were mammoth, nine-masted "treasure ships" with four decks capable of accommodating five hundred or more passengers, as well as huge stores of cargo. Measuring up to 124 meters (408 feet)

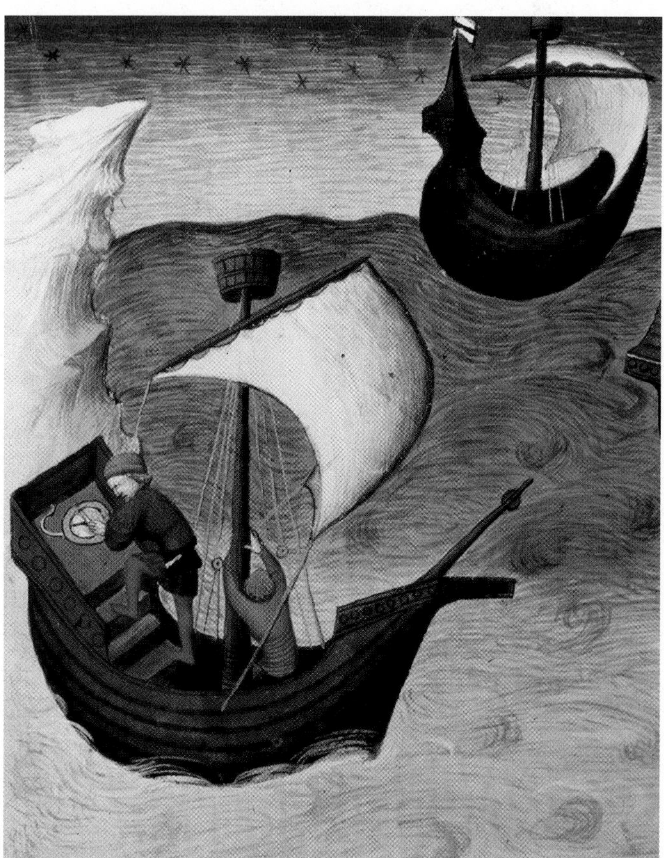

A fifteenth-century manuscript illustration depicts a mariner (left) using an astrolabe (an adapted version of an instrument from the Hellenistic Mediterranean) to determine his latitude while sailing on the Indian Ocean.

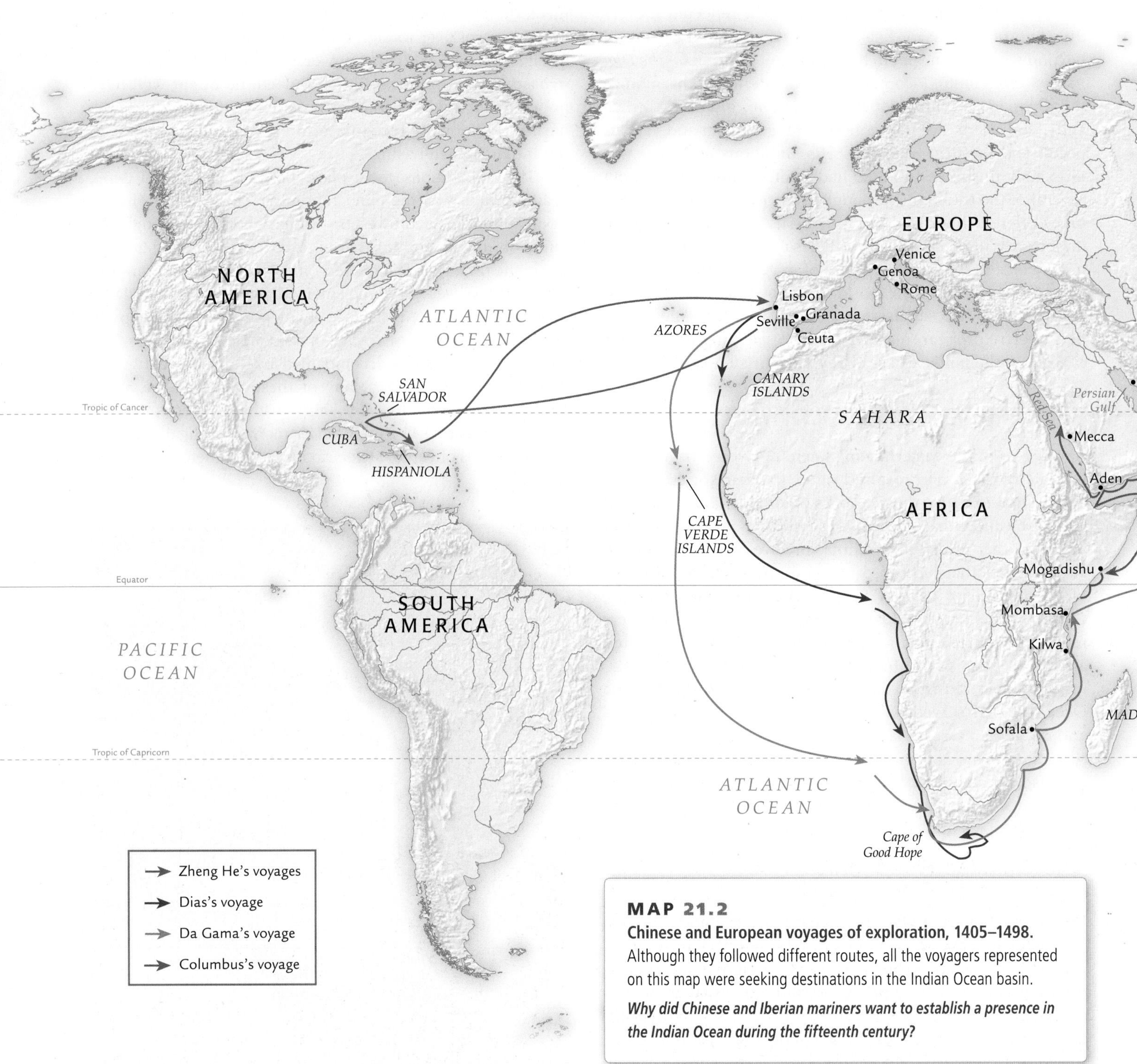

MAP 21.2
Chinese and European voyages of exploration, 1405–1498.
Although they followed different routes, all the voyagers represented on this map were seeking destinations in the Indian Ocean basin.
Why did Chinese and Iberian mariners want to establish a presence in the Indian Ocean during the fifteenth century?

long and 51 meters (166 feet) wide, these treasure ships were by far the largest marine craft the world had ever seen.

On the first three voyages, Zheng He took his fleet to southeast Asia, India, and Ceylon. The fourth expedition went to the Persian Gulf and Arabia, and later expeditions ventured down the east African coast, calling at ports as far south as Malindi in modern Kenya. Throughout his travels, Zheng He liberally dispensed gifts of Chinese silk, porcelain, and other goods. In return he received rich and unusual presents from his hosts, including African zebras and giraffes, which ended their days in the Ming imperial zoo. Zheng He and his companions paid respect to the local deities and customs they encountered, and in Ceylon they erected a monument honoring Buddha, Allah, and Vishnu.

Chinese Naval Power Zheng He generally sought to attain his goals through diplomacy. For the most part, his large contingents of armed troops overawed his hosts, and he had little need to engage in hostilities. But a contemporary reported that Zheng He walked like a tiger, and he did not shrink from violence when he considered it necessary to impress foreign peoples with China's military might. He ruthlessly suppressed pirates who had long plagued Chinese and southeast Asian waters. He also intervened in a civil disturbance to establish his authority in Ceylon, and he made displays of military force when local officials threatened his fleet in Arabia and east Africa. The seven expeditions established a Chinese presence and reputation in the Indian Ocean basin. Returning from his fourth voyage, Zheng He brought envoys from thirty states who traveled to China and paid their respects at the Ming court.

End of the Voyages Yet suddenly, in the mid-1430s, the Ming emperors decided to end the expeditions. Confucian ministers, who mistrusted Zheng He and the eunuchs who supported the voyages, argued that resources committed to the expensive expeditions would go to better uses if devoted to agriculture. Moreover, during the 1420s and 1430s the Mongols mounted a new military threat from the northwest, and land forces urgently needed financial support.

Thus in 1433, after Zheng He's seventh voyage, the expeditions ended. Chinese merchants continued to trade in Japan and southeast Asia, but imperial officials destroyed most of the nautical charts that Zheng He had carefully prepared and gave up any plans to maintain a Chinese presence in the Indian Ocean. The decommissioned treasure ships sat in harbors until they rotted away, and Chinese craftsmen forgot the technology of building such large vessels. Yet Zheng He's voyages demonstrated clearly that China could exercise military, political, and economic influence throughout the Indian Ocean basin.

European Exploration in the Atlantic and Indian Oceans

As Chinese fleets reconnoitered the Indian Ocean, European mariners were preparing to enter both the Atlantic and the Indian Ocean basins. Unlike Zheng He and his companions, Europeans did not venture onto the seas in the interests of diplomacy or in hopes of establishing a political and military reputation in foreign lands. Instead, they acted on two different but complementary motives: the desire to expand the boundaries of Roman Catholic Christianity and the desire to profit from commercial opportunities.

Portuguese Exploration The experience of Portugal illustrates that mixture of motives. Though Portuguese merchants were not especially prominent in trading circles, Portuguese fishermen had a long tradition of seafaring in the stormy Atlantic Ocean. Building on that experience, Portuguese mariners emerged as the early leaders in both Atlantic exploration and the search for a sea route to Asian markets through the Indian Ocean. During the fifteenth century Prince Henrique of Portugal, often called Prince Henry the Navigator, embarked on an ambitious campaign to spread Christianity and increase Portuguese influence on the seas. In 1415 he watched as Portuguese forces seized the Moroccan city of Ceuta, which guarded the Strait of Gibraltar from the south. He regarded his victory both as a blow against Islam

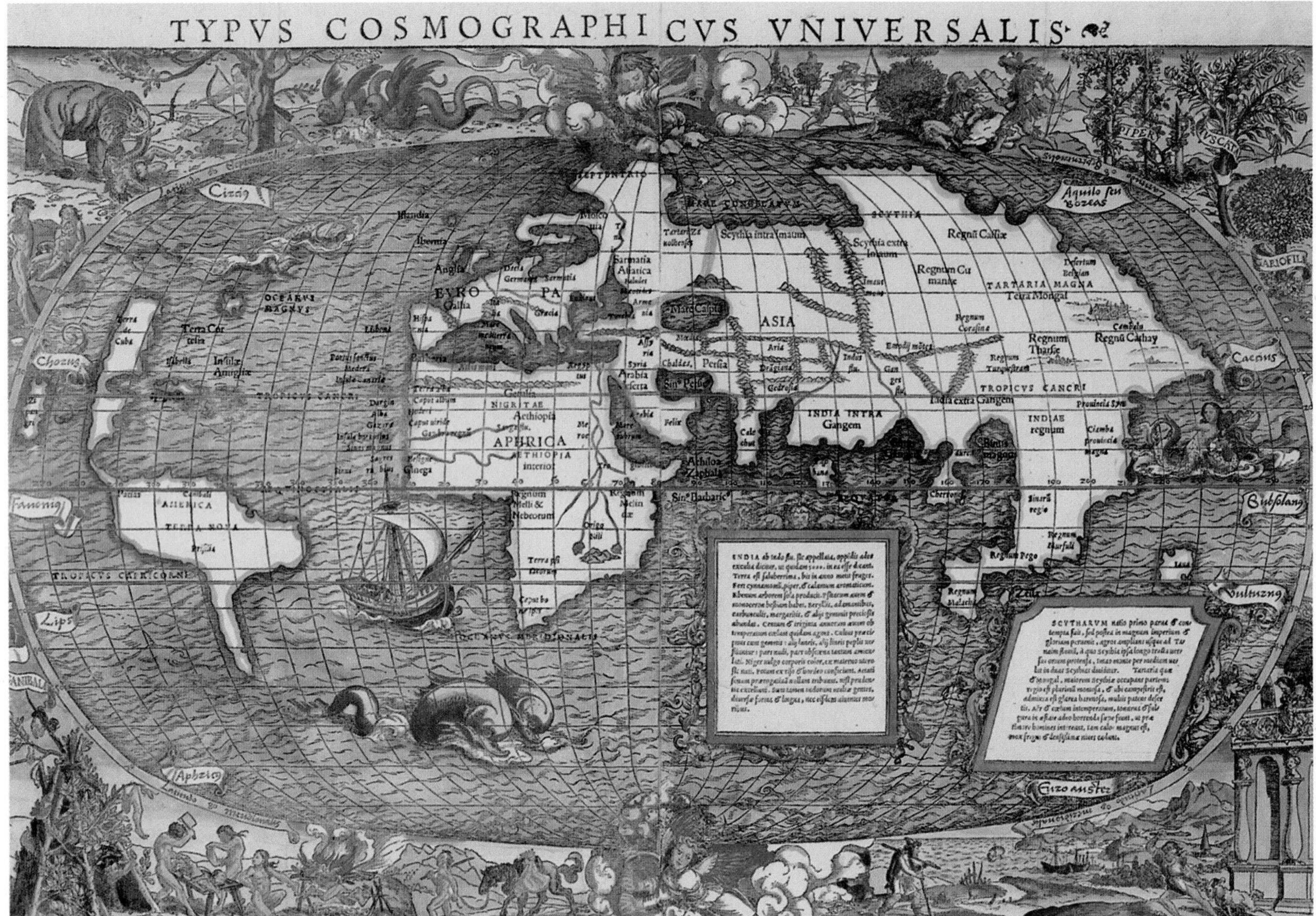

Although Christopher Columbus believed that he had sailed into Asian waters, later mariners soon realized that the Americas were continents unknown to geographers of the eastern hemisphere. This map, prepared in 1532 by the German cartographer Sebastian Münster, shows that by the early sixteenth century, European geographers had acquired a rough but accurate understanding of South America but had reconnoitered only the Atlantic coastline of North America.

and as a strategic move enabling Christian vessels to move freely between the Mediterranean and the Atlantic.

Colonization of the Atlantic Islands Following the capture of Ceuta, Henrique encouraged Portuguese mariners to venture into the Atlantic. During their voyages they discovered the Madeiras and Azores Islands, all uninhabited, which they soon colonized. They also made an unsuccessful effort to occupy the Canary Islands, inhabited by indigenous peoples but claimed since the early fifteenth century by the kingdom of Castile. Later discoveries included the Cape Verde islands, Fernando Po, São Tomé, and Principe off the west African coast. Because these Atlantic islands enjoyed fertile soils and a Mediterranean climate, Portuguese entrepreneurs soon began to cultivate sugarcane there, often in collaboration with Italian investors. Italians had financed sugar plantations in the Mediterranean islands since the twelfth century, and their commercial networks provided a ready means to distribute sugar to Europeans, who were rapidly developing a taste for sweets.

Slave Trade During the middle decades of the fifteenth century, a series of Portuguese fleets also explored the west African coast, each expedition proceeding a bit farther than its predecessor. Originally, the Portuguese traded guns, textiles, and other manufactured items for African gold and slaves. Portuguese traders took full advantage of the long-established African commerce in slaves, but they also changed the nature of the slave trade by dramatically increasing its volume and by sending slaves to new destinations. By the mid-fifteenth century, the Portuguese dispatched thousands of slaves annually from their forts on islands off the African coast. They delivered most of their human cargo to recently founded plantations in the Atlantic islands, where the slaves worked as laborers, although some worked as domestic servants in Europe. The use of African slaves to perform heavy labor on commercial plantations soon became common practice, and it fueled the development of a huge, Atlantic-wide trade that delivered as many as twelve million enslaved Africans to destinations in North America, South America, and the Caribbean region.

Indian Ocean Trade While some Portuguese mariners traded profitably in west Africa, others sought to enter the lucrative trade in Asian silk and spices. A sea route to Asian markets would enable Portuguese merchants to avoid Muslim and Italian intermediaries, through whom almost all Asian luxury goods reached European markets, and participate directly in the flourishing commercial world of the Indian Ocean basin. Toward the end of the fifteenth century, Portuguese mariners began to search seriously for a sea lane from Europe around Africa and into the Indian Ocean. By 1488 Bartolomeu Dias had sailed around the Cape of Good Hope and entered the Indian Ocean. Restless because of the long journey and distance from home, the crew forced Dias to return immediately to Portugal, but his voyage proved that it was possible to sail from Europe to the Indian Ocean. In 1497 Vasco da Gama departed Portugal with the intention of sailing to India. After rounding the Cape of Good Hope, he cruised up the east African coast and found a Muslim pilot who showed him how to take advantage of the seasonal monsoon winds to sail across the Arabian Sea to India. In 1498 he arrived at Calicut, and by 1499 he had returned to Lisbon with a hugely profitable cargo of pepper and spices.

During the following century, Portuguese merchants and mariners dominated trade between Europe and Asia. Indeed, they attempted to control all shipping in the Indian Ocean. Their ships, armed with cannons, were able to overpower the vessels of Arabs, Persians, Indians, southeast Asians, and others who sailed the Indian Ocean. They did not have enough ships to police the entire Indian Ocean, however, so most merchants easily evaded their efforts to control the region's commerce. Nevertheless, the entry of Portuguese mariners into the Indian Ocean signaled the beginning of European imperialism in Asia.

Christopher Columbus While Portuguese seafarers sought a sea route around Africa to India, the Genoese mariner Cristoforo Colombo, known in English as Christopher Columbus, conceived the idea of sailing west to reach Asian markets. Because geographers in the eastern hemisphere knew nothing of the Americas, Columbus's notion made a certain amount of good sense, although many doubted that his plan could lead to profitable trade because of the long distances involved. After the king of Portugal declined to sponsor an expedition to test Columbus's plan, the Catholic Kings, Fernando and Isabel of Spain, agreed to underwrite a voyage. In 1492 Columbus set sail. After a stop in the Canary Islands to take on supplies and make repairs, his fleet of three ships crossed the Atlantic Ocean, reaching land at San Salvador (Watling Island) in the Bahamas.

Columbus returned to Spain without the gold, silk, and spices that he had expected to find, but he persistently held that he had reached islands near the Asian mainland and the markets of China and Japan. Although he made three more voyages to the Caribbean region, Columbus never acknowledged that his expeditions had not reached Asia. News of his voyages spread rapidly, however, and by the end of the fifteenth century other mariners had explored the Caribbean and the American continents enough to realize that the western hemisphere constituted a world apart from Europe, Asia, and Africa.

inperspective

As European mariners ventured into the Indian and Atlantic Ocean basins, they unwittingly inaugurated a new era in world history. For millennia, peoples of different societies had traded, communicated, and interacted. As technologies of transportation improved, they dealt with peoples at increasingly greater distances. By 1500 the Indian Ocean served as a highway linking peoples from China to east Africa, and overland traffic kept the silk roads busy from China to the Mediterranean Sea. Trade goods, diplomatic missions, religious faiths, technological skills, agricultural crops, and disease pathogens all moved readily over the sea lanes and the silk roads, and they profoundly influenced the development of societies throughout the eastern hemisphere. In the western hemisphere, trading networks linked lands as distant as Mexico and the Great Lakes region, while Pacific islanders regularly traveled and traded between island groups.

Never before, however, had peoples of the eastern hemisphere, the western hemisphere, and Oceania dealt with one another on a regular and systematic basis. The voyages of European mariners during the fifteenth and following centuries initiated a long-term process—one that continues in the present day—that brought all regions and peoples of planet earth into permanent and sustained interaction. The formation and reconfiguration of global networks of power, communication, and exchange that followed from those interactions rank among the most prominent themes of modern world history. ●

CHRONOLOGY

1214	Creation of a Mongol artillery unit
1253–1324	Life of Marco Polo
1287–1288	Rabban Sauma's embassy to Europe
1291–1328	John of Montecorvino's mission to China
1304–1369	Life of Ibn Battuta
1304–1374	Life of Francesco Petrarca
1330s	First outbreaks of bubonic plague in China
1337–1453	Hundred Years' War
1347	Arrival of bubonic plague in the Mediterranean basin
1368–1644	Ming dynasty
1405–1433	Zheng He's expeditions in the Indian Ocean
1466–1536	Life of Desiderius Erasmus of Rotterdam
1488	Bartolomeu Dias's voyage around Africa
1492	Christopher Columbus's first voyage to the western hemisphere
1497–1498	Vasco da Gama's voyage to India

Assessing AP Themes

1. What were the changes and continuities from the now-extinct classical empires to the post-classical empires?
2. How did the empires of Mongols change the dynamics of the eastern hemisphere political and economic systems?
3. What state policies, mercantile practices, and innovations in transportation contributed to the intensification of cross-cultural exchanges?
4. Why could "the Indian Ocean Basin" be a more useful unit of analysis than the separate states of South and Southeast Asia (from ch. 15) and the Swahili states?
5. What kinds of cross-cultural interactions allowed or encouraged Western Europeans to engage in significant oceanic exploration and trade in the 15th and 16th centuries?
6. Should the histories of peoples in the Americas and Oceania be separated from the histories of the peoples and societies of the eastern hemisphere, or can they be incorporated?

For Further Reading

Janet L. Abu-Lughod. *Before European Hegemony: The World System, A.D. 1250–1350.* New York, 1989. An important study of long-distance trade networks during the Mongol era.

Jerry H. Bentley. *Humanists and Holy Writ: New Testament Scholarship in the Renaissance.* Princeton, 1983. Examines Renaissance humanists' efforts to prepare accurate texts, translations, and commentaries on the New Testament.

———. *Old World Encounters: Cross-Cultural Contacts and Exchanges in Pre-modern Times.* New York, 1993. Studies cultural and religious exchanges in the eastern hemisphere before 1500 C.E.

Timothy Brook. *The Confusions of Pleasure: Commerce and Culture in Ming China.* Berkeley, 1998. The best introduction to Ming China, with emphasis on social and cultural history.

Jerry Brotton. *The Renaissance Bazaar: From the Silk Road to Michelangelo.* Oxford, 2002. A provocative and well-illustrated study arguing that encounters in the larger world deeply influenced Renaissance cultural development in Europe.

Kenneth Chase. *Firearms: A Global History to 1700.* Cambridge, 2003. Offers a fresh interpretation of the invention and early diffusion of gunpowder weapons.

K. N. Chaudhuri. *Asia before Europe: Economy and Civilisation of the Indian Ocean from the Rise of Islam to 1750.* Cambridge, 1990. Controversial and penetrating analysis of economic, social, and cultural structures shaping societies of the Indian Ocean basin.

———. *Trade and Civilisation in the Indian Ocean: An Economic History from the Rise of Islam to 1750.* Cambridge, 1985. Brilliant analysis of the commercial life of the Indian Ocean basin by a prominent scholar.

Christopher Dawson, ed. *Mission to Asia.* Toronto, 1980. Translations of travel accounts and letters by European missionaries in central Asia and China during the Mongol era.

Michael W. Dols. *The Black Death in the Middle East.* Princeton, 1977. Careful, scholarly investigation of bubonic plague and its effects in southwest Asia.

Ross E. Dunn. *The Adventures of Ibn Battuta: A Muslim Traveler of the 14th Century.* Berkeley, 1986. Fascinating reconstruction of Ibn Battuta's travels and experiences.

Brian Fagan. *The Little Ice Age: How Climate Made History, 1300–1850.* New York, 2000. Popular account of the little ice age, with emphasis on its effects in Europe and North America.

Robert S. Gottfried. *The Black Death: Natural and Human Disaster in Medieval Europe.* New York, 1983. The best general study of bubonic plague and its effects in Europe.

Margaret L. King. *Women of the Renaissance.* Chicago, 1991. A lively and imaginative discussion of women's roles and experiences in Renaissance Europe.

John Larner. *Marco Polo and the Discovery of the World.* New Haven, 1999. Excellent study of Marco Polo and his significance, based on a thorough review of both textual evidence and recent scholarship.

Louise L. Levathes. *When China Ruled the Seas: The Treasure Fleet of the Dragon Throne, 1405–1433.* New York, 1994. Excellent popular account of Zheng He's voyages.

Lauro Martines. *Power and Imagination: City-States in Renaissance Italy.* New York, 1979. An attractive and thoughtful analysis of the Italian Renaissance.

William H. McNeill. *Plagues and Peoples.* Garden City, N.Y., 1976. A pioneering study of infectious and contagious diseases and their effects in world history.

Arnold Pacey. *Technology in World Civilization: A Thousand-Year History.* Oxford, 1990. A brief and insightful study that concentrates on processes of technological diffusion.

William D. Phillips Jr. and Carla Rahn Phillips. *The Worlds of Christopher Columbus.* New York, 1992. The best general work on Christopher Columbus.

Marco Polo. *The Travels.* Trans. by R. Latham. Harmondsworth, 1958. An accurate translation of Marco Polo's work based on reliable scholarship.

Sanjay Subrahmanyam. *The Career and Legend of Vasco da Gama.* Cambridge, 1997. Solid and thoughtful study of the important Portuguese navigator.

Frances Wood. *The Silk Road: Two Thousand Years in the Heart of Asia.* Berkeley, 2002. A brilliantly illustrated volume discussing the history of the silk roads from antiquity to the twentieth century.

State of the World

A World on the Point of Global Integration

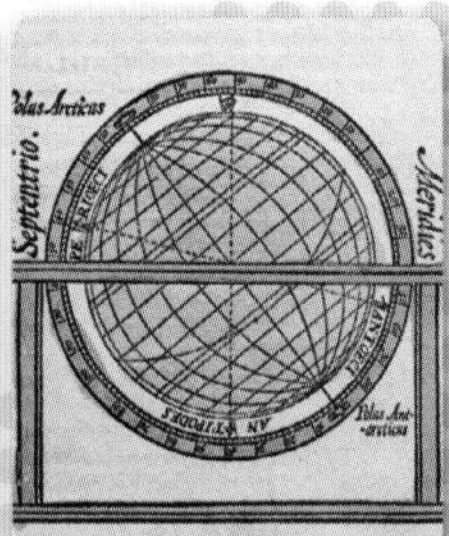

When Christopher Columbus and his crew sailed across the Atlantic Ocean in 1492, the world's peoples were no strangers to long-distance travels and meetings, nor were cross-cultural interactions and exchanges foreign experiences for them. Peoples of the world's three major geographic zones—the eastern hemisphere, the western hemisphere, and Oceania—had been dealing for thousands of years with counterparts from different societies. Even as they built their own distinctive political, social, economic, and cultural traditions, the world's peoples also engaged the larger world beyond their own societies. Their interactions were often hostile or unpleasant, taking the form of raids, wars, campaigns of imperial expansion, or transmissions of epidemic diseases. Yet their engagements also took more peaceful and beneficial forms, as trade, missionary activity, technological diffusion, and the spread of agricultural crops linked peoples of different societies.

Until 1492, however, long-distance travels and cross-cultural interactions took place mostly within the world's three broad regions. With rare and fleeting exceptions, peoples of the eastern hemisphere, the western hemisphere, and Oceania kept to their own parts of the world. They rarely possessed nautical technologies that would have enabled them to cross the earth's oceans regularly and carry on sustained relationships with peoples across the waters. Even when sufficient nautical technologies were available, the costs, dangers, and uncertain prospects of transoceanic voyaging mostly discouraged mariners from making efforts to venture beyond their own zones.

Developments of the era 1000 to 1500 were the immediate context for efforts to cross the world's largest bodies of water. Even as they carried out brutal campaigns of conquest, peoples of nomadic pastoral societies forged links between settled agricultural societies throughout Eurasia and created a demand for continuing relationships, particularly commercial relationships. While Turkish and Mongol peoples wielded more influence than any of their nomadic ancestors in Eurasia, Muslim Arab and Persian merchants drew the societies of sub-Saharan Africa increasingly into interaction with others of the eastern hemisphere. The region of the eastern hemisphere with the most to gain from transoceanic voyaging was western Europe, which otherwise had few good routes providing access to lands to the south and east. Thus, even though mariners from China, India, Persia, the Pacific islands, and other lands also possessed effective nautical technologies, it is not surprising that western European peoples most energetically and most systematically explored opportunities to establish maritime networks of travel, transport, trade, communication, and exchange.

In the year 1500 the world stood on the brink of a new era in the experience of humankind. Peoples of the world's three major geographic zones—the eastern hemisphere, the western hemisphere, and Oceania—were poised to enter into permanent and sustained interaction. The results of their engagements were profitable and beneficial for some peoples but difficult or disastrous for others. It is impossible to comprehend them except in context of the acceleration of cross-cultural interaction in the era 1000 to 1500.

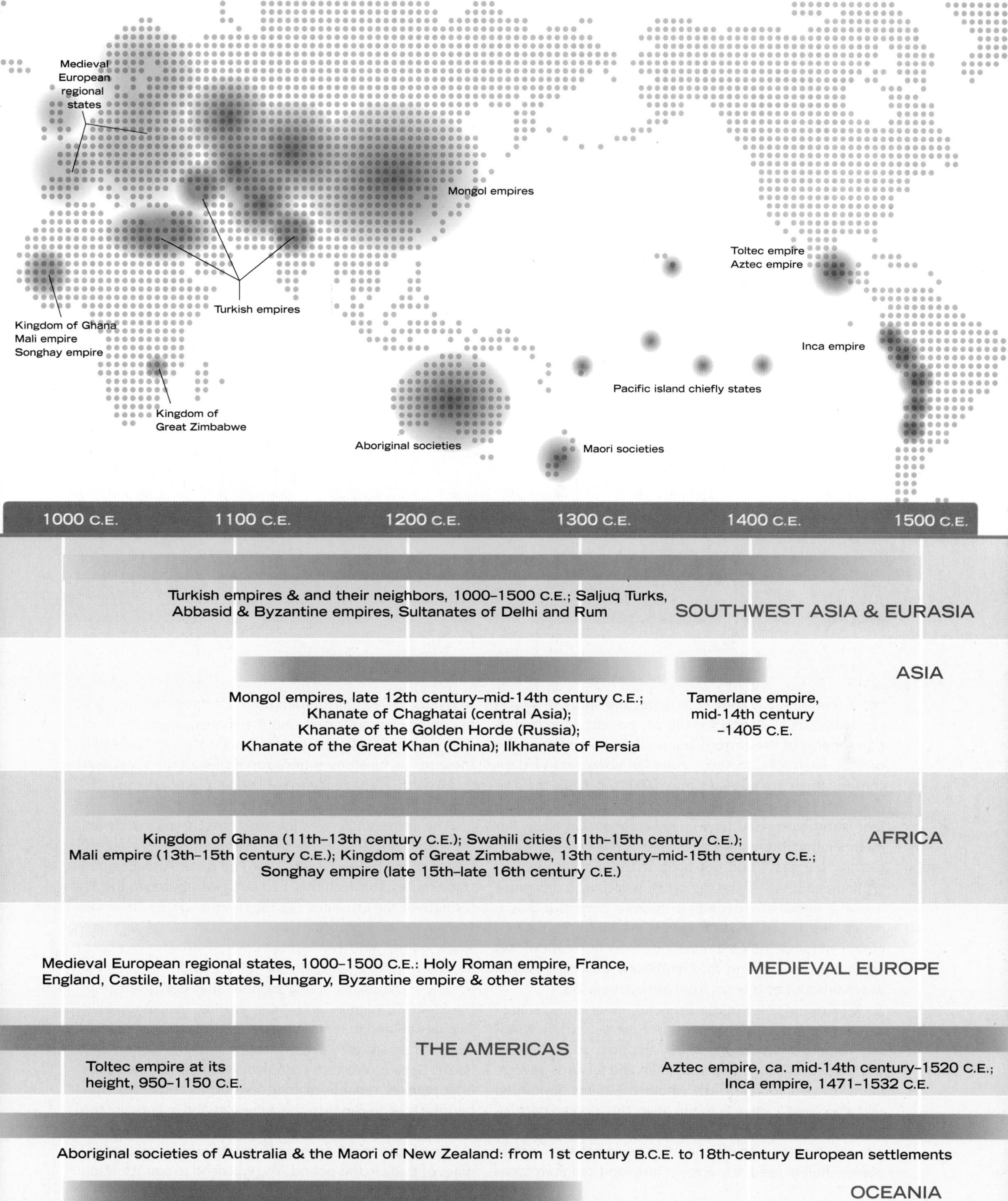
Medieval European regional states
Mongol empires
Toltec empire
Aztec empire
Turkish empires
Kingdom of Ghana
Mali empire
Songhay empire
Inca empire
Pacific island chiefly states
Kingdom of Great Zimbabwe
Aboriginal societies
Maori societies
1000 C.E.
1100 C.E.
1200 C.E.
1300 C.E.
1400 C.E.
1500 C.E.
Turkish empires & and their neighbors, 1000–1500 C.E.; Saljuq Turks, Abbasid & Byzantine empires, Sultanates of Delhi and Rum
SOUTHWEST ASIA & EURASIA
ASIA
Mongol empires, late 12th century–mid-14th century C.E.; Khanate of Chaghatai (central Asia); Khanate of the Golden Horde (Russia); Khanate of the Great Khan (China); Ilkhanate of Persia
Tamerlane empire, mid-14th century –1405 C.E.
AFRICA
Kingdom of Ghana (11th–13th century C.E.); Swahili cities (11th–15th century C.E.); Mali empire (13th–15th century C.E.); Kingdom of Great Zimbabwe, 13th century–mid-15th century C.E.; Songhay empire (late 15th–late 16th century C.E.)
Medieval European regional states, 1000–1500 C.E.: Holy Roman empire, France, England, Castile, Italian states, Hungary, Byzantine empire & other states
MEDIEVAL EUROPE
THE AMERICAS
Toltec empire at its height, 950–1150 C.E.
Aztec empire, ca. mid-14th century–1520 C.E.; Inca empire, 1471–1532 C.E.
Aboriginal societies of Australia & the Maori of New Zealand: from 1st century B.C.E. to 18th-century European settlements
OCEANIA
Pacific island (Samoa, Tonga, Society Islands) population growth (11th century C.E.) leads to emergence of Pacific island chiefly states (13th century C.E.)

part 5

THE ORIGINS OF GLOBAL INTERDEPENDENCE, 1500 TO 1800

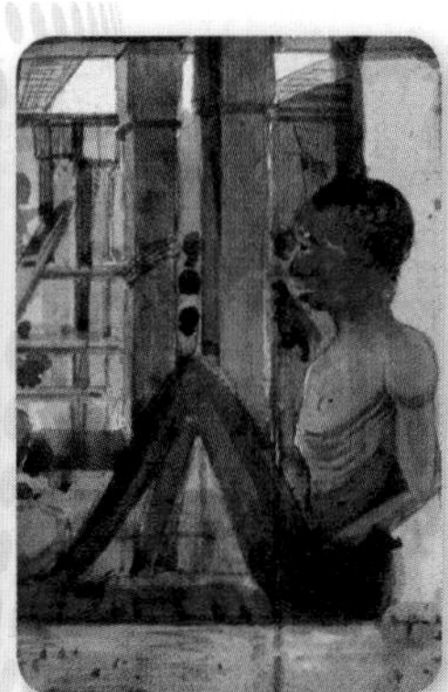

The enormous change that drives the study of World History in AP Period 4 is the permanent interconnection (finally) of the eastern and western hemispheres. Be careful, even though the Columbian voyages and their consequences are huge, from c. 1450 to c. 1750, the empires and states of East Asia, South Asia, and the Middle East (southwest Asia) remain powerful and wealthy. Remember that the western Europeans always wanted to get to "the East" and get hold of those luxury goods. HTS 4 Your main task in this period, however, is to recognize how the goods and peoples of four continents (Eurasia, Africa, North and South America) are integrated into a global network of exchanges and communication. Yet again, you are looking for "syntheses" (mixings) as well as continuities or themes from previous period.

HTS 4 Around the world, rulers of empires and states of varying sizes pursued strategies of centralization. Kings and emperors were trying to pull all power to make laws, war, and taxes away from noblemen and towards government officials (bureaucrats) whom the rulers appointed and who were loyal only to the ruler. This worked particularly well when rulers gave these important jobs to foreigners, thereby undercutting the power of their native nobles. Rulers used art, architecture, and religious ideas to reinforce (legitimize) their quests for power. They used tax money from farmers and merchants to pay for a lot of it. And of course, there were wars within and between these powerful empires because of their desire for power and wealth. HTS 3 Be ready to explain and compare the techniques various rulers used to centralize their power.

The increasingly-wealthy western Europeans craved the luxury goods (and the tax revenue they represented) traded in the Indian Ocean Basin and other Afro-Eurasian trade routes, to which they had been introduced in the aftermath of the Crusades. HTS 2 The creation of the Ottoman Empire in 1453 disrupted the European access to these trade goods, and sent governments, private investors, and merchants scrambling for sailing routes around the powerful Ottomans. Using technologies borrowed from the classical, Islamic, and Asian worlds, including tools, ship design and mapping, western Europeans sailed relatively safely around Africa, into the Indian, Atlantic, and Pacific Oceans. Western Europeans were by no means the only peoples capable of maritime exploration, but they had the luck to run into the Americas and eventually the force to take them over.

Royal chartered monopoly companies were the engines of trade in this period. You will need to pay attention to how they competed with each other for business, access to luxury goods, colonies, and influence in their respective European governments. Most of these chartered companies set up business offices (trading posts, or "factories") in Asian, African, and some American lands. Be sure to note that these companies were the new, minor players on the old Eurasian and African trade routes for centuries. Only a few European joint-stock companies set up permanent (settler) colonies in Africa or Asia. Eventually European states established new maritime empires in the Americas.

The new connections between the hemispheres resulted in the Columbian Exchange—a global exchange of biological goods. AP students must be able to track the positive and negative effects of this massive exchange of peoples, plants, animals, and diseases across time and place, right to the present day. In addition to biological goods, religions spread with the increased and intensified contacts made in this period—Islam to new settings in Asia and Africa, Christianity (in many forms after the Reformation) to the Americas, Buddhism within Asia. Native religions and these imported beliefs sometimes blended to produce a new, mixed or syncretic belief system. And let's not forget money. The silver from New Spain was the life blood of both the European and Asian economies for centuries, and the profits from sugar, the main American plantation crop, enriched the purses of Europeans, Asians, and Africans—from tax-collecting governments, to investors, to ship and warehouse owners, and finally slave traders. And then there was the mixing of peoples. Africans, Europeans, Asians, and Native Americans were brought together in the Americas resulting in new ethnic and racial groups and sometimes changing gender roles.

Even though trade seems to be the cutting edge in this period, the world's economic and productive systems were still heavily agricultural. The new crops, bigger populations, new markets, and new business practices caused all sorts of changes in traditional peasant-farmers agriculture, raised the demand for labor, and fueled the global demand for raw materials and finished products. AP students are often asked to compare labor sources and practices, especially forced or coerced labor (slaves, serfs, mit'a, indentured, or impressed). You need to ask the big questions such as: who wants the labor, how do they pay for it, who works, who decides who works, who profits from the labor?

This may seem obvious to you in the twenty-first century, but all the global conquests and new money-making opportunities meant the creation of newly-important and rich people, particularly businessmen and investors. These newly-important people wanted power and influence in their societies, and they tended to challenge the older land-based elites. Astute rulers took advantage of this conflict and played one group off the other. It was mostly the men who traveled on and profited from these global trade routes, but women were key players on the ground. Watch carefully for the role women played in the new global landscape: they were the mothers of mixed-ethnicity children in the Americas; they were the main merchants in Southeast Asia; they helped run the family businesses; and they took over important ruling functions when the men disappeared, such as in West Africa. In the AP World History course, we will use the terms "new social and political elites" and the "restructuring of racial and gender hierarchies" to describe this profound rearrangement of "who's up and who's down," or "the rearrangement of social, racial, and gender hierarchies."

Exploration, trade, and conquest cost money. Rulers came up with all sorts of ways to collect taxes and generate revenue so that they could continue to expand and consolidate their own power over their large states. In AP World History, you'll be asked to follow how some rulers managed to expand their empires to massive sizes and what the consequences of these expansions were for the conquerors and the conquered. Be ready to compare the strategies of those who acquired huge land-based empires (China, India, Ottomans, Russians) and those who established maritime empires (European states). And of course, all this competition over land and trade routes caused wars, revolts, and significant resistance to state power. As of c. 1750, AP World History looks a lot more modern, a lot more global, and a lot more complex.

Transocеanic Encounters and Global Connections

chapter 22

An unknown artist created a seventeenth-century portrait of Vasco da Gama, who established a sea route between Portugal and India.

EYEWITNESS:
Vasco da Gama's Spicy Voyage

On 8 July 1497 the Portuguese mariner Vasco da Gama led a small fleet of four armed merchant vessels with 170 crewmen out of the harbor at Lisbon. His destination was India, which he planned to reach by sailing around the continent of Africa and through the Indian Ocean. He carried letters of introduction from the king of Portugal as well as cargoes of gold, pearls, wool textiles, bronzeware, iron tools, and other goods that he hoped to exchange for pepper and spices in India.

Before there would be an opportunity to trade, however, da Gama and his crew had a prolonged voyage through two oceans. They sailed south from Portugal to the Cape Verde Islands off the west coast of Africa, where they took on water and fresh provisions. On 3 August they headed south into the Atlantic Ocean to take advantage of the prevailing winds. For the next ninety-five days, the fleet saw no land as it sailed through some six thousand nautical miles of open ocean. By October, da Gama had found westerly winds in the southern Atlantic, rounded the Cape of Good Hope, and entered the Indian Ocean. The fleet slowly worked its way up the east coast of Africa, engaging in hostilities with local authorities at Mozambique and Mombasa, as far as Malindi, where da Gama secured the services of an Indian Muslim pilot to guide his ships across the Arabian Sea. On 20 May 1498—more than ten months after its departure from Lisbon—the fleet anchored at Calicut in southern India.

In India the Portuguese fleet found a wealthy, cosmopolitan society. Upon its arrival local authorities in Calicut dispatched a pair of Tunisian merchants who spoke Spanish and Italian to serve as translators for the newly arrived party. The markets of Calicut offered not only pepper, ginger, cinnamon, and spices but also rubies, emeralds, gold jewelry, and fine cotton textiles. Alas, apart from gold and some striped cloth, the goods that da Gama had brought attracted little interest among merchants at Calicut. Nevertheless, da Gama managed to exchange gold for a cargo of pepper and cinnamon that turned a handsome profit when the fleet returned to Portugal in August 1499. Da Gama's expedition opened the door to direct maritime trade between European and Asian peoples and helped to establish permanent links between the world's various regions.

Cross-cultural interactions have been a persistent feature of historical development. Even in ancient times mass migration, campaigns of imperial expansion, and long-distance trade deeply influenced societies throughout the world. As a result of those interactions, Buddhism, Islam, and Christianity spread from their places of birth to the distant corners of the eastern hemisphere. Long before modern times, arteries of long-distance trade served also as the principal conduits for exchanges of plants, animals, and diseases.

After 1500 C.E., cross-cultural interactions took place on a much larger geographic scale, and encounters were often more disruptive than in earlier centuries. Equipped with advanced technologies and a powerful military arsenal, western European peoples began to cross the world's oceans in large numbers during the early modern era. At the same time, Russian adventurers built an enormous Eurasian empire and ventured tentatively into the Pacific Ocean.

Europeans were not the only peoples who actively explored the larger world during the early modern era. In the early fifteenth century the Ming emperors of China sponsored a series of seven massive maritime expeditions that visited all parts of the Indian Ocean basin. Although state-sponsored expeditions came to an end after 1435, Chinese merchants and mariners were prominent figures in east Asian and southeast Asian lands throughout the early modern era. In the sixteenth century Ottoman mariners also ventured into the Indian Ocean. Following the Ottoman conquest of Egypt in 1517, both merchant and military vessels established an Ottoman presence throughout the Indian Ocean basin. Ottoman subjects traveled as far as China, but they were most active in Muslim lands from east Africa and Arabia to India and southeast Asia, where they enjoyed especially warm receptions.

Although other peoples also made their way into the larger world, Europeans linked the lands and peoples of the eastern hemisphere, the western hemisphere, and Oceania. Because they traveled regularly between the world's major geographic regions, European peoples benefited from unparalleled opportunities to increase their power, wealth, and influence. The projection of European influence brought about a decisive shift in the global balance of power. During the millennium 500 to 1500 C.E., the world's most powerful societies were those organized by imperial states such as the Tang dynasty of China, the Abbasid dynasty in southwest Asia, the Byzantine empire in the eastern Mediterranean region, and the Mongol empires that embraced much of Eurasia. After 1500, however, European peoples became much more prominent than before in the larger world, and they began to establish vast empires that by the nineteenth century dominated much of the world.

The expansion of European influence also resulted in the establishment of global networks of transportation, communication, and exchange. A worldwide diffusion of plants, animals, diseases, and human communities followed European ventures across the oceans, and intricate trade networks gave birth to a global economy. Although epidemic diseases killed millions of people, the spread of food crops and domesticated animals contributed to a dramatic surge in global population. The establishment of global trade networks ensured that interactions between the world's peoples would continue and intensify.

THE EXPLORATION OF THE WORLD'S OCEANS

Between 1400 and 1800, European mariners launched a remarkable series of exploratory voyages that took them to all the earth's waters, with the exception of those in extreme polar regions. These voyages were very expensive affairs. Yet private investors and government authorities had strong motives to underwrite the expeditions and outfit them with advanced nautical technology. The voyages of exploration paid large dividends: they enabled European mariners to chart the world's ocean basins and develop an accurate understanding of world geography. On the basis of that knowledge, European merchants and mariners established global networks of communication, transportation, and exchange—and profited handsomely from their efforts.

Motives for Exploration

A complex combination of motives prompted Europeans to explore the world's oceans. Most important of these motives were the search for basic resources and lands suitable for the cultivation of cash crops, the desire to establish new trade routes to Asian markets, and the aspiration to expand the influence of Christianity.

Portuguese Exploration Mariners from the relatively poor and hardscrabble kingdom of Portugal were most prominent in the search for fresh resources to exploit and lands to cultivate. Beginning in the thirteenth century, Portuguese seamen ventured away from the coasts and into the open Atlantic Ocean. They originally sought fish, seals, whales, timber, and lands where they could grow wheat to supplement the meager resources of Portugal. By the early fourteenth century, they had discovered the uninhabited Azores and Madeiras Islands. They called frequently at the Canary Islands, inhabited by the indigenous Guanche people, which Italian and Iberian mariners had visited since the early fourteenth century. Because European demand for sugar was strong and increasing, the prospect of establishing sugar plantations on the Atlantic islands was very tempting. Italian entrepreneurs had organized sugar plantations in Palestine and the Mediterranean islands since the twelfth century, and in the fifteenth century Italian investors worked with Portuguese mariners to establish plantations in the Atlantic islands. Continuing Portuguese voyages also led to the establishment of plantations on more southerly Atlantic islands, including the Cape Verde Islands, São Tomé, Principe, and Fernando Po.

The Lure of Trade Even more alluring than the exploitation of fresh lands and resources was the goal of establishing maritime trade routes to the markets of Asia. During the era of the Mongol empires, European merchants often traveled overland as far as China to trade in silk, spices, porcelain, and other Asian goods. In the fourteenth century, however, with the collapse of the Mongol empires and the spread of bubonic plague, travel on the silk roads became much less safe than before. Muslim mariners continued to bring Asian goods through the Indian Ocean and the Red Sea to Cairo, where Italian merchants purchased them for distribution in western Europe. But prices at Cairo were high, and Europeans sought ever-larger quantities of Asian goods, particularly spices.

By the fourteenth century the wealthy classes of Europe regarded Indian pepper and Chinese ginger as expensive necessities, and they especially prized cloves and nutmeg from the spice islands of Maluku. Merchants and monarchs alike realized that by offering direct access to Asian markets

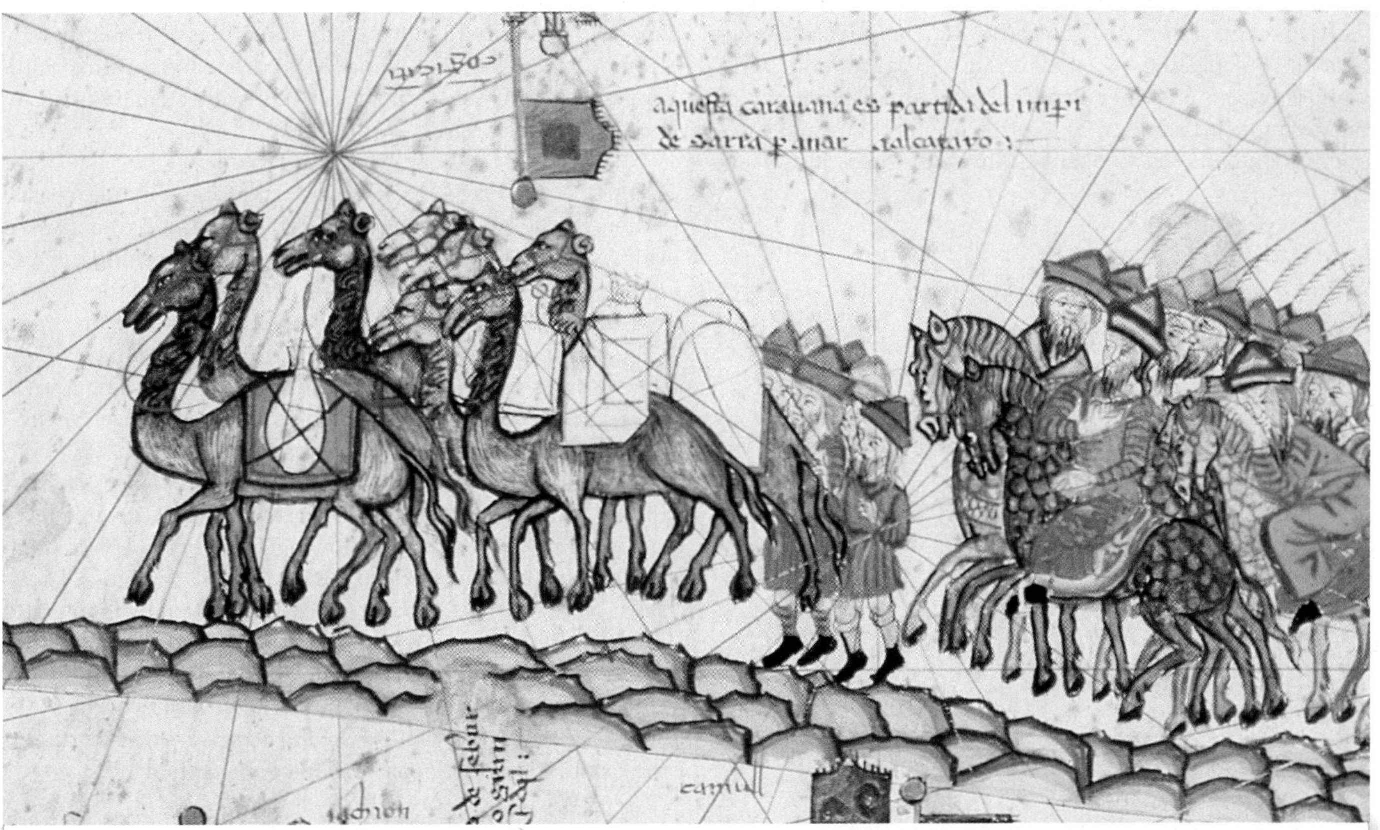

A detail from the Catalan Atlas, a magnificent illustrated representation of the known world produced about 1375, depicts a camel caravan traveling from China to Europe across the silk roads.

and eliminating Muslim intermediaries, new maritime trade routes would increase the quantities of spices and other Asian goods available in Europe—and would also yield enormous profits.

African trade also beckoned to Europeans and called them to the sea. Since the twelfth century, Europeans had purchased west African gold, ivory, and slaves delivered by the trans-Saharan camel caravans of Muslim merchants to north African ports. Gold was an especially important commodity because the precious metal from west Africa was Europeans' principal form of payment for Asian luxury goods. As in the case of Asian trade, maritime routes that eliminated Muslim intermediaries and offered more direct access to African markets would benefit European merchants.

Missionary Efforts Alongside material incentives, the goal of expanding the boundaries of Christianity also drove Europeans into the larger world. Like Buddhism and Islam, Christianity is a missionary religion. The New Testament specifically urged Christians to spread their faith throughout the world. Efforts to spread the faith often took peaceful forms. During the era of the Mongol empires, Franciscan and Dominican missionaries had traveled as far as India, central Asia, and China in search of converts. Yet the expansion of Christianity was by no means always a peaceful affair. Beginning in the eleventh century, western Europeans had launched a series of crusades and holy wars against Muslims in Palestine, the Mediterranean islands, and Iberia. Crusading zeal remained especially strong in Iberia, where the *reconquista* came to an end in 1492: the Muslim kingdom of Granada fell to Spanish Christian forces just weeks before Christopher Columbus set sail on his famous first voyage to the western hemisphere. Whether through persuasion or violence, overseas voyages offered fresh opportunities for western Europeans to spread their faith.

By using cross staffs to measure the angle of the sun or the pole star above the horizon, mariners could determine latitude.

In practice, the various motives for exploration combined and reinforced each other. Dom Henrique of Portugal, often called Prince Henry the Navigator, promoted voyages of exploration in west Africa specifically to enter the gold trade, discover profitable new trade routes, gain intelligence about the extent of Muslim power, win converts to Christianity, and make alliances against the Muslims with any Christian rulers he might find. When the Portuguese mariner Vasco da Gama reached the Indian port of Calicut in 1498, local authorities asked him what he wanted there. His reply: "Christians and spices." The goal of spreading Christianity thus became a powerful justification and reinforcement for the more material motives for the voyages of exploration.

The Technology of Exploration

Without advanced nautical technology and navigational skills, even the strongest motives would not have enabled European mariners to reconnoiter the world's oceans. Embarking on voyages that would keep them out of the sight of land for weeks at a time, mariners needed sturdy ships, navigational equipment, and sailing techniques that would permit them to make their way across the seas and back again. They inherited much of their nautical technology from Mediterranean and northern European maritime traditions and combined it imaginatively with elements of Chinese or Arabic origin.

Ships and Sails From their experiences in the coastal waters of the Atlantic, European sailors learned to construct ships strong enough to survive most adverse conditions. Beginning about the twelfth century, they increased the maneuverability of their craft by building a rudder onto the stern. (The sternpost rudder was a Chinese invention that had diffused across the Indian Ocean and probably became known to Europeans through Arab ships in the Mediterranean.) They outfitted their vessels with two main types of sail, both of which Mediterranean mariners had used since classical times. Square sails enabled them to take full advantage of a following wind (a wind blowing from behind), although these sails did not work well in crosswinds. Triangular lateen sails, on the other hand, were very maneuverable and could catch winds from the side as well as from behind. With a combination of square and lateen sails, European ships were able to use whatever winds arose. Their ability to tack—to advance against the wind by sailing across it—was crucial for the exploration of regions with uncooperative winds.

Navigational Instruments The most important navigational equipment on board these vessels were magnetic compasses and astrolabes (soon replaced by cross staffs and back staffs). The compass was a Chinese invention of the

Tang or Song dynasty that had diffused throughout the Indian Ocean basin in the eleventh century. By the mid-twelfth century, European mariners used compasses to determine their heading in Mediterranean and Atlantic waters. The astrolabe was a simplified version of an instrument used by Greek and Persian astronomers to determine latitude by measuring the angle of the sun or the pole star above the horizon. Portuguese mariners visiting the Indian Ocean in the late fifteenth century encountered Arab sailors using simpler and more serviceable instruments for determining latitude, which the Portuguese then used as models for the construction of cross staffs and back staffs.

European mariners' ability to determine direction and latitude enabled them to assemble a vast body of data about the earth's geography and to find their way around the world's oceans with tolerable accuracy and efficiency. (The measurement of longitude requires the ability to measure time precisely and so had to wait until the late eighteenth century, when dependable, spring-driven clocks became available.)

Knowledge of Winds and Currents

Equipped with advanced technological hardware, European mariners ventured into the oceans and gradually compiled a body of practical knowledge about the winds and currents that determined navigational possibilities in the age of sail. In both the Atlantic and the Pacific Oceans, strong winds blow regularly to create giant "wind wheels" both north and south of the equator, and ocean currents follow a similar pattern. Between about five and twenty-five degrees of latitude north and south of the equator, trade winds blow from the east. Between about thirty and sixty degrees north and south, westerly winds prevail. Winds and currents in the Indian Ocean follow a different, but still regular and reliable, pattern. During the summer months, generally between April and October, monsoon winds blow from the southwest throughout the Indian Ocean basin, whereas during the winter they blow from the northeast. Once mariners understood these patterns, they were able to take advantage of prevailing winds and currents to sail to almost any part of the earth.

The *volta do mar* Prevailing winds and currents often forced mariners to take indirect routes to their destinations. European vessels sailed easily from the Mediterranean to the Canary Islands, for example, since regular trade winds blew from the northeast. But those same trade winds complicated the return trip. By the mid-fifteenth century, Portuguese mariners had developed a strategy called the *volta do mar* ("return through the sea") that enabled them to sail from the Canaries to Portugal. Instead of trying to force their way against the trade winds—a slow and perilous business—they sailed northwest into the open ocean until they found westerly winds and then turned east for the last leg of the homeward journey.

Although the *volta do mar* took mariners well out of their way, experience soon taught that sailing around contrary winds was much faster, safer, and more reliable than butting up against them. Portuguese and other European mariners began to rely on the principle of the *volta do mar* in sailing to destinations other than the Canary Islands. When Vasco da Gama departed for India, for example, he sailed south to the Cape Verde Islands and then allowed the trade winds to carry him southwest into the Atlantic Ocean until he approached the coast of Brazil. There da Gama caught the prevailing westerlies that enabled him to sail east, round the Cape of Good Hope, and enter the Indian Ocean. As they became familiar with the wind systems of the world's oceans, European mariners developed variations on the *volta do mar* that enabled them to travel reliably to coastlines throughout the world.

Voyages of Exploration: from the Mediterranean to the Atlantic

Exploratory voyaging began as early as the thirteenth century. In 1291 the Vivaldi brothers departed from Genoa in two ships with the intention of sailing around Africa to India. They did not succeed, but the idea of exploring the Atlantic and establishing a maritime trade route from the Mediterranean to India persisted. During the fourteenth century Genoese, Portuguese, and Spanish mariners sailed frequently into the Atlantic Ocean and rediscovered the Canary Islands. The Guanche people had settled the Canaries from their original home in Morocco, but there had been no contact between the Guanches and other peoples since the time of the Roman empire. Iberian mariners began to visit the Canaries regularly, and in the fifteenth century Castilian forces conquered the islands and made them an outpost for further exploration.

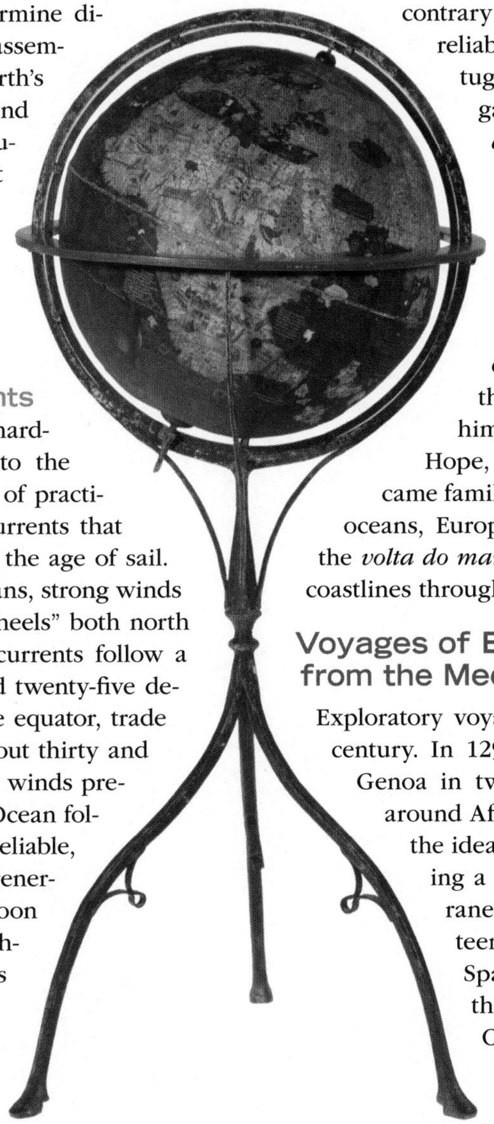

The earliest surviving world globe, produced in 1492 by the German cartographer Martin Behaim, depicts the eastern hemisphere quite accurately but shows almost no land west of Iberia except for east Asia.

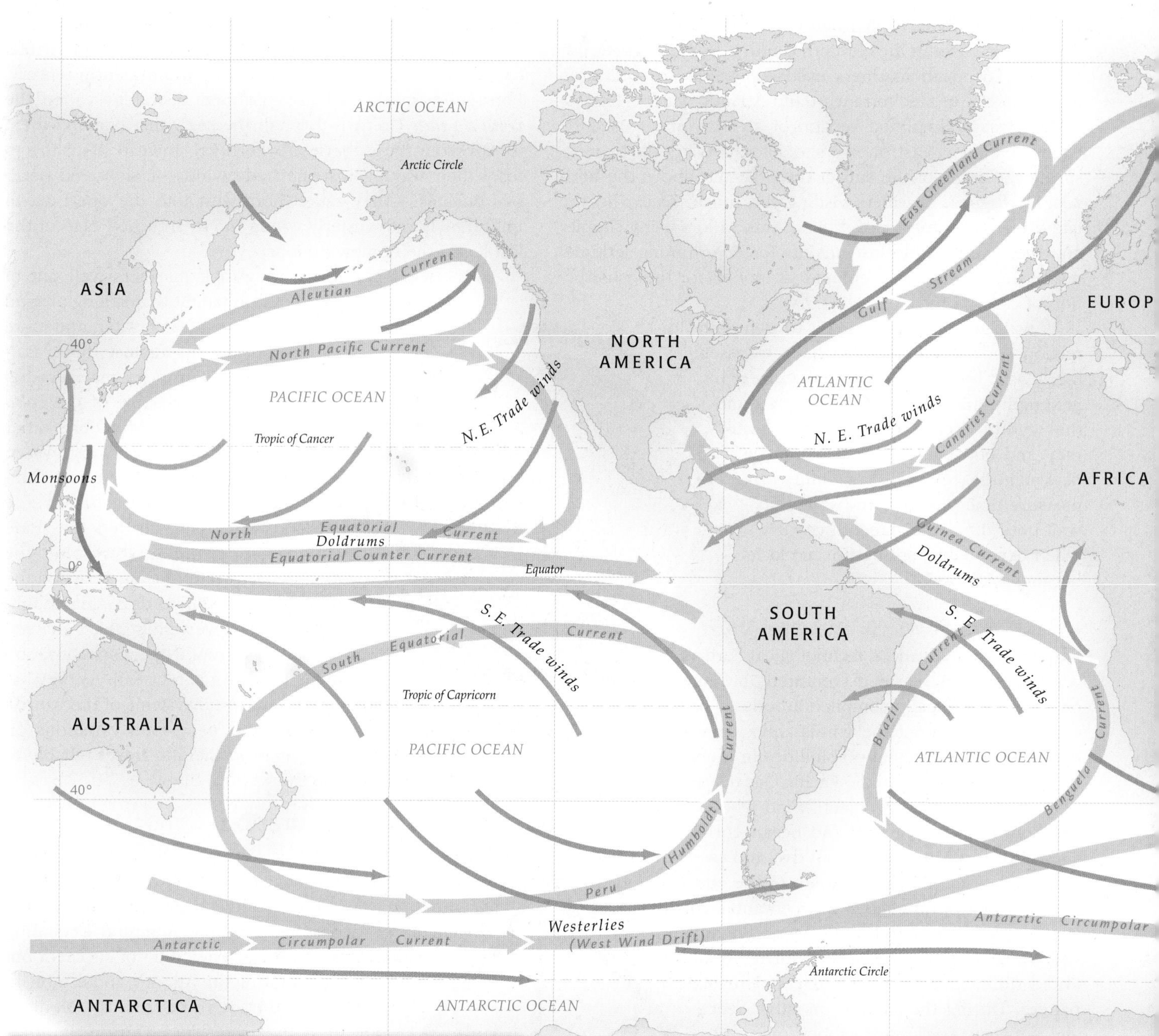

MAP 22.1
Wind and current patterns in the world's oceans.
Note how the winds of the Atlantic and Pacific resemble wind wheels, revolving clockwise north of the equator and counterclockwise south of the equator.

How crucial was an understanding of the world's wind patterns to the success of European overseas expansion?

Prince Henry of Portugal The pace of European exploration quickened after 1415 when Prince Henry of Portugal (1394–1460) conquered the Moroccan port of Ceuta and sponsored a series of voyages down the west African coast. Portuguese merchants soon established fortified trading posts at São Jorge da Mina (in modern Ghana) and other strategic locations. There they exchanged European horses, leather, textiles, and metalwares for gold and slaves. Portuguese explorations continued after Henry's death, and in 1488 Bartolomeu Dias rounded the Cape of Good Hope and entered the Indian Ocean. He did not proceed farther because of storms and a restless crew, but the route to India, China, and the spice-bearing islands of southeast Asia lay open. The sea route to the Indian Ocean offered European

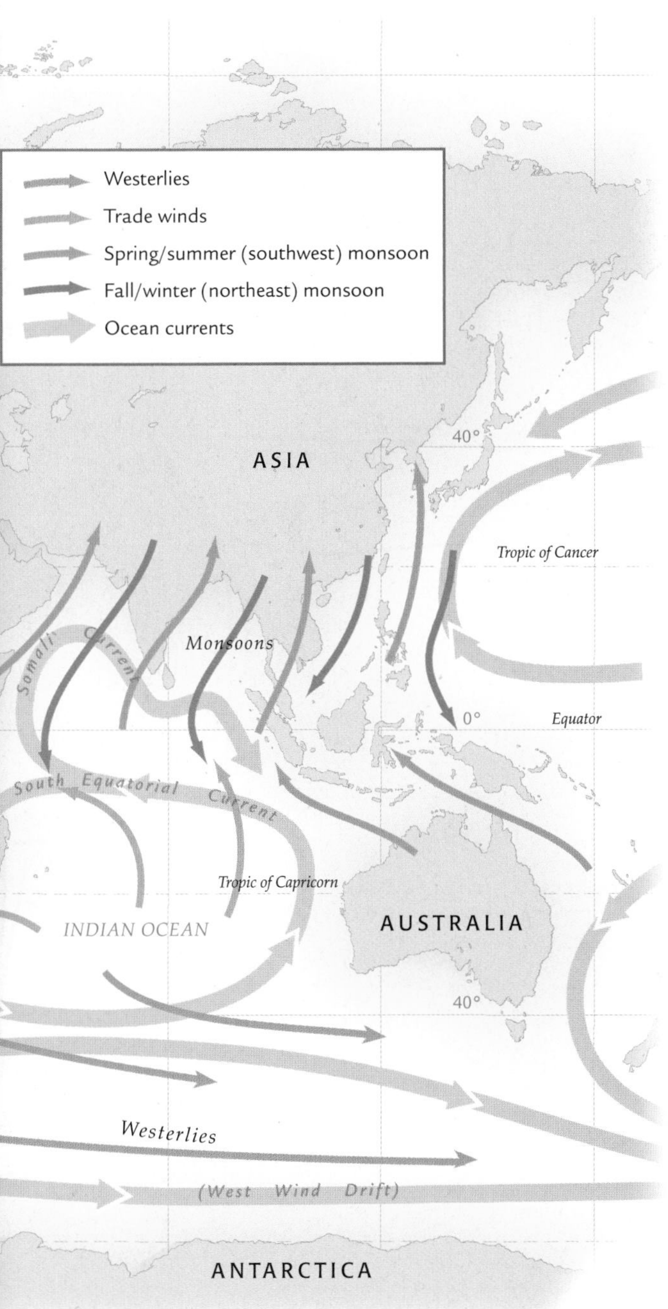

merchants the opportunity to buy silk, spices, and pepper at the source, rather than through Muslim intermediaries, and to take part in the flourishing trade of Asia described by Marco Polo.

Vasco da Gama Portuguese mariners did not immediately follow up Dias's voyage, because domestic and foreign problems distracted royal attention from voyages to Asia. In 1497, however, Vasco da Gama departed Lisbon with a fleet of four armed merchant ships bound for India. His experience was not altogether pleasant. His fleet went more than three months without seeing land, and his cargoes excited little interest in Indian markets. His return voyage was especially difficult, and less than half of his crew made it safely back to Portugal. Yet his cargo of pepper and cinnamon was hugely profitable, and Portuguese merchants began immediately to organize further expeditions. By 1500 they had built a trading post at Calicut, and Portuguese mariners soon called at ports throughout India and the Indian Ocean basin. By the late sixteenth century, English and Dutch mariners had followed the Portuguese into the Indian Ocean basin.

Christopher Columbus While Portuguese navigators plied the sea route to India, the Genoese mariner Cristoforo Colombo, known in English as Christopher Columbus (1451–1506), proposed sailing to the markets of Asia by a western route. On the basis of wide reading of literature on geography, Columbus believed that the Eurasian landmass covered 270 degrees of longitude and that the earth was a relatively small sphere with a circumference of about 17,000 nautical miles. (In fact, the Eurasian landmass from Portugal to Korea covers only 140 degrees of longitude, and the earth's circumference is almost 25,000 nautical miles.) By Columbus's calculations, Japan should be less than 2,500 nautical miles west of the Canary Islands. (The actual distance between the Canaries and Japan is more than 10,000 nautical miles.) This geography suggested that sailing west from Europe to Asian markets would be profitable, and Columbus sought royal sponsorship for a voyage to prove his ideas. The Portuguese court declined his proposal, partly out of skepticism about his geography and partly because Dias's voyage of 1488 already pointed the way toward India.

Although Fernando and Isabel of Spain eventually agreed to sponsor Columbus's expedition, Italian bankers actually financed the voyage. In August 1492 his fleet of three ships departed Palos in southern Spain. He sailed south to the Canaries, picked up supplies, and then turned west with the trade winds. On the morning of 12 October 1492, he made landfall at an island in the Bahamas that the native **Taíno** inhabitants called Guanahaní and that Columbus rechristened San Salvador (also known as Watling Island). Thinking that he had arrived in the spice islands known familiarly as the Indies, Columbus called the Taíno "Indians." In search of gold he sailed around the Caribbean for almost three months, and at the large island of Cuba he sent a delegation to seek the court of the emperor of China. When Columbus returned to Spain, he reported to his royal sponsors that he had reached islands just off the coast of Asia.

Hemispheric Links Columbus never reached the riches of Asia, and despite three additional voyages across the Atlantic Ocean, he obtained very little gold in the Caribbean.

Taíno (TEYE-noh)

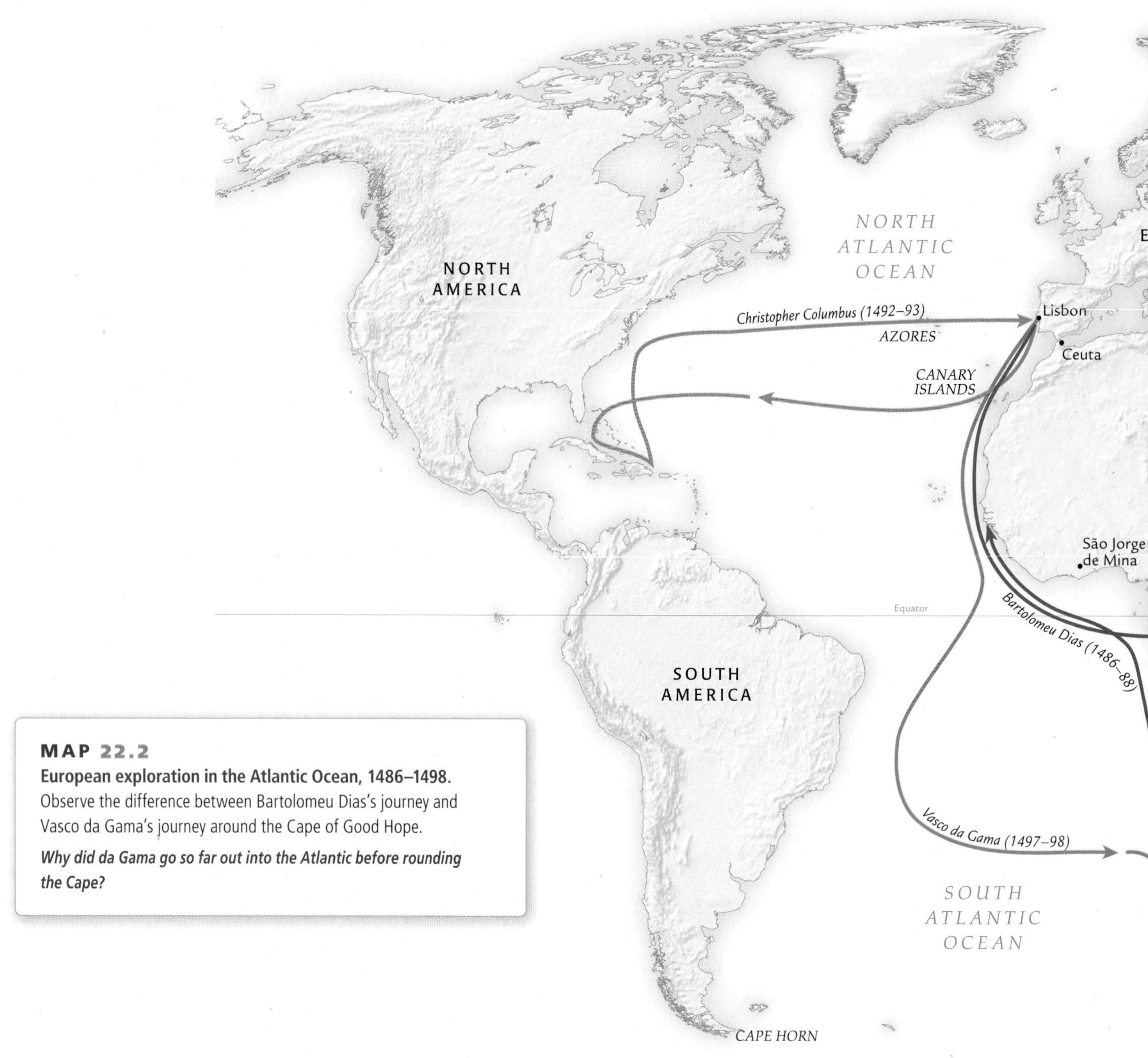

MAP 22.2
European exploration in the Atlantic Ocean, 1486–1498.
Observe the difference between Bartolomeu Dias's journey and Vasco da Gama's journey around the Cape of Good Hope.
Why did da Gama go so far out into the Atlantic before rounding the Cape?

Yet news of his voyage spread rapidly throughout Europe, and hundreds of Spanish, English, French, and Dutch mariners soon followed in his wake. Particularly in the early sixteenth century, many of them continued to seek the passage to Asian waters that Columbus himself had pursued. Over a longer term, however, it became clear that the American continents and the Caribbean islands themselves held abundant opportunities for entrepreneurs. Thus Columbus's voyages to the western hemisphere had unintended but momentous consequences, since they established links between the eastern and western hemispheres and paved the way for the conquest, settlement, and exploitation of the Americas by European peoples.

Voyages of Exploration: from the Atlantic to the Pacific

While some Europeans sought opportunities in the Americas, others continued to seek a western route to Asian mar-

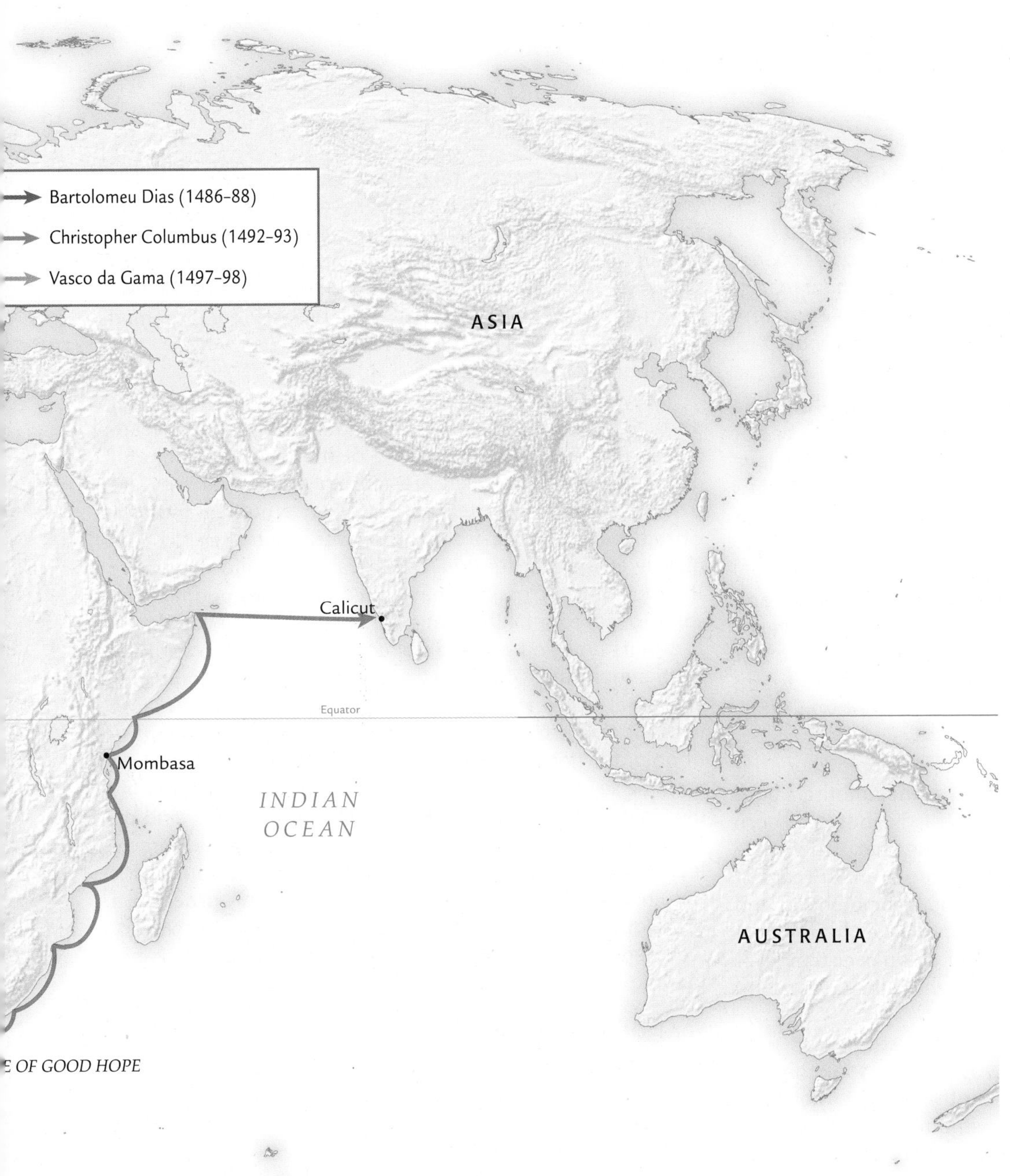

kets. The Spanish military commander Vasco Nuñez de Balboa sighted the Pacific Ocean in 1513 while searching for gold in Panama, but in the early sixteenth century no one knew how much ocean lay between the Americas and Asia. Indeed, no one even suspected the vast size of the Pacific Ocean, which covers one-third of the earth's surface.

Ferdinand Magellan The reconnaissance of the Pacific Ocean basin began with the Portuguese navigator Fernão de Magalhães (1480–1521), better known as Ferdinand Magellan. While sailing in the service of Portugal, Magellan had visited ports throughout the Indian Ocean basin and had traveled east as far as the spice islands of Maluku. He believed that the spice islands and Asian markets lay fairly close to the western coast of the Americas, and he decided to pursue Christopher Columbus's goal of establishing a western route to Asian waters. Because Portuguese mariners had already reached Asian markets through the Indian Ocean, they had little interest in Magellan's proposed western route. Thus, on his Pacific expedition Magellan sailed in the service of Spain.

sources from the past

Christopher Columbus's First Impressions of American Peoples

Christopher Columbus kept journals of his experiences during his voyages to the western hemisphere. The journal of his first voyage survives mostly in summary, but it clearly communicates Columbus's first impressions of the peoples he met in the Caribbean islands. The following excerpts show that Columbus, like other European mariners, had both Christianity and commerce in mind when exploring distant lands.

Thursday, 11 October [1492]. . . .

I . . . in order that they would be friendly to us—because I recognized that they were people who would be better freed [from error] and converted to our Holy Faith by love than by force—to some of them I gave red caps, and glass beads which they put on their chests, and many other things of small value, in which they took so much pleasure and became so much our friends that it was a marvel. Later they came swimming to the ships' launches where we were and brought us parrots and cotton thread in balls and javelins and many other things, and they traded them to us for other things which we gave them, such as small glass beads and bells. In sum, they took everything and gave of what they had willingly.

But it seemed to me that they were a people very poor in everything. All of them go as naked as their mothers bore them; and the women also, although I did not see more than one quite young girl. And all those that I saw were young people, for none did I see of more than 30 years of age. They are very well formed, with handsome bodies and good faces. Their hair [is] coarse—almost like the tail of a horse—and short. They wear their hair down over their eyebrows except for a little in the back which they wear long and never cut. . . .

They do not carry arms nor are they acquainted with them, because I showed them swords and they took them by the edge and through ignorance cut themselves. They have no iron. Their javelins are shafts without iron and some of them have at the end a fish tooth and others of other things. All of them alike are of good-sized stature and carry themselves well. I saw some who had marks of wounds on their bodies and I made signs to them asking what they were; and they showed me how people from other islands nearby came there and tried to take them, and how they defended themselves and I believed and believe that they come here from *tierra firme* [the continent] to take them captive. They should be good and intelligent servants, for I see that they say very quickly everything that is said to them; and I believe that they would become Christians very easily, for it seemed to me that they had no religion. . . .

Monday, 12 November. . . .

They are very gentle and do not know what evil is; nor do they kill others, nor steal; and they are without weapons and so timid that a hundred of them flee from one of our men even if our men are teasing them. And they are credulous and aware that there is a God in heaven and convinced that we come from the heavens; and they say very quickly any prayer that we tell them to say, and they make the sign of the cross. So that Your Highnesses ought to resolve to make them Christians: for I believe that if you begin, in a short time you will end up having converted to our Holy Faith a multitude of peoples and acquiring large dominions and great riches and all of their peoples for Spain. Because without doubt there is in these lands a very great quantity of gold; for not without cause do these Indians that I bring with me say that there are in these islands places where they dig gold and wear it on their chests, on their ears, and on their arms, and on their legs; and they are very thick bracelets. And also there are stones, and there are precious pearls and infinite spicery. . . . And also here there is probably a great quantity of cotton; and I think that it would sell very well here without taking it to Spain but to the big cities belonging to the Grand [Mongol] Khan.

For Further Reflection

- On the basis of Columbus's account, what inferences can you draw about his plans for American lands and peoples?

Source: Christopher Columbus. *The Diario of Christopher Columbus's First Voyage to America.* Trans. by Oliver Dunn and James E. Kelley Jr. Norman: University of Oklahoma Press, 1989, pp. 65–69, 143–45.

The Circumnavigation Magellan's voyage was an exercise in endurance. He left Spain in September 1519, and then began probing the eastern coast of South America in search of a strait leading to the Pacific. Eventually, he found and sailed through the tricky and treacherous strait, later to bear his name, near the southern tip of South America. After exiting the strait, his fleet sailed almost four months before taking on fresh provisions at Guam. During that period crewmen survived on worm-ridden biscuits, leather that they had softened in the ocean, and water gone foul. Ship's rats that were unfortunate enough to fall into the hands of famished sailors quickly became the centerpiece of a meal. A survivor reported in his account of the voyage that crewmen even ate ox hides, which they softened by dragging them through the sea for four or five days and then grilled on coals. Lacking fresh fruits and vegetables in their diet, many of the crew fell victim to the dreaded disease of scurvy, which caused painful rotting of the gums, loss of teeth, abscesses, hemorrhaging, weakness, loss of spirit, and in most cases death. Scurvy killed twenty-nine members of Magellan's crew during the Pacific crossing.

Conditions improved after the fleet called at Guam in March 1521, but its ordeal had not come to an end. From Guam, Magellan proceeded to the Philippine Islands, where he became involved in a local political dispute that took the lives of Magellan himself and 40 of his crew. The survivors continued on to the spice islands of Maluku, where they took on a cargo of cloves. Rather than brave the Pacific Ocean once again, they sailed home through the familiar waters of the Indian Ocean—and thus completed the first circumnavigation of the world—returning to Spain after a voyage of almost exactly three years. Of Magellan's five ships and 280 men, a single spice-laden ship with 18 of the original crew returned.

This color engraving features an idealized portrait of mariner Ferdinand Magellan.

Exploration of the Pacific The Pacific Ocean is so vast that it took European explorers almost three centuries to chart its features. Spanish merchants built on information gleaned from Magellan's expedition and established a trade route between the Philippines and Mexico, but they did not continue to explore the ocean basin itself. English navigators, however, ventured into the Pacific in search of an elusive northwest passage from Europe to Asia. In fact, a northwest passage exists, but most of its route lies within the Arctic Circle. It is so far north that ice clogs its waters for much of the year, and it was only in the twentieth century that the Norwegian explorer Roald Amundsen traveled from the Atlantic to the Pacific by way of the northwest passage. Nevertheless, while searching for a passage, English mariners established many of the details of Pacific geography. In the sixteenth century, for example, Sir Francis Drake scouted the west coast of North America as far north as Vancouver Island. By the mid-eighteenth century, French mariners had joined English seafarers in exploring the Pacific Ocean in search of a northwest passage.

Russian expansion was mostly a land-based affair in early modern times, but by the eighteenth century Russians also were exploring the Pacific Ocean. Russian officials commissioned the Danish navigator Vitus Bering to undertake two maritime expeditions (1725–1730 and 1733–1742) in search of a northeast passage to Asian ports. Bering sailed through the icy Arctic Ocean and the Bering Strait, which separates Siberia from Alaska, and reconnoitered northern Asia as far as the Kamchatka peninsula. Other Russian explorers made their way from Alaska down the western Canadian coast to northern California. By 1800, Russian mariners were scouting the Pacific Ocean as far south as the Hawaiian Islands. Indeed, they built a small fort on the island of Kaua`i and engaged in trade there for a few years in the early nineteenth century.

Captain James Cook Along with the Russian explorers and Magellan, one of the most important of the Pacific explorers was Captain James Cook (1728–1779), who led three expeditions to the Pacific and died in a scuffle with the indigenous people of Hawai`i. Cook charted eastern Australia and New Zealand, and he added New Caledonia, Vanuatu, and Hawai`i to European maps of the Pacific. He probed the frigid waters of the Arctic Ocean and spent months at a time in the tropical islands of Tahiti, Tonga, and Hawai`i, where he showed deep interest in the manners, customs, and languages of Polynesian peoples. By the time Cook's voyages had come to an end, European geographers had compiled a reasonably accurate understanding of the world's ocean basins, their lands, and their peoples.

TRADE AND CONFLICT IN EARLY MODERN ASIA

The voyages of exploration taught European mariners how to sail to almost any coastline in the world and return safely. Once they arrived at their destinations, they sought commercial opportunities. In the eastern hemisphere they built a series of fortified trading posts that offered footholds in regions where established commercial networks had held sway for centuries. They even attempted to control the spice trade in the Indian Ocean but with limited success. They mostly did not have the human numbers or military power to impose their rule in the eastern hemisphere, although Spanish and Dutch forces established small island empires in the Philippines and Indonesia, respectively. In a parallel effort involving expansion across land rather than the sea, Russian explorers and adventurers established a presence in central Asian regions formerly ruled by the Mongols and in the tundra and forests of Siberia, thus laying the foundations for a vast Eurasian empire. Commercial and political competition in both the eastern and the western hemispheres led to conflict between European peoples, and by the end of the Seven Years' War in 1763, English military and merchant forces had gained an initiative over their rivals that enabled

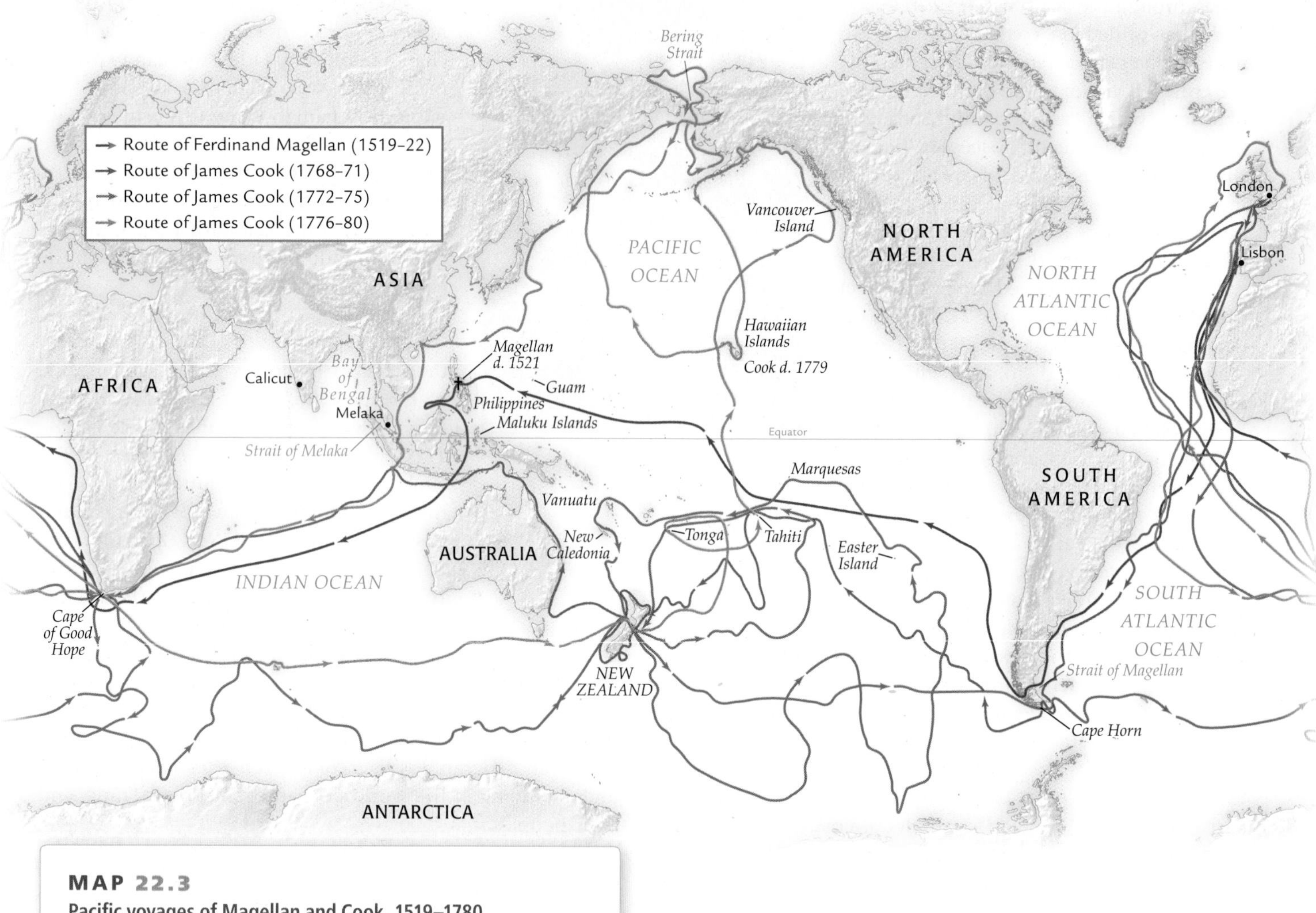

MAP 22.3

Pacific voyages of Magellan and Cook, 1519–1780.

What made exploration of the Pacific Ocean so daunting? What fate befell both Magellan and Cook?

them to dominate world trade and build the vast British empire of the nineteenth century.

Trading-Post Empires

Portuguese Trading Posts Portuguese mariners built the earliest trading-post empire. Their goal was not to conquer territories but, rather, to control trade routes by forcing merchant vessels to call at fortified trading sites and pay duties there. Vasco da Gama obtained permission from local authorities to establish a trading post at Calicut when he arrived there in 1498. By the mid-sixteenth century, Portuguese merchants had built more than fifty trading posts between west Africa and east Asia. At São Jorge da Mina, they traded in west African slaves, and at Mozambique they attempted to control the south African gold trade. From Hormuz they controlled access to the Persian Gulf, and from Goa they organized trade in Indian pepper. At Melaka they oversaw shipping between the South China Sea and the Indian Ocean, and they channeled trade in cloves and nutmeg through Ternate in the spice islands of Maluku. Posts at Macau and Nagasaki offered access to the markets of China and Japan.

Afonso d'Alboquerque Equipped with heavy artillery, Portuguese vessels were able to overpower most other craft that they encountered, and they sometimes trained their cannon effectively onshore. The architect of their aggressive policy was Afonso d'Alboquerque, commander of Portuguese forces in the Indian Ocean during the early sixteenth century. Alboquerque's fleets seized Hormuz in 1508, Goa in 1510, and Melaka in 1511. From these strategic sites, Alboquerque sought to control Indian Ocean trade by forcing merchant ships to purchase safe-conduct passes and present them at Portuguese trading posts. Ships without passes were subject to confiscation, along with their cargoes. Alboquerque's forces punished violators of his policy by executing

them or cutting off their hands. Alboquerque was confident of Portuguese naval superiority and its ability to control trade in the Indian Ocean. After taking Melaka, he boasted that the arrival of Portuguese ships sent other vessels scurrying and that even the birds left the skies and sought cover.

Alboquerque's boast was an exaggeration. Although heavily armed, Portuguese forces did not have enough vessels to enforce the commander's orders. Arab, Indian, and Malay merchants continued to play prominent roles in Indian Ocean commerce, usually without taking the precaution of securing a safe-conduct pass. Portuguese ships transported perhaps half the pepper and spices that Europeans consumed during the early and middle decades of the sixteenth century, but Arab vessels delivered shipments through the Red Sea, which Portuguese forces never managed to control, to Cairo and Mediterranean trade routes.

By the late sixteenth century, Portuguese influence in the Indian Ocean weakened. Portugal was a small country with a small population—about one million in 1500—and was unable to sustain a large seaborne trading empire for very long. The crews of Portuguese ships often included Spanish, English, and Dutch sailors, who became familiar with Asian waters while in Portuguese service. By the late sixteenth century, investors in other lands began to organize their own expeditions to Asian markets. Most prominent of those who followed the Portuguese into the Indian Ocean were English and Dutch mariners.

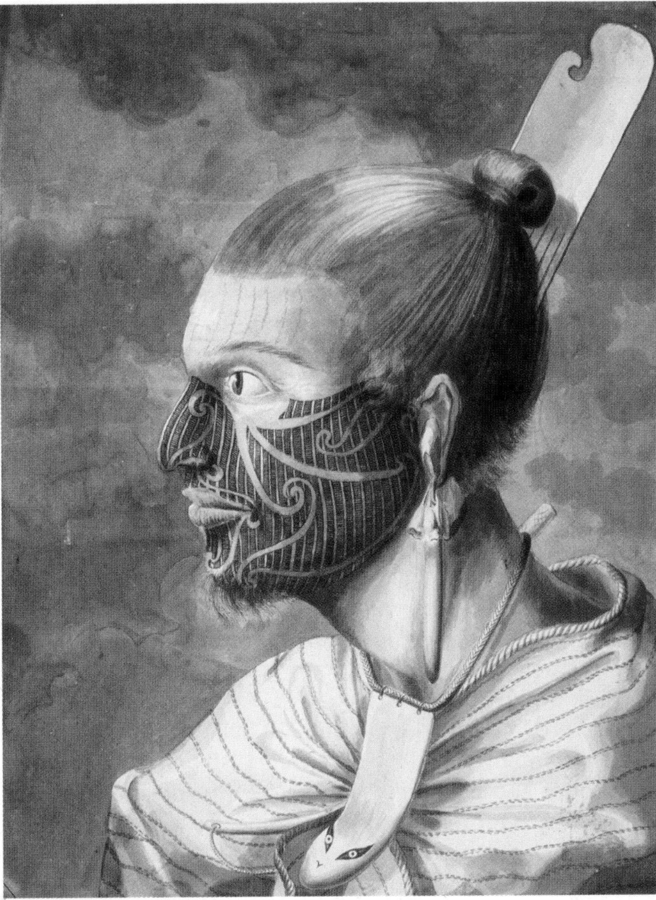

This European drawing from Captain James Cook's first voyage focuses on the exotic features of a Maori chief's son.

A portrait of Captain James Cook painted by William Hodges about 1775 depicts a serious and determined man.

English and Dutch Trading Posts Like their predecessors, English and Dutch merchants built trading posts on Asian coasts and sought to channel trade through them, but they did not attempt to control shipping on the high seas. They occasionally seized Portuguese sites, most notably when a Dutch fleet conquered Melaka in 1641. Yet Portuguese authorities held many of their trading posts into the twentieth century: Goa remained the official capital of Portuguese colonies in Asia until Indian forces reclaimed it in 1961. Meanwhile, English and Dutch entrepreneurs established parallel networks. English merchants concentrated on India and built trading posts at Bombay, Madras, and Calcutta, while the Dutch operated more broadly from Cape Town, Colombo, and Batavia (modern Jakarta on the island of Java).

sources from the past

Afonso D'Alboquerque Seizes Hormuz

Afonso d'Alboquerque the mariner had a son of the same name who in 1557 published a long set of historical Commentaries *on his father's deeds. His account of the battle for Hormuz vividly illustrates the effectiveness of Portuguese artillery as well as the chaos and confusion of sea battles in early modern times.*

As some time had passed since the king [of Hormuz] had received information about the [Portuguese] fleet and the destruction that the great Afonso d'Alboquerque had wrought along the [Arabian] coast, he began to prepare himself to fight with him. For this end he gave orders to detain all the ships that came into the port of Hormuz and added a force of sixty great vessels into which he draughted off many soldiers and much artillery with everything that was required for the undertaking. And among these great vessels there was one belonging to the king of Cambay [in India] . . . and another of the prince of Cambay. . . . And besides these ships there were in the harbor about 200 galleys, which are long ships with many oars. . . . There were also many barks full of small guns and men wearing sword-proof dress and armed from head to foot, most of them being archers. All this fleet was rigged out with flags and standards and colored ensigns, and made a very beautiful appearance. . . .

When Afonso d'Alboquerque perceived the gleaming of the swords and waving of the bucklers and other doings of the Moors [Muslims] on shore, . . . he understood by these signs that the king was determined to give him battle. . . . When morning broke, . . . he ordered a broadside to be fired. The bombardiers took aim so that with the first two shots they fired they sent two large ships which were in front of them, with all their men, to the bottom—one being the prince of Cambay's ship. . . . Afonso Lopez da Costa, who was stationed on the land side, vanquished and sent to the bottom some portion of the galleys and guard boats that his artillery could reach. Manuel Telez, after having caused great slaughter upon some vessels, . . . ran into a large vessel that lay close to him and killed a part of the men in it, while the rest threw themselves into the sea, and those who were heavy-armed went down at once. João da Nova too with his artillery did great execution among the ships that lay along the piles, as did also Antonio do Campo and Francisco de Tavora among the galleys that had surrounded them, and all night long they kept on hooking their anchors together in order to catch the galleys in the middle of them. And although the Moors endeavored to avenge themselves with their artillery, our men were so well fortified with their defenses that they did them no harm, except on the upper deck, and with their arrows they wounded some people.

The fight was so confused on this side and on that, both with artillery and arrows, that it lasted some time without either party seeing each other by reason of the smoke. As soon as this cleared off, . . . and when Afonso saw the discomfiture of the king's fleet and the unexpected victory that Our Lord had sent him and the Moors throwing themselves into the sea from fear of our artillery, thinking that they could escape in that way by swimming, . . . [Afonso] called out to the captains to take to their boats and follow up the victory.

For Further Reflection

- How might a Muslim commentator have described the battle for Hormuz?

Source: Afonso d'Alboquerque. *Commentaries of the Great Afonso Dalboquerque,* 4 vols. Trans. by Walter de Gray Birch. London: Hakluyt Society, 1875–84, 1:105, 112–14. (Translation slightly modified.)

English and Dutch merchants enjoyed two main advantages over their Portuguese predecessors. They sailed faster, cheaper, and more powerful ships, which offered both an economic and a military edge over their competitors. Furthermore, they conducted trade through an efficient form of commercial organization—the joint-stock company—which enabled investors to realize handsome profits while limiting the risk to their investments.

The Trading Companies English and Dutch merchants formed two especially powerful joint-stock companies: the English East India Company, founded in 1600, and its Dutch counterpart, the United East India Company, known from its initials as the VOC (Vereenigde Oost-Indische Compagnie), established in 1602. Private merchants advanced funds to launch these companies, outfit them with ships and crews, and provide them with commodities and money to trade. Although they enjoyed government support, the companies were privately owned enterprises. Unhampered by political oversight, company agents concentrated strictly on profitable trade. Their charters granted them the right to buy, sell, build trading posts, and even make war in the companies' interests.

The English and Dutch companies experienced immediate financial success. In 1601, for example, five English ships set sail from London with cargoes mostly of gold and silver

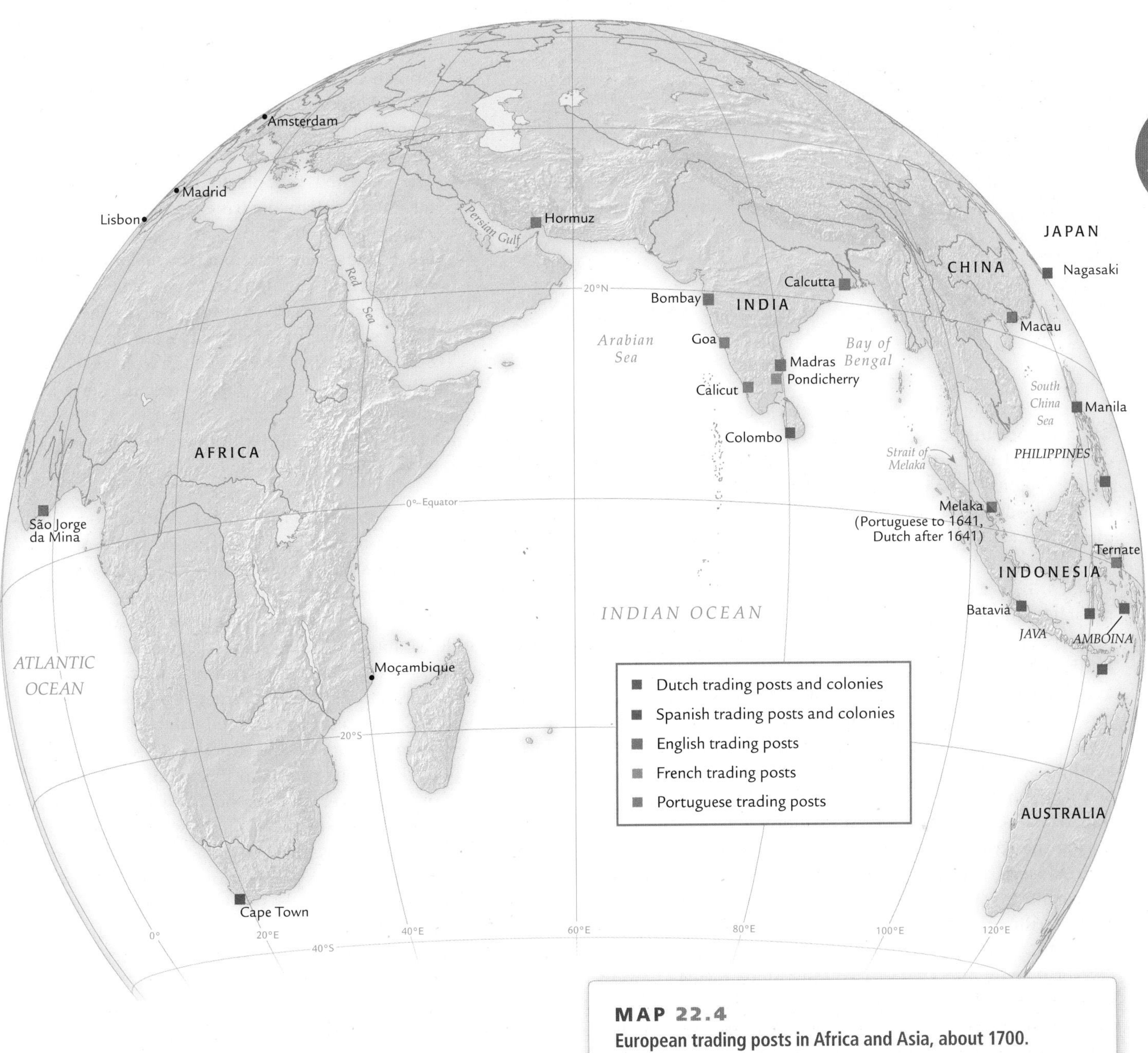

MAP 22.4
European trading posts in Africa and Asia, about 1700.
Note how many more trading posts there were in Asia than in Africa.
What accounts for the difference?

coins valued at thirty thousand pounds sterling. When they returned in 1603, the spices that they carried were worth more than one million pounds sterling. The first Dutch expedition did not realize such fantastic profits, but it more than doubled the investments of its underwriters. Because of their advanced nautical technology, powerful military arsenal, efficient organization, and relentless pursuit of profit, the English East India Company and the VOC contributed to the early formation of a global network of trade.

European Conquests in Southeast Asia

Following voyages of exploration to the western hemisphere, Europeans conquered indigenous peoples, built territorial empires, and established colonies settled by European migrants. In the eastern hemisphere, however, they were mostly unable to force their will on large Asian populations and powerful centralized states. With the decline of the Portuguese effort to control shipping in the Indian Ocean, Europeans mostly traded peacefully in Asian waters alongside Arab, Indian, Malay, and Chinese merchants.

Yet in two island regions of southeast Asia—the Philippines and Indonesia—Europeans conquered existing authorities and imposed their rule. Though densely populated,

thinking about ENCOUNTERS

Trading-Post Empires
Trading-post empires provided the most prominent spaces for cross-cultural interactions between Europeans, Africans, and Asians. Trading posts also limited European intrusion into Africa and Asia, especially in contrast to the settlement empires of the Americas. What characterized the relations between, for example, the Portuguese and the inhabitants of the Indian Ocean basin? Why were Europeans confined to such posts?

neither the Philippines nor Indonesia had a powerful state when Europeans arrived there in the sixteenth century. Nor did imperial authorities in China or India lay claim to the island regions. Heavily armed ships enabled Europeans to bring considerable force to bear and to establish imperial regimes that favored the interests of European merchants.

Conquest of the Philippines Spanish forces approached the Philippines in 1565 under the command of Miguel López de Legazpi, who named the islands after King Philip II of Spain. Legazpi overcame local authorities in Cebu and Manila in almost bloodless contests. Because the Philippines had no central government, there was no organized resistance to the intrusion. Spanish forces faced a series of small, disunited chiefdoms, most of which soon fell before Spanish ships and guns. By 1575 Spanish forces controlled the coastal regions of the central and northern islands, and during the seventeenth century they extended their authority to most parts of the archipelago. The main region outside their control was the southern island of Mindanao, where a large Muslim community stoutly resisted Spanish expansion.

Manila Spanish policy in the Philippines revolved around trade and Christianity. Manila soon emerged as a bustling, multicultural port city—an entrepôt for trade particularly in silk—and it quickly became the hub of Spanish commercial activity in Asia. Chinese merchants were especially prominent in Manila. They occupied a specially designated commercial district of the city, and they accounted for about one-quarter of Manila's forty-two thousand residents in the mid-seventeenth century. They supplied the silk goods that Spanish traders shipped to Mexico in the so-called Manila galleons. Their commercial success brought suspicion on their community, and resentful Spanish and Filipino residents massacred Chinese merchants by the thousands in at least six major eruptions of violence in 1603, 1639, 1662, 1686, 1762, and 1819. Nevertheless, Spanish authorities continued to rely heavily on the wealth that Chinese merchants brought to Manila.

Apart from promoting trade, Spanish authorities in the Philippines also sought to spread Roman Catholicism throughout the archipelago. Spanish rulers and missionaries pressured prominent Filipinos to convert to Christianity in hopes of persuading others to follow their example. They opened schools to teach the fundamentals of Christian doctrine, along with basic literacy, in densely populated regions throughout the islands. The missionaries encountered stiff resistance in highland regions, where Spanish authority was not as strong as on the coasts, and resistance drew support from opponents of Spanish domination as well as from resentment of the newly arrived faith. Over the long term, however, Filipinos turned increasingly to Christianity, and by the nineteenth century the Philippines had become one of the most fervent Roman Catholic lands in the world.

Conquest of Java Dutch mariners, who imposed their rule on the islands of Indonesia, did not worry about seeking converts to Christianity, but concentrated instead on the trade in spices, particularly cloves, nutmeg, and mace. The architect of Dutch policy was Jan Pieterszoon Coen, who in 1619 founded Batavia on the island of Java to serve as an entrepôt for the VOC. Batavia occupied a strategic site near the Sunda Strait, and its market attracted both Chinese and Malay vessels. Coen's plan was to establish a VOC monopoly over spice production and trade, thus enabling Dutch merchants to reap enormous profits in European markets. Coen brought his naval power to bear on the small Indonesian islands and forced them to deliver spices only to VOC merchants. On larger islands such as Java, he took advantage of tensions between local princes and authorities and extracted concessions from many in return for providing them with aid against the others. By the late seventeenth century, the VOC controlled all the ports of Java as well as most of the important spice-bearing islands throughout the Indonesian archipelago.

Dutch numbers were too few for them to rule directly over their whole southeast Asian empire. They made alliances with local authorities to maintain order in most regions, reserving for direct Dutch rule only Batavia and the most important spice-bearing islands such as clove-producing Amboina and the Banda Islands. They sought less to rule than to control the production of spices. The Dutch did not embark on campaigns of conquest for purposes of adding to their holdings, but they uprooted spice-bearing plants on islands they did not control and mercilessly attacked peoples who sold their spices to merchants not associated with the VOC. Monopoly profits from the spice trade not only enriched the VOC but also made the Netherlands the most prosperous land in Europe throughout most of the seventeenth century.

Workers are harvesting mace, a spice derived from nutmeg trees that are indigenous to the Banda Islands of Indonesia. Until the nineteenth century, these islands were the world's only source of this valuable spice.

Foundations of the Russian Empire in Asia

While western European peoples were building maritime empires, Russians were laying the foundations for a vast land empire that embraced most of northern Eurasia. This round of expansion began in the mid-sixteenth century, as Russian forces took over several Mongol khanates in central Asia. These acquisitions resulted in Russian control over the Volga River and offered opportunities for trade with the Ottoman empire, Iran, and even India through the Caspian Sea. Because of its strategic location on the Volga delta where the river flows into the Caspian Sea, the city of Astrakhan became a bustling commercial center, home to a community

A woodcut illustration depicts indigenous peoples of Siberia delivering fur tribute to Russian merchants in a walled, riverside fort.

of several hundred foreign merchants from as far away as northern India. During the seventeenth and eighteenth centuries, some of the Indian merchants regularly made their way up the Volga River to trade in Moscow and the Russian interior, while others devised plans (which they never realized) to extend their activities to the Baltic Sea and take their business to western Europe. In the eighteenth century, Russian forces extended their presence in the Caspian Sea region by absorbing much of the Caucasus, a vibrant multiethnic region embracing the modern-day states of Georgia, Armenia, and Azerbaijan.

Encounters in Siberia Far more extensive were Russian acquisitions in northeastern Eurasia. The frozen tundras and dense forests of Siberia posed formidable challenges, but explorers and merchants made their way into the region in a quest for fur. Throughout the early modern era, fur was a lucrative commodity that lured Russians eastward, just as North American fur attracted the interest of English, French, and Dutch merchants. Russian expansion in northeastern Eurasia began in 1581 when the wealthy Stroganov family hired a freebooting adventurer named Yermak to capture the khanate of Sibir in the Ural Mountains. In the following decades, Russian explorers pushed into the interior regions of Siberia by way of the region's great rivers. By 1639 they had made their way across the Eurasian landmass and reached the Pacific Ocean.

Native Peoples of Siberia Siberia was home to about twenty-six major ethnic groups that lived by hunting, trapping, fishing, or herding reindeer. These indigenous peoples varied widely in language and religion, and they responded in different ways to the arrival of Russian adventurers who sought to exact tribute from them by coercing them to supply pelts on a regular basis. Some groups readily accepted iron tools, woven cloth, flour, tea, and liquor for the skins of fur-bearing animals such as otter, lynx, marten, arctic fox, and especially the sleek sable. Others resented the ever-increasing demands for tribute and resisted Russian encroachment on their lands. Russian forces then

resorted to punishing raids and hostage taking to induce Siberian peoples to deliver furs. The Yakut people of the Lena and Aldan River valleys in central Siberia mounted a revolt against Russian oppression in 1642 and experienced a brutal retribution that continued for forty years, forcing many Yakut out of their settlements and reducing their population by an estimated 70 percent. Quite apart from military violence, the peoples of Siberia also reeled from epidemic diseases that reduced many populations by more than half.

As violence and disease sharply diminished the delivery of furs, the Russian government recognized that its interests lay in protection of the "small peoples," as state officials called the indigenous inhabitants of Siberia. Government-sponsored missionaries sought to convert Siberian peoples to Orthodox Christianity and bring them into Russian society, but they had little success. Few Siberians expressed an interest in Christianity, and those few came mostly from the ranks of criminals, abandoned hostages, slaves, and others who had little status in their own societies. Furthermore, once indigenous peoples converted to Christianity, they were exempt from obligations to provide fur tributes, so the Russian government demonstrated less zeal in its religious mission than did the Spanish monarchs, who made the spread of Roman Catholic Christianity a prime goal of imperial expansion. Although they managed to attract a few Siberian converts, Orthodox missionaries mostly served the needs of Russian merchants, adventurers, and explorers in Siberia. For their part, the indigenous peoples of Siberia continued to practice their inherited religions guided by native shamans.

The Russian Occupation of Siberia The settlers who established a Russian presence in Siberia included social misfits, convicted criminals, and even prisoners of war. Despite the region's harsh terrain, Russian migrants gradually filtered into Siberia and thoroughly altered its demographic complexion. Small agricultural settlements grew up near many trading posts, particularly in the fertile Amur River valley. Siberian landowners offered working conditions that were much lighter than those of Russia proper, so disgruntled peasants sometimes fled to settlements east of the Ural Mountains. Over time, Siberian trading posts with their garrisons developed into Russian towns with Russian-speaking populations attending Russian Orthodox churches. By 1763 some 420,000 Russians lived in Siberia, nearly double the number of indigenous inhabitants. In the nineteenth century, large numbers of additional migrants moved east to mine Siberian gold, silver, copper, and iron, and the Russian state was well on the way toward consolidating its control over the region.

Commercial Rivalries and the Seven Years' War

Exploration and imperial expansion led to conflicts not only between Europeans and Asians but also among Europeans themselves. Mariners competed vigorously for trade in Asia and the Americas, and their efforts to establish markets—and sometimes monopolies as well—led frequently to clashes with their counterparts from different lands.

Competition and Conflict Indeed, throughout the seventeenth and early eighteenth centuries, commercial and political rivalries led to running wars between ships flying different flags. Dutch vessels were most numerous in the Indian Ocean, and they enabled the VOC to dominate the spice trade. Dutch forces expelled most Portuguese merchants from southeast Asia and prevented English mariners from establishing secure footholds there. By the early eighteenth century, trade in Indian cotton and tea from Ceylon had begun to overshadow the spice trade, and English and French merchants working from trading posts in India became the dominant carriers in the Indian Ocean. Fierce competition again generated violence: in 1746 French forces seized the English trading post at Madras, one of the three principal centers of British operations in India.

Commercial competition led to conflict also in the Caribbean and the Americas. English pirates and privateers preyed on Spanish shipping from Mexico, often seizing vessels carrying cargoes of silver. English and French forces constantly skirmished and fought over sugar islands in the Caribbean while also contesting territorial claims in North America. Almost all conflicts between European states in the eighteenth century spilled over into the Caribbean and the Americas.

The Seven Years' War Commercial rivalries combined with political differences and came to a head in the Seven Years' War (1756–1763). The Seven Years' War was a global conflict in that it took place in several distinct geographic theaters—Europe, India, the Caribbean, and North America—and involved Asian and indigenous American peoples as well as Europeans. Sometimes called "the great war for empire," the Seven Years' War had deep implications for global affairs, since it laid the foundation for 150 years of British imperial hegemony in the world.

In Europe the war pitted Britain and Prussia against France, Austria, and Russia. In India, British and French forces each allied with local rulers and engaged in a contest for hegemony in the Indian Ocean. In the Caribbean, Spanish forces joined with the French in an effort to limit British expansion in the western hemisphere. In North America—where the Seven Years' War merged with a conflict already under way known as the French and Indian War (1754–1763)—British and French armies made separate alliances with indigenous peoples in an effort to outmaneuver each other.

British Hegemony British forces fought little in Europe, where their Prussian allies held off massive armies seeking to surround and crush the expansive Prussian state. Elsewhere, however, British armies and navies handily overcame their enemies. They ousted French merchants from

ATLANTIC OCEAN
ARCTIC
North Pole
0°
45°W
45°E
90°E
Baltic Sea
Barents Sea
Warsaw
POLAND
LITHUANIA
LATVIA
ESTONIA
Murmansk
Novgorod
Archangel
Kiev
UKRAINE
Moscow
Danube
THE CRIMEA
Black Sea
Volga
URAL MOUNTAINS
Ob
CAUCASUS MOUNTAINS
Astrakhan
Caspian Sea
Aral Sea
Yenisey
SIBERIA
Lena
Irkutsk
GOBI DESERT
INDIA
HIMALAYAS
CHINA

PART 5

MAP 22.5
Russian expansion, 1462–1795.
Observe how vast the empire became after it added the territory of Siberia.

How did Russians exert their control over such a huge and unforgiving territory?

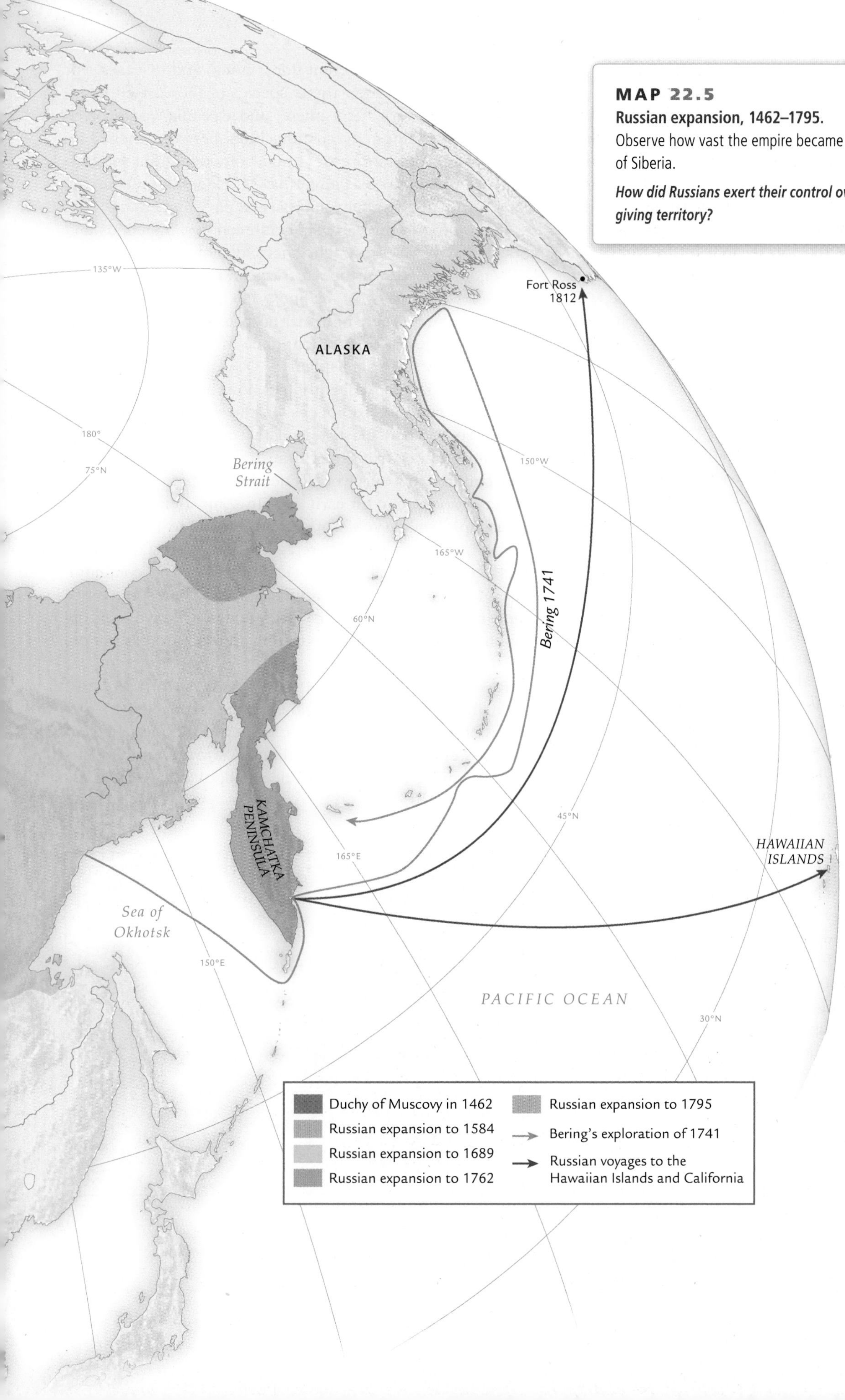

Fort Ross 1812
ALASKA
Bering Strait
Bering 1741
KAMCHATKA PENINSULA
HAWAIIAN ISLANDS
Sea of Okhotsk
PACIFIC OCEAN
135°W
180°
75°N
150°W
165°W
60°N
45°N
165°E
150°E
30°N

Duchy of Muscovy in 1462
Russian expansion to 1584
Russian expansion to 1689
Russian expansion to 1762
Russian expansion to 1795
Bering's exploration of 1741
Russian voyages to the Hawaiian Islands and California

India and took control of French colonies in Canada, although they allowed French authorities to retain most of their Caribbean possessions. They allowed Spanish forces to retain Cuba but took Florida from the Spanish empire. By no means did these victories make Britain master of the world, or even of Europe: both in Europe and in the larger world, powerful states challenged British ambitions. Yet victory in the Seven Years' War placed Britain in a position to dominate world trade for the foreseeable future, and "the great war for empire" paved the way for the establishment of the British empire in the nineteenth century. The war also suggested how close together earlier global exchanges had brought the peoples of the world.

ECOLOGICAL EXCHANGES

European explorers and those who followed them established links between all lands and peoples of the world. Interaction between peoples in turn resulted in an unprecedented volume of exchange across the boundary lines of societies and cultural regions. Some of that exchange involved biological species: plants, food crops, animals, human populations, and disease pathogens all spread to regions they had not previously visited. These biological exchanges had differing and dramatic effects on human populations, destroying some of them through epidemic diseases while enlarging others through increased food supplies and richer diets. Commercial exchange also flourished in the wake of the voyages of exploration as European merchants traveled to ports throughout the world in search of trade. By the late sixteenth century, they had built fortified trading posts at strategic sites in the Indian, Atlantic, and Pacific Ocean basins. By the mid-eighteenth century, they had established global networks of trade and communication.

The Columbian Exchange

Processes of biological exchange were prominent features of world history well before modern times. The early expansion of Islam had facilitated the diffusion of plants and food crops throughout much of the eastern hemisphere during the period from about 700 to 1100 C.E., and transplanted species helped spark demographic and economic growth in all the lands where they took root. During the fourteenth century the spread of bubonic plague caused drastic demographic losses when epidemic disease struck Eurasian and north African lands.

Biological Exchanges Yet the "Columbian exchange"—the global diffusion of plants, food crops, animals, human populations, and disease pathogens that took place after voyages of exploration by Christopher Columbus and other European mariners—had consequences much more profound than did earlier rounds of biological exchange. Unlike the earlier processes, the Columbian exchange involved lands with radically different flora, fauna, and diseases. For thousands of years the various species of the eastern hemisphere, the western hemisphere, and Oceania had evolved along separate lines. By creating links between these biological zones, the European voyages of exploration set off a round of biological exchange that permanently altered the world's human geography and natural environment.

Beginning in the early sixteenth century, infectious and contagious diseases brought sharp demographic losses to indigenous peoples of the Americas and the Pacific islands. The worst scourge was smallpox, but measles, diphtheria, whooping cough, and influenza also took heavy tolls. Before the voyages of exploration, none of these maladies had reached the western hemisphere or Oceania, and the peoples of those regions consequently had no inherited or acquired immunities to those pathogens. In the eastern hemisphere, these diseases had mostly become endemic: they claimed a certain number of victims from the ranks of infants and small children, but survivors gained immunity to the diseases through exposure at an early age. In some areas of Europe, for example, smallpox was responsible for 10 to 15 percent of deaths, but most victims were age ten or younger. Although its effects were tragic for individual families and communities, smallpox did not pose a threat to European society as a whole because it did not carry away adults, who were mostly responsible for economic production and social organization.

Epidemic Diseases and Population Decline When infectious and contagious diseases traveled to previously unexposed populations, however, they touched off ferocious epidemics that sometimes destroyed entire societies. Beginning in 1519, epidemic smallpox ravaged the Az-

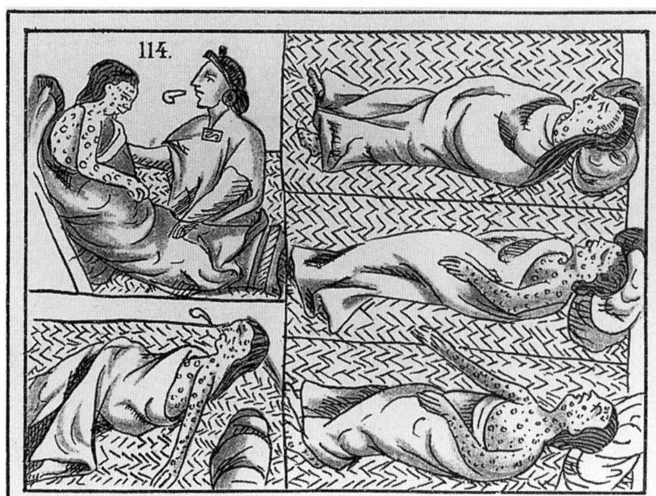

Smallpox victims in the Aztec empire. The disease killed most of those it infected and left disfiguring scars on survivors.

tec empire, often in combination with other diseases, and within a century the indigenous population of Mexico had declined by as much as 90 percent, from about 17 million to 1.3 million. By that time Spanish conquerors had imposed their rule on Mexico, and the political, social, and cultural traditions of the indigenous peoples had either disappeared or fallen under Spanish domination.

Imported diseases took their worst tolls in densely populated areas such as the Aztec and Inca empires, but they did not spare other regions. Smallpox and other diseases were so easily transmissible that they raced to remote areas of North and South America and sparked epidemics even before the first European explorers arrived in those regions. By the 1530s smallpox may have spread as far from Mexico as the Great Lakes in the north and the pampas of Argentina in the south.

When introduced to the Pacific islands, infectious and contagious diseases struck vulnerable populations with the same horrifying effects as in the Americas, albeit on a smaller scale. All told, disease epidemics sparked by the Columbian exchange probably caused the worst demographic calamity in all of world history. Between 1500 and 1800, upwards of 100 million people may have died of diseases imported into the Americas and the Pacific islands.

Food Crops and Animals Over the long term, however, the Columbian exchange increased rather than diminished human population because of the global spread of food crops and animals that it sponsored. In the long term, a better-nourished world was an important contributing factor in the growth of the world's population, which began in the eighteenth century and has continued to the present. Out of Eurasia to the western hemisphere traveled wheat, rice, sugar, bananas, apples, cherries, peaches, peas, and citrus fruits. Wheat in particular grew well on the plains of North America and on the pampas of Argentina, regions either too dry or too cold for the cultivation of indigenous maize (corn). Africa contributed yams, okra, collard greens, and coffee. Dairy and meat-yielding animals—horses, cattle, pigs, sheep, goats, and chickens—went from Europe to the Americas, where they sharply increased supplies of food and animal energy.

American Crops Food crops native to the Americas also played prominent roles in the Columbian exchange. American crops that took root in Africa, Asia, and Europe include maize, potatoes, beans, tomatoes, peppers, peanuts, manioc, papayas, guavas, avocados, pineapples, and cacao, to name only the most important. (A less nutritious transplant was tobacco.) Residents of the eastern hemisphere only gradually developed a taste for American crops, but by the eighteenth century maize and potatoes had contributed to a sharply increased number of calories in Eurasian diets. Maize became especially important in China because it grew in eco-niches unsuitable for rice and millet production. With the exception of Bengal (India), Asian lands proved less welcoming to the potato. It did eventually conquer most of northern Europe, from Ireland to Russia, because of its impressive nutritional qualities. American bean varieties added protein, and tomatoes and peppers provided vitamins and zesty flavors in lands from western Europe to China. Peanuts and manioc flourished in tropical southeast Asian and west African soils that otherwise would not produce large yields or support large populations. The Americas also supplied medicinal plants. Derived from the bark of the Peruvian cinchona tree, bitter-tasting quinine was the first effective treatment for malaria and proved vital to Europeans trying to survive mosquito-ridden tropics.

Population Growth The Columbian exchange of plants and animals fueled a surge in world population. In 1500, as Eurasian peoples were recovering from epidemic bubonic plague, world population stood at about 425 million. By 1600 it had increased more than 25 percent to 545 million. Human numbers increased less rapidly during the next century,

Tobacco was long used for religious and spiritual purposes in the Americas. After their arrival in the Americas, Europeans quickly popularized tobacco as a trade item and as a recreational drug to be smoked, snuffed, or chewed.

thinking about TRADITIONS

Local Foodways
For millennia, humans had generally relied on locally tended crops and foraged foods for their sustenance. How did the Columbian exchange alter those traditional foodways? What new crops and animals traveled between the eastern and western hemispheres—and what were the consequences?

reaching 610 million in 1700. But thereafter they increased at a faster rate than ever before in world history. By 1750 human population stood at 720 million, and by 1800 it had surged to 900 million, having grown by almost 50 percent during the previous century. Much of the rise was due to the increased nutritional value of diets enriched by the global exchange of food crops and animals.

Migration Alongside disease pathogens and plant and animal species, the Columbian exchange also involved the spread of human populations through transoceanic migration, whether voluntary or forced. During the period from 1500 to 1800, the largest contingent of migrants consisted of enslaved Africans transported involuntarily to South American, North American, and Caribbean destinations. A smaller but still sizable migration involved Europeans who traveled to the Americas and settled in lands depopulated by infectious and contagious diseases. During the nineteenth century, European peoples traveled in massive numbers mostly to the western hemisphere but also to south Africa, Australia, and Pacific islands where diseases had diminished indigenous populations, and Asian peoples migrated to tropical and subtropical destinations throughout much of the world. In combination, those migrations have profoundly influenced modern world history.

The Origins of Global Trade

The trading-post empires established by Portuguese, Dutch, and English merchants linked Asian markets with European consumers and offered opportunities for European mariners to participate in the carrying trade within Asia. European vessels transported Persian carpets to India, Indian cottons to southeast Asia, southeast Asian spices to India and China, Chinese silks to Japan, and Japanese silver and copper to China and India. By the late sixteenth century, European merchants were as prominent as Arabs in the trading world of the Indian Ocean basin.

Transoceanic Trade Besides stimulating commerce in the eastern hemisphere, the voyages of European merchant mariners encouraged the emergence of a genuinely global trading system. As Europeans established colonies in the Caribbean and the Americas, for example, trade networks extended to all areas of the Atlantic Ocean basin. European manufactured goods traveled west across the Atlantic in exchange for silver from Mexican and Peruvian mines and agricultural products such as sugar and tobacco, both of which were in high demand among European consumers. Trade in human beings also figured in Atlantic commerce. European textiles, guns, and other manufactured goods went south to west Africa, where merchants exchanged them for African slaves, who then went to the tropical and subtropical regions of the western hemisphere to work on plantations.

The Manila Galleons The experience of the Manila galleons illustrates the early workings of the global economy in the Pacific Ocean basin. For 250 years, from 1565 to 1815, Spanish galleons—sleek, fast, heavily armed ships capable of carrying large cargoes—regularly plied the waters of the Pacific Ocean between Manila in the Philippines and Acapulco on the west coast of Mexico. From Manila they took Asian luxury goods to Mexico and exchanged them for silver. Most of the precious metal made its way to China, where a thriving domestic economy demanded increasing quantities of silver, the basis of Chinese currency. In fact, the demand for silver was so high in China that European merchants exchanged it for Chinese gold, which they later traded profitably for more silver as well as luxury goods in Japan. Meanwhile, some of the Asian luxury goods from Manila remained in Mexico or went to Peru, where they contributed to a comfortable way of life for Spanish ruling elites. Most, however, went overland across Mexico and then traveled by ship across the Atlantic to Spain and European markets.

Environmental Effects of Global Trade As silver lubricated growing volumes of global trade, pressures fell on several animal species that had the misfortune to become prominent commodities on the world market. Fur-bearing animals came under particularly intense pressure, as hunters sought their pelts for sale to consumers in China, Europe, and North America. During the seventeenth century, an estimated two hundred to three hundred thousand sable pelts flowed annually from Siberia to the global market, and during the eighteenth century, more than sixteen million North American beaver pelts fed consumers' demands for fur hats and cloaks. Wanton hunting of fur-bearing animals soon drove many species into extinction or near-extinction, permanently altering the environments they had formerly inhabited. Quite apart from fur-bearing animals, early modern hunters harvested enormous numbers of deer, codfish, whales, walruses, seals, and other species as merchants

This is an artist's rendering of a Spanish galleon. Galleons were large, multidecked, highly stable and maneuverable sailing ships used by Europeans for war or commerce. The Spanish and the Portuguese built the largest types for their profitable overseas trade.

sought to supply skins, food, oil, ivory, and other animal products to global consumers.

By the late sixteenth century, conditions favored the relentless human exploitation of the world's natural and agricultural resources, as European mariners had permanently linked the world's port cities and created global trading networks. During the next two centuries, the volume of global trade expanded, as English, Dutch, French, and other merchants contributed to the development of global markets. During the seventeenth century, for example, Dutch merchants imported, among other commodities, wheat from south Africa, cowry shells from India, and sugar from Brazil. The wheat fed domestic consumers, who increasingly worked as merchants, bankers, or manufacturers rather than as cultivators. English, Dutch, and other merchants eagerly purchased the cowry shells—which served as currency in much of sub-Saharan Africa—and exchanged them for slaves destined for plantations in the western hemisphere. The sugar went on the market at Amsterdam and found its way to consumers throughout Europe. During the eighteenth century, world trade became even more intricate as mass markets emerged for commodities such as coffee, tea, sugar, and tobacco. By 1750 all parts of the world except Australia participated in global networks of commercial relations in which European merchant mariners played prominent roles.

in perspective

Global commercial and biological exchanges arose from the efforts of European mariners to explore the world's waters and establish sea lanes that would support long-distance trade. Their search for sea routes to Asia led them to the western hemisphere and the vast expanse of the Pacific Ocean. The geographic knowledge that they accumulated enabled them to link the world's regions into a finely articulated network of trade. But commercial exchange was not the only result of this global network. Food crops, animal stocks, disease pathogens, and human migrants also traveled the sea lanes and dramatically influenced societies throughout the world. Transplanted crops and animal species led to improved nutrition and increasing populations throughout the eastern hemisphere. Epidemics sparked by unfamiliar disease pathogens ravaged indigenous populations in the Americas and the Pacific islands. Massive migrations of human communities transformed the social and cultural landscape of the Americas and encouraged increased mingling of the world's peoples. The European voyages of exploration, transoceanic trade networks, and the Columbian exchange pushed the world's regions toward interdependence and global integration.

CHRONOLOGY	
1394–1460	Life of Prince Henry the Navigator of Portugal
1488	Bartolomeu Dias's voyage around the Cape of Good Hope into the Indian Ocean
1492	Christopher Columbus's first voyage to the western hemisphere
1497–1499	Vasco da Gama's first voyage to India
1500	Establishment of Portuguese trading post in Calicut, India
1519–1522	Ferdinand Magellan's circumnavigation of the world
1565–1575	Spanish conquest of the Philippines
1619	Establishment of Batavia by the Dutch on the island of Java
1756–1763	Seven Years' War
1768–1780	Captain James Cook's voyages in the Pacific Ocean

For Further Reading

David R. Abernathy. *The Dynamics of Global Dominance: European Overseas Empires, 1415–1980.* New Haven, 2000. A survey of the rise and decline of European overseas empires during a period of more than five hundred years.

Rene J. Barendse. *The Arabian Seas.* Eastgate, N.Y., 2002. A path-breaking and complex work that emphasizes the long predominance of Asia in the world economy.

Francisco Bethencourt and Diogo Curto, eds. *Portuguese Overseas Expansion.* New York, 2007. A collection of essays provides an overview of Portuguese maritime expansion between 1400 and 1800.

K. N. Chaudhuri. *Trade and Civilisation in the Indian Ocean: An Economic History from the Rise of Islam to 1750.* Cambridge, 1985. A brilliant analysis that places the European presence in the Indian Ocean in a larger historical context.

———. *The Trading World of Asia and the English East India Company, 1660–1760.* Cambridge, 1978. The best study of the English East India Company and its role in world trade.

Carlo Cipolla. *Guns, Sails, and Empires: Technological Innovation and the Early Phases of European Expansion, 1400–1700.* New York, 1965. A well-written study of the naval and military technology available to European mariners.

Christopher Columbus. *The Diario of Christopher Columbus's First Voyage to America.* Trans. by Oliver Dunn and James E. Kelley Jr. Norman, Okla., 1989. A careful translation.

Alfred W. Crosby. *The Columbian Exchange: Biological and Cultural Consequences of 1492.* Westport, Conn., 1972. Focuses on early exchanges of plants, animals, and diseases between Europe and America.

———. *Ecological Imperialism: The Biological Expansion of Europe, 900–1900.* Cambridge, 1986. An important study that examines the establishment of European biological species in the larger world.

Philip D. Curtin. *Cross-Cultural Trade in World History.* New York, 1984. Focuses on the roles of cross-cultural brokers in facilitating trade between different societies.

Stephen Frederic Dale. *Indian Merchants and Eurasian Trade, 1600–1750.* Cambridge, 1994. Scholarly analysis of Indian merchant communities trading in Russia, Persia, and central Asia in early modern times.

Andre Gunder Frank. *ReORIENT: Global Economy in the Asian Age.* Berkeley, 1998. Important and challenging analysis of global economic integration in the early modern world.

Jonathan L. Israel. *Dutch Primacy in World Trade, 1585–1740.* Oxford, 1989. A thorough examination of the Dutch seaborne empire at its height.

Michael Khodarkovsky. *Where Two Worlds Meet: The Russian State and the Kalmyk Nomads, 1600–1771.* Ithaca, 1992. One of the first major studies to look at Russian imperial expansion in Siberia through the eyes of colonized peoples.

Pablo E. Perez-Mallaina. *Spain's Men of the Sea: Daily Life on the Indies Fleet in the Sixteenth Century.* Trans. by Carla Rahn Phillips. Baltimore, 1988. Recounts shipboard life in vivid detail.

William H. McNeill. *Plagues and Peoples.* Garden City, N.Y., 1976. Examines the effects of infectious and contagious diseases in world history.

David Ormrod. *The Rise of Commercial Empires: England and the Netherlands in the Age of Mercantilism, 1650–1770.* New York, 2003. An important contribution to an understanding of European imperialism and colonialism that focuses on the issues surrounding Dutch decline and British ascendancy.

Anthony Pagden. *European Encounters with the New World: From Renaissance to Romanticism.* New Haven, 1993. Scholarly examination of early European responses to the peoples, societies, and environments they encountered in the Americas.

John H. Parry. *The Age of Reconnaissance.* Berkeley, 1982. Reliable and readable survey of European expansion.

M. N. Pearson. *The Portuguese in India.* Cambridge, 1987. A brief, lively discussion of the early Portuguese empire in India.

William D. Phillips Jr. and Carla Rahn Phillips. *The Worlds of Christopher Columbus.* Cambridge, 1992. The best general study of Christopher Columbus.

Antonio Pigafetta. *Magellan's Voyage: A Narrative Account of the First Circumnavigation.* 2 vols. Trans. by R. A. Skelton. New Haven, 1969. Valuable account by a crewman on Magellan's circumnavigation of the world.

Kenneth Pomeranz. *The Great Divergence: China, Europe, and the Making of the Modern World Economy.* Princeton, 2000. Pathbreaking scholarly study that illuminates the economic history of the early modern world through comparison of economic development in Asian and European lands.

——— and Steven Topik. *The World That Trade Created: Society, Culture, and the World Economy, 1400 to the Present.* Armonk, N.Y., 1999. Informative articles arguing the fundamental importance of trade and commerce in world history, both as a precursor to globalization and as a historically transformative force.

John F. Richards. *The Unending Frontier: An Environmental History of the Early Modern World.* Berkeley, 2003. Thoroughly explores the environmental effects of the global historical processes that shaped the early modern world.

Stuart B. Schwartz, ed. *Implicit Understandings: Observing, Reporting, and Reflecting on the Encounters between Europeans and Other Peoples in the Early Modern Era.* Cambridge, 1994. Fascinating collection of essays by specialists on cross-cultural perceptions in early modern times.

Yuri Slezkine. *Arctic Mirrors: Russia and the Small Peoples of the North.* Ithaca, 1994. Thoughtful analysis of Russian relations with the hunting, fishing, and herding peoples of Siberia.

Sanjay Subrahmanyam. *The Career and Legend of Vasco da Gama.* Cambridge, 1997. The best critical study of the famous Portuguese mariner.

———. *The Portuguese Empire in Asia, 1500–1700: A Political and Economic History.* London, 1993. A sophisticated analysis of the Portuguese trading-post empire.

Hugh Thomas. *Rivers of Gold: The Rise of the Spanish Empire, from Columbus to Magellan.* New York, 2003. Detailed narrative of a brief period in Spain's imperial outreach.

James D. Tracy, ed. *The Political Economy of Merchant Empires: State Power and World Trade, 1350–1750.* Cambridge, 1991. Essays on the interconnections between political, military, and commercial relationships in early modern times.

———. *The Rise of Merchant Empires: Long-Distance Trade in the Early Modern World, 1350–1750.* Cambridge, 1990. Essays by specialists on global trade in early modern times.

Immanuel Wallerstein. *The Modern World-System.* 3 vols. New York, 1974. A controversial but influential interpretation of global political and economic development in modern times.

Merry E. Wiesner-Hanks. *Christianity and Sexuality in the Early Modern World: Regulating Desire, Reforming Practice.* London, 2000. Pioneering comparative study of Christian sexuality in global context.

The Transformation of Europe

chapter 23

Martin Luther at age forty-two, depicted as a conscientious and determined man by the German painter Lucas Cranach in 1525.

EYEWITNESS:
Martin Luther Challenges the Church

In 1517 an obscure German monk posed a challenge to the Roman Catholic church. Martin Luther of Wittenberg denounced the church's sale of indulgences, a type of pardon that excused individuals from doing penance for their sins and thus facilitated their entry into heaven. Indulgences had been available since the eleventh century, but to raise funds for the reconstruction of St. Peter's basilica in Rome, church authorities began to market indulgences aggressively in the early sixteenth century. From their point of view, indulgences were splendid devices: they encouraged individuals to reflect piously on their behavior while also bringing large sums of money into the church's treasury.

To Martin Luther, however, indulgences were signs of greed, hypocrisy, and moral rot in the Roman Catholic church. Luther despised the pretentiousness of church authorities who arrogated to themselves powers that belonged properly to God alone: no human being had the power to absolve individuals of their sins and grant them admission to heaven, Luther believed, so the sale of indulgences constituted a huge fraud perpetrated on an unsuspecting public. In October 1517, following academic custom of the day, he offered to debate publicly with anyone who wished to dispute his views, and he denounced the sale of indulgences in a document called the *Ninety-Five Theses.*

Luther did not nail his work to the church door in Wittenberg, although a popular legend credited him with that heroic gesture, but news of the *Ninety-Five Theses* spread instantly: within a few weeks, printed copies were available throughout Europe. Luther's challenge galvanized opinion among many who resented the power of the Roman church. It also drew severe criticism from religious and political authorities seeking to maintain the established order. Church officials subjected Luther's views to examination and judged them erroneous, and in 1520 Pope Leo X excommunicated the unrepentant monk. In 1521 the Holy Roman emperor Charles V, a devout Roman Catholic, summoned Luther to an assembly of imperial authorities and demanded that he recant his views. Luther's response: "I cannot and will not recant anything, for it is neither safe nor right to act against one's conscience. Here I stand. I can do no other. God help me. Amen."

Martin Luther's challenge held enormous religious and political implications. Though expelled from the church, Luther still considered himself Christian—indeed, he considered his own faith true Christianity—and he held religious services for a community of devoted followers. Wittenberg became a center of religious dissent, which by the late 1520s had spread through much of Germany and Switzerland. During the 1530s dissidents known as Protestants—because of their protest against the established order—organized movements also in France, England, the Low Countries, and even Italy and Spain. By mid-century Luther's act of individual rebellion had mushroomed into the Protestant Reformation, which shattered the religious unity of western Christendom.

For all its unsettling effects, the Protestant Reformation was only one of several powerful movements that transformed European society during the early modern era. Another was the consolidation of strong centralized states, which took shape partly because of the Reformation. Between the sixteenth and the eighteenth centuries, monarchs in western Europe took advantage of religious quarrels to tighten control over their societies. By curbing the power of the nobility, expanding royal authority, and increasing control over their subjects, they built states much more powerful than the regional monarchies of the middle ages. By the mid-eighteenth century, some rulers had concentrated so much power in their own hands that historians refer to them as absolute monarchs.

Alongside religious conflict and the building of powerful states, capitalism and early modern science also profoundly influenced western European society in early modern times. Early capitalism pushed European merchants and manufacturers into unrelenting competition with one another and encouraged them to reorganize their businesses in search of maximum efficiency. Early modern science challenged traditional ways of understanding the world and the universe. Under the influence of scientific discoveries, European intellectuals sought an entirely rational understanding of human society as well as the natural world, and some sought to base European moral, ethical, and social thought on science and reason rather than Christianity.

Thus between 1500 and 1800, western Europe underwent a thorough transformation. Although the combination of religious, political, social, economic, intellectual, and cultural change was unsettling and often disruptive, it also strengthened European society. The states of early modern Europe competed vigorously and mobilized their human and natural resources in effective fashion. By 1800 several of them had become especially powerful, wealthy, and dynamic. They stood poised to play major roles in world affairs during the nineteenth and twentieth centuries.

THE FRAGMENTATION OF WESTERN CHRISTENDOM

In the third century C.E., Christian missionaries began to spread their faith from the Mediterranean basin throughout Europe, and by 1000 C.E. Christianity had established a foothold as far north as Scandinavia and Iceland. Although the peoples of western Europe spoke different languages, ate different foods, and observed different customs, the church of Rome provided them with a common religious and cultural heritage. During the sixteenth and seventeenth centuries, however, revolts against the Roman Catholic church shattered the religious unity of western Europe. Followers of Martin Luther and other Protestant reformers established a series of churches independent of Rome, and Roman Catholic leaders strengthened their own church against the challengers. Throughout early modern times, religious controversies fueled social tensions.

The Protestant Reformation

Roots of Reform The Protestant Reformation dates from the early sixteenth century, but many of the underlying conditions that prompted reformers to challenge the authority of the Roman Catholic church had existed for hundreds of years. Over the course of centuries, the church and its top officials had become deeply embroiled in the political affairs of western Europe. But political intrigues, combined with the church's growing wealth and power, also fostered greed and corruption, which undermined the church's spiritual authority and made it vulnerable to criticism. The blatant hedonism and crass materialism of church officials only further emphasized the perceived betrayal of Christian ideals. Although the church continued to enjoy the loyalty of most Christians, it faced a disapproval of its abuses that became increasingly strident in the decades before 1517. Alongside such criticism came a growing demand for a more personal involvement with the divine. Efforts by

church authorities to eliminate pre-Christian traditions and alternative kinds of spirituality only intensified the desire among laypeople for forms of devotion that would connect them more directly with God than the church allowed. Martin Luther coalesced these expressions of religious discontent into a powerful revolt against the church.

Martin Luther Martin Luther (1483–1546) attacked the sale of indulgences as an individual, but he soon attracted enthusiastic support from others who resented the policies of the Roman church. Luther was a prolific and talented writer, and he published scores of works condemning the Roman church. His cause benefited enormously from the printing press, which had first appeared in Europe in the mid-fifteenth century. A sizable literate public inhabited European cities and towns, and readers eagerly consumed printed works on religious as well as secular themes. Printed editions of Luther's writings appeared throughout Europe and sparked spirited debates on indulgences and theological issues. His supporters and critics took their own works to the printers, and religious controversies kept the presses busy churning out pamphlets and treatises for a century and more.

Luther soon moved beyond the issue of indulgences: he attacked the Roman church for a wide range of abuses and called for thorough reform of Christendom. He advocated the closure of monasteries, translation of the Bible from Latin into vernacular languages, and an end to priestly authority, including the authority of the pope himself. When opponents pointed out that his reform program ran counter to church policy, he rejected the authority of the church hierarchy and proclaimed that the Bible was the only source of Christian religious authority.

Luther's works drew an enthusiastic popular response, and in Germany they fueled a movement to reform the church along the lines of Luther's teachings. Lay Christians flocked to hear Luther preach in Wittenberg, and several princes of the Holy Roman Empire warmed to Luther's views—partly because of personal conviction but partly also because religious controversy offered opportunities for them to build their own power bases. During the 1520s and 1530s, many of the most important German cities—Strasbourg, Nuremberg, and Augsburg, among others—passed laws prohibiting Roman Catholic observances and requiring all religious services to follow Protestant doctrine and procedures.

Reform outside Germany By the mid-sixteenth century, about half the German population had adopted Lutheran Christianity, and reformers had launched Protestant movements and established alternative churches in other lands as well. By the late 1520s the prosperous cities of Switzerland—Zurich, Basel, and Geneva—had fledgling Protestant churches. The heavily urbanized Low Countries also responded enthusiastically to Protestant appeals. Protestants appeared even in Italy and Spain, although authorities in those lands handily suppressed their challenge to the Roman church.

In England a Reformation took place for frankly political as well as religious reasons. Lutherans and other Protestants worked to build a following in England from the 1520s, but they faced stout government resistance until King Henry VIII (reigned 1509–1547) came into conflict with the pope. Henry wanted to divorce his wife, who had not borne a male heir, but the pope refused to allow him to do so. Henry's response was to sever relations with the Roman church and make himself Supreme Head of the Anglican church—an English pope, as it were. While Henry reigned, the theology of the English church changed little, but under pressure of reformers, his successors replaced Roman Catholic with Protestant doctrines and rituals. By 1560 England had permanently left the Roman Catholic community.

John Calvin Meanwhile, an even more influential Reformation was taking shape in France and the French-speaking parts of Switzerland. The initiator was a French lawyer, John Calvin (1509–1564), who in the 1530s converted to Protestant Christianity. Because the French monarchy sought to suppress Protestants, Calvin slipped across the border to French-speaking Geneva in Switzerland. There he organized a Protestant community and worked with local officials to impose a strict code of morality and discipline on the city. Calvin also composed an influential treatise, *Institutes of the Christian Religion* (first published in 1536 and frequently reprinted with revisions), that codified Protestant teachings and presented them as a coherent and organized package.

Calvin's Geneva was not only a model Protestant community but also a missionary center. Calvinist missionaries were most active in France, where they attracted strong interest in the cities, but they ventured also to Germany, the Low Countries, England, Scotland, and even distant Hungary. They established churches in all these lands and worked for reform along Protestant lines. They were most successful in the Netherlands and Scotland. By the late sixteenth century, Lutherans, Anglicans, and Calvinists together had built communities large enough that a return to religious unity in western Christendom was inconceivable.

The Catholic Reformation

Partly in response to the Protestant Reformation, Roman Catholic authorities undertook an enormous reform effort within their own church. To some extent their efforts represented a reaction to Protestant success. Yet Roman Catholic authorities also sought to define points of doctrine so as to clarify differences between Roman and Protestant churches, to persuade Protestants to return to the Roman church, and to deepen the sense of spirituality and religious commitment in their own community. Taken together, their efforts constituted the Catholic Reformation.

The Council of Trent Two institutions were especially important for defining the Catholic Reformation and advancing its goals—the Council of Trent and the Society of Jesus.

The Council of Trent was an assembly of bishops, cardinals, and other high church officials who met intermittently between 1545 and 1563 to address matters of doctrine and reform. Drawing heavily on the works of the thirteenth-century scholastic theologian St. Thomas Aquinas, the council defined the elements of Roman Catholic theology in detail. The council acknowledged that abuses had alienated many people from the Roman church, and it took steps to reform the church. The council demanded that church authorities observe strict standards of morality, and it required them to establish schools and seminaries in their districts to prepare priests properly for their roles.

Under inspiration of the Catholic Reformation, many devout individuals sought mystic union with God. One of the most famous of the mystics was St. Teresa of Avila (in Spain), who founded a strict order of nuns and often experienced religious visions. A famous sculpture by the Italian artist Gianlorenzo Bernini depicts St. Teresa in an ecstatic trance accompanied by an angel.

St. Ignatius Loyola While the Council of Trent dealt with doctrine and reform, the Society of Jesus went on the offensive and sought to extend the boundaries of the reformed Roman church. The society's founder was St. Ignatius Loyola (1491–1556), a Basque nobleman and soldier who in 1521 suffered a devastating leg wound that ended his military career. While recuperating he read spiritual works and popular accounts of saints' lives, and he resolved to put his energy into religious work. In 1540, together with a small band of disciples, he founded the Society of Jesus.

The Society of Jesus Ignatius required that members of the society, known as Jesuits, complete a rigorous and advanced education. They received instruction not only in theology and philosophy but also in classical languages, literature, history, and science. As a result of that preparation—and their unswerving dedication to the Roman Catholic church—the Jesuits made extraordinarily effective missionaries. They were able to outargue most of their opponents and acquired a reputation for discipline and determination. They often served as counselors to kings and rulers and used their influence to promote policies that benefited the Roman church. They also were the most prominent of the early Christian missionaries outside Europe: in the wake of the European reconnaissance of the world's oceans, Jesuits attracted converts in India, China, Japan, the Philippines, and the Americas, thus making Christianity a genuinely global religion.

Witch-Hunts and Religious Wars

Europeans took religion seriously in the sixteenth century, and religious divisions helped to fuel social and political conflict. Apart from wars, the most destructive violence that afflicted early modern Europe was the hunt for witches, which was especially prominent in regions such as the Rhineland where tensions between Protestants and Roman Catholics ran high.

Like many other peoples, Europeans had long believed that certain individuals possessed unusual powers to influence human affairs or discover secret information such as the identity of a thief. During the late fifteenth century, theologians developed a theory that witches derived their powers from the devil. According to that theory, witches made agreements to worship the devil in exchange for supernatural powers, including the ability to fly through the night on brooms, pitchforks, or animals. Theorists believed that the witches regularly flew off to distant places to attend the "witches' sabbath," a gathering that featured devil worship, lewd behavior, and the concoction of secret potions, culminating in sexual relations with the devil himself.

Witch-Hunting Although the witches' sabbath was sheer fantasy, fears that individuals were making alliances with the devil sparked an intensive hunt for witches. Witchcraft became a convenient explanation for any unpleasant turn of events—failure of a crop, outbreak of a fire, an unexpected death, or inability to conceive a child. About 110,000 individuals underwent trial as suspected witches during the sixteenth and seventeenth centuries, and about 45,000 of them died either by hanging or by burning at the stake. As a rule, church courts tried large numbers of witches, but they usually imposed nonlethal penalties such as excommunication or imprisonment. It was secular courts that condemned and executed the vast majority of witches.

Witches and Gender Gender played an important role in the witch-hunts. Men were among the victims, and in places such as Finland they actually exceeded the number of women accused of witchcraft. Most convicted witches were women, however. Indeed, women may have accounted for 85 percent or more of the condemned. Many of the women were poor, old, single, or widowed—individuals who lived on the margins of their societies and were easy targets for accusers, since they had few protectors. Witch-hunting was mostly a European affair, but it also spread to European colonies in the Americas. The most intense witch-hunt in the Americas took place in seventeenth-century New England, where a population of about 100,000 colonists tried 234 individuals for witchcraft and executed 36 of them by hanging.

By 1700 the fear of witches had largely diminished. Accusations, trials, and executions occurred only sporadically thereafter. The last legal execution for witchcraft in Europe took place in Switzerland in 1782. For the better part of two centuries, however, the intermittent pursuit of witches revealed clearly the stresses and strains that afflicted European society during early modern times.

Religious Wars Religious tensions even led to outright war between Protestant and Roman Catholic communities. Religious wars racked France for thirty-six years (1562–1598), for example, and they also complicated relations between Protestant and Roman Catholic states. In 1588 King Philip II of Spain (reigned 1556–1598) attempted to force England to return to the Roman Catholic church by sending the Spanish Armada—a huge flotilla consisting of 130 ships and 30,000 men—to dethrone the Protestant Queen Elizabeth. The effort collapsed, however, when English forces disrupted the Spanish fleet by sending blazing, unmanned ships into its midst. Then a ferocious gale scattered Spanish vessels throughout the North Sea.

Religious convictions also aggravated relations between the Netherlands and Spain by fueling the revolt of the Dutch provinces from their overlord, the king of Spain. In 1567 Philip sent an army to tighten his control over the provinces and to suppress the Calvinist movement there. Resistance escalated into a full-scale rebellion. By 1610 the seven northern provinces (the modern Netherlands) had won their independence and formed a republic known as the United Provinces, leaving ten southern provinces (modern Belgium) under Spanish and later Austrian rule until the late eighteenth century.

The Thirty Years' War The religious wars culminated in a massive continental conflict known as the Thirty Years' War (1618–1648). The war opened after the Holy Roman emperor attempted to force his Bohemian subjects to return to the Roman Catholic church, and the main battleground was the emperor's territory in Germany. Other parties soon entered the fray, however, and by the time the war ended, Spanish, French, Dutch, German, Swedish, Danish, Polish, Bohemian, and Russian forces had taken part in the conflict.

The motives that prompted these states to enter the war were sometimes political or economic, but religious differences complicated the other issues and made them more difficult to resolve. Regardless of the motives, the Thirty Years' War was the most destructive European conflict before the twentieth century. Quite apart from violence and brutalities committed by undisciplined soldiers, the war damaged

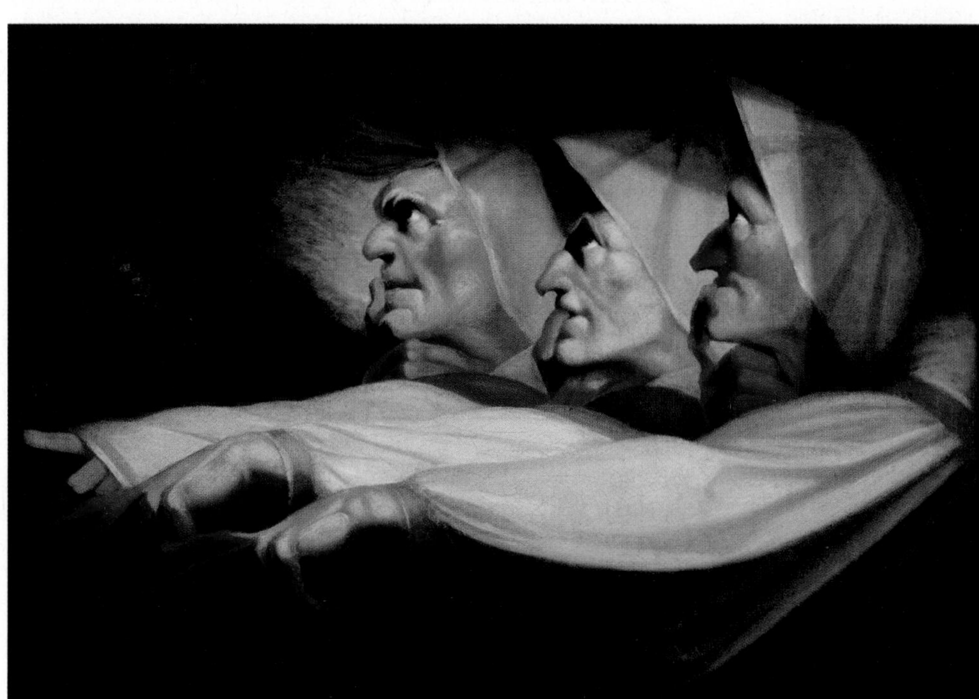

Henry Fuseli's 1783 painting offers a dramatic depiction of three witches. The painter based his image on the three witches who appear in William Shakespeare's play *Macbeth.* He titled his painting "The Weird Sisters" or "The Three Witches." Which physical features identify these women as "weird" witches?

Israel ex. Cum Priuil. Reg.
A la fin ces Voleurs infames et perdus,
Comme fruits malheureux a cet arbre pendus
Monstrent bien que le crime (horrible et noire engeance)
Est luy mesme instrument de honte et de vengeance,
Et que cest le Destin des hommes vicieux
Desprouuer tost ou tard la iustice des Cieux.
11

The Thirty Years' War offered abundant opportunity for undisciplined mercenary soldiers to prey on civilian populations. Only rarely, as in the mass hanging depicted in this engraving of 1633, did soldiers receive punishment for their criminal acts.

economies and societies throughout Europe and led to the deaths of about one-third of the German population. The destructiveness of the Thirty Years' War raised questions about the viability of Europe as a region of strong, independent, well-armed, and intensely competitive states.

THE CONSOLIDATION OF SOVEREIGN STATES

Although fundamentally a religious movement, the Reformation had strong political implications, and centralizing monarchs readily made use of religious issues in their efforts to strengthen their states and enhance their authority. Ruling elites had their own religious preferences, and they often promoted a Protestant or Roman Catholic cause out of personal conviction. Religious controversies also offered splendid opportunities for ambitious subordinates who built power bases by appealing to particular religious communities. Over the long run, centralizing monarchs profited most from religious controversy generated by the Reformation. While the Holy Roman Empire fell into disarray because of political and religious quarrels, monarchs in other lands augmented their revenues, enhanced their authority, and created powerful sovereign states. After the devastation of the Thirty Years' War, rulers of these states devised a diplomatic system that sought to maintain order among the many independent and competitive European states.

The Attempted Revival of Empire

After the dissolution of the Carolingian empire in the ninth century C.E., there was no effective imperial government in western Europe. The so-called Holy Roman Empire emerged in the tenth century, but its authority extended only to Germany and northern Italy, and even there the emperors encountered stiff opposition from powerful princes and thriving cities. During the early sixteenth century, it seemed that Emperor Charles V (reigned 1519–1556) might establish the Holy Roman Empire as the preeminent political authority in Europe, but by midcentury it was clear that there would be no revival of empire. Thus, unlike China, India, and Ottoman lands in southwest Asia and north Africa, early modern Europe developed as a region of independent states.

Charles V After 1438 the Habsburg family, with extensive dynastic holdings in Austria, dominated the Holy Roman Empire. Through marriage alliances with princely and royal families, the Habsburgs accumulated rights and titles to lands throughout Europe and beyond. Charles V inherited authority over the Habsburgs' Austrian domains as well as the duchy of Burgundy (including the wealthy provinces of the Low Countries) and the kingdom of Spain (including its possessions in Italy and the Americas). When he became emperor in 1519, he acquired authority over Germany, Bohemia, Switzerland, and parts of northern Italy. His empire stretched from Vienna in Austria to Cuzco in Peru.

Imperial Fragmentation In spite of his far-flung holdings, Charles did not extend his authority throughout Europe or even establish a lasting imperial legacy. Throughout his reign Charles had to devote much of his attention and energy to the Lutheran movement and to imperial princes who took advantage of religious controversy to assert their independence. Moreover, Charles did not build an administrative structure for his empire but, instead, ruled each of his lands according to its own laws and customs. He was able to draw on the financial resources of wealthy lands such as the Low Countries and Spain to maintain a powerful army. Yet Charles did not have the ambition to extend his authority by military force, but used his army mostly to put down rebellions.

Foreign Challenges Foreign difficulties also prevented Charles from establishing his empire as the arbiter of Europe. The prospect of a powerful Holy Roman Empire struck fear in the kings of France, and it caused concern among the sultans of the Ottoman empire as well. Charles's holdings surrounded France, and the French kings suspected that the emperor wanted to absorb their realm and extend his authority throughout Europe. To forestall that possibility, the French kings created every obstacle they could for Charles. Even though they were staunch Roman Catholics, they aided German Lutherans and encouraged them to rebel. The French kings even allied with the Muslim Ottoman Turks against the emperor.

MAP 23.1
Sixteenth-century Europe.
Note the extent of Habsburg territories and the wide boundaries of the Holy Roman Empire.
With such powerful territories, what prevented the Habsburgs from imposing imperial rule on most of Europe?

For their part, the Ottoman sultans did not want to see a powerful Christian empire threaten their holdings in eastern Europe and their position in the Mediterranean basin. With the encouragement of the French king, Turkish forces conquered Hungary in 1526, and three years later they even laid siege briefly to Vienna. Moreover, during the early sixteenth century Ottoman forces imposed their rule beyond Egypt and embraced almost all of north Africa. By midcentury, Turkish holdings posed a serious threat to Italian and Spanish shipping in the Mediterranean.

Thus numerous domestic and foreign problems prevented Charles V from establishing his vast empire as the supreme political authority in Europe. His inability to suppress the Lutherans was especially disappointing to Charles, and in 1556, after agreeing that imperial princes and cities could determine the religious faith observed in their jurisdictions, the emperor abdicated his throne and retired to a monastery in Spain. His empire did not survive intact. Charles bestowed his holdings in Spain, Italy, the Low Countries, and the Americas on his son, King Philip II of Spain, while his brother Ferdinand inherited the Habsburg family lands in Austria and the imperial throne.

The New Monarchs

In the absence of effective imperial power, guidance of public affairs fell to the various regional states that had emerged during the middle ages. The city-states of Italy were prominent because of their economic power: since the eleventh century they had been Europe's most important centers of trade, manufacturing, and finance. The most powerful European states, however, were the kingdoms of England, France, and Spain. During the late fifteenth and sixteenth centuries, rulers of these lands, known as the "new monarchs," marshaled their resources, curbed the nobility, and built strong centralized regimes.

Finance The new monarchs included Henry VIII of England, Louis XI and Francis I of France, and Fernando and Isabel of Spain. All the new monarchs sought to enhance their treasuries by developing new sources of finance. The French kings levied direct taxes on sales, households, and the salt trade. A new sales tax dramatically boosted Spanish royal income in the sixteenth century. For fear of provoking rebellion, the English kings did not introduce new taxes, but they increased revenues by raising fines and fees for royal services. Moreover, after Henry VIII severed ties between the English and Roman churches, he dissolved the monasteries and confiscated church wealth in England. This financial windfall enabled Henry to enhance royal power by increasing the size of the state and adding to its responsibilities. After the English Reformation, for example, the state provided poor relief and support for orphans, which previously had been responsibilities of churches and monasteries.

State Power With their increased income the new monarchs enlarged their administrative staffs, which enabled them to collect taxes and implement royal policies more reliably than before. The French and Spanish monarchs also maintained standing armies that vastly increased their power with respect to the nobility. Their armies with thousands of infantrymen were too large for individual nobles to match, and they equipped their forces with cannons that were too expensive for nobles to purchase. The English kings did not need a standing army to put down the occasional rebellion that flared in their island realm and so did not go to the expense of supporting one. Yet they too increased their power with respect to the nobles by subjecting them to royal justice and forcing them to comply with royal policy.

The debates and disputes launched by the Protestant Reformation helped monarchs increase their power. In lands that adopted Protestant faiths—including England, much of Germany, Denmark, and Sweden—rulers expropriated the monasteries and used church wealth to expand their powers. That option was not open to Roman Catholic kings, but Protestant movements provided them with a justification to mobilize resources, which they used against political as well as religious adversaries.

The Spanish Inquisition The Spanish Inquisition was the most distinctive institution that relied on religious justifications to advance state ends. Fernando and Isabel founded the Spanish Inquisition in 1478, and they obtained papal license to operate the institution as a royal agency. Its original task was to ferret out those who secretly practiced Judaism or Islam, but Charles V charged it with responsibility also for detecting Protestant heresy in Spain. Throughout the late fifteenth and sixteenth centuries, however, the Spanish Inquisition served political as well as religious purposes. Moreover, its reach extended well beyond the Iberian peninsula. Just as the fear of witchcraft crossed the Atlantic Ocean and inspired witch-hunts in England's North American colonies, concerns about heresy also made their way to the western hemisphere, where inquisitors worked to protect Spanish colonies from heretical teachings.

Inquisitors had broad powers to investigate suspected cases of heresy. Popular legends have created an erroneous impression of the Spanish Inquisition as an institution running amok, framing innocent victims and routinely subjecting them to torture. In fact, inquisitors usually observed rules of evidence, and they released many suspects after investigations turned up no sign of heresy. Yet, when they detected the scent of heresy, inquisitors could be ruthless. They sentenced hundreds of victims to hang from the gallows or burn at the stake and imprisoned many others in dank cells for extended periods of time. Fear of the inquisition intimidated many into silence, and a strict Roman Catholic orthodoxy prevailed in Spain. The inquisition deterred nobles from adopting Protestant views out of political ambition, and it used its influence on behalf of the Span-

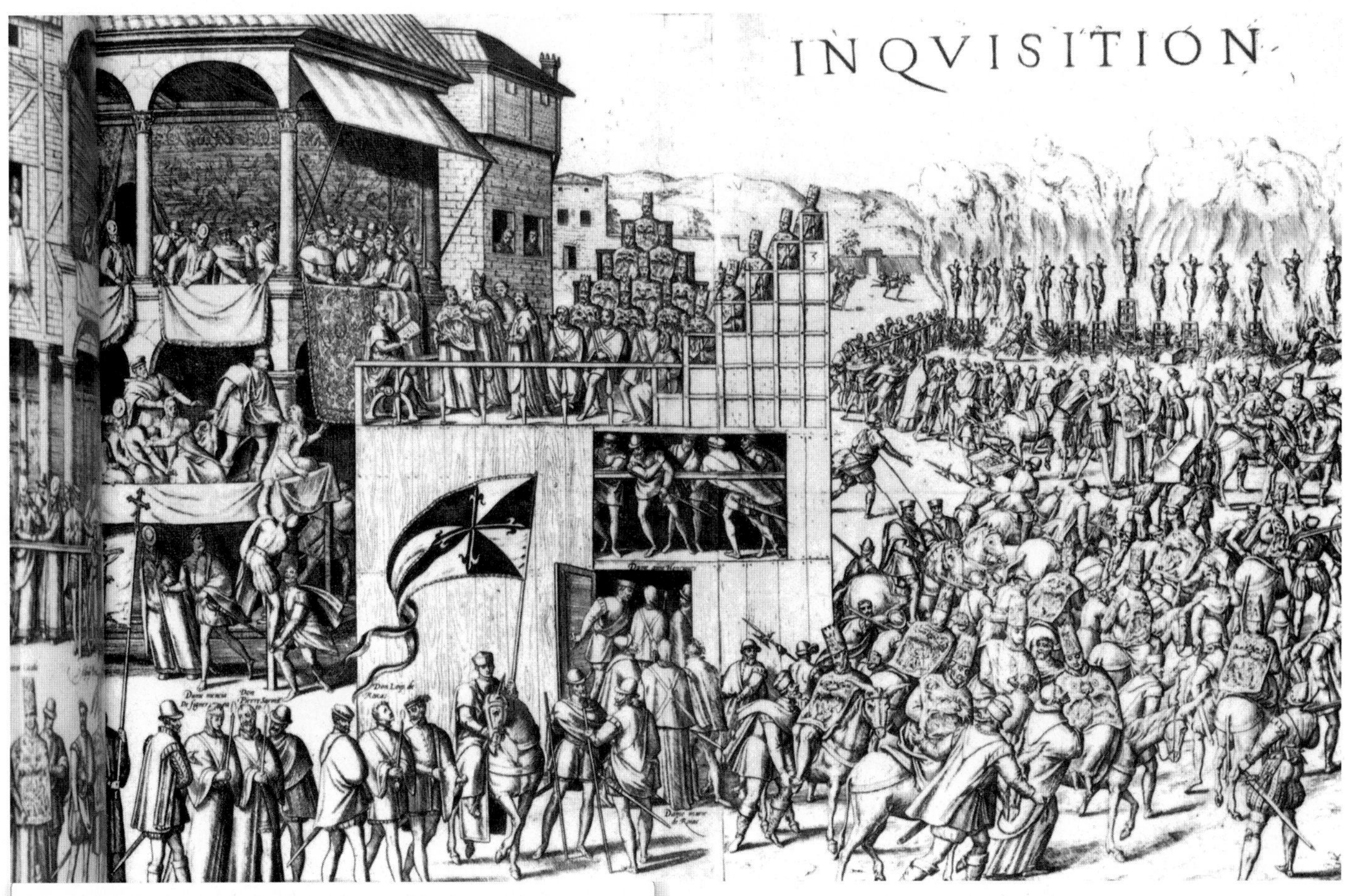

When the Spanish Inquisition detected traces of Protestant heresy, the punishment could be swift and brutal. In this engraving of about 1560, a large crowd observes the execution of heretics (top right) by burning at the stake.

ish monarchy. From 1559 to 1576, for example, inquisitors imprisoned the archbishop of Toledo—the highest Roman Catholic church official in all of Spain—because of his political independence.

Constitutional States

During the seventeenth and eighteenth centuries, as they sought to restore order after the Thirty Years' War, European states developed along two lines. Rulers in England and the Netherlands shared authority with representative institutions and created constitutional states, whereas monarchs in France, Spain, Austria, Prussia, and Russia concentrated power in their own hands and created a form of state known as absolute monarchy.

Constitutional States The island kingdom of England and the maritime Dutch republic did not have written constitutions specifying the powers of the state, but during the seventeenth century they evolved governments that claimed limited powers and recognized rights pertaining to individuals and representative institutions. Their constitutional states took different forms: in England a constitutional monarchy emerged, whereas the Netherlands produced a republic based on representative government. In neither land did constitutional government come easily into being: in England it followed a civil war, and in the Netherlands it emerged after a long struggle for independence. In both lands, however, constitutional government strengthened the state and provided a political framework that enabled merchants to flourish as never before in European experience.

The English Civil War Constitutional government came to England after political and religious disputes led to the English civil war (1642–1649). From the early seventeenth century, the English kings had tried to institute new taxes without approval of the parliament, which for more than three centuries had traditionally approved new levies. While royal financial policies generated political tensions, religious disagreements aggravated matters further. As Anglicans, the kings supported a church with relatively ornate ceremonies and a hierarchy of bishops working under authority of the monarchs themselves. Meanwhile, however, many of the boldest and most insistent voices within parliament belonged

In this contemporary painting, the executioner holds up the just-severed head of King Charles I of England. The spectacle of a royal execution overcomes one woman, who faints (at bottom). How does the image of a beheaded king reflect the ongoing political changes in Europe?

to zealous Calvinists known as Puritans because they sought to purify the English church of any lingering elements, such as ornate ceremonies and a hierarchy of bishops, suggestive of Roman Catholic Christianity. By 1641, King Charles I and parliament were at loggerheads, unable to cooperate or even communicate effectively with each other. Both sides raised armies. In the conflicts that followed, parliamentary forces under the leadership of Oliver Cromwell (1599–1658) captured Charles, tried him for tyranny, and in an act that shocked all of Europe, marched him up on a platform and beheaded him in 1649.

The Glorious Revolution In the absence of a king, Cromwell's Puritan regime took power but soon degenerated into a disagreeable dictatorship, prompting parliament to restore the monarchy in 1660. King and parliament, however, soon resumed their conflicts. The issue came to a head in a bloodless change of power known as the Glorious Revolution (1688–1689), when parliament deposed King James II and invited his daughter Mary and her Dutch husband, William of Orange, to assume the throne. The resulting arrangement provided that kings would rule in cooperation with parliament, thus guaranteeing that nobles, merchants, and other constituencies would enjoy representation in government affairs.

The Dutch Republic As in England, a potent combination of political and religious tensions led to conflict from which constitutional government emerged in the Netherlands. In the mid-sixteenth century, authority over the Low Countries, including modern-day Belgium as well as the Netherlands, rested with King Philip II of Spain. In 1567 Philip, a devout Roman Catholic, moved to suppress an increasingly popular Calvinist movement in the Netherlands—a measure that provoked large-scale rebellion against Spanish rule. In 1579 a group of Dutch provinces formed an anti-Spanish alliance, and in 1581 they proclaimed themselves the independent United Provinces. Representative assemblies organized local affairs in each of the provinces, and on this foundation political leaders built a Dutch republic. Spain did not officially recognize the independence of the United Provinces until the end of the Thirty Years' War in 1648, but the Dutch republic was effectively organizing affairs in the northern Low Countries by the early seventeenth century.

In many ways, the constitutional governments of England and the Dutch republic represented historical experiments. Apart from the Roman republic in classical times and a few Italian city-states of the medieval and Renaissance eras, European peoples had little experience with representative government. In their responses to political crises, popular leaders in both England and the Netherlands found it possible to mobilize support by appealing to the political and religious interests of broad constituencies and making a place for them in the government. The result was a pair of states that effectively harnessed popular support and used it to magnify state power.

In both England and the Dutch republic, merchants were especially prominent in political affairs, and state policy in both lands favored maritime trade and the building of commercial empires overseas. The constitutional states allowed entrepreneurs to pursue their economic interests with minimal interference from public authorities, and during the late seventeenth and eighteenth centuries, both states experienced extraordinary prosperity as a result of those policies. Indeed, in many ways the English and Dutch states represented an alliance between merchants and rulers that worked to the benefit of both. Merchants supported the state with the wealth that they generated through trade—especially overseas trade—while rulers followed policies that looked after the interests of their merchants.

Although best known as Louis XIII's "first minister," Cardinal Richelieu also gained fame for his patronage of the arts. Most notably, he founded the Académie Française, the learned society responsible for matters pertaining to the French language.

Absolute Monarchies

Whereas constitutional states devised ways to share power and authority, absolute monarchies found other ways to increase state power. Absolutism stood on a theoretical foundation known as the divine right of kings. This theory held that kings derived their authority from God and served as "God's lieutenants upon earth." There was no role in divine-right theory for common subjects or even nobles in public affairs: the king made law and determined policy. Noncompliance or disobedience merited punishment, and rebellion was a despicable act tantamount to blasphemy. In fact, absolute monarchs always relied on support from nobles and other social groups as well, but the claims of divine-right theory clearly reflected efforts at royal centralization.

The most conspicuous absolutist state was the French monarchy. The architect of French absolutism was a prominent church official, Cardinal Richelieu, who served as chief minister to King Louis XIII from 1624 to 1642. Richelieu worked systematically to undermine the power of the nobility and enhance the authority of the king. He destroyed nobles' castles and ruthlessly crushed aristocratic conspiracies. As a counterweight to the nobility, Richelieu built a large bureaucracy staffed by commoners loyal to the king. He also appointed officials to supervise the implementation of royal policy in the provinces. Finally, Richelieu attacked French Calvinists, who often allied with independent nobles, and destroyed their political and military power, although he allowed them to continue observing their faith. By midcentury France was under control of a tightly centralized absolute monarchy.

The Sun King

The ruler who best epitomized royal absolutism was King Louis XIV (reigned 1643–1715), who once reportedly declared that he was himself the state: *"l'état, c'est moi."* Known as *le roi soleil* ("the sun king"), Louis surrounded himself with splendor befitting one who ruled by divine right. During the 1670s he built a magnificent residence at **Versailles,** a royal hunting lodge near Paris, and in the 1680s he moved his court there. Louis's palace at Versailles was the largest building in Europe, with 230 acres of formal gardens and 1,400 fountains. Because Louis did not want to wait years for saplings to grow, he ordered laborers to dig up 25,000 fully grown trees and haul them to Versailles for transplanting.

The sun king was the center of attention at Versailles. Court officials hovered around him and tended to his every need. All prominent nobles established residences at Versailles for their families and entourages. Louis strongly encouraged them to live at court, where he and his staff

Versailles (vehr-SEYE)

The French painter Hyacinthe Rigaud, renowned for his portrait paintings of the royalty and nobility of Europe, created this vision of Louis XIV. Louis' reign, from 1643 to his death in 1715, lasted seventy-two years, three months, and eighteen days, and is the longest documented reign of any European monarch.

could keep an eye on them, and ambitious nobles gravitated there anyway in hopes of winning influence with the king. Louis himself was the arbiter of taste and style at Versailles, where he lavishly patronized painters, sculptors, architects, and writers whose creations met with his approval.

While nobles living at Versailles mastered the intricacies of court ritual and attended banquets, concerts, operas, balls, and theatrical performances, Louis and his ministers ran the state. In effect, Louis provided the nobility with luxurious accommodations and endless entertainment in exchange for absolute rule. From Versailles, Louis and his advisors promulgated laws and controlled a large standing army that kept order throughout the land. They also promoted economic development by supporting the establishment of new industries, building roads and canals, abolishing internal tariffs, and encouraging exports. Finally, they waged a series of wars designed to enlarge French boundaries and establish France as the preeminent power in Europe.

Absolutism in Russia Louis XIV was not the only absolute monarch of early modern Europe: Spanish, Austrian, and Prussian rulers embraced similar policies. The potential of absolutism to increase state power was particularly conspicuous in the case of Russia, where tsars of the Romanov dynasty (1613–1917) tightly centralized government functions. (*Tsar,* sometimes spelled *czar,* is a Russianized form of the term *caesar,* which Russian rulers borrowed from Byzantine emperors, who in turn had borrowed it from the classical Roman empire to signify their imperial status.) The Romanovs inherited a state that had rapidly expanded its boundaries since the mid-fourteenth century. Building on the foundation of a small principality around the trading city of Moscow, by 1600 Russia had become a vast empire extending from the Arctic seas in the north to the Caspian Sea in the south, with an increasing presence in the tundra and forests of Siberia as well.

Peter I Most important of the Romanov tsars was Peter I (reigned 1682–1725), widely known as Peter the Great, who inaugurated a thoroughgoing process of state transformation. Peter had a burning desire to make Russia, a huge but underpopulated land, into a great military power like those that had recently emerged in western Europe. In pursuit of that goal, he worked to transform Russia on the model of western European lands. In 1697–1698 he led a large party of Russian observers on a tour of Germany, the Netherlands, and England to learn about western European administrative methods and military technology. His traveling companions often behaved crudely by western European standards: they consumed beer, wine, and brandy in quantities that astonished their hosts, and King William III sent Peter a bill for damages done by his entourage at the country house where they lodged in England. (Among other things, Peter had ruined the gardens by having his men march through them in military formation.)

Upon return to Moscow, Peter set Russia spinning. He reformed the army by offering better pay and drafting peasants who served for life as professional soldiers. He provided his forces with extensive training and equipped them with modern weapons. He ordered aristocrats to study mathematics and geometry so that they could calculate how to aim cannons accurately, and he began the construction of a navy with an eye toward domination of the Baltic and other northern seas. He also overhauled the government bureaucracy to facilitate tax collection and improve administrative efficiency. His transformation of Russia even involved a cosmetic makeover, as he commanded his aristocratic subjects to wear western European fashions and ordered men to shave their traditional beards. These measures, which were extremely unpopular among conservative Russians, provoked spirited protest among those who resented the influence of western European ways. Yet Peter insisted on observance of his policies—to the point that he reportedly went into the streets and personally hacked the beards off

Tsar Peter the Great, with a pair of shears, readies himself to remove the beard of a conservative noble. Peter had traveled widely in Europe, and he wanted to impose newer European customs on his subjects. That included being more cleanly shaved. Nobles wishing to keep their beloved beards had to pay a yearly tax to do so.

recalcitrants' faces. Perhaps the best symbol of his policies was St. Petersburg, a newly built seaport that Peter opened in 1703 to serve as a magnificent capital city and haven for Russia's fledgling navy.

Catherine II and the Limits of Reform The most able of Peter's successors was Catherine II (reigned 1762–1796), also known as Catherine the Great. Like Peter, Catherine sought to make Russia a great power. She worked to improve governmental efficiency by dividing her vast empire into fifty administrative provinces, and she promoted economic development in Russia's towns. For a while, she even worked to improve the conditions of Russia's oppressed peasantry by restricting the punishments that noble landowners could inflict on the serfs who worked their lands. She sought to eliminate common penalties such as torture, beating, and the mutilation of individuals by cutting off their noses, ears, or tongues.

Yet her interest in social reform cooled rapidly when it seemed to inspire challenges to her rule. She faced a particularly unsettling trial in 1773 and 1774, when a disgruntled former soldier named Yemelian Pugachev mounted a rebellion

This is a regal Russian portrait of the German-born empress of Russia, Catherine II. Although admired by many Russians as a source of national pride, she is also remembered as a ruthless ruler who affirmed autocracy and extended serfdom on a large scale.

in the steppe lands north of the Caspian Sea. Pugachev raised a motley army of adventurers, exiles, peasants, and serfs who killed thousands of noble landowners and government officials before imperial forces crushed the uprising. Government authorities took the captured Pugachev to Moscow in chains, beheaded him, quartered his body, and displayed his parts throughout the city as a warning against rebellion. Thereafter, Catherine's first concern was the preservation of autocratic rule rather than the transformation of Russia according to western European models.

Thus, in Russia as in other European lands, absolutist policies resulted in tight centralization and considerable strengthening of the state. The enhanced power that flowed from absolutism became dramatically clear in the period 1772 to 1797, when Austria, Prussia, and Catherine II's Russia picked the weak kingdom of Poland apart. In a series of three "partitions," the predatory absolutist states seized Polish territory and absorbed it into their own realms, ultimately wiping Poland entirely off the map. The lesson of the partitions was clear: any European state that hoped to survive needed to construct an effective government that could respond promptly to challenges and opportunities.

The European States System

Whether they relied on absolutist or constitutional principles, European governments of early modern times built states much more powerful than those of their medieval predecessors. This round of state development led to difficulties within Europe, since conflicting interests fueled interstate competition and war. In the absence of an imperial authority capable of imposing and maintaining order in Europe, sovereign states had to find ways to resolve conflicts by themselves.

The Peace of Westphalia The Thirty Years' War demonstrated the chaos and devastation that conflict could bring. In an effort to avoid tearing their society apart, European states ended the Thirty Years' War with the Peace of Westphalia (1648), which laid the foundations for a system of independent, competing states. Almost all the European states participated in drafting the Peace of Westphalia, and by the treaty's terms they regarded one another as sovereign and equal. They also mutually recognized their rights to organize their own domestic affairs, including religious affairs. Rather than envisioning imperial or papal or some other sort of supreme authority, the Peace of Westphalia entrusted political and diplomatic affairs to states acting in their own interests. European religious unity had disappeared, and the era of the sovereign state had arrived.

The Peace of Westphalia did not bring an end to war. Indeed, war was almost constant in early modern Europe. Most conflicts were minor affairs inaugurated by monarchs seeking to extend their authority to new lands or to reclaim territories seized by others, but they nevertheless disrupted local economies and drained resources. A few wars, however, grew to sizable proportions. Most notable among them were the wars of Louis XIV and the Seven Years' War. Between 1668 and 1713, the sun king sought to expand his borders east into Germany and to absorb Spain and the Spanish Netherlands into his kingdom. That prospect prompted England, the United Provinces, and Austria to mount a coalition against Louis. Later, the Seven Years' War (1756–1763) pitted France, Austria, and Russia against Britain and Prussia, and it merged with conflicts between France and Britain in India and North America to become a global war for imperial supremacy.

The Balance of Power These shifting alliances illustrate the principal foundation of European diplomacy in early modern times—the balance of power. No ruler wanted to see another state dominate all the others. Thus, when any particular state began to wax strong, others formed coalitions against it. Balance-of-power diplomacy was risky business: it was always possible that a coalition might repress one strong state only to open the door for another. Yet, in playing balance-of-power politics, statesmen prevented the building of empires and ensured that Europe would be a land of independent, sovereign, competing states.

Military Development Frequent wars and balance-of-power diplomacy drained the resources of individual states but strengthened European society as a whole. European states competed vigorously and sought to develop the most expert military leadership and the most effective weapons for their arsenals. States organized military academies where officers received advanced education in strategy and tactics and learned how to maintain disciplined forces. Demand for powerful weapons stimulated the development of a sophisticated armaments industry that turned out ever more lethal products. Gun foundries manufactured cannons of increasing size, range, power, and accuracy as well as small arms that allowed infantry to unleash withering volleys against their enemies.

In China, India, and Islamic lands, imperial states had little or no incentive to encourage similar technological innovation in the armaments industry. These states possessed the forces and weapons they needed to maintain order within their boundaries, and they rarely encountered foreign threats backed up with superior armaments. In Europe, however, failure to keep up with the latest improvements in arms technology could lead to defeat on the battlefield and decline in state power. Thus Europeans continuously sought to improve

MAP 23.2
Europe after the Peace of Westphalia, 1648.
Compare this map with Map 23.1.
How have the boundaries of the Holy Roman Empire changed, and why?

their military arsenals, and as a result, by the eighteenth century European armaments outperformed all others.

EARLY CAPITALIST SOCIETY

While the Protestant Reformation and the emergence of sovereign states brought religious and political change, a rapidly expanding population and economy encouraged the development of capitalism, which in turn led to a restructuring of European economy and society. Technologies of communication and transportation enabled businessmen to profit from distant markets, and merchants and manufacturers increasingly organized their affairs with the market rather than local communities in mind.

Capitalism generated considerable wealth, but its effects were uneven and sometimes unsettling. Economic development and increasing prosperity were noticeable in western Europe, particularly England, France, Germany, and the Netherlands. Yet eastern Europe experienced much less economic ferment, as Poland and Russia increasingly became suppliers of grain and raw materials rather than centers of trade or production. Even in western Europe, early capitalism encouraged social change that sometimes required painful adjustments to new conditions.

Population Growth and Urbanization

American Food Crops The foundation of European economic expansion in early modern times was a rapidly growing population, which reflected improved nutrition and decreasing mortality. The Columbian exchange enriched European diets by introducing new food crops to European fields and tables. Most notable of the introductions was the potato, which during the sixteenth and seventeenth centuries enjoyed the reputation of being an aphrodisiac. Although potatoes probably did not inspire much romantic ardor, they provided a welcome source of carbohydrates for peasants and laborers who were having trouble keeping up with the rising price of bread. From Ireland to Russia and from Scandinavia to the Mediterranean, cultivators planted potatoes and harvested crops that added calories to European diets. American maize also made its way to Europe. Maize, however, served mostly as feed for livestock rather than as food for human consumption, although peasants sometimes used cornmeal to make bread or porridges like polenta. Other American crops, such as tomatoes and peppers, added vitamins and tangy flavor to European diets.

While recently introduced American crops improved European diets, old diseases lost some of their ferocity. Smallpox continued to carry off about 10 percent of Europe's infants, and dysentery, influenza, tuberculosis, and typhus claimed victims among young and old, rich and poor alike. Yet better-nourished populations were better able to resist those maladies. Bubonic plague, a virulent epidemic killer during the fourteenth and fifteenth centuries, receded from European society. After its initial onslaught in the mid-fourteenth century, plague made periodic appearances throughout the early modern era. After the mid-seventeenth century, however, epidemics were rare and isolated events. The last major outbreaks of plague in Europe occurred in London in 1660 and Marseilles in 1720. By the mid-seventeenth century, epidemic disease was almost negligible as an influence on European population.

Population Growth Although European birthrates did not rise dramatically in early modern times, decreasing mortality resulted in rapid population growth. In 1500 the population of Europe, including Russia, was about 81 million. During the sixteenth century, as Europe recovered from epidemic plague, the population rose to 100 million. The Thirty Years' War—along with the famine and disease that the war touched off—led to population decline from about 1620 to 1650, but by 1700 European population had rallied and risen to 120 million. During the next century it grew by an additional 50 percent to 180 million.

Urbanization Rapid population growth drove a process of equally rapid urbanization. Some cities grew because rulers chose them as sites of government. Madrid, for example, was a minor town with a few thousand inhabitants until 1561 when King Philip II decided to locate his capital there. By 1600 the population of Madrid had risen to 65,000, and by 1630 it had reached 170,000. Other cities were commercial and industrial as well as government centers, and their numbers expanded along with the European economy. In the mid-sixteenth century, for example, the population of Paris was about 130,000, and London had about 60,000 inhabitants. A century later the population of both cities had risen to 500,000. Other European cities also experienced growth, even if it was not so dramatic as in Madrid, Paris, and London: Amsterdam, Berlin, Copenhagen, Dublin, Stockholm, Vienna, and others became prominent European cities during the early modern era.

Early Capitalism and Protoindustrialization

The Nature of Capitalism Population growth and rapid urbanization helped spur a round of remarkable economic development. This economic growth coincided with the emergence of capitalism—an economic system in which private parties make their goods and services available on a free market and seek to take advantage of market conditions to profit from their activities. Whether they are single individuals or large companies, private parties own the land, machinery, tools, equipment, buildings, workshops, and raw materials needed for production. Private parties pursuing their own economic interests hire workers and decide for themselves what to produce: economic decisions are the prerogative of capitalist businessmen, not governments or social superiors. The center of a capitalist system is the market in which businessmen compete with one another, and the

forces of supply and demand determine the prices received for goods and services. If businessmen organize their affairs efficiently, they realize handsome profits when they place their goods and services on the market. Otherwise, they incur losses and perhaps even lose their businesses.

The desire to accumulate wealth and realize profits was by no means new. Ever since the introduction of agriculture and the production of surplus crops, some individuals and groups had accumulated great wealth. Indeed, for several thousand years before the early modern era, merchants in China, southeast Asia, India, southwest Asia, the Mediterranean basin, and sub-Saharan Africa had pursued commercial ventures in hopes of realizing profits. Banks, investors, and insurance underwriters had supported privately organized commercial ventures throughout much of the eastern hemisphere since the postclassical era (500–1500 C.E.).

Supply and Demand During early modern times, however, European merchants and entrepreneurs transformed their society in a way that none of their predecessors had done. The capitalist economic order developed as businessmen learned to take advantage of market conditions by building efficient networks of transportation and communication. Dutch merchants might purchase cheap grain from Baltic lands such as Poland or Russia, for example, store it in Amsterdam until they learned about a famine in

The Old Stock Exchange of Amsterdam, depicted here in a painting of the mid-seventeenth century, attracted merchants, investors, entrepreneurs, and businessmen from all over Europe. There they bought and sold shares in joint-stock companies such as the VOC and dealt in all manner of commodities traded in Amsterdam.

the Mediterranean, and then transport it and sell it in southern France or Spain. Their enormous profits fueled suspicions that they took advantage of those in difficulty, but their activities also supplied hungry communities with the necessities of life, even if the price was high.

Private parties organized an array of institutions and services to support early capitalism. Banks, for example, appeared in all the major commercial cities of Europe: they held funds on account for safekeeping and granted loans to merchants or entrepreneurs launching new business ventures. Banks also published business newsletters—forerunners of the *Wall Street Journal* and *Fortune* magazine—that provided readers with reports on prices, information about demand for commodities in distant markets, and political news that could have an impact on business. Insurance companies mitigated financial losses from risky undertakings such as transoceanic voyages. Stock exchanges arose in the major European cities and provided markets where investors could buy and sell shares in joint-stock companies and trade in other commodities as well.

Joint-Stock Companies Joint-stock companies were especially important institutions in early capitalist society. Large trading companies such as the English East India Company and its Dutch counterpart, the Vereenigde Oost-Indische Compagnie (VOC), spread the risks attached to expensive business enterprises and also took advantage of extensive communications and transportation networks. The trading companies organized commercial ventures on a larger scale than ever before. They were the principal foundations of the global economy that emerged in early modern times, and they were the direct ancestors of contemporary multinational corporations.

Politics and Empire Capitalism did not develop in a political vacuum. To the contrary, it emerged with the active support of government authorities who saw a capitalist order as the one best suited to their individual and collective interests. Merchants were especially influential in the affairs of the English and Dutch states, so it is not surprising that these lands adopted policies that were most favorable to capitalist enterprises throughout the early modern era. The English and Dutch states recognized individuals' rights to possess private property, enforced their contracts, protected their financial interests, and settled disputes between parties to business transactions. They also chartered joint-stock companies and authorized some of them to explore, conquer, and colonize distant lands in search of commercial opportunities. Thus early capitalism developed in the context of imperialism, as European peoples established fortified

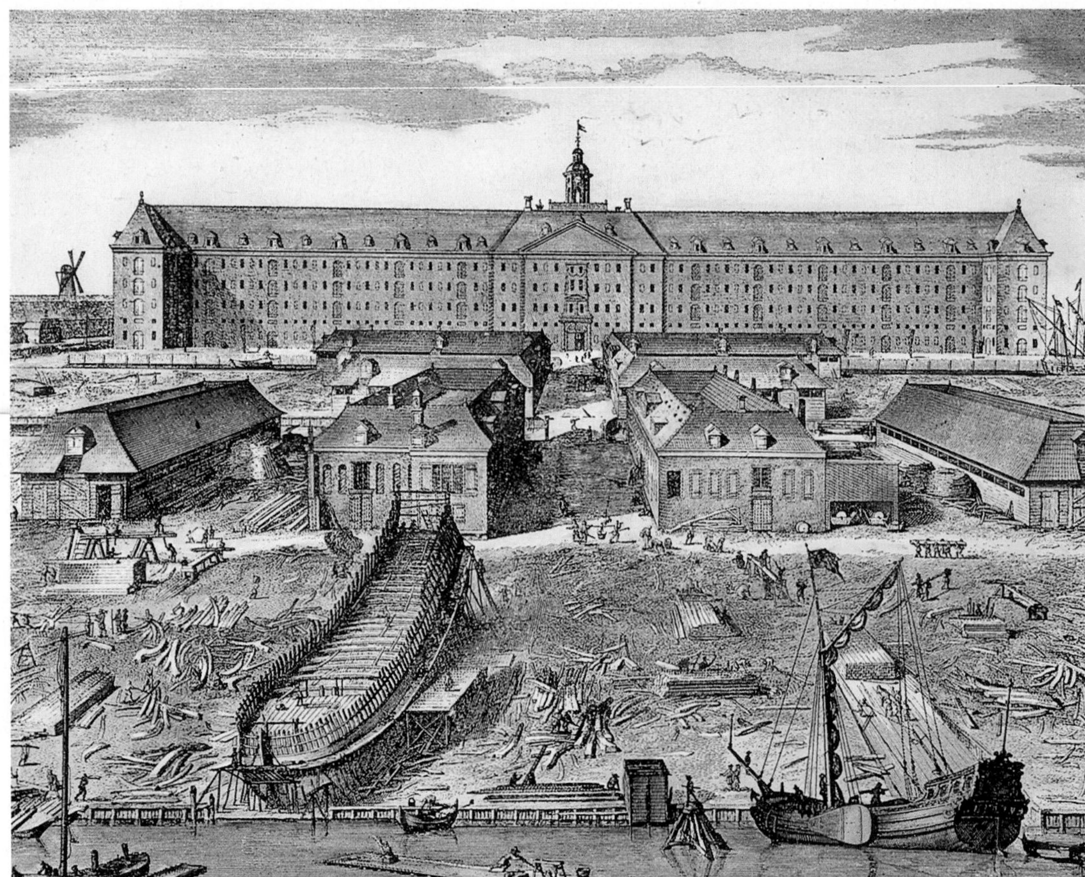

An anonymous engraver depicts activity in a Dutch shipyard where workers build a massive, oceangoing sailing ship. In the seventeenth century, Dutch ships were inexpensive to operate, yet they accommodated abundant cargoes. What kinds of cargoes were Dutch ships likely to carry in this period?

trading posts in Asia and colonial regimes in both southeast Asia and the Americas. Indeed, imperial expansion and colonial rule were crucial for the development of capitalism, since they enabled European merchants to gain access to the natural resources and commodities that they distributed so effectively through their transportation networks.

Quite apart from its influence on trade and the distribution of goods, capitalism encouraged European entrepreneurs to organize new ways to manufacture goods. For centuries, craft guilds had monopolized the production of goods such as textiles and metalwares in European towns and cities. Guilds fixed prices and wages, and they regulated standards of quality. They did not seek to realize profits so much as to protect markets and preserve their members' places in society. As a result, they actively discouraged competition and sometimes resisted technological innovation.

Putting-out System Capitalist entrepreneurs seeking profits found the guilds cumbersome and inflexible, so they sidestepped them and moved production into the countryside. Instead of relying on urban artisans to produce cloth, for example, they organized a "putting-out system" by which they delivered unfinished materials such as raw wool to rural households. Men and women in the countryside would then spin the wool into yarn, weave the yarn into cloth, cut the cloth according to patterns, and assemble the pieces into garments. The entrepreneur paid workers for their services, picked up the finished goods, and sold them on the market. During the seventeenth and eighteenth centuries, entrepreneurs moved the production of cloth, nails, pins, pots, and many other goods into the countryside through the putting-out system.

Because rural labor was usually plentiful, entrepreneurs spent relatively little on wages and realized handsome profits on their ventures. The putting-out system represented an early effort to organize efficient industrial production. Indeed, some historians refer to the seventeenth and eighteenth centuries as an age of "protoindustrialization." The putting-out system remained a prominent feature of European society until the rise of industrial factories in the nineteenth century.

thinking about ENCOUNTERS

Capitalism and Overseas Expansion

In the early modern era, Europeans consolidated previous economic developments into a new and profitable system of capitalism, where the central organizing form became the market. Capitalism provided the key tools for more efficient forms of overseas expansion. What were the signal capitalist institutions that underpinned overseas endeavors? How in turn did imperial expansion promote the further growth of capitalism?

Social Change in Early Modern Europe

Capitalist economic development brought unsettling change to European lands. The putting-out system, for example, introduced considerable sums of money into the countryside. Increased wealth brought material benefits, but it also undermined long-established patterns of rural life. The material standards of rural life rose dramatically: peasant households acquired more cabinets, furnishings, and tableware, and rural residents wore better clothes, ate better food, and drank better wine. Individuals suddenly acquired incomes that enabled them to pursue their own economic interests and to become financially independent of their families and neighbors. When young adults and women began to earn their own incomes, however, many feared that they might slip out of the control of their families and abandon their kin who continued to work at agricultural tasks.

The putting-out system did not become a prominent feature of production in eastern Europe, but early capitalism prompted deep social change there as well as in lands to the west. Eastern Europe had few cities in early modern times, so in expansive agrarian states such as Poland, Bohemia, and Russia, most people had no alternative to working in the countryside. Landlords took advantage of this situation by forcing peasants to work under extremely harsh conditions.

Serfdom in Russia Russia in particular was a vast but sparsely populated empire with little trade or manufacturing. Out of a concern to retain the allegiance of the powerful nobles who owned most of Russia's land, the Romanov tsars restricted the freedoms of most Russian peasants and tied them to the land as serfs. The institution of serfdom had emerged in the early middle ages as a labor system that required peasants to provide labor services for landowners and prevented them from marrying or moving away without their landlords' permission. After the fifteenth century, serfdom gradually came to an end in western Europe. In eastern Europe, however, landowners and rulers tightened restrictions on peasants during the sixteenth century, and in Russia the institution of serfdom survived until the nineteenth century. In effect, the Romanovs won the support of the Russian nobles by ensuring that laborers would be available to work their estates, which otherwise would have been worthless. In 1649 the government promulgated a law code that provided for tight state control over the Russian labor force by establishing a rigid, castelike social order that sharply restricted both occupational and geographic mobility. The law of 1649 did not turn serfs into chattel slaves, but during the late seventeenth and eighteenth centuries, landlords commonly sold serfs to one another as if they were indeed private property. Under those conditions, landlords operated estates with inexpensive labor and derived enormous incomes from the sale of agricultural products on the market.

These arrangements played crucial roles in the emergence of capitalism. In the larger economy of early modern Europe, eastern European lands relied on serfs to cultivate grains and provide raw materials such as timber for export to western Europe, where merchants and manufacturers were able to employ free wage labor in building a capitalist economy. Already by the early sixteenth century, consumers in the Netherlands depended for their survival on grains imported from Poland and Russia through the Baltic Sea. Thus it was possible for capitalism to flourish in western Europe only because the peasants and semifree serfs of eastern Europe provided inexpensive foods and raw materials that fueled economic development. From its earliest days, capitalist economic organization had implications for peoples and lands far removed from the centers of capitalism itself.

Profits and Ethics Capitalism also posed moral challenges. Medieval theologians had regarded profit-making activity as morally dangerous, since profiteers looked to their own advantage rather than the welfare of the larger community. Church officials even attempted to forbid the collection of interest on loans, since they considered interest an unearned and immoral profit. But profit was the lifeblood of capitalism, and bankers were not willing to risk large sums of money on business ventures without realizing returns on their investments in the form of interest. Even as it transformed the European economy, capitalism found advocates who sought to explain its principles and portray it as a socially beneficial form of economic organization. Most important of the early apostles of capitalism was the Scottish philosopher Adam Smith (1723–1790), who held that society would prosper when individuals pursued their own economic interests.

Nevertheless, the transition to capitalist society was long and painful. When individuals abandoned the practices of their ancestors and declined to help those who had fallen on hard times, their neighbors readily interpreted their actions as expressions of selfishness rather than economic prudence. Thus capitalist economic practices generated deep social strains, which often manifested themselves in violence. Bandits plagued the countryside of early modern Europe, and muggers turned whole sections of large cities into danger zones. Some historians believe that witch-hunting activities reflected social tensions generated by early capitalism and that accusations of witchcraft represented hostility toward women who were becoming economically independent of their husbands and families.

The Nuclear Family In some ways, capitalism favored the nuclear family as the principal unit of society. For centuries European couples had mostly married late—in their mid-twenties—and set up independent households. Early capitalism offered opportunities for these independent families to increase their wealth by cultivating agricultural crops or producing goods for sale on the market. As nuclear families became more important economically, they also became more socially and emotionally independent. Love between a man and a woman became a more important consideration in the making of marriages than the interests of the larger extended families, and affection between parents and their children became a more important ingredient of family life. Capitalism did not necessarily cause these changes in family life, but it may have encouraged developments that helped to define the nature and role of the family in modern European society.

SCIENCE AND ENLIGHTENMENT

While experiencing religious, political, economic, and social change, western Europe also underwent intellectual and cultural transformation. Astronomers and physicists rejected classical Greek and Roman authorities, whose theories had dominated scientific thought during the middle ages, and based their understanding of the natural world on direct observation and mathematical reasoning. During the seventeenth and eighteenth centuries, they elaborated a new vision of the earth and the larger universe. Scholars relied on observation and mathematics to transform the natural sciences in a process known as the scientific revolution. The results of early modern science were so powerful that some European intellectuals sought to overhaul moral, social, and political thought by adapting scientific methods and relying on reason rather than traditional cultural authorities. Their efforts weakened the influence of churches in western Europe and encouraged the development of secular values.

The Reconception of the Universe

The Ptolemaic Universe Until the seventeenth century, European astronomers based their understanding of the universe on the work of the Greek scholar Claudius Ptolemy of Alexandria. About the middle of the second century C.E., Ptolemy composed a work known as the *Almagest* that synthesized theories about the universe. Ptolemy envisioned a motionless earth surrounded by a series of nine hollow, concentric spheres that revolved around it. Each of the first seven spheres had one of the observable heavenly bodies—the sun, the moon, Mercury, Venus, Mars, Jupiter, and Saturn—embedded in its shell. The eighth sphere held the stars, and an empty ninth sphere surrounded the whole cosmos and provided the spin that kept all the others moving. Beyond the spheres Christian astronomers located heaven, the realm of God.

Following Ptolemy, astronomers believed that the heavens consisted of matter unlike any found on earth. Glowing like perfect jewels in the night skies, heavenly bodies were composed of a pure substance that did not experience change or corruption, and they were not subject to the physical laws that governed the world below the moon. They followed perfect circular paths in making their revolutions around the earth.

sources from the past

Adam Smith on the Capitalist Market

Adam Smith devoted special thought to the nature of early capitalist society and the principles that made it work. In 1776 he published a lengthy book entitled An Inquiry into the Nature and Causes of the Wealth of Nations, *a vastly influential work that championed free, unregulated markets and capitalist enterprise as the principal ingredients of prosperity. Smith's optimism about capitalism sprang from his conviction that society as a whole benefits when individuals pursue their own economic interests and trade on a free market.*

Every individual is continually exerting himself to find out the most advantageous employment for whatever capital he can command. It is his own advantage, indeed, and not that of the society, which he has in view. . . .

As every individual, therefore, endeavours as much as he can both to employ his capital in the support of domestic industry, and so to direct that industry that its produce may be of the greatest value, every individual necessarily labours to render the annual revenue of the society as great as he can. He generally, indeed, neither intends to promote the public interest, nor knows how much he is promoting it. By preferring the support of domestic to that of foreign industry, he intends only his own security; and by directing that industry in such a manner as its produce may be of the greatest value, he intends only his own gain, and he is in this, as in many other cases, led by an invisible hand to promote an end which was no part of his intention. Nor is it always the worse for the society that it was no part of it. By pursuing his own interest he frequently promotes that of the society more effectually than when he really intends to promote it. I have never known much good done by those who affected to trade for the public good. It is an affectation, indeed, not very common among merchants, and very few words need be employed in dissuading them from it.

What is the species of domestic industry which his capital can employ, and of which the produce is likely to be of the greatest value, every individual, it is evident, can, in his local situation, judge much better than any statesman or lawgiver can do for him. The statesman, who should attempt to direct private people in what manner they ought to employ their capitals, would not only load himself with a most unnecessary attention, but assume an authority which could safely be trusted, not only to no single person, but to no council or senate whatever, and which would nowhere be so dangerous as in the hands of a man who had folly and presumption enough to fancy himself fit to exercise it.

To give the monopoly of the home market to the produce of domestic industry, in any particular art or manufacture, is in some measure to direct private people in what manner they ought to employ their capitals, and must, in almost all cases, be either a useless or a hurtful regulation. If the produce of domestic industry can be brought there as cheap as that of foreign industry, the regulation is evidently useless. If it cannot, it must generally be hurtful. It is the maxim of every prudent master of a family, never to attempt to make at home what it will cost him more to make than to buy. The tailor does not attempt to make his own shoes, but buys them of the shoemaker. The shoemaker does not attempt to make his own clothes, but employs a tailor. The farmer attempts to make neither the one nor the other, but employs those different artificers. All of them find it for their interest to employ their whole industry in a way in which they have some advantage over their neighbours, and to purchase with a part of its produce, or, what is the same thing, with the price of a part of it, whatever else they have occasion for.

For Further Reflection

- To what extent do you think Adam Smith's analysis reflected the experiences of his own times, and to what extent did they represent universally valid observations?

Source: Adam Smith. *An Inquiry into the Nature and Causes of the Wealth of Nations.* Edinburgh: 1863, pp. 198–200.

Planetary Movement Although theoretically attractive, this earth-centered, or geocentric, cosmology did not mesh readily with the erratic movements of the planets—a term that comes from the Greek word *planetes,* meaning "wanderer." From the vantage point of the earth, the planets often followed regular courses through the skies, but they sometimes slowed down, stopped, or even turned back on their courses—motions that would be difficult to explain if the planetary spheres revolved regularly around the earth. Astronomers went to great lengths to explain planetary behavior as the result of perfect circular movements. The result was an awkward series of adjustments known as epicycles—small circular revolutions that planets made around a point in their spheres, even while the spheres themselves revolved around the earth.

The Copernican Universe As astronomers accumulated data on planetary movements, most of them sought to reconcile their observations with Ptolemaic theory by adding increasing numbers of epicycles to their cosmic maps.

In 1543, however, the Polish astronomer Nicolaus Copernicus published a treatise, *On the Revolutions of the Heavenly Spheres,* that broke with Ptolemaic theory and pointed European science in a new direction. Copernicus argued that the sun rather than the earth stood at the center of the universe and that the planets, including the earth, revolved around the sun.

Compared with Ptolemy's earth-centered universe, this new sun-centered, or heliocentric, theory harmonized much better with observational data, but it did not receive a warm welcome. Copernicus's ideas not only challenged prevailing scientific theories but also threatened cherished religious beliefs. His theory implied that the earth was just another planet and that human beings did not occupy the central position in the universe. To some it also suggested the unsettling possibility that there might be other populated worlds in the universe—a notion that would be difficult to reconcile with Christian teachings, which held that the earth and humanity were unique creations of God.

The Scientific Revolution

Although it was unpopular in many quarters, Copernicus's theory inspired some astronomers to examine the heavens in fresh ways. As evidence accumulated, it became clear that the Ptolemaic universe simply did not correspond with reality. Astronomers based their theories on increasingly precise observational data, and they relied on mathematical reasoning to organize the data. Gradually, they abandoned the Ptolemaic in favor of the Copernican model of the universe. Moreover, some of them began to apply their analytical methods to mechanics—the branch of science that deals with moving bodies—and by the mid-seventeenth century accurate observation and mathematical reasoning dominated both mechanics and astronomy. Indeed, reliance on

In this seventeenth-century engraving, Galileo Galilei faces the Inquisition, a Roman Catholic institution that prosecuted individuals accused of a wide variety of crimes related to heresy. At a trial in 1633, the Inquisition found Galileo "vehemently suspect of heresy," forced him to recant Copernicanism, and placed him under house arrest for the remainder of his life.

observation and mathematics transformed the study of the natural world and brought about the scientific revolution.

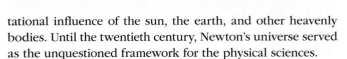

thinking about TRADITIONS

Science and the Enlightenment

Inspired by the advances in science, European intellectuals questioned long-standing beliefs concerning the nature and functioning of human society. What specific traditions did scientists and intellectuals challenge? How did religious tenets fare under such scrutiny?

Galileo Galilei The works of two scientists—Johannes Kepler of Germany and Galileo Galilei of Italy—rang the death knell for the Ptolemaic universe. Kepler (1571–1630) demonstrated that planetary orbits are elliptical, not circular as in Ptolemaic theory. Galileo (1564–1642) showed that the heavens were not the perfect, unblemished realm that Ptolemaic astronomers assumed but, rather, a world of change, flux, and many previously unsuspected sights. Galileo took a recently invented instrument—the telescope—turned it skyward, and reported observations that astonished his contemporaries. With his telescope he could see spots on the sun and mountains on the moon—observations that discredited the notion that heavenly bodies were smooth, immaculate, unchanging, and perfectly spherical. He also noticed four of the moons that orbit the planet Jupiter—bodies that no human being had ever before observed—and he caught sight of previously unknown distant stars, which implied that the universe was much larger than anyone had previously suspected.

In addition to his astronomical discoveries, Galileo contributed to the understanding of terrestrial motion. He designed ingenious experiments to show that the velocity of falling bodies depends not on their weight but, rather, on the height from which they fall. This claim brought him scorn from scientists who subscribed to scientific beliefs deriving from Aristotle. But it offered a better explanation of how moving bodies behave under the influence of the earth's gravitational pull. Galileo also anticipated the modern law of inertia, which holds that a moving body will continue to move in a straight line until some force intervenes to check or alter its motion.

Isaac Newton The new approach to science culminated in the work of the English mathematician Isaac Newton (1642–1727), who depended on accurate observation and mathematical reasoning to construct a powerful synthesis of astronomy and mechanics. Newton outlined his views on the natural world in an epoch-making volume of 1687 entitled *Mathematical Principles of Natural Philosophy.* Newton's work united the heavens and the earth in a vast, cosmic system. He argued that a law of universal gravitation regulates the motions of bodies throughout the universe, and he offered precise mathematical explanations of the laws that govern movements of bodies on the earth. Newton's laws of universal gravitation and motion enabled him to synthesize the sciences of astronomy and mechanics. They also allowed him to explain a vast range of seemingly unrelated phenomena, such as the ebb and flow of the tides, which move according to the gravitational pull of the moon, and the eccentric orbits of planets and comets, which reflect the gravitational influence of the sun, the earth, and other heavenly bodies. Until the twentieth century, Newton's universe served as the unquestioned framework for the physical sciences.

Newton's work symbolized the scientific revolution, but it by no means marked the end of the process by which observation and mathematical reasoning transformed European science. Inspired by the dramatic discoveries of astronomers and physicists, other scientists began to turn away from classical authorities and to construct fresh approaches to the understanding of the natural world. During the seventeenth and eighteenth centuries, anatomy, physiology, microbiology, chemistry, and botany underwent a thorough overhaul, as scientists tested their theories against direct observation of natural phenomena and explained them in rigorous mathematical terms.

Women and Science

In the sixteenth and seventeenth centuries, Europe's learned men challenged some of the most hallowed traditions concerning the nature of the physical universe and supplanted them with new scientific principles. Yet, when male scientists studied female anatomy, female physiology, and women's reproductive organs, they were commonly guided not by scientific observation but by tradition, prejudice, and fanciful imagination. William Harvey (1578–1657), the English physician who discovered the principles of the circulation of human blood, also applied his considerable talents to the study of human reproduction. After careful dissection and observation of female deer, chickens, and roosters, he hypothesized that women, like hens, served as mere receptacles for the "vivifying" male fluid. According to him, it was the male semen—endowed with generative powers so potent that it did not even have to reach the uterus to work its magic—from which the unfertilized egg received life and form. Anatomy, physiology, and limited reproductive function seemed to confirm the innate inferiority of women, adding a "scientific" veneer to the traditionally limited images, roles, and functions of women. With the arrival of printing, men were able to disseminate more widely those negative conclusions about women.

Émilie du Châtelet Despite prevailing critical attitudes, some women found themselves drawn to the new intellectual currents of the time. Women formulated their own

Émilie du Châtelet was perhaps the most exceptional female scientist of the Enlightenment. Although she had to contend with the conventional demands on women, she remained committed to her study of Newton and science.

theories about the natural world and published their findings. One of the most notable female scientists of her age was Émilie du Châtelet (1706–1749), a French mathematician and physicist. Long famous for being the mistress of the celebrated French intellectual Voltaire, she was in fact a talented intellectual and scientist in her own right. A precocious child, du Châtelet was apparently fluent in six languages at the age of twelve, and she benefited from having an unusually enlightened father who provided his rebellious daughter with an education more typical for boys. Her obvious intellectual abilities made her mother despair over her daughter's future, and her mother complained about a daughter who "flaunts her mind, and frightens away the suitors her other excesses have not driven off." Émilie du Châtelet nonetheless did marry, as was custom, and she had three children with her husband, the Marquis du Châtelet. She did this while also engaged in affairs of the intellect.

Du Châtelet established her reputation as a scientist with her three-volume work on the German mathematician Gottfried Leibniz (1646–1716) in 1740. Her crowning achievement, however, was her translation of Isaac Newton's monumental work *Principia Mathematica,* which has remained the standard French translation of the work. She did not simply render Newton's words into another language, however; rather, she explained his complex mathematics in graceful prose, transformed his geometry into calculus, and assessed the current state of Newtonian physics. She finished her work in the year of her death, at age forty-three, six days after giving birth to a child. Underscoring the difficulty of reconciling a woman's reproductive duties with her intellectual aspirations was her lover Voltaire's commentary. He declared in a letter to his friend Frederick II, King of Prussia (reigned 1740–1786), that du Châtelet was "a great man whose only fault was being a woman."

The Enlightenment

Newton's vision of the universe was so powerful and persuasive that its influence extended well beyond science. His work suggested that rational analysis of human behavior and institutions could lead to fresh insights about the human as well as the natural world. From Scotland to Sicily and from Philadelphia to Moscow, European and Euro-American thinkers launched an ambitious project to transform human thought and to use reason to transform the world. Like the early modern scientists, they abandoned Aristotelian philosophy, Christian theology, and other traditionally recognized authorities, and they sought to subject the human world to purely rational analysis. The result of their work was a movement known as the Enlightenment.

Science and Society

Enlightenment thinkers sought to discover natural laws that governed human society in the same way that Newton's laws of universal gravitation and motion regulated the universe. Their search took different forms. The English philosopher John Locke (1632–1704) worked to discover natural laws of politics. He attacked divine-right theories that served as a foundation for absolute monarchy and advocated constitutional government on the grounds that sovereignty resides in the people rather than the state or its rulers. Indeed, he provided much of the theoretical justification for the Glorious Revolution and the establishment of constitutional monarchy in England. The Scottish philosopher Adam Smith turned his attention to economic affairs and held that laws of supply and demand determine what happens in the marketplace. The French nobleman Charles Louis de Secondat, better known as the Baron de Montesquieu (1689–1755), sought to establish a science of politics and discover principles that would foster political liberty in a prosperous and stable state.

The center of Enlightenment thought was France, where prominent intellectuals known collectively as *philosophes* ("philosophers") advanced the cause of reason. The philo-

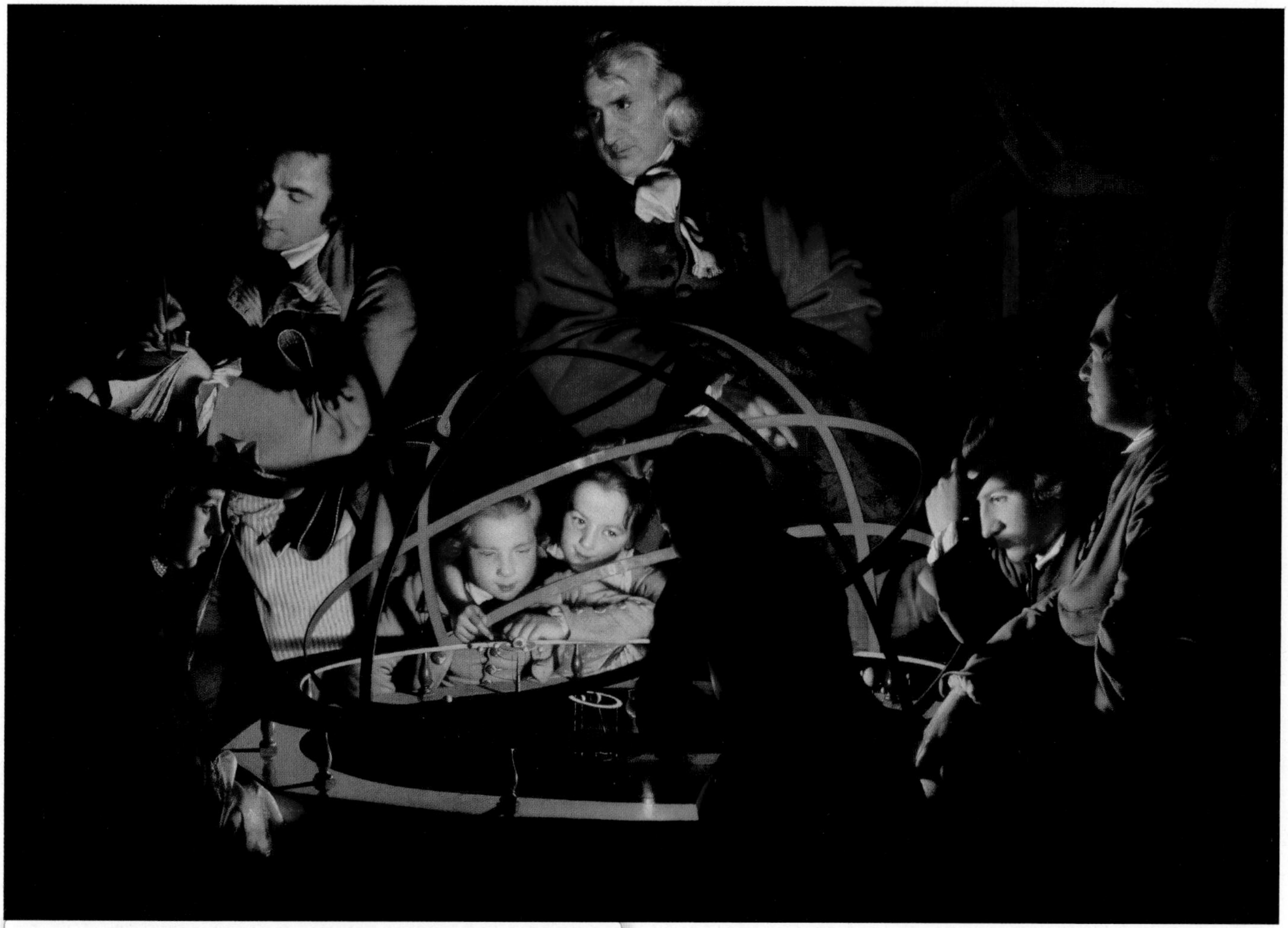

Joseph Wright of Derby's painting entitled "A philosopher gives a lecture on the orrery" centers on a three-dimensional image of the cosmos (the orrery); his use of light offers a metaphor for the Enlightenment and natural philosophy.

sophes were not philosophers in the traditional sense of the term so much as public intellectuals. They addressed their works more to the educated public than to scholars: instead of formal philosophical treatises, they mostly composed histories, novels, dramas, satires, and pamphlets on religious, moral, and political issues.

Voltaire More than any other philosophe, François-Marie Arouet (1694–1778) epitomized the spirit of the Enlightenment. Writing under the pen name Voltaire, he published his first book at age seventeen. By the time of his death at age eighty-four, his published writings included some ten thousand letters and filled seventy volumes. With stinging wit and sometimes bitter irony, Voltaire championed individual freedom and attacked any institution sponsoring intolerant or oppressive policies. Targets of his caustic wit included the French monarchy and the Roman Catholic church. When the king of France sought to save money by reducing the number of horses kept in royal stables, for example, Voltaire suggested that it would be more effective to get rid of the asses who rode the horses. Voltaire also waged a long literary campaign against the Roman Catholic church, which he held responsible for fanaticism, intolerance, and incalculable human suffering. Voltaire's battle cry was *écrasez l'infame* ("crush the damned thing"), meaning the church that he considered an agent of oppression.

Deism Some philosophes were conventional Christians, and a few turned to atheism. Like Voltaire, however, most of them were deists who believed in the existence of a god but denied the supernatural teachings of Christianity, such as Jesus' virgin birth and his resurrection. To the deists the universe was an orderly realm. Deists held that a powerful god set the universe in motion and established natural laws that govern it, but did not take a personal interest in its development or intervene in its affairs. In a favorite simile of the deists, this god was like a watchmaker who did not need

sources from the past

John Locke Claims People Are the Products of Their Environment

John Locke (1632–1704) was one of the leading intellectuals of his age. Although commonly recognized as an influential political theorist, he was also intensely curious about how humans acquired knowledge. In his seminal An Essay Concerning Human Understanding *(1690), Locke repudiates the prevailing view that knowledge—knowledge of certain moral truths or knowledge of the existence of God, for example—is innate, that is, imprinted on the human mind at birth. He argues instead that the foundation of all knowledge is sense experience (sensation), like the color of a flower, and awareness that one is thinking (reflection). These "ideas" provide the mind with knowledge.*

The way shown how we come by any knowledge, sufficient to prove it not innate. It is an established opinion amongst some men, that there are in the understanding certain innate principles; some primary notions, characters, as it were stamped upon the mind of man; which the soul receives in its very first being, and brings into the world with it. It would be sufficient to convince unprejudiced readers of the falseness of this supposition, if I should only show (as I hope I shall in the following parts of this Discourse) how men, barely by the use of their natural faculties, may attain to all the knowledge they have, without the help of any innate impressions; and may arrive at certainty, without any such original notions or principles. . . .

All ideas come from sensation or reflection. Let us then suppose the mind to be, as we say, white paper, void of all characters, without any ideas:—How comes it to be furnished? Whence comes it by that vast store which the busy and boundless fancy of man has painted on it with an almost endless variety? Whence has it all the materials of reason and knowledge? To this I answer, in one word, from Experience. In that all our knowledge is founded; and from that it ultimately derives itself. Our observation employed either, about external sensible objects, or about the internal operations of our minds perceived and reflected on by ourselves, is that which supplies our understandings with all the materials of thinking. These two are the fountains of knowledge, from whence all the ideas we have, or can naturally have, do spring.

The objects of sensation one source of ideas. First, our Senses, conversant about particular sensible objects, do convey into the mind several distinct perceptions of things, according to those various ways wherein those objects do affect them. And thus we come by those ideas we have of yellow, white, heat, cold, soft, hard, bitter, sweet, and all those which we call sensible qualities; which when I say the senses convey into the mind, I mean, they from external objects convey into the mind what produces there those perceptions. This great source of most of the ideas we have, depending wholly upon our senses, and derived by them to the understanding, I call Sensation.

The operations of our minds, the other source of them. Secondly, the other fountain from which experience furnisheth the understanding with ideas is,—the perception of the operations of our own mind within us, as it is employed about the ideas it has got;—which operations, when the soul comes to reflect on and consider, do furnish the understanding with another set of ideas, which could not be had from things without. And such are perception, thinking, doubting, believing, reasoning, knowing, willing, and all the different actings of our own minds;—which we being conscious of, and observing in ourselves, do from these receive into our understandings as distinct ideas as we do from bodies affecting our senses. This source of ideas every man has wholly in himself; and though it be not sense, as having nothing to do with external objects, yet it is very like it, and might properly enough be called internal sense. But as I call the other Sensation, so I Call this Reflection, the ideas it affords being such only as the mind gets by reflecting on its own operations within itself.

For Further Reflection

- What are the implications of Locke's claim for the development of human society that people are solely the products of their environment? How are those implications bound up with criticism of existing social structures?

Source: John Locke. *An Essay Concerning Human Understanding.* Kitchener, Ontario, Canada: Batoche Books, 1690, pp. 24, 73, 74. http://site.ebrary.com/lib/uhmanoa/Doc?id=2001993&ppg=24, 73, 74.

to interfere constantly in the workings of his creation, since it operated by itself according to rational and natural laws.

The Theory of Progress Most philosophes were optimistic about the future of the world and humanity. They expected knowledge of human affairs to advance as fast as modern science, and they believed that rational understanding of human and natural affairs would bring about a new era of constant progress. In fact, progress became almost an ideology of the philosophes, who believed that natural science would lead to greater human control over the world while rational sciences of human affairs would lead to indi-

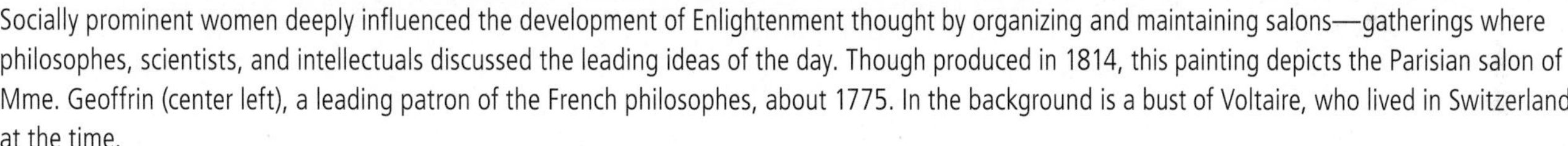

Socially prominent women deeply influenced the development of Enlightenment thought by organizing and maintaining salons—gatherings where philosophes, scientists, and intellectuals discussed the leading ideas of the day. Though produced in 1814, this painting depicts the Parisian salon of Mme. Geoffrin (center left), a leading patron of the French philosophes, about 1775. In the background is a bust of Voltaire, who lived in Switzerland at the time.

vidual freedom and the construction of a prosperous, just, and equitable society.

The philosophes' fond wishes for progress, prosperity, and social harmony did not come to pass. Yet the Enlightenment helped to bring about a thorough cultural transformation of European society. It weakened the influence of organized religion, although it by no means destroyed institutional churches. Enlightenment thought encouraged the replacement of Christian values, which had guided European thought on religious and moral affairs for more than a millennium, with a new set of secular values arising from reason rather than revelation. Furthermore, the Enlightenment encouraged political and cultural leaders to subject society to rational analysis and intervene actively in its affairs in the interests of promoting progress and prosperity. In many ways, the Enlightenment legacy continues to influence European and Euro-American societies.

inperspective

During the early modern era, European society experienced a series of profound and sometimes unsettling changes. The Protestant Reformation ended the religious unity of western Christendom, and intermittent religious conflict disrupted European society for a century and more. Centralizing monarchs strengthened their realms and built a society of sovereign, autonomous, and intensely competitive states. Capitalist entrepreneurs reorganized the production and distribution of manufactured goods, and although their methods led to increased wealth, their quest for efficiency and profits clashed with traditional values. Modern science based on direct observation and mathematical explanations emerged as a powerful tool for the investigation of the natural world, and its influence extended even to thought about human affairs. Some people rejected traditional religious beliefs altogether and worked toward the construction of a new moral thought based strictly on science and reason. At just the time that European merchants, colonists, and adventurers were seeking opportunities in the larger world, European society was becoming more powerful, more experimental, and more competitive than ever before. ●

CHRONOLOGY	
1473–1543	Life of Nicolaus Copernicus
1478	Foundation of the Spanish Inquisition
1483–1546	Life of Martin Luther
1491–1556	Life of Ignatius Loyola
1509–1547	Reign of King Henry VIII
1509–1564	Life of John Calvin
1517	Publication of the *Ninety-Five Theses*
1519–1556	Reign of Emperor Charles V
1540	Foundation of the Society of Jesus
1545–1563	Council of Trent
1556–1598	Reign of King Philip II
1564–1642	Life of Galileo Galilei
1571–1630	Life of Johannes Kepler
1588	Spanish Armada
1618–1648	Thirty Years' War
1632–1704	Life of John Locke
1642–1727	Life of Isaac Newton
1643–1715	Reign of King Louis XIV
1648	Peace of Westphalia
1689–1755	Life of the Baron de Montesquieu
1694–1778	Life of Voltaire
1706–1749	Life of Émilie du Châtelet
1723–1790	Life of Adam Smith

For Further Reading

Philip Benedict. *Christ's Churches Purely Reformed: A Social History of Calvinism.* New Haven, 2002. Impressive and very readable synthesis of the history of Calvinism and the general impact of the Protestant Reformation in Europe.

William J. Bouwsma. *John Calvin: A Sixteenth-Century Portrait.* New York, 1989. A penetrating examination of one of the principal Protestant reformers.

Fernand Braudel. *Civilization and Capitalism, 15th to 18th Century.* 3 vols. Trans. by S. Reynolds. New York, 1981–84. A rich analysis of early capitalist society by one of the greatest historians of the twentieth century.

Paul Dukes. *The Making of Russian Absolutism, 1613–1801.* 2nd ed. London, 1990. A succinct study of two disparate centuries, the seventeenth and eighteenth, and two influential tsars, Peter and Catherine.

Robert S. Duplessis. *Transitions to Capitalism in Early Modern Europe.* Cambridge, 1997. A valuable synthesis of research on early capitalism and protoindustrialization.

Elizabeth L. Eisenstein. *The Printing Press as an Agent of Change.* 2 vols. Cambridge, 1979. An insightful study that examines the significance of printing for the Protestant Reformation and the scientific revolution.

Patricia Fara. *Pandora's Breeches: Women, Science, and Power in the Enlightenment.* London, 2004. An engaging account of the contributions women made to science in the seventeenth and eighteenth centuries.

Peter Gay. *The Enlightenment: An Interpretation.* 2 vols. New York, 1966–69. A classic study making the case for the Enlightenment as a turning point in European cultural history.

Philip S. Gorski. *The Disciplinary Revolution: Calvinism and the Rise of the Early Modern State.* Chicago, 2003. Argues that the formation of strong European states was a result of religious and social control policies initiated by the Protestant Reformation.

Margaret Jacob. *The Cultural Meaning of the Scientific Revolution.* New York, 1989. Explores the larger cultural and social implications of early modern science.

Lisa Jardine. *Ingenious Pursuits: Building the Scientific Revolution.* New York, 1999. A close study of the messy context of the scientific revolution and of the ambiguous boundary between what have come to be thought of as the natural and the human sciences.

E. L. Jones. *The European Miracle: Environments, Economies, and Geopolitics in the History of Europe and Asia.* 2nd ed. Cambridge, 1987. Examines European politics and economic growth in comparative perspective.

———. *Growth Recurring: Economic Change in World History.* Oxford, 1988. Compares processes of economic growth in China, Europe, and Japan.

Leonard Krieger. *Kings and Philosophers, 1689–1789.* New York, 1970. A thoughtful analysis of European history during an age of absolutism and Enlightenment.

Thomas S. Kuhn. *The Structure of Scientific Revolutions.* 3rd ed. Chicago, 1997. An influential theoretical work that views scientific thought in larger social and cultural contexts.

Brian P. Levack. *The Witch-Hunt in Early Modern Europe.* New York, 1987. A compact but comprehensive survey of European witchcraft beliefs and pursuit of witches in the sixteenth and seventeenth centuries.

William H. McNeill. *The Pursuit of Power: Technology, Armed Force, and Society since A.D. 1000.* Chicago, 1982. Insightful analysis exploring the influence of sovereign states and early capitalism on military technology and organization.

Jerry Z. Muller. *The Mind and the Market: Capitalism in Modern European Thought.* New York, 2002. Broad history of the development of capitalism through the eyes of major European thinkers, including Adam Smith, Joseph Schumpeter, and Karl Marx.

Heiko A. Oberman. *Luther: Man between God and the Devil.* Trans. by E. Walliser-Schwartzbart. New Haven, 1989. A perceptive study of the first Protestant reformer by a foremost scholar.

Geoffrey Parker. *The Military Revolution: Military Innovation and the Rise of the West, 1500–1800.* Cambridge, 1988. A thoughtful essay on European military affairs in early modern times.

Kenneth Pomeranz. *The Great Divergence: China, Europe, and the Making of the Modern World Economy.* Princeton, 2000. Pathbreaking scholarly study that illuminates the economic history of the early modern world through comparison of economic development in Asian and European lands.

Roy Porter. *The Creation of the Modern World: The Untold Story of the British Enlightenment.* New York, 2000. An important work that returns the Enlightenment to Britain.

Eugene F. Rice Jr. and Anthony Grafton. *The Foundations of Early Modern Europe, 1460–1559.* 2nd ed. New York, 1994. Excellent introduction to political, social, economic, and cultural developments.

Jessica Riskin. *Science in the Age of Sensibility: The Sentimental Empiricists of the French Enlightenment.* Chicago, 2002. Study of the development of modern science not simply as a result of empiricism but also of sentimental, humanist sensibility.

Daniel Roche. *France in the Enlightenment.* Trans. by Arthur Goldhammer. Cambridge, Mass., 1998. Comprehensive account of the French Enlightenment and some of its most significant cultural, social, and political contexts.

Paolo Rossi. *The Birth of Modern Science.* Malden, Mass., 2001. Explores specific seventeenth-century value systems and traditions that were central to the rise of modern science.

Simon Schama. *The Embarrassment of Riches: An Interpretation of Dutch Culture in the Seventeenth Century.* New York, 1987. A marvelous popular study of the wealthy Dutch republic at its height.

Keith Thomas. *Religion and the Decline of Magic.* New York, 1971. A riveting analysis of popular culture in early modern times, especially strong on the explanation of magic and witchcraft.

James Van Horn Melton. *The Rise of the Public in Enlightenment Europe.* Cambridge, 2001. Work on the cultural aspects of the Enlightenment and the emergence of a public sphere in Britain, France, and German-speaking territories.

New Worlds: The Americas and Oceania

chapter 24

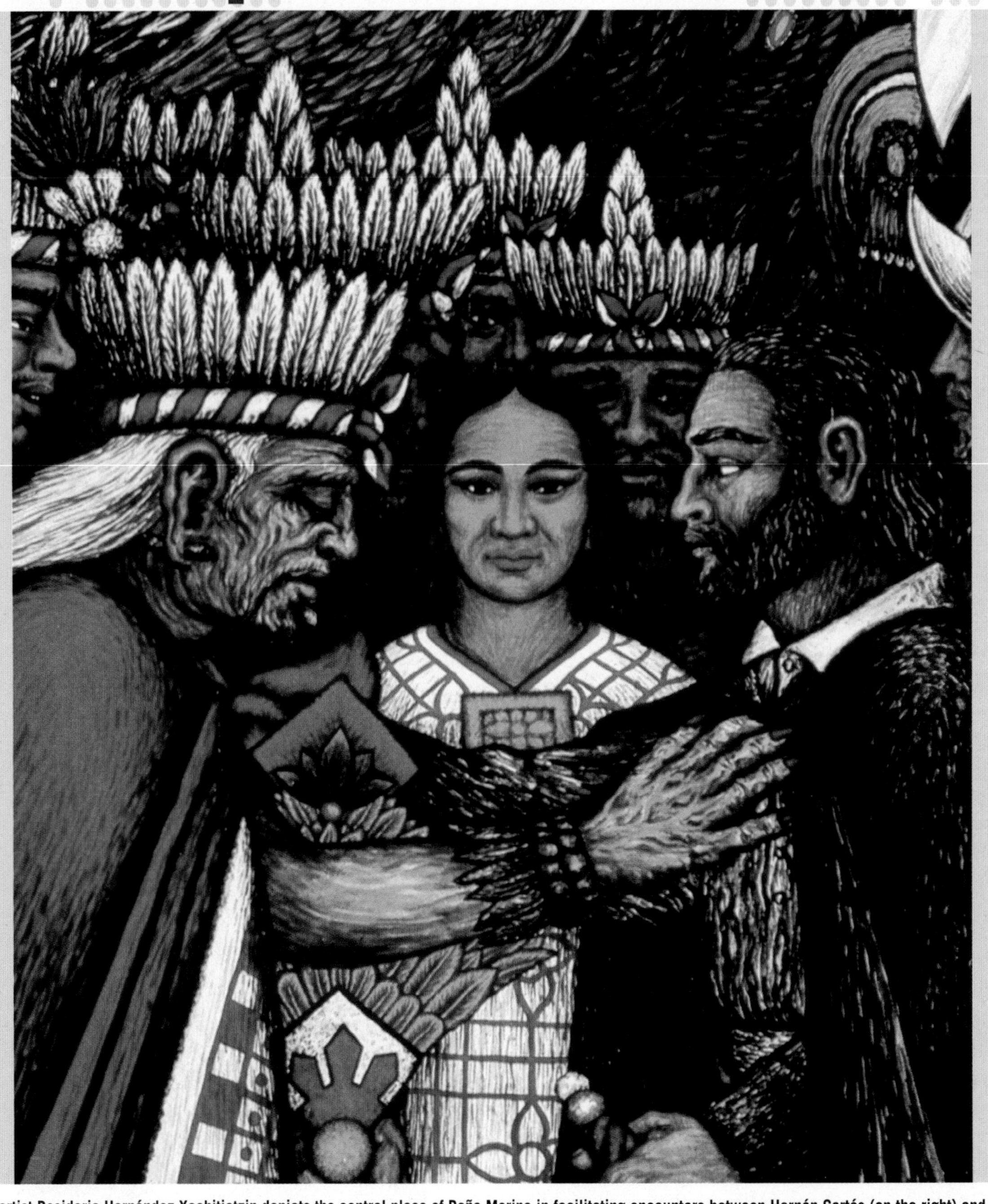

A mural by Tlaxala artist Desiderio Hernández Xochitiotzin depicts the central place of Doña Marina in facilitating encounters between Hernán Cortés (on the right) and the indigenous peoples of Mexico.

EYEWITNESS:
The Mysterious Identity of Doña Marina

A remarkable young woman played a pivotal role in the Spanish conquest of Mexico. Originally called Malintzin, over the years she has come to be better known as Doña Marina, the name bestowed on her by Spanish forces. Doña Marina was born about 1500 to a noble family in central Mexico. Her mother tongue was Nahuatl, the principal language of the Aztec empire. When she was a girl, Doña Marina's family sent her to the Mexican coast as a slave, and her new family later passed her on to their neighbors in the Yucatan peninsula. During her travels she became fluent in Maya as well as her native Nahuatl language.

When Hernán Cortés arrived on the Mexican coast in 1519, his small army included a Spanish soldier who had learned the Maya language during a period of captivity in the Yucatan. But he had no way to communicate with the Nahuatl-speaking peoples of central Mexico until a Maya chieftain presented him with twelve young women, including Doña Marina, when he entered into an alliance with the foreigner. Doña Marina's linguistic talents enabled Cortés to communicate through an improbable chain of languages—from Spanish to Maya to Nahuatl and then back again—while making his way to the Aztec capital of Tenochtitlan. (Doña Marina soon learned Spanish and thus eliminated the Maya link in the linguistic chain.)

Doña Marina provided Cortés with intelligence and diplomatic as well as linguistic services. On several occasions she learned of plans by native peoples to overwhelm and destroy the tiny Spanish army, and she alerted Cortés to the danger in time for him to forestall an attack. Once, she was able to report the precise details of a planned ambush because she played along with an effort to bring her into the scheme. She also helped Cortés negotiate with emissaries from Tenochtitlan and other major cities of central Mexico. Indeed, in the absence of Doña Marina's services, it is difficult to see how Cortés's small band could have survived to see the Aztec capital.

Precisely because of her pivotal role in aiding Cortés and forwarding his invasion of the Aztec empire, Doña Marina earned another name commonly bestowed on her in Mexican history: La Malinche, or the traitor. The belief that she betrayed her people by collaborating with the Spanish underscored how native Americans faced many challenges and conflicts in their encounters with Europeans. Other subjects of the Aztec empire also chose to ally themselves with the Spanish given their disaffection from Aztec imperial rule, so Doña Marina represented the existing divisions within Mesoamerican society as well as the demonstrated bravery, intelligence, and survival skills of a woman often harshly treated. Because of her symbolic richness, she has likewise attained the status of mother of the Mexican peoples.

Apart from facilitating the Spanish conquest of the Aztec empire, Doña Marina played a role in the formation of a new society in Mexico. In 1522, one year after the fall of Tenochtitlan, she gave birth to a son fathered by Cortés, and in 1526 she bore a daughter to a Spanish captain whom she had married. Her offspring were not the first children born in the western hemisphere of indigenous and Spanish parentage, but they symbolize the early emergence of a mestizo population in Mexico. Doña Marina died soon after the birth of her daughter, probably in 1527, but during her short life she contributed to the thorough transformation of Mexican society.

Until 1492 the peoples of the eastern and western hemispheres had few dealings with one another. About 1000 C.E. Norse explorers established a short-lived colony in modern Newfoundland, and sporadic encounters between European fishermen and indigenous peoples of North America probably occurred before Christopher Columbus undertook his first voyage across the Atlantic Ocean. It is likely, too, that an occasional Asian or Austronesian mariner reached the Pacific coast of North or South America before 1492. Yet travel between the eastern hemisphere, the western hemisphere, and Oceania was too irregular and infrequent to generate interaction between peoples of different societies until the fifteenth century.

After 1492, however, the voyages of European mariners led to permanent and sustained contact between the peoples of the eastern hemisphere, the western hemisphere, and Oceania. The resulting encounters brought profound and often violent change to both American and Pacific lands. European peoples possessed powerful military weapons, horses, and sailing ships that provided them with technological advantages over the peoples they encountered in the Americas and the Pacific islands. Moreover, most Europeans also enjoyed complete or partial immunity to diseases that caused demographic disasters when introduced to the western hemisphere and Oceania. Because of their technological advantages and the wholesale depopulation that followed from epidemic diseases, European peoples were able to establish a presence throughout the Americas and much of the Pacific Ocean basin.

The European presence did not lead to immediate change in Australia and the Pacific islands, although it laid a foundation for dramatic and often traumatic change in the nineteenth and twentieth centuries. In the western hemisphere, however, large numbers of European migrants helped to bring about a profound transformation of American societies in early modern times. In Mexico and Peru, Spanish conquerors established territorial empires that were ruled from Spain. In Brazil, Portuguese entrepreneurs founded sugar plantations and imported African slaves to perform the heavy labor required for their operation. In North America, French, English, and Dutch fur traders allied with indigenous peoples who provided them with animal skins, and their more sedentary compatriots founded settler societies concentrating on the production of cash crops for export. Throughout the western hemisphere, peoples of European, African, and American ancestry interacted to fashion new worlds.

COLLIDING WORLDS

When European peoples first sought to establish their presence in the Americas, they brought a range of technology unavailable to the peoples they encountered in the western hemisphere. Even more important than European technology, however, were the divisions between indigenous peoples that Europeans were able to exploit and the effects of epidemic diseases that devastated native societies. Soon after their arrival in the western hemisphere, Spanish conquerors toppled the Aztec and Inca empires and imposed their own rule in Mexico and Peru. In later decades Portuguese planters built sugar plantations on the Brazilian coastline. French, English, and Dutch migrants displaced indigenous peoples in North America and established settler colonies under the rule of European peoples.

One of the earliest European depictions of Native Americans was this engraving of 1505. The caption informed readers that American peoples lived in communal society, where men took several wives but none had private possessions, and that they routinely smoked and consumed the bodies of slain enemies. How might such representations have shaped European ideas about native Americans?

The Spanish Caribbean

The Taíno

The first site of interaction between European and American peoples was the Caribbean. When Spanish mariners arrived there, the Taíno (also known as Arawaks) were the most prominent people in the region. During the late centuries B.C.E., the ancestors of the Taíno had sailed in canoes from the Orinoco River valley in South America to the Caribbean islands, and by about 900 C.E. they had settled throughout the region. The Taíno cultivated manioc and other crops, and they lived in small villages under the authority of chiefs who allocated land to families and supervised community affairs. They showed interest in the glass, beads, and metal tools that Spanish mariners brought as trade goods and offered little initial resistance to the visitors.

Spanish Arrival

Christopher Columbus and his immediate followers made the island of Hispaniola (which embraces modern Haiti and the Dominican Republic) the base of Spanish operations in the Caribbean. There, Spanish settlers established the fort of Santo Domingo, and the city, officially founded in 1498, became the capital of the Spanish Caribbean. Columbus's original plan was to build forts and trading posts where merchants could trade with local peoples for products desired by European consumers. Within a few years of Spanish arrival, however, it became clear that the Caribbean region offered no silks or spices for the European market. If Spanish settlers wanted to maintain their presence in the Caribbean, they would need to find some way to make a living.

The settlers first attempted to support their society by mining gold. Spanish settlers were too few in number to mine

sources from the past

First Impressions of Spanish Forces

As the Spanish army made its way to Tenochtitlan, Motecuzoma dispatched a series of emissaries to communicate with Cortés and learn his intentions. The following document, based on indigenous accounts but filtered through imperial Spanish sensibilities, suggested that Motecuzoma reacted with fright when presented with reports that were less than reassuring, since they focused on fearsome weapons and animals of the Spanish. Given the martial response of the Aztecs to the Spanish invasion, it seems highly unlikely that Motecuzoma or the Aztecs would have expressed terror in such a humiliating fashion.

And when [Motecuzoma] had heard what the messengers reported, he was terrified, he was astounded. . . .

Especially did it cause him to faint away when he heard how the gun, at [the Spaniards'] command, discharged [the shot]; how it resounded as if it thundered when it went off. It indeed bereft one of strength; it shut off one's ears. And when it discharged, something like a round pebble came forth from within. Fire went showering forth; sparks went blazing forth. And its smoke smelled very foul; it had a fetid odor which verily wounded the head. And when [the shot] struck a mountain, it was as if it were destroyed, dissolved. And a tree was pulverized; it was as if it vanished; it was as if someone blew it away.

All iron was their war array. In iron they clothed themselves. With iron they covered their heads. Iron were their swords. Iron were their crossbows. Iron were their shields. Iron were their lances.

And those which bore them upon their backs, their deer [that is, horses], were as tall as roof terraces.

And their bodies were everywhere covered; only their faces appeared. They were very white; they had chalky faces; they had yellow hair, though the hair of some was black. Long were their beards; they also were yellow. They were yellow-headed. [The black men's hair] was kinky, it was curly.

And their food was like fasting food—very large, white, not heavy like [tortillas]; like maize stalks, good-tasting as if of maize stalk flour; a little sweet, a little honeyed. It was honeyed to eat; it was sweet to eat.

And their dogs were very large. They had ears folded over; great dragging jowls. They had fiery eyes—blazing eyes; they had yellow eyes—fiery yellow eyes. They had thin flanks—flanks with ribs showing. They had gaunt stomachs. They were very tall. They were nervous; they went about panting, with tongues hanging out. They were spotted like ocelots; they were varicolored.

And when Motecuzoma heard all this, he was much terrified. It was as if he fainted away. His heart saddened; his heart failed him.

For Further Reflection

- What did the Spanish and their indigenous allies hope to gain by presenting this image of Motecuzoma?

Source: Bernardino de Sahagún. *Florentine Codex: General History of the Things of New Spain,* 13 vols. Trans. by Arthur J. O. Anderson and Charles E. Dibble. Salt Lake City: University of Utah Press, 1950–82, 13:19–20. (Translation slightly modified.)

gold—and in any case they were not inclined to perform heavy physical labor—so the miners came largely from the ranks of the Taíno. Recruitment of labor came through an institution known as the ***encomienda,*** which gave Spanish *encomenderos* ("settlers") the right to compel the Taíno to work in their mines or fields. In return for labor, *encomenderos* assumed responsibility to look after their workers' health and welfare and to encourage their conversion to Christianity.

Conscription of Taíno labor was a brutal business. *Encomenderos* worked their charges hard and punished them severely when they did not deliver the expected quantities of gold or work sufficiently hard in the fields. The Taíno occasionally organized rebellions, but their bows, arrows, and slings had little effect against horse-mounted Spanish forces wielding steel swords and firearms. By about 1515, social disruption and physical abuse had brought decline to Taíno populations on the large Caribbean islands—Hispaniola, Jamaica, Puerto Rico, and Cuba—favored by Spanish settlers.

Smallpox Serious demographic decline set in only after 1518, however, when smallpox reached the Caribbean region and touched off devastating epidemics among the peoples of the western hemisphere. To replace laborers lost to disease, *encomenderos* launched raiding parties to kidnap and enslave the Taíno and other peoples. This tactic exposed additional victims to introduced diseases and hastened the decline of indigenous populations.

Under pressure of epidemic disease, the native population of the Caribbean plummeted from about four million in 1492 to a few thousand in the 1540s. Native societies

encomienda (ehn-KOH-mee-ehn-dah)

themselves also passed out of existence. Only a few Taíno cultural elements survived: *canoe, hammock, hurricane, barbecue, maize,* and *tobacco* all derive from Taíno words, but the society that generated them had largely disappeared by the middle of the sixteenth century.

From Mining to Plantation Agriculture Deposits of gold were thin in the Caribbean, but optimistic Spanish adventurers continued to seek treasure there for a century and more. After the mid-sixteenth century, however, when Spanish explorers located exceptionally rich sources of silver in Mexico and Peru, the Caribbean became a sleepy backwater of the Spanish empire. English pirates lurked in Caribbean waters hoping to intercept imperial fleets carrying American silver to Spain, but the region was not a center of production. Then, about the 1640s, French, English, and Dutch settlers began to flock to the Caribbean with the intention of establishing plantations. It became clear that even if the Caribbean islands lacked precious metals, they offered ideal conditions for the cultivation of cash crops, particularly sugar, which would fetch high prices in European markets. Later, tobacco also became a prime cash crop of the region. Meanwhile, because indigenous populations were extinct, planters lacked the labor they needed to operate their estates, so they imported several million slaves. By 1700 Caribbean society consisted of a small class of European administrators and large masses of African slaves.

The Conquest of Mexico and Peru

Spanish interest soon shifted from the Caribbean to the American mainland, where settlers hoped to find more resources to exploit. During the early sixteenth century, Spanish *conquistadores* ("conquerors") pressed beyond the Caribbean islands, moving west into Mexico and south into Panama and Peru. Between 1519 and 1521 Hernán Cortés and a small band of men brought down the Aztec empire in Mexico, and between 1532 and 1533 Francisco Pizarro and his followers toppled the Inca empire in Peru. Those conquests laid the foundations for colonial regimes that would transform the Americas.

In Mexico and Peru, Spanish explorers found societies quite different from those of the Caribbean islands. Both Mexico and Peru had been sites of agricultural societies, cities, and large states for more than a millennium. In the early fifteenth century, both lands fell under the sway of powerful imperial states: the Mexica people and their allies founded the Aztec empire that expanded to embrace most of Mesoamerica, while the Incas imposed their rule on a vast realm extending from modern Ecuador in the north to modern Chile in the south—the largest state South America had ever seen. The Aztec and Inca empires both had clear lines of political authority, and both had the means to mobilize massive populations, collect taxes or tribute to maintain their societies, and recruit labor for public works projects. (See chapter 20.)

Hernán Cortés The conquest of Mexico began with an expedition to search for gold on the American mainland. In 1519 Cortés led about 450 soldiers to Mexico and made his way from Veracruz on the Gulf coast to the island city of Tenochtitlan, the stunningly beautiful Aztec capital situated in Lake Texcoco. They seized the emperor Motecuzoma II, who died in 1520 during a skirmish between Spanish forces and residents of Tenochtitlan. Aztec forces soon drove the conquistadores from the capital, and Cuauhtémoc (ca. 1502–1525)—the nephew and son-in-law of Motecuzoma—emerged as the last Aztec emperor. Cortés built a small fleet of ships, placed Tenochtitlan under siege, and in 1521 starved the city into surrender. Cuauhtémoc stood up to the torture Cortés inflicted upon him in an attempt to uncover the whereabouts of Aztec gold and treasures, but he did not escape the execution ordered by Cortés in 1525.

Steel swords, muskets, cannons, and horses offered Cortés and his soldiers some advantage over the forces they met and help to account for the Spanish conquest of the Aztec empire. Yet weaponry alone clearly would not enable Cortés's tiny force to overcome a large, densely populated society. Quite apart from military technology, Cortés's expedition benefited from divisions among the indigenous peoples of Mexico. With the aid of Doña Marina, the conquistadores forged alliances with peoples who resented domination by the Mexica, the leaders of the Aztec empire, and who reinforced the small Spanish army with thousands of veteran warriors. Native allies also provided Spanish forces with logistical support and secure bases in friendly territory.

Epidemic Disease On the mainland, as in the Caribbean, epidemic disease aided Spanish efforts. During the siege of Tenochtitlan, smallpox raged through the city, killing inhabitants by the tens of thousands and fatally sapping the strength of defensive forces. Smallpox rapidly spread beyond the capital, raced through Mexico, and carried off so many people that Aztec society was unable to function. Only in the context of this drastic depopulation is it possible to understand the Spanish conquest of Mexico.

thinking about ENCOUNTERS

Conquest
Spaniards Hernán Cortés and Francisco Pizarro initiated the contacts with Mexico and Peru that resulted in the collapse of those previously strong imperial states. What was the nature of the initial relations between these Spaniards, the Aztecs, and the Incas? What factors altered the balance of power in these encounters?

This late-sixteenth-century painting idealized the Spanish conquest of the Aztec empire. Shown on the wall is Motecuzoma, captured by the Spaniards attacking his palace, and he is pleading with the Aztecs to surrender.

Francisco Pizarro Francisco Pizarro experienced similar results when he led a Spanish expedition from Central America to Peru. Pizarro set out in 1530 with 180 soldiers, later joined by reinforcements to make a force of about 600. The conquistadores arrived in Peru just after a bitter dispute between Huascar (1503–1532) and Atahualpa (ca. 1502–1533), two brothers within the Inca ruling house, and Pizarro's forces exploited the differences between those factions. Already by 1533 they had taken the Inca capital at Cuzco. Under pretext of holding a conference, they called the Inca ruling elites together, seized them, and killed most of them. They spared the Inca ruler Atahualpa until he had delivered a large quantity of gold to Pizarro. Then they strangled him and decapitated his body. The search for treasure continued after the end of Inca rule. Pizarro and his conquistadores looted gold and silver plaques from Cuzco's temples and public buildings, melted down statuettes fashioned from precious metals, and even filched jewelry and ornaments from the embalmed bodies of deceased Inca rulers.

Several considerations help to explain how Pizarro's tiny force was able to topple the Inca empire. Many subjects of the empire despised the Incas as overlords and tax collectors and put up little resistance to Pizarro's forces. Indeed, many allied with the Spanish invaders. Epidemic disease also discouraged resistance: smallpox had spread from Mexico and Central America to Peru in the 1520s, long before Pizarro's arrival, and had already taken a heavy toll among Andean populations. Pizarro and his army actually faced more threats from fresh Spanish interlopers than from native peoples. The conquest of Peru took longer than the conquest of Mexico, but by 1540 Spanish forces had established themselves securely as lords of the land.

Iberian Empires in the Americas

During the early days after the conquests, Cortés and Pizarro allocated lands and labor rights to their troops on their own authority. Gradually, however, the Spanish monarchy extended its control over the growing American empire, and

In this illustration from Peru-native Felipe Guaman Poma de Ayala's letter of complaint to the Spanish king—a record of grievances against Spanish overlords—conquistadores decapitate Atahualpa after executing him by strangulation in 1533.

by about 1570 the semiprivate regime of the conquistadores had given way to formal rule under the Spanish crown. Bureaucrats charged with the implementation of royal policy and the administration of royal justice replaced the soldiers of fortune who had conquered Mexico and Peru. The conquistadores did not welcome the arrival of the bureaucrats, but with the aid of Spanish lawyers, tax collectors, and military forces, royal officials had their way.

Spanish Colonial Administration Spanish administrators established two main centers of authority in the Americas—Mexico (which they called New Spain) and Peru (known as New Castile)—each governed by a viceroy who was responsible to the king of Spain. In Mexico they built a new capital, Mexico City, on top of Tenochtitlan. In Peru they originally hoped to rule from the Inca capital of Cuzco, but they considered the high altitude unpleasant and also found the Andean city too inaccessible for their purposes. In 1535 they founded Lima and transferred the government to the coast where it was accessible to Spanish shipping.

The viceroys were the king's representatives in the Americas, and they wielded considerable power. The kings of Spain, attempting to ensure that their viceroys would not build personal power bases and become independent, subjected them to the review of courts known as *audiencias* staffed by university-educated lawyers. The *audiencias* heard appeals against the viceroys' decisions and policies and had the right to address their concerns directly to the Spanish king. Furthermore, the *audiencias* conducted reviews of viceroys' performance at the end of their terms, and negative reviews could lead to severe punishment.

In many ways, Spanish administration in the Americas was a ragged affair. Transportation and communication difficulties limited the ability of viceroys to supervise their territories. In many regions, local administration fell to *audiencias* or town councils. Meanwhile, the Spanish monarchy exercised even less influence on American affairs than the viceroys. It often took two years for the central government in Spain to respond to a query from Mexico or Peru, and many replies simply asked for further information rather than providing firm directives. When viceroys received clear orders that they did not like, they found ways to procrastinate: they often responded to the king that "I obey, but I do not enforce," implying that with additional information the king would alter his decision.

New Cities Spanish rule in the Americas led to the rapid establishment of cities throughout the viceroyalties. Like their compatriots in Spain, colonists preferred to live in cities even when they derived their income from the agricultural production of their landed estates. As the numbers of migrants increased, they expanded the territory under Spanish imperial authority and built a dense network of bureaucratic control based in recently founded cities. The jurisdiction of the viceroyalty of New Spain reached from Mexico City as far as St. Augustine in Florida (founded in 1565). Administrators in Lima oversaw affairs from Panama (founded in 1519) to Concepción (founded in 1550) and Buenos Aires (founded in 1536).

Portuguese Brazil While Spanish conquistadores and administrators built a territorial empire in Mexico and Peru, Portuguese forces established an imperial presence in Brazil. The Portuguese presence came about by an odd twist of diplomatic convention. In 1494 Spain and Portugal signed the Treaty of Tordesillas, which divided the world along an imaginary north-south line 370 leagues west of the Azores and Cape Verde Islands. According to this agreement, Spain could claim any land west of that line, so long as it was not already under Christian rule, and Portugal gained the same rights for lands east of the line. Thus Portugal gained territory along the northeastern part of the South American continent, a region known as Brazil from the many brazilwood trees that grew along the coast, and the remainder of the western hemisphere fell under Spanish control.

The Portuguese mariner Pedro Alvares de Cabral stopped in Brazil briefly in 1500 while making a tack through the Atlantic Ocean en route to India. His compatriots did not

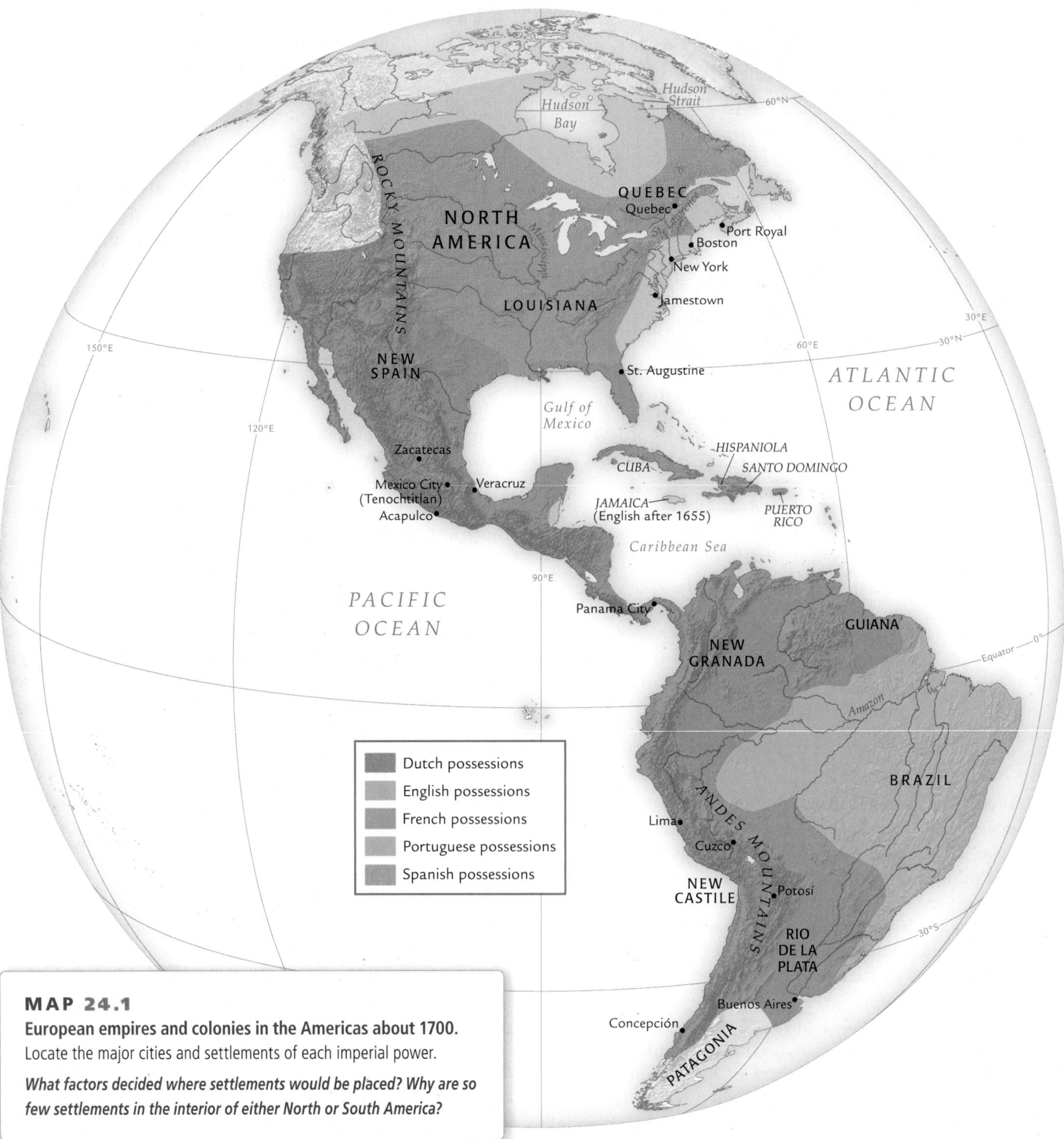

MAP 24.1

European empires and colonies in the Americas about 1700.
Locate the major cities and settlements of each imperial power.

What factors decided where settlements would be placed? Why are so few settlements in the interior of either North or South America?

display much immediate interest in the land. When French and Dutch mariners began to visit Brazilian shores, however, the Portuguese king decided to consolidate his claim to the land. He made vast land grants to Portuguese nobles in the expectation that they would develop and colonize their holdings, and later he dispatched a governor to oversee affairs and implement royal policy. Portuguese interest in Brazil rose dramatically after mid-century when entrepreneurs established profitable sugar plantations on the coast.

Colonial American Society The cities of the Spanish and Portuguese empires became centers of European-style society in the Americas: the spires of churches and cathedrals defined their skylines, and Spanish and Portuguese were the languages of government, business, and society. Beyond the urban districts, however, indigenous ways of life persisted. In the Amazon basin and Paraguay, for example, native peoples produced little agricultural surplus, and there were no mineral deposits to attract European migrants. The few Spanish and Portuguese colonists who ventured to those regions learned to adapt to indigenous societies and customs: they ate bread made of manioc flour, made use of native hammocks and canoes, and communicated in the Guaraní and Tupí languages. Indeed, indigenous languages flourish even today throughout much of Latin America: among the more prominent are Nahuatl in Mexico, K´iché in Guatemala, Guaraní in Paraguay, and Quechua in the Andean highlands of Peru, Ecuador, and Bolivia.

Spanish and Portuguese peoples saw the western hemisphere more as a land to exploit and administer than as a place to settle and colonize. Nevertheless, sizable contingents of migrants settled permanently in the Americas. Between 1500 and 1800, upwards of five hundred thousand Spanish migrants crossed the Atlantic, alongside one hundred thousand Portuguese. Their presence contributed to the making of a new world—a world characterized by intense interaction between the peoples of Europe, Africa, and the Americas—in the western hemisphere.

Settler Colonies in North America

Throughout the sixteenth century, Spanish explorers sought opportunities north of Mexico and the Caribbean. They established towns, forts, and missions from modern Florida as far north as Virginia on the east coast of North America, and they scouted shorelines off Maine and Newfoundland. On the west coast they ventured into modern Canada and established a fort on Vancouver Island. By mid-century, French, English, and Dutch mariners sailed the North Atlantic in search of fish and a northwest passage to Asia, and by the early seventeenth century they were dislodging Spanish colonists north of Florida. Their search for a northwest passage proved fruitless, but they harvested immense quantities of fish from the cod-filled banks off Labrador, Newfoundland, Nova Scotia, and New England.

Foundation of Colonies More important, in the early seventeenth century explorers began to plant permanent colonies on the North American mainland. French settlers established colonies at Port Royal (Nova Scotia) in 1604 and Quebec in 1608, and English migrants founded Jamestown in 1607 and the Massachusetts Bay Colony in 1630. Dutch entrepreneurs built a settlement at New Amsterdam in 1623, but the colony did not remain long in Dutch hands: an English fleet seized it in 1664, rechristened it New York, and absorbed it into English colonial holdings. During the seventeenth and eighteenth centuries, French migrants settled in eastern Canada, and French explorers and traders scouted the St. Lawrence, Ohio, and Mississippi Rivers, building forts all the way to the Gulf of Mexico. Meanwhile, English settlers established colonies along the east coast of the present-day United States of America.

Life in those early settlements was extremely difficult. Most of the settlers did not expect to cultivate food crops but, rather, hoped to sustain their communities by producing valuable commodities such as fur, pitch, tar, or lumber, if not silver and gold. They relied heavily on provisions sent from Europe, and when supply ships did not arrive as expected, they sometimes avoided starvation only because indigenous peoples provided them with food. In Jamestown, food shortages and disease became so severe that only sixty of the colony's five hundred inhabitants survived the winter of 1609–1610. Some settlers went so far as to disinter corpses and consume the flesh of their departed neighbors. One man even slaughtered and ate his wife.

Colonial Government The French and English colonies in North America differed in several ways from Spanish and Portuguese territories to the south. Whereas Iberian explorations had royal backing, private investors played larger roles in French and English colonial efforts. Individuals put up the money to finance expeditions to America, and they retained much more control over their colonies' affairs than did their Iberian counterparts. Although English colonies were always subject to royal authority, for example, they also maintained their own assemblies and influenced the choice of royal governors: there were no viceroys or *audiencias* in the North American colonies. At the conclusion of the Seven Years' War (1763), the French colony in Canada fell under British control, and it, too, soon acquired institutions of self-government.

Relations with Indigenous Peoples French and English colonies differed from Iberian territories also in their relationships with indigenous peoples. French and English migrants did not find large, centralized states like the Aztec and Inca empires. Nor did they encounter agricultural peoples living in densely settled societies. Although most of them spoke Algonquian, Iroquois, or Lakota languages, the peoples of eastern North America had formed dozens of distinct societies. Many of them practiced agriculture, but most also relied on hunting and consequently moved their villages frequently in pursuit of game. They did not claim ownership of precisely bounded territories, but they regularly migrated between well-defined regions.

When European settlers saw forested lands not bearing crops, they staked out farms and excluded the indigenous peoples who had frequently visited the lands during the course of their migrations. The availability of fertile farmland soon attracted large numbers of European migrants. Upwards of 150,000 English migrants moved to North America during the seventeenth century alone, and sizable French, German, Dutch, and Irish contingents joined them in the search for land.

European migrants took pains to justify their claims to American lands. English settlers in particular sought to

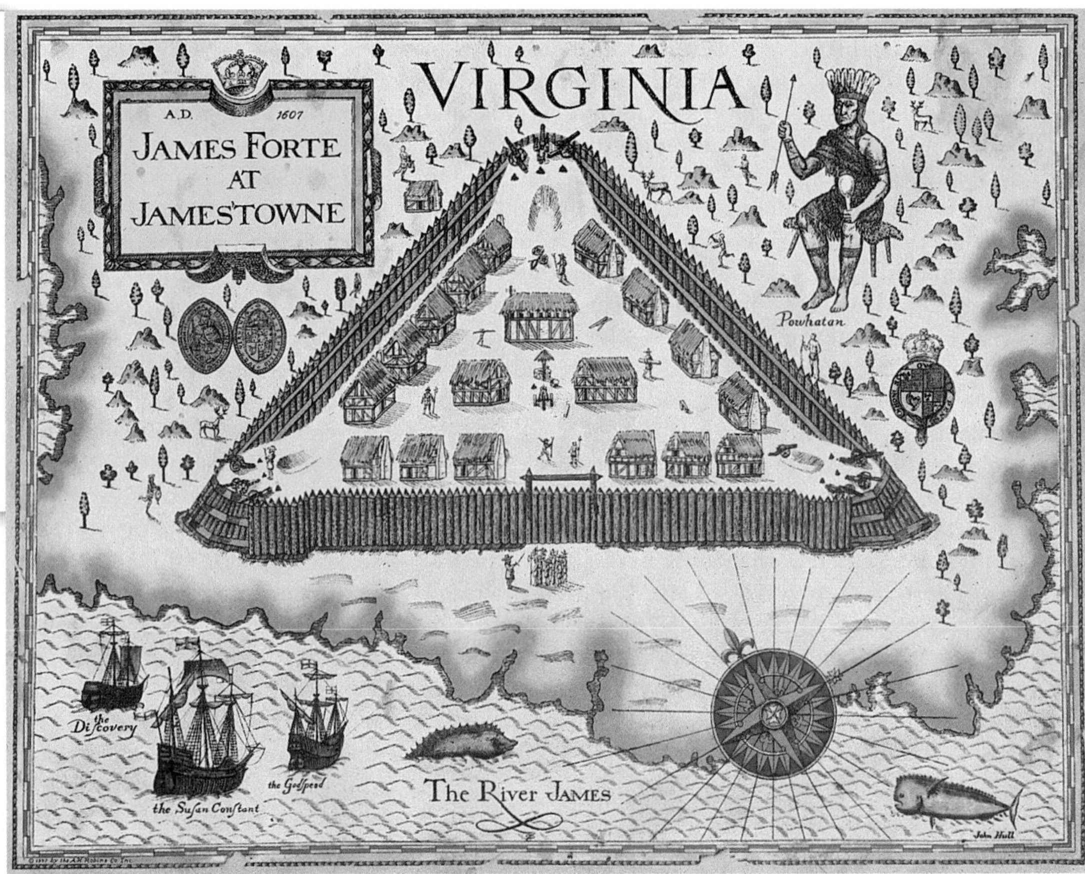

A painting of the English settlement at Jamestown in the early seventeenth century illustrates the precarious relations between European settlers and indigenous peoples. Note the heavy palisades and numerous cannons deployed within the fort, as well as the imposing figure of the native chief Powhatan depicted outside the settlement's walls.

provide legal cover for their expanding communities by negotiating treaties with the peoples whose lands they colonized. Quite apart from legal niceties, migrants also justified their occupation on the grounds that they made productive use of the land, whereas native peoples merely used it as a hunting park. In Europe, hunting was a pastime that only aristocratic and privileged classes could enjoy. Settlers did not recognize that hunting was a way of life, not a sport or a hobby, for the peoples of North America.

Conflict French and English settlers frequently clashed with native peoples who resented intrusions on their hunting grounds, but the conflicts differed from the campaigns of conquest carried out by the conquistadores in Mexico and Peru. English settlers negotiated rights to American lands by treaty, but native peoples did not appreciate the fine points of English law and frequently mounted raids on farms and villages. During an assault of 1622, for example, they massacred almost one-third of the English settlers in the Chesapeake region. Attacks on their communities brought reprisals from settlers, who ruthlessly destroyed the fields and villages of native peoples. Edward Waterhouse, who survived the raid of 1622, went so far as to advocate annihilation of the indigenous population: "Victorie may bee gained many waies: by force, by surprize, by [causing] famine [through] burning their Corne, by destroying and burning their Boats, Canoes, and Houses, by breaking their fishing Weares [nets], by assailing them in their huntings, whereby they get the greatest part of their sustenance in Winter, by pursuing and chasing them with our horses, and blood-Hounds to draw after them, and Mastives [mastiffs] to teare them."

Indeed, a combination of epidemic disease and violent conflict dramatically reduced the indigenous population of North America in early modern times. In 1492 the native population of the territory now embraced by the United States was greater than five million, perhaps as high as ten million. By the mid-sixteenth century, however, smallpox and other diseases had begun to spread north from Mexico and ravage native societies in the plains and eastern woodlands of North America. Between 1600 and 1800 about one million English, French, German, Dutch, Irish, and Scottish migrants crossed the Atlantic and sought to displace native peoples as they pursued economic opportunities in North America. By 1800, indigenous peoples in the territory of the present-day United States numbered only six hundred thousand, as against almost five million settlers of European ancestry and about one million slaves of African ancestry. Although the settler colonies of North America differed markedly from the Iberian territorial empires to the south, they too contributed greatly to the transformation of the western hemisphere.

COLONIAL SOCIETY IN THE AMERICAS

The European migrants who flooded into the western hemisphere interacted both with the native inhabitants and with African peoples whom they imported as enslaved laborers. Throughout the Americas, relations between individuals of American, European, and African ancestry soon led to the emergence of mestizo populations. Yet European peoples and their Euro-American offspring increasingly dominated political and economic affairs in the Americas. They mined precious metals, cultivated cash crops such as sugar and tobacco, and trapped fur-bearing animals to supply capitalist markets that met the voracious demands of European and Asian consumers. Over time they also established their Christian religion as the dominant faith of the western hemisphere.

The Formation of Multicultural Societies

Mestizo Societies Although their influence reached the American interior only gradually, European migrants radically transformed the social order in the regions where they established imperial states or settler colonies. All European territories became multicultural societies where peoples of varied ancestry lived together under European or Euro-American dominance. Spanish and Portuguese territories soon became not only multicultural but ethnically mixed as well, largely because of migration patterns. Migrants to the Iberian colonies were overwhelmingly men: about 85 percent of the Spanish migrants were men, and the Portuguese migration was even more male-dominated than the Spanish. Because of the small numbers of European women, Spanish and Portuguese migrants entered into relationships with indigenous women, which soon gave rise to an increasingly *mestizo* ("mixed") society.

Indigenous Zapotec painter Miguel Mateo Maldonado y Cabrera (1695–1768) created this domestic portrait of a multicultural family in the viceroyalty of New Spain, today's Mexico. A Spanish man gazes at his Mexican Indian wife and their mestizo daughter.

Most Spanish migrants went to Mexico, where there was soon a growing population of mestizos—those of Spanish and native parentage, like the children of Doña Marina. Women were more prominent among the migrants to Peru than to Mexico, and Spanish colonists there lived mostly in cities, where they maintained a more distinct community than did their counterparts in Mexico. In the colonial cities, Spanish migrants married among themselves and re-created a European-style society. In less settled regions, however, Spanish men associated with indigenous women and gave rise to mestizo society.

With few European women available in Brazil, Portuguese men readily entered into relations both with indigenous women and with African slave women. Brazil soon had large populations not only of mestizos but also of mulattoes born of Portuguese and African parents, *zambos* born of indigenous and African parents, and other combinations arising from these groups. Indeed, marriages between members of different racial and ethnic communities became common in colonial Brazil and generated a society even more thoroughly mixed than that of mestizo Mexico.

The Social Hierarchy In both Spanish and Portuguese colonies, migrants born in Europe known as ***peninsulares,*** those who came from the Iberian peninsula, stood at the top of the social hierarchy, followed by ***criollos,*** or *creoles,* those born in the Americas of Iberian parents. In the early days of the colonies, mestizos lived on the fringes of society. As time went on, however, the numbers of mestizos grew, and they became essential contributors to their societies, especially in Mexico and Brazil. Meanwhile, mulattoes, *zambos,* and others of mixed parentage became prominent groups in Brazilian society, although they were usually subordinate to European migrants, Euro-American creoles, and even mestizos. In all the Iberian colonies, imported slaves and conquered peoples stood at the bottom of the social hierarchy.

Sexual Hierarchies Race and ethnicity were crucial in shaping a person's position and role in colonial society. But

peninsulares (pehn-IHN-soo-LAH-rayz)
criollos (kree-OH-lohs)

the defining factor in both Spanish and Portuguese America was the existence of a clear sexual hierarchy that privileged men. Women lived in a patriarchal world, where men occupied positions of power and delineated the boundaries of acceptable female behavior. Only when it came to punishing disobedient slaves did society ignore gender—both male and female slaves could count on the same harsh punishment, which usually took the form of flogging. To the extent that women did exercise power, most of it was informal and limited to the confines of the home.

Gender alone, however, did not explain the diverse experiences of women in colonial society. Commonly, the ratio of men to women in a given community either enhanced or limited women's choices. Women's experiences also varied with the degree of prosperity and the nature of the local economy. As women moved from childhood through marriage and motherhood, to being widows or "spinsters," their experiences and roles in society likewise underwent change. Race and class usually figured as powerful forces shaping women's lives. Women of European descent, though under strict patriarchal control and under pressure to conform to the stereotype of female dependence and passivity, sometimes used their elite position to their advantage. By necessity, women of color and low class became part of the colonial labor force, performing tasks closely tied to the commercialization of traditional female work such as food preparation, laundering, and weaving. Although poor, these women were freer to move about in public and to interact with others than were their elite counterparts. The most disadvantaged women were black, mulatta, and zamba slaves, who were required to perform hard physical tasks such as planting and cutting cane or working as laundresses.

North American Societies The social structure of the French and English colonies in North America differed markedly from that of the Iberian colonies. Women were more numerous among the French and especially the English migrants than in Spanish and Portuguese communities, and settlers mostly married within their own groups. French fur traders often associated with native women and generated *métis* (French for "mixed") in regions around forts and trading posts. In French colonial cities such as Port Royal and Quebec, however, liaisons between French and native peoples were less common.

Mingling between peoples of different ancestry was least common in the English colonies of North America. Colonists disdained the native peoples they encountered and regarded them as lazy heathens who did not recognize private property and did not exert themselves to cultivate the land. Later, they also scorned imported African slaves as inferior beings. Those attitudes fueled a virulent racism, as English settlers attempted to maintain sharp boundaries between themselves and peoples of American and African ancestry.

Yet even English settlers interacted with American and African peoples, and they readily borrowed useful cultural elements from other communities. They learned about American plants and animals, for example, and they used native terms to refer to unfamiliar animals such as raccoons and opossums or trees such as hickory and pecan. They adapted moccasins and deerskin clothes, and they gave up European military customs of marching in massed ranks and announcing their presence with drums and flying colors. From their slaves they borrowed African food crops and techniques for the cultivation of rice. Yet, unlike their Iberian neighbors to the south, the English settlers strongly discouraged relationships between individuals of different ancestry and mostly refused to accept or even acknowledge offspring of mixed parentage.

Mining and Agriculture in the Spanish Empire

From the Spanish perspective the greatest attractions of the Americas were precious metals, which drew thousands of migrants from all levels of Spanish society. The conquistadores thoroughly looted the easily accessible treasures of the Aztec and Inca empires. Ignoring the artistic or cultural value of artifacts, the conquerors simply melted down silver and gold treasures and fashioned them into ingots. Their followers opened mines to extract the mineral wealth of the Americas in more systematic fashion.

Silver Mining Gold was not the most abundant American treasure. Silver far outweighed gold in quantity and value, and much of Spain's American enterprise focused on its extraction. Silver production concentrated on two areas: the thinly populated Mexican north, particularly the region around Zacatecas, and the high, cold central Andes, particularly the stunningly rich mines of Potosí (present-day Bolivia). Both sites employed large numbers of indigenous laborers. Many laborers went to Zacatecas voluntarily as their home villages experienced the pressures of conquest and disease. Over time they became professional miners, spoke Spanish, and lost touch with the communities of their birth.

Meanwhile, Spanish prospectors discovered a large vein of silver near Potosí in 1545 and began large-scale mining there in the 1580s. By 1600 Potosí was a boomtown with a population of 150,000. Rapid growth created an explosive demand for labor. As in the Mexican mines, Spanish administrators relied mostly on voluntary labor, but they also adapted the Inca practice of requisitioning draft labor, known as the *mita* system, to recruit workers for particularly difficult and dangerous chores that free laborers would not accept. Under the *mita* system, Spanish authorities annually required each native village to send one-seventh of its male population to work for four months in the mines at Potosí. Draft laborers received payment for their work, but wages were very low, and the conditions of work were extremely harsh. Some *mita* laborers hauled heavy baskets of silver ore up steep mine shafts, while others worked with toxic mercury, which miners used to separate the silver from

Mining operations at Potosí in South America gave rise to a large settlement that housed miners and others who supplied food, made charcoal, fashioned tools, and supported the enterprise. In this illustration from the mid-1580s, llamas laden with silver ore descend the mountain (background) while laborers work in the foreground to crush the ore and extract pure silver from it.

its ore. Death rates of draft laborers were high, and many native men sought to evade *mita* obligations by fleeing to cities or hiding in distant villages. Thus, even though at any given moment draft laborers represented only about 10 percent of the workforce at Potosí, the *mita* system touched a large portion of the indigenous population and influenced settlement patterns throughout the Andean region.

The Global Significance of Silver The mining industries of Mexico and Peru powered the Spanish economy in the Americas and even stimulated the world economy of early modern times. Silver produced profits for private investors and revenues for the crown. The Spanish government reserved a fifth of the silver production for itself. This share, known as the *quinto,* represented the principal revenue that the crown derived from its American possessions. American silver helped Spanish kings finance a powerful army and bureaucracy, but much of it also went well beyond Spain to lubricate the European and the larger world economies.

Most American silver made its way across the Atlantic to Spain and markets throughout Europe, and from there European merchants traded it for silk, spices, and porcelain in the markets of Asia. Some silver went from Acapulco on the west coast of Mexico across the Pacific to the Philippines in the Manila galleons, and from Manila it also made its way to Asian markets. No matter which direction it went or which oceans it crossed, American silver quickly traveled throughout the world and powerfully stimulated global trade.

The Hacienda Apart from mining, the principal occupations in Spanish America were farming, stock raising, and craft production. The organization of mining industries created opportunities for cultivators, herders, and artisans to provision mining towns with food, wine, textiles, tools, furniture, and craft items. By the seventeenth century the most prominent site of agricultural and craft production in Spanish America was the estate, or hacienda, which produced foodstuffs for its own use as well as for sale to local markets in nearby mining districts, towns, and cities. The products of the hacienda were mostly of European origin: wheat, grapes, and meat from pigs and cattle were the most prominent agricultural products. Bordering the large estates were smaller properties owned by Spanish migrants or creoles as well as sizable tracts of land held by indigenous peoples who lived in native villages and practiced subsistence agriculture.

Labor Systems The major source of labor for the haciendas was the indigenous population. Spanish conquerors first organized native workforces under the *encomienda* system. As originally developed in Spain during the era of the *reconquista* (see chapter 19), the *encomienda* system rewarded Spanish conquerors by allowing them to exact both labor and tribute from defeated Moorish populations, while requiring the *encomenderos* to look after the physical and spiritual welfare of their workers. Later, Spanish conquerors transferred the system to the Caribbean, Mexico, Central America, and Andean South America. From the 1520s to the 1540s, the *encomienda* system led to rampant abuse of indigenous peoples, as Spanish landowners overworked their laborers and skimped on their maintenance. After mid-century, *encomenderos* in agriculturally productive regions increasingly required their subject populations to provide tribute but not labor. Populations living under native leadership owned much of the land that they cultivated in villages. In some ways, their payments to Spanish colonists resembled the tributes their ancestors had provided to Aztec rulers.

As the *encomienda* system gradually went out of use, Spanish landowners resorted to a system of debt peonage to recruit labor for their haciendas. Under this system, landowners advanced loans to native peoples so that they could buy seeds, tools, and supplies. The debtors then repaid the loans with labor, but wages were so low that they were never able to pay off their debts. Because legal restrictions often prevented debtors from fleeing and escaping their obligations, landowners had in effect a captive labor force to work their estates.

Felipe Guaman Poma de Ayala depicted himself several times in his letter of complaint. Here, kneeling, he presents a copy of his work to the king of Spain. In fact, Guaman Poma never traveled to Spain, and his letter never reached the king. Nevertheless, Guaman Poma's illustrations offer remarkable images of early colonial Peru.

Resistance to Spanish Rule The Spanish regimes in the Americas met considerable resistance from indigenous peoples. Resistance took various forms: rebellion, half-hearted work, and retreat into the mountains and forests where Spanish power did not reach. In 1680, for example, after experiencing nearly a century of forced labor on Spanish estates, several native groups in northern Mexico (the modern-day American state of New Mexico) mounted a large uprising known as the Pueblo revolt. Led by a native shaman named Popé, the rebels attacked missions, killed priests and colonists, and drove Spanish settlers out of the region for twelve years. Spanish forces in Peru faced an even larger rebellion in 1780, when a force of about sixty thousand native peoples revolted in the name of Túpac Amaru, the last of the Inca rulers, whom Spanish conquistadores had beheaded in 1572. This Túpac Amaru rebellion raged for almost two years before Spanish forces suppressed it and executed thousands of its participants.

On some occasions, indigenous peoples turned also to Spanish law and administrators in search of aid against oppressive colonists. In 1615, for example, Felipe Guaman Poma de Ayala, a native of Peru, fired off a 1,200-page letter—accompanied by some four hundred hand-drawn illustrations—to King Philip III of Spain asking for protection for native peoples against rapacious colonists. Guaman Poma's letter went astray: the king never saw it. The missive somehow made its way to Denmark, where it remained unknown in a library until 1908.

Nevertheless, Guaman Poma's complaint serves as a record of grievances against Spanish overlords. The author wrote passionately of men ruined by overtaxation and women driven to prostitution, of Spanish colonists who grabbed the lands of native peoples and Spanish priests who seduced the wives of native men. Guaman Poma warned the king that the peoples of Peru were dying fast because of disease and abuse and that if Philip wanted anything to remain of his Andean empire, he should intervene and protect the indigenous peoples of the land.

Sugar and Slavery in Portuguese Brazil

Whereas the Spanish American empire concentrated on the extraction of silver, the Portuguese empire in Brazil depended on the production and export of sugar. The different economic and social foundations of the Spanish and Portuguese empires led to different patterns of labor recruitment. Spanish conquistadores subjugated sedentary peoples with effective administrative systems and compelled them to pro-

vide labor in the mines and estates of Mexico and Peru. Portuguese nobles and entrepreneurs established sugar plantations in regions without the administrative machinery to recruit workers and relied instead on imported African slaves as laborers. Indeed, Africans and their descendants became the majority of the population in Brazil, not simply an auxiliary labor force as in Spanish America.

The *Engenho* Colonial Brazilian life revolved around the sugar mill, or *engenho*. Strictly speaking, the term *engenho* (related to the English word *engine*) referred only to the mill itself, but it came to represent a complex of land, labor, buildings, animals, capital, and technical skills related to the production of sugar. Unlike other crops, sugarcane required extensive processing to yield molasses or refined sugar as a profitable export. Thus *engenhos* always combined agricultural and industrial enterprises. They depended both on heavy labor for the planting and harvesting of cane and on the specialized skills of individuals who understood the intricacies of the sugar-making process. As a result, *engenhos* were among the most complex business enterprises in the Americas.

In a colonial economy where sugar figured as the most important export, the Portuguese planters and owners of sugar mills were a privileged class, exercising political, social, and economic power. As long as they contributed to the government's revenues, they could usually count on strong royal support. The planters acted like landed nobility, but the nature of their enterprises required them to pay attention to affairs like businessmen. They operated on very small profit margins. Their exalted social position often disguised difficult financial predicaments, and turnover in the business was always high.

The Search for Labor Like their Spanish counterparts, Portuguese colonists first tried to enlist local populations as laborers. Unlike the inhabitants of Mexico and Peru, however, the peoples of Brazil were not sedentary cultivators. They resisted efforts to commandeer their labor, evaded Portuguese forces by retreating to interior lands, and took every opportunity to escape captors who managed to force them into servitude. From the Portuguese perspective, relying on native peoples as laborers had an additional drawback. In Brazil, as elsewhere in the Americas, epidemic diseases devastated indigenous populations. During the 1560s, smallpox and measles ravaged the whole Brazilian coast, making it difficult for Portuguese settlers even to find potential laborers, let alone force them to work.

Slavery Faced with those difficulties, the colonists turned to another labor source: the African slave. Portuguese plantation managers imported slaves as early as the 1530s, but they began to rely on African labor on a large scale only in the 1580s. The labor demands of cane cultivation and sugar production exacted a heavy toll from slave communities. Arduous working conditions, mistreatment, tropical heat, poor nutrition, and inadequate housing combined to produce high rates of disease and mortality: *engenhos* typically lost 5 to 10 percent of their slaves annually. In Brazil, as in most other plantation societies, the number of deaths in the slave population usually exceeded the number of births, so there was a constant demand for more slaves.

The system had its critics, but government officials mostly left matters of labor management to slave owners. To them the balance sheet of sugar production dictated practices that paid scant heed to the preservation of slaves' lives, as long as the owners realized profits. Indeed, if a slave lived five to six years, the investment of the average owner doubled and permitted him to purchase a new and healthy slave without taking a monetary loss. Hence owners had little economic incentive to improve conditions for slaves or to increase their birthrates. Children required financial outlays for at least twelve years, which from the perspective of the owner represented a financial loss. All told, the business of producing Brazilian sugar was so brutal that every ton of the sweet substance cost one human life.

Fur Traders and Settlers in North America

The Fur Trade European mariners first frequented North American shores in search of fish. Although fishing was a profitable enterprise, trade in furs became far more lucrative. The North American fur trade began when fishermen bartered for fur with local peoples. After explorers found a convenient entrance to rich fur-producing regions through the Hudson Strait and Hudson Bay, they began the systematic exploitation of the northern lands. Royal agents, adventurers, businessmen, and settlers began to connect large parts of the North American interior by a chain of forts and trading posts. Indigenous peoples trapped animals for Europeans and exchanged the pelts for manufactured goods such as wool blankets, iron pots, firearms, and distilled spirits. The hides went mostly to Europe, where capitalist markets experienced burgeoning demand for beaver skin hats and fur clothing.

Effects of the Fur Trade The fur trade generated tremendous conflict. American beaver populations, which were the chief targets of the trade, declined so rapidly that trappers constantly had to push farther inland in search of untapped beaver grounds. When hunting grounds became depleted, native peoples poached or invaded others' territories, which frequently led to war. Among the most brutal of those conflicts were the Beaver Wars of the seventeenth century, which pitted Iroquois against Hurons. The Iroquois sought to expand their hunting grounds at the expense of the Hurons and others, and thus monopolize the fur trade with Europeans.

The fur trade also took place in the context of competition between European states. This competitive atmosphere contributed to further conflict, as indigenous peoples became embroiled in their patrons' rivalries. During the mid-seventeenth century, for example, Iroquois peoples who were allies of Dutch fur traders in New Amsterdam launched a war against Hurons living north of the Great Lakes, who had allied themselves with the French. Equipped with firearms supplied by their Dutch allies, the Iroquois sought to exterminate the Hurons and extend their trapping to the northern lands. Hurons survived the war, although in greatly diminished numbers, but the Iroquois vastly increased their strength and destroyed Huron power.

Settler Society European settler-cultivators posed an even more serious challenge to native ways of life than did the fur traders, since they displaced indigenous peoples from the land and turned hunting grounds into plantations. The earliest colonists experienced difficult times, since European crops such as wheat did not grow well in their settlements. Indeed, many of the early colonies would have perished except for maize, game, and fish supplied by native peoples. Over time, however, French and especially English migrants stabilized their societies and distinguished them sharply from those of indigenous peoples.

Tobacco and Other Cash Crops As colonists' numbers increased, they sought to integrate their American holdings into the larger capitalist economy of the Atlantic Ocean basin by producing cash crops that they could market in Europe. In the English colonies of Virginia and Carolina, settlers concentrated on the cultivation of tobacco, a plant integral to the indigenous societies of the Americas. Christopher Columbus had observed the native Taíno smoking the leaves of a local plant through a pipe called a *tobago*—the origin of the word *tobacco.* Later, European visitors frequently observed tobacco consumption among indigenous peoples, who had used the plant as early as two thousand years ago for ritual, medicinal, and social purposes. Maya worshipers blew tobacco smoke from their mouths as offerings to the gods. Priests of the Aztec empire both smoked tobacco and took it in the form of snuff as an accompaniment to religious sacrifices.

The widespread popularity of this plant was due to the addictive nature of nicotine, an oily, toxic substance present in tobacco leaves and named after the French diplomat, Jean Nicot, who introduced tobacco use to Paris in 1560. Spanish and English promoters first touted the health benefits of tobacco to European consumers. Many physicians ascribed miraculous healing powers to tobacco, which they referred to as "the herb panacea," "divine tobacco," or the "holy herb nicotine." Merchants and mariners soon spread the use of tobacco throughout Europe and beyond to all parts of the world that European ships visited.

In 1612, English settlers cultivated the first commercial crop of tobacco in Virginia. By 1616, Virginia colonists exported 2,300 pounds of tobacco. European demand for the addictive weed resulted in skyrocketing exports amounting to 200,000 pounds in 1624 and three million pounds in 1638, and by the late seventeenth century, most consumers used tobacco socially and for pleasure, since tobacco's alleged health benefits never quite lived up to expectations. By the eighteenth century settlers in the southern colonies had established plantation complexes that produced rice and indigo as well as tobacco, and by the nineteenth century cotton also had become a prominent plantation crop.

European moralists often denounced tobacco as a noxious weed, and they associated its use with vices such as drunkenness, gambling, and prostitution. Nevertheless, its popularity surged in Europe, and later in Africa and Asia as well, after its introduction from the Americas.

Indentured Labor The plantations created high demand for cheap labor. Colonists in North America displaced indigenous peoples but could not subjugate them or induce them to labor in their fields. Planters initially met the demand for cheap labor by recruiting indentured servants from Europe. People who had little future in Europe—the chronically unemployed, orphans, political prisoners, and criminals—were often willing to sell a portion of their working lives in exchange for passage across the Atlantic and a new start in life. Throughout the seventeenth and eighteenth centuries, indentured servants streamed into the American colonies in hopes that after they had satisfied their obligation to provide four to seven years of labor they might become independent artisans or planters themselves. (The indentured labor trade in the Americas continued on a smaller scale even into the early twentieth century.) Some indentured servants went on to become prominent figures in colonial society, but many died of disease or overwork before completing their terms of labor, and others found only marginal employment.

Slavery in North America Most indentured servants eventually gained their freedom, but other suppliers of cheap labor remained in bondage all their lives. Like settlers in the Iberian colonies, English settlers in North America found uses for slave labor from Africa. In 1619 a group of about twenty Africans reached Virginia, where they worked alongside European laborers as indentured servants. Over time, some individual blacks fell into permanent servitude, others continued to work as indentured laborers, and some gained their freedom. In 1661, however, Virginia law recognized all blacks as slaves, and after 1680, planters increasingly replaced indentured servants with African slaves. By 1750 about 120,000 black slaves tilled Chesapeake tobacco, and 180,000 more cultivated Carolina rice.

Slave labor was not prominent in the northern colonies, principally because the land and the climate were not suitable for the cultivation of labor-intensive cash crops. Nevertheless, the economies of these colonies also profited handsomely from slavery. Many New England merchants traded in slaves destined for the West Indies: by the mid-eighteenth century, half the merchant fleet of Newport carried human cargo. The economies of New York and Philadelphia benefited from the building and outfitting of slave vessels, and the seaports of New England became profitable centers for the distillation of rum. The chief ingredient of this rum was slave-produced sugar from the West Indies, and merchants traded much of the distilled spirits for slaves on the African coast. Thus, although the southern plantation societies became most directly identified with a system that exploited African labor, all the North American colonies participated in and profited from the slave trade.

PART 5

Christianity and Native Religions in the Americas

Like Buddhists and Muslims in earlier centuries, European explorers, conquerors, merchants, and settlers took their religious traditions with them when they traveled overseas. The desire to spread Christianity was a prominent motive behind European ventures overseas, and missionaries soon made their way to the Americas as well as other lands where Europeans established a presence.

Spanish Missionaries From the beginning of Spanish colonization in Mexico and Peru, Roman Catholic priests served as representatives of the crown and reinforced civil administrators. Franciscan, Dominican, Jesuit, and other missionaries campaigned to Christianize indigenous peoples. In Mexico, for example, a group of twelve Franciscan missionaries arrived in 1524. They founded a school in Tlatelolco, the bustling market district of the Aztec capital of Tenochtitlan, where they educated the sons of prominent noble families in Latin, Spanish, and Christian doctrine. The missionaries themselves learned native languages and

An eighteenth-century engraving depicts work on a plantation: Several African slaves prepare flour and bread from manioc (left) while others hang tobacco leaves to dry in a shed (right). A male turkey—a fowl native to the Americas—ignores the bustle and displays his feathers (right foreground).

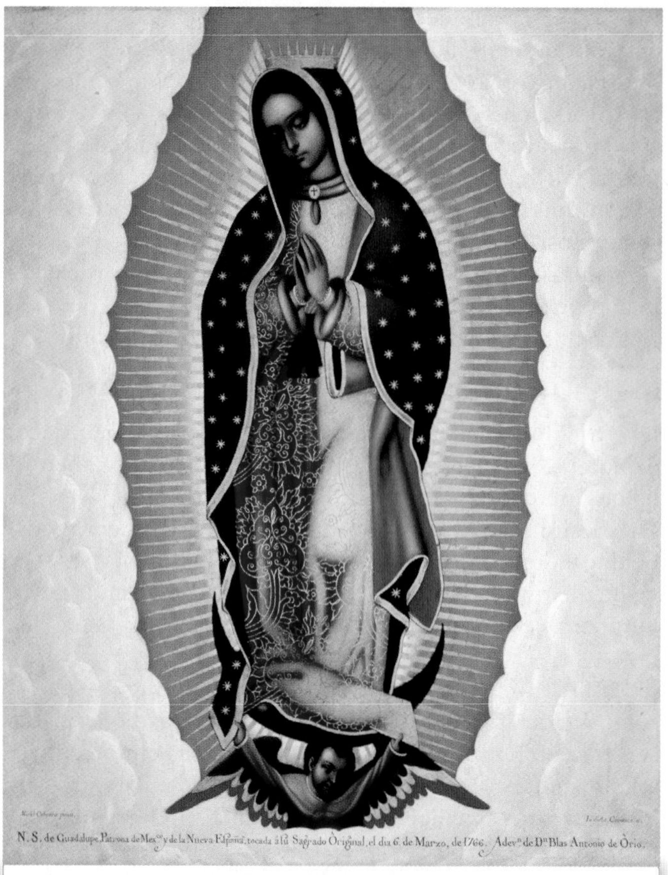

Famed Mexican painter Miguel Cabrera crafted this eighteenth-century depiction of the Virgin of Guadalupe. Recognized as the greatest painter in New Spain, he featured in this work one of Mexico's most powerful religious icons.

sought to explain Christianity in terms understandable to their audiences. They also compiled a vast amount of information about native societies in hopes of learning how best to communicate their message. The work of the Franciscan Bernardino de Sahagún was especially important. Sahagún preserved volumes of information about the language, customs, beliefs, literature, and history of Mexico before the arrival of Spanish forces there. His work remained largely unstudied until the twentieth century, but in recent times it has shed enormous light both on Aztec society and on the methods of early missionaries in Mexico.

Survival of Native Religions Christian missionaries encountered considerable resistance in the Americas. In both Mexico and Peru, indigenous peoples continued to observe their inherited faiths into the seventeenth century and beyond, even though Spanish authorities sponsored the Roman Catholic faith and tried to eliminate the worship of pagan deities. Native peoples honored idols in caves and inaccessible mountain sites, and they may have occasionally even continued to sacrifice human victims to their traditional gods.

Yet Christianity won adherents in Spanish America. In the wake of conquest and epidemic disease, many native leaders in Mexico concluded that their gods had abandoned them and looked to the missionaries for spiritual guidance. When native peoples adopted Christianity, however, they blended their own interests and traditions with the faith taught by Spanish missionaries. When they learned about Roman Catholic saints, for example, they revered saints with qualities like those of their inherited gods or those whose feast days coincided with traditional celebrations.

The Virgin of Guadalupe In Mexico, Roman Catholicism became especially popular after the mid-seventeenth century, as an increasingly mestizo society embraced the Virgin of Guadalupe almost as a national symbol. According to legends, the Virgin Mary appeared before the devout peasant Juan Diego on a hill near Mexico City in 1531. The site of the apparition soon became a popular local shrine visited mostly by Spanish settlers. By the 1640s the shrine attracted pilgrims from all parts of Mexico, and the Virgin of Guadalupe gained a reputation for working miracles on behalf of individuals who visited her shrine. The Virgin of Guadalupe, with her darker indigenous complexion, came to symbolize a distinctly Mexican faith and promise of salvation, and she became transformed as a result into a powerful symbol of Mexican nationalism. The popularity of the Virgin of Guadalupe helped to ensure not only that Roman Catholic Christianity would dominate cultural and religious matters in Mexico but also that Mexican religious faith would retain strong indigenous influences.

French and English Missions French and English missionaries did not attract nearly as many converts to Christianity in North America as their Spanish counterparts did in Mexico and Peru, partly because French and English colonists did not rule over conquered populations of sedentary cultivators: it was much more difficult to conduct missions among peoples who frequently moved about the countryside than among those who lived permanently in villages,

thinking about TRADITIONS

Women and Religion

Indigenous Mexican women and indigenous religious beliefs faced real challenges upon the arrival of the conquistadores and their Christian faith. How did European men and Christianity alter the fate of indigenous women and religion? How does the Virgin of Guadalupe speak to the survival of both?

towns, or cities. In addition, English colonists displayed little interest in converting indigenous peoples to Protestantism. The colonists did not discourage converts, but they made little effort to seek them, nor did they welcome native converts into their agricultural and commercial society. In contrast, Catholic French missionaries worked actively among native communities in the St. Lawrence, Mississippi, and Ohio River valleys and experienced modest success in spreading Christianity. Even though native peoples did not embrace Christianity, the burgeoning settlements of French and especially English colonists guaranteed that European religious traditions would figure prominently in North American society.

EUROPEANS IN THE PACIFIC

Though geographically distant from the Americas, Australia and the Pacific islands underwent experiences similar to those that transformed the western hemisphere in early modern times. Like their American counterparts, the peoples of Oceania had no inherited or acquired immunities to diseases that were common to peoples throughout the eastern hemisphere, and their numbers plunged when epidemic disease struck their populations. For the most part, however, Australia and the Pacific islands experienced epidemic disease and the arrival of European migrants later than did the Americas. European mariners thoroughly explored the Pacific basin between the sixteenth and eighteenth centuries, but only in Guam and the Mariana Islands did they establish permanent settlements before the late eighteenth century. Nevertheless, their scouting of the region laid a foundation for much more intense interactions between European, Euro-American, Asian, and Oceanic peoples during the nineteenth and twentieth centuries.

Australia and the Larger World

At least from the second century C.E., European geographers had speculated about *terra australis incognita* ("unknown southern land") that they thought must exist in the world's southern hemisphere to balance the huge landmasses north of the equator. As European mariners reconnoitered the Atlantic and Pacific Oceans during early modern times, they watched expectantly for a southern continent. Yet their principal interest was trade, and they rarely abandoned the pursuit of profit to sail out of their way in search of an unknown land.

Dutch Exploration When they visited the islands of southeast Asia in the quest for spices, however, they approached Australia from the west. Portuguese mariners most likely charted much of the western and northern coast of Australia as early as the 1520s, but Dutch sailors made the first recorded European sighting of the southern continent in 1606. The Dutch VOC authorized exploratory voyages, but mariners found little to encourage further efforts. In 1623, after surveying the dry landscapes of western Australia, the Dutch mariner Jan Carstenzs reported that his party had not seen "one fruit-bearing tree, nor anything that man could make use of: there are no mountains or even hills, so that it may be safely concluded that the land contains no metals, nor yields any precious woods," and he described the land as "the most arid and barren region that could be found anywhere on earth."

Nevertheless, Dutch mariners continued to visit Australia. By the mid-seventeenth century, they had scouted the continent's northern, western, and southern coasts, and they had ascertained that New Guinea and Tasmania were islands separate from Australia itself. Dutch explorers were so active in the reconnaissance of Australia that Europeans referred to the southern continent as "New Holland" throughout the seventeenth century. Yet neither Dutch nor any other European seamen visited the eastern coast until James Cook approached Australia from the southeast and charted the region in 1770, barely escaping destruction on the Great Barrier Reef.

Although European mariners explored Australian coastlines in the seventeenth and eighteenth centuries, they made only brief landfalls and had only fleeting encounters with indigenous peoples. The aboriginal peoples of Australia had formed many distinct foraging and fishing societies, but European visitors did not linger long enough to become familiar with either the peoples or their societies. Because they were nomadic foragers rather than sedentary cultivators, Europeans mostly considered them wretched savages. In the absence of tempting opportunities to trade, European mariners made no effort to establish permanent settlements in Australia.

British Colonists Only after Cook's charting of the eastern coast in 1770 did European peoples become seriously interested in Australia. Cook dropped anchor for a week at Botany Bay (near modern Sydney) and reported that the region was suitable for settlement. In 1788 a British fleet arrived at Sydney carrying about one thousand passengers, eight hundred of them convicts, who established the first European settlement in Australia as a penal colony. For half a century Europeans in Australia numbered only a few thousand, most of them convicts who herded sheep. Free settlers did not outnumber convicted criminal migrants until the 1830s. Thus exploratory voyages of the seventeenth and eighteenth centuries led to fleeting encounters between European and aboriginal Australian peoples, but only in the nineteenth and twentieth centuries did a continuing stream of European migrants and settlers link Australia more directly to the larger world.

The Pacific Islands and the Larger World

The entry of European mariners into the Pacific Ocean basin did not bring immediate change to most of the Pacific islands. In these islands, as in Australia, European merchants and settlers did not arrive in large numbers until the late eighteenth century. Guam and the Mariana Islands

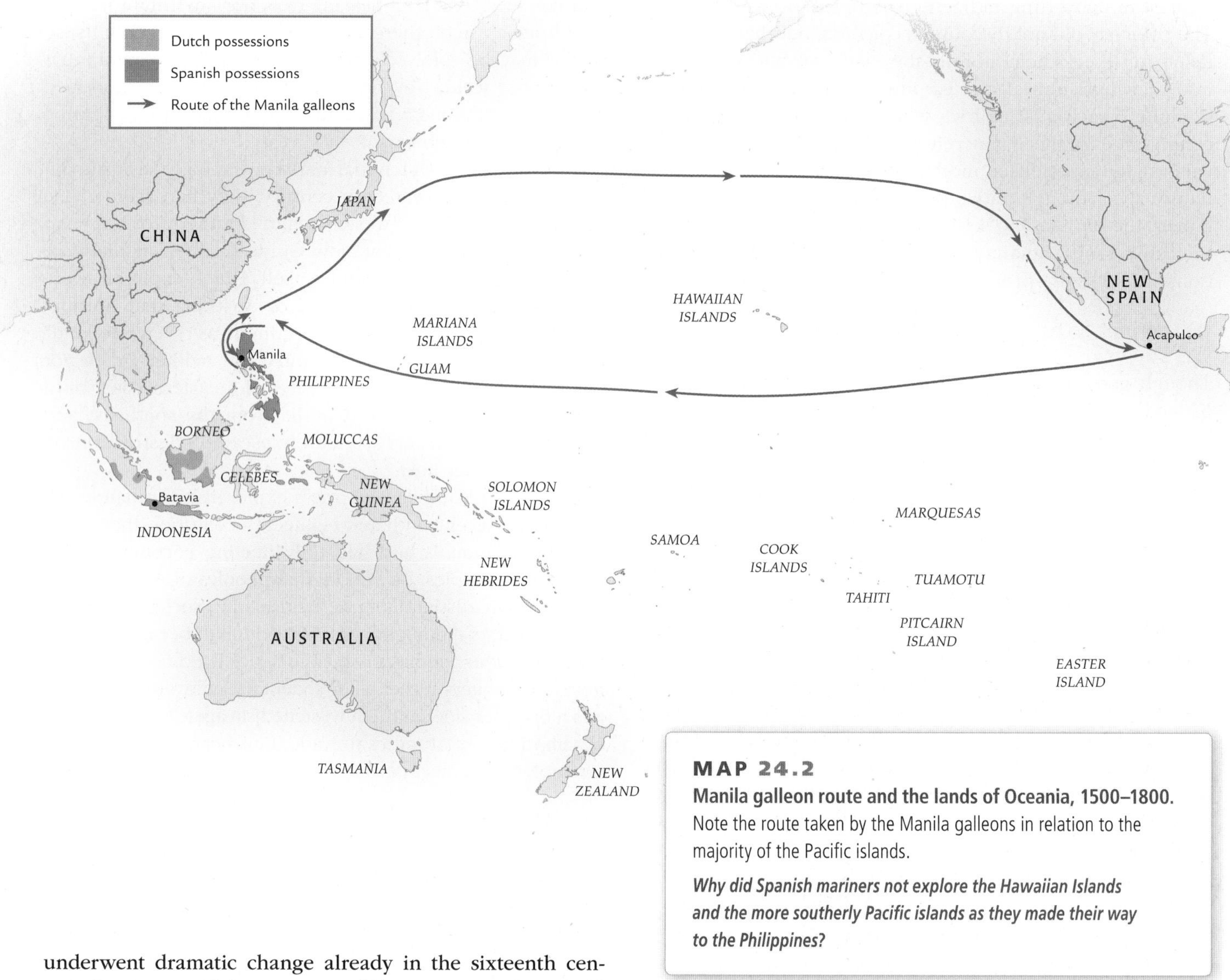

MAP 24.2
Manila galleon route and the lands of Oceania, 1500–1800.
Note the route taken by the Manila galleons in relation to the majority of the Pacific islands.
Why did Spanish mariners not explore the Hawaiian Islands and the more southerly Pacific islands as they made their way to the Philippines?

underwent dramatic change already in the sixteenth century, however, and the ventures of European merchants and explorers in the Pacific basin set the stage for profound upheavals in other island societies during the nineteenth and twentieth centuries.

Spanish Voyages in the Pacific In 1521 Ferdinand Magellan and his crew became the first Europeans to cross the Pacific Ocean. Before reaching the Philippines, they encountered only one inhabited island group—the Marianas, dominated by Guam. In 1565 Spanish mariners inaugurated the Manila galleon trade between Manila and Acapulco. Because their primary goal was to link New Spain to Asian markets, they rarely went out of their way to explore the Pacific Ocean or to search for other islands. Spanish vessels visited the Marquesas, Tuamotu, Cook, Solomon, and New Hebrides islands in the sixteenth century, and it is likely that one or more stray ships fetched up in Hawai`i. Yet Spanish mariners found little to interest them in most of the Pacific islands and did not establish regular communications with island peoples. They usually sailed before the trade winds from Acapulco to Manila on a route that took them south of Hawai`i and north of other Polynesian islands. On the return trip they sailed before the westerlies on a route that took them well north of all the Pacific islands.

Guam The only Pacific islands that attracted substantial Spanish interest in the sixteenth century were Guam and the northern Mariana Islands. Manila galleons called regularly at Guam, which lay directly on the route from Acapulco to Manila. For more than a century, they took on fresh provisions and engaged in mostly peaceful trade with the indigenous Chamorro people. During the 1670s and 1680s,

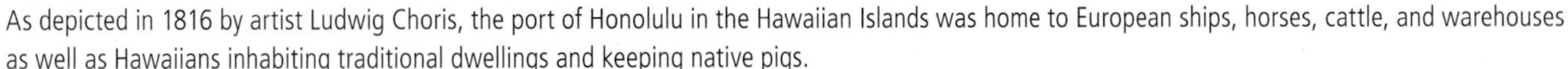
As depicted in 1816 by artist Ludwig Choris, the port of Honolulu in the Hawaiian Islands was home to European ships, horses, cattle, and warehouses as well as Hawaiians inhabiting traditional dwellings and keeping native pigs.

Spanish authorities decided to consolidate their position in Guam and bring the Mariana Islands under the control of the viceroy of New Spain in Mexico. They dispatched military forces to the islands to impose Spanish rule and subject the Chamorro to the spiritual authority of the Roman Catholic church. The Chamorro stoutly opposed those efforts, but a smallpox epidemic in 1688 severely reduced their numbers and crippled their resistance. By 1695 the Chamorro population had declined from about fifty thousand at mid-century to five thousand, partly because of Spanish campaigns but mostly because of smallpox. By the end of the seventeenth century, Spanish forces had established garrisons throughout the Mariana Islands and relocated surviving Chamorro into communities supervised by Spanish authorities.

Visitors and Trade Like the aboriginal peoples of Australia, the indigenous peoples of the Pacific islands had mostly fleeting encounters with European visitors during early modern times. By the late eighteenth century, however, growing European and Euro-American interest in the Pacific Ocean basin led to sharply increased interactions between islanders and mariners. English and French mariners explored the Pacific basin in search of commercial opportunities and the elusive northwest passage from Europe to Asia. They frequently visited Tahiti after 1767, and they soon began to trade with the islanders: European mariners received provisions and engaged in sexual relations with Tahitian women in exchange for nails, knives, iron tools, and textiles. Although trade was mostly peaceful, misunderstandings often led to minor skirmishes, and European captains occasionally trained their cannons on fleets of war canoes or villages in the Pacific islands.

**Captain Cook and Hawai`i** The experiences of Captain James Cook in Hawai`i illustrate a common pattern. In 1778, while sailing north from Tahiti in search of the northwest passage, Cook happened across the Hawaiian Islands. He immediately recognized Hawaiians as a people related to Tahitians and other Polynesians whose lands he had visited during his explorations of the Pacific Ocean since 1768, and he was able to communicate with Hawaiians on the basis of familiarity with Polynesian languages. Apart from some early concerns about thievery, Cook and his crew mostly got along well with Hawaiians, who readily traded pigs and provisions for iron wares. Sailors and island women avidly consorted with one another, resulting in the transmission of venereal diseases to Hawai`i, even though Cook had ordered infected crewmen to remain aboard ship. After a few weeks' stay in the islands, Cook resumed his northern course to seek the northwest passage. When he revisited Hawai`i late in 1779, he faced a very different climate, one in which islanders were less accommodating than before. Indeed, he lost his life when disputes over petty thefts escalated into a bitter conflict between his crew and islanders of Hawai`i.

Nevertheless, in the wake of Cook, whose reports soon became known throughout Europe, whalers began to venture into Pacific waters in large numbers, followed by missionaries, merchants, and planters. By the early nineteenth century, European and Euro-American peoples had become prominent figures in all the major Pacific islands groups. During the nineteenth and twentieth centuries, interactions among islanders, visitors, and migrants brought rapid and often unsettling change to Pacific islands societies.

sources from the past

Captain James Cook on the Hawaiians

Spanish mariners may well have been the first Europeans to visit the Hawaiian Islands, but Captain James Cook made the earliest surviving record of a European visit. His journal entries for the first few days of his visit depict a thriving society closely related to those of Tahiti and other Polynesian islands.

[Monday, 19 January 1778] There were three and four men in each [canoe] and we were agreeably surprised to find them of the same nation as the people of Otahiete [Tahiti] and the other [Polynesian] islands we had lately visited. It required but very little address to get them to come along side, but we could not prevail upon any one to come on board; they exchanged a few fish they had in the Canoes for any thing we offered them, but valued nails, or iron above every other thing; the only weapons they had were a few stones in some of the Canoes and these they threw overboard when they found they were not [needed]. . . . As soon as we made sail the Canoes left us, but others came off from the shore and brought with them roasting pigs and some very fine [sweet] Potatoes, which they exchanged, as the others had done, for whatever was offered them; several small pigs were got for a sixpenny nail or two apiece, so that we again found our selves in the land of plenty. . . .

[Tuesday, 20 January 1778] The next morning we stood in for the land and were met by several Canoes filled with people, some of them took courage and ventured on board. I never saw Indians so much astonished at the entering a ship before, their eyes were continually flying from object to object, the wildness of their looks and actions fully expressed their surprise and astonishment at the several new objects before them and evinced that they never had been on board of a ship before. However the first man that came on board did not with all his surprise forget his own interest, the first moveable thing that came in his way was the lead and line, which he without asking any questions took to put into his Canoe and when we stopped him said "I am only going to put it into my boat" nor would he quit it till some of his countrymen spoke to him. . . .

As there were some venereal complaints on board both the Ships, in order to prevent its being communicated to these people, I gave orders that no Women, on any account whatever were to be admitted on board the Ships, I also forbid all manner of connection with them, and ordered that none who had the venereal upon them should go out of the ships. But whether these regulations had the desired effect or not time can only discover. . . .

[Wednesday, 21 January 1778] As soon as every thing was settled to my satisfaction, I . . . took a walk up the Valley, accompanied by Dr. Anderson and Mr. Webber, conducted by one of the Natives and attended by a tolerable train. Our guide proclaimed our approach and every one whom we met fell on their faces and remained in that position till we passed. This, as I afterwards understood, is done to their great chiefs. Our road lay in among the Plantations, which were chiefly of Taro, and sunk a little below the common level so as to contain the water necessary to nourish the roots. . . .

At the beach I found a great crowd and a brisk trade for pigs, fowls and roots which was carried on with the greatest good order, though I did not see a man that appeared of more consequence than another if there was they did not show themselves to us. . . . No people could trade with more honesty than these people, never once attempting to cheat us, either ashore or along side the ships. Some indeed at first betrayed a thievish disposition, or rather they thought they had a right to any thing they could lay their hand upon but this conduct they soon laid aside.

For Further Reflection

- How does Cook's record of his first meeting with the Hawaiians compare and contrast with Christopher Columbus's account, presented earlier (in chapter 22), of his first encounter with indigenous American peoples?

Source: James Cook. *The Journals of Captain Cook.* Ed. by Philip Edwards. London: Penguin, 1999, pp. 530–34. (Translation slightly modified.)

in perspective

The Americas underwent thorough transformation in early modern times. Smallpox and other diseases sparked ferocious epidemics that devastated indigenous populations and undermined their societies. In the wake of severe depopulation, European peoples toppled imperial states, established mining and agricultural enterprises, imported enslaved African laborers, and founded colonies throughout much of the western hemisphere. Some indigenous peoples disappeared entirely as distinct groups. Others maintained their communities, identities, and cultural traditions but fell increasingly under the influence of European migrants and their Euro-American offspring. In Oceania only Guam and the Mariana

Islands felt the full effects of epidemic disease and migration in the early modern era. By the late eighteenth century, however, European and Euro-American peoples with advanced technologies had thoroughly explored the Pacific Ocean basin, and epidemic diseases traveled with them to Australia and the Pacific islands. As a result, during the nineteenth and twentieth centuries, Oceania underwent a social transformation similar to the one experienced earlier by the Americas. ●

CHRONOLOGY

1492	First voyage of Christopher Columbus to the western hemisphere
1494	Treaty of Tordesillas
1500	Brazil claimed for Portugal by Pedro Alvarez de Cabral
1518	Smallpox epidemic in the Caribbean
1519–1521	Spanish conquest of Mexico
1525	Execution of Cuauhtémoc
1532–1540	Spanish conquest of Peru
1545	Spanish discovery of silver near Potosí
1604	Foundation of Port Royal (Nova Scotia)
1607	Foundation of Jamestown
1608	Foundation of Quebec
1623	Foundation of New Amsterdam
1630	Foundation of the Massachusetts Bay Colony
1688	Smallpox epidemic on Guam
1754–1763	French and Indian war in North America
1763	Transfer of French Canadian possessions to British rule
1768–1779	Captain James Cook's exploration of the Pacific Ocean
1788	Establishment of first European colony in Australia

For Further Reading

Rolena Adorno. *Guaman Poma: Writing and Resistance in Colonial Peru.* Austin, 2000. A native Andean, who came of age after the fall of the Inca empire, tells Philip III of Spain of the evils of colonialism and the need for reform.

Alvar Nuñez Cabeza de Vaca. *Castaways.* Trans. by F. M. López-Morillas. Berkeley, 1993. Translation of Cabeza de Vaca's account of his shipwreck and travels through what is now the southwestern United States to Mexico.

Colin G. Callaway. *New Worlds for All: Indians, Europeans, and the Remaking of Early America.* Baltimore, 1997. Scholarly synthesis examining interactions and cultural exchanges between European and indigenous American peoples.

William Cronon. *Changes in the Land: Indians, Colonists, and the Ecology of New England.* New York, 1983. Brilliant study concentrating on the different ways English colonists and native peoples in colonial New England used the environment.

Philip D. Curtin. *The Rise and Fall of the Plantation Complex: Essays in Atlantic History.* 2nd ed. Cambridge, 1998. Examines plantation societies and slavery as institutions linking lands throughout the Atlantic Ocean basin.

Bernal Díaz del Castillo. *The Conquest of New Spain.* Trans. by J. M. Cohen. Harmondsworth, 1963. A conveniently available translation of Bernal Díaz's account of the conquest of Mexico from the viewpoint of a soldier.

John H. Elliot. *Empires of the Atlantic World: Britain and Spain in America 1492–1830.* New Haven, 2006. Excellent comparative study of Spanish and English colonies in the Americas.

K. R. Howe. *Where the Waves Fall: A New South Sea Island History from First Settlement to Colonial Rule.* Honolulu, 1984. A thoughtful survey of Pacific islands history emphasizing interactions between islanders and visitors.

Frances A. Karttunen. *Between Worlds: Interpreters, Guides, and Survivors.* New Brunswick, N.J., 1994. Reflective essays on Doña Marina and others who served as translators or interpreters between their society and the larger world.

John E. Kicza. *Resilient Cultures: America's Native Peoples Confront European Colonization, 1500–1800.* Upper Saddle River, N.J., 2002. A comprehensive comparative study assessing the impact of colonization on indigenous American peoples as well as native influences on American colonial history.

Karen Ordahl Kupperman. *Indians and English: Facing Off in Early America.* Ithaca, 2000. Fascinating reconstruction of the early encounters between English and indigenous American peoples, drawing on sources from all parties to the encounters.

Miguel León-Portilla. *The Broken Spears: The Aztec Account of the Conquest of Mexico.* Rev. ed. Boston, 1992. Offers translations of indigenous accounts of the Spanish conquest of the Aztec empire.

Kathleen Ann Meyers. *Neither Saints nor Sinners: Writing the Lives of Women in Spanish America.* New York, 2003. Examines female self-representation through the life writings of six seventeenth-century women in Latin America.

Gary B. Nash. *Red, White, and Black: The Peoples of Early America.* 3rd ed. Englewood Cliffs, N.J., 1992. Outstanding survey of early American history focusing on the interactions between peoples of European, African, and American ancestry.

James Pritchard. *The French in the Americas, 1670–1730.* Cambridge, 2004. Valuable study of French settlers and imperial policies in the Americas.

Matthew Restall, Lisa Sousa, and Kevin Terraciano, eds. *Mesoamerican Voices: Native Language Writings from Colonial Mexico, Yucatan, and Guatemala.* Cambridge, 2005. Composed between the sixteenth and eighteenth centuries, this collection of texts offers access to an important historical source.

Susan Migden Socolow. *The Women of Colonial Latin America.* Cambridge, 2000. An introductory survey of the female experience in the colonial societies of Spain and Brazil.

David J. Weber. *Bárbaros: Spaniards and Their Savages in the Age of Enlightenment.* New Haven, 2005. Pathbreaking and nuanced study of how Spanish administrators tried to forge a more enlightened policy toward native peoples.

———. *The Spanish Frontier in North America.* New Haven, 1992. A comprehensive study of Spanish efforts to explore and colonize lands north of Mexico.

Richard White. *The Middle Ground: Indians, Empires, and Republics in the Great Lakes Region, 1650–1815.* Cambridge, 1991. Insightful study of relations between French, English, and indigenous peoples in the Great Lakes region.

Africa and the Atlantic World

chapter 25

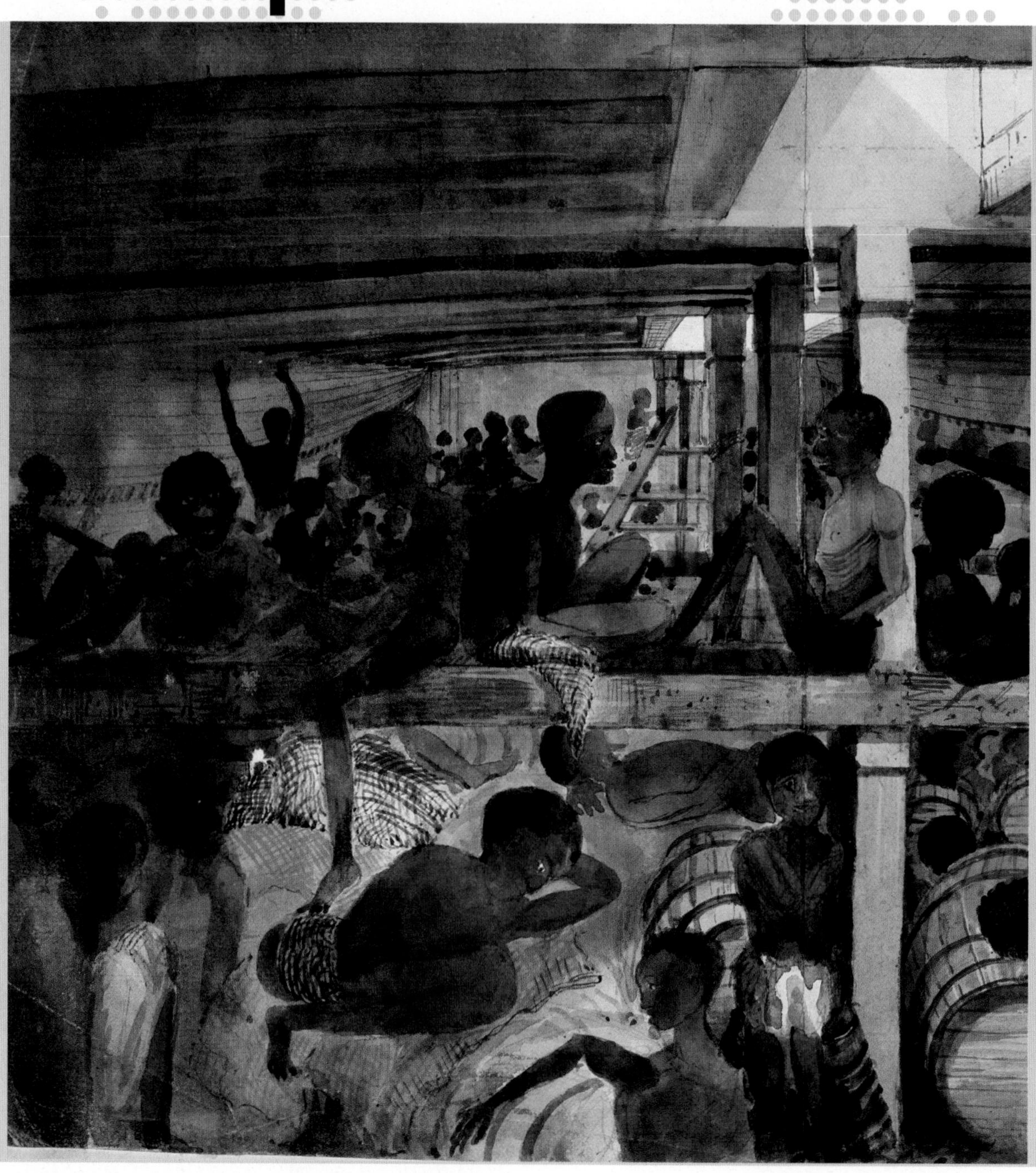

Below decks on an illegal slave ship seized by a British antislavery patrol in 1846.

EYEWITNESS:
A Slave's Long, Strange Trip Back to Africa

Between 1760 and 1792, a west African man known to history as Thomas Peters crossed the Atlantic Ocean four times. In 1760, slave raiders captured Peters, whose original African name is unknown, marched him to the coast, and sold him to French slave merchants. He traveled in a slave ship to the French colony of Louisiana, where he probably worked on a sugar plantation. But Peters was not a docile servant. He attempted to escape at least three times, and his master punished him by beating him, branding him with a hot iron, and forcing him to wear shackles around his legs. During the 1760s his French master sold Peters to an English planter, and about 1770 a Scottish landowner in North Carolina bought him.

During the 1770s, as English colonists in North America prepared to rebel against the British government in the interests of "life, liberty, and the pursuit of happiness," slaves of African ancestry considered their own prospects and looked for ways to obtain personal freedom. Peters was among them. When war broke out, he made his way with his wife and daughter to British lines and joined the Black Pioneers, a company of escaped slaves who fought to maintain British rule in the colonies. When the colonists won the war, Peters escaped to Nova Scotia with his family and many other former slaves.

Blacks were legally free in Nova Scotia, but the white ruling elites forced them to till marginal lands and live in segregated villages. In hopes of improving their lot, some two hundred black families designated Peters as their spokesman and sent him to London to petition the government for better treatment or resettlement in a more favorable land. In 1790 Peters sailed to England, where he promoted the establishment of a colony for former slaves in Sierra Leone. His efforts succeeded, and the next year he returned to Nova Scotia to seek recruits for the colony. In 1792 he led 1,196 blacks aboard a convoy of fifteen ships and began his fourth crossing of the Atlantic Ocean. The colonists arrived safely at Freetown, and Peters served as a leader of the black community there. His time in Freetown was tense and short—he experienced the great pressures of settlement and leadership and then died of malarial fever less than four months after arriving in Sierra Leone. Through his own life and experiences, Thomas Peters personified the links connecting the lands of the Atlantic Ocean basin.

For the most part, the peoples of sub-Saharan Africa continued to follow established patterns of life in early modern times. They built states and organized societies based on kinship groups as their Bantu-speaking predecessors had done for centuries. In west Africa and coastal east Africa, they also traded regularly with Muslim merchants from north Africa and southwest Asia.

Yet the establishment of global trade networks brought deep change to sub-Saharan Africa. Commercial opportunities drew European vessels to the coast of west Africa, and maritime trade soon turned west African attention to the Atlantic. Maritime commerce did not put an end to the trans-Saharan caravan trade that linked west Africa to the Mediterranean, but it helped promote the emergence of prosperous port cities and the establishment of powerful coastal kingdoms that traded through the ocean rather than the desert. In central Africa and south Africa, European merchants brought the first substantial opportunities for long-distance trade, since Muslim merchants had not ventured to those regions in large numbers.

Trade through the Atlantic profoundly affected African society because it included trade in human beings. African peoples had made a place for slavery within their societies for centuries, and they had also supplied slaves to Muslim merchants who transported them to markets in the Mediterranean and the Indian Ocean basin. The Atlantic slave trade, however, was vastly larger than the African and Islamic slave trades, and it had more serious consequences for African society. Between the fifteenth and the nineteenth centuries, it not only siphoned millions of people from their societies but also provoked turmoil in much of sub-Saharan Africa, as some peoples raided others' communities in search of captives for sale to slave traders.

The vast majority of Africans sold into the Atlantic slave trade went to destinations in the Caribbean or the Americas. Most worked on plantations cultivating cash crops for export, although some worked as domestic servants, miners, or laborers. Together they made up the largest forced migration in history before the nineteenth century and gave rise to an African diaspora in the western hemisphere. Under the restrictive conditions of slavery, they did not reconstitute African societies, but they also did not join European or Euro-American society. Instead, they preserved some African traditions and blended them with European and American traditions to create hybrid African-American societies.

AFRICAN POLITICS AND SOCIETY IN EARLY MODERN TIMES

For perhaps three millennia (2000 B.C.E. to 1000 C.E.), Bantu-speaking peoples migrated throughout sub-Saharan Africa. Many organized themselves into villages and clans governed by kinship groups rather than formal states. As their numbers grew, they devised political structures and built a series of chiefdoms and regional kingdoms. Muslim merchants, who ventured to sub-Saharan Africa after the eighth century, brought trade that encouraged the formation of large kingdoms and empires in west Africa and thriving city-states in east Africa.

African peoples continued to form states during the early modern era, but under the influence of maritime trade the patterns of state development changed. Regional kingdoms replaced the imperial states of west Africa as peoples organized their societies to take advantage of Atlantic as well as trans-Saharan commerce. The city-states of east Africa fell under the domination of Portuguese merchant-mariners seeking commercial opportunities in the Indian Ocean basin. The extension of trade networks also led to the formation of regional kingdoms in central Africa and south Africa. As the volume of long-distance trade grew, both Islam and Christianity became more prominent in sub-Saharan African societies.

The States of West Africa and East Africa

Between the eighth and the sixteenth centuries, powerful kingdoms and imperial states ruled the savannas of west Africa. The earliest was the kingdom of Ghana, which originated perhaps as early as the fourth or fifth century and established its dominance in the region in the eighth century. By controlling and taxing the trans-Saharan trade in gold, the kings of Ghana gained the financial resources they needed to field a large army and influence affairs in much of west Africa. In the thirteenth century the Mali empire replaced Ghana as the preeminent power in west Africa, but the Mali rulers continued the Ghana policy of controlling trans-Saharan trade.

The Songhay Empire By the fifteenth century the Mali empire had begun to weaken, and the expansive

Timbuktu, the commercial and cultural center of the Mali and Songhay empires, as sketched by a French traveler in 1828. Though long in decline, the city's mosques, mud-brick dwellings, and crowds of people bespeak a prosperous community.

state of Songhay emerged to take its place as the dominant power of the western grasslands. Based in the trading city of Gao, Songhay rulers built a flourishing city-state perhaps as early as the eighth century. In the early fifteenth century, they rejected Mali authority and mounted raids deep into Mali territory. In 1464 the Songhay ruler Sunni Ali (reigned 1464–1493) embarked on a campaign to conquer his neighbors and consolidated the Songhay empire (1464–1591). He brought the important trading cities of Timbuktu and Jenne under his control and used their wealth to dominate the central Niger valley.

Songhay Administration Sunni Ali built an elaborate administrative and military apparatus to oversee affairs in his realm. He appointed governors to oversee provinces and instituted a hierarchy of command that turned his army into an effective military force. He also created an imperial navy to patrol the Niger River, which was an extremely important commercial highway in the Songhay empire. Songhay military might enabled Sunni Ali's successors to extend their authority north into the Sahara, east toward Lake Chad, and west toward the upper reaches of the Niger River.

The Songhay emperors presided over a prosperous land. The capital city of Gao had about seventy-five thousand residents, many of whom participated in the lucrative trans-Saharan trade that brought salt, textiles, and metal goods south in exchange for gold and slaves. The emperors were all Muslims: they supported mosques, built schools to teach the Quran, and maintained an Islamic university at Timbuktu. Like the rulers of Ghana and Mali, the Songhay emperors valued Islam as a cultural foundation for cooperation with Muslim merchants and Islamic states in north Africa. Nevertheless, the Songhay emperors did not abandon traditional religious practices: Sunni Ali himself often consulted pagan diviners and magicians.

Fall of Songhay The Songhay empire dominated west Africa for most of the sixteenth century, but it was the last of the great imperial states of the grasslands. In 1591 a musket-bearing Moroccan army trekked across the Sahara and opened fire on the previously invincible Songhay military machine. Songhay forces withered under the attack, and subject peoples took the opportunity to revolt against Songhay domination.

As the Songhay empire crumbled, a series of small, regional kingdoms and city-states emerged in west Africa. The kingdom of Kanem-Bornu dominated the region around Lake Chad, and the Hausa people established thriving commercial city-states to the west. In the forests south of the grasslands, Oyo and Asante peoples built powerful

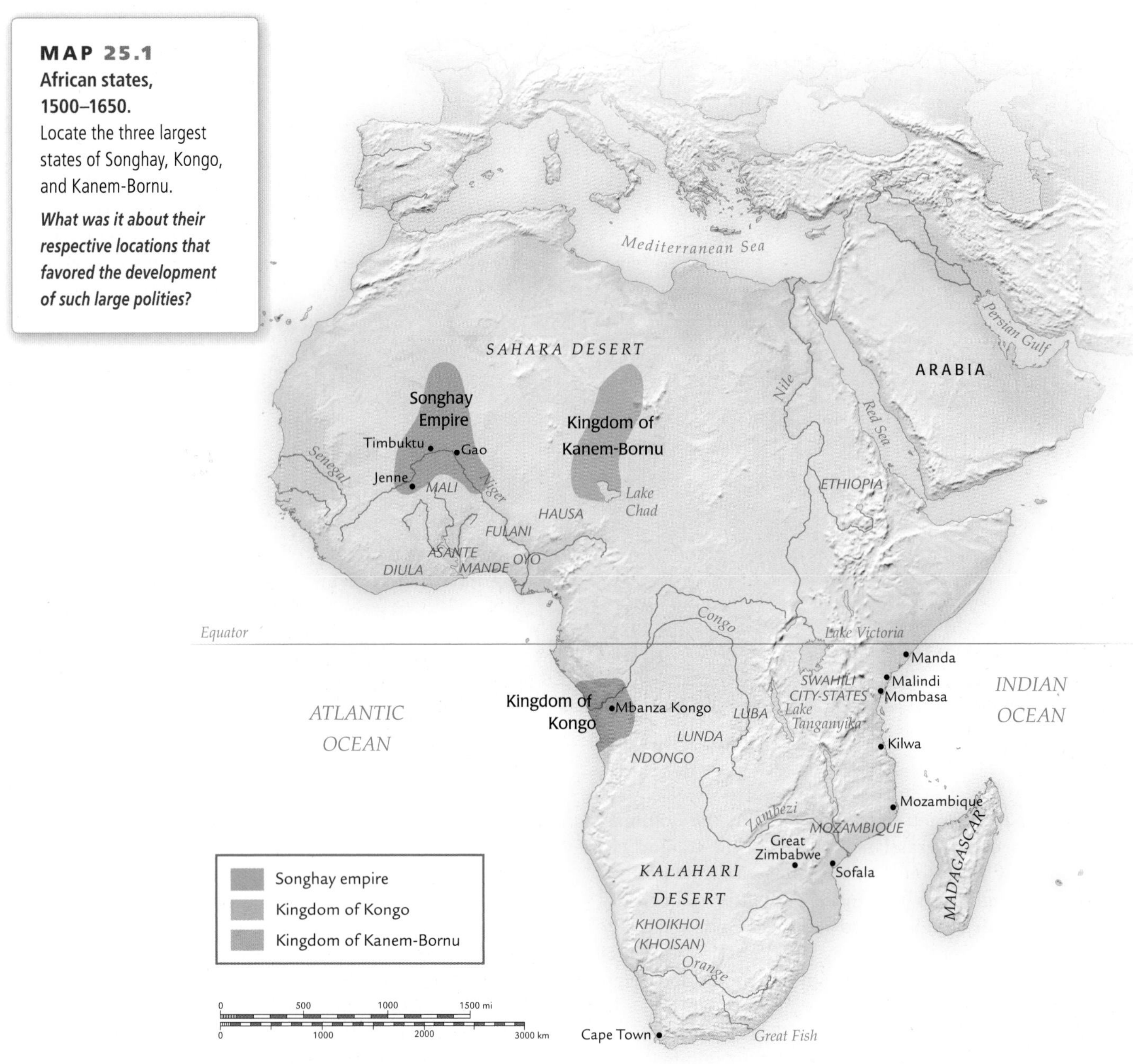

MAP 25.1
African states, 1500–1650.
Locate the three largest states of Songhay, Kongo, and Kanem-Bornu.
What was it about their respective locations that favored the development of such large polities?

regional kingdoms. On the coasts Diula, Mande, and other trading peoples established a series of states that entered into commercial relations with European merchant-mariners who called at west African ports after the fifteenth century. The increasing prominence of Atlantic trade in west African society worked against the interests of imperial states like Mali and Songhay, which had relied on control of trans-Saharan trade to finance their empires.

Swahili Decline While regional states displaced the Songhay empire in west Africa, the Swahili city-states of east Africa fell on hard times. When the Portuguese mariner Vasco da Gama made his way up the east African coast en route to India in 1497 and 1498, he skirmished with local forces at Mozambique and Mombasa. On his second voyage to India in 1502, he forced the ruler of Kilwa to pay tribute, and his followers trained their cannons on Swahili ports all along the east African coast. In 1505 a massive Portuguese naval expedition subdued all the Swahili cities from Sofala to Mombasa. Portuguese forces built administrative centers at Mozambique and Malindi and constructed forts throughout the region in hopes of controlling trade in east Africa.

They did not succeed in that effort, but they disrupted trade patterns enough to send the Swahili cities into a decline from which they never fully recovered.

The Kingdoms of Central Africa and South Africa

The Kingdom of Kongo As trade networks multiplied and linked all regions of sub-Saharan Africa, an increasing volume of commerce encouraged state building in central Africa and south Africa. In central Africa the principal states were the kingdoms of Kongo, Ndongo, Luba, and Lunda in the basin of the Congo River (also known as the Zaire River). Best known of them was the kingdom of Kongo, since abundant written records throw light on its experience in early modern times. The kingdom emerged in the fourteenth century. Its rulers built a centralized state with officials overseeing military, judicial, and financial affairs, and by the late fifteenth century Kongo embraced much of the modern-day Republic of Congo and Angola.

In 1483 a small Portuguese fleet reconnoitered the estuary of the Congo River and initiated commercial relations with the kingdom of Kongo. Within a few years, Portuguese merchants had established a close political and diplomatic relationship with the kings of Kongo. They supplied the kings with advisors, provided a military garrison to support the kings and protect Portuguese interests, and brought tailors, shoemakers, masons, miners, and priests to Kongo.

The kings of Kongo converted to Christianity as a way to establish closer commercial relations with Portuguese merchants and diplomatic relations with the Portuguese monarchy. The kings appreciated the fact that Christianity offered a strong endorsement of their monarchical rule. The new faith was convenient also because the saints of the Roman Catholic church were similar to spirits long recognized in Kongolese religion. King Nzinga Mbemba of Kongo, also known as King Afonso I (reigned 1506–1542), became a devout Roman Catholic and sought to convert all his subjects to Christianity. Portuguese priests in Kongo reported that he attended religious services daily and studied the Bible so zealously that he sometimes neglected to eat. The Kongo capital of Mbanza—known to Europeans as São Salvador—had so many churches during the sixteenth century that contemporaries referred to it as "Kongo of the Bell."

Slave Raiding in Kongo Relations with Portugal brought wealth and foreign recognition to Kongo but also led eventually to the destruction of the kingdom and the establishment of a Portuguese colony in Angola. In exchange for the textiles, weapons, advisors, and artisans that they brought to Kongo, Portuguese merchants sought high-value merchandise such as copper, ivory, and, most of all, slaves. They sometimes embarked on slaving expeditions themselves, but more often they made alliances with local authorities in interior regions and provided them with

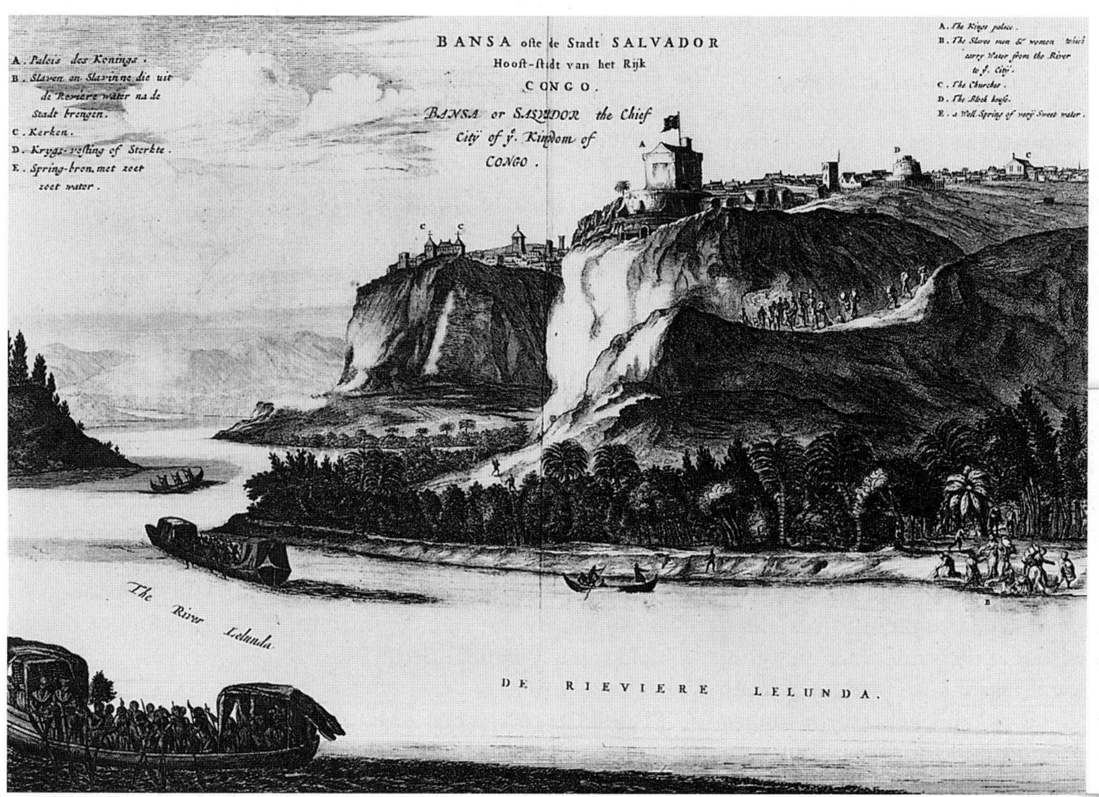

An engraving depicts São Salvador in Angola in the late seventeenth century. A flag flies over the royal palace while the Portuguese citadel (to the right of the palace) guards the city. Churches appear at the center and on the far right side of the engraving.

sources from the past

King Afonso I Protests Slave Trading in the Kingdom of Kongo

King Afonso I of Kongo wrote twenty-four official letters to his fellow monarchs, the kings of Portugal. The letters touch on many themes—relations between Portugal and Kongo, Afonso's devotion to Christianity, and the slave trade. The following excerpts come from two letters of 1526, when Portuguese slave trading was causing serious disruption in Kongo, prompting Afonso to request help in controlling the activities of Portuguese merchants.

And we cannot reckon how great the damage [caused by Portuguese merchants] is, since the mentioned merchants are taking every day our natives, sons of the land and the sons of our noblemen and vassals and our relatives, because the thieves and men of bad conscience grab them wishing to have the things and wares of this Kingdom which they are ambitious of; they grab them and get them to be sold; and so great, Sir, is the corruption and licentiousness that our country is being completely depopulated, and Your Highness should not agree with this nor accept it as in your service. And to avoid it we need from [your] Kingdoms no more than some priests and a few people to teach in schools, and no other goods except wine and flour for the holy sacrament. That is why we beg of Your Highness to help and assist us in this matter, commanding your factors that they should not send here either merchants or wares, because it is *our will that in these Kingdoms there should not be any trade of slaves nor outlet for them.* Concerning what is referred [to] above, again we beg of Your Highness to agree with it, since otherwise we cannot remedy such an obvious damage. . . .

Moreover, Sir, in our Kingdoms there is another great inconvenience which is of little service to God, and this is that many of our people, keenly desirous as they are of the wares and things of your Kingdoms, which are brought here by your people, and in order to satisfy their voracious appetite, seize many of our people, freed and exempt men, and very often it happens that they kidnap even noblemen and the sons of noblemen, and our relatives, and take them to be sold to the white men who are in our Kingdoms. . . .

And as soon as they are taken by the white men they are immediately ironed and branded with fire, and when they are carried to be embarked, if they are caught by our guards' men the whites allege that they have bought them but they cannot say from whom, so that it is our duty to do justice and to restore to the freemen their freedom, but it cannot be done if your subjects feel offended, as they claim to be.

And to avoid such a great evil we passed a law so that any white man living in our Kingdoms and wanting to purchase goods [i.e., slaves] in any way should first inform three of our noblemen and officials of our court whom we rely upon in this matter, . . . who should investigate if the mentioned goods are captives or free men, and if cleared by them there will be no further doubt nor embargo for them to be taken and embarked. But if the white men do not comply with it they will lose the aforementioned goods. And if we do them this favor and concession it is for the part Your Highness has in it, since we know that it is in your service too that these goods are taken from our Kingdom, otherwise we should not consent to this.

For Further Reflection

- On the basis of these letters, does it appear that King Afonso opposed all slave trading or only certain kinds of slave trading?

Source: Basil Davidson. *The African Past.* Boston: Little, Brown, 1964, pp. 191–93.

weapons in exchange for slaves. Some of their local allies were enemies of the kings of Kongo, while others were royal subordinates. In either case, Portuguese tactics undermined the authority of the kings, who appealed repeatedly but unsuccessfully for the Portuguese to cease or at least to limit their trade in slaves.

In spite of periodic invasions, Kongo remained strong until the mid-seventeenth century. Portuguese forces aided Kongo in expelling invaders, but at the same time they continued to trade in slaves. Some Portuguese merchants even settled in Kongo, took local wives, and henceforth looked more after the interests of their adoptive home than their native land. Over time, though, relations between Kongo and Portugal deteriorated, particularly after Portuguese agents began to pursue opportunities south of Kongo. By 1665 Portuguese colonists to the south even went to war with Kongo. Portuguese forces quickly defeated the Kongolese army and decapitated the king. Soon thereafter, Portuguese merchants began to withdraw from Kongo in search of more profitable business in the kingdom of Ndongo to the south. By the eighteenth century the kingdom of Kongo had largely disintegrated.

The Kingdom of Ndongo Meanwhile, Portuguese explorers were developing a brisk slave trade to the south in the kingdom of Ndongo, which the Portuguese referred

This is a martial portrait of the warrior Queen Nzinga, produced by European engravers who dubbed her "Anna Singa or Schmga." Queen Nzinga fought the Portuguese in Angola.

to as Angola from the title of the king, *ngola*. During the sixteenth century, Ndongo had grown from a small chiefdom subject to the kings of Kongo to a powerful regional kingdom, largely on the basis of the wealth it was able to attract by trading directly with Portuguese merchants rather than through Kongolese intermediaries. Portuguese merchants founded a small coastal colony in Ndongo as early as 1575. After 1611 they steadily increased their influence inland by allying with neighboring peoples who delivered increasing numbers of war captives to feed the growing slave trade. Over the next several decades, Portuguese forces campaigned in Ndongo in an effort to establish a colony that would support large-scale trading in slaves.

Queen Nzinga The conquest of Angola did not come easily. For forty years Queen Nzinga (reigned 1623–1663) led spirited resistance against Portuguese forces. Nzinga came from a long line of warrior kings. She dressed as a male warrior when leading troops in battle and insisted that her subjects refer to her as king rather than queen. She sometimes went so far in playing male roles as to travel with a group of "concubines"—young men dressed as women companions of the "king." She mobilized central African peoples against her Portuguese adversaries, and she also allied with Dutch mariners, who traded frequently on the African coast during the mid-seventeenth century. Her aim was to drive the Portuguese from her land, then expel the Dutch, and finally create a vast central African empire embracing the entire lower Congo basin.

The Portuguese Colony of Angola Although she was a cunning strategist and an effective military leader, Nzinga was unable to oust Portuguese forces from Ndongo. She stymied Portuguese efforts to extend their influence, but with their powerful arms and considerable wealth, Portuguese forces were able to exploit the political divisions that perennially plagued central Africa. When Nzinga died, Portuguese forces faced less capable resistance, and they both extended and tightened their control over Angola, the first European colony in sub-Saharan Africa.

Regional Kingdoms in South Africa Historical records do not shed as much light on the political structures of south Africa as they do on Kongo and Angola, but it is clear that in the south, as in central Africa, regional kingdoms dominated political affairs. Kingdoms had begun to emerge as early as the eleventh century, largely under the influence of trade. Merchants from the Swahili city-states of coastal east Africa sought gold, ivory, and slaves from the interior regions of south Africa. By controlling local commerce, chieftains increased their wealth, enhanced their power, and extended their authority. By 1300 rulers of one such kingdom had built a massive, stone-fortified city known as Great Zimbabwe, near the city of Nyanda in

thinking about ENCOUNTERS

Queen Nzinga

The Portuguese attempted to establish a colony in Angola in the seventeenth century to promote an even more robust slave trade. Their efforts did not go uncontested, however. What role did Queen Nzinga play in this conflict? What was the outcome of her efforts?

modern Zimbabwe, and they dominated the gold-bearing plain between the Zambesi and Limpopo rivers until the late fifteenth century.

European Arrival in South Africa After the fifteenth century a series of smaller kingdoms displaced the rulers of Great Zimbabwe, and Portuguese and Dutch mariners began to play a role in south African affairs. In search of commercial opportunities, Europeans struck alliances with local peoples and intervened in disputes with the aim of supporting their allies and advancing their own interests. They became especially active after Dutch mariners built a trading post at Cape Town in 1652. There they encountered the hunting and gathering Khoikhoi people, whom they referred to pejoratively as Hottentots. With the aid of firearms, they claimed lands for themselves and commandeered Khoikhoi labor with relative ease. By 1700 large numbers of Dutch colonists had begun to arrive in south Africa, and by mid-century they had established settlements throughout the region bounded by the Orange and the Great Fish rivers. Their conquests laid the foundation for a series of Dutch and British colonies, which eventually became the most prosperous European possessions in sub-Saharan Africa.

Islam and Christianity in Early Modern Africa

Indigenous religions remained influential throughout sub-Saharan Africa in early modern times. Although many African peoples recognized a supreme, remote creator god, they devoted most of their attention to powerful spirits who were thought to intervene directly in human affairs. African peoples associated many of these spirits with prominent geographic features such as mountains, waters, or forests. Others they thought of as the "living dead"—spirits of ancestors who roamed the world, not only distributing rewards to descendants who led worthy lives and who honored the memories of departed kin, but also meting out punishments to those who did not.

Islam in Sub-Saharan Africa Although most Africans continued to observe their inherited religions, both Islam and Christianity attracted increasing interest in sub-Saharan Africa. Islam was most popular in the commercial centers of west Africa and the Swahili city-states of east Africa. In the sixteenth century the trading city of Timbuktu had a prominent Islamic university and 180 schools that taught the Quran. Students flocked to Timbuktu by the thousands from all parts of west Africa.

Most African Muslims blended Islam with indigenous beliefs and customs. The result was a syncretic brand of Islam that not only made a place for African beliefs in spirits and magic but also permitted men and women to associate with each other on much more familiar terms than was common in north Africa, Arabia, and southwest Asia. Although it appealed to Africans, this syncretic Islam struck many devout Muslims as impure and offensive. Muslim merchants and travelers from north Africa and Arabia often commented on their shock at seeing women in tropical Africa who went out in public with bare breasts and socialized freely with men outside their own families.

The Fulani and Islam Some Muslims in sub-Saharan Africa also shared these concerns about the purity of Islam. Most important of them were the Fulani, originally a pastoral people who for centuries kept herds of cattle in the savannas of west Africa. By the late seventeenth century, many Fulani had settled in cities, where they observed a strict form of Islam like that practiced in north Africa and Arabia. Beginning about 1680 and continuing through the nineteenth century, the Fulani led a series of military campaigns to establish Islamic states and impose their own brand of Islam in west Africa.

The Fulani did not by any means stamp out African religions, nor did they eliminate indigenous elements from the syncretic Islam practiced in west Africa. But they founded powerful states in what is now Guinea, Senegal, Mali, and northern Nigeria, and they promoted the spread of Islam beyond the cities to the countryside. They even established schools in remote towns and villages to teach the Quran and Islamic doctrine. Their campaigns strengthened Islam in sub-Saharan Africa and laid a foundation for new rounds of Islamic state building and conversion efforts in the nineteenth and twentieth centuries.

"Although many African peoples recognized a supreme, remote creator god, they devoted most of their attention to powerful spirits who were thought to intervene directly in human affairs."

Christianity in Sub-Saharan Africa Like Islam, Christianity made compromises with traditional beliefs and customs when it spread in sub-Saharan Africa. The Portuguese community in Kongo and Angola supported priests and missionaries who introduced Roman Catholic Christianity to central Africa. They found strong interest among rulers such as King Afonso I of Kongo and his descendants, who eagerly adopted European-style Christianity as a foundation for commercial and political alliances with Portugal. Beyond the ruling courts, however, Christian teachings blended with African traditions to form syncretic cults. Some Africans regarded Christian missionaries as magicians and wore crosses and other Christian symbols as amulets to ward off danger from angry spirits.

The kings of Kongo retained their Christian faith even after their relations with European merchants and missionaries became strained in the seventeenth century. Here, King Garcia II—with European-style boots and a cross attached to his left sleeve—receives a Dutch embassy in 1642.

The Antonian Movement A particularly influential syncretic cult was the Antonian movement in Kongo, which flourished in the early eighteenth century, when the Kongolese monarchy faced challenges throughout the realm. The Antonian movement began in 1704 when an aristocratic woman named Dona Beatriz proclaimed that St. Anthony of Padua had possessed her and chosen her to communicate his messages. St. Anthony was a thirteenth-century Franciscan missionary and popular preacher. Born in Lisbon, St. Anthony died near Padua in Italy, where his followers built a large church in his honor. He was extremely popular among Portuguese Christians, who introduced his cult to Kongo. Dona Beatriz gained a reputation for working miracles and curing diseases, and she used her prominence to promote an African form of Christianity. She taught that Jesus Christ had been a black African man, that Kongo was the true holy land of Christianity, and that heaven was for Africans. She urged Kongolese to ignore European missionaries and heed her disciples instead, and she sought to harness the widespread popular interest in her teachings and use it to end the wars plaguing Kongo.

Dona Beatriz's movement was a serious challenge to Christian missionaries in Kongo. In 1706 they persuaded King Pedro IV of Kongo to arrest the charismatic prophetess on suspicion of heresy. Upon examining her, the missionaries satisfied themselves that Dona Beatriz was a false prophet and that she knowingly taught false doctrine. On their recommendation the royal government sentenced her to death and burned her at the stake. Yet the Antonian movement did not disappear: Dona Beatriz's disciples continued working to strengthen the monarchy and reconstruct Kongolese society. In 1708 an army of almost twenty thousand Antonians challenged King Pedro, whom they considered an unworthy ruler. Their efforts illustrate clearly the tendency of Kongolese Christians to fashion a faith that reflected their own needs and concerns as well as the interests of European missionaries.

Social Change in Early Modern Africa

Despite increased state-building activity and political turmoil, African society followed long-established patterns during the early modern era. Kinship groups, for example, the most important social units that emerged after the Bantu migrations, continued to serve as the basis of social organization and sometimes political organization as well. Within agricultural villages throughout sub-Saharan Africa, clans under the leadership of prominent individuals organized the affairs of their kinship groups and disciplined those who violated community standards. In regions where kingdoms and empires had not emerged, clan leaders consulted with one another and governed large regions. Indeed, even in lands ruled by formal states, clan leaders usually implemented state policy at the village level.

Yet interaction with European peoples brought change to African society in early modern times. Trade brought access to European textiles and metal goods. Africans had produced textiles and high-quality steel for centuries before the arrival of Portuguese mariners, but European products of different materials and styles became popular as complements to native African wares.

American Food Crops in Sub-Saharan Africa

Trade also brought new food crops to sub-Saharan Africa. In the mid-sixteenth century, American crops such as manioc, maize, and peanuts arrived in Africa aboard Portuguese ships. These crops supplemented bananas, yams, rice, and millet, the principal staple foods of sub-Saharan Africa. The most important American crop was manioc because of its high yield and because it thrived in tropical soils not well suited to cultivation of the other crops.

Population Growth By the eighteenth century, bread made from manioc flour had become a staple food in much of west Africa and central Africa, where it helped to underwrite steady population growth. In 1500 C.E. the population of sub-Saharan Africa was about thirty-four million. By 1600 it had increased by almost one-third to forty-four million, and it continued climbing to fifty-two million in 1700 and sixty million in 1800. This strong demographic expansion is all the more remarkable because it took place precisely when millions of Africans underwent an involuntary, forced migration to destinations in the Caribbean and the Americas. Despite that migration, American food crops supported expanding populations in all regions of sub-Saharan Africa during early modern times.

THE ATLANTIC SLAVE TRADE

Of all the processes that linked Africa to the larger Atlantic world in early modern times, the most momentous was the Atlantic slave trade. From the fifteenth to the nineteenth century, European peoples looked to Africa as a source of labor for sprawling plantations that they established in the western hemisphere. In exchange for slaves, African peoples received European manufactured products—most notably firearms, which they sometimes used to strengthen military forces that then sought further recruits for the slave trade. Only in the early nineteenth century did the Atlantic slave trade come to an end. During the course of the century, most states abolished the institution of slavery itself.

Foundations of the Slave Trade

Slavery in Africa The institution of slavery appeared in remote antiquity, and until the nineteenth century many settled agricultural peoples made some place for slaves in their societies. Slavery was common throughout Africa after the Bantu migrations spread agriculture to all parts of the continent. As in other societies, most slaves in Africa came from the ranks of war captives, although criminals and individuals expelled from their clans also frequently fell into slavery. Once enslaved, an individual had no personal or civil rights. Owners could order slaves to perform any kind of work, punish them at will, and sell them as chattel. African slaves usually worked as cultivators in societies far from their homes, although some worked as administrators, soldiers, or even highly placed advisors. The Songhay emperors, for example, often employed slaves as administrators and soldiers, since the rulers distrusted free nobles, whom they considered excessively ambitious and undependable. Agricultural plantations in the Songhay empire often had hundreds of slave laborers, many of them working under the management of slave administrators.

Law and society made African slavery different from bondage in Europe, Asia, and other lands. African law did not recognize private property but, rather, vested ownership of land in communities. Thus wealth and power in Africa came not from the possession of land but from control over the human labor that made the land productive. Slaves were a form of private investment, a type of heritable property, and a means of measuring wealth. Those who controlled large numbers of individuals were able to harvest more crops and accumulate more wealth than others. Africans routinely purchased slaves to enlarge their families and enhance their power. Often, they assimilated slaves into their kinship groups, so that within a generation a slave might obtain both freedom and an honorable position in a new family or clan.

The Islamic Slave Trade After the eighth century, Muslim merchants from north Africa, Arabia, and Persia sought African slaves for sale and distribution to destinations in the Mediterranean basin, southwest Asia, India, and even southeast Asia and China. This organized commerce found ready markets for slaves. When traditional sources proved insufficient to satisfy the demand for slaves, merchants created new supplies by raiding villages, capturing innocent individuals, and forcing them into servitude. State officials sometimes allied with the merchants by providing cavalry forces to mount lightning raids on undefended communities. Merchants then transported the freshly recruited slaves across the Sahara desert by camel caravan for distribution in the Mediterranean basin or boarded them on ships at the Swahili port cities of east Africa for delivery to destinations across the Indian Ocean. During a millennium and more of the Islamic slave trade, which lasted into the twentieth century, as many as ten million Africans may have left their homeland in servitude.

By the time Europeans ventured to sub-Saharan Africa in the fifteenth and sixteenth centuries, traffic in slaves was a well-established feature of African society, and a system for capturing, selling, and distributing slaves had functioned effectively for more than five hundred years. When Europeans began to pursue commercial interests in Africa and the Americas, the slave trade expanded dramatically. After 1450, European peoples tapped existing networks and expanded commerce in African slaves from the Mediterranean and the Indian Ocean to the Atlantic Ocean basin. This Atlantic slave trade brought about an enormous involuntary migration that influenced the development of societies throughout the Atlantic Ocean basin.

Human Cargoes

The Atlantic slave trade began small, but it grew steadily and eventually reached enormous proportions. The earliest European slave traders were Portuguese explorers who reconnoitered the west African coast in the mid-fifteenth century. In 1441 a raiding party seized twelve African men and took them to Portugal as slaves. Portuguese mariners encountered stiff resistance when they attempted to capture slaves, as African warriors fired thousands of poison-tipped arrows at gangs of would-be slave raiders. Soon, however, the mariners learned that they could purchase slaves rather than capturing them, and by 1460 they were delivering five hundred slaves per year to Portugal and Spain. In Europe, African slaves usually worked as miners, porters, or domestic servants, since free peasants and serfs cultivated the land.

The Early Slave Trade Slave traders also delivered their human cargoes to Portuguese island colonies in the Atlantic. There was no supply of labor to work plantations in the Azores, Madeiras, Cape Verde Islands, and São Tomé, all of which were uninhabited when explorers discovered them in the fifteenth century. The Portuguese population was too small to provide large numbers of colonists. Sugar planters on the island of São Tomé in particular called for slaves in increasing quantities. They relied on slave labor, and production soared along with the demand for sugar in Europe. By the 1520s some two thousand slaves per year went to São Tomé. Soon thereafter Portuguese entrepreneurs extended the use of slave labor to South America. During the 1530s Portuguese planters imported slaves directly from Kongo and Angola to Brazil, which eventually became the wealthiest of the sugar-producing lands of the western hemisphere.

A bronze plaque from Benin offers an early African view of Europeans: it depicts a Portuguese soldier armed with a musket and accompanied by a dog.

Meanwhile, Spanish explorers and conquerors also sought laborers to work lands in the Caribbean and the Americas. As imported diseases ravaged indigenous populations in the western hemisphere, the conquerors found themselves in possession of vast stretches of land but few laborers to work it. The Spanish attempted to harness the labor of those who survived the diseases, but native peoples frequently revolted against their overlords or simply escaped into the hinterlands. Gradually, Spanish settlers began to rely on imported African slaves as laborers. In 1518 the first shipment of slaves went directly from west Africa to the Caribbean, where they worked on recently established sugar plantations. During the 1520s Spanish authorities introduced slaves to Mexico, where they worked as cultivators and miners. By the early seventeenth century, English colonists had introduced slaves also to the North American mainland.

Triangular Trade The demand for labor in the western hemisphere stimulated a profitable commerce known as the triangular trade, since European ships often undertook voyages of three legs. On the first leg they carried horses and European manufactured goods—mostly cloth and metalwares, especially firearms—that they exchanged in sub-Saharan Africa for slaves. The second leg took enslaved Africans to Caribbean and American destinations. Upon arrival merchants sold their human cargoes to plantation owners for two to three times what they had cost on the African coast. Sometimes they exchanged slaves for cash, but in sugar-producing regions they often bartered slaves for sugar or molasses. Then they filled their vessels' hulls with American products before embarking on their voyage back to Europe.

At every stage of the process, the slave trade was a brutal and inhumane business. The original capture of slaves in Africa was almost always a violent affair. As European demand for slaves grew, some African chieftains organized raiding parties to seize individuals from neighboring societies. Others launched wars for the purpose of capturing victims for the slave trade. They often snatched individuals right out of their homes, fields, or villages: millions of lives changed instantly, as slave raiders grabbed their quarries and then immediately spirited them away in captivity. Bewilderment and anger was the lot not only of the captives but also of their family members, who would never again see their kin.

The Middle Passage Following capture, enslaved individuals underwent a forced march to the coast, where they lived in holding pens until a ship arrived to transport them to the western hemisphere. Then they embarked on the dreadful "middle passage," the trans-Atlantic journey aboard filthy and crowded slave ships. Enslaved passengers traveled below decks in hideously cramped quarters. Most ships provided slaves with enough room to sit upright, al-

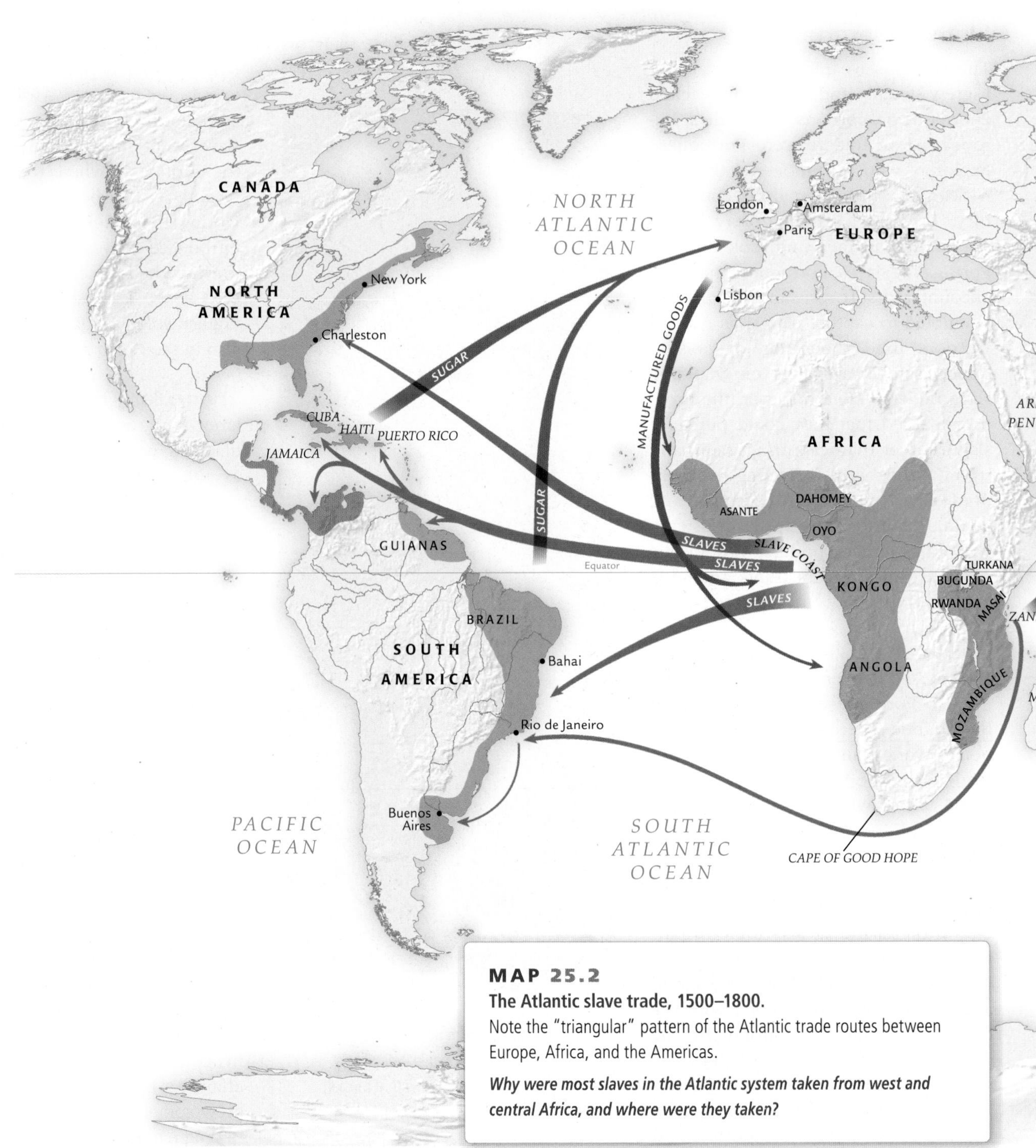

MAP 25.2
The Atlantic slave trade, 1500–1800.
Note the "triangular" pattern of the Atlantic trade routes between Europe, Africa, and the Americas.
Why were most slaves in the Atlantic system taken from west and central Africa, and where were they taken?

though not to stand, but some forced them to lie in chains on shelves with barely half a meter (twenty inches) of space between them. Conditions were so bad that many slaves attempted to starve themselves to death or mounted revolts. Ship crews attempted to preserve the lives of slaves, intending to sell them for a profit at the end of the voyage, but often treated the unwilling passengers with cruelty and contempt. Crew members used tools to pry open the mouths of those who refused to eat and pitched sick individuals into the ocean rather than have them infect others or waste limited supplies of food.

Barring difficulties, the journey to Caribbean and American destinations took four to six weeks, during which heat, cold, and disease levied a heavy toll on the human cargo. During the early days of the slave trade on particularly cramped ships, mortality sometimes exceeded 50 percent. As the volume of the trade grew, slavers built larger ships, carried more water, and provided better nourishment and facilities for their cargoes, and mortality eventually declined to about 5 percent per voyage. Over the course of the Atlantic slave trade, however, approximately 25 percent of individuals enslaved in Africa did not survive the middle passage.

INDIA

AN
AN

Slaves
Sugar
Manufactured goods
Source areas of African slaves
Slave settlement areas

The Impact of the Slave Trade in Africa

Volume of the Slave Trade Before 1600 the Atlantic slave trade operated on a modest scale. Export figures varied considerably from one year to the next, but on average about two thousand slaves left Africa annually during the late fifteenth and sixteenth centuries. During the seventeenth century, slave exports rose dramatically to twenty thousand per year, as European peoples settled in the western hemisphere and called for African labor to cultivate their lands. The high point of the slave trade came in the eighteenth century, when the number of slaves exported to the Americas averaged fifty-five thousand per year. During the 1780s slave arrivals averaged eighty-eight thousand per year, and in some individual years they exceeded one hundred thousand. From beginning to end, the Atlantic slave trade brought about the involuntary migration of about twelve million Africans to the western hemisphere. An additional four million or more died resisting seizure or during captivity before arriving at their intended destination.

The impact of the slave trade varied over time and from one African society to another. The kingdoms of Rwanda and Bugunda on the great lakes and the herding societies of the Masai and Turkana of east Africa largely escaped the slave trade, partly because they resisted it and partly because their lands were distant from the major slave ports on the west African coast. Other societies flourished during early modern times and benefited economically from the slave trade. Those Africans who raided, took captives, and sold slaves to Europeans profited handsomely from the trade, as did the port cities and the states that coordinated trade with European merchants. Asante, Dahomey, and Oyo peoples, for example, took advantage of the slave trade to obtain firearms from European merchants and build powerful states in west Africa. In the nineteenth century, after the abolition of slavery, some African merchants complained bitterly about losing their livelihood and tried to undermine the efforts of the British navy to patrol Atlantic waters and put an end to slave trading.

Social Effects of the Slave Trade On the whole, however, sub-Saharan Africa suffered serious losses from

sources from the past

Olaudah Equiano on the Middle Passage

Olaudah Equiano (1745–1797) was a native of Benin in west Africa. When he was ten years old, slave raiders seized him and his sister at home while their parents were tending the fields. He spent the next twenty-one years as a slave. Then Equiano purchased his freedom and worked against the slave trade for the rest of his life. In his autobiography of 1789, Equiano described the horrors of the middle passage.

The first object which saluted my eyes when I arrived on the coast was the sea, and a slave ship which was then riding at anchor and waiting for its cargo. These filled me with astonishment, which was soon converted into terror when I was carried on board. I was immediately handled and tossed up to see if I were sound by some of the crew, and I was now persuaded that I had gotten into a world of bad spirits and that they were going to kill me. . . .

I was not long suffered to indulge my grief; I was soon put down under the decks, and there I received such a salutation in my nostrils as I had never experienced in my life: so that with the loathsomeness of the stench and crying together, I became so sick and low that I was not able to eat, nor had I the least desire to taste anything. I now wished for the last friend, death, to relieve me; but soon, to my grief, two of the white men offered me eatables, and on my refusing to eat, one of them held me fast by the hands and laid me across I think the windlass and tied my feet while the other flogged me severely. I had never experienced anything of this kind before, and although not being used to the water I naturally feared that element the first time I saw it, yet nevertheless if I could have gotten over the nettings I would have jumped over the side, but I could not; and besides, the crew used to watch very closely over those of us who were not chained down to the decks, lest we should leap into the water: and I have seen some of these poor African prisoners most severely cut for attempting to do so, and hourly whipped for not eating. This indeed was often the case with myself. . . .

One day when we had a smooth sea and moderate wind, two of my wearied countrymen who were chained together (I was near them at the time), preferring death to such a life of misery, somehow made through the nettings and jumped into the sea: immediately another quite dejected fellow, who on account of his illness was suffered to be out of irons, also followed their example; and I believe many more would very soon have done the same if they had not been prevented by the ship's crew, who were instantly alarmed. Those of us that were the most active were in a moment put down under the deck, and there was such a noise and confusion amongst the people of the ship as I never heard before, to stop her and get the boat to go after the slaves. However, two of the wretches were drowned, but they got the other and afterwards flogged him unmercifully for thus attempting to prefer death to slavery. In this manner we continued to undergo more hardships than I can now relate, hardships which are inseparable from this accursed trade.

For Further Reflection

- On the basis of Equiano's account, what measures did the crews of slave ships take to ensure maximum profits from their business of transporting human cargoes?

Source: Olaudah Equiano. *The Interesting Narrative of the Life of Olaudah Equiano, or Gustavus Vassa, the African, Written by Himself.* 2 vols. London, 1789. (Translation slightly modified.)

the slave trade. The Atlantic slave trade alone deprived African societies of about sixteen million individuals, in addition to several million others consumed by the continuing Islamic slave trade during the early modern era. Although total African population rose during the early modern era, partly because American food crops enriched diets, several individual societies experienced severe losses because of the slave trade. West African societies between Senegal and Angola were especially vulnerable to slave raiding because of their proximity to the most active slave ports.

Gender and Slavery While diverting labor from sub-Saharan Africa to other lands, the slave trade also distorted sex ratios both in the Americas and in Africa. Approximately two-thirds of all slaves were young men between fourteen and thirty-five years of age. This reflected European preferences, because men in their physical prime had the best potential to repay their buyers' investments by providing heavy labor over an extended period of time. It also coincided with the desire of African slavers to retain female slaves for use in households. The resulting gender imbalance effectively militated against slaves reproducing in most places of colonial America. This, in turn, made it imperative for plantation owners and slavers to look constantly to Africa as a source for new slaves. This need to replenish the male slave populations was especially acute on Carib-

Armed escorts march a group of freshly captured Africans to the coast for sale on slave markets. Chained together are African men, women, and children. Why would some African peoples enslave other Africans?

bean sugar plantations, where death rates were especially high. The preference for male slaves also had implications for sub-Saharan societies. By the late eighteenth century, for example, women made up more than two-thirds of the adult population of Angola, encouraging Angolans to embrace polygyny, the practice of having more than one wife at a time. Women by necessity took on duties that earlier had been the responsibility of men.

Political Effects of the Slave Trade Apart from its demographic and social effects, the slave trade brought turmoil to African societies. During early modern times, African peoples fought many wars for reasons that had little or nothing to do with the slave trade, but it encouraged them to participate also in conflicts that might never have occurred in the absence of the trade.

Violence escalated especially after the late seventeenth century, when African peoples increasingly exchanged slaves for European firearms. When the kingdom of Dahomey obtained effective firearms, for example, its armies were able to capture slaves from unarmed neighboring societies and exchange them for more weapons. During the eighteenth century, Dahomey expanded rapidly and absorbed neighboring societies by increasing its arsenal of firearms and maintaining a constant flow of slaves to the coast. Indeed, the Dahomey army, which included a regiment of women soldiers, became largely a slave-raiding force. By no means did all African states take such advantage of the slave trade, but Dahomey's experience illustrates the potential of the slave trade to alter the patterns of African politics and society.

THE AFRICAN DIASPORA

Some slaves worked as urban laborers or domestic servants, and in Mexico and Peru many worked also as miners. The vast majority, however, provided agricultural labor on plantations in the Caribbean or the Americas. There they cultivated cash crops that made their way into commercial arteries linking lands throughout the Atlantic Ocean basin. Although deprived of their freedom, slaves often resisted their bondage, and they built hybrid cultural traditions compounded of African, European, and American elements. Most European and American states ended the slave trade and abolished slavery during the nineteenth century. By that time the African diaspora—the dispersal of African peoples and their descendants—had left a permanent mark throughout the western hemisphere.

Plantation Societies

Most African slaves went to plantations in the tropical and subtropical regions of the western hemisphere. When European peoples arrived in the Caribbean and the Americas, they found vast stretches of fertile land and soon began to envision huge profits from plantations that would satisfy the growing European demand for sugar and other agricultural commodities. Spanish colonists established the first of these plantations in 1516 on the island of Hispaniola (which embraces modern Haiti and the Dominican Republic) and soon extended them to Mexico as well. Beginning in the 1530s Portuguese entrepreneurs organized plantations in Brazil, and by the early seventeenth century English, Dutch, and French plantations had also appeared in the Caribbean and the Americas.

Cash Crops Many of these plantations produced sugar, which was one of the most lucrative cash crops of early modern times. But plantations produced other crops as well. During the seventeenth century, tobacco rivaled sugar as a profitable product. Rice also became a major plantation product, as did indigo. By the eighteenth century many plantations concentrated on the cultivation of cotton, and coffee had begun to emerge as a plantation specialty.

Regardless of the crops they produced, Caribbean and American plantations had certain elements in common. All of them specialized in the production of some agricultural crop in high demand. Plantations often maintained gardens that produced food for the local community, but their purpose was to profit from the production and export of commercial crops. In efforts to operate efficiently and profitably, plantations relied almost exclusively on slave labor. Plantation communities often included a hundred or more slaves, whose uncompensated labor services helped keep their agricultural products competitive. Plantations also featured a sharp, racial division of labor. Small numbers of European or Euro-American supervisors governed plantation affairs, and large numbers of African or African-American slaves performed most of the community's physical labor.

Regional Differences In spite of their structural similarities, plantation societies differed considerably from one

In an engraving of 1667, a European supervisor (lower right) directs slaves on a sugar plantation in Barbados as they haul cane, crush it to extract its juice, boil it to produce molasses, and distill the product into rum.

Slaves were vulnerable to cruel treatment that often provoked them to run away from their plantations or even mount revolts. A French visitor to Brazil in the early nineteenth century depicted a Portuguese overseer administering a brutal whipping to a bound slave on a plantation near Rio de Janeiro.

region to another. In the Caribbean and South America, slave populations usually were unable to sustain their numbers by natural means. Many slaves fell victim to tropical diseases such as malaria and yellow fever. On the plantations, they faced brutal working conditions and low standards of sanitation and nutrition. Moreover, slaves had low rates of reproduction because plantation owners mostly imported male slaves and allowed only a few to establish families. Thus, in the Caribbean and South America, plantation owners imported continuing streams of slaves from Africa to maintain their workforces. Of all the slaves delivered from Africa to the western hemisphere, about half went to the Caribbean, and about one-third went to Brazil. Smaller numbers went to other destinations in South America and Central America.

Only about 5 percent of enslaved Africans went to North American destinations. Diseases there were less threatening than in the Caribbean and Brazil, and in some ways the conditions of slaves' lives were less harsh than in the more southerly regions. North American planters imported larger numbers of female slaves and encouraged their slaves to form families and bear children. Their support for slave families was especially strong in the eighteenth century, when the prices of fresh slaves from Africa rose dramatically.

Resistance to Slavery No matter where they lived, slaves did not meekly accept their servile status, but like Thomas Peters resisted it in numerous ways. Some forms of resistance were mild but costly to slave owners: slaves often worked slowly for their masters but diligently in their own gardens, for example. They occasionally sabotaged plantation equipment or work routines. A more serious form of resistance involved running away from the plantation community. Runaways known as *maroons* gathered in mountainous, forested, or swampy regions and built their own self-governing communities. Maroons often raided nearby plantations for arms, tools, provisions, and even slaves to increase their own numbers or to provide labor for their communities. Many maroons had gained military experience in Africa, and they organized escaped slaves into effective military forces. Maroon communities flourished throughout slave-holding regions of the western hemisphere, and some of them survived for centuries. In present-day Suriname, for example, the Saramaka people maintain an elaborate oral tradition that traces their descent from eighteenth-century maroons.

Slave Revolts The most dramatic form of resistance to slavery was the slave revolt. Slaves far outnumbered others in most plantation societies, and they had the potential to organize and overwhelm their masters. Slave revolts brought stark fear to plantation owners and supervisors, and they often resulted in widespread death and destruction. Yet slave revolts almost never brought slavery itself to an end, because the European and Euro-American ruling elites had access to arms, horses, and military forces that extinguished most rebellions. Only in the French sugar colony of Saint-Domingue did a slave revolt abolish slavery as an institution (1793). Indeed, the slaves of Saint-Domingue declared independence from France, renamed the land Haiti, and established a self-governing republic (1804). The Haitian revolution terrified slave owners and inspired slaves throughout the western hemisphere, but no other slave rebellion matched its accomplishments.

Slavery and Economic Development The physical labor of African and African-American slaves made crucial contributions to the building of new societies in the Americas and also to the making of the early modern world as a whole. Slave labor cultivated many of the crops and extracted many of the minerals that made their way around the world in the global trade networks of the early modern era. Slaves themselves did not enjoy the fruits of their labors, which flowed disproportionately to European peoples and their Euro-American descendants. Except for the labor of enslaved African peoples and their African-American descendants, however, it would have been impossible for prosperous new societies to emerge in the Americas during the early modern era.

The Making of African-American Cultural Traditions

Enslaved Africans did not enjoy the luxury of maintaining their inherited cultural traditions in the western hemisphere. They often preserved African traditions, including languages and religions, but had to adapt to societies compounded of various European and American as well as African elements. When packed in slave ships for the middle passage, they found themselves in the company of Africans from societies other than their own. When sold to masters in the Caribbean and the Americas, they joined societies shaped by European and American traditions. In adapting to new circumstances, slaves constructed distinctive African-American cultural traditions.

African and Creole Languages European languages were the dominant tongues in the slave societies of the western hemisphere, but African languages also influenced communication. Occasionally, African slaves from a particular region were numerous enough to speak among themselves in their native tongues. More often, they spoke a creole tongue that drew on several African and European languages. In the low country of South Carolina and Georgia, for example, slaves made up about three-quarters of the population in the eighteenth century and regularly communicated in the creole languages Gullah and Geechee, respectively.

African-American Religions Like their languages, slaves' religions also combined elements from different societies. Some slaves shipped out of Africa were Christians, and many others converted to Christianity after their arrival in the western hemisphere. Most Africans and African-Americans did not practice European Christianity, however, but rather a syncretic faith that made considerable room for African interests and traditions. Because they developed mostly in plantation societies under conditions of slavery, these syncretic religions usually did not create an institutional structure or establish a hierarchy of priests and other church officials. Yet in several cases—most notably Vodou in Haiti, Santeria in Cuba, and Candomblé in Brazil—they became exceedingly popular among slaves.

All the syncretic, African-American religions drew inspiration from Christianity: they met in parish churches, sought personal salvation, and made use of European Christian paraphernalia such as holy water, candles, and statues. Yet they also preserved African traditions. They associated African deities with Christian saints and relied heavily on African rituals such as drumming, dancing, and sacrificing animals. Indeed, the core of these syncretic faiths was often participation in rituals like those observed in Africa. They also preserved beliefs in spirits and supernatural powers: magic, sorcery, witchcraft, and spirit possession all played prominent roles in African-American religions.

African-American Music As in their languages and religions, slaves relied on their African traditions in creating musical forms attuned to the plantation landscape. For many of these involuntary laborers, the playing of African music brought a sense of home and community to mind. It represented precisely what the slaves had lost—a sense of cultural grounding and belonging. African slaves in the Americas adapted African musical traditions, including both their rhythmic and their oratorical elements, to their new environments as a means of buffering the shock of transition, as a way to survive and to resist the horrid conditions of their new lives. In the process, they managed to create musical forms that made their influence felt not just in the slave quarters but also in the multicultural societies of the Caribbean and the Americas.

Slaves fashioned a new sense of identity and strength by bending west African instruments and musical traditions to European languages, Christian religion, and the work routines of American plantations. Slave musicians played drums and stringed instruments such as banjos that closely resembled traditional African instruments. They adapted west African call-and-response patterns of singing to the rhythms of field work on plantations. The call-and-response format also found its way into the music of spirituals that blended Christian, European, and African influences.

Many slave owners dismissed drumming and African-influenced music as heathenism, and some sought to ban music out of fear that it harbored subversive potential. Slave owners in South Carolina recalled, for example, that slaves had used drums to signal one another to rise up during the Stono rebellion of 1739. Despite efforts to suppress African influences, the music of slaves and later of their free de-

thinking about TRADITIONS

Creole Culture
The horrors of the institution of slavery made the preservation of African culture extremely difficult for those enslaved. African traditions nonetheless survived in blended or creole forms of culture in the Americas. What forms of culture best expressed this fusion? How did language and music in particular embody creole customs?

scendants survived and testified to the continuing relevance of music as a means of shaping community identity and resistance to oppression. From work songs and spirituals to the blues, jazz, and soul, African-American music evolved to mirror the difficult and often chaotic circumstances of black life in the Americas.

African-American Cultural Traditions African traditions also made their effects felt throughout much of the western hemisphere. Slaves introduced African foods to Caribbean and American societies and helped give rise to distinctive hybrid cuisines. They combined African okra, for example, with European-style sautéed vegetables and American shellfish to produce magnificent gumbos, which found their way to Euro-American as well as African-American tables. (*Okra* and *gumbo* are both African words.) Slaves introduced rice cultivation to tropical and subtropical regions, including South Carolina, Georgia, and Louisiana, and added variety to American diets. They also built houses, fashioned clay pots, and wove grass baskets in west African styles. In many ways, the African diaspora influenced the ways all peoples lived in plantation societies.

The End of the Slave Trade and the Abolition of Slavery

Almost as old as the Atlantic slave trade itself were voices calling for its abolition. The American and French revolutions stimulated the abolitionist cause. The American call for "life, liberty, and the pursuit of happiness" and the French appeal for "liberty, equality, and fraternity" suggested that there was a universal human right to freedom and equality.

Olaudah Equiano as depicted in the first edition of his autobiography (1789).

Olaudah Equiano Africans also took up the struggle to abolish commerce in human beings. Frequent slave revolts in the eighteenth and nineteenth centuries made the institution of slavery an expensive and dangerous business. Some freed slaves contributed to the abolitionist cause by writing books that exposed the brutality of institutional slavery. Most notable of them was the west African Olaudah Equiano (1745–1797), who in 1789 published an autobiography detailing his experiences as a slave and a free man. Captured at age ten in his native Benin (in modern Nigeria), Equiano worked as a slave in the West Indies, Virginia, and Pennsylvania. He accompanied one of his masters on several campaigns of the Seven Years' War before purchasing his freedom in 1766. Equiano's book became a best-seller, and the author traveled throughout the British isles giving speeches and denouncing slavery as an evil institution. He lobbied government officials and members of Parliament, and his efforts strengthened the antislavery movement in England.

The Economic Costs of Slavery Quite apart from moral and political arguments, economic forces contributed to the end of slavery and the slave trade. Plantations, slavery, and the slave trade continued to flourish as long as they were profitable, notwithstanding the efforts of abolitionists. Yet it gradually became clear that slave labor did not come cheap. The possibility of rebellion forced slave societies to maintain expensive military forces. Even in peaceful times slaves often worked unenthusiastically, but owners had to care for them throughout their lives no matter how hard they worked. Furthermore, in the late eighteenth century a rapid expansion of Caribbean sugar production led to declining prices. About the same time, African slave traders and European merchants sharply increased the prices they charged for fresh slaves.

As the profitability of slavery declined, Europeans began to shift their investments from sugarcane and slaves to newly emerging manufacturing industries. Investors soon found that wage labor in factories was cheaper than slave labor on plantations. As an additional benefit, free workers spent much of their income on manufactured goods. Meanwhile, European investors realized that leaving Africans in Africa where they could secure raw materials and buy manufactured goods in exchange was good business. Thus European entrepreneurs began to look upon Africa as something other than a source of slave labor.

End of the Slave Trade In 1803 Denmark abolished the trade in slaves, and other lands followed the Danish example: Great Britain in 1807, the United States in 1808, France in 1814, the Netherlands in 1817, and Spain in 1845. The end of the legal commerce in slaves did not abolish the institution of slavery itself, however, and as long as plantation slavery continued, a clandestine trade shipped slaves across the Atlantic. British naval squadrons sought to prevent this trade by patrolling the west coast of Africa and conducting search and seizure operations, so gradually the illegal slave trade ground to a halt. The last documented ship that carried slaves across the Atlantic arrived in Cuba in 1867.

The Abolition of Slavery The abolition of the institution of slavery itself was a long and drawn-out process: emancipation of all slaves came in 1833 in British colonies, 1848 in French colonies, 1865 in the United States, 1886 in Cuba, and 1888 in Brazil. Saudi Arabia and Angola abolished slavery in the 1960s. Officially, slavery no longer exists, but millions of people live in various forms of servitude even today. According to the Anti-Slavery Society for the Protection of Human Rights, debt bondage, contract labor, sham adoptions, servile marriages, and other forms of servitude still oppress more than two hundred million people, mostly in Africa, south Asia, and Latin America. Meanwhile, the legacy of the Atlantic slave trade remains visible throughout much of the western hemisphere, where the African diaspora has given rise to distinctive African-American communities.

inperspective

During the early modern era, the peoples of sub-Saharan Africa organized societies on the basis of kinship groups as they had since the early days of the Bantu migrations. They also built states and traded with Islamic societies as they had since the eighth century C.E. Yet African peoples also experienced dramatic changes as they participated in the formation of an integrated Atlantic Ocean basin. The principal agents of change were European merchant-mariners who sought commercial opportunities in sub-Saharan Africa. They brought European manufactured goods and introduced American food crops that fueled population growth throughout Africa. But they also encouraged a vast expansion of existing slave-trading networks as they sought laborers for plantations in the western hemisphere. The Atlantic slave trade violently removed sixteen million or more individuals from their home societies, and it led to political turmoil and social disruption throughout much of sub-Saharan Africa. Enslaved Africans and their descendants were mostly unable to build states or organize societies in the western hemisphere. But they formed an African diaspora that maintained some African traditions and profoundly influenced the development of societies in all slave-holding regions of the Caribbean and the Americas. They also collaborated with others to bring about an end to the slave trade and the abolition of slavery itself. ●

CHRONOLOGY

1441	Beginning of the Portuguese slave trade
1464–1493	Reign of Sunni Ali
1464–1591	Songhay empire
1506–1542	Reign of King Afonso I of Kongo
1623–1663	Reign of Queen Nzinga of Ndongo
1706	Execution of Dona Beatriz
1745–1797	Life of Olaudah Equiano
1793–1804	Haitian revolution
1807	End of the British slave trade
1865	Abolition of slavery in the United States

For Further Reading

Paul Bohannan and Philip D. Curtin. *Africa and Africans.* 3rd ed. Prospect Heights, Ill., 1988. General discussion of African society, religion, and history by an anthropologist and a historian.

Judith A. Carney. *Black Rice: The African Origin of Rice Cultivation in the Americas.* Cambridge, Mass., 2001. Fascinating study demonstrating how African slaves introduced a sophisticated agricultural technology to the low country of Carolina and Georgia.

Michael L. Conniff and Thomas J. Davis. *Africans in the Americas: A History of the Black Diaspora.* New York, 1994. A comprehensive survey of African-European relations, the slave trade, and the African diaspora.

Philip D. Curtin. *The Rise and Fall of the Plantation Complex: Essays in Atlantic History.* 2nd ed. Cambridge, 1998. Examines plantation societies and slavery as institutions linking lands throughout the Atlantic Ocean basin.

———, ed. *Africa Remembered: Narratives by West Africans from the Era of the Slave Trade.* Madison, 1967. Translations of works in which ten enslaved Africans recounted their memories of early modern Africa.

David Brion Davis. *Slavery and Human Progress.* New York, 1984. A rich and thoughtful book that places African slavery in a larger historical context.

Christopher Ehret. *The Civilizations of Africa: A History to 1800.* Charlottesville, Va., 2002. An important contribution that views Africa in the context of world history.

David Eltis. *The Rise of African Slavery in the Americas.* Cambridge, 1999. Emphasizes both the economic and the cultural foundations of Atlantic slavery.

Olaudah Equiano. *Equiano's Travels.* Ed. by Paul Edwards. Oxford, 1967. An abridged and conveniently available edition of Equiano's autobiography.

Leland Ferguson. *Uncommon Ground: Archaeology and Early African America, 1650–1800.* Washington, D.C., 1992. Enriches the understanding of slave society in the southeastern United States on the basis of archaeological discoveries.

Philip Gould. *Barbaric Traffic: Commerce and Antislavery in the Eighteenth-Century Atlantic World.* Cambridge, 2003. Compelling study of Anglo-American antislavery literature that suggests the discourse was less a debate over the morality of slavery than a concern with the commercial aspects of the slave trade.

Joseph E. Harris, ed. *Global Dimensions of the African Diaspora.* 2nd ed. Washington, D.C., 1993. A collection of scholarly essays on Africans in the Americas and the larger world.

Anne Hilton. *The Kingdom of Kongo.* Oxford, 1985. A valuable synthesis.

Patrick Manning. *Slavery and African Life: Occidental, Oriental, and African Slave Trades.* Cambridge, 1990. Concentrates on the impact of the slave trade on Africa.

Sidney W. Mintz. *Sweetness and Power: The Place of Sugar in Modern History.* New York, 1985. Important study of sugar, slavery, politics, and society by a prominent anthropologist.

——— and Richard Price. *The Birth of African-American Culture: An Anthropological Perspective.* Boston, 1992. A provocative study analyzing the forging of African-American cultural traditions under the influence of slavery.

Richard Price. *First-Time: The Historical Vision of an Afro-American People.* Baltimore, 1983. Fascinating reconstruction of the experiences and historical self-understanding of the Saramaka maroons of modern Suriname.

Elias N. Saad. *Social History of Timbuktu: The Role of Muslim Scholars and Notables, 1400–1900.* Cambridge, 1983. Emphasizes the role of Muslim scholars in one of west Africa's most important commercial and cultural centers.

Mechal Sobel. *The World They Made Together: Black and White Values in Eighteenth Century Virginia.* Princeton, 1987. Argues persuasively that African-American slaves deeply influenced the development of early American society.

James H. Sweet. *Recreating Africa: Culture, Kinship, and Religion in the African-Portuguese World, 1441–1770.* Chapel Hill, 2006. Engaging study of African slave culture in Portuguese Brazil and the process of creolization.

Robert Farris Thompson. *Flash of the Spirit: African and African-American Art and Philosophy.* New York, 1983. Fascinating study that documents and analyzes the maintenance and adaptation of African cultural traditions in the Americas.

John Thornton. *Africa and Africans in the Making of the Atlantic World, 1400–1800.* 2nd ed. New York, 1997. A rich analysis of African peoples and their roles in the Atlantic Ocean basin.

———. *The Kongolese Saint Anthony: Dona Beatriz Kimpa Vita and the Antonian Movement, 1684–1706.* Cambridge, 1998. Excellent scholarly study of Dona Beatriz and the Antonian movement in the kingdom of Kongo.

Dale W. Tomich. *Through the Prism of Slavery: Labor, Capital, and World Economy.* Lanham, Md., 2004. Brief overview of slavery's role in the development of global capitalism.

Jan Vansina. *Kingdoms of the Savanna.* Madison, 1966. The best history of central Africa in early modern times.

———. *Paths in the Rainforest: Toward a History of Political Tradition in Equatorial Africa.* Madison, 1990. A thoughtful analysis that considers both native traditions and external influences on African history.

Tradition and Change in East Asia

chapter 26

European-style buildings on the waterfront in eighteenth-century Guangzhou, where foreign merchants conducted their business.

EYEWITNESS:
Matteo Ricci and Chiming Clocks in China

In January 1601 a mechanical clock chimed the hours for the first time in the city of Beijing. In the early 1580s, devices that Chinese called "self-ringing bells" had arrived at the port of Macau, where Portuguese merchants awed local authorities with their chiming clocks. Reports of them soon spread throughout southern China and beyond to Beijing. The Roman Catholic missionary Matteo Ricci conceived the idea of capturing the emperor's attention with mechanical clocks and then persuading him and his subjects to convert to Christianity. From his post at Macau, Ricci let imperial authorities know that he could supply the emperor with a chiming clock. When the emperor Wanli granted him permission to travel to Beijing and establish a mission, Ricci took with him both a large mechanical clock intended for public display and a smaller, self-ringing bell for the emperor's personal use.

Chiming mechanical clocks enchanted Wanli and his court and soon became the rage in elite society throughout China. Wealthy Chinese merchants did not hesitate to pay handsome sums for the devices, and Europeans often found that their business in China went better if they presented gifts of self-ringing bells to the government officials they dealt with. By the eighteenth century the imperial court maintained a workshop to manufacture and repair mechanical clocks and watches. Most Chinese could not afford to purchase mechanical clocks, but commoners also had opportunities to admire self-ringing bells. Outside their residence in Beijing, Matteo Ricci and his missionary colleagues installed a large mechanical clock that regularly attracted crowds of curious neighbors when it struck the hours.

Chiming clocks did not have the effect that Ricci desired. The emperor showed no interest in Christianity, and the missionaries attracted only small numbers of Chinese converts. Yet, by opening the doors of the imperial court to the missionaries, the self-ringing bells symbolized the increasing engagement between Asian and European peoples.

By linking all the world's regions and peoples, the European voyages of exploration inaugurated a new era in world history. Yet transoceanic connections influenced different societies in very different ways. In contrast to sub-Saharan Africa, where the Atlantic slave trade bred instability and provoked turmoil, east Asian lands benefited greatly from long-distance trade, since it brought silver that stimulated their economies. East Asian societies benefited also from American plant crops that made their way across the seas as part of the Columbian exchange.

Unlike the Americas, where Europeans profoundly influenced historical development from the time of their arrival, east Asian societies largely controlled their own affairs until the nineteenth century. Europeans were active on the coastlines, but they had little influence on internal affairs in the region. Because of its political and cultural preeminence, China remained the dominant power in east Asia. Established during the Qin (221–206 B.C.E.) and Han (206 B.C.E.–220 C.E.) dynasties, long-standing political, social, and cultural traditions endowed Chinese society with a sense of stability and permanence. China was also a remarkably prosperous land. Indeed, with its huge population, enormous productive capacity, and strong demand for silver, China was a leading economic powerhouse driving world trade in early modern times. By the late eighteenth century, however, China was experiencing social and economic change that eventually caused problems both for state authorities and for Chinese society as a whole.

During the seventeenth and eighteenth centuries, Japan also underwent major transformations. The Tokugawa shoguns unified the Japanese islands for the first time and laid a foundation for long-term economic growth. While tightly restricting contacts and relations with the larger world, Tokugawa Japan generated a distinctive set of social and cultural traditions. Those developments helped fashion a Japan that would play a decisive role in global affairs by the twentieth century.

THE QUEST FOR POLITICAL STABILITY

During the thirteenth and fourteenth centuries, China experienced the trauma of rule by the Yuan dynasty (1279–1368) of nomadic Mongol warriors. Mongol overlords ignored Chinese political and cultural traditions, and they displaced Chinese bureaucrats in favor of Turkish, Persian, and other foreign administrators. When the Yuan dynasty came to an end, the Ming emperors who succeeded it sought to erase all signs of Mongol influence and restore traditional ways to China. Looking to the Tang and Song dynasties for inspiration, they built a powerful imperial state, revived the civil service staffed by Confucian scholars, and promoted Confucian thought. Rulers of the succeeding Qing dynasty were themselves Manchus of nomadic origin, but they too worked zealously to promote Chinese ways. Ming and Qing emperors alike were deeply conservative: their principal concern was to maintain stability in a large agrarian society, so they adopted policies that favored Chinese political and cultural traditions. The state that they fashioned governed China for more than half a millennium.

The Ming Dynasty

Ming Government When the Yuan dynasty collapsed, the Ming dynasty (1368–1644) restored native rule to China. Hongwu (reigned 1368–1398), founder of the Ming ("brilliant") dynasty, drove the Mongols out of China and built a tightly centralized state. As emperor, Hongwu made extensive use of mandarins, imperial officials who traveled throughout the land and oversaw implementation of government policies. He also placed great trust in eunuchs on the thinking that they could not generate families and hence would not build power bases that would challenge imperial authority. The emperor Yongle (reigned 1403–1424) launched a series of naval expeditions that sailed throughout the Indian Ocean basin and showed Chinese colors as far away as Malindi in east Africa. Yongle's successors discontinued the expensive maritime expeditions but maintained the tightly centralized state that Hongwu had established.

The Ming emperors were determined to prevent new invasions. In 1421 Yongle moved the capital from Nanjing in the south to Beijing so as to keep closer watch on the Mongols and other nomadic peoples in the north. The early Ming emperors commanded powerful armies that controlled the Mongols militarily, but by the mid-fifteenth century they had lost their effectiveness. Mongol forces massacred several Chinese armies in the 1440s, and in 1449 they captured the Ming emperor himself.

The Great Wall The later Ming emperors sought to protect their realm by building new fortifications, including the Great Wall of China, along the northern border. The Great Wall had precedents dating back to the fourth century B.C.E., and the first emperor of the Qin dynasty had ordered construction of a long defensive wall during the third century B.C.E. Those early walls had all fallen into ruin, however, and the Great Wall was a Ming-dynasty project. Workers by the hundreds of thousands labored throughout the late fifteenth and sixteenth centuries to build a formidable stone and brick barrier that ran some 2,500 kilometers (1,550 miles). The Great Wall was 10 to 15 meters (33 to 49 feet) high, and it featured watch towers, signal towers, and accommodations for troops deployed on the border.

The Ming emperors also set out to eradicate Mongol and other foreign influences and to create a stable society in the image of the Chinese past. With Ming encouragement,

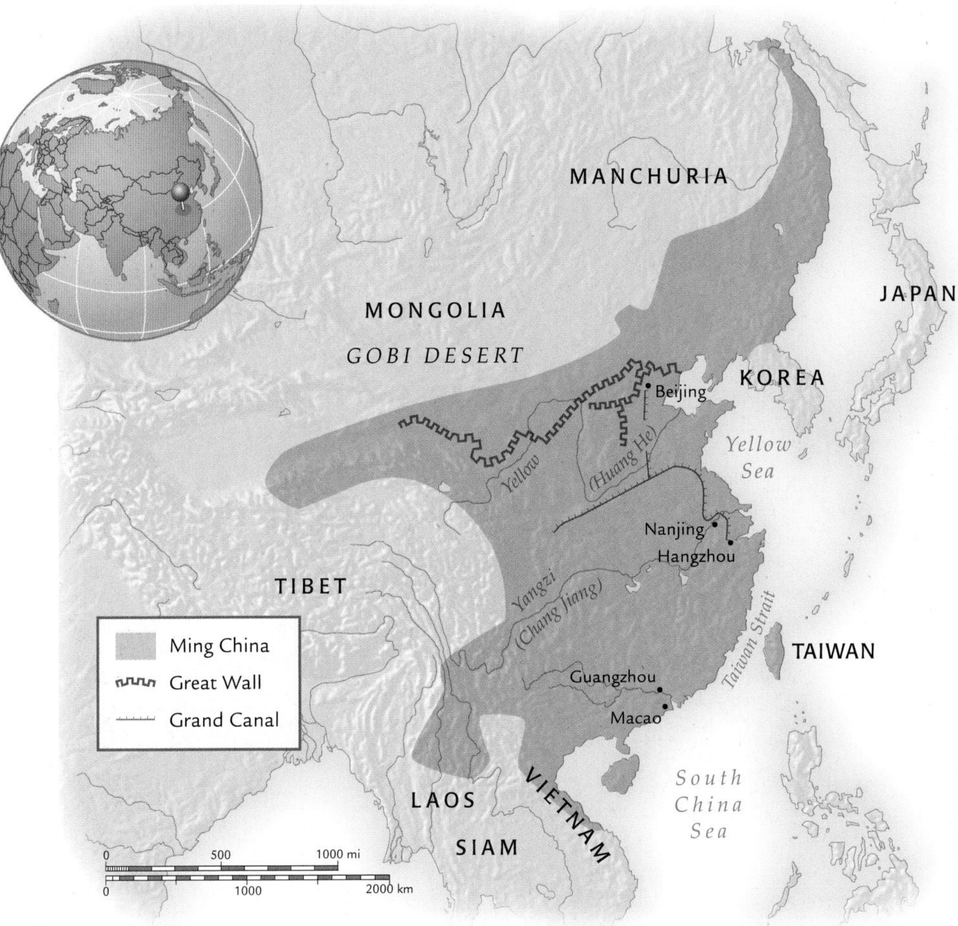

MAP 26.1
Ming China, 1368–1644.
Locate the old Ming capital at Nanjing and the new Ming capital at Beijing.
Why would the Ming emperors have wanted to move so far north?

for example, individuals abandoned the Mongol names and dress that many had adopted during the Yuan dynasty. Respect for Chinese traditions facilitated the restoration of institutions that the Mongols had ignored or suppressed. The government sponsored study of Chinese cultural traditions, especially Confucianism, and provided financial support for imperial academies and regional colleges. Most important, the Ming state restored the system of civil service examinations that Mongol rulers had neglected.

Ming Decline The vigor of early Ming rule did not survive beyond the mid-sixteenth century, when a series of problems weakened the dynasty. From the 1520s to the 1560s, pirates and smugglers operated almost at will along the east coast of China. (Although Ming officials referred to the pirates as Japanese, in fact most of them were Chinese.) Both the Ming navy and coastal defenses were ineffective, and conflicts with pirates often led to the disruption of coastal communities and sometimes even interior regions. In 1555, for example, a band of sixty-seven pirates went on a three-month rampage during which they looted a dozen cities in three provinces and killed more than four thousand people.

Suppression of pirates took more than forty years, partly because of an increasingly inept imperial government. The later Ming emperors lived extravagantly in the Forbidden City, a vast imperial enclave in Beijing, and received news about the outside world from eunuch servants and administrators. The emperors sometimes ignored government affairs for decades on end while satisfying their various appetites. Throughout his long reign, for example, the emperor Wanli (1572–1620) refused to meet with government officials. Instead, while indulging his taste for wine, he conducted business through eunuch intermediaries. Powerful eunuchs won the favor of the later Ming emperors by procuring concubines for them and providing for their amusement. The eunuchs then used their power and position to enrich themselves and lead lives of luxury. As their influence increased, corruption and inefficiency spread throughout the government and weakened the Ming state.

Ming Collapse When a series of famines struck China during the early seventeenth century, the government was unable to organize effective relief efforts. Peasants in famine-struck regions ate grass roots and tree bark. During the 1630s peasants organized revolts throughout China, and they

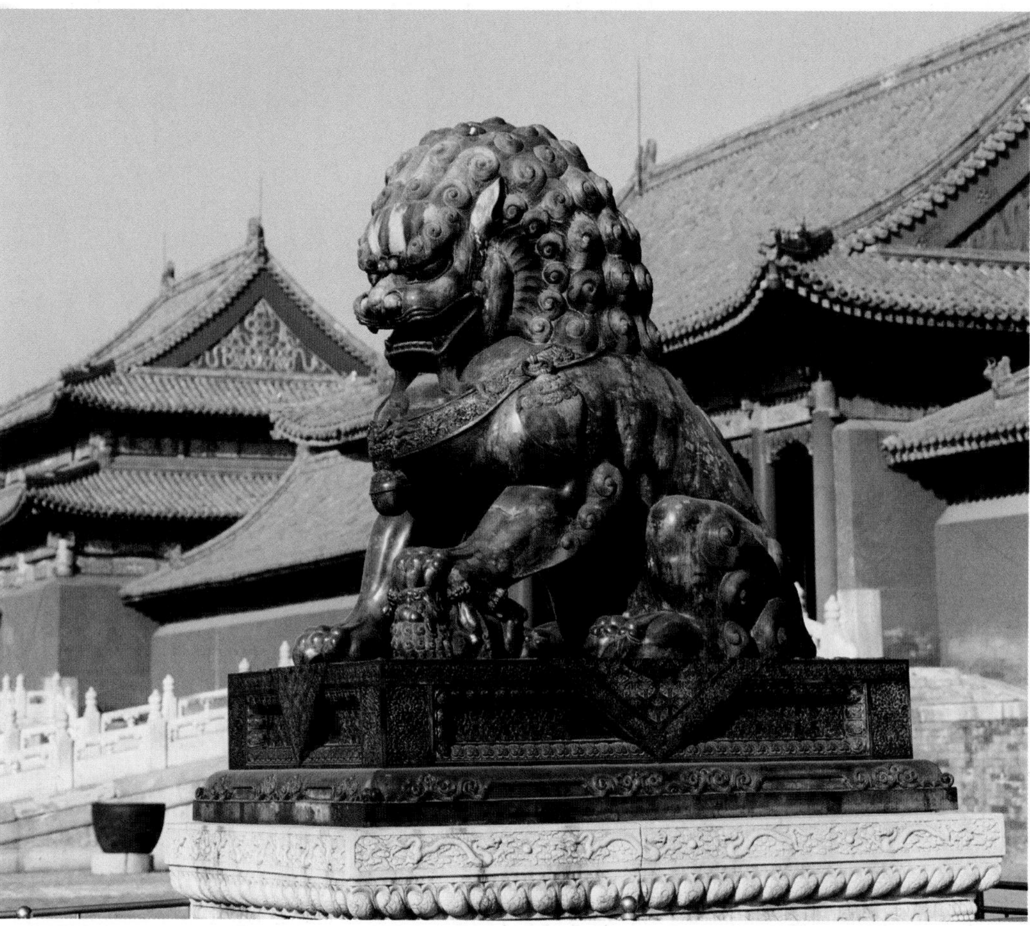

The emperor Yongle designed the Forbidden City as a vast, walled imperial retreat in central Beijing. Here a sculptured lion guards the Forbidden City's Gate of Supreme Harmony.

gathered momentum as one city after another withdrew its loyalty from the Ming dynasty. To complicate matters further, Manchu forces invaded from the north in search of opportunities for expansion in China. In 1644, rebel forces captured the Ming capital at Beijing. Manchu invaders allied with an army loyal to the Ming, crushed the rebels, and recovered Beijing. The Manchus portrayed themselves as avengers who saved the capital from dangerous rebels, but they neglected to restore Ming rule. Instead, they moved their own capital to Beijing and simply displaced the Ming dynasty.

The Qing Dynasty

The Manchus When the Ming dynasty fell, Manchus poured into China from their homeland of Manchuria north of the Great Wall. The victors proclaimed a new dynasty, the Qing ("pure"), which ruled China until the early twentieth century (1644–1911).

The Manchus mostly were pastoral nomads, although many had turned to agriculture and settled in the rich farmlands of southern Manchuria. Their remote ancestors had traded with China since the Qin dynasty, and they had frequently clashed with their neighbors over land and resources in northern China and southern Manchuria. During the late sixteenth and early seventeenth centuries, an ambitious chieftain named Nurhaci (reigned 1616–1626) unified Manchu tribes into a centralized state, promulgated a code of laws, and organized a powerful military force. During the 1620s and 1630s, the Manchu army expelled Ming garrisons in Manchuria, captured Korea and Mongolia, and launched small-scale invasions into China. After their seizure of Beijing in 1644, the Manchus moved to extend their authority throughout China. For almost forty years they waged campaigns against Ming loyalists and other rebels in southern China until by the early 1680s the Manchus had consolidated the Qing dynasty's hold throughout the land.

The establishment of the Qing dynasty was due partly to Manchu military prowess and partly to Chinese support for the Manchus. During the 1630s and 1640s, many Chinese generals deserted the Ming dynasty because of its corruption and inefficiency. Confucian scholar-bureaucrats also worked against the Ming, since they despised the eunuchs who dominated the imperial court. The Manchu ruling elites were schooled in Chinese language and Confucian thought, and they often enjoyed more respect from the scholar-bureaucrats than did the emperor and high administrators of the Ming dynasty itself.

The Manchus were careful to preserve their own ethnic and cultural identity. They not only outlawed intermarriage

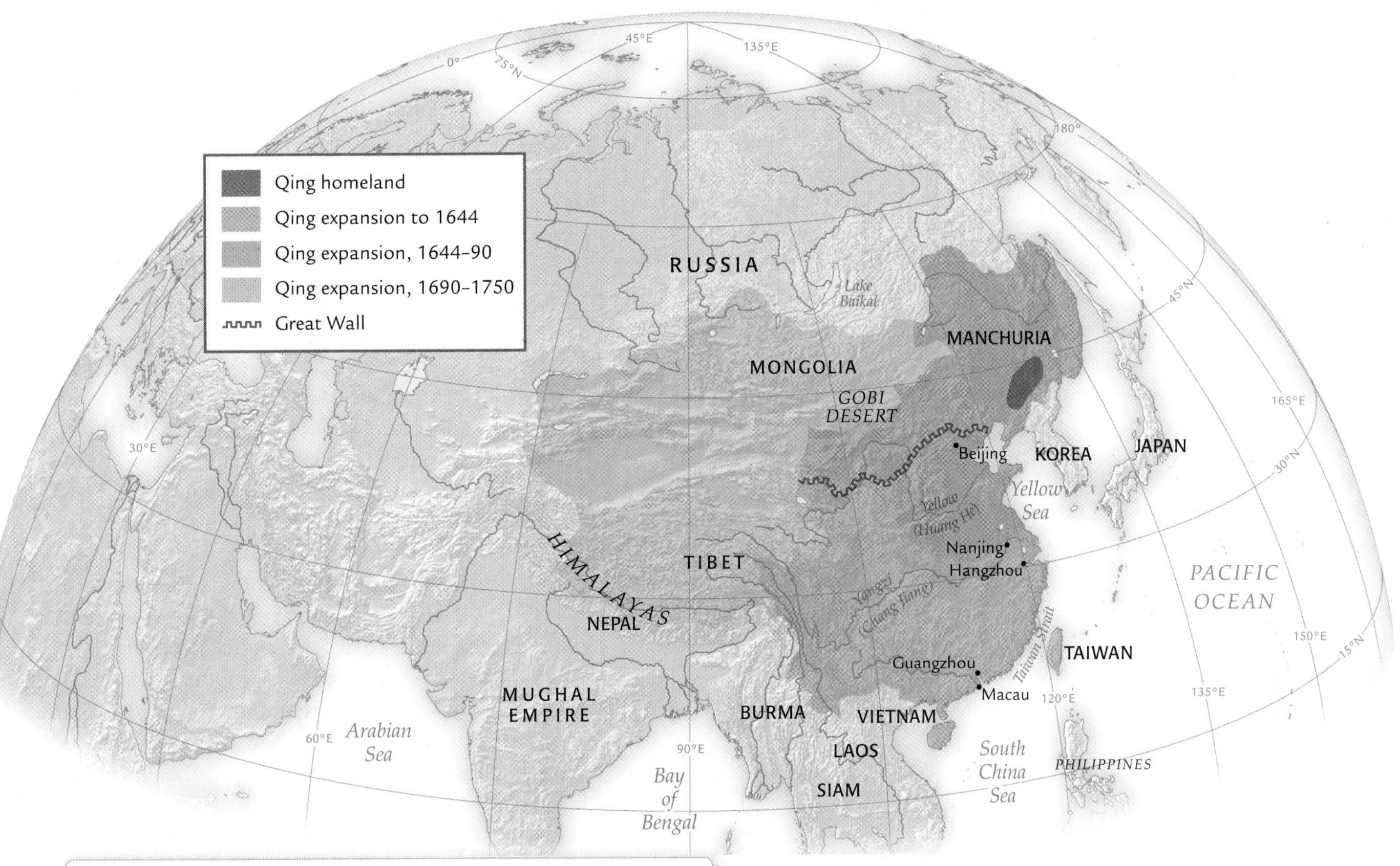

MAP 26.2
The Qing empire, 1644–1911.
Compare this map with Map 26.1.

Why would the Qing emperors have wanted to incorporate such extensive territories in Mongolia and Tibet into their empire?

between Manchus and Chinese but also forbade Chinese from traveling to Manchuria and from learning the Manchurian language. Qing authorities also forced Chinese men to shave the front of their heads and grow a Manchu-style queue as a sign of submission to the dynasty.

Kangxi and His Reign Until the nineteenth century, strong imperial leadership muted tensions between Manchu rulers and Chinese subjects. The long reigns of two particularly effective emperors, Kangxi (1661–1722) and Qianlong (1736–1795), helped the Manchus consolidate their hold on China. Kangxi was a Confucian scholar as well as an enlightened ruler. He was a voracious reader and occasionally composed poems. He studied the Confucian classics and sought to apply their teachings through his policies. Thus, for example, he organized flood-control and irrigation projects in observance of the Confucian precept that rulers should look after the welfare of their subjects and promote agriculture. He also generously patronized Confucian schools and academies.

Kangxi was also a conqueror, and he oversaw the construction of a vast Qing empire. He conquered the island of Taiwan, where Ming loyalists had retreated after their expulsion from southern China, and absorbed it into his empire. Like his predecessors of the Han and Tang dynasties, Kangxi sought to forestall problems with nomadic peoples by projecting Chinese influence into central Asia. His conquests in Mongolia and central Asia extended almost to the Caspian Sea, and he imposed a Chinese protectorate over Tibet. Kangxi's grandson Qianlong continued this expansion of Chinese influence. Qianlong sought to consolidate Kangxi's conquests in central Asia by maintaining military garrisons in eastern Turkestan (the territory now known as Xinjiang province in western China) and encouraging merchants to settle there in hopes that they would stabilize the region. Qianlong also made Vietnam, Burma, and Nepal vassal states of the Qing dynasty.

Qianlong and His Reign Qianlong's reign marked the height of the Qing dynasty. Like Kangxi, Qianlong was a sophisticated and learned man. He reportedly composed more than one hundred thousand poems, and he was a discriminating connoisseur of painting and calligraphy. During his long, stable, and prosperous reign, the imperial treasury bulged so much that on four occasions Qianlong cancelled tax collections. Toward the end of his reign, Qianlong paid less attention to imperial affairs and delegated many responsibilities to his favorite eunuchs. His successors continued that practice, devoting themselves to hunting and the harem, and by the nineteenth century the Qing dynasty faced serious difficulties. Throughout the reign of Qianlong, however, China remained a wealthy and well-organized land.

Though painted in the nineteenth century, this portrait depicts Kangxi in his imperial regalia as he looked at about age fifty. Kangxi reigned for sixty-one years, making him the longest-ruling emperor in Chinese history.

The Son of Heaven and the Scholar-Bureaucrats

Although Qing rulers usually appointed Manchus to the highest political posts, they relied on the same governmental apparatus that the Ming emperors had established. Both the Ming and the Qing dynasties presided over a tightly centralized state, which they administered through a bureaucracy staffed by Confucian scholars. For more than five hundred years, the autocratic state created by the Ming emperor Hongwu governed China's fortunes.

The Son of Heaven If the emperor of China during the Ming and Qing dynasties was not quite a god, he certainly was more than a mere mortal. Chinese tradition held that he was the "Son of Heaven," the human being designated by heavenly powers to maintain order on the earth. He led a privileged life within the walls of the Forbidden City. Hundreds of concubines resided in his harem, and thousands of eunuchs looked after his desires. His daily activities were carefully choreographed performances in the form of inspections, audiences, banquets, and other official duties. Everything about his person and the institution he represented conveyed a sense of awesome authority. The imperial wardrobe and personal effects bore designs forbidden to all others, for instance, and the written characters of the emperor's name were taboo throughout the realm. Individuals who had the rare privilege of a personal audience with the emperor had to perform the kowtow—three kneelings and nine head knockings. Those who gave even minor offense faced severe punishment. Even the highest official could have his bare buttocks flogged with bamboo canes, a punishment that sometimes brought victims to the point of death.

The Scholar-Bureaucrats Day-to-day governance of the empire fell to scholar-bureaucrats appointed by the emperor. With few exceptions these officials came from the class of well-educated and highly literate men known as the scholar-gentry. These men had earned academic degrees by passing rigorous civil service examinations, and they dominated China's political and social life.

Preparations for the examinations began at an early age. Sometimes they took place in local schools, which like the civil service examinations were open only to males. Wealthy families often engaged the services of tutors, who made formal education available also to girls. By the time students were eleven or twelve years old, they had memorized several thousand characters that were necessary to deal with the Confucian curriculum, including the *Analects* of Confucius and other standard works. They followed those studies with instruction in calligraphy, poetry, and essay composition. Diligent students also acquainted themselves with a large corpus of commentaries, histories, and literary works in preparing for civil service examinations.

Civil Service Examinations The examinations consisted of a battery of tests administered at the district, provincial, and metropolitan levels. Stiff official quotas restricted the number of successful candidates in each examination—only three hundred students could pass metropolitan examinations—and students frequently took the examinations several times before earning a degree.

Writing the examinations was a grueling ordeal. At the appointed hour, candidates presented themselves at the examination compound. Each candidate brought a water pitcher, a chamber pot, bedding, food, an inkstone, ink, and brushes. After guards had verified their identities and searched them for hidden printed materials, the new arrivals proceeded along narrow lanes to a honeycomb of small, cell-like rooms barely large enough to accommodate one man and his possessions. Aside from a bench, a makeshift bed, and boards that served as a desk, the rooms were empty. For the next three days and two nights, the cramped rooms were home to the candidates, who spent all their time writing "eight-legged essays"—literary compositions with eight distinct sections—on questions posed by the examiners. There were

Qiu Ying, a prominent Chinese artist of the sixteenth century, captured this image of candidates who had taken the civil service exams as they waited at the wall where officials would post the scores.

no interruptions, nor was there any communication between candidates. If someone died during the examination period, officials wrapped his body in a straw mat and tossed it over the high walls that ringed the compound.

The Examination System and Chinese Society

The possibility of bureaucratic service—with prospects for rich social and financial rewards—ensured that competition for degrees was ferocious at all levels. As a result, cheating candidates and corrupt examiners occasionally compromised the system. Yet a degree did not ensure government service. During the Qing dynasty the empire's one million degree holders competed for twenty thousand official civil service positions. Those who passed only the district exams had few opportunities for bureaucratic employment and usually spent their careers "plowing with the writing brush" by teaching in local schools or serving as family tutors. Those who passed the metropolitan examinations, however, could look forward to powerful positions in the imperial bureaucracy.

The examination system was a pivotal institution. By opening the door to honor, power, and rewards, the examinations encouraged serious pursuit of a formal education. Furthermore, since the system did not erect social barriers before its recruits, it provided an avenue for upward social mobility. Years of education and travel to examination sites were expensive, so candidates from wealthy families enjoyed advantages over others, but the exams themselves were open to all males regardless of age or social class. Finally, in addition to selecting officials for government service, the education and examination system molded the personal values of those who managed day-to-day affairs in imperial China.

By concentrating on Confucian classics and neo-Confucian commentaries, the examinations guaranteed that Confucianism would be at the heart of Chinese education and that Confucians would govern the state.

ECONOMIC AND SOCIAL CHANGES

By modeling their governmental structure on the centralized imperial states of earlier Chinese dynasties, the Ming and Qing emperors succeeded in their goal of restoring and maintaining traditional ways in China. They also sought to preserve the traditional hierarchical and patriarchal social order. Yet, while the emperors promoted conservative political and social policies, China experienced economic and social changes, partly as a result of influences from abroad. Agricultural production increased dramatically—especially after the introduction of new food crops from the Americas—and fueled rapid population growth. Meanwhile, global trade brought China enormous wealth, which stimulated the domestic economy by encouraging increased trade, manufacturing, and urban growth. These developments deeply influenced Chinese society and partly undermined the stability that the Ming and Qing emperors sought to preserve.

thinking about TRADITIONS

Chinese Women

Women had for long centuries lived under the strictures of a Confucian society. How did Confucian ideals in the Ming and Qing dynasties affect attitudes about women? What did the practice of foot binding suggest about gender relations in late imperial China?

The Patriarchal Family

Filial Piety Moralists portrayed the Chinese people as one large family, and they extended family values to the larger society. Filial piety, for example, implied not only duties of children toward their fathers but also loyalty of subjects toward the emperor. Like the imperial government, the Chinese family was hierarchical, patriarchal, and authoritarian. The father was head of the household, and he passed leadership of the family to his eldest son. The veneration of ancestors, which the state promoted as a matter of Confucian propriety, strengthened the authority of the patriarchs by honoring the male line of descent in formal family rituals. Filial piety was the cornerstone of family values. Children had the duty to look after their parents' happiness and well-being, and a crucial obligation was to support parents in their old age. Young children heard stories of sons who went so far as to cut off parts of their bodies to ensure that their parents had enough to eat!

The social assumptions of the Chinese family extended into patrilineal descent groups such as the clan. Sometimes numbering into the thousands, clan members came from all social classes, though members of the gentry usually dominated a given clan. Clans assumed responsibilities that exceeded the capacities of the nuclear family, such as the maintenance of local order, organization of local economies, and provision for welfare. Clan-supported education gave poor but promising relatives the opportunity to succeed in the civil service examinations. The principal motives behind this charity were corporate self-interest as well as altruism. A government position brought prestige and prosperity to the entire clan, so educational support was a prudent investment. Finally, clans served as a means for the transmission of Confucian values from the gentry leaders to all social classes within the clan.

Gender Relations Within the family, Confucian principles subjected women to the authority of men. The subordination of females began at an early age. Chinese parents preferred boys over girls. Whereas a boy might have the opportunity to take the official examinations, become a government official, and thereby bring honor and financial reward to the entire clan, parents regarded a girl as a social and financial liability. After years of expensive upbringing, most girls would marry and become members of other households. Under those circumstances it was not surprising that life was precarious for newborn girls, who were the primary victims of infanticide.

During the Ming and Qing dynasties, patriarchal authority over females probably became tighter than ever before in China. Since ancient times, relatives had discouraged widows from remarriage, but social pressures increased during the Ming dynasty. Friends and relatives not only encouraged widows to honor the memory of their departed husbands but also heaped posthumous honors on those who committed suicide and followed their spouses to the grave.

Foot Binding Moreover, foot binding, a custom that probably originated in the Song dynasty, became exceptionally popular during the late Ming and Qing dynasties. Tightly constrained and even deformed by strips of linen, bound feet could not grow naturally and so would not support the weight of an adult woman. Bound feet were small and dainty, and they sometimes inspired erotic arousal among men. The practice of foot binding became most widespread among the wealthy classes, since it demonstrated an ability to support women who could not perform physical labor, but commoners sometimes bound the feet of especially pretty girls in hopes of arranging favorable marriages that would enhance the family's social standing.

Marriage itself was a contractual affair whose principal purpose was to continue the male line of descent. A bride

To encourage widows to remain unmarried, the Ming and Qing governments constructed arches in honor of those who remained chaste. These arches erected during the Qing dynasty still stand in Anhui province in the Yangzi River valley.

became a member of the husband's family, and there was no ambiguity about her position in the household. On her wedding day, as soon as she arrived at her husband's home, the bride performed ritual acts demonstrating subservience to her husband and her new family. Women could not divorce their husbands, but men could put aside their wives in cases where there was no offspring or where the wife was guilty of adultery, theft, disobedience to her husband's family, or even being too talkative.

Thus custom and law combined to strengthen patriarchal authority in Chinese families during the Ming and Qing dynasties. Yet, while family life continued to develop along traditional lines, the larger Chinese society underwent considerable change between the sixteenth and the eighteenth centuries.

Population Growth and Economic Development

China was a predominantly agricultural society, a fact that meshed agreeably with the Confucian view that land was the source of everything praiseworthy. The emperor himself acknowledged the central importance of agriculture by plowing the first furrow of the season. Yet only a small fraction of China's land is suitable for planting: even today only about 11 percent is in cultivation. To feed the country's large population, China's farmers relied on intensive, garden-style agriculture that was highly productive. On its strong agrarian foundation, China supported a large population and built the most highly commercialized economy of the preindustrial world.

American Food Crops By intensively cultivating every available parcel of land, Chinese peasants increased their yields of traditional food crops—especially rice, wheat, and millet—until the seventeenth century. Beginning about the mid-seventeenth century, as peasants approached the upper limits of agricultural productivity, Spanish merchants coming by way of the Philippines introduced American food crops to China. American maize, sweet potatoes, and peanuts permitted Chinese farmers to take advantage of soils that previously had gone uncultivated. The introduction of new crops increased the food supply and supported further population growth.

Population Growth In spite of recurring epidemic diseases such as plague, which claimed the lives of millions, China's population rose rapidly from 100 million in 1500 to 160 million in 1600. Partly because of rebellion and war, it fell to 140 million in the mid-seventeenth century, but returned to 160 million by 1700 and then surged to 225 million by 1750, thus registering a more than 40 percent increase in half a century. This rapid demographic growth set the stage for economic and social problems, since agricultural production could not keep pace with population over a long term. Acute problems did not occur until the nineteenth century, but per capita income in China began to decline as early as the reign of Qianlong.

While an increasing population placed pressure on Chinese resources, the growing commercial market offered opportunities for entrepreneurs. Because of demographic

A Ming-era vase painting depicts a woman weaving silk as an attendant pours tea. Silk and tea were among the exports China produced for global trade.

expansion, entrepreneurs had access to a large labor force that was both occupationally and geographically mobile, so they were able to recruit workers readily at low cost. After the mid-sixteenth century, the Chinese economy benefited also from the influx of Japanese and American silver, which stimulated trade and financed further commercial expansion.

Foreign Trade Global trade brought prosperity to China, especially during the early Qing dynasty. Chinese workers produced vast quantities of silk, porcelain, lacquerware, and tea for consumers in the Indian Ocean basin, central Asia, and Europe. The silk industry was especially well organized: weavers worked in workshops for regular wages producing fine satins and brocades for export. Chinese imports were relatively few: they included spices from Maluku, exotic products such as birds and animal skins from tropical regions, and small quantities of woolen textiles from Europe. Compensation for exports came most importantly in the form of silver bullion, which supported the silver-based Chinese economy and fueled manufacturing.

Economic growth and commercial expansion took place mostly in an atmosphere of tight government regulation. During the early fifteenth century, the Ming emperor Yongle sought to establish a Chinese presence in the Indian Ocean basin, and he sponsored a series of seven massive maritime expeditions (1405–1433) led by the eunuch admiral Zheng He. The Chinese fleets included as many as 317 vessels and 28,000 men. Zheng He called at ports from Java to Malindi, suppressed pirates in southeast Asian waters, intervened in local conflicts in Sumatra and Ceylon, intimidated local authorities with shows of force in southern Arabia and Mogadishu, and made China's presence felt throughout the Indian Ocean basin.

After the reign of Yongle, however, the Ming government withdrew its support for expensive maritime expeditions and even tried to prevent Chinese subjects from dealing with foreign peoples. In its effort to pacify southern China during the later seventeenth century, the Qing government tried to end maritime activity altogether. An imperial edict of 1656 forbade "even a plank from drifting to the sea," and in 1661 the emperor Kangxi ordered evacuation of the southern coastal regions. Those policies had only a limited effect—small Chinese vessels continued to trade actively in Japan and southeast Asian ports—and when Qing forces pacified southern China in the 1680s, government authorities rescinded the strictest measures. Thereafter, however, Qing authorities closely supervised the activities of foreign merchants in China. They permitted Portuguese merchants to operate only at the port of Macau, and British agents had to deal exclusively with the official merchant guild in Guangzhou.

While limiting the activities of foreign merchants, government policies also discouraged the organization of large-scale commercial ventures by Chinese merchants. In the absence of government approval, it was impossible, for example, to maintain shipyards that could construct large sailing ships like the mammoth, nine-masted treasure ships that Zheng He had led throughout the Indian Ocean. Similarly, it was impossible to organize large trading firms like the English East India Company or the Dutch VOC.

Trade and Migration to Southeast Asia Nevertheless, thousands of Chinese merchants worked either individually or in partnerships, plying the waters of the China seas to link China with global trade networks. Chinese merchants were especially prominent in Manila, where they exchanged silk and porcelain for American silver that came across the Pacific Ocean with the Manila galleons. They were also frequent visitors at the Dutch colonial capital of Batavia, where they supplied the VOC with silk and porcelain in exchange for silver and Indonesian spices. Entrepreneurial Chinese merchants ventured also to lands throughout southeast Asia—the Philippines, Borneo, Sumatra, Malaya, Thailand, and elsewhere—in search of exotic tropical products for Chinese consumers. Indeed, the early modern era was an age when merchants established a prominent Chinese presence throughout southeast Asia.

sources from the past

Qianlong on Chinese Trade with England

Qing administrators tightly restricted foreign trade. Foreign merchants had to deal with government-approved agents outside the city walls of Guangzhou and had to depart as soon as they had completed their business. In 1793 a British diplomat representing King George III of England bestowed gifts on the emperor Qianlong and petitioned for the right to trade at ports other than Guangzhou. In a letter to King George, Qianlong outlined his views on Chinese trade with England. His letter also bespeaks clearly the importance of government policy for commerce and economic affairs in China.

You, O king, from afar have yearned after the blessings of our civilization, and in your eagerness to come into touch with our influence have sent an embassy across the sea bearing a memorandum. I have already taken note of your respectful spirit of submission, have treated your mission with extreme favor and loaded it with gifts, besides issuing a mandate to you, O king, and honoring you with the bestowal of valuable presents. . . .

Yesterday your ambassador petitioned my ministers to memorialize me regarding your trade with China, but his proposal is not consistent with our dynastic usage and cannot be entertained. Hitherto, all European nations, including your own country's barbarian merchants, have carried on their trade with our Celestial Empire at Guangzhou. Such has been the procedure for many years, although our Celestial Empire possesses all things in prolific abundance and lacks no product within its own borders. There was therefore no need to import the manufactures of outside barbarians in exchange for our own produce. But as the tea, silk, and porcelain which the Celestial Empire produces are absolute necessities to European nations and to yourselves, we have permitted, as a signal mark of favor, that trading agents should be established at Guangzhou, so that your wants might be supplied and your country thus participate in our beneficence. But your ambassador has now put forward new requests which completely fail to recognize our throne's principle to "treat strangers from afar with indulgence," and to exercise a pacifying control over barbarian tribes the world over. . . . Your England is not the only nation trading at Guangzhou. If other nations, following your bad example, wrongfully importune my ear with further impossible requests, how will it be possible for me to treat them with easy indulgence? Nevertheless, I do not forget the lonely remoteness of your island, cut off from the world by intervening wastes of sea, nor do I overlook your excusable ignorance of the usages of our Celestial Empire. I have consequently commanded my ministers to enlighten your ambassador on the subject, and have ordered the departure of the mission. . . .

If, after the receipt of this explicit decree, you lightly give ear to the representations of your subordinates and allow your barbarian merchants to proceed to Zhejiang and Tianjin, with the object of landing and trading there, the ordinances of my Celestial Empire are strict in the extreme, and the local officials, both civil and military, are bound reverently to obey the law of the land. Should your vessels touch the shore, your merchants will assuredly never be permitted to land or to reside there, but will be subject to instant expulsion. In that event your barbarian merchants will have had a long journey for nothing. Do not say that you were not warned in due time! Tremblingly obey and show no negligence! A special mandate!

For Further Reflection

- What considerations might have prompted the Chinese government to take such a restrictive approach to foreign trade?

Source: J. O. P. Bland. *Annals and Memoirs of the Court of Peking.* Boston: Houghton Mifflin, 1914, pp. 325–31. (Translation slightly modified.)

Government and Technology China's economic expansion took place largely in the absence of technological innovation. During the Tang and Song dynasties, Chinese engineers had produced a veritable flood of inventions, and China was the world's leader in technology. Yet by early Ming times, technological innovation had slowed. Imperial armed forces adopted European cannons and advanced firearms for their own uses—thus borrowing forms of gunpowder technology that had originated in China and that Europeans had refined and improved—but little innovation in agricultural and industrial technologies occurred during the Ming and Qing dynasties.

Part of the explanation for the slowdown has to do with the role of the government. During the Tang and Song dynasties, the imperial government had encouraged technological innovation as a foundation of military and economic strength. In contrast, the Ming and Qing regimes favored political and social stability over technological innovation, which they feared would lead to unsettling change. Alongside government policy, the abundance and ready availability of skilled workers also discouraged technological innovation. When employers wanted to increase production, they found that hiring additional workers was less costly than making large investments in new technologies. In the short term this tactic maintained relative prosperity in China while keeping most of the population gainfully employed. Over the longer term, however, it ensured that China lost technological ground to European peoples, who embarked on a round of stunning technological innovation beginning about the mid-eighteenth century.

This late-eighteenth-century drawing depicts Chinese men treading the pole of a device that raises irrigation water. The men all wear the braided queue that Manchus required of Chinese men.

Gentry, Commoners, Soldiers, and Mean People

Privileged Classes Except for the emperor and his family, scholar-bureaucrats and gentry occupied the most exalted positions in Chinese society. Because of their official positions, the scholar-bureaucrats ranked slightly above gentry. Nevertheless, scholar-bureaucrats had much in common with the gentry: they came largely from gentry ranks, and after leaving government service they usually rejoined gentry society. The scholar-bureaucrats and gentry functioned as intermediaries between the imperial government and local society. By organizing water control projects and public security measures, they played a crucial role in the management of local society.

Scholar-bureaucrats and gentry were easy to identify. They wore distinctive clothing—black gowns with blue borders adorned with various rank insignia—and commoners addressed them with honorific terms. They received favorable legal treatment that reflected their privileged status. As a rule, commoners could not call members of privileged classes to appear as witnesses in legal proceedings. They also enjoyed immunity from corporal punishment and exemption from labor service and taxes.

Most of the gentry owned land, which was their major source of income. As long as they did not have to perform physical labor, some gentry also supplemented their income by operating pawn and rice shops. Many of them were also silent business partners of merchants and entrepreneurs. Their principal source of income, however, came from the government service to which only they had access by virtue of their academic degrees. In contrast to landed elites elsewhere, who often lived on rural estates, China's gentry resided largely in cities and towns, where they tended to political, social, and financial affairs.

Working Classes Confucian tradition ranked three broad classes of commoners below the gentry: peasants, artisans or workers, and merchants. By far the biggest class consisted of peasants, a designation that covered everyone from day laborers to tenant farmers to petty landlords. Confucian principles regarded peasants as the most honorable of the three classes, since they performed honest labor and provided the food that supported the entire population.

The category of artisans and workers encompassed a wide spectrum of occupations. Despite their lower status, crafts workers, tailors, barbers, physicians, and workers in manufacturing plants generally enjoyed higher income than peasants did. Artisans and workers were usually employees of the state or of gentry and merchant families, but they also pursued their occupations as self-employed persons.

Merchants Merchants, from street peddlers to individuals of enormous wealth and influence, ranked at the bottom level of the Confucian social hierarchy. Because moralists looked upon them as unscrupulous social parasites, merchants enjoyed little legal protection, and government policy was always critically important to their pursuits. Yet Chinese merchants often garnered official support for their enterprises, either through bribery of government bureaucrats or through profit-sharing arrangements with gentry families. Indeed, the participation of gentry families in commercial ventures such as warehousing, money lending, and pawnbroking blurred the distinction between gentry and merchants. Merchants blurred the distinction further by providing their sons with an education that prepared them for government examinations, which in turn could result in promotion to gentry status and appointment to civil service positions.

The prominence of artisans and merchants pointed up the social and economic development of China since the time of Confucius. Although China was still a basically agri-

The elegant clothing of this Chinese merchant suggests the wealth and power of merchants in late imperial China.

cultural land, manufacturing and commerce had become much more economically important than in ancient times. As a result, those who could recognize and exploit opportunities had the potential to lead comfortable lives and even to climb into the ranks of the privileged gentry class. Yet Chinese merchants and artisans did not forge cooperative relationships with government authorities like the political-commercial alliances formed in the English and Dutch states in early modern times. Late Ming and Qing authorities permitted Chinese merchants to engage in small-scale commerce, and they allowed foreigners to trade through the official merchant guild in Guangzhou. Their principal concern, however, was to preserve the stability of a large agrarian society, not to promote rapid economic development through trade. Thus, unlike some of their European counterparts, Chinese authorities did not adopt policies designed to strengthen both merchants and the state by authorizing merchants to pursue their efforts aggressively in the larger world.

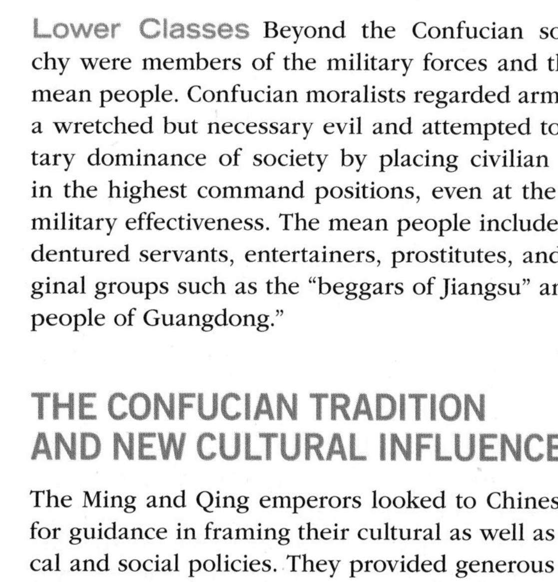

Lower Classes Beyond the Confucian social hierarchy were members of the military forces and the so-called mean people. Confucian moralists regarded armed forces as a wretched but necessary evil and attempted to avoid military dominance of society by placing civilian bureaucrats in the highest command positions, even at the expense of military effectiveness. The mean people included slaves, indentured servants, entertainers, prostitutes, and other marginal groups such as the "beggars of Jiangsu" and the "boat people of Guangdong."

THE CONFUCIAN TRADITION AND NEW CULTURAL INFLUENCES

The Ming and Qing emperors looked to Chinese traditions for guidance in framing their cultural as well as their political and social policies. They provided generous support for Confucianism, particularly in the form of neo-Confucianism articulated by the twelfth-century scholar Zhu Xi, and they ensured that formal education in China revolved around Confucian thought and values. Yet the Confucian tradition was not the only cultural alternative in Ming and Qing China. Demographic and urban growth encouraged the emergence of a vibrant popular culture in Chinese cities, and European missionaries reintroduced Roman Catholic Christianity to China and acquainted Chinese intellectuals with European science and technology as well.

Neo-Confucianism and Pulp Fiction

Imperial sponsorship of Chinese cultural traditions meant primarily support for the Confucian tradition, especially as systematized by the Song dynasty scholar Zhu Xi, the most prominent architect of neo-Confucianism. Zhu Xi combined the moral, ethical, and political values of Confucius with the logical rigor and speculative power of Buddhist philosophy. He emphasized the values of self-discipline, filial piety, and obedience to established rulers, all of which appealed to Ming and Qing emperors seeking to maintain stability in their vast realm. Cultural policies of the Ming and Qing dynasties made the neo-Confucian tradition the reigning imperial ideology from the fourteenth to the early twentieth century.

Confucian Education To promote Confucian values, the Ming and Qing emperors supported educational programs at several levels. They funded the Hanlin Academy, a research institute for Confucian scholars in Beijing, and maintained provincial schools throughout China where promising students could study for the civil service examinations. The exams themselves encouraged the cultivation of Confucian values, since they focused largely on Confucian texts and neo-Confucian commentaries.

Ming and Qing courts also provided generous funding for other projects emphasizing Chinese cultural traditions. The Ming emperor Yongle sponsored the compilation of the *Yongle Encyclopedia,* a vast collection of Chinese philosophical, literary, and historical texts that filled almost twenty-three thousand scrolls. During the Qing dynasty both Kangxi and Qianlong organized similar projects. Kangxi's *Collection of Books* was smaller than the *Yongle Encyclopedia,* but it was more influential because the emperor had it printed and distributed, whereas Yongle's compilation was available only in three manuscript copies. Qianlong's *Complete Library of the Four Treasuries* was too large to publish—it ran to 93,556 pamphlet-size volumes—but the emperor deposited manuscript copies in seven libraries throughout China.

Popular Culture While the imperial courts promoted Confucianism, a lively popular culture took shape in the cities of China. Most urban residents did not have an advanced education and knew little about Confucius, Zhu Xi, or other intellectual luminaries. Many of them were literate merchants, however, and they preferred entertainment and diversion more intellectually engaging than that found in local teahouses and wine shops. Popular novels met their needs.

Popular Novels Confucian scholars looked down on popular novels as crude fiction that had little to do with the realities of the world. Printing made it possible to produce books cheaply and in mass quantities, however, and urban residents eagerly consumed the fast-paced novels that flooded Chinese cities during the Ming and Qing eras. Many of the novels had little literary merit, but their tales of conflict, horror, wonder, excitement, and sometimes unconcealed pornography appealed to readers.

Yet many popular novels also offered thoughtful reflections on the world and human affairs. The historical novel *The Romance of the Three Kingdoms,* for example, explored the political intrigue that followed the collapse of the Han dynasty. *The Dream of the Red Chamber* told the story of cousins deeply in love who could not marry because of their families' wishes. Through the prism of a sentimental love story, the novel shed fascinating light on the dynamics of wealthy scholar-gentry families. In a different vein, *Journey to the West* dealt with the seventh-century journey to India of the famous Buddhist monk Xuanzang. In the popular novel, Xuanzang's traveling companion was a monkey with magical powers who among other things could jump 10,000 kilometers (6,215 miles) in a single bound. While promoting Buddhist values, *Journey to the West* also made the trickster monkey a wildly popular and celebrated character in Chinese literature. As recently as 1987, Chinese-American novelist Maxine Hong Kingston adapted this character to modern times in her novel *Tripmaster Monkey.*

Italian Jesuit Matteo Ricci (left) with Xu Quangqi, his most famous Chinese disciple. Both men wear the distinctive gowns of educated, refined scholar-gentry. A distinguished scholar who held an appointment at the Hanlin Academy, Xu helped Ricci translate Euclid's geometrical works into Chinese.

The Return of Christianity to China

Nestorian Christians had established churches and monasteries in China as early as the seventh century C.E., and Roman Catholic communities were prominent in Chinese commercial centers during the Yuan dynasty. After the outbreak of epidemic plague and the collapse of the Yuan dynasty in the fourteenth century, however, Christianity disappeared from China. When Roman Catholic missionaries returned in the sixteenth century, they had to start from scratch in their efforts to win converts and establish a Christian community.

Matteo Ricci The most prominent of the missionaries were the Jesuits, who worked to strengthen Roman Catholic Christianity in Europe and also to spread their faith abroad. Founder of the mission to China was the Italian Jesuit Matteo Ricci (1552–1610), who had the ambitious goal of converting China to Christianity, beginning with the Ming emperor Wanli. Ricci was a brilliant and learned man as well as a polished diplomat, and he became a popular figure at the Ming court. Upon arrival at Macau in 1582, Ricci immersed himself in the study of the Chinese language and the Confucian classics. He had a talent for languages, and his phenomenal memory enabled him to master the thousands of characters used in literary Chinese writing. By the time he first traveled to Beijing and visited the imperial court in 1601, Ricci was able to write learned Chinese and converse fluently with Confucian scholars.

Ricci's mastery of Chinese language and literature opened doors for the Jesuits, who then dazzled their hosts with European science, technology, and mechanical gadgetry. Ricci and his colleagues had an advanced education in mathematics and astronomy, and they were able to correct Chinese calendars that consistently miscalculated solar eclipses. The Jesuits also prepared maps of the world—with China placed diplomatically at the center—on the basis of geographic knowledge that Europeans had gained during their voyages through the world's seas. The Jesuits even supervised the casting of high-quality bronze cannons for Ming and early Qing armies.

Confucianism and Christianity The Jesuits piqued Chinese curiosity also with mechanical devices. Finely ground glass prisms became popular because of their refraction of sunlight into its component parts. Harpsichords also drew attention, and Jesuits with musical talents often composed songs for their hosts. Most popular of all, however, were the devices that Chinese called "self-ringing bells"—spring-driven mechanical clocks that kept tolerably accurate time, chimed the hours, and sometimes even struck the quarter hours as well.

The Jesuits sought to capture Chinese interest with European science and technology, but their ultimate goal was always to win converts. They portrayed Christianity as a faith very similar to Chinese cultural traditions. Ricci, for example, wrote a treatise entitled *The True Meaning of the Lord of Heaven* in which he argued that the doctrines of Confucius and Jesus were very similar, if not identical. Over the years, according to Ricci, neo-Confucian scholars had altered Confucius's own teachings, so adoption of Christianity by Chinese would represent a return to a more pure and original Confucianism. The Jesuits also held religious services in the Chinese language and allowed converts to continue the time-honored practice of venerating their ancestors.

In spite of their tolerance, flexibility, and genuine respect for their hosts, the Jesuits attracted few converts in China. By the mid-eighteenth century, Chinese Christians numbered about 200,000—a tiny proportion of the Chinese population of 225 million. Chinese hesitated to adopt Christianity partly because of its exclusivity: for centuries, Chinese had honored Confucianism, Daoism, and Buddhism at the same time. Like Islam, though, Christianity claimed to be the only true religion, so conversion implied that Confucianism, Daoism, and Buddhism were inferior or even fallacious creeds—a proposition most Chinese were unwilling to accept.

End of the Jesuit Mission Ultimately, the Roman Catholic mission in China came to an end because of squabbles between the Jesuits and members of the Franciscan and Dominican orders, who also sought converts in China. Jealous of the Jesuits' presence at the imperial court, the Franciscans and Dominicans complained to the pope about their rivals' tolerance of ancestor veneration and willingness to conduct Chinese-language services. The pope sided with the critics and in the early eighteenth century issued several proclamations ordering missionaries in China to suppress ancestor veneration and conduct services according to European standards. In response to that demand, the emperor Kangxi ordered an end to the preaching of Christianity in China. Although he did not strictly enforce the ban, the mission weakened, and by the mid-eighteenth century it had effectively come to an end.

The Roman Catholic mission to China did not attract large numbers of Chinese converts, but it nonetheless had important cultural effects. Besides making European science and technology known in China, the Jesuits made China known in Europe. In letters, reports, and other writings distributed widely throughout Europe, the Jesuits described China as an orderly and rational society. The Confucian civil service system attracted the attention of European rulers, who began to design their own civil service bureaucracies in the eighteenth century. The rational morality of Confucianism also appealed to the Enlightenment philosophes, who sought alternatives to Christianity as the foundation for ethics and morality. For the first time since Marco Polo, the Jesuits made firsthand observations of China available to Europeans and stimulated strong European interest in east Asian societies.

THE UNIFICATION OF JAPAN

During the late sixteenth and early seventeenth centuries, the political unification of Japan ended an extended period of civil disorder. Like the Ming and Qing emperors in China, the **Tokugawa** shoguns sought to lay a foundation for long-term political and social stability, and they provided generous support for neo-Confucian studies in an effort to promote traditional values. Indeed, the shoguns went even further than their Chinese counterparts by promoting conservative values and tightly restricting foreign influence in Japan. As in China, however, demographic expansion and economic growth fostered social and cultural change in Japan, and merchants introduced Chinese and European influences into Japan.

The Tokugawa Shogunate

From the twelfth through the sixteenth century, a *shogun* ("military governor") ruled Japan through retainers who received political rights and large estates in exchange for military services. Theoretically, the shogun ruled as a temporary stand-in for the Japanese emperor, the ultimate source of political authority. In fact, however, the emperor was nothing more than a figurehead, and the shogun sought to monopolize power. After the fourteenth century the conflicting ambitions of shoguns and retainers led to constant turmoil, and by the sixteenth century Japan was in a state of civil war. Japanese historians often refer to the sixteenth century as the era of *sengoku*—"the country at war."

Tokugawa Ieyasu Toward the end of the sixteenth century, powerful states emerged in several regions of Japan, and a series of military leaders brought about the unification of the land. In 1600 the last of these chieftains, Tokugawa Ieyasu (reigned 1600–1616), established a military government known as the Tokugawa *bakufu* ("tent government,"

Tokugawa (TOH-koo-GAH-wah)

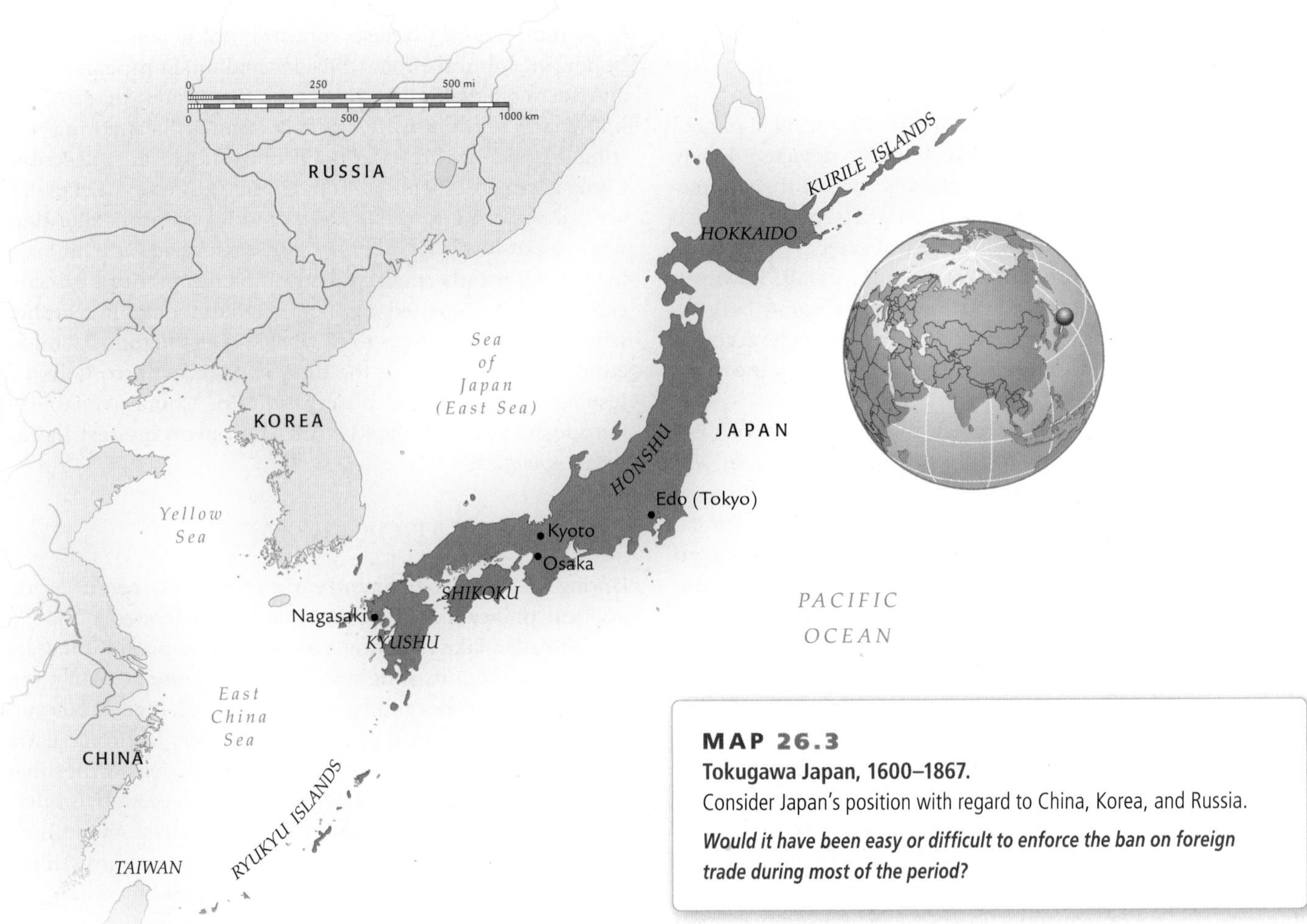

MAP 26.3
Tokugawa Japan, 1600–1867.
Consider Japan's position with regard to China, Korea, and Russia.
Would it have been easy or difficult to enforce the ban on foreign trade during most of the period?

since it theoretically was only a temporary replacement for the emperor's rule). Ieyasu and his descendants ruled the *bakufu* as shoguns from 1600 until the end of the Tokugawa dynasty in 1867.

The principal aim of the Tokugawa shoguns was to stabilize their realm and prevent the return of civil war. Consequently, the shoguns needed to control the ***daimyo*** ("great names"), powerful territorial lords who ruled most of Japan from their vast, hereditary landholdings. The 260 or so daimyo functioned as near-absolute rulers within their domains. Each maintained a government staffed by military subordinates, supported an independent judiciary, established schools, and circulated paper money. Moreover, after the mid-sixteenth century, many daimyo established relationships with European mariners, from whom they learned how to manufacture and use gunpowder weapons. During the last decades of the *sengoku* era, cannons and personal firearms had played prominent roles in Japanese conflicts.

daimyo (DEYEM-yoh)

Control of the Daimyo From the castle town of Edo (modern Tokyo), the shogun governed his personal domain and sought to extend his control to the daimyo. The shoguns instituted the policy of "alternate attendance," which required daimyo to maintain their families at Edo and spend every other year at the Tokugawa court. This policy enabled the shoguns to keep an eye on the daimyo, and as a side effect it encouraged daimyo to spend their money on lavish residences and comfortable lives in Edo rather than investing it in military forces that could challenge the *bakufu*. The shoguns also subjected marriage alliances between daimyo families to *bakufu* approval, discouraged the daimyo from visiting one another, and required daimyo to obtain permits for construction work on their castles. Even meetings between the daimyo and the emperor required the shogun's permission.

In an effort to prevent European influences from destabilizing the land, the Tokugawa shoguns closely controlled relations between Japan and the outside world. They knew that Spanish forces had conquered the Philippine Islands in the sixteenth century, and they feared that Europeans might jeopardize the security of the *bakufu* itself. Even if Europeans did not conquer Japan, they could cause serious problems by making alliances with daimyo and supplying them with weapons.

Control of Foreign Relations Thus during the 1630s the shoguns issued a series of edicts sharply restricting Japanese relations with other lands that remained in effect for more than two centuries. The policy forbade Japanese from going abroad on pain of death and prohibited the construction of large ships. It expelled Europeans from Japan, prohibited foreign merchants from trading in Japanese ports, and even forbade the import of foreign books. The policy allowed carefully controlled trade with Asian lands, and it also permitted small numbers of Chinese and Dutch merchants to trade under tight restrictions at the southern port city of Nagasaki.

During the seventeenth century, Japanese authorities strictly enforced that policy. In 1640 a Portuguese merchant ship arrived at Nagasaki in hopes of engaging in trade in spite of the ban. Officials beheaded sixty-one of the party and spared thirteen others so that they could relate the experience to their compatriots. Yet authorities gradually loosened the restrictions, and the policy never led to the complete isolation of Japan from the outside world. Throughout the Tokugawa period, Japan carried on a flourishing trade with China, Korea, Taiwan, and the Ryukyu Islands, and Dutch merchants regularly brought news of European and larger world affairs.

Economic and Social Change

By ending civil conflict and maintaining political stability, the Tokugawa shoguns set the stage for economic growth in Japan. Ironically, peace and a booming economy encouraged social change that undermined the order that the *bakufu* sought to preserve.

Economic growth had its roots in increased agricultural production. New crop strains, new methods of water control and irrigation, and the use of fertilizer brought increased yields of rice. Production of cotton, silk, indigo, and sake also increased dramatically. In many parts of Japan, villages moved away from subsistence farming in favor of production for the market. Between 1600 and 1700, agricultural production doubled.

Population Growth Increased agricultural production brought about rapid demographic growth: during the seventeenth century the Japanese population rose by almost one-third, from twenty-two million to twenty-nine million. Thereafter, however, Japan underwent a demographic transition, as many families practiced population control to maintain or raise their standard of living. Between 1700 and 1850 the Japanese population grew moderately, from twenty-nine million to thirty-two million. Contraception, late marriage, and abortion all played roles in limiting population growth, but the principal control measure was infanticide, euphemistically referred to as "thinning out the rice shoots." Japanese families resorted to those measures primarily because Japan was land poor. During the seventeenth century, populations in some areas strained resources, causing financial difficulties for local governments and distress for rural communities.

The Tokugawa era was an age of social as well as demographic change in Japan. Because of Chinese cultural influence, the Japanese social hierarchy followed Confucian precepts in ranking the ruling elites—including the shogun, daimyo, and samurai warriors—as the most prominent and privileged class of society. Beneath them were peasants and artisans. Merchants ranked at the bottom, as they did in China.

Social Change The extended period of peace ushered in by Tokugawa rule undermined the social position of the ruling elites. Since the twelfth century the administration of local affairs had fallen mostly to daimyo and samurai

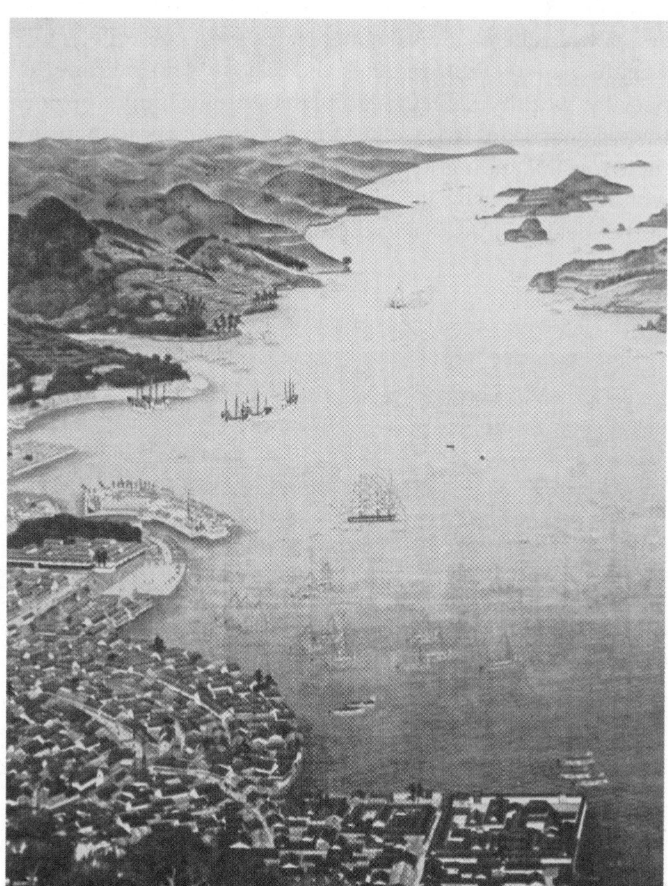

Dutch sailing ships and smaller Japanese vessels mingle in Nagasaki harbor. Dutch merchants conducted their business on the artificial island of Deshima, at left.

warriors. Once Japan was stable, however, the interest of Tokugawa authorities was to reduce the numbers of armed professional warriors, so they pushed daimyo and samurai to become bureaucrats and government functionaries. They even encouraged daimyo and samurai to turn their talents to scholarship, a pursuit that their martial ancestors would have utterly despised. As they lost their accustomed place in society, many of the ruling elite also fell into financial difficulty. Their principal income came in the form of rice collected from peasant cultivators of their lands. They readily converted rice into money through brokers, but the price of rice did not keep pace with other costs. Moreover, daimyo and samurai lived in expensive and sometimes ostentatious style—particularly daimyo who sought to impress others with their wealth while residing at Edo in alternate years. Many of them became indebted to rice brokers and gradually declined into genteel poverty.

Meanwhile, as in China, merchants in Japan became increasingly wealthy and prominent. Japanese cities flourished throughout the Tokugawa era—the population of Edo approached one million by 1700—and merchants prospered handsomely in the vibrant urban environment. Rice dealers, pawnbrokers, and sake merchants soon controlled more wealth than the ruling elites did. Those who became especially wealthy sometimes purchased elite ranks or contracted marriages with elite families in efforts to improve their social standing. Others did not go to such lengths but won respect anyway, in spite of occupations that ranked low in the ideal Confucian social order.

Neo-Confucianism and Floating Worlds

Japan had gone to school in China, and the influence of China continued throughout the Tokugawa era. Formal education began with study of Chinese language and literature. As late as the nineteenth century, many Japanese scholars wrote their philosophical, legal, and religious works in Chinese. The common people embraced Buddhism, which had come to Japan from China, and Confucianism was the most influential philosophical system.

Neo-Confucianism in Japan

Like the Ming and Qing emperors in China, the Tokugawa shoguns promoted the neo-Confucianism of Zhu Xi. With its emphasis on filial piety and loyalty to superiors, neo-Confucianism provided a respectable ideological underpinning for the *bakufu*. The shoguns patronized scholars who advocated neo-Confucian views, which figured prominently in the educational curriculum. All those who had a formal education—including the sons of merchants as well as offspring of government officials—received constant exposure to neo-Confucian values. By the early eighteenth century, neo-Confucianism had become the official ideology of the Tokugawa *bakufu*.

Native Learning

Yet even with Tokugawa sponsorship, neo-Confucianism did not dominate intellectual life in Japan. Although most scholars recognized Japan's debt to Chinese intellectual traditions, some sought to establish a sense of Japanese identity that did not depend on cultural kinship with China. Particularly during the eighteenth century,

The courtesan district of Kyoto hummed with activity in the mid-seventeenth century. In this woodblock print, courtesans await clients behind the wooden grill while urban residents fill the streets.

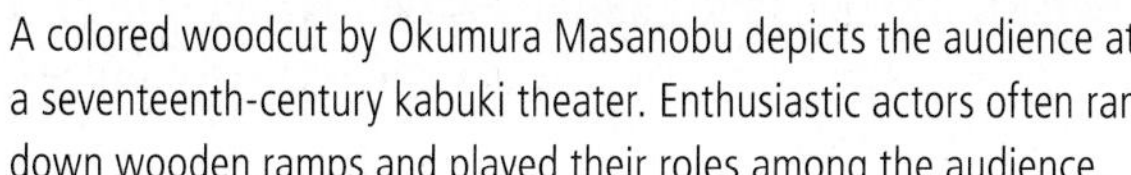

A colored woodcut by Okumura Masanobu depicts the audience at a seventeenth-century kabuki theater. Enthusiastic actors often ran down wooden ramps and played their roles among the audience.

scholars of "native learning" scorned neo-Confucianism and even Buddhism as alien cultural imports and emphasized instead the importance of folk traditions and the indigenous Shinto religion for Japanese identity. Many scholars of native learning viewed Japanese people as superior to all others and xenophobically regarded foreign influence as perverse. They urged the study of Japanese classics and glorified the supposed purity of Japanese society before its adulteration by Chinese and other foreign influences.

While scholars of neo-Confucianism and native learning debated issues of philosophy and Japanese identity, the emergence of a prosperous merchant class encouraged the development of a vibrant popular culture. During the seventeenth and eighteenth centuries, an exuberant middle-class culture flourished in cities such as Kyoto, the imperial capital; Edo, Japan's largest city and home to bureaucrats and daimyo; and Osaka, the commercial hub of the islands. In those and other cities, Japan's finest creative talents catered to middle-class appetites.

Floating Worlds The centers of Tokugawa urban culture were the *ukiyo* ("floating worlds"), entertainment and pleasure quarters where teahouses, theaters, brothels, and public baths offered escape from social responsibilities and the rigid rules of conduct that governed public behavior in Tokugawa society. In contrast to the solemn, serious proceedings of the imperial court and the *bakufu,* the popular culture of urban residents was secular, satirical, and even scatological. The main expressions of this lively culture were prose fiction and new forms of theater.

Ihara Saikaku (1642–1693), one of Japan's most prolific poets, helped create a new genre of prose literature, the "books of the floating world." Much of his fiction revolved around the theme of love. In *The Life of a Man Who Lived for Love,* for example, Ihara chronicled the experiences of a townsman who devoted his life, beginning at the tender age of eight, to a quest for sexual pleasure. Ihara's treatment of love stressed the erotic rather than the aesthetic, and the brief, episodic stories that made up his work appealed to literate urban residents who were not inclined to pore over dense neo-Confucian treatises.

Beginning in the early seventeenth century, two new forms of drama became popular in Japanese cities. One was *kabuki* theater, which usually featured several acts consisting of lively and sometimes bawdy skits where stylized acting combined with lyric singing, dancing, and spectacular staging. A crucial component of kabuki was the actor's ability to improvise and embellish the dialogue, for the text of plays served only as guides for the dramatic performance. The other new dramatic form was *bunraku,* the puppet theater. In bunraku, chanters accompanied by music told a story acted out by puppets. Manipulated by a team of three, each puppet could execute the subtlest and most intricate movements, such as brushing a tear from the eye with the sleeve of a kimono. Both kabuki and bunraku attracted enthusiastic audiences in search of entertainment and diversion.

thinking about ENCOUNTERS

Crucifixions in Japan

The Jesuits came to Japan in 1549 and enjoyed some success in their early efforts to convert the Japanese to Christianity. Their continued success over time had major repercussions for Japanese converts. How and why did the Tokugawa *bakufu* respond to this Christian influence? What measures did the Japanese government take to stem the conversions?

A seventeenth-century European painting provides an emotional representation of Franciscans being crucified in Nagasaki.

Christianity and Dutch Learning

Christian Missions

Alongside neo-Confucianism, native learning, and middle-class popular culture, Christian missionaries and European merchants contributed their own distinctive threads to the cultural fabric of Tokugawa Japan. The Jesuit Francis Xavier traveled to Japan in 1549 and opened a mission to seek converts to Christianity. In the early decades of their mission, Jesuits experienced remarkable success in Japan. Several powerful daimyo adopted Christianity and ordered their subjects to do likewise. The principal interest of the daimyo was to establish trade and military alliances with Europeans, but many Japanese converts became enthusiastic Christians and worked to convert their compatriots to the new faith. By the 1580s about 150,000 Japanese had converted to Christianity, and by 1615 Japanese Christians numbered about 300,000.

Although Christians were only a tiny minority of the Japanese population, the popularity of Christianity generated a backlash among government officials and moralists seeking to preserve Japanese religious and cultural traditions. The Tokugawa shoguns restricted European access to Japan largely because of concerns that Christianity might serve as a cultural bridge for alliances between daimyo and European adventurers, which in turn could lead to destabilization of Japanese society and even threats to the bakufu. Meanwhile, Buddhist and Confucian scholars resented the Christian conviction that their faith was the only true doctrine. Some Japanese converts to Christianity themselves eventually rejected their adopted faith out of frustration because European missionaries refused to allow them to become priests or play leadership roles in the mission.

Anti-Christian Campaign

Between 1587 and 1639, shoguns promulgated several decrees ordering a halt to Christian missions and commanding Japanese Christians to renounce their faith. In 1612 the shoguns began rigorous enforcement

sources from the past

Fabian Fucan Rejects Christianity

Fabian Fucan was a Japanese Buddhist who converted to Christianity and entered the Jesuit order as a novice in 1586. In the early seventeenth century, however, his relations with the Jesuits soured, and he eventually left the order. In 1620 he composed a treatise entitled Deus Destroyed *that leveled a spirited attack at Christianity and its God ("Deus" in Latin). His work reveals deep concerns about European imperial expansion as well as Christian doctrine.*

I joined this creed at an early age; diligently, I studied its teachings and pursued its practices. Due to my stupidity, however, I was long unable to realize that this was a perverse and cursed faith. Thus fruitlessly I spent twenty years and more! Then one day I clearly perceived that the words of the adherents of Deus were very clever and appeared very near reason—but in their teaching there was little truth. So I left their company. Some fifteen years have passed since: every morning I have lamented my desertion of the Great Holy True Law [of Buddhism]; every evening I have grieved over my adherence to the crooked path of the barbarians. All that effort to no effect! But I had a friend who remonstrated with me, saying: "'If you have made a mistake, do not be afraid of admitting the fact and amending your ways' [a Confucian precept]. Here, this is the Confucians' golden rule of life—act on it! Before, you learned all about the cursed faith of Deus; take pen in hand now, commit your knowledge to writing, and counter their teachings. Not only will you thereby gain the merit of destroying wickedness and demonstrating truth; you will also supply a guide toward new knowledge."

All right. Though I am not a clever man, I shall by all means try to act on this advice. I shall gather the important points about the teachings of the Deus sect and shall skip what is not essential; my aim is to write concisely. Thus shall I mount my attack; and I shall call my volume DEUS DESTROYED. . . .

Japan is the Land of the Gods. The generations of our rulers have received the Imperial Dignity from [the gods] Amaterasu Omikami, through U-gaya-fuki-awsezu no Mikoto and his August Child Jimmu Tenno, who became the progenitor of our Hundred Kings. The Three Divine Regalia [symbols of rule received from the gods] became the protectors of the Empire, so that among all the customs of our land there is not one which depends not on the Way of the Gods. . . .

And this, the adherents of Deus plan to subvert! They bide their time with the intent to make all of Japan into their own sectarians, to destroy the Law of Buddha and the Way of the Gods. Because the Law of Buddha and the Way of the Gods are planted here, the Royal Sway also flourishes; and since the Royal Sway is established here the glory of the Buddhas and the gods does grow. And therefore the adherents of Deus have no recourse but to subvert the Royal Sway, overthrow the Buddhas and the gods, eliminate the customs of Japan, and then to import the customs of their own countries; thus only will advance the plot they have concocted to usurp the country themselves.

They have dispatched troops and usurped such countries as Luzon [the Philippines] and Nova Hispania [Mexico], lands of barbarians with nature close to animal. But our land by far surpasses others in fierce bravery; and therefore the ambition to diffuse their faith in every quarter and thus to usurp the country, even if it take a thousand years, has penetrated down to the very marrow of their bones. Ah!—but what a gloomy prospect awaits them! For the sake of their faith they value their lives less than trash, than garbage. *Martyr,* they call this. When a wise sovereign rules the Empire good is promoted and evil is chastised. Rewards promote good and punishments chastise evil. There is no greater punishment than to take away life; but the adherents of Deus, without even fearing that their lives be cut, will not change their religion. How horrible, how awful it is!

For Further Reflection

- Discuss the various religious, cultural, historical, political, and social aspects of Fabian Fucan's attack on Christianity.

Source: George Elison. *Deus Destroyed: The Image of Christianity in Early Modern Japan.* Cambridge, Mass.: Harvard University Press, 1973, pp. 259–60, 283–84.

of those decrees. They tortured and executed European missionaries who refused to leave the islands as well as Japanese Christians who refused to abandon their faith. They often executed victims by crucifixion or burning at the stake, which Tokugawa authorities regarded as especially appropriate punishments for Christians. The campaign was so effective that even some European missionaries abandoned Christianity. Most notable of them was the Portuguese Jesuit Christovão Ferreira, head of the Jesuit mission in Japan, who gave up Christianity under torture, adopted Buddhism, and interrogated many Europeans who fell into Japanese hands in the mid-seventeenth century. By the late seventeenth century, the anti-Christian campaign had claimed tens of thousands of lives, and Christianity survived as a secret, underground religion observed only in rural regions of southern Japan.

Dutch Learning Tokugawa policies ensured that Christianity would not soon reappear in Japan, but they did not entirely prevent contacts between Europeans and Japanese. After 1639, Dutch merchants trading at Nagasaki became Japan's principal source of information about Europe and the world beyond east Asia. A small number of Japanese scholars learned Dutch in order to communicate with the foreigners. Their studies, which they called "Dutch learning," brought considerable knowledge of the outside world to Japan. After 1720, Tokugawa authorities lifted the ban on foreign books, and Dutch learning began to play a significant role in Japanese intellectual life.

European art influenced Japanese scholars interested in anatomy and botany because of its accurate representations of objects. Scholars translated Dutch medical and scientific treatises into Japanese and learned to draw according to the principles of linear perspective, which enabled them to prepare textbooks that were more accurate than the Chinese works they had previously used. European astronomy was also popular in Japan, since it enabled scholars to improve calendars and issue accurate predictions of eclipses and other celestial events. By the mid-eighteenth century, the Tokugawa shoguns themselves had become enthusiastic proponents of Dutch learning, and schools of European medicine and Dutch studies flourished in several Japanese cities.

inperspective

Both China and Japan controlled their own affairs throughout the early modern era and avoided the turmoil that afflicted societies in the Americas and much of sub-Saharan Africa. After driving the Mongols to the steppe lands of central Asia, rulers of the Ming dynasty built a powerful centralized state in China. They worked diligently to eradicate all vestiges of Mongol rule and restore traditional ways by reviving Chinese political institutions and providing state sponsorship for neo-Confucianism. In the interest of stability, authorities also restricted foreign merchants' access to China and limited the activities of Christian missionaries. The succeeding Qing dynasty pursued similar policies. The Ming and Qing dynasties both brought political stability, but China experienced considerable social and economic change in early modern times. American food crops helped increase agricultural production, which fueled rapid population growth, and global trade stimulated the Chinese economy, which improved the position of merchants and artisans in society. The experience of the Tokugawa era in Japan was much like that of the Ming and Qing eras in China. The Tokugawa *bakufu* brought political order to the Japanese islands and closely controlled foreign relations, but a vibrant economy promoted social change that enhanced the status of merchants and artisans. ●

CHRONOLOGY

1368–1644	Ming dynasty (China)
1368–1398	Reign of Hongwu
1403–1424	Reign of Yongle
1552–1610	Life of Matteo Ricci
1572–1620	Reign of Emperor Wanli
1600–1867	Tokugawa shogunate (Japan)
1616–1626	Reign of Nurhaci
1642–1693	Life of Ihara Saikaku
1644–1911	Qing dynasty (China)
1661–1722	Reign of Kangxi
1736–1795	Reign of Qianlong
1793	British trade mission to China

For Further Reading

Timothy Brook. *The Chinese State in Ming Society.* London and New York, 2004. An important collection of essays on commercialism and social networks, and the role they played in the development of a stable society.

———. *The Confusions of Pleasure: Commerce and Culture in Ming China.* Berkeley, 1998. Fascinating social and cultural analysis of Ming China focusing on the role of commerce as an agent of social change.

George Elison. *Deus Destroyed: The Image of Christianity in Early Modern Japan.* Cambridge, Mass., 1973. Scholarly study of the Jesuit mission in Japan and its end during the early Tokugawa era.

Mark C. Elliott. *The Manchu Way: The Eight Banners and Ethnic Identity in Late Imperial China.* Stanford, 2001. Important scholarly study focusing on relations between Manchus and Chinese during the Qing dynasty.

Benjamin A. Elman. *A Cultural History of Civil Examinations in Late Imperial China.* Berkeley, 2000. A meticulous study of one of the most important institutions in Chinese history.

Jacques Gernet. *China and the Christian Impact.* Trans. by J. Lloyd. Cambridge, 1985. A careful study of the Jesuit mission in China, concentrating on the cultural differences between Chinese and Europeans.

Harry D. Harootunian. *Things Seen and Unseen: Discourse and Ideology in Tokugawa Nativism.* Chicago, 1988. A challenging scholarly analysis of the efforts by Tokugawa thinkers to construct a distinctive Japanese identity.

Donald Keene. *The Japanese Discovery of Europe, 1720–1830.* Rev. ed. Stanford, 1969. A highly readable account of Japanese encounters with Europe by way of Dutch merchants.

Susan Mann and Yu-Ying Cheng, eds. *Under Confucian Eyes: Writings on Gender in Chinese History.* Berkeley, 2001. A rich anthology of primary texts documenting the lives of women in imperial China.

Ichisada Miyazaki. *China's Examination Hell: The Civil Service Examinations in Imperial China.* Trans. by Conrad Schirokauer. New Haven, 1981. Explores all aspects of the labyrinthine civil service examination system.

Susan Naquin and Evelyn S. Rawski. *Chinese Society in the Eighteenth Century.* New Haven, 1987. A lucid and well-organized discussion of Chinese social history.

Kenneth Pomeranz. *The Great Divergence: China, Europe, and the Making of the Modern World Economy.* Princeton, 2000. Pathbreaking scholarly study that illuminates the economic history of the early modern world through comparison of economic development in Asian and European lands.

Evelyn S. Rawski. *The Last Emperors: A Social History of Qing Imperial Institutions.* Berkeley, 1998. A nuanced study of the Manchu rulers and the politics of assimilation.

Jonathan D. Spence. *The Death of Woman Wang.* New York, 1978. Engaging reconstruction of life in rural China during the early Qing dynasty.

———. *Emperor of China: Self-Portrait of K'ang-Hsi.* New York, 1974. Outstanding introduction to the reign of Kangxi based partly on numerous documents, some written by the emperor himself.

Ronald P. Toby. *State and Diplomacy in Early Modern Japan: Asia in the Development of the Tokugawa Bakufu.* Princeton, 1984. An important study dealing with Japanese trade and relations with other lands under Tokugawa rule.

H. Paul Varley. *Japanese Culture.* 4th ed. Honolulu, 2000. Places the cultural history of the Tokugawa era in its larger historical context.

Arthur Waldron. *The Great Wall of China: From History to Myth.* Cambridge, 1990. Fascinating work that places the Great Wall of Ming China in the context of earlier efforts to build defensive walls.

The Islamic Empires

chapter 27

This equestrian portrait of Shah Jahan (reigned 1628–1658) is emblematic of the Mughal art promoted by Shah Jahan. Builder of the Taj Mahal, Shah Jahan here is shown in a rich and heroic light, symbolized by the ring of light, his clothing and weaponry, and the horse's exquisite appointments.

EYEWITNESS:
Shah Jahan's Monument to Love and Allah

In 1635 Shah Jahan, the emperor of Mughal India, took his seat on the Peacock Throne. Seven years in the making, the Peacock Throne is probably the most spectacular seat on which any human being has rested. Shah Jahan ordered the throne encrusted with ten million rupees' worth of diamonds, rubies, emeralds, and pearls. Atop the throne itself stood a magnificent, golden-bodied peacock with a huge ruby and a fifty-carat, pear-shaped pearl on its breast and a brilliant elevated tail fashioned of blue sapphires and other colored gems.

Yet, for all its splendor, the Peacock Throne ranks a distant second among Shah Jahan's artistic projects: pride of place goes to the incomparable Taj Mahal. Built over a period of eighteen years as a tomb for Shah Jahan's beloved wife, Mumtaz Mahal, who died during childbirth in 1631, the Taj Mahal is a graceful and elegant monument both to the departed empress and to Shah Jahan's Islamic faith.

The emperor and his architects conceived the Taj Mahal as a vast allegory in stone symbolizing the day when Allah would cause the dead to rise and undergo judgment before his heavenly throne. Its gardens represented the gardens of paradise, and the four water channels running through them symbolized the four rivers of the heavenly kingdom. The domed marble tomb of Mumtaz Mahal represented the throne of Allah, and the four minarets surrounding the structure served as legs supporting the divine throne. Craftsmen carved verses from the Quran throughout the Taj Mahal. The main gateway to the structure features the entire text of the chapter promising that on the day of judgment, Allah will punish the wicked and gather the faithful into his celestial paradise.

The Peacock Throne and the Taj Mahal testify to the wealth of the Mughal empire, and the tomb of Mumtaz Mahal bespeaks also the fundamentally Islamic character of the ruling dynasty. But the Mughal empire, which ruled most of the Indian subcontinent for more than three hundred years, was not the only well-organized Islamic empire of early modern times. The Ottoman empire was a dynastic Muslim state centered in what is today Turkey. At the height of its power, it controlled a vast area from southeastern Europe to western Asia and North Africa. It was also the longest-lived of the Muslim empires, not disbanding until the early twentieth century. On the eastern borders of the Ottoman empire lay the ancient lands of Persia, where yet another Muslim empire emerged during the early sixteenth century. Ruled by the Safavid dynasty, this state never expanded far beyond its heartland of present-day Iran, but its Shiite rulers challenged the Sunni Ottomans for dominance in southwest Asia. The Safavid realm prospered from its place in trade networks linking China, India, Russia, southwest Asia, and the Mediterranean basin.

All three Islamic empires of early modern times had Turkish ruling dynasties. The Ottomans, Safavids, and Mughals came from nomadic, Turkish-speaking peoples of central Asia who conquered the settled agricultural lands of Anatolia, Persia, and India, respectively. All three dynasties retained political and cultural traditions that their ancestors had adopted while leading nomadic lives on the steppes, but they also adapted readily to the city-based agricultural societies that they conquered. The Ottoman dynasty made especially effective use of the gunpowder weapons that transformed early modern warfare, and the Safavids and the Mughals also incorporated gunpowder weapons into their arsenals. All three dynasties officially embraced Islam and drew cultural guidance from Islamic values.

During the sixteenth and early seventeenth centuries, the three Islamic empires presided over expansive and prosperous societies. About the mid-seventeenth century, however, they all began to weaken. Their waning fortunes reflected the fact that they had ceased to expand territorially and gain access to new sources of wealth. Instead, each empire waged long, costly wars that drained resources without bringing compensating benefits. The empires also faced domestic difficulties. Each of them was an ethnically and religiously diverse realm, and each experienced tensions when conservative Muslim leaders lobbied for strict observance of Islam while members of other communities sought greater freedom for themselves. Furthermore, the Islamic empires made little investment in economic and technological development. By the mid-eighteenth century, the Safavid empire had collapsed, and the Ottoman and Mughal realms were rapidly falling under European influence.

FORMATION OF THE ISLAMIC EMPIRES

By the sixteenth century, Turkish warriors had transformed the major Islamic areas of the world into vast regional empires. Three empires divided up the greater part of the Islamic world: the Ottoman empire, which was distinguished by its multiethnic character; the Safavid empire of Persia, which served as the center of Shiite Islam; and the Mughal empire, which had been imposed over a predominantly Hindu Indian subcontinent. The creation of these durable and powerful political entities brought to an end a century and a half of Muslim political disunity.

The Islamic empires began as small warrior principalities in frontier areas. They expanded at varying rates and with varying degrees of success at the expense of neighboring states. As they grew, they devised elaborate administrative and military institutions. Under the guidance of talented and energetic rulers, each empire organized an effective governmental apparatus and presided over a prosperous society.

The Ottoman Empire

Osman The Ottoman empire was an unusually successful frontier state. The term *Ottoman* derived from Osman Bey, founder of the dynasty that continued in unbroken succession from 1289 until the dissolution of the empire in 1923. Osman was *bey* (chief) of a band of seminomadic Turks who migrated to northwestern Anatolia in the thirteenth century. Osman and his followers sought above all to become *ghazi,* Muslim religious warriors. In his encomium of the Ottomans, the poet Ahmadi described their ethos: "The Ghazi is the instrument of the religion of Allah, a servant of God who purifies the earth from the filth of polytheism; the Ghazi is the sword of God, he is the protector and the refuge of the believers. If he becomes a martyr in the ways of God, do not believe that he has died—he lives in beatitude with Allah, he has eternal life."

Ottoman Expansion The Ottomans' location on the borders of the Byzantine empire afforded them ample opportunity to wage holy war. Their first great success came in 1326 with the capture of the Anatolian city of Bursa, which became the capital of the Ottoman principality. Around 1352 they established a foothold in Europe when they seized the fortress of Gallipoli while aiding a claimant to the Byzantine throne. Numerous *ghazi,* many of them recent converts, soon flocked to join the Ottomans. The city of Edirne (Adrianople) became a second Ottoman capital and served as a base for further expansion into the Balkans. As warriors settled in frontier districts and pushed their boundaries forward, they took spoils and gathered revenues that enriched both the *ghazi* and the central government.

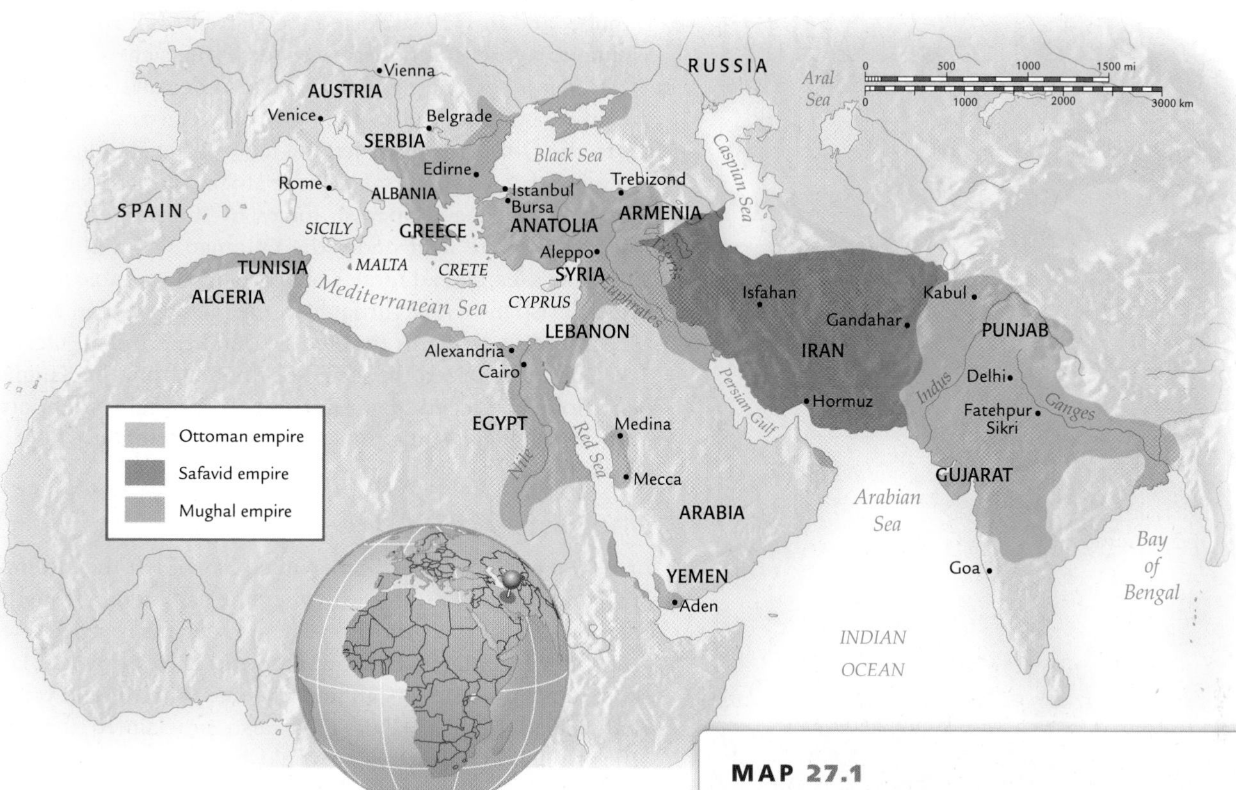

MAP 27.1
The Islamic empires, 1500–1800.
Locate the Ottoman capital of Istanbul, the Safavid capital of Isfahan, and the Mughal capital of Delhi.

What strategic or commercial purposes did each of these capitals fulfill, and how would their locations have aided or hindered imperial administration?

Bursa developed into a major commercial and intellectual center with inns, shops, schools, libraries, and mosques.

A formidable military machine drove Ottoman expansion. Ottoman military leaders initially organized *ghazi* recruits into two forces: a light cavalry and a volunteer infantry. As the Ottoman state became more firmly established, it added a professional cavalry force equipped with heavy armor and financed by land grants. After expanding into the Balkans, the Ottomans created a supremely important force composed of slave troops. Through an institution known as the *devshirme,* the Ottomans required the Christian population of the Balkans to contribute young boys to become slaves of the sultan. The boys received special training, learned Turkish, and converted to Islam. According to individual ability, they entered either the Ottoman civilian administration or the military. Those who became soldiers were known as Janissaries, from the Turkish *yeni cheri* ("new troops"). The Janissaries quickly gained a reputation for esprit de corps, loyalty to the sultan, and readiness to employ new military technology. Besides building powerful military forces, the Ottomans outfitted their forces with gunpowder weapons and used them effectively in battles and sieges.

Mehmed the Conqueror The capture of Constantinople in 1453 by Mehmed II (reigned 1451–1481)—known as Mehmed the Conqueror—opened a new chapter in Ottoman expansion. With its superb location and illustrious heritage, Constantinople became the new Ottoman capital, subsequently known as Istanbul, and Mehmed worked energetically to stimulate its role as a commercial center. With the capture of the great city behind him, Mehmed presented himself not just as a warrior-sultan but also as a true emperor, ruler of the "two lands" (Europe and Asia) and the "two seas" (the Black Sea and the Mediterranean). He laid the foundations for a tightly centralized, absolute monarchy, and his army faced no serious rival. He completed the conquest of Serbia, moved into southern Greece and Albania, eliminated the last Byzantine outpost at Trebizond, captured Genoese ports in the Crimea, initiated a naval war with Venice in the Mediterranean, and reportedly hoped to cross the Strait of Otranto, march on Rome, and capture the pope himself. Toward the end of his life, he launched an invasion of Italy and briefly occupied Otranto, but his successors abandoned Mehmed's plans for expansion in western Europe.

Süleyman the Magnificent The Ottomans continued their expansion in the early sixteenth century when

Sultan Süleyman (center, on horse) leads Ottoman forces as they march on Europe. How does this illustration promote the power and prominence of Süleyman and his Ottoman forces?

sultan Selim the Grim (reigned 1512–1520) occupied Syria and Egypt. Ottoman imperialism climaxed in the reign of **Süleyman** the Magnificent (reigned 1520–1566). Süleyman vigorously promoted Ottoman expansion both in southwest Asia and in Europe. In 1534 he conquered Baghdad and added the Tigris and Euphrates valleys to the Ottoman domain. In Europe he kept the rival Habsburg empire on the defensive throughout his reign. He captured Belgrade in 1521, defeated and killed the king of Hungary at the battle of Mohács in 1526, consolidated Ottoman power north of the Danube, and in 1529 subjected the Habsburgs' prized city of Vienna to a brief but nonetheless terrifying siege.

Süleyman (SOO-lee-mahn)

Under Süleyman the Ottomans also became a major naval power. In addition to their own Aegean and Black Sea fleets, the Ottomans inherited the navy of the Mamluk rulers of Egypt. A Turkish corsair, Khayr al-Din Barbarossa Pasha, who had challenged Spanish forces in Tunisia and Algeria, placed his pirate fleet under the Ottoman flag and became Süleyman's leading admiral. Thus Süleyman was able to challenge Christian vessels throughout the Mediterranean as well as Portuguese fleets in the Red Sea and the Indian Ocean. The Ottomans seized the island of Rhodes from the Knights of St. John, besieged Malta, secured Yemen and Aden, and even dispatched a squadron to attack the Portuguese fleet at Diu in India.

The Safavid Empire

In 1499 a twelve-year-old boy named Ismail left the swamps of Gilan near the Caspian Sea, where he had hidden from the enemies of his family for five years, to seek his revenge. Two years later he entered Tabriz at the head of an army and laid claim to the ancient Persian imperial title of shah. The young Shah Ismail (reigned 1501–1524) also proclaimed that the official religion of his realm would be Twelver Shiism, and he proceeded to impose it, by force when necessary, on the formerly Sunni population. Over the next decade he seized control of the Iranian plateau and launched expeditions into the Caucasus, Anatolia, Mesopotamia, and central Asia.

The Safavids

For propaganda purposes, Shah Ismail and his successors carefully controlled accounts of their rise to power—and expediently changed the story when circumstances warranted. They traced their ancestry back to Safi al-Din (1252–1334), leader of a Sufi religious order in northwestern Persia. Sufism, a mystical belief and practice, formed an important Islamic tradition. The goal of a Sufi mystic, such as Safi al-Din, was to recover the lost intimacy between God and the human soul, and to find the truth of divine knowledge and love through a direct personal experience of God. The famous tomb and shrine of Safi al-Din at Ardabil became the home of Shah Ismail's family (named "Safavids" after the holy man himself), the headquarters of his religious movement, and the center of a determined, deliberate conspiracy to win political power for his descendants. The Safavids changed their religious preferences several times in the hope of gaining popular support before settling on a form of Shiism that appealed to the nomadic Turkish tribes moving into the area in the post-Mongol era.

Twelver Shiism

Twelver Shiism held that there had been twelve infallible imams (or religious leaders) after Muhammad, beginning with the prophet's cousin and son-in-law Ali. The twelfth, "hidden," imam had gone into hiding around 874 to escape persecution, but the Twelver Shiites believed he was still alive and would one day return to take

sources from the past

Ghislain de Busbecq's Concerns about the Ottoman Empire

Ogier Ghislain de Busbecq was a diplomat who traveled to Istanbul in 1555 as a representative of Habsburg King Ferdinand of Hungary and Bohemia to negotiate a border dispute between Ferdinand and Sultan Süleyman the Magnificent. In a series of four letters to a friend, Ghislain commented on Ottoman state, society, customs, and military forces. His observations left him deeply concerned about the prospects of Christian Europe in the event of conflict with the Ottoman realm.

The Sultan, when he sets out on a campaign, takes as many as 40,000 camels with him, and almost as many baggage-mules, most of whom, if his destination is Persia, are loaded with cereals of every kind, especially rice. Mules and camels are also employed to carry tents and arms and warlike machines and implements of every kind. . . . They are careful, however, to avoid touching the supplies which they carry with them as long as they are marching against their foes, but reserve them, as far as possible, for their return journey, when the moment for retirement comes and they are forced to retrace their steps through regions which the enemy has laid waste, or which the immense multitude of men and baggage animals has, as it were, scraped bare, like a swarm of locusts. It is only then that the Sultan's store of provisions is opened, and just enough food to sustain life is weighed out each day to the Janissaries and the other troops in attendance upon him. The other soldiers are badly off, if they have not provided food for their own use; most of them, having often experienced such difficulties during their campaigns—and this is particularly true of the cavalry—take a horse on a leading-rein loaded with many of the necessities of life. These include a small piece of canvas to use as a tent, which may protect them from the sun or a shower of rain, also some clothing and bedding and a private store of provisions, consisting of a leather sack or two of the finest flour, a small jar of butter, and some spices and salt; on these they support life when they are reduced to the extremes of hunger. They take a few spoonfuls of flour and place them in water, adding a little butter, and then flavour the mixture with salt and spices. This, when it is put on the fire, boils and swells up so as to fill a large bowl. They eat of it once or twice a day, according to the quantity, without any bread, unless they have with them some toasted bread or biscuit. They thus contrive to live on short rations for a month or even longer, if necessary. . . .

All this will show you with what patience, sobriety, and economy the Turks struggle against the difficulties which beset them, and wait for better times. How different are our soldiers, who on campaign despise ordinary food and expect dainty dishes (such as thrushes and beccaficoes) and elaborate meals. If these are not supplied, they mutiny and cause their own ruin; and even if they are supplied, they ruin themselves just the same. . . . I tremble when I think of what the future must bring when I compare the Turkish system with our own; one army must prevail and the other be destroyed, for certainly both cannot remain unscathed. On their side are the resources of a mighty empire, strength unimpaired, experience and practice in fighting, a veteran soldiery, habituation to victory, endurance of toil, unity, order, discipline, frugality, and watchfulness. On our side is public poverty, private luxury, impaired strength, spirit, lack of endurance and training; the soldiers are insubordinate, the officers avaricious; there is contempt for discipline; licence, recklessness, drunkenness, and debauchery are rife; and worst of all, the enemy is accustomed to victory, and we to defeat. Can we doubt what the result will be?

For Further Reflection

- Why might Ghislain de Busbecq have assumed that conflict between Turkish and Habsburg forces was inevitable?

Source: Ghislain de Busbecq. *The Turkish Letters of Ogier Ghislain de Busbecq.* Trans. by E. S. Foster. Oxford: Clarendon Press, 1927, pp. 209–14.

power and spread his true religion. Ismail's father had instructed his Turkish followers to wear a distinctive red hat with twelve pleats in memory of the twelve Shiite imams, and they subsequently became known as the *qizilbash* ("red heads"). Safavid propaganda also suggested that Ismail was himself the hidden imam, or even an incarnation of Allah. Although most Muslims, including most Shiites, would have regarded those pretensions as utterly blasphemous, the *qizilbash* enthusiastically accepted them, since they resembled traditional Turkish conceptions of leadership that associated military leaders with divinity. The *qizilbash* believed that Ismail would make them invincible in battle, and they became fanatically loyal to the Safavid cause.

Battle of Chaldiran Shah Ismail's curious blend of Shiism and Turkish militancy gave his regime a distinctive identity, particularly since he made conversion to Shiite Islam mandatory for the largely Sunni population, but it also created some powerful enemies. Foremost among them were the staunchly Sunni Ottomans who detested the Shiite Safavids and feared the spread of Safavid propaganda among the nomadic Turks in their territory. As soon as Selim the Grim became sultan, he launched a persecution of Shiites in the Ottoman empire and prepared for a full-scale invasion of Safavid territory.

At the critical battle on the plain of Chaldiran (1514), the Ottomans deployed heavy artillery and thousands of Janissaries equipped with firearms behind a barrier of carts. Although the Safavids knew about gunpowder technology and had access to firearms, they declined to use devices that they saw as unreliable and unmanly. Trusting in the protective charisma of Shah Ismail, the *qizilbash* cavalry fearlessly attacked the Ottoman line and suffered devastating casualties. Ismail had to slip away, and the Ottomans temporarily occupied his capital at Tabriz. The Ottomans badly damaged the Safavid state but lacked the resources to destroy it, and the two empires remained locked in intermittent conflict for the next two centuries.

Shah Ismail and the *qizilbash*. This miniature painting from a Safavid manuscript depicts the shah and his *qizilbash* warriors wearing the distinctive red pleated cap that was their emblem of identity.

Later Safavid rulers recovered from the disaster at Chaldiran. They relied more heavily than Ismail had on the Persian bureaucracy and its administrative talents. Ismail's successors abandoned the extreme Safavid ideology that associated the emperor with Allah in favor of more conventional Twelver Shiism, from which they still derived legitimacy as descendants and representatives of the imams. They also assigned land grants to the *qizilbash* officers to retain their loyalty and give them a stake in the survival of the regime.

Shah Abbas the Great Shah Abbas the Great (reigned 1588–1629) fully revitalized the Safavid empire. He moved the capital to the more central location of Isfahan, encouraged trade with other lands, and reformed the administrative and military institutions of the empire. He incorporated "slaves of the royal household" into the army, increased the use of gunpowder weapons, and sought European assistance against the Ottomans and the Portuguese in the Persian Gulf. With newly strengthened military forces, Shah Abbas led the Safavids to numerous victories. He attacked and defeated the nomadic Uzbeks in central Asia, expelled the Portuguese from Hormuz, and harassed the Ottomans mercilessly in a series of wars from 1603 to the end of his reign. His campaigns brought most of northwestern Iran, the Caucasus, and Mesopotamia under Safavid rule.

The Mughal Empire

Babur In 1523 Zahir al-Din Muhammad, known as Babur ("the Tiger"), a Chaghatai Turk who claimed descent from both Chinggis Khan and Tamerlane, suddenly appeared in northern India. Unlike the Ottomans, who sought to be renowned *ghazis,* or the Safavids, who acted as champions of Shiism, Babur made little pretense to be anything more than an adventurer and soldier of fortune in the manner of his illustrious ancestors. His father had been the prince of Farghana, and Babur's great ambition was to transform his inheritance into a glorious central Asian empire. Yet envious relatives and Uzbek enemies frustrated his ambitions.

Never able to extend his authority much beyond Kabul and Qandahar and reduced at times to hardship and a handful of followers, Babur turned his attention to India. With the aid of gunpowder weapons, including both artillery and firearms, Babur mounted invasions in 1523 and 1525, and he took Delhi in 1526. Ironically, Babur cared little for the land he had conquered. Many in his entourage wanted to take their spoils of war and leave the hot and humid Indian climate, which ruined their finely crafted compound bows, but Babur elected to stay. He probably hoped to use the enormous wealth of India to build a vast central Asian empire like that of Tamerlane—an elusive dream that his successors would nonetheless continue to cherish. By the time of his death in 1530, Babur had built a loosely knit empire that

This colorful scene at a spring in Kabul highlights Babur (1483–1530), founder of the Mughal dynasty, who stands in a central position near the life-giving water.

This manuscript illustration from about 1590 depicts Akbar (at top, shaded by attendants) inspecting construction of a new imperial capital at Fatehpur Sikri.

stretched from Kabul through the Punjab to the borders of Bengal. He founded a dynasty called the *Mughal* (a Persian term for "Mongol"), which expanded to embrace almost all the Indian subcontinent.

Akbar The real architect of the Mughal empire was Babur's grandson Akbar (reigned 1556–1605), a brilliant and charismatic ruler. Akbar gathered the reins of power in his own hands in 1561 following an argument with Adham Khan, a powerful figure at the imperial court and commander of the Mughal army. Akbar threw Adham Khan out a window, then dragged him back from the palace courtyard, and tossed him out again to make sure he was dead. Thereafter Akbar took personal control of the Mughal government and did not tolerate challenges to his rule. He created a centralized administrative structure with ministries regulating the various provinces of the empire. His military campaigns consolidated Mughal power in Gujarat and Bengal. He also began to absorb the recently defeated Hindu kingdom of Vijayanagar, thus laying the foundation for later Mughal expansion in southern India.

Although he was a no-nonsense ruler, Akbar was also a thoughtful, reflective man deeply interested in religion and philosophy. He pursued a policy of religious toleration that he hoped would reduce tensions between Hindu and

sources from the past

A Conqueror and His Conquests: Babur on India

Babur was a talented writer as well as a successful warrior. His memoirs make fascinating reading and provide a unique perspective on early Mughal India. His writings include his reflections on the territories he conquered in India, which he compared unfavorably to his central Asian homeland, and on his decision to stay in India and found an empire.

Most of the inhabitants of India are infidels, called Hindus, believing mainly in the transmigration of souls; all artisans, wage-earners, and officials are Hindus. In our countries the desert dwellers get tribal names; here people settled in the cultivated villages also get tribal names. Again, every artisan follows the trade handed down to him from his forefathers.

India is a country of few charms. The people lack good looks and good manners. They have no social life or exchange of visits. They have no genius or intelligence, no polite learning, no generosity or magnanimity, no harmony or proportion in their arts and crafts, no lead-wire or carpenter's square. They lack good horses and good dogs; grapes, melons, and any good fruit; ice and cold water; good food or good bread in the markets. They have no baths and no advanced educational institutions. . . . There are no running streams in their gardens or residences, no waters at all except the large rivers and the swamps in the ravines and hollows. Their residences have no pleasant and salubrious breezes, and in their construction [there is] no form or symmetry. . . .

Among the charms that India does possess is that it is a large country, with large quantities of gold and silver. Its air in the rainy season is very fine. Sometimes it rains ten or fifteen or even twenty times a day, and in such torrents that rivers flow where no water was previously. While it rains, and throughout the rainy season, the air is remarkably fine, not to be surpassed for mildness and pleasantness. Its only fault is its great humidity, which spoils bows. . . .

It was the hot season when we came to Agra. All the inhabitants had run away in terror. We could find neither grain for ourselves nor corn for our horses. The villages, out of hostility and hatred for us, had taken to thieving and highway-robbery, and it was impossible to travel on the roads. We had not yet the opportunity to distribute the treasure and to assign men in strength to each district. Moreover, the year was a very hot one, pestilential simooms [sandstorms] were striking people down in heaps, and masses were beginning to die off.

For all these reasons, most of the best warriors were unwilling to stay in India; in fact, they determined to leave. . . .

When I discovered this unsteadiness among my people, I summoned all the leaders and took counsel. I said, "Without means and resources there is no empire and conquest, and without lands and followers there is no sovereignty and rule. By the effort of long years, through much tribulation and the crossing of distant lands, by flinging ourselves into battle and danger, we have through God's favor overcome so many enemies and conquered such vast lands. And now, what force compels us, what necessity has arisen, that we should, without cause, abandon a country taken at such risk of life? And if we returned to Kabul, we would again be left in poverty and weakness. Henceforth, let no well-wisher of mine speak of such things! But let not those turn back from going who cannot bear the hardship and have determined to leave." With such words I reasoned with them and made them, willy-nilly, quit their fears.

For Further Reflection

- What does Babur's reaction to India suggest about his views of his own central Asian homeland?

Source: Babur. *The Babur-nama in English (Memoirs of Babur).* Trans. by Annette Susannah Beveridge. London: Luzac, 1922. (Translation slightly modified.)

Muslim communities in India. Although illiterate (probably due to dyslexia), he was extremely intelligent and had books read to him daily. Instead of imposing Islam on his subjects, he encouraged the elaboration of a syncretic religion called the "divine faith" that focused attention on the emperor as a ruler common to all the religious, ethnic, and social groups of India.

Aurangzeb The Mughal empire reached its greatest extent under Aurangzeb (reigned 1659–1707). During his long reign, Aurangzeb waged a relentless campaign to push Mughal authority deep into southern India. By the early eighteenth century, Mughals ruled the entire subcontinent except for a small region at the southern tip.

Although he greatly expanded Mughal boundaries, Aurangzeb presided over a troubled empire. He faced rebellions throughout his reign, and religious tensions generated conflicts between Hindus and Muslims. Aurangzeb was a devout Muslim, and he broke with Akbar's policy of religious toleration. He demolished several famous Hindu temples and replaced them with mosques. He also imposed a tax on Hindus in an effort to encourage conversion to Islam.

His promotion of Islam appealed strongly to the Mughals themselves and other Indian Muslims as well, but it provoked deep hostility among Hindus and enabled local leaders to organize movements to resist or even rebel against Mughal authority.

IMPERIAL ISLAMIC SOCIETY

Despite their ethnically and religiously diverse populations, there were striking similarities in the development of Ottoman, Safavid, and Mughal societies. All relied on bureaucracies that drew inspiration from the steppe traditions of Turkish and Mongol peoples as well as from the heritage of Islam. They adopted similar economic policies and sought ways to maintain harmony in societies that embraced many different religious and ethnic groups. Rulers of all the empires also sought to enhance the legitimacy of their regimes by providing for public welfare and associating themselves with literary and artistic talent.

The Dynastic State

The Ottoman, Safavid, and Mughal empires were all military creations, regarded by their rulers as their personal possessions by right of conquest. The rulers exercised personal command of the armies, appointed and dismissed officials at will, and adopted whatever policies they wished. In theory, the emperors owned all land and granted use of it to peasant families on a hereditary basis in return for the payment of fixed taxes. The emperors and their families derived revenues from crown lands, and revenues from other lands supported military and administrative officials.

The Emperors and Islam In the Ottoman, Safavid, and Mughal empires, the prestige and authority of the dynasty derived from the personal piety and the military prowess of the ruler and his ancestors. The Safavids were prominent leaders of a Sufi religious order, and the Ottomans and Mughals associated closely with famous Sufis. Devotion to Islam encouraged rulers to extend their faith to new lands. The *ghazi* ideal of spreading Islam by fighting infidels or heretics resonated with the traditions of Turkish and Mongolian peoples: on the steppes fighting was routine, and successful warriors became charismatic leaders.

Steppe Traditions The autocratic authority wielded by the rulers of the Islamic empires also reflected steppe traditions. The early emperors largely did as they pleased, irrespective of religious and social norms. The Ottoman sultans, for example, unilaterally issued numerous legal edicts. The greatest of these were the many *kanun* ("laws") issued by Süleyman—Europeans called him Süleyman the Magnificent, but the Ottomans referred to him as Süleyman Kanuni, "the Lawgiver." Safavid and Mughal rulers went even further than the Ottomans in asserting their spiritual authority. Shah Ismail did not hesitate to force his Shiite religion on his subjects. Akbar issued a decree in 1579 claiming broad authority in religious matters, and he promoted his own eclectic religion, which glorified the emperor as much as Islam.

Steppe practices also brought succession problems. In the steppe empires the ruler's relatives often managed components of the states, and succession to the throne became a hot contest between competing members of the family. The Mughal empire in particular became tied up in family controversies: conflicts among Mughal princes and rebellions of sons against fathers were recurrent features throughout the history of the empire. The Safavids also engaged in murderous struggles for the throne. Shah Abbas himself lived in fear that another member of the family would challenge him. He kept his sons confined to the palace and killed or blinded relatives he suspected, almost wiping out his family in the process.

The early Ottomans assigned provinces for the sultan's sons to administer but kept the empire as a whole tightly unified. After the fifteenth century, however, the sultans moved to protect their position by eliminating family rivals. Mehmed the Conqueror decreed that a ruler could legally kill off his brothers after taking the throne. His successors observed that tradition in Turko-Mongol style—by strangling victims with a silk bow string so as not to shed royal blood—until 1595, when the new sultan executed nineteen brothers, many of them infants, as well as fifteen expectant mothers. After that episode, sultans confined their sons in special quarters of the imperial harem and forbade them to go outside except to take the throne.

Women and Politics Even though Muslim theorists universally agreed that women should have no role in public affairs and decried the involvement of women in politics as a sure sign of decadence, women played important roles in managing the Islamic empires. Many Ottoman, Safavid, and Mughal emperors followed the example of Chinggis Khan, who revered his mother and his first wife. In the Islamic empires the ruler's mother and his chief wife or favorite concubine enjoyed special privileges and authority. Ottoman courtiers often complained loudly about the "rule of women," thus offering eloquent testimony to the power that women could wield. Süleyman the Magnificent, for example, became infatuated with Hürrem Sultana (also known as Roxelana), a concubine of Ukrainian origin. Süleyman elevated her to the status of a legal wife, consulted her on state policies, and deferred to her judgment even to the point of executing his eldest son for treason when Hürrem wanted him eliminated to secure the succession of her own child. After Hürrem's death, Süleyman constructed a mausoleum for her next to his own in the courtyard of the great mosque in Istanbul.

Women also played prominent political roles in the Safavid and Mughal empires. In Safavid Persia, Mahd-e Olya, the wife of one shah, was the de facto ruler. Her efforts to limit the power of the *qizilbash* so enraged them that they murdered her. The aunt of another shah scolded the ruler for neglecting his duties and used her own money to raise an army to put down a revolt. The Mughal emperor Jahangir was content to let his wife Nur Jahan run the government, and even the conscientious Muslim Aurangzeb listened to his daughter's political advice. Shah Jahan's devotion to his wife, Mumtaz Mahal, has become world-famous because of the Taj Mahal.

Agriculture and Trade

Food Crops Productive agricultural economies were the foundations of all the Islamic empires. Each empire extracted surplus agricultural production and used it to finance armies and bureaucracies. Mostly the Islamic empires relied on crops of wheat and rice that had flourished for centuries in the lands they ruled. The Columbian exchange brought American crops to all the Islamic empires but without the same dramatic effects as in Europe, east Asia, and Africa. European merchants introduced maize, potatoes, tomatoes, and other crops to the Islamic empires, and the new arrivals soon found a place in regional cuisines. Potatoes appeared in the curries of southern India, and tomatoes enlivened dishes in the Ottoman empire as well as other Mediterranean lands. Maize did not appeal to human palates in the Islamic empires, but it became popular as feed for animal stocks, especially in the Ottoman empire.

The Columbian exchange strongly encouraged consumption of coffee and tobacco, especially in the Ottoman and Safavid empires. Although native to Ethiopia and cultivated in southern Arabia, coffee did not become popular in Islamic lands until the sixteenth century. Like sugar, it traveled to Europe and from there to the Americas, where plantations specialized in the production of tropical crops for the world market. By the eighteenth century, American producers and European merchants supplied Muslim markets with both coffee and sugar.

A bustling bazaar in Mughal India. At the center of this painting, a soothsayer attracts a crowd as he consults a manual while telling fortunes. Sacks of coins at his side suggest that he has done good business. Elsewhere in the market consumers buy watermelons, cloth, and peanuts.

Tobacco According to the Ottoman historian Ibrahim Pechevi, English merchants introduced tobacco around 1600, claiming it was useful for medicinal purposes. Within a few decades it had spread throughout the Ottoman empire. The increasing popularity of coffee drinking and pipe smoking encouraged entrepreneurs to establish coffeehouses where customers could indulge their appetites for caffeine and nicotine at the same time. The popularity of coffeehouses provoked protest from moralists who worried that these popular attractions were dens of iniquity that distracted habitués from their religious duties and attracted crowds of idlers and riffraff. Pechevi complained about the hideous odor of tobacco, the messy ashes, and the danger that smoking could cause fires, and religious leaders claimed that coffee was an illegal beverage and that it was worse to frequent a coffeehouse than a tavern. Sultan Murad IV went so far as to outlaw coffee and tobacco and to execute those who continued to partake. That effort, however, was a losing battle. Both pastimes eventually won widespread acceptance, and the coffeehouse became a prominent social institution in the Islamic empires.

Population Growth American food crops had less demographic effect in the Islamic empires than in other parts of the world. The population of India surged during early modern times, growing from 105 million in 1500 to 135 million in 1600, 165 million in 1700, and 190 million in 1800. But population growth in India resulted more from intensive agriculture along traditional lines than from the influence of new crops. The Safavid population grew less rapidly, from 5 million in 1500 to 6 million in 1600, and to 8 million in 1800. Ottoman numbers grew from 9 million in 1500 to 28 million in 1600, as the empire enlarged its boundaries to include populous regions in the Balkans, Egypt, and south-

In this anonymous painting produced about 1670, Dutch and English ships lie at anchor in the harbor of the busy port of Surat in northwestern India. Surat was the major port on the west coast of India, and it served as one of the chief commercial cities of the Mughal empire.

west Asia. After 1600, however, the Ottoman population declined to about 24 million, where it remained until the late 1800s. The decline reflected loss of territory more than a shrinking population, but even in the heartland of Anatolia, Ottoman numbers did not expand nearly as dramatically as those of other lands in early modern times. From 6 million in 1500, the population of Anatolia rose to 7.5 million in 1600, 8 million in 1700, and 9 million in 1800.

Trade The Islamic empires ruled lands that had figured prominently in long-distance trade for centuries and participated actively in global trade networks in early modern times. In the Ottoman empire, for example, the early capital at Bursa was also the terminus of a caravan route that brought raw silk from Persia to supply the Italian market. The Ottomans also granted special trading concessions to merchants from England and France to cement alliances against common enemies in Spain and central Europe. Aleppo became an emporium for foreign merchants engaged primarily in the spice trade and served as local headquarters for the operations of the English Levant Company.

Shah Abbas promoted Isfahan as a commercial center, extending trading privileges to foreign merchants and even allowing Christian monastic orders to set up missions there to help create a favorable environment for trade. European merchants sought Safavid raw silk, carpets, ceramics, and high-quality craft items. The English East India Company, the French East India Company, and the Dutch VOC all traded actively with the Safavids. To curry favor with them, the English company sent military advisors to introduce gunpowder weapons to Safavid armed forces and provided a navy to help them retake Hormuz in the Persian Gulf from the Portuguese.

The Mughals did not pay as much attention to foreign trade as the Ottomans and the Safavids did, partly because of the enormous size and productivity of the domestic Indian economy and partly because the Mughal rulers concentrated on their land empire and had little interest in maritime affairs. Nevertheless, the Mughal treasury derived significant income from foreign trade. The Mughals allowed the creation of trading stations and merchant colonies by Portuguese, English, French, and Dutch merchants. Meanwhile, Indian merchants formed trading companies of their own, ventured overland as far as Russia, and sailed the waters of the Indian Ocean to port cities from Persia to Indonesia.

Religious Affairs in the Islamic Empires

Religious Diversity All the Islamic empires had populations that were religiously and ethnically diverse, and imperial rulers had the daunting challenge of maintaining harmony between different religious communities. The Ottoman empire included large numbers of Christians and Jews in the Balkans, Armenia, Lebanon, and Egypt. The Safavid empire embraced sizable Zoroastrian and Jewish communities as well as many Christian subjects in the Caucasus. The Mughal empire was especially diverse. Most Mughal subjects were Hindus, but large numbers of Muslims lived alongside smaller communities of Jains, Zoroastrians, Christians, and devotees of syncretic faiths such as Sikhism.

Christian Mission in India Portuguese Goa became the center of a Christian mission in India. Priests at Goa sought to attract converts to Christianity and established schools that provided religious instruction for Indian children. In 1580 several Portuguese Jesuits traveled to the Mughal court at Akbar's invitation. They had visions of converting the emperor to Christianity and then spreading their faith throughout India, but their hopes went unfulfilled. Akbar received the Jesuits cordially and welcomed their participation in religious and philosophical discussions at his court, but he declined to commit to an exclusive faith that he thought would alienate many of his subjects.

Akbar's Divine Faith Indeed, Akbar was cool even to his Islamic faith. In his efforts to find a religious synthesis that would serve as a cultural foundation for unity in his diverse empire, he supported the efforts of the early Sikhs, who combined elements of Hinduism and Islam in a new syncretic faith. He also attempted to elaborate his own "divine faith" that emphasized loyalty to the emperor while borrowing eclectically from different religious traditions. Akbar never explained his ideas systematically, but it is clear that they drew most heavily on Islam. The divine faith was strictly monotheistic, and it reflected the influence of Shiite and Sufi teachings. But it also glorified the emperor: Akbar even referred to himself as the "lord of wisdom," who would guide his subjects to understanding of the world's creator god. The divine faith was tolerant of Hinduism, and it even drew inspiration from Zoroastrianism in its effort to bridge the gaps between Mughal India's many cultural and religious communities.

In a seventeenth-century painting, the emperor Akbar presides over discussions between representatives of various religious groups. Two Jesuits dressed in black robes kneel at the left.

Status of Religious Minorities The Islamic empires relied on a long-established model to deal with subjects who were not Muslims. They did not require conquered peoples to convert to Islam but extended to them the status of *dhimmi* ("protected people"). In return for their loyalty and payment of a special tax known as *jizya, dhimmi* communities retained their personal freedom, kept their property, practiced their religion, and handled their legal affairs. In the Ottoman empire, for example, autonomous religious communities known as *millet* retained their civil laws, traditions, and languages. *Millet* communities usually also assumed social and administrative functions in matters concerning birth, marriage, death, health, and education.

The situation in the Mughal empire was different, since its large number of religious communities made a *millet* system impractical. Mughal rulers reserved the most powerful military and administrative positions for Muslims, but in the day-to-day management of affairs, Muslims and Hindus cooperated closely. Some Mughal emperors sought to forge links between religious communities. Akbar in particular worked to integrate Muslim and Hindu elites. In an effort to foster communication and understanding among the different religious communities of his realm, he abolished the *jizya,* tolerated all faiths, and sponsored discussions and debates between Muslims, Hindus, Jains, Zoroastrians, and Christians.

thinking about TRADITIONS

Religious Diversity
An overarching feature of all three Islamic empires was the ethnic and religious diversity of the subject populations. What measures did the rulers of the Ottoman, Safavid, and Mughal states take to maintain harmony among the different ethnic and religious communities?

Promotion of Islam Policies of religious tolerance were not popular with many Muslims, who worried that they would lose their religious identity and that toleration might lead to their absorption into Hindu society as another caste. They therefore insisted that Mughal rulers create and maintain an Islamic state based on Islamic law. When Aurangzeb reached the Mughal throne in 1659, this policy gained strength. Aurangzeb reinstated the *jizya* and promoted Islam as the official faith of Mughal India. His policy satisfied zealous Muslims but at the cost of deep bitterness among his Hindu subjects. Tension between Hindu and Muslim communities in India persisted throughout the Mughal dynasty and beyond.

Cultural Patronage of the Islamic Emperors

As the empires matured, the Islamic rulers sought to enhance their prestige through public works projects and patronage of scholars. They competed to attract outstanding religious scholars, poets, artists, and architects to their courts. They lavished resources on mosques, palaces, government buildings, bridges, fountains, schools, hospitals, and soup kitchens for the poor.

Istanbul Capital cities and royal palaces were the most visible expressions of imperial majesty. The Ottomans beautified both Bursa and Edirne, but they took particular pride in Istanbul. Dilapidated and deserted after the conquest, it quickly revived and became a bustling, prosperous city of more than a million people. At its heart was the great Topkapi palace, which housed government offices, such as the mint, and meeting places for imperial councils. At its core was the sultan's residence with its harem, gardens, pleasure pavilions, and a repository for the most sacred possessions of the empire, including the mantle of the prophet Muhammad. Sultan Süleyman the Magnificent was fortunate to be able to draw on the talents of the architectural genius Sinan Pasha (1489–1588) to create the most celebrated of all the monuments of Istanbul. Sinan built a vast religious complex called the Süleymaniye, which blended Islamic and Byzantine architectural elements. It combined tall, slender minarets with large domed buildings supported by half domes in the style of the Byzantine church Hagia Sofia (which the Ottomans converted into the mosque of Aya Sofya).

Isfahan Shah Abbas made his capital, Isfahan, into the queen of Persian cities and one of the most precious jewels of urban architectural development anywhere in the world: its inhabitants still boast that "Isfahan is half the world." Abbas concentrated markets, the palace, and the royal mosque around a vast polo field and public square. Broad, shaded avenues and magnificent bridges linked the central city to its suburbs. Safavid architects made use of monumental entryways, vast arcades, spacious courtyards, and intricate, colorful decoration. Unlike the sprawling Ottoman and Mughal palaces, the Safavid palaces in Isfahan were relatively small and emphasized natural settings with gardens and pools. They were also much more open than Topkapi, with its series of

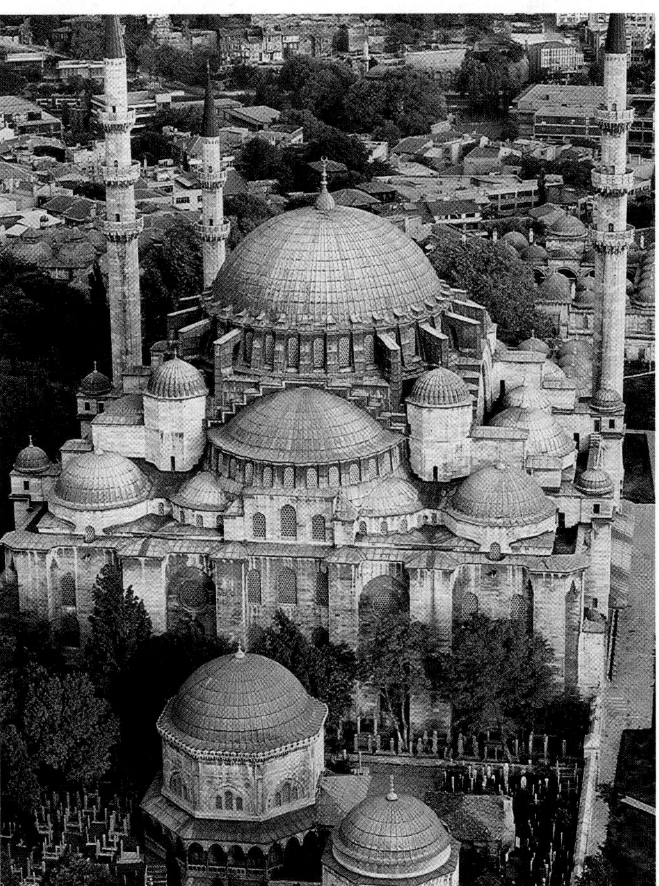

The massive Süleymaniye mosque built for Sultan Süleyman the Magnificent by the Ottoman architect Sinan Pasha in 1556.

Fatehpur Sikri, built by Akbar in the 1570s, commemorated the emperor's military conquests and housed the tomb of his religious guide. It included a palace, an audience hall where Akbar attended religious and philosophical debates, and a great mosque.

inner courts and gates. Ali Qapu, the palace on the square in Isfahan, had a striking balcony, and most of the palaces had large, open verandas. The point was not only to enable the shah to observe outside activities but also to emphasize his visibility and accessibility, qualities long esteemed in the Persian tradition of kingship.

To some extent, in accordance with steppe traditions, the early Mughals regarded the capital as wherever the ruler happened to camp. Yet they too came to sponsor urban development. Their work skillfully blended central Asian traditions with elements of Hindu architecture, and they built on a scale that left no doubt about their wealth and resources. They constructed scores of mosques, fortresses, and palaces and sometimes created entire cities.

Fatehpur Sikri The best example was Fatehpur Sikri, a city planned and constructed by Akbar that served as his capital from 1569 to 1585. It commemorated his conquest of the prosperous commercial province of Gujarat in a campaign that enabled Akbar to head off both Portuguese attacks and Ottoman intervention there. With its mint, records office, treasury, and audience hall, the new city demonstrated Akbar's strength and imperial ambitions. Fatehpur Sikri was also a private residence and retreat for the ruler, reproducing in stone a royal encampment with exquisite pleasure palaces where Akbar indulged his passions for music and conversation with scholars and poets. At yet another level, it was a dramatic display of Mughal piety and devotion, centered on the cathedral mosque and the mausoleum of Akbar's Sufi guru, Shaykh Salim Chisti. Despite their intensely Islamic character, many of the buildings consciously incorporated Indian elements such as verandas supported by columns and decorations of stone elephants. Even the tomb of Shaykh Chisti bore some resemblance to a Hindu shrine. Unfortunately, Akbar selected a poor site for the city and soon abandoned it because of its bad water supply.

The Taj Mahal The most famous of the Mughal monuments—and one of the most prominent of all Islamic edifices—was the Taj Mahal. Shah Jahan had twenty thousand workers toil for eighteen years to erect the exquisite white marble mosque and tomb. He originally planned to build a similar mausoleum out of black marble for himself, but his son Aurangzeb deposed him before he could carry out the project. Shah Jahan spent his last years confined to a small cell with a tiny window, and only with the aid of a mirror was he able to catch the sight of his beloved wife's final resting place.

THE EMPIRES IN TRANSITION

The Islamic empires underwent dramatic change between the sixteenth and the eighteenth centuries. The Safavid empire disappeared entirely. In 1722 a band of Afghan tribesmen marched all the way to Isfahan, blockaded the city until its starving inhabitants resorted to cannibalism, forced the shah to abdicate, and executed thousands of Safavid officials as well as many members of the royal family. After the death of Aurangzeb in 1707, Mughal India experienced provincial rebellions and foreign invasions. By mid-century the subcontinent was falling under British imperial rule. By 1700 the Ottomans, too, were on the defensive: the sultans lost control over remote provinces such as Lebanon and Egypt, and throughout the eighteenth and nineteenth cen-

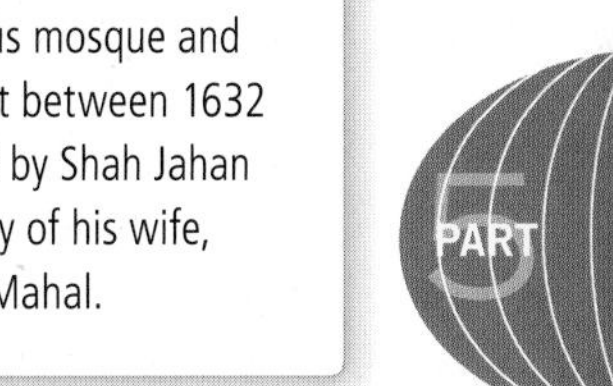

The Taj Mahal was a sumptuous mosque and tomb built between 1632 and 1649 by Shah Jahan in memory of his wife, Mumtaz Mahal.

turies European and Russian states placed political, military, and economic pressure on the shrinking Ottoman realm.

The Deterioration of Imperial Leadership

Strong and effective central authority was essential to the Islamic empires, and Muslim political theorists never tired of emphasizing the importance of rulers who were diligent, virtuous, and just. Weak, negligent, and corrupt rulers would allow institutions to become dysfunctional and social order to break down. The Ottomans were fortunate in having a series of talented sultans for three centuries, and the Safavids and Mughals produced their share of effective rulers as well.

Dynastic Decline Eventually, however, all three dynasties had rulers who were incompetent or more interested in spending vast sums of money on personal pleasures than in tending to affairs of state. Moreover, all three dynasties faced difficulties because of suspicion and fighting among competing members of their ruling houses. The Ottomans sought to limit problems by confining princes in the palace, but that measure had several negative consequences. The princes had no opportunity to gain experience in government, but they were exposed to plots and intrigues of the various factions maneuvering to bring a favorable candidate to the throne. Notorious examples of problem rulers included Süleyman's successor Selim the Sot (reigned 1566–1574) and Ibrahim the Crazy (reigned 1640–1648), who taxed and spent to such excess that government officials deposed and murdered him. Several energetic rulers and talented ministers attempted to keep the government on track. Nonetheless, after the late seventeenth century, weak rule increasingly provoked mutinies in the army, provincial revolts, political corruption, economic oppression, and insecurity throughout the Ottoman realm.

Religious Tensions Political troubles often arose from religious tensions. Conservative Muslim clerics strongly objected to policies and practices that they considered affronts to Islam. Muslim leaders had considerable influence in the Islamic empires because of their monopoly of education and their deep involvement in the everyday lives and legal affairs of ordinary subjects. The clerics mistrusted the emperors' interests in unconventional forms of Islam such as Sufism, complained bitterly when women or subjects who were not Muslims played influential political roles, and protested any exercise of royal authority that contradicted Islamic law.

In the Ottoman empire, disaffected religious students often joined the Janissaries in revolt. A particularly serious threat came from the Wahhabi movement in Arabia, which denounced the Ottomans as dangerous religious innovators who were unfit to rule. Conservative Muslims fiercely protested the construction of an astronomical observatory in Istanbul and forced the sultan to demolish it in 1580. In 1742 they also forced the closure of the Ottoman printing press, which they regarded as an impious technology.

The Safavids, who began their reign by crushing Sunni religious authorities, fell under the domination of the very Shiites they had supported. Shiite leaders pressured the shahs to persecute Sunnis, non-Muslims, and even the Sufis who had helped establish the dynasty. Religious tensions also afflicted Mughal India. Already in the seventeenth century, the conservative Shaykh Ahmad Sirhindi (1564–1624) fearlessly rebuked Akbar for his policy of religious tolerance and his interest in other faiths. In the mid-eighteenth century, as he struggled to claim the Mughal throne, Aurangzeb drew on Sirhindi's ideas when he required non-Muslims to pay the poll tax and ordered the destruction of Hindu temples. Those measures inflamed tensions between the various Sunni, Shiite, and Sufi branches of Islam and also fueled animosity among Hindus and other Mughal subjects who were not Muslims.

Economic and Military Decline

In the sixteenth century, all the Islamic empires had strong domestic economies and played prominent roles in global trade networks. By the eighteenth century, however, domestic economies were under great stress, and foreign trade had declined dramatically or had fallen under the control of European powers. The Islamic empires were well on their way to becoming marginal lands that depended on goods produced elsewhere.

Economic Difficulties The high cost of maintaining an expensive military and administrative apparatus helped

All the Islamic empires fought numerous wars, many of which exhausted resources without adding to the productive capacities of the empires. This illustration depicts Ottoman forces (right) clashing with heavily armored Austrian cavalry near Budapest in 1540.

to bring about economic decline in the Islamic empires. As long as the empires were expanding, they were able to finance their armies and bureaucracies with fresh resources extracted from newly conquered lands. When expansion slowed, ceased, or reversed, however, they faced the problem of supporting their institutions with limited resources. The long, costly, and unproductive wars fought by the Ottomans with the Habsburgs in central Europe, by the Safavids and the Ottomans in Mesopotamia, and by Aurangzeb in southern India, exhausted the treasuries of the Islamic empires without making fresh resources available to them. As early as 1589 the Ottomans tried to pay the Janissaries in debased coinage and immediately provoked a mutiny. The next 150 years witnessed at least six additional military revolts.

As expansion slowed and the empires lost control over remote provinces, officials reacted to the loss of revenue by raising taxes, selling public offices, accepting bribes, or resorting to simple extortion. All those measures were counterproductive. Although they might provide immediate cash, they did long-term economic damage. To make matters worse, the governments viewed foreign trade as just another opportunity to bring in revenue. The Ottomans expanded the privileges enjoyed by foreign merchants, and the Mughals encouraged the establishment of Dutch and English trading outposts and welcomed the expansion of their business in India. Imperial authorities were content to have foreign traders come to them. None made serious efforts to establish commercial stations abroad, although Indian merchants organized their own private trading companies.

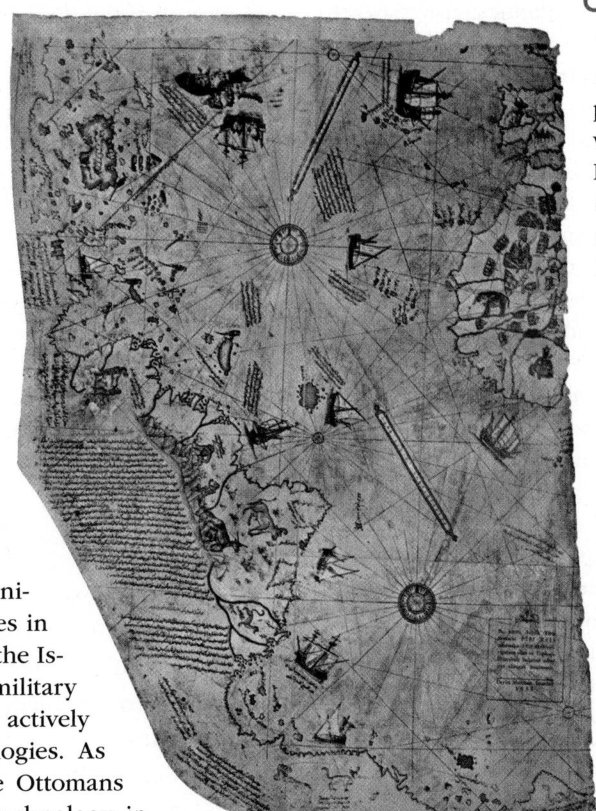

Ottoman cartographer Piri Reis drew on European charts when preparing this map of the Atlantic Ocean basin in 1513. Caribbean and South American coastlines are visible at left, while Iberian and west African coastlines appear in the upper right corner.

Military Decline As they lost initiative to western European peoples in economic and commercial affairs, the Islamic empires also experienced military decline because they did not seek actively to improve their military technologies. As early as the fifteenth century, the Ottomans had relied heavily on European technology in gunnery; indeed, the cannon that Mehmed the Conqueror used in 1453 to breach the defensive wall of Constantinople was the product of a Hungarian gun-founder. During the sixteenth and early seventeenth centuries, the Islamic empires were able to purchase European weapons in large numbers and attract European expertise that kept their armies supplied with powerful gunpowder weapons. In 1605, for example, the cargo of an English ship bound for Anatolia included seven hundred barrels of gunpowder, one thousand musket barrels, five hundred fully assembled muskets, and two thousand sword blades, alongside wool textiles and bullion.

By about the mid-seventeenth century, European military technology was advancing so rapidly that the Islamic empires could not keep pace. None of the empires had a large armaments industry, so they had to rely on foreign suppliers. They still were able to purchase European weapons and expertise, but their arsenals became increasingly dated, since they depended on technologies that European peoples had already replaced. By the late eighteenth century, the Ottoman navy, which had long influenced maritime affairs in the Mediterranean, Red Sea, Persian Gulf, and Arabian Sea, was closing its shipbuilding operations and ordering new military vessels from foreign shipyards.

Cultural Conservatism

While experiencing economic and military decline, the Islamic empires also neglected cultural developments in the larger world. Europeans who visited the Islamic empires attempted to learn as much as possible about the language, religion, social customs, and history of the host countries. They published accounts of their travels that became extremely popular in their homelands, and they advocated serious study of Islamic lands. In the early seventeenth century, for example, the English scholar William Bedwell described Arabic as the only important language of trade, diplomacy, and religion from Morocco to the China seas.

Piri Reis To some extent, information also flowed in the other direction. During the sixteenth century, just as European mariners were scouting Atlantic waters, Ottoman mariners reconnoitered the Indian Ocean basin from east Africa to Indonesia—a project that reflected military concerns about European and other naval forces in the region. Ottoman geographers also manifested great interest in European

thinking about ENCOUNTERS

Islamic Mapmaking

Muslims evinced a generalized wariness about knowledge deriving from European contacts. One notable exception to this was Piri Reis, an Ottoman cartographer. Why did he draw on European sources for his maps? Why were maps seen as so strategically useful in an age of cross-cultural contacts?

knowledge of geography, some of which had considerable military value. The Ottoman admiral and cartographer Piri Reis produced several large-scale maps and a major navigational text, the *Book of Seafaring,* which drew on reports and maps from European mariners and explorers. Piri Reis even managed to consult a copy of a chart drawn by Christopher Columbus during his first voyage to the western hemisphere. Some of Piri Reis's maps included the Atlantic coast of North America and the lands visited by Columbus, which the cartographer probably learned about from Spanish sailors captured in naval conflicts with Ottoman forces.

Cultural Confidence Yet few Muslims traveled willingly to the infidel lands of "the Franks." Muslim rulers and their Muslim subjects were confident of their superiority and believed that they had nothing to learn from Europeans. As a result, most Muslims remained largely oblivious to European cultural and technological developments. Not until 1703 was there an attempt to introduce European scientific instruments such as the telescope into astronomical observatories. Then conservative Muslim clerics soon forced the removal of the foreign implements, which they considered impious and unnecessary.

The Printing Press The early experience of the printing press in the Islamic empires illustrates especially well the resistance of conservative religious leaders to cultural imports from western Europe. Jewish refugees from Spain introduced the first printing presses to Anatolia in the late fifteenth century. Ottoman authorities allowed them to operate presses in Istanbul and other major cities as long as they did not print books in the Turkish or Arabic language. Armenian and Greek printers soon established presses in the Ottoman realm and published books in their own languages. Not until 1729 did government authorities lift the ban on the printing of books in the Turkish and Arabic languages. During the next thirteen years, a Turkish press published seventeen books dealing mostly with history, geography, and language before conservative Muslims forced its closure in 1742. Only in 1784 did a new Turkish press open, and printing spread throughout the Ottoman empire soon thereafter.

Printing also caught on slowly in Mughal India. Jesuit missionaries in Goa published books, including translations of the Bible into Indian and Arabic languages, as early as the 1550s. Yet Mughal rulers displayed little interest in the press, and printing did not become prominent in Indian society until the establishment of British colonial rule in Bengal in the eighteenth century.

To some extent, aesthetic considerations stood in the way of the printing press: particularly in the Ottoman and Safavid empires, as in many other Muslim lands, scholars and general readers alike simply preferred elegant handwritten books to cheaply produced printed works, especially when the book in question was the Quran. Yet resistance to printing also reflected the concerns of conservative religious leaders that readily available printed books would introduce all manner of new and dangerous ideas to the public—indeed, that an active publishing industry might spread inconvenient questions about the organization of Muslim societies or even about the Islamic faith itself.

Thus, like imperial China and Tokugawa Japan, the Islamic empires resisted the introduction of cultural influences from western European societies. Rulers of the Islamic empires readily accepted gunpowder weapons as enhancements to their military and political power, but they and their subjects drew little inspiration from European religion, science, or ideas. Moreover, under the influence of conservative religious leaders, Islamic authorities actively discouraged the circulation of ideas that might pose unsettling challenges to the social and cultural order of the Islamic empires. Like the Ming, Qing, and Tokugawa rulers, the Ottoman, Safavid, and Mughal emperors preferred political and social stability to the risks that foreign cultural innovations might bring.

inperspective

Like China and Japan, the Islamic empires largely retained control of their own affairs throughout the early modern era. Ruling elites of the Ottoman, Safavid, and Mughal empires came from nomadic Turkish stock, and they all drew on steppe traditions in organizing their governments. But the rulers also adapted steppe traditions to the needs of settled agricultural societies and devised institutions that maintained order over a long term. During the sixteenth and seventeenth centuries, all the Islamic empires enjoyed productive economies that enabled merchants to participate actively in the global trade networks of early modern times. By the early eighteenth century, however, these same empires were experiencing economic difficulties that led to political and military decline. Like the Ming, Qing, and Tokugawa rulers in east Asia, the Islamic emperors mostly sought to limit foreign and especially European influences in their realms. The Islamic emperors ruled lands that were religiously and ethnically diverse, and most of them worried that the expansion of foreign religious and cultural traditions would threaten political and social stability. They allowed their subjects to practice faiths other than Islam, and the Mughal emperor Akbar even promoted a syncretic religion in hopes that it would defuse tensions between Hindus and Muslims. For the most part, however, rulers of the Islamic empires followed the advice of conservative Muslim clerics, who promoted Islamic values and fought the introduction of foreign cultural imports, such as the printing press and European science, that might undermine their authority. By the late eighteenth century, the Safavid empire had collapsed, and economic difficulties and cultural insularity had severely weakened the Ottoman and Mughal empires. ●

CHRONOLOGY	
1289–1923	Ottoman dynasty
1451–1481	Reign of Mehmed the Conqueror
1453	Ottoman conquest of Constantinople
1501–1524	Reign of Shah Ismail
1501–1722	Safavid dynasty
1514	Battle of Chaldiran
1520–1566	Reign of Süleyman the Magnificent
1526–1858	Mughal dynasty
1556–1605	Reign of Akbar
1588–1629	Reign of Shah Abbas the Great
1659–1707	Reign of Aurangzeb

Assessing AP Themes

1. What were the global economic and demographic effects of the Columbian Exchange?
2. What were the global, economic, political, social, and cultural effects of the sugar plantation system in the Americas?
3. Compare the methods and successes of two states from two different regions in which the rulers attempted to consolidate their power and expand their empires.
4. Compare the political, economic, and cultural reasons for setting up a trading-post (non-settler) colony and settler colony.
5. To what extent (how much) did religions in Europe, Asia, Africa, and the Americas change in this time period? For those that changed, compare the reasons for the changes.
6. What effect did the global migrations of people have on those who migrated (emigrated) and those who stayed in their place of origin? Pick two regions and compare.
7. What new business arrangements came into existence because of the maritime explorations and colonial empires?

For Further Reading

Esin Atil. *The Age of Sultan Süleyman the Magnificent.* Washington, D.C., 1987. Richly illustrated volume that emphasizes Süleyman's role as a patron of the arts.

Franz Babinger. *Mehmed the Conqueror and His Time.* Trans. by R. Manheim. Princeton, 1978. A magisterial biography of the sultan who conquered Constantinople.

Jonathan P. Berkey. *The Formation of Islam: Religion and Society in the Near East, 600–1800.* New York, 2002. Broad survey of the history of Islam and Islamic civilization.

Stephen Frederic Dale. *Indian Merchants and Eurasian Trade, 1600–1750.* Cambridge, 1994. Examines the workings of an Indian trading community that conducted business in Persia, central Asia, and Russia.

Suraiya Faroghi. *Towns and Townsmen of Ottoman Anatolia.* Cambridge, 1989. A valuable contribution to an understanding of the Ottoman domestic economy.

Carter Vaughn Findley. *The Turks in World History.* New York, 2005. A highly readable account that connects the two-thousand-year history of the Turkic peoples with larger global processes.

Dina Le Gall. *A Culture of Sufism: Naqshbandis in the Ottoman World, 1450–1700.* Albany, N.Y., 2005. Study of the cultural practices and religious beliefs of an important Sufi brotherhood.

Halil Inalçik. *The Ottoman Empire: The Classical Age, 1300–1600.* New York, 1973. A reliable survey by the foremost historian of the early Ottoman empire.

——— and Donald Quataert, eds. *An Economic and Social History of the Ottoman Empire, 1300–1914.* Cambridge, 1994. An exhaustive survey of Ottoman economic history.

Çemal Kafadar. *Between Two Worlds: The Construction of the Ottoman State.* Berkeley, 1995. Studies the origins and early development of the Ottoman empire.

Kemal H. Karpat. *The Politicization of Islam: Reconstructing Identity, State, Faith, and Community in the Late Ottoman State.* New York, 2001. Scholarly study of the Ottoman state's role in constructing Muslim identity.

Bernard Lewis. *The Muslim Discovery of Europe.* New York, 1982. An important study that charts Muslim interest in European affairs.

Bruce Masters. *The Origins of Western Economic Dominance in the Middle East: Mercantilism and the Islamic Economy in Aleppo, 1600–1750.* New York, 1988. A stimulating case study of an important trading city caught between a central government in chaos and European mercantile pressure.

David Morgan. *Medieval Persia, 1040–1797.* London, 1988. A brief and insightful survey that examines Persian history through the Safavid dynasty.

Leslie Pierce. *The Imperial Harem: Women and Sovereignty in the Ottoman Empire.* Oxford, 1993. Challenges many stereotypes about the role of women in the imperial Ottoman elite.

Gabriel Piterberg. *An Ottoman Tragedy: History and Historiography at Play.* Berkeley, 2003. Analysis of the Ottoman empire in the seventeenth century that also examines the evolution of Ottoman historiography.

John F. Richards. *The Mughal Empire.* Cambridge, 1993. A concise and reliable overview of Mughal history, concentrating on political affairs.

Roger Savory. *Iran under the Safavids.* Cambridge, 1980. A rich and authoritative survey of Safavid history, especially interesting for its views on Safavid origins, culture, and commercial relations.

Madeline Zilfi. *The Politics of Piety: The Ottoman Ulema in the Postclassical Age, 1600–1800.* Minneapolis, 1988. Examines the influence and changing role of the Ottoman religious leadership.

State of the World

Changing Views of the World, Changing Worldviews

Whether signaled by a young Mexican woman serving as an interpreter for Spanish conquerors or by the sounds of chiming clocks in China, novel cross-cultural experiences—on both an intimately human and a coldly technological level—symbolized the intense global transformations taking place in the early modern world. One of the most stunning alterations after 1500 involved the very way humans could now envision a world so perilously and profitably interconnected. Mariners and voyagers from as far afield as east Asia, the Ottoman empire, and western Europe charted the vast expanses of the world's oceans and opened up new human vistas on a world where two previously isolated hemispheres coexisted in an ever-tightening web of global interaction. Detailed maps of the Americas, Oceania, the Indian Ocean basin, and western Africa added to the world's cartographic knowledge and stood as two-dimensional emblems of this changed view of the world—and of the changed worldviews impelled by that new world understanding.

Few societies could withstand the impulses of change emanating from this new, globally intertwined world. Western Europeans in the vanguard of global voyaging in the early modern era consolidated their global influence by establishing empires and settler colonies in the Americas and by setting off a complex process of voluntary and forced human migrations that changed both the world and the worldviews of those involved. Indigenous Americans and Pacific Islanders suffered mass die-offs from epidemics and the consequent dimming of their strength, while the African slaves who replaced them as laborers likewise had their worldviews rudely adjusted during their forced migrations through the Atlantic Ocean basin. And, as the far-flung travels of Thomas Peters suggested, Africans experienced exposure to a complex mixture of worldviews shaped by indigenous African, American, and European ideologies. In this early modern era of interconnectedness, worldviews took on an increasingly cross-cultural cast.

The imperative to change in this era had both external global and internal cultural elements. This was nowhere more evident than in western European societies, where intercontinental outreach was matched by an internal questioning of traditions, whether religious, intellectual, or political. In the age of revolution after 1750, the external and internal pulses of change in Europe would collide and provide it with even more explosive global power. The prosperous societies in the early modern era, such as China, Japan, and the Islamic empires, succeeded in shielding their traditions and their worldviews from the intensifying impulses of change through much of this period. The chimes of those clocks in China, however, served as harbingers of a more deafening weapons technology that threatened imperial intrusion and the further altering of worldviews.

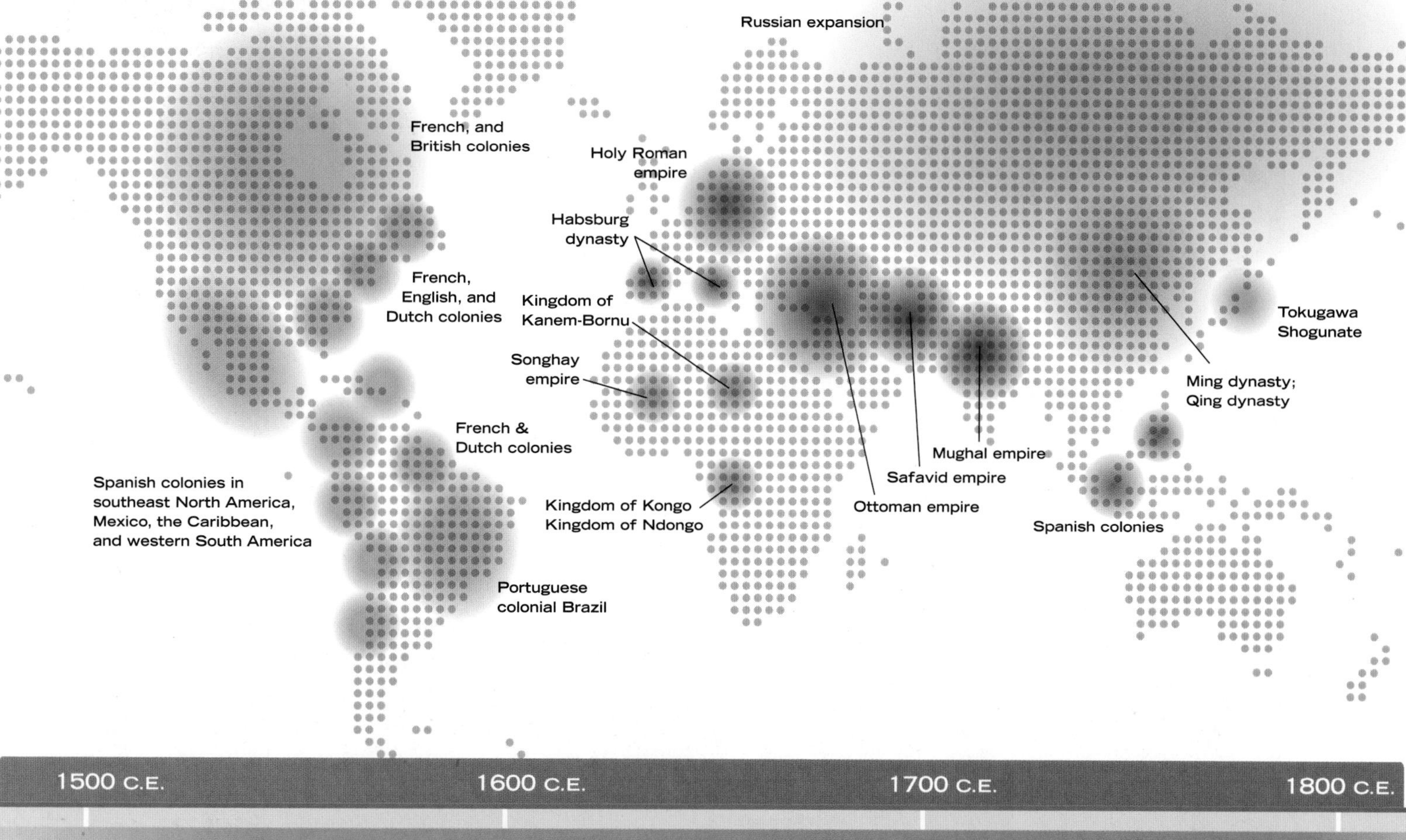

1500 C.E. | 1600 C.E. | 1700 C.E. | 1800 C.E.

CENTRAL & EAST ASIA

China: Ming dynasty, 1368–1644 C.E.
Russian expansion, 1462–1795 C.E.
Japan: Tokugawa Shogunate, 1600–1867 C.E.
China: Qing dynasty, 1644–1911 C.E.

EUROPE

Holy Roman Empire & Habsburg dynasty (including Spanish and Austrian territories), ca. 1519–1648 C.E.

SOUTH & SOUTHWEST ASIA

Ottoman empire, 1289–1923 C.E.
Safavid empire, 1501–1722 C.E.
Mughal empire, 1526–1858 C.E.

AFRICA

Songhay empire, 1464–1591 C.E.
Kingdom of Ndongo, early 16th century to 1671 C.E.
Decline of Swahili city-states after Portuguese raids, 1497–1505 C.E.
Kingdom of Kanem-Bornu, 9th century to 19th century C.E.; Kingdom of Kongo, 1396–1910 C.E.

THE AMERICAS

Spanish colonies in Mexico, the Caribbean, southeast North America, and western South America, 1492–18th century
Portuguese colonial Brazil, 1500–1822 C.E.
French, English, and Dutch colonies in North America, ca. 1600–late 18th century

OCEANIA

Spanish colonies in the Pacific, 1500–1800 C.E.

part 6

AP *Themes*

AN AGE OF REVOLUTION, INDUSTRY, AND EMPIRE, 1750 TO 1914

A lot of this period centers on the study of revolutions. Historians don't use the word "revolution" lightly. It implies drastic, 180° change, and humans don't do that very often. In the eighteenth and early nineteenth centuries, however, there were several significant and successful revolutions in the Atlantic World, in which peoples changed their rulers, economies, and social structures. AP students are asked to compare these revolutions in terms of their causes, participants, and outcomes. One of the significant causes of these changes was Enlightenment ideology. Enlightenment thinkers questioned established traditions in all areas of life, and as their ideas spread, they often propelled discontent with imperial rule and the status quo of European culture. The powerful ideas of nationalism, socialism, democracy, and human equality are found in Enlightenment writings. AP students will have to track these ideas from the eighteenth century to the present day.

Another type of revolution in this era was economic, and is known as the Industrial Revolution. Like the Neolithic Revolution at the beginning of this course, this huge shift proceeded slowly. Western European and North American states were the first to industrialize their economies, and students will need to explain why this occurred. AP students will be asked to look at how and by whom goods were produced, transported, and financed. Students will also have to follow the ways in which the Industrial Revolution changed the lives of people in different social classes, ages, and genders, living in different parts of the world. This is a huge topic, and one for which students are often asked to compare or to track changes and continuities over time. A few of the topics within this social history topic are: moving from rural to urban areas (migration); changes in gender relations and family structures; the development of new social classes and new forms of labor; and the effects of rapid urbanization.

The creation of industrialized economies in the West had a ripple-effect in international relations. The industrialized countries continued to expand and adapt their colonial empires. The mother countries needed access to cheap raw materials and labor forces, and to look for more peoples (in colonies and elsewhere) to buy their manufactured goods. AP students will be asked to evaluate how the lives, economies, and governments of colonial peoples were changed by these colonial incursions, as well as how the colonizers themselves were changed. And it wasn't just colonized peoples who had to deal with the newly-industrialized west. Rulers of well-established states such as Qing China, the Ottoman Empire, Russia, and the Japanese Tokugawa Shogunate had to decide whether or how much to industrialize in order to compete militarily or economically with the West. There were people in these societies, however, who feared industrialization because they feared the

foreign influences that would come with it. The tension of all these forces often led to deep political, social, and economic problems within these "societies at the crossroads." In the long run, competition over colonial empires becomes one of the key causes of the outbreak of a global war in 1914.

The third powerful force in this era is an intellectual force, rather than a political or economic force—the concepts of the Enlightenment and nationalism, arguably two of the most powerful sets of ideas in the modern world. Enlightenment philosophes' criticisms of existing traditions and authorities contributed to reformist and revolutionary movements in the eighteenth and nineteenth centuries. AP students will have to understand the basic ideas of Enlightenment philosophy and be able to trace the impact of those ideas as they are spread and the degree to which they are utilized by reformers or revolutionaries. The global spread of Enlightenment ideas contributed to new ideas of nationalism, human rights, and the proper role of governments in regions of the world far away from their Western European roots.

Industrialization and increasing global integration (globalization) changed the patterns of human migration in this period. The background to these migrations was a significant rise in global population due to increased food production and improved medical conditions. As the size of families and communities increased, there was often not enough land or work for the growing populations. Migration occurred on smaller scales as rural workers moved to urban areas to work in industrial economies. Migration also occurred on a transnational scale as workers chose to move or were coerced to move, often in search of work. The enormous numbers of the migrant peoples caused a wide variety of consequences to the lands they left and the lands to which they traveled. AP students should be able to evaluate and compare how families and communities on the giving and receiving ends of these migrations adapted to the addition or subtraction of the migrants, and how the migrants themselves adapted to their new surroundings. Migration, then and now, presented challenges to governments as they attempted to form national identities (or define their own nationalism), grow their national economies, and regulate the flow of people in their nation-states.

Revolutions and National States in the Atlantic World

chapter 28

Liberty, personified as a woman, leads the French people in a famous painting by Eugène Delacroix.

PART 6

EYEWITNESS:
Olympe de Gouges Declares the Rights of Women

Marie Gouze was a French butcher's daughter who educated herself by reading books, moved to Paris, and married a junior army officer. Under the name Olympe de Gouges, she won some fame as a journalist, actress, and playwright. Gouges was as flamboyant as she was talented, and news of her well-publicized love affairs scandalized Parisian society.

Gouges was also a revolutionary and a strong advocate of women's rights. She responded enthusiastically when the French revolution broke out in July 1789, and she applauded in August when revolutionary leaders proclaimed freedom and equality for all citizens in the *Declaration of the Rights of Man and the Citizen.* It soon became clear, however, that in the view of revolutionary leaders, freedom and equality pertained only to male citizens. They welcomed women's contributions to the revolution but withheld the right to vote and left women under the patriarchal authority of their fathers and husbands.

Gouges campaigned fervently to raise the standing of women in French society. She called for more education and demanded that women share equal rights in family property. She challenged patriarchal authority and appealed to Queen Marie Antoinette to use her influence to advance women's rights. In 1791 Gouges published a *Declaration of the Rights of Woman and the Female Citizen,* which claimed the same rights for women that revolutionary leaders had granted to men in August 1789. She asserted that freedom and equality were inalienable rights of women as well as men, and she insisted on the rights of women to vote, speak their minds freely, participate in the making of law, and hold public office.

Gouges's declaration attracted a great deal of attention but little support. Revolutionary leaders dismissed her appeal as a publicity stunt and refused to put women's rights on their political agenda. In 1793 they executed her because of her affection for Marie Antoinette and her persistent crusade for women's rights. Yet Gouges's campaign illustrated the power of the Enlightenment ideals of freedom and equality. Revolutionary leaders stilled her voice, but once they had proclaimed freedom and equality as universal human rights, they were unable to suppress demands to extend them to new constituencies.

Violence rocked lands throughout much of the Atlantic Ocean basin in the late eighteenth and early nineteenth centuries as a series of revolutions and wars of independence brought dramatic political and social change. Royal subjects attempted to restructure their societies—if necessary by violent means—by abolishing traditional social and political institutions and replacing them with novel ones. The notion of a divinely ordained division between ruler and ruled ceased to exist, as the politically activated masses not only sought to participate in government but also actually viewed it as their inherent right to do so. Each revolution broke out in its own context and had its own specific causes. Yet all derived, directly or indirectly, their inspiration and rationalization from the Enlightenment.

Revolution broke out first in the British colonies of North America, where colonists asserted their independence and founded a new republic. A few years later, revolutionaries abolished the French monarchy and thoroughly reorganized French society. Revolutionary ideas soon spread to other lands. They inspired popular movements throughout Europe and prompted Latin American peoples to seek independence from Spanish and Portuguese colonial rule. In Saint-Domingue, revolution led to the abolition of slavery as well as independence from French rule. By the 1830s, peoples had reorganized political and social structures throughout western Europe and the Americas.

Apart from affecting individual lands, the revolutions of the late eighteenth and early nineteenth centuries had two results of deep global significance. First, they helped to spread a cluster of Enlightenment ideas concerning freedom, equality, and popular sovereignty. Revolutionary leaders argued that political authority arose from the people and worked to establish states in the interests of the people rather than the rulers. Usually, they instituted republican forms of government, in which constituents selected delegates to represent their interests. In fact, early revolutionaries extended political rights to a privileged group of white men, but they justified their actions in general terms that invited new constituencies to seek enfranchisement. Ideas about freedom, equality, and popular sovereignty spread globally after the American and French revolutions as social reformers and revolutionaries struggled throughout the nineteenth and twentieth centuries to make freedom and equality a reality for oppressed groups and subject peoples throughout the world. By the mid-twentieth century, nearly every state in the world formally recognized the freedom and equality of all its citizens—even if they did not always honor their official positions—and claimed authority to rule on the basis of popular sovereignty.

While promoting Enlightenment values, revolutions also encouraged the consolidation of national states as the principal form of political organization. As peoples defended their states from enemies and sometimes mounted attacks on foreign lands, they developed a powerful sense of identity with their compatriots, and nationalist convictions inspired them to work toward the foundation of states that would advance the interests of the national community. During the nineteenth century, strong national identities and movements to build national states profoundly influenced the political experiences of European states. Strong nationalist sentiments created problems for multicultural states such as the Austrian empire, which embraced several distinct linguistic and ethnic communities, but also fueled movements to unify lands such as Italy and Germany, which previously had no national state. During the late nineteenth and twentieth centuries, efforts to harness nationalist sentiments and form states based on national identity became one of the most powerful and dynamic movements in world history.

POPULAR SOVEREIGNTY AND POLITICAL UPHEAVAL

Drawing on Enlightenment ideals, revolutionaries of the eighteenth and nineteenth centuries sought to fashion an equitable society by instituting governments that were responsive to the needs and interests of the peoples they governed. In justifying their policies, revolutionaries attacked monarchical and aristocratic regimes and argued for popular sovereignty—the notion that legitimate political authority resides not in kings but, rather, in the people who make up a society. In North America, colonists declared independence from British rule and instituted a new government founded on the principle of popular sovereignty. Soon thereafter, French revolutionaries abolished the monarchy and revamped the social order. Enlightenment ideals had given focus to a combination of social and political factors that motivated French revolutionaries, including their resentment of royal, noble, and clerical privileges as well as their own aspirations for freedom of religion, liberty, and republicanism. Yet revolutionaries in France were unable to devise a stable alternative to the monarchy, and French society experienced turmoil for more than twenty years. In the early nineteenth century, Napoleon Bonaparte imposed military rule on France and helped spread revolutionary ideas to much of western Europe.

Enlightened and Revolutionary Ideas

Throughout history, kings or emperors ruled almost all settled agricultural societies. Small societies occasionally instituted democratic governments, in which all citizens participated in political affairs, or republican governments, in which delegates represented the interests of various constituencies. Some societies, especially those with weak central leadership, also relied on aristocratic governments, in which privileged elites supervised public affairs. But hierarchical rule flowing from a king or an emperor was by far the most common form of government in settled agricultural societies.

In justifying their rule, kings and emperors throughout the world often identified themselves with deities or claimed divine sanction for their authority. Some rulers were priests, and most others cooperated closely with religious authorities. On the basis of their association with divine powers, kings and emperors claimed sovereignty—political supremacy and the authority to rule. In imperial China, for example, dynastic houses claimed to rule in accordance with the "mandate of heaven," and in early modern Europe centralizing monarchs often asserted a "divine right of kings" to rule as absolute monarchs.

Popular Sovereignty

During the seventeenth and eighteenth centuries, philosophes and other advocates of Enlightenment ideas (discussed in chapter 23) began to question long-standing notions of sovereignty. The philosophes rarely challenged monarchical rule, but sought instead to make kings responsible to the people they governed. They commonly regarded government as the result of a contract between rulers and ruled. The English philosopher John Locke (1632–1704) formulated one of the most influential theories of contractual government. In his *Second Treatise of Civil Government,* published in 1690, Locke held that government arose in the remote past when people decided to work together, form civil society, and appoint rulers to protect and promote their common interests. Individuals granted political rights to their rulers but retained personal rights to life, liberty, and property. Any ruler who violated those rights was subject to deposition. Furthermore, according to Locke, because individuals voluntarily formed society and established government, rulers derived their authority from the consent of those whom they governed. If subjects withdrew their consent, they had the right to replace their rulers. In effect, Locke's political thought relocated sovereignty, removing it from rulers as divine agents and vesting it in the people of a society.

Individual Freedom

Enlightenment thinkers addressed issues of freedom and equality as well as sovereignty. Philosophes such as Voltaire (1694–1778) resented the persecution of religious minorities and the censorship of royal officials, who had the power to prevent printers from publishing works that did not meet the approval of political and religious authorities. Philosophes called for religious toleration and freedom to express their views openly. When censors prohibited the publication of their writings in France, they often worked with French-speaking printers in Switzerland or the Netherlands who published their books and smuggled them across the border into France.

Political and Legal Equality

Many Enlightenment thinkers also called for equality. They condemned the legal and social privileges enjoyed by aristocrats, who in the philosophes' view made no more contribution to the larger society than a peasant, an artisan, or a crafts worker. They recommended the creation of a society in which all individuals would be equal before the law. The most prominent advocate of political equality was the French-Swiss thinker Jean-Jacques Rousseau (1712–1778), who identified with simple working people and deeply resented the privileges enjoyed by elite classes. In his influential book *The Social Contract* (1762), Rousseau argued that members of a society were collectively the sovereign. In an ideal society all individuals would participate directly in the formulation of policy and the creation of laws. In the absence of royalty, aristocrats, or other privileged elites, the general will of the people would carry the day.

Enlightenment thought on freedom, equality, and popular sovereignty reflected the interests of educated and talented men who sought to increase their influence and enhance their status in society. Most Enlightenment thinkers were of common birth but comfortable means. Although seeking to limit the prerogatives of ruling and aristocratic classes, they did not envision a society in which they would share political rights with women, children, peasants, laborers, slaves, or people of color.

Global Influence of Enlightenment Values

Nevertheless, Enlightenment thought constituted a serious challenge to long-established notions of political and social order. Revolutionary leaders in Europe and the Americas readily adopted Enlightenment ideas when justifying their efforts to overhaul the political and social structures they inherited. Over time, Enlightenment political thought influenced the organization of states and societies throughout the world. Enlightenment ideals did not spread naturally or inevitably. Rather, they spread when social reformers and revolutionaries claimed rights previously denied to them by ruling authorities and elite classes. Arguments for freedom, equality, and popular sovereignty originally served the interests of relatively privileged European and Euro-American men, but many other groups made effective use of them in seeking the extension of political rights.

The American Revolution

In the mid-eighteenth century there was no sign that North America might become a center of revolution. Residents of the thirteen British colonies there regarded themselves as British subjects: they recognized British law, read English-language books, and often braved the stormy waters of the North Atlantic Ocean to visit friends and family in England. Trade brought prosperity to the colonies, and British military forces protected colonists' interests. From 1754 to 1763, for example, British forces waged an extremely expensive conflict in North America known as the French and Indian War. This conflict merged with a larger contest for imperial supremacy, the Seven Years' War (1756–1763), in which British and French forces battled each other in Europe and India as well as North America. Victory in the Seven Years' War ensured that Britain would dominate global trade and that British possessions, including the North American colonies, would prosper.

In this painting by C. Y. Turner, Molly Pitcher, an imaginary heroine of the American revolution, is shown at the 1778 battle of Monmouth loading a cannon. Many historians regard Molly Pitcher as folklore, as a composite image inspired by the actions of a number of real women. The name itself may have originated as a nickname given to women who carried water to men on the battlefield.

Tightened British Control of the Colonies After the mid-1760s, however, North American colonists became increasingly disenchanted with British imperial rule, in some measure because colonists had become accustomed to a degree of autonomy. The geographic distance separating England and the colonies as well as the inevitable inefficiency of the imperial bureaucracy had weakened royal power. Nearly every colony had an elective legislative assembly that had gained control over legislation affecting taxation and defense and that ultimately controlled the salaries paid to royal officials. The colonists resisted once the British attempted to reinvigorate imperial control. Faced with staggering financial difficulties arising from the Seven Years' War, the British Parliament passed legislation to levy new taxes and bring order to a far-flung trading empire. Parliament expected that the North American colonies would bear a fair share of the empire's tax burden and respect imperial trade policies. But parliamentary legislation proved extremely unpopular in North America. Colonists especially resented the imposition of taxes on molasses by the Sugar Act (1764), on publications and legal documents by the Stamp Act (1765), on a wide variety of imported items by the Townshend Act (1767), and on tea by the Tea Act (1773). They objected to strict enforcement of navigation laws—some of them a century old, but widely disregarded—that required cargoes to travel in British ships and clear British customs. Colonists also took offense at the Quartering Act (1765), which required them to provide housing and accommodations for British troops.

In responding to British policies, the colonists argued that Parliament could do nothing in the colonies that it could not do in Britain because the Americans were protected by all the common-law rights of the British. The colonists in effect embraced legal traditions that were first demonstrated during the English Civil War (1641–1651), establishing the constitutional precedent that an English monarch cannot govern without Parliament's consent. This concept was legally enshrined in the Bill of Rights (1689), which established among other rights that the consent of Parliament is required for the implementation of any new taxes. Thus, the colonists responded to new parliamentary levies with the slogan "no taxation without representation." They boycotted British products, physically attacked British officials, and mounted protests such as the Boston Tea Party (1773), in which colonists dumped a cargo of tea into Boston harbor rather than pay duties under the Tea Act. They also organized the Continental Congress (1774), which coordinated the colonies' resistance to British policies. By 1775 tensions were so high that British troops and a colonial militia skirmished at the village of Lexington, near Boston. The war of American independence had begun.

The Declaration of Independence On 4 July 1776 the Continental Congress adopted a document entitled "The unanimous Declaration of the thirteen united States of America." This Declaration of Independence drew deep inspiration from Enlightenment political thought in justifying the colonies' quest for independence. The document asserted "that all men are created equal, that they are endowed by their Creator with certain unalienable Rights, that among these are Life, Liberty, and the pursuit of Happiness." It echoed John Locke's contractual theory of government in arguing that individuals established governments to secure those rights and in holding that governments derive their power and authority from "the consent of the governed." When any government infringes upon individuals' rights, the document continued, "it is the Right of the People to alter or abolish it, and to institute new Government." The Declaration of Independence presented a long list of specific abuses charged to the British crown and concluded by proclaiming the colonies "Free and Independent States" with "full Power to levy War, conclude Peace, contract Alliances, establish Commerce, and to do all other Acts and Things which Independent States may of right do."

Divided Loyalties It was one thing to declare independence, but a different matter altogether to make independence a reality. At the beginning of the war for independence, Britain enjoyed many advantages over the rebels: a strong government with clear lines of authority, the most powerful navy in the world, a competent army, a sizable population of loyalists in the colonies, and an overall colonial population with mixed sentiments about revolution. In their political views and attitudes, the colonial population was far from homogeneous. Political loyalties varied between and within regions and communities and frequently shifted during the course of the revolution. Although "patriots," those who supported the revolution, were in the majority, not every colonist favored a violent confrontation with the British empire. An estimated 20 percent of the white population of the colonies were "loyalists" or "Tories" who remained loyal to the

Washington Crossing the Delaware is an 1851 oil-on-canvas painting by German American artist Emanuel Leutze. It commemorates Washington's crossing of the Delaware on 25 December 1776, during the American revolutionary war. A copy of this painting hangs in the West Wing reception area of the White House.

British monarchy. A minority of people tried to stay neutral in the conflict, most notably the Religious Society of Friends of Pennsylvania, a religious movement better known as the Quakers. Native Americans were divided in their loyalties. Tribes that depended on colonial trade usually threw their weight behind the patriots, but most native Americans east of the Mississippi distrusted the colonists, and thus supported the British cause. African-Americans understood the political rhetoric of the times as promising freedom and equality, but their hopes were not realized. British promises of freedom for service were at best halfhearted. The British faced a dilemma: how to exploit the colonists' fear of slave revolts while also reassuring loyal slave owners and wealthy planters that their slave property would remain secure. Rather than advocating slave revolts, the British more commonly lampooned American advocates of independence for their hypocritical calls for freedom while many of their leaders were slave holders.

Nonetheless, Britain also faced some real difficulties in suppressing the revolution. Waging a war in a distant land full of opponents, Britain had to ship supplies and reinforcements across a stormy ocean. Meanwhile, the rebels benefited from the military and economic support of European states that were eager to chip away at British hegemony in the Atlantic Ocean basin: France, Spain, the Netherlands, and several German principalities contributed to the American quest for independence. Moreover, George Washington (1732–1799) provided strong and imaginative military leadership for the colonial army while local militias employed guerrilla tactics effectively against British forces.

By 1780 all combatants were weary of the conflict. In the final military confrontation of the war, American and French forces under the command of George Washington surrounded the British forces of Charles Cornwallis at Yorktown, Virginia. After a twenty-day siege, the British forces surrendered in October 1781, and major military hostilities ceased from that point forward. In September 1783 diplomats concluded the Peace of Paris, by which the British government formally recognized American independence.

Building an Independent State The leaders of the fledgling republic organized a state that reflected Enlightenment principles. In 1787 a constitutional convention drafted the blueprint for a new system of government—the Constitution of the United States—which emphasized the rights of

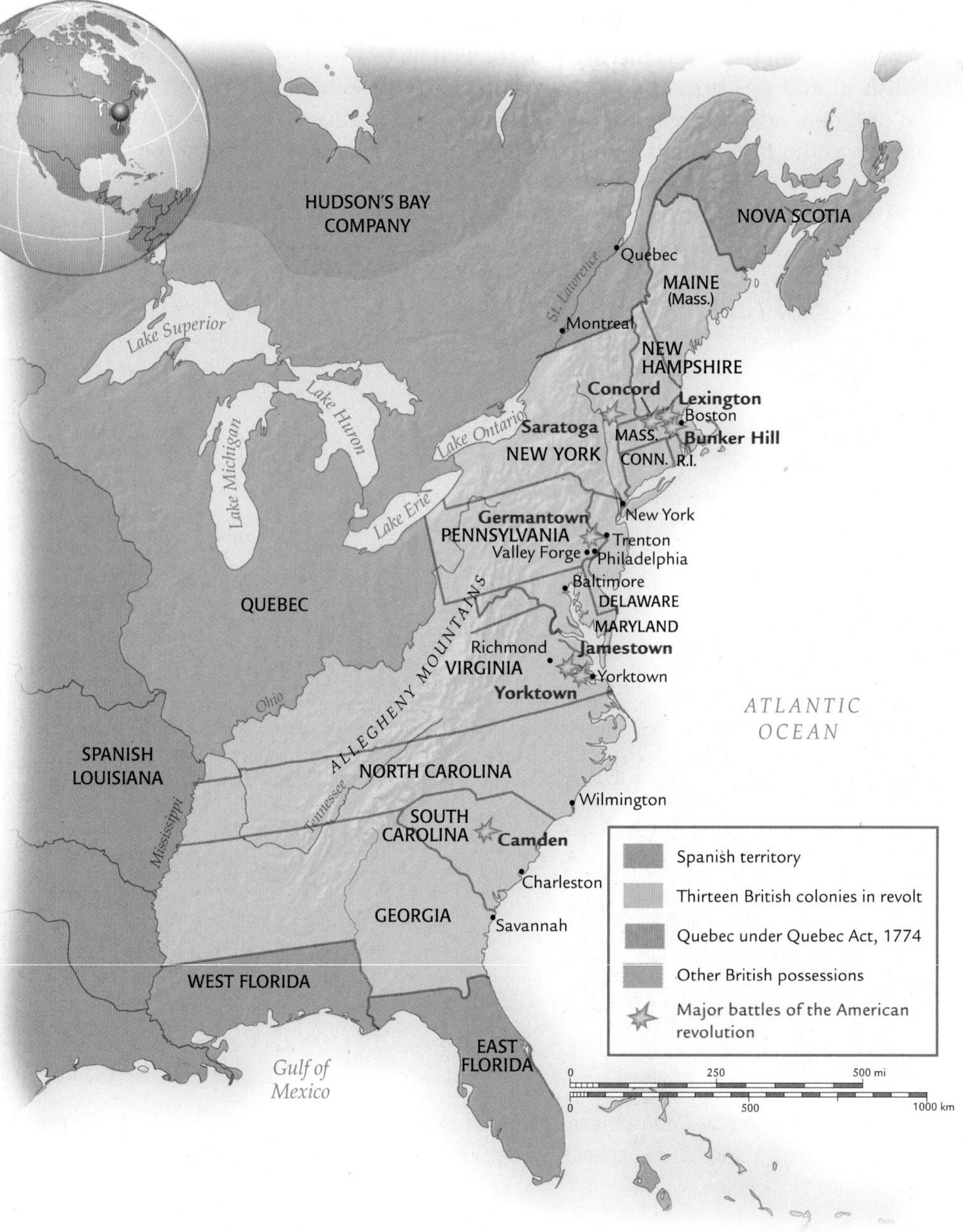

MAP 28.1
The American revolution.
Note both the location of the major towns and cities in the colonies and the location of the major battles that occurred during the revolution.

Why were both situated so close to the eastern coast?

individuals. American leaders based the federal government on popular sovereignty, and they agreed to follow this written constitution that guaranteed individual liberties such as freedom of speech, of the press, and of religion. They did not grant political and legal equality to all inhabitants of the newly independent land. They accorded full rights only to men of property, withholding them from landless men, women, slaves, and indigenous peoples. Over time, however, disenfranchised groups claimed and struggled for political and legal rights. Their campaigns involved considerable personal sacrifice and sometimes led to violence, since those in possession of rights did not always share them readily with others. With the extension of civil rights, American society broadened the implications of the Enlightenment values of freedom and equality as well as popular sovereignty.

The French Revolution

French revolutionaries also drew inspiration from Enlightenment political thought, but the French revolution was a more radical affair than its American counterpart. American revolutionary leaders sought independence from British imperial rule, but they were content to retain British law and much of their British social and cultural heritage. In contrast, French revolutionary leaders repudiated existing society, often referred to as the *ancien régime* ("old order"), and sought to replace it with new political, social, and cultural structures. But, unlike their American counterparts, French revolutionaries lacked experience with self-government.

The Estates General Serious fiscal problems put France on the road to revolution. In the 1780s approximately half of the French royal government's revenue went to pay off war debts—some of them arising from French support for colonists in the war of American independence—and an additional quarter went to French armed forces. King Louis XVI (reigned 1774–1793) was unable to raise more revenue from the overburdened peasantry, so he sought to increase taxes on the French nobility, which had long been exempt from many levies. Aristocrats protested that effort and forced Louis to summon the Estates General, an assembly that represented the entire French population through groups known as estates. In the ancien régime there were three estates, or political classes. The first estate consisted of about one hundred thousand Roman Catholic clergy, and the second included some four hundred thousand nobles. The third estate embraced the rest of the population—about twenty-four million serfs, free peasants, and urban residents ranging from laborers, artisans, and shopkeepers to physicians, bankers, and attorneys. Though founded in 1303, the Estates General had not met since 1614. The third estate had as many delegates as the other two estates combined, but that numerical superiority offered no advantage when the assembly voted on issues, because voting took place by estate—one vote for each—not by individuals.

In May 1789 King Louis called the Estates General into session at the royal palace of Versailles in hopes that it would authorize new taxes. Louis never controlled the assembly. Representatives of the third estate arrived at Versailles demanding political and social reform. Although some members of the lower clergy and a few prominent nobles supported reform, the first and second estates stymied efforts to push measures through the Estates General.

The National Assembly On 17 June 1789, after several weeks of fruitless debate, representatives of the third estate took the dramatic step of seceding from the Estates General

A contemporary print depicts the storming of the Bastille in 1789. The deeds of common people working in crowds became a favorite theme of artists after the outbreak of the French revolution.

sources from the past

Declaration of the Rights of Man and the Citizen

While developing their program of reform, members of the National Assembly consulted closely with Thomas Jefferson, the principal author of the American Declaration of Independence, who was the U.S. ambassador to France in 1789. Thus it is not surprising that the Declaration of the Rights of Man and the Citizen *reflects the influence of American revolutionary ideas.*

First Article. Men are born and remain free and equal in rights. Social distinctions may be based only on common utility.

Article 2. The goal of every political association is the preservation of the natural and inalienable rights of man. These rights are liberty, property, security, and resistance to oppression.

Article 3. The principle of all sovereignty resides essentially in the nation. No body and no individual can exercise authority that does not flow directly from the nation.

Article 4. Liberty consists in the freedom to do anything that does not harm another. The exercise of natural rights of each man thus has no limits except those that assure other members of society their enjoyment of the same rights. These limits may be determined only by law.

Article 6. Law is the expression of the general will. All citizens have the right to participate either personally or through their representatives in the making of law. The law must be the same for all, whether it protects or punishes. Being equal in the eyes of the law, all citizens are equally eligible for all public honors, offices, and occupations, according to their abilities, without any distinction other than that of their virtues and talents.

Article 7. No person shall be accused, arrested, or imprisoned except in the cases and according to the forms prescribed by law. Any one soliciting, transmitting, executing, or causing to be executed, any arbitrary order, shall be punished. But any citizen summoned or arrested in virtue of the law shall submit without delay, as resistance constitutes an offense.

Article 9. As all persons are held innocent until they shall have been declared guilty, if arrest shall be deemed indispensable, all harshness not essential to the securing of the prisoner's person shall be severely repressed by law.

Article 11. The free communication of thoughts and opinions is one of the most precious rights of man: every citizen may thus speak, write, and publish freely, but will be responsible for abuse of this freedom in cases decided by the law.

Article 13. For the maintenance of public military force and for the expenses of administration, common taxation is necessary: it must be equally divided among all citizens according to their means.

Article 15. Society has the right to require from every public official an accounting of his administration.

Article 16. Any society in which guarantees of rights are not assured and separation of powers is not defined has no constitution at all.

Article 17. Property is an inviolable and sacred right. No one may be deprived of property except when public necessity, legally determined, clearly requires it, and on condition of just and prearranged compensation.

For Further Reflection

- In what ways do the principles established in the Declaration reflect the political transformations taking place throughout the age of Atlantic revolutions?

Source: *Déclaration des droits de l'homme et du citoyen.* Translated by Jerry H. Bentley.

and proclaiming themselves to be the National Assembly. Three days later, meeting in an indoor tennis court, members of the new Assembly swore not to disband until they had provided France with a new constitution. On 14 July 1789 a Parisian crowd, fearing that the king sought to undo events of the previous weeks, stormed the Bastille, a royal jail and arsenal, in search of weapons. The military garrison protecting the Bastille surrendered to the crowd but only after killing many of the attackers. To vent their rage, members of the crowd hacked the defenders to death. One assailant used his pocketknife to sever the garrison commander's head, which the victorious crowd mounted on a pike and paraded around the streets of Paris. News of the event soon spread, sparking insurrections in cities throughout France.

Emboldened by popular support, the National Assembly undertook a broad program of political and social reform. The *Declaration of the Rights of Man and the Citizen,* which the National Assembly promulgated in August 1789, articulated the guiding principles of the program. Reflecting the influence of American revolutionary ideas, the *Declaration of the Rights of Man and the Citizen* proclaimed the equality of all men, declared that sovereignty resided in the people, and asserted individual rights to liberty, property, and security.

Liberty, Equality, and Fraternity Between 1789 and 1791 the National Assembly reconfigured French society. Taking "liberty, equality, and fraternity" as its goals, the Assembly abolished the old social order along with the many fees and labor services that peasants owed to their landlords. It dramatically altered the role of the church in French society by seizing church lands, abolishing the first estate, defining clergy as civilians, and requiring clergy to take an oath of loyalty to the state. It also promulgated a constitution that made the king the chief executive official but deprived him of legislative authority. France became a constitutional monarchy in which men of property—about half the adult male population—had the right to vote in elections to choose legislators. Thus far, the French revolution represented an effort to put Enlightenment political thought into practice.

The Convention The revolution soon took a radical turn. Efforts by the French nobility to mobilize foreign powers in support of the king and the restoration of the ancien régime gave the Assembly the pretext to declare war against Austria and Prussia in April 1792. Adding to the military burden of France, revolutionary leaders declared war in the following year on Spain, Britain, and the Netherlands. Fearing military defeat and counterrevolution, revolutionary leaders created the Convention, a new legislative body elected by universal manhood suffrage, which abolished the monarchy and proclaimed France a republic. The Convention rallied the French population by instituting the *levée en masse* ("mass levy"), or universal conscription that drafted people and resources for use in the war against invading forces. The Convention also rooted out enemies at home. It made frequent use of the guillotine, a recently invented machine that brought about supposedly humane executions by quickly severing a victim's head. In 1793 King Louis XVI and his wife, Queen Marie Antoinette, themselves went to the guillotine when the Convention found them guilty of treason.

Revolutionary chaos reached its peak in 1793 and 1794 when Maximilien Robespierre (1758–1794) and the radical Jacobin party dominated the Convention. A lawyer by training, Robespierre had emerged during the revolution as a ruthless but popular radical known as "the Incorruptible," and he dominated the Committee of Public Safety, the executive authority of the Republic. The Jacobins believed passionately that France needed complete restructuring, and they unleashed a campaign of terror to promote their revolutionary agenda. They sought to eliminate the influence of Christianity in French society by closing churches and forcing priests to take wives. They promoted a new "cult of reason" as a secular alternative to Christianity. They reorganized the calendar, keeping months of thirty days but replacing seven-day weeks with ten-day units that recognized no day of religious observance. The Jacobins also proclaimed the inauguration of a new historical era with the Year I, which began with the declaration of the First Republic on 22 September 1792. They encouraged citizens to display their revolutionary zeal by wearing working-class clothes. They granted increased rights to women by permitting them to inherit property and divorce their husbands, although they did not allow women to vote or participate in political affairs. The Jacobins also made frequent use of the guillotine: between the summer of 1793 and the summer of 1794, they executed about forty thousand people and imprisoned three hundred thousand suspected enemies of the revolution. Even the feminist Olympe de Gouges (1748–1793) was a victim of the Jacobins, who did not appreciate her efforts to extend the rights of freedom and equality to women.

The Directory Many victims of this reign of terror were fellow radicals who fell out of favor with Robespierre and the Jacobins. The instability of revolutionary leadership eventually undermined confidence in the regime itself. In July 1794 the Convention arrested Robespierre and his allies, convicted them of tyranny, and sent them to the guillotine. A group of conservative men of property then seized power and ruled France under a new institution known as the Directory (1795–1799). Though more pragmatic than previous revolutionary leaders, members of the Directory were unable to resolve the economic and military problems that plagued revolutionary France. In seeking a middle way between the ancien régime and radical revolution, they lurched from one policy to another, and the Directory faced constant challenges to its authority. It came to an end in November 1799 when a young general named Napoleon Bonaparte staged a coup d'état and seized power.

The Reign of Napoleon

Born to a minor noble family of Corsica, a Mediterranean island annexed by France in 1768, Napoleon Bonaparte (1769–1821) studied at French military schools and became an officer in the army of King Louis XVI. A brilliant military leader, he became a general at age twenty-four. He was a fervent supporter of the revolution and defended the Directory against a popular uprising in 1795. In a campaign of 1796–1797, he drove the Austrian army from northern Italy and established French rule there. In 1798 he mounted an invasion of Egypt to gain access to the Red Sea and threaten British control of the sea route to India, but the campaign ended in a complete British victory. Politically ambitious, Napoleon returned to France in 1799, overthrew the Directory, and set up a new government, the Consulate. Although ostensibly he shared power with two other consuls, it was Napoleon who was henceforth the real master of France. Having established a dictatorship, he crowned himself emperor in 1802.

Napoleonic France Napoleon brought political stability to a land torn by revolution and war. He made peace with the Roman Catholic church and in 1801 concluded an agreement with the pope. The pact, known as the Concordat, provided that the French state would retain church lands seized during the revolution, but the state agreed to pay clerics' salaries, recognize Roman Catholic Christianity as the preferred faith of France, and extend freedom of religion to Protestant Christians and Jews. This

The guillotine was an efficient killing machine. In this contemporary print the executioner displays the just-severed head of King Louis XVI to the crowd assembled to witness his execution.

measure won Napoleon a great deal of support from people who supported the political and social goals of the revolution but balked at radicals' efforts to replace Christianity with a cult of reason.

In 1804 Napoleon promulgated the Civil Code, a revised body of civil law, which also helped stabilize French society. The Civil Code affirmed the political and legal equality of all adult men and established a merit-based society in which individuals qualified for education and employment because of talent rather than birth or social standing. The code protected private property, and Napoleon allowed aristocratic opponents of the revolution to return to France and reclaim some of their lost property. The Civil Code confirmed many of the moderate revolutionary policies of the National Assembly but retracted measures passed by the more radical Convention. The code restored patriarchal authority in the family, for example, by making women and children subservient to male heads of households. French civil law became the model for the civil codes of Québec Province, Canada, the Netherlands, Italy, Spain, some Latin American republics, and the state of Louisiana.

Although he approved the Enlightenment ideal of equality, Napoleon was no champion of intellectual freedom or representative government. He limited free speech and routinely censored newspapers and other publications. He established a secret police force that relied heavily on spies and detained suspected political opponents by the thousands. He made systematic use of propaganda to manipulate public opinion. He ignored elective bodies and surrounded himself with loyal military officers who ensured that representative assemblies did not restrict his authority. When he crowned himself emperor, he founded a dy-

Jacques-Louis David's *Napoleon on Horseback at the St. Bernard Pass* (1800) presents a famously heroic image of Napoleon's attack on Italy in 1800. David's art clearly served the interests of Napoleon's political regime. The powerful and dynamic image was intended to convey Napoleon's greatness and his place in the history of conquering heroes.

nasty that set his family above and apart from the people in whose name they ruled.

Napoleon's Empire While working to stabilize France, Napoleon also sought to extend his authority throughout Europe. Napoleon's armies conquered the Iberian and Italian peninsulas, occupied the Netherlands, and inflicted humiliating defeats on Austrian and Prussian forces. Napoleon sent his brothers and other relatives to rule the conquered and occupied lands, and he forced Austria, Prussia, and Russia to ally with him and respect French hegemony in Europe. Napoleon's empire began to unravel in 1812, when he decided to invade Russia. Convinced that the tsar was conspiring with his British enemies, Napoleon led a Grand Army of six hundred thousand soldiers to Moscow. He captured the city, but the tsar withdrew and refused to surrender. Russians set Moscow ablaze, leaving Napoleon's massive army without adequate shelter or supplies.

The Fall of Napoleon Napoleon's disastrous Russian campaign emboldened his enemies. A coalition of British, Austrian, Prussian, and Russian armies converged on France and forced Napoleon to abdicate his throne in April 1814. The victors restored the French monarchy and exiled Napoleon to the tiny Mediterranean island of Elba, near Corsica. But Napoleon's adventure had not yet come to an end. In March 1815 he escaped from Elba, returned to France, and reconstituted his army. For a hundred days he ruled France again before a British army defeated him at Waterloo in Belgium. Unwilling to take further chances with the wily general, European powers banished Napoleon to the remote and isolated island of St. Helena in the South Atlantic Ocean, where he died of natural causes in 1821.

THE INFLUENCE OF REVOLUTION

The Enlightenment ideals promoted by the American and French revolutions—freedom, equality, and popular sovereignty—appealed to peoples throughout Europe and the Americas. In the Caribbean and Latin America, they inspired revolutionary movements: slaves in the French colony of Saint-Domingue rose against their overlords and established the independent republic of Haiti, and revolutionary leaders mounted independence movements in Mexico, Central America, and South America. The ideals of the American and French revolutions also encouraged social reformers to organize broader programs of liberation. Whereas the American and French revolutions guaranteed political and legal rights to white men, social reformers sought to extend those rights to women and slaves of African ancestry. During the nineteenth century all European and American states abolished slavery, but former slaves and their descendants remained an underprivileged and often oppressed class in most of the Atlantic world. The quest for women's rights also proceeded slowly during the nineteenth century.

The Haitian Revolution

The only successful slave revolt in history took place on the Caribbean island of Hispaniola in the aftermath of the French revolution. By the eighteenth century, Hispaniola was a major center of sugar production with hundreds of prosperous plantations. The Spanish colony of Santo Domingo occupied the eastern part of the island (modern Dominican Republic), and the French colony of Saint-Domingue occupied the western part (modern Haiti). Saint-Domingue was one of the richest of all European colonies in the Caribbean: sugar, coffee, and cotton produced there accounted for almost one-third of France's foreign trade.

Saint-Domingue Society On the eve of the Haitian revolution, the population of Saint-Domingue comprised three major groups. There were about forty thousand white colonials, subdivided into several classes: European-born Frenchmen who monopolized colonial administrative posts; a class of plantation owners, chiefly minor aristocrats who hoped to return to France as soon as possible; and lower-class

MAP 28.2

Napoleon's empire in 1812.

Observe the number of states dependent on or allied with Napoleon as opposed to those who were at war with him.

Were there geographic conditions that allowed some states to resist Napoleon's efforts at conquest better than others?

whites, which included artisans, shopkeepers, slave dealers, and day laborers. A second group comprised about twenty-eight thousand *gens de couleur* (French for "people of color"), most of whom were mulattoes and some of whom were black. Many of them were artisans, domestic servants, or overseers, but a small and influential proportion owned small plots of land and slaves. The remainder of the population made up the third group, consisting of some five hundred thousand slaves, some of whom were mulattoes but most of whom were African-born.

Most of the colony's slaves toiled in fields under brutal conditions. Planters worked their slaves so hard and pro-

Former slave and effective military leader, Toussaint Louverture led the Haitian revolution.

vided them with so little care that mortality was very high. Not surprisingly, white planters and black slaves frequently had violent conflicts. Aware that they were outnumbered by slaves by a factor of more than ten, plantation owners lived in constant fear of slave rebellion. Many slaves ran away into the mountains. By the late eighteenth century, Saint-Domingue had many large communities of maroons, who maintained their own societies and sometimes attacked plantations in search of food, weapons, tools, and additional recruits. As planters lost laborers, they imported new slaves from Africa and other Caribbean islands. This pattern continued throughout the eighteenth century, until prices of new slaves from Africa rose dramatically.

The American and French revolutions prepared the way for a violent political and social revolution in Saint-Domingue. Because French policy supported North American colonists against British rule, colonial governors in Saint-Domingue sent about five hundred *gens de couleur* to fight in the American war of independence. They returned to Saint-Domingue with the intention of reforming society there. When the French revolution broke out in 1789, white settlers in Saint-Domingue sought the right to govern themselves, but they opposed proposals to grant political and legal equality to the *gens de couleur.* By May 1791 civil war had broken out between white settlers and *gens de couleur.*

Slave Revolt The conflict expanded dramatically when a charismatic Vodou priest named Boukman organized a slave revolt. In August 1791 some twelve thousand slaves began killing white settlers, burning their homes, and destroying their plantations. Within a few weeks the rebels attracted almost one hundred thousand slaves into their ranks. Saint-Domingue quickly descended into chaos as white, *gens de couleur,* and slave factions battled one another. Many slaves were battle-tested veterans of wars in Africa, and they drew on their military experience to organize large armies. Slave leaders also found recruits and reinforcements in Saint-Domingue's maroon communities. Foreign armies soon complicated the situation: French troops arrived in 1792 to restore order, and British and Spanish forces intervened in 1793 in hopes of benefiting from France's difficulties.

Toussaint Louverture Boukman died while fighting shortly after launching the revolt, but slave forces eventually overcame white settlers, *gens de couleur,* and foreign armies. Their successes were due largely to the leadership of François-Dominique Toussaint (1744–1803), who after 1791 called himself Louverture—from the French *l'ouverture,* meaning "the opening," or the one who created an opening in enemy ranks. The son of slaves, Toussaint learned to read and write from a Roman Catholic priest. Because of his education and intelligence, he rose to the position of livestock overseer on the plantation and subsequently planted coffee on leased land with rented slaves. A free man since 1776, Toussaint was also an astute judge of human character. When the slave revolt broke out in 1791, Toussaint helped his masters escape to a safe place, then left the plantation and joined the rebels.

Toussaint was a skilled organizer, and by 1793 he had built a strong, disciplined army. He shrewdly played French, British, and Spanish forces against one another while also jockeying for power with other black and mulatto generals. By 1797 he led an army of twenty thousand that controlled most of Saint-Domingue. In 1801 he promulgated a constitution that granted equality and citizenship to all residents of Saint-Domingue. He stopped short of declaring independence from France, however, because he did not want to provoke Napoleon into attacking the island.

The Republic of Haiti Nevertheless, in 1802 Napoleon dispatched forty thousand troops to restore French authority in Saint-Domingue. Toussaint attempted to negotiate a peaceful settlement, but the French commander arrested him and sent him to France, where he died in jail of maltreatment in 1803. By the time he died, however, yellow fever had ravaged the French army in Saint-Domingue, and the black generals who succeeded Toussaint had defeated the

The slave rebellion in Saint-Domingue struck fear in the hearts of European and Euro-American peoples. This French print depicts outnumbered white settlers under attack on a plantation.

remaining troops and driven them out of the colony. Late in 1803 they declared independence, and on 1 January 1804 they proclaimed the establishment of Haiti, meaning "land of mountains," which became the second independent republic in the western hemisphere.

Wars of Independence in Latin America

Latin American Society Revolutionary ideals traveled beyond Saint-Domingue to the Spanish and Portuguese colonies in the Americas. Though governed by *peninsulares* (colonial officials from Spain or Portugal), the Iberian colonies all had a large, wealthy, and powerful class of Euro-American *criollos,* or creoles. In 1800 the *peninsulares* numbered about 30,000, and the creole population was 3.5 million. The Iberian colonies also had a large population—about 10 million in all—of less privileged classes. Black slaves formed a majority in Brazil, but elsewhere indigenous peoples and individuals of mixed ancestry such as mestizos and mulattoes were most numerous.

Creoles benefited greatly during the eighteenth century as they established plantations and ranches in the colonies and participated in rapidly expanding trade with Spain and Portugal. Yet the creoles also had grievances. Like British colonists in North America, the creoles resented administrative control and economic regulations imposed by the Iberian powers. They drew inspiration from Enlightenment political thought and occasionally took part in tax revolts and popular uprisings. The creoles desired neither social reform like that promoted by Robespierre nor the establishment of an egalitarian society like Haiti. Basically, they sought to displace the *peninsulares* but retain their privileged position in society: political independence on the model of the United States in North America struck them as an attractive alternative to colonial status. Between 1810 and 1825, creoles led

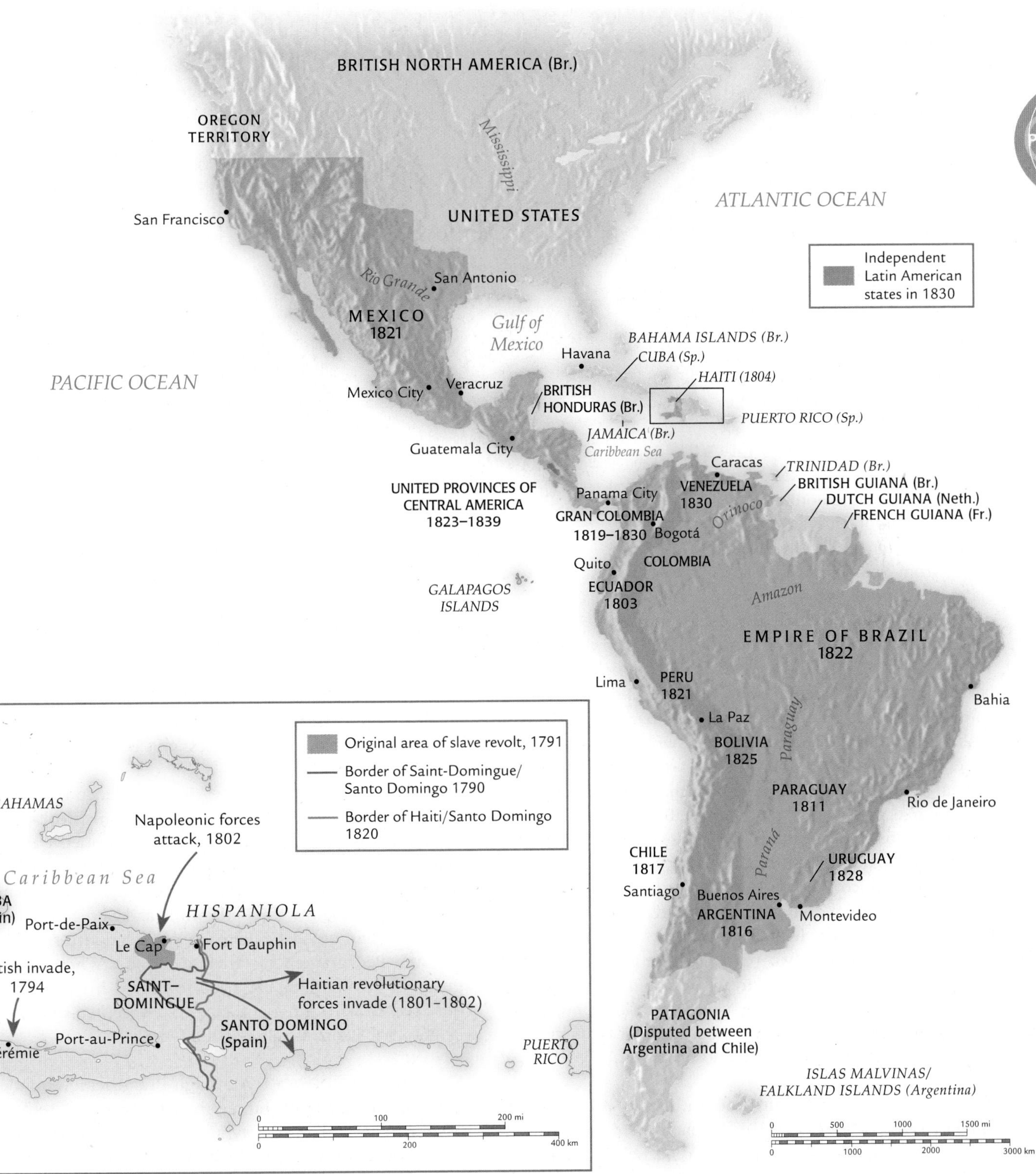

MAP 28.3

Latin America in 1830.

Note the dates each state won its independence.

Since most states became independent in very close succession, what conditions prevented Latin American states from joining together in a federation like that in the United States?

movements that brought independence to all Spanish colonies in the Americas—except Cuba and Puerto Rico—and established creole-dominated republics.

Simón Bolívar, creole leader of the independence movement in Latin America, was a favorite subject of painters in the nineteenth century. This portrait depicts him as a determined and farsighted leader.

Mexican Independence

The struggle for independence began in the wake of Napoleon's invasion of Spain and Portugal (1807), which weakened royal authority in the Iberian colonies. By 1810, revolts against Spanish rule had broken out in Argentina, Venezuela, and Mexico. The most serious was a peasant rebellion in Mexico led by a parish priest, Miguel Hidalgo y Costilla (1753–1811), who rallied indigenous peoples and mestizos against colonial rule. Many contemporaries viewed Hidalgo's movement for independence from Spanish rule as social and economic warfare by the masses against the elites of Mexican society, particularly since he rallied people to his cause by invoking the name of the popular and venerated Virgin of Guadalupe and by calling for the death of Spaniards. Conservative creoles soon captured Hidalgo and executed him, but his rebellion continued to flare for three years after his death. Hidalgo became the symbol of Mexican independence, and the day on which he proclaimed his revolt—16 September 1810—is Mexico's principal national holiday.

Colonial rule came to an end in 1821, when the creole general Augustín de Iturbide (1783–1824) declared independence from Spain. In the following year, he declared himself emperor of Mexico. Neither Iturbide nor his empire survived for long. Though an able general, Iturbide was an incompetent administrator, and in 1823 creole elites deposed him and established a republic. Two years later the southern regions of the Mexican empire declared their own independence. They formed a Central American Federation until 1838, when they split into the independent states of Guatemala, El Salvador, Honduras, Nicaragua, and Costa Rica.

Simón Bolívar In South America, creole elites such as Simón Bolívar (1783–1830) led the movement for independence. Born in Caracas (in modern Venezuela), Bolívar was a fervent republican steeped in Enlightenment ideas about popular sovereignty. Inspired by the example of George Washington, he took up arms against Spanish rule in 1811. In the early days of his struggle, Bolívar experienced many reversals and twice went into exile. In 1819, however, he assembled an army that surprised and crushed the Spanish army in Colombia. Later, he campaigned in Venezuela, Ecuador, and Peru, coordinating his efforts with other creole leaders, such as José de San Martín (1778–1850) in Argentina and Bernardo O'Higgins (1778–1842) in Chile. By 1825 creole forces had overcome Spanish armies and deposed Spanish rulers throughout South America.

Bolívar's goal was to weld the former Spanish colonies of South America into a great confederation like the United States in North America. During the 1820s independent Venezuela, Colombia, and Ecuador formed a republic called Gran Colombia, and Bolívar attempted to bring Peru and Bolivia (named for Bolívar himself) into the confederation. By 1830, however, strong political and regional differences had undermined Gran Colombia. As the confederation disintegrated, a bitterly disappointed Bolívar pronounced South America "ungovernable" and lamented that "those who have served the revolution have plowed the sea." Shortly after the breakup of Gran Colombia, Bolívar died of tuberculosis while en route to self-imposed exile in Europe.

Brazilian Independence Independence came to Portuguese Brazil at the same time as to Spanish colonies, but by a different process. When Napoleon invaded Portugal in 1807, the royal court fled Lisbon and established a government in exile in Rio de Janeiro. In 1821 the king returned to Portugal, leaving his son Pedro in Brazil as regent. The next year Brazilian creoles called for independence from Portugal, and Pedro agreed to their demands. When the Portuguese *Cortes* (parliament) tried to curtail his power, Pedro declared Brazil's independence and accepted appointment as Emperor Pedro I (reigned 1822–1834).

Creole Dominance Although Brazil achieved independence as a monarchy rather than a republic, creole elites dominated Brazilian society just as they did in former Spanish colonies. Indeed, independence brought little social change in Latin America. The *peninsulares* returned to Europe, but Latin American society remained as rigidly stratified as it had been in 1800. The newly independent states granted military authority to local charismatic strongmen, known as ***caudillos,*** allied with creole elites. The new states also permitted the continuation of slavery, confirmed the wealth and authority of the Roman Catholic church, and re-

caudillos (KAW-dee-ohs)

pressed the lower orders. The principal beneficiaries of independence in Latin America were the creole elites.

The Emergence of Ideologies: Conservatism and Liberalism

While inspiring revolutions and independence movements in other lands, the American and French revolutions also prompted political and social theorists to crystallize the modern ideologies of conservatism and liberalism. An *ideology* is a coherent vision of human nature, human society, and the larger world that proposes some particular form of political and social organization as ideal. Some ideologies seek to justify the current state of affairs, whereas others sharply criticize the status quo in arguing for movement toward an improved society. In all cases, ideologists seek to design a political and social order appropriate for their communities.

Conservatism The modern ideology of conservatism arose as political and social theorists responded to the challenges of the American and especially the French revolutions. Conservatives viewed society as an organism that changed slowly over the generations. The English political philosopher Edmund Burke (1729–1797) held, for example, that society was a compact between a people's ancestors, the present generation, and their descendants as yet unborn. While admitting the need for gradual change that came about by general consensus, Burke condemned radical or revolutionary change, which in his view could only lead to anarchy. Thus Burke approved of the American revolution, which he took as an example of natural change in keeping with the historical development of North American society, but he denounced the French revolution as a chaotic and irresponsible assault on society.

Liberalism In contrast to conservatives, liberals took change as normal and welcomed it as the agent of progress. They viewed conservatism as an effort to justify the status quo, maintain the privileges enjoyed by favored classes, and avoid dealing with injustice and inequality in society. For liberals the task of political and social theory was not to stifle change but, rather, to manage it in the best interests of society. Liberals championed the Enlightenment values of freedom and equality, which they believed would lead to higher standards of morality and increased prosperity for the whole society. They usually favored republican forms of government in which citizens elected representatives to legislative bodies, and they called for written constitutions that guaranteed freedom and equality for all citizens and that precisely defined the political structure and institutions of their societies.

The liberalism that emerged from the Atlantic revolutions was concerned about civil rights, less so about political and social rights. Most liberals, for example, held the view that voting was more of a privilege than a right, and therefore was legitimately subject to certain qualifications. Limitations on the franchise long characterized suffrage in postrevolutionary societies, with citizens being disenfranchised on the basis of class, age, gender, and race, among other factors. But as the nineteenth century passed, liberalism changed its character. As the masses of people became more assertive, liberalism could not concern itself mainly with interests of the more privileged strata of society. Consequently, there was a shift from early classical liberalism to a more democratic variety. Equality before the law was supplemented by equality before the ballot box. Liberalism's traditional emphasis on minimizing the role and power of government was reversed, and by the end of the nineteenth century, liberals started to look to government to minimize or correct the problems that accompanied industrialization.

The most prominent exponent of early liberalism was John Stuart Mill (1806–1873), an English philosopher, economist, and social reformer. Mill tirelessly promoted the freedom of individuals to pursue economic and intellectual interests. He tried to ensure that powerful minorities, such as wealthy businessmen, would not curb the freedoms of the poorly organized majority, but he also argued that it was improper for the majority to impose its will on minorities with different interests and values. He advocated universal suffrage as the most effective way to advance individual freedom, and he called for taxation of business profits and high personal incomes to forestall the organization of wealthy classes into groups that threatened individual liberties. Mill went further than most liberals in seeking to extend the rights of freedom and equality to women and working people as well as men of property.

Voting Rights and Restrictions As Mill recognized, the age of revolutions in the Atlantic world illustrated the centrality of suffrage in establishing a people's and a nation's sense of democratic legitimacy and political sovereignty. Defined as either the right or the privilege to vote, in order to elect public officials or to adopt laws, suffrage derived its revolutionary significance from Enlightenment notions about self-government and about governments deriving authority from the consent of the governed. Voting rights and restrictions evolved into powerful political concerns during and after the age of revolutions.

Testing the Limits of Revolutionary Ideals: Slavery

The Enlightenment ideals of freedom and equality were watchwords of revolution in the Atlantic Ocean basin. Yet different revolutionaries understood the implications of freedom and equality in very different ways. In North America revolution led to political independence, a broad array of individual freedoms, and the legal equality of adult white men. In France it destroyed the hierarchical social order of the ancien régime and temporarily extended political and legal rights to all citizens, although Napoleon and later rulers effectively curbed some of those rights. In Haiti revolution brought independence from French rule and the end of slavery. In South America it led to independence from Iberian rule and societies dominated by creole elites. In the wake of the Atlantic revolutions, social activists in Europe and the Americas considered the possibility that the ideals of freedom and equality might have further implications as yet unexplored. They turned their attention especially to the issues of slavery and women's rights.

thinking about TRADITIONS

Revolution and Slavery
North Atlantic political economies were organized at least in part around the institution of slavery. How did political revolutions in the Atlantic Ocean basin affect or alter the institution of slavery and the lives of slaves? What were the long-term consequences of revolutionary ideologies for peoples of color?

Movements to End the Slave Trade The campaign to end the slave trade and abolish slavery began in the eighteenth century. Freed slaves such as Olaudah Equiano (1745–1797) were among the earliest critics of slavery. Beginning in the 1780s European Christian moralists also voiced opposition to slavery.

Only after the American, French, and Haitian revolutions, however, did the antislavery movement gain momentum. The leading spokesman of the movement was William Wilberforce (1759–1833), a prominent English philanthropist elected in 1780 to a seat in Parliament. There he tirelessly attacked slavery on moral and religious grounds. After the Haitian revolution he attracted supporters who feared that continued reliance on slave labor would result in more and larger slave revolts, and in 1807 Parliament passed Wilberforce's bill to end the slave trade. Under British pressure, other states also banned commerce in slaves: the United States in 1808, France in 1814, the Netherlands in 1817, and Spain in 1845. The British navy, which dominated the North Atlantic Ocean, patrolled the west coast of Africa to ensure compliance with the law. But the slave trade died slowly, as illegal trade in African slaves continued on a small scale: the last documented ship to carry slaves across the Atlantic Ocean arrived in Cuba in 1867.

Movements to Abolish Slavery The abolition of slavery itself was a much bigger challenge than ending the slave trade because owners had property rights in their slaves. Planters and merchant elites strongly resisted efforts to alter the system that provided them with abundant supplies of inexpensive labor. Nevertheless, the end of the slave trade doomed the institution of slavery in the Americas. In Haiti the end of slavery came with the revolution. In much of South America, slavery ended with independence from Spanish rule, as Simón Bolívar freed slaves who joined his forces and provided constitutional guarantees of free status for all residents of Gran Colombia. In Mexico slavery was abolished in 1829, though not solely for humanitarian reasons. It served as a mechanism to stop the influx of residents from the southern United States coming in with their slaves to grow cotton.

Meanwhile, as they worked to ban traffic in human labor, Wilberforce and other moralists also launched a campaign to free slaves and abolish the institution of slavery itself. In 1833, one month after Wilberforce's death, Parliament provided twenty million pounds sterling as compensation to slave owners and abolished slavery throughout the British empire. Other states followed the British example: France abolished slavery in 1848, the United States in 1865, Cuba in 1886, and Brazil in 1888.

Freedom without Equality Abolition brought legal freedom for African and African-American slaves, but it did not bring political equality. In most lands other than Haiti, African-American peoples had little influence in society. Property requirements, literacy tests, poll taxes, and campaigns of intimidation effectively prevented them from voting. Nor did emancipation bring social and economic improvements for former slaves and their descendants. White creole elites owned most of the property in the Americas, and they kept blacks in subordination by forcing them to accept low-paying work. A few African-Americans owned small plots of land, but they could not challenge the economic and political power of creole elites.

Testing the Limits of Revolutionary Ideals: Women's Rights

Women participated alongside men in the movement to abolish slavery, and their experience inspired feminist social reformers to seek equality with men. They pointed out that women suffered many of the same legal disabilities as slaves: they had little access to education, they could not enter professional occupations that required advanced education, and they were legally deprived of the right to vote. They drew on Enlightenment thought in making a case for women's rights, but in spite of support from prominent liberals such as John Stuart Mill, they had little success before the twentieth century.

Enlightenment Ideals and Women Enlightenment thought called for the restructuring of government and society, but the philosophes mostly held conservative views on women and their roles in family and society. Rousseau, for example, advised that girls' education should prepare them to become devoted wives and mothers. Yet social reformers found Enlightenment thought extremely useful in argu-

Parisian women were the leaders of the crowd that marched to Versailles, protested high food prices, and forced the king and queen to return to Paris in October 1789. Although women in France would have to wait until the twentieth century for political rights fully equal to those of men, women laid a foundation for future gains by drawing on the ideas of the Enlightenment to argue for equality.

ing for women's rights. Drawing on the political thought of John Locke, for example, the English writer Mary Astell (1666–1731) suggested that absolute sovereignty was no more appropriate in a family than in a state. Astell also reflected Enlightenment influence in asking why, if all men were born free, all women were born slaves.

During the eighteenth century, advocates of women's rights were particularly active in Britain, France, and North America. Among the most prominent was the British writer Mary Wollstonecraft (1759–1797). Although she had little schooling, Wollstonecraft avidly read books at home and gained an informal self-education. In 1792 she published an influential essay entitled *A Vindication of the Rights of Woman*. Like Astell, Wollstonecraft argued that women possessed all the rights that Locke had granted to men. She insisted on the right of women to education: it would make them better mothers and wives, she said, and would enable them to contribute to society by preparing them for professional occupations and participation in political life.

Women and Revolution Women played crucial roles in the revolutions of the late eighteenth and early nineteenth centuries. Some women supported the efforts of men by sewing uniforms, rolling bandages, or managing farms, shops, and businesses. Others actively participated in revolutionary activities. In October 1789, for example, about six thousand Parisian women marched to Versailles to protest the high price of bread. Some of them forced their way into the royal apartments and demanded that the king and queen return with them to Paris—along with the palace's supply of flour. In the early 1790s, pistol-wielding members of the Republican Revolutionary Women patrolled the streets of Paris. The fate of Olympe de Gouges made it clear, however, that revolutionary women had little prospect of holding official positions or playing a formal role in public affairs.

Under the National Assembly and the Convention, the French revolution brought increased rights for women. The republican government provided free public education for girls as well as boys, granted wives a share of family property, and legalized divorce. Yet the revolution did not bring women the right to vote or to play major roles in public affairs. Under the Directory and Napoleon's rule, women lost even the rights that they had won in the early days of the revolution. In other lands, women never gained as much as they did in revolutionary France. In the United States and the independent states of Latin America, revolution brought legal equality and political rights only for adult white men, who retained patriarchal authority over their wives and families.

Women's Rights Movements Nevertheless, throughout the nineteenth century social reformers pressed for women's rights as well as the abolition of slavery. The American feminist Elizabeth Cady Stanton (1815–1902) was an especially prominent figure in this movement. In 1840 Stanton went to London to attend an antislavery conference but found that the organizers barred women from participation. Infuriated, Stanton returned to the United States and began to build a movement for women's rights. She organized a conference of feminists who met at Seneca Falls, New York, in 1848. The conference passed twelve resolutions demanding that lawmakers grant women rights equivalent to those

sources from the past

Declaration of the Rights of Woman and the Female Citizen

In 1791 Olympe de Gouges, a butcher's daughter and playwright of some note, wrote and published the Declaration of the Rights of Woman and the Female Citizen. *She directly challenged the inferiority presumed of women by the 1789* Declaration of the Rights of Man and the Citizen, *which limited citizenship to males. By publicly asserting the equality of women, Gouges breached barriers that most revolutionary leaders wanted to perpetuate. Charged with treason during the rule of the National Convention, Gouges went to the guillotine on 3 November 1793.*

Article 1. Woman is born free and lives equal to man in her rights. Social distinctions can be based only on the common utility.

Article 2. The purpose of any political association is the conservation of the natural and impresciptible rights of woman and man; these rights are liberty, property, security, and especially resistance to oppression.

Article 3. The principle of all sovereignty rests essentially with the nation, which is nothing but the union of woman and man; no body and no individual can exercise any authority which does not come expressly from it (the nation).

Article 4. Liberty and justice consist of restoring all that belongs to others; thus, the only limits on the exercise of the natural rights of woman are perpetual male tyranny; these limits are to be reformed by the laws of nature and reason.

Article 6. The law must be the expression of the general will; all female and male citizens must contribute either personally or through their representatives to its formation; it must be the same for all: male and female citizens, being equal in the eyes of the law, must be equally admitted to all honors, positions, and public employment according to their capacity and without other distinctions besides those of their virtues and talents.

Article 7. No woman is an exception; she is accused, arrested, and detained in cases determined by law. Women, like men, obey this rigorous law.

Article 11. The free communication of thoughts and opinions is one of the most precious rights of woman, since that liberty assures recognition of children by their fathers. Any female citizen thus may say freely, I am the mother of a child which belongs to you, without being forced by a barbarous prejudice to hide the truth; (an exception may be made) to respond to the abuse of this liberty in cases determined by law.

Article 13. For the support of the public force and the expenses of administration, the contributions of woman and man are equal; she shares all the duties and all the painful tasks; therefore, we must have the same share in the distribution of positions, employment, offices, honors, and jobs.

Article 14. Female and male citizens have the right to verify, either by themselves or through their representatives, the necessity of the public contribution. This can only apply to women if they are granted an equal share, not only of wealth, but also of public administration, and in the determination of the proportion, the base, the collection, and the duration of the tax.

Article 17. Property belongs to both sexes whether united or separate; for each it is an inviolable and sacred right; no one can be deprived of it, since it is the true patrimony of nature, unless the legally determined public need obviously dictates it, and then only with a just and prior indemnity.

For Further Reflection

- How does Olympe de Gouges's feminist restatement of the *Declaration of the Rights of Man and the Citizen* intensify its radical precepts?

Source: Darline Gay Levy, Harriet Branson Applewhite, and Mary Durham Johnson. *Women in Revolutionary Paris, 1789–1795.* Urbana: University of Illinois Press, 1979, pp. 90–92.

enjoyed by men. The resolutions called specifically for women's rights to vote, attend public schools, enter professional occupations, and participate in public affairs.

The women's rights movement experienced limited success in the nineteenth century. More women received formal education than before the American and French revolutions, and women in Europe and North America participated in academic, literary, and civic organizations. Rarely did they enter the professions, however, and nowhere did they enjoy the right to vote. Yet, by seeking to extend the promises of Enlightenment political thought to blacks and women as well as white men, social reformers of the nineteenth century laid a foundation that would lead to large-scale social change in the twentieth century.

THE CONSOLIDATION OF NATIONAL STATES IN EUROPE

The Enlightenment ideals of freedom, equality, and popular sovereignty inspired political revolutions in much of the Atlantic Ocean basin, and the revolutions in turn helped spread Enlightenment values. The wars of the French revolution and the Napoleonic era also inspired the development of a particular type of community identity that had little to do with Enlightenment values—nationalism. Revolutionary wars involved millions of French citizens in the defense of their country against foreign armies and the extension of French influence to neighboring states. Wartime experiences encouraged peoples throughout Europe to think of themselves as members of distinctive national communities. Throughout the nineteenth century, European nationalist leaders worked to fashion states based on national identities and mobilized citizens to work in the interests of their own national communities, sometimes by fostering jealousy and suspicion of other national groups. By the late nineteenth century, national identities were so strong that peoples throughout Europe responded enthusiastically to ideologies of nationalism, which promised glory and prosperity to those who worked in the interests of their national communities.

Nations and Nationalism

One of the most influential concepts of modern political thought is the idea of the nation. The word *nation* refers to a type of community that became especially prominent in the nineteenth century. At various times and places in history, individuals have associated themselves primarily with families, clans, cities, regions, and religious faiths. During the nineteenth century, European peoples came to identify strongly with communities they called nations. Members of a nation considered themselves a distinctive people born into a unique community that spoke a common language, observed common customs, inherited common cultural traditions, held common values, and shared common historical experiences. Often, they also honored common religious beliefs, although they sometimes overlooked differences of faith and construed the nation as a political, social, and cultural, rather than religious, unit.

A portrait of the Italian nationalist leader Giuseppe Mazzini as a disappointed but determined idealist. By the mid-nineteenth century, Mazzini's views had inspired nationalist movements not only in Italy but in other European lands as well.

Intense feelings of national identity fueled ideologies of nationalism. Advocates of nationalism insisted that the nation must be the focus of political loyalty. Zealous nationalist leaders maintained that members of their national communities had a common destiny that they could best advance by organizing independent national states and resolutely pursuing their national interests. Ideally, in their view, the boundaries of the national state embraced the territory occupied by the national community, and its government promoted the interests of the national group, sometimes through conflict with other peoples.

Cultural Nationalism Early nationalist thought often sought to deepen appreciation for the historical experiences of the national community and foster pride in its cultural accomplishments. During the late eighteenth century, for example, Johann Gottfried von Herder (1744–1803) sang the praises of the German *Volk* ("people") and their powerful and expressive language. In reaction to Enlightenment thinkers and their quest for a scientific, universally valid understanding of the world, early cultural nationalists such as Herder focused their attention on individual communities and relished their uniqueness. They emphasized historical scholarship, which they believed would illuminate the distinctive characteristics of their societies. They also valued the study of literature, which they considered the best guide to the *Volksgeist,* the popular soul or spirit or essence of their community. For that reason the German brothers Jakob and Wilhelm Grimm collected popular poetry, stories, songs, and tales as expressions of the German *Volk.*

Political Nationalism During the nineteenth century, nationalist thought became much more strident than the cultural nationalism of Herder or the brothers Grimm. Advocates of nationalism demanded loyalty and solidarity from members of the national group. In lands where they were minorities or where they lived under foreign rule, they sought to establish independent states to protect and advance the interests of the national community.

In Italy, for example, the nationalist activist Giuseppe Mazzini (1805–1872) formed a group called Young Italy that promoted independence from Austrian and Spanish rule and the establishment of an Italian national state. Mazzini likened the nation to a family and the nation's territory to the family home. Austrian and Spanish authorities forced Mazzini to lead much of his life in exile, but he used the opportunity to encourage the organization of nationalist movements in new lands. By the mid-nineteenth century, Young Italy had inspired the development of nationalist movements in Ireland, Switzerland, and Hungary.

While it encouraged political leaders to work toward the establishment of national states for their communities, nationalism also had strong potential to stir up conflict between different groups of people. The more nationalists identified with their own national communities, the more they distinguished themselves both from peoples in other lands and from minority groups within their societies.

thinking about ENCOUNTERS

Nationalism on the March

The Napoleonic wars that followed the French revolution brought both French troops and revolutionary ideals to the regions of Europe involved in those wars. What ideals were exported from France? How did clashes between the French and other peoples of Europe, such as the Italians and the Germans, reshape the nationalist sentiments of those peoples?

Nationalism and Anti-Semitism This divisive potential of nationalism helps to explain the emergence of Zionism, a political movement that holds that the Jewish people constitute a nation and have the right to their own national homeland. Unlike Mazzini's Italian compatriots, Jews did not inhabit a well-defined territory but, rather, lived in states throughout Europe and beyond. As national communities tightened their bonds, nationalist leaders often became distrustful of minority populations. Suspicion of Jews fueled anti-Semitism in many parts of Europe. Whereas anti-Semitism was barely visible in countries such as Italy and the Netherlands, it operated openly in those such as Austria-Hungary and Germany. In eastern Europe, anti-Semitism often turned violent. In Russia and in the Russian-controlled areas of Poland, the persecution of Jews climaxed in a series of pogroms. Beginning in 1881 and lasting into the early twentieth century, these massacres claimed the lives and property of thousands of Jews.

During the late nineteenth and twentieth centuries, millions of Jews migrated to other European lands or to North America to escape persecution and violence. Anti-Semitism was not as severe in France as in central and eastern Europe, but it reached a fever pitch there after a military court convicted Alfred Dreyfus, a Jewish army officer, of spying for Germany in 1894. Although he was innocent of the charges and eventually had the verdict reversed on appeal, Dreyfus was the focus of bitter debates about the trustworthiness of Jews in French society. The trial also became a key event in the evolution of Zionism.

A determined Theodor Herzl founded the Zionist movement, which sought to confront anti-Semitism in Europe by establishing a home for the Jews in Palestine.

Zionism Among the reporters at the Dreyfus trial was a Jewish journalist from Vienna, Theodor Herzl (1860–1904). As Herzl witnessed mobs shouting "Death to the Jews" in the land of enlightenment and liberty, he concluded that anti-Semitism was a persistent feature of human society that assimilation could not solve. In 1896 Herzl published the pamphlet *Judenstaat,* which argued that the only defense against anti-Semitism lay in the mass migration of Jews from all over the world to a land that they could call their own. In the following year, Herzl organized the first Zionist Congress in Basel, Switzerland, which founded the World Zionist Organization. The delegates at Basel formulated the basic platform of the Zionist movement, declaring that "Zionism seeks to establish a home for the Jewish people in Palestine," the location of the ancient Kingdom of Israel. During the next half century, Jewish migrants trickled into Palestine, and in 1948 they won recognition for the Jewish state of Israel. Although it arose in response to exclusive nationalism in Europe, Zionism in turn provoked a resentful nationalism among Palestinian Arabs displaced by Jewish settlers. Conflicts between Jews and Palestinians continue to the present day.

The Emergence of National Communities

The French revolution and the wars that followed it heightened feelings of national identity throughout Europe. In

The charming and polished courtier Prince Klemens von Metternich (standing at left center) dominated the Congress of Vienna. Here, delegates to the Congress are gathered at the Habsburg palace in Vienna.

France the establishment of a republic based on liberty, equality, and fraternity inspired patriotism and encouraged citizens to rally to the defense of the revolution when foreign armies threatened it. Revolutionary leaders took the tricolored flag as a symbol of the French nation, and they adopted a rousing marching tune, the "Marseillaise," as an anthem that inspired pride in and identity with the national community. In Spain, the Netherlands, Austria, Prussia, and Russia, national consciousness surged in reaction to the arrival of revolutionary and Napoleonic armies. Opposition to Napoleon and his imperial designs also inspired national feeling in Britain.

The Congress of Vienna After the fall of Napoleon, conservative political leaders feared that heightened national consciousness and ideas of popular sovereignty would encourage further experimentation with revolution and undermine European stability. Meeting as the Congress of Vienna (1814–1815), representatives of the "great powers" that defeated Napoleon—Britain, Austria, Prussia, and Russia—attempted to restore the prerevolutionary order. Under the guidance of the influential foreign minister of Austria, Prince Klemens von Metternich (1773–1859), the Congress dismantled Napoleon's empire, returned sovereignty to Europe's royal families, restored them to the thrones they had lost during the Napoleonic era, and created a diplomatic order based on a balance of power that prevented any one state from dominating the others. A central goal of Metternich himself was to suppress national consciousness, which he viewed as a serious threat to the multicultural Austrian empire that included Germans, Italians, Magyars, Czechs, Slovaks, Poles, Serbs, and Croats among its subjects.

The efforts of Metternich and the Congress of Vienna to restore the ancien régime had limited success. The European balance of power established at Vienna survived for almost a century, until the outbreak of a general continental and global war in 1914. Metternich and the conservative rulers installed by the Congress of Vienna took measures to forestall further revolution: they censored publications to prevent communication of seditious ideas and relied on spies to identify nationalist and republican activists. By 1815, however, it was impossible to suppress national consciousness and ideas of popular sovereignty.

Nationalist Rebellions From the 1820s through the 1840s, a wave of rebellions inspired by nationalist sentiments swept through Europe. The first uprising occurred in 1821 in the Balkan peninsula, where the Greek people sought independence from the Ottoman Turks, who had ruled the region since the fifteenth century. Many western Europeans sympathized with the Greek cause. The English poet Lord Byron even joined the rebel army and in 1824 died (of a fever) while serving in Greece. With the aid of Britain, France, and Russia, the rebels overcame the Ottoman forces in the Balkans by 1827 and won formal recognition of Greek independence in 1830.

In 1830 rebellion showed its face throughout Europe. In France, Spain, Portugal, and some of the German principalities, revolutionaries inspired by liberalism called for constitutional government based on popular sovereignty. In Belgium, Italy, and Poland, they demanded independence and the formation of national states as well as popular sovereignty. Revolution in Paris drove Charles X from the throne, while uprisings in Belgium resulted in independence from the

MAP 28.4

The unification of Italy and Germany.

The unification of Italy and Germany (see map on page 645) as national states in the nineteenth century fundamentally altered the balance of power in Europe.

Why did unification result from diplomacy and war conducted by conservative statesmen rather than popular nationalist action?

Netherlands. By the mid-1830s authorities had put down the uprisings elsewhere, but in 1848 a new round of rebellions shook European states. The uprisings of 1848 brought down the French monarchy and seriously threatened the Austrian empire, where subject peoples clamored for constitutions and independence. Prince Metternich resigned his office as Austrian foreign minister and unceremoniously fled Vienna as rebels took control of the city. Uprisings also rocked cities in Italy, Prussia, and German states in the Rhineland.

By the summer of 1849, the veteran armies of conservative rulers had put down the last of the rebellions. Advocates of national independence and popular sovereignty remained active, however, and the potential of their ideals to mobilize popular support soon became dramatically apparent.

The Unifications of Italy and Germany

The most striking demonstration of the power that national sentiments could unleash involved the unification of Italy and of Germany. Since the fall of the Roman empire, Italy and Germany had been disunited lands. A variety of regional kingdoms, city-states, and ecclesiastical states ruled the Italian peninsula for more than a thousand years, and princes divided Germany into more than three hundred semiautonomous jurisdictions. The Holy Roman Empire claimed authority over Germany and much of Italy, but the emperors were rarely strong enough to enforce their claims.

As they dismantled Napoleon's empire and sought to restore the ancien régime, delegates at the Congress of Vienna placed much of northern Italy under Austrian rule. Southern Italy was already under close Spanish supervision because of dynastic ties between the Kingdom of the Two Sicilies and the Spanish Bourbon monarchy. As national sentiment surged throughout nineteenth-century Europe, Italian political leaders worked to win independence from foreign rule and establish an Italian national state. Mazzini's Young Italy movement attracted discontented idealists throughout the peninsula. In 1820, 1830, and 1848, they mounted major uprisings that threatened but did not dislodge foreign rule in Italy.

Cavour and Garibaldi

The unification of Italy came about when practical political leaders such as Count Camillo di Cavour (1810–1861), prime minister to King Vittore Emmanuele II of Piedmont and Sardinia, combined forces with nationalist advocates of independence. Cavour was a cunning diplomat, and the kingdom of Piedmont and Sardinia was the most powerful of the Italian states. In alliance with France, Cavour expelled Austrian authorities from most of northern Italy in 1859. Then he turned his attention to south-

ern Italy, where Giuseppe Garibaldi (1807–1882), a dashing soldier of fortune and a passionate nationalist, led the unification movement. With an army of about one thousand men outfitted in distinctive red shirts, Garibaldi swept through Sicily and southern Italy, outmaneuvering government forces and attracting enthusiastic recruits. In 1860 Garibaldi met King Vittore Emmanuele near Naples. Not ambitious to rule, Garibaldi delivered southern Italy into Vittore Emmanuele's hands, and the kingdom of Piedmont and Sardinia became the kingdom of Italy. During the next decade the new monarchy absorbed several additional territories, including Venice, Rome, and their surrounding regions.

In Germany as in Italy, unification came about when political leaders harnessed nationalist aspirations. The Congress of Vienna created a German Confederation composed of thirty-nine states dominated by Austria. Metternich and other conservative German rulers stifled nationalist movements, and the suppression of the rebellions of 1848 left German nationalists frustrated at their inability to found a national state.

Otto von Bismarck In 1862 King Wilhelm I of Prussia appointed a wealthy landowner, Otto von Bismarck (1815–1898), as his prime minister. Bismarck was a master of *Realpolitik* ("the politics of reality"). He succinctly expressed his realistic approach in his first speech as prime minister: "The great questions of the day will not be settled by speeches or majority votes—that was the great mistake of 1848 and 1849—but by blood and iron."

It was indeed blood and iron that brought about the unification of Germany. As prime minister, Bismarck reformed and expanded the Prussian army. Between 1864 and 1870 he intentionally provoked three wars—with Denmark, Austria, and France—and whipped up German sentiment against the enemies. In all three conflicts Prussian forces quickly shattered their opponents, swelling German pride. In 1871 the Prussian king proclaimed himself emperor of the Second Reich—meaning the Second German Empire, following the Holy Roman Empire—which embraced almost all German-speaking peoples outside Austria and Switzerland in a powerful and dynamic national state.

Wearing a white jacket, Otto von Bismarck (center) witnesses the crowning of King Wilhelm I of Prussia as German emperor. The coronation followed the victory of Prussia over France in 1871, and it took place in the royal palace at Versailles.

The unification of Italy and Germany made it clear that when coupled with strong political, diplomatic, and military leadership, nationalism had enormous potential to mobilize people who felt a sense of national kinship. Italy, Germany, and other national states went to great lengths to foster a sense of national community. They adopted national flags to serve as symbols of unity, national anthems to inspire patriotism, and national holidays to focus public attention on individuals and events of special importance for the national community. They established bureaucracies that took censuses of national populations and tracked vital national statistics involving birth, marriage, and death. They built schools that instilled patriotic values in students, and they recruited young men into armies that defended national interests and sometimes went on the offensive to enhance national prestige. By the end of the nineteenth century, the national state had proven to be a powerful model of political organization in Europe. By the mid-twentieth century, it had become well-nigh universal as political leaders adopted the national state as the principal form of political organization throughout the world.

inperspective

The Enlightenment ideals of freedom, equality, and popular sovereignty inspired revolutionary movements throughout much of the Atlantic Ocean basin in the late eighteenth and early nineteenth centuries. In North America colonists threw off British rule and founded an independent federal republic. In France revolutionaries abolished the monarchy, established a republic, and refashioned the social order. In

Saint-Domingue rebellious slaves threw off French rule, established an independent Haitian republic, and granted freedom and equality to all citizens. In Latin America creole elites led movements to expel Spanish and Portuguese colonial authorities and to found independent republics. During the nineteenth century, adult white men were the main beneficiaries of movements based on Enlightenment ideals, but social reformers launched campaigns to extend freedom and equality to Africans, African-Americans, and women.

Meanwhile, as they fought each other in wars sparked by the French revolution, European peoples developed strong feelings of national identity and worked to establish states that advanced the interests of national communities. Nationalist thought was often divisive: it pitted national groups against one another and fueled tensions especially in large multicultural states. But nationalism also had strong potential to contribute to state-building movements, and nationalist appeals played prominent roles in the unification of Italy and Germany. During the nineteenth and twentieth centuries, peoples throughout the world drew inspiration from Enlightenment ideals and national identities when seeking to build or restructure their societies. ●

CHRONOLOGY

1632–1704	Life of John Locke
1694–1778	Life of Voltaire
1712–1778	Life of Jean-Jacques Rousseau
1744–1803	Life of Toussaint Louverture
1748–1793	Life of Olympe de Gouges
1753–1811	Life of Miguel Hidalgo y Costilla
1769–1821	Life of Napoleon Bonaparte
1773–1859	Life of Klemens von Metternich
1774–1793	Reign of King Louis XVI
1775–1781	American revolution
1783–1830	Life of Simón Bolívar
1789–1799	French revolution
1791–1803	Haitian revolution
1799–1814	Reign of Napoleon
1805–1872	Life of Giuseppe Mazzini
1807–1882	Life of Giuseppe Garibaldi
1810–1825	Wars of independence in Latin America
1810–1861	Life of Camillo di Cavour
1814–1815	Congress of Vienna
1815–1898	Life of Otto von Bismarck
1821–1827	War of Greek independence
1859–1870	Unification of Italy
1864–1871	Unification of Germany

For Further Reading

Benedict Anderson. *Imagined Communities: Reflections on the Origin and Spread of Nationalism.* Rev. ed. London, 1991. A pioneering work that analyzes the means and the processes by which peoples came to view themselves as members of national communities.

Bernard Bailyn. *The Ideological Origins of the American Revolution.* 2nd ed. Cambridge, Mass., 1992. A fundamental study of pamphlets and other publications that criticized British colonial policy in North America.

David A. Bell. *The Cult of the Nation in France: Inventing Nationalism, 1680–1800.* Cambridge, Mass., 2001. Looks at how patriotism and national sentiment were grafted onto religious forms of community in the context of the eighteenth century and the French revolution.

———. *The First Total War: Napoleon's Europe and the Birth of Warfare as We Know It.* Boston, 2007. A fine work that argues that nearly every "modern" aspect of war was born in the Revolutionary and Napoleonic wars.

Reinhard Bendix. *Kings or People: Power and the Mandate to Rule.* Berkeley, 1978. A challenging but important comparative study of popular sovereignty and its displacement of monarchical authority.

Linda Colley. *Britons: Forging the Nation, 1707–1837.* New Haven, 1992. A detailed analysis of the emergence of British national identity.

Laureant Dubois. *Avengers of the New World: The Story of the Haitian Revolution.* Cambridge, Mass., 2005. Comprehensive study of how the French slave colony of Saint-Domingue became a unique example of a successful black revolution that challenged the boundaries of freedom, citizenship, and empire.

Susan Dunn. *Sister Revolutions: French Lightning, American Light.* New York, 1999. An accessible and stimulating work that traces the different legacies of the American and French revolutions of the eighteenth century.

Geoffrey Ellis. *Napoleon.* New York, 1997. An excellent biography of a pivotal figure in modern European history.

Eric Hobsbawm. *Nations and Nationalism Since 1780: Programme, Myth, and Reality.* 2nd ed. Cambridge, 1992. A brief interpretation of nationalism in Europe and the larger world.

——— and Terence Ranger, eds. *The Invention of Tradition.* Cambridge, 1983. A fascinating collection of essays examining the rituals and other traditions that modern states have relied on to enhance their authority.

Lynn Hunt. *Politics, Culture, and Class in the French Revolution.* Berkeley and Los Angeles, 1984. Continues to be a touchstone for the history of the French revolution's political culture and of the meanings of the revolution's symbols to the course of events.

Colin Jones. *The Great Nation: France from Louis XV to Napoleon.* London and New York, 2003. An excellent economic and political history of a society opposed to absolutism.

Lester D. Langley. *The Americas in the Age of Revolution, 1750–1850.* New Haven, 1997. A comparative study of revolutions and wars of independence in the western hemisphere.

Mary Beth Norton. *Liberty's Daughters: The Revolutionary Experience of American Women, 1750–1800.* Boston, 1980. Focuses on the role of women in the American revolution and the early republic.

Robert Palmer. *The Age of the Democratic Revolution: A Political History of Europe and America, 1760–1800.* 2 vols. Princeton, 1959–64. A classic study of the American and French revolutions and their influence in Europe and the Americas.

Simon Schama. *Citizens: A Chronicle of the French Revolution.* New York, 1989. Detailed narrative of the French revolution focusing on the experiences and decisions made by individual actors.

Eric Van Young. *The Other Rebellion: Popular Violence, Ideology, and the Mexican Struggle for Independence, 1810–1821.* Stanford, 2001. An exhaustive account of Mexico's movement toward independence from Spain that stresses the importance of domestic struggles that pitted classes and ethnic groups against one another.

Gordon S. Wood. *The Radicalism of the American Revolution.* New York, 1991. A comprehensive synthesis emphasizing the role of republican and democratic ideas in the overthrow of monarchical institutions.

The Making of Industrial Society

chapter 29

Young woman at work in a mechanized mill in the 1830s.

EYEWITNESS:
Betty Harris, a Woman Chained in the Coal Pits

In 1827, shortly after marrying at the age of twenty-three, Betty Harris took a job as a drawer in a coal pit near Manchester, England. A drawer's job involved crawling down narrow mine shafts and hauling loads of coal from the bottom of the pit, where miners chipped it from the earth, to the surface. From there the coal went to fuel the steam engines that powered the factories and the mills of early industrial society. Drawers performed unskilled labor for low wages, but their work was essential for the emergence of industrial production.

While working, Harris wore a heavy belt around her waist. Hitched to the belt was a chain that passed between her legs and attached to the coal cart that she pulled through the mine shafts, often while creeping along on hands and knees. The belt strained against her body, and the mine shafts were steep and slippery. Yet every work day, even when she was pregnant, Harris strapped on her belt and chain at 6:00 A.M., removing her bindings only at the end of the shift twelve hours later.

Work conditions for Betty Harris were less than ideal. She labored in the coal pit with six other women and six boys and girls. All members of the crew experienced hardships and exploitation. Harris reported that drawing coal was "very hard work for a woman," and she did not exaggerate. She and her companions often had to crawl through water that collected in the mine shafts during rainstorms, and the men who mined coal in the pits showed scant respect for the lowly, ill-paid drawers. The belts and chains worn by drawers often chafed their skin raw, and miners contributed to their physical discomfort by beating them for slow or clumsy work. The miners, many of whom shed their clothes and worked naked in the hot, oppressive coal pits, also took sexual liberties with the women and girl drawers: Harris personally knew several illegitimate children conceived during forced sexual encounters in the coal pits.

Betty Harris faced her own sexual problems once she arrived home. Exhausted from twelve hours of work, with only a one-hour break for a midday meal consisting of bread and butter, she often tried to discourage her husband's advances. Her husband had little patience, however, and Harris remarked that "my feller has beaten me many a time for not being ready." Harris's work schedule made comfortable family life impossible. A cousin had to care for her two children during the day, and Harris tended to them and her husband at night. The grinding demands of the coal pit took a toll: at age thirty-seven, after fourteen years in the mines, Harris admitted that "I am not so strong as I was, and cannot stand my work so well as I used to."

Not all industrial workers suffered the indignities that coal drawers endured, but Betty Harris's experience nonetheless illustrates some of the deep changes that industrialization wrought in patterns of work and family life. Beginning in the late eighteenth century, workers and their families had to adjust to the sometimes harsh demands of the machine age. First in Britain, then in western Europe, North America, Russia, and Japan, machines and factories transformed agricultural societies into industrial societies. At the heart of this transformation were technological changes based on newly developed, inanimate sources of power that led to the extensive use of machinery in manufacturing. Machine production raised worker productivity, encouraged economic specialization, and promoted the growth of large-scale enterprise. Industrial machinery transformed economic production by turning out high-quality products quickly, cheaply, and efficiently. The process of industrialization encouraged rapid technological innovation and over the long term raised material standards of living in much of the world.

But the impact of industrialization went beyond economics, generating widespread and often unsettling social change as well. Early industrialists created a new work environment, the factory, which concentrated large numbers of workers under one roof to operate complicated machinery. The concentration of workers made it possible to rely on inanimate motive power such as waterwheels or steam engines. Factories also enabled managers to impose work discipline and closely supervise the quality of production at their plants. By moving work outside the home, however, factories drew fathers, mothers, and children in different directions, altered traditional patterns of domestic life, and strained family relations in the industrial era.

Industrialization encouraged rapid urbanization and migration. New cities mushroomed to house workers who left the countryside for jobs in factories. Millions of migrants traveled even farther, crossing the seas in search of opportunities in new lands. Often, however, early industrial workers found themselves living in squalor and laboring under dangerous conditions.

Social critics and reformers worked to alleviate the problems of early industrial society. Most scathing and influential of the critics were the German theorists Karl Marx and Friedrich Engels, who called for the destruction of capitalism and the establishment of a more just and equitable socialist society. Despite their appeals, capitalism and industrialization flourished and spread rapidly from Britain to continental Europe, North America, and Asia. Although industrialization spread unevenly around the globe, it profoundly influenced social and economic conditions throughout the world, since industrial societies created a new international division of labor that made most African, Asian, and American lands dependent on the export of raw materials.

PATTERNS OF INDUSTRIALIZATION

Industrialization refers to a process that transformed agrarian and handicraft-centered economies into economies distinguished by industry and machine manufacture. The principal features of this process were technological and organizational changes that transformed manufacturing and led to increased productivity. Critical to industrialization were technological developments that made it possible to produce goods by machines rather than by hand and that harnessed inanimate sources of energy such as coal and petroleum. Organizational changes accompanied technological developments. By the end of the nineteenth century, the factory had become the predominant site of industrial production in Europe, the United States, and Japan. Factory production strongly encouraged the emergence of new divisions of labor as interchangeable parts and belt-driven assembly lines made the mass production of goods a hallmark of industrialized societies. The need to invest in increasingly expensive equipment encouraged the formation of large businesses: by the mid-nineteenth century, many giant corporations had joined together to control trade through trusts and cartels.

Foundations of Industrialization

By the mid-eighteenth century, several areas of the world—Great Britain in western Europe, the Yangzi Delta in China,

Japan—exhibited growing and dynamic economies that shared many common features. High agricultural productivity in those regions resulted in significant population growth. High population densities in turn encouraged occupational specialization and permitted many individuals to work at tasks other than cultivation. Navigable rivers and networks of canals facilitated trade and transport, and cities and towns were home to sophisticated banking and financial institutions. At the same time, these commercially sophisticated economies ran up against difficult ecological obstacles—especially soil depletion and deforestation—that threatened continued population growth and consumption levels. First Great Britain and subsequently the other regions of western Europe transcended those ecological constraints by exploiting coal deposits fortuitously found at home and natural resources found abroad.

Coal and Colonies Coal played a crucial role in the industrialization of Great Britain. Until the eighteenth century, wood had served as the primary source of fuel for iron production, home heating, and cooking. Prodigious uses of wood, however, had also hastened deforestation, causing serious wood shortages. Geographic luck had placed some of western Europe's largest coal deposits in Great Britain, within easy reach of water transport, centers of commerce, and pools of skilled labor. The fortunate conjunction of coal deposits and the skills necessary to extract this fuel encouraged the substitution of coal for wood, thus creating a promising framework for industrialization. In the absence of easily accessible coal deposits, it was unlikely that the economy could have supported an expanding iron production and the application of steam engines to mining and industry—both crucial to the industrial process in Great Britain. In that respect, Britain's experience proved unique and differed from that of China, where the breakthrough to industrialization occurred at a later time. In China, geography conspired against an important early shift from wood to coal, because the main coal-producing regions of northwest China were too distant from the Yangzi Delta, economically China's most promising region.

Ecological Relief The unique economic relationship between Europe and the Americas gave Great Britain additional ecological relief. The conquered and colonized lands of the Americas lifted European land constraints by supplying European societies with a growing volume of primary products. During the eighteenth century the slave-based plantations of northeastern Brazil, the Caribbean islands, and later the southern United States supplied Europe with huge amounts of sugar and cotton; the former increased available food calories while the latter kept emerging textile industries going. Neither of these products could have been grown in Europe. The plantation economies of the Caribbean islands in particular also created significant markets for manufactured imports from Europe, the poverty of slaves notwithstanding. Almost one-half of the proceeds from sugar exports paid for the importation of manufactured goods from Europe, including cheap cotton cloth for slaves to wear. The significance of valuable American resources grew after 1830, when large amounts of grain, timber, and beef traveled across the Atlantic to European destinations. All these products grew on colonial acreage, which expanded Europe's land base. Later in the century, American lands also served as outlets for Europe's surplus population.

Access to coal deposits and the exploitation of overseas resources provided a context—one not yet available to societies such as China's—that increased the odds for an industrial breakthrough. This industrial expansion, in fact, started with Britain's textiles. Beginning about the mid-eighteenth century, consumer demand encouraged a transformation of the British cotton industry.

During the seventeenth century, English consumers had become fond of calicoes—inexpensive, brightly printed textiles imported from India. Cotton cloth came into demand because it was lighter, easier to wash, and quicker to dry than wool, which was the principal fabric of European clothes before the nineteenth century. Threatened by the popularity of cotton products, British wool producers persuaded Parliament to pass a series of laws to protect the domestic wool industry. The Calico Acts of 1720 and 1721 prohibited imports of printed cotton cloth and restricted the sale of calicoes at home. Parliament even passed a law requiring corpses to be buried in woolen shrouds, but legislation did not dampen consumers' enthusiasm for cotton. Consumer demand for cotton products drove the development of a British cotton textile industry.

Mechanization of the Cotton Industry Demand for cotton was so strong that producers had to speed up spinning and weaving to supply growing domestic and foreign markets. To increase production, they turned to inventions that rapidly mechanized the cotton textile industry. In the early 1730s, artisans began to develop labor-saving devices for spinning and weaving cotton, thereby moving away from hand-based techniques derived from the wool and linen industries. The first important technological breakthrough came in 1733 when Manchester mechanic John Kay invented the flying shuttle. This device speeded up the weaving process and stimulated demand for thread. Within a few years, competitions among inventors resulted in the creation of several mechanical spinning devices. The most important was Samuel Crompton's "mule," built in 1779. Adapted for steam power by 1790, the mule became the device of choice for spinning cotton. A worker using a steam-driven mule could produce a hundred times more thread than a worker using a manual spinning wheel.

The new spinning machines created an imbalance in manufacturing because weavers could not keep up with the production of thread, so innovators turned their attention next to weaving. In 1785 Edmund Cartwright, a clergyman

An 1835 engraving depicts female workers at a textile factory. The shift to machine-based manufacturing commonly started with the mechanization of the textile industries, not only in Great Britain, but also in other industrializing lands, such as the United States and Japan.

without training or experience in either mechanics or textiles, patented a water-driven power loom that inaugurated an era of mechanical weaving. Within two decades steam moved the power loom, and by the 1820s it had largely supplanted hand weavers in the cotton industry. Collectively, these technological developments permitted the production of textile goods in great volume and variety and at low cost. By 1830 half a million people worked in the cotton business, Britain's leading industry, which accounted for 40 percent of exports.

Steam Power The most crucial technological breakthrough of the early industrial era was the development of a general-purpose steam engine in 1765 by James Watt, an instrument maker at the University of Glasgow in Scotland. Steam engines burned coal to boil water and create steam, which drove mechanical devices that performed work. Even before Watt's time, primitive steam engines had powered pumps that drew water out of coal mines, but those devices consumed too much fuel to be useful for other purposes. Watt's version relied on steam to force a piston to turn a wheel, whose rotary motion converted a simple pump into an engine that had multiple uses. Watt's contemporaries used the term *horsepower* to measure the energy generated by his steam engine, which did the work of numerous animals. By 1800 more than a thousand of Watt's steam engines were in use in the British isles. They were especially prominent in the textile industry, where their application resulted in greater productivity for manufacturers and cheaper prices for consumers.

Iron and Steel Innovation did not stop with cotton production and steam engines. The iron and steel industries also benefited from technological refinement, and the availability of inexpensive, high-quality iron and steel reinforced the move toward mechanization. After 1709, British smelters began to use coke (a purified form of coal) rather than more expensive charcoal as a fuel to produce iron. Deforestation in England had made wood—the principal source of charcoal—scarce. Besides being cheaper than charcoal, coke made it possible for producers to build bigger blast furnaces and turn out larger lots of iron. As a result, British iron production skyrocketed during the eighteenth century, and prices to consumers fell. Inexpensive iron fittings and parts made industrial machinery stronger, and iron soon became common in bridges, buildings, and ships.

The nineteenth century was an age of steel rather than iron. Steel is much harder, stronger, and more resilient than iron, but until the nineteenth century it was very expensive to produce. Between 1740 and 1850 a series of improvements simplified the process. In 1856 Henry Bessemer built a refined blast furnace known as the Bessemer converter that made it possible to produce steel cheaply and in large quantities. Steel production rose sharply, and steel quickly began to replace iron in tools, machines, and structures that required high strength.

Transportation Steam engineering and metallurgical innovations both contributed to improvements in transportation technology. James Watt's steam engine did not adapt well to transportation uses because it consumed too much coal.

A woman working as a drawer in a British coal mine drags her coal cart with the aid of a belt and chain. Manually produced coal fueled the machines of early industrial society. What specific risks might have been associated with this kind of job?

After his patent expired, however, inventors devised high-pressure engines that required less fuel. In 1815 George Stephenson, a self-educated Englishman, built the first steam-powered locomotive. In 1829 his Rocket won a contest by reaching a speed of 45 kilometers (28 miles) per hour. Although they were more efficient than Watt's invention, Stephenson's engines still burned too much coal for use at sea. Sailing ships remained the most effective means of transport over the seas until the middle of the nineteenth century, when refined engines of high efficiency began to drive steamships.

Because they had the capacity to carry huge cargoes, railroads and steamships dramatically lowered transportation costs. They also contributed to the creation of dense transportation networks that linked remote interior regions and distant shores more closely than ever before. Between 1830 and 1870, British entrepreneurs laid about 20,000 kilometers (13,000 miles) of railroads, which linked industrial centers, coalfields, iron deposits, and port cities throughout the land—and also carried some 322 million passengers as well as cargoes of raw materials and manufactured goods. Steamships proved their own versatility by advancing up rivers to points that sailboats could not reach because of inconvenient twists, turns, or winds. Railroads and steamships benefited from the innovations that drove the industrialization process and in turn encouraged continuing industrialization by providing rapid and inexpensive transport.

George Stephenson's North Star engine of 1837. Although Stephenson did not invent the locomotive, his refinements of locomotive technology, his application of civil engineering to the development of efficient railroad lines, and his vision of the future impact of railway systems on commerce earned him the nickname "Father of the Railways."

The Factory System

In the emerging capitalist society of early modern Europe (discussed in chapter 23), most manufacturing took place under the putting-out system. To avoid guild restrictions on prices and wages, entrepreneurs in early modern Europe paid individuals to work on materials in their households. That protoindustrial system of production centered on the household and usually involved fewer than ten people. During the seventeenth and early eighteenth centuries, new and larger units of production supplemented the putting-out system. Rising demand for certain products such as textiles and the growing use of water and wind power led to the formation of protoindustrial factories, where workers performed specialized tasks under one roof. Nevertheless, the largest preindustrial workforces consisted of unskilled laborers in mines and slaves on plantations.

The Factory The factory system replaced both the putting-out system and protoindustrial factories and became the characteristic method of production in industrial economies. It began to emerge in the late eighteenth century, when technological advances transformed the British textile industry, and by the mid-nineteenth century most cotton production took place in factories. Many of the newly developed machines were too large and expensive for home use, and it became necessary to move work to locations where entrepreneurs and engineers built complicated machinery for large-scale production. This centralization of production brought together more workers doing specialized tasks than ever before. Most industrial workers hailed from the countryside. A combination of factors provided a plentiful supply of cheap labor for the burgeoning factories, including rural overpopulation, declining job opportunities, and the financial difficulties of small farmers who had to sell their land to large landowners.

The factory system with its new machines demanded a rational organization of job functions that differed from earlier forms of industrial organization. The factory became associated with a new division of labor, one that called for a production process in which each worker performed a single task, rather than one in which a single worker completed the entire job, as was typical of handicraft traditions. In the first chapter of the *Wealth of Nations* (1776), Adam Smith used a pin factory to describe the new system of manufacture. "One man draws out the wire, another straights it, a third cuts it, a fourth points it, a fifth grinds it at the top for receiving the head; . . . and the important business of making a pin is, in this manner, divided into about eighteen distinct operations." Factories also enabled managers to impose strict work discipline and closely supervise employees. Thus Josiah Wedgwood (1730–1795), an Englishman with a wooden leg and who owned a pottery plant, held his employees to high standards in an effort to produce the highest quality pottery. When he spotted inferior work, he frequently dumped it on the factory floor and crushed it with his peg leg saying, "This will not do for Josiah Wedgwood!"

Working Conditions With its new divisions of labor, the factory system allowed managers to improve worker productivity and realize spectacular increases in the output of manufactured goods. But the new environment also had unsettling effects on the nature of work. The factory system led to the emergence of an owner class whose capital financed equipment and machinery that were too expensive for workers to acquire. Industrial workers themselves became mere wage earners who had only their labor services to offer and who depended on their employers for their livelihood. In addition, any broad-range skills that workers may have previously acquired as artisans often became obsolete in a work environment that rewarded narrowly defined skills. The repetitious and boring nature of many industrial jobs, moreover, left many workers alienated or estranged from their work and the products of their labor.

Equally disturbing was the new work discipline and the pace of work. Those accustomed to rural labor soon learned that the seasons, the rising and setting of the sun, and fluctuations in the weather no longer dictated work routines. Instead, clocks, machines, and shop rules established new rhythms of work. Industrial workers commonly labored six days a week for twelve to fourteen hours daily. The factory whistle sounded the beginning and the end of the working day, and throughout the day workers had to keep pace with the monotonous movements of machines. At the same time, they faced strict and immediate supervision, which made little allowance for a quick nap or socializing with friends. Floor managers pressured men, women, and children to speed up production and punished them when they did not meet expectations. Because neither the machines nor the methods of work took safety into account, early industrial workers constantly faced the possibility of maiming or fatal accidents.

Industrial Protest In some instances, machine-centered factories sparked violent protest. Between 1811 and 1816, organized bands of English handicraft workers known as Luddites went on a rampage and destroyed textile machines that they blamed for their low wages and unemployment. They called their leader King Lud, after a legendary boy named Ludlam who broke a knitting frame to spite his father. The movement broke out in the hosiery and lace industries around Nottingham and then spread to the wool and cotton mills of Lancashire. The Luddites usually wore masks and operated at night. Because they avoided violence against people, they enjoyed considerable popular support. Nevertheless, by hanging fourteen Luddites in 1813, the government served notice that it was unwilling to tolerate violence even against machines, and the movement gradually died out.

The Early Spread of Industrialization

Industrialization and the technological, organizational, and social transformations that accompanied it might have originated in many parts of the world where abundant craft skills, agricultural production, and investment capital could support the industrialization process. For half a century, however, industrialization took place only in Great Britain. Aware of their head start, British entrepreneurs and government officials forbade the export of machinery, manufacturing techniques, and skilled workers.

Yet Britain's monopoly on industrialization did not last forever, because enterprising entrepreneurs recognized profitable opportunities in foreign lands and circumvented government regulations to sell machinery and technical know-how abroad. Moreover, European and North American businesspeople did their best to become acquainted with British industrial techniques and lure British experts to their lands. European and North American entrepreneurs

Workers tend to a massive steam hammer under dangerous conditions.

did not hesitate to bribe or even kidnap British engineers, and they also smuggled advanced machinery out of the British isles. Sometimes they got poor value for their investments: they found that it was difficult to attract the best British experts to foreign lands and had to make do with drunkards or second-rate specialists who demanded high pay but made little contribution to industrialization.

Industrialization in Western Europe Nevertheless, by the mid-nineteenth century, industrialization had spread to France, Germany, Belgium, and the United States. The French revolution and the Napoleonic wars helped set the stage for industrialization in western Europe by abolishing internal trade barriers and dismantling guilds that discouraged technological innovation and restricted the movement of laborers. The earliest continental center of industrial production was Belgium, where coal, iron, textile, glass, and armaments production flourished in the early nineteenth century. About the same time, France also moved toward industrialization. By 1830, French firms employed about fifteen thousand skilled British workers who helped establish mechanized textile and metallurgical industries in France. By the mid-nineteenth century, French engineers and inventors were devising refinements and innovations that led to greater efficiencies especially in metallurgical industries. Later in the century a boom in railroad construction stimulated economic development while also leading to decreased transportation costs.

German industrialization proceeded more slowly than did Belgian and French, partly because of political instability resulting from competition between the many German states. After the 1840s, however, German coal and iron production soared, and by the 1850s an extensive railroad network was under construction. After unification in 1871, Bismarck's government sponsored rapid industrialization in Germany. In the interests of strengthening military capacity, Bismarck encouraged the development of heavy industry, and the formation of huge businesses became a hallmark of German industrialization. The giant Krupp firm, for example, dominated mining, metallurgy, armaments production, and shipbuilding.

Industrialization in North America Industrialization transformed North America as well as western Europe in the nineteenth century. In 1800 the United States possessed abundant land and natural resources but few laborers and little money to invest in business enterprises. Both labor and investment capital came largely from Europe: migrants crossed the Atlantic in large numbers throughout the nineteenth century, and European bankers and businesspeople eagerly sought opportunities to invest in businesses that made use of American natural resources. American industrialization began in the 1820s when entrepreneurs lured British crafts workers to New England and built a cotton textile industry. By mid-century well over a thousand mills were producing fabrics from raw cotton grown in the southern states, and New England had emerged as a site for the industrial production also of shoes, tools, and handguns. In the 1870s heavy iron and steel industries emerged in areas such as western Pennsylvania and central Alabama where there were abundant supplies of iron ore and coal. By 1900 the United States had become an economic powerhouse, and industrialization had begun to spill over into southern Canada.

The vast size of the United States was advantageous to industrialists because it made abundant natural resources available to them, but it also hindered travel and communication between the regions. To facilitate transportation

MAP 29.1

Industrial Europe ca. 1850.

Locate the places marked as emerging industrial areas.

Are there any features those areas have in common? If so, what are they?

and distribution, state governments built canals, and private investors established steamship lines and railroad networks. By 1860 rails linked the industrial northeast with the agricultural south and the midwestern cities of St. Louis and Chicago, where brokers funneled wheat and beef from the plains to the more densely populated eastern states. As in other lands, railroad construction in the United States spurred industrialization by providing cheap transportation and stimulating coal, iron, and steel industries.

Industrial Capitalism

Mass Production Cotton textiles were the major factory-made products during the early phase of industrialization, but new machinery and techniques soon made it possible to extend the factory system to other industries. Furthermore, with refined manufacturing processes, factories could mass-produce standardized articles. An important contribution to the evolving factory system came from the American inventor Eli Whitney (1765–1825). Though best remembered as the inventor of the cotton gin (1793), Whitney also developed the technique of using machine tools to produce large quantities of interchangeable parts in the making of firearms. In conventional methods a skilled worker made a complete musket, forming and fitting each unique part; Whitney designed machine tools with which unskilled workers made only a particular part that fit every musket of the same model. Before long, entrepreneurs applied Whitney's method to the manufacture of everything from clocks and sewing machines to uniforms and shoes. By the middle of the nineteenth century, mass production of standardized articles was becoming the hallmark of industrial societies.

In 1913 Henry Ford improved manufacturing techniques further when he introduced the assembly line to automobile production. Instead of organizing production around a series of stations where teams of workers assembled each individual car using standardized parts, Ford designed a conveyor system that carried components past workers at the proper height and speed. Each worker performed a specialized task at a fixed point on the assembly line, which churned out a complete chassis every 93 minutes—a task that previously had taken 728 minutes. The subdivision of labor and the coordination of operations resulted in enormous productivity gains, enabling Ford Motor Company to produce half the world's automobiles in the early twentieth century. With gains in productivity, car prices plummeted, allowing millions of people to purchase automobiles. The age of the motor car had arrived.

Big Business As the factory evolved, so too did the organization of business. Industrial machinery and factories were expensive investments, and they encouraged businesses to organize on a large scale. Thus industrialization spurred the continuing development of capitalist business organization. Entrepreneurs in early modern Europe formed private businesses in the hopes of profiting from market-oriented production and trade. Some businesses, such as the English East India Company and other commercial concerns, organized joint-stock companies in the interests of spreading risk, achieving efficiency, and maximizing profits. With industrialization, manufacturers followed the lead of merchants by organizing on a large scale.

The Corporation During the 1850s and 1860s, government authorities in Britain and France laid the legal foundations for the modern corporation, which quickly became the most common form of business organization in industrial societies. By the late nineteenth century, corporations controlled most businesses requiring large investments in land, labor, or machinery, including railroads, shipping lines, and industrial concerns that produced iron, steel, and armaments. Meanwhile, an array of investment banks, brokerage firms, and other financial businesses arose to serve the needs of industrial capitalists organized in corporations.

Monopolies, Trusts, and Cartels To protect their investments, some big businesses of the late nineteenth century sought not only to outperform their competitors in the capitalist marketplace but also to eliminate competition. Business firms formed associations to restrict markets or establish monopolies in their industries. Large-scale business organizations formed trusts and cartels. The difference between the two was largely a technical one, and both shared a common goal: to control the supply of a product and hence its price in the marketplace. Some monopolists sought to control industries through vertical organization, by which they would dominate all facets of a single industry. The industrial empire of the American petroleum producer John D. Rockefeller, for example, which he ruled through Standard Oil Company and Trust, controlled almost all oil drilling, processing, refining, marketing, and distribution in the United States. Control over all aspects of the petroleum industry enabled Standard Oil to operate efficiently, cut costs, and undersell its competitors. Vertical organization of this kind offered large corporations great advantages over smaller companies.

Other monopolists tried to eliminate competition by means of horizontal organization, which involved the consolidation or cooperation of independent companies in the same business. Thus cartels sought to ensure the prosperity of their members by absorbing competitors, fixing prices, regulating production, or dividing up markets. The German firm IG Farben, the world's largest chemical concern until the middle of the twentieth century, grew out of a complex merger of chemical and pharmaceutical manufacturers that controlled as much as 90 percent of production in chemical industries. By the end of the nineteenth century, some governments outlawed these combinations and broke them up. Yet, when governments proved unwilling to confront large businesses, or when the public remained ignorant or indifferent, monopolistic practices continued well into the twentieth century.

This is a 1911 photograph of Standard Oil's refinery in Richmond, California. Established in 1870 as an Ohio corporation, Standard Oil was the largest oil refiner in the world and operated as a major company trust. It was one of the world's first and largest multinational corporations until it was broken up by the United States Supreme Court in 1911. John D. Rockefeller, the company's founder, became the richest man in history.

INDUSTRIAL SOCIETY

Industrialization brought material benefits in its train: inexpensive manufactured products, rising standards of living, and population growth. Yet industrialization also unleashed dramatic and often unsettling social change. Massive internal and external migrations took place as millions of people moved from the countryside to work in new industrial cities, and European migrants crossed the Atlantic by the tens of millions to seek opportunities in the less densely populated lands of the western hemisphere. Industrialization encouraged the emergence of new social classes—especially the middle class and the working class—and forced men, women, and children to adjust to distinctly new patterns of family and work life. Reformers sought to alleviate the social and economic problems that accompanied industrialization. The most influential critics were the socialists, who did not object to industrialization per se but worked toward the building of a more equitable and just society.

Industrial Demographics

Industrialization brought efficiencies in production that flooded markets with affordable manufactured goods. In 1851 the bounty of industry went on display in London at the Crystal Palace, a magnificent structure made of iron and glass that enclosed trees, gardens, fountains, and manufactured products from around the world. Viewers flocked to the exhibition to see industrial products such as British textiles, iron goods, and machine tools. Colt revolvers and sewing machines from the United States also attracted attention as representatives of the "American system of manufacture," which used interchangeable parts in producing large quantities of standardized goods at low prices. Observers marveled at the Crystal Palace exhibits and congratulated themselves on the achievements of industrial society.

In many ways, industrialization raised material standards of living. Industrial production led to dramatic reductions in the cost of clothing, for example, so individuals were able to add variety to their wardrobes. By the early nineteenth century, all but the desperately poor could afford several changes of clothes, and light, washable underwear came into widespread use with the availability of inexpensive manufactured cotton. Industrial factories turned out tools that facilitated agricultural work, while steam-powered locomotives delivered produce quickly and cheaply to distant markets, so industrialization contributed as well to a decline in the price of food. Consumers in early industrial Europe also filled their homes with more furniture, cabinets, porcelain, and decorative objects than any but the most wealthy of their ancestors.

Exhibitors from around the world displayed fine handicrafts and manufactured goods at the Crystal Palace exhibition of 1851 in London. Industrial products from Britain and the United States particularly attracted the attention of visitors to the enchanting and futuristic exhibition hall.

Population Growth The populations of European and Euro-American peoples rose sharply during the eighteenth and nineteenth centuries, and they reflected the rising prosperity and standards of living that came with industrialization. Between 1700 and 1800 the population of Europe increased from 105 million to 180 million, and during the nineteenth century it more than doubled to 390 million. Demographic growth in the western hemisphere—fueled by migration from Europe—was even more remarkable. Between 1700 and 1800 the population of North America and South America rose from 13 million to 24 million and then surged to 145 million by 1900. Demographic growth was most spectacular in the temperate regions of the western hemisphere. In Argentina, for example, population expanded from 300,000 in 1800 to 4.75 million in 1900—a 1,583 percent increase. In temperate North America—what is now the United States—population rose from 6 million to 76 million (1,266 percent) during the 1800s.

The rapid population growth in Europe and the Americas reflected changing patterns of fertility and mortality. In most preindustrial societies fertility was high, but famines and epidemics resulted in high mortality, especially child mortality, which prevented explosive population growth.

Medical advances over time supplied the means to control disease and reduce mortality. A case in point was smallpox, an ancient, highly contagious, and often fatal viral disease that had killed more people than any other malady in world history. The experiments of the English physician Edward Jenner dealt an effective blow against smallpox. Knowing that milkmaids often contracted cowpox, in 1797 Jenner inoculated an eight-year-old boy with cowpox and followed it six weeks later with the smallpox virus. The boy became ill but soon recovered fully, leading Jenner to deduce that cowpox conferred immunity against smallpox. Later called vaccination (from *vacca,* the Latin word for "cow"), Jenner's procedure not only created a powerful weapon in the war against smallpox but also laid the foundation for scientific immunology. Over time, physicians developed vaccines that prevented sickness and death from polio, tetanus, typhoid, whooping cough, and many other diseases that once plagued humankind.

High birthrates were common also in early industrializing societies, but death rates fell markedly because better diets and improved disease control reduced child mortality. Because more infants survived to adulthood, the population of early industrializing societies grew rapidly. By the late nineteenth century, better diets and improved sanitation led to declining levels of adult as well as child mortality, so populations of industrial societies expanded even faster. Britain and Germany, the most active sites of early industrialization, experienced especially fast population growth. Between 1800 and 1900 the British population increased from 10.5 million to 37.5 million while German numbers rose from 18 million to 43 million.

The Demographic Transition Beginning in the nineteenth century, industrializing lands experienced a social change known as the demographic transition, which refers to shifting patterns of fertility and mortality. As industrialization transformed societies, fertility began a marked decline. In the short run, mortality fell even faster than fertility, so the populations of industrial societies continued to increase. Over time, however, declining birthrates led to lower population growth and relative demographic stability. The principal reason for declining fertility in industrial lands was voluntary birth control through contraception.

Birth Control For thousands of years, people tried to find deliberate ways of preventing or reducing the probability of pregnancy resulting from sexual intercourse. Some of the methods, such as coitus interruptus, proved not to be particularly reliable, and others, such as sexual abstinence,

A French newspaper sponsored free smallpox vaccinations in 1905; the serum of a cow infected with cowpox is being injected into waiting Parisians.

turned out to be unrealistic. More ingenious methods of birth control such as vaginal depositories, cervical caps, or drinkable concoctions designed to prevent pregnancies or induce miscarriages usually carried serious health risks for women. Because none of those methods proved effective, people throughout the world had resorted to abortion or infanticide.

The first efficient means of contraception without negative side effects was the male condom. Initially made of animal intestines, it came into use in the seventeenth century. In reference to its place of origin, the Italian adventurer and womanizer Casanova called the condom an "English riding coat." The effectiveness and popularity of the condom soared in the mid-nineteenth century with the arrival of the latex condom, which served both as a contraceptive device and as a barrier against syphilis, a much-feared venereal disease. Since then, a plethora of contraceptive devices has become available.

Married couples might have chosen to have fewer offspring because raising them cost more in industrial than in agricultural societies or because declining child mortality meant that any children born were more likely to survive to adulthood. In any case, the demographic transition accompanied industrialization in western Europe, the United States, Japan, and other industrializing lands as well.

Urbanization and Migration

Industrialization and population growth strongly encouraged migration and urbanization. Within industrial societies, migrants flocked from the countryside to urban centers in search of work. Industrial Britain led the world in urbanization. In 1800 about one-fifth of the British population lived in towns and cities of 10,000 or more inhabitants. During the following century a largely rural society became predominantly urban, with three-quarters of the population working and living in cities. That pattern repeated itself in continental Europe, the United States, Japan, and the rest of the industrialized world. By 1900 at least 50 percent of the population in industrialized lands lived in towns with populations of 2,000 or more. The increasing size of cities reflected this internal migration. In 1800 there were barely twenty cities in Europe with populations as high as 100,000, and there were none in the western hemisphere. By 1900 there were more than 150 large cities in Europe and North America combined. With a population of 6.5 million, London was the largest city in the world, followed by New York with 4.2 million, Paris with 3.3 million, and Berlin with 2.7 million.

The Urban Environment With urbanization came intensified environmental pollution. Although cities had always been putrid and unsanitary places, the rapid increase in urban populations during the industrial age dramatically increased the magnitude and severity of water and air pollution. The widespread burning of fossil fuels, such as wood and coal, fouled the air with vast quantities of chemicals and particulate matter. This pollution led to typical occupational diseases among some trades. Chimney sweeps, for instance, contracted cancer of the scrotum from hydrocarbon deposits found in chimney soot. Effluents from factories and mills and an increasing amount of untreated sewage dirtied virtually every major river. No part of a city was immune to the constant stench coming from air and water pollution. Worse, tainted water supplies and unsanitary living conditions led to periodic epidemics of cholera and typhus, and dysentery and tuberculosis were also common maladies. Until the latter part of the nineteenth century, urban environments remained dangerous places in which death rates commonly exceeded birthrates, and only the constant stream of new arrivals from the country kept cities growing.

Income determined the degree of comfort and security offered by city life. The wealthy typically tried to insulate themselves the best they could from urban discomforts by retreating to their elegant homes in the newly growing suburbs. The working poor, in contrast, crowded into the centers of cities to live in shoddy housing constructed especially for them. The rapid influx of people to expanding industrial cities such as Liverpool and Manchester encouraged the quick but slipshod construction of dwellings close to the mills and factories. Industrial workers and their families occupied overcrowded tenements lacking in comfort and amenities. The cramped spaces in apartments obliged many to share the same bed, increasing the likelihood of incestuous relationships and the ease of disease transmission. The few open spaces outside the buildings were usually home to herds of pigs living in their own dung or were depositories for pools of stagnant water and human waste. Whenever possible, the inhabitants of such neighborhoods flocked to parks and public gardens.

By the later nineteenth century, though, government authorities were tending to the problems of the early industrial cities. They improved municipal water supplies, expanded sewage systems, and introduced building codes that outlawed the construction of rickety tenements to accommodate poorly paid workers. Those measures made city life safer and brought improved sanitation that helped to eliminate epidemic disease. City authorities also built parks and recreational facilities to make cities more livable.

Transcontinental Migration While workers moved from the countryside to urban centers, rapid population growth in Europe encouraged massive migration to the Americas, especially to the United States. During the nineteenth and early twentieth centuries, about fifty million Europeans migrated to the western hemisphere, and this flow of humanity accounts for much of the stunning demographic growth of the Americas. Many of the migrants intended to stay for only a few years and fully expected to return to their homelands with a modest fortune made in the Americas. Indeed, some did return to Europe: about one-third of Italian migrants to the Americas made the trip back across the Atlantic. The vast majority, however, remained in the western

sources from the past

Thomas Malthus on Population

The Reverend Thomas R. Malthus (1766–1834), English economist and pioneer of modern population study, generated controversy with his pessimistic predictions regarding the future of humanity. In his famous Essay on the Principle of Population *(1798, rev. ed. 1803), he insisted that poverty and distress are the inevitable consequences of unchecked population growth. Malthus argued that demand for food will invariably exceed the means of subsistence.*

The principal object of the present essay is to examine the effects of one great cause intimately united with the very nature of man; which, though it has been constantly and powerfully operating since the commencement of society, has been little noticed by the writers who have treated this subject. . . . The cause to which I allude is the constant tendency in all animated life to increase beyond the nourishment prepared for it.

This is incontrovertibly true. Through the animal and vegetable kingdoms Nature has scattered the seeds of life abroad with the most profuse and liberal hand; but has been comparatively sparing in the room and the nourishment necessary to rear them. The germs of existence contained in this earth, if they could freely develop themselves, would fill millions of worlds in the course of a few thousand years. Necessity, that imperious, all pervading law of nature, restrains them within the prescribed bounds. The race of plants and the race of animals shrink under this great restrictive law; and man cannot by any efforts of reason escape from it.

It may safely be pronounced, therefore, that population, when unchecked, goes on doubling itself every twenty-five years, or increases in a geometrical ratio. . . . It may fairly be pronounced, therefore, that considering the present average state of the earth, the means of subsistence, under circumstances the most favorable to human industry, could not possibly be made to increase faster than in an arithmetical ratio.

The ultimate check to population appears then to be want of food, arising necessarily from the different ratios according to which population and food increase. But this ultimate check is never the immediate check, except in the cases of actual famine.

The immediate check may be stated to consist in all those customs and diseases, which seem to be generated by a scarcity of the means of subsistence; and all those causes, independent of this scarcity, whether of a moral or physical nature, which tend prematurely to weaken and destroy the human frame.

These checks to population which are constantly operating with more or less force in every society, and keep down the number to the level of the means of subsistence, may be classed under two general heads—the preventative and positive checks.

The preventative check, as far as it is voluntary, is peculiar to man, and arises from that distinctive superiority in his reasoning faculties which enables him to calculate distant consequences. . . . These considerations are calculated to prevent, and certainly do prevent, a great number of persons in all civilised nations from pursuing the dictate of nature in an early attachment to one woman. . . . [T]he restraint from marriage which is not followed by irregular gratifications may properly be termed moral restraint.

The positive checks to population are extremely various, and include every cause, whether arising from vice or misery, which in any degree contributes to shorten the natural duration of human life. Under this head, therefore, may be enumerated all unwholesome occupations, severe labor and exposure to the seasons, extreme poverty, bad nursing of children, great towns, excesses of all kinds, the whole train of common diseases, and epidemics, wars, plague, and famine.

For Further Reflection

- Were Malthus's fears about a lack of food realized during the age of industrialization, or did aspects of the new industrial society in fact help to prevent those fears from being realized?

Source: Thomas R. Malthus. *An Essay on Population.* London: J. M. Dent, 1914, pp. 6–15.

hemisphere. They and their descendants transformed the Americas into Euro-American lands.

Most of the migrants came from the British isles in the early nineteenth century, from Germany, Ireland, and Scandinavia in the middle decades, and from eastern and southern Europe in the late nineteenth century. Migration reflected difficult political, social, and economic circumstances in Europe: British migrants often sought to escape dangerous factories and the squalor of early industrial cities, most Irish migrants departed during the potato famines of the 1840s, and millions of Jews left the Russian empire in the 1890s because of the tsar's anti-Semitic policies. Many of those migrants entered the workforce of the United States, where they settled in new industrial centers such as New York, Pittsburgh, and Cleveland. Indeed, labor from abroad made it possible for the United States to undergo rapid in-

Gustave Dore, a French book illustrator, sketched an image of Wentworth Street, Whitechapel, in London. By the middle of the nineteenth century, population shifts from rural areas to London made Whitechapel synonymous with poverty and overcrowding. Small dark avenues such as Wentworth Street contained the greatest suffering, filth, and danger.

dustrialization in the late nineteenth century.

Industry and Society

As millions of people moved from the countryside to industrial centers, society underwent a dramatic transformation. Before industrialization, the vast majority of the world's peoples worked in rural areas as cultivators or herders. Rulers, aristocrats, priests, and a few others enjoyed privileged status, and small numbers of people worked in cities as artisans, crafts workers, bureaucrats, or professionals. Many societies also made use of slave labor, occasionally on a large scale.

Industrialization radically altered traditional social structures. It encouraged the disappearance of slavery in lands undergoing industrialization, partly because the economics of industrial society did not favor slave labor. Slaves were generally poor, so they did not consume the products of industrial manufacturers in large quantities. Industrialists preferred free wage laborers who spent their money on products that kept their factories busy.

New Social Classes Industrialization also helped bring new social classes into being. Captains of industry and enterprising businesspeople became fabulously wealthy and powerful enough to overshadow the military aristocracy and other traditionally privileged classes. Less powerful than this new elite was the middle class, consisting of small business owners, factory managers, engineers, accountants, skilled employees of large corporations, and professionals such as teachers, physicians, and attorneys. Industrial production generated great wealth, and a large portion of it flowed to the middle class, which was a principal beneficiary of industrialization. Meanwhile, masses of laborers who toiled in factories and mines constituted a new working class. Less skilled than the artisans and crafts workers of earlier times, the new workers tended to machines or provided heavy labor for low wages. Concentrated in mining and industrial centers, the working class began to influence political affairs by the mid-nineteenth century.

Industrial Families The most basic unit of social organization—the family—also underwent fundamental change during the industrial age. In preindustrial societies the family was the basic productive unit. Whether engaged in agriculture, domestic manufacturing, or commerce, family members worked together and contributed to the welfare of the larger group. Industrialization challenged the family economy and reshaped family life by moving economic production outside the home and introducing a sharp distinction between work and family life. During the early years of industrialization, family economies persisted as fathers, mothers, and children pooled their wages and sometimes even worked together in factories. Over time, however, it became less common for family members to work in groups. Workers left their homes each day to labor an average of fourteen hours in factories, and family members led increasingly separate lives.

Work and Play Men gained increased stature and responsibility in the industrial age as work dominated public life. When production moved outside the home, some men became owners or managers of factories, although the majority served as wageworkers. Industrial work seemed to be far more important than the domestic chores traditionally carried out by women, or even the agricultural and light industrial work performed by women and children. Men's wages also constituted the bulk of their families' income. Upper-class and middle-class men especially enjoyed increased prestige at home, since they usually were the sole providers who made their families' comfortable existence possible.

Internalizing the work ethic of the industrial age, professional men dedicated themselves to self-improvement even in their leisure hours. They avidly read books and attended lectures on business or cultural themes. They also strove to instill their values in the industrial workforce and to impose work discipline on the laborers under their supervision. Threats of fines, beatings, and dismissal coerced workers into accepting factory rules against absenteeism, tardiness, and swearing. Through their support for churches and Sunday schools, factory owners sought to persuade workers to adopt middle-class norms of respectability and morality.

For their part, industrial workers often resisted the work discipline and moral pressures they encountered at the factory. They frequently observed "Holy Monday" and stayed home to lengthen their weekly break from work on Sundays. In their leisure time they flocked to sporting events: European soccer and American baseball both became popular sports during the industrial era. They also gambled, socialized at bars and pubs, and staged fights between dogs or roosters. The middle and upper classes tried to suppress these activities and established urban police forces to control workers' public behavior. But efforts at regulation had limited success, and workers persistently pursued their own interests.

Women at Home and Work Like men, women had worked long hours in preindustrial times. Agriculture and domestic manufacturing could easily accommodate women's dual role as mothers and workers, since the workplace

A small group of Englishmen find entertainment in a cockfight, a blood sport between two roosters. Cockfighting was a pastime already practiced in the Indus Valley by 2000 B.C.E. Banned out-right in England and Wales and in the British Overseas Territories with the Cruelty to Animals Act in 1835, it nonetheless remains a popular form of entertainment worldwide.

thinking about TRADITIONS

Family and Factory

Most families had for long centuries lived according to the rhythms of nature and agrarianism. The age of industrialization introduced a machine-driven world and radically altered family life. What transformations occurred once factories organized life and work? Did changes equally affect men, women, and children?

was either at home or nearby. Industrialization dramatically changed the terms of work for women. When industry moved production from the home to the factory, married women were unable to work unless they left their homes and children in someone else's care. By the late nineteenth century, industrial society neither expected nor wanted women to engage in labor but, instead, encouraged women to devote themselves to traditional pursuits such as the raising of children, the management of the home, and the preservation of traditional family values.

Working-Class Women Working-class women, however, typically were expected to work at least until marriage, and often even after marriage, usually to compensate for their husbands' insufficient wages. Since women commonly earned less money than men, working-class women rarely could support themselves, let alone their families. Although most women in the cities went into domestic service in middle-class households, an important minority labored in industry. Particularly during the early stages of industrialization, early manufacturers employed women in greater numbers than men. This was especially true for the flourishing low-wage textile industry, where labor-saving devices made their first appearance. Both inventors and manufacturers mistakenly believed that women (and also children) were best suited to operate the new machines because their small hands and fingers gave them superior dexterity. By the middle of the nineteenth century, women made up the majority of the British industrial workforce. Ironically, the labor-saving devices that initially increased female employment were also responsible for their elimination from the workforce. In the long term, most labor-saving devices replaced jobs women had done. The first spinning jenny, for example, replaced ten workers for every worker it employed. A similar pattern held for the power looms that replaced weavers.

Most working-class women found employment in domestic service. Industrialization increased the demand for domestic servants as the middle class grew in both numbers and wealth. One of every three European women became a domestic servant at some point in her life. Rural women sometimes had to move long distances to take positions in middle-class homes in cities, where they experienced adventure and independence from family control. Their employers replaced their parents as guardians, but high demand for servants ensured that women could switch jobs readily in search of more attractive positions. Young women servants often sent some of their earnings home, but many also saved wages for personal goals: amassing a dowry, for example, or building funds to start careers as clerks or secretaries.

Middle-Class Women Middle-class women generally did not work outside the home. For them, industrialization brought stringent confinement to the domestic sphere and pressure to conform to new models of behavior revolving around their roles as mothers and wives. In a book entitled *Woman in Her Social and Domestic Character* (1833), Mrs. John Sandford—who referred to herself by her husband's name rather than her own—described the ideal British woman. "Domestic life is the chief source of her influence," Sandford proclaimed, adding that "there is, indeed, something unfeminine in independence." (By *independence* Sandford meant taking a job or "acting the Amazon.") The model woman "knows that she is the weaker vessel" and takes pride in her ability to make the home a happy place for her husband and children.

Child Labor Industrialization profoundly influenced the childhood experience. Like their elders, children in preindustrial societies had always worked in and around the family home. Industrial work, which took children away from home and parents for long hours with few breaks, made child labor seem especially pitiable and exploitative. Early reports from British textile mills described sensational abuses by overseers who forced children to work from dawn until dark and beat them to keep them awake. Yet many families needed their children's wages to survive, so they continued to send their offspring to the factories and mines. By the 1840s the British Parliament began to pass laws regulating child labor and ultimately restricted or removed children from the industrial workforce. In the long term, industrial society was responsible for removing children from the labor process altogether, even in the home. Whereas agricultural settings continued to demand that children make a contribution to the family income, urban industrial societies redefined the role of children. Motivated in part by moral concerns and in part by the recognition that modern society demanded a highly skilled and educated labor force, governments established the legal requirement that education, and not work for monetary gain, was the principal task of childhood. In England, for instance, education for children age five to ten became mandatory by 1881.

The Socialist Challenge

Among the most vocal and influential critics of early industrial society were the socialists, who worked to alleviate the

This 1909 photograph shows a young girl being instructed by a male supervisor on how to use a spinning machine. Women, not men, made up the bulk of the early labor force in the textile industry, principally because women were presumed easier to discipline than men and because women's smaller hands allegedly made them better suited for working with machines.

social and economic problems generated by capitalism and industrialization. Socialists deplored economic inequalities, as represented by the vast difference in wealth between a captain of industry and a factory laborer, and they condemned the system that permitted the exploitation of laborers, especially women and children. Early socialists sought to expand the Enlightenment understanding of equality: they understood equality to have an economic as well as a political, legal, and social dimension, and they looked to the future establishment of a just and equitable society. Although most socialists shared this general vision, they held very different views on the best way to establish and maintain an ideal socialist society.

Utopian Socialists The term *socialism* first appeared around 1830, when it referred to the thought of social critics such as Charles Fourier (1772–1837) and Robert Owen (1771–1858). Often called utopian socialists, Fourier, Owen, and their followers worked to establish ideal communities that would point the way to an equitable society. Fourier spent most of his life as a salesman, but he loathed the competition of the market system and called for social transformations that would better serve the needs of humankind. He painstakingly planned model communities held together by love rather than coercion in which everyone performed work in accordance with personal temperament and inclination. Owen, a successful businessman, transformed a squalid Scottish cotton mill town called New Lanark into a model industrial community. At New Lanark, Owen raised wages, reduced the workday from seventeen to ten hours, built spacious housing, and opened a store that sold goods at fair prices. Despite the costs of those reforms, the mills of New Lanark generated profits. Out of the two thousand residents of the community, five hundred were young children from the poorhouses of Glasgow and Edinburgh, and Owen devoted special attention to their education. He kept young children out of the factories and sent them to a school that he opened in 1816. Owen's indictment of competitive capitalism, his stress on cooperative control of industry, and his advocacy of improved educational standards for children left a lasting imprint on the socialist tradition.

The ideas of the utopian socialists resonated widely in the nineteenth century, and their disciples established experimental communities from the United States to Romania. Despite the enthusiasm of the founders, most of the communities soon encountered economic difficulties and political problems that forced them to fold. By the mid-nineteenth century, most socialists looked not to utopian communities but to large-scale organization of working people as the best means to bring about a just and equitable society.

Marx and Engels Most prominent of the nineteenth-century socialists were the German theorists Karl Marx (1818–1883) and Friedrich Engels (1820–1895). They scorned the

Once held almost exclusively by men, clerical jobs increasingly went to women as industrial society matured. Men assumed positions as managers who supervised their female employees.

utopian socialists as unrealistic dabblers whose ideal communities had no hope of resolving the problems of the early industrial era. Marx and Engels believed that social problems of the nineteenth century were inevitable results of a capitalist economy. They held that capitalism divided people into two main classes, each with its own economic interests and social status: the capitalists, who owned industrial machinery and factories (which Marx and Engels called the means of production), and the proletariat, consisting of wageworkers who had only their labor to sell. Intense competition between capitalists trying to realize a profit resulted in ruthless exploitation of the working class. To make matters worse, according to Marx and Engels, the state and its coercive institutions, such as police forces and courts of law, were agencies of the capitalist ruling class. Their function was to maintain capitalists in power and enable them to continue their exploitation of the proletariat. Even music, art, literature, and religion served the purposes of capitalists, according to Marx and Engels, since they amused the working classes and diverted attention from their misery. Marx once referred to religion as "the opiate of the masses" because it encouraged workers to focus on a hypothetical realm of existence beyond this world rather than trying to improve their lot in society.

The *Communist Manifesto* Marx developed those views fully in a long, theoretical work called *Capital.* Together with Engels, Marx also wrote a short, spirited tract entitled *Manifesto of the Communist Party* (1848). In the *Manifesto* Marx and Engels aligned themselves with the communists, who worked toward the abolition of private property and the institution of a radically egalitarian society. The *Manifesto* asserted that all human history has been the history of struggle between social classes. It argued that the future lay with the working class because the laws of history dictated that capitalism would inexorably grind to a halt. Crises of overproduction, underconsumption, and diminishing profits would shake the foundations of the capitalist order. Meanwhile, members of the constantly growing and thoroughly exploited proletariat would come to view the forcible overthrow of the existing system as the only alternative available to them. Marx and Engels believed that a socialist revolution would result in a "dictatorship of the proletariat," which would abolish private property and destroy the capitalist order. After the revolution was secure, the state would wither away. Coercive institutions would also disappear, since there would no longer be an exploiting class. Thus socialism would lead to a fair, just, and egalitarian society infinitely more humane than the capitalist order.

The doctrines of Marx and Engels came to dominate European and international socialism, and socialist parties grew rapidly throughout the nineteenth century. Political parties, trade unions, newspapers, and educational associations all worked to advance the socialist cause. Yet socialists disagreed strongly on the best means to reform society. Revolutionary socialists such as Marx, Engels, and other communists urged workers to seize control of the state, confiscate the means of production, and distribute wealth equitably throughout society. Doubting that a revolution could

sources from the past

Marx and Engels on Bourgeoisie and Proletarians

Karl Marx and Friedrich Engels were the most scathing critics of early industrial society. Indeed, their critique extended to industrial capitalism in general. In their view, contemporary society pitted capitalists (whom they called the bourgeoisie in their Manifesto of the Communist Party*) against proletarians. Marx and Engels argued that in the short term capitalists would exploit the proletarians, but that over the longer term proletarians would become aware of their misery, rise up, and destroy capitalist society.*

The history of all hitherto existing society is the history of class struggles.

Freeman and slave, patrician and plebeian, lord and serf, guild-master and journeyman, in a word, oppressor and oppressed, stood in constant opposition to one another, carried on an uninterrupted, now hidden, now open fight, a fight that each time ended, either in a revolutionary reconstitution of society at large, or in the common ruin of the contending classes. . . .

The modern bourgeois society that has sprouted from the ruins of feudal society has not done away with class antagonisms. It has but established new classes, new conditions of oppression, new forms of struggle in place of the old ones.

Our epoch, the epoch of the bourgeoisie, possesses, however, this distinctive feature: it has simplified the class antagonisms. Society as a whole is more and more splitting up into two great hostile camps, into two great classes directly facing each other: Bourgeoisie and Proletariat. . . .

The bourgeoisie has stripped of its halo every occupation hitherto honoured and looked up to with reverent awe. It has converted the physician, the lawyer, the priest, the poet, the man of science, into its paid wage-labourers. . . .

The need for a constantly expanding market for its products chases the bourgeoisie over the whole surface of the globe. It must nestle everywhere, settle everywhere, establish connexions everywhere. . . .

The weapons with which the bourgeoisie felled feudalism to the ground are now turned against the bourgeoisie itself.

But not only has the bourgeoisie forged the weapons that bring death to itself; it has also called into existence the men who are to wield those weapons—the modern working class—the proletarians.

In proportion as the bourgeoisie, i.e., capital, is developed, in the same proportion is the proletariat, the modern working class, developed—a class of labourers, who live only so long as they find work, and who find work only so long as their labour increases capital. These labourers, who must sell themselves piecemeal, are a commodity, like every other article of commerce, and are consequently exposed to all the vicissitudes of competition, to all the fluctuations of the market. . . .

The advance of industry, whose involuntary promoter is the bourgeoisie, replaces the isolation of the labourers, due to competition, by their revolutionary combination, due to association. The development of Modern Industry, therefore, cuts from under its feet the very foundation on which the bourgeoisie produces and appropriates products. What the bourgeoisie, therefore, produces, above all, is its own grave-diggers. Its fall and the victory of the proletariat are equally inevitable.

For Further Reflection

- How did Marx and Engels's historical embrace of the concept of class struggle shape their understanding of the great forces clashing during this industrial age?

Source: Karl Marx and Friedrich Engels. *Manifesto of the Communist Party.* Trans. by Samuel Moore. London: W. Reeves, 1888.

succeed, evolutionary socialists placed their hopes in representative governments and called for the election of legislators who supported socialist reforms.

Social Reform Although socialists did not win control of any government until the Russian revolution of 1917, their critiques—along with those of conservatives and liberals—persuaded government authorities to attack the abuses of early industrialization and provide security for the working classes. Parliament prohibited underground employment for women, like the drawer Betty Harris, as well as for boys and girls under age ten and stipulated that children under age nine not work more than nine hours a day. The 1830s and 1840s saw the inception of laws that regulated women's working hours, while leaving men without protection and constraints. The intention behind this legislation was to protect women's family roles, but it also reduced women's economic opportunities on the grounds of their special frailty. Coming under pressure from the voting public and labor unions, governments increasingly accepted that the state was responsible for the social and economic welfare of its citizens. Beginning in the late nineteenth century, European countries, led by Germany, adopted social reform programs, including retirement pensions, minimum wage laws,

Contemporary photograph of Karl Marx, German political philosopher and founder of modern socialism. His most important theoretical work, *Das Kapital* (*Capital,* in the English translation), is an extensive treatise on political economy that offers a highly critical analysis of capitalism.

sickness, accident, and unemployment insurance, and the regulation of hours and conditions of work. These reforms of liberal capitalist society were a prelude to the modern welfare state.

Trade Unions Trade unions also sought to advance the quest for a just and equitable society. As governments regulated businesses and enhanced social security, trade unions struggled to eliminate abuses of early industrial society and improve workers' lives by seeking higher wages and better working conditions for their members. Through most of the nineteenth century, both employers and governments considered trade unions illegal associations whose purpose was to restrain trade. Tensions ran high when union members went on strike, especially when employers sought to keep their businesses going by hiring replacement workers. In those cases, violence frequently broke out, prompting government authorities to send in police or military forces to maintain order. Over the longer run, though, trade unions gradually improved the lives of working people and reduced the likelihood that a disgruntled proletariat would mount a revolution to overthrow industrial capitalist society. Indeed, trade unions became an integral part of industrial society because they did not seek to destroy capitalism but, rather, to make employers more responsive to their employees' needs and interests.

Global Effects of Industrialization

Early industrialization was a British, western European, and North American affair. By the late nineteenth century, Russia and Japan were beginning to industrialize (see chapter 31). Quite apart from its spread beyond western Europe, industrialization had deep global implications because industrial powers used their tools, technologies, business organization, financial influence, and transportation networks to obtain raw materials from preindustrial societies around the world. Many lands that possessed natural resources became increasingly oriented to exporting raw materials but maintained little control over them because representatives of industrial countries dominated the commercial and financial institutions associated with the trade. Some societies saw their home markets flooded with inexpensive manufactured products from industrial lands, which devastated traditional industries and damaged local economies.

The International Division of Labor Industrialization brought great economic and military strength to societies that reconfigured themselves and relied on mechanized production. Their power encouraged other societies to work toward industrialization. Before the mid-twentieth century, however, those efforts had limited results outside Europe, North America, and Japan. In India, for example, entrepreneurs established a thriving industry in the production of jute—a natural, hemplike fiber used for making carpets, upholstery, and burlap bags—as well as a small domestic steel

thinking about ENCOUNTERS

Class Struggle
The reconfiguration of an industrial economy resulted in the formation of antagonistic social and economic classes. What confrontations took place between industrial-capitalists and the working class? What institutions and ideologies arose to represent these opposing interests?

Robert Koehler's painting *The Strike* depicts a situation verging toward violence as workers mill about in a confrontation with factory owners and one angry laborer crouches to pick up a stone.

industry. But fledgling Indian industries lacked government support, and private investment capital was insufficient to bankroll industrialization on a large scale.

Nevertheless, industrialization had deep global ramifications. The industrialization process influenced the economic and social development of many societies because it promoted a new international division of labor. Industrial societies needed minerals, agricultural products, and other raw materials from sometimes distant regions of the world. Representatives of industrial societies searched the globe for raw materials to supply their factories.

Demand for Raw Materials Large-scale global trade in agricultural products was nothing new. From the sixteenth through the eighteenth century, European countries had imported sugar, spices, tobacco, tea, coffee, cotton, and other products grown mostly on plantations. In the nineteenth century, demand for these products increased sharply because of population growth. But industrial society fueled the demand for additional products as British, European, and U.S. industrialists sought the natural resources and agricultural products of Africa, the Americas, Asia, Australia, and eastern Europe. The mechanization of the textile industry, for example, produced a demand for large quantities of raw cotton, which came mostly from India, Egypt, and the southern rim of the United States. Similarly, new industrial technologies increased demand for products such as rubber, the principal ingredient of belts and tires that were essential to industrial machinery, which came from Brazil, Malaya, and the Congo River basin.

Economic Development In some lands, specialization in the production and export of primary goods paved the way for economic development and eventual industrialization. This pattern was especially noticeable in lands settled by European colonists, including Canada, Argentina, Uruguay, South Africa, Australia, and New Zealand, each of which experienced economic growth through the export of primary products and the infusion of foreign capital and labor. The same societies had an additional advantage in that they were high-wage economies. High incomes fostered economic development in two ways: they created flourishing markets, and

An Eastern Steamboat, a watercolor by Pavel Petrovich Svinin, depicted Robert Fulton's steamboat the *Paragon.* Steamboats transported passengers and cargo and helped spread industrialization around the world.

they encouraged entrepreneurs to counteract high wages and labor scarcity by inventing labor-saving technologies.

Economic Interdependence Other lands were less fortunate. The peoples of Latin America, sub-Saharan Africa, south Asia, and southeast Asia also exported primary products but attracted little foreign investment and developed little mechanical industry. Export-oriented agriculture dominated these lands, where the major cash crops were sugar, cotton, and rubber. Foreign owners controlled the plantations that produced these crops, and most of the profits went abroad, depriving domestic economies of funds that might otherwise have contributed to the building of markets and industries. The low wages of plantation workers made the situation worse by dampening demand for manufactured goods. The result was a concentration of wealth in the hands of small groups that contributed little to economic development through consumption or investment. To compound the problem, the dominant financial interests adopted free-trade policies allowing unrestricted entry of foreign manufactures, which supported continuing industrialization in foreign lands but sharply limited opportunities for indigenous industrialization.

The new geographic division of labor, in which some of the world's peoples provided raw materials while others processed and consumed them, increased the volume of world trade and led to increased transportation on both sea and land. Bigger ships, larger docks, and deeper canals facilitated trade and transport. The benefits of this new system flowed primarily to Europe, North America, and Japan. Other lands realized few benefits from the process of industrialization, but the process nevertheless increasingly linked the fortunes of all the world's peoples.

inperspective

The process of industrialization involved the harnessing of inanimate sources of energy, the replacement of handicraft production with machine-based manufacturing, and the generation of new forms of business and labor organization. Along with industrialization came demographic growth, large-scale migration, and rapid urbanization, which increased the demand for manufactured goods by the masses of working people. Societies that underwent industrialization enjoyed sharp increases in economic productivity: they produced large quantities of high-quality goods at low prices, and their increased productivity translated into higher material standards of living. Yet industrialization brought costs, in the form of unsettling social problems, as well as benefits. Family life changed dramatically in the industrial age as men, women, and children increasingly left their homes to work in factories and mines, often under appalling conditions. Socialist critics sought to bring about a more just and equitable society, and government authorities curtailed the worst abuses of the early industrial era. Governments and labor unions both worked to raise living standards and provide security for working people. Meanwhile, industrialization increasingly touched the lives of peoples around the world. Western European, North American, and Japanese societies followed Britain's lead into industrialization, while many African, Asian, and Latin American lands became dependent on the export of raw materials to industrial societies. ●

CHRONOLOGY

1730–1795	Life of Josiah Wedgwood
1733	John Kay develops the flying shuttle
1765	James Watt patents an improved steam engine
1765–1825	Life of Eli Whitney
1779	Samuel Crompton develops the spinning mule
1785	Edmund Cartwright develops the power loom
1797	Eli Whitney introduces interchangeable parts to the manufacturing process
1829	George Stephenson's locomotive, the Rocket, attains a speed of 45 kilometers (28 miles) per hour
1832	Reform Bill expands electorate to House of Commons
1833	Factory Act restricts employment of women and children in textile factories
1842	Mines Act restricts employment of women and children in mines
1848	Karl Marx and Friedrich Engels publish *Manifesto of the Communist Party*
1851	Crystal Palace exhibition in London
1856	Bessemer converter developed
1913	Henry Ford introduces the assembly line to the manufacture of automobiles

For Further Reading

Sean Patrick Adams. *Old Dominion, Industrial Commonwealth: Coal, Politics, and Economy in Antebellum America.* Baltimore, 2004. Shrewd and innovative analysis of the development of the coal industry in Virginia and Pennsylvania.

T. S. Ashton. *The Industrial Revolution, 1760–1830.* New York, 1968. A brief and readable survey of early industrialization in the British isles.

Jeffrey Auerbach. *The Great Exhibition of 1851: A Nation on Display.* New Haven, 1999. Analyzes the significance of the first world's fair and industrial exhibit held at London's Crystal Palace.

François Crouzet. *A History of the European Economy, 1000–2000.* Charlottesville, Va., 2000. A clear overview of European economic development that emphasizes European integration rather than the experiences of individual countries.

Daniel R. Headrick. *The Tentacles of Progress: Technology Transfer in the Age of Imperialism, 1850–1940.* New York, 1988. Concentrates on the political and cultural obstacles that hindered transfer of European technologies to colonial lands.

A. G. Kenwood and A. L. Lougheed. *Technological Diffusion and Industrialisation before 1914.* London, 1982. A balanced interpretation drawing on different theoretical perspectives raised by industrialization worldwide.

David S. Landes. *The Unbound Prometheus: Technological Change and Industrial Development in Western Europe from 1750 to the Present.* Cambridge, 1969. A comprehensive study of industrialization concentrating on the role of technological innovation.

———. *The Wealth and Poverty of Nations: Why Some Are So Rich and Some So Poor.* New York, 1998. A wide-ranging analysis arguing that social and cultural attitudes serve as the foundation of economic development.

Penelope Lane, Neil Raven, and K. D. M. Snell, eds. *Women, Work and Wages in England, 1600–1850.* Rochester, N.Y., 2004. Study of women's contributions to British industrialization and how it was rewarded.

Karl Marx and Friedrich Engels. *The Communist Manifesto.* Trans. by Samuel Moore. Harmondsworth, 1967. English translation of the most important tract of nineteenth-century socialism, with an excellent introduction by historian A. J. P. Taylor.

David R. Meyer. *The Roots of American Industrialization.* Baltimore, 2003. Interdisciplinary study that ties America's industrialization to increasing agricultural productivity of the antebellum period.

Joel Mokyr. *The Lever of Riches: Technological Creativity and Economic Progress.* New York, 1990. Examines European technological development in a comparative context.

Lawrence A. Peskin. *Manufacturing Revolution: The Intellectual Origins of Early American Industry.* Baltimore, 2003. The intellectual foundations of industrialization and economic growth take center stage.

Kenneth Pomeranz. *The Great Divergence: China, Europe, and the Making of the Modern World Economy.* Princeton, 2000. Argues that the fortuitous location of coal deposits and access to the resources of the Americas created a uniquely advantageous framework for English industrialization.

Mikulas Teich and Roy Porter, eds. *The Industrial Revolution in National Context: Europe and the USA.* Cambridge, 1996. A collection of essays by leading scholars who reappraise industrialization and explore the new approaches that have emerged.

E. P. Thompson. *The Making of the English Working Class.* New York, 1966. A classic work that analyzes the formation of working-class consciousness in England from the 1790s to the 1830s.

Louise A. Tilly. *Industrialization and Gender Inequality.* Washington, D.C., 1993. A brief historiographical survey of debates on gender and industrialization in England, France, Germany, the United States, Japan, and China.

The Americas in the Age of Independence

chapter 30

Chinese migrants toil at various tasks, from sifting soil and panning to carrying water, in their search for wealth in the California gold mines.

EYEWITNESS:
Fatt Hing Chin Searches for Gold from China to California

A village fish peddler, Fatt Hing Chin often roamed the coast of southern China in search of fish to sell at market. One day at the wharves, he heard a tale of mysterious but enticing mountains of gold beckoning young Chinese to cross the ocean. At nineteen years of age, Chin felt restless, and he longed for the glittering mountains. He learned that he could purchase passage on a foreign ship, but he also needed to be cautious. He did not want to alarm his parents, nor did he want to draw the attention of the authorities, who were reportedly arresting individuals seeking to leave China. Eventually, he reconciled his parents to his plans, and in 1849 he boarded a Spanish ship to sail to California and join the gold rush.

Chin felt some uncertainty once at sea. Surprised at the large number of young Chinese men crammed in with him in the ship's hold, he shared their dismay as they remained confined for weeks to the vomit-laden cargo areas of the ship. Ninety-five days and nights passed before the hills of San Francisco came into view. Upon arrival the travelers met Chinese veterans of life in the United States who explained the need to stick together if they were to survive and prosper.

Chin hired out as a gold miner and headed for the mountains of gold. After digging and sifting for two years, he had accumulated his own little pile of gold. He wrote to his brothers and cousins, urging them to join him, and thus helped fuel the large-scale overseas migration of workers. Having made his fortune, though, Chin decided to return to China. Wealthy, he traveled more comfortably this time around, with a bunk and other amenities—and temptations. He participated in the gambling that took place at sea and lost half his gold by the time the ship docked in Guangzhou. What remained still amounted to a small fortune. California gold provided him with the means to take a wife, build a house, and buy some land.

Although settled and prosperous, Chin remained restless and longed for the excitement of California. Leaving his pregnant wife, he sailed for California again after only a year in China. He returned to mining with his brother, but the gold was more difficult to find. Inspired by the luck of another migrant, Tong Ling, who managed to get one dollar for each meal he sold, Chin's cousins in San Francisco decided to open a restaurant. As one of them said, "If the foreign devils will eat his food, they will eat ours." Chin found the city much more comfortable than the mountains. "Let the others go after the gold in the hills," he said. "I'll wait for the gold to come to the city."

Fatt Hing Chin was one of the earliest Chinese migrants to settle in the Americas. His career path—from a miner in search of quick riches to an urban resident committed to a new homeland and hoping to profit from the service industry—was quite typical of Chinese migrants to the United States. Some went from mining to railroad construction or agricultural labor, but all contributed to the transformation of the Americas. Along with millions of others from Europe and Asia, Chinese migrants increased the ethnic diversity of American populations and stimulated political, social, and economic development in the western hemisphere.

During the late eighteenth and early nineteenth centuries, almost all the lands of the western hemisphere won their independence from European colonial powers. American peoples then struggled throughout the nineteenth century to build states and societies that realized their potential in an age of independence. The United States built the most powerful state in the western hemisphere and embarked on a westward push that brought most of the temperate regions of North America under U.S. control. Canada built a federal state under British Canadian leadership. The varied lands of Latin America built smaller states that often fell under the sway of local military leaders. One issue that most American peoples wrestled with, regardless of their region, was the legacy of the Enlightenment. The effort to build societies based on freedom, equality, and constitutional government was a monumental challenge only partially realized in lands characterized by enormous social, economic, and cultural diversity. Both the institution of slavery and its ultimate abolition complicated the process of building societies in the Americas, particularly in regard to defining and diversifying a new type of workforce for free and increasingly industrial economies. Asian and European migrants joined freed slaves and native-born workers in labor systems—from plantations and factories to debt peonage—that often betrayed American promises of welcome and freedom.

The age of independence for the United States, Canada, and Latin America was a contentious era characterized by continuous mass migration and explosive economic growth, occasionally followed by deep economic stagnation, and punctuated with civil war, ethnic violence, class conflict, and battles for racial and sexual equality. Independence did not solve all the political and social problems of the western hemisphere but, rather, created a new context in which American peoples struggled to build effective states, enjoy economic prosperity, and attain cultural cohesion. Those goals were elusive throughout the nineteenth century and in many ways remain so even in the present day. Nevertheless, the histories of these first lands to win independence from colonial powers inspired other peoples who later sought freedom from imperial rule, but they also served as portents of the difficulties faced by newly free states.

THE BUILDING OF AMERICAN STATES

After winning independence from Britain, the United States fashioned a government and began to expand rapidly to the west. By mid-century the new republic had absorbed almost all the temperate lands of North America. Yet the United States was an unstable society composed of varied regions with diverse economic and social structures. Differences over slavery and the rights of individual states as opposed to the federal government sparked a devastating civil war in the 1860s. That conflict resulted in the abolition of slavery and the strengthening of the federal state. The experience of Canada was very different from that of the United States. Canada gained independence from Britain without fighting a war, and even though Canada also was a land of great diversity, it avoided falling into a civil war. Although intermittently nervous about the possibility that the United States might begin to expand to the north, Canada established a relatively weak federal government, which presided over provinces that had considerable power over local affairs. Latin American lands were even more diverse than their counterparts to the north, and there was never any real possibility that they could join together in a confederation. Throughout the nineteenth century Latin America was a politically fragmented region, and many individual states faced serious problems and divisions within their own societies.

The United States: Westward Expansion and Civil War

After gaining independence the United States faced the need to construct a framework of government. During the 1780s leaders from the rebellious colonies drafted a constitution that entrusted responsibility for general issues to a federal government, reserved authority for local issues for individual states, and provided for the admission of new states and territories to the confederation. Although the Declaration of Independence had declared that "all men are created equal," most individual states limited the vote to men of property. But the Enlightenment ideal of equality encouraged political leaders to extend the franchise: by the late 1820s most property qualifications had disappeared, and by mid-century almost all adult white men were eligible to participate in the political affairs of the republic.

thinking about TRADITIONS

Vanishing Ways of Life

For millennia indigenous peoples throughout the Americas had established their own cultural and economic patterns of life. What happened to those traditions once the consolidating nation-states in North America and Latin America committed to an expansion of their territories? How did indigenous peoples resist such conquest?

Westward Expansion and Manifest Destiny

While working to settle constitutional issues, residents of the United States also began to expand rapidly to the west. After the American revolution, Britain ceded to the new republic all lands between the Appalachian Mountains and the Mississippi River, and the United States doubled in size. In 1803 Napoleon Bonaparte needed funds immediately to protect revolutionary France from its enemies, and he allowed the United States to purchase France's Louisiana Territory, which extended from the Mississippi River to the Rocky Mountains. Overnight the United States doubled in size again. Between 1804 and 1806 a geographic expedition led by Meriwether Lewis and William Clark mapped the territory and surveyed its resources. Settlers soon began to flock west in search of cheap land to cultivate. By the 1840s westward expansion was well under way, and many U.S. citizens spoke of a "manifest destiny." According to this idea, the United States was destined, even divinely ordained, to expand across the North American continent from the Atlantic seaboard to the Pacific and beyond. Manifest destiny was often invoked to justify U.S. annexations.

Conflict with Indigenous Peoples Westward expansion brought settlers and government forces into conflict with the indigenous peoples of North America, who resisted efforts to push them from their ancestral lands and hunting grounds. Native peoples forged alliances among themselves and also sought the backing of British colonial officials in Canada, but U.S. officials and military forces supported Euro-American settlers and gradually forced the continent open to white expansion. With the Indian Removal Act of 1830, the United States government determined to move all native Americans west of the Mississippi River into "Indian Territory" (Oklahoma). Among the tribes affected by this forced removal from the east were the Seminoles, some of whom managed to avoid capture and the long march to Oklahoma by resisting and retreating to Florida's swampy lowlands. The Cherokees also suffered a harrowing 800-mile migration from the eastern woodlands to Oklahoma

2. Sitting Bull, Head Chief at the Custer Massacre.

Sitting Bull (ca. 1831–1890) was a Hunkpapa Lakota Sioux holy man, who also led his people as a war chief during years of resistance to United States government policies. The Battle of the Little Bighorn, also known by the indigenous Americans as the Battle of Greasy Grass Creek, was the most famous action of the Great Sioux War of 1876–1877. It was an overwhelming victory for the Lakota and Northern Cheyenne, overseen by Sitting Bull.

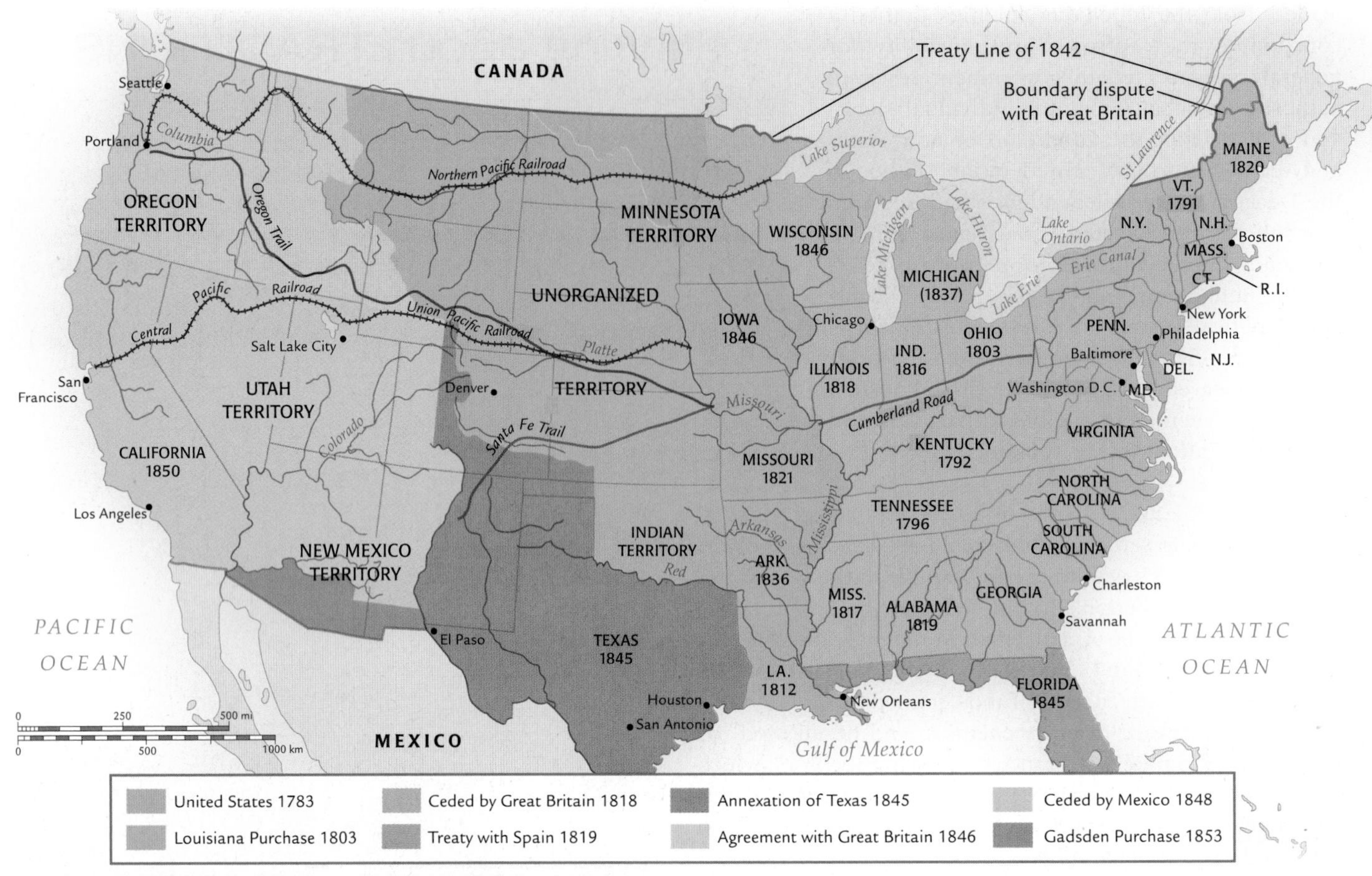

MAP 30.1
Westward expansion of the United States during the nineteenth century.
Note the large land claims ceded by Britain, France, and Mexico.
Why were there no portions of North America purchased from or ceded by native Americans?

on the Trail of Tears (1838–1839), so known because thousands died from disease, starvation, and the difficulties of relocation.

After 1840 the site of conflict between Euro-American and indigenous peoples shifted to the plains region west of the Mississippi River. Settlers and ranchers in the trans-Mississippi west encountered peoples such as the Sioux, Comanche, Pawnee, and Apache, who possessed firearms and outstanding equestrian skills. The native peoples of the plains offered effective resistance to encroachment by white settlers and at times celebrated powerful victories over U.S. forces. In 1876, for example, thousands of Lakota Sioux and their allies annihilated an army under the command of Colonel George Armstrong Custer in the battle of Little Big Horn (in southern Montana). Despite occasional successes in battle, native Americans on the plains ultimately lost the war against the forces of U.S. expansionism. The technologically sophisticated weaponry employed against native peoples included cannons and deadly, rapid-fire Gatling guns. Those weapons aided U.S. forces in breaking native resistance and opened the western plains to U.S. conquest.

One last forbidding and symbolic conflict took place in 1890 at Wounded Knee Creek in South Dakota. Frightened and threatened by the Sioux adoption of the Ghost Dance, an expression of religious beliefs that included a vision of an afterlife in which all white peoples disappeared, whites wanted these religious ceremonies suppressed. U.S. cavalry forces chased the Sioux who were fleeing to safety in the South Dakota Badlands. At Wounded Knee Creek, a Sioux man accidentally shot off a gun, and the cavalry overreacted badly, slaughtering more than two hundred men, women, and children with machine guns. Emblematic of harsh U.S. treatment of native peoples, Wounded Knee represented the place where "a people's dream died," as a later native leader put it.

The Mexican-American War Westward expansion also generated tension between the United States and Mexico, whose territories included Texas, California, and New Mexico (the territory that is now the American southwest). Texas declared independence from Mexico in 1836, largely because the many U.S. migrants who had settled there

This photograph of an 1890s Plains Indian camp in South Dakota offers an idealized, pastoral, and peaceful image of the disappearing indigenous societies in the United States.

wanted to run their own affairs. In 1845 the United States accepted Texas as a new state—against vigorous Mexican protest—and moved to consolidate its hold on the territory. Those moves led to conflicts that rapidly escalated into the Mexican-American War (1846–1848), or, as it is known in Mexico, *la intervención norteamericano* (the North American Intervention) or *la guerra del 47* (the War of 1847). U.S. forces instigated the war and then inflicted a punishing defeat on the Mexican army. By the Treaty of Guadalupe Hidalgo (1848), the United States took possession of approximately one-half of Mexico's territory, paying a mere fifteen million dollars in exchange for Texas north of the Rio Grande, California, and New Mexico. Thousands of U.S. and Mexican soldiers died in the conflict, and thousands of Mexican families found themselves stranded in the territories annexed by the United States. Some returned to Mexico, but most stayed put and attained U.S. citizenship. This conflict nonetheless fueled Mexican nationalism, as well as disdain for the United States.

While satisfying desires for the United States to realize its manifest destiny, westward expansion also created problems within the republic by aggravating tensions between regions. The most serious and divisive issue had to do with slavery, which had vexed American politics since independence. The Enlightenment ideal of equality clearly suggested that the appropriate policy was to abolish slavery, but the leaders of the American revolution and framers of the Constitution recognized the sanctity of private property, including slaves. U.S. independence initially promoted a surge of antislavery sentiment, as states from Delaware north abolished slavery within their jurisdictions. Abolition did not bring full equality for free blacks in northern states, but it hardened divisions between slave and free states. Westward expansion aggravated tensions further by raising the question of whether settlers could extend slavery to newly acquired territories.

Sectional Conflict Opponents of slavery had dreamed that the institution would die a natural death with the decline of tobacco cultivation. Their hopes faded, however, with the invigoration of the slave system by the rise of cotton as a cash crop in the early nineteenth century, followed by westward expansion. The U.S. slave population rose sharply, from five hundred thousand in 1770 to almost two million in 1820. As the numbers of slaves grew, antislavery forces fought to limit the spread of slavery to new territories. Beginning with the Missouri Compromise of 1820, a series of political compacts attempted to maintain a balance between slave and free states as the republic admitted new states carved out of western territories. Those compromises ultimately proved too brittle to endure, as proslavery and antislavery forces became more strident. Abraham Lincoln (1809–1865) predicted in 1858 that "a house divided against itself cannot stand," and he made the connection to slavery explicit: "I believe this government cannot endure permanently half *slave* and half *free*. . . . It will become *all* one thing, or *all* the other."

The election of Abraham Lincoln to the presidency in 1860 was the spark that ignited war between the states (1861–1865). Lincoln was an explicitly sectional candidate, was convinced that slavery was immoral, and was committed to free soil—territories without slavery. Although slavery stood at the center of the conflict, President Lincoln had insisted from the beginning of the war that his primary aim was the restoration of the Union, not the abolition of slavery. He was therefore reluctant to adopt an abolitionist policy. There were reasons for his hesitancy. Not only had Lincoln been elected on a platform of noninterference with slavery within the states, but he also doubted the constitutionality of any federal action. He was also concerned about the difficulties of assimilating four million freed slaves into the nation's social and political fabric. Most important, Lincoln feared that an abolitionist program would have the effect of inducing border states to join the Confederacy and upsetting the loyalty of Delaware, Maryland, Kentucky, and Missouri—the four slave states that remained in the Union. The Civil War also revolved around issues central to the United States as a society: the nature of the Union, states' rights as opposed to the federal government's authority, and the imperatives of a budding industrial-capitalist system against those of an export-oriented plantation economy.

This early-twentieth-century postcard offered an idealized depiction of Abraham Lincoln delivering his Gettysburg Address, which commemorated the Union soldiers who fell in that crucial battle.

The U.S. Civil War Eleven southern states withdrew from the Union in 1860 and 1861, affirming their right to dissolve the Union and their support for states' rights. Slavery and the cultivation of cotton as a cash crop had isolated the southern states from economic developments in the rest of the United States. By the mid-nineteenth century, the southern states were the world's major source of cotton, and the bulk of the crop went to the British isles. Manufactured goods consumed in the southern states came mostly from Britain, and almost all food came from the region's farms. Southerners considered themselves self-sufficient and believed that they did not need the rest of the United States. Northerners saw the situation differently. They viewed secession as illegal insurrection and an act of betrayal. They fought not only against slavery but also against the concept of a state subject to blackmail by its constituent parts. They also fought for a way of life—their emerging industrial society—and an expansive western agricultural system based on free labor.

The first two years of the war ended in stalemate. The war changed character, however, when Abraham Lincoln signed the Emancipation Proclamation, making the abolition of slavery an explicit goal of the war. As the war progressed, Lincoln increasingly viewed the destruction of slavery as the only way to preserve the Union. Five days after the Union victory at Antietam, President Lincoln issued a preliminary Emancipation

The grotesquely twisted bodies of dead northern soldiers lay near a fence outside Antietam, Maryland, in 1862. The Civil War was the most costly in U.S. history in terms of lives lost.

Proclamation. The final version, issued 1 January 1863, freed the slaves in those states that had rebelled. Ironically, in the states that remained loyal to the Union, slavery was protected by the U.S. Constitution. A looming problem was that the slaves freed by emancipation would have risked reenslavement after the war unless their liberty was quickly reaffirmed. The solution to this problem, one that Lincoln urged, was the Thirteenth Amendment to the Constitution, ratified in 1865, which completely abolished slavery throughout the United States.

Ultimately, the northern states prevailed in the Civil War, after the bloody battle at Gettysburg in July 1863 had turned the military tide against southern forces. The northern states brought considerable resources to the war effort—some 90 percent of the country's industrial capacity and approximately two-thirds of its railroad lines—but still they fought four bitter years against a formidable enemy. The victory of the northern states ended slavery in the United States. Moreover, it ensured that the United States would remain politically united, and it enhanced the authority of the federal government in the republic. Thus, as European lands were building powerful states on the foundations of revolutionary ideals, liberalism, and nationalism, the United States also forged a strong central government to supervise westward expansion and deal with the political and social issues that divided the nation. That strength came at a horrible cost for both sides, however, especially in terms of the enormous human casualties. About 1,556,000 soldiers served in the Union armies and suffered a total of over 634,000 casualties, 360,000 of whom died. Approximately 800,000 men served in the Confederate forces, which sustained approximately 483,000 casualties, including 258,000 dead.

The Canadian Dominion: Independence without War

Autonomy and Division Canada did not fight a war for independence, and in spite of deep regional divisions, it did not experience bloody internal conflict. Instead, Canadian independence came gradually as Canadians and the British government agreed on general principles of autonomy. The distinctiveness of the two dominant ethnic groups, the British Canadians and the French Canadians, ensured that the process of building an independent society would not be smooth, but intermittent fears of U.S. expansion and concerns about the possibility of an invasion from the south helped submerge ethnic differences. By the late nineteenth century, Canada was a land in control of its own destiny, despite continuing ties to Britain and the looming presence of the United States to the south.

Originally colonized by trappers and settlers from both Britain and France, the colony of New France passed into the British empire after the British victory in the Seven Years' War (1756–1763). Until the late eighteenth century, however, French Canadians outnumbered British Canadians, so imperial officials made large concessions to their subjects of French descent to forestall unnecessary strife. Officials recognized the Roman Catholic church and permitted continued observance of French civil law in Quebec and other areas of French Canadian settlement, which they governed through appointed councils staffed by local elites. British Canadians, in contrast, were Protestants who lived mostly in Ontario, followed British law, and governed themselves through elected representatives. After 1781 large numbers of British loyalists fled the newly formed United States to

MAP 30.2

The Dominion of Canada in the nineteenth century.

Note the provinces that make up the modern state of Canada and the dates in which they were incorporated into the Dominion.

At what date were eastern and western Canada geographically united?

the south and sought refuge in Canada, thus greatly enlarging the size of the English-speaking community there.

The War of 1812 Ethnic divisions and political differences could easily have splintered Canada, but the War of 1812 stimulated a sense of unity against an external threat. The United States declared war on Britain in retaliation for encroachments on U.S. rights during the Napoleonic wars, and the British colony of Canada formed one of the front lines of the conflict. U.S. military leaders assumed that they could easily invade and conquer Canada to pressure their foes. Despite the greater resources of the United States, however, Canadian forces repelled U.S. incursions. Their victories promoted a sense of Canadian pride, and anti-U.S. sentiments became a means for covering over differences among French Canadians and British Canadians.

After the War of 1812, Canada experienced an era of rapid growth. Expanded business opportunities drew English-speaking migrants, who swelled the population. That influx threatened the identity of Quebec, and discontent in Canada reached a critical point in the 1830s. The British imperial governors of Canada did not want a repeat of the American revolution, so between 1840 and 1867 they defused tensions by expanding home rule in Canada and permitting the provinces to govern their own internal affairs. Inspiring this imperial move toward Canadian autonomy was the Durham Report, issued in 1839 by John George Lambton (1782–1840), the first earl of Durham and the recent governor-general and lord high commissioner of Canada. He advocated a good deal of self-government for a united Canada, and his report became a model for British imperial policy and colonial self-rule in other states, including Australia and New Zealand.

Dominion Westward expansion of the United States and the U.S. Civil War pushed Canada toward political autonomy. Fear of U.S. expansion helped stifle internal conflicts among Canadians and prompted Britain to grant independence to Canada. The British North America Act of 1867 joined Quebec, Ontario, Nova Scotia, and New Brunswick and recognized them as the Dominion of Canada. Other provinces joined the Dominion later. Each province had its own seat of government, provincial legislature, and lieutenant governor representing the British crown. The act created a federal government headed by a governor-general who acted as the British representative. An elected House of Commons and appointed Senate rounded out the framework of governance. Provincial legislatures reserved certain political matters for themselves, whereas others fell within the purview of the federal government. Without waging war, the Dominion of Canada had won control over all Canadian internal affairs, and Britain retained jurisdiction over foreign affairs until 1931.

John A. Macdonald (1815–1891) became the first prime minister of Canada, and he moved to incorporate all of British North America into the Dominion. He negotiated the purchase of the huge Northwest Territories from the Hudson's Bay Company in 1869, and he persuaded Manitoba, British Columbia, and Prince Edward Island to join the Dominion. Macdonald believed, however, that Canada's Dominion would remain symbolic—a mere "geographic expression," as he put it—until the government took concrete action to make Canadian unity and independence a reality. To strengthen the union, he oversaw construction of a transcontinental railroad, completed in 1885. The railroad facilitated transportation and communications throughout Canada and eventually helped bring new provinces into the Dominion: Alberta and Saskatchewan in 1905 and Newfoundland in 1949. Internal conflicts never disappeared, but the Dominion provided a foundation for Canadian independence and unity. Although maintaining ties to Britain and struggling to forge an identity distinct from that of its powerful neighbor to the south, Canada developed as a culturally diverse yet politically unified society.

Latin America: Fragmentation and Political Experimentation

Political unity was short-lived in Latin America. Simón Bolívar (1783–1830), hailed as South America's liberator, worked for the establishment of a large confederation that would provide Latin America with the political, military, and economic strength to resist encroachment by foreign powers. The wars of independence that he led encouraged a sense of solidarity in Latin America. But Bolívar once admitted that "I fear peace more than war," and after the defeat of the common colonial enemy, solidarity was impossible to sustain. Bolívar's Gran Colombia broke into its three constituent parts—Venezuela, Colombia, and Ecuador—and the rest of Latin America fragmented into numerous independent states.

Creole Elites and Political Instability Following the example of the United States, creole elites usually established republics with written constitutions for the newly independent states of Latin America. Yet constitutions were much more difficult to frame in Latin America than in the United States. Before gaining independence, Latin American leaders had less experience with self-government because Spanish and Portuguese colonial regimes were far more autocratic than was the British imperial government in North America. Creole elites responded enthusiastically to Enlightenment values and republican ideals, but they had little experience putting their principles into practice. As a result, several Latin American lands lurched from one constitution to another as leaders struggled to create a machinery of government that would lead to political and social stability.

Creole elites also dominated the newly independent states and effectively prevented mass participation in public affairs. Less than 5 percent of the male population was active in Latin American politics in the nineteenth century, and millions of indigenous peoples lived entirely outside the political system. Without institutionalized means of expressing discontent or opposition, those disillusioned with the system had little choice beyond rebellion. Aggravating political instability were differences among elites. Whether they were urban merchants or rural landowners, Latin American elites divided into different camps as liberals or conservatives, centralists or federalists, secularists or Roman Catholics.

Conflicts with Indigenous Peoples One thing elites agreed on was the policy of claiming American land for agriculture and ranching. That meant pushing aside indigenous peoples and establishing Euro-American hegemony in Latin America. Conflict was most intense in Argentina and Chile, where cultivators and ranchers longed to take over the South American plains. During the mid-nineteenth century, as the United States was crushing native resistance to western expansion in North America, Argentine and Chilean forces brought modern weapons to bear in their campaign to conquer the indigenous peoples of South America. By the 1870s, they had pacified the most productive lands and forced indigenous peoples either to assimilate to Euro-American society or to retreat to marginal lands that were unattractive to cultivators and ranchers.

Caudillos Although creole elites agreed on the policy of conquering native peoples, division and discord in the

PART 6

MAP 30.3

Latin America in the nineteenth century. Date is year of independence.

Note the many states that emerged from the independence movements early in the century.

Why was it difficult for large, federated republics, such as the Republic of Colombia, founded by Simón Bolívar, to survive?

newly independent states helped caudillos, or regional military leaders, come to power in much of Latin America. The wars of independence had lasted well over a decade, and they provided Latin America with military rather than civilian heroes. After independence, military leaders took to the political stage, appealing to populist sentiments and exploiting the discontent of the masses. One of the most notable caudillos was Juan Manuel de Rosas, who from 1829 to 1852 ruled an Argentina badly divided between the cattle-herding and gaucho society of the pampas (the interior grasslands) and the urban elite of Buenos Aires. Rosas himself emerged from the world of cattle ranching, and he used his skills to subdue other caudillos and establish control in Buenos Aires. Rosas called for regional autonomy in an attempt to reconcile competing interests, but he worked to centralize the government he usurped. He quelled rebellions, but he did so in bloody fashion. Critics often likened Rosas to historically infamous figures, calling him "the Machiavelli of the pampas" and "the Argentine Nero," and they accused him of launching a reign of terror to stifle opposition. One writer exiled by the caudillo compiled a chart that counted the number of Rosas's victims and the violent ways they met their ends; of the 22,404 total victims killed, most met their end in armed clashes but others died by poisoning, hanging, and assassination.

Rosas did what caudillos did best: he restored order. In doing so, however, he made terror a tool of the government, and he ruled as a despot through his own personal army. Rosas also, however, embodied the winning personality traits most exemplified by caudillos. He attained great popularity through his identification with the people and with gauchos, and he demonstrated his physical strength and machismo. Although caudillo rule often limited freedom and undermined republican ideals, it sometimes also gave rise to an opposition that aimed to overthrow the caudillos and work for liberal reforms that would promote democratic forms of government.

Mexico: War and Reform Independent Mexico experienced a succession of governments, from monarchy to republic to caudillo rule, but it also generated a liberal reform movement. The Mexican-American War caused political turmoil in Mexico and helped the caudillo General Antonio López de Santa Anna (1797–1876) perpetuate his intermittent rule. After the defeat and disillusion of the war, however, a liberal reform movement attempted to reshape Mexican society. Led by President Benito Juárez (1806–1872), a Mexican of indigenous ancestry, La Reforma of the 1850s aimed to limit the power of the military and the Roman Catholic church in Mexican society. Juárez and his followers called for liberal reform, designed in part to create a rural middle class. The Constitution of 1857 set forth the ideals of La Reforma. It curtailed the prerogatives of priests and military elites, and it guaranteed universal male suffrage and other civil liberties, such as freedom of speech. Land reform efforts centered on dismantling corporate properties, which

Edouard Manet's painting depicts the execution by firing squad of Emperor Maximilian, whose death in 1867 ended attempted French rule in Mexico.

had the effect of parceling out communal Indian lands and villages as private property, much of which ended up in the hands of large landowners, not indigenous peoples.

Mexico: Revolution La Reforma challenged some of the fundamental conservatism of Mexican elites, who led spirited opposition to political, social, and economic reform. Liberals and conservatives in Mexico stayed bitterly divided, and conservatives forced the Juárez government out of Mexico City until 1861, when Juárez struggled to establish order in his country. To lessen Mexico's financial woes, Juárez chose to suspend loan payments to foreign powers, and that led to French, British, and Spanish intervention as Europeans sought to recover and protect their investments in Mexico. France's Napoleon III proved especially persistent and intrusive. His attempts to end Mexican disorder by re-creating a monarchy met unexpected resistance in Puebla, where Mexican forces beat back the French invaders on 5 May 1862, a date thereafter celebrated as Cinco de Mayo. Napoleon III then sent tens of thousands of troops and proclaimed a Mexican empire, although he had to withdraw those forces in 1867. A Mexican firing squad killed the man he had appointed emperor, the Austrian archduke Maximilian (1832–1867). Juárez managed to restore a semblance of liberal government, but Mexico remained beset by political divisions.

By the early twentieth century, Mexico was a divided land moving toward civil war. The Mexican revolution (1910–1920), a bitter and bloody conflict, broke out when middle-class Mexicans joined with peasants and workers to overthrow the powerful dictator Porfirio Díaz (1830–1915). The revolt in Mexico, which was the first major, violent effort in Latin America to attempt to topple the grossly unequal system of landed estates—whereby fully 95 percent of all peasants remained landless—turned increasingly radical as those denied land and representation armed themselves and engaged in guerrilla warfare against government forces. The lower classes took up weapons and followed the revolutionary leaders Emiliano Zapata (1879–1919) and Francisco (Pancho) Villa (1878–1923), charismatic agrarian rebels who organized massive armies fighting for *tierra y libertad* (land and liberty), which were Zapata's stated revolutionary goals. Zapata, the son of a mestizo peasant, and Villa, the son of a field worker, embodied the ideals and aspirations of the indigenous Mexican masses and enjoyed tremendous popular support. They discredited timid governmental efforts at reform and challenged governmental political control; Zapata confiscated hacienda lands and began distributing the lands to the peasants, while Villa attacked and killed U.S. citizens in retaliation for U.S. support of Mexican government officials—and succeeded in eluding capture by either U.S. or Mexican forces.

Despite the power and popularity enjoyed by Zapata and Villa, they were unable to capture Mexico's major cities, and they did not command the resources and wealth to which government forces had access. The Mexican revolution came to an end soon after government forces ambushed and killed Zapata in 1919. Villa was killed a few years later, assassinated in 1923 while driving in the town of Hidalgo de Parral, his car and body riddled with bullets. Government forces regained control over Mexico, a land battered and devastated by long years of war and by the death of as many as two million Mexicans. Although radicals such as Zapata and Villa were ultimately defeated, the Mexican Constitution of 1917 had already addressed some of the concerns of the revolutionaries by providing for land redistribution, universal suffrage, state-supported education, minimum wages and maximum hours for workers, and restrictions on foreign ownership of Mexican property and mineral resources. Although these constitutional provisions were not soon implemented, they provided important guarantees for the future.

Zapata, hailing from the southern state of Morelos, was the very picture of a revolutionary leader, heavily armed and sporting his dashing, trademark moustache.

In the form of division, rebellion, caudillo rule, and civil war, instability and conflict plagued Latin America throughout the nineteenth century. Many Latin American peoples lacked education, profitable employment, and political representation. Simón Bolívar himself once said that "independence is the only blessing we have gained at the expense of all the rest."

AMERICAN ECONOMIC DEVELOPMENT

During the nineteenth and early twentieth centuries, two principal influences—mass migration and British investment—shaped economic development throughout the Americas. But American states reacted in different ways to migration and foreign investment. The United States and

sources from the past

Ponciano Arriaga Calls for Land Reform

During the era of La Reforma in Mexico, the leftist liberal Ponciano Arriaga voiced demands for land reform on behalf of the Mexican masses, reflecting the broader problem of land control throughout Latin American societies. At the Constitutional Convention of 1856–1857, Arriaga spoke about the troubles resulting from an aristocratic monopoly on land and argued passionately for reform.

One of the most deeply rooted evils of our country—an evil that merits the close attention of legislators when they frame our fundamental law—is the monstrous division of landed property.

While a few individuals possess immense areas of uncultivated land that could support millions of people, the great majority of Mexicans languish in a terrible poverty and are denied property, homes, and work.

Such a people cannot be free, democratic, much less happy, no matter how many constitutions and laws proclaim abstract rights and beautiful but impracticable theories—impracticable by reason of an absurd economic system.

There are Mexican landowners who occupy (if one can give that name to a purely imaginary act) an extent of land greater than the area of some of our sovereign states, greater even than that of one or several European states.

In this vast area, much of which lies idle, deserted, abandoned, awaiting the arms and labor of men, live four or five million Mexicans who know no other industry than agriculture, yet are without land or the means to work it, and who cannot emigrate in the hope of bettering their fortunes. They must either vegetate in idleness, turn to banditry, or accept the yoke of a landed monopolist who subjects them to intolerable conditions of life. . . .

How can a hungry, naked, miserable people practice popular government? How can we proclaim the equal rights of men and leave the majority of the nation in conditions worse than those of helots or pariahs? How can we condemn slavery in words, while the lot of most of our fellow citizens is more grievous than that of the black slaves of Cuba or the United States? When will we begin to concern ourselves with the fate of the proletarians, the men we call Indians, the laborers and peons of the countryside, who drag the heavy chains of serfdom established not by Spanish laws—which were so often flouted and infringed—but by the arbitrary mandarins of the colonial regime? Would it not be more logical and honest to deny our four million poor Mexicans all share in political life and public offices, all electoral rights, and declare them to be things, not persons, establishing a system of government in which an aristocracy of wealth, or at most of talent, would form the basis of our institutions?

For one of two things is inevitable: either our political system will continue to be dominated for a long time to come by a *de facto* aristocracy—no matter what our fundamental laws may say—and the lords of the land, the privileged caste that monopolizes the soil and profits by the sweat of its serfs, will wield all power and influence in our civil and political life; or we will achieve a reform, shatter the trammels and bonds of feudal servitude, bring down all monopolies and despotisms, end all abuses, and allow the fruitful element of democratic equality, the powerful element of democratic sovereignty—to which alone authority rightfully belongs—to penetrate the heart and veins of our political institutions. The nation wills it, the people demand it; the struggle has begun, and sooner or later that just authority will recover its sway. The great word "reform" has been pronounced, and it is vain to erect dykes to contain those torrents of truth and light.

For Further Reflection

- In studies of life not just in Mexico but throughout the Americas, how can patterns of land ownership illuminate societies' economic and political power structures?

Source: "A Mexican Radical: Ponciano Arriaga." In Benjamin Keen, ed., *Latin American Civilization History and Society, 1492 to the Present,* 6th ed., revised and updated. New York: Westview Press, 1996, pp. 273–74.

Canada absorbed waves of migrants, exploited British capital, built industrial societies, and established economic independence. The fragmented states of Latin America were unable to follow suit, however, as they struggled with the legacies of colonialism, slavery, and economic dependence on single export crops. Migrants to Latin America mostly worked not in factories but on plantations. The importation of migrant laborers for agricultural work in South America and the Caribbean indicated some of the major alterations in labor systems taking place throughout the Americas in the wake of slavery's abolition. Freedom for slaves did not necessarily bring about freer forms of labor, because many migrants arrived under contract or as indentured laborers. Although some freed slaves became small landowning farmers, more found themselves still subject to landowning elite control in the form of debt peonage or sharecropping. Life and labor in the Americas, whether for

Italian migrants construct a railway in New York. Italians were just one of many European groups coming to the Americas in the nineteenth century.

freedmen and freedwomen, migrants, or industrial workers, often proved arduous and at times heartbreaking, even as those American workers contributed to the economic development of the region.

Migration to the Americas

Underpinning the economic development of the Americas was large-scale migration of European and Asian peoples to the United States, Canada, and Latin America. Internal migration within the Americas also contributed to a new economic landscape, particularly as Latin Americans journeyed to the United States in search of work and financial well-being. Gold discoveries drew prospectors hoping to make a quick fortune: the California gold rush of 1849 drew the largest crowd, but Canadian gold also lured migrants by the tens of thousands. Outnumbering gold prospectors were millions of European and Asian migrants who made their way to the factories, railroad construction sites, and plantations of the Americas. Following them were others who offered the support services that made life for migrant workers more comfortable and at the same time transformed the ethnic and cultural landscape of the Americas. Fatt Hing Chin's restaurant in San Francisco's Chinatown fed Chinese migrants, but it also helped introduce Chinese cuisine to American society. Migrants from other parts of the world found similar comforts as their foods, religious beliefs, and cultural traditions migrated with them to the Americas.

Industrial Migrants After the mid-nineteenth century, European migrants flocked to North America, where they filled the factories of the growing industrial economy of the United States. Their lack of skills made them attractive to industrialists seeking workers to operate machinery or perform heavy labor at low wages. By keeping labor costs down, migrants helped increase the profitability and fuel the expansion of U.S. industry.

In the 1850s European migrants to the United States numbered 2.3 million—almost as many as had crossed the Atlantic during the half century from 1800 to 1850—and the volume of migration surged until the early twentieth century. Increasing rents and indebtedness drove cultivators from Ireland, Scotland, Germany, and Scandinavia to seek opportunities in North America. Some of them moved to the Ohio and Mississippi River valleys in search of cheap and abundant land, but many stayed in the eastern cities and contributed to the early industrialization of the United

thinking about ENCOUNTERS

Mass Migration
The nineteenth century witnessed a mass migration of Asians and Europeans to the Americas. How did those migrants contribute to a redefinition of work and culture in the Americas? How in turn did their experience in the Americas—North, Central, and South—change migrants and their cultural practices?

States. By the late nineteenth century, most European migrants were coming from southern and eastern Europe. Poles, Russian Jews, Slavs, Italians, Greeks, and Portuguese were most prominent among the later migrants, and they settled largely in the industrial cities of the eastern states. They dominated the textile industries of the northeast, and without their labor, the remarkable industrial expansion that the United States experienced in the late nineteenth century would have been inconceivable.

Asian migrants further swelled the U.S. labor force and contributed to the construction of an American transportation infrastructure. Chinese migration grew rapidly after the 1840s, when British gunboats opened China to foreign influences. Officials of the Qing government permitted foreigners to seek indentured laborers in China and approved their migration to distant lands. Between 1852 and 1875 some two hundred thousand Chinese migrated to California. Some, like Fatt Hing Chin, negotiated their own passage and sought to make their fortune in the gold rush, but most traveled on indentured labor contracts that required them to cultivate crops or work on the Central Pacific Railroad. An additional five thousand Chinese entered Canada to search for gold in British Columbia or work on the Canadian Pacific Railroad.

Plantation Migrants Whereas migrants to the United States contributed to the development of an industrial society, those who went to Latin American lands mostly worked on agricultural plantations. Some Europeans figured among these migrants. About four million Italians sought opportunities in Argentina in the 1880s and 1890s, for example, and the Brazilian government paid Italian migrants to cross the Atlantic and work for coffee growers, who experienced a severe labor shortage after the abolition of slavery there (1888). Many Italian workers settled permanently in Latin America, especially Argentina, but some, popularly known as *golondrinas* ("swallows") because of their regular migrations, traveled back and forth annually between Europe and South America to take advantage of different growing seasons in the northern and southern hemispheres.

Other migrants who worked on plantations in the western hemisphere came from Asian lands. More than fifteen thousand indentured laborers from China worked in the sugarcane fields of Cuba during the nineteenth century, and Indian migrants traveled to Jamaica, Trinidad, Tobago, and Guyana. Laborers from both China and Japan migrated to Peru, where they worked on cotton plantations in coastal regions, mined guano deposits for fertilizer, and built railroad lines. After the middle of the nineteenth century, expanding U.S. influence in the Pacific islands also led to Chinese, Japanese, Filipino, and Korean migrations to Hawai`i, where planters sought indentured laborers to tend sugarcane. About twenty-five thousand Chinese went to Hawai`i during the 1850s and 1860s, and later 180,000 Japanese also made their way to island plantations.

Economic Expansion in the United States

British Capital British investment capital in the United States proved crucial to the early stages of industrial development by helping businesspeople establish a textile industry. In the late nineteenth century, it also spurred a vast expansion of U.S. industry by funding entrepreneurs, who opened coal and iron ore mines, built iron and steel factories, and constructed railroad lines. The flow of investment monies was a consequence of Britain's own industrialization, which generated enormous wealth and created a need for investors to find profitable outlets for their funds. Stable, white-governed states and colonies were especially fertile grounds for British investment, which often provided the impetus for industrial expansion and economic independence in those regions. In the case of the United States, it helped create a rival industrial power that would eventually outperform Britain's economy.

After the 1860s, U.S. businesses made effective use of foreign investment capital as the reunited land recovered from the Civil War. The war determined that the United States would depend on wage labor rather than slavery, and entrepreneurs set about tapping American resources and building a continental economy.

Railroads Perhaps the most important economic development of the later nineteenth century was the construction of railroad lines that linked all U.S. regions and helped create an integrated national economy. Because of its enormous size and environmental diversity, the United States offered an abundance of natural resources for industrial exploitation. But vast distances made it difficult to maintain close economic ties between regions until a boom in railroad construction created a dense transportation, communication, and distribution network. Before the Civil War the United States had about 50,000 kilometers (31,000 miles) of railroad lines, most of them short routes east of the Mississippi River. By 1900 there were more than 320,000 kilometers (200,000 miles) of track, and the U.S. rail network stretched from coast to coast. Most prominent of the new lines was a transcontinental route, completed in 1869, running from Omaha, where connections provided access to eastern states, to San Francisco.

Railroads decisively influenced U.S. economic development. They provided cheap transportation for agricultural commodities, manufactured goods, and individual travelers as well. Railroads hauled grain, beef, and hogs from the plains states, cotton and tobacco from the south, lumber from the northwest, iron and steel from the mills of Pittsburgh, and finished products from the eastern industrial cities. Quite apart from the transportation services they provided, railroads spurred the development of other industries: they required huge amounts of coal, wood, glass, and rubber, and by the 1880s some 75 percent of U.S. steel went to the railroad industry. Railroads also required the development of new managerial skills to operate large, complicated businesses. In 1850 few if any U.S. businesses had more than a thousand employees. By the early 1880s, however, the Pennsylvania Railroad alone employed almost fifty thousand people, and the size of the business called for organization and coordination on an unprecedented scale. Railroads were the testing grounds where managers developed the techniques they needed to run big businesses.

Space and Time Railroads led to drastic changes in the ways people organized and controlled space and time. Railroads altered the landscape in often extreme fashion, and the transformations consequent to the building of railroads—in land control and development, the transportation of migrants and settlers to the west, and the exploitation of natural resources—only furthered the environmental impact of the railroad. The westward expansion driven by the railroad led to broadscale land clearing and the extension of farming and mining lands, and brought about both human suffering for indigenous peoples and environmental damage through soil erosion and pollution. Irrigation and the politics of water also sparked trouble, especially as settlers and farmers entered the drier plains and even desert regions. The dark smoke emanating from railroad engines undoubtedly represented progress to industrial promoters, but it also symbolized an ever-widening intrusion into the natural environment.

Railroads even shaped the sense of time in the United States. Until rapid and regular rail transportation became available, communities set their clocks by the sun. As a result, New York time was eleven minutes and forty-five seconds behind Boston time. When the clock showed 12 noon in Chicago, it was 11:50 A.M. in St. Louis and 12:18 P.M. in Detroit. Those differences in local sun times created scheduling nightmares for railroad managers, who by the 1880s had to keep track of more than fifty time standards. Observance of local time also created hazards because a small miscalculation in scheduling could bring two massive trains

AMERICAN EXPRESS TRAIN.

In this lithograph of Frances F. Palmer's well-known painting *American Express Train* (ca. 1864), the railroad demonstrates its domination of the natural landscape and its role as the harbinger of change and industry.

hurtling unexpectedly toward each other on the same track. To simplify matters, in 1883 railroad companies divided the North American continent into four zones in which all railroad clocks read precisely the same time. The general public quickly adopted "railroad time" in place of local sun time, and in 1918 the U.S. government legally established the four time zones as the nation's official framework of time.

Economic Growth Led by railroads, the U.S. economy expanded at a blistering pace between 1870 and 1900. Inventors designed new products and brought them to market: electric lights, telephones, typewriters, phonographs, film photography, motion picture cameras, and electric motors all made their appearance during this era. Strong consumer demand for those and other products fueled rapid industrial expansion and suggested to observers that the United States had found the road to continuous progress and prosperity.

Yet the march of U.S. industrialization did not go entirely unopposed: large-scale labor unions emerged alongside big business in the period from 1870 to 1900, and confrontations between business owners seeking profits and workers seeking higher wages or job security sometimes grew ugly. A nationwide, coordinated strike of rail workers in 1877 shut down two-thirds of the nation's railroads. Violence stemming from the strike took the lives of one hundred people and resulted in ten million dollars' worth of property damage. Nevertheless, big business prevailed in its disputes with workers during the nineteenth century, often with support from federal or state governments, and by the early twentieth century the United States had emerged as one of the world's major industrial powers.

Canadian Prosperity

British investment deeply influenced the development of the Canadian as well as the U.S. economy in the nineteenth and early twentieth centuries. Canadian leaders, like U.S. leaders, took advantage of British capital to industrialize without allowing their economy to fall under British control. During the early nineteenth century, Britain paid relatively high prices for Canadian agricultural products and minerals, partly to keep the colony stable and discourage the formation of separatist movements. As a result, white Canadians enjoyed a high standard of living even before industrialization.

The National Policy After the establishment of the Dominion, politicians started a program of economic development known as the National Policy. The idea was to attract migrants, protect nascent industries through tariffs, and build national transportation systems. The centerpiece of the transportation network was the transcontinental Canadian Pacific Railroad, built largely with British investment capital and completed in 1885. The Canadian Pacific Railroad opened the western prairie lands to commerce, stimulated the development of other industries, and promoted the emergence of a Canadian national economy. The National Policy created some violent altercations with indigenous peoples who resisted encroachment on their lands and with trappers who resented disruption of their way of life, but it also promoted economic growth and independence. In Canada as in the United States, the ability to control and direct economic affairs was crucial to limiting the state's dependence on British capital.

As a result of the National Policy, Canada experienced booming agricultural, mineral, and industrial production in the late nineteenth and early twentieth centuries. Canadian population surged as a result of both migration and natural increase. Migrants flocked to Canada's shores from Asia and especially from Europe: between 1903 and 1914 some 2.7 million eastern European migrants settled in Canada. Fueled in part by this population growth, Canadian economic expansion took place on the foundation of rapidly increasing wheat production and the extraction of rich mineral resources, including gold, silver, copper, nickel, and asbestos. Industrialists also tapped Canadian rivers to produce the hydroelectric power necessary for manufacturing.

U.S. Investment Canada remained wary of its powerful neighbor to the south but did not keep U.S. economic influence entirely at bay. British investment dwarfed U.S. investment throughout the nineteenth century: in 1914 British investment in Canada totaled $2.5 billion, compared with $700 million from the United States. Nevertheless, the U.S. presence in the Canadian economy grew. By 1918, Americans owned 30 percent of all Canadian industry, and thereafter the U.S. and Canadian economies became increasingly interdependent. Canada began to undergo rapid industrialization after the early twentieth century, as the province of Ontario benefited from the spillover of U.S. industry in the northeastern states.

Latin American Investments

Latin American states did not undergo industrialization or enjoy economic development like that of the United States and Canada. Colonial legacies help explain the different economic development in Latin American lands. Even when Spain and Portugal controlled the trade and investment policies of their American colonies, their home economies were unable to supply sufficient quantities of the manufactured goods that colonial markets demanded. As a result, they opened the colonies to European trade, which snuffed out local industries that could not compete with British, French, and German producers of inexpensive manufactured goods. Moreover, both in colonial times and after independence, Latin American elites—urban merchants and large landholders—retained control over local economies. Elites profited handsomely from European trade and investment and thus had little incentive to seek different economic policies or work toward economic diversification. Thus foreign investment and trade had more damaging effects in Latin America than in the United States or Canada.

British Investment The relatively small size of Latin American markets limited foreign influence, which generally took the form of investment or what could be termed informal imperialism. British merchants had little desire to transform Latin American states into dependent trading partners for the simple reason that they offered no substantial market for British goods. Nevertheless, British investors took advantage of opportunities that brought them profits and considerable control over Latin American economic affairs. In Argentina, for example, British investors encouraged the development of cattle and sheep ranching. After the 1860s and the invention of refrigerated cargo ships, meat became Argentina's largest export. British investors controlled the industry and reaped the profits, however, as Argentina became Britain's principal supplier of meat. Between 1880 and 1914, European migrants labored in the new export industries and contributed to the explosive growth of urban areas such as Buenos Aires: by 1914 the city's population exceeded 3.5 million. Although migrant laborers rarely shared in the profits controlled by elites, the domination of urban labor by European migrants represented yet another form of foreign influence in Latin American economic affairs.

Attempted Industrialization In a few lands, ruling elites made attempts to encourage industrialization, but with only limited success. The most notable of those efforts came when the dictatorial general Porfirio Díaz ruled Mexico (1876–1911). Díaz represented the interests of large landowners, wealthy merchants, and foreign investors. Under his rule, railroad tracks and telegraph lines connected all parts of Mexico, and the production of mineral resources surged. A small steel industry produced railroad track and construction materials, and entrepreneurs also established glass, chemical, and textile industries. The capital, Mexico City, underwent a transformation during the Díaz years: it acquired paved streets, streetcar lines, and electric streetlights. But the profits from Mexican enterprises did not support continuing industrial development. Instead, they went into the pockets of the Mexican oligarchy and foreign investors who supported Díaz, while a growing and discontented urban working class seethed with resentment at low wages, long hours, and foreign managers. Even as agriculture, railroad construction, and mining were booming, the standard of living for average Mexicans had begun to decline by the early twentieth century. Frustration with that state of affairs helps explain the sudden outbreak of violent revolution in 1910.

Despite a large proportion of foreign and especially British control, Latin American economies expanded rapidly in the late nineteenth century. Exports drove that growth: copper and silver from Mexico, bananas and coffee from Central America, rubber and coffee from Brazil, beef and wheat from Argentina, copper from Chile, and tobacco and sugar from Cuba. Other areas in the world also developed many of those same products for export, however, and competition for markets often led to lower prices for those commodities. As in the United States and Canada, foreign investment in Latin America provided capital for development, but unlike the situation in the northern lands, control over industries and exports remained in foreign hands. Latin American economies were thus subject to decisions made in the interests of foreign investors, and unstable governments could do little in the face of strong foreign intervention. Controlled by the very elites who profited from foreign intervention at the expense of their citizens, Latin

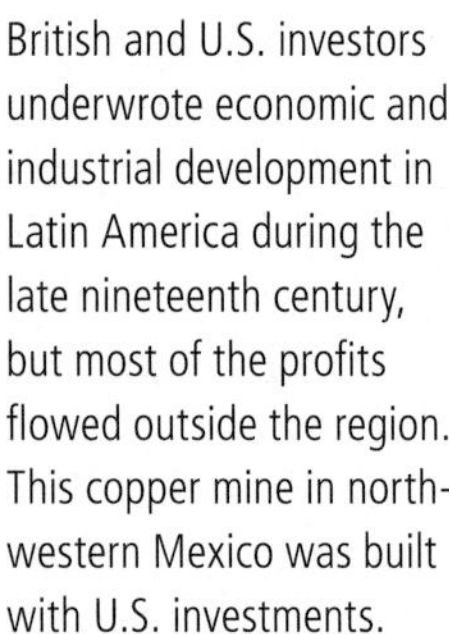

British and U.S. investors underwrote economic and industrial development in Latin America during the late nineteenth century, but most of the profits flowed outside the region. This copper mine in northwestern Mexico was built with U.S. investments.

American governments helped account for the region's slower economic development, despite growth in industrial and export economies.

AMERICAN CULTURAL AND SOCIAL DIVERSITY

In his "Song of Myself" (1855), a poetic celebration of himself as well as the vast diversity of his nation, U.S. poet Walt Whitman asked:

> Do I contradict myself?
> Very well then I contradict myself,
> (I am large, I contain multitudes.)

Much of the allure of the Americas derived from their vast spaces and diverse populations. The Americas were indeed large, and they contained multitudes. While diversity distinguished the Americas, it also provided abundant fuel for conflicts between ethnic groups, social classes, and those segregated into rigid castes based on race and gender. The social and cultural diversity of American societies challenged their ability to achieve cultural cohesion as well as political unity and democratically inclusive states. The lingering legacies of European conquest, slavery, migration, and patriarchy highlighted contradictions between the Enlightenment ideals of freedom and equality and the realities of life for native and African-American peoples as well as recent migrants and women. American societies experienced ample strife in the age of independence. In efforts to maintain their own position and preserve social stability, the dominant political forces in the Americas often repressed demands for recognition by dispossessed groups.

Societies in the United States

By the late nineteenth century, the United States had become a boisterous multicultural society—the most culturally diverse land of the western hemisphere—whose population included indigenous peoples, Euro-American settlers, African-American laborers, and growing numbers of migrants from Europe and Asia. Walt Whitman described the United States as "not merely a nation but a teeming nation of nations." Yet political and economic power rested almost exclusively with white male elites of European ancestry. The United States experienced tension and occasional conflict as members of various constituencies worked for dignity, prosperity, and a voice in society. During the nineteenth century, cultural and social tension swirled especially around indigenous peoples, African-American slaves and their descendants, women, and migrants.

Native Peoples As they expanded to the west, Euro-American settlers and ranchers pushed indigenous peoples

The Apache youths at the Carlisle Indian School offer stark faces to the camera, suggesting their discontent with reform efforts directed at assimilation through education.

onto reservations. Although promising to respect those lands, the U.S. government permitted settlers and railroads to encroach on the reservations and force native peoples into increasingly cramped and marginal territories. Begrudging native Americans even these meager lands, the United States embarked in the latter half of the nineteenth century on a policy designed to reduce native autonomy even further through laws and reforms aimed at assimilating tribes to the white way of life. The U.S. government and private citizens acted to undermine or destroy outright the bases of native cultural traditions. Native tribes on the plains, for example, had developed material cultures largely centered on the hunting of bison, or buffalo, and the skillful exploitation of those animal resources. Beginning in 1850 but accelerating after the Civil War, white migrants, railroad employees, hunters, and "wild west" men such as Buffalo Bill Cody shot and killed hundreds of thousands of bison, effectively exterminating the buffalo and the economy of the Plains Indians. Herds numbering at least 15 million had been reduced to a mere thousand by 1875.

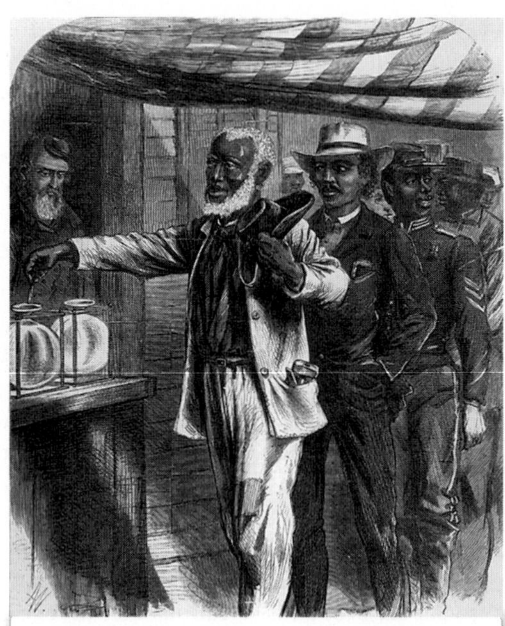
A lithograph from *Harper's Weekly* after the Civil War. A black artisan, a middle-class African-American, and a black Union soldier are in the process of voting, perhaps for the first time in their lives.

Other U.S. actions also attempted to sever native Americans' ties to their communal traditions and cultural practices. The Dawes Severalty Act of 1887 shifted land policies away from collective tribal reservations and toward individual tracts of land meant to promote the family farms once common in white U.S. society and now becoming increasingly less competitive. Even more traumatically, government officials removed native children from their families and tribes and enrolled them in white-controlled boarding schools. These schools, such as the Carlisle Indian School and the Toledo Indian School, illustrated the extent to which white society sought to eliminate tribal influences and inculcate Christian, U.S. values. Tribal languages as well as native dress and hair fashions were banned, further distancing the children from their cultures. Native Americans, however, resisted these forms of assimilation, often fleeing from boarding schools or refusing to agree to new governmental land policies. Native land control diminished as a result, but over the following decades tribes rebuilt and reaffirmed native identities.

Freed Slaves The Civil War ended slavery, but it did not bring about instant equality for freed slaves and their African-American descendants. In an effort to establish a place for freed slaves in American society, northern forces sent armies of occupation to the southern states and forced them to undergo a program of social and political Reconstruction (1867–1877). They extended civil rights to freed slaves and provided black men with voting rights. Black and white citizens in southern states elected biracial governments for the first time in U.S. history, and freed slaves participated actively in the political affairs of the republic.

After Reconstruction, however, the armies of occupation went back north, and a violent backlash soon dismantled the program's reforms. Freed slaves had not received land grants or any other means of economic support, so many had to work as sharecroppers for former slave owners. Under those circumstances it was relatively easy for white southerners to take away the political and civil liberties that former slaves had gained under Reconstruction. By the turn of the century, U.S. blacks faced violence and intimidation when they tried to vote. Southern states fashioned a rigidly segregated society that deprived the African-American population of educational, economic, and political opportunities. Although freedom was better than slavery, it was far different from the hopeful visions of the slaves who had won their emancipation.

Women Even before the Civil War, a small but growing women's movement had emerged in the United States. At the Seneca Falls Convention in 1848, feminists issued a "declaration of sentiments" modeled on the Declaration of Independence—"We hold these truths to be self-evident: that all men and women are created equal"—and they demanded equal political and economic rights for U.S. women:

> Now, in view of this entire disenfranchisement of one-half the people of this country, their social and religious degradation—in view of the unjust laws above mentioned, and because women do feel themselves aggrieved, oppressed, and fraudulently deprived of their most sacred rights, we insist that they have immediate admission to all the rights and privileges which belong to them as citizens of the United States.

Women fought for equal rights throughout the nineteenth century, and new opportunities for education and employment offered alternatives to marriage and domesticity. Women's colleges, reform activism, and professional in-

This photograph from the late nineteenth century captures the busy street life in San Francisco's Chinatown. Migrants flocked to urban centers and created ethnic enclaves such as Chinatown for comfort and protection, transforming the urban landscapes of the Americas in the process.

dustrial jobs allowed some women to pursue careers over marriage. Yet meaningful economic and political opportunities for women awaited the twentieth century.

Migrants Between 1840 and 1914 some twenty-five million European migrants landed on American shores, and in the late nineteenth century most of them hailed from southern and eastern European countries. Migrants introduced new foods, music, dances, holidays, sports, and languages to U.S. society and contributed to the cultural diversity of the western hemisphere. Yet white, native-born citizens of the United States began to feel swamped by the arrival of so many migrants. Distaste for foreigners often resulted in hostility to the migrants who flooded into the expanding industrial cities. Migrants and their families tended to concentrate in certain districts, such as Little Italy and Chinatown—partly out of choice, since they preferred neighbors with familiar cultural traditions, but partly also because native-born citizens discouraged the migrants from moving into other neighborhoods. Concerns about growing numbers of migrants with different cultural and social traditions eventually led to the exclusion of new arrivals from Asian lands: the U.S. government ordered a complete halt to migration from China in 1882 and from Japan in 1907.

Canadian Cultural Contrasts

Ethnic Diversity British and French settlers each viewed themselves as Canada's founding people. This cleavage, which profoundly influenced Canadian political development, masked much greater cultural and ethnic diversity in Canada. French and British settlers displaced the indigenous peoples, who remain a significant minority of Canada's population today. Slavery likewise left a mark on Canada. Slavery was legal in the British empire until 1833, and many early settlers brought their slaves to Canada. After the 1830s, escaped slaves from the United States also reached Canada by way of the Underground Railroad. Blacks in Canada were free but not equal, segregated and isolated from the political and cultural mainstream. Chinese migrants also came to Canada; lured by gold rushes such as the Fraser River rush of 1858 and by opportunities to work on the Canadian Pacific Railway in the 1880s, Chinese migrants lived mostly in segregated Chinatowns in the cities of British Columbia, and like blacks they had little voice in public affairs. In the late nineteenth and early twentieth centuries, waves of migrants brought even greater ethnic diversity to Canada. Between 1896 and 1914 three million migrants from Britain, the United States, and eastern Europe arrived in Canada.

Despite the heterogeneity of Canada's population, communities descended from British and French settlers dominated Canadian society, and conflict between the two communities was the most prominent source of ethnic tension throughout the nineteenth and twentieth centuries. After 1867, as British Canadians led the effort to settle the Northwest Territories and incorporate them into the Dominion, frictions between the two groups intensified. Westward expansion brought British Canadian settlers and cultivators into conflict with French Canadian fur traders and lumberjacks. The fur traders in particular often lived on the margins between European and indigenous societies. They frequently married or consorted with native women, giving rise to the métis, individuals of mixed European and indigenous ancestry.

The Métis and Louis Riel A major outbreak of civil strife took place in the 1870s and 1880s. Native peoples and métis had moved west throughout the nineteenth century to preserve their land and trading rights, but the drive of British Canadians to the west threatened them. Louis Riel (1844–1885) emerged as the leader of the métis and indigenous peoples of western Canada. A métis himself, Riel abandoned his studies for the priesthood in Montreal and

sources from the past

The Meaning of Freedom for an Ex-Slave

Even before the conclusion of the Civil War brought slavery to an end in the United States, Jourdan Anderson had taken the opportunity to run away and claim his freedom. After the war his former master, Colonel P. H. Anderson, wrote a letter asking him to return to work on his Tennessee plantation. In responding from his new home in Dayton, Ohio, Anderson respectfully refers to the colonel as "my old master" and addresses him as "sir." Yet Anderson's letter makes it clear that his family's freedom and welfare were his principal concerns.

I want to know particularly what the good chance is you propose to give me. I am doing tolerably well here; I get $25 a month, with victuals and clothing; have a comfortable home for Mandy (the folks here call her Mrs. Anderson), and the children, Milly, Jane and Grundy, go to school and are learning well; the teacher says Grundy has a head for a preacher. They go to Sunday-School, and Mandy and me attend church regularly. We are kindly treated; sometimes we overhear others saying, "Them colored people were slaves" down in Tennessee. The children feel hurt when they hear such remarks, but I tell them it was no disgrace in Tennessee to belong to Col. Anderson. Many darkies would have been proud, as I used to was, to call you master. Now, if you will write and say what wages you will give me, I will be better able to decide whether it would be to my advantage to move back again.

As to my freedom, which you say I can have, there is nothing to be gained on that score, as I got my free-papers in 1864 from the Provost-Marshal-General of the Department at Nashville. Mandy says she would be afraid to go back without some proof that you are sincerely disposed to treat us justly and kindly—and we have concluded to test your sincerity by asking you to send us our wages for the time we served you. This will make us forget and forgive old scores, and rely on your justice and friendship in the future. I served you faithfully for thirty-two years and Mandy twenty years. At $25 a month for me, and $2 a week for Mandy, our earnings would amount to $11,680. Add to this the interest for the time our wages has been kept back and deduct what you paid for our clothing and three doctor's visits to me, and pulling a tooth for Mandy, and the balance will show what we are in justice entitled to. Please send the money by Adams Express, in care of V. Winters, esq, Dayton, Ohio. If you fail to pay us for faithful labors in the past we can have little faith in your promises in the future. We trust the good Maker has opened your eyes to the wrongs which you and your fathers have done to me and my fathers, in making us toil for you for generations without recompense. Here I draw my wages every Saturday night, but in Tennessee there was never any pay day for the negroes any more than for the horses and cows. Surely there will be a day of reckoning for those who defraud the laborer of his hire.

In answering this letter please state if there would be any safety for my Milly and Jane, who are now grown up and both good-looking girls. You know how it was with poor Matilda and Catherine. I would rather stay here and starve and die if it comes to that than have my girls brought to shame by the violence and wickedness of their young masters. You will also please state if there has been any schools opened for the colored children in your neighborhood, the great desire of my life now is to give my children an education, and have them form virtuous habits.

For Further Reflection

- In what clever ways does Jourdan Anderson test the seriousness of his former owner's offer of employment, and what does his approach say about the meaning of black freedom?

Source: Leon F. Litwack. *Been in the Storm So Long: The Aftermath of Slavery.* New York: Knopf, 1979, pp. 334–35.

returned to his home in the Red River Settlement (in the southern part of modern Manitoba). Sensitive to his community's concern that the Canadian government threatened local land rights, Riel assumed the presidency of a provisional government in 1870. He led his troops in capturing Fort Garry (modern Winnipeg) and negotiated the incorporation of the province of Manitoba into the Canadian Dominion. Canadian government officials and troops soon outlawed his government and forced Riel into years of exile, during which he wandered through the United States and Quebec, even suffering confinement in asylums.

Work on the Canadian Pacific Railroad in the 1880s renewed the threat of white settlement to indigenous and métis society. The métis asked Riel to lead resistance to the railroad and British Canadian settlement. In 1885 he organized a military force of métis and native peoples in the Saskatchewan river country and led an insurrection known as the Northwest Rebellion. Canadian forces quickly subdued the makeshift army, and government authorities executed Riel for treason.

Although the Northwest Rebellion never had a chance of success, the execution of Riel nonetheless reverberated throughout Canadian history. French Canadians took it as an indication of the state's readiness to subdue individuals who were culturally distinct and politically opposed to the drive for a nation dominated by British Canadian elites. In the very year when completion of the transcontinental railroad signified for some the beginnings of Canadian national unity, Riel's execution foreshadowed a long term of cultural conflict between Canadians of British, French, and indigenous ancestry.

Engraving of Louis Riel, the rebellious Canadian métis. Riel fought through political and military means on behalf of the métis and indigenous peoples of western Canada.

Ethnicity, Identity, and Gender in Latin America

The heritage of Spanish and Portuguese colonialism and the legacy of slavery inclined Latin American societies toward the establishment of hierarchical distinctions based on ethnicity and color. At the top of society stood the creoles, individuals of European ancestry born in the Americas, while indigenous peoples, freed slaves, and their black descendants occupied the lowest rungs of the social ladder. In between were various groups of mixed ancestry, such as mestizos, mulattoes, zambos, and castizos. Although most Latin American states ended the legal recognition of these groups, the distinctions themselves persisted after independence and limited the opportunities available to peoples of indigenous, African, or mixed ancestry.

Migration and Cultural Diversity

Large-scale migration brought added cultural diversity to Latin America in the nineteenth century. Indentured laborers who went from Asian lands to Peru, Brazil, Cuba, and other Caribbean destinations carried with them many of their native cultural practices. When their numbers were relatively small, as in the case of Chinese migrants to Cuba, they mostly intermarried and assimilated into the working classes without leaving much foreign influence on the societies they joined. When they were relatively more numerous, however, as in the case of Indian migrants to Trinidad and Tobago, they formed distinctive communities in which they spoke their native languages, prepared foods from their homelands, and observed their inherited cultural and social traditions. Migration of European workers to Argentina brought a lively diversity to the capital of Buenos Aires, which was perhaps the most cosmopolitan city of nineteenth-century Latin America. With its broad avenues, smart boutiques, and handsome buildings graced with wrought iron, Buenos Aires enjoyed a reputation as "the Paris of the Americas."

Latin American intellectuals seeking cultural identity usually saw themselves either as heirs of Europe or as products of the American environment. One spokesperson who identified with Europe was the Argentine president Domingo Faustino Sarmiento (1811–1888). Sarmiento despised the rule of caudillos that had emerged after independence and worked for the development of the best society based on European values. In his widely read book *Facundo: Civilization and Barbarism* (1845), Sarmiento argued that it was necessary for Buenos Aires to bring discipline to the disorderly Argentine countryside. Deeply influenced by the Enlightenment, he characterized books, ideas, law, education, and art as products of cities, and he argued that only when cities dominated the countryside would social stability and genuine liberty be possible.

Gauchos

Sarmiento admired the bravery and independence of Argentina's *gauchos* ("cowboys"), but he considered it imperative that urban residents rather than ranchers make society's crucial decisions. Although the mystique of the gaucho did not extend throughout all of Latin America, observers did see gauchos as one symbol of Latin American identity. Most gauchos were mestizos or castizos, but there were also white and black gauchos. For all intents and purposes, anyone who adopted gaucho ways became a gaucho, and gaucho society acquired an ethnic egalitarianism rarely found elsewhere in Latin America. Gauchos were most prominent in the Argentine pampas, but their cultural practices linked them to the cowboys, or vaqueros, found throughout the Americas. As pastoralists herding cattle and horses on the pampas, gauchos stood apart from both the indigenous peoples and the growing urban and agricultural elites who gradually displaced them with large landholdings and cattle ranches that spread to the pampas.

Pedro Damian Alegre as an Argentinian gaucho, dressed traditionally and striking a solitary pose symbolic of gaucho individualism.

The gauchos led independent and self-sufficient lives that appealed broadly in hierarchical Latin American society. Gauchos lived off their own skills and needed only their horses to survive. They dressed distinctively, with sashed trousers, ponchos, and boots. Countless songs and poems lauded their courage, skills, and lovemaking bravado. Yet independence and caudillo rule disrupted gaucho life as the cowboys increasingly entered armies, either voluntarily or under compulsion, and as settled agriculture and ranches surrounded by barbed wire enclosed the pampas. The gauchos did not leave the pampas without resistance. The poet José Hernandez offered a romanticized vision of the gaucho life and protested its decline in his epic poem *The Gaucho Martín Fierro* (1873). Hernandez conveyed the pride of gauchos, particularly those who resisted assimilation into Euro-American society, by having Martín Fierro proclaim his independence and assert his intention to stay that way:

> I owe nothin' to nobody;
> I don't ask for shelter, or give it;
> and from now on, nobody
> better try to lead me around by a rope.

Nevertheless, by the late nineteenth century, gauchos were more echoes of the Latin American past than makers of a viable society.

Male Domination Even more than in the United States and Canada, male domination was a central characteristic of Latin American society in the nineteenth century. Women could not vote or hold office, nor could they work or manage estates without permission from their male guardians. In rural areas, women were liable to rough treatment and assault by gauchos and other men steeped in the values of *machismo*—a social ethic that honored male strength, courage, aggressiveness, assertiveness, and cunning. A few women voiced their discontent with male domination and machismo. In her poem "To Be Born a Man" (1887), for example, the Bolivian poet Adela Zamudio lamented bitterly that talented women could not vote, but ignorant men could, just by learning how to sign their names. Although Latin American lands had not yet generated a strong women's movement, they did begin to expand educational opportunities for girls and young women after the mid-nineteenth century. In large cities most girls received some formal schooling, and women usually filled teaching positions in the public schools that proliferated throughout Latin America in the late nineteenth century.

Female Activism Women did carve spaces for themselves outside or alongside the male world of machismo, and this was especially true in the home and in the marketplace, where Latin American women exerted great influence and control. In the early twentieth century, women served in conjunction with men in the Mexican revolution, most famously as Zapatistas, or followers of Emiliano Zapata. Many women supporting Zapata labored within the domestic realm to provide food for the soldiers, and others breached the domestic barrier to become soldiers and officers themselves. Although those women who became *soldaderas* (female soldiers or supporters of soldiers) demonstrated the most extreme forms of activism during the Mexican revolution, Mexican women on the whole made major contributions to the success of the revolution and shared in the radical spirit of change that characterized much of early-twentieth-century Latin America.

inperspective

After gaining independence from European colonial powers, the states of the western hemisphere worked to build stable and prosperous societies. The independent American states faced difficult challenges—including vast territories, diverse populations, social tensions, and cultural differences—as they sought to construct viable societies on the Enlightenment principles of freedom, equality, and constitutional government. The United States and Canada built large federal societies in North America, whereas a series of smaller states governed affairs in Latin America. The United States in particular was an expansive society, absorbing Texas, California, and the northern territories of Mexico while extending its authority from the Atlantic to the Pacific Ocean. Throughout the hemisphere, descendants of European settlers subdued indigenous American peoples and built societies dominated by Euro-American peoples. They established agricultural economies, exploited natural resources, and in some lands launched processes of industrialization. They accepted streams of European and Asian migrants, who contributed not only to American cultural diversity but also to the transformations in labor practices necessitated by the abolition of slavery and the rise of industry. All American lands experienced tensions arising from social, economic, cultural, and ethnic differences, which led occasionally to violent civil conflict and often to smoldering resentments and grievances. The making of independent American societies was not a smooth process, but it reflected the increasing interdependence of all the world's peoples. ●

CHRONOLOGY

1803	Louisiana Purchase
1804–1806	Lewis and Clark expedition
1812–1814	War of 1812
1829–1852	Rule of Juan Manuel de Rosas in Argentina
1838–1839	Trail of Tears
1846–1848	Mexican-American War
1848	Seneca Falls Convention
1849	California gold rush
1850s	La Reforma in Mexico
1861–1865	U.S. Civil War
1867	Establishment of the Dominion of Canada
1867	French troops withdraw from Mexico
1867–1877	Reconstruction in the United States
1869	Completion of the transcontinental railroad line in the United States
1876	Battle of Little Big Horn
1876–1911	Rule of Porfirio Díaz in Mexico
1885	Completion of the Canadian Pacific Railroad
1885	Northwest Rebellion
1890	Massacre at Wounded Knee
1910–1920	Mexican revolution

For Further Reading

Richard Buel Jr. *America on the Brink: How the Political Struggle over the War of 1812 Almost Destroyed the Young Republic.* New York, 2004. Scholarly examination of the conflicts between Federalists and Jeffersonians that culminated in the War of 1812.

Colin G. Calloway. *First Peoples: A Documentary Survey of American Indian History.* Boston, 1999. A fine text on native American history, written by a knowledgeable scholar in the field.

Roderic Ai Camp. *Politics in Mexico: The Democratic Transformation.* 4th ed. New York, 2004. The best introduction to Mexican politics.

William Cronon. *Nature's Metropolis: Chicago and the Great West.* New York, 1991. A valuable study exploring the role of Chicago in the economic development of the American west.

Ellen C. DuBois. *Feminism and Suffrage: The Emergence of an Independent Women's Movement in America, 1848–1869.* Ithaca, 1984. Traces the rise and character of the U.S. women's movement in the nineteenth century.

David Barry Gaspar and Darlene Clark Hine, eds. *Beyond Bondage: Free Women of Color in the Americas.* Chicago, 2004. Collection of essays on free black women and their unique abilities to negotiate social and legal institutions in the era of slavery.

Tom Holm. *The Great Confusion in Indian Affairs: Native Americans and Whites in the Progressive Era.* Austin, 2005. Study of native American resistance to the American government's attempts at subjugation.

Joseph Kinsey Howard. *Strange Empire: A Narrative of the Northwest.* Westport, Conn., 1974. An in-depth and often moving account of Louis Riel, the métis, and their struggles with the Canadian government.

Patricia Nelson Limerick. *The Legacy of Conquest: The Unbroken Past of the American West.* New York, 1987. A provocative work exploring the influences of race, class, and gender in the conquest of the American west.

James M. McPherson. *Battle Cry of Freedom: The Civil War Era.* New York, 1988. A balanced account of the Civil War by a renowned scholar.

J. R. Miller. *Skyscrapers Hide the Heavens: A History of Indian-White Relations in Canada.* Toronto, 1989. An important study of Canadian policies toward indigenous peoples.

Walter Nugent. *Crossings: The Great Transatlantic Migrations, 1870–1914.* Bloomington, 1992. Provides an overview and analysis of the mass migrations to North America in the nineteenth and twentieth centuries.

Marc Reisner. *Cadillac Desert: The American West and Its Disappearing Water.* Revised and updated ed. New York, 1993. An incisive analysis of water policies and politics from an engaging and environmentalist point of view.

Robert L. Scheina. *Latin American Wars.* Vol. 1: *The Age of the Caudillos, 1791–1899.* Washington, D.C., 2003. By examining the wars of independence, this work uncovers the reasons behind the failures of Latin American state building.

Ronald Takaki. *A Different Mirror: A History of Multicultural America.* Boston, 1993. A spirited account of the contributions made by peoples of European, African, Asian, and native American ancestry to the modern American society.

———. *Strangers from a Different Shore: A History of Asian Americans.* Boston, 1989. Fascinating survey of the experiences of Asian migrants who came to North America across the Pacific Ocean.

Richard White. *"It's Your Misfortune and None of My Own": A History of the American West.* Norman, Okla., 1991. Surveys the conquest, exploitation, and transformation of the American west.

Donald Worster. *Rivers of Empire: Water, Aridity, and the Growth of the American West.* New York, 1985. Focuses on the role of irrigation in the establishment of a Euro-American agricultural society in the arid west.

Jean Fagan Yellin. *Harriet Jacobs: A Life.* New York, 2003. Scholarly biography of an important figure in the abolitionist movement.

Societies at Crossroads

chapter 31

European portrait of China's Empress Dowager Cixi from 1903. Beginning her political career as a concubine in the harem of the Xianfeng emperor, she developed into a powerful and charismatic figure who became the de facto ruler of the Manchu Qing dynasty in China for over forty years, from 1861 until her death in 1908.

EYEWITNESS:
"Heavenly King" Hong Xiuquan, Empress Dowager Cixi, and Qing Reform

Hong Xiuquan, the third son of a poor family, grew up in a farming village in southern China about 50 kilometers (31 miles) from Guangzhou. Although he was arrogant and irritable, he showed intellectual promise. His neighbors made him village teacher so that he could study and prepare for the civil service examinations, the principal avenue to government employment, since a position in the Qing bureaucracy would bring honor and wealth to both his family and his village. Between 1828 and 1837, Hong took the exams three times but failed to obtain even the lowest degree. This outcome was not surprising, since thousands of candidates competed for a degree, which only a few obtained. Yet the disappointment was too much for Hong. He suffered an emotional collapse, lapsed into a delirium that lasted about forty days, and experienced visions.

Upon recovering from his breakdown, Hong resumed his position as village teacher. After failing the civil service examinations a fourth time in 1843, he began studying the works of a Chinese missionary who explained the basic elements of Christianity. As he pondered the religious tracts, Hong came to believe that during his illness he had visited heaven and learned from God that he was the younger brother of Jesus Christ. He believed further that God had revealed to him that his destiny was to reform China and pave the way for the heavenly kingdom. Inspired by these convictions, Hong baptized himself and worked to build a community of disciples.

Hong's personal religious vision soon evolved into a political program: Hong believed that God had charged him with the establishment of a new order, one that necessitated the destruction of the Qing dynasty, which had ruled China since 1644. In 1847 he joined the Society of God Worshipers, a religious group recently founded by disgruntled peasants and miners. Hong soon emerged as the group's guiding force, and in the summer of 1850 he led about ten thousand followers in rebellion against the Qing dynasty. On his thirty-seventh birthday, 11 January 1851, he assumed the title of "Heavenly King" and proclaimed his own dynasty, the **Taiping** tianguo ("Heavenly Kingdom of Great Peace"). Hong's followers, known as the Taipings, quickly grew from a ragtag band to a disciplined and zealous army of over one million men and women who pushed the Qing dynasty to the brink of extinction.

One of the more radical beliefs of the Taipings was the equality of men and women before God and on earth, and that belief was ironically illustrated in the political rise of a woman destined to be part of the Taipings' downfall: the Dowager Empress Cixi. Rising to behind-the-throne power in the early 1860s, Cixi helped to institute changes—putting Chinese, not Manchus, in charge of armies, for example—that worked to quell the Taiping rebels. Both the Hong-led Taiping rebellion and the imperial power of Cixi suggested the internal turmoil of a China reaching a crossroads in its history.

China was not the only land that faced serious difficulties in the nineteenth century: the Ottoman empire, the Russian empire, and Tokugawa Japan experienced problems similar to those of China during the late Qing dynasty. One problem common to the four societies was military weakness that left them vulnerable to foreign threats. The Ottoman, Russian, Qing, and Tokugawa armies all fought wars or engaged in military confrontations with the industrial lands of western Europe and the United States, and all discovered suddenly and unexpectedly that they were militarily much weaker than the industrial powers. European lands occasionally seized territories outright and either absorbed them into their own possessions or ruled them as colonies. More often, however, European and U.S. forces used their power to squeeze concessions out of militarily weak societies. They won rights for European and U.S. businesses to seek opportunities on favorable terms and enabled industrial capitalists to realize huge profits from trade and investment in militarily weak societies.

Another problem common to the four societies was internal weakness that was due to population pressure, declining agricultural productivity, famine, falling government revenue, and corruption at all levels of government. Ottoman, Russian, Chinese, and Japanese societies all experienced serious domestic turmoil, especially during the second half of the nineteenth century, as peasants mounted rebellions, dissidents struggled for reform, and political factions fought among themselves or conspired to organize coups. Military weakness often left leaders of the four societies unable to respond effectively to domestic strife, which sometimes provided western European powers and the United States with an excuse to intervene to protect their business interests.

Thus, by the late nineteenth century, the Ottoman empire, the Russian empire, Qing China, and Tokugawa Japan were societies at crossroads. Even if they undertook a program of thoroughgoing political, social, and economic reform, they might continue to experience domestic difficulties and grow progressively weaker in relation to industrial lands. Reformers in all four societies promoted plans to introduce written constitutions, limit the authority of rulers, make governments responsive to the needs and desires of the people, guarantee equality before the law, restructure educational systems, and begin processes of industrialization. Many reformers had traveled in Europe and the United States, where they experienced constitutional government and industrial society firsthand, and they sought to remodel their own societies along the lines of the industrial lands.

Vigorous reform movements emerged in all four lands, but they had very different results. In the Ottoman empire, the Russian empire, and Qing China, ruling elites and wealthy classes viewed reform warily and opposed any changes that might threaten their status. Reform in those three lands was halting, tentative, and sometimes abortive, and by the early twentieth century, the Ottoman, Romanov, and Qing dynasties were on the verge of collapse. In Japan, however, the Tokugawa dynasty fell and so was unable to resist change. Reform there was much more thorough than in the other lands, and by the early twentieth century, Japan was an emerging industrial power poised to expand its influence in the larger world.

Taiping (TEYE-pihng)

THE OTTOMAN EMPIRE IN DECLINE

During the eighteenth century the Ottoman empire experienced military reverses and challenges to its rule. By the early nineteenth century, the Ottoman state could no longer ward off European economic penetration or prevent territorial dismemberment. As Ottoman officials launched reforms to regenerate imperial vigor, Egypt and other north African provinces declared their independence, and European states seized territories in the northern and western parts of the Ottoman empire. At the same time, pressure from ethnic, religious, and nationalist groups threatened to fragment the polyglot empire. The once-powerful realm slipped into decline, its sovereignty maintained largely by the same European powers that exploited its economy.

By the latter part of the nineteenth century, European imperialism directly affected the fortunes of the Ottoman empire. This undated political cartoon shows England as a lion and Russia as a bear threatening Turkey (shown as a turkey). The illustration is labeled "Be my ally, or I'll give you the worst thrashing you ever had in your life."

The Nature of Decline

Military Decline By the late seventeenth century, the Ottoman empire had reached the limits of its expansion. Ottoman armies suffered humiliating defeats on the battlefield, especially at the hands of Austrian and Russian foes. Ottoman forces lagged behind European armies in strategy, tactics, weaponry, and training. Equally serious was a breakdown in the discipline of the elite Janissary corps, which had served as the backbone of the imperial armed forces since the fifteenth century. The Janissaries repeatedly masterminded palace coups during the seventeenth and eighteenth centuries and by the nineteenth century had become a powerful political force within the Ottoman state. The Janissaries neglected their military training and turned a blind eye to advances in weapons technology. As its military capacity declined, the Ottoman realm became vulnerable to its more powerful neighbors.

Loss of military power translated into declining effectiveness of the central government, which was losing power in the provinces to its own officials. By the early nineteenth century, semi-independent governors and local notables had formed private armies of mercenaries and slaves to support the sultan in Istanbul in return for recognition of autonomy. Increasingly these independent rulers also turned fiscal and administrative institutions to their own interests, collecting taxes for themselves and sending only nominal payments to the imperial treasury, thus depriving the central state of revenue.

Territorial Losses The Ottoman government managed to maintain its authority in Anatolia (present-day Turkey), the heart of the empire, as well as in Iraq, but it suffered serious territorial losses elsewhere. Russian forces took over poorly defended territories in the Caucasus and in central Asia, and the Austrian empire nibbled away at the western frontiers. Nationalist uprisings forced Ottoman rulers to recognize the independence of Balkan provinces, notably Greece (1830) and Serbia (1867).

Most significant, however, was the loss of Egypt. In 1798 the ambitious French general Napoleon invaded Egypt in hopes of using it as a springboard for an attack on the British empire in India. His campaign was a miserable failure: Napoleon had to abandon his army and sneak back to France, where he proceeded to overthrow the Directory. But the invasion sparked turmoil in Egypt, as local elites battled to seize power after Napoleon's departure. The ultimate victor was the energetic general Muhammad Ali, who built a powerful army modeled on European forces and ruled Egypt from 1805 to 1848. He drafted peasants to serve as infantry, and he hired French and Italian officers to train his troops. He also launched a program of industrialization, concentrating on cotton textiles and armaments. Although he remained nominally subordinate to the Ottoman sultan, by 1820 he had established himself as the effective ruler of Egypt, which was the most powerful land in the Muslim world. He even invaded Syria and Anatolia, threatening to capture Istanbul and topple the Ottoman state. Indeed, the Ottoman dynasty survived only because British forces intervened out of fear that Ottoman collapse would result in a sudden and dangerous expansion of Russian influence. Nevertheless, Muhammad Ali made Egypt an essentially autonomous region within the Ottoman empire.

Economic ills aggravated the military and political problems of the Ottoman state. The volume of trade passing through the Ottoman empire declined throughout the

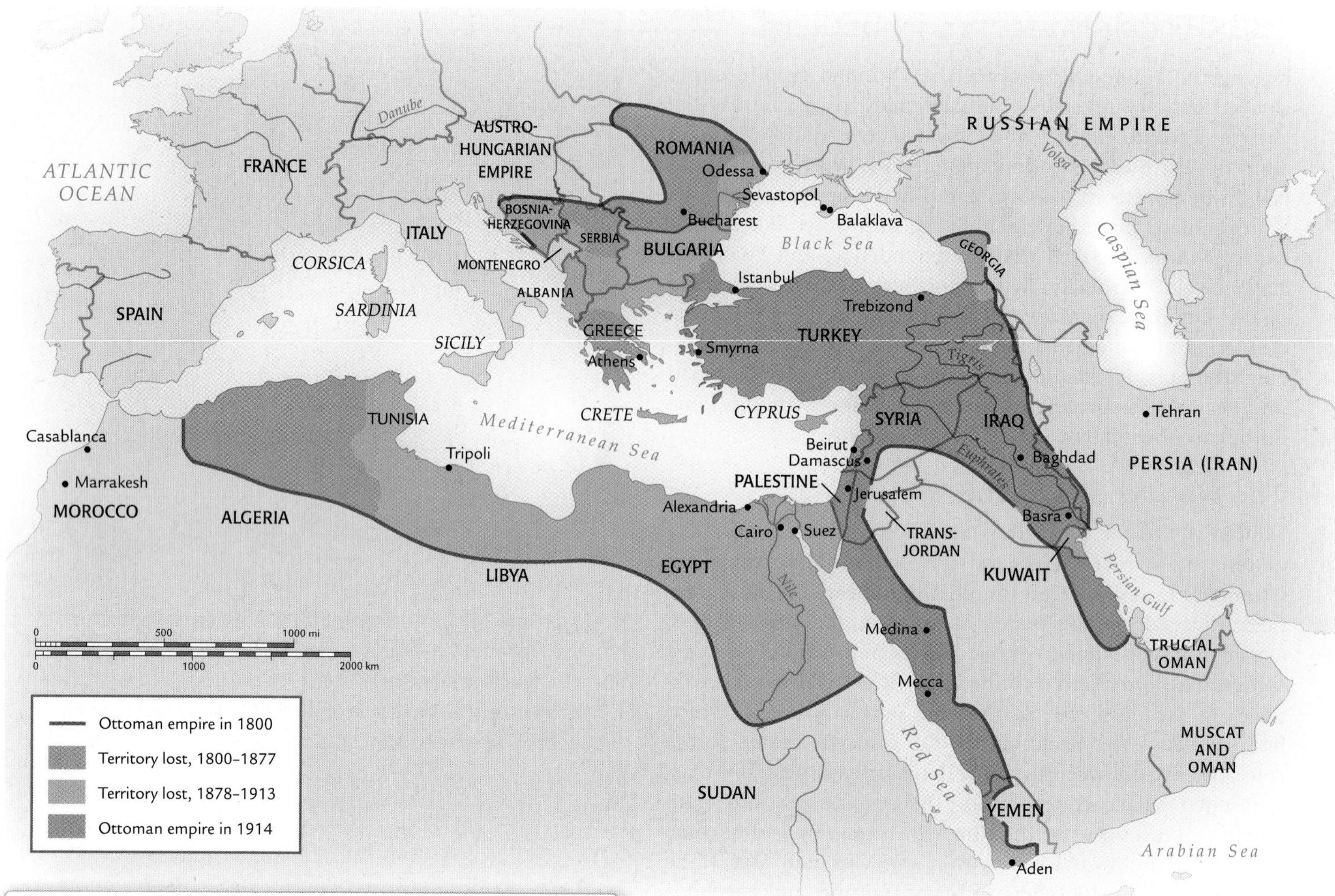

MAP 31.1
Territorial losses of the Ottoman empire, 1800–1923.
Compare the borders of the Ottoman empire in 1800 with what was left of the empire in 1914.
What might have been the strategic value of the remaining Ottoman territories?

later seventeenth and eighteenth centuries, as European merchants increasingly circumvented Ottoman intermediaries and traded directly with their counterparts in India and China. By the eighteenth century the focus of European trade had shifted to the Atlantic Ocean basin, where the Ottomans had no presence at all.

Economic Difficulties Meanwhile, as European producers became more efficient in the eighteenth and nineteenth centuries, their textiles and manufactured goods began to flow into the Ottoman empire. Because those items were inexpensive and high-quality products, they placed considerable pressure on Ottoman artisans and crafts workers, who frequently led urban riots to protest foreign imports. Ottoman exports consisted largely of raw materials such as grain, cotton, hemp, indigo, and opium, but they did not offset the value of imported European manufactures. Gradually, the Ottoman empire moved toward fiscal insolvency and financial dependency. After the middle of the nineteenth century, economic development in the Ottoman empire depended heavily on foreign loans, as European capital financed the construction of railroads, utilities, and mining enterprises. Interest payments grew to the point that they consumed more than half of the empire's revenues. In 1882 the Ottoman state was unable to pay interest on its loans and had no choice but to accept foreign administration of its debts.

The Capitulations Nothing symbolized foreign influence more than the capitulations, agreements that exempted European visitors from Ottoman law and provided European powers with extraterritoriality—the right to exercise jurisdiction over their own citizens according to their own laws. The practice dated back to the sixteenth century, when Ottoman sultans signed capitulation treaties to avoid the burden of administering justice for communities of foreign merchants. By the nineteenth century, however, Ottoman officials regarded the capitulations as humiliating intrusions on their sovereignty. Capitulations also served as instruments of economic penetration by European businesspeople who established tax-exempt banks and commercial enterprises in the Ottoman empire, and they permitted foreign governments to levy duties on goods sold in Ottoman ports.

By the early twentieth century, the Ottoman state lacked the resources to maintain its costly bureaucracy. Expenditures exceeded revenues, and the state experienced growing difficulty paying the salaries of its employees in the palace household, the military, and the religious hierarchy. Declining incomes led to reduced morale, recruitment difficulties, and a rise in corruption. Increased taxation designed to offset revenue losses only led to increased exploitation of the peasantry and a decline in agricultural production. The Ottoman empire was ailing, and it needed a major restructuring to survive.

> thinking about **TRADITIONS**
>
> **Reforming Traditions**
> Ottoman, Russian, and east Asian political leaders, long secure in their traditions, suddenly took up reform efforts in the nineteenth century to shore up the strength and the viability of their societies. How did those reforms challenge traditional precepts, and how effective were they?

Reform and Reorganization

In response to recurring and deepening crises, Ottoman leaders launched a series of reforms designed to strengthen and preserve the state. Reform efforts began as early as the seventeenth century, when sultans sought to limit taxation, increase agricultural production, and end official corruption. Reform continued in the eighteenth century, as Sultan Selim III (reigned 1789–1807) embarked on a program to remodel his army along the lines of European forces. But the establishment of a new crack fighting force, trained by European instructors and equipped with modern weapons, threatened the elite Janissary corps, which reacted violently by rising in revolt, killing the new troops, and locking up the sultan. When Selim's successor tried to revive the new military force, rampaging Janissaries killed all male members of the dynasty save one, Selim's cousin Mahmud II, who became sultan (reigned 1808–1839).

The Reforms of Mahmud II

The encroachment of European powers and the separatist ambitions of local rulers persuaded Mahmud to launch his own reform program. Politically savvy, Mahmud ensured that his reforms were perceived not as dangerous infidel innovations but, rather, as a restoration of the traditional Ottoman military. Nevertheless, his proposal for a new European-style army in 1826 brought him into conflict with the Janissaries. When the Janissaries mutinied in protest, Mahmud had them massacred by troops loyal to the sultan. That incident cleared the way for a series of reforms that unfolded during the last thirteen years of Mahmud's reign.

Sultan Abdül Hamid II ruled the Ottoman empire from 1876 to 1909, when the Young Turks deposed him and sent him into exile.

Mahmud's program remodeled Ottoman institutions along western European lines. Highest priority went to the creation of a more effective army. European drill masters dressed Ottoman soldiers in European-style uniforms and instructed them in European weapons and tactics. Before long, Ottoman recruits were studying at military and engineering schools that taught European curricula. Mahmud's reforms went beyond military affairs. His government created a system of secondary education for boys to facilitate the transition from mosque schools, which provided most primary education, to newly established scientific, technical, and military academies. Mahmud also tried to transfer power from traditional elites to the sultan and his cabinet by taxing rural landlords, abolishing the system of military land grants, and undermining the ulama, the Islamic leadership. To make his authority more effective, the sultan established European-style ministries, constructed new roads, built telegraph lines, and inaugurated a postal service. By the time of Mahmud's death in 1839, the Ottoman empire had shrunk in size, but it was also more manageable and powerful than it had been since the early seventeenth century.

Legal and Educational Reform Continuing defeats on the battlefield and the rise of separatist movements among subject peoples prompted the ruling classes to undertake more radical restructuring of the Ottoman state. The tempo of reform increased rapidly during the Tanzimat ("reorganization") era (1839–1876). Once again, the army was a principal target of reform efforts, but legal and educational reforms also had wide-ranging implications for Ottoman society. In designing their program, Tanzimat reformers drew considerable inspiration from Enlightenment thought and the constitutional foundations of western European states.

Tanzimat reformers attacked Ottoman law with the aim of making it acceptable to Europeans so they could have the capitulations lifted and recover Ottoman sovereignty. Using the French legal system as a guide, reformers promulgated a commercial code (1850), a penal code (1858), a maritime code (1863), and a new civil code (1870–1876). Tanzimat reformers also issued decrees designed to safeguard the rights of subjects. Key among them were measures that guaranteed public trials, rights of privacy, and equality before the law for all Ottoman subjects, whether Muslim or not. Matters pertaining to marriage and divorce still fell under religious law. But because state courts administered the new laws, legal reform undermined the ulama and enhanced the authority of the Ottoman state. Educational reforms also undermined the ulama, who controlled religious education for Muslims. A comprehensive plan for educational reform, introduced in 1846, provided for a complete system of primary and secondary schools leading to university-level instruction, all under the supervision of the state ministry of education. A still more ambitious plan, inaugurated in 1869, provided for free and compulsory primary education.

Opposition to the Tanzimat Although reform and reorganization strengthened Ottoman society, the Tanzimat provoked spirited opposition from several distinct quarters. Harsh criticism came from religious conservatives, who argued that reformers posed a threat to the empire's Islamic foundation. Many devout Muslims viewed the extension of legal equality to Jews and Christians as an act contrary to the basic principles of Islamic law. Even some minority leaders opposed legal equality, fearing that it would diminish their own position as intermediaries between their communities and the Ottoman state. Criticism arose also from a group known collectively as the Young Ottomans. Although they did not share a common political or religious program—their views ranged from secular revolution to uncompromising Islam—Young Ottomans agitated for individual freedom, local autonomy, and political decentralization. Many Young Ottomans desired the establishment of a constitutional government along the lines of the British system. A fourth and perhaps the most dangerous critique of Tanzimat emerged from within the Ottoman bureaucracy itself. In part because of their exclusion from power, high-level bureaucrats were determined to impose checks on the sultan's power by forcing him to accept a constitution and, if necessary, even to depose the ruler.

The Young Turk Era

Reform and Repression In 1876 a group of radical dissidents from the Ottoman bureaucracy seized power in a coup, formed a cabinet that included partisans of reform, and installed Abdül Hamid II as sultan (reigned 1876–1909). Convinced of the need to check the sultan's power, reformers persuaded Abdül Hamid to accept a constitution that limited his authority and established a representative government. Within a year, however, the sultan suspended the constitution, dissolved parliament, exiled many liberals, and executed others. For thirty years he ruled autocratically in an effort to rescue the empire from dismemberment by European powers. He continued to develop the army and administration according to Tanzimat

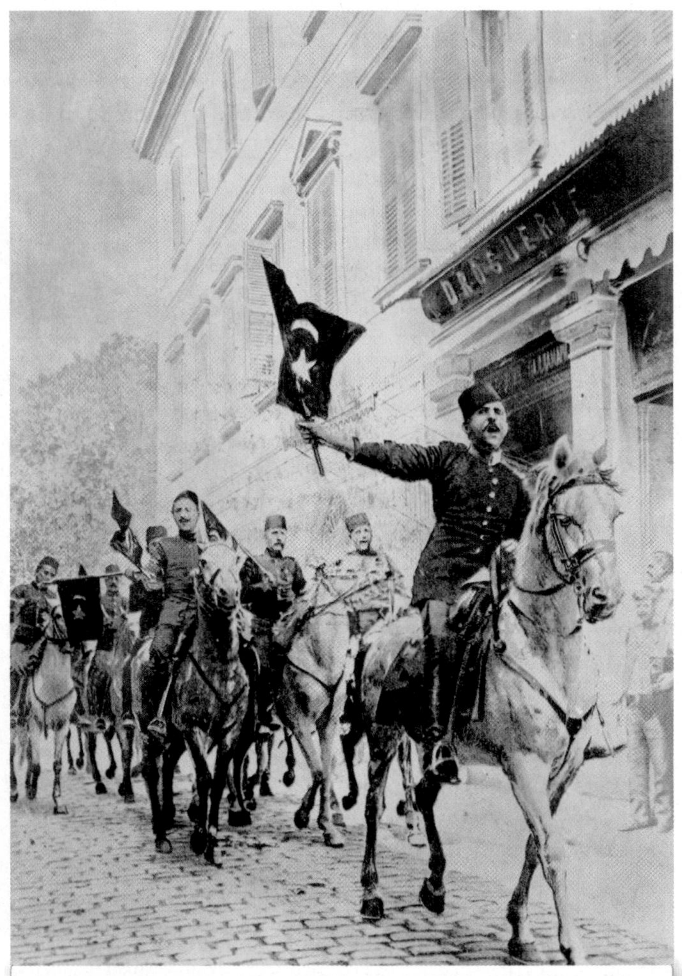

Young Turks celebrate the success of their coup, which forced the sultan to establish a constitutional government in 1908.

sources from the past

Proclamation of the Young Turks

Beginning in the 1890s the Ottoman Society for Union and Progress, better known as the Young Turk Party, started agitating for the resignation of the Ottoman sultan Abdül Hamid and the restoration of the constitution of 1876. After years of underground activity, the Young Turks forced the sultan to reestablish a parliamentary government and reinstate the constitution in 1908. Shortly thereafter the Young Turks outlined their plans for a new Turkish state.

1. The basis for the Constitution will be respect for the predominance of the national will. One of the consequences of this principle will be to require without delay the responsibility of the minister before the Chamber, and, consequently, to consider the minister as having resigned, when he does not have a majority of the votes of the Chamber.
2. Provided that the number of senators does not exceed one third the number of deputies, the Senate will be named (which is not provided for in article 62 of the Constitution) as follows: one third by the Sultan and two thirds by the nation, and the term of senators will be of limited duration.
3. It will be demanded that all Ottoman subjects having completed their twentieth year, regardless of whether they possess property or fortune, shall have the right to vote. Those who have lost their civil rights will naturally be deprived of this right.
4. It will be demanded that the right freely to constitute political groups be inserted in a precise fashion in the constitutional charter, in order that article 1 of the Constitution of 1293 (1876) be respected. . . .
7. The Turkish tongue will remain the official state language. Official correspondence and discussion will take place in Turk. . . .
9. Every citizen will enjoy complete liberty and equality, regardless of nationality or religion, and be submitted to the same obligations. All Ottomans, being equal before the law as regards rights and duties relative to the State, are eligible for government posts, according to their individual capacity and their education. Non-Muslims will be equally liable to the military law.
10. The free exercise of the religious privileges which have been accorded to different nationalities will remain intact. . . .
14. Provided that the property rights of landholders are not infringed upon (for such rights must be respected and must remain intact, according to the law), it will be proposed that peasants be permitted to acquire land, and they will be accorded means to borrow money at a moderate rate. . . .
16. Education will be free. Every Ottoman citizen, within the limits of the prescriptions of the Constitution, may operate a private school in accordance with the special laws.
17. All schools will operate under the surveillance of the state. In order to obtain for Ottoman citizens an education of a homogeneous and uniform character, the official schools will be open, their instruction will be free, and all nationalities will be admitted. Instruction in Turk will be obligatory in public schools. In official schools, public instruction will be free.

Secondary and higher education will be given in the public and official schools indicated above; it will use the Turkish tongue as a basis. . . . Schools of commerce, agriculture and industry will be opened with the goal of developing the resources of the country.

For Further Reflection

- How do the plans of the Young Turks privilege their own age cohort within the Ottoman empire, particularly in regard to voting rights and education?

Source: Rondo Cameron, ed. *Civilization since Waterloo: A Book of Source Readings.* Itasca, Ill.: F. E. Peacock, 1971, pp. 245–46.

principles, and he oversaw the formation of a police force, educational reforms, economic development, and the construction of railroads.

Abdül Hamid's despotic rule generated many liberal opposition groups. Though intended to strengthen the state, reform and reorganization actually undermined the position of the sultan. As Ottoman bureaucrats and army officers received an education in European curricula, they not only learned modern science and technology but also became acquainted with European political, social, and cultural traditions. Many of them fell out of favor with Abdül Hamid and spent years in exile, where they experienced European society firsthand. Educated subjects came to believe that the biggest problem of the Ottoman empire was the political structure that vested unchecked power in the sultan. For these dissidents, Ottoman society was in dire need of political reform and especially of a written constitution that defined and limited the sultan's power.

The Young Turks The most active dissident organization was the Ottoman Society for Union and Progress, better known as the Young Turk Party, although many of its members were neither young nor Turkish. Founded in 1889 by exiled Ottoman subjects living in Paris, the Young Turk Party vigorously promoted reform, and its members made effective use of recently established newspapers to spread their message. Young Turks called for universal suffrage, equality before the law, freedom of religion, free public education, secularization of the state, and the emancipation of women. In 1908 the Young Turks inspired an army coup that forced Abdül Hamid to restore parliament and the constitution of 1876. In 1909 they dethroned him and established Mehmed V Rashid (reigned 1909–1918) as a puppet sultan. Throughout the Young Turk era (1908–1918), Ottoman sultans reigned but no longer ruled.

While pursuing reform within Ottoman society, the Young Turks sought to maintain Turkish hegemony in the larger empire. They worked to make Turkish the official language of the empire, even though many subjects spoke Arabic or a Slavic language as their native tongue. Thus Young Turk policies aggravated tensions between Turkish rulers and subject peoples outside the Anatolian heartland of the Ottoman empire. Syria and Iraq were especially active regions of Arab resistance to Ottoman rule. In spite of their efforts to shore up the ailing empire, reformers could not turn the tide of decline: Ottoman armies continued to lose wars, and subject peoples continued to seek autonomy or independence. By the early twentieth century, the Ottoman empire survived principally because European diplomats could not agree on how to dispose of the empire without upsetting the European balance of power.

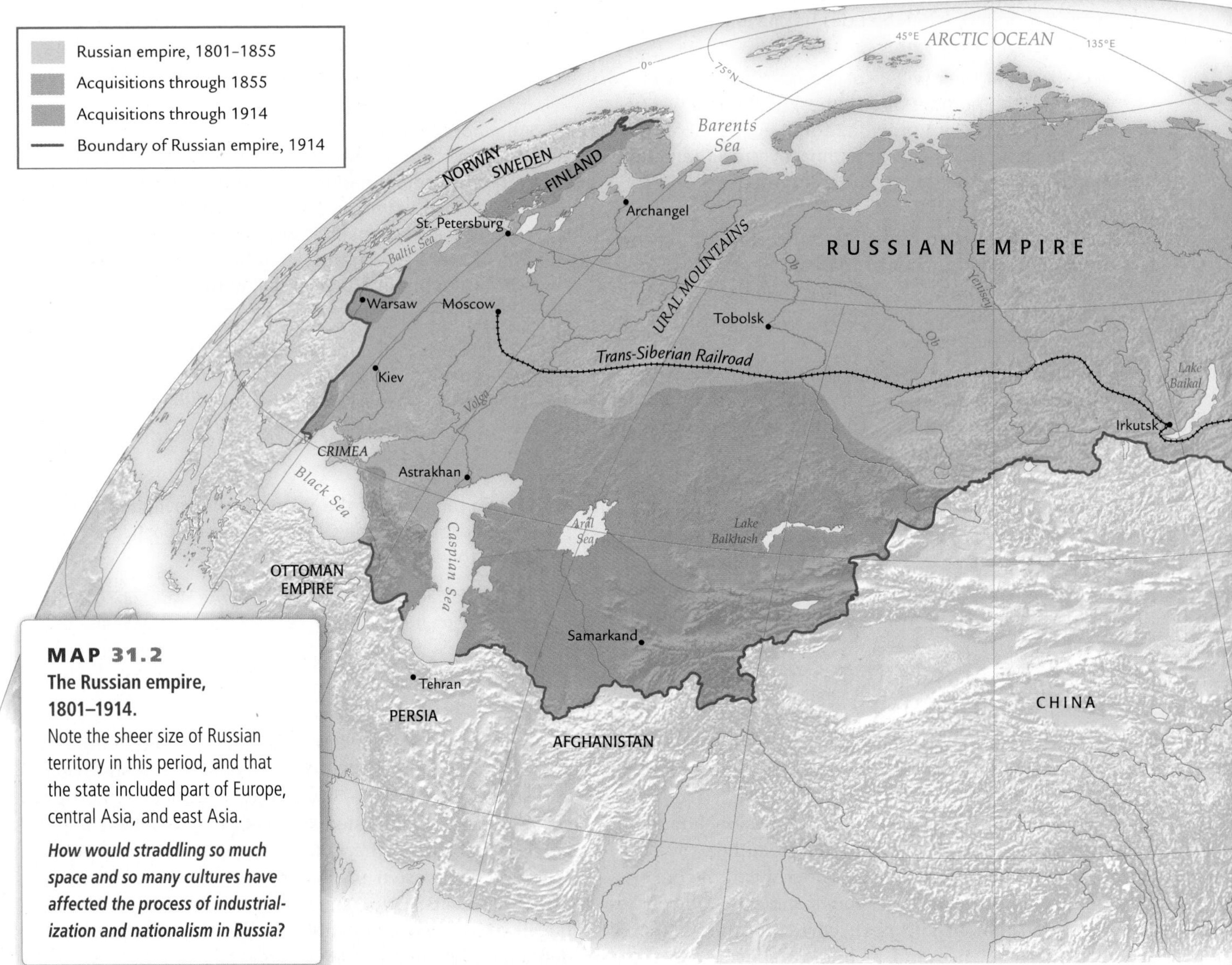

MAP 31.2
The Russian empire, 1801–1914.
Note the sheer size of Russian territory in this period, and that the state included part of Europe, central Asia, and east Asia.

How would straddling so much space and so many cultures have affected the process of industrialization and nationalism in Russia?

THE RUSSIAN EMPIRE UNDER PRESSURE

Like the Ottoman empire, the Russian empire experienced battlefield reverses that laid bare the economic and technological disparity between Russia and western European powers. Determined to preserve Russia's status as a great land power, the tsarist government embarked on a program of reform. The keystone of those efforts was the emancipation of the serfs. Social reform paved the way for government-sponsored industrialization, which began to transform Russian society during the last decades of the nineteenth century. Political liberalization did not accompany social and economic reform, because the tsars refused to yield their autocratic powers. The oppressive political environment sparked opposition movements that turned increasingly radical in the late nineteenth century. In the early twentieth century, domestic discontent reached crisis proportions and exploded in revolution.

Military Defeat and Social Reform

The nineteenth-century tsars ruled a multiethnic, multilingual, multicultural empire that stretched from Poland to the Pacific Ocean. Only about half the population spoke the Russian language or observed the Russian Orthodox faith. The Romanov tsars ruled their diverse and sprawling realm through an autocratic regime in which all initiative came from the central administration. The tsars enjoyed the support of the Russian Orthodox church and a powerful class of nobles who owned most of the land and were exempt from taxes and military duty. Peasants made up the vast majority of the population, and most of them were serfs bound to the lands that they cultivated. Serfdom was almost as cruel and exploitative as slavery, but most landowners, including the state, considered it a guarantee of social stability.

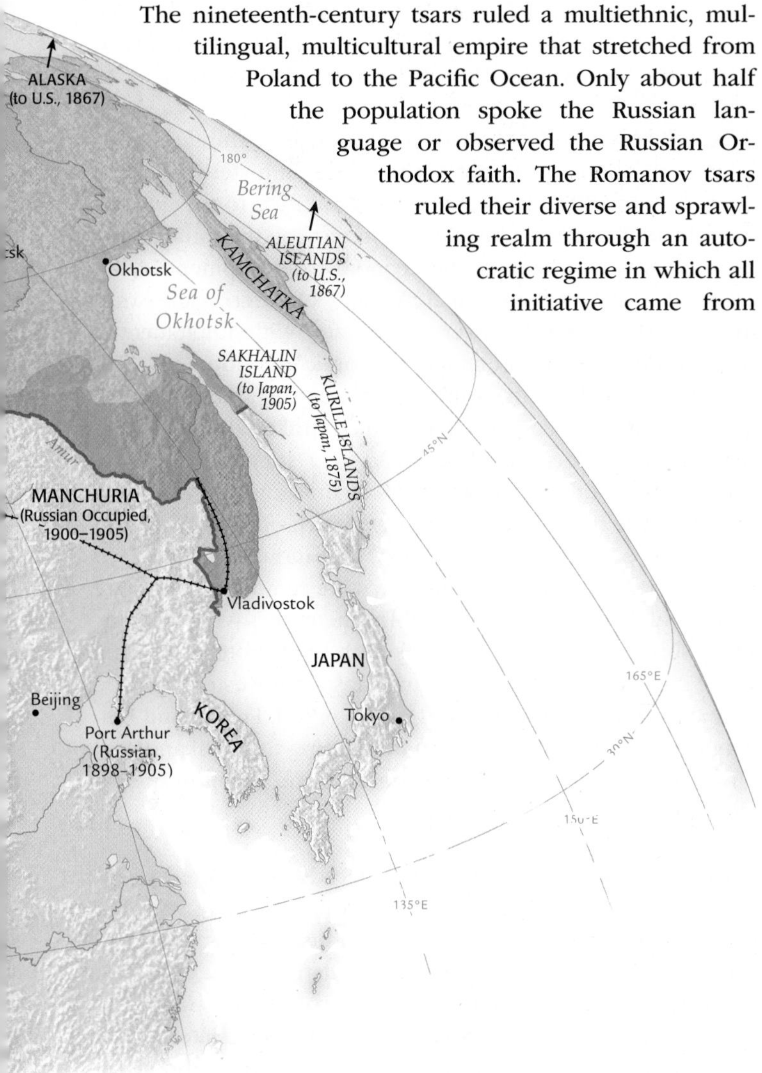

The Crimean War A respected and feared military power, Russia maintained its tradition of conquest and expansion. During the nineteenth century the Russian empire expanded in three directions: east into Manchuria, south into the Caucasus and central Asia, and southwest toward the Mediterranean. This last thrust led to interference in the Balkan provinces of the Ottoman empire. After defeating Turkish forces in a war from 1828 to 1829, Russia tried to establish a protectorate over the weakening Ottoman empire. This expansive effort threatened to upset the balance of power in Europe, which led to military conflict between Russia and a coalition including Britain, France, the kingdom of Sardinia, and the Ottoman empire. The Crimean War (1853–1856) clearly revealed the weakness of the Russian empire, which could hold its own against Ottoman and Qing forces, but not against the industrial powers of western Europe. In September 1854, allied forces mounted a campaign against Sevastopol in the Crimean peninsula, headquarters of Russia's Black Sea Fleet. Unable to mobilize, equip, and transport troops to defeat European forces that operated under a mediocre command, Russian armies suffered devastating and humiliating defeats on their own territory. Russia's economy could not support the tsars' expansionist ambitions, and the Crimean War clearly demonstrated the weakness of an agrarian economy based on unfree labor. Military defeat compelled the tsarist autocracy to reevaluate the Russian social order and undertake an extensive restructuring program.

Emancipation of the Serfs The key to social reform in Russia was emancipation of the serfs. Opposition to serfdom had grown steadily since the eighteenth century, not only among radicals, but also among high officials. Although some Russians objected to serfdom on moral grounds, many believed that it had become an obstacle to economic development and a viable state. Besides being economically inefficient, serfdom was a source of rural instability and peasant revolt: hundreds of insurrections broke out during the first four decades of the nineteenth century. As Tsar Alexander II (reigned 1855–1881) succinctly suggested to the nobility of Moscow, "It is better to abolish serfdom from above than to wait until the serfs begin to liberate themselves from below." Accordingly, in 1861 the tsar abolished the institution of serfdom, though it remained in practice for decades to come.

The government sought to balance the interests of lords and serfs, but on balance the terms of emancipation were unfavorable to most peasants. The government compensated landowners for the loss of their land and the serfs who had worked it. Serfs won their freedom, had their labor obligations gradually canceled, and gained opportunities to become landowners. But the peasants won few political rights, and they had to pay a redemption tax for most of the lands they received. Many disappointed peasants believed that their rulers forced them to pay for land that was theirs by right. A few peasants prospered and improved their position as the result of emancipation, but most found themselves in debt for the rest of their lives—a source of alienation and radicalization. Emancipation resulted in little if any increase in agricultural production.

Political and Legal Reform Other important reforms came in the wake of the serfs' emancipation. To deal with local issues of health, education, and welfare, the government created elected district assemblies, or *zemstvos,* in 1864. Although all classes, including peasants, elected representatives to these assemblies, the *zemstvos* remained subordinate to the tsarist autocracy, which retained exclusive authority over national issues, and the landowning nobility, which possessed a disproportionately large share of both votes and seats. Legal reform was more fruitful than experimentation with representative government. The revision of the judiciary system in 1864 created a system of law courts based on western European models, replete with independent judges and a system of appellate courts. Legal reforms also instituted trial by jury for criminal offenses and elected justices of the peace who dealt with minor offenses. These reforms encouraged the emergence of attorneys and other legal experts, whose professional standards contributed to a decline in judicial corruption.

Tsar Alexander II of Russia. After signing the Treaty of Paris in 1856, ending the Crimean War, Alexander abolished serfdom in the Russian empire.

Industrialization

Social and political reform coincided with industrialization in nineteenth-century Russia. Tsar Alexander II emancipated the serfs partly with the intention of creating a mobile labor force for emerging industries, and the tsarist government encouraged industrialization as a way of strengthening the Russian empire. Thus, although Russian industrialization took place within a framework of capitalism, it differed from western European industrialization in that the motivation for development was political and military and the driving force was government policy rather than entrepreneurial initiative. Industrialization proceeded slowly at first, but it surged during the last two decades of the nineteenth century.

The Witte System The prime mover behind Russian industrialization was Count Sergei Witte, minister of finance from 1892 to 1903. His first budget, submitted to the government in 1893, outlined his aims as "removing the unfavorable conditions which hamper the economic development of the country" and "kindling a healthy spirit of enterprise." Availing himself of the full power of the state, Witte implemented policies designed to stimulate economic development. The centerpiece of his industrial policy was an ambitious program of railway construction, which linked the far-flung regions of the Russian empire and also stimulated the development of other industries. Most important of the new lines was the trans-Siberian railway, which opened Siberia to large-scale settlement, exploitation, and industrialization. To raise domestic capital for industry, Witte remodeled the state bank and encouraged the establishment of savings banks. Witte supported infant industries with high protective tariffs while also securing large foreign loans from western Europe to finance industrialization. His plan worked. French and Belgian capital played a key role in developing the steel and coal industries, and British funds supported the booming petroleum industry in the Caucasus.

Industrial Discontent For a decade the Witte system played a crucial role in the industrialization of Russia, but peasant rebellions and strikes by industrial workers indicated that large segments of the population were unwilling to tolerate the low standard of living that Witte's policy entailed. Recently freed serfs often did not appreciate factory work, which forced them to follow new routines and adapt to the rhythms of industrial machinery. Industrial growth

Russian merchants in nineteenth-century Novgorod wear both western European and traditional Russian dress while taking tea. What does this mixed fashion suggest about the Russian society and its economic evolution?

began to generate an urban working class, which endured conditions similar to those experienced by workers in other societies during the early stages of industrialization. Employers kept wages of overworked and poorly housed workers at the barest minimum. The industrial sections of St. Petersburg and Moscow became notorious for the miserable working and living conditions of factory laborers. In 1897 the government limited the maximum working day to 11.5 hours, but that measure did little to alleviate the plight of workers. The government prohibited the formation of trade unions and outlawed strikes, which continued to occur in spite of the restrictions. Economic exploitation and the lack of political freedom made workers increasingly receptive to revolutionary propaganda, and underground movements soon developed among them.

Not everyone was dissatisfied with the results of intensified industrialization. Besides foreign investors, a growing Russian business class benefited from government policy that protected domestic industries and its profits. Russian entrepreneurs reaped rich rewards for their roles in economic development, and they had little complaint with the political system. In contrast to western European capitalists, who had both material and ideological reasons to challenge the power of absolute monarchs and the nobility, Russian businesspeople generally did not challenge the tsarist autocracy.

Repression and Revolution

Protest During the last three decades of the nineteenth century, antigovernment protest and revolutionary activity increased. Hopes aroused by government reforms gave impetus to reform movements, and social tensions arising from industrialization fueled protest by groups whose aims became increasingly radical. Peasants seethed with discontent because they had little or no land and, increasingly, mobile dissidents spread rebellious ideas between industrial cities. At the center of opposition were university students and a class of intellectuals collectively known as the intelligentsia. Their goals and methods varied, but they generally sought substantial political reform and thorough social change. Most dissidents drew inspiration from western European socialism, but they despised the individualism, materialism, and unbridled capitalism of western Europe and thus worked toward a socialist system more in keeping with Russian cultural traditions. Many revolutionaries were anarchists, who on principle opposed all forms of government and believed that individual freedom cannot be realized until all government is abolished. Some anarchists relied on terror tactics and assassination to achieve their goals. Insofar as they had a positive political program, the anarchists wanted to vest all authority in local governing councils elected by universal suffrage.

Repression Some activists saw the main potential for revolutionary action in the countryside, and between 1873 and 1876 hundreds of anarchists and other radicals traveled to rural areas to enlighten and rouse the peasantry. The peasants did not understand their impassioned speeches, but the police did and soon arrested the idealists. Tsarist authorities sentenced some to prison and banished others to the remote provinces of Siberia. Frightened by manifestations of radicalism, tsarist authorities resorted to repression: they censored publications and sent secret police to infiltrate and break up dissident organizations. Repression, however, only radicalized

Japanese infantry charging during the Russo-Japanese war.

revolutionaries further and encouraged them to engage in conspiratorial activities.

In the Baltic provinces, Poland, the Ukraine, Georgia, and central Asia, dissidents opposed the tsarist autocracy on ethnic as well as political and social grounds. In those lands, subject peoples speaking their own languages often used schools and political groups as foundations for separatist movements as they sought autonomy or independence from the Russian empire. Tsarist officials responded with a heavy-handed program of Russification to repress the use of languages other than Russian and to restrict educational opportunities to those loyal to the tsarist state. Throughout the Russian empire, Jews also were targets of suspicion, and tsarist authorities tolerated frequent pogroms (anti-Jewish riots) by subjects jealous of their Jewish neighbors' success in business affairs. To escape this violence, Jews migrated by the hundreds of thousands to western Europe and the United States in the late nineteenth century.

Terrorism In 1876 a recently formed group called the Land and Freedom Party began to promote the assassination of prominent officials as a means to pressure the government into political reform. In 1879 a terrorist faction of the party, the People's Will, resolved to assassinate Alexander II, who had emancipated the serfs and had launched a program of political and social reform. After several unsuccessful attempts, an assassin exploded a bomb under Alexander's carriage in 1881. The first blast did little damage, but as Alexander inspected his carriage, a second and more powerful explosion killed the reforming tsar. The attack brought the era of reform to an end and prompted the tsarist autocracy to adopt an uncompromising policy of repression.

In 1894 Nicholas II (reigned 1894–1917) ascended the throne. A well-intentioned but weak ruler, Nicholas championed oppression and police control. To deflect attention from domestic issues and neutralize revolutionary movements, the tsar's government embarked on expansionist ventures in east Asia. Russian designs on Korea and Manchuria clashed with similar Japanese intentions, leading to a rivalry that ended in war. The Russo-Japanese war began with a Japanese surprise attack on the Russian naval squadron at Port Arthur in February 1904 and ended in May 1905 with the destruction of the Russian navy.

The Revolution of 1905 Russian military defeats brought to a head simmering political and social discontent and triggered widespread disturbances. In January 1905 a group of workers marched on the tsar's Winter Palace in St. Petersburg to petition Nicholas for a popularly elected assembly and other political concessions. Government troops met the petitioners with rifle fire, killing 130. The news of this Bloody Sunday massacre caused an angry uproar throughout the empire that culminated in labor unrest, peasant insurrections, student demonstrations, and mutinies in both the army and the navy. Organizing themselves at the village level, peasants discussed seizing the property of their landlords. Urban workers created new councils known as soviets to organize strikes and negotiate with employers and government authorities. Elected delegates from factories and workshops served as members of these soviets.

Revolutionary turmoil paralyzed Russian cities and forced the government to make concessions. Sergei Witte, whom Nicholas had appointed to conduct peace negotiations with Japan, urged the tsar to create an elected legislative assembly. The tsar reluctantly consented and permitted the establishment of the Duma, Russia's first parliamentary institution. Although the Duma lacked the power to create or bring down governments, from the Romanov perspective this act was a major concession. Still, the creation of the Duma did not end unrest. Between 1905 and 1907 disorder continued, and violence flared especially in the Baltic provinces, Poland, the Ukraine, Georgia, and central Asia, where ethnic tensions added to revolutionary sentiments. Through bloody reprisals the government eventually restored order, but the hour was late for the Romanov dynasty.

THE CHINESE EMPIRE UNDER SIEGE

The Chinese empire and the Qing dynasty experienced even more difficulties than did the Ottoman and Russian empires during the nineteenth century. European powers inflicted military defeats on Qing forces and compelled China's leaders to accept a series of humiliating treaties. The provisions of these treaties undermined Chinese sovereignty, carved China into spheres of influence that set the stage for economic exploitation, and handicapped the Qing dynasty's ability to deal with domestic disorder. As the government tried to cope with foreign challenges, it also faced dangerous internal upheavals, the most important of which was the Taiping rebellion. Caught between aggressive foreigners and insurgent rebels, China's ruling elites developed reform programs to maintain social order, strengthen the state, and preserve the Qing dynasty. The reforms had limited effect, however, and by the early twentieth century, China was in a seriously weakened condition.

The Opium War and the Unequal Treaties

In 1759 the Qianlong emperor restricted the European commercial presence in China to the waterfront at Guangzhou, where European merchants could establish warehouses. There, Chinese authorities controlled not only European merchants but also the terms of trade. Foreign merchants could deal only with specially licensed Chinese firms known as *cohongs,* which bought and sold goods at set prices and operated under strict regulations established by the government. Besides the expense and inconvenience of the *cohong* system, European merchants had to cope with a market that had little demand for European products. As a result, European merchants paid for Chinese silk, porcelain, lacquerware, and tea largely with silver bullion.

The Opium Trade Seeking increased profits in the late eighteenth century, officials of the British East India Company sought alternatives to bullion to exchange for Chinese goods. They gradually turned to trade in a product that was as profitable as it was criminal—opium. Using Turkish and Persian expertise, the East India Company grew opium in India and shipped it to China, where company officials exchanged it for Chinese silver coin. The silver then flowed back to British-controlled Calcutta and London, where company merchants used it to buy Chinese products in Guangzhou. The opium trade expanded rapidly: annual imports of opium in the early nineteenth century amounted to about 4,500 chests, each weighing 60 kilograms (133 pounds), but by 1839 some 40,000 chests of opium entered China annually to satisfy the habits of drug addicts. With the help of this new commodity, the East India Company easily paid for luxury Chinese products.

Trade in opium was illegal, but it continued unabated for decades because Chinese authorities made little effort to enforce the law. Indeed, corrupt officials often benefited personally by allowing the illegal trade to go on. By the late 1830s, however, government officials had become aware that China had a trade problem and a drug problem as well. The opium trade not only drained large quantities of silver bullion from China but also created serious social problems in southern China. When government authorities took steps in 1838 to halt the illicit trade, British merchants started losing money. In 1839 the Chinese government stepped up its campaign by charging the incorruptible Lin Zexu with the task of destroying the opium trade. Commissioner Lin acted quickly, confiscating and destroying some 20,000 chests of opium. His uncompromising policy ignited a war that ended in a humiliating defeat for China.

The Opium War Outraged by the Chinese action against opium, British commercial agents pressed their government into a military retaliation designed to reopen the opium trade. The ensuing conflict, known as the Opium War (1839–1842), made plain the military power differential between Europe and China. In the initial stages of the conflict, British

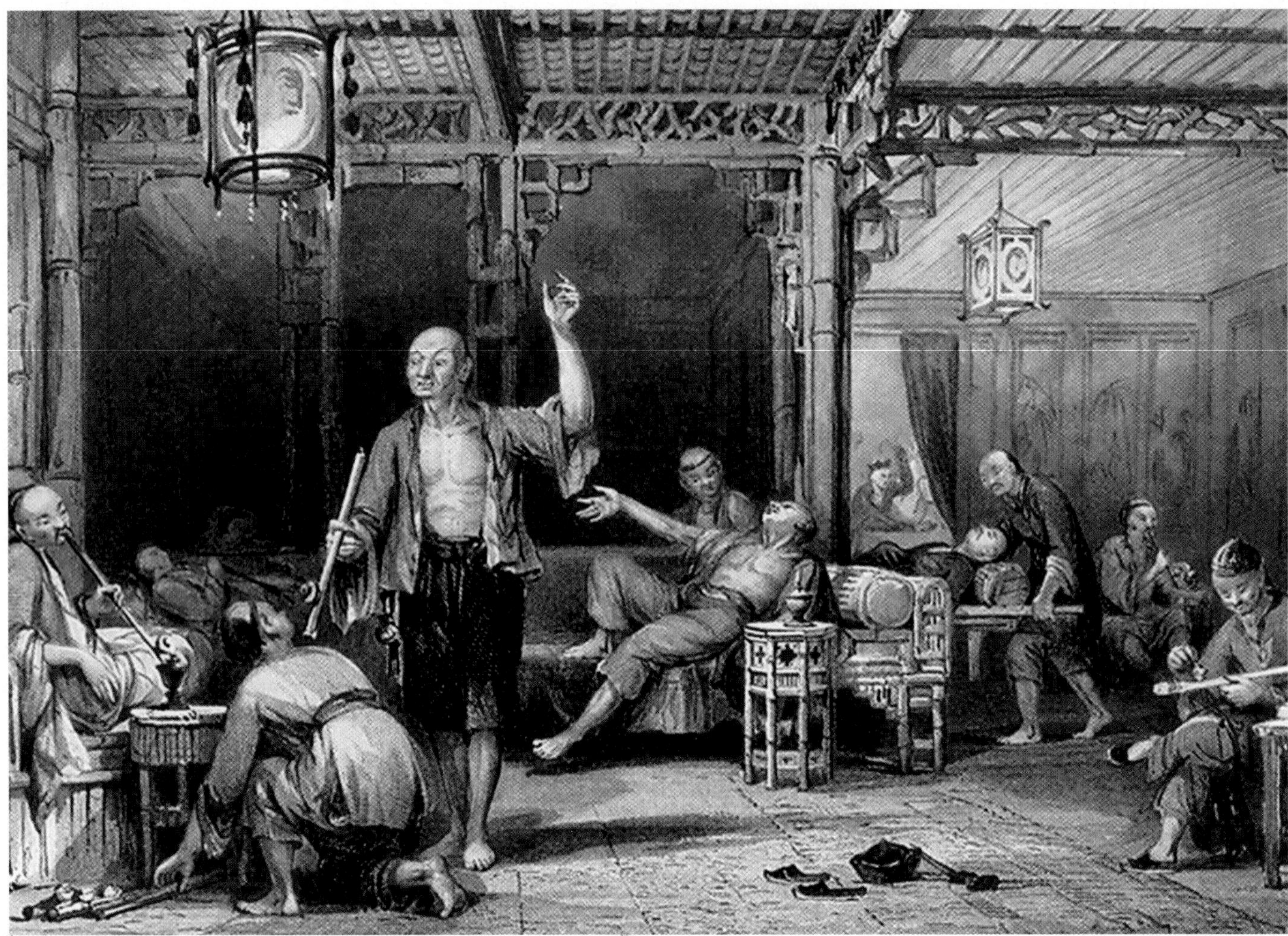

Chinese opium smokers. Chinese efforts to stop opium imports led to a humiliating defeat in the Opium War.

naval vessels easily demonstrated their superiority on the seas. Meanwhile, equipped only with swords, knives, spears, and occasionally muskets, the defenders of Chinese coastal towns were no match for the controlled firepower of well-drilled British infantry armed with rifles. But neither the destruction of Chinese war fleets nor the capture of coastal forts and towns persuaded the Chinese to sue for peace.

British forces broke the military stalemate when they decided to strike at China's jugular vein—the Grand Canal, which linked the Yangzi and Yellow River valleys—with the aid of steam-powered gunboats. Armed, shallow-draft steamers could travel speedily up and down rivers, projecting the military advantage that European ships enjoyed on the high seas deep into interior regions. In May 1842 a British armada of seventy ships—led by the gunboat *Nemesis*—advanced up the Yangzi River. The British fleet encountered little resistance, and by the time it reached the intersection of the river and the Grand Canal, the Chinese government had sued for peace. China experienced similar military setbacks throughout the second half of the nineteenth century in conflicts with Britain and France (1856–1858), France (1884–1885), and Japan (1894–1895).

Unequal Treaties In the wake of those confrontations came a series of pacts collectively known in China as unequal treaties, which curtailed China's sovereignty. Beginning with the Treaty of Nanjing, which Britain forced China to accept at the conclusion of the Opium War in 1842, these agreements guided Chinese relations with foreign states until 1943. The Treaty of Nanjing (1842) ceded Hong Kong Island in perpetuity to Britain, opened five Chinese ports—including Guangzhou and Shanghai—to commerce and residence, compelled the Qing government to extend most-favored-nation status to Britain, and granted extraterritoriality to British subjects, which meant they were not subject to Chinese laws. The Treaty of Nanjing governed relations only between Britain and China, but France, Germany, Den-

sources from the past

Letter of Lin Zexu to Queen Victoria

In 1838 Qing emperor Daoguang sent Lin Zexu to Guangzhou to put an end to imports of opium into China. A leading Confucian scholar, Lin worked to persuade Chinese and foreigners alike that opium was a harmful and evil drug. In 1839 he composed a letter to Great Britain's Queen Victoria seeking her support in halting the flow of opium. Although never delivered, the letter illustrates Lin's efforts to stem the flow of opium by reason and negotiation before he resorted to sterner measures.

You have traded in China for almost 200 years, and as a result, your country has become wealthy and prosperous.

As this trade has lasted for a long time, there are bound to be unscrupulous as well as honest traders. Among the unscrupulous are those who bring opium to China to harm the Chinese; they succeed so well that this poison has spread far and wide in all the provinces. You, I hope, will certainly agree that people who pursue material gains to the great detriment of the welfare of others can be neither tolerated by Heaven nor endured by men. . . .

I have heard that the areas under your direct jurisdiction such as London, Scotland, and Ireland do not produce opium; it is produced instead in your Indian possessions such as Bengal, Madras, Bombay, Patna, and Malwa. In these possessions the English people not only plant opium poppies that stretch from one mountain to another but also open factories to manufacture this terrible drug. As months accumulate and years pass by, the poison they have produced increases in its wicked intensity, and its repugnant odor reaches as high as the sky. Heaven is furious with anger, and all the gods are moaning with pain! It is hereby suggested that you destroy and plow under all of these opium plants and grow food crops instead, while issuing an order to punish severely anyone who dares to plant opium poppies again. If you adopt this policy of love so as to produce good and exterminate evil, Heaven will protect you, and gods will bring you good fortune. Moreover, you will enjoy a long life and be rewarded with a multitude of children and grandchildren! . . .

The present law calls for the imposition of the death sentence on any Chinese who has peddled or smoked opium. Since a Chinese could not peddle or smoke opium if foreigners had not brought it to China, it is clear that the true culprits of a Chinese's death as a result of an opium conviction are the opium traders from foreign countries. Being the cause of other people's death, why should they themselves be spared from capital punishment? A murderer of one person is subject to the death sentence; just imagine how many people opium has killed! This is the rationale behind the new law which says that any foreigner who brings opium to China will be sentenced to death by hanging or beheading. Our purpose is to eliminate this poison once and for all and to the benefit of all mankind. . . .

Our Celestial Empire towers over all other countries in virtue and possesses a power great and awesome enough to carry out its wishes. But we will not prosecute a person without warning him in advance; that is why we have made our law explicit and clear. If the merchants of your honorable country wish to enjoy trade with us on a permanent basis, they must fearfully observe our law by cutting off, once and for all, the supply of opium. Under no circumstance should they test our intention to enforce the law by deliberately violating it.

For Further Reflection

- How does Lin Zexu convey his distaste for opium in the descriptive terms he attaches to the drug, and how do the punishments inflicted on opium peddlers suggest Lin Zexu's perception of opium's threat to China?

Source: Dan J. Li. *China in Transition.* New York: Van Nostrand, 1969, pp. 64–67.

mark, the Netherlands, Spain, Belgium, Austria-Hungary, the United States, and Japan later concluded similar unequal treaties with China. Collectively these treaties broadened the concessions given to foreign powers; they legalized the opium trade, permitted the establishment of Christian missions throughout China, and opened additional treaty ports. To ease sales of foreign goods, various treaties also prevented the Qing government from levying tariffs on imports to protect domestic industries. By 1900 ninety Chinese ports were under the effective control of foreign powers, foreign merchants controlled much of the Chinese economy, Christian missionaries sought converts throughout China, and foreign gunboats patrolled Chinese waters. Several treaties also released Korea, Vietnam, and Burma (now known as Myanmar) from Chinese authority and thereby dismantled the Chinese system of tributary states.

The Taiping Rebellion

The debilitation of the Chinese empire at the end of the nineteenth century was as much a result of internal turmoil

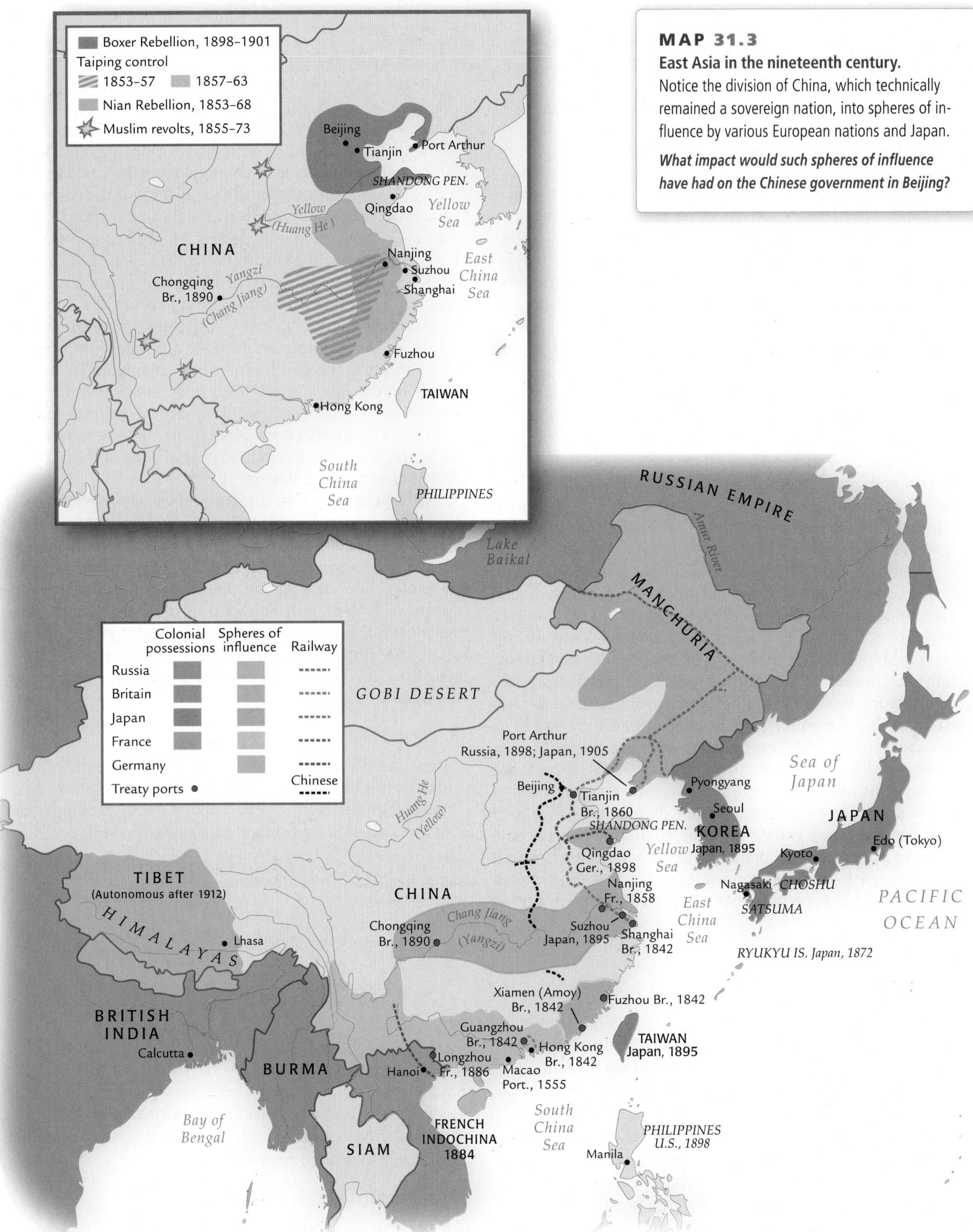

MAP 31.3
East Asia in the nineteenth century.
Notice the division of China, which technically remained a sovereign nation, into spheres of influence by various European nations and Japan. ***What impact would such spheres of influence have had on the Chinese government in Beijing?***

as it was a consequence of foreign intrusion. Large-scale rebellions in the later nineteenth century reflected the increasing poverty and discontent of the Chinese peasantry. Between 1800 and 1900 China's population rose by almost 50 percent, from 330 million to 475 million. The amount of land under cultivation increased only slowly during the same period, so population growth strained Chinese resources. The concentration of land in the hands of wealthy elites aggravated peasant discontent, as did widespread corruption of government officials and increasing drug addiction. After 1850, rebellions erupted throughout China: the Nian rebellion (1851–1868) in the northeast, the Muslim rebellion (1855–1873) in the southwest, and the Tungan rebellion (1862–1878) in the northwest. Most dangerous of all was the Taiping rebellion (1850–1864), which raged throughout most of China and brought the Qing dynasty to the brink of collapse.

The Taiping Program The village schoolteacher Hong Xiuquan provided both inspiration and leadership for the Taiping rebellion. His call for the destruction of the Qing dynasty and his program for the radical transformation of Chinese society appealed to millions of men and women. The Qing dynasty had ruled China since 1644, and Qing elites had adapted to Chinese ways, but many native Chinese subjects despised the Manchu ruling class as foreigners. The Taiping reform program contained many radical features that appealed to discontented subjects, including the abolition of private property, the creation of communal wealth to be shared according to needs, the prohibition of footbinding and concubinage, free public edcation, simplification of the written language, and literacy for the masses. Some Taiping leaders also called for the establishment of democratic political institutions and the building of an industrial society. Although they divided their army into separate divisions of men and women soldiers, the Taipings decreed the equality of men and women. Taiping regulations prohibited sexual intercourse among their followers, including married couples, but Hong and other high leaders maintained large harems.

After sweeping through southeastern China, Hong and his followers in the Society of God Worshipers took Nanjing in 1853 and made it the capital of their Taiping ("Great Peace") kingdom. From Nanjing they campaigned throughout China, and as the rebels passed through the countryside whole towns and villages joined them—often voluntarily, but sometimes under coercion. By 1855 a million Taipings were poised to attack Beijing. Qing forces repelled them, but five years later, firmly entrenched in the Yangzi River valley, the Taipings threatened Shanghai.

Taiping Defeat The radical nature of the Taiping program ensured that the Chinese gentry would side with the Qing government to support a regime dedicated to the preservation of the established order. After imperial forces consisting of Manchu soldiers failed to defeat the Taipings, the Qing government created regional armies staffed by Chinese instead of Manchu soldiers and commanded by members of the scholar-gentry class, a shift encouraged by the empress dowager Cixi (1835–1908), a former imperial concubine who established herself as effective ruler of China during the last fifty years of the Qing dynasty. With the aid of European advisors and weapons, these regional armies gradually overcame the Taipings. By 1862 Hong Xiuquan had largely withdrawn from public affairs, as he sought solace

The final assault on the Taipings at Nanjing by Qing forces in 1864, an operation that caught common people and their livestock in the crossfire.

in religious reflection and diversion in his harem. After a lingering illness, he committed suicide in June 1864. In the following months Nanjing fell, and government forces slaughtered some one hundred thousand Taipings. By the end of the year, the rebellion was over. But the Taiping rebellion had taken a costly toll. It claimed twenty million to thirty million lives, and it caused such drastic declines in agricultural production that populations in war-torn regions frequently resorted to eating grass, leather, hemp, and even human flesh.

Reform Frustrated

The Taiping rebellion altered the course of Chinese history. Contending with aggressive foreign powers and lands ravaged by domestic rebellion, Qing rulers recognized that changes were necessary for the empire to survive. From 1860 to 1895, Qing authorities tried to fashion an efficient and benevolent Confucian government to solve social and economic problems while also adopting foreign technology to strengthen state power.

The Self-Strengthening Movement Most imaginative of the reform programs was the Self-Strengthening Movement (1860–1895), which flourished especially in the 1860s and 1870s. Empowered with imperial grants of authority that permitted them to raise troops, levy taxes, and run bureaucracies, several local leaders promoted military and economic reform. Adopting the slogan "Chinese learning at the base, Western learning for use," leaders of the Self-Strengthening Movement sought to blend Chinese cultural traditions with European industrial technology. While holding to Confucian values and seeking to reestablish a stable agrarian society, movement leaders built modern shipyards, constructed railroads, established weapons industries, opened steel foundries with blast furnaces, and founded academies to develop scientific expertise.

Although it laid a foundation for industrialization, the Self-Strengthening Movement brought only superficial change to the Chinese economy and society. It did not introduce enough industry to bring real military and economic strength

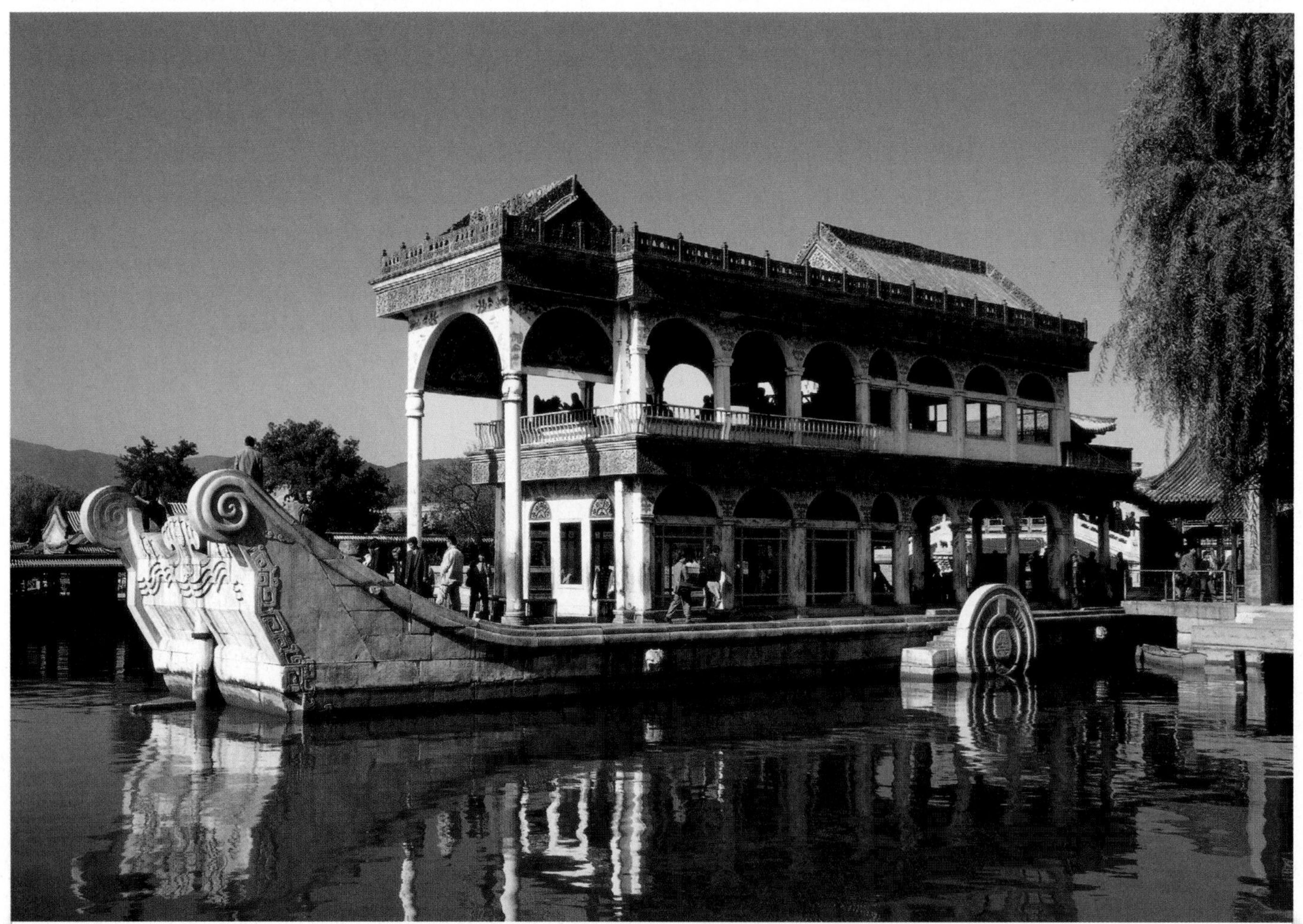

Empress Dowager Cixi diverted government funds intended for the construction of modern warships to the construction of a huge marble vessel to decorate a lake in the gardens of the Summer Palace near Beijing.

to China. It also encountered obstacles in the imperial government: the empress dowager Cixi diverted funds intended for the navy to build a magnificent marble boat to grace a lake in the imperial gardens. Furthermore, the movement foundered on a contradiction: industrialization would bring fundamental social change to an agrarian land, and education in European curricula would undermine the commitment to Confucian values.

Spheres of Influence In any case, the Self-Strengthening Movement also did not prevent continuing foreign intrusion into Chinese affairs. During the latter part of the nineteenth century, foreign powers began to dismantle the Chinese system of tributary states. In 1885 France incorporated Vietnam into its colonial empire, and in 1886 Great Britain detached Burma from Chinese control. In 1895 Japan forced China to recognize the independence of Korea and cede the island of Taiwan and the Liaodong Peninsula in southern Manchuria. By 1898 foreign powers had carved China into spheres of economic influence. Powerless to resist foreign demands, the Qing government granted exclusive rights for railway and mineral development to Germany in Shandong Province, to France in the southern border provinces, to Great Britain in the Yangzi River valley, to Japan in the southeastern coastal provinces, and to Russia in Manchuria. Only distrust among the foreign powers prevented the total dismemberment of the Middle Kingdom.

ÉVÉNEMENTS DE CHINE
Quatorze têtes de Boxers aux murs de Tchio-Tchao

A French journal discussing events in China included an illustration of the Chinese rebels' severed heads being displayed on a wall in 1900.

The Hundred Days Reforms Those setbacks sparked the ambitious but abortive Hundred Days reforms of 1898. The leading figures of the reform movement were the scholars Kang Youwei (1858–1927) and Liang Qichao (1873–1929), who published a series of treatises reinterpreting Confucian thought in a way that justified radical changes in the imperial system. Kang and Liang did not seek to preserve an agrarian society and its cultural traditions so much as to remake China and turn it into a powerful modern industrial society. Impressed by their ideas, the young and open-minded Emperor Guangxu launched a sweeping program to transform China into a constitutional monarchy, guarantee civil liberties, root out corruption, remodel the educational system, encourage foreign influence in China, modernize military forces, and stimulate economic development. The broad range of reform edicts produced a violent reaction from members of the imperial household, their allies in the gentry, and the young emperor's aunt, the ruthless and powerful empress dowager Cixi. After a period of 103 days, Cixi nullified the reform decrees, imprisoned the emperor in the Forbidden City, and executed six leading reformers. Kang and Liang, the spiritual guides of the reform movement, escaped to Japan.

The Boxer Rebellion Believing that foreign powers were pushing for her retirement, Cixi threw her support behind an antiforeign uprising known as the Boxer rebellion, a violent movement spearheaded by militia units calling themselves the Society of Righteous and Harmonious Fists. The foreign press referred to the rebels as Boxers. In 1899 the Boxers organized to rid China of "foreign devils" and their influences. With the empress dowager's encouragement, the Boxers went on a rampage in northern China, killing foreigners and Chinese Christians as well as Chinese who had ties to foreigners. Confident that foreign weapons could not harm them, some 140,000 Boxers besieged foreign embassies in Beijing in the summer of 1900. A heavily armed force of British, French, Russian, U.S., German, and Japanese troops quickly crushed the Boxer movement in bloody retaliation for the assault. The Chinese government had to pay a punitive indemnity and allow foreign powers to station troops in Beijing at their embassies and along the route to the sea.

Because Cixi had instigated the Boxers' attacks on foreigners, many Chinese regarded the Qing dynasty as bankrupt. Revolutionary uprisings gained widespread public support throughout the country, even among conservative Chinese gentry. Cixi died in November 1908, one day after the sudden, unexpected, and mysterious death of the emperor. In her last act of state, the empress dowager appointed the two-year-old boy Puyi to the imperial throne. But Puyi never had a chance to rule: revolution broke out in the autumn of 1911, and by early 1912 the last emperor of the Qing dynasty had abdicated his throne.

THE TRANSFORMATION OF JAPAN

In 1853 a fleet of U.S. warships steamed into Tokyo Bay and demanded permission to establish trade and diplomatic relations with Japan. Representatives of European lands soon joined U.S. agents in Japan. Heavily armed foreign powers intimidated the Tokugawa shogun and his government, the bakufu, into signing unequal treaties providing political and economic privileges similar to those obtained earlier from the Qing dynasty in China. Opposition forces in Japan used the humiliating intrusion of foreigners as an excuse to overthrow the discredited shogun and the Tokugawa bakufu. After restoring the emperor to power in 1868, Japan's new rulers worked for the transformation of Japanese society to achieve political and economic equality with foreign powers. The changes initiated during the Meiji period turned Japan into the political, military, and economic powerhouse of east Asia.

From Tokugawa to Meiji

Crisis and Reform By the early nineteenth century, Japanese society was in turmoil. Declining agricultural productivity, periodic crop failures and famines, and harsh taxation contributed to economic hardship and sometimes even led to starvation among the rural population. A few cultivators prospered during this period, but many had to sell their land and become tenant farmers. Economic conditions in towns and cities, where many peasants migrated in search of a better life, were hardly better than those in the countryside. As the price of rice and other commodities rose, the urban poor experienced destitution and hunger. Even samurai and daimyo faced hardship because they fell into debt to a growing merchant class. Under those conditions, Japan experienced increasing peasant protest and rebellion during the late eighteenth and early nineteenth centuries.

The Tokugawa bakufu responded with conservative reforms. Between 1841 and 1843 the shogun's chief advisor, Mizuno Tadakuni, initiated measures to stem growing social and economic decline and to shore up the Tokugawa government. Mizuno canceled debts that samurai and daimyo owed to merchants, abolished several merchant guilds, and compelled peasants residing in cities to return to the land and cultivate rice. Most of his reforms were ineffective, and they provoked strong opposition that ultimately drove him from office.

A Japanese view of an audience of the first U.S. consul, Townsend Harris, with the Tokugawa shogun and his officials in 1859.

Foreign Pressure Another problem facing the Tokugawa bakufu was the insistence on the establishment of diplomatic and commercial relations by foreign lands. Beginning in 1844, British, French, and U.S. ships visited Japan seeking to establish relations. The United States in particular sought ports where its Pacific merchant and whaling fleets could stop for fuel and provisions. Tokugawa officials refused all those requests and stuck to the policy of excluding all European and American visitors to Japan except for a small number of Dutch merchants, who carried on a carefully controlled trade in Nagasaki. In the later 1840s the bakufu began to make military preparations to resist potential attacks.

The arrival of a U.S. naval squadron in Tokyo Bay in 1853 abruptly changed the situation. The American commander, Commodore Matthew C. Perry, trained his guns on the bakufu capital of Edo (modern Tokyo) and demanded that the shogun open Japan to diplomatic and commercial relations and sign a treaty of friendship. The shogun had no good alternative and so quickly acquiesced to Perry's demands. Representatives of Britain, the Netherlands, and Russia soon won similar rights. Like Qing diplomats a few years earlier, Tokugawa officials agreed to a series of unequal treaties that opened Japanese ports to foreign commerce, deprived the government of control over tariffs, and granted foreigners extraterritorial rights.

The End of Tokugawa Rule The sudden intrusion of foreign powers precipitated a domestic crisis in Japan that resulted in the collapse of the Tokugawa bakufu and the restoration of imperial rule. When the shogun complied with the demands of U.S. and European representatives, he aroused the opposition of conservative daimyo and the emperor, who resented the humiliating terms of the unequal treaties and questioned the shogun's right to rule Japan as "subduer of barbarians." Opposition to Tokugawa authority spread rapidly, and the southern domains of Choshu and Satsuma became centers of discontented samurai. By 1858 the imperial court in Kyoto—long excluded from playing an active role in politics—had become the focal point for opposition. Dissidents there rallied around the slogan "Revere the emperor, expel the barbarians."

The Meiji Restoration Tokugawa officials did not yield power quietly. Instead, they vigorously responded to their opponents by forcibly retiring dissident daimyo and executing or imprisoning samurai critics. In a brief civil war, however, bakufu armies suffered repeated defeats by dissident militia units trained by foreign experts and armed with imported weapons. With the Tokugawa cause doomed, the shogun resigned his office. On 3 January 1868 the boy emperor Mutsuhito—subsequently known by his regnal name, Meiji ("Enlightened Rule")—took the reins of power. Emperor Meiji (1852–1912) reigned during a most eventful period in Japan's history.

Japanese artist Miyagawa Shuntei offered a late-nineteenth-century pointed contrast in fashion in his depiction of two women at the seaside. One wears European swimwear, and the other has donned a kimono.

Meiji Reforms

The Meiji restoration returned authority to the Japanese emperor and brought an end to the series of military governments that had dominated Japan since 1185. It also marked the birth of a new Japan. Determined to gain parity with foreign powers, a conservative coalition of daimyo, imperial princes, court nobles, and samurai formed a new government dedicated to the twin goals of prosperity and strength: "rich country, strong army." The Meiji government looked to the industrial lands of Europe and the United States to obtain the knowledge and expertise to strengthen Japan and win revisions of the unequal treaties. The Meiji government sent many students and officials abroad to study everything from technology to constitutions, and it also hired foreign experts to facilitate economic development and the creation of indigenous expertise.

thinking about ENCOUNTERS

Opening Doors

In 1853 Commodore Matthew Perry sailed into Edo Bay and inaugurated a new era in Japan's history. Why did the arrival of American forces prompt change in Japan? In what ways did the Japanese respond?

Foreign Influences Among the most prominent of the Meiji-era travelers were Fukuzawa Yukichi (1835–1901) and Ito Hirobumi (1841–1909). Fukuzawa began to study English soon after Perry's arrival in Japan, and in 1860 he was a member of the first Japanese mission to the United States. Later, he traveled in Europe, and he reported his observations of foreign lands in a series of popular publications. He lauded the constitutional government and modern educational systems that he found in the United States and western Europe, and he argued strongly for equality before the law in Japan. Ito ventured abroad on four occasions. His most important journey came in 1882 and 1883, when he traveled to Europe to study foreign constitutions and administrative systems, as Meiji leaders prepared to fashion a new government. He was especially impressed with recently united Germany, and he drew inspiration from the German constitution in drafting a governing document for Japan.

Abolition of the Social Order The first goal of the Meiji leaders was to centralize political power, a ticklish task that required destruction of the old social order. After persuading daimyo to yield their lands to the throne in exchange for patents of nobility, reformers replaced the old domains with prefectures and metropolitan districts controlled by the central government. Reformers then appointed new prefectural governors to prevent the revival of old domain loyalties. As a result, most daimyo found themselves effectively removed from power. The government also abolished the samurai class and the stipends that supported it. Gone as well were the rights of daimyo and samurai to carry swords and wear their hair in the distinctive topknot that signified their military status. When Meiji leaders raised a conscript army, they deprived the samurai of the military monopoly they had held for centuries. Many samurai felt betrayed by these actions, and Meiji officials sought to ease their discontent by awarding them government bonds. As the bonds diminished in value because of inflation, former warriors had to seek employment or else suffer impoverishment. Frustrated by these new circumstances, some samurai rose in rebellion, but the recently created national army crushed all opposition. By 1878 the national government no longer feared military challenges to its rule.

Revamping the Tax System Japan's new leaders next put the regime on secure financial footing by revamping the tax system. Peasants traditionally paid taxes in grain, but because the value of grain fluctuated with the price of rice, so did government revenue. In 1873 the Meiji government converted the grain tax into a fixed-money tax, which provided the government with predictable revenues and left peasants to deal with market fluctuations in grain prices. The state also began to assess taxes on the potential productivity of arable land, no matter how much a cultivator actually produced. This measure virtually guaranteed that only those who maximized production could afford to hold on to their land. Others had to sell their land to more efficient producers.

Constitutional Government The reconstruction of Japanese society continued in the 1880s under mounting domestic pressure for a constitution and representative government. Those demands coincided with the rulers' belief that constitutions gave foreign powers their strength and unity. Accordingly, in 1889 the emperor promulgated the Meiji constitution as "a voluntary gift" to his people. Drafted under the guidance of Ito Hirobumi, this document established a constitutional monarchy with a legislature, known as the Diet, composed of a house of nobles and an elected lower house. The constitution limited the authority of the Diet and reserved considerable power to the executive branch of government. The "sacred and inviolable" emperor commanded the armed forces, named the prime minister, and appointed the cabinet. Both the prime minister and the cabinet were responsible to the emperor rather than the lower house, as in European parliamentary systems. The emperor also had the right to dissolve the parliament, and whenever the Diet was not in session he had the prerogative of issuing ordinances. Effective power thus lay with the emperor, whom the parliament could advise but never control. The Meiji constitution recognized individual rights, but it provided that laws could limit those rights in the interests of the state, and it established property restrictions on the franchise, ensuring that delegates elected to the lower house represented the most prosperous social classes. In the elections of 1890 less than 5 percent of the adult male population was eligible to cast ballots. Despite its conservative features, the Meiji constitution provided greater opportunity for debate and dissent than ever before in Japanese society.

Remodeling the Economy Economic initiatives matched efforts at political reconstruction. Convinced that a powerful economy was the foundation of national strength, the Meiji government created a modern transportation, communications, and educational infrastructure. The establishment of telegraph, railroad, and steamship lines tied local

and regional markets into a national economic network. The government also removed barriers to commerce and trade by abolishing guild restrictions and internal tariffs. Aiming to improve literacy rates—40 percent for males and 15 percent for females in the nineteenth century—the government introduced a system of universal primary and secondary education. Universities provided advanced instruction for the best students, especially in scientific and technical fields. This infrastructure supported rapid industrialization and economic growth. Although most economic enterprises were privately owned, the government controlled military industries and established pilot programs to stimulate industrial development. During the 1880s the government sold most of its enterprises to private investors who had close ties to government officials. The result was a concentration of enormous economic power in the hands of a small group of people, collectively known as *zaibatsu,* or financial cliques. By the early twentieth century, Japan had joined the ranks of the major industrial powers.

This Japanese illustration of Emperor Mutsohito demonstrates the visual and martial transformations in Meiji Japan.

Costs of Economic Development Economic development came at a price, as the Japanese people bore the social and political costs of rapid industrialization. Japanese peasants, for example, supplied much of the domestic capital that supported the Meiji program of industrialization. The land tax of 1873, which cost peasants 40 to 50 percent of their crop yields, produced almost 90 percent of government revenue during the early years of Meiji development. Foreign exchange to purchase industrial equipment came chiefly from the export of textiles produced in a labor-intensive industry staffed by poorly paid workers.

The difficult lot of peasants came to the fore in 1883 and 1884 with a series of peasant uprisings aimed at moneylenders and government offices holding records of loans. The Meiji government deployed military police and army units to put down these uprisings, and authorities imprisoned or executed many leaders of the rebellions. Thereafter, the government did virtually nothing to alleviate the suffering of the rural population. Hundreds of thousands of families lived in destitution, haunted by malnutrition, starvation, and infanticide. Those who escaped rural society to take up work in the burgeoning industries learned that the state did not tolerate labor organizations that promoted the welfare of workers: Meiji law treated the formation of unions and the organization of strikes as criminal activities, and the government crushed a growing labor movement in 1901.

Nevertheless, in a single generation Meiji leaders transformed Japan into a powerful industrial society poised to play a major role in world affairs. Achieving political and economic equality with western European lands and the United States was the prime goal of Meiji leaders, who sought an end to humiliating treaty provisions. Serving as symbols of Japan's remarkable development were the ending of extraterritoriality in 1899, the conclusion of an alliance with Britain as an equal power in 1902, and convincing displays of military prowess in victories over the Chinese empire (1894–1895) and the Russian empire (1904–1905).

inperspective

During the nineteenth century, Ottoman, Russian, Chinese, and Japanese societies faced severe challenges on both foreign and domestic fronts. Confrontations with western European and U.S. forces showed that the agrarian societies were militarily much weaker than industrializing lands. Ottoman, Russian, Chinese, and Japanese societies suffered also from domestic weaknesses brought on by growing populations, the slowing of agricultural productivity, official corruption, and declining imperial revenues. All those societies embarked on ambitious reform programs that drew inspiration from western European and U.S. models to solve the crises caused by domestic discontent and foreign intrusions on their sovereignty. But reform programs had very different results in different lands. In the Ottoman, Russian, and Chinese empires, conservative ruling elites were able to limit the scope of reform: although they generally supported industrialization and military reform, they stifled political and social reforms that might threaten their positions in society. In Japan, however, dissent led to the collapse of the Tokugawa bakufu, and reformers had the opportunity to undertake a much more thorough program of reform than did their counterparts in Ottoman, Russian, and Chinese societies. By the early twentieth century, on the basis of reforms implemented by Meiji leaders, Japan was becoming a political, military, and economic powerhouse. ●

CHRONOLOGY

1805–1848	Reign of Muhammad Ali in Egypt
1808–1839	Reign of Sultan Mahmud II
1814–1864	Life of Taiping leader Hong Xiuquan
1839–1842	Opium War
1839–1876	Tanzimat era
1850–1864	Taiping rebellion
1853	Arrival of Commodore Perry in Japan
1853–1856	Crimean War
1855–1881	Reign of Tsar Alexander II
1860–1895	Self-Strengthening Movement
1861	Emancipation of the Russian serfs
1868	Meiji restoration
1876	Promulgation of the Ottoman constitution
1889	Promulgation of the Meiji constitution
1894–1917	Reign of Tsar Nicholas II
1898	Hundred Days reforms
1900	Boxer rebellion
1904–1905	Russo-Japanese war
1905	Revolution of 1905 in Russia
1908–1918	Young Turk era

For Further Reading

Michael R. Auslin. *Negotiating with Imperialism: The Unequal Treaties and the Culture of Japanese Diplomacy.* Cambridge, Mass., 2004. Diplomatic history that examines Japan's interaction with Western imperialism and the country's emergence as a world power.

David Anthony Bello. *Opium and the Limits of Empire: Drug Prohibition in the Chinese Interior, 1729–1850.* Cambridge, Mass., 2005. Explores Qing China's efforts at controlling and prohibiting the domestic opium trade.

William L. Blackwell. *The Industrialization of Russia: An Historical Perspective.* New York, 1982. A useful overview.

Carter V. Findley. *Bureaucratic Reform in the Ottoman Empire: The Sublime Porte, 1789–1922.* Princeton, 1980. An important scholarly work on bureaucratic reform and the development of the Ottoman civil service.

Yukichi Fukuzawa. *The Autobiography of Yukichi Fukuzawa.* Trans. by E. Kiyooka. New York, 1966. Fascinating autobiography of the former samurai who introduced Japan to the larger world on the basis of his travels in Europe and the United States.

Marius B. Jansen and Gilbert Rozman, eds. *Japan in Transition: From Tokugawa to Meiji.* Princeton, 1986. Important collection of essays exploring economic and social change during the era of the Meiji restoration.

Rebecca E. Karl. *Staging the World: Chinese Nationalism at the Turn of the Twentieth Century.* Durham, 2002. Intellectual history arguing that Chinese nationalism resulted from global interactions.

Peter Kolchin. *Unfree Labor: American Slavery and Russian Serfdom.* Cambridge, Mass., 1987. A remarkable and stimulating comparative study of American slavery and Russian serfdom.

Tetsuo Najita and J. Victor Koschmann, eds. *Conflict in Modern Japanese History: The Neglected Tradition.* Princeton, 1982. Explores the role of conflict rather than consensus in Japanese society.

Sevket Pamuk. *The Ottoman Empire and European Capitalism, 1820–1913: Trade, Investment, and Production.* Cambridge, 1987. Closely examines complex economic entanglements.

James M. Polachek. *The Inner Opium War.* Cambridge, Mass., 1992. A scholarly treatment of the Opium War and its effects in China.

Hans Rogger. *Russia in the Age of Modernisation and Revolution, 1881–1917.* New York, 1983. An important study of Russian social and economic development.

Jonathan D. Spence. *God's Chinese Son: The Taiping Heavenly Kingdom of Hong Xiuquan.* New York, 1996. A readable work on the Taiping rebellion.

John W. Steinberg, ed. *The Russo-Japanese War in Global Perspective: World War Zero.* Boston, 2005. Collection of essays that examines the Russo-Japanese War as a harbinger of World War I.

Conrad D. Totman. *The Collapse of the Tokugawa Bakufu, 1862–1868.* Honolulu, 1980. A detailed political history of the bakufu's decline and fall.

Arthur Waley. *The Opium War through Chinese Eyes.* Stanford, 1968. Fascinating perspective on the Opium War drawing on eyewitness accounts by Chinese participants and observers.

Francis William Wcislo. *Reforming Rural Russia: State, Local Society, and National Politics, 1855–1914.* Princeton, 1990. Beginning with emancipation of the serfs, this work traces agrarian and political problems in Russian society.

R. B. Wong. *China Transformed: Historical Change and the Limits of European Experience.* Ithaca, N.Y., 2002. A sophisticated work that explores similarities and differences between Chinese and European development over the long term.

Richard Wortman. *Scenarios of Power: Myth and Ceremony in the Russian Monarchy.* Princeton, 1995. An innovative study exploring the means by which Romanov rulers held on to their autocratic prerogatives despite fundamental changes in Russian society.

Peter Zarrow. *China in War and Revolution, 1895–1949.* New York, 2005. Study of the impact of Qing China's loss of Korea on the formation of modern China.

The Building of Global Empires

chapter 32

The battle of Omdurman on the Nile River, 2 September 1898.

PART 6

EYEWITNESS:

Cecil John Rhodes Discovers Imperial Diamonds Are Forever

Few Europeans had traveled to south Africa by the mid-nineteenth century, but the discovery of diamonds and rich gold deposits brought both European settlers and dramatic change to the region. European prospectors flocked to south Africa to seek their fortune.

Among the arrivals was Cecil John Rhodes, an eighteen-year-old student at Oxford University, who in 1871 went to south Africa in search of a climate that would relieve his tuberculosis. Rhodes was persistent, systematic, and ambitious. He carefully supervised African laborers who worked his claims in the diamond fields, and he bought the rights to others' claims when they looked promising. By 1889, at age thirty-five, he had almost completely monopolized diamond mining in south Africa, and he controlled 90 percent of the world's diamond production. With ample financial backing, Rhodes built up a healthy stake in the gold-mining business, although he did not seek to monopolize gold the way he did diamonds. He also entered politics, serving as prime minister (1890–1896) of the British Cape Colony.

Yet Rhodes's ambitions went far beyond business and local politics. In his vision the Cape Colony would serve as a base of operations for the extension of British control to all of Africa, from Cape to Cairo. Rhodes led the movement to enlarge the colony by absorbing territories to the north settled by Dutch farmers. Under Rhodes's guidance, the colony annexed Bechuanaland (modern Botswana) in 1885, and in 1895 it added Rhodesia (modern Zambia and Zimbabwe) to its holdings. But Rhodes's plan did not stop with Africa: he urged the expansion of the British empire until it embraced all the world, and he even hoped to bring the United States of America back into the British fold. Rhodes considered British society the most noble, moral, and honorable in the world, and he regarded imperial expansion as a duty to humankind: "We are the finest race in the world," he said in 1877, "and the more of the world we inhabit, the better it is for the human race." In his sense of superiority to other peoples as well as his restless energy, his compulsion to expand, and his craving to extract mineral wealth from distant parts of the world, Rhodes represented well the views of European imperialists who carved the world into colonies during the nineteenth century.

Throughout history strong societies have often sought to dominate their weaker neighbors by subjecting them to imperial rule. They have built empires for various reasons: to gain control over natural resources, to subdue potential enemies, to seize wealth, to acquire territory for expansion, and to win glory. From the days of ancient Mesopotamia and Egypt to the present, imperialism has been a prominent theme of world history.

During the second half of the nineteenth century, as the Ottoman and Qing empires weakened, a handful of western European states wrote a new chapter in the history of imperialism. Strong nationalist sentiments enabled them to mobilize their populations for purposes of overseas expansion. Industrialization equipped them with the most effective tools and the most lethal weapons available anywhere in the world. Three centuries of experience with maritime trade in Asia, Africa, the Americas, and Oceania provided them with unparalleled knowledge of the world and its peoples. With those advantages, western European peoples conquered foreign armies, overpowered local rulers, and imposed their hegemony throughout the world. Toward the end of the century, the United States and Japan joined European states as new imperial powers.

The establishment of global empires had far-reaching effects. In many ways, imperialism tightened links between the world's societies. Imperial powers encouraged trade between dominant states and their overseas colonies, for example, and they organized mass migrations of laborers to work in agricultural and industrial ventures. Yet imperialism also fostered divisions between the world's peoples. Powerful tools, deadly weapons, and global hegemony tempted European peoples to consider themselves superior to their subjects throughout the world: modern racism is one of the legacies of imperialism. Another effect of imperialism was the development of nationalism in subject lands. Just as the incursion of Napoleonic armies stimulated the development of nationalism in Europe, so the imposition of foreign rule provoked nationalist responses in colonized lands. Although formal empires almost entirely dissolved in the twentieth century, the influence of global imperialism continues to shape the contemporary world.

FOUNDATIONS OF EMPIRE

Even under the best of circumstances, campaigns to conquer foreign lands have always been dangerous and expensive ventures. They have arisen from a sense that foreign conquest is essential, and they have entailed the mobilization of political, military, and economic resources. In nineteenth-century Europe, proponents of empire advanced a variety of political, economic, and cultural arguments to justify the conquest and control of foreign lands. The imperialist ventures that they promoted enjoyed dramatic success partly because of the increasingly sophisticated technologies developed by European industry.

Motives of Imperialism

Modern Imperialism The building of empires is an old story in world history. By the nineteenth century, however, European observers recognized that empires of their day were different from those of earlier times. Accordingly, about mid-century they began to speak of *imperialism,* and by the 1880s the recently coined term had made its way into popular speech and writing throughout western Europe. In contemporary usage, imperialism refers to the domination of European powers—and later the United States and Japan as well—over subject lands in the larger world. Sometimes that domination came in the old-fashioned way, by force of arms, but often it arose from trade, investment, and business activities that enabled imperial powers to profit from subject societies and influence their affairs without going to the trouble of exercising direct political control.

Modern Colonialism Like the building of empires, the establishment of colonies in foreign lands is a practice dating from ancient times. In modern parlance, however, colonialism refers not just to the sending of colonists to settle new lands but also to the political, social, economic, and cultural structures that enabled imperial powers to dominate subject lands. In some lands, such as North America, Chile, Argentina, Australia, New Zealand, and south Africa, European powers established settler colonies populated largely by migrants from the home societies. Yet contemporary scholars also speak of European colonies in India, southeast Asia, and sub-Saharan Africa, even though European migrants did not settle there in large numbers. European agents, officials, and businesspeople effectively turned those lands into colonies and profoundly influenced their historical development by controlling their domestic and foreign policies, integrating local economies into the network of global capitalism, introducing European business techniques, transforming educational systems according to European standards, and promoting European cultural preferences.

During the second half of the nineteenth century, many Europeans came to believe that imperial expansion and colonial domination were crucial for the survival of their states and societies—and sometimes for the health of their personal fortunes as well. European merchants and entrepreneurs sometimes became fabulously wealthy from business ventures in Asia or Africa, and they argued for their home states to pursue imperialist policies partly to secure and enhance their own enterprises. After making his fortune mining diamonds and gold, for example, Cecil Rhodes (1853–1902) worked tirelessly on behalf of British imperial expansion.

Economic Motives of Imperialism It is not difficult to understand why entrepreneurs such as Rhodes would promote overseas expansion, but their interests alone could not have driven the vast imperialist ventures of the late nineteenth century. In fact, a wide range of motives encouraged European peoples to launch campaigns of conquest and control. Some advocates argued that imperialism was in the economic interests of European societies as well as individuals. They pointed out that overseas colonies could serve as reliable sources of raw materials not available in Europe that came into demand because of industrialization: rubber, tin, and copper were vital products, for example, and by the late nineteenth century petroleum had also become a crucial resource for industrialized lands. Rubber trees were indigenous to the Amazon River basin, but imperialists established colonial rubber plantations in the Congo River basin and Malaya. Abundant supplies of tin were available from colonies in southeast Asia and copper in central Africa. The United States and Russia supplied most of the world's petroleum in the nineteenth century, but the oil fields of southwest Asia attracted the attention of European industrialists and imperialists alike.

Proponents of imperialism also held that colonies would consume manufactured products and provide a haven for migrants in an age of rapidly increasing European population. In fact, manufactured goods did not flow to most colonies in large quantities, and European migrants went overwhelmingly to independent states in the Americas rather than to overseas colonies. Nevertheless, arguments arising from national economic interest generated considerable support for imperialism.

Political Motives of Imperialism As European states extended their influence overseas, a geopolitical argument for imperialism gained prominence. Even if colonies were not economically beneficial, imperialists held, it was crucial for political and military reasons to maintain them. Some overseas colonies occupied strategic sites on the world's sea lanes, and others offered harbors or supply stations for commercial and naval ships. Advocates of imperialism sought to gain those advantages for their own states and—equally important—to deny them to rivals.

Imperialism had its uses also for domestic politics. In an age when socialists and communists directly confronted industrialists, European politicians and national leaders sought to defuse social tension and inspire patriotism by focusing public attention on foreign imperialist ventures. Cecil Rhodes himself once observed that imperialism was an attractive alternative to civil war, and the German chancellor Otto von

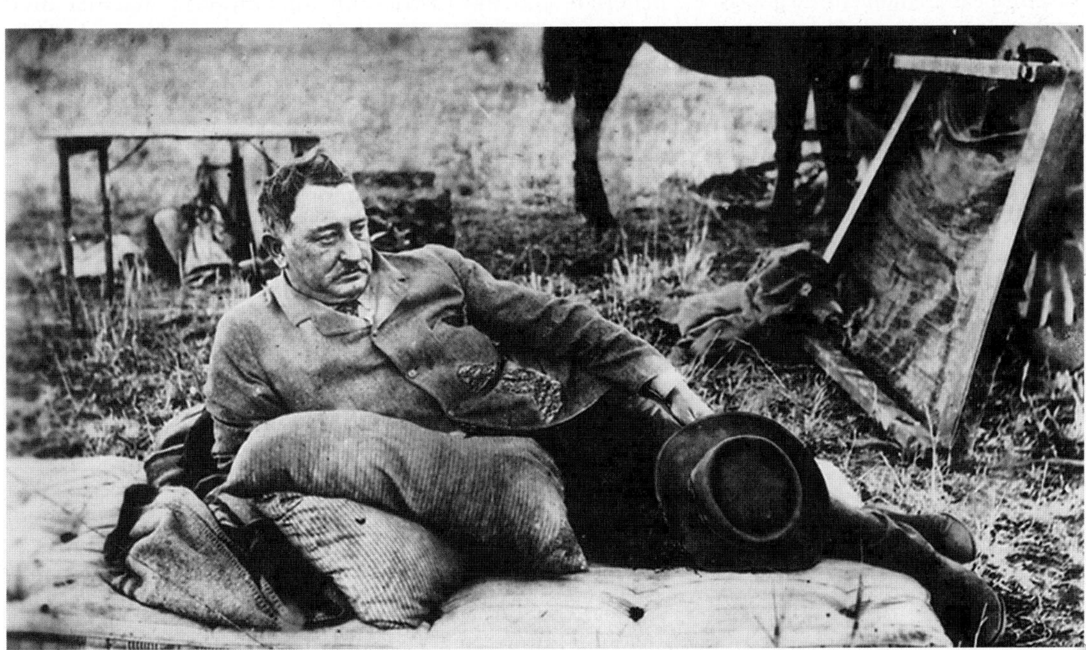

Cecil Rhodes resting in the goldfields of south Africa, about 1897. His dominating economic, cultural, and political influence on southern African territories for personal and British gain was a model of European imperialist values.

thinking about TRADITIONS

New Imperialism?
The building of empires stretched back historically as far as the beginning of written history. How did the so-called new imperialism of the nineteenth and twentieth centuries differ from earlier imperial traditions?

Bismarck worked to persuade both industrialists and workers that overseas expansion would benefit them all. By the end of the nineteenth century, European leaders frequently organized colonial exhibitions where subject peoples displayed their dress, music, and customs for tourists and the general public in imperial lands, all in an effort to win popular support for imperialist policies.

Cultural Justifications of Imperialism Even spiritual motives fostered imperialism. Like the Jesuits in the early modern era, missionaries flocked to African and Asian lands in search of converts to Christianity. Missionaries often opposed imperialist ventures and defended the interests of their converts against European entrepreneurs and colonial officials. Nevertheless, their spiritual campaigns provided a powerful religious justification for imperialism. Furthermore, missionaries often facilitated communications between imperialists and subject peoples, and they sometimes provided European officials with information they needed to maintain control of overseas colonies. Missionary settlements also served as convenient meeting places for Europeans overseas and as distribution centers for European manufactured goods.

While missionaries sought to introduce Christianity to subject peoples, other Europeans worked to bring them "civilization" in the form of political order and social stability. French imperialists routinely invoked the *mission civilisatrice* ("civilizing mission") as justification for their expansion into Africa and Asia, and the English writer and poet Rudyard Kipling (1864–1936) defined the "white man's burden" as the duty of European and Euro-American peoples to bring order and enlightenment to distant lands.

Tools of Empire

Even the strongest motives would not have enabled imperialists to impose their rule throughout the world without the powerful technological advantages that industrialization conferred on them. Ever since the introduction of gunpowder in the thirteenth century, European states had competed vigorously to develop increasingly powerful military technologies. Industrialization enhanced those efforts by making it possible to produce huge quantities of advanced weapons and tools. During the nineteenth century, industrialists devised effective technologies of transportation, communication, and war that enabled European imperialists to have their way in the larger world.

Transportation Technologies The most important innovations in transportation involved steamships and railroads. Small steamboats plied the waters of the United States and western Europe from the early nineteenth century. During the 1830s British naval engineers adapted steam power to military uses and built large, iron-clad ships equipped with powerful guns. These steamships traveled much faster than any sailing vessel, and as an additional advantage they could ignore the winds and travel in any direction. Because they could travel much farther upriver than sailboats, which depended on convenient winds, steamships enabled imperialists to project power deep into the interior regions of foreign lands. Thus in 1842 the British gunboat *Nemesis* led an expedition up the Yangzi River that brought the Opium War to a conclusion. Steam-powered gunboats later introduced European power to inland sites throughout Africa and Asia.

The construction of new canals enhanced the effectiveness of steamships. Both the Suez Canal (constructed 1859–1869) and the Panama Canal (constructed 1904–1914) facilitated the building and maintenance of empires by enabling naval vessels to travel rapidly between the world's seas and oceans. They also lowered the costs of trade between imperial powers and subject lands.

Once imperialists had gained control of overseas lands, railroads helped them to maintain their hegemony and organize local economies to their own advantage. Rail transportation enabled colonial officials and armies to travel quickly through the colonies. It also facilitated trade in raw materials and the distribution of European manufactured goods in the colonies.

Military Technologies European industrialists also churned out enormous quantities of increasingly powerful weapons. The most advanced firearms of the early nineteenth century were smoothbore, muzzle-loading muskets. When large numbers of infantry fired their muskets at once, the resulting volley could cause havoc among opponents. Yet it took a skilled musketeer about one minute to reload a weapon, and because of its smoothbore, the musket was not a very accurate firearm. By mid-century European armies were using breech-loading firearms with rifled bores that were far more accurate and reliable than muskets. By the 1870s Europeans were experimenting with rifled machine guns, and in the 1880s they adopted the Maxim gun, a light and powerful weapon that fired eleven bullets per second.

Those firearms provided European armies with an arsenal vastly stronger than any other in the world. Accurate rifles and machine guns devastated opposing overseas forces, enabling European armies to impose colonial rule almost at will. In 1898, for example, a British army with twenty ma-

sources from the past

Rudyard Kipling on the White Man's Burden

Rudyard Kipling lived in northern India for the first six years of his life. He grew up speaking Hindi, and he mixed easily with Indian subjects of the British empire. After attending a boarding school in England, he returned to India in 1882 and became a journalist and writer. Many of his works express his deep enchantment with India, but he also believed strongly in imperial rule. Indeed, he wrote his famous poem titled "The White Man's Burden" to encourage the United States to impose colonial rule in the Philippines. While recognizing the unpopularity of foreign rule, Kipling considered it a duty to bring order to colonial lands and to serve subject peoples.

Take up the White Man's burden—
Send forth the best ye breed—
Go bind your sons to exile
To serve your captives' need;
To wait in heavy harness,
On fluttered folk and wild—
Your new-caught, sullen peoples,
Half-devil and half-child.

Take up the White Man's burden—
In patience to abide,
To veil the threat of terror
And check the show of pride;
By open speech and simple,
An hundred times made plain,
To seek another's profit,
And work for another's gain.

Take up the White Man's burden—
The savage wars of peace—
Fill full the mouth of Famine
And bid the sickness cease;
And when your goal is nearest
The end for others sought,
Watch Sloth and heathen Folly
Bring all your hope to nought.

Take up the White Man's burden—
No tawdry rule of kings,
But toil of serf and sweeper—
The tale of common things.
The ports ye shall not enter,
The roads ye shall not tread,
Go make them with your living,
And mark them with your dead.

Take up the White Man's burden—
And reap his old reward:
The blame of those ye better,
The hate of those ye guard—
The cry of hosts ye humor
(Ah, slowly!) toward the light;—
"Why brought ye us from bondage,
"Our loved Egyptian night?"

Take up the White Man's burden—
Ye dare not stoop to less—
Nor call too loud on Freedom
To cloak your weariness;
By all ye cry or whisper,
By all ye leave or do,
The silent, sullen peoples
Shall weigh your Gods and you.

Take up the White Man's burden—
Have done with childish days—
The lightly proffered laurel,
The easy, ungrudged praise.
Comes now, to search your manhood
Through all the thankless years,
Cold, edged with dear-bought wisdom,
The judgment of your peers!

For Further Reflection

- Compare and contrast the sorts of adjectives Kipling uses to describe native peoples as opposed to Europeans; how does his very language usage convey his sense of white superiority?

Source: Rudyard Kipling. "The White Man's Burden." *McClure's Magazine* 12, no. 4 (1899): 290–91.

chine guns and six gunboats encountered a Sudanese force at Omdurman, near Khartoum on the Nile River. During five hours of fighting, the British force lost a few hundred men while machine guns and explosive charges fired from gunboats killed thousands of Sudanese. The battle of Omdurman opened the door for British colonial rule in Sudan.

Communications Technologies Communications also benefited from industrialization. Oceangoing steamships reduced the time required to deliver messages from imperial capitals to colonial lands. In the 1830s it took as long as two years for a British correspondent to receive a reply to a letter sent to India by sailing ship. By the 1850s, however, after the introduction of steamships, correspondence could make the round-trip between London and Bombay in four months. After the opening of the Suez Canal in 1869, steamships traveled from Britain to India in less than two weeks.

Thousands of spectators gathered on the banks of the Suez Canal in 1869 to watch a parade of ships that opened the canal by proceeding from the Mediterranean to the Red Sea. The Suez and Panama canals became the most strategic waterways in the world because they significantly shortened maritime routes both between Europe and the lands bordering the Indian and Pacific oceans and between one coast of North America and ports on the other side of South America.

The invention of the telegraph made it possible to exchange messages even faster. Telegraph wires carried communications over land from the 1830s, but only in the 1850s did engineers devise reliable submarine cables for the transmission of messages through the oceans. By 1870, submarine cables carried messages between Britain and India in about five hours. By 1902, cables linked all parts of the British empire throughout the world, and other European states maintained cables to support communications with their own colonies. Their monopoly on telegraphic communications provided imperial powers with distinct advantages over their subject lands. Imperial officials could rapidly mobilize forces to deal with troubles, and merchants could respond quickly to developments of economic and commercial significance. Rapid communication was an integral structural element of empire.

EUROPEAN IMPERIALISM

Aided by powerful technologies, European states launched an unprecedented round of empire building in the second half of the nineteenth century. Imperial expansion began with the British conquest of India. Competition between imperial powers led to European intrusion into central Asia and the establishment of colonies in southeast Asia. Fearful that rivals might gain control over some region that remained free of imperial control, European states embarked on a campaign of frenzied expansion in the 1880s that brought almost all of Africa and Pacific Ocean territories into their empires.

The British Empire in India

The British empire in south Asia and southeast Asia grew out of the mercantile activities of the English East India Company, which enjoyed a monopoly on English trade with India. The East India Company obtained permission from the Mughal emperors of India to build fortified posts on the coastlines. There, company agents traded for goods and stored commodities in warehouses until company ships arrived to transport them to Europe. In the seventeenth century, company merchants traded mostly for Indian pepper and cotton, Chinese silk and porcelain, and fine spices from southeast Asia. During the eighteenth century, tea and coffee became the most prominent trade items, and European consumers acquired a taste for both beverages that they have never lost.

Company Rule After the death of the emperor Aurangzeb in 1707, the Mughal state entered a period of decline, and many local authorities asserted their independence of Mughal rule. The East India Company took advantage of Mughal weakness to strengthen and expand its trading posts. In the 1750s company officials embarked on the outright conquest of India. Through diplomacy or military campaigns, the company conquered autonomous Indian kingdoms and reduced Mughal rule to only a small area around Delhi. Part of the British policy of expansion was the "doctrine of lapse," greatly resented by Indians. If an Indian ruler failed to produce a biological male heir to the throne, his territories lapsed to the company upon his death. By the mid-nineteenth century, the English East India Company had annexed huge areas of India and had established control over present-day Pakistan, Bangladesh, Burma, and Sri Lanka. Company rule was enforced by a small British army and a large number of Indian troops known as sepoys.

Indian Rebellion Not all of the Indian population was willing to cooperate with foreign rule, however, and the English East India Company faced a deadly uprising in 1857 that threatened the British empire in India. Sepoy discontent came to a head when rumors circulated among the troops that cartridges for newly issued rifles were lubricated with a mixture of pig and cow fat. To load their rifles, sepoys had to bite off the ends of the lubricated cartridges, thus making oral contact with a substance that was offensive and insulting to both Muslims and Hindus. In several isolated cases, soldiers refused to use these cartridges, but they were promptly convicted of mutiny.

In response to the harsh treatment meted out by the British, several sepoy regiments joined what became a large-scale mutiny, rapidly igniting a general anti-British revolution in central and north India. Sepoys were now joined by Indian princes and their followers, whose territories had been annexed by the British, and people whose ways of life and sources of income had been disrupted by British trade, missionary activities, and misguided social reforms. What had begun as a rebellion by Indian troops in the employ of the English East India Company turned into a full-fledged war of independence against British rule. In the course of the conflict, both sides committed widespread atrocities against combatants and noncombatants alike. After several months of inconclusive battles, British forces finally gained the upper hand by late 1857, and peace was officially declared on 8 July 1858.

British Imperial Rule The widespread but unsuccessful rebellion against British rule in India had far-reaching consequences. The British government officially abolished the Mughal empire and exiled the emperor Muhammad Bahadur Shah to Burma. To stabilize affairs and forestall future problems, the British crown abolished the East India Company in favor of the direct rule of India by the British government. In 1858 Queen Victoria (reigned 1837–1901) assigned responsibility for Indian policy to the newly established office of secretary of state for India. A viceroy represented British royal

A contemporary British print depicts what the British perceived as atrocities at Cawnpore. At left, independence-seeking sepoys kill British troops and men from the garrison, while women and children fall in the foreground.

authority in India and administered the colony through an elite Indian civil service staffed almost exclusively by the English. Indians served in low-level bureaucratic positions, but British officials formulated all domestic and foreign policy in India.

Under both the East India Company and direct colonial administration, British rule transformed India. As they extended their authority to all parts of India and Ceylon (modern Sri Lanka), British officials cleared forests, restructured landholdings, and encouraged the cultivation of crops, such as tea, coffee, and opium, that were especially valuable trade items. They built extensive railroad and telegraph networks that tightened links between India and the larger global economy. They also constructed new canals, harbors, and irrigation systems to support commerce and agriculture. British colonial authorities made little effort to promote Christianity, but they established English-style schools for the children of Indian elites, whom they sought as supporters of their rule.

Imperialism in Central Asia and Southeast Asia

As the East India Company and British colonial agents tightened their grip on India, competition among European states kindled further empire-building efforts. Beginning in the early nineteenth century, French and Russian strategists sought ways to break British power and establish their own colonial presence in India. The French bid stalled after the fall of Napoleon, but Russian interest in India fueled a prolonged contest for power in central Asia.

Russian forces had probed central Asia as early as the sixteenth century, but only in the nineteenth century did they undertake a systematic effort to extend Russian authority south of the Caucasus. The weakening of the Ottoman and Qing empires turned central Asia into a political vacuum and invited Russian expansion into the region. By the 1860s cossacks had overcome Tashkent, Bokhara, and Samarkand, the great caravan cities of the silk roads, and approached the ill-defined northern frontier of British India. For the next half century, military officers and imperialist adventurers engaged in a risky pursuit of influence and intelligence that British agents referred to as the "Great Game."

The Great Game Russian and British explorers ventured into parts of central Asia never before visited by Euro-

MAP 32.1
Imperialism in Asia, ca. 1914. Date is year of conquest.
Note the claims made by various industrial powers.
Which territories remained unclaimed, and why? Which power claimed the most imperial territory in Asia?

peans. They mapped terrain, scouted mountain passes, and sought alliances with local rulers from Afghanistan to the Aral Sea—all in an effort to prepare for the anticipated war for India. In fact, the outbreak of global war in 1914 and the collapse of the tsarist state in 1917 ensured that the contest for India never took place. Nevertheless, imperial expansion brought much of central Asia into the Russian empire and subjected the region to a Russian hegemony that persisted until the disintegration of the Soviet Union in 1991.

Competition among European powers led also to further imperialism in southeast Asia. The Philippines had come under Spanish colonial rule in the sixteenth century, and many southeast Asian islands fell under Dutch rule in the seventeenth century. As imperial rivalries escalated in the nineteenth century, Dutch officials tightened their control and extended their authority throughout the Dutch East Indies, the archipelago that makes up the modern state of Indonesia. Along with cash crops of sugar, tea, coffee, and tobacco, exports of rubber and tin made the Dutch East Indies a valuable and productive colony.

British Colonies in Southeast Asia In the interests of increasing trade between India, southeast Asia, and China, British imperialists moved in the nineteenth century to establish a presence in southeast Asia. As early as the 1820s, colonial officials in India came into conflict with the kings of Burma (modern Myanmar) while seeking to extend their influence to the Irrawaddy River delta. By the 1880s they had established colonial authority in Burma, which became a source of teak, ivory, rubies, and jade. In 1824 Thomas Stamford Raffles founded the port of Singapore, which soon became the busiest center of trade in the Strait of Melaka. Administered by the colonial regime in India, Singapore served as the base for the British conquest of Malaya (modern Malaysia) in the 1870s and 1880s. Besides offering outstanding ports that enabled the British navy to

Warships provide covering fire as British troops prepare to storm the Burmese port of Rangoon in 1824. By the 1880s the British had established colonial authority in Burma and were using it as a source of such valuable commodities as teak, ivory, rubies, and jade.

control sea lanes linking the Indian Ocean with the South China Sea, Malaya provided abundant supplies of tin and rubber.

French Indochina Although foiled in their efforts to establish themselves in India, French imperialists built the large southeast Asian colony of French Indochina, consisting of the modern states of Vietnam, Cambodia, and Laos, between 1859 and 1893. Like their British counterparts in India, French colonial officials introduced European-style schools and sought to establish close connections with native elites. Unlike their rivals, French officials also encouraged conversion to Christianity, and as a result the Roman Catholic church became prominent throughout French Indochina, especially in Vietnam. By century's end, all of southeast Asia had come under European imperial rule except for the kingdom of Siam (modern Thailand), which preserved its independence largely because colonial officials regarded it as a convenient buffer state between British-dominated Burma and French Indochina.

The Scramble for Africa

The most striking outburst of imperialism took place in Africa. As late as 1875, European peoples maintained a limited presence in Africa. They held several small coastal colonies and fortified trading posts, but their only sizable possessions were the Portuguese colonies of Angola and Mozambique, the French settler colony in northern Algeria, and a cluster of settler colonies populated by British and Dutch migrants in south Africa. After the end of the slave trade, a lively commerce developed around the exchange of African gold, ivory, and palm oil for European textiles, guns, and manufactured goods. This trade brought considerable prosperity and economic opportunity, especially to west African lands.

Between 1875 and 1900, however, the relationship between Africa and Europe dramatically changed. Within a quarter century, European imperial powers partitioned and colonized almost the entire African continent. Prospects of exploiting African resources and nationalist rivalries between European powers help to explain this frenzied quest for empire, often referred to as the "scramble for Africa."

Henry Morton Stanley spent a great deal of time in the field, but here he appears, along with his gun bearer Kalulu, in front of a painted backdrop in a photographer's studio.

European Explorers in Africa European imperialists built on the information compiled by a series of adventurers and explorers who charted interior regions of Africa that Europeans had never before visited. Some went to Africa as missionaries. Best known of them was Dr. David Livingstone, a Scottish minister, who traveled through much of central and southern Africa in the mid-nineteenth century in search of suitable locations for mission posts. Other travelers were adventurers such as the American journalist Henry Morton Stanley, who undertook a well-publicized expedition to find Livingstone and report on his activities. Meanwhile, two English explorers, Richard Burton and John Speke, ventured into east Africa seeking the source of the Nile River. The geographic information compiled by these travelers held great interest for merchants eager to exploit business opportunities in Africa.

Especially exciting was reliable information about the great African rivers—the Nile, Niger, Congo, and Zambesi—and the access they provided to inland regions. In the 1870s King Leopold II of Belgium (reigned 1865–1909) employed Henry Morton Stanley to help develop commercial ventures and establish a colony called the Congo Free State (modern-day Democratic Republic of the Congo) in the basin of the Congo River. To forestall competition from Belgium's much larger and more powerful European neighbors, Leopold announced that the Congo region would be a free-trade zone accessible to merchants and businesspeople from all European lands. In fact, however, he carved out a personal colony and filled it with lucrative rubber plantations run by forced labor. Working conditions in the Congo Free State were so brutal, taxes so high, and abuses so many that humanitarians protested Leopold's colonial regime. Predatory rule had culminated in the death of four to eight million Africans. In 1908 the Belgian government took control of the colony, known thereafter as Belgian Congo.

As Leopold colonized central Africa, Britain established an imperial presence in Egypt. As Muhammad Ali and other Egyptian rulers sought to build up their army, strengthen the economy, and distance themselves from Ottoman authority, they borrowed heavily from European lenders. In the 1870s crushing debt forced Egyptian officials to impose high taxes, which provoked popular unrest and a military rebellion. In 1882 a British army occupied Egypt to protect British financial interests and ensure the safety of the Suez Canal, which was crucial to British communications with India.

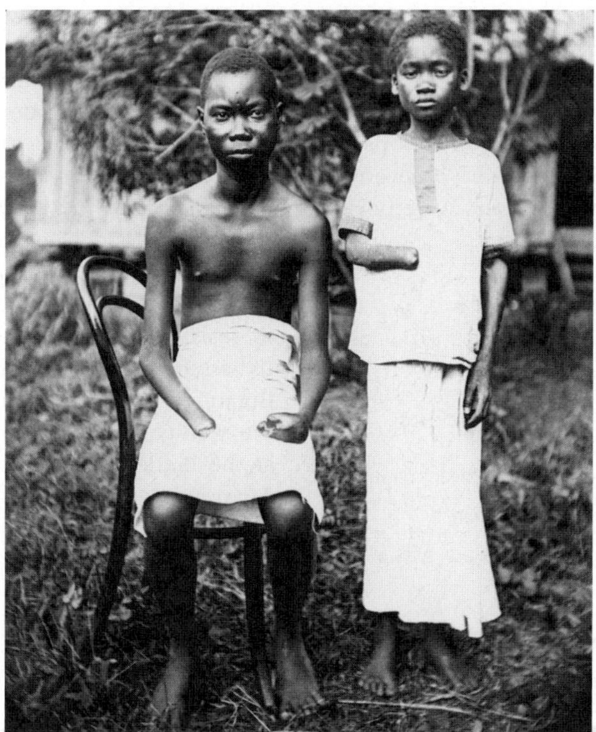

This 1912 photograph shows a stark portrait of the Belgian king's inhumane treatment of Africans in the Congo.

South Africa Long before the nineteenth-century scramble, a European presence had grown at the southern tip of the African continent, where the Dutch East India Company had established Cape Town (1652) as a supply station for ships en route to Asia. Soon after, former company employees plus newly arrived settlers from Europe moved into lands beyond company control to take up farming and ranching. Many of these settlers, known first as Boers (the Dutch word for "farmer") and then as Afrikaners (the Dutch word for "African"), believed that God had predestined them to claim the people and resources of the Cape. The area under white settler control expanded during the eighteenth century as a steady stream of European migrants—chiefly Dutch, Germans, and French Huguenots fleeing religious persecution—continued to swell the colony's population. As European settlers spread beyond the reaches of the original colony, they began encroaching on lands occupied by Khoikhoi and Xhosa peoples. Competition for land soon led to hostility, and by the early eighteenth century, warfare, enslavement, and smallpox epidemics had led to the virtual extinction of the Khoikhoi. After a century of intermittent warfare, the Xhosa too had been decimated, losing lives, land, and resources to European settlers.

The British takeover of the Cape during the Napoleonic Wars (1799–1815) encouraged further Afrikaner expansion into the interior of south Africa. The establishment of British rule in 1806 deeply disrupted Afrikaner society, for in its wake came the imposition of English law and language. The institution of slavery—a key defining feature of rural Afrikaner society—developed into the most contentious issue between British administrators and Afrikaner settlers. When the British abolished slavery in 1833, they not only eliminated the primary source of labor for white farmers but also dealt a crippling blow to Afrikaner financial viability and lifestyles. Chafing under British rule, Afrikaners started to leave their farms in Cape Colony and gradually migrated east in what they called the Great Trek. That colonial expansion sometimes led to violent conflict with indigenous peoples, but the superior firepower of Afrikaner *voortrekkers* (Afrikaans for "pioneers") overcame first Ndebele and then Zulu resistance. The colonizers interpreted their successful expansion as evidence that God approved of their dominance in south Africa. By the mid-nineteenth century, *voortrekkers* had created several independent republics: the Republic of Natal, annexed by the British in 1843; the Orange Free State in 1854; and the South African Republic (Transvaal territories) in 1860.

Britain's lenient attitude toward Afrikaner statehood took a drastic turn with the discovery of large mineral deposits in Afrikaner-populated territories—diamonds in 1867 and gold in 1886. The influx of thousands of British miners and prospectors led to tensions between British authorities and Afrikaners, culminating in the South African War (1899–1902; sometimes called the Boer War). Although the brutal conflict pitted whites against whites, it also took a large toll on black Africans, who served both sides as soldiers and laborers. The internment of 100,000 black Africans in British concentration camps, for example, left more than 10,000 dead. The Afrikaners conceded defeat in 1902, and by 1910 the British government had reconstituted the four former colonies as provinces in the Union of South Africa, a largely autonomous British dominion. British attempts at improving relations between English speakers and Afrikaners centered on shoring up the privileges of white colonial society and the domination of black Africans.

The Berlin Conference Tensions between those European powers who were seeking African colonies led to the Berlin West Africa Conference (1884–1885), during which the delegates of twelve European states as well as the United States and the Ottoman empire—not a single African was present—devised the ground rules for the colonization of Africa. Half the nations represented, including the United States, had no colonial ambitions on the continent, but they had been invited to give the proceedings a veneer of unbiased international approval. The Berlin Conference produced agreement for future claims on African lands: each colonial power had to notify the others of its claims, and each claim had to be followed up by "effective occupation" of the claimed territory. Occupation was commonly accomplished either by getting a signed agreement from a local African ruler or by military conquest. Conference participants also spelled out noble-minded objectives for colonized lands: an end to the slave trade, the extension of civilization and Christianity, and commerce and trade. Although the conference did not parcel out African lands among the participant nations, it nevertheless served public notice that European powers were poised to carve the continent into colonies.

During the next twenty-five years, European imperialists sent armies to consolidate their claims and impose colonial rule. Armed with the latest weapons technology, including the newly developed machine gun and artillery with explosive shells, they rarely failed to defeat African forces. All too often, battles were one-sided. In 1898, at Omdurman, a city in central Sudan near the junction of the White and Blue Nile rivers, British forces killed close to 20,000 Sudanese in a matter of hours while suffering only minor losses themselves. The only indigenous African state to resist colonization successfully was Ethiopia. In 1895, Italian forces invaded Ethiopia, anticipating an easy victory. But any designs to establish a colony were abandoned when the well-equipped Ethiopian army annihilated the Italians at the battle of Adwa in 1896. Besides Ethiopia, the only African state to remain independent was Liberia, a small

MAP 32.2
Imperialism in Africa, ca. 1914.
By 1914, only Ethiopia and Liberia remained free of European control.
How was it possible for Europeans to gain such domination?

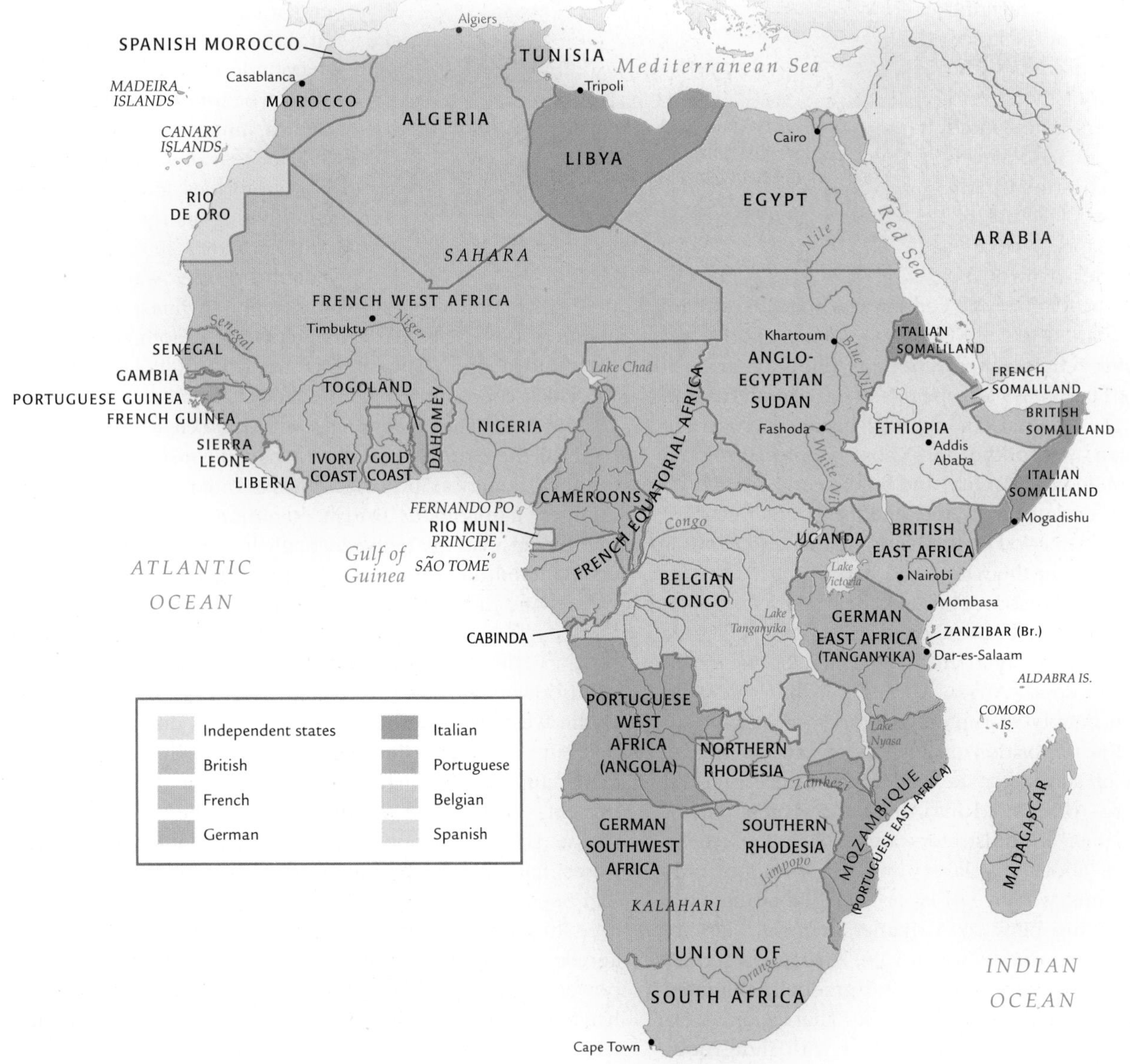

republic in west Africa populated by freed slaves that was effectively a dependency of the United States.

Systems of Colonial Rule In the wake of rapid conquest came problems of colonial occupation. Imperial powers commonly assumed that, following an initial modest investment, colonial administration would become financially self-sufficient. For decades, Europeans struggled to identify the ideal system of rule, only to learn that colonial rule in Africa could be maintained only through exceedingly high expenditures.

The earliest approach to colonial rule involved "concessionary companies." European governments typically granted private companies large concessions of territory and empowered them to undertake economic activities such as mining, plantation agriculture, or railroad construction. Concessionary companies also had permission to implement systems of taxation and labor recruitment. Although that approach allowed European governments to colonize and exploit immense territories with only a modest investment in capital and personnel, company rule also brought liabilities. The brutal use of forced labor, which provoked a public outcry in Europe, and profits smaller than anticipated persuaded most European governments by the early twentieth century to curtail the powers of private companies and to establish their own rule, which took the form of either direct rule, typical of French colonies, or indirect rule, characteristic of British colonies.

Under direct rule, colonies featured administrative districts headed by European personnel who assumed responsibility for tax collection, labor and military recruitment, and the maintenance of law and order. Administrative boundaries intentionally cut across existing African political and ethnic boundaries to divide and weaken potentially powerful indigenous groups. Direct rule aimed at removing strong kings and other leaders and replacing them with more malleable persons. Underlying the principle of direct rule was the desire to keep African populations in check and to permit European administrators to engage in a "civilizing mission." However, that approach to colonial rule presented its own difficulties. Key among them was the constant shortage of European personnel. For example, in French West Africa some thirty-six hundred Europeans tried to rule over an African population of more than nine million. The combination of long distances and slow transport limited effective communication between regional authorities and officials in remote areas. An inability to speak local languages and a limited understanding of local customs among European officials further undermined their effective administration.

The British colonial administrator Frederick D. Lugard (1858–1945) was the driving force behind the doctrine of indirect rule, which the British employed in many of their African colonies. In his book *The Dual Mandate in British Tropical Africa* (1922), he stressed the moral and financial advantages of exercising control over subject populations through indigenous institutions. He was particularly keen on using existing "tribal" authorities and "customary laws" as the foundation for colonial rule. Forms of indirect rule worked in regions where Africans had already established strong and highly organized states, but elsewhere erroneous assumptions concerning the "tribal" nature of African societies weakened the effectiveness of indirect rule. Bewildered by the complexities of African societies, colonial officials frequently imposed their own ideas of what constituted "tribal boundaries" or "tribal authorities." The invention of rigid tribal categories and the establishment of artificial tribal boundaries became one of the greatest obstacles to nation building and regional stability in much of Africa during the second half of the twentieth century.

European Imperialism in the Pacific

While scrambling for Africa, European imperial powers did not overlook opportunities to establish their presence in the Pacific Ocean basin. Imperialism in the Pacific took two main forms. In Australia and New Zealand, European powers established settler colonies and dominant political institutions. In most of the Pacific islands, however, they sought commercial opportunities and reliable bases for their operations but did not wish to go to the trouble or expense of outright colonization. Only in the late nineteenth century did they begin to impose direct colonial rule on the islands.

Settler Colonies in the Pacific European mariners reconnoitered Australia and made occasional landfalls from the early sixteenth century, but only after the Pacific voyages of Captain James Cook did Europeans travel to the southern continent in large numbers. In 1770 Cook anchored his fleet for a week at Botany Bay, near modern Sydney, and reported that the region would be suitable for settlement. In 1788 a British fleet with about one thousand settlers, most of them convicted criminals, arrived at Sydney harbor and established the colony of New South Wales. The migrants supported themselves mostly by herding sheep. Lured by opportunity, voluntary migrants outnumbered convicts by

thinking about ENCOUNTERS

Forays into the Pacific

Oceania had remained largely outside the purview of European and American imperialists until the nineteenth century. What resulted once European and American traders, missionaries, and settlers arrived on the shores of islands as far afield as Australia and Hawai`i? How did the indigenous peoples respond to these intruders?

sources from the past

The Royal Niger Company Mass-Produces Imperial Control in Africa

The 1880s proved a crucial time for sub-Saharan African societies and European imperial adventurers. European nations at the Berlin Conference set forth the rules by which they would partition and rule African states, and then those nations—such as Great Britain—commissioned companies like the Royal Niger Company to assert imperial prerogatives. To fend off French competitors in the Niger River delta, the British-controlled Royal Niger Company had local rulers sign its "standard treaty," a mass-produced, fill-in-the-blank document that essentially ceded trade and political control to the company, and thus to Britain, in what became the British colony of Nigeria.

We, the undersigned Chiefs of _________, with the view to the bettering of the condition of our country and our people, do this day cede to the Royal Niger Company, for ever, the whole of our territory from _________.

We also give to the said Royal Niger Company full power to settle all native disputes arising from any cause whatever, and we pledge ourselves not to enter into any war with other tribes without the sanction of the said Royal Niger Company.

We understand that the said Royal Niger Company have full power to mine, farm, and build in any portion of our country.

We bind ourselves not to have any intercourse with any strangers or foreigners except through the said Royal Niger Company.

In consideration of the foregoing, the said Royal Niger Company (Chartered and Limited) bind themselves not to interfere with any of the native laws or customs of the country, consistently with the maintenance of order and good government.

The said Royal Niger Company agree to pay native owners of land a reasonable amount for any portion they may require.

The said Royal Niger Company bind themselves to protect the said Chiefs from the attacks of any neighboring aggressive tribes.

The said Royal Niger Company also agree to pay the said Chiefs _________ measures native value.

We, the undersigned witnesses, do hereby solemnly declare that the _________ Chiefs whose names are placed opposite their respective crosses have in our presence affixed their crosses of their own free will and consent, and that the said _________ has in our presence affixed his signature.

Done in triplicate at _________, this _________ day of _________, 188__.

Declaration by interpreter I, _________, of _________, do hereby solemnly declare that I am well acquainted with the language of the country, and that on the _________ day of _________, 188__, I truly and faithfully explained the above Agreement to all the Chiefs present, and that they understood its meaning.

For Further Reflection

- What did this "standard treaty" promise to Nigerian leaders, and what was expected in return? Given language barriers and imperial greed, do you believe Nigerians received true and faithful explanations of the treaty's meaning?

Source: Alfred J. Andrea and James H. Overfield, eds. *The Human Record: Sources of Global History,* 3rd ed., vol. 2. Boston: Wadsworth, 1998, pp. 299–300.

the 1830s, and the discovery of gold in 1851 brought a surge in migration to Australia. European settlers established communities also in New Zealand. Europeans first visited New Zealand while hunting whales and seals, but the islands' fertile soils and abundant stands of timber soon attracted their attention and drew large numbers of migrants.

European migration rocked the societies of Australia and New Zealand. Diseases such as smallpox and measles devastated indigenous peoples at the same time that European migrants flooded into their lands. The aboriginal population of Australia fell from about 650,000 in 1800 to 90,000 in 1900, whereas the European population rose from a few thousand to 3.75 million during the same period. Similarly, the population of indigenous Maori in New Zealand fell from about 200,000 in 1800 to 45,000 a century later, while European numbers climbed to 750,000.

Increasing migration also fueled conflict between European settlers and native populations. Large settler societies pushed indigenous peoples from their lands, often following violent confrontations. Because the nomadic foraging peoples of Australia did not occupy lands permanently, British settlers considered the continent *terra nullius*—"land belonging to no one"—that they could seize and put to their own uses. They undertook brutal military campaigns to evict aboriginal

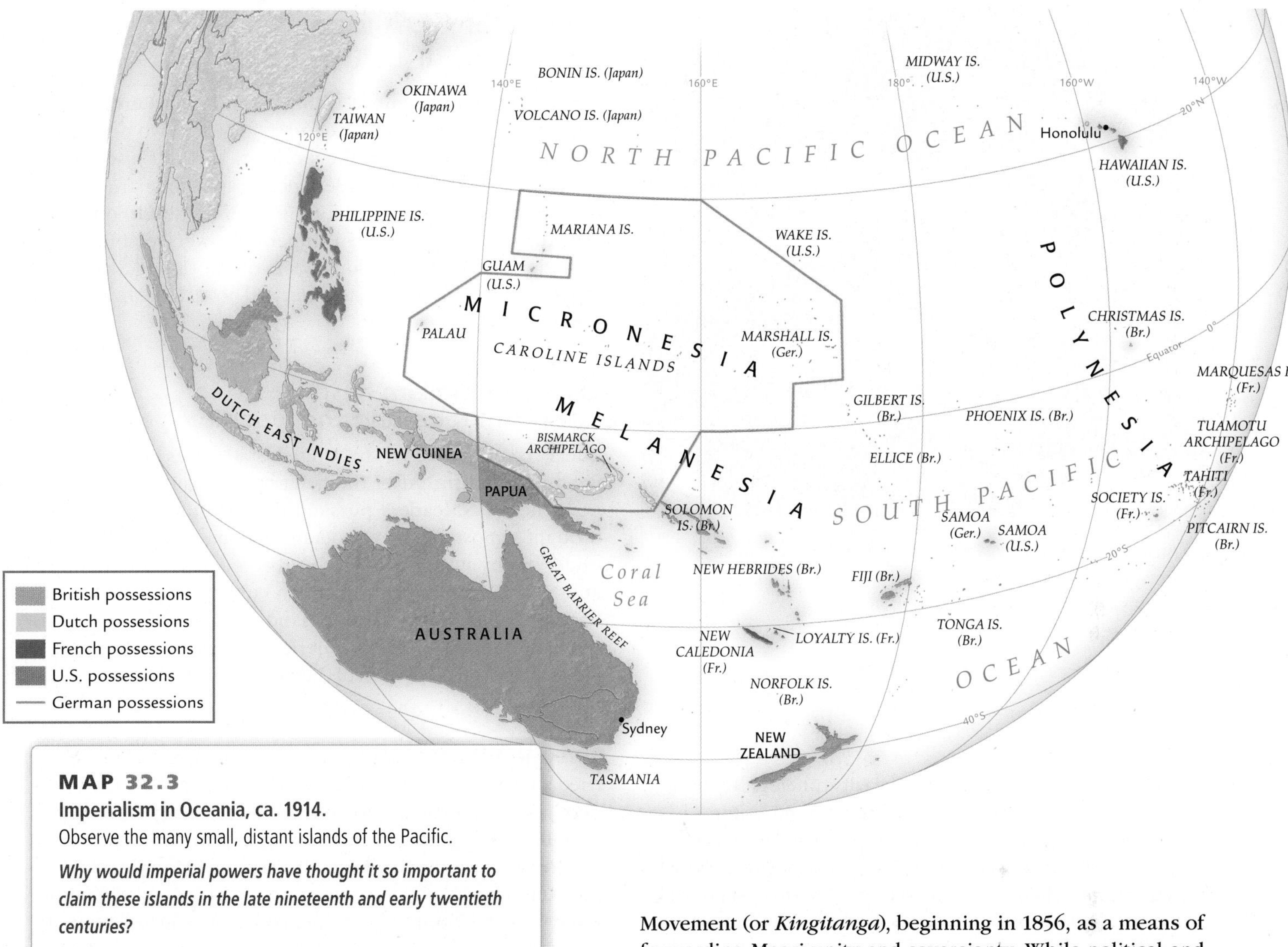

MAP 32.3
Imperialism in Oceania, ca. 1914.
Observe the many small, distant islands of the Pacific.
Why would imperial powers have thought it so important to claim these islands in the late nineteenth and early twentieth centuries?

peoples from lands suitable for agriculture or herding. Despite native resistance, by 1900 the British had succeeded in displacing most indigenous Australians from their traditional lands and dispersing them throughout the continent.

A similarly disruptive process transpired in New Zealand. Representatives of the British government encouraged Maori leaders in 1840 to sign the Treaty of Waitangi, presumably designed to place New Zealand under British protection. Interpreted differently by the British and the Maori, the treaty actually signaled the coming of official British colonial control in New Zealand (1841) and thereafter inspired effective and long-lasting Maori opposition to British attempts to usurp their land and sovereignty. Conflicts over land confiscations and disputed land sales, for example, helped to spark the New Zealand Wars, a series of military confrontations between autonomous Maori groups and British troops and settlers that extended from the mid- to the late nineteenth century. Various Maori also cooperated in the Maori King Movement (or *Kingitanga*), beginning in 1856, as a means of forwarding Maori unity and sovereignty. While political and military battles continued, the British managed by the end of the century to force many Maori into poor rural communities separated from European settlements.

Imperialists in Paradise Even though imported diseases ravaged indigenous populations, the Pacific islands mostly escaped the fate of Australia and New Zealand, where settlers overwhelmed and overpowered native populations. During the nineteenth century the principal European visitors to Pacific islands were whalers, merchants, and missionaries. Whalers frequented ports where they could relax, refit their ships, and drink rum. Merchants sought fragrant sandalwood and succulent sea slugs, both of which fetched high prices in China. Missionaries established both Roman Catholic and Protestant churches throughout the Pacific Ocean basin. Naval vessels sometimes made a show of force or intervened in disputes between islanders and Europeans—or between competing groups of Europeans. Through most of the nineteenth century, however, imperialist powers had no desire to establish direct colonial rule over Pacific islands.

An anonymous contemporary painting depicts the signing of the Treaty of Waitangi on 6 February 1840. British military and colonial officials look on as about fifty Maori chiefs put their names to the document.

That situation changed in the late nineteenth century. Just as nationalist rivalries drove the scramble for Africa, so they encouraged imperialist powers to stake their claims in the Pacific. In an era of global imperialism, European states sought reliable coaling stations for their steamships and ports for their navies. France established a protectorate in Tahiti, the Society Islands, and the Marquesas as early as 1841 and imposed direct colonial rule in 1880. France also annexed New Caledonia in 1853. Britain made Fiji a crown colony in 1874, and Germany annexed several of the Marshall Islands in 1876 and 1878. At the Berlin Conference, European diplomats agreed on a partition of Oceania as well as Africa, and Britain, France, Germany, and the United States proceeded to claim almost all of the Pacific islands. By 1900 only the kingdom of Tonga remained independent, and even Tonga accepted British protection against the possibility of encroachments by other imperial powers.

Quite apart from their value as ports and coaling stations, the Pacific islands offered economic benefits to imperial powers. Hawai`i and Fiji were the sites of productive sugarcane plantations. Samoa, French Polynesia, and many Melanesian and Micronesian islands were sources of copra—dried coconut, which produced high-quality vegetable oil for the manufacture of soap, candles, and lubricants. New Caledonia had rich veins of nickel, and many small Pacific islands had abundant deposits of guano—bird droppings that made excellent fertilizer.

THE EMERGENCE OF NEW IMPERIAL POWERS

Nineteenth-century imperialism was mostly a European affair. Toward the end of the century, however, two new imperial powers appeared on the world stage: the United States and Japan. Both lands experienced rapid industrialization in the late nineteenth century, and both built powerful armed forces. As European imperial powers planted their flags throughout the world, leaders of the United States and Japan decided that they too needed to establish a global imperial presence.

U.S. Imperialism in Latin America and the Pacific

The very existence of the United States was due to European imperialism. After the new republic had won its independence, U.S. leaders pursued their manifest destiny and brought almost all the temperate regions of North America under their authority. Like British migrants in Australia and New Zealand, Euro-American cultivators pushed indigenous peoples onto marginal lands and reservations. This domination of the North American continent represents a part of the larger story of European and Euro-American imperialism.

The Monroe Doctrine The fledgling United States also tried to wield power outside North America. In 1823 President James Monroe (in office 1817–1825) issued a proclamation that warned European states against imperialist designs in the western hemisphere. In essence Monroe claimed the Americas as a U.S. protectorate, and his proclamation, known as the Monroe Doctrine, served as a justification for later U.S. intervention in hemispheric affairs. Until the late nineteenth century, the United States mostly exercised informal influence in the Americas and sought to guarantee free trade in the region. That policy benefited U.S. entrepreneurs and their European counterparts who worked to bring the natural resources and agricultural products of the Americas to the world market.

As the United States consolidated its continental holdings, U.S. leaders became interested in acquiring territories beyond the temperate regions of North America. In 1867 the United States purchased Alaska from Russia and in 1875 it claimed a protectorate over the islands of Hawai`i, where U.S. entrepreneurs had established highly productive sugarcane plantations. The Hawaiian kingdom survived until 1893, when a group of planters and businesspeople overthrew the last monarch, Queen Lili`uokalani (reigned 1891–1893), and invited the United States to annex the islands. U.S. president Grover Cleveland (in office 1885–1889 and 1893–1897) opposed annexation, but his successor, William McKinley (in office 1897–1901), was more open to American expansion and agreed to acquire the islands as U.S. possessions in 1898.

The Spanish-Cuban-American War The United States emerged as a major imperial and colonial power after the brief Spanish-Cuban-American War (1898–1899). War broke out as anticolonial tensions mounted in Cuba and Puerto Rico—the last remnants of Spain's American empire—where U.S. business interests had made large investments. In 1898 the U.S. battleship *Maine* exploded and sank in Havana harbor. U.S. leaders claimed sabotage and declared war on Spain. The United States easily defeated Spain and took control and possession of Cuba and Puerto Rico. After the U.S. navy destroyed the Spanish fleet at Manila in a single day, the United States also took possession of Guam and the Philippines, Spain's last colonies in the Pacific, to prevent them from falling under German or Japanese control.

The United States quickly established colonial governments in most of its new possessions. Instability and disorder prompted the new imperial power to intervene also in the affairs of Caribbean and Central American lands, even those that were not U.S. possessions, to prevent rebellion and protect American business interests. U.S. military forces occupied Cuba, the Dominican Republic, Nicaragua, Honduras, and Haiti in the early twentieth century.

The consolidation of U.S. authority in the Philippines was an especially difficult affair. The Spanish-Cuban-American War coincided with a Filipino revolt against Spanish rule, and U.S. forces promised to support independence of the Philippines in exchange for an alliance against Spain. After the victory over Spain, however, President William McKinley decided to bring the Philippines under American control. The United States paid Spain twenty million dollars for rights to the colony, which was important to American businesspeople and military leaders because of its strategic position in the South China Sea. Led by Emilio Aguinaldo—known to his followers as the George Washington of his country—Filipino rebels turned their arms against the new intruders. The result was a bitter insurrection that raged until 1902 and flared sporadically until 1906. The conflict claimed the lives of 4,200 American soldiers, 15,000 rebel troops, and some 200,000 Filipino civilians.

Queen Lili`uokalani, last monarch of Hawai`i, before her deposition in 1893. Wearing a European dress, the queen sits on a throne covered with a traditional royal cape made of bird feathers.

The Panama Canal To facilitate communication and transportation between the Atlantic and the Pacific oceans, the United States sought to build a canal across some narrow stretch of land in Central America. Engineers identified the isthmus of Panama in northern Colombia as the best site for a canal, but Colombia was unwilling to cede land for the project. Under President Theodore Roosevelt (in office 1901–1909), an enthusiastic champion of imperial expansion, the United States supported a rebellion against Colombia in 1903 and helped rebels establish the breakaway state of Panama. In exchange for this support, the United States won the right to build a canal across Panama and to control the adjacent territory, known as the Panama Canal Zone. Given this expansion of U.S. interests in Latin America, Roosevelt added a corollary to the Monroe Doctrine in 1904. The "Roosevelt Corollary" exerted the U.S. right to intervene in the domestic affairs of nations within the hemisphere if they demonstrated an inability to maintain the security deemed necessary to protect U.S. investments. The Roosevelt Corollary, along with the Panama Canal when it opened in 1914, strengthened U.S. military and economic claims.

Imperial Japan

Strengthened by rapid industrialization during the Meiji era, Japan joined the ranks of imperial powers in the late nineteenth century. Japanese leaders deeply resented the unequal treaties that the United States and European powers forced them to accept in the 1860s. They resolved to eliminate the diplomatic handicaps imposed by the treaties and to raise Japan's profile in the world. While founding representative political institutions to demonstrate their trustworthiness to American and European diplomats, Japanese leaders also made a bid to stand alongside the world's great powers by launching a campaign of imperial expansion.

Early Japanese Expansion The Japanese drive to empire began in the east Asian islands. During the 1870s Japanese leaders consolidated their hold on Hokkaido and the Kurile Islands to the north, and they encouraged Japanese migrants to populate the islands to forestall Russian expansion there. By 1879 they had also established their hegemony over Okinawa and the Ryukyu Islands to the south.

In 1876 Japan purchased modern warships from Britain, and the newly strengthened Japanese navy immediately began to flex its muscles in Korea. After a confrontation between the Korean navy and a Japanese surveying vessel, Meiji officials dispatched a gunboat expedition and forced Korean leaders to submit to the same kind of unequal treaty that the United States and European states had imposed on Japan. As European and U.S. imperialists divided up the world in the 1880s and 1890s, Meiji political and military leaders made plans to project Japanese power abroad. They developed contingency plans for a conflict with China, staged maneuvers in anticipation of a continental war, and built a navy with the capacity to fight on the high seas.

The Sino-Japanese War Conflict erupted in 1894 over the status of Korea. Taking advantage of the unequal treaty of 1876, Japanese businesses had substantial interests in Korea. When an antiforeign rebellion broke out in Korea in 1893, Meiji leaders feared that the land might fall into anarchy and become an inviting target of European and U.S. imperialism. Qing rulers sent an army to restore order and reassert Chinese authority in Korea, but Meiji leaders were unwilling to recognize Chinese control over a land so important to Japanese business interests. Thus in August 1894 they declared war on China. The Japanese navy quickly gained control of the Yellow Sea and demolished the Chinese fleet in a battle lasting a mere five hours. The Japanese army then pushed Qing forces out of the Korean peninsula. Within a few months the conflict was over. When the combatants made peace in April 1895, Qing authorities recognized the independence of Korea, thus making it essentially a dependency of Japan. They also ceded Taiwan, the Pescadores Islands, and the Liaodong peninsula, which strengthened Japanese control over east Asian waters. Alongside territorial acquisitions, Japan gained unequal treaty rights in China like those enjoyed by European and American powers.

The unexpected Japanese victory startled European imperial powers, especially Russia. Tensions between Japan and Russia soon mounted, as both imperial powers had territorial ambitions in the Liaodong peninsula, Korea, and Manchuria. During the late 1890s Japanese military leaders vastly strengthened both their navy and their army with an eye toward a future conflict with Russia.

The Russo-Japanese War War broke out in 1904, and Japanese forces overran Russian installations before reinforcements could arrive from Europe. The enhanced Japanese navy destroyed the Russian Baltic fleet, which had sailed halfway around the world to support the war effort. By 1905 the war was over, and Japan won international recognition of its colonial authority over Korea and the Liaodong peninsula. Furthermore, Russia ceded the southern half

The Japanese painter Kobayashi Kiyochika celebrates a Japanese naval victory over the Chinese fleet. China's defeat in the Sino-Japanese war showed how the Qing dynasty had been weakened militarily, especially by the Opium War, and demonstrated how successful modernization had been for Japan since the Meiji restoration.

of Sakhalin island to Japan, along with a railroad and economic interests in southern Manchuria. Victory in the Russo-Japanese War transformed Japan into a major imperial power.

LEGACIES OF IMPERIALISM

Imperialism and colonialism profoundly influenced the development of world history. In some ways, they tightened links between the world's peoples: trade and migration increased dramatically as imperial powers exploited the resources of subject lands and recruited labor forces to work in colonies throughout the world. Yet imperialism and colonialism also brought peoples into conflict and heightened senses of difference between peoples. European, Euro-American, and Japanese imperialists all came to think of themselves as superior to the peoples they overcame. Meanwhile, foreign intrusion stimulated the development of national identities in colonized lands, and over time these national identities served as a foundation for anticolonial independence movements.

Empire and Economy

One of the principal motives of imperialism was the desire to gain access to natural resources and agricultural products. As imperial powers consolidated their hold on foreign lands, colonial administrators reorganized subject societies so they would become efficient suppliers of timber, rubber, petroleum, gold, silver, diamonds, cotton, tea, coffee, cacao, and other products as well. As a result, global trade in those commodities surged during the nineteenth and early twentieth centuries. The advantages of that trade went mostly to the colonial powers, whose policies encouraged their subject lands to provide raw materials for processing in the industrialized societies of Europe, North America, and Japan.

Economic and Social Changes Sometimes colonial rule transformed the production of crops and commodities that had long been prominent in subject societies. In India, for example, the cultivation of cotton began probably before 5000 B.C.E. For most of history, cultivators spun thread and wove their own cotton textiles or else supplied local artisans with raw materials. In the nineteenth century, however, colonial administrators reoriented the cultivation of cotton to serve the needs of the emerging British textile industry. They encouraged cultivators to produce cotton for export rather than for local consumption, and they built railroads deep into the subcontinent to transport raw cotton to the coast quickly, before rain and dust could spoil the product. They shipped raw cotton to England, where mechanized factories rapidly turned out large volumes of high-quality textiles. They also allowed the import of inexpensive British textiles, which undermined Indian cotton cloth production. The value of raw cotton exported from India went from 10 million rupees in 1849 to 60 million rupees in 1860 and 410 million rupees in 1913, whereas the value of finished cotton products imported into India rose from 50,000 rupees in 1814 to 5.2 million rupees in 1829 and 30 million rupees in 1890. Thus colonial policies transformed India from the world's principal center of cotton manufacture to a supplier of raw cotton and a consumer of textiles produced in the British isles.

In some cases, colonial rule led to the introduction of new crops that transformed both the landscape and the social order of subject lands. In the early nineteenth century, for example, British colonial officials introduced tea bushes from China to Ceylon and India. The effect on Ceylon was profound. British planters felled trees in much of the island, converted rain forests into tea plantations, and recruited Ceylonese women by the thousands to carry out the labor-intensive work of harvesting mature tea leaves. Consumption of tea in India and Ceylon was almost negligible, so increased supplies met the growing demand for tea in Europe, where the beverage became accessible to individuals of all social classes. The value of south Asian tea exports rose from about 309,000 pounds sterling in 1866 to 4.4 million pounds sterling in 1888 and 6.1 million pounds sterling in 1900. Malaya and Sumatra underwent a similar social

An engraving depicts the East India Railway about 1863. Though originally built to transport goods, railroads quickly became a popular means of passenger travel in India.

transformation after British colonial agents planted rubber trees there in the 1870s and established plantations to meet the growing global demand for rubber products.

Labor Migrations

Efforts to exploit the natural resources and agricultural products of subject lands led imperial and colonial powers to encourage mass migrations of workers during the nineteenth and early twentieth centuries. Two patterns of labor migration were especially prominent during the imperial and colonial era. European migrants went mostly to temperate lands, where they worked as free cultivators or industrial laborers. In contrast, migrants from Asia, Africa, and the Pacific islands moved largely to tropical and subtropical lands, where they worked as indentured laborers on plantations or manual laborers for mining enterprises or large-scale construction projects. Between them, these two streams of labor migration profoundly influenced the development of societies, especially in the Americas and the Pacific basin.

European Migration Between 1800 and 1914 some fifty million European migrants left their homes and sought opportunities overseas. Most of those migrants left the relatively poor agricultural societies of southern and eastern Europe, especially Italy, Russia, and Poland, although siz-

MAP 32.4

Imperialism and migration during the nineteenth and early twentieth centuries.

An unprecedented intercontinental migration of people characterized the age of imperialism.

What factors encouraged and facilitated migration on this extraordinary scale?

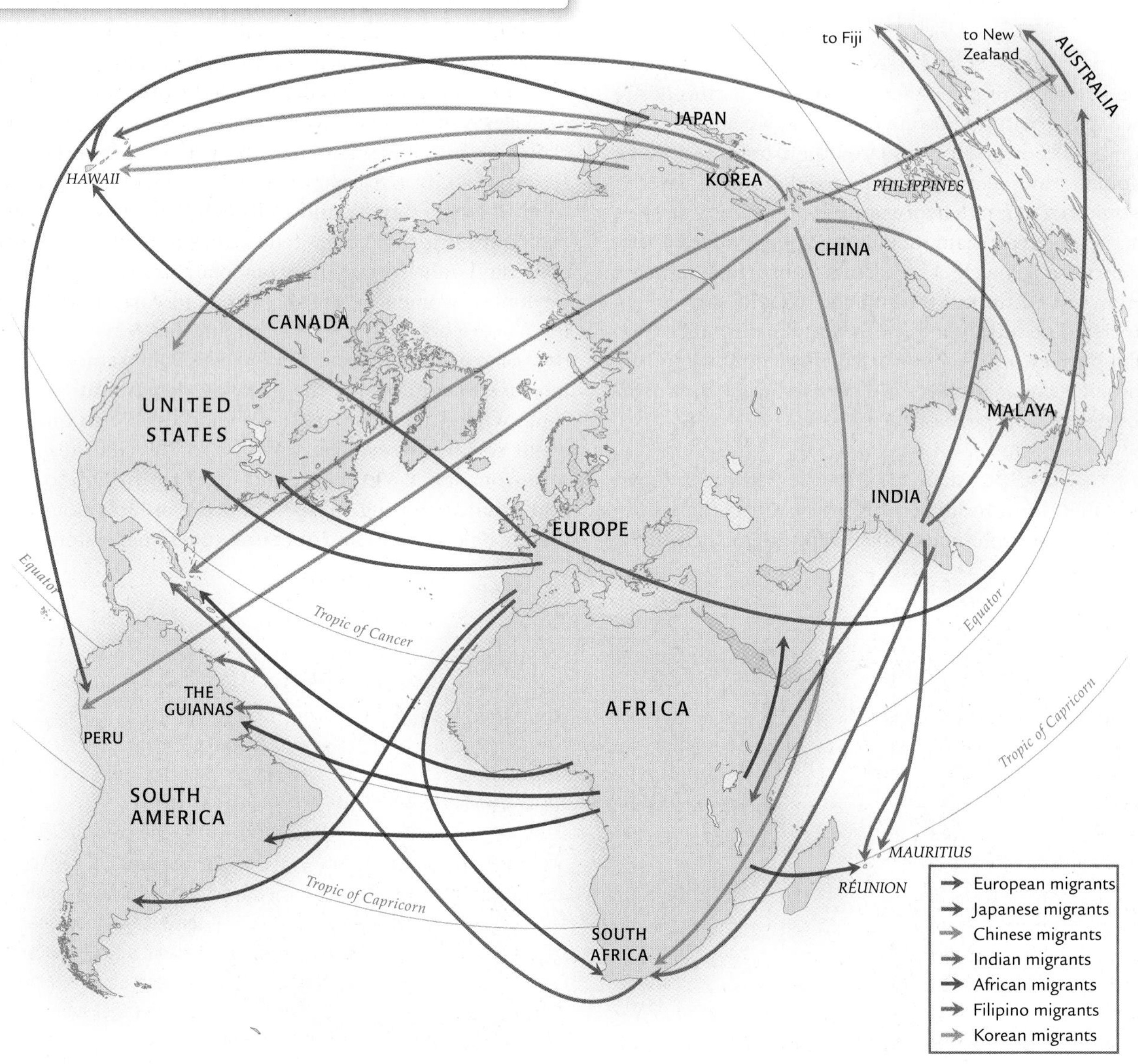

able numbers came also from Britain, Ireland, Germany, and Scandinavia. A majority of the migrants—about thirty-two million—went to the United States. Many of the early arrivals went west in search of cheap land to cultivate. Later migrants settled heavily in the northeast, where they provided the labor that drove U.S. industrialization after the 1860s. Settler colonies in Canada, Argentina, Australia, New Zealand, and south Africa also drew large numbers of European migrants, who mostly became free cultivators or herders but sometimes found employment as skilled laborers in mines or fledgling industries. Most European migrants traveled as free agents, but some went as indentured laborers. All of them were able to find opportunities in temperate regions of the world because of European and Euro-American imperialism in the Americas, south Africa, and Oceania.

Indentured Labor Migration In contrast to their European counterparts, migrants from Asia, Africa, and the Pacific islands generally traveled as indentured laborers. As the institution of slavery went into decline, planters sought large numbers of laborers to replace slaves who left the plantations. The planters relied primarily on indentured laborers recruited from relatively poor and densely populated lands. Between 1820 and 1914 about 2.5 million indentured laborers left their homes to work in distant parts of the world. Labor recruiters generally offered workers free passage to their destinations and provided them with food, shelter, clothing, and modest compensation for their services in exchange for a commitment to work for five to seven years. Sometimes recruiters also offered free return passage to workers who completed a second term of service.

The majority of the indentured laborers came from India, but sizable numbers also came from China, Japan, Java, Africa, and the Pacific islands. Indentured laborers went mostly to tropical and subtropical lands in the Americas, the Caribbean, Africa, and Oceania. The indentured labor trade began in the 1820s when French and British colonial officials sent Indian migrants to work on sugar plantations in the Indian Ocean islands of Réunion and Mauritius. The arrangement worked well, and large numbers of Indian laborers later went to work on rubber plantations in Malaya and sugar plantations in south Africa, the Pacific island of Fiji, the Guianas, and the Caribbean islands of Trinidad, Tobago, and Jamaica. After the Opium War, recruiters began to seek workers in China. Large numbers of Chinese laborers went to sugar plantations in Cuba and Hawai`i, guano mines in Peru, tin mines in Malaya, gold mines in south Africa and Australia, and railroad construction sites in the United States, Canada, and Peru. After the Meiji restoration in Japan, a large contingent of Japanese laborers migrated to Hawai`i to work on sugar plantations, and a smaller group went to work in guano mines in Peru. Indentured laborers from Africa went mostly to sugar plantations in Réunion, the Guianas, and Caribbean islands. Those from Pacific islands went mostly to plantations in other Pacific islands and Australia.

Empire and Migration All those large-scale migrations of the nineteenth century reflected the global influence of imperial powers. European migrations were possible only because European and Euro-American peoples had established settler societies in temperate regions around the world. Movements of indentured laborers were possible because colonial officials were able to recruit workers and dispatch them to distant lands where their compatriots had already established plantations or opened mines. In combination the nineteenth-century migrations profoundly influenced societies around the world by depositing large communities of people with distinctive ethnic identities in lands far from their original homes.

Empire and Society

Colonial Conflict The policies adopted by imperial powers and colonial officials forced peoples of different societies to deal with one another on a regular and systematic basis. Their interactions often led to violent conflicts between colonizers and subject peoples. The sepoy rebellion was the most prominent effort to resist British colonial authority in India, but it was only one among thousands of insurrections organized by discontented Indian subjects between the mid-nineteenth and the mid-twentieth centuries. Colonized lands in southeast Asia and Africa also became hotbeds of resistance, as subject peoples revolted against foreign rule, tyrannical behavior of colonial officials, the introduction of European schools and curricula, high taxation, and requirements that subject peoples cultivate certain crops or provide compulsory labor for colonists' enterprises.

Many rebellions drew strength from traditional religious beliefs, and priests or prophets often led resistance to colonial rule. In Tanganyika, for example, a local prophet organized the large-scale Maji Maji rebellion (1905–1906) to expel German colonial authorities from east Africa. Rebels sprinkled themselves with *maji-maji* ("magic water"), which they believed would protect them from German weapons. The magic water was ineffective, and as many as seventy-five thousand insurgents died in the conflict. Nevertheless, rebellion was a constant threat to colonial rule. Even when subject peoples dared not revolt, since they could not match European weaponry, they resisted colonial rule by boycotting European goods, organizing political parties and pressure groups, publishing anticolonial newspapers and magazines, and pursuing anticolonial policies through churches and religious groups.

Colonial policies also led to conflicts among peoples brought together artificially into multicultural societies. When indentured laborers from different societies congregated on plantations, for example, tensions quickly developed between workers and their supervisors and among different groups of workers themselves. In Hawai`i, one of the most diverse multicultural societies created by the labor migrations of the nineteenth century, workers on sugar plantations came primarily from China, Japan, and Portugal, but there were also sizable contingents from the Philippines, Korea, and other Pacific islands. Workers and their families normally lived in villages dominated by their own ethnic groups, but there were plentiful opportunities for individuals and groups to mix with one another at work, at play, or in the larger society. Although the various ethnic communities readily adopted their neighbors' foods and sometimes took spouses from other groups, linguistic, religious, and cultural differences provided a foundation for strong ethnic identities throughout the plantation era and beyond.

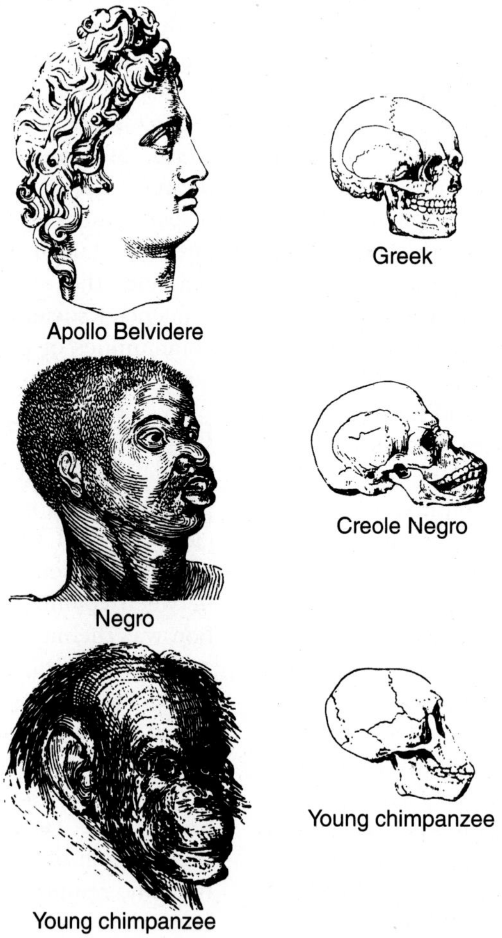

Scientific racists often argued that Europeans had reached a higher stage of evolution than other peoples. An illustration from a popular book by Josiah Clark Nott and G. R. Glidden, *Indigenous Races of the Earth,* deliberately distorted facial and skull features to suggest a close relationship between African peoples and chimpanzees.

Scientific Racism Social and cultural differences were the foundation of an academic pursuit known as scientific racism, which became prominent especially after the 1840s. Theorists such as the French nobleman Count Joseph Arthur de Gobineau (1816–1882) took race as the most important index of human potential. In fact, there is no such thing as a biologically pure race, but nineteenth-century theorists assumed that the human species consisted of several distinct racial groups. In his dense, four-volume *Essay on the Inequality of the Human Races* (1853–1855), Gobineau divided humanity into four main racial groups, each of which had its own peculiar traits. Gobineau characterized Africans as unintelligent and lazy; Asians as smart but docile; the native peoples of the Americas as dull and arrogant; and Europeans as intelligent, noble, and morally superior to others. Throughout the later nineteenth and early twentieth centuries, racist thinkers sought to identify racial groups on the basis of skin color, bone structure, nose shape, cranial capacity, and other physical characteristics. Agreeing uniformly that Europeans were superior to other peoples, race theorists clearly reflected the dominance of European imperial powers in the larger world.

After the 1860s, scientific racists drew heavily from the writings of Charles Darwin (1809–1882), an English biologist whose book *The Origin of Species* (1859) argued that all living species had evolved over thousands of years in a ferocious contest for survival. Species that adapted well to their environment survived, reproduced, and flourished, according to Darwin, whereas others declined and went into extinction. The slogan "survival of the fittest" soon became a byword for Darwin's theory of evolution. Theorists known as social Darwinists seized on those ideas, which Darwin had applied exclusively to biological matters, and adapted them to explain the development of human societies. The English philosopher Herbert Spencer (1820–1903) relied on theories of evolution to explain differences between the strong and the weak: successful individuals and races had competed better in the natural world and consequently evolved to higher states than did other, less fit peoples. On the basis of that reasoning, Spencer and others justified the domination of European imperialists over subject peoples as the inevitable result of natural scientific principles.

Popular Racism On a more popular level, there was no need for elaborate scientific theories to justify racist prejudices. Representatives of imperial and colonial powers routinely adopted racist views on the basis of personal experience, which seemed to teach their superiority to subject peoples. In 1896, for example, the British military officer Colonel Francis Younghusband reflected on differences between peoples that he noticed during his travels throughout China, central Asia, and India. He granted that Asian peoples were physically and intellectually equal to Europeans, but he held that

> no European can mix with non-Christian races without feeling his moral superiority over them. He feels, from the first contact with them, that whatever may be their relative positions from an intellectual point of view, he is stronger morally than they are. And facts show that this feeling is a true one. It is not because we are any cleverer than the natives of India, because we have more brains or bigger heads than they have, that we rule India; but because we are stronger morally than they

are. Our superiority over them is not due to mere sharpness of intellect, but to that higher moral nature to which we have attained in the development of the human race.

Racist views were by no means a monopoly of European imperialists: U.S. and Japanese empire builders also developed a sense of superiority over the peoples they conquered and ruled. U.S. forces in the Philippines disparaged the rebels they fought there as "gooks," and they did not hesitate to torture enemies in a conflict justified by President McKinley as an effort to "civilize and Christianize" the Filipinos. In the 1890s Japanese newspapers portrayed Chinese and Korean peoples as dirty, backward, stupid, and cowardly. Some scholars concocted speculative theories that the Japanese people were more akin to the "Aryans," who supposedly had conquered much of the Eurasian landmass in ancient times, than to the "Mongolians" who populated China and Korea. After their victory in the Russo-Japanese War, political and military leaders came to believe that Japan had an obligation to oversee the affairs of their backward neighbors and help civilize their little Asian brothers.

Nationalism and Anticolonial Movements

While imperialists convinced themselves of their racial superiority, colonial rule provoked subject peoples to develop a sense of their own identities. Just as Napoleon's invasions aroused national feelings and led to the emergence of nationalist movements in Europe, so imperial expansion and colonial domination prompted the formation of national identities and the organization of anticolonial movements in subject lands. The potential of imperialism and colonialism to push subject peoples toward nationalism was most evident in India.

Ram Mohan Roy During the nineteenth century, educated Indian elites helped forge a sense of Indian identity. Among the most influential of them was Ram Mohan Roy (1772–1833), a prominent Bengali intellectual sometimes called the "father of modern India." Roy argued for the construction of a society based on both modern European science and the Indian tradition of devotional Hinduism. He supported some British colonial policies, such as the campaign to end the practice of sati, and he worked with Christian social reformers to improve the status of women by providing them with education and property rights. Yet Roy saw himself as a Hindu reformer who drew inspiration from the Vedas and Upanishads and who sought to bring Hindu spirituality to bear on the problems and conditions of his own time. During the last two decades of his life, Roy tirelessly published newspapers and founded societies to mobilize educated Hindus and advance the cause of social reform in colonial India.

Reform societies flourished in nineteenth-century India. Most of them appealed to upper-caste Hindus, but some were Muslim organizations, and a few represented the interests of peasants, landlords, or lower castes. After mid-century, reformers increasingly called for self-government or at least greater Indian participation in government. Their leaders often had received an advanced education at British universities, and they drew inspiration from European Enlightenment values such as equality, freedom, and popular sovereignty. But they invoked those values to criticize the British colonial regime in India and to call for political and social reform.

The Indian National Congress The most important of the reform groups was the Indian National Congress,

Much of western India experienced severe famine in 1896–1897, and epidemics of bubonic plague broke out among weakened populations. British relief efforts were often heavy-handed and insensitive, and they did little to alleviate the problems.

founded in 1885, with British approval, as a forum for educated Indians to communicate their views on public affairs to colonial officials. Representatives from all parts of the subcontinent aired grievances about Indian poverty, the transfer of wealth from India to Britain, trade and tariff policies that harmed Indian businesses, the inability of colonial officials to provide effective relief for regions stricken by drought or famine, and British racism toward Indians. By the end of the nineteenth century, the congress openly sought Indian self-rule within a larger imperial framework. In 1916 the congress joined forces with the All-India Muslim League, the most prominent organization working to advance the political and social interests of Muslims, who made up about 25 percent of the Indian population.

Faced with increasing demands for Indian participation in government, in 1909 colonial authorities granted a limited franchise that allowed wealthy Indians to elect representatives to local legislative councils. By that time, however, the drive for political reform had become a mass movement. Indian nationalists called for immediate independence, mounted demonstrations to build support for their cause, and organized boycotts of British goods. A few zealous nationalists turned to violence and sought to undermine British rule by bombing government buildings and assassinating colonial officials. Going into the twentieth century, Indian nationalism was a powerful movement that would bring independence from colonial rule in 1947.

Although local experiences varied considerably, Indian nationalism and independence movements served as models for anticolonial campaigns in other lands. In almost all cases, the leaders of those movements were European-educated elites who absorbed Enlightenment values and then turned those values into an attack on European colonial rule in foreign lands.

inperspective

The construction of global empires in the nineteenth century noticeably increased the tempo of world integration. Armed with powerful transportation, communication, and military technologies, European peoples imposed their rule on much of Asia and almost all of Africa. They wielded enormous influence throughout the world, even where they did not establish imperial control, because of their wealth and economic power. Toward the end of the nineteenth century, the United States and Japan joined European states as global imperialists. All the imperial powers profoundly influenced the development of the societies they ruled. They shaped the economies and societies of their colonies by pushing them to supply natural resources and agricultural commodities in exchange for manufactured products. They created multicultural societies around the world by facilitating the movement of workers to lands where there was high demand for labor on plantations or in mines. They unintentionally encouraged the emergence of independence movements by provoking subject peoples to develop a sense of national identity. From the early twentieth century forward, much of global history has revolved around issues stemming from the world order of imperialism and colonialism.

CHRONOLOGY

1772–1833	Life of Ram Mohan Roy
1809–1882	Life of Charles Darwin
1816–1882	Life of Count Joseph Arthur de Gobineau
1824	Founding of Singapore by Thomas Stamford Raffles
1840	Treaty of Waitangi
1853–1902	Life of Cecil Rhodes
1857	Sepoy rebellion
1859–1869	Construction of the Suez Canal
1860–1864	Land wars in New Zealand
1865–1909	Reign of King Leopold II of Belgium
1884–1885	Berlin West Africa Conference
1885	Founding of the Indian National Congress
1894–1895	Sino-Japanese War
1897–1901	Term of office of U.S. president William McKinley
1898–1899	Spanish-Cuban-American War
1899–1902	South African War (Boer War)
1901–1909	Term of office of U.S. president Theodore Roosevelt
1904–1905	Russo-Japanese War
1904–1914	Construction of the Panama Canal
1905–1906	Maji Maji rebellion
1906	Founding of All-India Muslim League

Assessing AP Themes

1. Why did parts of Europe and North America develop industrialized economies in the early 19th century while prominent empires like China did not?
2. What complex array of factors facilitated the growth of the western capitalist, industrialized economies in the 19th century?
3. Compare the social, political, and intellectual responses to industrialization in non-Western countries (the societies at the crossroads in Asia, Africa, and Latin America).
4. Analyze the connections between industrialization and imperialism.
5. Explain how the spread of Enlightenment ideas and increased discontent with imperial rule propelled reformist and revolutionary movements in the late 18th and 19th centuries.
6. How much or in what ways were migration patterns changed because of the developments of transoceanic empires and a global capitalist economy?
7. Evaluate the consequences of large-scale migration for the migrants and for the existing populations to which they migrated and from which they came.

For Further Reading

Michael Adas. *Machines as the Measure of Men: Science, Technology, and Ideologies of Western Dominance.* Ithaca, 1988. Argues that European imperialists judged other peoples on the basis of their technological expertise.

———. *Prophets of Rebellion: Millenarian Protest Movements against the European Colonial Order.* Cambridge, 1987. Fascinating study focusing on five rebellions against European colonial rule led by religious leaders.

Benedict Anderson. *Imagined Communities: Reflections on the Origin and Spread of Nationalism.* Rev. ed. London, 1991. Examines the emergence of nationalism in Europe and its spread to other parts of the world during the era of imperialism.

A. Adu Boahen. *African Perspectives on Colonialism.* Baltimore, 1987. A valuable synthetic work that examines African responses to imperial intrusions and colonial regimes.

Sugata Bose. *A Hundred Horizons: The Indian Ocean in the Age of Global Empires.* Cambridge, Mass., 2006. A bold interregional history that argues that the peoples of the Indian Ocean littoral shared a common historical destiny.

H. V. Bowen. *The Business of Empire: The East India Company and Imperial Britain, 1756–1833.* Cambridge, 2006. Detailed history of the company's rise to power in India.

Jane Burbank and Frederick Cooper. *Empires in World History: Power and the Politics of Difference.* Princeton, 2010. A major study that considers modern empires in historical context.

John M. Carroll. *Edge of Empires: Chinese Elites and British Colonials in Hong Kong.* Cambridge, Mass., 2005. Study of the commercial and social interaction between Chinese and British in the formation of Hong Kong.

Ken S. Coates. *A Global History of Indigenous Peoples: Struggle and Survival.* Houndmills, 2004. Stressing the active role of indigenous peoples, this work examines the dynamics of colonial encounters.

Bernard S. Cohn. *Colonialism and Its Forms of Knowledge: The British in India.* Princeton, 1996. Insightful essays on the cultural and intellectual manifestations of imperialism.

Philip D. Curtin. *The World and the West: The European Challenge and the Overseas Response in the Age of Empire.* Cambridge and New York, 2000. A work that focuses on cultural change as it examines how various peoples have responded to the establishment of European empires.

Ranajit Guha and Gayatri Chakravorty Spivak, eds. *Selected Subaltern Studies.* New York, 1988. A collection of essays dealing with the experiences of women, minorities, peasants, workers, rebels, and subordinate groups in colonial India.

Daniel R. Headrick. *The Tentacles of Progress: Technology Transfer in the Age of Imperialism, 1850–1940.* New York, 1988. Argues that imperial powers reserved the benefits of technological innovation for themselves by limiting the expertise that they shared with subject peoples.

———. *The Tools of Empire: Technology and European Imperialism in the Nineteenth Century.* New York, 1981. Surveys the role of transportation, communication, military, and medical technologies in the making of global empires.

Adam Hochschild. *King Leopold's Ghost: A Story of Greed, Terror, and Heroism in Colonial Africa.* Boston, 1998. A ghastly story of nearly forgotten greed and crime.

Peter H. Hoffenberg. *An Empire on Display: English, Indian, and Australian Exhibitions from the Crystal Palace to the Great War.* Berkeley, 2001. An imaginative work that shows how exhibitions shaped culture and society within and across borders of the British empire.

Zine Magubane. *Bringing the Empire Home: Race, Class, and Gender in Britain and Colonial South Africa.* Chicago, 2004. Study of the ways that colonial England used racial stereotypes to justify its own social hierarchies as well as the colonial project.

David Northrup. *Indentured Labor in the Age of Imperialism, 1834–1922.* Cambridge, 1995. Careful study of indentured labor migrations and working conditions.

Thomas Pakenham. *The Scramble for Africa, 1876–1912.* New York, 1991. Detailed popular history of empire building in sub-Saharan Africa.

H. L. Wesseling. *The European Colonial Empires: 1815–1919.* New York, 2004. Puts the process of colonization into a comparative and long-term perspective.

Kathleen Wilson, ed. *A New Imperial History: Culture, Identity, and Modernity in Britain and the Empire, 1660–1840.* New York, 2004. Study of the cultural impact of colonialism on Britain.

Louise Young. *Japan's Total Empire: Manchuria and the Culture of Wartime Imperialism.* Berkeley, 1988. An important work that analyzes the transforming power imperialism had on both the colonized and the colonizer.

State of the World

The World Turned Upside Down

At the 1781 British surrender to colonial American troops in Yorktown, the British band reputedly played the march "The World Turned Upside Down." Whether that is a true story or not, the tune's title offered an appropriate commentary on how the state of the world was indeed experiencing dramatic changes, not just by political revolutions, but also by industrialization and the new imperialism. When the much-underrated colonial and guerrilla forces defeated the brash, imperial army of Great Britain, the most powerful nation in the world, that world did indeed seem upside down. A subject population of the British empire had bested its rulers and overthrown monarchy in favor of a republican form of government.

As "the people" became the source for national sovereignty in much of the Atlantic basin, revolution brought about the beheading of a king and a queen in France and the elevation of slaves to the status of national leaders in Haiti. Throughout Europe, the Caribbean, and Latin America, old governments fell under the pressure of revolutionary ideals and a new sort of nationalism. Similarly, the economic transformations linked to industrialization contributed to a world seemingly upended, whereby machines, factories, and inanimate sources of power and energy ruled over human life and nature. Industrialization likewise promoted mass migrations of Europeans and Asians to the Americas, literally repositioning human populations across hemispheres. Migrants, indigenous peoples, freed slaves, and women agitated for their democratic rights and equality in these new industrial and expansionist national states, but most of the world did not immediately undergo revolution inspired by Enlightenment of ideals of liberty, equality, and popular sovereignty.

Some of the oldest, most prestigious, and most powerful territories in the world, from the Ottoman empire and Africa to Russia, China, and Japan, found themselves challenged by the upstart new imperialists in Europe and the United States, their sovereignty and freedom impinged upon by the powerful combination of nationalism, industry, and militarism. Resistance to this world turned upside down persisted, however. On the foundation of thoroughgoing reform, Japan managed to attain parity with European empires. Colonial subjects from India to Africa engaged in large-scale rebellion and small acts of resistance. What North American colonists began in the late eighteenth century, colonial peoples in Africa and Asia finished in the twentieth century. After Europe imploded from within during two cataclysmic world wars, colonized peoples would turn the world upside down once again.

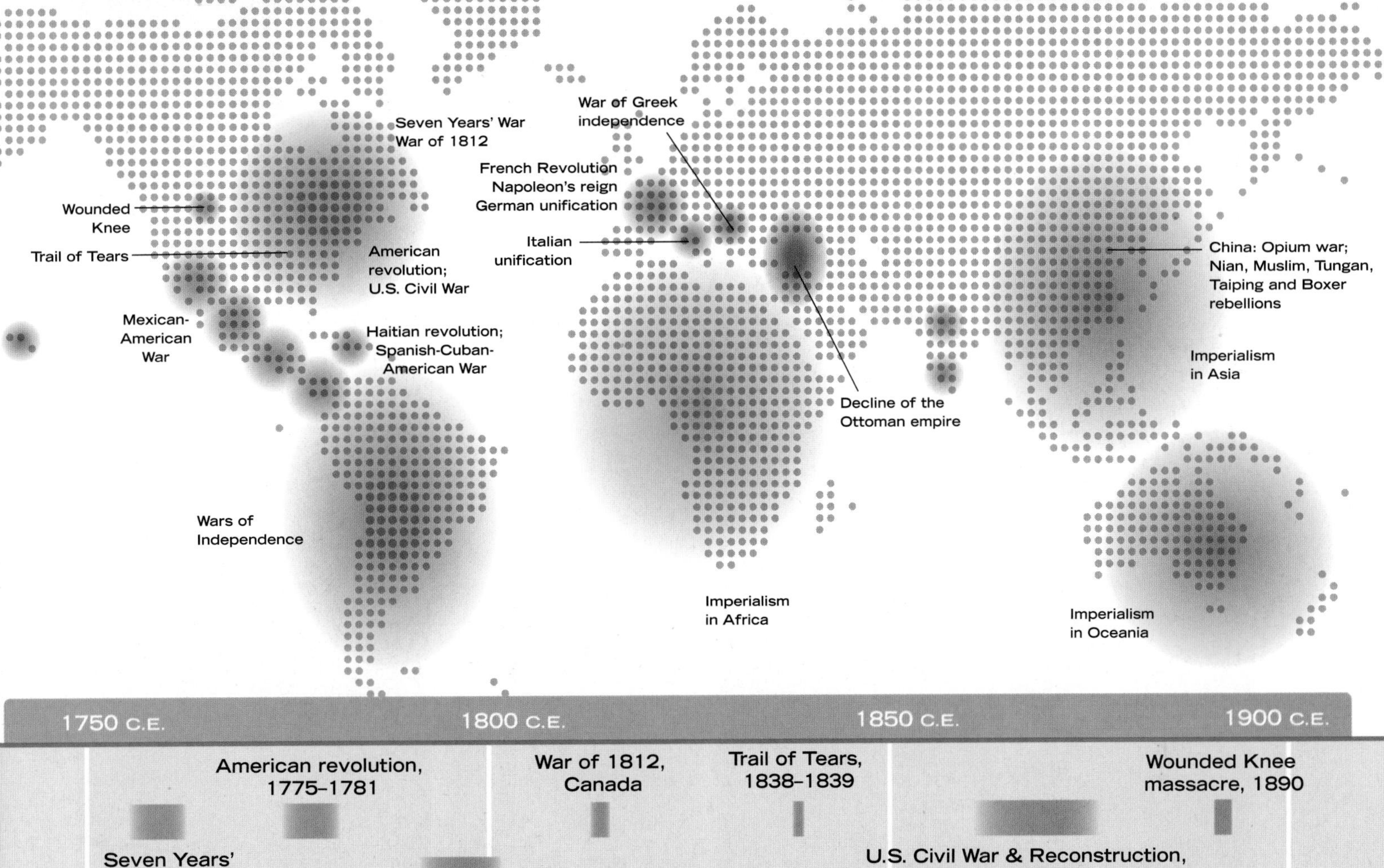

1750 C.E. | 1800 C.E. | 1850 C.E. | 1900 C.E.

THE AMERICAS

Seven Years' War, 1756–1763

American revolution, 1775–1781

Haitian revolution, 1791–1803

War of 1812, Canada

Wars of independence in Latin America, 1810–1825

Trail of Tears, 1838–1839

Mexican-American War, 1846–1848

U.S. Civil War & Reconstruction, 1861–1865; 1867–1877

Wounded Knee massacre, 1890

Spanish-Cuban-American War, 1898–1899

EUROPE

French revolution, 1789–1799
Napoleon's reign, 1799–1814

War of Greek independence, 1821–1827

Italian unification, 1859–1870
German unification, 1864–1871

SOUTHWEST ASIA

Decline of Ottoman empire, 1800–1923 (southwest Asia & northern Africa)

EAST ASIA

China: Opium War, 1839–1842; Nian, Muslim, Tungan and Taiping rebellions, 1851–1878; Boxer rebellion, 1898–1901;

Meiji Japan, 1868–1912; Imperialism in Asia, ca. 1914. Territories claimed by Britain, France, the U.S., Japan, Russia, and Portugal.

AFRICA

Imperialism in Africa, ca. 1914. Territories claimed by Belgium, Britain, France, Germany, Italy, Portugal, and Spain.

OCEANIA

Imperialism in Oceania, ca. 1914. Territories claimed by Britain, France, Germany and the U.S.

part 7

CONTEMPORARY GLOBAL REALIGNMENTS, 1914 TO THE PRESENT

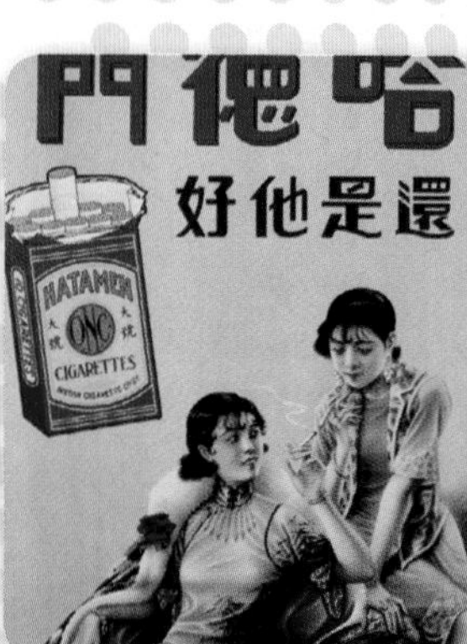

One of the greatest difficulties in studying the very recent past is that there hasn't been enough time for historians to figure out the long-term significance of recent events. It's hard to take "two steps back" and see the big picture. Another related difficulty is that we have too much information. So, without a sense of long-term significance, how can historians determine what's important and what is not, in our world filled to the brim with print, audio-visual, and computer-based information? One of the ways world historians try to make sense of the recent past is to tie events into the themes and key concepts of the early eras of human history. So as you go through this last period of world history, be sure you do this, and be sure you stay global, and don't focus exclusively on the West.

The global conflicts of the twentieth-century are only one-third of the AP Curriculum in this modern era, so it's important for AP classes not to dwell exclusively on these wars. The AP focus should be, first on the global causes of World War I and II, including great power rivalries, imperialist expansion, the economic crises caused by the Great Depression, ethnic conflicts and nationalist-inspired ideas. The "total war" aspects of these conflicts should be explored in great detail, since the all-consuming involvement of peoples on all continents changed the shape of much of the global community in the twentieth century. HTS 3 The consequences of the global conflict were and continue to be enormous for the modern world. The European-dominated global political order collapsed as empires dissolved due to nationalist and transnational movements, as well as the inability of European countries to maintain their possessions. Five empires collapsed, and colonial peoples negotiated or fought for their independence.

HTS 1 The ensuing Cold War and independence/de-colonization movements were intertwined. The United States and USSR represented the new global balance of power, and AP students should be able to link conflicts in Asia, Africa, and Latin America to the competing superpowers' conflicts. Some peoples and nations opposed the entire bi-polar-world concept, and AP students will need to explain the alternative positions offered by groups such as the Non-Aligned Movement. New institutions, created in response to the horrific warfare and near collapse of the world's economy, were also essentially opposed to a bi-polar world. International governing organizations like the United Nations (UN), humanitarian organizations like the World Health Organization, and economic institutions like the IMF, the European Union, and even Coca-Cola worked to create transnational or multinational economies, not merely nation-based ones.

These political changes were accompanied by major demographic and social consequences. Individual people and whole societies, not just governments, were affected by the wars. Twentieth-century wars and modern military technologies frequently led to ethnic genocides and enormous wartime casualties. Violent conflicts and the redrawing of colonial boundaries forced people to move or be moved to new places—often the main cities of the former imperial powers (imperial metropoles)—to look for housing and work. HTS 3 Individual lives and entire human populations were altered on an unprecedented scale. Modern transportation technologies made the transmission of epidemics faster and easier than ever before in human history. Diseases associated with poverty and poor living conditions persisted in some areas of the world, while life-improving medicines and technologies flourished in the wealthier countries of the world. On the other hand, the notion of human rights gained traction throughout the world, and more effective forms of artificial birth control gave women greater control over their own fertility and the ability to plan the size of their families. HTS 2 AP students will need to watch carefully for the continuities (conflict, migration, epidemics, globalization, for example) and changes (technologies, medical advances, role of women, for example) as they study how whole populations were or were not changed in the twentieth and early twenty-first centuries.

Rapid advances in science in the twentieth century altered everything from our understanding of the universe to how food is grown, from great advances in human life-spans to threats to destroy the delicate ecologies on which human life depends. HTS 2 Again, since you and your fellow AP students are living daily with the miracles of modern science, it takes some conscious effort to step back and understand both the continuities and changes that modern science represents. HTS 4 Journalists tend to use the term "globalization" to describe the closely-knit world of international business and finance, but AP students know this is not a new phenomenon, but a continuation of human migration, trade, and cultural interconnections over the last 10,000 years. For those who have access to it, new modes of communication and transportation have virtually eliminated the problem of geographic space. Increased interactions among diverse peoples have led to formations of new cultural identities, new forms of spirituality, and increasingly, a global popular culture. HTS 1 Music, film, social networking sites, and sports can reach and engage people on a global scale (if they have access to the technologies necessary), entertaining people and being adapted by them far from the place of origin.

HTS 4 The effects of increasing globalization are not always seen as good. Some people see increasing global contact as the homogenization or the destruction of their indigenous cultures or beliefs. Others protest against the economic inequalities or unevenness of the global economy, while still others focus on the destructive effects of the spread of modern technologies on the environment. AP students will need to be alert to the opinions of a wide variety of people, and not impose their own values and viewpoints on these situations.

The Great War: The World in Upheaval

chapter 33

This 1914 painting depicts the assassination of Archduke Francis Ferdinand and his wife, the Duchess Sophie. The gun in the killer's hand triggered what became the bloodiest war in history to date.

EYEWITNESS:
A Bloodied Archduke and a Bloody War

Archduke Francis Ferdinand (1863–1914) was aware that his first official visit to Sarajevo was fraught with danger. That ancient city was the capital of Bosnia-Herzegovina, twin provinces that had been under Ottoman rule since the fifteenth century and then occupied in 1878 and finally annexed by Austria-Hungary in 1908. These provinces became the hotbed of pan-Serbian nationalism. Ferdinand was on record as favoring greater autonomy for the provinces, but his words carried little weight with most Serbian nationalists, who hated the dynasty and the empire represented by the heir to the throne of Austria-Hungary.

It was a warm and radiant Sunday morning when Ferdinand's motorcade made its way through the narrow streets of Sarajevo. Waiting for him along the designated route were seven assassins armed with bombs and revolvers. The first would-be assassin did nothing, but the next man in line had more resolve and threw a bomb into the open car. Glancing off Ferdinand's arm, the bomb exploded near another vehicle and injured dozens of spectators. Trying to kill himself, the bomb thrower swallowed cyanide and jumped into a nearby river. The old poison only made him vomit, and the water was too shallow for drowning.

Undeterred, Ferdinand went on to a reception at city hall; after the reception he instructed his driver to take him to the hospital where those wounded in the earlier attack were being treated. While Ferdinand was on his way to the hospital, a young Bosnian Serb named Gavrilo Princip (1894–1918) lunged at the archduke's car and fired a revolver. The first bullet blew a gaping hole in the side of Ferdinand's neck. A second bullet intended for the governor of Bosnia went wild and entered the stomach of the expectant Duchess Sophie, the wife of the archduke. Turning to his wife, the archduke pleaded: "Sophie dear! Don't die! Stay alive for our children!" By the time medical aid arrived, however, the archduke and the duchess were dead.

In the meantime, Princip swallowed poison, which also only made him sick. When he tried to turn the gun on himself, a crowd intervened. After rescuing Princip from the mob, the police inflicted their own torture on the assassin: they kicked him, beat him, and scraped the skin from his neck with the edges of their swords. Three months later a court found Princip guilty of treason and murder, but because he committed his crime before his twentieth birthday, he could not be executed. Sentenced to twenty years in prison, Princip died in April 1918 from tuberculosis.

The assassination on 28 June 1914 brought to a head the tensions between the Austro-Hungarian empire and the neighboring kingdom of Serbia. As other European powers took sides, the stakes far outgrew Austro-Serbian conflicts. Nationalist aspirations, international rivalries, and an inflexible alliance system transformed that conflict into a general European war and ultimately into a global struggle involving thirty-two nations. Twenty-eight of those nations, collectively known as the Allies and the Associated Powers, fought the coalition known as the Central Powers, which consisted of Germany, Austria-Hungary, the Ottoman empire, and Bulgaria. The shell-shocked generation that survived the carnage called this clash of arms the Great War. Sadly, though, a subsequent generation of survivors renamed the conflict World War I, because it was only the first of two wars that engulfed the world in the first half of the twentieth century.

The Great War lasted from August 1914 to November 1918 and ushered in history's most violent century. In geographic extent the conflict surpassed all previous wars, compelling men, women, and children on five continents to participate directly or indirectly in a struggle that many did not understand. The Great War also had the distinction of being the first total war in human history, as governments mobilized every available human and material resource for the conduct of war. This scope contrasted with those of past wars, which, though frequently waged with ruthlessness and savage efficiency, were less destructive because they rarely engaged the passions of entire nations. Moreover, total war depended on industrial nations' capacity to fight with virtually unlimited means and to conduct combat on a vast scale. The industrial nature of the conflict meant that it was the bloodiest in the annals of organized violence. It took the lives of millions of combatants and civilians, physically maimed untold multitudes, and emotionally scarred an entire generation. The military casualties passed a threshold beyond previous experience: approximately fifteen million soldiers died, and an additional twenty million combatants suffered injuries.

The war of 1914–1918 did more than destroy individual lives. It seriously damaged national economies. The most visible signs of that damage were huge public debts and soaring rates of inflation. The international economy witnessed a shift in power away from western Europe. By the end of the conflict, the United States loomed as an economic world power that, despite its self-imposed isolation during the 1920s and 1930s, played a key role in global affairs in the coming decades. Politically, the war led to the redrawing of European boundaries and caused the demise of four dynasties and their empires—the Ottoman empire, the Russian empire, the Austro-Hungarian empire, and the German empire. The Great War also gave birth to nine new nations: Yugoslavia, Austria, Hungary, Czechoslovakia, Poland, Lithuania, Latvia, Estonia, and Finland. The war helped unleash the Bolshevik Revolution of 1917, which set the stage for an ideological conflict between capitalism and communism that endured to the end of the twentieth century. Finally, the Great War was responsible for an international realignment of power. It undermined the preeminence and prestige of European society, signaling an end to Europe's global primacy.

THE DRIFT TOWARD WAR

The catalyst for war was the assassination of Archduke Francis Ferdinand, heir to the throne of the Austro-Hungarian empire, by a Serbian nationalist. Yet without deeper underlying developments, the assassin's bullets would have had limited effect. The underlying causes for the war of 1914–1918 were many, including intense nationalism, frustrated national ambitions and ethnic resentments, the pursuit of exclusive economic interests, abrasive colonial rivalries, and a general struggle over the balance of power in Europe and in the world at large. Between 1871 and 1914, European governments adopted foreign policies that increased steadily the danger of war. So as to not find themselves alone in a hostile world, national leaders sought alignments with other powers. The establishment and maintenance in

Europe of two hostile alliances—the Allies and the Central Powers—helped spread the war from the Balkans.

Nationalist Aspirations

The French revolution and subsequent Napoleonic conquests spread nationalism throughout most of Europe (see chapter 28). Inherent in nationalism was the idea that peoples with the same ethnic origins, language, and political ideals had the right to form sovereign states; this concept is termed *self-determination.* The dynastic and reactionary powers that dominated European affairs during the early nineteenth century either ignored or opposed the principle of self-determination, thereby denying national autonomy to Germans, Italians, and Belgians, among others. Before long, however, a combination of powerful nationalistic movements, revolutions, and wars allowed Belgians to gain independence from the Netherlands in 1830, promoted the unification of Italy in 1861, and secured the unification of Germany in 1871. Yet at the end of the nineteenth century, the issue of nationalism remained unresolved in other areas of Europe, most notably in eastern Europe and the Balkans. There the nationalist aspirations of subject minorities threatened to tear apart the multinational empires of the Ottoman, Habsburg, and Russian dynasties and with them the regional balance of power. In those instances, opposition to foreign rule played a large role in the construction of national identities and demands for self-determination.

The Ottoman empire had controlled the Balkan peninsula since the fifteenth century, but after 1829 the Turkish empire shriveled. European powers, especially Austria and Russia, were partly responsible for the shrinking of Ottoman territories in Europe, but the slicing away of Turkish territory resulted mostly from nationalist revolts by the sultan's subjects. Greece was the first to gain independence (in 1830), but within a few decades Serbia, Romania, and Bulgaria followed suit.

As the Ottoman territories succumbed to the forces of nationalism, Austria-Hungary confronted the nationalist aspirations of Slavic peoples—Poles, Czechs, Slovaks, Serbs, Croats, and Slovenes. Most menacing and militant were the Serbs, who pressed for unification with the independent kingdom of Serbia. Russia added fuel to this volatile situation by promoting Pan-Slavism, a nineteenth-century movement that stressed the ethnic and cultural kinship of the various Slav peoples of eastern and east central Europe and that sought to unite those peoples politically. Pan-Slavism, as advocated by Russian leaders, supported Slav nationalism in lands occupied by Austria-Hungary. The purpose behind that policy was to promote secession by Slav areas, thereby weakening Austrian rule and perhaps preparing territories for future Russian annexation. Russia's support of Serbia, which supported Slav nationalism, and Germany's backing of Austria-Hungary, which tried desperately to counter the threat of national independence, helped set the stage for international conflict.

National Rivalries

Aggressive nationalism was also manifest in economic competition and colonial conflicts, fueling dangerous rivalries among the major European powers. The industrialized nations of Europe competed for foreign markets and engaged in tariff wars, but the most unsettling economic rivalry involved Great Britain and Germany. By the twentieth century, Germany's rapid industrialization threatened British economic predominance. In 1870 Britain, the first industrial nation, produced almost 32 percent of the world's total industrial output, compared with Germany's share of 13 percent, but by 1914 Britain's share had dropped to 14 percent, roughly equivalent to that of Germany. British reluctance to accept the relative decline of British industry vis-à-vis German industry strained relations between the two economic powers.

The Naval Race

An expensive naval race further exacerbated tensions between the two nations. Germans and Britons convinced themselves that naval power was imperative to secure trade routes and protect merchant shipping. Moreover, military leaders and politicians saw powerful navies as a means of controlling the seas in times of war, a control they viewed as decisive in determining the outcome of any war. Thus, when Germany's political and military leaders announced their program to build a fleet with many large battleships, they seemed to undermine British naval supremacy. The British government moved to meet the German threat through the construction of super battleships known as *dreadnoughts.* Rather than discouraging the Germans from their naval buildup, the British determination to retain naval superiority stimulated the Germans to build their own flotilla of dreadnoughts. This expensive naval race contributed further to international tensions and hostilities between nations.

Colonial Disputes

Economic rivalries fomented colonial competition. During the late nineteenth and early twentieth centuries, European nations searched aggressively for new colonies or dependencies to bolster economic performance. In their haste to conquer and colonize, the imperial powers stumbled over each other, repeatedly clashing in one corner of the globe or another: Britain and Russia faced off in Persia (modern-day Iran) and Afghanistan; Britain and France in Siam (modern-day Thailand) and the Nile valley; Britain and Germany in east and southwest Africa; Germany and France in Morocco and west Africa.

Virtually all the major powers engaged in the scramble for empire, but the competition between Britain and Germany and that between France and Germany were the most intense and dangerous. Germany, a unified nation only since 1871, embarked on the colonial race belatedly but aggressively, insisting that it too must have its "place in the sun." German imperial efforts were frustrated, however, by the simple fact that British and French imperialists had already carved up most of the world. German-French antagonisms and German-British rivalries went far toward shaping the international alliances that contributed to the spread of war after 1914.

Between 1905 and 1914, a series of international crises and two local wars raised tensions and almost precipitated a general European war. The first crisis resulted from a French-German confrontation over Morocco in 1905. Trying to isolate the French diplomatically, the German government announced its support of Moroccan independence, which French encroachment endangered. The French responded to German intervention by threatening war. An international conference in Algeciras, Spain, in the following year prevented a clash of arms, but similar crises threatened the peace in subsequent years. Contributing to the growing tensions in European affairs were the Balkan wars. Between 1912 and 1913, the states of the Balkan peninsula—including Bulgaria, Greece, Montenegro, Serbia, and Romania—fought two consecutive wars for possession of European territories held by the Ottoman empire. The Balkan wars strained European diplomatic relations and helped shape the tense circumstances that led to the outbreak of the Great War.

Public Opinion Public pressure also contributed to national rivalries. Characteristic of many European societies was a high degree of political participation and chauvinism on the part of citizens who identified strongly with the state. These citizens wanted their nation to outshine others, particularly in the international arena. New means of communication nourished the public's desire to see their country "come in first," whether in the competition for colonies or in the race to the South Pole. The content of cheap, mass-produced newspapers, pamphlets, and books fueled feelings

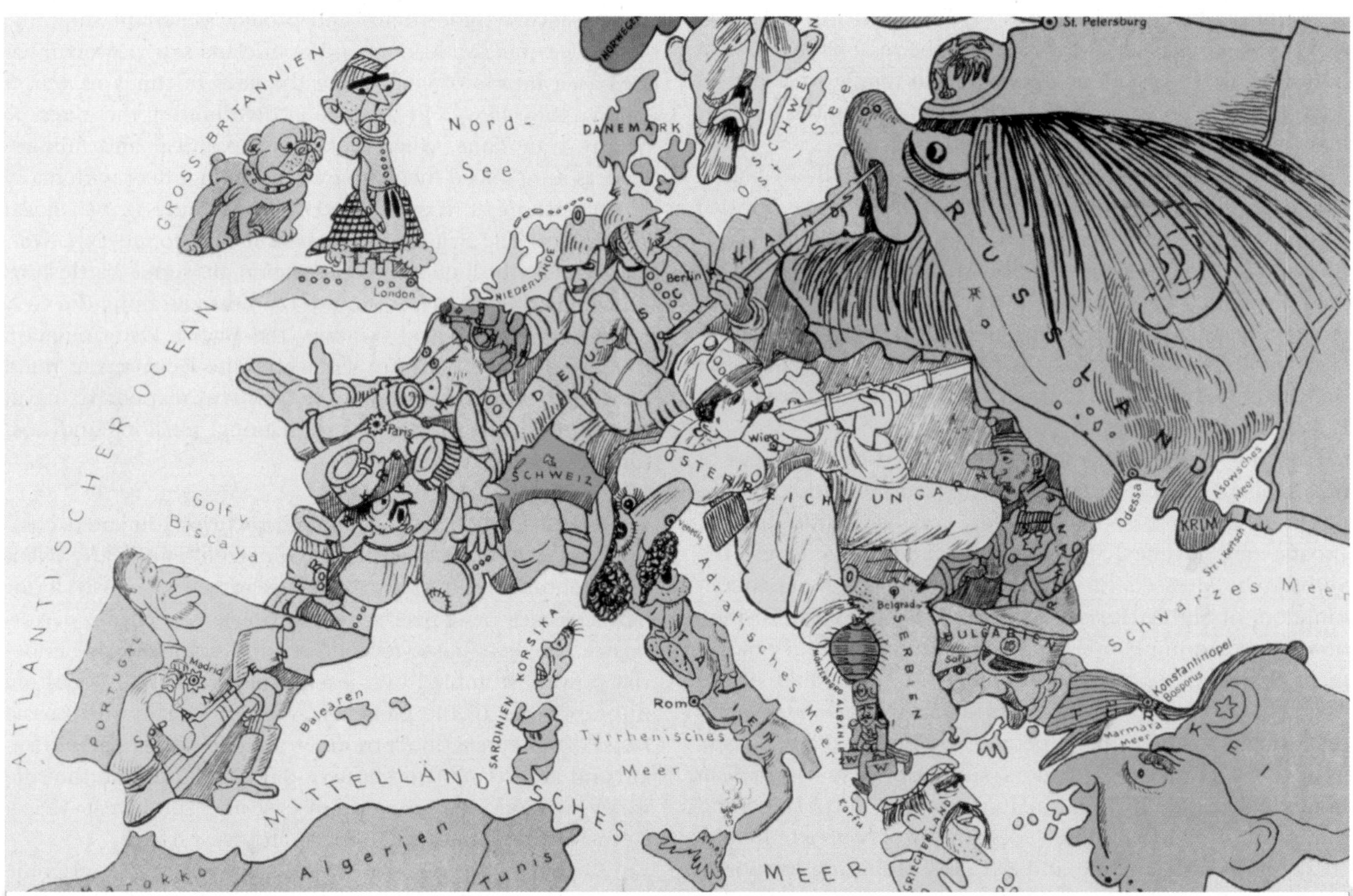

Dissident cartoonist Walter Trier's satirical map of Europe in 1914. Trier's work stands in stark contrast to the press of the time, which fueled the chauvinist desires of competing national publics. What message was Trier trying to convey with this map?

of national arrogance and aggressive patriotism. However, public pressure calling for national greatness placed policymakers and diplomats in an awkward situation. Compelled to achieve headline-grabbing foreign policy successes, these leaders ran the risk of paying for short-lived triumphs with long-lasting hostility from other countries.

Understandings and Alliances

In addition to a basic desire for security, escalating national rivalries and nationalist aspirations of subject minorities spawned a system of entangling alliances. While national interests guided the search for allies, each nation viewed its fulfillment of treaty obligations as crucial to self-preservation. Moreover, the complexity of those obligations could not hide the common characteristic underlying all the alliances: they outlined the circumstances under which countries would go to war to support one another. Intended to preserve the peace, rival alliance systems created a framework whereby even a small international crisis could set off a chain reaction leading to global war. Thus by 1914 Europe's major powers had transformed themselves into two hostile camps—the Triple Alliance and the Triple Entente.

The Central Powers The Triple Alliance, also known as the Central Powers, grew out of the close relationship that developed between the leaders of Germany and Austria-Hungary during the last three decades of the nineteenth century. In 1879 the governments of the two empires formed the Dual Alliance, a defensive pact that ensured reciprocal protection from a Russian attack and neutrality in case of an attack from any other power. Fear of a hostile France motivated Germans to enter into this pact, whereas Austrians viewed it as giving them a free hand in pursuing their Balkan politics without fear of Russian intervention. Italy, fearful of France, joined the Dual Alliance in 1882, thereby transforming it into the Triple Alliance. From the outset, however, the Italian policy of aggrandizement at the expense of the Ottoman empire and Italy's rivalry with Austria-Hungary in the Balkans threatened to wreck the alliance. Thus the Italian declaration of war on the Ottoman empire in 1911 and the subsequent drive to annex the Tripoli region of northern Africa strained the Triple Alliance because the German government tried to cultivate friendly relations with the Turks.

The Allies The Central Powers sought to protect the political status quo in Europe, but the leaders of other nations viewed this new constellation of power with suspicion. This response was especially true of French leaders, who neither forgot nor forgave France's humiliating defeat during the Franco-Prussian War of 1870–1871. The French government was determined to curb the growing might of Germany.

The tsarist regime of Russia was equally disturbed by the new alignment of powers, especially by Germany's support of Austria, and British leaders were traditionally suspicious of any nation that seemed to threaten the balance of power on the Continent. The result was that the most unlikely bedfellows formed the Triple Entente, a combination of nations commonly referred to as the Allies. The Triple Entente originated in a series of agreements between Britain and France (1904) and between Britain and Russia (1907) that aimed to resolve colonial disputes. Between 1907 and 1914 cooperation between the leaders of Britain, France, and Russia led to the signing of a military pact in the summer of 1914. Reciprocal treaty obligations, which the governments felt compelled to honor lest they face the risk of being alone in a hostile world, made it difficult for diplomats to contain what otherwise might have been relatively small international crises.

War Plans The preservation of peace was also difficult because the military staffs of each nation had devised inflexible military plans and timetables to be carried out in the event of war. For example, French military strategy revolved around Plan XVII, which amounted to a veritable celebration of offensive maneuvers. The French master plan could be summed up in one word, *attack,* to be undertaken always and everywhere. This strategy viewed the enemy's intentions as inconsequential and gave no thought to the huge number of casualties that would invariably result. German war plans in particular played a crucial role in the events leading to the Great War. Germany's fear of encirclement encouraged its military planners to devise a strategy that would avoid a war on two fronts. It was based on a strategy developed in 1905 by General Count Alfred von Schlieffen (1833–1913). The Schlieffen plan called for a swift knockout of France, followed by defensive action against Russia. German planners predicated their strategy on the knowledge that the Russians could not mobilize their soldiers and military supplies as quickly as the French, thus giving German forces a few precious weeks during which they could concentrate their full power on France. However brilliantly conceived, the Schlieffen plan raised serious logistical problems, not the least of which was moving 180,000 soldiers and their supplies into France and Belgium on five hundred trains, with fifty wagons each. More important, Germany's military strategy was a serious obstacle to those seeking to preserve the peace. In the event of Russian mobilization, Germany's leaders would feel compelled to stick to their war plans, thereby setting in motion a military conflict of major proportions.

GLOBAL WAR

War came to Europe during harvest time, and most ordinary people heard the news as they worked in the fields. They reacted not with enthusiasm but with shock and fear. Other people, especially intellectuals and young city dwellers, met the news with euphoria. Many of them had long expected

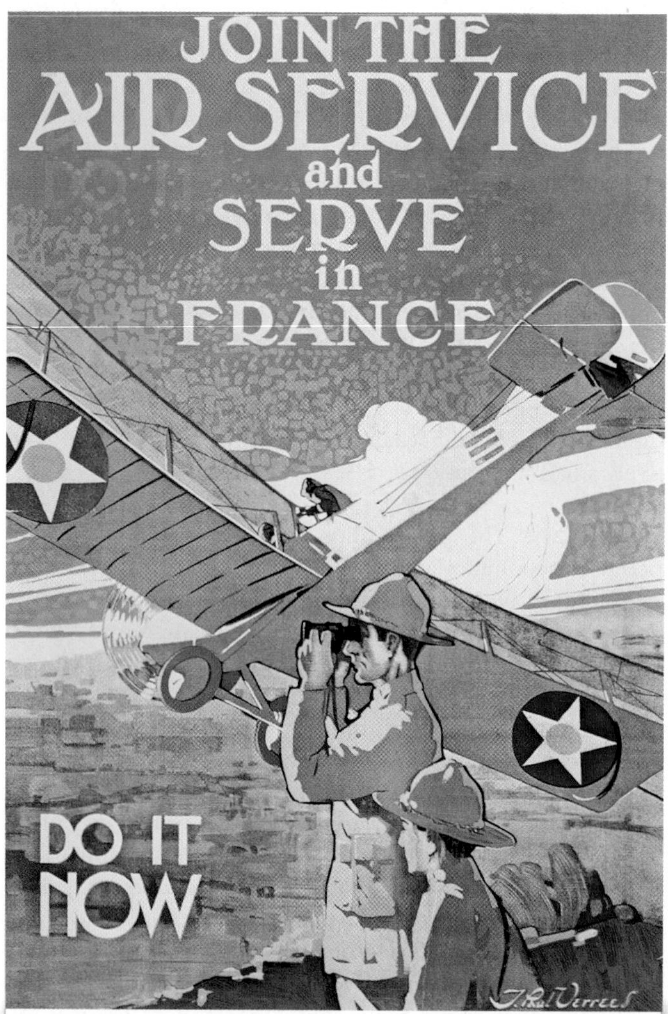

This British recruiting poster reflects the enthusiasm that many British people felt at the beginning of the Great War, when they believed it would be a short and glorious adventure—an expectation that was very quickly dashed.

war and saw it as a liberating release of pressure that would resolve the various political, social, and economic crises that had been building for years. The philosopher Bertrand Russell observed that the average Englishman positively wanted war, and the French writer Alain-Fournier noted that "this war is fine and just and great." In the capitals of Europe, people danced in the streets when their governments announced formal declarations of war. When the first contingents of soldiers left for the front, jubilant crowds threw flowers at the feet of departing men, who expected to return victorious after a short time.

Reality crushed any expectations of a short and triumphant war. On most fronts the conflict quickly bogged down and became a war of attrition in which the firepower of modern weapons slaughtered soldiers by the millions. For the first time in history, belligerent nations engaged in total war. Even in democratic societies, governments assumed dictatorial control to marshal the human and material resources required for continuous war. One result was increased participation of women in the labor force. Total war had repercussions that went beyond the borders of Europe. Imperial ties drew millions of Asians, Africans, and residents of the British dominions into the war to serve as soldiers and laborers. Struggles over far-flung colonies further underlined the global dimension of this war. Last, the war gained a global flavor through the entry of Japan, the United States, and the Ottoman empire, nations whose leaders professed little direct interest in European affairs.

The Guns of August

The shots fired from Gavrilo Princip's revolver on that fateful day of 28 June 1914 were heard around the world, for they triggered the greatest war in human history up to that point. By July, Austrian investigators had linked the assassins to a terrorist group known as the Black Hand. Centered in neighboring Serbia, this organization was dedicated to the unification of all south Slavs, or Yugoslavs, to form a greater Serbia. As far as Serbian nationalists were concerned, the principal obstacle to Slavic unity was the Austro-Hungarian empire, which explains why the heir to the Habsburg throne was a symbolic victim. This viewpoint also explains Austria's unyielding and violent response to the murder.

Declarations of War The assassination set in motion a flurry of diplomatic activity that quickly escalated into war. Austrian leaders in Vienna were determined to teach the unruly Serbs a lesson, and on 23 July the Austrians issued a nearly unacceptable ultimatum to the government of Serbia. The Serbian government accepted all the terms of the ultimatum except one, which infringed on its sovereignty. The ultimatum demanded that Austrian officials take part in any Serbian investigation of persons found on Serbian territory connected to the assassination of Francis Ferdinand. On 28 July, after declaring the Serbian reply to be unsatisfactory, Austria-Hungary declared war on Serbia. The war had begun, and politicians and generals discovered that it could not be easily arrested. The subsequent sequence of events was largely determined by two factors: complex mobilization plans and the grinding logic of the alliance system. Mobilization called for the activation of military forces for imminent battle and the redirection of economic and social activities to support military efforts. Thus military planners were convinced that the timing of mobilization orders and adherence to precise timetables were crucial to the successful conduct of war.

On 29 July the Russian government mobilized its troops to defend its Serbian ally and itself from Austria. The tsar of Russia then ordered mobilization against Germany. Nicholas II (1868–1918) took that decisive step reluctantly and only after his military experts had convinced him that a partial mobilization against the Austrians would upset complex

This photograph from August 1914 documents the famous "guns of August" that sparked the Great War. Dogs carted this machine gun to the front in Belgium.

military plans and timetables. Delayed mobilization might invite defeat, they advised, should the Germans enter the war. That action precipitated a German ultimatum to Russia on 31 July, demanding that the Russian army cease its mobilization immediately. Another ultimatum addressed to France demanded to know what France's intentions were in case Germany and Russia went to war. The Russians replied with a blunt "impossible," and the French never answered. Thus on 1 August the German government declared war on Russia, and France started to mobilize.

After waiting two more days, the Germans declared war on France, on 3 August. On the same day, German troops invaded Belgium in accordance with the Schlieffen plan. Key to this plan was an attack on the weak left flank of the French army by a massive German force through Belgium. The Belgian government, which had refused to permit the passage of German troops, called on the signatories of the treaty of 1839, which guaranteed Belgium's neutrality. On 4 August the British government, one of the signatories, sent an ultimatum to Germany demanding that Belgian neutrality be respected. When Germany's wartime leaders refused, the British immediately declared war. A local conflict had become a general European war.

Mutual Butchery

Everyone expected the war to be brief. In the first weeks of August 1914, twenty million young men donned uniforms, took up rifles, and left for the front. Many of them looked forward to heroic charges, rapid promotions, and a quick homecoming. Some dreamed of glory and honor, and they believed that God was on their side. The inscription on the belt buckle of German recruits read *Gott mit uns* ("God is with us"), a sentiment echoed by Russian troops, who fought for "God and Tsar," and British soldiers, who went into battle "For God, King, and Country." Several years later Americans felt called on to "make the world safe for democracy." Similar attitudes prevailed among the political and military leaders of the belligerent nations. The war strategies devised by the finest military thinkers of the time paid little attention to matters of defense. Instead, they were preoccupied with visions of sweeping assaults, envelopments, and, above all, swift triumphs.

The Western Front The German thrust toward Paris in August 1914 came to a grinding halt along the river Marne, and both sides then undertook flanking maneuvers, a "race to the sea" that took them to the Atlantic coast. For the next three years, the battle lines remained virtually stationary, as both sides dug in and slugged it out in a war of attrition that lasted until the late autumn of 1918. Each belligerent tried to wear down the enemy by inflicting continuous damage and casualties, only to have their own forces suffer heavy losses in return. Trenches on the western front ran from the English Channel to Switzerland. Farther south, Italy left the Triple Alliance in favor of neutrality but entered the war on the side of the Allies in 1915. By the terms of the Treaty

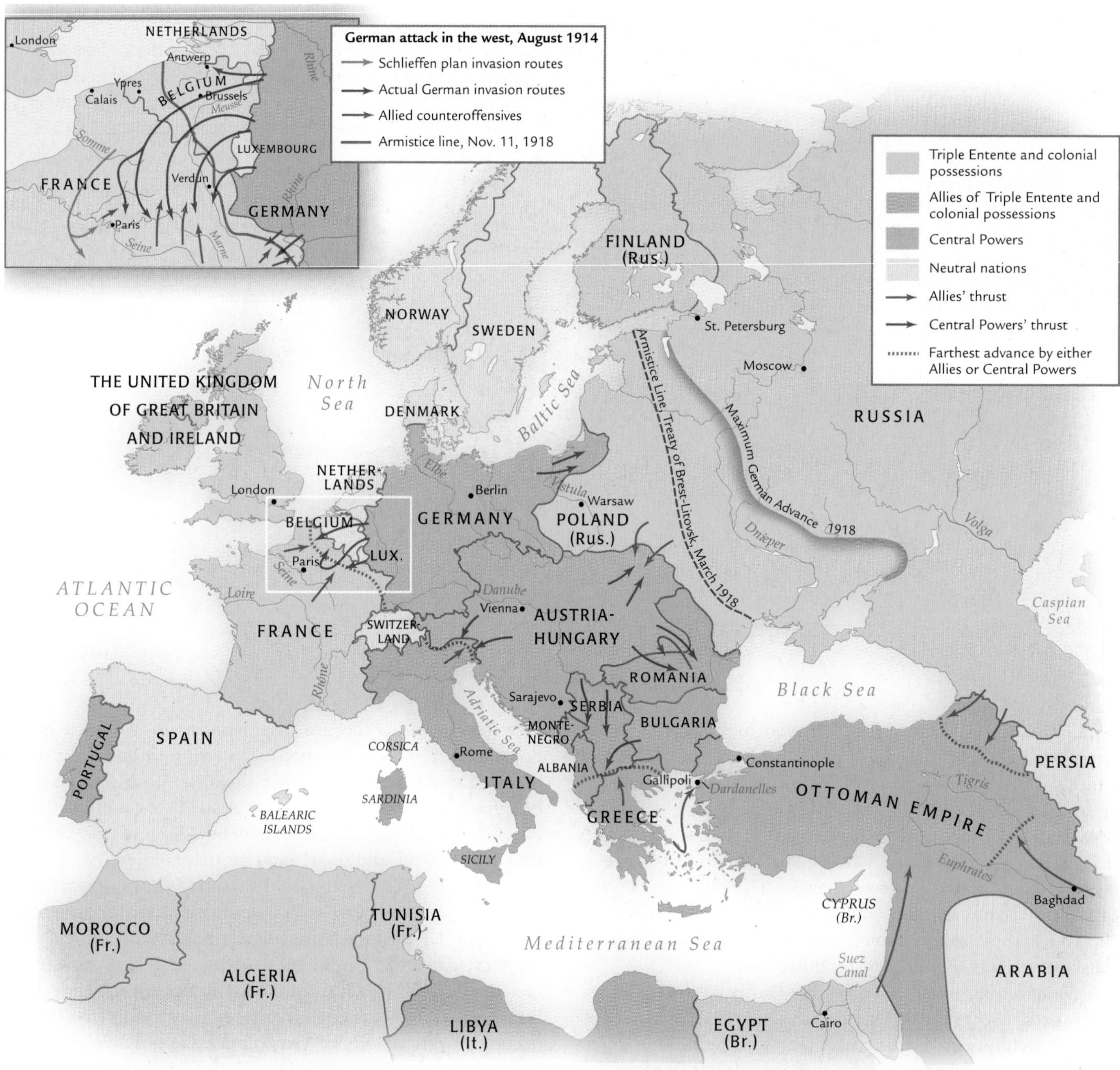

MAP 33.1

The Great War in Europe and southwest Asia, 1914–1918.
Note the locations of both the eastern and the western fronts in Europe during the war.

Why didn't the same kind of trench warfare immobilize opposing armies on the eastern front the way it did on the western front?

of London, the Allies promised, once victory was secured, to cede to Italy Austro-Hungarian-controlled territories, specifically south Tyrol and most of the Dalmatian coast. Allied hopes that the Italians would pierce Austrian defenses quickly faded. After the disastrous defeat at Caporetto in 1917, Italian forces maintained a defensive line only with the help of the French and the British.

Stalemate and New Weapons The stalemate on the western and southern fronts reflected technological developments that favored defensive tactics. Barbed wire, which had confined cattle on America's Great Plains, proved highly effective in frustrating the advance of soldiers across "no-man's-land," the deadly territory between opposing trenches. The rapid and continuous fire of machine guns further contributed to the battlefield stalemate, turning in-

thinking about TRADITIONS

Heroic War?
Before the Great War, Europeans in battle usually adhered to certain military traditions and had expectations that conflicts could be settled quickly. How did the Great War alter time-honored military codes of conduct and dash hopes for a quick end to the war? What role did new technologies play in the process of changing the understanding of war?

fantry charges across no-man's-land into suicide missions. First deployed by Confederate troops during the U.S. Civil War, the machine gun had been a key weapon for overcoming resistance to colonial expansion before Europeans trained the weapon on one another during the Great War. The machine gun represented one of the most important advances in military technology and compelled military leaders on all sides to rethink their battlefield tactics.

The immobility of trench warfare and the desire to reintroduce movement to warfare prompted the development of weapons that supplied the power necessary to break the deadly stalemate. Industrial societies subsequently gave birth to many new and potent weapons. The most unconventional weapon was poisonous gas, first used by German troops in January 1915. Especially hated and much feared by troops in the trenches was mustard gas, a liquid agent that, when exposed to air, turned into a noxious yellow gas, hence its name. The effects of mustard gas did not appear for some twelve hours following exposure, but then it rotted the body from both within and without. After blistering the skin and damaging the eyes, the gas attacked the bronchial tubes, stripping off the mucous membrane. Death could occur in four to five weeks. In the meantime, victims endured excruciating pain and had to be strapped to their beds. Like the machine gun, gas proved a potent weapon, and both sides suffered heavy casualties totaling about 1.2 million soldiers. Such destructiveness convinced military leaders of the effectiveness of chemical agents, yet gas attacks failed to deliver the promised strategic breakthroughs, and the anticipated return to more fluid battle lines never materialized.

Other novel weapons developed during the war included tanks and airplanes. The British first introduced tanks in late 1915, and the Allies deployed them to break down defensive trenches and to restore fighting. Despite its proven short-term effectiveness during the final offenses of the war, the tank did not produce the longed-for strategic advantage. As a rule, German counterattacks quickly regained the ground won by tanks. Also of recent origin was the airplane, still in its infancy in 1914. Constantly refined and improved as the war progressed, the airplane by the end of the war showed dramatic improvements in speed, range, and altitude. However, because airplanes could not carry enough weapons to do serious damage to troops or installations on the ground, their real asset during the Great War was aerial reconnaissance. It was, in effect, an attempt to prevent the enemy from conducting aerial reconnaissance that led to the much publicized and glamorized aerial combat of the Great War featuring "ace fighters" and "dogfights." The plane and the tank figured more prominently as important strategic weapons during the Second World War. Other weapons systems, such as the submarine, had made earlier appearances in warfare but did not play a significant role until the Great War. It was not until the Great War, when the German navy deployed its diesel-powered submarine fleet against Allied commercial shipping, that the submarine proved its military effectiveness. Although the German navy relied more heavily on submarines, the allied navies of Great Britain and the United States deployed their own fleets of diesel-powered submarines.

Air-raid warden in helmet and gas mask, holding a wooden gas attack rattle in his gloved hand. The deployment of poison gas represented a technological development of horrific dimension that was designed to break the stalemate of trench warfare by killing, on a massive scale, soldiers otherwise difficult to reach.

No-Man's-Land The most courageous infantry charges, even when preceded by pulverizing artillery barrages and clouds of poisonous gas, were no match for determined defenders. Shielded by the dirt of their trenches and by barbed wire and gas masks, they unleashed a torrent of lethal metal with their machine guns and repeating rifles. In every sector of the front, those who fought rarely found the glory they sought. Instead, they encountered death. No-man's-land was strewn with shell craters, cadavers, and body parts. The grim realities of trench warfare—the wet, cold, waist-deep mud, gluttonous lice, and corpse-fed rats—contrasted sharply with the ringing phrases of politicians and generals justifying the unrelenting slaughter. War had ceased to be a noble and sporting affair, if it ever was.

A dogfight between German and British planes during the Great War. Dogfights as a new type of combat resulted from the attempt of each contestant to prevent the enemy from conducting aerial reconnaissance.

The Eastern Front In eastern Europe and the Balkans, the battle lines were more fluid. After a staunch defense, a combination of Austrian and German forces overran Serbia, Albania, and Romania. Farther north, Russia took the offensive early by invading Prussia in 1914. The Central Powers recovered quickly, however, and by the summer of 1915 combined German-Austrian forces drove the Russian armies out of East Prussia and then out of Poland and established a defensive line extending from the Baltic to the Ukraine. Russian counterattacks in 1916 and 1917 collapsed in a sea of casualties. Those Russian defeats undermined the popularity of the tsar and his government and played a significant role in fostering revolutionary ferment within Russian society.

Bloodletting Many battles took place, but some were so horrific, so devastating, and so futile that their names are synonymous with human slaughter. The casualty figures attested to this bloodletting. In 1916 the Germans tried to break the deadlock with a huge assault on the fortress of Verdun. The French rallying cry was "They shall not pass," and they did not—but at a tremendous cost: while the victorious French counted 315,000 dead, the defeated Germans suffered a loss of 280,000. Survivors recovered fewer than 160,000 identifiable bodies. The rest were unrecognizable or had been blown to bits by high explosives and sucked into the mud. To relieve the pressure on Verdun, British forces counterattacked at the Somme, and by November they had gained a few thousand yards at the cost of 420,000 casualties. The Germans suffered similar losses, although in the end neither side gained any strategic advantage.

New Rules of Engagement Dying and suffering were not limited solely to combatants: the Great War established rules of engagement that made civilians targets of warfare. Because they were crucial to the war effort, millions of people out of uniform became targets of enemy military operations. On 30 August 1914, Parisians looked up at the sky and saw a new weapon of war, a huge, silent German zeppelin (a hydrogen-filled dirigible) whose underbelly rained bombs, eventually killing one person. That event heralded a new kind of warfare—air war against civilians. A less novel but more effective means of targeting civilian populations was the naval blockade. Military leaders on both sides used blockades to deny food to whole populations, hoping that starving masses would force their governments to capitulate. The British blockade of Germany during the war contributed to the deaths of an estimated half-million Germans.

Total War: The Home Front

Helmuth Karl von Moltke (1800–1891), former chief of the Prussian General Staff, showed an uncanny insight long before 1914 when he predicted that future wars would not end with a single battle, because the defeat of a nation would not be acknowledged until the whole strength of its people was broken. He was right. As the Great War ground on, it became a conflict of attrition in which the organization of material and human resources was of paramount importance. War became total, fought between entire societies, not just between armies; and total victory was the only acceptable outcome that might justify the terrible sacrifices made by all sides. The nature of total war created a military front and a home front. The term *home front* expressed the important reality that the outcome of the war hinged on how effectively each nation mobilized its economy and activated its noncombatant citizens to support the war effort.

The Home Front As the war continued beyond Christmas 1914 and as war weariness and a decline in economic capability set in, the response of all belligerents was to limit individual freedoms and give control of society increasingly over to military leaders. Because patriotism and courage alone could not guarantee victory, the governments of belligerent nations assumed control of the home front. Initially, ministers and generals shrank from compulsive measures, even conscription of recruits, but they quickly changed their minds. Each belligerent government eventually militarized civilian war production by subordinating private enterprises to governmental control and imposing severe discipline on the labor process.

Economic measures were foremost in the minds of government leaders because the war created unprecedented demands for raw materials and manufactured goods. Those material requirements compelled governments to abandon long-cherished ideals of a laissez-faire capitalist market economy and to institute tight controls over economic life. Planning boards reorganized entire industries, set production quotas and priorities, and determined what would be produced and consumed. Government authorities also established wage and price controls, extended work hours, and in some instances restricted the movement of workers. Because bloody battlefields caused an insatiable appetite for soldiers, nations responded by extending military service. In Germany, for example, men between the ages of sixteen and sixty were eligible to serve at the front. By constantly tapping into the available male population, the war created an increasing demand for workers at home. Unemployment—a persistent feature of all prewar economies—vanished virtually overnight.

Mutilated body on the western front. So tremendous was the number of the dead—over a half-million French and German soldiers perished in the battle of Verdun alone—that many were never recovered or identified.

Women at War As men marched off to war, women marched off to work. Conscription took men out of the labor force, and wartime leaders exhorted women to fill the gaps in the workforce. A combination of patriotism and high wages drew women into formerly "male" jobs. The lives of women changed as they bobbed their hair and left home or domestic service for the workplace. Some women took over the management of farms and businesses left by their husbands, who went off to fight. Others found jobs as postal workers and police officers. Behind the battle lines, women were most visible as nurses, physicians, and communications clerks.

Perhaps the most crucial work performed by women during the war was the making of shells. Several million women, and sometimes children, put in long, hard hours in munitions factories. This work exposed them to severe dangers. The first came from explosions, because keeping sparks away from highly volatile materials was impossible. Many women died in these incidents, although government censorship during the war made it difficult to know how many women perished in this fashion. The other, more insidious danger came from working with TNT explosives. Although the authorities claimed that this work was not dangerous, exposure to TNT caused severe poisoning, depending on the length of exposure. Before serious illnesses manifested themselves, TNT poisoning marked its victims by turning their skin yellow and their hair orange. The accepted though ineffectual remedy for TNT poisoning was rest, good food, and plenty of fresh milk.

Middle- and upper-class women often reported that the war was a liberating experience, freeing them from older attitudes that had limited their work and their personal lives. At the least, the employment of upper-class women spawned a degree of deliverance from parental control and gave women a sense of mission. They knew that they were important to the war effort. The impact of the Great War on the lives of working-class women, in contrast, was relatively minor. Working-class women in cities had long been accustomed to earning wages, and for them war work proved less than liberating. Most of the belligerent governments promised equal pay for equal work, but in most instances that promise remained unfulfilled. Although women's industrial wages rose during the war, measurable gaps always remained between the incomes of men and women. In the end, substantial female employment was a transitory phenomenon. With few exceptions, the Great War only briefly suspended traditional patterns of work outside the home. Nevertheless, the extension of voting rights to women shortly after the war, in Britain (1918, for women thirty years and older), Germany (1919), and Austria (1919), was in part due to the role women assumed during the Great War. Later in the century, war and revolution continued to serve as at least temporary liberating forces for women, especially in Russia (1917) and China (1949), where new communist governments discouraged the patriarchal family system and supported sexual equality, including birth control.

Propaganda To maintain the spirit of the home front and to counter threats to national unity, governments resorted to the restriction of civil liberties, censorship of bad news, and vilification of the enemy through propaganda campaigns. While some government officials busily censored war news, people who had the temerity to criticize their nation's war

sources from the past

Dulce et Decorum Est

The Great War produced a wealth of poetry. The poetic response to war covered a range of moods, from early romanticism and patriotism to cynicism, resignation, and the angry depiction of horror. Perhaps the greatest of all war poets was Wilfred Owen (1893–1918), whose poems are among the most poignant of the war. Owen, who enlisted for service on the western front in 1915, was injured in March 1917 and sent home. Declared fit for duty in August 1918, he returned to the front. German machine-gun fire killed him on 7 November, four days before the armistice, when he tried to cross the Sambre Canal.

Bent double, like old beggars under sacks,
Knock-kneed, coughing like hags, we cursed through sludge,
Till on the haunting flares we turned our backs
And towards our distant rest began to trudge.
Men marched asleep. Many had lost their boots
But limped on, blood-shod. All went lame; all blind;
Drunk with fatigue; deaf even to the hoots
Of gas-shells dropping softly behind.

Gas! GAS! Quick, boys!—An ecstasy of fumbling,
Fitting the clumsy helmets just in time;
But someone still was yelling out and stumbling
And floundering like a man in fire or lime.—
Dim, through the misty panes and thick green light
As under a green sea, I saw him drowning.

In all my dreams, before my helpless sight,
He plunges at me, guttering, choking, drowning.
If in some smothering dreams you too could pace
Behind the wagon that we flung him in,
And watch the white eyes writhing in his face,
His hanging face, like a devil's sick of sin;
If you could hear, at every jolt, the blood
Come gargling from the froth-corrupted lungs,
Obscene as cancer, bitter as the cud
Of vile, incurable sores on innocent tongues,—
My friend, you would not tell with such high zest
To children ardent for some desperate glory,
The old Lie: Dulce et decorum est
Pro patria mori.*

*Author's note: "Sweet and fitting is it to die for one's country" comes from a line by the Roman poet Horace (65–8 B.C.E.)

For Further Reflection

- How does Owen poetically describe the effects of a gas attack? Is his literary depiction more or less effective than detached descriptions of war's effects?

Source: Edmund Blunden, ed. *The Poems of Wilfred Owen.* London: Chattus & Windus, 1933, p. 66.

effort were prosecuted as traitors. In France, for example, former prime minister Joseph Caillaux spent two years in prison awaiting trial because he had publicly suggested that the best interest of France would be to reach a compromise peace with Germany.

The propaganda offices of the belligerent nations tried to convince the public that military defeat would mean the destruction of everything worth living for, and to that end they did their utmost to discredit and dehumanize the enemy. Posters, pamphlets, and "scientific" studies depicted the enemy as subhuman savages who engaged in vile atrocities. While German propaganda depicted Russians as semi-Asiatic barbarians, French authorities chronicled the atrocities committed by the German "Hun" in Belgium. In 1917 the *Times* of London published a story claiming that Germans converted human corpses into fertilizer and food. With much less fanfare a later news story admitted that this information resulted from a sloppy translation: the German word for *horse* had been mistakenly translated as "human." German propaganda stooped equally low. One widely distributed poster invoked images of bestial black Allied soldiers raping German women, including pregnant women, to suggest the horrors that would follow if the nation's war effort failed. Most atrocity stories originated in the fertile imagination of propaganda officers, and their falsehood eventually engendered public skepticism and cynicism. Ironically, public disbelief of wartime propaganda led to an inability to believe in the abominations perpetrated during subsequent wars.

Conflict in East Asia and the Pacific

To many Asian and African peoples, the Great War was a murderous European civil war that quickly turned into a global conflict. There were three reasons for the war's expansion. First, European governments carried their animosities into their colonies, embroiling them—especially

Women at work in an English munitions factory. The Great War drew huge numbers of men out of the workforce at a time of great industrial need. Women replaced them, for the first time assuming traditionally "male" jobs.

"The Heroes of Belgium 1914." French propaganda poster expresses outrage at the German invasion of Belgium.

African societies—in their war. Second, because Europe's human reserves were not enough to satisfy the appetite of war, the British and the French augmented their ranks by recruiting men from their colonies. Millions of Africans and Asians were drawn into the war. Behind their trenches the French employed laborers from Algeria, China, and French Indochina, and the British did not hesitate to draft Indian and African troops for combat. The British in particular relied on troops furnished by the dominion lands, including Australia, New Zealand, Canada, Newfoundland, and South Africa. Third, the Great War assumed global significance because the desires and objectives of some principal actors that entered the conflict—Japan, the United States, and the Ottoman empire—had little to do with the murder in Sarajevo or the other issues that drove the Europeans to battle.

Japan's Entry into the War On 15 August 1914 the Japanese government, claiming that it desired "to secure firm and enduring peace in Eastern Asia," sent an ultimatum to Germany demanding the handover of the German-leased territory of Jiaozhou (northeastern China) to Japanese authorities without compensation. The same note also demanded that the German navy unconditionally withdraw its warships from Japanese and Chinese waters. When the Germans refused to comply, the Japanese entered the war on the side of the Allies on 23 August 1914. Japanese forces took the fortress of Qingdao, a German-held port in China's Shandong Province, in November 1914, and between August and November of that year took possession of the German-held Marshall Islands, the Mariana Islands, Palau, and the Carolines. Forces from New Zealand and Australia joined in the Japanese quest for German-held islands in the Pacific, capturing German-held portions of Samoa in August 1914 and German-occupied possessions in the Bismarck Archipelago and New Guinea.

The Twenty-one Demands After seizing German bases on the Shandong peninsula and on Pacific islands, Japan shrewdly exploited Allied support and European preoccupation to advance its own imperial interests in China.

On 18 January 1915 the Japanese presented the Chinese government with twenty-one secret demands. The terms of that ultimatum, if accepted, would have reduced China to a protectorate of Japan. The most important demands were that the Chinese confirm the Japanese seizure of Shandong from Germany, grant Japanese industrial monopolies in central China, place Japanese overseers in key government positions, give Japan joint control of Chinese police forces, restrict their arms purchases to Japanese manufacturers, and make those purchases only with the approval of the Tokyo government. China submitted to most of the demands but rejected others. Chinese diplomats leaked the note to the British authorities, who spoke up for China, thus preventing total capitulation. The Twenty-one Demands reflected Japan's determination to dominate east Asia and served as the basis for future Japanese pressure on China.

An Indian gun crew in the Somme area, 1916. During the Great War, colonial powers relied on millions of Asian and African men to fight or labor for their respective sides.

Battles in Africa and Southwest Asia

The geographic extent of the conflict also broadened beyond Europe when the Allies targeted German colonies in Africa. When the war of 1914–1918 erupted in Europe, all of sub-Saharan Africa (except Ethiopia and Liberia) consisted of European colonies, with the Germans controlling four: Togoland, the Cameroons, German Southwest Africa, and German East Africa. Unlike the capture of German colonies in the Pacific, which Allied forces accomplished during the first three months of the war with relative ease, the conquest of German colonies in Africa was difficult. Togoland fell to an Anglo-French force after three weeks of fighting, but it took extended campaigns ranging over vast distances to subdue the remaining German footholds in Africa. The Allied force included British, French, and Belgian troops and large contingents of Indian, Arab, and African soldiers. Fighting took place on land and sea; on lakes and rivers; in deserts, jungles, and swamps; and in the air. Germs were frequently more deadly than Germans; tens of thousands of Allied soldiers and workers succumbed to deadly tropical diseases. The German flag did not disappear from Africa until after the armistice took effect on 11 November 1918.

Gallipoli The most extensive military operations outside Europe took place in the southwest Asian territories of the Ottoman empire, which was aligned with the Central Powers at the end of 1914. Seeking a way to break the stalemate on the western front, Winston Churchill (1874–1965), first lord of the Admiralty (British navy), suggested that an Allied strike against the Ottomans—a weak ally of the Central Powers—would hurt the Germans. Early in 1915 the British navy conducted an expedition to seize the approach to the Dardanelles Strait in an attempt to open a warm-water supply line to Russia through the Ottoman-controlled strait. After bombing the forts that defended the strait, Allied ships took damage from floating mines and withdrew without accomplishing their mission. After withdrawing the battleships, the British high command decided to land a combined force of English, Canadian, Australian, and New Zealand soldiers on the beaches of the Gallipoli peninsula. The campaign was a disaster. Turkish defenders, ensconced in the cliffs above, quickly pinned down the Allied troops on the beaches. Trapped between the sea and the hills, Allied soldiers dug in and engaged in their own version of trench warfare. The resulting stalemate produced a total of 250,000 casualties on each side. Despite the losses, Allied leaders took nine months to admit that their campaign had failed.

Gallipoli was a debacle with long-term consequences. Although the British directed the ill-fated campaign, it was mostly Canadians, Australians, and New Zealanders who suffered terrible casualties. That recognition led to a weakening of imperial ties and paved the way for emerging national identities. In Australia the date of the fateful landing, 25 April 1915, became enshrined as Anzac Day (an acronym for Australian and New Zealand Army Corps) and remains the country's most significant day of public homage. On the other side, the battle for the strait helped launch the political career of the commander of the Turk-

thinking about ENCOUNTERS

From Civil War to Total War

Many observers considered the Great War a civil war among Europeans. How did the war draw in peoples outside Europe, and what form did contacts between Europeans, Asians, and Africans take?

ish division that defended Gallipoli. Mustafa Kemal (1881–1938) went on to play a crucial role in the formation of the modern Turkish state.

Armenian Massacres The war provided the pretext for a campaign of extermination against the Ottoman empire's two million Armenians, the last major non-Muslim ethnic group under Ottoman rule seeking autonomy and eventual independence. Friction between Christian Armenians and Ottoman authorities went back to the nineteenth century, when distinct nationalist feelings stirred many of the peoples who lived under Ottoman rule.

Initially, Armenians had relied on government reforms to prevent discrimination against non-Muslim subjects by corrupt officials and extortionist tax collectors. When abuses persisted, Armenians resorted to confrontation. Armenian demonstrations against Ottoman authorities in 1890 and 1895 led to reprisals by a government that had become increasingly convinced that the Armenians were seeking independence, as other Christian minorities of the Balkans had done in previous decades.

After 1913 the Ottoman state adopted a new policy of Turkish nationalism intended to shore up the crumbling imperial edifice. The new nationalism stressed Turkish culture and traditions, which only aggravated tensions between Turkish rulers and non-Turkish subjects of the empire. In particular, the state viewed Christian minorities as an obstacle to Turkism. During the Great War, the Ottoman government branded Armenians as a traitorous internal enemy, who threatened the security of the state, and then unleashed a murderous campaign against them. Forced mass evacuations, accompanied by starvation, dehydration, and exposure, led to the death of tens of thousands of Armenians. An equally deadly assault on the Armenians came by way of government-organized massacres that claimed victims through mass drowning, incineration, or assaults with blunt instruments.

Those wartime atrocities that took place principally between 1915 and 1917 have become known as Armenian genocide. Best estimates suggest that close to a million Armenians perished. Although it is generally agreed that the Armenian genocide did occur, the Turkish government in particular rejects the label of genocide and claims that Armenian deaths resulted not from a state-sponsored plan of mass extermination but from communal warfare perpetrated by Christians and Muslims, disease, and famine.

The Ottoman Empire After successfully fending off Allied forces on the beaches of Gallipoli in 1915 and in Mesopotamia in 1916, Ottoman armies retreated slowly on all fronts. After yielding to the Russians in the Caucasus, Turkish troops were unable to defend the empire against invading British armies that drew heavily on recruits from Egypt, India, Australia, and New Zealand. As the armies smashed the Ottoman state—one entering Mesopotamia and the other advancing from the Suez Canal toward Palestine—they received significant support from an Arab revolt against the Turks. In 1916, abetted by the British, the nomadic bedouin of Arabia under the leadership of Ibn Ali Hussain, sherif of Mecca and king of the Hejaz (1856–1931), and others rose up against Turkish rule. The motivation for the Arab revolt centered on securing independence from the Ottoman empire and subsequently creating a unified Arab nation spanning lands from Syria to Yemen. The British government did not keep its promise of Arab independence after the war.

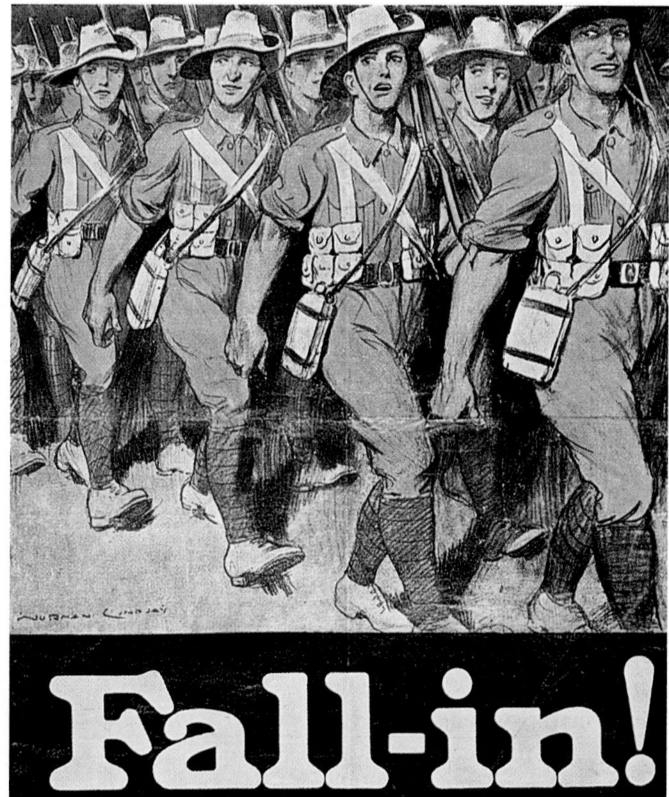

Australian recruiting poster. The British were keen to augment their forces by recruiting Australians and others to help defeat the Ottoman empire, which had allied itself with the Central Powers.

THE END OF THE WAR

The war produced strains within all the belligerent nations, but most of them managed, often ruthlessly, to cope with food riots, strikes, and mutinies. In the Russian empire, the war amplified existing stresses to such an extent that the Romanov dynasty was forced to abdicate in favor of a provisional government in the spring of 1917. Eight months later, the provisional government yielded power to **Bolshevik** revolutionaries, who took Russia out of the war early in 1918. This blow to the Allies was more than offset by the entry of

Bolshevik (BOHL-sheh-vihk)

the United States into the conflict in 1917, which turned the tide of war in 1918. The resources of the United States finally compelled the exhausted Central Powers to sue for peace in November 1918.

In 1919 the victorious Allies gathered in Paris to hammer out a peace settlement that turned out to be a compromise that pleased few of the parties involved. The most significant consequence of the war was Europe's diminished role in the world. The war of 1914–1918 undermined Europe's power and simultaneously promoted nationalist aspirations among colonized peoples who clamored for self-determination and national independence. For the time being, however, the major imperialist powers kept their grip on their overseas holdings.

Revolution in Russia

The March Revolution The Great War had undermined the Russian state. In the spring of 1917, disintegrating armies, mutinies, and food shortages provoked a series of street demonstrations and strikes in Petrograd (St. Petersburg). The inability of police forces to suppress the uprisings, and the subsequent mutiny of troops garrisoned in the capital, persuaded Tsar Nicholas II (reigned 1894–1917) to abdicate the throne. Thus Russia ceased to be a monarchy, and the Romanov dynasty disappeared after more than three hundred years of uninterrupted rule. The March revolution—the first of two revolutions in 1917—was an unplanned and incomplete affair.

The Struggle for Power After its success in Petrograd, the revolution spread throughout the country, and political power in Russia shifted to two new agencies: the provisional government and the Petrograd soviet of Workers' and Soldiers' Deputies. Soviets, which were revolutionary councils organized by socialists, appeared for the first time during the Russian revolution of 1905 (see chapter 31). In 1917, soviets of Workers' and Soldiers' Deputies surfaced all over Russia, wielding considerable power through their control of factories and segments of the military. The period between March and November witnessed a political struggle between the provisional government and the powerful Petrograd soviet. At first the new government enjoyed considerable public support as it disbanded the tsarist police; repealed all limitations on freedom of speech, press, and association; and abolished laws that discriminated against ethnic or religious groups; but it failed to satisfy popular demands for an end to war and for land reform. It claimed that, being provisional, it could not make fundamental changes such as confiscating land and distributing it among peasants. Any such change had to be postponed for decision by a future constituent assembly. The government also pledged itself to "unswervingly carry out the agreements made with the Allies" and promised to continue the war to a victorious conclusion. The Petrograd soviet, in contrast, called for an immediate peace. Such radicals were the only ones in Russia determined to end the war and hence gained more support from the people of Russia.

Lenin Into this tense political situation stepped Vladimir Ilyich Lenin (1870–1924), a revolutionary Marxist who had been living in exile in Switzerland. Born into a warm and loving family, Lenin grew up in the confines of a moderately prosperous family living in the provincial Russian town of Simbirsk. In 1887, shortly after his father's death, the police arrested and hanged his older brother for plotting to assassinate the tsar, an event that seared Lenin's youth. Following a brief career as a lawyer, Lenin spent many years abroad, devoting himself to studying Marxist thought and writing political pamphlets. In contrast to Marx, Lenin viewed the in-

Vladimir Lenin makes a speech in Red Square on the first anniversary (1918) of the Bolshevik revolution.

dustrial working class as incapable of developing the proper revolutionary consciousness that would lead to effective political action. To Lenin the industrial proletariat required the leadership of a well-organized and highly disciplined party, a workers' vanguard that would serve as the catalyst for revolution and for the realization of a socialist society.

In a moment of high drama, the German High Command transported Lenin and other revolutionaries in 1917 to Russia in a sealed train, hoping that this committed antiwar activist would stir up trouble and bring about Russia's withdrawal from the war. Lenin headed the Bolsheviks, the radical wing of the Russian Social Democratic Party. In April he began calling for the transfer of legal authority to the soviets and advocated uncompromising opposition to the war. Initially, his party opposed his radicalism, but he soon succeeded in converting his fellow Bolsheviks to his proposals.

The November Revolution The Bolsheviks, who were a small minority among revolutionary working-class parties, eventually gained control of the Petrograd soviet. Crucial to that development was the provisional government's insistence on continuing the war, its inability to feed the population, and its refusal to undertake land reform. Those policies led to a growing conviction among workers and peasants that their problems could be solved only by the soviets. The Bolsheviks capitalized on that mood with effective slogans such as "All Power to the Soviets" and, most famous, "Peace, Land, and Bread." In September, Lenin persuaded the Central Committee of the Bolshevik Party to organize an armed insurrection and seize power in the name of the All-Russian National Congress of Soviets, which was then convening in Petrograd. During the night of 6 November and the following day, armed workers, soldiers, and sailors stormed the Winter Palace, the home of the provisional government. By the afternoon of 7 November, the virtually bloodless insurrection had run its course, and power passed from the provisional government into the hands of Lenin and the Bolshevik Party. The U.S. journalist John Reed (1887–1920), who witnessed the Bolshevik seizure of power, understood the significance of the events when he referred to them as "ten days that shook the world." Lenin and his followers were poised to destroy the traditional patterns and values of Russian society and challenge the institutions of liberal society everywhere.

Treaty of Brest-Litovsk The Bolshevik rulers ended Russia's involvement in the Great War by signing the Treaty of Brest-Litovsk with Germany on 3 March 1918. The treaty gave the Germans possession or control of much of Russia's territory (the Baltic states, the Caucasus, Finland, Poland, and the Ukraine) and one-quarter of its population. The terms of the treaty were harsh and humiliating, but taking Russia out of the war gave the new government an opportunity to deal with internal problems. Russia's departure from the war meant that Germany could concentrate all its resources on the western front.

U.S. Intervention and Collapse of the Central Powers

The year 1917 was crucial for another reason: it marked the entry of the United States into the war on the side of the Allies. In 1914 the American public firmly opposed intervention in a European war. Woodrow Wilson (1856–1924) was reelected president in 1916 because he campaigned on a nonintervention platform. That sentiment soon changed. After the outbreak of the war, the United States pursued a neutrality that favored the Allies, and as the war progressed, the United States became increasingly committed economically to an Allied victory.

Economic Considerations During the first two years of the war, the U.S. economy coped with a severe business recession that saw thousands of businesses fail and unemployment reach 15 percent. Economic recovery became dependent on sales of war materials, especially on British orders for munitions. Because U.S. companies sold huge amounts of supplies to the Allies, insistence on neutrality seemed hypocritical at best. With the war grinding on, the Allies took out large loans with American banks, which persuaded some Americans that an Allied victory made good financial sense. Moreover, by the spring of 1917, the Allies had depleted their means of paying for essential supplies from the United States and probably could not have maintained their war effort had the United States remained neutral. An Allied victory and, hence, the ability to pay off Allied war debts could be accomplished only by direct U.S. participation in the Great War.

Submarine Warfare The official factor in the United States' decision to enter the war was Germany's resumption of unrestricted submarine warfare in February 1917. At the outset of the war, U.S. government officials asserted the traditional doctrine of neutral rights for American ships because they wanted to continue trading with belligerents, most notably the British and the French. With the German surface fleet bottled up in the Baltic, Germany's wartime leaders grew desperately dependent on their submarine fleet to strangle Britain economically and break the British blockade of the Central Powers. German military experts calculated that submarine attacks against the ships of Great Britain and all the ships headed to Great Britain would bring about the defeat of Great Britain in six months. German subs often sank neutral merchant ships without first giving a warning as required by international law. On 7 May 1915, a German submarine sank the British passenger liner *Lusitania* off the Irish coast with a loss of 1,198 lives, including 128 U.S. citizens. Technically, the ship was a legitimate target, because it carried 4,200 cases of ammunition and traveled through a declared war zone. Nevertheless, segments of the American public were outraged, and during the next two years the country's mood increasingly turned against Germany. Allied

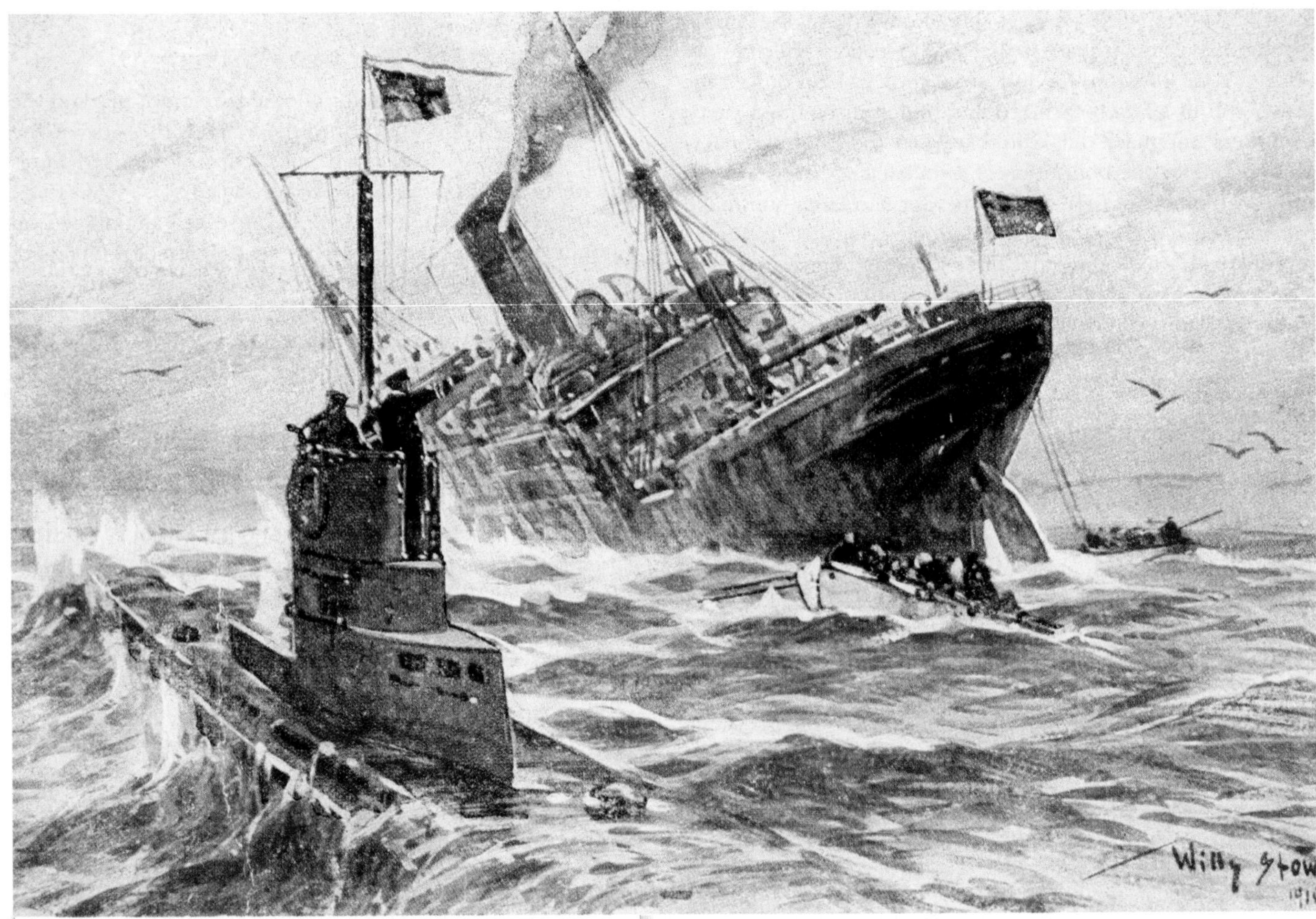

In 1915 artist Willy Stower depicted a ship sinking as a result of a submarine attack. The Germans used submarines to great effect to disrupt the shipping of essential supplies to Great Britain.

propaganda, especially British manipulation of information, also swayed public opinion.

America Declares War Even though the British naval blockade directed at the Central Powers constantly interfered with American shipping, Woodrow Wilson nonetheless moved his nation to war against Germany. In January 1917, with his country still at peace, Wilson began to enumerate U.S. war aims, and on 2 April he urged the Congress of the United States to adopt a war resolution. In his ringing war message, Wilson equated German "warfare against commerce" with "warfare against mankind," intoning that "the world must be made safe for democracy." Republican senator George W. Norris, arguing for U.S. neutrality, countered by saying "I feel that we are about to put the dollar sign upon the American flag." That protest was to no avail, and on 6 April 1917 the United States declared war against Germany. The U.S. entry proved decisive in breaking the stalemate.

Collapsing Fronts The corrosive effects of years of bloodletting showed. For the first two years of the conflict, most people supported their governments' war efforts, but the continuing ravages of war took their toll everywhere. In April 1916 Irish nationalists mounted the Great Easter Rebellion, which attempted unsuccessfully to overthrow British rule in Ireland. The Central Powers suffered from food shortages as a result of the British blockade, and increasing numbers of people took to the streets to demonstrate against declining food rations. Food riots were complemented by strikes as prewar social conflicts reemerged. Governments reacted harshly to those challenges, pouncing on strikers, suppressing demonstrators, and jailing dissidents. Equally dangerous was the breakdown of military discipline. At the German naval base in Kiel, sailors revolted in the summer of 1917 and again, much more seriously, in the fall of 1918. In the wake of another failed offensive during the spring of 1917, which resulted in ghastly casualties, French soldiers lost confidence in their leadership. When ordered to attack once again, they refused. The extent of the mutiny was enormous: 50,000 soldiers were involved, resulting in 23,385 courts-martial and 432 death sentences. So tight was

German prisoners taken in France in the autumn of 1918. Millions of soldiers had been captured and imprisoned by war's end, and many more had died or been wounded. Over fifteen million had been killed and twenty million wounded by the time of the armistice on 11 November 1918.

French censorship that the Germans, who could have taken advantage of this situation, did not learn about the mutiny until the war was over.

Against the background of civilian disillusionment and deteriorating economic conditions, Germany took the risk of throwing its remaining might at the western front in the spring of 1918. The gamble failed, and as the offensive petered out, the Allies broke through the front and started pushing the Germans back. By that time Germany had effectively exhausted its human and material means to wage war. Meanwhile, Bulgaria capitulated to the invading Allies on 30 September, the Ottomans concluded an armistice on 30 October, and Austria-Hungary surrendered on 4 November. Finally, the Germans accepted an armistice, which took effect on 11 November 1918. At last the guns went silent.

After the War

The immediate effects of the Great War were all too obvious. Aside from the physical destruction, which was most visible in northern France and Belgium, the war had killed, disabled, orphaned, or rendered homeless millions of people. Conservative estimates suggest that the war killed fifteen million people and wounded twenty million others. In the immediate postwar years, millions more succumbed to the effects of starvation, malnutrition, and epidemic diseases.

The Influenza Pandemic of 1918 The end of the Great War coincided with the arrival of one of the worst pandemics ever recorded in human history. No one knows its origins or why it vanished in mid-1919, but by the time this virulent influenza disappeared, it had left more than twenty million dead. The disease killed more people than did the Great War, and it hit young adults—a group usually not severely affected by influenza—with particular ferocity. Contemporaries called it the Spanish flu because the first major documented outbreak of the disease occurred in Spain in late 1918.

The Great War did not cause the flu pandemic of 1918–1919, but wartime traffic on land and sea probably contributed to the spread of the infection. It killed swiftly wherever it went. From the remotest villages in Arctic climates and crowded cities in India and the United States to the battlefields of Europe, men and women were struck down by high fever. Within a few days they were dead. One estimate puts deaths in India alone at seven million. In Calcutta, the postal service and the legal system ground to a halt. In the United States, the flu killed more Americans than all the wars fought in the twentieth century put together. In cutting a swath across west Africa, it left in its deadly path more than one million victims. The Pacific islands suffered worst of all as the flu wiped out up to 25 percent of their entire population.

The influenza plague never discriminated. It struck the rich as fiercely as the poor. It decimated men and women equally. It did not distinguish between the hungry and the well nourished, and it took the sick as well as the healthy. The presence or absence of doctors and nurses never made any difference. There was no cure for the flu of 1918.

The Paris Settlement Before the costs of the war were assessed fully, world attention shifted to Paris. There, in 1919, the victorious powers convened to arrange a postwar settlement and set terms for the defeated nations. At the outset, people on both sides of the war had high hopes for the settlement, but in the end it left a bitter legacy. Because the twenty-seven nations represented at Paris had different and often conflicting aims, many sessions of the conference deteriorated into pandemonium. Ultimately, Georges Clemenceau (1841–1929), Lloyd George (1863–1945), and Woodrow Wilson—the representative leaders of France, Great Britain, and the United States—dominated the deliberations. The Allies did not permit representatives of the Central Powers to participate. In addition, the Allies threatened to renew the war if the terms they laid down were not accepted. Significantly, the Soviet Union was not invited to the conference.

Throughout this time the British blockade of Germany remained in effect, adding a sense of urgency to the proceedings. That situation later gave rise to the charge of a dictated peace, especially because no foreign troops set foot on German soil.

Wilson's Fourteen Points One year before the opening of the Paris Peace Conference in January 1918, U.S. president Woodrow Wilson forwarded a proposal for a just and enduring postwar peace settlement. Wilson's postwar vision had subsequently prompted the defeated Central Powers to announce their acceptance of his so-called Fourteen Points as the basis for the armistice. They also expected the Allies to use them as the foundation for later peace treaties. Key among Wilson's Fourteen Points were the following recommendations: open covenants (agreements) of peace, openly arrived at; absolute freedom of navigation on the seas in peace and war; the removal of all economic barriers and the establishment of an equality of trade conditions among all nations; adequate guarantees for a reduction in national armaments; adjustments of colonial disputes to give equal weight to the interests of the controlling government and the colonial population; and a call for "a general association of nations." The idealism expressed in the Fourteen Points gave Wilson a position of moral leadership among the Allies. Those same allies also opposed various points of Wilson's peace formula, because those points compromised the secret wartime agreements by which they had agreed to distribute among themselves territories and possessions of the defeated nations. The defeated powers, in turn, later felt betrayed when they faced the harsh peace treaties that so clearly violated the spirit of the Fourteen Points.

The Peace Treaties The final form of the treaties represented a series of compromises among the victors. The hardest terms originated with the French, who desired the destruction or the permanent weakening of German power. Thus, in addition to requiring Germany to accept sole responsibility and guilt for causing the war, the victors demanded a reduction in the military potential of the former Central Powers. For example, the Treaty of Versailles (1919) denied the Germans a navy and an air force and limited the size of the German army to 100,000 troops. In addition, the Allies prohibited Germany and Austria from entering into any sort of political union. The French and the British agreed that the defeated Central Powers must pay for the cost of the war and required the payment of reparations either in money or in kind. Although the German government and the public decried the Treaty of Versailles as being excessively harsh, it was no more severe in its terms than the Treaty of Brest-Litovsk that the Germans imposed on Russia in 1918.

Political leaders sign the Treaty of Versailles, which, among other provisions, controversially compelled the Germans to accept sole responsibility for causing the war.

The Paris peace conference resulted in several additional treaties. Bulgaria accepted the Treaty of Neuilly (1919), ceding only small portions of territory, because the Allies feared that major territorial changes in the Balkans would destabilize the region. That view did not apply to the dual monarchy of Austria-Hungary, whose imperial unity disintegrated under the impact of the war. The peacemakers recognized the territorial breakup of the former empire in two separate treaties: the Treaty of St. Germain (1919), between the Allies and the Republic of Austria, and the Treaty of Trianon (1920), between the Allies and the kingdom of Hungary. Both Austria and Hungary suffered severe territorial losses, which the Allies claimed were necessary in order to find territorial boundaries that accorded closely with the principle of self-determination. For example, the peace settlement reduced Hungarian territory to one-third of its prewar size and decreased the nation's population from 28 to 8 million people.

Arrangements between the defeated Ottoman empire and the Allies proved to be a more complicated and protracted affair. The Treaty of Sèvres (1920) effectively dissolved the empire, calling for the surrender of Ottoman Balkan and Arab provinces and the occupation of eastern and southern Anatolia by foreign powers. The treaty was acceptable to the government of sultan Mohammed VI, but not to Turkish nationalists who rallied around their wartime hero Mustafa Kemal. As head of the Turkish nationalist movement, Mustafa Kemal set out to defy the Allied terms. He organized a national army that drove out Greek, British, French, and Italian occupation forces and abolished the sultanate and replaced it with the Republic of Turkey, with Ankara as its capital. In a great diplomatic victory for Turkish nationalists, the Allied powers officially recognized the Republic of Turkey in a final peace agreement, the Treaty of Lausanne (1923).

Atatürk As president of the republic, Mustafa Kemal, now known as Atatürk ("Father of the Turks"), instituted an ambitious program of modernization that emphasized economic development and secularism. Government support of critical industries and businesses, and other forms of state intervention in the economy designed to ensure rapid economic development, resulted in substantial long-term economic progress. The government's policy of secularism dictated the complete separation between the existing Muslim religious establishment and the state. The policy resulted in the replacement of religious with secular institutions of education and justice, the emancipation of women, including their right to vote, the adoption of European-derived law, Hindu-Arabic numerals, the Roman alphabet, and Western clothing. Theoretically heading a constitutional democracy, Atatürk ruled Turkey as a virtual dictator until his death in 1938.

Turkey's postwar transformations and its success in refashioning the terms of peace proved to be something of an exception. In the final analysis, the peace settlement was strategically weak because too few participants had a stake in maintaining it and too many had an interest in revising it. German expansionist aims in Europe, which probably played a role in the nation's decision to enter the Great War, remained unresolved, as did Italian territorial designs in the Balkans and Japanese influence in China. Those issues virtually ensured that the two decades following the peace settlement became merely a twenty-year truce, characterized by power rivalries and intermittent violence that led to yet another global war.

The League of Nations

In an effort to avoid future destructive conflicts, the diplomats in Paris created the League of Nations. The League was the first permanent international security organization whose principal mission was to maintain world peace. At the urging of U.S. president Woodrow Wilson, the Covenant of the League of Nations was made an integral part of the peace treaties, and every signatory to a peace treaty had to accept this new world organization. Initially, the League seemed to be the sign of a new era: twenty-six of its forty-two original members were countries outside Europe, suggesting that it transcended European interests.

The League had two major flaws that rendered it ineffective. First, though designed to solve international disputes through arbitration, it had no power to enforce its decisions. Second, it relied on *collective security* as a tool for the preservation of global peace. The basic premise underlying collective security arrangements was the concept that aggression against any one state was considered aggression against all the other states, which had pledged to aid one another. Shared deterrence could assume different forms, such as diplomatic pressure, economic sanctions, and, ultimately, force. However, the basic precondition for collective security—participation by all the great powers—never materialized, because at any given time one or more of the major powers did not belong to the League. The United States never joined the organization because the U.S. Senate rejected the idea. Germany, which viewed the League as a club of Allied victors, and Japan, which saw it as an instrument of imperialism, left the League of Nations in 1933, as did some smaller powers. Italy, chastised by the League for imperial adventures in Ethiopia, withdrew from it in 1937. The Soviet Union, which regarded the League as a tool of global capitalism, joined the organization in 1934, only to face expulsion in 1940. Although its failure to stop aggression in the 1930s led to its demise in 1940, the League established the pattern for a permanent international organization and served as a model for its successor, the United Nations.

Self-Determination

One of the principal themes of the peacemaking process was the concept of self-determination, which was promoted most intensely by Woodrow Wilson. Wilson believed that self-determination was the key to international peace and cooperation. With respect to Europe, that principle sometimes translated into reality. For example, Poland, Czechoslovakia, and Yugoslavia (kingdom of Serbs, Croats, and Slovenes until 1929) already existed as sovereign states by 1918, and by the end of the conference, the principle of self-determination had triumphed in many areas that were previously under the control of the Austro-Hungarian and Russian empires. Yet in other instances peacemakers pushed the principle aside for strategic and security reasons, such as in Austria and Germany, whose peoples were denied the right to form one nation. At other times, diplomats violated the notion of self-determination because they found it impossible to redraw national boundaries in accordance with nationalist aspirations without creating large minorities on one side or the other of a boundary line. Poland was one case in point; one-third of the population did not speak Polish. A more complicated situation existed in Czechoslovakia. The peoples who gave the republic its name—the Czechs and the Slovaks—totaled only 67 percent of the population, with the remaining population consisting of Germans (22 percent), Ruthenes (6 percent), and Hungarians (5 percent). On the surface, the creation of Yugoslavia ("Land of the South Slavs") represented a triumph of self-determination, because it politically united related peoples who for centuries had chafed under foreign rule. Beneath that unity, however, there lingered the separate national identities embraced by Serbs, Croats, and Slovenes.

The Mandate System

However imperfect the results, the peacemakers at Paris tried to apply the principle of self-determination and nationality throughout Europe. Elsewhere, however, they did not do so. The unwillingness to apply the principle of self-determination became most obvious when the victors confronted the issue of what to do with Germany's former colonies and the Arab territories of the Ottoman empire. Because the United States rejected the establishment of old-fashioned colonies, the European powers came up with the enterprising idea of trusteeship. Article 22 of the Covenant of the League of Nations referred to the colonies and territories of the former Central Powers as areas

MAP 33.2
Territorial changes in Europe after the Great War.
Observe the territories ceded by the Central Powers and the Soviet Union.
Which power lost the most territory, and why?

"inhabited by peoples not yet able to stand by themselves under the strenuous conditions of the modern world." As a result, "The tutelage of such peoples should be entrusted to the advanced nations who . . . can best undertake this responsibility." The League divided the mandates into three classes based on the presumed development of their populations in the direction of fitness for self-government. The administration of the mandates fell to the victorious powers of the Great War.

The Germans interpreted the mandate system as a division of colonial booty by the victors, who had conveniently forgotten to apply the tutelage provision to their own colonies. German cynicism was more than matched by Arab outrage. The establishment of mandates in the former ter-

sources from the past

Memorandum of the General Syrian Congress

Article 22 of the League of Nations Covenant established a system of mandates to rule the colonies and territories of the defeated powers, including parts of the former Ottoman empire (comprising present-day Syria, Lebanon, Jordan, and Israel). The mandate system essentially substituted European mandates for Ottoman rule. The news of this arrangement came as a shock to the peoples of the defeated Ottoman empire who had fought alongside the English and the French during the Great War and expected their independence. They quickly denounced the mandate system. The following selection is a memorandum addressed to the King Crane Commission, which was responsible for overseeing the transfer of Ottoman territory.

We the undersigned members of the General Syrian Congress, meeting in Damascus on Wednesday, July 2nd 1919, . . . provided with the credentials and authorizations by the inhabitants of our various districts, Moslems, Christians, and Jews, have agreed upon the following statement of the desires of the people of the country who have elected us. . . .

1. We ask absolutely complete political independence for Syria. . . .
2. We ask that the Government of this Syrian country should be a democratic civil constitutional Monarchy on broad decentralization principles, safeguarding the rights of minorities, and that the King be the Emir Feisal, who carried on a glorious struggle in the cause of liberation and merited our full confidence and entire reliance.
3. Considering that the Arabs inhabiting the Syrian area are not naturally less gifted than other more advanced races and that they are by no means less developed than the Bulgarians, Serbians, Greeks, and Romanians at the beginning of their independence, we protest against Article 22 of the Covenant of the League of Nations, placing us among the nations in their middle stage of development which stand in need of a mandatory power.
6. We do not acknowledge any right claimed by the French Government in any part whatever of our Syrian country and refuse that she should assist us or have a hand in our country under any circumstances and in any place.
7. We oppose the pretensions of the Zionists to create a Jewish commonwealth in the southern part of Syria, known as Israel, and oppose Zionist migration to any part of our country; for we do not acknowledge their title but consider them a grave peril to our people, from the national, economical, and political points of view. Our Jewish compatriots shall enjoy our common rights and assume the common responsibilities.

For Further Reflection

- For what specifically was the Syrian Congress asking? Do you think the European powers expected this response to the League of Nations Covenant?

Source: *Foreign Relations of the United States: Paris Peace Conference,* vol. 12. Washington, D.C.: Government Printing Office, 1919, pp. 780–81. Cited in Philip F. Riley et al., *The Global Experience. Readings in World History,* vol. 2. Englewood Cliffs, N.J.: Prentice Hall, 1992, pp. 193–94.

ritories of the Ottoman empire violated promises (made to Arabs) by French and British leaders during the war. They had promised Arab nationalists independence from the Ottoman empire and had promised Jewish nationalists in Europe a homeland in Palestine. Where the Arabs hoped to form independent states, the French (in Lebanon and Syria) and the British (in Iraq and Palestine) established mandates. The Allies viewed the mandate system as a reasonable compromise between the reality of imperialism and the ideal of self-determination. To the peoples who were directly affected, the mandate system smacked of continued imperial rule draped in a cloak of respectability.

Challenges to European Preeminence

The Great War changed Europe forever, but to most Europeans the larger world and the Continent's role in it remained essentially unchanged. With the imperial powers still ruling over their old colonies and new protectorates, it appeared that European global hegemony was more secure. Yet that picture did not correspond to reality. The Great War did irreparable damage to European power and prestige and set the stage for a process of decolonization that gathered momentum during and after the Second World War. The war of 1914–1918 accelerated the growth of nationalism in the European-controlled parts of the world, fueling desires for independence and self-determination.

Weakened Europe The decline in European power was closely related to diminished economic stature, a result of the commitment to total war. In time, Europe overcame many war-induced economic problems, such as high rates of inflation and huge public debts, but other economic dislocations

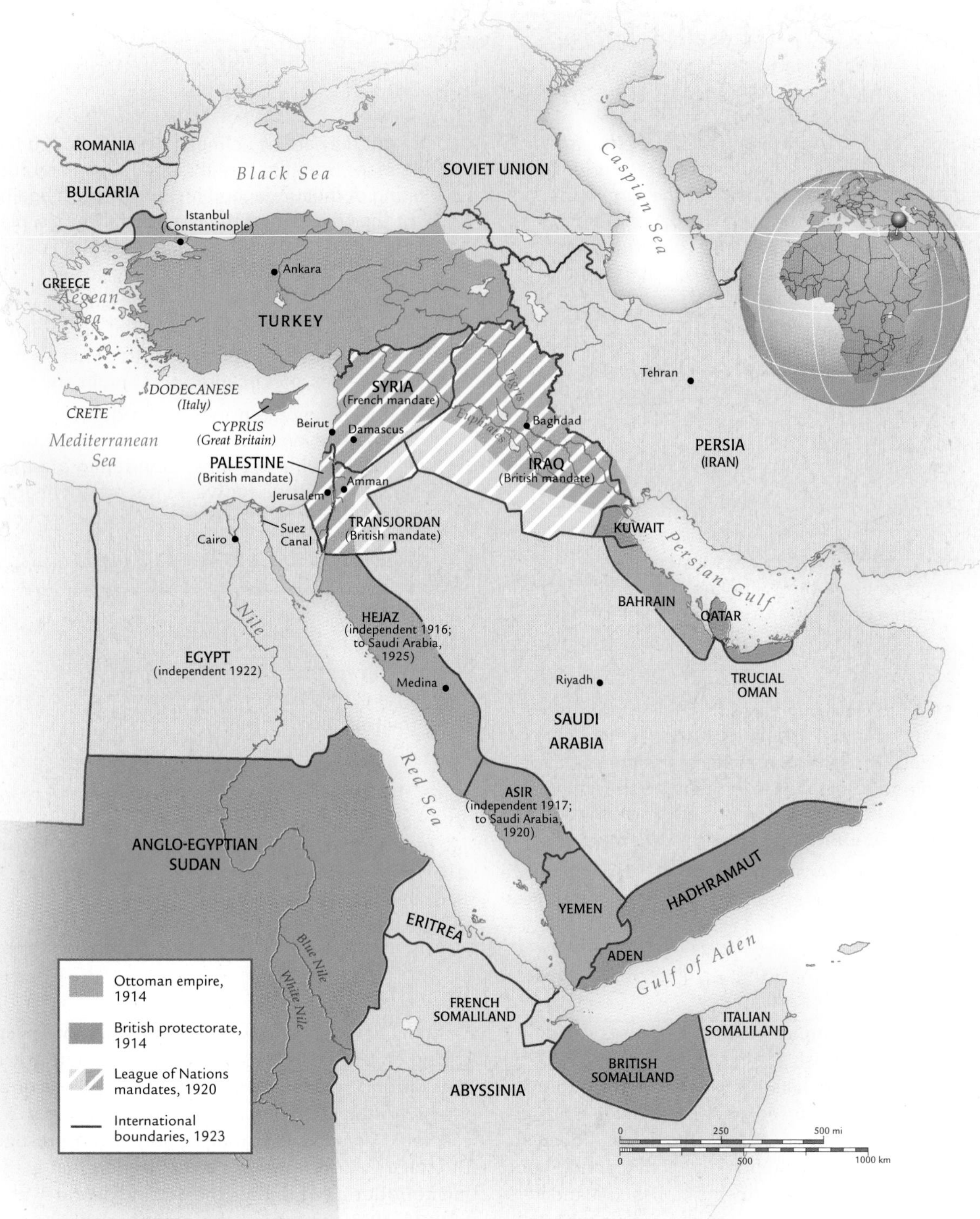

MAP 33.3

Territorial changes in southwest Asia after the Great War.

The Great War completed the process of disintegration of the Ottoman empire and left much of the region in limbo.

What was the reaction in the region when European statesmen assigned former Ottoman territories to French or British control under the League of Nations mandates?

were permanent and damaging. Most significant was the loss of overseas investments and foreign markets, which had brought huge financial returns. Nothing is more indicative of Europe's reduced economic might than the reversal of the economic relationship between Europe and the United States. Whereas the United States was a debtor nation before 1914, owing billions of dollars to European investors, by 1919 it was a major creditor.

A loss of prestige overseas and a weakening grip on colonies also reflected the undermining of Europe's global hegemony. Colonial subjects in Africa, Asia, and the Pacific often viewed the Great War as a civil war among the European nations, a bloody spectacle in which the haughty bearers of an alleged superior society vilified and slaughtered one another. Because Europe seemed weak, divided, and vulnerable, the white overlords no longer appeared destined to rule over colonized subjects. The colonials who returned home from the war in Europe and southwest Asia reinforced those general impressions with their own firsthand observations. In particular, they were less inclined to be obedient imperial subjects.

Revolutionary Ideas The war also helped spread revolutionary ideas to the colonies. The U.S. war aims spelled out in the Fourteen Points raised the hopes of peoples under imperial rule and promoted nationalist aspirations. The peacemakers repeatedly invoked the concept of self-determination, and Wilson publicly proposed that in all colonial questions "the interests of the native populations be given equal weight with the desires of European governments." Wilson seemed to call for nothing less than national independence and self-rule. Nationalists struggling to organize anti-imperialist resistance also sought inspiration from the Soviet Union, whose leaders denounced all forms of imperialism and pledged their support to independence movements. Taken together, these messages were subversive to imperial control and had a great appeal for colonial peoples. The postwar disappointments and temporary setbacks experienced by nationalist movements did not diminish their desire for self-rule and self-determination.

inperspective

The assassination of the Austrian archduke Francis Ferdinand had a galvanizing effect on a Europe torn by national rivalries, colonial disputes, and demands for self-determination. In the summer of 1914, inflexible war plans and a tangled alliance system transformed a local war between Austria-Hungary and Serbia into a European-wide clash of arms. With the entry of the Ottoman empire, Japan, and the United States, the war of 1914–1918 became a global conflict. Although many belligerents organized their societies for total war and drew on the resources of their overseas empires, the war remained at a bloody stalemate until the United States entered the conflict in 1917. The tide turned, and the combatants signed an armistice in November 1918. The Great War, a brutal encounter between societies and peoples, inflicted ghastly human casualties, severely damaged national economies, and discredited established political and cultural traditions. The war also altered the political landscape of many lands as it destroyed four dynasties and their empires and fostered the creation of several new European nations. In Russia the war served as a backdrop for the world's first successful socialist revolution. In the end the Great War sapped the strength of European colonial powers while promoting nationalist aspirations among colonized peoples. ●

CHRONOLOGY	
1914	Assassination of Archduke Francis Ferdinand
1915	German submarine sinks the *Lusitania*
1915	Japan makes Twenty-one Demands on China
1915	Gallipoli campaign
1916	Battles at Verdun and the Somme
1917	German resumption of unrestricted submarine warfare
1917	United States declaration of war on Germany
1917	Bolshevik Revolution
1918	Treaty of Brest-Litovsk
1918	Armistice suspends hostilities
1919	Paris Peace Conference
1920	First meeting of the League of Nations
1923	Atatürk proclaims Republic of Turkey

For Further Reading

Jonathan W. Daly. *The Watchful State: Security Police and Opposition in Russia, 1906–1917.* DeKalb, Ill., 2004. Study of the Russian secret police and their policies toward early revolutionary activities.

Belinda Davis. *Home Fires Burning: Food, Politics, and Everyday Life in World War I Berlin.* Chapel Hill, 2000. Effectively covers daily life in wartime and also offers insights into how government policies during the war affected the reconstruction of society following it.

Modris Eckstein. *Rites of Spring: The Great War and the Birth of the Modern Age.* Boston, 1989. An imaginative cultural study that ranges widely.

Niall Ferguson. *The Pity of War: Explaining World War I.* New York, 2000. A stimulating example of revisionist history that shifts the blame for the war away from Germany and onto England.

Paul Fussell. *Great War and Modern Memory.* Oxford, 1975. An original and deeply moving piece of cultural history.

Peter Gatrell. *Russia's First World War: A Social and Economic History.* London, 2005. Traces the impact of World War I on Russian society before the revolution.

Felix Gilbert. *The End of the European Era, 1890 to the Present.* New York, 1979. An information-laden study that argues that the Great War destroyed Europe's centrality in the world.

Paul G. Halpern. *A Naval History of World War I.* Annapolis, 1994. Unlike most other treatments, this work covers all participants in all major theaters.

Margaret Randolph Higonnet et al. *Behind the Lines.* New Haven, 1990. Women's work and the war industry take center stage.

James Joll. *The Origins of the First World War.* 2nd ed. London, 1991. The most lucid and balanced introduction to a complex and controversial subject.

John Keegan. *The First World War.* New York, 1999. A comprehensive and a stunningly vivid account of the Great War.

John Maynard Keynes. *The Economic Consequences of the Peace.* New York, 1920. A classic and devastating critique of the Versailles treaty.

John H. Morrow. *The Great War. An Imperial History.* New York, 2003. A global history of the Great War that places the conflict squarely in the context of imperialism.

Michael S. Neiberg. *Fighting the Great War.* Cambridge, Mass., 2005. A good blend of narrative and analysis, this work highlights the global reach of the conflict.

Richard Pipes. *The Russian Revolution 1899–1919.* 2nd ed. London, 1992. An up-to-date and well-argued interpretation.

Erich Remarque. *All Quiet on the Western Front.* New York, 1958. A fictional account of trench warfare.

Hew Strachan. *The First World War.* Vol. 1: *To Arms.* New York, 2001. The first of three anticipated volumes, this is a masterly work that treats the war in global rather than European terms.

Barbara Tuchman. *The Guns of August.* New York, 1962. Spellbinding narrative of the coming of the war.

Robert Wohl. *The Generation of 1914.* Cambridge, 1979. Elegantly captures the ideas and attitudes of the generations that experienced the Great War.

An Age of Anxiety

chapter 34

Probing Cultural Frontiers
- Postwar Pessimism
- Revolutions in Physics and Psychology
- Experimentation in Art and Architecture

Global Depression
- The Great Depression
- Despair and Government Action
- Economic Experimentation

Challenges to the Liberal Order
- Communism in Russia
- The Fascist Alternative
- Italian Fascism
- German National Socialism

EYEWITNESS:
The Birth of a Monster

Born on a lovely spring day in 1889, in a quaint Austrian village, he was the apple of his mother's eye. He basked in Klara's warmth and indulgence as a youth, enjoying the fine life of a middle-class child. As he grew older, he sensed a tension that long stayed with him, a vague anxiety that stemmed from the competing expectations of his parents. Contented with the dreamy indolence allowed by Klara, he bristled at the demands of his father, Alois. Alois expected him to follow in his footsteps, to study hard and enter the Austrian civil service. He had no desire to become a bureaucrat. In fact, he envisioned a completely different life for himself. He wanted to be an artist. His school grades slipped, and that seemed an appropriate way to express his discontent and sabotage his father's pedestrian plans for his future.

Alois's unexpected death in 1903 freed him from that awful future. He now had the time and the familial sympathy to daydream and indulge his imagination. He left school in 1905, not at all dissatisfied with having achieved only a ninth-grade education, because now he could pursue his heart's desire: an education as an artist. He followed his ambitions to Vienna, only to find bitter disappointment when the Vienna Academy of Fine Arts rejected him as an art student in 1907. His beloved Klara died the following year, and he meandered the city streets of Vienna, living off a pension and the money he inherited from his mother. He immersed himself in Vienna, admiring the architecture of the city and attending the opera when his funds permitted. He especially enjoyed the music of Richard Wagner, whose embrace of heroic German myth matched his own imaginative predilections.

Having finally run through all of his money, he hit bottom and began staying at a homeless shelter. It was interesting, though, to hear the different political points of view spouted by the shelter's other inhabitants. They discussed compelling issues of the day, such as race, and he listened intently to those who hailed the supremacy of the Aryan race and the inferiority of the Jews. He immersed himself in reading, particularly the newspapers and pamphlets that gave him more information about those disturbing political issues. He came to hate Jews and Marxists, whom he thought had formed an evil union with the goal of destroying the world. He also despised liberalism and democracy, and in cheap cafés

This is one of the few known photographs of a young Adolf Hitler, taken in 1923.

he began directing political harangues at anyone who would listen.

Still, he had his art, and he found he could just barely survive on the earnings he made from selling his pretty postcards covered with painted replicas of famous works or his original sketches of Viennese buildings. He believed, too, that his political and social life had become much more exciting, as he was now publicly debating issues and learning to speak up about the concerns of the day—and what anxious, perilous, but interesting times these were. He felt compelled to leave Vienna in 1913, however, if only to avoid the Austrian military draft. He was not willing to serve or die for what he believed was a decaying Austria-Hungary empire.

He found refuge in Munich, Germany, and there volunteered for service in the German army, which had just embarked on its crusade in the greatest war ever fought. He discovered in himself a real talent for military service, and he remained in the army for the duration of the war, 1914–1918. Twice wounded and decorated for bravery, he nonetheless found himself in despair at war's end. He languished in a military hospital, temporarily blinded by the mustard gas that had enveloped him during his last days of fighting. An impotent rage coursed through him when he learned of Germany's defeat. He knew with all his being that the Jews were responsible for this humiliation, and he also knew what he had to do: he had to enter the political arena in his chosen fatherland and save the nation. Adolf Hitler had finally found his mission in life.

Affected by and in turn affecting the anxiety and malaise of the early decades of the twentieth century, Hitler (1889–1945) stood as just one personification of Europe's age of anxiety. Torn between divergent visions of his future and embittered by a sense of dislocation and fear stemming from the drastic changes engulfing the society around him, Hitler dedicated himself to discovering a way out of the anxiety for the nation he had adopted. His solutions ultimately brought about more rather than less anxiety, but the novelty and cruelty of his political and military agendas reflected brilliantly the traumatic consequences of the Great War and the Great Depression.

Just as Adolf Hitler changed as a result of his life experiences in the early twentieth century, so too did European society as a whole. Badly shaken by the effects of years of war, Europeans experienced a shock to their system of values, beliefs, and traditions. Profound scientific and cultural transformations that came to the fore in the postwar decades also contributed to a sense of loss and anxiety. As peoples in Europe and around the world struggled to come to terms with the aftermath of war, an unprecedented economic contraction gripped the international community.

Against the background of the Great Depression, dictators in Russia, Italy, and Germany tried to translate blueprints for utopias into reality. While Joseph Stalin and his fellow communists recast the former tsarist empire into a dictatorship of the proletariat, Benito Mussolini and his fascists along with Adolf Hitler and his Nazi party forged new national communities. These political innovations unsettled many Europeans and much of the world, contributing significantly to the anxiety of the age. Such shifts in political thought matched in their radicalness, however strangely, the vast alterations taking place in the intellectual and cultural realms of European society after the Great War.

PROBING CULTURAL FRONTIERS

The Great War discredited established social and political institutions and long-held beliefs about the superiority of European society. Writers, poets, theologians, and other intellectuals lamented the decline and imminent death of their society. While some wrote obituaries, however, others embarked on bold new cultural paths that established the main tendencies of contemporary thought and taste. Most of these cultural innovators began their work before the war, but it was in the two decades following the war that a revolution in science, psychology, art, and architecture attained its fullest development and potency.

The discoveries of physicists undermined the Newtonian universe, in which a set of inexorable natural laws governed events, with a new and disturbing cosmos. Uncertainty governed this strange universe, which lacked objective reality. Equally discomforting were the insights of psychoanalysis, which suggested that human behavior was fundamentally irrational. Disquieting trends in the arts and architecture paralleled the developments in science and psychology. Especially in painting, an aversion to realism and a pronounced preference for abstraction heralded the arrival of new aesthetic standards.

Postwar Pessimism

"You are all a lost generation," noted Gertrude Stein (1874–1946) to her fellow American writer Ernest Hemingway (1899–1961). Stein had given a label to the group of American intellectuals and literati who congregated in Paris in the postwar years. This "lost generation" expressed in poetry and fiction the malaise and disillusion that characterized U.S. and European thought after the Great War. The vast majority of European intellectuals rallied enthusiastically to the war in 1914, viewing it as a splendid adventure. The brutal realities of industrialized warfare left no room for heroes, however, and most of these young artists and intellectuals quickly became disillusioned. During the 1920s they spat out their revulsion in a host of war novels such as Ernest Hemingway's *A Farewell to Arms* (1929) and Erich Maria Remarque's *All Quiet on the Western Front* (1929), works overflowing with images of meaningless death and suffering.

Postwar writers lamented the decline of Western society. A retired German schoolteacher named Oswald Spengler (1880–1936) made headlines when he published *The Decline of the West* (1918–1922). In this work, which might have been seen as an obituary of civilization, Spengler proposed that all societies pass through a life cycle of growth and decay comparable to the biological cycle of living organisms. His analysis of the history of western Europe led him to conclude that European society had entered the final stage of its existence. All that remained was irreversible decline, marked by imperialism and warfare. Spengler's gloomy predictions provided a kind of comfort to those who sought to rationalize their postwar despair, as did his conviction that all the nations of the world were equally doomed. In England the shock of war caused the historian Arnold J. Toynbee (1889–1975) to begin his twelve-volume classic, *A Study of History* (1934–1961), that sought to discover how societies develop through time. In this monumental comparative study, Toynbee analyzes the genesis, growth, and disintegration of twenty-six societies.

Religious Uncertainty Theologians joined the chorus of despair. In 1919 Karl Barth (1886–1968), widely recognized as one of the most notable Christian theologians, published a religious bombshell entitled *Epistle to the Romans*. In his work Barth sharply attacked the liberal Christian theology that embraced the idea of progress, that is, the tendency of European thinkers to believe in limitless improvement as the realization of God's purpose. Other Christians joined the fray, reminding a generation of optimists that Christ's kingdom is not of this world. The Augustinian, Lutheran, and Calvinist message of original sin—the depravity of human nature—fell on receptive ears as many Christians refused to accept the idea that contemporary human society was in any way a realization of God's purpose. The Russian orthodox thinker Niokolai Berdiaev (1874–1948) summed up these sentiments: "Man's historical experience has been one of steady failure, and there are no grounds for supposing it will be ever anything else."

Attacks on Progress The Great War destroyed long-cherished beliefs such as belief in the universality of human progress. Many idols of nineteenth-century progress came under attack, especially science and technology. The scientists' dream of leading humanity to a beneficial conquest of nature seemed to have gone awry, because scientists had spent the war making poisonous gas and high explosives. Democracy was another fallen idol. The idea that people should have a voice in selecting the leaders of their government enjoyed widespread support in European societies. By the early twentieth century, the removal of property and educational restrictions on the right to vote resulted in universal male suffrage in most societies. In the years following the Great War, most European governments extended the franchise to women. Those developments led to an unprecedented degree of political participation as millions of people voted in elections and referendums, but many intellectuals abhorred what they viewed as a weak political system that championed the tyranny of the average person. Because they viewed democracy as a product of decay and as lacking in positive values, many people idealized elite rule. In Germany a whole school of conservatives lamented the "rule of inferiors." Common people, too, often viewed democracy as a decaying political system because they associated it with corrupt and ineffective party politics. However, antidemocratic strains were not confined to Germany. The widely read essay "Revolt of the Masses" (1930) by the Spanish philosopher José Ortega y Gasset (1883–1955) warned readers

One of the best-known faces of the twentieth century, Albert Einstein was the symbol of the revolution in physics.

about the masses who were destined to destroy the highest achievements of Western society.

Revolutions in Physics and Psychology

The postwar decade witnessed a revolution in physics that transformed the character of science. Albert Einstein (1879–1955) struck the first blow with his theory of special relativity (1905), showing that there is no single spatial and chronological framework in the universe. According to the theory, it no longer made sense to speak of space and time as absolutes, because the measurement of those two categories always varies with the motion of the observer. That is, space and time are relative to the person measuring them. To the layperson such notions—usually expressed in incomprehensible mathematical formulas—suggested that science had reached the limits of what could be known with certainty. A commonsense universe had vanished, to be replaced by a radically new one in which reality or truth was merely a set of mental constructs.

The Uncertainty Principle More disquieting even than Einstein's discoveries was the theory formulated by Werner Heisenberg (1901–1976), who in 1927 published a paper, "About the Quantum-Theoretical Reinterpretation of Kinetic and Mechanical Relationships," which established the "uncertainty principle." According to Heisenberg, it is impossible to specify simultaneously the position and the velocity of a subatomic particle. The more accurately one determines the position of an electron, the less precisely one can determine its velocity, and vice versa. In essence, scientists cannot observe the behavior of electrons objectively, because the act of observation interferes with them. The indeterminacy of the atomic universe demanded that the exact calculations of classical physics be replaced by probability calculations.

It quickly became evident that the uncertainty principle had important implications beyond physics. It also carried broader philosophical ramifications. Heisenberg's theory called into question established notions of truth and violated the fundamental law of cause and effect. Likewise, objectivity as it was understood was no longer a valid concept, because

A striking painted portrait of Sigmund Freud. Freud formulated psychoanalysis, a theory and clinical practice to explore the mind and, by extension, its creations, such as literature, religion, art, and history.

Paul Gauguin, *Nafea Fan Ipoipo* ("When are you to be married?"; 1892). Gauguin sought the spiritual meaning for his art in the islands of the South Pacific. This painting of two Tahitian women revealed his debt to impressionism, but also showed his innovations: strong outlines, flat colors, and flattened forms.

the observer was always part of the process under observation. Accordingly, any observer—an anthropologist studying another society, for instance—had to be alert to the fact that his or her very presence became an integral part of the study.

Freud's Psychoanalytic Theory Equally unsettling as the advances in physics were developments in psychology that challenged established concepts of morality and values. In an indeterminate universe governed by relativity, the one remaining fixed point was the human psyche, but the insights of Sigmund Freud (1856–1939) proved disturbing as well. Beginning in 1896, the medical doctor from Vienna embarked on research that focused on psychological rather than physiological explanations of mental disorders. Through his clinical observations of patients, Freud identified a conflict between conscious and unconscious mental processes that lay at the root of neurotic behavior. That conflict, moreover, suggested to him the existence of a repressive mechanism that keeps painful memories or threatening events away from the conscious mind. Freud believed that dreams held the key to the deepest recesses of the human psyche. Using the free associations of patients to guide him in the interpretation of dreams, he identified sexual drives and fantasies as the most important source of repression. For example, Freud claimed to have discovered a so-called Oedipus complex in which male children develop an erotic attachment to their mother and hostility toward their father.

From dreams Freud analyzed literature, religion, politics, and virtually every other type of human endeavor, seeking always to identify the manifestations of the repressed conscious. He was convinced that his theory, known as *psychoanalysis,* provided the keys to understanding all human behavior. In the end, Freudian doctrines shaped the psychiatric profession and established a powerful presence in literature and the arts. During the 1920s, novelists, poets, and painters acknowledged Freud's influence as they focused on the inner world—the hidden depths of memory and emotion—of their characters. The creators of imaginative literature used Freud's bold emphasis on sexuality as a tool for the interpretation and understanding of human behavior.

Experimentation in Art and Architecture

The roots of contemporary painting go back to nineteenth-century French avant-garde artists who became preoccupied with how a subject should be painted. The common denominator among the various schools was disdain for realism and concern for freedom of expression. The aversion to visual realism was heightened by the spread of photography. When everyone could create naturalistic landscapes or portraits with a camera, it made little sense for artists to do so laboriously with paint and brush. Thus painters began to think of canvas not as a reproduction of reality but as an end in itself. The purpose of a painting was not to mirror reality but to create it.

By the beginning of the twentieth century, the possibilities inherent in this new aesthetic led to the emergence of a bewildering variety of pictorial schools, all of which promised an entirely new art. Regardless of whether they called themselves *les fauves* ("wild beasts"), expressionists, cubists, abstractionists, dadaists, or surrealists, artists generally agreed on a program "to abolish the sovereignty of appearance." Paintings no longer depicted recognizable objects from the everyday world, and beauty was expressed in pure color or shape. Some painters sought to express feelings and emotions through violent distortion of forms and the use of explosive colors; others, influenced by Freudian psychology, tried to tap the subconscious mind to communicate an inner vision or a dream.

Artistic Influences The artistic heritages of Asian, Pacific, and African societies fertilized various strains of contemporary painting. Nineteenth-century Japanese prints, for

Pablo Picasso's *Les Demoiselles d'Avignon* (1907) was the first of what would be called cubist works. This image had a profound influence on subsequent art.

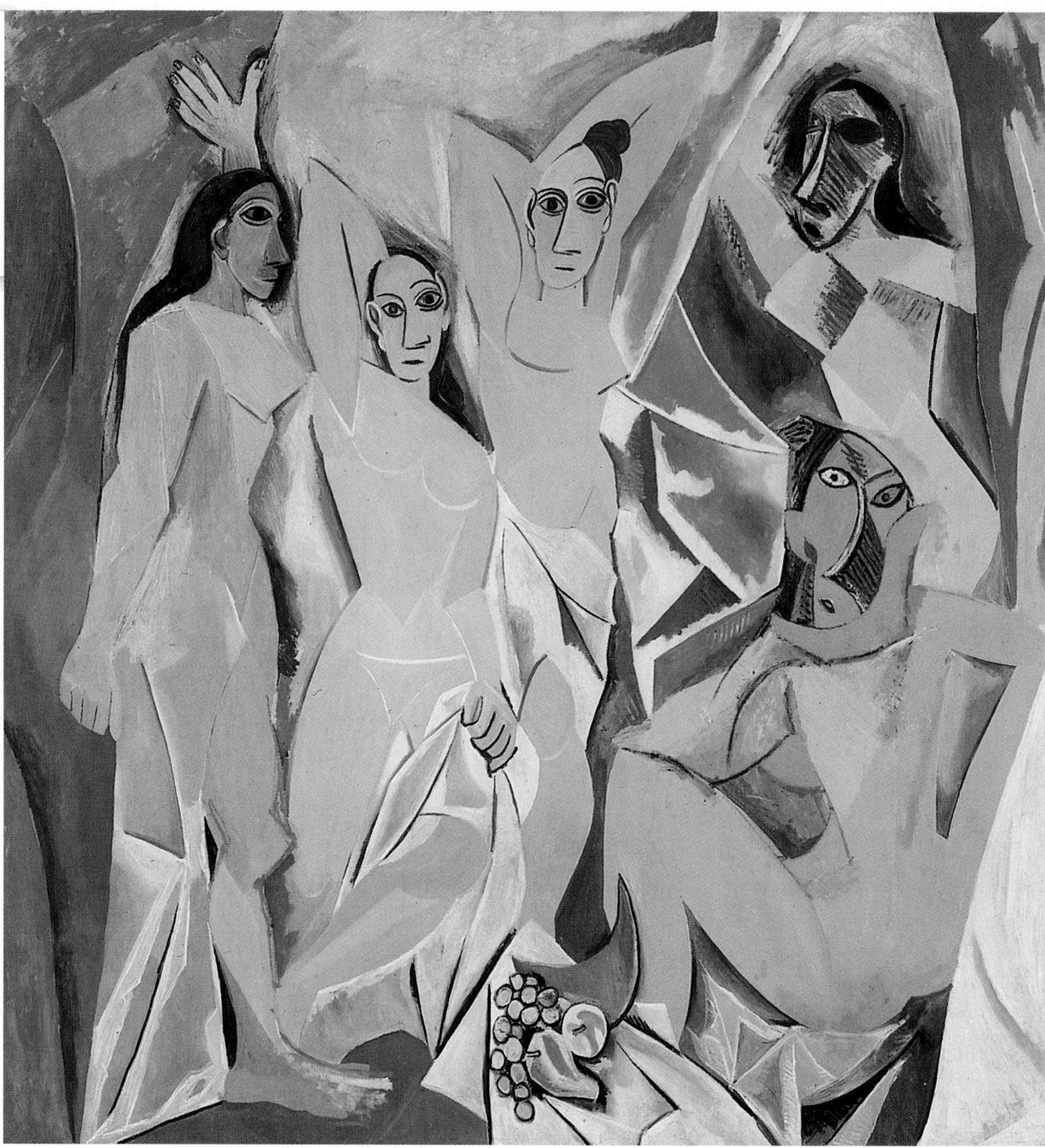

example, influenced French impressionists such as Edgar Degas (1834–1917), whose study of them led him to experiment with visual angles and asymmetrical compositions. The deliberate violation of perspective by Japanese painters and their stress on the flat, two-dimensional surface of the picture, their habit of placing figures off center, and their use of primary colors, encouraged European artists to take similar liberties with realism. In a revolt against rational society, the postimpressionist painter Paul Gauguin (1848–1903) fled to central America and Tahiti. He was inspired by the "primitive" art he found there, claiming that it held a sense of wonder that "civilized" people no longer possessed. In Germany a group of young artists known as the "Bridge" made a point of regularly visiting the local ethnographic museum to be inspired by the boldness and power of indigenous art. The early works of Pablo Picasso (1881–1973), the leading proponent of cubism, displayed the influence of African art forms.

By the third decade of the twentieth century, it was nearly impossible to generalize about the history of contemporary painting. All artists were acknowledged to have a right to their own reality, and generally accepted standards that distinguished between "good" and "bad" art disappeared.

Bauhaus During the first decades of the twentieth century, architecture underwent a revolutionary transformation as designers deliberately set out to create a completely different building style that broke with old forms and traditions. The modernistic trends in architecture coalesced with the opening of the *Bauhaus,* an institution that brought together architects, designers, and painters from several countries. Located first in Weimar and then Dessau, Germany, the Bauhaus

Designed by Walter Gropius in 1925, this building introduced the functional international style of architecture that dominated for the next half century.

was a community of innovators bent on creating a building style and interior designs that were uniquely suited to the urban and industrial landscape of the twentieth century.

The first director of the Bauhaus was Walter Gropius (1883–1969), whose theory of design became the guiding principle first of the Bauhaus and subsequently of contemporary architecture in general. To Gropius, design was functional, based on a marriage between engineering and art. The buildings Gropius designed featured simplicity of shape and extensive use of glass and always embodied the new doctrine that form must follow function. The second director of the Bauhaus, Ludwig Mies von der Rohe (1886–1969), exerted an equally profound influence on modern architecture. He experimented with steel frames around which he stretched non-load-bearing walls of glass. His designs became the basis for the ubiquitous glass-box skyscrapers that first adorned cities such as Chicago and New York and later dominated the skylines of most major cities.

The style initiated by the Bauhaus architects, the international style, gradually prevailed after 1930 because its functionalism was well suited to the construction of large apartment and office complexes. The work of the world-famous Swiss-French architect Le Corbusier (Charles Édouard Jeanneret, 1887–1965) proved the broad appeal of the new architecture. At the request of Jawaharlal Nehru (1889–1964), India's first prime minister, Le Corbusier laid out the new capital city of the Punjab, Chandigarh, and designed for it three concrete government buildings. Governments and businesses eagerly embraced the new style, but the public never quite warmed to the glass box, a cold and impersonal structure that seemed to overwhelm the individual.

GLOBAL DEPRESSION

After the horrors and debilitating upheavals of the Great War, much of the world yearned for a return to normality and prosperity. By the early 1920s the efforts of governments and businesses to rebuild damaged economies seemed to bear fruit. Prosperity, however, was short-lived. In 1929 the world plunged into economic depression that was so long-lasting, so severe, and so global that it has become known as the Great Depression. The old capitalist system of trade and finance collapsed, and until a new system took its place after 1945, a return to worldwide prosperity could not occur.

The Great Depression

By the middle of the 1920s, some semblance of economic normality had returned, and most countries seemed on the way to economic recovery. Industrial productivity had returned to prewar levels as businesses repaired the damages the war had inflicted on industrial plants, equipment, and transportation facilities. But that prosperity was fragile, perhaps false, and many serious problems and dislocations remained in the international economy.

Economic Problems The economic recovery and well-being of Europe, for example, were tied to a tangled financial system that involved war debts among the Allies, reparations paid by Germany and Austria, and the flow of U.S. funds to Europe. In essence, the governments of Austria and Germany relied on U.S. loans and investment capital to finance reparation payments to France and England. The French and British governments, in turn, depended on those reparation payments to pay off loans taken out in the United States during the Great War. By the summer of 1928, U.S. lenders and investors started to withdraw capital from Europe, placing an intolerable strain on the financial system.

There were other problems as well. Improvements in industrial processes reduced worldwide demand for certain raw materials, causing an increase in supplies and a drop in prices. Technological advances in the production of automobile tires, for instance, permitted the use of reclaimed rubber. The resulting glut of natural rubber had devastating consequences for the economies of the Dutch East Indies, Ceylon, and Malaysia, which relied on the export of rubber. Similarly, the increased use of oil undermined the coal industry, the emergence of synthetics hurt the cotton industry, and the growing adoption of artificial nitrogen virtually ruined the nitrate industry of Chile.

One of the nagging weaknesses of the global economy in the 1920s was the depressed state of agriculture, the result of overproduction and falling prices. During the Great War, when Europe's agricultural output declined significantly, farmers in the United States, Canada, Argentina, and Australia expanded their production. At the end of the war, European farmers resumed their agricultural activity, thereby contributing to worldwide surpluses. Above-average global harvests between 1925 and 1929 aggravated the situation. As production increased, demand declined, and prices collapsed throughout the world. By 1929 the price of a bushel of wheat was at its lowest level in 400 years, and farmers everywhere became impoverished. The reduced income of farm families contributed to high inventories of manufactured goods, which in turn caused businesses to cut back production and to dismiss workers.

The Crash of 1929 The United States enjoyed a boom after the Great War: industrial wages were high, and production and consumption increased. Many people in the United States invested their earnings and savings in speculative ventures, particularly the buying of stock on margin—putting up as little as 3 percent of a stock's price in cash and borrowing the remainder from brokers and banks or by mortgaging their homes. By October 1929, hints of a worldwide economic slowdown and warnings from experts that stock prices were overvalued prompted investors to pull out of the market. On Black Thursday (24 October), a wave of panic selling on the New York Stock Exchange caused stock prices to plummet. Investors who had overextended themselves in a frenzy of speculative stock purchases watched in agony. Thousands of people, from poor widows to industrial tycoons, lost their life savings, and by the end of the day eleven financiers had committed suicide. The crisis deepened when lenders called in loans, thereby forcing more investors to sell their securities at any price.

Economic Contraction Spreads In the wake of this financial chaos came a drastic decrease in business activity, wages, and employment. Consumer demand no longer sufficed to purchase all the goods that businesses produced, and when businesses realized that they could not sell their inventories, they responded with cutbacks in production and additional layoffs. With so many people unemployed or underemployed, demand plummeted further, causing more business failures and soaring unemployment. In 1930 the slump deepened, and by 1932 industrial production had fallen to half of its 1929 level. National income had dropped by approximately half. Forty-four percent of U.S. banks were out of business, and the deposits of millions of people had disappeared. Because much of the world's prosperity depended on the export of U.S. capital and the strength of U.S. import markets, the contraction of the U.S. economy created a ripple effect that circled the globe.

Most societies experienced economic difficulties throughout the 1930s. Although the severity of the economic contraction varied in intensity, virtually every industrialized society saw its economy shrivel. Nations that relied on exports of manufactured goods to pay for imported fuel and food—Germany and Japan in particular—suffered the most. The depression also spread unevenly to primary producing economies in Latin America, Africa, and Asia. Hardest hit were countries that depended on the export of a few primary products—agricultural goods, such as coffee, sugar, and cotton, and raw materials, such as minerals, ores, and rubber.

Industrial Economies U.S. investors, shaken by the collapse of stock prices, tried to raise money by calling in loans and liquidating investments, and Wall Street banks refused to extend short-term loans as they became due. Banking houses in Austria and Germany became vulnerable to collapse, because they had been major recipients of U.S. loans. Devastated by the loss of U.S. capital, the German economy experienced a precipitous economic slide that by 1932 resulted in 35 percent unemployment and a 50 percent decrease in industrial production. As the German economy ground to a virtual halt, the rest of Europe—which was closely integrated with the German economy—sputtered and stalled. Although Germany lost the Great War, it remained a leading economic power throughout the postwar years. Because no military engagements took place on German soil, the national economy—its natural resources, infrastructure, and productive capacity—was spared the physical destruction that seriously disrupted the economies of other lands such as France or Russia. Germany did not escape the ravages of the depression. The situation in Europe deteriorated further when businesses, desperate to raise capital by exporting goods to the United States, found that U.S. markets had virtually disappeared behind tariff walls. Foreign trade fell sharply between 1929 and 1932, causing further losses in manufacturing, employment, and per capita income. Because of its great dependence on the U.S. market, the Japanese economy felt the depression's effects almost immediately. Unemployment in export-oriented sectors of the economy skyrocketed as companies cut back on production.

In January 1932, ten thousand hunger strikers marched on Washington, D.C., seeking government relief for their misery.

Economic Nationalism The Great Depression destroyed the international financial and commercial network of the capitalist economies. As international cooperation broke down, governments turned to their own resources and practiced economic nationalism. By imposing tariff barriers, import quotas, and import prohibitions, politicians hoped to achieve a high degree of economic self-sufficiency. In an age of global interdependence, such goals remained unobtainable, and economic nationalism invariably backfired. Each new measure designed to restrict imports provoked retaliation by other nations whose interests were affected. After the U.S. Congress passed the Smoot-Hawley Tariff in 1930, which raised duties on most manufactured products to prohibitive levels, the governments of dozens of other nations immediately retaliated by raising tariffs on imports of U.S. products. The result was a sharp drop in international trade. Instead of higher levels of production and income, economic nationalism yielded the opposite. Between 1929 and 1932, world production declined by 38 percent and trade dropped by more than 66 percent.

Despair and Government Action

By 1933 unemployment in industrial societies reached thirty million, more than five times higher than in 1929. Men lost their jobs because of economic contraction, and a combination of economic trends and deliberate government policy caused women to lose theirs also. Unemployment initially affected women less directly than men because employers preferred women workers, who were paid two-thirds to three-quarters the wages of men doing the same work. But before long, governments enacted policies to reduce female employment, especially for married women. The notion that a woman's place was in the home was widespread. In 1931 a British royal commission on unemployment insurance declared that "in the case of married women as a class, industrial employment cannot be regarded as the normal condition." More candid was the French Nobel Prize–winning physician Charles Richet (1850–1935), who insisted that removing women from the workforce would solve the problem of male unemployment and increase the nation's dangerously low birthrate.

Personal Suffering The Great Depression caused enormous personal suffering. The stark, gloomy statistics documenting the failure of economies do not convey the anguish and despair of those who lost their jobs, savings, and homes, and often their dignity and hope. For millions of people the struggle for food, clothing, and shelter grew desperate. Shantytowns appeared overnight in urban areas, and breadlines stretched for blocks. Marriage, childbearing, and divorce rates declined, while suicide rates rose. The acute physical and social problems of those at the bottom of the economic ladder often magnified social divisions and class hatreds. Workers and farmers especially came to despise the wealthy, who, despite their reduced incomes, were shielded from the worst impact of the economic downturn and continued to enjoy a comfortable lifestyle. Adolescents completing their schooling faced an almost nonexistent job market.

That the Great Depression deflated economies and hope was especially noticeable in the literature of the period. Writers castigated the social and political order, calling repeatedly for a more just society. The U.S. writer John Steinbeck (1902–1968) chillingly captured the official heartlessness and the rising political anger inspired by the depression. In *The Grapes of Wrath* (1939), the Joad family, prototypical "Okies," migrated from Oklahoma to California to escape the dust bowl. In describing their journey Steinbeck commented on the U.S. government's policy of "planned scarcity," in which surplus crops were destroyed

Soup kitchens and breadlines became commonplace in the United States during the earliest, darkest years of the Great Depression. They fed millions of starving and unemployed people.

to raise prices while citizens starved. In one of the novel's most famous passages, Steinbeck portrayed the nation's rising political anguish:

> The people come with nets to fish for potatoes in the river and the guards hold them back; they come in rattling cars to get the dumped oranges, but the kerosene is sprayed. And they stand still and watch potatoes float by, listen to the screaming pigs being killed in a ditch and covered with quicklime, watch the mountains of oranges slop down to a putrefying ooze; and in the eyes of the people there is the failure; and in the eyes of the hungry there is a growing wrath. In the souls of the people the grapes of wrath are filling and growing heavy, growing heavy for the vintage.

Human faces of the Great Depression: children bathing in the Ozark Mountains, Missouri, 1940.

Economic Experimentation

Classical economic thought held that capitalism was a self-correcting system that operated best when left to its own devices. Governments responded to the economic crisis in one of two ways. Initially, most governments did nothing, hoping against all odds that the crisis would resolve itself. When the misery spawned by the depression sparked calls for action, some governments assumed more active roles, pursuing deflationary measures by balancing national budgets and curtailing public spending. In either case, rather than lifting national economies out of the doldrums, the classical prescriptions for economic ills worsened the depression's impact and intensified the plight of millions of people. Far from self-correcting, capitalism seemed to be dying. Many people called for a fundamental revision of economic thought.

sources from the past

Franklin Delano Roosevelt: Nothing to Fear

Franklin Delano Roosevelt (1882–1945) assumed the presidency of the United States on 4 March 1933, during the very depths of the Great Depression. In his inaugural address to the nation, he conveyed both the anxiousness of the times and the seemingly unquenchable optimism that carried him—and his nation—through hard times. A vastly wealthy man serving as president during a time of devastating penury, Roosevelt nonetheless gained the admiration and respect of his people because of his warm eloquence and compassion. Although he hid his condition quite successfully during his time in public, FDR had contracted polio in the 1920s and had lost the use of his legs. This "crippled" president became a metaphor for the United States' economic collapse, but also for its ability to overcome fear itself.

I am certain that my fellow Americans expect that on my induction into the Presidency I will address them with a candor and a decision which the present situation of our Nation impels. This is preeminently the time to speak the truth, the whole truth, frankly and boldly. Nor need we shrink from honestly facing conditions in our country today. This great Nation will endure as it has endured, will revive and will prosper. So, first of all, let me assert my firm belief that the only thing we have to fear is fear itself—nameless, unreasoning, unjustified terror which paralyzes needed efforts to convert retreat into advance. In every dark hour of our national life a leadership of frankness and vigor has met with that understanding and support of the people themselves which is essential to victory. I am convinced that you will again give that support to leadership in these critical days.

In such a spirit on my part and on yours we face our common difficulties. They concern, thank God, only material things. Values have shrunken to fantastic levels; taxes have risen; our ability to pay has fallen; government of all kinds is faced by serious curtailment of income; the means of exchange are frozen in the currents of trade; the withered leaves of industrial enterprise lie on every side; farmers find no markets for their produce; the savings of many years in thousands of families are gone.

More important, a host of unemployed citizens face the grim problem of existence, and an equally great number toil with little return. Only a foolish optimist can deny the dark realities of the moment. . . .

Happiness lies not in the mere possession of money; it lies in the joy of achievement, in the thrill of creative effort. The joy and moral stimulation of work no longer must be forgotten in the mad chase of evanescent profits. These dark days will be worth all they cost us if they teach us that our true destiny is not to be ministered unto but to minister to ourselves and to our fellow men.

For Further Reflection

- How does Roosevelt believe U.S. citizens can profit from the dark days of the Great Depression, and why is it that all they have to fear is fear itself?

Source: Franklin D. Roosevelt, First Inaugural Address, 4 March 1933, available at The Avalon Project at http://www.yale.edu/lawweb/avalon/president/inaug/froos1.htm.

Keynes John Maynard Keynes (1883–1946), the most influential economist of the twentieth century, offered a novel solution. His seminal work, *The General Theory of Employment, Interest, and Money* (1936), was his answer to the central problem of the depression—that millions of people who were willing to work could not find employment. To Keynes the fundamental cause of the depression was not excessive supply, but inadequate demand. Accordingly, he urged governments to play an active role and stimulate the economy by increasing the money supply, thereby lowering interest rates and encouraging investment. He also advised governments to undertake public works projects to provide jobs and redistribute incomes through tax policy, an intervention which would result in reduced unemployment and increased consumer demand, which would lead to economic revival. Such measures were necessary even if they caused governments to run deficits and maintain unbalanced budgets.

The New Deal Although Keynes's theories did not become influential with policymakers until after World War II, the administration of U.S. president Franklin Delano Roosevelt (1882–1945) applied similar ideas. Roosevelt took aggressive steps to reinflate the economy and ease the worst of the suffering caused by the depression. His proposals for dealing with the national calamity included legislation designed to prevent the collapse of the banking system, to provide jobs and farm subsidies, to give workers the right to organize and bargain collectively, to guarantee minimum wages, and to provide social security in old age. This program of sweeping economic and social reforms was called the "New Deal." Its fundamental premise, that the federal government was justified in intervening to protect the social and economic welfare of the people, represented a major shift in U.S. government policy and started a trend toward social reform legislation that continued long after the depression years. Ultimately, the

thinking about ENCOUNTERS

Poverty, People, and the State

The Great Depression radically transformed the role of government in nations as divergent as the Soviet Union and the United States, and the people had more contact with government representatives and programs than ever before. How did the Great Depression reconfigure the relationships between governments and citizens?

enormous military spending during World War II did more to end the Great Depression in the United States and elsewhere than did the specific programs of the New Deal or similar approaches.

CHALLENGES TO THE LIBERAL ORDER

Amid the gloom and despair of the Great Depression, some voices proclaimed the promise of a better tomorrow. Marxists believed that capitalist society was on its deathbed, and they had faith that a new and better system based on rule by the proletariat was being born out of the ashes of the Russian empire. The new rulers of Russia, Vladimir Ilyich Lenin and then Joseph Stalin, transformed the former tsarist empire into the world's first socialist society, the Union of Soviet Socialist Republics (1922).

Other people, uncomfortable with the abolition of private property and the "dictatorship of the proletariat," found solace in activist political movements that claimed to have an alternative formula for the reconstruction of society. Fascist movements across Europe promoted their alternatives to socialism and offered revolutionary answers to the economic, social, and political problems that seemed to defy solution by traditional liberal democratic means. Among those fascist movements, the Italian and German ones figured most prominently.

Communism in Russia

In 1917 Lenin and his fellow Bolsheviks had taken power in the name of the Russian working class, but socialist victory did not bring peace and stability to the lands of the former Russian empire. After seizing power, Lenin and his supporters had to defend the world's first dictatorship of the proletariat against numerous enemies, including dissident socialists, anti-Bolshevik officers and troops, peasant bands, and foreign military forces.

Civil War Opposition to the Bolshevik Party—by now calling itself the Russian Communist Party—erupted into a civil war that lasted from 1918 to 1920. Operating out of its new capital in Moscow, Lenin's government began a policy of crushing all opposition. The communists began the Red Terror campaign in which suspected anticommunists known as Whites were arrested, tried, and executed. The secret police killed some 200,000 opponents of the regime. In July 1918 the Bolsheviks executed Tsar Nicholas II, Empress Alexandra, their five children, and their remaining servants because they feared that the Romanov family would fall into the hands of the Whites, thereby strengthening counterrevolutionary forces. White terror was often as brutal as Red terror. The peasantry, although hostile to the communists, largely supported the Bolsheviks, fearing that a victory by the Whites would result in the return of the monarchy. However, foreign military intervention supported White resistance to the communist takeover. Russia's withdrawal from the Great War and anticommunist sentiment inflamed Russia's former allies (notably Britain, France, Japan, and the United States), who sent troops and supplies to aid White forces. Although their numbers were negligible, the foreigners' presence sometimes had the effect of bonding otherwise hostile groups to the Reds. Poorly organized and without widespread support, the Whites were defeated by the Red Army in 1920. Estimates place the number of lives lost in the civil war at ten million, with many more people dying from disease and starvation than from the fighting. The political system that emerged from the civil war bore the imprint of political oppression, which played a significant role in the later development of the Soviet state.

War Communism The new rulers of Russia had no plans to transform the economy, but in the course of the civil war they embarked on a hasty and unplanned course of nationalization, a policy known as *war communism.* After officially annulling private property, the Bolshevik government assumed control or ownership of banks, industry, and other privately held commercial properties. Landed estates and the holdings of monasteries and churches became national property, although the Bolsheviks explicitly exempted the holdings of poor peasants from confiscation. The abolition of private trade was unpopular, and when the party seized crops from peasants to feed people in the cities, the peasants drastically reduced their production. By 1920 industrial production had fallen to about one-tenth of its prewar level and agricultural output to about one-half its prewar level.

In 1921, as the Reds consolidated their military victories, Lenin faced the daunting prospect of rebuilding a society that had been at war since 1914. The workers, in whose name he had taken power, were on strike. Other problems included depopulated cities, destroyed factories, and an army that demobilized soldiers faster than the workforce could absorb them. Lenin and the party tried to take strict control of the country by crushing workers' strikes, peasant rebellions, and a sailors' revolt. Yet Lenin recognized the need to make peace with those whose skills would rekindle industrial production. Faced with economic paralysis, in the spring of 1921 he decided on a radical reversal of war communism.

The New Economic Policy Demonstrating his pragmatism and willingness to compromise, Lenin implemented the New Economic Policy (NEP), which temporarily restored the market economy and some private enterprise in Russia. Large industries, banks, and transportation and communications facilities remained under state control, but the government returned small-scale industries (those with fewer than twenty workers) to private ownership. The government also allowed peasants to sell their surpluses at free market prices. Other features of the NEP included a vigorous program of electrification and the establishment of technical schools to train technicians and engineers. Lenin did not live to see the success of the NEP. After suffering three paralytic strokes, he died in 1924. His death was followed by a bitter struggle for power among the Bolshevik leaders.

Joseph Stalin Many old Bolsheviks continued to argue for a permanent or continuous revolution, asserting that socialism in Russia would fail if socialism did not move from a national to an international stage. Others in the Politburo, the central governing body of the Communist Party, favored establishing socialism in one country alone, thus repudiating the role of the Union of Soviet Socialist Republics as torchbearer of worldwide socialist revolution. Joseph Stalin (1879–1953), who served in the unglamorous bureaucratic position of general secretary, promoted the idea of socialism in one country. A Georgian by birth, an Orthodox seminarian by training, and a Russian nationalist by conviction, Stalin indicated his unified resolve to gain power in his adopted surname, which meant "man of steel." Speaking Russian with a heavy accent, he was an intellectual misfit among the Bolshevik elite. However, by 1928, Stalin lived up to his name and completely triumphed over his rivals in the party, clearing the way for an unchallenged dictatorship of the Soviet Union.

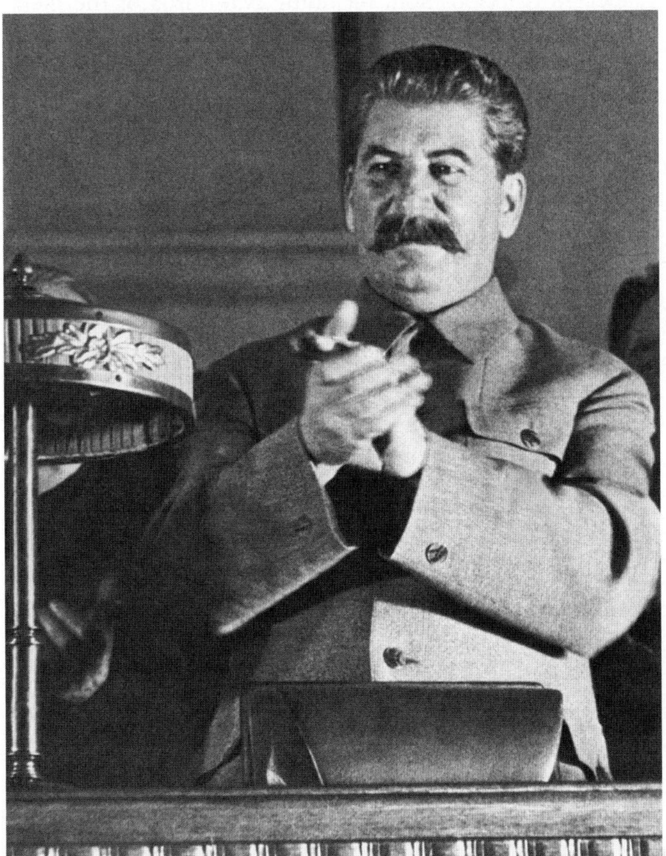

Joseph Stalin at a Soviet congress in 1936. By 1928 Stalin had prevailed over his opponents to become the dictator of the Soviet Union, a position he held until his death in 1953.

First Five-Year Plan Stalin decided to replace Lenin's NEP with an ambitious plan for rapid economic development known as the First Five-Year Plan. The basic aims of this and subsequent five-year plans, first implemented in 1929, were to transform the Soviet Union from a predominantly agricultural country to a leading industrial power. The First Five-Year Plan set targets for increased productivity in all spheres of the economy but emphasized heavy industry—especially steel and machinery—at the expense of consumer goods. Through Gosplan, the central state planning agency, Stalin and the party attempted to coordinate resources and the labor force on an unprecedented scale. As the rest of the world teetered on the edge of economic collapse, this blueprint for maximum centralization of the entire national economy offered a bold alternative to market capitalism. Stalin repeatedly stressed the urgency of this monumental endeavor, telling his people, "We are 50 to 100 years behind the advanced countries. Either we do it, or we shall go under."

Collectivization of Agriculture Integral to the drive for industrialization was the collectivization of agriculture. The Soviet state expropriated privately owned land to create collective or cooperative farm units whose profits were shared by all farmers. The logic of communist ideology demanded the abolition of private property and market choices, but more practical considerations also played a role. Stalin and his regime viewed collectivization as a means of increasing the efficiency of agricultural production and ensuring that industrial workers would be fed. Collectivization was enforced most ruthlessly against *kulaks*—relatively wealthy peasants who had risen to prosperity during the NEP but accounted for only 3 to 5 percent of the peasantry.

In some places, outraged peasants reacted to the government's program by slaughtering their livestock and burning their crops. Millions of farmers left the land and migrated to cities in search of work, thereby further taxing the limited supplies of housing, food, and utilities. Unable to meet production quotas, peasants often starved to death on the land

Men and women drive tractors out of one of the Soviet Union's Machine Tractor Stations to work fields where mechanization had been a rare sight.

they once owned. When Stalin called a halt to collectivization in 1931, proclaiming the policymakers "dizzy with success," half the farms in the Soviet Union had been collectivized. Estimates of the number of peasant lives lost have fluctuated wildly, but even the most cautious place it at three million.

The First Five-Year Plan set unrealistically high production targets. Even so, the Soviet leadership proclaimed success after only four years. The Soviet Union industrialized under Stalin even though the emphasis on building heavy industry first and consumer industries later meant that citizens postponed the gratifications of industrialization. Before refrigerators, radios, or automobiles became available, the government constructed steelworks and hydroelectric plants. The scarcity or nonexistence of consumer goods was to some degree balanced by full employment, low-cost utilities, and—when available—cheap housing and food. Set against the collapse of the U.S. stock market and the depression-ridden capitalist world, the ability of a centrally planned economy to create more jobs than workers could fill made it appear an attractive alternative.

The Great Purge Nevertheless, the results of Stalin's First Five-Year Plan generated controversy as the Communist Party prepared for its seventeenth congress in 1934, the self-proclaimed "Congress of Victors." The disaster of collectivization and the ruthlessness with which it was carried out had raised doubts about Stalin's administration. Although themes of unity and reconciliation prevailed, Stalin learned of a plan to bring more pluralism back into leadership. The Congress of Victors became the "Congress of Victims" as Stalin incited a civil war within the party that was climaxed by highly publicized trials of former Bolshevik elites for treason and by a purge of two-thirds of the delegates. Between 1935 and 1938 Stalin removed from posts of authority all persons suspected of opposition, including two-thirds of the members of the 1934 Central Committee and more than one-half of the army's high-ranking officers. The victims faced execution or long-term suffering in labor camps. In 1939 eight million Soviet citizens were in labor camps, and three million were dead as a result of the "cleansing," as Stalin's supporters termed this process.

The outside world watched the events unfolding within the Soviet Union with a mixture of contempt, fear, and admiration. Most observers recognized that the political and social upheavals that transformed the former Russian empire were of worldwide importance. The establishment of the world's first dictatorship of the proletariat challenged the values and institutions of liberal society everywhere and seemed to demonstrate the viability of communism as a social and political system.

The Fascist Alternative

While socialism was transforming the former Russian empire, another political force swept across Europe after the Great War. Fascism, a political movement and ideology that sought to create a new type of society, developed as a reaction against liberal democracy and the spread of socialism and communism. The term *fascism* derives from the *fasces,* an ancient Roman symbol of punitive authority consisting of a bundle of wooden rods strapped together around an axe. In 1919 Benito Mussolini adopted this symbol for the Italian Fascist movement that governed Italy from 1922 to 1943. Movements comparable to Italian fascism subsequently developed and sometimes dominated political life in many European societies, most notably in Germany in the guise of National Socialism (Nazism). Although fascism enjoyed

sources from the past

Goals and Achievements of the First Five-Year Plan

In the aftermath of war, revolution, and civil strife, Vladimir Lenin in 1921 adopted the New Economic Policy (NEP) to prevent the collapse of the Russian economy. In the main, the NEP was successful, but it rankled Marxist purists because it permitted the return of a limited form of capitalism. Lenin's successor, Joseph Stalin, was determined to build "socialism in one country" by replacing the NEP with a planned economy, whereby a centralized bureaucracy guided and regulated production. To that end, Stalin launched a series of Five-Year Plans designed to transform the Soviet Union into a modern, powerful state. In the following report, delivered to the Central Committee of the Communist Party of the Soviet Union in January 1933, Stalin outlined the goals and the achievements of the First Five-Year Plan.

The fundamental task of the five-year plan was to convert the U.S.S.R. from an agrarian and weak country, dependent upon the caprices of the capitalist countries, into an industrial and powerful country, fully self-reliant and independent of the caprices of world capitalism.

The fundamental task of the five-year plan was, in converting the U.S.S.R. into an industrial country, to completely oust the capitalist elements, to widen the front of socialist forms of economy, and to create the economic basis for the abolition of classes in the U.S.S.R., for the building of a socialist society.

The fundamental task of the five-year plan was to transfer small and scattered agriculture on to the lines of large-scale collective farming, so as to ensure the economic basis of socialism in the countryside and thus to eliminate the possibility of the restoration of capitalism in the U.S.S.R.

Finally, the task of the five-year plan was to create all the necessary technical and economic prerequisites for increasing to the utmost the defensive capacity of the country, enabling it to organize determined resistance to any attempt at military intervention from abroad, to any attempt at military attack from abroad.

What are the results of the five-year plan in four years in the sphere of industry?

> We did not have an iron and steel industry, the basis for the industrialization of the country. Now we have one.
>
> We did not have a tractor industry. Now we have one.
>
> We did not have an automobile industry. Now we have one.
>
> We did not have a machine-tool industry. Now we have one.
>
> We did not have a big and modern chemical industry. Now we have one.
>
> We did not have a real and big industry for the production of modern agricultural machinery. Now we have one.
>
> We did not have an aircraft industry. Now we have one.
>
> In output of electric power we were last on the list. Now we rank among the first.
>
> In output of oil products and coal we were last on the list. Now we rank among the first.
>
> And as a result of all this the capitalist elements have been completely and irrevocably ousted from industry, and socialist industry has become the sole form of industry in the U.S.S.R.

Let us pass to the question of the results of the five-year plan in four years in the sphere of agriculture. The Party has succeeded in the course of some three years in organizing more than 200,000 collective farms and about 5,000 state farms devoted to grain growing and livestock raising, and at the same time it has succeeded during four years in expanding the crop area by 21 million hectares. The Party has succeeded in getting more than 60 per cent of the peasant farms to unite into collective farms, embracing more than 70 per cent of all the land cultivated by peasants; this means that we have fulfilled the five-year plan three times over. The Party has succeeded in converting the U.S.S.R. from a country of small-peasant farming into a country of the largest-scale agriculture in the world. Do not all these facts testify to the superiority of the Soviet system of agriculture over the capitalist system?

Finally, as a result of all this the Soviet Union has been converted from a weak country, unprepared for defense, into a country mighty in defense, a country prepared for every contingency, a country capable of producing on a mass scale all modern means of defense and of equipping its army with them in the event of an attack from abroad.

For Further Reflection

- What were the fundamental aims and achievements of the First Five-Year Plan? What benefits, if any, did the peoples of the Soviet Union derive from this economic experiment in a planned economy?

Source: J. V. Stalin. "The Results of the First Five-Year Plan. Report Delivered at the Joint Plenum of the Central Committee and the Central Control Commission of the C.P.S.U.(B.), January 7, 1933." From J. V. Stalin, *Problems of Leninism.* Peking: Foreign Languages Press, 1976, pp. 578–630.

thinking about **TRADITIONS**

Challenges to the Liberal Order
In the years following the Great War, new political ideologies emerged in European societies. What were those new ideologies, and how did they overturn traditional ideals of political democracy and capitalism?

widespread popularity in many European countries, it rarely threatened the political order and, with the exception of Italy and Germany, never overthrew a parliamentary system. Political and economic frustrations made fertile ground for fascist appeals outside Europe, and potential fascist movements sprang up during the 1930s in Japan, China, and South Africa; in Latin American societies such as Brazil and Argentina; and in several Arab lands. Nevertheless, that potential for fascism never reproduced the major characteristics of European fascism, and fascism remained basically a European phenomenon of the era between the two world wars.

Defining Fascism During the 1920s and 1930s, fascism attracted millions of followers and proved especially attractive to middle classes and rural populations. These groups became radicalized by economic and social crises and were especially fearful of class conflict and the perceived threat from the political left. Fascism also proved attractive to nationalists of all classes, who denounced their governments for failing to realize the glorious objectives for which they had fought during the Great War. Asserting that society faced a profound crisis, fascists sought to create a new national community, which they defined either as a nation-state or as a unique ethnic or racial group. As part of their quest, fascist movements commonly dedicated themselves to the revival of allegedly lost national traditions and, hence, differed widely. Nevertheless, most fascist movements shared certain common features, such as the veneration of the state, a devotion to a strong leader, and an emphasis on ultranationalism, ethnocentrism, and militarism.

Fascist ideology consistently invoked the primacy of the state, which stood at the center of the nation's life and history and which demanded the subordination of the individual to the service of the state. Strong and often charismatic leaders, such as Benito Mussolini in Italy or Adolf Hitler in Germany, embodied the state and claimed indisputable authority. Consequently, fascists were hostile to liberal democracy, its devotion to individualism, and its institutions, which they viewed as weak and decadent. Fascism was also extremely hostile to class-based visions of the future promoted by socialism and communism. Fascist movements emphasized chauvinism (a belligerent form of nationalism) and xenophobia (a fear of foreign people), which they frequently linked to an exaggerated ethnocentrism. Some fascist leaders, accordingly, viewed national boundaries as artificial restraints limiting their union with ethnic or racial comrades living in other states. The typical fascist state embraced *militarism,* a belief in the rigors and virtues of military life as an individual and national ideal. In practice, militarism meant that fascist regimes maintained large and expensive military establishments, tried to organize much of public life along military lines, and generally showed a fondness for uniforms, parades, and monumental architecture.

Italian Fascism

The first fascist movement grew up in Italy after the Great War. Conditions conducive to the rise of fascism included a widespread disillusionment with uninspired political leadership and ineffective government, extensive economic turmoil and social discontent, and a growing fear of socialism. In addition, there was vast disappointment over Italy's skimpy territorial spoils from the peace settlement after the Great War.

Italian dictator Benito Mussolini strikes a dramatic pose on horseback in 1940. Such images of Mussolini and Adolf Hitler (see page 807) testify to the importance that the fascist leaders placed on propaganda.

A 1924 painting of Hitler as a knight in shining armor, as the standard-bearer for National Socialism, became the state-sanctioned Hitler portrait for 1938; reproductions in poster and postcard form proved very popular.

Benito Mussolini The guiding force behind Italian fascism was Benito Mussolini, a former socialist and, from 1912 to 1914, editor of Italy's leading socialist daily *Avanti!* ("Forward!"). In 1914 he founded his own newspaper, *Il Popolo d'Italia* ("The People of Italy"), which encouraged Italian entry into the Great War. Mussolini was convinced that the war represented a turning point for the nation. The soldiers returning from the front, he argued, would spearhead the thorough transformation of Italian society and create a new type of state. After the Great War, the one-time socialist advanced a political program that emphasized virulent nationalism, demanded repression of socialists, and called for a strong political leader. In 1919 he established the *Fasci Italiani di Combattimento* (Italian Combat Veteran League).

Mussolini's movement gained widespread support after 1920, and by 1921 his league managed to elect thirty-five fascists to the Italian parliament. Much of the newly found public support resulted from the effective use of violence against socialists by fascist armed squads known as Blackshirts. The Italian socialist party had organized militant strikes throughout Italy's northern industrial cities, causing considerable chaos. By early 1921 Italy was in a state of incipient civil war. In 1922, Mussolini and his followers decided the time was ripe for a fascist seizure of power, and on 28 October, they staged a march on Rome. While Mussolini stayed safely in Milan awaiting the outcome of events, thousands of his blackshirted troops converged on Rome. Rather than calling on the military to oppose the fascist threat, King Victor Emmanuel III hastily asked Mussolini on 29 October to become prime minister and form a new government. Mussolini inaugurated a fascist regime in 1922.

The Fascist State Between 1925 and 1931, Italy's fascists consolidated their power through a series of laws that provided the legal basis for the nation's transformation into a one-party dictatorship. In 1926 Mussolini seized total power as dictator and subsequently ruled Italy as *Il Duce* ("the leader"). The regime moved quickly to eliminate all other political parties, curb freedom of the press, and outlaw free speech and association. A Special Tribunal for the Defense of the State, supervised by military officers, silenced political dissent. Marked as antifascist subversives, thousands of Italians found themselves imprisoned or exiled on remote islands, and some faced capital punishment. Allying himself and his movement with business and landlord interests, *Il Duce* also crushed labor unions and prohibited strikes. In an effort to harmonize the interests of workers, employers, and the state, the regime tried to establish a corporatist order. This order was based on the vague fascist concept of corporatism, which viewed society as an organic entity through which the different interests in society came under the control of the state. Thus, in theory, a National Council of Corporations settled labor disputes and supervised wage settlements; but, in reality, this scheme was little more than a propaganda effort. In 1932, on the tenth anniversary of the fascist seizure of power, Mussolini felt confident enough to announce "that the twentieth century will be a century of fascism, the century of Italian power."

Racism and anti-Semitism were never prominent components of Italian fascism, but in 1938 the government suddenly issued anti-Semitic laws that labeled Jews unpatriotic, excluded them from government employment, and prohibited all marriages between Jews and so-called Aryans. This development may have been occasioned by Mussolini's newfound friendship with fellow dictator Adolf Hitler. In 1936 Mussolini told his followers that from now on, world history would revolve around a Rome-Berlin Axis. In May 1939 the leaders of fascist Italy and Nazi Germany formalized their political, military, and ideological alliance by signing a ten-year Pact of Steel. This Pact of Steel illustrated the strong links between the Italian and German variants of fascism.

German National Socialism

Hitler and the Nazi Party

After his postwar political awakening, Adolf Hitler came into contact with an obscure political party sympathetic to his ideas. In 1921 he became chairman of the party now known as the National Socialist German Workers' Party. National Socialism (the Nazi movement) made its first major appearance in 1923 when party members and Hitler attempted to overthrow the democratic Weimar Republic that had replaced the German empire in 1919. The revolt quickly fizzled under the gunfire of police units; Hitler was jailed, and the Nazi movement and its leader descended into obscurity. When Hitler emerged from prison in 1924, he resolved to use new tactics. Recognizing the futility of armed insurrection, he reorganized his movement and launched it on a "path of legality." Hitler and his followers were determined to gain power legally through the ballot box and, once successful, to discard the very instrument of their success.

The Struggle for Power

National Socialism made rapid gains after 1929 because it had broad appeal. Hitler attracted disillusioned people who felt alienated from society and frightened by the specter of socialist revolution. A growing number of people blamed the young German democracy for Germany's misfortunes: a humiliating peace treaty—the Treaty of Versailles—that identified Germany as responsible for the Great War and assigned reparation payments to the Allies; the hyperinflation of the early 1920s that wiped out the savings of the middle class; the suffering brought on by the Great Depression; and the seemingly unending and bitter infighting among the nation's major political parties. Adolf Hitler promised an end to all those misfortunes by creating a new order that would lead to greatness for Germany. By stressing racial doctrines, particularly anti-Semitism, the Nazis added a unique and frightening twist to their ideology. Although the Nazis avoided class divisions by recruiting followers from all strata of society, National Socialism in the main appealed to the members of the lower-middle classes: ruined shopkeepers and artisans, impoverished farmers, discharged white-collar workers, and disenchanted students.

The impact of the Great Depression and political infighting led to bloody street battles, shaking the foundations of Germany's fragile young democracy. The leaders of the nation's democratic and liberal parties groped for solutions to mounting unemployment but were hindered by lack of consensus and the public's loss of faith in the democratic system. The electorate became radicalized. Fewer and fewer Germans were willing to defend a parliamentary system they considered ineffective and corrupt. Between 1930 and 1932 the Nazi party became the largest party in parliament, and the reactionary and feeble president, Paul von Hindenburg (1847–1934), decided to offer Hitler the chancellorship. Promising to gain a majority in the next elections, Hitler lost little time in transforming the dying republic into a single-party dictatorship. He promised a German *Reich,* or empire, that would endure for a thousand years.

Consolidation of Power

Under the guise of a state of national emergency, the Nazis used all available means to impose their rule. They began by eliminating all working-class and liberal opposition. The Nazis suppressed the German communist and socialist parties and abrogated virtually all constitutional and civil rights. Subsequently, Hitler and his government outlawed all other political parties, made it a crime to create a new party, and made the National Socialist Party the only legal party. Between 1933 and 1935 the regime replaced Germany's federal structure with a highly centralized state that eliminated the autonomy previously exercised by state and municipal governments. The National Socialist state then guided the destruction of trade unions and the elimination of collective bargaining, subsequently prohibiting strikes and lockouts. The Nazis also purged the judiciary and the civil service, took control of all police forces, and removed enemies of the regime—both real and imagined—through incarceration or murder.

The Racial State

Once securely in power, the Nazi regime translated racist ideology, especially the notions of racial superiority and racial purity, into practice. The leaders of the Third Reich pursued the creation of a race-based national community by introducing eugenic measures designed to improve both the quantity and the quality of the German "race." Implicit in this racial remodeling was the conviction that there was no room for the "racially inferior" or for "biological outsiders."

Women and Race

Alarmed by declining birthrates, the Nazis launched a campaign to increase births of "racially valuable" children. This battle against the empty cradle meshed agreeably with Nazi ideology, which relegated women primarily to the role of wife and mother. Through tax credits, special child allowances, and marriage loans,

"Mother and Child" was the slogan on this poster, idealizing and encouraging motherhood. The background conveys the Nazi predilection for the wholesome country life, a dream that clashed with the urban reality of German society.

the authorities tried to encourage marriage and, they hoped, procreation among young people. Legal experts rewrote divorce laws so that a husband could get a divorce decree solely on the ground that he considered his wife sterile. At the same time, the regime outlawed abortions, closed birth control centers, restricted birth control devices, and made it difficult to obtain information about family planning. The Nazis also became enamored with a relatively inexpensive form of propaganda: pronatalist (to increase births) propaganda. They set in motion a veritable cult of motherhood. Annually on 12 August—the birth date of Hitler's mother—women who bore many children received the Honor Cross of the German Mother in three classes: bronze for those with more than four children, silver for those with more than six, and gold for those with more than eight. By August 1939 three million women carried this prestigious award, which many Germans cynically called the "rabbit decoration." In the long term, however, any efforts by the Nazis to increase the fecundity of German women failed, and the birthrate remained below replacement level. German families were unwilling to change their reproductive preferences for fewer children.

Nazi Eugenics The quantity of offspring was not the only concern of the new rulers, who were obsessed with quality. Starting in 1933, the regime initiated a compulsory sterilization program for men and women whom the regime had identified as having "hereditarily determined" sicknesses, including schizophrenia, feeblemindedness, manic depression, hereditary blindness, hereditary deafness, chronic alcoholism, and serious physical deformities. Between 1934 and 1939 more than thirty thousand men and women underwent compulsory sterilization. Beginning in 1935 the government also sanctioned abortions—otherwise illegal in Germany—of the "hereditary ill" and "racial aliens." The mania for racial health culminated in a state-sponsored euthanasia program that was responsible for the murder of approximately two hundred thousand women, men, and children. Between 1939 and 1945 the Nazis systematically killed—by gassing, lethal injections, or starvation—those people judged useless to society, especially the physically and mentally handicapped. Nazi eugenics measures served as a precursor to the wholesale extermination of peoples classified as racial inferiors, such as gypsies and Jews.

Anti-Semitism Anti-Semitism, or prejudice against Jews, was a key element in the designs to achieve a new racial order and became the hallmark of National Socialist rule. Immediately after coming to power in 1933, the Nazis initiated systematic measures to suppress Germany's Jewish population. Although Nazi anti-Semitism was based on biological racial theories dating to the nineteenth century, government

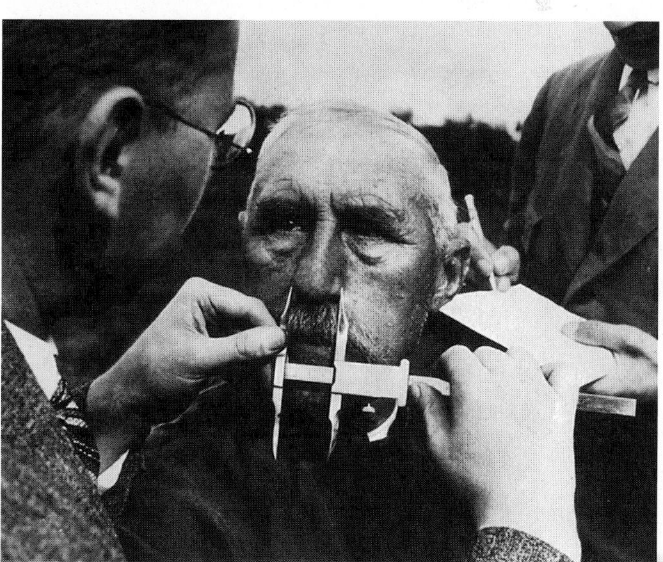

A Nazi "racial expert" uses a caliper to measure the racial purity of a German.

authorities used religious descent to determine who was a Jew. A flood of discriminatory laws and directives designed to humiliate, impoverish, and segregate Jews from the rest of society followed. In 1935 the notorious Nuremberg Laws deprived German Jews of their citizenship and prohibited marriage and sexual intercourse between Jews and other Germans. The Nazi party, in cooperation with government agencies, banks, and businesses, took steps to eliminate Jews from economic life and expropriate their wealth. Jewish civil servants lost their jobs, and Jewish lawyers and doctors lost their gentile, or non-Jewish, clients. Party authorities also supervised the liquidation of Jewish-owned businesses or argued for their purchase—at much less than their true value—by companies owned or operated by gentiles.

The official goal of the Nazi regime was Jewish emigration. Throughout the 1930s thousands of Jews left Germany, depriving the nation of many of its leading intellectuals, scientists, and artists. The exodus gained urgency after what came to be known as *Kristallnacht* ("the night of broken glass"). During the night of 9–10 November 1938, the Nazis arranged for the destruction of thousands of Jewish stores, the burning of most synagogues, and the murder of more than one hundred Jews throughout Germany and Austria. This *pogrom* (Yiddish for "devastation") was a signal that the position of Jews in Hitler's Reich was about to deteriorate dramatically. Although they had difficulty finding refuge, approximately 250,000 Jews left Germany by 1938. Those staying behind, especially the poor and the elderly, contemplated an uncertain destiny.

inperspective

In the decades after the Great War, European intellectuals questioned and challenged established traditions. While scientists and social thinkers conceived new theories that reshaped human knowledge and perceptions, artists forged a contemporary aesthetic. In an age of global interdependence, the U.S. stock market crash of 1929 ushered in a period of prolonged economic contraction and social misery that engulfed much of the world. As most of the industrialized world reeled under the impact of the Depression, the leadership of the Soviet Union embarked on a state-sponsored program of rapid industrialization. Though causing widespread human suffering, a series of five-year plans transformed the Soviet Union into a major industrial and military power.

Italians under the leadership of Mussolini rebuilt their state through fascist policies and imperial expansion. In Germany the effects of the Great Depression paved the way for the establishment of the Nazi state, which was based on the principle of racial inequality. Although many peoples suffered under the racist regime, Jews were the principal victims. Adolf Hitler's mission in life, envisioned in the wake of the Great War, was coming to a spectacular conclusion that culminated in another world war. That war brought both the fulfillment and the destruction of the goals and dreams he had crafted in an age of anxiety. ●

CHRONOLOGY	
1905	Einstein publishes special theory of relativity
1907	Picasso paints *Les Demoiselles d'Avignon*
1918–1920	Civil war in Russia
1919	Mussolini launches fascist movement in Italy
1919	Walter Gropius founds the Bauhaus
1921–1928	Lenin's New Economic Policy
1927	Heisenberg establishes the uncertainty principle
1928–1932	First Soviet Five-Year Plan
1929	U.S. stock market crash
1929	Beginning of Great Depression
1929	Hemingway and Remarque publish antiwar novels
1933–1945	Hitler rules Germany
1935–1938	Stalin's Great Purge in the Soviet Union
1939	Steinbeck publishes *The Grapes of Wrath*

For Further Reading

Malcolm Bradbury and James McFarlane, eds. *Modernism, 1890–1930.* Atlantic Highlands, N.J., 1978. A comprehensive survey of the new trends in literature.

Michael Burleigh. *The Third Reich: A New History.* New York, 2000. A new treatment of the Nazi dictatorship that stresses the tacit consent of the German people.

Peter Conrad. *Modern Times, Modern Places.* New York, 1999. Evocative appraisal of twentieth-century art and thought.

Sarah Davies and James Harris, eds. *Stalin: A New History.* New York, 2005. Reassessment of the Soviet leader based on newly available sources.

Richard Evans. *The Coming of the Third Reich.* New York, 2004. The first of a three-volume series, this work chronicles the Nazi movement's rise to power.

———. *The Third Reich in Power, 1933–1939.* New York, 2005. The second work in a three-volume series, this book starts with the Nazis' assumption of power, and ends at the beginning of World War II in Europe.

Sheila Fitzpatrick. *The Russian Revolution, 1917–1932.* 2nd ed. New York, 1984. This work stands out for the author's ability to make complex processes accessible to the general reader and still instruct the specialist.

George Gamow. *Thirty Years That Shook Physics.* Garden City, N.Y., 1966. A leading physicist engagingly tells the story of modern physics.

Peter Gay. *Freud: A Life for Our Time.* New York, 1988. A balanced biography of one of the most influential social thinkers of the twentieth century.

George Heard Hamilton. *Painting and Sculpture in Europe, 1880–1940.* 6th ed. New Haven, 1993. A classic that presents a discerning overview of the subject.

Ian Kershaw. *Hitler: 1889–1936: Hubris.* New York, 1999.

———. *Hitler: 1936–1945: Nemesis.* New York, 2000. One of the foremost historians of the Nazi era pens the definitive biography of Adolf Hitler.

Charles Kindleberger. *The World in Depression, 1929–1939.* London, 1973. A sophisticated analysis that focuses on developments in the United States and Europe.

A. J. H. Latham. *The Depression and the Developing World, 1914–1939.* London, 1981. One of the few works that looks beyond the industrialized world to give a global perspective on the subject.

Michael Mann. *Fascists.* New York, 2004. Comparative analysis of fascist movements in interwar Europe.

Colleen McDannell. *Picturing Faith: Photography and the Great Depression.* New Haven, 2004. Examination of depression-era photographs as evidence of the importance of religion in American life.

Robert Paxton. *The Anatomy of Fascism.* New York, 2004. A groundbreaking and fascinating history of fascism.

Nikolaus Pevsner. *Pioneers of Modern Design: From William Morris to Walter Gropius.* Rev. ed. New York, 1964. This work chronicles the rise of the international style in architecture.

Richard Pipes. *The Russian Revolution.* New York, 1990. When the Communist Party collapsed in 1991, this sweeping study was quickly translated into Russian and became a national bestseller.

Eli Zaretsky. *Secrets of the Soul: A Social and Cultural History of Psychoanalysis.* New York, 2004. Flawed but useful history of the broad social impacts of Freud's theories.

Nationalism and Political Identities in Asia, Africa, and Latin America

chapter 35

In this cigarette advertisement from 1935, Chinese women are shown challenging traditions. They are "new women," affected by the radical changes in identity and behavior taking place after the Great War and during the Great Depression.

EYEWITNESS:
Shanfei Becomes a New and Revolutionary Young Woman in China

Shanfei lived in politically exciting times. The daughter of a wealthy landowning man of the Chinese gentry, she grew up with luxuries and opportunities unknown to most girls. Her father allowed her to attend school, and her mother clothed her in beautiful silk dresses. Shanfei, however, matured into a woman who rejected the rich trappings of her youth. Her formative years were marked by political ferment and the unsettling cultural changes that engulfed the globe in the wake of the Great War. The rise of nationalism and communism in China after the revolution of 1911 and the Russian revolution in 1917 guided the transformation of Shanfei—from a girl ruled by tradition and privilege, she became an active revolutionary dedicated to the cause of women and communism.

With the exception of Shanfei's father, the members of her family in Hunan province took in the new spirit of the first decades of the twentieth century. Her brothers returned from school with strange and compelling ideas, including some that challenged the subordinate position of women in China. Shanfei's mother, to all appearances a woman who accepted her subservience to her husband, proved instrumental to Shanfei's departure from the common destiny of Chinese girls. She listened quietly to her sons as they discussed new views, and then she applied them to her daughter. She used every means at her disposal to persuade her husband to educate their daughter. She wept, begged, and cajoled. He relented but still insisted that Shanfei receive an old-fashioned education and submit to foot binding and childhood betrothal.

When Shanfei was eleven years old, her father suddenly died, and his death emboldened her mother. She ripped the bandages off Shanfei's feet and sent her to a modern school far from home. In the lively atmosphere of her school, Shanfei bloomed into an activist. At sixteen she incited a student strike against the administration of her school, transferred to a more modern school, and became famous as a leader in the student movement. She went to school with men and broke tradition in her personal and political life. In 1926 Shanfei abandoned her studies to join the Communist Youth, and she gave up her fiancé for a free marriage to the man she loved: a peasant leader in the communist movement.

The twists of fate that altered the destiny of Shanfei had parallels throughout the colonial world after 1914. Two major events, the Great War and the Great Depression, defined much of the turmoil of those years. Disillusion and radical upheaval marked areas as distinct as Asia, Africa, and Latin America. As peoples around the world struggled to come to terms with the aftermath of war, an unprecedented economic contraction gripped the international economy. The Great Depression complicated peoples' struggles for national sovereignty and financial solvency, especially in Asia, where Japan's militarist leaders sought to build national strength through imperial expansion. Latin American states worked to alter the economic domination of its "good neighbor" to the north while African peoples suffered a contraction in living standards along with the economically weakened imperial industrialists.

European empires still appeared to dominate global relations, but the Great War had opened fissures within the European and U.S. spheres of influence. Beneath colonial surfaces, nationalist and communist ferment brewed. Nationalist and anti-imperial movements gathered strength, and in the postwar years resistance to foreign rule and a desire for national unity were stronger than ever. This situation was especially true in India and China, where various visions of national identity competed, but it also pertained to those in Africa and Latin America who struggled against the domination of imperial powers. While peoples in Africa worked to become independent of outright imperial control, those in Latin America had to fight off the more indirect economic effects of postindependence colonialism, usually termed *neocolonialism.* The roots of all of these developments lay in the global storm of a world war that shook the foundations of established traditions, which crumbled in Shanfei's home in Hunan as much as in the Kikuyu highlands and Mexico City.

ASIAN PATHS TO AUTONOMY

The Paris peace settlement had barely altered the prewar colonial holdings of Europeans, yet indirectly the Great War affected relations between Asian peoples and the imperial powers. In the decades following the Great War, nationalism developed into a powerful political force in Asia, especially in India and China, where growing numbers of people were influenced by the self-determination concept that was one of the legacies of the Paris Peace Conference. Achieving the twin ideals of independence from foreign powers and national unity became a dream of intellectuals and a goal of new political leaders. Even as foreign control was being rejected, Asian leaders availed themselves of European ideologies such as nationalism and socialism, but in their search for new identities untainted by the dependent past, Asians either transformed or adapted those ideologies to fit indigenous traditions. In that sense, peoples in India and China followed in the footsteps of Japan, which had already adapted European and U.S. economic strategies to its advantage. Still dissatisfied with its status, Japan used militarism and imperial expansion in the interwar years to enhance its national identity.

Indian, Chinese, and Japanese societies underwent a prolonged period of disorder and struggle until a new order emerged. In India the quest for national identity focused on gaining independence from British rule, a pursuit that was complicated by sectarian differences between Hindus and Muslims. The Chinese path to national identity was fraught with foreign and civil war as two principal groups—the Nationalist and Communist Parties—contended for power. Deeply divided by ideologies, both parties opposed foreign domination, rejected the old Confucian order, and sought a unified Chinese state. Japanese militarists made China's quest for national unity more difficult, because Japan struggled to overcome its domestic problems through conquests that focused on China.

India's Quest for Home Rule

By the beginning of the twentieth century, Indian nationalism threatened the British empire's hold on India. The construction of a vast railway network across India to facilitate the export of raw materials contributed to the idea of national unity by bringing the people of the subcontinent within easy reach of one another. Moreover, because it was impossible for a small group of foreigners to control and administer such a vast country, the British had created an elite of educated Indian administrators to help in this task. A European system of education familiarized the local middle-class intelligentsia with the political and social values of European society. Those values, however—democracy, individual freedom, and equality—were the antithesis of empire, and they promoted nationalist movements.

Indian National Congress Of all the associations dedicated to the struggle against British rule, the greatest and most influential was the Indian National Congress, founded in 1885. This organization, which enlisted the support of many prominent Hindus and Muslims, at first stressed collaboration with the British to bring self-rule to India, but after the Great War the congress pursued that goal in opposition to the British. The formation of the Muslim League, established in 1906 with the encouragement of the British government, added a new current into the movement for national liberation. Both organizations were dedicated to achieving independence for India, but members of the Muslim League increasingly worried that Hindu oppression and continued subjugation of India's substantial Muslim minority might replace British rule.

During the Great War, large numbers of Indians—Hindus and Muslims—rallied to the British cause, and nationalist movements remained inactive. But as the war led to scarcities of goods and food, social discontent increasingly focused on the British colonizer. Indian nationalists also drew encouragement from ideas emanating from Washington, D.C., and St. Petersburg. They read Woodrow Wilson's Fourteen Points, which called for national self-determination, and Lenin's appeal for a united struggle by proletarians and colonized peoples. The British government responded to the upsurge of nationalist activity that came in the wake of the peace settlement with a series of repressive measures that precipitated a wave of violence and disorder throughout the Indian subcontinent.

Mohandas K. Gandhi Into this turmoil stepped Mohandas Karamchand Gandhi (1869–1948), one of the most remarkable and charismatic leaders of the twentieth century. Gandhi grew up in a prosperous and pious Hindu household, married at thirteen, and left his hometown in 1888 to study law in London. In 1893 he went to South Africa to accept a position with an Indian firm, and there he quickly became involved in organizing the local Indian community against a system of racial segregation that made Indians second-class citizens. During the twenty-five years he spent in South Africa, Gandhi embraced a moral philosophy of *ahimsa* (tolerance and nonviolence) and developed the technique of passive resistance that he called *satyagraha* ("truth and firmness"). His belief in the virtue of simple living led him to renounce material possessions, dress in the garb of a simple Indian peasant, and become a vegetarian. He renounced sex—testing his willpower by chastely sleeping with various comely young women—and extolled the virtues of a daily saltwater enema. He also spent an hour each morning in careful study of the Bhagavad Gita (Sanskrit for "The Lord's Song"), one of the most sacred writings of Hinduism, which he regarded as a spiritual dictionary.

Returning to India in 1915, Gandhi became active in Indian politics. He succeeded in transforming the Indian National Congress from an elitist body of anglicized gentlemen into a mass organization that became an effective instrument of Indian nationalism. Although the reform program of the congress appeared remote from the needs of common people, Gandhi spoke in a language that they could understand. His unique mixture of spiritual intensity and political activism appealed to a broad section of the Indian population, and in the eyes of many he quickly achieved the stature of a political and spiritual leader, their Mahatma, or "great soul." Although he was a member of the merchant caste, Gandhi was determined to eradicate the injustices of the caste system. He fought especially hard to improve the status of the lowest classes of society, the casteless Untouchables, whom he called *harijans* ("children of God").

Under Gandhi's leadership the congress launched two mass movements: the Non-Cooperation Movement of 1920–1922 and the Civil Disobedience Movement of 1930. Convinced that economic self-sufficiency was a prerequisite for self-government, Gandhi called on the Indian people to boycott British goods and return to wearing rough homespun cotton clothing. He disagreed with those who wanted India to industrialize, advocating instead manual labor and the revival of rural cottage industries. Gandhi furthermore admonished his people to boycott institutions operated by the British in India, such as schools, offices, and courts. Despite Gandhi's cautions against the use of force, violence often accompanied the protest movement. The British retaliated with arrests. That the British authorities could react brutally was shown in 1919 in the city of Amritsar in Punjab, where colonial troops freely used their rifles to disperse an unarmed crowd, killing 379 demonstrators.

The India Act When repressive measures failed to quell the movement for self-rule, the British offered a political compromise. After years of hesitation and deliberation, the British parliament enacted the Government of India Act, which gave India the institutions of a self-governing state. The legislation allowed for the establishment of autonomous legislative bodies in the provinces of British India, the creation of a bicameral (two-chambered) national legislature, and the formation of an executive arm under the control of the British government. On the urging of Gandhi, the majority of Indians approved the measure, which went into effect in 1937.

The India Act proved unworkable, however, because India's six hundred nominally sovereign princes refused to cooperate and because Muslims feared that Hindus would dominate the national legislature. Muslims had reason for concern because they already faced economic control by Hindus, a fact underlined during the Great Depression, which had a severe impact on India. On top of Indians suffering the typical devastations associated with agricultural economies during depression, they had to cope with added hurdles erected by an imperial government that did not respond with energetic efforts to mitigate the effects of the economic crisis. Moreover, the Great Depression exacerbated conflict between Muslims and Hindus, as Muslims constituted the majority of indebted tenant farmers, who found themselves increasingly unable to pay rents and debts. Their landlords were mainly Hindus. Muslims felt keenly what they perceived as economic exploitation by Hindus, and their recognition of this economic discrimination bolstered calls for a separate Muslim state. Muhammad Ali Jinnah (1876–1948), an eloquent and brilliant lawyer who headed the Muslim League, warned that a unified India represented nothing less than a threat to the Muslim faith and its Indian community. In place of one India, he proposed two states, one of which would be the "land of the pure," or Pakistan. Jinnah's proposal reflected an uncomfortable reality that society in India was split by hostility between Hindus and Muslims, making national unification an illusory goal.

China's Search for Order

As Shanfei's life story suggested, during the first half of the twentieth century China was in a state of almost continual revolutionary upheaval. The conflict's origins dated from the nineteenth century, when the Chinese empire came under relentless pressure from imperialist powers that rushed in to fill the vacuum created by China's internal political disintegration (see chapter 31). As revolutionary and nationalist uprisings gained widespread support, a revolution in 1911 forced the Xuantong emperor, still a child (also known as Puyi), to abdicate. The Qing empire fell with relative ease. Dr. Sun Yatsen (1866–1925), a leading opponent of the old regime, proclaimed a Chinese republic in 1912 and briefly assumed the office of president. The dynasty was dead, but there remained the problems of how to bury it and what to put in its place.

The Republic The revolution of 1911 did not establish a stable government. Indeed, the republic soon plunged into a state of political anarchy and economic disintegration marked by the rule of warlords, who were disaffected generals from the old imperial Chinese army, and their troops. While the central government in Beijing ran the post office and a few other services, the warlords established themselves as provincial or regional rulers. Because the warlords were responsible for the neglect of irrigation projects crucial to the survival of farmers, for the revival of the opium trade, which they protected, and for the decline of crucial economic investments, they contributed to the deterioration of Chinese society. They never founded a new dynasty, nor did they create the semblance of a stable central state. Yet warlords were just one symbol of the disintegration of the political order. The fragmented relationship between native authority and foreign powers was another. Since the nineteenth century, a collection of treaties, known in China as the unequal treaties, had guided Chinese relations with foreign countries. Those treaties had established a network of foreign control over the Chinese economy that effectively prevented economic development. The continued sway of unequal treaties and other concessions permitted foreigners to intervene in Chinese society. Foreigners did not control the state, but through their privileges they impaired its sovereignty.

Chinese Nationalism After the Great War, nationalist sentiment developed rapidly in China. Youths and intellectuals, who in the previous decade had looked to Europe and the United States for models and ideals for the reform of China, eagerly anticipated the results of the 1919 Peace Conference in Paris. They expected the U.S. government to support the termination of the treaty system and the restoration of full Chinese sovereignty. Those hopes were shattered, however, when the peacemakers approved increasing Japanese interference in China. That decision gave rise to the May Fourth Movement. Spearheaded by students and intellectuals in China's urban areas, the movement galvanized the country, and all classes of Chinese protested against foreign, especially Japanese, interference. In speeches, newspapers, and novels, the movement's leaders pledged themselves to rid China of imperialism and reestablish national unity. Student leaders such as Shanfei rallied their comrades to the cause.

Disillusioned by the cynical self-interest of the United States and the European powers, some Chinese became interested in Marxist thought as modified by Lenin (see chapter 33) and the social and economic experiments under way in the Soviet Union. The anti-imperialist rhetoric of the Soviet leadership struck a responsive chord, and in 1921 the Chinese Communist Party (CCP) was organized in Shanghai. Among its early members was Mao Zedong (1893–1976), a former teacher and librarian who viewed a Marxist-inspired social revolution as the cure for China's problems. Mao's political radicalism extended to the issue of women's equality, which he and other communists championed. As Shanfei's personal experience suggested, Chinese communists believed in divorce, opposed arranged marriages, and campaigned against the practice of foot binding.

Sun Yatsen The most prominent nationalist leader at the time, Sun Yatsen, did not share the communists' enthusiasm for a dictatorship of the proletariat and the triumph of communism. Sun's basic ideology, summarized in

thinking about TRADITIONS

Chinese Revolutions

In the period before, during, and after the Great War, Chinese political thinkers and leaders questioned contemporary Chinese political and cultural practices. How did Chinese nationalism and communism promote challenges to long-standing Chinese political and cultural traditions, such as those pertaining to peasants and women?

sources from the past

"Self-Rule Is My Birthright"

Bal Gangadhar Tilak (1856–1920) was a fiery Indian nationalist who galvanized public support for India's independence movement. Although he was a great Sanskrit scholar and a very successful journalist, people best remember Tilak as a political activist who sought a Hindu revival and independence from Great Britain. His slogan, "Swaraj (Self-Rule) is my birthright," inspired millions of Indians. Whereas the British labeled him the "Father of Indian Unrest," Mohandas K. Gandhi more generously called him the "Maker of Modern India." What follows is an excerpt from Tilak's address to the Indian National Congress in 1907, calling for a boycott of British goods and resistance to British rule.

One fact is that this alien government has ruined the country. In the beginning, all of us were taken by surprise. We were almost dazed. We thought that everything that the rulers did was for our good and that this English Government has descended from the clouds to save us from the invasions of Tamerlane and Chingis Khan, and, as they say, not only from foreign invasions but from internecine warfare. We felt happy for a time, but it soon came to light that the peace which was established in this country did this . . . —that we were prevented from going at each other's throats, so that a foreigner might go at the throat of us all. Pax Britannica has been established in this country in order that a foreign Government may exploit the country. That this is the effect of this Pax Britannica is being gradually realized in these days. It was an unhappy circumstance that it was not realized sooner. . . . English education, growing poverty, and better familiarity with our rulers, opened our eyes. . . . Your industries are ruined utterly, ruined by foreign rule; your wealth is going out of the country and you are reduced to the lowest level which no human being can occupy. In this state of things, is there any other remedy by which you can help yourself? The remedy is not petitioning but boycott. We say prepare your forces, organize your power, and then go to work so that they cannot refuse you what you demand. . . . Every Englishman knows that they are a mere handful in this country and it is the business of every one of them to befool you in believing that you are weak and they are strong. This is politics. We have been deceived by such policy so long. What the new party wants you to do is realize the fact that your future rests entirely in your own hands. . . . We shall not give them assistance to collect revenue and keep peace. We shall not assist them in fighting beyond the frontiers or outside India with Indian blood and money. We shall not assist them in carrying on the administration of justice. We shall have our own courts, and when time comes we shall not pay taxes. Can you do that by your united efforts? If you can, you are free from to-morrow. . . .

For Further Reflection

- What does Tilak suggest the British duped Indians into believing, and how would an Indian boycott let the British know that Indians would no longer be fooled?

Source: Bal Gangadhar Tilak. *Bal Gangadhar Tilak: His Writings and Speeches.* Madras: Ganesh and Co., 1923, pp. 56–65.

his *Three Principles of the People,* called for elimination of special privileges for foreigners, national reunification, economic development, and a democratic republican government based on universal suffrage. To realize those goals, he was determined to bring the entire country under the control of his Nationalist People's Party, or *Guomindang.* In 1923, members of the small CCP began to augment the ranks of the Guomindang and by 1926 made up one-third of the Guomindang's membership. Both organizations availed themselves of the assistance offered by the Soviet Union. Under the doctrine of Lenin's democratic centralism—stressing centralized party control by a highly disciplined group of professional revolutionaries—Soviet advisors helped reorganize the Guomindang and the CCP into effective political organizations. In the process, the Soviets bestowed on China the basis of a new political system.

Civil War After the death of Sun Yatsen in 1925, the leadership of the Guomindang fell to Jiang Jieshi (Chiang Kai-shek, 1887–1975), a young general who had been trained in Japan and the Soviet Union. In contrast to the communists, he did not hold a vision for social revolution that involved the masses of China. Before long, Jiang Jieshi launched a political and military offensive, known as the Northern Expedition, that aimed to unify the nation and bring China under Guomindang rule. Toward the end of his successful campaign, in 1927, Jiang Jieshi brutally and unexpectedly turned against his former communist allies, bringing the alliance of convenience between the Guomindang and the CCP to a bloody end. In the following year, nationalist forces occupied Beijing, set up a central government in Nanjing, and declared the Guomindang the official government of a unified and sovereign Chinese state. Meanwhile, the badly mauled communists

MAP 35.1
The struggle for control in China, 1927–1936.
Compare the continental territories controlled by Japan and the Guomindang in 1934.
How would the size of Japan's territories in Manchuria and Korea influence Chinese abilities to challenge Japanese expansion?

retreated to a remote area of southeastern China, where they tried to reconstitute and reorganize their forces.

The nationalist government had to deal with many concerns, but Chinese leaders evaded one major global crisis—the Great Depression. China's large agrarian economy and small industrial sector were connected only marginally to the world economy. Foreign trade in such items as tea and silk, which did decline, made up only a small part of China's economy, which was otherwise dominated by its large domestic markets. Although the new government in China generally avoided having to contend with global economic devastation, it did have to confront three major problems during the 1930s. First, the nationalists actually controlled only part of China, leaving the remainder of the country in the hands of warlords. Second, by the early 1930s communist revolution was still a major threat. Third, the Guomindang faced increasing Japanese aggression. In dealing with those problems, Jiang Jieshi gave priority to eliminating the CCP and its Red Army.

Adversaries in the struggle for power in China: at left, Jiang Jieshi (Chiang Kai-shek); at right, Mao Zedong.

No longer able to ward off the relentless attacks of nationalist forces, the communists took flight in October 1934 to avoid annihilation. Bursting through a military blockade around their bases in Jiangxi province in southeastern China, some eighty-five thousand troops and auxiliary personnel of the Red Army began the legendary Long March, an epic journey of 10,000 kilometers (6,215 miles). After traveling across difficult terrain and fighting for survival against hunger, disease, and Guomindang forces, the marchers arrived in a remote area of Shaanxi Province in northwestern China in October 1935 and established headquarters at Yan'an. Although thousands had died in this forced retreat, the Long March inspired many Chinese to join the Communist Party. During the Long March, Mao Zedong emerged as the leader and the principal theoretician of the Chinese communist movement. He came up with a Chinese form of Marxist-Leninism, or Maoism, an ideology grounded in the conviction that peasants rather than urban proletarians were the foundation for a successful revolution. Village power, Mao believed, was critical in a country where most people were peasants.

Imperial and Imperialist Japan

After the Great War, Japan achieved great power status and appeared to accept the international status quo that the major powers fashioned in the aftermath of war. After joining the League of Nations as one of the "big five" powers, the Japanese government entered into a series of international agreements that sought to improve relations among countries with conflicting interests in Asia and the Pacific. As a signatory to several Washington Conference treaties in 1922, Japan agreed to limit naval development, pledged to evacuate Shandong Province of China, and guaranteed China's territorial integrity. In 1928 the Japanese government signed the Kellogg-Briand Pact, which renounced war as an instrument of national policy. Concerns about earlier Japanese territorial ambitions, highlighted by the Twenty-one Demands on China in 1915, receded from the minds of the international community.

Japan's limited involvement in the Great War gave a dual boost to its economy. Japanese businesses profited from selling munitions and other goods to the Allies throughout the war, and they gained a bigger foothold in Asia as the war led Europe's trading nations to neglect Asian markets. Economic prosperity was short-lived, however, as the postwar economy of Japan faced serious challenges. Rapid inflation and labor unrest appeared by 1918, followed by a series of recessions that culminated in a giant economic slump caused by the Great Depression. Like the economies of other industrial nations tied into the global economy, Japan's economy experienced plummeting industrial production, huge job layoffs, declining trade, and financial chaos. Economic contraction set the stage for social unrest and radical politics.

Public demands for sweeping political and social reforms, including a broadening of the franchise, protection for labor unions, and welfare legislation, figured prominently in Japanese domestic politics throughout the 1920s. Yet conservatives blocked any major advances beyond the suffrage law of 1925, which established universal male suffrage. By the early 1930s an increasingly frustrated public blamed its government for the nation's continuing economic problems and became more disenchanted with leading politicians tainted by bribery scandals and corrupt connections to business conglomerates. Right-wing political groups called for an end to party rule, and xenophobic nationalists dedicated themselves to the preservation of a unique Japanese culture and the eradication of Western influences. A campaign of assassinations, targeting political and business leaders, culminated in the murder of Prime Minister Inukai Tsuyoshi (1855–1932).

Politicians who supported Japan's role in the international industrial-capitalist system faced increasing opposition from those who were inclined toward a militarist vision of a self-sufficient Japan that would dominate east Asia. The hardships of the depression undermined support for the internationalist position, and the militarists were able to benefit from Japanese martial traditions and their own unwillingness to be constrained by international cooperation. China's unification, aided by international attempts to reinstate its sovereignty, threatened Japan's economic interests in Manchuria. Moreover, political instability, the result of nationalists and communists vying for power, made China an inviting target. Manchuria had historically been Chinese territory, but by the twentieth century it was a sphere of influence where Japan maintained the Manchurian Railroad (built in 1906), retained transit rights, and stationed troops. In 1931 Japan's military forces in Manchuria acted to assert control over the region.

The Mukden Incident On the night of 18 September 1931, Japanese troops used explosives to blow up a few feet of rail on the Japanese-built South Manchuria Railway north of Mukden. They accused the Chinese of attacking their railroad. This "Mukden incident" became the pretext for war between Japanese and Chinese troops. Although the civilian government in Japan tried to halt this military incursion, by 1932 Japanese troops controlled all of Manchuria, thereby ensuring Japan preeminence and protecting its long-term economic and industrial development of the region. The Japanese established a puppet state called Manchukuo, but in reality Japan had absorbed Manchuria into its empire, challenged the international peace system, and begun a war. In response to the Manchurian invasion, the Guomindang (Nationalist Party) leader Jiang Jieshi appealed to the League of Nations to halt Japanese aggression. After a lengthy investigation, the league called for the withdrawal of Japanese forces and for the restoration of Chinese sovereignty. The Japanese responded by leaving the league, and, although China gained the moral high ground in international eyes, nothing was done to stop the aggression. This reaction set the pattern for future responses to the actions of expansionist nations such as Japan. Embarking on conquests in east Asia, Japanese militarists found a sure means to promoting a new militant Japanese national identity. They also helped provoke a new global conflagration.

"The persistence of colonialism led to the development of African nationalism and the birth of embryonic nationalist movements."

The Great War and the Great Depression made signal contributions to the ongoing nationalist and political upheavals taking place throughout Asia. New ideologies and old conflicts intersected to complicate the processes of independence and national unification in India and China. The global economic crisis led to some lessening of European imperial influence, while it prompted an industrialized Japan to exert its imperial will on the Asian sphere. Only the aftermath of another world war brought any resolution to the turmoil within and among Asian nations.

AFRICA UNDER COLONIAL DOMINATION

The Great War and the Great Depression similarly complicated quests for national independence and unity in Africa. The colonial ties that bound African colonies to European powers ensured that Africans became participants in the Great War, willing or not. European states transmitted their respective animosities and their military conflicts to African soil and drew on their colonies for the recruitment of soldiers and carriers. The forced recruitment of military personnel led some Africans to raise arms against their colonial overlords, but Europeans generally prevailed in putting down those uprisings. African contributions to the Great War and the wartime rhetoric of self-determination espoused by U.S. President Woodrow Wilson led some Africans to anticipate a different postwar world. The peacemakers in Paris, however, ignored African pleas for social and political reform.

Rather than retreating, colonialism consolidated its hold on the African continent. In the decades following the peace settlement of 1919, the European powers focused on the economic exploitation of their colonies. The imposition of a rapacious form of capitalism destroyed the self-sufficiency of many African economies and turned the resulting colonial economies into extensions of those of the colonizing powers. As a result, African economic life became enmeshed in the global economy. The persistence of colonialism led to the development of African nationalism and the birth of embryonic nationalist movements. During the decades following the Great War, African intellectuals searched for new national identities and looked forward to the construction of nations devoid of European domination and exploitation.

Africa and the Great War

The Great War had a profound impact on Africa. The conflict of 1914–1918 affected Africans because many belligerents were colonial powers who ruled over the greater part of Africa. Except for Spanish-controlled territories, which remained neutral, every African colony took sides in the war. In practice this meant that the German colonial administration faced the combined colonial forces of Great Britain, France, Belgium, Italy, and Portugal. Even the last remaining independent states on the continent—Liberia and Ethiopia—did not avoid involvement. Whereas Lij Iyasu (reigned 1913–1916), the uncrowned, pro-Muslim boy emperor of Ethiopia, aligned his nation with Turkey until he was overthrown by

A Senegalese regiment of the French Colonial Infantry on parade in Africa during the Great War. Over a million African soldiers participated in military campaigns in Africa.

pro-Christian nobles in 1916, Liberia joined the Allies in 1917 when the United States entered the war.

War in Africa Although Germany had been a latecomer in the race for overseas colonies, German imperialists had managed to carve out a rudimentary colonial empire in Africa that included Togo, Cameroon, German South-West Africa, and German East Africa. Thus, one immediate consequence of war for Africans in 1914 was that the Allies invaded those German colonies. Specific strategic interests among the Allies varied. British officers and soldiers, trying to maintain naval supremacy, attempted to put German port facilities and communications systems out of action. The British also anticipated that victory in the German colonies would bring victors' spoils after the war. France's objective was to recover territory in Cameroon that it had ceded to Germany in 1911. The Germans, in contrast, simply tried to hold on to what they had. Outnumbered ten to one, the Germans could not hope to win the war in Africa. Yet, by resorting to guerrilla tactics, some fifteen thousand German troops tied sixty thousand Allied forces down and postponed defeat until the last days of the war.

More than one million African soldiers participated directly in military campaigns, in which they witnessed firsthand the spectacle of white people fighting one another. Colonial "masters" sent them to fight on African soil, in the lands of southwest Asia, and on the western front in Europe. The colonial powers also encouraged their African subjects in uniforms to kill the enemy "white man," whose life until now had been sacrosanct because of his skin color. Even more men, as well as women and children, served as carriers to support armies in areas where supplies could not be hauled by conventional methods such as road, rail, or pack animal. The colonial powers raised recruits for fighting and carrier services in three ways: on a purely voluntary basis; in levies supplied by African chiefs that consisted of volunteer and impressed personnel; and through formal conscription. In French colonies, military service became compulsory for all males between the ages of twenty and twenty-eight, and by the end of the war more than 480,000 colonial troops had served in the French army. The British also raised recruits in their African colonies. In 1915 a compulsory service order made all men aged eighteen to twenty-five liable for military service. In the Congo, the Belgians impressed more than half a million porters. Ultimately, more than 150,000 African soldiers and carriers lost their lives, and many more suffered injury or became disabled.

thinking about ENCOUNTERS

Colonial Legacies of the Great War

During the Great War, Europeans relied on the military service and conscripted labor of many in their colonial empires. How did African participation in the Great War, for example, alter African expectations for their political future?

Challenges to European Authority While the world's attention was focused on the slaughter taking place in European lands between 1914 and 1918, Africans mounted bold challenges to European colonial authority. As the war dragged on, European commercial and administrative personnel began to leave the colonies in large numbers, whether for combat in Europe or for enlistment in locally based units for campaigns in Africa. That spread an already thin European presence even thinner, a fact not missed by colonial subjects. Africans took the opportunity to stage armed uprisings and other forms of protest. When they could least afford trouble, colonial regimes had no choice but to divert scarce military resources to meet those challenges.

The cause of widespread revolts varied. In some cases, as in Libya, revolts simply represented continued resistance to European rule. In other cases, the departure of European personnel, which seemed to signal a weakening of power, encouraged those who had previously only contemplated revolt. In yet other instances, pan-Islamic opposition to the war manifested itself in uprisings. The British had nervous moments, for example, when the Sufi brotherhood, based in Libya and still busy battling Italian occupation there, responded to a Turkish call for holy war and invaded western Egypt. The Mumbo cult in Kenya targeted Europeans and their Christian religion, declaring that "all Europeans are our enemies, but the time is shortly coming when they will disappear from our country." The major inspiration for most revolts, however, stemmed from the resentment and hatred engendered by the compulsory conscription of soldiers and carriers. No matter the cause, colonial authorities responded ruthlessly and succeeded in putting down all the revolts.

The Colonial Economy

The decades following the Great War witnessed a thorough transformation of African economic life. Colonial powers pursued two key economic objectives in Africa: they wanted to make sure that the colonized paid for the institutions—bureaucracies, judiciary, police, and military forces—that kept them in subjugation; and they developed export-oriented economies characterized by the exchange of unprocessed raw materials or minimally processed cash crops for manufactured goods from abroad. In pursuit of those goals, colonial authorities imposed economic structures that altered, subordinated, or destroyed previously self-sufficient African economies. In their place came colonial economies, tightly integrated into and dependent on a European-dominated global economy. The Great Depression of the 1930s exposed the vulnerability of dependent colonial economies. As international markets for primary products shrank under the impact of the depression, European companies that controlled the export of African products suffered accordingly. Trade volume often fell by half, and commodity prices dropped even more sharply.

Infrastructure Africa's economic integration required investment in infrastructures. Thus, during the early twentieth century, the new colonial economy first became visible in the form of port facilities, roads, railways, and telegraph

This poster, produced by the Empire Marketing Board, presented an idealized image of the dominant European role in forwarding African economic progress.

wires. Efficient transportation and communication networks not only facilitated conquest and rule but also linked the agricultural or mineral wealth of a colony to the outside world. Although Europeans later claimed that they had given Africa its first modern infrastructure, Europeans and their businesses were usually its main beneficiaries. It was Africans who paid for the infrastructure with their labor and taxes, yet Europeans never considered the needs of local African economies.

Farming and Mining Colonial taxation was an important tool designed to drive Africans into the labor market. To earn the money to pay the taxes levied on land, houses, livestock, and people themselves, African farmers had to become cash crop farmers or seek wage labor on plantations and in mines. Cash crop farming embraced the largest proportion of Africans. In most colonies, farmers who kept their land specialized in one or two crops, generally destined for export to the country governing them. African farmers grew a variety of cash crops for the international marketplace, among them peanuts from Senegal and northern Nigeria, cotton from Uganda, cocoa from the Gold Coast, rubber from the Congo, and palm oil from the Ivory Coast and the Niger delta. In areas with extensive white settlement, such as in Kenya, Rhodesia, and South Africa, settler agriculture was most prominent. Production of agricultural commodities intended for overseas markets remained in the hands of white settlers, whose governments saw to it that they received large and productive areas of land. In British-controlled Kenya, for example, four thousand white farmers seized the Kikuyu highlands, which comprised seven million acres of the colony's richest land. In South Africa, the government reserved 88 percent of all land for whites, who made up just 20 percent of the total population.

Colonial mining enterprises relying on African labor loomed large in parts of central and southern Africa. Engaged in the extraction of mineral wealth such as copper, gold, and diamonds, these enterprises recruited men from rural areas and paid them minimal wages. The recruitment practices set in motion a vast pattern of labor migration that persisted throughout the twentieth century. The absence of male labor and the payment of minimal wages had the effect of impoverishing the rural areas. In many cases, the wives left behind could not grow enough food to feed their children and elderly relatives.

Labor Practices Where taxation failed to create a malleable native labor force, colonial officials resorted to outright forced labor. Indeed, forms of forced labor and barely disguised variants of slavery were prominent features of the colonial economy. A white settler in Kenya candidly expressed the view held by many colonial administrators: "We have stolen his land. Now we must steal his limbs. Compulsory labor is the corollary to our occupation of the country." Much of the labor abuse originated with concessionary companies, which were authorized by their governments to exploit a region's resources with the help of their own system of taxation and labor recruitment. Frequently, the conduct of such companies with respect to labor practices was downright brutal. For example, the construction of railways and roads often depended on forced labor regimes. When the French undertook the construction of the Congo-Ocean railway from Brazzaville to the port at Point-Noir, they rounded up some ten thousand workers annually. Within a few years, between fifteen and twenty thousand African laborers had perished from starvation, disease, and maltreatment.

African Nationalism

In the decades following the Great War, European powers consolidated their political control over the partitioned continent and imposed economies designed to exploit Africa's natural and labor resources. Many Africans were disappointed that their contributions to the war went unrewarded. In place of anticipated social reforms or some degree of greater political participation came an extension and consolidation of the colonial system. Nevertheless, ideas concerning self-determination, articulated by U.S. President Woodrow Wilson during the war, and the notion of the accountability of colonial powers that had been sown during the war gained adherents among a group of African nationalists. Those ideas influenced the growth of African nationalism and the development of incipient nationalist movements. An emerging class of native urban intellectuals, frequently educated in Europe, became especially involved in the formation of ideologies that promised freedom from colonialism and promoted new national identities.

Africa's New Elite Colonialism prompted the emergence of a novel African social class, sometimes called the "new elite." This elite derived its status and place in society from employment and education. The upper echelons of Africa's elite class contained high-ranking civil servants, physicians, lawyers, and writers, most of whom had studied abroad either in western Europe or sometimes in the United States. A case in point was Jomo Kenyatta (1895–1978), who spent almost fifteen years in Europe, during which time he attended various schools and universities, including the London School of Economics. An immensely articulate nationalist, Kenyatta later led Kenya to independence from the British. Even those who had not gone abroad had familiarized themselves with the writings of European authors. Below them in status stood teachers, clerks, and interpreters who had obtained a European-derived primary or secondary education. Although some individuals were self-employed, such as lawyers and doctors, most of them held jobs with colonial governments, with foreign companies, or with Christian missions. In short, these were the Africans who spoke and understood the language of the colonizer, moved with ease in the world of the colonizer, and outwardly adopted the cultural norms of the colonizer such as

sources from the past

Africa for Africans

Marcus Garvey (1887–1940) is best remembered as a pivotal figure in black nationalism, one who inspired nationalist movements as well as many African leaders. A powerful orator, Garvey preached the greatness of the African heritage and called on European colonial powers to leave Africa. Convinced that blacks in the diaspora could never secure their rights as minorities, this "Black Moses" rejected the idea of integration and instead championed a "Back to Africa" movement. According to Garvey, a Jamaican who garnered notoriety during his time in the United States, only in ancestral Africa would it be possible to establish an autonomous black state that featured its own unique culture.

George Washington was not God Almighty. He was a man like any Negro in this building, and if he and his associates were able to make a free America, we too can make a free Africa. Hampden, Gladstone, Pitt and Disraeli were not the representatives of God in the person of Jesus Christ. They were but men, but in their time they worked for the expansion of the British Empire, and today they boast of a British Empire upon which "the sun never sets." As Pitt and Gladstone were able to work for the expansion of the British Empire, so you and I can work for the expansion of a great African Empire. Voltaire and Mirabeau were not Jesus Christs, they were but men like ourselves. They worked and overturned the French Monarchy. They worked for the Democracy which France now enjoys, and if they were able to do that, we are able to work for a democracy in Africa. Lenin and Trotsky were not Jesus Christs, but they were able to overthrow the despotism of Russia, and today they have given to the world a Social Republic, the first of its kind. If Lenin and Trotsky were able to do that for Russia, you and I can do that for Africa. Therefore, let no man, let no power on earth, turn you from this sacred cause of liberty. I prefer to die at this moment rather than not to work for the freedom of Africa. If liberty is good for certain sets of humanity it is good for all. Black men, Colored men, Negroes have as much right to be free as any other race that God Almighty ever created, and we desire freedom that is unfettered, freedom that is unlimited, freedom that will give us a chance and opportunity to rise to the fullest of our ambition and that we cannot get in countries where other men rule and dominate.

We have reached the time when every minute, every second must count for something done, something achieved in the cause of Africa. . . . It falls to our lot to tear off the shackles that bind Mother Africa. Can you do it? You did it in the Revolutionary War. You did it in the Civil War; You did it at the Battles of the Marne and Verdun; You did it in Mesopotamia. You can do it marching up the battle heights of Africa. Let the world know that 400,000,000 Negroes are prepared to die or live as free men. Despise us as much as you care. Ignore us as much as you care. We are coming 400,000,000 strong. We are coming with our woes behind us, with the memory of suffering behind us—woes and suffering of three hundred years—they shall be our inspiration. My bulwark of strength in the conflict of freedom in Africa, will be the three hundred years of persecution and hardship left behind in this Western Hemisphere.

For Further Reflection

- In his speech, how does Marcus Garvey convey the significance of Africa for both Africans and those involved in the black diaspora?

Source: Amy Jacques Garvey, compiler. *Philosophy and Opinions of Marcus Garvey or Africa for Africans.* London: Frank Cass and Co., 1967, pp. 73–74.

wearing European-style clothes or adopting European names. It was within the ranks of this new elite that ideas concerning African identity and nationhood germinated.

Because colonialism had introduced Africans to European ideas and ideologies, African nationalists frequently embraced the European concept of the nation as a means of forging unity among disparate African groups. As they saw it, the nation as articulated by European thinkers and statesmen provided the best model for mobilizing their resources and organizing their societies, and it offered the best chance to mount effective resistance to colonialism. Although the concept of the nation proved a useful general framework for African nationalists, there remained differences as to what constituted a nation or a people's national identity.

Forms of Nationalism Some nationalists in search of a national identity looked to the precolonial past for inspiration. There they found identities based on ethnicity, religion, and languages, and they believed that any future nation must reconstitute institutions crucial to those identities, such as distinctively African forms of spiritual and political authority. Race had provided colonial powers with one rationale for conquest and exploitation; hence it was not surprising that some nationalists used the concept of an African race as a founda-

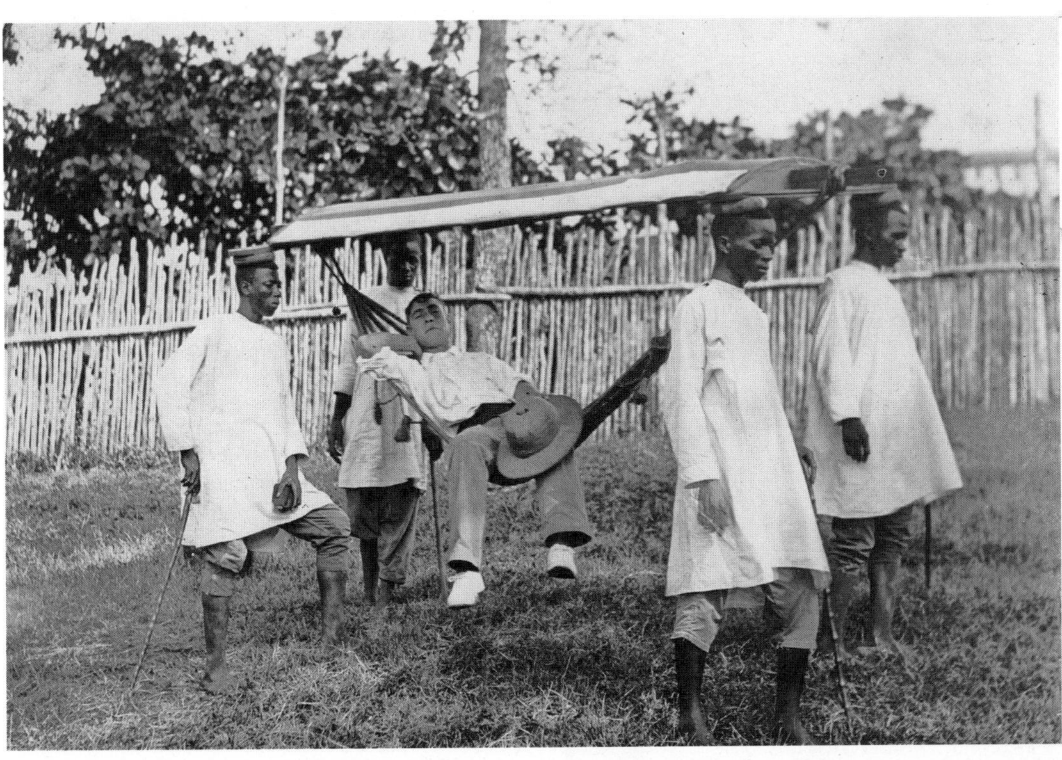

A European colonialist takes advantage of African labor and is "Traveling in Hammock," as this 1912 photograph's title suggests.

tion for identity, solidarity, and nation building. Race figured as an important concept in another important strain of African nationalism, which originated in the western hemisphere among the descendants of slaves. Typically it was U.S. blacks and Afro-Caribbean intellectuals who thought of themselves as members of a single race and who promoted the unification of all people of African descent into a single African state. Representatives of this Pan-Africanism were the black U.S. activist and intellectual W. E. B. DuBois (1868–1963) and the Jamaican nationalist leader Marcus Garvey (1887–1940), who preached black pride and called on blacks living in the African diaspora to go "Back to Africa." Still other nationalists discarded the concept of a unique racial identity altogether and looked rather for an African identity rooted in geography. This approach commonly translated into a desire to build the nation on the basis of borders that defined existing colonial states. Collectively these ideas influenced the development of nationalist movements during the 1930s and 1940s, but it took another world war before these ideas translated into demands for independence from colonialism.

LATIN AMERICAN STRUGGLES WITH NEOCOLONIALISM

The postcolonial history of Latin American states in the early twentieth century offered clues about what the future might hold for those areas in Asia and Africa still chafing under colonial dominion but seeking independence. Having gained their independence in the nineteenth century, most sovereign nations in Latin America thereafter struggled to achieve political and economic stability in the midst of interference from foreign powers. The era of the Great War and the Great Depression proved crucial to solidifying and exposing to view the neocolonial structures that guided affairs in Latin America. Generally seen as an indirect and more subtle form of imperial control, neocolonialism usually took shape as foreign economic domination but did not exclude more typically imperial actions such as military intervention and political interference. In Central and South America, as well as in Mexico and the Caribbean, this new imperial influence came not from former colonial rulers in Spain and Portugal but, rather, from wealthy, industrial-capitalist powerhouses such as Great Britain and especially the United States. Neocolonialism impinged on the independent political and economic development of Latin American states, but it did not prevent nationalist leaders from devising strategies to combat the newfound imperialism.

The Impact of the Great War and the Great Depression

Reorientation of Political and Nationalist Ideals

The Great War and the Russian revolution, along with the ongoing Mexican revolution, spread radical ideas and the promise of new political possibilities throughout Latin America. The disparate ideals emerging from this time of political ferment found receptive audiences in Latin America before but especially during the global economic crisis of the Great Depression. Marxism, Vladimir Lenin's theories on

Diego Rivera's *Imperialism* was one in a series of paintings on the United States and offered a visual critique of U.S. neocolonialism in Latin America.

capitalism and imperialism, and a growing concern for the impoverished Indian masses as well as exploited peasants and workers in Latin American societies informed the outlooks of many disgruntled intellectuals and artists. Although those revolutionary doctrines did not achieve full-scale adoption by Latin American states during the interwar era, their increasing popularity and perceived viability as political options suggested the alternatives open to nations in the future. The Enlightenment-derived liberalism that had shaped independence movements and the political systems of many postindependence nations no longer served as the only form of political legitimacy.

University Protests and Communist Parties The Great War had propelled the United States into a position of world economic leadership. The peoples of Latin America came to experience most intensely this new U.S. economic power, and it was probably no coincidence that the capitalism embraced by the United States came under attack. One of the first institutions in Latin America to witness this rebelliousness was the university. Taking their inspiration from two revolutions inimical to ideals of the United States, university students hailed the Mexican and Russian revolutions and in the 1920s began to demand reforms. Students wanted more representation within the educational system, and their political activism resulted in the long-term politicization of the student bodies at Latin American universities. Universities thereafter became training grounds for future political leaders, including Fidel Castro (1926–), and the ideas explored within an academic setting—from Marxism to anti-imperialism—exerted great influence on those budding politicians.

The currency of radicalism also expressed itself in the formation of political parties that either openly espoused communism or otherwise adopted rebellious agendas for change. Peruvians, for example, created a number of radical new political parties, many of which had connections to a self-educated young Marxist intellectual, José Carlos Mariátegui (1895–1930). Mariátegui felt particular concern for the poor and for the Indians, who constituted approximately 50 percent of Peru's population. He castigated Peru's leaders in journals and newspapers for not helping the downtrodden, and he suffered exile to Europe as a result. He came back from Europe a dedicated Marxist and in 1928 established the Socialist Party of Peru. Mariátegui continued to write and rally in support of laborers, and he was in the midst of helping to create the Peruvian Communist Party when he died from cancer in 1930.

The same agitation that filled José Carlos Mariátegui affected others in Peru and led in the 1920s and 1930s to violence and strikes. The *Alianza Popular Revolucionaria Americana* (Popular American Revolutionary Alliance, or APRA) gave another voice to those critical of Peru's ruling system. This party's followers, known as *Apristas,* advocated indigenous rights and anti-imperialism among other causes. *Aprismo* offered a radical but noncommunist alternative to Peruvians, and it stemmed from the ideas of Victor Raúl Haya de la Torre (1895–1979). Haya de la Torre began his political activism as a student protester and as a supporter of a workers' movement. Exiled like Mariátegui, Haya de la Torre nonetheless imparted his eclectic views to APRA, including both staunch anti-imperialism and a plan for capitalist development that had peasants and workers cooperating with the middle class. The more traditional power of the military and landed elites in Peru managed to contain these rebellious movements, but the cultural and political popularity of radicalism and its intellectual proponents persisted.

Diego Rivera and Radical Artistic Visions The ideological transformations apparent in Latin America be-

came stunningly and publicly visible in the murals painted by famed Mexican artist Diego Rivera (1886–1957). Artistically trained in Mexico in his youth, Rivera went to study in Europe in 1907 and did not return to Mexico until 1921. Influenced by the art of both Renaissance artists and cubists, Rivera also experienced the turmoil and shifting political sensibilities taking place during the Great War and its aftermath. He blended his artistic and political visions in vast murals that he intended for viewing and appreciation by the masses. He believed that art should be on display for working people. Along with other Mexican muralists, such as David Alfaro Siqueiros (1896–1974) and José Clemente Orozco (1883–1949), Rivera shaped the politicized art of Mexico for decades.

Diego Rivera celebrated indigenous Mexican art and pre-Columbian folk traditions, and he incorporated radical political ideas in his style and approach to mural painting. The government commissioned him in the late 1920s and 1930s to create large frescoes for public buildings, and Rivera artistically transcribed the history of Mexico, replete with its social ills, on the walls of such structures as the National Palace and the Ministry of Education in Mexico City. An activist in the Mexican Communist Party, he taught briefly in Moscow in the late 1920s. In the early 1930s the Detroit Institute of Arts commissioned him to paint murals for a U.S. audience, and this migration of his art to the United States soon caused a controversy.

In 1933 Rivera received a request to paint murals for the RCA building in Rockefeller Center in New York City. He included in one panel a portrait of Vladimir Lenin, which outraged those who had commissioned the work. His mural was destroyed. Rivera in turn undertook a series of twenty-one paintings on United States history titled *Portrait of America.* He labeled one of the most pointed and critical paintings *Imperialism,* which visualized and advertised the economic interference and political repressiveness engendered by U.S. neocolonialism in Latin America. Rivera depicted massive guns and tanks extending over the New York Stock Exchange. In the foreground and at the edges of the Stock Exchange are a variety of Latin American victims of this monied-military oppression, including Central Americans laboring for the United Fruit Company and others toiling for the Standard Oil Company. Overlooking all of this in the upper-right corner is Augusto César Sandino (1893–1934), the martyred nationalist hero who opposed U.S. intervention in Nicaragua. Rivera made visible the impact of U.S. imperialism on Latin American societies, and by doing so he helped spread political activism in the Americas.

The Evolution of Economic Imperialism

United States Economic Domination Latin American states were no strangers to foreign economic domination in the nineteenth and early twentieth centuries. Their export-oriented economies had long been tied to global finances and had long been subject to controls imposed by foreign investors, largely those from Great Britain and the United States. The major evolution in economic neocolonialism during this period concerned the growing predominance of the United States in the economic affairs of Latin American nations. The Great War sealed this transition to U.S. supremacy, and U.S. investments in Latin America soared in the 1920s. Between 1924 and 1929, U.S. banks and businesses more than doubled their financial interests in Latin America as investments grew from $1.5 billion to $3.5 billion. Much of that money went toward the takeover of businesses extracting vital minerals, such as copper-mining firms in Chile and oil-drilling concerns in Venezuela.

Dollar Diplomacy That U.S. neocolonialism was meant to be largely economic became evident in the policies of President William Howard Taft (1857–1931). In his final address to Congress in 1912, Taft argued that the United States should substitute "dollars for bullets" in its foreign policy. He wanted businesses to develop foreign markets through peaceful commerce and believed that expensive military intervention should be avoided as much as possible. Likewise, by replacing European investments with U.S. investments, the United States would face fewer tests of the Monroe Doctrine or its 1904 Roosevelt corollary, which justified direct intervention in Latin American nations deemed unstable by the United States. This new vision of U.S. expansion abroad, dubbed "dollar diplomacy" by critics, encapsulated the gist of what those in Latin America perceived as "Yankee imperialism."

Economic Depression and Experimentation The economic crisis of the Great Depression demonstrated the extent to which Latin America had become integrated in the world economy. With some exceptions, exports had continued in the interwar period to help nations achieve basic solvency and even enough economic expansion to institute social reforms. The Great Depression, however, halted fifty years of economic growth in Latin America and illustrated the region's susceptibility to global economic crises. The increasing U.S. capital investments for nascent industries and other financial concerns during the 1920s could not be maintained during this catastrophic economic downturn. Most Latin American states, because they exported agricultural products or raw materials, were further vulnerable to the effects of the depression. The prices of sugar from the Caribbean, coffee from Brazil and Colombia, wheat and beef from Argentina, tin from Bolivia, nitrates from Chile, and many other products fell sharply after 1929. Attempts by producers to raise prices by holding supplies off the market—Brazilians, for example, set fire to coffee beans or used them in the construction of highways—failed, and throughout Latin America unemployment rates increased rapidly. The drastic decline in the price of the region's exports and the drying-up of foreign capital prompted Latin American governments to raise tariffs on foreign products and impose various other restrictions on foreign trade. Those same conditions also

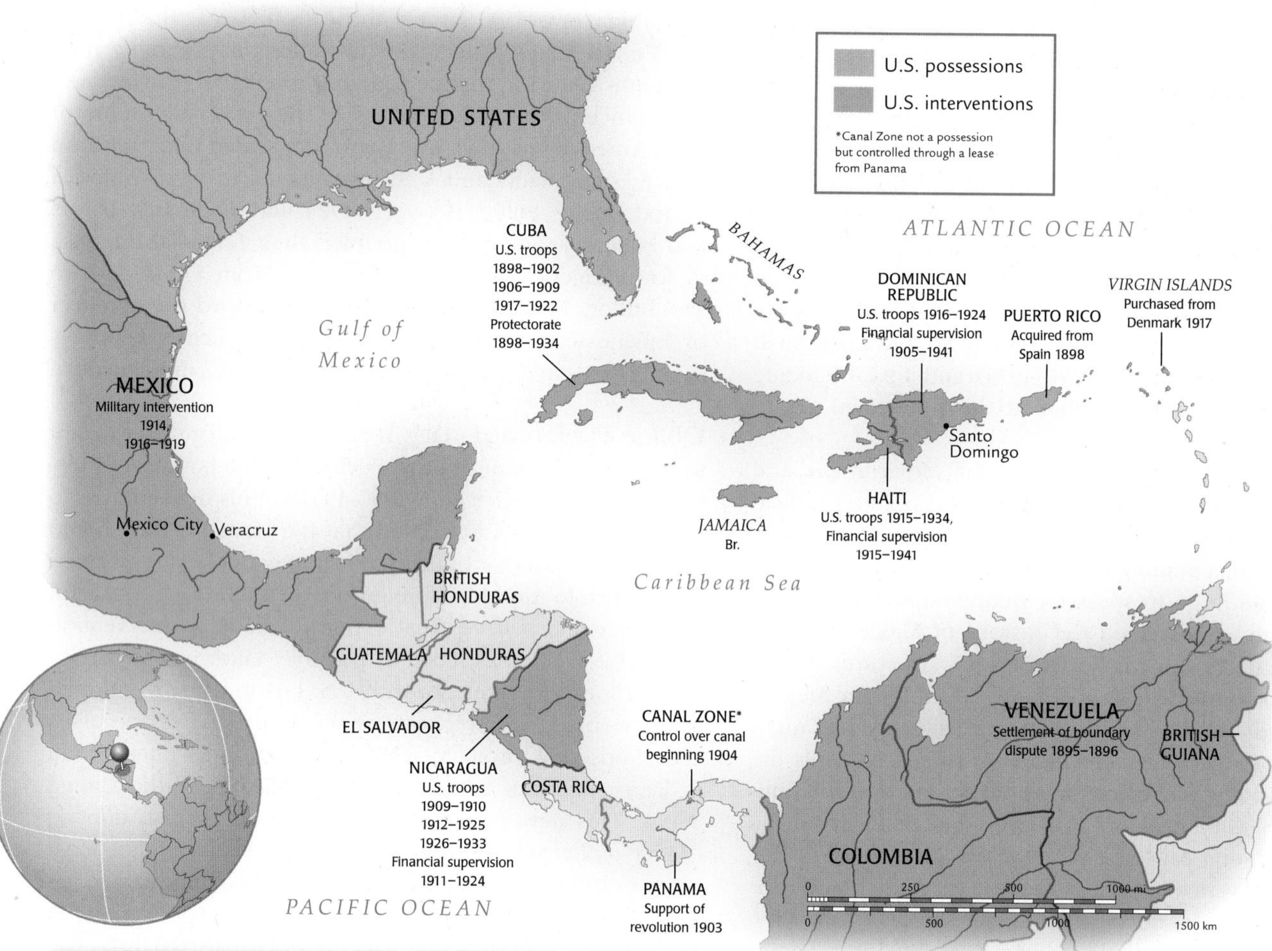

MAP 35.2
The United States in Latin America, 1895–1941.
Note the number of Latin American states where U.S. troops intervened in local politics.
On what basis did U.S. policymakers justify those interventions?

encouraged domestic manufacturing, which made important gains in many Latin American nations.

Although the weaknesses of export-oriented economies and industrial development financed by foreigners became evident during the Great Depression, the international crisis also allowed Latin American nations to take alternative paths to economic development. Economic policy stressing internal economic development was most visible in Brazil, where dictator-president (1930–1945, 1950–1954) Getúlio Dornelles Vargas (1883–1954) turned his nation into an *estado novo* (new state). Ruling with the backing of the military but without the support of the landowning elite, Vargas and his government during the 1930s and 1940s embarked on a program of industrialization that created new enterprises. Key among them was the iron and steel industry. The Vargas regime also implemented protectionist policies that shielded domestic production from foreign competition, which pleased both industrialists and urban workers. Social welfare initiatives accompanied industrial development, protecting workers with health and safety regulations, minimum wages, limits on working hours, unemployment compensation, and retirement benefits. The Great Depression contributed in many ways to the evolution of both economic neocolonialism and economic experimentation within Latin American states.

Conflicts with a "Good Neighbor"

The "Good Neighbor Policy" The pressures of the Great Depression and the instability of global politics led to a reassessment of U.S. foreign policy in Latin America during the late 1920s and 1930s. U.S. leaders realized the costliness and the ineffectiveness of their previous direct interventions in Latin America, especially when committing U.S. Marines as peacekeeping forces. To extricate U.S. military forces and rely more fully on dollar diplomacy, policymakers instituted certain innovations that nonetheless called into question any true change of heart among U.S. neocolonialists. They approved "sweetheart treaties" that guaranteed U.S. financial control in the Caribbean economies of Haiti and the Dominican Republic, for example, and the U.S. Marines provided training for indigenous police forces to keep the peace and maintain law and order. These national guards tended to be less expensive than maintaining forces of U.S. Marines, and the guards' leaders usually worked to keep cordial relations with the United States. This revamped U.S. approach to relations with Latin America became known as the "Good Neighbor Policy," and it was most closely associated with the administration of Franklin D. Roosevelt (1882–1945). Although Roosevelt appeared more well-intentioned in his exercise of the policy, events in Nicaragua before and during the beginning of his administration highlighted the limits of U.S. neighborliness.

A 1920s photograph of Nicaraguan patriot leader Augusto César Sandino. Sandino opposed the presence of the United States in Nicaragua and fought to expel U.S. Marines in his country. He was murdered by officers from the U.S.-friendly National Guard in 1934.

Nicaragua and the *Guarda Nacional* U.S. financial interests had long influenced the economy of Nicaragua, and those substantial investments—whether in the transportation industry or in bananas—served to justify U.S. intervention when revolts or civil wars broke out. The mid- and late 1920s again witnessed the outbreak of civil war in Nicaragua and the repeated insertion of the Marines to restore order. Leading the opposition to Nicaraguan conservatives and the occupation of Nicaragua by U.S. Marines was Augusto César Sandino, a nationalist and liberal general who refused to accept any peace settlement that left Marines on Nicaraguan soil.

As part of a plan to remove U.S. forces, the United States established and trained the *Guarda Nacional,* or National Guard, in Nicaragua. The U.S.-supervised elections of 1932 brought Juan Batista Sacasa (president, 1932–1936) into power, and U.S. troops departed, having positioned the brutal but trusted Anastacio Somoza Garcia (1896–1956) as commander of the Guard. Even though conflicts between Sandino's forces and Somoza's Guard persisted, Sandino explored options with Sacasa and Somoza for ending the rebellion given the departure of the Marines. Officers from the National Guard murdered Sandino in 1934, and Somoza soon after fulfilled his ambitions and became president of his country. Somoza endeavored successfully to maintain the loyalty of the National Guard and to prove himself a good neighbor to the United States. He visited Washington, D.C., in 1939 and renamed the Nicaraguan capital city's main thoroughfare after Roosevelt. He also began to collect what became the largest fortune in Nicaragua's history and to establish a political dynasty that ruled the nation for decades to come. In the meantime, Sandino gained heroic status as a martyr who died in part because he fought the good neighbor to the north.

Cárdenas' Mexico However flawed, the Good Neighbor Policy evolved under Roosevelt into a more conciliatory U.S. approach to Latin American relations. The interventionist corollary to the Monroe Doctrine enunciated previously by President Theodore Roosevelt (1859–1919) was formally renounced in December 1933, when Secretary of State Cordell Hull attended the Seventh International Conference of American States in Montevideo, Uruguay. Hull signed the "Convention on the Rights and Duties of States," which held that "no state has the right to intervene in the internal or external affairs of another." That proposition faced a severe challenge in March 1938 when Mexican president Lázaro Cárdenas (1895–1970) nationalized the oil industry, much of which was controlled by foreign investors from the United States and Great Britain.

Given the history of tempestuous relations between the United States and Mexico, including multiple U.S. military incursions into Mexico during the revolution, there was little

This Hollywood publicity photo of Carmen Miranda features the type of lively costuming that made her a colorful favorite in both the United States and Latin America.

panies, and his nationalization of the oil industry proved popular with the Mexican people.

Neighborly Cultural Exchanges Although the nationalization crisis in Mexico ended in a fashion that suggested the strength of the Good Neighbor Policy, a good deal of the impetus for that policy came from economic and political concerns associated with the Great Depression and the deterioration of international relations in the 1930s. The United States wanted to cultivate Latin American markets for its exports, and it wanted to distance itself from the militarist behavior of Asian and European imperial powers. The U.S. government knew it needed to improve relations with Latin America, if only to secure those nations' support in the increasingly likely event of another global war. Widespread Mexican migration to the United States during and after the Great War suggested the attractiveness of the United States for at least some Latin Americans. Filling the migration void left by Europeans prevented from coming to the United States by the war and by the U.S. immigration restriction laws of the 1920s, Mexican men, women, and children entered the United States in the hundreds of thousands to engage in agricultural and industrial work. The migrants suffered the animosity of some U.S. citizens, who considered them "cheap Mexican labor," but the political power of agribusinesses prevented the government from instituting legal restrictions on Mexican migration. Federal and local officials managed, however, to deport thousands of Mexicans during the Great Depression.

Trying to contribute to the repairing of relations and the promoting of more positive images of Latin American and U.S. relations, Hollywood adopted a Latin American singing and dancing sensation, Carmen Miranda (1909–1955). Born in Portugal but raised from childhood in Brazil, Miranda found fame on a Rio de Janeiro radio station and recorded hundreds of hit songs. A Broadway producer lured her to the United States, but she gained her greatest visibility in such films as *Down Argentine Way* (1940) and many others produced during World War II. Carmen Miranda appeared as an exotic Latin American woman, usually clothed in sexy, colorful costumes that featured amazing headdresses adorned with the

chance for a peaceful resolution to this provocative move on the part of Cárdenas. The reluctance of U.S. and British oil companies to adhere to an arbitration decree granting concessions to Mexican oil workers prompted him to this drastic act. His radical persuasions also drove Cárdenas to this extreme, as did his intent to implement some of the progressive provisions of the Constitution of 1917. Despite calls for a strong U.S. and British response, Roosevelt and his administration officials resisted the demands of big businesses and instead called for a cool, calm response and negotiations to end the conflict. This plan prevailed, and the foreign oil companies ultimately had to accept only $24 million in compensation rather than the $260 million that they initially demanded. Cárdenas cleverly based the compensation price on the tax value claimed by the oil com-

Chiquita Banana, an advertising icon used to promote a good image of the United Fruit Company, was a replica in fruit of the singing and acting sensation Carmen Miranda.

fruits grown in Latin America—such as bananas. She softened representations of Latin Americans for audiences in the United States, providing a less threatening counterpoint to laboring migrants or women guerrilla fighters in Mexico's revolution. She also became a source of pride for Brazilians, who reveled in her Hollywood success. Hollywood's espousal of Roosevelt's Good Neighbor Policy proved a success.

Equally successful as a marketing device, although one that illustrated the continued limitations of the Good Neighbor Policy, was the United Fruit Company's appropriation of Carmen Miranda's image for the selling of the bananas that symbolized U.S. economic control of regions throughout Central America and the Caribbean. The United Fruit Company owned 160,000 acres of land in the Caribbean by 1913, and already by 1918 U.S. consumers bought fully 90 percent of Nicaragua's bananas. Not content with such market control, the United Fruit Company's advertising executives in 1944 crafted "Chiquita Banana," a female banana look-alike of Carmen Miranda. In singing radio commercials, Chiquita Banana taught U.S. consumers about the storage and various uses of bananas ("I'm Chiquita Banana / And I've come to say / Bananas have to ripen / In a certain way"). This singing banana promoted the sales of United Fruit Company bananas, and for consumers in the United States, it gave the prototypical neocolonial company in Latin America a softer, less threatening image—one that challenged, for example, the more ideologically raw representation in Diego Rivera's *Imperialism*.

in perspective

In the decades after the Great War, and in the midst of the Great Depression, intellectuals and political activists in Asia, Africa, and Latin America challenged the ideological and economic underpinnings of empire and neocolonialism. Often embracing the ideas and theories that disseminated around the globe as a result of the war, including self-determination, socialism, communism, and anti-imperialism, radicals and nationalists revised understandings of political identity in the colonial and neocolonial worlds.

Japanese and U.S. imperial practices incited military and civil discord within their respective spheres, while European colonial rulers continued to limit, often brutally, the freedom of peoples in India and Africa. Like Shanfei, young intellectuals and older political leaders alike emerged transformed in these years. Their efforts to inspire nationalism and to achieve economic and political autonomy came to fruition later—after another world war had come and gone. ●

CHRONOLOGY

1912	Taft establishes dollar diplomacy as U.S. foreign policy
1914–1918	2.5 million African troops and carriers serve in the Great War
1919	May Fourth Movement in China
1920	Non-Cooperation Movement in India
1921	Rivera returns to Mexico to paint
1928	Socialist Party of Peru is founded
1929	Beginning of Great Depression
1930	Civil Disobedience Movement in India
1930s–1940s	Vargas's *Estado Novo* in Brazil
1931	Japanese invasion of Manchuria
1933	Roosevelt begins practice of the Good Neighbor Policy
1934	Long March by Chinese Communists
1934	Sandino is murdered in Nicaragua
1935	Government of India Act
1938	Cárdenas nationalizes oil industry in Mexico

For Further Reading

A. Adu Boahen, ed. *Africa under Colonial Domination, 1880–1935.* Berkeley, 1985. Part of the ambitious UNESCO General History of Africa (vol. 7), this work reflects how different Africans view their history.

Judith Brown. *Modern India: The Origins of Asian Democracy.* 2nd ed. Oxford, 1994. This survey is a good introduction to the past two hundred years of Indian history.

Victor Bulmer-Thomas, John H. Coatsworth, and Robert Cortés Conde, eds. *The Cambridge Economic History of Latin America.* Vol. 2: *The Long Twentieth Century.* Cambridge, 2006. Scholarly collection of essays that outlines the region's main economic trends and developments.

Ian Buruma. *Inventing Japan, 1853–1964.* New York, 2003. A respected journalist compresses a century of complex history into a short and elegant book.

Prasenjit Duara. *Sovereignty and Authenticity: Manchukuo and the East Asian Modern.* Lanham, Md., 2003. Using the Japanese puppet state of Manchukuo as a focal point, this is a technical and highly demanding but impressive study of imperialism, nationalism, and modernity.

Cynthia Enloe. *Bananas, Beaches & Bases: Making Feminist Sense of International Politics.* Berkeley, 1989. A gendered analysis of U.S. and other foreign policies through such categories as tourism and diplomats' spouses.

William Gould. *Hindu Nationalism and the Language of Politics in Late Colonial India.* New York, 2004. Political history of India on the eve of independence.

Robert E. Hannigan. *The New World Power: American Foreign Policy, 1898–1917.* Philadelphia, 2002. A detailed account of U.S. foreign relations that links class, race, and gender influences to policymakers.

Lawrence James. *Raj: The Making and Unmaking of British India.* New York, 1998. A sweeping, narrative account of the Raj and British influence in the Indian subcontinent.

Robert W. July. *A History of the African People.* 5th ed. Long Grove, Ill., 1997. A critically acclaimed survey that explores themes that cut across time and place.

Patrick Marnham. *Dreaming with His Eyes Wide Open: A Life of Diego Rivera.* Berkeley, 2000. An engaging and well-received biography, which includes an appendix with reprints of Rivera's major mural paintings.

Jim Masselos. *Indian Nationalism: A History.* 3rd ed. Columbia, 1998. A keen work that remains the standard, most readable introduction to Indian leaders and movements.

Michael C. Meyer, William L. Sherman, and Susan M. Deeds. *The Course of Mexican History.* 6th ed. Oxford, 1999. An updated survey of Mexican history from pre-Columbian to modern times.

Roland Oliver and Anthony Atmore. *Africa since 1800.* 4th ed. Cambridge, 1994. An updated version of a well-regarded survey.

Anthony Read and David Fisher. *The Proudest Day: India's Long Road to Independence.* New York, 1998. Written for the general reader, this is a compelling and colorful account of India's road to freedom.

Elizabeth Schmidt. *Mobilizing the Masses: Gender, Ethnicity, and Class in the Nationalist Movement in Guinea, 1939–1958.* Portsmouth, N.H., 2005. Details the emergence of lesser-known but powerful subaltern anticolonial networks that preceded formal nationalist organizations in French West Africa.

Vera Schwarcz. *The Chinese Enlightenment: Intellectuals and the Legacy of May Fourth Movement of 1919.* Berkeley, 1986. A gracefully written, thoughtful work.

Steve Striffler and Mark Moberg, eds. *Banana Wars: Power, Production, and History in the Americas.* Durham, 2003. Interdisciplinary analysis of the transformative impact of the banana industry on global trade and the consequences for Latin American societies and economies.

Odd Arne Westad. *Decisive Encounters: The Chinese Civil War, 1946–1950.* Stanford, 2003. An engagingly written work that introduces the reader to the salient political and military events that led to the eventual defeat of the Guomindang.

New Conflagrations: World War II and the Cold War

chapter 36

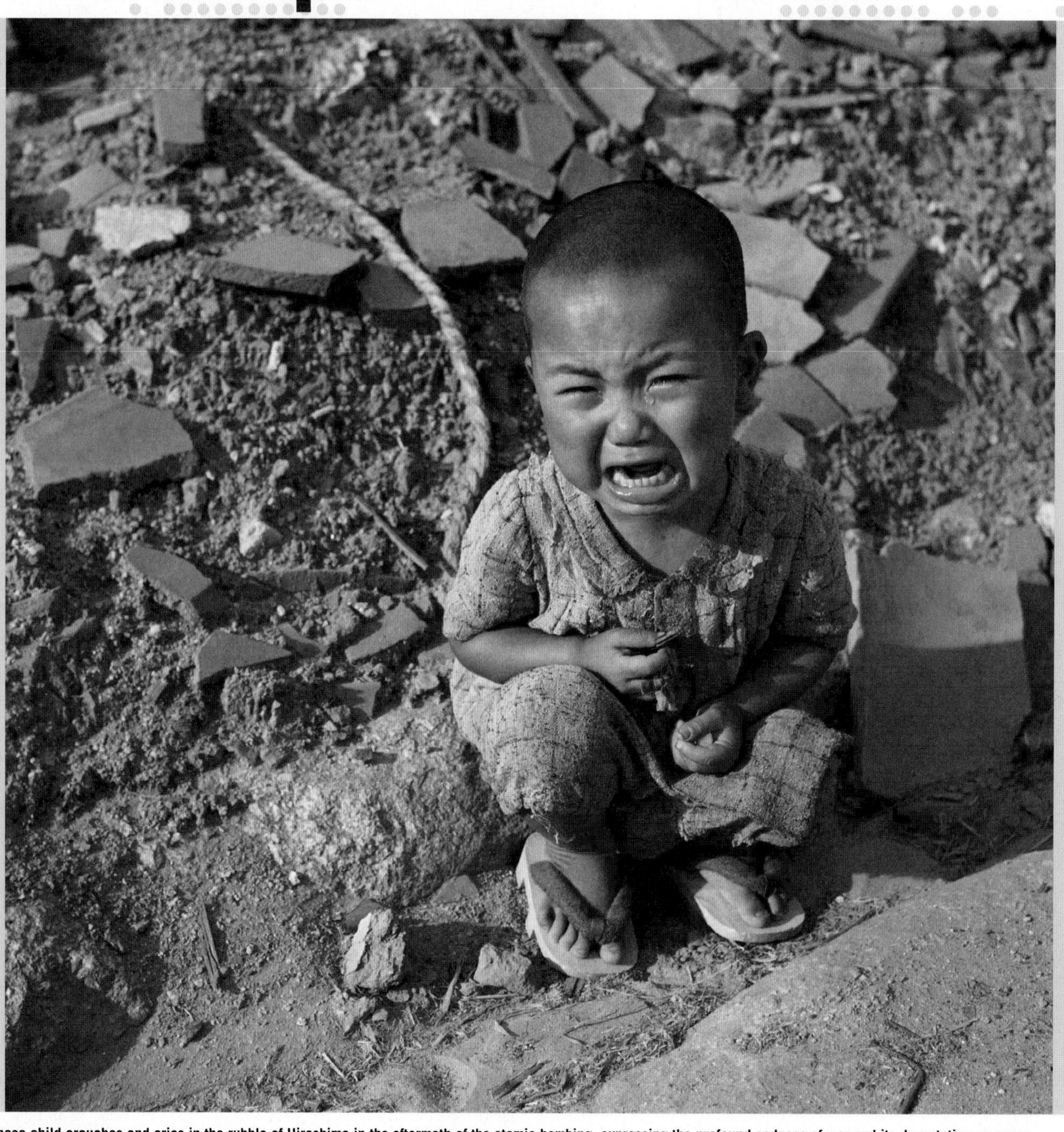

A Japanese child crouches and cries in the rubble of Hiroshima in the aftermath of the atomic bombing, expressing the profound sadness of war and its devastating weapons.

EYEWITNESS:
Victor Tolley finds Tea and Sympathy in Nagasaki

On 6 August 1945, as he listened to the armed services radio on Saipan (a U.S.-controlled island in the north Pacific), U.S. marine Victor Tolley heard the news: the president of the United States announced that a "terrible new weapon" had been deployed against the city of Hiroshima, Japan. Tolley and the other marines rejoiced, realizing that the terrible new weapon—the atomic bomb—might end the war and relieve them of the burden of invading Japan. A few days later Tolley heard that the city of Nagasaki had also been hit with an atomic bomb. He remembered the ominous remarks that accompanied the news of this atomic destruction: radio announcers suggested it might be decades before the cities would be inhabitable.

Imagine Tolley's astonishment when a few weeks later, after the Japanese surrender, he and his buddies were assigned to the U.S. occupation forces in Nagasaki. Assured by a superior officer that Nagasaki was "very safe," Tolley lived there for three months, during which he became very familiar with the devastation wrought by the atomic bomb. On his first day in Nagasaki, Tolley investigated the city. As he noted, "It was just like walking into a tomb. There was total silence. You could smell this death all around ya. There was a terrible odor."

Tolley also became acquainted with some of the Japanese survivors in Nagasaki, which proved to be an eye-opening experience. After seeing "young children with sores and burns all over," Tolley, having become separated from his unit, encountered another young child. He and the boy communicated despite the language barrier between them. Tolley showed the child pictures of his wife and two daughters. The Japanese boy excitedly took Tolley home to meet his surviving family, his father and his pregnant sister. Tolley recalled,

> This little kid ran upstairs and brought his father down. A very nice Japanese gentleman. He could speak English. He bowed and said, "We would be honored if you would come upstairs and have some tea with us." I went upstairs in this strange Japanese house. I noticed on the mantel a picture of a young Japanese soldier. I asked him, "Is this your son?" He said, "That is my daughter's husband. We don't

know if he's alive. We haven't heard." The minute he said that, it dawned on me that they suffered the same as we did. They lost sons and daughters and relatives, and they hurt too.

Before his chance meeting with this Japanese family, Tolley had felt nothing except contempt for the Japanese. He pointed out, "We were trained to kill them. They're our enemy. Look what they did in Pearl Harbor. They asked for it and now we're gonna give it to 'em. That's how I felt until I met this young boy and his family." But after coming face-to-face with his enemies, Tolley saw only their common humanity, their suffering, and their hurt. The lesson he learned was that "these people didn't want to fight us."

The civility that reemerged at the end of the war was little evident during the war years. The war began and ended with Japan. In 1931 Japan invaded Manchuria, thereby ending the post–Great War peace, and the United States concluded hostilities by dropping atomic bombs on Hiroshima and Nagasaki. Between 1931 and 1945 the conflict expanded well beyond east Asia. By 1941 World War II was a truly global war. Hostilities spread from east Asia and the Pacific to Europe, north Africa, and the Atlantic, and large and small nations from North America, Asia, Europe, Africa, and Australia came into close contact for the duration of the war. Beyond its immense geographic scope, World War II exceeded even the Great War (1914–1918) in demonstrating the willingness of societies to make enormous sacrifices in lives and other resources to achieve complete victory. At least sixty million people perished in the war, and civilian deaths likely outnumbered military casualties. In this total war, contacts with enemies, occupiers, and liberators affected populations around the world. World War II redefined gender roles and relations between colonial peoples and their masters, as women contributed to their nations' war efforts and as colonial peoples exploited the war's weakening of imperial nations.

The atomic age and cold war that began as World War II ended complicated the task of postwar recovery. The cold war, over time, illustrated how deep the rift between the United States of America and the Union of Soviet Socialist Republics (USSR) had grown since 1945, and signaled a major realignment in international relations and the global balance of power. The cold war was a strategic struggle that developed after World War II between the United States and its allies on the one hand and the USSR and its allied communist countries on the other. It was this clash between the forces of democratic capitalism and communism, each armed with increasingly powerful nuclear weapons, that gave rise to a new set of global relationships, shaping the foreign policies, economic systems, and political institutions of nations throughout the world. The hostility between these new adversaries resulted in a divided world. First Europe, and Germany in particular, split into separate blocs and states. Then the cold war became global in scale as the superpowers came into conflict in nations as far afield as Korea and Cuba. Over the course of four decades, the cold war evolved from mutual hostility to peaceful coexistence and détente, finally coming to a close near the end of the twentieth century.

ORIGINS OF WORLD WAR II

In 1941 two major alliances squared off against each other. Japan, Germany, and Italy, along with their conquered territories, formed the Axis powers, the name of the alignment between Nazi Germany and Fascist Italy that had been formed in October 1936. The term was used later to include Germany's other allies in World War II, especially Japan. The Allied powers included France and its empire; Great Britain and its empire and Commonwealth allies (such as Canada, Australia, and New Zealand); the Soviet Union; China; and the United States and its allies in Latin America. The construction of these global alliances took place over the course of the 1930s and early 1940s.

Driven in part by a desire to revise the peace settlements that followed the Great War and affected by the economic distress of the worldwide depression, Japan, Italy, and Germany engaged in a campaign of territorial expansion that ultimately broke apart the structure of international cooperation that had kept the world from violence in the 1920s. These *revisionist powers,* so called because they revised, or overthrew, the terms of the post–Great War peace, confronted nations that were committed to the international system and to the avoidance of another world war. To expand their global influence, the revisionist nations remilitarized and conquered territories they deemed central to their needs and to the spread of their imperial control. The Allies acquiesced to the revisionist powers' early aggressive actions,

Japanese soldiers execute Chinese prisoners. In the Japanese invasion of China, four hundred thousand Chinese died when the Japanese used them for bayonet practice or executed them.

but after they had been attacked, in the late 1930s and early 1940s, the Allies engaged the Axis powers in a total war.

Japan's War in China

The global conflict opened with Japan's attacks on China in the 1930s: the conquest of Manchuria between 1931 and 1932 was the first step in the revisionist process of expansionism and aggression. Within Japan a battle continued between supporters and opponents of the aggressive policies adopted in Manchuria, but during the course of the 1930s the militarist position dominated, and for the most part civilians lost control of the government and the military. In 1933, after the League of Nations condemned its actions in Manchuria, Japan withdrew from the league and followed an ultranationalist and promilitary policy.

Seeing territorial control as essential to its survival, Japan launched a full-scale invasion of China in 1937. A battle between Chinese and Japanese troops at the Marco Polo Bridge in Beijing in July 1937 was the opening move in Japan's undeclared war against China. Japanese troops took Beijing and then moved south toward Shanghai and Nanjing, the capital of China. Japanese naval and air forces bombed Shanghai, killing thousands of civilians, and secured it as a landing area for armies bound for Nanjing. By December 1937 Shanghai and Nanjing had fallen, and during the following six months Japanese forces won repeated victories.

The Rape of Nanjing China became the first nation to experience the horrors of World War II: brutal warfare against civilians and repressive occupation. During the invasion of China, Japanese forces used methods of warfare that led to mass death and suffering on a new, almost unimaginable, level. Chinese civilians were among the first to feel the effects of aerial bombing of urban centers; the people of Shanghai died by the tens of thousands when Japanese bombers attacked the city to soften Chinese resistance. What became known as the Rape of Nanjing demonstrated the horror of the war as the residents of Nanjing became victims of Japanese troops inflamed by war passion and a sense of racial superiority. Over the course of two months, Japanese soldiers raped seven thousand women, murdered hundreds of thousands of unarmed soldiers and civilians, and burned one-third of the homes in Nanjing. Four hundred thousand Chinese lost their lives as Japanese soldiers used them for bayonet practice and machine-gunned them into open pits.

Chinese Resistance Despite Japanese military successes and the subsequent Japanese occupation of Chinese lands, Chinese resistance persisted throughout the war. Japanese aggression aroused feelings of nationalism among the Chinese that continued to grow as the war wore on. By September 1937 nationalists and communists had agreed on a "united front" policy against the Japanese, uniting themselves into standing armies of some 1.7 million soldiers. Although Chinese forces failed to defeat the Japanese, who retained naval and air superiority, they tied down half the Japanese army, 750,000 soldiers, by 1941.

Throughout the war, the coalition of nationalists and communists threatened to fall apart. Although neither side was willing to risk open civil war, the two groups engaged in numerous military clashes as their forces competed for both control of enemy territory and political control within China. Those clashes rendered Chinese resistance less effective, and while both sides continued the war against Japan, each fought ultimately for its own advantage. The nationalists suffered major casualties in their battles with Japanese forces, but they kept the Guomindang government alive by moving inland to Chongqing. Meanwhile, the communists carried on guerrilla operations against the Japanese invaders. Lacking air force and artillery, communist guerrillas staged hit-and-run operations from their mountain bases, sabotaged bridges and railroads, and harassed Japanese troops. The guerrillas did not defeat the Japanese, but they captured the loyalty of many Chinese peasants through their resistance to the Japanese and their moderate policies of land reform. At the end of the war, the communists were poised to lead China.

Japanese soldiers in 1938 engaged in strenuous physical education and kept fit in order to fight the Chinese.

The Japanese invasion of China met with intense international opposition, but by that time Japan had chosen another path—and it was an auspicious time to further its attack on the international system. Other world powers, distracted by depression and military aggression in Europe, could offer little in the way of an effective response to Japanese actions. The government of Japan aligned itself with the other revisionist nations, Germany and Italy, by signing the Tripartite Pact, a ten-year military and economic pact, in September 1940. Japan also cleared the way for further empire building in Asia and the Pacific basin by concluding a neutrality pact with the Soviet Union in April 1941, thereby precluding hostilities on any other front, especially in Manchuria. Japan did not face determined opposition to its expansion until December 1941, when conflict with the United States created a much broader field of action for Japan and its growing empire.

Italian and German Aggression

Italy's expansionism helped destabilize the post–Great War peace and spread World War II to the European continent. Italians suffered tremendously in World War I. Six hundred thousand Italian soldiers died, and the national economy never recovered sufficiently for Italy to function as an equal to other European military and economic powers. Many Italians expected far greater recompense and respect than they received at the conclusion of the Great War. Rather than being treated as a real partner in victory by Britain and France, Italy found itself shut out of the divisions of the territorial spoils of war.

Italy Benito Mussolini promised to bring glory to Italy through the acquisition of territories that it had been denied after the Great War. Italy's conquest of Ethiopia in 1935 and 1936, when added to the previously annexed Libya, created an overseas empire. Italy also intervened in the Spanish Civil War (1936–1939) on the side of General Francisco Franco (1892–1975), whose militarists overthrew the republican government, and annexed Albania in 1939. (Mussolini viewed Albania as a bridgehead for expansion into the Balkans.) The invasion and conquest of Ethiopia in particular infuriated other nations; but, as with Japan's invasion of Manchuria, the League of Nations offered little effective opposition.

What angered nonrevisionists about Italy's conquest of Ethiopia was not just the broken peace. The excessive use of force against the Ethiopians also rankled. Mussolini sent an army of 250,000 soldiers armed with tanks, poison gas, artillery, and aircraft to conquer the Ethiopians, who were entirely unprepared for the assault. The mechanized troops mowed them down. Italy lost 2,000 soldiers while 275,000 Ethiopians lost their lives. Despite its victories in Ethiopia, Italy's prospects for world glory never appeared quite as bright as Japan's, especially since few Italians wanted to go to war. Throughout the interwar years, Italy played a diplomatic game that kept European nations guessing as to its future intentions, but by 1938 it was firmly on the side of the Axis.

Germany Japan and Italy were the first nations to challenge the post–World War I settlements through territorial conquest, but it was Germany that systematically undid the Treaty of Versailles and the fragile peace of the interwar years. Most Germans and their political leaders deeply resented the harsh terms imposed on their nation in 1919, but even the governments of other European nations eventually recognized the extreme nature of the Versailles treaty's terms and turned a blind eye to the revisionist actions of Adolf Hitler (1889–1945) and his government. Hitler came to power in 1933, riding a wave of public discontent with Germany's postwar position of powerlessness and the suffering caused by the Great Depression. Hitler referred to the signing of the 1918 armistice as the "November crime" and blamed it on those he viewed as Germany's internal enemies: Jews, communists, and liberals of all sorts. Neighboring European states—Poland, France, Czechoslovakia, Yugoslavia, Hungary, and Austria—also shared in the blame. Hitler's scheme for ridding Germany of its enemies and reasserting its power was remilitarization—which was legally denied to Germany under the Versailles treaty. Germany's dictator abandoned the peaceful efforts of his predecessors to ease the provisions of the treaty and proceeded unilaterally to destroy it step-by-step. Hitler's aggressive foreign policy helped relieve the German public's feeling of war shame

Ethiopian soldiers train with outmoded equipment that proves no match for Italian forces. At the end of the Great War, Italy, under Benito Mussolini, sought to redress perceived wrongs that denied it territorial gain by conquering Ethiopia with an army of a quarter-million soldiers.

and depression trauma. After withdrawing Germany from the League of Nations in 1933, his government carried out an ambitious plan to strengthen the German armed forces. Hitler reinstated universal military service in 1935, and in the following year his troops entered the previously demilitarized Rhineland that bordered France. Germany joined with Italy in the Spanish Civil War, during which Hitler's troops, especially the air force, honed their skills. In 1938 Hitler began the campaign of expansion that ultimately led to the outbreak of World War II in Europe.

Germany's forced *Anschluss* ("union") with Austria took place in March 1938. Hitler justified this annexation as an attempt to reintegrate all Germans into a single homeland. Europe's major powers, France and Britain, did nothing in response, thereby enhancing Hitler's reputation in the German military and deepening his already deep contempt for the democracies. Soon thereafter, using the same rationale, the Nazis attempted to gain control of the Sudetenland, the western portion of Czechoslovakia. This region was inhabited largely by ethnic Germans, whom Hitler conveniently regarded as persecuted minorities. Although the Czech government was willing to make concessions to the Sudeten Germans, Hitler in September 1938 demanded the immediate cession of the Sudetenland to the German Reich. Against the desires of the Czechoslovak government, the leaders of France and Britain accommodated Hitler and allowed Germany to annex the Sudetenland. Neither the French nor the British were willing to risk a military confrontation with Germany to defend Czechoslovakian territory.

Peace for Our Time At the Munich Conference held in September 1938, European politicians consolidated the policy that came to be known throughout the 1930s as *appeasement*. Attended by representatives of Italy, France, Great Britain, and Germany, the meeting revealed how most nations outside the revisionist sphere had decided to deal with territorial expansion by aggressive nations, especially Germany. In conceding demands to Hitler, or "appeasing" him, the British and French governments extracted a promise that Hitler would cease further efforts to expand German territorial claims. Their goal was to keep peace in Europe, even if it meant making major concessions. Because of public opposition to war, the governments of France and Britain approved the Munich accord. Britain's prime minister, Neville Chamberlain (1869–1940), arrived home from Munich to announce that the meeting had achieved "peace for our time." Unprepared for war and distressed by the depression, nations sympathetic to Britain and France also embraced peace as an admirable goal in the face of aggression by the revisionist nations.

Hitler, however, refused to be bound by the Munich agreement, and in the next year German troops occupied most of Czechoslovakia. As Hitler next threatened Poland, it became clear that the policy of appeasement was a practical and moral failure, which caused Britain and France to abandon it by guaranteeing the security of Poland. By that time Joseph Stalin (1879–1953) was convinced that British and French leaders were conspiring to deflect German aggression toward the Soviet Union. Despite deep ideological differences that divided communists from Nazis, Stalin accordingly sought an accommodation with the Nazi regime. In August 1939 the foreign ministers of the Soviet Union and Germany signed the Russian-German Treaty of Nonaggression, an agreement that shocked and outraged the world. By the terms of the pact, the two nations agreed not to attack each other, and they promised neutrality in the event that either of them went to war with a third party. Additionally, a secret protocol divided eastern Europe into German and Soviet spheres of influence. The protocol provided for German control over western Poland while granting the Soviet Union a free hand in eastern Poland, eastern Romania, Finland, Estonia, Latvia, and Lithuania. Hitler was ready to conquer Europe.

German dive-bombers like this one dominated the early air war in World War II and played a significant role in Blitzkrieg.

TOTAL WAR: THE WORLD UNDER FIRE

Two months after the United States became embroiled in World War II, President Franklin Roosevelt (1882–1945) delivered one of his famous radio broadcasts, known as fireside chats. In it he explained the nature of the war: "This war is a new kind of war," he said. "It is warfare in terms of every continent, every island, every sea, every air lane." There was little exaggeration in FDR's analysis. Before World War II was over, almost every nation had participated in it. Battles raged across the vast Pacific and Atlantic oceans, across Europe and northern Africa, and throughout much of Asia. Virtually every weapon known to humanity was thrown into the war. More than the Great War, this was a conflict where entire societies engaged in warfare and mobilized every available material and human resource.

The war between Japan and China had already stretched over eight years when European nations stormed into battle. Between 1939 and 1941, nations inside and outside Europe were drawn into the conflict. They included the French and British colonies in Africa, India, and the British Dominion allies: Canada, Australia, and New Zealand. Germany's stunning military successes in 1939 and 1940 focused attention on Europe, but after the Soviet Union and the United States entered the war in 1941, the conflict took on global proportions. Almost every nation in the world had gone to war by 1945.

Blitzkrieg: Germany Conquers Europe

During World War II it became common for aggressor nations to avoid overt declarations of war. Instead, the new armed forces relied on surprise, stealth, and swiftness for their conquests. Germany demonstrated the advantages of that strategy in Poland. German forces, banking on their air force's ability to soften resistance and on their *Panzer* ("armored") columns' unmatched mobility and speed, moved into Poland unannounced on 1 September 1939. Within a month they subdued its western expanses while the Soviets took the eastern sections in accordance with the Nazi-Soviet pact. The Germans stunned the world, especially Britain and France, with their *Blitzkrieg* ("lightning war") and sudden victory.

While the forces of Britain and France coalesced to defend Europe without facing much direct action with Nazi forces, the battle of the Atlantic already raged. This sea confrontation between German *Unterseeboote* ("U-boats," or submarines) and British ship convoys carrying food and war matériel proved decisive in the European theater of war. The battle of the Atlantic could easily have gone either way—to the German U-boats attempting to cut off Britain's vital imports or to the convoys devised by the British navy to protect its ships from submarine attacks. Although British intelligence cracked Germany's secret code to the great advantage of the Allies, advance knowledge of the location of submarines was still not always available. Moreover, the U-boats began traveling in wolf packs to negate the effectiveness of convoys protected by aircraft and destroyers.

The Fall of France As the sea battle continued, Germany prepared to break through European defenses. In April 1940 the Germans occupied Denmark and Norway, then launched a full-scale attack on western Europe. Their offensive against Belgium, France, and the Netherlands began in May, and again the Allies were jolted by Blitzkrieg tactics. Belgium and the Netherlands fell first, and the French signed an armistice in June. The fall of France convinced Italy's Benito Mussolini that the Germans were winning the war, and it was time to enter the conflict and reap any potential benefits his partnership with the Germans might offer.

Before the battle of France, Hitler had boasted to his staff, "Gentlemen, you are about to witness the most famous victory in history!" Given France's rapid fall, Hitler was not far wrong. Field Marshal Erwin Rommel put it more colorfully: "The war has become practically a lightning Tour de France!" In a moment of exquisite triumph, Hitler had the French sign their armistice in the very railroad car in which the Germans had signed the armistice in 1918. Trying to rescue some Allied troops before the fall of France, the British engineered a retreat at Dunkirk, but it could not hide the bleak failure of the Allied troops. Britain now stood alone against the German forces.

The Battle of Britain The Germans therefore launched the Battle of Britain, led by its air force, the *Luftwaffe*. They hoped to defeat Britain almost solely through air attacks. "The Blitz," as the British called this air war, rained bombs on heavily populated metropolitan areas, especially London, and killed more than forty thousand British civilians. The Royal Air Force staved off defeat, however, forcing Hitler to abandon plans to invade Britain. By the summer of 1941, Hitler's conquests included the Balkans, and the battlefront extended to north Africa, where the British fought both the Italians and the Germans. The swastika-bedecked Nazi flag now waved from the streets of Paris to the Acropolis in Athens, and Hitler had succeeded beyond his dreams in his quest to reverse the outcome of World War I.

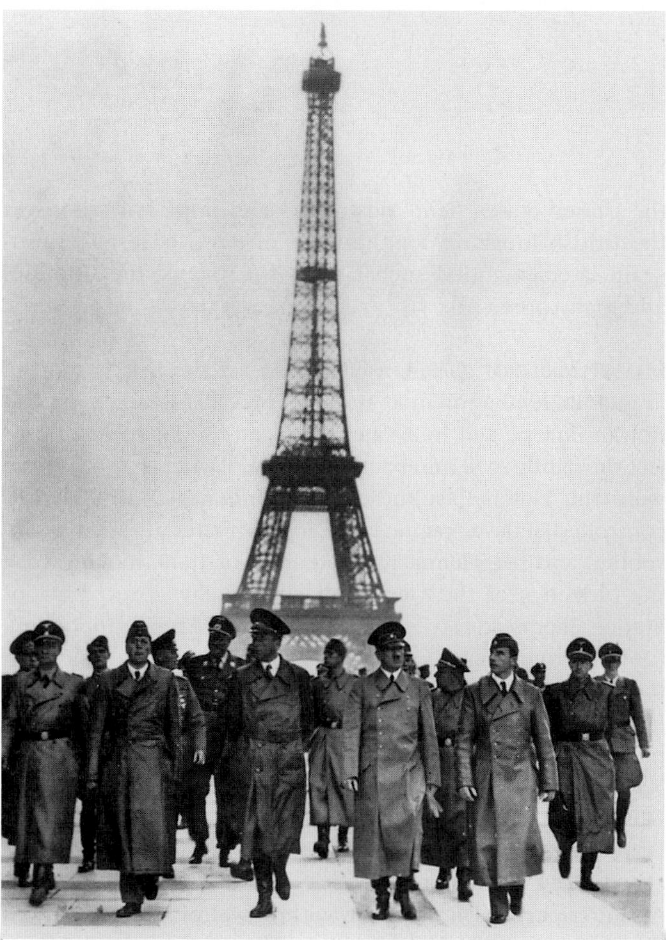

Adolf Hitler proudly walks through conquered Paris in 1940, with the Eiffel Tower as a backdrop.

The German Invasion of the Soviet Union

Flush with victory in the spring of 1941, Hitler turned his sights on the Soviet Union. This land was the ultimate German target, from which Jews, Slavs, and Bolsheviks could be expelled or exterminated to create more *Lebensraum* ("living space") for resettled Germans. Believing firmly in the bankruptcy of the Soviet system, Hitler said of Operation Barbarossa, the code name for the June invasion of the Soviet Union, "You only have to kick in the door, and the whole rotten structure will come crashing down."

Operation Barbarossa On 22 June 1941, Adolf Hitler ordered his armed forces to invade the Soviet Union. For the campaign against the Soviet Union, the German military assembled the largest and most powerful invasion force in history, attacking with 3.6 million soldiers, thirty-seven hundred tanks, and twenty-five hundred planes. The governments of Hungary, Finland, and Romania declared war on the Soviet Union and augmented the German invasion force with their own military contingents totaling about thirty divisions. The invasion, along a front of 3,000 kilometers (1,900 miles), took Stalin by surprise and caught the Red Army off guard. By December 1941 the Germans had captured the Russian heartland, Leningrad had come under siege, and German troops had reached the gates of Moscow. Germany seemed assured of victory.

However, German Blitzkrieg tactics that had earlier proved so effective in Poland and western Europe failed the Germans in the vast expanses of Russia. Hitler and his military leaders underestimated Soviet personnel reserves and industrial capacity. Within a matter of weeks, the 150 German divisions faced 360 divisions of the Red Army. Also, in the early stages of the war Stalin ordered Soviet industry to relocate to areas away from the front. About 80 percent of firms manufacturing war matériel moved to the Ural Mountains between August and October 1941. As a result, the capacity of Soviet industry outstripped that of German industry. The Soviets also received crucial equipment from their allies, notably trucks from the United States. By the time the German forces reached the outskirts of Moscow, fierce Soviet resistance had produced eight hundred thousand German casualties.

The arrival of winter—the most severe in decades—helped Soviet military efforts and prevented the Germans from capturing Moscow. So sure of an early victory were the Germans that they did not bother to supply their troops with winter clothing and boots. One hundred thousand soldiers suffered frostbite, and two thousand of them underwent amputation. The Red Army, in contrast, prepared for winter and

The devastation caused by German bombardments is visible in the wreckage of a London neighborhood in 1944.

found further comfort as the United States manufactured thirteen million pairs of felt-lined winter boots. By early December, Soviet counterattacks along the entire front stopped German advances.

German forces regrouped and inflicted heavy losses on the Red Army during the spring. The Germans briefly regained the military initiative, and by June 1942 German armies raced toward the oil fields of the Caucasus and the city of Stalingrad. As the Germans came on Stalingrad in September, Soviet fortunes of war reached their nadir. At this point the Russians dug in. "Not a step back," Stalin ordered, and he called on his troops to fight a "patriotic" war for Russia. Behind those exhortations lay a desperate attempt to stall the Germans with a bloody street-by-street defense of Stalingrad until the Red Army could regroup for a counterattack.

Battles in Asia and the Pacific

Before 1941 the United States was inching toward greater involvement in the war. After Japan invaded China in 1937, Roosevelt called for a quarantine on aggressors, but his plea fell mostly on deaf ears. However, as war broke out in Europe and tensions with Japan increased, the United States took action. In 1939 it instituted a cash-and-carry policy of supplying the British, in which the British paid cash and carried the materials on their ships. More significant was the lend-lease program initiated in 1941, in which the United States "lent" destroyers and other war goods to the British in return for the lease of naval bases. The program later extended such aid to the Soviets, the Chinese, and many others.

Pearl Harbor German victories over the Dutch and the French in 1940 and Great Britain's precarious military position in Europe and in Asia encouraged the Japanese to project their influence into southeast Asia. Particularly attractive were the Dutch East Indies (now Indonesia) and British-controlled Malaya, regions rich in raw materials such as tin, rubber, and petroleum. In September of 1940, moving with the blessings of the German-backed Vichy government of France, Japanese forces began to occupy French Indochina (now Vietnam, Laos, and Cambodia). The government of the United States responded to that situation by freezing Japanese assets in the United States and by imposing a complete embargo on oil. Great Britain, the Commonwealth of Nations, and the independent colonial government of the Dutch East Indies supported the U.S. oil embargo. Economic pressure, however, did not persuade the Japanese to accede to U.S. demands, which included the renunciation of the Tripartite Pact and the withdrawal of Japanese forces from China and southeast Asia. To Japanese militarists, given the equally unappetizing alternatives of succumbing to U.S. demands or engaging the United States in war, war seemed the lesser of two evils. In October 1941, defense

Flames consumed U.S. battleships in Pearl Harbor after the Japanese attack on 7 December 1941.

minister general Tojo Hideki (1884–1948) assumed the office of prime minister, and he and his cabinet set in motion plans for war against Great Britain and the United States.

The Japanese hoped to destroy American naval capacity in the Pacific with an attack at Pearl Harbor and to clear the way for the conquest of southeast Asia and the creation of a defensive Japanese perimeter that would thwart the Allies' ability to strike at Japan's homeland. On 7 December 1941, "a date which will live in infamy," as Franklin Roosevelt concluded, Japanese pilots took off from six aircraft carriers to attack Hawai`i. More than 350 Japanese bombers, fighters, and torpedo planes struck in two waves, sinking or disabling eighteen ships and destroying more than two hundred. Except for the U.S. aircraft carriers, which were out of the harbor at the time, American naval power in the Pacific was devastated.

On 11 December 1941, though not compelled to do so by treaty, Hitler and Mussolini declared war on the United States. That move provided the United States with the only reason it needed to declare war on Germany and Italy. The United States, Great Britain, and the Soviet Union came together in a coalition that linked two vast and interconnected theaters of war, the European and Asian-Pacific theaters, and ensured the defeat of Germany and Japan. Adolf Hitler's gleeful reaction to the outbreak of war between Japan and the United States proved mistaken: "Now it is impossible for us to lose the war: We now have an ally who has never been vanquished in three thousand years." More accurate was Winston Churchill (1874–1965), prime minister of Britain, who expressed a vast sense of relief and a more accurate assessment of the situation when he said, "So we had won after all!"

Japanese Victories After Pearl Harbor the Japanese swept on to one victory after another. The Japanese coordinated their strike against Pearl Harbor with simultaneous attacks against the Philippines, Guam, Wake Island, Midway Island, Hong Kong, Thailand, and British Malaya. For the next year the Japanese military maintained the initiative in southeast Asia and the Pacific, capturing Borneo, Burma, the Dutch East Indies, and several Aleutian Islands off Alaska. Australia and New Zealand were now in striking distance. The Japanese navy emerged almost unscathed from these campaigns. The humiliating surrender of British-held Singapore in February 1942 dealt a blow to British prestige and shattered any myths of European military invincibility.

Singapore was a symbol of European power in Asia. The slogan under which Japan pursued expansion in Asia was

After the Pearl Harbor attack, Americans expressed great hostility toward the Japanese nationals and Japanese Americans living in the United States, primarily on the west coast. In 1942 President Franklin Roosevelt authorized the forcible removal of approximately 120,000 Japanese and Japanese Americans to relocation or internment camps. This photograph from Seattle in March 1942 shows both the gloom and the patriotism of those on a train bound for a camp; the family is flashing the World War II "V for victory" sign while a boy holds the American flag.

"Asia for Asians," implying that the Japanese would lead Asian peoples to independence from the despised European imperialists and the international order they dominated. In this struggle for Asian independence, Japan required the region's resources and therefore sought to build a "Greater East Asia Co-Prosperity Sphere." The appeal to Asian independence at first struck a responsive chord, but conquest and brutal occupation made it soon obvious to most Asians that the real agenda was "Asia for the Japanese." Proponents of the Greater East Asia Co-Prosperity Sphere advocated Japan's expansion in Asia and the Pacific while cloaking their territorial and economic designs with the idealism of Asian nationalism.

Defeat of the Axis Powers

The entry of the Soviet Union and the United States into the war in 1941 was decisive, because personnel reserves and industrial capacity were the keys to the Allied victories in the European and Asia-Pacific theaters. Despite the brutal exploitation of conquered territories, neither German nor Japanese war production matched that of the Allies, who outproduced their enemies at every turn. The U.S. automotive industry alone, for instance, produced more than four million armored, combat, and supply vehicles of all kinds during the war. Not until the United States joined the struggle in 1942 did the tide in the battle in the Atlantic turn in favor of the Allies. Although German submarines sank a total of 2,452 Allied merchant ships and 175 Allied warships in the course of six years, U.S. naval shipyards simply built more "Liberty Ships" than the Germans could sink. By the end of 1943, sonar, aircraft patrols, and escort aircraft from carriers finished the U-boat as a strategic threat.

Allied Victory in Europe By 1943, German forces in Russia lost the momentum and faced bleak prospects as the Soviets retook territory. Moscow never fell, and the battle for Stalingrad, which ended in February 1943, marked the first large-scale victory for Soviet forces. Desperate German counteroffensives failed repeatedly, and the Red Army, drawing on enormous personnel and material reserves, pushed the German invaders out of Russian territory. By 1944 the Soviets had advanced into Romania, Hungary, and Poland, reaching the suburbs of Berlin in April 1945. At that point, the Soviets had inflicted more than six million casualties on the German enemy—twice the number of the original German invasion force. The Red Army had broken the back of the German war machine.

With the Eastern front disintegrating under the Soviet onslaught, British and U.S. forces attacked the Germans from north Africa and then through Italy. In August 1944 the Allies forced Italy to withdraw from the Axis and to

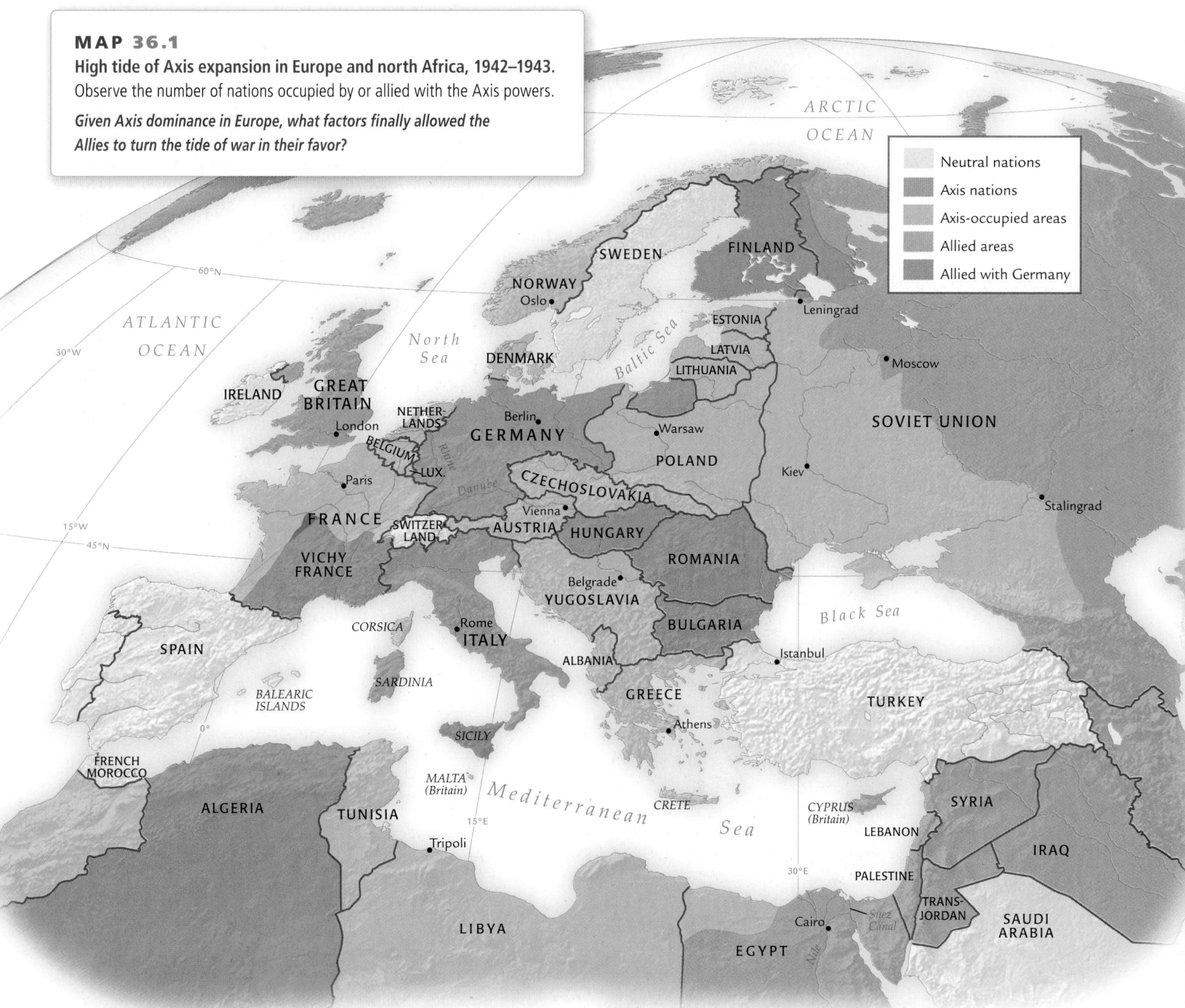

MAP 36.1
High tide of Axis expansion in Europe and north Africa, 1942–1943.
Observe the number of nations occupied by or allied with the Axis powers.
Given Axis dominance in Europe, what factors finally allowed the Allies to turn the tide of war in their favor?

join them. In the meantime, the Germans also prepared for an Allied offensive in the west, where the British and U.S. forces opened a front in France. On D-Day, 6 June 1944, British and U.S. troops landed on the French coast of Normandy. Although the fighting was deadly for all sides, the Germans were overwhelmed. With the two fronts collapsing around them and round-the-clock strategic bombing by the United States and Britain leveling German cities, German resistance faded. Since early 1943, Britain's Royal Air Force had committed itself to area bombing in which centers of cities became the targets of nighttime raids. U.S. planes attacked industrial targets in daytime. The British firebombing raid on Dresden in February 1945 literally cooked German men, women, and children in their bomb shelters: 135,000 people died in the firestorm. A brutal street-by-street battle in Berlin between Germans and Russians, along with a British and U.S. sweep through western Germany, forced Germany's unconditional surrender on 8 May 1945. A week earlier, on 30 April, as fighting flared right outside his Berlin bunker, Hitler committed suicide, as did many of his Nazi compatriots. He therefore did not live to see the Soviet red flag flying over the Berlin *Reichstag,* Germany's parliament building.

Turning the Tide in the Pacific The turning point in the Pacific war came in a naval engagement near the Midway Islands on 4 June 1942. The United States prevailed there partly because U.S. aircraft carriers had survived the attack on Pearl Harbor. Although the United States had few carriers, it did have a secret weapon: a code-breaking operation known as *Magic,* which enabled a cryptographer monitoring Japanese radio frequencies to discover the plan to attack Midway. On the morning of 4 June, thirty-six carrier-launched dive-bombers attacked the Japanese fleet, sinking three Japanese carriers in one five-minute strike and a fourth one later in the day. This victory changed the character of the war in the Pacific. Although there was no immediate shift in Japanese fortunes, the Allies took the offensive. They adopted an island-hopping strategy, capturing islands from which they could make direct air assaults on Japan. Deadly, tenacious fighting characterized these battles in which the United States and its allies gradually retook islands in the Marianas and the Philippines and then, early in 1945, moved toward areas more threatening to Japan: Iwo Jima and Okinawa.

MAP 36.2
World War II in Asia and the Pacific.
Compare the geographic conditions of the Asian-Pacific theater with those of the European theater.

What kinds of resources were necessary to win in the Asian-Pacific theater as opposed to the European theater?

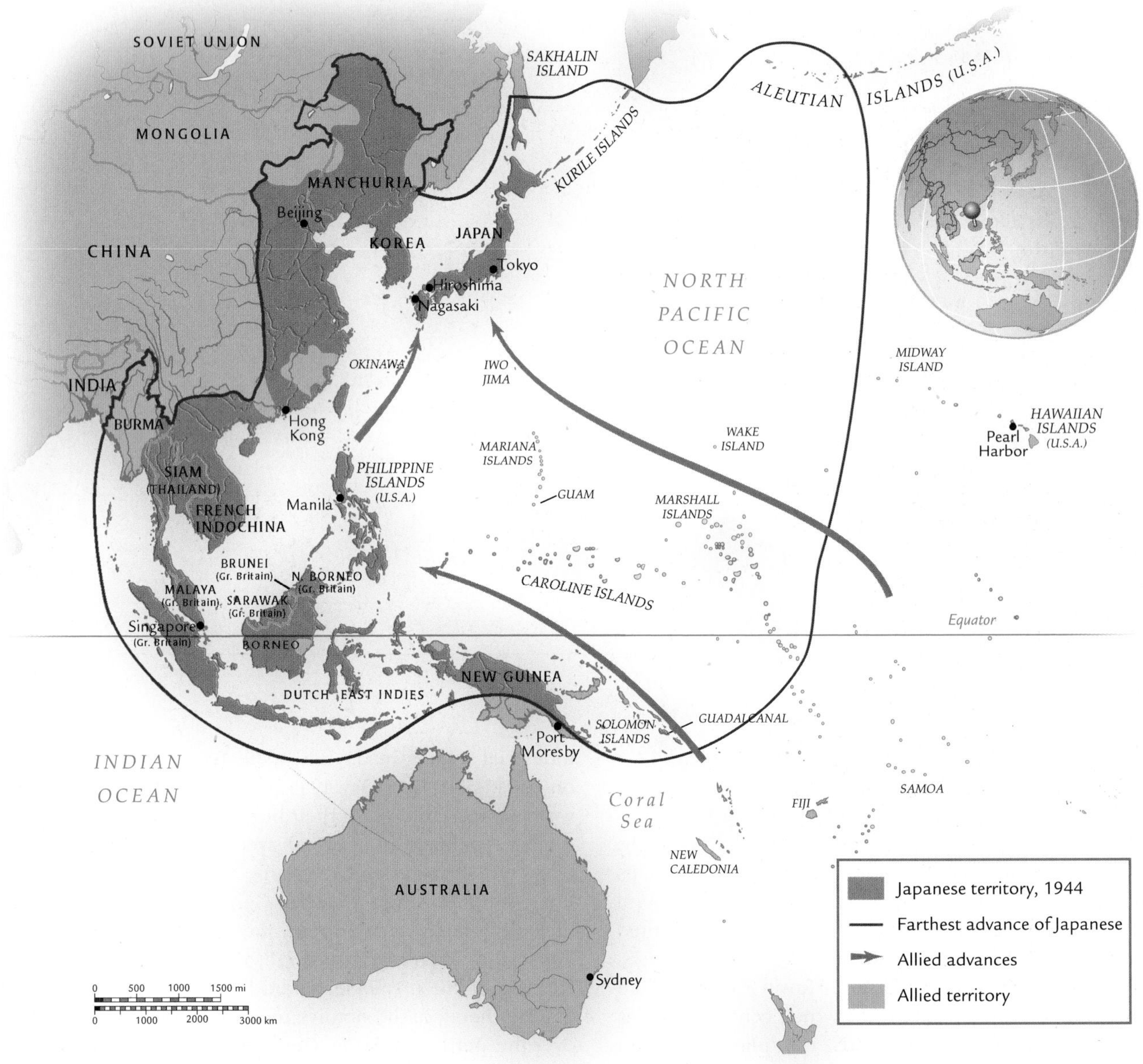

sources from the past

A Hiroshima Maiden's Tale

Yamaoka Michiko, at fifteen years of age, worked as an operator at a telephone exchange in Hiroshima and attended girls' high school. Many young women had been mobilized for work during World War II, and they viewed even civilian work on telephone exchanges as a means of helping to protect Japan during wartime. On the morning of 6 August 1945, when the first U.S. atomic bomb used in battle devastated Hiroshima, Yamaoka Michiko had just started off for work.

That morning I left the house at about seven forty-five. I heard that the B-29s [U.S. bomber planes] had already gone home. Mom told me, "Watch out, the B-29s might come again." My house was one point three kilometers from the hypocenter [the exact point of the atomic bomb's impact in Hiroshima]. My place of work was five hundred meters from the hypocenter. I walked toward the hypocenter. . . . I heard the faint sound of planes. . . . The planes were tricky. Sometimes they only pretended to leave. I could still hear the very faint sound of planes. . . . I thought, how strange, so I put my right hand above my eyes and looked up to see if I could spot them. The sun was dazzling. That was the moment.

There was no sound. I felt something strong. It was terribly intense. I felt colors. It wasn't heat. You can't really say it was yellow, and it wasn't blue. At that moment I thought I would be the only one who would die. I said to myself, "Goodbye, Mom."

They say temperatures of seven thousand degrees centigrade hit me. You can't really say it washed over me. It's hard to describe. I simply fainted. I remember my body floating in the air. That was probably the blast, but I don't know how far I was blown. When I came to my senses, my surroundings were silent. There was no wind. I saw a threadlike light, so I felt I must be alive. I was under stones. I couldn't move my body. I heard voices crying, "Help! Water!" It was then I realized I wasn't the only one. . . .

"Fire! Run away! Help! Hurry up!" They weren't voices but moans of agony and despair. "I have to get help and shout," I thought. The person who rescued me was Mom, although she herself had been buried under our collapsed house. Mom knew the route I'd been taking. She came, calling out to me. I heard her voice and cried for help. Our surroundings were already starting to burn. Fires burst out from just the light itself. It didn't really drop. It just flashed. . . .

My clothes were burnt and so was my skin. I was in rags. I had braided my hair, but now it was like a lion's mane. There were people, barely breathing, trying to push their intestines back in. People with their legs wrenched off. Without heads. Or with faces burned and swollen out of shape. The scene I saw was a living hell.

Mom didn't say anything when she saw my face and I didn't feel any pain. She just squeezed my hand and told me to run. She was going to rescue my aunt. Large numbers of people were moving away from the flames. My eyes were still able to see, so I made my way toward the mountain, where there was no fire, toward Hijiyama. On this flight I saw a friend of mine from the phone exchange. She'd been inside her house and wasn't burned. I called her name, but she didn't respond. My face was so swollen she couldn't tell who I was. Finally, she recognized my voice. She said, "Miss Yamaoka, you look like a monster!" That's the first time I heard that word. I looked at my hands and saw my own skin was hanging down and the red flesh exposed. I didn't realize my face was swollen up because I was unable to see it. . . .

I spent the next year bedridden. All my hair fell out. When we went to relatives' houses later they wouldn't even let me in because they feared they'd catch the disease. There was neither treatment nor assistance for me. . . . It was just my Mom and me. Keloids [thick scar tissue] covered my face, my neck. I couldn't even move my neck. One eye was hanging down. I was unable to control my drooling because my lip had been burned off. . . .

The Japanese government just told us we weren't the only victims of the war. There was no support or treatment. It was probably harder for my Mom. Once she told me she tried to choke me to death. If a girl had terrible scars, a face you couldn't be born with, I understand that even a mother could want to kill her child. People threw stones at me and called me Monster. That was before I had my many operations.

For Further Reflection

- What did Yamaoka Michiko's psychological and physical reaction to the atomic bombing of Hiroshima suggest about the nature of these new weapons? Why did friends and relatives treat her as if she were a "monster"?

Source: Yamaoka Michiko. "Eight Hundred Meters from the Hypocenter." In Haruko Taya Cook and Theodore F. Cook, *Japan at War: An Oral History.* New York: The New Press, 1992, pp. 384–87.

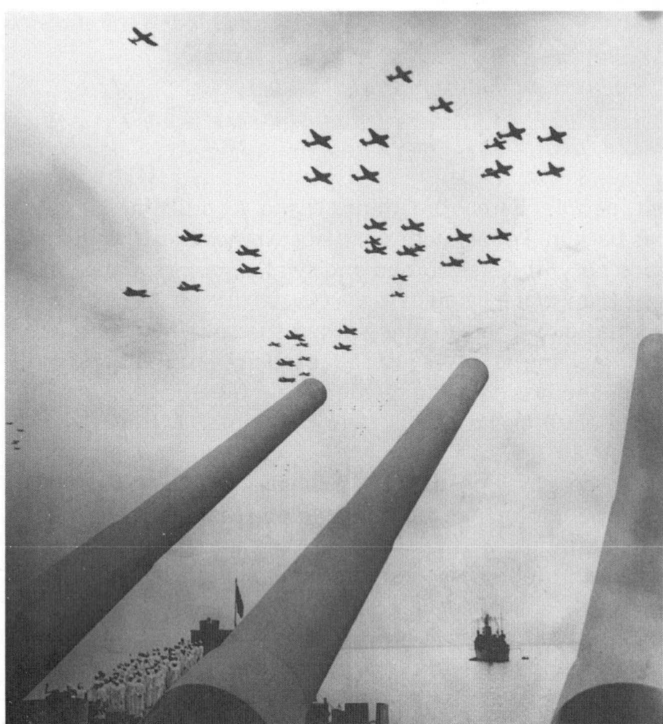

A photograph titled "Planes over Tokyo Bay," taken from the U.S.S. *Missouri,* visually captured a sense of U.S. power and victory on V-J Day, 1945.

Iwo Jima and Okinawa The fighting on Iwo Jima and Okinawa was savage. Innovative U.S. amphibious tactics were matched by the vigor and sacrifice of Japanese soldiers and pilots. On Okinawa the Japanese introduced the ***kamikaze***—pilots who "volunteered" to fly planes with just enough fuel to reach an Allied ship and dive-bomb into it. In the two-month battle, the Japanese flew nineteen hundred kamikaze missions, sinking dozens of ships and killing more than five thousand U.S. soldiers. The kamikaze, and the defense mounted by Japanese forces and the 110,000 Okinawan civilians who died refusing to surrender, convinced many people in the United States that the Japanese would never capitulate.

Japanese Surrender The fall of Saipan in July 1944 and the subsequent conquest of Iwo Jima and Okinawa brought the Japanese homeland within easy reach of U.S. strategic bombers. Because high-altitude strikes in daylight failed to do much damage to industrial sites, military planners changed tactics. The release of napalm firebombs during low-altitude sorties at night met with devastating success. The firebombing of Tokyo in March 1945 destroyed 25 percent of the city's buildings, annihilated approximately one hundred thousand people, and made more than a million homeless. The final blows came on 6 and 9 August 1945, when the United States used its revolutionary new weapon, the atomic bomb, against the cities of Hiroshima and Nagasaki. The atomic bombs either instantaneously vaporized or slowly killed by radiation poisoning upward of two hundred thousand people.

The Soviet Union declared war on Japan on 8 August 1945, and this new threat, combined with the devastation caused by the bombs, persuaded Emperor Hirohito (1901–1989) to surrender unconditionally. The Japanese surrendered on 15 August, and the war was officially over on 2 September 1945. When Victor Tolley sipped his conciliatory cup of tea with a Nagasaki family, the images of ashen Hiroshima and firebombed Tokyo lingered as reminders of how World War II brought the war directly home to millions of civilians.

kamikaze (KAH-mih-kah-zee)

LIFE DURING WARTIME

The widespread bombing of civilian populations during World War II, from its beginning in China to its end in Hiroshima and Nagasaki, meant that there was no safe home front during the war. So too did the arrival of often brutal occupation forces in the wake of Japanese and German conquests in Asia and Europe. Strategic bombing slaughtered men, women, and children around the world, and occupation troops forced civilians to labor and die in work and extermination camps. In this total war, civilian death tolls far exceeded military casualties. Beside the record of the war's brutality can be placed testimony to the endurance of the human spirit personified in the contributions of resistance groups battling occupying forces, in the mobilized women, and in the survivors of bombings or concentration camps.

Occupation, Collaboration, and Resistance

Axis bombardments and invasion were followed by occupation, but the administration imposed on conquered territories by Japanese and German forces varied in character. In territories such as Manchukuo, Japanese-controlled China, Burma, and the Philippines, Japanese authorities installed puppet governments that served as agents of Japanese rule. Thailand remained an independent state after it aligned itself with Japan, for which it was rewarded with grants of territory from bordering Laos and Burma. Other conquered territories either were considered too unstable or unreliable for self-rule or were deemed strategically too important to be left alone. Thus territories such as Indochina (Laos, Cambodia, and Vietnam), Malaya, the Dutch East Indies, Hong Kong, Singapore, Borneo, and New Guinea came under direct military control.

In Europe, Hitler's racist ideology played a large role in determining how occupied territories were administered. As a rule, Hitler intended that most areas of western and northern Europe—populated by racially valuable people, according to him—would become part of a Greater Germanic Empire. Accordingly, Denmark retained its elected government and monarchy under German supervision. In Norway and Holland, whose governments had gone into exile, the

Germans left the civilian administration intact. Though northern France and the Atlantic coast came under military rule, the Vichy government remained the civilian authority in the unoccupied southeastern part of the country. Named for its locale in central France, the Vichy government provided a prominent place for those French willing to collaborate with German rule. The Germans had varying levels of involvement in eastern European and Balkan countries, but most conquered territories came under direct military rule as a prelude for harsh occupation, economic exploitation, and German settlement.

Exploitation Japanese and German authorities administered their respective empires for economic gain and proceeded to exploit the resources of the lands under their control for their own benefit regardless of the consequences for the conquered peoples. The occupiers pillaged all forms of economic wealth that could fuel the German and Japanese war machines. The most notorious form of economic exploitation involved the use of slave labor. As the demands of total war stimulated an insatiable appetite for workers, Japanese and German occupation authorities availed themselves of prisoners of war (POWs) and local populations to help meet labor shortages. By August 1944, more than seven million foreign workers labored inside the Third Reich. In China alone, the Japanese military mobilized more than ten million civilians and prisoners of war for forced labor. These slave laborers worked under horrific conditions and received little in the way of sustenance. Reaction to Japanese and German occupation varied from willing collaboration and acquiescence to open resistance.

Atrocities The treatment of POWs by German and Japanese authorities spoke to the horrors of the war as well. The death rate among soldiers in Japanese captivity averaged almost 30 percent, and the mortality rate among Chinese POWs was even higher. The racial ideologies of Hitler's regime were reflected in the treatment meted out to Soviet prisoners of war in particular. By February 1942, 2 million out of the 3.3 million Soviet soldiers in German custody had died from starvation, exposure, disease, or shootings.

Beyond the callous mistreatment of POWs, both German and Japanese authorities engaged in painful and often deadly medical experiments on thousands of unwilling subjects. In China, special Japanese military units, including the most infamous Unit 731, conducted cruel experiments on civilians and POWS. Victims, for example, became the subject of vivisection (defined as surgery conducted on a living organism) or amputation without anesthesia. Tens of thousands of Chinese became victims of germ warfare experiments, dying of bubonic plague, cholera, anthrax, and other diseases. German physicians carried out similarly unethical medical experiments in concentration camps. Experimentation ranged from high-altitude and hypothermia investigations by air force medical personnel, designed to facilitate the survival of German military personnel, to bone-grafting surgeries without anesthesia and exposing victims to phosgene and mustard gas to test possible antidotes. German doctors also directed painful serological experiments to determine how different "races" withstood various contagious diseases.

Collaboration The majority of people resented occupation forces but usually went on with life as much as possible. That response was especially true in many parts of Japanese-occupied lands in Asia, where local populations found little to resent in the change from one colonial administration to another. In Asia and Europe, moreover, local notables often joined the governments sponsored by the conquerors because collaboration offered them the means to gain power. In many instances, bureaucrats and police forces collaborated because they thought it was better that natives rule than Germans or Japanese. Businesspeople and companies often collaborated because they prospered financially from foreign rule. Still other people became collaborators and assisted occupation authorities by turning in friends and neighbors to get revenge for past grievances. In western Europe, anticommunism motivated Belgians, French, Danish, Dutch, and Norwegians to join units of Hitler's elite military formations, the Waffen SS, creating in the process a multinational army tens of thousands strong. In China several Guomindang generals went over to the Japanese, and local landowners and merchants in some regions of China set up substantial trade networks between the occupiers and the occupied.

Resistance Occupation and exploitation created an environment for resistance that took various forms. The most dramatic forms of resistance were campaigns of sabotage, armed assaults on occupation forces, and assassinations. Resistance fighters as diverse as Filipino guerrillas and Soviet partisans harassed and disrupted the military and economic activities of the occupiers by blowing up ammunition dumps, destroying communication and transportation facilities, and sabotaging industrial plants. More quietly, other resisters gathered intelligence, hid and protected refugees, or passed on clandestine newspapers. Resistance also comprised simple acts of defiance such as scribbling anti-German graffiti or walking out of bars and restaurants when Japanese soldiers entered. In the Netherlands, people associated the royal House of Orange with national independence and defiantly saluted traffic lights when they turned orange.

German and Japanese citizens faced different decisions about resistance than conquered peoples did. They had no antiforeign axe to grind, and any form of noncompliance constituted an act of treason that might assist the enemy and lead to defeat. Moreover, many institutions that might have formed the core of resistance in Japan and Germany, such as political parties, labor unions, or churches, were weak or had been destroyed. As a result, there was little or no opposition to the state and its policies in Japan, and in

Germany resistance remained generally sparse and ineffective. The most spectacular act of resistance against the Nazi regime came from a group of officers and civilians who tried to kill Adolf Hitler on 20 July 1944. The plot failed when their bomb explosion killed several bystanders but inflicted only minor injuries on Hitler.

Attempts to eradicate resistance movements in many instances merely fanned the flames of rebellion because of the indiscriminate reprisals against civilians. Despite the deadly retaliation meted out to people who resisted occupation, widespread resistance movements grew throughout the war. Life in resistance movements was tenuous at best and entailed great hardship—changing identities, hiding out, and risking capture and death. Nevertheless, the resisters kept alive their nations' hopes for liberation.

The Holocaust

By the end of World War II, the Nazi regime and its accomplices had physically annihilated millions of Jews, Slavs, Gypsies, homosexuals, Jehovah's Witnesses, communists, and others targeted as undesirables. Jews were the primary target of Hitler's racially motivated genocidal policies, and the resulting Holocaust epitomized the tragedy of conquest and occupation in World War II. The Holocaust, the near destruction of European Jews by Germany, was a human disaster on a scale previously unknown.

The murder of European Jews was preceded by a long history of vilification and persecution of Jews. For centuries Jewish communities had been singled out by Christian society as a "problem," and by the time the Nazi regime assumed power in 1933, anti-Semitism had contributed significantly to the widespread tolerance for anti-Jewish measures. Marked as outsiders, Jews found few defenders in their societies. Nazi determination to destroy the Jewish population and Europeans' passive acceptance of anti-Semitism laid the groundwork for genocide. In most war-torn European countries, the social and political forces that might have been expected to rally to the defense of Jews did not materialize.

Titled "Abyss of Human Horror," this photograph shows a survivor of the concentration camp at Nordhausen, Germany, on its liberation by Allies in 1945.

Initially, the regime encouraged Jewish emigration. Although tens of thousands of Jews availed themselves of the opportunity to escape from Germany and Austria, many more were unable to do so. Most nations outside the Nazi orbit limited the migration of Jewish refugees, especially if the refugees were impoverished, as most of them were because Nazi authorities had previously appropriated their wealth. This situation worsened as German armies overran Europe, bringing an ever-larger number of Jews under Nazi control. At that point Nazi "racial experts" toyed with the idea of deporting Jews to Nisko, a proposed reservation in eastern Poland, or to the island of Madagascar, near Africa. Those ideas proved to be impractical and threatening. The concentration of Jews in one area led to the dangerous possibility of the creation of a separate Jewish state, hardly a solution to the so-called Jewish problem in the Nazi view.

The Final Solution

The German occupation of Poland in 1939 and invasion of the Soviet Union in the summer of 1941 gave Hitler an opportunity to solve what he considered the problem of Jews in Germany and throughout Europe. When German armies invaded the Soviet Union in June 1941, the Nazis also dispatched three thousand troops in mobile detachments known as SS *Einsatzgruppen* ("action squads") to kill entire populations of Jews and Roma (or Gypsies) and many non-Jewish Slavs in the newly occupied territories. The action squads undertook mass shootings in ditches and ravines that became mass graves. By the spring of 1943, the special units had killed over one million Jews, and tens of thousands of Soviet citizens and Roma.

Sometime during 1941 the Nazi leadership committed to the "final solution" of the Jewish question, a solution that entailed the attempted murder of every Jew living in Europe. At the Wannsee Conference on 20 January 1942, fifteen leading Nazi bureaucrats gathered to discuss and coordinate the implementation of the final solution. They agreed to evacuate all Jews from Europe to camps in eastern Poland, where they would be worked to death or exterminated. Soon German forces—aided by collaborating authorities in foreign countries—rounded up Jews and deported them to specially constructed concentration camps in occupied Poland. The victims from nearby Polish ghettos and distant assembly points all across Europe traveled to their destinations by train. On the way the sick and the elderly often perished in overcrowded freight cars. The Jewish victims packed into these suffocating railway cars never knew their destinations, but rumors of mass deportations and mass deaths nonetheless spread among Jews remaining at

sources from the past

"We Will Never Speak about It in Public"

On 4 October 1943, Heinrich Himmler, leader of the SS and chief of the German police, gave a three-hour speech to an assembly of SS generals in the city of Posen (Poznan), in what is now Poland. In the following excerpt, Himmler justified Nazi anti-Jewish policies that culminated in mass murder. The speech, recorded on tape and in handwritten notes, was entered into evidence at the Nuremberg war crimes trials in 1945.

I also want to speak to you here, in complete frankness, of a really grave chapter. Amongst ourselves, for once, it shall be said quite openly, but all the same we will never speak about it in public. . . .

I am referring here to the evacuation of the Jews, the extermination of the Jewish people. This is one of the things that is easily said: "The Jewish people are going to be exterminated," that's what every Party member says, "sure, it's in our program, elimination of the Jews, extermination—it'll be done." And then they all come along, the 80 million worthy Germans, and each one has his one decent Jew. Of course, the others are swine, but this one, he is a first-rate Jew. Of all those who talk like that, not one has seen it happen, not one has had to go through with it. Most of you men know what it is like to see 100 corpses side by side, or 500 or 1,000. To have stood fast through this and except for cases of human weakness to have stayed decent, that has made us hard. This is an unwritten and never-to-be-written page of glory in our history. . . .

The wealth they possessed we took from them. I gave a strict order, which has been carried out by SS *Obergruppenfuehrer* Pohl, that this wealth will of course be turned over to the Reich in its entirety. We have taken none of it for ourselves. Individuals who have erred will be punished in accordance with the order given by me at the start, threatening that anyone who takes as much as a single Mark of this money is a dead man. A number of SS men, they are not very many, committed this offense, and they shall die. There will be no mercy. We had the moral right, we had the duty towards our people, to destroy this people that wanted to destroy us. But we do not have the right to enrich ourselves by so much as a fur, as a watch, by one Mark or a cigarette or anything else. We do not want, in the end, because we destroyed a bacillus, to be infected by this bacillus and to die. I will never stand by and watch while even a small rotten spot develops or takes hold. Wherever it may form we will together burn it away. All in all, however, we can say that we have carried out this most difficult of tasks in a spirit of love for our people. And we have suffered no harm to our inner being, our soul, our character. . . .

For Further Reflection

- Himmler argued that SS officers and soldiers "stayed decent" while overseeing the extermination of the Jews; why then does he focus so much attention on punishing those who took money from the dead Jews?

Source: International Military Tribunal. *Trial of the Major War Criminal,* Nuremberg, Germany, 1948; volume 29, Document 1919-PS. Translation Copyright 2002 Yad Vashem.

large and among the Allied government leaders, who were apparently apathetic to the fate of Jews.

In camps such as Kulmhof (Chelmno), Belzec, Majdanek, Sobibòr, Treblinka, and Auschwitz, the final solution took on an organized and technologically sophisticated character. Here, the killers introduced gassing as the most efficient means for mass extermination, though other means of destruction were always retained, such as electrocution, phenol injections, flamethrowers, hand grenades, and machine guns. The largest of the camps was Auschwitz, where at least one million Jews perished. Nazi camp personnel subjected victims from all corners of Europe to industrial work, starvation, medical experiments, and outright extermination. The German commandant of Auschwitz explained proudly how his camp became the most efficient at killing Jews: by using the fast-acting crystallized prussic acid Zyklon B as the gassing agent, by enlarging the size of the gas chambers, and by lulling victims into thinking they were going through a delousing process. At Auschwitz and elsewhere, the Germans also constructed large crematories to incinerate the bodies of gassed Jews and hide the evidence of their crimes. This systematic murder of Jews constituted what war crime tribunals later termed a "crime against humanity."

Jewish Resistance The murder of European Jewry was carried out with the help of the latest technology and with the utmost efficiency. For most of the victims, the will to resist was sapped by prolonged starvation, disease, and mistreatment. Nevertheless, there was fierce Jewish resistance throughout the war. Thousands of Jews joined anti-Nazi partisan groups and resistance movements while others led rebellions in concentration camps or participated in ghetto uprisings from Minsk to Krakow. The best-known uprising took place in the Warsaw ghetto in the spring of

MAP 36.3
The Holocaust in Europe, 1933–1945.
Observe the geographic locations of the concentration and extermination camps.
Why were there more concentration camps in Germany and more extermination camps in Poland?

1943. Lacking adequate weapons, sixty thousand Jews who remained in the ghetto that had once held four hundred thousand rose against their tormentors. It took German security forces using tanks and flamethrowers three weeks to crush the uprising. Approximately 5.7 million Jews perished in the Holocaust.

Women and the War

Observing the extent to which British women mobilized for war, the U.S. ambassador to London noted, "This war, more than any other war in history, is a woman's war." A poster encouraging U.S. women to join the WAVES (Women Appointed for Volunteer Emergency Service in the navy) mirrored the thought: "It's A Woman's War Too!" While hundreds of thousands of women in Great Britain and the United States joined the armed forces or entered war industries, women around the world were affected by the war in a variety of ways. Some nations, including Great Britain and the United States, barred women from engaging in combat or carrying weapons, but Soviet and Chinese women took up arms, as did women in resistance groups. In fact, women often excelled at resistance work because they were women: they were less suspect in the eyes of occupying security forces and less subject to searches. Nazi forces did not discriminate, though, when rounding up Jews for transport and extermination: Jewish women and girls died alongside Jewish men and boys.

Women's Roles Women who joined military services or took jobs on factory assembly lines gained an independence and confidence previously denied them, but so too did women who were forced to act as heads of household in the absence of husbands killed or away at war, captured as prisoners of war, or languishing in labor camps. Women's roles changed during the war, often in dramatic ways, but those new roles were temporary. After the war, women war-

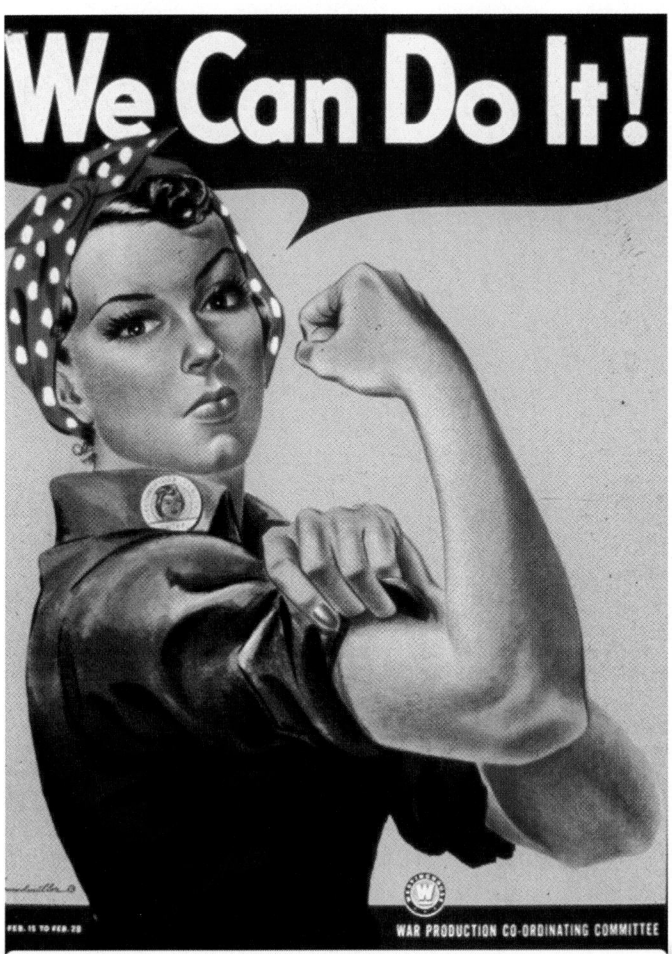

This famous 1942 poster of an idealized woman war worker in the United States featured the archetypal "Rosie the Riveter" and coined the motto for women meeting the challenges of the war: "We Can Do It!"

riors and workers were expected to return home and assume their traditional roles as wives and mothers. In the meantime, though, women made the most of their opportunities. In Britain, women served as noncombatant pilots, wrestled with the huge balloons and their tethering lines designed to snag Nazi aircraft from the skies, drove ambulances and transport vehicles, and labored in the fields to produce foodstuffs. More than 500,000 women joined British military services, and approximately 350,000 women did the same in the United States.

Comfort Women Women's experiences in war were not always ennobling or empowering. The Japanese army forcibly recruited, conscripted, and dragooned as many as two hundred thousand women age fourteen to twenty to serve in military brothels, called "comfort houses" or "consolation centers." The army presented the women to the troops as a gift from the emperor, and the women came from Japanese colonies such as Korea, Taiwan, and Manchuria and from occupied territories in the Philippines and elsewhere in southeast Asia. The majority of the women came from Korea and China.

Once forced into this imperial prostitution service, the "comfort women" catered to between twenty and thirty men each day. Stationed in war zones, the women often confronted the same risks as soldiers, and many became casualties of war. Others were killed by Japanese soldiers, especially if they tried to escape or contracted venereal diseases. At the end of the war, soldiers massacred large numbers of comfort women to cover up the operation. The impetus behind the establishment of comfort houses for Japanese soldiers came from the horrors of Nanjing, where the mass rape of Chinese women had taken place. In trying to avoid such atrocities, the Japanese army created another horror of war. Comfort women who survived the war experienced deep shame and hid their past or faced shunning by their families. They found little comfort or peace after the war.

THE COLD WAR

The end of World War II produced moving images of peace, such as Soviet and U.S. soldiers clasping hands in camaraderie at the Elbe River, celebrating their victory over the Germans. But by the time Germany surrendered in the spring of 1945, the wartime alliance between the Soviet Union, the United States, and Great Britain was disintegrating. The one-time partners increasingly sacrificed cooperation for their own national interests. Within two years the alliance forged by mutual danger gave way to a cold war between two principal rivals. It was a contest in which neither side gave way; yet, in the end, a direct clash of arms was always avoided, hence the term *cold war.*

The cold war became a confrontation for global influence principally between the United States and the Soviet Union. It was a tense encounter between rival political and economic systems—between liberal democracy and capitalism on the one hand and international communism and one-party rule on the other. The

thinking about TRADITIONS

The "Home" Front

Many observers during World War II acknowledged the significant role women played in the war effort. Traditionally bound to the home, women worked both on the home front and in the armed forces to support their nations' fight. In what ways did women transform their roles during the war? What sorts of jobs symbolized those changes?

British women handle a balloon used for defense in the Battle of Britain.

geopolitical and ideological rivalry between the Soviet Union and the United States and their respective allies lasted almost five decades and affected every corner of the world. The cold war was responsible for the formation of military and political alliances, the creation of client states, and an arms race of unprecedented scope. It engendered diplomatic crises, spawned military conflicts, and at times brought the world to the brink of nuclear annihilation. Among the first manifestations of the cold war was the division of the European continent into competing political, military, and economic blocs—one dependent on the United States and the other subservient to the USSR—separated by what Winston Churchill in 1946 called an "iron curtain."

Origins of the Cold War

The United Nations Despite their many differences, the Allies were among the nations that agreed to the creation of the United Nations (UN) in October 1945, a supranational organization dedicated to keeping world peace and security. The commitment to establish a new international organization derived from Allied cooperation during the war. Unlike its predecessor, the League of Nations (1920), which failed in its basic mission to prevent another world war, the United Nations created a powerful Security Council responsible for maintaining international peace. Recognizing that peace could be maintained only if the great powers were in agreement, the UN founders made certain that the Security Council consists of five permanent members and six rotating elected members. The United States, the Soviet Union, Great Britain, France, and China—the members of the full Allied alliance in World War II—are the five permanent powers, and their unanimous vote is required on all substantive matters. The decisions of the Security Council are binding on all members.

Despite this initial cooperation, the wartime unity of the former Allies began to crack. Even before the defeat of Germany, the Allies had expressed differences over the future of Poland and eastern European nations liberated and subsequently occupied by the Soviet Red Army. On the surface, all sides agreed at the wartime conference at Yalta to "the earliest possible establishment through free elections of governments responsive to the will of the people." A determined Joseph Stalin, however, insisted on "friendly" governments that were controlled by the Soviet Union in order to safeguard against any future threat from Germany. From the American and British perspectives, Stalin's intentions signaled the permanent Soviet domination of eastern Europe and the threat of Soviet-influenced communist parties coming to power in the democracies of western Europe. Their worst fears were realized in 1946 and 1947, when the Soviets helped bring communist governments to power in Romania, Bulgaria, Hungary, and Poland. Communists had previously gained control in Albania and Yugoslavia in 1944 and 1945.

Truman Doctrine The enunciation of the Truman Doctrine on 12 March 1947 crystallized the new U.S. perception of a world divided between "free" (democratic) and "enslaved" (communist) peoples. Articulated partly in response to crises in Greece and Turkey, where communist movements seemed to threaten democracy and U.S. strategic interests, the Truman Doctrine starkly drew the battle lines of the cold war. As President Harry Truman (1884–1972) explained to the U.S. Congress: "At the present moment in world history nearly every nation must choose between alternative ways of life. I believe that it must be the policy of the United States to support free peoples who are resisting attempted subjugation by armed minorities or by outside pressures." The United States then committed itself to an interventionist foreign policy, dedicated to the "containment" of communism, which meant preventing any further expansion of Soviet influence.

Marshall Plan As an economic adjunct to the Truman Doctrine, the U.S. government developed a plan to help shore up the destroyed infrastructures of western Europe. The European Recovery Program, commonly called the

MAP 36.4
Occupied Germany, 1945–1949.
Locate the city of Berlin in Soviet-controlled territory.
How was it possible for the British, American, and French to maintain their zones of control in Berlin, given such geographic distance from western Germany?

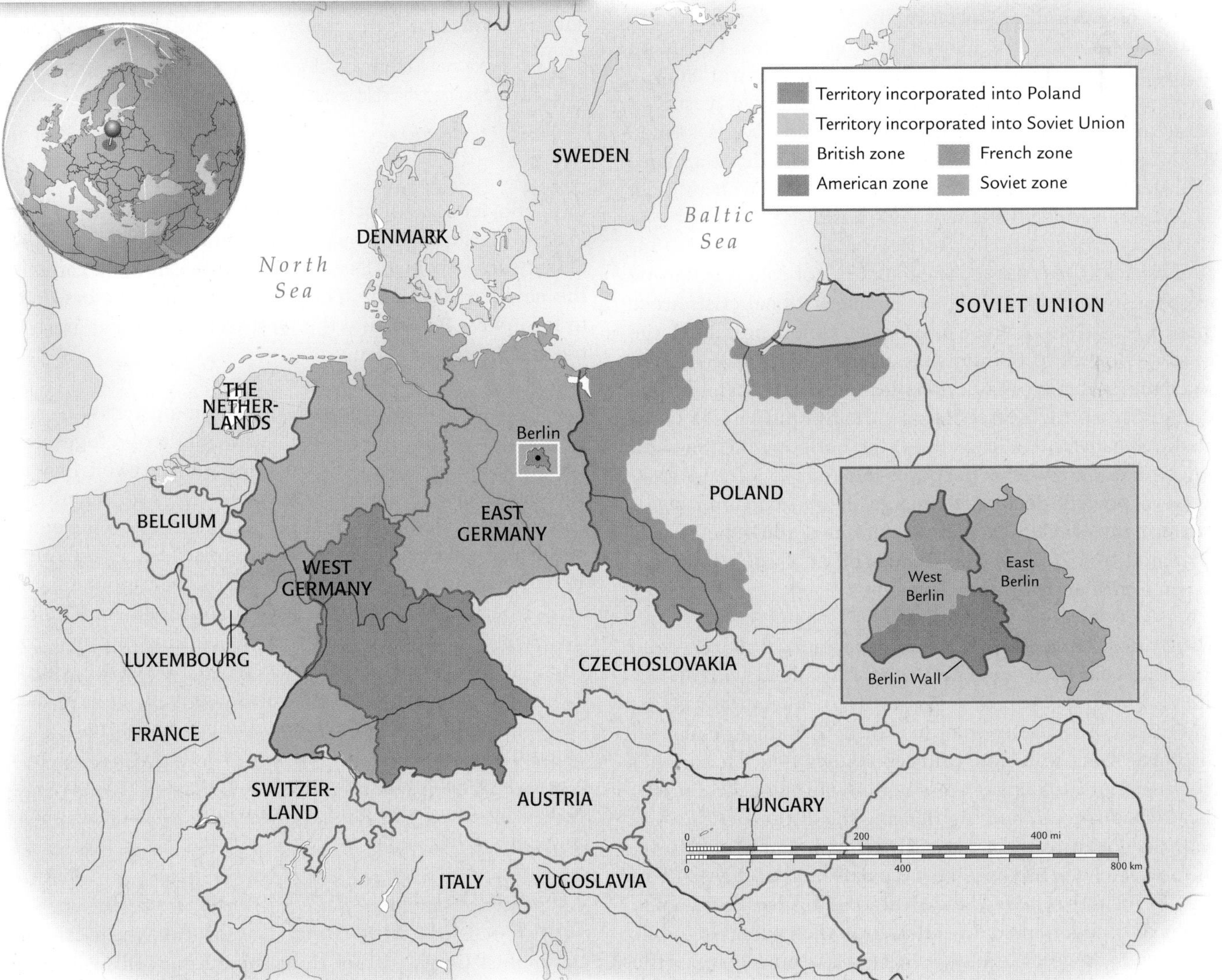

Marshall Plan after U.S. Secretary of State George C. Marshall (1880–1959), proposed to rebuild European economies through cooperation and capitalism, forestalling communist or Soviet influence in the devastated nations of Europe. Proposed in 1947 and funded in 1948, the Marshall Plan provided more than $13 billion to reconstruct western Europe. Although initially included in the nations invited to participate in the Marshall Plan, the Soviet Union resisted what it saw as capitalist imperialism and countered with a plan for its own satellite nations. The Soviet Union established the Council for Mutual Economic Assistance (COMECON) in 1949, offering increased trade within the Soviet Union and eastern Europe as an alternative to the Marshall Plan.

Military Alliances The creation of the U.S.-sponsored North Atlantic Treaty Organization (NATO) and the Soviet-controlled Warsaw Pact signaled the militarization of the cold war. In 1949 the United States established NATO as a regional military alliance against Soviet aggression. The original members included Belgium, Canada, Denmark, France, Great Britain, Iceland, Italy, Luxembourg, the Netherlands, Norway, Portugal, and the United States. The intent of the alliance was to maintain peace in postwar Europe through collective defense. When NATO admitted West Germany and allowed it to rearm in 1955, the Soviets formed the Warsaw Pact as a countermeasure. A military alliance of seven communist European nations, the Warsaw Pact matched the collective defense policies of NATO.

A Divided Germany The fault lines of cold war Europe were most visible in Germany. An international crisis arose there in 1948–1949 when the Soviet Union pressured the western powers to relinquish their jurisdiction over Berlin. After the collapse of Hitler's Third Reich, the forces of the United States, the Soviet Union, Britain, and France occupied Germany and its capital, Berlin, both of which they divided for administrative purposes into four zones. When the western powers decided to merge their occupation zones in Germany—including their sectors in Berlin—the Soviets retaliated by blockading all road, rail, and water links between Berlin and western Germany.

Blockade and Airlift In the first serious test of the cold war, the Americans and the British responded with an airlift designed to keep West Berlin's inhabitants alive, fed, and warm. For eleven months, in a daunting display of airpower, American and British aircrews flew around-the-clock missions to supply West Berlin with the necessities of life. Tensions remained high during the airlift, but the cold war did not turn hot. Stymied by British and U.S. resolve, the Soviet leadership called off the blockade in May 1949. In the aftermath of the blockade, the U.S., British, and French zones of occupation coalesced to form the Federal Republic of Germany (West Germany) in May 1949. In October the German Democratic Republic (East Germany) emerged out of the Soviet zone of occupation. A similar process repeated itself in Berlin, which was deep within the Soviet zone. The Soviet sector formed East Berlin and became the capital of the new East Germany. The remaining three sectors united to form West Berlin, and the West German capital moved to the small town of Bonn.

Barbed wire and a concrete wall in front of the Brandenburg Gate in Berlin symbolized the cold war division of Europe.

The Berlin Wall By 1961 the communist East German state was hemorrhaging from a steady drain of refugees who preferred life in capitalist West Germany. Between 1949 and 1961 nearly 3.5 million East Germans—many of them young and highly skilled—left their homeland, much to the embarrassment of East Germany's communist leaders. In August 1961 the communists reinforced their fortification along the border between East and West Germany, following the construction of a fortified wall that divided the city of Berlin. The wall, which began as a layer of barbed wire, quickly turned into a barrier several layers deep, replete with watchtowers, searchlights, antipersonnel mines, and border guards ordered to shoot to kill. The Berlin Wall accomplished its purpose of stemming the flow of refugees, though at the cost of shaming a regime that obviously lacked legitimacy among its own people.

The Globalization of the Cold War

The People's Republic of China The birth of a communist China further transformed the cold war, ostensibly enhancing the power of the Soviet Union and its communist allies. With the defeat of Japan in 1945, the civil war in China had resumed. By mid-1948 the strategic balance favored the communists, who inflicted heavy military defeats on the nationalists throughout 1948 and 1949, forcing the national government under Jiang Jieshi (Chiang Kai-shek) to seek refuge on the island of Taiwan. In the meantime, Mao Zedong, the chairman of the Chinese Communist Party (CCP), proclaimed the establishment of the People's Republic of China on 1 October 1949. This declaration brought to an end the long period of imperialist intrusion in China and spawned a close relationship between the world's largest and most powerful socialist states.

Fraternal Cooperation Moscow and Beijing drew closer during the early years of the cold war. This relationship was hardly astonishing, because the leaders of both communist states felt threatened by a common enemy, the United States, which sought to establish anticommunist bastions throughout Asia. Most disconcerting to Soviet and Chinese leaders was the American-sponsored rehabilitation of their former enemy, Japan, and the forming of client states in South Korea and Taiwan. The Chinese-Soviet partnership matured during the early 1950s and took on a distinct form when Beijing recognized Moscow's undisputed authority in world communism in exchange for Russian military equipment and economic aid.

Confrontations in Korea In conjunction with the communist victory in China, the unforeseen outbreak of hostilities on the Korean peninsula in the summer of 1950 shifted the focus of the cold war from Europe to east Asia. At the end of World War II, the leaders of the Soviet Union and the United States had partitioned Korea along the thirty-eighth parallel of latitude into a northern Soviet zone and a southern U.S. zone. Because the superpowers were unable to agree on a framework for the reunification of the country, in 1948 they consented to the establishment of two separate Korean states: in the south, the Republic of Korea, with Seoul as its capital, and in the north, the People's Democratic Republic of Korea, with Pyongyang as its capital. After arming their respective clients, each of which claimed sovereignty over the entire country, U.S. and Soviet troops withdrew.

On the early morning of 25 June 1950, the unstable political situation in Korea came to a head. Determined to unify Korea by force, the Pyongyang regime ordered more than one hundred thousand troops across the thirty-eighth parallel in a surprise attack, quickly pushing back South Korean defenders and capturing Seoul on 27 June. Convinced that the USSR had sanctioned the invasion, the United States persuaded the United Nations to adopt a resolution to repel the aggressor. Armed with a UN mandate and supported by small armed forces from twenty countries, the U.S. military went into action, and within months had pushed the North Koreans back to the thirty-eighth parallel. However, sensing an opportunity to unify Korea under a pro-U.S. government, they pushed on into North Korea and within a few weeks had occupied Pyongyang. Subsequent U.S. advances toward the Yalu River on the Chinese border resulted in Chinese intervention in the Korean conflict. A combined force of Chinese and North Koreans pushed U.S. forces and their allies back into the south, and the war settled into a protracted stalemate near the original border at the thirty-eighth parallel. After two more years of fighting that raised the number of deaths to three million—mostly Korean civilians—both sides finally agreed to a cease-fire in July 1953. The failure to conclude a peace treaty ensured that the Korean peninsula would remain in a state of suspended strife that constantly threatened to engulf the region in a new round of hostilities.

Beyond the human casualties and physical damage it wrought, the Korean conflict also encouraged the globalization of the U.S. strategy of containment. Viewing the North Korean offensive as part of a larger communist conspiracy to conquer the world, the U.S. government extended military protection and economic aid to the noncommunist governments of Asia. It also entered into security agreements that culminated in the creation of the Southeast Asian Treaty Organization (SEATO), an Asian counterpart of NATO. By 1954 U.S. President Dwight D. Eisenhower (1890–1969), who had contemplated using nuclear weapons in Korea, asserted the famous "domino theory." This strategic theory rationalized worldwide U.S. intervention on the assumption that if one country became communist, neighboring ones would collapse to communism the way a row of dominoes falls sequentially until none remains standing. Subsequent U.S. administrations extended the policy of containment to areas beyond the nation's vital interests and applied it to local or imagined communist threats in Central and South America, Africa, and Asia.

Cracks in the Soviet-Chinese Alliance Despite the assumptions of U.S. leaders, there was no one monolithic communist force in global politics, as was demonstrated by the divisions between Chinese and Soviet communists that appeared over time. The Chinese had embarked on a crash program of industrialization, and the Soviet Union rendered valuable assistance in the form of economic aid and technical advisors. By the mid-1950s the Soviet Union was China's principal trading partner, annually purchasing roughly half of all Chinese exports. Before long, however, cracks appeared in the Soviet-Chinese alliance. From the Chinese perspective, Soviet aid programs were far too modest and had too many strings attached. By the end of 1964, the rift between the Soviet Union and the People's Republic of China became embarrassingly public, with both sides engaging in name-calling. In addition, both nations openly competed for influence in Africa and Asia, especially in the nations that had recently gained independence. The fact that the People's Republic had conducted successful nuclear tests in 1964 enhanced its prestige. An unanticipated outcome of

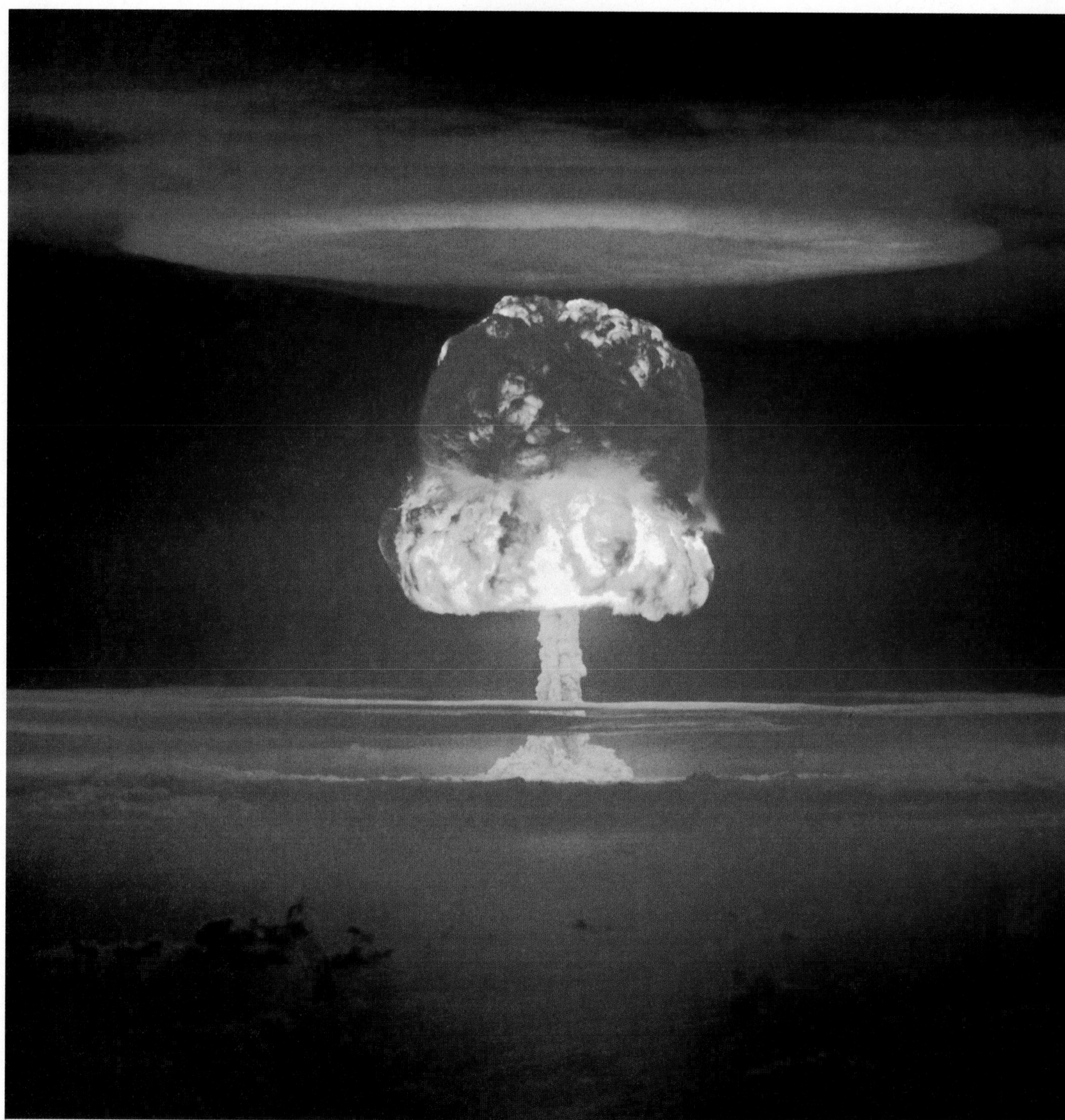

The visceral beauty of nuclear explosions, such as this one in the Marshall Islands in 1954, masked the terror and the tensions that beset the Soviet Union, the United States, and the rest of the world during the cold war.

the Chinese-Soviet split was that many countries gained an opportunity to pursue a more independent course by playing capitalists against communists and by playing Soviet communists against Chinese communists.

The Nuclear Arms Race A central feature of the cold war world was a costly arms race and the terrifying proliferation of nuclear weapons. The Soviet Union had broken the U.S. monopoly on atomic weaponry by testing its own atomic bomb in 1949, but because the United States was determined to retain military superiority and because the Soviet Union was equally determined to reach parity with the United States, both sides amassed enormous arsenals of nuclear weapons and developed a multitude of systems for deploying those weapons. In the 1960s and beyond, the superpowers acquired so many nuclear weapons that they reached the capacity for mutually assured destruction, or MAD. This balance of terror, while often frightening, tended to restrain the contestants and stabilize their relationship, with one important exception.

Cuba: Nuclear Flashpoint Ironically, the cold war confrontation that came closest to unleashing nuclear war took place not at the expected flashpoints in Europe or Asia but on the island of Cuba. In 1959 a revolutionary movement headed by Fidel Castro Ruz (1926–) overthrew the autocratic Fulgencio Batista y Zaldivar (1901–1973), whose regime had gone to great lengths to maintain the country's traditionally subservient relationship with the United States, especially with the U.S. sugar companies that controlled Cuba's economy. Fidel Castro's new regime gladly accepted a Soviet offer of massive economic aid—including an agreement to purchase half of Cuba's sugar production—and arms shipments. In return for the Soviet largesse, Castro declared his support for the USSR's foreign policy. In December 1961 he confirmed the U.S. government's worst suspicions when he publicly announced: "I have been a Marxist-Leninist all along, and will remain one until I die."

Bay of Pigs Invasion Cuba's alignment with the Soviet Union spurred the U.S. government to action. Newly elected president John F. Kennedy (1917–1963) authorized a clandestine invasion of Cuba to overthrow Castro and his supporters. In April 1961 a force of fifteen hundred anti-Castro Cubans trained, armed, and transported by the Central Intelligence Agency (CIA) landed on Cuba at a place called the Bay of Pigs. The arrival of the invasion force failed to incite a hoped-for internal uprising, and when the promised American air support failed to appear, the invasion quickly fizzled. Within three days, Castro's military had either captured or killed the entire invasion force. The Bay of Pigs fiasco diminished U.S. prestige, especially in Latin America. It also, contrary

This propaganda poster celebrated the leadership of Fidel Castro during his rise to revolutionary power in Cuba.

thinking about ENCOUNTERS

Cold War in Cuba
The very definition of the cold war meant that the two superpowers, the United States and the Soviet Union, avoided direct military confrontations and struggled instead on a largely ideological plane. Why did this "cold" version of war turn potentially so hot in Cuba in 1962? What made this superpower contest in Cuba so frightening?

to U.S. purposes, actually strengthened Castro's position in Cuba and encouraged him to accept the deployment of Soviet nuclear missiles in Cuba as a deterrent to any future invasion.

On 26 October 1962 the United States learned that Soviet technicians were assembling launch sites for medium-range nuclear missiles on Cuba. The deployment of nuclear missiles that could reach targets in the United States within minutes represented an unacceptable threat to U.S. national security. Thus President John F. Kennedy issued an ultimatum, calling on the Soviet leadership to withdraw all missiles from Cuba and stop the arrival of additional nuclear armaments. To back up his demand, Kennedy imposed an air and naval quarantine on the island nation. The superpowers seemed poised for nuclear confrontation, and for two weeks the world's peoples held their collective breath. After two weeks, finally realizing the imminent possibility of nuclear war, the Soviet government yielded to the U.S. demands. In return, Soviet Premier Nikita Khrushchev (1894–1971) extracted an open pledge from Kennedy to refrain from attempting to overthrow Castro's regime and a secret deal to remove U.S. missiles from Turkey. The world trembled during this crisis, awaiting the apocalypse that potentially lurked behind any superpower encounter.

Dissent, Intervention, and Rapprochement

De-Stalinization Even before the Cuban missile crisis, developments within the Soviet Union caused serious changes in eastern Europe. Within three years of Joseph Stalin's death in 1953, several communist leaders startled the world when they openly attacked Stalin and questioned his methods of rule. The most vigorous denunciations came from Stalin's successor, Soviet Premier Nikita Khrushchev, who embarked on a policy of de-Stalinization, that is, the end of the rule of terror and the partial liberalization of Soviet society. Government officials removed portraits of Stalin from public places, renamed institutions and localities bearing his name, and commissioned historians to rewrite textbooks to deflate Stalin's reputation. The de-Stalinization period, which lasted from 1956 to 1964, also brought a "thaw" in government control and resulted in the release of millions of political prisoners. With respect to foreign policy, Khrushchev emphasized the possibility of "peaceful coexistence" between different social systems and the achievement of communism by peaceful means. This change in Soviet doctrine reflected the recognition that a nuclear war was more likely to lead to mutual annihilation than to victory.

Soviet Intervention The new political climate in the Soviet Union tempted communist leaders elsewhere to experiment with domestic reforms and seek a degree of independence from Soviet domination. Eastern European states also tried to become their own masters, or at least to gain a measure of autonomy from the Soviet Union. The nations of the Soviet bloc did not fare well in those endeavors. The most serious challenge to Soviet control came in 1956 from nationalist-minded communists in Hungary. When the communist regime in Hungary embraced the process of de-Stalinization, large numbers of Hungarian citizens demanded democracy and the breaking of ties to Moscow and the Warsaw Pact. Soviet leaders viewed those moves as a serious threat to their security system. In the late autumn of 1956, Soviet tanks entered Budapest and crushed the Hungarian uprising.

Twelve years after the Hungarian tragedy, Soviets again intervened in eastern Europe, this time in Czechoslovakia. In 1968 the Communist Party leader, Alexander Dubček (1921–1992), launched a "democratic socialist revolution." He supported a liberal movement known as the "Prague Spring" and promised his fellow citizens "socialism with a human face." The Czechs' move toward liberal communism aroused fear in the Soviet Union because such ideas could lead to the unraveling of Soviet control in eastern Europe. Intervention by the Soviet army brought an end to the Prague Spring. Khrushchev's successor, Leonid Ilyich Brezhnev (1906–1982), justified the invasion of Czechoslovakia by the Doctrine of Limited Sovereignty. This policy, more commonly called the "Brezhnev doctrine," reserved the right to invade any socialist country that was deemed to be threatened by internal or external elements "hostile to socialism." The destruction of the dramatic reform movement in Czechoslovakia served to reassert Soviet control over its satellite nations in eastern Europe and led to tightened controls within the Soviet Union.

Détente Amid those complications of the cold war and the challenges issuing from allies and enemies alike, Soviet and U.S. leaders began adjusting to the reality of an unmanageable world—a reality they could no longer ignore. By the late 1960s the leaders of the Soviet Union and the United States agreed on a policy of *détente,* or a reduction in hostility, trying to cool the costly arms race and slow their competition in developing countries. Although détente did not resolve the deep-seated antagonism between the superpowers, it did signal the relaxation of cold war tensions and prompted a new spirit of cooperation. The spirit of détente was most visible in negotiations designed to reduce the threat posed by strategic nuclear weapons. The two cold war antagonists cooperated despite the tensions caused by the U.S. incursion into Vietnam, Soviet involvement in Angola and other African states, and continued Soviet repression of dissidents in eastern Europe. Likewise symbolic of this rapprochement between democratic and communist nations were the state visits in 1972 to China and the Soviet Union made by U.S. President Richard Nixon (1913–1994). Nixon had entered politics in 1946 on the basis of his service in World War II and his staunch belief in anticommunism, and his trips to the two global centers of communism suggested a possible beginning to the end of World War II and cold war divisions.

inperspective

At the end of World War II, it was possible for a U.S. marine to enjoy the hospitality of a Japanese family in Nagasaki, but not for Soviet and U.S. troops to continue embracing in camaraderie. World War II was a total global war that forced violent encounters between peoples and radically altered the political shape of the world. Beginning with Japan and China in 1931, this global conflagration spread to Europe and its empires and to the Pacific Ocean and the rest of Asia. Men, women, and children throughout the world became intimate with war as victims of civilian bombing campaigns, as soldiers and war workers, and as slave laborers and comfort women. When the Allies defeated the Axis powers in 1945, destroying the German and Japanese empires, the world had to rebuild as another war began. The end of the war saw the breakup of the alliance that had defeated Germany and Japan, and within a short time the United States and the Soviet Union and their respective allies squared off against each other in a cold war, a rivalry waged primarily on political, economic, and propaganda fronts. A longer-lasting realignment in world politics came about after World War II as colonial nations gained independence through the process of decolonization. ●

CHRONOLOGY	
1937	Invasion of China by Japan
1937	The Rape of Nanjing
1939	Nazi-Soviet Pact
1939	Invasion of Poland by Germany
1940	Fall of France, Battle of Britain
1941	German invasion of the Soviet Union
1941	Attack on Pearl Harbor by Japan
1942	U.S. victory at Midway
1943	Soviet victory at Stalingrad
1944	D-Day, Allied invasion at Normandy
1945	Capture of Berlin by Soviet forces
1945	Atomic bombing of Hiroshima and Nagasaki
1945	Establishment of United Nations
1947	Truman Doctrine
1948	Marshall Plan
1949	Division of Berlin and Germany
1949	Establishment of the People's Republic of China
1950–1953	Korean War
1961	Construction of Berlin Wall
1962	Cuban missile crisis

For Further Reading

Gar Alperovitz. *Atomic Diplomacy: Hiroshima and Potsdam.* Rev. ed. New York, 1985. The classic account of the atomic origins of the cold war.

Christopher Bayly and Tim Harper. *Forgotten Armies: The Fall of British Asia, 1941–1945.* Cambridge, 2005. Broad study of the impact of World War II on Britain's Asian empire.

Herbert P. Bix. *Hirohito and the Making of Modern Japan.* New York, 2001. A groundbreaking, unvarnished biography that details the strong and decisive role the emperor played in wartime operations during World War II.

Christopher R. Browning with contributions by Jürgen Matthäuss. *The Origins of the Final Solution: The Evolution of Nazi Jewish Policy, September 1939–March 1942.* Lincoln, Neb., and Jerusalem, 2004. Standard work on the evolution of Nazi anti-Jewish policies from persecution to mass murder.

Ian Buruma. *The Wages of Guilt: Memories of War in Germany and Japan.* New York, 1995. A moving account of how societies deal with the war crimes of World War II.

Winston Churchill. *The Second World War.* 6 vols. New York, 1948–60. An in-depth account of the war from one of the major players.

Dwight Eisenhower. *Crusade in Europe.* New York, 1948. An account of the European war from the military point of view of the supreme Allied commander.

John Lewis Gaddis. *The Cold War: A New History.* New York, 2005. A fresh and concise history of the cold war by the dean of cold war historians.

Tsuyoshi Hasegawa. *Racing the Enemy: Stalin, Truman, and the Surrender of Japan.* Cambridge, Mass., 2005. Impressive international history of the end of World War II in the Pacific that argues the Soviet threat was the decisive factor in Japan's surrender, not Truman's use of nuclear weapons.

Brian Masaru Hayashi. *Democratizing the Enemy: The Japanese American Internment.* Princeton, 2004. Important account of the experience of Japanese Americans in World War II.

Margaret Higgonet, Jane Jenson, Sonya Michel, and Margaret Weitz, eds. *Behind the Lines: Gender and the Two World Wars.* New Haven, 1987. A penetrating series of articles on women in both world wars, focusing generally on U.S. and European experiences.

Raul Hilberg. *The Destruction of the European Jews.* New York, 1967. One of the most important works on the Holocaust.

Akira Iriye. *The Cold War in Asia: A Historical Interpretation.* Englewood Cliffs, N.J., 1974. A leading diplomatic historian provides an excellent introduction to the subject.

———. *The Origins of the Second World War in Asia and the Pacific.* New York, 1987. An examination of the Asian and Pacific origins of the war by one of the field's leading scholars.

John Keegan. *The Second World War.* New York, 1989. An exhaustive military history.

Williamson Murray and Alan R. Millet. *A War to Be Won: Fighting in the Second World War, 1937–1945.* Cambridge, Mass., 2000. A fine single-volume history focusing on military operations.

Martin Sherwin. *A World Destroyed: The Atomic Bomb and the Grand Alliance.* New York, 1975. A classic study of how the bomb influenced the end of the war.

You-Li Sun. *China and the Origins of the Pacific War, 1931–1941.* New York, 1993. An account of the origins of the war in which China takes center stage.

William Taubman. *Stalin's American Policy: From Entente to Détente to Cold War.* New York, 1982. An important work that focuses on the Soviet perspective of the cold war.

Studs Terkel. *"The Good War": An Oral History of World War II.* New York, 1984. A valuable collection of oral histories on the war from a U.S. perspective.

Gerhard L. Weinberg. *Visions of Victory: The Hopes of Eight World War II Leaders.* Cambridge, 2005. A close examination of eight political leaders and their visions for the postwar world.

The End of Empire

chapter 37

This saintly image of Mohandas K. Gandhi captures his spiritual significance to the independence movement in India both before and after his death.

Independence in Asia
India's Partitioned Independence
Nationalist Struggles in Vietnam
Arab National States and the Problem of Palestine
Decolonization in Africa
Forcing the French out of North Africa
Black African Nationalism and Independence
Freedom and Conflict in Sub-Saharan Africa
After Independence: Long-Term Struggles in the Postcolonial Era
Communism and Democracy in Asia
Islamic Resurgence in Southwest Asia and North Africa
Colonial Legacies in Sub-Saharan Africa
Politics and Economics in Latin America

EYEWITNESS:
Mohandas Gandhi's Saintly Last Words

"Hé Ram" were the last words that escaped his lips after three bullets savagely ripped through his frail body. Roughly translated, he uttered, "O! God," and then died. It had begun as a day much like any other in the life of Mohandas K. Gandhi (1869–1948), or "Bapuji" as he was fondly called—a dear father of the country of India. On 30 January 1948, a few months after India gained its independence from Great Britain, he awakened at Birla House in Delhi at an early hour, 3:00 A.M., to continue his work hammering out solutions to the problems that plagued his land. That morning, he labored on a draft of a new constitution for the Indian National Congress, stressing as usual his major concerns for his newly independent and strife-ridden nation: that villages be empowered, that discrimination based on the caste system be abolished, that religious intolerance and violence between Hindus and Muslims cease. Still distraught over the partitioning of his land into a Hindu India and Muslim Pakistan, he had weakened himself after independence through fasts and hunger strikes staged as *satyagraha,* or "truth and firmness," protests against the killings of Hindus and Muslims and the mistreatment of Pakistan. He weighed a mere 107 pounds that day.

Alternating between working, talking with visitors, and napping, Gandhi finally took a meal at 4:30 P.M. He nibbled on raw and cooked vegetables and oranges, and drank goat's milk and a special brew made with aloe juice, lemons, ginger, and strained butter. A little over half an hour later, he made his way to the evening prayer meeting he was to lead. A bit late, the skies already darkening, he took a shortcut across the emerald green, finely trimmed lawns of Birla House to reach the dais where he would speak. As he approached the dais, he stopped to press his palms together, offering the traditional Hindu greeting to the crowd waiting at the meeting. At that moment, out of the crowd stepped a large and impatient man who suddenly pulled a Beretta pistol from his pants pocket and fired the three shots that ended the life of the man many credited with Indian independence, the man seen as the very soul and conscience of India. The force of the shots crumpled Gandhi's thin body, his chest and abdomen riddled by bullets. As he slumped to the ground, his glasses fell from his face, his sandals slipped from his feet, and large crimson blood stains spread starkly over his white homespun shawl. After he whispered "Hé Ram," his breathing stilled.

Two days before he was assassinated by the Hindu extremist Nathuram Godse, Gandhi prophetically said, "If I am to die by the bullet of a mad man, I must do so smiling. There must be no anger within me. God must be in my heart and on my lips." Gandhi died as he had wanted, and as he lived, without anger and with God on his lips. His assassination, however, stood in bleak contrast to the nonviolence embraced by Gandhi throughout his life. Gandhi could have been forgiven some anger given the apparent failure of his nonviolence doctrine in the days after independence—a failure made publicly evident in communal killings after partition and personally evident in his violent death. Not all Hindus agreed with Gandhi's rejection of violence and avowal of religious tolerance for Muslims. Before he was executed by hanging in 1949, his assassin Godse declared Gandhi a "curse for India, a force for evil."

Gandhi's murder suggested the troubles and traumas faced by nations and peoples adjusting to independence from colonial rule, but his martyrdom also enshrined his principles of nonviolence and religious tolerance in Indian life after independence. Gandhi's death discredited Hindu extremism and halted communal violence, for a time. He became a more mythic hero in India, a new national symbol to be invoked in times of trouble and violence. His life and death spoke to the promise and perils of independence and its aftermath. Despite the hazards of life in a world without empires, peoples in the colonial world fought tenaciously for independence and then for national unity after World War II.

The expansion of European power since 1500 is one of the principal themes of world history. For over four centuries, European colonies and empires dominated large parts of the planet. Beginning in the early twentieth century, however, a series of developments undermined Europe's global hegemony. The catalyst for change was the Great War (World War I), which sapped the strength and the prestige of the major colonial powers such as Great Britain and France. The Great Depression further undermined the strength of the imperialist nations, and by the end of World War II the same nations were so exhausted, so economically debilitated, and so demoralized that any realistic attempt to assert or reassert control over colonies was simply out of the question. Europe's palsied condition was not lost on leaders of independence movements in Asia and Africa, and they lost little time in taking advantage of Europe's unparalleled weakness. Many intellectual and political leaders of independence movements (Gandhi, Nehru, Nkrumah, and Ho Chi Minh) had been educated in Europe and the United States, where they had been exposed to ideals of freedom, self-determination, and national sovereignty. In the decades after 1945, peoples in the colonial world fought tenaciously for independence and then for national unity, and by 1990, nationalist movements had swept away colonial rule and given birth to over ninety new nations.

This process of decolonization was aided by several factors. It became increasingly apparent that there was a significant growth of democratic and anti-imperialist sentiments within imperial countries themselves, and political leaders could no longer count on a war-weary public to make serious sacrifices to maintain overseas colonies. The short-lived Japanese empire contributed to colonial revolutions throughout Asia, where European military prestige had been severely and permanently damaged after the Japanese defeated the British in Burma and Malaya, the French in Indochina, the Dutch in Indonesia, and the United States in the Philippines. With the emergence of the two postwar superpowers, the United States and the Soviet Union, both of which opposed European colonialism, the stage was set for a drastic overturning of colonial rule. The end of empire was one of the most important outcomes of World War II.

Peoples in the former colonial world labored to build national identities, balancing their traditions against demands for development. Such difficulties were true for nations in areas of the world where independence came long ago and in areas where peoples achieved independence from colonial or imperial rule recently. Despite all the complications of decolonization and its aftermath, colonial peoples in Asia and Africa fought for freedom and then for security. The desire of nations to seek peace and stability after independence seemed reasonable, especially because independence often led to numerous problems. Freedom did not remain elusive for the nations of Asia, Africa, and Latin America, but peace often did—a fact Gandhi acknowledged in the days after Indian independence and on the day of his death.

INDEPENDENCE IN ASIA

In the wake of World War II, the power of Asian nationalism was irrepressible. New nations emerged throughout Asia, from India and Pakistan in south Asia to diverse Arab nations in southwest Asia and to Vietnam, Cambodia, and Laos in southeast Asia. These lands encountered different conditions in their quests for independence and freedom from imperial control, but everywhere Asian nationalists rallied their people against colonialism and imperialism. Whether fighting against colonial powers, which established formal political and territorial control, or against imperial powers, which often exercised a more informal and indirect control, Asians were successful. The result of their efforts, measured in years or decades, was independence and the end of empire in Asia.

India's Partitioned Independence

In the 1930s Great Britain had granted numerous reforms in response to the tireless campaign of Mohandas K. Gandhi and the Congress Party, as well as Muhammad Ali Jinnah and the Muslim League. The gradual trend toward Indian self-rule, as in the India Act of 1935, faced challenges in the form of increasing calls for independent yet separate Hindu and Muslim states. World War II, however, interrupted the drive for any sort of self-rule.

The Coming of Self-Rule Under the leadership of Winston Churchill, who despised Gandhi and vowed never "to preside over the liquidation of the British empire," measures for home rule were suspended, and India was ordered to support the war effort. British recalcitrance about Indian independence evaporated after the war, however. The British people voted Churchill out of office. His conservative government was replaced with a Labour government more inclined to dismantle the empire. The economic devastation of the war made it unrealistic for Britain to continue bearing the financial burden of empire in India.

The issue of Muslim separatism grew in importance as the probability of Indian independence became more pronounced, and Muslims increasingly feared their minority status in a free India dominated by Hindus. Muhammad Ali Jinnah (1876–1948), leader of the Muslim League, felt no qualms about frankly expressing Muslim concerns and desires for a separate Muslim state, even as Congress Party leaders such as Jawaharlal Nehru (1889–1964) and Gandhi urged all Indians to act and feel as one nation, undivided

Jawaharlal Nehru (left) and Mohandas K. Gandhi, Hindu leaders of India's independence movement. Gandhi's nonviolent resistance powerfully contributed to the end of the British rule of India. Nehru promoted a strategy of nonalignment for the newly independent nation.

by what came to be known as communalism—emphasizing religious over national identity. In August 1946, in the midst of negotiations with the British to reach terms regarding independence, the Muslim League called for a Day of Direct Action, even though the league's leaders recognized that Muslim demonstrations might lead to rioting and fighting between Muslims and Hindus. Some six thousand people died in the Great Calcutta Killing that resulted, further fueling communal feeling and adding weight to Jinnah's claim: "The only solution to India's problem is Pakistan."

Partition and Violence The idea of partition, the division of India into separate Hindu and Muslim states, violated the stated ideals of men such as Gandhi and Nehru, who sickened at the prospect and only reluctantly came to accept the notion of a divided and independent India. Gandhi nonetheless condemned the division of his homeland as a "vivisection," using a term that refers to the cutting up of a living body. He avoided the celebrations on 15 August 1947 that accompanied independence for India and Pakistan, glumly prophesying that "rivers of blood" would flow in the wake of partition. His vision came true as the terms of partition were announced and hundreds of thousands of Muslim and Hindu refugees migrated either to Muslim Pakistan (divided between parts of Bengal in the east and Punjab in the west) or to Hindu India. By mid-1948 an estimated ten million refugees made the torturous journey to one state or the other, and between half a million and one million people died in the violence that accompanied those massive human migrations. The hostility between migrating Hindus and Muslims spilled over into the enmity between the two states, complicating efforts to build their independent nations.

Though mired in violence, Indian independence became a reality with momentous consequences for the process of decolonization. India was the jewel in the crown of the British empire, and its breakaway marked a significant turning point. Just as Gandhi's nonviolent resistance to British rule inspired nationalists around the globe before and after World War II, independence in India and Pakistan further encouraged anti-imperial movements throughout Asia and Africa. Another way in which Indian independence inspired nations and set a pattern for grappling with decolonization in the midst of a cold war was through Nehru's promotion of a nonalignment strategy. Nehru proved instrumental in fashioning a compelling position for newly independent nations caught in the cold war and in the superpower tug-of-war contests for the loyalties of new nations. He became one of the impassioned defenders of nonalignment, especially at the Bandung Conference, where he was one of the most visible participants.

Nonalignment Leaders of new African and Asian countries first discussed nonalignment at the Bandung Conference. In April 1955, leaders from twenty-three Asian and six African nations met in Bandung, Indonesia, partly to find a "third path," an alternative to choosing either the United States or the Soviet Union. Besides neutrality in the cold war, the Bandung Conference stressed the struggle against colonialism and racism, and Indonesian president Achmad Sukarno (1901–1970) proudly proclaimed Bandung "the first international conference of coloured peoples in the history of mankind." Bandung was the precursor of the broader Nonaligned Movement, which held occasional meetings so that its members could discuss matters of common interest, particularly their relations with the United States and the Soviet Union. The movement's primary goal was to maintain formal neutrality. However, the Nonaligned Movement suffered from a chronic lack of unity among its members and ultimately failed to present a genuinely united front. Although theoretically nonaligned with either cold war superpower, many member states had close ties to one or the other, and that situation caused dissension within the movement.

Nationalist Struggles in Vietnam

In contrast to India, Vietnam over time had more difficulty in keeping its nationalist struggle for independence separate from the complications of the cold war. In its fight for independence, Vietnam became deeply enmeshed in the cold war, but immediately after World War II the Vietnamese first engaged in a battle to free themselves from French colonial control. Vietnam's nationalist communist leader, Ho Chi Minh (1890–1969), had exploited wartime conditions to advance the cause of Vietnamese independence.

Fighting the French After the Japanese conquest of Vietnam, which effectively ended French rule, Ho helped oust the Japanese from Vietnam in the waning days of World War II. He then issued the Vietnamese Declaration of Independence, which was modeled on the U.S. declaration. However, the French, humiliated by their country's easy defeat and occupation by the Germans, sought to reclaim their world-power status through their imperial possessions. Armed with British and U.S. weapons, the French recaptured Saigon and much of southern Vietnam in 1945. Faced with the hostility of the northern nationalist communists, organized as the Viet Minh, the French retook the north brutally, bombing Hanoi and Haiphong and killing

thinking about TRADITIONS

Independence and Nonviolence
Mohandas Gandhi embodied the modern principle of nonviolence, which had a deep and long history of acceptance in Indian society. What happened to this traditional belief as India gained its independence from Great Britain?

sources from the past

Muhammad Ali Jinnah on the Need for a Muslim Pakistan

Muhammad Ali Jinnah (1876–1948) served as the most visible and articulate leader of India's Muslims during the first half of the twentieth century. Like Mohandas K. Gandhi, he initially promoted cooperation and unity among Muslims and Hindus in order to achieve freedom from British rule. He came to feel strongly, however, that Muslims in an independent but Hindu-controlled India would only suffer from the discrimination they already faced from the Hindu majority. In the following speech to the Muslim League in 1940, Jinnah formulated some of the reasons why Muslims indeed deserved and already constituted their own nation.

It is extremely difficult to appreciate why our Hindu friends fail to understand the real nature of Islam and Hinduism. They are not religions in the strict sense of the word, but are, in fact, different and distinct social orders, and it is a dream that the Hindus and Muslims can ever evolve a common nationality, and this misconception of one Indian nation has gone far beyond the limits and is the cause of most of your troubles and will lead India to destruction if we fail to revise our notions in time. The Hindus and Muslims belong to two different religious philosophies, social customs, literatures. They neither intermarry nor interdine together and, indeed, they belong to two different civilizations which are based mainly on conflicting ideas and conceptions. Their aspects on life and of life are different. It is quite clear that Hindus and Mussalmans [Muslims] derive their inspiration from different sources of history. They have different epics, different heroes, and different episodes. Very often the hero of one is the foe of the other and, likewise, their victories and defeats overlap. To yoke together two such nations under a single state, one as a numerical minority and the other as a majority, must lead to growing discontent. . . .

[W]e know that the history of the last twelve hundred years has failed to achieve unity and has witnessed, during the ages, India always divided into Hindu India and Muslim India. The present artificial unity of India dates back only to the British conquest and is maintained by the British bayonet, but termination of the British regime, which is implicit in the recent declaration of His Majesty's government, will be the herald of the entire break-up with worse disaster than has ever taken place during the last one thousand years under Muslims. Surely that is not the legacy which Britain would bequeath to India after one hundred fifty years of her rule, nor would Hindu and Muslim India risk such a sure catastrophe. Muslim India cannot accept any constitution which must necessarily result in a Hindu majority government. Hindus and Muslims brought together under a democratic system forced upon the minorities can only mean Hindu raj [rule]. . . .

Mussalmans are a nation according to any definition of a nation, and they must have their homelands, their territory, and their state. We wish to live in peace and harmony with our neighbors as a free and independent people. We wish our people to develop to the fullest our spiritual, cultural, economic, social, and political life in a way that we think best and in consonance with our own ideals and according to the genius of our people. Honesty demands and the vital interests of millions of our people impose a sacred duty upon us to find an honorable and peaceful solution, which would be just and fair to all.

For Further Reflection

- How does Jinnah employ the idea of "difference" to justify his calls for a separate Muslim state in an independent India?

Source: Muhammad Ali Jinnah, "Hindus and Muslims: Two Separate Nations," from *Sources of Indian Tradition,* 2nd ed., vol. 2, edited by Stephen Hay. New York, 1988, pp. 228–31.

at least ten thousand civilians. By 1947 the French appeared to have secured their power, especially in the cities, but that security proved to be temporary. Much like the Chinese communists in their battles against the Japanese and then against the nationalists in the postwar years, the Vietnamese resistance forces, led by Ho Chi Minh and General Vo Nguyen Giap (1912–), took to the countryside and mounted a campaign of guerrilla warfare. The Vietnamese communists grew increasingly influential in the anti-imperial war, especially after 1949 when communist China sent aid and arms to the Viet Minh. Thus strengthened, they defeated the French at their fortress in Dienbienphu in 1954. The French had to sue for peace at the conference table.

The Geneva Conference and Partial Independence The peace conference, held in Geneva in 1954, determined that Vietnam should be temporarily divided at the seventeenth parallel; North Vietnam would be controlled by Ho Chi Minh and the communist forces, whereas South Vietnam would remain in the hands of noncommunists. The communist affiliation of Ho and his comrades, along with the globalization of the cold war that accompanied the Korean

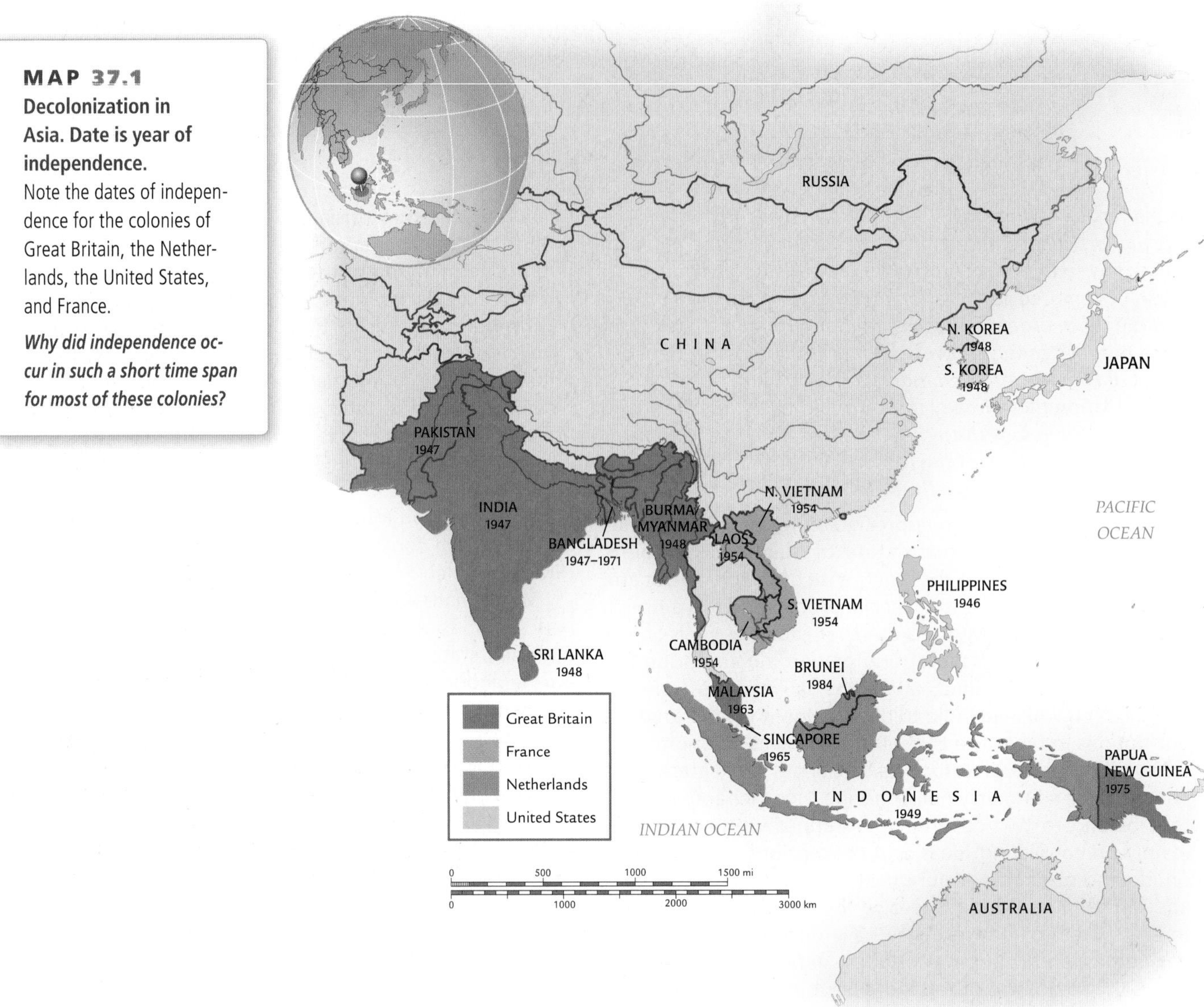

MAP 37.1
Decolonization in Asia. Date is year of independence.
Note the dates of independence for the colonies of Great Britain, the Netherlands, the United States, and France.
Why did independence occur in such a short time span for most of these colonies?

War, persuaded the United States to lend its support first to the French war effort and then to the government of South Vietnam. U.S. president Dwight Eisenhower applied the domino theory to Vietnam. Violating the terms of the Geneva Agreements, which required elections that would likely have brought Ho to power, South Vietnam's leaders, with U.S. support, avoided elections and sought to build a government that would prevent the spread of communism in South Vietnam and elsewhere in Asia. Ngo Dinh Diem (1901–1963), the first president of the Republic of (South) Vietnam, and other South Vietnamese leaders did not garner popular support with the people, however, and growing discontent sparked the spread of guerrilla war in the south.

In 1960, Vietnamese nationalists formed the National Liberation Front (NLF) to fight for freedom from South Vietnamese rule. Although Vietnamese from the south made up the majority in this organization, it received direction, aid, weapons, and ultimately troops from the north also. In turn, the government in the north received economic and military assistance from the Soviet Union and China, and a cold war stalemate ensued.

Vietnam's "American War" Given the lack of popular support for Diem and U.S.-style democratic reforms, the nationalist communist attacks against the South Vietnamese government met with continued success. In 1965 President Lyndon Johnson (1908–1973) embarked on a course of action that exponentially increased U.S. involvement in Vietnam. He ordered a bombing campaign against North Vietnam and sent U.S. ground troops to augment the South Vietnamese army. Yet, even with the overwhelming firepower and military personnel, the best the United States and South Vietnam could achieve against the Viet Cong was a draw. North Vietnam found a stalemate quite acceptable. Vietnamese forces fought for freedom from outside interference of any sort and could show patience while making progress toward independence.

Vietnamese Victory Their patience was rewarded as opposition to the war grew in the United States. Recognizing his country's distaste for the Vietnam War, presidential candidate Richard Nixon pledged in 1968 to end the war. After his election, he implemented his strategy of turning the war over to the South Vietnamese—termed *Vietnamization*—by escalating the conflict. Nixon extended the war into Cambodia through bombing and invasion in 1969 and 1970, and he resumed the heavy bombing of North Vietnam. He also opened diplomatic channels to the Soviet Union and China, hoping to get them to pressure North Vietnam into a negotiated end to the war. U.S. troops gradually withdrew from the conflict, and in January 1973 the "American War," as the Vietnamese termed it, ended with the negotiated Paris Peace Accords. War itself did not end, as forces from North Vietnam and the NLF continued their struggle to conquer South Vietnam and unite the nation. They achieved their goals with the military defeat of South Vietnam in 1975 and with national reunification in 1976.

Ho Chi Minh, leader of North Vietnam from 1945 to 1969 and one of southeast Asia's most influential communist leaders.

Arab National States and the Problem of Palestine

With the exception of Palestine, the Arab states of southwest Asia had little difficulty freeing themselves from the colonial powers of France and Britain by the end of World War II. Before the war, Arab states agitated for concessions under the mandate system, which limited Arab nationalist aspirations after the Great War. In fact, Egypt had almost complete autonomy from British rule, an autonomy limited by British military control of the strategic Suez Canal and the oil-rich Persian Gulf.

Arab Independence After the war, although Syria, Iraq, Lebanon, and Jordan gained complete independence, significant vestiges of imperial rule impeded Arab sovereignty. The battle to rid southwest Asia of those remnants of imperialism took some twists and turns as the superpowers interfered in the region, drawn by its vast reserves of oil, the lifeblood of the cold war's military-industrial complexes. Throughout, one ambiguous legacy of imperialism—Palestine—absorbed much of the region's energies and emotions.

Palestine Great Britain served as the mandate power in Palestine after the Great War and, before and during its mandate, made conflicting promises to the Palestinian Arabs and to the Jews migrating to Palestine to establish a secure homeland where they could avoid persecution. With the Balfour Declaration of 1917, the British government committed itself to the support of a homeland for Jews in Palestine, a commitment engendered in part by the vibrant Zionist movement that had been growing in Europe since the 1890s. Zionists were dedicated to combating the violent anti-Semitism prevailing in central and eastern Europe by establishing a national Jewish state. The Zionist dream of returning to Palestine, considered the site of the original Jewish homeland, received a boost from the Balfour Declaration and from the Allies' support for it at the Paris Peace Conference in 1919. Thus the British were compelled to allow Jewish migration to Palestine under their mandate, but they also had to allay the fears of those in possession of the land—the Palestinian Arabs. The British therefore limited the migration and settlement of Jews and promised to protect the Arabs' political and economic rights.

At the end of World War II, a battle brewed. As Arab states around Palestine gained their freedom from imperial rule, they developed a pan-Arab nationalism sparked by support for their fellow Arabs in Palestine and opposition to the possibility of a Jewish state there. The Holocaust, along with the British policy of limiting Jewish migration to Palestine after the war, intensified the Jewish commitment to build a state capable of defending the world's remaining Jews—and the tens of thousands of Palestinian Jews who had fought in the British army during the war were seen as potential defenders of the new state.

The Creation of Israel The British could not adjudicate the competing claims of the Arabs and the Jews in Palestine. While the Arabs insisted on complete independence under Arab rule, in 1945 the Jews embarked on a course of violent resistance to the British to compel recognition of Jewish demands for self-rule and open immigration. The British gave up in 1947, stating that they intended to withdraw from Palestine and turn over the region to the newly created United Nations. Delegates to the UN General Assembly debated the idea of dividing Palestine into two states, one Arab and the other Jewish. The United States and the Soviet Union lent their support to that notion, and in November 1947 the General Assembly announced a proposal for the division of Palestine into two distinct states. Arabs inside and outside Palestine found that solution unacceptable, and in late 1947 civil war broke out. Arab and Jewish troops battled each other as the British completed their withdrawal from Palestine, and in May 1948 the Jews in Palestine proclaimed the creation of the independent state of Israel.

Israel's proclamation of statehood provoked a series of military conflicts between Israeli and various Arab forces spanning five decades, most notably in 1948–49, 1956, 1967, 1973, and 1982. As a result of those wars, Israel substantially increased the size of its territory beyond the area granted to it by the original UN partition, and hundreds of thousands of Palestinians became refugees outside the state of Israel. Because Arabs and Israelis failed to reach a comprehensive and permanent peace agreement, hostilities continued. Beginning in 1987 a popular mass movement known as the *intifada* initiated a series of demonstrations, strikes, and riots against Israeli rule in the Gaza Strip and other occupied territories. Violence continued well into the twenty-first century, and the future of the occupied territories remains undetermined.

Egypt and Arab Nationalism Egyptian military leaders, under the direction of Gamal Abdel Nasser (1918–1970), committed themselves to opposing Israel and taking command of the Arab world. Forsaking constitutional government and democratic principles, they began a political revolution and campaign of state reform through militarism, suppressing the ideological and religious opposition organized by communists and the Muslim Brotherhood. In July 1952 Nasser and other officers staged a bloodless coup that ended the monarchy of Egypt's King Farouk. After a series of complicated intrigues, Nasser named himself prime minister in 1954 and took control of the government. He then labored assiduously to develop Egypt economically and militarily and make it the fountainhead of pan-Arab nationalism.

In his efforts to strengthen Egypt, Nasser adopted an internationalist position akin to Nehru's nonalignment policy in India. Nasser's neutralism, like Nehru's, was based on the belief that cold war power politics were a new form of imperialism. Nasser condemned states that joined with foreign powers in military alliances, such as the Baghdad Pact, a British- and U.S.-inspired alliance that included Turkey, Iraq, and Iran. Nevertheless, he saw in the new cold

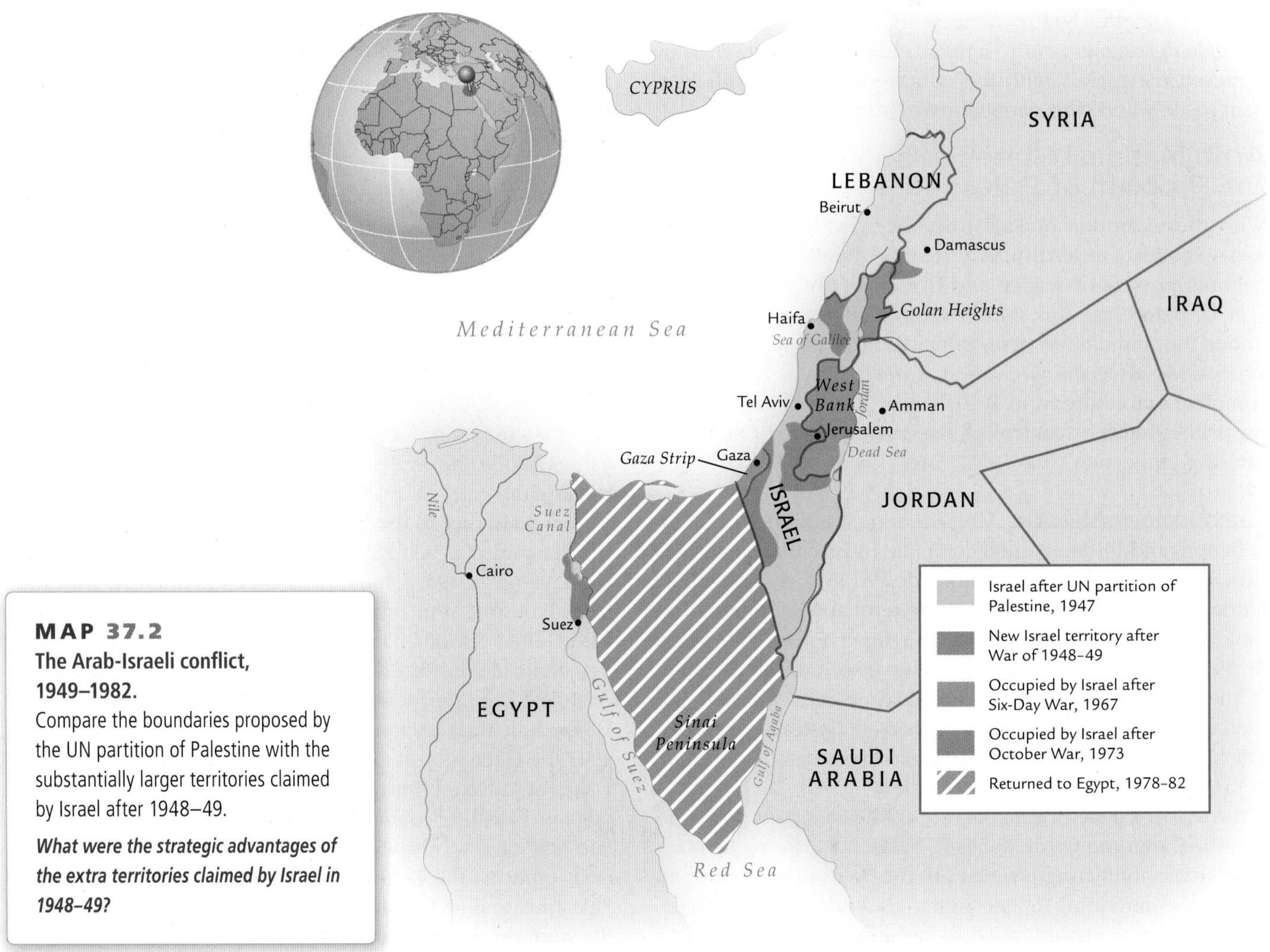

MAP 37.2
The Arab-Israeli conflict, 1949–1982.
Compare the boundaries proposed by the UN partition of Palestine with the substantially larger territories claimed by Israel after 1948–49.

What were the strategic advantages of the extra territories claimed by Israel in 1948–49?

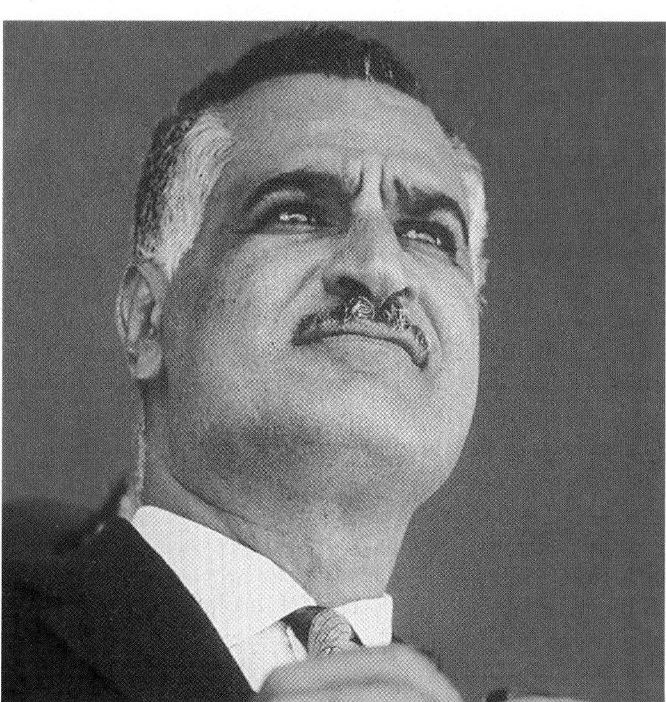

Gamal Abdel Nasser was president of Egypt from 1954 until his death in 1970. He successfully demonstrated how newly independent nations could avoid alignment with the cold war powers. Nasser also sought to rid Egypt and the Arab world of lingering imperialist influences. In particular, he sought the destruction of the state of Israel.

war world, opportunities that could be exploited for the advancement of Egypt, and he used his political savvy to extract pledges of economic and military assistance from the United States and the Soviet Union. Nasser demonstrated how newly independent nations could evade becoming trapped in either ideological camp and could force the superpowers to compete for influence.

Nasser also dedicated himself to ridding Egypt and the Arab world of imperial interference, which included destroying the state of Israel. He gave aid to the Algerians in their war against the French. Nasser did not neglect the remaining imperial presence in Egypt: he abolished British military rights to the Suez Canal in 1954. Through such actions and through his country's antipathy toward Israel, he laid claim to pan-Arab leadership throughout southwest Asia and north Africa.

The Suez Crisis Nasser sealed his reputation during the Suez crisis, which left him in a dominant position in the Arab world. The crisis erupted in 1956, when Nasser decided to nationalize the Suez Canal and use the money collected from the canal to finance construction of a massive dam of the Nile River at Aswan. When he did not bow to international pressure to provide multinational control of the vital Suez Canal, British, French, and Israeli forces combined to wrest control of the canal away from him. Their military campaign was successful, but they failed miserably on the diplomatic level and tore at the fabric of the cold war world system. They had not consulted with the United States, which strongly condemned the attack and forced them to withdraw. The Soviet Union also objected forcefully, thereby gaining a reputation for being a staunch supporter of Arab nationalism. Nasser gained tremendous prestige, and Egypt solidified its position as leader of the charge against imperial holdovers in southwest Asia and north Africa.

Despite Nasser's successes, he did not manage to rid the region of Israel, which was growing stronger with each passing year. More wars were fought in the decades to come, and peace between the Arab states and Israel seemed not only elusive but at times impossible. Although the partition that took place in Palestine appeared to lend itself to manipulation by the superpowers, the region of southwest Asia confused, complicated, and undermined elements of bipolarism. The strategic importance of oil dictated that both superpowers vie for favor in the Arab states, and while the United States became a firm ally of Israel, the Soviet Union also supported Israel's right to exist. The Suez crisis further tangled cold war power politics because it divided the United States and its allies in western Europe. Southwest Asia proved successful at ousting almost all imperial control and at challenging the bipolar worldview.

DECOLONIZATION IN AFRICA

Agitation for independence in sub-Saharan Africa took many forms—some peaceful and some violent—and decolonization occurred at different paces in different nations. Complicating the decolonization process were internal divisions in African societies, which undermined attempts to forge national or pan-African identities. Tribal, ethnic, religious, and linguistic divides within and between state boundaries, all of which colonial rulers had exploited, posed a challenge to African leaders, particularly once independence came and the imperial outsider departed. In colonies where imperial rule had the support of European settlers, as in Algeria or Kenya, for example, decolonization became mired in violence. In many instances, African nations symbolized and sealed their severance from imperial control by adopting new names that shunned the memory of European rule and drew from the glory of Africa's past empires. Ghana set the pattern, and the map of Africa soon featured similar references to precolonial African places such as Zambia, Malawi, and Zimbabwe.

Forcing the French out of North Africa

In Africa as in southeast Asia, the French resisted decolonization. In Algeria the French fought a bloody war that began in 1954, the year France suffered its defeat at Dienbienphu. Somewhat ironically, while it focused its efforts on Algeria in the 1950s and 1960s, France allowed all its other territories in Africa to gain independence. In 1956 France granted

This 1960 photograph served as the identity-card portrait for an Algerian woman. During the war for Algerian independence, colonial French authorities forced such documentation, which included having women violate Muslim practices of remaining veiled in public.

independence to its colonies in Morocco and Tunisia, and thirteen French colonies in west and equatorial Africa won their independence in 1960, a year that came to be known as "the year of Africa."

France in Africa France's concessions to its other African colonies illustrated its determination to control Algeria at all costs. The French people expressed differing opinions on the Algerian conflict, being less determined than their government leaders. French settlers demanded that the government in Paris defend their cause in north Africa. Two million French settled or were born there by the mid-1940s. The end of World War II, however, marked the beginning of a revitalized nationalist movement in Algeria, fueled by desire for independence from France and freedom from domination by white settlers. The event that touched off the Algerian revolt came in May 1945. French colonial police in the town of Sétif fired shots into an otherwise peaceful demonstration in support of Algerian and Arab nationalism. Algerian rioting and French repression of the disturbances took place in the wake of the incident. In the resulting melee more than eight thousand Algerian Muslims died, along with approximately one hundred French.

War in Algeria The Algerian war of liberation began in 1954 under the command of the Front de Libération Nationale (FLN, or National Liberation Front). The FLN adopted tactics similar to those of nationalist liberation groups in Asia, relying on bases in outlying mountainous areas and resorting to guerrilla warfare. The French did not realize the seriousness of the challenge they faced until 1955, when the FLN moved into more urbanized areas. France sent thousands of troops to Algeria to put down the revolution, and by 1958 it had committed half a million soldiers to the war. The war became ugly: Algerians serving with the French had to kill fellow Algerians or be killed by them; Algerian civilians became trapped in the crossfire of war, often accused of and killed for aiding FLN guerrillas; thousands of French soldiers died. By the war's end in 1962, when the Algerians gained independence from France, hundreds of thousands of Algerians had died.

Frantz Fanon One ideological legacy for Africa stemmed from Algeria's war of independence. Frantz Fanon (1925–1961) gained fame as an Algerian revolutionary and as an influential proponent of national liberation for colonial peoples through violent revolution. Born in Martinique in the West Indies, Fanon studied psychiatry and medicine in France, went to Algeria to head a hospital's psychiatric department, and then participated in Algeria's battle to free itself from French rule. Fanon furthered his fame and provided ideological support for African nationalism and revolution in his writings. In works such as *The Wretched of the Earth* (1961), he urged the use of violence against colonial oppressors as a means of overcoming the racist degradation experienced by peoples in developing or colonial nations outside the Soviet-U.S. sphere. Fanon died shortly before Algerians achieved independence, but his ideas influenced the independence struggles ongoing in Africa.

Black African Nationalism and Independence

Before and during World War II, nationalism flourished in sub-Saharan Africa. African nationalists celebrated their blackness and Africanness in contrast to their European colonial rulers. Drawing from the pan-African movements that emerged in the United States and the Caribbean, African intellectuals, especially in French-controlled west Africa, established a movement to promote *Négritude* ("Blackness"). Reviving Africa's great traditions and cultures, poets and writers expressed a widely shared pride in Africa.

Growth of African Nationalism This celebration of African culture was accompanied by grassroots protests against European imperialism. A new urban African elite slowly created the sorts of associations needed to hold demonstrations and fight for independence. Especially widespread, if sporadic, were workers' strikes against oppressive labor practices and the low wages paid by colonial overlords in areas such as the Gold Coast and Northern Rhodesia. Some independent Christian churches also provided

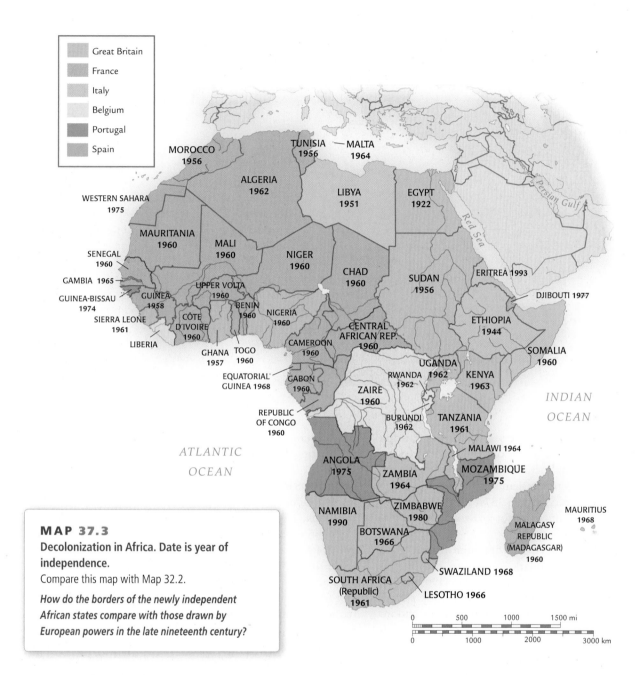

MAP 37.3
Decolonization in Africa. Date is year of independence.
Compare this map with Map 32.2.
How do the borders of the newly independent African states compare with those drawn by European powers in the late nineteenth century?

avenues for anticolonial agitation, as prophets such as Simon Kimbangu in the Belgian Congo promised his churchgoers that God would deliver them from imperial control. In the years after World War II, African poets associated with the *Négritude* movement continued to express their attachment to Africanness and encourage Africans to turn away from European culture and colonial rule.

African Independence The dreams and hopes of African nationalists frequently had to be placed on hold in the early years after World War II. Often assuming that black Africans were incapable of self-government, imperial powers planned for a slow transition to independence. The presence of white settlers in certain African colonies also complicated the process of decolonization. The politics of the cold war allowed imperial powers to justify oppressive actions in the name of rooting out a subversive communist presence. Despite the delays, however, sub-Saharan states slowly but surely won their independence as each newly independent nation inspired and often aided other lands to win their freedom.

Freedom and Conflict in Sub-Saharan Africa

Ghana was the first sub-Saharan country to achieve independence from colonial rule. Located in west Africa, its

Roadside portraits of Queen Elizabeth II and Kwame Nkrumah in Accra. The British monarch made a postindependence visit to Ghana in November 1961.

people had been engaged in direct sea trade with Europe since the fifteenth century. Trading originally centered on gold but then shifted to the lucrative slave trade in the seventeenth century. By the time Ghana became part of the British empire as a Crown colony in 1874, its economy had developed into an important center for growing and exporting cacao.

Ghana's success in achieving its freedom from British rule in 1957 served as a hallmark in Africa's end of empire. Under the leadership of Kwame Nkrumah (1909–1972), political parties and strategies for mass action took shape. Although the British subjected Nkrumah and other nationalists to jail terms and repressive control, gradually they allowed reforms and negotiated the transfer of power in their Gold Coast colony.

Ghana After it became independent in 1957, Ghana emboldened and inspired other African nationalist movements. More than thirty other African countries followed Ghana's example and declared their own independence within the next decade. Nkrumah, as a leader of the first sub-Saharan African nation to gain independence from colonial rule, became a persuasive spokesperson for pan-African unity. His ideas and his stature as an African leader symbolized the changing times in Africa. In preparation for the 1961 visit of Britain's Queen Elizabeth II (1926–), the people of Ghana erected huge side-by-side posters of the queen and their leader, Nkrumah. Those roadside portraits offered a stunning vision of newfound equality and distinctiveness. Ex-colonial rulers, dressed in royal regalia, faced off against new African leaders, clothed in traditional African fabrics, the once-dominating white faces matched by the proud black faces.

Anticolonial Rebellion in Kenya The process of attaining independence did not always prove as nonviolent as in Ghana. The battle that took place in the British colony of Kenya in east Africa demonstrated the complexity and difficulty of African decolonization. The situation in Kenya turned tense and violent in a clash between powerful white settlers and nationalists, especially the Kikuyu, one of Kenya's largest ethnic groups. Beginning in 1947, Kikuyu rebels embarked on an intermittently violent campaign against Europeans and alleged traitorous Africans. The settlers who controlled the colonial government in Nairobi refused to see the uprisings as a legitimate expression of discontent with colonial rule. Rather, they branded the Kikuyu tribes as radicals bent on a racial struggle for primacy. As one settler put it, "Why the hell can't we fight these apes and worry about the survivors later?" Members of the militant nationalist movements were labeled by the British government as Mau Mau subversives or communists.

In reality, Kikuyu radicalism and violence had much more to do with nationalist opposition to British colonial rule, especially land policies in Kenya. Kikuyu resentment of the British stemmed from their treatment in the 1930s and 1940s, when white settlers pushed them off the most fertile highland farm areas and reduced them to the status of wage slaves or relegated them to overcrowded "tribal reserves." Resistance began in the early 1940s with labor strikes and violent direct action campaigns designed to force or frighten

sources from the past

Kwame Nkrumah on African Unity

As the leader of the first African nation to gain independence, Kwame Nkrumah (1909–1972) became a respected spokesperson for African unity as a strategy for dealing with decolonization during the cold war. In his book I Speak of Freedom: A Statement of African Ideology *(1961), Nkrumah made an eloquent case for an African solution for the problems of African independence during a global cold war.*

It is clear that we must find an African solution to our problems, and that this can only be found in African unity. Divided we are weak; united, Africa could become one of the greatest forces for good in the world.

Never before have a people had within their grasp so great an opportunity for developing a continent endowed with so much wealth. Individually, the independent states of Africa, some of them potentially rich, others poor, can do little for their people. Together, by mutual help, they can achieve much. But the economic development of the continent must be planned and pursued as a whole. A loose confederation designed only for economic cooperation would not provide the necessary unity of purpose. Only a strong political union can bring about full and effective development of our natural resources for the benefit of our people.

The political situation in Africa today is heartening and at the same time disturbing. It is heartening to see so many new flags hoisted in place of the old; it is disturbing to see so many countries of varying sizes and at different levels of development, weak and, in some cases, almost helpless. If this terrible state of fragmentation is allowed to continue it may well be disastrous for us all.

Critics of African unity often refer to the wide differences in culture, language and ideas in various parts of Africa. This is true, but the essential fact remains that we are all Africans, and have a common interest in the independence of Africa. The difficulties presented by questions of language, culture and different political systems are not insuperable. If the need for political union is agreed by us all, then the will to create it is born; and where there's a will there's a way.

The greatest contribution that Africa can make to the peace of the world is to avoid all the dangers inherent in disunity, by creating a political union which will also by its success, stand as an example to a divided world. A union of African states will project more effectively the African personality. It will command respect from a world that has regard only for size and influence.

We have to prove that greatness is not to be measured in stockpiles of atom bombs. I believe strongly and sincerely that with the deep-rooted wisdom and dignity, the innate respect for human lives, the intense humanity that is our heritage, the African race, united under one federal government, will emerge not as just another world bloc to flaunt its wealth and strength, but as a Great Power whose greatness is indestructible because it is not built on fear, envy and suspicion, nor won at the expense of others, but founded on hope, trust, friendship and directed to the good of all mankind.

For Further Reflection

- How does Nkrumah's call for African unity rather than fragmentation reflect the tensions between decolonization and the ongoing cold war?

Source: Kwame Nkrumah. *I Speak of Freedom: A Statement of African Ideology.* New York: Frederick A. Praeger, 1961, pp. x–xii.

the white settlers off their lands. In the 1950s, attacks on white settlers and black collaborators escalated, and in 1952 the British established a state of emergency to crush the anticolonial guerrilla movement through detention and counterinsurgency programs. Unable or unwilling to distinguish violent activism from nonviolent agitation, the British moved to suppress all nationalist groups and jailed Kenya nationalist leaders, including Jomo Kenyatta (1895–1978) in 1953. Amid growing resistance to colonial rule, the British mounted major military offenses against rebel forces, supporting their army troops with artillery, bombers, and jet fighters. By 1956 the British had effectively crushed all military resistance in a conflict that claimed the lives of twelve thousand Africans and one hundred Europeans.

Despite military defeat, Kikuyu fighters broke British resolve in Kenya and gained increasing international recognition of African grievances. The British resisted the radical white supremacism and political domineering of the settlers in Kenya and instead responded to calls for Kenya independence. In 1959 the British lifted the state of emergency, and as political parties formed, nationalist leaders like Kenyatta reemerged to lead those parties. By December 1963 Kenya had negotiated its independence.

Internal Colonialism in South Africa As elsewhere in Africa, the presence of large numbers of white settlers in South Africa long delayed the arrival of black freedom. South Africa's black population, though a majority, remained

These Kikuyu children were photographed in 1952 in a British government prison camp, where rebel nationalists and their families were detained.

dispossessed and disfranchised. Anticolonial agitation thus was significantly different in South Africa than in the rest of sub-Saharan Africa: it was a struggle against internal colonialism, against an oppressive white regime that denied basic human and civil rights to tens of millions of South Africans.

Apartheid The ability of whites to resist majority rule had its roots in the South African economy, the strongest on the continent. That strength had two sources: extraction of minerals and industrial development, which received a huge boost during World War II. The growth of the industrial sector opened many jobs to blacks, creating the possibility of a change in their status. Along with black activism and calls for serious political reform after World War II, these changes struck fear into the hearts of white South Africans. In 1948 the Afrikaner National Party, which was dedicated to quashing any move toward black independence, came to power. Under the National Party the government instituted a harsh new set of laws designed to control the restive black population; these new laws constituted the system known as apartheid, or "separateness."

The system of apartheid asserted white supremacy and institutionalized the racial segregation established in the years before 1948. The government designated approximately 87 percent of South Africa's territory for white residents. Remaining areas were designated as homelands for black and colored citizens. Nonwhites were classified according to a variety of ethnic identifications—colored or mixed-race peoples, Indians, and "Bantu," which in turn was subdivided into numerous distinct tribal affiliations (for example, Zulu, Xhosa, Sotho). As other imperial powers had done in Africa, white South Africans divided the black and colored population in the hope of preventing the rise of unified liberation movements. The apartheid system, complex and varied in its composition, evolved into a system designed to keep blacks in a position of political, social, and economic subordination.

Dispossessed peoples all found in apartheid an impetus for resistance to white rule. The African National Congress (ANC), formed in 1912, gained new young leaders such as Nelson Mandela (1918–), who inspired direct action campaigns to protest apartheid. In 1955 the ANC published its Freedom Charter, which proclaimed the ideal of multiracial democratic rule for South Africa. Because its goals directly challenged white rule, the ANC and all black activists in South Africa faced severe repression. The government declared all its opponents communists and escalated its actions against black activists. Protests increased in 1960, the so-called year of Africa, and on 21 March 1960 white police gunned down black demonstrators in Sharpeville, near Johannesburg. Sixty-nine blacks died and almost two hundred were wounded. Sharpeville instituted a new era of radical activism.

When the white regime banned black organizations such as the ANC and jailed their adherents, international opposition to white South African rule grew. Newly freed nations in Asia and Africa called for UN sanctions against South Africa, and in 1961 South Africa declared itself a republic, withdrawing from the British Commonwealth. Some leaders of the ANC saw the necessity of armed resistance, but in 1963 government forces captured the leaders of ANC's military unit, including Nelson Mandela. The court sentenced them to life in prison, and Mandela and others became symbols of oppressive white rule. Protests against the system persisted in the 1970s and 1980s, spurred especially by student activism and a new black-consciousness movement. The combined effects of widespread black agitation and a powerful international anti-apartheid boycott eventually led to reform and a growing recognition that, if it was to survive, South Africa had to change.

The End of Apartheid When F. W. de Klerk (1936–) became president of South Africa in 1989, he and the National Party began to dismantle the apartheid system. De Klerk released Mandela from jail in 1990, legalized the ANC, and worked with Mandela and the ANC to negotiate the end of white minority rule. Collaborating and cooperating, the National Party, the ANC, and other African political groups created a new constitution and in April 1994 held elections that were open to people of all races. The ANC won overwhelmingly, and Mandela became the first black president of South Africa. In 1963, at the trial that ended in his jail sentence, Mandela proclaimed, "I have cherished the ideal of a democratic and free society in which all persons live

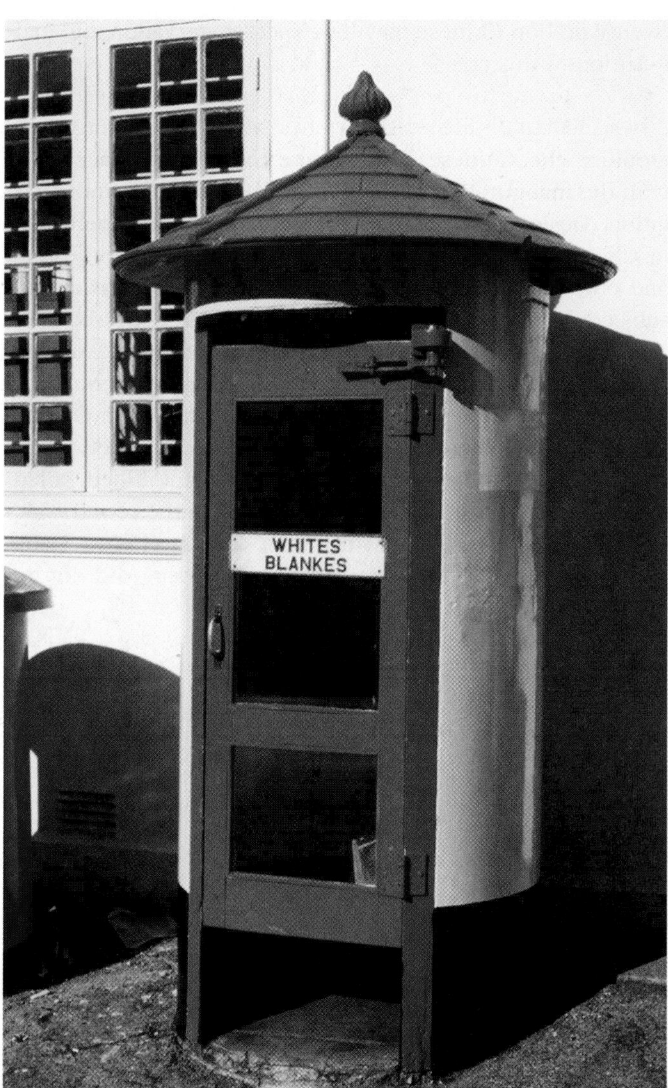

Whites telephone kiosk. The South African system of apartheid institutionalized racial segregation.

together in harmony and with equal opportunities. It is an ideal which I hope to live for and to achieve. But if needs be, it is an ideal for which I am prepared to die." Mandela lived to see his ideal fulfilled. In 1994, as president, he proclaimed his nation "free at last."

AFTER INDEPENDENCE: LONG-TERM STRUGGLES IN THE POSTCOLONIAL ERA

Political and economic stability proved elusive after independence, particularly in those developing nations struggling to build political and economic systems free from the domination of more powerful nations. The legacies of imperialism, either direct or indirect, hindered the creation of democratic institutions in many parts of the world—in recently decolonized nations, such as those of Africa, and in some of the earliest lands to gain independence, such as those of Latin America. Continued interference by the former colonial powers, by the superpowers, or by more developed nations impeded progress, as did local elites with ties to the colonial powers. The result was an unstable succession of governments based on an authoritarian one-party system or on harsh military rule. South Africa and India, however, transformed themselves into functioning democracies despite deep racial and religious divides. In Asia and the Islamic world, some governments kept order by relying on tightly centralized rule, as in China, or on religion, as in Iran after the 1979 revolution. Few developing or newly industrialized countries, however, escaped the disruption of war or revolution that also characterized the postcolonial era.

Communism and Democracy in Asia

Except for Japan and India, the developing nations in south, southeast, and east Asia adopted some form of authoritarian or militarist political system, and many of them followed a communist or socialist path of political development. Under Mao Zedong (1893–1976), China served as a guide and inspiration for those countries seeking a means of political development distinct from the ways of their previous colonial masters.

Mao's China Mao reunified China for the first time since the collapse of the Qing dynasty, transforming European communist ideology into a distinctly Chinese communism. After 1949 he embarked on programs designed to accelerate development in China. The economic and social transformation of Chinese society centered on rapid industrialization and the collectivization of agriculture (making landownership collective, not individual). Emulating earlier Soviet experiments, the Chinese introduced their first Five-Year Plan in 1955. Designed to speed up economic development, the Five-Year Plan emphasized improvements in infrastructure and the expansion of heavy industry at the expense of consumer goods. A series of agrarian laws promoted an unprecedented transfer of wealth among the population, virtually eliminating economic inequality at the village level. After confiscating the landholdings of rich peasants and landlords, the government redistributed the land so that virtually every peasant had at least a small plot of land. After the government took over the grain market and prohibited farmers from marketing their crops, though, collective farms replaced private farming. Health care and primary education anchored to collectives permitted the extension of social services to larger segments of the population. In the wake of economic reforms came social reforms, many of which challenged and often eliminated Chinese family traditions. Supporting equal rights for women, Chinese authorities introduced marriage laws that eliminated practices such as child or forced marriages, gave women equal access to divorce, and legalized abortion. Foot binding, a symbol of women's subjugation, also became a practice of the past.

A 1966 poster shows Mao Zedong inspiring the people to launch the Great Proletarian Cultural Revolution.

Continuing China's push for development were the Great Leap Forward (1958–1961) and the Great Proletarian Cultural Revolution (1966–1976). These were far-reaching policies that contrarily hampered the very political and economic development that Mao sought.

Mao envisioned his Great Leap Forward as a way to overtake the industrial production of more developed nations, and to that end he worked to collectivize all land and to manage all business and industrial enterprises collectively. Private ownership was abolished, and farming and industry became largely rural and communal. The Great Leap Forward—or "Giant Step Backward" as some have dubbed it—failed. Most disastrous was its impact on agricultural production in China: the peasants, recalcitrant and exhausted, did not meet quotas, and a series of bad harvests also contributed to one of the deadliest famines in history. Rather than face reality, Mao blamed the sparrows for the bad harvests, accusing these counterrevolutionaries of eating too much grain. He ordered tens of millions of peasants to kill the feathered menaces, leaving insects free to consume what was left of the crops. Between 1959 and 1962 as many as twenty million Chinese may have died of starvation and malnutrition in this crisis.

The Cultural Revolution In 1966 Mao tried again to mobilize the Chinese and reignite the revolutionary spirit with the inauguration of the Great Proletarian Cultural Revolution. Designed to root out the revisionism Mao perceived in Chinese life, especially among Communist Party leaders and others in positions of authority, the Cultural Revolution subjected millions of people to humiliation, persecution, and death. The elite—intellectuals, teachers, professionals, managers, and anyone associated with foreign or bourgeois values—constituted the major targets of the Red Guards, youthful zealots empowered to cleanse Chinese society of opponents to Mao's rule. Victims were beaten and killed, jailed, or sent to corrective labor camps or to toil in the countryside. The Cultural Revolution, which cost China years of stable development and gutted its educational system, did not die

The student democracy movement in Tiananmen Square, Beijing, June 1989. Many Chinese students had been encouraged by the government to study abroad. Their exposure to democratic societies prompted protests for change at home that were violently suppressed.

down until after Mao's death in 1976. It fell to one of Mao's political heirs, Deng Xiaoping, to heal the nation.

Deng's Revolution Although he was a colleague of Mao, Deng Xiaoping (1904–1997) suffered the same fate as millions of other Chinese during the Cultural Revolution: he had to recant criticisms of Mao, identify himself as a petit-bourgeois intellectual, and labor in a tractor-repair factory. When a radical faction failed to maintain the Cultural Revolution after Mao's death, China began its recovery from the turmoil. Deng came to power in 1981, and the 1980s are often referred to as the years of "Deng's Revolution." Deng moderated Mao's commitment to Chinese self-sufficiency and isolation and engineered China's entry into the international financial and trading system, a move that was facilitated by the normalization of relations between China and the United States in the 1970s.

Tiananmen Square To push the economic development of China, Deng opened the nation to the influences that were so suspect under Mao—foreign, capitalist values. His actions included sending tens of thousands of Chinese students to foreign universities to rebuild the professional, intellectual, and managerial elite needed for modern development. Those students were exposed to the democratic societies of western Europe and the United States. When they staged prodemocracy demonstrations in Beijing's Tiananmen Square in 1989, Deng, whose experiences in the Cultural Revolution made him wary of zealous revolutionary movements, approved a bloody crackdown. Not surprisingly, Deng faced hostile world opinion after crushing the student movement. The issue facing China as it entered the global economy was how (or whether) to reap economic benefits without compromising its identity and its authoritarian political system. This issue gained added weight as Hong Kong, under British administration since the 1840s and in the throes of its own democracy movement, reverted to Chinese control in 1997. Chinese leaders in the twenty-first century have managed to maintain both centralized political control over China and impressive economic growth and development. The evidence of China's increasing global power and prominence became especially visible during the 2008 summer Olympics in Beijing.

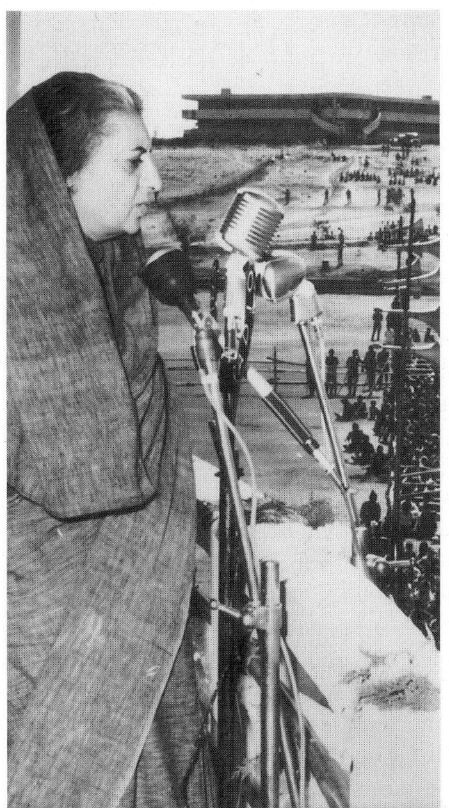

Indira Gandhi delivers a speech in 1972. Gandhi led India into the "green revolution," which sought to increase agricultural production to help feed the country's eight hundred million people. The campaign's mixed results, among other reasons, led to her temporarily losing power in 1977 before regaining it in 1980.

Indian Democracy The flourishing of democracy in India stands in stark contrast to the political trends in many other developing nations. Whereas other nations turned to dictators, military rule, or authoritarian systems, India maintained its political stability and its democratic system after gaining independence in 1947. Even when faced with the crises that shook other developing nations—ethnic and religious conflict, wars, poverty, and overpopulation—India remained committed to free elections and a critical press. Its first postindependence prime minister, Jawaharlal Nehru, guided his nation to democratic rule.

In 1966 Indira Gandhi (1917–1984), Nehru's daughter (and no relation to Mohandas K. Gandhi), became leader of the Congress Party. She served as prime minister of India from 1966 to 1977 and from 1980 to 1984, and under her leadership India embarked on the "green revolution" that increased agricultural yields for India's eight hundred million people. Although the new agricultural policies aided wealthier farmers, the masses of peasant farmers fell deeper into poverty. Beyond the poverty that drove Indians to demonstrations of dissatisfaction with Gandhi's government, India was beset by other troubles—overpopulation and continuing sectarian conflicts.

Those problems prompted Indira Gandhi to take stringent action to maintain control. To quell growing opposition to her government, she declared a national emergency (1975–1977) that suspended democratic processes. She used her powers under the emergency to forward one of India's most needed social reforms, birth control. But rather than persuading or tempting Indians to control the size of their families (offering gifts of money for those who got vasectomies, for example), the government engaged in repressive birth control policies, including involuntary sterilization. A record eight million sterilization operations were performed in 1976 and 1977. The riots that ensued, and the fear of castration among men who might be forced to undergo vasectomies, added to Gandhi's woes.

When Indira Gandhi allowed elections to be held in 1977, Indians voted against her because of her abrogation of democratic principles and her harsh birth control policies. She returned to power in 1980, however, and again faced great difficulty keeping the state of India together in the face of religious, ethnic, and secessionist movements. One such movement was an uprising by Sikhs who wanted greater autonomy in the Punjab region. The Sikhs, representing perhaps 2 percent of India's population, practiced a religion that was an offshoot of Hinduism, and they had a separate identity—symbolized by their distinctive long hair and headdresses—and a history of militarism and self-rule. Unable or unwilling to compromise in view of the large number of groups agitating for a similar degree of autonomy, Indira Gandhi ordered the army to attack the sacred Golden Temple in Amritsar, which harbored armed Sikh extremists. In retaliation, two of her Sikh bodyguards—hired for their martial skills—assassinated her a few months later in 1984.

Indira Gandhi's son Rajiv Gandhi (1944–1991) took over the leadership of India in 1985 and offered reconciliation to the Sikhs. He was assassinated by a terrorist in 1991 while attempting to win back the office he lost in 1989. Despite those setbacks, however, Nehru's heirs maintained democracy in India and continued to work on the problems plaguing Indian development—overpopulation, poverty, and sectarian division. The legacy of Mohandas K. Gandhi lived on in the form of brutal assassinations and continued quests for peace and religious tolerance.

thinking about ENCOUNTERS

Islamism and the World

Given the multiple encounters between Muslims, Europeans, Americans, and Israelis in the decades after World War II, Muslims turned away from the peoples and ways of life outside the Islamic sphere. How did that rejection of the non-Muslim world manifest itself?

Islamic Resurgence in Southwest Asia and North Africa

The geographic convergence of the Arab and Muslim worlds in southwest Asia and north Africa encouraged the development of Arab nationalism in states of those regions that gained independence in the year after World War II. Whether in Libya, Algeria, or Egypt in north Africa or in Syria, Saudi Arabia, or Iraq in southwest Asia, visions of Arab nationalism, linked to the religious force of Islam, dazzled nations that wished to fend off European and U.S. influence. In north Africa, Egypt's Gamal Abdel Nasser provided the leadership for this Arab nationalism, and Arab-Muslim opposition to the state of Israel held the dream together.

The hopes attached to pan-Arab unity did not materialize. Although Arab lands shared a common language and religion, divisions were frequent and alliances shifted over time. The cold war split the Arab-Muslim world; some states allied themselves with the United States, and others allied with the Soviet Union. Some countries also shifted between the two, as Egypt did when it left the Soviet orbit for the U.S. sphere in 1976. Governments in these nations included military dictatorships, monarchies, and Islamist revolutionary regimes. Religious divisions also complicated the attainment of Arab unity, because Sunni and Shia Muslims followed divergent theologies and foreign policies.

Islamism

In the 1970s, Muslims in many countries began to seek, sometimes violently, the revival of Islamic values in the political and social sphere. Leading Islamic thinkers called for the rigorous enforcement of the *sharia* (Islamic law), emphasized pan-Islamic unity, and urged the elimination of non-Muslim economic, political, or cultural influences in the Muslim world. In the view of many proponents, the Muslim world had been slipping into a state of decline, brought about by the abandonment of Islamic traditions. Many Muslims had become skeptical about European and American models of economic development and political and cultural norms, which they blamed for economic and political failure as well as for secularization and its attendant breakdown of traditional social and religious values. Disillusionment and even anger with European and American societies, and especially with the United States, became widespread. The solution to the problems faced by Muslim societies lay, according to Islamists, in the revival of Islamic identity, values, and power. The vast majority of Islamic activists have sought to bring about change through peaceful means, but an extremist minority has claimed a mandate from God that calls for violent transformations. Convinced that the Muslim world is under siege, extremists used the concept of *jihad*—the right and duty to defend Islam and the Islamic community from unjust attack—to rationalize and legitimize terrorism and revolution.

The Iranian Revolution

The Arab-Muslim world was divided on a number of issues, but the revolution that took place in Iran in 1979 demonstrated the power of Islam as a means of staving off secular foreign influences. Islamist influences penetrated Iran during the lengthy regime of Shah Mohammed Reza Pahlavi (1919–1980), whom the CIA helped bring to power in 1953. The vast sums of money that poured in from Iran's oil industry helped finance industrialization, and the United States provided the military equipment that enabled Iran to become a bastion of anticommunism in the region. In the late 1970s, however, opposition to the shah's government coalesced. Shia Muslims despised the shah's secular regime, Iranian small businesses detested the influence of U.S. corporations on the economy, and leftist politicians rejected the shah's repressive policies. The shah fled the country in early 1979 as the revolution gained force, and power was captured by the Islamist movement under the direction of Ayatollah Ruhollah Khomeini (1900–1989).

The revolution took on a strongly anti-U.S. cast, partly because the shah was allowed to travel to the United States for medical treatment. In retaliation, Shia militants captured sixty-nine hostages at the U.S. embassy in Tehran, fifty-five of whom remained captives until 1981. In the meantime, Iranian leaders shut U.S. military bases and confiscated U.S.-owned economic ventures. This Islamic power play against a developed nation such as the United States inspired other Muslims to undertake terrorist actions. The resurgent Islam of Iran did not lead to a new era of solidarity, however. Iranian Islam was the minority sect of Shia Islam, and one of Iran's neighbors, Iraq, attempted to take advantage of the revolution to invade Iran.

By the late 1970s Iraq had built a formidable military machine, largely owing to oil revenues and the efforts of Saddam Hussein (1937–2006), who became president of Iraq in 1979. Hussein launched his attack on Iran in 1980, believing that victory would be swift and perhaps hoping to become the new leader of a revived pan-Arab nationalism. (Iran is Muslim in religion, but not ethnically Arab, as are Iraq, Kuwait, and Saudi Arabia.) Although they were initially successful, Iraqi troops faced a determined counterattack by Iranian forces, and the conflict became a war of attrition that did not end until 1988.

The Iran-Iraq War The Iran-Iraq War killed as many as one million soldiers. In Iran the human devastation is still visible, if not openly acknowledged, in a nation that permits little dissent from Islamist orthodoxy. Young people are showing signs of a growing discontent caused by the war and by the rigors of a revolution that also killed thousands. Signs of recovery and a relaxation of Islamist strictness appeared in Iran in the late 1990s, but the destruction from war also remained visible. Islamism has reemerged in twenty-first-century Iran and has aroused some international concern, particularly for the United States. A conservative supreme leader, the Ayatollah Khamenei (1939–), and a conservative president, Mahmoud Ahmadinejad (1956–), represented this trend. Ahmadinejad took office in 2005 and touted Iran's nuclear program and his antipathy to the state of Israel, which had the effect of increasing his status in the Islamic world while intensifying tensions with the United States.

Iraqis continued on a militant course. Two years after the end of the Iran-Iraq War, Hussein's troops invaded Kuwait (1990) and incited the Gulf War (1991). The result was a decisive military defeat for Iraq, at the hands of an international coalition led by the United States, and further hardships for the Iraqi people.

Colonial Legacies in Sub-Saharan Africa

The optimism that accompanied decolonization in sub-Saharan Africa faded as the prospects for political stability gave way to civil wars and territorial disputes. This condition largely reflected the impact of colonialism. As European powers departed their decolonized lands, they left behind territories whose borders were artificial conveniences that did not correspond to any indigenous economic or ethnic divisions. Historically hostile communities found themselves jammed into a single "national" state. In other instances, populations found themselves in newly independent states whose borders were unacceptable to neighboring states. As a result, decolonization was frequently accompanied or followed by civil wars and border disputes that resisted resolution.

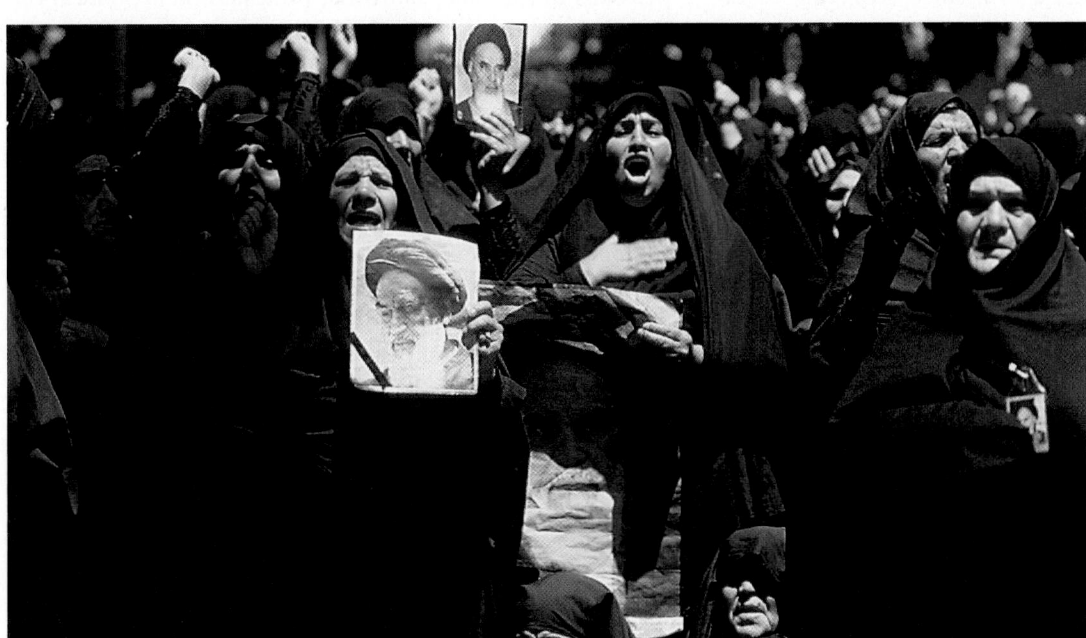

Iranians show their devotion to the Ayatollah Khomeini at his funeral in 1989.

The Organization of African Unity (OAU), created in 1963 by thirty-two member states, recognized some of those problems and attempted to prevent conflicts that could lead to intervention by former colonial powers. The artificial boundaries of African states, though acknowledged as problematic, were nonetheless held inviolable by the OAU to prevent disputes over boundaries. International law too treated postcolonial borders as inviolable. The OAU also promoted pan-African unity, at least in the faction headed by Kwame Nkrumah, as another way for African states to resist interference and domination by foreign powers. But although national borders have increasingly held, unity has not. African nations have been unable to avoid internal conflicts. Nkrumah, the former president of Ghana, is a case in point: he was overthrown in 1966, and Ghanaians tore down the statues and photographs that celebrated his leadership. Thus in Ghana, as in many other sub-Saharan states, politics evolved into dictatorial one-party rule, with party leaders forgoing multiparty elections in the name of ending political divisiveness. Several African nations fell prey to military rule in a large number of unsettling coups.

As political institutions foundered, the grinding poverty in which many African peoples lived increased tensions and made the absence of adequate administration and welfare programs more glaring. Poverty also prevented nations from accumulating the capital that could have contributed to a sound political and economic infrastructure. Africa's economic prospects after decolonization were not always so bleak, however. The continent is rich in mineral resources, raw materials, and agricultural products, and the postwar period saw a growing demand for Africa's commodity exports. Because many newly independent nations lacked the capital, the technology, and the foreign markets to exploit their natural wealth, they developed or maintained financial links with ex–colonial powers to finance economic development. After the 1970s many nations faced similar crises: falling commodity prices, rising import costs, and huge foreign debts. Africa's burdens were complicated by droughts, famines, and agricultural production that could not keep pace with population growth. Leaders of African nations were among the strongest supporters of the New International Economic Order that was called for by a coalition of developing nations. These states sought a more just allocation of global wealth, especially by guaranteeing prices and markets for commodities. Nevertheless, African states have continued to attempt wider integration into the global economy, despite the dependency that this move often entails.

Politics and Economics in Latin America

The uneasy aftermath of independence visible throughout Asia and Africa also affected states on the other side of the world—states that gained their freedom from colonial rule more than a century before postwar decolonization. Nations in Central and South America along with Mexico grappled with the conservative legacies of Spanish and Portuguese colonialism, particularly the political and economic power of the landowning elite of European descent. Latin America moreover had to deal with neocolonialism, because the United States not only intervened militarily when its interests were threatened but also influenced economies through investment and full or part ownership of enterprises such as the oil industry. In the nineteenth century Latin American states may have looked to the United States as a model of liberal democracy, but by the twentieth century U.S. interference provoked negative reactions. That condition was true after World War I, and it remained true during and after World War II.

Mexico Only President Lázaro Cárdenas (in office 1934–1940) had substantially invoked and applied the reforms guaranteed to Mexicans by the Constitution of 1917. The constitution's provisions regarding the state's right to redistribute land after confiscation and compensation, as well as its claim to government ownership of the subsoil and its products, found a champion in Cárdenas. He brought land reform and redistribution to a peak in Mexico, returning forty-five million acres to peasants, and he wrested away control of the oil industry from foreign investors. Cárdenas's nationalization of Mexico's oil industry allowed for the creation of the *Petróleos Mexicanos* (PEMEX), a national oil company in control of Mexico's petroleum products. The revenues generated by PEMEX contributed to what has been called "El Milagro Mexicano," or the Mexican economic miracle, a period of prosperity that lasted for decades. Conservative governments thereafter, controlled by the one-party rule of the Institutional Revolutionary Party (PRI), often acted harshly and experimented with various economic strategies that decreased or increased Mexico's reliance on foreign markets and capital. The PRI came under attack in the 1990s as Mexican peasants in the Chiapas district protested their political oppression. Cuauhtemoc Cárdenas, the son of Lázaro Cárdenas, took on the leadership of an opposition party, the Democratic Revolutionary Party (PRD), and this shift to democratic political competition and multiparty elections has continued into the twenty-first century.

Argentina Mexico served as one model for political development in Latin America, and Argentina seemed to be another candidate for leadership in South America. It had a reasonably expansive economy based on cattle raising and agriculture, a booming urban life, the beginnings of an industrial base, and a growing middle class in a population composed mostly of migrants from Europe. Given its geographic position far to the south, Argentina remained relatively independent of U.S. control and became a leader in the Latin American struggle against U.S. and European economic and political intervention in the region. A gradual shift to free elections and a sharing of political power beyond that exercised by the landowning elite also emerged. Given the military's central role in its politics, however, Argentina be-

In this 1950 photo taken in Buenos Aires, Eva Perón waves to adoring *descamisados,* or shirtless ones, to whose poverty she ceaselessly ministered. Although many thought of Eva Perón as a "saint," others viewed her own extravagant lifestyle as a sign of her opportunism.

came a model of a less positive form of political organization: the often brutal and deadly sway of military rulers.

Juan Perón During World War II, nationalistic military leaders gained power in Argentina and established a government controlled by the army. In 1946 Juan Perón (1895–1974), a former colonel in the army, was elected president. Although he was a nationalistic militarist, his regime garnered immense popularity among large segments of the Argentine population, partly because he appealed to the more downtrodden Argentines. He promoted a nationalistic populism, calling for industrialization, support of the working class, and protection of the economy from foreign control.

Evita However opportunistic Perón may have been, his popularity with the masses was real. His wife, Eva Perón (1919–1952), helped to foster that popularity, as Argentinians warmly embraced their "Evita" (little Eva). She rose from the ranks of the desperately poor. An illegitimate child who migrated to Buenos Aires at the age of fifteen, she found work as a radio soap-opera actress. She met Perón in 1944, and they were married shortly thereafter. Reigning in the Casa Rosada (the Pink House) as Argentina's first lady from 1946 to 1952, Eva Perón transformed herself into a stunningly beautiful political leader, radiant with dyed gold-blonde hair and clothed in classic designer fashions. While pushing for her husband's political reforms, she also tirelessly ministered to the needs of the poor, often the same *descamisados,* or "shirtless ones," who formed the core of her husband's supporters. Endless lines of people came to see her in her offices at the labor ministry—asking for dentures, wedding clothes, medical care, and the like. Eva Perón accommodated those demands and more: she bathed lice-ridden children in her own home, kissed lepers, and created the Eva Perón Foundation to institutionalize and extend such charitable endeavors. When she died of uterine cancer at the age of thirty-three, the nation mourned the tragic passing of a woman who came to be elevated to the status of "Santa Evita."

Some saw Eva Perón not as a saint but as a grasping social climber and a fascist sympathizer and saw her husband as a political opportunist, but after Juan Perón's ouster from office in 1955, support for the Perónist party remained strong. However, with the exception of a brief return to power by Perón in the mid-1970s, brutal military dictators held sway for the next three decades. Military rule took a sinister turn in the late 1970s and early 1980s when dictators approved the creation of death squads that fought a "dirty war" against suspected subversives. Between six thousand and twenty-three thousand people disappeared between 1976 and 1983. Calls for a return to democratic politics increased in the aftermath of the dirty war, demands that were intensified by economic disasters and the growth of the poor classes.

Guatemala and Nicaragua The political models and options open to states in Latin America were rather diverse, even though cold war issues complicated some political choices made after World War II. The establishment of communist and socialist regimes in Central and South America—or the instigation of programs and policies that hinted of progressive liberalism or anti-Americanism—regularly provoked a response from the United States. The United States did not need the impetus of a communist threat to justify its intervention in Latin America, because the northern neighbor had upheld the right to make southern incursions since the enunciation of the Monroe Doctrine in 1823. Moreover, one hundred years later, Latin America had become the site of fully 40 percent of U.S. foreign investments. Nonetheless, cold war imperatives shaped many U.S. actions in Latin America in the postwar years, especially in the Central American nations of Guatemala and Nicaragua.

Democratically elected president of Guatemala in 1951, Jacobo Arbenz Guzmán (1913–1971) publicly announced in 1953 a government seizure of hundreds of thousands of acres of uncultivated land owned by the United Fruit Company, a private enterprise controlled mainly by U.S. investors. Foreign companies such as the United Fruit Company dominated Guatemala's economy and its major export crop of bananas. President Arbenz was attempting to reassert Guatemala's control over its economy and its lands—for redistribution to the peasants. He offered monetary compensation to the company, based on the land's declared value for tax payments, but both the company and the United States government found that amount insufficient. U.S. officials also believed Arbenz's policies to be communist inspired, and they feared a spread of such radical doctrines throughout Central America.

President Dwight Eisenhower therefore empowered the CIA to engineer the overthrow of Arbenz's government. The United States sent arms to Guatemala's neighbors, Nicaragua and Honduras, to shore up their defenses against communism, and the CIA trained noncommunist Guatemalans under Colonel Carlos Castillo Armas (1914–1957) to attack and weaken the Arbenz government. With a continued supply of U.S. weapons and air support, Castillo Armas and his troops forced the fall of Arbenz in 1954. Castillo Armas established a military government, returned land to the United Fruit Company, and ruthlessly suppressed opponents with methods that included torture and murder. After his assassination in 1957, Guatemalans plunged into a civil war that did not end until the 1990s.

Anastacio Somoza Garcia (1896–1956) served as president of Nicaragua in 1954, just as the CIA was helping Guatemalan rebels overthrow what many believed was a communist-inspired government. During that time, Somoza demonstrated himself to be a staunch anticommunist U.S. ally. He had funneled weapons to Guatemalan rebels opposing Arbenz, and he outlawed the communist party in Nicaragua during the cold war. Somoza first grasped power in the 1930s, when members of his Nicaraguan National Guard killed nationalist Augusto Cesar Sandino (1893–1934), who had led a guerrilla movement aimed at ending U.S. interference in Nicaragua. After murdering Sandino, Somoza and his sons, Luis Somoza Debayle (d. 1967) and Anastacio Somoza Debayle (1928–1980), controlled Nicaraguan politics for more than forty years, aided by U.S. financial and military support.

The brutality, corruption, and pro-U.S. policies of the Somoza family—which extended to allowing the United States to use Nicaragua as a staging place during the Bay of Pigs attack on Cuba in 1961—alienated other Latin American nations as well as Nicaraguans. In the early 1960s, a few Nicaraguans created the Sandinista Front for National Liberation, in honor of the murdered Augusto Sandino. The Sandinistas, as they became known, launched guerrilla operations aimed at overthrowing the Somozas, and they finally took power in 1979. Although the administration of U.S. president Jimmy Carter (1924–) recognized the Sandinistas, the fervent anticommunist president Ronald Reagan (1911–2004), who came to the presidency in 1981, abandoned and reversed Carter's policies. Because Reagan believed that the Sandinistas were abetting communist rebels elsewhere in Central America, such as in El Salvador, he halted aid to Nicaragua and instituted an economic boycott of the country. By 1983 Reagan offered increasing support—monetary and military—to the Contras, a CIA-trained counterrevolutionary group dedicated to overthrowing the Sandinistas and engaging over time in such activities as the bombing of oil facilities and the mining of harbors.

In the face of U.S. efforts to destabilize Sandinista rule in Nicaragua, Central American leaders decided to take action themselves on their region's troubles. President Oscar Arias Sánchez (1940–) of Costa Rica became especially influential in promoting a negotiated end to the Contra war in Nicaragua. A 1989 agreement provided for the presence of a UN peacekeeping force, for monitored elections, and for the disarming of the Contras. Elections in the following decade brought new political parties to the forefront, and the Sandinistas worked to form coalition governments with opposition parties. Sandinista power was weakened but not eliminated despite the overwhelming interference of the United States, and democratic politics and a normalization of relations with the United States emerged in Nicaragua in the late twentieth century.

Nicaragua's experiences after World War II suggested clearly the political complications associated with continued U.S. interference in Latin America. The economic and political conditions in South and Central America nonetheless made experiments with revolutionary doctrines and Marxist programs attractive to many of the region's peoples. These interested people included members of normally conservative institutions such as the Catholic Church; numerous priests in Latin America embraced what was called "liberation theology," a mixture of Catholicism and Marxism meant to combat the misery and repression of the masses through revolutionary salvation. Brutal regimes ordered the assassinations of hundreds of priests preaching this message of liberation, including Archbishop Oscar Romero in El Salvador in 1980.

Liberation for Nations and Women Revolutionary ideologies and political activism also provided opportunities for Latin American women to agitate for both national and women's liberation. Nicaraguan women established the Association of Women Concerned about National Crisis in 1977 and fought as part of the FSLN to rid their nation of Somoza's rule. In 1979 they renamed the organization the Luisa Amanda Espinoza Association of Nicaraguan Women

(AMNLAE) to honor the first woman who died in the battle against Somoza. The group's slogan—"No revolution without women's emancipation: no emancipation without revolution"—suggested the dual goals of Nicaraguan women. By the mid-1980s, AMNLAE had over eighty thousand members. Despite facing problems typical to women's movements trying to navigate between national and personal needs, AMNLAE has been credited with forwarding women's participation in the public and political spheres, an impressive accomplishment in a region where women's suffrage had often been delayed. Although women in Ecuador attained voting rights in 1929, women in Nicaragua could not vote until 1955; Paraguay's women waited for suffrage rights until 1961, when that nation became the last in Latin America to incorporate women into the political process.

The Search for Economic Equity The late twentieth century witnessed a revival of democratic politics in Latin America, but economic problems continued to limit the possibility of widespread change or the achievement of economic and social equity. In many Latin American nations, the landowning elites who gained power during the colonial era were able to maintain their dominant position, which resulted in societies that remained divided between the few rich, usually backed by the United States, and the masses of the poor. It was difficult to structure such societies without either keeping the elite in power or promoting revolution on behalf of the poor, and the task of fashioning workable state and economic systems was made even more troublesome given the frequency of foreign interference, both military and economic. Despite the difficulties, the mid-twentieth century offered economic promise. During World War II, many Latin American nations took advantage of world market needs and pursued greater industrial development. Profits flowed into these countries during and after the war, and nations in the region experienced sustained economic growth through expanded export trade and diversification of foreign markets. Exports included manufactured goods and traditional export commodities such as minerals and foodstuffs such as sugar, fruits, and coffee.

Dependency Theory Latin American nations realized the need to reorient their economies away from exports and toward internal development, but the attempts to do so fell short. One influential Argentine economist, Raul Prebisch (1901–1985), who worked for the United Nations Commission for Latin America, explained Latin America's economic problems in global terms. Prebisch crafted the "dependency" theory of economic development, pointing out that developed industrial nations—such as those in North America and Europe—dominated the international economy and profited at the expense of less developed and industrialized nations burdened with the export-oriented, unbalanced economies that were a legacy of colonialism. To break the unequal relationship between what Prebisch termed the "center" and the "periphery," developing nations on the periphery of international trade needed to protect and diversify domestic trade and to use strategies of import-substituting industrialization to promote further industrial and economic growth.

Prebisch's theories about the economic ills of the developing world, though influential at the time, have since declined in currency. Latin American economies have shown resilience in the late twentieth and early twenty-first centuries, and Latin American nations have maintained links to global markets and money. Their economies appeared strong enough to limit the effects of their export-oriented systems and their use of foreign investment monies, and further economic growth should aid in the search for a social and economic equity that have been elusive in Latin America from colonial times.

inperspective

In the years immediately before and after World War II, a few nations controlled the political and economic destiny of much of the world. The imperial and colonial encounters between European elites and indigenous peoples defined much of the recent history of the world before the mid-twentieth century. The decades following 1945 witnessed the stunning reversal of that state of affairs, as European empires fell and dozens of newly independent nations emerged. Decolonization changed the world's political, economic, and social landscape in often radical ways, and the peoples of these newly free countries thereafter labored to reshape their national identities and to build workable political and economic systems. The effervescence of liberty and independence at times gave way to a more sober reality in the days, years, and decades after liberation. Religious and ethnic conflict, political instability, economic challenges, and neoimperialism dampened spirits and interfered with the ability of nations to achieve peace and stability. Nothing, however, could ever truly diminish the historic significance of what transpired in the colonial world after World War II. The global balance of power had been irrevocably altered by this attainment of worldwide independence and pointed to the emergence of a new kind of world order: one without borders. ●

CHRONOLOGY

1947	Partition of India
1948	Creation of Israel
1948–1989	Apartheid in South Africa
1954	Overthrow of Arbenz in Guatemala
1954	French defeat at Dienbienphu
1954–1962	Algerian war of liberation
1955	Bandung Conference
1956	Suez crisis
1957	Ghana gains independence
1958–1961	Great Leap Forward in China
1963	Founding of Organization of African Unity
1973	Arab-Israeli War
1976	Reunification of Vietnam
1979	Revolution in Iran
1979	Sandinistas in power in Nicaragua
1980–1988	Iran-Iraq War
1990–1991	Gulf War
1997	Transfer of British Hong Kong to People's Republic of China

For Further Reading

David Anderson. *Histories of the Hanged: The Dirty War in Kenya and the End of Empire.* New York, 2005. History of Kenya's Kikuyu insurrection as a consequence of British colonial violence and land appropriation.

Franz Ansprenger. *The Dissolution of the Colonial Empires.* New York, 1989. A discerning and thorough treatment of the dismantling of European empires and colonies.

Mark Borthwick, ed. *Pacific Century: The Emergence of Modern Pacific Asia.* Boulder, 1992. An excellent source for an overview of southeast and east Asia.

Greg Campbell. *Blood Diamonds: Tracing the Deadly Path of the World's Most Precious Stones.* New York, 2002. A look at the dark side of the Sierra Leone–centered diamond trade.

M. E. Chamberlain. *Decolonization: The Fall of European Empires.* Oxford, 1985. A brief but competent summary of the demise of empires.

Gloria Chuku. *Igbo Women and Economic Transformation in Southeastern Nigeria, 1900–1960.* New York, 2004. Study of the impact of colonial policies on gender relations in postcolonial Nigeria from economic and political perspectives.

Nancy L. Clark and William H. Worger. *South Africa: The Rise and Fall of Apartheid.* New York, 2004. A survey of the history of the apartheid regime from 1948 to its collapse in the 1990s.

Michael J. Cohen. *Palestine and the Great Powers 1945–48.* 2nd ed. Princeton, 1992. An evenhanded assessment of the role played by the great powers in the partition of Palestine and the creation of Israel.

Basil Davidson. *The Black Man's Burden: Africa and the Curse of the Nation State.* New York, 1992. A critical postindependence account that emphasizes the shortcomings of nationalism and the national state.

Prasenjit Duara, ed. *Decolonization (Rewriting Histories).* New York, 2004. The perspective of the colonized is privileged through a selection of writings by leaders of the colonizing countries.

Carlene J. Edie. *Politics in Africa: A New Beginning?* New York, 2002. Examines the domestic and external pressures that have transformed postcolonial African states and societies.

Caroline Elkins. *Imperial Reckoning: The Untold Story of Britain's Gulag in Kenya.* New York, 2004. Powerful study of British atrocities in late colonial Kenya.

Robert Hardgrave Jr. and Stanley A. Hardgrave. *India: Government and Politics in a Developing Nation.* 4th ed. San Diego, 1986. A work that centers on Indian postindependence politics.

Sunil Khilani. *The Idea of India.* New York, 1988. A lively and incisive analysis of the many meanings of India.

Phyllis M. Martin and Patrick O'Meara, eds. *Africa.* 3rd ed. Bloomington, 1995. An insightful collection of articles addressing the cultural, social, economic, and political development of Africa.

Mark Mathabane. *Kaffir Boys: The True Story of a Black Youth's Coming of Age in Apartheid South Africa.* New York, 1986. A gripping real-life story.

Robert A. Mortimer. *The Third World Coalition in International Politics.* New York, 1980. Surveys the political evolution of the non-aligned world.

Timothy H. Parsons. *The 1964 Army Mutinies and the Making of Modern East Africa.* Westport, Conn., 2003. Detailed analysis of soldiers' anticolonial protests in Tanganyika, Uganda, and Kenya.

Thomas E. Skidmore and Peter H. Smith. *Modern Latin America.* New York, 1992. Excellent overview covering the region from the 1880s to the 1980s and supported by an extensive bibliography.

Thomas W. Walker. *Nicaragua: Living in the Shadow of the Eagle.* 4th ed. Boulder, 2003. Best and most comprehensive treatment of the nation in the past two decades.

A World without Borders

chapter 38

This stunning digitally crafted photograph, called "Omnipotent Technology" (1999), blurs the boundaries between art and reality. Its composition of an ethnically fluid face from computer chips and hardware suggests how global identity has morphed and how computers have breached borders between humans and machines.

EYEWITNESS:
Kristina Matschat and a Falling Wall

On 9 November 1989, Kristina Matschat felt excitement and tension in the night air of Berlin. She had joined thousands of other East Germans at Checkpoint Charlie, one of the most famous crossing points in the Berlin Wall. Anticipating that some momentous event was soon to occur at the wall, that the wall might come down that night, she also shivered in fear at the proximity of the *Volkspolizei* ("people's police")—the same officers who since 1961 gunned down East Germans attempting to scale the wall and escape to freedom in West Berlin. She wore running shoes in case she needed to sprint away if shooting broke out or tanks rumbled through East Berlin to prevent the destruction of the wall.

She remembered that "everybody was full of fear—but also full of hope." Bitter memories flooded her consciousness as she recalled not being allowed to study what she wanted in school, not being able to speak freely of her discontent in case her friends were government spies, and not being able to locate disgruntled colleagues whom the government had condemned as "unwanted elements." Her hope overcame her fears, though, as she chanted with her fellow compatriots, "Tear the wall down! Open the gates!" She could see that on the other side of the wall massive crowds of West Berliners had gathered to join their demonstration. Thrilled by this open protest against the most salient symbol of the cold war, she was nonetheless psychologically unprepared for victory when it came. Just before midnight East German soldiers suddenly began not only opening gates in the Wall but also gently helping East Germans cross to the West, often for the first time in their lives. Her near disbelief at the swift downfall of Berlin's decades-old barricade registered in the word she heard shouted over and over again by those passing through the wall: *Wahnsinn* ("craziness").

Kristina Matschat remained at the wall until 3:00 or 4:00 A.M., celebrating with the hundreds of thousands of other Berliners who now mingled, drinking champagne and dancing on top of the wall. While celebrating the fall of the barbed wire and mortar structure, she became aware of the significance of a world without borders: "Suddenly we were seeing the West for the first time, the forbidden Berlin we had only seen on TV or heard about from friends. When we came home at dawn, I felt free for the first time in my life. I had never been happier." The fall of the Berlin Wall brought down one of the world's most notorious borders and symbolized the breaching of all sorts of boundaries in the contemporary world.

Along with decolonization, the fall of the Berlin Wall, and the end of the cold war, many other forces were at work to create a new, more open, world. One pronounced feature of this world was an increased level of economic interaction between countries and a tighter economic integration of the world. The forces driving the world economy in this direction, often referred to as *globalization,* included advances in communication technology, an enormous expansion of international trade, and the emergence of new global enterprises as well as governments and international organizations that favored market-oriented economics.

Although certain formal national borders changed only after decolonization and the end of the cold war, cultural and technological developments since World War II had steadily broken down the distances between countries and peoples. Cultural integration resulted from the never-ending stream of ideas, information, and values spreading from one society to another. Consumer goods, popular culture, television, computers, and the Internet all spread outward from advanced capitalist and industrialized nations, particularly Europe and the United States, and other societies had to come to terms with this breakdown of cultural and technological barriers. Cultural traditions from Europe and the United States were challenged as often as they were accepted, as most of the world's peoples attempted to blend foreign traditions with their own.

The world's peoples themselves underwent changes in a world with fewer barriers. Women struggled to close the divide between the sexes, at times fighting for equal economic, social, and political rights and at other times abiding by gender expectations while waiting for new opportunities to improve their condition. As populations grew at often alarming rates, women spent much of their time at the traditional female task of child rearing, but both women and men embarked on migrations when their societies could no longer adequately support their growing populations. They moved to the cities or to other nations either to escape suffering or to seek new fortunes.

The populations moving around the globe revealed the diminishing significance of national boundary lines, but they also posed problems that could not be solved by any one state acting alone. International organizations such as the United Nations acknowledged that global problems needed global solutions, underscoring anew the tenuousness of borders in the contemporary world. The global troubles posed by epidemic diseases, labor servitude, terrorism, and human rights also crossed national boundaries and prompted international cooperation. Not everyone experienced the ecstasy Kristina Matschat felt at the Berlin Wall when that most restrictive border disappeared, but global interconnectedness made it more difficult to maintain boundaries among the peoples and countries of the world.

THE END OF THE COLD WAR

Between 1989 and 1991, the Soviet system in Europe collapsed with indecent haste. This was partly encouraged by U.S. President Ronald Reagan (in office 1981–1989), who reinvigorated cold war animosities, zeroing in on communism and the USSR, which he called "the evil empire." Beyond adopting this rhetorical fervor, Reagan advocated enormous military spending. Reagan's cold war rhetoric and budgets challenged détente and the Soviet ability to match U.S. spending, but internal changes in the Soviet Union and eastern Europe worked most effectively to end communism and the cold war. Whether forced by internal dissent or by the horrendous military and economic costs of the cold war, the superpowers soon backed down from their traditional polarizing division of the world. The result was the collapse of the cold war world, whose disintegration began in eastern Europe and the Soviet Union. Between 1989 and 1990, through a series of mostly nonviolent revolutions, the peoples of eastern and central Europe regained their independence, instituted democratic forms of government, and adopted market-based economies.

The downfall of communist regimes in Europe was the direct consequence of interrelated economic and political developments. The economic weakness of the communist regimes in eastern and central Europe and the Soviet Union became so apparent as to require reforms. The policies espoused by a new Soviet leader, Mikhail S. Gorbachev (1931–), who came to power in 1985, represented an effort to address this economic deterioration, but they also unleashed a tidal wave of revolution that brought down communist governments. As communism unraveled throughout eastern and

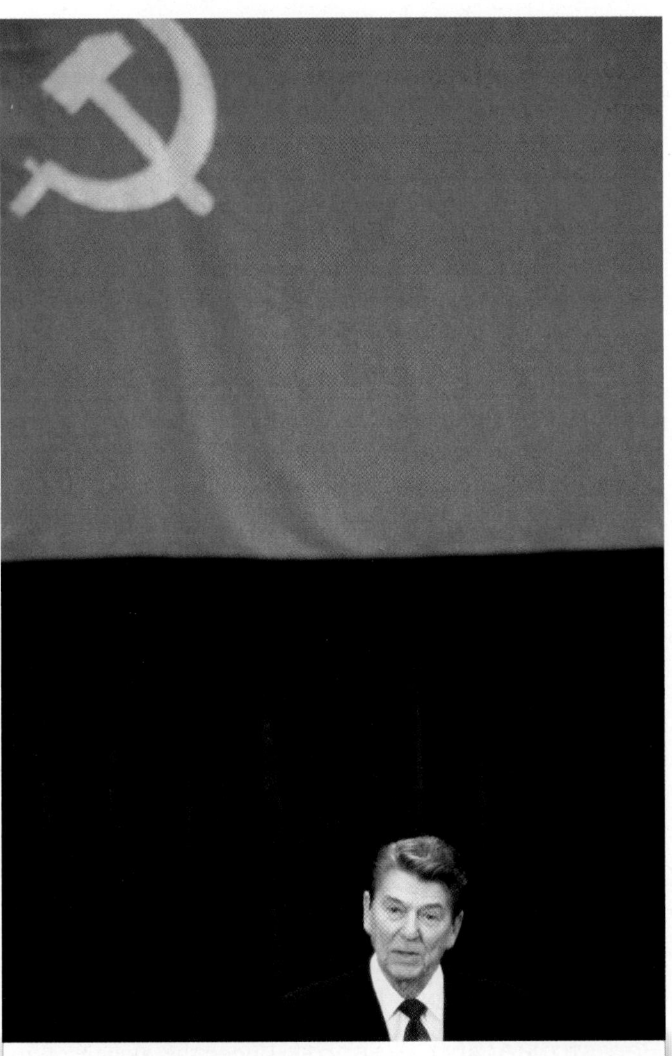
At a U.S./U.S.S.R. summit in 1985, a Soviet flag served as a dramatic backdrop and counterpoint to U.S. President Ronald Reagan's speech.

central Europe, Gorbachev desperately tried to save the Soviet Union from disintegration by restructuring the economy and liberalizing society. Caught between the rising tide of radical reforms and the opposition of entrenched interests, however, there was little he could do except watch as events unfolded beyond his control. By the time the Soviet Union collapsed in 1991, the Soviet vision of socialism had ceased to inspire either fear or emulation. The cold war system of states and alliances became irrelevant to international relations.

Revolutions in Eastern and Central Europe

The inability to connect communism with nationalism left communist regimes vulnerable throughout eastern and central Europe. Those regimes were born in Moscow, transplanted by the Soviet army, and shored up by tanks and bayonets. To most eastern and central Europeans, the Soviet-imposed governments lacked legitimacy from the beginning, and despite the efforts of local communist leaders, the regimes never became firmly established. The Polish intellectual Leszek Kolakowski echoed the sentiments of many when he bitterly complained in 1971 that "the dead and by now also grotesque creature called Marxist-Leninism still hangs at the necks of the rulers like a hopeless tumor."

Despite economic stagnation, an accelerated arms race with the United States that further strained the Soviet economy, and obvious signs of discontent, the rulers of eastern and central Europe were too reluctant to confront the challenge and restructure their ailing systems. It remained for Gorbachev to unleash the forces that resulted in the disappearance of the Soviet empire in Europe. By the time Gorbachev visited East Berlin in 1989 on the fortieth anniversary of the founding of the German Democratic Republic, he had committed himself to a restructuring of the Soviet Union and to unilateral withdrawal from the cold war. In public interviews he surprised his grim-faced hosts with the announcement that the Brezhnev Doctrine was no longer in force and that from then on each country would be responsible for its own destiny. As one observer put it, the "Sinatra doctrine" ("I did it my way") replaced the Brezhnev Doctrine. The new Soviet orientation led in rapid succession to the collapse or overthrow of regimes in Poland, Bulgaria, Hungary, Czechoslovakia, Romania, and East Germany.

Poland, Bulgaria, and Hungary The end of communism came first in Poland, where Solidarity—a combined trade union and nationalist movement—put pressure on the crumbling rule of the Communist Party. The Polish government legalized the previously banned Solidarity movement and agreed to multiparty elections in 1989 and 1990. The voters favored Solidarity candidates, and Lech Walesa (1943–), the movement's leader, became president of Poland. In Bulgaria popular unrest forced Todor Zhivkov (1911–1998), eastern Europe's longest-surviving communist dictator, to resign in November 1989. Two months later a national assembly began dismantling the communist state. Hungarians tore down the Soviet-style political system during 1988 and 1989. In 1990 they held free elections and launched their nation on the rocky path toward democracy and a market economy.

Velvet and Violent Revolutions The disintegration of communism continued elsewhere in eastern Europe. In Czechoslovakia a "velvet revolution" swept communists out of office and restored democracy by 1990. The term *velvet revolution* derived from the fact that aside from the initial suppression of mass demonstrations, little violence was associated with the transfer of power in societies formerly ruled by an iron fist. The communist leadership stood by and watched events take their course. In 1993, disagreements over the time frame for shifting to a market economy led to a "velvet divorce," breaking Czechoslovakia into two new

Berliners climb the wall after it fell on 9 November 1989.

nations, the Czech Republic and Slovakia. In Romania, by contrast, the regime of dictator Nicolae Ceauşescu (1918–1989) refused to acknowledge the necessity of reform. In 1989 *Securitate,* a brutal secret police force, savagely repressed demonstrations, setting off a national uprising that ended within four days and left Ceauşescu and his wife dead.

Fall of the Berlin Wall East Germany had long been a staunchly communist Soviet satellite. Its aging leader, Erich Honecker (1912–1994), openly objected to Gorbachev's ideas and clung to Stalinist policies. When he showed genuine bewilderment at the fact that East German citizens fled the country by the thousands through openings in the iron curtain in Hungary and Czechoslovakia, his party removed him from power. It was too late for anything other than radical changes, and when the East German regime decided to open the Berlin Wall to intra-German traffic on 9 November 1989, the end of the German Democratic Republic was in sight. The end to a divided Berlin was also in sight, literally, as thousands of east and west Berliners tore down the Berlin Wall in the last weeks of 1989. In 1990 the two Germanies, originally divided by the cold war, formed a united nation.

The Collapse of the Soviet Union

The desire to concentrate attention and resources on urgent matters at home motivated Gorbachev's decision to disengage his nation from the cold war and its military and diplomatic extensions. When he came to power in 1985, Gorbachev was keenly aware of the need for economic reform and the liberalization of Soviet society, although he never intended to abolish the existing political and economic system. Yet it proved impossible to fix parts of the system without undermining the whole.

Gorbachev's Reforms Gorbachev's reform efforts focused on the ailing economy. Antiquated industrial plants, obsolete technologies, and inefficient government control of production resulted in shoddy and outmoded products. The diversion of crucial resources to the military made it impossible to produce enough consumer goods—regardless of their quality. The failure of state and collective farms to feed the population compelled the Soviet government to import grains from the United States, Canada, and elsewhere. By 1990 the government imposed rationing to cope with the scarcity of essential consumer goods and food. Economic stagnation in turn contributed to the decline of the Soviet standard of living. Ominous statistics documented the disintegration of the state-sponsored health care system: infant mortality increased while life expectancy decreased. Funding of the educational system dropped precipitously, and pollution threatened to engulf the entire country. Demoralization affected ever larger numbers of Soviet citizens as divorce rates climbed, corruption intensified, and alcoholism became more widespread.

Perestroika and Glasnost Under the slogan of *uskorenie,* or "acceleration," Gorbachev tried to shock the economy out of its coma. Yet the old methods of boosting production and productivity through bureaucratic exhortation and harassment paid few dividends; in fact, they called attention to the drawbacks of centralized economic control. Gorbachev then contemplated different kinds of reform, using the term *perestroika,* or "restructuring," to describe his efforts to decentralize the economy. To make perestroika work, the Soviet leader linked it to *glasnost,* a term that referred to the opening of Soviet society to public criticism and admission of past mistakes.

Perestroika proved more difficult to implement than Gorbachev imagined, and glasnost unleashed a torrent of criticism that shook the Soviet state to its foundations. When Gorbachev pushed economic decentralization, the profit motive and the cost-accounting methods he instituted engendered the hostility of those whose privileged positions depended on the old system. Many of Gorbachev's comrades and certain factions of the military objected to perestroika and worked to undermine or destroy it. Glasnost also turned out to be a two-edged sword, since it opened the door to public criticism of party leaders and Soviet institutions in a way unimaginable a short time earlier. While discontent with Soviet life burst into the open, long-repressed ethnic and nationalist sentiments bubbled to the surface, posing a threat to the multiethnic Soviet state. Only half of the 285 million Soviet citizens were Russian. The other half included numerous ethnic minorities, most of whom never fully reconciled themselves to Soviet dominance.

The pressures on the Soviet system were exacerbated by an ill-considered and costly Soviet military intervention in 1979 to save a Marxist regime in Afghanistan. For nine years well-equipped Soviet forces fought a brutal, unsuccessful campaign against *Afghan mujahideen,* or Islamic warriors, who gradually gained control of most of the countryside. Weapons and money from the United States, Saudi Arabia, Iran, Pakistan, and China sustained the mujahideen in their struggle. The Central Intelligence Agency of the United States supplied the decisive weapons in the war: ground-to-air Stinger missiles, which could be used to shoot down heavily armored Soviet helicopters, and thousands of mules to haul supplies from Pakistan. In 1986 the Kremlin decided to pull its troops out of the costly, unpopular, and unwinnable war. A cease-fire negotiated by the United Nations in 1988 led to a full Soviet withdrawal in 1989.

Collapse By the summer of 1990, Gorbachev's reforms had spent themselves. As industrial and agricultural production continued their downward slide against a backdrop of skyrocketing inflation, the Soviet economy disintegrated. Inspired by the end of the Soviet empire in eastern and central Europe, many minorities now contemplated secession from the Soviet Union. The Baltic peoples—Estonians, Latvians, and Lithuanians—were first into the fray, declaring their independence in August 1991. In the following months the remaining twelve republics of the Soviet Union followed suit. The largest and most prominent of the Soviet republics, the Russian Soviet Federated Socialist Republic, and its recently elected president, Boris N. Yeltsin (1931–2007), led the drive for independence. Soviet leaders vacillated between threats of repression and promises of better

MAP 38.1
The collapse of the Soviet Union and European communist regimes, 1991.
Note the number of states suddenly created by the breakup of the Soviet Union.
How would this affect the ability of each to survive, both economically and politically?

treatment, but neither option could stop the movement for independence.

Although the pace of reform was neither quick nor thorough enough for some, others convinced themselves that they had gone too far. While Gorbachev was vacationing in the Crimea in August 1991, a group of conspirators—including discontented party functionaries, disillusioned KGB (secret police) officials, and dissatisfied military officers—decided to seize power. Gorbachev's former friend and ally, the flamboyant Boris Yeltsin, crushed the coup with the help of loyal Red Army units. Gorbachev emerged unscathed from house arrest, but his political career had ended. He watched from the sidelines as Yeltsin dismantled the Communist Party and pushed the country toward market-oriented economic reforms. As the Soviet system disintegrated, several of its constituent regions moved toward independence. On 25 December 1991 the Soviet flag fluttered for the last time atop the Kremlin, and by the last day of that year the Union of Soviet Socialist Republics ceased to exist.

Toward an Uncertain Future In many ways, the cold war provided comfort to the world—however cold that comfort seemed at the time. World War II left most of the major imperialist, fascist, and militarist nations in shambles, and the United States and the Soviet Union stepped into what could have been an uncomfortable vacuum in global leadership. Perilous and controlling it may have been, but the cold war that resulted from the ideological contest between the superpowers had ordered and defined the world for almost fifty years. The cold war also shaped how the nations and peoples of the world perceived themselves—as good capitalists fighting evil communists, as progressive socialists battling regressive capitalists, or as nonaligned peoples striving to follow their own paths. Although those perceptions placed constraints on the choices open to them, particularly given the control exerted by the United States and the USSR at the peak of their power, the choices nonetheless were familiar. At the end of the cold war, those easy choices disappeared. The end of the cold war suggested the possibility of a radical shift in power relations, a global realignment that marked a new era of world history devoid of the categories embraced during the cold war.

THE GLOBAL ECONOMY

The global economy came into public view after the spectacular collapse of communism in 1990. Economists pointed to a new economic order characterized by the expansion of trade between countries, the growth of foreign investments, the unfettered movement of capital, the privatization of former state enterprises, a wave of deregulation that undermined the control that national governments once exercised over economic activity, and the emergence of a new breed of corporations. Supporting the new global economy were technological developments in communications; semiconductors, fiber-optic cables, and satellites have virtually eliminated geographic distances, causing an ever-faster integration of the market economy. The forces driving the world economy toward increased economic integration have been responsible for a process termed *globalization*.

Economic Globalization

Globalization is a widely used term that can be defined in a number of ways. There is general agreement, however, that in an economic context, globalization refers to the reduction and removal of barriers between national borders to facilitate the flow of goods, capital, services, and labor. Global economic interaction and integration is not a new phenomenon. Ancient Rome and China, for example, controlled and economically integrated vast regions of the ancient world. In more recent centuries, the nations of western Europe—through their global outreach and encounters with far-flung societies—created worldwide empires in which goods and people moved with relative ease. The more recent phenomenon of globalization, however, has been different and unprecedented in both scope and speed, and it has the potential to transform the social and political as well as the economic contours of the world.

Free Trade International trade proved to be a key driving force behind economic globalization. Trade across long distances especially has figured prominently in the shaping of human history, and for at least the past five hundred years it has served as an integrating force. Of more recent origin is the phrase *free trade,* meaning freedom from state-imposed limits and constraints on trade across borders. The issue of free trade engendered a debate about the extent to which free trade enhances the prosperity of a society. In the aftermath of World War II, leaders from industrialized nations, especially from the United States, took a decisive stand on the issue.

GATT and WTO U.S. politicians and business leaders wanted to establish an international trading system that suited their interests, and they pushed for the elimination of restrictive trading practices that stood in the way of free trade. The main vehicle for the promotion of unrestricted global trade was the General Agreement on Tariffs and Trade (GATT), which was signed by the representatives of 23 noncommunist nations in 1947. In 1994, the member nations of GATT signed an agreement to establish the World Trade Organization (WTO), which took over the activities of GATT in 1995. The WTO has developed into a forum for settling international trade disputes, with the power to enforce its decisions. The WTO has 153 member nations, which account for 97 percent of all world trade.

Global Corporations The emergence of a new breed of corporation played another key role in the development of the new economic order. Global corporations have in-

This image of a "Balanced World Economy" (1996) artistically expresses the precariousness of economic globalization.

creasingly replaced the more traditional international or multinational forms of corporate enterprises. International companies were born out of the desire to extend business activities across borders in pursuit of specific activities such as importation, exportation, and the extraction of raw materials. International companies evolved into multinationals, which conducted their business in several countries but had to operate within the confines of specific laws and customs of a given society. During the past twenty-five years, the transformation of the corporate landscape has resulted in the birth of some fifty thousand global corporations. In contrast to the multinational, the typical global corporation relies on a small headquarters staff while dispersing all other corporate functions across the globe in search of the lowest possible operating costs. Global corporations treat the world as a single market and act as if the nation-state no longer exists. Many multinational corporations, such as General Motors, Siemens AG, and Nestlé, have transformed themselves into global enterprises, both benefiting from and contributing to the ongoing process of globalization.

Global corporations have become the symbols of the new economy. They also have begun to transform the political and social landscape of many societies. During the past fifty-five years, major corporations throughout the developed world have been operating under the constraints of a social compact with their employees and communities. Through a combination of collective bargaining agreements, tax laws, and environmental regulations, these companies had to contribute to the welfare of their respective home communities. Highly mobile global corporations that are no longer bound to any particular location have managed, however, to escape those obligations and break the social compact. Competing with companies around the world, the global corporation has moved jobs from high-wage facilities to foreign locations where wages are low and environmental laws are weak or nonexistent.

Economic Growth in Asia

Globalization and the speeding up of worldwide economic integration also benefited from economic developments in east and southeast Asia, where the economies of Japan, China, and the so-called Asian tigers underwent dramatic economic growth. This Asian "economic miracle" was largely a result of economic globalization.

Japan U.S. policies jump-started Japan's economic revival after its defeat in 1945, and by 1949 the Japanese economy had already attained its prewar level of productivity. Just as western European countries had benefited from the Marshall Plan, so Japan benefited from direct U.S. financial aid ($2 billion), investment, and the timely abandonment of war reparations. In addition, there were no restrictions on the entry of Japanese products into the U.S. market. The United States, in its role as Japan's military protector, contributed to long-term economic growth as well. Because a 1952 mutual defense treaty stipulated that Japan could never spend more than 1 percent of its gross national product on defense, Japan's postwar leaders channeled the nation's savings into economic development.

At first sight, Japan's economy was ill equipped for intensive economic growth. Japan had lost its overseas empire and was hampered by a large population and a lack of natural resources. Japan's economic planners sidestepped many of those disadvantages by promoting an economic policy that emphasized export-oriented growth supported by low wages. The large and mostly compliant workforce, willing to endure working conditions and wages considered intolerable by organized labor in western Europe and the United States, gave Japanese employers a competitive edge over international rivals. Although Japanese industries had to pay for the import of most raw materials, the low cost of Japanese labor ensured the production of goods that were cheap enough to compete on the basis of price.

Initially, the Japanese economy churned out labor-intensive manufactured goods such as textiles, iron, and steel slated for export to markets with high labor costs, particularly the United States. During the 1960s Japanese companies used their profits to switch to more capital-intensive manufacturing and produced radios, television sets, motorcycles, and automobiles. In the 1970s Japanese corporations took advantage of a highly trained and educated workforce and shifted their economic resources toward technology-intensive products such as random access memory chips, liquid crystal displays, and CD-ROM drives. By that time the label "Made in Japan," once associated with cheap manufactured goods, signified state-of-the-art products of the highest quality. Japan's economic achievements gave its banks, corporations, and government an increasingly prominent voice in global affairs. By the 1980s Japan seemed poised to overtake the United States as the world's largest economy. In the 1990s, however, it became clear that postwar growth rates were not sustainable, and the Japanese economy sputtered into a recession that has continued into the twenty-first century. Nevertheless, the Japanese success story served as an inspiration for other Asian countries.

The Little Tigers The earliest and most successful imitators of the Japanese model for economic development were Hong Kong, Singapore, South Korea, and Taiwan. Their remarkable and rapid growth rates earned them the sobriquet of the "four little tigers," and by the 1980s these newly industrializing countries had become major economic powers. Like Japan, all four countries suffered from a shortage of capital, lacked natural resources, and had to cope with overpopulation. But like Japan a generation earlier, they transformed apparent disadvantages into advantages through a program of export-driven industrialization. By the 1990s the four little tigers were no longer simply imitators of Japan but had become serious competitors. As soon as new Japanese products had carved out market niches, corporations based in the four little tigers moved in and undercut the original item with cheaper versions. Before long, Indonesia, Thailand, and Malaysia joined the original tigers in their quest for economic development and prosperity.

Perils of the New Economy For the supporters of the new global economy, the spectacular economic development of so many Asian societies was proof that globalization could deliver on the promise of unprecedented prosperity. By the late 1990s, however, critics could point to the perils of the new global economy as many of the Asian tigers went from boom to bust economies.

At the center of this bust was a financial crisis that came to a head in 1997. In the preceding twenty years, the developing Asian economies had started to embrace the market, opening their borders to imports and courting foreign investments. After years of generous lending and growing national debts, the international investment community suddenly lost confidence in the booming economies and withdrew support. The crisis began in Thailand in mid-1997, when investments that once easily poured into the country now left it equally quickly, causing the value of the baht (Thai national currency) to plummet. In quick succession, the Thai stock market lost 75 percent of its value, and the country found itself in the grip of a depression. For no obvious reason, the financial panic—and with it economic contraction—then moved to Malaysia, Indonesia, the Philippines, and South Korea. In each instance, the rise and fall of the individual economies resulted from their integration in the new global economy, which rewarded and punished its new participants with equal ease.

BRICs Contrary to all expectations, the nations hit so hard by the financial crisis recovered quickly. Their recovery was matched by other emerging economies, often identified as BRICs because they include the fast-growing and developing economies of Brazil, Russia, India, and China. (South Korea and Mexico are usually classified as developed economies.) In the aftermath of the cold war, the governments composing the BRICs initiated political and economic reforms that embraced capitalism and allowed their countries to join the world economy. To make these nations more competitive, their leaders have simultaneously emphasized education, domestic entrepreneurship, foreign investment, and domestic consumption. Predictions point to China and India becoming the dominant global suppliers of manufactured goods and services, with Brazil and Russia becoming similarly dominant suppliers of raw materials. Among these emerging economies, China already figures as an economic titan.

The Rise of China China's leaders launched economic reforms in the late 1970s that reversed some earlier policies and opened Chinese markets to the outside world, encouraged foreign investment, and imported foreign technology. With the economy growing dramatically, the government in 1992 signaled the creation of a socialist market economy. In effect, the planned economic system of the past gave way to a market economy, where demand for goods and services determined production and pricing, and where the role of the government was limited to providing a stable but competitive environment. Besides acting as a major exporter, China benefited from its large pool of cheap labor and its enormous domestic markets have made the Chinese economy the destination of choice for foreign investment capital. In December 2001 China became a member of the World Trade Organization and moved to global economic superpower status.

Emerging nations scour the earth for raw materials, are responsible for a steep rise in world energy demand and consumption, and cause an alarming increase in emissions of greenhouse gases and air pollution. The once-poor world is not only getting richer but also increasingly making its weight felt in international organizations on everything from trade issues to membership in the United Nations Security Council. What all this means is that the rich developed countries no longer dominate the global economy the way they did during the nineteenth and twentieth centuries. This shift is not as astonishing as it first seems, as some of today's emerging economies are simply regaining their former preeminence. Until the late nineteenth century, for example, China and India were the world's biggest economies.

MAP 38.2

European Union membership, 2007.

In 2007 the European Union celebrated the fiftieth anniversary of its founding as a supranational and intergovernmental organization that encompasses twenty-seven member states.

What major challenge faced the European Union in the twenty-first century?

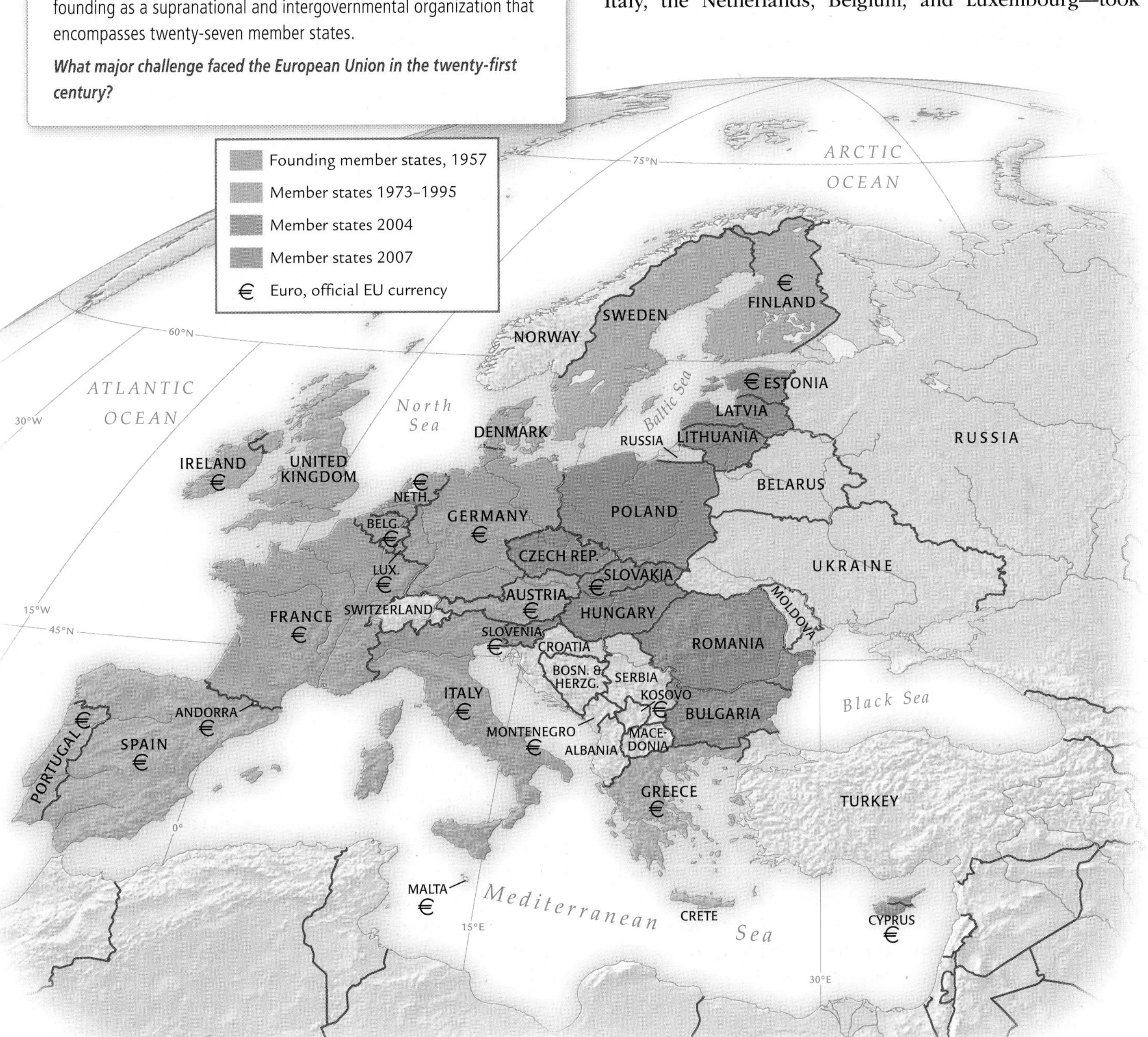

Trading Blocs

Accepting free trade and open markets meant acknowledging global economic interdependence; no single economic power could fully control global trade and commerce. In the rapidly changing global economy, groups of nations have therefore entered into economic alliances designed to achieve advantages and greater strength for their partners in the competitive global economy.

European Union The most famous and most strongly integrated regional bloc is the European Union, which is characterized by a common market and free trade. In March 1957, representatives of six nations—France, West Germany, Italy, the Netherlands, Belgium, and Luxembourg—took a significant step in this direction by signing the Treaty of Rome. This treaty established the European Economic Community—renamed the European Community in 1967. At the heart of this new community of nations lay the dismantling of tariffs and other barriers to free trade among member nations. Subsequent treaties creating political institutions such as the Council of Ministers and the European Parliament facilitated the long-range goal of European political integration. The development of a supranational organization dedicated to increasing European economic and political integration culminated in the Maastricht Treaty of 1993, which established the European Union. Twenty-seven European nations have submerged much of their national sovereignty in the European Union, and since 1999 sixteen members have adopted a common currency. In the future, this tight economic integration is expected to lead to a European Political Union.

OPEC One of the earliest and most successful economic alliances was the Organization of Petroleum Exporting Countries (OPEC), a producer cartel established in 1960 by the oil-producing states of Iran, Iraq, Kuwait, Saudi Arabia, and Venezuela, and later joined by Qatar, Libya, Indonesia, Abu Dhabi, Algeria, Nigeria, Ecuador, and Gabon. The mostly Arab and Muslim member states of OPEC sought to raise the price of oil through cooperation, but OPEC demonstrated during the Arab-Israeli War of 1973 that cooperation had political as well as economic potential. The cartel ordered an embargo on oil shipments to the United States, Israel's ally, and quadrupled the price of oil between 1973 and 1975. The huge increase in the cost of petroleum triggered a global economic downturn, as did a curtailment of oil exports in the later 1970s. OPEC's policies therefore contributed to the global recession and debt crisis that hurt many developing nations, but its members—also developing nations—demonstrated how the alliance could exert control over the developed world and its financial system. OPEC's influence diminished in the 1980s and 1990s as a result of overproduction and dissension among its members over the Iran-Iraq War and the Gulf War.

ASEAN Another well-established economic partnership is the Association of Southeast Asian Nations, or ASEAN. Established in 1967 by the foreign ministers of Thailand, Malaysia, Singapore, Indonesia, and the Philippines, its principal objectives were to accelerate economic development and promote political stability in southeast Asia. Originally conceived as a bulwark against the spread of communism in the region, the economic focus of ASEAN became sharper after it signed cooperative agreements with Japan in 1977 and the European Community in 1980. In 1992 member states agreed to establish a free-trade zone and to cut tariffs on industrial goods over a fifteen-year period.

Globalization and Its Critics The global economy is still very much a work in progress, and it is not clear what the long-term effects will be on the economies and societies it touches. To its supporters, the global economy delivers markets that operate with maximum efficiency, speedily directing goods and services wherever there is demand for them and always expecting the highest returns possible. Proponents of globalization also argue that the new economy is the only way to bring prosperity—the kind previously enjoyed only by industrialized nations—to the developing world. To its critics—nongovernmental organizations ranging from labor unions to tribal-rights activists—the global economy is an untamed juggernaut that is neither inevitable nor desirable, a force that rewards the few and impoverishes the many. The specific charges leveled by antiglobalization groups and coalitions are many. They assert that globalization diminishes the sovereignty of local and national governments and transfers the power to shape economic and political destinies to transnational corporations and global institutions such as the WTO. Detractors of globalization also claim that the hallmark of globalization—rapid economic development—is responsible for the destruction of the environment, the widening gap between rich and poor societies, and the worldwide homogenization of local, diverse, and indigenous cultures. It is certain that globalization has been accompanied by serious social and economic problems. It is less certain, however, if anyone can succeed in taming its power.

CROSS-CULTURAL EXCHANGES AND GLOBAL COMMUNICATIONS

The demise of European colonial empires, the fall of the Berlin Wall, and the end of the cold war brought down the most obvious political barriers of the post–World War II world. Long before then, however, cultural and technological developments had started a similar process of breaching boundaries. By showcasing the consumer goods of capitalist societies and spreading news of each new chapter in the fall of communism, television in fact had helped spur the revolutions that ended the cold war. As Kristina Matschat testified, before the Berlin Wall fell she had seen West Berlin only on television. One of the first products of the global consumer culture imbibed by East Germans was Coca-Cola, served to them by store owners in West Berlin.

Like trade and business organizations, cultural practices have also become globalized, thriving on a continuous flow of information, ideas, tastes, and values. At the turn of the twentieth century, local traditions—commonly derived from gender, social class, or religious affiliation—still determined the cultural identity of the vast majority of people. At the end of the twentieth century, thanks in part to advances in technology and communications, information and cultural practices were becoming truly global. Their impact was summarized in a jingle popularized by the Walt Disney corporation during the 1964–1965 World's Fair in New York City: "It's a small world after all."

Consumption and Cultural Interaction

New communications media have tied the world together and have promoted a global cultural integration whose hallmark is consumption. Beginning in the eighteenth century, industrialization and the subsequent rise in per capita income gave birth to a type of society in which the consumption of goods and services satisfied wants and desires rather than needs or necessities. Although the desire to consume is hardly novel, the modern consumer culture means more than simple consumption. It implies that consumers want more than they need and that the items they consume take on symbolic value. Consumption, in other words, has become a means of self-expression as well as a source for personal identity and social differentiation. The peculiar shape of this consumer culture resulted from two seemingly contradictory trends: a tendency toward homogenization of cultural products and heightened awareness of local tastes and values. Critics sometimes refer to the homogenizing aspect of global culture as the "Americanization" or "McDonaldization" of the world.

Those terms suggest that the consumer culture that developed in the United States during the mid-twentieth century has been exported throughout the world, principally through advertising. Thus it is no accident that young people clad in blue jeans and T-shirts sing the same Usher or Eminem lyrics in San Francisco, Sarajevo, and Beijing. Still, nothing symbolizes the global marketing of U.S. mass culture more than the spread of its food and beverage products. While Pepsi and Coca-Cola fight battles over the few places on earth that their beverages have not yet dominated, fast-food restaurants such as Burger King, McDonald's, and Pizza Hut sell their standardized foods throughout the world. The closing of many bistros and cafés in France, for instance, is the result of more French people opting for fashionable fast food instead of taking the time for more traditional and lengthy lunches. So successful has the global spread of U.S. mass culture been that it seems to threaten local or indigenous cultures everywhere.

The export of U.S. products and services is not the sole determinant of global cultural practices, however. Because the contemporary consumer culture stresses minute differences between products and encourages consumers to make purchase decisions based on brand names designed to evoke particular tastes, fashion, or lifestyle, it also fosters differentiation. Indeed, global marketing often emphasizes the local or indigenous value of a product. Genuinely Australian products, such as Drizabone wet-weather gear and Foster's Lager, have become international commodities precisely because they are Australian in origin. Likewise, young upwardly mobile consumers continue to prefer Rolex watches from Switzerland, Armani clothes from Italy, miniature electronics from Japan, and Perrier mineral water from France.

Pan-American Culture The experiences in the Americas demonstrate that U.S. patterns of cultural consumption have not simply dominated the globe without competition or critical evaluation. For example, as she was dying, the Argentine political and cultural icon Eva Perón is reputed to have said, "I will return and I will be millions." Her prophecy has come true in the images of her that continually appear around the world, especially in the Americas. In Buenos Aires, city housing projects are named after her, a new Argentine film about her life played in 1996, and her face appears on souvenir T-shirts sold in the streets. In an Argentine supper club, the show's cast members sing "Don't Cry for Me, Argentina" as their grand finale, and audiences rise to their feet applauding. The song is from the musical *Evita* by Sir Andrew Lloyd Webber and Tim Rice, which was first performed in London and subsequently became a hit on Broadway (1979). While Argentine performers sing a Euro-American song, their Evita has become an icon in the United States and Europe, not only in the musical, but also in the 1996 film *Evita* starring Madonna.

Although Latin American critics often decry the spell cast by North American popular culture on Latin American audiences, Evita-mania has indicated that the sharing or imposing of cultural practices is a two-way phenomenon. A trend in Latin America is Music Television (MTV) Latino, perceived by many critics as another case of foreign cultural intrusion, whereby Latin video deejays speak "Spanglish" or "Chequenos" ("check us out"), mixing Spanish and English. Yet, whereas Latin Americans once had called for protection against such alien influence, by the 1990s many had relaxed their guard. They see evidence of increased cultural sharing among Latin societies, noting that MTV and cable television have come to serve as a means of communication and unity by making the nations of Latin America more aware of one another. While the sheer dominance and size of the U.S. entertainment-technology industry keeps cultural sharing lopsided, cultural dominance is

thinking about ENCOUNTERS

Coca-Cola and MTV

The process of globalization as it relates to culture has often been reduced to the notion of the Americanization of the globe—or to the idea of a "McWorld," given the spread of McDonald's restaurants around the world. Were cultural exchanges so one-sided? How did the globalization of culture reveal a more complicated sharing of images, ideas, and products?

also limited by those societies' ability to blend and absorb a variety of foreign and indigenous practices.

The Age of Access

Throughout history, technological advances such as in shipbuilding provided the means to dissolve boundaries between localities and peoples and thus allowed cultural transmission to take place. Today virtually instantaneous electronic communications have dissolved time and space. Contemporary observers have labeled our era "the age of access." Communication by radio, telephone, television, fax machine, and networked computers has spawned a global village that has swept away the social, economic, and political isolation of the past. However, because it takes capital to purchase the necessary equipment, maintain and upgrade it, and train people to use it, many societies find it difficult to plug into the global village. The existing gulf between the connected and the unconnected has the potential therefore to become one border in a world without borders.

Preeminence of the English Language This new world of global interconnectedness is not without its detractors. Critics have charged, for instance, that mass media are a vehicle for cultural imperialism because most electronic media and the messages they carry emanate from advanced capitalist societies. A specific consequence is that English is becoming the primary language of global communications systems, effectively restricting vernacular languages to a niche status.

The Internet reinforces the contemporary fact that English has become the universal tongue of the twenty-first century. As a result of British colonialism, subjugated peoples the world over had been compelled to learn English and become at least bilingual, speaking their own languages along with those of the colonizer. In more recent times, many peoples have voluntarily adopted the language of a politically and economically preeminent English-speaking society, especially the United States. In this fashion, English has almost become a universal language, enjoying acceptance in scientific, diplomatic, and commercial circles. However understandable, English-language dominance on the Internet rankles some users. Xia Hong, a manager for an Internet access provider in Shanghai, articulates this concern:

> There's no question about it: the Internet is an information colony. From the moment you go online, you're confronted with English hegemony. It's not merely a matter of making the Net convenient for users in non-English-speaking countries. People have to face the fact that English speakers are not the whole world. What's the big deal about them, anyway? Our ideal is to create an exclusively Chinese-language network. It will be a Net that has Chinese characteristics, one that is an information superhighway for the masses.

Such sentiments apparently reflect the thinking of Chinese political leaders, for authorities are going to great lengths to ensure that China and its communications sys-

A citizen of Kuwait lugs a television through streets filled with European and U.S. consumer products. From tennis shoes to automobiles to English-language signs, cultural interpenetration is occurring around the globe.

tem do not become a spiritual colony of capitalist powers such as the United States. Accordingly, officials of China's Public Security Bureau—an agency that concerns itself with crimes ranging from murder to cultural espionage—are trying to contain the influence of the Internet by erecting around China a so-called "firewall" or *fanghuo qiang* (a direct translation from the English). The more prevailing and popular phrase for it is *wangguan* (literally, "net wall"), a name that invokes many centuries of Chinese efforts to repulse foreign invaders. However, because the original Great Wall had limited success, the fate of its digital successor remains an open question.

Adaptations of Technology Some societies have managed to adapt European and U.S. technology to meet their needs while opposing cultural interference. Television, for example, has been used to promote state building around the world, since most television industries are state controlled. In Zaire, for example, the first television picture residents saw each day was of Mobutu Sese Seko. He especially liked to materialize in segments that pictured him walking on clouds—a miraculous vision of his unearthly power. The revolution in electronic communications has been rigidly controlled in other societies—including Vietnam and Iraq—where authorities limit access to foreign servers on the Internet. They thus harness the power of technology for their own purposes while avoiding cultural interference.

GLOBAL PROBLEMS

By the end of the twentieth century, many traditional areas of state responsibility—whether pertaining to population policies, health concerns, or environmental issues—needed to be coordinated on an intergovernmental level. Global problems demanded global solutions, and together they compelled the governments of individual states to surrender some of their sovereignty to larger international organizations such as the United Nations. Issues concerning labor servitude, poverty, epidemic diseases, terrorism, and human rights demanded attention and action on a scale greater than the nation-state.

Population Pressures and Climate Change

The past hundred years or so have been accompanied by vast population increases. As the result of advances in agriculture, industry, science, medicine, and social organization, the world experienced a fivefold population increase over a period of three hundred years: from 500 million people in 1650 to 2.5 billion in 1950. After World War II the widespread and successful use of vaccines, antibiotics, and insecticides, along with improvements in water supplies and increased agricultural yields, caused a dramatic decline in worldwide death rates. The rapid decline in mortality among people who also maintained high levels of fertility led to explosive population growth in many areas of Asia and Africa. In some developing nations, population growth now exceeds 3.1 percent, a rate that ensures the doubling of the population within twenty-three years. In 2005 roughly 6.5 billion people shared the planet, and the population division of the United Nations has estimated that the earth's population will stabilize around 9 billion in 2050. In the meantime, 75 million people are joining the world's total population each year, and unless fertility declines to replacement levels—that is, two children per woman—the world's population will grow forever.

More optimistic voices, however, have pointed out that the odds of a population explosion and its dreaded consequences are exaggerated and are in fact receding. In part this decline is the result of the AIDS crisis, which is taking a heavy demographic toll in societies where fertility rates are high. More important, fertility rates have been falling fast in the past two decades, both in rich and in poor societies.

TABLE 38.1 Population (in Millions) for Major Areas of the World, 1900–2050

Major Area	1900	1950	1975	2005	2050
Africa	133	224	416	906	1937
Asia	947	1396	2395	3905	5217
Europe	408	547	676	728	653
Latin America	74	167	322	561	783
North America	82	172	243	331	438
Oceania	6	13	21	33	48
World (total)	1650	2519	4074	6465	9076

Source: *World Population Prospects: The 2004 Revision. Highlights.* New York: United Nations, 2005.

The same optimists also argue that despite rapid population growth, wages have risen and the cost of everything extracted or grown from the earth has declined. Equally significant is the fact that food production has more than kept pace with the growing population.

The Planet's Carrying Capacity A large population changes the earth and its environment, raising an important question: How many people can the earth support? The exact carrying capacity of the planet is, of course, a matter of debate, but by many measures the earth seems to strain already to support the current population. Scientists and concerned citizens have become increasingly convinced that human society cannot infinitely expand beyond the physical limits of the earth and its resources. Beginning in 1967 a group of international economists and scientists—dubbed the Club of Rome—attempted to specify the limits of both economic and population growth in relation to the capacity of the planet to support humanity. Praised by some observers as the conscience of the world and decried by others as being excessively negative, the club issued a report in 1972 with the subtitle "The Limits to Growth." Because the world's physical resources are in finite supply, the Club of Rome concluded, any transgression of those limits would be calamitous. Two decades later, fifteen hundred scientists, including ninety-nine Nobel laureates and representatives from a dozen of the world's most prestigious academies, signed a document titled "Warning to Humanity" (1992). The report sounded a clear alarm, stating that "human beings and the natural world are on a collision course . . . [that] may so alter the living world that it will be unable to sustain life in the manner that we know."

The prophets of doom are not without their detractors, who have eagerly pointed out that the predictions of the Club of Rome and similar ones by other organizations and by concerned governments have not been borne out by the facts. For example, the Club of Rome predicted that the global reserves of oil, natural gas, silver, tin, uranium, aluminum, copper, lead, and zinc were approaching exhaustion and that prices

Smokestacks in Siberia releasing carbon dioxide emissions into the atmosphere. Most scientists argue that emissions such as these, along with other hydrocarbon emissions and methane, contribute to global warming, the increases of world temperatures that are having a negative impact on the world's economy and natural environment.

would rise steeply. In every case but tin, reserves have actually grown since 1972. Eight years later the prices for virtually all minerals—excepting only zinc and manganese—had dropped and continue to do so. The Club of Rome's inaccurate predictions have not diminished its dystopian confidence. In a more recent and widely acclaimed work, *Beyond the Limits* (1999), the Club of Rome, while acknowledging that its earlier predictions had been too pessimistic, persisted in being equally pessimistic about the future.

Climate Change The problem is not simply one of depleting nonrenewable resources or expanding populations. The prodigious growth of the human population is at the root of many environmental problems. As people are born, pollution levels increase, more habitats and animal and plant species disappear, and more natural resources are consumed. In recent decades one environmental issue has taken center stage: climate change. In the context of environmental debates and policymaking, climate change usually refers to a human-induced climate change known as global warming.

Global warming is the phenomenon of increasing average air temperature near the surface of the earth over the past two centuries. On the basis of detailed observations, scientists have concluded that the influence of human activities since the beginning of industrialization have altered the earth's climate. More specifically, most scientists are convinced that most of the observed temperature increases since the middle of the twentieth century are caused by increasing concentrations of greenhouse gases, which prevent solar heat from escaping from the earth's atmosphere. Like the glass panes in a greenhouse, hydrocarbon emissions from automobiles, and methane emitted from the stool of farm animals, trap heat within the atmosphere, leading to a rise in global temperatures. Climate model projections indicate that the global surface temperature is likely to rise a further 1.1°C–6.4°C (2.0°F–11.5°F). An average rise of global temperature by more than 2°C (3.6°F), however, would cause significant economic and ecological damage.

A vigorous debate is in progress over the extent and seriousness of rising surface temperatures, their consequences for the environment, and the necessity to limit further warming. In the ancient Japanese capital of Kyoto, at a conference dedicated to climate change, the delegates from 187 nations agreed in 1997 to cut greenhouse emissions blamed for global warming. The Kyoto protocol went into force in 2005 and imposed targets for carbon emission reductions on developed countries until 2012. The protocol did not require developing countries—some of them major polluters, such as India and China—to reduce their emissions. The world's second largest polluter after China, the United States, did not sign the protocol because it required nothing of developing countries. Since Kyoto, global carbon-dioxide emissions have risen by a third.

International efforts in dealing with climate change have been hampered by a split between developed and developing countries; only the former committed themselves to cutting emissions. Developing countries made no such promise and insisted that the rich world bear the costs of reducing emissions. In 2009, delegates from 193 countries gathered in Copenhagen, Denmark, to renew the Kyoto protocol beyond 2012, with tougher limits on emissions. They struggled to find a way to a new protocol that would include commitments from developing countries. The Copenhagen conference ended without a new protocol or binding extensions to the Kyoto agreements. The only positive outcome was that developing as well as developed countries agreed to an international monitoring of any emissions reductions they promised to pursue.

Population Control For decades the issue of population control was highly politicized. Political leaders in developing countries, for example, charged representatives of industrialized countries with racism when they raised concerns regarding overpopulation. Industrialized nations were also accused of trying to safeguard their outrageous consumption patterns of the world's nonrenewable resources. Some leaders, such as Mexico's Luis Echeverría, went so far as to promote pronatalist measures (to increase births), urging his fellow citizens to have numerous children. The problems caused by rapid population growth eventually persuaded many governments to take action to control fertility. By that time, the old pervasive notion that a large population is a source of national power had given way to the idea that the best way to promote the health and well-being of a population is to control its growth.

As death rates declined persistently throughout the world during the latter part of the twentieth century, reducing birthrates became a central concern of many governments, and to date some eighty countries have adopted birth control programs. The United Nations and two of its specialized agencies, the World Health Organization and the UN Fund for Population Activities, have aided many countries in organizing and promoting family-planning programs. However, the availability and promotion of contraceptives does not guarantee effective control of fertility. Whereas China has, however stringently, significantly reduced its population growth rate and some Latin American societies also have a decline in their birthrates, people in other societies have resisted efforts to reduce birthrates. In some instances, resistance stems from both religious and political motives. In India, for example, the Hindu emphasis on fertility has impeded birth control efforts. Thus global attempts to prevent excessive population growth have had mixed results.

Economic Inequities and Labor Servitude

The unequal distribution of resources and income, and the resulting poverty, have materialized as key concerns of the contemporary world. Several hundred million people, especially in the developing areas of eastern Europe, Africa, Latin America, and Asia, struggle daily for sufficient food,

sources from the past

Climate Change: An Inconvenient Truth

Premiering in 2006, An Inconvenient Truth *is a documentary film, directed by Davis Guggenheim, about the campaign waged by former United States vice president Al Gore (1948–) to educate the public about the severity of the climate crisis and especially global warming. Gore discusses the scientific opinion on climate change, as well as the present and future effects of global warming, and stresses that climate change "is really not a political issue, so much as a moral one." The selection below is taken from the introduction to the book by the same title, released in conjunction with the film, which elaborates upon the same overall message. Gore and the Intergovernmental Panel on Climate Change were jointly awarded the Nobel Peace Prize in 2007, and the film won an Academy Award the same year.*

Some experiences are so intense while they are happening that time seems to stop altogether. When it begins again and our lives resume their normal course, those intense experiences remain vivid, refusing to stay in the past, remaining always and forever with us.

Seventeen years ago my youngest child was badly—almost fatally—injured. This is a story I have told before, but its meaning for me continues to change and to deepen.

That is also true of the story I have tried to tell for many years about the global environment. It was during that interlude 17 years ago when I started writing my first book, *Earth in the Balance.* It was because of my son's accident and the way it abruptly interrupted the flow of my days and hours that I began to rethink everything, especially what my priorities had been. Thankfully, my son has long since recovered completely. But it was during that traumatic period that I made at least two enduring changes: I vowed always to put my family first, and I also vowed to make the climate crisis the top priority of my professional life.

Unfortunately, in the intervening years, time has not stood still for the global environment. The pace of destruction has worsened and the urgent need for a response has grown more acute.

The fundamental outline of the climate crisis story is much the same now as it was then. The relationship between human civilization and the Earth has been utterly transformed by a combination of factors, including the population explosion, the technological revolution, and a willingness to ignore the future consequences of our present actions. The underlying reality is that we are colliding with the planet's ecological system, and its most vulnerable components are crumbling as a result.

I have learned much more about this issue over the years. I have read and listened to the world's leading scientists, who have offered increasingly dire warnings. I have watched with growing concern as the crisis gathers strength even more rapidly than anyone expected.

In every corner of the globe—on land and in water, in melting ice and disappearing snow, during heat waves and droughts, in the eyes of hurricanes and the tears of refugees—the world is witnessing mounting and undeniable evidence that nature's cycles are profoundly changing.

I have learned that, beyond death and taxes, there is at least one absolutely indisputable fact: Not only does human-caused global warming exist, but it is also growing more and more dangerous, and at a pace that has now made it a planetary emergency.

This digitized photograph offers a stunning image of global warming through its depiction of the earth afire.

For Further Reflection

- Al Gore suggests in this passage that his concern for the global environment coincided with the trauma of his six-year-old son's near-deadly accident. (He was hit by a car while crossing a street.) Why do you think the personal and the political, or the local and the global, intersected for Gore? How does Gore's thinking compare with Aung San Suu Kyi's thoughts in the other selection for Sources from the Past in this chapter?

Source: Al Gore. *An Inconvenient Truth: The Planetary Emergency of Global Warming and What We Can Do About It* (New York: Rodale Books, 2006), p. 8.

A poster advertising China's one-child family rule.

clean water, adequate shelter, and other basic necessities. Poverty is a lack of basic human necessities, and its effects are as wide-ranging as they are devastating. Malnutrition among the poor has led to starvation and death. As one of the most persistent effects of poverty, malnutrition is also responsible for stunted growth, poor mental development, and high rates of infection. Typically, vitamin and mineral deficiencies accompany malnutrition, causing mental disorders, organ damage, and vision failure among poor children and adults. Because of inadequate shelter, lack of safe running water, and the absence of sewage facilities, the poor have been exposed disproportionally to bacteria and viruses carried by other people, insects, and rodents. Poverty has correlated strongly with higher-than-average infant mortality rates and lower-than-average life expectancies.

The Causes of Poverty The division between rich and poor has been a defining characteristic of all complex societies. Although relative poverty levels within a given society remain a major concern, it is the continuing division between rich and poor societies that has attracted the attention of the international community. A worldwide shortage of natural resources as well as the uneven distribution of resources have figured as major causes of poverty and have divided nations into the haves and have-nots. Excessively high population densities and environmental degradation have caused the depletion of available resources, leading to shortages of food, water, and shelter and ultimately to poverty. The other major cause of poverty, the unequal distribution of resources in the world economy, resulted from five hundred years of colonialism, defined by the appropriation of labor and natural resources. Pervasive poverty characterizes many former colonies and dependencies. All of these developing societies have tried to raise income levels and eliminate poverty through diversified economic development, but only a few, such as South Korea, Singapore, Malaysia, and Indonesia, have accomplished their aims. In the meantime, economic globalization has generated unprecedented wealth for developed nations, creating an even deeper divide between rich and poor countries.

Labor Servitude Poor economic conditions have been closely associated with forms of servitude similar to slavery. Although legal slavery ceased to exist when Saudi Arabia and Angola abolished slavery officially in the 1960s, forced and bonded labor practices continue to affect millions of poor people in the developing world. Of particular concern is child-labor servitude. According to the International Labor Organization, a specialized agency of the United Nations, more than 250 million children between ages five and fourteen work around the world, many in conditions that are inherently harmful to their physical health and emotional well-being. Child-labor servitude is most pronounced in south and southeast Asia, affecting an estimated 50 million children in India alone. Most child labor occurs in agriculture, domestic service, family businesses, and the sex trade, making it difficult to enforce existing prohibitions and laws against those practices. Many children are born into a life of bonded labor because their parents have worked in debt bondage, a condition whereby impoverished persons work for very low wages, borrow money from their employer, and pledge their labor as security.

Trafficking A growing and related global problem that touches societies on every continent is the trafficking of persons. In this insidious form of modern slavery, one to two million human beings annually are bought and sold across international and within national boundaries. Trafficking has appeared in many forms. In Russia and the Ukraine, for example, traffickers lure victims with the promise of well-paying jobs abroad. Once the victims arrive in the countries of their destination, they become captives of ruthless traffickers who force them into bonded labor, domestic servitude, or the commercial sex industry through threats and physical brutality—including rape, torture and starvation, incarceration, and death. Most of the victims of trafficking are girls and women, which is a reflection of the low social and economic status of women in many countries. In south Asia, for instance, it is common for poverty-stricken parents or other relatives to sell young women to traffickers for the sex trade or forced labor. The trafficking industry is one of the fastest growing and most lucrative criminal enterprises in the world, generating billions of dollars annually in profits.

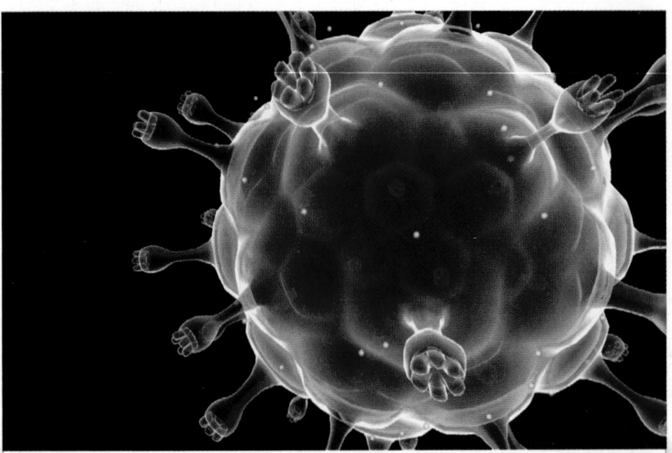
This is a microscopic vision of the human immunodeficiency virus (HIV).

Global Diseases

Since the dawn of history, disease has played a significant role in the development of human communities. Its impact has been as dramatic as it has been destructive. For example, the most devastating impact of the Columbian exchange (see chapter 22) came in the wake of diseases that Europeans introduced into the Americas following the voyages of Christopher Columbus and others. The introduction of diseases to populations that lacked any form of immunity killed perhaps as many as 90 percent of native Americans in the span of 150 years. More recently, an influenza pandemic that swept the globe in 1918 and 1919 killed between twenty and forty million people, far more than died as the result of the Great War that had just ended. Since then, medical experts, public health officials, and scientists scored major victories in their fight against diseases, eradicating smallpox and diphtheria, for example. Buoyed by those successes, the United Nations in 1978 called for the elimination of all infectious diseases by the year 2000. That goal was unrealistic and, in the meantime, ancient diseases once thought under control, such as malaria and tuberculosis, are on the rise again. Equally ominous, public health officials have identified new lethal diseases such as HIV/AIDS.

HIV/AIDS The most serious epidemic threat comes from acquired immunodeficiency syndrome (AIDS). This fatal disorder of the immune system is caused by the human immunodeficiency virus (HIV), which slowly attacks and destroys the immune system, leaving the infected individual vulnerable to diseases that eventually cause death. AIDS is the last stage of HIV infection, during which time these diseases arise. The HIV infection is spread through sexual contact with an infected person, contact with contaminated blood, and transmission from mother to child during pregnancy and, after birth, through breast feeding. Factors contributing to the spread of AIDS include poverty, ignorance, the prohibitive cost of drugs, and sexual promiscuity.

Medical experts identified AIDS for the first time in 1981 among homosexual men and intravenous drug users in New York and San Francisco. Subsequently, evidence for an epidemic appeared among heterosexual men, women, and children in sub-Saharan Africa, and rather quickly AIDS developed into a worldwide epidemic that affected virtually every nation. At the end of 2008, the number of people living with HIV/AIDS was 33.4 million, and over 25 million AIDS deaths had occurred since the beginning of the epidemic.

AIDS in Africa The AIDS epidemic is a serious public health threat throughout the world, but the disease has struck the developing world hardest, especially sub-Saharan Africa. Statistics paint a grim picture. Of the 33.4 million people identified with HIV/AIDS worldwide, 22.4 million of them currently live in sub-Saharan Africa. If current trends persist, AIDS deaths and the loss of future population from the demise of women in childbearing ages will lead to a 70-million drop in population by 2010. Between 2005 and 2010, the life expectancy in the region is expected to decline from fifty-nine years to forty-five. Africa is also home to 80 percent of the children who are living with HIV/AIDS worldwide. AIDS has touched children in two ways: as a disease infecting children and as a disease that leaves them orphans. Thus far the epidemic has orphaned over 14 million children in sub-Saharan Africa, and unless this pattern is reversed Africa will have 40 million AIDS orphans, most of whom will grow up with little or no social nurturing.

The AIDS epidemic threatens to overwhelm the social and economic fabric of African societies, rolling back decades of progress toward a healthier and more prosperous future. The health infrastructure of some African nations cannot cope with the impact of the AIDS epidemic. Although sophisticated palliative treatments—not cures—are available, only the wealthy can afford them. Most Afri-

Adults and children estimated to be living with HIV/AIDS as of December 2008

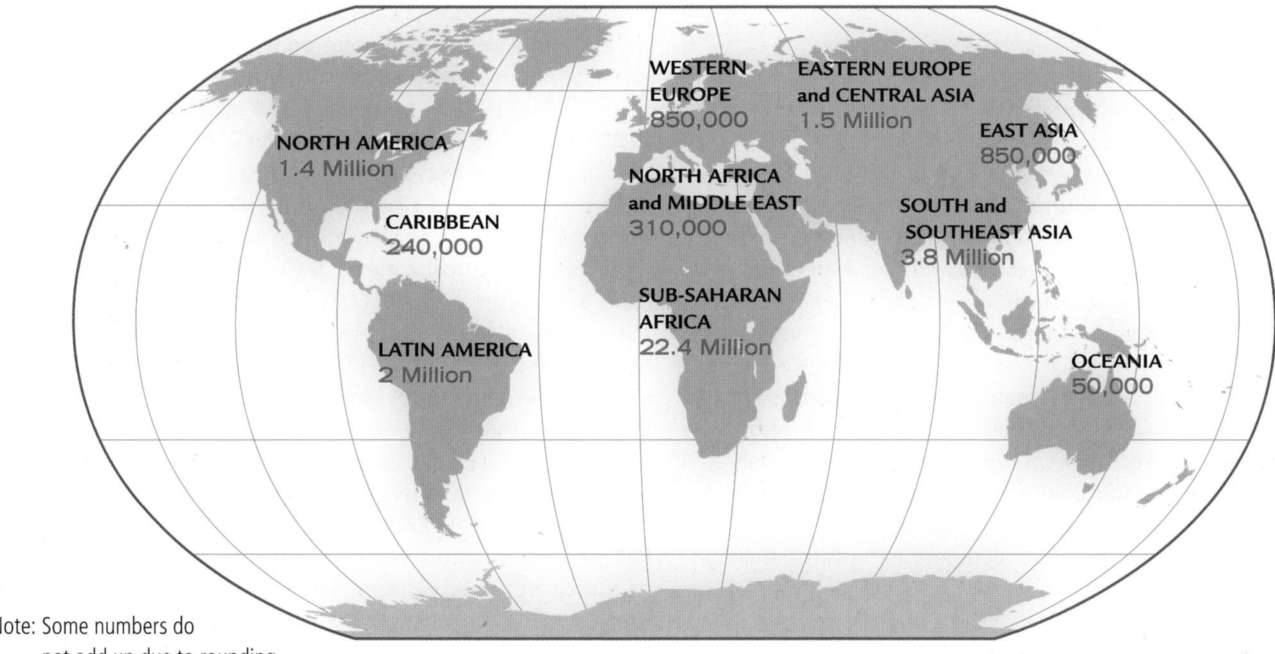

MAP 38.3

Global estimates of HIV/AIDS.

HIV infection in humans is one of the most destructive pandemics in recorded history. The virus has infected nearly 60 million people and has claimed 25 million lives since scientists first identified it in 1981. Slow progress has been made since then; for example, the life expectancy of people with HIV has increased dramatically with the advent of antiretroviral therapies. Still, the epidemic continues to spread at disturbingly high levels. The annual number of HIV/AIDS-related deaths has gone down slightly since 2004 but still exceeds 2 million, and the number of new annual infections remains high—2.7 million in 2008, of which 430,000 were children under age fifteen. Moreover, the number of people living with HIV continues to increase, rising 20 percent since 2000.

What regions of the world have been most affected by HIV/AIDS?

cans are desperately poor. As the AIDS epidemic deepens, it leaves an economically weakened continent in its wake. Families who must care for a member who is ill with AIDS often deplete financial resources that would otherwise be used to cover necessities or to invest in children's futures. When AIDS claims the lives of people in their most productive years, grieving orphans and elders must contend with the sudden loss of financial support, communities must bear the burden of caring for those left behind, and countries must draw on a diminishing number of trained and talented workers.

There are signs that HIV incidence may stabilize in sub-Saharan Africa. So many people in the sexually active population have been affected that only a small pool of people is still able to acquire the infection. In addition, successful prevention programs in a small number of countries, notably in Uganda, have reduced infection rates and contributed to a regional downturn of the epidemic.

The good news from Africa is tainted by bad news from Asia. Although infection rates in Asia remain low, health officials fear that the disease will spread faster as it traverses India, the world's second most populous nation. There is fear that the infection rate will escalate during the next decade, causing the epidemic in India to dwarf the problems seen in Africa. Although no vaccine has yet emerged to prevent or cure HIV infection, some advances have been made. When scientists first identified AIDS, there was no treatment for the disease. Existing antiviral drugs at best delayed the inevitable and at worst failed completely. By 1995, though, researchers succeeded in developing a new class of drugs known as protease inhibitors and, in combination with some of the older drugs, they produced what is now known as highly active antiretroviral therapy, or HAART. In most cases, HAART can prolong life indefinitely. The high cost of these sophisticated drugs initially prevented poor people from sharing in their benefits, but this too is changing. By 2007 over one million people in sub-Saharan Africa routinely received anti-AIDS drugs, and optimistic estimates suggest that, soon, effective AIDS drugs will be available to all who might benefit from them.

Global Terrorism

Terrorism has become a persistent feature of the globalized world. Although not a recent phenomenon, since it has been practiced throughout history, terrorism attained its greatest impact in a world distinguished by rapid technological advances in transportation, communications, and weapons development. Heightened media awareness, especially the ubiquity of worldwide television coverage, has exposed the grievances and demands of terrorists to millions of viewers, but it has also transformed the practice of terrorism. Acts of terror therefore punctuated the era following World War II, as individuals and groups the world over attempted to destabilize or overthrow political systems within or outside the borders of their countries. Terrorism figured prominently in anticolonial conflicts in Algeria and Vietnam; in struggles over a homeland between national groups such as Israelis and Palestinians; in clashes between religious denominations such as Protestants and Catholics in Northern Ireland; and between revolutionary forces and established regimes in lands such as Indonesia, Iran, and Nicaragua.

Defining Terrorism No universally agreed-on definition of terrorism exists, but experts agree that a key feature of terrorism is the deliberate and systematic use of violence against civilians, with the aim of advancing political, religious, or ideological causes. Terrorists use violent means—from hijackings and hostage-taking to assassinations and mass murder—to magnify their influence and power. In contrast to the populations and institutions they fight, terrorists and their organizations are limited in size and resources. Despite their ability to destabilize societies, terrorist organizations have rarely if ever realized their stated goals. In fact, terrorist tactics have more commonly discredited otherwise potentially worthy and commendable causes. During the last decades of the twentieth century and the first decade of the twenty-first century, terrorism increasingly assumed a global character because sustained terror campaigns require sophisticated financial support networks, a reliable and sustained supply of weapons technology, and places of

This smoky image of New York City's skyline on 12 September 2001 reveals the void and the airborne debris left by the collapse of the World Trade Center's two towers.

sanctuary. Aside from regional initiatives such as those emanating from the European Union, however, the international community did not respond to the threat of global terrorism in a coherent or unified manner. The thorny issues of what constitutes terrorism and how to respond to it gained renewed attention, however, as a result of the terror attacks against the United States in September 2001.

11 September On the morning of the second Tuesday in September, New York City and Washington, D.C., became the targets of a coordinated terrorist attack that was unprecedented in scope, sophistication, and destructiveness. Hijackers seized four passenger jetliners and used them as guided missiles. Two of the planes crashed into the World Trade Center towers, causing the collapse of the two towers, the ancillary destruction of adjacent skyscrapers, and thousands of deaths. Before the morning was over, another plane crashed into the Pentagon, the nerve center of the U.S. military in Washington, D.C., and the fourth jet crashed into a field outside Pittsburgh, Pennsylvania. Intended for another Washington, D.C., landmark, the fourth jet was thwarted in its mission when passengers stormed the hijackers. As millions around the world watched events unfold on television, the U.S. government launched an intensive investigation and identified the Islamic militant Osama bin Laden (1957–) as the mastermind behind the attacks. Officials also accused bin Laden of directing previous attacks on U.S. interests in Africa and southwest Asia. Before the dust of the collapsed World Trade towers had settled, U.S. President George W. Bush (1946–) declared war on Osama bin Laden and global terrorism itself.

Osama bin Laden headed *al-Qaeda* ("the base"), the core of a global terrorist network. He became a popular figure in the U.S.-backed effort to aid mujahideen (Islamic warriors) who fought Soviet forces in Afghanistan. By the end of the Persian Gulf War (1990–1991), however, he began to regard the United States and its allies with unqualified hatred. The stationing of U.S. troops on the holy soil of Saudi Arabia, the bombing of Iraq, and supporting Israeli oppression of Palestinians, bin Laden claimed, were tantamount to a declaration of war against God. Convinced that he was carrying out God's will, bin Laden in 1998 publicly called on every Muslim to kill Americans and their allies "wherever he finds them and whenever he can." Viewed by many as the personification of evil, yet admired by some for his convictions and aims, Osama bin Laden has moved to the forefront of Islamist violence.

War in Afghanistan and Iraq Another related radical manifestation of Islam's resurgence was the creation of the Islamic State of Afghanistan in 1996 by the Taliban movement. The Taliban emerged out of the disorder and devastation of the Afghan-Soviet war (1979–1988) and the later civil war. Promoting itself as a new force for unity and determined to create an Islamic state according to its own austere interpretation of Islam, the Taliban proclaimed its followers the liberators who brought peace to Afghanistan. In that pursuit of the purest Muslim state on earth, Taliban intolerance figured prominently, and Islamist strictures quickly alienated people both inside and outside Afghanistan. Dominated by Pashtuns—the majority ethnic group of Afghanistan—the Taliban under its leading *mullah* (male religious leader), Mohammed Omar, fought a series of holy wars against other ethnic and Muslim groups, such as Afghanistan's Shia minority. At the same time, the Taliban provided sanctuary and training grounds for Islamist fighters in southwest and central Asia, most notably for Osama bin Laden and al-Qaeda.

The Taliban espoused a strict brand of Islam that barred women from education and the workplace. As all forms of European and American dress became taboo, women had to be completely veiled in *burkas,* and men had to eschew neckties and grow full, untrimmed beards. The stringent form of Taliban-promoted Islam also called for a ban on television, movie theaters, photographs, and most styles of music. Some of those rules had little to do with pure Islam, but a religious police, the Ministry of the Promotion of Virtue and Prevention of Vice, enforced them with an extremely harsh code of justice. The United Nations and most governments in the world withheld recognition of the Taliban as Afghanistan's legitimate government. De jure recognition came instead to a Taliban opposition force, the Northern Alliance, composed of the country's smaller religious and ethnic groups, mainly Tajiks, Uzbeks, and Hazaras. The Northern Alliance became a crucial ally of the United States in its mission to find and punish those responsible for the 11 September attacks.

When the United States government announced its war against global terrorism it also pointedly targeted "those harboring terrorists," that is, governments and states that supported and provided sanctuary for terrorists. The refusal of the Taliban government to surrender Osama bin Laden prompted the United States and its allies on 7 October 2001 to begin military operations against Taliban military positions and terrorist training camps. The U.S. military and its international allies generally limited their operations to intelligence missions and massive air strikes, fighting the war on the ground through Afghan proxies, most notably the forces of the Northern Alliance. By November, U.S.-led bombardments permitted Northern Alliance troops to capture Kabul and other key Afghan cities. The United States' coalition hampered both the Taliban and al-Qaeda, but conflicts continued. The war against terrorism beyond Afghanistan also promised to be a long-term struggle necessitating a great deal of international cooperation.

Another international action against terrorism came in March 2003, when President Bush coordinated what he termed "Operation Iraqi Freedom." A multinational coalition force some three hundred thousand strong, largely made up of U.S. and British troops but also including those from

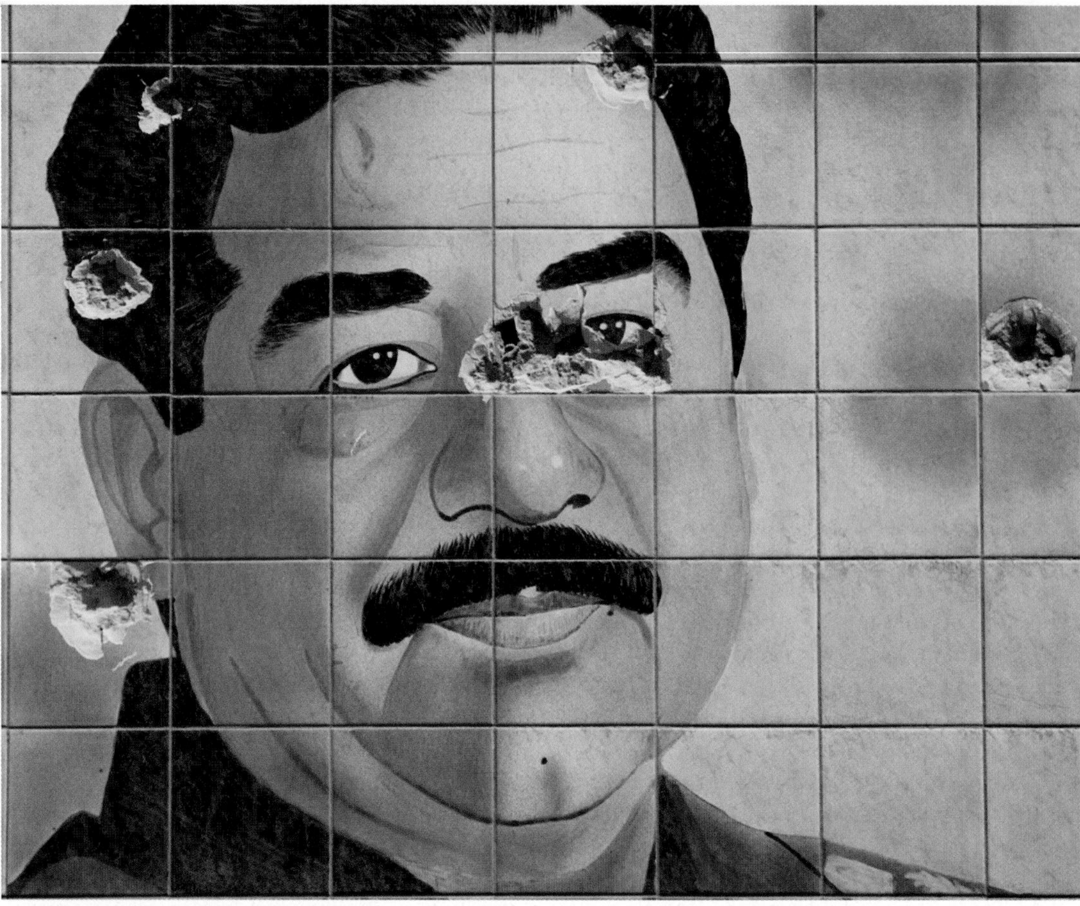

A photographer captured the ruin of Saddam Hussein in this image of a tiled mural pitted and pocked by the destruction in Baghdad as a result of Operation Iraqi Freedom.

approximately two dozen other nations, carried out an invasion of Iraq designed to wage further war on terrorism by ousting the regime of Saddam Hussein and creating a democratic state. One special target was Hussein's suspected stockpile of chemical and biological weapons, otherwise termed "weapons of mass destruction," devastating implements of war that could presumably be employed by global terrorists to wreak destruction on a scale even greater than that of 11 September 2001. Hussein himself made another special target, although he eluded capture for months. Coalition forces managed to establish their military supremacy in Iraq, but they did not uncover any such cache of weapons nor did they immediately control Hussein. President Bush declared an end to major battle operations on 1 May 2003, and coalition forces since that time struggled in their efforts to occupy and stabilize Iraq. Hussein was finally caught in December 2003 and executed in 2006, but deadly resistance in Iraq persisted.

The costs of the Iraq War climbed in terms of both casualties and expenditures. Tens of thousands of Iraqi military personnel and civilians have died, as have over 4,700 coalition soldiers by mid-2010. The United States has spent approximately $4 billion per month to maintain troops in Iraq. While President Bush sustained the United States' willingness to pay such a price, some critics in the United States and around the globe balked at the president's aggressive approach to the war on terrorism. Dubbed by some the "Bush Doctrine of Deterrence," his preemptive strike against Iraq—which had not overtly committed a terrorist act or been proven to harbor terrorists—set a troubling precedent in U.S. foreign policy. Moreover, the increased presence of foreign military personnel in Iraq may only serve to intensify the sort of Islamist fervor already fanned by Osama bin Laden. U.S. President Barack Obama (1961–), elected in 2008, has shifted the war on terror away from Iraq and toward Afghanistan and bin Laden.

Coping with Global Problems: International Organizations

Although the world's nations and peoples are becoming increasingly interdependent, governments still operate on the basis of the territorially delimited state. Because global economic and cultural interdependence demands that political activity focus on cross-societal concerns and solutions, nations are under pressure to surrender portions of their sovereignty. Moreover, as national borders become less important in the face of new economic and cultural connections, the effectiveness of national governments has declined. The widespread recognition that the national state is ill equipped to handle problems of a global magnitude has led to an increase in the number of organizations dedicated to solving global problems through international coordination and action. Often categorized as nongovernmental international organizations and governmental international organizations, these institutions are important because they have the potential to tackle problems that do not respect territorial boundaries and are beyond the reach of national governments.

Nongovernmental Organizations Contemporary efforts at global cooperation have antecedents in the past. A prototypical nongovernmental organization (NGO) is the Red Cross, an international humanitarian agency. Founded on the initiative of the Swiss philanthropist Jean Henri Dunant (1828–1910), this agency was originally dedicated to alleviating the sufferings of wounded soldiers, prisoners of war, and civilians in time of war. In 1864 the representatives of twelve nations signed the first Geneva Convention, which laid down the rules for the treatment of the wounded and the protection of medical personnel and hospitals. The convention adopted the red cross as a symbol of neutral aid. (Most Muslim countries use a red crescent.) Later protocols—signed by most nations—revised and amended the original principles enunciated in the first Geneva Convention to include protection for noncombatants as well. The Red Cross ultimately extended its mission to peacetime, rendering medical aid and other help for victims of natural disasters such as floods, earthquakes, and famines.

The United Nations The premier international governmental organization is the United Nations, which superseded the League of Nations (1920–1946). This association of sovereign nations attempts to find solutions to global problems and to deal with virtually any matter of concern to humanity. Unlike a national parliament, the UN does not legislate. Yet, in its meeting rooms and corridors, representatives of the vast majority of the world's countries have a voice and a vote in shaping the international community of nations.

Under its charter a principal purpose of the UN is "to maintain international peace and security." Cynics are quick to point to the UN's apparent inability to achieve that goal, citing as evidence the eight-year war between Iraq and Iran, the civil war in Somalia, and the many years of bloodshed in Afghanistan. However flawed its role as an international peacemaker and a forum for conflict resolution, the UN has compiled an enviable record with respect to another role defined in its charter, namely, "to achieve international cooperation in solving international problems of an economic, social, cultural, or humanitarian character." Quietly and without attracting attention from the news media, the specialized agencies of the UN have achieved numerous successes. For example, in 1980 the World Health Organization proclaimed the worldwide eradication of smallpox as a result of its thirteen-year global program. On other fronts, UN efforts resulted in more than a 50 percent decrease in both infant and child mortality rates in developing countries between 1960 and 2002. The organization's efforts also promoted an increase in female literacy, especially in Africa, where for the first time in history the majority of women—50.8 percent in 2000—were deemed to be literate. The UN as well worked to provide access to safe water for over one billion people living in rural areas.

Human Rights Governmental and nongovernmental organizations have focused much of their attention on the protection of human rights, the notion that all persons are entitled to some basic rights, especially rights that protect an individual against state conduct prohibited by international law or custom. The concept of human rights originated with Greco-Roman natural law doctrines and subsequently evolved into specific efforts to protect the rights of humanity such as the abolition of slavery and the implementation of universal suffrage. Universal recognition and acceptance of the concept of human rights came in the aftermath of World War II, especially with the exposure of crimes that the Nazi regime unleashed on its own citizens and all those that had come under Nazi control during the war. The Nuremberg war crimes trials, designed to bring Nazi leaders to justice, challenged the notion of unlimited national sovereignty and created the concept of "crimes against humanity," which warranted international judgment and punishment. In the charter establishing the United Nations in 1945, fifty member nations pledged to achieve "universal respect for, and observance of, human rights, and fundamental freedoms." In 1948, the National Assembly of the UN adopted the Universal Declaration of Human Rights, which contributed to the codification of international human rights laws. The declaration singled out specific human rights violations such as extrajudicial or summary executions, arbitrary arrest and torture, and slavery or involuntary servitude as well as discrimination on racial, sexual, or religious grounds. The concern for human rights is shared by nongovernmental organizations such as Amnesty International and the Human Rights Watch, which bring the pressure of world public opinion to bear on offending governments. By the late 1980s, human rights had emerged as one of the principal themes of global politics.

Given the present level of global interaction, international coordination to solve global problems is a necessity. However, collaboration within and between international organizations has often been inadequate. Meetings, talks, and consultations have frequently deteriorated into arguments. At the height of the cold war, this situation hampered progress in finding solutions to crucial problems. Contentious issues have sometimes paralyzed the UN and its affiliated organizations, because societies at different stages of economic development have pursued sometimes conflicting social and political goals. Cultural diversity continues to make it difficult for people to speak a common language. Despite the shortcomings of international organizations, however, for the present they represent the closest thing humanity has to a global system of governance that can help the world's peoples meet the challenges of international problems.

CROSSING BOUNDARIES

Human populations also underwent radical transformations. Peoples throughout the world challenged gender definitions and embarked on large-scale migrations. Women in Europe, the United States, China, and the Soviet Union gained greater equality with men, partly by advocating women's liberation and a nonbiological or culturally defined understanding of gender. Elsewhere, women continued to follow their societies' dictates for acceptable female behavior, although extraordinary circumstances propelled some women to prominence even in countries that resisted the feminist revolution. Both women and men also experienced either forced or voluntary migrations and in the process helped to create an increasingly borderless world.

Women's Traditions and Feminist Challenges

The status of women began changing after World War II. Women gained more economic, political, social, and sexual rights in highly industrialized states than in developing nations, but nowhere have they achieved full equality with men. Although women have increasingly challenged cultural norms requiring their subordination to men and confinement in the family, attainment of basic rights for women has been slow. Agitation for gender equality is often linked to women's access to employment, and the industrialized nations have the largest percentage of working women. Women constitute 40 to 50 percent of the workforce in industrial societies, compared with only 20 percent in developing countries. In Islamic societies, 10 percent or less of the workforce is composed of women. In all countries, women work primarily in low-paying jobs designated as female—that is, teaching, service, and clerical jobs. Forty percent of all farmers are women, many at the subsistence level. Rural African women, for example, do most of the continent's subsistence farming and produce more than 70 percent of Africa's food. Whether they are industrial, service, or agricultural workers, women earn less than men earn for the same work and are generally kept out of the highest-paid professional careers.

Feminism and Equal Rights The discrimination that women faced in the workplace was a major stimulus for the feminist movement in industrialized nations. Women in most of those nations had gained the right to vote after the Great War, but they found that political rights did not guarantee economic or sexual equality. After World War II, when more and more women went to work, women started to protest job discrimination, pay differentials between women and men, and their lack of legal equality. In the 1960s those complaints expanded into a feminist movement that criticized all aspects of gender inequality. In the United States, for example, the civil rights movement that

Women belonging to the U.S. feminist group the National Organization for Women (NOW) march for equal rights in Washington, D.C., in 1992. Although American and European women have experienced many gains with respect to achieving full equality with men, they remain less powerful in many areas. Pressures against equality for women remain strong in many developing areas of the world.

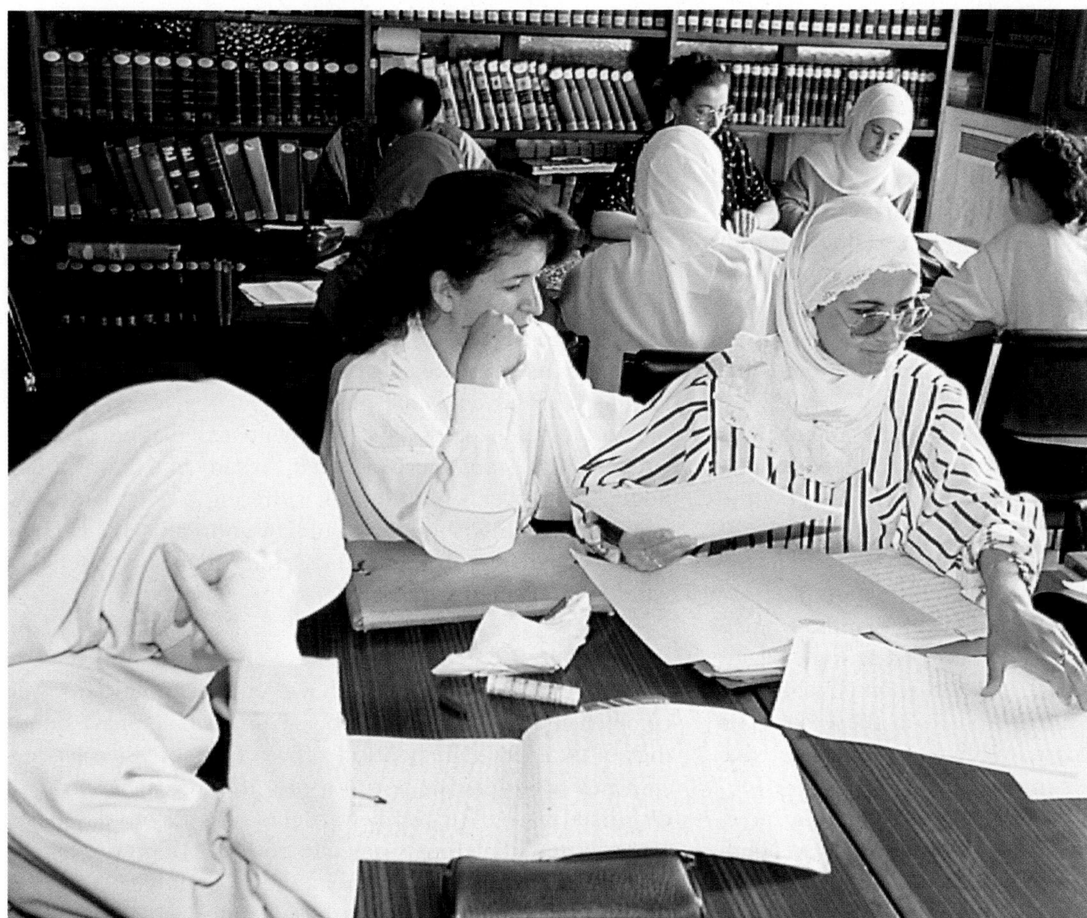

Education offers hope for the future of Muslim and Arab women.

demanded equality for African-Americans influenced the women's movement and provided a training ground for many women activists.

Women started to expose the ways in which a biologically determined understanding of gender led to their oppression. In addition to demanding equality in the workplace, women demanded full control over their bodies and their reproductive systems. Access to birth control and abortion became as essential to women's liberation as economic equality and independence. Only with birth control measures would women be able to determine whether or when to have children and thus avoid the notion that "biology is destiny." The U.S. Civil Rights Act of 1964 prohibited discrimination on the basis of both race and sex, and the introduction of the birth control pill in the 1960s and legal protection of abortion in the 1970s provided a measure of sexual freedom. The gender equality that an Equal Rights Amendment would have secured never materialized, however, because the amendment failed to achieve ratification before the 1982 deadline.

Gender Equality in China Some socialist or communist societies transformed their legal systems to ensure basic equality. Legally, the position of women most closely matched that of men in communist or formerly communist countries such as the Soviet Union, Cuba, and China. "Women hold up half the sky," Mao Zedong had declared, and that eloquent acknowledgment of women's role translated into a commitment to fairness. The communist dedication to women's rights led to improvement in the legal status of Chinese women once the communists gained power in China. In 1950, communist leaders passed a marriage law that declared a "new democratic marriage system, which is based on free choice of partners, on monogamy, on equal rights for both sexes, and on protection of the lawful interests of women and children." The law abolished patriarchal practices such as child betrothal and upheld equal rights for men and women in the areas of work, property ownership, and inheritance.

Critics argue that despite such laws China's women have never gained true equality. Certainly, few women have gained high status in the Communist Party's leadership. And although most women in China have full-time jobs outside the home, they do not receive wages equal to those of men. They do most of the work at home as well. Nevertheless, they are able to enter most professions, although most Chinese women engage in menial work. Long-standing

Confucian values continue to degrade the status of women, especially in rural areas. Parents almost universally prefer boys over girls. One unintended consequence of China's population policies, which limits couples to one child, is the mysterious statistical disappearance of a large number of baby girls. Demographers estimate that annually more than one-half million female births go unrecorded in government statistics. Although no one can with certainty account for the "missing" girls, some population experts speculate that a continued strong preference for male children causes parents to send baby girls away for adoption or to be raised secretly or, in some cases, to single them out for infanticide.

Domesticity and Abuse Although girls and women in industrial and communist nations are guaranteed basic if not fully equal legal rights and are educated in roughly the same numbers as boys and men, women in other areas of the world have long been denied access to education. Expected to stay at home, girls and women have high illiteracy rates in these societies. In Arab and Muslim lands, women are twice as likely as men to be illiterate, and in some places nine of ten women are illiterate. This situation is beginning to change. Fifty years ago most women in these societies were illiterate, but in the past twenty-five years girls have begun to catch up with boys in education.

The same cannot be said for girls and women in India, despite some real advances made during the late twentieth century. By 2001 female literacy had reached 54 percent, and yet women remained largely confined to the home. Labor force participation remained low. Less than one-quarter of women of all ages were engaged in work, while the birthrate remained high even with the greater availability of birth control measures. This condition has ensured a life of domesticity for many Indian women. The issue that has most dramatically illustrated the perilous status of women in south Asia, though, is the prevalence of dowry deaths. What makes the birth of girl children in India so burdensome is the custom of paying dowries (gifts of money or goods) to the husband and his family upon a woman's marriage, a requirement that is difficult for many Indian families to meet. If the husband and his family perceive the dowry as inadequate, if the husband wants a new wife without returning his first wife's dowry, or even if the wife has simply annoyed the husband or her in-laws, the wife is doused with kerosene and set on fire—so that her death can be explained as a cooking accident. In 1995 the government of India reported six thousand dowry deaths, though unofficial estimates put the number closer to twenty-five thousand.

This form of domestic abuse has not been restricted to India and Hindu women, but has spread through south Asia. In Pakistan more than five hundred husbands set fire to their wives between 1994 and 1997. The motives for burnings go beyond dowry, because husbands have set fire to wives who overcooked or oversalted the men's food. The victims themselves, some of whom survive, voice perhaps the saddest aspect of this treatment: resignation to their fate. One Pakistani survivor noted, "It's my fate. From childhood, I have seen nothing but suffering." These attitudes may be changing, though, as Indian and Pakistani women activists challenge these practices and establish shelters for women threatened with burning.

Women Leaders Around the world most women have the right to vote. They do not, however, exert political power commensurate with their numbers. Some women have nonetheless attained high political offices or impressive leadership positions. The same south Asia that revealed so many continued barriers to women's rights on a day-to-day basis also elevated numerous women to positions of power, breaking down other political barriers. Indira Gandhi (1917–1984) and Benazir Bhuto (1953–2007) led India and Pakistan as effective politicians, having been raised by fathers who themselves were prominent in politics. In 1994 Chandrika Bandaranaike Kumaratunga (1945–) became the first female president of Sri Lanka. Both her parents had previously served as prime ministers; her mother, Sirimavo Bandaranaike (1916–2000), became the first elected woman prime minister in 1960. As president, Kumaratunga appointed her mother to serve a third term as prime minister.

In Myanmar (formerly Burma), Aung San Suu Kyi (1945–) has emerged as a leader, also deriving her political authority from her father, Aung San, assassinated in 1947. Assuming the leadership of the democracy movement after her return from exile in 1988, Suu Kyi called for a nonviolent revolution against Myanmar's "fascist government." The government placed her under house arrest from 1989 to 1995, during which time she created a new political institution, the "gateside meeting," speaking to her followers from behind the gates of her home. In the 1990 elections Suu Kyi and her party won a landslide victory, but they were not allowed to come to power. Awarded the Nobel Peace Prize for her efforts in 1991, she could not accept the award personally because she was still under house arrest. She remained in detention or under house arrest for much of the next two decades.

thinking about TRADITIONS

Female Freedom and Subjugation
Despite the major transformations in the lives of women after World War II, the practice of limiting the freedom of women persisted in many areas of the world. Why was the feminism evident in Europe and the Americas less effective and applicable elsewhere? How did women in Asia and Africa experience both freedom and subjugation?

Opposition leader and Nobel Prize winner Aung San Suu Kyi at a gateside meeting in Rangoon, Myanmar. The government of Myanmar placed Suu Kyi under house arrest as a leader of a democracy movement, thus restricting her meetings with followers to the gates of her home.

Women demonstrated their leadership abilities in a variety of ways. They became highly visible political figures, as in south Asia, or they more anonymously joined organizations or participated in activities designed to further the cause of women's rights. The United Nations launched a Decade for Women program in 1975, and since then global conferences on the status of women have been held regularly, attracting large crowds. Even in Iran, where the Islamic revolution severely limited opportunities for women, internal forces could radically transform the image and role of women. Today revolutionary patrols walk the streets of Tehran making sure that women conform to the society's rule of dress and behavior, but during the war with Iraq, Iranian women became revolutionaries, picking up guns and receiving weapons training. They protected their national borders while defying gender boundaries.

Migration

Migration, the movement of people from one place to another, is as old as humanity and has shaped the formation and identity of societies throughout the world. The massive influx of outsiders has transformed the ethnic, linguistic, and cultural composition of indigenous populations. With the advent of industrialization during the eighteenth century, population experts distinguished between two types of migration: internal migration and external or international migration. Internal migration describes the flow of people from rural to urban areas within one society, whereas external migration describes the movement of people across long distances and international borders. Both types of migration result from push factors, pull factors, or a combination of the two. Lack of resources such as land or adequate food supplies, population pressure, religious or political persecution, or discriminatory practices aimed at ethnic minorities push people to move. Conversely, opportunities for better employment, the availability of arable land, or better services such as health care and education pull people to move. In the most general sense, migration is caused by differences, and because differences among societies are widening, the potential for migration has increased.

Internal Migration The largest human migrations today are rural-urban flows. During the last half of the twentieth century, these internal migrations led to rapid urbanization in much of the world. Today the most highly urbanized societies are those of western and northern Europe, Australia, New Zealand, and temperate South America and North America. In these societies the proportion of people living in urban areas exceeds 75 percent; in some countries, such as Belgium, it exceeds 97 percent. (A more recent phenomenon visible in developed countries is a reverse migration, from the city to the country.) The societies of tropical Latin America are in an intermediate stage of urbanization, with 50 to 65 percent of the population living in cities. In many countries in Africa and Asia, the process of urbanization has just begun. Although most people still reside in rural areas, the rate of urbanization is very high.

Urbanization Urbanization has proved to be a difficult and challenging transformation for rural folk who have chosen or been forced to adjust to a new way of life. In Latin America, Africa, and south Asia, large numbers of people have migrated to metropolitan areas in search of relief from rural poverty. Once in the cities, though, they often find

sources from the past

Politics and Family: The Hope of and for Girl Children

Since the late 1980s, Aung San Suu Kyi (1945–), the girl child of the assassinated Burmese independence leader Aung San, has remained a beacon of democratic hope for the nation now known as Myanmar. Leader of the political opposition to a military-ruled government, she has been arrested, jailed, and placed under house arrest during most of her residence in the country. Despite that, she managed to win the Nobel Peace Prize in 1991, and she has likewise managed to communicate her political messages and hopes. In the following passage, from one of many letters written to a Japanese newspaper in 1996, Suu Kyi discusses the meaning of the birth of her friends' first grandchild, a girl, and meditates on the political future of Myanmar's children through health care and education. She in fact committed her Nobel Peace Prize money, equal to US $1.3 million, to a trust in support of these causes for her people.

A couple of weeks ago some friends of mine became grandparents for the first time when their daughter gave birth to a little girl. The husband accepted his new status as a grandfather with customary joviality, while the wife, too young-looking and pretty to get into the conventional idea of a cosily aged grandmother, found it a somewhat startling experience. . . . I was told the paternal grandfather was especially pleased because the baby had been born in the Burmese month of *Pyatho*—an auspicious time for the birth of a girl child.

In societies where the birth of a girl is considered a disaster, the atmosphere of excitement and pride surrounding my friends' granddaughter would have caused astonishment. In Burma there is no prejudice against girl babies. In fact, there is a general belief that daughters are more dutiful and loving than sons and many Burmese parents welcome the birth of a daughter as an assurance that they will have somebody to take care of them in their old age. . . .

Babies, I have read somewhere, are specially constructed to present an appealingly vulnerable appearance aimed at arousing tender, protective instincts: only then can tough adults be induced to act as willing slaves to demanding little beings utterly incapable of doing anything for themselves. It is claimed that there is something about the natural smell of a baby's skin that invites cuddles and kisses. Certainly I like both the shape and smell of babies, but I wonder whether their attraction does not lie in something more than merely physical attributes. Is it not the thought of a life stretching out like a shining clean slate on which might one day be written the most beautiful prose and poetry of existence that engenders such joy in the hearts of the parents and grandparents of a newly born child? The birth of a baby is an occasion for weaving hopeful dreams about the future.

However, in some families parents are not able to indulge in long dreams over their children. The infant mortality rate in Burma is 94 per 1000 live births, the fourth highest among the nations of the East Asia and Pacific Region. The mortality rate for those under the age of five too is the fourth highest in the region, 147 per 1000. And the maternal mortality rate is the third highest in the region at the official rate of 123 per 100,000 live births. (United Nations agencies surmise that the actual maternal mortality rate is in fact higher, 140 or more per 100,000.)

The reasons for these high mortality rates are malnutrition, lack of access to safe water and sanitation, lack of access to health services, and lack of caring capacity, which includes programmes for childhood development, primary education, and health education. Yet government expenditure in both sectors, as a proportion of the budget, has been falling steadily. . . .

Some of the best indicators of a country developing along the right lines are healthy mothers giving birth to healthy children who are assured of good care and a sound education that will enable them to face the challenges of a changing world. Our dreams for the future of the children of Burma have to be woven firmly around a commitment to better health care and better education.

For Further Reflection

- How did Aung San Suu Kyi make the leap from personal observations about her friends' granddaughter to political issues central to the future of Burma/Myanmar? Can you make similar connections back in time to Suu Kyi's birth and its symbolic meaning for the country?

Source: Aung San Suu Kyi, *Letters from Burma* (New York: Penguin, 1996), pp. 55–57, as cited in Kevin Reilly, ed., *Worlds of History: A Comparative Reader,* vol. 2, 2nd ed. Boston: Bedford/St. Martin's, 2004, pp. 512–13.

Seeking relief from rural poverty, large numbers of people throughout the developing world have migrated to urban areas ill equipped to meet their needs and have had to settle in slums such as this one in Rio de Janeiro.

themselves equally destitute. Life is bleak in the slums outside Mumbai; in the shantytowns around Kinshasa or Nairobi; and in the *barriadas, barrios,* and *villas miserias* of Lima, Mexico City, and Buenos Aires. More than ten million people cram the environs of cities such as Calcutta, Cairo, and Mexico City, straining those cities' resources. The few services originally available to the slum dwellers—potable water, electricity, and medical care—have diminished with the continuous influx of new people. Among the unemployed or underemployed, disease runs rampant, and many suffer from malnutrition.

External Migration A combination of voluntary and forced international migrations has transformed the human landscape, especially during the past five hundred years. Between the sixteenth and the twentieth centuries, more than sixty million European migrants, for example, colonized the Americas, Australia, Oceania, and the northern half of Asia. Between 1820 and 1980, in the course of the Atlantic migration, thirty-seven million migrants of European descent made their home in the United States. Slave migrations supplemented those voluntary movements of people. Between the sixteenth and the nineteenth centuries, slave traders consigned about twelve million Africans to the Americas, though many died in the appalling conditions of the Atlantic voyages.

During World War II the Nazi regime initiated the largest mass expulsions of the twentieth century, deporting eight million people to forced-labor sites and extermination camps. Following the war, the Soviet regime expelled ten million ethnic Germans from eastern and central Europe and transported them back to Germany. The largest migrations in the second half of the twentieth century have consisted of refugees fleeing war. For example, the 1947 partition of the Indian subcontinent into two independent states resulted in the exchange of six million Hindus from Pakistan and seven million Muslims from India. More recently, three million to four million refugees fled war-torn Afghanistan during the 1980s. According to UN estimates, at the end of 2003 there were some ten million refugees who lived outside their countries of origin and who could not return because of fear of persecution.

Afghan refugees fled to Iran in 1986, joining the ranks of the hundreds of thousands of forced displaced persons in the contemporary world.

Many of these migrants left their home countries because they wanted to escape the ravages of war, but economic inequities between societies have caused most international migration. That is, people leave their country of birth in search of better jobs and more readily available health care, educational opportunities, and other services provided by the new society. Thus most contemporary mass migrations involve movement from developing countries to developed ones. Since 1960 some 13 million "guest workers" from southern Europe, Turkey, and northern Africa have taken up permanent residence in western Europe, and more than 10 million permanent migrants—mostly from Mexico—have entered the United States. Foreigners currently make up more than half the working population in the oil-producing countries of southwest Asia. Approximately 130 million people currently live outside their country of citizenship, collectively constituting a "nation of migrants" equivalent in size to Japan, the world's eighth most populous nation.

Migrant Communities International mass migrations have accelerated and broadened the scope of cross-cultural interaction. After their arrival on foreign shores, migrants established cultural and ethnic communities that maintained their social customs and native languages. The sounds of foreign languages as well as the presence of ethnic foods, arts, and music have transformed especially large cities into multicultural environments. Although the arrival of migrants has enriched societies in many ways, it has also sparked resentment and conflict. People in host countries often believe that foreigners and their ways of life undermine national identity, especially if defined by language and other cultural characteristics. Beyond that, many citizens of host societies view migrants, who are often willing to work for low wages and not join labor unions, as competitors for jobs. When unemployment rates climb, there is a tendency to look for scapegoats, and all too frequently the blame falls on migrants. In many countries, governments have come under pressure to restrict immigration or even expel foreign residents. Moreover, xenophobia, or an unreasonable fear of foreigners, has sometimes produced violence and racial tension, as when skinheads (shaved-head youths) in England assaulted members of ethnic minority groups or when neo-Nazis in Germany bombed the community centers of Turkish workers. Thus, while migrants are reshaping the world outside their home countries, international mass migration poses challenges both to the migrants themselves and to the host society.

Transient Migrants A more recent and transient form of migration is tourism. Although travelers have established cultural links between societies since the beginning of recorded history, travel for a long time took place mainly in connection with military conquest, religious pilgrimage, trade, or diplomacy. If more people did not take to travel, it was because most had little incentive to leave their homes, especially when transport was slow, expensive, and inconvenient. So risky was travel that most people regarded travelers as either very courageous or very foolish. Industrial society gave birth to mass tourism by providing both safer and faster transport and by institutionalizing two modern features of social life—leisure and travel.

In the early and mid-1800s, it became fashionable in Europe for the affluent to vacation, often for extended periods, and then later in the century working people began to copy the fashions of the wealthy. Working-class families took to the road during holidays to escape the grimy drudgery of the industrial city and, in the process, created working-class pleasure zones such as seaside resorts in Britain, Coney Island in the United States, or Varna at the Black Sea. People journeyed for pleasure and engaged in activities they normally did not do, such as breathing fresh air, wearing oddly colorful clothes, or taking long walks for no reason at all. By the twentieth century, leisure travel took on added symbolic value when travelers could show off the special clothes required for their journeys, such as ski apparel or bikinis. Others established that they had traveled through changes in their physical appearance, which could include varying degrees of sunburn or a leg encased in plaster. After World War II, companies created the packaged tour, which enabled millions of tourists to swarm across the world. Today middle-class tourists, new age travelers, and ecotourists—often weighted down by duty-free goods—busily crisscross the entire planet in their search for rarely visited sites.

Effects of Mass Tourism Travel and tourism have become the largest industry on the planet. The industry is sustained by growing personal wealth, which continues to produce more tourists, and by cheaper and more efficient transport, especially the jet plane. According to World Travel and Tourism Council estimates, the total economic value of goods and services attributable to tourism in 2010 was $5.7 trillion, or 9.2 percent of the gross global product. The tourism business also provided work for approximately 255 million people. The attraction of an industry that generates wealth and jobs relatively quickly—and often with minimal investment compared with establishing a manufacturing industry, for example—has served as a powerful incentive for both governments and businesses in the developed and the developing worlds to further promote tourism. On the downside, tourism most often creates low-paying jobs, and most of the profits flow to the developed world, where the majority of tourism businesses are located. The travel boom has also sparked concerns connected to the cultural impact of mass tourism. Tourism has acted as a globalizing influence, sometimes initiating dramatic and irreversible changes within the cultural traditions of host communities. Large numbers of visitors have the tendency to transform local cultural traditions into commodities, which are then consumed like any other commodity. Religious rituals, ethnic rites, and festivals are reduced and sanitized to conform to tourist expectations, resulting in a "reconstructed ethnicity."

inperspective

The decades following World War II were largely dominated by cold war politics and by nations seeking their independence from colonial rule. Borders created by the cold war world and European empires dissolved and reshaped the world's landscape. Another barrier-crushing development that became visible at the end of the century was economic globalization, a process responsible for the unprecedented integration of the global economy. A growing share of the world's societies embraced market-oriented economies and thus hitched their fortunes to the vagaries of the global marketplace.

Globalization pointed to the new relevance of international organizations and to the increasing irrelevance of national boundaries; it signified the arrival of a world without borders. Technological and cultural developments likewise combined to break down barriers and create a global village that connected diverse peoples. Although many societies resisted cultural influences from Europe and the United States, the prevalence of communications technology and cultural diffusion made interactions and encounters inevitable. Women's efforts to achieve greater equality with men also collided with cultural traditions; and, although many barriers to women's liberation remain, others have fallen. The global movement of human populations crisscrossed boundaries, both internal and external, and contributed to global problems that could be solved only through international cooperation. In the borderless world of contemporary times, nothing less is acceptable. ●

CHRONOLOGY

1947	Establishment of GATT
1948	UN adopts Universal Declaration of Human Rights
1950	World population at 2.5 billion
1960	Introduction of birth control pill
1960	Creation of OPEC
1967	Establishment of ASEAN
1967	Birth of European Community
1981	Identification of AIDS
1982	Defeat of Equal Rights Amendment in U.S.
1989	Fall of Berlin Wall
1991	Collapse of the Soviet Union
1992	Beginning of socialist market economy in China
1995	WTO supersedes GATT
2000	World population at 6 billion
2001	China joins WTO
2001	Terrorist attacks against the United States
2003	Operation Iraqi Freedom

Assessing AP Themes

1. How or in what ways did advances in science, technology, and warfare fundamentally change demographic patterns and the relationships of humans with Earth's environment?
2. How and why did the Western Europeans lose their place of preeminence in global politics in the 20th century?
3. To what extent were ideals of nationalism and internationalism products of the world wars?
4. What sort of challenges do international political, economic, and social organizations present to the 19th- and 20th-centuries' concepts of the nation-state?
5. In what ways do various parts of a global popular culture (sports, music, toys, clothes, movies, New Age, etc.) challenge traditional assumptions about race, class, gender, and religion?
6. Analyze the causes and the rationales of modern terrorist movements.
7. Has the end of the Cold War changed the international balance of power or has it instituted a new global political pattern?

For Further Reading

Peter Baldwin. *Disease and Democracy: The Industrialized World Faces AIDS.* Berkeley, 2005. Probing comparative history of the public health policies implemented by Western democracies to contain domestic AIDS epidemics in the 1980s and 1990s.

Jagdish Bhagwati. *In Defense of Globalization.* New York, 2004. A convincing rebuttal to popular fallacies about global economic integration.

Joel E. Cohen. *How Many People Can the Earth Support?* New York, 1997. An author who treads where few demographers dare to go.

Tim Flannery. *The Weather Makers: How Man Is Changing the Climate and What It Means for Life on Earth.* New York, 2006. A passionate and clear account that looks at the connection between human-made climate change and global warming.

Thomas L. Friedman. *The Lexus and Olive Tree.* New York, 1999. A readable overview that does justice to the complexities of globalization.

Kevin J. Gaston and John I. Spicer. *Biodiversity: An Introduction.* 2nd ed. Oxford, 2004. A simple and concise overview of biodiversity—what it is and why it is important.

Karl Gerth. *China Made: Consumer Culture and the Creation of the Nation.* Cambridge, Mass., 2003. Links notions of nationalism and consumerism in twentieth-century China.

Andrei Grachev. *Gorbachev's Gamble: Soviet Foreign Policy and the End of the Cold War.* Boston, 2008. A penetrating account of the end of the cold war, as seen from the Soviet side.

Francis Harris, ed. *Global Environmental Issues.* New York, 2004. A clear, nontechnical introduction to a broad range of environmental issues.

Margaret Jean Hay and Sharon Stichter. *African Women South of the Sahara.* Boston, 1984. An analysis of social and economic change and how it affected African women in the twentieth century.

Michael J. Hogan, ed. *The End of the Cold War: Its Meaning and Implications.* Cambridge and New York, 1997. A thoughtful collection of essays by leading academics about the end of the cold war.

Nikki R. Keddie and Beth Baron, eds. *Women in Middle Eastern History: Shifting Boundaries in Sex and Gender.* New Haven, 1992. A sensitive selection of articles by the leading scholars in the field.

Naomi Klein. *No Space, No Choice, No Jobs, No Logo: Taking Aim at the Brand Bullies.* New York, 2000. Part cultural analysis and part political manifesto, this work makes an angry case against multinational corporations.

Joanna Liddle and Rama Doshi. *Daughters of Independence: Gender, Caste, and Class in India.* New Delhi, 1986. A work on the contemporary women's movement that covers the Indian caste system, British colonial rule, and class structure.

J. R. McNeill. *Something New under the Sun: An Environmental History of the Twentieth-Century World.* New York, 2000. A brilliant but dark tale of the past century's interaction between humans and the environment.

Julian L. Simon. *Population Matters: People, Resources, Environment, and Immigration.* New Brunswick, N.J. 1990. Broad and general treatment of demographic, environmental, and economic problems.

Joseph Stiglitz. *Globalization and Its Discontents.* New York, 2002. A former chief economist at the World Bank and 2002 Nobel Prize winner takes aim at the institutions that govern globalization, especially the IMF.

Wang Gungwu, ed. *Global History and Migrations.* Boulder, 1997. A fine collection of essays on topics that range from the Atlantic slave trade to diasporas and their relationship to the nation-state.

Martin Wolf. *Why Globalization Works.* 2nd ed. New Haven, 2005. A sophisticated defense of the global market economy and free trade.

State of the World

A World Destroyed / A World Reborn

The global history of the twentieth century catalogued staggering numbers of human deaths and massive amounts of material destruction. It was, to date, the world's most violent century, and that violence announced itself in assassinations of figures as diverse as the Austro-Hungarian Archduke Francis Ferdinand and the nationalist Indian hero Mohandas Gandhi. Those assassinations also symbolized the forces responsible for destroying the world as it had existed at the turn of the century: world wars of unprecedented scope and horror and the final dismantling of colonial empires in a process of decolonization that was at once liberating and sobering for those seeking national independence. Tens of millions of soldiers and civilians on both sides of mighty European and global alliances died often horrid deaths, from weapons as mundane as guns to those as bewilderingly new and appallingly destructive as the atomic bombs that demolished Hiroshima and Nagasaki. The imperial and industrial power amassed by European and North American states dissipated as a result of the human and economic cost of world wars and the relatively short-lived cold war that followed those wars. That power also diminished as colonial peoples in Asia and Africa fought for their freedom and independence and thus destroyed as surely as the world wars had the global domination of imperial nations.

The geopolitical alliances that had shaped wars and divided peoples from the time of the Great War through the cold war evaporated one by one, leaving in their wake a seemingly borderless world of both promise and peril. No longer contained by European imperial hegemony, newly independent nations from India to Ghana, from Indonesia to Vietnam, contributed to the rebirth of a world free of empire. The tearing down of literal barriers between people, such as the Berlin Wall, was matched by the fall of figurative barriers between peoples as ushered in by the process of globalization. The disintegration of the world as it existed at the beginning of this era of contemporary global realignments led to a new sort of integration at the end of the century and into the twenty-first century, led by technological and economic forces that broke through national boundaries and connected the world's peoples through a complex web of communications, transportation, and economic interconnectedness. Resisted by some, and criticized by many, globalization has nonetheless remade the world and undermined old divisions, underscoring in its own way the commonality of human experience.

Destruction and disaster have not disappeared in the twenty-first century, and indeed, vast natural disasters have devastated societies and reminded humans of their vulnerability to the forces of nature—a vulnerability that ties twenty-first-century humans to their earliest ancestors. The devastating Indian Ocean earthquake and tsunami in 2004 and the Haitian earthquake of 2010 have suggested anew that fragility of human existence. What is different about these natural disasters is the new globalized world, wherein intricate networks of communications and transportation can be used to support and help those humans in desperate need, wherein the world's common humanity can be reasserted and reaffirmed, and wherein massive destruction can be countered to some extent by a human cooperation little witnessed at the beginning of this era of contemporary global realignments.

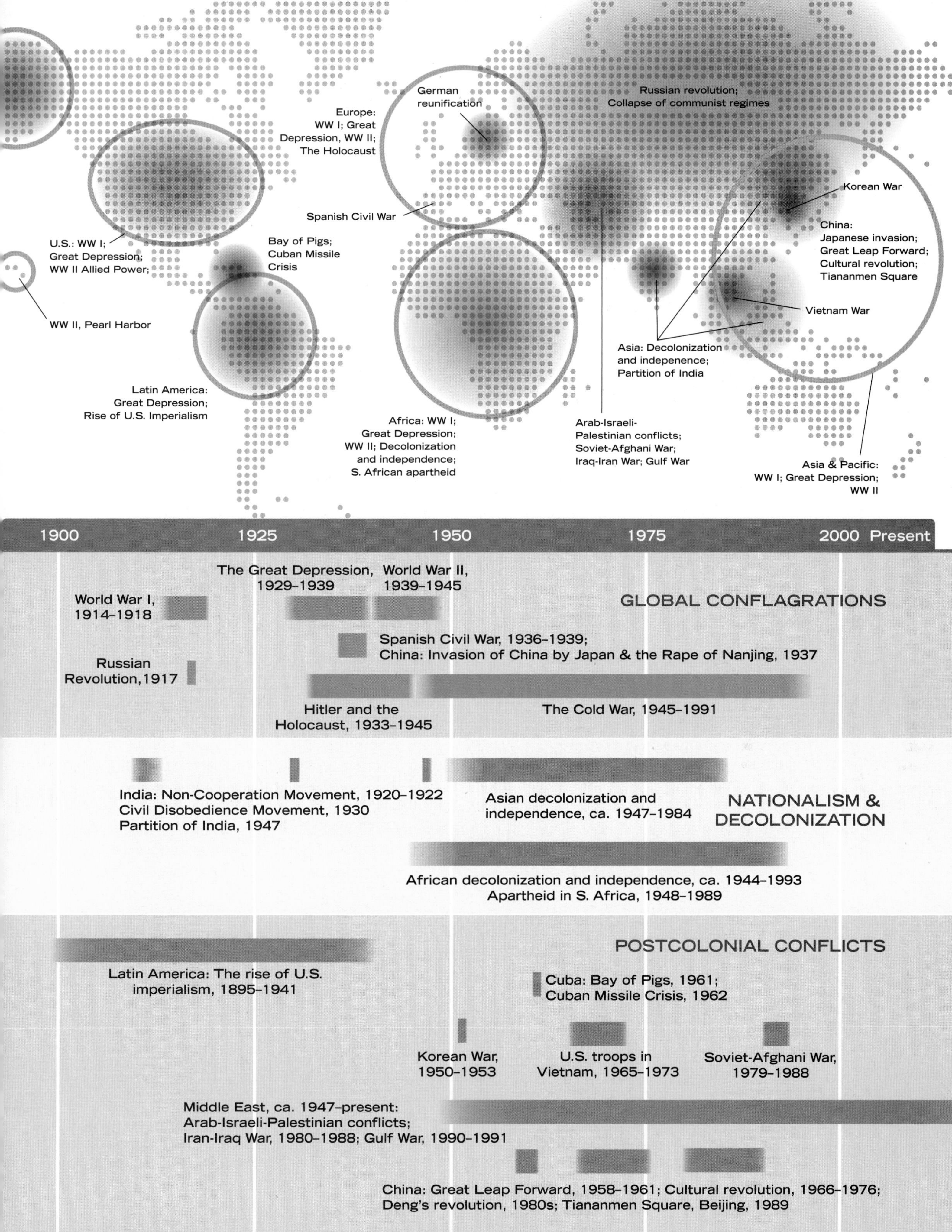
German reunification
Russian revolution; Collapse of communist regimes
Europe: WW I; Great Depression, WW II; The Holocaust
Korean War
Spanish Civil War
China: Japanese invasion; Great Leap Forward; Cultural revolution; Tiananmen Square
U.S.: WW I; Great Depression; WW II Allied Power;
Bay of Pigs; Cuban Missile Crisis
Vietnam War
WW II, Pearl Harbor
Asia: Decolonization and indepenence; Partition of India
Latin America: Great Depression; Rise of U.S. Imperialism
Africa: WW I; Great Depression; WW II; Decolonization and independence; S. African apartheid
Arab-Israeli-Palestinian conflicts; Soviet-Afghani War; Iraq-Iran War; Gulf War
Asia & Pacific: WW I; Great Depression; WW II
1900
1925
1950
1975
2000 Present
The Great Depression, 1929–1939
World War II, 1939–1945
World War I, 1914–1918
GLOBAL CONFLAGRATIONS
Spanish Civil War, 1936–1939;
China: Invasion of China by Japan & the Rape of Nanjing, 1937
Russian Revolution, 1917
Hitler and the Holocaust, 1933–1945
The Cold War, 1945–1991
India: Non-Cooperation Movement, 1920–1922
Civil Disobedience Movement, 1930
Partition of India, 1947
Asian decolonization and independence, ca. 1947–1984
NATIONALISM & DECOLONIZATION
African decolonization and independence, ca. 1944–1993
Apartheid in S. Africa, 1948–1989
POSTCOLONIAL CONFLICTS
Latin America: The rise of U.S. imperialism, 1895–1941
Cuba: Bay of Pigs, 1961;
Cuban Missile Crisis, 1962
Korean War, 1950–1953
U.S. troops in Vietnam, 1965–1973
Soviet-Afghani War, 1979–1988
Middle East, ca. 1947–present:
Arab-Israeli-Palestinian conflicts;
Iran-Iraq War, 1980–1988; Gulf War, 1990–1991
China: Great Leap Forward, 1958–1961; Cultural revolution, 1966–1976;
Deng's revolution, 1980s; Tiananmen Square, Beijing, 1989

glossary & pronunciation key

AH *a* sound, as in *car, father*
IH short *i* sound, as in *fit, his, mirror*
OO long *o* sound, as in *ooze, tool, crew*
UH short *u* sound, as in *up, cut, color*
A short *a* sound, as in *asp, fat, parrot*
EE long *e* sound, as in *even, meet, money*
OH long *o* sound, as in *open, go, tone*
EH short *e* sound, as in *ten, elf, berry*
AY long *a* sound, as in *ape, date, play*
EYE long *i* sound, as in *ice, high, bite*
OW diphthong *o* sound, as in *cow, how, bow*
AW diphthong *a* sound, as in *awful, paw, law*

Note on emphasis: Syllables in capital letters receive the accent. If there is no syllable in capitals, then all syllables get equal accent.

Abbasid (ah-BAH-sihd) Cosmopolitan Arabic dynasty (750–1258) that replaced the Umayyads; founded by Abu al-Abbas and reached its peak under Harun al-Rashid.

Abolitionism Antislavery movement.

Absolutism Political philosophy that stressed the divine right theory of kingship: the French king Louis XIV was the classic example.

Abu Bakr (ah-BOO BAHK-uhr) First caliph after the death of Muhammad.

Achaemenid empire (ah-KEE-muh-nid) First great Persian empire (558–330 B.C.E.), which began under Cyrus and reached its peak under Darius.

Aeschylus (ES-kuh-luhs) Greek tragedian, author of the *Oresteia.*

Age grades Bantu institution in which individuals of roughly the same age carried out communal tasks appropriate for that age.

Ahimsa (uh-HIM-suh) Jain term for the principle of nonviolence to other living things or their souls.

Ahura Mazda (uh-HOORE-uh MAHZ-duh) Main god of Zoroastrianism who represented truth and goodness and was perceived to be in an eternal struggle with the malign spirit Angra Mainyu.

Al-Andalus (al-ANN-duh-luhs) Islamic Spain.

Ali'i nui Hawaiian class of high chiefs.

Allah (AH-lah) God of the monotheistic religion of Islam.

Amon-Re (AH-muhn RAY) Egyptian god, combination of the sun god Re and the air god Amon.

Angkor (AHN-kohr) Southeast Asian Khmer kingdom (889–1432) that was centered on the temple cities of Angkor Thom and Angkor Wat.

Anti-Semitism Term coined in the late nineteenth century that was associated with a prejudice against Jews and the political, social, and economic actions taken against them.

Antonianism African syncretic religion, founded by Dona Beatriz, that taught that Jesus Christ was a black African man and that heaven was for Africans.

Apartheid (ah-PAHR-teyed) South African system of "separateness" that was implemented in 1948 and that maintained the black majority in a position of political, social, and economic subordination.

Appeasement British and French policy in the 1930s that tried to maintain peace in Europe in the face of German aggression by making concessions.

Arianism Early Christian heresy that centered on teaching of Arius (250–336 C.E.) and contained the belief that Jesus was a mortal human being and not coeternal with God; Arianism was the focus of Council of Nicaea.

Artha Hindu concept for the pursuit of economic well-being and honest prosperity.

Arthashastra (AR-thah-sha-strah) Ancient Indian political treatise from the time of Chandragupta Maurya; its authorship was traditionally ascribed to Kautalya, and it stressed that war was inevitable.

Aryans (AIR-ee-anns) Indo-European migrants who settled in India after 1500 B.C.E.; their union with indigenous Dravidians formed the basis of Hinduism.

Association of Southeast Asian Nations (ASEAN.) Regional organization established in 1967 by Thailand, Malaysia, Singapore, Indonesia, and the Philippines; the organization was designed to promote economic progress and political stability; it later became a free-trade zone.

Assyrians (uh-SEAR-ee-uhns) Southwest Asian people who built an empire that reached its height during the eighth and seventh centuries B.C.E.; it was known for a powerful army and a well-structured state.

Astrolabe Navigational instrument for determining latitude.

Aten Monotheistic god of Egyptian pharaoh Akhenaten (r. 1353–1335 B.C.E.) and a very early example of monotheism.

Audiencias Spanish courts in Latin America.

Australopithecus (ah-strah-loh-PITH-uh-kuhs) "Southern ape," oldest known ancestor of humans; it lived from around four million down to around one million years ago, and it could walk on hind legs, freeing up hands for use of simple tools.

Austronesians People who as early as 2000 B.C.E. began to explore and settle islands of the Pacific Ocean basin.

Avesta Book that contains the holy writings of Zoroastrianism.

Axum African kingdom centered in Ethiopia that became an early and lasting center of Coptic Christianity.

Aztec empire Central American empire constructed by the Mexica and expanded greatly during the fifteenth century during the reigns of Itzcoatl and Motecuzoma I.

Balfour Declaration British declaration from 1917 that supported the creation of a Jewish homeland in Palestine.

Bantu (BAN-too) African peoples who originally lived in the area of present-day Nigeria; around 2000 B.C.E. they began a centuries-long migration that took them to most of sub-Saharan Africa; the Bantu were very influential, especially linguistically.

Bedouins (BEHD-oh-ihnz) Nomadic Arabic tribespeople.

Benefice Grant from a lord to a vassal, usually consisting of land, which supported the vassal and signified the relationship between the two.

Berlin Conference Meeting organized by German chancellor Otto von Bismarck in 1884–1885 that provided the justification for European colonization of Africa.

Bezant Byzantine gold coin that served as the standard currency of the Mediterranean basin from the sixth through the twelfth century.

Bhagavad Gita (BUH-guh-vahd GEE-tuh) "Song of the Lord," an Indian short poetic work drawn from the lengthy *Mahabharata* that was finished around 400 C.E. and that expressed basic Hindu concepts such as karma and dharma.

Bhakti (BAHK-tee) Indian movement that attempted to transcend the differences between Hinduism and Islam.

Black Hand Pre–World War I secret Serbian society; one of its members, Gavrilo Princip, assassinated Austrian archduke Francis Ferdinand and provided the spark for the outbreak of the Great War.

Blitzkrieg German style of rapid attack through the use of armor and air power that was used in Poland, Norway, Denmark, Belgium, the Netherlands, and France in 1939–1940.

Bodhisattvas (BOH-dih-SAT-vuhs) Buddhist concept regarding individuals who had reached enlightenment but who stayed in this world to help people.

Bolshevik (BOHL-shih-vehk) Russian communist party headed by Lenin.

Bourgeoisie Middle class in modern industrial society.

Brahmins (BRAH-minz) Hindu caste of priests.

Brezhnev Doctrine Policy developed by Leonid Brezhnev (1906–1982) that claimed for the Soviet Union the right to invade any socialist country faced with internal or external enemies; the doctrine was best expressed in Soviet invasion of Czechoslovakia.

Buddha (BOO-duh) The "enlightened one," the term applied to Siddhartha Gautama after his discoveries that would form the foundation of Buddhism.

Buddhism (BOO-diz'm) Religion, based on Four Noble Truths, associated with Siddhartha Gautama (563–483 B.C.E.), or the Buddha; its adherents desired to eliminate all distracting passion and reach nirvana.

Bunraku (boon-RAH-koo) Japanese puppet theater.

Byzantine Empire (BIHZ-ann-teen) Long-lasting empire centered at Constantinople; it grew out of the end of the Roman empire, carried the legacy of Roman greatness, and was the only classical society to survive into the early modern age; it reached its early peak during the reign of Justinian (483–565).

Caesaropapism Concept relating to the mixing of political and religious authority, as with the Roman emperors, that was central to the church-versus-state controversy in medieval Europe.

Cahokia (kuh-HOH-kee-uh) Large structure in modern Illinois that was constructed by the mound-building peoples; it was the third largest structure in the Americas before the arrival of the Europeans.

Caliph (KAL-ihf) "Deputy," Islamic leader after the death of Muhammad.

Capetian (cah-PEE-shuhn) Early French dynasty that started with Hugh Capet.

Capitalism An economic system with origins in early modern Europe in which private parties make their goods and services available on a free market.

Capitulation Highly unfavorable trading agreements that the Ottoman Turks signed with the Europeans in the nineteenth century that symbolized the decline of the Ottomans.

Carolingians Germanic dynasty that was named after its most famous member, Charlemagne.

Carthage Northern African kingdom, main rival to early Roman expansion, that was defeated by Rome in the Punic Wars.

Çatal Hüyük Important Neolithic settlement in Anatolia (7250–6150 B.C.E.).

Cathars Medieval heretics, also known as the Albigensians, who considered the material world evil; their followers renounced wealth and marriage and promoted an ascetic existence.

Catholic Reformation Sixteenth-century Catholic attempt to cure internal ills and confront Protestantism; it was inspired by the reforms of the Council of Trent and the actions of the Jesuits.

Caudillos (KAW-dee-ohs) Latin American term for nineteenth-century local military leaders.

Central Powers World War I term for the alliance of Germany, Austria-Hungary, and the Ottoman empire.

Chaghatai One of Chinggis Khan's sons, whose descendants ruled central Asia through the Chaghatai khanate.

Chan Buddhism (CHAHN BOO-diz'm) Influential branch of Buddhism in China, with an emphasis on intuition and sudden flashes of insight instead of textual study.

Chanchan (chahn-chahn) Capital of the pre-Incan, South American Chimu society that supported a large population of fifty thousand.

Chavín cult Mysterious but very popular South American religion (1000–300 B.C.E.).

Chimu Pre-Incan South American society that fell to Incas in the fifteenth century.

Chinampas Agricultural gardens used by Mexica (Aztecs) in which fertile muck from lake bottoms was dredged and built up into small plots.

Chivalry European medieval code of conduct for knights based on loyalty and honor.

Chola Southern Indian Hindu kingdom (850–1267), a tightly centralized state that dominated sea trade.

Chucuito Pre-Incan South American society that rose in the twelfth century and fell to the Incas in the fifteenth century.

City-state Urban areas that controlled surrounding agricultural regions and that were often loosely connected in a broader political structure with other city-states.

Cohong Specially licensed Chinese firms that were under strict government regulation.

Collectivization Process beginning in the late 1920s by which Stalin forced the Russian peasants off their own land and onto huge collective farms run by the state; millions died in the process.

COMECON The Council for Mutual Economic Assistance, which offered increased trade within the Soviet Union and eastern Europe; it was the Soviet alternative to the United States' Marshall Plan.

Communalism A term, usually associated with India, that placed an emphasis on religious rather than national identity.

Communism Philosophy and movement that began in middle of the nineteenth century with the work of Karl Marx; it has the same general goals as socialism, but it includes the belief that violent revolution is necessary to destroy the bourgeois world and institute a new world run by and for the proletariat.

Confucianism (kuhn-FYOO-shuhn-iz'm) Philosophy, based on the teachings of the Chinese philosopher Kong Fuzi (551–479 B.C.E.), or Confucius, that emphasizes order, the role of the gentleman, obligation to society, and reciprocity.

Congress of Vienna Gathering of European diplomats in Vienna, Austria, from October 1814 to June 1815. The representatives of the "great powers" that defeated Napoleon—Britain, Austria, Prussia, and Russia—dominated the proceedings, which aimed to restore the prerevolutionary political and social order.

Conquistadores (kohn-KEE-stah-dohr-ayz) Spanish adventurers such as Cortés and Pizarro who conquered Central and South America in the sixteenth century.

Constitutionalism Movement in England in the seventeenth century that placed power in Parliament's hands as part of a constitutional monarchy and that increasingly limited the power of the monarch; the movement was highlighted by the English Civil War and the Glorious Revolution.

Containment Concept associated with the United States and specifically with the Truman Doctrine during the cold war that revolved around the notion that the United States would contain the spread of communism.

Corporation A concept that reached mature form in 1860s in England and France; it involved private business owned by thousands of individual and institutional investors who financed the business through the purchase of stocks.

Corpus iuris civilis (KOR-puhs yoor-uhs sih-VEE-lihs) *Body of the Civil Law,* the Byzantine emperor Justinian's attempt to codify all Roman law.

Criollos (kree-OH-lohs) Creoles, people born in the Americas of Spanish or Portuguese ancestry.

Cross staff Device that sailors used to determine latitude by measuring the angle of the sun or the pole star above the horizon.

Cuneiform Written language of the Sumerians, probably the first written script in the world.

Daimyo (DEYEM-yoh) Powerful territorial lords in early modern Japan.

Dao Key element in Chinese philosophy that means the "way of nature" or the "way of the cosmos."

Daodejing (DOW-DAY-JIHNG) Book that is the fundamental work of Daoism.

Daoism (DOW-i'zm) Chinese philosophy with origins in the Zhou dynasty; it is associated with legendary philosopher Laozi, and it called for a policy of noncompetition.

Dar al-Islam The "house of Islam," a term for the Islamic world.

Declaration of Independence Drafted by Thomas Jefferson in 1776; the document expressed the ideas of John Locke and the Enlightenment, represented the idealism of the American rebels, and influenced other revolutions.

Declaration of the Rights of Man and the Citizen Document from the French Revolution (1789) that was influenced by the American Declaration of Independence and in turn influenced other revolutionary movements.

Decolonization Process by which former colonies achieved their independence, as with the newly emerging African nations in the 1950s and 1960s.

Deism (DEE-iz'm) An Enlightenment view that accepted the existence of a god but denied the supernatural aspects of Christianity; in deism, the universe was an orderly realm maintained by rational and natural laws.

Descamisados "Shirtless ones," Argentine poor who supported Juan and Eva Perón.

Détente A reduction in cold war tension between the United States and the Soviet Union from 1969 to 1975.

Devshirme Ottoman requirement that the Christians in the Balkans provide young boys to be slaves of the sultan.

Dharma (DAHR-muh) Hindu concept of obedience to religious and moral laws and order; also, the basic doctrine of Buddhism.

Dhimmi (dihm-mee) Islamic concept of a protected people that was symbolic of Islamic toleration during the Mughal and Ottoman empires.

Dhow Indian, Persian, and Arab ships, one hundred to four hundred tons, that sailed and traded throughout the Indian Ocean basin.

Diaspora People who have settled far from their original homeland but who still share some measure of ethnic identity.

Dionysus Greek god of wine, also known as Bacchus; Greek plays were performed in his honor.

Dravidians Peoples who produced the brilliant Harappan society in India, 3000–1500 B.C.E.

Dreadnoughts A class of British battleships whose heavy armaments made all other battleships obsolete overnight.

Duma Russian parliament, established after the Revolution of 1905.

Dutch learning European knowledge that reached Tokugawa Japan.

East India Company British joint-stock company that grew to be a state within a state in India; it possessed its own armed forces.

Eight-legged essay Eight-part essays that an aspiring Chinese civil servant had to compose, mainly based on a knowledge of Confucius and the Zhou classics.

Encomienda (ehn-KOH-mee-ehn-dah) System that gave the Spanish settlers *(encomenderos)* the right to compel the indigenous peoples of the Americas to work in the mines or fields.

Engenho Brazilian sugar mill; the term also came to symbolize the entire complex world relating to the production of sugar.

Enlightenment Eighteenth-century philosophical movement that began in France; its emphasis was on the preeminence of reason rather than faith or tradition; it spread concepts from the Scientific Revolution.

Epicureans (ehp-ih-kyoo-REE-uhns) Hellenistic philosophers who taught that pleasure—as in quiet satisfaction—was the greatest good.

Equal-field system Chinese system during the Tang dynasty in which the goal was to ensure an equitable distribution of land.

Essenes Jewish sect that looked for the arrival of a savior; they were similar in some of their core beliefs to the early Christians.

Etruscans (ih-TRUHS-kuhns) Northern Italian society that initially dominated the Romans; the Etruscans helped convey Greek concepts to the expanding Romans.

Eunuchs (YOO-nihks) Castrated males, originally in charge of the harem, who grew to play major roles in government; eunuchs were common in China and other societies.

European Community (EC) Organization of European states established in 1957; it was originally called the European Economic Community and was renamed the EC in 1967; it promoted economic growth and integration as the basis for a politically united Europe.

European Union Established by the Maastricht Treaty in 1993, a supranational organization for even greater European economic and political integration.

Fascism Political ideology and mass movement that was prominent in many parts of Europe between 1919 and 1945; it sought to regenerate the social, political, and cultural life of societies, especially in contrast to liberal democracy and socialism; fascism began with Mussolini in Italy, and it reached its peak with Hitler in Germany.

Five Pillars The foundation of Islam: (1) profession of faith, (2) prayer, (3) fasting during Ramadan, (4) almsgiving, and (5) pilgrimage, or hajj.

Five-year plans First implemented by Stalin in the Soviet Union in 1928; five-year plans were a staple of communist regimes in which every aspect of production was determined in advance for a five-year period; five-year plans were opposite of the free market concept.

Four Noble Truths The foundation of Buddhist thought: (1) life is pain, (2) pain is caused by desire, (3) elimination of desire will bring an end to pain, (4) living a life based on the Noble Eightfold Path will eliminate desire.

Front de Libération Nationale (FLN) The Algerian organization that fought a bloody guerrilla war for freedom against France.

Fulani (foo-LAH-nee) Sub-Saharan African people who, beginning in the seventeenth century, waged a series of wars designed to impose their own strict interpretation of Islam.

Gathas (GATH-uhs) Zoroastrian hymns believed to be compositions by Zarathustra.

Gauchos (GOW-chohz) Argentine cowboys, highly romanticized figures.

General Agreement on Tariffs and Trade (GATT) Free-trade agreement first signed in 1947; by 1994 it had grown to 123 members and formed the World Trade Organization (WTO).

Ghana (GAH-nuh) Kingdom in west Africa during the fifth through the thirteenth century whose rulers eventually converted to Islam; its power and wealth was based on dominating trans-Saharan trade.

Ghazi (GAH-zee) Islamic religious warrior.

Ghaznavids Turkish tribe under Mahmud of Ghazni who moved into northern India in the eleventh century and began a period of greater Islamic influence in India.

Gilgamesh Legendary king of the Mesopotamian city-state of Uruk (ca. 3000 B.C.E.), subject of the *Epic of Gilgamesh,* world's oldest complete epic literary masterpiece.

Glasnost (GLAHS-nohst) Russian term meaning "openness" introduced by Mikhail Gorbachev in 1985 to describe the process of opening Soviet society to dissidents and public criticism.

Globalization The breaking down of traditional boundaries in the face of increasingly global financial and cultural trends.

Global warming The emission of greenhouse gases, which prevents solar heat from escaping the earth's atmosphere and leads to the gradual heating of the earth's environment.

Golden Horde Mongol tribe that controlled Russia from the thirteenth to the fifteenth century.

Greater East Asia Co-Prosperity Sphere Japanese plan for consolidating east and southeast Asia under their control during World War II.

Great Game Nineteenth-century competition between Great Britain and Russia for the control of central Asia.

Great Zimbabwe Large sub-Saharan African kingdom in the fifteenth century.

Greenpeace An environmental organization founded in 1970 and dedicated to the preservation of earth's natural resources.

Guomindang (GWOH-mihn-dahng) Chinese nationalist party founded by Sun Yatsen (1866–1925) and later led by Jiang Jieshi; it has been centered in Taiwan since the end of the Chinese civil war.

Gupta (GOOP-tah) Indian dynasty (320–550 C.E.) that briefly reunited India after the collapse of the earlier Mauryan dynasty.

Hacienda (HAH-see-ehn-dah) Large Latin American estates.

Hagia Sophia (HAH-yah SOH-fee-uh) Massive Christian church constructed by the Byzantine emperor Justinian and later converted into a mosque.

Hajj (HAHJ) Pilgrimage to Mecca.

Hammurabi's Code (hahm-uh-RAH-beez) Sophisticated law code associated with the Babylonian king Hammurabi (r. 1792–1750 B.C.E.).

Harappan (hah-RAP-puhn) Early brilliant Indian society centered in Harappa and Mohenjo-daro.

Harijans "Children of God," Gandhi's term for the Untouchables.

Hebrews Semitic-speaking nomadic tribe influential for monotheistic belief in Yahweh.

Heian (HAY-ahn) Japanese period (794–1185), a brilliant cultural era notable for the world's first novel, Murasaki Shikibu's *The Tale of Genji.*

Hellenistic Era Phase in Greek history (328–146 B.C.E.), from the conquest of Greece by Philip of Macedon until Greece's fall to the Romans; this era was a more cosmopolitan age facilitated by the conquests of Alexander the Great.

Hieroglyphics (heye-ruh-GLIPH-iks) Ancient Egyptian written language.

Hijra Muhammad's migration from Mecca to Medina in 622, which is the beginning point of the Islamic calendar and is considered to mark the beginning of the Islamic faith.

Hinayana (HEE-nah-yah-nuh) Branch of Buddhism known as the "lesser vehicle," also known as Theravada Buddhism; its beliefs include strict, individual path to enlightenment, and it is popular in south and southeast Asia.

Hinduism Main religion of India, a combination of Dravidian and Aryan concepts; Hinduism's goal is to reach spiritual purity and union with the great world spirit; its important concepts include dharma, karma, and samsara.

Holocaust German attempt in World War II to exterminate the Jews of Europe.

Home front Term made popular in World War I and World War II for the civilian "front" that was symbolic of the greater demands of total war.

Hominid (HAWM-ih-nihd) A creature belonging to the family Hominidae, which includes human and humanlike species.

Homo erectus (HOH-MOH ee-REHK-tuhs) "Upright-walking human," which existed from two million to two hundred thousand years ago; *Homo erectus* used cleavers and hand axes and learned how to control fire.

Homo sapiens (HOH-MOH SAY-pee-uhns) "Consciously thinking human," which first appeared around two hundred fifty thousand years ago and used sophisticated tools.

Huitzilopochtli (wee-tsee-loh-pockt-lee) Sun god and patron deity of the Aztecs.

Hundred Days of Reform Chinese reforms of 1898 led by Kang Youwei and Liang Qichao in their desire to turn China into a modern industrial power.

Hyksos (HICK-sohs) Invaders who seized the Nile delta and helped bring an end to the Egyptian Middle Kingdom.

Iconoclasts (eye-KAHN-oh-klasts) Supporters of the movement, begun by the Byzantine Emperor Leo III (r. 717–741), to destroy religious icons because their veneration was considered sinful.

Ilkhanate (EEL-kahn-ate) Mongol state that ruled Persia after abolition of the Abbasid empire in the thirteenth century.

Imperialism Term associated with the expansion of European powers and their conquest and colonization of African and Asian societies, mainly from the sixteenth through the nineteenth century.

Inca empire Powerful South American empire that would reach its peak in the fifteenth century during the reigns of Pachacuti Inca and Topa Inca.

Indentured labor Labor source for plantations; wealthy planters would pay the laboring poor to sell a portion of their working lives, usually seven years, in exchange for passage.

Indo-Europeans Tribal groups from southern Russia who, over a period of millennia, embarked on a series of migrations from India through western Europe; their greatest legacy was the broad distribution of Indo-European languages throughout Eurasia.

Indra Early Indian god associated with the Aryans; Indra was the king of the gods and was associated with warfare and thunderbolts.

Intifada Palestinian mass movement against Israeli rule in the Gaza Strip and other occupied territories.

Investiture (ihn-VEHST-tih-tyoor) One aspect of the medieval European church-versus-state controversy, the granting of church offices by a lay leader.

Iroquois (EAR-uh-kwoi) Eastern American Indian confederation made up of the Mohawk, Oneida, Onondaga, Cayuga, and Seneca tribes.

Islam Monotheistic religion announced by the prophet Muhammad (570–632); influenced by Judaism and Christianity, Muhammad was considered the final prophet because the earlier religions had not seen the entire picture; the Quran is the holy book of Islam.

Jainism (JEYEN-iz'm) Indian religion associated with the teacher Vardhamana Mahavira (ca. 540–468 B.C.E.) in which every physical object possessed a soul; Jains believe in complete nonviolence to all living beings.

Jati Indian word for a Hindu subcaste.

Jizya (JIHZ-yuh) Tax in Islamic empires that was imposed on non-Muslims.

Joint-stock companies Early forerunner of the modern corporation; individuals who invested in a trading or exploring venture could make huge profits while limiting their risk.

Ka'ba (KAH-buh) Main shrine in Mecca, goal of Muslims embarking on the hajj.

Kabuki (kah-BOO-kee) Japanese theater in which actors were free to improvise and embellish the words.

Kama Hindu concept of the enjoyment of physical and sexual pleasure.

Kamikaze (KAH-mih-kah-zee) A Japanese term meaning "divine wind" that is related to the storms that destroyed Mongol invasion fleets; the term is symbolic of Japanese isolation and was later taken by suicide pilots in World War II.

Kanun (KAH-noon) Laws issued by the Ottoman Süleyman the Magnificent, also known as Süleyman Kanuni, "the Lawgiver."

Kapu Hawaiian concept of something being taboo.

Karma (KAHR-mah) Hindu concept that the sum of good and bad in a person's life will determine his or her status in the next life.

Khoikhoi South African people referred to pejoratively as the Hottentots by Europeans.

Kongo Central African state that began trading with the Portuguese around 1500; although their kings, such as King Affonso I (r. 1506–1543), converted to Christianity, they nevertheless suffered from the slave trade.

Koumbi-Saleh Important trading city along the trans-Saharan trade route from the eleventh to the thirteenth century.

Kshatriayas (KSHAHT-ree-uhs) Hindu caste of warriors and aristocrats.

Kulaks Land-owning Russian peasants who benefited under Lenin's New Economic Policy and suffered under Stalin's forced collectivization.

Kush Nubian African kingdom that conquered and controlled Egypt from 750 to 664 B.C.E.

Lamaist Buddhism (LAH-muh-ihst BOO-diz'm) Branch of Buddhism that was similar to shamanism in its acceptance of magic and supernatural powers.

La Reforma Political reform movement of Mexican president Benito Juárez (1806–1872) that called for limiting the power of the military and the Catholic church in Mexican society.

Latifundia (LAT-ih-FOON-dee-uh) Huge state-run and slave-worked farms in ancient Rome.

League of Nations Forerunner of the United Nations, the dream of American president Woodrow Wilson, although its potential was severely limited by the refusal of the United States to join.

Lebensraum (LAY-behnz-rowm) German term meaning "living space"; the term is associated with Hitler and his goal of carving out territory in the east for an expanding Germany.

Legalism Chinese philosophy from the Zhou dynasty that called for harsh suppression of the common people.

Levée en masse (leh-VAY on MASS) A term signifying universal conscription during the radical phase of the French revolution.

Lex talionis (lehks tah-lee-oh-nihs) "Law of retaliation," laws in which offenders suffered punishments similar to their crimes; the most famous example is Hammurabi's Laws.

Li (LEE) Confucian concept, a sense of propriety.

Linear A Minoan written script.

Linear B Early Mycenaean written script, adapted from the Minoan Linear A.

Luddites Early-nineteenth-century artisans who were opposed to new machinery and industrialization.

Machismo (mah-CHEEZ-moh) Latin American social ethic that honored male strength, courage, aggressiveness, assertiveness, and cunning.

Madrasas (MAH-drahs-uhs) Islamic institutions of higher education that originated in the tenth century.

Magyars (MAH-jahrs) Hungarian invaders who raided towns in Germany, Italy, and France in the ninth and tenth centuries.

Mahabharata (mah-hah-BAH-rah-tah) Massive ancient Indian epic that was developed orally for centuries; it tells of an epic civil war between two family branches.

Mahayana (mah-huh-YAH-nah) The "greater vehicle," a more metaphysical and more popular northern branch of Buddhism.

Majapahit (MAH-ja-PAHT) Southeast Asian kingdom (1293–1520) centered on the island of Java.

Mali (MAH-lee) West African kingdom founded in the thirteenth century by Sundiata; it reached its peak during the reign of Mansa Musa.

Manchus Manchurians who conquered China, putting an end to the Ming dynasty and founding the Qing dynasty (1644–1911).

Mandate of Heaven Chinese belief that the emperors ruled through the mandate, or approval, of heaven contingent on their ability to look after the welfare of the population.

Mandate system System that developed in the wake of World War I when the former colonies ended up mandates under European control, a thinly veiled attempt at continuing imperialism.

Manichaeism (man-ih-KEE-iz'm) Religion founded by the prophet Mani in the third century C.E., a syncretic version of Zoroastrian, Christian, and Buddhist elements.

Manor Large estates of the nobles during the European middle ages, home for the majority of the peasants.

Maori (mow-ree) Indigenous people of New Zealand.

Marae Polynesian temple structure.

Marathon Battlefield scene of the Athenian victory over the Persians in 490 B.C.E.

Maroons Runaway African slaves.

Marshall Plan U.S. plan, officially called the European Recovery Program, that offered financial and other economic aid to all European states that had suffered from World War II, including Soviet bloc states.

Mauryan empire Indian dynasty (321–185 B.C.E.) founded by Chandragupta Maurya and reaching its peak under Ashoka.

Maya (Mye-uh) Brilliant Central American society (300–1100) known for math, astronomy, and a sophisticated written language.

May Fourth Movement Chinese movement that began 4 May 1919 with a desire to eliminate imperialist influences and promote national unity.

Medes (meeds) Indo-European branch that settled in northern Persia and eventually fell to another branch, the Persians, in the sixth century B.C.E.

Meiji Restoration (MAY-jee) Restoration of imperial rule under Emperor Meiji in 1868 by a coalition led by Fukuzawa Yukichi and Ito Hirobumi; the restoration enacted western reforms to strengthen Japan.

Melaka (may-LAH-kah) Southeast Asian kingdom that was predominantly Islamic.

Mesopotamia Term meaning "between the rivers," in this case the Tigris and Euphrates; Sumer and Akkad are two of the earliest societies.

Mestizo (mehs-TEE-zoh) Latin American term for children of Spanish and native parentage.

Métis (may-TEE) Canadian term for individuals of mixed European and indigenous ancestry.

Millet An autonomous, self-governing community in the Ottoman empire.

Ming Chinese dynasty (1368–1644) founded by Hongwu and known for its cultural brilliance.

Minoan (mih-NOH-uhn) Society located on the island of Crete (ca. 2000–1100 B.C.E.) that influenced the early Mycenaeans.

Missi dominici (mihs-see doh-mee-nee-chee) "Envoys of the lord ruler," the noble and church emissaries sent out by Charlemagne.

Mithraism (MITH-rah-iz'm) Mystery religion based on worship of the sun god Mithras; it became popular among the Romans because of its promise of salvation.

Mochica (moh-CHEE-kuh) Pre-Incan South American society (300–700) known for their brilliant ceramics.

Moksha Hindu concept of the salvation of the soul.

Monotheism (MAW-noh-thee-iz'm) Belief in only one god, a rare concept in the ancient world.

Monroe Doctrine American doctrine issued in 1823 during the presidency of James Monroe that warned Europeans to keep their hands off Latin America and that expressed growing American imperialistic views regarding Latin America.

Mughals (MOO-guhls) Islamic dynasty that ruled India from the sixteenth through the eighteenth century; the construction of the Taj Mahal is representative of their splendor; with the exception of the enlightened reign of Akbar, the increasing conflict between Hindus and Muslims was another of their legacies.

Muhammad (muh-HAH-mehd) Prophet of Islam (570–632).

Muslim A follower of Islam.

Mycenaean (meye-seh-NEE-uhn) Early Greek society on the Peloponnese (1600–1100 B.C.E.) that was influenced by the Minoans; the Mycenaeans' conflict with Troy is immortalized in Homer's *Odyssey*.

Nara era Japanese period (710–794), centered on the city of Nara, that was the highest point of Chinese influence.

National Policy Nineteenth-century Canadian policy designed to attract migrants, protect industries through tariffs, and build national transportation systems.

NATO The North Atlantic Treaty Organization, which was established by the United States in 1949 as a regional military alliance against Soviet expansionism.

Ndongo (n'DAWN-goh) Angolan kingdom that reached its peak during the reign of Queen Nzinga (r. 1623–1663).

Neandertal (nee-ANN-duhr-tawl) Early humans (100,000 to 35,000 years ago) who were prevalent during the Paleolithic period.

Negritude (NEH-grih-tood) "Blackness," a term coined by early African nationalists as a means of celebrating the heritage of black peoples around the world.

Neo-Confucianism (nee-oh-kuhn-FYOO-shuhn-iz'm) Philosophy that attempted to merge certain basic elements of Confucian and Buddhist thought; most important of the early Neo-Confucianists was the Chinese thinker Zhu Xi (1130–1200).

Neolithic New Stone Age (10,000–4000 B.C.E.), which was marked by the discovery and mastery of agriculture.

Nestorian (neh-STOHR-ee-uhn) Early branch of Christianity, named after the fifth-century Greek theologian Nestorius, that emphasized the human nature of Jesus Christ.

New Economic Policy (NEP) Plan implemented by Lenin that called for minor free-market reforms.

Nirvana (nuhr-VAH-nuh) Buddhist concept of a state of spiritual perfection and enlightenment in which distracting passions are eliminated.

Noble Eightfold Path Final truth of the Buddhist Four Noble Truths that called for leading a life of balance and constant contemplation.

North American Free Trade Agreement (NAFTA) Regional accord established in 1993 between the United States, Canada, and Mexico; it formed world's second largest free-trade zone.

Nubia (NOO-bee-uh) Area south of Egypt; the kingdom of Kush in Nubia invaded and dominated Egypt from 750 to 664 B.C.E.

Oceania Term referring to the Pacific Ocean basin and its lands.

Olmecs Early Mesoamerican society (1200–100 B.C.E.) that centered on sites at San Lorenzo, La Venta, and Tres Zapotes and that influenced later Maya.

Oracle bones Chinese Shang dynasty (1766–1122 B.C.E.) means of foretelling the future.

Organization of African Unity (OAU) An organization started in 1963 by thirty-two newly independent African states and designed to prevent conflict that would lead to intervention by former colonial powers.

Organization of Petroleum Exporting Countries (OPEC) An organization begun in 1960 by oil-producing states originally for purely economic reasons but that later had more political influence.

Osiris Ancient Egyptian god that represented the forces of nature.

Ottoman empire Powerful Turkish empire that lasted from the conquest of Constantinople (Istanbul) in 1453 until 1918 and reached its peak during the reign of Süleyman the Magnificent (r. 1520–1566).

Paleolithic Old Stone Age, a long period of human development before the development of agriculture.

Palestinian Liberation Organization (PLO) Organization created in 1964 under the leadership of Yasser Arafat to champion Palestinian rights.

Paris Peace Accords Agreement reached in 1973 that marked the end of the United States' role in the Vietnam War.

Parsis (pahr-SEES) Indian Zoroastrians.

Parthians Persian dynasty (247 B.C.E.–224 C.E.) that reached its peak under Mithradates I.

Pater familias (PAH-tur fuh-MEE-lee-ahs) Roman term for the "father of the family," a theoretical implication that gave the male head of the family almost unlimited authority.

Patriarch (PAY-tree-ahrk) Leader of the Greek Orthodox church, which in 1054 officially split with the Pope and the Roman Catholic church.

Patricians Roman aristocrats and wealthy classes.

Pax Romana (pahks roh-MAH-nah) "Roman Peace," a term that relates to the period of political stability, cultural brilliance, and economic prosperity beginning with unification under Augustus and lasting through the first two centuries C.E.

Peninsulares (pehn-IHN-soo-LAH-rayz) Latin American officials from Spain or Portugal.

Perestroika (PAYR-eh-stroy-kuh) "Restructuring," a Russian term associated with Gorbachev's effort to reorganize the Soviet state.

Pharaohs (FARE-ohs) Egyptian kings considered to be gods on earth.

Plebians (plih-BEE-uhns) Roman common people.

Polis (POH-lihs) Greek term for the city-state.

Popol Vuh (paw-pawl vuh) Mayan creation epic.

Prehistory The period before the invention of writing.

Proletariat Urban working class in a modern industrial society.

Protestant Reformation Sixteenth-century European movement during which Luther, Calvin, Zwingli, and others broke away from the Catholic church.

Ptolemaic (TAWL-oh-may-ihk) Term used to signify both the Egyptian kingdom founded by Alexander the Great's general Ptolemy and the thought of the philosopher Ptolemy of Alexandria (second century C.E.), who used mathematical formulas in an attempt to prove Aristotle's geocentric theory of the universe.

Putting-out system Method of getting around guild control by delivering unfinished materials to rural households for completion.

Qadi Islamic judge.

Qanat (kah-NAHT) Persian underground canal.

Qi (chee) Chinese concept of the basic material that makes up the body and the universe.

Qin (chihn) Chinese dynasty (221–207 B.C.E.) that was founded by Qin Shihuangdi and was marked by the first unification of China and the early construction of defensive walls.

Qing (chihng) Chinese dynasty (1644–1911) that reached its peak during the reigns of Kangxi and Qianlong.

Qizilbash (gih-ZIHL-bahsh) Term meaning "red heads," Turkish tribes that were important allies of Shah Ismail in the formation of the Safavid empire.

Quetzalcoatl (keht-zahl-koh-AHT'l) Aztec god, the "feathered serpent," who was borrowed originally from the Toltecs; Quetzalcoatl was believed to have been defeated by another god and exiled, and he promised to return.

Quinto (KEEN-toh) The one-fifth of Mexican and Peruvian silver production that was reserved for the Spanish monarchy.

Quipu (KEE-poo) Incan mnemonic aid comprised of different-colored strings and knots that served to record events in the absence of a written text.

Quran (koo-RAHN) Islamic holy book that is believed to contain the divine revelations of Allah as presented to Muhammad.

Ramayana (rah-mah-yah-nah) Ancient Indian masterpiece about the hero Rama that symbolized the victory of *dharma* (order) over *adharma* (chaos).

Rape of Nanjing Japanese conquest and destruction of the Chinese city of Nanjing in the 1930s.

Realpolitik (ray-AHL-poh-lih-teek) The Prussian Otto von Bismarck's "politics of reality," the belief that only the willingness to use force would actually bring about change.

Reconquista (ray-kohn-KEE-stah) Crusade, ending in 1492, to drive the Islamic forces out of Spain.

Reconstruction System implemented in the American South (1867–1877) that was designed to bring the Confederate states back into the union and also extend civil rights to freed slaves.

Romanov (ROH-mah-nahv) Russian dynasty (1610–1917) founded by Mikhail Romanov and ending with Nicholas II.

Rubaiyat (ROO-bee-aht) "Quatrains," famous poetry of Omar Khayyam that was later translated by Edward Fitzgerald.

Safavid (SAH-fah-vihd) Later Persian empire (1501–1722) that was founded by Shah Ismail and that became a center for Shiism; the empire reached its peak under Shah Abbas the Great and was centered on the capital of Isfahan.

Sakk Letters of credit that were common in the medieval Islamic banking world.

Saljuqs (sahl-JYOOKS) Turkish tribe that gained control over the Abbasid empire and fought with the Byzantine empire.

Samsara (sahm-SAH-ruh) Hindu term for the concept of transmigration, that is, the soul passing into a new incarnation.

Samurai (SAM-uhr-eye) A Japanese warrior.

Sasanids (suh-SAH-nids) Later powerful Persian dynasty (224–651) that would reach its peak under Shapur I and later fall to Arabic expansion.

Sati (SUH-TEE) Also known as *suttee,* Indian practice of a widow throwing herself on the funeral pyre of her husband.

Satraps (SAY-traps) Persian administrators, usually members of the royal family, who governed a satrapy.

Satyagraha (SAH-tyah-GRAH-hah) "Truth and firmness," a term associated with Gandhi's policy of passive resistance.

Scholasticism Medieval attempt of thinkers such as St. Thomas Aquinas to merge the beliefs of Christianity with the logical rigor of Greek philosophy.

Scientific racism Nineteenth-century attempt to justify racism by scientific means; an example would be Gobineau's *Essay on the Inequality of the Human Races.*

Seleucids (sih-LOO-sihds) Persian empire (323–83 B.C.E.) founded by Seleucus after the death of Alexander the Great.

Self-determination Belief popular in World War I and after that every people should have the right to determine their own political destiny; the belief was often cited but ignored by the Great Powers.

Self-Strengthening Movement Chinese attempt (1860–1895) to blend Chinese cultural traditions with European industrial technology.

Semitic (suh-miht-ihk) A term that relates to the Semites, ancient nomadic herders who spoke Semitic languages; examples of Semites were the Akkadians, Hebrews, Aramaics, and Phoenicians, who often interacted with the more settled societies of Mesopotamia and Egypt.

Sepoys Indian troops who served the British.

Serfs Peasants who, though not chattel slaves, were tied to the land and who owed obligation to the lords on whose land they worked.

Shamanism (SHAH-mah-niz'm) Belief in shamans or religious specialists who possessed supernatural powers and who communicated with the gods and the spirits of nature.

Shari'a (shah-REE-ah) The Islamic holy law, drawn up by theologians from the Quran and accounts of Muhammad's life.

Shia (SHEE-ah) Islamic minority in opposition to the Sunni majority; their belief is that leadership should reside in the line descended from Ali.

Shintoism (SHIHN-toh-iz'm) Indigenous Japanese religion that emphasizes purity, clan loyalty, and the divinity of the emperor.

Shiva (SHEE-vuh) Hindu god associated with both fertility and destruction.

Shogun (SHOH-gun) Japanese military leader who ruled in place of the emperor.

Shudras (SHOO-druhs) Hindu caste of landless peasants and serfs.

Siddhartha Gautama (sih-DHAR-tuh GOW-tau-mah) Indian *kshatriya* who achieved enlightenment and became known as the Buddha, the founder of Buddhism.

Sikhs (SIHKS) Adherents of an Indian syncretic faith that contains elements of Hinduism and Islam.

Silk roads Ancient trade routes that extended from the Mediterranean in the west to China in the east.

Social Darwinism Nineteenth-century philosophy, championed by thinkers such as Herbert Spencer, that attempted to apply Darwinian "survival of the fittest" to the social and political realm; adherents saw the elimination of weaker nations as part of a natural process and used the philosophy to justify war.

Socialism Political and economic theory of social organization based on the collective ownership of the means of production; its origins were in the early nineteenth century, and it differs from communism by a desire for slow or moderate change compared with the communist call for revolution.

Solidarity Polish trade union and nationalist movement in the 1980s that was headed by Lech Walesa.

Song (SOHNG) Chinese dynasty (960–1279) that was marked by an increasingly urbanized and cosmopolitan society.

Soviets Russian elected councils that originated as strike committees during the 1905 St. Petersburg disorders; they represented a form of local self-government that went on to become the primary unit of government in the Union of Soviet Socialist Republics. The term was also used during the cold war to designate the Soviet Union.

Spanish Inquisition Institution organized in 1478 by Fernando and Isabel of Spain to detect heresy and the secret practice of Judaism or Islam.

Srivijaya (sree-VIH-juh-yuh) Southeast Asian kingdom (670–1025), based on the island of Sumatra, that used a powerful navy to dominate trade.

Stateless societies Term relating to societies such as those of sub-Saharan Africa after the Bantu migrations that featured decentralized rule through family and kinship groups instead of strongly centralized hierarchies.

Stoics (STOH-ihks) Hellenistic philosophers who encouraged their followers to lead active, virtuous lives and to aid others.

Strabo (STRAH-boh) Greek geographer (first century C.E.).

Strategic Arms Limitations Talk (SALT) Agreement in 1972 between the United States and the Soviet Union.

Stupas (STOO-pahs) Buddhist shrines.

Sufis (SOO-fees) Islamic mystics who placed more emphasis on emotion and devotion than on strict adherence to rules.

Sui (SWAY) Chinese dynasty (589–618) that constructed the Grand Canal, reunified China, and allowed for the splendor of the Tang dynasty that followed.

Süleyman (SOO-lee-mahn) Ottoman Turkish ruler Süleyman the Magnificent (r. 1520–1566), who was the most powerful and wealthy ruler of the sixteenth century.

Sumerians (soo-MEHR-ee-uhns) Earliest Mesopotamian society.

Sundiata (soon-JAH-tuh) Founder of the Mali empire (r. 1230–1255), also the inspiration for the *Sundiata,* an African literary and mythological work.

Sunni (SOON-nee) "Traditionalists," the most popular branch of Islam; Sunnis believe in the legitimacy of the early caliphs, compared with the Shiite belief that only a descendant of Ali can lead.

Suu Kyi, Aung San (SOO KEY, AWNG SAHN) Opposition leader (1945–) in Myanmar; she was elected leader in 1990 but she was not allowed to come to power; she was a Nobel Peace Prize recipient in 1991.

Swahili (swah-HEE-lee) East African city-state society that dominated the coast from Mogadishu to Kilwa and was active in trade.

Taino (TEYE-noh) A Caribbean tribe who were the first indigenous peoples from the Americas to come into contact with Christopher Columbus.

Taiping rebellion (TEYE-pihng) Rebellion (1850–1864) in Qing China led by Hong Xiuquan, during which twenty to thirty million were killed; the rebellion was symbolic of the decline of China during the nineteenth century.

Taliban Strict Islamic organization that ruled Afghanistan from 1996 to 2002.

Tang Taizong (TAHNG TEYE-zohng) Chinese emperor (r. 627–649) of the Tang dynasty (618–907).

Tanzimat "Reorganization" era (1839–1876), an attempt to reorganize the Ottoman empire on Enlightenment and constitutional forms.

Temüjin (TEM-oo-chin) Mongol conqueror (ca. 1167–1227) who later took the name Chinggis Khan, "universal ruler."

Tenochtitlan (the-NOCH-tee-tlahn) Capital of the Aztec empire, later Mexico City.

Teotihuacan (tay-uh-tee-wah-KAHN) Central American society (200 B.C.E.–750 C.E.); its Pyramid of the Sun was the largest structure in Mesoamerica.

Teutonic Knights Crusading European order that was active in the Baltic region.

Third Rome Concept that a new power would rise up to carry the legacy of Roman greatness after the decline of the Second Rome, Constantinople; Moscow was referred to as the Third Rome during the fifteenth century.

Three Principles of the People Philosophy of Chinese Guomindang leader Sun Yatsen (1866–1925) that emphasized nationalism, democracy, and people's livelihood.

Tian (TEE-ehn) Chinese term for heaven.

Tikal (tee-KAHL) Maya political center from the fourth through the ninth century.

Timur-i lang (tee-MOOR-yee LAHNG) "Timur the Lame," known in English as Tamerlane (ca. 1336–1405), who conquered an empire ranging from the Black Sea to Samarkand.

Tokugawa (TOH-koo-GAH-wah) Last shogunate in Japanese history (1600–1867); it was founded by Tokugawa Ieyasu who was notable for unifying Japan.

Toltecs Central American society (950–1150) that was centered on the city of Tula.

Trail of Tears Forced relocation of the Cherokee from the eastern woodlands to Oklahoma (1837–1838); it was symbolic of U.S. expansion and destruction of indigenous Indian societies.

Triangular trade Trade between Europe, Africa, and the Americas that featured finished products from Europe, slaves from Africa, and American products bound for Europe.

Triple Alliance Pre–World War I alliance of Germany, Austria-Hungary, and Italy.

Triple Entente (ahn-TAHNT) Pre–World War I alliance of England, France, and Russia.

Truman Doctrine U.S. policy instituted in 1947 by President Harry Truman in which the United States would follow an interventionist foreign policy to contain communism.

Tsar (ZAHR) Old Russian term for king that is derived from the term *caesar.*

Twelver Shiism (SHEE'i'zm) Branch of Islam that stressed that there were twelve perfect religious leaders after Muhammad and that the twelfth went into hiding and would return someday; Shah Ismail spread this variety through the Safavid empire.

Uighurs (WEE-goors) Turkish tribe.

Ukiyo Japanese word for the "floating worlds," a Buddhist term for the insignificance of the world that came to represent the urban centers in Tokugawa Japan.

Ulaanbaatar (OO-lahn-bah-tahr) Mongolian city.

Ulama Islamic officials, scholars who shaped public policy in accordance with the Quran and the *sharia.*

Umayyad (oo-MEYE-ahd) Arabic dynasty (661–750), with its capital at Damascus, that was marked by a tremendous period of expansion to Spain in the west and India in the east.

Umma (UM-mah) Islamic term for the "community of the faithful."

United Nations (UN) Successor to the League of Nations, an association of sovereign nations that attempts to find solutions to global problems.

Upanishads (oo-PAHN-ee-shahds) Indian reflections and dialogues (800–400 B.C.E.) that reflected basic Hindu concepts.

Urdu (OOR-doo) A language that is predominant in Pakistan.

Uruk (OO-rook) Ancient Mesopotamian city from the fourth millennium B.C.E. that was allegedly the home of the fabled Gilgamesh.

Vaishyas (VEYES-yuhs) Hindu caste of cultivators, artisans, and merchants.

Vaqueros (vah-KEHR-ohs) Latin American cowboys, similar to the Argentine gaucho.

Varna (VAHR-nuh) Hindu word for caste.

Varuna (vuh-ROO-nuh) Early Aryan god who watched over the behavior of mortals and preserved the cosmic order.

Vedas (VAY-duhs) "Wisdom," early collections of prayers and hymns that provide information about the Indo-European Aryans who migrated into India around 1500 B.C.E.; *Rig Veda* is the most important collection.

Velvet revolution A term that describes the nonviolent transfer of power in Czechoslovakia during the collapse of Soviet rule.

Venta, La (VEHN-tuh, lah) Early Olmec center (800–400 B.C.E.).

Venus figurines Small Paleolithic statues of women with exaggerated sexual features.

Vernacular (ver-NA-kyoo-lar) The language of the people; Martin Luther translated the Bible from the Latin of the Catholic church into the vernacular German.

Versailles (vehr-SEYE) Palace of French King Louis XIV.

Viet Minh North Vietnamese nationalist communists under Ho Chi Minh.

Vietnamization President Richard Nixon's strategy of turning the Vietnam War over to the South Vietnamese.

Vijayanagar (vee-juh-yah-NAH-gahr) Southern Indian kingdom (1336–1565) that later fell to the Mughals.

Vikings A group that raided the British Isles from their home at Vik in southern Norway.

Vishnu (VIHSH-noo) Hindu god, preserver of the world, who was often incarnated as Krishna.

Vodou (voh-DOW) Syncretic religion practiced by African slaves in Haiti.

Volksgeist (FOHLKS-geyest) "People's spirit," a term that was coined by the German philosopher Herder; a nation's volksgeist would not come to maturity unless people studied their own unique culture and traditions.

Volta do mar (VOHL-tah doh MAHR) "Return through the sea," a fifteenth-century Portuguese sea route that took advantage of the prevailing winds and currents.

Voltaire (vohl-TAIR) Pen name of French philosophe François-Marie Arouet (1694–1778), author of *Candide.*

Waldensians Twelfth-century religious reformers who criticized the Roman Catholic church and who proposed that the laity had the right to preach and administer sacraments; they were declared heretics.

Walesa, Lech (WAH-lehn-sah, LEHK) Leader of the Polish Solidarity movement.

Wanli (wahn-LEE) Chinese Ming emperor (r. 1572–1620) whose refusal to meet with officials hurried the decline of the Ming dynasty.

War Communism The Bolshevik policy of nationalizing industry and seizing private land during the civil war.

Warsaw Pact Warsaw Treaty Organization, a military alliance formed by Soviet bloc nations in 1955 in response to rearmament of West Germany and its inclusion in NATO.

Wind wheels Prevailing wind patterns in the Atlantic and Pacific Oceans north and south of the equator; their discovery made sailing much safer and quicker.

Witte, Sergei (VIHT-tee, SAYR-gay) Late-nineteenth-century Russian minister of finance who pushed for industrialization.

World Health Organization (WHO) United Nations organization designed to deal with global health issues.

World Trade Organization (WTO) An organization that was established in 1995 with more than 120 nations and whose goal is to loosen barriers to free trade.

Wuwei (woo-WAY) Daoist concept of a disengagement from the affairs of the world.

Xia (shyah) Early Chinese dynasty (2200–1766 B.C.E.).

Xianyang (SHYAHN-YAHNG) Capital city of the Qin empire.

Xiao (SHAYOH) Confucian concept of respect for one's parents and ancestors.

Xinjiang (shin-jyahng) Western Chinese province.

Xuanzang (SHWEN-ZAHNG) Seventh-century Chinese monk who made a famous trip to India to collect Buddhist texts.

Yahweh (YAH-way) God of the monotheistic religion of Judaism that influenced later Christianity and Islam.

Yangshao (YAHNG-show) Early Chinese society (2500–2200 B.C.E.).

Yangzi (YAHNG-zuh) River in central China.

Yongle (YAWNG-leh) Chinese Ming emperor (r. 1403–1424) who pushed for foreign exploration and promoted cultural achievements such as the *Yongle Encyclopedia.*

Young Turks Nineteenth-century Turkish reformers who pushed for changes within the Ottoman empire, such as universal suffrage and freedom of religion.

Yu (yoo) Legendary founder of the Xia dynasty (ca. 2200 B.C.E.).

Yuan (yoo-AHN) Chinese dynasty (1279–1368) that was founded by the Mongol ruler Khubilai Khan.

Yucatan (yoo-kuh-TAN) Peninsula in Central America, home of the Maya.

Yurts (yuhrts) Tents used by nomadic Turkish and Mongol tribes.

Zaibatsu (zeye-BAHT-soo) Japanese term for "wealthy cliques," which are similar to American trusts and cartels but usually organized around one family.

Zambos (ZAHM-bohs) Latin American term for individuals born of indigenous and African parents.

Zamudio, Adela (ZAH-moo-dee-oh, ah-DEH-lah) Nineteenth-century Bolivian poet, author of "To Be Born a Man."

Zarathustra (zar-uh-THOO-struh) Persian prophet (ca. sixth century B.C.E.) who founded Zoroastrianism.

Zemstvos (ZEHMST-voh) District assemblies elected by Russians in the nineteenth century.

Zen Buddhism Japanese version of Chinese Chan Buddhism, with an emphasis on intuition and sudden flashes of insight instead of textual study.

Zhou (JOH) Chinese dynasty (1122–256 B.C.E.) that was the foundation of Chinese thought formed during this period: Confucianism, Daoism, Zhou Classics.

Zhu Xi (ZHOO-SHEE) Neo-Confucian Chinese philosopher (1130–1200).

Ziggurats (ZIG-uh-rahts) Mesopotamian temples.

Zimbabwe (zihm-BAHB-way) Former colony of Southern Rhodesia that gained independence in 1980.

Zoroastrianism (zohr-oh-ASS-tree-ahn-iz'm) Persian religion based on the teaching of the sixth-century-B.C.E. prophet Zarathustra; its emphasis on the duality of good and evil and on the role of individuals in determining their own fate would influence later religions.

credits

PART 1

Photo Credits p. 2L, Courtesy Ministere de la Culture et de la Communication, Direction Régionale des Affaires Culturelles de Rhône-Alpes, Service Régional de Archéologie; **p. 2ML,** © Erich Lessing/Art Resource, NY; **p. 2MR,** © James Morris/Art Resource, NY; **p. 2R,** © Josephine Powell photograph, courtesy of Photograph Collections, Fine Arts Library, Harvard College Library.; **p. 3L,** © Bridgeman-Giraudon/Art Resource, NY; **p. 3R,** © SEF/Art Resource, NY.

CHAPTER 1

Text Credits p. 11, From *The Making of Mankind* by Richard E. Leakey (Michael Joseph, 1981). Copyright © Sherma B.V. 1981. Reprinted with permission of Richard E. Leakey. **Photo Credits p. 4,** Courtesy Ministere de la Culture et de la Communication, Direction Régionale des Affaires Culturelles de Rhône-Alpes, Service Régional de Archéologie; **p. 7,** © John Reader/Photo Researchers, Inc.; **p. 12T,** © Damian Andrus/Maxwell Museum, University of New Mexico; **p. 12B,** © The Field Museum, Neg. #76851c; **p. 13,** © Victor Boswell/NGS Image Collection; **p. 14,** © Charles & Josette Lenars/Corbis; **p. 15T,** © Francois Ducasse/Photo Researchers, Inc.; **pp. 15B, 16,** © Erich Lessing/Art Resource, NY; **p. 20,** © Arlette Mellaart; **p. 21,** © Dorling Kindersley/Getty Images.

CHAPTER 2

Text Credits p. 36, Pritchard, James B.: *Ancient Near Eastern Texts Relating to the Old Testament.* © 1950 Princeton University Press, 1978 renewed, 2nd Edition 1955, 1983 renewed PUP. Reprinted by permission of Princeton University Press. **Photo Credits p. 24,** © Erich Lessing/Art Resource, NY; **p. 28,** © Georg Gerster/Photo Researchers, Inc.; **p. 29,** © Iraq Museum, Baghdad/Hirmer Fotoarchiv; **p. 31,** © Réunion des Musées Nationaux/Art Resource, NY; **p. 32,** © Werner Foreman/Corbis; **p. 33,** © Nik Wheeler; **p. 34,** © The Trustees of The British Museum/Art Resource, NY; **p. 36,** © The British Museum; **p. 37,** © Bildarchiv Preussischer Kulturbesitz/Art Resource, NY; **p. 39,** © Erich Lessing/Art Resource, NY; **p. 40,** © Réunion des Musées Nationaux/Art Resource, NY; **p. 43,** © ullstein bild - Archiv Gerstenberg/The Image Works; **p. 46,** © DeA Picture Library/Art Resource, NY.

CHAPTER 3

Text Credits p. 56, Miriam Lichtheim, ed., *Ancient Egyptian Literature,* Volume I: *The Old and Middle Kingdoms,* Copyright © 1973 Regents of the University of California. Published by the University of California Press. Used by permission of the Regents of the University of California; **p. 64,** Miriam Lichtheim, ed., *Ancient Egyptian Literature,* Volume I: *The Old and Middle Kingdoms,* Copyright © 1973 Regents of the University of California. Published by the University of California Press. Used by permission of the Regents of the University of California. **Photo Credits p. 48,** © James Morris/Art Resource, NY; **p. 52,** © Erich Lessing/Art Resource, NY; **p. 53,** © Werner Forman/Art Resource, NY; **p. 54,** Stela of the Nubian soldier Nenu, Egypt (Geblein), about 2130–1980 BC First Intermediate Period; Limestone, painted: 14 5/8 × 17 3/4 in. (37.1 × 45 cm). Purchased by A.M. Lythgoe, 03.1848. Courtesy, Museum of Fine Arts, Boston. Reproduced with permission. © 2010 Museum of Fine Arts, Boston. All rights reserved.; **p. 57,** © Robert Partridge/The Ancient Egypt Picture Library; **p. 58,** © The British Museum, London/Bridgeman Art Library; **p. 60T,** © Michael Holford; **p. 60B,** © Werner Foreman/Art Resource, NY; **p. 61,** © HIP/Art Resource, NY; **p. 62,** © Erich Lessing/Art Resource, NY; **p. 65T,** © The British Museum, London/Bridgeman Art Library; **p. 65B,** © Bildarchiv Preussischer Kulturbesitz/Art Resource, NY.

CHAPTER 4

Text Credits p. 82, From *The Upanishads,* translated by Juan Mascaró (Penguin Classics, 1965). Copyright © Juan Mascaró, 1965. **Photo Credits p. 70,** © Josephine Powell photograph, courtesy of Photograph Collections, Fine Arts Library, Harvard College Library.; **p. 74,** © MacQuitty International Collection; **p. 75T,** © National Museum of India, New Delhi, India/The Bridgeman Art Library; **p. 75B,** © National Museum of India, New Delhi/Bridgeman Art Library; **p. 77,** © The British Museum; **p. 80,** Digital Image © 2009 Museum Associates/LACMA/Art Resource, NY; **p. 81,** © The British Library; **p. 83,** © V.I. Thayil/DPA/VIT/The Image Works.

CHAPTER 5

Photo Credits p. 86, © Bridgeman-Giraudon/Art Resource, NY; **p. 89,** Cultural Relics Publishing House, Beijing; **p. 91,** © ChinaStock; **p. 92,** © 1995 Wang Lu/ChinaStock; **p. 92,** © Wang Lu/ChinaStock; **p. 93,** Cultural Relics Publishing House, Beijing; **p. 94,** © The British Museum; **p. 96,** Ritual vessel (chia), Chinese, Shang Dynasty, 12th century BC, Bronze, 52.8 × 30.5 cm. Freer Gallery of Art, Smithsonian Institution, Washington, DC: Purchase F1923.1; **p. 97,** Wang-go Wen, Inc.; **p. 98,** Cultural Relics Publishing House, Beijing; **p. 100,** © Werner Foreman Archive/Art Resource, NY; **p. 103,** © Keren Su/Corbis.

CHAPTER 6

Text Credits p. 122, Low, Drury, and Timi Koro, "The Story of Ru's Canoe and the Discovery and Settlement of Aitutaki," *Journal of the Polynesian Society* 43 (1934): 17–24. Reprinted by permission of The Polynesian Society, University of Auckland. **Photo Credits p. 106,** © SEF/Art Resource, NY; **p. 110,** © Andrew Rakaczy/Photo Researchers, Inc.; **p. 111,** Courtesy Department of Library Services, American Museum of Natural History, Neg. #1298(3).

Photo by Denis Finnin; **p. 112,** © Paul C. Pet/Corbis; **p. 113,** © SEF/Art Resource, NY; **p. 114,** © Justin Kerr; **p. 116T,** Courtesy Arthur A. Demarest; **p. 116B,** © Robert Frerck/Stone/Getty Images; **p. 119,** © ÖNB/Vienna, F4213, p. 148; **p. 121,** © John Noble/Corbis; **p. 122T,** © The British Library (ADD. 23921 fol. 20); **p. 122B,** © Carl Bento/The Australian Museum; **p. 126L,** © PhotoLink/Getty Images; **p. 126ML,** © Digital Vision/PunchStock; **p. 126MR,** © ImageShop/Corbis; **p. 126R,** © Digital Vision Ltd./Getty Images.

PART 2

Photo Credits p. 128L, © Erich Lessing/Art Resource, NY; **p. 128ML,** Bibliotheque Nationale, Paris, France/© The Bridgeman Art Library; **p. 128MR,** © Borromeo/Art Resource, NY; **p. 128R,** © Erich Lessing/Art Resource, NY; **p. 129L,** © Scala/Art Resource, NY; **p. 129R,** © Getty Images

CHAPTER 7

Photo Credits p. 130, © Erich Lessing/Art Resource, NY; **p. 134,** © Oriental Institute Museum, University of Chicago; **p. 135,** © Fred J. Maroon/Photo Researchers, Inc.; **p. 136,** © Oriental Institute Museum, University of Chicago; **p. 137,** Courtesy Museum of Fine Arts, Boston. Reproduced with permission. Gift of Mrs. George M. Brett. © 2010 Museum of Fine Arts, Boston. All rights reserved.; **p. 138,** The State Hermitage Museum, St. Petersburg, Russia; **p. 140,** © Fred J. Maroon/Photo Researchers, Inc.; **p. 141,** © Oriental Institute Museum, University of Chicago; **p. 143,** The State Hermitage Museum, St. Petersburg, Russia; **p. 145,** © HIP/Art Resource, NY.

CHAPTER 8

Photo Credits p. 148, Bibliotheque Nationale, Paris, France/© The Bridgeman Art Library; **p. 151,** © akg-images; **p. 154,** © Burstein Collection/Corbis; **p. 157,** © O. Louis Mazzatenta/NGS Image Collection; **p. 158,** © Rolf Richardson/Alamy; **p. 160,** © ChinaStock; **p. 163,** The Nelson-Atkins Museum of Art, Kansas City, Missouri, Purchase: Nelson Trust; **p. 164T,** Tales from History and Legends (detail: single male figure), late 1st century BC China; Western Han Dynasty. Hollow tiles of a tomb lintel and pediment; ink and color on whitened ground. Total 73.8 × 204.7 cm. Denman Waldo Ross Collection. 25.10–13. Courtesy Museum of Fine Arts, Boston. Reproduced with permission. © 2010 Museum of Fine Arts, Boston. All rights reserved.; **p. 164B,** © Erich Lessing/Art Resource, NY; **p. 165,** Wang-go Wen, Inc.; **p. 166,** Cultural Relics Publishing House, Beijing.

CHAPTER 9

Text Credits p. 183, Strong, John S., *The Legend of King Asoka.* © 1983 Princeton University Press. Reprinted by permission of Princeton University Press. **Photo Credits p. 168,** © Borromeo/Art Resource, NY; **p. 172,** Sarnath, Uttar Pradesh, India/© The Bridgeman Art Library; **p. 173,** © The British Library; **p. 174,** Buddha, Coin of Kaniska, 2nd century AD, India, gold. Seth K. Sweetser Fund. Courtesy Museum of Fine Arts, Boston. (31.895). Reproduced with permission. © 2010 Museum of Fine Arts, Boston. All rights reserved.; **p. 175,** © Borromeo/Art Resource, NY; **p. 176,** The Art Archive; **p. 177,** © SEF/Art Resource, NY; **p. 178,** © The British Museum; **p. 179,** © Lindsay Hebberd/Corbis; **p. 181,** Foto Features; **p. 182,** © Borromeo/Art Resource, NY; **p. 184,** Pakistan, Gandharan region, A Bodhisattva, 2nd/3rd century, Gray Schist, 150.5 × 53.3 × 19 cm (59 1/4 × 21 × 7 1/2 in.), The James W. and Marilynn Alsdorf Collection, 198.1997, The Art Institute of Chicago. Photography © The Art Institute of Chicago.

CHAPTER 10

Text Credits p. 199, From *The Campaigns of Alexander* by Arrian, translated by Aubrey de Sélincourt, revised by J.R. Hamilton (Penguin Classics 1958, Revised edition 1971). Copyright © the Estate of Aubrey de Sélincourt, 1958, 1971. **Photo Credits pp. 188, 190,** © Erich Lessing/Art Resource, NY; **p. 191,** © Walter S. Clark/Photo Researchers, Inc.; **p. 193,** © Réunion des Musées Nationaux/Art Resource, NY; **p. 194,** © Scala/Art Resource, NY; **p. 195,** © The British Museum; **p. 197T,** © Corbis; **p. 197B,** © C.M. Dixon/Ancient Art & Architecture Collection; **pp. 202, 203, 204,** © The British Museum; **p. 206,** © Corbis.

CHAPTER 11

Text Credits p. 220, From *The Annals of Imperial Rome* by Tacitus, translated by Michael Grant (Penguin Classics 1956, Sixth revised edition 1989). Copyright © Michael Grant Publications Ltd, 1956, 1956, 1971, 1973, 1975, 1977, 1989. **Photo Credits p. 210,** © Scala/Art Resource, NY; **p. 213,** © Hirmer Fotoarchiv; **p. 214,** © David Epperson/Photographer's Choice/Getty Images; **p. 216T,** © C.M. Dixon/Ancient Art & Architecture Collection; **p. 216B,** © Vatican Museum/Robert Harding Picture Library; **pp. 217, 221, 222,** © Erich Lessing/Art Resource, NY; **p. 223,** © Michael Holford; **p. 224T,** © C.M. Dixon/Ancient Art & Architecture Collection; **p. 224B,** © Alinari/Art Resource, NY; **p. 225,** © Scala/Art Resource, NY; **p. 226,** © Alinari/Art Resource, NY.

CHAPTER 12

Photo Credits p. 232, © Getty Images; **p. 235,** Stair-riser with Parthian men, Pakistan, Gandharan school. With permission of the Royal Ontario Museum. © ROM (939.17.19); **p. 236,** Cultural Relics Publishing House, Beijing; **p. 238T,** © The British Museum; **p. 238B,** With permission of the Royal Ontario Museum. © ROM (910.159.644); **p. 239,** © Scala/Art Resource, NY; **p. 240,** © akg-images; **p. 242,** © Bildarchiv Preussischer Kulturbesitz/Art Resource, NY; **p. 246,** Cultural Relics Publishing House, Beijing; **p. 247,** © Michael Holford; **p. 249,** © Deutsches Archaeologisches Institut, Rome; **p. 250,** © Erich Lessing/Art Resource, NY; **p. 251,** © Ancient Art & Architecture Collection; **p. 254L,** PIXFOLIO/Alamy; **p. 254ML,** PhotoDisc/Getty Images; **p. 254MR,** Anton Robert/Getty Images; **p. 254R,** © S. Stoltzfuss/Iconotec.

PART 3

Photo Credits p. 256L, © The British Library (Ms. add. 27261, f. 363a); **p. 256ML,** © Bibliotheque Nationale, Paris, France/Lauros/Giraudon/The Bridgeman Art Library; **p. 256MR,** © The British Museum; **p. 256R,** © Erich Lessing/Art Resource, NY.

CHAPTER 13

Text Credits p. 263, *Al-Qur'an: A Contemporary Translation.* Trans. By Ahmed Ali. Princeton University Press, 1984; **p. 276,** Al-Muqaddasi, *The Best Divisions for Knowledge of the Regions.* Trans. by Basil Anthony Collins. Reading: Garnet, 1994. **Photo Credits p. 258,** © The British Library (Ms. add. 27261, f. 363a); **p. 261,** © Robert Harding Picture Library; **p. 262,** Reproduced by kind permission of the Trustees of the Chester Beatty Library, Dublin; **p. 264,** © Art Resource, NY; **p. 267,** © Salmer Imagen; **p. 269T,** © Art Resource, NY; **p. 269B,** © akg-images; **p. 270,** The Art Archive/Bodleian Library Oxford; **p. 271,** © akg-images; **p. 272,** © Benjamin Rondel; **p. 273,** Bibliotheque

Nationale, Paris, France/Archives Charmet/The Bridgeman Art Library; **p. 274,** Sultan Muhammad. Heavenly and Earthly Drunkenness (painting, recto), folio from a Divan of Hafiz, c. 1526–1527. Ink, color, gold and silver on paper; actual 28.7 × 35.5 cm (11⁵⁄₁₆ × 14 in.) Harvard Art Museums, Arthur M. Sackler Museum, Promised Gift of Mr. and Mrs. Stuart Cary Welch, Jr. Partially owned by the Metropolitan Museum of Art and the Arthur M. Sackler Museum, Harvard University, 1988. In honor of the students of Harvard University and Radcliffe College, 1988.460.3. Art © Dedalus Foundation, Inc./Licensed by VAGA, New York, NY. Photo: Allan Macintyre © President and Fellows of Harvard College; **p. 275,** The Art Archive/University Library Istanbul/Gianni Dagli Orti; **p. 277,** © Topkapi Palace Museum, Istanbul, Turkey/The Bridgeman Art Library.

CHAPTER 14

Text Credits p. 286, "A Song of War Chariots" by Du Fu, from *Anthology of Chinese Literature,* Vol. 1, edited by Cyril Birch, copyright © 1965 by Grove Press, Inc. Used by permission of Grove/Atlantic, Inc. **Photo Credits p. 280,** © Bibliotheque Nationale, Paris, France/Lauros/Giraudon/The Bridgeman Art Library; **p. 284,** © Dean Conger/Corbis; **p. 285,** Cultural Relics Publishing House, Beijing; **p. 288,** Freer Gallery of Art, Smithsonian Institution, Washington, DC, Purchase, F1954.21 detail; **p. 289,** © The Granger Collection, New York; **p. 291,** © The British Library (OR. 8210 fol. 2); **p. 292,** © National Palace Museum, Taipei, Taiwan, Republic of China; **pp. 293, 295,** Cultural Relics Publishing House, Beijing; **pp. 296, 297,** © Fujita Museum of Art; **p. 300,** © Victoria & Albert Museum, London/Art Resource, NY; **p. 301,** © Museum of Fine Arts, Boston, Massachusetts, USA/Fenollosa-Weld Collection/The Bridgeman Art Library.

CHAPTER 15

Text Credits p. 319, From *Sources of Indian Tradition,* Volume 1, pp. 325–26, 328 edited by Ainslie T. Embree and Stephen Hay. © 1988 Columbia University Press. Used by permission. **Photo Credits p. 304,** © The British Museum; **p. 308,** Edinburgh University Library (Or. ms. 20, fol. 121); **p. 309,** © Macduff Everton/Corbis; **p. 310,** © DPA/NMK/The Image Works; **p. 312,** © Adam Woolfit/Robert Harding Picture Library; **p. 314,** © George Holton/Photo Researchers, Inc.; **p. 315,** © The British Library (AS10 5809); **p. 317,** © Victoria & Albert Museum, London/Art Resource, NY; **p. 318,** © The New York Public Library/Art Resource, NY; **p. 320,** © The British Library (J-55[3]); **p. 323T,** © Werner Forman/Art Resource, NY; **p. 323B,** © Alain Evrard/Photo Researchers, Inc.

CHAPTER 16

Photo Credits p. 326, © Erich Lessing/Art Resource, NY; **p. 330,** © Scala/Art Resource, NY; **p. 331,** © Robert Frerck/Odyssey; **p. 332,** © The Granger Collection, New York; **p. 333,** © Erich Lessing/Art Resource, NY; **p. 335T,** © Werner Foreman/Art Resource, NY; **p. 335B,** © The Pierpont Morgan Library/Art Resource, NY; **p. 337,** The Art Archive/Sucevita Monastery Moldavia Romania/Alfredo Dagli Orti; **p. 338,** © Biblioteca Medicia Lorenziana, Florence/Index S.A.S; **p. 340,** © Art Resource, NY; **p. 344,** © State Historical Museum, Moscow. Khkudov Psalter 129 D (f. 67). GIM 86795; **p. 345,** © Erich Lessing/Art Resource, NY; **p. 346,** © The Pierpont Morgan Library/Art Resource, NY; **p. 348L,** © Digital Vision Ltd.; **p. 348ML,** Getty Images; **p. 348MR,** © GOODSHOOT/Alamy; **p. 348R,** © Pixtal/age footstock.

PART 4

Photo Credits p. 350L, © National Palace Museum, Taipei, Taiwan/The Bridgeman Art Library International; **p. 350ML,** The Metropolitan Museum of Art, Gift of Mr. and Mrs. Klaus G. Perls, 1990 (1990.332). Image copyright © The Metropolitan Museum of Art/Art Resource, NY; p. 350MR, © Bibliotheque Nationale de France, Paris (Rcc 677); p. 350R, Neg. #5004(2) Cat. No. B/1619, Courtesy Department of Library Services, American Museum of Natural History. Photo by John Bigelow Taylor; **p. 351,** © National Palace Museum, Taipei, Taiwan, Republic of China.

CHAPTER 17

Text Credits p. 356, William of Rubruck, *The Mission of Friar William of Rubruck.* Trans. by Peter Jackson. Ed. By Peter Jackson with David Morgan. London: Hakluyt Society, 1990. **Photo Credits p. 352,** © National Palace Museum, Taipei, Taiwan/The Bridgeman Art Library International; **p. 355,** © Topkapi Palace Museum, Istanbul, Turkey/The Bridgeman Art Library; **p. 357,** Cultural Relics Publishing House, Beijing; **p. 358,** © The Nasser D. Khalili Collection of Islamic Art (POT 1310); **p. 360T,** © National Palace Museum, Taipei, Taiwan, Republic of China; **p. 360B,** © Bibliotheque Nationale de France, Paris (Ms. Persan Suppl. 1113 f.49); **p. 363,** © Bibliotheque Nationale de France, Paris (Ms. Persan Suppl. 1113 f.180v); **p. 365,** © National Palace Museum, Taipei, Taiwan, Republic of China; **p. 367,** © Art Resource, NY; **p. 368,** © Bibliotheque Nationale de France, Paris (Ms. fr. 9087, v. 207 Rcc 286).

CHAPTER 18

Text Credits p. 378, From D T Niane, *Sundiata: An Epic of Old Mali,* pp. 80–82. © Pearson Education Limited, 1965. Used by permission of Pearson Education Limited; **p. 381,** H.A.R. Gibb, trans. *The Travels of Ibn Battuta,* A.D. *1325-1354.* 4 vols., Hakluyt Society, 1958–1994, vol. 2. Used by permission. **Photo Credits p. 370,** The Metropolitan Museum of Art, Gift of Mr. and Mrs. Klaus G. Perls, 1990 (1990.332). Image copyright © The Metropolitan Museum of Art/Art Resource, NY; **p. 374,** © Dirk Bakker; **p. 375,** From *Travels in North and Central America* by Heinrich Barth, 1857–58, vol. 4, plate facing pg. 404; **p. 377T,** © Werner Forman Archive/Art Resource, NY; **p. 377B,** © HIP/Art Resource, NY; **p. 380T,** © Werner Foreman Archive/Art Resource, NY; **p. 380B,** © Ariadne van Zandbergen/Africa Image Library; **p. 382,** © The British Museum; **p. 383,** © Georg Gerster/Photo Researchers, Inc.; **p. 385,** © Marc and Evelyne Bernheim/Woodfin Camp and Associates; **p. 386,** © Peter Guttman/Corbis; **p. 387,** © C.J. Lenars/Photo Researchers, Inc.

CHAPTER 19

Text Credits p. 408, Marion A. Habig, ed. *St. Francis of Assisi: Writings and Early Biographies.* English Omnibus of Sources for the Life of St. Francis. Quincy, IL: Franciscan Press, 2000, pp. 229–31, 288–92. **Photo Credits p. 390,** © Scala/Art Resource, NY; **p. 394,** © Erich Lessing/Art Resource, NY; **p. 395,** Bibliotheque Nationale, Paris, France/© The Bridgeman Art Library; **p. 396,** © Erich Lessing/Art Resource, NY; **p. 397,** © Scala/Art Resource, NY; **p. 399,** © Bodleian Library, University of Oxford (MS Bodl. 264, fol. 218r); **p. 400,** © The British Library(Add. Ms 27, 695, f. 8); **p. 403,** © Escorial Monastery, Madrid/Oroñoz; p. 404, © Bibliotheque Nationale de France, Paris (RCB 4189); **p. 405,** © Bildarchiv Preussischer Kulturbesitz/Art Resource, NY; **p. 406,** © Peter Willi, Notre-Dame Cathedral, Evreux, France/The Bridgeman Art Library; **p. 407,** © Scala/Art Resource, NY; **p. 411,** Bibliotheque

Nationale, Paris, France/© The Bridgeman Art Library; **p. 412,** © Erich Lessing/Art Resource, NY.

CHAPTER 20

Text Credits p. 420, Bernardino de Sahagún, *Florentine Codex: General History of the Things of New Spain,* 13 vols. Trans. by Arthur J. O. Anderson and Charles E. Dibble. Salt Lake City: University of Utah Press, 1950–82, 13: 19–20. Used by permission; **p. 431,** Teuira Henry and others, Dennis Kawaharada, ed., *Voyaging Chiefs of Havai'i.* Copyright 1995. pp. 138–39, 144–46. Kalamaku Press. **Photo Credits p. 414,** Neg. #5004(2) Cat. No. B/1619, Courtesy Department of Library Services, American Museum of Natural History. Photo by John Bigelow Taylor; **p. 418,** © Robert Frerck/Woodfin Camp and Associates; **p. 419,** Bodleian Library, University of Oxford (MS Arch. Selden, A.1, fol. 31r); **p. 421,** © Biblioteca Apostolica Vaticana/Index S.A.S.; **p. 422,** © Biblioteca Nazionale Centrale, Florence/Index S.A.S.; **p. 423,** © Georg Gerster/Photo Researchers, Inc.; **p. 425,** Neg. #3614(2). Courtesy Department of Library Services, American Museum of Natural History. Photo by Perkins/Becket; **pp. 426, 427,** Det Kongelige Bibliotek, Copenhagen; **p. 429,** Honolulu Academy of Arts, Gift of George R. Carter, 1927 (5945); **p. 430,** © Douglas Peebles/Corbis.

CHAPTER 21

Text Credits p. 441, H.A.R. Gibb, trans. *The Travels of Ibn Battuta, A.D. 1325–1354.* 4 vols. Hakluyt Society, 1958–1994, vol. 4. Used by permission. **Photo Credits p. 434,** © National Palace Museum, Taipei, Taiwan, Republic of China; **p. 437,** © Christine Osborne/Corbis; **p. 440,** © Art Resource, NY; **p. 444,** Biblioteca Monasterio del Escorial, Madrid, Spain/Index/The Bridgeman Art Library International; **p. 445,** © The British Library (MS 14 E IV f. 23); **p. 446,** © Bibliotheque Nationale de France, Paris (RCC9816); **p. 447,** White porcelain with under glaze blue decoration. China Ming dynasty, early 15th century. With permission of the Royal Ontatio Museum © ROM (925.25.15a-b); **p. 449,** © Scala/Art Resource, NY; **p. 450T,** © Sylvain Grandadam/Photo Researchers, Inc.; **p. 450B,** © Scala/Art Resource, NY; **p. 452,** Courtesy Ryukoku University Library; **p. 453,** © Bibliotheque Nationale, Paris, France/The Bridgeman Art Library; **p. 456,** World map engraving, 1532, Typus Comsmographicus Universalis by Münster, Sebastian. With permission of the Royal Ontario Museum © ROM (956.186.2); **p. 460L,** Library of Congress, Prints and Photographs Division (LC-USZC2-1687); **p. 460ML,** Fototeca Storica Nazionale/Getty Images; **p. 460MR,** © Creatas/PunchStock; **p. 460R,** © BananaStock/PunchStock.

PART 5

Photo Credits p. 462L, © Stapleton Collection/Corbis; **p. 462ML,** © Scala/Art Resource, NY; **p. 462MR,** Benson Latin American Collection, General Libraries, University of Texas at Austin; **p. 462R,** © National Maritime Museum, London, #A1818; **p. 463L,** Peabody Essex Museum. Photo by Mark Sexton; **p. 463R,** © Francis G. Mayer/Corbis

CHAPTER 22

Text Credits p. 474, From *Diario of Christopher Columbus's First Voyage to America,* 1492–1493, translated and edited by Oliver C. Dunn and James E. Kelley, Jr. Published by the University of Oklahoma Press, 1989. Used by permission. **Photo Credits p. 464,** © Stapleton Collection/Corbis; **p. 467,** © Bildarchiv Preussischer Kulturbesitz/Art Resource, NY ; **p. 469,** © Germanisches Nationalmuseum, Nuremberg, Germany/The Bridgeman Art Library; **p. 475,** © Stefano Bianchetti/Corbis; **p. 477T,** © HIP/Art Resource, NY; **p. 477B,** © National Maritime Museum, Greenwich, London; **p. 481,** © Maritiem Museum, Rotterdam. P-2161-31; **p. 482,** © Oregon Historical Society (OrHi 97421); **p. 486,** Peabody Museum, Harvard University (2004.24.29636); **p. 487,** © Stapleton Collection/Corbis; **p. 489,** © Bettmann/Corbis.

CHAPTER 23

Photo Credits pp. 492, 496, © Scala/Art Resource, NY; **p. 497,** © Erich Lessing/Art Resource, NY; **p. 498,** Anne S.K. Brown Military Collection, Brown University Library; **p. 501,** © Bibliotheque National de France, Paris; **p. 502,** © The Granger Collection, New York; **p. 503,** © The Art Archive/Corbis; **p. 504,** © Superstock/Getty Images; **p. 505,** © akg-images; **p. 506,** © The Art Archive/Corbis; **p. 509,** Amsterdam Historisch Museum (INV. NR.SA3025); **p. 510,** © The Granger Collection, New York; **p. 514,** © Stefano Bianchetti/Corbis; **p. 516,** © The Gallery Collection/Corbis; **pp. 517, 519,** © Erich Lessing/Art Resource, NY.

CHAPTER 24

Text Credits p. 526, Bernardino de Sahagún, *Florentine Codex: General History of the Things of New Spain,* 13 vols. Trans. By Arthur J. O. Anderson and Charles E. Dibble. Salt Lake City: University of Utah Press, 1950–82, 13:19–20. Used by permission; **p. 544,** James Cook, *The Journals of Captain Cook.* Ed. By Philip Edwards. London: Penguin, 1999. **Photo Credits p. 522,** Benson Latin American Collection, General Libraries, University of Texas at Austin; **p. 525,** © Spencer Collection, The New York Public Library, Astor, Lenox and Tilden Foundations/Art Resource, NY; **p. 528,** © The Gallery Collection/Corbis; **p. 529,** Biblioteca del ICI, Madrid, Spain/Index/The Bridgeman Art Library; **p. 532,** Courtesy of Whitehall-Robins Company, Photograph by Don Eiler; **p. 534,** © The Gallery Collection/Corbis; **p. 535,** Courtesy of the Hispanic Society of America, New York; **p. 536,** Det Kongelige Bibliothek, Copenhagen; **pp. 538, 539,** © Arents Collection, New York Public Library, Astor, Lenox and Tilden Foundations/Art Resource, NY; **p. 540,** © Christie's Images/Corbis; **p. 543,** Honolulu Academy of Arts, Gift of the Honolulu Art Society, 1944 (12,161).

CHAPTER 25

Text Credits p. 554, Basil Davidson, *The African Past.* Boston: Little, Brown, 1964. Copyright © 1964 by Basil Davidson. Reprinted by permission of Curtis Brown, Ltd. **Photo Credits p. 548,** © National Maritime Museum, London, #A1818; **p. 551,** © The Art Archive/Bibliothèque Nationale Paris; **p. 553,** © Rare Books Division, New York Public Library, Astor, Lenox and Tilden Foundations/Art Resource, NY; **p. 555,** From Description de l'Afrique by Olifert Dapper, 1686; **p. 557,** © Rare Books Division, New York Public Library, Astor, Lenox and Tilden Foundations/Art Resource, NY; **p. 559,** © The British Museum; **p. 563,** © North Wind Picture Archives; **p. 564,** © Arents Collection, New York Public Library, Astor, Lenox and Tilden Foundations/Art Resource, NY; **p. 565,** From Debret, *Voyages Pittoresque et Historiques au Bresil,* 1816–1831; **p. 567,** © Manuscripts, Archives and Rare Books Division, Schomberg Center for Research in Black Culture, New York Public Library, Astor, Lenox and Tilden Foundations/Art Resource, NY.

CHAPTER 26

Text Credits p. 591, George Elison, *Deus Destroyed: The Image of Christianity in Early Modern Japan.* Cambridge, Mass.: Harvard University, Council on East Asian Studies, 1973, pp. 259–60, 283–84. © 1973 The President and Fellows of Harvard College. **Photo Credits p. 570,** Peabody Essex Museum. Photo by Mark Sexton; **p. 574,** © Manfred Gottschalk/Workbook Stock/ Getty Images; **p. 576,** © The Metropolitan Museum of Art/Art Resource, NY; **p. 577,** © National Palace Museum, Taipei, Taiwan, Republic of China; **p. 579,** © Dennis Cox/ ChinaStock; **p. 580,** Golestan Palace, Tehran, Iran/© Giraudon/Bridgeman Art Library; **p. 582,** © Bettmann/Corbis; **p. 583,** © Christie's Images/Corbis; **p. 584,** © Rare Books Division, New York Public Library, Astor, Lenox and Tilden Foundations/Art Resource, NY; **p. 587,** Art Archive/Kobe Municipal Museum/Granger Collection; **p. 588,** Scenes from the Pleasure Quarters of Kyoto, 17th Century, Edo Period. One of a pair of 6-panel folding screens. Denman Waldo Ross Collection. Courtesy Museum of Fine Arts, Boston. Photograph © 2001 Museum of Fine Arts, Boston. All rights reserved.; **p. 589,** © The British Museum; **p. 590,** © Erich Lessing/Art Resource, NY.

CHAPTER 27

Text Credits p. 599, Ghislain de Busbecq. *The Turkish Letters of Ogier Ghislain de Busbecq.* Trans. By E.S. Foster. Oxford: Clarendon Press, 1927. **Photo Credits p. 594,** © Francis G. Mayer/Corbis; **p. 598,** © Giraudon/Art Resource, NY; **p. 600,** © The British Library (OR.3248, f. 55v); **p. 601L,** © Angelo Homak/Corbis; **p. 601R,** © Victoria & Albert Museum, London/Art Resource, NY; **p. 604,** © Aga Khan Trust for Culture, Geneva. AKM00288 fol. 103, from Akhlaq-e Nasiri ("Ethics of Nasir") by Nasir al-Din Tusi; **p. 605,** © Rijksmuseum Amsterdam; **p. 606,** Reproduced by kind permission of the Trustees of the Chester Beatty Library; **p. 607,** © Harvey Lloyd; **p. 608,** © Byron Crader/Ric Ergenbright Photography; **p. 609,** © Andrea Pistolesi/The Image Bank/Getty Images; **p. 610,** © Art Resource, NY; **p. 611,** © INTERFOTO/Alamy; **p. 616L,** © Digital Vision/Getty Images; **p. 616ML,** © Hemera Technologies/Alamy; **p. 616MR,** Library of Congress Prints & Photographs Division [LC-DIG-jpd-00292]; **p. 616R,** Library of Congress.

PART 6

Photo Credits p. 618L, © Bridgeman-Giraudon/Art Resource, NY; **p. 618ML,** © Corbis; **p. 618MR,** © Bettmann/Corbis; **p. 618R,** Chinese School/© The Bridgeman Art Library/Getty Images; **p. 619** The Art Archive.

CHAPTER 28

Text Credits p. 640, From *Women in Revolutionary Paris, 1789–1795: Selected Documents Translated With Notes And Commentary.* Translated with notes and commentary by Darline Gay Levy, Harriet Branson Applewhite, and Mary Durham Johnson. Copyright 1979 by the Board of Trustees of the University of Illinois. Used with permission of the editors and the University of Illinois Press. **Photo Credits p. 620,** © Bridgeman-Giraudon/Art Resource, NY; **p. 624,** © Bettmann/Corbis; **p. 625,** © Lebrecht Music & Arts/Corbis; **p. 627,** © Bulloz/Agence Réunion des Musées Nationaux/Art Resource, NY; **p. 630,** Private Collection/Archives Charmet/© The Bridgeman Art Library; **p. 631,** © The Gallery Collection/Corbis; **p. 633,** © Snark/Art Resource, NY; **p. 634,** © The Granger Collection, New York; **p. 636,** © Van Butcher/ Photo Researchers, Inc.; **p. 639,** © Réunion des Musées Nationaux/Art Resource, NY; **p. 641,** © The Granger Collection, New York; **p. 642,** © Erich Lessing/Art Resource, NY; **p. 643,** © akg-images; **p. 646,** Schloss Friedrichsruhe/© The Bridgeman Art Library.

CHAPTER 29

Photo Credits p. 650, © Corbis; **p. 654,** © Bettmann/Corbis; **p. 655T,** © Corbis; **p. 655B,** Science Museum, London/© The Bridgeman Art Library; **p. 657,** © Ann Ronan Picture Library/HIP/The Image Works; **p. 660,** © Corbis; **p. 661,** Guildhall Library, Corporation of London/© The Bridgeman Art Library; **p. 662,** © HIP/Art Resource, NY; **p. 665,** © Stapleton Collection/Corbis; **p. 666,** © Hulton-Deutsch Collection/Corbis; **p. 668,** © Bettmann/Corbis; **p. 669,** © Museum of the City of New York; **p. 671,** © Bettmann/ Corbis; **p. 672,** Deutsches Historisches Museum, Berlin, Germany/© DHM Arne Psille/ The Bridgeman Art Library; **p. 673,** The Metropolitan Museum of Art, Rogers Fund, 1942 (42.95.7). Image copyright © The Metropolitan Museum of Art/Art Resource, NY.

CHAPTER 30

Text Credits p. 689, "A Mexican Radical: Ponciano Arriaga." In Benjamin Keen, ed., *Latin American Civilization History and Society, 1492 to the Present,* 6th ed., revised and updated. Westview Press, 1996, pp. 273–74. Used by permission of Perseus Books; **p. 698,** From *Been in the Storm So Long* by Leon F. Litwack, copyright © 1979 by Leon F. Litwack. Used by permission of Alfred A. Knopf, a division of Random House, Inc. **Photo Credits p. 676,** © Bettmann/Corbis; **p. 679,** © Smithsonian Institution/Corbis; **p. 681,** © The Granger Collection, New York; **p. 682,** © PoodlesRock/Corbis; **p. 683,** Library of Congress; **p. 687,** © Erich Lessing/ Art Resource, NY; **p. 688,** © Lake County Museum, Corbis; **p. 690,** © Micael Maslan Historic Photographs/Corbis; **p. 692,** © Museum of the City of New York/Corbis; **p. 694,** Courtesy of the Arizona Historical Society, Tuscon. #97329; **pp. 695, 696,** © Corbis; **p. 697** © California Historical Society, San Francisco (FN-23115 [OV]); **p. 699,** © Bettmann/Corbis; **p. 700,** © Yann Arthus-Bertand/Corbis.

CHAPTER 31

Text Credits p. 711, Rondo Cameron, ed. *Civilization since Waterloo: A Book of Source Readings.* Itasca, Ill.: F.E. Peacock, 1971. Used by permission; **p. 719,** Dan J. Li, *China in Transition.* New York: Van Nostrand, 1969. **Photo Credits p. 704,** Chinese School/© The Bridgeman Art Library/Getty Images; **p. 707,** © Bettmann/ Corbis; **p. 709,** © W. & D. Downey/Getty Images; **p. 710,** © Culver Pictures; **p. 714,** © Michael Nicholson/Corbis; **p. 715,** © Hulton Archive/Getty Images; **p. 716,** © Chris Hellier/Corbis; **p. 718,** © Corbis; **p. 721,** © 2005 Roger-Viollet/The Image Works; **p. 722,** © David Ball/Alamy; **p. 723,** © Leonard deSelva/Corbis; **p. 724,** Art Archive/Private Collection/Granger Collection; **p. 725,** © Asian Art & Archaeology, Inc./Corbis; **p. 727,** © Lebrecht Authors/ Lebrecht Music & Arts/Corbis.

CHAPTER 32

Text Credits p. 744, From Alfred Andrea, *The Human Record: Sources of Global History,* 3rd Ed., Vol. 2, 1998, Wadsworth, a part of Cengage Learning, Inc. Reproduced by permission. www.cengage.com/ permissions. **Photo Credits p. 730,** The Art Archive; **p. 733,** © Baldwin H. Ward/

Corbis; **p. 736,** © Mary Evans Picture Library/Alamy; **p. 737,** © Bildarchiv Preussischer Kulturbesitz/Art Resource, NY; **p. 739,** The Art Archive/India Office Library/Eileen Tweedy; **p. 740,** © Hulton Archive/Getty Images; **p. 741,** © Anti-Slavery International/Panos; **p. 746,** © Mary Evans Picture Library/Alamy; **p. 747,** © Brown Brothers; **p. 748,** © Philadelphia Museum of Art/Corbis; **p. 749,** © The Granger Collection, NY; **p. 753,** Illustration of comparative physiognomy. From *Indigenous Races of the Earth* by J.C. Nott and G.R. Glidden, 1868; **p. 755,** © Royal Geographic Society; **p. 758L,** Library of Congress, Prints and Photographs Division (LC-USZC4-4969); **p. 758ML,** © DEA/G.Dagli Orti/Getty Images; **p. 758MR,** Library of Congress Prints & Photographs Division [LC-DIG-jpd-00820]; **p. 758R,** Library of Congress.

PART 7

Photo Credits p. 760ML, Photo © Erich Lessing/Art Resource, NY. © 2010 Artists Rights Society (ARS), New York/VG Bild-Kunst, Bonn; **pp. 760L, 760MR,** © Swim Ink/Corbis; **pp. 760R, 761L,** © Bettmann/Corbis; **p. 761R,** © Sanford/Agliolo/Corbis.

CHAPTER 33

Photo Credits p. 762, © Bettmann/Corbis; **p. 766,** © Christel Gersetenberg/Corbis; **p. 768,** The Art Archive/Musée des 2 Guerres Mondiales Paris/Gianni Dagli Orti; **p. 769,** © Bettmann/Corbis; **p. 771,** © Imperial War Museum, London; **p. 772,** © Bettmann/Corbis; **p. 773,** © akg-images; **p. 775L,** The Art Archive; **pp. 775R, 776,** National Archives; **p. 778,** © Hulton-Deutsches Collection/Corbis; **p. 780,** © Bettmann/Corbis; **p. 781,** The Art Archive/Imperial War Museum; **p. 782,** © National Portrait Gallery, Smithsonian Institution/Art Resource, NY.

CHAPTER 34

Text Credits p. 805, From Alfred Andrea, *The Human Record: Sources of Global History,* 3rd Ed., Vol. 2, 1998, Wadsworth, a part of Cengage Learning, Inc. Reproduced by permission. www.cengage.com/permissions. **Photo Credits p. 792,** © Bettmann/Corbis; **p. 794T,** © Corbis; **p. 794B,** © Bettmann/Corbis; **p. 795,** Rudolf Staechelin Collection on loan to the Kunstmuseum, Basel; **p. 796,** © The Museum of Modern Art/Licensed by SCALA/Art Resource, NY. © 2010 Estate of Pablo Picasso/Artists Rights Society (ARS), New York; **p. 797,** © akg-images; **pp. 799, 800T,** © Bettmann/Corbis; **p. 800B,** Library of Congress; **p. 803,** © Bettmann/Corbis; **p. 804,** © Karl Liebknecht/Sovfoto; **p. 806,** © Hulton-Deutsch Collection/Corbis; **p. 807,** © Erich Lessing/Art Resource, NY; **p. 809T,** © akg-images; **p. 809B,** © Henry Guttmann/Getty Images.

CHAPTER 35

Text Credits p. 824, *The Philosophy and Opinions of Marcus Garvey.* Edited by Amy Jacques Garvey. New Preface by Tony Martin. The Majority Press Inc., Dover, MA, pp. 73–74. **Photo Credits p. 812,** © Swim Ink/Corbis; **p. 819L,** © UPI/Corbis; **pp. 819R, 821,** © Bettmann/Corbis; **p. 822,** © HIP/Art Resource, NY; **p. 825,** © Hulton-Deutsch Collection/Corbis; **p. 826,** © 2010 Banco de México Diego Rivera Frida Kahlo Museums Trust, Mexico, D.F./Artists Rights Society (ARS), New York; **p. 829,** © Bettmann/Corbis; **p. 830T,** TM and Copyright © 20th Century Fox Film Corp. All rights reserved. Courtesy Everett Collection; **p. 830B,** Miss Chiquita Banana Figure is a registered trademark of Chiquita Brands L.L.C. in the United States and other countries and is used with permission. No other use of Miss Chiquita Banana Figure is permitted without the prior, written permission of Chiquita Brands L.L.C.

CHAPTER 36

Text Credits p. 847, Copyright © 1992 *Japan at War: An Oral History* by Haruko Taya Cook and Theodore F. Cook. Reprinted by permission of The New Press; **p. 851,** *International Military Tribunal, Trial of the Major War Criminal, Nuremberg Germany, 1948;* volume 29, Document 1919-PS. Translation Copyright © 2002 Yad Vashem. Reprinted by permission of Yad Vashem. **Photo Credits p. 834,** © Bettmann/Corbis; **p. 837,** © Hulton-Deutsch Collection/Corbis; **p. 838,** © Bettmann/Corbis; **p. 839,** © Popperfoto/Robertstock; **p. 840,** © Bettmann/Corbis; **p. 841,** © Harwood/Getty Images; **p. 842,** © Imperial War Museum, London; **p. 843,** © Bettmann/Corbis; **p. 844,** © Corbis; **p. 848,** © Hulton-Deutsch Collection/Corbis; **p. 850,** © Bettmann/Corbis; **p. 853,** © Hulton Archive/Getty Images; **p. 854,** © Imperial War Museum, London; **p. 856,** © Fritz Henle/Photo Researchers, Inc.; **p. 858,** © Corbis; **p. 859,** © Michael Nicholson/Corbis.

CHAPTER 37

Text Credits p. 869, Muhammad Ali Jinnah, from *Sources of Indian Tradition,* 2nd ed., Vol. 2, edited by Stephen Hay (New York, 1988), Columbia University Press. Used by permission; **p. 877,** Kwame Nkrumah, *I Speak of Freedom: A Statement of African Ideology.* New York: Frederick A. Praeger, 1961. **Photo Credits p. 864,** © Bettmann/Corbis; **p. 867,** © UPI/Corbis; **p. 871,** © Baldwin H. Ward/Corbis; **p. 873,** © UPI/Corbis; **p. 874,** © Marc Garanger/Corbis; **p. 876,** © Express Newspapers/Getty Images; **p. 878,** © Hulton-Deutsch Collection/Corbis; **p. 879,** © Martin Jones/Corbis; **p. 880L,** © Sovfoto; **p. 880R,** © Getty Images; **p. 881,** © Corbis; **p. 883,** © Alexandra Avakian/Woodfin Camp and Associates; **p. 885,** © Keystone/Getty Images.

CHAPTER 38

Text Credits p. 906, Reprinted from: *An Inconvenient Truth* by Al Gore. Copyright © 2006 by Al Gore. Permission granted by Rodale, Inc., Emmaus, PA 18098 and The Wylie Agency; **p. 918,** Aung San Suu Kyi, *Letters from Burma,* Penguin, 1996. **Photo Credits p. 890,** © Sanford/Agliolo/Corbis; **p. 893,** © Peter Turnley/Corbis; **p. 894,** © Tom Stoddart/Katz Pictures/Woodfin Camp and Associates; **p. 897,** © William Whitehurst/Corbis; **p. 902,** © Bruno Barbey/Magnum Photos; **p. 904,** © David & Peter Turnley/Corbis; **p. 906,** © William Radcliffe/Science Faction/Corbis; **p. 907,** © J.P. Laffont; **p. 908,** © MedicalRF.com/Corbis; **p. 910,** © Reuters/Corbis; **p. 912,** © AP Images; **p. 914,** © Brad Markel/Getty Images; **p. 915,** © Francois Perri/Woodfin Camp and Associates; **p. 917,** © Jan Banning/Panos; **p. 919,** © Vittoriano Rastelli/Corbis; **p. 920,** © A. Hollmann/United Nations High Commissioner for Refugees; **p. 924L,** National Archives and Records Administration, NAIL Control Number: NWDNS -208-N-43888; **p. 924ML,** National Archives and Records Administration; **p. 924MR,** © Jupiter Images; **p. 924R,** US Department of Defense.

index

120°
160°
120°
80°
40°
80°
ARCTIC OCEAN
GREENLAND (Denmark)
RUSSIA
ALASKA
CANADA
40°
UNITED STATES
JAPAN
NORTH PACIFIC OCEAN
Midway Islands (U.S.)
Tropic of Cancer
MEXICO
BAHAMAS
CUBA
Wake Islands (U.S.)
Hawaiian Islands
JAMAICA
DOMINICAN REPUBLIC
Puerto Rico (to U.S.)
BELIZE
HONDURAS
HAITI
Lesser Antilles
GUATEMALA
EL SALVADOR
NICARAGUA
COSTA RICA
TRINIDAD AND TOBAGO
VENEZUELA
GUYANA
SURINAME
Marshall Islands
PANAMA
COLOMBIA
FRENCH GUIANA
0°
Nauru
Galapagos Islands
ECUADOR
PAPUA NEW GUINEA
Solomon Islands
Tuvalu
PERU
Samoa
BRAZIL
Vanuatu
Fiji
BOLIVIA
Tonga
Tropic of Capricorn
PARAGUAY
New Caledonia (Fr.)
AUSTRALIA
Easter Island
CHILE
URUGUAY
SOUTH PACIFIC OCEAN
ARGENTINA
40°
NEW ZEALAND
Falkland Islands
Antarctic Circle
120°
160°
120°
80°
40°

0°
40°
80°
120°
160°
80°
Arctic Circle
NORWAY
SWEDEN
FINLAND
RUSSIA
EST.
LATVIA
LITH.
RUSS.
DENMARK
UNITED KINGDOM
BELARUS
NETH.
BELG.
LUX.
GERMANY
POLAND
CZECH.
SLOVAK.
AUSTRIA
UKRAINE
MOLDOVA
FRANCE
SWITZ.
HUNG.
ROM.
SLOVN.
CRO.
BOS.
SERB.
KOSOVO
BULG.
ITALY
MONT.
ALB.
MACE.
GREECE
SPAIN
GEORGIA
ARMENIA
AZERB.
TURKEY
KAZAKHSTAN
MONGOLIA
UZBEKISTAN
TURKMENISTAN
KYRGYZSTAN
TAJIKISTAN
N. KOREA
S. KOREA
JAPAN
CHINA
40°
TUNISIA
MOROCCO
ALGERIA
LIBYA
EGYPT
LEBANON
ISRAEL
SYRIA
IRAQ
IRAN
JORDAN
KUWAIT
AFGHANISTAN
PAKISTAN
NEPAL
BHUTAN
INDIA
SAUDI ARABIA
QATAR
U.A.E.
OMAN
YEMEN
TAIWAN
Tropic of Cancer
HONG KONG
MYANMAR
LAOS
BANGLADESH
THAILAND
VIETNAM
CAMBODIA
PHILIPPINES
PACIFIC OCEAN
MALI
NIGER
CHAD
SUDAN
ERITREA
DJIBOUTI
ETHIOPIA
SOMALIA
BURKINA FASO
NIGERIA
IVORY COAST
GHANA
TOGO
BENIN
CAMEROON
CENTRAL AFRICAN REP.
EQUATORIAL GUINEA
SAO TOME AND PRINCIPE
GABON
CONGO
UGANDA
KENYA
DEMOCRATIC REPUBLIC OF THE CONGO
RWANDA
BURUNDI
TANZANIA
SEYCHELLES
SRI LANKA
INDIAN OCEAN
BRUNEI
MALAYSIA
INDONESIA
0°
PAPUA NEW GUINEA
Solomon Islands
EAST TIMOR
ANGOLA
ZAMBIA
MALAWI
MOZAMBIQUE
NAMIBIA
ZIMBABWE
MADAGASCAR
MAURITIUS
RÉUNION
BOTSWANA
SWAZILAND
SOUTH AFRICA
LESOTHO
Vanuatu
New Caledonia (Fr.)
AUSTRALIA
Tropic of Capricorn
Tasmania
40°
NEW ZEALAND
Abbreviations
ALB. ALBANIA
AZERB. AZERBAIJAN
BELG. BELGIUM
BOS. BOSNIA-HERZEGOVINA
BULG. BULGARIA
CRO. CROATIA
CZECH. CZECH REPUBLIC
EST. ESTONIA
HUNG. HUNGARY
LITH. LITHUANIA
LUX. LUXEMBOURG
MACE. MACEDONIA
MONT. MONTENEGRO
NETH. NETHERLANDS
ROM. ROMANIA
RUSS. RUSSIA
SERB. SERBIA
SLOVAK. SLOVAKIA
SLOVN. SLOVENIA
SWITZ. SWITZERLAND
U.A.E. UNITED ARAB EMIRATES
Antarctic Circle
0°
40°
80°
120°
160°